Reliance of the Traveller

*In accordance with the real nature of things
it is the human that must conform to the Divine
and not the Divine to the human.*

—Seyyed Hossein Nasr

Reliance of the Traveller

Revised Edition

The Classic Manual of Islamic Sacred Law 'Umdat al-Salik
by Ahmad ibn Naqib al-Misri (d. 769/1368) in Arabic with
Facing English Text, Commentary, and Appendices
Edited and Translated by Nuh Ha Mim Keller

amana publications
Beltsville, Maryland U.S.A

© *Nuh Ha Mim Keller 1991 and 1994*

Published 1991. Revised Edition 1994,

This new edition 1997
published by amana publications
10710 Tucker Street, Suite B
Beltsville, Maryland 20705-2223 USA
Tel. (301) 595-5777 Fax (301) 595-5888
Website: www.amana-publications.com
Email: igamana@erols.com

The Arabic calligraphy for this volume was done by
the Syrian calligrapher Salih Nasab. The front cover
ornament is a radial pattern from 4th/10th-century Persia,
by courtesy of Dover Publications Inc., from Persian Designs
and Motifs for Artists and Craftsmen, by Ali Dowlatshahi

Library of Congress Cataloging-in-Publication Data

Ibn al-Naqīb, Aḥmad ibn Lu'lu', d. 1368.
    ['Umdat al-sālik wa-'uddat al-nāsik. English & Arabic]
    Reliance of the traveller : a classic manual of Islamic sacred law
/ by Ahmad ibn Naqib al-Miṣri ; in Arabic with facing English text,
commentary, and appendices, edited and translated by Nuh Ha Mim
Keller. — Rev. ed.
      p.   cm.
    Includes bibliographical references (pp. 97) and indexes.
    ISBN 0–915957–72–8
    1. Islamic law—Early works to 1800.   2. Shafiites—Early works to
1800.   I. Keller, Nuh Ha Mim. II. Title
IN PROCESS
340.5'9—dc21   97-27651
                                                     CIP

Printed in the United States of America

CONTENTS

A comprehensive table of contents precedes each section.

INTRODUCTION

Praise to Allah Most High, who inspired His slave Muhammad the Koran and Wisdom, as a mercy unto the worlds. Allah bless him and give him peace.

The four Sunni schools of Islamic law, Hanafi, Maliki, Shafi'i, and Hanbali, are identical in approximately 75 percent of their legal conclusions, while the remaining questions, variances within a single family of explainers of the Holy Koran and prophetic sunna, are traceable to methodological differences in understanding or authentication of the primary textual evidence, differing viewpoints sometimes reflected in even a single school. The present volume, *'Umdat al-salik* [The reliance of the traveller], represents one of the finest and most reliable short works in Shafi'i jurisprudence, a school with perhaps fewer scholarly differences on rulings than others because its main resource is the recension of Imam Nawawi, the great thirteenth-century Shafi'i hadith scholar and jurisprudent who upgraded the work of previous generations in terms of the authenticity and application of hadith evidence. The author of *'Umdat al-salik*, Ibn Naqib, closely follows the order and conclusions of Nawawi's encyclopedic *al-Majmu': sharh al-Muhadhdhab* [The compendium: an exegesis of "The rarefaction"] with its addendum, *al-Takmila* [The completion], by Ibn Naqib's own sheikh, Taqi al-Din Subki. The present volume is virtually an index of the conclusions of the *Majmu'*, and readers interested in the evidence from Koran and hadith for the rulings of the present volume can find them there, or, Allah willing, in a forthcoming sister-work to be called *The Guidance of the Traveller*.

In an age when some Muslims are calling for an end to the four schools of jurisprudence in order to make way for a single school exclusively taken, it is claimed, from the texts of the Koran and hadith, it might be wondered: why offer Muslims a book from a particular school at all? The answer, in part, is that each school does not merely comprise the work of a single Imam, but rather represents a large collectivity of scholars whose research in Sacred Law and its ancillary disciplines has been characterized by considerable division of labor and specialization over a very long period of time. Among the specialists in the field of hadith, for example, who were Shafi'is are such scholars as Bukhari, Muslim, Tirmidhi, Nasa'i, Ibn Majah, Abu Dawud, Ibn Kathir, Dhahabi, and Nawawi; while the school has also had many Koranic exegetes, scholars of the sciences of Arabic, and legal specialists, most of whom were actively involved in contributing to the school's jurisprudence. The result of this division of labor has been a body of legal texts that are arguably superior in evidence, detail, range, and in sheer usefulness to virtually any recent attempt to present Islam as a unified system of human life. For most nontraditional works seen up to the present have been one-man efforts, while the classic texts have been checked and refined by a large number of scholars, and the difference is manifest. At the same time, it is fairly safe to say that there is no single work from any of the schools that has everything, and an impartial student of jurisprudence must surely feel that the research of the schools should not only be learned and transmitted, but also sorted out and recast into a form accessible and suited to Muslim needs today.

Regarding this need for relevance, it will be noticed that the basic text *'Umdat al-salik* is by no means the only thing in the present work. Three introductory sections in the form of a "user's guide to Sacred Law" precede the basic text, which is likewise followed by eight major appendices on subjects ranging from personal ethics and character (akhlaq) to Islamic spirituality and tenets of faith, while a final biographical section tells readers who the figures mentioned throughout the book's legal texts are. Though these separate parts cover a considerable range of topics within the Islamic ethic, the aim in gathering them has been to achieve a unitary reference work that is eclectic in neither subject matter nor scholarly sources.

As for subject matter, the emphasis of the book is on the path we now travel, to paradise or hell, and it is this that unites the work and determines the relative importance of the questions treated; why, for example, a legal discussion from Nawawi's *Kitab al-adhkar* [The book of the remembrances of Allah] on unlawful slander (ghiba) must be given equal weight to a section on the sunnas of ablution (wudu) from *'Umdat al-salik,* and so on.

As for sources, the authors translated are, with few exceptions, well-known scholars of the Shafi'i school of jurisprudence and Ash'ari school of tenets of faith, as appears in their biographies. The many who were Sufis were of the strictest observance of the Sacred Law. While such affiliations, and indeed much of what can be termed traditional Sunni Islam, have not been spared the criticism of certain post-caliphal Muslim writers and theorists, the authors of the present volume and their positions do represent the orthodox Muslim intellectual and spiritual heritage that has been the strength of the Community for over a thousand years, and the means through which Allah has preserved His religion, in its purest and fullest sense, to the present day.

THE INTERPRETIVE METHOD

The style of translating the basic text is an explanative one with interlinear commentary. The reason for commentary, briefly, is that this book, like others in Islamic law, is less the achievement of a particular author than the shared effort of a whole school of research and interpretation in explaining rules of divine origin. The cooperative nature of this effort may be seen in the *multilayered* character of its texts, whose primary authors often merely state the ruling of an act, lawful or unlawful, leaving matters of definition, conditions, and scriptural evidence for the commentator to supply, who in turn leaves important details for both writers of marginal notes and for living sheikhs to definitively interpret when teaching the work to their students. The sheikhs form a second key resource of textual commentary, a spoken one parallel to the written, and in previous centuries of traditional Islamic learning it was well known that no student could dispense with it. Living teachers were and are needed to explain terminological difficulties, eliminate ambiguities, and correct copyists' mistakes. The present translator was no exception to the need for instructors, but went to sheikhs to learn, studying with them during the course of preparing the translation, asking, and listening to their explanations of matters of Sacred Law, many of which are recorded below. The entire book's Arabic texts have been reviewed separately with each of the scholars, Sheikh 'Abd al-Wakil Durubi and Sheikh Nuh 'Ali Salman. Both ably represent the tradition, links in an unbroken succession of masters leading back to the founder of the school himself. Sheikh 'Abd al-Wakil acquired his Shafi'i jurisprudence in the course of eighteen years of instruction with his own teacher, Ibrahim al-Ghazzi, before becoming imam of the Darwishiyya in Damascus, while Sheikh Nuh spent a similar number of years reading and studying the law with various sheikhs before his appointment as mufti in Jordan. Few Western vocations require as much specialized learning. If it be objected that their comments are not part of the original text, or even intrusive, the reply is that such teaching is recommended by long Islamic tradition with good reason, as may be seen by readers who compare the clarity, for example, of the present work's sections on estate division (L4 to L10) with any English translation of comparable sections from other works. Moreover, care has been taken throughout the volume to assign each statement to the person who said it. Finally, close contact with these scholars as Muslims leaves one with a firm impression of godfearingness, the first condition of real knowledge and its most important fruit.

Some Points About the Book

Ahmad ibn Naqib al-Misri (d. 769/1368) is the author of the basic text, *'Umdat al-salik wa 'uddat al-nasik* [The reliance of the traveller and tools of the worshipper] (y89), which is vowelled in the Arabic. Not a single omission has been made from it, though rulings about matters now rare or nonexistent have been left untranslated unless interesting for some other reason. Parts untranslated are enclosed in brackets.

'Umar Barakat (d. after 1307/1890) wrote the text's commentary, *Fayd al-Ilah al-Malik fi hall alfaz 'Umdat al-salik wa 'uddat al-nasik* [The outpouring of the Sovereign Divinity: an interpretation of the words of "The reliance of the traveller and tools of the worshipper"] (y27), from which excerpts have been selected and introduced into the basic text by the translator. These are parenthesized in the Arabic and unvowelled, and distinguished in the English by parentheses and the capital letter O. Similarly, the comments of Sheikh Nuh 'Ali Salman are parenthesized in both languages, in the Arabic unvowelled and introduced by the letter ha' (ح), and in the English by the letter N. The comments of Sheikh 'Abd al-Wakil Durubi are presented in the same way, but marked in the English with the capital letter A, and in the Arabic, where given, by the letter 'ayn (ع). Notes from the sheikhs that are not given in the Arabic text are from discussions (often partly in colloquial Arabic) recorded at the time in English alone, whose precise classical Arabic wording the translator did not try to reconstruct, though they have been well understood, and the English, Allah willing, adequately conveys their meaning. The translator's own remarks are parenthesized, and introduced by a lowercase *n* in the English and by the letter ta' (ت) if given in Arabic.

Other supplementary texts begin with the author's name at the first of the quote, and finish with the source's title, volume, and page number at the end of it, with the addition in the English of the work's reference number from the present volume's bibliographical section, book y. All works cited about Islamic faith or practice are by Muslim authors. Biographical information on those quoted or mentioned throughout the present work is given in book x, where they are listed alphabetically, first name first.

The rulings of the text have been *numbered* both to increase the work's accessibility to users of the tables of contents and to facilitate cross-reference, since the definition and range of many important terms are governed by conditions and stipulations classical authors typically mention but once, their students mastering such definitional points by prodigious memories, for which a system of cross-reference is, in our own times, perhaps the only effective substitute.

Within the rulings themselves, columns of necessary *conditions* or *integrals*, meaning that all of them must be present for the ruling to hold true, are itemized by letters: (a), (b), (c), etc. An example is the conditions for the validity of the prayer, which must all be met for the prayer to be valid. Columns of *examples* or *instances* of a ruling's applicability are itemized by numbers: (1), (2), (3), etc., indicating that not all need exist but any one of them suffices to apply the ruling, such as the things which invalidate fasting, the existence of any of which invalidates it.

EDITING THE TEXTS

The editorial preferences of *The Chicago Manual of Style* have generally been followed in preparing the texts of the present volume, though by the nature of their special challenges, the manner of citing the texts differs from the manual's recommendations for handling quotations in the following ways:

(1) The old Arabic texts were free of need for any punctuation because of the language's syntactic precision, and were originally written without it, while it was introduced in a somewhat haphazard manner in comparatively recent times, attested to by the books printed within the last hundred years in the Arab world, which show wide discrepancies in both the extent to which punctuation is used and in the meaning of such devices as quotation marks, commas, semicolons, parentheses, brackets, and the rest. In editing the Arabic of the present volume, the translator has standardized its punctuation according to the practice of most Arab publishers in the 1980s, with the exception of the use of parentheses and brackets, which Arab writers often use for emphasis, while the translator has employed them as in English, for the purposes of interlinear commentary and indicating untranslated passages, as described above.

(2) The Arabic chapter and section titles extant in the original texts have been shortened to the name of the topic alone, for example, from *Bab al-Hiba* ("Chapter of Gift Giving") to *al-Hiba* ("Gift Giving"), and so forth.

Passages introducing a new topic that is not separately distinguished in the original Arabic, or merely distinguished by the word *fasl* ("section") have been separated into sections and given English titles, such as section n6, "Doubts About the Fact of Having Divorced," and subsection titles have been added where expedient, such as before j17.9, "Hunting." The reason for this retitling and regrouping was to improve the work's accessibility to English-speaking users, to whom an effective reference tool is worth more than a well-kept antique. The Arabic titles of such sections were supplied by Sheikh Nuh after their English titles had been written, according to the expressions he felt best summarized the sections' contents, not by way of translating the English titles, so there is not always a strict correspondence between the titles of the two languages. "Hunting," for example, became "The Rulings of Hunting" (Ahkam al-Sayd) in Arabic, and so forth.

As for major regroupings, books *d* through *o* of the present volume correspond to the books of *'Umdat al-salik* with only three exceptions: book d, "The Author's Introduction"; the sections of book L on bequests (L1–3), which have been moved there from book k ("Trade"); and "The Book of Dowry" (Kitab al-Sadaq), originally from m8 to n12, from which book n ("Divorce") has been separated, since it seemed fitter to include dowry, wife support, and so forth, under the rubric of marriage, and place matters connected with divorce in a separate book.

(3) As previously mentioned, parts of the Arabic left untranslated into English are distinguished in the Arabic alone by square brackets. For the sake of fluency and readability, such untranslated portions are not marked by ellipsis points (...) in the English, as the existence of the contents of the ellipsis in the parallel column of Arabic was felt to suffice in their stead. The occasional use of ellipsis points in the English has been confined to indicating editorial omissions in the Arabic, and where such an ellipse is not indicated in the English, the ellipsis points appear in brackets in the facing column of Arabic alone.

(4) In the course of editing the commentary and some of the supplementary material of the present volume, though not the basic text, the sequence of some passages has occasionally been altered for the sake of coherence of argumentation, the need for which will not be lost on anyone familiar with medieval Arabic texts, whose authors sometimes seem to have not reedited their work with a view towards logical sequencing or eliminating digressions. Passages in which this has been done have been reviewed and checked by both Sheikh 'Abd al-Wakil and Sheikh Nuh, like the other texts of the present work, and are indicated at the end of their Arabic texts by the words *bi taqdim wa ta'khir* ("put ahead and behind") as is done by Muslim scholars when a passage is quoted in this way.

OTHER DETAILS

As an aid to non-Arabic-speakers, transliteration section w1 has been added to help people pronounce the supplications (du'a') and invocations (dhikr) mentioned in the course of the book, with the observation that it is best to also tape-record a native speaker of Arabic reading the texts so as to master them by imitating the tape, and to facilitate this there is an index of the relevant Arabic texts at w2.

The untranslatability of the Holy Koran is fully acknowledged by the translator, whose only effort where it is quoted in the present volume has been to explain the significance of its verses, giving a *map* as it were to the wide lands of its magnificent Arabic. The English by no means purports to be or to imitate the word of Allah Most High.

It is related that Imam Shafi'i (Allah have mercy on him) rechecked his masterpiece on legal principles, *al-Risala*, forty times before he finally said, "Allah has refused to give divine protection from error ('isma) to anyone besides His prophets." The matter is as he said, and one can only strive one's utmost for accuracy and ask Allah to forgive one's mistakes and oversights. If readers benefit from these pages, perhaps they will pray for those who had a hand in them and thank Allah Most High, who attributes all that exists to Himself by saying,

"This is Allah's creation, so show me what those besides Him have created." (Koran 31:11). ﴿هَـٰذَا خَلْقُ اللهِ فَأَرُونِي مَاذَا خَلَقَ الَّذِينَ مِنْ دُونِهِ﴾ [لقمان : ١١].

May Allah Most High bless His beloved, Muhammad, and give him peace, and his folk and Companions one and all.

*

DOCUMENTS

Documents

بسم الله الرحمن الرحيم

الحمد لله رب العالمين وصلى الله على سيدنا محمد وعلى آله وصحبه
وسلم يقول راقم هذه الاحرف عبدالوكيل الدروبي قد سمع
مني الاخ فلو هم كلر جميع أبواب هذا الكتاب الذي اصله
عمدة السالك وعدة الناسك مع ما اضافه هو الى المتن
من الشرح المسمى بفيض الآله المالك ومع أبواب أخرى
في الاصول والفروع اثبتها قبل المتن وبعده وأنه يفهم
نصوص هذا المصنف وأنه أهل لشرحه ونقله الى لغته
الانكليزية وذلك في مجالس اولها في شهر رجب من
سنة ١٤٠٥ه وآخرها في شهر شعبان من سنة
١٤٠٨ه كتبه العبد الفقير الى الله تعالى

عبدالوكيل الدروبي   شهر شعبان ١٤٠٨
امام جامع درويش
باشا بدمشق   شهد بذلك
الشام   الفقير الى الله تعالى
ياسين عرفه

شهد بما شرح عرفه   اشهد على ما رقمه
الاستاذ ايتيما سيمة عرفه الاستاذ الشيخ عبدالوكيل
الدروبي حفظه الله تعالى
انا العبد الفقير عبدالرحمن
الشاغوري   عبدالكريم

Documents

[WARRANT OF SHEIKH NUH 'ALI SALMAN]

IN THE NAME OF ALLAH, MOST MERCIFUL AND COMPASSIONATE

Praise be to Allah, Lord of the Worlds. May Allah bless our liegelord Muhammad and give him peace, and his folk and Companions one and all.

To commence: I have read all the chapters of this book, whose basic text is *'Umdat al-salik wa 'uddat al-nasik*, made notes on some matters of it, and reviewed it with brother **Nuh Ha Mim** Keller in numerous sessions, the first of which was in the month of Safar, A.H. 1405, and the last of which was in the month of Jumada II, A.H. 1409; during which I found the above-mentioned brother knowledgeable in what it contains and qualified to expound it and translate it into his native English, and I observed his accuracy and integrity in quoting the texts he has added before and after the main work, of principles of law and faith (usul) and particular rulings (furu'). He has interspersed the texts of the above-mentioned work with passages from its commentary entitled *Fayd al-Ilah al-Malik*, and he was successful in this, choosing passages needed to clarify the text and distinguishing the latter from the commentary with symbols. I ask Allah to give him success, reward him the best reward for it, and to benefit him and benefit others through him.

May Allah bless our liegelord Muhammad and give him peace, and his folk and Companions. Composed in Jumada II, A.H. 1409 [February, 1989] and written by:

Nuh 'Ali Salman [signed]
Mufti of the Jordanian Armed Forces

Witnessed by Yunus Hamdan [signed].

Witnessed by 'Adil Yusuf Rayhan [signed].

Witnessed by Kamal 'Abd al-Majid Muhammad [signed].

بسم الله الرحمن الرحيم

الحمد لله رب العالمين ، وصلى الله وسلم على سيدنا
محمد وعلى آله وصحبه أجمعين .

أما بعد : فقد قرأت جميع أبواب هذا الكتاب
الذي أصله كتاب «عمدة السالك و عدة الناسك»
وعلقت على بعض مسائله ، وراجعته مع الأخ
نوح حتم كلر في مجالس متعددة ، أولها في
شهر صفر ١٤٠٩هـ وآخرها في شهر جمادى الآخرة
١٤٠٩هـ ، ومن خلال ذلك وجدت الأخ المذكور
متقناً لما فيه وأهلاً لشرحه ونقله الى لغته
الانكليزية ، ولا حظت دقته و أمانته في نقل
النصوص التي أثبتها قبل المتن وبعده من أصول
و فروع ، وقد مزج نصوص الكتاب المذكور بنصوص
من شرح للكتاب اسمه «فيض الإله المالك ،
وكان موفقاً في ذلك لأنه اختار نصوصاً لابد منها
لتوضيح الأصل ، وميز بين عبارات الأصل والشرح
بإشارات ، وأسأل الله أن يوفقه ويجزيه على
ذلك خير الجزاء ، وأن ينفعه وينفع به .
وصلى الله وسلم على سيدنا محمد وآله وصحبه .
حرر في شهر جمادى الآخرة ١٤٠٩

وكتبه : نوح علي سلمان

شهد به
يوسي حمدان

نفع الله
مفتي العدوان المسلم الأردني

شهد به
كمال عبد الجيد محمد

شهد به
عادل يوسف بركان

Documents

IN THE NAME OF ALLAH, MOST MERCIFUL AND COMPASSIONATE

1 Jumada II 1411/18 December 1990

Report on the English translation of '*Umdat al-salik* by Ahmad ibn Naqib al-Misri al-Shafi'i undertaken by the scholar Nuh Ha Mim Keller:

(1)   There is no doubt that this translation is a valuable and important work, whether as a textbook for teaching Islamic jurisprudence to English-speakers, or as a legal reference for use by scholars, educated laymen, and students in this language.

(2)   As for the correctness of the translation, its accuracy, and its fidelity to the meanings and objects, we had our colleague in the Research Department of the International Institute of Islamic Thought, the scholar Yusuf Talal DeLorenzo, member of the Fiqh Council of North America and former chief of the Translation Bureau at the International Islamic University, Islamabad, review its texts and check it against the Arabic original. He found that the translation presents the legal questions in a faithful and precise idiom that clearly delivers the complete meaning in a sound English style. The translation is far from literalism, but does not exceed the author's intent, thereby demonstrating the translator's knowledge of Sacred Law and ability in jurisprudence as well as his complete command of both the Arabic and English languages.

(3)   In view of the utility of this eminent work of Islamic jurisprudence and its rank among well known standard Shafi'i legal texts, its translation into English is regarded as a useful, auspicious step, as is the translator's work, which, in clarifying fine shades of meaning and abstruse legal questions, succeeds in serving the book, making its objects accessible, and rendering it of general benefit to both followers of the Shafi'i school and others of the Muslim community. The book will be of great use in Southeast Asia in particular, and in America, Britain, and Canada.

(4)   From a purely academic point of view, this translation is superior to anything produced by orientalists in the way of translations of major Islamic works, in that while faithfully maintaining the required scholarly level, its aim is to imbue the consciousness of the non-Arabic-speaking Muslim with a sound understanding of Sacred Law, and the success of the translator lies in the notes, commentaries, appendices, and indexes he has added that help give the Muslim access to what will benefit him in his religion and this-worldly concerns and earn him the pleasure of Allah Most High. And this is the great triumph.

Dr. Taha Jabir al-'Alwani [signed]
President of the International Institute of Islamic Thought
Member of Islamic Fiqh Academy at Jedda
President of the Fiqh Council of North America

INTERNATIONAL
INSTITUTE OF
ISLAMIC
THOUGHT

P.O. Box 669, 555 Grove Street, Herndon, VA 22070 U.S.A. Telephone: (703) 471-1133 Telex: 901153 IIIT WASH Fax: (703) 471-3922

١ جمادى الآخرة ١٤١١هـ الموافق ١٨ ديسمبر ١٩٩٠م

تقرير عن : <u>الترجمة الانجليزية لعمدة السالك</u>

<u>لأحمد بن النقيب المصري الشافعي التي قام بها الأستاذ نوح حاميم كيلر</u>

أولا : لاشك أن هذه الترجمة عمل مهم ومفيد إما ككتاب دراسي يستخدم في تدريس الفقه للناطقين بالانجليزية أو كمرجع فقهي يعتمده الباحث والمثقف والطالب في هذه اللغة .

ثانيا : أما بالنسبة لصحة الترجمة ودقتها ووفائها بالمعاني والمطالب فقد كلفنا زميلنا في قسم البحوث بالمعهد العالمي للفكر الإسلامي الأستاذ يوسف طلال اللورينزي ، عضو المجلس الفقهي لشمال أمريكا ورئيس قسم الترجمة بالجامعة الإسلامية العالمية بإسلام آباد سابقا ، بمراجعة نصوصها ومقابلتها بالأصل العربي ، فوجد الترجمة تقدم المسائل الفقهية في عبارة دقيقة وأمينة تؤدي المعنى الكامل بوضوح في أسلوب انجليزي سليم . فالترجمة بعيدة عن الحرفية ومع ذلك لا تتجاوز حدود ما أراد المؤلف رحمه الله . ومن هنا تدل الترجمة على تفقه المترجم وملكته الفقهية بالإضافة إلى تمكنه التام من اللغتين العربية والانجليزية .

ثالثا : ونظرا إلى فائدة هذا الكتاب الفقهي الجليل وإلى مكانته بين المتون الفقهية الشافعية المعروفة فإن ترجمته إلى اللغة الانجليزية تعتبر خطوة مباركة نافعة ، كما أن عمل المترجم في توضيح المعاني الدقيقة والمسائل العويصة عمل مجد يهدف خدمة الكتاب وتسهيل مطالبه وتعميم فائدته لاتباع الفقه الشافعي ولغيرهم من أبناء الأمة . وسوف يكون الكتاب عظيم الفائدة في جنوب شرق آسيا بصفة خاصة وكل من أمريكا وبريطانيا وكندا .

رابعا : من الناحية الأكاديمية البحتة فإن هذه الترجمة تفوق ، كل ما قدمه المستشرقون من ترجمات لأمهات كتب التراث الإسلامي ، وذلك لأن هذه الترجمة ـ مع وفائها بالمستوى العلمي المطلوب ـ فإنها تهدف إلى توعية المسلم غير الناطق بالعربية توعية فقهية سليمة ، ونجاح المترجم فإن فيما أضاف من التعليقات والهوامش والملاحق والفهارس التي تساعد المسلم في الحصول على ما ينفعه في دينه ودنياه ، ويكسب له رضا الله تعالى . وهذا هو الفوز الكبير .

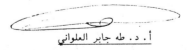

أ . د . طه جابر العلواني

رئيس المعهد العالمي للفكر الإسلامي
وعضو مجمع الفقه الإسلامي بجدة ورئيس المجلس الفقهي لشمال أمريكا

Documents

IN THE NAME OF ALLAH, MOST MERCIFUL AND COMPASSIONATE

al-Azhar
Islamic Research Academy
General Department for Research, Writing, and Translation

Mr. Nuh Ha Mim Keller
Amman, Jordan

Peace be upon you, and the mercy of Allah and His blessings.

To commence: In response to the request you have submitted concerning the examination of the English translation of the book *'Umdat al-salik wa 'uddat al-nasik* by Ahmad ibn Naqib in the Shafi'i school of jurisprudence, together with appendices by Islamic scholars on matters of Islamic law, tenets of faith, and personal ethics and character: we certify that the above-mentioned translation corresponds to the Arabic original and conforms to the practice and faith of the orthodox Sunni Community (Ahl al-Sunna wa al-Jama'a). There is no objection to printing it and circulating it.

The stamping of the pages of the above-mentioned work with the seal of the department has been completed.

May Allah give you success in serving Sacred Knowledge and the religion. Peace be upon you, and the mercy of Allah and His blessings.

Composed on 26 Rajab 1411 A.H./11 February 1991 A.D.

General Director of Research, Writing, and Translation
Fath Allah Ya Sin Jazar [signed]

Muhammad 'Umar Muhammad 'Umar [signed]

Seal of al-Azhar [stamped]
General Department for Research, Writing, and Translation

بسم الله الرحمن الرحيم

AL-AZHAR
ISLAMIC RESEARCH ACADEMY
GENERAL DEPARTMENT
For Research, Writing & Translation

الأزهـــــر
مجمـــع البحـــوث الاســـلامية
الادارة العـــــامة
للبحـوث والتـأليف والترجمـــة

السيد / نوح حايم كلر

عمان / الاردن

السلام عليكم ورحمة الله وبركاته   وبعد .

فبناء على ماجاء بطلبكم بشأن فحص الترجمة الانجليزية لكتـاب؛

(عمدة السالك وعدة الناسك) لاحمد بن النقيب في الفقه الشافعـى

مضافا اليه ملاحق لبعض العلماء في مادة الفقه والعقيدة والاخـــلاق

نفيد بأن الترجمة المذكورة مطابقة للاصل العربى وموافقة لمنهـج

وعقيدة أهل السنة والجماعة ولامانع من طبعها وتداولها .

وقد تم ختم صفحات الكتاب سالف الذكر بخاتم الادارة .

ونفعكم الله لخدمة العلم والديـن .

والسلام عليكم ورحمة الله وبركاته

٢٦ من رجب ١٤١١هـ

تحريرا فى ١١ من فبراير ١٩٩١ م

مدير عام
البحوث والتأليف والترجمة

فتح الله بن جـــزر

ABBREVIATIONS

A: .... comment by Sheikh 'Abd al-Wakil Durubi
Ar. ... Arabic
ca. .... approximately
cm. ... centimeters
d. ..... died
def: ... defined at another ruling
dis: ... discussed at another ruling
ibid. .. from the work previously cited
km. ... kilometers
lit. .... literally
mi. ... miles
N: .... comment by Sheikh Nuh 'Ali Salman
n: ..... remark by the translator
O: .... excerpt from the commentary of Sheikh 'Umar Barakat
par. .. paragraph
pl. .... plural
syn. ...a synonym for

BOOK A

SACRED KNOWLEDGE

CONTENTS:

a1.0   THE KNOWLEDGE OF GOOD AND BAD

a1.1   ('Abd al-Wahhab Khallaf:) There is no disagreement among the scholars of the Muslims that the source of legal rulings for all the acts of those who are morally responsible is Allah Most Glorious.

a1.2   The question arises, Is it possible for the mind alone, unaided by Allah's messengers and revealed scriptures, to know rulings, such that someone not reached by a prophet's invitation would be able through his own reason to know Allah's rule concerning his actions? Or is this impossible?

a1.3   The position of the Ash'aris, the followers of Abul Hasan Ash'ari, is that the mind is unable to know the rule of Allah about the acts of those morally responsible except by means of His messengers and inspired books.

For minds are in obvious disagreement about acts. Some minds find certain acts good, others find them bad. Moreover, one person can be of two minds about one and the same action. Caprice often wins out over the intellect, and considering something good or bad comes to be based on mere whim. So it cannot be said that an act which the mind deems good is therefore good in the eyes of Allah, its performance called for and its doer rewarded by Allah; or that whatever the mind feels to be bad is thus bad in the eyes of Allah, its nonperformance called for and its doer punished by Allah.

a1.4   The basic premise of this school of thought is that the *good* of the acts of those morally responsible is what the Lawgiver (syn. Allah or His messenger (Allah bless him and give him peace)) has indicated is good by permitting it or asking it be done. And the *bad* is what the Lawgiver has indicated is bad by asking it not be done. The good is not what reason considers good, nor the bad what reason considers bad. The measure

معرفة الحسن   a1.0
والقبح

a1.1   (عبـد الـوهـاب خلّاف:) لا خلاف بين علماء المسلمين في أن مصدر الأحكام الشرعية لجميع أفعال المكلفين هو الله سبحانه.

a1.2   وهـل يمكن العقـل أن يعرفها بنفسه من غير وسـاطـة رسل الله وكتبه بحيث أن من لم تبلغـه دعـوة رسـول يستطيـع أن يعرف حكم الله في أفعـاله بعقله أم لا يمكن؟

a1.3   مذهب الأشـاعـرة، أتباع أبي الحسن الأشعـري هو أنـه لا يمكن العقل أن يعرف حكم الله في أفعال المكلفين إلا بواسطة رسله وكتبه.

لأن العقول تختلف اخـتـلافـاً بيناً في الأفعـال، فبعض العقـول يستحسن بعض الأفعـال وبعضهـا يستقبحهـا، بل عقـل الـشـخص الـواحـد يختلف في الفعـل الـواحـد، وكثيراً ما يغلب الهـوى على العقـل فيكـون التحسين أو التقبيـح بنـاء على الهوى فعلى هذا لا يمكن أن يقال ما رآه العقـل حسنـاً فهـو حسن عنـد الله ومطلوب لله فعله، ويثـاب علـيـه من الله فاعله، ومـا رآه العقل قبيحاً فهو قبيح عند الله، ومطلوب لله تركه، ويعاقب من الله فاعله.

a1.4   وأسـاس هذا الـمـذهب أن الـحـسن من أفعـال المكلفين هو ما دل الشـارع على أنـه حسن بإبـاحـته أو طلب فعله، والقبيح هو ما دل الشـارع على أنه قبيـح بطلبه تركـه وليس الحسن ما رآه العقل حسنـاً ولا القبيـح ما رآه العقـل قبيحـاً. فمقيـاس الحسن والقبح في هذا

of good and bad, according to this school of thought, is the Sacred Law, not reason (dis: w3).

المذهب هو الشرع لا العقل [. . .].

a1.5   According to this school, a person is not morally obligated by Allah to do or refrain from anything unless the invitation of a prophet and what Allah has legislated have reached him (n: w4 discusses Islam's relation to previous prophets' laws). No one is rewarded for doing something or punished for refraining from or doing something until he knows by means of Allah's messengers what he is obliged to do or obliged to refrain from.

So whoever lives in such complete isolation that the summons of a prophet and his Sacred Law do not reach him is not morally responsible to Allah for anything and deserves neither reward nor punishment.

And those who lived in one of the intervals after the death of a prophet and before a new one had been sent were not responsible for anything and deserve neither reward nor punishment.

This view is confirmed by the word of Allah Most High,

"We do not punish until We send a messenger" (Koran 17:15).

('Ilm usul al-fiqh (y71), 96–98)

a1.5   وعلى هذا المذهب لا يكون الإنسان مكلفاً من الله بفعل شيء أو ترك شيء إلّا إذا بلغته دعوة رسول وما شرعه الله . ولا يثـاب أحد على فعل شيء ولا يعـاقب على ترك أو فعل ، إلا إذا علم من طريق رسـل الله ما يجب عليه فعله ومـا يجب عليه تركه .

فمن عاش في عزلة تامـة بحيث لم تبلغه دعوة رسول ولا شرعه فهو غير مكلف من الله بشيء ولا يستحق ثواباً ولا عقاباً . و[أهل الفترة وهم] من عاشوا بعد موت رسـول وقبـل مبعث رسـول غير مكلفين بشيء ولا يستحقون ثواباً ولا عقاباً .

ويؤيد هذا المذهب قوله سبحانه : ﴿وَمَا كُنَّا مُعَذِّبِينَ حَتَّىٰ نَبْعَثَ رَسُولاً﴾ [الإسراء : ١٥] . [محرّر من علم أصول الفقه : ٩٦ـ٩٨].

*

a2.0   THE SUPERIORITY OF SACRED KNOWLEDGE OVER DEVOTIONS

a2.0   ترجيح الاشتغـال بالعلم

a2.1   (Nawawi:) Allah Most High says:

(1) "Say, 'Are those who know and those who do not know equal?' " (Koran 39:9).

(2) "Only the knowledgeable of His slaves fear Allah" (Koran 35:28).

(3) "Allah raises those of you who believe and those who have been given knowledge whole degrees" (Koran 58:11).

a2.1   (الإمام النووي :)

ـ قال الله تعـالى : ﴿قُلْ هَلْ يَسْتَوِي الَّـذِينَ يَعْلَمُـونَ وَالَّـذِينَ لاَ يَعْلَمُـونَ﴾ [الزمر : ٩] .

ـ وقـال تعـالى : ﴿إِنَّمَـا يَخْشَى اللهَ مِنْ عِبَادِهِ العُلَمَاءُ﴾ [فاطر : ٢٨] .

ـ وقال تعالى : ﴿يَرْفَعِ اللهُ الَّذِينَ آمَنُوا مِنْكُمْ وَالَّـذِينَ أُوتُـوا العِلْمَ دَرَجَـاتٍ﴾ [المجادلة : ١١] :

a2.2   The Prophet (Allah bless him and give him peace) said:

(1) "Whoever Allah wishes well, He gives knowledge of religion."

(2) "The superiority of the learned Muslim over the devotee is as my superiority over the least of you."

Then the Prophet (Allah bless him and give him peace) said,

"Allah and His angels, the inhabitants of the heavens and the earth, the very ant in its anthill and the fish bless those who teach people what is good."

(3) "When a human being dies his work comes to an end except for three things: ongoing charity, knowledge benefitted from, or a pious son who prays for him."

(4) "A single learned Muslim is harder on the Devil than a thousand worshippers."

(5) "Whoever travels a path seeking knowledge Allah makes easy for him a path to paradise.
"Angels lower their wings for the seeker of knowledge out of pleasure in what he seeks.
"Those in the heavens and the earth, and the very fish in the water ask Allah to forgive the person endowed with Sacred Knowledge.
"The superiority of the learned Muslim over the devotee is like the superiority of the moon over all the stars.
"The learned are the heirs of the prophets. The prophets have not bequeathed dinar nor dirham, but have only left Sacred Knowledge, and whoever takes it has taken an enormous share."

(6) "He who calls others to guidance shall receive the like of the reward of those who follow him without this diminishing their own reward in the slightest. And he who calls others to misguidance shall bear the like of the sins of those who follow him without this diminishing their own sins."

(7) "He who goes forth to seek Sacred

[وعن معاوية رضي الله عنه
قال :] قال رسول الله ﷺ: «من يُرد الله به
خيراً يفقّههُ في الدين» [رواه البخاري
ومسلم] .

[وعن أبي أمامة الباهلي رضي الله عنه
قال : قال رسول الله ﷺ :] «فضل العالم
على العابد كفضلي على أدناكم» ثم قال
رسول الله ﷺ : «إن الله وملائكته وأهل
السماوات والأرض حتى النملة في
جحرها وحتى الحوت ليصلون على
معلمي الناس الخير» [رواه الترمذي وقال
حديث حسن] .

[وعن أبي هريرة رضي الله عنه أن
رسول الله ﷺ قال :] «إذا مات ابن آدم
انقطع عمله إلا من ثلاث صدقة جارية أو
علم ينتفع به أو ولد صالح يدعو له» [رواه
مسلم] .

[وعن ابن عباس رضي الله عنهما أن
رسول الله ﷺ قال :] «فقيه واحد أشد
على الشيطان من ألف عابد» [رواه
الترمذي] .

[وعن أبي الدرداء رضي الله عنه قال :
سمعت رسول الله ﷺ يقول :] «من سلك
طريقاً يلتمس فيه علماً سهّل الله له طريقاً
إلى الجنة ، وإن الملائكة لتضع أجنحتها
لطالب العلم رضاً بما يطلب ، وإن العالم
ليستغفر له من في السماوات ومن في
الأرض حتى الحيتان في الماء ، وفضل
العالم على العابد كفضل القمر على سائر
الكواكب ، وإن العلماء ورثة الأنبياء إن
الأنبياء لم يورّثوا ديناراً ولا درهماً وإنما
ورّثوا العلم فمن أخذه أخذ بحظ وافر»
[رواه أبو داود والترمذي وغيرهما] .

[وعن أبي هريرة رضي الله عنه قال :
قال رسول الله ﷺ :] «من دعا إلى هدى
كان له من الأجر مثل أجور من تبعه لا
ينقص ذلك من أجورهم شيئاً ، ومن دعا
إلى ضلالة كان عليه من الإثم مثل آثام من
تبعه لا ينقص ذلك من آثامهم شيئاً» [رواه
مسلم] .

[وعن أنس رضي الله عنه قال : قال
رسول الله ﷺ :] «من خرج في طلب

Knowledge is in the way of Allah [syn. *jihad*, def: o9] until he returns."

(8) "This world and what is in it are accursed [dis: w5] except for the remembrance of Allah, that which Allah loves, someone with Sacred Knowledge, or someone learning it."

a2.3 'Ali ibn Abi Talib (Allah be well pleased with him) said,

"The religious scholar is greater in reward than the fighter in the way of Allah who fasts the day and prays the night."

a2.4 Abu Darda' (Allah be well pleased with him) said,

"Teaching Sacred Knowledge for a brief time is better than spending a night in prayer."

a2.5 Yahya ibn Abi Kathir said,

"Studying Sacred Knowledge is a prayer."

a2.6 Sufyan al-Thawri and Shafi'i said,

"There is nothing after what is obligatory that is superior to seeking Sacred Knowledge."

a2.7 (Nawawi:) There are similar statements from whole groups of early Muslims I have not mentioned that are like those I have quoted, the upshot of which is that they concur that devoting one's time to Sacred Knowledge is better than devoting it to voluntary fasting or prayer, better than saying "Subhan Allah" (lit. "Exalted is Allah above any limitation"), or other supererogatory devotions.
     Among the proofs for this, besides the foregoing, is that:

(1) the benefit of Sacred Knowledge affects both its possessor and the Muslims, while the

العلم فهو في سبيل الله حتى يرجع» [رواه الترمذي].

[وعن أبي هريرة رضي الله عنه قال: سمعت رسول الله ﷺ يقول:] «الـدنـيـا ملعونةٌ ما فيها إلا ذكر الله وما والاه وعـالمـاً ومتعلماً» [رواه الـترمـذي وقال حديث حسن].

a2.3 وعـن علي رضي الله عنـه: «العـالم أعظم أجراً من الصـائم القائم الغازي في سبيل الله».

a2.4 وعن أبي الـدرداء: «مذاكرة العلم ساعة خير من قيام ليلة».

a2.5 وعـن يحيى بن أبي كثيـر: «دراسة العلم صلاة».

a2.6 وعـن سفـيـان الـثـوري والشـافعي: «ليس شيء بعـد الفرائض أفضل من طلب العلم».

a2.7 (الـنــووي:) وجـاء عـن جماعات من السلف ممن لم أذكره نحو ما ذكرته. والحاصل أنهم متفقون على أن الاشتغال بالعلم أفضل من الاشتغال بنوافـل الصوم والصـلاة والتسبيح ونحو ذلـك من نوافـل عبـادات البـدن. ومن دلائله سوى ما سبق: أن نفـع العلم يعم صاحبه والمسلمين، والنـوافـل المذكورة

above-mentioned supererogatory works are confined to oneself;

(2) Sacred Knowledge validates, so other acts of worship require it, though not vice versa;

(3) scholars are the heirs of the prophets, while devotees are not characterized as such;

(4) the devotee follows the scholar, being led by and imitating him in worship and other acts, obeying him being obligatory and not the other way around;

(5) the benefit and effect of Sacred Knowledge remain after its possesser departs, while supererogatory works cease with the death of their doer;

(6) knowledge is an attribute of Allah Most High;

(7) Sacred Knowledge, meaning the knowledge we are discussing, is a communal obligation (def: c3.2), and it is thus better than the supererogatory. The Imam of the Two Sanctuaries (A: Juwayni) says in his book *al-Ghiyathi* that "the communal obligation is superior to the personal obligation in that the person performing it fulfills the need of the Islamic Nation (Umma) and lifts the obligation from it, while the obligation of the individual is restricted to himself." And success is through Allah (*al-Majmu‘* (y108), 1.18–22).

*

a3.0   THE BLAMEWORTHINESS OF SEEKING SACRED KNOWLEDGE FOR OTHER THAN ALLAH

a3.1   (Nawawi:) Know that what we have mentioned about the merit of seeking Sacred Knowledge only applies to the seeker who thereby intends Allah Himself, not some end concerned with this world.

مختصة به .

ولأنّ العـلم مصحـح ، فغيـره من العبادات مفتقر إليه ولا ينعكس .

ولأن العلمـاء ورثة الأنبياء ولا يوصف المتعبدون بذلك .

ولأن العـابـد تابع للعالم مقتدٍ به مقلد له في عبـادتـه وغيـرها واجب عليه طاعته ولا ينعكس .

ولأن العلم تبقى فائـدتـه وأثـره بعـد صاحبه ، والنوافل تنقطع بموت صاحبها .

ولأن العلم صفة لله تعالى .

ولأن العلم فرض كفـايـة أعني العلم الـذي كلامنا فيه فكان أفضل من النافلة وقـد قال إمـام الحرمين [رحمـه الله] في كتـابـه الغيـاثي : «فرض الكفاية أفضل من فرض العين من حيث أن فاعله يسدّ مسدّ الأمة ويسقط الحرج عن الأمة ، وفرض العين قاصر عليه» . وبالله التوفيق [محرر من المجموع : ١/ ١٨ـ٢٢؛ بتقديم وتأخير] .

a3.0   ذم من أراد بطـلب العلم غير الله تعالى

a3.1   (النووي :) اعلم أن ما ذكرناه من الفضل في طلب العلم إنما هو في من طلبه مريداً به وجه الله تعالى ، لا لغرض من الـدنيـا . ومَن أراده لغـرض دنيوي

6

Whoever seeks it for a worldly aim such as money, leadership, rank, prestige, fame, people inclining towards him, defeating opponents in debate, or similar motive, is blameworthy.

(A: When the basic reason is Allah but other motives play a role, they diminish the merit in the proportion that they enter into it.)

a3.2 Allah Most High says:

(1) "Whoever wants to cultivate the afterlife We shall increase for him his tillage, while whoever wants to cultivate this world, we shall give him of it, but he will have no share in the next" (Koran 42:20).

(2) "Whoever wants the present world We hasten for him therein whatever We will, for whomever We want, and then consign him to hell, roasting in it condemned and rejected" (Koran 17:18).

(3) "Verily, your Lord is ready at ambush" (Koran 89:14).

(4) "They were not ordered except to worship Allah, making their religion sincere unto Him as pure monotheists" (Koran 98:5).

a3.3 The Prophet (Allah bless him and give him peace) said:

(1) "The first person judged on Resurrection Day will be a man martyred in battle.

"He'll be brought forth, Allah will reacquaint him with His blessings upon him and the man will acknowledge them, whereupon Allah will say, 'What have you done with them?' to which the man will respond, 'I fought to the death for you.'

"Allah will reply, 'You lie. You fought in order to be called a hero, and it has already been said.' Then he will be sentenced and dragged away on his face to be flung into the fire.

"Then a man will be brought forward who learned Sacred Knowledge, taught it to others, and who recited the Koran. Allah will remind him of His gifts to him and the man will acknowledge

قال الله تعالى : ﴿مَنْ كَانَ يُرِيدُ حَرْثَ الآخِرَةِ نَزِدْ لَهُ فِي حَرْثِهِ وَمَنْ كَانَ يُرِيدُ حَرْثَ الدُّنْيَا نُؤْتِهِ مِنْهَا وَمَا لَهُ فِي الآخِرَةِ مِنْ نَصِيبٍ﴾ [الشورى : ٢٠].

وقال تعالى : ﴿مَنْ كَانَ يُرِيدُ العَاجِلَةَ عَجَّلْنَا لَهُ فِيهَا مَا نَشَاءُ لِمَنْ نُرِيدُ ثُمَّ جَعَلْنَا لَهُ جَهَنَّمَ يَصْلَاهَا مَذْمُومَاً مَدْحُوراً﴾ [الإسراء : ١٨].

وقال تعالى : ﴿إِنَّ رَبَّكَ لَبِالْمِرْصَادِ﴾ [الفجر : ١٤].

وقال تعالى : ﴿وَمَا أُمِرُوا إِلَّا لِيَعْبُدُوا اللهَ مُخْلِصِينَ لَهُ الدِّينَ حُنَفَاءَ﴾ [البينة : ٥].

a3.3 [وروينا في صحيح مسلم عن أبي هريرة رضي الله عنه قال : سمعت رسول الله ﷺ يقول :] «إن أول الناس يقضى يوم القيامة عليه رجل استشهد فأتي به فعرَّفه نعمه فعرفها . قال : فما عملت فيها؟ قال : قاتلت فيك حتى استشهدت . قال : كذبت لكنك قاتلت ليقال جريء فقد قيل . ثم أمر به فسحب على وجهه حتى ألقي في النار . ورجل تعلّم العلم وعلّمه وقرأ القرآن فأتي به فعرَّفه نعمه فعرفها . قال : فما عملت فيها؟ قال :

them, and then Allah will say, 'What have you done with them?' The man will answer, 'I acquired Sacred Knowledge, taught it, and recited the Koran, for Your sake.'

"Allah will say, 'You lie. You learned so as to be called a scholar, and read the Koran so as to be called a reciter, and it has already been said.' Then he will be sentenced and dragged away on his face to be flung into the fire."

(2) "Anyone who seeks Sacred Knowledge to argue with fools, vie with scholars, or draw people's attention to himself, will take a place in hell."

(3) "The most severely tortured on Resurrection Day shall be the scholar who did not benefit from his knowledge."

a3.4   Sufyan al-Thawri said,

"No servant increased in knowledge and then in desire for the things of this world, save that he increased in distance from Allah."

(Ibid., 1.23–24)

*

a4.0   PERSONALLY OBLIGATORY KNOWLEDGE

a4.1   (Nawawi:) There are three categories of Sacred Knowledge. The first is the *personally obligatory* (fard al-'ayn, def: c2.1), which is a morally responsible individual's learning the knowledge that the obligatory acts he must perform cannot be accomplished without, such as how the ablution (wudu) and prayer are done and so forth.

Its obligatory character is how groups of scholars have interpreted the hadith in the *Musnad* of Abu Ya'la al-Mawsuli, from Anas, who relates that the Prophet (Allah bless him and give him peace) said,

تعلَّمت العلم وعلّمتـه وقـرأت فيـك القرآن . قال : كذبت ولكنـك تعلمت ليقـال عالم وقرأت القرآن ليقـال قارىء فقـد قيـل . ثم أمـر به فسحب على وجهه حتى ألقي في النار» .

[وعن أنس وحـذيفـة قالا : قال رسول الله ﷺ :] «مـن طلب الـعلم ليمـاريَ به السفهـاء ويكـاثر به العلماء أو يصرف به وجوه النـاس إليه فليتبوأ مقعده من النار» [رواه الترمذي] .

[وعـن أبي هريـرة رضي الله عنـه أن رسول الله ﷺ قال :] «أشـد النـاس عذاباً يوم القيامة عالم لا ينتفع بعلمه» .

a3.4   وعن سفيـان «مـا ازداد عبـد علمـاً فازداد في الـدنيـا رغبة إلا ازداد من الله بُعـداً» [محـررٌ من المرجع المذكور : ١/ ٢٣-٢٤] .

a4.0   العلم الذي هو فرض عين

a4.1   (النـووي:) أقسـام العلم الشرعي ثلاثـة : الأول فرض العين وهو تعلُم المكلف مالا يتأدى الـواجب الـذي تعين عليـه إلا به ككيفيـة الـوضوء والصلاة ونحوهما وعليه حمل جماعات الحـديث المـروي في مسند أبي يعلى الموصلي عن أنس عن النبي ﷺ : «طلب

"Seeking knowledge is an obligation upon every Muslim."

The meaning of this hadith, though the hadith itself is not well authenticated (A: being *weak* (dis: p9.5)), is true.

العلم فريضة على كل مسلم». وهـذا الحديث وإن لم يكن ثابتاً فمعناه صحيح.

a4.2   As for the basic obligation of Islam, and what relates to tenets of faith, it is adequate for one to believe in everything brought by the Messenger of Allah (Allah bless him and give him peace) and to credit it with absolute conviction free of any doubt. Whoever does this is not obliged to learn the evidences of the scholastic theologians. The Prophet (Allah bless him and give him peace) did not require of anyone anything but what we have just mentioned, nor did the first four caliphs, the other prophetic Companions, nor others of the early Muslim community who came after them.

Rather, what befits the common people and vast majority of those learning or possessing Sacred Knowledge is to refrain from discussing the subtleties of scholastic theology, lest corruption difficult to eliminate find its way into their basic religious convictions. Rather, it is fitter for them to confine themselves to contentment with the above-mentioned absolute certainty.

Our Imam Shafi'i (Allah Most High have mercy on him) went to the greatest possible lengths in asserting that engaging in scholastic theology is forbidden. (A: What he meant thereby was the heretical scholastic theology that proliferated in his time and put rationalistic theories ahead of the Koran and sunna, not the science of theology ('ilm al-tawhid) by which Ash'ari and Maturidi scholars (dis: x47) have clarified and detailed the tenets of faith of Sunni Islam, which is an important part of the Islamic sciences.) He insistently emphasized its unlawfulness, the severity of the punishment awaiting those who engage in it, the disgrace of doing it, and the enormity of the sin therein by saying,

"For a servant to meet Allah with any other sin than idolatry (shirk) is better than to meet Him guilty of anything of scholastic theology."

a4.2   وأمـا أصل واجب الإسلام وما يتعلق بالعقائد فيكفي فيه التصديق بكل ما جاء به رسول الله ﷺ واعتقاده اعتقاداً جازماً سليماً من كل شك. ولا يتعين على من حصل له هذا تعلم أدلة المتكلمين [...] فإن النبي ﷺ لم يطالب أحـداً بشيء سوى ما ذكرناه، وكذلك الخلفاء الراشدون ومن سواهم من الصحابة فمن بعـدهم من الصـدر الأول. بل الصـواب للعـوام وجمـاهير المتفقهين والفقهاء الكف عن الخـوض في دقـائق الكـلام مخافة من اختلال يتطرق إلى عقائدهم يصعب عليهم إخراجه. بل الصواب لهم الاقتصـار على ما ذكـرناه من الاكتفاء بالتصـديق الجـازم [وقـد نص على هذه الجملة جمـاعـات من حذاق أصحـابنا وغيـرهم] وقـد بالغ إمامنا الشافعي رحمه الله تعـالى في تحريم الاشتغـال بعلم الكـلام أشـد المبالغة وأطنب في تحريمه وتغليـظ العقوبـة لمتعـاطيه وتقبيح فعله وتعظيم الإثم فيـه فقـال: «لأن يلقى الله العبد بكل ذنب ما خلا الشرك خير من أن يلقاه بشيء من الكـلام». وألفـاظـه بهذا

His other statements expressing the same meaning are numerous and well known.

But if someone has doubts (Allah be our refuge) about any of the tenets of faith in which belief is obligatory (def: books u and v), and his doubt cannot be eliminated except by learning one of the theologians' proofs, then it is obligatory for him to learn it in order to remove the doubt and acquire the belief in question.

المعنى كثيرة مشهورة .

ولو تشكك والعباذ بالله في شيء من أصول العقائد مما لا بد من اعتقاده ولم يزل شكه إلا بتعلم دليل من أدلة المتكلمين وجب تعلم ذلك لإزالة الشك وتحصيل ذلك الأصل .

a4.3   Scholars disagree about the Koranic verses and hadiths that deal with the attributes of Allah (n: such as His 'hand' (Koran 48:10), His 'eyes' (52:48), or His 'nearness' (50:16)) as to whether they should be discussed in terms of a particular *figurative interpretation* (ta'wil, def: w6) or not.

Some say that they should be figuratively interpreted as befits them (n: interpreting His 'hand,' for example, as an allusion to His omnipotence). And this is the more well known of the two positions of the scholastic theologians.

Others say that such verses should not be given a definitive interpretation, but rather their meaning should not be discussed, and the knowledge of them should be consigned to Allah Most High, while at the same time believing in the transcendence of Allah Most High, and that the characteristics of created things do not apply to Him. For example, it should be said we believe that

"the All-merciful is 'established' [Ar. istawa, dis: v1.3] on the Throne" (Koran 20:5),

but we do not know the reality of the meaning of that, nor what is intended thereby, though we believe of Allah Most High that

"there is nothing whatsoever like unto Him" (Koran 42:11),

and that He is above indwelling in created things (hulul, dis: w7), or having the characteristics of temporal, contingent existence (huduth, dis: w8). And this is the path of the early Muslims, or the vast majority of them, and is the safest, for a person is not required to enter into discussions about

a4.3   اختلفوا في آيات الصفات وأخبارها هل يخاض فيها بالتأويل أم لا فقال قائلون تتأول على ما يليق بها وهذا أشهر المذهبين للمتكلمين . وقال آخرون لا تتأول بل يمسك عن الكلام في معناها ويوكل علمها إلى الله تعالى ويعتقد مع ذلك تنزيه الله تعالى وانتفاء صفات الحادث عنه . فيقال مثلاً نؤمن بأن ﴿الرَّحْمَنُ عَلَى الْعَرْشِ اسْتَوَى﴾ ولا نعلم حقيقة معنى ذلك والمراد به مع أنّا نعتقد أن الله تعالى ﴿لَيْسَ كَمِثْلِهِ شَيْءٌ﴾ وأنه منزه عن الحلول وسمات الحدوث . وهذه طريقة السلف أو جماهيرهم وهي أسلم إذ لا يطالب الإنسان بالخوض في

this. When one believes in Allah's transcendence above created things, there is no need for debate on it, or for taking risks over what there is neither pressing necessity nor even any real call for.

But if the need arises for definitive interpretations to refute someone making unlawful innovations and the like, then the learned may supply them, and this is how we should understand what has come down to us from scholars in this field. And Allah knows best.

ذلك . فإذا اعتقد التنزيه فلا حاجة إلى الخـوض في ذلك والمخـاطـرة فيمـا لا ضرورة بل لا حاجة إليه .

فإن دعت الحـاجـة إلى التأويـل لرد مبتدع ونحوه تأولـوا حينئـذ ، وعلى هذا يحمل ما جاء عن العلماء في هذه ، والله أعلم .

a4.4   A person is not obliged to learn how to perform ablution, the prayer, and so forth, until the act itself is obligatory for him.

As for trade, marriage, and so forth, of things not in themselves obligatory, the Imam of the Two Sanctuaries (A: Juwayni), Ghazali, and others say that learning their means and conditions is personally obligatory for anyone who wants to do them.

It has also been said that one should not call this knowledge "personally obligatory," but rather say, "It is unlawful to undertake them until one knows the conditions for their legal validity." And this expression is more accurate.

a4.4   لا يلزم الإنسـان تعلَّمُ كيفيـة الوضوء والصلاة وشبههما إلا بعد وجوب ذلك الشيء .

أمـا البيع والنكـاح وشبههمـا ممـا لا يجب أصله فقـال إمـام الحرمين والغزالي وغيرهما يتعين على من أراده تعلم كيفيته وشـرطه . وقيـل لا يقـال يتعين بل يقـال يحرم الإقدام عليه إلا بعد معرفة شرطه . وهذه العبارة أصح .

a4.5   It is obligatory for one to know what is permissible and what is unlawful of food, drink, clothing, and so forth, of things one is unlikely to be able to do without. And likewise for the rulings on treatment of women if one has a wife.

a4.5   تلزمـه معرفة ما يحل وما يحرم من المأكـول والمشـروب والملبـوس ونحوها مما لا غنى له عنه غالباً . وكذلك أحكام عشرة النساء إن كانت له زوجة .

a4.6   Shafi'i and colleagues (Allah have mercy on them) say that fathers and mothers must teach their children what will be obligatory for them after puberty. The guardian must teach the child about purification, prayer, fasting, and so forth; and that fornication, sodomy, theft, drinking, lying, slander, and the like are unlawful; and that he acquires moral responsibility at puberty and what this entails.

It has been said that this education is merely recommended, but in fact it is obligatory, as the plain content of its scriptural basis (n: mentioned below) shows. Just as it is mandatory for a guardian to wisely manage his charge's property,

a4.6   قال الـشـافعي والأصحـاب رحمهم الله على الآبـاء والأمهـات تعليم أولادهم الصغـار مـا سيتعين عليهم بعـد البلوغ . فيعلمه الـولي الطهـارة والصلاة والصـوم ونحوهـا ويعـرّفه تحريم الزنا واللواط والسرقة وشرب المسكر والكذب والغيبة وشبهها ، ويعرّفه أن بالبلوغ يدخل في التكليف ويعرّفه ما يلغ به . وقيل هذا التعليم مستحب والصحيـح وجوبـه وهو ظاهـر نصـه . وكمـا يجب عليـه النظر في

this is even more important. The merely recommended is what exceeds this, such as teaching him the Koran, Sacred Law, etiquette, and teaching him what he needs to earn a living.

The evidence for the obligation of teaching a young child is the word of Allah Mighty and Majestic,

"O you who believe, protect yourselves and families from a fire" (Koran 66:6).

'Ali ibn Abi Talib (Allah be well pleased with him), Mujahid, and Qatada say it means, "Teach them that with which they can save themselves from hell."

a4.7   As for knowledge of the heart, meaning familiarity with the illnesses of the heart such as envy, pride, and the like (dis: books p, r, and s), Ghazali has said that knowledge of their definitions, causes, remedy, and treatment is personally obligatory.

(A: And this is what Ghazali meant when he said that Sufism (Tasawwuf, dis: w9) is personally obligatory for every Muslim. He did not mean that taking a *way* (tariqa) and a sheikh are obligatory, but rather the elimination of unlawful inner traits, which one could conceivably accomplish through the companionship of a single sincere brother.)

Others hold that if the morally responsible individual is endowed with a heart free of all these unlawful diseases, it suffices him, and he is not obliged to learn what will cure them. But if not safe from them, he must reflect: if he can purify his heart from them without instruction then he must purify it, just as he must shun fornication and the like without learning the evidence proving he must. But if he cannot rid himself of these unlawful traits except through learning the above-mentioned knowledge, then he is personally obliged to. And Allah knows best (*al-Majmu'* (y108), 1.24–26).

ماله وهذا أولى . وإنما المستحب ما زاد على هذا من تعليم القرآن وفقه وأدب ، ويعرِّفه ما يصلح به معاشه .

ودليل وجوب تعليم الولد الصغير [والمملوك] قول الله عز وجل : ﴿يا أيها الذين آمنوا قوا أنفسكم وأهليكم ناراً﴾ [التحريم : ٦] .

قال علي بن أبي طالب رضي الله عنه ومجاهد وقتادة معناه علموهم ما ينجُون به من النار .

a4.7   أما علم القلب وهو معرفة أمراض القلب كالحسد والعجب وشبهها فقال الغزالي : معرفة حدودها وأسبابها وطبها وعلاجها فرض عين .

وقال غيره : إن رُزق المكلف قلباً سليماً من هذه الأمراض المحرمة كفاه ذلك ولا يلزمه تعلم دوائها . وإن لم يسلم نظر : إن تمكن من تطهير قلبه من ذلك بلا تعلم لزمه التطهير كما يلزمه ترك الزنا ونحوه من غير تعلم أدلة الترك . وإن لم يتمكن من الترك إلا بتعلُّم العلم المذكور تعيَّن حينئذ والله أعلم [محرر من المجموع : ١/ ٢٤–٢٦] .

*

a5.0 COMMUNALLY OBLIGATORY KNOWLEDGE

a5.1 (Nawawi:) The second category (n: of Sacred Knowledge) is what is *communally obligatory* (fard al-kifaya, def: c3.2), namely the attainment of those Sacred Sciences which people cannot do without in practicing their religion, such as memorizing the Koran and hadith, their ancillary disciplines, methodological principles, Sacred Law, grammar, lexicology, declension, knowledge of hadith transmitters, and of *scholarly consensus* (ijma', def: b7) and nonconsensus.

a5.2 As for learning which is not Sacred Knowledge but is required to sustain worldly existence, such as medicine and mathematics, it too is a communal obligation (ibid., 1.26).

*

a6.0 RECOMMENDED KNOWLEDGE

a6.1 (Nawawi:) The third category is the *supererogatory* (def: c4.2), such as in-depth research into the bases of evidences, and elaboration beyond the amount required by the communal obligation, or such as an ordinary Muslim learning the details of nonobligatory acts of worship for the purpose of performing them; though not the work of scholars in distinguishing the obligatory from the nonobligatory, which is a communal obligation in respect to them. And Allah knows best (ibid., 1.27).

*

a7.0 SUBJECTS THAT ARE NOT SACRED KNOWLEDGE

a7.1 (Nawawi:) Having mentioned the categories of Sacred Knowledge, the subjects it

a5.0 العلم الذي هو فرض كفاية

a5.1 (النووي:) القسم الثاني فرض الكفاية وهو: تحصيل ما لا بد للناس منه في إقامة دينهم من العلوم الشرعية كحفظ القرآن والأحاديث وعلومها والأصول والفقه والنحو واللغة والتصريف ومعرفة رواة الحديث والإجماع والخلاف.

a5.2 وأما ما ليس علماً شرعياً ويحتاج إليه في قوام أمر الدنيا كالطب والحساب ففرض كفاية أيضاً [نقل من المرجع المذكور: ٢٦/١].

a6.0 العلم المندوب

a6.1 (النووي) القسم الثالث النفل وهو كالتبحر في أصول الأدلة والإمعان فيما وراء القدر الذي يحصل به فرض الكفاية، وكتعلم العامي نوافل العبادات لغرض العمل، لا ما يقوم به العلماء من تمييز الفرض من النفل، فإنّ ذلك فرض كفاية في حقهم والله أعلم [نقل من المرجع المذكور: ٢٧/١].

a7.0 العلم غير الشرعي

a7.1 (النووي:) قد ذكرنا أقسام العلم الشرعي. ومن العلوم الخارجة عنه

excludes are those that are unlawful, offensive, or permissible.

ما هو محرم أو مكروه أو مباح .

a7.2   *Unlawful* knowledge includes:

(1)   learning sorcery (dis: p3), since according to the most reliable position, it is unlawful, as the vast majority of scholars have decisively stated;

(2)   philosophy (dis: w10);

(3)   magic (sha'badha, meaning sleight of hand, etc.);

(4)   astrology (dis: p41);

(5)   the sciences of the materialists (dis: w11);

(6)   and anything that is a means to create doubts (n: in eternal truths). Such things vary in their degree of unlawfulness.

a7.2   فالمحرم كتعلم السحر . فإنه حرام على المـذهب الصحيح وبـه قطع الجمهور [. . .] وكـالفلسفـة والشعبذة والتنجيم وعلوم الطبـائعيين وكـل ما كان سببـاً لإثـارة الشكوك . ويتفاوت في التحريم .

a7.3   *Offensive* knowledge includes such things as post-classical poetry which contains romance and uselessness.

a7.3   والمكـروه كأشعـار المولـدين التي فيها الغزل والبطالة .

a7.4   *Permissible* knowledge includes post-classical poetry which does not contain stupidity or anything that is offensive, incites to evil, hinders from good; nor yet that which urges one to do good or helps one to do it (n: as the latter would be recommended) (ibid., 1.27).

a7.4   والمبـاح كأشعـار المـولـدين التي ليس فيهـا سخف ولا شيء مما يكره ولا ما ينشـط إلى الشــر ولا ما يثبط عن الخير ولا ما يحث على خير أو يستعان به عليه [نقل من المرجع المذكور: ١ / ٢٧] .

*

BOOK B

THE VALIDITY OF FOLLOWING
QUALIFIED SCHOLARSHIP

CONTENTS:

b1.0 INTRODUCTION	المقدمة b1.0
b1.1 (Muhammad Sa'id Buti:) What is the proof that it is legally valid and even obligatory to accept the authority of qualified scholarship (taq-	b1.1 (محمـد سعيـد البــوطي:) [. . .] فمـا الدليل على مشروعية التقليد

15

lid) when one is not capable of issuing expert legal opinion (ijtihad) on matters of Sacred Law? There are several aspects to it (n: discussed in the sections that follow) (*al-Lamadhhabiyya akhtar bid'a tuhaddidu al-shari'a al-Islamiyya* (y33), 70).

وجـوبه عند عدم التمكن من الاجتهاد؟ الـدليـل من وجـوه [نقـل من الـلامذهبية أخطر بدعة تهدد الشريعة الإسلامية : . [٧٠

b1.2   (n:) For the key term *qualified to issue expert legal opinion* (Ar. *mujtahid*, this ability being *ijtihad*), please turn to book o and read o22.1(d), the qualifications of an Islamic judge (qadi). The difference between the qualifications for the Imam of a school and those for a judge or a mufti is that the former's competence in giving opinion is absolute, extending to all subject matters in the Sacred Law, while the competence of the judge or mufti is limited respectively to judging court cases or to applying his Imam's *ijtihad* to particular questions.

No age of history is totally lacking people who are competent in *ijtihad* on particular questions which are new, and this is an important aspect of Sacred Law, to provide solutions to new ethical problems by means of sound Islamic legal methodology in applying the Koranic and hadith primary texts. But while in this specific sense the door of *ijtihad* is not and cannot be closed, Islamic scholarship has not accepted anyone's claims to absolute *ijtihad* since Imams Abu Hanifa, Malik, Shafi'i, and Ahmad. If one studies the intellectual legacy of these men under scholars who have a working familiarity with it, it is not difficult to see why.

As for those who decry "hidebound conservatism" and would open the gate of *ijtihad* for themselves while lacking or possibly not even knowing the necessary qualifications, if such people have not studied the rulings of a particular school and the relation between these rulings, the Koranic and hadith primary texts, and the school's methodological principles, they do not know how *ijtihad* works from an observer's standpoint, let alone how to employ it. To ask them, for example, which of two equally authenticated primary texts that conflict on a legal question should be given precedence, and why, is like asking an aspiring drafting student for the particulars of designing a suspension bridge. Answers may be forthcoming, but they will not be the same as those one could get from a qualified contractor. To urge that a *mujtahid* is not divinely protected from error (ma'sum) is as of little relevance to his work as the fact that a major physicist is not divinely protected from simple errors in calculus; the probability of finding them in his published work is virtually negligible. Regarding other, long-dead schools, such as the Zahiriyya, the difference between their work and that of the four living schools is firstly one of quality, as their positions and evidence have not been reexamined and upgraded by succeeding generations of first-rank scholars like those of the four schools (dis: w12), and secondly the lack of verification of the actual positions of their *mujtahid*s through reliable chains of transmitters, as described below at b7.6.

*

b2.0 THE KORANIC EVIDENCE FOR FOLLOWING SCHOLARS	الأدلة القرآنية b2.0

b2.1   (Muhammad Sa'id Buti:) The first aspect of it is the word of Allah the Majestic,

"Ask those who recall if you know not" (Koran 16:43).

By consensus of all scholars (ijma', def: b7), this verse is an imperative for someone who does not know a ruling in Sacred Law or the evidence for it to follow someone who does. Virtually all scholars of fundamentals of Islamic law have made this verse their principle evidence that it is obligatory for the ordinary person to follow the scholar who is a *mujtahid*.

b2.1   (محمـــد سعيـــد البـــوطي :) الـوجـه الأول قوله جل جلاله : ﴿فَاسْأَلُوا أَهْلَ الذِّكْرِ إِنْ كُنْتُمْ لَا تَعْلَمُونَ﴾ [النحل : ٤٣].

أجمع العلماء على أن الآية أمر لمن لا يعلـم الـحكـم ولا دليله باتبـاع من يعلم ذلك . وقد جعل عامة علماء الأصول هذه الآيـة عمـدتهم الأولى في أن على العامي تقليد العالم المجتهد.

b2.2   Similar to the above verse in being evidence for this is the word of Allah Most High:

"Not all of the believers should go to fight. Of every section of them, why does not one part alone go forth, that the rest may gain knowledge of the religion to admonish their people when they return, that haply they may take warning" (Koran 9:122).

Allah Most High prohibited the people to go out altogether in military expeditions and jihad, and ordered a segment of them to engage solely in becoming knowledgeable in the religion of Allah, so that when their brothers returned to them, they would find someone qualified to give them legal opinion on the lawful and unlawful and to explain the rule of Allah the Glorious and Exalted (ibid., 71).

b2.2   ومثـــل هذه الآيــة في نفس الـدلالة قوله تعالى : ﴿وَمَا كَانَ الْمُؤْمِنُونَ لِيَنْفِرُوا كَافَّةً ، فَلَوْلَا نَفَرَ مِنْ كُلِّ فِرْقَةٍ مِنْهُمْ طَائِفَةٌ لِيَتَفَقَّهُوا فِي الدِّينِ وَلِيُنْذِرُوا قَوْمَهُمْ إِذَا رَجَعُوا إِلَيْهِمْ لَعَلَّهُمْ يَحْذَرُونَ﴾ [التوبة : ١٢٢].

فقد نهى الله تعالى أن ينفر الناس كافة للغـزو والجهـاد ، وأمـر ببقاء طائفة منهم يتفرغون للتفقه في دين الله حتى إذا عاد إخوانهم إليهم وجدوا فيهم من يفتيهم في أمـر الـحلال والحرام وبيان حكم الله عز وجل [نقل من المرجع المذكور : ٧١].

*

b3.0 THE PRACTICE OF THE PROPHETIC COMPANIONS (SAHABA)	طريـــق الصحــابـــة b3.0 رضوان الله عليهم

b3.1   (Muhammad Sa'id Buti:) A second aspect is the consensus of scholars that the Companions

b3.1   (محمـــد سعيـــد البـــوطي :) الـوجـه الثاني ما يدل عليه الإجماع من أن

of the Prophet (Ar. Sahaba, anyone who personally met the Prophet (Allah bless him and give him
peace) and died while believing in Islam) were at
various levels of knowledge in religion; not all of
them were capable of giving formal legal opinion
(fatwa), as Ibn Khaldun has noted, nor was the
religion taken from all of them.

أصحاب رسول الله ﷺ كانوا يتفاوتون
في العلم ولم يكن جميعهم أهل فتيا
ـ كما قال ابن خلدون ـ ولا كان الدين
يؤخذ عن جميعهم .

b3.2   Rather, there were those of them capable
of legal opinion and *ijtihad*, and these were a small
minority in relation to the rest, and there were
those of them who sought legal opinion and followed others therein, and these were the vast
majority of them.

(n: Suyuti, in *Tadrib al-rawi*, quotes Ibn
Hazm's report that most of the Companions' legal
opinions came from only seven of them: 'Umar,
'Ali, Ibn Mas'ud, Ibn 'Umar, Ibn 'Abbas, Zayd
ibn Thabit, and 'A'isha; and this was from
thousands of the Companions (*Tadrib al-rawi fi
sharh Taqrib al-Nawawi* (y109), 2.219).)

b3.2   بل كان فيهم المفتي
المجتهد، وهم قلة بالنسبة لسائرهم،
وفيهم المستفتي المقلد وهم الكثرة
الغالبة فيهم . (ت: نقل السيوطي في
تدريب الراوي عن ابن حزم أن أكثر
فتاوى الصحابة صدرت عن سبعة : عمر
وعلي وابن مسعود وابن عمر وابن عباس
وزيد بن ثابت وعائشة . وذلك من آلاف
الصحابة [تدريب الراوي : ٢/ ٢١٩])).

b3.3   Nor did the individual Companion giving
a legal opinion necessarily mention the evidence
for it to the person who had asked about it. Al-
Amidi notes in his book *al-Ihkam*: "As for scholarly consensus [ijma', dis: b7.2], it is that ordinary
people in the times of the Companions and those
who immediately followed them, before there
were dissenters, used to seek the opinion of *mujtahid*s and would follow them in rules of
Sacred Law.

"The learned among them would unhesitat-
ingly answer their questions without alluding to
mention of evidence. No one censured them for
doing this; a fact that establishes scholarly consensus on the absolute permissibility of the ordinary
person following one capable of *ijtihad*."

b3.3   ولم يكن المفتي من الصحابة
يلتزم مع ذكر الحكم بيان دليله
للمستفتي .
قال الآمدي في كتابه الإحكام «وأما
الإجماع فهو أنّه لم تزل العامة في زمن
الصحابة والتابعين قبل حدوث
المخالفين يستفتون المجتهدين ،
ويتبعونهم في الأحكام الشرعية والعلماء
منهم يبادرون إلى إجابة سؤالهم من غير
إشارة إلى ذكر الدليل . ولا ينهونهم عن
ذلك من غير نكير. فكان إجماعاً على
جواز اتباع العامي للمجتهد مطلقاً» .

b3.4   The Prophet (Allah bless him and give
him peace) used to dispatch the most knowledgeable of the Companions to places whose inhabitants knew nothing more of Islam than its five
pillars. The latter would follow the person sent to
them in everything he gave his judgement upon
and had them do, of works, acts of worship, deal-

b3.4   وقد كان الرسول ﷺ يبعث
الفقيه من الصحابة إلى المكان الذي لا
يعلم سكانه من الإسلام إلا عقيدته
والاعتقاد بأركانه ، فيتبعونه بكل ما يفتيهم
به ويحملهم عليه من الأعمال والعبادات

ing with one another, and all matters of the lawful and unlawful.

Sometimes such a person would come across a question on which he could find no evidence in the Koran or sunna, and he would use his own personal legal reasoning and furnish them an answer in light of it, and they would follow him therein.

b3.5   As for the era of those who came after them (Ar. tabi'in, those who had personally learned from one or more of the Companions but not the Prophet himself (Allah bless him and give him peace)), the scope of legal reasoning had expanded, and the Muslims of this time followed the same course as had the Companions of the Prophet (Allah bless him and give him peace), except that the legal efforts were represented by the two main schools of thought, that of *juridical opinion* (ra'y) and that of *hadith* (n: the former in Iraq, the latter in Medina) because of the methodological factors we previously mentioned when we quoted Ibn Khaldun....

There were sometimes discussions and sharp disputes between leading representatives of the two schools, but the ordinary people and learners not at the main figures' level of understanding were unconcerned with this disagreement, and followed whomever they wanted or whomever was near to them without anyone censuring them for this (*al-Lamadhhabiyya akhtar bid'a tuhaddidu al-shari'a al-Islamiyya* (y33), 71–73).

*

b4.0   THE RATIONAL EVIDENCE
FOR FOLLOWING SPECIALISTS

b4.1   (Muhammad Sa'id Buti:) A third aspect is the obvious rational evidence, which we express in the words of Sheikh 'Abdullah Diraz, who says: "The logical proof is that, assuming that a person does not have the qualifications for *ijtihad*, when an instance of a particular religious ruling arises, he will either not worship by any means at all, which all concur is impermissible, or, if he wor-

والمعاملات وعامة شؤون الحلال والحرام .

وربما اعترضه أمر لم يجد فيه دليلاً من كتاب ولا سنة فيجتهد فيه ويفتيهم بما هداه إليه اجتهاده فيقلدونه في ذلك .

b3.5   أما في عهد التابعين فقد اتسعت دائرة الاجتهاد ، وسلك المسلمون في هذا العهد نفس الطريق الذي سلكه أصحاب رسول الله ﷺ . إلّا أنّ الاجتهاد تمثـل في مذهبين رئيسيين هما مذهب الـرأي والحـديث بسبب العوامل الاجتهادية التي ذكرناها عندما نقلنا كلام ابن خلدون . . .

وقد كان بين أقطاب هذين المذهبين مناقشـات وخصومـات حادة في بعض الأحيان ولكن العـوام والمتعلمين ممن كانـوا دونـهم في العلم والفقـه لم يكن يعنيهم شأن تلك الخصـومة إذ كانـوا يقلدون من شاءوا أو من كان قريباً منهم دون أي إنكار من أحد عليهم [محرّر من اللامـذهبية أخطر بدعة تهدد الشريعة الإسلامية : ٧١ ـ ٧٣] .

b4.0   الدليل العقلي

b4.1   (محمـد سعيـد البـوطي :) الـوجه الثـالث هو الدليل العقلي البين ، ونعبر عنه بما قاله العلامة الشيخ عبد الله دراز «[. . .] والدليل المعقول هو أن من لم يكن عنده أهلية الاجتهاد إذا حدثت به حادثة فرعية ، فإمـا أن لا يكون متعبـداً بشيء أصلاً ، وهو خلاف الإجماع ، وإن

ships by means of something, it will either be by examining the proof that verifies the ruling or by following a competent authority.

"The former is inadmissible because it would lead, in respect to him and all others like him, to in-depth examination of the evidences for all such instances, preoccupation with which would obviate the earning of livelihoods, disrupting trades and occupations, ruining the world by neglect of tillage and offspring, and preventing anyone's following another's *ijtihad*, placing everyone under the most extreme hardship. The sole remaining alternative is to follow another, which is the means through which one must worship in such a case" (ibid., 73).

*

b5.0   THE OBLIGATORINESS OF FOLLOWING QUALIFIED SCHOLARSHIP

b5.1   (Muhammad Sa'id Buti:) Because scholars accept the evidence from Koran, sunna, and reason as complete and intersubstantiative that the ordinary person or learned one not at the level of textual deduction and *ijtihad* is not entitled but to follow a qualified *mujtahid* who has a comprehensive grasp of the evidence—they say that a formal legal opinion (fatwa) from a *mujtahid* is in relation to the ordinary person just as a proof from the Koran and sunna is in relation to the *mujtahid*. For the Koran, just as it obligates the scholar thoroughly versed in it to hold to its evidences and proofs, also obligates (n: in the verse quoted above at b2.1) the uninformed person to adhere to the formal legal opinion of the scholar and his *ijtihad* (ibid., 73).

*

b6.0   WHY QUALIFIED SCHOLARS DIFFER ON LEGAL QUESTIONS

b6.1   (Salih Mu'adhdhin:) Muslims of the Sunna and Community are in agreement that we

كان متعبداً بشيء فإما بالنظر في الدليل المثبت للحكم أو بالتقليد.

والأول ممتنع لأن ذلك مما يفضي في حقه وحق الخلق أجمع إلى النظر في أدلة الحوادث والاشتغال عن المعايش وتعطيل الحرف والصناعات وخراب الدنيا بتعطيل الحرث والنسل ورفع التقليد رأساً وهو منتهى الحرج فلم يبق إلا التقليد وأنه هو المتعبد به عند ذلك الفرض». [نقل من المرجع المذكور: ٧٣].

وجوب التقليد   b5.0

b5.1   (محمد سعيد البوطي :) ولما رأى العلماء تكامل كل من دليل الكتاب والسنة والعقل على أن العامي أو العالم الذي لم يبلغ درجة الاستنباط والاجتهاد ليس له إلا أن يقلد مجتهداً متبصراً بالدليل ـ قالوا إن فتوى المجتهد بالنسبة للعامي مثل دليل الكتاب والسنة بالنسبة للمجتهد لأن القرآن كما يلزم العالم به التمسك بدلائله وبراهينه ، فقد ألزم الجاهل بالتمسك بفتوى العالم واجتهاده [نقل من المرجع المذكور: ٧٣].

b6.0   لمحة موجزة عن سبب اختلاف الفقهاء

b6.1   (صالح مؤذن:) إن من المجمع عليه عند جمهور أهل السنة

have arrived at all the rulings of Sacred Law through evidence that is either of *unquestionably established transmission* (qat'i al-wurud) or *probabilistically established transmission* (zanni al-wurud).

The suras of the Koran, all of its verses, and those hadiths which have reached us by so many channels of transmission that belief in them is obligatory (mutawatir, def: o22.1(d(II))) are all of unquestionably established transmission, since they have reached us by numerous means, by generation from generation, whole groups from whole groups, such that it is impossible that the various channels could all have conspired to fabricate them.

As for the evidentiary character of these texts, regardless whether they are of unquestionably or probabilistically established transmission, they are of two types.

The first type, *unquestionable as evidence* (qat'i al-dalala), is a plain text that does not admit of more than one meaning, which no mind can interpret beyond its one meaning, and which there is no possibility to construe in terms of other than its apparent sense. This type includes Koranic verses that deal with fundamental tenets of faith in the oneness of Allah, the prayer, zakat, and fasting; in none of which is there any room for disagreement, nor have any differences concerning them been heard of or reported from the Imams of Sacred Law. Everything in this category is termed *unquestionable as evidence*.

The second type, *probabilistic as evidence* (zanni al-dalala), is a text that can bear more than one meaning, whether because it contains a word that can lexically have two different meanings, or because it was made by way of figure of speech or metaphor, or because it can be interpreted in other than its apparent sense in the context without this contradicting what was intended by the Wise Lawgiver. It is here that we find scope for scholarly difference of opinion to a greater or lesser extent depending on the number of meanings a text can imply, how much interpretation it will bear, and so forth.

All of the derivative rulings of Sacred Law are of this type, probabilistic as evidence, so we naturally find differences among Islamic legal scholars as to their interpretation, each scholar interpreting them according to his comprehension

والجماعـة أن الأحكـام الشـرعيـة كلهـا وصلت إلينـا إمـا بدليـل قطعي الورود أو دليل ظني الورود.

فسـور القـرآن الكـريم وآيـاتـه كلهـا والأحـاديث الشريفة المتواترة كلها قطعية الـورود لأنهـا نُقلت إلينا بالتواتر جيلاً عن جيـل وجمعاً عن جمع يستحيل تواطؤهم على الكذب.

أمـّا دلالة هذه النصـوص سواء كانت قطعية الورود أو ظنية الورود فإنها على قسمين:

آ: قطعي الدلالة: وهو النص الذي لا يحتمـل أكثر من معنى واحد ولا يمكن لأي عقل أن يحمِّله أكثر من معناه الواحد ولا مجال لتأويله على غير ظاهره والآيات التي تبحث في أصل العقيـدة من توحيـد وصلاة وزكاة وصيام [. . .] مما لا مجال للاختـلاف فيـه ولم يسمـع أو ينقل فيهـا خلاف بين أئمة الفقه كلها من هذا القبيل «قطعي الدلالة».

ب: ظني الـدلالة: وهـو النص الذي يحتمـل أكثر من معنى واحد إما لأنه لفظ مشترك بين معنيين في أصل اللغة أو لأنه جاء على سبيـل الكنايـة والاستعـارة أو يمكن صرفـه عن ظاهـره إلى معنى آخر بقـرينة دون أن ينبني على ذلك إخـلال بمقصود الشارع الحكيم. وهنا نرى أن المجال للاختلاف يتسع ويضيق بقدر ما يحتمل هذا النص من المعاني أو بحسب ما يحتمله من التأويل وما شابه ذلك.

وسائر الأحكـام الشرعية الفرعية هي من هذا القبيل «ظني الدلالة»، فنجد فيها خلافـاً بين الفقهاء في تفسيرها فكلٌ يفسِّر بحسب فهمه وسعة أفقه دون أن يحمِّل

and the broadness of his horizons, while not giving the text a reading it does not imply, and then corroborating his interpretation with evidence acceptable to scholars. Scholarly differences are thus something natural, even logically necessary, as a result of the factors we have just described.

Allah Mighty and Majestic has willed that most texts of the Sacred Law be probabilistic as evidence because of a wisdom He demands, namely, to give people more choice and leave room for minds to use *ijtihad* in understanding His word and that of His messenger (Allah bless him and give him peace).

b6.2   We conclude this short summary with an example to clarify what we have said. Consider the word of Allah,

"Divorced women shall wait by themselves for three periods" (Koran 2:228),

as opposed to His saying, in the same sura,

"Those who forswear their women have a wait of four months" (Koran 2:226).

Allah's saying "three" in the former and "four" in the latter are texts that are decisive as evidence, in that neither admits of more than one interpretation, namely, the well-known numbers.

But in contrast with this, when Allah says "periods" (Ar. quru') in the first, and "months" (ashhur) in the second, we find that the former word can have more than one sense in its Arabic lexical root meaning, while *months* cannot, the latter being decisive in meaning and incapable of bearing another interpretation. Concerning this question, Imam Qurtubi says in his Koranic exegesis: "Scholars differ about the word *periods*. Those of Kufa hold that it means menstrual periods, and this is the position of 'Umar, 'Ali, and Ibn Mas'ud. But those of the Hijaz hold it means the intervals of purity between menstrual periods, and this is the view of 'A'isha, Ibn 'Umar, and Shafi'i."

Considering this, is it not natural that there should be various opinions about understanding the verse "three periods" but only one about

النص ما لا يحتمل ومؤيداً فهمه بدليل من الأدلة المعتبرة لدى العلماء .

فكان الخلاف أمراً طبيعياً بل حتمياً نتيجة لما قلنا .

ولقد اختار الله عز وجل أن تكون أكثر النصوص الشرعية ظنية الدلالة لحكمة اقتضاها وهي التوسعة على الناس وفسح المجال أمام العقول لتجتهد في كلامه وكلام رسوله ﷺ .

b6.2   ونختم هذه اللمحة الموجزة بمثال يوضح ما ذكرنا : قوله تعالى [في سورة البقرة] : ﴿وَالمُطَلَّقَاتُ يَتَرَبَّصْنَ بِأَنْفُسِهِنَّ ثَلَاثَةَ قُرُوءٍ﴾ .

لنقابله مع قوله عز وجل في نفس السورة : ﴿وَلِلَّذِينَ يُؤْلُونَ مِنْ نِسَائِهِمْ تَرَبُّصُ أَرْبَعَةِ أَشْهُرٍ﴾ .

فقوله في الآية الأولى ﴿ثلاثة﴾ وفي الأخرى ﴿أربعة﴾ نص قطعي لا يحتمل أكثر من معنى واحد وهو العدد المعروف .

وبمقارنة ذلك مع قوله عز وجل في الأولى ﴿قُرُوءٍ﴾ وفي الأخرى ﴿أَشْهُرٍ﴾ نجد أن اللفظة الأولى ﴿قُرُوءٍ﴾ تحتمل أكثر من معنى واحد في الوضع اللغوي العربي خلافاً للفظة ﴿أَشْهُرٍ﴾ فإنها قطعية المعنى لا تحتمل أكثر من معنى واحد . وفي هذا يقول الإمام القرطبي في تفسيره : «اختلف العلماء في الأقراء . فقال أهل الكوفة هي الحيض وهو قول عمر ، وعلي ، وابن مسعود [...] وقال أهل الحجاز هي الأطهار ، وهو قول عائشة وابن عمر والشافعي» . اهـ . أليس بعد هذا أن يكون من الطبيعي أن تتعدد الآراء في فهم هذه الآية الكريمة ﴿ثَلَاثَةَ قُرُوءٍ﴾ وتتحد في فهم

understanding Allah's saying "four months"? If Allah had wanted all opinions to coincide on this question, He might have said, for example, "three menstrual periods" (hiyad), or "three intervals of purity between menstrual periods" (athar), just as He said "four months." And all the texts of Sacred Law that can bear more than one meaning are comparable to this example (*'Umdat al-salik* (y90), 11–13).

قوله تعالى ﴿أَرْبَعَةَ أَشْهُرٍ﴾؟ فلو أراد الله عز وجل أن تتوحد الآراء في هذه المسألة لقال مثلاً «ثلاث حِيَض»، أو «ثلاثة أطهار» كما قال ﴿أَرْبَعَةَ أَشْهُرٍ﴾. ويقاس على ذلك جميع النصوص الشرعية المحتملة لأكثر من معنى واحد [محرر من مقدمة عمدة السالك: ١١ـ١٣].

*

b7.0   SCHOLARLY CONSENSUS (IJMA')

الإجماع   b7.0

b7.1   (*'Abd al-Wahhab Khallaf:*) *Scholarly consensus* (ijma') is the agreement of all the *mujtahids* (def: o22.1(d)) of the Muslims existing at one particular period after the Prophet's death (Allah bless him and give him peace) about a particular ruling regarding a matter or event. It may be gathered from this that the integral elements of scholarly consensus are four, without which it is invalid:

(a) that a number of *mujtahids* exist at a particular time;

(b) that all *mujtahids* of the Muslims in the period of the thing or event agree on its ruling, regardless of their country, race, or group, though non*mujtahids* are of no consequence;

(c) that each *mujtahid* present his opinion about the matter in an explicit manner, whether verbally, by giving a formal legal opinion on it, or practically, by giving a legal decision in a court case concerning it;

(d) and that all *mujtahids* agree on the ruling, for if a majority of them agree, consensus is not effected, no matter how few those who contradict it, nor how many those who concur.

b7.1   (عبد الوهاب خلّاف:) الإجماع [في اصطلاح الأصوليين] هو اتفاق جميع المجتهدين من المسلمين في عصر من العصور بعد وفاة الرسول على حكم شرعي في واقعة [...]. ومن هذا يؤخذ أن أركان الإجماع التي لا ينعقد شرعاً إلا بتحققها أربعة:

الأول: أن يوجد في عصر وقوع الحادثة عدد من المجتهدين [...].

الثاني: أن يتفق على الحكم الشرعي في الواقعة جميع المجتهدين من المسلمين في وقت وقوعها بصرف النظر عن بلدهم أو جنسهم أو طائفتهم [...] ولا عبرة بغير المجتهدين.

الثالث: أن يكون اتفاقهم بإبداء كل واحد منهم رأيه صريحاً في الواقعة سواء أكان إبداء الواحد منهم رأيه قولاً بأن أفتى في الواقعة بفتوى، أو فعلاً بأن قضى فيها بقضاء [...].

الرابع: أن يتحقق الاتفاق من جميع المجتهدين على الحكم، فلو اتفق أكثرهم لا ينعقد باتفاق الأكثر إجماعاً مهما قل عدد المخالفين وكثر عدد المتفقين.

b7.2   When the four necessary integrals of consensus exist, the ruling agreed upon is an

b7.2   إذا تحققت أركان الإجماع الأربعة [ت: والمؤلف يكررها هنا

authoritative part of Sacred Law that is obligatory to obey and not lawful to disobey. Nor can *mujtahid*s of a succeeding era make the thing an object of new *ijtihad*, because the ruling on it, verified by scholarly consensus, is an absolute legal ruling which does not admit of being contravened or annulled.

b7.3   The proof of the legal authority of scholarly consensus is that just as Allah Most Glorious has ordered the believers, in the Koran, to obey Him and His messenger, so too He has ordered them to obey *those of authority* (ulu al-amr) among them, saying,

"O you who believe, obey Allah and obey the Prophet and those of authority among you" (Koran 4:59),

such that when those of authority in legal expertise, the *mujtahid*s, agree upon a ruling, it is obligatory in the very words of the Koran to follow them and carry out their judgement.

And Allah threatens those who oppose the Messenger and follow other than the believers' way, saying,

"Whoever contraverts the Messenger after guidance has become clear to him and follows other than the believers' way, We shall give him over to what he has turned to and roast him in hell, and how evil an outcome" (Koran 4:115).

b7.4   A second evidentiary aspect is that a ruling agreed upon by all the *mujtahid*s in the Islamic Community (Umma) is in fact the ruling of the Community, represented by its *mujtahid*s, and there are many hadiths that have come from the Prophet (Allah bless him and give him peace), as well as quotes from the Companions, which indicate that the Community is divinely protected from error, including his saying (Allah bless him and give him peace):

(1) "My Community shall not agree on an error."

[. . .] كان هذا الحكم المتفق عليه قانوناً شرعياً واجباً اتباعه ولا يجوز مخالفته، وليس للمجتهدين في عصر تالٍ أن يجعلوا هذه الواقعة موضع اجتهاد، لأن الحكم الثابت فيها بهذا الإجماع حكم شرعي قطعي لا مجال لمخالفته ولا نسخه.

b7.3   والبرهان على حجية الإجماع [ما يأتي:] أولاً أن الله سبحانه في القرآن كما أمر المؤمنين بطاعته وطاعة رسوله أمرهم بطاعة أولي الأمر منهم [ولفظ الأمر معناه الشأن] فقال تعالى: ﴿يَا أَيُّهَا الَّذِينَ آمَنُوا أَطِيعُوا اللَّهَ وأَطِيعُوا الرَّسُولَ وَأُولِي الأْمْرِ مِنْكُمْ﴾ [. . .]، فإذا أجمع أولو الأمر في التشريع وهم المجتهدون على حكم وجب اتباعه وتنفيذ حكمهم بنص القرآن [. . .]. وتوعَّد سبحانه من يشاقق الرسول ويتبع غير سبيل المؤمنين، فقال عزَّ شأنه: ﴿وَمَنْ يُشَاقِقِ الرَّسُولَ مِنْ بَعْدِ مَا تَبَيَّنَ لَهُ الْهُدَى وَيَتَّبِعْ غَيْرَ سَبِيلِ الْمُؤْمِنِينَ نُوَلِّهِ مَا تَوَلَّى وَنُصْلِهِ جَهَنَّمَ وَسَاءَتْ مَصِيراً﴾.

b7.4   وثانياً: أن الحكم الذي اتفقت عليه آراء جميع المجتهدين في الأمة الإسلامية هو في الحقيقة حكم الأمة ممثلة في مجتهديها. وقد وردت عدة أحاديث عن الرسول، وآثار عن الصحابة تدل على عصمة الأمة من الخطأ منها قوله ﷺ:

«لا تجتمع أمتي على خطأ». وقوله:

(2) "Allah is not wont to make my Community concur on misguidance."

(3) "That which the Muslims consider good, Allah considers good."

('Ilm usul al-fiqh (y71), 45–47)

b7.5   (n: Another hadith that scholars quote in connection with the validity of scholarly consensus is the following, given with its commentary.)

The Prophet (Allah bless him and give him peace) said,

"Allah's hand is over the group, and whoever dissents from them departs to hell."

Allah's hand is over the group
(al-'Azizi:) Munawi says, "Meaning His protection and preservation of them, signifying that the collectivity of the people of Islam are in Allah's fold, so be also in Allah's shelter, in the midst of them, and do not separate yourselves from them." The rest of the hadith, according to the one who first recorded it (n: Tirmidhi), is,
and whoever dissents from them departs to hell.
Meaning that whoever diverges from the overwhelming majority concerning what is lawful or unlawful and on which the Community does not differ has slipped off the path of guidance and this will lead him to hell (al-Siraj al-munir sharh al-Jami' al-saghir (y18), 3.449).

b7.6   (n: In addition to its general interest as a formal legal opinion, the following serves in the present context to clarify why other than the four Sunni schools of jurisprudence do not necessarily play a role in scholarly consensus.)

('Abd al-Rahman Ba'alawi:) Ibn Salah reports that there is scholarly consensus on its being unlawful to follow rulings from schools other than those of the four Imams, meaning in one's personal works, let alone give court verdicts

---

«لـم يكـن الـله ليجمـع أمتي على الضلالة» [ت: أخرجه الحاكم ١/ ١١٦ بسنـد صحيح ولفظه: لا يجمع الله أمتي على ضلال أبداً، ويد الله على الجماعة]. وقوله:
«مـا رآه المسلمون حسناً فهو عند الله حسن» [ت: من حديث أخرجـه أحمد رقم (٣٦٠٠) وإسناده حسن] [محرر من علم أصول الفقه: ٤٥-٤٧].

b7.5   قال النبي ﷺ: «يـد الله على الجماعة ومن شذ شذ إلى النار» [رواه الترمذي].
قال الشـارح الـعـزيزي في حديث يد الله على الجماعة: (قال المناوي: أي حفظه وكـلاءته عليهم يعني أن الجماعة أهـل الإسـلام في كنف الله فأقيمـوا في كنف الله بين ظهرانيهم ولا تفـارقـوهم. وتمـامه عند مخرجـه:) ومن شذ شذ إلى النار (أي من خرج من السواد الأعظم في الحـلال والحـرام الـذي لم تختلف فيـه الأمة فقد زاغ عن سبيل الهـدى وذلك يؤديه إلى دخول النار). [رواه الترمذي عن ابن عباس، وقال العلقمي بجانبه علامة الحسن] [نقل من السـراج المنير شرح الجامع الصغير: ٣/ ٤٤٩].

b7.6   (عبد الرحمن باعلوي:) نقل ابن الصلاح الإجماع على أنـه لا يجوز تقليد غير الأئمة الأربعة، أي حتى العمل لنفسه فضـلاً عن القضاء والفتوى، لعدم

or formal legal opinions to people from them, because of the untrustworthiness of the ascription of such rulings to the scholars who reportedly gave them, there being no channels of transmission which obviate the possibility of textual corruption and spurious substitutions.

The Zaydis, for example, who trace themselves to Zayd ibn 'Ali ibn Husayn (n: son of 'Ali and Fatima), the beatitude of Allah be upon them, despite the fact that Zayd was one of the Imams of the religion and a renowned figure well qualified to give guidance to those seeking it, his followers identify him with extreme permissiveness on many questions, ascriptions based on failure to check as to what his positions actually were (n: by naming the intermediate transmitters and establishing their reliability). It is quite otherwise with the four schools, whose Imams (Allah reward them) have spent themselves in checking the positions of their schools, explaining what could be rigorously authenticated as the position of the person it was attributed to; and what could not be. Their scholars have thus achieved safety from textual corruption and have been able to discern the genuine from the poorly authenticated (*Bughya al-mustarshidin fi talkhis fatawa ba'd al-a'imma min al-muta'akhkhirin* (y19), 8).

الثقـة بنسبتهـا إلى أربـابهـا بأسانيد تمنع التحريف والتبديل كمـذهب الزيديين المنسـوبين إلى الإمـام زيـد بن علي بن الحسين السبط رضـوان الله عليهم وإن كان هو إماماً من أئمة الدين وعلماً صالحاً للمستـرشـدين غير أن أصحابه نسبوه إلى التسـاهـل في كثير لعدم اعتنائهم بتحرير مذهبـه بخـلاف المـذاهب الأربعـة فإن أئمتهم جزاهم الله خيـراً بذلـوا نفـوسهم في تحرير أقوالها وبيان ما ثبت عن قائلها وما لم يثبت. فأمن أهلها التحريف وعلم الصحيـح من الضعيف [نقـل من بغيـة المستـرشـدين في تلخيص فتـاوى بعض الأئمة من المتأخرين: ٨].

*

BOOK C

THE NATURE OF LEGAL RULINGS

CONTENTS:

c1.0   KINDS OF RULINGS

c1.0   أنواع الحكم

c1.1   ('Abd al-Wahhab Khallaf:) A *legal ruling* is a statement from the Lawgiver (syn. Allah or His messenger (Allah bless him and give him peace)) concerning the acts of those morally responsible which:

(1) requires something;

(2) allows a choice;

(3) or gives stipulations.

c1.1   (عبـد الـوهـاب خلّاف:) الـحكم الشـرعي هو خطـاب الشـارع المتعلق بأفعـال المكلفين طلبـاً أو تخييراً أو وضعاً.

c1.2   An *injunctive* ruling is one that enjoins the morally responsible individual to either do or refrain from an act, or gives him an option to do or refrain from it.
     An example of enjoining one to *do* an act is Allah's saying,

     "People owe Allah to make pilgrimage to the House" (Koran 3:97).

     An example of enjoining one to *refrain* from an act is His saying,

     "Let no people mock another people" (Koran 49:11).

     And an example of *giving an option* to do or refrain from an act is His saying,

c1.2   فالـحـكم الـتـكـليـفي هو ما اقتضى طلب فعـل من المكلف، أو كفه عن فعل ،أو تخييره بين فعل والكف عنه . فمثـال ما اقـتـضى طلب فعـل من المكلف قوله تعالى : ﴿وَلِلَّهِ عَلَىٰ النَّاسِ حِجُّ البَيْتِ﴾ .
   ومثـال ما اقتضى طلب الكف عن فعل قوله تعالى : ﴿لا يَسْخَرْ قَوْمٌ مِنْ قَوْمٍ﴾ .
   ومثـال ما اقتضى تخيـر المكلف بين فعـل والكف عنه قوله تعـالى : ﴿فَإِذَا

"When the prayer is finished, go forth in the land" (Koran 62:10).

قُضِيَتِ الصَّلاةُ فَانْتَشِرُوا فِي الأَرْضِ ﴾.

c1.3   As for *stipulatory* rulings, they entail that something is made a legal reason (sabab) for another thing, a condition (shart) for it, or a preventive (mani') of it.

c1.3   وأمـا الحكـم الـوضعي فهـو ما اقتضى وضع شيء سبباً لشيء أو شرطاً له أو مانعاً منه.

An example of being stipulated as a *reason* for something is Allah's saying,

فمثـال مـا اقتضى وضـع شيء سببـاً لشيء قوله تعالى: ﴿يَا أَيُّها الَّذِينَ آمَنُوا إِذَا

"O believers, when you go to pray, wash your faces and wash your forearms to the elbows" (Koran 5:6),

قُمْتُمْ إِلَى الصَّلاةِ فَاغْسِلُوا وُجُـوهَكُمْ وَأَيْـدِيَكُمْ إِلَى المَـرَافِقِ﴾ اقتضى وضع

which stipulates wanting to pray as a reason for the obligation of performing *ablution* (wudu).

إرادة إقامة الصلاة سبباً في إيجاب الوضوء.

An example of something being made a *condition* for another thing is His saying,

ومثـال مـا اقتضى وضـع شيء شرطاً لشيء قوله تعالى: ﴿وَلِلَّهِ عَلَى النَّاسِ حِجُّ

"People owe Allah to make pilgrimage to the House, whoever is able to find a way" (Koran 3:97),

البَيْتِ مَنْ اسْتَطَاعَ إِلَيهِ سَبِيلاً﴾ اقتضى أن استطاعة السبيل إلى البيت شرط لإيجاب

which implies that the ability to get to the House (n: Kaaba) is a condition for the obligatoriness of one's pilgrimage. Another example is the Prophet's saying (Allah bless him and give him peace),

حجه. وقولـه ﷺ: «لا نكـاح إلا بشـاهدين» اقتضى أن حضور الشاهدين شرط لصحة الزواج.

"There is no marriage unless there are two witnesses,"

which means the presence of two witnesses is a condition for the validity of a marriage.

ومثـال مـا اقتضى جعل شيء مانعاً من شيء قوله ﷺ: «ليس للقـاتِـل ميراثٌ﴾

An example of being made a *preventive* of something is the Prophet's saying (Allah bless him and give him peace),

اقتضى جعـل قتل الوارث مورثه مانعاً من إرثه [محرر من علم أصول الفقه:

"The killer does not inherit,"

١٠٠-١٠٢].

which entails that an heir's killing the deceased is preventive of his inheriting an estate division share from him (*'Ilm usul al-fiqh* (y71), 100–102).

*

c2.0 TYPES OF HUMAN ACT	c2.0 أقسام الحكم التكليني

c2.1   (N:) The *obligatory* (fard) is that which the Lawgiver strictly requires be done. Someone who performs an obligatory act out of obedience to Allah is rewarded, while a person who refrains from it without excuse deserves to be punished.

(A: In the Shafi'i school there is no difference between *obligatory* (fard) and *requisite* (wajib) except in the pilgrimage, where nonperformance of a requisite does not invalidate the pilgrimage, but necessitates an expiation by slaughtering. For any act of worship, obligatory or nonobligatory, all conditions necessary for its validity and all of its *integrals* (rukn, pl. arkan) are obligatory, since it is unlawful to intentionally perform an invalid act of worship.)

c2.1   (ح:) الفرض ما طلبه الشارع طلباً جازماً. وفاعل الفرض طاعةً لله يثاب، وتاركه بلا عذر يستحق العقاب.

(ع: لا فرق عند الشافعية بين الفرض وبين الـواجب إلا في باب الحـج؛ حيث ترك واجب لا يفسـد الحـج ولكنـه يجبر بالـدم. وفي كل عبـادة، واجبـة كانت أو نافـلة، يجب القيـام بجميـع شروطهـا وأركانها، إذ لا يجوز أداء عبادة فاسدة).

c2.2   The *sunna* (n: or *recommended* (mandub)) is that which the Lawgiver asks be done, but does not strictly require it. Someone who performs it out of obedience to Allah is rewarded, though someone who refrains from it is not punished.

c2.2   السنة ما طلبه الشارع طلباً غير جازم. ومن فعلها طاعـة لله يثـاب، ومن تركها لا يعاقب.

c2.3   The *permissible* (mubah) is what the Lawgiver has neither requested nor prohibited, so the person who does it is not rewarded or punished. Rather, doing or not doing it are equal, though if a person does it to enable him to perform an act of obedience to Allah, or refrains from it for that reason, then he is rewarded for it. And if he does such an act to enable him to perform an act of disobedience, he is sinning.

c2.3   المبـاح ما لم يطلبه الشارع ولم ينه عنه. فلا يثاب فاعله ولا يعاقب. بل يستـوي فعله وتـركـه لكن لو فعله الإنسـان ليستعين علـى طاعة الله كان له ثواب، وكـذا لو تركه لذلك. ولـو فعله ليستعين على معصية كان آثماً.

c2.4   The *offensive* (makruh) is that which the Lawgiver has interdicted but not strictly forbidden. A person who refrains from such an act out of obedience to Allah is rewarded, while the person who commits it does not deserve to be punished.

c2.4   المكروه ما نهى عنه الشارع نهياً غير جازم ومن تركه طاعة لله يثاب ومن فعله لا يستحق العقاب.

c2.5   The *unlawful* (haram) is what the Lawgiver strictly forbids. Someone who commits an unlawful act deserves punishment, while one who

c2.5   الحـرام ما نهى عنه الشارع نهيـاً جازماً. ومن فعله يستحق العقـاب

refrains from it out of obedience to the command of Allah is rewarded.

ومن تركه امتثالًا لأمر الله يثاب .

(n: Scholars distinguish between three levels of the unlawful:

(1) *minor sins* (saghira, pl. sagha'ir), which may be forgiven from prayer to prayer, from one Friday prayer (jumu'a) to another, and so forth, as is mentioned in hadith;

(2) *enormities* (kabira, pl. kaba'ir), those which appear by name in the Koran or hadith as the subject of an explicit threat, prescribed legal penalty, or curse, as listed below at book p;

(3) and *unbelief* (kufr), sins which put one beyond the pale of Islam (as discussed at o8.7) and necessitate stating the Testification of Faith (Shahada) to reenter it.

Repentance (def: p77) is obligatory for all three (*al-Zawajir 'an iqtiraf al-kaba'ir* (y49), 1.5–9).)

c2.6   (Nawawi:) There is no doubt that the merit of an act varies. Fasting, for example, is unlawful on 'Eid Day, obligatory before it, and recommended after it. The prayer is highly desirable most of the time, but offensive at some times and situations, such as when restraining oneself from using the lavatory. Reciting the Koran is desirable, but offensive when bowing in the prayer or prostrating. Dressing one's best is good on the 'Eid or on Friday, but not during the drought prayer. And so forth.

Abul Qasim al-Junayd (Allah have mercy on him) said, "A sincere person changes forty times a day, while the hypocritical show-off stays as he is forty years."

The meaning of this is that the sincere person moves with what is right, wherever it may lead, such that when prayer is deemed better by the Sacred Law, then he prays, and when it is best to be sitting with the learned, or the righteous, or guests, or his children, or taking care of something a Muslim needs, or mending a broken heart, or whatever else it may be, then he does it, leaving aside what he usually does. And likewise for fasting, reciting the Koran, invoking Allah, eating or drinking, being serious or joking, enjoying the good life or engaging in self-sacrifice, and so on. Whenever he sees what is preferred by the Sacred Law under the circumstances, he does it, and is

c2.6   (النـووي:) ولا شك في اختـلاف أحـوال الشيء في الأفضلية فإن الصوم حرام يوم العيد واجب قبله مسنون بعـده . والصـلاة محبـوبـة في معظم الأوقـات وتكـره في أوقـات وأحـوال كمدافعة الأخبثين . وقراءة القرآن محبوبة وتكره في الركوع والسجود [وغير ذلك] . وكـذلـك تحسين اللبـاس يوم الجمعة والعيد وخلافه يوم الاستسقاء . وكذلك ما أشبه هذه .

قال أبـو القـاسـم الجنيـد بن محمد رحمـه الله إن الصـادق يتقلب في اليـوم أربعين مرة والمـرائي يثبت على حالـة واحـدة أربعين سنـة (قلت) معنـاه أن الصادق يدور مع الحق حيث دار فإذا كان الفضل الشرعي في الصـلاة مثلًا صلى وإذا كان في مجالسة العلماء والصالحين والضيفـان والعيـال وقضاء حاجـة مسلم وجبـر قلب مكسـور ونحو ذلك فَعَلَ ذلك الأفضـل وتـرك عادتـه . وكـذلك الصوم والقراءة والذكر والأكل والشرب والجد والمـزح والاختـلاط والاعتـزال والتنعم والابتـذال ونحوها . فحيث رأى الفضيلة الشرعية في شيء من هذا فعلُه ولا يرتبط

not bound by a particular habit or kind of devotion as the show-off is. The Prophet (Allah bless him and give him peace) did various things, of prayer, fasting, sitting for Koran recital and invocation, eating and drinking, dressing, riding, lovemaking with his wives, seriousness and jest, happiness and wrath, scathing condemnation for blameworthy things, leniency in punishing those who deserved it and excusing them, and so on, according to what was possible and preferable for the time and circumstances (*al-Majmu'* (y108), 1.17–18).

بعـادة ولا بعبـادة مخصوصـة كمـا يفعله المـراءي . وقـد كانت لرسـول الله ﷺ أحـوال في صلاتـه وصيامه وأوراده وأكله وشـربه ولبسه وركوبه ومعاشرة أهله وجده ومـزحـه وسـروره وغضبه وإغـلاظه في إنكـار المنكر ورفقه في عقوبته مستحقي التعـزير وصفحه عنهم وغير ذلك بحسب الإمكان والأفضل في ذلك الوقت والحال [محـرر من المجمـوع : ١ / ١٧ـ١٨ ، بتقديم وتأخير] .

*

c3.0   OBLIGATORY ACTS

c3.0   الواجب

c3.1   ('Abd al-Wahhab Khallaf:) Obligatory acts are distinguished in four ways, according to various considerations.

     One distinction is whether current performance is time-restricted or non-time-restricted.

     A *time-restricted* obligatory act is one the Lawgiver demands be done at a particular time, such as the five obligatory prayers, for each of which the time for current performance is set, such that the particular prayer is not obligatory before it, and the individual is guilty of serious sin if he delays it past its time without excuse.

     A *non-time-restricted* obligatory act is one which the Lawgiver strictly demands, but does not specify a time for its current performance, such as the expiation obligatory for someone who swears and oath and breaks it (def: o20).

c3.1   (عبـد الـوهـاب خلّاف :) ينقسم الـواجب إلى أربعة تقسيمـات باعتبـارات مختلفـة .
     التقسيم الأول : الـواجب من جهـة وقت أدائه ، إما مؤقت وإما مطلق عن التوقيت .
     فالواجب المؤقت هو ما طلب الشارع فعـله حتمـاً في وقت معين كالصلوات الخمس ، حدد لأداء كل صلاة منهـا وقتـاً معينـاً بحيث لا تجب قبله ويأثم المكلف إن أخرها عنه بغير عذر .
     والـواجب المطلق عن التـوقيت هو ما طلب الشارع فعله حتماً ولم يعين وقتـاً لأدائـه ، كالكفـارة الواجبة على من حلف يمينـاً وحنث .

c3.2   A second distinction between obligatory acts is made on the basis of who is called upon to perform them, namely, whether an act is personally obligatory or communally obligatory.

     A *personally obligatory* (fard al-'ayn) act is what the Lawgiver requires from each and every morally responsible person. It is insufficient for someone to perform such an act on another's behalf, such as the prayer, *zakat* (def: h1.0), pilgrimage, keeping agreements, and avoiding wine or gambling.

c3.2   التقسيم الثـاني : ينقسم الـواجب من جهـة المطـالب بأدائـه إلى واجب عيني وواجب كفائي .
     فالواجب العيني هو ما طلب الشارع فعلـه من كل فرد من أفـراد المكلفين ولا يجزيء قيـام مكلف به عن آخر كالصلاة والـزكـاة والحج والوفاء بالعهود واجتناب الخمر والميسر .

A *communally obligatory* (fard al-kifaya) act is what the Lawgiver requires from the collectivity of those morally responsible, not from each one of them, such that if someone undertakes it, then the obligation has been fulfilled and the sin and responsibility (n: of nonperformance) is lifted from the rest, while if no one undertakes it, then all are guilty of serious sin for neglecting the obligation. Examples include commanding the right and forbidding the wrong (def: book q), praying over the dead, building hospitals, lifesaving, fire fighting, medicine, industries people require, the existence of Islamic courts and judges, issuing formal legal opinions, responding to someone who says "as-Salam 'alaykum," and testifying in court. The Lawgiver requires that these obligatory acts exist in the Islamic Community regardless of who does them. But He does not require they be done by each person, or some particular one, since the interests of the Community are realized by the existence of these things through the efforts of some of those morally responsible, and do not entail every particular person's performance of them.

Someone able through himself or his property to perform the communally obligatory act is obliged to perform it, and someone unable to do it himself is obliged to urge and have the person do it who can. If the obligatory act is done, all are cleared of the sin, and if neglected, all are guilty of serious sin. The person capable of it is guilty because he neglected a communally obligatory act he could have done, and the rest are guilty because they neglected to urge him and have him perform the obligatory act he was capable of.

When an individual is the only one available who can perform a communally obligatory act, it becomes personally obligatory for him.

c3.3   A third way obligatory acts are distinguished is by the amount of them required, that is, whether the act is of a defined amount or an undefined amount.

Obligatory acts of *defined amount* are those for which the Lawgiver has determined a particular quantity, such that the subject is not free of the obligation until he has done the amount stipulated by the Lawgiver, as with the five obligatory

والواجب الكفائي هو ما طلب الشارع فعله من مجموع المكلفين لا من كل فرد منهم ، بحيث إذا قام به بعض المكلفين سقط الإثم والحرج عن الباقين ، وإذا لم يقم به أي فرد من أفراد المكلفين أثموا جميعاً بإهمال هذا الواجب .

كالأمر بالمعروف والنهي عن المنكر والصلاة على الموتى وبناء المستشفيات وإنقاذ الغريق وإطفاء الحريق والطب والصناعات التي يحتاج إليها الناس والقضاء والإفتاء ، ورد السلام وأداء الشهادة . فهذه الواجبات مطلوب للشارع أن توجد في الأمة أياً كان من يفعلها . وليس المطلوب للشارع أن يقوم كل فرد أو فرد معين بفعلها . لأن المصلحة تتحقق بوجودها من بعض المكلفين ولا تتوقف على قيام كل مكلف بها .

فالقادر بنفسه أو ماله على أداء الواجب الكفائي عليه أن يقوم به وغير القادر على أدائه بنفسه عليه أن يحث القادر ويحمله على القيام به .

فإذا أدي الواجب سقط الإثم عنهم جميعاً ، وإذا أهمل أثموا جميعاً : أثم القادر لإهماله واجباً قدر على أدائه وأثم غيره لإهماله حث القادر وحمله على فعل الواجب المقدور له .

وإذا تعين فرد لأداء الواجب الكفائي كان واجباً عينياً عليه .

c3.3   التقسيم الثالث : ينقسم الواجب من جهة المقدار المطلوب منه إلى محدد وغير محدد .

فالواجب المحدد هو ما عين له الشارع مقداراً معلوماً بحيث لا تبرأ ذمة المكلف من هذا الواجب إلا إذا أداه على ما عين الشارع كالصلوات الخمس

prayers, or zakat.

Obligatory acts of *undefined amount* are those which the Lawgiver has not stipulated the amount of, but rather demands them from the subject in an undetermined quantity, such as spending in the way of Allah, cooperating with one another in good works, feeding the hungry, helping those in distress, and so forth.

c3.4   A fourth distinction between obligatory acts is whether an act is a specific obligation, or an obligation to choose between certain alternatives.

Specific obligations are those in which the Lawgiver demands the act itself, such as the prayer, fasting in Ramadan, paying for merchandise, rent from a tenant, or returning something wrongfully taken; such that the individual is not free of the obligation until he does that very act.

An obligation to choose between certain *alternatives* is when the Lawgiver requires the performance of one of a given number of actions, such as one of the options in expiating a broken oath, where Allah Most High requires the person who has broken his oath to feed ten poor people, clothe them, or free a slave ('abd, def: w13), and the obligation consists of doing any of these three things (*'Ilm usul al-fiqh* (y71), 106, 108–11).

*

c4.0   RECOMMENDED ACTS

c4.1   ('Abd al-Wahhab Khallaf:) Recommended acts are divided into three categories.

The first is recommended acts whose demand is *confirmed*. Someone who neglects such an act does not deserve punishment, but does deserve censure and blame. This includes the sunnas and recommended acts that are legally considered to complete obligatory acts, such as the call to prayer (adhan) or performing the five obligatory prayers in a group, as well as all religious matters that the Prophet (Allah bless him and give him peace) diligently performed and did not omit except once or twice to show that they were not obligatory, like

والزكاة .

والواجب غير المحدد هو ما لم يعين الشارع مقداره بل طلبه من المكلف بغير تحديد ، كالإنفاق في سبيل الله والتعاون على البر وإطعام الجائع وإغاثة الملهوف وغير ذلك .

c3.4   التقسيـم الـرابـع : ينقسم الواجب إلى واجب معين وواجب مخيّر .

فالواجب المعين ما طلبه الشارع بعينه كالصلاة والصيام وثمن المشتري وأجر المستأجر ورد المغصوب ، ولا تبرأ ذمة المكلف إلا بأدائه بعينه .

والـواجـب المخير ما طلبه الشارع واحداً من أمور معينة ، كأحد خصال الكفارة فإن الله تعـالى أوجب على من حنث في يمينه أن يطعم عشرة مساكين أو يكسوهم أو يعتق رقبة فالواجب أي واحد من هذه الأمور الثلاثة [محرر من علم أصول الفقه : ١٠٦ـ١١١].

المندوب   c4.0

c4.1   (عبد الـوهـاب خلّاف :) المندوب ينقسم إلى ثلاثة أقسام .

مندوب مطلوب فعله على وجه التأكيد ولا يستحق تاركه العقاب ولكن يستحق اللـوم والـعـتـاب . ومن هذا السـنـن والمنـدوبـات التي تعـد شرعـاً مكملة للواجبـات كالأذان وأداء الـصلوات الخمس جماعة . ومنه كل ما واظب عليه الرسول ﷺ من شؤونه الدينية ، ولم يتركه إلا مرة أو مرتين ليـدل على عدم تحتيمه

rinsing out the mouth when performing ablution, or reciting a *sura* or some verses of the Koran after the *Fatiha* during the prayer. This category is called the *confirmed sunna* (sunna mu'akkada) or *sunna of guidance*.

كالمضمضة في الوضوء وقراءة سورة أو آية بعد الفاتحة في الصلاة . ويسمى هذا القسم السنة المؤكدة أو سنة الهدى .

c4.2 The second category is those acts whose performance is sanctioned by Sacred Law such that the person who performs them is rewarded, though someone who omits them deserves neither punishment nor blame. This includes acts the Prophet (Allah bless him and give him peace) did not diligently perform, but did one or more times and then discontinued. It also includes all voluntary acts, like spending on the poor, fasting on Thursday of each week, or praying *rak'as* (units) of prayer in addition to the obligatory and confirmed sunna prayers.

This category is called the *extra sunna* or *supererogatory* (nafila).

c4.2 ومندوب مشروع فعله وفاعله يثاب وتاركه لا يستحق عقاباً ولا لوماً . ومن هذا ما لم يواظب الرسول ﷺ على فعله بل فعله مرة أو أكثر وتركه . ومنه جميع التطوعات كالتصدق على الفقير أو صيام يوم الخميس من كل أسبوع أو صلاة ركعات زيادة عن الفرض وعن السنة المؤكدة . ويسمى هذا القسم السنة الزائدة أو النافلة .

c4.3 The third category consists of the superlatively recommended, meaning those acts considered part of an individual's perfections. It includes following the Prophet (Allah bless him and give him peace) in ordinary matters that proceeded from him as a human being, as when a person eats, drinks, walks, sleeps, and dresses like the Prophet used to. Following the example of the Prophet (Allah bless him and give him peace) in these and similar matters is an excellence and considered among one's refinements, as it shows one's love for the Prophet and great attachment to him. But someone who does not follow the Prophet (Allah bless him and give him peace) in matters like these is not considered a wrongdoer, because they are not part of his lawgiving (A: though such acts are rewarded when one thereby intends to follow the Prophet (Allah bless him and give him peace), and every desirable practice one performs means a higher degree in paradise which the person who neglects it may not attain to).

Acts of this category are called *desirable* (mustahabb), *decorum* (adab), or *meritorious* (ibid., 112).

c4.3 ومندوب زائد أي يعد من الكماليات للمكلف . ومن هذا الاقتداء بالرسول ﷺ في الأمور العادية التي تصدر عنه بصفته إنساناً كأن يأكل ويشرب ويمشي وينام ويلبس على الصفة التي كان يسير عليها الرسول فإن الاقتداء بالرسول في هذه الأمور وأمثالها كمالي ، ويعد من محاسن المكلف لأنه يدل على حبه للرسول ﷺ وفرط تعلقه به . ولكن من لم يقتد بالرسول ﷺ في مثل هذه الأمور لا يعد مسيئاً، لأن هذه ليست من تشريعه ﷺ . ويسمى هذا القسم مستحباً وأدباً وفضيلة [نقل من المرجع المذكور: ١١٢].

*

c5.0   UNLAWFUL ACTS

c5.0   المحرم

c5.1   ('Abd al-Wahhab Khallaf:) The unlawful is of two kinds.

The first is the *originally unlawful in itself*, meaning the Sacred Law forbids it from the outset, such as adultery, theft, prayer without ritual purity, marrying a member of one's unmarriageable kin while knowing them to be such, selling unslaughtered dead animals, and so forth, of things that are intrinsically unlawful because they entail damage and harm, the prohibition applying from the outset to the very act.

The second is the *unlawful because of an extrinsic reason*, meaning that the initial ruling of an act was that it was obligatory, recommended, or permissible, but an extrinsic circumstance became linked with it that made it unlawful, such as a prayer performed in a garment wrongfully taken, or a sale in which there is fraud, or a marriage whose sole purpose is to allow the woman to remarry her previous husband who has pronounced a threefold divorce against her, or fasting day after day without breaking the fast at night, or an unlawfully innovated divorce (def: n2.3), and so forth, of things unlawful because of an external circumstance. The prohibition is not due to the act itself, but because of something extrinsic to the act; meaning the act is not damaging or harmful in itself, but something has happened to it and become conjoined with it that makes it entail damage or harm.

c5.2   One consequence of the above distinction is that an *intrinsically* unlawful act is uncountenanced by the Law to begin with, so it cannot be a legal cause or reason, or form the basis for further legal consequences. Rather, it is *invalid*. Because of this, prayer without ritual purity is invalid, marriage to a close unmarriageable relative when one knows them to be such is invalid, and the sale of an unslaughtered dead animal is invalid. And something legally invalid is without other legal efficacy.

But an act that is unlawful because of an *extrinsic* circumstance is intrinsically lawful, and can thus be a legal reason and form the basis for

c5.1   (عبد الـوهـاب خلّاف:)
المحـرم قسمان: محرم أصالة لذاته، أي أنـه فعـل حكمه الشرعي التحريم من الإبتـداء، كالـزنـا والسـرقة والصلاة بغير طهارة وزواج إحـدى المحارم مع العلم بالحرمـة وبيع الميتة وغير ذلك مما حرم تحـريماً ذاتياً لما فيه من مفاسد ومضار، فالتحريم وارد ابتداءً على ذات الفعل.

ومحـرم لعـارض أي أنـه فعـل حكمه الشرعي ابتـداءً الـوجوب أو النـدب أو الإبـاحـة ولكن اقتـرن به عارض جعله محـرماً كالصلاة في ثوب مغصوب والبيع الذي فيه غش والزواج المقصود به مجرد تحليـل الـزوجة لمطلقها ثلاثاً وصـوم الـوصـال والطلاق البدعي وغير ذلك مما عرض له التحـريم لعـارض، فليس التحريم لذات الفعل ولكن لأمر خارجي أي أن ذات الفعل لا مفسدة فيه ولا مضرة ولكن عرض له واقتـرن به ما جعـل فيه مفسدة أو مضرة.

c5.2   ومما يبنى على هذا التقسيم أن المحرم أصالة غير مشروع أصلاً، فلا يصلح سبباً شرعياً ولا تترتب أحكـام شرعيـة عليه، بل يكون باطلاً. ولهـذا كانت الصلاة بغير طهارة باطلة. وزواج إحـدى المحارم مع العلم بالحرمة باطلاً. وبيع الميتة باطلاً. والبـاطـل شرعـاً لا يترتب عليه حكم.

وأمـا المحـرم لعـارض فهـو في ذاتـه مشـروع فيصلح سبباً شرعياً وتترتب عليه

further legal consequences, since its prohibition is accidental to it and not essential. Because of this, a prayer while wearing a garment wrongfully taken is legally *valid,* though the person is guilty of serious sin for having taken it; a sale in which there is fraud is legally valid (N: though the buyer has the option to cancel the sale and return the merchandise for a full refund); and an unlawfully innovated divorce is legally effective.

The reason for this is that the prohibition of an act because of an extrinsic event or circumstance does not vitiate either the basis of its being a legal cause or its identity, provided all its integrals and conditions exist. As for intrinsic unlawfulness, it negates the basis of an act's being a legal cause and vitiates its identity by the nonexistence of one of its integrals or conditions, so that it is no longer something that is of legal consideration (ibid., 113–14).

آثاره، لأن التحريم عارض له وليس ذاتياً. ولهذا كانت الصلاة في ثوب مغصوب صحيحة ومجزئة وهو آثم للغصب. والبيع الذي فيه غش صحيح. والطلاق البدعي واقع.

والعلة في هذا أن التحريم لعارض لا يقع به خلل في أصل السبب ولا في وصفه مادامت أركانه وشروطه مستوفاة. وأما التحريم الذاتي فهو يجعل الخلل في أصل السبب ووصفه بفقد ركن أو شرط من أركانه وشروطه فيخرج عن كونه مشروعاً [نقل من المرجع المذكور: ١١٣-١١٤].

*

c6.0 DISPENSATION (RUKHSA) AND STRICTNESS ('AZIMA)

c6.0   الرخصة والعزيمة

c6.1   ('Abd al-Wahhab Khallaf:) *Strictness* is what Allah initially legislates, of general rulings not concerned with one circumstance rather than another, or one individual rather than another.

c6.1   (عبد الوهاب خلّاف:) العزيمة هي ما شرعه الله أصالة من الأحكام العامة التي لا تختص بحال دون حال ولا بمكلف دون مكلف.

c6.2   *Dispensation* is when what is normally forbidden is made permissible because of necessity or need.

For example, if someone is forced to make a statement of unbelief (kufr) it is made permissible, to ease his hardship, for him to do so as long as faith remains firm in his heart. Likewise with someone who is forced to break his fast in Ramadan, or forced to destroy the property of another; the normally prohibited act which he is forced to do becomes permissible for him, to ease the hardship. And it is made permissible for someone forced by extreme hunger or severe thirst to eat from an unslaughtered dead animal or drink wine. (A: The latter is not permissible even under such

c6.2   والرخصة هي إباحة المحظور للضرورة أو الحاجة. فمن أكره على التلفظ بكلمة الكفر أبيح له ترفيهاً عنه أن يتلفظ بها وقلبه مطمئن بالإيمان. وكذا من أكره على أن يفطر في رمضان أو يتلف مال غيره أبيح له المحظور الذي أكره عليه ترفيهاً عنه. ومن اضطرّه الجوع الشديد والظمأ الشديد إلى أكل الميتة أو شرب الخمر أبيح له أكلها وشربها.

conditions in the Shafi'i school.)

Dispensation also includes being permitted to omit an obligatory act when an excuse exists that makes its performance a hardship (dis: c7.2, second par.) upon the individual. Thus, someone who is ill or travelling in Ramadan is permitted not to fast. And someone who is travelling is permitted to shorten prayers of four rak'as to only two rak'as (ibid., 121–22).

ومن الـرخص إبـاحـة ترك الواجب إذا وجـد عذر يجـعـل أداءه شاقـاً على المكلف . فمن كان في رمضان مريضاً أو على سفـر أبيـح له أن يفطـر . ومن كان مسافـراً أبيح له قصر الصلاة الرباعية أي أداؤهـا ركعتين بدل أربـع . [محـرّر من علم أصول الفقه].

c6.3   (n:) Since it is permissible for a Muslim to follow any of the four Imams in any of his acts of worship, comparison of their differences opens another context for discussing dispensation and strictness, a context in which classical scholars familiar with various schools often use the term "dispensation" to refer to the ruling of the school easiest on a particular legal question, and "strictness" to refer to the ruling of the school that is most rigorous. Which school this is varies from question to question. The following entry discusses how and when it is permissible for ordinary Muslims to use dispensations in the sense of following easier rulings from a different school, while entry c6.5 discusses the *way of greater precaution* (al-ahwat fi al-din) taken by those Muslims who purposely select the strictest school of thought on each legal question because of its being more precautionary and closer to godfearingness (taqwa).

c6.4   Scholars frequently acknowledge that the difference of the Imams is a mercy, and their unanimity is a decisive proof. Sheikh 'Umar Barakat, the commentator of *'Umdat al-salik*, says:

"It is permissible to follow each of the four Imams (Allah be well pleased with them), and permissible for anyone to follow one of them on a legal question, and follow a different one on another legal question. It is not obligatory to follow one particular Imam on all legal questions" (*Fayd al-Ilah al-Malik* (y27), 1.357).

(الشيخ عمر بركات :) يجوز تقليد كل واحد من الأئمة الأربعة رضي الله عنهم ويجـوز لكل واحد أن يقلد واحداً منهم في مسـألـة ويقلد إمـامـاً آخـر في مسـألة أخرى ولا يتعين تقليد واحد بعينه في كل المسائل [نقل من فيض الإله المالك : ١ / ٣٥٧].

This does not, however, imply that it is lawful to indiscriminately choose dispensations from each school, or that there are no conditions for the abovementioned permissibility. Imam Nawawi was asked for a formal legal opinion on whether pursuing dispensations in such a manner was permissible:

(Question:) "Is it permissible for someone of a particular school to follow a different school in matters that will be of benefit to him, and to seek out dispensations?"

He answered (Allah be well pleased with him), "It is not permissible to seek out dispensations [A: meaning it is unlawful, and the person who does is corrupt (fasiq)], and Allah knows best" (*Fatawa al-Imam al-Nawawi* (y105), 113).

(مسألة :) هل يجوز لمن تمذهب أن يقلد مذهباً آخر فيما يكون به نفع ، ويتبع الرخص؟

(أجـاب رضي الله تعـالى عنـه :) لا يجوز تتبُّع الرخص، والله أعلم [نقل من فتاوى الإمام النووي : ١١٣].

But when forced by necessity or hardship to take such a dispensation (A: even retroactively, as when one has finished the action, and then makes the intention to have followed another Imam's school of thought on the question), then there is nothing objectionable in it, provided that one's act of worship together with its prerequisites is valid in at least one of the schools. One may not simply *piece together* (talfiq) constituent parts from various schools in a single act of worship, if none of the schools would consider the act valid. An example is someone who performs an ablution that is minimally valid in the Shafi'i school by wetting only a few hairs of his head in the ablution sequence, something not permitted by Hanafis, and then prays behind an imam without himself reciting the Fatiha, something permitted by Hanafis but not Shafi'is. His ablution, the necessary condition for his prayer, is inadequate in the Hanafi school, and his performance of the prayer is inadequate in the Shafi'i school, with the result that neither considers his prayer valid, and in fact it is not. Whoever follows a ruling mentioned in this volume from another school must observe the conditions given at w14, and make sure his worship is valid in at least one school, which for prayer can best be achieved by performing *all recommended measures* in the present volume relating to purity, for example, e5, e11, and so on, as if *obligatory*.

c6.5   A second way to use differences between schools is to take the *way of greater precaution* by following whoever is most rigorous on a given question. For example, when performing the *purificatory bath* (ghusl), rinsing the mouth and nostrils with water is a nonobligatory, sunna measure according to the Shafi'i school, but obligatory and necessary for the purificatory bath's validity according to Hanafis. The way of greater precaution is for the Shafi'i to perform it as diligently as if it were obligatory, even though omitting it is permitted by his school.

('Abd al-Wahhab Sha'rani:) My brother, when you first hear of the two levels of this scale (n: dispensation and strictness), beware of jumping to the conclusion that there is absolute free choice between them, such that an individual may without restriction choose either dispensation or strictness in any ruling he wishes. It does not befit a person able to perform the stricter ruling to stoop to taking a dispensation permissible to him. (A: The more rigorous is always preferable in the Shafi'i school, even when the dispensation is permissible.) For as you know, my brother, I do not say that the individual is free to choose between taking the dispensation or taking the stricter ruling when he is able to perform the stricter ruling obligatory for him. I take refuge in Allah from saying such a thing, which is like making a game of religion. Of an absolute certainty, dispensations are only for someone unable to perform the stricter ruling, for in such a case, the dispensation *is* the stricter ruling in relation to him.

Moreover, I hold that mere sincerity and

(عبـد الـوهـاب الشعراني:) إيـاك يا أخي أن تبـادر أول سمـاعـك لمـرتبتي الـميـزان إلى فهم كون المـرتبتين على التخييـر مطلقاً حتى أن المكلف يكـون مخيراً بين فعل الرخصة والعزيمة في أي حكـم شاء [. . .] وليس الأولى لمن قدر على فعـل العـزيمـة أن ينـزل إلى فعـل الـرخصـة الـجـائزة [. . .] فقد علمت يا أخي أنني لا أقـول بتخييـر المكلف بين العمل بالرخصة والعزيمة مع القدرة على فعـل العـزيمـة المتعينة عليه معاذ الله أن أقول بذلك فإنه كالتلاعب بالدين [كما مرّ في الميزان]. إنما تكون الرخصة للعاجز عن فعـل العـزيمـة الـمـذكـورة قطعاً لأنه حينئذ تصير الرخصة في حقه عزيمة. بل أقـول إن من الـواجب على كل مقلد من

honesty demand of anyone who follows a particular school not to take a dispensation that the Imam of his school holds is permissible unless he is someone who needs to; and that he must follow the stricter ruling of a different Imam when able to, since rulings fundamentally refer back to the word of the Lawgiver, no one else; this being especially necessary when the other Imam's evidence is stronger, as opposed to what some followers do.

We find among the dictums of the Sufis that one should not follow a position in Sacred Law for which the evidence is weaker except when religiously more precautionary than the stronger position. For example, the Shafi'i opinion that (n: a male's) ablution is nullified by touching a girl who is a child or touching the nails or hair of a woman: though this position is considered weaker by them (n: than the position given at e7.3), it is religiously more precautionary, so performing ablution for the above-mentioned things is better (*al-Mizan al-kubra* (y123), 1.10–11).

(A: Because more rigorous rulings necessarily meet the requirements of less rigorous ones (though not vice versa), following more rigorous rulings from another school is unconditionally valid, unlike following its dispensations. And Allah knows best.)

*

c7.0   THINGS ONE MAY BE HELD LEGALLY RESPONSIBLE FOR

c7.1 ('Abd al-Wahhab Khallaf:) Three conditions must exist in any act that it is legally valid to make an individual responsible for.

The first is that the act be well enough known to the individual that he can perform it in the way required of him. It should be noted that the individual's *knowledge* of what he is responsible for means *the possibility of his knowing it*, not his actual knowledge of it. Whenever a person reaches puberty, of sound mind and capable of knowing the rulings of Sacred Law by himself or by asking those familiar with them, then he is considered to know what he is responsible for, and rulings are carried out on him, their consequences exacted of him, and the excuse of being ignorant

طريق الإنصاف أن لا يعمل برخصة قال بها إمام مذهبه إلا إن كان من أهلها وأنه يجب عليه العمل بالعزيمة التي قال بها غير إمامه . حيث قدر عليها لأن الحكم راجع إلى كلام الشارع بالأصالة لا إلى كلام غيره لا سيما إن كان دليل الغير أقوى ، خلاف ما عليه بعض المقلدين [. . .] وفي كلام القوم لا ينبغي لأحد العمل بالقول المرجوح إلا إن كان أحوط في الدين من القول الأرجح كالقول بنقض الطهارة عند الشافعية بلمس الصغيرة والشعر والظفر . فإن هذا القول وإن عندهم ضعيفاً فهو أحوط في الدين فكان الوضوء منه أولى اهـ [محرر من الميزان الكبرى : ١/ ١٠-١١].

c7.0   المحكوم فيه

c7.1 (عبد الوهاب خلّاف :) يشترط في الفعل الذي يصح شرعاً التكليف به ثلاثة شروط .

أولها : أن يكون معلوماً للمكلف علماً تاماً حتى يستطيع المكلف القيام به كما طلب منه . ويلاحظ أن المراد بعلم المكلف بما كلف به إمكان علمه به ، لا علمه به فعلاً . فمتى بلغ الإنسان عاقلاً قادراً على أن يعرف الأحكام الشرعية بنفسه أو بسؤال أهل الذكر عنها ، اعتبر عالماً بما كلف به ونفذت عليه الأحكام وألزم بآثارها ولا يقبل منه الاعتذار

of them is not accepted from him.

The second condition is that it is known that the ruling has been imposed by someone who possesses the authority to do so and whose rules the individual is obliged to observe, since it is through this knowledge that the individual's will can be directed to obey him. This is the reason that in any proof for a ruling of Sacred Law the first point discussed is why it is legally binding for individuals.

The third condition is that the act the subject is responsible for be possible and within the capacity of the subject to do or to refrain from. This condition in turn implies two things: first, that it is legally invalid to impose something impossible, whether impossible in itself or impossible because of another thing; and second, that it is invalid to ask that a particular individual be responsible for someone else's performing an act or refraining from one, since someone else's action or inaction is not within the individual's own capacity. Hence, a person is not responsible for his father's paying zakat, his brother's performing the prayer, or his neighbor's refraining from theft. As regards others, all a person is obliged to do is to advise, to command the right and forbid the wrong, for these are acts he is capable of.

Nor is it legally valid to make a person responsible for various innate human states which are the results of natural causes that are not of the person's acquisition or choice, such as emotional arousal when angry; turning red when embarrassed; love, hate, grief, elation, or fear when reasons for them exist; digestion; breathing; being short or tall, black or white; and other innate traits with which people are born and whose presence or absence is subject to natural laws, not to the individual's will and choice, and which are thus beyond his capacity and not among the things possible for him. And if some primary texts have reached us that apparently show that there is responsibility for some of the things that are not within a person's capacity, these are not as they seem. For example, the order of the Prophet (Allah bless him and give him peace),

"Do not become angry,"

is outwardly an order to refrain from something natural and unacquired, namely, anger when

بجهلها .

وثانيها : أن يكون معلوماً أن التكليف به صادر ممن له سلطان التكليف ، وممن يجب على المكلف اتباع أحكامه لأنه بهذا العلم تتجه إرادته إلى امتثاله . وهذا هو السبب في أن أول بحث في أي دليل شرعي هو حجيته على المكلفين .

وثالثها : أن يكون الفعل المكلف به ممكناً أو يكون في قدرة المكلف أن يفعله أو أن يكف عنه . ويتفرع عن هذا الشرط أمران : أحدهما أنه لا يصح شرعاً التكليف بالمستحيل سواء أكان مستحيلاً لذاته أم مستحيلاً لغيره . وثانيهما أنه لا يصح شرعاً تكليف المكلف بأن يفعل غيره فعلاً أو يكف غيره عن فعل ، لأن فعل غيره أو كف غيره ليس ممكناً له هو . وعلى هذا لا يكلف إنسان بأن يزكي أبوه أو يصلي أخوه أو يكف جاره عن السرقة . وكل ما يكلف به الإنسان مما يخص غيره هو النصح والأمر بالمعروف والنهي عن المنكر ، وهذا من فعله المقدور له .

وكذلك لا يصح شرعاً أن يكلف الإنسان بأمر من الأمور الجبلية للإنسان التي هي مسببات لأسباب طبيعية ولا كسب للإنسان فيها ولا اختيار ، كالانفعال عند الغضب ، والحمرة عند الخجل ، والحب والبغض ، والحزن والفرح ، والخوف حين وجود أسبابها ، والهضم والتنفس ، والطول والقصر ، والسواد والبياض ، وغير ذلك من الغرائز التي فطر عليها الناس ووجودها وعدمها خاضع لقوانين خلقية وليس خاضعاً لإرادة المكلف واختياره . فهي خارجة عن قدرته وليس من الممكنات له .

وإذا ورد في بعض النصوص ما يدل ظاهره على أن فيه تكليفاً بما ليس مقدوراً للإنسان من هذه الأمور فهو ليس على ظاهره . مثلاً قوله ﷺ : «لا تغضب» ظاهره التكليف بالكف عن أمر طبيعي غير كسبي وهو الغضب عند وجود داعيته

motives for it exist. But the real meaning is "Control yourself when angry and restrain yourself from its bad consequences."

c7.2   From the condition that an act must be within the individual's capacity before he can be held accountable for it, one should not jump to the conclusion that this implies there will not be any hardship whatsoever for the individual in the act. There is no contradiction between an act's being within one's capacity and its being hard. Nothing a person is responsible for is completely free of hardship, since moral responsibility is being obliged to do that in which there is something to bear with, and some type of difficulty.

Hardship, however, is of two types. The first is that which people are accustomed to bear, which is within the limits of their strength, and were they to continue bearing it, it would not cause them harm or damage to their persons, possessions, or other concerns. The second is that which is beyond what people are accustomed to bear and impossible for them to continually endure because they would be cut off, unable to go on, and damage and harm would affect their persons, possessions, or one of their other concerns. Examples include fasting day after day without breaking it at night, a monastic life, fasting while standing in the sun, or making the pilgrimage on foot. It is a sin for someone to refuse to take a dispensation and insist on the stricter ruling when this will probably entail harm (*'Ilm usul al-fiqh* (y71), 128–33).

*

c8.0   WHO MAY BE HELD RESPONSIBLE

c8.1   ('Abd al-Wahhab Khallaf:) Two conditions must exist in an individual for it to be legally valid to hold him responsible.

The first condition is that he is able to understand the evidence that he is responsible for something, such that it is within his capacity to

فالمراد اضبط نفسك حين الغضب وكفها عن آثاره السيئة .

c7.2   ولا يتبادر إلى الذهن من اشتراط أن يكون الفعل مقدوراً للمكلف لصحة التكليف به شرعاً أن هذا يستلزم أن لا تكون في الفعل أية مشقة على المكلف ، لأنه لا منافاة بين كون الفعل مقدوراً وكونه شاقاً . وكل ما يكلف به الإنسان لا يخلو من نوع مشقة ، لأن التكليف هو الإلزام بما فيه كلفة ونوع مشقة .

غير أن المشقة نوعان : النوع الأول مشقة جرت عادة الناس أن يحتملوها وهي في حدود طاقتهم ولو داموا على احتمالها لا يلحقهم أذى ولا ضرر لا في نفس ولا في مال ولا في أي شأن من شؤونهم . النوع الثاني مشقة خارجة عن معتاد الناس ولا يمكن أن يداوموا على احتمالها ، لأنهم إذا داوموا عليها انبتوا وانقطعوا ونالهم الضرر والأذى في أنفسهم ونالهم أو أموالهم أو أي شأن من شؤونهم ، كالمشقة في صوم الوصال والمثابرة على قيام الليل والترهب والصيام قائماً في الشمس والحج ماشياً . وحُكم بإثم من ترك الرخص واستمسك بالعزيمة محتملاً ما فيه من ضرر [محرر من علم أصول الفقه : ١٢٨ـ١٣٣] .

c8.0   المحكوم عليه

c8.1   (عبد الوهاب خلّاف :) يشترط في المكلف لصحة تكليفه شرعاً شرطان :

أولهما : أن يكون قادراً على فهم دليل التكليف بأن يكون في استطاعته أن يفهم

understand legal texts from the Koran and sunna by which the ruling is imposed, whether by himself or through another (dis: b5.1). Since human reason is something hidden, unobservable by outward sense perception, the Lawgiver has conjoined responsibility for rulings with something manifest and perceptible to the senses from which reason may be inferred, namely, puberty. Whoever reaches puberty without showing signs of impaired intellectual faculties, his capacity for responsibility exists. And conversely, neither an insane person nor child are responsible, because of their lack of intellect, which is the means of understanding the evidence that something is a ruling. Nor are those responsible who are in a state of absentmindedness or sleeping, because while they are heedless or asleep it is not within their capacity to understand. The Prophet (Allah bless him and give him peace) said,

"The pen has been lifted from three: the sleeper until he awakens, the child until his first wet dream, and the insane person until he can reason."

The second condition (n: for the legal validity of holding someone responsible) is that he be legally eligible for the ruling. Eligibility is of two types, eligibility for *obligation,* and eligibility for *performance.*

c8.2   *Eligibility for obligation* is the capacity of a human being to have rights and duties. This eligibility is established for every person by the mere fact of being human, whether male, female, fetus, child, of the age of discrimination, adolescent, intelligent, foolish, sane or insane, healthy or ill; because its basis is an innate attribute found in man. Every human being, whoever he or she may be, has eligibility for obligation and none lacks it because one's eligibility for obligation is one's humanness.

There are only two human states in relation to eligibility for obligation, partial and full. One could have *partial eligibility for obligation* by being entitled to possess rights over others but not have obligations towards them, like a fetus in its mother's womb, which has rights, since it can be

النصوص القانونية التي يكلف بها من القرآن والسنة بنفسه أو بالواسطة .

ولما كان العقل أمراً خفياً لا يدرك بالحس الظاهر ، ربط الشارع التكليف بأمر ظاهر يدرك بالحس هو مظنة للعقل وهو البلوغ . فمن بلغ الحلم من غير أن تظهر عليه أعراض خلل بقواه العقلية فقد توافرت فيه القدرة على أن يكلف . وعلى هذا لا يكلف المجنون ولا الصبي لعدم وجود العقل الذي هو وسيلة فهم دليل التكليف . ولا يكلف الغافل والنائم لأنهم في حال الغفلة أو النوم [. . .] ليس في استطاعتهم الفهم . ولهذا قال رسول الله ﷺ : «رفع القلم عن ثلاثة : النائم حتى يستيقظ ، وعن الصبي حتى يحتلم ، وعن المجنون حتى يعقل» .

وثانيهما : أن يكون أهلاً لما كلف به . فالأهلية تنقسم إلى قسمين : أهلية الوجوب وأهلية الأداء .

c8.2   فأهلية الوجوب هي صلاحية الإنسان لأن تثبت له حقوق وتجب عليه واجبات . [. . .] وهذه الأهلية أي أهلية الوجوب ثابتة لكل إنسان بوصف أنه إنسان سواء أكان ذكراً أم أنثى ، وسواء أكان جنيناً أم طفلاً أم مميزاً أم بالغاً أم رشيداً أم سفيهاً ، عاقلاً أو مجنوناً ، صحيحاً أو مريضاً ، لأنها مبنية على خاصة فطرية في الإنسان . فكل إنسان أياً كان له أهلية الوجوب ولا يوجد إنسان عديم أهلية الوجوب لأن أهليته للوجوب هي إنسانيته . والإنسان بالنسبة لأهلية الوجوب له حالتان اثنتان فقط : فقد تكون له أهلية وجوب ناقصة إذا صلح لأن تثبت له حقوق لا لأن تجب عليه واجبات

43

an heir, inherit a bequest, and the proceeds of an endowment (waqf) can accrue to it, but it does not have any obligations to others. *Full eligibility for obligation* means a person has rights upon others and obligations towards them. Every human being acquires it at birth.

c8.3   *Eligibility for performance* is the capacity of an individual for words and actions that are legally significant, such that if an agreement or act proceeds from him, it legally counts and entails the rulings applicable to it. If he prays, fasts, makes the pilgrimage, or does anything obligatory, it is legally acknowledged and discharges the obligation. And if he commits a crime against another's person, possessions, or honor, he is held accountable for his crime and is bodily or financially penalized.

So eligibility for performance is *responsibility,* and its basis in man is intellectual discrimination. There are three states which a person may have in relation to eligibility for performance:

(1) a person could *completely lack or lose eligibility for performance,* like a young child during his childhood or an insane person during his insanity (regardless of his age), neither of whom has eligibility for performance because they lack human reason, and for neither of whom are there legal consequences entailed by their words or actions. Their agreements and legal dispositions are null and void, the limit of which is that if either of them commits a crime against another's person or possessions, he is responsible for paying the indemnity out of his own property, but not subject to retaliation in his own person. This is the meaning of the scholars' expression, "The intentional act of a child or insane person is an honest mistake."

(2) A person could have *partial eligibility for performance,* an example of which is the child who has reached the age of mental discrimination (def: f1.2) but not puberty (k13.8), or the retarded person, who is not disturbed in intellect nor totally bereft of it, but rather is weak-minded and lacking

كالجنين في بطن أمـه فإنه تثبت له حقوق لأنـه يرث ويوصى لـه ويستحق في ريـع الـوقف، لكـن لا تجـب عليــه لغيــره واجبـات. وقـد تكـون لـه أهليـة وجـوب كاملة إذا صلح لأن تثبت له حقوق وتجب عليه واجبات. وهذه تثبت لكل إنسان من حين ولادته.

c8.3   وأمـا أهـليـة الأداء: فهـي صلاحيـة المكلف لأن تعتبر شرعاً أقواله وأفعاله بحيث إذا صدر منه عقد أو تصرف كان معتبراً شرعاً وترتبت عليه أحكامه، وإذا صلى أو صام أو حج أو فعـل أي واجب كان معتبـراً شرعاً ومسقطاً عنـه الواجب. وإذا جنى على غيره في نفس أو مال أو عرض أخـذ بجنايته وعوقب عليها بدنيـاً ومالياً. فأهليـة الأداء هي المسؤولية وأساسها في الإنسان التمييـز بالعقـل. والإنسان بالنسبة لأهلية الأداء له حالات ثلاث:

١ـ قد يكـون عديـم الأهليـة للأداء أصلاً أو فاقـدهـا أصلاً. وهذا هو الطفل في زمن طفوليته والمجنون في أي سن كان، فكل منهما لكونه لا عقل له لا أهلية أداء له وكـل منهمـا لا تترتب آثار شرعية على أقـوالـه ولا على أفعالـه، فعقـوده وتصـرفـاتـه باطلة، غايـة الأمـر إذا جنى أحدهمـا على نفس أو مال يؤاخذ مالياً لا بدنيـاً [...] وهـذا معنى قول الفقهاء «عمد الطفل أو المجنون خطأ».

٢ـ وقـد يكـون ناقص الأهليـة للأداء وهو المميز الـذي لم يبلغ الحلم وهذا يصدق على الصبي في دور التمييـز قبل البلـوغ ويـصـدق على المعتـوه، فإن المعتوه ليس مختل العقل ولا فاقده بل ضعيف العقـل ناقصـه، فحكمـه حكم

in intellect, so that the Sacred Law treats him as it does the child with discrimination.

Because each of these two possesses the basis of eligibility for performance by the fact of having discrimination, those of their legal actions which are absolutely beneficial to them, such as accepting gifts or alms, are valid without their guardian's permission.

As for those of their legal actions which are wholly harmful to them, such as giving donations or waiving their rights to something, these are not in any way valid, even with the guardian's permission. The gift, bequest, endowment, and divorce of such persons are not valid, and the guardian's permission is irrelevant to these actions.

The legal actions of the child with discrimination or the retarded person which are between absolute benefit and absolute harm to him are valid, but only on condition that the guardian gives his permission for them. If the guardian gives permission for the agreement or disposition, it is implemented, and if he does not permit it, the action is invalid.

(3) Or a person could have *full eligibility for performance* by the fact of having reached puberty sound of mind.

Events, however, may befall this eligibility. They include those that happen to a person without affecting his eligibility for performance by eliminating or diminishing it, but which alter some rulings concerning him because of considerations and interests that arise through these events, not because of loss or lessening of eligibility for performance. Examples include the foolhardy and the absentminded person. Both have reached puberty with normal intelligence and have full eligibility for performance, but to protect their own property from loss and prevent them from becoming a financial burden on others, they are declared legally incompetent in financial dealings such that neither their financial transactions nor donations are valid. This is not because of a lack or lessening of their eligibility for performance, but rather to protect their own property.

A debtor has likewise reached puberty with normal intelligence and possesses full eligibility for performance, but to protect the rights of his creditors, he is declared legally incompetent to

الصبي المميـز . وكل منهما لوجود وثبوت أصل أهليــة الأداء له بالتمييـز تصـح تصرفاتـه النـافعة له نفعاً محضاً كقبولـه الهبات والصدقات بدون إذن وليه .

وأمـا تصرفاتـه الضارة بمـا لـه ضرر محض كتبرعـاتـه وإسقاطـاتـه فلا تصح أصـلاً ولو أجازهـا وليـه ، فهبته ووصيته ووقفه وطلاقـه [وإعتاقه] كل هذه باطلة ولا تلحقهـا إجـازة وليـه . وأمـا تصرفاته الدائرة بين النفع له والضرر به فتصح منه ولكنهـا تكـون موقوفة على إذن وليه بها . فإن أجاز وليه العقد أو التصرف نفذ ، وإن لم يجزه بطل .

٣ـ وقد يكون كامل الأهلية للأداء وهو من بلغ الحـلم عاقـلاً ، فأهليـة الأداء الكـاملة تتحقق ببلوغ الإنسـان عاقـلاً [. . .] غير أن هذه الأهلية قد تعرض لها عوارض [. . .] منهـا ما يعـرض للإنسان فلا يؤثر في أهليتـه لا بإزالتها ولا بنقصها ولكن يغيـر بعض أحكـامـه لاعتبـارات ومصالـح قضت بهذا التغير لا لفقد أهلية أو نقصهـا . كالسفه والغفلة فكـل من السفيه وذي الغفلة بالغ عاقل له أهلية أداء كاملة ولكن محافظـة على مال كل منهما من الضياع ومنعاً من أن يكون كل منهما عالـة على غيـره حجـر عليـهـمـا في التصرفات المالية فلا تصح معاوضة مالية منهـا ولا تبـرعات مالية لا لفقد أهليتهما أو نقصها ولكن محافظة على مالهما .

وكـذلـك المـدين بالغ عاقل له أهلية أداء كاملة ، ولكن محـافظـة على حقـوق دائنيـه حجـر عليـه أن يتصرف في ماله بما

make transactions with his money that infringe on the rights of his creditors, such as charitable donations (*'Ilm usul al-fiqh* (y71) 134–40).

يضـر بحقـوق الـدائنين كالتبـرعـات .
[محرر من علم أصول الفقه:
١٣٤-١٤٠].

*

BOOK D

AUTHOR'S INTRODUCTION TO 'UMDAT AL-SALIK

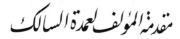

CONTENTS:

---

d1.0 AUTHOR'S INTRODUCTION

المقدمة d1.0

---

d1.1   In the name of Allah, Most Merciful and Compassionate.

    Praise be to Allah, Lord of the Worlds. Allah bless our liegelord Muhammad, his folk, and his Companions one and all.

d1.1 بِسْمِ اللَّهِ الـرَّحْمٰنِ الـرَّحِيمِ
الحمـدُ للَّهِ ربِّ العالمينَ وصَلَّى اللَّهُ على سيِّدِنا محمَّدٍ وعلى آلِهِ وصحبِهِ أجمعينَ.

---

d1.2   This is a summary of the school of Imam Shafi'i (the mercy and bliss of Allah Most High be upon him) in which I have confined myself to the most dependable positions (al-sahih) of the school according to Imam Rafi'i and Imam Nawawi, or according to just one of them. I may mention a difference of opinion herein, this being when their recensions contend (dis: w12), giving Nawawi's position first (O: as he is the foremost reference of the school), and then as opposed to it, that of Rafi'i (n: generally left untranslated because it is the weaker position where mentioned).

d1.2 هٰذا مختـصـرٌ على مذهب الإمام الشافعيِّ رحمةُ اللَّهِ عليْهِ ورضوانُهُ اقتصرتُ فيه على الصحيح مِنَ المذهب عنـدَ الـرّافعيِّ والنـوويِّ أوْ أحـدهمَا وقدْ أذْكُـرُ فيـهِ خلافـاً، وذلـكَ إذَا اخْتَلَفَ تصحيحُهُما مقدِّماً لتصحيح النـوويِّ (لأنَّـه العمدة في المذهب) فَيَكُونُ مقابلُهُ تصحيحَ الرّافعيِّ.

47

d1.3   I have named it *The Reliance of the Traveller and Tools of the Worshipper.*

(O: *Reliance* means that which is depended upon, since the author meant that this text should be a reliable resource work for whoever goes by it, because it contains the most dependable positions of the school and omits the weak ones.

Traveller (salik) derives from *travel* (suluk), meaning to proceed along, the allusion being to the spiritual journey, meaning one's seeking knowledge of the rules of religion with seriousness and effort, to thereby reach Allah Most High and be saved from perdition.

Tools are physical instruments their owner depends on in his work, like those of a carpenter. The tools here are knowledge of the rules of Sacred Law found in this text which the validity of worship depends upon.)

d1.4   I ask Allah to give benefit through it, and He is my sufficiency, and best to rely on.

د1.3   وَسَمَّيْتُهُ «عُمْدَةَ السَّالِكِ وعُدَّةَ النَّاسِكِ». (والعمدة ما يعتمد عليه فأراد المصنِّف أن يكون هذا المتن عمدة لمن تمسـك به لأنـه قد اشتمـل على المسائل المعتمـدة في المـذهب دون الضعيفـة. والسـالك من السلوك وهو السير والمراد منـه هنـا السير المعنوي وهو طلبه لمعرفة أحكام الدين بالجد والاجتهاد فيصل بهذا إلى الله تعـالى وينجو حينئذ من الهلاك. والعـدة اسم للآلـة الحسيـة التي يعتمـد عليها صاحبها في أشغاله كآلة النجار مثلاً وتلك الآلة هي معرفة ما في هذا المتن من الأحكـام الشرعيـة التي تتـوقف صحة العبادة عليها).

د1.4   واللَّهَ أَسْـأَلُ أَنْ يَنْفَعَ بِه وهـوَ حسبي وَنِعْمَ الوكيلُ.

*

BOOK E

PURIFICATION

كتاب الطهارة

CONTENTS:

---

e1.0 WATER	**أقسام المياه e1.0**
e1.1 Water is of various *types*:	المياهُ أقسامٌ، طهورٌ وطاهرٌ e1.1 ونجسٌ.
(1) purifying;	
(2) pure;	
(3) and impure.	
e1.2 *Purifying* means it is pure in itself and it purifies other things. (O: *Purification* (Ar. tahara) in Sacred Law is lifting a state of *ritual impurity* (hadath, def: e7), removing *filth* (najasa, e14), or matters similar to these, such as purificatory baths (ghusl) that are merely sunna or renewing ablution (wudu) when there has been no intervening ritual impurity.)	فالطهورُ هو الطاهرُ في نفسِهِ e1.2 المطَهِّرُ لغيرهِ. (والطهارةُ [. . .] شرعاً رفع حدث أو إزالة نجس أو ما في معناهما كـ[التيمم و] الأغسال المسنونة وتجديد الوضوء).
e1.3 *Pure* means it is pure in itself but cannot purify other things (O: such as water that has already been used to lift a state of ritual impurity).	والطاهـرُ هو الطاهرُ في نفسِهِ e1.3 ولا يُطَهِّرُ غَيْرَهُ (كالماء المستعمل في رفع حدث).
e1.4 *Impure* means it is neither purifying nor pure. (O: Namely:	والنَّجِسُ غَيْرُهُمَا. (وهو الذي e1.4

(1) less than *216 liters of water* (qullatayn) which is contaminated by filth (najasa), even when none of the water's *characteristics* (n: i.e. taste, color, or odor) have changed;

(2) or 216 liters or more of water when one of its characteristics of taste, color, or odor have changed (n: through the effect of the filth. As for the purity of water that has been used to wash away filth, it is discussed below at e14.14).)

e1.5   It is not permissible (O: or valid) to lift a state of ritual impurity or remove filth except with *plain water* (O: not *used* water (def: (2) below), or something other than water like vinegar or milk), meaning purifying water as it comes from nature, no matter what quality it may have (O: of taste, such as being fresh or saline (N: including sea-water); of color, such as being white, black, or red; or of odor, such as having a pleasant smell).

e1.7   It is not permissible to purify (def: e1.2(O:)) with:

(1) water that has changed so much that it is no longer termed *water* through admixture with something pure like flour or saffron which could have been avoided;

(2) less than 216 liters of water that has already been used for the obligation (dis: c2.1(A:), end) of lifting a state of ritual impurity, even if only that of a child;

(3) or less that 216 liters of water that has been used to remove filth, even if this resulted in no change in the water.

e1.8   It is permissible to purify with water:

(1) (non-(1) above) that has been only slightly changed by saffron or the like;

حلَّت فيه نجاسة وهو دون القلتين ولو لم يتغير أحد أوصافه، أو كان قلتين فأكثر وتغير أحد أوصافه من طعم أو لون أو ريح).

e1.5   فَلا يجـوزُ (ولا يصـح) رفـعُ حدثٍ ولا إزالـةُ نجسٍ إلا بالماء المطلقِ (لا بغيـره من المـاء المستعمـل ولا بغير المـاء كالخـل واللبن)، وهُوَ الطهورُ على أيِّ صفةٍ كانَ مِنْ أصلِ الخِلقة (من طعم ككونه حلواً أو ملحاً، أو لون ككونه أبيض أو أسـود أو أحمـر، أو ريح كأن كان له رائحة طيبة).

e1.6   [وَيُكرَهُ بالمشمَس في البـلاد الحـارَة في الأواني المنطبعـة وهِيَ مَا يُطْرَقُ بالمطارق، إلَّا الذهبَ والفضةَ، وتزُولُ بالتبريدِ].

e1.7   وإذا تَغَيَّـرَ المـاءُ تَغَيُّـراً كثِيراً بحيثُ يُسلَبُ عنهُ اسمُ المـاءِ بمخـالطةِ شيءٍ طاهـرٍ يُمْكِنُ الصـونُ عنـهُ كدقيقٍ وزعـفـرانٍ أو استُعْمـلَ دونَ القلتين في فرض طهـارةِ الحـدثِ ولَـوْ لِصبِيٍّ أو لنجسٍ ولوْ لمْ يَتَغَيَّرْ لمْ تَجُزِ الطهارةُ بهِ.

e1.8   فإنْ تَغَيَّـرَ بالـزعفـرانِ ونحوِه

(2) that has been changed by proximity with something such as aloes or oil that are (O: i.e. even if) fragrant;

(3) that has been changed by something impossible to prevent, such as algae, tree leaves falling in it, dust, or the effects of standing too long;

(4) (non-(2) of the previous ruling) that has already been used for a nonobligatory use such as the sunnas of rinsing out the mouth, renewing ablution when there has been no intervening state of ritual impurity, or a sunna purificatory bath;

(5) or water that has already been used (n: to lift a state of ritual impurity) and has now been added together until it amounts to 216 liters or more.

e1.9   With less than 216 liters, if a person performing ablution (after washing his face once) or the purificatory bath (after making intention for it) makes the intention in his heart to use his hands to scoop up the water, then the introduction of his hands into this amount of water does not make the water used. But if not (O: if he does not make this intention at all, or does so after putting his hands in the water, which is less than 216 liters), then the rest of the water is considered as already used (n: and no longer purifying. But in the Maliki school (dis: c6.4(end)), it is valid (though offensive) to lift a state of ritual impurity with water that has already been used for that purpose (al-Sharh al-saghir 'ala Aqrab al-masalik ila madhhab al-Imam Malik (y35),1.37)).

e1.10   As for 216 liters or more of water, even if two or more persons in a state of *major ritual impurity* (janaba, def: e10) are immersed in it, whether simultaneously or serially, their impurity is lifted and the water does not thereby become used (n: but remains purifying).

e1.11   *Qullatayn* (lit. "two great jars") roughly equal five hundred Baghdad *ritl*s, and their vol-

يسيراً أوْ بمجاورة (بسببها) كعودٍ ودُهْنٍ (ولو كانا) مطيَّبيْن أوْ بما لاَ يُمْكنُ الصوْنُ عنـهُ كطُحْلُبٍ ووَرَقِ شجـرٍ تَنَـاثَرَ فيـهِ وبتـرابٍ وطـولِ مكثٍ أو استُعْملَ في النفلِ كمضمضةٍ وتجديدٍ وضوءٍ وغسلٍ مسنــونٍ أوْ جُمِعَ المستعمَلُ فَبَلَغَ قلتيْنِ جازتِ الطهارة به .

e1.9   ولوْ أُدْخَـلَ مُتـوضّيءٌ يَدَهُ بعدَ غسـلِ وجهِـه مرَّةً أوْ جُنُبٌ بعـدَ النيـةِ في دونِ القلتيْنِ فاغْتَـرَفَ ونَوَى الاغترافَ لمْ يَضُـرَّهُ . وإلاّ (أي وإن لم ينـوِ الاغتـراف أصـلاً أو أتى بهـذهِ النية بعد أن أدخل يده في الماء القليل) صَارَ الباقِي مستعْمَلاً . (ت : أي : وغيـر مطهّـرٍ . لكن في المـذهب المـالكي يجـوز رفع الحدث بالماء المستعمـل، مع الكراهة [الشرح الصغير على أقرب المسالك إلى مذهب الإمام مالك : ١/ [٣٧]) .

e1.10   ولوِ انْغَمَسَ جُنُبانِ فاكثَرُ دُفعَةً أوْ واحـداً بعـدَ واحدٍ في قلتين ارْتَفَعَتْ جَنَابتُهُمْ ولا يَصيرُ مُسْتَعْمَلاً .

e1.11   والقلتـانِ خَمْسُمائةِ رطلٍ

ume is one and a quarter *dhira‘* in height, width, and length.

(n: The definition of *qullatayn* as being 216 liters is based on estimating the *dhira‘* at forty-eight centimeters. Metric equivalents of Islamic weights and measures are given at w15.)

بغـداديَّـةٍ تقـريـباً ومساحتُهُمَا ذراعٌ وربعُ طولاً وعرضاً وعمقاً.

e1.12   Two hundred and sixteen liters of water does not become impure by mere contact with filth, but only becomes so by changing (n: in taste, color, or smell) because of it, even when (O: this change is) only slight.

e1.12   فالقلتــانِ لا تَنْجُسُ بِمُجَـرَّدِ مُلاَقَاةِ النجـاسَـةِ بل بالتَّغُيـرِ بها ولَوْ (كان التغير بالنجاسة) يسيراً.

e1.13   If such change (n: in 216 liters or more of water) disappears by itself (O: such as through standing at length) or by water (O: added to it, even if the additional water is used or impure) then the water is again purifying.

e1.13   ثُمَّ إنْ زَالَ التغيُّرُ بنفسِهِ (وذلك كطــول مكثٍ) أوْ بمـاءٍ (انضم إليـه ولـو مستعملاً ولو متنجساً) طَهُرَ.

e1.14   But the 216 liters of water does not become purifying if the change disappears by (O: putting) such things as musk (O: in it, or amber-gris, or camphor, which mask the scent; or putting saffron and the like in it which mask the color) or vinegar (O: which masks the taste) or earth.

e1.14   أوْ (بـوضـع) نحـوِ مِسْكٍ (فيه وعنبر وكافور وغيرهما مما يستر الريح ووضع زعفران وغيره فيه مما يستر اللون) أوْ بِخَلّ (مما يستر الطعم) أوْ بترابٍ فَلاَ.

e1.15   Less than 216 liters becomes impure by mere contact with filth, whether the water changes or not, unless filth falls into it whose amount (N: before it falls in is so small that it) is indiscernible by eyesight (A: *eyesight*, here and for all rulings, meaning an average look, not a negligent glance nor yet a minute inspection), or if something dead falls into it of creatures without flowing blood, such as flies and the like, in both of which cases it remains purifying. This is equally true of running or still water.

e1.15   ودونَهُمَا يَنْجُسُ بمجرَّدِ ملاقاة النجـاسَـةِ وإنْ لـمْ يَتَغَيَّـرْ إلاَّ أنْ يَقَـعَ فيـه نجسٌ لا يَرَاهُ البصرُ أوْ ميتةٌ لا دم لَهَا سائلٌ كذباب ونحوِه فَلاَ يَضُرُّ، وسواءُ الجاري والراكدُ.

e1.16   When less than 216 liters of impure water is added to (O: even if with impure water) until it amounts to 216 liters or more and no change (def: below) remains in it, then it is (O: has become) purifying.

e1.16   فإنْ كُوثِرَ القليلُ النجسُ (ولو بماء نجس) فَبَلَغَ قلتين ولا تَغَيُّرَ طَهُرَ (أي صار طهوراً).

e1.17 *Change,* resulting from something pure or impure, means in color, taste, or smell.

(N: But the least change caused by filth makes water (n: even if more than 216 liters) impure, while change caused by something pure does not hurt as long as it can still be termed *water.* For example, when sugar and tea leaves have been added to water and it is called *tea,* it has become *pure but not purifying.* As for a slight discoloration by tea leaves, or a slight sweetness from sugar, this does not negate water's being purifying.)

e1.17 والمـراد بالتغيُّر بالطاهـر أو بالنجس إمَّا اللونُ أو الطعمُ أو الـريـحُ (ح: لكن أدنى تغير بالنجاسة يجعل الماء نجساً، والتغير بالطاهر لا يضر ما لم يمنع إطلاق اسم الماء عليه، كالماء إذا وضع فيه سكر وشاي فصار اسمه شاياً وصار طاهراً غير مطهَّر. أما قليل من لون الشاي أو حلاوة السكر فلا يسلب الطهورية).

e1.18 [ويُنْدَبُ تغطيةُ الإناء، فلَوْ وَقَعَ في أحدِ الإناءين نجسٌ تَوَضَّأَ من أحدِهِمَا باجتهادٍ وظهور علامةٍ سواءٌ قَدَرَ على طاهرٍ بيقينٍ أمْ لا . فإن تَحَيَّرَ أَرَاقَهُمَا وتيَمَّمَ بلا إعادةٍ . والأعمى يَجْتَهِدُ . فإنْ تَحَيَّرَ قَلَّدَ بصيراً . ولو اشتبه طهورُ ماءٍ وردٍ تَوَضَّأَ بكلِّ واحدٍ مرةً . أو بيولٍ أَرَاقَهُمَا وتَيَمَّمَ].

*

e2.0 CONTAINERS AND UTENSILS

e2.0 الأوانـي التي تجــوز الطهارة فيها

e2.1 Purification is permissible with water from any pure container, except those of gold or silver, or those to which enough gold or silver has been applied that any of it could be collected from the vessel by heating it with fire (N: meaning that if the vessel were exposed to fire, the metallic coat would melt and separate from the container, even if not drop by drop). Such containers or utensils are unlawful for men or women to use in purification, eating, drinking, or other use (O: of any type whatever). It is unlawful to acquire such a container or utensil even if one does not use it. Even a small eye-liner stick of silver is unlawful.

e2.1 تَحِـلُّ الطهـارةُ من كلِّ إنـاءٍ طاهرٍ إلَّا الـذَّهَبَ والـفِضَّـة والمطْلِيَّ بأحـدِهِمَا بحيثُ يَتَحَصَّلُ منْهُ شيءٌ بالنار (ح: يعني لوْ عرض الإنـاء المطلي على النار لذاب الطلاء وانفصل عن الإناء وإن لم يتقـاطـر) . فَيَحـرُمُ استعمالُهُ على الـرجـالِ والنسـاءِ في الطهـارةِ والأكـلِ والشـرب وغير ذلك (من سائـر وجوه الاسـتـعـمـالات) وكـذا اقـتـنـاؤُهُ بلا استعمالٍ ، حتى الميلُ من الفضَّةِ .

e2.2 Vessels soldered with gold are absolutely unlawful.

It is unlawful to use a vessel to which *much* (def: f4.5) silver solder has been applied by way of decoration; permissible to use a vessel to which only a little silver solder has been applied by way of a needed repair; and offensive but not unlawful to use a vessel to which only a little silver has been applied for decoration, or much out of necessity.

e2.2 المـضـبَّـبُ بالـذَهَبِ حرامٌ مطلقاً . [وقيلَ كالفضةِ] وبـالفضةِ إنْ كانتْ كبيرةً للزينةِ فهيَ حرامٌ . أوْ صغيرةً للحـاجةِ حَلَّ . أوْ صغيرة للزينة أوْ كبيرة للحـاجةِ كُرِهَ ولمْ يَحْرُمْ . ومعنى التضبيب

Solder means that a part of the vessel has been broken and then silver is put there to hold it together.

أنْ يَنْكَسِرَ موضِعٌ مِنْهِ فَيَجْعَلَ موضِعَ الكِسْرِ فضةً تُمْسِكُهُ بِهَا .

e2.3　It is offensive to use the vessels of non-Muslims (N: before washing them) (O: to be certain of the purity of the vessels used, since non-Muslims are not as concerned about purity as Muslims are) or wear their clothes (O: for the same reason).

e2.3　وَتُكْرَهُ أواني الكُفَّارِ (حرصاً على يقين الطهارة والكفار لا يحافظون على الطهارة كالمسلمين) وثيابُهُمْ (لما مَرّ) .

e2.4　It is permissible to use a vessel made of any precious gem, such as a ruby or emerald.

e2.4　وَيُبَاحُ الإناءُ مِنْ كلِّ جوهرٍ نفيسٍ كياقوتٍ وزمرِدٍ .

*

e3.0　USING A TOOTHSTICK (SIWAK)
　　(O: In Sacred Law it refers to the use of a twig or the like on the teeth and around them to remove an unpleasant change in the breath or similar, together with the intention (n: of performing the sunna).)

e3.0　السواك
(. . وهو شرعاً استعمال عود ونحوه في الأسنان وما حولها لإذهاب التغير ونحوه بنية) .

e3.1　Using a *toothstick* is recommended any time, except after noon for someone who is fasting, in which case it is offensive. (A: Using toothpaste is also offensive then, and if any reaches the stomach of someone fasting, it is unlawful (n: if the fast is obligatory, as this breaks a fast).)

e3.1　يُنْدَبُ السواكُ في كلِّ وقتٍ إلا لصائمٍ بعدَ الزوالِ فيُكرَهُ .

e3.2　It is especially desirable to use the toothstick for every prayer, for reading (O: the Koran, hadith, or a lesson), ablution, yellowness of teeth, waking from sleep, entering one's house, and for any change of breath from eating something with a bad odor or from not eating.
　　(A: When there exists a demand for an act, such as using the toothstick before reading the Koran, and an equal demand not to, as when it is after noon on a fast-day, then the proper course is not to do it.)

e3.2　وَيَتَأَكَّدُ استحبابُهُ لكلِّ صلاةٍ وقراءةٍ (أي للقرآن أو للحديث أو للدرس) ووضوءٍ وصفرةِ أسنانٍ واستيقاظٍ مِنَ النومِ ودخولِ بيتِهِ وتغيُّرِ الفمِ مِنْ أكلِ كلِّ كريهِ الريحِ وتركِ أكلٍ .
(ع : إذا استوى طلبُ فعلٍ ، كندب السواكِ للقرآن، وتركُ فعلٍ ، ككراهية السواكِ للصائمِ بعد الزوالِ، فالترك أولى) .

e3.3   Anything coarse is adequate (n: to fulfill the sunna) except rough fingers, though the best is a twig from the *arak* (n: a desert shrub) that is dried (N: meaning previously cut from the shrub long enough to have dried) and then moistened.

e3.3 ويُجْزِىءُ بكـلِّ خشـنٍ إلا إصبعُهُ الخَشنةَ. والأفضلُ بأراكٍ ويابسٍ (ح: أي قطع من الشجرة قبلَ مدة بحيث يبس) ندي.

e3.4   It is best to clean the teeth laterally, beginning on the right and paying particular attention to the bases of the back teeth, and to intend the sunna thereby.

e3.4 وأنْ يَسْتَاكَ عرضاً ويَبْدَأ بجانبه الأيمن ويتَعَهّدَ كراسيَّ أضراسه ويَنْوِيَ به السنة.

*

e4.0   THE BODY

e4.0 بعض السـنـن التي تتعلق بالبدن

e4.1   It is sunna:

(1) to trim the fingernails and toenails;

(2) to clip one's mustache (O: when it grows long. The most one should clip is enough to show the pink of the upper lip. Plucking it out or shaving it off is offensive.) (A: Shaving one's beard is unlawful according to all Imams except Shafi'i, who wrote two opinions about it, one that it is offensive, and the other that it is unlawful. A weak chain of narrators ascribes an opinion of offensiveness to Imam Malik. It is unbelief (kufr) to turn from the sunna in order to imitate non-Muslims when one believes their way to be superior to the sunna);

(3) for those used to it, to pluck away the hair of the underarms and nostrils, though if plucking the underarms is a hardship, then shaving them; and to shave the pubic hair;

(4) and to line the eyes with *kohl* (n: an antimonic compound that one should be careful to see contains no lead), each eye an odd number of times, preferably three.

e4.1 ويُسَـنُّ قلمُ ظفـرٍ، وقصُّ شاربٍ (طَالَ وغـايـتُهُ بدو حمرة الشفة ويكـرهُ استئصالـه وكذا حلقه)، ونتفُ إبـطٍ، وأنفٍ لمَن آعْتَادَهُ، فإنْ شَقَّ نتفُ الإبـطِ حلَقَهُ، وحَلْقُ عانـةٍ، والاكتحـالُ وتـراً ثلاثـاً في كلِّ عينٍ [وغسلُ البراجمِ وهيَ عقدُ ظهورِ الأصابعِ].

e4.2   It is offensive to shave part of the head and leave part unshaven (A: though merely cutting

e4.2 ويُكْرَهُ القزعُ وهوَ حلقُ بعضِ الـرأسِ وتـركُ بعضِهِ ولَا بأسَ بحلقِ كلِّهِ

some of the hair shorter than another part is not objectionable). There is no harm in shaving it all off (O: but it is not recommended except for the rites of *hajj* and *'umra* (n: the greater and lesser pilgrimages)).

e4.3 Circumcision is obligatory (O: for both men and women. For men it consists of removing the prepuce from the penis, and for women, removing the prepuce (Ar. bazr) of the clitoris (n: not the clitoris itself, as some mistakenly assert). (A: Hanbalis hold that circumcision of women is not obligatory but sunna, while Hanafis consider it a mere courtesy to the husband.)

e4.4 It is unlawful for men or women to dye their hair black, except when the intention is jihad (O: as a show of strength to unbelievers). Plucking out gray hair is offensive. It is sunna to dye the hair with yellow or red. (N: It is unlawful for a woman to cut her hair to disfigure herself (n: e.g. for mourning), though if done for the sake of beauty it is permissible.) It is sunna for a married woman to dye all of her hands and feet with *henna* (n: a red plant dye), but it is unlawful for men to do so unless it is needed (N: to protect from sunburn, for example).

*

e5.0 ABLUTION (WUDU)
(N: Meaning to wash certain parts of the body with water, with the intention of worship.)
(O: The legal basis for ablution, prior to scholarly consensus, is the word of Allah Most High,

"O believers, when you go to pray, wash your faces, and wash your forearms to the elbows, wipe your heads, and [wash] your feet to the two anklebones" (Koran 5:6),

and the hadith related by Muslim,

"A prayer is not accepted without purification.")

THE INTEGRALS OF ABLUTION	أركان الوضوء

e5.1   Ablution has six obligatory integrals:

    (a) to have the intention when one starts washing the face;

    (b) to wash the face;

    (c) to wash the arms up to and including the elbows;

    (d) to wipe a little of the head with wet hands;

    (e) to wash the feet up to and including the anklebones;

    (f) and to do these things in the order mentioned.

The sunnas of ablution are all its actions besides the above. (N: The obligatory minimum is to perform (b), (c), (d), and (e) once, though the sunna is to perform them each three times.)

e5.1 فروضُهُ ستةٌ: النيةُ عندَ غَسلِ الوجهِ، وغسلُ الوجهِ، وغسلُ اليدَيْنِ إلى المـرفِـقَيْن، ومسـحُ القليـلِ منَ الـرأسِ، وغسلُ الرجلَيْنِ إلى الكعبَيْنِ، والترتيبُ على مَا ذَكَرْنَا. وسننُهُ ما عَدَا ذلك.

THE INTENTION

النية

e5.2   The person performing ablution intends:

    (1) to lift a state of lesser ritual impurity (hadath) (O: since the purpose of ablution is to eliminate that which prevents prayer and the like);

    (2) to purify for the prayer;

    (3) or to purify for something not permissible without purification, such as touching a Koran, or something else.

    (N: The simple intention to perform the obligation of ablution suffices in place of all the above.)

e5.2 فَيَنْـوي المتـوضِّىءُ رفـعَ الحدثِ (لأن القصد من الوضوء رفع مانع الصـلاة ونحـوهـا) أوْ الطهـارةَ للصلاةِ أوْ لأمـرٍ لا يُسـتَبَـاحُ إلّا بالطهـارةِ كَمَسِّ المصحفِ أوْ غـيرِهِ. (ح: ويغني عن كل هذا أن ينوي فرض الوضوء).

e5.3   The above intentions are not used by three types of people when performing ablution:

(1) a woman with chronic vaginal discharge (def: e13.6);

(2) a person unable to hold back intermittent drops of urine coming from him (n: or with some similar state of chronic annulment of ablution (e13.7));

(3) or a person intending to perform dry ablution (tayammum, def: e12).

Such people merely intend permission to perform the obligation of the prayer as they begin their ablution.
(O: The intention to lift a state of minor ritual impurity is inadequate for these people because their state of impurity is not lifted.) (n: Rather, the Sacred Law gives them a dispensation to perform the prayer and so forth without lifting it.)

e5.4   The necessary condition of ablution is that the intention for it exist in the heart and that it accompany one's washing the first part of the face.
It is recommended to pronounce it aloud, and that it be present in the heart from the first of ablution (O: during the preliminary sunnas before washing the face, so as to earn their reward). It is obligatory that this intention persist in the heart until one washes the first part of the face (O: as that is the first integral). If one confines oneself to making the intention when washing the face, it suffices, but one is not rewarded for the previous sunnas of rinsing the mouth and nostrils and washing the· hands (N: provided that one merely intended cleanliness or something else by them, and the intention of worship did not come to one's mind).

HOW TO PERFORM ABLUTION

e5.5   It is recommended to begin ablution by mentioning (n: in Arabic, like the other invocations in this volume (def: w1)) the name of Allah

e5.3   إلا المستحاضةَ ومَنْ بِهِ سَلَسُ البـولِ ومتيممـاً فَيَنْـوي استبـاحةَ فرضِ الصلاةِ (فلا يكفي كل واحد من هؤلاء نية رفع الحدث [...] لأن حدثهم لا يرتفع).

e5.4   وشـــرطُـهُ النيـــةُ بالقلبِ وأنْ تَقْتَـــرِنَ بغسـلِ أوَّلِ جزءٍ مِنَ الـوجهِ. ويُنْـدَبُ أنْ يَتَلَفَّظَ بها وأنْ تَكُونَ مِنْ أولِ الوضـوء (حتى يـثـاب على جميـع السنن المطلوبـة قبـل غسـلِ الـوجهِ). وَيَجِبُ استصحـابُهـا (أي استدامتها بالقلب) إلى غسلِ أولِ الوجهِ (لأنه أول الفروض).
فإن اقْتَصَرَ على النيةِ عندَ غسلِ الوجهِ كَفَـى لكـنْ لا يُثَـابُ على مَا قبـلَهُ مِنْ مضمضةٍ واستنشاقٍ وغسلِ كفٌّ (ح: إن كان قد نوى مجرد النظـافـة أو غيرها ولم يخطر بباله قصد العبادة).

كيفية الوضوء

e5.5   ويُنْـدَبُ أنْ يُسَمِّيَ اللهَ تَعَـالى

Most High (O: by saying "In the name of Allah," which is the minimum.

The optimum is to say, "In the name of Allah, Most Merciful and Compassionate." Before this, it is sunna to say, "I take refuge in Allah from the accursed Devil," and to add after the *Basmala*: "Praise to Allah for Islam and its blessings. Praise to Allah who made water purifying and Islam a light. My Lord, I take refuge in You from the whispering of devils and take refuge in You lest they come to me." It is sunna to say all the above to oneself.)

If one intentionally or absentmindedly omits saying the name of Allah (n: at the first of ablution), then one pronounces it during it (O: by saying, "In the name of Allah, first to last").

e5.6   It is recommended to wash the hands three times.

(O: By saying "three times," the author indicates the sunna character of performing such acts thrice, and that it is an independent sunna (N: rewarded apart from the sunnas it is conjoined with).)

If one has doubts as to whether or not one's hands are free of filth, it is offensive to dip them into less than 216 liters of water without first washing them three times. (O: When sure they are pure, it is not offensive to immerse them. When sure they are impure, it is unlawful to dip them into this amount of water (N: since it spoils it by making it impure).)

e5.7   One next uses the toothstick (def: e3), and then rinses the mouth and nose out three times, with three handfuls of water. One takes in a mouthful from a handful of water and snuffs up some of the rest of the handful into the nostrils (n: swishing the water around the mouth, and expelling the water of the mouth and the nose simultaneously), then again rinses the mouth and then the nostrils from a second handful of water, followed by rinsing the mouth and then the nostrils from a third handful of water.

One lets the water reach as much of the mouth and nostrils as possible, unless fasting, when one goes lightly.

(بأن يقول «بسم الله وهو أقلها فإن أراد الأكمل قال بسم اللّه الرّحمن الرّحيم». ويسن التعـوّذ قبلها وأن يزيـد بعـدهـا: «الْحَمْـدُ للّهِ عَلَى الإِسْلام وَنعمَتِه الْحَمْدُ للّه الّذي جَعَل الماءَ طَهُوراً والإِسلام نُوراً ربِّ أعُوذُ بكَ مِنْ هَمَزَاتِ الشّياطِين وأعُوذُ بكَ ربِّ أَنْ يَحْضُـرُونِ» ويسن الإسرار بهـا) فإنْ تَرَك التسميـة عمداً أو سهْواً أتى بهَا في أثنائِه (فيقول: «بسْم اللّه أوّلَه وآخرَهُ»).

e5.6   وأنْ يَغْسِـلَ كفّيْـه ثلاثاً (فأشار المصنّف بقوله ثلاثاً إلى سنية التثليث وأنه سنة مستقلة).

فإنْ شَكَّ في نجاسَةِ يدِه كُرِهَ غَمْسُهـا في دُونِ القلتين قبْلَ غَسلِها ثلاثاً (فإن تيقن طهـرهـا لم يكـره له الغمس، وإن تيقن نجـاستها حرم عليـه غمسها في ماء قليل) (ح: لأنه يفسده بالتنجيس).

e5.7   ثمَّ يَسْتَـاكُ ويَتَمَضْـمَضُ ويَسْتَنْشِقَ ثلاثـاً وبثـلاث غَرَفَـات فَيَتَمَضْمَضُ مِنْ غَرْفَـةٍ ثُمَّ يَسْتَنْشِقُ ثُمَّ يَتَمَضْمَضُ مِنْ أُخْـرَى ثُمَّ يَسْتَنْشِقُ ثمَّ يَتَمَضْمَضُ مِنَ الثـالثـةِ ثُمَّ يَسْتَنْشِقُ ويُبَالِغُ فيهِمَا إلّا أَنْ يَكُونَ صائماً فَيُرْفِقُ.

e5.8   Then one washes the face three times, *face* meaning from the point where the hairline usually begins to the chin in height, and from ear to ear in width.

e5.9   It is obligatory to wash all facial hair—inner, outer, and the skin beneath, whether the hair is thick or thin—such as eyebrows, mustache, and so forth; except for the beard, since:

(1) if it is thin, its inner and outer hair and the skin beneath must be washed;

(2) but if thick, then the outer hair is enough, though it is recommended to saturate it by combing it from beneath with wet fingers.

It is obligatory to cause the water to flow over the outer (O: hair of the) part of the beard that hangs below the chin (O: though not its inner hair).

It is obligatory to wash part of the head in every direction beyond the bounds of the face, to make sure everything has been completely covered.

It is sunna to use new water to saturate one's beard (O: if it is thick) by combing it from beneath with the fingers.

e5.10   Then one washes the hands up to and including the elbows three times.

(If the arm has been amputated between the hand and elbow, it is necessary to wash the remaining forearm and the elbow. If amputated at the elbow, then the end of the upper arm must be washed. If it has been amputated between the elbow and shoulder, then it is recommended to wash the rest of the upper arm.)

e5.11   Then one wipes the head with wet hands, beginning at the front of the head, sliding the paired hands back to the nape of the neck, and then returning them to where one began. (O: This is an explanation of the best way, for otherwise,

---

e5.8   ثُمَّ يَغْسِلُ وجهَهُ ثلاثاً وهوَ مَا بينَ منابتِ شعرِ الـرأسِ في العـادةِ إلى الـذقنِ طولاً ومنَ الأذنِ إلى الأذنِ عرضـاً [فمنْـه موضعُ الغممِ وهوَ ما تحتَ الشعرِ الذي عَمَّ الجبهةَ أوْ بعضَها].

e5.9   ويَجبُ غسلُ شعورِ الـوجهِ كلِّها ظاهرهَا وبـاطنهَا والبشـرةَ تحتَها خفيفةً كَانتْ أوْ كثيفةً كالحـاجبِ والشـاربِ [والعنفقةِ والعـذارِ والهدبِ وشعرِ الخدِّ] إلا اللحيةَ [والعارضَيْنِ] فإنَّه يجبُ غسلُ ظاهرهمَا وباطنهِما والبشرة تحتَهمـا عندَ الخفَّةِ، فظاهرُ هما فقطْ عندَ الكثافةِ لكنْ يُنْدَبُ التخليلُ حينئذٍ.

ويَجبُ إفـاضـةُ المـاءِ على ظاهـرِ (الشعـرِ) النـازلِ منَ اللحيةِ عنِ الـذقنِ (أي دون باطنه).

ويَجبُ غسلُ جزءٍ منَ الـرأسِ وسائرِ مَا يُحيطُ بالوجهِ ليتحقَّقَ كمالُهُ.

ويُسَنُّ أنْ يُخَلَّلَ اللحيـةَ (الكثيفة) مِنْ أسفلِها بماءٍ جديدٍ.

e5.10   ثمَّ يَغسِلُ يدَيهِ مَعَ مِرْفَقَيْهِ ثلاثاً.

فإنْ قُطعَتْ منَ السـاعـدِ وَجَبَ غسلُ البـاقي أوْ مِنْ مفصـلِ المـرفقِ لزمَهُ غَسلُ رأسِ العضدِ أوْ منَ العضدِ نُدِبَ غسلُ باقيهِ.

e5.11   ثمَّ يَمسَحُ رأسَهُ فَيَبْدَأُ بمقدَّمِ رأسِهِ فَيـذْهَبُ بيـدَيْهِ إلى قفاهُ ثُمَّ يَرُدُّهُمَا إلى المكـانِ الـذي بَدَأ مِنْـهُ (هـذا بيانِ الأفضـلِ وإلا فالفـرضُ لا يتـوقف على

---

fulfilling the obligation does not depend on starting at the front, but may be from any part of the head.) One does this three times.

If one is bald, or one's hair never grew, or is long, or braided, then it is not recommended to slide the hands back to the front.

Each of the following suffices as *wiping the head:*

(1) to place the hand on the head without moving it so that one wets any of what is referred to by "wiping the head," the minimum of which is part of a single hair, provided this part does not hang below the limits of the head;

(2) to drip water on the head without making it flow over it;

(3) or to wash the head.

(If it is difficult to remove one's turban, then after wiping the minimum of the head required, one may finish by wiping the turban.)

e5.12   One then wipes the ears inside and out with new water, three times, and then the ear canals with one's little fingers with more new water, three times (O: though this second sunna is not separately mentioned in the more well known books, which speak of the two sunnas together, making "wiping the ears" include the ear canals).

e5.13   Then one washes the feet up to and including the anklebones three times.

e5.14   If one does not know whether one washed a particular limb or the head three times (N: as is sunna), then one assumes one has washed it the least number that one is sure of, and washes as many additional times as it takes to be certain one has reached three.

e5.15   One begins with the right when washing arms and legs, but not the hands, cheeks, and ears, which are washed right and left simultaneously.

مسح المقدم بَل يحصل مِن أي جانب مِن جوانب الرأس). يُفْعَلُ ذلِكَ ثلاثاً.

فإنْ كانَ أقرعَ أوْ ما نَبَتَ شعرهُ أوْ كانَ طويلاً أوْ مضفوراً لمْ يُنْدَبْ الردُّ.

فلَوْ وَضَعَ يدَهُ بَلا مدٍّ بحيــثُ بَلَّ ما يَنْطَلِقُ علَيْهِ الاسمُ وهُوَ بعضُ شعرةٍ لمْ تَخْرُجْ بالمدِّ عنْ حَدِّ الرأسِ، أوْ قَطَرَ ولمْ يُسِلْ، أوْ غَسَلَهُ، كَفَى.

فإنْ شَقَّ نزْعُ عمامتِهِ كَمَّلَ علَيْها بعدَ مَسْحِ ما يَجِبُ.

e5.12   ثمَّ يَمْسَحُ أذنيـهِ ظاهراً وباطناً بماءٍ جديدٍ ثلاثاً ثمَّ صماخَيْهِ بماءٍ جديدٍ ثلاثاً فَيُـدخِلُ خنصرَيْهِ فيهمَا (وهي غير مذكـورة في الكتب المشهورة استقـلالاً وقــد جمعـوا في عبـاراتهم بين السنتين وجعلوا مسـح الأذنين شامـلاً لهمـا أي لمسح الصماخين).

e5.13   ثمَّ يَغْسِلُ رِجْلَيْهِ معَ كعبَيْهِ ثلاثاً.

e5.14   فلَوْ شَكَّ في تثليثِ عضوٍ أخَذَ بالأقلِّ فيُكَمِّلُ ثلاثاً يقيناً.

e5.15   ويُقَـدَّمُ اليمنى مِنْ يدٍ ورجْـلٍ لا كفٍّ وخدٍّ وأذنٍ فيُطَهِّرُهُمَا دُفْعَةً.

e5.16   One washes more than is obligatory of the face by adding part of the head and neck, and likewise with the arms and legs by washing above the elbows and ankles, the maximum of which is the whole upper arm or lower leg.

e5.16   وَيُطِيلُ الغُرّةَ بِأَنْ يَغْسِلَ مَعَ وجهِهِ مِنْ رَأسِهِ وعنقِهِ زائداً عَنِ الفرضِ ، والتحجيلِ بِأَنْ يَغْسِلَ فوقَ مرفقَيْهِ وكَعْبَيْهِ وغايتُهُ استيعابُ العضدِ والساقِ .

e5.17   One washes the parts of the body successively and without pausing between them (O: such that in normal weather the last part would not dry before one began the next), though if one pauses between them, even for a long time, one's ablution is still valid without renewing the intention.

e5.17   وَيُوالِي الأعضاءَ (بحيثُ لا يجفُّ الأولُ قبلَ الشروعِ في الثاني مع اعتدالِ الهواءِ والمزاجِ) فإنْ فَرّقَ ولَوْ طويلاً صَحَّ بغيرِ تجديدِ نيةٍ .

e5.18   After finishing, one says: "I testify that there is no god but Allah, alone, without partner, and I testify that Muhammad is His slave and messenger. O Allah, make me one of the oft-repentant, one of the purified, one of Your goodly slaves. O Allah, I declare Your exaltedness above every imperfection and Your praise. I testify there is no god but You. I ask Your forgiveness and turn to You in repentance."

There are supplications said for each limb washed, but these are not authenticated as being of the sunna.

e5.18   ويقولُ بعدَ فراغِهِ : «أشهدُ أنْ لا إلهَ إلاّ اللّهُ وَحْدَهُ لا شريكَ لَهُ ، وأشْهَدُ أنّ محمداً عبدُهُ ورسولُهُ ، اللّهُمّ اجْعَلْني مِنَ التّوّابينَ ، واجْعَلْني مِنَ المُتَطَهّرينَ ، واجْعَلْني مِنْ عِبادِكَ الصّالحينَ سُبْحانَكَ اللّهُمّ وبِحَمْدِكَ أشْهَدُ أنْ لا إلهَ إلاّ أنْتَ ، أسْتَغْفِرُكَ وأَتُوبُ إليكَ» .

وللأعضاءِ أدْعِيةً تُقالُ عندَها لا أصْلَ لَهَا .

OTHER RECOMMENDED MEASURES

آدابُ الوضوء

e5.19   Other recommended measures (adab) include:

(1)   facing the direction of prayer;

(2)   not to talk during ablution for other than a necessity;

(3)   and to begin with the top of the face and not slap water upon it.

e5.19   وآدابُهُ استقبالُ القِبْلَةِ ، ولا يَتَكَلّمُ لغيرِ حاجةٍ ويَبْدَأُ بأعلى وجهِهِ ، ولا يَلْطِمُهُ بالماءِ .

e5.20   If another person is pouring one's water (N: or if using a tap) one begins washing the arms from the elbows, and the feet from the anklebones. If pouring one's own water (N: from

e5.20   فإنْ صَبَّ عليـهِ غيـرُهُ بَدَأَ بمرفقَيْهِ وكعبَيْهِ . وإنْ صَبَّ على نفسِهِ بَدَأَ

a jug, for example), one begins washing the arms from the fingers and the feet from the toes.

e5.21 One should take care that water reaches the inner corners of the eyes, and the heels (N: up to the level of the anklebones) and similar places it is feared one may neglect, especially during the winter.

e5.22 One moves one's ring when washing the hand to allow water to reach the skin beneath. (O: If the water cannot otherwise get under it, it is obligatory to move the ring.)

e5.23 One saturates between the toes using the little finger of the left hand. One begins with the little toe of the right foot, coming up through the toes from beneath, and finishes with the little toe of the left.

THINGS OFFENSIVE IN ABLUTION

e5.24 It is offensive:

(1) to have another person wash one's limbs, unless there is some excuse (O: such as old age or the like);

(2) to wash the left before the right;

(3) or to waste water.

e5.25 It is recommended:

(1) not to use less than *0.51 liters* (mudd) of water for ablution;

(2) not to use less than *2.03 liters* (sa') of water for the purificatory bath (ghusl);

(3) not to dry off the parts washed in ablution (N: unless there is an excuse such as illness or cold weather) or shake the water off one's hands;

بأصابِعِهِ .

e5.21 ويَتَعَهَّدُ أماقِيَ عينيهِ وعقبيْهِ ونحوهِمَا مما يُخاف إغفالَهُ سِيّمَا في الشتاءِ .

e5.22 ويُحرِّكُ خاتماً لِيَدْخُلَ الماءُ تحتَهُ (وأمَّا إذا لم يصل الماء إلى ما تحته إلّا بالتحريك فيجب حينئذ) .

e5.23 ويُخَلِّلُ أصابعَ رجليْهِ بخنصر يدِهِ اليسرى يَبْدَأ بخنصر رجلِهِ اليمنى مِنْ أسْفَلَ ويَخْتِمُ بخنصر اليسرى .

مكروهات الوضوء

e5.24 ويُكرَهُ أنْ يَغْسِلَ غيرُهُ أعضاءَهُ إلّا لعـذرٍ (ككبـرِ سن أو نحوه) وتقـديمُ يسارِهِ والإسرافُ في الماءِ .

e5.25 ويُـنْـدَبُ أنْ لا يَنْـقُصَ ماءَ الوضوءِ عنْ مدٍّ [وهوَ رطلٌ وثلثٌ بغداديٌّ] ولا يَنْقُصَ ماءُ الغسلِ عن صاعٍ [والصاعُ خمسـةُ أرطالٍ وثلثُ رطلٍ بالعراقيِّ] ولا يُنَشِّفَ أعضـاءَهُ رح : إلا لعـذرٍ كمرضٍ أو

(4) not to ask another to pour water for one's ablution;

(5) and not to wipe the neck.

OTHER PROVISIONS

e5.26   If dirt under the nails prevents the water (O: of ablution or the purificatory bath from reaching the skin beneath) then the ablution (O: or bath) is not valid.

(N: The same is true of waterproof glue, paint, nail polish, and so forth on the nails or skin: if it prevents water from reaching *any part* of the nails or skin, no matter how small, one's ablution or purificatory bath is not valid.)

e5.27   If one has doubts during the course of the ablution that one has washed a particular limb or the head, then it is obligatory to wash it again and everything that follows it in the ablution sequence.

But if these doubts arise after one has finished ablution, one need not repeat anything. (A: The same is true of the purificatory bath (ghusl).)

e5.28   It is recommended to renew the ablution (N: when there has been no intervening state of minor ritual impurity) when one has performed any prayer, obligatory or nonobligatory, with it.

e5.29   Ablution is recommended for someone in a state of major ritual impurity (janaba) who wishes to eat, drink, sleep, or make love again.

And Allah knows best.

*

e6.0   WIPING FOOTGEAR
(N: Wiping one's *footgear* (Ar. khuff) with wet hands is a dispensation that can take the place

برد)، ولا يَنْفُضَ يدَيْه، ولا يَسْتَعِينَ بأحدٍ يَصُبُّ عليْهِ، ولا يَمْسَحَ الرقبةَ.

أحكام أخرى

e5.26   ولَوْ كانَ تحتَ أظفارِه وَسَخٌ يَمْنع وُصُول الماءِ (أي ماء الوضوءِ أو الغسل إلى ما تحتها من البشرة) لمْ يصحَّ الوضوءُ (ولا الغسل).

e5.27   ولو شكَّ في أثناءِ الوضوءِ في غسلِ عضوٍ لزِمَهُ مَعَ ما بعدَهُ، أوْ بعدَ فراغِهِ لمْ يَلْزَمْهُ شيءٌ (ع: وكذلك الغسل).

e5.28   ويُنْدَبُ تجديدُ الوضوءِ لِمَنْ صلَّى بِهِ فرضاً أوْ نفلاً.

e5.29   ويُنْدَبُ الوضوءُ لجنبٍ يريدُ أكلاً، أوْ شرباً أوْ نوماً أوْ جماعاً آخَرَ، واللَّهُ أعلمُ.

المسح على الخفين   e6.0

of the fifth ablution integral of washing the feet. The footgear Muslims generally use for this are ankle-high leather socks that zip up and are worn inside the shoes.)

e6.1   Wiping footgear is permissible for 72 hours (lit. "three days and nights") to a traveller on a lawful trip (N: one not undertaken for purposes of disobeying Allah) that fulfills the conditions permitting one to shorten prayers on journeys (def: f15.1–5).

Wiping them is permissible to a nontraveller for 24 hours (lit. "a day and a night"). (n: At the end of these periods, one removes the footgear to perform ablution, or, if one has ablution at the time, to wash the feet, before putting them on again and starting a new period of permissibility, as at e6.7.)

The beginning of the period is reckoned from the time of the first minor ritual impurity (hadath) that occurs after having put them on while in a state of ablution.

Wiping footgear is permissible for only 24 hours:

(1)   when one has wiped both of a pair of footgear for ablution or just one of the pair (n: leaving the other for later) when not on a trip, and then begun travelling;

(2)   or (O: when one has wiped both of a pair of footgear or just one) when on the trip and then finished travelling;

(3)   or when one is in doubt as to whether one first wiped one's footgear for ablution while travelling or whether it was while not travelling.

Wiping footgear is permissible for 72 hours if one's ablution is nullified when not travelling and one then lifts that state of minor ritual impurity by wiping them for the ablution while travelling.

e6.2   When one doubts as to whether or not the permissible period for wiping them has expired, then one may not wipe them while the doubt exists. (A: Because dispensations cannot be taken

e6.1   يَجُوزُ المَسحُ علىٰ الخُفَّيْنِ في الوُضوءِ للمُسافِرِ سفراً مباحاً تُقصَرُ فيهِ الصلاةُ ثلاثةَ أيامٍ ولياليهنَّ، وللمقيمِ يوماً وليلةً.

وآبتداءُ المدةِ مِنَ آلحدثِ بعدَ اللبسِ.

فإنْ مَسَحَهُما أوْ أحدَهُما حضراً ثمَّ سافَرَ، أوْ (مسحهما أوْ أحدهما) سفراً ثمَّ أقامَ، أوْ شَكَّ هلِ ابْتَدأَ المسحَ سفراً أوْ حضراً أتَمَّ مَسْحَ مُقيمٍ فَقَطْ.

وَلَوْ أحْدَثَ حضراً وَمَسَحَ سفراً أتَمَّ مدة مسافرٍ [سواءٌ مَضَى عليْهِ وقتُ الصلاةِ بكمالِهِ في الحضرِ أمْ لا].

e6.2   فإنْ شَكَّ في انقضاءِ المدةِ لمْ يَمْسَحْ في مدةِ الشكِّ (ع: لأنَّ الرخصةَ لا

unless one is certain (N: of their necessary conditions).) If one has doubts (n: when near the end of the permissible period for wiping them, for example, and uncertain exactly when it began) about whether one nullified one's ablution at the time of the noon prayer, or whether it was at the time of the midafternoon prayer, then one proceeds on the assumption that it was at the time of the noon prayer.

يصار إليها إلا بيقين) .

فإنْ شُكَّ هَلْ أُحْـدَثَ وقتَ الظهـرِ أو العصرِ بَنى أَمْرَهُ على أنَّهُ الظهْرُ .

e6.3　If a state of major ritual impurity (janaba) occurs during the permissible period for wiping footgear, then one must take them off for the purificatory bath (ghusl).

e6.3　ولَـوْ أَجْنَبَ في المـدةِ وَجَبَ النزعُ للغُسلِ .

e6.4　The conditions for the permissibility of wiping footgear are:

(a) that one have full ablution when one first puts them on;

(b) that they be free of filth;

(c) that they cover the whole foot up to and including the anklebones;

(d) that they prevent water (N: if dripped on them drop by drop from directly) reaching the foot (O:—if water reaches the foot through the holes of a seam's stitches, it does not affect the validity of wiping them, though if water can reach the foot through any other place, it violates this condition);

(e) and that they be durable enough to keep walking around upon as travellers do in attending to their needs (O: when encamping, departing, etc.);

—no matter whether they are of leather, felt, layers of rags (N: including thick, heavy wool socks that prevent water from reaching the foot (A: not modern dress socks (n: due to non-(d) and (e) above), which are not valid to wipe in any school, even if many are worn in layers)), wood, or other; nor whether they have a cleavage laced up with eyelets (O: provided none of the foot

e6.4　وشـرطُهُ أَنْ يَلْبَسَهُ على وضوءٍ كامـلٍ ، وأنْ يَكُـونَ طاهـراً ساتراً لجميعِ محلِّ الفرضِ (ح : لو نقـط عليـه ، أن يصل مباشرة) (فلو وصل المـاء من موضع الخرز لا يضر في صحة المسح ، وأما وصول الماء إلى الرجل من أي موضعٍ كان من غيرِ محلِ الخرز فإنه يضرَّ) يُمْكِنُ متابعةُ المشي عليْهِمَا لتردُّدِ مسافرٍ لحاجاتِه (عند الحط والترحال وغيرهما) .

سواءٌ كانَ مِنْ جِلْدٍ أَوْ لبـدٍ أَوْ خرقٍ مطبقـةٍ أَوْ خشبٍ أوْ غيـرِ ذلكَ ، أَوْ مشقوقاً شُدَّ بشـرجٍ (على أنـه لا يظهر شيءٌ من محل الفرض) .

shows).

One may not wipe footgear if wearing just one of a pair, washing the other foot. Nor if any of the foot shows through a hole in them.

ولَـوْ لَبِسَ خفّـاً في رجـلٍ لِيَمْسَحَهُ ويَغْسِـلَ الأخرى، أوْ ظَهَـرَ مِنَ الـرجـلِ شيءٌ وإنْ قَلَّ مِنْ خرقٍ في الخفِّ لَمْ يَجُزْ.

e6.5   [والجرموقُ هوَ خفٌّ فوقَ خفٍّ، فإنْ كانَ الأعلى قوياً والأسفلُ مخرّقاً فلَهُ مسحُ الأعلى، وإن كانا قويين أو القويُّ الأسفلَ لمْ يَكْفِ مسحُ الأعلى إذا لم يصل البلل من الأعلى إلى الأسفل). فإنْ وَصَلَ البللُ منهُ إلى الأسفلِ كَفَى سواءٌ قَصَدَ مسحَهُمَا أو الأسفلَ (بـالمسح على الأعلى) فقطْ أو أَطْلَقَ (المسح أي لم يقصد واحداً بعينه)، لا إنْ قَصَدَ الأعلى فقطْ].

e6.6   It is sunna to wipe the footgear on the top, bottom, and heel in lines (N: as if combing something with the fingers), without covering every part of them or wiping them more than once.

One puts the left hand under the heel and the right hand on top of the foot at the toes, drawing the right hand back towards the shin while drawing the left along the bottom of the foot in the opposite direction towards the toes.

It is sufficient as *wiping the footgear* to wipe any part of their upper surface (N: with wet hands), from the top of the foot up to the level of the anklebones. It is not sufficient to only wipe some of the bottom, heel, side of the foot, or some of the footgear's inner surface that faces the skin.

e6.6   ويُسَـنُّ مسـحُ أعلى الخفِّ وأسفلِه وعقبِه خطـوطاً بِلا استيعاب ولا تكـرارٍ فيَضَـعُ يَدَهُ البُسْـرَى تحتَ عقبِهِ ويمنـاهُ عند أصابعِهِ وَيُمِرُّ اليمنى إلى الساقِ واليسرى إلى الأصابعِ. فإنِ اقْتَصَرَ على مسحٍ أقلَّ جزءٍ مِنْ ظاهِرِ أعلاهُ محاذياً لمحلِّ الفرضِ كَفَى. وإنِ اقْتَصَـرَ على الأسْفَـلِ أو العقبِ أو الحرفِ أو الباطنِ مِمَّا يلي البشرةَ فلَا.

e6.7   When on an ablution that was performed by wiping the footgear, and then some part of the foot shows because of taking them off, or through a hole, it's sufficient (N: to complete one's ablution) to merely wash the feet again (O: without repeating the ablution).

e6.7   ومتى ظَهَرَتِ الرجلُ بنزعٍ أو بخرقٍ وهـو بوضوءِ المسـحِ كَفـاهُ (ح: لإتمـام وضوءِه) غَسلُ القدمين فقطْ (أي من غيرِ إعادة للوضوءِ).

*

e7.0   THE FOUR CAUSES OF MINOR RITUAL IMPURITY (HADATH)

(N: Meaning the things that nullify one's ablution.)

e7.0   أسبـاب الأحـداث الأربعة

(ح: أي نواقض الوضوء).

ANYTHING THAT EXITS FROM THE
PRIVATE PARTS

الخارج من القبل أو الدبر

e7.1   The first is anything that exits from the
front or rear private parts, whether a substance
(O: such as urine or feces) (N: or the mucus that
exits from the vagina with or without sexual stimu-
lation, though not a woman's sexual fluid that
appears through orgasm, discussed below) or
wind, and whether something usual or something
uncommon such as a worm or stones. But not a
male's sperm or female's sexual fluid (Ar. maniyy,
that which exits with orgasmic contractions,
whether a man's or a woman's (def: e10.4)), which
necessitates the purificatory bath (N: as it causes
major ritual impurity) but does not necessarily
nullify ablution, an example of this being someone
firmly seated (dis: e7.2, second paragraph) who
sleeps and has a wet dream, or someone who looks
at something lustfully and sperm or sexual fluid
come. Otherwise, if one makes love to one's
spouse, or has an orgasm while lying asleep, ablution is nullified (n: respectively) by touching the
spouse's skin (e7.3) or by sleep (below).

e7.1   أحدُها الخارجُ مِنْ قبلٍ أوْ دبرٍ [أوْ ثقبةٍ تحتَ السرةِ مَعَ انسدادِ المخرج المعتادِ] عيناً (كالبول والغائط) أوْ ريحاً، معتـاداً أو نادراً كدودةٍ وحصـاةٍ، إلّا المنيّ فإنّـهُ يوجبُ الغسـلَ ولا يَنْقضُ الـوضوءَ وصورةُ ذلك أنْ يَنامَ مُمَكِّناً مَقْعَدَهُ فَيَحْتَلِمَ أوْ يَنْظُـرَ بشهـوةٍ فَيُنْزِلَ، وإلّا فلَوْ جَامَعَ أوْ نَامَ مضطجعاً فَأَنْزَلَ انْتَقضَ باللمسِ وبالنومِ.

LOSS OF INTELLECT THROUGH SLEEP ETC.

زوال العقل

e7.2   The second cause of minor ritual impurity
is loss of intellect (O: meaning the loss of the ability to distinguish, whether through insanity,
unconsciousness, sleep, or other. *Loss of intellect*
excludes drowsing and daydreaming, which do
not nullify ablution. Among the signs of *drowsing*
is that one can hear the words of those present,
even if uncomprehendingly).

Sleep while *firmly seated* on the ground (A:
or any other surface firm enough to prevent a person's breaking wind while seated on it asleep)
does not nullify ablution, whether riding
mounted, leaning on something which if removed
would cause one to fall, or otherwise seated.

If one sleeps when firmly seated and one's
rear moves from its place before one awakens, this
nullifies one's ablution. But not if:

(1) one's rear moved after or during awaken-

e7.2   الثـاني زوالُ عقلِه (والمراد به زوالُ التمييـز سواء كان زوالـه بجنـون أو إغمـاء أو نوم أو غيرهـا، وخـرج بزوال العقـل النعاس وحديث النفس فلا ينقض بهمـا. ومن علامـات النعاس سماع كلام الحاضرين وإن لم يفهمه) إلا النومُ قاعداً ممكِّنـاً مقْعـدَهُ مِنَ الأرضِ سواءَ الراكبُ والمستندُ ولوْ لشيءٍ لوْ أُزِيلَ لَسَقَطَ وغيرُهُما.

فلوْ نامَ ممكِّنـاً فزالَتْ أليتاهُ قبلَ انتباهِه انْتَقضَ. أوْ بعدَهُ أوْ مَعَهُ أوْ شكَّ أوْ سقطَتْ

ing, or if one is uncertain about whether it happened before awakening or during;

(2) one's arm dropped to the ground while one was firmly seated;

(3) or when one drowses while not firmly seated, hearing but not comprehending, or if one is uncertain as to whether one drowsed or slept, or uncertain as to whether one slept while firmly seated or not firmly seated.

CONTACT OF MAN AND WOMAN'S SKIN

التقاء بشرتي رجل وامرأة

يدُهُ على الأرضِ وهـوَ نائمٌ ممكّنٌ مقعدُهُ أوْ نَعَسَ وهـوَ غيـرُ ممكّنٍ وهـوَ يَسْمـعُ ولا يَفْـهَمُ، أوْ شَكَّ هلْ نام أوْ نَعَسَ أوْ هَلْ نَامَ ممكّناً أوْ غير ممكّنٍ فلا يَنْقُضُ.

e7.3   The third cause of minor ritual impurity is when any, no matter how little, of the two skins of a man and woman touch (N: husband and wife, for example) when they are not each other's unmarriageable kin (Ar. mahram, def: m6), even if they touch without sexual desire, or unintentionally, and even if with tongue or a nonfunctional or surplus limb; though *touching* does not include contact with teeth, nails, hair, or a severed limb.

Ablution is also nullified by touching an aged person or a corpse (N: of the opposite sex) but not by touching a member of one's unmarriageable kin, or a child who is younger than the age that usually evokes sexual interest.

One's ablution is not nullified when one is uncertain about:

(1) whether one touched a male or female;

(2) whether one touched hair or skin;

(3) or whether the person one touched was of one's unmarriageable kin or not.

e7.3   الثالثُ التقاءُ شيءٍ وإنْ قَلَّ منْ بَشَـرتَيْ رجلٍ وامرأةٍ أجنبيّيْنِ، ولـوْ بغيرِ شهـوةٍ وقصـدٍ، حتّى اللسـانِ والأشـلِّ والزائدِ إلا سِنّاً وظفْراً وشعراً وعضواً مقطوعاً.

ويَنْقُضُ هرمٌ وميّتٌ لا مَحْـرَمٌ وطفلٌ لا يُشْتَهَى في العادةِ.

فلوْ شَكَّ هلْ لَمَسَ امـرأةً أمْ رجُـلاً، أوْ شعراً أوْ بشرةً، أوْ أجنبيةً أوْ محرماً لَمْ يَنْقُضْ.

TOUCHING HUMAN PRIVATE PARTS WITH HAND

مس الفرج

e7.4   The fourth cause of minor impurity is touching human private parts with the *palm or inner surface of the fingers only* (N: i.e. those parts which touch when the hands are put together palm

e7.4   الـرابـعُ مَسُّ فرجِ الآدمـيِّ بباطنِ الكَفِّ والأصابعِ خاصةً، ولوْ سهواً

to palm), whether one touches the private parts:

(1) absentmindedly;

(2) without sexual desire;

(3) in the front or rear;

(4) of a male or female;

(5) of oneself or another, even if deceased, or a child;

—but not if one touches them with one's fingertips, the skin between the fingers, with the outer edge of the hand, or touches the corresponding parts of an animal.

أوْ بلاَ شهـوةٍ قُبُـلاً أوْ دبراً ذكراً أوْ أنْثى من نفسِهِ أوْ غيرهِ ولوْ من ميتٍ وطفلٍ [ومحلِّ جبٍّ وإنْ اكـتـسى جلداً أوْ أشـلَّ ولـوْ مقطـوعـاً وبـيـدٍ شلاءَ]، لا برؤوسِ الأصابعِ ومَا بينَهَا وحـرفِ الكفِّ ولا فرجِ بهيمةٍ.

e7.5   Ablution is not nullified by vomiting, letting blood, nosebleed, laughing during the prayer, eating camel meat, or other things (N: not discussed above).

e7.5   ولاَ يَنْقُضُ قَيْءٌ وفصدٌ ورُعافٌ وقهقهةُ مُصَلٍّ وأكلُ لحمِ جزورٍ وغيرُ ذلكَ.

e7.6   When certain that a minor ritual impurity has occurred, but uncertain whether one subsequently lifted it (N: with ablution), then one is in a state of minor ritual impurity (A: because in Sacred Law, a state whose existence one is certain about does not cease through a state whose existence one is uncertain about).

When certain that one had ablution, but uncertain that it was subsequently nullified, then one still has ablution.

e7.6   ومَنْ تَيَقَّنَ حدثاً وشـكَّ في ارتفـاعِهِ فهوَ مُحْدِثٌ (ع: لأنَّ في الشرعِ اليقين لا يزول بالشك)، ومَنْ تَيَقَّنَ طهراً وشكَّ في ارتفاعِهِ فهوَ متطهرٌ.

e7.7   [وإنْ تَيَقَّنَهُمَا وشكَّ في السابقِ مِنْهُمَا فإنْ لمْ يَعْرفْ مَا كانَ قَبْلَهُمَا، أوْ عَرَفَهُ وكانَ طهراً وكانتْ عادتُهُ تجديدَ الوضوءِ لزمَهُ تجديدُ الوضوءِ، فإنْ لمْ يَكُنْ عادتُهُ تجديدَ الوضوءِ، أوْ كانَ حدثاً فهوَ الآنَ متطهرٌ].

*

e8.0   ACTIONS UNLAWFUL DURING MINOR RITUAL IMPURITY

e8.0   محرمات الحدث

e8.1   The following are unlawful for someone in a state of minor ritual impurity:

e8.1   ومَـنْ أُحْـدَثَ حَرُمَ عليْــه الصـلاةُ، وسجـــودُ التـــلاوة والشكـر، والطـوافُ، وحملُ المصحف ولوْ بعلاقتِه أوْ في صنـدوقِه وَمَسُّهُ سواءٌ المكتوبُ ومَا بين الأسطرِ والحواشي وجلدُهُ وعـلاقتُه وخريطتُهُ وصندوقُهُ وهو فيِهمَا.

(1) to perform the prayer;

(2) to prostrate when reciting the Koran at verses in which it is sunna to do so (def: f11.13);

(3) to prostrate out of thanks (f11.19);

(4) to circumambulate the Kaaba (j5);

(5) or to carry a Koran, even by a strap or in a box, or touch it, whether its writing, the spaces between its lines, its margins, binding, the carrying strap attached to it, or the bag or box it is in.

(n: Other aspects of proper manners (adab) towards the Book of Allah are treated below at w16.) (A: The opinion expressed in *Fiqh al-sunna* that it is permissible to touch the Koran without ritual purity is a deviant view contrary to all four schools of jurisprudence and impermissible to teach (dis: r7.1(3), except to explain that it is aberrant.) (n: Though in the Hanafi school, it is permissible for someone in a state of minor ritual impurity to touch or carry a Koran that is inside a cover not physically attached to it, such as a case or bag, as opposed to something joined to it, like a binding (*al-Lubab fi sharh al-Kitab* (y88), 1.43). And Allah knows best.)

e8.2   It is also unlawful (n: when without ablution) to touch or carry any of the Koran written for the purpose of study, even a single verse or part of one, as when written on a slate or the like.

e8.2   وكَـذَا يَحْـرُمُ مَسُّ وحملُ ما كُتِبَ لدراسةٍ ولوْ آيَةٍ (ولو بعضها) كاللوح وغـيرِه (وحل لغير الدراسة كما إذا قصد للتميمة ولو مع القرآن فلا يحرم مسها ولا حملهـا وإن اشتملت على سور بل قال الشيخ الخطيب وإن اشتملت على جميع القرآن).
ويَحِلُ حملُ مصحفٍ في أمتعةٍ، وحَلَّ حملُ دراهمَ ودنـانيرَ وخاتمٍ وثوبٍ كُتِبَ عَلَيْهِنَّ قرآنٌ.
وكُتب فقهٍ وحديثٍ وتفسيرٍ فيهَا قرآنٌ بشَرْطِ أنْ يَكُونَ غيرُ القرآنِ أكثَرَ (لأن غير

(O: But this is permissible for nonstudy purposes such as when the Koran is intended to be an amulet (def: w17). It is not prohibited to touch or carry such an amulet even if it contains whole suras, or even, as Sheikh (N: Shirbini) al-Khatib has said, if it contains the whole Koran.)

It is permissible to carry a Koran in one's baggage and to carry money, rings, or clothes on which Koran is written.

It is permissible to carry books of Sacred Law, hadith, or Koranic exegesis which contain Koran, provided that most of their text is not Koran (O: because the non-Koranic part is the purpose, though this is unlawful if half or more is Koran).

Boys who have reached the age of discrimination (def: f1.2(O:)) may touch or carry the Koran while in a state of minor ritual impurity (O: because of the need to learn it and the hardship of their keeping ablution, and likewise for young girls, though this is for study alone, as opposed to nonstudy, when it is unlawful. As for children under this age, their guardian may not give a Koran to them) (A: as this is an insult to it. Also, teachers should remind children that it is unlawful to moisten one's fingers with saliva to turn its pages).

Someone in a state of minor or major impurity may write Koran if he does not touch or carry what he has written.

القرآن هو المقصود فإن كان القرآن أكثر أو مساوياً حرم ذلك).

وَيُمَكَّنُ الصبيُّ (أي المميز) المحدث مِنْ حملِهِ ومسِّهِ (لحاجة تعلمه ومشقة استمراره متطهراً ومثل الصبي في هذا الحكم الصبية وهـذا إذا كان لدراسـة بخلاف ما إذا كان لغيرها فإنه يمنع، أما غير المميز فلا يجوز للولي تمكينه من ذلك).

ولـوْ كَتَبَ محدثٌ أوْ جنبٌ قرآناً ولمْ يَمَسَّهُ ولم يَحْمِلْهُ جازَ.

e8.3   When one fears that a Koran may burn, get soaked, that a non-Muslim may touch it, or that it may come into contact with some filth, then one must pick it up if there is no safe place for it, even if one is in a state of minor or major ritual impurity, though performing the dry ablution (tayammum, def: e12) is obligatory if possible.

e8.3   ولوْ خَافَ على المصحفِ مِنْ حرقٍ أوْ غرقٍ أوْ يدِ كافرٍ أوْ نجاسةٍ وَجَبَ أخذُهُ مَعَ الحدثِ والجنابةِ إنْ لمْ يَجِدْ مستودعاً لَهُ لكنْ يَتَيَمَّمَ (وجوباً) إنْ قَدَرَ

e8.4   It is unlawful to use a Koran or book of Islamic knowledge as a pillow (O: except for fear of theft, when it is permissible to do so).

And Allah knows best.

e8.4   ويَحْرُمُ تَوَسُّدُهُ وغيره مِنْ كتب العلم (إلا إن خاف عليه من سرقة فيجوز حينئذ) واللهُ أعلمُ.

*

e9.0   GOING TO THE LAVATORY

e9.0   آداب الذهاب إلى الخلاء

e9.1   It is recommended when one intends to use the lavatory:

(1)   to put something on one's feet, unless there is an excuse (O: such as not having shoes);

(2)   to cover the head (O: even if only with a handkerchief or other);

e9.1   يُنْدَبُ لمريد الخلاءِ أنْ يَنْتَعِلَ إلا لعذرٍ (كأن لا يجد النعل).
ـ ويَسْتُرَ رأسَهُ (ولو بمنديل أو غير ذلك).

(3) to set aside anything on which there is the mention of Allah Most High, His messenger (Allah bless him and give him peace), or any revered name (O: like those of prophets or angels). If one enters with a ring (O: on which something worthy of respect is written), one closes one's hand around it;

(4) to ready stones (N: or other suitable material (def: e9.5)) (O: if one uses them) to clean oneself of filth (N: though water alone is sufficient);

(5) to say before entering:

"In the name of Allah. O Allah, I take refuge in You from demons, male and female,"

and after leaving,

"[O Lord,] Your forgiveness. Praise be to Allah who rid me of the hurt and gave me health";

(6) to enter with the left foot first and depart with the right foot first (and this, together with (3) and (5) above, are not only for indoors, but recommended outdoors as well);

(7) not to raise one's garment until one squats down to the ground (O: to keep one's nakedness covered as much as possible) and to lower it before one stands up;

(8) to put most of one's weight on the left foot while squatting;

(9) not to spend a long time;

(10) not to speak;

(11) when finished urinating, for men to squeeze the penis with the left hand from base to head (O: recommended because this is where the urethra is, and for women to squeeze their front between thumb and forefinger) (N: so urine does not exit later and nullify one's ablution) pulling lightly three times (O: this being recommended when one thinks the urine has stopped, though if one thinks it has not, this is obligatory);

ـ وَيُنَحِّي مَا فِيهِ ذِكْرُ اللهِ ورسولهِ وكلِّ اسمٍ معظمٍ (كأسماء الأنبياء والملائكة) فإنْ دَخَلَ بالخاتم (الذي كتب عليه شيء معظم) ضَمَّ كَفَّهُ عَلَيْهِ.

ـ وَيُهَيِّئُ أحجـارَ الاستنجـاء (إنْ كان يستنجي بها).

ـ وَيَقُـولُ عندَ الدخولِ: «بِسْمِ اللَّهِ، الـلّٰهُـمَّ إنِّي أَعُـوذُ بِكَ مِنَ الـخُـبُـثِ والخَبَائِثِ» وعندَ الخروجِ: «غُفْرَانَكَ، الحَمْدُ للَّهِ ٱلَّذِي أَذْهَبَ عَنِّي الأَذى وَعَافَانِي».

ـ وَيُقَـدِّمُ داخـلاً يسـارَهُ وخارجاً يمينَهُ، ولا يَخْتَصُّ ذِكْرُ الـدخـولِ للخـلاءِ والخـروجِ، وتقـديمُ البُسـرَى واليمنى وتنحيـةُ ذكرِ اللهِ تعالى ورسولهِ بالبنيانِ، بلْ يُشْرَعُ بالصحراءِ أيضاً.

ـ ولا يَرْفَعُ ثوبَهُ (محافظة على الستر ما أمكن) حتّى يَدْنُوَ مِنَ الأرضِ، وُيرْخِيه قبلَ انتصابهِ.

ـ ويَعْتَمِدُ في الجلوسِ على يسارِهِ.

ـ ولا يُطِيلَ.

ـ ولا يَتَكَلَّمَ.

ـ فإذا انْقَطَعَ البـولُ مَسَحَ بيسارِه مِنْ دبـرِه إلى رأسِ ذكـرِه (نـدباً لأن هذا المكان مجرى البول، وأما المرأة فتعصر عانتها) وَيَنْتُرَ بلطفٍ ثلاثاً (فإذا غلب على ظنه انقطـاعه فيكـون مندوباً وإذا غلب على ظنه عدم الانقطاع فيكون حينئذ وجوباً).

(12) not to urinate while standing (O: which is offensive) unless there is an excuse (N: such as when standing is less likely to spatter urine on one's clothes than sitting, or when sitting is a hardship);

(13) not to clean oneself with water in the same place one relieved oneself, if it might spatter, though if in a lavatory one need not move to a different place;

(14) to distance oneself from others if outdoors and to screen oneself;

(15) not to urinate into holes, on hard places, where there is wind, in waterways, where people gather to talk, on paths, under fruit trees, near graves, in still water, or in less than 216 liters of running water;

(16) and not to relieve oneself with one's front or rear facing the sun, moon, or the Sacred Precinct in Jerusalem.

e9.2   It is unlawful to urinate on anything edible, bones, anything deserving respect, a grave, or in a mosque, even if into a receptacle.

e9.3   It is unlawful to urinate or defecate with one's front or rear towards the direction of prayer when outdoors and there is no barrier to screen one, though it is permissible when outdoors or indoors within a meter and a half of a barrier at least 32 cm. high, or in a hole that deep. When one is not this close to such a barrier, it is not permissible except in a lavatory, where, if the walls are farther from one than the maximal distance or are shorter than the minimal height, relieving oneself with front or rear towards the direction of prayer is permissible, though offensive.

e9.4   It is obligatory to clean oneself of every impure substance coming from one's front or rear, though not from gas, dry worms or stones, or excrement without moisture.

- ولا يَبُولَ قائماً (فيكرهُ له حينئذٍ وذلك) بلا عذرٍ .
- ولا يَسْتَنْجيَ بالمـاءِ في موضعِه إنْ خاف ترشُّشاً، ولا يَنْتَقِلَ في المراحيض .
- ويُبعَد في الصحراءِ ويَسْتَتِرَ .
- وَلا يَبُولَ في جحـرٍ، ومـوضـعٍ صلبٍ، ومَهَبِّ ريحٍ، ومورِدٍ، ومُتَحدَّثٍ للنـاسِ، وطريقٍ، وتحتَ شجرةٍ مثمرةٍ وعنـدَ قبرٍ وفي الماءِ الراكدِ وقليلٍ جارٍ، ولا مستقبِـلِ الشمسِ والقمـرِ وبيتِ المقدِسِ ومستديرَه .

e9.2   ويَحـرُمُ البـولُ عَلى مطعـومٍ وعظمٍ ومعظَّمٍ وقبرٍ وفي مسجدٍ ولوْ في إناءٍ .

e9.3   ويَحرُمُ استقبـالُ القِبلةِ واستدبـارُها ببولٍ أوْ غائطٍ في الصحراءِ بلا حائـلٍ، ويُباحانِ في البنيانِ إذا قَرُبَ مِنَ السـاتِـرِ نحوَ ثلاثةِ أذرعٍ، ويَكْفي مرتفعُ ثلثَيْ ذراعٍ مِنْ جدارٍ ووهدةٍ [ووهدةٍ وذيلِهِ المرخِيِّ قبالةَ القِبلةِ، والاعتبارُ في الصحراءِ والبنيانِ بالستـرةِ فحيثُ قَرُبَ منها على ثلاثةِ أذرعٍ وهيَ ثلثا ذراعٍ جازَ فيهمَـا]. وإلا فلا. إلا في المـراحيضِ فيَجُوزُ مَعَ كراهةٍ وإنْ بَعُدَ جدارُها أوْ قَصُرَ .

e9.4   ويَجِبُ الاستنجـاءُ مِنْ كلِّ عينٍ ملوِّثةٍ خارجـةٍ مِنَ السبيلينِ لا ريحٍ ودودةٍ وحصاةٍ وبعرةٍ بلا رطوبةٍ .

e9.5   Stones suffice to clean oneself, though it is best to follow this by washing with water. Anything can take the place of stones that is a solid, pure, removes the filth, is not something that deserves respect or is worthy of veneration, nor something that is edible (O: these being five conditions for the validity of using stones (N: or something else) to clean oneself of filth without having to follow it by washing with water).

But it is obligatory to wash oneself with water if:

(1) one has washed away the filth with a liquid other than water, or with something impure;

(2) one has become soiled with filth from a separate source;

(3) one's waste has moved from where it exited (n: reaching another part of one's person) or has dried;

(4) or if feces spread beyond the inner buttocks (N: meaning that which is enfolded when standing), or urine moved beyond the head of the penis, though if they do not pass beyond them, stones suffice.

It is obligatory (N: when cleaning oneself with a dry substance alone) to both remove the filth, and to wipe three times, even when once is enough to clean it, doing this either with three pieces (lit. "stones") or three sides of one piece. If three times does not remove it, it is obligatory to (N: repeat it enough to) clean it away (O: as that is the point of cleaning oneself. Nawawi says in al-Majmu' that cleaning oneself (N: with a dry substance) means to remove the filth so that nothing remains but a trace that could not be removed unless one were to use water) (N: and when this has been done, any remaining effects of filth that could have only been removed with water are excusable). An odd number of strokes is recommended. One should wipe from front to back on the right side with the first piece, similarly wipe the left with the second, and wipe both sides and the anus with the third. Each stroke must begin at a point on the skin that is free of impurity.

e9.5   وَيَكْفِي الأحجارُ [وَلَوْ فِي نادِرِ كدمٍ] وتعقيبُهَا بالماءِ أفضلُ ويُغْنِي عن الحجرِ كلُّ جامدٍ طاهرٍ قالعٍ للنجاسةِ غيرِ محترمٍ ومطعومٍ (فهذه خمسةُ قيودٍ لصحةِ الاستنجاءِ بالأحجارِ من غيرِ أن يتبعها بالماءِ) [كجلدِ المذكَّى قبلَ الدباغِ].

فلو اسْتُعْمِلَ مائعاً غيرَ الماءِ، أوْ نجساً، أوْ طَرَأَتْ نجاسةٌ أجنبيةٌ، أو انتقلَ ما خَرَجَ منهُ عن موضِعِهِ، أوْجَفَّ، أو انْتَشَرَ حالَ خروجِهِ وجَاوَزَ الأليةَ (ح: والمقصودُ صفحةُ الأليةِ من الداخلِ وهو ما انضمُّ من الأليتينِ عندَ القيامِ) أو الحشفةِ، تَعَيَّنَ الماءُ. فإنْ لمْ يُجاوِزْهُمَا كَفَى الحجرُ.

ويَجِبُ إزالةُ العينِ واستيفاءُ ثلاثِ مَسَحَاتٍ إما بثلاثةِ أحجارٍ، أوْ بحجرٍ لهُ ثلاثةُ أحرفٍ، وإنْ أَنْقَى بدونها. فإنْ لمْ تُنْقِ الثلاثةُ وَجَبَ الإنقاءُ (لأنه المقصودُ من الاستنجاءِ والإنقاءِ قال في المجموعِ هو أنْ يزيلَ العينَ حتى لا يبقى إلا أثرٌ لا يزيلهُ إلا الماءُ).

ونُدِبَ إيتارٌ. ويُنْدَبُ أنْ يَبْدَأَ بالأولِ من مقدمِ صفحةِ اليمنى وَيُمِرَّهُ إلى موضعٍ ابتدائِهِ ثمَّ يَعْكِسَ بالثاني ثمَّ الثالثِ على الصفحتينِ والمسربةِ وَجَبَ وضعُهُ أولاً بموضعٍ طاهرٍ ثُمَّ يُمِرُّهُ.

It is offensive to use the right hand to clean oneself of filth.

ويُكْرَهُ الاستنجاءُ بيمينهِ [فَلْيَأْخُذِ الحجرَ بيمينهِ والذكرَ بشمالهِ ويُحَرّكُهَا].

e9.6   It is best to clean oneself of filth before ablution, though if one waits until after it to clean, the ablution is nevertheless valid (N: provided that while cleaning, the inside surface of the hand (def: e7.4) does not touch the front or rear private parts).

e9.6   والأفضلُ تقديمُ الاستنجاءِ على الــوضوءِ فإنْ أخَّرَهُ عنهُ صَحَّ (ح) لكن بشرط أن لا يلمس بباطن كفه القبل أو الدبر)، أوْ عنِ التيمّم فَلَا.

If one waits until after one's dry ablution (tayammum, def: e12) to clean away filth, the dry ablution is not valid (A: because lack of filth is a condition for it).

*

e10.0   MAJOR RITUAL IMPURITY (JANABA)

e10.0   الجنابة ومحرماتها

e10.1   The purificatory bath (ghusl, def: e11) is obligatory for a male when:

(1)   sperm exits from him;

(2)   or the head of his penis enters a vagina;

and is obligatory for a female when:

(1)   sexual fluid (def: below) exits from her;

(2)   the head of a penis enters her vagina;

(3)   after her menstrual period;

(4)   after her postnatal lochia stops or after a child is born in a dry birth.

(n: The Arabic term *maniyy* used in all these rulings refers to both male sperm and female sexual fluid, i.e. that which comes from orgasm, and both sexes are intended by the phrase *sperm or sexual fluid* wherever it appears below.)

e10.1   يَجِبُ الغسلُ على الرجُلِ منْ خروجِ المنيِّ ومِنْ إيـلاجِ الحشفةِ في [أيّ] فرجٍ [كانَ قبلًا أوْ دبراً ذكراً أوْ أنثى ولـوْ بهيمـةً (ت: وهـذه الصـور الشـاذة محرمـة شديدة التحريم كما سيأتي بيانه في كتـاب الكبائر، وإنما ذكرت هنا على سبيل الاستيعاب لأسباب الجنابة، وذلك لاعتنـاء العلمـاء القـدمـاء بالشمـول في البحـوث الشرعية، ولو في نوادر الوقائع) أوْ صغيـراً في صغيـرةٍ]. ويَجِبُ على المرأة منْ خروجِ منّهَا ومنْ أيّ ذكرٍ دَخَلَ في قبلهَا [أو دبرهَا ولوْ أشلَّ أوْ مِنْ صبيٍّ أوْ بهيمـةٍ] ومِنَ الحيضِ والنفاسِ وخروجِ الولدِ جافاً.

e10.2   ولوْ رأى منياً في ثوبٍ أوْ فراشٍ يَنَامُ فيه مَعَ مَنْ يُمْكِنُ كونُهُ منْهُ نَدَبَ لَهُمَا الغُسلُ (ح) ولا يَجِبُ (ح: لأن كلاً منهما لم يجزمْ بأن المني منه ولا يجب الغسل إلا بعد الجزم) ولا يَقْتَدِي أحدُهُمَا بالآخر (ح: لأن كلاً منهما يعتقد أن الآخر

جنب) فإنْ لمْ يَنَمْ فيه غيرُهُ لزِمَهُ الغسلُ ويجِبُ إعادةُ كلِّ صلاةٍ لا يُحتَمَلُ حُدوثُ المنيِّ بعدَها، لكنْ يُنْدَبُ إعادةُ ما أمْكَنَ كونُها بعدَهُ].

e10.3　When a woman who has been made love to performs the purificatory bath, and the male's sperm afterwards leaves her vagina, then she must repeat the ghusl if two conditions exist:	e10.3　ولــوْ جُومِـعَـتْ في قبـلِهَـا فاغْتَـسَـلَتْ ثمَّ خَرَجَ منيُّـهُ منْهَـا لزِمَهَا غسلٌ آخـرُ بشـرطَيْنِ: أحـدُهُمَـا أنْ تَكُونَ ذاتَ شهـوةٍ لا صغـيرةً، الثاني أنْ تَكُونَ قضَتْ شهوَتَها لا نائمةً ومكرهةً.

(a) that she is not a child, but rather old enough to have sexual gratification (A: as it might otherwise be solely her husband's sperm);

(b) and that she was fulfilling her sexual urge with the lovemaking, not sleeping or forced.

e10.4　Male sperm and female sexual fluid are recognised by the fact that they:	e10.4　ويُعْرَفُ المنيُّ بتـدفُّقٍ أوْ تلذُّذٍ أوْ ريحٍ [طَلْعٍ أوْ] عجينٍ إذَا كانَ رطباً أوْ بياضِ بيضٍ إذَا كانَ جافاً. فمَتَى وُجـدَ واحدٌ منها كانَ منياً موجباً للغسلِ. ومَتَى فُقِـدَتْ كلُّها لمْ يكنْ منياً، ولا يُشْتَـرَطُ البياضُ والثخانةُ في منيِّ الرجلِ ولا الصفرةُ والرقّةُ في منيِّ المرأةِ.

(a) come in spurts (n: by contractions);

(b) with sexual gratification;

(c) and when moist, smell like bread dough, and when dry, like egg-white.

When a substance from the genital orifice has any one of the above characteristics, then it is sperm or sexual fluid and makes the purificatory bath obligatory. When not even one of the above characteristics is present, it is not sperm or sexual fluid. Being white or thick is not necessary for it to be considered male sperm, and being yellow or thin is not necessary for it to be considered female sexual fluid.

e10.5　The purificatory bath is not obligatory:	e10.5　ولا غسـلَ في مَذيٍ وهـوَ ماءٌ أبيضُ رقيقٌ لزِجٌ يَخْـرُجُ بلا شهـوةٍ عنْـدَ المـلاعبةِ. ولا في وَديٍ وهُـوَ ماءٌ أبيضُ كدرٌ ثخينٌ يخْـرُجُ عقِبَ البـولِ. (أوْ عنْـدَ حمل شيءٍ ثقيل).

(1) when there is an unlustful discharge of thin, sticky, white fluid (madhy) caused by amorous play or kissing;

(2) or when there is a discharge of the thick, cloudy white fluid (wady) that exits after urinating (O: or carrying something heavy).

e10.6   If one does not know whether one's discharge is sperm or whether it is *madhy* (def: (1) above), then one may either:

(1)   consider it sperm, and perform the purificatory bath (O: in which case washing the portions of clothes and so forth affected with it is not obligatory, as it is legally considered a pure substance);

(2)   or consider it *madhy,* and wash the affected portions of the body and clothes (N: which is obligatory, as it is legally considered filth), and perform ablution, though not the purificatory bath.

The best course in such cases of uncertainty is to do all of the above (O: of bathing, washing the affected portions, and ablution, so as to take due precaution in one's worship).

e10.7   All things unlawful for someone in minor ritual impurity (def: e8.1) are also unlawful for someone in a state of major ritual impurity (N: or menstruation). In addition, it is likewise unlawful for such a person:

(1)   to remain in a mosque;

(2)   or to recite any of the Koran, even part of a single verse, though it is permissible to use its invocations (dhikr) when the intention is not Koran recital (O: such as saying in disasters, "Surely we are Allah's, and unto Him we will return," and the like). If one intends Koran recital, it is disobedience, but if one intends it primarily as invocation (dhikr), or as nothing in particular, it is permissible.

It is permissible to pass through a mosque (A: though not to enter and leave by the same door (Ar. taraddud), which is unlawful) when one is in a state of major ritual impurity, but this is offensive when there is no need.

e10.6   فإنْ شَكَّ هَلِ الخـــارِجُ مَنِيٌّ أوْ مَذِيٌ تَخَيَّرَ إنْ شاءَ جَعَلَهُ مَنِياً واغْتَسَلَ فقط (ولا يجب عليه حينئذ غسل ما أصابه من ذلك الخارج لأنه محكوم عليه بالطهارة) وإنْ شاءَ جَعَلَهُ مَذِياً وغَسَلَ ما أَصابَ بَدَنَهُ وثِوْبَهُ مِنْهُ وتَوَضَّأَ ولاَ يَغْتَسِلَ .

والأفضلُ أنْ يَفْعَلَ جميعَ ذلكَ (من الاغتسـال، وغسل ما أصاب بدنه وثوبه، والوضوء احتياطاً للعبادة) .

e10.7   ويَحْـرُمُ بالـجنـابـة (ح: والحيض) ما حَرُمَ بالحدثِ، وكَذا اللبثُ في المسجِدِ وقِراءةُ القرآنِ، ولَوْ بعضَ آيةٍ، ويُبَاحُ أذكارُهُ لا بِقصدِ القرآنِ (وذلك كقـوله عند المصيبة إنَّـا للهِ وإنَّـا إلَيْـهِ رَاجِعُونَ) فإنْ قَصَدَ القرآنَ عَصَى أو الذكرَ أوَّلاً أوْ لاَ شيءَ جَازَ . ولَـهُ الـمـرورُ في المسجِدِ، ويُكْرَهُ لغيرِ حاجةٍ .

*

e11.0 HOW TO PERFORM THE PURIFICATORY BATH (GHUSL)

e11.0 كيفية الغسل

e11.1   When performing the purificatory bath, one:

(1) begins by saying, "In the name of Allah, Most Merciful and Compassionate";

(2) removes any unclean matter on the body (O: pure or impure);

(3) performs ablution (wudu) as one does before the prayer;

(4) pours water over the head three times, intending to lift a state of major ritual impurity (janaba) or menstruation, or to be permitted to perform the prayer, and running the fingers through one's hair to saturate it;

(5) and then pours water over the body's right side three times, then over the left side three times, ensuring that water reaches all joints and folds, and rubbing oneself.

(6) If bathing after menstruation, a woman uses some musk to eliminate the afterscent of blood (O: by applying it to a piece of cotton and inserting it, after bathing, into the vagina as far as is obligatory (def: (b) below) for her to wash). (N: What is meant thereby is a substance that removes the traces of filth, by any means, and it is fine to use soap.)

Two things (N: alone) are obligatory for the validity of the purificatory bath:

(a) having the intention ((4) above) when water is first applied to the parts that must be washed;

(b) and that water reaches all of the hair and skin (N: to the roots of the hair, under nails, and the outwardly visible portion of the ear canals, though unlike ablution the sequence of washing the parts is not obligatory), even under the foreskin of the uncircumcised man, and the private

e11.1 يَبْـدَأ المغتسـلُ بالتسميـة ثمَّ بإزالة قذرٍ (طاهراً كان أوْ نجساً) ثمَّ وضوءٍ كوضوء الصلاة ثمَّ يُفيضُ الماء على رأسِه ثلاثاً ناوياً رَفْعَ الجنابـة أو الحيض أوِ استبـاحـة الصلاة، ويُخَلِّلُ شعرَهُ ثمَّ على شقِّـه الأيمن ثلاثاً ثمَّ الأيسر ثلاثاً ويتعهَّدُ معاطفَهُ ويَدْلُكُ جَسَدَهُ.

وفي الحيض تُتبِعُ إثـرَ الـدم فرصـة مسكٍ (بأن تجعله على قطنة وتـدخلهـا فرجهـا بعد اغتسـالهـا إلى المحل الذي يجب غسله) [فـإنْ لَمْ تَجدْهُ فطيباً غيـرَهُ فإنْ لَمْ تَجـدْهُ فطينـاً فإنْ لَمْ تَجـدْهُ كفى المـاءُ] (ح: والمـراد به مادة تقلع أثـر النجاسة بأي أسلوب كان، فإن استعملت الصابون فحسن).

والـواجبُ منـهُ شيئان: النيةُ عندَ أولِ غُسـلٍ مفـروضٍ، وتعميمُ شعرِه وبشرِه بالمـاء حتّى مَا تَحْتَ قُلْفَةِ غيـرِ المختونِ

parts of the nonvirgin woman which are normally disclosed when she squats to relieve herself.

(n: In the Hanafi school, rinsing out the mouth and nostrils (def: e5.7) is obligatory for the validity of the purificatory bath (*al-Lubab fi sharh al-Kitab* (y88), 1.14). It is religiously more precautionary for a Muslim never to omit it, and Allah knows best.)

e11.2   If one begins the purificatory bath while on ablution (wudu) but nullifies it (def: e7) before finishing, one simply completes the bath (N: though one needs a new ablution before praying).

e11.3   If there is filth (najasa) on the body, one washes it off by pouring water on it and then performs the purificatory bath, though washing oneself a single time suffices for both removing it and for the purificatory bath.

e11.4   When a woman who is obliged to both lift a state of major ritual impurity (janaba) and purify after menstruation performs the purificatory bath for either of these, it suffices for both.

Whoever performs the bath one time with the intention to (n: both) lift a state of major ritual impurity and fulfill the sunna of the Friday prayer bath has performed both, though if he only intends one, his bath counts for that one but not the other.

e11.5   The purificatory bath is sunna:

(1) for those who want to attend the Friday prayer (def: f18) (O: the bath's time beginning at dawn);

(2) on the two 'Eids (f19) (O: the time for it beginning from the middle of the night);

(3) on days when the sun or moon eclipse;

(4) before the drought prayer (f21);

وما يَظْهَرُ مِنْ فرج الثيّبِ إذا قَعَدَتْ لحاجَتِها .

(ت : في الـمـذهـب الـحنفي يجب المضمضة والاستنشاق لصحة الغسل [اللبـاب في شرح الكتاب : ١/ ١٤]، والأحـوط للمسلم في دينـه أن لا يهملهما أبداً والله أعلم) .

e11.2   ولـوْ أَحْـدَثَ في أثنـائِهِ تَمَّمَهُ . [ولـوْ تَلَبَّدَ شعرُهُ وَجَبَ نَقْضُهُ إنْ لـمْ يَصِل الماءُ إلى باطِنِهِ] .

e11.3   ومَنْ عليْهِ نجاسةٌ يَغْسِلُها ثُمَّ يَغْتَسِلُ ويَكْفِي لَهُمَا غسلةٌ [في الأصحّ] .

e11.4   ولـوْ كان عليْهَا غسلُ جنابة وغسـلُ حيض فاغْتَسَلَتْ لأحـدِهِمَا كَفَى عَنْهُمَا . ومَنِ اغْتَسَلَ مرةً واحدةً بنية جنابة وجُمُعَةٍ حَصَلا أوْ نِيةِ أحدِهِمَا حَصَلَ دونَ الآخَرِ .

e11.5   ويُسَنُّ غسلُ الجمعةِ (ووقته من الفجر)، والعيدَيْن (ويدخل وقت هذا الغسـلِ بنصفِ الليـلِ)، والكسـوفَيْنِ، والاستسقاءِ، ومِنْ غسل الـميتِ (ويسن

(5) after washing the dead (O: and it is sunna to perform ablution (wudu) after touching a corpse);

(6) after recovering one's sanity or regaining consciousness after having lost it;

(7) (N: before) entering the state of pilgrim sanctity (ihram, def: j3), when entering Mecca, for standing at 'Arafa (j8), for circumambulating the Kaaba (j5) and going between Safa and Marwa (j6), for entering Medina, at al-Mash'ar al-Haram (j9.2), and for each day of stoning at Mina (j10) on the three days following 'Eid al-Adha.

الـوضـوء من مسه)، والمجنونِ والمغمَى عليهِ إذا أفاقا وللإحرام ولدخول مكةَ المشـــرّفـة وللوقـوف بعـرفـة وللطـواف والسعي ولـدخـول مدينـةٍ [رسـول الله صلَّى اللهُ عليهِ وسَلَّمَ] وبالمشعر الحرام وثلاثةٌ لرمي الجمار أيامَ التشريقِ.

*

e12.0   DRY ABLUTION (TAYAMMUM)

(N: When unable to use water, dry ablution is a dispensation to perform the prayer or similar act without lifting one's minor or major impurity, by the use of earth for one's ablution.)

e12.0 التيمم

(ح: هو رخصــة عنــد العجــز عن استعمــال المــاء لأداء نحـو الصــلاة باستعــمـال تراب التـيمم بدل المــاء الطهور؛ لكنـه لا يرفـع الحدث الأصغر ولا الأكبر).

e12.1   Three conditions must be met for the legal validity of performing dry ablution.

(a) The first is that it take place after the beginning of the prayer's time if it is for an obligatory prayer or a nonobligatory one that has a particular time. The act of lifting earth to the face and arms (N: the first step of dry ablution) must take place during that time. If one performs dry ablution when unsure that the prayer's time has come, then one's dry ablution is invalid, even if it coincides with the correct time (dis: e6.2(A:)). If one performs dry ablution in the midmorning for the purpose of making up a missed obligatory prayer, but the time for noon prayer comes before one has made up the missed obligatory prayer, then one may pray it (N: the noon prayer) with that dry ablution (N: because one did not perform dry ablution for it before its time, but rather performed dry ablution for a different prayer in that prayer's time, which clarifies why this does not

e12.1   شروطُ التيمم ثلاثةٌ:

ـ أحدُها أنْ يَقَعَ بَعْدَ دُخولِ الوقتِ إنْ كانَ لفرضٍ أوْ نفلٍ مؤقّتٍ بَلْ يَجِبُ نقلُ التــراب في الـوقتِ. فلوْ تَيَمَّمَ شاكّـاً في الـوقتِ لـمْ يَصِحَّ وإنْ صَادَفَه. ولـوْ تَيَمَّمَ لفـائـتـةٍ ضَحْوَةً فلَمْ يُصَلّها حتّى حَضَرَتِ الظهـرُ فلهُ أنْ يُصَلّيَهـا (ح: أي صلاة الظهر) به (ح: لأنه لم يتيمم لها قبل وقتها بل تيمم لغيـرهـا في وقتها وبذلك يتضح

violate the conditions of praying with dry ablution), or one could pray a different missed prayer with it (O: as one is not required to specify which obligatory prayer the dry ablution is for).

(b) The second condition is that dry ablution must be performed with plain, purifying earth that contains dust, even the dust contained in sand; though not pure sand devoid of dust; nor earth mixed with the likes of flour; nor gypsum, pottery shards (O: which are not termed *earth*), or earth that has been previously used, meaning that which is already on the limbs or has been dusted off them.

(c) The third condition is inability to use water. The person unable to use water performs dry ablution, which suffices in place of lifting all forms of ritual impurity, permitting the person in a state of major ritual impurity (janaba) or woman after her menstrual period to do everything that the purificatory bath (ghusl) permits them to do. If either of them subsequently has a minor ritual impurity (hadath), then only the things prohibited on minor impurity are unlawful for them (def: e8.1) (N: not those prohibited on major impurity (e10.7), that is, *until they can again obtain water* to lift their state of major impurity, when they must, for the dry ablution is only a dispensation to pray and so forth while in states of impurity and is nullified by finding water).

e12.2   *Inability to use water* has (O: three) causes (n: lack of water, fear of thirst, and illness).

LACK OF WATER

e12.3   The first is lack of water. When one is sure there is none, one performs dry ablution without searching for it. If one thinks there might be some, one must look through one's effects and inquire until one has asked all of one's party or (N: if too numerous) there is no time left except for the prayer. One does not have to ask each person individually, but may simply call out, "Who has water, even for a price?" Then one looks around,

أنـه لا مخـالفـة لشـروط التيمم) أوْفائتـةً أخرى (ولا يشترط تعيين الفرض الذي يتيمم له) .

ـ الثاني أنْ يكونَ بترابٍ طاهرٍ خالصٍ مطلقٍ لـهُ غبـارٌ ولـوْ بغبـارِ رمـلٍ لا رملٍ متمحّضٍ ولا بترابٍ مختلطٍ بدقيقٍ ونحوِهِ ولا بجصٍّ وسحـاقـةِ خزَفٍ (وكـلِّ من الجص وسحاقة الخزف لا يسمى تراباً) ومستعملٍ وهو مَا على العضوِ أوْ تَنَاثَرَ عنْـهُ .

ـ الثالثُ العجزُ عَن استعمالِ الماءِ . فيَتَيَمَّمُ العـاجـزُ عن استعمالِه ويَكُونُ عَن الأحـداثِ كُلِّهـا ويَسْتَبيـحُ به الجنبُ والحـائضُ ما يَسْتبيحـانِ بالغسـلِ . فإنْ أَحْدَثَا بعدَهُ حَرُمَ عَلَيهِمَا ما يَحْرُمُ بالحدثِ (الأصغـر) . (ح : أي : حتى يقـدرا على رفعِ الحدثِ الأكبرِ بالماءِ ، فحينئذ يتعين عليهمـا الغسـلُ ؛ لأن التيمم رخصةٌ لأداءِ الصلاةِ ونحوِها عنـد العجـزِ عن الماءِ ويبطل بالقدرةِ على استعمالِه) .

e12.2   وللعجزِ أسبابٌ (ثلاثة) :

فقد الماء

e12.3   أحدُهـا فقدُ الماءِ . فإنْ تَيَقَّنَ عدمَهُ تَيَمَّمَ بلا طلبٍ . وإنْ تَوَهَّمَ وجودَهُ وجَبَ طلبُـهُ مِنْ رَحْـلِه ورفقتِـهِ حتّى يَسْتـوْعِبَهُمْ أوْلا يَبْقَى مـن الـوقتِ إلا مَا يَسَـعُ الصلاةَ . ولا يَجبُ الطلبُ مِنْ كلِّ واحـدٍ بعينِه بلْ يُنَـادِي : «مَنْ مَعَهُ ماءٌ ولوْ بالثـمنِ» . ثم يَنْظُـرُ حوالَيْـهِ إنْ كانَ في

85

if on level ground. If not level, one checks on foot within the range at which one's group could be expected to respond to a cry for help, provided there is no threat to life or property. Or one may climb a nearby hill.

The search for water must occur after the particular prayer's time has come.

When one checks, does not find water, performs dry ablution, (N: prays an obligatory prayer with it,) and remains at the place, one need not search again before performing dry ablution for another obligatory prayer (N: when the next prayer's time comes), provided one made sure there was no water the first time, and nothing has happened to change one's mind. But if one did not make sure, or if something has happened to suggest that there might now be water, like the appearance of rain clouds or riders, one is obliged to check again for water.

أرضٍ مستويةٍ وإلا تَرَدَّد إلى حدِّ الغَوثِ وهُـوَ بحيـث مَا لو استغـاثَ برفقتِهِ [مع اشتغـالهمْ بأقـوالهمْ وأفعالهمْ] لأغاثُوهُ إنْ لَمْ يَخَفْ ضَرَرَ نفسٍ أوْ مالٍ أوْ صَعَـدَ جبلاً صغيراً قريباً.

ويجبُ أنْ يَقَعَ الطلبُ بعدَ دخول الوقتِ.

فإنْ طَلَبَ فلَمْ يَجِـدْهُ وتَيَـمَّمَ ومَكَثَ مَوْضِعَهُ وأرادَ فرضاً آخرَ فإنْ لَمْ يَحْدُثْ مَا يُوهِمُ ماءً وكانَ تَيَقَّنَ العدمَ بالطلبِ الأول تَيَمَّمَ بلا طلب.

وإنْ لَمْ يَتَيَقَّنْـهُ أوْ وجَـدَ ما يُوهِمُـهُ كسحابٍ وركبٍ وَجَبَ الطلبُ الآنَ [إلَّا مِنْ رحلِهِ].

e12.4   [وإنْ تَيَقَّنَ وجودَ الماء على مسافةٍ يَتَرَدَّدُ إليها المسافرُ للاحتطابِ والاحتشاشِ وهِيَ فوقَ حدِّ الغَوثِ أوْ عَلِمَ أنـهُ يَصِلُهُ بحفرٍ قريبٍ وَجَبَ قصدُهُ إنْ لَمْ يَخَفْ ضرراً (ويشترط أيضاً الأمن على خروج الوقتِ). وإنْ كانَ فوقَ ذلكَ فلهُ التيممُ].

e12.5   When sure that one can obtain water by waiting until the last of a prayer's time, then it is better to wait. But if one thinks otherwise, then it is better to perform dry ablution (n: and pray) at the first of the time.

e12.5   ولكنْ إنْ تَيَقَّنَ أنَّهُ لوْ صَبَرَ إلى آخـرِ الـوقتِ وجَدَهُ فانتظارُهُ أفضلُ. وإنْ ظَنَّ غيرَ ذلكَ فالأفضلُ التيممُ أولَ الوقتِ.

e12.6   (N: This entry's rulings apply equally to obtaining water for purification and to obtaining clothing to fulfill the prayer's condition of covering one's nakedness (def: f5).)

If a person gives or loans one water, or loans one a bucket (O: when it is the sole means of obtaining the water) then one must accept it, though not if the person loans or gives one the price of these things (O: because of the burden of accepting charity that it involves).

If one finds water or a bucket for sale at the usual price for that locality and time, then one is obliged to buy it, provided one's money is in excess of one's debts, even if they are not due until a future date; and provided one's money exceeds the amount required for the journey's expenses,

e12.6   (ح: يَنطبـقُ ما يأتـي من الأحكـام على المحتـاج لمـاء الطهـارة والمحتاج لستر العورة على حد سواء).

ولوْ وَهَبَ إنساناً ماءً أوْ أَقْرَضَهُ إيَّاهُ أوْ أعارَهُ دلواً (ولم يمكن تحصيل الماء إلا به) لَزِمَـهُ القبـولُ وإنْ وَهَبَهُ أوْ أَقْرَضَهُ ثمنَهُمَا فَلَا (يلزمه القبول لثقل المنة في ذلك).

وإنْ وَجَدَ المـاءَ والـدلوَ يُبَاعَانِ بثمنِ مثلِهِ وهُوَ ثمنُهُ في ذلكَ الموضع وذلكَ الوقتِ لزِمَهُ شراؤُهُ إنْ وَجَدَ ثمنَهُ فاضلاً عَنْ دَيْنٍ ولَوْ مؤجَّلاً ومؤنةِ سفرهِ ذهاباً

round trip.

When someone has water he does not need but will not sell, one may not simply take it from him by force, except when compelled by thirst (N: provided the water's owner is not also suffering from thirst, and provided one pays him the normal price for it in that locality and time, because one's need does not eliminate another's rights).

e12.7   If one finds some water, but not enough to complete purification, one must use it as far as it will go, and then perform dry ablution in place of the rest. For minor ritual impurity, one uses the water on the face, then the arms, and so forth, in the usual ablution sequence. For major ritual impurity (janaba), one begins wherever one wishes, though it is recommended to start at the top of the body.

FEAR OF THIRST

e12.8   The second cause of inability to use water is fear of one's own thirst, or that of worthy companions and animals with one, even if in the future (O: *worthy* meaning those whose killing is unlawful, such as a trained hunting dog or other useful animal, while *unworthy* includes non-Muslims at war with the Muslims, apostates from Islam (def: o8), convicted married adulterers, pigs, and biting dogs).

Ablution (N: as well as the purificatory bath (ghusl)) is unlawful in such a case. One should conserve one's water for oneself and others, and may perform dry ablution for prayer with no need to make up the prayer later (A: provided lack of water predominates in that place (dis: e12.19(N:))).

ILLNESS

e12.9   The third cause is an ailment from which one fears (N: that performing a normal ablution or purificatory bath would cause):

ورجوعاً.

فإن امتَنَعَ مِنْ بيعِهِ وهو مستغنٍ عنْهُ لمْ يأخُذْهُ غصباً إلَّا لعطشٍ (ح: بشرط أن لا يكون صاحب الماء عطشان، ويضمن قيمة المثل في ذلك المكان والزمان لأن الاضطرار لا يبطل حق الغير).

e12.7   ولـوْ وَجَدَ بعضَ ماءٍ لا يَكْفِي طهـارتَهُ لَزِمَهُ استعمالُهُ ثمَّ تَيـمَّمَ للباقي. فالمحـدثُ يُطَهِّـرُ وجهَـهُ ثمَّ يدَيْـهِ على الترتيب والجنبُ يَبْدأ بِمـا شـاءَ ويُنْدَبُ أعالي بدنِهِ.

خوف العطش

e12.8   الثـاني خوفُ عطشٍ نفسِـهِ ورفقتِـهِ وحيـوانٍ محتـرم مَعَهُ ولـوْ في المستقبل (والمحترم هو الذي يحرم قتله ومنه كلب ينتفع به ونحوه وغير المحترم منه الحربي والمرتد والزاني المحصن والخنزير والكلب العقور).

ويَحْـرُمُ الـوضوءُ (ح: والغسل) حينئذٍ فَيَزوُدُ لرفقتِه ويَتَيَمَّمُ بلا إعادةٍ.

المرض

e12.9   الثالثُ مرضٌ يُخافُ مَعَهُ تلفٌ

(1) harm to life or limb;

(2) disability;

(3) becoming seriously ill;

(4) an increase in one's ailment;

(5) a delay in recovering from one's illness;

(6) considerable pain;

(7) or (n: a bad effect from the water such as) a radical change in one's skin color on a visible part of the body.

One may depend on one's own knowledge (N: as to whether one of the above is to be apprehended) (O: if one is knowledgeable in medicine) (N: though it is not a condition that one be knowledgeable in medicine, for one's own previous experience may be sufficient to establish the probability that one of them will occur if a full ablution or bath (ghusl) is performed. Or one may depend on a physician whose information concerning it is acceptable (A: meaning one with skill in medicine whose word can be believed, even if he is not a Muslim).

النفسِ أوْ عضـوٍ أوْ فواتَ منفعـةِ عضـوٍ أوْ
حدوثَ مرضٍ مَخُوفٍ أوْ زيادةَ مرضٍ أوْ
تأخيرَ البرءِ أوْ شدةَ ألمٍ أوْ شيناً فاحشاً في
عضو ظاهرٍ.
ويَعْتَمِدُ فيـهِ معـرفتَـهُ (إن كان عالمـاً
بالطب) أوْ طبيباً يُقْبَلُ فيهِ خبرُهُ.

e12.10 (n: Rulings e12.11–13 below have been left in Arabic and deal with a person who has injuries that prevent a normal ablution or bath for one of the above reasons. Strictness on the question ('azima) is to follow the Shafi'is, while dispensation (rukhsa) is to follow the Hanafi school ((2) below).

(1) The Shafi'i school is the hardest in this matter, insisting on a full ablution except for the injured part, where a full dry ablution must be performed at the proper point in the ablution sequence in place of washing the injured part, as at e12.11 below.

If someone has a cast or dressing harmful to remove, as at e12.12, it must be first applied when one has ablution, and thereafter one must wipe it with water when one comes to it in the ablution sequence in addition to performing a complete dry ablution at that point.

Finally, when someone with such a bandage on the members of dry ablution (the face or arms) recovers and has his cast or dressing removed, he is obliged to make up (repray) all the prayers he performed with such an ablution, as at e12.13(O:).

(2) The Hanafi school requires someone with an injury who wants to pray to

make a complete ablution (N: or bath, if needed). But if this would entail harm, such as one of the things mentioned above at e12.9, then when he comes to the injury in the ablution sequence, he is merely required to wipe it with wet hands so as to cover more than half of the injury. If this would also entail harm, or if he has a bandage that cannot be removed without harm, or he cannot reapply the dressing by himself and has no one to help him to do so, then he simply wipes more than half the bandage when he comes to it in his ablution. He may pray with such an ablution and need not repeat the prayer later *(al-Hadiyya al-'Ala'iyya (y4) (43–44)*.

It is not necessary that he be free of minor or even major impurity (janaba) at the time the dressing is applied *(al-Lubab fi sharh al-Kitab (y88), 1.41)*.

(3) (N: There is strong evidence for performing dry ablution (tayammum) in place of washing such an injury. To add it at the proper point of the ablution sequence as a precautionary measure (dis: c6.5) would not interfere with the validity of following the Hanafi position just discussed.)

e12.11 [فإنْ خافَ منْ جرحٍ ولا ساترٍ عليه غَسلُ الصحيحِ بأقصى الممكنِ . فلا يتْركُ إلا ما لوْ غَسلَهُ تَعَدَّى إلَى الجرحِ وتيَمَّم للجرحِ في الوجهِ واليدينِ (ح : أي يتيمم بمسح وجهِ ويديه بالتراب سواء كانت الجراحة فيهما أو في غيرهما) في وقتِ جوازِ غسلِ العليلِ ، فالجنبُ يَتَيَمَّمُ متَى شاءَ ، والمحدِثُ لا يَنْتقلُ عنْ عضوٍ حتَّى يَكْمُلَ غسلاً وتيمماً، مقدماً ما شاءَ . فإنْ جُرحَ عضواهُ فتيَمُّمان . ولا يجبُ مسحُ الجرحِ بالماءِ وإنْ لمْ يضُرَّهُ (المسحُ وإنمايتلطف بوضع خرقة مبلولة بقربه ويتحامل عليها لينغسل بالمتقاطرِ منها ما حواليه من غير أن يسيل إليه) . فإنْ كانَ الجرحُ على عضوِ التيمم وَجَبَ مسحُهُ بالترابِ (ما أمكن (ح : فإن لم يمكنه لكونه يتضرر بالتراب لم يجب مسحه) وهو غير مستور لأن مسحه بالتراب بدل عن غسله بالماء)] .

e12.12 [فإن اُحْتاجَ لعصابةٍ أوْ لصوقٍ أوْ جبيرةٍ وَجَبَ وضعُها على طهرٍ (ح : وطهر كل عضو بحسب فطهارة أعضاء الوضوء عدم الحدث الأكبر والأصغر وطهارة بقية الجسم عدم الجنابة وهذا عند الإمكان) ولا يَسْتُرُ إلا ما لا بُدَّ منْهُ . فإنْ خافَ منْ نزعِها ضرراً وَجَبَ المسحُ علَيْها كلُّها بالماءِ معَ غسلِ الصحيحِ والتيمم كمَا تَقَدَّمَ . فإنْ كانتْ (ح : الجراحة) في غيرِ عضوِ التيمم لمْ يجبْ مسحُها بترابٍ . فإنْ أرادَ أنْ يُصَلِّيَ فرضاً آخرَ لمْ يُعِدِ الجنبُ غسلاً (للصحيح بعد تيممه ، لبقاء طهره) وكَذا المحدِثُ (لا يعيد غسلاً للصحيح ولا مسحاً للساتر لأن طهارته باقية فلم ترتفع بإرادة صلاةٍ أخرى ، وإنما وجب عليه إعادة التيمم) وقيلَ ما بعدَ عليهِ .

وإنْ وُضِعَ بلا طهرٍ وَجَبَ النزعُ . فإنْ خافَ فَعَـلَ ما تَقَدَّمَ وهوَ آثمُ (وهذا الإثم إثم الابتداء (ح : إن كان بإمكانه أن يتطهر فلم يفعل كما تقدم وإلا فلا إثم) وأما إثم الاستمرار فقد زال عنه لوجود العذر وهو خوف الضرر) ويُعيدُ الصلاة (وجوباً سواء كان في أعضاء الوضوء أو في أعضاء التيمم)] .

e12.13 [ولا يُعيدُ إنْ وُضِعَ على طُهرٍ ولمْ يكنْ في أعضاء التيمم (فإن كان فيها وجبت الإعادة مطلقاً سواء وضع على طهر أم لا وسواء أخذ الساتر شيئاً من الصحيح أم لا ، لنقصان البدل والمبدل) ولا مَنْ تَيَمَّم لمرضٍ أوجرح بلا ساتر إلاَّ مَنْ بجرحِهِ دمٌ كثيرٌ يخافُ منْ غسلِهِ فيُعيدُ] .

e12.14 If it is so cold that one fears an illness or one of the things previously mentioned (e12.9) | e12.14 ولوْ خافَ منْ شدةِ البرد مرضاً

89

from the use of water and one lacks means of heating the water or warming one's limbs up afterwards, then one performs the dry ablution (N: prays), and repeats the prayer later.

e12.15 When one lacks both water and earth, one is obliged to pray the obligatory prayer by itself, and later make up the prayer when one again finds water or finds earth, if in a place where dry ablution suffices as purification for a prayer that need not be made up later (N: such as in the desert (dis: e12.19(N:))).

THE INTEGRALS OF DRY ABLUTION

e12.16 Dry ablution has seven obligatory integrals:

(a) the intention, one intending permission to perform the obligation of the prayer, or that which requires dry ablution (N: such as carrying the Koran when there is no water for ablution). It is inadequate to intend to lift a state of minor ritual impurity (dis: e5.3(O:)) or intend the obligation of dry ablution.

If one is performing dry ablution for an obligatory prayer, one must intend its being obligatory, though need not specify whether, for example, it is for the noon prayer or the midafternoon prayer. If one were to intend it for the obligation of performing the noon prayer, one could (N: instead) pray the midafternoon prayer with it (N: though not both, as at e12.20).

If one intends a dry ablution for both an obligatory prayer and a nonobligatory prayer, then both may be prayed with that same dry ablution. But if one's intention is merely for a nonobligatory prayer, a funeral prayer (janaza), or simply *prayer,* then one may not pray an obligatory prayer with that dry ablution. If one intends an obligatory prayer, one may pray nonobligatory prayers only, or pray them before and after an obligatory prayer during the obligatory prayer's time, or after the obligatory prayer's time has expired.

The intention must occur when one conveys

مِمّــا تَقَـدَّمَ ولمْ يَقْـدِرْ على تسخينِ المـاءِ وتدفئةِ عضوٍ تَيَمَّمَ وأعَادَ .

e12.15 ومَنْ فَقَـدَ ماءً وتـراباً وَجَبَ أنْ يُصَلّيَ الفرضَ وحدَهُ ويُعيدَ إذا وَجَدَ الماءَ أو التراَب حيثُ يُسْقِطُ التيممُ الإعادةَ [فلا يُعيدُ إذا وَجَدَ تراباً في الحضرِ] .

واجبات التيمم

e12.16 وواجباتُهُ سبعةٌ :
ـ النيـةُ فَيْنـوي استباحةَ فرضِ الصلاةِ أو استبـاحةَ مفتقرٍ إلى التيممِ . ولاَ يَكْفي نيّـةُ رفعِ الحدثِ ولاَ فرضِ التيمم فإنْ تَيَمَّمَ لفـرضٍ وَجَبَ نيـةُ الفـرضيّـةِ ، لا تعيينُـهُ مِنْ ظهـرٍ أوْ عصرٍ بلْ لوْ نَوَى فرضَ الظهرِ استبـاحَ بِه العصرَ ، ولوْ نَوَى فرضاً ونفـلاً أبِيحَـا ، أوْ نفـلاً أوْ جنازةً أو الصلاةَ لمْ يَسْتَبِـحْ الفـرضَ أوْ فرضاً فلَهُ النفـلُ مُنْفَرِداً وكَذَا النفلُ قبْلَهُ وبعدَهُ في الوقتِ وبعدَهُ .

ويجبُ قرنُهـا بالنقْـلِ واستدامتُها إلى

the earth (O: meaning when one first strikes the earth) and must continue until one wipes part of the face;

(b and c) that one's hands contact the earth and convey it (N: up to the face and arms, after having shaken the excess dust from one's hands);

(d and e) to wipe the face (N: not missing under the nose) and arms including the elbows;

(f) to do the above in the order mentioned;

(g) and that the dry ablution be performed by striking the earth twice, once for wiping the face, and a second time for wiping the arms.

It is not obligatory to make the earth reach under the hair (N: of the arms and face).

THE SUNNAS OF DRY ABLUTION

e12.17　The sunnas of dry ablution are:

(1) to say, "In the name of Allah, Most Merciful and Compassionate";

(2) to wipe the upper face before the lower;

(3) to wipe the right arm before the left;

(4) and for wiping the arms, (N: holding the palms up,) to place the left hand crosswise under the right with the left hand's fingers touching the backs of the fingers of the right hand, sliding the left hand up to the right wrist. Then, curling the fingers around the side of the right wrist, one slides the left hand to the right elbow, then turns the left palm so it rests on the top of the right forearm with its thumb pointed away from one before sliding it back down to the wrist, where one wipes the back of the right thumb with the inside of the left thumb. One then wipes the left arm in the same manner, followed by interlacing the fingers, rubbing the palms together, and then dusting the hands off lightly.
(N: This method is not obligatory, but rather any way will suffice that wipes all of both arms.)

مسحِ شيءٍ منَ الوجه (والمرادُ بالنقل الضرب).

ـ الثاني والثالثُ قصدُ الترابِ ونقلُهُ. [فلَوْ كانَ على وجهِه ترابٌ فمسحَ بهِ لـم يكُف. ولـوْ أمـرَ غيرُهُ حتى يَمَّمَهُ جازَ وإنْ كانَ قادراً على الأظهر].

ـ الرابعُ والخامسُ مسحُ وجهِه ويَدَيْهِ مَع مرفقَيْهِ.

ـ السادسُ الترتيبُ.

ـ السابعُ كونُهُ بضربَتَيْن ضربةٍ للوجهِ وضربـةٍ لليدَيْن. [وقيلَ إنْ أمكن بضربةٍ كفى كخرقةٍ ونحوِه].

ولا يجِبُ إيصالُهُ باطنَ شعرٍ خفيفٍ.

سنن التيمم

e12.17 وسنتُهُ التسميةُ وتقديمُ يمينِه، وأعلى وجهِه، وفي البـدِ يضَـعُ أصابـعَ اليسرى سوَى الإبهام على ظهورِ أصابعِ اليـمْنَى سوَى الإبهام ويُمِـرُّهَـا إلى الكـوعِ، ثمَّ يَضُمُّ أطرافَ أصابعِه إلى حرفِ الـذّراعِ ويمرُّهَـا إلى المرفقِ ثمَّ يُديـرُ بطنَ كفّـهِ إلى بطنِ الـذراعِ ويُمِرُّهَا وإبهامُـهُ مرفـوعةٌ، فإذَا بَلَغَ الكوعَ مَسَحَ بطنَ إبهامِ اليسـرَى ظَهْرَ إبهامِ اليمنَى، ثمَّ يَمْسَـحُ اليسـرَى باليمنَى كذلكَ، ثمَّ يُخَلِّلُ أصابعَهُ ويَمْسَحُ إحْدَى الراحتَيْن بالأخـرَى، ويُخَفِّفُ الغبـارَ (ح): وهـذه الكيفِيـة ليست واجبـة بل تكفِي كل كيفية تؤدي إلى تعميم اليدين بالمسح).

e12.18 One separates the fingers when striking the earth each of the two times, and must remove one's ring for the second (N: before wiping the arms).

18 ‎e12 وُيفَرِّقُ أصابعَهُ عندَ الضرب على التـراب فيهما، ويَجبُ نزعُ الخاتمِ في الثانية.

THINGS WHICH NULLIFY DRY ABLUTION

مبطلات التيمم

e12.19 Dry ablution is nullified by both the things which nullify ablution (def: e7) and by the mere belief that one can now obtain water when this belief occurs before one begins praying, such as by seeing a mirage or a troop of riders.

This belief also nullifies dry ablution when it occurs during one's prayer if the prayer is one which must be later made up, like that of someone at home who performs dry ablution for lack of water (N: because if one performs dry ablution in a place where water is generally available during the whole year, it is obligatory to make up one's prayer, in view of the fact that the dry ablution has been performed for a rare excuse. The rule is that whoever performs the prayer without full ritual purity because of a rare excuse is obliged to make up his prayer, as when the water of a city or village is cut off for a brief period of time during which those praying perform dry ablution, while if one has performed it in a place where water is seldom available during the year, it is not obligatory to make up one's prayer, as when one performs dry ablution in the desert). But if not of those prayers that must be made up later, such as that of a (N: desert) traveller who has performed dry ablution, then it (N: the belief that one can now obtain water, when it occurs during prayer) does not (N: nullify one's dry ablution) and one finishes the prayer, which is adequate, though it is recommended to interrupt it in order to begin again after one has performed ablution.

‎e12.19 وَيَبْطُلُ التيممُ عن الـوضـوءِ بنواقض الوضوء وبتوهُّم قدرتِه على ماءٍ يجبُ استعمالُه كرؤية سراب أوْ ركب قبلَ الصلاة أوْ فيها وكانَتْ مِمَّا تُعَادُ (بأنْ كانت في محل يغلب فيه وجـود الماء) كتيمم حاضرٍ لفقدِ الماء (ح: لأنه إذا تيمم في موضعٍ يغلب فيه وجود المـاء طيلة أيام السنة فإن الإعادة واجبة، نظراً لأن التيمم هنـا لعـذرٍ نادر، والقـاعـدة أن من يصلي بغير طهارة كاملة لعـذرٍ نادر وجب عليـه الإعـادة. وذلك كمـا لو انقطع الماء في مدينة أو قرية فترة وجيزة من الوقت فتيمم المصلون خلالهـا. فإن كان قد تيمم في موضعٍ يغلب فيه عدم وجود الماء طيلة أيام السنة لم يجب عليـه الإعـادة وذلك كمـا لو تيمم في الصحراء). فإنْ لمْ تُعَدْ كتيمم مسـافـرٍ فلَا (ح: أي لا تبطِـل الصلاة) ويُتمُّها وتُجزئُهُ لكنْ يُنْدَبُ قطعُها ليَسْتَـأنِفَهـا بوضـوءٍ. [وإنْ رآهُ في نفـلٍ ونَوَى عدداً أَتَمَّهُ، وإلَّا فركعتين].

e12.20 One may not perform more than one obligatory prayer with one dry ablution, whether one of the prescribed obligatory prayers or one vowed (def: j18), though one may pray any number of nonobligatory prayers or funeral prayers with it.

‎e12.20 ولا يَجـوزُ بتيمم أكثـرُ مِنْ فريضةٍ واحدةٍ مكتوبةٍ أوْ منذورةٍ، و[ح: له أنْ يصلي)] ما شاءَ مِنَ النوافِل والجنائز.

e13.0 THE MENSTRUAL PERIOD

e13.1   The minimal age for menstruation is about 9 full years. There is no maximal age for the end of it, as it is possible until death.

The minimal menstrual period is a day and a night. It generally lasts 6 or 7 days. The maximal period is 15 days.

The minimal interval of purity between two menstruations is 15 days. There is no maximal limit to the number of days between menstruations.

e13.2   Whenever a woman who is old enough notices her bleeding, even if pregnant, she must avoid what a woman in her period avoids (def: e13.4). If it ceases in less than 24 hours (lit. "the minimum"), then it is not considered menstruation and the woman must make up the prayers she has omitted during it. If it ceases at 24 hours, within 15 days, or between the two, then it is menstruation. If it exceeds 15 days, then she is a woman with chronic vaginal discharge (dis: e13.6).

Yellow or dusky colored discharge is considered menstrual flow.

If a woman has times of intermittent bleeding and cessation during an interval of 15 days or less, and the times of bleeding collectively amount to at least 24 hours, then the entire interval, bleeding and nonbleeding, is considered menstruation.

e13.3   Postnatal bleeding (nifas) lasts at least a moment, generally 40 days, and at most 60. If it exceeds this, the woman is considered to have chronic vaginal discharge (dis: e13.6).

e13.4   All things unlawful for someone in a state of major ritual impurity (janaba) (dis: e10.7) are unlawful for a woman during her menstruation and postnatal bleeding. It is also unlawful for her to fast then, and the (N: obligatory) fast-days she misses must be made up later, though not missed prayers.

It is unlawful for her:

e13.0   الحيض

e13.1   أقـلُّ سنٍّ تَحيضُ فيهِ المـرأةُ استكمـالُ تسـعِ سنينَ تقريباً. [فلوْ رأتْهُ قبـلَ تسـعِ سنينَ لزمنٍ لا يَسَـعُ طهـراً وحيضـاً فهـوَ حيضٌ، وإلّا فَلا]. ولا حَدَّ لآخرهِ، فَيُمْكِنُ إلى الموتِ.

وأقلُّ الحيضِ يومٌ وليلةٌ وغالبُهُ ستُّ أو سبعٌ وأكثرُهُ خمسـة عشـرَ يوماً. وأقـلُّ الطهـرِ بينَ الحيضتينِ خمسـةَ عشرَ يوماً، ولا حَدَّ لأكثرِه.

e13.2   فمتـى رأتْ دمـاً في سنِّ الحيضِ ولوْ حاملاً وَجَبَ تركُ ما تَتـرُكُ الحـائضُ. فإنِ انْقَطَعَ لدونِ أقلّهِ تَبَيّنَ أنّهُ غيرُ حيضٍ فَتَقْضي الصلاةَ. فإنِ انْقَطَعَ لأقلّهِ أوْ أكثـرهِ أوْ ما بينهمـا فهـوَ حيضٌ. وإنْ جَاوَزَ أكثرَهُ فهيَ مستحاضةٌ [ولهـا أحكامٌ طويلةٌ مذكورةٌ في كتبِ الفقهِ]. والصُفرةُ والكُدْرةُ حيضٌ.

وإنْ رأتْ وقتاً دماً ووقتاً نقاءً ووقتاً دماً وهكـذا ولمْ يُجَـاوزِ الخمسـةَ عشـرَ ولمْ يَنْقُصْ مجمـوعُ الـدمـاءِ عنْ يومٍ وليلةٍ فالدماءُ والنقاءُ المتخلّلُ كلّها حيضٌ.

e13.3   وأقلُّ النفاسِ لحظةٌ وغالبُهُ أربعـونَ يوماً، وأكثـرُهُ ستـونَ يوماً. فإنْ جَاوَزَهُ فمستحاضةٌ.

e13.4   ويَحْرُمُ بالحيضِ والنفاسِ مَا يَحْرُمُ بالجنابةِ. وكَذا الصومُ ويَجِبُ قضاؤهُ دونَ الصلاةِ.

ويَحْرُمُ عبورُ المسجدِ إنْ خافَتْ تلويثهُ

(1) to pass through a mosque when she thinks some of her blood might contaminate it (N: and it is unlawful for her to *remain* in the mosque under any circumstances (n: when menstruating or during postnatal bleeding));

(2) to make love, or take sexual enjoyment from what is between her navel and knees;

(3) to be divorced;

(4) or to perform purification with the intention to raise a state of ritual impurity.

When her bleeding ceases, then fasting, divorce, purification, and passing through the mosque are no longer unlawful for her, though the other things remain unlawful for her until she performs the purificatory bath (ghusl, def: e11).

e13.5   If a woman claims to be having her period, but her husband does not believe her, it is lawful for him to have sexual intercourse with her.

e13.6   A woman with chronic vaginal discharge (N: preparing to pray) should wash her private parts, apply something absorbent to them and a dressing, and then perform ablution (N: with the intention discussed above at e5.3). She may not delay (N: commencing her prayer) after this except for reasons of preparing to pray such as clothing her nakedness, awaiting the call to prayer (adhan), or for a group to gather for the prayer. If she delays for other reasons, she must repeat the purification.

She is obliged to wash her private parts, apply a dressing, and perform ablution before each obligatory prayer (N: though she is entitled, like those mentioned below, to perform as many nonobligatory prayers as she wishes, carry and read the Koran, etc. until the next prayer's time comes (n: or until her ablution is broken for a different reason), when she must renew the above measures and her ablution).

e13.7   People unable to hold back intermittent drops of urine coming from them must take the

(ح) : ويحرم عليها المكث فيه مطلقاً) والـوطء والاستمتـاع فيمـا بين السـرة والركبة، والطلاقُ، والطهارةُ بنية رفع الحدثِ .

فإِنِ انْقَطَعَ الدمُ ارْتَفَعَ تحريمُ الصومِ والطلاق والطهارة وعبورِ المسجدِ ويَبْقَى الباقي حتَّى تَغْتَسِلَ .

e13.5   ولـو ادَّعَتِ الحيضَ ولمْ يَقَعْ في قلبه صِدْقُهَا حَلَّ لَهُ وطؤُهَا .

e13.6   وتَغْسِلُ المستحـاضَـةُ فرجَهَا وتَشُدُّهُ وتَعْصِبُهُ ثمَّ تَتَوَضَّأُ ولاَ تُؤَخِّرُ بعدَ الطهارة إِلَّا للاشتغـال بأسبـاب الصلاة كَسَتْرِ عورةٍ وأذانٍ وانتظارِ جمـاعةٍ . فإِنْ أخَّرَتْ لغير ذلك اسْتأنَفَتِ الطهارة .

ويَـجِبُ غسـلُ الفـرجِ وتعصيبُـهُ والوضوءُ لكلِّ فريضةٍ .

(ح) : ولكن لهـا أن تصلي [بـذلـك الـوضـوء] ما شاءت من النـوافـل وتحمل المصحف وتتلو القرآن ونحوها (ت : ما لم ينتقض وضـوؤهـا بسبب آخر) حتى دخـول وقت صلاة ثانيـة، فعنـدئذ يتعين تجـديد الـوضوء مع هذه الإجراءات . وكذلك أصحاب الأعذار التي سيأتي ذكرها) .

e13.7   ومَـنْ به سَلَسُ البـول

same measures (def: above) that a woman with chronic vaginal discharge does. (N: And likewise for anyone in a state of chronic annulment of ablution, such as continually breaking wind, excrement, or *madhy* (def: e10.5), though washing and applying an absorbent dressing are only obligatory when filth exits.)

(A: If a person knows that drops of urine will not stop until the time for the next prayer comes, then he takes the above measures and performs the prayer at the first of its time.)

كالمستحـاضة فِيمَا تَقَدَّمَ . (ح : وكذا كل صاحب حدث دائم ، كمن يخـرج منــه ريـح دائماً ، أو غائط أو مذي لكن الغسل والتعصيب لا يجب إلا في سلس النجاسة) .

(ع : فإن علم استمــرار سلس البـول حتى دخـول وقت صلاة ثانيـة فعل ما ذكر وأدّى صلاته في أول وقتها) .

*

e14.0 FILTH (NAJASA)

النجاسات   e14.0

e14.1 *Filth* means:

e14.1 الــنـجــاسـةُ هِيَ البـولُ، والغـائـطُ، والـدمُ، والقيـحُ، والقيءُ، والخمرُ، [والنبيذُ]، وكلُ مسكرٍ مائعٍ .

(1) urine;

(2) excrement;

(3) blood;

(4) pus;

(5) vomit;

(6) wine;

(7) any liquid intoxicant (n: including, for the Shafi'i school, anything containing alcohol such as cologne and other cosmetics, though some major Hanafi scholars of this century, including Muhammad Bakhit al-Muti'i of Egypt and Badi al-Din al-Hasani of Damascus, have given formal legal opinions that they are pure (tahir) because they are not produced or intended as intoxicants.(N: Other scholars hold they are not pure, but their use is excusable to the extent strictly demanded by necessity.) While it is religiously more precautionary to treat them as filth, the dispensation exists when there is need, such as for postoperative patients who are unable for some time after their surgery to wash away the alcohol used to sterilize sutures. And Allah knows best.)

(N: As for solid intoxicants, they are not filth, though they are unlawful to take, eat, or drink);

(ح : وأمـا الجـامد فليس بنجس لكن يحرم تعـاطيـه وأكله وشربه) ، والكلبُ والخنـزيـرُ، وفـرعُ أحـدِهِمَـا، والوديُ،

(8) dogs and pigs, or their offspring;

(9) *wady* and *madhy* (def: e10.5);

(10) slaughtered animals that (N: even when slaughtered) may not be eaten by Muslims (def: j16);

(11) unslaughtered dead animals other than aquatic life, locusts, or humans (A: which are all pure, even when dead, though amphibious life is not considered aquatic, and is filth when dead);

(12) the milk of animals (other than human) that may not be eaten;

(13) the hair of unslaughtered dead animals;

(14) and the hair of animals (other than human) that may not be eaten, when separated from them during their life (N: or after their death. As for before it is separated from them, the hair is the same as the particular animal, and all animals are pure during their life except dogs and swine).

(n: In the Hanafi school, the hair of an unslaughtered dead animal (other than swine), its bones, nails (hoofs), horns, rennet, and all parts unimbued with life while it was alive (A: including its ivory) are pure (tahir). That which is separated from a living animal is considered as if from the unslaughtered dead of that animal (*Hashiya radd al-muhtar 'ala al-Durr al-mukhtar sharh Tanwir al-absar* (y47), 1.206–7).)

e14.2 Rennet (n: a solidifying substance used in cheese-making) is pure if taken from a slaughtered (def: j17) suckling lamb or kid that has eaten nothing except milk.

e14.3 That which comes from the mouth of a sleeping person is impure if from the stomach, but pure if from the saliva ducts.

والمَذيُّ، ومَا لاَ يُؤْكَلُ لحمُهُ إذَا ذُبِحَ، والميتةُ إلا السَّمكَ والجَرادَ والآدميَّ، ولَبَنُ مَا لاَ يُؤْكَلُ لحمُهُ غيرَ الآدميِّ وشعرُ الميتةِ، وشعرُ غيرِ المأكولِ إذَا انْفَصَلَ (ح: أما قبل انفصاله عن الحيوان فحكمه حكم ذلك الحيوان، والحيوانات كلها طاهرة في حياتها إلا الكلب والخنزير) في حياتِهِ (ح: وكذا إذا انفصل بعد موته) إلَّا الآدمي، [ومنيُّ الكلب والخنزير].

(ت: في المذهب الحنفي شعر الميتة (غيرِ الخنزيرِ) وعظمها وحافرها وقرنها وكـل مـا لا تحله الحيـاة، حتى الأنفحة (ع: والعاج) طاهرٌ. والمنفصل من الحي كميتتـه [حـاشيـة رد المحتـار على الـدر المختار: ١/ ٢٠٧ ـ ٢٠٨]).

e14.2   والأنفحةُ طاهرةٌ إنْ أُخِذَتْ مِنْ سخلةٍ مذكاةٍ لمْ تأكُلْ غيرَ اللبنِ.

e14.3   ومـا يَسيلُ مِنْ فَمِ النـائمِ إنْ كانَ مِنَ المعـدةِ [بأن كانَ لاَ يَنْقطِعُ إذَا طَالَ نومُـهُ] نجسٌ وإنْ كانَ مِنَ اللهَـواتِ [بأنْ كانَ يَنْقطِعُ] فطاهرٌ.

e14.4   [والعضـوُ المنفصـلُ من الحيّ حكمُـهُ حكم ميتـةِ ذلـكَ الحيـوانِ، إنْ كانَتْ طاهـرةً كالسمكِ فطاهرٌ وإلَّا كالحمار فنجسٌ].

e14.5   The following are pure:

(1) seminal fluid that has reached the stages of gestation in the womb, becoming like a bloodclot and then becoming flesh;

(2) the moisture (N: mucus) of a woman's private parts (O: as long as it remains inside the area that need not be washed in the purificatory bath (def: e11.1(b), end), though if it exits, it is impure);

(3) the eggs of anything;

(4) the milk, fur, wool, or feathers of all animals that may be eaten, provided they are separated from the animal while living or after properly slaughtered;

(5) human milk, male sperm, and female sexual fluid (def: e10.4).

e14.6   No form of filth can become pure, except:

(1) wine that becomes vinegar;

(2) the hide of an unslaughtered dead animal that is tanned;

(3) new animate life that comes from filth (O: such as worms that grow in carrion);

(4) (n: and for the Hanafis, filth which is transformed [molecularly changed] into a new substance, such as a pig becoming soap, etc. (*al-Hadiyya al-'Ala'iyya* (y4), 54)).

Wine that becomes vinegar without anything having been introduced into it is pure, as are the sides of the container it touched when it splashed or boiled. But if anything was introduced into the wine before it became vinegar, then turning to vinegar does not purify it. (A: In the Hanafi school it is considered pure whether or not anything has been introduced into it.)

Tanning means removing from a hide all excess blood, fat, hair, and so forth by using an acrid substance, even if impure. Other measures

e14.5 والعَلَقَةُ والمُضغَةُ ورطوبةُ فرجِ المرأةِ (ما لم تخرجْ مِن محلٍ لا يجبُ غسلُه وإلا فهيَ نجسةٌ)، وبيضُ [المأكولِ وغيرِه] ولبنُه وشعرُه وصوفُه [ووبرُه] وريشُه إذا انفَصَلَ في حياتِه أوْ بعدَ ذكاتِه، [وعَرَقُ الحيوانِ الطاهرِ طاهرٌ حتّى الفأرةِ] وريقُه ودمعُه] ولبنُ الآدميِّ ومنيُّه غيرُ نجسٍ [وكذا منيُّ غيرِه غيرَ الكلبِ والخنزيرِ وقيلَ نجسٌ].

e14.6 ولا يَطْهُرُ شيءٌ مِنَ النجاساتِ إلا الخمرُ إذا تَخَلَّلَ والجلدُ إذا دُبِغَ، ونجساً يَصيرُ حيواناً (كالدودِ المتولدِ مِن نحوِ الجيفِ).

فإذا تَخَلَّلَتِ الخمرُ بغيرِ إلقاءِ شيءٍ فيها [إمّا بنفسِها أوْ بنقلِها مِنَ الشمسِ إلى الظلِّ وعكسِه أوْ بفتحِ رأسِها] طَهُرَتْ معَ أجزاءِ الدنِّ الملاقيةِ لها وما فوقَها ممّا أصابتْه عندَ الغليانِ. وإنْ أُلْقِيَ فيها شيءٌ فلا.

والدبغُ هوَ نزعُ الفضلاتِ بكلِّ حِرّيفٍ ولَوْ نجساً ولا يَكفي ملحٌ وترابٌ وشمسٌ.

such as using salt, earth, or sunlight, are insufficient. Water need not be used while tanning, though the resultant hide is considered like a garment affected with filth, in that it must be washed with purifying water before it is considered pure. Hides of dogs or swine cannot be purified by tanning. Any hair that remains after tanning has not been made pure, though a little is excusable.

وَلاَ يَجِبُ استعمالُ ماءٍ في أثنائِهِ لكنَّهُ بعـدَ الدباغِ كثوبٍ متنجِّسٍ فَيَجِبُ غسلُهُ بماءٍ طهورٍ.
وَلاَ يَطْهُرُ بهِ جلدُ كلبٍ وخنزيرٍ.
ولَـوْ كانَ على الجلدِ شعـرٌ لَمْ يَطْهُرِ الشعرُ بالدباغِ ويُعْفَى عنْ قليلِهِ.

e14.7   Something that becomes impure by contact (def: below) with something from dogs or swine does not become pure except by being washed seven times, one of which (recommended not to be the last) must be with purifying earth (def: e12.1(b)) mixed with purifying water, and it must reach all of the affected area. One may not substitute something else like soap or glasswort in place of earth.

e14.7   ومَا تَنَجَّسَ بمـلاقاةِ شيءٍ مِنَ الكلبِ والخنزيرِ لَمْ يَطْهُرْ إلاّ بغسلِهِ سبعاً إحداهنَّ بترابٍ طاهرٍ يَسْتَوْعِبُ المحلَّ ويَجِبُ مَزْجُهُ بماءٍ طهورٍ ويُنْدَبُ جعلُهُ في غيـرِ الأخيـرةِ ولاَ يَقُـومُ غيـرُ الترابِ مقامَهُ كصابونٍ وأشنانٍ.

(n: The contact referred to is restricted, in the Shafi'i school, to contamination by traces of *moisture* from dogs or swine, whether saliva, urine, anything moist from them, or any of their dry parts that have become moist (*Mughni al-muhtaj ila ma'rifa ma'ani alfaz al-Minhaj* (y73), 1.83). (A: If something dry such as the animal's breath or hair touches one's person, it need only be brushed away.) In the Maliki school, every living animal is physically pure, even dogs and swine (*al-Fiqh 'ala al-madhahib al-arba'a* (y66), 1.11) (A: and they consider the above sevenfold washing as merely a sunna). While more precautionary to follow the Shafi'i school, the dispensation exists for those who have difficulty in preventing contamination from dogs, provided their prayer with its prerequisites is considered valid in the Maliki school (dis: c6.4(end) and w14.1(6)). And Allah knows best.)

e14.8   [ولوْ رأى هرةً تأْكُلُ نجاسةً ثمَّ شربَتْ مِنْ ماءٍ دونَ قلتينِ قبلَ أنْ تغيبَ عنْهُ نجَّسَتْهُ. وإنْ غابَتْ زمناً يُمْكِنُ فيهِ ولوغُها في قلتينِ شربَتْ مِنَ القليلِ لَمْ تُنَجِّسْهُ.

ودخـانُ النجاسـةِ نجسٌ ويُعْفَى عنْ يسيـرِهِ. فإنْ مُسِحَ كثيرُهُ عنْ تنورٍ بخرقةٍ يابسةٍ فزالَ طَهُرَ، أوْ رطبةٍ فلاَ. فإنْ خُبِزَ عليْهِ فطاهرٌ وأسفلُ الرغيفِ نجسٌ].

e14.9   The urine of a baby boy who has fed on nothing but human milk can be purified from clothes by sprinkling enough water on the spot to wet most of it, though it need not flow over it. The urine of a baby girl must be washed away as an adult's is.

e14.9   ويَكْفي في بولِ الصبيِّ الـذي لَمْ يأْكُـلْ غيـرَ اللبنِ الـرشُّ مَعَ غلبةِ الماءِ ولاَ يُشْتَـرَطُ سيـلانُهُ. وبولُ الصبيةِ [وكَذا الخنثى] يُغْسَلُ كالكبيرةِ.

WASHING AWAY FILTH

تطهير المتنجس

e14.10 As for kinds of filth that are "without substance" (N: i.e. *without discernible characteristic* (najasa hukmiyya) such as a drop of dry urine on a garment that can not be seen), it is sufficient (N: to purify it) that water flow over it.

But if it is a substance (N: *with discernible characteristic* (najasa 'ayniyya')), it is obligatory to remove all taste of it, even if difficult, and to remove both color and odor if not difficult. If the odor alone is difficult to remove, or the color alone, then the fact that one of these two remains does not affect a spot's purity, though if both the odor and color of the filth remain in the spot, it is not considered pure.

e14.10 وما سوى ذلك من النجاسات إنْ لم يكنْ لهُ عينٌ كفى جريُ الماء عليه. وإنْ كانَ لهُ عينٌ وجَبَ إزالةُ طعمٍ وإنْ عسُرَ، ولونٍ وريحٍ إنْ سهُلا. فإنْ عسُرَ إزالةُ الريحِ وحدَهُ أو اللونِ وحدَهُ لم يضُرَّ بقاؤُهُ. وإنِ اجتَمَعا ضَرّا.

e14.11 When using less than 216 liters of water to purify a spot affected by filth, it is obligatory that the water *flow* over it (N: and it may not be simply immersed in the water (dis: e1.15), though this would be permissible with more than 216 liters), but is not obligatory to wring it out. After one purifies it, it is recommended to wash it a second and third time.

e14.11 ويُشتَرطُ ورودُ الماءِ القليل على المحلِّ لا العصرُ. ويُنْدَبُ بعدَ طهارتِه غسلُه ثانيةً وثالثةً.

e14.12 When the ground (A: or floor, or carpet) is affected with liquid filth (A: like wine or urine), it is enough to drench the place with water and is not necessary that the filth sink into the ground. If the effects of sun, fire, or wind remove the traces of the filth, the ground is still not pure until one drenches it with water.

e14.12 ويَكفِي في أرضٍ نجسةٍ بذائب المكاثرةُ بالماءِ ولا يُشتَرطُ نضوبُهُ. ولوْ ذَهَبَ أثرُ نجاسةِ الأرض بشمسٍ أوْ نارٍ أوْ ريحٍ لم تَطُهْر حتّى تُغْسَل.

e14.13 Liquids other than water, such as vinegar or milk, cannot be purified after they become affected with filth. But if a solid is affected, such as shortening, one discards the filth that fell into it and the shortening around it, and the remainder is pure.

e14.13 وكلُّ مائعٍ غيرِ الماءِ كخلٍّ ولبنٍ إذا تَنَجَّسَ لا يُمْكِنُ تطهيرُهُ. فإنْ كانَ جامداً كالسمنِ الجامدِ ألْقى النجاسةَ وما حولَها والباقي طاهرٌ.

e14.14 Water used to wash away filth is impure when:

e14.14 وما غُسِلَ به النجاسةُ إنْ تغَيَّرَ

(1) it changes (def: e1.17);

(2) its weight increases;

(3) (O: or if neither of the above have oc-curred, but some trace (N: i.e. an inexcusable amount (def: e14.10, second par.)) of filth remains on the place to be purified);

—but if none of the above occurs, then it is not impure (O: i.e. then the water is pure but not purifying to other things); though if it amounts to (N: or is added to until it amounts to) 216 or more liters (dis: e1.16), then it is purifying. If less, it is considered the same as the spot it washed: if the spot is pure (N: i.e. an inexcusable trace does not remain) then the water is pure, but if the spot is still impure, then the water is impure.

أوْ زَادَ وزنُهُ (أوْ لم يزد وزنه ولمْ يتغير لكن المحلّ لم يطهر بأن بقي عليـه شيء من أوصـاف النجاسة) فنجسٌ . وإلا فَلاَ (أي فلا ينجس ذلك المـاء، بل يحكم عليـه بأنه طاهر في نفسه غير مطهّر لغيره) . فإنْ بَلَغَ قلتين فمطهّـرُ . وإلا فحكمُهُ حكمُ المحـلّ بعدَ الغسل بهِ، إنْ كَانَ قدْ حُكِمَ بطهارتهِ فطاهرٌ . وإلا فنجسٌ .

e14.15 (n: In the Hanafi school, if a garment's damp spot of filth, whose quantity is too slight to wring out any drops, touches another dry, pure garment, the latter does not become impure (*Maraqi al-falah sharh Nur al-idah* (y126), 31).)

*

BOOK F

THE PRAYER (SALAT)

CONTENTS:

f1.0   WHO MUST PRAY

(O: The legal basis for the prayer, prior to scholarly consensus, is Koranic verses such as the word of Allah Most High,

"And perform the prayer" (Koran 2:43),

and hadiths such as the word of the Prophet (Allah bless him and give him peace):

"On the night I was taken from Mecca to Jerusalem [dis: Koran 17:1], Allah imposed fifty obligatory prayers upon my Community. So I kept petitioning Him in the matter, asking they be lightened, until He made them but five each day and night";

a hadith related by Bukhari, Muslim, and others.)

f1.0 المخاطب بوجوب الصلاة

(والأصـل فيهـا قبـل الإجمـاع آيـات كقـولـه تعـالى : ﴿وَأَقِيمُوا الصَّلَاةَ﴾ [البقـرة : ٤٣]، وأخبـار كقـولـه ﷺ : «فَـرَضَ اللَّهُ على أمـتي ليـلةَ الإسـراء خمسينَ صلاةً فلم أزلْ أراجعـهُ وأسألهُ التخفيفَ حتّى جعلهَا خمساً في كلِّ يوم وليلةٍ» رواه الشيخان وغيرهما).

f1.1   The prayer is only obligatory for Muslims who have reached puberty, are sane, and in purity (O: meaning not during menstruation or postnatal bleeding).

Those who lose their reason through insanity or illness do not have to make up the prayers they miss while in this state, and nor do converts to Islam (N: make up prayers from before their Islam).

An apostate from Islam (murtadd, def: o8) who then returns must make up every prayer missed. (n: w18 discusses why making up prayers missed without excuse is obligatory.)

f1.2   When a child with discrimination (O: meaning he can eat, drink, and clean himself after using the toilet unassisted) is seven years of age, he is ordered to perform the prayer, and when ten, is beaten for neglecting it (N: not severely, but so as to discipline the child, and not more than three blows).

f1.3   Someone raised among Muslims who denies the obligatoriness of the prayer, zakat, fasting Ramadan, the pilgrimage, or the unlawfulness of wine and adultery, or denies something else upon which there is scholarly consensus (ijma', def: b7) and which is necessarily known as being of the religion (N: *necessarily known* meaning things that any Muslim would know about if asked) thereby becomes an unbeliever (kafir) and is executed for his unbelief (O: if he does not admit he is mistaken and acknowledge the obligatoriness or unlawfulness of that which there is scholarly consensus upon. As for if he denies the obligatoriness of something there is not consensus upon, then he is not adjudged an unbeliever).

f1.4   A Muslim who holds the prayer to be obligatory but through lack of concern neglects to perform it until its proper time is over has not committed unbelief (dis: w18.2).

Rather, he is executed, washed, prayed over, and buried in the Muslim's cemetery (O: as he is one of them. It is recommended, but not obligatory, that he be asked to repent (N: and if he does, he is not executed)).

f1.1   إِنَّما تَجِبُ (ت: الصلاة) على كلِّ مسلم بالغٍ عاقلٍ طاهرٍ (فلا تجب على الحائض والنفساء) .

فلا قضاءَ على مَنْ زالَ عقلُهُ بجنونٍ أو مرضٍ ، وكافرٍ أصليٍّ . ويَقْضِي المرتدُّ .

f1.2   ويُؤْمَرُ الصبيُّ المميزُ بها لسبعٍ (والمميز هو الذي يأكل وحده ويشرب وحده ويستنجي وحده) ويُضْرَبُ عليها لعشرٍ (ح : ضرباً غير مبرح ، أي غير شديد ، على وجه التأديب ، ولا يزيد على ثلاث ضربات) .

f1.3   ومَنْ نَشَأَ بينَ المسلمينَ وجَحَدَ وجوبَ الصلاةِ أو الزكاةِ أو الصومِ أو الحجِّ أوْ تحريمَ الخمرِ أو الزنَا أوْ غيرَ ذلكَ ممَّا أُجْمِعَ على وجوبِهِ أوْ تحريمِهِ وكانَ معلوماً مِنَ الدينِ بالضرورةِ (ح : وهـو الـذي لو سُئِلَ أي مسلم عنه يعرفه) كَفَـرَ وقُتِـلَ بكفـره (إن لم يرجع ويقرّ بالوجوب ويعتقد تحريم المجمع على تحريمه . وأما إذا أنكر شيئاً لم يجمع على وجوبه فلا يحكم عليه بالكفر) .

f1.4   ومَنْ تَرَكَ الصلاةَ تهاوناً مَعَ اعتقادِ وجوبِها حتّى خرَجَ وقتُها [وضاق وقتُ ضرورتها] لم يَكْفُرْ .

بلْ يُضْرَبُ عنقُهُ ويُغَسَّلُ ويُصَلَّى عليه ويُدْفَنُ في مقابرِ المسلمينَ (لأنه منهم . والمعتمد أنه) يستتاب ندباً لا وجوباً (ح : وإن تاب فلا يقتل)) .

f1.5   No one has an excuse to delay the prayer beyond its time except:

(1) someone asleep (N: when its time first came who remained so until the time ended);

(2) someone who forgot it;

(3) or someone who delayed it to combine two prayers during a journey (dis: f15.12).

*

f2.0   PRAYER TIMES AND MAKING UP MISSED PRAYERS

PRAYER TIMES

f2.1   The prescribed prayers are five:

(1) The time for the *noon prayer* (zuhr) begins after the sun's zenith for that day, and ends when an object's shadow, minus the length of its shadow at the time of the sun's zenith, equals the object's height.

(2) The time for the *midafternoon prayer* ('asr) begins at the end of the noon prayer's time, and ends at sunset, though when an object's shadow (N: minus the length of its shadow at the sun's zenith) is twice as long as the object's height, the preferred time is over and the merely permissible time remains.

(3) The time for the *sunset prayer* (maghrib) begins when the sun has completely set. It only lasts long enough to perform ablution (wudu), clothe one's nakedness, make the call to prayer (adhan) and call to commence (iqama) and to pray five moderate-length rak'as (units) of prayer. It is a sin to delay commencing the sunset prayer beyond this, and if one does, one is making up a missed prayer (O: i.e., according to the position the author has adopted, which contradicts the more reliable opinion that one's prayer is not a

ولاَ يُعْذَرُ أحدٌ في التأخير إلا **f1.5** نائماً (ح): من دخول الوقت إلى خروجه أَوْ ناسياً أوْ مَنْ أَخَّرَ لأجلِ الجمع في السفر.

f2.0   أوقــات الــصّـــلاة وقضاء الفوائت

مواقيت الصلاة

f2.1   المكتوباتُ خمسٌ:

ـ الظهــرُ وأولُ وقـتِـهـا إذا زَالَتِ الشمسُ، وآخرُهُ مصيرُ ظلِّ كلِّ شيء مثلَهُ سِوَى ظلِّ الزوال.

ـ والعصرُ وأولُهُ آخِرُ الظهـرِ، وآخرُهُ الغروبُ لكنْ إذا صارَ ظلُّ كلِّ شيء مثلَيْهِ خَرَجَ وقتُ الاختيار وبقيَ الجوازُ.

ـ والمَغْربُ وأولهُ تكامُلُ الغروبِ. ثمَّ يَمْتَدُّ بقدرِ وضوءٍ وسترِ عورةٍ وأذانٍ وإقامةٍ وخمسِ ركعاتٍ متوسطاتٍ. فإنْ أَخَّرَ الـدخـولَ فيها عنْ هذا القدرِ عَصَى وهيَ قضاءٌ (على ما ذهب إليـه المصنف وهـو خلاف المعتمـد والصحيـح أنها لا تكون

makeup until after the red has disappeared from the sky), though if one begins it within the right time, one may continue until the red disappears from the sky.

(4) The time for the *nightfall prayer* ('isha) begins when the red of sunset leaves the sky, and ends at true dawn (n: *true dawn* being when the sky around the horizon begins to grow light. Before this, a dim light sometimes appears over-head for some minutes, followed by darkness, and is termed the *deceptive dawn* (al-fajr al-kadhib) (*al-Iqna' fi hall alfaz Abi Shuja'* (y7), 1.95). But after a third of the night has passed, the preferred time for nightfall prayer has ended and the merely permissible remains.

(5) And the time for the *dawn prayer* (subh) begins at true dawn and ends at sunrise, though the preferred time for it ends when it becomes light outside, after which the merely permissible remains.

(n: Prayer times vary a little each day with the season and the year, and from one town to another through the effects of latitude and longitude. One can keep abreast of the changes by obtaining the whole year's times in a printed calendar from one's local Muslim association or mosque, or by using the pocket computer mentioned below at w19, which discusses how one fasts and prays at northerly latitudes (including much of North America and Europe during the summer months) lacking the features that legally define the true prayer and fasting times, such as nightfall or true dawn.)

f2.2   It is best to pray every prayer at the first of its time, taking the necessary steps at its outset, such as purification, clothing one's nakedness, giving the call to prayer (adhan) and call to commence (iqama), and then praying.

f2.3   If less than one rak'a of one's prayer occurs within the proper time (A: meaning that one does not lift one's head from the second prostration of the rak'a before the time ends) and the

قضـــاء إلا إذا غاب الشفــق الأحمــر) وإنْ دَخَـــلَ فيهــا فَلَهُ استــدامَتُهـا إلى غيبــوبــة الشفق الأحمر.

ـ والعِشاءُ وأوّلُهُ غيبوبةُ الشفق الأحمر وآخـــرُهُ الفجرُ الصادقُ. لكنْ إذا مَضى ثلثُ الليل خَرَجَ وقتُ الاختيار وبَقِيَ الجوازُ.

ـ والصُّبْـحُ وأولُـهُ الفجرُ الصادقُ، وآخـــرُهُ طلوعُ الشمس، لكنْ إذا أَسْفَـرَ خَرَجَ وقتُ الاختيار وبَقِيَ الجوازُ.

f2.2   والأفـضـلُ أنْ يُصـلّيَ أولَ الـوقت، ويَحْصُلُ بأنْ يَشْتَغِلَ أولَ دخوله بالأسبـاب كطهـارةٍ وستـر عورةٍ وأذانٍ وإقامةٍ ثمَّ يُصَلّيَ. [ويُسْتَثْنَى الظهرُ فيُسَنُّ الإبـرادُ بَهـا في شدةِ الحرِّ ببلدٍ حارٍ لمنْ يَمْضي إلى جمـاعـةٍ بعيـدةٍ، وليَسَ في طريقـهِ كنُّ يُظلّهُ. فَيُـؤخِّـرُ حتَّى يَصيرَ للحيطان ظلٌّ يُظلُّهُ فإنْ فُقِدَ شرطٌ منْ ذلك نُدبَ التعجيلُ].

f2.3   ولَوْ وَقَعَ في الوقتِ دونَ ركعةٍ

remainder takes place after it, then the whole prayer is considered a makeup. If one rak'a or more takes place within the prayer's time and the remainder is after it, then the prayer is considered a current performance, though it is unlawful to intentionally delay the prayer until part of it occurs after the time is finished.

والباقي خارجَهُ فكلُّها قضاء. أو ركعةً فأكثرَ والباقي خارجَهُ فكلُّها أداءً. لكنْ يَحْرُمُ تعمُّدُ التأخيرِ عن الوقتِ حتَّى يَقَعَ بعضُها خارجَ الوقتِ.

f2.4　[ومَنْ جَهِلَ دخولَ الـوقتِ (لغيمٍ أو حبس ببيتٍ مظلم) فأخْبَرَهُ ثقةٌ عنْ مشاهدةٍ وَجَبَ قبولُهُ. أوْ عنِ اجتهادٍ فلا. فللأعمى أو البصيرِ العاجزِ عنِ الاجتهادِ تقليدُهُ لا القادرِ عليهِ].

f2.5　It is permissible to rely (N: for knowledge that a prayer's time has come) on a knowledge-able, dependable *muezzin* (caller to prayer). If one lacks someone to inform one of the time, then one may reason on the basis of reciting a scheduled period of invocation or Koran recital (Ar. wird) (n: referring to those whose *wird*s normally take the whole time between two prescribed prayers such that when they finish, they know the time for the second prayer has come. The legal basis of *wird*s is discussed at w20), and the like (N: including modern clocks, and prayer time calendars issued by experts on the times in various localities).

f2.5　ويَجُوزُ اعتمـادُ مؤذنٍ ثقـةٍ عارفٍ [وديـكٍ مجـرَّبٍ]. فإنْ فَقَـدَ [الأعمى أو البصيرُ] مخبراً اجْتَهَـدَ بوردٍ ونحوه (ح: ومنه الساعـات الحديثة والتقـويمـات التي يصـدرها الخبراء بالمواقيت في مختلف الأزمنة والأمكنة)، [وإنْ أمْكَنَهُمَا اليقينُ بالصبرِ، فإنْ تَحَيَّرا صَبَـرَا حتَّى يَظُنَّا، فإنْ صَلَّيَا بلا اجتهادٍ أعادَا، وإنْ أصَابَا].

MAKING UP MISSED PRAYERS

قضاء الفوائت

f2.6　When enough of a prayer's time has elapsed to have performed the prayer during it, and someone who has not yet prayed loses their reason or their menstrual period begins, they are obligated to make up that missed prayer (O: as soon as they are able).

f2.6　وإنْ مَضَى مِنْ أولِ الـوقتِ مَا يُمْكِنُ فيهِ الصلاةُ فَجُنَّ أوْ حاضَتْ وَجَبَ القضاءُ (لما فاته فوراً).

f2.7　Whenever a prescribed prayer is missed for a valid reason (def: f1.5), it is recommended to make it up immediately.

If missed without a valid reason, it is obligatory to make it up (dis: w18) immediately (A: meaning during all one's time that is not occupied by necessities. In the Shafi'i school, it is not even permissible for such a person to perform sunna prayers (N: before having finished making up the

f2.7　ومَتَى فَاتَتِ المكتـوبـةُ بعذرٍ نُدِبَ الفورُ في القضاءِ.
وإنْ فَاتَتْ بغيرِ عذرٍ وَجَبَ الفورُ (ع: يعني في جميعِ الـوقتِ الـذي يزيـدُ عن ضروريـاته ولا يجوزُ له عند الشافعية أنْ

missed ones)). The same applies to making up missed obligatory fasts (N: by fasting a day in place of each day missed), and it is unlawful to delay doing so until the following Ramadan (dis: i1.33).

يصلي السنة) والصـومُ كالصـلاةِ ويَحْـرُمُ تراخيهِ لرمضانَ القابلِ .

f2.8   It is recommended that missed prayers be made up in the order they were missed. (n: The call to prayer (adhan) and call to commence (iqama) when making up missed prayers are discussed at f3.5, and whether to recite prayers aloud or to oneself at f8.25.)

f2.8   ويُنْدَبُ ترتيبُ الفوائتِ .

f2.9   It is recommended to make up missed prescribed prayers before performing the current one, unless one fears its time will pass, in which case it is obligatory to pray the current one first.

If one begins making up a missed prayer thinking that there will be time for both it and the current prescribed prayer, but finds that there is only enough time left for the latter, then one must discontinue the makeup in order to perform the current one.

f2.9   وتقـديمُهـا علـى الحاضرة إلا أنْ يَخْشَى فواتَ الحاضرة فَيَجِبُ تقديمُها.
وإنْ شَرَعَ في فائتـةٍ ظانّـاً سعـةَ الوقتِ فَبَانَ ضيقُهُ وَجَبَ قَطْعُها وفَعَلَ الحاضرة .

f2.10   If one has a prayer to make up and finds the current prayer being performed by a group, it is recommended to perform the makeup by oneself before praying the current one.

f2.10   ومنْ عليـهِ فائتـةٌ فوجدَ جماعةَ الحاضرة قائمةً نُدبَ تقديمُ الفائتة منفرداً ثمَّ الحاضرة .

f2.11   If one misses one or more of the five prayers but does not remember which of them it was, then one must pray all five, intending for each one making up the missed prayer.

f2.11   ومن نَسِيَ صلاةً فأكْــرَ مِنَ الخمسِ ولَمْ يَعْـرفْ عَيْنَهـا لَزِمَهُ الخمسُ ويَنْوي بكلِ واحدةٍ الفائتةَ .

f2.12   (n: If someone finds he has been consistently mistaken day after day in praying, for example, the dawn prayer (subh) before its time, or some similar timing error, then each prayer performed after the first day of the whole series of prayers thus mistakenly prayed is considered the makeup of the day before it, and when such a person discovers the error, he has only one prayer to make up, namely the one on the last day prior to learning of the mistake (*Mughni al-muhtaj ila ma'rifa ma'ani alfaz al-Minhaj* (y73), 1.127).)

*

f3.0   THE CALL TO PRAYER (ADHAN) AND CALL TO COMMENCE (IQAMA)

الأذان والإقامة   f3.0

f3.1   The call to prayer (adhan) and call to commence (iqama) are two sunnas for the prescribed prayers, even when praying alone or in the second group to pray (N: in a mosque, for example), such that there is public cognizance (O: of both the call to prayer and to commence, whether in a large or small town).

f3.1   هُمَـا سنتـانِ في المكتوبـات حتَّى لمنفردٍ وجماعـةٍ ثانيةٍ بحيث يَظْهَرُ الشِّعَار (بهما في البلد الكبيرة والصغيرة).

f3.2   To give the call to prayer (adhan) is better than being the imam for a group prayer (O: though to be imam is superior to giving the call to commence (iqama)).

f3.2   والأذانُ أفضـلُ مِنَ الإمـامـةِ (وهي أي الإمـامـة أفضـل من الإقـامةِ) [وقِيلَ عكسُهُ].

f3.3   When praying alone in a mosque where a group has already prayed, one does not raise one's voice in giving the call to prayer, though if no group has yet prayed, one raises it. The same applies to a second group to pray: they do not raise their voice.

f3.3   فإنْ أذَّنَ المنفـردُ في مسجدٍ صُلِّيَتْ فيـه جماعـةٌ لمْ يَرْفَعْ صوتَهُ وإلاَّ رَفَعَ. وكذا الجماعةُ الثانيةُ لا يَرْفَعُونَ صوتَهُمْ.

f3.4   It is sunna for a group of women who are praying together to give the call to commence without giving the call to prayer.

f3.4   ويُسَنُّ لجماعةِ النساءِ الإقامةُ دونَ الأذانِ.

f3.5   When making up one or more missed prescribed prayers, one gives the call to prayer only for the first (N: in the series), but gives the call to commence for each one.

f3.5   [ولا يُؤَذَّنُ للفـائتـةِ في الجديد ويُـؤَذَّنُ لَهَا في القديم الأظهرِ] فإنْ فَاتَتْهُ صلواتٌ لمْ يُؤَذِّنْ لِمَـا بعـدَ الأُولى [وفي الأُولى الخلافُ]. ويُقِيمُ لكلِّ واحدةٍ.

f3.6   The words of the call to prayer and call to commence are well known.
    (n: The words of the call to prayer mean: "Allah is greatest, Allah is greatest. Allah is greatest, Allah is greatest. I testify there is no god but Allah. I testify there is no god but Allah. I testify that Muhammad is the Messenger of Allah. I testify that Muhammad is the Messenger of Allah. Come to the prayer. Come to the prayer. Come to success. Come to success. [n: At this point,

f3.6   وألفاظُ الأذانِ والإقامةِ معروفةٌ
(ت: وهي: «اللهُ أكبـرُ اللهُ أكبـرُ اللهُ أكبـرُ اللهُ أكبـرُ، أشْهَدُ أنْ لاَ إلَهَ إلاَّ اللهُ، أشْهَدُ أنْ لا إلَهَ إلاَّ اللهُ، أشْهَدُ أنَّ مُحَمَّداً رَسُـولُ اللهِ، أشْهَدُ أنَّ مُحَمَّداً رَسُولُ اللـهِ، حَيَّ على الصَّـلاةِ، حَيَّ على الصَّـلاةِ، حَيَّ على الفَـلاحِ، حَيَّ على

before the dawn prayer only, one adds: "Prayer is better than sleep. Prayer is better that sleep."] Allah is greatest, Allah is greatest. There is no god but Allah."

The words of the call to commence mean: "Allah is greatest, Allah is greatest. I testify there is no god but Allah. I testify that Muhammad is the Messenger of Allah. Come to the prayer. Come to success. The prayer is commencing. The prayer is commencing. Allah is greatest, Allah is greatest. There is no god but Allah.")

f3.7   Each word (N: of both of them) must be recited in the order mentioned above.

If one remains silent for long or speaks at length between the words of the call to prayer (O: or call to commence), it is not valid and must be begun again, though a short remark or silence while calling it does not invalidate it.

When giving the call to prayer or call to commence by oneself, the minimal audibility permissible is that one can hear oneself. The minimum when calling them for a group is that all their contents can be heard by at least one other person.

f3.8   It is not valid to give the call to prayer before a prayer's time has come, except for the dawn prayer, when it is permissible to give the call to prayer from the middle of the night onwards (N: as is done in Mecca and Medina).

f3.9   When giving the call to prayer and call to commence, it is recommended to have ablution (wudu), stand, face the direction of prayer, and to turn the head (not the chest or feet) to the right when saying, "Come to the prayer," and to the left when saying, "Come to success."

It is offensive to give the call to prayer while in a state of minor ritual impurity (hadath), more offensive to do so in a state of major ritual impurity (janaba), and even worse to give the call to commence (iqama) while in either of these two states.

It is recommended:

(1) to give the call to prayer from a high place near the mosque;

الفَلاحِ ، (وقبل الصبح فقط : «الصلاة خيرٌ مِنَ النَّوْمِ ، الصلاةُ خيرٌ مِنَ النَّوْمِ ») اللهُ أَكْبَرُ اللهُ أَكْبَرُ ، لاَ إِلَهَ إِلَّا اللهُ) .

(ت) : وألفاظُ الإقامةِ هي : اللهُ أَكْبَرُ اللهُ أَكْبَرُ ، أَشْهَدُ أَنْ لاَ إِلَهَ إِلَّا اللهُ ، أَشْهَدُ أَنَّ مُحَمَّداً رَسُولُ الـلـهِ ، حَيَّ على الصلاةِ ، حَيَّ على الفَلاحِ ، قَدْ قَامَتِ الصلاةُ قَدْ قَامَتِ الصلاةُ اللهُ أَكْبَرُ اللهُ أَكْبَرُ لاَ إِلَهَ إِلَّا اللهُ) .

f3.7   وَيَجِبُ تَرْتِيبُهُمَا (ح : أي ترتيب ألفاظ كل منهما) .

فإِنْ سَكَتَ أَوْ تَكَلَّمَ في أثنائِهِ طويلاً بَطَلَ أذانُهُ (ومثل الأذان الإقامة في ذلك) فَيَسْتَأْنِفُهُ . وإِنْ قَصُرَ فَلاَ .

وأَقَلُّ مَا يَجِبُ أَنْ يُسْمِعَ نفسَهُ إِنْ أَذَّنَ وأقامَ لنفسِهِ . فإِنْ أَذَّنَ وأقامَ لجماعةٍ وَجَبَ إسماعُ واحدٍ جميعِهِمَا .

f3.8   ولا يَصِحُّ الأذانُ قبلَ الوقتِ ، إلَّا الصبحَ فإِنَّهُ يَجُوزُ أَنْ يُؤَذَّنَ لَهَا بعدَ نصفِ الليلِ .

f3.9   وَيُنْدَبُ الطهارةُ والقيامُ واستقبالُ القبلةِ والالتفاتُ في الحيعلتَيْنِ في الأولى يميناً وفي الثانية شمالاً فَيَلْوِي عنقَهُ ولا يُحَوِّلُ صدرَهُ وقدميْهِ .

ويُكْرَهُ للمحدِثِ ، وكراهةُ الجنبِ أشدُّ ، وفي الإقامةِ أغلظُ .

وأَنْ يُؤَذَّنَ على موضعٍ عالٍ وبقربِ

(2) to put one's fingertips in one's ears while calling it;

(3) to take one's time in giving the call to prayer (A: pausing for an interval after each sentence equal to the sentence's length) (O: except for repetitions of "Allah is Greatest," which are said in pairs);

(4) and to give the call to commence rapidly, without pause.

f3.10   It is obligatory for the muezzin (O: or person giving the call to commence):

(a) to be Muslim;

(b) to have reached the age of discrimination (def: f1.2);

(c) to be sane;

(d) and if calling for a men's group prayer, to be male.

It is recommended that he be *upright* (def: o24.4) and have a strong, pleasant voice.

It is offensive for a blind person to give the call to prayer unless a sighted person is with him (O: to tell him when the time has come).

f3.11   When one hears the call to prayer (N: or call to commence), it is recommended to repeat each phrase after the muezzin, even if in a state of major ritual impurity (janaba), during menstruation, or when reciting the Koran (N: and *a fortiori* when reading or reciting something else).

One does not repeat the phrases "Come to the prayer" or "Come to success," but rather says after them, "There is no power or strength except through Allah." And at the call to prayer at dawn, one does not repeat "Prayer is better than sleep," but instead says, "You have spoken the truth, and piously."

When the person giving the call to commence says, "The prayer is commencing," one replies, "May Allah establish it and make it endure as long

المسجد ويجعَل إصبعَيْه في صماخَيْه ويُرَتِّلَ الأذانَ (إلا التكبير فيجمع فيه بين كل تكبيرتين بصوت) ويُدرِج الإقامة .

f3.10   ويُشْتَرَطُ كونُ المؤذِّنِ (ومثله المقيم) مسلماً عاقلاً مميِّزاً ذكراً إنْ أذَّنَ للرجال .
ونُدِب كونُهُ [حراً] عدلاً صيِّتاً حَسَنَ الصوت [منْ أقارب مؤذني النبيِّ ﷺ] . ويُكْرَهُ للأعمى إلَّا أَنْ يَكُونَ مَعَهُ بصيرٌ (يخبره بدخول الوقت) .

f3.11   ويُنْدَبُ لسامِعِهِ ولَوْ جنباً أو حائضاً أوْ في قراءةٍ (ح : أي قراءة القرآن وقارىء غير القرآن من باب الأولى) أَنْ يَقُولَ مثلَ قوله (ح : أي المؤذن والمقيم) عقبَ كلِّ كلمةٍ .
وفي الحيعلتَيْنِ : «لا حَوْلَ وَلاَ قُوَّةَ إلَّا بالله» . . وفي «الصلاةُ خيرٌ مِنَ النوم » : «صَدَقْتَ وبَرَرْتَ» .
وفي كلمتْيْ الإقامة : «أقَامَها اللَّه

as the heavens and earth, and make me one of the righteous of its folk."

If one hears it while making love, going to the lavatory, or performing the prayer, one says the words when finished.

وأداممهـــا مَادامَـتِ الـسَّمــواتُ والأرْضُ وجَعَلني مِنْ صَالحي أَهْلِها» .

فإنْ كانَ مجــامِعــاً أوْعلى الخلاء أوْ مُصلِّياً أجابَ بعدَ فراغِهِ .

f3.12   It is recommended for the muezzin, after he finishes, and those hearing him to bless the Prophet (Allah bless him and give him peace). (A: It is unobjectionable in the Shafi'i school for the muezzin to do so as loudly as the call to prayer.) Then one adds, "O Allah, Lord of this comprehensive invitation and enduring prayer, grant our liegelord Muhammad a place near to You, an excellence and exalted degree, and bestow on him the praiseworthy station that You have promised him."

f3.12   ويُنْدَبُ للمـؤذِّنِ وسامِعِهِ بعدَ فراغِـه الصلاةُ على النبيِّ ﷺ ثمَّ يَقـولُ: «اللَّهُمَّ رَبَّ هَذِه الـدَّعـوَة الـتَّامَّة والصَّلاة القَـائمَـة آتِ سَيِّدَنَا مُحَمَّداً الـوَسيلَةَ والفَضيلَةَ والـدَّرَجَـةَ الـرَّفيعَةَ وابْعَثْهُ مَقَاماً مَحْمُوداً الَّذِي وَعَدْتَهُ» .

*

f4.0   PURITY OF BODY, CLOTHES, AND PLACE OF PRAYER

f4.0   طهارة البدن والثوب وموضع الصلاة

f4.1   It is a necessary condition (shart) for the validity of prayer that one have purity (N: absence of filth (najasa, def: e14.1)) in:

(a) body;

(b) clothing, whether or not it moves with the person (N: who is praying);

(c) anything that touches the body or clothing (O: though if one's chest overhangs something impure while prostrating without touching it, this does not hurt);

(d) and the place on which one is standing during the prayer.

f4.1   وطهارةُ البدنِ والملبوسِ وإنْ لَمْ يَتَحَرَّكْ بحركتِهِ (ح: أي المصلي) ومَا يُمَسُّـهُمَـا (فـإنْ حاذى صدرَه في حال سجوده نجاسة مع عدم المماسة لم يضر) ومـوضِـع الصـلاة (أي موضع الـوقوف فيها) شَرْطٌ لصِحَّة الصلاة .

f4.2   One's prayer is invalid if one is holding the end of a rope connected with something impure.

One's prayer is valid if performed on the pure portion of a rug which is affected with some filth

f4.2   ولـو قَبَضَ طرفَ حبـلِ [أوْ رَبَطَهُ مَعَهُ] وطرفُهُ الآخَرُ متصلٌ بنجسٍ لَمْ تَصِحَّ صلاتُهُ . ولو تَنَجَّسَ بعضُ بِسَاطٍ

(N: on another part) or on a bed whose legs rest on something impure, even if the rug or bed moves when one's own portion moves. (N: The rule illustrated by these examples is that it is not permissible for the person praying to support or carry something affected by filth, but is permissible for him to be supported by it, provided he is not in direct contact with the filth.)

فَصَلَّى على موضِعٍ طاهِرٍ منهُ وتَحَرَّكَ الباقي بحركتِهِ (ح : أي حركة البِساطِ) أَوْ على سريرٍ قوائمُهُ على نجسٍ وَيَتَحَرَّكُ بحركتِهِ (ح : أي السرير) صَحَّتْ صلاتُهُ .

f4.3 Impure substances (najasa) other than blood (dis: below) that are indiscernible by (A: average) vision are excusable, though if visually discernible, they are inexcusable. (A: That which is seen by a normal look is not excusable, while that which can only be seen by minute scrutiny is excusable.)

f4.3   والنجاسةُ غيرُ الدم إنْ لم يُدرِكْهُ طرفٌ (ع : معتدل) يُعْفى عنها . وإنْ أَدْرَكَها لَمْ يُعْفَ عنها (ع : فإن أدركها بصرٍ معتدلٍ يضر، وإن أدركها بصرٍ حادٍّ فلا) . [إلاَّ عنْ دمِ براغيثَ وقَمْلٍ وغيرِهِما ممّا لا نفسَ لهُ سائلةً (أي دمٌ سائلٌ فالنفسُ هنا بمعنى دمٍ) فيُعْفى عن قليلِهِ وكثيرِهِ، وإنْ اِنْتَشَرَ بعرقٍ].

f4.4 As for blood or pus, if it is from another, (O: human or otherwise,) then only a *little* (def: below) is excusable, though if from the person praying, it is excusable whether much or little, regardless if from a squeezed pimple, a boil, a sore, being bled, cupped, or something else.

f4.4   وأمّا الدمُ والقيحُ، فإنْ كانَ مِنْ أجنبيٍّ (من إنسانٍ وغيرِه) عُفِيَ عن يسيرِهِ، وإنْ كان مِنَ المصلّي عُفِيَ عن قليلِهِ وكثيرِهِ سواءٌ خَرَجَ مِنْ بثرةٍ عَصَرَها أوْ مِنْ دُمَّلٍ أوْ قرحٍ أوْ فصدٍ أوْ حجامةٍ أوْ غيرِها .

f4.5 (N: In rulings of Sacred Law, the application of key descriptive terms like *little, much, near, far, briefly, at length,* and so forth, is governed by the concept of *common acknowledgement* ('urf). To know whether something is *little* or *much,* which could be stipulations in a particular ruling, we stop to reflect whether it is commonly acknowledged as such, namely, whether most people would describe it as such when speaking about it.

Common acknowledgement also takes into consideration what is normal or expected under the circumstances. For example, a few drops of animal blood on the clothes of a butcher would be little, while the same amount on the clothes of a student would be *much.*)

f4.6   [وأمّا ماءُ القروحِ والنفاطاتِ إنْ كانَ لهُ رائحةٌ كريهةٌ فهوَ نجسٌ (ح : لكن له حكم الدم فيعفى عن قليله وكثيره إن كان من المصلي) وإلّا فَلا].

f4.7 If one prays with (N: an inexcusable amount of) something impure (N: on one's per-

f4.7   ولوْ صَلَّى بنجاسةٍ جَهِلَها أوْ

son, place, or clothes) that one did not know of or forgot, and notices it after finishing, one must repeat the prayer. It invalidates the prayer if noticed during it.

f4.8   If one gets some mud on oneself from the street and but is not certain it contains filth, then it is is considered pure (N: the rule being that the initial presumption for all things is that they are pure, as long as their impurity has not been decisively established).

f4.9   Someone unable to remove filth from his person or who is being held in an impure place must pray and later make up the prayer when capable of purity.

(N: When being held in an impure place,) one bows the head as close to the ground as possible without actually contacting the filth, which is unlawful to place the forehead upon.

f4.10   If one loses track of a spot of filth on a garment, then all of it must be washed without trying to decide where the spot might be, though if someone reliable knows where it is and informs one, one may accept this.

f4.11   If a spot of filth is on one of two garments (N: one of which the person wants to pray in) and the person is not sure which, then he may reason and choose the one he believes is pure (N: to pray in), regardless of whether another pure one is available or whether he can wash one to use. (N: But it is not obligatory to try to decide which is pure. Rather, he may wash one, or both, and pray in them, or pray in some other garment.)

If one washes the garment believed to have filth on it, then one may pray wearing both garments, or pray in each garment alone, though if one makes no attempt to decide which garment is impure, but rather performs a prayer in each one separately, then neither prayer is valid.

نَسِيَهَا ثُمَّ رَآهَا بعدَ فَراغِهِ أعادَهَا . أوْ فِيهَا بَطَلَتْ .

f4.8   ولوْ أصَابَهُ طينُ الشارِعِ ، فإنْ لَمْ يَتَحَقَّقْ نجَاسَتُـهُ فهـوَ طاهِـرٌ . (ح : والقاعدة أن الأصل في الأشياء الطهارة ما لم يقطع بنجاستها) . [وإنْ تَحَقَّقَهَا عُفِيَ عَنْ قليلِهِ عُرْفاً وَهُوَ مَا يَتَعَذَّرُ الاحترازُ مِنْهُ ، وَيَخْتَلِفُ بالـوقتِ كأنْ كَانَ أيـامَ الأمطارِ ، وبمـوضِعِهِ مِنَ البدنِ والثوبِ (فيعفى عنه في أسفل الثوب ما لا يعفى في أعلاه) ولاَ يُعْفَى عَنْ كثيرِه] .

f4.9   ومَنْ عَجَـزَ عنْ إزالـةِ نجـاسـةٍ ببـدنِهِ أوْ حُبِسَ في موضِعٍ نجسٍ صَلَّى (وجوباً) وأعادَ ويَنْحَنِي لسجودِهِ بحيثُ لوْ زادَ أصَابَها ، ويَحْرُمُ وَضْعُ الجبهةِ عَلَيْهَا . [ولوْ عَجَزَ عنْ تطهيرِ ثوبِهِ صَلَّى عِرياناً بلا إعادةٍ . ولوْ لَمْ يَجِدْ إلاَّ حريراً صَلَّى فيهِ] .

f4.10   وإنْ خَفِيَتِ النجـاسةُ في ثوبٍ وَجَبَ غسلُهُ كلُّهُ ولاَ يَجْتَهِـدُ . فإنْ أخْبَـرَهُ ثقةٌ بموضِعِهِ اعْتَمَدَهُ .

f4.11   وإنِ اشْتَبَـهَ طاهِـرٌ بمتنجسٍ اجْتَهَـدَ (ح : إن أراد الصـلاة بأحدهما) ، وإنْ أمْكَـنَ طاهِـرٌ بيقينٍ أوْ (ح : أمكنَ) غَسْلُ أحدِهِمَا (أي اجتهاد وإن أمكن الخ) (ح : ولا يجب عليـه الاجتهـاد بل له أن يغسلهمـا أو أحـدهمـا ويصلي في غيرهمـا) . [فإنْ تَحَيَّرَ صَلَّى عِرياناً وأعادَ إنْ لَمْ يُمْكِنْهُ غسلُ ثوبِهِ ، فإنْ أمْكَنَ وَجَبَ] .

وإذا غَسَـلَ مَا ظَنَّهُ نجسـاً صَلَّى فيهِمَا معـاً أوْ في كلِّ منفـرداً . ولـوْ صَلَّى بلا اجتهادٍ في كلِّ ثوبٍ مرةً لمْ تَصِحَّ .

119

f4.12 If one loses track of the location of filth on the ground in open country, one may pray wherever one wishes.

But if one loses track of its location on a small plot of ground or in a room (*bayt*, lit. "house," meaning a one-room dwelling), then all the ground or floor must be washed (def: e14.12) before one may pray on any of it.

f4.12 ولوْ خَفِيَتِ النجاسةُ في فلاةٍ صَلَّى حيثُ شَاءَ بلا اجتهادٍ. أوْ في أرضٍ صغيرةٍ أوْ في بيتٍ وَجَبَ غسلُ الكلِّ. [ولو اشْتَبَهَ بيتانِ اجْتَهَدَ].

f4.13 [ولا تَصِحُّ في مقبرةٍ عَلِمَ نبشَهَا واختلاطَهَا بصديدِ الموتى (وذلك بغير حائل بينه وبينها وأما مع وجود الحائل فالصلاة فيها صحيحة مع الكراهة). فإنْ لمْ يُعْلَمْ نبشُهَا (بأَنْ حفرت الأرض ولم يدفن فيها أحد) كُرِهَتْ وصَحَّ].

f4.14 It is offensive to pray:

(1) in a bathhouse or its outer room where clothes are removed;

(2) in the middle of a path;

(3) at a rubbish dump;

(4) at a slaughterhouse;

(5) in a church;

(6) in places where taxes (dis: p32) are gathered or taken;

(7) in places likely to be contaminated by wine;

(8) on top of the Kaaba;

(9) or towards a tomb (dis: w21).

f4.14 وتُكْـرَهُ في حمـامٍ ومسلخةٍ [(أي المكان الـذي تلقى الثياب فيه عند إرادة الدخول للاغتسال)] وقارعة الطريق (أي في وسطه) ومـزبلةٍ ومجزرةٍ وكنيسةٍ وموضعِ مكسٍ وخمرٍ وظهرِ الكعبةِ وإلى قبرٍ مُتَـوَجِّهاً إلَيـهِ. [وأعطانِ الإبلِ، لا مراحِ غنمٍ].

f4.15 Prayer is unlawful in a garment or on land wrongfully taken, being legally valid (dis: c5.2), but without reward.

f4.15 وتَـحْـرُمُ في ثوبٍ وأرضٍ مغصوبَيْنِ وتَصِحُّ بلا ثوابٍ.

*

f5.0   CLOTHING ONE'S NAKEDNESS

ستر العورة   f5.0

f5.1 Clothing one's nakedness (O: from the eyes of men as well as *jinn* (def: w22) and angels, for these too see people in this world) is obligatory, by scholarly consensus (ijma', b7), even when alone, except when there is need to undress. (O: Zarkashi states (A: and it is the authoritative position for the school) that the nakedness it is obligatory to clothe when alone consists solely of the front and rear private parts for men, and of that which is between the navel and the knees for women.)

f5.2 Clothing one's nakedness is a necessary condition for the validity of the prayer (O: when one is able).

Seeing a hole in one's clothes after a prayer is like seeing a spot of filth (n: meaning the prayer must be repeated, as at f4.7, unless one covers the hole immediately, as below at f5.5).

f5.3 The *nakedness* of a man (O: *man* meaning the counterpart of the female, including young boys, even if not yet of the age of discrimination) consists of the area between the navel and knees. The nakedness of a woman (O: even if a young girl) consists of the whole body except the face and hands.

(N: The *nakedness* of women is that which invalidates the prayer if exposed (dis: w23). As for looking at women, it is not permissible to look at any part of a woman who is neither a member of one's unmarriageable kin (mahram, def: m6.1) nor one's wife, as is discussed below in the book of marriage (m2).)

f5.4 It is a necessary condition that one's clothing:

(a) prevent the color of the skin from being perceptible (n: Nawawi notes, "A thin garment beneath which the blackness or whiteness of the skin may be seen is not sufficient, nor a garment of thick, gauzelike fabric through which part of the nakedness appears" (al-Majmu' (y108), 3.170));

f5.1 هوَ واجبٌ بالإجماع (عن أعين الناس ومثل الناس في ذلك الجن والملك فيطلب سترها عن أعينهم لأنهم يرون بني آدم في الدنيا حتى في الخلواتِ إلّا لحاجةٍ. قال الزركشي والعورة التي يجب سترها في الخلوة السوأتان فقط من الرجل وما بين السرة والركبة من المرأة) (ع: وعليه الاعتماد في المذهب).

f5.2 وهوَ شرطٌ لصحةِ الصلاةِ (عند القدرة).

فإنْ رأى في ثوبِهِ بعدَ الصلاةِ خرقاً فكرؤيةِ النجاسةِ.

f5.3 وعورةُ الرجل (والمراد بالرجل ما قابل المرأة فيدخل الصبي ولو غير مميز) [والأمة] ما بينَ السرة والركبة. وعورةُ الحرةِ (ولو صغيرةٍ) كلُّ بدنِها إلّا الوجهَ والكفين. (ح: عورة النساء ما تبطل الصلاة بانكشافه، وأما في حق النظر فلا يجوز النظر إلى شيء من بدن الأجنبية ـ غير المحرم والزوجة ـ كما سيأتي في كتاب النكاح).

f5.4 وشرطُ الساترِ أنْ يَمْنَعَ لونَ البشرةِ [فلا يَكْفي زجاجٌ وماءُ صافٍ ويَكْفي التطيينُ ولو مَعَ وجودِ الثوبِ ويَجِبُ عندَ فقدِهِ]. (ت: قال النووي: «... فلا يكفي ثوب رقيق يشاهَد من ورائه سواد البشرة أو بياضها، ولا يكفي أيضاً الغليظ المهلهل النسج الذي يظهر بعض العورةِ من خلله» [نقل من

(b) enclose the body as a garment, for a prayer performed without clothes in a small tent would not be valid;

(c) and conceal the nakedness from view on all sides and above, though it need not do so from below.

المـجـمـوع: ٣/ ١٧٠] وأنْ يَشْـمَـلَ المستورَ لُبْساً فلوْ صَلَّى في خيمةٍ ضيقةٍ عرياناً لمْ تَصحَّ وَيُشْتَرَطُ السترُ مِنَ الأعلى والجـوانب لا الأسفل [فلوْ صَلَّى مرتفعاً بحيثُ تُرى عورتُهُ مِنَ الأسفل (جازَ)].

f5.5   One's prayer is valid when there is a tear through which one's nakedness shows that one covers with one's hand (A: immediately, i.e. one must do so before enough time passes to say "Subhan Allah") (O: that is, one must cover it with one's hand when not prostrating, at which point not covering it is excusable).

f5.5   أوْ كانَ في سترتِه خرقٌ فَسَتَرَهُ بيدِه جازَ (أي يستر الخرق بيده إذا لم يسجد وعند إرادة السجود يغتفر له عدم ستره عند عدم السترة لذلك الخرق).

f5.6   It is recommended for a woman to wear a covering over her head (khimar), a full length shift, and a heavy slip under it that doesn't cling to the body. (O: She should not wrap it so tightly about herself that it hinders standing, sitting, and other postures connected with the actions of prayer. She is recommended to pray in three garments even though the headcover and shift alone are sufficient as a covering.)

f5.6   ويُنْدَبُ لامرأةٍ خِمارٌ وقميصٌ ومِلْحَفَةٌ غليظةٌ وَتَجَافيهَا (لا تجعلها ضيقة ملتصقة بها بحيث يعسر عليها حينئـذ القيام والجلوس وغيـرهمـا مما يتعلق بأفعـال الصلاة، وتصلي المرأة في ثلاثـة أثـواب على سبيل الندب وإن كان الخمار مع القميص كافياً في الستر).

f5.7   It is recommended for a man to pray in his best clothes, and to wear an ankle-length shirt and a turban (O: and a shawl over head and shoulders, a mantle, and a wraparound or loose drawers (N: under the ankle-length shirt)). If he does not wear all of these, it is desirable to wear two, namely the ankle-length shirt with either the mantle, the wraparound, or the loose drawers.

f5.7   ولرجلٍ أحسنُ ثيابِه ويَتَقَمَّصُ ويَـتَـعَمَّمُ (وأن يتطيلس وأن يرتـدي وأن يتـزر أو يتسرول). فإنِ اقْتَصَرَ فثوبان: قميصٌ مَعَهُ رداءٌ أو إزارٌ أو سراويلُ.

f5.8   If only wearing enough to clothe one's nakedness, one's prayer is valid, though it is recommended to place something on one's shoulders, even if only a piece of rope.

One if does not have clothes but is able to conceal part of one's nakedness, one must cover the front and rear private parts. If only one of these two can be covered, it must be the front. If one has no clothes at all, then one performs the prayer without clothes and need not make it up later.

f5.8   فإنِ اقْتَصَرَ على ستـرِ العـورةِ جازَ لكنْ يُنْدَبُ لَهُ وَضْعُ شيءٍ على عاتقِه ولوْ حبلاً.
فإن فَقَـدَ ثوباً وأمْكَنَ ستـرُ بعضِ العورةِ وَجَبَ ويَسْتُرُ السوأتين حتماً. فإنْ أمْكَنَ أحـدُهُمَا فقطْ تَعَيَّنَ القبـلُ. فإنْ فَقَدَهَا بالكلية صَلَّى عرياناً بلا إعادةٍ.

f5.9 [فإنْ وَجَدَ السترةَ في الصلاةِ وهي بقربِه سَتَرَ وبَنَى، إنْ لمْ يَعْدِلْ عن القبلةِ (ح: بصدرِه). أو بعيدةً سَتَرَ واسْتَأنَف. وتُنْدَبُ الجماعةُ للعراةِ. ويَقِفُ إمامُهُمْ وسطَهُمْ. وإنْ أُعِيرَ ثوباً لَزِمَهُ القبولُ. فإنْ لمْ يَقْبَلْ وصَلَّى عريانًا لمْ تصِحَّ. وإنْ وَهَبَهُ لمْ يَلْزَمْهُ القبولُ. وسَبَقَ في التيمم (e12.6) مسائلُ فيَعُودُ مثلُها ههُنَا].

*

f6.0   FACING THE DIRECTION OF PRAYER (QIBLA)

f6.0   استقبال القبلة

f6.1   Facing the *direction of prayer* (qibla) is a necessary condition for the prayer's validity, with the sole exceptions of praying in extreme peril (dis: f16.5) and nonobligatory prayers performed while travelling.

f6.1   هوَ شرطٌ لصحةِ الصلاةِ، إلّا في شدةِ الخوفِ ونفلِ السفرِ.

f6.2   (N: The rulings below deal with nonobligatory prayers, not the five prescribed ones, which must be performed while facing the proper direction for prayer (qibla) whether one is riding in a vehicle or not (dis: w24).)

A traveller may perform nonobligatory prayers riding or walking, even on short trips.

When riding and able to face the direction of prayer, prostrate, and bow, as when on a ship, one is obligated to. If not able, then one is only required to face the direction of prayer during the first Allahu Akbar of the prayer, provided this is not difficult, as when one's mount is stationary or when one can turn oneself or one's mount the proper direction. If it *is* difficult, as when one's mount is not properly saddle broken, or if the reins are not in one's hands, as when riding in a pack train with each animal tied to the one ahead of it, then it is not obligatory to face the direction of prayer at any point of the prayer's performance, and one merely nods in the direction of travel instead of bowing and prostrating. One's nod for prostration must be deeper than the nod for bowing. One does not have to bow to the limit of one's capacity, nor bow the forehead until it touches the mount's back, though this is permissible if one troubles oneself to do so.

When praying while walking, one must stop to bow and prostrate on the ground (O: if easy,

f6.2   فللمسافرِ التنفُّلُ راكباً وماشياً وإنْ قَصُرَ سفرُه.
فإنْ كَانَ راكباً وأمْكَنَ استقبالُهُ وإتمامُ الركوعِ والسجودِ في [محملٍ وَ] سفينةٍ لَزِمَهُ وإنْ لمْ يُمْكِنْـهُ لَزِمَهُ الاستقبالُ عندَ التحرُّمِ فقطْ إنْ سَهُلَ بأنْ كانَتْ واقفةً وأمْكَنَ انحرافُهُ أوْ تحريكُهُ [أو سائرةً سهلةً زمامُها بيدِه]. وإنْ شَقَّ بأنْ كانَتْ عَسِرَةً أوْ مقطورةً فَلَا (يلزمه حينئذ الاستقبال لا في التحـرم ولا في غيـره) ويُـومِـىءُ إلى مقصدِهِ بركوعِهِ وسجودِهِ. ويَجِبُ كونُهُ أخفضَ، ولَا يَجِبُ غايةُ وسعِهِ ولَا وضعُ الجبهةِ على الدابةِ فلوْ تَكَلَّفَ جَازَ.
والماشِي يَرْكَعُ ويَسْجُدُ على الأرضِ

though if walking in mud, water, or snow, one may simply nod), and may walk during the rest of the prayer, though it is obligatory to face the direction of prayer during the first Allahu Akbar, and at each bowing and prostration.

Such prayers (O: whether riding or walking) are only valid on condition:

(a) that one's journey continue for the prayer's duration;

(b) and that one not turn from the direction of travel towards anything but the direction of prayer.

If one reaches home while thus praying, or the destination, or a town where one intends to stay, then one must face the direction of prayer, and bow and prostrate on the ground or on one's mount if stopped.

(أي إن سهل عليه ذلك فلوكان يمشي في وحـل أو ماء أو ثلج فالأوجـه أنـه بكفيـه الإيمـاء) ويَمْشي في البـاقي . ويُشْتَـرَطُ الاسـتقبـالُ في الإحرام والـركـوعِ والسجود فقطْ .

ويُشْتَـرَطُ دوامُ سفـرِه (سواء كان راكباً أو ماشياً) ولزومُ جهة مقصدِه إلّا إلى القبلة .

فإنْ بَلَغَ في أثنائهـا منزلَهُ أوْ مقصدَهُ أوْ بلداً ونـوَى الإقـامـةَ بِه وَجَب إتمـامُهـا بركـوعٍ وسجودٍ واستقبالٍ على الأرض أوْ دابةٍ واقفةٍ .

f6.3   When at the Kaaba, one must pray directly towards the Kaaba itself. One's prayer is invalid if one merely faces the semicircular wall (N: Hijr Isma'il) that is to one side of it, or directs any part of the body outside the outline of the Kaaba, unless one is standing at the end of a long row of people praying at the periphery of al-Masjid al-Haram (n: the mosque of the Kaaba), a row which, if the people in it were to advance, some of them would be facing outside the Kaaba's outline. To pray in such a row is valid for everyone in it.

f6.3   ومَنْ حَضَـرَ الـكعبـةَ لَزِمَـهُ اسْتِقْبَالُ عينهَا فلو اسْتقبَلَ الحِجْرَ (ح : أي حجر إسماعيل) أوْ خَرَجَ بَعْضُ بدنِه عنهَا لم تَصِحَّ، إلّا أنْ يَمْتَدَّ صفٌّ بعيدٌ في آخر المسجد الحرام ولوْ قَرُبُوا لخَرَجَ بعضُهُمْ فإنّهُ يَصِحُّ للكلّ .

f6.4   [ومَنْ صَلَّى داخـلَ الكعبـةِ واسْتَقْبَـلَ جدارَهَـا أوْ بابَهَا المردودَ أو المفتوحَ وعتبُّهُ ثلثا ذراعٍ تقريباً صَحَّ . وإلّا فلا . وإنْ كانَ بمكـةَ وبينَـهُ وبينَ الكعبـةِ حائـلٌ خلقيٌّ أوْ طارئٍ فلهُ الاجتهادُ . وإنْ وَضَعَ محرابَهُ على العِيانِ صَلَّى إليه أبداً ، ومنْ غَابَ عنهَا فأخْبَرَهُ بها مقبولُ الروايةِ عنْ مشاهدٍ وجَبَ قبولُه] .

f6.5   For knowledge of the proper direction it is obligatory to rely on the *prayer niche* (mihrab) of a mosque in a city or village through which many people pass.

At every place the Prophet (Allah bless him and give him peace) faced to pray and established where he stood, it is obligatory to pray facing as he did, without reconsidering the direction of prayer,

f6.5   وكـذا يَجِبُ اعتمـادُ محرابِ بلدٍ أوْ قريةٍ يَكْثُرُ طُارِقُهَا .

وكلُّ مكانٍ صَلَّى إليْهِ النبيُّ ﷺ وضَبطَ موقفَهُ متعيَّنٌ لا يَجْتهِـدُ فيـه لا بتيامُن ولا

or turning right or left, though in other places one may use personal reasoning as to whether to turn right or left.

بتياسُر. وَيَجْتَهِدُ فيهِمَا في غيرِهِ مِن المحاريبِ.

f6.6 If one does not find an informant to tell one of the proper direction of prayer by having seen the Kaaba in that direction, then one employs personal reasoning, using other evidence.

f6.6 وإنْ لمْ يَجِـدْ مَنْ يُخْبِـرُهُ عن مشاهدةٍ اجْتَهَدَ بالدلائلِ.

(n: To establish the direction of prayer in cities far from Mecca one may use a world globe and a piece of string, since in North America, Australia, and other regions, using a flat world map will yield the wrong direction because of the curvature of the earth, and the error factor is often considerable. One puts the end of the string on the position of Mecca on the globe, the other end on one's own city, and pulls the string taut, observing the bearing of the string and drawing a line in the same direction on a local map, which can be oriented with a compass and used to indicate the proper direction to pray.)

If one does not know how to use other evidence, (O: and it is a communal obligation (def: c3.2) for someone to know,) or one is blind, then one follows another (O: reliable sighted person acquainted with the evidence).

فإنْ لمْ يَعرِفْها (والأدلة فرض كفاية) أوْ كانَ أعمَى قلَّد (بصيراً ثقة عارفاً بأدلتها).

f6.7 If, after praying, one becomes certain one was mistaken, then the prayer must be repeated.

(n: In the Hanafi, Maliki, and Hanbali schools, the criterion for *facing the direction of prayer* is merely that some portion of the person's face be directed towards the Kaaba (*al-Fiqh 'ala al-madhahib al-arba'a* (y66), 1.195). (A: This takes in 180 degrees, from far left to far right, such that when the Kaaba is anywhere between, one is considered to be facing the direction of prayer.))

f6.7 وإنْ تَيَقَّنَ الخطأَ بعـدَ الصلاة بالاجتهادِ أعـادَ. (ت: وقال الحنفيـة والمـالكيـة والحنـابلة إن ضابط استقبال جهـة الكعبة هو أن يكون جزء من سطح الـوجـه مقابـلاً لها (الفقه على المذاهب الأربعـة: ١/ ١٩٥] (ع) رع: وذلك يشمـل نصف دائرة، من أقصى يساره إلى أقصى يمينه. فإن كانت الكعبة بجهة ضمنها فهو مستقبل القبلة).

*

f7.0 PLACING A BARRIER IN FRONT OF ONE'S PRAYER PLACE

f7.0 السترة

f7.1 It is recommended to put a barrier at least 32 cm. high in front of oneself when performing the prayer, or to spread out a mat, or if one cannot, to draw a line (N: on the ground, straight out, perpendicular to one's chest) about a meter and a

f7.1 يُنْدَبُ للمصلّي أنْ يَكُونَ بينَ يدَيْهِ سترةٌ ثلثَا ذراع أوْ يَبْسُطَ مصلّى فإنْ عَجَزَ خَطَّ خطًّا علَى [ح: بُعدِ]] ثلاثة

125

half (O: or less) in front of one. It is then unlawful for anyone to pass (O: between the person praying and such a barrier, even when there is no other way to pass (dis: p75.27)).

أَذْرع (فَأَقَلَ) فَيَحْـرُمُ المرورُ حينئذٍ (بين المصلِّي وبين السترة المذكورة وإن لم يجد المار سبيلًا).

If someone tries to pass between oneself and the barrier, it is recommended to gently push him back. If he persists, one may push him back as hard as necessary, as one would an attacker (def: o7.3). Were he to die as a result, one would not be subject to retaliation (o3) or have to pay an indemnity (o4) to his kin.

وَيُنْدَبُ دفعُ المارِّ بالأسهلِ ويَزيدُ قدرَ الحاجةِ كالصائلِ . فإنْ مَاتَ فَهْدَرٌ .

f7.2   If there is no barrier, or if the person praying is farther than a meter and a half from it, then passing in front of him is merely offensive, and the person praying is not entitled to push him.

f7.2   فإنْ لَمْ يكنْ ستـرةٌ أَوْ تَبَـاعَـدَ عنْها كُرِهَ المرورُ وليَّسَ لهُ الدفعُ .

f7.3   (A: *Passing in front* of a person without a barrier, in a mosque for example, is limited to the length of his prostration, and it is not unlawful or offensive to pass in front of him when farther than that.)

f7.4   When one notices a gap in a row of people performing a group prayer, one is entitled to pass in front of others to fill it.

f7.4   ولـوْ وَجَـدَ في صفٍّ فرجـةً فلهُ المرورُ ليَسْتُرَها .

*

f8.0   DESCRIPTION OF THE PRAYER

f8.0   صفة الصلاة

f8.1   (n: Special vocabulary:

Allahu Akbar: Allah is greatest.

Ameen: a one-word supplication meaning "Answer our prayer."

as-Salamu 'alaykum: Peace be upon you.

Fatiha: the opening sura of the Koran.

Follower: someone praying in group behind an imam.

Integral (rukn): one of the legally essential elements found within an action that compose it.

Imam: someone leading a group prayer.

Rak'a: one complete cycle of the words and actions of the prayer.

Sura: a chapter of the Koran.

Ta'awwudh: to say in Arabic, "I take refuge in Allah from the accursed Devil.")

MEASURES RECOMMENDED BEFORE PRAYER

سنن ما قبل الصلاة

f8.2   It is recommended:

(1) to stand for the prayer after the end of the call to commence (iqama);

(2) to be in the first row;

(3) to make the rows straight, especially if one is the imam (O: when one should order the group to do so);

(4) and to fill up the first row first, then the second, and so on (O: meaning there should not be a second row when the first one is not full (A: as to pray in such a second row is the same as not praying with a group, and is rewarded as if one had prayed alone), nor gaps within one row, nor a distance in excess of a meter and a half between rows).

It is superior to stand on the imam's right (A: though the sunna is for the imam to be in the middle) (N: and if one arrives at a group prayer in which the row extends to the right, one's reward is greater for standing on the left, since one is performing the sunna).

f8.2   يُنْدَبُ أَنْ يَقُومَ لهَا بعدَ فراغ الإقـامة ويُنْدَبُ الصفُ الأولُ وتسـويةُ الصـفـوفِ وللـإمـام آكَـدُ (بأن يأمـر المأمـومين بتسـوية الصفـوف) وإتمـامُ الصفِّ الأولِ فالأولِ (أي لا ينبغي جعل صف ثان إلا بعد إكمال الصف وكذلك تقطيـع الصفـوف بأن يجعلوا فرجـاً بين الصف الـواحد وكـذلك تباعُد الصفوف بعـضهـا عن بعض بأن يزيـد ما بين كل صف على ثلاثـة أذرع) . وجهـةُ يميـن الإمام أفضلُ .

THE INTENTION

النية

f8.3   Then one makes the intention with one's heart.

If it is for an obligatory prayer, one must intend performing the prayer, and that it is obligatory, and know which one it is, such as the

f8.3   ثمَّ يَنْوي بقلبِهِ . فإنْ كانَ فريـضةً وَجَبَ نيـةُ فعـل الصلاةِ وكـونهـا فرضاً وتعيينها ظهراً أوْ

noon, midafternoon, or Friday prayer. The intention must coincide with one's first Allahu Akbar, obligatorily existing in the mind and recommended to be uttered with the tongue (N: before the first Allahu Akbar) as well. One intends it from the first of the phrase ''Allahu akbar'' to the last of it. It is not obligatory to specify the number of rak'as, or that it is for Allah Most High, or whether it is a current performance or a makeup prayer, though specifying these is recommended.

(A: some scholars hold that the mere determination to perform a particular prayer existing in the mind beforehand is sufficient. Such an intention could be expressed, for example, by walking to the mosque after hearing the call to the noon prayer (dis: w25).)

If the intention is for a nonobligatory prayer that has a particular time, one must intend which one it is, such as for 'Eid, the eclipse prayer, assuming the state of pilgrim sanctity (ihram), the sunna prayers before and after the noon prayer, and so forth.

If it is for a nonobligatory prayer that is wholly supererogatory, unconnected with a particular time, one may simply intend to perform *prayer*.

عصراً أو جمعةً وَيِجبُ قرنُ ذلكَ بالتكبير فَيُحضِرُهُ في ذهنِهِ حتماً وَيَتَلَفَّظُ بهِ ندباً ويَقصِدُهُ مقارِناً لأولِ التكبير وَيَسْتَصْحِبُهُ حتّى يُفـرِغَـهُ. ولا يجبُ التعرُّضُ لعـدد الـركعـاتِ ولا الإضافة إلى اللهِ تعالى ولا الأداء أو القضاء بلْ يُنْدَبُ ذلكَ.

وإنْ كَانَتْ نافلةً مؤقتـةً وَجَبَ التعيينُ كعيدٍ وكسوفٍ وإحرامٍ وسنةِ الظهر وغيرِ ذلكَ.

وإنْ كَانَتْ نافلةً مطلقةً أجزأُه نيّةُ الصلاة.

f8.4   [ولوْ شَكَّ بعدَ التكبير في النيةِ أوْ في شرطِها فَيُمْسِكُ فإنْ ذَكَرَهَا قَبْلَ ركنٍ وقَصُرَ الفصلُ (أي لم يمض مقدار فعل ركن) لَمْ تَبْطُلْ. وإنْ طَالَ أوْ بَعْدَ ركنٍ قوليٍّ أوْ فعليٍّ بَطَلَتْ].

f8.5   It immediately invalidates one's prayer:

(1) to cease to intend praying;

(2) to decide that one will cease to;

(3) not to know whether one has ceased to or not (O: meaning one hesitates in one's heart, saying, ''Shall I stop intending or continue?'' The mere thought of how it would be if one were to hesitate during the prayer is of no consequence, but rather the occurrence of doubt that negates one's resolve and certainty);

(4) to intend during the first rak'a to stop when one reaches the second;

f8.5   ولـوْ قَطَـعَ النيـةَ أوْ عَزَمَ على قطعهَـا أوْ شَكَّ هلْ قَطَعَهَا (بأن تردد في قلبـه وقـال هل أقطعها أو استمـر فيهـا والمراد أن يطرأ له الشك المناقض للجزم واليقين ولا عبـرة بمـا يجري في الفكر أنه لوْ تردد في الصـلاة كيف يكـون) أوْ نَوى في الركعةِ الأولى قَطْعَهَا في الثانيةِ أوْ عَلَّقَ

(5) or to decide to interrupt one's prayer if such and such a thing happens, regardless whether the event will definitely occur during the prayer or whether it merely *may* happen, such as, "I'll stop if Zayd comes in."

الخـروجَ بمـا يُوْجَـدُ فـي الصلاةِ يقيناً أَوْ توهماً كدخولِ زيدٍ بَطَلَت في الحالِ .

f8.6 If one knowingly begins the noon prayer (N: for example) before its time has come, one's prayer is not legally considered to have begun. If one does so unknowingly, it is validly begun, but counts as a nonobligatory prayer.

f8.6 ولـوْ أَحـرَمَ بالظهرِ قبلَ الزوالِ عالماً لمْ تَنْعَقِدْ . أَوْ جاهلاً انْعَقَدَتْ نفلاً .

THE OPENING ALLAHU AKBAR

تكبير الإحرام

f8.7 The Allahu Akbar (n: an integral) that begins the prayer can only be in Arabic and must be pronounced "Allāhu akbar" or "Allāhul-akbar."

One's prayer is not legally considered to have begun if one omits any of its letters, pauses between the two words, adds the letter waw (و) between them, or says "Allahu akbār" with a long *a* between the final *b* and *r*.

If unable to pronounce it because of being a mute or similar, one must move the tongue and lips according to one's capacity.

f8.7 ولفظُ التكبيـرِ متعينٌ بالعربيةِ وهوَ اللهُ أَكْبَرُ أو اللهُ الأَكْبَرُ .
ولـوْ أَسْقَـطَ حرفـاً منـهُ أَوْ سَكَتَ بينَ كلمتَيْـهِ ، أَوْ زَادَ بينهمـا واواً ، أَو بينَ البـاءِ والراءِ ألفاً ، لمْ تَنْعَقِدْ .
فإنْ عَجَـزَ لخـرسٍ ونحـوِهِ وَجَبَ تحريكُ لسانِهِ وشفتَيْهِ طاقتَهُ .

f8.8 [فإنْ لمْ يَعرفِ العربيةَ كَبَّرَ بأيِّ لغةٍ شاءَ وعليهِ أَنْ يَتَعَلَّمَ إنْ أَمْكَنَهُ . فإنْ أَهْمَلَ مَعَ القدرةِ وضاقَ الوقتُ تَرْجَمَ وأعادَ الصلاةَ] .

f8.9 The minimal valid audibility for saying "Allahu akbar," reciting the Koran, and all invocations (dhikr), is that one can hear them oneself, given normal hearing and lack of extraneous noise.

The imam speaks aloud (def: below) every time he says "Allahu akbar" in the prayer.

f8.9 وأقـلُّ التكبيـرِ والقـراءةِ وسائرِ الأذكـارِ أَنْ يُسْمِـعَ نفسَهُ إذا كانَ صحيحَ السمـعِ بلا عارضٍ .
ويَجْهُرُ الإمامُ بالتكبيراتِ كلِّهَا .

f8.10 (A: Throughout the rulings, *aloud* (jahran) means that someone beside or behind the speaker could distinguish his words, while *to oneself* (sirran) means that the speaker can distinguish his own words, but such a person could not.)

f8.11 It is obligatory that one be standing when one opens an obligatory prayer with "Allahu akbar." If a single letter of it occurs while not standing, the prayer is not considered to have validly begun as an obligatory prayer, but is considered to have begun as a supererogatory prayer, provided one is ignorant that it is unlawful, though not if one knows. (N: The latecomer to a group prayer should take careful note of this, and not bow or make other prayer movements until he has completed the opening Allahu Akbar while standing.)

f8.12 It is recommended to lift the hands to shoulder level when one says "Allahu akbar" (O: meaning that one's fingertips are even with the tops of the ears, thumbs with the earlobes, and palms with one's shoulders), fingers slightly outspread. If one intentionally or absentmindedly does not lift the hands at the first of saying "Allahu akbar," one may do so during it, though not afterwards. The palms face the direction of prayer (qibla) and the hands are uncovered.

After the opening Allahu Akbar, one places the hands between the chest and navel, grasping the left wrist with the right hand, and fixing one's gaze on the place where one's forehead will prostrate. (O: One does this when not reciting the Testification of Faith (Tashahhud, def: f8.45), where one only looks at the place of prostration until one says "except Allah," and then looks at the index finger.)

(A: It is offensive to close one's eyes while praying unless it is more conducive to awe and humility towards Allah.)

THE OPENING SUPPLICATION (ISTIFTAH)

f8.13 Then one recites (N: to oneself) the Opening Supplication (Istiftah), which means: "I turn my face to Him who created the heavens and earth, a pure monotheist, in submission, and am not of those who associate others with Him. My prayer, worship, life, and death are for Allah, Lord of the Worlds, who has no partner. Thus I have been commanded, and I am of those who

---

f8.11 وَيُشْتَرَطُ أَنْ يُكَبِّرَ قائماً في الفَرْض . فإنْ وَقَعَ منهُ حرفٌ في غيرِ القيامِ لم تَنْعَقِدْ فرضاً وتَنْعَقِدْ نَفلاً لجاهلِ التحريمِ دونَ عالِمِهِ . (ح : وينبغي أن يلاحظ هذا المسبوق فلا يهوي للركوع أو غيره ما لم يتم التكبيرة قائماً) .

f8.12 وَيُنْدَبُ رَفْعُ يدَيْهِ حذوَ مَنكِبَيْهِ (بأن تحاذي أطرافُ أصابعه أعلى أذنَيْهِ وإبهاماه شحمتي أذنيه وراحتاه مَنكِبَيه) مفرَّقةَ الأصابعِ مَعَ التكبيرِ . فإنْ تَرَكَهُ عمداً أوْ سهواً أتَى بِهِ في أثناءِ التكبير لا بعدَهُ . وتَكُونُ كفَّاهُ إلى القِبلةِ مكشوفَتَيْنِ . ويَحُطُّهُمــا بعــدَ التكبيــرِ إلى تحت صدرِهِ وفـوقَ سُرتِهِ ويَقْبِضُ كوعَهُ الأيسَرَ بكفِّهِ الأيمَنِ، ويَنْظُرُ إلى موضعِ سجودِهِ . (وهـذا في غير التشهد وأما فيه فينظــر إلى محلِّ سجـوده أيضـاً إلى أن يقـــول : إلا الــله» فيَنظــر حيــنئـذ إلى السبـابة) . (ع : ويكره إغماض عينه إلا إذا كان أخشع) .

دعاء الاستفتاح

f8.13 ثُمَّ يقرأُ دعـاءَ الاستفتاح وهُوَ «وَجَّهْتُ وَجْهِي للّذي فطَرَ السَّمــوات والأرضَ حَنِيفـاً مُسْلِمـاً ومَا أنَـا مِنَ المُشْــركينَ إنَّ صَلاتِي ونُسُكِي ومَحْيـايَ ومَمَــاتِي للّهِ رَبِّ العَـالَمينَ لاَ شَريكَ لَهُ وبِذلِكَ أُمِرْتُ وأَنَا مِنَ المُسْلِمينَ» .

submit."

This is recommended for anyone performing an obligatory or supererogatory prayer, even if seated; no matter whether a child, woman, or traveller (O: alone or in a group, imam or follower), though not for a funeral prayer.

وَيُنْدَبُ ذلك لكلِّ مصلٍّ مفترضٍ ومتنفلٍ وقاعدٍ وصبيٍّ وامرأةٍ ومسافرٍ (وسواءٌ كان منفرداً أو في جماعةٍ ، إماماً أو مأموماً) لا في جنازةٍ .

f8.14 If one intentionally or absentmindedly omits the Opening Supplication (Istiftah) and begins saying "I take refuge, etc." (Ta'awwudh), one may not return to the Opening Supplication.

f8.14 ولوْ تَرَكَهُ عمداً أوْ سهواً وشَرَعَ في التعوذِ لمْ يَعُدْ إليهِ .

f8.15 When (N: joining a group that has already begun, and) the imam says "Ameen" just after one's opening Allahu Akbar, one says "Ameen" with him and then recites the Opening Supplication (Istiftah).

If one says the opening Allahu Akbar and the imam finishes the prayer with Salams before one has sat down with the group, then one recites the Opening Supplication (Istiftah). But if one has already sat down when the imam finishes with Salams and one rises (N: to finish one's prayer), then one does not recite it (O: the Opening Supplication).

If one joins the group while the imam is standing, and one knows it is possible (O: to recite the Opening Supplication) together with saying "I take refuge," and so on (Ta'awwudh) and the Fatiha (N: all before the imam will finish his recital and bow), then one may recite the Opening Supplication, though if one has doubts (N: that there is enough time), one omits both the Opening Supplication and Ta'awwudh, and begins reciting the Fatiha. If the imam bows before one finishes (O: the Fatiha), one bows with him, provided one has omitted the Opening Supplication and Ta'awwudh, though if one did not omit them, then one must recite as much (A: as many letters) of the Fatiha as one recited of them, since if one bows before having recited that much, it invalidates one's prayer.

If one recites what we have just said is enough of the Fatiha to permit one to bow with the imam (n: when one is a latecomer, for otherwise it is obligatory to recite it all, as at f12.17(O:)), but one holds back from bowing with him without

f8.15 ولوْ أحْرَمَ فأمَّنَ الإمامُ عَقِبَهُ أمَّنَ معَهُ ثمَّ اسْتَفْتَحَ .

ولوْ أحْرَمَ فَسَلَّمَ الإمامُ قبلَ قعودِه اسْتَفْتَحَ .

وإنْ قَعَدَ [[المأمومُ المذكورُ في هذه الحالةِ معه]] فَسَلَّمَ [[الإمام]] فقامَ [[المأموم المذكور]] فَلا (يستفتح) .

ولوْ أدْرَكَ الإمامَ قائماً وعَلِمَ إمكانَهُ (أي يمكنه الإتيانُ بدعاء الافتتاح) معَ التعوذِ والفاتحةِ أتَى به . فإنْ شَكَّ لمْ يَسْتَفْتِحْ ولمْ يَتَعَوَّذْ ، بلْ يشْرَعُ في الفاتحةِ . فإنْ رَكَعَ الإمامُ قبلَ أنْ يُتِمَّهَا (أي الفاتحة) رَكَعَ معَهُ إن لم يَكُنِ اسْتَفْتَحَ ولا تَعَوَّذَ . وإلاّ قَرَأَ بقدرِ ما اشْتَغَلَ به . فإنْ رَكَعَ ولمْ يَقْرَأْ بقدرِه بَطَلَتْ صلاتُهُ . وإنْ قَرَأَ حيثُ قلنا

excuse, then if the imam straightens up from bowing before one has oneself bowed, one has missed that rak'a (N: and must rise after the group has finished to perform it).

يَرْكَعُ فَتَخَلَّفَ بلا عذرٍ فإنْ رَفَعَ الإمامُ قبلَ ركوعِهِ فاتَتْهُ الركعةُ.

SAYING "I TAKE REFUGE, ETC." (TA'AWWUDH)

التعوذ

f8.16 After the Opening Supplication, it is recommended to recite the *Ta'awwudh*, saying, "I take refuge in Allah from the accursed Devil."

It is said in every rak'a and especially recommended in the first, whether one is imam, follower, or praying by oneself, and whether the prayer is obligatory, supererogatory, or even a funeral prayer. It is said to oneself in both the prayers recited to oneself and those recited aloud.

f8.16 ويُنْدَبُ بعدَهُ: «أعُوذُ باللَّهِ مِنَ الشَّيطانِ الرَّجيمِ».
ويتَعَوَّذُ في كلِّ ركعـةٍ وفي الأُولى آكدُ سواءً الإمامُ والمأمومُ والمنفردُ والمفترضُ والمتنفِّـلُ حتَّى الجنــازةِ. ويُسِرُّ بِهِ في السريةِ والجهريةِ.

THE FATIHA

الفاتحة

f8.17 Then one recites the Fatiha (def: w1.16) in every rak'a (n: an integral), whether one is imam, follower, or praying alone.

The *Basmala* (n: the words "In the name of Allah, Most Merciful and Compassionate") is one of its verses. (n: In the other three schools, it is recited to oneself even when the rest is recited aloud (*Sharh al-sunna* (y22), 3.54).)

It is obligatory to recite the Fatiha's verses in order and without interruption. It is considered to be interrupted and must be begun again if one deliberately pauses at length during it, or pauses briefly but thereby intends to cease reciting, or mixes with it some words of invocation (dhikr) or Koran that are not in the interests of the prayer.

One's recital of the Fatiha is not considered to be interrupted if one speaks words during it that are in the interests of the prayer, such as saying "Ameen" in response to the imam's Ameen, or reminding him of the right words when he errors, or prostrating with him as a sunna for his Koran recital (def: f11.14). Nor is it interrupted if one forgetfully falls silent during it or absentmindedly adds some words of invocation (dhikr).

f8.17 ثُمَّ يَقْرَأُ الفـاتحـةَ في كلِّ ركعةٍ سواءً الإمامُ والمأمومُ والمنفردُ.
والبسملةُ آيةٌ مِنها [ومِن كلِّ سورةٍ غير براءةَ].
ويجبُ ترتيبُها وتـواليهـا. فإنْ سَكَتَ فيهـا عمداً وَطالَ، أوْ قَصُرَ وقَصَدَ قطعَ القراءةِ، أوْ خَلَّلَها بذكرٍ أوْ قراءةٍ مِنْ غيرِها ممَّـا لَيْسَ مِنْ مصلحةِ الصلاةِ، انْقَطَعَتْ قراءتُهُ ويَسْتَأْنِفُها.
وإنْ كانَ مِنْ مصلحةِ الصلاةِ كتأمينِهِ لتأمينِ إمامـهِ، أوْ فتحـهِ عليـهِ إذَا غَلِطَ أوْ سجودِهِ لتلاوتِهِ ونحوِهِ، أوْ سَكَتَ أوْ ذَكَرَ ناسياً، لَمْ يَنْقَطِعْ.

f8.18 If one omits one of the Fatiha's letters (Ar. *harf,* a consonant or long vowel (A: mistakes in a short vowel (haraka) do not harm as long as they do not alter the meaning)), fails to double a letter that should be doubled, or substitutes a wrong letter for the right one, it invalidates (O: one's recital of that particular word, and one must recite the word again (dis: s3.3). But it does not invalidate one's prayer unless it changes the meaning and was done deliberately).

SAYING "AMEEN"

f8.19 After reciting (n: the last words of the Fatiha) "nor of the lost," one says "Ameen" to oneself in prayers spoken to oneself and aloud in those recited aloud.

When following an imam, one says "Ameen" when he does, and then a second time (N: to oneself) when finished with one's own recital of the Fatiha.

RECITING A SURA

f8.20 If one is the imam or praying by oneself, it is recommended in the first and second rak'as only to recite one complete sura (O: even if short) after the Fatiha.

It is recommended to recite:

(1) the suras from al-Hujurat (Koran 49) to al-Naba' (Koran 78) for the dawn (subh) and noon (zuhr) prayers;

(2) the suras from al-Naba' (Koran 78) to al-Duha (Koran 93) for the midafternoon ('asr) and nightfall ('isha) prayers;

(provided that there are a restricted number of followers (O: meaning no others are praying behind the imam) who do not mind the length of these ((1) and (2) above) recitations, though if otherwise, the imam should be brief)

(3) the suras from al-Duha (Koran 93) to the end (Koran 114) for the sunset prayer (maghrib);

(4) al-Sajda (Koran 32) for the dawn prayer on Friday (n: in the first rak'a, when the group may prostrate during the recital, as at f11.14), and al-Insan (Koran 76) (n: in the second rak'a);

(5) and al-Kafirun (Koran 109) (n: in the first rak'a) and al-Ikhlas (Koran 112) (n: in the second) for the sunna prayers that accompany the sunset and dawn prayers (def: f10.2), for the two rak'as after circumambulating the Kaaba (j5), and for the *guidance prayer* (istikhara, f10.12).

الضحى إلى الآخـر) إنْ رَضِيَ بطـوالِـه وأوسـاطِـه مأمـومـونَ محصورونَ (أي لا يصلي وراء الإمام غيرهم). وإلّا خَفَّفَ. ولصبح الجمعةِ ألَم تنـزيـل وهَلْ أتَى ، ولسنةِ المغرب ولسنةِ الصبح ، وركعتي الطوافِ والاستخارةِ قلْ يا أيُّها الكافرونَ والإخلاصُ.

f8.21   It is recommended to recite the Koran in a distinct, pleasant way (tartil) (O: i.e. to recite it as revealed by Allah, observing the proper rules of Koranic recitation) and to reflect upon its lessons and meanings (dis: w26).

f8.21   ويُنْـدَبُ الترتيل (وهو أن يقرأ على الـوجـه الـذي نزل من عنـد الله بأن يُدْغِمَ ويُغِنَّ ويُمِدَّ في محل كل منهـا) والتَدَبُّر.

f8.22   It is offensive for a follower to recite a sura when praying behind an imam whose recital is audible to him, though it is recommended for the follower to recite the sura during prayers that are not recited aloud, or those recited aloud if he cannot hear the imam's recital due to the distance or poor hearing, or can hear it, but uncomprehendingly.

f8.22   وتُكْرَهُ السورةُ لمأمومٍ يَسْمَعُ قراءةَ الإمام . فإنْ كانَتْ سريةً، أوْ جهريةً ولمْ يَسْمَعْ لبُعدٍ أوْ صممٍ نُدِبَتْ لهُ أيضاً وكذَا لوْ كانَ يَسْمَعُ قراءةَ الإمام ولمْ يَفْهَم [على الأصحّ].

f8.23   One recites a longer sura in the first rak'a than in the second.

f8.23   ويُطَوَّلُ الأولى على الثانية .

f8.24   If a latecomer to a group prayer misses the first two rak'as with the group and then performs them alone after the imam has finished the group prayer with Salams, he is recommended to recite the suras to himself during them.

f8.24   ولـوْ فَاتَ المسبوقَ ركعتـانِ فَتَداركَهُمـا بعـدَ السـلامِ نُدِبَتِ السورةُ فيهمَا سرّاً.

f8.25   The imam (or person praying by himself) recites the Fatiha and suras aloud for the dawn prayer (subh), Friday prayer (jumu'a), prayer on the two 'Eids (def: f19), drought prayer (f21), lunar eclipse prayer (f20), the group prayer that is

f8.25   ويَجْهَـرُ الإمـامُ والمنفـردُ في الصبـح والجمعةِ والعيـدَيْن والاستسقاء وخسـوف القمرِ والتراويح والأُوْلَيَيْن مِنَ

sunna on the nights of Ramadan (tarawih, f10.5), and for the first two rak'as of the sunset (maghrib) and nightfall ('isha) prayers.

In other prayers, the Fatiha and suras are recited to oneself.

When making up at night (*layl*, from sunset to true dawn) a prayer that one missed during the day or night, one recites aloud. When making up in the daytime (*nahar*, from dawn to sunset) a prayer that one missed during the day or night, one recites to oneself. At dawn, however (N: from true dawn to sunrise), all makeup prayers are recited aloud. (N: The upshot is that one recites aloud in all prayers that are made up at times when one normally recites aloud, and recites to oneself at the times one normally recites to oneself.)

المغرب والعشاء.

ويُسَرُّ في البَاقِي . فإن قَضَى فائتَــة اللّيل أو النهار لَيـلاً جهـر. أوْ فائتَـة النهـار أو اللّيـل نهـاراً أَسَـرَّ. إلّا الصبـح فإنّـه يجْهـرُ بقضـائهـا مطلقـاً [(أي بالقضاء في وقتها . وعبارة المصنف كعبارة الروضة توهم أن الصبح يجهر في قضائها مطلقاً ولـو نهـاراً)] . (ح : والحـاصل أنّـه يجهـر في وقت الجهرية ويسر في وقت السرية سواء كانت الفائتة جهرية أم سرية) .

f8.26   [ومَنْ لاَ يُحْسِنُ الفـاتحـة لَزمَهُ تعلُّمُهَـا . وإلّا فَقـراءَتُهَـا من مصحفٍ (وتـرجمـة القـرآن ليست قرآناً بإجماع المسلمين) . فإنْ عَجزَ لعدم ذلكَ أوْ لَمْ يَجِدْ معلماً أوْ ضَاقَ الوقتُ حَرُمَتْ بالعجمية . فإنْ أَحْسَنَ غيرَهَا لَزمَهُ سبعُ آياتٍ لا تَنْقُصُ حروفُهـا عنْ حروفِ الفـاتحـة (وحـروف الفاتحة بالبسملة مائة وستة وخمسون حرفاً) فإنْ لَمْ يُحْسِنْ قرآناً لَزمَهُ سبعُ أذكـارٍ بعـددِ حروفهـا . فإنْ أَحْسَنَ بعضَ الفـاتحـةِ قـرأهُ وأتَى بَدَلـهُ من قرآنٍ أوْ ذكـرٍ . فإنْ حَفِظَ الأولَ قرأهُ ثمَّ أتَى بالبدلِ . أو الآخِرَ أتَى بالبدلِ ثمَّ قَرأهُ . فإنْ لَمْ يُحْسِنْ شيئاً وَقَفَ بقدرِ الفاتحةِ ولا إعادةٍ عليهِ] .

STANDING

القيام

f8.27   Standing is an integral in all obligatory prayers (O: for anyone who can stand, whether by himself or assisted by another, though it is not an integral in nonobligatory prayers).

Standing requires that the spine be upright. One is not standing if one inclines forward so that the backbone is no longer straight, or bends so that one is closer to *bowing* (def: f8.29) than to standing. If a person's back is bowed with age or the like so that his normal posture resembles someone bowing, then he stands as he is, but must bend a little further for bowing if able to.

It is offensive in prayer to stand on one foot, for both feet to be held together (A: though this is sunna for women), or for one foot to be ahead of the other.

To stand at length (A: reciting the Koran in prayer) is better than to prostrate or bow at length (A: therein).

f8.27   والقيامُ ركنٌ في المفروضةِ (لا في النافلة، للقادر عليه إما بنفسه أو غيره) .

وشـرطُـهُ أنْ يَنْصِبَ فقـارَ ظهـرِه . فإنْ مَالَ بحيـثُ خَرَجَ عَن الـقيـام (أي عن ضابطه المـذكور) أو انْحَنَى وصَـارَ إلى الـركوعِ أقربَ لمْ يَجُزْ . ولوْ تَقَوَّسَ ظهرُهُ لكبرٍ أوْ غيـرِه حتى صَارَ كراكـعٍ وَقَفَ كذلكَ ثمَّ زَادَ انحناءً للركوعِ إنْ قَدَرَ .

ويُكرَهُ أنْ يَقومَ على رِجْلٍ واحدةٍ وأن يَلْصِقَ قدميهِ وأن يُقَدِّمَ إحداهُمَا على الأخرى .

وتطويلُ القيـامِ أفضـلُ مِنْ تطـويلِ السجودِ والركوعِ .

f8.28 It is permissible to pray nonobligatory prayers seated (O: any way one wishes, though the *iftirash* (def: f8.37) style of sitting is best) or lying down, even when able to stand (A: but the merit is less than to do so standing).

BOWING

f8.29 Then one bows from the waist (n: an integral).

The minimum is to bow as far as an average size person needs to when he wants to put his hands on his knees. It is obligatory that one *repose* therein, minimally meaning to remain motionless for a moment after having moved. It is also obligatory that one intend nothing by the motion but bowing.

f8.30 The optimal way is to raise one's hands and say "Allahu akbar" so that one begins raising the hands as one starts saying it, and when the hands are at shoulder level, one bows.

Whenever one says "Allahu akbar" during a movement from one prayer posture to another, it is recommended to prolong the words until one reaches the next posture (A: so that one's prayer is not devoid of invocation (dhikr) at any point).

Then one puts the hands on the knees, fingers apart, with back and neck extended, legs straight, and elbows out, though women keep them close.

One then says, "My Lord Most Great is exalted above all limitation," three times, the least that is optimal. If praying alone, or the imam of a limited number of followers who do not mind the extra length, one may increase the number of times one says this to five, seven, nine, or eleven.

When finished, (O: however many times one has said it,) it is recommended to say, "O Allah, to You I bow, in You I believe, to You I submit. My hearing, sight, mind, bones, nerves, and all that my feet bear up are humbled before You."

STRAIGHTENING UP

f8.31 Then one lifts one's head, the minimum of which is to return to standing as one was before

---

f8.28 وَيُبَاحُ النفلُ قاعداً (على أي هيئـة من هيئـات القعـود لكن الافتـراش أفضـل من غيـره) ومضطجعـاً مَعَ القدرةِ على القيامِ.

الركوع

f8.29 ثمَّ يَرْكَعُ.

وأقلُّهُ أنْ يَنْحَنِيَ بحيثُ لوْ أرادَ وضـعَ راحتَيْهِ على ركبتيـهِ مَعَ اعتـدالِ الخلقـةِ لقـدَرَ. ويجبُ الطمأنينـةُ وأقلُهـا سكونٌ بعدَ حركةٍ. وأن لا يَقصِدَ بهويِّهِ غيرَ الركوعِ.

f8.30 وأكمـلُ الركوعِ أنْ يُكَبِّرَ رافعاً يدَيْـهِ فَيَبْتَدِىءُ الرفعَ مَعَ التكبيرِ فإذا حَاذَى كفاهُ منكبَيْهِ انْحَنَى.

ويَمُدُّ تكبيراتِ الانتقالاتِ.

ويَضَـعُ يدَيْـهِ على ركبتَيْـهِ مفـرقـةَ الأصابـعِ ويمُـدُّ ظهـرَهُ وعنقَهُ ويَنْصِبُ ساقيْهِ ويُجَافِي مرفقَيْـهِ عن جنبيْهِ وتَضُمُّ المـرأةُ. ويقـولُ «سُبْحـانَ ربِّيَ العظيمِ» ثلاثـاً وهـو أدْنَى الكمالِ. ويَزيدُ المنفردُ وكـذا الإمـامُ إنْ رَضِيَ المأمـومونَ وهُمْ محصـورونَ خامسـةً وسابعـةً وتـاسعـةً وحاديَ عشَرَ.

ثـمَّ (بعد التسبيح المذكور قليلاً كان أو كثيراً) يقـولُ «اللهُمَّ لَكَ رَكَعْتُ وبِكَ آمَنْتُ ولَكَ أسْلَمْتُ خشـعَ لَكَ سَمعِي وبَصَري وَمُخِّي وعظمِي وعَصَبِي وما اسْتَقَلَّتْ بِهِ قَدَمِي».

الاعتدال

f8.31 ثمَّ يَرْفـعُ رأسَـهُ، وأقلُّهُ، أن يَعـودَ إلى ما كانَ عليـهِ قبـلَ الـركـوعِ،

bowing, and then remain motionless for a moment. (n: Each is an integral.) It is obligatory to intend nothing by one's movement except straightening up.

f8.32 The optimal way is to raise the hands (A: lifting them from the knees as one starts straightening up, raising them to shoulder level) and the head together, saying, "Allah hears whoever praises Him." This is said whether one is imam, follower, or praying alone. When one is standing upright, one says, "Our Lord, all praise is Yours, heavensful, earthful, and whatever-else-You-will-full."

(O: If following an imam or praying alone, one says this to oneself. If imam, one says "Allah hears whoever praises Him" aloud, but the rest to oneself.)

Those we have previously mentioned who wish to add to the words of bowing may add here, "O You who deserve praise and glory, the truest thing a slave can say (and all of us are Your slaves) is, 'None can withhold what You bestow, none can bestow what You withhold, and the fortune of the fortunate avails nothing against You.' "

PROSTRATION

f8.33 Then one prostrates (n: an integral). The conditions for its validity are:

(a) that an uncovered portion of the forehead touch a part of the place of prayer (N: it is not obligatory that any of the other limbs of prostration be uncovered);

(b) that one remain motionless for a moment while prostrating;

(c) that the place of prostration bear the weight of the head;

(d) that one's rear be higher than one's head;

(e) that one not prostrate on something joined to one's person that moves with one's motions, such as a sleeve or turban;

وَيَطْمَئِنَّ وَيَجِبُ أَنْ لا يَقْصِدَ غيرَ الاعتدالِ . [فَلَوْ رَفَعَ فزعاً مِنْ حيةٍ ونحوِهَا لَمْ يُجْزِئْهُ] .

f8.32   وأَكْمَلُهُ أَنْ يَرْفَعَ يدَيْهِ حَالَ ارتفاعِهِ [أَي يكون رفع اليدين مقارناً لرفع رأسه)] قائلاً «سَمِعَ اللَّهُ لِمَنْ حَمِدَهُ» سواءُ الإمامُ والمأمومُ والمنفردُ . فإذَا انْتَصَبَ قائماً قَالَ : «رَبَّنَا لَكَ الحَمْدُ مِلْءَ السمواتِ ومِلْءَ الأرضِ ومِلءَ مَا شِئْتَ مِنْ شيءٍ بَعْدُ» .

(ويكون القول سراً من المأموم والمنفرد، والإمام يجهر بسمع الله لمن حمده ويسر بما بعده) .

ويزيد مَنْ قُلْنَا يزيدُ في الركوعِ «أَهْلَ الثَّناءِ والمَجْدِ أَحَقُّ مَا قَالَ العَبْدُ وكُلُّنَا لَكَ عَبْدُ لَا مَانِعَ لِمَا أَعْطَيْتَ ولاَ مُعْطِي لِمَا مَنَعْتَ ولاَ يَنْفَعُ ذا الجَدِّ مِنْكَ الجَدُّ» .

السجود

f8.33   ثُمَّ يَسْجُدُ .

وشروطُ إجزائِهِ أَنْ يُبَاشِرَ مُصَلَّاهُ بجبهتِهِ أَوْ بعضِها مكشوفاً (ح : ولا يجب كشف غيرها من أعضاء السجود) ويَطْمَئِنَّ ، وأَنْ يَنَالَ مُصَلَّاهُ ثِقَلَ رأسِهِ وأَنْ تَكُونَ عجيزتُهُ أعلى مِنْ رأسِهِ وأَنْ لَا يَسْجُدَ على مُتَّصِلٍ بِهِ يَتَحَرَّكُ بحركتِهِ ككمٍّ وعمامةٍ ، وأَنْ لَا يَقْصِدَ بهوِيِّهِ غيرَ

(f) that nothing but prostration be intended by one's motion;

(g) and that part of each knee, the bottom of the toes of each foot, and the fingers of each hand be placed on the ground.

(O: In our school, it is not obligatory that the nose touch the ground in prostration, though it is desirable.)

f8.34   If one cannot fully prostrate so that one's forehead touches the ground (N: a pregnant woman, for example), then it is not necessary to stack up pillows on the place of prostration to touch the forehead on them. One merely bows as low as one can.

If one has put a bandage on the forehead because of an injury that affects all of it, and there is hardship in removing it (O: severe enough to permit dry ablution (tayammum) (def: e12.9)), then one may prostrate upon it and need not make up the prayer.

f8.35   The optimal way to prostrate is to say "Allahu akbar" and:

(1) to put the knees down first, then the hands, and then the forehead and nose (O: the order is called for, and any other order is offensive);

(2) to prostrate with the hands directly under one's shoulders, fingers together, extended towards the direction of prayer (qibla), hands uncovered;

(3) for men to keep 1 span (n: about 23 cm.) between the two knees and two feet (O: though a woman's are kept together);

(4) for men to keep the stomach apart from the thighs, and forearms from sides, though women keep them together;

(5) and to say three times, "My Lord Most High is exalted above all limitation."

السجــود، وأنْ يَضَعَ جزءاً مِنْ ركبتيْهِ وبطُــونِ أصـــابـــعِ رجلَيْـهِ وكفَّيْـه على الأرضِ . (ومـذهبنا أنه لا يجب السجود على الأنف وإنما يستحب) .

f8.34   ولـوْ تَعَـذَّرَ التنكيسُ لمْ يَجِبْ وضـعُ وسادةٍ لِيَضـعَ الجبهةَ عليْهَـا بلْ يَخْفِضُ القدرَ الممكنَ .
ولوْ عَصَبَ جبهتَهُ لجراحةٍ عمّتْهَا وشَقَّ إزالتُها (مشقة شديدة تبيح التيمم) سَجَدَ عليْهَا بلاَ إعادةٍ .

f8.35   وأكملُهُ أنْ يُكَبِّرَ ويَضعَ ركبتيْهِ ثمَّ يدَيْهِ ثمَّ جبهتَهُ وأنفَهُ دفعةً (والترتيب بين المـذكورات مطلوب وخلافه مكروه) ويَضعَ يدَيْهِ حذوَ منكبَيْهِ منشورةَ الأصابع نحوَ القبلةِ مضمومـةً مكشـوفـةً ويُفَـرِّقُ ركبتيْـهِ وقـدمَيْـهِ قدرَ شبرٍ (هـذا إن كان المصلي رجـلاً وإلا ضمَّ ركبتيـه) ويَـرْفَعُ الرجلُ بطنَهُ عنْ فخذيْهِ وذراعَيهِ عنْ جنبيْهِ وتضُمُّ المـرأةُ ويَقـولَ: «سُبْحَـانَ رَبِّيَ الأعلى» ثلاثاً .

Those we have previously mentioned who wish to add to the words of bowing may increase the number of times this is said as previously described (O: namely, in odd numbers up to eleven) and add: "O Allah, I prostrate myself to You, believe in You, and surrender to You. My face prostrates to Him who created it and gave it form, who opened its hearing and vision by His power and strength. Allah is exalted in perfection, the Best of Creators."

It is commendable to supplicate Allah while prostrating.

SITTING BETWEEN PROSTRATIONS

f8.36   Then one raises the head (N: and sits back before prostrating a second time. Sitting at this point is an integral). It is obligatory to sit motionlessly for at least a moment and to intend nothing but sitting by one's movement.

ويـزيـدُ مَنْ قُلْنَا يَزيدُ في الـركـوع تسبيحـاً كَمَـا سَبَقَ (أي في أكمله وهـو إحـدى عشرة تسبيحـة) في الـركـوع ثمَّ «اللَّهُمَّ لَكَ سَجَـدْتُ وبِـكَ آمَنْتُ ولـك أسلمتُ سَجَدَ وَجْهي للّذي خلقَهُ وصَوَّرَهُ وشَقَّ سَمْعَهُ وبَصَرَهُ بِحَوْلِهِ وقُوَّتِه تَبَارَكَ اللَّهُ أَحْسَنُ الخَالِقِين». وإنْ دَعَا فَحَسَنٌ.

الجلوس بين السجدتين

f8.36   ثمَّ يَرْفَـعُ رأسَـهُ، ويَـجِبُ الجلوسُ مطمئناً وأنْ لا يَقْصِدَ برفعِهِ غيرَهُ.

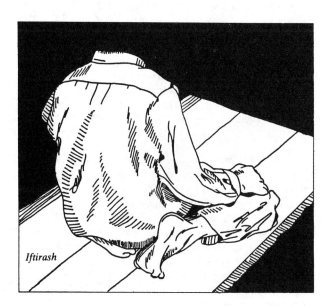

Iftirash

f8.37   The optimal way is:

(1) to say "Allahu akbar" (N: as one raises the head);

(2) to sit in iftirash, which is to place the left foot on its side and sit upon it while keeping the

f8.37   وأكمـلُهُ أنْ يُكَبِّـرَ ويَـجْلِسَ مفتـرشـاً يَفْرِشُ يسـراهُ ويَجْلِسُ علَيْهَـا

right foot resting on the bottom of its toes, heel up;

    (3) to place one's two hands on the thighs near the knees, fingers extended and held together;

    (4) and to say, "O Allah, forgive me, have mercy on me, pardon me, set me right, guide me, and sustain me."

وَيَنْصِبَ يمناهُ وَيَضَعَ يديْهِ على فَخِذَيْهِ بقربِ رُكبتيْهِ منشورةً مضمومةَ الأصابع وَيَقُولَ: «اللّهُمَّ اغْفِرْ لي، وَارْحَمْني، وعَافِني، وَاجْبُرْني، وَاهْدِني، وَارْزُقْني».

f8.38   There are two other ways of sitting back (iq‘a’) (O: between the two prostrations, or at the first and second Testifications of Faith (Tashahhud, def: f8.45)).

    One way is to sit back on the heels with the bottom of the toes and knees upon the ground. This is rcommended between the two prostrations, though *iftirash* (def: f8.37) is better.

    The other way is to simply sit on the ground, palms down, and knees drawn up. This is offensive in any prayer.

f8.38   والإقْعـاءُ ضربـانِ (بـيـن السجدتين أو في التشهد الأولِ أو الأخير).

أحدُهُمـا أنْ يَضَعَ ألِيَتَيْهِ على عقِبَيْهِ، ورُكبتيْهِ وأطرافَ أصابِعِهِ بالأرضِ وهوَ مندوبٌ بينَ السجدتين ولكنِ الافتراشُ أفضلُ.

والثـاني أنْ يَضَعَ ألِيَتَيْهِ ويديْهِ بالأرضِ وَيَنْصِبَ ساقيْهِ وهذا مكروهٌ في كلِّ صلاةٍ.

f8.39   Then one prostrates again just as before. (O: The first rak‘a is only completed when one has performed the second prostration, because each prostration is a separate integral, as is the moment of motionlessness in each.)

f8.39   ثُمَّ يَسْجُدَ سجدةً أخرَى مثلَ الأولى. (وقـد تمت الـركعـة الأولى من ركعـات الصـلاة بالسجدتين لأن كل سجدة ركن مستقل من أركان الصلاة مع طمأنينة كل منهما).

f8.40   After this one raises the head, saying "Allahu akbar" (O: as one first raises it, drawing out the words until one is standing upright).

    It is sunna, here and in each rak‘a that is not followed by the Testification of Faith (Tashahhud), to briefly rest in the *iftirash* style of sitting (f8.37) before rising. Then one (O: quickly) rises, helping oneself up with both hands (O: palms down), and prolonging the Allahu Akbar until standing. If the imam omits this brief sitting, the follower performs it anyway. It is not done after a Koran recital prostration (def: f11.13).

f8.40   ثُمَّ يَرْفَعَ رأسَـهُ مُكَبِّراً (مع ابتداء الرفع المذكور يمدّه إلى أن ينتصب قائماً).

ويُسَنُّ أنْ يَجْلِسَ مفترشاً جلسةً لطيفةً للاستـراحةِ عَقِيبَ كلِّ ركعةٍ لاَ يَعْقُبُهـا تشهُّدُ ثُمَّ يَنْهَضَ (أي يسرع إلى القيام) معتمـداً على يدَيْـهِ (أي على بطن كفّيْـهِ منهمـا) ويَمُـدُّ التكبيرَ إلى أنْ يقومَ وإنْ تَرَكَهَا الإمـامُ جَلَسَهَا المأمـومُ ولا تُشْرَعُ لرفعٍ مِنْ سجود التلاوة.

f8.41   Then one performs the second rak‘a of the prayer just like the first, except for the initial intention, the opening Allahu Akbar, and Opening Supplication (Istiftah).

f8.41   ثُمَّ يُصَلِّي الـركعـة الثـانيـةَ كالأولى إلاَّ في النيةِ والإحرامِ والاستفتاحِ.

f8.42   If one's prayer exceeds two rak'as, one sits in *iftirash* (def: f8.37) after the first two rak'as and recites the Testification of Faith (Tashahhud, f8.45) and the Blessings on the Prophet (Allah bless him and give him peace), though not upon his family (N: which is done only in the final Testification of Faith at the end of the prayer).

Then one rises, saying "Allahu akbar" and leaning on one's hands (n: as before). When standing, one lifts the hands to shoulder level (A: which one does here, but not after rising from the first or third rak'a), and then goes on to perform the remainder of the prayer as one did the second rak'a, except that one recites the Fatiha to oneself and does not recite a sura after it.

TESTIFICATION OF FAITH (TASHAHHUD)

f8.43   One sits back (n: an integral) at the last of one's prayer for the Testification of Faith in the *tawarruk* style of sitting, with one's (O: left) posterior on the ground and left foot on its side, emerging from under the right, which is vertical.

f8.42   فإنْ زَادَتْ صلاتُهُ على ركعتَيْن جَلَسَ بعدَهُما مفترشاً وتشهَّدَ وصَلَّى على النبيِّ صَلَّى اللهُ عَلَيْهِ وسَلَّمَ وحدَهُ دونَ آلهِ.

ثمَّ يَقُومُ مُكَبِّراً معتمـداً على يدَيْهِ فإذا قامَ رَفَعَهُمـا حذوَ منكبَيْهِ ويُصَلِّيْ مَا بَقِيَ كالثانيةِ إلَّا في الجَهْرِ والسورةِ.

التشهد

f8.43   ويَجْـلِسُ في آخِـرِ صلاتِـهِ للتشهدِ متـوركاً يَفْرِشُ يسـراهُ ويَنْصِبُ يمناهُ ويُخْـرِجُهَا مِنْ تحتِهِ ويُفْضِي بوركِهِ إلى الأرضِ (أي يلصق وركـه الأيسـر

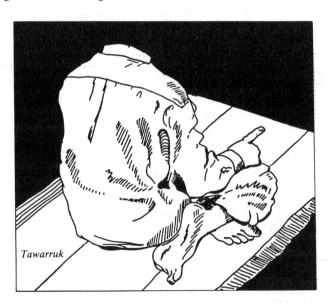

Tawarruk

(O: The wisdom in the difference between the ways of sitting during the two Testifications of Faith, namely, *iftirash* (f8.37) in the first and

بالأرضِ. والحكمـة في المخـالفـة بين التـشهـدين في الجلوس فيهمـا وهـو الافتـراش في الأول والتـورك في الأخيـر

tawarruk in the second, is that a latecomer to group prayer may know by observing the former that the prayer has not finished, and by the latter that it nearly has.

Imam Malik holds the sunna in both testifications to be the *tawarruk* style of sitting; while Abu Hanifa holds that the *iftirash* style is sunna for both. May Allah have mercy on them all for explaining the Deity's command without the slightest loss.)

However one sits here (O: in the final Testification of Faith (Tashahhud)) and in the foregoing (O: Testification of Faith, and between the two prostrations, and before rising) is permissible, though *iftirash* and *tawarruk* are sunna.

A latecomer to a group prayer sits in *iftirash* at the end of his imam's prayer and sits in *tawarruk* at the end of his own.

Similarly, the person who must perform a forgetfulness prostration (def: f11) sits in *iftirash* for his last Testification of Faith, prostrates for forgetfulness, and then sits in *tawarruk* for his Salams.

f8.44 In the two Testifications of Faith, one's left hand rests on the left thigh near the knee, its fingers extended and held together. The right hand is similarly placed, but is held closed with its thumb touching the side of the index finger, which alone is left extended. One lifts the index finger and points with it when one says the words "except Allah." One does not move it while it is thus raised (O: following the sunna from a hadith related by Abu Dawud. It is offensive to move it here, though some hold that it is recommended, the evidence for which is also from the sunna, in a hadith related by Bayhaqi, who states that both hadiths are rigorously authenticated (sahih). Precedence is given to the former hadith, which negates moving the finger, over the latter hadith, which affirms it, because scholars hold that what is sought in prayer is lack of motion, and moving it diminishes one's humility. The Prophet's moving it (Allah bless him and give him peace) was merely to teach people that it was permissible (A: as it was the Prophet's duty (Allah bless him and give him peace) to distinguish for his Community the acts that were offensive from those that were

ليعلم المسبوق أن الصلاة لم تفرغ في حال الافتراش، وقد فرغت في التورك.

ويسن التورك عند الإمام مالك مطلقاً، ويسن الافتراش عند أبي حنيفة مطلقاً. رحم الله الجميع حيث بينوا حكم الإله بلا تضييع).

وكيفَ قَعَدَ هنَا (أي الجلوس الأخير) وفيمَا تَقَدَّمَ (أي في الجلوس للتشهد وفي الجلوس بين السجدتين وللاستراحة) جازَ وهيئةُ الافتراش والتوركِ سنةٌ.

ويَفتَرِشُ المسبوقُ في آخرِ صلاة الإمام ويَتَوَرَّكُ آخرَ صلاةِ نفسِه.

وكذا يَفترِشُ هنا مَنْ عليه سجودُ سهوٍ وإذا سَجَدَ تَوَرَّكَ وسَلَّمَ.

f8.44 ويَضَعُ في التشهدَينِ يسراهُ على فخذِهِ عندَ طرفِ ركبتيهِ مبسوطةً مضمومةً ويَقبِضُ يمناهُ ويُرسِلُ المسبِّحَة ويَضَعُ إبهامَه على حرفِها ويَرفَعُ المسبحة مشيراً بها عندَ قولِهِ: «إلاّ اللهُ». ولا يُحَرِّكُها عندَ رفعِها (للاتباع رواه أبو داود. فلو حركها ـ كره. وقيل إن تحريكها مندوب، ودليل الندب الاتباع أيضاً رواه البيهقي وقال الحديثان صحيحان. وتقديم الأول النافي على الثاني المثبت لما قام عندهم في ذلك وهو أن المطلوب في الصلاة عدم الحركة أو لأن التحريك يذهب الخشوع وتحريكه ﷺ لبيان

unlawful, and he was given the reward of the obligatory for doing such offensive acts). Moreover, Bayhaqi says that the meaning of *moving it* in the latter hadith is simply *raising* it, so there is no actual contradiction).

f8.45 The minimal Testification of Faith (Tashahhud) is to say: "Greetings to Allah. Peace be upon you, O Prophet, and the mercy of Allah and His blessings. Peace be upon us and upon Allah's righteous slaves. I testify there is no god except Allah, and that Muhammad is the Messenger of Allah."

The optimal way is to say: "Greetings, blessings, and the best of prayers to Allah. Peace be upon you O Prophet, and the mercy of Allah and His blessings. Peace be upon us and upon Allah's righteous slaves. I testify that there is no god except Allah, and that Muhammad is the Messenger of Allah."

Its words (N: minimal or optimal) are obligatory (O: i.e. when one can recite the Arabic, one may not use other words) and their order is a condition. If one cannot say it, one must learn. If one cannot learn (O: because there is no teacher, or there is, but one is unable), then one may translate it (O: to any language one wishes).

One then says the Blessings on the Prophet (Allah bless him and give him peace) (n: an integral after the final Testification of Faith, but merely sunna after the first one, as at f9.15 below).

The minimum is to say, "O Allah, bless Muhammad." (n: One confines oneself to this minimum at the first Testification of Faith, as mentioned above at f8.42.)

The optimal way is to say: "O Allah, bless Muhammad and the folk of Muhammad as You blessed Ibrahim and the folk of Ibrahim. And show grace to Muhammad and the folk of Muhammad as You did to Ibrahim and the folk of Ibrahim in the worlds, for You are truly the Most Praiseworthy and Noble."

(A: It is desirable to add before each mention of the names *Muhammad* and *Ibrahim* the word *sayyidina* ("our liegelord"). The hadith "Do not liegelord me in the prayer" is a forgery containing corrupt Arabic.)

f8.46 It is recommended afterwards (O: after the second Testification of Faith (Tashahhud) of the prayer, though not after the first) to supplicate Allah for any permissible thing one wishes concerning one's religion or this world. One of the best supplications is: "O Allah, forgive me what I have done and what I may do, what I have hidden and what I have made known, my excesses and what You know better than I. Only You put one ahead or behind. There is no god but You."

It is recommended (O: if one is imam) that such supplications be briefer than the Testification of Faith with its Blessings on the Prophet (Allah bless him and give him peace) (O: though if one is alone, one may supplicate as long as one wishes, if not afraid of forgetting (N: that one is still in the prayer)).

CLOSING THE PRAYER WITH SALAMS

f8.47 Then one says the final *Salams* (n: an integral). The minimum is to say "as-Salamu 'alaykum" (peace be upon you), and it must occur while one is sitting. (O: It is inadequate to say "Salam 'alaykum" without the first word being definite (n: i.e. *as*-Salamu), since this has not reached us through any hadith texts, and invalidates the prayer if done intentionally.)

The optimal way is to say, "Peace be upon you, and the mercy of Allah" (O: though to add the words "and His grace" (wa barakatuhu) is not sunna) and to turn the head to the right enough to show the right cheek (N: to those behind). One thereby intends to finish the prayer and intends greetings of peace to the angels and Muslims (whether human or jinn (def: w22)) on the right. One then turns one's head to the left and repeats the Salam, intending to greet those on the left. A follower intends one of the two Salams as a response to the imam's, depending on which side the imam is on, or if the follower is directly behind him, he may intend either Salam as a response to him.

f8.48 When one is a latecomer to a group prayer, it is recommended not to stand up to finish

---

٨.٤٦ ويُنْدَبُ بعدَهُ (أي بعد الفراغ من التشهد الأخير أما التشهد الأول فلا يُسَنُّ بعده الدعاء) الدعاءُ بِمَا يَجوزُ مِنْ أمر الدين والدنيا ومِنْ أفضلِهِ «اللَّهُمَّ اغْفِرْ لي مَا قَدَّمْتُ وَمَا أَخَّرْتُ وَمَا أَسْرَرْتُ وَمَا أَعْلَنْتُ وَمَا أَسْرَفْتُ وَمَا أَنْتَ أَعْلَمُ به مِنِّي أَنْتَ المُقَدِّمُ وأَنْتَ المُؤَخِّرُ لَا إلَهَ إلَّا أَنْتَ».

ويُنْدَبُ كونُهُ أقَلَّ مِنَ التشهد والصلاةِ على النبيِّ ﷺ. (هذا بالنسبة للإمام وأما المنفـرد فيطيـل ما أراد ما لم يخف من التطويل الوقوع في سهو).

السلام

٨.٤٧ ثمَّ يُسَلِّمُ وأَقَلُّهُ «السـلامُ عَلَيْكُمْ» ويُشْتَرَطُ وقوعُهُ في حال القعودِ. (ولا يجـزىء «سـلام عليكم» بتنكيـر المبتدأ لعدم وروده. بل هو مبطل إن تعمد).

وأكملُهُ السَّـلامُ عَلَيْكُمْ وَرَحْمَـةُ اللَّهِ (ولا يسنُّ هنا زيادة «وبركاته») ملتفتاً عَنْ يمينِهِ حتَّى يُرى خدُّهُ الأَيمنُ. ويَنْوي به الخروجَ مِنَ الصلاةِ والسلامَ على مَنْ عَنْ يمينِهِ مِنَ الملائكة ومسلمي إنسٍ وجنٍّ. ثمَّ أُخْـرَى عن يسارهِ كذلـكَ حتَّى يُرى خدُّهُ الأَيسرُ يَنْوي بها السلامَ على مَنْ عن يسارهِ مِنْهُمْ. والمأمومُ يَنْوي الردَّ على الإمام بالأولى إنْ كان عنْ يسارهِ وبالثانية إنْ كان عنْ يمينهِ ويَتَخَيَّرُ إنْ كان خَلْفَهُ.

٨.٤٨ ويُنْدَبُ أنْ لَا يَقُومَ المسبوقُ

144

one's missed rak'as until the imam has said both Salams. It is permissible to stand after he has said just one, but if one stands before he has said the first Salam it invalidates one's prayer, unless one purposely intended to cease participation in the group prayer before doing so.

A latecomer, if making his first Testification of Faith while the group is making their last one, may sit at length (O: for *dhikr* or supplications) after the imam's Salams before he stands up to finish his own rak'as, though it is offensive. If he does this when not at the point of his first Testification of Faith, it invalidates his prayer if intentional.

f8.49   Someone who is not a latecomer to a group prayer may sit as long as he wishes after the imam's Salams to supplicate, finishing with his own Salams whenever he wants (O: because the imam's leadership ends with the imam's first Salam, so there is no harm in the follower taking his time, as he is now praying alone, and someone praying alone may do so as long as he likes).

f8.50   It is recommended to invoke Allah Most High (dhikr) to oneself and to supplicate after the prayer.

(O: Shafi'i says in *al-Umm*, "I prefer that the imam and follower invoke Allah (dhikr) after the Salams, and do so silently, unless the imam wants to be learned from, in which case he says the invocations aloud until he believes that he has been learned from, after which he says them to himself.")

(n: The following invocations are listed in the commentary and have been written in full and vowelled by the translator in the facing column of Arabic. Their order is sunna, as the commentator notes below.

(1) Ayat al-Kursi (Koran 2:255) (said once);

(2) al-Ikhlas (Koran 112) (once);

(3) al-Falaq (Koran 113) (once);

(4) al-Nas (Koran 114) (once);

إلَّا بعدَ تسليمتَيْ إمامِهِ. فإنْ قامَ المسبوقُ بعـدَ التسليمـةِ الأولى جازَ أوْ قبلَها بَطَلَتْ صلاتُهُ إنْ لَمْ ينوِ المفارقة.

ولـوْ مَكَثَ المسبوقُ بعدَ سلام إمامِهِ (مشـتغلاً بذكر ودعاء) وأطالَ جازَ إنْ كانَ موضعَ تشهدِهِ لكنْ يُكْرَهُ وإلَّا بَطَلَتْ إنْ تَعَمَّدَ.

f8.49   ولغيـرِ المسبوقِ بعـدَ سلام الإمـامِ إطالةُ الجلوسِ للدعاءِ ثمَّ يُسَلِّمُ مَتـى شاءَ (لأن الـقـدوةَ قد انـقـطـعـت بالتسليمـةِ الأولى فلا يضر تخلفـه لذلك لأنـه صار منفرداً والمنفرد يطيل ما شاء). [ولـوِ اقْتَصَـرَ الإمـامُ على تسليمـةٍ سَلَّمَ المأمومُ ثِنتَيْنِ].

f8.50   ويُنـدَبُ ذكـرُ اللـهِ تعـالـى والـدعـاءُ سِراً عَقِيبَ الصـلاةِ (وقـال الشـافعي في الأم: «أختار للإمام والمأموم أن يَذْكُرا الله بعـد السـلام من الصـلاة ويخفيا الـذكر إلا أن يكون إماماً يريد أن يتعلم منـه فيجهر حتى يرى أنـه قد تعلم منه، ثم يسر»)

(١) ﴿اللَّهُ لَا إِلَـٰهَ هُوَ الحَيُّ القَيُّومُ لَا تَأْخُذُهُ سِنَةٌ ولَا نَوْمٌ لَهُ مَا في السَّمٰواتِ ومَا في الأرضِ مَنْ ذَا الَّذِي يَشْفَعُ عِنْدَهُ إلَّا بإذْنِهِ يَعْلَمُ مَا بَيْنَ أَيْدِيهِمْ ومَا خَلْفَهُمْ ولَا يُحِيطُونَ بِشيْءٍ مِنْ عِلْمِهِ إلَّا بِمَا شَاءَ وَسِعَ كُرْسِيُّـهُ السَّمـٰواتِ والأرْضَ ولَا يَؤُودُهُ حِفْظُهُمَا وهُوَ العَلِيُّ العَظِيمُ﴾.

(٢) ﴿بِسْمِ اللَّهِ الـرَّحْمٰنِ الرَّحِيمِ قُلْ هُوَ اللَّهُ أَحَدٌ اللَّهُ الصَّمَدُ لَمْ يَلِدْ ولَمْ يُولَدْ ولَمْ يَكُنْ لَهُ كُفُواً أَحَدٌ﴾.

(٣) ﴿بِسْمِ اللَّهِ الـرَّحْمٰنِ الرَّحِيمِ قُلْ أَعُوذُ بِرَبِّ الفَلَقِ مِنْ شَرِّ مَا خَلَقَ ومِنْ شَرِّ غَاسِقٍ إذا وَقَبَ ومِنْ شَرِّ النَّفَّـاثَـاتِ في

(5) "I ask Allah's forgiveness" (three times);

(6) "O Allah, You are peace, from You is peace, You are exalted through Yourself above all else, O You of Majesty and Beneficence";

(7) "O Allah, none can withhold what You bestow, none can bestow what You withhold, and the fortune of the fortunate avails nothing against You";

(8) "Allah is exalted above any limitation or imperfection" (thirty-three times);

(9) "Praise be to Allah" (thirty-three times);

(10) "Allah is greatest" (thirty-three (A: or thirty-four) times);

(N: (8), (9), and (10) above are also recommended before going to sleep at night, in which case "Allah is greatest" is said thirty-four times)

(11) and "There is no god but Allah, alone, without partner. His is the dominion, His the praise, and He has power over all things.")

(O: It is recommended to begin the supplications with the Koran when called for, like Ayat al-Kursi and so forth, then (5) through (10) above.) One should invoke the Blessings on the Prophet (Allah bless him and give him peace) at the beginning (O: and middle) and end of one's supplications.

f8.51 The imam turns for (N: postprayer) invocation and supplications so that his right side is towards the group and his left side towards the direction of prayer (qibla). He leaves his place as soon as he finishes, if there are no women (N: in which case he waits for them to leave first). It is recommended that the followers remain seated until the imam stands.
(A: In the Shafi'i school, the invocations are recommended to precede the postprayer sunna rak'as.)

f8.52 It is recommended for those who perform nonobligatory prayers after the prescribed prayer

العُقَدِ وَمِنْ شَرِّ حَاسِدٍ إِذَا حَسَدَ﴾ .

(٤) ﴿بِسْمِ اللَّهِ الرَّحْمنِ الرَّحِيمِ قُلْ أَعُوذُ بِرَبِّ النَّاسِ مَلِكِ النَّاسِ إِلهِ النَّاسِ مِنْ شَرِّ الوَسْوَاسِ الخَنَّاسِ الَّذِي يُوَسْوِسُ فِي صُدُورِ النَّاسِ مِنَ الجِنَّةِ والنَّاسِ﴾ .

(٥) أَسْتَغْفِرُ اللَّهَ .

(٦) اللَّهُمَّ أَنْتَ السَّلَامُ وَمِنْكَ السَّلَامُ تَبَارَكْتَ يَاذَا الجَلَالِ والإِكْرَامِ .

(٧) اللَّهُمَّ لَا مَانِعَ لِمَا أَعْطَيْتَ وَلَا مُعْطِيَ لِمَا مَنَعْتَ وَلَا يَنْفَعُ ذَا الجَدِّ مِنْكَ الجَدُّ .

(٨) سُبْحَانَ اللَّهِ (٣٣) .

(٩) الحَمْدُ لِلَّهِ (٣٣) .

(١٠) اللَّهُ أَكْبَرُ (٣٣) .

(١١) لَا إِلهَ إِلَّا اللَّهُ وَحْدَهُ لَا شَرِيكَ لَهُ، لَهُ المُلْكُ وَلَهُ الحَمْدُ وَهُوَ عَلَى كُلِّ شَيْءٍ قَدِيرٌ .

(ويندب أن يقدم في الدعاء القرآن إن طلب كآية الكرسي ثم الاستغفار ثلاثاً ثم اللهم أنت السلام الخ، ثم اللهم لا مانع الخ، ثم التسبيح وما معه) .

ويُصَلِّي على النبيِّ ﷺ أولَهُ (ووسطه) وآخِرَهُ .

f8.51 ويَلْتَفِتُ الإمامُ للذكر والدعاءِ فيَجْعَلُ يمينَهُ إليهم ويسارَهُ إلى القبلة . ويُفَارِقُ الإمامُ مصلاهُ عقيبَ فراغِهِ إنْ لم يكُنْ ثَمَّ نساءٌ . ويَمْكُثُ المأمومُ (ندباً) حتى يقوم الإمامُ .

f8.52 ومَنْ أرادَ نفلاً بعدَ فرضِهِ نُدِبَ

to first wait till after some conversation; it being better to pray them elsewhere, and best to perform them in one's home. (O: However, it is better to perform certain nonobligatory prayers in the mosque, such as those before the Friday prayer, those after circumambulating the Kaaba, and those before entering the state of pilgrim sanctity (ihram) if there is a mosque at the site. (A: Others that are better in the mosque include:

(1) the midmorning nonobligatory prayer (duha, def: f10.6);

(2) the guidance prayer (istikhara, f10.12);

(3) the two rak'as that are sunna before departing on a journey and when arriving from one;

(4) prayers performed during a period of spiritual retreat in a mosque (i'tikaf, i3);

(5) confirmed sunna prayers (sunna mu'akkada, f10.2) that one is afraid of missing if one does not pray them in the mosque;

(6) and the sunna rak'as before the sunset prayer.))

f8.53   While performing the dawn prayer (subh) it is sunna to lift one's hands and supplicate after straightening up from bowing in the second rak'a.

One says: "O Allah, guide me among those You guide, grant me health and pardon among those You grant health and pardon, look after me among those You look after, grant me grace in what You have given me, and protect me from the evil [A: here, one turns the palms down for a moment] of what You have ordained; for You decree and none decrees against You, and none is abased whom You befriend. O our Lord, who are above all things sacred and exalted, all praise is Yours for what You decree. I ask Your forgiveness and turn to You in repentance."

It is commendable to add "and none is exalted whom You are at enmity with" (A: after the above words "and none is abased whom You befriend").

الفصـلُ بكـلامٍ أو انتقـالٍ وهـو أفضـلُ، وفي بيتِـهِ أفضـلُ (ويستثنى نفـل يوم الجمعة قبلهـا وركعتـا الطـواف وركعتـا الإحرام حيث كان في الميقـات مسجـد [والمراد بنفل يوم الجمعة القبلية بخلاف البعـديـة]). (ع: ويستثنى أيضاً صلاة الضحى والاستخارة والركعتان قبل السفر وبعـده، ونفـل الاعتكـاف، وعند خوف فوات الرواتب، والركعتان قبل صلاة المغرب).

f8.53   فإنْ كانَ في الصبح فالسنةُ أن يقنُتَ في اعتدال الـركعـة الثـانية فيقـولَ «اللّهُمَّ اهـدِني فيمَنْ هَدَيْتَ وعَافِني فيمَنْ عَافَيْتَ وتَوَلَّني فيمَنْ تَوَلَّيْتَ وبارِكْ لي فيمَا أَعْطَيْتَ وقِني شرَّ ما قَضَيْتَ، فإنَّكَ تَقْضي ولاَ يُقْضى عَلَيْكَ وإنَّـهُ لاَ يَذِلُّ مَن وَالَيْتَ تَبارَكْتَ رَبَّنا وتَعَالَيْتَ فلَكَ الحمدُ على ما قَضَيْتَ، أَسْتَغْفِرُكَ وأتوبُ إلَيْكَ». ولَوْ زادَ «ولا يَعِزُّ مَنْ عَادَيْتَ» فحسنٌ.

If one is imam, one pluralizes the singular pronominal suffix so that, for example, *ihdini* ("guide me") becomes *ihdina* ("guide us") and so forth (dis: w1.27).

The words of this supplication are not set and may be accomplished by pronouncing any supplication (O: and praise) or Koranic verse containing a supplication, such as the last verses of al-Baqara (Koran 2:285-86), though the above words are better.

After this, one invokes the Blessings on the Prophet (Allah bless him and give him peace).

It is recommended to raise one's hands throughout the supplication (O: palms up when asking the good, palms down when asking Allah to avert affliction). One does not stroke the face or chest with one's hands after the supplication (O: as opposed to other supplications, for which it is recommended to wipe the face with the hands, as is mentioned in hadith).

The imam says the supplications aloud. The follower says "Ameen" after each supplication that is audible to him and participates in the praises and so forth by responding with similar expressions. If the imam is inaudible, the follower himself says the supplication. When praying alone one says it to oneself.

When disasters (O: such as drought or an epidemic) befall the Muslims, they similarly supplicate in every prescribed prayer (O: after straightening up from bowing in the last rak'a).

فإنْ كَانَ إمـامـاً أتَى بلفـظِ الجمـعِ
«اللهم آهدنا» إلى آخرهُ.

ولا تَتَعَيَّنُ هذهِ الكلماتُ فَيَحْصُلُ بكلِّ
(لفظ اشتمل على) دعاءٍ (وثناء) وبآيةٍ فيها
دعاءٌ كآخرِ البقرة لكنْ هٰذهِ الكلماتُ
أفضلُ.

ثُمَّ يُصَلِّي على النبيِّ ﷺ.

ويُنْـدَبُ رفعُ يديهِ (أي يرفع بطونهما
عنـد إرادةِ نزول الخيـر وظهورهمـا عنـد
إرادةِ دفـعِ البـلاء) دون مسـحِ وجههِ أو
صدرهِ (بخـلاف دعـاء غيـر القنـوت فإنه
يندب بعـد الفراغِ من الدعاء مسح وجهه
بهما وذلك لوروده).

ويَجْهَرُ به الإمامُ فَيُؤَمِّنُ مأمومٌ يَسْمَعُهُ
للدعاء ويُشارِكُ في الثناء. وإنْ لـم يَسْمَعْهُ
قَنَتَ. والمنفردُ يُسِرُّ به.

وإنْ نَزَلَ بالمسلمين نازلةٌ (كقحطٍ أو
وبـاء) قنتـوا (في اعتدال الركعة الأخيرة)
في جميعِ الصلواتِ.

*

f9.0   WHAT INVALIDATES, IS OFFENSIVE, OR OBLIGATORY IN PRAYER

f9.0   مفسـدات الصـلاة
ومكروهاتها وواجباتها

EXTRANEOUS SPEECH

الكلام

f9.1   The prayer is invalidated (if one has no excuse (def: below)) by uttering two or more letters, or when two or more letters worth of sounds such as laughter, crying, groaning, clearing the throat, blowing, sighing, or similar are audible.

f9.1   متَى نَطَقَ بلا عذرٍ بحرفينِ [أو
بحرفٍ مفهم مثـل «قِ» مِنَ الـوقـايـةِ،
و«لِ» مِنَ الـولايـةِ] بَطَـلَتْ صلاتُـهُ.
والضحـكُ والبكـاءُ والأنينُ والتنحنـحُ

It is also invalidated by much (O: i.e. more than six words worth of) sound, even when there *is* a valid excuse such as blurting out words unthinkingly, laughter or coughing overcoming one, absentmindedly speaking, or when one speaks because as a new Muslim one does not know it is unlawful during the prayer; though with such an excuse a slight amount of speech does not invalidate the prayer.

One's prayer is invalid if one speaks knowing that it is unlawful but ignorant of the fact that it invalidates the prayer, and is also invalid if one says "Aah" during it out of fear of hell.

When it is impossible to recite the Fatiha (N: to oneself) (A: or the final Testification of Faith (Tashahhud) or Salams) except by clearing one's throat, one may do so even when it approximates two letters, though if it is merely impossible to recite *aloud*, then one may not clear one's throat, but must instead recite to oneself.

(A: Some things which are not commonly known to invalidate the prayer, such as clearing the throat, do not invalidate the prayer of ordinary people, whose ignorance of them is excusable, though a scholar has no such excuse.)

f9.2   If one notices (N: during the prayer) a blind person about to fall into a well, or the like, then one must speak up to alert him if there is not a nonverbal means of warning him of it.

f9.3   No form of invocation of Allah (dhikr) invalidates the prayer unless it is a direct address such as "Allah have mercy on you" or "And upon you be peace"; though it does not invalidate the prayer if it refers to someone not present, such as "Allah have mercy on Zayd" (O: nor is it invalidated by addressing Allah or the Prophet (Allah bless him and give him peace)).

f9.4   When something happens to one during the prayer (O: such as someone asking permission to enter, or having to remind the imam that he has forgotten something), then if one is male, one says "Subhan Allah" (O: intending only invocation (dhikr) thereby, as one may not merely intend to

والنفخُ والتأوُّهُ ونحوُهُما يُبْطِلُ الصلاةَ إنْ بانَ حرفانِ.

فإنْ كانَ عذرٌ بأنْ سَبَقَ لسانُهُ أوْ غَلَبَهُ ضحكٌ أوْ سعالٌ ، أوْ تَكَلَّمَ ناسياً أوْ جاهلاً تحريمَهُ لقربِ عهدِهِ بالإسلامِ وكثُرَ عرفاً (بأن زادَ على ستِّ كلماتٍ) أَبْطَلَ . وإنْ قلَّ فَلا.

ولوْ عَلِمَ التحريمَ وجَهِلَ كونَهُ مبطلاً ، أو قال مِنْ خوفِ النارِ «آهِ» بَطَلَتْ .

ولوْ تَعَذَّرَتِ الفاتحةُ (ح: سراً) إلاَّ بالتنحنحِ تَنَحْنَحَ لَها وإنْ بانَ حرفانِ، وإنْ تَعَذَّرَ الجهرُ بها إلاَّ بهِ (أي بالتنحنحِ) تَرَكَهُ (أي الجهرَ بالقراءةِ) وأَسَرَّ بها ولا يَتَنَحْنَحُ لَهُ.

f9.2   ولوْ رأى أعْمَى يَقَعُ في بئرٍ ونحوِهِ وجَبَ إنذارُهُ بالنطقِ إنْ لمْ يُمْكِنْ بغيرِهِ (أي بغيرِ النطقِ).

f9.3   ولا تَبْطُلُ بالذكرِ، وتَبْطُلُ بالدعاءِ خطاباً كَرحِمَكَ اللهُ، وعليكَ السلامُ، لا غَيْبَةَ كَرحِمَ اللهُ زيداً (ولا تبطل بخطابِ اللهِ ورسولِه).

f9.4   ولوْ نابَهُ شيءٌ في الصلاةِ (كإذنِهِ في دخولِ الدارِ لمنْ يستأذِنُ أو كتنبيهِ إمامٍ إذا سها) سَبَّحَ الرجلُ (فيقول سبحانَ اللهِ بقصدِ الذكرِ فقطْ وأما إذا

149

inform, nor lack any particular intention thereby, for these invalidate the prayer), or if female, one claps the right palm on the back of the left hand, not palm to palm.

If one recites a Koranic expression such as "O Yahya, take the book" (Koran 19:12), intending only to inform (O: without intending invocation) or not intending anything in particular, this invalidates the prayer, though not if the intention is Koran recital, or recital and informing together.

قصـد الإعـلام فقـط أوْ أطلق فتبطـل الصـلاة) وصَفَّقَت المـرأة بيطن كفٍ على ظهر أخرى لا بطناً لبطنٍ.
ولـوْ تَكَلَّم بنظم القـرآن كيا يَحْيَى خُذ الكتـاب وقَصَد إعـلامَهُ فقط (أي من غير قصـد الـذكـر) أوْ أطْلَقَ بَطَلَت. أو تلاوة فقطْ أو تلاوةً وإعلاماً فلا.

A SUBSTANCE REACHING THE BODY CAVITY

وصول عين إلى الجوف

f9.5   The prayer is invalidated when any (even if a little) substance (A: other than saliva) reaches the body cavity intentionally. It also invalidates the prayer if it occurs absentmindedly or in ignorance of its prohibition, provided the amount of the substance is commonly acknowledged to be much (def: f4.5), though not if it is little.

f9.5   وتَبْطُلُ بوصولِ عينٍ وإنْ قَلَّت إلى جوفـه عمـداً وكَذَا سهـواً أوْ جهـلاً بالتحريمِ إنْ كَثُرَ عُرْفاً لا إنْ قَلَّت.

EXTRANEOUS MOTION

الحركة

f9.6   Adding a surplus action that is an integral, such as bowing, invalidates the prayer if done intentionally, but does not invalidate it if done because one has forgotten (O: that one has already performed it).

The prayer is not invalidated by intentionally or absentmindedly adding a surplus *spoken* integral such as repeating one's recital of the Fatiha or the Testification of Faith (Tashahhud) or reciting them in the wrong place.

f9.6   وتَبْطُلُ بزيـادة ركنٍ فِعْليٍّ كركـوعٍ عمـداً لا سهـواً (أي ساهياً في إتيانه به).
ولا بقـوليٍّ عمـداً كتكـرار الفـاتحةِ أوْ التشهـد أوْ قراءتهـما في غير محلِّهما.

f9.7   The prayer is invalidated by adding, even if absentmindedly, a motion that is not one of the actions of prayer, provided it is both (O: considered by common acknowledgement (def: f4.5) to be) much and uninterruptedly consecutive, such as three steps (O: or successively moving three separate body parts like the head and two hands, though an up-and-down motion is considered just one) or three or more consecutive motions.

f9.7   وتَبْطُلُ بزيـادة فعلٍ ولوْ سهواً مِنْ غيـر جنس الصـلاة إنْ كَثُرَ (عـرفـاً) متـوالياً كثـلاثِ خطواتٍ (وكتحريك ثلاثة أعضـاء على التـوالي كرأسِـه ويـديـه و[المعتمد أن] النقل لجهة العلوِ ثم لجهة السفلِ خطوة واحدة) أوْ ضرباتٍ متواليـاتٍ.

The prayer is not invalidated by action that is not much, such as two steps, or is much but is separated so that the subsequent motion is considered to be unconnected with the preceding one. But if a (O: slight) action is grossly improper, such as jumping, it invalidates the prayer.

لَا إِنْ قَلَّ كخطــوتَيْن، أَوْ كَثُرَ وتَفَـرَّقَ
بحيْثُ يُعَدُّ الثاني منقطعاً عَنِ الأوَّلِ، فإِنْ
فَحُشَ (أي الفعل القليل) كوثبةٍ بَطَلَتْ.

f9.8 Slight actions such as scratching oneself, or turning a rosary (subha, dis: w27) do not affect the validity of the prayer, nor does remaining silent at length.

f9.8 ولَا تَضُـرُّهُ حركــاتٌ خفيفـةٌ
كحَــكّ بأصـابعـهِ وإدارةِ سُبحةٍ، ولا
سكوتٌ طويلٌ، [وإشارةٌ مفهمةٌ من
أخرسَ].

مكروهات الصلاة

f9.9 It is offensive to perform the prayer while one is holding back from urinating or defecating. (O: If enough time remains to perform the prayer, the sunna is to relieve oneself first, even when one fears missing praying with a group, since it diminishes one's awe and humility in prayer.)

f9.9 وتُكْرَهُ (ح: الصـلاة) وهـوَ
يُدافِعُ الأخبثيْن (وهما البـول والغـائط.
فالسنة تفريغ نفسه من ذلك لأنه يخل
بالخشوع وإن خاف فوت الجماعة حيث
كان الوقت متسعاً).

f9.10 It is offensive to pray in the presence of food or drink one would like to have, unless one fears that the prayer's time will end.

It is offensive during the prayer:

(1) to interlace the fingers;

(2) to turn (N: the head when there is no need. As for turning the chest from the direction of prayer (qibla), it invalidates the prayer except when there is an excuse such as in extreme peril, or when performing a nonobligatory prayer during a journey);

(3) to look to the sky;

(4) to look at something distracting;

(5) to gather one's clothes or hair with the hand, tuck one's hair under a turban, or wipe the dust from one's forehead;

(6) to yawn, though if it overcomes one, one should cover the mouth with the hand;

f9.10 وبحضــرةِ طعــامٍ أَوْ شرابٍ
يَتُوقُ إِلَيْهِ إِلَّا أَنْ خَشِيَ خروجَ الوقتِ.
ويُكْرَهُ تشبيكُ أصابعِهِ والالتفاتُ (ح:
بوجهــهِ، أمــا تحـول الصـدر عن القبلة
فمبطـل للصـلاة إلا لعـذر كشدة الخوف
وصـلاة النـافلة في السفر) لغيـر حاجةٍ
ورفعُ بصرهِ إلى السمـاءِ، والنظَرُ إِلَى مَا
يُلْهِيـهِ، وكفُّ ثوبِهِ وشعرِهِ ووضعُهُ تحتَ
عمـامَتِهِ ومسحُ الغبارِ عَنْ جبهتِهِ والتثاؤُبُ
فإِنْ غَلَبَهُ وَضَعَ يدَهُ على فمِهِ، والمبالغةُ

(7) to exaggerate in lowering one's head while bowing;

(8) or to put one's hands on the hips.

في خفض الـرأس فـي الـركـوع ووضعُ يدِهِ على خاصرتِهِ .

f9.11   It is offensive during the prayer to spit to the front of one or to the right. Rather, one should expectorate to the left, in the hem of one's garment, or under the foot (N: when one is praying in a desert or similar). (O: It is unlawful to spit in a mosque except into the left hem of one's garment (N: or a handkerchief. The slight motions necessary to take out one's handkerchief and return it do not harm, as they are inconsiderable).)

f9.11   والبصـاقُ قِبَـلَ وجهِهِ ويمينـه بـل عـنْ يسـارِهِ فـي ثوبِهِ أوْ تحتَ قدمِه (ح : إن كان في صحراء ونحـوها) (وأما إذا كان المصلي في المسجـد فلا يبصق فيه فإنه حرام بل يبصق في طرف ثوبه من جانبـه الأيسر) (ح : أو في منديل ولا تضر الحـركـة اللطيفـة الـلازمـة لاستخراج المنديل ورده لأنها ليست كثيرة) .

THINGS OBLIGATORY IN PRAYER

واجبات الصلاة

f9.12   The prayer has conditions (def: f9.13), integrals (f9.14), main sunnas (f9.15), and ordinary sunnas.

f9.12   وللصـلاةِ شروطٌ وأركـانٌ وأبعاضٌ وسُنَنٌ .

THE CONDITIONS OF PRAYER

شروط الصلاة

f9.13   The prayer's *conditions* are eight:

(a) purification from minor and major ritual impurity (hadath and janaba) (A: through ablution (wudu, def: e5) and the purificatory bath (ghusl, e11) respectively, as well as from menstruation and postnatal bleeding by bathing after them);

(b) that one be free of filth (najasa, e14) (A: in body, clothes, and place of prayer (f4));

(c) that one's nakedness be clothed (f5);

(d) that one be facing the direction of prayer (qibla, f6);

(e) that one avoid the actions prohibited in prayer, i.e. extraneous speech, eating, and excessive motion (f9.1–7);

f9.13   فشـروطُها ثمانيةٌ : طهارةُ الـحـدثِ والنجس ، وستـرُ العـورةِ ، واستقبـالُ القبلةِ ، واجتنـابُ المنـاهي المـذكـورةِ وهيَ الكـلامُ والأكلُ والفعلُ

(f) knowing or believing that the prayer's time has come (f2);

(g) knowing that the prayer is obligatory;

(h) and knowing how it is performed.

Whenever one violates any of these conditions, one's prayer is invalidated, such as:

(1) (non-(a) above) when a state of ritual impurity occurs during the prayer, even if absentmindedly;

(2) (non-(b)) when some filth containing moisture affects a garment during the prayer, but one does not immediately shed the garment; or when some dry filth affects it, but one throws it off with the hand or sleeve (O: since in that case one is supporting it and in contact with it (dis: f4.2(N:)));

(3) (non-(c)) when the wind discloses a part of one' nakedness and its cover gets beyond reach;

(4) or (non-(g)) when one believes that some elements of the prayer are obligatory and some are merely recommended, but does not know which are obligatory.

One's prayer is not invalidated if one thinks that all the prayer's parts are obligatory, or ((2) above) if one immediately sheds the garment affected by moist filth, brushes off dry filth, or ((3) above) immediately re-covers one's nakedness.

THE INTEGRALS OF PRAYER

أركان الصلاة

f9.14 The prayer's *integrals* (rukn, pl. arkan) are seventeen:

(a) the intention (def: f8.3);

(b) the opening Allahu Akbar (f8.7);

(c) standing (f8.27);

الكثيرُ، ومعرفةُ دخولِ الوقتِ ولوْ ظنّاً، والعلمُ بفرضية الصلاةِ وبكيفيتها .

فمتى أخَلَّ بشرطٍ منها بَطَلَتْ الصلاةُ، مثلُ أنْ يَسْبِقَهُ الحـدثُ فيها ولوْ سهواً أوْ تُصيبَهُ نجـاسـةً رطبـةً ولمْ يُلْقِ الثـوبَ أوْ يابسةً فيُلْقِيهَا بيـدهِ أو كُمِّـهِ (لأنه في هذه الحـالـة حامل للنجـاسة ومتصل بها) أوْ تَكْشِفَ الـريـحُ عورتَـهُ وتَبْعُـدَ السترةُ أوْ يَعْتَقِـدَ بَعْضَ أفعـالها فرضاً وبعضَها سنَّةً ولمْ يُمَيِّزْهُما .

فلوِ اعْتَقَـدَ أنَّ جميعَهَـا فرضٌ أوْ بادَرَ بإلقاءِ الثـوبِ النجسِ وبنفضِ اليـابسـةِ وستر العورةِ لمْ تَبْطُلْ .

f9.14 وأركـانُهَـا سَبْعَةَ عَشَرَ: النيةُ، وتكبيـرةُ الإحـرامِ، والقيـامُ، والفاتحةُ،

(d) the Fatiha (f8.17);

(e) bowing (f8.29);

(f) remaining motionless a moment therein;

(g) straightening back up after bowing (f8.31);

(h) remaining motionless a moment therein;

(i) prostration (f8.33);

(j) remaining motionless a moment therein;

(k) sitting back (f8.36) between the two prostrations;

(l) remaining motionless a moment therein;

(m) the prayer's final Testification of Faith (Tashahhud) (f8.45);

(n) sitting therein (f8.43);

(o) the Blessings on the Prophet (Allah bless him and give him peace) after the prayer's final Testification of Faith (f8.45);

(p) saying "as-Salamu 'alaykum" the first of the two times it is said at the end of the prayer (f8.47);

(q) and the proper sequence of the above integrals.

THE MAIN SUNNAS OF PRAYER

f9.15   The prayer's *main sunnas* (A: meaning those which if omitted call for a *forgetfulness prostration* (def: f11)) are six:

(a) the prayer's first Testification of Faith (Tashahhud) (N: in prayers that have two);

(b) sitting during it;

والـركـوعُ، والطمأنينةُ، والاعتـدالُ، والطمأنينـةُ، والسجـودُ، والطمأنينـةُ، والجلوسُ بينَ السجـدتَيْن، والطمأنينـةُ، والتشهدُ الأخيرُ، وجلوسُهُ، والصلاةُ على النبيِّ ﷺ فيه، والتسليمةُ الأولى، وترتيبُها هكذَا.

أبعاض الصلاة

f9.15   وأبعـاضُهـا ستةٌ التشهدُ الأولُ وجلوسُـهُ وصـلاةٌ على النبيِّ ﷺ فيــه،

(c) the Blessings on the Prophet (Allah bless him and give him peace) after it (f8.45);

(d) the blessings on his family in the prayer's final Testification of Faith (Tashahhud);

(e) the supplication (f8.53) after bowing in the final rak'a of the dawn prayer (subh);

(f) and standing therein.

OTHER SUNNAS

ور (ح: الصلاة على) آلهِ في (ح: التشهد الأخيرِ، والقنوتِ، وقيامُهُ.

سنن أُخرى

f9.16 All other parts of the prayer are ordinary sunnas (O: and missing one is not compensated by a forgetfulness prostration).

f9.16 وما عَدا ذلكَ سننٌ (فلا يجبر تركها بسجود السهو).

*

f10.0 SUPEREROGATORY PRAYER

صلاة التطوع f10.0

f10.1 The prayer is the best of the body's spiritual works (O: *prayer* referring to the prescribed prayer, and *body* excluding worship connected with the heart, such as faith in Allah, which is better than the works of the body), and supererogatory prayers are the best of voluntary spiritual works (O: though scholarly work in Islamic religious knowledge, meaning beyond what is obligatory to ensure the validity of one's worship, is superior to nonobligatory prayer because it fulfills a communal obligation (fard al-kifaya, def: c3.2)).

Supererogatory prayers that the Sacred Law stipulates be prayed in groups, such as the prayer on the two 'Eids (f19), the prayer at solar and lunar eclipses, and the drought prayer, are better than those it does not stipulate be prayed in groups, namely, all others besides these. But the sunna rak'as before and after the prescribed prayers (O: whether confirmed sunna (sunna mu'akkada, def: below) or otherwise) are superior to the group prayer that is sunna on the nights of Ramadan (tarawih).

f10.1 أفضلُ عباداتِ البدنِ الصلاةُ (والمراد منها المكتوبة فخرج بالبدن العبادة المتعلقة بالقلب فهي أفضل منها كالإيمان بالله)، ونفلُها أفضلُ النفلِ. (والاشتغال بالعلم أفضل من صلاة النافلة والمراد منه ما زاد على ما تتوقف عليه صحة العبادة لأنه حينئذ يكون فرض كفاية).

وما شُرِعَ لهُ الجماعةُ وهوَ العيدانِ، والكسوفانِ، والاستسقاءُ أفضلُ ممَّا لا يُشْرَعُ لهُ الجماعةُ وهوَ ما سِوَى ذلكَ لكنِ الرواتبُ (مطلقاً مؤكداً وغيره) مَعَ الفرائضِ أفضلُ مِنَ التراويحِ.

THE SUNNA PRAYERS BEFORE AND
AFTER THE PRESCRIBED PRAYERS

الرواتب

f10.2 It is sunna to diligently perform the nonobligatory prayers that are offered before and after the prescribed ones.

The optimal number of these is two rak'as before the dawn prayer (subh), four before and after the noon prayer (zuhr), four before the midafternoon prayer ('asr), two after the sunset prayer (maghrib), and two after the nightfall prayer ('isha).

The confirmed sunnas (dis: c4.1) of these (O: *confirmed* (mu'akkada) meaning those which the Prophet (Allah bless him and give him peace) did not omit whether travelling or at home) consist of ten rak'as:

(1) two before the dawn prayer (subh);

(2) two before and after the noon prayer (zuhr);

(3) two after the sunset prayer (maghrib);

(4) and two after the nightfall prayer ('isha).

It is recommended to pray two rak'as before the sunset prayer.

The sunnas of the Friday prayer (jumu'a) are the same as those of the noon prayer (zuhr) (dis: w28.1).

The time for the nonobligatory rak'as that come before prescribed prayers is that of the prescribed prayers. It is proper (adab) to pray such a sunna before the prescribed prayer, though if prayed after it, it is still a current performance (A: not a makeup, and one must intend it, for example, as the sunna before noon prayer (zuhr)). The time for nonobligatory rak'as that come after the prescribed prayer begins when one has performed the prescribed prayer and ends with the end of the prayer's time.

WITR (THE FINAL PRAYER AT NIGHT)

f10.3 The minimal performance for *witr* (lit. "odd number") is one rak'a (O: even if one omits

f10.2 والسنةُ أنْ يُوَاظِبَ على رواتبِ الفرائضِ .

وأكملُهَا : ركعتَان قبلَ الصبح وأربعٌ قبلَ الظهر وأربعٌ بعدها وأربعٌ قبلَ العصر وركعتانِ بعدَ المغرب وركعتانِ بعدَ العشاء .

والمـؤكَّـدُ (والمؤكد هو الذي لم يتركه ﷺ لا سفـراً ولا حضـراً) مِنْ ذلكَ عشْرُ ركعـاتٍ : ركعتانِ قبـلَ الصبـح والظهر وبعدَها وبعدَ المغرب والعشاء .

ويُنْدَبُ ركعتانِ قبلَ المغربِ .

والجمعـةُ كالظهـر . ومَا قبلَ الفريضة وَقْتـهُ وقتُ الفـريضـة وتقديمُهُ عليْهَا أدبُ وهـوَ بعـدَهـا أداءً ، ومَا بعدَهَا يَدْخُلُ وَقْتُهُ بفعلِهَا ويَخْرُجُ بخروجِ وقتِهَا .

صلاة الوتر

f10.3 وأقـلُ الـوترِ ركعـةٌ (وإن لم

the sunnas after the nightfall prayer ('isha). (A: A *witr* of at least three rak'as is obligatory (wajib) in the Hanafi school, and one should never omit it.)

The optimal way is to perform eleven rak'as, and (O: if one performs more than three) one should finish with Salams (def: f8.47) after every pair. The least considered optimal is three rak'as, (O: and one separates them by) finishing two times with Salams (N: i.e. by finishing two rak'as with Salams and then performing the final rak'a). One recites al-A'la (Koran 87) in the first rak'a, al-Kafirun (Koran 109) in the second, and al-Ikhlas, al-Falaq, and al-Nas (Koran 112, 113, and 114) in the third.

It is permissible to (n: serially) join all the rak'as of any *witr* prayer that has from three to eleven rak'as by finishing them once with Salams (O: in the final rak'a. In that case and also when one's *witr* is only a single rak'a, one merely intends *witr*, whereas in other *witr*s prayed in pairs (n: until one reaches the last one), one intends each pair as *two rak'as of witr*).

When joining the rak'as of *witr* one may limit oneself to a single Testification of Faith (Tashahhud) (A: in the final rak'a), or may recite two Testifications, one in the last rak'a and one in the next to the last, and to thus recite two Testifications is superior (A: if one separates the final two rak'as from one another by finishing the next to the last rak'a with Salams (N: before praying the final rak'a by itself), for otherwise it is better to recite a single Testification, as making *witr* resemble the sunset prayer (maghrib) is offensive). More than two Testifications (A: in a joined *witr*) invalidates the whole prayer.

f10.4 The best time for *witr* is just after the sunna rak'as that follow the nightfall prayer ('isha), unless one intends to offer the *night vigil prayer* (tahajjud; to rise at night after having slept, to pray some nonobligatory rak'as), in which case it is best to pray *witr* after the night vigil prayer (A: provided that one usually manages to get up when one has made such an intention. If not, then it is better to perform *witr* after the sunnas of the nightfall prayer ('isha)).

When one has already performed *witr*, but

يتقدمه سنة العشاء).

وأكملُهُ إحـدىٰ عشـرةَ وَ(إذا زاد على ثلاث فـ) يُسَـلَّمُ مِنْ كلّ ركـعـتَين، وأدنىٰ الكمـال ثلاثٌ (ويفصـل بين الثلاث) بسلامَين (وهو أفضل من الوصل) يَقْرَأ في الأولىٰ: ﴿سَبِّـحِ اسمَ ربِّـكَ الأعلىٰ﴾، وفي الثـانيـة: ﴿قُـلْ يَا أيُّهَا الكافرونَ﴾، وفي الثالثةِ: ﴿قُلْ هُوَ اللَّهُ أحدٌ﴾، والمعوذتَين.

ولَـهُ وصـلُ الثـلاثِ والإحـدَىٰ عَشَـرَةَ (ركعةً وما بينهما) بتسليمةٍ (واحدة آخرها وينوي الوتر في ذلك وفيما اقتصر فيه على ركعـة، وإن أوتـر بأكثـر وسلم من كل ركعتين نوى بكلِّ ركعتين من الوتر).

ويَجُـوزُ بتشهـدٍ (واحـد) و(وصله) بتـشـهـدَين في الأخيـرة والتي قبلهـا، وبتشهـدَين أفضلَ (ع: إن فصل بينهما بسلام. وإلا فالوصل بتشهد واحد أفضل لأن تشبيه الـوتـر بالمغرب مكروه). فإنْ زَادَ على تشهدَين بطَلَتْ صلاتُهُ.

f10.4 والأفضـلُ تقـديمُهُ عقيبَ سنة العشـاء، إلّا أنْ يَكُـونَ لهُ تَهجُّدُ فالأفضل تأخيرُهُ لِيوترَ بعدَه.

ولـوْ أوْتَـرَ ثمَّ أراد تهجُّـداً صَلّىٰ مثنىٰ

decides to pray the night vigil prayer (tahajjud), one performs the latter's rak'as two by two, and there is no need to repeat the *witr*, or "make it an even number" by performing one rak'a before the night vigil prayer. However, it is recommended not to intend performing prayers between *witr* and dawn.

مَثْنَى ولا يُعيدُهُ ولاَ يَحْتاجُ إلى نقضِه بركعةٍ قبلَ التهجدِ ويُنْدَبُ أَنْ لا يَتَعَمَّدَ بعدَهُ صلاةٍ .

TARAWIH

صلاة التراويح

f10.5 It is recommended to perform *tarawih*, which is twenty rak'as of group prayer on each night of Ramadan. (O: As well as being sunna to pray *tarawih* alone, it is also sunna to pray it in a group.) One finishes each pair of rak'as with Salams.

f10.5   ويُنْدَبُ التراويحُ وهيَ كلُّ ليلةٍ مِنْ رمضانَ عشرونَ ركعةً في الجماعة (والتراويح كما تسن فرادى تسن أن تكون واقعة في الجماعة) ويُسَلَّمُ مِنْ كلِّ ركعتين .

It is recommended to pray *witr* in a group after *tarawih*, unless one intends the night vigil prayer (tahajjud), in which case one should postpone *witr* until after it. During the second half or Ramadan, in the last rak'a (N: of *witr*), it is recommended to supplicate as one does in the dawn prayer (def: f8.53), and then one adds: "O Allah, we ask Your help, Your forgiveness, and Your guidance. In You we believe, on You we rely, You we praise with every good, we are grateful to You and not ungrateful, and disown and abandon him who commits outrages against You. O Allah, You alone do we worship, to You we pray and prostrate, You we strive for and hasten to obey, hoping for Your mercy and fearing Your punishment. Truly, Your earnest punishment shall overtake the unbelievers."

ويُوتِرُ بعدَها جماعةً إلاَّ لمنْ يَتَهَجَّدُ فيُؤَخِّرُهُ. ويُقْنَتُ في الأخيرة (ح : من الوتر) في النصف الأخيــر (ح : من رمضان) بقنــوتِ الصبح ثُمَّ يَزيــدُ «اللهُمَّ إنــا نَسْتعينُكَ ونَسْتَغْفِرُكَ ونَسْتَهـديكَ ونُؤْمِنُ بكَ ونتَوكَّلُ عَلَيْكَ ونُثني عَلَيْكَ الخيرَ كلَّهُ نَشْكُــرُكَ ولاَ نَكْفِــرُكَ ونَخْلَعُ ونَتْـــرُكَ مَنْ يَفْجُــرُكَ، اللَّهُمَّ إيَّـاكَ نَعْبُدُ ولَكَ نُصَلِّي ونَسْجُــدُ وإليـكَ نَسْعَى ونَحْفِـدُ، نَرْجُـو رَحْمَتَكَ ونَخْشَى عَذَابَكَ إنَّ عَذَابَكَ الجِدَّ بالكُفَّار مُلْحِقٌ» .

The time for *witr* and *tarawih* is between the nightfall prayer ('isha) and dawn.

ووقتُ الـوتـرِ والـتـراويح مَا بَيْنَ صلاة العشاءِ والفجرِ .

THE MIDMORNING PRAYER (DUHA)

صلاة الضحى

f10.6 It is recommended to pray the midmorning prayer (duha), which minimally consists of two rak'as, is optimally eight rak'as, and maximally twelve. One finishes each pair of rak'as with Salams.

f10.6   ويُصَلِّي الـضُّـحَى وأقلُّهـا ركعتان وأكملُهَا ثمانٍ وأكثرُهَا اثنتا عَشْرَةَ ويُسَلِّمُ مِن كلِّ ركعتَيْن .

Its time is after the sun is well up until just before the noon prayer (zuhr). (O: The preferable

ووقتُهَا مِنْ ارتفــاعِ الشمسِ إلى الزوال (ووقتها المختار إذا مضى ربع

time for its performance is after a quarter of the day has passed.)

النهار).

f10.7 When one misses (O: even intentionally) any supererogatory prayer that has a specified time, such as the two 'Eids, *duha, witr,* or the sunnas before and after the prescribed prayers, it is recommended to make it up at any time afterwards.

f10.7 وكـلُّ نفـلٍ مؤقتٍ كالعيـد والضُحَى والـوتـر ورواتب الفـرائض إذا فاتَ (ولو تركه عمداً) نُدِبَ قضاؤُهُ أبداً

If one misses a supererogatory prayer that is contingent upon some passing event, such as the eclipse prayer, drought prayer, greeting the mosque, or the prayer for guidance (istikhara, def: f10.12), one does not make it up.

وإنْ فُعـلَ لعـارضٍ كالكـسـوف والاستسقاء والتحية والاستخارة لـمْ يُقْضَ.

THE NIGHT VIGIL PRAYER (TAHAJJUD)

التهجد

f10.8 Supererogatory prayer at night is a confirmed sunna (def: f10.2(O:)), even if one can only do a little. *Wholly supererogatory* prayers (O: meaning those unconnected with a particular time or reason) at night are better than during the day.

f10.8 والنفـلُ في الليـل متأكّدٌ وإنْ قَلَّ، والنفـلُ المطلقُ (وهـو مالا يتقيـد بوقـت ولا سبب) في الليـل أفْضَـلُ من المطلق في النهار.

If one divides the night into six parts, the fourth and fifth part are the best for prayer. If divided in half, the second half is best. If divided into thirds, the middle part is best. Praying the entire night, every night, is offensive.

وأفضلُهُ السـدسُ الـرابعُ والخامسُ إنْ قَسَمَهُ أسـداساً فإنْ قَسَمَهُ نصفيْن فأفضلُهُ الأخيـرُ، أوْ أثـلاثـاً فالأوسط. ويُكرَهُ قيامُ كلِّ الليل دائماً.

It is recommended to begin one's night vigil prayers (tahajjud) with two brief rak'as, to have intended the night vigil prayer before going to sleep, and not to make a practice of more prayer than one can regularly perform without harm to oneself.

ويُنْـدَبُ افـتتـاحُ التهجـد بركعتيْن خفيفَتيْن ويَنْـوي التهجـدَ عنـد نومِهِ ولا يَعْتَادُ منْهُ إلَّا ما يُمْكِنُهُ الدوامُ عليْهِ بلا ضرر.

(A: It is sunna to recite the suras of the night vigil prayer sometimes aloud, sometimes to oneself.)

f10.9 One (O: who is performing wholly supererogatory prayers, whether in the night or day) finishes every two rak'as with Salams, though one may also:

f10.9 ويُسَلِّمُ (المصلي للصلاة النافلة المطلقة في الليل أوْ في النهار) منْ كلِّ ركعتيْن فإنْ جَمَعَ ركعاتٍ بتسليمةٍ أوْ

(1) join three or more rak'as by finishing but once with Salams;

159

(2) pray a single supererogatory rak‘a by itself;

(3) recite the Testification of Faith (Tashahhud) every two rak‘as (O: without finishing them with Salams), or every three, or every four, even if the Testifications of Faith grow very numerous (A: before finishing the series of rak‘as with Salams). (N: This is if not praying *witr* (dis: f10.3, end));

(4) or confine oneself to just one Testification of Faith (Tashahhud) in the final rak‘a (O: in which case one recites a sura in each of the rak‘as and finishes with Salams after the above-mentioned final Testification of Faith), though it is not permissible to recite the Testification of Faith in every rak‘a (O: without finishing with Salams).

When one's intention (N: in a wholly supererogatory prayer) is to perform a specific number of rak‘as (O: four or more), then one may change one's mind as to the number and pray fewer rak‘as, or more, provided one changes the intention before (O: having added or subtracted any). Thus, it is permissible to intend four but finish after two, if one intends to subtract two, though it invalidates the prayer to purposely finish it after two without having made the intention to curtail the planned four rak‘as. If one absentmindedly finishes with Salams, one goes on to complete the four and performs the forgetfulness prostration (def: f11) at the end.

GREETING THE MOSQUE

f10.10 It is recommended for whoever enters a mosque to *greet the mosque* by praying two rak‘as each time he enters, even if many times within an hour. One is no longer entitled to pray it after sitting. It is accomplished anytime one enters a mosque and prays two rak‘as, whether one intends merely performing two supererogatory rak‘as, fulfilling a vow, the sunna rak‘as before or after a prescribed prayer, the prescribed prayer alone, or the prescribed prayer together with the

تَطَوَّعَ بركعةٍ جَازَ ولَهُ التشهـدُ في كلِّ ركعتَيْن (أي من غيـر سلام) أوْ ثلاثٍ أوْ أربعٍ وإنْ كَثُرَتْ التشهـداتُ (ح : وهذا في غيـر الـوتـر) ولَهُ أنْ يَقْتَصِرَ على تشهِدٍ واحـدٍ في الأخيرة (وعليه يقرأ السورة في جميـع الركعات ويسلم عقب التشهد المذكور) ولَا يَجُوزُ في كلِّ ركعةٍ (من غير سلام).

وإذا نَوَى (ح : في النـفـل المطلق) عدداً (أربعةً فأكثرَ) فلَهُ الـزيادةُ والنقصُ بشـرطِ أنْ يُغيِّرَ النية قبلَهُمَا (أي قبل فعل الـزيادة وقبـل النقص). فوْ نَوَى أربعـاً فَسَلَّم مِنْ ركعتَيْن بنية النقص جَازَ. أوْ بلا نيـةٍ عمـداً بَطَلَتْ. أوْ سهـواً أَتَمَّ أربعـاً وسَجَدَ للسهوِ.

تحية المسجد

f10.10 ويُنْدَبُ لمنْ دَخَلَ المسجدَ أنْ يُصَلِّيَ ركعتَيْن تحيتَـهُ كلَّمـا دَخَلَ وإنْ كَثُرَ دخـولُـهُ في ساعـةٍ. وتَفُوتُ بالقعود. ولوْ نَوَى ركعتين مطلقـاً أوْ منـذورةً أوْ راتبةً أوْ فريضةً فقط أو الفرض والتحية حَصَلا.

intention of greeting the mosque.

(O: If one enters the mosque when one does not have ablution (wudu), it is sunna to say four times, "Allah is far exalted above any limitation, praise be to Allah, there is no god but Allah, Allah is greatest.")

f10.11 It is offensive to begin any nonobligatory prayer, whether greeting the mosque, the sunna rak'as before a prescribed prayer, or other, when the imam has begun the prescribed prayer or the muezzin has begun the call to commence (iqama).

THE GUIDANCE PRAYER (ISTIKHARA)

f10.12 (n: the translator has added the following text from Imam Nawawi's *Riyad al-salihin:*)

Jabir (Allah be well pleased with him) relates that "the Prophet (Allah bless him and give him peace) used to teach us the *guidance prayer* (istikhara) for all matters, as he would a sura of the Koran, saying:

" 'When a matter concerns one of you, pray two nonobligatory rak'as [dis: f8.20(5)] and say: "O Allah, I ask You to show me what is best through Your knowledge, and bring it to pass through Your power, and I ask You of Your immense favor; for You are all-powerful and I am not, You know and I do not, and You are the Knower of the Unseen. O Allah, if You know this matter to be better for me in my religion, livelihood, and *final outcome* [or perhaps he said, "the short and long term of my case"], then bring it about and facilitate it for me, and bless me with abundance therein. And if You know this matter to be worse for me in my religion, livelihood, and *final outcome* [or perhaps he said, "the short and long term of my case"], then keep it from me, and keep me from it, and bring about the good for me whatever it may be, and make me pleased with it," and then one should mention the matter at hand.' "

(*Riyad al-salihin* (y107), 325–26)

(فـإذا دخـل بغـير الـوضوء يسن له أن يقـول: «سبحـان الله، والحمد لله، ولا إله إلا الله، والله أكبر»، أربع مرات).

f10.11 وإذا دَخَلَ الإمامُ في المكتوبة أوْ شَرَعَ المؤذنُ في الإقامةِ كُرِهَ افتتاحُ كلِّ نفلٍ التحيةُ والرواتبُ وغيرُهُما.

صلاة الاستخارة

f10.12 (ت: قد أضــاف الـمتـرجم حديث صلاة الاستخـارة إلى المتن هنـا من كتاب رياض الصالحين للإمام النووي:)

«عن جابـرٍ رضي الله عنه قال: كان رسـولُ الله ﷺ يُعَلِّمُنَـا الاسْتِخـارَةَ في الأمورِ كُلِّها كالسورةِ مِنَ القرآنِ، يَقُولُ: «إذا هَمَّ أحدُكُم بالأمر فَلْيَركَعْ ركعتيِّن مِنْ غيـرِ الفريضـةِ، ثمَّ ليَقُلْ: اللَّهُمَّ إنِّي أَسْتَخِيرُكَ بِعِلْمِكَ وَأَسْتَقْدِرُكَ بِقُدْرَتِكَ، وَأَسْـأَلُكَ مِنْ فَضْلِكَ العَظيمِ، فإنَّك تَقْدِرُ ولاَ أَقْـدِرُ، وتَعْلَمُ ولاَ أَعْلَمُ، وأَنْتَ عَلاّمُ الـغُيُـوبِ. اللَّهُمَّ إنْ كُنْتَ تَعْلَمُ أَنَّ هذا الأمْـرَ خيرً لي في ديني ومَعَـاشِي وعَـاقِبَةِ أَمْـري» أوْ قال: «عـاجِـلِ أمري وآجِلِهِ، فَأَقْـدُرْهُ لي ويَسِّـرْهُ لي، ثُمَّ بَارِكْ لي فِيـهِ، وإنْ كُنْتَ تَعْلَمُ أَنَّ هذا الأَمْـرَ شرٌّ لي في ديني ومَعَـاشِي وعَـاقِبَةِ أَمْـري» أوْ قال: «عـاجِـلِ أمْـري وآجِلِهِ، فَأَصْرِفْـهُ عَنِّي وآصرِفْنِي عَنْهُ، وَأَقْدُرْ لي الخيرَ حَيْثُ كَانَ، ثُمَّ رَضِّني بِهِ» قال: ويسمِّي حاجتَـه [رواه الـبخـاري] (نُقـل من ريـاض الصالحين: ٣٢٥ ـ ٣٢٦).

f10.13 A nonobligatory prayer at home is superior to one performed at the mosque (dis: f8.52).

f10.13 والنفلُ في بيتِه أفضلُ مِنَ المسجدِ.

f10.14 It is offensive for one to single out the night before Friday (lit. "night of Friday," i.e. Thursday night, since in Arabic the night of a given date comes before its day) as a special night for prayer.

f10.14 ويُكْرَهُ تخصيصُ ليلةِ الجمعةِ بصلاةٍ.

f10.15 It is an offensive, blameworthy innovation (bid'a, def: w29) to perform any of the following spurious prayers:

(1) twelve rak'as between the sunset prayer (maghrib) and nightfall prayer ('isha) on the first Thursday night of the month of Rajab;

(2) one hundred rak'as in the middle of the month of Sha'ban;

(3) (O: two rak'as after each of three times of reciting Ya Sin (Koran 36) on the night of mid-Sha'ban;

(4) or the so-called prayer of 'Ashura' on 10 Muharram.)

f10.15 وصلاةُ الرغائب (وهي ثنتا عشـرة ركعة تفعـل ليلة أول جمعة بين المغـرب والعشـاءُ) في رجب وصـلاةُ نصف شعبـان بِدْعتـانِ مكـروهتـانِ (والصلاة في نصف شعبان هي مائة ركعة تفعل، وكذلك ما يفعل ليلة نصف شعبان من صلاة ركعتين عقب قراءة سورة يس ثلاث مرات وكذلك الصلاة الواقعة في يوم عاشوراء: كل ذلك بدعة قبيحة).

*

f11.0 PROSTRATIONS OF FORGETFULNESS, KORAN RECITAL, OR THANKS

f11.0 السجـود للسهـو وللتلاوة وللشكر

THE FORGETFULNESS PROSTRATION

سجود السهو

f11.1 The two reasons for the forgetfulness prostration are nonperformance of something called for (O: such as a main sunna (f9.15)), or performance of something uncalled-for (O: such as absentmindedly adding a rak'a to one's prayer).

f11.1 لَهُ سببـانِ: تركُ مأمـورٍ بِه (كتـرك بعض من أبعـاضهـا المأمور بها) وارتكابُ مُنْهِيٍّ عَنْهُ (كزيادة ركعة ناسياً).

f11.2 (n: As for nonperformance,) if one misses an integral of the prayer (def: f9.14) and does not

f11.2 فإنْ تَرَكَ ركناً واشْتَغَلَ بِمَا بعدَهُ

remember it until doing what comes after it, then one must (A: if still in the same rak'a) go back to it, perform it and what comes after it, and (A: it is sunna to) prostrate for it at the end of one's prayer (O: provided one is not a follower. As for a follower who misses an integral, he continues following the imam until the imam finishes with Salams, and then the follower rises alone and performs a makeup rak'a.

One is only obliged to reperform a missed integral (A: in the same rak'a, i.e. when praying by oneself) if one's forgetfulness of it doesn't continue (A: until the next rak'a). If one's forgetfulness continues and one goes on to perform the integral (A: during the course of the subsequent rak'a) then the same integral (A: of the following rak'a) takes the missed integral's place (A: in which case the rak'a containing the omission does not count and one does not return to it, but performs the rest of the prayer and then adds a makeup rak'a at the end, after which one performs the forgetfulness prostration before one finishes with Salams)).

f11.3   (O: If there is a surplus action, such as when one absentmindedly goes from standing to prostration without having bowed, but then remembers, in such a case one stands up and bows, and performs the forgetfulness prostration (N: at the end of the prayer). This (N: having stood twice before bowing) is a surplus action.

One does not prostrate for forgetfulness when there is no surplus action, as when one omits the final prostration of the prayer, but remembers it before one finishes with Salams and performs it, in which case one does not prostrate for it because there has not been an addition.)

f11.4   If one misses a main sunna (def: f9.15), even purposely, one performs a forgetfulness prostration.

If one misses anything besides an integral or main sunna, then one does not prostrate for it.

f11.5   One does not prostrate for (A: either intentionally or absentmindedly) doing an uncalled-

ثُمَّ ذَكَرَ تَدَارَكَهُ (أي فعل ذلك المتروك وجوباً إن لم يكن مأموماً. وأما هو فيتدارك بعد سلام إمامه بركعة. ومحل كونه يتدارك إن لم يستمر على سهوه فإن استمر وفعل المتروك قام المفعول مقامه) وأتى بِمَا بعدَهُ [[أي بما بعد المتروك وهو باقي صلاته)] وسَجَدَ للسهو.

f11.3   (إن كان هناك زيادة كأن سجد قبل ركوعه سهواً ثم تذكر فإنه يقوم ويركع ويسجد للسهو. فهذه زيادة.

وإن لم يكن هناك زيادة لم يسجد للسهو كأن ترك السجدة الأخيرة ثم تذكر قبل سلامه فإنه يأتي بها ولا يسجد للسهو لعدم الزيادة).

f11.4   ولوْ تَرَكَ بعضاً ولوْ عمداً سَجَدَ.

ولو تَرَكَ غيرَهُمَا لمْ يَسْجُدْ.

f11.5   وإن ارْتَكَبَ منهياً فإنْ لمْ يُبطِلْ

for action of the type which when done intentionally does not invalidate the prayer (O: such as turning the head, or taking one or two steps), though reciting a part or all of the Fatiha or Testification of Faith (Tashahhud) at the wrong place in the prayer are exceptions to this, in that, although intentionally reciting them at the wrong place does not invalidate the prayer, it does call for a forgetfulness prostration.

f11.6　One performs a forgetfulness prostration for unintentionally doing an uncalled-for action of the type which when done intentionally invalidates the prayer (O: such as a small amount of extraneous speech), provided it is not the type of action whose *unintentional* performance also invalidates the prayer (O: such as much extraneous speech or action (def: f9)) (N: since doing it would in any case invalidate the prayer and obviate the need for a forgetfulness prostration).

Straightening back up after bowing (f8.31), and sitting between prostrations (f8.36) are two brief integrals. To intentionally make them lengthy invalidates one's prayer, though to do so absentmindedly merely calls for a forgetfulness prostration.

(A: An exception to this is standing at length after bowing in the final rak'a of any prayer, as this does not invalidate the prayer even when done intentionally, and even if one does not supplicate therein.)

f11.7　If one forgets the first Testification of Faith (Tashahhud) and stands up, it is unlawful to return to it. If one intentionally returns to it, this invalidates one's prayer (O: because one has interrupted an obligatory act (A: the *integral* of standing) for the sake of something nonobligatory (A: the *main sunna* of the first Testification of Faith (Tashahhud))).

But if one returns to it absentmindedly or out of ignorance, one merely prostrates for it, though one must (O: interrupt the Testification of Faith that one has returned to, and) stand up as soon as one remembers.

If one (A: has omitted the first Testification of Faith and started to rise, but) checks oneself

عمدُهُ الصلاةَ (وذلك كالالتفات رح : بالوجه) والخطوة والخطوتين) لَمْ يَسْجُدْ . ويُسْتَثْنَى [مِمَّا لا يُبْطِلُ عمدُهُ] مَا إذا قَرَأَ الفَاتِحةَ أو التشهدَ أوْ بعضَهُمَا في غيرِ موضِعِهِ فإنَّهُ يَسْجُدُ لسهوِهِ ولاَ يُبْطِلُ عمدُهُ .

f11.6　وإنْ أَبْطَلَ (أي عمـده وذلـك كقليـل كلام) سَجَدَ لسهـوه إنْ لمْ يُبْطِلْ سهـوُهُ أيضاً (أي كما يبطل عمده كالكلام والعمل الكثيرين) .

والاعتدالُ مِن الركوع والجلوسُ بَيْنَ السجـدتَيْن ركنـانِ قصيرانِ تُبْطُلُ الصلاةَ بإطالتِهِمَا عمداً، فإنْ طَوَّلَهُمَا سهواً سَجَدَ.

f11.7　ولـوْ نَسِيَ التشهدَ الأولَ فَذَكَرَهُ بعـد انتصابـه حَرُمَ العـودُ إلَيْـه . فإنْ عَادَ عمداً بَطَلَتْ (لقطعه فرضاً لنفل) . أوْ سهـواً أوْ جاهلاً سَجَدَ ويَلْزَمُهُ القيامُ (عن التشهد في هذه الحالة) إذا ذَكَرَهُ . وإنْ عَادَ قبْلَهُ (أي قبـل الانتصاب) لَمْ

before standing and sits down again, this does not call for a forgetfulness prostration (O: as it is not a full surplus action (def: f11.3)). But if one intentionally rises and then returns to sitting after having been closer to standing, one's prayer is invalid. If not (O: i.e. if one had not yet been that close, or had, but returned absentmindedly or in ignorance of its prohibition), it is not (O: invalid).

The same applies to omitting the supplication of the dawn prayer (f8.53), where placing the forehead on the ground is as *standing up* is in the above rulings (N: that is, one may return to the omitted supplication as long as one has not yet completed one's (A: first) prostration).

f11.8   When praying behind an imam who misses the first Testification of Faith (Tashahhud) by standing, the follower may not remain seated to recite it by himself (O: as this is a gross contravention of his leadership and invalidates the prayer when done purposely and in awareness of its prohibition) unless he has made the intention to cease his participation in the group prayer and finish alone.

But if the imam omits the first Testification of Faith (Tashahhud) and the follower stands up with him, and then the imam sits down, it is unlawful for the follower to follow him therein. Rather, the follower should either cease his participation in the group prayer, or else remain standing and wait for the imam to rise before they continue the prayer together. If the follower intentionally sits back down when the imam does (O: knowing it is unlawful) then his prayer is invalid.

If the imam is sitting for the Testification of Faith and the follower absentmindedly stands up, then he must sit again, in deference to his imam's leadership (O: because following him in what is correct takes priority over starting an obligatory integral, which is also why the latecomer to group prayer may omit both standing and reciting the Fatiha (n: to bow when the imam bows, as above at f8.15)).

f11.9   One does not perform the forgetfulness prostration when one is uncertain (A: i.e. does not know or believe) that one did something that calls

يَسْجُدْ (لعدم الزيادة) . ولوْ نَهَضَ عامداً ثُمَّ عَادَ بعـدَ ما صَارَ إلى القيـام أقـرَبَ بَطَلَتْ . وإلّا (أي إن لم يصل إلى المحل المتقـدم، أو وصـل وعـاد ناسياً أو جاهلاً بالتحريم) فَلَا (تبطل صلاته) .

والقنـوتُ كالتشهدِ ووضـعُ الجبهـةِ بالأرضِ كالانتصابِ (ح: أي فيعود إليه ما لم يتم سجوده) .

f11.8   ولـوْ نَهَضَ الإمـامُ لَمْ يَجُـزْ للمأمـوم القعودُ لهُ (لفحش المخالفة فتبطـل صلاته حينئـذ إن تخلف عامـداً عالماً، إلّا أنْ يَنْوِيَ مفارقتَهُ .

فلو انْتَصَبَ مَعَ الإمام فَعَادَ الإمامُ إليهِ حَرُمَتْ موافقتُهُ . بلْ يُفارقُهُ أو يَنْتَظِرُهُ قائماً فإنْ وافَقَـهُ عمـداً (أي متعمـداً عالمـاً بالتحريم) بَطَلَتْ .

ولـوْ قَعَدَ الإمامُ وقَامَ المأمومُ سهواً لَزِمَهُ العـودُ لموافقةِ إمامِهِ (لأن المتابعة آكد من التلبس بالفرض ولـذلك سقط القيام عن المسبوق وكذلك الفاتحة) .

f11.9   ولـوْ شَكَّ هَلْ سَهَـا (أي هل حصـل منه ما يقتضي سجود السهو)، أوْ

for a forgetfulness prostration, or that one added a surplus integral, or did something uncalled-for. But if uncertain whether one omitted a main sunna (def: f9.15), or performed the forgetfulness prostration, or whether one prayed three rak'as or four (A: and this includes being uncertain (N: i.e. not knowing or believing it probable) that one performed one or more of a rak'a's integrals, since without all seventeen integrals (def: f9.14), the rak'a remains unperformed), then one proceeds on the assumption that one did not yet do it (O: returning to the original basis, which was that one had not done it) and one finishes with a forgetfulness prostration.

When one's doubt (A: that one has performed an extra rak'a) is resolved before finishing the prayer with Salams, one also prostrates for forgetfulness because of the rak'a one prayed while uncertain, which was presumed to have possibly been extra (A: i.e. the final rak'a, which one performed thinking it might be extra). But if performing it would have been obligatory in any case, as when one is uncertain during the third rak'a (A: of a four-rak'a prayer) as to whether it is the third or fourth rak'a (A: both of which would be obligatory for the prayer in any case), but one remembers during it that it is the third, then one does not prostrate for one's forgetfulness, though if one did not remember which it was until rising for the fourth rak'a (A: which one presumed might be the fifth), one prostrates for forgetfulness. (A: The same applies to prayers of less than four rak'as.)

f11.10 The forgetfulness prostration, even if there are numerous reasons for it in one prayer, is only two prostrations.

f11.11 If one comes late to a group prayer and the imam performs a forgetfulness prostration at the end of the group's prayer, one performs it with the group, and once again at the end of one's own prayer.

A follower does not prostrate for forgetfulness when he makes an individual mistake (A: the imam did not make) while following (n: unless he omits an integral, as discussed above at

هَلْ زَادَ رَكَناً أوْ هَلِ ارْتَكَبَ مِنها لَمْ يَسْجُدْ.

أوْ هَلْ تَرَكَ بعضاً معيّناً أوْ هَلْ سَجَدَ للسهو أوْ هَلْ صَلّى ثلاثاً أوْ أربعاً بَنى على أنّهُ لَمْ يَفْعَلْهُ (فيرجع في ذلك إلى الأصل وهو عدم الفعل) ويَسْجُدُ.

لكِنْ إنْ زَالَ شكُّهُ قبلَ السلام يَسْجُدُ أيضاً لِمَا صَلّاه متردّداً وَاحْتِملَ أنّهُ زائدٌ، وإنْ وَجَبَ فِعْـلُهُ على كلِّ حالٍ لمْ يَسْجُدْ، مثالُهُ شَكَّ في الثالثة أهيَ ثالثةٌ أمْ رابعةٌ فَتَذَكَّرَ فِيها لمْ يَسْجُدْ، أوْ بعدَ قيامِهِ للرابعة سَجَدَ.

f11.10 وسجودُ السهوِ وإنْ تَعَدَّدَتْ أسبابُهُ سَجْدَتَان.

f11.11 ولوْ سَجَدَ المسبوقُ مَعَ إمامِهِ أعادَهُ في آخِرِ صلاتِهِ.
وإنْ سَهَا خَلْفَ الإمام لَمْ يَسْجُدْ. فإنْ

f11.2(O:)), though he does prostrate if his mistake occurred before joining the group or after the imam finished with Salams.

If the imam makes a mistake, even if it was before one joined the group prayer, then one must prostrate for it with the group out of deference to the imam's leadership. If one does not, it invalidates one's prayer. If the imam neglects to perform a forgetfulness prostration, the follower does so anyway.

If one comes late to group prayer, absentmindedly finishes with Salams with the imam, and then remembers (O: the rest of the prayer that one has to complete), one performs the remainder and prostrates for forgetfulness.

f11.12　The forgetfulness prostration is a sunna. It is performed before one's final Salams, whether the reason is a surplus action or an omitted one.

One is no longer entitled to perform it if one deliberately finishes with Salams before it, or absentmindedly finishes with Salams and there is a lengthy interval before one recalls that one was supposed to have performed it; though if this interval is brief and one wishes, then one may prostrate, and one has thereby returned to the prayer and must again finish it with Salams.

THE KORAN RECITAL PROSTRATION

f11.13　To prostrate for recital of appropriate verses of the Koran is sunna for the person reciting, listening, or merely hearing.

f11.14　One prostrates for one's own recital if praying by oneself or if one is imam (O: but it invalidates one's prayer to intentionally and with knowledge of its prohibition recite a verse for the purpose of prostrating during the prayer (N: if one prostrates therein), except for al-Sajda (Koran 32) recited in the dawn prayer (subh) on Friday. (A: Though if such a verse merely occurs in the course of one's prayer, as when one is reciting a particular sura containing it, one may prostrate)). But if either of them prostrates upon hearing someone

سَهَا قبلَ الاقتداءِ بِهِ أوْ بعدَ سلامِ الإمامِ سَجَدَ .

ولوْ سَهَا الإمامُ ولوْ قبلَ الاقتداءِ بِهِ وَجَبَ متابعتُهُ في السجودِ. فإنْ لمْ يُتابِعْ بَطَلتْ صلاتُهُ. فإنْ تَرَكَ الإمامُ سَجَدَ المأمومُ.

ولو نَسِيَ المسبوقُ فَسَلَّمَ مَعَ الإمامِ ثمَّ ذَكَرَ (أي تذكر ما عليهِ من بقيةِ صلاتهِ) تَدَارَكَ وسَجَدَ للسهوِ.

f11.12　وسجودُ السهوِ سنةٌ. ومحلُّهُ قبلَ السلامِ سواءٌ سَهَا بزيادةٍ أوْ نقصٍ. فإنْ سَلَّمَ قبلَهُ عمداً مطلقاً أوْ سهواً وطَالَ الفصلُ فاتَ وإنْ قَصُرَ وأرَادَ السجودَ سَجَدَ وكانَ عائداً إلى الصلاةِ فَيُعيدُ السلامَ.

سجود التلاوة

f11.13　سجودُ التلاوةِ سنةٌ للقارىءِ والمستمعِ والسامعِ.

f11.14　ويَسْجُدُ المصلّي المنفردُ والإمامُ لقراءةِ نفسِهِ (وإذا قرأ آيةَ السجدةِ بقصدِ السجودِ في غيرِ «آلم تنزيل» في صبحِ يومِ الجمعةِ بطلتْ (ح: صلاتهِ إن سجدَ) إن كانَ عامـداً عالماً بالتحريمِ). فإنْ سَجَدَا لقراءةِ غيرِهِمَا بَطَلتْ

else's recital, it invalidates their prayer.

A follower prostrates with his imam. The follower's prayer is invalid if he prostrates for his own recital, the recital of someone besides the imam, or prostrates without the imam, or does not prostrate when the imam does.

صلاتُهُما .

ويَسْجُدُ المأمومُ لقراءةِ إمامِهِ مَعَهُ . فلوْ سَجَدَ لِقِراءةِ نفسِهِ أوْ غيرِ إمامِهِ أوْ سَجَدَ دونَهُ أوْ تَخَلَّفَ عنهُ بَطَلَتْ .

f11.15   There are fourteen prostration verses, two of them in al-Hajj (Koran 22). They do not include the prostration at Sad (Koran 38:24), which is a prostration of thanks, not of Koran recital, and is only performed outside of prayer. To purposely prostrate for it during the prayer invalidates the prayer.

f11.15   وهوَ أربعَ عشرةَ سجدةً منها ثنتان في الحجِّ . وليَسَ منْها سجدةُ صٍ بلْ هِيَ سجدةُ شكرٍ تُفْعَلُ خارجَ الصلاةِ . ويُبْطِلُ تعمّدُهَا الصلاةَ .

f11.16   When one prostrates for reciting while in the prayer, it is recommended to say "Allahu akbar" before prostrating and again when rising. It is obligatory to stand again after it (O: or to sit up again if performing a nonobligatory prayer seated) and recommended to then recite more of the Koran before one bows.

When one prostrates for reciting while outside of the prayer, it is obligatory to say an opening Allahu Akbar (O: and to finish with Salams. The four integrals of both the prostration of Koran recital (A: outside of prayer) and of the prostration of thanks are:

(a) the intention;

(b) the opening Allahu Akbar;

(c) the prostration;

(d) and the final Salams (A: which can only be performed in a sitting position).

Whether in or out of the prayer, the things that invalidate a normal prayer invalidate the prostrations of recital or thanks, and the conditions of the prayer, i.e. ablution (wudu), clothing nakedness, the entry of the proper time—which is when the last letter of a prostration verse has been recited—facing the direction of prayer (qibla), and so forth, are also conditions of these prostrations).

f11.16   وإذا سَجَدَ في الصلاةِ كَبَّرَ للسجودِ والرفعِ ندباً ويَجبُ أنْ يَنْتَصبَ قائماً (وأنْ يقعد عقبه إن صلى من قعود) ويُنْدَبُ أنْ يَقْرَأَ شيئاً ثمّ يَركَعَ .

وفي غيرِ الصلاةِ تَجبُ تكبيرةُ الإحرامِ (والسلامِ والحاصلِ أنّ لسجودِ التلاوةِ والشكرِ أركاناً أربعةً : النيةِ والتكبيرةِ للإحرامِ والسجودِ والسلام .

ويبطلُ هاتين السجدتين ما يبطلُ غيرهما من مبطلاتِ الصلاةِ، وشرطهما شرطُ غيرهما من الصلاةِ وذلك كالطهارةِ وسترِ العورةِ ودخولِ الوقتِ وهو فراغهُ من القراءةِ لآيتها ولو بقيَ حرفٌ واحدٌ لم يسجدْ حتى يتمها واستقبالِ القبلةِ وغيرُ ذلك من شروطِ الصلاةِ) .

It is recommended to say "Allahu akbar" when one prostrates and rises, though not to recite the Testification of Faith (Tashahhud) therein.

وتُنَّدَبُ تكبيرةُ السجودِ والرفعِ لا التشهدُ.

f11.17 If one delays the recital prostration past its time and the interval is brief (O: meaning less than the time of two brief, medium-length rak'as) then one is still entitled to prostrate. If longer than that, one does not make it up.

When one repeats a prostration verse within one sitting or within one rak'a and one has missed the prostration at its first mention, then it is accomplished by a single prostration (O: though if one prostrates for the first, one still prostrates for the subsequent times, as the reason to do so has been renewed).

f11.17 وإنْ أَخَّرَ السجودَ وقَصَّرَ الفصلُ (وضبط قصر ذلك في العرف بأن لا يزيدَ على قدر ركعتين بأخف ممكن من الوسط المعتدل) سَجَدَ وإلّا لَمْ يَقْضِ.

ولَوْ كَرَّرَ آيةً في مجلس أوْ ركعةٍ ولمْ يَسْجُدْ للأولى كَفَتْهُ سجدةٌ (فلو سجد للأولى سجد لما بعدها لتجدد السبب).

f11.18 When reciting the Koran, whether during the prayer or not, it is recommended to ask Allah for mercy at the verses mentioning mercy, and to seek refuge in Him (Ta'awwudh) at verses mentioning punishment.

f11.18 ويُنْدَبُ لِمَنْ قَرَأَ في الصلاةِ وغيرِها آيةَ رحمةٍ أنْ يَسْأَلَ اللهَ الرحمةَ، أوْ آيةَ عذابٍ أنْ يَتَعَوَّذَ منهُ.

THE PROSTRATION OF THANKS

سجود الشكر

f11.19 Whenever a manifest blessing appears in one's life (O: such as a child, wealth, or prestige), it is recommended to prostrate out of thanks to Allah, and likewise when an affliction is averted (O: such as being saved from drowning, regaining health, or the reappearance of someone lost (A: or the death of a tyrant)), or when one sees someone Allah has afflicted with disobedience or illness, though in the latter case one should prostrate in private (O: so as not to sadden the person).

The prostration of thanks is the same as the Koran recital prostration outside of the prayer (O: regarding its integrals and conditions (def: f11.16)). It invalidates one's prayer if performed during it.

f11.19 و(يندب) لِمَنْ تَجَدَّدَ لهُ نعمةٌ ظاهرةٌ (كحدوث ولد ومال وجاه مثلاً) أو انْدَفَعَتْ عنهُ نقمةٌ ظاهرةٌ (كنجاة من غرق وشفاء مريض وقدوم غائب) ومنهُ رؤيةُ مُبْتَلىً بمعصيةٍ أوْ مرضٍ أنْ يَسْجُدَ شكراً للهِ تعالى ويُخْفِيَهَا (لئلا ينكسر خاطره) [إلّا لفاسقٍ فَيُظْهِرُهَا لِيَرْتَدِعَ إنْ لمْ يَخَفْ ضرراً].

وهيَ كسجودِ التلاوةِ (في الأركان والشروط) خارجَ الصلاةِ. وتَبْطُلُ بفعلِهَا الصلاةُ.

f11.20 It is unlawful to prostrate without occasion merely to humble oneself to Allah to draw

f11.20 ولَوْ خَضَعَ فَتَقَرَّبَ للهِ بسجدةٍ

near to Him (O: because it is a reprehensible innovation (bid'a, def: w29.3))).

منفردةٍ بلَا سبب حَرُم (فإنه بدعة) .

f11.21   The recital prostration's requirements of facing the direction of prayer (qibla), purity, and clothing nakedness are the same as those of nonobligatory prayers.

f11.21 وحكمُ سجـود التـلاوة حكمُ صلاةِ النفل في القبلةِ والطهارة والستارة .

*

f12.0   GROUP PRAYER AND THE IMAM

f12.0 صلاة الـجمـاعـة وصفة الإمام

GROUP PRAYER

صلاة الجماعة

f12.1   Group prayer is a communal obligation (def: c3.2) upon all male nontravellers for the five current prescribed prayers, such that the rite of the prayer be public. (O: In a small town, it is enough to merely gather somewhere and pray. In a city, the prayer must be held in public places such that the manifestations of obedience to Allah's command are evident. If held in houses where the rite of prayer is not public, the obligation remains unfulfilled (A: though a house with a sign on it is sufficient).)

f12.1   هيَ فرضُ كفـايـةٍ في حقِّ الـرجـالِ المقيمينَ في المكتـوبـاتِ الخمس المؤدياتِ بحيثُ يَظْهَرُ الشعارُ (في البلد أو في محل إقامتها . ففي القرية الصغيرة يكفي إقـامتهـا في محـل وفي الكبيرة والبلد تقـام في محال يظهر بها الشعـار فلو أُطبقوا على إقامتها في البيوت ولم يظهر بها الشعار لم يسقط الفرض) .

f12.2   Group prayer is sunna for women, travellers, and for makeup prayers in which the imam and followers are performing the same type of prayer; though it is not sunna for a follower's makeup prayer to be performed behind an imam's current prescribed prayer, or for a makeup prayer to be performed behind a different type of makeup (O: such as a follower making up the noon prayer (zuhr) behind an imam who is making up the midafternoon prayer ('asr)).

f12.2   وتُسَنُّ للنسـاءِ والمسـافـرينَ وللمقضيـة خلفَ مثلِهـا لَا خلفَ مؤداةٍ ومقضيةٍ غيرها (كظهر خلف عصر) .

f12.3   It is personally obligatory to perform the Friday prayer (jumu'a) in a group (A: for every male Muslim who is not travelling).

f12.3   وهيَ في الجمعةِ فرضُ عينٍ .

f12.4   The group prayer for which the demand is the strongest is the dawn prayer (subh), then the nightfall prayer ('isha), and then the midafternoon prayer ('asr).

The minimal number of people for a group prayer is an imam and a follower.

It is best for men to perform group prayer at the mosque (O: as the act of going to the mosque makes the group prayer evident). The best mosque in which to pray is the one with the most people. If there is a nearby mosque attended by few people, then it is better to go to a distant one attended by more, unless the imam there commits reprehensible innovations (bid'a, def: w29.3), is immoral, does not consider one of the integrals of the prayer to be an integral (n: though this does not matter if it is the result of the imam's following a different school of jurisprudence, as below at f12.29(N:)), or if one's going to the farther mosque will make group prayer impossible at the one nearby (A: as when one is one of the only two people who are likely to come), in all of which cases it is better to pray at the nearby mosque.

It is better for women to pray at home than at the mosque (A: whether they are young or old). It is offensive for an attractive or young woman to come to the mosque to pray (O: or for her husband to permit her), though not offensive for women who are not young or attractive when this is unlikely to cause temptation. (N: The author's words here must be interpreted in the light of the following details: If a woman's going to group prayer or elsewhere will definitely lead to temptation between the sexes, it is unlawful for her to go. If such temptation can be definitely prevented, her going to attend group prayer remains sunna, as is attested to by the hadiths that have reached us on the subject. If temptation is feared but not certain to occur, her going becomes offensive. Whether such temptation is likely to occur is something that differs with different times, places, and people. An old woman is not like a young one, nor a righteous society like one in which temptation between the sexes is the rule; nor is a special prayer place set aside for women at a mosque like a prayer place which they share with men. This is why 'A'isha (Allah be well pleased with her) said,

"Had the Prophet (Allah bless him and give

f12.4   وآكدُ الجماعاتِ الصبحُ ثمَّ العشاءُ ثمَّ العصرِ. وأقلُّها إمامٌ ومأمومٌ.

وهيَ للرجالِ في المساجدِ أفضلُ (وفي الذهابِ إلى المسجدِ إظهارُ شعارِ الجماعةِ) وأكثرُها جماعةً أفضلُ. فإنْ كانَ بجوارِه مسجدٌ قليلُ الجمعِ فالبعيدُ الكثيرُ الجمعِ أولى إلاّ أنْ يكونَ إمامُه مبتدعاً أوْ فاسقاً أوْ لا يعتقدَ بعضَ الأركانِ أوْ يتعطَّلَ بذهابِه إلى البعيدِ جماعةُ مسجدِ الجوارِ فمسجدُ الجوارِ أولى.

وللنساءِ في بيوتهنَّ أفضلُ ويُكرَهُ حضورُ المسجدِ لمشتهاةٍ أوْ شابةٍ (ويكره لزوجها تمكينها منه) لا غيرهمَا عندَ أمنِ الفتنةِ.

(ح : كلام المصنف هنا يجب أن يحمل على التفصيل التالي : إذا ترتب على خروجِ المرأةِ لصلاةِ الجماعةِ وغيرها فتنة مؤكدة صار خروجها محرماً. وإذا انتفت الفتنة بصورة مؤكدة ظل خروجها للجماعةِ مسنوناً بمقتضى الأحاديث الواردة في الموضوعِ. وإذا خشيت الفتنة فلم تنتف ولم تتأكد صار خروجها مكروهاً. وهذا يختلف باختلاف الأزمنة والأمكنة والأشخاص فليس العجوز كالشابة، ولا المجتمع الصالح كالمجتمع الذي تغلب فيه الفتنة، ولا المصلى الخاص بالنساء في المسجد كالمصلى المشترك مع الرجال. ولهذا قالت عائشة رضي الله عنها :

«لو أن رسول الله ﷺ رأى ما أحدث

him peace) seen what women do now, he would
have forbidden them the mosque as the women of
Bani Isra'il were forbidden,''

a hadith reported by Bukhari and Muslim.

The temptation between the sexes whose
occurrence is to be feared when they intermingle
is of various degrees, the least of which is a person's appreciating and admiring the other, then
being attracted to and enamored with the other,
and finally, those indecencies which are not hidden from anyone. Islam is eager to eliminate evil
at its inception and extirpate temptation from its
outset, and the word of Allah Most High,

"Tell believers to lower their eyes and to
guard their private parts" (Koran 24:30),

explains both the starting point and final outcome
of the temptation of men through women and the
temptation of women through men.)

f12.5   There is no demand to go to group prayer
(O: whether communally obligatory (dis: f12.1),
personally obligatory (f12.3), or sunna (f12.2)),
when there is a valid excuse not to, such as:

(1) hardship due to rain or snow that soaks
clothing;

(2) hardship due to heavy mud (O: from getting soiled or slipping when walking through it);

(3) (O: severe) winds at night (O: or dawn);

(4) severe heat or cold (O: because of the
hardship of moving in them, and likewise intense
darkness at night, which is an excuse not to
attend);

(5) being in the presence of food or drink
that one wants to have (O: as they obviate the awe
and humility befitting the prayer. One should eat
enough to take the edge off one's hunger (A: and
then go to join the group));

(6) holding back from going to the toilet or
breaking wind (O: as one should relieve oneself
first, even if one fears missing the group prayer);

(7) hazard to one's person;

(8) hazard to one's property (O: from theft or seizure, whether it belongs to oneself or to another whose property one is obliged to protect. It also includes bread one has put in the oven that would burn if one were to leave and attend the prayer);

(9) hardship from an ailment (O: even when one is able to attend, if it entails a hardship comparable to that of walking in the rain. If one is suffering from a slight indisposition such as a toothache or the like, it is not an excuse);

(10) taking care of a sick person (O: who would suffer harm if one left to pray, whether a relative, friend, or total stranger) or taking care of someone ill who is strongly attached to one's staying with him;

(11) the death of a relative, friend, (O: or spouse);

(12) fear of missing the impending departure of the party one intends to travel with;

(13) having eaten something with a bad odor (O: such as raw onions or garlic, though not if cooked, as this eliminates the smell);

(14) or fear of meeting someone who will try to collect a debt one owes him and one is unable to pay.

(O: The demand for group prayer is not eliminated by other than the above excuses.)

f12.6 It is a condition of a valid group prayer that the follower intend to follow the imam (O: whether at the opening Allahu Akbar or thereafter). If the follower neglects to do so, his prayer is as if he had performed it alone. It invalidates one's prayer to purposely omit the intention to follow the imam while at the same time praying behind him and following his motions by awaiting them at length, though awaiting them shortly or performing one's own prayer simultaneously with his does

على نفسٍ أوْ مالٍ (من سرقته ونهبه سواء كان له أو لمن يلزمه الذب عنه [من ظالم أو غيـره]) ويـدخـل في المـال الخبـز إذا وضعه في الفـرن فإذا تركه وحضر لصلاة الجمـاعـة فيحتـرق فيكون ذلك عذر في ترك الـجمـاعـة) أوْ مرض (وإن كان الحضـور ممكنـاً لكن بمشقـة بأن تلحقه مشقة كمشقة مشيه في المطر. فإن كان مرضه يسيراً كوجع ضرسٍ فليس بعذرٍ) أوْ تمـريض مَنْ يُخَافُ ضيـاعَـهُ (بحيث لو تركه من يريـد حضـور الجمـاعة لتضرر بغيبته سواء كان المتمـرض قريـاً أو صديقـاً أو غريـباً لا معـرفـة له به) أوْ كانَ يأنَسُ به، أوْ حضـور موتِ قريـبٍ أوْ صديقٍ (أو زوجته) أوْ فوت رفقةٍ تَرْحَلُ أوْ أكـلٍ ذِي رائحـةٍ كريهةٍ (كبصل وثوم نيء كل منهما بخلاف المطبوخ لزوال ريحه) أوْ ملازمـةِ غريمِهِ وهوَ معسرٌ. (ولا تسقط الجماعة بلا عذر من هذه الأعذار).

f12.6 وشـروطُ الجمـاعـةِ أنْ يَنْـوِيَ الـمأمـومُ الاقتـداءَ (أي مع التحـرم أو بعـده). فإنْ أهْمَلَهُ انْعَقَدَتْ فُرادَى. فإنْ تَابَعَ بَلا نية بَطَلَتْ صلاتُهُ إن انْتَظَرَ أفعالَهُ انتظاراً طويلاً. فإنْ قلَّ أو اتَّفَقَ فَلَا.

not invalidate it.

It invalidates one's prayer to take a follower as one's imam when the follower is concurrently praying behind an imam (O: though if his imam finishes with Salams and the follower is still praying, he may then be taken as one's imam).

ولـو اقْتَدَى بمأموم خالَ اقتدائِه بَطَلَت صلاتُـهُ. (وأمـا بعد انقطاع القدوة فيصح الاقتداء به).

f12.7   The imam intends leading the prayer as imam. If he neglects this intention then his own prayer counts as if he had prayed alone (N: though his followers' prayer counts as a group prayer), the imam having lost the reward for praying in a group.

In the Friday prayer (jumu'a), it is a necessary condition for the prayer's validity that the imam intend leading as imam.

f12.7   وَلْيَنْـوِ الإمام الإمامةَ فإنْ أهملَهُ انْعَقَـدَتْ فرادَى وصحَّ الاقتـداءُ بِه (ح: وكـانت للمقتـدين جمـاعة) وفاتَ الإمامَ ثوابُ الجماعة.
ويُشْتَرَطُ نيةُ الإمامة في الجمعة.

f12.8   When going to a group prayer, it is recommended to walk with tranquillity. (O: It is sunna not to gambol about, speak of disapproved things, or engage in acts which are offensive in the prayer itself, such as looking right or left.)

It is recommended to diligently seek the spiritual merit of being at the group prayer's opening Allahu Akbar, meaning that one says it just after the imam does.

f12.8   ويُنْـدَبُ لقاصِدِ الجمـاعـةِ المشيُ بسكينـةٍ. (السنـة أن لا يعبث في مشيه إلى الصلاة ولا يتكلم بمستهجن ولا يتعاطى ما يكره في الصلاة كالالتفات).
ويُحَـافِـظُ على إدراكِ فضيلةِ تكبيـرةِ الإحرام وتَحْصُـلُ بأنْ يَشْتَغِـلَ بالتحرُّم عقب تحرُّمِ الإمام.

f12.9   If one has begun a nonobligatory prayer when the call to commence (iqama) is given, one should finish it before joining the group, as long as one does not fear the group will finish before one can join them. If afraid they will, then one interrupts the nonobligatory prayer to join them.

If one has begun praying a prescribed prayer alone and the call to commence (iqama) is given for a group prayer, it is recommended to turn one's prayer into a supererogatory prayer of two rak'as, and pray the prescribed prayer with the group. Were one to merely change one's intention to that of following their imam, it would count as a valid group prayer for one, but it is offensive. In such a case if one reaches the end of one's prayer before the group, one may either wait for them to finish with one while sitting in the final Testification of Faith (Tashahhud), or else finish with Salams as soon as one reaches the end of one's

f12.9   ولـوْ دَخَـلَ في نفـلٍ فأُقيمَت الـجمـاعـةُ أَتَمَّـهُ إنْ لمْ يَخشَ فواتَ الجماعة. وإلاَّ قَطَعَهُ.
ولـوْ دَخَـلَ في الفرضِ منفرداً فأُقيمَت الجماعـةُ نُدِبَ قَلْبُـهُ نفلاً ركعتَيْنِ ثُمَّ يَقْتَـدِي. فإنْ لمْ يَفْعَلْ ونَوَى الاقتداءَ في أثناءِ الصلاةِ صحَّ وكُرِهَ [ولزمَهُ المتابعةُ]. فإنْ تَمَّت صلاةُ المقتـدي أولاً انْتَظَـرَ في التشهـدِ أوْ سَلَّمَ (ولم يجز أن يتابع الإمام

prayer. (O: One may not follow the imam in what is in excess of one's own prayer.)

فيما زاد على صلاته) .

f12.10 It is permissible to start praying with a group, and then cease one's participation in praying with them (A: by a silent intention) and finish one's prayer alone, though this is offensive when there is no excuse. (O: It is not offensive to do so when there is an excuse, such as being ill, or unable to endure the imam's lengthy Koran recital because of weakness or having business to attend to (N: or a pressing emergency).)

f12.10 وَلَوْ أَحْرَمَ مَعَ الإمام ثُمَّ أَخْرَجَ نَفْسَهُ مِنَ الجماعةِ وأتَمَّ منفرداً جَازَ لكِنْ يُكْرَهُ بلا عذرٍ. (وأما قطعها لعذر كمرض وتطويل إمام القراءة لمن لم يصبر لضعف أو شغــل (ح : أو أمـرٍ طارىء مهـم) فلا كراهة في المفارقة حينئذ) .

f12.11 When one arrives late to a group prayer in which the imam is already bowing, it is obligatory for one to say the opening Allahu Akbar while standing upright, after which one says a second Allahu Akbar before one bows to join the group (O: though if one only says it once, intending the opening Allahu Akbar thereby, then omitting the second Allahu Akbar of bowing does no harm, as it is sunna). If any part of one's opening Allahu Akbar occurs when one is not standing upright (def: f8.27), one's prayer is invalid.

A latecomer is considered to have performed the rak'a if he manages to say ''Allahu akbar,'' bow, and remain motionless a moment therein before the imam straightens up beyond the definitional limit of *bowing* (f8.29). If one is uncertain as to whether the imam straightened up past the limits of bowing before one reached that position, or whether it was after, then one has not performed the rak'a (O: as one assumes, when uncertain, that one had not yet reached it). Nor does the rak'a count for such a follower when it does not count for the imam, such as when the imam nullifies his ablution (wudu), or has overlooked something impure on his person, or has mistakenly added a fifth rak'a to his prayer.

If one does not join the group until the imam has straightened up from bowing, or thereafter, then one follows his motions, saying ''Allah akbar'' with him and repeating ''Subhan Allah'' and the Testification of Faith (Tashahhud) when he does, even when this does not correspond to the rak'a in which one's own Testification of Faith would be if one were praying alone.

f12.11 وَلَوْ وَجَدَ الإمـامَ راكعـاً أَحْرَمَ منتصباً ثُمَّ كَبَّرَ للركـوع (فلوكبر واحدة ونوى بها التحرم فقط انعقدت صلاته ولا يضـر ترك تكبيرة الركوع لأنها سنة) . فإنْ وَقَعَ بعضُ تكبيرةِ الإحرامِ في غير القيام لَمْ تَنْعَقِدْ.

فإنْ وَصَلَ إلى حدِّ الركوعِ المجزىء واطْمَأَنَّ قبلَ رفعِ الإمامِ عنْ حدِّ الركوع المجـزىءِ حَصَلَتْ لَهُ الركعةُ فإنْ شَكَّ هَلْ رَفَعَ الإمامُ عَنِ الحدِّ المجزىءِ قبلَ وصــولِهِ إلى الحـدِّ المجـزىءِ أوبعـدَهُ ((ح : لم يدرك) لأن الأصلَ في الشـك عدم الإدارك) أوْ كَانَ الـركــوعُ غيـرَ محسوبٍ للإمام كمحدثٍ وكَذَا مـن بِه نجاسةٌ خفيةٌ أوْ ركوعِ خامسةٍ لم يُدْرِكْ. ومتَى أَدْرَكَ الاعتـدالَ فَمَـا بعـدَهُ انْتَقَلَ مَعَهُ مكبراً وُيسَبِّحُ ويَتَشَهَّدُ مَعَهُ في غيرِ موضعِهِ.

If one joins the group just as the imam is prostrating or sitting in the final Testification of Faith, then one prostrates or sits with him (N: after having recited one's opening Allahu Akbar while standing) without (A: a second) Allahu Akbar (O: though one does say "Subhan Allah" in prostration and recite the Testification of Faith with the imam, in deference to his leadership).

If the final Testification of Faith of the imam coincides with one's own first Testification, then when the imam finishes with Salams, one stands up with an Allahu Akbar to finish one's prayer; though if the imam's final Testification does not coincide with one's first Testification, one rises to finish without an Allahu Akbar.

ولـوْ أَدْرَكـهُ ساجداً أو متشهداً سَجَدَ أوْ جَلَسَ (ح: بعد تكبيرة الإحرام قائماً) بلا تكبيـر (لكنـه يأتي بالتسبيـح في الأول وبالتشهّد في الثاني للمتابعة).

ولـوْ سَلَّمَ الإمـامُ وهـوَ موضعُ جلوس الـمسبـوق [(ح: بأن كان المقتـدي في التشهـد الأول من صلاتـه والإمـام في التشهـد الأخيـر)] قام (ح: المقتـدي) مكبراً فإنْ لَمْ يكُنْ موضعُهُ فَلا تكبيرَ.

f12.12 Whenever one joins the group before the imam finishes with Salams, one has attained the merit of the group prayer. (N: But it is less than the merit of praying with the group from the beginning or joining them in the middle, though joining them at the end is better than praying alone.)

f12.12 وإنْ أَدْركَ الإمام قبلَ أنْ يُسَلِّمَ أَدْركَ فضيلَة الجمـاعـة (ح: لكنـه ليس كفـضيلة من أدرك الصـلاة من أولهـا أو وسطها بل هذا أفضل من صلاة المنفرد).

f12.13 The rak'as one performs before the imam finishes with Salams are the first rak'as of one's prayer, and those performed after the imam finishes are the last. Hence, if the imam performs the dawn prayer's supplication (def: f8.53) in the rak'a in which one joins the group, one repeats it in one's own second rak'a.

f12.13 ومـا أَدْركَهُ فهوَ أولُ صلاتِه ومَا يأتي به بعـدَ سلام الإمام فهوَ آخرُ صلاتِه فيُعيدُ فيه القنوتَ.

f12.14 It is obligatory for one to follow the imam's leadership in prayer actions, such that each of one's movements begins after the imam begins it and before he finishes (N: the following integral). (O: It is highly desirable that) one follows the imam's spoken integrals in the same way, with the sole exception of saying "Ameen" (def: f8.19), which should be simultaneous with his.

It invalidates one's prayer to say one's opening Allahu Akbar simultaneously with the imam, or to be uncertain as to whether one did so or not. It is offensive to perform some other part of the prayer simultaneously with the imam, and one thereby loses the merit of group prayer.

f12.14 ويجِبُ متـابعـةُ الإمـام في الأفعـال وَلْيَكُنِ ابتداءُ فعلِه متأخراً عَن ابتدائِه ومتقدماً علي فراغِه (ح: من الركن الذي انتقل إليه) ويُتابعُهُ في الأقوال أيضاً (أي كمـا يجب عليه أن يتابعه في الأفعال يستحب أن يتابعه في الأقوال) إلّا التأمينَ فيُقارِنُهُ فيه.

ولـوْ قارَنـهُ في تكبيرة الإحرام أوْ شَكَّ هلْ قارنـهُ لَمْ تنْعقِـدْ أوْ في غيرِه كرِه وفاتَتْهُ فضيلةُ الجماعة.

GETTING AHEAD OF THE IMAM

f12.15 It is offensive to proceed to an integral ahead of the imam, as when one bows before he does, and one is recommended to return to following him.

(N: An "integral" in rulings concerning the person who gets ahead of the imam or lags behind him refers to integrals that are physical *actions,* such as standing, bowing, straightening up, prostrating, or sitting up between prostrations. It does not refer to spoken integrals such as reciting the Fatiha, or to remaining motionless for a moment in the various positions.)

It is unlawful, though it does not invalidate the prayer, to completely finish an integral before the imam comes to it, as when one bows, straightens up, and then waits for him to straighten up.

It invalidates one's prayer to completely finish two integrals before the imam does, if one does so intentionally (O: and knowing it is unlawful). If one does so absentmindedly (O: or in ignorance of its prohibition), it does not invalidate the prayer, but the rak'a does not count (O: and one must add an additional rak'a after the imam finishes with Salams).

LAGGING BEHIND THE IMAM

f12.16 If there is no excuse (def: below), it is offensive to lag behind the imam until he completely finishes an *integral* (def: f12.15(N:)) ahead of one, and it invalidates one's prayer to lag behind the imam until he finishes two integrals.

If the imam bows and straightens up while (N: without excuse) one has not yet bowed, it does not invalidate one's prayer until the imam actually begins going down towards prostration and one still has not bowed (O: since *lagging* means that the imam has finished two integrals before the follower has reached the first of them). This invalidates one's prayer even before the imam reaches prostration, as he has completed two integrals.

f12.17 When one lags behind the imam for a valid reason, such as one's slow recital (O: the imam

---

من سبق الإمام

f12.15 وإنْ سَبَقَهُ إلى ركنٍ بأن رَكَعَ قَبْلَهُ كُرِهَ ونُدِبَ العودُ إلى متابعتِهِ .

(ح : والمراد بركنٍ في أحكام مَن سَبَقَ الإمام أو تخلف عنه هو الـركن الفعلي ، كالقيـام والـركـوع والاعتـدال والسجـود والجلوس بين السجـدتين ، وليس المراد به الركن القولي كقراءة الفاتحة ، ولا الطمأنينة) .

وإنْ سَبَقَـهُ بركنٍ بأنْ رَكَـعَ ورفَعَ ثمَّ مَكَثَ حتّى رفعَ الإمامُ حَرُمَ ولمْ يَبْطُلْ .

أو بركنينِ (أي فعليين ولو غير طويلين سبقاً) عمداً (وحال كونه عالماً بالتحريم) بَطَلَتْ أوْ سهواً (أو سبقه بهما لكنه جاهل بالتحـريم) فَلَا ، ولَا يُعْتَدُّ بهـذِهِ الـركعـةِ (فيأتي بعد سلام إمامه بركعة) .

التخلف عن الإمام

f12.16 وإنْ تَخَـلَّفَ بركـنٍ بلَا عذرٍ كُرِهَ . أو بركنينِ بَطَلَتْ فإنْ رَكَـعَ واعْتَدَلَ والمأمـوم بعـدُ قائمٌ لمْ تَبْطُلْ ، فإنْ هوى لِيَسْجُدَ وهـوَ بعدُ قائمٌ بَطَلَتْ (لأن المراد بالتخلف بهمـا فـراغ الإمام منهمـا قبـل لحـوق المأمـوم ، وإنْ لمْ يَبْلُغِ السجودَ لأنّهُ كمَّلَ الركنينِ) .

f12.17 وإنْ تَخَلَّفَ بعذرٍ كبطءِ قراءتِهِ (أي والإمام سريعٌ في قراءتـه) لعجـزٍ لَا

being fast in his recital) due to one's inability (A: whether natural inability or being a non-Arabic-speaker), not merely to unfounded misgivings (waswasa, def: s3.3), and the imam bows, then it is obligatory for one to finish the Fatiha (O: one is not entitled in such a case to simply omit the rest of the Fatiha and bow with the imam, as a latecomer is entitled to do (dis: f8.15, third par.)), after which one rapidly performs the elements of the prayer to catch up with the imam, provided the imam is not more than three (O: long) integrals ahead of one. (O: *Long* excludes the integrals of straightening up after bowing and sitting between prostrations, which are short. Rather, the imam's being *three integrals ahead* of one means he has bowed, prostrated once, and begun the second prostration, while the follower still has not bowed.)

If one is further behind than that (O: as when he has started to stand up while one is still standing for recital), then one follows from where one is (N: the number of rak'as one has done) and performs the ones missed after the imam finishes with Salams.

f12.18 When the imam is bowing or in the final Testification of Faith (Tashahhud), and becomes aware of someone coming to join the group prayer, it is recommended that he wait for the latecomer (N: so the *rak'a* counts for him if they are bowing, or so the *group prayer* counts for him if they are in the final Testification of Faith), provided:

(a) that the person has entered the mosque or place of prayer;

(b) that the wait is not excessively long;

(c) and that the imam's intention is obedience to Allah, not to give distinction or honor to the latecomer, such as by waiting for the noble but not the lowly.

Waiting for a latecomer is offensive in other than bowing and the final Testification of Faith.

لوسوسةٍ حتّى رَكَعَ الإمامُ لَزِمَهُ إتمامُ الفاتحةِ ويَسْمَعُ خلفَهُ [(أي يجري المأموم بعد إتمام فاتحته على نظم صلاته ويـلحـق الإمـام] ولا يقـاس هذا على المسبوق حيث يسقط عنه باقيها) مَا لم يَسْبِقْهُ بأكثَرَ مِنْ ثلاثةِ أركانٍ . (طويلة فلا يُعدُّ منهـا الاعتـدال ولا الجلوس بين السجدتين لأنهما ركنان قصيران فيحصل السبق بالـركـوع والسجـود الأول وتلبُّسه بالسجود الثاني) .

فإنْ زادَ (بأن رفع الإمام رأسه وشرع في القيـام إلى الثـانية مثـلًا والمأموم قائم للقـراءة) وافقَهُ فيمـا هوَ فيه ثمَّ يَتَدَارَكُ مَا فاتَهُ بعدَ سلامِه .

f12.18 وإذَا أَحَسَّ الإمامُ بداخلٍ وهوَ راكعٌ أوْ في التشهـدِ الأخيـرِ نُدِبَ انْتِظَارُهُ (ح : ليـدرك الـركعـة في الحـالـة الأولى ويدرك الجماعة في الحالة الثانية) بشرطِ أنْ يكونَ قدْ دَخَلَ المسجدَ وأنْ لا يَفْحُشَ الطـول وأنْ يَقْصِـدَ الطـاعـة لا تمييـزَهُ وإكرامَهُ بأنْ يَنْتَظِرَ الشريفَ دونَ الحقيرِ . ويُكْرَهُ في غير الركوع والتشهدِ .

f12.19 When a mosque has an imam assigned to it (O: by the person in charge of the mosque, or as a condition of an endowment (waqf, def: k30)), and the mosque is not in a busy location, it is offensive for another to commence the group prayer without the imam's permission (O: because the imamate is his, no one else's, and because of the alienation and hurt feelings it involves). It is not offensive for another to do so in a mosque at a busy location or one to which no imam has been assigned.

f12.19 ولوْ كـان لمسجـدٍ إمامُ راتبٌ (وهو من ولاه الناظر أو كان بشرط الوقف) ولمْ يَكُنْ مطروقاً كُرهَ لغيرِه إقامةُ الجماعة فيـه بغير إذنِه (لأن الإمامة له لا لغيره ولما في ذلـك من الإيحاش وإيذاء القلوب) . وإنْ كان مطروقاً أوْ لا إمام لَهُ لمْ يُكْرَهْ .

f12.20 When one has already performed one's prescribed prayer alone or in a group, and finds another group prayer being performed, it is recommended to repeat one's prayer with them, intending the obligatory prayer. (A: The first fulfills one's obligation of the prescribed prayer, but one intends repeating, e.g., the noon prayer (zuhr).) Its reward is that of a supererogatory prayer.

f12.20 ومـنْ صَلَّى منـفـرداً أوْ في جمـاعـةٍ ثمّ وَجـدَ جماعةً تُصَلِّي نُدِبَ أنْ يُعيدَ مَعهُمْ بنِّيَّةِ الفريضة . وتَقَعُ نفلاً .

f12.21 The imam is recommended to keep his recital of the sura brief (O: not necessarily the absolute minimum, but not the maximum desirable for someone praying alone).

When leading a group composed solely of those who do not mind lengthy prayers, he is recommended to lengthen the recital.

(O: The imam should not prolong the recital when he does not know how everyone feels, and of those present some generally prefer lengthy rak‘as and some do not, or when praying in a mosque at a busy location where people often join the prayer after the imam has begun.)

f12.21 ويُنَدَبُ للإمام التخفيفُ (ولا يقتصـر على الأقـل ولا يستـوفي الأكمـل المستحب للمنفرد) .
فإنْ عَلمَ رضـا محصـورينَ بالتطويل نُدِبَ حينئذٍ .
(فـإن جهل حالهم وكان فيهم من يؤثر التطويل وفيهم من لا يؤثره لم يطول . ولو كانـوا يؤثـرون التطويـل ولكن المسجد مطـروق بحيث يدخـل في الصـلاة من حضره بعد دخول الإمام فيها لم يطول) .

f12.22 When the imam stops reciting the Koran because of uncertainty, it is recommended for the follower to remind him of what comes next. (N: When he does not stop but merely hesitates, the follower does not remind him, so as not to fluster him.) If the imam forgets an invocation (dhikr), the follower says it so the imam can hear. If he forgets an *action*, the follower should remind him of it by saying "Subhan Allah" (n: with the intention of invocation, as at f9.4(O:)). If the imam

f12.22 ويُنْدَبُ تلقينُ إمامِه إنْ وَقَفَتْ قراءتُـهُ . (ح) . وأمـا إذا لم يقف بل كان يتـردد فلا يلقنه حتى لا يشـوش عليه) . وإنْ نَسيَ ذكـراً جَهَـرَ بِه المأمومُ لِيُسْمَعَهُ . أوْ فعلاً سَبَّحَ .

remembers having missed the action, he performs it. But if he does not remember having missed it, it is not permissible for him to perform it just because the followers or others are reminding him, even if they are numerous. (A: The more reliable opinion is that if their number reaches four or more, he must act upon it.)

فإنْ تَذَكَّـرَهُ الإمـامُ عَمِلَ بِه . وإنْ لمْ يَتَـذَكَّـرْهُ لمْ يَجُزْ العملُ بقولِ المأمومينَ ولا غيرِهمْ وإنْ كَثُرُوا .

f12.23 If the imam omits an obligatory element of the prayer (O: and does not return to it and perform it), then it is obligatory for the follower to cease his participation (def: f12.10) in the group prayer.

If the imam omits a sunna that the follower cannot add without considerably lagging behind, such as the first Testification of Faith (Tashahhud), then it is unlawful for the follower to perform the missing sunna (O: rather, he must follow the imam). If he performs it anyway (O: intentionally and knowing it is unlawful), it invalidates his prayer, though he is entitled to cease his participation in the group prayer to perform the sunna in the course of finishing his own prayer alone. If the sunna omitted by the imam can be done without much of a lag, such is sitting briefly before rising for a new rak‘a (def: f8.40), then the follower may add it without ceasing his participation in the group. (O: This also applies to when the imam omits the dawn prayer's supplication (f8.53), which the follower may perform it he can catch up with the imam before the imam lifts his head from the second prostration, though if the imam lifts his head before the follower has prostrated even once and the follower has not intended to cease his participation in the group prayer, then the follower's prayer is invalid.)

f12.23 وإنْ تَرَكَ فرضاً (ولم يرجع إلى الصواب) وَجَبَ فِراقُهُ . أوْ سنـةً لا تُفْعَـلُ إلّا بتَخَلُّفٍ فاحشٍ كتشهدِ حَرُمَ فعلُها (بـل يتـابـع المأمـوم الإمـام) . فإنْ فَعَلَهـا (عـامِـداً عالمـاً بالتحريم) بَطَلَتْ صلاتُـهُ ولَـهُ فِراقُـهُ لِيَفْعَلَهـا . فإنْ أُمْكَنَتْ قريبـاً كجلسـةِ الاستـراحةِ فَعَلَهـا . (والقنـوت كجلسـة الاستـراحة إذا تركه الإمام، وللمأموم أن يفعله إذا لحقه في السجـدة الأولى أو في السجـدة الثانيـة مادام متلبسـاً بها قبل أن يرفع رأسه منها فإذا رفع رأسه من السجود الثاني ولم ينو المأموم المفارقة بطلت) .

f12.24 Whenever the imam ceases his prayer because of his ablution (wudu) being nullified, or another reason, he may choose a successor to finish leading the prayer, provided the successor is eligible (def: f12.27) to lead the group. If the group performs a whole integral (f12.15(N:)) after the imam has stopped leading, then he may no longer choose a successor.

Any follower may be picked as the successor (O: even if he came late to the group prayer). If a

f12.24 ومتى قَطَعَ الإمـامُ صلاتَـهُ بحدثٍ أوْ غيـرِه فلَهُ استخلافُ منْ يُتِمُهَا بشرطِ صلاحيتِه لإمامةِ هذه الصلاة . فإنْ فَعَلُوا ركناً قبلَ الاستخلافِ امْتَنَعَ الاستخلافُ . فإنْ كانَ الخليفةُ مأموماً جَازَ استخلافُهُ مطلقاً (سواء كان موافقاً أو مسبوقاً) .

latecomer, he leads the group beginning at the same point in the prayer where the imam left off. When he finishes leading them in their prayer, he stands (O: to finish his own), and indicates to them to cease following his leadership, or better yet, indicates for them to remain waiting for him (A: in their final Testification of Faith (Tashahhud)) until he comes to it after finishing his own rak'as. If he does not know which rak'a the imam was in, then he should observe (O: by looking left or right to see if the followers are sitting or) whether they are ready to rise. If they are, he rises, and if not, then he sits in a Testification of Faith.

It is permissible for the successor to be someone who has not been praying with the group, provided he is picked in the first or third rak'a (if the prayer has four rak'as), though he may not be picked in the second or fourth rak'a (A: because the order of the person's prayer will not correspond to theirs, for such a person is not committed to the imam's order).

The followers need not intend to follow the successor. They may each simply break off and finish alone. If the imam chooses someone but they put forward someone else, their choice takes precedence.

THE IMAMATE

f12.25 The one with the best right to be imam (N: in order of preference, when there is a disagreement) is:

(1) the most learned in Sacred Law (A: i.e. the rulings concerned with prayer) (O: even if he has not memorized any of the Koran except the Fatiha, since the need in prayer for knowledge of its rules is practically unlimited, while the only Koran recital required is the Fatiha);

(2) he who has memorized the most Koran;

(3) the most godfearing (O: because leading the prayer is an embassage between the servant and Allah Most High, and best befits him most honored by Allah);

ويراعي المسبوقُ نظمَ الإمام فإذا فَرَغَ مِنْهُ قامَ (يتمم صلاتـه) وأشار ليفارقُوهُ أَوْ يَنْتَظِـرُوهُ وهـوَ أَفضَـلُ. وإنْ جَهِـلَ نظمَ الإمام راقَبَهُمْ (أي نظر جهة يمينه وجهة شماله). فإنْ هَمُّوا بالقيام قامَ وإلّا قَعَدَ.

وإنْ كانَ الخليفـةُ غيـرَ مأمـوم جازَ في الأولى وفي الثـالثـة مَنَ الـربـاعيـةِ لاَ في الثانيةِ والرابعةِ.

ولا تَجبُ نيّةُ الاقتـداءِ بالخليفـةِ، بلْ لهمْ أَنْ يُتِمُّـوا فرادَى. ولـوْقَدَّمَ الإمـامُ واحداً والقومُ آخَرَ فمُقَدَّمُهُمْ أولى.

الإمامة

f12.25 أولى النـاس بالإمـامةِ الأفقهُ (وإن لم يحفظ من القرآن إلا الفاتحة لأن افتقار الصـلاة للفقه لا ينحصـر بخلاف القـرآن المتعلق بالصـلاة فهـو محصـور ومخصوص بالفاتحة) ثمَّ الأقرأ ثُمَّ الأورعُ (لأن الإمـامة سفـارة بين العبد وبين الله تعالى والأولى بها الأكرم عنده) [ثمَّ الأقدمُ

(4) he who has been a Muslim longest;

(5) the noblest in lineage;

(6) he with the best life history or reputation;

(7) the cleanest in person and clothes;

(8) he with the best voice;

(9) and the most handsome.

When only one of the above is present, he is chosen. If all people present or some of them possess one or more of these characteristics, then someone from the first of the list takes priority over those listed after him. If two are equal and each insists on being the imam, they draw lots.

(N: It is permissible for a less qualified person to lead, even when a better qualified one is present.)

The imam assigned to a mosque or a person living in the house where the prayer takes place, even if only renting, takes precedence over everyone on the list, from the most learned on down, though he may select anyone else he wishes to lead the prayer. The sultan and those under him, of Islamic judges, regional governors, and so on, take precedence over even the imam of the mosque, the householder, and others.

The following take precedence even when the latter is more learned in Sacred Law:

(1) a nontraveller over a traveller;

(2) an upright person (def: o24.4) over a corrupt one;

(3) and an adult over a child.

A sighted and a blind person are equally eligible to lead the prayer.

f12.26 It is offensive for someone to lead a group at prayer when most of the group dislike him for a reason recognized by Sacred Law (O: such as wrongdoing, not taking precautions against filth (najasa), having a blameworthy income, keeping

هجرةً وولدُهُ] ثمَّ الأسنُّ في الإسلام، ثمَّ النسيبُ، ثمَّ الأحسنُ سيرةً ثمَّ الأحسنُ ذكراً [(والظاهر هو أن المراد به هو المراد بما قبله)] ثمَّ الأنظفُ بدناً وثوباً ثمَّ الأحسنُ صوتاً ثمَّ الأحسنُ صورةً.

فمتى وُجدَ واحدٌ من هؤلاء قُدِّمَ. وإن اجتَمعُوا أوْ بعضُهُمْ رتَّبوا هكذا. فإن استَوَيا وتَشاحَّا أُقرِعَ.

(ح: ويجوز إمامة المفضول مع وجود الفاضل.)

وإمامُ المسجدِ وساكنُ البيتِ ولوْ بإجارةٍ مقدمانِ على الأفقهِ ومَا بعدَهُ. ولهمَا تقديمُ مَنْ أرَادَا. والسلطانُ والأعلى فالأعلى منَ القُضاةِ والولاةِ يُقَدَّمُونَ على الساكنِ وإمام المسجدِ وغيرِهِما.

ويُقَدَّمُ حاضرٌ [وحرٌّ] وعدلٌ وبالغٌ على مسافرٍ [وعبدٍ] وفاسقٍ وصبيٍّ، وإنْ كانوا أفقه.

والبصيرُ والأعمى سواءٌ.

f12.26 ويُكرَهُ أنْ يؤُمَّ قوماً مَنْ يَكرَهُهُ أكثرُهُمْ بسببٍ شرعيٍّ (كظلمٍ أو عدم توقي نجاسةٍ أو تعاطي معيشةٍ مذمومةٍ أو

the company of oppressors or the immoral, and so forth. If a minority dislike him, it is not offensive, for nobody lacks someone who dislikes him).

معـاشـرة الظلمـة والفسقـة . أما إذا كرهه أقلهم فلا كراهة إذ لا يخلو أحد عمن يكرهه) .

f12.27 It is not permissible (O: or valid) to follow an imam who is non-Muslim, insane, in a state of ritual impurity (def: e7, e10), or who has filth (najasa) on his clothing or person, or is a woman leading men, or someone who omits or mispronounces (def: f8.18) a letter of the Fatiha leading someone who knows it, or a mute, or someone who slurs the words so the letters are indistinct from one another, or someone with a lisp.

If after the prayer one finds out that the imam was one of the above, then one must make up the prayer, unless the imam had filth upon him that was concealed, or he was in a state of ritual impurity (N: in which cases one need not make it up).

f12.27 ولاَ يَجُوزُ (ولا يصح) الاقتداءُ بكـافـر ولا مجنـون ولا محـدثٍ ولا ذي نجـاسـةٍ ولا رجُل [وختنَى] بامرأةٍ ولا مَنْ يَحْفَظُ الفـاتحـة بمَنْ يُخِلُّ بحرفٍ مِنْها أوْ بأْخْرَسَ أوْ أرَتَّ أوْ ألثغَ .

فإنْ ظَهَرَ بعـدَ الصـلاةِ أنَّ إمامَهُ واحدٌ مِنْ هؤلاءِ لزمَهُ الإعـادةُ إلاَّ إذَا كانَ علَيْـهِ نجـاسـةٌ خفيـةٌ أوْ كانَ محـدثـاً [في غيـر الجمعـةِ أوْ فيهـا وهـوَ زائدٌ على الأربعينَ فإنْ كَمَلَتْ به الأربعونَ وجَبَتْ الإعادةُ] .

f12.28 The group prayer is valid:

(1) when the imam is performing a supererogatory prayer and the follower is performing a prescribed prayer, or vice versa;

(2) when the imam is performing the noon prayer (zuhr) and the follower is praying the dawn prayer (subh) (A: i.e. when the type of prayer differs), or vice versa;

(3) when the imam is praying while sitting and the follower is praying standing, or vice versa;

(4) and when the imam is performing a makeup prayer and the follower is performing a current one, or vice versa.

(n: But a person shortening his prayer because of travelling may not pray behind an imam who is performing the full number, as at f15.8(f).)

f12.28 ويَـصِـحُّ فرضٌ خلفَ نفـلٍ وصبـحٌ خلفَ ظهـرٍ وقـائمٌ خلفَ قاعـدٍ وأداءٌ خلفَ قضاءٍ وبالعكس [(أي عكس ما تقدم من ابتداء قوله ويصح فرض الخ)] .

f12.29 It is valid for a Shafi'i to follow the leadership of an imam who follows a different school of jurisprudence whenever the follower is not certain that the imam has omitted an obligatory element

f12.29 ولو اقْتَدَى بغيرِ شافعيٍّ صَحَّ إنْ لم يَتَيَقَّنْ أنَّـهُ أخَـلَّ بواجِبٍ . وإلاَّ فَلاَ .

of the prayer, though if certain the imam has omitted one, it is not valid to follow him. The validity is based solely on the belief of the follower as to whether or not something obligatory has been omitted.

(N: One should mention the position of the Malikis and Hanbalis here, which is that the criterion for the validity of following the imam is the *imam's* school of jurisprudence, such that if his prayer is valid in his own school, it is permissible to follow him as imam. How close this is to the spirit of the Law, which strives for Muslim unity.)

f12.30 It is offensive to take an immoral person (def: o24.3(A:)) as imam (O: because he might not be concerned about the things that are obligatory in the prayer), or someone who stutters over the letter *f* or the letter *t*, or who makes inconsequential mistakes in the Arabic vowelling (O: that do not change the meaning).

RULES AND CONDITIONS OF FOLLOWING

f12.31 When there are two or more male followers, it is sunna for them to stand behind the imam. A single male follower stands on the imam's right, and if a second follower arrives, the newcomer stands to the imam's left and says his opening Allahu Akbar, after which the two followers move back (O: little by little). If they cannot move back (O: for lack of room) then the imam moves forward.

f12.32 When there are men, boys, and women present, the men form the front row or rows, then the boys, and then the women. (A: This is also the rule for husband and wife: the wife prays in a separate row behind the husband.)

(O: If the men's back row is incomplete, it **should** be completed with boys (A: and a latecomer may not remove the boys to make a **place** for himself unless they are directly behind the imam). Those who form a new row behind a row that is incomplete do not attain the merit of group prayer.)

والاعتبارُ باعتقادِ المأمومِ .

(ح : ومن الجدير بالإشارة هنا مذهب المالكية والحنابلة إذ يرون أن العبرة بمذهب الإمام ، فإذا كانت صلاته صحيحة في مذهبه جاز الاقتداء به ، وما أقرب هذا إلى روح الشريعة الحريصة على جمع الكلمة) .

f12.30 ويُكْرَهُ وراءَ فاسقٍ (لأنه يخاف منه أن لا يحافظ على الواجبات) وفأفاءٍ وتمتامٍ ولاحنٍ (لما لا يغير المعنى) .

شروط القدوة وآدابها

f12.31 السنة أنْ يَقِفَ الذَكَـرانِ فصاعـداً خلفَ الإمـام . والذَكرُ الواحدُ عنْ يمينهِ ، فإنْ جاءَ آخرُ أحْرَمَ عنْ يساره ثمَّ يَتَـأَخَـرانِ (شيئاً فشيئاً) إنْ أمْكَن . وإلاَّ (أي وإن لم يمكن التأخر لضيق المكان) تَقَدَّم الإمامُ .

f12.32 وإنْ حَضَـرَ رجـالٌ وصبيـانٌ ونسـاءٌ تَقَـدَّمَ الـرجـالُ ثمَّ الصبيـانُ ثمَّ النسـاء . (وهذا كله إن استوعب الرجال الصف وإلا فيكمـل صفهم بالصبيـان كلهـم أو ببـعـضهـم . وتـفـوت فضيلة الجماعة إذا وقف صف قبل تمام ما أمامه) .

A woman leading women in prayer stands in the middle of their first row.

وتَقِفُ إمامةُ النساءِ وسَطَهُنَّ.

f12.33 It is offensive for the imam's place to be higher or lower than the followers' unless the imam wishes to teach the followers the actions of prayer. If the imam and follower are not in a mosque, it is obligatory that part of the imam's body be level with part of the follower's when both are of average height.

f12.33 ويُكْرَهُ أنْ يَرْتَفِعَ موقِفُ الإمام على المأمومِ وعكسُهُ إلّا أن يُريدَ الإمامُ تعليمَهُمْ أفعالَ الصلاةِ [أوْ يَكُونَ المأمومُ مبلغاً عنِ الإمامِ فيُنْدَبُ]. لكنْ إنْ كانَا في غيـرِ مسجـدٍ وَجَبَ أنْ يُحَـاذِيَ الأسفـلُ الأعلى ببعضِ بَدَنِه بشرْطِ اعْتِدَالِ الخِلقةِ.

f12.34 A latecomer to a group prayer who does not find a place in the last row should stand behind it, begin his prayer with the opening Allahu Akbar, and then indicate to someone in the row to stand with him, by drawing him back; and it is recommended that the person selected cooperate by stepping back (A: this is only if the latecomer does not expect anyone else to come).

f12.34 ومنْ لمْ يجِدْ في الصفِّ فُرْجَةً أحْرَمَ ثمَّ يَجْذِبُ لنفسِه واحداً منَ الصفِّ ليقِف مَعَهُ ويُنْدَبُ لذلكَ مساعدتُهُ.

f12.35 The follower's prayer is invalid if his heel is farther forward than the imam's. (O: He should be farther back than the imam's heel, even if only a little, but not more than 1.44 meters, for otherwise the merit of group prayer is lost (A: i.e. unrewarded, though not legally invalid).)

f12.35 ولوْ تَقَدَّمَ عَقِبُ المأمومِ على عقِبِ الإمامِ لمْ تَصِحَّ صلاتُهُ (فينبغي أن يتأخرَ عن عقِبِه ولـو قليلاً بحيث لا يبعد عنه أكثرَ من ثلاثةِ أذرعٍ وإلا فاتت الفضيلة).

f12.36 Whenever an imam leads a follower in a mosque, the group prayer is valid no matter if they are at a distance from each other, and no matter whether they are in the same chamber or not, as when one of them is on the roof (even if the door is closed) and the other is in the mosque's well, provided that (O: both places open onto the mosque, and that) the follower can know when the imam is performing the motions of the prayer, whether by seeing the imam, or hearing his *backup man* (muballigh, the person who repeats the imam's Allahu Akbars and Salams in a loud voice so people can hear).

Multiple interconnected mosques opening onto each other are considered as one mosque (O: and so are the mosque's outer courtyards, even when there is a walkway between the courtyard and mosque).

f12.36 ومتى اجْتَمَعَ المأمومُ والإمامُ في مسجِدٍ صَحَّ الاقتِداءُ مطلقاً وإنْ تَباعَدا أو اخْتَلَفَ البناءُ مثلَ أنْ يَقِفَ أحدُهُما في السطحِ والآخَرُ في بئرٍ في المسجدِ وإنْ أُغْلِقَ بابُ السطحِ (بشرطِ أنْ يكونَ كل من البئرِ والسطحِ نافذاً إليه) لكنْ يُشْتَرطُ العلمُ بانتقالاتِ الإمامِ إمَّا بمشاهدةٍ أو سماعِ مبلغٍ.
والمسـاجـدُ المتـلاصِقةُ المتنـافـذةُ كمسجـدٍ واحـدٍ (ورحبةُ المسجـد لهـا حكمـه سواء كان بينهـا وبين المسجـد طريق أم لا).

MAXIMAL DISTANCES BETWEEN
THE IMAM AND FOLLOWERS

المسافة بين الإمام والمأموم

f12.37   When the imam and follower are not in a mosque, but are in an open expanse such as a desert or large house, their group prayer is valid as long as the distance between them does not exceed approximately 144 meters. If farther apart than this, their group prayer is not valid. If there are rows of people behind the imam, this distance is the maximum that is valid between each row and the one in front of it, even if there are miles between the imam and the last row, or a fire, river that would have to be swum to reach him, or busy street between them.

　　If the imam is in one building and the follower in another, such as two houses, or if there is a house, inn, or school where the imam is in a courtyard and the follower is under a covered porch, or vice versa, then the maximum allowable distance is the same as for outdoors (def: above), provided that there is nothing between the imam and follower that obstructs passage to the imam, such as a latticework window (O: and provided that there is nothing that prevents the follower from seeing him, such as a closed door).

　　The group prayer is valid when the imam is in a mosque and the follower is in an adjoining space, provided that there is 144 meters or less between the follower and the edge of the mosque, and that between the follower and the mosque there is not a barrier lacking a breach in it, *breach* meaning, for example, when the follower is standing before a wall's open gate. If such a person's group prayer with the imam is thus valid, then the prayer of those behind him or in the row with him is also valid, even when (O: these others are numerous, and) the group extends beyond the area fronting the gate. Such a person's group prayer is not valid if he turns from the gate, or if the wall of the mosque, a window, or a closed door (locked or not) lies between him and the imam.

f12.37   ولوْ كانَـا في غيـرِ مسجدٍ في فضاءٍ كصحراءَ أوْ بيتٍ واسعٍ صحَّ اقتداءُ المأمومِ بالإمامِ إنْ لمْ يزدْ ما بينَهُمَا على ثلثمائة ذراعٍ تقريباً. وإلاَّ فَلا . ولوْ صلَّى خلفَـهُ صفـوفٌ اعتُبـرَتْ الأذرعُ بين كلِّ صفٍ والصفِّ الذي قدامَهُ وإنْ بلَغَ ما بيْنَ الأخيرِ والإمامِ أميالٌ سواءٌ حَالَ بينَهُما نارٌ أوْ بحـرٌ يُحـوجُ إلى سبـاحـةٍ أوْ شارعٌ مطروقٌ أم لا .

ولوْ وقَفَ كلُ منهُمَا في بناءٍ كبيتيْن أوْ أحدُهُمَـا في صحنٍ والآخـرُ في صُفَّةٍ منْ دارٍ أوْ خانٍ أوْ مدرسَـةٍ فَحُكـمُـهُ حكمُ الفضـاءِ بشـرط أنْ لا يحـولَ ما يَمْنـعُ الاستطـراقَ كشبـاكٍ (أو الـرؤيـة كبابٍ مردود) [وقيـلَ إنْ كانَ بناءُ المأمـومِ عنْ يمينِهِ أوْ شمالِهِ وجَبَ الاتصالُ بحيث لا يبْقَى ما يسَعُ واقفاً . وإنْ كان خلفَهُ وجَبَ أنْ لا يزيدَ على ثلاثةِ أذرعٍ] .

ولوْ وَقَفَ الإمامُ في المسجدِ والمأمومُ في فضاءٍ متصلٍ بهِ صحَّ إنْ لمْ يزدْ ما بينَهُ وبينَ آخرِ المسجدِ على ثلثمائة ذراعٍ ولمْ يحُـلْ حائـلٌ مثل أنْ يقِفَ قبالةَ البابِ وهو مفتـوحٌ فإذا صحَّتْ لهـذا صحَّتْ لمن خلفَهُ أو اتَّصَـلَ بهِ وإنْ (كثرُوا و) خَرَجُوا عنْ قبـالةِ البابِ فإنْ عَدَلَ عنْ قبالةِ البابِ أوْ حَالَ جدارُ المَسجـدِ أوْ شبـاكُـهُ أوْ بابُهُ المردودُ وإنْ لمْ يُقْفَلْ لمْ تَصِحَّ .

*

f13.0 TIMES WHEN THE PRAYER IS FORBIDDEN

f13.0 الأوقـات الـتي نهي عن الصلاة فيها

f13.1 (O: The rules below apply to prayers that are wholly supererogatory, i.e. which are not performed for any particular occasion or reason, and apply to prayers performed for a reason that will occur after the prayer, such as the two sunna rak'as before entering the state of pilgrim sanctity (ihram).)

f13.1 (أي النـافلة المطلقـة التي لا سبب لهـا أصلاً أوْ لها سبب متأخر عن الصلاة وذلك كسنة الإحرام).

f13.2 The prayer is unlawful and invalid:

(1) from sunrise until the sun is *a spear's length* above the horizon (N: meaning when a distance equal to the sun's diameter appears between the sun and the horizon);

(2) from the time the sun is at its highest point in the sky until it moves on;

(3) from when the sun yellows before sunset until after it has set;

(4) after praying the current dawn prayer (subh);

(5) and after praying the current midafternoon prayer ('asr).

f13.2 تَحْـرُمُ الصـلاةُ ولاَ تَنْعَقِـدُ عندَ طلوع الشمس حتَّى تَرْتَفِـعَ قدرَ رمـح وعنـدَ الاسـتـواء حتـى تَزُولَ، وعنـدَ الاصـفـرار حتَّى تَغْـرُبَ، وبعـدَ صلاة الصبح وبعدَ صلاة العصرِ.

f13.3 It is permissible at the above times to offer nonobligatory prayers that are performed for a particular reason, such as the funeral prayer, greeting the mosque (def: f10.10), or the two rak'as that are sunna after ablution (wudu); and is also permissible to make up missed prayers; though one may not perform the two rak'as that are sunna before entering the state of pilgrim sanctity (ihram).

f13.3 ولا يَحْـرُمُ فيهَـا مَا لهُ سبـبٌ كجنـازةٍ وتحيـةِ مسجـدٍ وسنةٍ وضـوءٍ وفائتةٍ، لا ركعتَيْ الإحرام.

f13.4 It is not offensive to pray within the Meccan Sacred Precinct (Haram) at any time.
Nor is it offensive to pray when the sun is at its zenith on Fridays (N: whether in the Sacred Precinct or elsewhere).

f13.4 ولا تُكْرَهُ الصلاةُ في حرم مكةَ مطلقاً.
ولا عندَ الاستواء يوم الجمعةِ.

f14.0 THE PRAYER OF A SICK PERSON	f14.0 صلاة المريض

f14.1   Someone unable to stand may pray the prescribed prayer seated (O: and need not make it up), *unable* meaning that standing involves manifest hardship, will cause illness or the worsening of a present illness, or cause vertigo, as when one is on a ship.

Such a person may sit for the prayer any way he likes, though the *iftirash* style of sitting (def: f8.37) is recommended. It is offensive in prayer to simply sit on the ground, palms down and knees drawn up, or to sit with legs outstretched (A: when there is no excuse).

f14.1   للعـاجز صلاةُ الفرض قاعداً (ولا إعـادة عليـه) والمـراد مِن العجـز أن يَشُقَّ عليْهِ القيامُ مشقةً ظاهرةً أوْ يَخَافَ منهُ مرضاً أوْ زيادتَهُ أوْ دورانَ الرأسِ في سفينةٍ.

ويَقْعُـدُ كيفَ شاءَ ويُنْـدَبُ الافتـراشُ ويُكْرَهُ الإقعاءُ ومدُّ رِجلِهِ.

f14.2   When seated for the prayer, the minimal *bowing* is to incline until the forehead is farther forward than the knees. The optimal way is to incline until the forehead is as far forward as the place where the head rests in prostration.

When unable to bow or prostrate, one comes as close to the ground with the forehead as one can. When unable to do this, one performs them by nodding.

f14.2   وأقلُّ ركوعـهِ محـاذاةُ جبهتِهِ قدّامَ ركبتيْهِ وأكملُهُ محاذاتُها موضعَ سجوده.

فإنْ عَجَـزَ عنْ ركوعٍ وسجودٍ فَعَل نهـايـةَ الممكن مِنْ تقريب الجبهةِ مِنَ الأرضِ فإنْ عَجَزَ أوْمَأ بهِمَا.

f14.3   If an abscess or the like prevents one from sitting, then one "sits" standing (A: meaning ordinary standing, with the intention of sitting (N: so that one stands between prostrations and for the Testification of Faith (Tashahhud))).

f14.3   ولـوْ عَجـزَ عن القعـود فقـطْ لدملٍ ونحوِه أتى بالقعودِ قائماً.

f14.4   If one is capable of standing but suffers from a painful swelling of the eyes or something similar (O: such as a wound that can be treated by having the patient remain lying down) and a reliable physician (O: in terms of knowledge and expertise in medicine, who can be believed) tells one that praying while on one's back will enable one to be treated, then it is permissible to pray while lying down (O: without having to make up the prayer).

f14.4   ولـوْ أمْكَنَـهُ القيـامُ وبـهِ رمدٌ أوْ غيـرُهُ (أي كجراحـةٍ يمكن علاجها مع إدامـة الاستلقاء) فَقَالَ لَهُ طبيبٌ معتمـدٌ (بسبب معرفتِه وحذقِه في صنعة الطب أهـل للروايـة) «إنْ صَلَّيْتَ مستلقياً أمْكَنَ مداواتُكَ» جَازَ الاستلقاءُ (ولا إعادة عليه).

f14.5   If unable to stand and unable to sit, one lies on one's right side (O: the right is recom-

f14.5   ولـوْ عَجَـزَ عنْ قيـامٍ وقعـودٍ اضْطَجَعَ على جنبِهِ الأيمن (ندباً) مستقبلاً

mended) facing the direction of prayer (qibla) with the face and front of one's body, though one must bow and prostrate if possible (O: meaning one stands up enough to bow, then bows, then prostrates; or else sits up and bows).

If this is not possible, one bows and prostrates by merely nodding one's head (O: bringing one's forehead as near to the ground as possible), deeper for prostration than for bowing.

If unable to even nod, one merely glances down with the eyes for bowing and prostration. If one cannot, one goes through the integrals of the prayer in one's mind. If unable to speak (O: to recite the Fatiha) one recites it in one's heart.

The obligation of prayer exists as long as one is able to reason (dis: f1.1, second par.).

بوجهِهِ ومقـدم بدنِهِ ويَركَعُ ويَسْجُدُ (أي يقـوم إلى حد الـركـوع ويـركـع ثم يهوي للسجـود أو يقعـد ويـركـع) ثم يهـوي للسجود أو يقعد ويركع) إنْ أمْكَنَ .

وإلّا أوْمَـأ برأسِهِ (ويقـرب جبهتـه من الأرض بحسب الإمكان) والسجودُ أخفضُ .

فإنْ عَجـزَ فبطرفِهِ . فإنْ عَجـزَ فبقلبِهِ (أي بإجراء الأركان عليه) فإنْ خَرِسَ (ولمْ يقدر على قراءة الفاتحة بلسانه) قَرَأ بقلبِهِ .

ولا تَسْقُطُ الصلاةُ مَادامَ يَعْقِلُ .

f14.6 If one is standing during the prayer and becomes unable to remain standing, one sits to finish the prayer. If this occurs during the Fatiha, one may not interrupt reciting it, but must continue to do so as one proceeds to sit.

If one's condition improves enough (O: i.e. if seated during a prescribed prayer because of illness and a recovery of strength enables one to now stand), then one must stand to complete the prayer.

f14.6 فإنْ عَجـزَ في أثنـائِهـا قَعَـدَ . ويجِبُ الاستمرار في الفاتحةِ إنْ عَجزَ في أثنائِها .

وإنْ خَفَّ (أي ممـا به من المـرض في أثنـاء صلاتِه قاعداً بحيث صار قادراً على القيام) قَامَ .

f14.7 [فإنْ كانَ في أثناء الفاتحة وَجَبَ الإمساكُ لِيَقْرأ قائماً . فإنْ قَرأ في نهوضِهِ لمْ يُعْتَدَ بِهِ . وإنْ خَفَّ بعدَ الفاتحة قَامَ لِيَرْكَعَ منهُ . أو في الركوعِ قبلَ الطمأنينةِ ارْتَفَعَ راكماً، فإنِ انْتَصَبَ بَطَلَتْ، أو بعدَها اعْتَدَلَ قائماً ثُمَّ يَسْجُدُ . أو في اعتدالِهِ قبلَ الطمأنينةِ قامَ لِيَعْتَدِلَ . أو بعدَها سَجَدَ ولا يَقوُمُ] .

*

f15.0 SHORTENING OR JOINING PRAYERS FOR TRAVEL OR RAIN

(A: The two travel dispensations of shortening and joining prayers have no effect on each other: one may take both together, either, or none. It is superior in our school not to take dispensations that are permissible.)

f15.0 القـصـر والجمـع للسفر أو المطر

(ع: القصـر والجمـع للمسـافـر رخصتـان منفصلتـان؛ فيجـوز الأخـذ بإحداهما فقط، أو بهما معاً، أو تركهما . والأفضل ترك الرخص الجائزة) .

SHORTENING PRAYERS WHILE TRAVELLING

شروط القصر

f15.1   It is permissible to shorten the current prescribed prayers of noon (zuhr), midafternoon ('asr), and nightfall ('isha) to two rak'as each, when one:

(a) is travelling for a reason that is not disobedience to Allah (O: as there is no dispensation to shorten prayers on such a trip);

(b) on a journey of at least 48 Hashemite miles (n: approximately 81 km./50 mi.) one way.

One may also shorten the above prayers when one both misses them and makes them up on the trip, though one must pray the full number if one misses them while not travelling and makes them up on the trip, or misses them on the trip and makes them up while not travelling.

f15.1   إذا سافَرَ في غيرِ معصيةٍ (فلا يباح القصر معها) سفراً تَبْلُغُ مسيرتُهُ ذهاباً ثمانيةً وأربعينَ ميلاً بالهاشميِّ [وهو يومان بلا ليليهما بسير الأثقال]، فلهُ أنْ يصلِّيَ الظهرَ والعصرَ والعشاءَ ركعتَينِ إذا كانَتْ مؤدياتٍ، أوْ فائتةً في السفرِ فَقَضاهَا في السفرِ. فإنْ فاتَتْهُ في الحضرِ فَقَضاهَا في السفرِ أوْ عكسُهُ أتَمَّ.

f15.2   This distance (n: 81 km./50 mi. one way) holds for travel by water as well as by land. If such a distance is traversed in an instant (O: preternaturally, because of a miracle (karama, def: w30)), one may still shorten the prayer. (O: The brevity of the time taken to travel the distance is of no consequence.)

f15.2   وفي البحرِ تُعْتَبَرُ هذهِ المسافةُ كَمَا في البرِّ فَلَوْ قَطَعَهَا في لحظةٍ (على خلافِ العادةِ للكرامةِ) قَصَرَ (فلا يؤثر قطعها في زمن يسير).

f15.3   When there are two routes to a destination and one of them is less than the distance that permits shortening prayers but one chooses the longer way for a legitimate purpose such as safety, convenience, or recreation (O: provided that recreation is merely the reason for taking that route, not the reason for the trip itself, which must have some other legitimate purpose such as trade, for an *outing* is not a legitimate purpose) then one may shorten prayers. But if the only reason for choosing the longer way is to take the dispensation, then doing so is not valid and one must pray the full number.

(A: Purely recreational trips whose purpose is not disobedience are permissible, but there are no travel dispensations in them, though if undertaken in order to gain religious knowledge, to visit

f15.3   ولوْ قَصَدَ بلداً لَهُ طريقانِ أحدُهُما دونَ مسافةِ القصرِ فَسَلَكَ الأبعدَ لغرضٍ كأمنٍ وسهولةٍ ونزهةٍ قَصَرَ (والحالَ أن التنزه هو الحامل على سلوك ذلك الطريق وليس حاملاً على أصل السفر بل الحامل عليه غيره كالتجارة مثلاً ولا بدَّ أن يكون الحامل على السفر غرضاً صحيحاً وليس التنزه منه) وإنْ قَصَدَ مُجَرَّدَ

a fellow Muslim, or visit the grave of a righteous or learned Muslim (dis: g5.8), these and similar purposes are legitimate and permit the dispensations.)

القصرُ أتَمَّ .

f15.4   The journey's destination must be known. If a wife travelling with her husband or a soldier with his leader does not know the destination, they may not shorten their prayers (N: as long as they have not yet travelled the distance that permits shortening. When they have travelled it, then they may). If they know the destination and the journey meets the conditions (def: f15.1), then they may shorten their prayers (N: from the beginning of the journey).

f15.4   ولا بدَّ مِنْ مقصِدٍ معلوم فلوْ [طَلَبَ آبقاً لا يَعْرفُ موضعَهُ أوْ] سَافَرَ [عبدٌ و] امرأةٌ وجنديٌّ مع [سيدٍ و] زوجٍ وأميرٍ ولمْ يَعْرفوا المقصدَ لمْ يَقْصُرُوا (ح: ما لم يقطعــوا مســافةَ القصرِ فإذا قطعوها قصروا) . وإنْ عَرَفُوا قَصَرُوا (ح: من أول السفر) بشرطِهِ .

f15.5   Someone whose journey constitutes an act of disobedience, such as a woman travelling against her husband's wishes, may not shorten their prayer but must pray the full number. (O: The same applies to someone who undertakes a legitimate trip and then changes the purpose of it to disobedience.) (N: Though shortening prayers is permissible for someone who commits an act of disobedience while *on* a legitimate trip, as when someone travels for trade, but then sins by drinking wine, for example.)

f15.5   والعــاصِي بسفرِه كـ[آبقٍ و] ناشـزةٍ يُتِمُ (وكـذا لو أنشأه مبـاحاً ثم قلبه معصية) (ح: أمـا لو عصى في السفر فله القصر كما لو سافر لتجارة فعصى بشرب الخمر مثلاً) .

THE BEGINNING OF THE JOURNEY

ابتداء السفر

f15.6   If one's city has walls, one may begin shortening prayers as soon as one has passed them, whether or not there are other buildings outside them. If there are no walls, one may shorten one's prayers after passing beyond the last buildings, excluding farms, orchards, and cemeteries. (N: When the buildings of a city extend to the next city, one's journey begins at the former's city limits, or at what people commonly acknowledge (def: f4.5) to be the edge of town.) A desert dweller may begin shortening prayers when he passes beyond his people's tents. (O: A person living in a valley begins shortening prayers when he has traversed the distance of the valley's width. Someone living on a hill begins when he comes down

f15.6   ثمَّ إنْ كَان للبــلدِ سورٌ قَصَـرَ بمجـرد مجاوزتِه سواءٌ كانَ خارجُهُ عمارة أمْ لا . وإنْ لمْ يَكُنْ لهُ سورٌ فبمجـاوزة العمران كلِه ولا يُشْتَرطُ مجاوزةُ المزارع والبســاتيـن والمقـابـــر . والمقيمُ في الصحراء يَقْصُرُ بمفارقةِ خيام قومِهِ . (وإن سكن وادِيـاً وسـافـر منه اشتـرط مجاوزة عرضه ، وإن كان نازلاً في ربوة

from it. A person living in a gorge begins when he climbs up out of it.)

اشـترط أن يهـبط منها أوفي وهدة اشترط أن يقصد إلى أعلاها).

THE END OF THE JOURNEY

انتهاء السفر

f15.7   When the trip ends one must pray the full number of rak'as for each prayer.

A trip *ends* when one reaches one's hometown. It also ends:

(1) by the mere intention to stay in a place at least 4 full days, not counting the day one arrives or the day one departs;

(2) or by staying that long without the intention, so that after one has stayed 4 full days, not counting the days of arrival and departure, one prays the full number of rak'as, unless one is staying in a place in order to fulfill a purpose that one expects to accomplish and intends to leave as soon as one does. As long as this is the case, one may shorten one's prayers for up to 18 days. If longer than this, one prays the full number. This holds for both jihad (def: o9) and other purposes.

When one reaches one's destination and intends to stay there for a significant amount of time (O: 4 days), one must pray the full number of rak'as, but if not (O: as when not intending to stay at all, or intending 3 days or less), then one may continue shortening prayers for either 4 days (O: if one learns that one cannot accomplish one's purpose during them), or 18, if one can expect one's purpose to be accomplished at any moment.

f15.7   ثُمَّ إذا انْتَهَى السفرُ أتَمَّ. ويَنْتَهِي بوصـولِه إلى وطنِه أو بنيةِ إقامةِ أربعةِ أيام غيرَ يومَي الدخولِ والخروج أوْ بنفسِ الإقامةِ وإنْ لمْ ينوِهَا، فمتَى أقامَ أربعةَ أيام غيرَ يومَي الدخولِ والخروج أتَمَّ. [اللهم،] إلاَّ أنْ يُقيمَ لحـاجةٍ يَتوَقَّعُ نجـازَهَا ويَنْوِي الارتحال إذا انْقَضَتْ فإنَّه يَقْصُرُ إلى ثمـانيـة عَشَـر يوماً فإنْ تَأخَّرَتْ عنْهَا أتَمَّ وسواءٌ الجهادُ وغيرُه. ولوْ وَصَلَ مقصدَهُ فإنْ نَوَى الإقـامةَ المـؤثرةَ (وهيَ أربعـةَ أيام) أتَمَّ وإلاَّ (أي وإن لم ينوِ الإقامةَ أصلاً أو نوى إقـامةَ ثلاثـة أيـام فأقل) قَصَرَ إلى أربعةِ أيام (إن علم أن حاجتـه لم تنقض فيهـا) أوْ ثمـانيةَ عَشَـر إنْ تَوَقَّعَ حاجتَهُ كلَّ وقتٍ.

THE CONDITIONS FOR SHORTENING THE PRAYER

شروط القصر

f15.8   The conditions for shortening the prayer while travelling are:

(a) (O: that the trip be legitimate (def: f15.5);

(b) that it be at least 81 km./50 mi. one way;

f15.8   وشـروطُ القصـر (الأول عبر عنـه بقوله إذا سافر في غير معصية والثاني عبر عنه بقوله تبلغ مسيرته ثمانية وأربعين ميـلاً والثالـث عبـر عنـه بقـوله ولا بد من

(c) that the destination be known (f15.4));

(d) that the prayer take place from start to finish while on the trip (A: if one's vehicle arrives before the prayer is finished, one prays the full number);

(e) that the intention to shorten the prayer coincide with the opening Allahu Akbar (O: it not being valid if made after this);

(f) that no portion of the prayer be performed while following an imam who is praying the full number of rak'as;

(g) (O: that one be aware of the permissibility of shortening prayers for travel;

(h) and that the intention be free of things which nullify it (A: such as vacillation or doubts (dis: below))).

One must pray the full number of rak'as if:

(1) (non-(d) above) the intention to stay at the place for 4 days occurs during the prayer;

(2) (non-(h)) one is uncertain whether one's intention was to shorten, but one soon recalls that one did intend it;

(3) (non-(h)) one vacillates in the intention between shortening the prayer or not doing so;

(4) or (non-(f)) one does not know whether one's imam is shortening or not, though if one does not know the imam's intention, it is valid to intend that if the imam shortens the prayer, one will shorten, and if he prays the full number, one will pray the full number, and then to do this.

JOINING TWO PRAYERS DURING A JOURNEY

f15.9 It is permissible to join the noon prayer (zuhr) and midafternoon prayer ('asr) during the time of either of them (N: or the Friday prayer (jumu'a) and midafternoon prayer in the time of

مقصـد معلوم و) وقـوعُ الصــلاة كلّهـا في السفـر ونيـةُ القصر في الإحـرام (أي مع تكبيـرة التحـرم فلو نوى بعـدَها لم ينفعه) وأن لاَ يَقْتَـدِيَ بمُتِمّ في جزءٍ منَ الصـلاة (وعلمه بجواز القصر وتحرزه عما ينافي نيته) .

فلَوْ نَوَى الإقـامـةَ في الصـلاةِ أوْشَكَّ هلْ نَوَى القصرَ أمْ لاَ ثمَّ ذَكَرَ قريباً أنَّهُ نَوَاهُ أوْ تَرَدَّدَ هلْ يُتِمُّ أمْ لاَ أوْ هل إمـامُهُ مقيمٌ أمْ لاَ أتَمَّ . ولـوْ جَهِلَ نية إمامِهِ فنَوَى إنْ قَصَرَ قَصَرْتُ وإن أتَمَّ أتْمَمْتُ صَحَّ ، فإنْ قَصَرَ قصَرَ وإنْ أتَمَّ أتَمَّ .

الجمع في السفر

f15.9 يَجُـوزُ الجمـعُ بينَ الظهـرِ والعصـرِ في وقتِ أحدِهِمَا وبينَ المغرب

the Friday prayer), and permissible to similarly join the sunset prayer (maghrib) and nightfall prayer ('isha) during the time of either, provided one joins them during a journey in which prayer may be shortened (def: f15.8(a,b,c,d)).

If one stops travelling (A: to rest, for example) during the time of the first of the two prayers, then this is the best time to join them, but if one is travelling steadily during the first's time, the time of the second is better.

f15.10 The conditions for joining two prescribed prayers on a trip in the time of the first of them are:

(a) that the trip continue (A: until one finishes both prayers);

(b) that the first of the two be prayed first;

(c) that the intention to join the two prayers occur before finishing the first, either coinciding with the opening Allahu Akbar, or occurring during the prayer;

(d) and that one not separate the two prayers by waiting between them, though a short interval (A: meaning one that could contain two rak'as of the briefest possible) is of no consequence, nor is a brief search for water (dis: e12.3) by someone who has performed dry ablution (tayammum).

If one prays the second of the two prayers before the first (non-(b) above), then that prayer is invalid (O: and must be repeated after the first, if one still wants to join them).

One must wait to perform the second of the two prayers until its own time if:

(1) (non-(a) above) one finishes one's journey before performing the second prayer;

(2) (non-(c)) one neglects to intend joining them during the first prayer;

(3) or (non-(d)) one waits at length between them.

والعشاءِ كذلكَ في كلِّ سفرٍ تُقْصَرُ الصلاةُ فيه

فإنْ كَانَ نازلاً في وقتِ الأولى فالتقديمُ أفضلُ وإنْ كَانَ سائراً فالتأخيرُ أفضلُ .

f15.10 وإذا جَمَعَ تقديماً فشرطُهُ دوامُ السفـرِ وتقـديـمُ الأولى ونيـةُ الجمـع قبـلَ فراغِ الأولى إمّا في الإحرام أوْ في أثنائهَا وأنْ لَا يُفَـرِّقَ بينَهُـما فإنْ فَرَّقَ يسيراً (ع : وضابطها أن يسع ما بينهما ركعتين بأقل ما يمكن) لمْ يَضُرَّ فَيُغْتَفَرُ للمتيمم طلبُ خفيفٌ .

فإنْ قَدَّمَ الثـانيـةَ فبـاطلةٌ (فيحتـاج إلى إعادتها إن أراد الجمع) .

وإنْ أَقَـامَ قبـلَ شروعِهِ في الثانية أوْ لمْ ينـوِ الجمعَ في الأولى أوْ فَرَّقَ كثيراً وَجَبَ تأخيرُ الثانيةِ إلى وقتِها .

f15.11 If one has performed both prayers and the journey subsequently ends (A: whether in the time of the first prayer or the time of the second), they are and remain valid.

f15.11 وإنْ أَقَامَ بعـدَ فراغِهِمَـا مَضَتَا على الصحةِ.

f15.12 The necessary condition for joining two prayers in the time of the second of them (A: in addition to f15.8(a,b,c,d)) is that one make the intention to do so before the end of the first prayer's time (O: by an interval which could contain at least one rak'a). If one neglects this intention, one has sinned, and praying the first prayer during the second prayer's time is considered making it up.

f15.12 وإذَا جَمَعَ تأخيراً لـمْ يَلْزِمْهُ إلّا أنْ يَنْوِيَ قبلَ خروجِ وقتِ الأولى بقدرِ ما يَسَعُ فِعْلَهَا (أي ذلك الزمن الذي بقي من وقت الأولى أداءهـا، والأداء هو أن تقع ركعـة منهـا في الوقت) أنّهُ يُؤَخِّرُ لِيَجْمَعَ. فلَوْ لمْ يَنْوِه أَثِمَ وكَانَتْ قضاءً.

f15.13 When joining two prayers in the time of the second, it is recommended (A: not obligatory):

f15.13 ويُنْدَبُ الترتيبُ والموالاةُ ونيةُ الجمع في الأولى [(أي التي بدأ بها)].

(1) to pray the first one before the second;

(2) to not pause at length between them;

(3) and that the intention to join them be present during the prayer one performs first.

JOINING PRAYERS BECAUSE OF RAIN

الجمع للمطر

f15.14 It is permissible for a nontraveller to pray the noon prayer (zuhr) and the midafternoon prayer ('asr) at the time of the noon prayer (N: or the Friday prayer (jumu'a) and midafternoon prayer at the time of the Friday prayer), and to similarly pray the sunset prayer (maghrib) and nightfall prayer ('isha) at the time of the sunset prayer if:

f15.14 ويَجُوزُ للمقيمِ الجمعُ تقديماً لمطرٍ يبُلُّ الثـوبَ (ومثله الثلج والبرد إذا ذابـا) بشـرطِ أنْ يَقْصِدَ جماعةً في مسجدٍ (والمـراد منه مكان صلاة الجماعة سواء كان مسجداً أوغيـره) بعيدٍ (أي عن بابِ

(a) it is raining hard enough to wet one's clothing (O: and like rain in this is melted snow or hail);

(b) one is praying with a group in a mosque (O: or other place of prayer);

(c) the mosque is far (O: from one's door, i.e. far by common acknowledgement (def: f4.5));

(d) it is raining when the first prayer begins, when it ends, and when the second prayer begins;

(e) and conditions f15.10(b,c,d) exist.

داره عرفاً) وأنْ يُوجَدَ المطرُ عندَ افتتاح الأولى والفـراغ منهـا وافتتـاح الثانيـة ويُشْتَرطُ مَعَ ذلكَ ما تَقَدَّمَ في جمعِ السفرِ تقديماً .

f15.15 (A: If one arrives during the second of two prayers joined because of rain and does not finish one's own first prayer before the group finishes their second, then one is no longer entitled to join one's prayers for rain. It is a necessary condition that one pray at least part of the second prayer with them, though one may hurry through one's own first prayer alone to catch up with and join them during their second.)

f15.16 If the rain stops after one finishes the two prayers or during the second one, both prayers are and remain valid.

f15.16 فإن انقَطَعَ بعدَهُما أوْ في أثناءِ الثانية مَضَتا على الصحة .

f15.17 It is not permissible to join two prayers in the time of the second of them because of rain.

f15.17 ولاَ يَجوزُ الجمعُ بالمطرِ تأخيراً

f15.18 (n: In the Shafi'i school, there are no valid reasons other than travel or rain for joining prayers, though others exist in the Hanbali school, as discussed in what follows.)

('Abd al-Rahman Jaziri:) The Hanbalis hold that the above-mentioned joining between the noon prayer (zuhr) and midafternoon prayer ('asr), or between the sunset prayer (maghrib) and nightfall prayer ('isha) is permissible, whether in the time of the first prayer of each of these two pairs, or in the time of the second prayer of each of them, though it is superior not to join them.

It is a necessary condition for the permissibility of joining them that the person praying be:

(1) a traveller on a trip in which shortening prayers is permissible;

(2) a sick person for whom not to join prayers would pose a hardship;

(3) a woman who is nursing an infant, or who has chronic vaginal discharge (dis: e13.6), since she is permitted to join prayers to obviate the hardship of purification for every single prayer;

f15.18 (ت : في المذهب الشافعي لا يُترخص في الجمعِ لغير السفر والمطر ؛ ويترخص فيه لغيرهما عند الحنابلة كما يأتي) .

(عبـد الـرحمن الجزيري :) الحنابلة قالـوا : الجمـع المــذكـور بين الظهر والعصـر ، أو المغرب والعشاء ، تقديماً أو تأخيراً مباحٌ وتركه أفضل [. . .] ويشترط في إبـاحـة الجمـع أن يكـون المصلي مسـافراً سفراً تقصر فيه الصلاة ، أو يكون مريضاً تلحقه مشقـة بترك الجمـع ، أو تكـون امرأة مرضعـة أو مستحاضة ، فإنه . . رزّ لها الجمع دفعاً لمشقة الطهارة عند كل صلاة ، ومثـل المستحـاضة المعذور

(4) someone with an excuse similar to the woman with chronic discharge, such as a person unable to prevent intermittent drops of urine coming from him (e13.7);

(5) or someone who fears for himself, his property, or his reputation, or who fears harm in earning his living if he does not join prayers; the latter giving leeway to workers for whom it is impossible to leave their work.

(*al-Fiqh 'ala al-madhahib al-arba'a* (y66), 1.487)

كمن به سلس البـول [. . .] وكـذا يبـاح الجمــع لمن خاف على نفسـه أو مالـه أو عرضه، ولمن يخاف ضرراً يلحقه بتركه في ذلك سعة للعمال الذين في ذلك يستحيل عليهم ترك أعمـالهم . [محـرّر من الفقه على المذاهب الأربعة: [٤٨٧ / ١].

PRAYING THE SUNNA RAK'AS WHEN ONE JOINS PRAYERS

كيفية أداء الرواتب عند الجمع

f15.19 (O: When one wants to join the midafternoon prayer ('asr) and noon prayer (zuhr) in the time of the noon prayer, one first prays the sunnas that come before the noon prayer, followed by the noon prayer, the midafternoon prayer, the sunnas that come after the noon prayer, and then the sunnas that come before the midafternoon prayer.

Similarly, when one joins the nightfall prayer ('isha) with the sunset prayer (maghrib), one prays the sunnas that come before the sunset prayer, and postpones those that follow the sunset prayer until after one has prayed the nightfall prayer, after which one prays the sunnas that come before and after the nightfall prayer, and then *witr*. Their order is sunna.)

f15.19 (وإذا أراد أن يجمــع العصـر مع الظهـر تقـديماً فيصلي أولاً سنة الظهر القبليـة [المـؤكدة وغيرها] ثم يصلي سنة الظهر البعـديـة [المـؤكدة وغيرها] بعد العصر ثم يصلي سنة العصر القبلية . وهكذا العشاء مع المغرب أي فيصلي سنته القبلية ويـؤخر سنتـه البعـدية بعد العشـاء ثم يصلي سنـة العشـاء القبلية والبعدية ثم الوتر . ويسن ترتيب السن هنا) .

*

f16.0   THE PRAYER OF PERIL

f16.0   صلاة الخوف

f16.1   The prayer of peril may be performed when the Muslims are engaged in permissible fighting (O: whether obligatory, as when fighting non-Muslims or highwaymen whom the caliph (def: o25) is fighting, or permissible, as when fighting someone who is trying to take one's property or that of others).

f16.1   إذا كَانَ القتـالُ مبـاحاً (سواء كان واجباً كقتال الكفار وقطاع الطريق إذا قاتلهم الإمـام أو مبـاحاً مستوي الطرفين كقتال من قصد مال الإنسان أو مال غيره) .

f16.2 When the enemy is not in the direction of prayer (qibla), the imam divides the Muslim force into two groups. One group faces the enemy while the other prays a rak'a behind the imam. When the imam rises for the second rak'a, the group makes the intention to cease following his leadership in the prayer and then finishes their second rak'a alone as individuals while the imam remains standing at the beginning of his second rak'a, reciting the Koran and awaiting the second group.

Then this first group goes to relieve the others in facing the enemy, and the others come and begin their group prayer behind the imam, who is still standing and who remains so long enough for the second group to recite the Fatiha and a short sura. At the end of this rak'a when the imam sits in the Testification of Faith (Tashahhud), the group rises and performs their second rak'a without him (while he remains sitting at the end of his second rak'a waiting for them to reach the same point in their own prayer). When they catch up with him, he closes the prayer with Salams.

If this prayer is the sunset prayer (maghrib), the first group prays two rak'as following the imam's lead, and the second group follows him in the third rak'a. If it is a prayer with four rak'as, then each group follows the imam for two rak'as. The imam may also divide the Muslim force into four groups and have each group pray one rak'a behind him.

f16.3 When the enemy is visible in the direction of prayer (qibla) and the Muslims are numerous, the imam arranges them in two or more rows, opens the group prayer with "Allahu akbar," and (O: after reciting the Fatiha with all of them) he bows and straightens up with everyone following his lead. Then he prostrates together with the row nearest him, while the other row remains standing. When the imam and his row stand after their second prostration, the other row performs its own prostrations and rises to catch up with the imam and his row, who have remained standing waiting for them.

In the second rak'a all bow and straighten up together, but when the imam prostrates, the second row, who remained standing on guard before, prostrate with him while the row nearest him

f16.2 والعَدوُّ في غيرِ جهةِ القبلةِ فَرَّقَ الإمامُ الناسَ قِرْقَتَيْنِ فِرْقَةً في وجهِ العَدوِّ ويُصَلّي بفِرقةٍ ركعةً فإذا قامَ إلى الثانيةِ نَوَوْا مفارقَتَهُ وأتَمُّوا منفردِينَ وذهَبُوا إلى وجهِ العَدوِّ وجاءَ أولئكَ إلى الإمامِ وهوَ قائمٌ في الصلاةِ يَقْرَأُ فَيُحرِمُونَ ويَمْكُثُ لَهُمْ بقدرِ الفاتحةِ وسورةٍ قصيرةٍ فإذا جلَسَ للتشهدِ قامُوا وأتَمُّوا لأنفسِهِمْ ويُطيلُ هوَ التشهدَ ثمَّ يُسَلِّمُ بِهِمْ.

فإنْ كانَت مغرباً صَلّى بالأُولى ركعتَيْنِ وبالثانيةِ ركعةً. أوْ رباعيةً صَلّى بكلِّ فِرقةٍ ركعتَينِ. فإنْ فرَّقَهم أربـعَ فِرقٍ وصَلّى بكلِّ فِرقةٍ ركعةً صحَّ.

f16.3 وإنْ كانَ العــدوُّ في القـبـلةِ يُشاهدُونَ في الصلاةِ وفي المسلمِينَ كثرةٌ صَفَّهُمْ صفَّيْنِ فأكثـرَ وأحْـرَمَ ورَكَـعَ (بعدَ الفراغِ من الفاتحةِ بهم جميعاً) ورَفَعَ بالكلِّ فإذا سَجَدَ سَجَدَ معهُ الصفُّ الذي يليهِ واسْتَمَرَّ الصفُّ الآخَرُ قائماً فإذا رَفَعُوا رؤوسَهُمْ سَجَدَ الصفُّ الآخَرُ.

ثمَّ يرْكَعُ ويرْفَعُ بالكلِّ فإذا سَجَدَ سَجَدَ معـهُ الصفُّ الـذي حرَسَ أولاً وحرَسَ

remain standing on guard. When those who have prostrated with the imam sit back (O: after their prostration, for the Testification of Faith (Tashahhud)) then the row nearest him (O: who have been standing on guard) prostrate (O: and catch up with the others in the Testification of Faith (Tashahhud)).

الصفُّ الآخَرُ. فإذا رَفَعُوا (أي من سجد مع الإمام رؤوسهم من السجود واستقروا جالسين للتشهد) سَجَدَ الصفُّ الآخَرُ (الذي كان واقفاً ولحقوه في التشهد).

f16.4   It is recommended to remain armed during the prayer of peril.

f16.4   وَيُنْـدَبُ حمـلُ السـلاحِ في صلاةِ الخوف.

f16.5   When the peril is great, in actual combat, Muslims may pray walking or riding, facing the direction of prayer (qibla) or not, in a group or singly, and nodding in place of bowing and prostration when they are unable to perform them, nodding more deeply for prostration than for bowing. If forced to strike blow after blow during the prayer, this is permissible. Shouting is not.

f16.5   وإذا اشْتَـدَّ الخـوفُ والْتَحَمَ القتـالُ صَلُّوا رجـالاً وركبانـاً إلى القبلة وغيرِهَا جماعةً وفرادى وَيُوْمِئُون بالركوع والسجــود إنْ عَجَـزُوا والسجـودُ أخفض وإنِ اضْطَـرُوا إلى الضَـرب المتـابـع ضَرَبُوا ولا إعادةَ علَيهِمْ، ولا يَجُوزُ الصياحُ.

*

f17.0   UNLAWFUL CLOTHING AND JEWELRY

f17.0   ما يحرم لبسه

f17.1   (A: It is offensive for men to wear tight clothing that discloses the size of the parts of their body which are nakedness (def: f5.3), and this is unlawful for women.)

f17.2   It is unlawful for men to wear silk or use it in any way, even to line clothing, though it is permissible to use it as padding in a cloak, pillow, or mattress.

f17.2   يَحْـرُمُ على الـرجـل لبسُ الحرير وسائرُ وجوه استعمالِهِ ولوْ بطانةً، ويَجُوزُ حشْوُ جبةٍ ومخدةٍ وفرشٍ بِه.

f17.3   Women may wear and use silk, and it is permissible for a guardian to dress a child in it before puberty.

f17.3   ويَجُـوزُ للنسـاءِ استعمالُـهُ [وقِـلَ يَحْـرُمُ علَيهِنَّ افتراشُـهُ] ويَجُوزُ للولِيِّ إلباسُه للصبيِّ مَا لمْ يَبْلُغْ.

f17.4   It is permissible for men to use fabric composed partly of silk as long as the weight of the silk is half or less of the weight of the fabric; to

f17.4   والمـركَّبُ مِنْ حرير وغيره إنْ زَادَ وزنُ الحـريـر حَرُمَ وإن اسْتَوَيَا جَازَ.

embroider with silk thread where (O: the width of) the design does not exceed four fingers (O: though the length does not matter); to have a silk fringe on a garment; or a silk collar; or to cover a silk mattress with a handkerchief or the like and sit on it.

It is also permissible for men to use silk when there is need to in severe heat or cold, to clothe their nakedness with it for the prayer when there is nothing else, or to use it when suffering from itching or for protection from lice. (O: The upshot is that when there is real need for it, one may use it. Otherwise, it is an enormity (def: c2.5(2)). Imam Ghazali attributes its prohibition to its effeminacy and softness, which are unbecoming of men.)

f17.5 It is permissible to wear a garment affected by something impure (najasa, def: e14.1) when not in prayer (O: or other activites requiring purity, provided one is not in a mosque. As for wearing such a garment in a mosque, one may not, since it is not permissible to carry something impure into the mosque when there is not some need, such as having to take one's shoes inside).

It is unlawful to wear leather taken from the carcass of an unslaughtered animal (n: before tanning, as at e14.6) except when there is pressing need, such as in the event of a sudden outbreak of war (A: when there is nothing else) and the like.

f17.6 It is unlawful for men to wear gold jewelry, even the teeth of a ring's setting that holds its stone. (O: Unlike silk, there is no difference for the prohibition of gold between small and large amounts.) Nor may men wear objects painted or plated with gold, though if these tarnish so that the gold is no longer apparent, then they are permissible.

f17.7 It is permissible to repair teeth with gold.

ويَجُوزُ مطرَّزٌ بِهِ لا يُجَاوِزُ أَرْبَعَ أصابعَ (عـرضـاً وإن زَادَ طولاً) ومطرَّفٌ ومجيَّبٌ معتـادٌ [(والمجيب هو المطوق)] ولهُ أَنْ يَبْسُطَ على فرشِ الحريرِ منديلاً ونحوَهُ ويَجْلِسَ فوقَهُ.

ويَجُوزُ لِبْسُهُ لحَـرٍّ وبـردٍ مهلكين [(وليس بقيـد بل عند الحـاجـة أيضاً)] وستر عورة [ومفاجأةِ حرب] إذا فُقِدَ غيرُهُ ولحكةٍ ودفع قملٍ . (فـالحاصل متى دعت حاجة إلى لبسه جاز [ولـو من غير ضرورة....،] وهـذه الـحـرمـة من الكبـائر، وقد علل الإمام الغزالي الحرمة بأن في الحريرِ خنوثة أي نعومة وليونة لا تليق بشهـامـة الرجـال) [ويَجُوزُ ديباجٍ ثخينٌ لا يَقُومُ غيرُهُ مقامَهُ في الحربِ].

f17.5 ويَجُوزُ لِبْسُ ثوبٍ نجسٍ في غيرِ الصلاةِ (ونحوهـا ممـا يتوقف على طهـارة ويشترط أن يكـون واقعـاً في غير المسجـد أمـا لبسه فيـه فلا يجوز لأنه لا يجـوز إدخال النجاسة فيه لغير حاجة كما في النعل).

ويَحْرُمُ جلدُ ميتةٍ إلا لضرورةٍ كمفاجأة حرب ونحوِهِ [ويَجُوزُ أَنْ يُلْبِسَ دابَّتَهُ الجلدَ النجسَ سِوَى جلدِ الكلبِ والخنزير].

f17.6 ويَحْـرُمُ على الرجـالِ حُليُ الـذهبِ حتى سِنُّ الخاتمِ (ولا فرق في الـذهبِ بين قليله وكثيره بخلاف الحريرِ) والمطليُّ به فلَوْ صَدِىءَ بحيثُ لَا يَبِينُ جَازَ.

f17.7 ويُبَـاحُ شَدُّ سنٍ [وأنـملةٍ] بذهبٍ [واتخـاذُ أنفٍ وأنملةٍ منـهُ ويَجُوزُ درعُ نُسِجَتْ بذهبٍ وخـوذةٍ طُلِيَتْ به لمفاجأةِ حرب ولمْ يجدْ غيرَهما].

f17.8   It is lawful (A: for both sexes) to wear a silver ring (A: the sunna for men being to do so on the little finger, of either hand), and (A: for men) to decorate battle weapons with silver, but not riding gear such as saddles and the like, nor an inkwell, writing utensil case, work knife, penknife, or lamp fixture—even if in a mosque—nor to have silver jewelry other than rings, such as a necklace, armband, bracelet (O: because these resemble the habits of women and it is unlawful for men to imitate women), or a crown.

It is not permissible to use silver (A: or gold) to embellish the ceiling or walls of a house or mosque (O: even those of the Kaaba, because it is wasteful, and no one has reported that the early Muslims did so), though if the amount is so slight that none could be melted off by applying fire, then it may remain. If more than that, then not (O: i.e. it must be removed).

f17.9   (O: It is offensive to use cloth for interior decoration in houses (A: meaning that if curtains and the like are used merely for decoration, it is offensive, though there is nothing wrong with using them to screen a room from view), even for shrines at the tombs of the righteous and learned. It is unlawful to decorate walls with pictures (n: of animate life, as at p44).)

f17.10   It is permissible for both men and women to decorate copies of the Koran and to embellish writing with silver (O: out of reverence for it). It is permissible for women to have copies of the Koran decorated with gold, but this is unlawful for men.

f17.11   All gold jewelry is permissible for women, even on shoes and woven into fabric, provided it is not wasteful. But if a woman is wasteful, such as when she has a 720-gram anklet of gold (O: meaning that it (N: i.e. the *weight* of a piece, though there is no limit to the *number* of average-weight pieces) exceeds the customary), then it is unlawful (O: since gold is only permitted to women for the sake of beauty, and when gold exceeds what is

f17.8   ويَجُوزُ خاتمُ الفضةِ وتحليةُ آلــةِ الحـربِ بهــا [كسيفٍ ورمحٍ وطبرٍ وسهمٍ ودرعٍ وجـوشنٍ وخـوذةٍ وخفٍّ] لا سرجٍ [ولجــامٍ وركــابٍ وقــلادةٍ وطـرفِ سيـورٍ] ودواةٍ ومقلمـةٍ وسكينِ مهنةٍ ودواةٍ وتعليقِ قنـديلٍ ولو بمسجدٍ وغير الخاتمِ مِنَ الحليِّ كطوقٍ ودملجٍ وسوارٍ (لما فيه من التشبه بالنساء والتشبه بهن حرام) وتاجٍ .

وفي سقفِ البـيتِ والمـسجـدِ وجدارِنهِمَا (حتى سقف الكعبة وجدرانها لمــا فيـه من السرف مع كونه لم ينقل عن أحــدٍ من السلف) فلو استُهْلِكَ بحيثُ لا يَجْمَعُ منـهُ (أي من ذلك الذهب) شيءٌ بالسبكِ جَازَتْ الاستدامةُ وإلا فَلا (بل تجب إزالته) .

f17.9   (ويكـره تزيـينِ البـيـوت [للرجـال وغيرهم] حتى مشاهد الصلحاء والعلماء بالثياب . ويحرم تزيينها بالصور) .

f17.10   ويَجُوزُ تحليةُ المصحفِ والكتب [(والنسـاء في الكتب ساكنة فهو مصـدر بمعنى الكتـابـة وليس جمعـاً لكتاب)] بالفضة للمرأةِ والرجلِ (تعظيماً له) ويَجُـوزُ تحليةُ المصحفِ بالـذهبِ للمرأةِ ويَحْرُمُ على الرجلِ .

f17.11   ويَجُوزُ للمرأةِ حليُّ الـذهبِ كلُّه حتى النعلِ والمنسوجُ به بشرط عدم الإســرافِ فإنِ أسْـــرَفَتْ (فـي الـحـلـي وجـاوزت العـادة) كخلخـالٍ مائتَـا دينارٍ حَرُمَ (لأن جواز الحلي لها إنمـا هو لأجل الـزينة وإذا جاوزت العادة صار في غاية

normal it is repulsive and devoid of beauty (A: and zakat must be paid on such wasteful jewelry (n: as opposed to jewelry that is not wasteful, on which no zakat is due (dis: h4.4)))).

القباحة ولا زينة فيه). [وَيَحْرُمُ عَلَيْهِنَّ تحليةُ آلةِ الحربِ ولَوْ بالفضةِ].

*

f18.0   THE FRIDAY PRAYER (JUMU‘A)

f18.0   صلاة الجمعة

f18.1   (O: Attending the Friday prayer is personally obligatory. It is the finest of prayers, and its day, Friday, is the best day of the week. Its integrals and conditions are the same as other prayers (def: f9.13–14).)

f18.1   (وهي [بشـروطها] فرض عين وهي أفضـل الصلوات ويـومها أفضل أيام الأسبـوع وأما من حيث الأركان والشروط فهي كغيرها من باقي الصلوات).

f18.2   Anyone obliged to pray the noon prayer (zuhr) is obliged to pray the Friday prayer (jumu‘a), except for women and for travellers on a trip that is not disobedience (def: f15.5), even if the trip is less that 81 km./50 mi. one way (n: though one's departure for the journey must have taken place before dawn on Friday, as at f18.6).

Valid excuses for not attending group prayer (def: f12.5), such as illness or taking care of a sick person, excuse one from attending the Friday prayer (jumu‘a).

f18.2   مَنْ لَزِمَهُ الظهرُ لَزِمَتْهُ إلّا [العبدَ و] المـرأةَ والمسـافـرَ في غيـرِ معصيةٍ ولوْ سفراً قصيراً.
وكـلُّ مَا أَسْقَـطَ الجمـاعـةَ أَسْقَطَهَا كالمرضِ والتمريضِ وغيرِ ذلكَ.

f18.3   Eligible Muslims living in a village where there are not forty men (n: the minimum required for a valid Friday prayer, as at f18.7(e)) must go to a larger town for the Friday prayer when the two places are close enough that the call to prayer (adhan) from the larger town is audible to them under normal circumstances, given a calm wind and no interference. *Audible* means that the call of a man with a loud voice standing in the larger town on the side facing the village could be heard by a man with normal hearing standing on the side of the village facing the town. If such a call would be inaudible, then the villagers are not obliged to go to pray the Friday prayer (A: but merely pray the noon prayer (zuhr)).

f18.3   والمقيم بقـريـةٍ ليسَ فيهـا أربعـونَ كاملونَ فإنْ كَانَ بحيثُ لوْ نَادَى رجلٌ عالي الصوتِ بطرفِ بلدِ الجمعة الـذي في جهةِ القريةِ والأصواتُ والرياحُ ساكنةٌ لَسَمِعَهُ مصغٍ صحيحُ السمعِ واقفٌ بطرفِ القريـةِ الذي مِنْ جهةِ بلدِ الجمعـةِ لَزِمَتِ الجمعةُ كلَّ أهلِ القريةِ. وإنْ لمْ يَسْمَعْ فَلَا تَلْزَمُهُمْ.

f18.4   A Muslim present at the mosque who is not obliged to pray the Friday prayer may leave

f18.4   ومَنْ لَا تَلْزَمُهُ إذا حَضَرَ الجامعَ لَهُ الانصرافُ إلّا المـريضَ الذي لَا يَشُقُّ

(A: instead of participating in it, such as a traveller merely wanting to pray the noon prayer (zuhr) and go), except for the following, who must pray the Friday prayer:

(1) someone with an illness for whom waiting for the Friday prayer poses no hardship, provided that he has arrived after its time has begun (O: namely noon, for if he arrives before this, or if waiting is a hardship, then he may leave);

(2) someone who is blind;

(3) or someone whose excuse is muddy terrain (dis: f12.5(2)).

Those present at the mosque who are not obliged to pray the Friday prayer (A: other than the above-mentioned) may choose between performing the Friday prayer and the noon prayer (zuhr) (O: even when the fact that they are present eliminates their excuse). If they want to perform the noon prayer (zuhr) in a group (O: as is sunna) and their excuse from the Friday prayer is not obvious to onlookers, then they should conceal their group prayer rather than display it (O: which would be offensive under the circumstances).

If a person is not obliged to perform the Friday prayer, but believes the reason for his excuse may disappear, such as sick person (A: hoping to recover before the prayer ends), then he should postpone his noon prayer (zuhr) until he can no longer hope to attend the Friday prayer. But if one's excuse from the obligation of attending the Friday prayer is not expected to cease, such as being a woman, then it is recommended to pray the noon prayer (zuhr) at the first of its time.

f18.5 The noon prayer (zuhr) of someone obliged to perform the Friday prayer is not valid until he has missed the Friday prayer (A: by its having finished without his having attended).

f18.6 It is unlawful for someone (O: obliged to pray the Friday prayer) to travel after dawn (A: on Friday before having prayed it) unless:

عليهِ الانتظارُ وجاءَ بعـدَ دخولِ الوقتِ (وهـو زوالِ الشمسِ أمـا إذا حضـر قبـل الـوقت فله الانصـراف وأمـا إن شق عليه الانـتـظـار لم يلزمـه بل له الانصـراف) والأعمَى ومَنْ في طريقهِ وحلٌ فَتَلْزَمُهُمُ الجمعة.

ومنْ لاَ تَلْزَمُهُ (أي الجمعة مطلقاً سواء زال عذره بالحضـور أم لا) مخيّـرٌ بينهَـا وبين الظهر ويُخفونَ الجماعةَ في الظهر إنْ خَفِيَ عُذْرُهُمْ (وأرادوا صلاتهـا جماعة وهي مسنونة ويكره لهم إظهارها).

ويُـنْـدَبُ لمَـنْ يَرْجُـو زوالَ عذرِه كمريض [وعبد] تأخيرُ الظهر إلى اليأس مِنَ الجمعةِ. وإنْ لم يَرْجُ زوالَـهُ كالمرأةِ فَيُنْدَبُ تعجيلُهُ (أي الظهر).

f18.5 ومنْ لَزِمَتْهُ الجمعـةُ لمْ يَصِحَّ ظهرُهُ قبلَ فواتِ الجمعةِ.

f18.6 ويَـحْـرُمُ عليهِ (أي على من لزمته الجمعة) السفرُ مِنْ طلوعِ الفجرِ إلاَّ

(1) there is a place on his route where the Friday prayer will take place;

(2) or he is going to travel with a group (O: of people not obliged to pray the Friday prayer) who are departing, such that his staying behind would entail harm for him.

أَنْ يَكُونَ فِي طَرِيقِهِ مَوْضِعُ جمعةٍ أَوْ تَرْحَلَ رفقتُهُ (وهـو معهم وكـانوا ممن لا تلزمهم الجمعة) ويَتَضَرَّرَ بالتخلُّفِ.

f18.7 In addition to the usual conditions for the prayer (def: f9.13), a valid Friday prayer (jumu'a) also requires:

(a) that it be a group prayer;

(b) that it take place during the time of noon prayer (zuhr);

(c) that it follow two sermons (khutba, def: f18.9);

(d) that its site be located among the dwellings of the community;

(e) that there be a minimum of forty participants who are male, have reached puberty, are sane, and are local residents, meaning they live there and do not leave except when they need to (n: though the minimum according to Abu Hanifa is three participants besides the imam (al-Lubab fi sharh al-Kitab (y88), 1.111));

(f) and that, in places where it is no hardship for everyone to pray at one location, there be no other Friday prayer prior to or simultaneous with it (O: i.e. in the opening Allahu Akbar of the prayer (dis: below)).

The imam is counted as one of the forty ((e) above).

A group performing the Friday prayer must finish it as a noon prayer (zuhr) if:

(1) (non-(e) above) the number of participants diminishes during it to less than forty;

(2) or (non-(b)) if its time ends during the prayer (O: with the coming of the midafternoon

f18.7   وشـروطُ صحـةِ الجمعـةِ بعدَ شروطِ الصلاةِ ستةٌ أَنْ تُقَـامَ جمـاعةً فِي وقتِ الظهـرِ بعـدَ خطبتَيْنِ فِي خُطَّةِ أبنيـةٍ مجتمعةٍ بأربعينَ رجـلاً [أحـراراً] بالغينَ عقـلاءَ مستوطِنينَ حيثُ تُقَامُ الجمعةُ لَا يَظْعَنُونَ عنهُ إلّا لحاجةٍ وأنْ لا تَسْبِقَهَا (بتحرم) ولا تُقَارِنَهَا جمعةٌ أخرَى حيثُ لَا يَشُقُّ الاجتماعُ فِي موضعٍ واحدٍ.

والإمامُ واحدٌ مِنْ أربعينَ.

فلوْ نَقَصُوا فِي الصلاةِ عن الأربعينَ أوْ خَرَجَ الـوقتُ (بأن دخل وقت العصر) فِي

prayer's time). If the group has doubts before starting the Friday prayer that they will be able to finish it within its time, then they must begin it as a noon prayer (zuhr).

f18.8 In places where having everyone assemble in one location is a hardship, as in Cairo or Baghdad, it is valid to hold as many Friday prayers as are needed. In places where it poses no hardship, such as Mecca or Medina, if two Friday prayers are held, the first of them (A: to open with ''Allahu akbar'') is the Friday prayer, and the second is invalid (A: and must be reprayed as a noon prayer). If two are held in such a place and it is not clear which was first, they should start over together as one Friday prayer.

THE SERMON (KHUTBA)

f18.9   The integrals of the sermon (khutba) are five (O: and their order is sunna) (n: (a), (b), and (c) below are required in each of the two sermons, while (d) may be in either, and (e) must occur in the second, as mentioned below):

(a)   saying ''al-Hamdu lillah'' (praise be to Allah), this particular utterance being prescribed;

(b)   the Blessings on the Prophet (Allah bless him and give him peace), which is also a prescribed utterance;

(c)   enjoining godfearingness (taqwa), for which a particular expression is not prescribed, it being sufficient to say ''Obey Allah'';

(the above (O: integrals (a), (b), and (c)) are obligatory in each of the two sermons)

(d)   reciting one verse of the Koran (O: that conveys an intended meaning, such as a promise, threat, exhortation, or similar) in at least one of the two sermons;

(e)   and to supplicate for believers (O: male and female) in the second of the two sermons (O:

أثنـائهـا أَتَمُّوهـا ظهـراً، ولـوْ شَكُّـوا قبلَ افتتاحِها في بقاءِ الوقتِ صَلُّوا ظهراً.

f18.8   وإنْ شَقَّ الاجتمـاعُ بمـوضعٍ كمصـرَ وبغـدادَ جَازَتْ زيـادةُ الجُمَـعِ بحسبِ الحـاجـةِ. وإنْ لمْ يَشُقَّ كمكةَ والمـدينةِ فأقيمَتْ جمعتـانِ فالجمعةُ هيَ الأولى والثـانيـةُ باطلةٌ. وإنْ وَقَعَتـا معاً أوْ جُهِلَ السبقُ اسْتُؤْنِفَتْ جمعةً.

الخطبة

f18.9   وأركانُ الخطبةِ خمسةٌ (وسن ترتـيبُ أركـانِ الـخطبتينِ) الحمدُ للّهِ والصـلاةُ علىٰ رسولِ اللّهِ ﷺ، والوصيةُ بتقوىٰ اللّهِ، ويَجِبُ ذلك (أي ما ذكر من الأركـانِ) في كلِ مِنَ الـخطبتَّينِ ويَتَعَيَّنُ لفظُ الحمدُ للّهِ والصـلاةُ ولا يَتَعَيَّنُ لفظُ الـوصيةِ فيكفي «أطيعُوا اللّهَ» والـرابعُ قراءةُ آيةٍ (مفهمةٍ معنى مقصوداً كالوعد والوعيد والوعظ ونحو ذلك) في إحداهُما والخامسُ الدعاءُ للمؤمنينَ (وللمؤمنات) في (الخطبـةِ) الـثـانيـةِ (ويتعين كونـه

which must be for their *hereafter*, as supplications for this world alone do not fulfill the integral).

(n: The following sermon, added here by the translator from the commentary at m2, has been related by two chains of transmission, one ascribing it to Ibn Mas'ud, and the other through him to the Prophet (Allah bless him and give him peace):

"Praise is truly Allah's. We praise Him, seek His help, and ask His forgiveness. We seek refuge in Allah from the evils of our selves and our bad actions. Whomever Allah guides none can lead astray, and whomever He leads astray has no one to guide him. I testify that there is no god but Allah alone, without any partner, and that Muhammad is His slave and messenger. Allah bless him and give him peace, with his folk and Companions. O you who believe: fear Allah as He should be feared, and do not die other than as Muslims.

" 'O people, fear your Lord who created you from one soul and created its mate from it, and spread forth from them many men and women. And be mindful of your duty to Allah, by whom you ask of one another, and to the wombs [that bore you], for verily, Allah is vigilant over you' " (Koran 4:1).

(n: This sermon fulfills conditions (a), (b), (c), and (d) above (A: and the rest of the sermon may be in any language), and after sitting briefly, one rises and says, "al-Hamdu lillah," the Blessings on the Prophet (Allah bless him and give him peace), enjoins the people to fear Allah, and must add a supplication for the Muslims ((e) above), such as saying, "O Allah, forgive the believers" (Ar. Allahumma-ghfir lil-mu'minin wal-mu'minat).)

f18.10   The conditions of the two sermons are:

(a) that the speaker be in a state of purity (O: from minor (def: e7) and major (e10) ritual impurity and from filth (najasa, e14.1));

(b) that his nakedness be clothed;

بأخروي فلا يكفي الدنيوي) .

(ت : هذه الخطبـة نقلها المترجم من شرح كتاب النكاح من هذا المجلد ، وهي ما روي عن ابن مسعود موقوفاً ومرفوعاً :)

«إِنَّ الحمـدَ للَّهِ ، نَحْمَـدُهُ ونَسْتَعِينُـهُ ونَسْتَغْفِرُهُ ، ونَعُوذُ باللَّهِ مِنْ شُرُورِ أَنْفُسِنَا ومِنْ سَيِّئَـاتِ أَعْمَـالِنَا مَنْ يَهْـدِهِ اللَّهُ فَلا مُضِلَّ لَهُ ومَنْ يُضْلِلْ فَلا هَادِيَ لَهُ وأَشْهَـدُ أَنْ لَا إِلـهَ إِلَّا الـلَّهُ وَحْـدَهُ لَا شَرِيـكَ لَهُ وأَشْهَدُ أَنَّ مُحَمَّداً عَبْدُهُ وَرَسُولُهُ ﷺ وَعَلى آلِهِ وأَصْحَابِهِ ، ﴿يَا أَيُّهَا الَّذِينَ آمَنُوا اتَّقُوا اللَّهَ حَقَّ تُقَـاتِـهِ ولاَ تَمُـوتُنَّ إلّا وأنْـتُمْ مُسْلِمُونَ﴾ ﴿يَا أَيُّهَا النَّاسُ اتَّقُوا رَبَّكُمُ الَّذِي خَلَقَكُمْ مِنْ نَفْسٍ وَاحِدَةٍ وَخَلَقَ مِنْهَا زَوْجَهَا وَبَثَّ مِنْهُمَا رِجَالاً كَثِيراً ونِسَاءً وَاتَّقُوا اللَّهَ الَّذِي تَسَاءَلُونَ بِه والأَرْحَامَ إِنَّ الـلَّهَ كَانَ عَلَيْـكُـمْ رَقِيبـاً﴾ [سـورة النساء : ١].

f18.10 وشرطُهُمَا الطهارةُ (عن حدث أصغـر وأكبـر وعن نجسٍ والستـارةُ

(c) that the two sermons occur during the noon prayer's time (zuhr) before performing the two rak'as of the Friday prayer;

(d) that the speaker be standing during them (O: if able);

(e) that he sit down between the two;

(f) and that his voice be loud enough for the forty required participants (def: f18.7(e)) to hear (O: the sermons' integrals).

f18.11 The sunnas of the sermon include:

(1) that the speaker stand on a pulpit (minbar) or high place (O: and that it be to the right of the prayer niche (mihrab) and that the speaker stand on the right side of the pulpit);

(2) that he say "as-Salamu 'alaykum" to those present when he enters the mosque and (O: again) when he ascends the pulpit (O: and reaches his seat there);

(3) that he sit until the muezzin has finished (A: the second (dis: w28.2) call to prayer (adhan));

(4) that when speaking, he lean on a sword, bow, or stick (O: which is in his left hand. It is desirable for him to put his other hand on the pulpit. If he does not have a sword or the like, he keeps his hands still by placing the right upon the left, or dropping them to his sides. He does not move them or fidget with one, as the aim is stillness and humility);

(5) and that he face the group during both sermons (O: and not turn to the right or left during them, for it is a reprehensible innovation. It is desirable for the listeners to face the speaker).

DESCRIPTION OF THE FRIDAY PRAYER

f18.12 The Friday prayer (jumu'a) consists of two rak'as. It is sunna for the imam to recite al-Jumu'a

ووقـوعُهُمَـا في وقتِ الظهـر قبـلَ الصلاةِ والقيامُ فيهِمَا (للقادر عليه) والقعودُ بَيْنَهُمَا ورفْـعُ الصـوتِ بحيثُ يَسْمَعُـهُ أربعـونَ تَنْعَقِدُ بهـمُ الجمعةُ (والمراد سماعهم الأركان).

f18.11 وسُنَتُهُمَـا منْبَـرٌ أوْ موضعٌ عالٍ (ويسن كون ذلـك عن يمين المحـراب ويسن أن يقف الخطيب على يمينه) وأنْ يُسَلِّمَ إذا دَخَـلَ (المسجد) و(يسلم أيضاً إذا صَعَـدَ (المنبر أي انتهى إليـه [ووصل إلى الـدرجة المسماة بالمستراح]) وَ(سن أنْ يَجْلِسَ حَتَّى يُؤذِّنَ (المؤذن ويفرغ من أذانـه) ويَعْتَمـدَ على سيفٍ أوْ قوسٍ أوْ عصًـا (أي يشغـل يسـاره بذلك ويستحب أن يشغـل يده الأخرى بأن يضعهـا على المنبر فإن لم يجد سيفاً ونحوه سكن يديه بأن يضع اليمنى على اليسرى أو يرسلهما ولا يحـرّكهمـا ولا يعبث بواحـدة منهمـا والمقصـود الخشـوع) ويُقْبـلَ علَيْهِمْ في جميعِهما (ولا يلتفت في شيء منهما يميناً ولا شمـالاً لأنـه بدعـة. ويستحب للقوم الإقبال بوجوههم على الخطيب).

صفة صلاة الجمعة

f18.12 والجمعـةُ ركعتـانِ يَقْـرأُ في

207

(Koran 62) in the first rak'a (A: meaning the entire sura, the sunna being to make the sermon brief and the rak'as long, though wisdom must be used in deciding how much those present will accept) and al-Munafiqun (Koran 63) in the second rak'a (O: following the sunna from a hadith reported by Muslim, who also reported that the Prophet (Allah bless him and give him peace) sometimes recited al-A'la (Koran 87) in the first rak'a of the Friday prayer and al-Ghashiya (Koran 88) in the second).

f18.13   A latecomer who joins the group prayer in time to bow and remain motionless a moment therein while the imam is still bowing in the second rak'a is legally considered to have attended the Friday prayer (A: though such a person must rise after the imam has finished with Salams to pray the rak'a he missed). If the latecomer joins the group after this point, he has missed the Friday prayer, but (O: obligatorily) intends performing the Friday prayer anyway and follows the imam (O: in case the imam has omitted an integral and has to repeat a rak'a, in which event the latecomer will have attended the Friday prayer). (N: But if this does not happen, then) when the imam finishes with Salams, the latecomer rises and completes his prayer as a noon prayer (zuhr).

RECOMMENDED MEASURES FOR THOSE
ATTENDING THE FRIDAY PRAYER

f18.14   It is recommended to perform a purificatory bath (ghusl) (O: and offensive not to) before going to the Friday prayer, though it may be performed anytime after dawn. If one is unable to bathe, one may perform the dry ablution (tayammum).

It is also recommended to clean the teeth with a toothstick (siwak, def: e3), trim the nails, remove (O: bodily) hair, eliminate offensive odors, wear perfume and one's finest clothes (white being the best), and for the imam to dress better than anyone else. (A: Because of the time taken by these measures, it is offensive to visit others on Friday mornings.)

الأولى الجمعة وفي الثانية المنافقون (للإتباع رواه مسلم وروى أيضاً أنه ﷺ كان يقرأ في الجمعة ﴿سَبِّحِ اسْمَ رَبِّكَ الأَعْلَى﴾ و﴿هَلْ أَتَاكَ حَدِيثُ الغَاشِيَةِ﴾).

f18.13   ومنْ أُدْرَكَ معَ الإمام ركوعَ الثانية وآطمأنَّ فقَدْ أدْرَكَ الجمعةَ. وإنْ أدْرَكَهُ بعدَهُ وفاتَتْهُ الجمعةُ فينْوي الجمعةَ (وجوباً) خلفَهُ (باحتمال كون الإمام قد سها بترك ركن فيتذكر ويأتي به قبل أن يسلم وحينئذ أدرك المأموم الجمعة). فإذا سلَّمَ أتَمَّ الظهرَ.

سنن وآداب الجمعة

f18.14   ويُنْدَبُ لمريدها أنْ يَغْتَسِلَ عندَ الذهابِ (ويكره تركه) ويَجُوزُ منَ الفجرِ. فإنْ عَجَزَ تَيَمَّمَ.

وأنْ يَتَنَظَّفَ بسواكٍ وأخذِ ظفرٍ (أي قصة وإزالته) وشعرٍ (أي إزالته والظاهر أن المراد به غير شعر الرأس) وقطع رائحةٍ كريهةٍ ويتطَيَّبَ وبَلْبَسَ أحسنَ ثيابِهِ، وأفضلُها البيضُ، والإمامُ يزيدُ عليهم في الزينة.

It is offensive for women who attend the Friday prayer to wear perfume or fine clothes.

It is recommended:

(1) to arrive early (O: which is recommended for everyone besides the imam, so as to take a seat and wait for the prayer), the best time being from dawn on;

(2) to come on foot in tranquility and dignity, and not to ride to the mosque unless there is an excuse (O: such as old age, weakness, or being so far from the mosque that the fatigue of walking would obviate one's humility and presence of mind in the prayer);

(3) to sit near to the imam;

(4) and to invoke Allah (dhikr) (O: both on the way and at the mosque before the sermon), and to recite the Koran and invoke Blessings (O: on the Prophet (Allah bless him and give him peace)).

f18.15 It is offensive (O: for anyone but the imam, when there is no need) to step over people to reach a place among them, unless one sees a vacant spot that cannot be reached otherwise.

It is unlawful to make someone sitting in the mosque rise and then sit in his place, though if someone voluntarily rises it is permissible (O: for another to sit there).

f18.16 It is offensive to give another person one's place in the front row, in closeness to the imam, or to put others ahead of oneself in performing any act of worship (O: as is proved by the rigorously authenticated (sahih) hadith,

"People keep staying behind until Allah keeps them behind."

As for Allah's saying,

"... preferring others to themselves, though poverty be their lot" (Koran 59:9),

ويُكْرَهُ للمـرأةِ إذا حَضَـرَتْ الطيبُ وفاخِرُ الثياب .

و(يندب أن) يُبَكِّرَ (وسنية البكور تكـون لغير الإمام ليأخـذوا مجـالسهم ويتنظروا الصلاة) وأفضلُهُ مِنَ الفجـرِ، ويَمْشِيَ بسكينـةٍ ووقارٍ ولا يَرْكَبُ إلّا لعذر (قـام به من أجـل هرم أو ضعف أو بعـد الدار بحيث يمنعه ما يناله من التعب من الخشـوع والحضـور في الصلاة)، ويَدْنُوَ مِنَ الإمـام ، ويَشْتَغِلَ بالذكرِ (في طريقه وفي حضـوره قبـل الخطبـة) والتـلاوة والصلاةِ (على النبي ﷺ) .

f18.15 ولا يَتَخَطَّى رقابَ الناس (فإن تخطى لغير حاجة وكان غير إمام كره) فإذا وَجَدَ فرجةً لا يَصِلُ إلَيْها إلّا بالتَخَطِّي لَمْ يُكْرَهْ.

ويَحْرُمُ أنْ يُقيمَ رجلاً ويَجْلِسَ مكانَهُ . فإنْ قامَ باختيارِهِ جازَ (لغيره الجلوس) .

f18.16 ويُكْـرَهُ أنْ يُؤْثِـرَ غيرَهُ بالصفِّ الأولِ أوْ بالقربِ مِنَ الإمام ، وبكلِّ قربةٍ (أي الطاعات غير ما ذكر) وقد استدل له بالحديث الصحيح «لا يزال قوم يتأخرون حتى يؤخرهم الله». وأمـا قولـه تعـالى: ﴿وَيُـؤْثِـرُونَ على أَنْفُسِهِمْ وَلَوْ كَانَ بِهِمْ خَصَـاصَـةٌ﴾ فالمـراد به في خصوص

it refers to things that relate to the physical self, such as feeding a hungry person when one needs the food, in which case preferring another to oneself is desirable, without a doubt).

It is permissible to send someone to the mosque to save a place for oneself there by spreading something out (O: such as a rug, for no one else may pray on it), though it is permissible for another to move it aside and sit down in its place.

f18.17 It is offensive, though not unlawful, for someone sitting in the mosque to speak or to rise and perform the prayer while the imam is giving the sermon (khutba). (O: The more reliable position is that prayer is unlawful during the sermon (N: for the person already sitting in the mosque, as opposed to someone who has just arrived, as next discussed).)

A latecomer who arrives (O: when the imam is speaking or seated on the pulpit) should pray two brief rak'as to greet the mosque (O: if the prayer is being held in a mosque. If held elsewhere, one should intend them as the two rak'as that are sunna before the Friday prayer, though if one has already prayed these at home, one should simply sit down without praying.

It is offensive for a latecomer to simply omit the two rak'as of greeting the mosque, though if one enters the mosque at the end of the imam's sermon and believes that praying them will prevent one's participating in the opening Allahu Akbar with the group, then one should remain standing until they rise and incorporate one's greeting the mosque into the obligatory prayer (dis: f10.10)).

f18.18 It is recommended to recite al-Kahf (Koran 18) and invoke Blessings on the Prophet (Allah bless him and give him peace) on the night before Friday and during its day.

f18.19 It is recommended to supplicate Allah much on Fridays, seeking the moment when prayers are answered (O: in view of the hadith related by Bukhari and Muslm,

النفوس كإطعام شخص جائع مع احتياجه هو إلى الطعام فإن إيثار نفس الغير على نفسه مستحب بلا شك).

ويجُوزُ أَنْ يَبْعَثَ مَنْ يَأْخُذُ لهُ موضعاً يَبْسُطُ شيئاً فيهِ (كسجادة ونحوها، ولا يجوز لشخص آخر أن يصلي على ذلك الشيء المبسُوط) ولكنْ لغيرِه إزالتُـه والجلوسُ مكانَهُ.

f18.17   ويُكْرَهُ الكلامُ والصلاةُ حالَ الخطبـةِ (للجـالـس في المسجـد من المأمومين) ولاَ يَحْرُمَانِ (والمعتمـد أن إنشاء الصلاة في حال الخطبة يحرم).

فإنْ دَخَلَ (الشخص والإمام يخطب أو وهو جالس على المنبر) صَلَّى التحيَة فقطْ (نوى بصلاته عند دخوله تحية المسجد] إن كان هناك مسجد. وإلا نوى بها سنة الجمعة القبلية إن لم يصلها في بيته وإلا جلس بلا صلاة) ويُخَفِّفُهَا (ويكره ترك هاتين الـركعتين لكن إذا دخل والإمام في آخـر الخطبـة وغلب على ظنـه أنـه لو صلاهما فاتته تكبيرة الإحرام مع الإمام لم يصلهمـا بل يقف حتى تقـام الصـلاة وتندرج هذه التحية في صلاة الفرض).

f18.18   ويُنْدَبُ «الكهف» والصلاةُ على النبيِّ ﷺ ليلة الجمعة ويومَهَا.

f18.19   ويُكْثِرُ في يومِهَا الدعاءَ رجاءَ ساعةِ الإجابةِ (لما رواه الشيخان من قوله

"There is a moment on Friday when the slave shall not ask Allah for anything save that He will give it to him"),

which lies between the time the imam first sits on the pulpit and when the prayer finishes. (A: Others hold that the moment occurs after the midafternoon prayer ('asr).)

*

ﷺ : «إن يوم الجمعة فيه ساعة لا يوافقها عبد يسأل الله شيئاً إلا أعطاه» وهيَ مَا بينَ جلوسِ الإمام على المنبر إلى فراغِ الصلاة (ع : وقيل بعد صلاة العصر) .

f19.0 THE PRAYER ON THE TWO 'EIDS

(N: Meaning *'Eid al-Fitr* at the end of Ramadan, and *'Eid al-Adha* on 10 Dhul Hijja.)

f19.0   صلاة العيدين

(ح : يعني عيـد الفطـر بعـد نهايـة رمضان وعيد الأضحى في العاشر من ذي الحجة) .

f19.1   The prayer on the two 'Eids is a confirmed sunna (def: c4.1) and is recommended to be prayed in a group.

Its time begins at sunrise, and it is recommended to take place after the sun is a spear's length (def: f13.2(1)) above the horizon (O: the time for its current performance continuing) until noon.

f19.1   هيَ سنةٌ مؤكدةٌ ويُنْدَبُ لهَا الجماعةُ .

ووقتُهـا مِن طلوع الشمس ويُنْدَبُ مِنَ ارتفـاعِهـا قدرَ رمحٍ (ويستمر وقت أدائها) إلى الزوال .

f19.2   It is best to perform it in the mosque if there is room, though if there is not, then it is better to hold it outdoors.

f19.2   وفعلُهـا في المسجدِ أفضلُ إن اتَّسَعَ . فإنْ ضَاقَ فالصحراءُ أفضلُ .

RECOMMENDED MEASURES FOR THE 'EID PRAYER

سنن وآداب صلاة العيد

f19.3   It is recommended not to eat anything on 'Eid al-Adha until one performs the prayer, though one should eat an odd number of dates before the prayer on 'Eid al-Fitr.

f19.3   ويُنْـدَبُ أَنْ لَا يَأْكُـلَ في الأضحى حتَّى يُصَلِّيَ ويَـأْكُـلَ في الفطر قبلَ الصلاة تمراتٍ وتراً .

f19.4   It is recommended to perform the purificatory bath (ghusl) after dawn, even if one does not attend the prayer, though it may be performed from midnight on. It is recommended to wear perfume, dress one's best, for young boys to

f19.4   ويَغْتَسِـلَ بعـدَ الفجر وإنْ لمْ يُصَلِّ ويجُوزُ مِنْ نصفِ الليـل ويَتَطَيَّبَ ويلْبَسَ أحْسَنَ ثيـابِهِ ويُنْـدَبُ حضورُ

come in their good clothes, and for women who do not attract men's attention to attend, though without wearing perfume or fine clothes. It is offensive for an attractive woman to attend (dis: f12.4(N:)).

It is sunna:

(1) to come early after the dawn prayer (subh) on foot;

(2) to return home by a different route (N: than one came);

(3) for the imam to delay his arrival until the time of the prayer;

(4) and to call the people to prayer with the words "The prayer is gathering," as one also does for the eclipse prayer (def: f20) and the drought prayer (f21).

DESCRIPTION OF THE 'EID PRAYER

f19.5 The 'Eid prayer consists of two rak'as.

(A: In addition to the opening Allahu Akbar,) one says "Allahu akbar" seven times in the first rak'a after the Opening Supplication (Istiftah, def: f8.13) and before saying "I take refuge, etc." (Ta'awwudh, f8.16); and five times in the second rak'a, not counting the Allahu Akbar for rising from prostration, before saying the Ta'awwudh.

One raises one's hands (f8.12) each time one says "Allahu akbar."

One invokes Allah Most High (N: to oneself) between each Allahu Akbar (O: saying "Glory be to Allah, praise be to Allah, there is no god but Allah, Allah is greatest"), placing the right hand upon the left (A: each time one says this invocation).

Missing or adding repetitions of "Allahu akbar" does not necessitate a forgetfulness prostration at the end of one's prayer. If one forgets them and proceeds directly to the Ta'awwudh, one does not return to them.

f19.6 It is recommended to recite Qaf (Koran 50) in the first rak'a and al-Qamar (Koran 54) in

الصبيانِ بزينتِهِم ومَنْ لاَ تُشْتَهَى مِنَ النساءِ بغيرِ طيبٍ ولا زينةٍ . ويُكْرَهُ لمشتهاةٍ . ويُكْرَهُ بعـدَ الفجـرِ ماشيـاً ويَرْجِـعَ في غيـرِ طريقِـهِ (ح : التي ذهب فيها) ويَتَأَخَّر الإمـامُ إلى وقتِ الصـلاةِ ويُنـادَى لهَـا وللكسوفِ والاستسقاءِ «الصلاةُ جامعةٌ» .

صفة صلاة العيد

f19.5   وهيَ ركعتانِ .

ويُكَبِّرُ في الأولى بعدَ الاستفتاحِ وقبلَ التعوذ سبعَ تكبيراتٍ وفي الثـانيـة قبـلَ التعوذ خمساً غيرَ تكبيرة القيامِ يَرْفَعُ فيهَا اليدين ويَذْكُرُ اللهَ تعالَى بينَهُنَّ (بأن يقول سبحـانَ اللهِ، والحمـدُ للهِ، ولاَ إلَـهَ إلاَّ اللهُ، واللهُ أكبـرُ) ويَضَـعُ اليمنَى على اليسرَى . ولوْ تَرَكَ التكبيـرَ أوْ زَادَ فيـهِ لمْ يَسْجُدْ للسهوِ، ولوْ نَسِيَهُ وشَرَعَ في التعوذِ فَاتَ .

f19.6   ويَقْـرَأ في الأولى ﴿قَ﴾ وفي الثانية ﴿اقْتَرَبَتْ﴾؛ وإنْ شَاءَ قَرَأَ ﴿سَبِّحْ

the second. Or if one wishes, one may recite al-A'la (Koran 87) in the first rak'a and al-Ghashiya (Koran 88) in the second. (A: Or one may recite al-Kafirun (Koran 109) in the first rak'a and al-Ikhlas (Koran 112) in the second.)

اسْمَ رَبِّكَ الأعْلَى﴾ و﴿الغَاشِيَةَ﴾ .

f19.7   After the two rak'as, the imam gives two sermons (khutba) like those of the Friday prayer (O: in integrals (def: f18.9), not conditions (n: which here exclude f18.10(c,d,e))).

It is recommended to open the first sermon by saying "Allahu akbar" nine times and to open the second by saying it seven times.

It is permissible for the imam to sit during the sermons.

f19.7   ثمَّ يَخْطُبُ بعـدَهُمـا خطبتين كالجمعةِ (في الأركان لا في الشروط) . ويَفْتَتِحُ الأولى ندباً بتسع تكبيراتٍ والثانية بسبع .

ولوْ خطَبَ قاعداً جَازَ .

f19.8   There are two types of Allahu Akbars (A: said for the 'Eids), unrestricted and restricted.

The *unrestricted,* meaning those not confined to a particular circumstance but rather recited in mosques, homes, and the street, are sunna to recite from sunset on the night before each 'Eid until the imam commences the 'Eid prayer with the opening Allahu Akbar.

The *restricted,* meaning those recited after prayers (O: whether the five prescribed prayers or the nonobligatory), are sunna for 'Eid al-Adha only, from the noon prayer (zuhr) on 'Eid day until the dawn prayer (subh) on the last of the three days that follow it, which is the fourth day of the 'Eid. (N: The more reliable position is that the time for them begins from dawn of the Day of 'Arafa (n: 9 Dhul Hijja) and ends at the midafternoon prayer ('asr) on the last of the three days that follow 'Eid al-Adha.) They are recited (O: by men, by women (who say them to themselves), by both nontravellers and travellers, and whether one is praying by oneself or in a group) after the current prescribed prayers or making up prescribed prayers missed during the 'Eid or before, and after prayers performed to fulfill a vow, funeral prayers (janaza), and supererogatory prayers. If one misses a prayer during the 'Eid but does not make it up until after the 'Eid, then one does not recite "Allahu akbar" after it.

One says, "Allahu akbar, Allahu akbar, Allahu akbar" (N: and then, "there is no god but

f19.8   والتكبيرُ مرسلٌ ومقيدٌ .
فالمرسلُ وهوَ ما لا يَتَقَيَّدُ بحالٍ بلْ في المسـاجـدِ والمنـازلِ والـطـرقِ يُسَنُّ في العيدينِ منْ غروبِ الشمسِ ليلتَي العيدِ إلى أنْ يُحْرِمَ الإمامُ بصلاةِ العيدِ .
والـمـقَـيَّـدُ وهـوَ مـا يُؤْتَى بِهِ عَقِيبَ الصلوات (الخمس وغيرهـا من صلاةِ النافلة) يُسَنُّ في النحر فقط من صلاةِ ظهر النحر إلى صلاةِ صبح آخر التشريق وهو رابـعُ العيدِ . (ح : والمعتمد أنه من صبح عرفة إلى العصر من آخر أيام التشريق) .
يُكَبِّرُ (رجلاً كان أو امرأة وهي تسر بقدر سماع نفسها، مقيماً كان أو مسافراً وسواء كان منـفـرداً أو في جمـاعـةٍ) خلفَ الفرائض المـؤداةِ والمقضيةِ مِنَ المـدةِ وقبلهَا والمنذورة والجنازة والنوافل ، ولوْ قَضَى فوائتَ المدة بعدَهَا لمْ يُكَبِّرْ .
وصيغتُهُ : اللهُ أكبـرُ اللهُ أكبرُ اللهُ أكبرُ (ح : لا إلهَ إلَّا اللهُ واللهُ أكبرُ اللهُ أكبرُ وللهِ

Allah. Allahu akbar, Allahu akbar, praise be to Allah''). It is commendable to add, as people are accustomed to, "Allah is ever greatest, etc." (O: namely: "Much praise be to Allah. Glory to Him morning and evening. There is no god but Allah. Him alone we worship, making our religion sincerely His though the unbelievers be averse. There is no god but Allah alone. He fulfilled His promise, gave victory to His slave, strengthened His army, and vanquished the Confederates alone. There is no god but Allah. Allah is ever greatest'').

الحمدُ) فإنْ زادَ ما اعْتادَهُ الناسُ فحسنٌ وهـو اللهُ أكبـرُ كبيـراً وسبحـانَ اللهِ بُكْـرَةً وأصِيـلًا لا إلـهَ إلَّا اللهُ ولا نَعْبُـدُ إلَّا إيَّـاهُ مخلصينَ لهُ الـدينَ ولـوْ كَرِهَ الكَافِرُونَ لا إلَه إلَّا اللهُ وحدَهُ صَدَقَ وَعْدَهُ ونَصَرَ عَبْدَهُ وأعَزَّ جُنْدَهُ وهزَمَ الأحْزَابَ وَحْدَهُ لا إلَه إلَّا اللهُ واللهُ أكبرُ».

f19.9   It is recommended to say "Allahu akbar" on the first ten days of Dhul Hijja whenever one sees a head of livestock (O: out of reverence for its Creator).

f19.9   ولـوْ رأَى في عَشْرِ ذِي الحجةِ شيئاً مِنَ الأنعامِ فَلْيُكَبِّرْ (حينئذ تعظيماً لخالقها).

*

f20.0   THE ECLIPSE PRAYER
(O: *Eclipse* refers to both that of the moon and sun.)

f20.0   صلاة الكسوف
(والكسوف يقال للقمر كما يقال للشمس)

f20.1   The eclipse prayer is a confirmed sunna (def: c4.1) (O: and missing it is not permissible, but rather is offensive).

f20.1   هي سنةٌ مؤكدةٌ (وتركها لا يباح بل هو مكروه).

f20.2   (O: Like the drought prayer, it has no call to prayer (adhan) (n: besides that mentioned at f19.4(4)).)

f20.2   (ولا أذان لها كصلاة الاستسقاء).

f20.3   It is recommended to be performed in a group at the mosque.
    It is recommended for women without attractive figures to attend (O: in their household clothes, that is, women advanced in years and the like. As for women who have attractive figures, it is desirable for them to perform it in their homes (dis: f12.4(N:))).

f20.3   ويُنْدَبُ لَها الجماعةُ في الجامعِ.
ويَحْضُـرُهَـا مَنْ لا هيئـةَ لَهَـا مِنْ النساءِ (يحضـرن بثياب بذلة كالعجوز ونحوها. وذوات الهيئات يستحب لهن فعلها في بيوتهن).

DESCRIPTION OF THE ECLIPSE PRAYER	صفة صلاة الكسوف

f20.4 The eclipse prayer consists of two rak'as. The minimum is:

(a) to open with "Allahu akbar";

(b) to recite the Fatiha;

(c) to bow;

(d) to straighten up;

(e) to recite the Fatiha again;

(f) to bow again;

(g) to (O: straighten up and) remain motionless a moment;

(h) and to prostrate, then sit up, and then prostrate again.

This is one rak'a, comprising standing twice, reciting (O: the Fatiha) twice, and bowing twice.
One then prays the second rak'a like the first.
It is not permissible to lengthen the amount of time one stands or bows merely because the eclipse has not yet passed, or to shorten the rak'as to less (O: than the above way after having intended it) because the eclipse has passed.

f20.5 The optimal way is that after reciting the Opening Supplication (Istiftah, def: f8.13), the Ta'awwudh (f8.16), and the Fatiha, one:

(a) recite al-Baqara (Koran 2) for the first Koran recital;

(b) recite Al 'Imran (Koran 3) after the second time one recites the Fatiha (A: in the first rak'a);

(A: then, in the second rak'a:)

(c) recite al-Nisa (Koran 4) for the third recital;

f20.4 وأقلُّها أنْ يُحرمَ فَيَقرأَ الفاتحةَ ثمَّ يَركعَ ثمَّ يَرفعَ فَيقرأَ الفاتحةَ ثمَّ يَركعَ (ثم يرفع رأسَه من هذا الـركوع الثاني) فَيطمَئنَّ ثمَّ يَسجُدَ سجدتين فهـذِه ركعةٌ فيهـا قيـامـانِ وقـراءتـانِ (للفـاتحة) وركوعانِ. ثمَّ يُصلِّي الثانيةَ كذلكَ.
ولا يَجـوزُ زيادةُ قيام وركوع لتمادِي الـكسـوف ولاَ يَجـوزُ النقصُ (عن هذه الكيفية بعد نيتها) لتجليةٍ.

f20.5 وأكملُهـا أنْ يَقرأَ بعدَ الافتتاح والتعـوذ والفاتحةِ البقرةَ في القيام الأولِ وآلَ عمرانَ في الثـاني والنساءَ في الثالثِ

(d) and recite al-Ma'ida (Koran 5) for the fourth recital.

Or one may recite comparable amounts of the Koran in place of the above suras.

One bows and says "Subhana Rabbiya al-'Adhim" ("How far above any limitation is my Lord Most Great") after the first of the four Koran recitals for a period equal to reciting one hundred verses of al-Baqara (N: about 20 minutes); after the second recital for the length of eighty of its verses; after the third for the length of seventy verses; and after the fourth for the length of fifty verses.

The other parts of the eclipse prayer are the same as other prayers.

f20.6   After praying, it is recommended that the imam give two sermons like those of the Friday prayer (O: in integrals (def: f18.9) and conditions (f18.10), except that here the sermons follow the prayer, as opposed to those of the Friday prayer, which precede it).

f20.7   One may no longer perform the eclipse prayer if one has not yet begun it when the eclipse passes, when the sun sets while still eclipsed, or when the sun rises while the moon is still eclipsed. But if one has begun the prayer and the eclipse passes or the sun sets while still in eclipse, one nevertheless completes the prayer.

*

f21.0   THE DROUGHT PRAYER

f21.1   The drought prayer is a confirmed sunna (def: c4.1) (O: even for someone travelling, or praying alone), and is recommended to be prayed in a group.

f21.2   When the land is parched or the water supply is cut off or diminished, the imam (A: i.e. the

والمائدةَ في الرابع أوْ نحوَ ذلك.

ويُسَبِّحُ في الـركوع الأولِ بقدرِ مائة آيةٍ منَ البقرة وفي الثاني بقدرِ ثمانين وفي الثالثِ بقدرِ سبعين وفي الرابعِ بقدرِ خمسينَ.

وباقيها كغيرهَا منَ الصلواتِ.

f20.6   ثمَّ يَخْطُبُ خطبتين (نــدبـاً) كالجمعــةِ (في الأركــان والشـروط إلا كونهمـا بعـد الصـلاة بخـلاف خطبتي الجمعة فإنهما قبل الصلاة).

f20.7   فإنْ لمْ يُصَلِّ حتَّـى تَجَـلَّى الجميـعُ أوْغَابَتْ (الشمس حال كونِها) كاسفةً أوْ طَلَعَتِ الشمسُ والقمرُ خاسفٌ لمْ يُصَلِّ. ولـوْ أحْرَمَ فَتَجَلَّتْ أوْغَابَتْ كاسفةً أتَمَّهَا.

f21.0   صلاة الاستسقاء

f21.1   هيَ سنةٌ مؤكدةٌ (ولولمسافرٍ ومنفردٍ) ويُنْدَبُ لها الجماعةُ.

f21.2   فإذَا أجْـدَبَـتِ الأرضُ أو انْقطَعَتِ المياهُ أوْ قَلَّتْ وَعَظَ الإمامُ الناسَ

caliph (def: o25) or his representative) warns people against wrongdoing and orders them to repent for their sins, give charity (O: because this influences the acceptance of prayers), settle their differences with enemies (O: if the enmity is not for Allah's sake. Otherwise, it is not objectionable, for severing ties with the corrupt is something that one should do), and fast for three days (O: which must be consecutive, for this is obligatory if the caliph orders it). Then, on the fourth day while still fasting, they come out to an empty expanse (lit. "desert") in their work clothes, accompanied by those of the women who do not have attractive figures (dis: f12.4(N:)), livestock, men and women advanced in years, infants and small children, the pious, and those related to the Messenger of Allah (Allah bless him and give him peace); and they ask Allah to give them rain because of those present (O: i.e. by virtue of their spiritual grace (baraka), interceding through them). Each mentions to himself the good works he has done and intercedes through them.

Non-Muslim subjects of the Islamic state who attend are not hindered from doing so, but may not mix with us.

DESCRIPTION OF THE DROUGHT PRAYER

f21.3   The drought prayer consists of two rak'as like those of the 'Eid (def: f19.5).

The imam then gives two sermons like those of the 'Eid, except that in place of each Allahu Akbar (f19.7), the imam says, "I ask forgiveness of Allah Most Great, whom there is no god but He, the Living, the Ever Subsistent, and I turn to Him in repentance."

During the sermons, the imam frequently asks Allah's forgiveness (istighfar), blesses the Prophet (Allah bless him and give him peace), supplicates Allah, and recites the verses,

"Ask forgiveness of your Lord—verily He is oft-forgiving—and He will loose the sky upon you in torrents, aid you with wealth and sons, and make gardens and rivers yours" (Koran 71:10–12).

وأَمَرَهُمْ بالتوبة والصدقة (لأن لذلك أثراً في إجابة الدعاء) ومصالحة الأعداء (أي في عداوة لغير الله تعالى وأما هي فلا بأس بها لأن هجر الفاسق مطلوب) وصوم ثلاثة أيام (ويجب تتابع الصوم لأنه صار فرضاً عليهم بأمر الإمام لهم) ثم يَخْرُجُونَ في الرابع إلى الصحراء صياماً في ثياب بذلةٍ [(أي ما يلبس من ثياب المهنة وقت العمل)] ويَخْرُجُ غيرُ ذواتِ الهيئة من النساء والبهائم والشيوخ والعجائز والأطفال (الرضع) والصغار والصلحاء وأقاربُ رسولِ الله ﷺ، وَيَسْتَسْقُونَ بِهِمْ (أي يطلبون السقيا من الله) [ببركتهم ويستشفعون بهم) ويَذْكُرُ كلُّ في نفسه صالحَ عملِه ويَسْتَشْفِعُ بِه.

وإنْ خَرَجَ أهلُ الذمةِ لم يُمْنَعُوا لكنْ لَا يَخْتَلِطُونَ بنا.

صفة صلاة الاستسقاء

f21.3   وهي ركعتانِ كالعيد.

ثُمَّ يَخْطُبُ خطبتين كالعيدِ إلَّا أنَّهُ يَفْتَتِحُهُمَا (أي خطبتي الاستسقاء) بالاستغفار بدلَ التكبير (وصيغته في ابتداء الخطبة هي قوله «أَسْتَغْفِرُ اللهَ العظيمَ الذي لا إله إلَّا هوَ الحيّ القيّومَ وأتوبُ إليْهِ» يقول ذلك بدل كل تكبيرة).

ويُكْثِرُ فيهما من الاستغفار والصلاة على النبيِّ ﷺ والدعاء ومن ﴿اسْتَغْفِرُوا رَبَّكُمْ إنَّهُ كَانَ غَفَّاراً﴾ (الآيات وتمامها ﴿يُرْسِلِ السَّمَاءَ عَلَيْكُمْ مِدْرَاراً وَيُمْدِدْكُمْ بِأَمْوَالٍ وَبَنِينَ وَيَجْعَلْ لَكُمْ جَنَّاتٍ وَيَجْعَلْ لَكُمْ أَنْهَاراً﴾).

In the second sermon (O: about a third of the way through it) the imam turns toward the direction of prayer (qibla) and switches his cloak around (O: by putting the right side of it on his left and vice versa. It is also sunna to turn it upside down. Both sunnas can be effected by putting the lower left corner on the right shoulder and lower right corner on the left shoulder. The wisdom therein is the favorable portent of a change of state). The people do likewise.

He should supplicate to his utmost, both to himself and aloud. (O: Those present raise their hands with the backs of the hands up. The sunna supplication is: "O Allah, send us rain, raining wholesomely, healthily, torrentially, widespread, pouringly, in sheets, drenchingly, continuously till Judgement Day. O Allah, give us rain and make us not of those who despair. O Allah, servants and cities are in distress, hunger, and want, from which we can ask none but You for relief. O Allah, make the crops grow and the milk of the livestock flow, and send down the sky's blessings upon us and bring forth for us the blessings of the earth. Raise from us the affliction that none but You can lift.")

If they pray but are not given any rain, they repeat the prayer (O: until given rain). If they prepare (O: and gather), but are given rain before the prayer, they pray in thanks and ask for more.

f21.4   It is recommended for those whose land is flourishing to supplicate after prayers for those whose land is parched. (O: This being the middle course. The minimum is to make a supplication, while the optimum is to take the above measures of performing two rak'as with the two sermons, the supplications, and asking for forgiveness.)

f21.5   At the first rainfall of the year, it is recommended to uncover part of the body for the rain to strike.

f21.6   It is recommended to glorify Allah when thunder is heard (O: saying, "Glory to Him the thunder and the angels glorify, in awe of Him,") and when lightning is seen (O: saying, "Glory to

ويَسْتَقْبِلُ القِبلةَ في أثناء الخطبةِ الثانية (أي من نحـو ثلثها) ويُحَـوِّلُ رداءَهُ (بأن يجعـل يمين ردائـه يسـاره وعكسه ويسن الـتـنـكـيس بأن يجعـل أعـلاه أسفله، ويحصلان معـاً بجعل الطرف الأسفل الـذي على شقه الأيسر على عاتقه الأيمن والطرف الأسفل الذي على شقه الأيمن على عاتقه الأيسر. والحكمة فيها التفاؤل بتغير الحال) ويَفْعَلُ الناسُ كذلك.

ويُبَـالِـغُ في الدعاءِ سراً وجهراً (ويرفع الحاضـرون أيـديهم في الدعاء مشيرين بظهـور أكفهم إلى السماء والدعاء الوارد «اللَّهُمَّ أسْقِنا غَيْثاً مُغِيْثاً هَنِيْئاً مَرِيئاً سَحّاً عَامّـاً غَدَقـاً طَبَقـاً مُجَلّلاً دائـماً إلى يَوْم الدِّين اللَّهُمَّ أسْقِنا الغَيْثَ ولا تَجْعَلْنا مِنَ القَـانِطِينَ. اللَّهُمَّ إنّ بالعبَاد والبـلاد مِنَ الجَهْدِ والجُوع والضَّنْكِ ما لا نَشْكُو إلّا إلـيْـكَ اللَّهُمَّ أنْبِتْ لَنـا الـزَّرْعَ وأدِرَّ لَنَا الضَّـرْعَ وأنْـزِلْ عَلَيْنا مِنْ بَركَاتِ السَّماء وأنْبِتْ لَنَا مِنْ بَركَاتِ الأرْض. واكْشِفْ عَنّا مِنَ البَلاءِ ما لا يَكْشِفُهُ غَيْرُكَ»).

فإنْ صَلَّوْا ولمْ يُسْقَـوْا أَعَـادُوهَا (أي الصلاةَ وتكرر حتى يسقوا). وإنْ تأهَّبُوا (أي تهيـؤوا) واجتمعـوا] فَسُقُوا قبـلَ الصلاةِ صَلَّوْا شكراً وسَألُوا الزيادة.

f21.4   ويُنْـدَبُ لأهـل الخصب أنْ يَدْعُـوا لأهـل الجـدب خلفَ الصلوات (وهذا هو الوسط فيها وأدناه الدعاء وأعلى منهما يحصل بما تقدم من صلاة الركعتين مع الخطبتين والدعاء والاستغفار).

f21.5   ويُنْدَبُ أنْ يَكْشِفَ بعض بدنِه لِيُصِيبَهُ أولُ مطرٍ يَقَعُ في السنة.

f21.6   ويُسَبِّـحُ للرعـد (ويقـول «سُبْحـانَ الَّـذي يُسَبِّـحُ الـرَّعْـدُ بحَمْـدِه والمـلائكـةُ مِنْ خِيفَتِـه») والبـرق (ويقال

Him who shows you the lightning that you may have fear and hope").

عنده «سُبْحَانَ مَنْ يُرِيكُمُ البَرْقَ خَوْفاً وَطَمَعاً».

f21.7   If it rains so much that harm is feared, it is recommended to supplicate as has come in the sunna: "O Allah, around us, not upon us. O Allah, upon the hills and bluffs, the valley floors and copses of trees."

f21.7   وإذا كَثُرَ المَطَرُ وخُشِيَ ضَرَرُهُ دَعَـا بِرَفِعِـهِ بِمَـا وَرَدَ في السنةِ «اللهُمَّ حَوَالَيْنَـا وَلَا عَلَيْنا» إلى آخرهِ (أي إلى آخر الـدعـاء الـوارد وهو «اللّهُمَّ عَلَى الظِّرابِ والآكَامِ وبُطُونِ الأَوْدِيةِ وَمَنابتِ الشَّجَرِ»).

*

BOOK G

THE FUNERAL PRAYER (JANAZA)

CONTENTS:

g1.0   VISITING THE SICK AND DYING

g1.0   عيـادة الــمـريض وتلقين المحتضر

g1.1 It is recommended for everyone to frequently remember death, particularly if one is ill, and to prepare for it by repenting (def: p77) (O: because of the hadith,

"Remember often the Ender of Pleasures,"

meaning death, a hadith related by Tirmidhi, Ibn Hibban, and Hakim, the latter two classifying it as rigorously authenticated (sahih). Nasa'i's version has the addition,

"for truly, it is not remembered in a plentitude save it diminishes it, and not remembered in a dearth save it increases it,"

"plentitude" meaning of wives and this-worldly goods, and "dearth" meaning of spiritual works).

g1.1 يُنْدَبُ لكـلِّ أحدٍ أنْ يُكْثِرَ ذكرَ الموتِ والمريضُ آكدُ وَيَسْتَعِدَّ (كل أحد) لهُ بالتـوبـة (لخبـر «أكثـروا من ذكـر هاذم اللذات» يعني المـوت رواه الترمذي وابن حبـان والحاكم وصححاه وزاد النسائي : «فـإنـه ما ذكر في كثير إلا قلله ولا قليل إلا كثره» أي كثير من الأهل والدنيا وقليل من العمل) .

g1.2   It is recommended to visit the ill, even if the malady is only sore eyes, whether the person is a friend or enemy.

　　　If the sick person is a non-Muslim subject of the Islamic state (dhimmi, def: o11) then if he is a relative or neighbor, visiting him is recommended. If not, visiting him is merely permissible.

g1.3   It is offensive to sit lengthily with a sick person. It is recommended not to continuously visit (O: but only from time to time) unless one is a relative or similar person (O: of his friends) whom the sick person is fond of, or someone (O: of the righteous) from whose presence others derive spiritual blessing (baraka), for any of whom visiting the sick person is recommended at any time as long as there is no objection (O: by the sick person to long visits).

g1.4   If the visitor has hopes that the patient will survive, he supplicates for him (O: saying, "O Allah, Lord of Men, remove the harm and heal—for You are the Healer besides whom there is no other—with a cure that will not leave behind pain or sickness,") and then leaves. But if the visitor sees little hope of a recovery, he should encourage the sick person to repent and to make his bequests (def: L1–3) (O: by telling him, e.g. "You should repent of all your sins so that Allah Most High heals you, for repentance is reason for cures. And you should make some provision for bequests, as it prolongs one's life. A person should make bequests while alive and only die after having done so, for there is no one who does not pass on").

INSTRUCTING THE DYING PERSON

g1.5   If the visitor sees the person is dying, he should make him desirous of Allah's mercy (O: since hope should predominate over fear in this state) and should turn him to face the direction of prayer (qibla) by laying him on his right side, or if impossible, on his left. If this too is impossible, he is laid on his back (O: with his face and feet

g1.2   ويَعُودَ المريضَ ولَوْ مِنْ رَمَدٍ ويَعُمَّ بها العدوَّ والصديقَ.
فإنْ كانَ ذِمِّيَّاً فإنِ اقْتَـرَنَ به قرابةٌ أوْ جوارٌ نُدِبَتْ عيادتُهُ وإلَّا أُبِيحَتْ.

g1.3   ويُكْرَهُ إطالةُ القعودِ عنـدَهُ ونُـنْـدَبُ غِبَّاً (أي وقتاً وقتاً لا على الدوام) إلَّا لأقـاربِه ونَحْوِهِمْ ممن يَأْنَسُ (هو بهم من الأصدقاء) أوْ (كان الزائر ممن) يَتَبَرَّكُ به (من أهل الصلاح) فَـ] (حينئذ تندب الـزيـارة)] كلَّ وقتٍ ما لم يُنْـهَ (المـريض عن الإطالة).

g1.4   فإنْ طَمِـعَ في حيـاتـهِ دَعَـا (الـزائـرُ) له وانْصَرَفَ (فيقـول في دعائه «اللهُمَّ رَبَّ النّـاسِ أَذْهِبِ البَـأْسَ اشفِ وأنتَ الشَّـافِي لَا شَافِيَ إلَّا أنتَ شفاءً لَا يُغَـادِرُ أَلَماً ولَا سَقماً) وإلَّا رَغَّبَهُ في التوبة والـوصـيـة (بأن يقول له عليك بالتوبة من جميع الـذنـوب حتى يعـافيك الله تعالى والتـوبـة سبب للشفـاء. وعليك بالوصية فإن الـوصيـة تطيل العمر وينبغي للحي أن يوصي وأن يمـوت على وصيـة لأنه ما من أحد إلا ويموت).

تلقين المحتضر

g1.5   وإنْ رَآهُ مَنـزولاً به أَطْمَعَهُ في رحمـة اللهِ (لأنـه ينبغي له تقديم الـرجاء على الخوف في هذه الحالة) وَوَجَّهَهُ إلى القبلة على جنبـه الأيمنِ فإنْ تَعَذَّرَ فالأيسر فإن تَعَـذَّرَ فقفـاهُ (ووجهه وأخمصاه للقبلة

towards the direction of prayer (qibla) by propping up his head a little, *feet* meaning the bottoms of them).

The visitor should then instruct the dying person to say "There is no god but Allah," letting him hear it (N: so he can repeat it) but without irritating insistence, and without telling him "Say ...." When he says it, then he is let be until he himself speaks of something else.

It is recommended that the person instructing him to say it be neither his heir nor enemy.

IMMEDIATE MEASURES AFTER DEATH

g1.6   When he dies, it is recommended that the kindliest to him of his unmarriageable kin (mahram) close his eyes. It is recommended:

(1) to close his jaws (O: with a wide bandage tied above his head so his mouth is not left open);

(2) to make his joints flexible (O: by bending the forearm to the upper arm, calf to thigh, thigh to stomach, and then straightening them, and to similarly flex the fingers in order to facilitate washing and shrouding him. If the joints are flexed at this point, they remain flexible, but if not, it becomes impossible afterwards);

(3) to (O: gently) remove his clothes, and to cover him with a light cloth (O: tucking the edge under his head and feet so they do not become uncovered);

(4) and to place something heavy on his stomach (O: to prevent bloating).

g1.7   It is recommended to hasten in paying off the debts of the deceased (dis: L4.2–3) or having them waived (n: by creditors). It is recommended to hurry in implementing his bequests, and in readying him for burial (O: haste being recommended (N: in readying him and burying him) when it is unlikely that the body will rapidly change, but obligatory when this is likely).

بأن يرفــع رأسـه قليـلاً والأخمصـان هنـا أسفل الرجلين) .

وَلَقَّنَهُ قولَ لَا إلَـهَ إلَّا اللهُ لِيَسْمَعَهَـا فَيَقُـولَهَـا بلا إلحاحٍ ولاَ يَقُلْ قُلْ فإذا قَالَها تُركَ حَتَّى يَتَكَلَّمَ بغيرهَا .

(وَينـدب) أنْ يَكُونَ الملقِّنُ غيـرَ مُتَّهمٍ بإرثٍ وعداوةٍ .

ما يندب إذا مات

g1.6   فإذا مَاتَ نُدِبَ لأرفقِ محارمِهِ تغميضُهُ (أي تغميض عينيه) وَ(ندب) شَدُّ (أي ربط) لَحْيَيْهِ (بعصابة عريضة تربط فوق رأسه لئلا يبقى فمه منفتحاً وتليينُ مفـاصلِهِ (فيـرد ساعـده إلى عضده وساقه إلى فخذه وفخذه إلى بطنه ثم تمد وتليين أصـابعه تسهيـلاً لغسله وتكفينه فإذ لينت المفـاصـل حينئـذ لانت وإلا فلا يمكن تليينها بعد) ونَـزْعُ ثيابِهِ (ويتلطف في نزعهـا) ثمَّ يُسْتَـرُ بثـوبٍ خفيفٍ (ويجعل طرفـاه تحت رأسـه ورجليه لئلا ينكشـف) ويُجْعَلُ على بطنِهِ شيءٌ ثقيلٌ (لئلا ينتفخ) .

g1.7   ويُبَادَرُ (ندباً) إلى قضاءِ دَيْنِهِ أوْ إبرائِه منـهُ و(ينـدب إلى) تنفيذ وصيتِهِ وتجهيزِهِ (هذا إن لم يخف تغيره وإلا فيجب أن يبـادر إلى ذلك (ح : أي إلى تجهيزه ودفنه)) .

g1.8   When someone dies suddenly (O: or is believed to have died), the body is left until it is certain he is dead (O: by a change in odor or the like).

g1.8   فإذا مَاتَ (أوْ ظنّ موتــه) فجأةً تُرك لِيُتَيَقَّنَ موتُهُ (بتغير الرائحة ونحوها).

g1.9   Washing the dead person, shrouding him, praying over him, carrying him, and burying him are communal obligations (def: c3.2).

g1.9   وغسلُهُ وتكفينُـهُ والصلاةُ عليه وحملُهُ ودفنُهُ فروضُ كفايةٍ.

*

g2.0   WASHING THE BODY

g2.0   غسل الميت

g2.1   Then the body is washed (O: obligatorily).

g2.1   ثُمَّ يُغَسَّلُ (وجوباً).

WHO SHOULD WASH THE BODY

الأولى بغسله

g2.2   When the deceased is male, the best suited to wash the body (A: anyone may wash it, but it is not permissible (N: being offensive) for a non-Muslim to wash the body of a Muslim, and non-Muslim relatives are as though nonexistent in the following priority list) is:

g2.2   فإذا كَانَ رجلًا فالأولى بغسلِه الأبُ ثمَّ الجَدُّ (أبـو الأب) ثمَّ الابنُ (ثم ابـن الابن) ثمَّ الأخُ ثمَّ العمُّ ثمَّ ابنُـهُ (أي ابـن الـعم) على ترتيب العصبــاتِ ثمَّ

(1) the father of the deceased;

(2) the father's father;

(3) the son;

(4) the son's son;

(5) the brother;

(6) the father's brother;

(7) the son of the father's brother;

(8) those named in the sequence given at L10.6(12–14);

(9) men related to the deceased;

(10) men not related to him;

(11) his wife;

(12) and his unmarriageable female relatives (mahram, def: m6.1).

الـرجـالُ الأقاربُ ثمَّ الأَجانبُ ثمَّ الزوجةُ ثمَّ النساءُ المحارمُ.

g2.3 If the deceased is female, the best suited to wash the body is:

(1) one of her female relatives (O: meaning the women of her immediate family, such as her daughter or mother);

(2) other women;

(3) her husband;

(4) and then a member of her unmarriageable male relatives (mahram, def: m6.2) (O: in the above (g2.2) order).

g2.3 وإنْ كَانَ امـرأةً غَسَّلَهـا النساءُ الأقاربُ (وهن محارمها كالبنت والأم) ثمَّ الأجـانبُ ثمَّ الـزوجُ ثمَّ الـرجالُ المحارمُ (على الترتيب).

g2.4 If the deceased is a non-Muslim, then his non-Muslim relatives are better suited to wash him.

g2.4 وإنْ كَانَ كافراً فأقاربُهُ الكفارُ أحقُّ.

g2.5 It is recommended that the washer be trustworthy (O: so that he can be relied on to wash the deceased completely and so forth. If he notices something good, it is sunna to mention it, but if he notices something bad, it is unlawful to mention it, as this is slander (ghiba, def: r2.2)).

g2.5 ويُنْدَبُ كونُ الغـاسـلِ أمينـاً (ليوثق به في تكميل غسله وغيره فإن رأى خيراً سن ذكره أو رأى ضده حرم ذكره لأنه غيبة).

HOW TO WASH THE BODY

كيفية غسل الميت

g2.6 It is obligatory for the washer to keep the nakedness (def: f5.3) of the deceased clothed (f5.4) while washing him.

It is sunna that no one be present except the washer and his assistant. (O: It is preferable that the body be washed while clothed in an ankle-length shirt into which the washer inserts his hand from the sleeve if ample enough, while pouring water over the garment and washing the body

g2.6 ويُسْتَـرُ الميتُ في الغسـلِ [أي وجب على الغاسل أن يستر عورة الميت)].

وَ(سن أن) لاَ يَحْضُـرَ سِوَى الغـاسـلِ ومعينِـهِ (ويستحب أن يغسل في قميص ويـدخـل الغـاسـل يده في كمـه إن كان واسعـاً ويصب المـاء من فوق القميص ويغسل من تحته فإن لم يكن كم القميص

under it. If the sleeve is not wide enough for this, he tears open the seam from the side under the arm. It is obligatory that the body be covered from navel to knees.) Incense should be burned from the start of washing to the finish (O: as is sunna).

It is best to wash the body under a roof, and best that cold water be used, except when necessary (O: to heat it, such as to clean away filth that could not otherwise be removed, or when the weather is cold, since the deceased suffers from it just as a living person would).

واسعـاً فتق رؤوس الـدخـاريص ويجب تغطيـة ما بين سرتـه وركبتيـه) وَ(سن أن) يُبَخَّرَ مِنْ أولِ غسلِهِ إلى آخرِهِ .

والأوْلَى تحتَ سقف وبمـاءٍ بارِدٍ إلّا لحـاجةٍ (إلى الماء المسخن كإزالة وسخ لا يزول إلا بالمسخن وبــرد شديــد لأن الميت يتأذى مثل ما يتأذى به الحي) .

g2.7   It is unlawful to look at the nakedness of the deceased (def: f5.3) or touch it, except with a cloth (O: or similar, since direct contact without there being something in between is not permissible). It is recommended not to look at or directly touch the other parts of the body save with a cloth.

g2.7   ويَحْرُمُ نظرُ عورتِهِ ومسُّهَا إلّا بخرقةٍ (ونحوها فلا يجوز المس بغير حائل) .

ويُنْدَبُ أنْ لَا يَنْظُرَ إلى غيرِهَا ولَا يَمَسَّهُ إلّا بخرقة .

g2.8   It is recommended:

(1)   to force out waste from the stomach;

(2)   to clean the private parts of filth (O: which is recommended when one is not certain anything has exited from those parts, though if it has, cleaning is obligatory);

(3)   to give the body ablution (wudu) (O: like the ablution of a living person, turning the head when rinsing the mouth and nostrils so that no water reaches the stomach);

(4)   to make the intention of performing the purificatory bath (ghusl), and then to wash the head, beard, and body each three times with water infused (with *sidr* (n: i.e. lote tree (*Rhamus spina christi*) leaves), taking care each time to press the hand on the stomach (N: in a downward stroke) (O: leaning on it to force its contents out, but gently so as not to hurt the deceased. If the hair of the head or beard is matted, it should be gently combed with a wide-toothed comb so as not to pull any out. If hair comes out as a result, the washer should return it and place it in the shroud to be buried with the deceased).

g2.8   ويُخرِجُ (ندباً) مَا في بطنِهِ منَ الـفـضـلاتِ ويَسْتَنْجِيـهِ (إن لم يتحقق خروج شيء من دبره وإلا وجب) ويُوَضِّئُهُ (كـوضـوءِ الحي ويميـل رأسـه عنـد المضمضة والاستنشاق لئلا يصل الماء إلى جوفه) ويَنْوِي غسلَهُ ويَغْسِلُ رَأَسَهُ ولحيتَهُ وجسدَهُ بماءٍ وسدرٍ ثلاثاً يَتَعَهُّدُ كلَّ مرةٍ إمرارَ اليد على البطنِ (أي يجعل يده تمر في كل مرة على بطنه ويتكىء عليه حتى يخرج ما فيه لكن بالرفق بحيث لا يتأذى وإذا كان هناك شعر متلبد من رأسه أوْ لحيته سرحـه بمشط واسع الأسنان ويـرفق في ذلك حتى لا ينتتف منه شيء . فإذا خرج بسبب ذلك شعر رده الغـاسل وجعله في كفنه ليدفن معه) .

g2.9   (O: It is sunna:

(1) that the place of washing be on an incline so the head is highest and the water flows down away from it;

(2) that there be an incense burner present with incense in it;

(3) to put one's right hand on the shoulder of the deceased with the thumb on the nape of his neck so that the head does not loll, and brace his back up against one's right knee;

(4) to have the helper pour abundant water during the process to obviate offensive odors from waste leaving the body;

(5) to stroke the stomach firmly and effectively with one's left hand;

(6) and when finished, to lay the deceased down again on his back with his feet towards the direction of prayer (qibla).)

g2.10   If the body is not clean after three times, one washes it again, reaching an odd number of washings. (O: If clean after an even number of washings, it is sunna to add another. If clean after an odd number, one does not add any.)

It is sunna to add a little camphor to the water, especially for the last washing.

The obligatory minimum for this purificatory bath (ghusl) is that water reach all external parts of the body (O: and it is obligatory to remove any filth (najasa, def: e14.1), if present).

The body should be dried with a cloth afterwards.

If anything leaves the body after washing, only the affected area need be washed. (O: It is not necessary to repeat the ablution (wudu) or bath (ghusl), even if the excretion is from the front or rear private parts.)

g2.9 (السنـة أن يكـون المـوضـع منحـدراً بحيث يكون رأسه أعلى لينحدر عنـه الماء ويكـون عنده مجمرة فيها بخور ويضـع يده اليمنى على كتفـه وإبهامه في نقرة قفاه لئلا يميل رأسه ويسند ظهره إلى ركبتـه اليمنى ويصب علیـه المعین ماء كثيراً لئلا يظهر رائحة ما يخرج منه ويمر يده اليسرى على بطنه إمراراً بليغاً ثم يَرده هيئة الاستلقاء ويلقيه على ظهره ورجلاه إلى القبلة) .

g2.10 فإنْ لَمْ يَنْظُفْ زَادَ وتـراً . (ولـو حصلت النظافة بالشفع سن الوتر، ولو حصل الإنقاء بالوتر فلا يزاد بعده) .

ويَجْعَـلُ في المـاء قلیـلَ كافـورٍ وفي الأخيرَة آكَدُ .

وواجبُـهُ تعمیـم البـدنِ بالمـاءِ (وإن كانت النجاسة عینیة فلا بد من زوال عينها) .

ثُمَّ يُنَشِّفُ بثوب .

فإنْ خَرَجَ مِنـهُ شيءٌ بعـدَ الغسلِ كَفَاهُ غسـلُ المحـلّ . (ولا يجب وضـوء ولا غسل وإن خرج من أحد السبيلين) .

*

g3.0   SHROUDING THE BODY

g3.0   كفن الميت

g3.1   Then the body is shrouded (O: obligatorily).

g3.1   ثمَّ يُكَفَّنُ (وجوباً).

g3.2   If the deceased is male it is recommended that he be wrapped in three washed (O: not new) white shrouds, without an ankle-length shirt or turban, each shroud covering the whole body (O: unless the deceased was in a state of pilgrim sanctity (ihram), in which case the head of the male or face of the female must be left uncovered). It is permissible to add (O: beneath the shrouds) an ankle-length shirt and a turban. It is unlawful to use silk (N: to shroud a man).

If the deceased is a woman it is recommended that she be dressed in a wraparound, headcover, and a shift, and that she be wrapped in two shrouds (O: like those used for men in being white and washed), each of which covers her (O: entire body). It is offensive for a woman's shroud to be made of silk, or fabric dyed with saffron or safflower.

The obligatory minimum for shrouding a man or woman is to completely cover their nakedness. (O: For a man it is obligatory to cover the navel, the knees, and what lies between them, and for a woman, her entire body.)

g3.2   فإنْ كانَ رجـلاً نُدِبَ لهُ ثلاثُ لفـائفَ بيضٍ مغسولةٍ (لا جديـدة) كلُّ واحدةٍ تَسْتُرُ كلَّ البدنِ (أي تعمه غير رأس المحـرم ووجه المحرمة) لا قميصَ فيهَا ولا عمـامـةً فإنْ زَادَ عَلَيْهَا قميصاً وعمامةً جاز (وتـكـون هذه الـزيـادة تحـت اللفائف). ويَحْرُمُ الحريرُ.

و(يندب) للمرأةِ إزارٌ وخمارٌ وقميصٌ ولفـافتـانِ (موصوفتان بما وصف به كفن الرجل من البياض والغسل) سابغتانِ (أي يعمـان جميع بدنهـا). ويُكْرَهُ لها حريرٌ ومزعفرٌ ومعصفرٌ (وهو الثوب المصبوغ بالعصفر).

والـواجبُ في الـرجل والمرأةِ ما يَسْتُرُ العـورة. (وهي بالنسبة للرجل ما بين السـرة والـركبـة فالـواجب في حقه ما يسترهما وما بينهما وبالنسبة للمرأة جميع بدنها).

g3.3   It is recommended:

(1)   to scent the shrouds with incense (O: from aloes and the like);

(2)   to sprinkle them with hunut (O: an aromatic compound of camphor, reed perfume, and red and white sandalwood) and camphor;

(3)   to place cotton and hunut on the apertures of the body (O: such as the eyes, mouth, nostrils, and ears) and on places that touch the ground in prostration (O: the forehead, nose, palms, bottoms of the feet, and the knees);

(4)   and it is commendable to perfume the entire body.

g3.3   ويُبَخَّرُ الكفنُ (بـالعود ونحوه [بأن تنصب مجمرة ويوضع عليها الكفن ليصيبها دخان العود]) ويُذَرُّ عليْهِ الحنوطُ (وهـو نوع من الطيب مركب من الكـافور وذريـرة الـقـصـب والصنـدل الأحـمـر والأبيض) والكـافورُ ويَجْعَلُ قطناً بحنوطٍ على منافذِه (كعينيه وفمه ومنخريه وأذنيه) ومـواضع السجودِ (وهي الجبهة والأنف وبـاطن الكفين وبـاطن القـدمين وعلى الركبتين) ولوْ طَيَّبَ جميعَ بدنِه فحسنٌ.

g3.4   If a person dies while in a state of pilgrim sanctity (ihram, def: j3), it is unlawful to scent the body, to dress it in a garment with any sewing in it (A: if male), and to cover the head of a male's body or the face of a female's.

فإنْ مَاتَ مُحرماً حَرُمَ الطيبُ والمخيطُ وتغطيةُ رأسِ الرجلِ ووجهِ المرأةِ.   g3.4

g3.5   It is not recommended to prepare a shroud for oneself, unless to ensure that it comes from a lawful source or from the effects of a virtuous person (O: meaning those who worship much, or religious scholars who apply their knowledge in their lives. In such a case, one may procure it for the blessing therein (tabarruk, dis: w31)).

ولا يُنْدَبُ أنْ يُعِدَّ لنفسِهِ كفناً إلاَّ أنْ يَقْطَعَ بحلِّهِ أوْ مِنْ أثرِ أهلِ الخير (وأهل الخير هم العباد والعلماء العاملون فحينئذ يعده ويهيئه لأجل التبرك به).   g3.5

*

g4.0   THE PRAYER OVER THE DEAD

الصلاة على الميت   g4.0

g4.1   Then the deceased is prayed over (O: obligatorily).
    The obligation is fulfilled if a single Muslim male (O: who has reached the age of discrimination) prays over the deceased. It is not fulfilled by a prayer of women alone when there is a male available, though if there is no one besides women, they are obliged to pray and their prayer fulfills the obligation.

ثمَّ يُصَلَّى عليْهِ (وجوباً). ويَسْقُطُ الفرضُ بذكَرٍ واحدٍ (وهذا بشرط التمييـز) دونَ النسـاءِ إن حَضَرَهُنَّ رجـلٌ [(وصلين فلا تسقط صلاة الجنازة بهن مع وجـود الـذكر)] فإنْ لمْ يُوجَدْ غيرُهُنَّ لزمَهُنَّ ويَسْقُطُ الفرضُ بهنَّ.   g4.1

g4.2   It is recommended to perform the funeral prayer in a group. It is offensive to pray it at a cemetery (O: though not in a mosque, which is preferable).

وتُنْدَبُ فيهـا الجمـاعةُ وتُكْرَهُ في المقبـرةِ (ولا تكره في المسجـد بل تستحب فيه).   g4.2

WHO SHOULD LEAD THE FUNERAL PRAYER

أوْلى الناس بالصلاة

g4.3   The person best suited to lead the funeral prayer as imam is the one who is best suited to wash the deceased (dis: g2.2) except for women, who have no right to lead (dis: f12.27). The family member responsible for the deceased is given preference in leading the prayer even over the sultan (O: or imam of the mosque).

وأوْلى الناس بالصلاةِ أولاهُمْ بالغسلِ مِنْ أقاربِهِ إلاَّ النساءَ فلاَ حقَّ لهُنَّ [(لعـدم أهليتهن لإمـامتها)] ويُقَدَّمُ الوليُّ على السلطانِ (ويلزم منه تقديمه على إمام المسجـد أيضـاً) والأسنُّ (في الإسلام   g4.3

The older of two persons (O: meaning more years in Islam, provided he is upright (def: o24.4)) takes precedence over the more learned in Sacred Law (O: when they are at the same level (n: of the g2.2 precedence order), such as two sons or two brothers, since the purpose is to pray for the deceased, and the supplication of an older person is more likely to be answered) and (n: the older) is given precedence over any others (A: at that level), though if they are of the same age, then one is chosen according to the order used for the imamate of other prayers (def: f12.25).

The responsible family member is given precedence in leading the funeral prayer even when the deceased has stipulated some other nonfamily member to be the imam.

PLACING THE BODY FOR THE FUNERAL PRAYER

g4.4   It is recommended (N: in the funeral prayer itself, where the deceased, enshrouded, is on a bier in front of the imam and lying on his right side facing the direction of prayer (qibla)) that the imam stand by the head of the deceased, if male, and by the posterior, if female (O: because this better screens her from view).

g4.5   If there are several bodies, it is best to perform a separate funeral prayer for each individual, though it is permissible to pray for all of them in a single prayer by putting the biers directly in front of the imam (O: one after another (N: parallel with the rows of worshippers), each body facing the direction of prayer (qibla)). The closest body to the imam (O: if the dead differ in gender) should be an adult male, then a boy, then a woman (O: though if all are male, all female, or all boys), then the best Muslim, then the next best (O: in piety, abstinence from this world, godfearingness, and all praiseworthy traits), and so forth.

If bodies are brought successively, the first one brought is placed closest to the imam, even if a prior arrival is less virtuous or is a boy, though not if a female, whose body should be placed further from the imam than that of a male brought subsequently.

العـدل) على الأفقـه (منـه وهـذا عنـد استـوائهمـا في درجـة واحـدة كابنين أو أخـوين لأن الغـرض هنـا الـدعـاء ودعاء الأسن أقـرب إلى الإجـابـة) وغيـره فإن اسْتَوَوا في السنِّ رُتِّبُوا كباقي الصلاة.
ولـوْ أوصى أنْ يُصَلّيَ عليـه أجنبيّ قُدِّمَ الوَليُّ عليه.

وضع الجنائز للصلاة

g4.4   ويَقِفُ الإمـامُ (نـدباً) عنـد رأس الرجل وعجيزة المرأة (لأنه أستر لها).

g4.5   فإن اجْتَمَعَ جنائزُ فالأفضـلُ إفرادُ كلِّ واحدٍ بصلاةٍ، ويَجُوزُ أنْ يُصَلّيَ عليهمْ دفعـةً واحـدةً ويَضَعَهُمْ بيْنَ يَدَيْـهِ بعضُهُمْ خلفَ بعضٍ هكذا (أي مصطفين واحـداً خلف واحد وموجهين إلى القبلة) ويليـهِ (أي المصلي على الجنائز) الرجل ثمَّ (يقـدم) الصبيُّ (على غيره من الجنائز المختلفة الجنس) ثمَّ المرأةُ ثمَّ (إذَا كانوا كلهم ذكوراً أو إناثاً أو صبيـاناً قدم إليه) الأفضـلُ فالأفضـلُ (بـالـورع والـزهد والتقـوى وسائر الخصال الحميدة [ولا اعتبارَ بالرِّقِّ والحرية]).
ولـوْ جَاءَ واحـدٌ بعد واحدٍ قُدِّمَ إلى الإمـام (أي إلى ما يليه) الأسبقُ ولوْ (كان السـابقُ) مفضـولاً وصبيـاً إلّا المرأة فتُؤَخَّر للذكر المتأخِّر مجيئُهُ.

DESCRIPTION OF THE FUNERAL PRAYER

صفة الصلاة على الميت

g4.6   Then one intends to perform the prayer. One must keep in mind its obligatory character, though need not explicitly intend it as a communal obligation (def: c3.2). (O: One may confine oneself to merely intending to pray four Allahu Akbars over the particular deceased person as an obligatory act, without intending its being in fulfillment of a communal obligation. The intention must coincide with one's opening Allahu Akbar.)

It is valid for someone to perform a funeral prayer for a dead person who is absent (dis: g4.18) while following an imam who is praying over a dead person who is present.

g4.6   ثُمَّ يَنْـوي ويَـجبُ التعــرُّضُ للفـرضيــة دونَ فرضِ الكفـايةِ (بل له أن يقتصـر على قولـه أصلي على هذا الميت أربـع تكبيرات فرضاً من غيـر التعرض لذكر الكفاية ويجب كون النية مقرونة مع التكبير).

ولــوْ صَلَّى على غائبٍ خَلفَ مَنْ (أي إمام) يُصَلِّي على حاضرٍ صَحَّ.

g4.7   One says "Allahu akbar" four times in the funeral prayer, raising one's hands (O: to shoulder level) at each one, and it is recommended between each one to fold the right hand over the left. The funeral prayer is not invalidated by adding a fifth Allahu Akbar, even intentionally, though if the imam adds one the follower does not do likewise, but simply waits to finish with him when he says his Salams.

g4.7   ويُكَبِّـرُ أربعاً رافعاً يديْهِ (حذو منكبيهِ) ويَضَعُ يمناهُ على يسراهُ (ندباً) بين كلِّ تكبيـرتَيْنِ . فإنْ كَبَّرَ خمساً ولـوْ عمداً لمْ تَبْطُلْ لكِنْ (لوكبر الإمام خمساً) لا يُتَـابِعُهُ المأمـومُ في الخامسة بلْ يَنْتَظِرُهُ لِيُسَلِّمَ مَعَهُ.

g4.8   After the first Allahu Akbar it is obligatory to recite the Fatiha. It is recommended to say "I take refuge, etc." (Ta'awwudh, def: f8.16) before it and "Ameen" after it, though not to recite the Opening Supplication (Istiftah, f8.13) or a sura therein.

(A: It is obligatory that the Fatiha be recited in the funeral prayer and that the other spoken elements be uttered, but as for each occurring after its respective Allahu Akbar, the only one which must obligatorily be in its place is the Blessings on the Prophet (Allah bless him and give him peace), which must come after the second Allahu Akbar.)

g4.8   ويَقْـرَأُ الفـاتحـةَ (وجوباً) بعدَ الأولى ويُنْــدَبُ الـتعـوُّذُ والتأمينُ دونَ الاستفتاحِ والسورة.

(ع : يجب قراءة الفـاتحـة وغيرها من الأركـان القولية في الصلاة على الميت . أما وقوع كل منها بعد تكبيرته فإنما يجب ذلـك في حق الـصــلاة على الـنـبي ﷺ فيجب أن تكون بعد التكبيرة الثانية).

g4.9   After the second Allahu Akbar (N: and one remains standing throughout the funeral prayer), it is obligatory to say the Blessings on the Prophet (Allah bless him and give him peace),

g4.9   ويُصَلِّي (وجـوبـاً) على النبيِّ ﷺ بعـدَ الثـانيـةِ ثُمَّ يَدْعـو (المصلي بعد

after which it is sunna to supplicate for the believers. (O: It is also sunna to bless the folk of the Prophet after the blessings upon him (Allah bless him and give him peace) and to say "al-Hamdu lillah" before it.)

الصلاة على النبي ﷺ) للمؤمنين (وهذا الدعاء على سبيل السنة لا على طريق الوجوب وكذلك تسن الصلاة على الآل عقبها والحمد قبل الصلاة على النبي ﷺ.)

g4.10   After the third Allahu Akbar one supplicates for the deceased. The recommended supplication is: "O Allah, this is Your slave, and son of Your slave. He has left the zephyr of this world and its spaciousness, in which were the things and people he loved, for the darkness of the grave and that which he will meet. He testified that there is no god but You alone without a partner, and that Muhammad is Your slave and messenger. You know him better than we. O Allah, he has gone to remain with You, and You are the best to remain with. He is now in need of Your mercy, and You have no need to torment him. We come to You in desire for You, interceding for him. O Allah, if he did well, treat him the better, and if he did wrong, disregard it and through Your mercy show him Your good pleasure and protect him from the trial and torment of the grave. Make his grave spacious for him and distance the earth from his sides, and through Your mercy protect him from Your torment until You raise him and send him safely to Your paradise, O Most Merciful of the Merciful." (n: This is the optimal supplication. The minimum is mentioned below at g4.13(f).)

g4.10   ثم يَدْعو للميت بعد الثالثة فيقول اللَّهُمَّ هذا عَبْدُكَ وَابْنُ عَبْدِكَ خَرَجَ مِنْ رَوحِ الدُّنْيا وسِعَتِها (أي نسيم ريحها واتساعها) ومَحْبوبُـهُ وأحِبّاؤُهُ فيها إلى ظُلْمَةِ القبر ومَا هُوَ لاَقِيهِ. كَانَ يَشْهَدُ أنْ لاَ إلهَ إلاَّ أنْتَ وَحـدَكَ لاَ شَريـكَ لَكَ وَأنَّ مُحَمّـداً عَبْدُكَ وَرَسُـولُكَ وأنْتَ أَعْلَمُ بِه مِنّا. اَللَّهُمَّ إنّـهُ نَزَلَ بِكَ [(أي صَار ضيفاً عنـدك)] وأنْتَ خيرُ مَنْـزُولٍ بِه وأصْبَحَ فَقيراً إلى رَحْمَتِكَ وأنْتَ غَنيُّ عَن عذابِه وقـدْ جِئْنَاكَ راغبين إلَيْكَ شُفَعاءَ لَهُ اللَّهُمَّ إنْ كَانَ مُحْسِناً فَزِدْ في إحْسانِـه وإنْ كَانَ مُسيئاً فَتَجـاوَزْ عَنْـهُ ولَقِّه بِرَحْمَتِكَ رِضَاكَ وَقِه فِتْنَـةَ القَبر وعَذابَهُ وَأفْسَحْ لَهُ في قَبْرِه وجـاف الأرْضَ عَنْ جَنْبَيْـه ولَقّـه بِرَحْمَتِكَ الأمْنَ مِنْ عَذابِـكَ حَتَّى تَبْعَثـهُ آمِناً إلى جَنّتِكَ يا أرْحَمَ الراحمينَ.

g4.11   It is commendable to say before the above: "O Allah, forgive those of us who are alive and those who are dead, those present and those absent, those who are young and those who are old, those who are male and those who are female. O Allah, let those of us You give life live by Islam, and let those of us You take back die in a state of faith."

If it is the funeral of a child, one may add to this: "O Allah, send him ahead to smoothe the way for his parents, and make him a reason for reward, a treasure, admonition, reflection, and intercessor. Make the scales of their good deeds heavy through him, and fill their hearts with patience."

g4.11   وحَسُنَ أَنْ يُقـدَّمَ عليْـه «اللَّهُمَّ اغْفِرْ لِحَيِّنَا ومَيِّتِنَا وشاهِدِنا (أي حاضرنا) وغـائِبِنَا وصَغيرِنا وكَبيرِنَا وذَكَرِنَا وأنْثَانَا. اللهُمَّ مَنْ أحْيَيْتَـهُ مِنَّا فَأَحْيِه على الإسلام ومَنْ تَوَفَّيْتَهُ مِنّا فَتَوَفّه على الإيمانِ» ويَقُولُ في الصلاة على الطفـل [(ومثله المميـز الـذي لم يبـلغ)] مَعَ هذا الثـانِي «اللَّهُمَّ اجْعَلْهُ فَرَطـاً لأبَـوَيْـه [(أي سابقاً مهيئاً لمصالحهما في الآخرة)] وسَلَفاً وذُخْراً وعظَةً وَاعْتِبَاراً وشَفِيعاً وثَقِّلْ بِه مَوَازِينَهُما وأفْرِغِ الصَّبْرَ على قُلوبِهِمَا».

g4.12   After the fourth Allahu Akbar, it is sunna to say, "O Allah, do not withhold from us his recompense, nor try us after him, but forgive us and him."

Then one says "as-Salamu 'alaykum" twice (O: the first one being obligatory and the second sunna).

g4.13   The integrals of the funeral prayer are seven:

(a) the intention;

(b) standing;

(c) saying "Allahu akbar" four times;

(d) the Fatiha;

(e) the Blessings on the Prophet (Allah bless him and give him peace);

(f) the supplication for the deceased, the minimum being "O Allah, forgive this deceased";

(g) and the first of the two times one says "as-Salamu 'alaykum" to finish the prayer.

g4.14   The conditions of the funeral prayer are the same as other prayers (def: f9.13), but in addition require:

(a) that the deceased's body has been washed before the prayer;

(b) and that the imam and those praying do not stand ahead of the body during the prayer (N: i.e. closer to the direction of prayer (qibla)).

It is offensive to perform the funeral prayer over a body before it has been shrouded.

If someone dies under a pile of rubble, and it is impossible to take out the body and wash it (non-(a) above), then he is not prayed over.

g4.15   A latecomer to the funeral prayer whom the imam has preceded by having already said

g4.12   وَيَقُـولُ بعـدَ الـرابعـةِ (على سبيـل السنيـة) «اللَّهُمَّ لَا تَحْرِمْنَا أُجْرَهُ ولاَ تَفْتِنَّا بَعْدَهُ وَاغْفِرْ لَنَا ولَهُ» .

ثُمَّ يُسَلِّمُ تسليمتَيْنِ (﴿وهذا هو﴾ الركن [السادس و] هو التسليمة الأولى والثانية سنة) .

g4.13   وواجبـاتُهَـا سبعةٌ النيةُ والقيامُ وأربـعُ تكبيراتٍ والفـاتحةُ والصَلاةُ علَى النبيِّ ﷺ وأدنى الـدعـاءِ وهوَ «اللَّهُمَّ اغْفِرْ لِهٰذَا الميِّتِ» والتسليمةُ الأُولَى .

g4.14   وشـرطُهَا كغيرِهَا ويَزيدُ تقديمَ الغسل وأنْ لَا يَتَقَدَّمَ (المصلي) علَى الجنازة .
وتُكْرَهُ (الصلاة على الميت) قبلَ الكفن .
فإِنْ مَاتَ [فـي بِئـرٍ أوْ] تحـتَ هدْمٍ وتعَذَّرَ إخْرَاجُهُ وغسلُهُ لَمْ يُصَلَّ عليهِ .

g4.15   ومَنْ سَبَقَـهُ الإمـامُ ببعض

"Allahu akbar" a number of times recites (O: the Fatiha) after his own opening Allahu Akbar, and then says "Allahu akbar" each time the imam does, though he performs the integrals in order from the point at which he began (O: reciting the Fatiha after his first Allahu Akbar, the Blessings on the Prophet (Allah bless him and give him peace) after the second, and the supplication for the deceased after his third), and when the imam finishes with Salams, the latecomer goes on to complete his remaining number of times of saying "Allahu akbar" and the other spoken elements, and then finishes with his own Salams.

It is recommended that the body not be lifted until the latecomer finishes his prayer.

If the latecomer joins the group with his opening Allahu Akbar, and the imam immediately says the (O: second) Allahu Akbar (N: before the latecomer has had a chance to recite the Fatiha), then the latecomer (N: omits the Fatiha and) says "Allahu akbar" with the imam. Here, the latecomer has performed the first two Allahu Akbars (O: both the second one which he performed with them, and the first one which lacked the Fatiha), and he is no longer obliged to recite the Fatiha. If the imam's Allahu Akbar occurs while such a latecomer is reciting the Fatiha, he discontinues it and says "Allahu akbar" with the imam.

If the imam says "Allahu akbar" and the follower does not say it until the imam has said it a second time, it invalidates the follower's prayer.

REPEATING THE FUNERAL PRAYER

g4.16   When one has performed a funeral prayer over someone, it is recommended that one not repeat it.

g4.17   Someone who has missed praying (O: a funeral prayer until after the deceased has been buried) may pray it at the grave (O: and such a prayer is legally valid whether the deceased was buried before the funeral prayer had been performed over him, or whether after, though it is unlawful to bury a Muslim before his funeral prayer, and anyone who knows of it is guilty of a sin), but only on condition that the person praying at the grave had reached puberty and was sane on the day the deceased died (O: as he was thus one of those responsible for the communal obligation of praying over the deceased). Otherwise, he may not pray there.

حرام ويأثـم كل من علم به) إنْ كَانَ يومَ موتِه بالغاً عاقلاً (فالمصلي حينئذ من أهل الفرض) وإلَّا فَلَا .

PRAYING OVER THE DEAD WHO ARE NOT PRESENT

الصلاة على الغائب

g4.18 It is permissible to perform the funeral prayer for an absent person whose body is out of town, even if not far (O: and even if the body is not in the direction of prayer (qibla) which the person praying faces (non-(g4.14(b)))). But such a prayer does not lift the communal obligation from the people of the town where the deceased died).

It is not permissible to perform the funeral prayer over someone who is absent (O: from the place of prayer) when the body is in the same town (A: though this is permissible if it is at the edge of a large city and is a problem to reach).

g4.18 ويَجُوزُ على الغائب عن البلد وإنْ قَرُبَتْ مسافتُه (ولو في غير جهة القبلة والـمصلي مستقبلهـا لكنهـا لا تسقـط الفرض أي عن أهل البلد) .

ولاَ يَجُوزُ على غائبٍ (عـن محـل الصلاة وهو في البلدِ) .

g4.19 If part of the body of a person whose death has been verified is found, then it is obligatory to wash, shroud, and pray over it (O: even if the part is a fingernail or hair, as there is no difference between a little and a lot (A: provided that the part was separated from him after death (N: and provided the rest of him has not been prayed over, for if it has, then it is not obligatory to pray over the part))).

g4.19 ولـوْ وُجدَ بعضُ مَنْ تُيُقِّنَ موتُه غُسِّلَ وكُفِّنَ وصُلِّيَ علَيْهِ (وجوباً وإن كان ذلك الجزء ظفراً أو شعراً فلا فرق فيه بين القليـل والكثيـر) (ح : هذا إذا لـم يصـل على الأصل وإلا فلا يجب) .

BURYING MARTYRS

دفن الشهيد

g4.20 It is unlawful to wash the body of a martyr (O: even if in a state of major ritual impurity (janaba) or the like) or perform the funeral prayer over him. A martyr (shahid) means someone who died in battle with non-Muslims (O: from fighting them, as opposed to someone who died otherwise, such as a person killed out of oppression when not in battle, or who died from fighting non-

g4.20 ويَحْرُمُ غسلُ الشهيدِ (ولوجنباً ونحـوه) وَ(تحـرم) الصلاةُ عليْهِ، وهوَ مَنْ مَاتَ في معركةِ الكفار بسبب قتالِهم (كأن قتله كافـر [أو كان موتـه بسبب الحـرب] بخلاف من مات بغير ذلك كالمقتول في غير القتال ظلماً أو مات بسبب القتال لكنه

polytheists, such as (N: Muslim) transgressors).

It is recommended that war gear be removed from the body (O: such as a breastplate and the like), and it is best to bury the martyr in the rest of his bloodstained clothes (O: since it is the effect of worship), though the responsible family member may nevertheless remove the garments and shroud the body before burial.

BURYING THE STILLBORN

g4.21   A premature baby (A: meaning one born before six full months) that dies is treated as an adult if it gave a cry (O: sneeze, or cough when it left the mother) or showed movement (O: *treated as an adult* meaning it is obligatory to wash, shroud, pray over, and bury the baby, since its life and death have been verified). If it did not, then:

(1) if it had reached four months in the womb (O: which is the time at which the spirit is breathed into it) then it is washed before burial but not prayed over;

(2) but if it had not, it is only obligatory to bury it.

CARRYING THE DECEASED TO THE GRAVE

g4.22   The burial should take place immediately after the funeral prayer and not be delayed to wait for anyone besides the responsible family member, provided he is (O: reasonably) nearby, if it is not to be feared that the condition of the body will change (O: though if this is feared, then the family member is not awaited).

f4.23   It is best that the bier be carried by its poles, sometimes by four (O: men) (N: one pole on the shoulder of each, the poles being parallel with the bier and supporting it, two ends forward and two ends aft) and sometimes by five, the fifth man between the two forward poles. It is recommended that the bearers walk faster than usual, though they should not trot.

غيـر قتـال المشـركين كقتـال أهـل البغي (ح: من المسلمين)).

فَتُنْـزَعُ عنْـهُ ثيـابُ الحـربِ (كـدرع ونحـوه [ونـزع ذلـك على سبيل النـدب]) ثم الأفضـلُ أنْ يُدْفنَ ببقيـةِ ثيابه الملطَّخةِ بالدم (لأنه أثر عبادة) وللوليِّ نزعُها وتكفينُهُ.

دفن السقط

g4.21   والسقطُ إنْ بَكَى (أي إن ظهر منه صياح حال نزوله أو عطاس أو سعال) أو اخْتَلَجَ فحكمُهُ حكمُ الكبير (في جميع ما تقدم من وجوب غسله وتكفينه والصلاة عليـه ووجوب دفنه لتيقن حيـاته وموتـه) وإلَّا فإن بَلَغَ أربعـةَ أشهر (وهي زمن نفخ الـروح فيـه) غُسِـلَ ولمْ يُصَـلَّ عليْه وإلَّا وَجَبَ دفنُهُ فقطْ.

حمل الميت

g4.22   وَلْيُبَادَرْ بالدفنِ بعدَ الصلاةِ ولا يُنتَظَرُ (أي لا يؤخر لأحـد) إلَّا الـوليُّ إن قَرُبَ (عرفاً) ولمْ يُخْشَ تغيُّر الميتِ (فإن خشي ذلك لم ينتظر).

g4.23   والأفضـلُ أنْ يُحْمـلَ الجنـازَةَ تارةً أربعةٌ (من الرجال) منْ قوائمِها وتارةً خمسةٌ والخـامِسُ يَكُونُ بين العمـودَيْنِ المقـدَّمَيْن. ويُنْـدَبُ الإسراعُ فوقَ العادة دونَ الـخببِ [إنْ لمْ يَضُـرَّ الميتَ وإنْ خِيفَ انفجارُهُ زِيدَ على الإسراع].

g4.24   It is recommended for men to follow the bier to the place of burial close enough behind to be considered part of the funeral procession. It is offensive to follow it with fire or incense burners, which are likewise offensive at the burial.

g4.24 وَيُنْدَبُ للرجالِ اتّباعُها إلى الـدفنِ بقربِها بحيثُ يُنْسَبُ إلَيْهَا . وَيُكْرَهُ اتبـاعُهـا بنارٍ والبخورِ في المجمرة وكذا عندَ الدفنِ .

*

g5.0   BURIAL

g5.0   الدفن

g5.1   Then the deceased is buried (O: obligatorily). It is best to bury him in the cemetery.

It is unlawful to bury someone where another person has been buried unless the previous body is completed disintegrated (O: such that nothing of it remains, neither flesh nor bone).

It is also unlawful to bury two people in the same grave unless absolutely necessary, as when there has been much killing or death, in which case a wall of earth is made between the two bodies as a barrier. If the bodies differ in gender, this is even more imperative, especially when two people (O: of the same gender or not) are not related.

If someone dies on a ship and it is impossible to bury him on land, the body is placed (O: tightly lashed) between two planks (O: to obviate bloating) and thrown into the sea (O: so that it reaches shore, even if the inhabitants are non-Muslims, since a Muslim might find the body and bury it facing the direction of prayer (qibla)).

g5.1 ثمَّ يُدْفَنُ (وجوباً) وفي المقبرة أفضلُ .

ولا يُدْفَنُ ميتٌ على ميتٍ إلّا أنْ يَبْلَى الأولُ كلُّهُ (أي بحيث لا يبقى منه شيء لا اللحم ولا العظم ، فيحرم قبل ذلك) .

ولا ميتـانِ في قبـرٍ واحدٍ إلّا لضرورةٍ كثرةِ القتل والفناءِ ويُجْعَلُ بينَهُمَا حائلٌ منْ ترابٍ وبينَ المـرأةِ والـرجلِ آكدُ (أي أشـدُّ طلبـاً سيّمَا الأجنبيّينِ (مطلقاً اتحد الجنس أو اختلف) .

ولوْ مَاتَ في سفينةٍ ولمْ يُمْكِنْ دفنُهُ في البرِّ جُعِـلَ بينَ لوحَيْنِ (وشـدَّ عليه برباط شديـدٍ لئـلا يتنفـخ) وألْقِيَ في البحرِ (أي ليصـل إلى السـاحـل ولـوكان أهله كفاراً فقد يجده مسلم فيدفنه إلى القبلة) .

حفر القبر

g5.2   The obligatory minimum for a grave is that it conceal the odor of the body and that it protect it from (O: being dug up and eaten by) animals.

It is recommended to dig the grave wider than the obligatory minimum and that its depth equal the height of an average man with his arm fully extended upward.

g5.2 وأقـلُّ القبـرِ مَا يَكْتُمُ الـرائحـةَ ويَمْنَـعُ السبـاعَ (أي حفـرة تمنـع نبش السباع لها فتأكل الميت) .

ويُنْدَبُ توسيعُهُ وتعميقُهُ قامةً وبسطةً [(أي الـزيادة في حفره لجهة الأسفل قدر قامة رجل معتدل وقدر بسطة يده إلى الأعلى)] .

237

A *lahd* (O: i.e. a grave with a lateral hollow large enough for the body dug into the side of the bottom of the grave that is towards the direction of

واللحدُ أفضلُ مِنَ الشقِّ (واللحد بفتح اللام وضمها أن يحفر في أسفل جانب

The *Lahd*
in Cross Section

prayer (qibla)) is superior to a *shaqq* (O: meaning a simple trench dug down into the middle of the floor of the grave with low block walls raised along the trench's sides, in which the deceased is placed before the walls are ceilinged with blocks (N: and the earth is shovelled back into the grave on top of them)), unless the earth is soft, in which case the *shaqq* is preferable (O: so as not to cave in on the deceased).

It is offensive to bury the deceased in a coffin (O: or to put in a pillow for him, because all of this wastes money without being of any benefit) unless the earth is soft (O: quick to fall) or moist (O: in which cases it is not offensive. If otherwise, then even if a coffin was stipulated by the deceased in his will, it is not provided).

القبرِ القبلي قدر ما يسع الميت، والشقِّ هو أن يحفر في وسط أرض القبر كالنهر تبنى حافتاه باللبن [أو غيره] ويوضع بينهما ويسقف عليه باللبن [أو غيره]) إلاَّ أنْ تكـونَ الأرضُ رخـوةً فَيُنـدَبُ الشقِّ (حينئذ لئلا ينخسف القبر على الميت).

ويُكْرَهُ في تابوتٍ (وهو الصندوق، وكـره أن يجعـل له مخـدة فراش لأن في ذلك كله إضاعـة مال بلا فائـدة) إلاَّ أنْ تكـونَ الأرضُ رخوةً (سريعة السقوط) أوْ نديةً (أي رطابـة فلا يكـره ما ذكر ولا تنفذ وصيته إلا حينئذ).

BURYING THE BODY

دفن الميت

g5.3 Men should bury the dead, even if the deceased is female, in which case the best suited is the husband, if able, and then (n: for either sex) those listed in the funeral prayer preference order

g5.3 ويَتَـوَلَّاُ (أي دفـن الـميت) الـرجـالُ ولوْ لامـرأةٍ وأولاهُمُ الـزوجُ إنْ صَلَحَ للدفن ثمَّ أولاهُـمْ بـالصـلاةِ لكن

(g4.3), except that (A: when two are on the same level, such as two sons or brothers) the most learned in Sacred Law is preferred to the oldest, unlike the order for the prayer (O: the purpose thereof being knowledge of the rules of burial, which a learned person is likely to know better than others).

It is recommended that the number of men (O: burying the deceased) be an odd number.

g5.4   It is preferable to conceal it (O: the grave) with a cloth while placing the body in it (N: a blanket is stretched over the grave about half a meter above the level of the ground, helpers holding each corner, while another person stands down in the grave at the foot end, ready to take the body from the bier). (O: This is especially necessary when burying a female, and is done because something might be disclosed of the deceased that is desirable to conceal.)

The head of the deceased is placed near the foot of the grave (O: *foot* meaning the end which will accomodate the feet when the body is in place), and the body is slid from the bier head-first.

It is recommended for the person burying the deceased (N: who is standing in the grave taking the body, and there may be more than one):

(1) to say (O: to the deceased), "In the name of Allah and according the religion of the Messenger of Allah (Allah bless him and give him peace)";

(2) to supplicate Allah for (O: the forgiveness of) the deceased;

(3) to place a block as a pillow for him, and to pull back the shroud enough to lay his cheek directly on the surface of the block (O: as it is more expressive of lowliness);

(4) and to place the deceased upon his right side.

It is obligatory that the body be placed facing the direction of prayer (qibla) (O: and this is absolutely necessary. If buried facing the other way, or

الأفقَهُ مقـدَّمٌ على الأسَنِّ عكسُ الصـلاةِ (فـالغرض منـه المعرفـة بأحكـام الدفن والأفقـه أعـرف من غيـره في ذلـك).

ويُنْدَبُ أنْ يكُونُوا (أي من يدفنونه) وتراً.

g5.4   ويُغَطَّى (أي القبـر استحبـاباً بثـوب عنـد الدفن (وهو للأنثى) آكد لأنه ربما ينكشف من الميت ما يستحب إخفاؤه).

ويُـوضَـعُ رأسُـهُ عنـدَ رِجْـلِ القبـر (والمراد برجل القبر المؤخر الذي سيصير عنـد أسفـله رجـل الميت) ويُسَـلُّ (أي يخرج الميت من النعش) منْ جهةِ رأسِهِ.

ويَقُـولُ الـدافنُ (للميت) «بسم اللهِ وعلى مِلَّةِ رسولِ اللهِ ﷺ» ويَدْعُوله (أي للميت بالمغفرة) ويُوَسّـدُهُ لبنةً ويُفْضِي بخدِّهِ إلى الأرض (بعد كشف الكفن عنه لأنه أبلغ في إظهـار الـذل) ويُوْضَعُ على جنبـهِ الأيمن ندبـاً مستقبـلَ القبلةِ حتمـاً (وكونه مستقبل القبلة لازم محتم لا بد منه فلو دفن مستدبراً لها أو مستلقياً على ظهره

239

lying on his back, he is disinterred and reburied facing the direction of prayer).

نبش ووضع للقبلة).

g5.5   The lateral hollow dug into the side of the grave (N: in the *lahd* (def: g5.2)) for the body is walled up with blocks (A: after the body has been placed in it, before filling in the grave. It is sunna to use nine blocks).

g5.5   وَيُنْصَبُ عَلَيْهِ [(أي على باب القبر المفتوح)] اللبِنُ .

g5.6   The person at the graveside sprinkles three scoops of earth (O: using two hands) into the grave. (O: it is sunna to say with the first, "Of it We created you all," with the second, "To it We shall make you all return," and with the third, "And from it We shall bring you forth again" (Koran 20:55).)

Then the grave is filled in, using shovels, after which one stays for a moment:

(1) to instruct the deceased (dis: w32) (N: the answers he will need to know when Munkar and Nakir (u3.3) question him in the grave as to his Lord, religion, and prophet);

(2) to supplicate for him (O: such as to say: "O Allah, make him steadfast. O Allah, teach him his plea");

(3) and to ask forgiveness for him.

g5.6   وَيَحْثُو مَنْ دَنَا ثلاثَ حثياتٍ (من التـراب بيـديـه ويسن أن يقول مع الأولى ﴿مِنْهَا خَلَقْنَاكُمْ﴾ ومع الثانية ﴿وَفِيهَا نُعِيدُكُمْ﴾ ومع الثالثة ﴿وَمِنْها نُخْـرِجُـكُمْ تَارَةً أُخْـرَى﴾) ثمَّ يُهَـالُ بالمساجي ويَمْكُثُ ساعةً بعدَ الدفنِ يُلَقِّنُهُ ويَدْعُـو لَهُ (كأن يقول: «اللَّهُمَّ ثَبِّتْهُ اللَّهُمَّ لَقِّنْهُ حُجَّتَهُ)ويَسْتَغْفِرُ لَهُ .

THE FINISHED GRAVE

القبر

g5.7   One should raise the grave's surface (O: up to) 1 span (n: about 23 cm.) above the ground (O: so that it can be known, visited, and respected), except in countries at war with the Muslims (O: where it is not raised but rather concealed, so as not to be meddled with), and to make its top flat is better (O: than mounding it). No earth should be added (O: when levelling it) to what was excavated from it. It is recommended to sprinkle water over the grave and to put pebbles on it.

It is offensive:

g5.7   وَيُـرْفَـعُ القبرُ (وغـايتـه في الارتفـاع أن يصير شبراً لأجل أن يعرف فيـزار ويحتـرم) إلّا في بلاد الحـرب (فلا يرفع بل يخفى لئلا يتعرضوا له) وتسطيحُهُ أفضـلُ (من تسنيمه) ولاَ يُزَادُ فيهِ (أي في التسطيح) على ترابِهِ (فقط وهو ما خرج منـه) وبُـرَشُ عَلَيْـهِ المـاءُ (على طريق الندب) ويُوْضَعُ عَلَيْهِ حَصىً .

وَيُـكْـرَهُ تجصيصٌ [(أي تبـييضه

(1) to whiten the grave with plaster;

(2) to build (O: a cupola or house) over it;

(3) to put *khaluq* (O: a perfume) on the grave (O: as it is of no benefit and wastes money) or rose water;

(4) to place an inscription on it (O: whether it is the name of the deceased or something other, on a board at the head of the grave or on something else; unless the deceased is a friend of Allah (wali, def: w33) or religious scholar, in which case his name is written so that he may be visited and honored, it then not being offensive);

(5) or to put a pillow or mattress under the deceased.

VISITING GRAVES

g5.8   It is recommended for men to visit graves (dis: w34) (O: of Muslims, especially on Fridays. As for visiting graves of non-Muslims, it is merely permissible. The spirit of the dead person has a connection with his grave that is never severed, but is stronger from the midafternoon prayer ('asr) on Thursday until sunrise on Saturday, which is why people often visit graves on Friday and on Thursday afternoon).

There is no harm in wearing one's shoes when visiting (O: to walk between graves). The visitor walks up to the grave as close as he would if the deceased were alive, and says, "Peace be unto you, abode of a believing folk; Allah willing, we will be joining you."

It is sunna to recite (O: as much of the Koran as is easy) and to supplicate Allah (O: to forgive the deceased, while facing the direction of prayer, as supplications benefit the dead and are more likely to be answered if made after reciting the Koran). (n: w35 discusses whether the spiritual reward for reciting the Koran may be donated to the deceased.)

g5.9   It is offensive for women to visit graves (O: because of their lack of fortitude and exces-

بالجص وهو الجبس)] وبناءٌ (على القبر كقبة أو بيت) وَ(كره وضع) خَلُوقٍ (على القبر وهو نوع من الطيب لأنه لا فائدة فيه بل فيه إضاعة مال) وماءُ وردٍ وكتابةٌ (على القبر سواء كتب عليه اسم صاحبه أم غيره في لوح عنـد رأسـه أم في غيره إلا إذا كان ولياً أو عالماً وكتب اسمه ليزار ويحترم فلا كراهة حينئذ) ومخدةٌ ومضربةٌ تحتَهُ .

زيارة القبور

g5.8   ويُنـدَبُ للرجالِ زيارةُ القبور (أي قبور المسلمين أما زيارة قبور الكفار فمبـاحـة، ويتأكـد ذلك يوم الجمعة [(فائدة)] روح الميت لها ارتباط في قبره ولا تفارقه أبـداً لكنها أشد ارتباطاً به من عصـر يوم الـخـميس إلى شمس السبت ولـذلك اعتـاد الناس الزيارة يوم الجمعة وفي عصر الخميس) .

ولا بأسَ بمـشـيـهِ في الـنـعـل (بين القبور). ويَـدْنُـو مِنْـهُ (أي لا كراهة في قرب الزائر من المزور) كحياتِهِ ويَقولُ إذا زارَ «سلامٌ علَيْكُمْ دارَ قوم مؤمنينَ وإنَّا إنْ شَاءَ اللهُ بكُمْ لَاحِقُونَ». و(سن أن) يَقْرَأَ (بما تيسر من القـرآن) ويَـدْعُـو لَهُمْ (بـالمغفرة بعـد توجهه للقبلة لأن الدعاء ينفع الميت وهو عقب القراءة أقرب إلى الإجابة) .

g5.9   ويُكْرَهُ للنسـاءِ (لفقد صبر الأنثى وكثرة جزعها، وهذا في غير زيارة

sive grief, though this does not apply to visiting the Prophet's tomb (Allah bless him and give him peace) which they should do. And like the Prophet (Allah bless him and give him peace) in this is their visiting the graves of the prophets, righteous, and learned).

قبره ﷺ وأما هي فمطلوبة لهن ومثل النبي ﷺ قبور الأنبياء والصلحاء والعلماء).

*

g6.0   CONSOLING NEXT OF KIN

g6.0   التعزية

g6.1   It is recommended to console all the relatives of the deceased, except young women who are not (O: the consoler's) unmarriageable kin (O: since only her unmarriageable relatives (mahram, def: m6.2) may console her, *console* meaning to enjoin steadfastness and encourage it by mentioning the reward in the hereafter, to warn against overburdening oneself with grief, and to pray for forgiveness for the deceased and the lightening of the burden of those bearing the misfortune) when there has been a death in the family, for approximately three days after the burial.

It is offensive to sit for it (O: that is, for the extended family of the deceased to be seated and gather in one place for people to come and console them, because it is an innovation (muhdath, syn. bid'a, def: w29.3) that the Prophet (Allah bless him and give him peace) did not do, nor those after him. It is offensive for either men or women).

If one is absent (O: whether one is the consoler or person to be consoled) and then arrives after a period (O: of three days), one should console (N: the deceased's relatives) or be consoled (N: if one of them).

g6.1   ويُنْـدَبُ تعـزيـةُ كلَّ أقـارب الميت إلاَّ الشـابّـةَ الأجنبيـةَ (من المعزي فلا يعـزيها إلا محارمها وهي الأمر بالصبر والحمـل عليـه بوعد الآخرة والتحذير من الـوزر بالجـزع والـدعاء للميت بالمغفرة وللمصاب بجبر المصيبة) مِنَ المـوت إلى ثلاثة أيام تقريباً بعدَ الدفن.
ويُكـرَهُ الجلوسُ لَهَـا (أي جلوس أهل الميت واجتماعهم في مكان واحد ليأتيهم النـاس للتعزية لأنه محدث ما فعله النبي ﷺ ولا من بعده. وسواء في ذلك الرجال والنساء).
فلَوْ كَانَ (المعـزي أو المعـزى) غائبـاً فَقَـدِمَ (أي من كان غائباً منهمـا) بعـد مدةٍ (وهي ثلاثة أيام) عَزّاهُ [(أي عزى الحاضر القادم أو عزى القادم الحاضر)].

g6.2   It is recommended to say:

(1) to a Muslim who has lost a Muslim relative, "May Allah greaten your reward, perfect your consolation, and forgive your deceased";

(2) to a Muslim who has lost a non-Muslim

g6.2   ويَقُـولُ في تعـزيـة المسلم بالمـسـلم (أي بالميت المسلم) «أعْظَمَ اللهُ أُجْـرَكَ وأحْـسَنَ عَزاءَكَ وغَفَـرَ لمَيِّـتِكَ» وفي (تعـزيـة) المسلم بالكـافر (يعني أن

242

relative, "May Allah greaten your reward and perfect your consolation";

(3) and to a non-Muslim who has lost a Muslim relative, "May Allah perfect your consolation and forgive your deceased."

g6.3   It is permissible to weep before someone dies, but better not to afterwards (O: since the Prophet (Allah bless him and give him peace) wept for his son Ibrahim before his death. It is only considered better not to weep afterwards because it is sorrow for something that has already passed).

g6.4   It is unlawful to eulogize the dead, lament in a raised voice, slap one's cheeks (n: as a display of grief), rend one's garments, or dishevel one's hair.

g6.5   It is recommended for distant relatives and neighbors to prepare enough food for the deceased's close family relatives to suffice them for a day and night, and to urge them to eat.

g6.6   For the deceased's family to prepare food and gather people over it is an unpraiseworthy innovation (bid'a, def: w29.3).

*

الميت كافر أَعْظَمَ اللهُ أَجْـرَكَ وأَحْسَنَ عَزاءَكَ وفي الكـافـر بالمسلم أَحْسَنَ اللهُ عَزاءَكَ وغَفَرَ لِمَيِّتِكَ [وفي الكافر بالكافر أَخْلَفَ اللهُ عليكَ ولا نَقَصَ عَدَدُكَ ويَنْوي بِه تكثيرَ الجزية (وهذا مشكل لأنه دعاء له ببقاء الكفر واستمراره فالمختار تركه)].

g6.3   والبكـاءُ قبـلَ المـوتِ جائـزٌ وبعـدَهُ خلافَ الأَوْلَى (لأنه ﷺ بكى على ولـده إبراهيم قبـل موتـه وإنما كان بعده خلافَ الأَوْلَى لأنه حينئذ يكون أسفاً على ما فات).

g6.4   ويَحْرُمُ النَّدبُ [(على الميت وهـو عد محاسنه)] والنياحةُ واللطمُ وشقُّ الثوب ونشرُ الشعر.

g6.5   ويُنْـدَبُ لأقـارب المـيتِ البعـداءِ وجيرانِه أَنْ يُصْلِحُوا طعاماً لأهل المـيتِ الأَقـربين يَكْفيهِم يومَهُمْ وليلتَهُمْ ويُلحَّ عليْهِمْ لِيَأْكُلوا.

g6.6   ومـا يَفْعَلُهُ أهـلُ الميتِ منْ إصلاح طعام وجمع الناس علَيْه بدعةٌ غيرُ حسنةٍ.

BOOK H

ZAKAT

كتاب الزكاة

CONTENTS:

---

h1.0   WHO MUST PAY ZAKAT

((Muhammad Shirbini Khatib:) Lexically, *zakat* means growth, blessings, an increase in good, purification, or praise. In Sacred Law it is the name for a particular amount of property that must be payed to certain kinds of recipients under the conditions mentioned below. It is called zakat because one's wealth grows through the blessings of giving it and the prayers of those who receive it, and because it purifies its giver of sin and extolls him by testifying to the genuineness of his faith (*al-Iqna' fi hall alfaz Abi Shuja'* (y7), 1.183).)

h1.1   Zakat is obligatory:

(a) for every free Muslim (O: male, female, adult, or child);

(b) who has possessed a *zakat-payable amount* (Ar. nisab, the minimum that necessitates zakat, def: for livestock h2.4–5; for grain and dried foodstuffs h3.4; for gold, silver, and other money h4.2; and for trade goods h5.1);

(c) for one lunar year.

h1.2   Non-Muslims are not obliged to pay zakat, nor apostates from Islam (murtadd, def: o8) unless they return to Islam, in which case they must pay for the time they spent out of Islam, though if they die as non-Muslims their property is not subject to zakat (N: because their property is considered to belong to the *Muslim common fund* (bayt al-mal) from the moment such people leave Islam).

h1.0   المخاطب بوجوب الزكاة

(محمد الشربيني الخطيب: وهي لغة النمو والبركة وزيادة الخير [. . .] وتطلق على التطهير [. . .] وتطلق أيضاً على المدح. وشرعاً اسم لقدر مخصوص من مال مخصوص يجب صرفه إلى أصناف مخصوصة بشرائط تأتي. وسميت بذلك لأن المال ينمو ببركة إخراجها ودعاء الآخذ لها ولأنها تطهر مخرجها من الإثم وتمدحه حتى تشهد له بصحة الإيمان [محرر من كتاب الإقناع في حل ألفاظ أبي شجاع: ١ / ١٨٣]).

h1.1   تَجِبُ الـزكـاةُ على كلّ حرّ (سواء كان ذكراً أو أنثى كبيراً أو صغيراً) تَمَّ ملكُهُ على نصابٍ حَوْلاً.

h1.2   فلا تَلْزَمُ [المكاتبَ ولاَ] الكافرَ وأمـا المـرتـدُّ فإنْ رَجَعَ إلى الإسلام لَزِمَهُ لِمَـا مَضَى وإنْ مَاتَ مرتداً فَلَا (ح): لأن مالـه يعتبر فيئاً لبيت مال المسلمين من حين الردة).

h1.3   The guardian of a child or insane person is obliged to pay zakat from their property (N: if they owe any). It is a sin for the guardian not to pay the zakat due on their property, and when the child or insane person becomes legally responsible (O: upon reaching puberty or becoming sane), he is obliged to pay the amount that his guardian neglected to pay (O: of zakat in the past).

h1.4   Zakat is due from the owner of property that has been:

(1) wrongfully seized from him;

(2) stolen;

(3) lost;

(4) fallen into the sea;

(5) or loaned to someone who is tardy in repayment;

—only if the owner regains possession of it, whereupon he must pay zakat on it for the whole time it was out of his hands (O: for the year or years that no zakat was paid on the absent property, since his having regained it establishes that it belonged to him the whole time, and his ownership of it is not vitiated by the mere fact of its not having been in his possession during these years, provided that it has remained a zakat-payable amount (nisab) during them. If it has diminished through expenditure to less than the zakat-payable amount, then no zakat need be paid on it). If the owner cannot regain the property, there is no zakat on it.

h1.5   If a landlord rents someone a house for two years for 40 dinars, which he accepts in advance and retains possession of until the end of the two years, then at the end of the first of the two years he only pays zakat on 20 dinars, but at the end of the second year he pays one year's zakat on the 20 which he paid zakat on at the end of the first year (N: as the 20 has now been in his possession a second year) and pays two years' zakat on the 20

h1.3   ويَلْزَمُ الوليَّ إخراجُها مِنْ مال الصبيِّ والمجنـونِ فإنْ لمْ يُخـرِجْ عَصى ويَلْزَمُ الصبيَّ والمجنونَ إذا صَارا مكلفَيْن (بـالبلوغ والإفـاقـة) إخراجُ مَا (أي القدر الذي) أَهْمَلَهُ الوليُّ (من الزكاة في المدة الماضية).

h1.4   ولـوْ غُصِبَ مالُـهُ أوْ سُرِقَ أوْ ضَاعَ أوْ وقَعَ في البحر أوْ كانَ لهُ دَيْنٌ على مماطِل فإنْ قَدَرَ عَلَيهِ بعدَ ذلكَ لَزِمَهُ زكاةُ مَا مَضَى (من حول وأحـوال من غـير زكاة لذلك المـال الـذاهب لأنه تبين برجوعه إليـه أنـه بـاق على ملكـه له ولا يضـر عدم كونـه تحت يده في هذه الأحوال الماضية بشـرط بقـاء النصـاب في هذه الأحـوال، وإن نقص عن النصاب بسبب الإنفاق منه فلا يزكى) وإلّا [(أي وإن لم يقـدر على رده ودخوله تحت يده)] فلا (زكاة عليه).

h1.5   ولـوْ آجَـرَ دارًا سنتيْـن بأربعين دينـارًا وقَبَضَهـا وبَقِيَتْ في ملكِـه إلى آخر سنتيـن فإذا حَالَ الـحـولُ الأولُ زَكَّى عشرينَ فقطْ وإذا حَالَ الحولُ الثاني زَكَّى العشرينَ التي زكَّاها لسنةٍ وزَكَّى العشرينَ

for which he did not previously pay zakat (N: as it has remained in his possession for two full years).

التي لَمْ يُزَكِّها لسنتين .

h1.6 Someone with only the zakat-payable amount (O: of gold or silver) must pay zakat on this amount even when he is in debt for an amount equal to it, for debts do not remove the obligation of zakat.

h1.6   ولَوْ مَلَكَ نصاباً (ذهباً أو فضة) فقط وعلَيْهِ مِنَ الدَّيْنِ مثلُهُ لَزِمَهُ زكاةُ مَا بيدِهِ (من النصاب) والدينُ لاَ يَمْنَعُ الوجوبَ .

h1.7 Zakat is not due on anything besides:

(1) livestock (def: h2.1);

(2) (n: some) food crops (h3.2);

(3) gold and silver (A: or their monetary equivalents);

(4) trade goods;

(5) mined wealth (n: meaning gold or silver exclusively, as at h6.1);

(6) and wealth from treasure troves (A: buried in pre-Islamic times).

h1.7   .ولاَ تَجِبُ الزكـاةُ إلاَّ في المـواشِي والنبـاتِ والـذهب والفضـة وعروض التجارة ومَا يُوجَدُ مِنَ المعدنِ والرُّكازِ .

h1.8 Zakat is paid from the property itself, though it is permissible to take it from another lot of property (N: on condition that the amount paid is from the same type of property (n: of the five types mentioned above) that the zakat is due on, such that one may not, for example, pay *money* for zakat due on *wheat* (n: but must pay wheat. An exception to this is trade goods, which are appraised, and zakat may be paid on them with money, as at h5.1(O:) below)).

h1.8   وتَجِبُ الزكاةُ في عينِ المالِ لكنْ لَوْ أَخْـرَجَ من غيـرِهِ جَازَ (ح : لكن يشتـرط أنْ يكـون الـمخـرج من نوع الواجب فلا يخرج نقوداً عن القمح مثلاً) .

THE ZAKAT YEAR

الحول

h1.9 By the mere fact that a full lunar year transpires (O: i.e. begins and ends while zakat-payable property is in the owner's possession), the poor now own the portion of it that the owner is obliged to pay as zakat. Thus, if someone has had

h1.9   فبمجـرَّدِ حَوَلاَنِ الحولِ (أي دخـولـهِ وتمامهِ والمالُ المزكى باقٍ تحت يدِهِ) يَمْلِكُ الفـقـراءُ مِنَ المـالِ قَدْرَ الفـرضِ حتى لَوْ مَلَكَ مائتَيْ درهمٍ فقـط

200 dirhams (n: the minimal zakat-payable amount of silver) in his possession for years without paying zakat, he is only obliged to pay zakat on it for the first year (O: because after that year, the amount owned by the poor (n: 5 dirhams) has diminished the money he possesses to less than the zakat-payable amount).

ولم يُزَكِّها أحوالاً لَزِمَهُ الزكاةُ للسنةِ الأولى فقطْ (وإنما وجبتِ الزكاة في السنة الأولى دون غيرها لأنه بمجرد حولان الحول اشترك الفقراء في المائتين فنقص النصاب عن تمامه).

h1.10 If all one's property were destroyed after having been in one's possession a full year but before it was possible to pay zakat (O: to deserving recipients), then there is no obligation to pay zakat on it (O: because it was destroyed through no fault of the owner); but if only part of the property has been destroyed, such that this diminishes the rest to less than the zakat-payable amount, then one must take the percentage due on the original amount (n: 2.5 percent, for example) from the remaining property, and no zakat is paid on the amount destroyed.

If all or part of one's property is destroyed after having been in one's possession a full year and after it was possible to have paid zakat on it (O: by there being both property and recipients), then one must pay the zakat due on both the remainder and the property destroyed.

h1.10 ولو تَلِفَ مالُهُ كلُّهُ بعدَ الحولِ وقبلَ التمكنِ منَ الإخراجِ (من مالِ الزكاةِ لمستحقيه) سَقَطَتِ الزكاةُ (لوجودِ التلفِ من غيرِ تقصيرٍ من المالكِ). وإنْ تَلِفَ بعضُهُ بحيثُ نَقَصَ عنِ النصابِ لَزِمَهُ بقسطِ الباقي وسَقَطَ بقسطِ التالفِ.

وإنْ تَلِفَ مالُهُ كلُّهُ أوْ بعضُهُ بعدَ الحولِ والتمكُّنِ (من أدائها بأن وجدَ المالَ ووجدَ الفقراءَ) لَزِمَهُ زكاةُ الباقي والتالفِ.

h1.11 Zakat is not obligatory if a person's ownership of the property ceases during the year, even if only for a moment, and it then returns to his possession; or if it does not return; or if the person dies during the year.

h1.11 ولوْ زَالَ ملكُهُ في الحولِ ولوْ لحظةً ثمَّ عادَ إلى ملكِهِ في الحولِ أوْ لمْ يَعُدْ أوْ مَاتَ في أثناءِ الحولِ سَقَطَتِ الزكاةُ.

h1.12 The zakat year begins on property purchased or inherited when the buyer or inheritor takes possession of it, though if a person relinquishes his ownership of property during the zakat year merely to avoid paying zakat on it, this is offensive (O: as the learned differ about its unlawfulness). The more reliable opinion is that it is unlawful, though the transaction would be legally valid (dis: c5.2). But if such a person sells the property after possessing it a full year and before paying zakat on it (O: as when he sells it all, or sells part and the rest is not enough to require zakat), then the sale of the proportion of the prop-

h1.12 ويَبْتَدِىءُ المشتري والوراثُ الحولَ من حينِ ملكِ المالِ، لكنْ لوْ أزالَ ملكَهُ في الحولِ فراراً منَ الزكاةِ فإنَّهُ يكرَهُ (لما فيه من خلافِ العلماءِ) والأصحُّ أنه حرامٌ ويصحُّ البيعُ. ولو باعَ بعدَ الحولِ وقبلَ الإخراجِ (أي ولم يبقَ شيئاً بأن باع الجميعَ أو البعضَ والباقي لا يفي بقدر

erty that was owed as zakat is invalid (O: because it belonged to someone else (n: i.e. the recipients, as at h1.9), and it is not valid to sell another's property without his consent), although the sale of the proportion of the property that was not owed as zakat is valid.

الـزكـاة) بَطَلَ (البيع) في قدر الـزكـاة (الواجبة لأنه حق الغير ولا يصح بيع ملك الغير بغير إذنه) وصحّ في الباقي .

*

h2.0   ZAKAT ON LIVESTOCK

h2.1   Zakat on livestock is restricted to camels, cattle, sheep, and goats.

h2.2   Zakat is obligatory when one has owned:

(a) a zakat-payable number of livestock;

(b) for one year;

(c) and has been grazing them (n: on unowned open range, as discussed below) for the entire year.

There is no zakat on work animals, for example, those trained to plow or bear loads (O: since the purpose in having them is utility, like clothes or household furnishings, and is not production).

Grazing means they have been grazed on open range pasturage (O: *open range* excluding pasturage growing on land that a person owns (A: as it would then be considered fodder)). If the livestock have been given fodder for a period long enough that they would have been unable to survive had they not eaten during it, then there is no zakat on them, though if fed with it for less than such a period, then this does not affect the necessity of paying zakat on them. (A: There is no zakat on cattle that have been solely fed fodder or grain, even if they could have otherwise been grazed.)

(n: It is religiously more precautionary (def: c6.5) and of greater benefit to the poor to follow Imam Malik on this question. Malik holds that zakat is obligatory whenever one has possessed a

زكاة المواشي   h2.0

h2.1   لَا تَجِبُ الـزكـاةُ إلَّا في الإبل والبقرِ والغنمِ .

h2.2   فمتى مَلَكَ منها نصابـاً حولاً كاملاً وأسَامَهُ كلَّ الحولِ لَزِمَتْهُ الزكاةُ إلَّا أنْ تَكُونَ ماشيتُهُ عاملةً مثل أنْ تَكُونَ معدةً للحراثـة أو الحمـلِ فَلا زكـاةَ فيهـا (لأن القصـد منها حينئـذ الاستعمـال لا النماء كثيـاب البـدن وأمتعـة الـدار) . والمـرادُ بالإسـامـة أنْ تَرعى مِنَ الكـلإ المبـاح (خـرج به الكـلأ الـمملوك كأن نبت في أرضٍ مملوكة لشخصٍ) فلوْ عَلَفَهَا زمانًا لَا تَعِيشُ دونـهُ لوْ تَرَكَتِ الأكـلَ سَقَطَتْ الزكاةُ وإنْ كَانَ أقلَّ فَلا يُؤَثِّرُ (ذلك العلف في وجوب الزكاة) .

(ت: اتّبـاع الإمـام مالـك في هذه المسألـة أحوط في الدين وأنفع للفقراء، فقـد ذهب الإمـام إلى وجوب الـزكاة في المـاشيـة إذا بلغت النصـاب وحال عليها

250

zakat-payable number of livestock for a year, whether or not they are work animals, and whether they have been grazed on open pasturage or fed with fodder for the entire year (al-Sharh al-saghir 'ala Aqrab al-masalik ila madhhab al-Imam Malik (y35), 1.592).)

الحـول سواء العـاملة وغـيرهـا، وسـواء أكـانت سائمة أم معلوفة في السنة كلها [الشرح الصغير على أقرب المسالك إلى مذهب الإمام مالك: ١/ ٥٩٢]).

ZAKAT ON CAMELS

زكاة الإبل

h2.3   [وأولُ نصابِ الإبلِ خمسٌ فَتَجِبُ فيها شاةٌ من غنمِ البلدِ وهي جذعةٌ منَ الضأنِ وهيَ ما لها سنةٌ أوْ ثنيةٌ منَ المعزِ وهيَ ما لها سنتانِ وبجزئُ الذكرُ أناثاً ولوْ كانتِ الإبلُ ذكوراً أناثاً وفي عشر شياتان وفي خمسةَ عشرَ ثلاثُ شياهٍ وفي عشرينَ أربعُ شياهٍ فإنْ أخرَجَ عن العشرينَ فما دونها بعيراً يُجزئُ عن خمسٍ وعشرينَ قُبلَ منهُ وفي خمسٍ وعشرينَ بنتُ مخاضٍ وهيَ التي لها سنةٌ ودخلَت في الثانيةِ فإنْ لمْ يكُنْ في إبلهِ بنتُ مخاضٍ أوكانتْ وهيَ معيبةٌ قُبلَ منهُ ابنُ لبونٍ ذكراً أوْ أنثى وهوَ ما لهُ سنتانِ ودخلَ في الثالثةِ ولوْ مَلَكَ بنتَ مخاضٍ كريمةً أوْ يُسْمَحُ بالكريمةِ إنْ شاءَ وفي ستٍ وثلاثينَ بنتُ لبونٍ وفي ستٍ وأربعينَ حقةٌ وهيَ التي لها ثلاثُ سنينَ ودخلَت في الرابعةِ وفي إحدى وستينَ جذعةٌ وهيَ التي لها أربعُ سنينَ ودخلَت في الخامسةِ وفي ستٍ وسبعينَ بنتا لبونٍ وفي إحدى وتسعينَ حقتانِ وفي مائةٍ وإحدى وعشرينَ ثلاثُ بناتِ لبونٍ فإنْ زادَت إبلُهُ على ذلكَ وجَبَ في كلِّ أربعينَ بنتُ لبونٍ وفي كلِّ خمسينَ حقةٌ ففي مائةٍ وثلاثينَ حقةٌ وبنتا لبونٍ وفي مائةٍ وأربعينَ بنتُ لبونٍ وحقتانِ وفي مائةٍ وخمسينَ ثلاثُ حقاقٍ وفي مائتينِ أربعُ حقاقٍ وخمسينَ وخمسُ بناتِ لبونٍ فإنْ كانَ في ملكهِ خمسُ بناتِ لبونٍ وأربعُ حقاقٍ لزمَهُ الأغبطُ للفقراءِ فإنْ فقدَهُما حصَلَ ما شاءَ منهما وإنْ كانَ في ملكهِ أحدُ الصنفينِ دونَ الآخرِ دفعَهُ ومَنْ لزمَهُ سنٌ وليسَ عندَهُ صعدَ درجةً واحدةً وأخذَ شاتينِ تُجزئانِ في عشرٍ منَ الإبلِ أو عشرينَ درهماً أو نزَلَ درجةً ودفعَ شاتينِ أو عشرينَ درهماً ولوْ أرادَ أنْ ينزلَ أو يصعدَ درجتينِ فجبرانينِ فإنْ فقدَ أيضاً الدرجةَ القربى جازَ وإنْ وجدَها فلا والاختيارُ في الصعودِ والنزولِ للمزكي وفي الغنمِ والدراهمِ لمَنْ أعطاهُ ولا يَدخُلُ الجبرانُ في الغنمِ والبقرِ].

ZAKAT ON CATTLE

زكاة البقر

h2.4   For cattle, the minimum on which zakat is payable is 30 head, for which it is obligatory to pay a yearling, meaning a male calf in its second year (A: though a female may take its place, being worth more).

The zakat due on 40 head is a two-year-old female that has entered its third year (A: a male will not suffice).

The zakat on 60 head is 2 yearling males. Zakat on additional numbers is figured in the same way: on 30 head, a yearling male, and on 40 head, a two-year-old female (N: according to which of the two alternatives accommodates the last 10 head (dis: h2.6)).

h2.4   وأولُ نصابِ البقرِ ثلاثونَ فَيجِبُ فيها تبيعٌ وهوَ ما لهُ سنةٌ ودخلَ في الثانيةِ، وفي أربعينَ مسنةٌ وهيَ ما لهَا سنتانِ ودخلَت في الثالثةِ، وفي ستينَ تبيعانِ وعلى هذا أبـداً: في كلِّ ثلاثينَ تبيعٌ وفي كلِّ أربعينَ مسنةٌ.

| ZAKAT ON SHEEP AND GOATS | زكاة الغنم |

h2.5 For sheep or goats (n: the Arabic *ghanam* meaning both), the minimum on which zakat is payable is 40, on which it is obligatory to pay a *shah*, meaning either a one-year-old sheep (O: in its second year) or a two-year-old goat (O: in its third year). The zakat on 121 sheep or goats is 2 *shahs*, on 201 sheep or goats is 3, on 400 sheep or goats is 4, and for every additional 100 the zakat is 1 *shah*.

h2.5   وأولُ نصابِ الغنم أربعونَ فتجِبُ فيهـا شاةً جَذَعَـةُ ضأنٍ (لهـا سنـة مضت من عمرها) أوْ ثنيةُ معز (مضى لها من عمرِها سنتان وشرعت في الثالثة) وفي مائةٍ وإحدَى وعشرينَ شاتانِ وفي مائتينِ وواحدةٍ ثلاثُ شياهٍ وفي أربعمـائةٍ أربعُ شياهٍ ثمَّ هكذَا أبداً في كلِّ مائةِ شاةٍ .

| CALCULATING THE NUMBER OF ANIMALS | تقدير الأنصاب |

h2.6 Numbers (O: of camels, cattle, or sheep) which are between zakat quantities (N: i.e. which number more than the last relevant zakat quantity but do not amount to the next highest one) are not counted, and no zakat is due on them.

h2.6   وهـذِهِ الأوقـاصُ ([وهو ما بين الفـرضين] من الإبل والبقر والغنم) التي بين النُصُب عفوٌ لا شيءَ فيهَا .

h2.7 New offspring of a zakat-payable quantity of livestock that are born during the year are counted for the zakat of the year their mothers are currently in, no matter whether their mothers survive or die. Thus, if one owned 40 sheep or goats which gave birth to 40 young a month before the year's end, but then the 40 mothers died, one's zakat on the offspring would be 1 *shah*.

h2.7   ومَا يَنْتُجُ مِنَ النصاب في أثناءِ الحـولِ يُزَكَّى لحـولِ أصلِهِ وإنْ لمْ يَمْض عليهِ حولٌ ، سواءً بَقِيَتِ الأمهـاتُ أوْ مَاتَتْ كلها . فلوْ مَلَكَ أربعيـنَ شاةً فوَلَدَتْ قبـل تمـام الحولِ بشهرٍ أربعينَ ومَاتَتِ الأمهاتُ لَزِمَهُ شاةٌ للنتاج .

h2.8   [فإنْ كَانَتْ ماشيتُهُ مراضاً أخَـذَ مِنهـا مريضـةً متوسطةً . أوْ صحاحاً أخَذَ منها صحيحةً . أوْ بعضها صِحاحاً وبعضهـا مراضاً أخَـذَ صحيحـةً بالقسط . فإذا مَلَكَ أربعين نصفُها صحاحٌ قُلْنَا لوْ كَانَتْ كلهَا صحاحاً كمْ تُساوي واحدةٌ منهَا ، فإذَا قِيلَ أربعةُ دراهمَ مثلاً قُلْنَا لوْ كَانَتْ كلها مراضاً كمْ تُساوي واحدةً منها ، فإذَا قيل درهمين مثلاً قُلْنَا لهُ حَصَّلَ لنا شاةً صحيحةً بثلاثةِ دراهمَ . ولوْ كانَتِ الصحـاحُ ثلاثينَ لَزِمَهُ شاةٌ تُساوي ثلاثة دراهمَ ونصفاً . ومَتَى قَوَّمَ (من في ملكِه صحاح ومراض) الجملة وأخْرَجَ صحيحـةً تُساوي ربعَ عشرِ كَفَى . نَعَمْ لوْ كَانَ الصحيحُ فيهـا دون الواجب (أي لو كانت الشـاةُ الصحيحـة دون الشـاة الـواجبة وهي المريضة في القيمة) أجْزَأهُ صحيحـةٌ ومريضةٌ (فجاز إخراجها أي الصحيحة لصحتها ، وجاز إخراج المريضة لأنها أعلى من الصحيحة في القيمة)] .

h2.9 If a group of livestock are all female, or are both male and female, then only a female animal may be paid as zakat, except as mentioned

h2.9   وإنْ كَانَتْ إناثاً أوْ ذكوراً وإناثاً لمْ يُؤْخَـذْ في فرضِهَا إلَّا أنثى إلَّا مـا تَقَـدَّمَ [في خمسٍ وعشـريـنَ عنـدَ فقـدِ بنتِ

above (h2.4) for 30 cattle, where a yearling male is acceptable.

مخـاض و] في ثلاثين بقرةً [وفي خمس مِنَ الإبل] فإنَّهُ يُجزِىءُ [ابنُ لبونٍ و] تبيعُ [وجَـذَعُ ضأنٍ أو ثنيُّ معـزٍ (في الاستثناء الثالث وهو قوله وفي خمس من الإبل)].

h2.10   If a group of livestock are all male, then a male animal may be paid as zakat.

h2.10   وإنْ تَمَحَّضَتْ ذكـوراً أجْـزَأهُ الـذكـرُ مطلقـاً. [لكنْ يُؤْخَـذُ في سِتٍ وثـلاثينَ ابنُ لبـونٍ أكثرُ قيمةً مِنَ ابنِ لبونٍ يُؤْخَذُ في خمسٍ وعشرينَ بالتقويم والنسبةِ].

h2.11   If all the livestock are below the minimum age that may be given as zakat (def: h2.4–5), then one of them is given anyway. But if the herd is mixed, with only some of them underage, then only an animal of the acceptable age may be paid.

h2.11   وإنْ كَانَتْ كلُّها صغـاراً دونَ سِنَّ الفـرض (أي لم تبلغ سنـه الـذي تجزِىء فيه) أخَذَ منها صغيرةً [ويجتهِدُ بحيثُ لا يُسَـوِّي بينَ القليـل والكثيـر فتفصيـلُ سِتٍ وثـلاثينَ يَكـونُ خيـراً من فصيل خمس وعشرينَ] وإنْ كَانَتْ كباراً وصغاراً لزمَهُ كبيرةٌ وهوَ سِنُّ الفرض المتقدم.

h2.12   If the animals of the herd are defective, an animal is taken which is of the average defectiveness (O: of the group, *defective* meaning with defects that permit return for refund when sold as merchandise (def: k5.3)).

h2.12   وإنْ كَانَتْ معيبةً أخَذَ الأوسطَ في العيب ((بـاعتبار عيب البقية] والمراد بالعيب ما يثبت به الرد في المبيع).

h2.13   If the herd is composite, such as sheep and goats, then either kind may be paid as zakat, though the value of the animal given must correspond to the average value of the members of the herd.

h2.13   وإنْ كَانَتْ أنـواعاً كضأنٍ ومعزٍ أخذ مِنْ أيِّ نوعٍ شَاءَ بالقسطِ (أي باعتبار القيمـة) [فيُقَالَ لوْ كَانَتْ كلُّهـا ضأنـاً كمْ تُسَاوِي واحدةٌ منها إلى آخرِ مَا تَقَدَّمَ].

h2.14   The following are not taken as zakat unless the owner wishes to give them:

   (1) a pregnant female (O: because of its superiority);

   (2) one that has given birth (O: because of the high yield of milk);

   (3) a stud (O: as it is for insemination, and the owner would suffer its loss);

h2.14   ولا يُؤْخَـذُ الحامِلُ (في الزكاة لأنها من الخيار) ولاَ التي وَلَدَتْ (لكثرة لبنها) ولا الفحـلُ (لأنه للضراب فيتضرر

(4) a superior quality animal;

(5) or one fattened for eating.

المـالك بأخـذه) ولَا الخيارُ ولَا المسمنةُ
للأكل إلاَّ أنْ يرْضَى المالكُ.

ZAKAT ON JOINTLY OWNED PROPERTY OR VENTURES WITH SHARED FACILITIES

زكاة النصاب المشترك

h2.15 Two people pay zakat jointly as a single person if:

(1) they jointly own a zakat-payable amount of livestock or something else (O: such as fruit, grain, money, or trade goods), as when two people inherit it;

(2) or when the property is not jointly owned, as when each owner has, for example, 20 head of sheep (N: of a herd amounting to the zakat minimum of 40), but they share the same place to bed them down, to gather them before grazing, to pasture, water, or milk them, or share the same stud, employ the same shepherd, or similar, such as having the same watchman (O: for orchards and fields), the same drying or threshing floor (O: for fruit or grain), the same store, or the same warehouse.

h2.15 ولوْ كانَ بين نفسين منْ أهـل
الزكاة نصابٌ مشتركٌ منَ الماشية أوْ غيرهَا
(من الثمر والزرع والنقد وعرض التجارة)
مثْلَ أنْ يرثاهُ أوْ غيرَ مشترَك بلْ لكلٍّ منهمَا
عشرونَ شاةً مثـلاً مميَّزةً إلاَّ أنَّهمَا اشتركَا
في المـراح والمـسْـرَح والمـرعى
والمشـرَب وموضع الحلب والفحل
والـراعِي وفي غيرهَا منَ النـاطورِ (أي
حافظ الشجر والزرع) والجرينِ (أي
موضع تجفيف الثمر وتخليص الحب)
والـدكَّانِ (أي المـوضع الـذي توضع
الأقمشة والأمتعة فيه) ومكان الحفظ زكيًا
زكاة الرجل الواحد.

*

h3.0   ZAKAT ON CROPS

h3.0   زكاة النبات

h3.1 (N: The rulings of this section apply to the farmers who raise the crops. As for those who buy agricultural produce with the intention to sell it, their produce is no longer considered as crops are, but is rather a type of trade goods, and the zakat on it must be paid accordingly (def: h5).)

h3.2 There is no zakat on grains or legumes except the staple types that people cultivate, dry, and store, such as wheat, barley, millet, rice, lentils, chickpeas, broad beans, grass peas, and Sana'i wheat.

There is no zakat on fruit except for raw dates and grapes (O: the zakat on grapes being taken in

h3.2 لا تَجبُ الـزكاةُ في الزرع إلاَّ
فيما يقْتاتُ من جنس مَا يسْتنْبتُهُ الآدميونَ
ويَيبسُ ويُـدَّخَرُ كحنطةٍ وشعيرٍ وذرةٍ وأرزٍ
وعدسٍ وحمصٍ وباقلاء وجلبانٍ
وعلسٍ.
ولا تَجبُ في الثمـار إلاَّ في الـرطب

raisins, and on dates, in cured dates). There is no zakat on vegetables. Nor is there zakat on seasonings such as cumin or coriander (O: since the aim in using them is preparation of food, not nourishment).

والعنب (وتُؤخذ زكاته زبيباً كما تؤخذ زكاة النخل تمراً). ولا تَجبُ في الخضروات ولا الأبازير مثلَ الكمون (لأن القصد منها إصلاح الطعام لا القوت) والكزبرة.

h3.3 One is obliged to pay zakat as soon as one possesses the zakat-payable amount (def: below) of grain, or when the ripeness and wholeness of a zakat-payable amount of dates or grapes is apparent. Otherwise, one is not obliged.

h3.3 فَمَن انْعَقَد في ملكِه نصابُ حب أوْ بَدَا صلاحُ نصابِ رطبٍ أوْ عنبٍ لَزِمَتْهُ الزكاةُ وإلَّا فَلا.

THE ZAKAT-PAYABLE AMOUNT OF CROPS

نصاب النبات

h3.4 The minimal quantity on which zakat is payable for crops is 609.84 kilograms of net dried weight, free of husks or chaff, though for rice and Sana'i wheat, which are stored in the kernal, the zakat minimum, including husks, is 1219.68 kilograms of dried weight.

h3.4 والنصابُ أنْ يَبْلُغَ جافاً خالصاً من القشرِ والتبنِ خمسةَ أوسق وهوَ ألفٌ وستمائةِ رطلٍ بغداديةٍ، إلَّا الأرزَ والعلسَ وهوَ صنفٌ من الحنطة يُدَّخَرُ مَعَ قشرِه فنصابُهُمَا عشرةُ أوسقٍ بقشرِهِمَا.

Zakat is not taken from grain until it has been winnowed (O: made free of straw), nor from fruits until they are dried (n: made into raisins and dates).

ولا تُخْرَجُ الزكاةُ في الحب إلَّا بعدَ التصفيةِ (من التبن) ولا في الثمرةِ إلَّا بعدَ الجفاف.

The produce for the entire year (N: i.e. the agricultural year) is added together in calculating the zakat minimum (N: when, for example, the season's first crop alone is less than the zakat minimum). When one crop is harvested after another—due to varietal differences or the location of the two fields—in the same year, and of the same kind of crop (n: such as spring wheat and winter wheat), zakat is payed from them as if they were a single quantity. Different varieties of grain are also calculated additively when harvested at the same time, though the fruit or grain of one year is not added to the fruit or grain of a different year.

وتُضَمُّ ثمرةُ العامِ الواحدِ بعضُها إلى بعضٍ في تكميلِ النصاب حتّى لوْ أطْلَعَ البعضُ بعدَ جذاذِ البعض لاختلافِ نوعِه أوْ بلدِه والعامُ واحدٌ والجنسُ واحدٌ ضَمَّهُ إلَيْهِ في تكميلِ النصابِ ويُضَمُّ أنواعُ الزرعِ بعضُهُ إلى بعضٍ في النصاب إن اتَّفَقَ حصادُهُمَا في عام واحدٍ ولاَ تُضَمُّ ثمرةُ عام أوْ زرعُهُ إلى ثمرةِ عام آخَرَ أوْ زرعِه.

Grapes are not calculated cumulatively with dates, nor wheat with barley (O: as they are different from one another).

ولاَ عنبٌ لرطبٍ ولاَ برُّ لشـعـيــرٍ (لاختلاف الجنس).

h3.5 The zakat for crops that have been watered without effort, as by rain and the like, is 10 percent of the crop (N: i.e. of the net dried stor-

h3.5 ثمَّ الواجبُ العشرُ إنْ سُقِيَ بلاَ مؤنةٍ كالمطرِ ونحوِه ونصفُ العشرِ إنْ

age weight of the grain, raisins, or dates). The zakat for crops that have been watered with effort, such as on land irrigated by ditches (O: or a water-wheel) is 5 percent of the crop.

If a crop has been raised without irrigation for part of the year and irrigated for part of it, then the zakat is adjusted (O: according to the period, meaning how much of the time the fruit or crops were growing). (N: It is more reliable to consult agricultural experts as to how much of the crop's water came from rain and how much came from irrigation. If 50 percent of the water came from each, for example, one would pay 7.5 percent of the crop as zakat, as this is the mean between the above two percentages.)

سُقِيَ بمـؤنـةٍ كسـاقيةٍ ونحوهَا (وكتاعورة) والقسـطُ إنْ سُقِيَ بهمَا (باعتبار المدة أي مدة عيش الثمر والزرع ونمائهما).

(ح: الأولى أن يستشار خبراء الزراعة في نسبـة المـاء الذي من المطر، والنسبة التي من الـري. فإن كان مثلاً ٥٠٪ من كل منهمـا فالـواجب ٧,٥٪ لأنه المعدل بين العشر وبين نصف العشر).

h3.6   After one has paid zakat once on a crop (N: if one is the farmer), there is nothing further due on it (O: as there is no repetition of zakat on one's crops when they are in storage, unlike the repetition of it on money), even if it remains in one's possession for years.

h3.6   ثمّ (بعد إخراج زكاته) لَا شيءَ فيهِ (لأن زكـاة النبـات لا تتكـرر كل عام كتكرر زكاة النقد) وإنْ دَامَ في ملكِه سنينَ.

h3.7   It is unlawful for the grower to consume dates or grapes or otherwise dispose of them or sell them before they have been assessed (O: i.e. estimated as to how much there is, and the owner made responsible for the portion to be paid as zakat), and if he does, he is responsible for the loss (O: since part of it belongs to the poor (dis: h1.9)).

h3.7   ويَحـرُمُ على المـالكِ أنْ يأْكُلَ شيئـاً من الثمـرة أوْيَتَصَـرَّفَ فيهَـا ببيع وغيـره قبلَ الخرص (أي الحزر والتقدير وقبل التضمين للمالك في ذمته) فإنْ فَعَلَ ضَمِنَهُ (لأن فيه حق الفقراء).

h3.8   [ويُنْـدَبُ للإمـام أنْ يَبْعَثَ خارصـاً (له معرفـة بكميـة ما يخرج من الثمر ظناً) عدلاً (وأما اتصاف المبعوث بهذين الوصفين فهو شرط فلا يصح بعث جاهل به ولا غير عدل) يَخْرُصُ الثمارَ ومعناهُ أنّهُ يَدُورُ حول النخلةِ فَيَقُولُ: فيهَا منَ الرطب كذا ويأتي منهُ منَ الثمر كذا.

ويَضْمَنُ المالكُ نصيبَ الفقراء (لينتقل الحق من العين إلى الذمة تمراً أو زبيباً ليخرجه بعد جفافه. والخرص خاص بالرطب والزبيب فلا خرص للزرع لأنه لا يؤكل غالباً رطباً بخلاف التمر) بحسابه (أي بقدر ما قدره الخارص) في ذمتِهِ ويَقْبَلُ المالكُ ذلكَ فَيَنْتَقِلُ حينئذٍ حقُّ الفقراء منهُ إلى ذمتِه ولهُ بعدَ ذلك التصرفُ].

h3.9   If an act of God destroys the fruit after assessment, there is no zakat on it.

h3.9   فإنْ تَلِفَ بآفةٍ سمـاويـةٍ بعـدَ ذلك سَقَطَتِ الزكاةُ.

*

h4.0 ZAKAT ON GOLD, SILVER, AND OTHER MONEY

h4.0 زكاة الذهب والفضة

h4.1 Zakat is obligatory for anyone who has possessed the zakat-payable amount of gold or silver for one year.

h4.1 مَنْ مَلَكَ مِنَ الذهبِ والفضةِ نصاباً حولاً لَزِمَتْهُ الزكاةُ.

THE ZAKAT-PAYABLE AMOUNTS OF GOLD, SILVER, AND OTHER MONEY

نصاب الذهب والفضة

h4.2 The zakat-payable minimum for gold is 84.7 grams, on which 2.1175 grams (2.5 percent) is due. The zakat-payable minimum for silver is 592.9 grams, on which 14.8225 grams (2.5 percent) is due. There is no zakat on less that this.

(N: One must pay zakat (n: 2.5 percent) on all money that has been saved for a year if it equals at least the market value of 592.9 grams of silver (n: that is current during the year). While there is a considerable difference between the value of the gold zakat minimum and the silver zakat minimum, the minimum for monetary currency should correspond to that of silver, since it is better for the poor.)

h4.2 ونصابُ الذهب عشرونَ مثقالاً وزكاتُهُ نصفُ مثقالٍ، ونصابُ الفضةِ مائتا درهمٍ خالصةٍ وزكاتُهُ خمسةُ دراهمَ خالصةً، ولا زَكاةَ فيمَا دونَ ذلكَ. (ح: تجب الزكاة على من ملك عملة ما حولاً كاملاً إذا ساوت قيمتها نصاب الفضة. وإنما قدرنا بالفضة دون الذهب مع الفارق في قيمة نصابيهما لأن ذلك أنفع للفقراء).

h4.3 Zakat is exacted proportionately (2.5 percent) on any amount over these minimums, whether the gold or silver is in coins, ingots, jewelry prepared for uses that are unlawful or offensive (dis: f17.6,8,11), or articles which are permanent acquisitions.

h4.3 وتجبُ فيمَا زادَ على النصاب بحسابِهِ سواءً في ذلكَ المضروبُ والسبائكُ والحليُّ المعَدُّ (أي المهيأ) لاستعمالٍ محرّمٍ أوْ مكروهٍ أوْ للقنيةِ.

h4.4 There is no zakat on (n: gold or silver) jewelry that is for permissible use.

h4.4 فإنْ كانَ الحليُ معَدّاً لاستعمالٍ مباحٍ فلا زكاةَ فيهِ.

*

h5.0 ZAKAT ON TRADE GOODS

h5.0 زكاة العروض

h5.1 A zakat of 2.5 percent (O: like that of gold and silver, as merchandise is assessed according to its value in them) is obligatory for anyone who:

h5.1 إذا مَلَكَ عرضاً حولاً وكانَ

(a) has possessed trade goods for a year (n: whether the merchandise itself remains, or whether there is sale and replacement, as below at h5.4–5);

(b) whose value (n: at the zakat year's end, as at h5.3) equals or exceeds the zakat minimum (N: 592.9 grams of silver if bought with monetary currency or silver, and 84.7 grams of gold if bought with gold, these being reckoned according to the values of silver and gold existing during the year);

provided:

(c) that the trade goods have been acquired through a transaction (O: such as a purchase, or acquired by a woman as her marriage payment (mahr, def: m8), or received as a gift given in return for something else (dis: k31.4), or such as articles rented from someone in order to rent them out to others at a profit, or land rented from someone in order to rent it out to others at a profit);

(d) and that at the time of acquisition, the owner intended to use the goods for trade.

There is no zakat on trade goods if (non-(c) above) the owner acquired them by estate division (irth, def: L1) or received them as a gift, or if (non-(d)) he acquired them by purchase but at the time did not intend using them for trade.

THE BEGINNING OF THE ZAKAT YEAR FOR TRADE GOODS

h5.2   When the owner buys trade goods that cost (N: at least) the gold or silver zakat minimum, the year of the merchandise's possession is considered to have begun at the beginning of the gold or silver's zakat year (N: so that a merchant's zakat is figured yearly on his total business capital and goods).
But the year of the merchandise's possession is considered to have begun at the moment of purchase if:

قيمتُهُ في آخرِ الحولِ نصاباً لزمتْهُ زكاتُهُ وهيَ ربعُ العُشْرِ (كما في الذهب والفضة لأن العـــرض المـــذكـــور يقـــوَّم بهمـــا) بشـرطيـنِ : أنْ يَتَمَلَّكَهُ بمعـاوضةٍ (كشراء وإصداق وهبة بثواب واكتراء كأن يستأجر الأعيان ويؤجرها بقصد التجارة أو يستأجر أرضاً ثمَّ يؤجرها بقصد التجارة) وأنْ يَنْوِيَ حالَ التملكِ التجارة .
فلوْ مَلَكَهُ بإرثٍ أوْ هبةٍ أوْ بيعٍ ولمْ يَنْوِ التجارةَ فلا زكاةَ .

ابتداء الحول

h5.2   فإنِ اشْتَـرَاهُ بنصابٍ كاملٍ مِنَ النقديْنِ بَنَى حولَهُ على حولِ النقد . وإنِ اشْتَرَاهُ بغيرِ ذلكَ إمَّا بدونِ نصابٍ

(1) the owner has bought the merchandise for less than the zakat minimum (O: provided the price of the new merchandise plus his remaining money do not amount to the zakat minimum);

(2) or he has bought it (N: in exchange) for nonmonetary goods (N: provided these are not also trade goods, as at h5.4, for if they are, the zakat year continues from the zakat year of the previous goods).

ESTIMATING WHETHER THE VALUE OF ONE'S TRADE GOODS AMOUNTS TO THE ZAKAT MINIMUM OR NOT

(أي ولم يكن عنده باقيه من النقد) أوْ بغير نقدٍ فحولُهُ منَ الشراءِ.

تقدير نصاب العروض

h5.3   Merchandise is appraised (A: at its current market value) at the end of the zakat year:

(1) in terms of the same type of money that it was purchased with, if bought with money (N: i.e. if purchased with silver or monetary currency, we see if the merchandise's market value at the year's end has reached the silver zakat minimum (def: h5.1(b)); or if with gold, we see if its market value has reached the gold minimum) even if it had been purchased for less than the zakat minimum (N: at the beginning of the year) (O: so that if it has now reached the value of the zakat minimum, one pays zakat on it, and if not, then there is no zakat);

(2) or in terms of its value in local monetary currency, if the merchandise was acquired by other than paying money for it (O: such as in exchange for goods, or acquired by a woman as her marriage payment (mahr), or by a husband in exchange for releasing his wife from marriage (def: n5)). If its value equals the zakat minimum (h5.1(b)), then zakat is paid. But if not, then there is no zakat on it until the end of the next year, when it is reappraised and zakat is paid if its value amounts to the zakat minimum, and so on (N: in the following years).

It is not a condition that the value of the trade goods amount to the zakat minimum except at the *end* of the year (O: not at the beginning, middle, or during the whole of the year).

h5.3   ويُقَوَّمُ مال التجـارة آخِـرَ الحـول بمَـا اشْتَراهُ به إن اشتراهُ بنقدٍ ولوْ بدونِ النصابِ (فإن بلغ نصابَ الـزكاة زكاه وإن لم يبلغ به نصاباً فلا زكاة). فإن اشتراهُ بغيـر نقدٍ (كعرض ونكاح وخلع) قَوَّمَهُ بنقـدِ البلدِ. فإذا بَلَغَ نصـاباً زَكَـاهُ وإلاَّ فلا زكاةَ حتَّى يَحُولَ علَيْهِ حولٌ آخَـرُ فيَقَـوَّمُ ثانيـاً وهكـذا ولاَ يُشْتَرَطُ كونُهُ نصاباً إلاَّ في آخِرِ الحولِ فقطْ (لا في أوله ولا وسطه ولا في جميع الحول).

h5.4 If trade goods are exchanged for other trade goods during the course of the year, this does not interrupt their possession (O: because zakat on merchandise is based on the value, and the value of the previous merchandise and the new merchandise is the same, so the year of its possession is not interrupted by merely transferrring it from one set of goods to another), though the zakat year of the funds which a professional money changer exchanges for other funds is interrupted by each exchange (N: and he pays no zakat as long as he keeps changing his business capital).

h5.5 If merchandise is sold during the zakat year at a profit and its price is kept until the end of the year, then zakat on the merchandise's original value is paid at the end of that zakat year, but the zakat on the profit is not paid until the profit has been possessed for a full year.

(n: A second position in the Shafi'i school is that the zakat on the profit is simply paid in the current zakat year of the merchandise, just as one pays zakat on the offspring of livestock (dis: h2.7) in the current year of their mothers (*Mughni al-muhtaj ila ma'rifa ma'ani alfaz al-Minhaj* (y73), 1.399).)

*

h6.0   ZAKAT ON MINES AND TREASURE TROVES

h6.1 A zakat of 2.5 percent is immediately due on:

(a) the zakat minimum or more of gold or silver (def: h4.2) (O: *gold or silver* excluding anything else, such as iron, lead, crystal, turquoise, cornellian, emerald, antimony, or other, on which there is no zakat);

(b) extracted from a mine (O: i.e. a site at which Allah has created gold or silver) located on land permissible for the miner to work or owned by him;

h5.4 ولوْ بَاعَ عرضَ التجــارةِ في الحولِ بعرضٍ تجارةٍ لمْ يَنْقطعِ الحولُ (لأن زكـاة التجارة تتعلق بالقيمـة وقيمـة الثـاني والأول واحـدة فلا ينقطـع الحول لانتقالها من سلعة إلى سلعة).
ولوْ بَاعَ الصيرفيُّ النقودَ بعضَها ببعضٍ في الحولِ للتجارةِ انْقطَعَ.

h5.5 ولوْ بَاعَ في الحــولِ بنقـدٍ وربحٍ وأمْسَكَهُ [(أي المذكور من النقد والربح)] إلى آخـرِ الحولِ زكَّى الأصلَ بحولهِ والربحَ بحولهِ [وأولُ حولِ الربحِ مِنْ حينِ نضوضِهِ لا مِنْ حينِ ظهورِهِ].
(ت: وفي قول آخـر عند الشـافعيـة يزكّى الأصل والربح بحول الأصل كما يزكّى نتـاج نصـاب المـاشية لحول أصله [مغني المحتاج إلى معرفة معاني ألفاظ المنهاج: ١/ ٣٩٩]).

h6.0 زكاة المعدن والركاز

h6.1 إذَا اسْتَخْـرِجَ مِنْ معـدنٍ (أي مكـان خلق الله فيـه الذهب والفضة) في أرضٍ مباحةٍ أوْ مملوكةٍ لهُ نصابَ ذهبٍ أوْ فضةٍ (فخرج بالذهب أو الفضة غيره من الحـديـد والرصـاص والبلور والفيـروز والعقيق والزمرد والكحل وغيرها فلا زكاة

(c) and that this amount of ore has been gathered by working the site one time, or several times uninterrupted by abandoning or neglecting the project.

The zakat is only paid after the ore is refined into metal.

If the person stops working the site for a justifiable reason, such as to travel (O: not for recreation, but for something such as an illness) or to fix equipment, then he adds (O: the ore collected after the interruption to that collected before, in calculating the zakat minimum).

Ore found on someone else's land belongs to the owner of the land.

ZAKAT ON TREASURE TROVES

h6.2   An immediate zakat of 20 percent is due when one finds a treasure trove that was buried in pre-Islamic times (N: or by non-Muslims, ancient or modern) if it amounts to the zakat minimum (def: h4.2) and the land is not owned. If such a treasure is found on owned land, it belongs to the owner of the land. If found in a mosque or street, or if it was buried in Islamic times, it is considered as a lost and found article (def: k27).

*

h7.0   THE ZAKAT OF 'EID AL-FITR

WHO MUST PAY IT

h7.1   The zakat of 'Eid al-Fitr is obligatory for every free Muslim, provided:

(a) that one has the necessary amount (O: 2.03 liters of food);

(b) and that on the night before the 'Eid and on the 'Eid itself, this is in excess of what one needs to feed oneself and those whom one is

فيهَا) في دفعةٍ أَوْ دفعاتٍ لمْ يَنْقَطِعْ فيهَا عن العمـل بتــركٍ أَوْ إهمـالٍ، ففيـهِ في الحـالِ، ربعُ العُشْـر ولا تُخْـرَجُ إلاّ بعـدَ التصفيـةِ. فإنْ تركَ العمـلَ بعـذرٍ كسفـرٍ (لغيـر تنـزه وكمـرض) وإصلاح آلةٍ ضُمَّ (أي ذلك النيل الثاني للأول في إكمال النصاب).

وإنْ وَجَدَ في أرضِ الغيرِ فهوَ لصاحِبها.

زكاة الركاز

h6.2   وإنْ وَجـدَ ركـازاً منْ دفيـنِ الجـاهليـةِ وهـوَ نصـابُ ذهبٍ أَوْ فضةٍ في أرضٍ مواتٍ ففيه الخمسُ في الحالِ. وإنْ وَجَدَهُ في مِلكٍ فهوَ لصاحبِ الملكِ. أَوْ في مسجـدٍ أَوْ في شارعٍ أَوْ كانَ منْ دفينِ الإسلامِ فهوَ لُقَطَةٌ.

زكاة الفطر   h7.0

المخاطب بوجوبها

h7.1   تجـبُ على كلِّ حرٍّ مسلمٍ إذا وجـدَ ما يُؤَدِّيهِ (وهـو الصـاعِ) في (زكاة) الفطر فاضلاً عنْ قوتِهِ وقوتِ منْ تلْزَمُهُ

obliged to support (def: m12.1), what one needs to clothe them, and in excess of one's debts and housing expenses.

If one's excess amounts to only part of the required zakat, one must pay as much of it as one has.

PAYING THE ZAKAT OF 'EID AL-FITR FOR ONE'S DEPENDENTS

نفقتُهُ وكسوتهمْ ليلةَ العيدِ ويومَهُ [(كلّ منهمـا متعلق بقـولـه فاضـلاً)] وعنْ دينٍ ومسكنٍ [وعبدٍ يَحْتَاجُهُ].

فلوْ فَضَلَ بعضُ مَا يُؤدِّيهِ لَزِمَهُ إخراجُهُ.

إخراج الفطرة عمن يعول

h7.2   Someone obligated to pay the zakat of 'Eid al-Fitr must also pay it for every person he is obliged to support, such as his wife and family (O: e.g. his young son, grandson, father, or mother), if they are Muslim and if he has enough food (O: 2.03 liters per person above his own expenses and theirs), though he is not obliged to pay it for his father's wife when supporting his father because of the father's financial difficulties, even though he is obliged to support her (dis: m12.5).

h7.2   ومَنْ لَزِمَتْـهُ فطرتُـهُ لَزِمَتْهُ فطرةُ كلِّ مَنْ تَلْزَمُـهُ نفقتُـهُ من زوجةٍ وقريبٍ (كـابنٍ صغيـرٍ أو ابنِ ابنٍ كذلك أو أبٍ أو أمٍ) [ومملوكٍ] إنْ كانُوا مسلمينَ ووَجَدَ مـا يُؤدِّي عَنْهُمْ (وهو الصاع عن كل شخصٍ فاضـلاً عن نفقتـه ونفقتِهم) لكنْ لَا تَلْزَمُهُ فطـرةُ زوجـةِ الأبِ المعسـرِ [ومستولدتِه] وإنْ لَزِمَتْهُ نفقتُها.

h7.3   If one is obligated to pay the zakat of 'Eid al-Fitr but only has enough to pay part of it, then one begins by paying one's own, then that of one's wife, young child, father, mother, and then one's adult son (O: without an income, as when he is chronically ill or insane, for otherwise one is not obliged to support him).

h7.3   ومَنْ لَزِمَهُ فطرةٌ ووَجَدَ بعضَها بَدَأ بنفسِهِ ثمَّ زوجتِهِ ثمَّ ابنِه الصغيـرِ ثمَّ أبيـهِ ثمَّ أمِّهِ ثمَّ ابنِه الكبيرِ (الذي لا كسب له وهو زمنٌ أو مجنونٌ فإن لم يكن كذلك لم تجب نفقتُه).

h7.4   A wealthy woman married to a man too poor to pay her 'Eid al-Fitr zakat is not obliged to pay her own (A: though it is sunna for her to pay this and all forms of zakat to her husband, even if he spends it on her).

h7.4   ولوْ تَزَوَّجَ معسرٌ بموسرةٍ [أوْ بأمةٍ لَزِمَتْ سيدَ الأمةِ فطرةُ لأمتِه وَ] لَا تَلْزَمُ الحرةَ فطرةُ نفسِها [وقيلَ تَلْزَمُهَا].

h7.5   The zakat of 'Eid al-Fitr becomes obligatory when the sun sets on the night before the 'Eid (n: meaning on the evening of the last day of Ramadan).

h7.5   وسبـبُ الـوجـوبِ إدراكُ غروبِ الشمسِ ليلةَ الفطرِ [فلوْ وُلدَ له ولـدٌ أو تَزَوَّجَ أو اشْتَـرَى قَبْـلَ الغروبِ ومـاتَ عَقِبَ الغروبِ لَزِمَتْهُ فطرتُهم وإن وُجدُوا بعدَ الغروبِ لَمْ تَجِبْ فطرتُهم].

النوع الواجب من الطعام

h7.6   The zakat of 'Eid al-Fitr consists of 2.03 liters of the main staple of the area in which it is given, of the kinds of crops on which zakat is payable (def: h3.2). (A: If the main staple is bread, as in many countries, only *wheat* may be given, and is what is meant by the expression *giving food* here and in all texts below dealing with expiations (e.g. j3.22(2)).) (N: The Hanafi school permits paying the poor the wheat's value in *money,* both here and for expiations.) It is permissible to give the best quality of the staple food of the area, but not to give less than the usual quality (O: such as by giving barley where wheat is the main staple).

h7.6   ثُمَّ الـواجِـبُ صاعٌ عنْ كلِّ شخصٍ [وهـو خمسـةُ أرطـالٍ وثلثُ بغـداديةٍ وبالمصريِّ أربعةٌ ونصفٌ ورُبْعُ وسُبْعُ أُوقيةٍ] من الأقواتِ التي تَجِبُ فيها الـزكـاةُ منْ غالبِ قوتِ البلد [ويُجْـزِىءُ الأقِطُ واللبنُ لمنْ قوتُهُم ذلك] فإنْ أخْرَجَ منْ أعلى قوتِ بلدِهِ أجْـزأهُ، أوْ دونِهِ (بأن كانوا يقتاتون البر وأخرج من الشعير) فَلَا.

h7.7   It is permissible to give the zakat of 'Eid al-Fitr (N: to deserving recipients (dis: h8.26)) anytime during Ramadan, though the best time is on the day of 'Eid al-Fitr before the prayer (def: f19.1). It is not permissible to delay giving it until after the day of the 'Eid (O: that is, one may give it until sunset), and is a sin to delay until after this, and one must make it up (N: by paying it late).

h7.7   ويَجُـوزُ الإخـراجُ في جميع رمضـانَ والأفضـلُ يومَ العيدِ قبلَ الصلاةِ ولَا يَجُـوزُ تأخيرُهَـا عنْ يوم الفطرِ (وهو يومَ العيدِ أي فتكـون أداء إلى الغـروب) فإنْ أخَّرَ عنْهُ أثِمَ ولزِمَهُ القضاءُ.

*

h8.0   GIVING ZAKAT TO DESERVING RECIPIENTS

h8.0   قسم الصدقات

h8.1   It is unlawful to delay paying what is due from a zakat-payable amount of property when:

(a) it has been possessed for one year;

(b) one can find the (O: eight) categories (O: of eligible recipients, or some of them) so as to be able to pay it;

(c) and the property is present (O: within 81 km./50 mi.);

—unless one is awaiting a poor person more deserving than those present, such as a relative

h8.1   مَتَى حَالَ الحـولُ وقَـدَرَ على الإخـراج (أي إخراج الـزكـاة) بأنْ وَجَدَ الأصنـافَ (الثمانية المستحقين للزكاة أو وجد بعضهم) ومالُـهُ حاضـرٌ (عنده غير غائب مسافة القصر) حَرُمَ عليْهِ التأخيرُ إلّا أنْ يَنْتَظِـرَ فقيـراً أحقَّ منَ المـوجـودينَ

(O: of the person paying zakat whom he is not obliged to support), a neighbor, or a more righteous or needy person (O: than those present. Under these circumstances it is not unlawful to delay giving it because there is an excuse, unless withholding it involves considerable harm for those present).

كقريب (للمزكي لم تجب نفقته عليه) وجار (له فقير) وأصلح وأحوج (من الحاضر فلا يحرم التأخير حينئذ للعذر إلا إذا اشتد ضرر الحاضرين).

PAYING ZAKAT IN ADVANCE

تقديم الزكاة على الحول

h8.2   Zakat, on all types of property that a year's possession of the zakat minimum makes giving obligatory, may be payed for the current year (A: alone) before the year's end whenever the property owner possesses the zakat minimum.

This zakat in advance is considered valid only when the year ends and:

(a) the recipient it still among the types eligible for zakat (O: meaning, for example, that his state has not changed from poverty to wealth);

(b) the zakat giver is still obliged to pay it;

(c) and the property is still as it was (O: i.e. the zakat minimum still exists and has not been destroyed or sold).

The zakat in advance is not valid if (N: before the end of the year):

(1) (non-(a) above) the poor person who accepted it dies, or becomes financially independent for some other reason than having accepted the zakat;

(2) (non-(b)) the giver dies;

(3) or (non-(c)) the property diminishes to less than the zakat minimum by more than the amount given in advance (O: such as when the giver takes out 5 dirhams as zakat in advance from 200 dirhams, but his holdings are subsequently reduced by 10 (N: to 190 dirhams, which is less than the zakat minimum)), even when this reduction is because of sale.

h8.2   وكلُّ مالٍ وَجَبَتْ زكاتُهُ بحولٍ ونصابٍ جازَ تقديمُ الزكاةِ على الحولِ بعد ملكِ النصاب لحولٍ واحدٍ وإذا حالَ الحولُ والقابضُ بصفةِ الاستحقاقِ (أي لم يتغير حاله من الفقر إلى الغنى مثلاً) والدافعُ بصفةِ الوجوب والمالُ بحالِهِ (أي يشترط بقاء النصاب بحاله بأن لم يحصل له تلف أو بيع) وقَعَ المعجَّلُ عن الزكاةِ. وإنْ كانَ مَاتَ الفقيرُ أو استَغْنَى بغير (أخذ) الزكاة، أوْ مَاتَ الدافعُ أوْ نَقَصَ مالُـهُ عن النصابِ بأكثرَ منَ المعجَّلِ (متعلق بنقص كأن عجل خمسة من مائتي درهم وقد نقص ماله عشرة) ولوْ ببيع لمْ يقَعِ المعجَّلُ عنِ الزكاةِ، ويَسْتَردُّهُ إنْ بَيَّنَ

When the zakat in advance is not valid, the giver may take it back if he has explained that the money has been given in advance (O: by merely having said, "This is my zakat in advance," or if the recipient knows it). If what was given as zakat still exists, the recipient gives it back together with any increment organically connected with it, such as additional weight gained by a head of livestock while in the recipient's possession. But the property owner is not entitled to take back an increment that is not organically connected to the zakat, such as its offspring (O: born from the animal while in the recipient's possession).

If the zakat given in advance no longer exists, then the giver is entitled to take back a substitute (O: whether it be the substitute for a commodity that is fungible (mithli, def: k20.3(1)), such as silver dirhams, or whether for a nonfungible (mutaqawwim) commodity such as sheep or goats, in which case its price is the market value at the time the zakat in advance was *accepted*, not the time it ceased to exist).

After the return of the zakat in advance, the zakat giver pays the zakat from his wealth again if he is still obliged to.

The zakat in advance that is paid from the zakat-payable amount (nisab) is considered as if still part of the giver's property (O: only in respect to calculating whether the giver's total property equals the zakat-payable amount. It is not actually considered as still belonging to the zakat giver, since the recipient is entitled to dispose of it by sale or otherwise while it is in his possession). Thus, if the zakat giver paid a sheep in advance as zakat on 120 head, and one of the sheep then gave birth to a new lamb, the giver would now be obliged to pay another sheep (O: it being as if he owns the (N: next highest) zakat-payable amount of 121 head (dis: h2.5)).

AUTHORIZING ANOTHER TO DISTRIBUTE ONE'S ZAKAT

h8.3   It is permissible for the zakat giver to personally distribute his zakat to eligible recipients or to authorize an agent (wakil, def: k17) to do so.

It is permissible for the zakat giver to pay his

(أي الـدافـع له) أنَّهُ معجّلٌ (كأن قال هذه زكـاتي المعجلة فقط أو علم القابض أنها معجلة). فإنْ كانَ (ذلك المعجـل) باقياً رَدَّهُ بزيادتِه المتصلة كالسمنِ. لا (يستردّه بزيادته) المنفصلة كالولدِ (الحاصل عند المستحق). وإنْ تَلِفَ أخَـذَ بدلَهُ (المثلي كالـدراهم والمتقـوم كالغنم والعبرة بقيمة وقت القبض لا وقت التلف). ثمَّ يُخرِجُ ثانياً إنْ كَانَ بصفةِ الوجوبِ. ثمَّ المخرَجُ (أي أن الـمـخـرج من يد الـمـالـك للمستحقين هو) كالبـاقي على ملكِهِ (أي في تكميل النصابِ به وليس المـراد أنه باق حقيقـة فإن للقـابض أن يتصـرف فيـه بالبيـع وغيـره). ولـوْ عَجّلَ شاةً عنْ مائةٍ وعشرينَ ثمَّ وُلِدَ لهُ سخلةٌ لَزِمَهُ شاةٌ أخرىٰ (فكأنه ملك نصاباً قدره مائة وإحدى وعشرون).

جواز الوكالة في تفريق زكاته

h8.3   ويَجـوزُ أنْ يُفَرَّقَ زكاتَهُ بنفسِهِ أوْ بوكيلِهِ.

ويَجـوزُ أنْ يَدْفَعَهَا إلى الإمـام وهـو

265

zakat to the imam (A: i.e. the caliph (o25) or his representative), and this is superior unless the imam is unjust, in which case it is better to distribute it oneself.

THE PRAYER OF THE RECIPIENT FOR THE ZAKAT GIVER

h8.4   It is recommended for the poor person (O: receiving zakat when the owner is distributing it) or the agent assigned to deliver the zakat to recipients (N: if the imam has gathered it by means of agents to distribute to the poor) to supplicate for the giver, saying, "May Allah reward you for what you have given, bless you in what you have retained, and purify it for you."

THE INTENTION OF ZAKAT

h8.5   Making the intention of zakat is a necessary condition for the validity of giving it. The intention is made when zakat is paid to the poor person or the one being authorized to distribute it, and one must intend giving it as the zakat of one's property. (O: It is permissible to make the intention before paying the money.) When the owner has made this intention, it is not necessary that the agent distributing it also make an intention before giving it (O: because the owner's intention is sufficient, whether the agent is an ordinary individual or is the ruler. It is also permissible for the owner to authorize an agent to both make the intention and distribute the zakat).

h8.6   It is recommended that the imam dispatch a zakat worker, (O: to collect zakat funds from those obliged to pay, to make this easier for them. Such an agent must be) an upright Muslim (def: o24.4) who knows the rulings of zakat, and who is not of the Hashimi or Muttalibi clans of Quraysh.

THE EIGHT CATEGORIES OF RECIPIENTS

h8.7   It is obligatory to distribute one's zakat among eight categories of recipients (O: meaning

أفضَـلُ إلّا أنْ يَكُـونَ جائِـراً (غيـر عادل) فتفريقُهُ بنفسِهِ أفضلُ.

دعاء الآخذ للمعطي

h8.4   ويُنْدَبُ للفقير (الآخذ للزكاة إن فرق المـالـك) والسـاعي (ح: إن جمعها الإمام بواسطة السعاة ليفرقها على الفقراء) أنْ يَدْعُو للمعطي فَيَقُولُ «آجَرَكَ اللهُ فيمَـا أَعْطَيْتَ وبَـارَكَ لَكَ فيمَا أَبْقَيْتَ وَجَعَلَهُ لَكَ طَهُوراً».

نية الزكاة

h8.5   ومِنْ شرطِ الإجـزاءِ النيـةُ. فَيَنْـوي عنـدَ الـدفـعِ إلى الفقير أو إلـى الوكيل أنَّ هذِهِ زكاةَ مالي (ويجوز تقديم النية على دفع المال) فإذَا نَوَى المالكُ لمْ تَجِب نيـةُ الـوكيـلِ عندَ الدفع ([للفقراء] اكتفـاء بنية المالك سواء كان الوكيل من آحاد الناس أو كان هو السلطان وإن وكله بالنية وبالدفع جاز).

h8.6   ويُنْدَبُ للإمام أنْ يَبْعَثَ عاملاً (على الزكواتِ بأن يأخذها من أربابها أي ممن وجبت عليه تسهيلاً عليهم، ولا بد أن يكون العـامـل) مسلمـاً [حراً] عدلاً فقيهاً في الزكاة غيرَ هاشميٍ ومطلبيٍ.

أصناف المستحقين الثمانية

h8.7   ويجـبُ صرفُ الـزكـاةِ إلى ثمـانيـة أصنـاف (والمـراد أن الـزكاة لا

that zakat goes to none besides them), one-eighth of the zakat to each category.

(n: In the Hanafi school, it is valid for the giver to distribute his zakat to all of the categories, some of them, or to confine himself to just one of them (*al-Lubab fi sharh al-Kitab* (y88), 1.155).)

THE POOR

تخــرج عنـهم [فهي مقصـورة عليهم لا تتجاوزهم]) لكلِّ صنفٍ ثمنُ الزكاةِ.

الفقراء

h8.8   The first category is the *poor*, meaning someone who:

(a) does not have enough to suffice himself (O: such as not having any wealth at all, or having some, but (N: he is unable to earn any, and) what he has is insufficient to sustain him to the end of his probable life expectancy if it were distributed over the probable amount of remaining time; *insufficient* meaning it is less than half of what he needs. If he requires ten dirhams a day, for example, but the amount he has when divided by the time left in his probable life expectancy is four dirhams a day or less, not paying for his food, clothing, housing, and whatever he cannot do without, to a degree suitable (dis: f4.5) to someone of his standing without extravagance or penury, then he is *poor*—all of which applies as well to the needs of those he must support (def: m12.1).) (N: A mechanic's tools or scholar's books are not sold or considered part of his money, since he needs them to earn a living);

(b) and is either:

(1) unable to earn his living by work suitable to him (O: such as a noble profession befitting him (N: given his health and social position), as opposed to work unbefitting him, which is considered the same as not having any. If such an individual were an important personage unaccustomed to earning a living by physical labor, he would be considered "poor." This also includes being able to do work suitable to one, but not finding someone to employ one);

(2) or is able to earn his living, but to do so would keep him too busy to engage in attaining

h8.8   أحدُها الفقراءُ؛ والفقيرُ:

- مَنْ لا يَقْــدرُ على مَا يَقَــع موقعـاً مِنْ كفايتِهِ (بأن لم يكن له مال أصلاً أو له مال لا يقع موقعاً من كفايته العمر الغالب عند توزيعه عليه أي أنه لا يسد مسداً بحيث لا يبلغ النصف كأن يحتـاج إلى عشـرة، ولو وزع المال الذي عنده على العمر الغالب لخص كل يوم أربعة أو أقل وهي لا تكفيه من المطعم والملبس والمسكن وسـائر ما لا بد منــه على ما يليق بحـالــه من غير إسراف ولا تقتير وكـل ذلك لنفسه ولمن تلزمه نفقته).

- وعَجَــزَ عن كسب يَليقُ به (كصنعـة شريفة تليق به بخـلاف صنعـة لا تليق به فهي كالعدم حتى لو كان من الناس الكبار الــذين لا يعتـادون التكسب بالبـدن فهو فقير. ومن جملة العجـز أنه إذا قدر على صنعـة تليق به لكن لا يجد من يستعمله في تلك الصنعة فيعد فقيراً).

أوْ شَغَلَهُ الكسبُ عنِ الاشتغـالِ بعلمٍ

knowledge of Sacred Law. (n: Nawawi notes, "If able to earn a living at work befitting him except that he is engaged in attaining knowledge of some subject in Sacred Law such that turning to earning a living would prevent the acquisition of this knowledge (dis: w36), then it is permissible for him to take zakat because the attainment of knowledge is a communal obligation, though zakat is not lawful for someone able to earn a living who cannot acquire knowledge, even if he lives at a school. What we have just mentioned is the most correct and well known position. Darami mentions three positions concerning someone engaged in attaining religious knowledge:

—that he deserves charity even when able to earn a living;

—that he does not deserve it;

—and that if he is an outstanding student who can be expected to develop a good comprehension of the Sacred Law and benefit the Muslims thereby, then he deserves charity, but if not, then he does not.

"Darami mentioned this in the chapter of 'Voluntary Charity' " (*al-Majmu'* (y108), 6.190–91).)

But if one's religious devotions are what keeps one too busy to earn a living, one is not considered poor.

h8.9   Someone separated from his money by at least 81 km./50 mi. is eligible for zakat. (N: This was in the past. In our day it is fitter to say that he must be *far* from his money in terms of common acknowledgement (def: f4.5).) (O: Such a person's absent property is as if nonexistent, and his "poverty" continues until the money is present. Likewise, someone owed money on a debt not yet due who does not have any other money is given zakat when it is distributed (N: to suffice him) until the debt becomes due.)

h8.10   People whose needs are met by the expenditures of those who are obliged to support them

شرعيٍ . (ت: قال النـووي : ولـو قدر على كسب يليق بحـالـه إلا أنه مشتغـل بتحصيل بعض العلوم الشرعية بحيث لو أقبـل على الكسب لانقطع عن التحصيل حلت له الـزكـاة لأن تحصيل العلم فرض كفاية ، وأما من لا يتأتى منه التحصيل فلا تحـل له الـزكاة إذا قدر على الكسب وإن كان مقيمـاً بالمـدرسـة . هذا الذي ذكرناه هو الصحيح المشهور وذكر الدارمي في المشتغل بتحصيل العلم ثلاثـة أوجـه : [أحـدهـا] يستحق وإن قدر على الكسب [الثاني] لا [والثالث] إن كان نجيباً يرجى تفقهـه ونفـع المسلمين به استحق وإلا فلا . ذكـرهـا الـدارمي في باب صدقة التطوع» . [نقل من كتاب المجموع] .
فإنْ شَغَلَهُ التعَبُّدُ فلَيْسَ بفقيرٍ .

h8.9   ولـوْ كانَ لهُ مالٌ غائبٌ بمسافةٍ القـصـر أُعطيَ (ح: هذا في زمـانـهـم والأولى أن يقـال له مال بعيد عرفاً) (ومالـه الغائب كالعـدم فيستمر فقره إلى حضور مالـه . ومثله من له دين مؤجل وليس عنده غيره فيعطى وقت تفرقة الزكاة حتى يحل الأجل) .

h8.10   وإنْ كَانَ مستغنيـاً بنفقـةٍ مـنْ تَلْزَمُهُ نَفَقَتُهُ مِنْ زوجٍ وقريبٍ فلَا .

such as their husbands or families are not given zakat (N: for poverty) (O: though it is permissible for a third party to give zakat to such a dependent by virtue of the dependent's belonging to some category other than the poor or those short of money (def: below), as when the person belongs to a category such as travellers needing money (h8.18) or those whose hearts are to be reconciled (h8.14)).

THOSE SHORT OF MONEY

h8.11 The second category is people *short of money*, meaning someone who has something to spend for his needs but it is not enough, as when he needs five dirhams, but he only has three or four. The considerations applicable to the poor person also apply to someone short of money (O: namely, that he is given zakat if he cannot earn a living by work befitting him (def: h8.8(b)), or if he can earn a living but attainment of knowledge of Sacred Law prevents his doing so; though if he is able to earn a living but extra devotions prevent him from doing so, then he may not take zakat).

HOW MUCH THE POOR ARE GIVEN

h8.12 A person who is poor or short of money is given as much as needed of tools and materials (O: if he has a trade, such as the tools of a carpenter) with which he can earn a living, or property with which he can engage in trade (O: if a merchant), each according to the demands of his profession. This amount varies, depending on whether, for example, he is a jeweller, clothier, grocer, or other.

If the recipient has no trade (O: i.e. is unable to do any work, whether for wages, by trading, or other), then he is given enough zakat to fulfill his needs from the present till the end of his probable life expectancy (O: based on (N: the average life-span for someone like him in) that locality). Another position is that such a person is given enough for just one year.

These measures are obligatory when abun-

(ويجوز أن يدفع الأجنبي إلى المكفى بنفقة غيره باسم غير الفقراء والمساكين إذا كان بتلك الصفة كصفة ابن السبيل أو المؤلفة قلوبهم).

المساكين

h8.11 الثاني المساكين ؛ والمسكينُ مَنْ وَجَدَ مَا يَقَعُ موقعاً مِنْ كفايتِهِ ولا يكفيهِ مثلِ أَنْ يُريدَ خمسةً فَيجِدَ ثلاثةً أَوْ أربعةً . ويَأْتِي فيـه مَا قيـلَ في الفقيـر (وهو أنه إن عجـز عن كسب يليق به أو لم يعجـز لكنه يشغله عن علم شرعي فإنه يعطى حينئـذ فإن شغله الكسب عن التعبـد دون العلم فلا يعطى).

ما يعطى الفقراء

h8.12 وبُعْطَى الفقيـرُ والمسكينُ مَا يُزيـلُ حاجَتَهُمَا مِنْ عدةٍ يَكْتَسِبُ بهَا (كل منهمـا إن كان من أصحاب الصنائع كآلة النجارة مثلاً) أوْ مالٍ يَتَّجِرُ بِه (كل منهما إن كانـا من أهلِ التجارة) على حسب مَا يَليقُ به فيَتَفَاوَتُ بين الجـوهـريِّ والبـزازِ والبقالِ وغيرِهمْ.
فإنْ لمْ يَحْتَـرِفْ (أي بأن لم يحسن صنعة مـن الصنائـع لا بكسب ولا تجارة ولا غيرهمـا) أُعْطِيَ كفـايةَ العمر الغالب (في بلده) لمثلِهِ وقيلَ كفايةَ سنةٍ فَقَطْ. وهـذا مفـروضٌ مَعَ كثرة الزكاة إما بأنْ

dant zakat funds are available, whether the imam distributes them or a property owner. But if there is not much zakat available (O: meaning if the owner or imam distributes funds that are too little to last the poor person for his probable life expectancy or for even one year), it is distributed as is, an eighth to each category.

فَرَّقَ الإمامُ الـزكـاةَ أَوْرَبُّ المالِ وكـانَ المـالُ كثيراً . وإلّا (أي وإن فرقها ربُّ المـال أو الإمـام وكان المال قليلاً جداً لا يكفي لغـايـةِ العمـر الغالب أوكفايةِ سنةٍ) فكلُّ صنفٍ الثمنُ كيفَ كانَ .

ZAKAT WORKERS

العاملون

h8.13   The third category consists of *zakat workers*, the above-mentioned agents (h8.6) dispatched by the imam. These include the person collecting it, the clerk (O: recording what the owners give), the person who matches the payees to recipients, and the one who distributes it to recipients.

The zakat workers receive an eighth of the zakat funds. If this amount is more than it would cost to hire someone to do their job, then they return the excess for distribution to the other categories of recipients. But if less (N: than the cost of hiring someone), then enough is taken from the zakat funds to make up the difference. All of this applies only if the imam (A: caliph) is distributing the zakat (O: and has not allotted a fee to the zakat workers from the Muslim common fund (bayt al-mal)). If the property owner is distributing the zakat (O: or if the imam has allotted the workers a fee from the common fund) then the zakat funds are divided solely among the other categories of recipients.

h8.13   الثالثُ العاملونَ وهمْ الذينَ يَبْعَثُهُمْ الإمامُ كَمَا تَقَدَّمَ فمِنْهُمْ السـاعِي (وهو الذي يجمعها) والكاتبُ (وهو الذي يكتب ما أعطـاه أرباب الأموال) والحاشرُ (وهـو الـذي يجمـعهم أو يجمـع ذوي السهمـان) والقـاسمُ [(وهو الذي يقسمها على أربـابهـا المستحقين)] . فَيُجْعَـلُ للعـامـلِ الثمنُ فإنْ كانَ الثمنُ أكثرَ منْ أجرتـهِ (لـو استؤجر) ردَّ الفاضلَ على البـاقينَ وإنْ كانَ أقلَّ كَمَّلَهُ منَ الزكاة هذا إذا فَرَّقَ الإمامُ (ولم يجعـل للعامل جعلاً من بيت المال) فإن فَرَّقَ المالكُ (أوجعل الإمام للعامل جعلاً من بيت المال) قَسَّمَ على سبعةٍ وسَقَطَ العاملُ .

THOSE WHOSE HEARTS ARE TO BE RECONCILED

المؤلفة قلوبهم

h8.14   The fourth category is *those whose hearts are to be reconciled*. If they are non-Muslims, they are not given zakat, but if Muslims, then they may be given it (O: so that their certainty may increase, or if they are recent converts to Islam and are alienated from their kin).

Those to be reconciled include:

(1) the chief personages of a people (O: with weak Islamic intentions) whose Islam may be

h8.14   الـرابعُ المؤلفةُ قلوبُهم . فإنْ كانُوا كفاراً لمْ يُعْطَوا وإنْ كانوا مسلمينَ أعطُـوا (ليتقـوى يقينهم أوكانوا قريبي العهد بالإسلام بأن كان عندهم وحشة في أهلهم) والمـؤلفـةُ قومٌ أشـرافٌ (نيتهم ضعيـفـة في الإسـلام) يُرْجَى حسنُ

expected to improve, or whose peers may be expected to enter Islam;

(2) or the heads of a people who collect zakat for us from Muslims living near them who refuse to pay it, or who fight an enemy for us at considerable expense and trouble to themselves.

إسلامِهِم أو إسلامُ نظرائِهِم أوْ يَجْبُونَ (لَنا) الزكاةَ مِنْ مانِعيها بقربِهِم أوْ يُقاتِلُونَ عنّـا عدواً يُحْتَـاجُ في دفعِهِ إلى (صرف) مؤنةٍ ثقيلةٍ.

THOSE PURCHASING THEIR FREEDOM

الرقاب

h8.15 The fifth category is slaves who are purchasing their freedom from their owners. They are given enough to do so if they do not have the means.

h8.15 الـخـامـسُ الـرقـابُ وهُـمُ المكـاتبـونَ فَيُعْطَوْنَ ما يُؤَدُّونَ إنْ لَمْ يَكُنْ مَعهُمْ ما يُؤَدُّونَ.

THOSE IN DEBT

الغارمون

h8.16 The sixth category is those who have debts (O: and they are of three types):

(1) A person who incurs debts in order to settle trouble (O: between two people, parties, or tribes) involving bloodshed (O: as when there has been a killing but it is not known who the killer is, and trouble has arisen between the two sides) or to settle trouble concerning property (O: such as bearing the expense when trouble occurs over it) is given zakat even if he is affluent.

(2) A person who incurs debts to support himself or his dependents is given zakat if he is poor, but not if affluent. If he incurs a debt (O: for something lawful) but spends it on something unlawful, and then repents (O: and is felt to be sincere in this, and the original reason is known to have been something lawful), then he is given zakat.

(3) (O: And a third type, not mentioned by the author, which (n: given persons P, Q, and R) is when R incurs a debt by guaranteeing (daman, def: k15) to P that Q will pay P (n: what Q owes him). If R finds that neither he nor Q can pay, then R is given zakat (n: because he has gone into debt in order to guarantee Q's debt), even if the

h8.16 السادسُ الغارمونَ (وهم ثلاثة أقسـام) فإنْ غرِمَ لإصلاح (بين شخصين أو طائفتين أو قبيلتين) بأنْ اسْتَدانَ دينـاً لتسكين فتنة دم (أي قتيل ولم يظهر قاتله وقـد وقع التنـازع بين من ذكر) أوْ مالٍ (كتحمـل قيمةٍ وقد وقع التنازع أيضاً في هذه القيمة لأجل تسكين تلك الفتنة) دُفِعَ إليْهِ مَعَ الغِنَى.

وإن اسْتَدانَ لنفقتِهِ ونفقـةِ عيالِهِ دُفِعَ إليْهِ مَعَ الفقر دونَ الغِنَى.

وإنِ استدانَ (في مبـاح) وصَـرَفَـهُ في معصيةٍ وتَـابَ (وظن صدقه في توبته وقد عرف قصـد الإبـاحـة) دُفِعَ إليْـهِ [في الأصـحّ]. (ولم يذكـر المصنف القسم الثالث وهو من استدان لضمان فيعطى من الزكاة إن أعسر مع الأصيل وإن لم يكن

271

reason R agreed to guarantee Q was not charity (N: but was rather that Q would pay him back).)

متبرعاً).

THOSE FIGHTING FOR ALLAH

في سبيل الله

h8.17   The seventh category is *those fighting for Allah,* meaning people engaged in Islamic military operations for whom no salary has been allotted in the army roster (O: but who are volunteers for jihad without remuneration). They are given enough to suffice them for the operation, even if affluent; of weapons, mounts, clothing, and expenses (O: for the duration of the journey, round trip, and the time they spend there, even if prolonged. Though nothing has been mentioned here of the expense involved in supporting such people's families during this period, it seems clear that they should also be given it).

h8.17   السابعُ في سبيلِ اللهِ. وهمُ الغزاةُ الذينَ لَا حَقَّ لَهُمْ في الديوانِ ([أي في دفتـر العسكـر بل] هم متطـوعـون بالجهـاد بلا مقـابلة شيء) فَيُعْطَوْنَ مَعَ الغِنَى مَا يكفيهِمْ لِغـزوِهِم مِنْ سلاحٍ وفرس وكسوةٍ ونفقةٍ (مدة الذهاب والإيـاب ومـدة الإقـامـة وإن طالت، وسكتوا عن نفقة عياله والظاهر أنه يعطاها).

TRAVELLERS NEEDING MONEY

ابن السبيل

h8.18   The eighth category is *the traveller in need of money,* meaning one who is passing among us (O: i.e. through a town in Muslim lands where zakat is collected), or whose journey was not undertaken for the purpose of disobeying Allah. If such a person is in need, he is given enough to cover his personal expenses and transportation, even if he possesses money back home.

h8.18   الثـامنُ ابنُ السبيـل. وهـوَ المسافرُ المجتازُ بنَا (أي في بلد الزكاة من بلاد المسلمين) أو المنشىءُ للسفـر في غيـر معصيةٍ فَيُعْطَى نفقةً ومـركـوبـاً مَعَ الحاجةِ وإنْ كَانَ لهُ في بلدِهِ مالٌ.

PAYING ZAKAT TO RECIPIENTS

الدفع للمستحقين

h8.19   A person who qualifies as a member of two or more of the above categories is only given zakat for one of them.

h8.19   ومَنْ فيه سببانِ لمْ يُعْطَ إلَّا بأحدِهِمَا.

h8.20   When the (N: eight) categories of recipients exist in the town where zakat is collected, it is unlawful and invalid to give it to recipients elsewhere (O: as it must be paid to those present if the property owner is distributing his own zakat. The other schools of jurisprudence permit giving it

h8.20   فمَتَى وُجِدَت هذِه الأصنافُ في بلد المالِ فنقلُ الزكاةِ إلى غيرِهَا حرامٌ ولمْ يُجْزِ (فيتعين صرفها لهم وهذا كله إن فرق المالكُ. بخـلاف بقيـة المذاهب

elsewhere). But if the imam (A: caliph) is distributing the zakat, he may give it to recipients in a different place.

If the zakat giver's property is in the desert, or none of the eight categories of eligible zakat recipients exist in his own town, then the zakat should be distributed in the nearest town.

فيجـوز نقلهـا عندهـم) إلاّ أنْ يُفَرِّقَ الإمام فلَهُ النقل .

وإنْ كانَ مالُهُ بباديةٍ أوْ فُقِدَتِ الأصنافُ كلُّهَا ببلدِهِ نَقَلَ إلى أقربِ بلدٍ إلَيْهِ .

h8.21   Each category of recipients must receive an equal share, one-eighth of the total (dis: h8.7(n:)) (A: though one may give various individuals within a particular category more or less), except for zakat workers, who receive only their due wage (def: h8.13).

If one of the categories does not exist in one's town, their eighth is distributed over the other categories such that each of them gets one-seventh. If two categories of recipients do not exist in the town, then each of the remaining categories receive a sixth of the zakat, and so on (O: such that if there were only one category in town, all the zakat would be paid to it).

It is obligatory to give zakat to every individual member of a category if the owner is distributing zakat and the individuals are of a limited, known number, or if the imam is distributing zakat and it is possible to give it out person by person and include them all because of the abundance of funds.

If the owner is distributing zakat and the recipients in each category are not of a limited, known number, then the fewest permissible for him to give to in one category is three people, except for the category of zakat workers, in which a single person is enough.

h8.21   ويَجِبُ التسويةُ بينَ الأصنافِ لكـلِّ صنفٍ الثمنُ إلاّ العـامـلَ فقـدرُ أجـرتِـهِ . فإنْ فُقِدَ صنفٌ في بلدِهِ فَرَّقَ نصيبَهُ على البـاقينَ فيُعْطي لكلِّ صنفٍ السبعَ . أوْ صنفانِ فلكلِّ صنفٍ السدسُ وهكَذا (حتى لو لم يوجد إلا صنف واحد دفع إليه جميعها) .

فإنْ قَسَّمَ المـالـكُ وآحـادُ الصنفِ محصـورونَ (بـالعـدد) أوْ قَسَّمَ الإمامُ مطلقـاً وأمْكَنَ الاستيعـابُ لكثرة المال وَجَـبَ [(أي يجـب على كل منـهـمـا استيعاب الأفراد إن أمكن للإمام ذلك وانحصرت في صورة قسمة المالك)] .

وإنْ قَسَّمَ المـالـكُ وهمْ (أي أفراد كل صنف) غيـرُ محصورينَ فأقلُّ مَا يَجُوزُ أنْ يَدْفَعَ إلى ثلاثةٍ مِنْ كلِّ صنفٍ إلاّ العاملَ فيَجُوزُ واحدٌ .

h8.22   It is recommended to give one's zakat to relatives other than those one is obliged to support (def: m12.1).

h8.22   ويُنْدَبُ الصرفُ (أي صرف الزكاة) لأقاربِهِ الذينَ لَا تلزمُهُ نفقتُهُمْ .

h8.23   It is recommended to distribute zakat to recipients in proportion to their needs, giving someone who needs 100 dirhams, for example, half of what one gives to someone who needs 200.

h8.23   وأنْ يُفَرَّقَ على قدرِ الحـاجـةِ فيُعْطي مَنْ يَحْتَاجُ إلى مائةٍ مثلاً قدرَ نصفِ مَنْ يَحْتَاجُ مائتينِ .

h8.24   It is not permissible to give zakat to a non-Muslim, or to someone whom one is obliged to support (def: m12.1), such as a wife or family member.

ولا h8.24 وَلا يَجُـوزُ أَنْ يَدْفَعَ لكافرٍ [ولا لبني هاشمٍ وبني المطّلب] ولا لمَنْ تلزمُهُ نفقتُهُ كزوجةٍ وقريبٍ .

h8.25   It is not valid for one to give zakat to a poor person on condition that he return it to one to pay off a debt he owes, or to tell the recipient, "I hereby make the money you owe me zakat, so keep it for yourself." But it is permissible:

(1) for the giver to pay his zakat (O: to a poor person who owes him money) when the giver's intention is that the recipient should pay him back with it;

(2) for the zakat giver to tell the poor person, "Pay me the money you owe me so that I can give it to you as zakat";

(3) or for the poor person to tell his creditor, "Give me (O: zakat) so that I can pay it back to you (O: for the debt I owe you)";

though it is not obligatory to fulfill these promises (O: meaning the outcomes alluded to in (2) and (3) above).

h8.25 ولـو دَفَـعَ لفقيرٍ وشَرَطَ أَنْ يَرُدَّهُ عليْـهِ مِنْ دَيْنٍ لهُ عليْـهِ أَوْ قَالَ جَعَلْتُ مالي (الـذي هو) في ذمّتِكَ زكـاةً فَخُذْهُ (عنها لنفسك) زكاة) لَمْ يُجزِ .

وإنْ دَفَـعَ إلَيْـهِ (أي إلى الفقيـر الـذي عليـه الـدين شيئـاً بنيـةِ أنـهُ (أي الفقير) يَقْضِيـه منهُ (أي يقضي صاحب الدين أي يؤديه له) أَوْ قَالَ اقضِ مالي لأُعْطِيَكَهُ زكاةً أَوْ قَالَ المـديـونُ أَعْطِني (من الـزكاة) لأُقْضِيَكَهُ (عن دينك الذي هو علي) جَازَ .

ولا يَلْزَمُ الـوفاءُ بِهِ (أي بالشرط الموعود به في الصورتين الأخيرتين) .

h8.26   All of the above rulings concerning zakat (h8.2–25) apply to the zakat of 'Eid al-Fitr (def: h7) (O: in details, in giving it to deserving recipients (N: the eight categories described in this section), and in giving it in advance). It is permissible for a group of people to pool their zakat of 'Eid al-Fitr, mix it, and collectively distribute it, or for one of them to distribute it with the others' permission. (O: The author mentions this to inform people that anyone can distribute their zakat of 'Eid al-Fitr to all categories of recipients, no matter how little it is.)

h8.26 وزكـاةُ الفطـرِ في جميـعِ مَا ذَكَـرْنـاهُ (من التفصيل ومن إعطائها لمن يستحقهـا ومن تعجيلها) كزكاة المالِ منْ غيـرِ فرقٍ، فَلَوْ جَمَعَ جماعـةٌ فطـرتَهُمْ وخَلَطُوهـا وفرَّقُوهَا أَوْ فرَّقَهَا أَحَدُهُمْ بإذنِ البـاقينَ جَازَ . (وخص هذا الفـرع بالذكر لمـا فيـه من التنبيه على أنه لا يتعذر على الإنسـان تفرقة زكاة فطره وإن كانت قليلة على الأصناف كلهم) .

*

h9.0   VOLUNTARY CHARITY

h9.1   Giving voluntary charity is recommended at all times; especially during Ramadan, before praying for something one needs, (O: when there is an eclipse, illness, or journey,) and at all noble times and places (O: e.g. times such as the first ten days of Dhul Hijja or the days of 'Eid, and places such as Mecca or Medina).

h9.2   It is superior to give charity to righteous people (O: meaning those who give Allah and His slaves their due), to one's relatives (A: which is better than giving to the righteous), even those of them who are one's enemies (A: and this is better than giving to one's friends among them), and to give from the best of one's wealth (O: meaning that which is lawful, which is better than giving what is from a doubtful source, or giving what is of poor quality, either of which are offensive to give as charity. It is unlawful to give property that has been unlawfully obtained (N: if one knows its rightful owner. If not, one *must* give it as charity (A: or taxes (def: p32)) to remove it from one's possession)).

h9.3   It is unlawful to give as charity money needed to support one's dependents or needed to pay a debt that is currently due (O: because supporting one's dependents or paying a current debt are obligatory, and obligatory acts take precedence over recommended ones).

h9.4   It is recommended to give away in charity everything one owns that is in excess (O: of personal expenses and the expenses of those one is obliged to support), provided one can be patient with the resultant poverty. (O: But if one cannot be patient, it is offensive to give away what is in excess of one's needs.)

h9.5   It is offensive to ask for anything besides paradise with the words "For the sake [lit. "By the countenance (O: i.e. entity)"] of Allah," though if someone does, it is offensive not to give to him.

h9.0   صدقة التطوع

h9.1   تُنْدَبُ صدقةُ التطوع كلَّ وقتٍ وفي رمضانَ وأمامَ الحاجاتِ ([أي في ابتداء طلبها] وعند الكسوف والمرض والسفرِ وكلَّ وقتٍ شريفٍ (كعشرِ ذي الحجة وأيام العيد) ومكانٍ شريفٍ (كمكة والمدينة) آكَدُ .

h9.2   وللصلحاءِ ([جمع صالح] وهو القائم بحقوق الله وحقوق العباد) وأقاربِهِ وعدوِّه منهم، وبأطيب مالِهِ (أي الحلالِ منه) أفضلُ (من التصدق بالمشبوه ومثله الرديء، فالتصدق به مكروه وبالمالِ الحرام حرام (ح : إن عرف صاحبه . وإلا فيجب التصدق به ليخرجه من ملكه)) .

h9.3   ويَحْرُمُ التصدقُ بما يُنفِقُهُ على عيالِهِ أو يَقْضي به دَيْنَهُ الحالَّ (لأن النفقة على عياله وقضاء الدين الحالّ كل منهما من الواجب وهو مقدم على المندوب) .

h9.4   ويُنْدَبُ بكلَّ ما فَضَلَ (وزاد على نفقته ونفقة من تلزمه نفقته) إنْ صَبَرَ على الإضافة ([أي على الشدة بعد التصدق] وأما إذا لم يصبر على ذلك فتكره بما فضل عن حاجته) .

h9.5   ويُكْرَهُ أنْ يَسْأَلَ بوجهِ اللهِ (أي بذاته) غيرَ الجنة وإذا سَأَلَ سائلٌ بوجهِ الله شيئاً كُرِه ردُّه .

h9.6   It is unlawful to remind a recipient of charity that one has given him (mann, dis: p36), and it eliminates the reward.

والمنُ بالصدقةِ حرامٌ ويُبْطِلُ   h9.6
ثوابَهَا.

h9.7   (O: It is permissible to give charity to a person not in need, or to a relative of the Prophet (Allah bless him and give him peace). It is offensive for a person not in need to accept charity, and preferable that he avoid it. It is unlawful for such a person to accept it if he pretends to be needy, and is unlawful for him to ask for charity.

It is permissible to give charity to a non-Muslim (n: but not zakat, as above at h8.24).)

(وتحـل الصـدقـة لغني ولذي   h9.7
قربى للنبي ﷺ ويكــره للغني التعــرض
لأخـذها ويستحب له التنزه عنها بل يحرم
أخـذهـا إن أظهـر الفـاقـة بل يحرم سؤاله
أيضاً. وتحل لكافر).

*

BOOK I

FASTING

CONTENTS:

i1.0   FASTING RAMADAN

(O: The month of the fast is the best of months, and it is one of the distinctive features of this Community (Umma); that is, as now practiced, a fact not contradicted by the word of Allah Most High,

"Fasting is prescribed for you, as it was prescribed for those before you" (Koran 2:183),

the resemblance interpreted as referring to *fasting* without other qualification, not to its amount and time. Fasting Ramadan is one of the pillars of Islam (def: u2) by scholarly consensus (ijma'). Bukhari and Muslim relate that the Prophet (Allah bless him and give him peace) said,

"Islam is built upon five: testifying there is no god but Allah and that Muhammad is the messenger of Allah, performing the prayer, giving zakat, making the pilgrimage to the House [Kaaba], and fasting Ramadan.")

WHO MUST FAST RAMADAN

i1.1   Fasting Ramadan is obligatory for:

(a) every Muslim (O: male or female) who:

(b) has reached puberty;

i1.0   صوم رمضان

(وشهـره أفضــل الشهــور وهو من خصــائص هذه الأمــة أي بهـذه الكيفية المـوجـودة الآن فلا ينـافي قولـه تعـالى : ﴿كُتِبَ عَلَيْكُمُ الصِّيَامُ كَمَا كُتِبَ عَلَى الَّذِينَ مِنْ قَبْلِكُمْ﴾ [البقرة : ١٨٣]، فإن التشبيه محمـول على مطلق الصوم دون قدره وزمنـه . وصوم رمضـان أحد أركان الإسـلام بالإجمـاع وروى الشيخـان أنه ﷺ قال : «بُنـي الإسـلامُ علىٰ خَمسٍ شَهادَةِ أن لا إلٰه إلّا الله وأنَّ محمداً رَسولُ الله ، وإقامِ الصلاة ، وإيتاءِ الزكاة ، وحَجِّ البيت ، وصومِ رمضان) .

المخاطب بوجوب الصوم

i1.1   يَجِبُ صومُ رمضـانَ علىٰ كلِّ مسلمٍ (سـواء كان ذكـراً أو أنثى) بالغٍ

(c) is sane;

(d) is capable of bearing the fast;

(e) and if female, is not in the period of menstruation or postnatal bleeding (nifas).

عاقلٍ قادرٍ على الصومِ مَعَ الخلوِّ عنْ حيضٍ ونفاسٍ .

THOSE NOT OBLIGED TO FAST RAMADAN

من لا يجب عليه الصوم

i1.2   The following are not required to fast:

(1) (non-(a) above) a non-Muslim (O: meaning that we do not ask him to, nor would it be valid if he did (N: though he is punished in the next life for not doing so));

(2) (non-(b)) a child;

(3) (non-(c)) someone insane;

(4) or (non-(d)) someone whom fasting exhausts because of advanced years or having an illness from which he is unlikely to recover.

None of the above-mentioned is obliged to fast or to make up missed fast-days, though someone who misses a fast because of (4) above must give 0.51 liters of food (def: h7.6(A:)) for each fast-day he misses.

i1.2   فلاَ يُخَـاطَبُ به كافرٌ (بمعنى أننا لا نطالبه بأدائه أي ولا يصح منه أيضاً (ح): لكنه يعذب على تركه في الآخرة)) وصبيٌّ ومجنـونٌ وَلا يخـاطب به) مَنْ أَجْهَـدَهُ الصـومُ [(أي أتعبـه)] لكبرٍ أوْ مرضٍ لاَ يُرْجَى بُرؤُهُ (لا بأداءٍ ولاَ بقضاءٍ لكنْ يَلْزَمُ مَنْ أَجْهَدَهُ الصومُ لكلِّ يومٍ مدُّ طعامٍ .

i1.3   The following are not required to fast, though they are obliged to make up fast-days missed (A: *making up*, according to our school, meaning that one fasts a single day for each obligatory fast-day missed):

(1) those who are ill (N: the *illness* that permits not fasting being that which fasting would worsen, delay recovery from, or cause one considerable harm with; the same dispensation applying to someone who needs to take medicine during the day that breaks the fast and that he can not delay taking until night);

(2) those who are travelling (def: i1.7);

(3) a person who has left Islam (murtadd, def: o8);

i1.3   ويُخَـاطَبُ المـريضُ (ح): والمـرض المبيح للإفطار هو الذي يزيد بالصيـام أو يتأخر شفاؤه أو يتضرر صاحبه بالصيـام ضرراً شديـداً . وكـذا إذا كان يحتاج إلى تناول دواء مفطر في النهار ولا يمكن تأخيره إلى الليـل)، والمسـافرُ والمـرتدُّ والحائضُ والنفساءُ بالقضاءِ دونَ

(4) or a woman who is in her menses or period of postnatal bleeding.

If the ill person or traveller take it upon themselves to fast, it is valid, though a fast by someone who has left Islam, or a woman in menstruation or period of postnatal bleeding is not valid.

When not fasting on a day of Ramadan, if a non-Muslim becomes a Muslim, an insane person regains his sanity, or a child reaches puberty, it is recommended but not obligatory that they fast the rest of that day and make up the fast later. A child who reaches puberty while fasting on a day of Ramadan is obliged to fast the rest of the day, and is recommended to make it up.

A woman whose period ends during a day of Ramadan is recommended to fast the rest of the day and is obliged to make up the fast (O: and the fast-days prior to it missed during her period or postnatal bleeding).

i1.4 If the testimony of a witness (O: that the new moon has been seen during the previous night) is made during a day (N: that was initially) uncertain as to whether it was the the first of Ramadan, then it is obligatory (O: for people) to fast the rest of the day and to make it up later.

i1.5 A child of seven is ordered to fast, and at ten is beaten for not fasting (N: with the reservations mentioned at f1.2).

i1.6 Excessive hunger or thirst, meaning likely to cause death or illness, are legitimate excuses not to fast, even when they occur on a day one has already begun to fast, as soon as the fast becomes a hardship.

i1.7 It is permissible not to fast when travelling, even when the intention to fast has been made the night before, provided that the journey is at least 81 km./50 mi. one way, and that one leaves town (def: f15.6) before dawn. If one leaves after dawn, one is not entitled to omit the fast. It is preferable for travellers not to fast if fasting

الأداءِ. فإنْ تَكَلَّفَ المـريضُ والمسافـرُ وصامَا صَحَّ دونَ المرتدِّ والحائضِ والنفساءِ.

فإنْ أَسْلَمَ أَوْ أَفَـاقَ أَوْ بَلَغَ مفطـراً في أثنـاء النهارِ نُدِبَ الإمسـاكُ والقضاءُ ولا يَجِبـان. وإنْ بَلَغَ صائماً لَزِمَـهُ الإمسـاكُ ونُدِبَ القضاءُ.

ولَـوْ طَهُرَتِ الحائضُ (في أثناء النهارِ) أَمْسَكَتْ نَدباً وقَضَتْ حتماً (مع ما قبله من أيام الحيض والنفاس).

i1.4 ولَـوْ قَامَتِ البَيِّنـةُ برؤيةِ يومِ الشـكِّ (والمعنى لو شهـدت البينة يوم الشك برؤية الهـلال ليلتهِ) وَجَبَ (على الناس) إمساكُ بَقِيَّتِهِ وقضاؤُهُ.

i1.5 ويُـؤْمَـرُ الـصبيُّ به لسبـعٍ ويُضْرَبُ لعشرٍ.

i1.6 ويُبِيـحُ الفطرَ غلبـةُ الجوعِ والـعطش بحيـثُ يُخْـشَى الهـلاكُ أو المرضُ ولوْ طَرَأَ في أثناءِ اليومِ إذا شَقَّ الصومُ.

i1.7 وسفرُ القصرِ إنْ فَارَقَ العمرانَ قبلَ الفجرِ وإنْ نَوَاهُ مِنَ الليلِ. فإنْ سَافَرَ بعدَهُ فَلَا. والفطرُ للمسافرِ أفضلُ إنْ ضَرَّهُ

would harm them, though if not, then fasting is better.

الصومُ وإلَّا فالصومُ أفضلُ .

i1.8   A woman who is breast-feeding a baby or is pregnant and apprehends harm to herself or her child may omit the fast and make it up later, though if she omits it because of fear (A: of harm) for the child alone (O: not for herself) then she must give 0.51 liters of food (def: h7.6(A:)) in charity for each day missed, as an expiation (A: in addition to making up each day).

i1.8   ولــوْ خَافَتْ مرضـعٌ أوْ حامـلٌ على أنفسِهمَا أوْ ولـدَيْهِمَا أفْطَرَتَا وقَضَتَا ، لكنْ تُفْدِيَانِ عنـدَ الخوفِ على الولدِ (فقط أي من غيـر الخـوفِ على أنفسهمـا) لكلِّ يومٍ مداً .

SIGHTING THE NEW MOON

رؤية الهلال

i1.9   Fasting Ramadan is only obligatory when the new moon of Ramadan is sighted (O: i.e. in respect to the person who sees it, though for those who do not see it, it only becomes obligatory when the sighting is established by the testimony of an upright witness (def: o24.4)). If it is too overcast to be seen, then (n: the preceding lunar month of) Sha'ban is presumed to last for thirty days, after which people begin fasting Ramadan. If the new moon is sighted during the day (O: before noon on the last of the thirty days), it is considered as belonging to the following night (O: and the ruling for that day does not change).

If the moon is seen in one city but not another, then if the two are close (O: i.e. in the same region), the ruling (n: that the new month has come) holds for both. But if the two are not close, then not (O: i.e. the people far from the place where it was seen are not obligated to fast), *not close* meaning in different regions, such as the Hijaz, Iraq, and Egypt.

i1.9   ولا يَجبُ صومُ رمـضـانَ إلَّا برؤيـةِ الـهــلالِ (أي في حق من رآه أو بثبـوتها في حق من لم يره بشهادة عدل) فإنْ غُمَّ وَجَبَ استكمالُ شعبانَ ثلاثينَ ثُمَّ يَصُـومُونَ . فإنْ رُؤيَ نهاراً (أي قبل الـزوال في اليـومِ المتمم للثـلاثين) فهـوَ لليلةِ المستقبلةِ (فلا يتغير حكم ذلك النهار) .

وإنْ رُؤيَ في بلدٍ دون بلدٍ فإنْ تقـاربـا (بـاتحـاد المطلع) عَمَّ الحكمُ . وإلَّا فَلا (أي فلا يلزم أهل البلد البعيد عن محل الـرؤية الصوم) والبعدُ باختلافِ المطالع كالحجازِ والعراقِ ومصرَ [وقيل بمسافة القصر] .

i1.10   The testimony of a single witness (N: that the new moon has been seen) is sufficient to establish that the month of Ramadan has come, provided the witness is upright (def: o24.4), male, and responsible for the duties of Islam (O: which excludes boys who have reached the age of discernment but not puberty).

i1.10   ويُقْبَلُ في رمضانَ بالنسبةِ إلى الصـوم عدلٌ واحدٌ ذكرٌ [حرٌ] مكلَّفٌ (والتكليف مخرِج للصبي المميز) [ولا يُقْبَلُ في سائرِ الشهورِ إلَّا عدلانِ] .

i1.11   If a person knows by calculations of lunar movements or the positions of the stars that the next day is Ramadan, fasting is nevertheless not obligatory (O: for him or the public), though it is permissible for him alone.

i1.11   ولَـوْ عَرَفَ رجلٌ بالحساب والنجـوم أن غداً مِنْ رمضـانَ لَمْ يَجِب الصـوم (عليه ولا على عامة الناس) لكنْ يَجوزُ للحاسب والمنجم فَقَطْ.

i1.12   If it is difficult to learn which month it is, for someone imprisoned or the like (O: such as someone being held in a dark place who cannot tell night from day, or someone who does not know when Ramadan has come because of being in a land without habitations or people who know when it is), then such a person is obliged to reckon Ramadan as best he can and to fast it. Such a fast is valid if it remains unknown as to whether the month fasted actually coincided with Ramadan, or if it *did* coincide with it, or if the month fasted occurred after it, though if the month fasted was before Ramadan, it is not valid.

i1.12   وإنِ اشْـتَـبَهَتِ الشهـورُ على أسيرٍ ونحوِه (كالمحبوس في محل مظلم لا يعرف الليل من النهار ومثل المحبوس من في أرض خاليـة عن العمـران وعمن يعرف رمضانَ فلم يدر رمضان من غيره) اجْتَهَدَ وجـوباً وصـامَ فإن اسْتَمَرَّ الإشكالُ أوْ وَافَـقَ رمضـانَ أوْ مَا بعـدَه صَحَّ. وإنْ وَافَقَ مَا قبْلَهُ لم يَصِحَّ.

THE CONDITIONS OF A VALID FAST

شروط الصوم

i1.13   The conditions of a valid fast are:

(a) the intention;

(b) and refraining from things which break the fast.

i1.13   وشرطُ الصوم النيةُ والإمساكُ عن المفطِّراتِ.

THE INTENTION

النية

i1.14   One must make the intention to fast for each day one fasts. If the intended fast is obligatory, then the intention must:

(a) be specific (O: as to the fast being for Ramadan, a vow, an expiation, or whatever);

(b) and be made in the night prior to dawn. (n: For Hanafis, the intention for a day of Ramadan (but not a makeup) is valid if made before midway between true dawn and sunset of the day itself (*al-Hadiyya al-'Ala'iyya* (y4), 171).)

i1.14   فَنْـوي لكـلِّ يومٍ. فإنْ كَانَ فرضاً وَجَبَ تعيينُهُ (أي صوم الفرض من كونـه عن رمضـان أوعن نذر أوعن كفارة أو غير ذلك) وتبييتُهُ مِنَ الليلِ.

The optimal way is to intend (O: in one's heart) to fast the following day as a current performance of the obligation of Ramadan in the present year for Allah Most High (O: *fast* and *of Ramadan* being unanimously considered as integral to the intention, though scholars differ concerning the obligatoriness of intending it as a current performance, an obligation, or for Allah Most High).

وأكملُهُ أنْ يَنْوي (بقلبه) صومَ غدٍ عن أداءِ فرضِ رمضانَ هذِهِ السنـةَ للهِ تعالى (فأمـا الصومُ وكونُهُ عن رمضانَ فلا بد منه بلا خلافٍ، وأمـا الأداءُ والـفـرضيـة والإضافةُ إلى الله تعالى ففيها خلافٌ).

i1.15 One's intention is valid if on the night before a day of uncertainty (N: as to whether it will be the first day of Ramadan), someone one trusts but who does not have all the qualifications of an acceptable witness (def: i1.10) informs one of having seen the new moon, and relying on this information one intends to fast the next day to fulfill the obligation of Ramadan, and the next day turns out to be Ramadan. But one's fast is not valid if one makes the intention without anyone having informed one of sighting the new moon, no matter whether if one's intention is firm or whether undecided, as when one intends that if the following day is Ramadan, one will fast, but if not, one will not.

i1.15 ولـوْ أخْبَـرَهُ بالرؤيةِ ليلةَ الشكِّ منْ يَثِقُ به مِمَّنْ لاَ يَقْبَلُهُ الحاكمُ [منْ نسوةٍ وعبيدٍ وصبيانٍ] فَنَوى بناءً على ذلك فكانَ منـهُ صحَّ. وإنْ نَوَاهُ منْ غيرِ إخبارِ أحدٍ فكانَ منهُ لم يَصحَّ سواءٌ جَزَمَ النيةَ أوْ تَرَدَّدَ فقالَ: «إنْ كانَ غداً منْ رمضانَ فأنَا صائمٌ وإلاَّ فمفطرٌ».

i1.16 One's fast is valid if on the night before 30 Ramadan, one intends that if the following day is of Ramadan, one will fast, but if not, one will not, and then the next day is of Ramadan (O: since it already is Ramadan, and the initial presumption is that it will remain so (dis: e7.6(A:))).

i1.16 ولـوْ قَالَ ليلةَ الـثـلاثينَ منْ رمضـانَ: «إنْ كانَ غداً منْ رمضانَ فأنَا صائمٌ وإلاَّ فمفطرٌ» فكانَ منْ رمضانَ صحَّ (لأن الأصل بقاء رمضان وقد كان من رمضان).

i1.17 Nonobligatory fasts are valid by merely making the intention to fast before noon (O: without needing to specify the type of fast).

i1.17 ويَصِحُّ النفلُ بنيةٍ مطلقةٍ (عن التعيين) قبلَ الزوالِ.

THINGS WHICH INVALIDATE THE FAST

مفسدات الصوم

i1.18 Each of the following things invalidates the day's fast when one knows they are unlawful (A: during an obligatory fast) and remembers one is fasting (A: but does them deliberately anyway);

i1.18 وإنْ أَكَـلَ أو شَرِبَ (ح): أو شِربِ الـدخـان) أوِ اسْتَعَطَ (أي أدخـل

and they obligate one to both make up the fast-day later and fast the remainder of that day:

(1) eating;

(2) drinking (N: and smoking (A: though not if there is some smoke in the air that one unintentionally inhales));

(3) taking snuff (O: up the nose that reaches the sinuses, a ruling likewise applicable to oil or water preparations);

(4) suppositories (O: vaginal or anal);

(5) pouring (O: water, oil, or other) into the ears until it reaches the eardrum;

(6) inserting a finger or something else into the anus or vagina further than the area disclosed when one squats (O: to relieve oneself);

(7) anything that enters the body cavity, whether stabbed into it (O: such as a knife or spear thrust which penetrates it) or whether medicine (N: though intramuscular or intravenous injections of medicine do not break one's fast);

(8) vomiting (N: if it is deliberate and one is able to prevent it, though if nausea overcomes one, vomiting does not break one's fast);

(9) sexual intercourse (O: if deliberate, even if there is no orgasm), or orgasm from stroking a nongenital region or from masturbation (O: no matter whether such orgasm is produced by unlawful means, like one's own hand (dis: w37), or whether by lawful means, such as the hand of one's wife);

(10) using so much water to rinse out the nose and mouth (O: in ablution (wudu) or the purificatory bath (ghusl)) that some reaches the stomach (O: i.e. if any reaches the body cavity because of using an abundance of water, it breaks the fast, though if some water slips down when an abundance has not been used, it does not break it);

السعوط الذي هو النشوق في أنفه مع جذبه بواسطة النفس إلى الخيشوم ومثل السعوط دهن أو ماء في هذا الحكم) أو احْتَقَن (والحقنة دواء يحقن به المريض في قبل أو دبر) أوْ صَبَّ (ماء أو دهناً أو نحوه) في أذنِه فَوَصَلَ دماغَهُ أوْ أدْخَلَ إصبعاً أوْ غيرَهُ في دبره أوْ قبلهَا وراءَ ما يَبْدُوا عندَ القعدة (أي القعود لقضاء الحاجة) أوْ وصَلَ إلى جوفهِ شيءٌ مِنْ طعنةٍ (أي ضربة بسكين أو رمح وقد وصلت إلى الجوف) أوْ دواءٍ (ح: ولا يفطر الصائم إذا حقن بدواء بواسطة الإبرة الطبية في العضل أو الوريد) أوْ تَقَيَّأ (ح: ويشترط فيه العمد والقدرة على منعه، فلو غلب القيء الصائم لم يفطر) أوْ جَامَعَ (الصائم ولو لم ينزل) أو باشَرَ فيما دونَ الفرج فأنْزَلَ أو اسْتَمْنَى فأنْزَلَ (محرماً كان الإنزال كإخراجه بيده أو غير محرم كإخراجه بيد زوجته)، أوْ بالَغَ في المضمضة (في الوضوء أو الغسل) أو الاستنشاق فنزل جوفهُ (فإذا نزل إلى الجوف شيء من أجلها ضر بخلاف ما إذا سبق ماء المضمضة من غير مبالغة فلا يضر. [قال ابن عبد الحق: لا يضر بلع ريقه إثر ماء المضمضة وإن أمكنه مجه]) أوْ أخْرَجَ ريقَهُ مِنْ فمهُ (ثم

(11) swallowing saliva that has left the mouth, such as when threading a needle and one moistens the end of the thread, and then remoistens it, swallowing some of the saliva that the thread had been previously wetted with;

(12) swallowing saliva that has been qualitatively altered, such as when threading a needle and one wets the end, and some dye from the thread remains in the mouth and is swallowed (A: so people who use toothpaste should take care to eliminate it from the mouth before dawn on fast-days);

(13) swallowing saliva that has been made impure by contact with filth (najasa), such as when one's mouth is bloodied and one spits out the saliva until it is clear and colorless, but neglects to wash one's mouth out (O: before swallowing the saliva, which breaks the fast because the mouth is still affected by impurity (n: and water is necessary to purify it, as at e14.10));

(14) allowing phlegm or mucus at the back of the mouth to be swallowed when one could have spit them out (n: though in the Hanafi school this does not break the fast, even if intentional (al-Hadiyya al-'Ala'iyya (y4), 180));

(15) or to continue making love, even for a moment, after dawn has arrived.

THE CRITERION FOR THINGS WHICH
INVALIDATE THE FAST

i1.19 The criterion as to whether something invalidates the fast is (N: whether it comes under any one of three headings):

(1) a substance, even if not much, that reaches the body cavity through an open passage-way (O: *substance* excluding odors, and *open* excluding anything else, such as absorption through pores). (N: The deliberate introduction of anything besides air or saliva into the body cavity breaks the fast, though if the person fasting does so absentmindedly or under compulsion, it does not break it);

ابتلعه ثانياً) كَمَا إذا جَرَّ الخيطَ في فمِهِ عنـدَ فتلِهِ فَانْفَصَلَ علَيْهِ (أي على الخيط) ريقٌ ثمَّ ردَّهُ وبَلعَ ريقَهُ أوْ بَلعَ ريقَهُ متغيِّراً كَمَا إذا فَتَـلَ خيطاً فتَغَيَّـرَ بصِبْغِهِ أوْ كانَ (ذلك الـريق) نجساً كَمَا إذا دَمِيَ فمُهُ فبَصَقَ حتّى صَفَا ريقُهُ (عن التغير أي صار خالـصاً من لون الـحـمـرة) ولمْ يَغْسِلْهُ (فيضر حينئذ ابتلاعه لأن الفم متنجس في هذه الحالـة) أو ابْتَلَعَ نخامـةً منْ أقصَى الفم إنْ قَدَرَ على قطعِهـا ومَجِّهـا فَتـركَهَا حتّى نَزَلَتْ أوْ طَلَعَ الفجـرُ وهـوَ مجـامِـعٌ فَاسْتَـدَامَ ولوْ لحظـةً وهوَ في جميع ذلك ذاكـرٌ للصـوم عالمٌ بالتحريم ، بَطَـلَ صوْمُهُ وعليهِ قضاءً وإمساكٌ بقية النهار.

ضابط المفطر

i1.19 وضابطُ المفطرِ وصولُ عينٍ وإنْ قلَّتْ مِنْ منفـذٍ مفتـوحٍ إلى جوفٍ (وخـرج بالعين وصـول الـريـح وخرج بالمنفتح غيره كالتشرب من المسام) (ح : ويفطر وصول الشيء إلى الجوف عمداً إلا الهـواء والريق، فلوفعل الصائم ذلك ناسيـاً أو مكـرهـاً لم يبطـل صومـه به)

(2) sexual intercourse (O: meaning inserting the head of the penis into the vagina);

(3) or orgasm, whether as the result of touching (O: such as kissing, contact, lying between the other's thighs, or something else), or because of masturbation;

—provided that one is aware that these acts are unlawful and that one remembers one is fasting (N: and provided they are done deliberately and voluntarily).

والجمـاعُ (أي وضـابـط المفطـر إدخـال الحشفـة في فرج [قبـلاً كان أو دبراً])، والإنـزالُ عنْ مبـاشـرةٍ (كتقبيـل ولمس ومفـاخـذة وغيـر ذلك) أو استمناءٍ، عالماً بالتحريم ذاكـراً للصـوم ﴿ح: ويشترط فيها أيضاً العمد والاختيار﴾.

THE EXPIATION FOR VITIATING A FAST-DAY BY SEXUAL INTERCOURSE

كفارة الإفساد بالجماع

i1.20   In addition to making up the fast, an expiation is obligatory for fast-days of Ramadan that are (A: deliberately) vitiated by sexual intercourse. (O: The legal occasion of the offense is the particular day of fasting, so that if it were committed on two separate days, two separate expiations would be necessary, though if it were committed twice in one day there would be only one expiation.)

The expiation consists of freeing a sound Muslim slave (dis: k32), or if not possible, then to fast the days of two consecutive months. (A: In our school the expiation is only for sexual intercourse, though the Hanafis hold it is obligatory for vitiating the fast for other reasons as well.) If this is not possible, then the expiation is to feed sixty unfortunates (N: 0.51 liters of food (def: h7.6(A:)) to each unfortunate). If one is unable to do this, the expiation remains as an unperformed obligation upon the person concerned.

The woman who is made love to is not obliged to expiate it.

i1.20   ويَلْزَمُهُ لإفسـادِ الصـومِ في رمضـان بالجماعِ مَعَ القضاءِ الكفـارةُ (والإثم بسبب الصـوم، حتى لو جامع في يومين أو أيـام وجب لكـل يوم كفارة وإن جامع في يوم مرتين لم تلزمه للثاني كفارة) وهيَ عتقُ رقبةٍ مؤمنةٍ سليمةٍ منَ العيوب المضـرة. فإنْ لمْ يَجِدْ فصيـامُ شهرَيْن متتـابعَيْن. فإنْ لمْ يَسْتَطِعْ فإطعـامُ ستينَ مسكينـاً (ح: لكـل مسكين مد طعام) فإنْ عَجِزَ ثَبَتَ في ذمّتِه.
ولا يَجِبُ على الموطوءةِ كفارةٌ.

THINGS THAT DO NOT BREAK THE FAST

ما لا يفسد الصوم

i1.21   The fast remains valid if any of the things which break it are done absentmindedly (O: not remembering the fast), out of ignorance (O: that doing the things which break the fast are unlawful,

i1.21   فإنْ فَعَلَ جميعَ ذلكَ ناسياً (للصوم) أوْ جاهلاً بالتحريمِ (أي تحريم تنـاول المفطـرات بأن كان قريب العهـد

whether this is due to being a new Muslim, or to being born and raised far from Islamic scholars), or under compulsion. Nor is it broken by:

(1) involuntary vomiting;

(2) having a wet dream, or orgasm as a result of thinking or looking at something (A: unless the latter two usually cause orgasm, in which case one has broken one's fast by not avoiding them);

(3) some water reaching the body cavity as a result of rinsing out the mouth or nose, (dis: i1.18(10)), provided not much water was used;

(4) saliva carrying down some food particles from between one's teeth, provided this is after having cleaned between them (O: after eating, by using a toothpick or the like between them), if one is unable to spit them out;

(5) gathering saliva in the mouth and swallowing it, bringing saliva as far forward as the tongue (O: but not to the lips) and then swallowing it, or coughing up phlegm from the throat and spitting it out;

(6) the arrival of dawn when there is food in one's mouth which one spits out;

(7) the arrival of dawn when one is lovemaking and one immediately disengages;

(8) or when sleeps all day or has lost consciousness, provided one regains consciousness for at least a moment of the day.

EATING OR DRINKING WHEN UNCERTAIN OF THE TIME OF DAWN OR SUNSET

i1.22 Making up the fast-day is obligatory if one eats, thinking it is night, but then finds that it is day; or eats, presuming (N: but uncertain) that the sun has set, and the question (O: as to whether one ate before sunset or after) continues and remains unresolved (dis: e7.6(A:)).

بالإسلام أو نشأ بعيداً عن العلماء) أو مكرهاً أوْ غَلَبَهُ القيءُ أوْ أنْزَلَ باحتلام أوْ عنْ فكرٍ أوْ نظرٍ أوْ نَزَلَ جوفُهُ بمضمضةٍ أو استنشاقٍ بلا مبالغةٍ أوْ جَرَى الريقُ بِمَا يبقى من الطعام في خلال أسنانِهِ بعدَ تخليلِهِ (أي أثرِ الطعامِ بأن خلله بعود ونحوه) وعَجَزَ عنْ مجِّهِ أوْ جَمَعَ ريقَهُ في فمِهِ وابْتَلَعَهُ صِرفاً أوْ أخْرَجَهُ على لسانِهِ ثمَّ ردَّهُ وبَلَعهُ (ولم يخرج ذلك الريق إلى الشفتين) أو اقْتَلَعَ نخامةً منْ باطنِهِ ولَفَظَها أوْ طَلَعَ الفجرُ وفي فمِهِ طعامٌ فَلَفَظَهُ أوْ كَانَ مجامعاً فنَزَعَ في الحالِ أوْ نَامَ جميعَ النهارِ أوْ أُغْمِيَ عليْهِ فيهِ وأفَاقَ لحظةً منْهُ لمْ يضُرَّهُ في جميع ذلك ويصحُّ صومُهُ.

حكم تعاطي المفطرات عند الشك في طلوع الفجر أو غروب الشمس

i1.22 وإذا أكَلَ معتقداً أنهُ ليلٌ وبَانَ أنهُ نهارٌ أوْ أكَلَ ظانّاً للغروب واستَمَرَّ الإشكالُ (وهو أنه أكل وقت الغروب أو قبله) وَجَبَ القضاءُ.

It is not obligatory to make up a fast-day on which one ate on the presumption that dawn had not yet come, and the question (O: as to what the case was) remains unresolved (A: since the initial certainty was that it was night).

وإنْ ظَنَّ أنَّ الفجرَ لمْ يَطْلُعْ فأكَـلَ واسْتَمَرَّ الإشكالُ (أي عدم ظهور الحال) فلا قضاءَ .

INVOLUNTARY ACTS WHICH INVALIDATE
THE FAST

مفسدات الصوم غير الاختيارية

i1.23   A fast-day is invalidated by:

   (1) insanity, even for a moment;

   (2) being unconscious the entire day;

   (3) or the appearance of menstrual or post-natal flow.

   (N: The insane person is not obliged to make up such a day's fast, while the others are.)

i1.23   وإنْ طَرَأ في أثناءِ اليومِ جنونٌ ولـوْ في لحظـةٍ منـه أو اسْتَغْـرَقَ نهـارَهُ بالإغمـاءِ أو طَرَأ حيضٌ أوْ نفـاسٌ بَطَـلَ الصومُ (ح: لكن لا يجب القضـاء على من جنَّ لذلـك اليـوم ويجب على غيره ممن ذكر) .

RECOMMENDED MEASURES WHILE FASTING

ما يندب للصائم

i1.24   A predawn meal is recommended, even if it is slight or consists of water alone (O: and the time for it begins from the middle of the night onwards). It is best to delay it to just before dawn, as long as one does not apprehend dawn's arrival while still eating (O: though when one does not know when dawn is, it is not the sunna to thus delay it).

i1.24   ويُنْـدَبُ السحورُ وإنْ قَلَّ ولوْ بمـاءٍ (ووقته من نصف الليل) والأفضلُ تأخيرُهُ ما لمْ يَخِف الصبحَ (فإذا خفي عليه الصبح فلا يسن تأخيره) .

i1.25   It is best to hasten breaking the fast when one is certain that the sun has set. One should break it with an odd number of dates, though if one has none, water is best. It is recommended to say after doing so, "O Allah, for You I fasted, and upon Your bounty I have broken the fast."

i1.25   والأفضـلُ تعجيلُ الفطـرِ إذا تحقق الغـروبَ ويُفْطِرُ علـى تمراتٍ وِتراً . فإنْ لمْ يجدْ فالماءُ أفضلُ ويَقُولُ: «اللهُمَّ لكَ صُمْتُ وعَلى رِزْقِكَ أفْطَرْتُ» .

i1.26   It is recommended in Ramadan:

   (1) to be especially generous (O: in giving charity);

i1.26   ويُنْـدَبُ كثرةُ الجودِ (أي فعل الخيـر من الصـدقـة) وصلةُ الرحمِ وكثرةُ

(2) to improve one's relations with family and relatives;

(3) to recite the Koran much;

(4) to spend periods of spiritual retreat (i'tikaf, def: i3) in the mosque, especially during the last ten days of Ramadan;

(5) to break the fast of others after sunset, even if only with water (O: because of the hadith related by Tirmidhi that the Prophet (Allah bless him and give him peace) said,

"He who breaks another's fast earns the same reward as the one who fasted without diminishing the latter's reward in the slightest");

(6) and if in a state of major ritual impurity (janaba), to perform the purificatory bath (ghusl) before dawn.

i1.27   It is recommended to avoid:

(1) slander (def: r2.2), lying, and foul language (N: which are always unlawful, but even worse when fasting);

(2) the pleasures of the senses (O: i.e. those that do not break the fast, such as smelling fragrant plants or looking at them, because of the gratification therein which is incompatible with the wisdom of the fast, even though they are permissible when not fasting) (A: and while it is recommended not to use perfume during a fast-day, it does not hurt to use it on the night before);

(3) and medicinal bloodletting (N: or blood donating) or cupping (O: as these, like the fast, weaken a person and could have a synergistic debilitating effect).

If someone abuses one while fasting, one should say to him, "I am fasting."

تلاوة القرآن والاعتكافُ سيمَا العشر الأواخر وأنْ يُفطِّرَ الصوّام (فقـد روى الترمذي وقال حسن صحيح أن النبي ﷺ قال: «من فطَّر صائماً فله مثـل أجره ولا ينقص من أجر الصائم شيء») ولوْ بماءٍ وتقديمُ غسلِ الجنابةِ على الفجرِ.

i1.27   وتـركُ الغيبـة والكـذب والفحش (ح: وهي محرمـة دائماً لكنْ يتأكـد تحـريـمهـا في حق الصـائم) والشهـوات (التي لا تبطل الصوم كشم الـريـاحين والنظر إليها لما فيها من الترفه الـذي لا يناسب حكمة الصوم وإنْ كانت مباحة في غير الصوم) والفصدِ والحجامة (لأن ذلـك يضعِف والصـوم مضعِف فيجتمـع على الصـائم مضعِفـان) فإنْ شوتِمَ فلْيَقُلْ: «إنِّي صائمٌ».

THINGS THAT ARE UNLAWFUL OR
OFFENSIVE WHILE FASTING

محرمات الصوم ومكروهاته

i1.28   It is unlawful to kiss (O: or embrace, or pet with the hand) on fast-days for those it sexually arouses.

i1.28   وتَحْـرُمُ الـقُـبلةُ لـمَن حَرَّكَتْ شهـوتَهُ (وفي معنى القبلة في هذا الحكم المعانقة والمباشرة باليد) .

i1.29   It is unlawful not to eat or drink anything (wisal) between fast-days, though it is not unlawful if one has some water, even a mouthful, before dawn.

i1.29   والـوصـالُ بأنْ لا يَتَنَـاوَلَ في الليل شيئاً فلوْ شَرِبَ ماءً ولـوْ جرعةً عندَ السحورِ فلا تحريمَ .

i1.30   It is offensive during the fast to taste food, or to use a toothstick (def: e3) after noon.

i1.30   ويُكْرَهُ ذوقُ الطعام [وعلكُ] وسواكُ بعدَ الزوالِ .

i1.31   It is not offensive during the fast to line the eyes with *kohl* (def: e4.1(4)) or to bathe.

i1.31   لَا كحلٌ واستحمامٌ .

i1.32   It is offensive (dis: w38) for anyone (O: whether fasting or not) to keep silent all day until night (O: when there is no need to) (A: *need* including the necessity of restraining the tongue from useless talking (dis: r1.1)).

i1.32   ويُكْرَهُ لكـلِّ أحدٍ صمتُ يومٍ إلى الليـلِ (من غيـر حاجـة سواء كان صائماً أم لا) .

MAKING UP MISSED FAST-DAYS

قضاء الصوم

i1.33   Someone obliged to make up some fast-days of Ramadan is recommended to do so consecutively and immediately.
It is not permissible for a person with some unperformed fast-days of Ramadan to delay making them up until the next Ramadan unless there is an excuse (N: for delaying). If one delays until the next Ramadan, one must pay 0.51 liters of food (def: h7.6(A:)) (N: to the poor) for each fast-day missed, in addition to making it up. If making up a fast-day is delayed until a second Ramadan comes, then one must pay double this amount for each day. And so forth: every year that passes upon an unfulfilled fast-day adds 0.51 liters to be paid for that day. (O: But if one's excuse for not performing them persists, such as travel or illness,

i1.33   ومَـنْ لَزِمَـهُ قضـاءُ شيءٍ من رمضانٍ يُنْدَبُ لـه أنْ يَقْضِيَه متتابعاً علىْ الفورِ .
ولاَ يَجُوزُ أنْ يُؤَخِّرَ القضاءَ إلى رمضانٍ آخَـرَ بغيـر عذرٍ . فإنْ أخَّرَ لزِمَهُ مَعَ القضاءِ عنْ كلِّ يومٍ مُدَّ طعـامٍ فإنْ أخَّرَ رمضانَيْنِ فمـدانِ وهكَذا يَتَكَرَّرُ بتكرُّرِ السنينَ (وأما إذا دام العـذرُ كالسفـرِ والمـرض جازَ له

then it is permissible for one to delay making them up as long as the excuse is present, even if it lasts for years. One is not obliged to pay the penalty fee for this delay even if several Ramadans go by, but is merely obliged to make up the missed fast-days).

If someone dies with unperformed fast-days which he could have fasted but did not, then each fast-day is paid for (N: by the responsible family member) with 0.51 liters of food (N: or he can fast for him (A: in place of paying for each day)). (O: As for someone who dies after two Ramadans elapse upon his missed fast-days, each fast is paid for with 1.02 liters (n: double the above) of food (N: or the family member can both fast a day and pay 0.51 liters for each day (A: i.e. the family member may fast in the deceased's stead for the initial nonperformance of the fast-day, though he cannot fast in place of paying the 0.51 liters of food for each year that making up a fast-day was delayed before the deceased's death, because this is the legal expiation for the delay). As for someone who died before his excuse (n: for not fasting) ceased to exist, nothing at all is obligatory for him).)

*

i2.0   VOLUNTARY FASTING

DAYS ON WHICH FASTING IS RECOMMENDED

i2.1   It is recommended to fast:

(1) on six days of the month of Shawwal, and that they be the six consecutive days immediately following 'Eid al-Fitr (O: their being consecutive and their immediately following the 'Eid are two separate sunnas), though it is permissible to fast them nonconsecutively;

(2) on 9 and 10 Muharram;

(3) on the full moon (lit. "white") days of every lunar month, which are the thirteenth and the two days that follow it;

التأخير مادام عذره ولو بقي سنين ولا تلزمه الفدية لهذا التأخير وإن تكرر عليه رمضان وإنما عليه القضاء فقط) .

ومنْ مَاتَ وعليْـه صومٌ تَمَكّنَ مِنْ فعلِه أطْعَمَ عنْـهُ (ح : وليُـهُ) عنْ كل يوم مدّ طعام (ح : وله أن يصوم عنه) (ومن مات بعد مضي رمضان الثاني أطعم عنه لكل يوم مدّين (ح : أو يصوم يوماً ويطعم مداً عن كل يوم، أما لو مات قبل انقضاء العذر الذي أفطر بسببه فلا يجب شيء)) .

i2.0   صوم التطوع

أيام يندب الصوم فيها

i2.1   يُنْدَبُ صومُ ستـةٍ مِنْ شوالٍ وتُنْدَبُ متتـابعةً تَلي العيدَ (فهاتان سنتان وهمـا التتابـع والعقبية) فإنْ فرَّقَهـا جَازَ وتاسوعاءَ وعاشوراءَ وأيام البيض في كل شهرٍ : الثـالثَ عشـرَ وتـاليَيْـه والاثنين

(4) on Mondays and Thursdays;

(5) on the first nine days of Dhul Hijja;

(6) during the inviolable months, which are four: Dhul Qa‘da, Dhul Hijja, Muharram, and Rajab;

(7) (n: and on every other day, a fast described by the Prophet (Allah bless him and give him peace) as "the most beloved fast to Allah" (*Riyad al-salihin* (y107), 466)).

The best fast-days, after Ramadan, are those of Muharram, then Rajab, then Sha‘ban. (O: In general, the best month for fasting, after Ramadan and the inviolable months, is Sha‘ban (A: there being no objection to fasting an entire month or just part of one).)

It is recommended to fast on the Day of ‘Arafa (O: 9 Dhul Hijja), unless one is a pilgrim present at ‘Arafa (def: j8), when it is better not to fast. It is not offensive for such a person to fast, though it is better for him not to.

FASTS THAT ARE OFFENSIVE OR UNLAWFUL

i2.2   It is offensive to fast every day of the year (O: besides the two ‘Eids and the three days following ‘Eid al-Adha (n: these being unlawful to fast (dis: below) rather than offensive)) if this harms one (O: in body or mind) or causes one not to do something one should do (O: for oneself or others, even if merely recommended). If not, then it is not offensive.

i2.3   It is unlawful and not valid to fast (O: whether voluntarily, as a vow, or as a makeup) on the two ‘Eids or the three days following ‘Eid al-Adha.

i2.4   It is also unlawful and invalid to fast on a day of uncertainty (N: as to whether it is the first day of Ramadan), meaning that on 30 Sha‘ban, someone who does not have the necessary qualifi-

والخميس وعشر ذي الحجة [ح: يريد به تسع ذي الحجة)] والأشهر الحرم وهي أربعة ذو القعدة وذو الحجة والمحرم ورجب.

وأفضل الصوم بعد رمضان المحرم ثمّ رجب ثمّ شعبان. (وبالجملة فأفضل الأشهر للصوم بعد رمضان وبعد الأشهر الحرم شهر شعبان).

وصوم يوم عرفة (وهو تاسع ذي الحجة) إلا للحاجّ بعرفة ففطره أفضل فإن صام لم يُكرَه لكنّهُ تَركَ الأولى.

ما يكره أو يحرم من الصيام

i2.2   ويُكرَهُ صومُ الدهر (غير عيدي الفطر والأضحى وأيام التشريق) إن ضَرَّهُ (الصوم في بدن أو عقل) أو فَوَّتَ حقاً (له أو لغيره ولو مندوباً) وإلَّا لمْ يُكرَهُ.

i2.3   ويَحرُمُ ولا يَصِحُّ أصلاً (لا تطوعاً ولا عن نذر ولا عن قضاء) صومُ العيدَينِ وأيام التشريق وهيَ ثلاثةٌ بعدَ الأضحى.

i2.4   ويومُ الشكِّ وهو أنْ يَتَحَدَّثَ بالرؤية يوم الثلاثين مِنْ شعبانَ مَن لَا

cations of a witness (def: i1.10) mentions having seen the new moon of Ramadan. Otherwise (O: when no one has mentioned seeing it, or when an acceptable witness has), then it is not considered a day of uncertainty.

Fasting on a day of uncertainty is not valid as a day of Ramadan, though it can validly fulfill a vow or a makeup fast. Voluntary fasting on such a day is only valid when one would have fasted anyway because it falls on a day one habitually fasts, or when one has been fasting each day since before mid-Sha'ban. If neither of these is the case, then it is unlawful and invalid to fast on it.

It is unlawful to fast during the days after mid-Sha'ban unless one would have fasted anyway because they fall on days one habitually fasts, or unless one has been fasting each day since before mid-Sha'ban.

i2.5   (Nawawi: (n: with commentary by Muhammad Shirbini Khatib)) It is offensive to single out Fridays or Saturdays ((Shirbini:) or Sundays for fasting, i.e. to single out one of the above-mentioned days when they do not coincide with days one normally fasts. The fast of someone who usually fasts every other day and whose fast coincides with one of these days or with a day of uncertainty is *not* offensive, because of the hadith related by Muslim,

"Do not single out Friday for fasting unless it happens to coincide with a fast one of you performs,"

similar days being analogous to Fridays in this respect) (*Mughni al-muhtaj ila ma'rifa ma'ani alfaz al-Minhaj* (y73), 1.447)).

i2.6   Once begun, it is unlawful to interrupt either an obligatory fast-day or an obligatory prayer, whether it is current, a makeup, or vowed; though if it is nonobligatory (O: whether wholly supererogatory or linked with a particular event or time), then one may interrupt it (O: but it is offensive to do so if there is no excuse).

يَثْبُتُ (هلالُ رمضان) بقولِه [مِنْ عبيدٍ وفسقةٍ ونسوةٍ] وإلاَّ (أي وإن لم يتحدث أحد برؤيته أصلاً أو تحدث برؤيته من يقبل قوله) فليس بيومِ شكٍّ، فلا يَصِحُّ صومُه عن رمضان بل (يصح صومه) عَنْ نذرٍ وقضاءٍ وأمّا التطوُّعُ به فإنْ وَافَقَ عادةً لَهُ أَوْ وَصَلَهُ بِمَا قبلَ نصفِ شعبانَ صَحَّ وإلاَّ حَرُمَ ولمْ يَصِحَّ .

ويَحْرُمُ صومُ مَا بعدَ نصفِ شعبانَ إنْ لم يُوَافِقْ عادةً ولمْ يَصِلْهُ بما قبلَهُ .

i2.5   (الإمام النووي (ت: بشرح الشربيني الخطيب) :) وَيُكْرَهُ إفرادُ (يوم) الجمعةِ (بالصوم)، وإفرادُ السبتِ (أو الأحدِ بالصوم [. . .] ومحل كراهة إفراد ما ذكر إذا لم يوافق عادة له، فإنْ [كان له عادة كأنْ] اعتادَ صوم يوم وفطر يوم فوافق صومه يوماً منها لم يكره في صوم يوم الشكِ، لخبـر مسلم «لا تخصـوا يوم الجمعة بصيام من بين الأيام إلاّ أن يكون في صوم يصومه أحدكم» وقيس بالجمعة الباقي) [محرّر من كتاب مغني المحتاج إلى معرفة معاني ألفاظ المنهاج: ١/٤٤٧] .

i2.6   ومَنْ دَخَـلَ في صومٍ وصلاةٍ فرضاً أداءً كَانَ أَوْ قضاءً أَوْ نذراً حَرُمَ قطعُهُمَا . فإذَا كَانَ نفلاً (مطلقاً أو ذا سبب أو ذا وقت) جَازَ قطعُهُمـا (لكن الجـواز المذكور مقيد بالكراهة من غير عذرٍ) .

*

i3.0   SPIRITUAL RETREAT (I'TIKAF)

i3.1   It is sunna, at any time, to make spiritual retreat (i'tikaf) in the mosque.

LAYLAT AL-QADR

i3.2   Spiritual retreat (i'tikaf) is especially recommended in Ramadan, particularly in the last ten days of it, seeking *Laylat al-Qadr* (lit. "the Night of the Divine Decree") (O: which is, as Allah Most High says,

"better than a thousand months" (Koran 97:3),

meaning that spiritual works therein are better than works of a thousand months lacking Laylat al-Qadr. Indicating its excellence, the Prophet (Allah bless him and give him peace) said,

"He who prays on Laylat al-Qadr in faith and expectation of its reward will be forgiven his previous sins").

Laylat al-Qadr could be on any night of Ramadan (n: or any other month of the year, according to some (dis: w39)). It probably occurs within the last ten nights, more likely on the odd-numbered ones (N: remembering that the night of an Islamic date comes before the day of that date), the twenty-first and twenty-third of which are the likeliest (n: though most scholars hold it to be the twenty-seventh (*Mughni al-muhtaj ila ma'rifa ma'ani alfaz al-Minhaj* (y73), 1.450)). On Laylat al-Qadr it is recommended to frequently repeat, "O Allah, You are oft-relenting and love to forgive, so forgive me."

HOW TO PERFORM SPIRITUAL RETREAT

i3.3   At minimum, spiritual retreat (i'tikaf) consists of:

(a)   staying, with the intention of spiritual

---

i3.0   الاعتكاف

i3.1   الاعتكاف سنةٌ في كلِّ وقتٍ.

ليلة القدر

i3.2   ورمضانُ آكَدُ والعشرةُ الأخيرةُ آكَدُ لطلب ليلة القـدر (التي هي كما قال تعــالى: ﴿خَيْرٌ مِنْ أَلْفِ شَهْرٍ﴾ أي العمل فيهـا خير من العمل في ألف شهـر ليس فيهـا ليلة القـدر وقال ﷺ استدلالاً على فضلهـا «من قامَ ليلة القدر إيماناً واحتساباً غُفِرَ له ما تَقَدَّمَ من ذنبه» [رواه البخاري ومسلم].

ويُمْكِنُ أنْ تكونَ في جميعِ رمضانَ وفي العشـرة الأخيـرة أَرْجَى وفي أوتـاره أَرْجَى وفي الحـادي والثـالثِ والعشرينَ أَرْجَى. ويُكْثِرُ في ليلةِ القدرِ: «اللّهُمَّ إنّكَ عفوٌ تُحِبُّ العَفْوَ فَاعْفُ عَنِّي».

كيفية الاعتكاف

i3.3   وأقلُّ الاعتكافِ لبثٌ وإنْ قَلَّ بشـرطِ النيةِ وزيـادتِه على أقلِّ الطمأنينةِ

retreat, for more than the least amount of time that can be considered *repose* (A: i.e. a moment);

(b) while being Muslim, sane, conscious, and free of major ritual impurity (O: i.e. of menstruation, postnatal bleeding, and major impurity (janaba));

(c) in a mosque, even when this stay is no more than entering the periphery and then leaving by the same entrance (taraddud), though to merely pass through is insufficient.

Optimally, the spiritual retreat (i'tikaf) should be accompanied by fasting, take place in the Friday congregational mosque (O: because of the size of the group prayer therein, and so as not to have to leave to attend the Friday prayer), and be no less than a day.

VOWING SPIRITUAL RETREAT IN
PARTICULAR MOSQUES

وكـونـه (أي المعتكف) مسلمـاً عاقـلاً صاحيـاً خاليـاً مِنَ الحدثِ الأكـبر (وهـو الحيض والنفـاس والجنابة) وفي المسجـد ولوْ مترددا في جوانبِه ولاَ يَكْفي مجرَّدُ المرورِ.

والأفضـل كونُه بصـومٍ وفي الجـامع (لكثرة الجماعـة فيـه ولئلا يحتـاج إلى الخروج للجمعة) وأن لاَ يَنْقُصَ عنْ يومٍ.

نذر الاعتكاف في مساجد معينة

i3.4   If one vows (def: j18) to make spiritual retreat (i'tikaf) in:

(1) al-Masjid al-Haram (n: in Mecca);

(2) al-Masjid al-Aqsa (n: in Jerusalem);

(3) or Masjid al-Medina;

then the vow cannot be fulfilled elsewhere. Spiritual retreat (i'tikaf) in al-Masjid al-Haram fulfills a vow to make spiritual retreat in either of the other two (n: al-Aqsa or Medina), but not vice versa (N: they do not fulfill a vow to make a spiritual retreat in al-Masjid al-Haram). Spiritual retreat in Masjid al-Medina fulfills a vow to do so in al-Masjid al-Aqsa, but not vice versa. If one vows to make a spiritual retreat in any mosque besides these three, the vow can be fulfilled in any mosque whatever (O: since none besides these three is superior to any other).

i3.4   ولـوْ نَذَرَ الاعـتـكـافَ في المسجـد الحرامِ أو الأقصَى أو مسجـد المـدينـة تَعَيَّن لكنْ يُجْزِىءُ المسجـدُ الحرامُ عنهُمَا بخلاف العكس ويُجْزِىءُ مسجـدُ المـدينـةِ عن الأقصَى بخـلاف العكس ولـوْ عَيَّنَ مسجـداً غيـرَ ذلـك لمْ يَتَعَيَّنْ (إذ لا مزية لبعضها على غيره).

i3.5   Spiritual retreat (i'tikaf) is invalidated by lovemaking and by orgasm as a result of touching.

i3.5   ويَفْسُدُ الاعتكافُ بالجماع والإنزال عنْ مباشرةٍ.

VOWS TO SPEND A CERTAIN CONSECUTIVE
PERIOD IN SPIRITUAL RETREAT

الاعتكاف المنذور لمدة متتابعة

i3.6   If one vows to make spiritual retreat for a
consecutive period, then one is obligated to do so.
The consecutiveness of such a period is not nullified by leaving the mosque for something necessary such as eating (even when it is possible to do
so in the mosque), drinking (provided it is not possible to do so in the mosque), using the lavatory,
attending to an illness, the onset of a menstrual
period, or similar things; though one's spiritual
retreat is interrupted by leaving the mosque to
visit a sick person, perform a funeral prayer
(janaza), or attend the Friday prayer (jumu'a).

i3.6   وإنْ نَذَرَ مدةً متتــابعةً لَزِمَهُ.
فإنْ خَرَجَ لِمَا لاَ بُدَّ منهُ كأكلٍ وإنْ أَمْكَنَ
في المسجــدِ وشـــرب إنْ لَمْ يُمْكِنْ فيهِ
وقضـاء حاجةِ الإنسانِ (من بول وغائط)
والمــرض والحيض ونحو ذلكَ لَمْ يَبْطُلْ
(أي التتــابــع) وإنْ خَرَجَ منَ المسجـدِ
لزيــارةِ مريضٍ أو صلاةِ جنــازةٍ أوْ صلاةِ
جمعةٍ بَطَلَ اعتكافُهُ.

i3.7   [وإنْ خَرَجَ لمنارةِ المسجدِ وهيَ خارجةٌ عنهُ لِيُؤَذِّنَ جَازَ إنْ كانَ هوَ المؤذنَ الراتبَ وإلاَّ فَلاَ. وإنْ خَرَجَ لِمَا لاَ
بُدَّ منهُ فَسَأَلَ عنِ المريضِ وهوَ مارٌّ ولمْ يُعَرِّجْ جَازَ (إن لمْ يطل وقوفه عنده) وإنْ عَرَّجَ لأجلِهِ (أوْ طال وقوفه) بَطَلَ].

i3.8   Touching another with sexual desire is
unlawful for someone in spiritual retreat (i'tikaf).

i3.8   وتَحْرُمُ المباشرةُ بشهوةٍ.

i3.9   It is not permissible for a wife to make
spiritual retreat without her husband's permission.

i3.9   ويَحْرُمُ على [العبدِ وَ] الزوجةِ
دونَ إذنِ [سيدٍ وَ] زوجٍ.

*

BOOK J

THE PILGRIMAGE

CONTENTS:

---

j1.0   WHO MUST PERFORM HAJJ AND 'UMRA

(O: Hajj and 'umra are obligatory because of the word of Allah Most High:

j1.0   المخـاطب بوجـوب
الحج والعمرة

(وهمـا فرضـان لقـوله تعالى : ﴿وَللّهِ

"People owe Allah to make pilgrimage to the House, whoever is able to find a way" (Koran 3:97),

and,

"Complete the hajj and 'umra for Allah" (Koran 2:196),

meaning, "Perform both of them completely.")

عَلَى النَّاسِ حِجُّ البَيْتِ مَنِ اسْتَطَاعَ إِلَيْهِ سَبِيلاً﴾ [آل عمران: ٩٧]، وقوله تعالى: ﴿وَأَتِمُّوا الحَجَّ وَالعُمْرَةَ لِلَّهِ﴾ [البقرة: ١٩٦]، أي ائتوا بهما تامين) .

j1.1   (n: This section uses the following special vocabulary, in addition to some of the terms previously mentioned at f8.1:

'Arafa: (syn. 'Arafat) the name of a plain about thirteen miles to the east-southeast of Mecca.

Hajj: the pilgrimage to Mecca.

Ihram: the state of consecration that pilgrims enter for hajj and 'umra.

Labbayk: a litany meaning, "Ever at Your service, O Allah, ever at Your service."

al-Masjid al-Haram: the Holy Mosque in Mecca that encompasses the Kaaba.

Safa and Marwa: two hillocks connected by a course adjoining al-Masjid al-Haram.

'Umra: the lesser pilgrimage or *visit* to Mecca that may be performed at any time of the year.)

j1.2   Both hajj and 'umra are obligatory, though neither is obligatory more than once in a person's lifetime unless one vows (def: j18) more than that.

j1.2   الحَجُّ والعمــرةُ فرضــانِ ولا يَجِبانِ في العمر إلَّا مرةً واحدةً إلَّا أنْ يُنْذَرَا .

j1.3   They are only obligatory for someone who:

j1.3   وإنَّمـا يَلْزَمَانِ مسلماً بالغـاً عاقلاً [حراً] مستطيعاً .

(a) is Muslim;

(b) has reached puberty;

(c) is sane;

(d) and is able (def: j1.6–10) to make them.

301

j1.4 The hajj or 'umra of someone considered unable (non-(d) above) is valid (O: i.e. if he undertakes the hardship, travels, and stands at 'Arafa (def: j8), it fulfills the obligation), though not that of a non-Muslim, or a child below the age of discrimination (f1.2) who is unaccompanied by a guardian.

It is valid for a child of the age of discrimination to enter the state of ihram with his guardian's permission (O: *guardian* meaning the person with lawful disposal over the child's property).

It is also valid for the guardian to enter ihram on behalf of an insane person or a child below the age of discrimination, in which case the guardian has his charge do as much as he is able, by having him (O: telling him to) perform the purificatory bath (ghusl), remove clothing that has seams, and put on hajj garments; and forbidding him the things prohibited while in the state of ihram, such as perfumes and the like (def: j3.5), after which he takes him to the various places of the hajj rites (O: it being insufficient for the guardian to go alone), and performs the acts that the charge cannot do himself, such as entering into ihram (n: which the charge, lacking discrimination, is unable to make a legally valid intention for), the two rak'as after circumambulating the Kaaba, and stoning at Mina. (N: But the hajj of someone who has not reached puberty does not fulfill the obligation Islam imposes, since even though it is valid, it is supererogatory.)

WHO IS CONSIDERED ABLE TO PERFORM THE HAJJ

j1.5 Those able to perform the hajj are of two types: those able to perform the hajj in person, and those able to fulfill the hajj by sending someone in their stead.

THOSE ABLE TO PERFORM THE HAJJ IN PERSON

j1.6 The conditions for being considered able to perform the hajj in person are:

---

j1.4 وَيَصِحُّ حَجُّ [العَبْدِ وَ] غيرِ المستطيعِ (إذا تكلف وارتكب المشقة وسافر وأدرك الوقوف وقع له عن فرض الإسلام) ولا يَصِحُّ مِنْ الكافرِ وغيرِ المميز استقلالاً.

فإنْ أَحْرَمَ الصبيُّ المميزُ بإذن الوليِّ (وهو المتصرف في ماله) أوْ أَحْرَمَ الوليُّ عن المجنـون أو الطفـل الـذي لا يُمَيِّزُ جَازَ. ويُكَلِّفُهُ الـوليُّ ما يَقْدِرُ عليهِ فيغْسِلُهُ (أي الـولي أي يأمره عنـد إرادة الإحرام بالغسـل) ويُجَـرِّدُهُ عن المخيـطِ ويُلْبِسُـهُ ثيـابَ الإحرام (من إزار ورداء ونعلين) ويُجَـنِّبُـهُ المحظـورَ كالطيب ونحـوه ويُحْضِرُهُ المشاهـدَ (ولا يكفي حضـور الـولي لها) ويَفْعَـلُ عنـهُ مَا لاَ يُمْكِنُ منـهُ كالإحرام وركعتي الطوافِ والرميِ (ح: وحـج غيـر البـالـغ لا يسقط عنـه حجة الإسلام وإن صح، فهو نافلة).

معنى الاستطاعة

j1.5 والمستطيـعُ اثنـانِ مستطيعٌ بنفسِه ومستطيعٌ بغيرِه.

المستطيع بنفسه

j1.6 أمّـا الأول فهـوَ أَنْ يَكُـونَ

(a) to be healthy (O: enough to ride there without serious harm);

(b) to be able to obtain provisions for the trip;

(c) to have enough money to afford water at the going price at the places people travel through because of the water there;

(d) to have transportation suitable to someone like oneself (O: though if one cannot find any, or if it is more than the usual price (A: *usual* meaning that the fare to the hajj is no more than the fare to another destination of comparable distance), then one is not obliged to perform the hajj);

(all of the above (O: (b), (c), and (d)) apply equally to the journey there and back)

(e) to be able to pay for (b), (c), and (d), round trip, with money one has that is in excess of the amount one requires to support the members of one's family and clothe them while one is travelling there and back, and obtain lodgings for oneself; and that is in excess of any money one owes for debts, even those not yet due (O: scholars concur that a debtor is not obliged to perform the hajj even when his creditor does not mind postponing the debt until after the hajj, and that a person is not obliged to perform the hajj when someone is willing to loan him the money to do so (N: though such a person's hajj would be valid, as previously discussed (j1.4)));

(f) and that a route exist that is safe for one's person and property from predators and enemies, whether the latter be non-Muslims or whether highwaymen wanting money, even when the amount is inconsiderable (A: including so-called hajj fees, which are not countenanced by Sacred Law). If there is no route except by sea, then one must take it if it is usually safe, but if not, then it is not obligatory.

(N: These are the conditions for the obligatoriness of the hajj or 'umra, meaning that if one of them is lacking, the hajj and 'umra are not obligatory for that year, though if one performs them

صحيحاً (أي بأن يثبت على مركوب بلا ضرر شديد) وواجداً للزاد والماء بثمنِ مثلِهِ في المواضع التي جَرَتِ العادةُ بكونه فيها وراحلةٍ تَصْلُحُ لمثلِهِ (فإن لم يجدها أصلاً أو وجدها بأكثر من أجرة المثل لم يجب عليه) (إنْ كانَ منْ مكةَ على مسافة القصر وإنْ أطاقَ المشيَ وكذا دونَها إنْ لمْ يُطِقْهُ ومحملاً إنْ شقَّ عليهِ ركوبُ القتب وشريكاً يُعادِلُهُ] يُشْتَرَطُ ذلكَ كلُّهُ ذاهباً وراجعاً (أي يشترط وجود الزاد وما بعده) وأنْ يكونَ ذلكَ فاضلاً عنْ نفقةِ عيالِهِ وكسوتهمْ ذهاباً وإياباً وعنْ مسكنٍ [يُناسِبُهُ وخادمٍ يليقُ بهِ (ويحتاج إليه) لمنصبٍ أوْ عجزٍ] وعنْ دينٍ ولوْ مؤجلاً (ولوْ رضي صاحبه بتأخيره إلى ما بعد الحج لم يلزمه الحج بلا خلاف ولو وجد من يقرضه ما يحج به لم يجب الحج بلا خلاف (ح: لكن يصح حجه كما سبق)) وأنْ يجدَ طريقاً آمناً يأمنُ فيها على نفسِه ومالِه من سبُعٍ وعدوٍّ كافراً أوْ صداً يريدُ مالاً وإنْ قَلَّ (ذلك المال) وإنْ لمْ يجدْ طريقاً إلاّ في البحرِ لزِمَهُ إنْ غَلَبَتِ السلامةُ وإلاّ فَلا.

(ح): هذه شروط لوجوب الحج أو العمرة بمعنى لو فُقِد واحد منها لا يجب الحج أو العمرة في تلك السنة، لكن إن

anyway, one's performance validly fulfills the rites which Islam imposes, as mentioned above at j1.4.)

أَدَاهَا أَسْقَطَ عَنْهُ فَرْضَ الإِسْلامِ كما سبق).

j1.7 The above conditions apply equally to a woman, who in addition requires someone to accompany her to protect her, such as a husband, an unmarriageable male relative (mahram, def: m6.2), or some (O: two or more) reliable women, even if they are not accompanied by any of their unmarriageable male relatives.

j1.7 والمرأةُ في كلِّ ذلكَ كالرجلِ وتَزِيدُ بأَنْ يَكُونَ مَعَها مَنْ تَأْمَنُ معهُ على نفسِهَا مِنْ زوجٍ أَوْ محرمٍ أَوْ نسوةٍ ثقاتٍ (ثنتين فأكثر) وإنْ لَمْ يَكُنْ مَعَ إحداهنَّ محرمٌ.

j1.8 If the above conditions are met, but there is no longer time to reach Mecca, then the hajj is not obligatory. But if time remains, it is obligatory.

j1.8 فمتَى وُجِدَتْ هذِهِ الشروطُ ولمْ يُدْرِكْ زمناً يُمْكِنُ فيهِ الحجُّ على العادةِ لَمْ يَلْزِمْهُ. وإنْ أَدْرَكَ ذلكَ لَزِمَهُ.

j1.9 It is recommended to perform hajj as soon as possible (N: i.e. to perform it the first year that one is able to, and likewise for 'umra). One is entitled to delay it, but if one dies without performing it after having been able to, one dies in disobedience, and it is obligatory to take out the cost for it from the deceased's estate (n: just as debts are, as at L4.3(1)) to pay for someone to make it up (A: in the deceased's place (dis: below)).

j1.9 ويُنْدَبُ المبادرةُ بهِ (ح: أي بالنسك من حج وعمرة بأن يأتي بالحج في عام الاستطاعة وبالعمرة عند الاستطاعة) ولهُ التأخيرُ لكن لوْ مَاتَ بعدَ التمكنِ قبلَ فعلِهِ مَاتَ عاصياً ووَجَبَ قضاؤُهُ مِنْ تركتِهِ.

THOSE ABLE TO PERFORM THE HAJJ BY SENDING SOMEONE IN THEIR STEAD

المستطيع بغيره

j1.10 The second type of being able to perform hajj is when one may fulfill it by sending another in one's place, the necessary conditions for which are:

(a) that one is unable to ride there (O: at all, or is able, but with great difficulty) because of chronic illness or old age;

(b) and that one either has the money (n: to hire someone to go in one's place) or (N: if lacking the money) has someone to obey one (O: by agreeing to perform the rites of hajj for one (N: at their own expense, as a charitable donation)),

j1.10 وأمَّا المستطيعُ بغيرِه فهوَ مَنْ لا يَقْـدِرُ على الثبـوتِ (أصـلاً أو يقـدِر بمشقـةٍ شديـدةٍ) لزمنٍ أَوْ كِبَرٍ ولهُ مالٌ، أو (ح: ليس له مال ولكـن له) مَنْ يُطيعُـهُ (بـالإتيان بالنسـك (ح: على نفقتـه أي المتبـرع)) ولـوْ أجنبياً. فَيَلْزَمُهُ أَنْ يَسْتَأْجِرَ

even if not a family member—in which case one is obliged to either hire someone (N: in the former instance) or give permission to someone (N: in the latter instance) to perform hajj in one's place.

One may also have someone perform a nonobligatory hajj for one under such conditions.

THE PRIORITY OF THE OBLIGATORY HAJJ
OVER ANY OTHER

j1.11   It is not permissible for someone who has not yet performed his own obligatory hajj:

(1) to perform the hajj for someone else;

(2) to perform a nonobligatory hajj;

(3) or to perform hajj in fulfillment of a vow, or as a makeup.

(N: If he does any of these, it counts instead as his own obligatory hajj).

j1.12   The order of performing hajj (O: or 'umra) must be:

(1) the obligatory hajj first;

(2) then a makeup hajj (def: j3.14:(c)) if any is due;

(3) then a hajj in fullfillment of a vow, if any has been made;

(4) and then a supererogatory hajj, or one in another person's place.

If one tries to change this order, for example, by commencing a hajj with the intention for a supererogatory performance or a vow when one has not yet made the obligatory hajj, the intention is invalid, and the hajj counts instead as fulfilling the obligatory one. The same is true for the other types (A: i.e. if one intends any of the types in the order just mentioned when a prior type exists

بمـالِـهِ (ح : في الحـال الأول) أوْ يَأْذَنَ للمطيـع في الحجِّ عنـهُ (ح : في الحـال الثاني) . ويَجُوزُ أنْ يُحَجَّ عنهُ تطوعاً (أي حج التطوع) أيضاً .

أولوية حجة الإسلام على غيرها

j1.11   ولاَ يَجُـوزُ لِمَنْ عليْـهِ فرضُ الإسلام أنْ يَحُجَّ عن غيرِه ولاَ أنْ يَتَنَفَّلَ ولاَ أنْ يَحُجَّ نذراً ولا قضاءً (ح : فإن فعل وقع حجه عن حجة الإسلام في كل هذه الصور) .

j1.12   فَيَحُـجُّ أولاً الفـرضَ (ومثله العمرة) وبعدَهُ القضاءَ إنْ كانَ عليه وبعدَهُ النفلَ أو النيابة .
فإنْ غَيَّرَ هذا الترتيبَ فنَوَى التطوعَ أو النـذرَ مثلاً وعليه فرضُ الإسلامِ لَغَتْ نيّتُهُ ووَقَعَ عن حِجَّة الإسلامِ وقِسْ علَيْهِ .

unperformed, then one's hajj counts as fulfilling the prior one, regardless of the intention).

WAYS OF PERFORMING THE HAJJ

j1.13 It is permissible to enter ihram with the intention for any of four ways of performing the hajj, which are, in order of superiority:

(1) hajj before 'umra (ifrad);

(2) 'umra first (tamattu');

(3) hajj and 'umra simultaneously (qiran);

(4) and the unconditional intention to perform hajj and 'umra (itlaq).

HAJJ BEFORE 'UMRA (IFRAD)

j1.14 *Hajj before 'umra* (ifrad) means to perform hajj (O: i.e. enter ihram for hajj) first (O: before subsequently entering ihram for 'umra) at the ihram site for people from one's country (def: j2), then (O: after having completed one's hajj) to go outside the Sacred Precinct (Haram) and enter ihram for 'umra. (O: There is no special place for the second ihram: if one went to the closest place outside of the Sacred Precinct, it would suffice for this ihram of 'umra.) (N: People generally go to the Mosques of 'A'isha (Allah be well pleased with her) at al-Tan'im because it is close.)

'UMRA FIRST (TAMATTU')

j1.15 *'Umra first* (tamattu') (N: perhaps the easiest and most practical way to perform hajj in our times, since one does not have to remain in a state of ihram throughout the week or more that one is generally there between the initial 'umra and subsequent hajj) means to perform the 'umra first (O: before the hajj) by:

كيفية الدخول في النسك

j1.13 يَجوزُ الإحرامُ بالحجِّ إفراداً وتمتعاً وقراناً وإطلاقاً وأفضلُ ذلك الإفرادُ ثمَّ التمتعُ ثمَّ القرانُ ثمَّ الإطلاقُ.

الإفراد

j1.14 فالإفرادُ أنْ يَحُجَّ (أي أن يحرم بالحج) أولاً (أي قبـل الإحـرام بالعمرة) مِنْ ميقاتِ بلدِه ثمَّ (بعد فراغه منه) يَخْرُجَ (من الحرم) إلى الحِلَّ فَيُحْرِمَ بالعمرةِ (ولا يتعين عليه مكان في الإحرام بل إذا خرج إلى أدنى مكــان منـــه من أرض الحرم كان كافياً في الإحرام بالعمرة (ح: وقـد اعتـاد النـاس الخـروج إلى مسجـد عائشة رضي الله عنها في التنعيم لقرب المسافة)).

التمتع

j1.15 والتمتعُ أنْ يَعْتَمِرَ أولاً (أي قبل الإتيـان بعمـل الحج) مِنْ ميقاتِ بلدِه في

(a) entering ihram for it from the ihram site for people of one's own country;

(b) during the hajj months (def: j1.19);

(c) and then (O: after finishing the 'umra) performing hajj within the same year from Mecca (O: meaning to intend hajj from Mecca (n: by entering ihram there), if one wants to have to slaughter (n: in expiation, as at j12.6(I)), which relieves one of the necessity to return to the ihram site of people of one's country, though if one returns to that site to enter ihram for hajj, then one is no longer obliged to slaughter and one's ihram is valid).

It is recommended to enter ihram for hajj on 8 Dhul Hijja if one is performing 'umra first (tamattu') and has an animal to slaughter. But if one does not have an animal, (O: one enters ihram) on 6 Dhul Hijja (O: so that one's (N: three-day expiatory) fast (N: in place of slaughtering (def: j12.6(I))) takes place before standing at 'Arafa (A: since in the Shafi'i school, being in ihram for hajj is obligatory during these three days of fasting, though for the Hanafi school, these days may be fasted before entering ihram for hajj, after one's 'umra), thus fasting on the sixth, seventh, and eighth, and not on the Day of 'Arafa (N: the ninth) if one was able to fast on the sixth, though if not, then fasting the Day of 'Arafa is mandatory because of the previous inability. If one does not fast it, it is a sin and the delayed fast-day is a makeup, as its obligatory time is before the Day of 'Arafa). One enters ihram for hajj in Mecca from the door of one's lodgings. Then one proceeds in a state of ihram to al-Masjid al-Haram as a Meccan would (O: to perform a farewell circumambulation (tawaf al-wada', def: j11.2) of the Kaaba, which is desirable (mustahabb) for non-Meccans who are leaving Mecca to go to 'Arafa. For Meccans, the farewell circumambulation is obligatory when leaving Mecca, even for a short distance).

HAJJ AND 'UMRA SIMULTANEOUSLY (QIRAN)

j1.16 *Hajj and 'umra simultaneously* (qiran) means to enter ihram intending both (O: hajj and

أشهر الحج ثم يَحُجَّ مِنْ عامِهِ مِنْ مكةَ (أي ينـوي حجه منها إن أراد لزوم الـدم ولا يجب عليـه العــود إلى ميقـات بلده فإن رجـع إليه سقط الدم عنه وصح إحرامه) . ويُنْـدَبُ أنْ يُحْـرِمَ المتمتعُ إنْ كَانَ واجداً للهَدي بالحجّ ثامنَ ذِي الحجةِ وإلّاَ (أي وإن لم يكن واجداً له) فـ (يحرم) سادسَهُ (أي سادس ذي الحجـة لأجـل أن يقع الصوم قبل الوقوف فيصومه وما بعده وهو السـابع والثامن ويكون يوم عرفة مفطراً ما لم يتضيق عليـه الصوم بأن لم يصم يوم السادس فيتعين عليه حينئذ صوم يوم عرفة للتضيق المـذكـور وإلا كان آثمـاً بتأخيـر صوم يوم من هذه الثلاثة عن وقت الوقوف ويصير المـؤخـر قضـاءً لأن وقت صومها قبل الوقوف وجوباً) [ت : فيحرم المتمتع بحجـه] في مكـة مِنْ باب داره فَيَـأتـي المسجدَ (أي مسجد الحرام) محـرمـاً (لطواف الوداع لأنه يستحب للخارج إلى عرفة وهي ليست وطناً ولو كانت وطناً له لوجب بمفـارقة مكة طواف الـوداع ولـو كانت المسافة قصيرة) كالمكيِّ .

القِران

j1.16 والقِرَانُ أنْ يُحْرِمَ بهمَا معاً (أي بالحج والعمرة) مِنْ ميقات بلدِه ويُقْتَصَرَ

'umra) at the ihram site for people of one's country, and then perform only the rites of hajj. (O: Such that one does not perform an additional circumambulation or a second going between Safa and Marwa (def: j6), but rather once is sufficient to fulfill the obligation of both hajj and 'umra, because the actions of the 'umra have been incorporated into the actions of the hajj. The author mentions a second way of performing hajj and 'umra simultaneously (qiran) by saying:)

Or the person may enter ihram first for 'umra, and then before beginning his circumambulation (O: even if only by a single step), incorporate into his intention for 'umra the intention to perform hajj, this taking place in the months of hajj.

THE OBLIGATION TO SLAUGHTER OR FAST FOR THOSE PERFORMING THE 'UMRA FIRST (TAMATTU') OR HAJJ AND 'UMRA SIMULTANEOUSLY (QIRAN)

j1.17 A Person performing 'umra first (tamattu') or performing hajj and 'umra simultaneously (qiran) is obliged to slaughter (N: a *shah* (def: h2.5) or to fast, as mentioned below), though if the person performing hajj and 'umra simultaneously (qiran) lives within the Sacred Precinct (Haram) or within 81 km./50 mi. of it, or if the person performing 'umra first (tamattu') returns to the ihram site for people of his country (N: after his 'umra) to enter ihram for hajj, or lives within 81 km./50 mi. of the Sacred Precinct—in any of these cases he is not obliged to slaughter.

If one (O: performing 'umra first (tamattu') or hajj and 'umra simultaneously (qiran)) is obliged to slaughter but:

(1) lacks an animal there (O: i.e. in the Sacred Precinct (Haram), which is the place of the obligation to slaughter, *lacks* meaning absolutely, as when there is not an animal available that meets slaughter specifications (def: j14.2));

(2) or (O: there is an animal, but one lacks) its price (O: or has the price but needs the money for expenses and the like);

على أفعـال الحجّ فقطْ (فلا يزيد لأجل العمـرة طوافـاً آخـر ولا سعيـاً ثانيـاً بل الطـواف الـواحد كاف عنهمـا وكـذلـك السعي فقـد انـدرجت أفعـال العمرة في أفعـال الحـج وقـد أشـار المصنف إلى الصـورة الثانية للقـران بقـوله) أوْ يُحْرِم بالعمـرة أولاً ثمَّ أنْ قبلَ أنْ يَشْرَعَ في طوافها (ولو بخطوة) يُدْخِل عليها الحجَّ في أشهره .

فدية التمتع والقران

j1.17 ويَلْزَمُ المتمتـعَ والقـارنَ دمٌ، ولا يجبُ على القارن إلاّ أنْ لا يكونَ مِنْ حاضـري المسجدِ الحرام وهمْ أهـلُ الحرمِ ومَنْ كـان منـهُ على دونِ مسافة القصرِ، ولاَ على المتمتع إلاّ أنْ لا يَعُودَ لإحـرامِ الحجِّ إلى الميقاتِ وأنْ لا يَكُونَ مِنْ حاضري المسجدِ الحرامِ .

فإنْ فَقَدَ (كـل من القـارن والمتمتع) الدمَ هناكَ (أي في أرض الحرم لأنها محل وجوب الذبح (أي فقده أصلاً بأن لم يوجد ما يجزىء في الذبح) أوْ (وجده لكن فقد) ثمنَـهُ (أو وجده وكان محتاجاً إليه لنفقة أو

(3) or finds that it is being sold for more than the normal price for that locality and time;

—then one must fast three days of the hajj. (O: For our school it is insufficient to fast them before the hajj, as opposed to the school of Abu Hanifa, in which it is permissible to fast them before the hajj (A: i.e. when performing the 'umra first (tamattu'), fasting them after having finished the initial 'umra and before entering ihram for hajj).) It is recommended that these days be before the Day of 'Arafa (O: time permitting, as when one fasts from 1 Dhul Hijja after having entered ihram for hajj. It is unlawful to delay these fast-days till after the Day of 'Arafa), and one must fast seven additional days after returning home (n: making a total of ten fast-days).

The time for current performance of the three fast-days ends after the Day of 'Arafa (O: and it is not permissible to fast any of them on 'Eid al-Adha or on the three days following the 'Eid), and if one thus delays them, it is obligatory to make them up before the other seven fast-days, by an interval between the three and seven fast-days equal to the interval that would have separated them had they been a current performance, namely, the time taken by the trip (O: from Mecca to home) plus four days (O: equal to the 'Eid and the three days that follow it).

THE UNCONDITIONAL INTENTION TO PERFORM HAJJ AND 'UMRA (ITLAQ)

j1.18 The *unconditional intention to perform hajj and 'umra* (itlaq) means to merely intend entering into the performance of rites, without specifying at the time of ihram that it is for hajj, 'umra, or hajj and 'umra simultaneously (qiran). After this, one may use it (O: the ihram, made unconditional by the intention) as one wishes (O: meaning to perform hajj only, 'umra only, or hajj and 'umra simultaneously (qiran) (A: though one may not use the unconditional intention as a way to perform 'umra first (tamattu') without having to either return to the ihram site to enter ihram for hajj, or to slaughter or fast (def: j1.17))).

غيرها) أَوْ وَجَدَهُ يُبَاعُ بِأَكثَرَ مِنْ ثمن مثلِهِ صامَ ثلاثـةَ أيّـامٍ في الحـجِّ (ولا يكفي صومهـا قبله عنـدنـا بخـلاف مذهب أبي حنيفة فإنه يجـوز صومهـا قبـل التلبس بالحج) ويُنْدَبُ كونُها قبلَ يوم عرفةَ (من حيث اتساع الوقت كأن يصوم من أول ذي الحجة بعد التلبس بالإحرام به ويحرم تأخيرها عن يوم عرفة) وسبعةً إذا رَجَعَ إلى أهلِهِ (أي إلى وطنه) .

وتَفُوتُ الثلاثةُ بتأخيرهَا عن يوم عرفة (ولا يجوز صوم شيء منها في (النحر ولا في أيـام التشـريق) ويَجبُ قضـاؤُهـا قبـل السبعة ويُفَرَّقُ بينها وبين السبعة بمَا كَانَ يُفَـرَّقُ في الأداءِ وهـوَ مدةُ السير (من مكة إلى وطنه) وزيـادةُ أربعـةِ أيّـامٍ (هي يوم العيد وأيام التشريق) .

الإطلاق

j1.18 والإطـلاقُ أنْ يَنـوِيَ الدخولَ في النسك مِنْ غير أنْ يُعَيِّنَ حالةَ الإحرام أنـهُ حجٌّ أَوْ عمـرةٌ أَوْ قِرانٌ ثمَّ له بعـدَ ذلكَ صرفُهُ (أي الإحرام المطلق بالنية) لِمَا شاءَ (أي الحج فقط أو العمرة فقط أو هما معاً) .

الميقات الزماني للحج والعمرة

j1.19   It is not permissible to enter ihram for hajj other than during its months, namely, Shawwal, Dhul Qa'da, and the first ten nights of Dhul Hijja (A: with their days). If one enters ihram for hajj during non-hajj months, one's ihram counts for 'umra.

Entering ihram for 'umra is valid at any time of the year except for a person on hajj encamped at Mina for stoning (def: j10).

j1.19   ولا يَجُوزُ الإحرامُ بالحَجِّ إلا في أشهره وهي شوالٌ وذو القعدةِ وعشرُ ليالٍ منْ ذي الحجةِ . فإنْ أحرَمَ به في غيرهَا انْعَقَد عمرةٌ .

وينْعَقِدُ الإحرامُ بالعمرةِ كلَّ الوقتِ إلا للحاجِّ المقيم للرمي بمنىً .

*

j2.0   SITES FOR ENTERING IHRAM

j2.0   الميقات

j2.1   The sites for entering ihram for hajj or 'umra are as follows:

j2.1   ميقاتُ الحــجِّ والعمرةِ : ذُو الحليفةِ لأهلِ المـدينةِ والجحفةِ للشام ومصرَ والمغربِ ويلملمُ لتهامةِ اليمنِ وقرنٌ لنجدِ اليمنِ ونجدِ الحجازِ وذاتِ عِرقٍ للعراقِ وخراسانَ والأفضلُ لهُ العقيقُ .

(1) (N: people going to hajj from the West by plane must enter ihram before boarding it, or during the flight before it passes the airspace that is even (def: j2.3) with the city of Rabigh, on the western coast of the Arabian Peninsula, this generally being announced on the plane);

(2) Medina residents (N: or those travelling through Medina to Mecca) enter ihram at Dhul Hulayfa;

(3) residents of the Syria-Palestine region, Egypt, and North Africa enter ihram at al-Juhfa;

(4) residents of al-Tihama in Yemen enter ihram at Yalamlam;

(5) residents of the Najd of Yemen and the Najd of the Hijaz enter ihram at Qarn;

(6) and residents of Iraq and Khurasan enter ihram at Dhat 'Irq, preferably at al-'Aqiq.

j2.2   Someone at Mecca, even if merely passing through, enters ihram for hajj in Mecca, and for

j2.2   ومَنْ في مكةَ ولَوْ مارّاً ميقاتُ حجِّه مكةُ وميقاتُ عمرتِه أدنَى الحلِّ

'umra must go (N: at least) to the nearest place outside of the Sacred Precinct (Haram), of which the best is al-Ji'rana, then al-Tan'im, and then al-Hudaybiya.

Someone residing closer to Mecca than the ihram site is to Mecca should enter ihram (O: for hajj or 'umra) at his residence.

والأفضل من الجعرانة ثم التنعيم ثم الحديبية.

ومن مسكنُهُ أقربُ من الميقات إلى مكة فميقاتُهُ (للحج أو العمرة) موضعُهُ (أي موضع إقامته).

j2.3   When coming by a route lacking an ihram site, one enters ihram when even with (O: on the left or right) the ihram site that is nearest.

j2.3   ومن سلك طريقاً لا ميقات فيه أحرم إذا حاذى (من جهة اليمين أو اليسار) أقربَ المواقيتِ إليهِ.

j2.4   For someone residing farther from Mecca than the ihram site is, to enter ihram at the ihram site is superior (A: than for him to enter ihram at his own residence).

j2.4   ومن دارُهُ أبعدُ من الميقات إلى مكة فالأفضل أن لا يُحرم إلا من الميقاتِ [وقيل من دارِهِ].

THE EXPIATION FOR NEGLECTING TO ENTER IHRAM AT THE PROPER SITE

فدية تجاوز الميقات من غير إحرام

j2.5   Someone intending hajj, 'umra, or both, who passes the ihram site (O: intentionally, absentmindedly, or in ignorance of it) and enters ihram somewhere closer to Mecca, is obliged to slaughter (def: j12.6(I)), though if he returns to the proper site and enters ihram there before having performed a single rite, he is no longer obliged to slaughter.

j2.5   ومن جاوز الميقات وهو يُريدُ النسكَ (سواء كان حجاً أو عمرة أو هما معاً وسواء جاوز عامداً أو ناسياً أو جاهلاً) وأحرم دونَهُ لزمَهُ دمٌ فإن عاد إليه محرماً قبل التلبس بنسكٍ سَقَطَ الدمُ.

*

j3.0   IHRAM (THE STATE OF PILGRIM SANCTITY)

j3.0   الإحرام

MEASURES RECOMMENDED PRIOR TO IHRAM

ما يندب قبل الإحرام

j3.1   When one wishes to enter ihram, it is recommended (even for a woman in menstruation) to perform the purificatory bath (ghusl), intending bathing for ihram. If there is not much water, one merely performs ablution (wudu).

j3.1   إذا أراد أن يُحرم اغتسل (ندباً) ولو حائضاً بنية غسل الإحرام. فإن قلَّ ماؤُهُ توضأ فقط [وإن فَقَدَهُ بالكلية

It is also recommended to shave pubic hair, pluck the underarms, clip the mustache, (O: trim the nails,) clean oneself of dirt, and wash the head.

تَيَمَّمَ]. وَيَتَنَظَّفُ بحلقِ العانة ونتف الإبط وقصِّ الشـارب (وقلمِ الأظفـار) وإزالـة الوسخِ بأنْ يَغْسِلَ رأسَهُ [بسدرٍ ونحوه].

OBLIGATORY MEASURES BEFORE IHRAM

ما يجب قبل الإحرام

j3.2   Then (O: if male) one:

j3.2   ثُمَّ يَتَجَـرَّدُ (الــرجــل) عن المخيط (والتجرد في الإحرام واجب لا يتم إلا بالتجـرد قبله) وَيَلْبَسُ إزاراً ورداءً أبيـضَـيْـن نظيفيْن ونعلَيْن غيـر محيطَيْن (بـالـرجـل بأن تظهـر أصابـع الـرجلين والعقب منهما لا ما يغطي الأصابـع ، وإلا لزمتـه الفـدية) وُيُطَيِّبُ بدنَـهُ (نـدباً) ولاَ يُطَيِّبُ ثيابَهُ [(يراد من النفي عدم الندب)].

(a) sheds any garments that have sewing in them (O: taking them off being obligatory for ihram, which is incomplete if one does not remove them before entering it);

(b) puts on a clean white *mantle* (Ar. rida', the rectangular piece of cloth worn over the shoulders that covers the upper body of a man in ihram) and *wraparound* (izar, the cloth worn around the lower body), and sandals (O: that do not enclose the foot, but rather reveal the toes and heels, as opposed to sandals that cover the toes, for wearing such sandals obliges one to slaughter (def: j12.6(II)));

(c) and it is recommended to perfume the body, though not one's clothes.

والمرأةُ في ذلك كالرجلِ إلا في نزع المخيط فإنّها لا تَنْزِعُهُ (ويجب عليها ستر سائر بدنها إلا الوجه والكفين فإنهما ليسا بعـورة في الإحـرام كمـا في الصـلاة) وتَخْضِبُ كَفَّيْهَـا كِلَيْهِمَـا بالحنـاء (وهـذا الخضب على سبيل الاستحباب والندب لا يترتب على تركه شيء) وتُلَطِّخُ بها وجهَهَا.

The above measures (j3.1) apply equally to women, although women do not divest themselves of sewn garments (O: a woman being obliged to cover all of her body except the face and hands, which, in ihram as well as in prayer, are not considered nakedness). It is recommended that she dye her hands and face with henna (O: a measure that is desirable, and whose nonperformance is without consequence). (A: But women do not use perfume.)

هذا كلُّه قبلَ الإحرام .

All of the foregoing are done before entering ihram.

ENTERING IHRAM

الشروع في الإحرام

j3.3   One then prays two rak'as, provided it is not a time when the prayer is forbidden (def: f13), intending the sunna of ihram. (O: It is sunna to

j3.3   ثُمَّ يُصَلِّي ركعتَيْن في غير وقت الكـراهة ينْوي بهمَا سنة الإحرام (ويسن

recite al-Kafirun (Koran 109) in the first rak'a, and al-Ikhlas (Koran 112) in the second.)

Then one rises to start travelling to Mecca. As soon as one begins travelling to Mecca, one has entered ihram.

Ihram (O: which is an integral of hajj and 'umra) is the intention to enter into the performance of the rites (O: of hajj, 'umra, or both (qiran)). One intends in one's heart to perform the hajj for Allah Most High, if one wants to perform hajj; or to perform 'umra if one wants to; or both together if one wants to perform them simultaneously (qiran). It is recommended that one also pronounce this intention with the tongue.

CHANTING "LABBAYK"

j3.4   Then one chants "Labbayk" (n: as described below), raising the voice (O: enough to (N: at least) hear oneself, the *raising* being relative. For the duration of the time one is in ihram one raises it enough for those nearby to hear), though a woman should lower her voice when saying it (O: as raising the voice is offensive for a woman) saying: "Ever at Your service, O Allah, ever at Your service. Ever at Your service, You have no partner, ever at Your service. Verily, all praise, blessings, and dominion are Yours. You have no partner" (O: saying this three times).

Then (O: after chanting the above) one recites the Blessings on the Prophet (Allah bless him and give him peace) in a softer voice, asking Allah Most High for paradise (O: saying, "O Allah, I ask You for paradise and its blessings," and asking for His good pleasure and acceptance (ridwan)) and seeking refuge in Him from hell (O: saying, "I take refuge in You from Your wrath, and hell," and asking Him for whatever one wishes of the good of this world and the next).

It is desirable to chant "Labbayk" for the duration of one's ihram, whether standing, sitting, riding, walking, lying down, and even in a state of major ritual impurity (janaba), or for a woman in menstruation. It is particularly desirable when:

(1) changing from one state, time, or place to another, such as when going uphill or down, or getting on or off a vehicle;

أن يقرأ في الركعة الأولى قُلْ يا أيُّها الكافرونَ وفي الثانية سورة الإخلاص) .

ثمَّ يَنْهضُ في السير (إلى جهة مكة) فإذا شَرَعَ فيه أَحْرَمَ حينئذٍ .

والإحرامُ (الذي هو ركن من أركان الحجِّ والعمرة) هو نيةُ الدخولِ في النسكِ (من حج أو عمرة أو هما المسمى بالقران) فَيَنْوي بقلبه الدخولَ في الحجِّ للهِ تعالى إنْ كان يُريدُ حجاً أو العمرة إنْ كان يُريدُها أو الحجَّ والعمرة إنْ كان يُريدُ القرانَ . ويُنْدَبُ أنْ يَتَلَفَّظَ بذلك أيضاً بلسانه .

التلبية

j3.4   ثمَّ يُلَبِّي رافعاً صوتَهُ (فيكون رفع صوته بقدر ما يسمع نفسه (ح : على الأقل) فالرفع نسبي وأما في دوام إحرامه فيرفع بحيث يسمع من بقربه) والمرأة تَخْفِضُهُ (فيكره لها الرفع) فَيقولُ: «لَبَّيْكَ اللهمَّ لَبَّيْكَ، لَبَّيْكَ لا شَريكَ لَكَ لَبَّيْكَ، إنَّ الحمدَ والنعمةَ لَكَ والملكَ لا شريكَ لك» (ثلاثاً) . ثمَّ (بعد فراغه من التلبية) يُصَلِّي على النبيِّ ﷺ بصوتٍ أخفضَ مِنْ ذلكَ ويَسْأَلَ اللهَ تعالى الجنةَ (بأن يقول : «اللهمَّ إنِّي أسألُكَ الجنةَ ونعيمَها» ويسأله رضوانه) ويَسْتَعيذُ بهِ مِنَ النارِ (بأن يقول : «وأعوذُ بكَ مِنْ سَخَطِكَ والنارِ» ويدعو بما شاء وأحب من خيري الدنيا والآخرة) . ويُكْثِرُ التلبية في دوام إحرامِهِ (استحباباً) قائماً وقاعداً وراكباً وماشياً ومضطجعاً وجنباً وحائضاً ويتأكَّد استحبابُها عند تغيُّرِ الأحوالِ والأزمانِ والأماكنِ كصعودٍ وهبوطٍ وركوبٍ ونزولٍ واجتماع رفاقٍ .

(2) meeting groups of people;

(3) at the approach of dawn, night, or daytime;

(4) after prayer;

(5) and in all mosques.

One does not chant "Labbayk" while circumambulating the Kaaba or going between Safa and Marwa (O: as these have their own particular invocations). It is undesirable to stop chanting it in order to speak, though if someone greets one with "as-Salamu 'alaykum," it is recommended (O: but not obligatory) to return his greeting.

When one sees something pleasing (O: or displeasing) during ihram, it is recommended to say, "Ever at Your service, truly, the real life is the life of the hereafter" (O: and if one sees the like while not in ihram, one says, "O Allah, truly, the real life is the life of the hereafter," without saying "Labbayk."

وعندَ السَّحَرِ وإقبالِ الليلِ والنهارِ وأدبارِ الصلاةِ وفي سائرِ المساجدِ ولا يُلَبِّي في طوافِهِ وسعيِهِ (لأنَّ لهما أذكاراً خاصة) ولا يَقطَعُ التلبيةَ بكلام (استحباباً) فإنْ سَلَّمَ عليهِ إنسانٌ رَدَّ عليهِ (ندباً لا وجوباً) فإذا رأى شيئاً فأعْجَبَهُ (أوكرهه) قالَ: (على سبيل النـدب) «لَبَّيْكَ إنّ العيشَ عيْشُ الآخرة» ([هـذا إذا كان الـرائي محرماً] وإلا قال: «اللهمَّ إنّ الـعـيشَ عيْشُ الآخرة» من غير ذكر لبيك).

محرمات الإحرام

j3.5   Five things are unlawful (dis: j12.6) when one has entered ihram. (n: Namely:

j3.5   وإذا أَحْرَمَ حَرُمَ عليه خمسةُ أشياء.

(1) sewn garments on men (dis: j3.6);

(2) using perfume (j3.7);

(3) removing hair or nails (j3.8);

(4) sexual intercourse or foreplay (j3.13);

(5) and hunting (j3.21).)

SEWN GARMENTS ON MEN

لبس المخيط

j3.6   The first thing unlawful in ihram is wearing sewn clothing such as shirts, trousers, moccasins (khuff, def: e6), anything else sewn (N: sewn meaning that which is for wearing, not just any

j3.6   أحـدُهـا لبسُ الـمـخـيـطِ كالقميص والسراويل والخفَّ [والعَباءِ] وكـلِّ مخيط (ح: فالمـراد بالمخيط ما

sewing, as a patched mantle or wraparound are permissible), and anything that encircles the body as sewn garments do, such as (N: those seamed) by being woven or felted together and the like.

It is unlawful to cover the head with anything, sewn or unsewn, that is generally considered a headcover (O: such as a hat, cloth, bandage (N: or blanket while sleeping)).

It is permissible while in ihram to carry a (N: sewn) bag or the like, or to tote a basket (O: on one's head, though it is unlawful if one intends it as a headcover). (A: It is permissible to carry an umbrella held in the hand for protection against the sun.)

It is not permissible to fasten one's mantle by tucking part of it through a hole, tying it together, passing a string through one end and then the other, or by tying a string to each of the two ends (N: though it is permissible to fasten it together with safety pins).

It is permissible to tie one's wraparound (O: one end to the other) or tie a string over it (O: so that it holds it fast, like a drawstring, and one may likewise use a waistband) (N: the reason for the permissibility (n: of tying the *wraparound* but not the mantle) being that if the wraparound were to fall it would reveal one's nakedness, unlike the mantle). (n: Safety pins are permissible to fasten the wraparound, and are useful to make pleats at the waistline by safety-pinning two or three tucks of cloth there to gather the wraparound at the waist and leave more freedom of movement for the legs below.) (A: A belt may also be used to hold one's wraparound at the waist.)

PERFUME

j3.7 The second thing that is unlawful after entering ihram is using perfume, such as musk, camphor, or saffron on one's clothing, body, or bedding. It is also unlawful to smell roses, violets, lilies, or anything fragrant; to sprinkle rose water or flower water about; or to use scented oils (N: or scented bar soap), whether to smell them or to apply them to any part of the body.

It is also unlawful:

صنع بشكل خاص للبس، لا كل ما خيط، إذ لا يضر إزار أو رداء مرقع) وما استدارتُه كاستدارة المخيط بنسج وتلبيد ونحو ذلك.

ويَحْرُمُ عليْهِ أيضاً سترُ رأسِهِ بمخيط وغيرِهِ مما يُعَدُّ في العادة ساتراً (كقلنسوة، وخرقة وعصابة).

فَلا يَضُرُّهُ [الاستظلالُ بالمحمل وَ] حملُ عِدْلٍ وزنبيلٍ (على رأسِهِ، وإن قصدَ بحمل القفة ونحوِه السترَ حرم) ونحو ذلك.

ولَيْسَ لهُ أنْ يَزُرَّ رداءَهُ (بأن يدخل رداءه في العرى) ولا أنْ يَعْقِدَهُ ولا أنْ يُخِلَّهُ بخلالٍ (بأن يدخل مخيطاً في طرفه وينفذه في الطرف الآخر) ولا أنْ يَرْبِطَ خيطاً في طرفِه ثمَّ يَرْبِطَهُ بالطرف الآخر.

ولهُ عقدُ الإزار (بأن يعقد طرفه بطرفه الآخر) وشَدُّ خيطٍ عليهِ (أي على الإزار من فوقه حتى يستمسك وأن يجعله مثل الحِجزة، ويدخل فيها التكة بكسر التاء) (ح: لأن سقوط الإزار يؤدي إلى انكشاف العورة وليس الرداء كذلك).

الطيب

j3.7 الثاني: يَحْرُمُ بعدَ الإحرام الطيبُ في الثوب والبدنِ والفراشِ كالمسكِ والكافورِ والزعفرانِ وشمِّ الورد والبنفسج والنيلوفر وكلِّ مشمومٍ طيّبٍ.

ويَحْرُمُ رثُّ ماءِ الوردِ وماءِ الزهرِ، وكذلك الدُّهْنُ المطيَّبُ يَحْرُمُ شمُّهُ ودهْنُ جميعِ بدنِه بِهِ [كدهن الورد والبنفسج وما أشْبَهَ ذلك].

(1) to apply unscented oils like olive, sesame, and so on to the beard or scalp, unless one is bald (A: in which case it can be used on the skin of the head), though it is permissible to smell them or apply them to any of the body (O: except the hair of the head and face);

(2) to eat food in which the use of a cosmetic is manifest, whether in taste, color, or scent, such as the scent of rose water, the color of saffron or its taste, or the taste of ambergris in cooked grain and the like;

(3) or to use scented perspiration deodorant or eyeliner.

REMOVING HAIR OR NAILS

j3.8   The third thing that is unlawful while in ihram (O: for both men and women, but only if one does so deliberately, knowing that it is unlawful, voluntarily, and remembering that one is in ihram) is:

(1) cutting or plucking hair (O: i.e. removing it by any means whatever), even if only part of a single hair (by shortening it), and whether from the head, underarms, pubes, mustache, or any other part of the body (A: the obligatory expiation for one hair is to give 0.51 liters of food to the poor in Mecca, and for two hairs, twice that amount. For three or more, a full expiation (def: j12.6(II)) is obligatory);

(2) or clipping fingernails or toenails, even if only part of one (A: my above remark on expiations also applies to nails).

THE EXPIATION FOR VIOLATING THE CONDITIONS OF IHRAM

j3.9   It is necessary to slaughter a *shah* (def: h2.5) (n: or perform one of the other alternatives mentioned below at j12.6(II)) when one is in ihram and one:

وإنْ كانَ غيـرَ مطيبٍ كزيتٍ وشيـرج ونحـوهِ حَرُمَ أنْ يَدْهُنَ بهِ لحيتَهُ ورأسَهُ إلّا أنْ يكُونَ أصلعَ، ولاَ يَحْـرُمُ شَـمُّـهُ ودهنُ جميـع بدنِه (ما عدا شعر الرأس واللحية وشعور الوجه).

ويَحْرُمُ عليْهِ أكلُ طعامٍ فيهِ طيبٌ ظاهرٌ طعمُهُ أوْ لونُهُ أوْ ريحُهُ كرائحةِ ماءِ الورد ولونِ الـزعفرانِ وطعمِهِ وطعمِ العنبرِ في الجوارِشِ ونحوِهِ.

ويَـحْـرُمُ دواءُ العَـرَقِ (أي ما يزيـل رائحته الكريهة منه) والكحلِ المطيّبيْنِ.

إزالة الشعر أو قلم الأظفار

j3.8   الثالثُ: يَحْرُمُ (على المحرم ذكراً كان أو أنثى بشرط كونِه عامداً عالماً بالتحريم مختاراً ذاكراً للإحرام) حلقُ شعرِه ونتفُهُ (والمراد إزالته بأي نوع كان) ولوْ بعضَ شعرةٍ تقصيراً مِنْ رأسِهِ أوْ إبطِهِ أوْ عانتِهِ أوْ شاربِهِ وسائرِ جسدِه، وتقليمُ أظافرِه ولوْ بعضَ ظفرٍ.

فدية محظورات الإحرام

j3.9   فإذا تَطَيَّـبَ أوْ لَبِسَ أوْ حَلَقَ

(1) uses perfume;

(2) wears a prohibited garment (def: j3.6);

(3) removes three or more hairs, fingernails, or toenails (def: j12.6(II(1–2)));

(4) touches another person with desire in a nongenital area;

(5) or applies unscented oil to one's hair (dis: j3.7).

ثلاثَ شعراتٍ أَوْ قَلَّمَ ثلاثَ أظفارٍ أَوْ بَاشَرَ فيمَا دونَ الفرجِ بشهوةٍ أَو دَهَنَ لَزِمَهُ شاةٌ .

j3.10 A person obliged to perform such an expiation may fulfill it (A: any time thereafter) in any of the following ways:

(1) by slaughtering a *shah* (def: h2.5) (O: and distributing its meat to the poor and those short of money in the Sacred Precinct);

(2) by distributing 6.09 liters of food (def: h7.6) to the poor in charity, giving 1.015 liters to each person;

(3) or by fasting three days (O: even if unconsecutive).

j3.10 وهــوَ مُخَيَّــرٌ بينَ ذَبحِهَـا (أي الشـاة) وتفرقـة لحمِها على فقراءِ الحرمِ ومسـاكينه) وبينَ أَنْ يُطْعِمَ ثلاثـةَ آصعٍ لكـلِّ مسكـينٍ نصفُ صاعٍ وبينَ صومِ ثلاثةِ أيامٍ (ولو مفرقة) .

ACCIDENTALLY REMOVING A HAIR

فدية إزالة الشعر والظفر

j3.11 It is unlawful during ihram to comb one's beard (N: or hair) or run one's fingers through it if one knows that hair will be pulled out.

When one runs the fingers through one's beard or washes the face and then notices hair in one's hand, then if one knows one pulled it out while doing this, an expiation (def: j12.6(II)) must be paid, though if one knows that it came out by itself, or does not know whether it did or not, then one is not obliged to expiate.

j3.11 فإنْ عَلِمَ أنهُ إنْ سَرَّحَ لحيتَهُ أَوْ خَلَّلَها انْتَتَفَ شعرٌ حَرُمَ ذلك . فلوْ خَلَّلَ أو غَسَـلَ وجهَـهُ فرأَى في كفِّه شعراً وعَلِمَ أنهُ هوَ الـذي نَتَفَـهُ حينَ غَسَـلَ وجهَهُ أَوْ خَلَّلَ لزِمَهُ الفـدية . وإنْ عَلِمَ أنهُ كانَ قد انْتَتَفَ بنفسِهِ أَوْ لمْ يَعْلَمْ هذا ولاَ ذاكَ فلا شيءَ عَلَيْهِ .

j3.12 The following things necessitate the expiation (def: j12.6(II)), but when done out of need, are not unlawful:

j3.12 وإنِ احْتَـاجَ إلى حلقِ الشعرِ

(1) having to cut one's hair because of illness, heat, or lice;

(2) having to wear something sewn because of intense heat or cold;

(3) or having to cover one's head.

SEXUAL INTERCOURSE OR FOREPLAY

j3.13   The fourth thing unlawful while in ihram is sexual intercourse or touching a nongenital area with sexual desire, such as kissing, hugging, or touching lustfully.

j3.14   If one intentionally has sexual intercourse before finishing one's 'umra, or while on hajj before partial release from ihram (def: j9.13), then:

(a) this nullifies the hajj or 'umra;

(b) it is nonetheless obligatory to complete the hajj or 'umra from the point at which it was spoiled to the end;

(c) it is obligatory to make it up as soon as possible, even if the spoiled hajj or 'umra was merely supererogatory;

(d) and it is obligatory to pay the expiation (def: below) (O: for the male, not the female, who need not do anything, though it is a sin if she participated willingly) (A: the more reliable position is that if the woman was unwilling, none of the above ((a), (b), (c), or (d)) apply to her, though if willing, (a), (b), and (c) apply to her but not (d)).

j3.15   The expiation for the above (j3.14) is to slaughter (A: and distribute to the poor of the Sacred Precinct, immediately):

(1) a camel (O: i.e. a male or female that meets slaughter specifications (def: j14.2)), but if this is not possible (N: within the days of that hajj), then one must slaughter:

لمـرضٍ أوْحَرٍّ وكثـرةِ قمل ٍ أواحْتَاجَ إلى لبس المخيطِ للحرِّ أو البردِ أوْ إلى تغطيةِ الرأس ِ فلَهُ ذلكَ ويَفْدي [شاة مجزئة في الأضحية وهي للتخيير كما مرّ].

الجماع في الفرج والمباشرة فيما دونه

j3.13   الــرابــعُ: يَحْـرُمُ الجمـاعُ في الفرجِ والمباشرةُ فيمَا دونَ الفرج بشهوةٍ كالقُبلةِ والمعانقةِ واللمس ِ بشهوةٍ.

j3.14   فإنْ جَامَعَ عمـداً في العمـرةِ قبــلَ فراغِهــا أوْفي الحـجِّ قبــلَ التحلُّل الأول ِ فَسَدَ نسكُهُ ويَجبُ علَيْهِ إتمامُهُ كمَا كانَ يُتمُّهُ لوْلمْ يُفْسِـدْهُ، والقضـاءُ علـى الفـورِ، وإنْ كَانَ الفاسدُ تطوعاً، و(يجب على الـواطىء وخرج بقولنا على الواطىء المـوطـوءةِ فلا شيء عليهـا غيـر الإثم إن كانت مطاوعة له) الكفارةُ.

j3.15   وهيَ بدنةٌ (أي واحد من الإبل ذكراً كان أو أنثى بصفة الأضحية) فإنْ لمْ

(2) a cow, but if not possible, then:

(3) seven *shah*s (def: h2.5), but if not possible, then:

(4) one estimates the cost of a camel and how much food (def: h7.6) this would buy, and then gives that much food (N: to the poor in Mecca), but if not possible, then:

(5) one fasts one day for every 0.51 liters of food that would have been given had (4) been done. (N: One may fast anywhere, but it is not permissible to delay it without an excuse.)

يَجِدْ فبقرةً فإنْ لمْ يَجِدْ فسبعَ شياهٍ فإنْ لمْ يَجِدْ قَوَّمَ البَدَنةَ دراهِمَ والدارهِمَ طعاماً ويَتَصَدَّقُ بهِ فإنْ لمْ يَجِدْ صَامَ عن كلِّ مُدٍّ يوماً.

j3.16 A person making up a hajj or 'umra nullified by sexual intercourse must enter ihram for the makeup hajj or 'umra at the same ihram site as the original (n: nullified) hajj or 'umra, though if one entered ihram for it at a location closer to Mecca (N: than the ihram site (dis: j2.5)), one must enter ihram for the makeup at the (O: prescribed) site (N: for those of one's country).

j3.16 ويجبُ أنْ يُحْـرِمَ بالقضـاءِ مِنْ حيثُ أَحْرَمَ بالأداءِ (أي قبَل الفساد) فإنْ كانَ أَحْرَمَ بهِ مِنْ دونِ المِيقاتِ (ح: أي من مكانٍ أقربَ منهُ إلى الحرمِ) أَحْرَمَ بالقضاءِ مِنَ الميقاتِ (الشرعيِّ).

j3.17 When someone (O: in ihram who intends to make up a nullified hajj) is accompanied on the makeup hajj by the wife he made love to, he is recommended to separate himself from her while they are at the place where they had intercourse.

(N: Such a makeup counts as the original hajj or 'umra would have counted: if it was obligatory, it counts as the obligatory one; if supererogatory, as supererogatory; and if vowed, as vowed.)

j3.17 ويُنْدَبُ (للمحرم الذي أراد أن يقضي الحج الفاسد) أنْ يُفارِقَ الموطوءةَ في المكانِ الذي وَطِئَها فيهِ إنْ قَضَى وهيَ مَعَـهُ. (ح: ويقـع القضـاء عن النسـك الفاسد فإن كان فرضاً وقع فرضاً وإن كان نفلاً وقع نفلاً وكذا المنذور).

j3.18 If a man has sexual intercourse after partial release from ihram (def: j9.13), it does not nullify his hajj (n: i.e. does not entail j3.14(a,b,c,d)), though he must pay an expiation (O: of the type discussed at j12.6(II)).

j3.18 وإنْ جَامَـعَ بعـدَ التـحـلـلِ الأولِ لمْ يَفْسُـدْ وعلَيْـهِ شاةٌ (ودم الشـاة المذكورة على التخيير والتقدير [كما مرَّ]).

j3.19 If one has sexual intercourse absentmindedly (O: forgetting one is in ihram or out of ignorance of its prohibition or because of being forced), then one is not obliged to do anything (A: i.e. none of j3.14(a,b,c,d)).

j3.19 وإنْ جَامَـعَ ناسِـاً (للإحرام أو جاهلاً بالتحريم أو مكرهاً) فَلا شيءَ علَيْهِ.

THE PROHIBITION OF MARRYING WHILE
IN IHRAM

تحريم عقد النكاح في الإحرام

j3.20   It is unlawful while in ihram to marry, or
to marry someone to another (zawwaja, def:
m3.2(a)) (O: whether one does so oneself or
through an agent). If one does so, the marriage
contract is invalid.

j3.20   ويَحْــرُمُ علَيْــهِ أنْ يَتَــزَوَّجَ أوْ
يُزَوِّجَ (إمــا بنفســه أو بوكـالـة) فإنْ فَعَـلَ
فالعقدُ باطلٌ .

It is offensive while in ihram to get engaged to
marry, or to serve as a witness for a marriage contract.

ويُكْــرَهُ لهُ أنْ يَخْطُبَ امـرأةً وأنْ يَشْهَدَ
على نكاحٍ .

HUNTING

الصيد

j3.21   The fifth thing that is unlawful while in
ihram is:

j3.21   الخــامسُ يَحْرُمُ أنْ يَصْطَادَكلَّ
صيـدٍ بريٍّ مأكولٍ أوْ مَا تَوَلَّدَ مِنْ مأكولٍ
وغيرِ مأكولٍ .

(1) to kill any wild game that may be eaten by
Muslims;

فإنْ مَاتَ في يدِهِ أوْ أتْلَفَهُ أوْ أتْلَفَ جزأَهُ
لَزِمَهُ الجزاءُ .

(2) or to kill the offspring of matings between game animals that may be eaten by
Muslims and game animals that may not be eaten
by Muslims.

Someone in ihram is obliged to pay the expiation (def: below) whenever such an animal dies at
his hands, is destroyed by an act of his, or is
injured, in which case one must expiate in proportion to the part damaged.

THE EXPIATION FOR HUNTING

فدية الصيد

j3.22   If the animal killed has a domestic counterpart, one may fulfill the expiation in any of the
following ways:

j3.22   فإنْ كانَ لهُ (أي للصــيـد
المقتـول) مثلٌ مِنَ النعم (والمراد بالمثل
التقـريب لا حقيقة الممـاثلة وتراعى في
الصــورة لا في القيمــة فيفـدى الكبير
والصغيـر والصحيـح والمريض والسمين
والهـزيـل والمعيب بمثله رعـاية للمماثلة

(1) to slaughter a head of domestic livestock
that is like the wild animal which was killed (O:
like meaning an approximation, not actual
resemblance. The criterion is the condition of the
animal, not its value. One expiates a game animal
that was, for example, large, small, healthy,
diseased, fat, thin, or defective, with a head of

livestock of the same description, heeding the correspondences. It is a necessary condition that the wild animal and the head of livestock share, if the animal was defective, the same type of defect, such as blindness (N: though it is permissible, indeed superior, to pay a healthy one for a defective one or a whole one for one that is lacking some part));

(2) to estimate the value of the like head of livestock, and distribute an equal value of food (def: h7.6) to the poor;

(3) or to fast one day for every 0.51 liters of food (N: that would have been bought had (2) been done).

j3.23   If the animal killed does not have a domestic counterpart, then one may fulfill the expiation in any of the following ways:

(1) to distribute funds to the poor which equal the value of the game animal, although if the animal was a pigeon, one is obliged to slaughter a *shah* (def: h2.5) (O: which is obligatory for killing even a single pigeon);

(2) to buy food equal to the animal's value and distribute it as charity;

(3) or to fast one day for each 0.51 liters of food (N: that would have been bought had (2) been done).

j3.24   The prohibition of all things unlawful while in ihram applies to both men and women, except for not wearing sewn clothing (def: j3.6) and not covering the head, which are restricted to men.

A woman, however, may not veil her face in ihram (dis: (j12.6(II(3)))). If she wants to conceal it from people, she may drape something in front provided it does not touch her face (N: such as a veil worn over a cap's visor), though if it touches it without her intention, it is of no consequence.

بشرط اتحاد جنس العيب كالعور) (ح) ويجوز إخراج الصحيح عن معيب والكامل عن الناقص بل هو أفضل) وَجَبَ مثلُهُ منَ النعم يُخَيَّرُ بينَهُ وبين طعامٍ بقيمتِهِ (أي قيمةِ المثل وبينَ صومٍ لكلِّ مدٍّ يومٌ.

j3.23   وإنْ لَمْ يكنْ لهُ مثـلٌ وَجَبَتِ القيمةُ إلَّا الحمـامَ [وما عَبَّ وهَدَرَ] فشاةٌ (تجب في قتل حمامة واحدة) ثمَّ إنْ شاءَ يُخْرجُ بالقيمةِ طعاماً أَوْ يَصُومُ لكلِّ مدٍّ يوماً.

j3.24   ويَحرُمُ ذلك كلُهُ على الرجل والمـرأةِ إلَّا فعـلَ التجـرد منَ المخيـط وكشفَ الرأس فَيَخْتَصُّ وجوبُهُ بالرجل. لكنْ يَلْزَمُ المرأةَ كشفُ وجهِها فإنْ أَرادَتِ السترَ عنِ النّاسِ سَدَلَتْ علَيْهِ شيئاً بشرطِ أنْ لا يَمَسَّ وجهَهـا. فإنْ مَسَّهُ مِنْ غيـرِ اختيارِها لَمْ يَضُرَّ.

j3.25   It is permissible when in ihram to scratch one's head or body with one's fingernails as long as this does not remove any hair.

It is also permissible in ihram to kill lice (N: or other insects harmful to humans), though if one kills a louse, it is recommended to expiate its death by giving charity, even if only a single bite of food.

j3.25   وللمُحْرِم حكُّ رأسِه وجسدِه بأظفارِه بحيثُ لَا يَقْطَعُ شعراً.

ولهُ قتلُ القملِ [لكنْ يُكْرَهُ أنْ يَفْلِيَ المحرمُ رأسَهُ] فإنْ قَتَلَ منها قملةً نُدِبَ أنْ يَتَصَدَّقَ ولوْ بلقمةٍ.

*

j4.0   ENTERING MECCA

j4.1   It is recommended when one wants to enter Mecca:

(1) to perform the purificatory bath (ghusl) outside of the city with the intention of entering Mecca;

(2) to enter in the daytime, and from the Mu'alla gate of Thaniyyat Kada' (N: a pass from the direction of Jedda);

(3) to walk barefoot, provided one does not apprehend something unclean (najasa);

(4) not to annoy anyone by jostling;

(5) and after entering, to proceed to al-Masjid al-Haram.

j4.0   سنن دخول مكة

j4.1   إذا أرادَ دخولَ مكةَ اغْتَسَلَ (نـدباً) خارجَ مكةَ بنيـة دخـولِ مكـةَ ويـدْخُلُ بالنهـار منْ باب المُعَلَّى منْ ثنيّةِ كداءَ ماشياً حافياً إنْ لمْ يَخفْ نجاسةً ولا يُؤْذي أحـداً بمـزاحمـةٍ وَلْيَمْضِ نحـوَ المسجدِ الحرامِ.

WHEN ONE FIRST SEES THE KAABA

j4.2   When one first sees the Kaaba, it is recommended to lift the hands and say: "O Allah, increase this house in nobility, honor, reverence, and dignity. Increase those going on hajj or 'umra who honor and reverence it in honor, reverence, and piety. O Allah, You are Peace, the Source of Peace; O Lord, raise us after death in peace." And then one asks Allah for whatever one wishes of religious matters or those of this world.

الدعاء عند رؤية البيت

j4.2   فإذا وَقَعَ بصرُهُ على البيتِ رَفَعَ يديْهِ حينئذٍ [وهوَ يَرَاهُ منْ خارج المسجدِ منْ موضـعٍ يقـالُ لَهُ رأسُ الـردم فهنـاكَ يَقفُ ويرْفَعُ يديْهِ] ويَقُولُ: «اللهُمَّ زِدْ هذا البيتَ تشـريفـاً وتكريمـاً وتعظيماً ومهابةً وزِدْ مَنْ شَرَّفَهُ وعَظَّمَهُ ممَّنْ حَجَّهُ واعْتَمَرَهُ تشـريفاً وتكريماً وتعظيماً وبراً اللهُمَّ أنتَ السـلامُ ومنـكَ السـلامُ فَحيِّنـا ربَّنـا بالسلام»، ويَدْعُو بِمَا أَحَبَّ منْ أُمْر الدينِ والدنيا.

j5.0   CIRCUMAMBULATING THE KAABA (TAWAF)

j5.1   Then one enters al-Masjid al-Haram from the Bani Shayba door (O: even if it is out of one's way, as it is sunna) prior to getting one's luggage down or finding a place to stay and so forth (O: such as deciding to rest or to eat; all this should be put off until after circumambulating the Kaaba). Rather (n: by turns), some of one's party should stay with the luggage while others go to the mosque (O: to circumambulate), and after they finish, they return to watch the luggage so the rest can go.

(O: The arrival circumambulation (tawaf al-qudum) is desirable for anyone who enters al-Masjid al-Haram, whether in ihram or not.)

j5.1   ثُمَّ يَدْخُـلُ المسجـدَ مِنْ باب بني شيبةَ (وإنْ لَمْ يكنْ في طريقه للاتباع) قبـلَ أنْ يشتغـلَ بحطّ رحله وكراء منزل وغيـر ذلك (كتعويل على استراحة أو أكل فإنه يؤخر كل ذلك عن الطواف) بلْ يَقِفُ بعض الـرفقـة عند المتَاع وبعضُهُمْ يأتي المسجـدَ (للطـواف) بالنـوبـة (وطـواف القدوم مستحب لكل داخل محرماً كان أو غير محرم).

HOW TO CIRCUMAMBULATE THE KAABA

كيفية الطواف

j5.2   Prior to circumambulating the Kaaba one proceeds to the Black Stone (diagram: 1) (O: next

j5.2   ويَقْصِدُ (عند ابتداء الطواف) الحجرَ الأسودَ (وهو في الركن الذي يلي

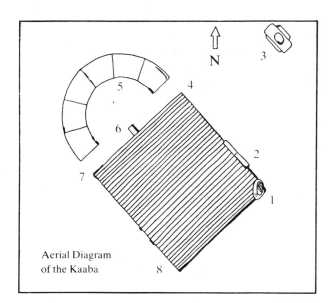

Aerial Diagram of the Kaaba

to the Kaaba's door, on the east corner), drawing near to it, if one can do so without hurting others

باب الكعبة من جانب المشـرق) ويَـدْنُو منـهُ بشـرط أنْ لا يُؤْذِيَ أحـداً بمـزاحمة

by jostling. One faces the Black Stone, places the hand on it, and without a word, kisses the stone thrice and touches the forehead upon it thrice. (O: Touching, kissing, and placing the forehead on the stone are only sunna for women when the circumambulation area is vacant, whether in the night or day.)

j5.3   One ceases to chant "Labbayk" at this point, not to resume until after having finished both circumambulating the Kaaba and going between Safa and Marwa (def: j6). One puts the center (N: of the top edge) of one's mantle under the right arm and its two ends over the left shoulder so that the right shoulder is left bare (dis: j5.13, second par.).

One begins circumambulating by first standing facing the Kaaba with the Black Stone on one's right and the Yamani corner (diagram: 8) on one's left, standing back from the stone a little towards the Yamani corner (n: i.e. behind the black stripe in the marble pavement, extending out from the stone, that marks the beginning of one's circumambulation). One should intend performing the circumambulation for Allah Most High (O: though this intention is only necessary for a supererogatory or a departure circumambulation, not for an obligatory or an arrival circumambulation, since the intention to perform the rites of hajj or 'umra (def: j3.3) includes the intention for the latter two types of circumambulation).

Then one:

(1) places the hand on the Black Stone, and then kisses it and places the forehead on it thrice, as mentioned above (A: i.e. it is done again here to begin the circumambulation, just as it was done before circumambulation (j5.2));

(2) says "Allahu akbar" three times;

(3) and adds, "O Allah, out of faith in You and to affirm Your book, fulfill Your covenant, and follow the sunna of Your prophet Muhammad (Allah bless him and give him peace)."

j5.4   Then one moves sideways (A: as is recommended) to the right, passing in front of all of the

فَيَسْتَقْبِلُهُ (بصدره ويستلمه بيده) ثُمَّ يُقَبِّلُهُ بلا صوتٍ وَيَسْجُـدُ عليهِ وُيُكَرِّرُ التقبيلَ والسجودَ عليهِ ثلاثاً [(والمراد بالسجود عليه وضع الجبهة عليه للاتباع]) وإنما يسن الاستلام والتقبيل والسجود للمرأة إذا خلا المطاف ليلاً أو نهاراً).

j5.3   ومِنْ هنا يَقْطَعُ التلبيةَ ولا يُلَبِّي في طوافٍ ولا سعيٍ حتَّى يَفْرُغَ منْهُما.

ثُمَّ يَضْطَبِعُ فَيَجْعَلُ وسطَ ردائِه تحت عاتِقِـه الأيمنِ ويطرَحُ طرفَيْـه على عاتِقِه الأيسر ويَتْرُكُ مَنكِبَهُ الأيمنَ مكشوفاً.

ثُمَّ يَشْـرَعُ في الطوافِ فَيَقِفُ مستقبلَ البيتِ ويكونُ الحجرُ الأسودُ من جهةِ يمينِه والـركن اليمانيُّ من جهةِ شمالِه ويَتَأخَّرُ عن الحجرِ قليلاً إلى جهةِ الركنِ اليمانيِّ.

فَيَنْـوي الطوافَ للهِ تعالى (وهذه النية إنمــا تكــون في طوافِ النفل أو طوافِ الوداع لا في طوافِ الفرض ولا في طوافِ القـدوم لشمـول نية النسك لهذه الأنواع) ثُمَّ يَسْتَلِمُ الحجـرَ بيـدِه ثمَّ يُقَبِّلُهُ وَيَسْجُدُ عليـهِ ثلاثاً كَما تَقَدَّمَ وُيُكَبِّرُ ثلاثاً ويَقُولُ: «اللهُمَّ إيمـاناً بك وتصديقاً بكتابِك ووفاءً بعهـدِك واتِّباعاً لسنةِ نبيِّك ﷺ» [(وإيماناً وما بعده مفعول لأجله]).

j5.4   ثُمَّ يَمْشي إلى جهةِ يمينِه مارّاً على جميعِ الحجرِ الأسودِ بجميعِ بدنِه

Black Stone with all of the body, while facing it. When past the stone, one turns (O: from facing it) so that the Kaaba is on one's left and then proceeds to circumambulate it. (O: If one did this (N: kept the Kaaba on one's left while passing the stone) from the beginning and neglected to face the stone, it would likewise be permissible.)

وهو مستقبله فإذا جاوزه انفتل (عن الاستقبال) وجعل البيت عن يساره ويطوف (ولو فعل هذا من أول الأمر وترك الاستقبال جاز).

j5.5   At the Kaaba's door (diagram: 2) one says, "O Allah, verily this house is Your house, the sanctuary Your sanctuary, the safety Your safety, and this is the station of him who took refuge in You from fire" (N: i.e. the Station of Ibrahim (diagram: 3), though some hold the words mean "him who *takes* refuge," alluding to oneself).

j5.5   ويقول عند الباب: «اللهم إن هذا البيت بيتك والحرم حرمك والأمن أمنك وهذا مقام العائذ بك من النار».

j5.6   When one reaches the corner (diagram: 4) by the opening of the Hijr (n: a semicircular wall that stands apart from the Kaaba (diagram: 5)), one says, "O Allah, I take refuge in You from doubt, from ascribing partners to You, from discord, hypocrisy, evil traits, and from bad turns of fortune in money, spouse, and children."

j5.6   فإذا وصل إلى الركن الذي عند فتحة الحجر قال: «اللهم إني أعوذ بك من الشك والشرك والشقاق والنفاق وسوء الأخلاق وسوء المنقلب في المال والأهل والولد».

j5.7   When even with the rainspout (N: called the Spout of Mercy (Mizab al-Rahma), at the top of the Kaaba (diagram: 6)), one says: "O Allah, shade me in Your shade on a day when there is no shade but Yours. Give me to drink from the cup of Your prophet Muhammad (Allah bless him and give him peace), a wholesome drink after which I will never thirst."

j5.7   ويقول قبالة الميزاب: «اللهم أظلني في ظلك يوم لا ظل إلا ظلك واسقني بكأس نبيك محمد ﷺ مشرباً هنيئاً لا أظمأ بعده أبداً».

j5.8   Between the third corner (diagram: 7) and the Yamani corner (diagram: 8), one should say, "O Allah, make this a pious hajj, a rewarded effort, an accepted work, and a transaction that will never perish, O All-powerful and Oft-forgiving one."

j5.8   ويقول بين الركن الثالث واليماني: «اللهم اجعله حجاً مبروراً وسعياً مشكوراً وعملاً مقبولاً وتجارة لن تبور يا عزيز يا غفور».

j5.9   When one reaches the Yamani corner, one does not kiss it, but touches it and then kisses one's hand.

j5.9   فإذا بلغ الركن اليماني لم يقبله بل يستلمه ويقبل يده بعد ذلك.

j5.10 One does not kiss any of the Kaaba (O: meaning that it is not required, though if one kisses any of its parts, it is not offensive, but rather is good) except the Black Stone. Nor does one touch any of it except the Yamani corner, which is the one before the Black Stone.

j5.11 When one reaches the Black Stone, one has completed a single round (O: provided its conditions (def: j5.16) have been met).

j5.12 One goes around the Kaaba seven times (O: the seventh ending where one began, at the Black Stone. One's circumambulation is incomplete as long as even a span remains between oneself and the place even with the stone).

TROTTING FOR THE FIRST THREE ROUNDS

j5.13 It is sunna in the first three rounds of circumambulation to hasten one's gait (N: if one can do so without harming others) (O: taking close steps, without running) which is termed *trotting* (ramal) (O: and which is desirable for men only, not women).

Both trotting and baring the right shoulder (def: j5.3) are only called for in circumambulations that are followed by going between Safa and Marwa (def: j6). If one wishes to go between Safa and Marwa after one's arrival circumambulation, then one does the two sunnas (O: both trotting and baring the shoulder at this point, but when one later performs one's going-forth circumambulation (tawaf al-ifada, def: j9.10), one does not do these two sunnas because that circumambulation is not followed by going between Safa and Marwa (N: if one has already gone between them before)).

But if one wishes to go between Safa and Marwa after the going-forth circumambulation (O: which is superior), one postpones the two (O: sunnas of trotting and baring the shoulder) until then.

While trotting, one says, "O Allah, make this a pious hajj, a rewarded effort, and forgive my

ولاَ يُقَبِّلُ شيئاً مِنَ البيتِ **j5.10** (أي لا يطلب تقبيله فلو قبل شيئاً من أجزائه لم يكره بل هو حسن) إلاَّ الحجرَ الأسودَ ولاَ يَستَلِمُ شيئاً إلاَّ اليمانِيَّ وهوَ الـذي قبـلَ الحجرِ الأسودِ.

j5.11 ثمَّ إذا وَصَـلَ إلـى الـحجـرِ الأسودِ فقَـدْ كَمَلَتْ لهُ طوفةٌ (واحدة مع الإتيان بشرطها).

j5.12 يَفْعَلُ ذلكَ سبعاً (من المرات والسابعـة تنتهي بمـا ابتدأ به وهو الحجر فلا يتم طوافه ما بقي عليـه مقدار شبر من الطواف قبل الوصول إليه).

الرمل

j5.13 ويُسَـنُّ في الثـلاثة الأُوَلِ مِنها الإسراع (ح: بشرط عدم إيذاء الآخرين) (بأن تكـون الخطـا متقاربة من غير عدو) ويُسَمَّى الـرمـلَ (وهو مستحب للذكـر لا للمرأة) وإنمـا يُشْـرَعُ هوَ والاضطبـاعُ في طوافٍ يَعْقُبُـه سعيٌ فإنْ رَام السعيَ عَقبَ طوافِ القـدومِ فعلهُمَـا (أي الـرمـل والاضطبـاع ولا يفعلهمـا بعـد طواف الإفاضـة لأنه طواف لا يعقبه سعي) وإنْ رَام عقبَ طوافِ الإفـاضـةِ (وهو الأفضل) أخَّرَهُمَا (أي الرمل والاضطباع) إلَيْهِ.

ويقُولُ في رملِهِ: «اللهمَّ اجْعَلْهُ حَجّاً مبروراً وسَعْياً مشكوراً وذنباً مغفوراً».

sins."

In the last four rounds of one's circumambulation, it is sunna to proceed at one's normal pace, while saying: "My Lord, forgive me, show me mercy, and pardon that which You know. Verily You are the All-powerful and the Most Generous. Our Lord, give us what is good in this world and the next, and keep us from the torment of hell." This supplication is particularly recommended in the odd-numbered rounds of the circumambulation (O: as they are superior. Reciting the Koran while circumambulating is better than making supplications that have not reached us through prophetic hadith, though supplications from hadith are superior to reciting the Koran during it).

وأنْ يَمْشِيَ على مهلِهِ في الأربعةِ الأخيرةِ ويَقُـولُ فيها: «ربِّ اغفرْ وارْحَمْ واعْفُ عَمَّا تَعْلَمُ إنَّـكَ أنْتَ الأعَـزُّ الأكرمُ ﴿رَبَّنَا آتِنَا في الدُّنْيَا حَسَنَةً [الآية (التي هي] وفي الآخِرةِ حَسَنَةً وَقِنَا عَذَابَ النَّارِ﴾» وهو في الأوتارِ آكَدُ (لأنها أفضل وقـراءةِ القـرآن في الطوافِ أفضل من الدعاء غير المأثور وأما المأثور فهو أفضل منها) .

j5.14   It is recommended to kiss the Black Stone in each round (O: and to place the forehead on it, each three times) and to touch the Yamani corner, particularly in the odd-numbered rounds.

If it is not possible to kiss the Black Stone because of crowds or because one fears to hurt people (O: or be hurt) by jostling, one may touch it with one's hand and then kiss the hand. If this is not possible, one may touch it with a stick (O: or the like, such as a scarf) and kiss the stick. If this too is impossible, then one points to it (O: or the Yamani corner) with the hand (O: and it is sunna to kiss one's hand).

j5.14   ويُقَبِّلُ الحجرَ الأسودَ في كلَّ طوفةٍ (ويندب أيضاً وضع الجبهة عليه كذلك ثلاثاً ثلاثاً) وكذا يَسْتَلِمُ اليمانيَّ، وفي الأوتارِ آكَدُ.

فإنْ عَجَـزَ عن تقبيـلِهِ (أي الحجـر الأسودَ) لرحمةٍ أوْ خَافَ أنْ يُؤْذِيَ الناسَ (أو يتأذى هو منهم) اسْتَلَمَهُ بيـدِهِ وقَبَّلَهَا فإنْ عَجَـزَ اسْتَلَمَهُ بعصاً (ونحوه كمنديل) وقَبَّلَها فإنْ عَجَزَ أَشَارَ إلَيْهِ (وكذا أشار إلى الركن اليماني) بيدِهِ (ويسن تقبيل يده إذا أشار إليه بها) .

j5.15   A noteworthy detail here is that there is a *buttress* at the base of the Kaaba that resembles a ledge and slide. It is part of the Kaaba, and when one kisses the stone, one's head is in the space above the buttress. So one is obliged to keep one's feet motionless until one finishes kissing the stone and straightens up, after which one continues circumambulating. (N: One may not move one's feet as part of the circumambulation while one's head is within the space above the buttress, as it nullifies that particular round because of the condition (dis: j5.16(i)) that circumambulation be done *around* the Kaaba, and not within its confines.) If, when leaning over to kiss the stone, one's feet move even a finger's width towards the Kaaba's

j5.15   وهنَا دقيقةٌ وهـوَ أنَّ بجـدار البيتِ شاذرواناً كالصفـة والزلاقة وهو منَ البيتِ فعنـدَ تقبيل الحجـر يكونُ الرأسُ في هواء الشاذروان فيَجِبُ أنْ يُثْبِتَ قَدَمَيْهِ إلى فراغِهِ منَ التقبيل ويَعْتَـدِلَ قائماً ثمَّ بعدَ ذلك يَمُرَّ.

فإن انْتَقَلَتْ قدمـاهُ إلى جهة البابِ وهوَ متطامِنٌ في التقبيل ولوْ قدرَ إصبع ومَضى

door, and after this, one continues circumambulating, then that particular round does not

كَمـا هوَ لَمْ تَصِحَّ تلكَ الطوفةُ (أي ومـا

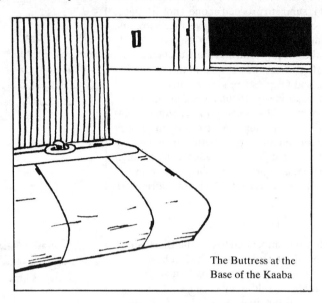

The Buttress at the
Base of the Kaaba

count (O: nor do the others that come after it, if
one limits oneself to just those seven, considering
the spoiled one as a valid round. But if one adds an
extra round (N: to make up for the invalid one),
then one's circumambulation is valid).

It is more precautionary when one has
straightened up from kissing the stone, to step
back to the left towards the Yamani corner (j5.2
diagram: 8) enough to ensure that one is where
one was before kissing the stone. (N: The same is
true of touching the Yamani corner with one's
hand.)

بعـدهـا إنْ اقتصر على هذه السبعـة مع
جعـل الفـاسـدة طوفة . وأما إذا زاد على
الفـاسـدة طوفة أخرى صح الطواف)
فالاحتيـاط إذَا اعْتَـدَلَ مِنَ التقبيـل أنْ
يَرْجِعَ إلى جهـةِ يسارِهِ وهيَ جهةُ الركنِ
اليمانيّ قدراً يَتَحَقَّقُ به أنَهُ كَمَا كَانَ قبلَ
التقبيلِ .

THE CONDITIONS OF A VALID
CIRCUMAMBULATION

شروط الطواف

j5.16   The conditions of a valid circumambulation (O: of any kind, obligatory or nonobligatory)
are:

    (a)   that one's nakedness (def: f5.3) be
clothed, because the round is invalid whenever
any of one's nakedness shows, even a single hair of
a woman's head (O: meaning that the particular

j5.16   وواجبـاتُ الطـوافِ (بأنـواعه
من فرض ونفل [وأراد بالواجبات الشروط
لأن هذه المـذكورات كلها شروط]) ستـرُ
العورة فمَتَى ظَهَرَ شيءٌ منهَا ولوْ شعرةً مِنْ
شعـرِ رأسِ المـرأةِ لَمْ تَصِحَّ (هذه الطوفة

round in which it showed is invalid, provided it was done intentionally. If it happened inadvertently and the woman immediately covered it (A: *immediately* meaning after no more than the time required to say "Subhan Allah"), then it does not invalidate that round, though if she does not cover it until after it is showing, the subsequent round takes the place of the above-mentioned invalid one);

(b) ritual purity (O: from minor (hadath) and major (janaba) impurity) (n: though for Hanafis. touching a marriageable member of the opposite sex (N: despite being unlawful) does not nullify one's ablution (*Maraqi al-falah sharh Nur al-idah* (y126), 17), and considering the difficulty of avoiding it at a contemporary hajj, taking the dispensation seems a virtual necessity);

(c) to be free from impure substances (najasa) on one's person, clothing, and the place of walking while circumambulating;

(d) that it take place within al-Masjid al-Haram;

(e) that one's circumambulation comprise seven full rounds;

(f) that it begin from the Black Stone. as described above, and that one pass by all of the stone with all of one's body, for if one begins from another part of the Kaaba. then the round does not count until one reaches the stone, from whence it begins;

(g) that one keep the Kaaba on one's left and move towards the door (j5.2 diagram: 1–2);

(h) that each round be outside of the Hijr (diagram: 5) such that one does not enter the opening between the Hijr and the Kaaba and then exit through the other opening;

(i) and that all of the body of the person circumambulating be exterior to all parts of the Kaaba. such that while walking around it, one does not put one's hand in the space above the buttress previously mentioned (j5.15). which viol-

التي ظهرت فيها؛ هذا مع العمد، فإذا ظهر منها ذلك مع نسيان وسترها حالاً فلا تبطل تلك الطوفة وأما إذا سترتها بعد ظهورها فيقال ما بعد هذه الطوفة يقوم مقامها وتلغى هي أي الطوفة المذكورة) وطهارةُ الحدثِ (سواء كان الحدث أصغر أو أكبر) والنجس في البدنِ والثوب وموضعِ الطوافِ، وأنْ يَطُوفَ داخلَ المسجدِ الحرام، وأنْ تُسْتَكْمَلَ سبعُ طوفاتٍ، وأنْ يَبْتَدِيءَ طوافَهُ من الحجر الأسودِ كما تَقَدَّمَ وأنْ يَمُرَّ عليْهِ بكلِّ بدنِه فإنْ بدأ منْ غيرِه لمْ يَعْتَدَّ بذلك إلى أنْ يصلَ إليْهِ فمنْهُ ابتداءُ طوافِه، وأنْ يَجْعَلَ البيتَ على يسارِه ويَمُرَّ إلى جهةِ البابِ وأنْ يطُوفَ خارجَ الحِجرِ ولا يَدْخُلَ منْ إحدى فتحَتيْه ويخْرُجَ منَ الأخرى، وأنْ يَكُونَ كلُهُ خارجاً عنْ كلِّ البيتِ فإذا طافَ لا يَجْعَلُ يدَهُ في هواءِ الشاذروانِ فَيَكُونُ

ates the condition of being wholly outside all of the Kaaba while making one's rounds.

ما خَرَجَ بكلِّهِ عن كلِّ البيتِ .

j5.17   Everything besides the above conditions is sunna (N: not obligatory), such as trotting in the first three rounds, the various supplications, and the other things previously mentioned.

j5.17   وما سوى ذلكَ سُنَنٌ كالرمل والدعاء وغيرِهما مما تَقَدَّمَ .

TWO RAK'AS AFTER CIRCUMAMBULATION

ركعتا الطواف

j5.18   When one has finished circumambulating, and after putting one's mantle over both shoulders, it is recommended to pray two rak'as for the sunna of circumambulation (O: and it is best to perform them) behind the Station of Ibrahim (j5.2 diagram: 3). In the first rak'a, one recites al-Kafirun (Koran 109), and in the second, al-Ikhlas (Koran 112).

After this, one supplicates Allah from behind the station (O: if one prays there. Otherwise, one may perform the two rak'as (N: in order of superiority) in the Hijr (diagram: 5), al-Masjid al-Haram, the Sacred Precinct, or whenever and wherever one wishes to pray them, and they remain a current performance until the day one dies. It is sunna to recite the suras aloud in these two rak'as if performed at night, and to recite them to oneself if performed during the day. It is desirable to make the supplication related by Jabir, who said that the Prophet (Allah bless him and give him peace) prayed two rak'as behind the station (N: of Ibrahim) and then said;

"O Allah, this is Your city, and al-Masjid al-Haram, and Your inviolable house, and I am Your slave, the son of Your slave and bond-woman. I have come to You with many sins, mistakes, and wicked acts, and this is the station of him who took refuge in You from the fire; so forgive me, verily You are the All-forgiving and Compassionate. O Allah, You have called Your servants to Your inviolable house, and I have come, asking for Your mercy and seeking what pleases You, and You are the Rewarder, so forgive me and have mercy on me, verily You have power over everything").

j5.18   ثم إذا فَرَغَ من الطواف صَلَّى ركعتين سنةَ الطوافِ خلفَ المقام (أفضل) ويُرزِلُ هيئةَ الاضطباع فيهما ويقرأ في الأولى بعدَ الفاتحة ﴿قُلْ يا أيُّها الكافِرُونَ﴾ وفي الثانية ﴿قُلْ هُوَ اللَّهُ أَحَدٌ﴾ .

ثم يَدعو خلفَ المقام (إن صلاهما فيه فإن لم يفعلهما خلفَ المقام ففي الحِجر ففي المسجد ففي الحرم فحيثُ شاء متى شاء ولا يفوتان إلا بموته . ويسن أن يجهر بهما ليلاً ويسر فيما عدا ذلك ويستحب أن يدعوبما روي عن جابر أن النبي ﷺ صلَّى خلفَ المقام ثم قال : «اللهُمَّ هذا بَلَدُكَ والمسجِدُ الحرامُ وبيتُكَ الحرامُ وأنا عَبْدُكَ ابنُ عبدِكَ وابنُ أمَتِكَ أتَيْتُكَ بذنوبٍ كثيرةٍ وخطايا جَمَّةٍ وأعمالٍ سيئةٍ وهذا مقامُ العائذِ بكَ من النارِ فاغْفِرْ لي إنَّكَ أَنْتَ الغفورُ الرحيمُ . اللهُمَّ إنَّكَ دعوتَ عبادَكَ إلى بيتِكَ الحرام وقد جئتُ طالباً رَحْمَتَكَ مُتَبِعاً مرضاتِكَ وأنت مُثِيبٌ فاغْفِرْ لي وارْحَمْني إنَّكَ على كلِّ شيءٍ قديرٌ») .

Then one returns to the Black Stone and touches it (O: kisses it, and bows one's head upon it).

ثُمَّ يَرْجِعُ فَيَسْتَلِمُ الحجرَ الأسودَ (ويقبله ويسجد عليه).

*

j6.0   GOING BETWEEN SAFA AND MARWA (SA'Y)

j6.0   السعي بين الصفا والمروة

j6.1   Then it is recommended to exit through the Safa door of al-Masjid al-Haram if one wishes to go between Safa and Marwa immediately. (O: It is necessary for the validity of going between Safa and Marwa (N: for hajj) prior to the Day of 'Arafa that one do so after one's arrival circumambulation (tawaf al-qudum) (N: though one may not do so on an 'umra first (tamattu') hajj, for which the initial circumambulation and going between Safa and Marwa are part of one's 'umra (dis: j12.2(c))), nor do so after a supererogatory or farewell circumambulation.) One may postpone it until after the going-forth circumambulation (tawaf al-ifada, def: j9.10) (O: which is superior).

j6.1   ثُمَّ يَخْرُجُ مِنْ باب الصفا (ندباً) إنْ أرادَ أنْ يَسْعَى الآنَ (فالشرط في صحة تقديم السعي أن يكون بعد طواف قدوم لا بعد نفل أو وداع). وله تأخيرُهُ إلى بعدَ طوافِ الإفاضةِ (وهو أفضل [من تقديمه لوقوعه بعد الوقوف وبعد طواف مفروض]).

HOW TO GO BETWEEN SAFA AND MARWA

كيفية السعي

j6.2   One begins from Safa. It is recommended:

(1) for men (O: not women) to climb upon Safa the height of a person, so that one can see the Kaaba through the mosque's door, and to face the Kaaba;

(2) to say: "La ilaha illa Llah, Allahu akbar," and "There is no god but Allah alone, without partner. His is the dominion, His the praise, He gives life and causes to die, all good is in His hand, and He has power over everything. There is no god but Allah alone, without partner. He kept His promise, give His slave the victory, and routed the Confederates alone. There is no god but Allah. We worship none but Him, making our religion sincerely for Him, though unbelievers be averse";

j6.2   فَيَبْدَأُ بالصفا. فَيَرْقَى عليها الرجلُ (لا المرأة) قدرَ قامةٍ حتَّى يَرَى البيتَ مِنْ باب المسجدِ فَيَسْتَقْبِلُ القبلةَ ويُهَلِّلُ ويُكَبِّرُ ويقولُ: «لَا إِلَهَ إِلَّا اللهُ وحدَهُ لَا شريكَ لهُ المُلكُ ولهُ الحمدُ يُحْيي ويُميتُ بيـدِهِ الخيرُ وهـوَ على كلّ شيءٍ قديرٌ، لَا إله إِلَّا اللهُ وحدَهُ لَا شريكَ لهُ أنْجَزَ وعْدَهُ ونَصَرَ عبدَهُ وهزَمَ الأحزابَ وحدَهُ لَا إِلَـهَ إِلَّا اللهُ ولَا نَعْبُـدُ إِلَّا إِيَّاهُ مخلصينَ لهُ الدين ولوْ كرهَ الكافرونَ» ثُمَّ

(3) to supplicate for whatever one wishes (O: which is called for here because it is one of the places where prayers are answered. 'Umar (Allah be well pleased with him) used to supplicate lengthily here);

(4) and to repeat (2) and (3) a second and third time.

يَدْعُو بِمَا أَحَبَّ (وإنما طلب الدعاء هنا لأنه من جملة الأمكنة المستجاب فيها الـدعاء وكان عمر يطيل الدعاء هنالك). ثُمَّ يُعِيدُ هذا الذكرَ كُلَّهُ والدعاءَ ثانياً وثالثاً.

j6.3 Then one descends from Safa and walks (O: towards Marwa) at one's normal pace until within three meters of the first green marker suspended from the left wall. Here one runs (N: women walk) until midway to the second green marker, at which midpoint one resumes one's usual pace until one reaches Marwa. One climbs Marwa and says the same invocation as was said at Safa. This is *once*.

Then one descends from Marwa and returns, walking and running at the proper places, until one reaches Safa. This is twice.

At Safa one says the same invocation and supplication, and then goes back to Marwa, which is three times.

One repeats the process until one has completed seven times, finishing at Marwa.

j6.3 ثُمَّ يَنْـزِلُ مِنَ الصَّفـا فَيَمْشِي (متـوجهاً إلى المـروة) على هيئتِهِ حتّى يَبْقَى بينـهُ وبين الميـل الأخضـر المعلق بركن المسجد على يسارِهِ قدرُ ستةِ أذرع فحينئـذٍ يَسْعَى سعياً شديـداً حتى يَتَوَسَّطَ بين الميلين الأخضرين [الـذَيْـنِ أحدُهُمَا في ركن المسجـدِ والآخـرُ متصلٌ بدار العباسِ] فحينئـذٍ يَتْـرُكُ السعيَ الشديدَ ويَمْشِي على هيئتِـهِ حتّى يأتِيَ المـروةَ فيَصْعَدَ عليها ويأتي بالذكر الذي قِيلَ على الصفا والدعاء فهذه مرةٌ. ثُمَّ يَنْـزِلُ فَيَمْشِي في موضـعِ مشيِهِ ويَسْعَى في موضعِ سعيِهِ إلى الصفا فهذِهِ مرتانِ. فَيُعِيدُ الـذكرَ والـدعاءَ ثُمَّ يَذْهَبُ إلى المروة فهذِهِ ثلاثةٌ يُفْعَلُ ذلك حتّى تَكْمُلَ سبعاً يَخْتِمُ بالمروةِ.

THE OBLIGATORY ELEMENTS OF GOING BETWEEN SAFA AND MARWA

واجبات السعي

j6.4 The obligatory elements (O: i.e. conditions for the validity) of going between Safa and Marwa are four:

(a) to begin at Safa. If one begins at Marwa and walks to Safa, this does not count and one's going between them is not considered to have begun until one reaches Safa;

(b) to traverse the entire distance. It would be invalid if one neglected even a single span or less of the distance. One must begin by putting one's heel against the wall at Safa, and finish at

j6.4 وواجبـاتُ السعيِ (أي شروط صحته) أربعـةٌ أحدُهَا أنْ يَبْدَأَ بالصفَا فلوْ بَدَأ بالمـروةِ إلى الصفـا لمْ تُحْسَبْ هذِه المـرةُ وحينئـذٍ (حين إذ بلغ الصفـا) ابْتَدَأ السعيَ، الثاني: قطعُ جميع المسافةِ فلوْ تَرَكَ شبراً أوْ أقـلَّ منْـهُ لمْ يَصِحّ فيجِبُ أنْ يُلصِقَ عقبَهُ بحائطِ الصفا، فإذا انْتَهَى إلى

Marwa by putting the toes against the wall there (N: the course has now been enlarged and paved so that one's going between them is complete without having to reach the walls that are currently there. Rather, between the two sides of the paved track (n: the lanes for going and coming) there is a smaller track for wheelchair patients, and the ends of this smaller track currently represent the minimal distance);

(c) to complete seven times: from Safa to Marwa equals one, from Marwa to Safa is another one, and so on, as mentioned above. If doubts arise while going between them as to how many times it has been—or while circumambulating the Kaaba, how many rounds have been done—then one assumes one has done the least number one is sure of and completes the rest (O: though if the doubts arise after finishing, one need not do anything);

(d) and that going between Safa and Marwa take place after the going-forth circumambulation (tawaf al-ifada, def: j9.10) or else after one's arrival circumambulation, provided that standing at 'Arafa does not intervene between the arrival circumambulation and going between Safa and Marwa (dis: j6.1).

THE SUNNAS OF GOING BETWEEN SAFA
AND MARWA

j6.5   The sunnas of going between Safa and Marwa are those previously mentioned (j6.2–3), to have ablution (wudu), that one's nakedness (def: f5.3) be clothed, and to say while between Safa and Marwa: "My Lord, forgive, show mercy, and overlook that which You know. Verily You are the Most Powerful and Generous. O Allah, our Lord, give us what is good in this world and the next, and protect us from the torment of hell."

If one recites the Koran (A: while going between them) it is better (O: than anything besides the invocations that have reached us in hadith (A: i.e. the above), which are better here than reciting the Koran).

المروة أَلْصَقَ رؤوسَ الأصابعِ بحائطِ المروة [ثُمَّ إذا ابْتَدَأَ الثانيةَ أَلْصَقَ عقبَهُ بحائطِ المروة ورؤوسَ أصابعِهِ بحائطِ الصفا وهكذا أبداً يُلْصِقُ عقبَهُ بما يَذْهبُ منهُ ورؤوسَ أصابعِهِ بما يَذْهَبُ إلَيْهِ]، الثالثُ: استكمالُ سبعِ مراتٍ بحسب ذهابِهِ من الصفا إلى المروة مرةً ومنَ المروة إلى الصفا مرةً وهكـذا كَمَا تَقَدَّمَ فلوْ شَكَّ فيهِ أوْ في أعـدادِ الطوفاتِ أخَذَ بالأقـلِّ وكَمَّلَ (ولو شك بعد الفراغ منها فلا شيء عليه)، الرابعُ: أن يَسْعَى بعدَ طوافِ الإفاضةِ أو القـدوم بشرطِ أنْ لا يَفْصِـلَ بينَهُمَا (أي بين طواف القـدوم والسعي) الوقوفُ بعرفةَ.

سنن السعي

j6.5   وسنتهُ ما تَقَدَّمَ وأنْ يكونَ على طهارةٍ وسِتارةٍ ويقُولُ بينَهُمَا: «ربِّ اغْفِرْ وارْحَمْ وتَجَاوَزْ عمَّا تَعْلَمُ إنكَ أنتَ الأعَزُّ الأكرمُ اللهُمَّ ربَّنَا آتِنَا في الدُّنْيا حَسَنَةً وفي الآخرَةِ حَسَنَةً وقِنَا عذابَ النَّارِ.

ولـوْ قَرَأ القرآنَ فهـو أفضـلُ (من غيـر الـذكر الوارد وأما الذكر الوارد فهو أفضل من قراءة القرآن).

j6.6 It is not recommended to repeat going between Safa and Marwa.	ولا يُنْدَبُ تكرارُ السعيِ . j6.6

*

j7.0   THE WAY TO 'ARAFA

الخروج إلى عرفة   j7.0

j7.1   On 7 Dhul Hijja it is recommended for the imam (A: i.e. the caliph or his representative) to give a sermon after the noon prayer (zuhr) in Mecca (O: at the Kaaba), instructing the pilgrims about the rites they will soon perform, and ordering them to go forth on the following day (O: the morning of the eighth) to Mina.

j7.1   فإذا كَانَ سابعُ ذي الحجة نُدِبَ للإمام أَنْ يَخْطُبَ خطبةً واحدةً بعدَ صلاةِ الظهرِ بمكةَ (عند الكعبة) يُعَلِّمُهُم فيها ما بين أيديهم من المناسك ويأمُرُهُمْ بالخروج إلى منىً من الغدِ (أي في أول النهار يوم الثامن) .

j7.2   The imam goes forth with them after the dawn prayer (subh) on 8 Dhul Hijja.

He prays the noon, midafternoon, sunset, and nightfall prayers with them at Mina, and they spend the night and pray the following dawn prayer there. When the sun rises over the mountain at Mina that is called Thabir, they proceed to 'Arafa.

Spending the night and staying at Mina during this time are a sunna (O: and not part of the hajj rites. If one does not spend the night at Mina at all, or go there, it does not entail any consequences) that many people no longer do, but come to 'Arafa at the end of the night with lighted candles. This lighting of candles is a disgraceful innovation (O: as is their coming there a day or two before 9 Dhul Hijja, a mistake that contravenes the sunna, and through which they miss many other sunnas).

j7.2   ثُمَّ يَخْرُجُ يوم الثامن بعدَ صلاةِ الصبحِ إلى منىً فَيُصَلِّي (الإمام بهم) الظهرَ والعصرَ والمغربَ والعشاءَ بمنىً ويَبيتُ [(أي الإمام ومن معه)] بها ويُصَلِّي الصبحَ . فإذا طَلَعَتِ الشمسُ على جبلٍ بمنىً يُسَمَّى ثبيراً سارَ إلى الموقفِ وهذا المبيتُ بمنىً والإقامةُ بها إلى هذا الوقتِ سنةٌ (ليس من المناسك في شيءٍ فلو لم يبيتوا بها أصلاً ولم يدخلوها فلا شيءَ عليهم) قَدْ تَرَكَهَا كثيرٌ منَ الناسِ فإنَّهُم يأتونَ الموقفَ سَحَراً (آخر الليل) بالشمعِ الموقَدِ وهذا الإيقادُ بدعةٌ قبيحةٌ (ومن البدعة دخولهم قبل يوم التاسعِ بيومٍ أو يومين فهو خطأٌ مخالفٌ للسنة وتفوتهم بسبب ذلك سنن كثيرة) .

j7.3   It is sunna on the way to 'Arafa to say: "O Allah, to You I betake myself, seeking Your noble countenance. Forgive me my sins, make my hajj a pious one, show me mercy, and do not disappoint me"; and to do much of chanting "Labbayk," invocation (dhikr), supplication, and Blessings on the Prophet (Allah bless him and give him peace).

j7.3   ويَقُولُ في مسيرِه : «اللهُمَّ إليكَ توجَّهْتُ ولِوَجْهِكَ الكريمِ [(والوجه الذات)] أَرَدْتُ فاجْعَلْ ذنْبي مغفوراً وحَجِّي مبروراً وارْحَمْني ولا تُخَيِّبْني» . ويُكْثِرُ التلبيةَ والـذكرَ والدعاءَ والصلاة على النبيِّ ﷺ .

j7.4   When the pilgrims reach a place called Namira (N: the site of a large mosque) just before 'Arafa, they stop, and do not immediately enter 'Arafa. When the time for the noon prayer comes, it is sunna for the imam to give two sermons before the prayer, and then they pray, joining the noon and midafternoon prayers together. This too is a sunna that few follow.

*

j8.0   STANDING AT 'ARAFA

j8.1   Then they enter 'Arafa after the sunna bath (ghusl) for standing at 'Arafa, chanting "Labbayk" in lowliness and humility.

THE SUNNAS OF STANDING AT 'ARAFA

j8.2   It is recommended to stand exposed to the sun (O: and not take shade beneath a tent, umbrella, or other, unless there is an excuse such as harm from exposure) facing the direction of prayer (qibla) with one's heart fully attentive and not occupied with this-worldly matters, and to do much of chanting "Labbayk," reciting the Blessings on the Prophet (Allah bless him and give him peace), asking Allah's forgiveness, supplicating, and weeping, for here tears are shed and mistakes annulled.

The greater part of one's words should be: "There is no god but Allah alone, without partner. His is the dominion, His the praise, and He has power over everything." And one should pray for one's family, friends, and all Muslims.

j8.3   It is recommended to stand (O: if possible without hurting anyone) by the large round boulders that lie at base of the hill called Jabal al-Rahma (lit. "Mount of Mercy"). As for climbing Jabal al-Rahma, which lies in the middle of 'Arafa, there is no merit in doing so (O: above the merit of standing in other parts of 'Arafa). Stand-

j7.4   فإذا وَصَلوا إلى موضع يُسَمَّى نمِرَة قبلَ دخولِ عَرَفَةَ نزَلُوا هناكَ ولا يَدْخلُونَ حينئذٍ عرفةَ . فإذا زَالَتِ الشمسُ فالـسـنـةُ أنْ يَخْطُبَ الإمـامُ خطبتَيْن ثم يُصَلّي الظهرَ والعصرَ جمعاً . وهيَ سنةً قلَّ مَنْ يَفْعَلُهَا أيضاً .

j8.0   الوقوف بعرفة

j8.1   ثمَّ يَدْخُـلُونَ عرفةَ بعـدَ أنْ يَغْتَسِلُوا للوقوفِ مُلَبِّينَ خاضِعينَ .

سنن الوقوف

j8.2   ويُـنْـدَبُ أنْ يَقِـفَ بارزاً للشـمسِ (ولا يستظل تحت خيمـةٍ أو تحت شمسيةٍ أو تحت غيرهمـا إلا لعذر بأن يتضررَ إنْ برزَ) مستقبلَ القبلةِ حاضرَ القلبِ فارغـاً مِنَ الـدنْيا ويُكثِرَ التلبيةَ والصلاةَ على النبيِّ والاستغفارَ والـدعاءَ والبكاءَ فثَمَّ تُسْكَبُ العبراتُ وتُقَالُ العثراتُ .

ولْيَكُنْ أكثـرُ قولِـهِ : «لَا إلـهَ إلَّا اللهُ وحدَهُ لَا شَريكَ لَهُ لَهُ الملكُ ولَهُ الحمدُ وهـوَ على كلّ شيءٍ قديرٌ» ولْيَـدْعُ لأهلِهِ وأصحابِهِ ولسائرِ المسلمينَ .

j8.3   ويُـنْـدَبُ أنْ يَقِـفَ عنـدَ الصخراتِ الكبارِ المفروشةِ أسفَلَ جبل الرحمةِ (على حسب الإمكـان بحيث لا يؤذي أحـداً) وأمـا الصعـودُ إلى جبـل الرحمةِ الـذي في وسطِ عرفةَ فلَيْسَ في طلوعِـهِ فضيلـةٌ زائـدةٌ (على الوقوفِ بغيره

ing is valid anywhere in the whole expansive plain, and this bluff is merely a part of it, the same as any other, though standing by the boulders below is better (A: as the Prophet (Allah bless him and give him peace) did so).

It is better to be mounted, and not fasting.

It is best for women to sit at the edge of the crowd (O: not in the middle of it, because men should not randomly mix with women).

THE OBLIGATORY ELEMENTS OF STANDING AT 'ARAFA

j8.4   The obligatory elements of standing at 'Arafa are:

(a) to be present (O: while in ihram) in some portion of 'Arafa;

(b) while sane and in full possession of one's faculties;

(c) at some point between the noon prayer (zuhr) on 9 Dhul Hijja and dawn of the following day. (O: It is sunna to remain at 'Arafa until sunset so as to include both night and day.) Anyone who is present and sane during any of this time, even if merely passing through for a moment, has accomplished the hajj (O: as the Prophet (Allah bless him and give him peace) said,

"The pilgrimage is 'Arafa,"

meaning that most of it is 'Arafa).

Someone who misses standing at 'Arafa or who spends it unconscious has missed the hajj, and he releases himself from ihram by performing the rites of 'umra; that is, by circumambulating, going between Safa and Marwa, and cutting his hair, and he is thus released from his ihram.

Such a person is obliged to make up the hajj and to slaughter as do those who perform an 'umra first (tamattu') hajj (def: j12.6(I)).

*

من بقية أجزاء عرفة] فالوقوفُ صحيحٌ في جميـع تلك الأرض المتسعـة وذلـك الجبل جزءٌ منها هوَ وغيرُهُ سواءٌ والوقوفُ عندَ الصخراتِ أفضلُ .

والأفضلُ أنْ يكونَ راكباً مفطراً .

والأفضلُ للمرأةِ الجلوسُ في حاشيةِ النـاس (لا في وسطهـم لأنـه لا يليق اختلاط الرجال بالنساء) .

واجبات الوقوف بعرفة

j8.4   وواجبـاتُ الـوقـوفِ [(بعرفة ثلاثـة الأول)] حضـورُ جزءٍ منْ عرفـاتٍ (أي حضـور المحرم) عاقـلاً [[(وهذا هو الـواجب الثاني)] ووقتُـهُ مِنَ الزوالِ إلى طلوع الـفجـر الثـاني منْ يومِ النحـر (ويسن المكث في عرفـة إلى الغـروب لأجل الجمع بين الليـل والنهـار) فمَنْ حضَـر بعرفةَ في شيءٍ منْ هذا الوقتِ وهوَ عاقلٌ ولوْ مارّاً في لحظةٍ فقَدْ أدْرَكَ الحج (كما قال ﷺ «الحج عرفة» أي معظمه عرفة) .

ومنْ فاتَهُ ذلك أوْ وقَفَ مغمىً عليْهِ فقَدْ فاتَهُ الحجُّ فيتَحَلَّلُ بفعـلِ عمرةٍ فيطُوفُ ويسْعى ويَحلِقُ وقـدْ حَلَّ من إحرامِهِ . ويَجِبُ عليْهِ القضاءُ ودمُ الفواتِ مثلَ دمِ التمتع .

j9.0   MUZDELIFA, MINA, AND THE GOING-FORTH CIRCUMAMBULATION

j9.0 المزدلفة ومنى وطواف الإفاضة

المزدلفة

MUZDELIFA

j9.1 When the sun sets on 9 Dhul Hijja, those on hajj go forth to Muzdelifa, occupied with invocation (dhikr), chanting "Labbayk," proceeding with tranquility and dignity, not jostling or injuring others (though if the way is clear it is desirable to hurry), and they join the sunset and nightfall prayers in the time of the nightfall prayer ('isha) at Muzdelifa. (O: It is necessary to have made the intention to join the prayers while in the time of the sunset prayer.)

When they reach Muzdelifa, they stop, pray, and spend the night there (O: which is best, and optimal. If one cannot spend the night, then the obligation to be present at Muzdelifa can be met by coming there, even for a brief moment, during the second half of the night, for *spending the night* merely means to be present there during the second half of the night, not actually staying overnight, as opposed to spending the night at Mina (dis: j10.4), which must be for the greater part of the night. If someone misses spending the night at Muzdelifa in the above-mentioned sense, does not return there before dawn, and has no excuse (N: of those given below), then he is obliged to slaughter as one does for an 'umra first (tamattu') hajj (def: j12.6(I)). But if he misses spending the night there for one of the same reasons which justify not spending the night at Mina (def: j10.10), then he is not obliged to slaughter. Other valid excuses for not spending the night at Muzdelifa include:

(1) being occupied with standing at 'Arafa because of not having arrived there until after sunset, since it is more important than Muzdelifa;

(2) or going forth from 'Arafa after the middle of the night to Mecca in order to perform the (A: obligatory) going-forth circumambulation (tawaf al-ifada), missing Muzdelifa because of being occupied with it, since it too is more important than Muzdelifa.

j9.1 فإذا غَرَبَتِ الشمسُ أفَـاضُـوا إلى مزدلفـةَ ذاكـرينَ مُلَبِّيَنَ بسكينـةٍ ووقارٍ بغير مزاحمةٍ وإيذاءٍ [وضرب دوابّ] فمَنْ وَجَدَ فرجةً أَسْـرَعَ وَيُـؤَخِّـرُونَ المغربَ ولْيَجْمَعُـوهَا بمزدلفةَ مَعَ العشاءِ. (ولا بد من نية جمع التأخير في وقت الأولى). فإذا وَصَلُوا نَزَلُـوا وَصَلُّوا وبَـاتُـوا بهَا (وهـو الأفضـل والأكمـل وإلا فالـواجب يحصـل بالحضـور ولـو لحظـة صغيرة في نصف الليل الثاني فالمراد من المبيت بهـا الحضـور فيهـا في نصـف الليـل الثاني لا حقيقـة المبيـت بخـلاف المبيـت الواجب بمنى فهو هناك معظم الليل ومن ترك هذا المبيت المذكور ولم يعد إليها قبل الفجر وكان ذلك لغير عذر من الأعذار المسقطة للمبيت فعليـه دم كدم التمتـع ولا دم على من تركه لعذر من الأعذار [الآتية] في ترك المبيت بمنى ومن العـذر هنـا الاشتغـال بالـوقوف بأن انتهى إلى عرفة ليلة النحر، لاشتغاله بالأهم. ولو أفاض من عرفة إلى مكة لطواف الركن بعد نصف الليل وفات المـبيت لأجـل ذلـك لم يلزمـه شيء لاشتغـالـه بالطواف كاشتغاله بالوقوف).

In either of these two cases, one does not have to slaughter (A: for having missed Muz-delifa)).

In the morning, the pilgrims pray the dawn prayer at the first of its time.

They also pick up seven pebbles, not one stone broken into seven (O: which is offensive), to throw at the stoning site (Ar. jamra, the enclosed round space with a pillar in the middle of it) at Mina, and it is best that these be the size of a broadbean (N: i.e. about the size of a thumbprint).

STOPPING AT AL-MASH‘AR AL-HARAM

j9.2   After the dawn prayer, it is sunna to stop by a hill at the last of Muzdelifa (O: in the direction of Mina) called al-Mash‘ar al-Haram (lit. "the Sanctuary Landmark"), which it is recommended to climb if possible. (A: Others hold that *al-Mash‘ar al-Haram* refers to all of Muzdelifa.) It is desirable to face the direction of prayer (qibla), to do much of chanting "Labbayk," supplication, and invocation (dhikr), and to say, "O Allah, as You have brought us to stand in it and shown us to it, so too, give us success in Your remembrance, as You have guided us. Forgive us, and show us the mercy You have promised us by saying (and Your word is the truth):

" ‘And when you move on from ‘Arafa, remember Allah at al-Mash‘ar al-Haram. Remember Him, for He has guided you though you were astray. And then go forth from where the people go forth, and seek Allah's forgiveness. Truly Allah is Oft-relenting and Most Compassionate' (Koran 2:198–99).

"Our Lord, give us what is good in this world and the next, and keep us from the torment of hell."

j9.3   When the day lightens considerably, the pilgrims proceed to Mina with gravity and tranquility before the sun rises.

وصلُّوا الصبحَ أولَ الوقتِ ويأخُذونَ منها حَصَى الجمـارِ سبـعَ حصياتٍ لقطاً لَا تكسيـراً (أي يكـره تكسيـر الأحجـار) والأفضلُ بقدرِ الباقلَاءِ .

الوقوف على المشعر الحرام

j9.2   ويقِفـونَ بعـدَ الصلاةِ على المشعر الحرام وهوَ جبلٌ صغيرٌ في آخر المـزدلفةِ (منْ جهةِ مِنى) ويُنْدَبُ صعودُهُ إنْ أمْكَنَ [وهناك بناءٌ محدثٌ يَقُولُ العوامُ إنـهُ المشعـرُ الحـرامُ وليَسَ كذَلـكَ] . ويُكْثِـرُونَ التلبيـةَ والدعـاءَ والـذكرَ مستقبلينَ القبلةَ (وكـل هذا على سبيـل الاستحبـاب) ويَقُـولُـونَ : «اللهُمَّ كَمَـا أوقفتَنـا فيـه وأرَيْتَنـا إِيَّاه فوَفِّقْنَا لِذِكْرِكَ كَمَا هَدَيْتَنـا وَاغْفِرْ لَنـا وَارْحَمْنَـا كَمَا وَعَـدْتَنا بقـولِكَ وقولُكَ الحقُّ ﴿فإذَا أفَضْتُمْ من عرفـاتٍ [إلى قولِـهِ غفورٌ رحيمٌ (أي] ﴿فـاذْكُـرُوا اللهَ عنـدَ المشعـرِ الحرام وَاذْكُـرُوه كَمَا هَدَاكُمْ وإِن كُنْتُمْ منْ قبلِه لمِنَ الضالينَ ثمَّ أفيضوا منْ حَيْثُ أفاضَ النـاسُ واسْتَغْفِرُوا اللهَ إنَّ اللهَ غفـورٌ رحيمٌ﴾) ﴿رَبَّنـا آتِنـا في الدنيا حسنةً وفي الآخرةِ حسنةً وقِنا عذابَ النارِ﴾) .

j9.3   فإذا أسْفَرَ جِدّاً سَارُوا إلى مِنىً بوقارٍ وسكينةٍ قبلَ طلوعِ الشمسِ .

RELEASE FROM IHRAM:
THE INITIAL STONING AT MINA

التحلل : الرمي بمنى

j9.4 When the pilgrims reach the valley of Muhassir near Mina, it is sunna to quicken their step for a distance of a stone's throw. Then they take the middle way which leads to (N: one of the three stoning sites called) Jamrat al-'Aqaba. They stone it as they are when they arrive (O: i.e. if mounted, they stone it mounted, and if on foot, they stone it on foot) with the seven stones picked up from Muzdelifa. These may be picked up from anywhere, not necessarily Muzdelifa, though it is offensive to take them from the stoning sites themselves, latrines (O: or other unclean places), or around mosques (O: which is not merely offensive but rather unlawful if they are taken from grounds included in the endowment (waqf, def: k30) for the mosque).

j9.4 فإذا وَصَلوا إلى وادِي محسِّــر وهُـو بقرب منّى أسرَعُوا قدرَ رميةِ حجر. ثُمَّ يَسْلُكُــونَ الطريقَ الـوسطى التي تَرْميهم على جَمْرَة العقبةِ فكَمَـا يأتونَها وهُمْ ركبانٌ يَرْمُونَ جمرة العقبة (فإن كانوا ركبانـاً أتـوها ركبـاناً فيرمونها حال كونهم كذلك وإن أتوهـا مشاة فيرمونها كذلك) بتلكَ الحصيـاتِ السبـعِ الملتقطـةِ مِنَ المـزدلفة، ومِنْ أيِّ مكانِ التُقِطَ الحصَى جازَ مِن المزدلفة وغيرِها لكنْ يُكْرَهُ أخذُها مِنَ المَـرْمَى والحشِ (وهـو بيت الخلاء ومـثله كل مكـان نجس) والمـسجـد (وكراهـة الرمي بحصى المسجد إن لم يكن داخلاً في الوقفية ، وإلا فيحرم الرمي به).

j9.5 When one begins to stone Jamrat al-'Aqaba, one ceases chanting "Labbayk," and does not resume it thereafter (O: as its time is over, which was the period of ihram, and stoning Jamrat al-'Aqaba is the first step to release from ihram).

The (O: optimal) way to stone Jamrat al-'Aqaba is to stand in the middle of the valley after the sun is up so that 'Arafa lies to the right, Mecca to the left, and the stoning-site before one, and to throw the pebbles one by one (O: as throwing them two at a time or all at once counts as having thrown one pebble) with the right hand, saying "Allahu akbar" with each pebble, lifting the arms high enough when throwing (O: if male, though not if female) that the underarm shows, and to actually *throw* the pebbles (O: meaning hard enough to be considered throwing), not merely flick them off the thumb with the forefinger. (n: The minimal conditions for the validity of stoning are given at j10.8.)

j9.5 وكَمَـا [[فالكاف بمعنى عند]] يُشْرَعُ في الرميِ يَقْطَعُ التلبيةَ ولا يُلَبّي بعـدَ ذلـك (لأنـه فات وقتها وهو دوام الإحرام والرمي أول أسباب التحلل) . وصـورة الرمي (الفاضلة) أنْ يقِفَ ببطن الوادي بعد ارتفاع الشمس بحيثُ تَكُونُ عرفةُ عن يمينِهِ ومكةَ عن يسارِه ويَسْتَقْبِلَ الجمرةَ ويَرْمِيَ حصـاةً حصاةً (فإذا رمى ثنتين أو أكثـر دفعـة واحـدة حسبت واحـدة) بيمينِـهِ ويُكَبِّـرُ مَعَ كل حصـاةٍ ويرفَعَ يديهِ حتّى يُرى بياضُ إبطِهِ (ولا ترفع المرأة) ويَرْمِيَ رمياً (أي شديداً أي بحيث يعد رمياً) ولاَ يَنْقُدَ نقداً .

j9.6 When finished stoning (N: Jamrat al-'Aqaba), one slaughters a voluntary sacrifice animal (hady) driven to hajj or one due by reason of

j9.6 فإذا فَرَغَ مِنَ الرميِ ذَبَحَ هَدْياً

hajj (dis: j12.6); or other sacrifice animal (udhiya, def: j14).

إِنْ كَانَ مَعَهُ أَوْ ضَحَّى.

RELEASE FROM IHRAM: CUTTING THE HAIR

التحلل : الحلق

j9.7 Then men have their entire head shaved, which is optimal, though one may confine oneself to (O: removing (A: by any means)) three hairs thereof (O: i.e. from the head, not something else such as the beard or mustache), or may merely shorten it, for which the optimal is to clip a little less than two centimeters from all the hair.

As for women, it is optimal for them to shorten their hair in the latter way (O: it being offensive for a woman to shave her head).

j9.7 ثُمَّ يَحْلِقَ الرجلُ جميعَ رأسِهِ هٰذا هوَ الأفضلُ ولـهُ أنْ يَقْتَصِـرَ على (إزالة) ثلاثِ شعراتٍ منهُ (أي من الرأس لا من غيـرِهِ كاللحيـةِ والشــارب) أوْ تقصيرِهَا والأفضلُ في التقصيرِ قدرُ أنملةٍ مِنْ جميعِ شعرِهِ.
وأمَّا المرأةُ فالأفضلُ لهَا التقصيرُ على هٰذا الوجهِ (فالحلق لها مكروه).

j9.8 While having one's hair cut it is best:

(1) to face the direction of prayer (qibla);

(2) to say "Allahu akbar" (O: that is, "Allahu akbar, Allahu akbar, Allahu akbar, wa lillahi l-hamd");

(3) for the person shaving to start from the right;

(4) and to bury the hair afterwards (O: a measure recommended for any parts separated from a living being).

j9.8 ويكـونُ حالَ الحلقِ مستقبـلَ القبلةِ مُكَبِّـراً (أي قائـلًا الله أكبر الله أكبر الله أكبـر ولله الحمـد) ويبـدَأُ الحالقُ (استحباباً) بشقِّـهِ الأيمن ويَـدْفِنُ شعرَهُ (ندباً كسائر الأجزاء المنفصلة من الحي).

j9.9 Cutting the hair is an integral without which the hajj remains unfinished (O: and which may not be compensated for by merely slaughtering), and a person remains in ihram until it is done. Someone without hair can simply pass a razor over his head (O: which is recommended, not obligatory, because it is a rite whose condition is the existence of a particular site, as is also the case with washing a hand (n: for ablution) when the hand has been amputated (A: i.e. it need not be done if the site does not exist).

After one's hair, has been cut, it is sunna to say, "O Allah, for each hair reckon for me a good deed, annul a bad one, and raise me a degree. For-

j9.9 والحلقُ ركنٌ لَا يَتِمُّ الحجُّ إلَّا بِهِ (ولا يجبر تركه بدم) ويَبْقَى مُحْرِماً إِلَى أَنْ يَأْتِيَ بِهِ، ومَنْ لا شعرَ لهُ أَمَـرَّ الموسى على رأسِهِ (ندباً ولا يجب لأنه قربة تتعلق بمحل فتسقط بفـواتـه كغسـل اليـد إذا قطعت، وسن أَنْ يقـول بعـد فراغـه: «اللهُمَّ آتِني بكـلِّ شَعْرَةٍ حَسَنَةً وَامْحُ عَنِّي بهَا سَيِّئَةً وَارْفَعْ لي بهَا درجةً وَاغْفِرْ لي

give me, those who shave their hair, those who shorten it, and all the Muslims").

وللمُحَلِّقينَ والمُقصِّرينَ ولجميع المسلمينَ).

RELEASE FROM IHRAM: THE GOING-FORTH CIRCUMAMBULATION (TAWAF AL-IFADA)

التحلل : طواف الإفاضة

j9.10   On the same day (A: 10 Dhul Hijja) one enters Mecca and performs the going-forth circumambulation (tawaf al-ifada), which is an integral without which the hajj remains unfinished (O: the author's expression "without which the hajj remains unfinished" meaning that it may not be compensated for by merely slaughtering, though the time it may be performed is anytime thereafter, according to our school. The Hanafis hold it must be done by sunset on 12 Dhul Hijja, and if the sun sets and one has not performed it, this obliges one to slaughter), and one remains in ihram until one does it. Its obligatory features are as described above (dis: j5.16).

After it, one prays two rak'as (O: intending the sunna of circumambulation (def: j5.18)).

j9.10   ثُمَّ يأتي مكةَ في يومِهِ فَيَطُوفُ طوافَ الإفاضةِ وهوَ رُكنٌ لاَ يَتِمُّ الحجُّ إلاَّ بِهِ (وأفاد قوله إنه لا يتم الحج إلا به أنه لا يجبر بدم ووقته موسع إلى ما لا نهاية عندنا بخلاف بقية المذاهب فعند الحنفية يبقى إلى غروب شمس يوم النفر الأول فإذا غربت ولم يطف وجب عليه دم) وَيَبْقَى محرماً إلى أنْ يَأتِي بِهِ وصفتُهُ كَمَا تَقَدَّمَ.

ثُمَّ يُصَلِّي ركعتَيْن (وينوي بهما مصليهما سنة الطواف).

j9.11   Then, if one has already gone between Safa and Marwa after the arrival circumambulation (dis: j6.1), one does not repeat it, though if one has not yet done it, one must do so, since going between Safa and Marwa is also an integral without which the hajj is unfinished, and one remains in ihram (O: legally, regarding one's relations with women (dis: j9.13)) until it is performed.

j9.11   ثُمَّ إنْ كانَ سَعَـى مَعَ طوافِ القُدومِ لمْ يُعِدْهُ وإلاَّ سَعَى (وجوباً لأنَّ السـعيَ أيضـاً ركنٌ لا يَتِمُّ الحجُّ إلاَّ بِهِ وَيَبْقَى محرماً (حكماً بالنسبة لما يتعلق بالنساء) إلى أنْ يَأتِيَ بِهِ.

RELEASE FROM IHRAM: GENERAL PROVISIONS

التحلل : أحكامه العامة

j9.12   The best order in which to perform:

(1) stoning Jamrat al-'Aqaba;

(2) cutting the hair;

(3) and the going-forth circumambulation (tawaf al-ifada);

j9.12   [وَاعْلَمْ أنَّ] الـرميَ، والحلقَ وطوافَ الإفـاضةِ (كل منها يسن فعله في هذا اليـوم و) الأفضـلُ (في ترتيبها) تقديمُ الـرميِ ثُمَّ الحلقُ ثُمَّ الطوافُ (والمـراد

is (1), (2), and (3) (O: and the sunna is to do all three on this day), though it is valid to do them in some other order.

The time for these three begins at the middle of the night (A: between sunset of 9 Dhul Hijja and dawn of the tenth) on 'Eid al-Adha (O: though it is best for the stoning to take place after sunrise). The (O: preferred) time for stoning Jamrat al-'Aqaba ends at the end of the day of the 'Eid (O: at sunset. As for the permissible time, it lasts until the end of the three days after the 'Eid. The best time to stone on 'Eid al-Adha finishes at noon. Thus, the stoning has three times: the best, the preferred, and the merely permissible), while the time for cutting one's hair and the going-forth circumambulation lasts indefinitely, even if years.

j9.13   The release from ihram in hajj is in two stages, partial (lit. "first") and full ("second").

Partial release from ihram occurs when any two of the three rites of stoning, cutting the hair, and the going-forth circumambulation are performed, whether cutting the hair and stoning, cutting the hair and circumambulation, or stoning and circumambulation. Doing any two of them accomplishes partial release from ihram, rendering permissible all the things that were made unlawful by ihram (def: j3.5) except those relating to women, such as sexual intercourse, getting married, or touching with desire.

Full release from ihram occurs when all three rites have been performed, and it renders permissible everything made unlawful by ihram (O: though one still has to stone at the three stoning sites and stay overnight at Mina during the days following the 'Eid (Ayam al-Tashriq)).

*

j10.0 ENCAMPMENT AND STONING AT MINA ON THE DAYS AFTER 'EID

j10.1   When finished with the going-forth circumambulation (tawaf al-ifada) and going between Safa and Marwa (O: i.e. doing the latter if

بالرمي رمي جمرة العقبة) فلو أُتِيَ بها على غير هذا الترتيب فَقَدَّمَ وأَخَّرَ جَازَ.

ويَدْخُلُ وقتُ الثلاثة بنصف الليل مِنْ ليلةِ النحرِ (والأفضلُ أنْ يكـون الرمي واقعاً بعد طلوع الشمس) ويَخْرُجُ وقتُ رمي جمرةِ العقبةِ (أي وقت الاختيـار) بخـروجِ يوم النحرِ (بغروب شمسها. وأمـا وقتُ الجوازِ فيمتـد إلى آخر أيـام التشريق. ووقت الفضيلة لرمي يوم النحر ينتهي بالـزوال. فيكـون لرميـه ثلاث أوقات: وقت فضيلة ووقت اختيار ووقت جواز) ويَبْقَـى وقتُ الحلقِ والطـوافِ متراخياً ولو إلى سنينَ.

j9.13   وللحـجِّ تحلُّلانِ أولُ وثانٍ. فالأولُ يَحْصُلُ باثنينِ مِنْ هذه الثلاثةِ أيُّها كانَ، إمّـا حلقٌ ورميٌ أو حلقٌ وطـوافٌ أو رميٌ وطوافٌ فمتَى فَعَلَ اثنينِ منها حَصَلَ التحللُ الأولُ ويَحِـلُّ به جميـعُ ما حَرُمَ عليـه ما عَدَا النسـاءَ مِنْ وطءٍ وعقدِ نكاحٍ ومباشـرةٍ فإذا فَعَلَ الثـالثَ حَلَّ لهُ كلُّ مَا حَرَّمَهُ الإحرامُ (ويجب عليه أن يأتي بما بقي عليه من الرمي لأيام التشريق والمبيت).

j10.0 المبيت والرمي بمنى لأيام التشريق

j10.1   فإذا فَرَغَ مِنْ طواف الإفـاضـة والسـعي (إن لم يكن سعى بعـد طواف

one had not previously performed it after the arrival circumambulation (dis: j6.1)), one is obliged to return to Mina (O: to stay overnight there and stone on the days following the 'Eid (Ayam al-Tashriq). It is desirable to arrive before noon to perform the noon prayer there as the Prophet did (Allah bless him and give him peace)), and one spends the night there.

One picks up twenty-one pebbles from Mina on the days after the 'Eid (the first of which is the second day of the 'Eid), taking care to shun the three places mentioned above (dis: j9.4(end)).

القـدوم) رَجَعَ إلى مِنى (وجوباً لأجل المبيت بها والـرمي لأيـام التشـريق ويستحب كون الرجوع قبل الظهر بحيث يدرك الصلاة فيها اقتداء به ﷺ) وَبَات بِها.

ويُلْتَقـطُ في أيـام التشـريق وهـوَ ثاني العيـد إحـدى وعشـرينَ حصـاةً مِنْ مِنى ويَتَجَنَّبُ المواضِعَ الثلاثةَ المتقدمةَ.

j10.2   After the time for the noon prayer has come (O: on 11 Dhul Hijja, the first day after the 'Eid) one stones with the pebbles before performing the noon prayer.

j10.2   فإذَا زَالَتِ الشمسُ (أي شمس يوم الحـادي عشـر الـذي هو أول أيـام التشريق) رَمى بها قبلَ الصلاةِ.

(N: It is well to mention some rulings about stoning that enable one to avoid the crowding at Mina on a contemporary hajj. The time for stoning on each of the three days that follow the 'Eid (Ayam al-Tashriq) begins at *noon of that day* and ends at *sunset on the third day* after the 'Eid. This means that one may postpone all of one's stoning until the afternoon of the third day, having remained at Mina until then. But in such a case, the correct order is still obligatory: one must begin by stoning with the intention of performing it for the first day, starting at the first stoning site (Jamrat al-Kubra), then the second site (Jamrat al-Wusta), and then the third (Jamrat al-'Aqaba). Then one stones with the intention of performing it for the second day, the first stoning site first, then the second, then the third. And then one stones for the third day, observing the same order.)

THE PROPER SEQUENCE FOR STONING

ترتيب رمي الجمار

j10.3   The first site one stones (O: called Jamrat al-Kubra) is the one closest to al-Khayf mosque. One (A: optimally) walks up to it, keeping it on one's left and facing the direction of prayer (qibla), stones it pebble by pebble as mentioned above (j9.5), and turns from the direction of prayer to avoid others' pebbles, after which one puts the stoning site behind one and again turns to the direction of prayer, to supplicate and invoke Allah humbly and imploringly for as much time as it takes to recite al-Baqara (Koran 2) (N: about an hour).

One then proceeds to the second site (O: called Jamrat al-Wusta), repeats the stoning procedure, and when finished, supplicates (O: and

j10.3   فيَـرْمِي الـجمـرةَ الأولى (وتسمى الجمـرة الكبرى) وهيَ التي تَلي مسجدَ الخيف فَيَصْعَدُ إليهَا ويَجْعَلُهَا عن يسارِه ويَسْتَقْبِلُ القِبلةَ ويَرْمِيهَا بسبعِ حصياتٍ حصـاةً حصـاةً كَمَـا تَقـدَّمَ ثمَّ يَنْحَرِفُ قليلًا [(أي عن استقبال القِبلة ويمشي قليلًا وهذا معنى التقدم)] بحيثُ لا يَنَالُهُ الحصى الذي يَرْمِيهِ الناسُ وتَبْقَى الجمـرةُ خلفَهُ ويَسْتَقْبِـلُ القِبلةَ ويَـدْعُـو ويَذْكُرُ بخشوعٍ وتضرعٍ بقدرِ سورةِ البقرةِ.

ثمَّ يأتي الجمـرةَ الثـانيـةَ (وتسمى الجمـرة الـوسطى) فَيَفْعَلُ كَمَـا فَعَـلَ في

343

invokes Allah Most High) for as long as it takes to recite al-Baqara.

Then one goes to the third site, which is Jamrat al-'Aqaba that was previously stoned with seven pebbles on 'Eid al-Adha, and stones it as one did at that time (dis: j9.5), facing it with the direction of prayer (qibla) to the left, though when finished, one does not stand there.

الأولى فإذا فَرَغ منهَا وَقَفَ ودَعا (وذكر الله تعالى) قدرَ سورة البقرة .

ثمَّ يَأْتي الجمــرةَ الثـالثـةَ وهيَ جمرةُ العقبة التي رَمَاهَا يومَ النحر فَيَرْميهَا بسبع كَمَا فَعَلَ يومَ النحر فَيَسْتَقْبِلُهَا والقبلةَ عَن يسارِهِ فإذا فَرَغ لا يَقِفُ عندَهَا .

THE SECOND DAY AFTER THE 'EID

اليوم الثاني من أيام التشريق

j10.4 One is obliged to spend the night at Mina (A: that evening, after sunset on 11 Dhul Hijja).

The following day, the second day after the 'Eid (A: i.e. 12 Dhul Hijja), one picks up twenty-one pebbles, and after the noon prayer's time has come, one stones the three stoning sites as described above, seven pebbles at each site. It is not permissible to stone for each of the days after the 'Eid until after the noon prayer's time arrives.

The correct sequence of stoning the sites is obligatory: the one closest to al-Khayf mosque first, the middle one second, and Jamrat al-'Aqaba third.

j10.4   وَيبيتُ بمنَى .

ثمَّ يَلْتَقِطُ مِنَ الغــدِ وهـوَ ثاني أيــام التشريق إحدى وعشرينَ حصاةً فَيَرْمي بهَا الجمراتِ الثـلاثَ كلَّ جمرةٍ بسبع بعدَ الزوالِ كَمَا تَقَدَّمَ .

ولا يَجُـــوزُ رَمْيُ الـجمــارِ في أيــام التشريق إلاّ بعدَ الزوالِ .

ويَجِبُ الـتـرتيبُ فَيَرْمي ما يَلي مسجدَ الخيف أولاً والوسطَى ثانياً والعقبةَ ثالثاً .

j10.5 It is recommended to take a bath (ghusl) each day for stoning.

j10.5   ويُنْدَبُ الغسلُ كلَّ يومٍ للرمي .

THE PERMISSIBILITY OF LEAVING MINA ON THE SECOND DAY

جواز النفر في ثاني التشريق

j10.6 After stoning on the second day after the 'Eid, it is recommended for the imam to give a sermon informing people about the permissibility of leaving early (A: on the second day rather than the third) (O: which is permissible provided:

(a) that one's departure takes place after the noon prayer's time has come;

(b) after having stoned the three stoning sites;

(c) that one's departure is from Mina itself,

j10.6   فإذا رَمَى في ثانِي التشـــريق نُدِبَ للإمــام أنْ يَخْطُبَ خطبــةً يُعَلِّمُهُمْ فيهـا جوازُ النفـر (وهو أن يكون واقعاً بعد الـزوال وأن يكون بعـد الرمي وأن يكون النفر من منى فلا يصح النفر من غيرها

as it is not permissible to leave directly from Jamrat al-'Aqaba, in view of the position that it is not part of Mina;

(d) that one intends leaving while within the boundries of Mina;

(e) and that one leaves before sunset).

Then the imam bids them farewell.

كمن ينفـر من جمـرة العقبـة على القـول بأنها ليست منى وأن ينويه منها وأن يكون قبل الغروب) وَيُوَدِّعُهُمْ.

j10.7   One then has a choice between leaving early on the second day after the 'Eid, or waiting (A: until having stoned on the third day). If one wishes to leave early, one may do so, provided the departure from Mina occurs before sunset. If the sun sets and one is still at Mina, it is not permissible to leave early, and one is obliged to spend the night there and stone the sites the next day.

If one does not wish to leave early, one stays overnight at Mina, picking up twenty-one pebbles and stoning the sites on the following day after the time of the noon prayer has begun, as previously mentioned.

j10.7   ثُمَّ يَتَخَيَّـرُ بينَ أنْ يَتَعَمَّـلَ في يومين وبينَ أنْ يَتَأَخَّـرَ فإذا أرادَ التعجيـلَ فَلْيَنْفِـرْ بشـرطِ أنْ يَرْتَحِلَ منْ منىً قبـلَ الغـروب فإنْ غَرَبَتْ وهـوَ بمنىً امْتَنَـعَ التعجيـلُ ولَزِمَهُ المبيتُ ورميُ الغدِ. وإنْ لمْ يُردِ التعجيـلَ بَاتَ بمنىً والْتَقَطَ إحدَى وعشـرينَ حصاةً يَرْميهـا مِنَ الغـدِ بعـدَ الزوالِ كَمَا تَقَدَّمَ.

CONDITIONS FOR THE VALIDITY OF STONING

شروط صحة الرمي

j10.8   (O: Having mentioned the conditions for stoning in various rulings above, it is well to enumerate all seven together:

(a) that seven pebbles be used;

(b) that they be thrown one by one;

(c) that one's action may be termed *throwing,* not merely putting the pebbles into the throwing place;

(d) that what is thrown be some form of stone;

(e) that it be done with the hand, as a bow or foot would be inadequate;

(f) that one aim at the throwing place;

j10.8   (تنبيـه في حاصـل شـروط الرمـي إجمالاً بعـد ذكرها مفصلة مشتتة وهي سبعـة: الأول كون الـرمي بسبـع حصيـات، والثـاني كونها واحدة واحدة، والثالث أن يسمى رمياً بحيث يصدق عليه مسمى الـرمي لا بوضـع الحصـاة في المرمى، والرابع كون المرمي حجراً بأي نوع كان من أنـواعـه فكل ما يصدق عليه اسم الحجـر يصـح الـرمي به، والخامس كونـه باليـد لا بغيـرهـا فلا يكفي بقـوس ورجـل، والسـادس قصـد المـرمى وهـو المكـان الـذي يجتمـع الحصى فيـه،

345

(g) that one be certain that the pebble reaches it, even if it falls out again, for if one doubts that the stone reached it, then that stone does not count;

(the above seven conditions hold for both 'Eid al-Adha (dis: j9.5) and for the days following the 'Eid, though the days following the 'Eid require two additional conditions:)

(h) that the stoning be done after the time for the noon prayer arrives;

(i) and that one stone the three sites in the proper sequence (dis: j10.3).)

j10.9   Then one (O: who has (n: remained at Mina and) stoned on the third day after the 'Eid) leaves (O: after stoning. None of the conditions for leaving early (def: j10.6) are necessary to leave at this point).

VALID EXCUSES FOR NOT SPENDING THE NIGHT AT MINA

j10.10 (O: If there is an acceptable excuse for not spending the night at Mina, then not doing so does not entail any consequences. Excuses include:

(1) having property one fears to lose were one to stay overnight;

(2) fearing for one's person or the funds with one;

(3) having a sick person with one who requires care;

(4) having an illness that makes spending the night a hardship;

(5) or a similar excuse,

People in such circumstances do not have to spend the night, and may leave on the second day after the 'Eid, even after sunset.

والسابع تحقق إصابته بالحجر وإن لم يبق فيه كأن تدحرج وخرج منه فلو شك في إصابته لم يحسب ولا يعتد به . فهذه سبعة شروط تكون عامة لرمي يوم النحر ولرمي أيام التشريق، ويزاد عليه شرطان لرمي أيام التشريق : [الأول] أن يكون الـرمـي واقعـاً بعـد الـزوال و[الثاني] أن يكون مرتباً وتقدم معنى الترتيب) .

j10.9   ثمَّ (بعـد رمي يوم الثالث) يَنْفِرُ (ولا يشتـرط لهـذا النفـر الثـاني شيء مما يشترط للأول) .

أعذار لترك المبيت

j10.10 (وتـرك المبيت لعـذر لا شيء فيه كمن له مال يخـاف ضياعه لو اشتغل بالمبيت أو يخاف على نفسه أو مال معه أو له مريض يحتـاج إلى تعهـده أو يكـون به مرض يشق معـه المبيت أو نحـو ذلـك فالصحيح أنه يجوز لهم ترك المبيت ولهم أن ينفروا بعـد الغروب ولا شيء عليهم

These excuses, which permit one to not spend the night at Mina, likewise permit not spending the night at Muzdelifa, in connection with which some other excuses have been previously mentioned (dis: j9.1(1–2)).)

فهـذه الأعذار المذكورة كما تكون عـذراً لتـرك المبيت بمنى تكـون عذراً لتـرك المبيت بمزدلفة وتقدم بعضها هناك).

j10.11　It is recommended (N: after leaving Mina) to spend the night at al-Muhassab, which is by the mountain near the cemetery of Mecca, one's hajj now being finished.

j10.11　ويُنْـدَبُ أنْ يَنْـزِلَ المُحَصَّبَ وهوَ عندَ الجبل الذي عندَ مقابر مكةَ وقَدْ فَرَغَ مِنْ حجِّهِ.

*

j11.0　THE FAREWELL CIRCUMAMBULATION AND FINAL MEASURES

j11.0　طواف الوداع والرحيل

j11.1　If one wishes to perform the 'umra, one may do so (O: i.e. enter ihram for it) from any point outside of the Sacred Precinct (Haram), as mentioned below in the description of 'umra (def: j12).

j11.1　وإذا أرادَ الاعتمـارَ اعْتَمَرَ (أي أحرم بها) منَ الحلِّ كَمَا سَيَأْتِي في صفةِ العمرةِ.

THE FAREWELL CIRCUMBULATION

طواف الوداع

j11.2　When one wants to return home, one comes to Mecca and performs the farewell circumambulation (tawaf al-wada') (O: as is obligatory. It is disobedience to Allah to leave without the farewell circumambulation, and one must return to Mecca to perform it if still within 81 km./ 50 mi. of it. If farther than this, one is not obliged to return, but must slaughter (def: j12.6(I)) (N: i.e. if one goes by the position that the farewell circumambulation is obligatory, though slaughtering is sunna if one goes by the position (A: the weaker position in the Shafi'i school) that the farewell circumambulation is merely sunna). The integrals and conditions of the farewell circumambulation are the same as the obligatory circumambulation (def: j5.16).

The farewell circumambulation is not only for those performing hajj or 'umra, but is required

j11.2　فإذَا أرادَ الـرجـوعَ إلى بلدِهِ [(والحـال أنـه بمنى أو في المحصب)] أتَى مكـةَ وطَـافَ للوداع (فلو خرج بلا وداع عصى ولـزمه العود ما لم يبلغ مسافة القصر من مكة فإن بلغها لم يجب العود بعـد ذلـك ولكن تستقـر عليه الفدية (ح: على القول بأنه واجب وتسن على القول بأنه سنة)، ومـا وَجَبَ وشُرطَ في طواف الفـرض يجب في طواف الوداع، وطواف الوداع لا يختص بمن حج واعتمر بل يؤمر

347

from (A: i.e. obligatory for) anyone leaving Mecca a considerable distance, no matter whether intending to return or not).

به كل من أراد فراق مكة إلى مسافة بعيدة سواء نوى أنه يرجع إلى مكة أم لا) .

j11.3   After the farewell circumambulation, one prays two rak‘as (O: a sunna in our school) and stands at the place between the Black Stone and the door of the Kaaba, and supplicates: "O Allah, the house is Your house, the servant Your servant and son of Your two servants. You have carried me on a creature You have made submissive to me, bringing me to Your city and showing me Your grace that I might fulfill Your rites. If You are pleased with me then be the more so, and if not, then bless me now before my residence and the place where I am visited grow far from Your house. Now is the time I depart if You permit me, who seek none but You and no other than Your house, and am not averse to You or Your house. O Allah, give me good health in body and protect me in my religion. Make my affairs turn out well and give me the sustenance of obedience to You as long as You let me live. Give me the best of this world and the next, for truly, You have power over everything." One blesses the Prophet (Allah bless him and give him peace), and then walks away normally (O: turning one's back on the Kaaba) without backing away from it (O: while facing it, as many people do, which is offensive because it is a reprehensible innovation (bid‘a, def: w29.3)).

j11.3   ثُمَّ رَكَعَ ركعتين (وهي عـندنا سنة) وَوَقَفَ في الملتــزم بينَ الحجـر الأسـود والباب وَقَـالَ : «اللهمَّ إنَّ البيت بيتُكَ والعبدَ عبدُكَ وابنُ عبدَيْكَ حَمَلْتَنِي على ما سَخَّـرْتَ لي مِن خَلْقِـكَ حتّـى صَيَّـرْتَني في بلادكَ وبَلَّغتِني بنعمتِكَ حتّى أَعَنْتَني على قضـاءِ منـاسِكَـكَ فإنْ كنتَ رَضِـيْتَ عني فازْدَدْ عني رضـاً وإلّا فَمُنَّ الآنَ قبـلَ أنْ تَنْـأى عن بيتِكَ داري ويَبْعُدَ عنـكَ وَلَا عَنْ بيتِـكَ، اللهُمَّ فأصْحِبْنِي العـافيــةَ في بَدَني والعصمــةَ في ديني وأحْسِنْ مُنْقَلَبِي وَارْزُقْني العمـلَ بطاعَتِكَ مَا أَبْقَيْتَني وَاجْمَـعْ لي خيـرَي الـدنيـا والآخرةِ إنّـكَ على كلّ شيءٍ قديرٌ» . ثُمَّ يُصَـلّي على النبيّ ﷺ . ثُمَّ يَمضي على عادتِـه (من جعل ظهرَه للبيت) ولا يَرْجِعُ القهقرى (وجهه للبيت كما يفعله كثير من الناس فإنه مكروه لأنه بدعة) .

j11.4   One then immediately prepares for departure. If one stops to stand (O: lengthily), or becomes involved in something unconnected with travel (O: like shopping, paying a debt, visiting a friend or sick person, and so forth), then one's farewell circumambulation is invalid (A: though such things do not nullify it in the Hanafi school) and it is obligatory to repeat it. But if one's activity concerns travelling, such as making one's baggage fast or buying travel provisions and the like (O: such as a rope with which to tie up one's baggage) then it is permissible.

j11.4   ثُمَّ يُعَجِّـلُ الرحيلَ . فإنْ وَقَفَ بعـدَ ذلكَ (أي وقـوفاً طويلاً) أَوْ تَشاغَلَ بشيءٍ لَا تَعَلُّقَ لهُ بالرحيل (كشراء متاع أو قضاء دين أو زيارة صديق أو عيادة مريض أو نحـو ذلك) لَمْ يُعْتَدَّ بطوافِه عن الوداع وتَلْزَمُهُ إعادتُه . فإنْ تَعَلَّقَ بالرحيل كشدِّ رَحْـلٍ وشراءِ زادٍ ونحوِه (أي الزاد كشراء حبل يشد به الرحل) لَمْ يَضُرَّ .

j11.5   A woman in her monthly period may depart without a farewell circumambulation, and

j11.5   وللحائض أنْ تَنْفِـرَ بلا وداع

need not slaughter in expiation (O: though it is sunna for her to come to the door of the mosque and say the supplication mentioned above (j11.3)).

RECOMMENDED MEASURES FOR THOSE STAYING IN MECCA

j11.6   It is recommended to do much of:

(1) performing 'umra (O: the whole time one is in Mecca, especially in Ramadan);

(2) looking at the Kaaba (O: as it is said that Allah Most High sends down one hundred and twenty mercies day and night upon the Noble House, sixty for those circumambulating, forty for those praying there, and twenty for those looking at it);

(3) drinking the water of the Well of Zamzam for whatever intention one wishes, religious or this-worldly (O: as the Prophet (Allah bless him and give him peace) said,

"The water of Zamzam is for whatever it is drunk for."

It is sunna to face the Kaaba while drinking, to breathe three times, and say "al-Hamdu lillah" and "Bismillah" each time one drinks), drinking one's fill of it;

(4) and visiting the noble places of Mecca (O: which are many, such as the birthplace of the Prophet (Allah bless him and give him peace) and that of 'Ali (Allah be well pleased with him).

j11.7   It is unlawful to take the slightest bit of the earth of the Sacred Precinct or its stones, or take cups or jugs made from the clay of the Sacred Precinct of Medina.

*

ولا دم عليْهَا (لكن يسن لها أن تأتي على باب المسجد وتقول الدعاء المتقدم) .

ما يندب للمقيم بمكة

j11.6   وَيُنْـدَبُ أَنْ [يَـدْخُلَ البيتَ حافياً إنْ لَمْ يُؤذ أحـداً بمـزاحمةٍ ونحوِهَا فإذا دَخَلَ مَشى تلقاءَ وجهِهِ حتى يَبْقَى بينَهُ وبينَ الجدارِ المقابِل للبابِ ثلاثةُ أذرع فهناكَ يُصَلِّي فهوَ مصلَّى النبيِّ ﷺ وَاَ يُكْثِرَ مِنَ الاعتمارِ (مدة إقامته بمكة وخصوصاً في رمضـان) والنظرِ إلى البيتِ (ويقال إن الله تعـالى ينـزل على البيت الشريف في كل يوم وليلة مائـة وعشـرين رحمة ستون للطائفين وأربعـون للمصلين وعشـرون للناظرين) وشُرْب ماءِ زمزمَ لِمَا أَحَبَّ مِنْ أمـر الـدين والـدنْيَا (فقد قال عليه الصلاة والسـلام : «ماء زمزم لما شرب له» ويسن في شربه استقبال الكعبة وأن يتنفس ثلاثاً وفي كل مرة يحمـد الله ويسمـل عنـد الـشـرب) وأنْ يَـتَـضَـلَّع منـهُ وأنْ يَزُورَ المـواضـع الشـريفـة بمكـة (وهي كثيـرة كمولد النبي ﷺ ومولد علي رضي الله عنه) .

j11.7   وَيَحْـرُمُ أخـذُ شيءٍ مِنْ [طيب الكعبـةِ و] تراب الحـرـم وأحجـارِهِ ولا يَسْتَصْحِبُ شيئـاً مِنَ الأكـوزة والأبـاريق المعمولة مِنْ حَرَم المدينة أيضاً.

j12.0 THE OBLIGATORY FEATURES OF HAJJ AND 'UMRA

j12.0 واجبات الحج والعمرة

A DESCRIPTION OF 'UMRA

صفة العمرة

j12.1   The 'umra consists of entering ihram as one does for hajj (def: j3) (O: resembling the hajj in the obligatoriness of the intention when one enters ihram, in the sunna of bathing (ghusl) for it, and in the necessity of divesting oneself of sewn clothing before or after the intention). If one is a Meccan (N: or a temporary resident (dis: j2.2)), one must go to (n: enter ihram from at least as far as) the nearest place outside of the Sacred Precinct. If one is from outside (O: meaning a stranger travelling towards Mecca), then one enters ihram at the ihram site (O: which one passes, meaning the hajj ihram sites (def: j2.1)), as previously mentioned. All of the things unlawful while in ihram for hajj (def: j3.5) are unlawful while in ihram for 'umra.

j12.1   صفةُ العمرةِ أنْ يُحرِمَ بها كَما يُحْرِمُ بالحجِّ (مشبه بإحرام الحج في وجوب النيَّة عند الإحرام وفي سنيَّة الاغتسال لها وفي وجوب التجرد بعد النية أو قبلِها). فإنْ كانَ مكيّاً فمِنْ أدنَى الحلِّ. وإنْ كانَ آفاقياً (أي غريباً متوجهاً إلى مكة) فمنَ الميقاتِ (التي يمر عليها وهي مواقيت الحج) كَما تَقَدَّمَ. ويَحْرُمُ بإحرامِها جميعُ ما يَحْرُمُ بإحرام الحجِّ.

Then one enters Mecca and performs the circumambulation (def: j5.16) of 'umra, though the arrival circumambulation (tawaf al-qudum) is not called for by Sacred Law (O: at all, since one is performing an obligatory circumambulation).

ثمَّ يَدْخُلَ مكةَ فيَطُوفَ طوافَ العمرةِ ولا يُشْرَعُ لَها طوافُ قدوم (من أصله لدخول طوافها المفروض).

One then goes between Safa and Marwa (j6), and finally shaves the head or shortens the hair (def: j9.7) (O: the former being preferable for men and the latter for women). When this has been done, one is released from the ihram of 'umra.

ثمَّ يَسْعَى.
ثمَّ يَحْلِقَ رأسَهُ أوْ يُقَصِّرَ (والأول أفضل للرجل والثاني أفضل للمرأة) وَحينئذ قدْ حَلَّ مِنْها.

THE INTEGRALS OF HAJJ AND 'UMRA

أركان الحج والعمرة

j12.2   The integrals of 'umra are:

(a) ihram (def: j3);

(b) circumambulation (def: j5.16);

(c) going between Safa and Marwa (def: j6.4);

(d) shaving or shortening the hair (def: j9.7);

j12.2   فأركانُها إحرامٌ وطوافٌ وسعيٌ وحلقٌ (وترتيب وبه تصير الأركان

(O: and performing them in the order given, which is a fifth integral).

خمسة) .

j12.3   The integrals of hajj are these four (n: (a), (b), (c), and (d) above) plus standing at 'Arafa (def: j8.4).

j12.3   وأركانُ الحجِّ هذِهِ الأربعةُ والـوقـوفُ وواجبـاتُـهُ كونُ الإحـرامِ منَ الميقـاتِ ورميُ الجمار والمبيتُ بمزدلفة

The hajj's other *requisites* (wajibat, dis: c2.1(A:)) are:

وليالي مِنّى وطوافُ الوداعِ .
وما عَدَا ذلكَ سننٌ .

(a) that one enter ihram at the proper site (def: j2.1–2);

(b) stoning the stoning sites at Mina (def: j9.4, j10);

(c) staying the night at Muzdelifa (def: j9.1) (N: another position is that this is sunna and not obligatory);

(d) staying the nights following the 'Eid at Mina (def: j10.1,4,7);

(e) and the farewell circumambulation (def: j11.2).

Everything besides the above is sunna.

THE NONPERFORMANCE OF AN OBLIGATORY FEATURE OF HAJJ OR 'UMRA

ترك ركن أو واجب

j12.4   Someone who does not perform an integral (N: of hajj or 'umra) remains in ihram until he performs it.

j12.4   فإنْ تَرَكَ ركنـاً لمْ يَحـلَّ مِنْ إحرامِهِ حتّى يَأتيَ بِه ومَنْ تَرَكَ واجباً لَزِمَهُ

Someone who does not perform some other obligatory feature of them must slaughter in expiation (def: j12.6(I)) (O: if he does not return and perform it before its time is finished, as in such cases as:

دمُ (إن لم يعـد إليـه ويفعله كأن يعود إلى الميقـات قبـل التلبس بالطواف وإلا فلا ينفعـه العـود فإنـه قد استقر الدم عليه فلا يسقـط عنه بالعود إلى الميقات حينئذ أي حين إذ شرع في الطواف ؛ وكترك المبيت

(1) returning to enter ihram at the proper site before one starts circumambulating (dis: j2.5), though if one returns after having begun circumambulating, it does not lift the obligation to slaughter;

(2) not spending the night at Muzdelifa

(j9.1), which necessitates slaughtering if one does not return before sunrise, though to do so after sunrise does not lift the obligation to slaughter;

(3) or not spending most of the night at Mina, if one does not return to it before most of the time has passed, though if one does (n: return while most of it remains), then one need not slaughter.

And similarly for the other requisites). Someone who does not perform a sunna is not obliged to do anything.

BEING PREVENTED BY OTHERS FROM COMPLETING THE INTEGRALS OF HAJJ OR 'UMRA AFTER HAVING ENTERED IHRAM

بمـزدلفـة فإنـه يجب عليـه الدم ما لم يعد إليهـا قبـل طلوع الشمس وإلا فلا ينفعـه العـود، وكتـرك المبيت بمنى معظم الليل أي أكثـره ما لم يعد إليهـا قبل مضي قبل أكثر الليل وإلا سقـط عنـه الدم وغير ذلك من الواجبات) ومَنْ تَرَكَ سنةً لَمْ يَلْزَمْهُ شيءٌ.

الإحصار

j12.5   Someone prevented by an enemy (O: non-Muslim or Muslim) from entering Mecca (O: and fulfilling the integrals (A: of hajj or 'umra, including being barred from performing the obligatory circumambulation (tawaf al-ifada) or going between Safa and Marwa) when there is no alternative route, releases himself from ihram by intending release from it, shaving his head, and slaughtering a sacrifice animal at the place he has been prevented, if an animal is available. If not (O: such as when unable to find an animal at all, or finding one for more than the going price of similar animals at that place and time), one gives the animal's value in food (A: wheat) (O: as charity to the poor and those short of money in the Sacred Precinct (N: or place one is prevented)); or if unable (O: to give food), one fasts a single day for each 0.51 liters of food (A: wheat) that would have been given had the latter been done (O: fasting the days wherever one wishes. When fasting is the only option possible, one is immediately released from ihram after shaving one's head with the intention of releasing oneself).

If such a hajj or 'umra was to have been supererogatory, one is not obliged to make it up.

j12.5   ومَنْ أَحْصَـرَهُ عدوٌ (والعـدو المذكور يشمل المسلم والكافر) عنْ مكةَ (وعن إتمـام الأركـان) ولمْ يَكُنْ لَهُ طريقٌ آخَرُ تَحَلَّلَ بأنْ يَنْويَ التحللَ ويَحْلِقَ رأسَهُ ويُـريقَ دمـاً مكانَهُ إنْ وَجَدَهُ. وإلَّا (إن لم يجـده أصـلًا أو وجـده لكن زاد ثمنه عن ثمن المثـل) أَخْـرَجَ طعامـاً بقيمتِـه (ويتصدق به على فقراء الحرم ومساكينه) وإنْ عَجَـزَ (عن إخراج الطعام) صَامَ لكلِّ مدٍّ يوماً (في أي مكـان شاء. وإذا انتقـل إلى الصوم تحلل حالاً بما تقدم من الحلق مع النية) ولا قضاءَ إنْ كان تطوعاً.

| A FULL SUMMARY OF THE EXPIATIONS CONNECTED WITH HAJJ AND 'UMRA | محصل دماء الحج والعمرة |

j12.6   (n: Muhammad 'Abdullah Jurdani distinguishes between four categories of expiations relating to hajj and 'umra.

(I)   The first category consists of *alternatives in a fixed precedence order and predetemined amount* (dam tartib wa taqdir), meaning that one must either slaughter a *shah* (def: h2.5) meeting sacrifice specifications (def: j14.2), distribut- ing its meat to the poor and those short of money (def: h8.11) in the Sacred Pre- cinct; or if unable to slaughter (N: from lack of money (def: j1.17(2)) while on the hajj, even if one has enough money back home), then one must fast three days during the hajj and seven more at home, making ten days. (N: If this expiation is for something that should have been performed after standing at 'Arafa (n: (4), (5), (6), or (9) below), the three days "during the hajj" may be fasted after one's release from ihram while still in Mecca, or if one fails to do so while there (A: as is obligatory), they become a makeup fast that must be performed before the other seven fasted at home (A: by an interval equal to the days of one's journey home).)

There are nine things which necessitate this type of expiation:

(1) performing an 'umra first (tamattu') hajj (def: j1.15,17);

(2) performing hajj and 'umra simultaneously (qiran, def: j1.16,17);

(3) not standing at 'Arafa (def: j8.4);

(4) to miss stoning (def: j10.8) at the stoning sites of Mina on the three days after the 'Eid, the time for which ends at sunset on the third day (dis: j10.2(N:)) if one does not leave early (def: j10.6);

(5) to miss all three nights at Mina after the 'Eid (def: j10.1,4,7), though if one only misses a single night, one distributes 0.51 liters of wheat to the poor of the Sacred Precinct, and if two nights, then double this amount;

(6) to miss spending the night at Muzdelifa (def: j9.1, second par.);

(7) not entering ihram at the proper site (dis: j2.5);

(8) breaking one's vow (def: j18.5);

(9) or not performing the farewell circumambulation (tawaf al-wada', def: j11.2).

(II)   The second category consists of expiations in which one is *free to choose one of three predetermined alternatives* (dam takhyir wa taqdir), namely: to slaughter and distribute a *shah* as described above (I); to fast three days, even if unconsecutive, wherever one wishes; or to give 1.015 liters of wheat to each of six of the poor or those short of money at the Sacred Precinct.

There are eight things which necessitate this type of expiation:

(1) removal of three hairs (dis: j3.8) at one time and place, meaning that the interval between removing each is not considered *long* (dis: f4.5), and one has remained at the same place, though if their removal does not occur at a single time and place, one must pay 0.51 liters of wheat to the poor or fast one day for each hair, even if their number exceeds three;

(2) trimming three nails at one time and place, with the same rules and restrictions as just mentioned;

(3) men wearing sewn garments or covering their head (dis: j3.6), or women covering their faces (dis: j3.24);

(4) using oil (def: j3.7(1));

(5) using scent (j3.7);

(6) sexual foreplay (n: other than intercourse) (dis: j3.13);

(7) having sexual intercourse a second time after having spoiled one's hajj (dis: j3.14) by an initial sexual intercourse;

(8) or having sexual intercourse between partial and full release (def: j9.13) from ihram.

(III)   The third category consists of expiations in a *fixed precedence order of alternatives involving estimate-based substitutes* (dam tartib wa ta'dil). It is necessitated by two things.

(1) The first is being prevented by another from completing all the integrals of the hajj or 'umra (def: j12.5), in which case one must release oneself from ihram by slaughtering and distributing a *shah* as described above (I); or if unable to slaughter, one estimates its value, buys food for that amount, and distributes it to the poor of the Sacred Precinct (N: or place one is prevented); or if unable to give food, one fasts one day for each 0.51 liters of wheat that would have been given if one had been able to.

(2) The second is having spoiled one's hajj or 'umra by sexual intercourse (def: j3.14), in which case one must slaughter a camel, or if unable to, one must perform the alternative one is capable of, of those mentioned at j3.15.

(IV)   The fourth category involves *choosing between alternatives consisting of estimate-based substitutes* (dam takhyir wa ta'dil). It is necessitated by two things.

(1) The first is killing a game animal while in ihram, where if there is a domestic animal of similar value (lit. "like"), one has a choice between the alternatives mentioned at j3.22, though if there is not, then those mentioned at j3.23.

(2) The second is destroying a tree of the Sacred Precinct, where, if it is large in relation to other trees of its kind, one slaughters and distributes a cow, and if small, one slaughters a sheep. In either case, one has a choice between slaughtering it and distributing its meat to the poor of the Sacred Precinct, estimating its cost and buying wheat to distribute to the poor of the Sacred Precinct, or fasting a day for each 0.51 liters of wheat that would have been bought had the latter been done.

(*Mufid 'awam al-Muslimin ma yajibu 'alayhim min ahkam al-din* (y67), 230–38))

(N: Throughout the above, whenever one is obliged to slaughter an animal, it is permissible to commission (wakala, def: k17) another person to do so by means of the written contracts readily available at a modern hajj, simply paying an amount of money and signing the agreement. They then slaughter for one in the early morning of the 'Eid and distribute the meat to deserving recipients. Secondly, giving *food* or *wheat* to the poor, wherever it is mentioned in connection with expiations, means giving them the type of food that is valid for the zakat of 'Eid al-Fitr (def: h7.6), and the remarks made in that section about the Hanafi school permitting other than wheat apply equally here.) (n: In the Hanafi school, slaughtering must take place in the Sacred Precinct, though one may distribute both the meat and other expiations anywhere (*al-Lubab fi sharh al-Kitab* (y88), 1.212, 1.224).)

*

j13.0   VISITING THE TOMB OF THE PROPHET (ALLAH BLESS HIM AND GIVE HIM PEACE)

j13.0   زيارة قبر النبي ﷺ

j13.1   It is recommended when one has finished the hajj to visit the tomb of the Prophet (Allah bless him and give him peace) (n: in Medina). (O: One should enter his mosque with the right foot first, as in any mosque, and say the well-known supplication: "In the name of Allah, praise be to Allah. O Allah, bless our liegelord Muhammad, his folk and his Companions, and give them peace. O Allah, open unto me the gates of Your mercy.")

j13.1   يُنْدَبُ إذا فَرَغَ مِنْ حَجِّهِ زيارة قبر النبيِّ ﷺ (فإذا دخل المسجد فليقدم رجله اليمنى كمـا في سائـر المسـاجـد وحينئذ فليقـل الـدعـاء المشهـور وهو: «بـسم الله والحمـدُ لله اللهُمّ صلّ على سـيـدنا محمدٍ وعلى آلهِ وأصحابه وسلّم، اللهُمَّ افْتَحْ لي أبوابَ رَحْمَتِك»).

كيفية زيارة القبر الشريف

j13.2 It is recommended to pray two rak'as to greet his mosque, and then approach the noble and honored tomb and stand at the head of it with one's back to the direction of prayer (qibla). One bows one's head and summons to mind reverent awe and humility, then greets the Prophet (Allah bless him and give him peace) and blesses him in a normal voice (O: saying: "Peace be upon you, O Messenger of Allah. Peace be upon you, O Prophet of Allah. Peace be upon you, O Chosen One of Allah. Peace be upon you, O Best of Allah's Creation. Peace be upon you, O Beloved of Allah''), after which one supplicates Allah for whatever one wishes. Then one steps half a meter to the right to greet Abu Bakr, and again to the right to greet 'Umar (Allah be well pleased with them). Then it is recommended to return to one's original place and do much of supplicating Allah, turning to Allah through the Prophet (tawassul, def: w40) (O: concerning one's aims and goals, since he is the greatest intermediary, in intercession and other things), and invoking blessings upon him (Allah bless him and give him peace), after which one supplicates beside the pulpit (minbar) and in the Rawda (N: which is the space designated by the white pillars between the chamber containing the noble tomb and the pulpit).

j13.3 It is unlawful to circumambulate the tomb.

It is offensive to nudge the wall around the tomb with one's back or front, to kiss it, or touch it (O: with one's hand. Proper conduct here is to stand back from it as one would if present during his life (Allah bless him and give him peace). This is what is right, and what scholars have said and are agreed upon. One should not be deceived by what some common people do in their ignorance of proper manners, for it is reprehensible innovation (bid'a, def: w29.3)).

One of the most disgraceful innovations is the eating of dates in the Rawda.

j13.2 فَيُصَلّي تحيـةَ مسجدِه ثمَّ يأتي القبرَ الشريفَ المكـرَّمَ فَيَسْتَـدْبِـرُ القبلةَ (ويَجْعَـلُ قنديـلَ القبلةِ الذي عندَ رأسِ القبر على رأسِهِ] وَيُطْرِقُ رأسَهُ وَيَسْتَحْضِرُ الهيبـة والخشـوع ثمَّ يُسَلِّمُ وُيُصَلّي على النبيِّ ﷺ بصوتٍ متوسطٍ (وصيغة السلام هي قول المسلِم : «السـلامُ عليـكَ يا رسولَ الله ، السلامُ عليـكَ يا نبيَّ الله ، السلامُ عليكَ يا خِيرَةَ الله ، السلامُ عليكَ يا خَيْرَ خلقِ الله السـلامُ عليكَ يا حبيبَ الله») وَيَدْعو بِمَا أَحَبَّ ثمَّ يَتَأَخَّرُ إلى جهةِ يمينِـه قدرَ ذراعٍ فَيُسَلِّمُ على أبي بَكرٍ ثمَّ يَتَـأَخَّـرُ قدرَ ذراعٍ فَيُسَلِّمُ على عُمَـرَ رَضِيَ اللهُ عنهُمَا .

ثمَّ يَرْجِـعُ إلى موقفِـه الأول ويُكْثِـرُ الـدعـاءَ والتوسـلَ (بـه ﷺ في مطلوبِـه ومقصـودِه لأنـه الـوسيلة العظمى في الشفاعة وغيرها) والصلاة علَيْهِ .

ثمَّ يَدْعُو عندَ المنبر وفي الروضةِ .

j13.3 ولاَ يَجُوزُ الطوافُ بالقبرِ .

ويُكْـرَهُ إلصاقُ الظهـر والبطنِ بِه ولا يُقَبِّلُهُ (أي الجـدار) ولا يَسْتَلِمُـهُ (بيـدِه والأدب أن يبعد منه كما يبعد منه لو حضر في حياتِهِ ﷺ هذا هو الصواب وهو الذي قاله العلماء وأطبقوا عليـه ولا تغتر بما يفعله العـوام لجهلِهم بالأدب فهـذا من البـدع المحدثـة) ومِن أقبح البدع أكلُ التمرِ في الروضةِ .

j13.4   It is recommended to visit al-Baqi' (O: the cemetery of Medina. It is desirable to go to it every day, for buried there are the wives of the Prophet (Allah bless him and give him peace), some of his children, his father's brother 'Abbas, our liegelord 'Uthman ibn 'Affan the successor of the Messenger of Allah (Allah bless him and give him peace), a number of his Companions (Sahaba), and Imam Malik, founder of the Maliki school of jurisprudence, the bliss and benefaction of Allah be upon them all).

j13.5   When one desires to travel, one bids farewell to the mosque by praying two rak'as, and to the noble tomb with a visit and supplication. And Allah knows best.

*

j14.0   SACRIFICES ON 'EID AL-ADHA
(O: *Sacrifices* are the livestock slaughtered in worship of Allah Most High between 'Eid al-Adha and the last of the three days that follow it. They are a general hospitality from Allah to believers (A: to whom the meat is distributed. It is unlawful to give any of it to non-Muslims).)

j14.1   'Eid al-Adha sacrifices are a confirmed sunna (def: c4.1) (N: which is considered obligatory in the Hanifi school) (O: being sunna for those able to slaughter, though uncalled-for from the poor person who is unable).
It is recommended for someone who intends to sacrifice not to cut his hair or trim his nails on 10 Dhul Hijja until he slaughters (O: these being offensive until he does). The time for slaughtering begins when it is long enough after sunrise to have performed the 'Eid prayer (def: f19) with its two sermons (A: i.e. about forty minutes) (O: even if one does not attend it) and it ends at (A: sunset on) the last of the three days following the 'Eid.

j13.4   ويَـزورُ البقيـعَ (وهـو مقابـر المـدينـة فيستحب أن يخـرج إليه كل يوم لأن فيه نساء رسول الله ﷺ وبعض أولاده وفيهـا العبـاس عم رسول الله ﷺ وسيدنا عثمـان بن عفان خليفة رسـول الله ﷺ وجملة من الصحابة وفيها قبر الإمام مالك صاحب المذهب رضوان الله عليهم أجمعين).

j13.5   فإذا أرادَ الرحيلَ ودّعَ المسجدَ بركعتين والقبرَ الكريمَ بالزيارة والدعاءِ. واللهُ أعلمُ.

j14.0   بابُ الأضحية
(وهي ما يذبح من النعم تقرباً إلى الله تعـالى من يوم عيـد النحر إلى آخر أيـام التشـريق والأضحيـة ضيافة عامة من الله تعالى للمؤمنين).

j14.1   هيَ سنةٌ مؤكدةٌ [[وطلبها على سبيل الندب] مقيد بكون الفاعل لها قادراً فلا تطلب من الفقير العاجز عنها). يُنْدَبُ لمنْ أرادَهـا أن لا يَحْلِقَ شعَـرهُ ولا يُقَلِّمَ ظفـرَهُ في عشـرِ ذي الحجـةِ (فتستمـر الكراهة) حتّى يُضَحّيَ. ويَدْخُلُ وقتُها إذا طَلَعَتِ الشمسُ ومضى قدرُ صلاة العيـد والخطبتين (وإن لم يفعـل ذلك) ويَخْرُجُ بخروجِ أيامِ التشريقِ [وهي ثلاثةٌ بعدَ العيدِ].

SACRIFICE ANIMAL SPECIFICATIONS	ما يجزىء في الأضحية

j14.2 Only camels, cattle, sheep, or goats may be slaughtered. At the youngest, camels must be over five full years, cattle and goats over two full years, and sheep over one full year.

A single camel or cow fulfills the sunna for seven (A: men and their families), though a *shah* (def: h2.5) only fulfills it for one. It is superior to slaughter a single *shah* than to have a share in slaughtering a camel.

The best animal to sacrifice is a camel, then a cow, then a sheep, and then a goat. The best kind of *shah* (h2.5) to slaughter is white, then tawny-colored, then black and white, and then a black one.

It is a necessary condition that a sacrifice animal be free of defects that diminish (A: the quality of) its meat. It is invalid to slaughter:

(1) a lame animal (O: that has an obvious walking problem that hinders its going to pasture and thus weakens it);

(2) a blind or one-eyed animal (O: whose defect is manifest, as this diminishes its ability to graze);

(3) a sick animal (O: whose infirmity is plain);

(though if these defects are slight, the animal will suffice. It is likewise invalid to sacrifice an animal that is:)

(4) deranged by malnutrition or insane;

(5) mangy or scabrous (O: even when it is not obvious);

(6) with an ear that has been cut off or a piece of it separated, even if not much (O: or one born without an ear);

(7) or missing a considerable part of the haunch or similar meat-bearing portion (O: though not if it is a slight amount).

j14.2 ولا تَجُوزُ إلّا بإبلٍ أوْ بقرٍ أوْ غنمٍ . وأقلُّ سنهِ في الإبلِ خمسُ سنينَ ودَخَـلَ في السـادسـةِ وفي البقـرِ والمعـزِ سنتانِ ودَخَلَت في الثالثةِ وفي الضأنِ سنةً ودَخَلَ في الثانيةِ .

وتُجـزىء البدنةُ عنْ سبعةٍ والبقرةُ عنْ سبعةٍ ولا تُجزىء شاةً إلّا عنْ واحدٍ وشاةً أفضـلُ منْ شركـةٍ في بدنةٍ وأفضلُها البدنةُ ثمَّ البقرةُ ثمَّ الضأنُ ثمَّ المعزُ .

وأفضلُهَـا (أي الشـاةِ) البيضـاءُ ثمَّ الصفراءُ ثمَّ البلقاءُ ثمَّ السوداءُ .

وتُشْتَـرَطُ سلامةُ الأضحيةِ عنِ العيوبِ التي تَنْقِصُ اللحمَ .

فلا تُجْزىء العرجاءُ (أي البيّن عرجها بأن يمنعهـا من ذهابهـا إلى المـرعى فتضعف بسبب ذلك) والعوراءُ (أي البيّن عورهـا لأنـه يضـعفهـا عن المـرعى) والمـريضةُ (أي البيّن مرضها) . فإنْ قَلَّت هذهِ الأشياءُ جَازَ. ولا تُجْـزىء العجفـاءُ [(وهي ذاهبةُ المـخّ من شدة هزالهـا)] والمجنـونةُ والجـربـاءُ (وإن لم يكن بيناً) والـتي قُطِـعَ بعض أذنـهَـا وأبـينَ (أي انفصل) وإنْ قَلَ (ولا مخلوقة بلا أذن) أوْ قطعةٌ منْ فخـذِهَا ونحوهِ إنْ كَانَتْ كبيرةً (بخـلاف الفلقـة اليسيرة منـه) وتُجْزىءُ

It is permissible to sacrifice an animal with a slit in its ear (O: a measure for identification that does not diminish the meat) or one with part or all of a horn broken off.

مشروطةُ الأذَنِ (لأنه وسم لا ينقص لحماً) ومكسورةُ كلِّ القرنِ أوْ بعضِهِ .

HAVING ANOTHER SLAUGHTER FOR ONE

التوكيل في الذبح

j14.3   It is best to slaughter (def: j17.4) the animal oneself (O: if one can slaughter well. If not, then it is obligatory to have someone who can slaughter properly do it for one). If unable to slaughter well, it is recommended to be present when it is done.

j14.3   والأفضلُ أنْ يَذْبَحَ بنفسِهِ (إن أحسن الـذبح فإن لم يحسنه فليوكل من يحسن الـذبح وجوباً) . فإنْ لمْ يُحْسِنْ فَلْيَحْضُرْ (ندباً) .

THE INTENTION

النية

j14.4   The intention to sacrifice must be made at the time of slaughtering. (O: It suffices the person who is having another slaughter for him to make the intention when he authorizes the other to do so.)

j14.4   ويجبُ أنْ يَنْوِيَ عندَ الذبح (والنية تكفي من الموكل عند التوكيل) .

DISTRIBUTING THE MEAT

توزيع اللحم

j14.5   It is recommended that a third of the animal sacrificed be eaten, a third be given away (O: even if to wealthy Muslims), and a third be given as charity (O: raw, not cooked).

It is obligatory to give away some of the (O: raw) meat as charity, even if it is not much (O: it suffices to give it to one Muslim), and the hide is given in charity or used at home.

It is not permissible to sell the hide or meat (O: all of the above applying to sunna or voluntary sacrifices). It is not permissible for a person who has vowed (def: j18) a sacrifice to eat any of the animal slaughtered.

j14.5   ويُنْـدَبُ أنْ يأْكُـلَ الـثـلـثَ ويُهْدِي الثلثَ (ولو لأغنِياء المسلمِين) ويَتَصَدَّقَ بالثلثِ (أي نيئاً لا مطبوخاً) . ويجبُ التصدُّقُ بشيءٍ (أي نيئاً أيضاً وإنْ قلَّ (ويكفِي تمليكهُ لمسلم واحدٍ والجلدُ يَتَصَدَّقُ بهِ أوْ يَنْتَفِعُ بهِ في البيتِ . ولا يَجُـوزُ بَيْـعُـهُ ولاَ بيـعُ شيءٍ منَ اللحمِ (هـذا كلّه في الأضحيةِ المندوبة أو المتطـوع بهـا) ولاَ يُجـوزُ لهُ الأكلُ منَ الأضحيةِ المنذورة .

*

j15.0 SACRIFICE FOR A NEWBORN ('AQIQA) AND NAME-GIVING

(O: Lexically, 'aqiqa means the hair on a baby's head at birth. In Sacred Law, it means the animal sacrificed when the baby's hair is cut, which is a confirmed sunna (def: c4.1).)

j15.0 العقيقة

(وهي لغة الشعر الذي على رأس الولد حين ولادته وشرعـاً ما يذبح عنـد حلق شعره وهي سنة مؤكدة).

SUNNAS AFTER BIRTH

ما يندب بعد الولادة

j15.1   It is recommended for anyone to whom a child is born to shave its hair on the seventh day thereafter (O: meaning any newborn, whether male or female; a baby girl should also have her hair shaved) and give away in charity gold or silver equal to the weight of the hair.

It is also recommended (N: when the baby is first born) to give the call to prayer (adhan, def: f3.6) in its right ear and the call to commence (iqama) in its left.

j15.1   يُنْـدَبُ لِمَنْ وُلِـدَ لهُ ولدٌ أَنْ يَحْلِقَ رأْسَهُ يومَ السابعِ (والـولد معناه المـولـود ولـو أُنثى فإنه يسن حلق راسها) ويَتَصدّقَ بوزنِ شعره ذهباً أَوْ فضةً .

وأَنْ يُؤذّنَ في أَذنِهِ اليمنَى ويُقيمَ في اليسرَى .

THE SACRIFICE

الذبح عن المولود

j15.2   If the baby is male, it is recommended to slaughter two *shahs* (def: h2.5) that meet 'Eid Sacrifice specifications (def: j14.2), while if the baby is female, it is recommended to slaughter one.

(O: The person called-upon to slaughter for a newborn is the one obliged to support the child (dis: m12.1).)

After slaughtering, the *shah* is cooked (O: as at any feast) in sweet sauce, but none of its bones are broken (A: it is cut at the joints), and it is recommended to distribute the meat to the poor.

j15.2   ثمَّ إنْ كانَ غلامـاً ذُبـحَ عنـهُ شاتانِ تُجزِيانِ في الأضحيةِ ، وإنْ كانَتْ جاريـةً فشـاةً (والمخـاطب بالـذبح عن المولود هو من تلزمه نفقته) .

وتُطْبَـخُ (العقيقـة كسائر الولائم) بحلوٍ ولاَ يُكْسَـرُ العظمُ ويُفـرّقُ (نـدبـاً لحمها) على الفقراءِ .

NAME-GIVING

تسمية المولود

j15.3   It is sunna to give the child a good name such as *Muhammad* or *'Abd al-Rahman*. (O: It is desirable to name a child even if it dies before being named.) (A: It is sunna for a new Muslim to take a good name like the above, or one of the names of the prophets (def: u3.5) (Allah bless them and give them peace).)

j15.3   ويُسَمّيَهُ باسمٍ حسنٍ كمحمدٍ وعبـدِ الـرحمن (ولو ماتَ قبـل التسميـة استحب تسميته).

j16.0   FOODS

(O: This section is an explanation of what is lawful (halal) and unlawful (haram), the knowledge of which is among the most important concerns of the religion, since knowing it is personally obligatory for every Muslim.)

AVOIDING DOUBTFUL FOODS

j16.1   (n: The following hadith and its commentary have been added here by the translator.)

Anas (Allah be well pleased with him) relates that the Prophet (Allah bless him and give him peace) found a date in his path, and said,

"But for fear that it was charity, I would have eaten it."

(*Riyad al-salihin* (y107), 277)

(Muhammad ibn 'Allan Bakri:) The hadith shows that when a person doubts that something is permissible, he should not do it. The question arises, Is refraining from it in such a case obligatory, or recommended?—to which our Imams explicitly reply that it is the latter, because a thing is initially assumed to be permissible and fundamentally not blameworthy, as long as some prior reason for considering it unlawful is not known about it that one doubts has been removed. For example, when one doubts that one of the conditions for valid slaughtering (def: j17.2–4) has been met, conditions which make (N: a particular piece of meat) lawful, the assumption is that it remains unlawful (N: since initially the animal was alive, a state in which it is unlawful to eat, while it only becomes lawful by a specific procedure, i.e. Islamic slaughtering), so that the meat does not become lawful except through certainty (A: that it has been slaughtered. The case of meats is exceptional in this, since most other foods are initially permissible, and one assumes they remain so unless one is certain something has occurred which has made them unlawful).

In cases of doubt, only likely possibilities are taken into consideration, since it appears probable (n: in the above hadith) that dates for charity

j16.0   الأطعمة

(أي بيـان مـا يحـل منهـا ومـا يحرم. ومعـرفتهمـا من آكـد مهمـات الـدين لأن معرفة الحلال والحرام فرض عين).

ترك الشبهات

j16.1   (ت: قد أضـاف الـمتـرجم الحديث التالي وشرحه هنا لعموم فائدته).

ـ وعـن أنس رضي الله عنـه أنَّ النبيَّ ﷺ، وَجَدَ تمرةً في الطريق، فقال: «لَوْلاَ أنِّي أَخافُ أنْ تكونَ منَ الصدقةِ لأَكَلْتُها» [متفقٌ عليه] (حـديث ٥٨٧ من كتـاب رياض الصالحين للنووي).

(محمـد بن علان البكـري:) [...] يؤخـذ من الحـديث أنه ينبغي للإنسان إذا شك في إبـاحـة شيء ألا يفعله لكن هل التـرك حينئـذ واجب أو منـدوب؟ [وتقدم فيه الخلاف في حديث النعمان]. وكلام أئمتنا مصرح بالثاني لأن الأصل الإباحة والبـراءة الأصليـة مـا لم تعلم جهة محرمة قبل ذلك في شيء بعينه ويشك في زوالها كأن يشـك في شرط من شروط الـذبح المبيح هل وجـد أم لا لأن الأصـل حينئذ بقاء الحرمة فلا يحل إلا بيقين. ثم لا يراعى من الاحتمال في ذلك إلا القريب لأن الظاهر أن تمر الصدقة كان موجوداً إذ

were present at the time. As for remote possibilities, taking them into consideration only leads to a blameworthy extremism and departure from how the early Muslims were, for the Prophet (Allah bless him and give him peace) was given some cheese and a cloak (A: by members of a non-Muslim Arab tribe) and he ate the one and wore the other without considering whether they might have mixed the former with pork, or whether the wool came from a slaughtered or unslaughtered animal. Were one to take such possibilities into consideration, one would not find anything lawful on the face of the earth. This is why our colleagues say, "Complete certainty that something is lawful is only conceivable about rainwater falling from the sky into one's hand" (*Dalil al-falihin li turuq Riyad al-salihin* (y25), 5.37–38).

ANIMALS LAWFUL AND UNLAWFUL TO EAT

j16.2   It is permissible to eat the oryx, zebra, hyena, fox, rabbit, porcupine, daman (n: a Syrian rock badger), deer, ostrich, or horse.

j16.3   It is unlawful to eat:

(1)   (N: any form of pork products);

(2)   cats or disgusting small animals that creep or walk on the ground such as ants, flies, and the like (O: *disgusting* being used here to exclude inoffensive ones such as the jerboa, locust, and hedgehog, which are small creeping animals, but are recognized as wholesome, and are pure);

(3)   predatory animals that prey with fangs or tusks, such as the lion, lynx, leopard, wolf, bear, simians, and so forth (O: including the elephant and weasel);

(4)   those which hunt with talons, such as the falcon, hawk, kite, or crow, except for the barnyard crow, which may be eaten;

(5)   or the offspring of an animal permissible

ذاك .

أما الاحتمال البعيد فتؤدي مراعاته إلى التنطع المذموم والخروج عما عرف من أحوال السلف فقد أتِيَ ﷺ بجبنة وجبة فأكل ولبس ولم ينظر لاحتمال مخالطة الخنزير لهم ولا إلى صوفها من مذبوحة أو ميتة . ولو نظر أحد للاحتمال المذكور لم يجد حلالاً على وجه الأرض . ومن ثم قال أصحابنا لا يتصور الحلال بيقين إلا في ماء المطر النازل من السماء المتلقى باليد [محرر من دليل الفالحين لطرق رياض الصالحين : ٥/ ٣٧ ـ ٣٨].

ما يحل وما يحرم من الحيوان

j16.2   يُؤْكَلُ بقرُ الوحشِ وحمارُ الوحشِ والضبعُ والثعلبُ والأرنبُ والقنفذُ والوبرُ والظبيُّ [والضبُّ] والنعامةُ والخيلُ .

j16.3   ولا يُؤْكَلُ السنورُ ولا الحشراتُ المستخبِثةُ كالنمل والذباب ونحوهما (ووصف الحشرات بالاستخباث يخرج ما ليس خبيثاً منها كاليربوع [والضب] والجراد فإنها داخلة في مسماها مع أنها مستطابة فهي طاهرة) .

ولا ما يَتَقَوّىٰ (أي يعدو) بنابه كالأسد والفهدِ والنمرِ والذئبِ والدبِّ والقردِ ونحوِها (كالفيل والنمس) .

وما يَصْطَادُ بالمخلبِ كالصقرِ والشاهين والحدأة والغرابِ إلا غرابَ الزرع فيُؤْكَلُ .

وما تولَّدَ مِنْ مأكولٍ وغير مأكولٍ لاَ

to eat and one not permissible to eat, such as a mule (O: which is a cross between one eaten, the horse, and one not eaten, the donkey).

يُؤكَلُ كالبغل (فهو متولد من مأكول وهو الفرس وغير مأكول وهو الحمار الأهلي) [واليعفور].

j16.4   It is permissible to eat any aquatic game (sayd al-bahr) except frogs and crocodiles.

j16.4   ويُؤكَلُ كلُّ صيدِ البحرِ إلّا الضفدعَ والتمساحَ

OTHER SUBSTANCES UNLAWFUL TO EAT

ما يحرُم أكلُه

j16.5   It is unlawful to eat anything harmful, such as poison, glass, or earth. (A: If something has been proven harmful, it is unlawful to consume, while if suspected to be harmful, it is offensive to.) (n: w41 discusses cigarette smoking.)

j16.5   وكـلُّ ما ضَرَّ أكـلُهُ كالسـمِّ والزجاجِ والترابِ [(لا يحل أكله)].

j16.6   It is unlawful to eat anything impure (najasa, def: e14.1) (O: whether impure in itself, or because of being affected with something impure, as is the case with (N: befouled) milk, vinegar, or honey).
    It is also unlawful to eat substances which are pure, but generally considered repulsive, such as saliva or sperm.

j16.6   أوْ كانَ نجسـاً (نجاسة عين أو كانت نجاسـة عارضـة كاللبن والخل والعسلِ (ح: إذا تنجست))، أوْ طاهراً مستقذراً كالبصاقِ والمنيّ، لا يَحلُّ أكلُهُ.

j16.7   If forced to eat from a unslaughtered dead animal (O: out of fear of losing one's life or fear of an illness growing worse), then one may eat enough (O: the necessary minimum) to avert destruction (O: meaning enough to keep life from ending. One may not eat to repletion from a dead animal unless one believes that confining oneself to the survival minimum entails dangerous consequences, in which case it is obligatory to take the edge off one's hunger). If circumstances force one to choose between a dead animal and some permissible food belonging to someone else (O: who is not present), one is obliged to eat of the dead animal.

j16.7   فإن اضْطَـرَّ إلى أكـل الميتـةِ (بأن خاف على نفسـه الهـلاك أو زيادة المرض) أكَلَ منهَا ما (أي شيئاً قليلاً) يَسُدُّ رمقَهُ (أي يقي روحه من الهلاك ولا يشبع من أكل الميتـة إلا إن خاف من اقتصاره على سد الـرمق محذوراً فإنه يشبع وجوباً بأن يأكـل حتى يكسر سورة الجـوع أي شدته وحدته).
    فإنْ وَجَدَ ميتـةً وطعامَ الغير (أي طعاماً مسلوكـاً لغيره وصاحبه غـائب) [أو ميتةً وصيداً وهوَ مُحْرِم] أكَلَ الميتةَ (وجوباً في الصورة الأولى والثانية).

*

j17.0   HUNTING AND SLAUGHTERING

j17.0   الصيد والذبائح

j17.1   It is not permissible to eat any animal (O: that Muslims are permitted to eat) until it has been properly slaughtered, the only exceptions to which are fish (def: j16.4) and locusts, which are permissible to eat even when they die unslaughtered.

j17.1   لَا يَحِلُّ الحيوانُ (المأكول) إلَّا بالذكاة [(أي إلا بالذبح)] . إلَّا السمكَ والجرادَ فَيَحِلُّ ميتتُهُمَا .

j17.2   It is unlawful to eat meat slaughtered by a Zoroastrian, someone who has left Islam (murtadd, def: o8), or an idol worshipper, (O: included with whom are those (zanadiqa) with corrupt convictions about tenets of faith that are well-known as essential parts of Islam (def: books u and v),) or a Christian of the desert Arab tribes (O: the upshot of which is that it is a necessary condition that the slaughterer be of a people whose women we are permitted to marry, whether Muslims, Jews, or Christians).

j17.2   ويَحْرُمُ ما ذَبَحَهُ مجوسيٌّ ومرتدٌ وعابدُ وثنٍ (والزنادقة ملحقة بعبدة الأوثان في عدم حل ذبيحتهم) ونصرانيُّ العرب ([ونصارى العرب هم بهز وتنوخ وتغلب] والحاصل أنه يشترط في الذابح حِل نكاحنا لأهل ملته بأن يكون مسلماً أو كتابياً) .

j17.3   It is permissible to slaughter with anything that has a cutting edge; but not a tooth, bone, or claw, whether human or otherwise, attached to the body or not.

j17.3   ويَجُوزُ الذبحُ بكلِّ ما لهُ حدٌّ يَقْطَعُ إلَّا السنَّ والعظمَ والظفرَ من الآدميِّ وغيره متصلاً أو منفصلاً .

j17.4   The necessary condition for slaughtering any animal which is within one's capacity to slaughter (O: domesticated or wild) is to cut both the windpipe and the gullet (O: *windpipe* meaning the channel of breath, and *gullet* meaning the channel of food and drink which lies beneath the windpipe.

It is not necessary for the validity of slaughtering to cut the carotid arteries, which are two blood vessels on the sides of the neck encompassing the windpipe.

If the slaughterer neglects to cut any part of either the windpipe or gullet and the animal dies, it is considered an unslaughtered dead animal, as is an animal with nothing but purely reflexive movement left when one finishes cutting a part of the windpipe or gullet previously missed. If the slaughterer cuts from the back of the neck until he severs the windpipe and gullet, it is a sin because

j17.4   ومَا قُدِرَ على ذبحِهِ (أي الحيوان إنسياً كان أو وحشياً) اشْتُرطَ قطعُ حلقومِهِ ومريئِهِ (والحلقوم هو مجرى النفس والمريء هو مجرى الطعام والشراب وهو تحت الحلقوم، ولا يشترط في صحة الذبح قطع الودجين وهما عرقان في صفحتي العنق يحيطان بالحلقوم، فلو ترك من الحلقوم والمريء شيئاً ومات الحيوان فهو ميتة وكذا لو انتهى إلى حركة المذبوح فقط بعد ذلك المتروك فهو ميتة . ولو قطع من القفا حتى وصل إلى الحلقوم والمريء عصى بزيادة

of the excess pain caused (A: though it is valid as slaughtering. Chopping off heads of chickens with a hatchet is offensive, though the meat is lawful).

The slaughterer should cut swiftly and not take his time such that he has to cut two or more times. If he does, and there is no life remaining in the animal on the second swipe, then the animal (A: has died unslaughtered and) is impermissible to eat. The determining factor is whether life remains in the animal when the knife is applied at the beginning of the last stroke (A: the one which successfully severs both the windpipe and gullet), no matter whether this is the second or third).

j17.5 It is recommended when slaughtering:

(1) to turn the animal towards the direction of prayer (qibla);

(2) to sharpen the knife;

(3) to cut rapidly (O: even faster than is obligatory, such that it does not take two or more swipes, as mentioned above);

(4) to mention Allah's name (O: for the spiritual grace therein, saying "Bismillah," as is sunna) (A: this is obligatory in the Hanafi school);

(5) to bless the Prophet (Allah bless him and give him peace);

(6) and to cut the large blood vessels (O: on either side of the neck).

j17.6 It is recommended to slaughter camels by thrusting the knife (O: into the hollow at the base of the neck (A: between the two collarbones) above the chest so that one severs them (A: the windpipe and gullet) in this concavity, since it is easier than cutting the throat, for it speeds the exit of the spirit from the body by bypassing the length of the neck, being the preferable way to slaughter any animal with a long neck, such as a duck, goose, ostrich, or giraffe), with the camel left standing, one foreleg bound up.

الإيـــلام . وينبغي للذابــح أن يســرع في القطع ولا يتأنى في القطع بحيث يقطع ما ذكـر في دفعتين فأكثـر فإذا كان كذلك فلا يحـل المـذبوح حينئذ إذا لم توجد الحياة المستقرة عند الدفعة الثانية أما إذا وجدت الحيـاة المستقرة عند الدفعة الثانية فيحل المـذبـوح ، فالشرط في وجود الحيـاة المستقرة في ابتـداء وضـع السكين على الذبح آخر مرة سواء كانت الثانية أم الثالثة) .

j17.5 ويُنـــدَبُ أنْ يُوَجَّـــهَ إلى القبلة وأنْ يُحِدَّ الشفرةَ (والمـراد هنا السكين) ويُسْرِع إمرارَها (والمراد أن يسـرع إسراعاً زائداً على ما يجب بحيث لا يكون الذبح بدفعتين أو دفعات كما تقدم) ويُسَمِّيَ اللهَ تعالى (لأجل حصول البركة فيقول «بسم الـله» للاتبـاع) ويُـصَلِّيَ على النبيِّ ﷺ ويَقْطَعَ الأوداجَ كُلَّها ([والمراد بالجمع ما فوق الواحد لأن كل حيوان له ودجان] أي عرقان في صفحتي عنقه) .

j17.6 وأنْ يَنْحَرَ الإبلَ (في لبتها وهي أسفل العنق وفوق الصدر [وتسمى ثغرة النحـر] بأن يقطعهـا بالسكين في هذه الوهـدة لأنـه أسهل من ذبحها لأنه أسـرع لخروج الروح بسبب طول عنقه ويشـارك الإبل في هذا كل مأكول طال عنقه كالبط والـوز والنعامة والزرافة) قائمةً مُعَقَّلَةً (أي حال كونها مربوطة إحدى يديها) .

j17.7   It is recommended to slaughter other than camels (O: such as cattle, sheep, goats, or horses (A: by drawing the knife) across the throat at the top of neck) after laying them on their left side. (O: Slaughtering them this way is only called for to easily enable the slaughterer to hold the knife in his right hand and the animal's head with his left. It is also sunna for the animal's legs to be bound, except the right hind leg, so the animal will not jerk during slaughtering and cause the slaughterer to miss his mark. The right hind leg is left free in order to pacify the animal by giving it something to move).

j17.8   It is a necessary condition that the slaughterer not raise his knife-hand while slaughtering (O: while drawing it across the neck). If he lifts it before completely severing both the windpipe and gullet, and then returns to cut them, the animal is not lawful to eat.

HUNTING

j17.9   As for hunting, a game animal is lawful to eat whenever one hits it with an arrow (A: or according to the Maliki school, shoots it with a rifle or shotgun) or brings it down with a trained hunting animal (A: such as a falcon or dog) (O: but only if trained), and it dies before one can slaughter it (O: that is, provided that one did not reach it when there was any life left in it besides reflexive motion. If one reaches it while it is alive or any life remains, then one must properly slaughter it), provided that the hunter is not blind, is of a people whose slaughtered food Muslims may eat (def: j17.2), and provided that the animal does not die from being struck by the mere weight of the arrow, but rather dies by its edge (O: meaning that it hits the animal point-first, wounding it).

If the game was brought down by a trained hunting animal, it is a necessary condition that the animal ate nothing of the game.

If the game animal dies from being struck by the weight of the trained hunting animal (A: as in falconing), then the game is lawful to eat.

j17.7   وَيُذْبَحَ ما عداها (من نحو بقر كغنم وخيـل في حلقٍ وهـو أعلى العنق) مضطجعةً على جنبها الأيسر (وإنما طلب ذبحهـا مع هذه الحـالـة لسـهـولتـه على الـذابـح لأخذه السكين باليمين وإمساكه الـرأس باليسار، ويسّر أن تكون مشدودة القـوائم غير الرجل اليمنى لئلا تضطرب حالة الذبح فيخطىء الذابح المذبح وإنما تركت الـرجـل اليمنى بلا شد لتستـريـح بتحـريكها) [ولا يَكْسِرَ عنقَها ولا يَسْلَخَها حتّى تَمُوتَ].

j17.8   ويُشْتَـرَطُ أَنْ لا يَرْفَـعَ يدَهُ في أثنـاء الـذبـح (أي في أثنـاء جرّ آلته على المـذبـح) فإنْ رَفَعَهَا قبـل تمـام قطع الحلقوم والمريء ثمَّ قَطَعَهُمَا لمْ تَحِلَّ.

أحكام الصيد

j17.9   وأمَّا الصيدُ فحيثُ أصابَهُ السهمُ أو الجارحةُ المعلمةُ (قيـد لا بد منه) فَمَاتَ قبـلَ القـدرة على ذبحِه حَلَّ (بشرط أنه لم يدركه حياً أو لم يبق فيه إلا حركـة مذبوح فإن أدركه حياً ذكاه أو وجد فيـه حياة مستقرة فلا بد حينئذ من تذكيته) إذا أرْسَلَهُ بصيـرٌ تَحِـلُّ ذكـاتُـهُ ولمْ يَمُتْ الصيدُ بثِقل السهم بلْ بحدِّه (أي سقط السهم على الصيد من جهة حده الجارح له) ولاَ أَكَلَتِ الجارحةُ منهُ شيئاً. فإنْ مَاتَ بثقل الجارحةِ حَلَّ.

j17.10　A game animal is not lawful to eat if:

(1)　an arrow hits it and it then drops into water (O: because of the likelihood that it died from drowning (N: if that is probable) rather than from being shot);

(2)　it is brought down on a peak which it then falls from (O: because of the likelihood that it died from the fall);

(3)　or if it disappears after having been wounded and is found dead (O: because it might have died for some other reason than being wounded (N: though if it is obvious that it died from the wound, it is lawful to eat)).

j17.11　A camel or other (O: domestic animal such as a cow, sheep, goat, or horse) that strays and cannot be retrieved, or that falls into a well and cannot be gotten out may be made lawful to eat by shooting it (O: because of the impossibility of slaughtering it), no matter where one hits its body (N: provided one mortally wounds it).

And Allah knows best.

*

j18.0　VOWS (NADHR)

(O: Lexically, the word *vow* means any promise. It is legally defined as making obligatory some act of worship that was not originally obligatory in Sacred Law, such as a supererogatory prayer or fast, and the like. There is a difference of opinion among scholars whether a vow in itself is an act of worship or whether it is offensive. The strongest position is that it is an act of worship when made to perform a pious act (A: since Allah Most High describes the pious as "fulfilling their vows" (Koran 76:7)), for it is an intimate discourse with Allah Most High; though it is offensive in the heat of an argument.)

(A: The advantage of a vow is that one may obtain the reward of an obligatory act by fulfilling it. Its drawback is that unlike broken oaths, which may be expiated (dis: o20), there is no way to lift

j17.10　وَإِنْ أَصَابَهُ السهمُ فَوَقَعَ في ماءٍ أَوْ على جبلٍ ثمَّ تَرَدَّى منهُ فَمَاتَ أَوْ غَابَ عنهُ بعدَ أَنْ جُرِحَ ثمَّ وَجَدَهُ ميتاً لمْ يَحِلَّ (في الصورةِ الأولى لاحتمالِ موتِه بسببِ الغَرَقِ لا بسببِ الجَرْحِ، وفي الصورةِ الثانيةِ لاحتمالِ موتِه بالتردِّي، وفي الثالثةِ لاحتمالِ موتِه بسببٍ غيرِ الجرحِ).

j17.11　وإذا نَدَّ بعيرٌ ونحوُهُ (من كلِّ حيوانٍ إنسيٍّ كبقرةٍ وشاةٍ وفرسٍ) وتَعَذَّرَ رَدُّهُ أَوْ تَرَدَّى في بئرٍ وتَعَذَّرَ إخراجُهُ فرَماهُ بحَدِيدَةٍ في أيِّ موضعٍ كانَ منْ بدنِه فَمَاتَ حَلَّ (ح) لكن بشرطِ أنْ يجرحه جرحاً مزهقاً للروحِ (لتعذرِ ذكاتِه). واللهُ أعلمُ.

j18.0　النذر

(وهو لغةً الوعدُ مطلقاً وتعريفه شرعاً التزامُ قربةٍ لم تلزم بأصلِ الشرعِ كالنوافلِ من الصلاةِ والصومِ وغيرهما وفي كونِه قربةً أو مكروهاً خلافٌ والراجحُ أنه قربةٌ في نذرِ التبررِ لأنه مناجاةٌ لله تعالى مكروهٌ في نذرِ اللجاجِ).

(ع : فائدةُ النذرِ أن ثوابَه ثوابُ الفرضِ. لكن من جانبٍ آخرَ، لا سبيلَ

367

the vowed action: it remains obligatory unless one is physically unable (N: in which case one performs an alternative (n: e.g. giving food in place of fasting) if there is one in Sacred Law). For this reason, many pious and learned Muslims avoid making vows.)

THE CONDITIONS FOR THE LEGAL VALIDITY OF A VOW

j18.1   A vow (O: to perform some pious act) is only valid:

(a) if made by a Muslim who is legally responsible (mukallaf, def: c8.1);

(b) when it concerns some act of worship (A: meaning, for the Shafi'is, any recommended act, though for the Hanafi school it can only be an act that is similar in kind to an *obligatory* form of worship (n: such as prayer, fasting, or hajj));

(c) and is stated in words such as "I hereby owe Allah to perform such and such," or "I am hereby obliged to do such and such."

(O: A vow to do something that is merely permissible, such as standing, sitting, eating, or sleeping, is not legally valid because these are not acts of worship; the reason being the hadith related by Bukhari that the Prophet (Allah bless him and give him peace) passed a man standing in the sun without seeking shade, whom he inquired about and was told that it was Abu Isra'il, who had vowed to stand while fasting without sitting, taking shade, or speaking; to which he replied,

"Pass by him and have him sit in the shade and speak, but let him finish fasting."

By *act of worship*, our author means acts that are supererogatory and not obligatory, since an oath to undertake an obligatory act is invalid whether it involves performance of something, such as an obligatory prayer or fast, or nonperformance of something, such as vowing to abstain from wine or fornication and the like. Such vows are not valid to begin with, as Allah has made

لرفع موجَبه ، فيبقى في الـذمة إلا عنـد العجز الفعلي (ح : فحينئذ يصار إلى بدل إن كان له بدل في الشــرع)؛ بخــلاف اليمين ، فلهـا كفارة . ولذلك يجتنب كثير من أهل الورع والعلم النذور) .

شروط صحة النذر

j18.1   لاَ يَصِحُّ النذرُ (للتبرر) إلاَّ مِنْ مسلمٍ مكلَّفٍ في قربةٍ (أي طاعة) باللفظ وهوَ للهِ علَيَّ كذا أو علَيَّ كَذَا . (ولا يصح نذر المباح كالقيام والقعود لأنه ليس بقربة والأكل والنوم لما رواه البخاري أن النبي ﷺ مرّ برجل قائم في الشمس لا يستظل فسأل عنـه فقالوا هذا أبو إسرائيل نذر أن يقف ولا يقعـد ولا يستظـل ولا يتكلم ويصوم فقـال : «مروه فليقعـد وليستظل وليتكلم وليتم صومه» . ومراد المصنف من القربة النوافل منها لا الفرائض لأنه لا يصح نذر الـواجـب سواء كان فعـلاً كالصلاة الواجبة والصوم كذلك أو تركاً كأن نذر أن يشـرب الـخمـر ولا يزني وهكـذا فلا ينعقـد نذره كذلـك لأن الله

these obligatory and "obligating oneself to do them" is meaningless.

The obligatory acts which are not valid to vow are restricted to the personally obligatory. As for the communally obligatory (def: c3.2), a vow to do such an act obliges one to fulfill it, because it is an act of worship not originally obligatory in the law, meaning not initially called for from any particular person.)

GENERAL PROVISIONS REGARDING VOWS

j18.2   A valid vow to do an act of worship makes the act obligatory.

j18.3   One must fulfill a vow that one has made conditional upon the occurrence of some event, such as by saying, "If Allah heals my sick friend, I am obliged to do such and such" (O: of fasting, praying, or charity), which becomes obligatory if the sick person regains his health.

j18.4   If someone makes a vow by way of argument and in anger, saying, for example, "If I speak to Zayd, I am obliged to do such and such," then if he speaks to Zayd, he has a choice between doing what he has vowed, or else paying the expiation for a broken oath (def: o20).

j18.5   If one vows to perform the hajj riding but instead does so on foot, or vows to perform it on foot but then does so riding, this accomplishes the vow, though one is obliged to slaughter (O: as one does for an 'umra first (tamattu') hajj (def: j12.6(I)).

(N: Because the vowed walking or riding has become one of the obligatory elements of one's hajj, the expiation for its nonperformance is as other unperformed obligatory acts of hajj, and if such a person lacks a shah (def: h2.5) or lacks the money for it, he may fast. As for a person who vows to do something unconnected with the hajj and finds he cannot fulfill it, he performs a valid alternative if one exists in Sacred Law (dis:

أوجــب فعــل الـواجبـات فلا معـنى لالتزامها. والمراد بالواجب الـذي لا يصح نذره الـواجب العيني وأمـا الكفائي فيصــح نذره ويلزمـه فعله لأنـه قـربـة لم تتعيـن بأصـل الشـرع أي لم يطلب من شخص معين).

أحكام عامة تتعلق بالنذر

j18.2   فَيَلْزَمُهُ الإتيانُ بِهِ.

j18.3   ومَنْ عَلَّقَ النــذرَ على شيءٍ فقال إنْ شَفَى اللهُ مريضي فَعَلَيَّ كَذَا (أي أن أصوم أو أصلي أو أتصدق) لَزِمَهُ الوفاءُ بمَا التزَمَهُ عند الشفاءِ.

j18.4   ومَنْ نَذَرَ على وجـهِ اللجـاج والغضب فقالَ إنْ كَلَّمْتُ زيداً فَعَلَيَّ كَذَا فهـو بالخيارِ إذا كَلَّمَـهُ بينَ الـوفاءِ وبين كفارة اليمين.

j18.5   فإنْ نَذَرَ الحـجَّ راكبـاً فَحَجَّ ماشياً أوْ نَذَرَ الحَجَّ ماشياً فَحَجَّ راكباً أجْزَأَهُ وعليه دمٌ (كدم التمتع). (ح: لأن المشي أو الـركـوب المنذور قد صار واجبـاً من واجبـات الحـج، فإن فقـد شاة أو ثمنهـا أجـزأه الصـوم. أما من نذر ما لا يتعلق بالحج ثم عجز عن فعله، فإن كان له بدل

j18.0(A:)). If there is no valid alternative in Sacred Law, he remains responsible for performing the vowed act.)

(O: If one does not fulfill a vow because of being unable to or because of forgetfulness, it is not a sin, but one must slaughter, an obligation that incapacity or forgetfulness does not lift. To summarize, the sin (A: of not fulfilling one's vow) only exists when one is capable of fulfilling it, not when one is incapable, though someone who does not fulfill a vow because of incapacity must slaughter a *shah* meeting sacrifice specifications (def: j14.2).)

في الشرع أتى به ، وإلا بقي في ذمته) .

(وإن ترك المنذور عجزاً فلا إثم عليه والـدم لازم على كل حال لأن العجــز لا يسقط الـدم وكـذلك إذا تركه نسياناً له لا يسقطه أيضاً وإن لم يكن آثماً . فالحاصل أن الإثم يكـون مع القـدرة دون العجـز فيجب على تارك ما ذكر شاة مجزئة في الأضحية) .

j18.6   If one vows to go to the Kaaba, Masjid al-Medina, or al-Masjid al-Aqsa (n: in Jerusalem), then one is obliged to. If one vows to go to the Kaaba, then one must perform hajj or 'umra (O: because hajj and 'umra are what is fundamentally intended in Sacred Law by going to the Sacred Precinct, and the vow is interpreted according to this convention of the Law as a vow to perform either hajj or 'umra). If one vows to go to Masjid al-Medina or al-Masjid al-Aqsa, then one must either perform the prayer or else spend a period of spiritual retreat (i'tikaf, def: i3) in the mosque (O: i.e. one is entitled to choose between prayer or spiritual retreat).

If one vows to go to some other mosque, the vow does not oblige one to do so (dis: i3.4(end)) (O: since travelling to other mosques is not an act of worship (N: that is, if intended for itself, though if one intends it in order to perform the prayer or for spiritual retreat therein, it is an act of worship)).

j18.6   وإنْ نَذَرَ المضيَّ إلى الكعبةِ أوْ مسجدِ المدينةِ أو الأقصَى لزِمَهُ ذلك ويجبُ أنْ يَقْصِدَ الكعبـةَ بحجٍّ أوْ عمرةٍ (لأن ذلك هو المقصود شرعاً بالأصالة من إتيــان الحـرم فصـار محمولاً في عرف الشرع عليه أي على ذلك النسك من حج أو عمرة) وأنْ يُصَلِّيَ في مسجدِ المدينة أو الأقصى أوْ يَعْتَكِفَ (فهـو مخير فيهما بين الصلاة والاعتكاف) .

وإنْ نَذَرَ الـمـضيَّ إلـى غيـرهَـا مِنَ المسـاجدِ لمْ يَلْزَمْـهُ (لأنه ليس في قصده قربـة (ح : أي قصده لذاتـه أما القصـد للصلاة أو الاعتكاف فقربة)) .

j18.7   If one vows to fast for the whole of a particular year, one does not have to make up days not fasted on the two 'Eids or the three days following 'Eid al-Adha (dis: i2.3), or the days fasted during Ramadan, or the days a woman misses during her monthly period or postnatal bleeding.

j18.7   ومَنْ نَذَرَ صومَ سنةٍ بعينِهـا لمْ يَقضِ أيامَ العيدِ والتشريقِ ورمضانَ وأيامَ الحيضِ والنفاسِ .

j18.8   Someone who vows to perform the prayer (A: but does not specify how much) must pray two rak'as.

j18.8   ومن نَذَرَ صلاةً لَزِمَـهُ ركعتـانِ [أو عتقاً أجْزَأَهُ ما يَقَعُ عليْهِ الاسمُ] .

BOOK K

TRADE

CONTENTS:

---

k1.0 SALE

(O: The legal basis for sale, prior to scholarly consensus (ijma'), is such Koranic verses as the word of Allah Most High,

"Allah has made sale lawful..." (Koran 2:275).

The more reliable of the two positions reported from our Imam (Allah Most High be well pleased with him) is that this verse is general in meaning, referring to all sales except those specifically excluded by other evidence. For the Prophet (Allah bless him and give him peace) forbade various sales but did not explain the permissible ones, his not doing so proving that the initial presumption for the validity of a sale is that it is lawful. This is also borne out by hadiths such as the one in which the Prophet (Allah bless him and give him peace) was asked what type of earning was best,

k1.0 صفة البيع وعقده

(والأصل فيه قبل الإجماع آيات كقوله تعـــالى: ﴿وَأَحَلَّ اللَّهُ البَيْعَ﴾ [البقرة: ٢٧٥]. [. . .] وأفهم قولي إمامنـا رضي الله تعالى عنه أن هذه الآيـة عامة تتناول كل ما خرج بدليل فإنه ﷺ نهى عن بيوع ولم يبين الجائز أي فدل عدم بيانه على أن الأصل في البيع الحل [. . .] وأخبار كخبر سئل النبي ﷺ أي كسب أطيب فقال: «عمل

and he answered,

"The work of a man's own hand, and every pious sale,"

meaning sales free of cheating and deceit. Hakim related this hadith, which he classified as rigorously authenticated (sahih).

Lexically, *sale* means to transact something for something else. In Sacred Law it means to exchange an article of property for other property in a particular way. Its integrals are six:

(a) the seller;

(b) the buyer;

(c) the price;

(d) the article purchased;

(e) the spoken offer;

(f) and the spoken acceptance.)

(N: *Sale* (bay'), wherever it is used in the rulings below, refers to both exchanging goods for money and exchanging them for other goods (n: i.e. barter).)

THE SPOKEN OFFER AND ACCEPTANCE

k1.1 A sale is not valid unless there is a spoken offer (O: by the seller) and spoken acceptance (O: by the buyer). *Offer* means the statement of the seller or his agent (wakil, def: k17) "I sell it to you" or "I make it yours." *Acceptance* means the statement of the buyer or his agent "I buy it" or "I take possession of it" or "I accept."

(A: Regarding *mu'atah*, which is giving the seller the price and taking the merchandise without speaking, as when buying something whose cost is well known, Bajuri notes, "Nawawi and a group of scholars have adopted the position that sales conducted by it [A: mu'atah] are valid for all transactions that people consider sales, since the determining factor therein is the acceptance of

الرجـل بيده وكل بيع مبرور» أي لا غش فيه ولا خيانة رواه الحاكم وصححه .

والبيـع لغـة مقابلة شيء بشيء وشرعاً مقابلة مال بمال على وجه مخصوص وأركانه [كما في المجموع ثلاثة وهي في الحقيقـة] ستـة وهي : [عـاقـد :] بائـع ومـشتـر ، [ومـعـقـود :] ثمن ومثمن ، [وصيغة :] إيجاب وقبول) .

(ح : وحيث تطلق كلمـة البيـع فيمـا يأتي من الأحكام فهي تشمل مقابلة سلعة بعملة مالية ، ومقابلة سلعة بسلعة) .

الإيجاب والقبول

k1.1 لا يَصِحُّ إلّا بالإيجـاب (من البـائـع) والـقبـول (من المشتـري) فالإيجابُ هوَ قولُ البائع أوْ وكيلِهِ بِعْتُكَ أوْ مَلَّكْتُكَ . والقبولُ هوَ قولُ المشتري أوْ وكيـلِهِ : اشْتَـرَيْتُ أوْ تَمَلَّكْتُ أوْ قَبِلْتُ .

(ع : وأما المعاطاة وهي دفع الثمن وقبض المبيع دون التلفظ بإيجاب وقبول ، كأن يكون الثمن معتاداً معـروفاً ، فقـد قال البـاجوري : «واختـار النـووي وجماعة صحة البيع بها [ع : أي بالمعاطاة] في كل ما يعده الناس بيعاً لأن المدار فيه على

both parties, and there is no decisively authenticated primary text stipulating that it be spoken, so common acknowledgement ['urf, def: f4.5] is the final criterion [A: as to what legally constitutes *acceptance*]" (*Hashiya al-Shaykh Ibrahim al-Bajuri* (y5), 1.355).)

(N: The category of *mu'atah* also includes sales conducted by means of vending machines (A: provided it is clear what one is buying before one puts the money in the machine).)

It is permissible for the buyer's acceptance to precede the offer, such as his saying, "I buy it for so-and-so much," and for the seller to reply, "I sell it to you." It is also permissible to say, "Sell it to me for so-and-so much," and for the seller to reply, "I sell it to you." All of these are unequivocal expressions. Sales can likewise be effected, if the intention exists, by equivocal expressions such as "Take it for so-and-so much," or "I consider it yours for so-and-so much," thereby intending a transaction with the buyer, who then accepts. If one does not intend a transaction by such expressions, then the sale is nothing (O: but empty words, and the buyer is obliged to return the merchandise to its owner if it still exists, or replace it if used up while in his possession).

It is obligatory (O: for the validity of the sale agreement that other conditions be met, among them):

(a) that the interval between the offer and its acceptance not be longer than what is customary (O: the criterion being whether it gives the impression that one is averse to accepting, not merely a brief interval. Other conditions include:

(b) that conversation extraneous to the agreement by either of the two parties not intervene between the offer and acceptance, even if inconsiderable, since it gives the impression of nonacceptance;

(c) that the offer and its acceptance correspond, for if the offered price is one thousand, and the buyer "accepts" for five hundred, the transaction is invalid;

(d) that neither the offer nor acceptance be made conditional (ta'liq) upon an event extrane-

رضــا المتعاقـدين ولم يثبت اشتراط لفظ فيــرجع فيه إلى العرف» [نقل من حاشية الشيخ إبراهيم الباجوري: ١/ ٣٥٥].

وَيَجُوزُ أَنْ يَتَقَدَّمَ لَفظُ المشتري مثلَ أَنْ يَقُــولَ: اشْتَـرَيْتُ بِكَــذَا، فَيَقُـولَ: بِعْتُــكَ. وَيَجُوزُ أَنْ يَقُـولَ: بِعْني بِكَـذَا فَيَقُـولُ: بِعْتُـكَ. فهـذِه صرائـحُ وَيَنْعَقـدُ أيضاً بالكِنَـايةِ مَعَ النيةِ مثلُ: خُذْهُ بِكَذَا، أوْ: جعلتُهُ لكَ بِكَذَا، وَيَنْوي بذلكَ البيعَ فَيَقْبَـلُ (المشتري). فإنْ لَمْ يَنْـوِ بِه البيعَ فَلَيْسَ بشيءٍ (فـهـو لغـو فيجـب على المشتري رده على مالكـه إن كان باقياً أو بدله إن تلف تحت يده).

وَيَجِبُ (أي يشتـرط في صحةِ عقدِ البيع شروط منها) أَنْ لَا يَطُولَ الفصلُ بينَ الإيجـابِ والقبـولِ عُرْفاً (وضابط الطول هو ما أشعر بإعراضه عن القبول بخلاف اليسير، ومنها أن لا يتخللهما كلام أجنبي عن العقد ممن يريد أن يتمه ولو يسيراً لأن فيـه إعراضاً عن القبول، ومنها أن يتوافقا أي الإيجـاب والقبـول معنى فلو أوجب بألف صحيحة وقبل نصفه بخمسمائة لم يصح العقد، ومنها عدم تعليق لا يقتضيه

ous to the agreement, such as saying, "I sell it to you, should my father die";

(e) and that the sale not be subject to time stipulations (ta'qit) such as saying, "I sell it to you for a period of one month";

—because both (d) and (e) vitiate the necessary intention).

A mute's gesture is as binding as a speaker's words.

THE BUYER AND SELLER

k1.2   The conditions that must exist in the buyer and seller are:

(a) having reached puberty (A: Imam Ahmad permits the buying and selling of minor items by children, even before they have reached the age of discrimination (def: f1.2) and without their guardian's permission);

(b) sanity;

(c) that one's disposal over one's property not be suspended (def: k13);

(d) and that one not be unjustly forced to make the sale. (O: The agreement of someone unjustly forced to sell his property is invalid because of lack of consent, though it is valid if he is justly forced, as when he is ordered to sell his property to repay a debt.)

(e) If a Koran is being purchased for someone, it is obligatory that the person be Muslim. (O: The same is true of books of hadith and books containing the words and deeds of the early Muslims. "Koran" in this context means any work that contains some of the Koran, even a slight amount.) (A: This ruling holds for any religious books, even the *Tabaqat* of Sha'rani (n: a collection of biographical sketches of Muslims), though the Hanafi school permits non-Muslims to buy or be given the Koran and other Islamic books.)

(f) It is a condition that someone buying weapons be of a people who are not at war with Muslims.

السيد. ولاَ يُقْبَلُ فيه قولُ العبد. والعبدُ لاَ يَمْلِكُ شيئاً وإنْ مَلَّكَهُ سيدُهُ].

THE OPTION TO CANCEL A SALE AT THE TIME OF THE AGREEMENT

خيار المجلس

k1.3   When a sale is effected, both buyer and seller have the *option to cancel at the time of the agreement* (khiyar al-majlis), meaning the right to nullify the agreement at any time before they (O: physically) part company, or both waive the right to cancel, or until one of them cancels the sale.

(O: The option to cancel at the time of the agreement exists at every sale, and for its duration, the ownership of the articles exchanged is suspended (def: k1.5).)

k1.3   وإذا انْعَقَدَ البيعُ ثَبَتَ لكلٍ مِنَ البـائـعِ والمشتري خيارُ المجلس مَا لمْ يَتَفَرَّقَا (أي مدة عدم تفرقهما بأبدانهما) أو يخْتَـارَا الإمضـاءَ جميعاً [(ح : أي يختارا لزوم العقـد وعـدم فسخه)] أوْ يَفْسَخُـهُ أحدُهُمَا (وخيار المجلس يثبت في كل بيع والملك في زمن الخيار موقوف).

STIPULATING AN OPTION TO CANCEL PERIOD

شرط الخيار

k1.4   Both the buyer and seller have the right to stipulate an *option to cancel period,* an interval during which either party may cancel the agreement, of up to three days (O: provided the days are consecutive. The option to cancel period is not valid if the two parties stipulate an indeterminate period, or leave it open-ended by merely stipulating "an option to cancel" (A: though the buyer has the right to return the article because of defects (dis: k5) regardless of what they stipulate), or when the period is determinately known, but exceeds three days). The option to cancel may be given (A: depending on what the buyer and seller agree upon) to both parties, or just one of them (O: and not the other, or they may give the option to a third party, since the need for this might arise. In any case, both buyer and seller must agree to the conditions). But such a period may not be stipulated for transactions in which it is unlawful to part company before taking possession of the commodities exchanged (O: by one or both parties) as is the case in exchanging the kinds of foodstuffs and moneys in which usurious gain (riba, dis: k3.1–2) is present, or in buying in advance (salam, dis: k9.2(a)).

k1.4   ولكـلٍ مِنَ البـائـعِ والمشتري شرطِ الخيار في البيع ثلاثة أيامٍ فَمَا دونَهَا (بشـرط أن تكـون متـوالِيـة فلو شرطا مدة مجهـولـة أو أطلقا الشرط بأن قالا بشرط الخيار أوكانت المدة معلومة لكنها زادت على الثـلاثـة فلا يصح الشـرط) لهُمَـا أوْ لأحدِهمَا (شرطه دون الآخر ولأجنبي لأن الحاجة قد تدعو إلى ذلك. وبكل حال لا بد من اجتماعهما عليه) إلاَّ إذَا كَانَ العقدُ مِمَّا يَحْرُمُ فيه التفرُّقُ قبلَ القبضِ (للمبيع إمـا من الجانبين معاً أو من أحدهما فقط) كَمَا في الربَا والسَّلَم .

k1.5 If the option to cancel is given to the seller alone, then the merchandise is considered his property during this period (O: meaning that he owns the proceeds earned by the property, and its increments such as its milk, eggs, or fruit, and he is obliged to cover its maintenance and other expenses).

If the option to cancel is given to the buyer alone, then the merchandise is considered his property during this period (O: and the above increments and expenses are his).

If the option to cancel is given to both buyer and seller, then the ownership of the merchandise during this period is *suspended,* meaning that if the transaction is finalized, it is established that it belonged to the buyer (O: from the time the agreement was first made, together with its increments and expenses), but if the transaction is cancelled, it is established that it belonged to the seller (O: meaning that it never left his ownership).

*

k2.0 THE THINGS EXCHANGED IN A TRANSACTION

(N: *Things* here refers to both the merchandise and its price.)

k2.1 Five conditions must exist in any article transacted. It must:

(a) be pure (O: in itself, or if affected with filth, it must be capable of being purified by washing);

(b) be useful;

(c) be deliverable (O: by the seller to the buyer, meaning that the buyer is able to take possession of it);

(d) be the property of the seller or the person whom the seller has been authorized to represent;

(e) and be determinately known (ma'lum) (O: to the buyer and seller, as to which particular

k1.5 ثُمَّ إذَا كَانَ الخِيـارُ للبـائــع وحـدَهُ فالمبيـعُ في زمنِ الخيـارِ ملكُـهُ (فيكــون له أكســابــه وزوائــده كاللبن والبيض والثمرة ويكون عليه النفقة) .

وإنْ كَانَ للمشتـري وحدَهُ فالمبيعُ في زمنِ الخيارِ ملكُهُ (فيكون له وعليه ما تقدم من الزوائد والنفقة) .

وإنْ كَانَ لَهُمَا فالمِلْكُ فيهِ موقوفٌ : إنْ تَمَّ البيعُ تَبَيَّنَ لَنَا أنَّـهُ كَانَ مِلْكُ المشتري (من حين العقـد مع توابعـه من فوائـده [(ت :] ونفقتـه)) وإنْ فُسِخَ البيعُ تَبَيَّنَ أنَّهُ كَانَ ملكاً للبائع (بمعنى أنه لم يخرج عن ملكه) .

k2.0 المبيع

(ح : وكلمة المبيع تشمل السلعة ومقابلتها) .

k2.1 للمبيــع شروطٌ خمسـةٌ أنْ يَكُـونَ طاهراً (أي طاهر العين أو متنجس يطهر بالغسل) ، مُنْتَفَعاً بِهِ ، مقدوراً على تسليـمِهِ (أي تسليم البــائـع المبيـع للمشتـري أو على تسلمــه من البــائــع والمـدار على التسلم) ، مملوكاً للعـاقـد (وهـو البـائـع) أوْ لِمَنْ نَابَ العـاقدُ عنْهُ ، معلومـاً (للمتعـاقـدين عينـاً وقـدراً وصفة

thing it is, how much it is, and what kind it is, in order to protect against chance or risk (gharar), because of the hadith related by Muslim that the Prophet (Allah bless him and give him peace) forbade the transaction of whatever involves chance or risk). (n: w42 discusses buying and selling insurance policies.)

حَذراً من الغرر لمـا روى مسلم أنـه ﷺ نهى عن بيع الغرر).

PURITY

كون المبيع طاهراً

k2.2 It is invalid to transact something that is impure in itself (najasa, def: e14.1) such as a dog, or something affected with filth that cannot be purified (O: by washing), like milk or shortening, though if it can be, like a garment, then it may be transacted.

k2.2   فلاَ يَصِّحُ بيـعُ عين نجسـةٍ كالكلب أو متنجسـةٍ ولمْ يُمْكِنْ تطهيـرُهَـا (أي بالغسـل) كاللبنِ والـدهنِ مثلاً. فإنْ أمْكَنَ كثوبٍ متنجسٍ جَازَ.

USEFULNESS

كون المبيع منتفعاً به

k2.3 It is invalid to transact something which is not useful (O: whether the reason for invalidity is the article's baseness or the smallness of the amount being dealt with,) such as vermin, a single grain of wheat, or unlawful musical instruments (dis: r40) (O: such as the mandolin or flute, since there is no lawful benefit in them).

k2.3   ولاَ يَصِحُّ بيـعُ مَا لاَ يُنْتَفَعُ بِه (وعـدم صحته إمـا لخسته أو لقلتـه) كالحشـراتِ وحبةِ حنطةٍ وآلاتِ الملاهي المحرمةِ (كطنبور ومزمار إذ لا نفع بها شرعاً).

DELIVERABILITY

كون المبيع مقدوراً تسليمه

k2.4 It is invalid to transact something undeliverable, such as a bird on the wing or something that a third party has wrongfully taken from one, though if one sells the latter to a buyer who is able to take it back from the third party, the sale is valid; while if the buyer is unable to take it from him, then the buyer has the option to either declare the sale binding or cancel it.

It is invalid to transact a particular half of a whole object such as a vessel, sword, or garment (O: since the buyer cannot take possession of that part without breaking or cutting the article, involving the lessening and loss of property), or part of anything whose value is diminished by cut-

k2.4   ولاَ بيعُ مَا لاَ يَقْدِرُ على تسليمِه كَـ [عبدٍ آبقٍ و] طير طائر ومغصوب لكنْ إنْ بَاعَ المغصوبَ مِمَّنْ يُقْدِرُ على انتزاعِه جَازَ. فإنْ تَبَيَّنَ عجزُهُ (أي عجز المشتري عن الانتـزاع من يد الغـاصب) فلَهُ (أي للمشتري) الخيارُ (بين إمضاء لزوم البيع والفسخ).

ولاَ بيعُ نصفٍ مُعَيَّنٍ منْ إنـاءٍ أوْ سيفٍ أوْ ثوبٍ (لأن التـسلم فيـه لا يمكن إلا بالكسر أو القطع وفيه نقص وتضييع مال) وكَـذا كل ما تَنْقُصُ قيـمتُـه بالقطع

ting or breaking, though if it does not diminish its value, as with a bolt of heavy cloth, such portions may be sold.

والكسر. فإنْ لَمْ تَنْقُصْ كثوبٍ نَخينٍ جازَ.

LAWFUL DISPOSAL OVER THE PROPERTY

التصرف في المبيع

k2.5 It is not valid for the owner of an article that has been put up as collateral (def: k11) to sell it without the permission of the person to whom the collateral has been given.

Nor is it valid to sell property belonging to another, unless the seller is the owner's guardian (def: k13.2) or authorized representative (def: k17).

k2.5 ولاَ يَجُوزُ بيعُ المرهونِ دونَ إذنِ المرتهنِ [(أي ولا يصح)].

ولاَ [بيعُ الفضوليِّ وهُوَ] أنْ يَبيعَ مالَ غيرِه بغيرِ ولايةٍ ولاَ وكالةٍ.

BEING DETERMINATELY KNOWN

كون المبيع معيناً

k2.6 It is not valid to sell property not determinately identified such as "one of these two garments" (O: since "one of them" is not an identification. Likewise with saying, "I sell you one of these sheep." It makes no difference whether all the objects are of equal or unequal value).

It is not valid to transact a particular thing that is not in view (O: meaning that it has not been seen by both buyer and seller or by one of them) such as saying, "I sell you the Mervian robe I have up my sleeve," or "the black horse that is in my stable." But if the buyer has seen it before and the article is something that does not generally change within the time that has elapsed since it was last seen, then such sales are valid.

It is permissible to sell something like a pile of wheat that is in plain view when its weight is unknown, or to sell something for a heap of silver that is visible when the silver's weight is unknown, for seeing is sufficient.

The selling and buying of a blind person are not valid. He must commission another to buy and sell for him (A: though the Hanafi, Maliki, and Hanbali schools permit him to buy and sell for himself). It is valid for a blind person to buy in advance (def: k9) or for another to buy in advance from him, provided the payment is forwarded to and held by the person being bought from in advance.

k2.6 ولاَ يبيعُ مَا لَمْ يُعَيَّنْ كأحــدِ [العبدينِ (أو] الثوبينِ فإن الأحد منها غير معين ومثل ذلــك: بعتك شاة من هذه الشياه. ولا فرق بين أن تتساوى القيمة في جميع ذلك أو تختلف).

ولاَ يبيعُ عينٍ غائبةٍ عنْ عينٍ (أي التي لم تشاهد للمتعاقدين ولا لأحدهما) مثـل: بعْتُكَ الثوبَ المروزيَّ الذي في كُمِّي والفرسَ الأدهمَ (أي الأسود) الذي في اصطبلي. فإنْ كانَ المشتري رآها من قبل ذلكَ وهيَ مِمّا لاَ يَتَغَيَّرُ في مدةِ الغِيبة غالباً جازَ.

ولـوْ بَاعَ عُرْمَةَ حنطةٍ ونحوهـا وهيَ مشاهَدةً ولمْ يُعْلَمْ كيلُها أوْ بَاعَ شيئاً بعرمة فضةٍ مشاهَدةٍ ولمْ يُعْلَمْ وزنُها جازَ وتَكْفِي الرؤيةُ.

ولا يَصِحُّ بيـعُ الأعـمـى ولا شراؤُهُ وطريقُهُ التوكيلُ ويَصِحُّ سلمُهُ في بعوضٍ في ذمتِه.

k3.0 USURIOUS GAIN (RIBA)

(O: The word *riba* lexically means *increment*. In Sacred Law it is (N: of two types, the first being usurious gain (riba) in selling, which is) an agreement for a specific recompense whose equivalence to the merchandise is unknown (def: k3.1(a)) according to the standards of the Law at the time of the transaction, or in which the exchange of the two properties transacted is delayed, or one of them is delayed. (N: The second type concerns loans, and consists of any loan by which the lender obtains some benefit (dis: k10.5).) The basis for its unlawfulness, prior to scholarly consensus (ijma', def: b7), is such Koranic verses as:

"Allah permits trade but forbids usurious gain" (Koran 2:275),

and,

"Fear Allah and relinquish what remains of usury, if you are believers" (Koran 2:278),

and such hadiths as that related by Muslim,

"The Messenger of Allah (Allah bless him and give him peace) cursed whoever eats of usurious gain (riba), feeds another with it, writes an agreement involving it, or acts as a witness to it."

Another hadith, in *al-Mustadrak* (n: by Hakim), relates that the Prophet (Allah bless him and give him peace) said,

"Usurious gain is of seventy kinds, the least of which is as bad as a man marrying his mother.")

(n: w43 discusses taking interest in enemy lands (dar al-harb).)

USURIOUS GAIN IN SALES OF FOODSTUFFS, GOLD, AND SILVER

k3.1 Gain is not unlawful except in certain exchanges involving (O: human) foodstuffs, gold, and silver (A: or other money) (N: which is the ruling for usurious gain in sales. As for usurious

k3.0 الربا

(وهو لغة الزيادة وشرعاً عقد على عوض مخصوص غير معلوم التماثل في معيار الشرع حالة العقد أو مع تأخير في البدلين أو أحدهما. (ح: الربا نوعان: الأول في باب البيع كما تقدم والنوع الثاني في باب القرض وهو كل قرض جر نفعاً للمقرض). والأصل في تحريمه قبل الإجماع آيات كآية: ﴿وَأَحَلَّ اللَّهُ الْبَيْعَ وَحَرَّمَ الرِّبَا﴾ [البقرة: ٢٧٥]، و﴿اتَّقُوا اللَّهَ وَذَرُوا مَا بَقِيَ مِنَ الرِّبَا إِنْ كُنْتُمْ مُؤْمِنِينَ﴾ [البقرة: ٢٧٨]، وأخبار كخبر مسلم: «لعن رسول الله ﷺ آكل الربا وموكله وكاتبه وشاهده». وفي المستدرك عن النبي ﷺ الربا سبعون باباً أيسرها مثل أن ينكح الرجل أمه».

الربا في بيع المطعومات والذهب والفضة

k3.1 لا يَحْرُمُ الرِّبَا إلَّا في المطعومات (مطعوم الآدميين) والذهب والفضة (ح: هذا ربا البيع أما ربا القرض

gain or *interest* from loans, it is unlawful for any type of property whatever). The determining factor in the prohibition of usurious gain in foodstuffs is their being edible, and in gold and silver, their being the value of things.

When a foodstuff is sold for a foodstuff of the same kind, such as wheat exchanged for wheat (O: or when gold is traded for gold), three conditions are obligatory:

(a) exact equivalence in amount (def: k3.5) (O: which must be made certain of, this stipulation precluding exchanges of foodstuffs, gold, or silver in which the amounts are not known, for such sales are not valid even if the two quantities transacted subsequently turn out to be equal, because of the ignorance of their equivalence at the time of the transaction, since ignorance of it is the same as actual nonequivalence);

(b) that the properties transacted be in the respective possession of buyer and seller before they part company;

(c) and immediacy (N: such that the agreement does not mention any delay in the exchange, even if brief).

k3.2   When foodstuffs are sold for foodstuffs of a different kind, such as wheat for barley (O: or when gold is sold for silver), only two conditions are obligatory:

(a) that the exchange be immediate;

(b) and that the properties exchanged be in the respective possession of buyer and seller before they part company.

If these two conditions are met, the two commodities exchanged may differ in amount.

TRANSACTING GOLD AND SILVER

k3.3   When gold is exchanged for gold, or silver for silver, conditions k3.1(a,b,c) are obligatory. If

---

فيحرم في كل الأموال).

والعلةُ في تحريمِ المطعوماتِ الطعمُ وفي تحريمِ الذهبِ والفضةِ كونُهُما قيمَ الأشياءِ.

فإذا بيعَ مطعومٌ بمطعومٍ مِنْ جنسِهِ كبرٍّ ببرٍّ (أي وكذهبٍ بذهبٍ) اشْتُرطَ ثلاثةُ أمورٍ المماثلةُ في القدرِ (يقيناً خرج بهذا القيدِ ما لوباعَ ربوياً بجنسِه جزافاً فلا يصح وإن خرجـا سواء للجهل بالمماثلة حالة البيع. والجهل بالمماثلة كحقيقة المـفــاضلة) والتقــابُضُ قبــلَ التفـرُّقِ والحلولُ (ح: بأن لا يذكر في العقد أجل وإن كان قصيراً).

k3.2   وإنْ كَانَ مِنْ غيرِ جنسِهِ كبرٍّ بشعيرٍ (أي وذهبٍ بفضةٍ) اشْتُرطَ شرطانِ الحلولُ والتقــابُض قبــلَ التفـرُّقِ وجَازَ (حينئذٍ) التفاضُلُ.

بيع الذهب والفضة

k3.3   وإنْ بَاعَ نقداً بجنسِهِ كذهبٍ بذهبٍ اشْتُرطَ الشروطُ الثلاثةُ المتقدمةُ.

gold is exchanged for silver, their amounts may differ, but conditions k3.2(a,b) are obligatory.

وإنْ بَاعَ بغيرِ جِنسِهِ كذهبٍ بفضةٍ اشْتُرِطَ الشرطانِ وجَازَ التفاضلُ.

k3.4   When foodstuffs are sold for gold or silver, the transaction is unconditionally valid (O: meaning none of the above conditions are necessary).

k3.4   وإنْ بَاعَ مطعــوماً بنقدٍ صَحَّ مطلقاً (والمعنى أنـه لا يشتـرط شيء من الشروط السابقة).

k3.5   *Equivalence in amount* for commodities customarily sold by volume is reckoned according to volume (O: even if weights differ), and for articles customarily sold by weight according to weight. Thus, it is invalid to sell a pound of wheat for a pound of wheat when there is a difference between the two's volume, though it is valid to sell a bushel of wheat for a bushel of wheat even when their weights differ.

Customarily transacted by weight or volume means according to the prevalent custom in the Hijaz during the time of the Messenger of Allah (Allah bless him and give him peace). If this is unknown, then according to the custom of the town where the transaction takes place. If the foodstuff is of a kind not customarily exchanged by either weight or volume, and it has no dried storage state, such as cucumbers, quinces, or citrons, then it may not be traded for its own sort.

Equivalence in amount is not applicable to foodstuffs until they are completed, meaning, for fruits, in the dried storage state. It is invalid to trade fresh dates for fresh dates, fresh dates for dried dates, fresh grapes for fresh grapes, or fresh grapes for raisins. Types of dates and grapes not sold as dried dates and raisins may not be exhanged for their own sort. It is also invalid (A: because of ignorance of their equivalence) to exchange:

(1) flour for flour (O: when they are of the same type);

(2) flour for wheat;

(3) bread for bread (O: when of the same type);

(4) a pure foodstuff for a mixed one;

k3.5   ويُعْتَبَرُ التماثلُ في المكيلِ بالكيلِ (وإن اختلفا وزناً) وفي الموزونِ بالوزنِ فلا يَصِحُّ رطلٌ برٍّ برطلٍ برٍّ إذَا كَانَ يَتَفَاوَتُ بالكيلِ ويَجُوزُ إردبُ بإردبٍ وإنْ تَفَاوَتَ الـوزنُ. والمرادُ ما كَانَ يُوزَنُ أو يُكَالُ في الحجـازِ في عهـدِ رسـولِ اللهِ ﷺ. فإنْ جُهِلَ حالُهُ اعْتُبِرَ بِلدِ البيعِ. وإنْ كَانَ (المبيـع الـربـوي) مِمَّا لا يُوزَنُ ولا يُكَالُ في العـادةِ ولا جَفافَ لهُ كالقثاءِ والسفرجَلِ والأُتْرُجِّ لَمْ يَصِحَّ بيعُ بعضِهِ ببعضٍ.

[فَلَوْ بَاعَ برّاً ببرٍّ جزافاً لَمْ يَصِحَّ وإنْ ظَهَرَ مِنْ بعدِ تساويهِمَا كيلاً]. وإنمَا تُعْتَبَرُ الممـاثلةُ حالةَ الكمالِ. فحالةُ كمالِ الثمـرةِ حالةُ الجفافِ، فلا يَصِحُّ رطبٌ برطبٍ أو رطبٌ بتمرٍ وكذا عنبٌ بعنبٍ أو بزبيبٍ وإنْ تَمَـاثَـلا. فإنْ لَمْ يَجيءْ مِنْهُ تمرٌ ولا زبيبٌ لَمْ يَصِحَّ بيعُ بعضِهِ ببعضٍ.

ولاَ يُبَاعُ دقيقٌ بدقيقٍ (أي عنـد اتحاد الجنسِ) ولا بـرٌّ ولا خبـزٌ بخبـزٍ (أي إن اتحــد الجنسِ) ولا خالصٌ بمشـوبٍ ولا

(5) cooked food for uncooked, or cooked food for other cooked food, unless the cooking is very slight, such as separating honey (O: from the comb) or milkfat (O: from milk).

It is not permissible to exchange (N: for example) a measure of dates plus one dirham for two dirhams, or for two measures of dates, or for a measure of dates and a dirham. Nor is it permissible to exchange a measure of dates and a garment for two measures, nor a dirham and a garment for two dirhams.

It is invalid to transact meat for a live animal (O: even when the two are not of the same kind of animal).

مطبـوخٌ بنيءٍ ولا مطبــوخٍ إلّا أنْ يَخِفَّ الطبخُ كتميـيـزِ العسـلِ (أي من الشمـعِ) والسمنِ (أي من اللبن). ولا يجــوزُ مدُّ عجوةٍ ودرهـمٍ بدرهمَيْنِ أوْ بمدَّينِ ولا مدُّ ودرهـمٍ بمـدٍّ ودرهـمٍ، ولا مدٌّ وثـوبٌ بمدَّينِ، ولا درهمٌ وثوبٌ بدرهمَيْنِ، ولا يَصِحُّ بيعُ اللحمِ بالحيوانِ (ولو غير جنسه).

*

(dis: c5.2)

k4.0 SOME PROHIBITED KINDS OF TRANSACTIONS

(O: Prohibited transactions may be invalid, as is usually the case with the prohibited, for prohibition generally entails invalidity; or not, such that the transaction is valid despite being prohibited (dis: c5.2).)

k4.0 البيوع المحرمة

(إما مع البطلان وهو الغالب فيما نهى عنـه لأن النهي عن الشيءِ يقتضي الفسـاد غالباً وإما مع عدمه بأن يصح البيع مع الحرمة).

SELLING THE OFFSPRING OF EXPECTED OFFSPRING

بيع نتاج النتاج

k4.1 It is invalid to sell the offspring of (A: expected) offspring, such as saying, "When my she-camel gives birth, and her offspring in turn gives birth to a camel, I hereby sell you that camel" (O: i.e. the offspring of the offspring. The reason for invalidity is that it is a transaction of an article that is not owned, known, or deliverable). Nor is it valid to sell something for a price whose payment is deferred to a time similar to the above (O: that is, till the time the offspring of an offspring is born, because the date of payment is not known).

k4.1 لَا يَصِحُّ بَيْعُ نَتَاجِ النتاجِ كقـولِهِ: إذَا وَلَدَتْ نَاقَتِي وَوَلَدَ وَلَدُهَا فَقَدْ بِعْتُكَ الولدَ (أي ولد الولد لأنه بيع ما ليس بمـمـلوكٍ ولا معـلومٍ ولا مقـدورٍ على تسليمه) ولا أنْ يَبِيعَ شيئـاً ويُؤَجَّلَ الثمنَ بذلك (أي لزمنِ نتاجِ النتاجِ لأنه إلى أجلٍ مجهول) [ولا بيع الملامسةِ والمنابذةِ والحصاةِ].

EITHER-OR SALES

بيعتان في بيعة

k4.2 It is invalid to make a transaction whose terms include two different possible deals (A: without specifying which has been agreed upon) such as saying, "I sell you this for either one thousand in cash or two thousand in deferred payment" (O: which is invalid because the price is not known), or such as saying, "I sell you my robe for a thousand, provided you sell me your sword for five hundred" (O: which is invalid because of the invalid stipulation (dis: below)).

k4.2   ولا بَيْعَتانِ في بَيْعَةٍ كقولكَ: بِعْتُكَ هذا بألفٍ نقـداً أوْ بألفَيْنِ مُؤَجَّـلاً (للجهـل بالعـوض)، أوْ: بِعْتُكَ ثوبي بألفٍ على أنْ تَبيعَني [عبـدَك] (ت: سيفَكَ) بخمسمائةٍ (وعـدم الصحة في هذا للشرط الفاسد).

SALES WITH EXTRANEOUS STIPULATIONS

بيع وشرط

k4.3 It is not valid to make a transaction that includes an invalid stipulation (A: such as a condition that is extraneous to the original agreement which adds to its price) (O: because the Prophet (Allah bless him and give him peace) forbade transactions with such conditions, like stipulating a loan or a second transaction), saying, for example, "I hereby sell it to you [n: for a thousand] provided you loan me a hundred" (O: or "provided you sell me your house for such and such a price" (A: or "provided you do not sell it to So-and-so"). Its invalidity is due to considering both the thousand and the accompanying second deal as the price. Stipulating this invalidates the transaction, and paying this "price" is void, it not being determinately known (def: k2.1(e))). (A: The invalidating factor is *stipulating* a second transaction, not the mere fact that it accompanies the first transaction, for it is permissible to join two transactions, as discussed at k4.12 below.)

k4.3   ولا بيعٌ وشرطٌ (لنهيه ﷺ عن بيعٍ وشرط كشرط قرض أو بيع) مثلُ: بِعْتُك بشرط أنْ تَقْرِضَني مائةً (أوْ على أن تبيعَني دارك بكـذا وعـدم الصحة في هذا لكونه جعل الألف ورفق العقد الثاني ثمناً واشتراطـه فاسد فبطـل مقابله من الثمن وهو مجهول).

SALES WITH VALID STIPULATIONS

صحة بيع مع شرط في بعض الصور

k4.4 The following types of conditions do not invalidate transactions that stipulate them:

(1) a condition to postpone payment, though this requires that the date of payment be specified;

k4.4   ويَصِحُّ بيعٌ وشـرطٌ في صورٍ وهي شرطُ الأجـلِ في الثمن بشرط أنْ يَكـونَ الأجلُ معلوماً وأنْ يَرْهَنَ به رهناً أوْ

(2) a condition that collateral (def: k11) be put up as security (N: for payment of the price or for delivery of the merchandise);

(3) a condition that a particular individual will guarantee (def: k15) payment;

(4) or other conditions (O: from the seller, the buyer, or both) that the deal requires, such as an option to return the merchandise if defective, and so forth.

It is valid for the seller to stipulate that he is free of responsibility for defects in the merchandise. By doing so, he is not held responsible for an animal's internal defects which he does not know of, though he remains responsible for all other kinds of defects. (O: The conditions for this ruling are that the defect be internal, be found in an animal, be unknown to the seller, and that it exist at the time of the agreement.)

يَضْمَنُهُ بِهِ زيدٌ [أوْ أنْ يُعْتِقَ العَبَدَ المبيعَ] أوْ شَرَطَ (أي البَائِعِ أوِ المشتري أوكل منهما) مَا يَقْتَضِيهِ العقدُ كالردُّ بالعيب ونحوه.

فإِنْ باعَ وشَــرَطَ البَـراءةَ مِنَ العيوبِ صَحَّ وبَـريءَ مِنْ كل عيبٍ باطنٍ في الحيوان لَمْ يَعْلَمْ بهِ البائعُ ولا يُبْرَأُ مِمَّا سِواهُ (فَالعيبُ البَـاطنُ قيـد أول، وفي الحيوان قيـد ثانٍ، ولم يعلمه قيد ثالثٌ، ويزاد قيد رابع على هذه الثلاثة وهو وجود العيب في الحيوان حال العقد).

PAYING NONREFUNDABLE DEPOSITS

بيع العربون

k4.5   It is not valid to pay a nonrefundable deposit towards the price of an article, such as paying a dirham for piece of merchandise on the basis that if the buyer decides to keep it, the dirham is part of the price, but if he does not, then the seller keeps the dirham for free.

(A: The school of Imam Ahmad permits nonrefundable deposits.)

k4.5   ولا يَصِحُّ بيعُ العربونِ بأنْ يَشْتَري سلعةً ويَدْفَعَ درهماً على أنَّهُ إِنْ رَضِيَ بالسلعـةِ فالدرهمُ مِنَ الثمنِ وإلَّا فهوَ للبائع مجاناً. [ولوْ فَرَّقَ بينَ الجاريةِ وولدِهَا قبلَ سِنّ التمييزِ ببيعٍ أوْ هبةٍ بطَلَ العقدُ وبعدَ التمييزِ يَصِحُّ].

k4.6   [ويَحْـرُمُ أنْ يَبيـعَ حاضِرٌ لبـادٍ بأنْ يَقُولَ الحاضرُ للبدويِّ الذي قَدِمَ بسلعةٍ وهيَ مِمَّا يُحتَاجُ إليهَا في البلدِ: لا تبعِ الآنَ حتَّى أبيعَهَا لكَ قليلاً قليلاً بثمنٍ غالٍ. وأنْ يَتَلَقَّى الركبانَ فيُخْبِرَهُمْ بكسادِ ما مَعَهُمْ لِيشْتَرِيَ منهم بغبنٍ].

UNDERCUTTING ANOTHER'S DEAL

السوم على سوم أخيه

k4.7   It is unlawful to undercut a brother's deal (A: or a non-Muslim's, since there is no difference between Muslims and non-Muslims in rulings concerning commercial dealings) that he has made with a customer, after they have settled on the

k4.7   وأنْ يَسُـومَ على سَوْمِ أخيـهِ (ع: ولوْ غيرِ مسلمٍ إذا لا فرقَ بين مسلم وكـافرٍ في المعـاملاتِ) بأنْ يَزيـدَ في السلعةِ بعدَ استقرارِ الثمنِ (بأن يقولَ لمن

price (O: meaning to say to someone who has accepted something with the intention to buy it for so-and-so much, "Return it to its owner and I'll sell you a better one for the same price or less," or tell the seller, "Take it back from him and I'll pay you more for it." The above restriction *after they have settled on the price* excludes someone going around taking bids from those who are increasing them, as auctioneers do, which is not unlawful).

It is also unlawful to undercut a brother's price (O: that is, during the option to cancel at the time of the agreement (def: k1.3), or during a stipulated option to cancel period (def: k1.4)) by telling the buyer, "Cancel the deal and I'll sell you one cheaper." (O: This also holds for other contracts, such as renting or lending the use of something.)

BIDDING UP MERCHANDISE

k4.8   It is unlawful to bid up the price of a piece of merchandise that one is not really interested in, to fool another bidder.

SELLING GRAPES TO A WINEMAKER

k4.9   It is unlawful to sell grapes to someone who will make wine from them. (O: Like grapes in this is the sale of dates, bread, wheat, or barley, whenever one knows that this (A: i.e. alcoholic drink) will result, or thinks it will. If there is doubt or if one merely imagines it, then the transaction is merely offensive. (N: *Think* (zann) means to believe it probable, *doubt* (shakk) means one is undecided, and *imagine* (wahm) means to merely consider it possible.) Selling in such cases is unlawful or offensive because it is a means to disobedience, whether certain or suspected (A: *means* meaning an instrumental cause, as opposed to something which is not instrumental, such as renting a house to a drunkard, which is not unlawful because it is not a cause, though it is unlawful to rent a building to someone who intends to open a bar, for example). Tirmidhi relates that the Prophet (Allah bless him and give him peace)

اخذ شيئاً ليشتريه بكذا : رده على صاحبه حتى أبيعك خيـراً منه بهذا الثمن أو بأقل منه . أو يقـول لمـالكه : استرده لأشتريه منك بأكثر . وخـرج بقـوله بعد استقرار الثمن ما يطاف به على من يزيد كالدلالين فلا يحرم) .

وأنْ يَبيعَ على بيعِ أخيهِ (وذلك في زمن خيارِ المجلس أو الشرط) بأنْ يَقُولَ للمشتـري : افْسَـخِ البيعَ وأنَـا أبيعُـكَ بأرْخَصَ منهُ . (ومثـل البيع في هذا غيره من بقية العقود كالإجارة والعارية) .

النجش

k4.8   وأنْ يَنْـجُشَ بأنْ يَزيـدَ في السلعةِ وهوَ غيرُ راغبٍ فيها ليُغِرَّ بَهَا غيرَهُ .

بيع عنب ممن يتخذه خمراً

k4.9   وأنْ يَبيـعَ العنبَ ممّنْ يَتَّخـذُهُ خمراً . (ومثـل العنب الـرطب والخبـز والحنطة والشعيـر بأن يعلم ذلـك منـه أو يظنـه فإن شك فيـه أو توهمـه منه فالبيع له مكـروه . وإنمـا حـرم أوكـره لأنـه سبب لمعصيـة محققـة أو مظنـونة . وروى الترمـذي أنه ﷺ لعن شاربها وسـاقيها

cursed whoever drinks wine, gives it to others to drink, sells it, buys it, presses it for another, transports it, receives it, or eats its price.)

وبـائعهـا ومبتـاعهـا وعاصرهـا ومعتصرها وحاملها والمحمولة إليه وآكل ثمنها) .

k4.10 If one makes any of the above unlawful transactions (k4.6–9), the agreement is valid (dis: c5.2).

k4.10 فإنْ بَاعَ في هٰذهِ الصورِ كلّهَا المحرمةِ صَحَّ البيعُ .

A VALID SALE COMBINED WITH AN
INVALID SALE

الجمع بين بيع صحيح وبيع فاسد
في عقد واحد

k4.11 If one combines something valid to sell with something invalid to sell in one transaction, such as selling one's own garment together with someone else's without his permission, or such as selling wine and vinegar, then the transaction is valid for the portion of the price that covers the valid sale (O: no matter whether the person knew what the case was, or whether he did not and believed the sale permissible, thinking at the time, e.g. that the wine was vinegar) and is invalid for the portion of the price that was not valid (A: and the portion must be refunded to the buyer). The buyer has the option to cancel the whole agreement if, at the time the deal was made, he did not know it included something impermissible.

k4.11 وإنْ جَمَعَ في عقدٍ واحدٍ مَا يَجُوزُ وما لا يَجُوزُ [ع : ويُحمل الجواز هنـا على الصحة)] مثلُ [عبدِهِ وعبدِ] (ت: ثوبِه وثوبٍ) غيره بغير إذنِه أو خمرٍ وخـلٍّ صَحَّ فيمَا يَجُوزُ بقسطِه منَ الثمنِ ([باعتبار قيمتِه] سواء علم الحال أم جهل وأجـاز البيع ويقدر الخمر عند البيع خلاً) وبَطَـلَ فيمَا لاَ يَجُوزُ . وللمشتري الخيارُ إنْ جَهِلَ .

JOINING TWO TYPES OF TRANSACTIONS IN ONE
CONTRACT

الجمع بين عقدين مختلفي
الحكم

k4.12 It is valid to join two contracts of different kinds (O: for example, a sale with a rent agreement) such as saying, "I sell you my horse and rent you my house for a year for such and such an amount" (O: though it is not necessary that they be different kinds, for the ruling also applies to two contracts of the same type, such as a partnership (def: k16) linked with financing a profit-sharing venture (qirad, def: k22)), or such as saying, "I marry you my daughter and sell you her house [N: as her proxy, the proceeds being hers] for so-and-so much," and the price is considered as proportionately distributed over the two transactions.

k4.12 وإنْ جَمَعَ عقـدَيْن مختلفَي الحكمِ (كـالبيـع والإجـارة) مثل : بعْتُكَ [عبـدِي] (ت : فَرَسَي) وآجَـرْتُـكَ داري سنةً بكَذَا (والاختلاف ليس بقيد بل مثله المتحـدان فيه كالشـركـة والقـراض) ، وزَوَّجْتُـكَ ابنتي وبِعْتُكَ [عبـدها] (ت : دارَها) بكَذَا صَحَّ وقُسِّطَ العوضُ عليهمَا .

k5.0   THE RETURN OF MERCHANDISE BECAUSE OF A DEFECT

(O: The criterion for *defect* is based on something that is expected to exist (n: in merchandise), whether this expectation results from:

(1) stipulations agreed upon (dis: k4.4(4));

(2) the customary level of quality (dis: f4.5) for merchandise of its type;

(3) or outright deception by the seller.

The author does not mention (1) in this section, but confines himself to (2) and (3).)

INFORMING A PROSPECTIVE BUYER OF DEFECTS IN MERCHANDISE

k5.1   Whoever knows of a defect in the article (O: he is selling) is obliged to disclose it. If he does not, he has cheated (O: the buyer, which is prohibited by the Prophet's statement (Allah bless him and give him peace),

"He who cheats us is not one of us"),

though the transaction is valid (A: provided the buyer accepts it, as discussed below).

RETURNING DEFECTIVE MERCHANDISE

k5.2   When a buyer notices a defect in the merchandise that existed when the seller had it, he is entitled to return it (O: though if he is content to accept the defect, he does not have to return it. He may also return it when the defect occurred after the sale but before the merchandise was delivered, since the merchandise is the seller's responsibility during this period).

k5.3   The criterion (O: of *defectiveness*) is:

(a) any flaw that diminishes the article or its value to a degree that hinders a valid purpose;

---

k5.0   رد المبيع بالعيب

(وهـو ما يتـوقف على شيء مظنـون الحصول نشأ ذلك الظن من التزام شرطي أو قضـاء عرفي أو تغرير فعلي . ولم يذكر المصنف القسم الأول وذكر الثاني والثالث) .

التنبيه على عيب السلعة

k5.1   مَنْ عَلِمَ بالسلعة عيباً لَزِمَهُ (أي البـائـع) أنْ يُبَيِّنَهُ . فإنْ لمْ يُبَيِّنْ فَقَـدْ غَشَّ (المشتري وهو منهي عنه لقوله ﷺ : «من غشنا فليس منا») والبيعُ صحيحٌ .

رد المبيع

k5.2   فإذا اطَّلَعَ المشتري على عيب كَانَ عندَ البائع فلَهُ الردُّ (فإن رضي به فلا يجب رده، وله أن يرده بالعيب الحـادث بعـد العقـد وقبـل القبض لأن المبيـع في تلك الحالة من ضمان البائع) .

k5.3   وضـابـطُهُ (أي ضابـط العيب هو) مَا نَقَصَ العينَ أو القيمةَ نقصاناً يُفوتُ بِه غرضٌ صحيـحٌ والغـالبُ في مثل ذلك

(b) provided that such an imperfection does not usually exist in similar merchandise.

(O: The former restriction excludes such things as amputation of a surplus digit or a minor nick from the animal's thigh or hock that is inconsequential and does not obviate its purpose, in which case there is no option to return it. The latter restriction excludes defects not generally absent in similar merchandise, such as missing teeth in older animals. There is no option to return such merchandise, even if the value is diminished.)

المبيع عدمُهُ (وخرج بالقيد الأول قطع إصبع زائدة أو فلقة يسيرة من فخذ أو ساق لا تؤثر شيئاً ولا تفوت غرضاً فلا خيار به وبالثاني ما لا يغلب فيه ما ذكر كقلع سن في الكبير فلا خيار به وإن نقصت القيمة به) [فَيُرَدُّ إنْ بَانَ العبدُ خصياً (والخصاء حرام وقال ابن القاسم الظاهـر أنـه من الكبائر) أوْ سارقاً أوْ يَبُولُ في الفراش وهوَ كبيرٌ].

k5.4 If the buyer notices a defect in the merchandise after it has been destroyed (O: whether physically, such as an animal being killed, a garment worn out, or food eaten; or whether *legally* finished, by being no longer permissible to transfer from person to person, as when a site has been made an endowment (waqf, def: k30))—then a compensation (A: from the seller to the buyer) is obligatory. (O: The buyer is entitled to it because of the impossibility of returning the article due to its no longer existing. *Compensation* means a part of the article's price whose relation to the whole price is the same as the relation of the value which the defect diminished to the full value of the article if it had been without defect. (N: The difference between price and value is that the *value* is how much money an article is worth in the marketplace, while the *price* is whatever the sale agreement specifies, whether this be more or less than the value.) The value in such a case is fixed at the lowest value (A: for articles of its type current in the marketplace) between the time the deal was made and the time the buyer took possession of it.)

The buyer is no longer entitled to seek compensation for such a defect if (O: he notices the defect after) he no longer owns the article because of having sold it or otherwise disposed of it. But if such an article returns to the buyer's possession after this (O: i.e. after having left his ownership, whether as a gift, or returned (A: from a subsequent buyer) because it was defective, or because of a cancelled deal, or he buys it back), then he is entitled to return it (A: to the person who originally sold it to him).

k5.4 فلو اطَّلَعَ (المشتـري) على العيب بعدَ تلف المبيع (حساً كأن قتل أو أتلف الثوب أو أكـل الطعـام أو شرعـاً بأن خرج عن قبـول النقـل من شخص إلى شخص كمـا إذا أوقف المكـان) تَعَيَّنَ (على المشتـري أخـذ) الأرش (لتعـذر الـرد لفـوات المبيـع. والأرش جزء من الثمن نسبته إليه كنسبة ما نقص المعيب من القيمة إلى تمامها لو كان سليماً. (ح: والفرق بين الثمن والقيمـة أن القيمـة ما تساويه السلعة في السوق من النقود؛ وأما الثمن فمـا وقع عليه العقد سواء كان أكثر أم أقـل من القيمة). والأصح اعتبار أقل قيمـة المبيـع من حين العقـد إلى حين القبض) أو (اطلع على العيب) بعدَ زوال الملك عنْهُ (ببيـع أو غيره لمْ يَكُنْ لَهُ (أي للمشتري) طلبُ الأرش الآنَ. فإنْ رَجَعَ إليـهِ بعـدَ ذلكَ (أي بعد زواله عنه إما بهبة أو برد بعيب أو إقـالـة أو شراء) فلَهُ (أي للمشتـري الأول الـذي وجـد بالمبيع عيباً) الردُّ.

k5.5   If an additional defect occurs in an article (O: other than the above-mentioned defect (A: that existed before the buyer received the article)) while it is in the buyer's possession, then the buyer is only entitled to take a compensation (O: from the seller, to compensate for the original defect) and is not entitled to (A: insist that the seller accept) return (A: of the article for a full refund).

But if the original seller is willing to accept it back with the (O: new) defect, (A: refunding the original price,) then the buyer is not entitled to (A: keep the article and) demand compensation (O: for the original defect. Rather, the buyer is told, "Either return it, or else be content with it as it is and you get nothing"; for the harm to the original seller which is what prevents (A: it being obligatory for him to accept) its return no longer exists if the seller is content to take it back, and the merchandise is as if the additional defect never occurred.

Their agreement is implemented if buyer and seller agree upon:

(1) the seller taking it back with (A: the seller refunding the original price, and the buyer giving him) compensation for the new additional defect;

(2) or the buyer keeping the merchandise, and the seller paying him compensation for the original defect;

since either of these options might satisfy the interests of the two parties. If the buyer and seller disagree about which of these two options should be implemented, the decision goes to whichever of them requests option (2), whether this person is the buyer or the seller, since it confirms the original contract).

k5.6   If the new defect which occurs while the article is in the buyer's possession is the sole means of disclosing the old defect, such as breaking open a (A: spoiled) watermelon or eggs, and so forth, then the new defect does not prevent (A: the obligation of the seller to accept) its return. But if the new damage exceeds the extent that was necessary to reveal the original defect, then the seller is no longer compelled to accept it back.

k5..5   وإنْ حَدَثَ عنـدَ المـشتـري عيبٌ آخرُ (غيـر العيب المتقدم) [مثلُ أنْ يَفْضَ البكـرَ] تَعَيَّنَ الأرشُ (من البـائـع لأجـل الـعيب القـديم) وامْتَنَـعَ الـرّدُّ (القهـري) فإنْ رَضِيَ البـائـعُ بالعيب (الحـادث) لَمْ يَكُنْ للمـشتـري طلبُ الأرش (للعيب القـديم بل يقـال له : إما أن ترده وإما أن تقنع به ولا شيء لك ؛ لأن المـانـع من الـرد هو ضـرر البائع وقد زال برضاه فصار كما لو لم يحدث فيه عيب . ولو توافقا على الرد مع الأرش الحادث أو الإمساك مع الأرش القـديم فُعِلَ لما فيه من الجمـع بين المصلحتين ومـراعـاة الجانبين . وإن تنازعـا فيما يفعل منهما أجيب من طلب إمساك المبيـع مع أرش القـديم بائعـاً كان أو مشتـرياً لما فيه من تقرير العقد) .

k5.6   فإنْ كانَ الـعيبُ الحـادثُ لا يُعْرَفُ العيبُ القديمُ إلّا به ككسر البطيخ والبيض ونحـوِهِمَـا لَمْ يَمْنَـعْ (العيب الحـادثُ) الـرّدَ . فإنْ زادَ على ما يُمْكِنُ المعرفةُ به فلا ردَّ [(أي سقط الرد القهري)].

k5.7 It is a necessary condition for (A: cases where the buyer seeks a refund for something he is) returning (O: because of a defect) that the buyer return it immediately upon noticing the defect (O: and his option to return it is cancelled if he delays without an excuse). On his way back to the seller, he should have two witnesses affirm that he is cancelling the agreement (A: so if the seller is unavailable at the time, the buyer is nevertheless able to prove that he went to return it immediately). If the defect is noticed while one is praying, eating, using the lavatory, or at night (A: if the night presents a problem in returning it), then one is entitled to delay returning it until the hindrance preventing one from doing so is no longer present, provided one stops using and benefiting from it. If the buyer delays returning it when capable of doing so, then the seller is no longer obliged to accept the article back for a refund, or no longer obliged (A: in cases like k5.5 above) to compensate the buyer for the original defect (O: because the delay gives the impression that the buyer is satisfied with the defect).

k5.7 وشـرطُ الـردِّ (بـالعيبِ) أنْ يكُــونَ علـى الفـور (فيبطـلُ بالتأخيـرِ بلا عذرٍ) ويُشْهِـدُ في طريقِه أنَّـهُ فسَخَ . فلْو عَرَفَ العيبَ وهوَ يُصَلّي أوْ يأكُلُ أوْ يَقْضي حاجـةً أوْ ليـلاً فلَهُ الـتأخيـرُ إلى زوالِ العـارضِ بشـرطِ تركِ الاستعمـالِ والانتفـاعِ فإنْ أخَّـرَ (الـردَّ) متمكناً (منه) سَقَطَ الردُّ (أي القهري) والأرشُ (للإشعار التأخير بالرضا) .

k5.8 [وتَحرُمُ التصريةُ وهيَ أنْ يشُدَّ البائعُ أخلافَ البهيمةِ ويتْركَ حلبَها أياماً ليغُرَّ غيرَهُ بكثرةِ اللبن . فإذا اطَّلَعَ عليه المشتري فلهُ الردُّ مطلقاً . فإنْ كانَ بعدَ حلبِها وتلِفَ اللبنُ رَدَّ صاعاً منْ تمرٍ بدلَ اللبنِ إنْ كانَ الحيوانُ مأكولاً ويُلْحَقُ بالتصريةِ في الردِّ تحميرُ وجهِ الجاريةِ وتسويدُ الشعرِ ونحوُهُمَا] .

k5.9 (A: The term *murabaha* applies to sales where the seller states the price in terms of "the original price plus such and such an amount as profit," whether by *original price* he means the amount he originally paid for the whole lot, or whether he means the proportion of that price represented by the percentage of the lot which he is now selling.)

The seller in *murabaha* (O: meaning an agreement where the price consists of the original price plus increment) is obliged to inform the buyer of any defect that occurred in the merchandise while in his possession, such as by saying, "I bought it for ten [O: or "bought it for one hundred and sell it to you at what I bought it for, plus one dirham's profit on every ten"] but such and such a defect happened to it while I had it." (O: He is likewise obliged to say, for example, "Such and

k5.9 (ع: كلمةُ المرابحةِ تنسحب على البيعِ الذي يعبّر البائعُ عن الثمنِ فيه بنحوِ قولِه : ثمنُ التكلفةِ زائدٌ كذا ؛ سواء عنى بالـزائـد مقـداراً زائـداً على ثمنِ التكلفةِ أو نسبة مأويةٍ منها) .

ويَلْزَمُ البائعَ أنْ يُخْبِرَ في بيعِ المرابحةِ (وهي عقدٌ يبقى الثمنُ فيـه على ثمنِ المبيـعِ الأولِ مع زيـادةٍ) بالعيبِ الـذي حَدَثَ عندهُ فيقُولُ : اشْتَـرَيْتُـهُ بعشرةٍ ؛ مثلًا (أي أو: بمائةٍ وبعتكه بما اشتريته أي بمثله وربح درهمٍ لكـل عشـرةٍ) لكنْ حَدَثَ عنـدي العيبُ الفـلانيُّ (ومثل هذا

such a defect appeared in it that was from the previous owner, and I accepted this.")

The seller in *murabaha* is also obliged to explain how much time he was given to pay the original price (A: since deferring payment generally
raises the price, and merely stating such a raised
price without mentioning that it was deferred
would give the new buyer a false impression).

(O: The author should have mentioned (A:
that telling the prospective buyer the above information is also obligatory in sales of) *discount* (A:
on a lot of goods or portion thereof), as when the
seller tells someone, "I sell it to you for what I
bought it for, minus one from every eleven."
These rulings likewise apply to agreements stated
in terms of, "I sell you it at the same price the original deal was made for.")

أن يقول ظهر به عيب قديم ورضيت به) .
وبُيِّنَ الأجَـلَ (وكـان على المصنف أن
يذكر المحـاطـة أيضاً [من الحط وهـو
النقص] كقـول من ذكر لغيره : بعتك بما
اشـتـريت وحـط واحـد من كل أحـد
عشـر ؛ ويـدخـل في : بعت بما اشتريت
ثمنه الذي استقر عليه العقد فقط) .

*

k6.0   SELLING FRUIT AND CROPS

k6.1   It is not permissible (O: or valid) to sell the
fruit alone from a tree (A: without the tree, while
still on it) before it is ripe, unless the agreement
stipulates immediate picking of the fruit. But such
a sale is valid without restriction if made after the
fruit is *ripe,* meaning, for fruits that do not change
color, to become fit to eat; and for fruits whose
color changes, to start to turn the color of ripeness.

If both the tree and the fruit are sold
together, the sale is permissible without stipulating that the fruit be picked.

k6.2   Grain, when green, is subject to the same
rulings as fruit before it is ripe: it may not be sold
(O: nor would the sale be valid) unless the agreement stipulates immediate harvest, though there
are no restrictions on sales made after the grain is
solid and firm.

k6.3   It is not permissible to sell grain when still
in the husk, or to sell unripe nuts, almonds, or

k6.0   بيع الثمار والزرع

k6.1   بيـعُ الثمـرة وحـدَهَا على
الشجـرة إنْ كانَ قبلَ بدوِّ الصلاح لمْ يَجُزْ
(ولم يصح) إلّا بشرط القطع . وإنْ كان
بعـدَهُ (أي بعد بدوِّ الصلاح) جَازَ مطلقاً .
وبـدوُّ الصـلاح هوَ أنْ يَطيبَ أكلُهُ فيمَا لا
يَتَلَوَّنُ أوْ يأْخُذَ (أي يشرع) بالتلوين فيما
يَتَلَوَّنُ .
وإنْ بَاعَ الشجـرة وثمرتَها جازَ منْ غير
شرط القطع .

k6.2   والزرعُ الأخضرُ كالثمرة قبلَ
بدوِّ الصلاح : لا يَجُوزُ (البيع ولا يصح
فيـه) إلّا بشـرط القطع . وبعـد اشتـداد
الحبِّ يَجُوزُ مطلقاً .

k6.3   ولا يَجُوزُ بيعُ الحبِّ في سنبله
ولا الجـوزِ واللوزِ والبـاقـلّاء الأخضـر

broadbeans when these are in the shell. (A: When the latter three are dried, they may be sold in the shell.)

[(صفة لكـل من هذه الثـلاثـة أي الجوز الأخضر وما بعده)] في القشرين .

*

k7.0 MERCHANDISE BEFORE THE BUYER TAKES POSSESSION OF IT

k7.0   قبض المبيع وضمانه

k7.1 Merchandise is the responsibility of the seller before the buyer has taken possession (def: k7.3) of it. If such merchandise is destroyed (Ar. talifa, to be finished off or used up) by itself or through an act of the seller, then the agreement is cancelled and no payment is due for it. If the buyer destroys such merchandise, he must pay its price, and his destroying it is considered as having taken possession of it. If a third party destroys such merchandise, the deal is not cancelled but rather the buyer is given a choice to either:

(1) cancel the agreement and make the value (def: k5.4(N:)) (O: of what the third party destroyed) a debt that the third party owes to the seller;

(2) or effect the deal, paying the seller the price (O: if he agrees to effect the deal) and making the third party liable to pay the value (O: to the buyer).

k7.1   المبيعُ قبـلَ قبضهِ من ضمان البائع . فإنْ تَلِفَ (المبيعُ بنفسه) أوْ أتْلَفَهُ البائعُ انْفَسَخَ البيعُ وسَقَطَ الثمنُ .

وإنْ أتْلَفَهُ المشتري استقرَّ عليه الثَّمنُ ويكونُ إتلافُهُ قبضاً .

وإنْ أتْلَفَهُ أجنبيٌّ لمْ يَنْفَسِخْ بـلْ يُخَيَّرُ المشتـري بيـن أنْ يَفْسَخَ فيَغْـرَمَ الأجنبيُّ للبائعِ القيمةَ (أي قيمة ما أتلفه) أوْ يُجيزَ (أي عقد البيع) ويُعْطيَ الثمنَ (للبائعِ إن أجاز العقد) ويُغْرَّمَ الأجنبيُّ القيمةَ (للمشتري) .

k7.2 When one buys something, it is not permissible (O: or valid) to sell it until one has taken possession of it. (O: The invalidity of selling it likewise applies to all transactions disposing of it (A: such as renting it, giving it away, and so forth).

It is also invalid for the seller to dispose of the price in any way before it has been received from the buyer, unless the new transaction is with the same buyer and involves the very same (A: article that is the) price.)

But if the price is a financial obligation (N: that is, an amount of money, unspecified as to which particular pieces of money it is), the seller may ask for a different sort of payment, provided

k7.2   وإذا اشْتَرَى شيئاً لمْ يَجُزْ (أي ولم يصحّ) أنْ يَبيعَهُ حتّى يَقْبِضَهُ . (ومثل عدم صحـة بيعـه بيعه قبل قبضه الثمن فلا يصح للبـائـع التصرف فيه قبل قبضه من المـشتـري في جميـع ما تقـدم إلا مع المشتري إذا كان بعين المقابـل) . لكنْ للبـائـع إذا كانَ الثمنُ في الذمةِ (ح : أي نقـداً غيـر معين) أنْ يَسْتَبْدِلَ عنهُ (أي عن

he has not already accepted the payment, as when he sells something for dirhams, but then accepts gold, a garment, or something else instead of them.

k7.3 *Taking possession* means:

(1) for transportable things such as wheat or barley, that they be transported (N: by the buyer or his representative) (O: that is, when he moves the merchandise to a place not belonging to the seller, such as the street or the buyer's house);

(2) for things dealt with by hand, such as a garment or book, that they be taken in hand;

(3) and for other things, such as a house or land, that they be given over (O: i.e. the seller give the buyer control over them, such as by handing the key to him or moving others' belongings off the property).

*

k8.0 DISPUTES OVER WHAT THE TERMS OF A TRANSACTION WERE

k8.1 When two parties agree on the validity of a transaction but disagree on its terms, and there is no proof, then they each swear an oath (dis: k8.2) affirming their side of the story. Such a disagreement could be:

(1) the seller saying that he sold it for immediate payment, while the buyer asserts that payment was to be deferred;

(2) the seller stating that he sold for ten, while the buyer maintains it was five;

ذلك الثمنَ قبلَ قبضِهِ (من المشتري) مثلَ أنْ يبيعَ بدراهمَ فيعْتاضَ عنها ذهباً أوْ ثوباً ونحوَ ذلك .

k7.3 والقبضُ فيما يُنْقَلُ النقلُ (ح) : من قبلِ المشتري أو نائبه) مثلَ القمحِ والشعيرِ (إذا نقلَه إلى مكانٍ لا يختص به بائعٍ كشارعٍ أو دارٍ للمشتري) وفيما يُتَناوَلُ باليدِ التناوُلُ مثلَ الثوبِ والكتابِ . وفيما سواهُمَا التخليةُ مثلَ الدارِ والأرضِ (بأن يمكنه البائعُ منه ويسلمه المفتاح وأن يفرغه عن متاع غيره أي غير المشتري) .

k7.4 [فلوْ قالَ البائعُ : لا أُسَلِّمُ المبيعَ حتّى أقْبِضَ الثمنَ ؛ وقالَ المشتري : لا أُسَلِّمُ الثمنَ حتّى أقْبِضَ المبيعَ ؛ فإنْ كانَ الثمنُ في الذمةِ أُلْزِمَ البائعُ بالتسليم أولاً ثمَّ يُلْزَمُ المشتري بالتسليمِ ، وإنْ كانَ الثمنُ معيناً أُلْزِمَا معاً بأنْ يُؤْمَرَا فَيُسَلِّمَا إلى عدلٍ ثمَّ العدلُ يُعطي لكلِّ واحدٍ حقَّهُ] .

k8.0 الاختلاف في كيفية العقد

k8.1 إذا اتّفقا على صحةِ العقدِ واختَلَفَا في كيفيتِه بأنْ قالَ البائعُ : بعْتُكَ بحالٍ ؛ فقـالَ (أي الـمـشـتـري) : بلْ بمـؤجّـلٍ ؛ أوْ : بعْتُكَ بعشرةٍ ؛ فقالَ : بلْ بخمسةٍ ؛ أوْ : بعتُـكَ بشـرطِ الخيارِ ؛

(3) the seller saying he sold it to the buyer on condition that there be an option to cancel period (def: k1.4), while the buyer asserts that no such option was stipulated;

or similar disputes.

فَقَالَ: بَلْ بِلَا خِيَارٍ؛ ومَا أَشْبَهَ ذلكَ ولمْ يَكُنْ ثَمَّ بَيِّنَةٌ تَحَالَفَا.

k8.2   (N: Swearing an oath (def: o18) is a means for urging one's case when there is no proof, meaning no witnesses. When rulings mention, for example, that "So-and-so's word is believed;" or "So-and-so's word is accepted," it means that his word is accepted when he swears an oath in cases where there is no proof presented by either of the two parties. If there is proof, whether from the plaintiff or defendant, it is given precedence over an oath.)

k8.2   (ح: واليَمين تكـون حجـة حيث لا بَيِّنة. والبَيِّنة الشهود. وإذا قيل صدق فلان أو القـول قول فلان فمعنـاه قبـل قوله مع يمينه حيث لا بيّنة لأحـد الطـرفين. فإنْ كانت بيّنـة قدمت على اليمين سواء كانت للمدعي أو المدعي عليه).

k8.3   In the oath for such cases, the seller swears first, saying, for example, "By Allah, I did not sell it to you for such and such an amount, but rather for such and such an amount." Then the buyer swears, "By Allah, I did not buy it for such and such, but rather bought it for such and such." It consists of one oath (A: from each party) which joins the denial of the other's claim with the affirmation of one's own claim, and in which the denial is recommended to precede the affirmation.

k8.3   فيَبْدَأ البائعُ فيَقُولُ: واللهِ ما بِعْتُك بكـذا ولقَدْ بِعْتُك بكذ؛ ثمَّ يَقُولُ المشتري: واللهِ ما اشْتَرَيْتُ بكـذا ولقد اشْتَرَيْتُ بكذا؛ وهيَ يمينٌ واحدةٌ يَجْمَعُ فيهـا بين نفي قول صاحبه وإثبـات قوله ويُقَدَّمُ النفي (استحباباً).

k8.4   When the buyer and seller have sworn, but subsequently reach a solution that both accept, the agreement is not cancelled. But if they cannot reach an accord, they cancel the agreement, or one of them cancels it, or the Islamic magistrate does (O: to end the trouble between them. When the agreement is cancelled, each returns whatever he has accepted from the other).

k8.4   فإذا تَحَالَفَا فإنْ تَرَاضِيَا بعـدَ ذلك فلا فسخَ للعقد. وإلّا فَيَفْسَخَانِه أوْ أحـدُهُمَـا أو الحـاكِم (قطعاً للنزاع بينهما وإذا حصل الفسخ فكل واحد منهما يرد ما قبضه من العوضين على الآخر).

k8.5   If either the buyer or seller testifies that a particular agreement is invalid, but the other party says it is valid, then the word of whichever of them asserts it is valid is accepted if he swears an oath (dis: k8.2).

If the buyer comes to the seller with a piece of merchandise that he wants to return because of a

k8.5   فلوْ ادَّعَى أحـدُهُمـا شيئـاً يَقْتَضِي أنَّ البيـعَ وَقَـعَ فاسداً وكَذَبَهُ الآخرُ صُدِّقَ مُدَّعي الصحة بيمينِه.

ولوْ جَاءَ (المشتري) بمعيب لِيَرُدَّهُ فقالَ

defect, but the seller says that it is not the one he sold him, then the seller's word is accepted (O: when he swears).

If the buyer and seller disagree about a defect in an article that could have occurred while it was in the buyer's possession, but each party asserts that the defect occurred while in the other's possession, then the seller's word is accepted (O: when he swears).

الـبـائـعُ: لَيْسَ هوَ الـذي بِعْتُكَهُ؛ صُدِّقَ البائعُ (بيمينه).

ولوِ اخْتَلَفا في عيبٍ يُمْكِنُ حدوثُهُ عندَ المشتري فقـالَ البـائـعُ: حَدَثَ عندَكَ؛ وقـالَ المشتـري: بلْ كَانَ عنـدَكَ؛ صُدِّقَ البائعُ (بيمينه).

*

k9.0   BUYING IN ADVANCE (SALAM)

السلم   k9.0

k9.1   *Buying in advance* means the sale of described merchandise which is under (A: the seller's) obligation (A: to deliver to the buyer at a certain time).

هوَ بيعُ موصوفٍ في الذمةِ.   k9.1

THE CONDITIONS FOR THE VALIDITY OF BUYING IN ADVANCE

شروط صحة السلم

k9.2   In addition to the conditions for valid sales (def: k1.1–2, k2.1), other conditions (O: seven of them) must be met for buying in advance to be valid:

(a) that the price of the merchandise be received when the agreement is first made. It is sufficient to merely see the price that is being accepted, even when its exact amount is unknown;

(b) that the merchandise bought in advance be a *financial obligation* (dayn) (O: owed by the seller (N: meaning that buying in advance is not valid for particular individual articles ('ayn) (A: i.e. "this one" and no other)) which the seller will deliver when its time comes). Its delivery may be due from the present onwards, or may be due later through deferment (O: by clearly stating whether it is to be due immediately or deferred) to a specific date (O: which specificity is a necessary condition for the validity of deferring payment). It

k9.2   ويُشْتَرَطُ فيهِ مَعَ شروطِ البيع أمـورٌ (أي شروط سبعـة) أحـدُهـا قبضُ الثمنِ في المجلس وتَكْفِي رؤيـةُ الثمن وإنْ لَمْ يعْـرفْ قدرَهُ، والـثـانـي كونُ المسلم فيه ديناً (أي في ذمة المسلم إليه يحضـره وقت حلول الأجـل) (ح): فلا يصح السلم إذا كان المبيع معيناً ويَجُوزُ حالاً ومؤجلاً (بأن يصرح بهما) إلى أجلٍ معلومٍ (شـرط في صحته مؤجلاً) فلْوْ قَالَ

is not permissible to say, "I advance you these dirhams for that particular horse" (O: which is invalid because of the condition that the merchandise bought in advance be a financial obligation (dayn), which the above-mentioned horse is not, but is rather a particular individual article ('ayn));

(c) that the location to which the merchandise is to be delivered be clearly stipulated (A: though this is only a condition) in cases in which the buyer pays for it at a place where it cannot be delivered, such as the wilderness; or to which the merchandise can be delivered, but transporting it there involves considerable difficulty;

(d) that the merchandise bought in advance be determinately known by volume, weight, quantity, or yardage in terms of a familiar measure. It is not valid for someone to say "the weight of this stone," or "the capacity of this basket," if the (O: stone's) weight or basket's capacity is not known;

(e) that the merchandise be within the seller's power to deliver (def: k2.4) when the time for delivery arrives;

(f) that the merchandise not be generally subject to unavailability. If it is something rare (O: such as a great quantity of the season's first fruits of a particular kind of produce) or something not typically safe from unavailability, such as "the fruit of this particular date palm," then its sale in advance is not permissible;

(g) that those characteristics of the merchandise over which the buyer and seller might be at cross-purposes be expressly delineated by clear specifications. It is not permissible (O: to buy things in advance which cannot be defined by clear criteria, such as) for jewels or composites like meat pastry (O: composed of wheat, meat, and water, all of which are expected but not delineable in terms of minimal or maximal amounts), *ghaliya* perfume (O: composed of musk, ambergris, aloes, and camphor), or slippers (O: composed of outer and inner layers and padding), nor articles whose top randomly differs from their bottom, like a lamp or pitcher (O: the top of which is some-

أَسْلَمْتُ إلَيْكَ هٰذِهِ الـدراهِمَ في هٰذا [العبدِ] (ت: الحصانِ) لَمْ يَجُزْ (أي لم يصح العقد لفقد الشرط وهو كونه دَيناً لأن [العبدَ] (ت: الحصانَ المـذكورَ ليس دَيـناً بل هو عين)، الثـالثُ إذا أَسْلَمَ في موضعٍ لاَ يَصْلُـحُ للتسليم (أي تسليم المسلم فيـه) مثـلَ البـريةِ أوْ يَصْلُحُ ولكِنْ لنقلِه إلـيـه مؤنـةٌ اشْتُـرِطَ بيـانُ موضـعِ التسليم وشـروطُ المسلم فيه كونُهُ معلومَ القـدر كيـلاً أوْ وزنـاً أوْ عدداً أوْ ذرعـاً بمـقـدارٍ معـلومٍ . فلَوْ قالَ : زِنـةَ هٰذِهِ الصخرةِ ؛ أوْ: مِلءَ هٰذا الزنبيلِ ؛ولاَ يَعرف وزنَها (أي الصخرة) ولا ما يَسَعُ الزنبيل لَمْ يَصِحَّ، وأَنْ يَكُونَ مقـدوراً عليه عند وجـوبِ التسليم مأمونَ الانقطاعِ فإِنْ كَانَ عزيـزَ الـوجـودِ (كقـدرٍ كثيرٍ من البـاكـورةِ) [كجـاريـةٍ وبنتِها] أوْ لا يُؤْمَنُ انقطاعُهُ كثمرةِ نخلةٍ بعينِها لمْ يَجُزْ، وأنْ يُمْكِنَ ضبطُـهُ [كـالأدقـةِ والمـائـعـاتِ والحيـوانِ واللحم والقطن والحـديـدِ والأحجارِ والأخشابِ ونحوِ ذلك] فيُشْتَرَطُ ضبطُهُ بالصفاتِ التي يَخْتَلِفُ بها الغرضُ (أي غرض المتعـاقـدين) [فيَقُـولُ مثلاً: أَسْلَمْتُ إلَيْكَ في عبدٍ تركيٍّ أبيضَ رباعيِّ السِّنِّ طولُـه وُسِمنُـه كَذا ؛ ونحوُ ذلك] فلا يَجُـوزُ (السلم فيمـا لا ينضبط بالصفات كالسلم) في الجـواهـرِ والمختلطـاتِ كالهـريسةِ (فـإنها مركبة من قمح ولحم وماء وهي أجزاء مقصودة لا تنضبط بالقلة والكثرة) والغـاليـةِ (وهي مركبة من مسك وعنبر وعـود وكـافـورٍ) والخفـافِ (وهي مركبة من ظِهارةٍ وبطانةٍ وحشوٍ) وكذا مَا اخْتَلَفَ أعلاهُ وأسفلُهُ كمنارةٍ وإبريقٍ (فإن

401

times wider than the bottom, or vice versa) (N: though the Hanafi school permits such agreements, calling them *made to order* (istisna'), which they hold includes whatever is customarily bought in this way. They affirm the buyer's option to cancel the agreement when he sees the merchandise, and it is obligatory that the article be described very precisely), nor something substantially processed and altered by fire (A: meaning heat), such as bread or roast meat, since describing it (A: i.e. how much cooking it takes) is impossible in a precise way.

أعلى ما ذكر تارة يكون أعرض من أسفله وتارة بالعكس) (ح: وأجازَ الحنفية هذه العقـود وسمـوها الاستصناع وهو عندهم فيمـا جرت به العـادة، وأثبتـوا للمشتري خيار الرؤية، وأوجبوا أن يضبط المشترى بوصف دقيق) أو ما دَخَلَتْهُ نارٌ قويةٌ كالخبز والشواءِ إذْ لا يُمْكِنُ ضبطُ ذلك بالصفةِ .

k9.3 It is not permissible for the buyer to sell something he has bought in advance until he has received it.

k9.3 ولا يَجوزُ بيعُ المسلمِ فيهِ قبلَ قبضِهِ .

k9.4 It is not permissible to take some other type of merchandise in place of the article bought in advance (A: that is, when the buyer demands the substitute before the delivery of the original is due, though they may agree on it after that).

If the seller delivers the merchandise specified, or better (O: than what was specified), the buyer must accept it (O: since it is apparent that the seller could not find a way to fulfill his obligation save through this means. If the seller delivers merchandise that is inferior to what was specified, then the buyer may accept it, as this is voluntarily refraining from demanding his due, but he is not obliged to, because of the loss therein).

k9.4 ولا الاستبدالُ .

وإذا أَحْضَرَهُ مثلَ ما شَرَطَ أَوْ أَجْوَدَ (مما شرطه) وَجَبَ قبولُهُ (لأن ظاهر حاله أنه لم يجـد سبيـلاً إلى براءة الذمة إلا بذلك ولو أحضـر أردأ منه جاز قبـوله لأنه نزول عن حقه ولم يجب لتضرره بذلك) .

*

k10.0 PERSONAL LOANS (QARD)
(A: A *loan* means repayable financial aid. It does not refer to lending a particular article ('ayn) for someone to use and then return after use, which is termed an *'ariyya* (def: k19).)

k10.0 القرض
(ع: كلمـة القـرض إنمـا تنطبق على مسـاعـدة ماليـة في ذمـة المستقرض. فتخرج به إعـارة الأعيان لتستعمل وترد إلى صاحبها فإنها تسمَّى عاريّة) .

k10.1 Loaning (O: meaning to give something to the borrower on the basis that he will return its equal) is recommended.

k10.1 القرضُ (وهـو تمليك الشيء على أن يرد المقترض مثله) مندوبٌ إليهِ .

k10.2   A loan is effected through a spoken offer and acceptance (def: k1.1), such as saying, "I loan you this," or, "I advance you it."

k10.3   It is permissible to give as a personal loan any article that may be bought in advance (def: k9.2(b,d,e,f,g)) and nothing else (A: though this restriction does not apply to *lending for use* ('ariyya, dis: k10.0(A:))).

k10.4   It is not permissible for the lender to impose as a condition that the loan be repaid on a certain date (N: though for the Maliki school, to stipulate that repayment is obligatory on a certain date is valid and legally binding).

k10.5   It is not permissible for the lender to impose some condition that will enable him to benefit from the loan, such as a condition that the borrower must return superior to what was loaned, or such as saying, "on condition that you sell me your horse for such and such an amount," for these are usurious gain (riba). But it is permissible for the borrower to return superior to what was loaned without this having been stipulated.

k10.6   It is permissible for the loan agreement to include the condition of collateral (O: meaning for the recipient to give the lender something as collateral (def: k11) for what he borrows) or the condition of a guarantor (O: such that the recipient brings someone to guarantee that the loan will be repaid (def: k15)).

k10.7   The recipient of a loan is obliged to repay the equal of what was lent, though it is permissible for the lender to accept something other than the (A: type of) thing loaned. If the lender gives the recipient a loan and later meets him in another town and asks for it back, the recipient must repay it if it was gold or silver and the like, though if the loaned commodity was something troublesome to carry, such as wheat or barley, then the recipient is not obliged to pay it back (A: in kind) but is merely obliged to pay back its value.

k10.2 (ويحصل بإيجابٍ وقبولٍ مثلَ : أقرِضْكَ (هذا) ؛ أوْ: أسلَفتُكَ .

k10.3 ويجـوزُ قرضُ كلَّ مَا يجـوزُ السلمُ فيه . وما لَا فلا .

k10.4 ولا يجـوزُ فيـهِ (أي القرض) شرطُ الأجـل (ح : ولكن عنـد المـالكية شرطُ الأجل صحيح لازم) .

k10.5 ولا شرطُ جرِّ منفـعـةٍ (للمقـرض) كرَدِّ الأجـود أوْ: على أنْ تبيعَني [عبدَك] (ت : حصانَـك) بكذَا ؛ فإنَّه رباً . فإنْ ردَّ عليْهِ المقترضُ أجودَ مِنْ غيرِ شرطٍ جازَ .

k10.6 ويجـوزُ شرطُ الـرهنِ (أي بأن يعطي المقتـرض للمقـرض رهنـاً على ما يأخذه) والضـامنُ (أي أن المقترض يأتي بمن يضمنه على أن يرد ما اقترض) .

k10.7 ويجبُ على المقتـرض ردُّ المثـل . وإنْ أخَذَ (المقرض) عنه عوضاً (عن الشيء المقرض) جازَ . وإنْ أقرَضَهُ ثمَّ لقيَهُ في بلدٍ آخرَ فطَـالَبَهُ لَزِمَهُ (أي لزم المقترض) الدفعُ (للمقرض) إنْ كَانَ ذهباً أوْ فضةً ونحوَهُمَا . وإنْ كانَ لحملِهِ مؤنةٌ نحوَ حنطةٍ وشعيرٍ فلا ، بلْ تَلزَمُهُ القيمةُ .

k11.0 PUTTING UP COLLATERAL (RAHN)

(O: In Sacred Law *collateral* is a piece of saleable property put up as security for a financial obligation to cover the amount if it should prove impossible to repay.)

CONDITIONS FOR THE VALIDITY OF PUTTING UP COLLATERAL

k11.1 Putting up collateral is only valid when done by someone with full disposal over his own property, as security for a financial obligation (dayn, dis: k9.2(b)) that is currently due, such as the price (O: due for merchandise after its delivery), or a personal loan, or for a financial obligation that is currently becoming due (N: such as something's price) during the option to cancel period (def: k1.4). (O: The collateral's being security for a *financial obligation* is one restriction on its validity, and for one that is *currently due* is another. It is not valid to put up collateral for a particular individual article ('ayn) or the use of an article, since (A: the obligation to deliver) a particular article is not a *financial* obligation (dayn), as the selfsame article cannot be obtained by selling the collateral.)

Putting up collateral is not valid in cases in which the financial obligation is not yet due, such as collateral accepted (O: by a lender) as security for a loan that he will make (O: in the future).

It is necessary (O: for the validity of putting up collateral) that there be a spoken offer (O: by the person putting up the collateral) and spoken acceptance (O: from the person accepting it, just as it is necessary for sales, the conditions mentioned in connection with sales (k1.1) applying equally here).

The agreement is not legally binding until the collateral has been taken possession of with the permission of the person putting it up, who is entitled to cancel the agreement (A: at any point) before the collateral has been taken possession of (def: k7.3).

When the agreement has been effected, if the two parties (A: the collateral's giver and receiver) agree that the collateral should be kept with either

k11.0 الرهن

(وهو شرعاً جعل عين مالية وثيقة بدين يستوفى منها عند تعذر وفائه).

شروط صحة الرهن

k11.1 لا يَصِحُّ إلا مِنْ مُطلَقِ التصرف بدينٍ لازمٍ كالثمن (أي للمبيع بعد قبضِه) والقرضِ أوْ يَؤُولُ (ذلك الدين) إلى اللزوم في مدة الخيارِ. (فالدينُ قيدٌ وكونه لازماً قيدٌ أيضاً. فلا يصح الرهن بعين ولا بمنفعتها لأنها ليست ديناً لأنها لا تستوفى من ثمن المرهون).

فإنْ لمْ يَلْزَمْهُ الدينُ بعدُ مثلُ أنْ يرْهَنَ (أي يأخذ المرتهن رهناً) على ما سيُقرِضُهُ (في المستقبل) لمْ يصِحَّ.

وشـرطُهُ (أي شرط صحة الرهن) إيجـابٌ (من الـراهـن) وقبـولٌ (من المرتهن. فافتقر إليهما كالبيع فيأتي فيهما ما تقدم في البيع).

ولا يلْزَمُ (أي الرهن) إلا بالقبض بإذنِ الراهِنِ، فيجُوزُ للراهِنِ فسْخُهُ قبلَ القبضِ.

وإذا لزِم فإن اتّفَقَـا أن يُوْضَـعَ عنـدَ

of them, or with a third party, this is done. If not (O: if they do not agree), the Islamic magistrate has it kept with an upright person (def: o24.4) (O: to end the disagreement. But the magistrate is not entitled to place it with either of the two parties without the other's permission).

أحَدِهِمَا أوْ ثَالِثٍ وُضِعَ وإلاَّ (أي وإن لم يتفقا) وَضَعَهُ الحَاكِمُ عِنْدَ عَدِلٍ (قَطْعاً للنِّزاعِ. وليسَ له أن يُسلِّمَهُ لأحَدِهِمَا بدون إذن الآخَرِ).

GENERAL PROVISIONS CONCERNING
COLLATERAL

أحكام عامة تتعلق بالرهن

k11.2   The collateral must be an article that is permissible to sell (def: k2.1).

None of the collateral may be separated from the rest of it until the financial obligation has been entirely paid off.

The person who put up the collateral is not entitled to dispose of it in any way which infringes upon the right of the person who has received it as collateral (O: such as transferring its ownership to another) by selling it or giving it away (O: or putting it up as collateral for another person), or to dispose of it in any way that diminishes its value, such as wearing (O: a garment put up that would depreciate by being worn), though he may use it in ways that do not harm (O: the interests of the person who has received it) such as riding it, or living (O: in a house that has been put up as collateral).

k11.2   وشرطُ المرهونِ أنْ يكُونَ عيناً يجُوزُ بيْعُها.

ولا يَنْفكُّ مِنَ الرهنِ شيءٌ حتَّى يقْضِيَ جميع الدين.

وليسَ للراهنِ أنْ يتَصَرَّفَ فيه [(أي في الرهنِ)] بمَا يُبْطِلُ حقَّ المرتهنِ (وينقل الملك في المرهون إلى غيره) كبيعٍ وهبةٍ (أو رهنِهِ عنْدَ رجلٍ آخَرَ) أوْ [(كان التصرُّف)] ينْقصَ قيمتَهُ كاللبس (للثوب المــرهــونِ) إذا كان ينـقص باللبس [والوطءِ]. ويَجُوزُ [(للراهنِ التصرف فيه)] بمَا لا يَضُرُّ (المرتهنَ) كركُوبٍ وسُكْنَى (للدار المرهونة).

k11.3   An article put up as collateral for a financial obligation may not (A: at the same time) be put up as collateral for a second financial obligation, even when the second obligation is with the same person who has accepted the article (A: for the first one).

k11.3   ولا يَجُوزُ رهنُهُ بدينٍ آخَرَ ولوْ عند المرتهن.

k11.4   The expenses for maintaining an article put up as collateral (O: such as fodder for livestock, or the wages of a person watering trees) are the responsibility of the person who put it up, and he may be compelled to pay them to protect the rights of the person receiving it (O: lest it be destroyed). The person who put it up is entitled to the increments produced by it (O: that are separable from it) such as milk or fruit.

k11.4   وعلى الــراهنِ مؤنـةُ الـرهنِ (كعلف دابة وأجرة سقي أشجارٍ) ويُلْزَمُ [(أي الراهن)] بهَا صيانةً لحقّ المرتهن (عن التلف) ولَهُ (أي للراهن) زوائدُهُ (أي المرهون أي الأشياء التي تنفصـل منه) كلبنٍ وثمرةٍ.

k11.5   If the article is destroyed while in the possession of the person who received it as collateral without negligence on his part (A: meaning he took the precautions normal for similar articles), then he is not obliged to pay anything for its loss. But if destroyed because of his negligence, then he is obliged to pay the article's value to the person who put it up, though its destruction does not eliminate any of the original financial obligation for which the destroyed collateral was put up. (O: When the collateral has been destroyed and the two parties are at a disagreement,) the final word as to how much the article was worth (A: when there is no proof (dis: k8.2)) belongs to the person who received it as collateral (O: provided he swears an oath as to how much it was). But the final word as to whether the collateral has been returned (A: to its owner after his financial obligation has been paid) belongs to the person who put it up (A: when there is no proof, and he swears).

k11.5   وإنْ هَلَكَ عنـدَ المـرتهن بلا تفريط لمْ يَلْزَمْهُ شيءٌ. أوْ بتفريطٍ ضَمِنَهُ. ولا يَسْقُـطُ بتلفِهِ شيءٌ منَ الـدين والقولُ في القيمةِ قولُهُ (أي المرتهن فيما إذا أتلفه وتنـازعا في قدرها فيصدق المرتهن بيمينه في قدرها) وفي الردِّ قولُ الراهن ..

k11.6   The benefit of collateral is that the article is sold (A: by the person who put it up) when there is need to pay the amount which is due. If the person who put it up refuses (O: to sell the article when the person who has received it as collateral asks him to), then the Islamic magistrate has him either pay the original obligation or else sell the article. (O: He is given a choice between the two alternatives.) If he continues to refuse (O: to sell), then the Islamic magistrate sells it for him. (O: If the person who put it up is absent, then this is established by proof to the magistrate, who sells it for him and gives the person who accepted the collateral his due. If there is no Islamic magistrate and no proof (A: that there is a financial obligation for which the collateral has been put up), then the person who accepted it as collateral is entitled to sell it himself.)

k11.6   وفائـدةُ الرهن بيعُ العين عندَ الحاجةِ إلى وفاء الحقِّ.
فإن امْتَنَعَ الـراهنُ منـهُ (أي من البيع عنـد طلب المـرتهن البيع) أَلْزَمَهُ الحاكمُ إمَّا الـوفـاءَ أو البيع (فهو مخير بين هذين الأمـرين) فإنْ أَصَـرَّ (أي الـراهن على الامتناع من البيع) بَاعَهَا الحاكمُ (فإن كان الـراهن غائبـاً أثبت ذلـك عنـد الحاكم فيبيعه عليه ويعطي المرتهن حقه، فإن لم يكن حاكم ولم تكن بينة فله بيعه بنفسه).

*

k12.0   BANKRUPTCY (TAFLIS)
(O: Bankruptcy occurs when the Islamic magistrate makes a debtor bankrupt by (N: declaring him so and) forbidding him to dispose of

k12.0   التفليس
(وهـو جعل الحـاكم المديون مفلساً
(ح: أي بأن يحكم عليه بذلك) بمنعه من

his property (N: such that if he disposes of it, his disposition is not effected).)

k12.1 When someone obliged to pay a current debt is being asked to pay it, and he claims that he is unable to (O: while his creditors deny this), then if it is known that he has saleable property, he is kept under arrest until he provides evidence that he cannot pay. If not (O: i.e. if it is not known that he has saleable property), then he swears an oath (O: that there is no property), and (O: when it is established that he is unable to pay, whether through evidence, or through his oath) he is released (O: and given time) until his circumstances allow him to pay (O: and his creditors may not keep after him, because of Allah's word,

"If there be someone in difficulties, let him have respite until things are easier" (Koran 2:280)).

k12.2 But if he has saleable property (O: such as real estate, home furnishings, or livestock) and refuses to pay his debt, then the Islamic magistrate sells it for him and pays his debt. If the proceeds of the sale are insufficient to cover the debt, and he or his creditor asks the magistrate that he be suspended from dealing in his property, then this is done (O: obligatorily, if requested). When the person is *suspended,* his disposal over his own saleable property is not legally binding or effective, and the magistrate pays the person's expenses and those of his family (O: whom he is obliged to support (def: m12.1)) out of this (O: suspended) property if he is unable to earn enough to pay his expenses.

Then (O: after the person has been suspended) the magistrate sells the property in the most profitable manner and divides the proceeds according to the percentage of the total debt which is owed to each creditor.

k12.3 If one of the creditors is owed money on a debt which is not yet due, he is not entitled to be paid from the proceeds. (N: Rather, if the bankrupt does not agree to pay the person

التصرف في ماله (ح : فلو تصرف لم ينفذ تصرفه)) .

k12.1 إذا لَزِمَـهُ دِيـنٌ حالٌّ فَطُـولِبَ فادَّعَى الإعسارَ (وأنكر غرماؤه ذلك) فإنْ عُهِدَ [(أي علم)] لَهُ مالٌ حُبِسَ حتَّى يُقِيمَ بينةً على إعساره وإلّا (أي وإن لم يعلم له مال) حَلَفَ (على نفي المال) وإذا أثبت إعساره بالبينة أو باليمين) خُلِّي سبيلُهُ (ترك بلا حبس وينتظر إلى أنْ يُوسِرَ (ولا يلزمه غريمه حينئذ لقوله تعالى : ﴿وَإِنْ كَانَ ذُو عُسْرَةٍ فَنَظِرَةٌ إِلَى مَيْسَرَةٍ﴾) .

k12.2 فإنْ كَانَ له مالٌ (كـالـعـقـار والأمتعة والبهائم) وامْتَنَعَ مِنَ الوفاءِ بَاعَهُ الحاكمُ ووفّى عنهُ .

فإنْ لمْ يَفِ مالُـهُ بدينـهِ وسـأَلَ هوَ أوْ غرماؤُهُ الحاكمَ الحجرَ حَجَرَ عليْهِ (وجوباً عند الطلب) فإذا حَجَرَ لمْ يَنْفُذْ تصرفُهُ في المالِ ويُنْفِقُ (أي الحاكم) عليهِ وعلى عيالِهِ (الذين يلزمه نفقتهم) منهُ (أي من المالِ المحجورِ عليه) إنْ لمْ يَكُنْ لهُ كسبٌ . ثُمَّ (بعد الحجرِ) يَبيعُـهُ الحاكمُ ويحْتاطُ ويُقَسِّمُهُ على قدرِ ديونهم .

k12.3 وإنْ كانَ فيهِمْ مَنْ دَينُهُ مؤجَّلٌ لمْ يُقْضَ (ح : بل يجعل الحاكم نصيبه

immediately, the magistrate keeps this person's share until the debt is due (A: and then pays him).)

تحت يده حتى يحل الأجل ما لم يرض المفلس بالتعجيل) .

k12.4   If one of the creditors has accepted an article of the bankrupt's property as collateral from him for a debt, he is paid the amount owed to him from the sale of the collateral (O: and if there is money from its sale in excess of what was owed to him, it is distributed among the other creditors).

k12.4   أوْ مَنْ عِنْدَهُ بِدينِهِ رهنٌ خُصَّ مِنْ ثمنِه بقدرِ دينِه (وما زاد من ثمنه يوزع على باقي الغرماء) .

k12.5   If one of the creditors finds the very piece of merchandise he sold to the bankrupt person, he may choose between selling it and dividing the profits with the other creditors, or cancelling the deal and taking back the piece of merchandise, provided there is nothing to prevent taking it back such as it being subject to preemption by a part owner (shuf'a, def: k21), or the bankrupt person having made it collateral to another person, or the merchandise's being mixed with merchandise better than it, or some similar objection.

k12.5   ولوْ وَجَدَ أحدُهُمْ عينَ مالِه التي باعَها لهُ فإنْ شَاء ضَارَبَ مَع الغرماء وإنْ شَاء فَسَخَ البيعَ ورجَعَ فيهَا إلَّا أنْ يَمْنَعَ مانعُ مِنَ الرجوعِ فيهَا مثلُ أنْ تُسْتَحَقَّ بشفعةٍ أوْ رهنٍ أوْ خُلِطَتْ بأجودَ ونحو ذلكَ .

k12.6   The bankrupt person is permitted to keep a suitable set of clothes and enough food for himself and his dependents to suffice for the day on which his saleable property is divided up. (N: If the bankrupt is then earning enough to suffice himself and his dependents, he is left as is. If not, then he is supported by the Muslim common fund (bayt al-mal), like all poor people. If there is no common fund, he must be supported by all the Muslims.)

k12.6   ويُتْرَكُ للمفلس دستُ ثوبٍ يَليقُ به وقوتُهُ وقوتُ عيالِهِ يوم القسمةِ (ح: ثم إن كان المفلس مكتسباً ما يكفيه وعيالَه فيها، وإلَّا أنفق عليه من بيت المال كسائر الفقراء. فإن لم يكن بيت مال فنفقته على عامة المسلمين) .

*

k13.0   THE SUSPENSION OF CHILDREN AND THE INSANE FROM DEALINGS

(O: Suspension is of two types:

(1)   The first has been established in Sacred Law for the interests of others, such as the suspension of a bankrupt person in the interests of his creditors, or the suspension of the person putting

k13.0   الحجر

(والحجر نوعان: نوع شرع لمصلحة الغيـر كالحجـر على المفلس للغرمـاء

up collateral from dealing in it, in the interests of the person who has accepted it.

(2) The second has been established in Sacred Law in the interests of the suspended person, which is the type of suspension our author refers to in the following.)

k13.1 It is not permissible for a child or insane person to dispose of their own property (N: and their doing so is considered legally invalid) (O: to protect them from loss. The fact that a person is a child, male or female, even if at the age of discrimination (def: f1.2), negates the legal efficacy of whatever he says, as well as his legal authority over others, both in respect to transactions such as sale, and in respect to religion, such as Islam. His Islam is not valid, since it requires full capacity for legal responsibility (taklif, dis: c8.1). And this state continues until he reaches puberty. Insanity similarly negates the legal efficacy of whatever the insane person says, as well as his legal authority over others. His Islam is not valid, nor his leaving Islam (def: o8), nor are his dealings, as previously mentioned).

(A: Also suspended from commercial dealings is the *foolhardy* person (safih), meaning a spendthrift who is chronically careless with his money. In the schools of Shafi'i and Ahmad, this class also includes those who are careless about their religious obligations, as they too are considered too foolish to deal in their own property.)

k13.2 A guardian conducts such a charge's affairs, the *guardian* being:

(1) the charge's father;

(2) the father's father, if the father is deceased;

(O: it is a necessary condition that they be upright (def: o24.4), at least outwardly, though they need not be Muslim unless the child is Muslim)

(3) if neither of them is alive, then the person designated by the guardian's will (wasiyya, def: L3) to take custody of the charge;

والراهن للمرتهن في المرهون، ونوع شرع لمصلحة المحجور عليه نفسه، وقد أشار له المصنف بقوله:)

k13.1 لا يَجُوزُ تصرُّفُ الصبيِّ والمجنون في مالهِمَا (ح: ويعتبر باطلاً شرعاً) (أي حفظاً لهما عن الضياع فالصبا القائم بالشخص ذكراً أو أنثى ولو مميزاً يسلب العبارة والولاية أي في المعاملة كالبيع وفي الدين [بكسر الدال] كالإسلام أي فلا يصح إسلامه لتوقفه على التكليف ويستمر ذلك إلى البلوغ. والجنون كذلك أي يسلب العبارة والولاية فلا يصح الإسلام منه ولا الارتداد ولا معاملته كما تقدم)

k13.2 ويَتَصَرَّفُ لهُمَا الوليُّ وهوَ الأبُ أو الجدُّ أبو الأب عنـدَ عدمِـهِ (ويشترط ظهور عدالتهما ولا يشترط إسلامهما إلا أن يكون الولد مسلماً) ثُمَّ

(4) or if no one has been designated by the will, then the Islamic magistrate or his representative.

الـوصيُّ ثمَّ الحـاكمُ (الشـرعي) أوْ أمينُـهُ [[معطوف على الحاكم)]] .

THE GUARDIAN'S DISPOSAL OF HIS CHARGE'S PROPERTY

تصرف الولي في مال المحجور عليه

k13.3   The guardian deals with the charge's property to the charge's best financial advantage (O: and is entitled to sell it for needs that arise, such as when he does not have enough to cover his charge's expenses and clothing).

k13.3   وَيَتَصـرَّفُ لهُمَـا بالغبطـةِ (وله بيـع المـال لحـاجـة مثـل أن لا يجـد له ما يصرفه عليه من نفقة وكسوة) .

k13.4   If the guardian claims to have spent his charge's property to cover the charge's expenses, or claims that the property has been destroyed (O: by an act of God (A: and not through his negligence)), then his word is accepted (O: about it without having to swear an oath). But if the guardian claims to have given the property to the charge (O: i.e. to the child who has reached maturity or the insane person who has regained his sanity), then his word is not accepted (O: because of the ease with which he could have legally established that he gave the property to his charge at the time of doing so. If he did not obtain witnesses to observe the property being handed over, he is guilty of remissness for neglecting to have it witnessed).

k13.4   فإنْ ادَّعَى أنَّهُ أنْفَقَ عليهِ مالَهُ أوْ (ادعى أنـه) تَلِفَ (أي المال بآفة سماوية) قُبِـلَ (ادعـاؤه ذلـك بلا يمين) أوْ أنَّهُ دَفعَهُ إليـهِ (أي إلى الصبي أو المجنـون الـذي بلغ رشـده أو الـذي أفاق من الجنـون) فَلَا (يقبـل قولـه بالـدفع له لسهولة البينة عند الدفع إليه فإذا لم يشهد عليه عند الدفع له فيكون مفرطاً بترك الإشهاد) .

k13.5   Suspension from dealings ends (O: without a ruling from the judge) when a child reaches puberty and mental maturity, meaning that he:

(a) is physically mature;

(b) shows religious sincerity;

(c) and is competent to handle his own property.

(O: For an insane person, suspension ends when he regains his sanity, shows religious sincerity, and displays competence in handling his property. Religious sincerity means that a person

k13.5   فإذَا بَلَغَ [أوْ أفَـاقَ] رشيـداً بأنْ بلغ مصلحـاً لدينِهِ ومالِهِ (وأفاق المجنون مصلحـاً لدينه ومـاله وذلـك بأن يفعـل

performs acts of obedience and avoids disobedience and the unlawful. *Competence in handling one's property* means that one does not waste it by losing it, for example, in buying something outrageously overpriced. Both of these traits ((b) and (c)) are the criteria for maturity according to Imam Shafi'i, as opposed to Abu Hanifa and Malik, who hold that competence in handling property is sufficient.)

k13.6   A charge is not given his property until his competence in handling it has been tested before puberty in a manner appropriate to him. (O: Thus a merchant's son is tried at striking a bargain in dealings, having been given money to do this, though not actually concluding the deal, which is done by the guardian. A farmer's son is tested at agriculture and managing the expenditures connected with it. An examination is also made of the charge's religion, by observing whether he performs acts of worship, avoids acts of disobedience, shuns the unlawful, and is wary of things that are doubtful (dis: j16.1).

It is necessary that this testing be repeated one or more times.)

k13.7   If the suspended person reaches puberty or regains his sanity but is corrupt in his religion or incompetent in financial dealings, then his suspension continues and he is not permitted to deal in his property by selling or anything else, with or without his guardian's permission, though if the guardian permits him to marry, the marriage is valid.

If the suspended person reaches puberty with religious sincerity and financial competence, but subsequently squanders his wealth, then he is resuspended by the Islamic magistrate, not the guardian. But if the person becomes morally corrupt (A: after having reached puberty), he is not resuspended (N: provided his corruption does not involve spending money on what is unlawful, though if it does, he is suspended from dealing).

k13.8   *Puberty* applies to a person after the first wet dream, or upon becoming fifteen (O: lunar)

الطاعات ويتجنب المحرمات والمعاصي ولا يبـذر مالـه بتضييعـه باحتمـال غبن فاحش وتفسيـر الرشـد هو عنـد إمامنـا الشـافعي خلافـاً لأبي حنيفة ومالك حيث اعتبرا إصـلاح المـال فقط) انْفَكَّ الحجرُ (فينفك بغير القاضي) .

k13.6   ولاَ يُسَلَّمُ إليـهِ المـالُ إلاَّ بالاختبار فيمَا يَليقُ به قبلَ البلوغِ (فيختبر ولد تاجر بمماكسة في شأن معاملة ويسلم له المـال ليماكس لا ليعقـد والعـاقـد هو الـولي . ويختبر ولد الزراع بزراعة ونفقة عليهـا . والاختبار المـذكـور يكـون في الـدين أيضاً وذلك كإقبال المحجور عليه على الـعبـادات وتـجـنب المعـاصي والمحظورات وتوقي الشبهات . ويشترط تكرار الاختبار مرة أو مرتين أو أكثر) .

k13.7   وإنْ بَلَغَ أوْ أَفَاقَ مفسداً لدينه أو مالِهِ اسْتُديمَ الحجرُ عليـهِ ولاَ يَجُوزُ تصرفُهُ في المال ببيعٍ وغيرِه [(من سائر التصرفـات)] سواءٌ أَذِنَ الوليُّ أمْ لا . فإنْ أَذِنَ لهُ في نكاحٍ صَحَّ .

فإنْ بَلَغَ رشيـداً ثُمَّ بَذَّرَ حَجَـرَ عليـهِ الحـاكمُ لا الوليُّ . وإنْ فَسَقَ لَمْ يُعِدْ عليهِ الحجــرَ (ح : إن كان فسقه بغيـر إنفـاق مال ، فإن كان بإنفاق مال على المحرمات حجر عليه) .

k13.8   والبـلوغُ بالاحـتـلام أوْ باستكمالِ خمسَ عشـرةَ سنةً (قمرية) أوْ

| years old, or when a girl has her first menstrual period or pregnancy. | بالحيض والحبل في الجارية [(أي الأنثى) والله أعلم]. |

*

k14.0 TRANSFERRING THE RIGHT TO COLLECT A DEBT (HAWALA)

(O: In Sacred Law, a transfer is an agreement that moves a debt from one person's responsibility to another's.)

(n: Given three persons, X (al-muhtal), Y (al-muhil), and Z (al-muhal 'alayhi) (A: where X loans Y a dirham, and Z already owes Y a dirham, so Y transfers the right to collect the old debt (that Z owes him) to X, instead of repaying X for the new debt. Such transfers have six integrals:

(a) Y;

(b) X;

(c) Z;

(d) Y's debt to X;

(e) Z's debt to Y;

(f) Y's spoken offer and X's spoken acceptance).)

k14.0 الحوالة

(وهي في الشرع عقد يقتضي نقل دين من ذمة إلى ذمة).

(ت: يمثل لها بثلاثة أشخاص: زيد (المحتال) وعمرو (المحيل) وبكر (المحال عليه) (ع): حيث يقرض زيد لعمرو درهماً. ولعمرو وعلى بكر درهم. فجعل عمرو وحق استيفاء الدين القديم لزيد بدلاً من أن يدفع لزيد الدين الجديد. وأمثال هذه الحوالة لها ستة أركان: محيل، ومحتال، ومحال عليه، ودين للمحتال على المحيل، ودين للمحيل على المحال عليه، والصيغة)).

k14.1 It is a necessary condition for the validity of transferring a debt that Y wishes to do so, and that X accepts. It is not necessary that Z wishes it.

(O: The agreement also requires a form, which is the spoken offer and acceptance (def: k1.1), meaning Y's offer and X's acceptance.)

k14.1 يُشتَرطُ فيها رضا المحيل وقبول المحتال دون رضا المحال عليه. (ولا بد من صيغة للعقد وهي إيجاب وقبول أي إيجاب من المحيل وقبول من المحتال).

k14.2 Such a transfer is not valid unless Z owes Y a debt and Y owes X a debt.

A transfer is valid respecting a legally binding debt (O: owed to X) for another legally binding debt (O: Z owes to Y), provided:

(a) that X and Y know what is being transferred (A: gold, silver, or wheat, for example) for what;

k14.2 ولا تصحُ على مَنْ لا دَيْنَ عليهِ (أي لا للمحيل على المحال عليه ولا للمحتال على المحيل).

وتصحُّ بدين لازم (للمحتال) على دين لازم (للمحيل على المحال عليه) بشرط العلم (أي علم المحتال والمحيل بما يُحالُ به و)(بشرط العلم بما

(b) that X and Y know that the two debts are homogeneous in type (A: such as money for money, or wheat for wheat) and in amount (O: though if Y owes X five, and Z owes Y ten, and Y transfers (A: the right to collect) five of it to X, then this is valid);

(c) and that X and Y know whether the debts are currently due or payable in the future (A: the two debts may differ in this respect if both parties agree).

k14.3   (O: The validity of a transfer is not affected by the existence of collateral (def: k11) or of a guarantor (def: k15) as security for one of the debts, but the occurrence of the transfer eliminates (A: either form of) security, the guarantor being relieved of any responsibility and the collateral no longer being collateral.)

k14.4   Through a valid transfer, Y no longer owes X a debt, Z no longer owes Y a debt, and the debt owed to X becomes the responsibility of Z. If X is unable to collect the debt from Z because Z is bankrupt or denies the existence of the debt or for some other reason (O: such as Z's death), then X is not entitled to go back to Y (A: to collect it) (N: but rather it is as though X has accepted for the debt a remuneration which was subsequently destroyed in his possession).

*

k15.0   GUARANTEEING PAYMENT (DAMAN)

(O: *Guarantee* lexically means ensuring implementation, and in Sacred Law means to ensure a financial obligation which is another's or ensure the appearance of a particular person whose presence is required.)

(n: Given three persons, P (al-madmun lahu), Q (al-madmun 'anhu), and R (al-damin) (A: where P loans Q a dirham, and R guarantees

يُحـال عليهِ وتساويهِمَا جنساً وقدراً (ولو كان لبكـر على زيـد خمسـة ولـزيـد على عمرو عشرة فأحال زيد بكراً بخمسة منها صح) [وصحة وتكسيراً] وحلولاً وأجلاً .

k14.3   (ولـو كان بأحـد الدينين توثق برهن أو ضامن لم يؤثر في صحة الحوالة ولم ينتقل بصفة التوثق بل يسقط التوثق بل يبرأ الضامن وينفك الرهن بها) .

k14.4   ويَبْـرَأُ بهـا المحيـلُ عنْ دين المحتال، والمحالُ عليه عنْ دين المحيل ويَتَحَوَّلُ حقُّ المحتال إلى ذمةِ المحالِ عليه .
فإنْ تَعَـذَّرَ على المحتـالِ أخـذُهُ مِن المحـالِ عليه لفلس المحـالِ عليهِ أوْ جحدِهِ أوْ غيـرِ ذلـك (وذلك كالموت) لمْ يَرْجِعْ (أي المحتـال) إلى المحيل (ح: كما لو أخذ عوضاً عن الدين فتلف في يده) .

k15.0   الضمان
(وهـو لغة الالتزام وشرعاً يقال الالتزام بدين ثابت في ذمـة الـغيـر أو بدن من يستحق حضوره) .
(ت: ويمثل له بثلاثة أشخاص: زيد (المضمون له) وعمرو (المضمون عنه) وبكـر (الضامن) (ع): حيث يقرض زيد لعمـرو درهماً فيضمن بكر لزيد أن عمراً

to P that either Q will repay it or else he, R, will repay it. Such guarantees have five integrals:

(a) R;

(b) P;

(c) Q;

(d) the debt covered;

(e) and the form of the agreement).)

GUARANTEEING ANOTHER'S FINANCIAL OBLIGATION

ضمان دين الغير

k15.1 It is a necessary condition for the validity of guaranteeing payment that R have full right to manage his own property. It is not valid from a child, someone insane, or a foolhardy person (def: k13.1(A:)), though it is valid from someone suspended for bankruptcy.

k15.1 يَصِحُّ ضمانُ مَنْ يَصِحُّ تصرفُهُ في مالِهِ فلا يَصِحُّ مِنْ صبيٍّ ومجنونٍ وسفيهِ [وعبدٍ لمْ يأذَنْ لهُ سيدُهُ] ويَصِحُّ مِنْ محجورٍ عليه بفلسٍ [ومن عبدٍ أذِنَ له سيدُهُ].

k15.2 It is a condition for the validity of a guarantee that R know P, though it is not necessary that P agree to it.

It is not necessary that Q agree, or that R know Q.

k15.2 ويُشْتَرَطُ معرفةُ المضمونِ لَهُ [(أي معرفة الضامن عين المضمون له)] ولاَ يُشْتَرَطُ رضَاهُ.
ولاَ رضَا المضمونِ عنهُ ولاَ معرفتُهُ.

k15.3 It is necessary that the guaranteed debt be a financial obligation (dayn, dis: k9.2(b)) that is existent (O: since it is not valid to guarantee a debt before it exists, such as "tomorrow's expenses") and is determinately known (O: in terms of amount, type, and description).

k15.3 ويُشْتَرَطُ أنْ يَكُونَ المضمونُ دينًا ثابتًا معلومًا (قدرًا وجنسًا وصفة، فلا يصح الضمان قبل ثبوته كنفقة الغد).

k15.4 It is necessary that R make the guarantee in words (O: or their written equivalent, with the intention) that imply he is effecting it, such as "I guarantee your debt [O: that So-and-so owes you]," or "I will cover it," or the like. (O: These are explicit expressions in that they mention the guaranteed financial obligation. When it is not mentioned, the expression is allusive, which is

k15.4 وأنْ يأتِيَ (أي الضامن) بلفظٍ (وما يقوم مقامه من الكتابة مع النية) يَقْتَضِي الالتزامَ كَضَمِنْتُ دَيْنَكَ (الذي على فلان) أوْ تَحَمَّلْتُهُ ونحوَ ذلكَ. (وهذه الألفاظ صريحة لذكر المال فيها وإذا لم يذكر المال فهي كناية فإذا نوى المال

valid provided the financial obligation is what is intended, and the speaker knows how much it is. Otherwise, allusive expressions are not valid.)

It is not valid to base the implementation of a guarantee on a condition, such as saying, "When Ramadan comes, I hereby guarantee it." (O: Nor is it valid to make it subject to time stipulations, such as saying, "I guarantee what So-and-so owes for one month, after which I no longer guarantee it.")

k15.5   When a seller has accepted the price of something, it is valid (O: for someone) to guarantee the buyer his money back if the merchandise should prove to belong to another or to be defective. (O: It is likewise valid for someone to guarantee to the seller that the merchandise will be returned if the price paid for it should turn out to belong to someone other than the buyer.)

k15.6   P is entitled to collect the guaranteed debt from R and Q (O: by asking both of them or either for the full amount, or one of them for part of it and the other for the rest of it).

If another guarantor guarantees the debt for R (O: by saying (A: to P), "I guarantee Q's debt [A: to you] for R"), then P is entitled to collect it from all (A: from Q, R, and the new guarantor).

k15.7   If P asks for payment from R, then R is entitled to ask Q to pay the debt, provided that Q had given his permission to R before R guaranteed it.

k15.8   If P cancels the debt Q owes him, then R is also free of the obligation to pay P. But if P cancels R's obligation to cover Q's debt, then Q is not thereby free of the debt he owes P.

k15.9   If R pays Q's debt to P, then R can collect it from Q, provided that Q had given his permission to R before R guaranteed it. But if Q had not (O: given his permission to R to guarantee), then R is not now entitled to collect it from Q, no

وعرف قدره صح وإلا فلا) .

ولا يَجُوزُ تعليقُهُ على شرطٍ مثل : إذا جاء رمضانُ فقَـدْ ضَمِنْت . (ولا يصح توقيته نحو : أنا ضامن ما على فلان إلى شهر فإذا مضى برئت) .

k15.5   ويصحُّ ضمانُ الـدرك بعـد قَبْضِ الثمن (وبـالعكس أي بعـد قبض المشـتـري المبيـع) وهـو أَنْ يَضْمَنَ (شخص) للمشتـري الثمن إنْ خَرَجَ المبيـع مستحقاً أو معيباً . (أوأن يضمن للبائع المبيع إن خرج الثمن مستحقاً) .

k15.6   وللمضمون لَهُ مطالبةُ الضامن والمضمـون عنـه (بأن يطالبهما جميعاً أو يطالب أيهمـا شاء بالجميـع أو يطالب أحدهما ببعضه والآخر بباقيـه) . فإن ضمِن عن الضامن ضامنٌ آخرُ (بأن قال ذلك الآخـر : أنـا أضمن المضمون عنه عن هذا الضامن) طَالَبَ الكلَّ .

k15.7   وإنْ طَالَبَ الضـامنَ فللضامن مطالبةُ الأصيل بتخليصِهِ إنْ ضَمِنَ بإذْنِه .

k15.8   فإنْ أَبْـرَأ (أي مستحق الـدين) الأصيل بَرِئ الضامنُ . وإنْ أَبْرَأ الضامنَ لمْ يَبْرَإ الأصيلُ .

k15.9   وإنْ قَضَى الضـامنُ الـدينَ رجــع به على الأصيـل إنْ كان ضَمِنَ بإذنِه . وإلّا (أي وإن لم يكن ضمن بإذنه)

matter whether R paid it off with Q's leave or without it.

فلا (رجوع له) سواءٌ قَضاهُ بإذنِهِ أمْ لا .

k15.10 It is not valid to guarantee delivery of particular articles ('ayn) (A: as they are not *financial obligations* (dis: k9.2(b)), such as something wrongfully taken, or articles loaned for use (O: i.e. "guaranteeing" they will be returned to their owner).

k15.10 ولا يَصِحُّ ضمـانُ الأعيـان كالمغصـوب (فـالمـراد ضمـان ردهـا لمالكها) والعواري .

GUARANTEEING ANOTHER'S APPEARANCE

الكفالة

k15.11 It is permissible for R to guarantee that Q will appear in person (O: in court) provided:

(a) that Q owes someone something or is liable to punishment for a crime against another person, such as when the other is entitled to retaliate (def: o1–o3) against Q, or when Q has charged someone with adultery without evidence (def: o13);

(b) and that Q gives R permission to guarantee his appearance.

It is not valid to guarantee Q's appearance if (non-(a) above) Q's crime is against Allah Most High (O: such as drinking, adultery, or theft).

k15.11 وتَصِحُّ الكفـالةُ ببدنِ مَنْ عليْهِ مالٌ (أي يكفـل إحضاره مجلس الحكم) أوْ عقـوبةٌ لآدميٍّ كالقصاص وحدِّ القذفِ بإذْنِ المَكفولِ . وإنْ كانَ عليْهِ حقُّ اللهِ تعالى فلا تَصِحُّ (الكفالة وذلك كحد خمر وزنا وسرقة) .

k15.12 If R guarantees Q's appearance but does not specify when, he is required to produce Q at once. But if R stipulates a certain time, then he is required to do so at that time.
If Q disappears and his whereabouts is unknown, R is not required to produce Q until he knows where Q is.
(A: When R knows where Q is, then) R is given time to travel to where Q is and return. If R does not bring Q, then he is under arrest, though he is not responsible for Q's (A: unfulfilled) financial obligations.
If Q dies, the guarantee is nullified, though if R is asked to produce Q's body before burial to verify its identity, he is obliged to if able.

k15.12 ثمَّ إذا صَحَّتِ الكفالةُ فأُطْلَقَ طُولِبَ (أي الكفيل) به في الحالِ . وإنْ شُرطَ أجَـلٌ طُولِبَ به عنـدَ الأجَلِ . وإن انْقَطَـعَ خَبَرُهُ لمْ يُطَالَبْ به حتى يَعْرِفَ (الكفيل) مكـانَـهُ ، ويُمْهَلُ مدةَ الذهاب والعـود . فإنْ لمْ يُحْضِرْهُ حُبِسَ ولا تَلْزَمُهُ غرامةُ ما عليـهِ . وإنْ ماتَ المـكفـولُ سَقَطَتِ الكفالةُ لكنْ إنْ طُولِبَ بإحضاره قبلَ الدفنِ لِيُشْهَدَ على عينِه وأمْكَنَهُ ذلكَ لَزِمَهُ .

k16.0 PARTNERSHIPS (SHARIKA)

k16.0 الشركة

k16.1 Partnership is valid with anyone having full right to dispose of his own property.

k16.1 تَصِحُّ مِنْ كلِّ جائزِ التصرف .

COOPERATIVE PARTNERSHIP

شركة العنان

k16.2 There are four kinds of partnership (dis: k16.9) of which one alone, cooperative partnership, is valid. It consists of each of the two (A: or more) partners putting up capital, which must be either money or a fungible commodity typically transacted measure for measure (mithli, def: k20.3(1)) (O: as opposed to goods appraised and sold as particular pieces of merchandise (mutaqawwim), which cannot form the basis of a partnership because it is impossible to mix each partner's share with the other's (dis: below)).

k16.2 وهي أنواعٌ أربعةٌ . وإنَّما تَصِحُّ مِنْها شركةُ العنانِ خاصةً وهي أنْ يأتيَ كلُّ منهُمـا بمالٍ وتصِحُّ علـى النقـودِ وعلى مثليٍّ (بخـلافِ المتقـومـاتِ فلا تجوزُ الشركة عليها لأنه لا تمكن الخلطة فيها) .

k16.3 It is a condition for the validity of a cooperative partnership that the two shares of capital put up by the partners be intermixed such that it is impossible to tell them apart.

k16.3 ويُشْتَـرَطُ أنْ يُخْلَطَ المـالانِ بحيثُ لا يَتَميَّزانِ .

k16.4 [وأنْ يَكُونَ مالُ أحَـدِهِمـا مِنْ جنسِ مالِ الآخرِ وعلى صفتِهِ . فلَوْ كانَ لهذا ذهبٌ ولهذا فضةٌ أوْ لهذا حنطةٌ ولهذا شعيرٌ أوْ لهذا صحيحٌ ولهذا مكسَرٌ لَمْ يَصِحَّ] .

k16.5 It is a necessary condition that each partner give the other his permission to handle the capital (O: that they have put up in common).
Each partner must deal in a way that realizes their common capital's best advantage and maximal safety. Thus, neither partner may travel with it (O: i.e. the shared capital, because of the danger in travelling) or sell for postponed payment (N: unless the other partner gives him permission, in which case (A: either of) these are permissible).

k16.5 ويُشْتَـرَطُ أنْ يأْذَنَ كلُّ منهُمـا للآخرِ في التصرف (في المال المعقود عليه) .
فيَتَصَـرَّفُ كلُّ منهُمـا بالنظـرِ [(فيمـا يصلح للمـال المشترك)] والاحتيـاطِ فلا يُسَـافِرُ به (أي بالمـال المشترك لأن السفر فيـه خطر) ولا يَبيعُ بمؤجَّلٍ (ح : إلا بإذن صاحبه فإن أذن جاز) .

k16.6 It is not necessary that the two shares of capital put up by the partners be equal in amount.
Both profits and losses are divided between the two partners in proportion to the percentage

k16.6 ولا يُشْتَرَطُ تساوي المالينِ .
ويكُونُ الـربحُ والخسرانُ بينهُمَا على

of the shared capital each of them put up (O: even if there is a difference in the amount of work that each does). If they stipulate otherwise, the partnership is not valid (O: such as stipulating that the partner who put up one hundred, for example, gets two-thirds, while the partner who put up two hundred gets one-third; or stipulating that each gets an equal share, despite having put up unequal amounts). (N: This is in the Shafi'i school. The Hanafis and Hanbalis hold that it is permissible for the distribution of profits to be disproportionate (A: to the amount of capital each invests), corresponding to the disproportionate amount of work each puts into the venture (A: or any other division of the profits which they both agree upon).)

k16.7   If partner A forbids partner B to handle the shared capital, then B is not entitled to handle it, though A is still entitled to (O: handle both shares, one of which is his by ownership, and the other by permission of his partner) until B forbids him to handle it.

k16.8   Each partner is entitled to cancel the partnership whenever he wants (O: and it is also cancelled by the death or insanity of either or both partners).

k16.9   The following types of partnerships are not valid:

(1) *manual partnership* (sharika al-abdan), such as the partnership of two porters or other workers agreeing to divide their earnings between them (N: though this type of partnership is valid in the Maliki, Hanafi, and Hanbali schools);

(2) *well-known partner partnership* (sharika al-wujuh) (n: such as of two individuals who put up no capital, but have good reputations among people which create confidence and enable them to purchase trade goods for deferred payment, the profits from the sale of which they agree to divide between them (*Mughni al-muhtaj ila ma'rifa ma'ani alfaz al-Minhaj* (y73), 2.212)).

قدر المـالين (وإن تفـاوت الشـريكان في العمل) فـإنْ شَـرطَا خلافَ ذلكَ (بأن شرطا أن لصـاحب المـائة مثلاً ثلثين ولصاحب المـائتين ثلثاً، أو شرطا التساوي فيهما مع التـفـاوت) بَطَلَتْ. (ح: هذا مذهب الشـافعيـة وذهب الحنفيـة والحنـابلة إلى جواز التفاوت بتفاوت العمل في الشركة).

k16.7   فإنْ عَزَلَ أحـدُهُمـا الآخرَ عن التصرف انْعَـزَلَ وللآخر التصرفُ (في المالين ماله بطريق الملكية ومال الآخر بطريق الإذن) إلى أنْ يَعزلَهُ صاحبُه.

k16.8   ولكـل منهمَا فسخُهَا متى شَاءَ (وتنفسـخ بمـوتهمـا وبمـوت أحـدهمـا وبجنونهما أو أحدهما).

k16.9   وأمَّـا شركةُ الأبـدانِ فبـاطلةٌ كشــركةِ الحمـالين وغيـرهمـا مِنْ ذوي الحـرف علـى أنْ يكـونَ الكسبُ بينُهُمَـا (ح: وأجازها المالكية والحنفية والحنابلة).

وشركةُ الوجوهِ والمفاوضةِ أيضاً باطلتـان. (ت: وشـركـة الـوجوه هي أن الـوجيهين (عند النـاس) لا يأتيان بالنقد لكن يتفقـان ليبتـاع كلُ واحـدٍ بمـؤجـلٍ لهمـا، فإذا باعـا كان الفاضلُ عن الأثمان

(3) and *comprehensive partnership* (sharika al-mufawada) (n: an agreement by which the partners share whatever they each earn from their respective (A: separate) funds and labor, mutually covering the financial liabilities incurred by either (ibid., 2.212)).

*

k17.0 COMMISSIONING ANOTHER TO DO SOMETHING (WAKALA)

(n: Given persons X (al-muwakkil) and Y (al-wakil) (A: where X gives Y an article to sell for him. This section deals with commissioning others to carry out such requests, which have four integrals:

(a) X;

(b) Y;

(c) the act that is being commissioned (al-muwakkal fihi);

(d) and the words by which X commissions Y to do it).)

k17.1 It is a necessary condition that both X and Y have full right to perform the act being commissioned, though it is permissible to commission a child to let people into one's house or take a gift to someone.

THINGS ONE MAY COMMISSION OTHERS TO DO

k17.2 X may commission Y:

(1) to conclude contracts on X's behalf (O: such as a sale, gift, putting up collateral, conducting a marriage contract, guaranteeing payment, or transferring a debt);

(2) to cancel contracts on X's behalf (O: such as cancelling a sale or returning defective merchandise);

بينهما . وشركة المفاوضة أن يكون بينهما كسبُهُمـا وعليهمـا ما يَعْـرِضُ من غُرْمٍ [مغني المحتـاج إلى معـرفة معاني ألفاظ المنهاج : ٢/ ٢١٢]).

الوكالة k17.0

(ت : يمثـل لهـا بشخصين : زيــد (الموكِّل) وعمرو (الوكيل) (ع : حيث يعطي زيد لعمرو سلعة فيوكله أن يبيعها له . وأمثـال هذه الوكالة لها أربعة أركان : الموكِّل، والوكيل، والموكَّل فيـه، والصيغة)) .

k17.1 يُشْتَرَطُ في الموكِّل والوكيل أَنْ يَكُونا جائزَي التصرف فيمَا يُوكَّلُ فيه وتَصِحُّ وكالةُ الصبيِّ في الإذنِ في دخول الدار وحملِ الهدية [والعبدِ في قبولِ النكاحِ] .

ما يجوز التوكيل فيه

k17.2 ويَجُوزُ التوكيلُ في العقـود (كعقـد بيع وهبـة ورهن ونكـاح وضمان وحوالة) والفسـوخ (كإقالة ورد بعيب)

(3) to conduct X's divorce;

(4) to make claims (A: by lawsuit against others, as lawyers do);

(5) to ensure fulfillment of established claims (O: from whoever owes them to X, after they have been established by proof);

(6) or to take possession of something that is free to take, such as wild game, pasturage, or water (O: by Y conveying it from land which X is permitted to take it from, since this is a way of gaining property just as sale is).

والطـلاق [والـعتق] وإثبـاتِ الحقـوقِ واستيفـائهـا (ممن هي عليـه بعـد إثبـاتها بالبيـنة) وفي تمليـكِ المبـاحـاتِ كالصيد والحشيشِ والميـاه (بأن ينقله الوكيل من أرض مباحة للموكل لأن ذلك أحد أسباب الملك كالشراء).

k17.3   It is not permissible for Y to undertake obligations of worship that X owes Allah Most High, except for:

(1) distributing zakat to deserving recipients (O: or giving food or alms as an expiation, or voluntary charity);

(2) performing hajj (O: or 'umra, which another may perform on the behalf of an invalid or a deceased person);

(3) and slaughtering sacrifices (dis: j12.6(end), j14.3).

k17.3 وأمَّـا حقـوقُ اللهِ تعـالى فإنْ كانتْ عبـادةً لمْ تَجُـزْ إلَّا في تفرقةِ الزكاةِ (والكفـارة فإنـه يصـح التـوكيل فيها ومثل الزكاة فيما ذكر صدقة التطوع) والحجِّ (أو العمـرة، فإنـه يصـح التـوكيـل فيـه عن المعضوب وعن الميت) وذبحِ الأضحية.

k17.4   It is permissible to commission Y to perform an obligation (O: to Allah) that consists of inflicting a prescribed legal penalty (hadd) (O: such as the penalties for the crimes of accusing another of adultery without proof (def: o13), adultery, or drinking), but is not permissible to commission Y to establish that such an obligation exists (O: such as by X telling Y, "I commission you to affirm [A: in court, by Y submitting X's testimony] that So-and-so has committed adultery," or "that So-and-so has drunk wine").

k17.4 وإنْ كَانَ (حـق الله) حدّاً (أي حد قذف وزنـا وشـرب خمـر) جَازَ في استيفـائـه دونَ إثبـاتـه (وذلك بأن يقـول شخص لآخر: وكلتك في إثبات زنا فلان أو إثبات شربه الخمر).

k17.5   It is a necessary condition for the validity of X's commissioning Y that there be:

(a) a spoken proposal (O: indicating X's wish for Y to handle some matter for him) that

k17.5 وشـرطُهـا الإيجابُ باللفـظ (الـدال على رضـا المـوكل بتصرف الغير

does not restrict the (A: fact of there being a) commission by giving conditions under which the commission takes effect (O: such as saying, "If So-and-so comes, I hereby commission you," which is invalid) (A: but rather, a valid commission must be) such as saying, "I commission you," or "Sell this garment for me";

(b) and an acceptance (O: by Y, whether this be) in word or deed, i.e. by Y simply doing what he has been asked to. It is not necessary that his acceptance take place immediately.

k17.6 When X validly commissions Y to do something, X may include stipulations about how it is to be carried out, such as saying, "I commission you, but don't sell it till after a month." (A: The previous ruling prohibits stipulations restricting the *fact* of Y being commissioned, while here X has already commissioned Y and his stipulations merely govern *how* Y is to do it.) (O: A temporary commission, such as saying, "I commission you for one month," is also valid.)

k17.7 Y may not commission another to perform what X has commissioned Y to do unless X either gives Y permission to commission another, or Y cannot undertake the task (O: because he is unable to, or it does not befit him) or is incapable of it because it is too much (A: for a single person to perform).

THE AGENT'S DISCRETIONARY POWERS

k17.8 Y is not entitled to sell an article (A: he has been comissioned to sell) to himself or his underage son, nor (O: is it valid) to sell it:

(1) for less than the current price of similar articles;

(2) for deferred payment;

(3) or for other than the type of money used locally;

له) مِنْ غيـر تعليـقٍ (كقـولـه : إذا قدم زيد فقـد وكلتك بكـذا ؛ فلا يصـح عقـدهـا حيـنـئـذٍ) كوَكَّلْتُـكَ أوْبِعْ هذا الثـوب ؛ والقبولُ (من الوكيل إما) باللفظ أو الفعل وهو امتثالُ ما وُكِّل به ولا يُشْتَرَطُ الفورُ في القبول .

k17.6 فإنْ نَجَّـزَهـا وعلَّقَ التصرفَ على شرطٍ جازَ كقـولـه : وَكَلّتُـكَ ولا تَبِعْ إلى شهرٍ (وتصح الوكالة المؤقتة كقوله : وكلتك إلى شهر) .

k17.7 وليَسَ للوكيل أنْ يُوَكِّلَ (أحداً فيمـا وكـل فيـه) إلَّا بإذنٍ (أي للموكل) أو (إلّا إن) كَانَ (ح : المـوكــل به) ممّـا لا يَتَوَلَّاهُ (الوكيل) بنفسِه (لكونِه لا يحسنه أو لا يليق به) أو لا يَتَمَكَّنُ مِنْهُ لكثرتِهِ .

ما يصح وما لا يصح من تصرفات الوكيل

k17.8 وليَسَ لهُ أنْ يَبِيـعَ ما وُكِّلَ فيـه لنفسِه أوْ لِولايِه الصغير ولا (يصح أن يبيع المـوكل فيه) بدون ثمن مثلِه ولا بمؤجلٍ ولا بغيـرِ نقـدِ البلدِ إلَّا أنْ يَأْذَنَ لهُ في ذلك

though Y may do these (O: (1), (2), or (3)) if X grants him permission to.

（المذكور من دون ثمن المثل وما بعده）.

k17.9   Y's sale of the commissioned article is not valid when X specifies the type of funds he wants as its price, but Y sells it for a different type, such as when X says, "Sell it for a thousand dirhams," but Y sells it for a thousand dinars. But Y's selling it is valid if X specifies the amount he wants and Y sells it for more, provided the type of funds is the same, as when X says, "Sell it for a thousand," but Y sells it for two thousand—unless X has specifically prohibited this (O: in which case the sale would not be valid, as it contravenes X's commission).

k17.9   ولَوْ نَصَّ لهُ على جنس الثمن فخالفَ لمْ يَصحَّ البيعُ كبِعْ بألفِ درهمٍ ، فبَاعَ بألفِ دينارٍ . وإنْ نَصَّ على القدرِ فزادَ من الجنس صَحَّ كبِعْ بألفٍ ، فبَاعَ بألفين إلَّا أنْ ينْهَـاهُ ((المـوكل عن هذه الزيادة)) فلا يصح البيع للمخالفة）.

k17.10   If X commissions Y to "buy such and such a thing for a hundred," but Y buys one worth a hundred for less than a hundred, then the purchase is valid. But if Y buys one for two hundred that is worth two hundred (A: when X has commissioned him to buy one for a hundred), then the purchase is not valid. If X tells Y, "Buy a sheep with this dinar," (O: and describes it in type and so forth, since without such a description, the commission would not be valid), but Y buys two sheep (A: with that dinar) of which each one is worth a dinar, then the purchase is valid and both sheep belong to X, though if the sheep are not each worth a dinar, then the purchase is not valid.

k17.10   ولوْ قالَ : اشْترِ بمائةٍ ؛ فاشْتَرَى ما يُسَاوِيها بدون مائةٍ صَحَّ . وإن اشْتَرَى بمائتين ما يُسَـاوِي مائتين فَلا [(يصح الشراء للمخالفـة في الثمن لأنه اشترى بمـائتين ما يساويهمـا بلا إذن في زيـادة الثمن على المـائـة)] . وإنْ قَالَ : اشْترِ بهذا الدينار شاةً ؛ (ووصفها بصفة بأن بين نوعهـا وغيـره وإلا لم يصح التـوكيـل) فاشْتَـرَى به شاتين تُسَـاوِي كلَّ واحـدةٍ دينـاراً صَحَّ وكَـانَتا للمـوكل . فإنْ لمْ تُسَاوِ كلُّ واحدةٍ ديناراً لمْ يَصحَّ العقدُ .

k17.11   When X commissions Y to sell something to a particular person, it is not permissible (O: or valid) for Y to sell it to another.

k17.11   وإنْ قَالَ : بِعْ لِزَيْـدٍ ؛ فبَـاعَ لغيره لمْ يَجُزْ (أي ولم يصح) .

k17.12   When X tells Y, "Buy this [A: particular] garment," and Y buys it and X finds it is defective, then Y may return it for a refund (O: and so may X, since he is its owner). But when X merely tells Y to "buy a garment" (O: without further restriction), then it is not permissible for Y to buy a defective one (O: because the lack of further restrictions is understood to mean being free of defects, and if Y buys a defective one, the purchase is invalid).

k17.12   وإنْ قَالَ : اشْترِ هذا الثوبَ ؛ فأشْتراهُ (الوكيل) فَوَجَدَهُ (الموكل) معيباً فلهُ (أي للوكيل) الـردُ (وللمـوكل كذلك لأنه المالك) . أوْ : اشْترِ ثوباً ؛ (وأطلقه) لمْ يَجُـزْ (للوكيـل) شراءُ (ثـوب) معيب (لأن الإطـلاق يحمـل على السـلامة من العيب فإذا اشتراه فالشراء باطل) .

k17.13 It is a necessary condition that the thing Y is being commissioned to do is determinately known (O: to X and Y) in some respects. Thus, if X says, "I commission you to sell my property and conduct the divorce of my wives," his commission is valid, though if he merely commissions Y to "handle everything, large or small," or "all of my affairs," it is not valid.

k17.14 Y's responsibility in a commission is that of someone who has been given a trust (O: since he represents X, and his possession of the article is like X's), meaning that if (O: X's) property is destroyed without negligence while in Y's possession, Y does not have to pay for it. (O: But when Y is to blame and negligent, as when he uses the article himself or keeps it in a place lacking the normal precautions for safeguarding similar articles, then he must pay for its loss, as with any trust.)

k17.15 Y's word (dis: k8.2) is accepted over X's when there is a dispute:

(1) concerning the commissioned article's destruction;

(2) as to whether the article was or was not returned to X;

(3) or whether Y betrayed his trust.

k17.16 Either X or Y may cancel the commission at any time. If X relieves Y of his commission, but Y does not learn of this and performs it, then what he has done is not legally binding or effective (O: because he did not have the right to handle the matter).

k17.17 The commission is cancelled when X or Y dies, loses his sanity, or loses consciousness (Ar. ughmiya 'alayhi, i.e. through other than falling asleep).

*

k17.13 وَيُشْتَرَطُ كونُ المـوكَّلِ فيهِ معلوماً (لهما) مِنْ بعض الوجوه فلَوْ قَالَ: وَكَّلْتُكَ في بيـعِ مالي [وعتق عبـدي] وطلاق زوجاتي؛ صَحَّ، أَوْ: في كلِّ قليلٍ وكثيرٍ، أَوْ: في كلِّ أموري. ؛ لَمْ يَصِحَّ.

k17.14 ويدُ الـوكيلِ يدُ أمـانةٍ (لأنه قائم مقام المـوكل فكانت يده كيده) فمَا يَتْلَفُ مَعَهُ (من المـال المـوكـل فيـه) بلا تفريطٍ لا يَضْمَنُهُ (فإذا فرّط وتعدّى كأن استعمـل العين أو وضعهـا في غير حرز مثلها ضمن كسائر الأمناء).

k17.15 والقـولُ في الهـلاكِ (للموكل فيـه) والـردِّ (أي على المــوكـل أي رد المـوكل فيه عليه) ومَا يُدَّعَى عليْهِ (أي على الوكيل) مِنَ الخيانة (في الموكل فيه) قولُهُ [(أي فالقـول في هذه المـذكورات قول الوكيل بيمينه)].

k17.16 ولكلٍّ منهُمَا الفسخُ متى شَاءَ. فإنْ عزلـهُ (أي عزل الموكل الـوكيل) والـوكيل المعزول) لَمْ يَعْلَمْ فتَصَرَّفَ لَمْ يَصِحَّ التصرفُ (لأنه غير مالك للتصرف).

k17.17 وإنْ مَاتَ أحدُهُمَا أَوْ جُنَّ أَوْ اُغْمِيَ عليْهِ انْفَسَخَتْ.

k18.0 DEPOSITS FOR SAFEKEEPING (WADI‘A)

(n: Given persons P (al-mudi‘) and Q (al-wadi‘) (A: where P deposits an article with Q for safekeeping until such time as P should want it back. Such deposits have four integrals:

(a) the article (al-wadi‘a);

(b) the verbal agreement;

(c) P;

(d) and Q).)

(O: The appropriateness of mentioning deposits for safekeeping after having discussed commissioning others is plain, namely that both the person commissioned and the person with whom something is deposited are bearers of a trust, and do not pay for the loss or destruction of the article in their care unless the destruction is the result of their wrongdoing (A: or remissness in taking normal precautions).)

k18.1 Deposits for safekeeping are only valid when both P and Q have full right to handle their own property.

Thus, if a child or a foolhardy person (def: k13.1(A:)) deposits something for safekeeping with an adult, he should not accept it. If he does, then he is responsible for it (O: and must cover the cost if it is destroyed) and is not free of the responsibility until he returns it to the child's guardian. He is not free of the responsibility if he merely returns it to the child.

If an adult deposits something for safekeeping with a child (A: or other person without full disposal over their affairs), then the child is not responsible if the article is destroyed through negligence or otherwise (O: as when an act of God befalls it), though if the child *destroys* the article, he is financially responsible for it.

k18.2 It is unlawful for Q to accept a deposit for safekeeping when he is not able to protect it. It is offensive for him to accept it if he is able to protect

k18.0 الوديعة

(ت: يمثل لها بشخصين: زيد (المودع) وعمرو (الوديع) (ع: حيث يودع زيد عيناً عند عمرو أمانةً إلى أن يطلبها زيد. وأمثال هذه الودائع لها أربعة أركان: عين الوديعة، وصيغة العقد، والمودع، والوديع)).

(ومناسبة ذكرها عقب الوكالة ظاهرة وهي أن كلاً من الوكيل والوديع أمين لا يضمن إلا بالتعدي).

k18.1 لا تصحُّ إلاّ مِنْ جائزِ التصرف عند جائز التصرف. فإنْ أوْدَعَ صبيٌّ أوْ سفيهٌ عند بالغ شيئاً فلا يَقْبَلُه. فإنْ قَبِلَه دَخَل في ضمانِه ولا يَبْرأُ (الوديع المذكور من الضمان) إلاّ بدفعه لوليّه. فلوْ ردَّه للصبيِّ لمْ يَبْرأْ. وإنْ أوْدَعَ بالغٌ عند صبيٍّ فتَلِف عند الصبيِّ لتفريط أوْ غيره (كآفة سماوية نزلت على الشيء المودع) لمْ يضْمنْه الصبيُّ. وإنْ اتْلفَه ضَمِنَه.

k18.2 ومَنْ عَجَزَ عن حفظِ الوديعة حَرُمَ عليْه قبولُها.
وإنْ قَدَر ولمْ يثِقْ بأمانة نفسِه وخاف

it but cannot trust himself and fears he may betray the responsibility. But if he can trust himself, it is desirable and praiseworthy for him to accept it.

k18.3 If Q accepts a deposit for safekeeping, he is obliged to keep it in a place meeting the normal specifications for safeguarding similar articles (A: for his town and times) (O: which varies according to the nature of the article deposited, as each thing has precautions proper to safeguarding it (dis: o14.3)).

k18.4 If Q plans to travel or fears he may die, he must return the deposited article to P. If Q cannot find P or someone commissioned by P (A: to manage P's affairs), then he must deliver it to the Islamic magistrate (A: to keep for P). If there is none, Q leaves it with a trustworthy person (O: and he is not obliged to delay his trip), though if he deposits the article with a trustworthy person when there *is* an Islamic magistrate, he is still financially responsible for it.

If Q fails to take the above measures (A: of returning it to the owner or next most appropriate person available) and he dies without having provided in his will for returning the article, or he travels with it, then he is financially responsible for it, unless he dies suddenly, or looting or fire breaks out in the city, and he travels with it because of being unable to give it to any of the above persons

k18.5 Whenever P asks for the deposited article, Q is obliged to return it by allowing P to take it (O: i.e. by relinquishing possession of it, though this does not mean he has to transport it to P).

k18.6 Q is financially responsible for the deposited article if:

(1) without excuse, he delays allowing P to take it;

(2) he deposits the article for safekeeping with a third party, without having had to travel and when there was no need;

أَنْ يَخُونَ كُرِهَ لَهُ أَخْذُهَا . فَإِنْ وَثِقَ اسْتُحِبَّ .

k18.3 ثُمَّ يَلْزَمُهُ (أي الوديعَ) الحفظُ [(أي حفظ الوديعة)] في حِرْز مِثلِهَا (وهو يختلف باختلاف الـوديعـة فكل شيء له حرز يليق به) .

k18.4 فإنْ أرادَ (الـوديعَ) السفرَ أوْ خاف المـوتَ فَلْيَـرُدَّهَا إلى صاحِبِهَا . فإنْ لمْ يَجِـدْهُ ولا وكيلَهُ سَلَّمَهَا إلى الحاكم . فإنْ فُقِـدَ فإلى أمـينٍ (ولا يكلف تأخيـر السفـر) فإنْ سَلَّمَهَا إلى أمينٍ مَعَ وجودِ الحاكمِ ضَمِنَ .

فإنْ لمْ يَفْعَلْ فمَاتَ ولمْ يُوصِ بهَا أوْ سَافَرَ بهَا ضَمِنَها، إلّا أنْ يَمُوتَ فجأةً أوْ يَقَـعَ في البـلدِ نهبٌ أوْ حريقٌ ولمْ يَتَمَكَّنْ مِنْ شيءٍ مِنْ ذلك فسافَرَ بهَا .

k18.5 ومتى طَلَبَهـا المـالـكُ لَزِمَهُ (الوديعَ) الردُّ بأنْ يُخَلِّي بينَهُ (أي المالك) وبينَهـا (أي الـوديعـة بأن يرفع الوديع يده عنها وليس المراد أنه يلزمه حملها له) .

k18.6 فإنْ أَخَّـرَ بلا عذرٍ أوْ أوْدَعَهـا عنـد غيـرِه بلا سفرٍ ولا ضرورةٍ أوْ خَلَطَها

(3) he mixes the deposited property with his own property or with some of P's other property such that the deposited property is no longer distinguishable from what it has been mixed with (O: as opposed to when the deposited property can be easily distinguished and has not depreciated as a result of being mixed);

(4) he takes the article out of the place of safekeeping to use, even if he did not use it (O: because merely taking it out with such an intention is a betrayal of his trust);

(5) he does not keep it in a place meeting the normal specifications for safeguarding similar articles;

(6) or if P has told him, "Keep it in such and such a particular place for safeguarding," but he instead puts it in a different place less protected (O: than the one P indicated), even when this second place meets the normal specifications for safeguarding similar articles (O: though if Q puts it in a different place with protection equal or superior to the place P has indicated, Q is not responsible for it).

k18.7   Either party may cancel the deposit for safekeeping agreement at any time. The agreement is also annulled when either party dies, loses his sanity, or loses consciousness (Ar. ughmiya 'alayhi, i.e. through other than falling asleep).

k18.8   Q's responsibility in accepting a deposit for safekeeping is that of someone who has been given a trust (O: meaning that his claims when he swears an oath (N: and neither side has proof (dis: k8.2)) are accepted, as he is a trustee). His word is accepted over P's when there are disputes about:

(1) whether the deposit for safekeeping was actually made (O: When P claims that it was);

(2) whether the article was returned to P;

(3) or whether and how the article was destroyed (O: when Q claims it was).

(أي الوديعة) بمالٍ لَهُ (أي للوديع) أوْ للمودع أيضاً بحيثُ لا يَتَمَيَّزُ (بخلاف ما إذا تميز بسهولة ولم تنقص الوديعة بهذا الخلط) أو اسْتَعْمَلَهَا أوْ أخْـرَجَهَـا مِنَ الحرز ليَنْتَفعَ بها فلمْ يَنْتَفعْ (لأن الإخراج على هذا القصـد خيـانـة) أوْ حَفظَهَـا في دونِ جِرْزهَا أوْ قال لَهُ المـالكُ: احْفَظْهَا في هٰذا الحرز؛ فَوَضَعَهَـا في دونهِ (أي أقل في الحرز مما أمره) وهوَ حرزُهَا أيضاً ضَمِنَهَا. (ولو وضع الـوديعـة في مثـل الحرز الأول أو أعلى منه في الحرز فلا ضمان).

k18.7   ولكلٍّ منهُمَا الفسخُ مَتَى شَاءَ. فإنْ مات أحدُهُمَا أوْ جُنَّ أوْ أُغْمِيَ عليْهِ انْفَسَخَتْ.

k18.8   ويـدُ المـودَع [(بفتـح الـدال بمعنى الـوديع)] أمانةٌ (فيصدق بما يدعيه بيمينه (ح: حيث لا بينة لأحد الطرفين) لأنه أمين) فالقولُ في أصل الإيداع (إذا ادعاه المـالك) أوْ في الردِّ أو التلف (إذا ادعـاه الوديع) قولُهُ. فلوْ قَالَ: مَا أوْدَعْتَنِي

Thus if Q says, "You did not deposit anything with me," or "I returned it to you," or "It was destroyed without negligence on my part," then his word is accepted when he swears.

شيئاً، أو: رَدَدْتُها إليكَ، أوْ: تَلِفَتْ بلا تفريطٍ، صُدِّقَ بيمينِه.

k18.9 It is a necessary condition for the validity of a deposit for safekeeping that P states it in words such as "I entrust it to you to keep," or "I entrust it to you to protect." It is not necessary that Q give a spoken reply to this, but is sufficient for him to simply accept the article.

k18.9 وَيُشْتَرَطُ لفظٌ مِنَ المُودِع كأسْتَوْدَعْتُكَ، أوْ: آسْتَحْفَظْتُكَ، ولا يُشْتَرَطُ القبولُ (لفظاً من الوديع) بلْ يَكْفي القبضُ.

                           *

k19.0 LENDING SOMETHING FOR USE ('ARIYYA)

    (n: Given persons A (al-muʿir) and B (al-mustaʿir) (A: where A lends B an article to use and return after use. This section discusses such loans, which have four integrals:

    (a) the article (al-ʿariyya);

    (b) the verbal agreement;

    (c) A;

    (d) and B).)

k19.0 العاريةُ
(ت: يمثّل لها بشخصين: زيد (المعير) وعمرو (المستعير) (ع: حيث يعير زيد لعمرو عيناً ليستعملها ويردها بعد الاستعمال. وأمثال هذه المعاملة لها أربعةُ أركانٍ: العاريّة [وهي العين المعارة]، وصيغة العقد، والمعير، والمستعير)).

k19.1 A's lending an article for B to use is valid if A possesses full disposal over his own property and has the lawful right to the article's use, even if he is only renting it (n: though not if someone else has lent him the article without giving him permission to relend it, as at k19.8).

k19.1 تَصِحُّ مِنْ كُلِّ جائزِ التصرفِ مالكٍ للمنفعةِ ولوْ بإجارةٍ.

k19.2 It is permissible to lend anything that can be benefited from while the article itself still remains (O: such that B gets some use out the article, as is usually the case, or else he materially gains from it, as when he borrows a sheep for its milk or its expected offspring, or borrows a tree for its fruit. It is not valid to lend something of no lawful benefit such as a musical instrument (dis:

k19.2 ويجوزُ إعارةُ كلِّ ما يُنْتَفَعُ بِه مَعَ بقاءِ عينِه (بأن يستفيد المستعير منفعةً من الشيءِ المعارِ وهو الأكثرُ أو يستفيد عيناً منه كما لو استعار شاةً ليأخذ درها ونسلها أو شجرة ليأخذ ثمرها. ولا يصح إعارةُ ما يحرمُ الانتفاعُ به كآلة لهوٍ. ولا

r40), or such things as edibles, which do not them-selves exist after use, since their use consists solely in their consumption). (A: The latter would be a *loan* (qard, def: k10) repayable in kind, and hence not included in *lending for use*.)

يعـــار المطعـوم ونحـوه من كل ما لا تبقى عينه لأن الانتفاع إنما هو باستهلاكه) .

k19.3 It is necessary for the validity of lending something for use that either A or B state the agreement in words. (O: The loan is not valid except by either A or B stating it, such as by B telling A, "Loan me such and such," and then A giving it to him. The action alone, between A and B, is insufficient.)

k19.3 . بشرط لفظٍ مِنْ أحدِهمَا . (أي لا تصح العارية إلا به من أحد المتعاقدين بأنْ يقول المستعير للمعير : أعِرني الشيء الفـلاني ؛ فيـدفعـه المعيـر له . ولا يكفي الفعل من الطرفين) .

k19.4 B may then use the article according to the permission given. He may:

(1) do what A has given him permission to;

(2) or do the equivalent (O: in respect to the wear and tear on the article involved) or some-thing less, though not if A has forbidden B to do other than what he has specifically given him per-mission to do.

If A tells B, "Plant wheat," (A: on land lent), then it is permissible for B to plant barley, though not vice versa (O: since wheat is harder on the soil than barley), while if A merely permits B to *plant*, without further restriction, then B may plant whatever he wishes.

k19.4 ويْنتفِـعُ بِحسب الإذْن فَيَفْعَـلُ المأذونَ فيـه أوْ مثلَهُ (أي مثل المأذون فيه في الضرر) أوْ دونَهُ إلاَّ أنْ يَنْهَاهُ عن الغير . فإنْ قَالَ : ارْزَعْ حنطةً ؛ جَازَ الشعيرُ لا عكسُـهُ (لأن البر أعظم ضرراً من الشعير في الأرض) . فإنْ قَالَ : ازْرَعْ ؛ وأطْـلَقَ زَرَعَ مَا شَاءَ [فإنْ رَجَعَ قبلَ الحصادِ بَقِيَ إلى الحصــادِ لكنْ بأجـرةٍ إنْ أذَنَ مطلقـاً وبغيرِها إنْ أذَنَ في معيّنٍ فَزَرَعَهُ] .

k19.5 When A permits B to plant an orchard or build buildings on property he lends B, but later wants the land back, then:

(1) if A had stipulated that B would have to remove the trees or buildings, then B removes them (O: obligatorily, performing what was stipu-lated, for if B will not, then A may remove them);

(2) but if A had not stipulated this, then if B wishes, he may remove them, though if B does not (O: but rather chooses to keep them there), then A has a choice between leaving them on the land for rent (O: from B for the land), or else removing

k19.5 وإنْ قَالَ : اغْـرِسْ ؛ أوِ : ابْنِ ؛ ثمَ رَجَـعَ (في الأرض المأذونِ فيهـا) فإنْ كانَ (قد) شَرَطَ عليهِ القلعَ قَلَعَ . (أي قلعه المستعير بمعنى أنه يجب عليه ذلك عملاً بالشـرط . فإن امتنع قلعه المعير) وإنْ لمْ يشْـرُطْ واخْتَـار المستعيرُ القلعَ قَلَعَ . وإنْ لمْ يَخْتَـرْ (بأن اختـار الإبقـاء) فالمعيـرُ بالخِيـارِ بيـنَ تبقيتِـهِ بأجـرةٍ (للأرض المستعارة يدفعها المستعير له) وبينَ قلعِهِ

them (O: the trees or buildings) and being obliged to pay B a compensation for the loss of value (O: to the trees (A: or buildings)) caused by removal.

A is entitled to take back the article lent at any time he wishes.

k19.6 B is financially liable for the article lent (N: even if it is destroyed by an act of God). If it is destroyed while B is using it for other than what A gave him permission to do with it, even if not through B's negligence, then B is responsible to A for the article's value (A: at the market price current for similar articles on) the day of its destruction (O: and he may either replace it or pay A for it).

But if the loaned article wears out through being used in the way that A gave permission to use it, then B is not financially responsible for it (N: as when B borrows a garment to wear which becomes worn out through use alone).

k19.7 B is responsible for the measures entailed in returning the article to A.

k19.8 B may not loan (O: the article lent to him) to a third party (O: without permission).

*

k20.0 THE RETURN OF WRONGFULLY TAKEN PROPERTY (GHASB)

(O: Taking another's property is an enormity (dis: p20), the scriptural basis for its prohibition being Koranic verses such as the word of Allah Most High,

"Do not consume each other's property through falsehood" (Koran 2:188).)

(n: Given persons X and Y (A: where X takes an article belonging to Y. This section presents the details of X's obligation (dis: p77.3) to restore Y his property).)

(أي الـغـراس والبنـاء) و(على المعيـر حيـنـئـذ) ضمـان أرش مَا نَقَصَ (مـن الغراس) بالقلع .

ولهُ الرجوعُ في الإعارة متى شاءَ [إلّا أنْ يُعيـرَ أرضاً للدفن فإنّهُ لا يَرْجعُ فيها مَا لمْ يَبْلَ الميّتُ].

k19.6 والعـاريةُ مضمـونـةٌ (ح). ولو هلكت بآفة سمـاويـة). فإنْ تَلفَتْ بغيـر الاستعمال المأذون فيهِ ولوْ بغير تفريط (من المستعير) ضَمِنَها بقيمتِها يومَ التلف (بدلاً أو أرشاً).

فإنْ تَلفَتْ بالاستعمال المأذون فيه لمْ يَضْمَنْ (ح: كأن استعار ثوباً ليلبسه فبلي باللبس لا بشيء آخر).

k19.7 ومؤنةُ الردِّ على المستعير.

k19.8 وليـسَ لهُ أنْ يُعيـرَ (الـشـيء المعار بغير إذن).

k20.0 الغصب

(هـو كبيرة من الكبـائـر. والأصل في تحريمه آيات كقوله تعالى: ﴿وَلَا تَأْكُلُوا أَمْوَالَكُم بَيْنَكُم بِالْبَاطِلِ﴾ [أي لا يأكل بعضكم مال بعض بالباطل]).

(ت: يمثل له بشخصين: زيد (الغاصب) وعمرو (المغصوب منه) (ع: حيث يغصب زيد عيناً من عمرو. هذا البـاب يبيـن واجب زيـد في رد العين المغصوبة لصاحبها عمرو [ح: وما يترتب على عدم الرد])).

429

k20.1 *Wrongfully taking* (ghasb) means to appropriate what is another's right (O: even if this consists of the right to use something, such as forcing someone sitting in a mosque or marketplace to get up from his place) unjustly.

k20.1 هُوَ الاستيلاءُ على حقِّ الغيرِ (ولو كان ذلك الحق منفعة كإقامة من قعد بمسجد أو سوق) عدواناً [(أي تعدياً وظلماً)].

k20.2 When X wrongfully takes anything of value from Y, even if the value is inconsiderable, he is obliged to return it unless this involves destruction to life or lawful property, as when X takes a plank and nails it over a leak in the hull of a ship at sea that is bearing others' property or worthy people or animals (N: meaning those not obligatory to kill (def: e12.8(O:))).

k20.2 فَمَنْ غَصَبَ شيئاً لهُ قيمةٌ وإنْ قَلَّتْ لَزِمَهُ ردُّهُ إلاَّ أنْ يَتَرَتَّبَ على ردِّه تلفُ حيوانٍ أوْ مالٍ معصومَيْن مثلُ أن غَصَبَ لوحاً فَسَمَّرَهُ على خرق سفينةٍ في وسطِ البحر وفيهَا مالٌ لغير الغاصبِ أوْ حيوانٌ معصومٌ (ح: وهو مالا يجب قتله).

k20.3 If the article taken is destroyed while in X's possession or X himself destroys it, then:

(1) if it was *fungible* (mithli, a homogeneous commodity transacted by weight or measure, an equal amount of which precisely supplies the place of another), then X is financially responsible for replacing it with an equal amount, *fungible* meaning that which is measured by volume or weight, and which can be validly sold in advance (def: k9.2(b,d,f,g)) such as grain, gold or silver, and so forth, while *nonfungible* (mutaqawwim, commodities appraised and transacted as particular pieces of merchandise) means everything else, such as livestock and articles of heterogeneous composition, like meat pastry, and so forth;

(2) if the article was fungible (mithli) but it is no longer possible for X to obtain an equal amount to return to Y, then X owes Y its value, which is reckoned at its highest market value between the time X seized it and the time of its subsequent unavailability;

(3) but if the article was nonfungible (mutaqawwim), X owes Y its highest market value during the interval between X's taking it and the time of its destruction.

(N: The foregoing apply to when X has appropriated a physical article or commodity ('ayn). As for when he has wrongfully appro-

k20.3 فإنْ تلفَ عنـدَهُ أوْ أتْلَفَـهُ فإنْ كان مثلياً ضَمِنَـهُ بمثلِه. والمثليُّ هوَ ما حَصَـرَهُ كيـلٌ أوْ وزنٌ وجَـازَ فيـه السلمُ كالحبـوب والنقـود وغير ذلك. والمتقومُ غيـرُ ذلك كالحيوانـاتِ والمختلطـات كالهريسـةٍ وغير ذلك. فإنْ تَعَذَّرَ المثلُ فالـقيمـةُ أكثـرُ مـا كانَتْ مِنَ الغصبِ إلى تعـذرِ المثـل. وإنْ كانَ متقـوماً ضَمِنَـهُ بقيـمتِـه أكثـرَ مـا كانَتْ مِنَ الغصبِ إلى الـتلفِ [حتّى لوْ زَادَ عنـدَ الغـاصبِ بأنْ سَمِنَ لَزِمَهُ قيمتُـهُ سميـناً سواءٌ هَزَلَ بعـدَ ذلكَ أمْ لاَ]. (ح: هذا إذا كان المغصوبُ عيناً أما المنفعة، فـ [الأصح أنها] تضمن

priated the use of something, the obligation consists of repaying Y the cost of renting a similar article for a similar amount of time.)

k20.4 X's word (O: provided he swears an oath (N: and neither side has proof (dis: k8.2))) is accepted over Y's when there is a dispute about the destroyed article's value (O: when both agree that it has been destroyed) or about its destruction (A: as to when it occurred, for example). But Y's word is accepted over X's when there is a dispute about whether or not X returned the article to Y.

k20.5 If the property returned by X is materially diminished or has depreciated in value because of some new defect, or both, then X is obliged to pay Y compensation for the loss of value (O: while still being obliged to return the rest).

But if the article has diminished in value solely because its market price is now less, then X is not required to pay anything.

k20.6 If the article possesses a utility (O: meaning a rentable utility, as a house does), then X owes Y its rent for the period that X had it, no matter whether he used it or not.

k20.7 Anyone who obtains the wrongfully appropriated article from X, or subsequently obtains it from the person who got it from X, and so forth, on down, is financially responsible (def: k20.2–6) to Y for it, no matter whether such a person knows of its having been wrongfully appropriated or not.

k20.8 (N: Given persons X, Y, and Z, where X has wrongfully taken something from Y, and then Z obtains it from X. This ruling describes the compensation due to Y when the article has been damaged or destroyed in Z's possession.)

Y is entitled to demand restoration or payment for the loss or depreciation of the article from either X or Z. The obligation to cover this

بأجرة المثل) .

k20.4 فإن اخْتَلَفَا في قدرِ القيمة (أي بعـد اتفـاقِهما على تلفه) أوْ في التلفِ فالقـولُ قولُ الغاصِب (بيمينه (ح : حيث لا بينة لأحد الطرفين)) أوْ في الردّ فقولُ المالكِ .

k20.5 وإنْ ردَّهُ ناقصَ العينِ أو القيمة لعيب أوْ ناقصَهُما ضَمِنَ الأرشَ (مع لزوم رد الباقي من العين) .

وإنْ نَقَصَتِ القيمةُ بانخفاضِ السعرِ فقطْ لمْ يَلْزَمْهُ شيءٌ .

k20.6 وإنْ كانَتْ لهُ منفعـةٌ (تقـابـل بأجـرة كدار) ضَمِنَ أجـرتَهُ للمدة التي قَام في يدِهِ سواءٌ انْتَفَعَ به أمْ لا [لكنْ لا يَلْزَمُهُ مهرُ الجارية المغصوبة إلَّا أنْ يَطأَها وهيَ غيرُ مطاوعةٍ] .

k20.7 وكـلُّ يدٍ تَرَتَّبَـتْ على يدِ الغـاصِب فهيَ يدُ ضمـانٍ سواءٌ عَلِمَتْ بالغصبِ أمْ لا .

k20.8 فللمـالـكِ أنْ يُضَمِّنَ الأولَ (الـذي هو الغاصِب) والثانيَ (الذي تلقى الملك فيهِ من الغـاصِب) لكنْ إنْ كانَتْ

becomes Z's own financial liability—meaning that if Y asks Z for compensation, Z may not in turn demand it from X; though if Y asks X for it, X may it turn demand it from Z—in the following cases:

(1) when Z obtained it knowing that it had been wrongfully appropriated;

(2) when Z obtained it not knowing that it had been wrongfully appropriated, but the means by which Z obtained it would have made him financially responsible for its destruction anyway, as when Z himself wrongfully appropriated it or borrowed it for use (def: k19) from X. (O: Z is also financially liable if he bought it from X);

(3) or when Z obtained it not knowing it had been wrongfully taken, and the means by which he got it from X would not otherwise have made him responsible for its destruction except for the fact that he himself precipitated its destruction (A: as when X deposits it with Z for safekeeping and Z destroys it).

*

k21.0 PREEMPTING THE SALE OF A CO-OWNER'S SHARE TO ANOTHER (SHUF‘A)

(n: Given P, Q, and R (A: where P and Q each own part of some dividable piece of real estate, and P sells his part to R, a third party. In such a case, Q can legally force R to sell the part to him by right of preemption (N: whose purpose is to prevent the harm to Q that would result if R were to subsequently go to the Islamic magistrate and demand that the property be divided to distinguish his property from Q's)).)

k21.1   Preemption is only legally binding:

(a) on a portion of real estate (A: that belonged to P and Q) which can be divided without loss of value;

(b) when P has sold his part (A: to R) for recompense.

اليدُ الثانيةُ عالمةً بالغصب أوْ جاهلةً وهيَ يدُ ضمانٍ كغصب (من غاصبٍ) أوْ عاريةٍ (من الغـاصب ومثلهمـا المشتري منه) أوْ لمْ تكنْ (يـده يد ضمـانٍ) وبـاشـرتْ الإتلاف فقرارُ الضمانِ على الثاني أي إذا غرَمَـهُ المالكُ لا يَرْجِـعُ (الثـاني) على الأول وإن غَرِمَ الأولُ (وهـو الغـاصب) رَجَـع عليه (أي على الثاني) [وإنْ جَهلَتْ (يـد الثـاني) الغصبَ وهيَ يدُ أمانةٍ (لا يد ضمـان) كوديعـةٍ فالقـرارُ (في الضمـان) على الأول أي إذا غَرِمَ الثـاني رَجَـع على الأول وإن غَرِمَ الأولُ فلَا (يـرجـع على الثاني) وإنْ غَصَبَ كلباً فيه منفعةً أوْ جلدَ ميتةٍ أوْ خمراً من ذميٍّ أوْ منْ مسلم وهيَ محتـرمـةً لزمَـهُ الـردُّ فإنْ أتْلفَ ذلكَ لمْ يَضْمَنْـهُ فإنْ دَبغَ الجلدَ أوْ تَخَلَّلتِ الخمرة فهما للمغصوب منه].

k21.0 الشفعة

(ت: يمثل لها بثلاثة أشخاص: زيد وعمرو وبكر (ع: حيث يشترك كل من زيـد وعـمـرو في ملك جزء من أرض تحتمل القسمة فيبيع زيد جزأه لبكر؛ فعندئذ يجوز شرعاً لعمر وأن يجبر زيداً على بيـع الجـزء له (أي لعمـرو) بالشفعة (ح: وفـائـدتهـا حمـايـة عمـرو ومن ضرر يحصـل لو اشتـرى بكـر الجـزء فطالب القـاضي بقسمـة الأرض ليميـز جزأه من جزء عمرو))).

k21.1   إنَّمَا تجبُ في جزءٍ مشاعٍ منْ أرضٍ تحْتَمِـلُ الـقـسمـةَ إذا مُلِكَتْ بمعـاوضةٍ فيَأخُذُهَا الشريكُ أو الشركاءُ

In such a case, Q may preempt its being sold to R by buying R's share for the price that P and R agreed on. If there are several co-owners in place of Q, they each buy a part of the share proportionate to the percentage of the whole property they respectively own.

(A: If there is disagreement between the parties as to how much P sold it to R for, and there is no proof, then) R is the one to say (A: when he swears (def: k8.2)) how much the price of the part was.

على قدر حصصِهِمْ بالعِـوضِ الـذي اسْتَقَرَّ عليهِ العقدُ. والقولُ قولُ المشتري في قدرِه.

k21.2   It is a necessary condition for the preemptive sale that Q effect it with words such as "I hereby appropriate this property by preemption."

It is also necessary that Q give R the price, that R agree to let Q pay it later, or that the Islamic magistrate rule that Q may buy the property by preemption; in any of which cases Q takes possession of it.

If R paid P with something fungible (mithli, def: k20.3(1)), then Q must pay R an equal amount. If R paid with something nonfungible, then Q must pay its value (A: in the marketplace on) the day of the sale.

k21.2   ويُشْتَرَطُ اللفظُ كَتَمَلَّكْتُ [أوْ أخَذْتُ] بالشفعةِ. ويُشْتَرَطُ مَعَ ذلك إمّا تسليمُ العِوضِ إلى المشتري أوْ رضاهُ بكونِهِ في ذمةِ الشفيعِ أوْقضاءُ القاضي لهُ بالشفعةِ فحينئـذٍ يَمْلكُ. فإنْ كَانَ ما بَذَلَهُ المشتري مثلياً دَفَعَ مثلَهُ وإلا فقيمتُهُ حَالَ البيعِ.

k21.3   There is no preemption if:

(1)   the property is divided (N: already, by boundary markers or similar);

(2)   the building and trees on the land are sold separately from it;

(3)   the property cannot be divided without eliminating its usefulness (non-k21.1(a)), such as a cistern or a narrow walkway;

(4)   R acquired it without paying a price for it, as when it has been given to him as a gift;

(5)   or if R bought it with a price whose amount was not known (A: such as "for this pile of silver you see").

k21.3   أمّا الملكُ المقسومُ أوِ البنـاءُ والغـراسُ إذا بيعـا منفـردَيْنِ أوْ ما تَبْطُـلُ بالقسمةِ منفعتُهُ المقصودةُ كالبئرِ والطريقِ الـضـيـقِ أوْ ما مُلِكَ بغيـرِ معـاوضـةٍ كالمـوهـوبِ أوْ مَا لمْ يُعْلَمْ قدرُ ثمنـِهِ فلا شفعة فيه.

k21.4   If the building and trees have been sold with the land (A: for one price), then Q also takes them as part of the land he preempts.

وإنْ بِيعَ البِناءُ والغِراسُ مَعَ k21.4
الأرضِ أخَذَهُ بالشفعةِ تبعاً .

k21.5   Preemption must occur immediately (A: upon Q's learning of P's having sold the property to R). When Q learns of it, he must preempt at once (def: f4.5). If he delays without excuse, he no longer has the right to preempt, unless R bought the property from P for postponed payment, in which case Q has a choice between buying it at once, or waiting until payment is due and then buying it.

If Q learns of the sale while ill, or being detained, he must commission someone (def: k17) to preempt for him. If he does not, he loses the right to preempt, unless he was unable to commission someone, or the person who informed him of the sale was a child or someone unreliable, or he was informed of it while travelling and then started returning in order to preempt; in all of which cases he may still preempt.

والشفعةُ على الفورِ فإذا علِمَ k21.5
فَلْيُبَادِرْ على العـادةِ فإنْ أخَّـرَ بلا عذرٍ
سقَطَتْ إلّا أنْ يكـونَ الثمنُ مؤجلاً فيَتَخَيَّرُ
إنْ شاءَ عَجَّـلَ وأخَـذَ وإنْ شاءَ صَبَـرَ حتى
يحِـلَّ ويأخُذَ . ولوْ بَلَغَهُ الخبرُ وهوَ مريضٌ
أو محبوسٌ فَلْيُوَكِّلْ . فإنْ لمْ يَفْعَلْ بطَلَتْ .
فإنْ لمْ يَقْـدِرْ أوْ كانَ المُخْبِـرُ صبياً أوْ غيرَ
ثقةٍ أوْ أُخبِرَ وهوَ مسافرٌ فَسَافَرَ في طلبِهِ فهوَ
على شفعتِهِ .

k21.6   If R has built, or planted trees (A: before Q could preempt), then Q has a choice between paying R the value of the new buildings (A: or trees) and taking possession of them, or else removing them and paying R for the loss of value (A: to them as a result of being removed).

If R has given away the part of the property (A: that he bought from P), made it a charitable endowment (waqf, def: k30), sold it, or returned it to P because of a defect, then Q may annul any of these transactions that R has effected.

Q also has the right to take the property from the person who bought it from R, by paying this person the amount for which he bought it.

وإنْ تَصَرَّفَ المشتري فبَنَى أوْ k21.6
غَرَسَ تَخَيَّـرَ الشفيـعُ بينَ تملَّكِ مَا بَنَـاهُ
بالقيمةِ وبينَ قلعِهِ وضمانِ أرشِهِ .
وإنْ وهَبَ المشتري الشقصَ أوْ وقَفَهُ
أوْ باعَهُ أوْ ردَّهُ بالعيب فلهُ أنْ يفْسَخَ ما فعَلَهُ
المشتري ، ولهُ أنْ يأخُـذَ منَ المشتري
الثاني بمَا اشْتَرَى بِهِ .

k21.7   If Q dies (A: before he is able to preempt), his heirs can preempt. If some of them decline to do so, the rest of the heirs may still preempt the entire portion, or may relinquish the right to preempt any of it.

وإذا ماتَ الـشفيـعُ فللورثـةِ k21.7
الأخـذُ . فإنْ عَفَـا بعضُهُمْ أخَـذَ البـاقونَ
الكلَّ أوْ يَدَعونَ .

*

k22.0 FINANCING A PROFIT-SHARING VENTURE (QIRAD)

(n: Given persons X (al-malik) and Y (al-'amil) (A: where X gives Y a sum of money for Y to do business with, on the basis that X will take a percentage of the profits. Such ventures have six integrals:

(a) X;

(b) Y;

(c) the work performed by Y;

(d) the profit (n: divided between them at a given percentage);

(e) the spoken form;

(f) and the venture's capital (n: which is put up by X)).)

k22.1 *Financing a profit-sharing venture* (qirad) means for X to give Y money with which to trade, the profits to be shared between them. (O: It is not valid to finance such a venture on the basis that a third party gets any of the profit.)

It is only valid when both parties have full right to manage their own property. It also requires that there be:

(a) a spoken proposal (O: by X, such as "I finance you," or "I engage you," or "Take these dirhams [N: as a trade loan]");

(b) an acceptance (O: by Y in words. It is insufficient for him to begin working without saying anything);

and that the invested capital be:

(c) money (lit. "gold or silver" (A: money taking their place in these rulings));

(d) of known amount;

(e) physically existent (A: i.e. it can be seen and handled, not merely a debt or financial obligation to be collected);

القراض k22.0

(ت : يمثـل له بشـخصـين : زيــد (المـالك) وعمرو (العامل) (ع : حيث يدفع زيد إلى عمرو ومبلغاً من المال ليتجر عمرو به على أن يأخذ زيد نسبة معينة من الـربـح . ولمثل هذه المعاملة ستة أركان : المـالك، والعـامل، والعمل، والربح، والصيغة، والمال)) .

k22.1 هوَ أنْ يَدْفَـعَ (المـالك) إلى رجـلٍ (وهـو العـامـل) مالاً ليَتَجـرَ فيـه ويَكـونَ الـربحُ بينهمَا (فلا يصح على أن لغيرهما شيئاً) .

ويَجُوزُ من جائزِ التصرف مَع جائزِ التصرف .

وشـرطُـهُ إيجـابٌ (أي من المـالك كقـارضتك وعـاملتك وخذ هذه الدراهم (ح : مقـارضة)) وقبولٌ (من العامل لفظاً فلا يكـفـي الشـروع في العـمـل مع السكـوت) وكـونُ المـال نقـداً [خالصاً مضـروبـاً] معلومَ القـدر معيَّناً مسلَّماً إلى

(f) delivered to Y (O: it is not valid to finance a profit-sharing venture on condition that the funds be held by someone other than Y, such as X holding them and paying for what Y buys, since Y might not find X when he needs him);

(g) (A: and that Y be given the funds) in return for (A: X's receiving) a known fraction of the entire profit, such as a half or a third.

Financing a profit-sharing venture is not valid when:

(1) (non-(c) above) the capital put up consists of commodities;

(2) (non-(f)) X holds the funds;

(3) (non-(g)) it is stipulated that either X or Y be specifically entitled to the profits from a certain part of the business (O: such as saying, "You get the profits from the clothing, and I get the profits from the livestock");

(4) (non-(g)) either X or Y is guaranteed (N: for example) ten dirhams of the profit (O: since they might not make more than ten, in which case the second partner would get nothing) (A: rather, they must specify the percentage that each will take);

(5) (non-(g)) it is stipulated that one of them be entitled to all of the profit;

(6) or (non-(f)) it is stipulated that X work with Y in the business.

k22.2   Y's role is to conduct business and related matters with consideration for their best financial advantage and with circumspection. Y may not sell at a loss, sell for deferred payment, or travel with the capital, and so forth, without X's permission.

k22.3   The agreement between X and Y is nullified whenever X stipulates (O: something that is not obligatory for Y in such ventures, such as) that

العـامـل (فـلا يصح القراض بشرط كون المـال بيـد غير العامل كالمالك ليوفي منه ثمن ما اشتراه العـامـل، لأنه قد لا يجده عنـد الحـاجـة) بجزءٍ معلومٍ مِنَ الربح كالنصف والثلث.

فلا يَجُوزُ على عروضٍ [ومغشوش وسبيكـةٍ] ولا على أنْ يكـونَ المـالُ عنـدَ المـالك ولا على أنَّ لأحدِهِمَا ربحَ صنفٍ معيَّن (كأن يقـول لك ربحُ الثيـاب ولي ربح الدواب) ولا عشرةَ دراهمَ (لأنه قد لا يربح إلا العشـرة فيبقى الآخر بلا شيء) ولا على أنَّ الـربحَ كلَّهُ لاحدِهِمَا ولا على (شرط) أنَّ المالكَ يَعْمَلُ معَهُ.

k22.2 ووظيفـةُ العـامـل التجارةُ وتـوابعهـا بالنظر والاحتياطِ فلا يَبِيعُ بغبنٍ ولا نسيئةٍ ولا يُسَافرُ بلا إذنٍ ونحو ذلكَ.

k22.3 فلوْ شرَطَ (المـالك) عليهِ (أي على العـامـل ما ليس عليه وذلك مثل) أنْ

Y buy wheat, mill it, and bake it; that Y buy yarn, weave it, and sell it; that Y not deal except in such and such a rare commodity; or that Y deal exclusively with So-and-so.

يَشْتَري حِنْطَةً فَيَطْحَنَ ويَخْبِزَ، أَوْغَزْلاً فَيَنْسِجَ ويَبِيعَ، أَوْ أَنْ لا يَتَصَرَّفَ إلّا في كَذَا وهُوَ عَزِيزُ الوجودِ، أَوْ لا يُعَامِلَ العَامِلُ إلا زَيداً، فَسَدَ.

k22.4 When such an agreement is invalid, the transactions Y has conducted are valid, and Y is paid the wages that are usual for such work, unless X had stipulated, "I get all the profits," in which case he takes all of it and Y gets nothing (O: since he worked without expecting anything).

k22.4 فحيثُ فَسَدَ نَفَذَ تصرُّفُ العَامِلِ بِأجرةِ المِثلِ وكُلُّ الرِّبحِ للمالكِ إلّا إذا قَالَ المالكُ الرِّبحُ كلُّهُ لي فلا شيءَ للعاملِ (لأنه عمِل غيرَ طامِعٍ في شيءٍ).

k22.5 When either X or Y cancels the agreement, loses his sanity, or loses consciousness (Ar. ughmiya 'alayhi, i.e. through other than falling asleep), then the agreement is annulled and Y is obliged to liquidate the holdings (A: by changing them back into funds).

k22.5 ومتى فَسَخَهُ أحدُهُما أوْ جُنَّ أو أُغمِيَ عليهِ انْفَسَخَ العقدُ فيَلزَمُ العَامِلَ تنضيضُ رأسِ المالِ.

k22.6 (A: When neither party has proof,) Y's word (O: if he swears (dis: k8.2)) is accepted over X's when there are disputes:

k22.6 والقولُ قولُ العاملِ (بيمينه) في قدرِ رأسِ المالِ وفي ردِّه وفيمَا يَدَّعي مِنْ هلاكٍ وفيمَا يُدَّعَى عليه مِنَ الخيانةِ.

(1) concerning the amount of capital originally put up;

(2) as to whether or not the capital was restored to X;

(3) concerning the destruction of the holdings;

(4) or as to whether Y betrayed his trust.

k22.7 If X and Y dispute as to how much of the profit was stipulated (O: as Y's share, as when for example Y says, "You stipulated half for me," and X replies, "To the contrary, it was one-third"), then each party swears an oath supporting his own claim (O: and when they have sworn, X gets all the profit, and Y receives the wages customary for the work he did).

k22.7 وإن اخْتَلَفا في قدرِ الرِّبحِ المشروطِ (للعاملِ كأن قال شرطتَ لي النصفَ فقال المالكُ بل الثلثَ مثلاً) تَحالَفا (وإذا تحالفا كان جميعُ الرِّبحِ للمالكِ وللعاملِ أجرةُ المثلِ لما عمل).

k22.8 Y does not own his share of the profit until the venture's final division. (O: His possession of

k22.8 ولا يَملِكُ العامِلُ حصّتَهُ مِنَ الرِّبحِ إلّا بالقِسمةِ (وإنما يستقرُّ ملكُه

437

it is only finalized by dividing the profits when the holdings are liquidated and the agreement is terminated.)

بالقسمة إن نض رأس المال وفسخ العقد).

*

k23.0   WATERING GRAPES OR DATES FOR PART OF THE CROP

k23.0   المساقاة

k23.1   [تَصِحُّ ممّنْ يَصِحُّ قراضُهُ على كرمٍ ونخلٍ خاصةً مغروسَيْن إلى مدةٍ يَبقَى فيها الشجرُ ويُثمِرُ غالباً بجزءٍ معلومٍ مِنَ الثمرةِ كثلثٍ وربعٍ كالقراض ويَمْلِكُ حصتَهُ مِنَ الثمرةِ بالظهور. ووظيفتُهُ أَنْ يَعْمَلَ مَا فيه صلاحُ الثمرةِ كتلقيحٍ وسقيٍ وتنقيةِ ساقيةٍ وقطعِ حشيشٍ مضرٍ ونحوهِ وعلى المالكِ مَا يَحْفَظُ الأصلَ كبناءِ حائطٍ وحفرِ نهرٍ ونحوهِ. والعامِلُ أمينٌ فإنْ ثَبَتَتْ خيانتُهُ ضُمَّ إليه مشرفٌ لأنَّ المساقاةَ لازمةٌ لَيْسَ لأحدِهِما فسخُها كالإجارةِ. فإنْ لَمْ يَتَحَفَّظْ بالمشرفِ اسْتُؤْجِرَ عليه مَنْ يَعْمَلُ عَنْهُ].

*

k24.0   SHARECROPPING (MUZARA'A)

k24.0   المزارعة

(n: Sharecropping means to farm someone's land for a share of the harvest. In the Shafi'i school, it is not permissible or valid except on strips of land between date groves under certain conditions, such as:

(a) that the landowner provide the seed;

(b) that it be unfeasible to separate working the trees from working the ground;

(c) and that the sharecropper be currently working the trees also, under the above (k23) arrangement.

This section has been left in Arabic below, and rulings from the Hanafi school, which permits sharecropping, have been added by the translator.)

k24.1   [العملُ في الأرضِ ببعضِ مَا يَخْرُجُ منها إنْ كَانَ البذرُ مِن المالكِ سُمِّيَ مزارعةً أَوْ مِنَ العاملِ سُمِّيَ مخابرةً وهمَا باطلتَانِ إلّا أَنْ يَكُونَ بينَ النخيلِ بياضٌ وإنْ كَثُرَ فتَصِحُّ المزارعةُ عليه تبعاً للمساقاةِ على النخيلِ وإنْ تَفَاوَتَ المشروطُ في المساقاةِ والمزارعةِ بشرطِ أَنْ يتَّحِدَ العاملُ في الأرضِ والنخيلِ ويَعْسُرَ إفرادُ النخيلِ بالسقيِ والبياضِ بالعمارةِ وأَنْ يُقَدَّمَ لفظُ المساقاةِ فيَقُولُ: سَاقَيْتُكَ وزَارَعْتُكَ، وأَنْ لا يَفْصِلَ بينَهُمَا. ولا تَجُوزُ المخابرةُ تبعاً للمساقاةِ].

k24.2 (Ahmad Quduri:) Abu Hanifa (Allah have mercy on him) holds that sharecropping, for one-third or one-fourth of the harvest (or any-

k24.2 (أحمـد القـدوري): قال أبـو حنيفة رحمـه الله: المـزارعـةُ بالثلثِ

thing less or more), is invalid, though Abu Yusuf and Muhammad (A: the colleagues of Abu Hanifa) hold it to be valid.

Sharecropping, in the view of the latter two, is of four types (A: three of them valid and one invalid). (n: Given persons X and Y, and the four agricultural variables: land, seed, labor, and oxen (i.e. the means of plowing):)

(1) X provides the land and seed, and Y provides the labor and oxen; which is permissible;

(2) X provides the land, and Y provides the labor, oxen, and seed; which is permissible;

(3) X provides the land, oxen, and seed, and Y provides the labor; which is permissible;

(4) or X provides the land and oxen, and Y provides the seed and labor; which is not valid.

A sharecropping agreement is only valid if the period of the agreement is determinately specified (lit. "known"), and it requires that the total produce be divided between the partners (A: not a specific number of bushels to one, for example, or on condition that the produce from one part of the land belong to one of them and the produce from another part belong to the other) (*al-Lubab fi sharh al-Kitab* (y88), 2.228–30).

*

k25.0 RENTING THINGS AND HIRING PEOPLE'S SERVICES (IJARA)

(n: Given persons P and Q, where Q rents a pack animal from P, or hires P as a guide. The title of this section, *Ijara*, has the dual significance of renting an article and hiring a person's services.)

(O: Lexically, *rent* is a name for the rental fee. In Sacred Law it means to take possession of a utility or service for payment under certain conditions. It has four integrals:

(a) the spoken form;

(b) the fee;

والـربـع (أو أقـل أو أكثر) باطلةٌ وقال أبو يوسف ومحمدٌ : جائزةٌ .

وهي عـنـدهُمَـا على أربعـةِ أوجهٍ : إنْ كَانَت الأرضُ والبذرُ لواحدٍ والعملُ والبقرُ لواحـدٍ جَازَت المــزارعــةُ . وإنْ كَانَت الأرضُ لواحدٍ والعملُ والبقرُ لآخرَ جَازَتْ . وإنْ كَانَتْ الأرضُ لواحدٍ والبذرُ والعملُ لآخرَ فهِيَ باطلةٌ .

ولا تَصِـحُّ الـمــزارعــةُ إلّا على مدةٍ معلومةٍ ، ومِنْ شرائطِها أنْ يَكُونَ الخارجُ مشـاعـاً بينهمـا [نقل من اللباب في شرح الكتاب : ٢ / ٢٢٨ ـ ٢٣٠] .

k25.0 الإجارة

(وهي لغـة اسم للأجرة وشرعاً تمليك منفعة بعوض بشروط . وأركـانها أربعة :

(c) the utility or service;

(d) and the persons making the agreement.)

k25.1   A rental agreement is only valid between two persons entitled to conduct sales (def: k1.2). It requires both a spoken offer, such as "I rent this to you," or "the use of it"; and a spoken acceptance. (O: The agreement must also specify how much the rental fee is.)

k25.2   There are two types of rental agreements:

(1) renting anticipated utilities or services described in advance and under obligation to deliver (ijara dhimma);

(2) or renting the use or services of an identified thing or individual who is present (ijara 'ayn).

Rental of something anticipated (ijara dhimma) consists of Q saying, for example, "I am renting from you a pack animal of such and such a description," or "I am hiring you to tailor a garment for me," or "to provide me with transportation to Mecca."
Rental of something identified and present (ijara 'ayn) consists of Q saying, for example, "I rent this animal from you," or "I hire you to sew this particular garment for me."

k25.3   It is a necessary condition for a valid rental of something anticipated (ijara dhimma) that P accepts the fee for it at the time the agreement is made.

k25.4   The necessary conditions for a valid rental of something identified and present (ijara 'ayn) are:

(a) that the article (or person whose services are) being rented be a particular individual (O: meaning visible to the eye, as in sales);

صيغة وأجرة ومنفعة وعاقد).

k25.1   نَصِحُّ مِمَّنْ يَصِحُّ بَيْعُهُ. رَشرطُها إيجابٌ مثلُ: آجَرْتُكَ هذا أو منافعَهُ، [أوْ: أَكْرَيْتُكَ،] وقبولٌ. (ولا بد في الصيغة من بيان الأجرة).

k25.2   وهي على قسمَيْن: إجارةُ ذمةٍ وإجارةُ عينٍ.
وإجارةُ الذمةِ أَنْ يَقُولَ: اسْتَأْجَرْتُ منك دابةً صفتُها كذا، أو: اسْتَأْجَرْتُكَ لتُحَصِّلَ لي خياطة ثوبٍ، أو ركوبي إلى مكةَ.
وإجارةُ العينِ مثلُ: اسْتَأْجَرْتُ منك هذه الدابة، أو اسْتَأْجَرْتُكَ لتخيط لي هذا الثوبَ.

k25.3   وشرطُ إجارةِ الذمةِ قبضُ الأجرة في المجلسِ.

k25.4   وشرطُ إجارةِ العينِ أَنْ تَكُونَ العينُ معيَّنةً (أي مشاهدة بالعين مثل البيـع)، مقـدوراً على تسليمِهـا يُمْكِنُ

440

Renting Things and Hiring People's Services (Ijara)   k25.5

(b) that the article (or person's service) be within P's power to deliver such that Q can utilize it as intended (O: *within one's power to deliver* including both the actual ownership of an article and the possession of the right to use it, such that if Q is renting it from P, Q may in turn rent it out to a third party);

(c) that Q have the right to utilize the article (or services of the person hired) as soon as the deal is made;

(d) that the utility for which the article is being rented not entail the article's destruction;

(e) and that the agreement specify a rental period that the rented article will probably outlast, even if it be a hundred years, as in the case of land.

Thus, rental of something identified and present (ijara 'ayn) is invalid when it consists of:

(1) (non-(a) above) hiring the services of "one of these two servants";

(2) (non-(a)) hiring someone absent (A: from the place where the agreement is made);

(3) (non-(b)) renting land for agricultural use when the land is without water and the area's rainfall is insufficient for crops;

(4) (non-(c)) P renting out something (A: that he is already renting to Q) to a third party for the year following the current one, though Q may rent if for the following year (O: since his rental period is unexpired and the two periods are contiguous);

(5) (non-(d)) wax for fuel;

(6) (non-(e)) or renting out an article unlikely to last, for example, more than a year, for a period longer than that.

k25.5 (O: Additional) conditions for rental of something identified and present (ijara 'ayn) (O:

استيفاءُ المنفعة المذكورة منْها (والقدرة على التسليم يشمل ملك العين وملك منفعتها ليدخل المستأجر فإن له أن يؤجر) ويتصل استيفاءُ منفعتها بالعقد، ولا يتضمَّنُ الانتفاعُ استهلاكُ عينها وأنْ يُعْقَد إلى مدةٍ تَبقى فيها العينُ غالباً ولوْ مائةِ سنةٍ في الأرض.

فلا تصحُّ إجارةُ أحدِ العبدَيْن ولا غائب [وآبق] وأرضٍ لا ماءَ لها ولا يَكْفيها المطرُ للزرع [وحائضٍ لكنسِ مسجدٍ ومنكوحةٍ للرضاع بلا إذنِ زوجٍ] ولا استئجارُ العام المستقبل لغير المستأجرِ (لأن مدة المستأجر الأول لم تفـرغ) ويجـوزُ لهُ (أي لذلك المستأجرِ الأول لاتصالِ المدتين) ولا الشمعِ للوقودِ ولا ما لا يَبْقى إلا سنةً مثلاً أكثرَ منها.

k25.5 وشرطُها (أي شرط الإجارة العينية زيادة على الشروط السابقة بالنسبة

relating to its use or service) are that its utility be:

    (a) permissible in Sacred Law;

    (b) of some value;

    (c) determinately known (O: as to which one it is, its amount, and its utility, meaning that both P and Q know these things), such as saying, "I rent you this land to raise crops on," or "to build on," or "[A: I rent you this pack animal] to carry such and such a quantity of iron," or "of cotton";

    (d) for a period known (O: to both P and Q);

    (e) and for a fee known (O: to both P and Q, in type and amount), even when it is merely seen in bulk, or when it consists of the use of some other utility or service.

Thus, rental of something identified and present (ijara 'ayn) is not valid when the utility for which it is being hired or rented consists of:

    (1) (non-(a) above) playing a flute;

    (2) (non-(a)) transporting wine, other than to pour it out;

    (3) (non-(b)) a hawker's cry that does not require any effort, even if it increases the demand for the merchandise;

    (4) (non-(c)) carrying such and such a quantity (O: on a pack animal) when the nature of the load is unspecified;

    (5) (non-(d)) being rented for "one dirham per month" when the total period (A: of occupancy, for example) is unspecified (A: though one may renew a valid rent agreement each month, and in such a case the landlord has the right to ask for it in advance);

    (6) or (non-(e)) hiring someone for the "fee" of providing him with food and clothing.

k25.6   The particulars of the utility (N: such as its precise duration) might not become determi-

للمنفعة) أَنْ تَكُونَ المنفعةُ مباحةً متقومةً (أي لها قيمةً) معلومةً (عيناً وقدراً ومنفعةً، والمراد أن كلاً من المتعاقدين يعلم ذلك) كقوله: آجَرْتُكَ لِتَزْرَعَ، أَوْ تَبْنِيَ أَوْ تَحْمِلَ قنطارَ حديدٍ أَوْ قطنٍ في مدةٍ معلومةٍ (للمتعاقدين) وبأجرةٍ معلومةٍ (لهما أيضاً جنساً وقدراً) ولَوْ بالرؤية جزافاً أَوْ منفعةً أخرى.

فلا تَصِحُّ على زمرٍ وحملِ خمرٍ لغير إراقتِها وكلمةِ بياعٍ لا كلفةَ فيهَا وإنْ رَوَّجَتِ السلعةَ و(لا تصح الإجارة أي إجارة الدابة لـ) حملِ قنطارٍ لَمْ يُعَيَّنْ ما هوَ، وكلِّ شهرٍ بدرهمٍ ولَمْ يُبَيِّنْ جملةَ المدةِ، ولا بالطعمةِ والكسوةِ.

k25.6   ثمَّ المنفعةُ قَدْ لا تُعْـرَفُ إلّا

nately known except through the passage of time, as when renting a house or hiring a wet nurse. In such cases the time must be preestimated (A: when the agreement is made, as a condition for its validity). Similarly, the utility or service might not become determinately known except through the work itself, such as when hiring someone to perform hajj in one's place (dis: j1.10) or the like, in which case the amount of work involved must be preestimated.

If the utility requires both time and work to become determinately known, as is the case with tailoring, building, or teaching someone the Koran, then the utility is preestimated (A: i.e. stated in the rental agreement) with regard to one of these two variables alone. It is not valid to estimate the utility with regard to both, such as Q saying, "[O: I hire you to] tailor this garment for today's daylight hours" (O: since the work involved might take more or less time than that).

k25.7 The necessary things required by Q in order to utilize the article, such as the key (A: to a house), or the reins, girth, or saddle (A: of a mount), are P's responsiblility to provide. Things that merely *enhance* or improve the utility for which Q has rented the article are Q's responsibility.

k25.8 Q is entitled to normal use of the article in obtaining the utility for which he has rented it or an equivalent utility (A: riding it in a different direction, for example, the same distance as that agreed upon and under the same conditions). If Q travels farther than the agreed upon destination, then he is obligated to pay the rental fee agreed upon, plus the amount customarily paid for a distance comparable to the excess.

k25.9 It is permissible (O: only when renting something identified and present (ijara 'ayn)) for Q to pay in advance or to defer payment to the future. If neither party states whether it is to be paid in advance or whether in the future, then it is

بالزمان كالسكنى والرضاع فَتُقَدَّرُ به . وقد لا تُعْرَفُ إلا بالعمل كالحجِّ ونحوه فَتُقَدَّرُ به . وقد تُعْرَفُ بهما كالخياطةِ والبناء وتعليم القرآن فَتُقَدَّرُ بأحدِهما، فإن قُدِرَتْ بهما فقال (المستأجِر استأجرتك لتخيطَ لي هذا الثوبَ بياض هذا اليوم لَمْ يَصِحّ (لأن العمل فيها قد يتقدم وقد يتأخر) . [وتُشْتَرَطُ معرفةُ الراكبِ (في إجارةِ دابةٍ للركوبِ) بمشاهدةٍ أوْ وصفٍ تامٍ وكذا ما يُرْكَبُ عليه مِنْ محملٍ وغيره . وفي إجارةِ الذمة ذكرُ جنسِ الدابةِ ونوعِها وكونِها ذكراً أوْ أنثى في الاستئجارِ للركوبِ لا للحملِ إلا أنْ يَكُونَ لنحوِ زجاجٍ .]

k25.7 وما يُحْتَاجُ إليه للتمكنِ منَ الانتفاعِ كالمفتاحِ والزمامِ والحزامِ [والقتبِ] والسرجِ فهوَ على المكري . أوْ لكمالِ الانتفاعِ [كالمحملِ والغطاءِ والدلوِ والحبلِ] فعلى المكتري . [وعلى المكري في إجارةِ الذمةِ الخروجُ معهُ والتحملُ والحطُّ وإركابُ الشيخِ وإبراكُ لجملٍ للمرأةِ والضعيفِ].

k25.8 وللمكتري أنْ يَسْتَوْفِيَ المنفعةَ بالمعروفِ أوْ مثلِها [إمّا بنفسِه أوْ مثلِه فإذا اسْتَأْجَرَ ليَزْرَعَ حنطةً زَرَعَ مثلَها أوْ ليَرْكَبَ أُرْكَبَ مثلَهُ] وإنْ جاوَزَ المكانَ المكترَى إليه لَزِمَهُ المسمَّى في المكانِ وأجرةُ المثلِ للزائدِ .

k25.9 ((وقد أشارَ المصنفُ إلى حكمٍ مختصٍ بالإجارةِ العينيةِ [بقولِه]:) ويَجُوزُ تعجيلُ الأجرةِ وتأجيلُهَا . فإنْ

payable in advance.

When renting anticipated utilities or services (ijara dhimma), it is permissible to let Q use the utility prior to the agreed upon period, or to delay use until after the period.

أُطْلَقَ تَعَجَّلَتْ. وَيَجُوزُ فِي إِجَارةِ الذمةِ تعجيلُ المنفعةِ وتأجيلُهَا.

k25.10 (O: When renting something identified and present (ijara 'ayn)), if the article being rented is destroyed, the agreement is thereafter cancelled (O: with respect to the future, since the article to be utilized is no longer available then, as opposed to the period that has transpired after the article's delivery, for which Q must pay an appropriate proportion of the agreed upon fee, based on the current market value of similar utilities or services).

k25.10 وإنْ تَلِفَتِ العينُ المستأجرةُ (إجـارة عين) انْفَسَخَتْ فِي المسـتقبـل (أي بالنسبة للمدة المستقبلة لفوات محل المنفعة فيه بخلاف المدة الماضية بعد قبض العين فيقـابلها قسط من المسمى باعتبار أجرة المثل).

(O: When renting an identified and present utility or service (ijara 'ayn),) if a defect occurs (O: in the article being rented, and the defect obviously entails a discrepancy in the rental fee), then Q has the option to cancel the agreement (O: unless P immediately undertakes to correct or repair the defect, for if he does, Q is not entitled to cancel it). But if the rental agreement concerns an anticipated utility or service (ijara dhimma) (O: and the rented article has been destroyed after its delivery), then the agreement is not nullified and Q may not cancel it, but is only entitled to ask P to replace the article so that Q can obtain the utility anticipated.

وإنْ تَعَيَّبَتْ (العين المستأجـرة بعيب يؤثر تأثيـراً يظهـر به تفاوت الأجرة) تَخَيَّرَ (ومحـل التخيير ما لم يبـادر المـؤجر إلى الإصلاح في الحال. فإن وقع ذلك سقط خيـار المستأجـر) هذا إذا كانت الإجارة عينيـة) فإنْ كَانَتِ الإجارةُ فِي الذمةِ (وقد تلفت العين المسلمـة) لمْ تَنْفَسِـخْ ولمْ يَتَخَيَّـرْ (المستأجـر) بلْ لهُ طلبُ بَدَلِهَـا لِيَسْتَوْفِي المنفعة.

k25.11 If the material Q has hired P to work on (A: e.g. when Q hires P to tailor a garment from material Q has given him) is destroyed in P's possession without his negligence, then P is not obliged to pay for its loss.

If Q has rented an article from P and it is ruined in Q's possession without his negligence, then Q is not obliged to pay for its loss.

k25.11 وإنْ تَلِفَتِ العينُ التي اسْتُؤْجِرَ على العمـل فيهَا في يد الأجير، أوِ العينُ المستأجرة في يد المستأجر بلا عدوانٍ لمْ يَضْمَنْها.

k25.12 If P or Q dies while the rental agreement is in effect, it is not cancelled. (O: Rather, if P has died, Q finishes using the article, while if Q has died, then Q's heirs finish utilizing it. Neither party has the right to cancel the agreement in such a case when the article itself still exists.) (A: The

k25.12 وإنْ مَاتَ أحـدُ المتكـاريين والعين المستأجـرةُ باقيـةٌ لمْ تَنْفَسِخْ ([أي الإجارة] فيستوفي المكتري مدته إن كان المكـري هو الـذي قد مات وإن كان المكتري هو الـذي قد مات فيقـوم ورثه

death of either party is considered by the Hanafi school to nullify the agreement.)

مقـامه في الاستيفاء المـذكور ولا تخيير فيهما مع بقاء العين).

k25.13 When the rental period is over, Q must return the article rented and is responsible for the measures (A: and the expenses) entailed in returning it.

k25.13 إذا انْـقَـضَـتِ الـمـدةُ لَزمَ المستأجر رَدُّ العين وعليه مؤنةُ الردِّ.

k25.14 When P or Q stipulates a particular rental period or a specific use for the article, then when P has delivered the article to Q, and the period stipulated elapses, or a period elapses that is sufficient for the utility stipulated to have been obtained from the article (O: even if it has not in fact been obtained), then the rental fee is due (O: from Q, who rented the article under such stipulations), and the article must be returned. (O: This ruling holds for both renting something identified and present (ijara 'ayn) and renting something anticipated (ijara dhimma).)

k25.14 وإذا عَقَـدَ (أي أحـد المكتـريين) على مدةٍ (معينة) أو منفعةٍ معيّنة فسَلَّم (المكري) العينَ (للمكتري) وانْقضَتِ المـدةُ (المعينة) أو زمنٌ يُمْكنُ فيـه استيفاءُ المنفعـة (وإن لم يستوف بالـفعـل) اسْتَقـرَّتِ (أي الأجـرة على المستأجـر بهـذه القيود المذكورة) الأجرةُ ووجَبَ ردُّ العين (وهـذا الحكم المذكور عام للإجارتين العينية والذمية).

k25.15 In an invalid agreement, Q owes P the amount typically paid for renting similar utilities, due whenever he would have owed P the fee agreed upon had the agreement been valid.

k25.15 وتَسْتَقـرُّ في الإجـارة الفاسدة أجرةُ المثل حيث يَسْتَقرُّ المسمَّى في الصحيحة.

*

k26.0   JOB WAGES (JA'ALA)
(n: Given persons X and Y, where X offers Y a dirham to do a certain job.)

k26.0   الجعالة

k26.1   When X says, "I owe whoever builds me a wall a dirham" (A: or makes a similar offer), this is termed *job wages*. It is permissible that (A: the particulars of) such a job be unknown, though not the amount of the wage. Whoever then builds the wall for X is entitled to the amount stated, even if they are a group of people.

k26.1   إذا قال: مَنْ بَنى لي حائطاً فلَهُ (عـليّ) درهمٌ [أو مَنْ رَدَّ لي آبقي لـهُ كذا] فهذه جعالةٌ يُغْتَفَرُ فيها جهالةُ العمل دونَ جهالة العوض. فمَنْ بَنَى (الحائط) [أَوْ رَدَّ إليـه الآبَق] ولوْ جماعةً اسْتَحَقَّ الجُعْلَ (المشروط له).

k26.2   Whoever works when no wage has been stipulated does not deserve anything. If X gives Y

k26.2   ومـنْ عَمِـلَ بلا شرطِ لـمْ يـسْتحقَّ شيئاً. فلوْ دفع ثوباً لغسّالٍ فقالَ:

a garment to clean, saying, "Wash it," but does not mention a wage, and Y washes it, then Y deserves nothing (N: unless it is a well known, customary usage that Y should receive a fee, as when Y is a barber or presses clothes and the like). If Y says, "You stipulated a wage for me," but X denies it, then X's word is accepted (A: when there is no proof (dis: k8.2)) (O: if he swears an oath).

اغْسِلْهُ، ولمْ يُسَمِّ لهُ أجرةً فغَسَلَهُ لمْ يَسْتَحِقَّ شيئاً (ح: إلّا إذا اقتضى العرف أجرة كالحلاق والكوّاء وغيرهما). فإنْ قال: شَرَطْتَ لي عوضاً، فأنْكَرَ فالقولُ قولُ المنكر (بيمينه).

k26.3   Both X and Y are entitled to cancel their agreement (O: before the job is finished), but if X cancels it after Y has begun work, then X is obliged to pay Y an appropriate portion of the wage agreed upon (O: such that if the job is half done, then X owes Y half the amount, and so forth).

Otherwise (O: if X cancels it before Y has begun, or if Y cancels it himself after having begun), Y gets nothing.

k26.3   ولكلٍّ منهُمَا فسخُها (أي قبل تمام العمل) لكنْ إنْ فَسَخَ صاحبُ العملِ بعدَ الشروع لزمَهُ قسطُهُ من العوض (فإن كان العمل نصفاً فيستقر له نصف العوض وعلى هذا القياس): وفيمَا سوَى ذلك (أي بأن كان الفسخ الملتزم قبل الشروع في العمل أو فسخ العامل بعد الشروع لا شيءَ للعامل.

*

k27.0 LOST AND FOUND (LUQTA)
       (n: Given Z, who finds an article lying on the ground and picks it up.)

k27.0   اللقطة

k27.1   When a responsible adult finds a lost and found article it is permissible for him to take (O: or leave) it.

k27.1   إذَا وَجَدَ [الحرُّ] الرشيدُ لقطةً جَازَ التقاطُهَا (وتركها).

k27.2   If he can trust himself to take the proper measures for such articles (dis: below), it is recommended that he pick it up, though if he cannot depend on himself not to betray the trust (A: by simply appropriating the article without telling anyone), then it is offensive for him to take it.

k27.2   فإنْ وَثِقَ بأمانة نفسهِ نُدِبَ، وإنْ خَافَ الخيانة كُرِهَ.

k27.3   It is recommended that the finder determine the type, description, and amount of the article he has found, its container, and the string with which it was tied (O: it being preferable that he record this in writing so as not to forget), and

k27.3   ثمَّ يُنْـدَبُ أنْ يَعْرِفَ جنسهَا وصفتَهَا وقـدرَهَا ووعـاءَها ووكاءَها وهوَ الخيط الذي رُبِطَتْ بِه (ويستحب أن يقيد ذلك بالكتابة خشية النسيان) و(يندب) أنْ

for him to have witnesses attest to his having found it.

k27.4 The following two kinds of articles are permissible to pick up for safekeeping (def: k27.5) but unlawful to pick up as lost and found (A: to be advertised and then appropriated (def: k27.6)), and should he do the latter, Z is financially responsible for the article:

(1) something lost and found within the Meccan Sacred Precinct (Haram);

(2) or an animal unmenaced by small predators, such as a camel or a horse lost and found on open range.

In other than these two cases it is permissible for Z to pick up the article, either for safekeeping, or to be advertised and then appropriated.

k27.5 If Z picks up the article for safekeeping, he is not obliged to advertise having found it, and it remains in his care as a trust (def: k17.14) which he is never entitled to dispose of in any way until he finds its owner, in which case he gives it to him. If Z wishes to deliver it to the Islamic magistrate, the latter must accept it.

If Z picks up the article within the Meccan Sacred Precinct (Haram) for safekeeping, he is obliged to advertise his having found it (n: as below).

k27.6 If Z picks up an article intending to appropriate it if he cannot find the owner, then he is obliged to advertise its having been found for a (O: full) year on the doors of mosques, in the marketplaces, and the vicinity where he found it, in the manner customary for advertising such things. At the first of the period he should publicize it morning and evening, then subsequently once a day, then once a week, then once a month, such that the first advertisement is not forgotten and that it is realized that the subsequent notices are repetitions of it (O: and this is what is meant by the *customary manner* mentioned above). Z should

يُشهَدَ عليها.

k27.4 ثُمَّ إِنْ كَانَ الالتقاطُ في الحرم (المكي) [أَوْ كَانَتِ اللقطةُ جاريةً يَحِلُّ له وطؤُها بِملكٍ أو نكاحٍ] أوْ وَجَدَ في بريّةٍ حيـواناً يَمْتَنِعُ مِنْ صِغـار السبـاع كبعير وفرس [وأرنب وظبيٍّ وطيـر] فلا يَجـوزُ في هذه المـواضع أنْ يُلْتَقـط إلاّ للحفظ على صاحبِها. فإِنِ الْتَقَطَ (شيئاً من ذلك) للتملكِ حَرُمَ وكَانَ ضامناً.

وفيمَا عَدَا ذلكَ يَجُوزُ للحفظ والتملّك.

k27.5 وإِنِ الْتَقَطَ للحفـظ لمْ يَلْزَمْـهُ تعريفُها وتكُونُ عندَهُ أمانةً لا يَتَصَرَّفُ فيهـا أبـداً إلى أنْ يَجِدَ صاحبَهـا فَيَدْفَعهَا إليه. وإِنْ دَفَعَهَا إلى الحاكم [((وهو القاضي))] لَزِمَهُ القبولُ.

نَعَمْ لُقَطَةُ الحرم مَعَ كونِها للحفظ يَجِبُ تعريفُها.

k27.6 وإِنِ الْتَقَطَ للتملكِ وَجَبَ أَنْ يُعرّفَها سنةً (كاملة) على أبواب المساجد والأسـواق والمـواضـع التي وَجَدَها فيها على العـادةِ ثم في أول الأمر يُعَرّفُ طرَفَي النهـار ثُمَّ في كلِّ يوم مرّةً ثُمَّ في كلِّ أسبوع ثُمَّ في كلِّ شهر مرّةً بحيثُ لا يُنْسَى التعـريفُ الأوّلُ (وهـذا هو معنى العـادةِ فيمـا تقدم) ويُعْلَمُ أنَّ هذا تكرارُ له فيَذْكُرُ

mention some of the article's characteristics in the advertisement, but not all of them (A: so that a would-be claimant is able to prove ownership by describing it in detail) (O: for if Z divulges them all (A: and a pretender takes it), then Z is financially responsible for its loss (A: if the real owner should appear and the pretender cannot be found)).

If the lost and found item is not something major, meaning something unlikely to cause much regret and which will probably be unsought after its loss, then it is not obligatory to advertise it for a whole year, though one must advertise it long enough that its owner will probably have ceased to be concerned about it (N: and this latter is the criterion for advertising most lost and found things, which need not be advertised for a whole year).

بعضَ أوصــافهــا ولاَ يَسْتَــوْعِبُهَا (فـإن استوعبها ضمن) .

وإنْ كَانَت اللقطةُ يسيرةً وهيَ مِمَّا لا يَتَأَسَّفُ عليهِ ويُعْرَضُ عنهُ غالباً إذَا فُقِدَ لمْ يَجِبْ تعريفُهَا سنةً بلْ (يعرفها وجوباً) زمناً يُظَنُّ أنَّ فاقِدَهَا أعْرَضَ عَنْهَا .

k27.7 When Z advertises a lost and found article for a year, it does not enter his possession until he chooses to appropriate it with a formal statement to that effect (O: and not by the mere intention. The statement consists of saying, "I take possession of it," or the like). Z takes possession of it when he chooses to do so (O: by uttering the above words). If it is destroyed before he chooses to appropriate it, Z is not financially responsible for its loss.

k27.7 ثمَّ إذا عَرَّف سنةً لمْ تَدْخُلْ في ملكِــه حتَّى يَخْتَــارَ التملكَ باللفــظ (لا بالنيــة، وصيغة التملك هي أن يقــول الملتقِط: تملكتها، ونحوه) فإذا اختارهُ (أي التملك بالصيغة المــذكـورة) مَلَكَهُ حتَّى لوْ تلِفَتْ قبلَ أنْ يَخْتَارَ لمْ يَضْمَنْهُ .

k27.8 If Z has appropriated the article (N: which thus enters his financial liability), and the owner one day appears, then the owner is entitled to take:

(1) the article itself, if it still exists;

(2) an equal quantity (O: if it was fungible (mithli, def: k20.3(1)));

(3) its market value (O: if it was nonfungible (mutaqawwim), where *market value* refers to the going price for similar articles on the day Z formally appropriated it);

(4) or, if the article still exists but some defect has occurred in it, then the owner takes it

k27.8 وإذَا تَمَلَّكَهَا (ح: ودخلت في ضمانـه) ثمَّ جاءَ صاحبُهَا يوماً منَ الدهر فلهُ أخــذُهَـا بعينهَا إنْ كَانَتْ باقيـةً وإلاَّ فمثلُهَا (إن كانت مثليـة) أوْ قيمتَهَا (إن كانت متقـومـة والمعتبر قيمة يوم التملك) وإنْ تَعَيَّبَتْ أخــذَهَا مَعَ الأرشِ (للنقص

back with an appropriate compensation (def: k5.4) (O: for the new defect that occurred while Z had it).

k27.9 It is offensive for a corrupt person (def: o24.3) to pick up a lost and found article. If he does, the article is taken from him and deposited with someone trustworthy, and a reliable person is dispatched to oversee the corrupt person's advertising (def: k27.6) of the find, after which the corrupt person may appropriate it.

k27.10 In cases where safekeeping the article is not practicable, as when it is a watermelon or similar, Z may choose to either eat it or sell it (A: in either case covering the cost if the owner subsequently appears), after which he advertises finding it for a year (O: if it is something major, or less than a year (dis: k27.6, second par.) if minor).

If it is possible to preserve the article, as when it consists of dates (A: which are conserved by drying), then if it is to the owner's advantage to sell it, Z sells it, while if it is to the owner's advantage to dry it, then Z dries it. (O: In such a case, if Z wants to simply donate the cost of drying it to the owner, he does so. Otherwise, he sells part of the lot to cover the cost of drying the rest, in the owner's interests. The difference between this and an animal found, of which all is sold, is that an animal's maintenance requires repeated expenditures that may add up to more than it is worth.)

*

k28.0 A FOUNDLING CHILD (LAQIT)

(O: Meaning a child found abandoned without anyone to care for it. The scriptural basis for these rulings is Allah's word:

"And do what is good" (Koran 22:77),

and,

"Cooperate with one another in [works of] piety and godfearingness" (Koran 5:2).)

بسبب العيب الحادث عنده) .

k27.9 ويُكرَهُ التقاطُ الفاسقِ ويُنزَعُ منهُ ويُسلَّمُ إلى ثقةٍ ويُضَمُّ إلى الفاسقِ ثقةٌ يُشرِفُ عليهِ في التعريفِ ثمَّ يَتَمَلَّكُها الفاسقُ [ولا يَصحُّ لقطُ العبدِ فإنْ أخَذَها السيدُ منهُ كانَ السيدُ ملتقطاً] .

k27.10 وإذا لمْ يُمكِنْ حفـظُ اللقطةِ كالبطيخِ ونحوهِ يُخَيَّرُ بينَ أكلِهِ وبيعِهِ ثمَّ يُعـرِّفُ سنةً (إنْ كان جسيماً عظيماً أو أقل من سنةٍ إنْ كان حقيـراً) وإنْ أمـكـنَ إصلاحُهُ كالـرطبِ فإنْ كانَ الحظُّ [أي الأنفـعُ للمـالكِ)] في بيعِهِ باعَهُ أو في تجفيفِهِ جَفَّفَهُ [ثم إن تبـرع الملتقط بتجفيفِهِ فذاك وإلا فيبيع بعضه لتجفيف باقيه محافظة على المصلحة والفرق بينه وبين الحيوان حيث يبـاع جميعه أن نفقة الحيوان تتكرر فيؤدي إلى أن يأكل نفسه) .

k28.0 اللقيط

(وهو اسم للطفل الذي يوجد مطروحاً لا متعهد له . والأصل فيه قوله تعالى : ﴿ . . . وَافْعَلُوا الخَيْرَ﴾ [الحـج : ٧٧]، وقوله تعالى : ﴿وَتَعَـاوَنُـوا عَلَى البِـرِّ والتَّقْـوَىٰ﴾ [المائدة : ٢)] .

449

k28.1   To pick up a foundling is a communal obligation (def: c3.2). A child that is found (N: in a Muslim town) is considered a Muslim, and likewise if found in a non-Muslim town if there is a single Muslim therein, even if he denies the child is his (N: because the religion of someone whose religion is unknown is considered to be that of the people of his own city, and in this case there are two religions, with Islam given precedence, as it always surpasses and is never surpassed. Moreover, considering the child a Muslim is a cause for his own happiness and salvation, as he will be raised in Islam).

k28.1   التقاط المنبوذ فرضُ كفاية .
فإذا وُجدَ لقيطٌ (ح : في بلد مسلمين) حُكِم [بحريته وكذا] بإسلامِهِ (ح : وكذا إنْ وُجِدَ في بلدٍ (ح : كافر) فيه مسلمٌ وإنْ نفـاهُ (ح : لأن من جُهِـل دينـه ينسب إلى دين أهـل بلده وهنا وجد دينان فيقـدم الإسـلام لأنـه يعـلو ولا يعـلى عليـه ، والحكم بإسلامه سبب لسعادته إذ سينشأ على ذلك) .

k28.2   If money is found with the child or under his head, it belongs to him.

k28.2   فإنْ كَانَ معـهُ مالٌ متصلٌ بِهِ أَوْ تَحتَ رأسِهِ فهوَ لَهُ .

k28.3   If the finder is a resident, trustworthy, and Muslim, then the child remains with him, and he is obliged to have witnesses attest to his having found the child and whatever was found with him (O: such as clothing or money).

The finder spends the money found with the child for its own expenses with the permission of the Islamic magistrate. If there is no Islamic magistrate, then the finder spends it anyway, but has witnesses attest to the amount of the expenditures. If no money was found with the child, then its expenses are paid for by the Muslim common fund. If there is no money in the Muslim common fund (N: or no Muslim common fund), then the finder may borrow money to cover its expenses as a financial obligation to be later repaid by the child.

If the finder is a corrupt person (def: o24.3(A:)) or a non-Muslim, then if the child is considered a Muslim (dis: k28.1), he is taken from the finder.

If two people find the child and disagree about whom the child should remain with, then the one who is a resident and wealthy is given preference.

k28.3   فإذَا الْتَقَطَهُ [حرٌّ] مسلمٌ أمينٌ مقيمٌ أقـرَّ في يدِه ويَلْزَمُهُ الإشهادُ عليـه وعلى مَا مَعَهُ (من ملبوس ودنانير) . ويُنْفَقُ عليـهِ مِنْ مالِهِ بإذنِ الحاكمِ فإنْ لَمْ يكنْ حاكمٌ أَنْفقَ منْهُ وأَشْهَدَ فإنْ لَمْ يَكُنْ لَهُ مالٌ فَمِنْ بيتِ المـالِ وإلاَّ (أي وإن لم يكن مال في بيـتِ الـمـال (ح : أو لم يكن للمسلمين بيت مال)) اقْتَرَضَ على ذمةِ الطفل .
وإنْ أَخَـذَهُ [عبـدٌ أَوْ] فاسقٌ [أو مَنْ يَظْعَنُ بِهِ من الحضـرِ إلى الـبـاديـة] وكَـذَا كافرٌ وهوَ محكومٌ بإسلامِهِ انْتُزِعَ منهُ .
وإنْ الْتَقَطَهُ اثنـانِ وتَنَـازَعَـا فالمـوسِرُ المقيمُ أولى .

k28.4   (A: Adoption is unlawful in Islam when it means giving a child one's own name, a share of one's estate division (irth, def: L1.0), and so on. But when it merely means giving the child a home and other advantages provided by family life until it grows up, then it is a charitable act rewarded by Allah. And Allah knows best.)

*

k29.0 GAMES, CONTESTS, AND PRIZES

(O: The scriptural basis for competitions and races entailing prize money is the word of Allah Most High,

"And make ready against them whatever force and lines of horses you can" (Koran 8:60).

Muslim relates from 'Uqba ibn 'Amir that the Prophet (Allah bless him and give him peace) said,

"Force means marksmanship,"

repeating this three times.)

RACES FOR PRIZE MONEY

k29.1   Races with prize money for the winner are permissible between horses, mules, donkeys, camels, or elephants, provided that the animals competing are of the same species, though it is not, for example, permissible to have such a race between a camel and a horse.

It is a necessary condition for such a race that the participants know which animals will be ridden, the amount of the prize, and the distance to be run.

k29.2   The prize money may be put up by both contestants, either one, or by a third party. If the prize money is put up by either contestant or by a third party, then the race is unconditionally permissible, and the winner takes all (N: regardless whether he was the one who put up the money or whether it was the other person).

But if the prize money is put up by both con-

k29.0   المسابقة

(والأصل فيها قوله تعالى :
﴿وَأَعِدُّوا لَهُمْ مَا اسْتَطَعْتُمْ مِنْ قُوَّةٍ وَمِنْ رِبَاطِ الْخَيْلِ﴾ [الأنفال : ٦٠].
وروى مسلم عن عقبة بن عامر: «إن القوة الرمي» كرّرها ثلاثاً).

المسابقة

k29.1   تَجُوزُ على العِوَضِ بينَ الخيلِ والبغالِ والحميرِ والإبلِ والفيلةِ بشرطِ اتحادِ الجنسِ فلا تَجُوزُ بين بعيرٍ وفرسٍ.
ويُشْتَرَطُ معرفةُ المركوبيْنِ وقدرِ العوضِ والمسافةِ.

k29.2   ويَجُوزُ أَنْ يَكُونَ العِوَضُ منهما أوْ مِنْ أحدِهِما أوْ مِنْ أجنبيٍّ. فإنْ كانَ مِنْ أحدِهِما أوْ مِنْ أجنبيٍّ جازَ بلا شرطٍ فمَنْ سَبَقَ أخَذَهُ (ح: سواء سبق من دفع المال أو سبق صاحبه).
وإنْ كانَ منهُما اشْتُرِطَ أَنْ يَكُونَ معهُما

testants, then it is a necessary condition that a third rider enter the contest with a mount equal to theirs (A: in speed, stamina, and so forth,) who puts up no money (N: so that it may be distinguished from gambling. If all three put up the money, then it is necessary that there be a fourth contestant with them who does not pay, and so on). (A: Similarly, bets from one side alone, such as saying, "I will give you ten dinars if what you have said proves to be correct," are lawful when the other party bets nothing.)

Here, the winner takes all. If two riders finish together, they divide the prize.

COMPETITIONS IN MARKSMANSHIP FOR PRIZE MONEY

المناضلة

k29.3 It is also permissible to compete for prize money in competitions of skill at archery, spear throwing, or other military weaponry, when the prize is put up by both contestants, either one, or a third party, though if put up by both, it is necessary that a third marksman enter the contest, as mentioned above (A: meaning one comparable to the others in marksmanship, who puts up nothing).

It is a necessary condition for the validity of such a competition that the following details be specified before the contest:

(a) who will be shooting;

(b) the number of shots per bout, how many shots are needed to win, and the criterion for a hit (A: that is, in archery, whether the arrow must stick or whether it need merely leave a mark);

(c) the distance to the target;

(d) and which of the contestants is to begin.

k29.4 It is not permissible to conduct contests for prize money that involve birds, footracing, or wrestling (O: since they are not military weaponry or equipment).

مُحَلَّلُ وهــوَ ثالــثُ على مركــوبٍ كفءٍ لمركــوبَيهمـا لا يُخْرجُ عوضاً (ح: حتى يتميز هذا عن القمار، وإن كان المال من الثلاثة اشترط أن يكــون معهم رابع لم يخــرج عوضــاً وهكــذا) فمَنْ سَبَقَ من الثلاثة أخَذَ. وإنْ سَبَقَ اثنانِ اشْترَكا فيه.

k29.3   ويجُــوزُ على النشابِ والرمح وآلاتِ الحــرب والعــوضُ منهمـا أوْ مِنْ أحدِهمَا أوْ مِنْ أجنبيٍّ والمحلَّلُ معهُمَا إذا كانَ منهُمَا على مَا تقَدَّمَ.
ويُشْتَرطُ تعيينُ الــرمـاةِ وعــددِ الرشقِ والإصابـةِ وصفـةِ الــرمي والمسـافةِ ومَن البادىءُ منهُمَا.

k29.4   ولا يَجُــوزُ بالــعــوضِ على الطيــورِ والأقــدام والصــراع (لأن هذه المذكورات ليست من آلاتِ الحرب).

k29.5　(N: As for games:

(1) every game played by two or more people that relies on luck, conjecture, and guessing is unlawful, no matter whether money is stipulated or not;

(2) paying prize money in every game that encourages and assists fighting for Allah (jihad, def: o9) is permissible if the terms of the competition conform to the rulings discussed above in this section (k29.1–4);

(3) every game not of the preceding two types is permissible if no money is paid therein;

(4) and any of the above-mentioned things which are permissible become unlawful if they prevent one from performing a religious or this-worldly duty.)

*

k30.0 ESTABLISHING AN ENDOWMENT (WAQF)

(O: Lexically, *waqf* means to be retained. In Sacred Law, it refers to the retention of any property that can be benefited from while the property itself still remains, by suspending disposal of it; with the financial proceeds of it going to some permissible expenditure. The scriptural basis for it is the hadith related by Muslim that the Prophet (Allah bless him and give him peace) said,

"When a human being dies, his work comes to an end, except for three things: ongoing charity, knowledge benefited from, or a pious son who prays for him,"

from which scholars understand *ongoing charity* as meaning an endowment (waqf).)
(n: Given persons P (al-waqif) and Q (al-mawquf 'alayhi) (A: where P owns, for example, an apartment building that he makes an endow-

أحكام الألعاب

k29.5　(ح : وأما الألعاب فكما يلي :

ـ كل لعب بين اثنين فأكثر اعتمد على الحظ والحزر والتخمين فهو حرام سواء كان بشرط مال أم لا ؛

ـ كل لعب يعين على الجهاد جاز فيه بذل المال إن وافق الأحكام التي تقدمت في هذا الباب ؛

ـ كل لعب ليس من النوع الأول ولا الثاني فهو جائز بشرط عدم بذل المال فيه ؛

ـ كل ما تقدم مما حكم بجوازه يصير حراماً إذا شغل عن واجب ديني أو دنيوي) .

k30.0 الوقف

(هو لغة الحبس وشرعاً حبس مال يمكن الانتفاع به مع بقاء عينه بقطع التصرف في رقبته على مصرف مباح والأصل فيه خبر مسلم «إذا مات ابن آدم انقطع عمله إلا من ثلاث : صدقة جارية أو علم ينتفع به أو ولد صالح يدعوله» والصدقة الجارية محمولة عند العلماء على الوقف) .

(ت : يمثل له بشخصين : زيد (الواقف) وعمرو (الموقوف عليه) (ع : حيث يملك زيد عمارة شقق مثلاً فيجعلها وقفاً [ح : على عمرو ثم

ment (waqf), the rent of which will henceforth go to Q, and P stipulates that Q must supervise the upkeep of the building. This section deals with such endowments).)

k30.1   Establishing an endowment is an act of worship.

k30.2   Establishing an endowment is not valid unless the following conditions are met:

(a) that P have full right to manage his own property (O: *full right to manage his own property* including the non-Muslim, whose endowment is legally valid, even if it is for a mosque);

(b) that the endowment concern a particular identified article ('ayn) (O: it being invalid to make the mere "right to use something" an endowment, because it is not a particular article);

(c) that the article have a (O: lawful) use;

(d) that it remain existent (O: for a period in which it would be feasible to rent or hire it out), such as real estate or an animal (O: or clothing, weapons, Korans, or books. It is not permissible to make an endowment of something that cannot be utilized except by using it up, such as food);

(e) that the beneficiary be some particular party (O: such as the poor, for example) besides P himself, whether the endowment is an act of worship, as when the beneficiary is mosques (O: or Islamic schools), one's relatives, or the general good; or whether it is merely permissible, such as an endowment that benefits the wealthy, or Jewish and Christian subjects of the Islamic state;

(f) and that the endowment be formally established by words that effect it such as "I make it an endowment," or "I restrict [O: such and such a thing to benefit So-and-so]," or "I give [A: such and such] as nonsaleable charity."

k30.3   When the endowment has been made, the ownership of the article belongs to Allah Most

الفقراء)] ويشترط أن يستلم عمرو وأجرتها ويقوم بصيانتها [(ح : ويكون الباقي له ثم للفقراء من بعده)]. وهذا الباب يتناول مثل هذا الوقف)).

k30.1   هو قربةٌ.

k30.2   ولا يَصِحُّ إلاّ مِنْ مطلق التصرف (ويدخل في قوله مطلق التصرف الكافر فيصح وقفه ولو مسجداً في عين معيّنة (فلا يصح وقف منفعة لأنها ليست عيناً) يُنْتَفَعُ بها (نفعاً مباحاً) مع بقاء عينها دائماً (أي مدة يصح استئجارها فيها) كالعقار والحيوان (أي والثياب والسلاح والمصاحف والكتب لا ما لا يفيد نفعاً إلا بفواته كطعام) على جهة معينةٍ (كالفقراء مثلاً) وغير نفسِهِ غير محرمةٍ إمّا قربة كالمساجِد (والمدارس) والأقارب وسبيل الخير وإمّا مباحةٌ كالأغنياء وأهل الذمة باللفظ المنجَز وهو: وَقَفْتُ وحَبَسْتُ [وسَبَّلْتُ] (كذا على كذا) أوْ تَصَدَّقْتُ صدقةً لا تباعُ.

k30.3   فحينئذٍ يَنْتَقِلُ الملكُ في الرقبة إلى اللهِ تعالى (فلا يكون الملك للواقف

High (O: not P or Q) (N: meaning that even though everything is the property of Allah, the article is now dissevered from its metaphorical human ownership), while Q owns the proceeds from it and its utilities (O: and all the benefits that come from it after the endowment has been made, such as rent, the fruit of trees, or offspring. Q may dispose of these as an owner would, as this is the purpose of the endowment. He may utilize the endowment either personally, or through another by loaning it for use or renting it out).

k30.4   The interests of the endowment (O: i.e. its concerns, condition, upkeep (N: and supervision)) are looked after by whoever P stipulates, whether himself or Q or a third party. If P does not stipulate (O: that anyone in particular look after it), then the responsibility belongs to the Islamic authority (N: by himself, or through the person he appoints to do so).

k30.5   The proceeds of the endowment (O: such as the produce of an acreage endowment, or the rent of a property endowment) are disposed of as P stipulates, in terms of (A: for example):

(1)   proportionality of shares (O: between recipients as to the amount each receives, such as having stipulated twice as much for males as females, or vice versa, or equal shares for each);

(2)   precedence (O: in some receiving the proceeds before others when they are a group, through a condition that determines who deserves to receive it);

(3)   inclusiveness (O: of (A: all) recipients, as by saying, "I make this an endowment for my children and their children," where the word *and* implies that each person must be given a share);

(4)   priority (O: such as saying, "I make this an endowment for the benefit of Islamic scholars, without restriction, and after that [A: if there are no more to be given a share] to the poor," or "I make this an endowment for the benefit of Zayd, and then 'Amr," where if one dies, the next one receives his share);

ولا للموقوف عليه (ح : وكل شيء ملك لله لكن المعنى هنا ينفك عنه ملك الآدميين المجازي) ويَمْلِكُ الموقوفُ عليه غَلَتَهُ ومنفعتَهُ (وجميع الفوائد الحادثة بعد الوقف كالأجرة وثمرة الأشجار وولد، ويتصرف الموقوف عليه في هذه المذكورات تصرف المالك لأن ذاك هو المقصود. فيستوفي منافعه بنفسه وغيره بإعارة وإجارة) [إلا الوطءَ إنْ كانَتْ جاريةً].

k30.4   ويَنْظُرُ فيه (أي في شأنه وحاله وحفظه (ح : وإدارته) مَنْ شَرَطَ الواقفُ إما بنفسِه أو الموقوف عليه أوْ غيرِهما [(بأن شرطَه لأجنبي)] فإنْ لَمْ يَشْــرِطْ (الواقف النظارة لأحد) فالحاكمُ (ح : إما بنفسه أو بمن يعيّنه لذلك).

k30.5   وتُصْــرَفُ الـغَـلَّةُ (أي غلة ما يخرج من الأرض الموقوفة وأجرة الأماكن الموقوفة) على ما شَرَطَ من المفاضلةِ (بين الموقف عليهم في قدر الاستحقاق كأن يشرط للذكر ضعف ما للأنثى أو بالعكس أو التسوية فيه) والتقديم (أي تقديم بعضهم على بعض في أخذ الغلة إن كانوا جماعةً، بوجود شرط الاستحقاق) والجمع (بينهم كأن يقول وقفت هذا على أولادي وأولاد أولادي فالعطف هنا اقتضى إعطاء لكل) والترتيب (كوقفت هذا على العلماء مطلقاً ثم من بعدهم على الفقراء أو وقفت هذا على زيد ثم من بعده على عمر فإذا مات أحدهما صرف نصيبه للآخر) وغيرِ ذلك

(5) or other conditions (O: such as the proceeds going to those most closely related to P (N: of his offspring), and then the less closely related).

k30.6 (n: The following are examples of invalidity of establishing an endowment due to lack of one of the conditions mentioned at k30.2 above.) An endowment is not valid when it consists of:

(1) (non-k30.2(b)) a debt (N: that someone owes to P);

(2) (non-(b)) "One of these two houses";

(3) (non-(d)) food;

(4) (non-(d)) sweet basil (A: which used to be spread on floors as an air freshener) (O: since it quickly deteriorates) (N: i.e. if it is uprooted, though if it is growing, it is valid to make it an endowment);

(5) (non-(e)) when its beneficiary is unidentified by P, or unknown (O: since the endowment cannot be implemented. It is thus invalid if P stipulates "whoever Zayd says" as the beneficiary), or is P himself (O: including P stipulating that the proceeds of the endowment be used to pay off his debts, or when P eats of its produce, or utilizes the endowment for his own benefit, any of which invalidates the endowment);

(6) (non-(c)) when the proceeds are directed to an unlawful use, such as building a church (dis: o11.5(7)) (O: or purchasing lamps for a church, or building walls around it, since this assists disobedience to Allah. Rafi'i says, "The same is true of an endowment for printing the Torah or New Testament, which is invalid because the Jews and Christians have altered the texts and interpolated spurious material, it not being permissible to occupy oneself with printing their scriptures because doing so is to participate in their disobedience to Allah");

(7) (non-(f)) when the beginning or end of the endowment's being in effect are subject to conditions such as saying, "I make it an endow-

كالأعلى فالأعلى (ح: من فروع الذرية)).

k30.6 وإنْ وَقَفَ شيئاً في الـذمـةِ أو إحـدى الـدارين أو مطعـومـاً أو ريحـانـاً (لسـرعـة فسـاده) (ح: مقلوعـاً وأمـا المـزروع فيصح وقفه) أوْ وَقَفَ ولمْ يُعيِّنْ المصرفَ أوْ وَقَفَ علىٰ مجهولٍ (لتعذر تنفيـذ الـوقف، ولـو قال: وقفت على من شاء زيد، كان باطلاً) أوْ علىٰ نفسِهِ (ومنه ما لو شرط أن يقضى من ريع الوقف ديونه أو يأكـل من ثماره أو يستنفع به فكل ذلك يبطـل الـوقف) أوْ علىٰ محـرَّمٍ كعمـارةِ كنيسةٍ (وكـذا على قنـاديلها وحصرها لم يصـح لمـا فيه من الإعانة على المعصية. قال الـرافـعي وكـذا لو وقف على كتبـة التـوراة والإنجيـل لا يصـح لأنهم حرفـوا وبـدلوا فيهما والاشتغال بكتبها حينئذٍ غير جائـز فيصـير من جملة المعصية) أوْ عَلَّقَ [(أي علّق صيغة الوقف)] ابتداءَهُ وانتهاءَهُ على شرطٍ كقولِهِ إذَا جَاءَ رأسُ الشهرِ فقدْ

ment starting from the first of next month,'' or "for one year,'' or "provided that I am entitled to sell it'' (O: or "on condition that I may take it back whenever I wish'');

(8) or (non-(e)) when (n: P stipulates, as a priority order of beneficiaries, "Q, then R,'' and) Q is not an eligible recipient—such as P stipulating himself as the first beneficiary—but R *is* an eligible recipient, as when P stipulates (A: after himself) "and then the poor.''

k30.7 If P designates a particular recipient (O: or group of recipients), it is a necessary condition for the validity of the endowment that the recipient accept it. If he refuses it, this invalidates the endowment.

k30.8 If P designates a particular person (lit. "Zayd'') as an endowment's beneficiary, but does not stipulate anyone after him, then the endowment is valid, and after the particular person is gone, its beneficiaries are the poor of P's relatives.

*

k31.0 GIFT GIVING (HIBA)
(n: As when X gives Y a gift.)

k31.1 Gift giving is recommended. It is superior to give gifts to one's relatives than to nonrelatives. When giving gifts to one's children, it is recommended to give each child the equal of what the others are given.

k31.2 Gift giving is only valid under the following conditions:

(a) that X have full right to manage his own property;

(b) that the gift be something permissible to sell (def: k2.1);

وَقَفْتُ أَوْ وَقَفْتُهُ إلى سنةٍ أَوْ على أنَّ لي بيعَهُ (أو على أن أرجع عنه متى شئت) أو على مَنْ لا يَجُوزُ ثُمَّ على مَنْ يَجُوزُ كَعلى نفسِهِ ثُمَّ للفقراءِ بَطَلَ.

k30.7 ولوْ وَقَفَ على (شخص) معين (وكذا على جماعة معينين) اشتُرِطَ قبولُهُ فإنْ ردَّهُ بَطَلَ.

k30.8 وإنْ وَقَفَ على زيدٍ ولمْ يَقُلْ وبعدَهُ إلى كذا صَحَّ ويُصرَفُ بعدَ زيدٍ لفقراءِ أقارب الواقف [وإنْ وَقَفَ على العبد نفسِهِ بَطَلَ. وإنْ أَطْلَقَ فهوَ لسيدِهِ].

k31.0 الهبة

k31.1 هيَ منـدوبـةٌ، وللأقـارب أفضـلُ. وتُنْـدَبُ التسـويةُ فيها بينَ أولادِهِ [حتّى بينَ الذكر والأنثى].

k31.2 وإنَّـمـا تَصِـحُّ مِنْ مطـلقِ التصرف فيمَا يَجُوزُ بيعُهُ بإيجابٍ منجَّزٍ

(c) that X give it with spoken words that effect it;

(d) and that Y accept it with a spoken reply.

وقَبُولٍ .

k31.3 Y does not own the gift until he takes possession (def: k7.3) of it, before which X may take it back. It is not valid for Y to take possession of the gift without X's permission. In cases where X gives Y an article that is already being kept with Y (O: as when Y has it as a trust for safekeeping, or has borrowed it), or X has put up the article as collateral for Y, and now simply gives Y the article, then it is necessary that Y obtain X's permission to take possession of the gift, and that enough time elapse for Y to reach the gift (O: if it is distant) and take possession of it.

Once Y has taken possession of the gift, X is no longer entitled to take it back. An exception to this is when one gives a gift to one's child, or their descendant, in which case one may take the gift back, unless such a receiver has sold it in the meantime, and the article has subsequently returned to him (O: by sale or gift), in which case one may no longer take it back.

k31.3 ولا تُمْلَكُ إلّا بالقبضِ فلَهُ الرجوعُ قبلَه . ولا يصحُّ القبضُ إلّا بإذنِ الواهِبِ فلَوْ وَهَبَهُ شيئاً عندَهُ (أي عند الموهوب له بأن كان عنده على سبيلِ الأمانة أو الوديعة أو العارية) أو رَهَنَهُ [(رهن الواهب الموهوب له الشيء الذي وهبه)] إيّاهُ فلا بدَّ منَ الإذنِ في قبضه ومُضيِّ زمنٍ يَتأتَّى فيه قبضُهُ والمضيُّ إليِه (إن كان الموهوب بعيداً) .

فإذا مَلَكَ لمْ يكُنْ للواهب الرجوعُ إلّا أنْ يَهَبَ لولدِه أوْ ولدِ ولدِه [وإن سَفَل] فلَهُ الرجوعُ فيه بعدَ قبضه [بزيادتِه المتصلة كالسمن لا المنفصلة كالولد] فلَوْ [حُجِرَ على الولدِ بفلسٍ أوْ] باعَ (الولدَ) الموهوبَ ثمَّ عادَ إليِه (أي إلى الولد إمّا بشراء أو هبة له) فلا رجوعَ .

k31.4 If X gives Y something and stipulates that Y give him something determinately known in return, this is valid, but is a sale (A: not a gift). If X stipulates that Y give him something in return that is not determinately known, then the gift is invalid. If X does not stipulate that anything be given him in return, then Y is under no obligation to him.

k31.4 فإنْ وَهَبَ وشَرَطَ ثواباً معلوماً صحَّ وكان بيعاً . أو مجهولاً بَطَلَ . وإنْ لمْ يَشْرُطْهُ لمْ يَلْزَمْ .

*

k32.0 MANUMISSION ('ITQ)

k32.0 العتق

(n: This section, which begins, "To free a slave is an act of worship," deals with a system of ownership that Islam did not invent but found fully established and not possible to instantly abolish, so it rather encouraged its elimination in steps, with incentives. It closed all avenues for obtaining new slaves except the capture of war prisoners, the soldiers of whom the caliph had the option to enslave or not; it encouraged the freeing of slaves by the tremendous reward from Allah Most High; and it materially helped slaves to purchase their freedom by providing them the money to do so from zakat funds (dis: h8.15). Like previous references to slaves, the following four sections have been left untranslated because the issue is no longer current, unlike the times of our author Ibn Naqib, whose rulers, the Mamelukes of Egypt, were themselves slaves who legally belonged to the Islamic state, a fact sufficient to show the fallacy of understanding slavery in the Islamic milieu in terms of the institution that existed in nineteenth-century America and elsewhere in the West (dis: w13).)

k32.1 [هـو قربـةٌ لَا يَصـحُّ إلَّا مِنْ مطلقِ التصـرف ويَصـحُّ بالصريـح بلا نيـةٍ وبـالكنايـة مع النية . فصريحُهُ العتقُ والحريـةُ وفَكَكْتُ رقبـتَـكَ والكنـايـة لا مِلْكَ لي عليـكَ ولا سلطانَ لي عليـكَ وأنتَ للهِ وحبلُكَ على غارِبكَ وشبُهُ ذلك . ويَجُوزُ تعليقُهُ على شرطٍ مثـلُ إذا جاءَ زيدٌ فأنتَ حرٌّ . فإذا عَلَّقَ بصفةٍ لم يَمْلِكْ الرجوعَ فيه بالقول ، ويَجُوزُ الرجوعُ بالتصـرف كالبيـع ونحوِه فإنْ اشْتَـرَاهُ بعدَ ذلك لم تَعُد الصفةُ . ويَجُوزُ في العبدِ وفي بعضِه . فإنْ أعتَقَ بعض عبدِه عَتَقَ كلُّه . فإنْ كان عبداً بين اثنينِ فعَتَقَ أحدُهُمَـا نصيبَـه عَتَقَ . ثمَّ إنْ كان موسِراً عَتَقَ عليه نصيبُ شريكِه في الحالِ ولزِمَهُ قيمتُه حينئذٍ . وإنْ كان معسِراً عَتَقَ نصيبُه فقطْ . ومَنْ مَلَكَ أحدَ الوالدينِ وإنْ عَلَوا أو المولودينَ وإنْ سَفَلُوا عَتَقَ عليه . وإنْ مَلَكَ بعضَه فإنْ كانَ برضَاهُ وهـوَ موسِرٌ قُوِّمَ عليه الباقي وعَتَقَ وإلَّا فلا . ولَوْ أعتَقَ الحاملَ عَتَقَتْ هيَ وحملُهَا . أوْ أعتَقَ الحملَ عَتَقَ دونَها . ولوْ قَالَ أعْتَقْتُكَ على ألفٍ أوْ بِعتُكَ نفسَك بألفٍ عَتَقَ وقَبِلَ وَلزِمَهُ الألفُ .]

k32.2 [(التـدبيـر) التدبيرُ قربةٌ وهوَ أنْ يَقُولَ : «إذا مُتُّ فأنتَ حرٌّ أوْ دَبَّرْتُكَ أوْ أنتَ مُدَبَّرٌ ويُعْتَبَرُ مِنَ الثلثِ . ويَصِحُّ مِنْ مطلقِ التصرفِ وكَذَا من مبذِّرٍ لا صبيٍّ . ويَجُوزُ تعليقُه على صفةٍ مثلَ إنْ دَخَلْتَ الدارَ فأنتَ حرٌّ بعدَ موتي فَيُشْتَرَطُ الـدخـولُ قبـلَ المـوتِ . وإنْ دَبَّرَ بعضَ عبدِه أوْكلَّ ما يَمْلِكُهُ مِنَ العبدِ المشتَرَكِ لم يَسْرِ إلى الباقي . ويَجُوزُ الرجوعُ فيه بالتصـرفِ لا بالقولِ . ولوْ أَتَت المدبَّرةُ بولدٍ لم يَتْبَعْها في التدبيرِ .]

k32.3 [(الكتابة) الكتابةُ قربةٌ تُعْتَبَرُ في الصحةِ مِنْ رأسِ المالِ وفي مرضِ الموتِ مِنَ الثلثِ ولا تَصِحُّ إلَّا مِنْ جائزِ التصرفِ مع عبدٍ بالغٍ عاقلٍ على عوضٍ في الذمةِ معلومِ الصفةِ في نجمَيْنِ فأكثَرَ يَعْلَمُ ما يؤدِّي في كلِّ نجمٍ بإيجابٍ منجزٍ وهوَ : كاتَبْتُكَ على كذَا تُؤدِّيهِ في نجمَيْنِ كلَّ نجمٍ كذَا فإذَا أدَّيْتَ فأنتَ حرٌّ ، وقبولٍ . ولا يَجُوزُ كتابةُ بعضِ عبدٍ إلَّا أنْ يَكُونَ باقيهِ حراً ولا تُسْتَحَبُّ إلَّا لِمَنْ يُعْرَفُ كسبُه وأمانتُه وللعبدِ فسخُها متى شاءَ . وليسَ للسيدِ فسخُها إلَّا أنْ يَعْجَزَ المكـاتبُ عن الأداءِ . وإنْ ماتَ العبدُ انْفَسَخَتْ أو السيدُ فلا . ويَلْزَمُ السيدَ أنْ يَحُطَّ عنهُ جزءاً مِنَ المالِ وإنْ قَلَّ قبلَ العتقِ أوْ يَدْفَعهُ إليهِ وفي النجمِ الأخيرِ أَلْيَقُ . ويُنْدَبُ الربعُ . فإنْ لم يَفْعَلْ حَتَّى قَبَضَ المالَ ردَّ عليهِ بعضَه . ولا يَعْتِقُ المكاتبُ ولا شيءٌ منهُ ما بَقِيَ عليهِ شيءٌ ويَمْلِكُ بالعقدِ منافِعَهُ واكتِسابَهُ وهوَ مَعَ السيدِ كالأجنبيِّ . ولا يَتَزَوَّجُ ولا يَهَبُ ولا يَعْتِقُ ولا يُحابي إلَّا بإذنِ السيدِ ولا يَجُوزُ بيعُ المكاتبِ ولا بيعُ ما في ذمتِهِ مِنَ النجومِ وولدُ المكاتبةِ يَعتِقُ إذا عَتَقَتْ .]

k32.4 [(فصـل) إذا أوْلَدَ جاريتَـهُ أوْ جاريـةً يَمْلِكُ بعضَهـا أوْ جاريـةَ ابنِه فالولدُ حرٌّ والجاريـةُ أمُّ ولدٍ لـهُ فَتَعْتِقُ بموتِه ويَمْتنِعُ بيعُها وهبتُهَا ويَجُوزُ استخدامُها وإجارتُها وتزويجُها . وكسبُها للسيدِ وسواءً أوْلَدَتْهُ حياً أوْ ميتاً لكنْ لوْ لمْ يُتَصَوَّرْ فيه خلقُ آدميٍّ لمْ تَصِرْ أمَّ ولدٍ . ولوْ أوْلَدَ جاريةَ أجنبيٍّ بنكاحٍ أوْ زناً فالولدُ مِلْكٌ لسيدِهَا . أوْ بشبْهةٍ فهو حرٌّ . فلوْ مَلَكَها بعدَ ذلك لمْ تَصِرْ أمَّ ولدٍ .]

*

459

BOOK L

INHERITANCE

CONTENTS:

L1.0   BEQUESTS (WASIYYA)

الوصية   L1.0

(n: Sections L1, L2, and L3 have been moved here from their original place at the end of last book. They deal with bequests, meaning testamentary disposition of one's property (wasiyya) such as to say, "I bequeath such and such to So-and-so"; while sections L4 through L10 form the original content of book L, and deal with estate division (irth).)

(A: The difference between bequests (wasiyya) and estate division (irth) is that a *bequest* is the act of a living person disposing of his own property, even if it is to be implemented after his death, while *estate division* occurs after his death according to the Koranic rules of inheritance. Because a bequest is the act of a living person with his own money, it is legally valid for a Muslim to bequeath up to a third of his property to a non-Muslim (dis: L3.13(1)) and similarly valid for a non-Muslim to bequeath his property to a Muslim. Nawawi says:

"A bequest is legally valid from any legally responsible free person, even if non-Muslim" (*Mughni al-muhtaj ila ma'rifa ma'ani alfaz al-Minhaj* (y73), 3.39).

(النـووي:) تَصِحُّ وصيةُ كلِّ مكلفٍ حرٍّ وإنْ كَانَ كافـراً. [نـقـل من مغني المحتاج: ٣/ ٣٩].

But it is invalid and unlawful for a non-Muslim to inherit property through *estate division* from a Muslim (dis: L5.2), or vice versa. The determining factor in the permissibility of a Muslim and non-Muslim inheriting from each other is whether the property comes by way of a bequest (wasiyya) made by the deceased before his death, in which case it is permissible, or whether it comes by way of estate division (irth) made after the deceased's death according to the Koranic rules of inheritance, in which case the difference between their respective religions prevents it.)

(O: Our author only mentions bequests at this point (n: at the end of book k, as mentioned above) before estate division because of the fact that a person first makes bequests, then dies, and then the estate is divided. The scriptural basis for the validity of bequests, prior to the consensus of scholars, is the word of Allah Most High,

(إنمـا ذكـرهـا المصنف هنـا قبـل الفرائض نظراً إلى أن الشخص يوصي ثم يمـوت ثم تقسم تركته. والأصل فيها قبل الإجماع قوله تعالى:
﴿مِنْ بَعْدِ وَصِيَّةٍ يُوْصَى بِهَا أوْ دَيْنٍ﴾
[النساء: ١٢]).

"... after any bequest which has been made, and after any debts" (Koran 4:12).)

(n: Given persons X (al-musi), Y (al-wasiyy), and Z (al-musa lahu) (A: where X has made provision in his will for Z to receive a bequest (wasiyya) of a sum of money, and X appoints Y as his executor to make sure this is done).)

L1.1   A bequest made by X is valid if he is legally responsible (mukallaf, def: c8.1), even if he is a spendthrift.

تَصِحُّ مِنَ المكلفِ [الحرِّ] ولوْ مبذراً .   L1.1

L1.2   The discussion is in two parts (n: namely, section L2, on X's appointing Y as the executor, and section L3, on the bequest itself).

ثمَّ الكلامُ في فصلَيْن .   L1.2

*

L2.0   THE BEQUEST'S EXECUTOR
(O: *Appointing an executor* means for X to put Y in charge of his property and young children, bequests, paying his debts, or collecting his property from others. The verbal form is, "I appoint So-and-so to execute such and such a bequest.")

الوصي   L2.0
[أحـدُهُمـا في نصب الـوصيِّ] (أي إقـامتـه على أمر ماله وصغار أولاده وتنفيذ الـوصيـة ومـا عليـه من الدين وقبض ماله على النـاس، فيقـال في صيغته «أوصيت لفلان بكذا») .

L2.1   The necessary conditions for the validity of X appointing Y as the executor of his bequest are that Y be:

(a) legally responsible (mukallaf, def: c8.1);

(b) upright (def: o24.4) (O: meaning the uprightness of Islam, as it is not valid under any circumstances for Y to be a non-Muslim if X is a Muslim);

(c) and that Y have the knowledge and capacity to properly undertake the bequest.

وشـرطُـهُ التكليفُ [والحرية]   L2.1
والعـدالةُ (والمراد بالعدالة عدالة الإسلام فلا يصـح إيصـاء المسلم إلى الكـافـر مطلقاً) والإهتداءُ للموصى به .

L2.2   The following examples of X appointing Y as the executor of his bequest are legally valid:

(1) when X appoints Y as his executor at a time when Y is not legally eligible to be it, but by the time of X's death, Y is eligible (O: by fulfilling all the above (L2.1) conditions);

فلوْ أوْصَى لغيـرِ أهـلٍ فصَـارَ   L2.2
عند الموتِ أهلاً (للإيصاء بأن صار كاملاً متصفـاً بالشـروط المـذكـورة) أوْ أوْصَى

(2) when X appoints a group of two or more people as his executors (O: and if he does so, then if he does not stipulate that each of them must manage their respective role, but rather says that they are to manage the legacy collectively, or does not say anything, then they must cooperate and not manage the work, maintenance, and dealings as separate individuals. *Cooperate* in such a case means that their acts proceed from the decision of the group, and does not mean, for example, that when they buy something they must all conduct the transaction together. Rather, if all agree to permit something, it is sufficient for one of them to take the matter in hand and carry it out);

(3) when X appoints (n: for example,) W, and then after him, Y (N: or vice versa) (O: saying, "I appoint W as executor until Y comes, but when Y arrives, he is the executor," or "I make W executor for one year, and when it has passed, then Y is the executor");

(4) or when X appoints Y as executor, authorizing him to appoint in turn whomever he chooses as executor of the bequest (O: if the person fulfills the conditons (L2.1)).

L2.3   X's appointing Y as the executor of his bequest is not legally effective until Y accepts this responsibility after X's death, even if this acceptance is not immediately thereafter.

Both X and Y are entitled to cancel the appointment of Y as executor of the bequest whenever they wish (O: unless (A: after X's death) Y feels it almost certain that the property will be lost through a wrongdoer appropriating it, in which case Y may not withdraw as executor, meaning it is unlawful for him to do so. In such a case, if Y withdraws of his own choice, he is not thereby free of having to execute the bequest, though he is not obliged to continue therein without remuneration, but does so for a fee.)

L2.4   It is not legally valid to appoint an executor unless the bequest consists of some good work or pious act such as paying off a debt, mak-

لجماعةٍ (فإن لم يشترط الموصي الإنفراد بالتصرف لكل واحد على حدته بل شرط الاجتماع عليه أو أطلق وجب عليهم التعاون في الموصى عليه ولا ينفرد واحد بالعمل والحفظ والتصرف والمراد بالاجتماع على ما ذكر صدور الشيء عن رأي الجميع وليس المراد أنهم عند عقد البيع مثلاً يتلفظون معاً بل إن حصل الرضا أو الإذن منهم بأن يتولى أمر الشيء واحد منهم ويباشره كان كافياً) أوْ لزيدٍ ثمَّ مِنْ بعدِهِ لعَمْرو (كأن قال أوصيت لزيد إلى قدوم عمرو فإذا قدم فهو الوصي أو أوصيت إلى زيد سنة فإذا مضت فعمرو وهو الوصي) أوْ جَعَلَ للوصيِّ أَنْ يُوصيَ مَنْ يَخْتَارَ (الوصي من شخص عدل حر إلى آخر ما تقدم من الشروط السابقة في الوصي الأصلي) صَحَّ.

L2.3   ولا يَتِمُّ إلَّا بالقبولِ بعدَ موتِ الموصي ولوْ على التراخي.
ولكلٍّ منهمَا [(أي من الموصي والوصي)] العزلُ متَى شاءَ (إلا أن يغلب على ظن الوصي تلف المال باستيلاء ظالم عليه فليس له الرجوع أي يحرم عليه ولو عزل نفسه لم ينعزل لكن لا يلزم ذلك مجاناً بل بالأجرة).

L2.4   ولا تَصِحُّ الوصيةُ (بمعنى الإيصاء) إلَّا في معروفٍ أوْ برٍ كقضاءِ دين

ing up a hajj (dis: j1.9), looking after the welfare of one's children, and so forth (O: excluding actions that are not dispositions of property, such as marrying off the children) (A: and excluding acts of disobedience such as those mentioned above at k30.6(6)).

وحجٍ والنظرِ في أمرِ الأولادِ وشبهِه (وخرج ما لم يكن تصرفاً مالياً كتزويج الأولادِ).

L2.5 When X's father is still alive and fit for guardianship (def: m13.2), X may not appoint Y to look after the welfare of his children.

L2.5 وليسَ لهُ أنْ يوصيَ على الأولادِ وصياً والجدُّ أبو الأبِ حيٌّ أهلٌ للولايةِ. [والفصلُ الثاني في]:

*

L3.0   THE BEQUEST

L3.0   الموصى به

L3.1 X may devote one-third or less of his financial resources to bequests, but not more than this, *one-third* meaning a third of his property as it stands at the time of his death (O: not before or afterwards).

L3.1 تجوزُ الوصيةُ [(أي تصح الوصيةُ)] بثلثِ المالِ فَما دونَهُ ولا تجوزُ [(أي لا تصح)] بالزيادةِ عليهِ والمرادُ ثلثُهُ عندَ الموتِ (لا قبلَه ولا بعدَه).

(A: If there are no Muslim heirs, or if the existent Muslim heirs do not deserve the whole estate, such as when the sole eligible estate division heir is a husband or wife (dis: L6.3–4), then the Hanafi school permits disposing of more than a third of one's property in bequests (dis: w44), *more than a third* meaning everything in excess of what one's eligible heirs deserve by estate division (irth).) (n: The ruling in the Shafi'i school is that such an excess may not be disposed of in bequests, but rather is given to the Muslim common fund (bayt al-mal) if it exists, as mentioned below (L3.3(O:) and L9.1).)

L3.2 If X's heirs (def: L4.4) are not poor, it is recommended for X to devote a full one-third to bequests, but if not (O: i.e. if his heirs are not well off, as when they do not have any money at all, or have some, but not enough for their expenses, and the other two-thirds (A: of the estate that constitutes their obligatory shares) which they deserve is insufficient), then it is not recommended for X to devote a full one-third to bequests.

L3.2 فإنْ كانَ ورثتُهُ أغنياءَ نُدِبَ استيفاءُ الثلثِ [(أي ينـدب حينئـذ للموصي أن لا ينقص عن الثلث بل يستوفيه بالوصية)] وإلاَّ (أي بأن لم تكن ورثته أغنياء بأن لم يكن لهم مال أصلاً أو لهم ولكن لا يغنيهم ولا يكفيهم الثلثان الباقيان لهم) فَلاَ [(يندب له استيفاء الثلث)].

L3.3 If X wills more than one-third in bequests, then his dispositions are not valid regarding the portion in excess of one-third when he has no one (O: in particular) to lawfully inherit the rest (A:

L3.3 فإنْ زادَ عليهِ بَطَلَتْ في الزائدِ إنْ لمْ يكُنْ لهُ وارثٌ (خـاصٌ لأنَّ الـحقَّ

who, if they existed, could give permission for the excess, as discussed below). (O: In cases where there are no heirs, the Muslim people have better right to X's property, and no one may waive this right.)

Nor are X's bequests in excess of one-third valid when he has an heir, but the heir refuses to authorize the excess, though if the heir (N: or group of heirs unanimously) permits it, such a bequest is valid. It is not valid for the heir to authorize the excess or refuse to do so until after X's death.

L3.4   Charitable expenditures made by X in his will (O: such as an endowment (waqf, def: k30), gift, and so forth) are considered as part of the bequeathable one-third.

L3.5   Bequests concerning obligatory expenditures are also considered from the bequeathable one-third, provided that X has stipulated that they come from it. (O: Though if the bequeathable third does not cover these (A: despite X having stipulated that they come from it), then the excess is paid from the remaining two-thirds. *Obligatory expenditures* include such things as paying debts, making up the hajj (dis: j1.9), paying zakat (A: for any year that the deceased neglected to pay it), expiations, and the fulfillment of vows that would have been binding had X been well.) But if X did not stipulate (O: that these obligatory expenditures come from the bequeathable one-third), then they come directly from the other two-thirds.

L3.6   Current charitable dispositions of property made by X during his life, such as establishing an endowment (waqf, k30), giving a gift, or others, are considered as personal expenditures of his own money (O: and he could spend it all without any objection) if made while he was in sound health. But if X makes such current dispositions under any of the following circumstances, when these are linked with his death, then the dispositions are considered as having come from the bequeathable one-third:

للمسلمين فلا مجيـز) وكـذا إنْ كَانَ وَرَدَّ الـزائدُ. فإنْ أجَازَهُ (أي أجازَ الـوارث الخـاص المطلق التصـرف الـزائـد على الثلث) صَحَّ ولا تصحُّ الإجازةُ والرَّدُ (له من الوارث المذكور) إلاَّ بعدَ الموتِ.

L3.4   ومـا وَصَّى به مِنَ التبـرعـات تُعْتَبَرُ مِنَ الثلث. (وذلك كوقف وهبة وغيرهما).

L3.5   وكذا مِنَ الواجبات (أي فيعتبر من الثلث أيضاً فإن لم يوف الثلث بها تمـمـت من الثلثين كالـديـن وأداء فرض الحج والزكاة والكفارة والنذر اللازم له في الصحـة) إنْ قَيَّـدَهُ (أي قيـد الـواجب) بالثلث. فإنْ أطْلَقَهُ (أي أطلق الوصية ولم يقيده بالثلث) فمِنْ رأسِ المال.

L3.6   ومـا نجَّـزَهُ في حيـاتـه من النبرعات كالوقف [والعتق] والهبة وغيرها فإنْ فَعَلَهُ في الصحـة اعْتُبِـرَ مِنْ رأسِ المـال. (فلو تصرف فيه كله فلا حرج عليه) وإنْ فَعَلَهُ في مرضِ الموتِ أوْ في

(1) in the final illness which brought about X's death;

(2) in military combat;

(3) while travelling on rough seas in a storm;

(4) as a final request before being killed;

(5) or (O: if female) X dies while giving birth, or afterwards before separation of the placenta.

If otherwise, (O: meaning if the current charitable disposition was not made under any of the above circumstances, or was, but the circumstance was not linked with X's death,) then the disposition is not taken from the bequeathable one-third.

حال التحـام الحرب أوْ تَمَوّج البحر أو التقديم للقتل أوْ (فعلته المرأة في حال) الطّلْق (أي وجع الـولادة) أوْ بعـدَ الولادة قبل انفصـال المشيمـة وَاتَصَلَتْ هذه الأشيـاء بالمـوت اعْتُبرَ من الثلث. وإلّا (أي وإن لم يكن ذلك التبرع في حال من الأحوال المتقدمة أو وقع في هذه الأحوال ولم يتصل بالموت) فلا (أي فلا يحسب من الثلث).

L3.7   (N: We distinguish between the above-mentioned current dispositions (n: such as gifts, endowments, and donations), and between bequests by noting that current dispositions are effective before X's death, while bequests are effective after. Current dispositions are normally implemented even if X uses up all his money, while bequests—unless X's heirs unanimously agree to allow otherwise—are restricted to one-third of the estate. An exception to permitting current dispositions to amount to as much of X's property as he wishes is when they are effected during his death illness (n: or other L3.6 circumstance), in which case they are limited to one-third of the estate, just as bequests are.)

If one-third of the estate does not cover the cost of the (N: current) dispositions which X made during his (N: final) illness, then (O: if these have been given in some order) they are implemented first thing first, then second, then third, and so on.

فإنْ عَجـزَ الـثـلثُ عمَّـا نَجـزَهُ في المـرض (وكـانت هذه التبـرعات مرتبة) بُدِىءَ بالأول فالأول.

(N: Thus, if during his death illness, X said to his three friends P, Q, and R, "I give P a gift of 100 dinars, Q 100 dinars, and R 100 dinars," but it turns out that X's total estate is only 600 dinars, then his gifts to P and Q are valid, but we take back his gift to R, which is not valid because it exceeds the 200 dinars that is a third of the 600 dinars constituting the whole estate. This is what is meant by implementing them *in order*.)

L3.8   The bequeathable one-third of the estate is divided (O: proportionally (N: if shares vary)) between all the recipients X designates when:

(1) (N: in cases of death illness current dispositions, such as gifts) X did not state them in any

L3.8   فإنْ وَقَعَتْ دفعةً أوْ عَجزَ الثلثُ

particular order (N: such as by saying (n: in a situation like the above example) to P, Q, and R, "I give you each a hundred dinars," in which case the bequeathable one-third is divided between them);

(2) or (N: in cases where X has explicitly made bequests) the bequeathable one-third will not cover all the bequests, whether they were made separately or not.

(N: All of the above (L3.6–8) only holds if the heirs do not agree to permit more than one-third of the estate for bequests or current dispositions, since if they unanimously agree, it may exceed a third, even if it takes the whole estate.)

L3.9   Bequests made to nonspecific individuals such as *the poor* are effective when X dies. (O: They own the property without the fact of ownership depending on their accepting it.)

L3.10   When X bequeaths something to Z, a particular individual, the ownership of the article bequeathed is *suspended,* meaning that if Z accepts it after X's death, even if after some time has passed, then Z has owned it from the moment X died; but if Z declines to accept it, then X's heirs own it. If Z accepts it, but then refuses it before having taken possession of it (def: k7.3), this cancels his ownership of it, though if he refuses after having taken possession of it, it does not cancel his ownership (O: as his refusal is meaningless in such a case).

L3.11   It is permissible to make the implementation of a bequest subject to a condition, whether the condition is something occuring before X's death (O: such as his saying, "If Z enters So-and-so's house, I bequeath to him such and such of my property,") or after (O: such as his saying, "If Z enters So-and-so's house after my death, I bequeath to him such and such of my property").

عن الوصايا متفرقةً كانَتْ أوْ دفعةً قُسِّمَ الثلثُ بينَ الكلِّ (ووزع عليها) [سواءً كان ثَمَّ عتقٌ أمْ لا].

L3.9   وتَلزَمُ الوصيةُ بالموتِ إنْ كانتْ لغيرِ مُعَيَّنٍ كالفقراءِ (فإنهم يملكون الموصى به ولا يتوقف ذلك على القبول).

L3.10   فإنْ كَانَتْ لمعَيَّنٍ [كـزيـدٍ] فالملْكُ موقوفٌ فإنْ قَبِـلَ بعدَ الموتِ ولوْ متراخياً حُكِمَ بأنَّهُ ملْكُهُ مِنْ حين الموتِ. وإنْ رَدَّهُ حُكِمَ بالملكِ للوارث. وإنْ قَبِلَ [(أي الموصى له الموصى به)] ورَدَّ قبلَ القبضِ سَقَط الملكُ [(أي ملك الموصى له الموصى به)] أوْ بعدَهُ فَلا (فـلا عبـرة لرده حينئذ).

L3.11   ويَجـوزُ تعليقُ الوصيـةِ على شرطٍ في الحياةِ (كإن دخل زيد دار فلان فقـد أوصيت له بكـذا من مالي) أوْ بعـد الموتِ (كإن دخـل زيـد دار فلان بعـد موتي فقد أوصيت له بكذا من مالي).

THINGS WHICH MAY BE BEQUEATHED	ما يوصى به

L3.12 It is permissible to bequeath any of the following:

(1) the right to utilize something (O: while not bequeathing the actual thing);

(2) particular things;

(3) something not yet existent, such as "what this tree will bear";

(4) something not determinately known (O: whether it be an unknown thing (A: such as "the contents of this box"), or something unknown in amount);

(5) something undeliverable (non-k2.4);

(6) something not currently owned (O: at the time the bequest is made, but which X owns at the time of his death);

(7) or something impure (najasa, def: e14.1) that has a lawful use, such as a (O: trained hunting) dog, or oil contaminated with impurity; though not something impure that is without lawful use, such as wine or pigs.

L3.12 وَيَجُوزُ بالمنافع (فقط دون العين) والأعيان وبالمعدوم كالوصيةِ بمَا تَحْمِلُ هذِه [الجاريةُ أَو] الشجرةُ وبالمجهول (كشيء أو كأن يكون مجهول القدر) وبِمَا لا يُقْدَرُ على تسليمِهِ [كالآبق] وبِمَا لا يَمْلِكُهُ الآن (أي عند الوصية ثم يملكه عند الموت) وبِمَا يَجُوزُ الانتفاعُ به من النجاساتِ كالكلب (المعلم للصيد) والزيتِ النجس لا بِمَا لا يُنْتَفَعُ به (من النجاسات) كالخمر والخنزير.

THOSE TO WHOM BEQUESTS ARE VALID	لمن يوصى

L3.13 It is permissible for X to bequeath something to Z even if Z is:

(1) a non-Muslim at war with Muslims (A: and with still better right when Z is an ordinary non-Muslim);

(2) a Jewish or Christian subject of the Islamic state;

(3) an apostate from Islam;

(4) the person who kills X;

L3.13 وَيَجُوزُ الوصيةُ للحربيِّ والذميِّ والمرتدِّ ولقاتلِهِ وكَذَا لوارثِهِ عندَ

469

(5) X's heir (def: L4.4), provided X's other heirs permit him to receive it (O: though if they do not, then the bequest is not carried out);

(6) or to a person yet unborn, in which case the bequest is paid to the person (O: i.e. guardian) who knows of the unborn's existence at the time X makes the bequest, provided that the child is either born alive within six months of the time the bequest is made, or is born alive more than six months and less than four years after the bequest is made, during which time the mother has had no husband (O: from whom the pregnancy could have resulted).

CANCELLING ONE'S BEQUESTS

الرجوع عن الوصية

L3.14   If X makes some article a bequest but then changes his mind, his taking it back is valid, annulling his bequest. X's doing any of the following is also considered *taking it back* (A: and cancels the bequest):

(1) X's loss of ownership (O: of the bequeathed article) such as by sale or gift;

(2) X's subjecting the article to loss of ownership by putting it up as collateral, offering it for sale, or making another bequest that stipulates that it be sold;

(3) or when the name of the article changes, such as wheat being ground into flour, flour made into dough, yarn woven into fabric, or when X mixes a particular article with other goods.

L3.15   If Z dies before X, then X's bequest to him is invalid. If Z dies after X but before Z accepts the bequest, then Z's heirs may accept or reject it.

*

L4.0   ESTATE DIVISION (IRTH)
   (O: *Estate division* refers to the share allotted to each heir by Sacred Law. The scriptural basis

المــوت إنْ أَجَـازَهُ بقيــةُ الورثة (وأما إذا لم يجيزوا فلا تنفذ الوصية) وللحمل فَتُدْفَعُ لمَنْ (أي لوليّ) عَلِمَ وجـودَهُ (أي الحمل) عند الوصية إذا انْفَصَلَ حيّاً بأنْ تَلِدَ لدون ستة أشهر مِن الوصية أوْ فوقَها ودونَ أربعة سنينَ ولا زوج لَهـا [ولا سيـدَ يَطَؤُهـا] (أمكن كون الحمـل منـه) [وإنْ أوْصَى لعبدٍ فَقبِل دُفع إلى سيدِه].

L3.14   وإنْ وصَّى بشيءٍ ثمَّ رجَعَ عن الوصية صحَّ الرجوعُ وبَطلَت الوصيةُ. وإزالةُ الملْك فيه (أي في الموصى به) كالبيـع والهبة أوْ تعـريضُـهُ (أي تعرض الموصي) لزوالِه (أي زوال ملك الموصى به) بأنْ [دبَّـرَهُ أوْ كاتَبَـهُ أوْ] رهنَهُ أوْ عرَضَهُ على البيـع أوْ أوْصَى ببيعـه أوْ أزالَ اسمَهُ بأنْ طحَنَ القمحَ أوْ عجَنَ الدقيق أوْ نَسَجَ الغزلَ أوْ خلَطَهُ إذا كان معيّناً بغيرِه رجوعٌ.

L3.15   وإنْ مات الــموصى لُه قبْـلَ الموصي بطلت الوصيةُ. وإنْ مات (المـوصى له) بعـدَهُ وقبـلَ القبول فلوارثة قبولُه وردُّهُ.

L4.0   [كتاب] الفرائض
(وهـو نصيب مقـدر شرعـاً للوارث)

for estate division, prior to the consensus of scholars, consists of the Koranic verses on inheritance (Koran 4:11–12, 4:176) and hadiths such as the one related by Bukhari and Muslim that the Prophet (Allah bless him and give him peace) said,

"Give the obligatory shares of the estate to those who deserve them, and the rest belongs to the closest male to the deceased."

Encouragement to master the knowledge of estate division comes from such hadiths as the one from Ibn Mas'ud (Allah be well pleased with him) that the Prophet (Allah bless him and give him peace) said,

"Learn estate division and teach it to people, for I am someone who will be taken from you, and this knowledge will be taken from you and calamities will ensue, until two men will one day disagree about the obligatory apportionment and will not find anyone to judge between them.")

والأصل في كتاب الفرائض قبل الإجماع آيـات الــمـواريـث وأخبـار كخبـر الصحيحين : «ألحقـوا الفرائض بأهلهـا فمـا بقي فلأولى رجـل ذكـر» وقـد ورد الحث على تعلم علم الفرائض كحديث ابن مسـعـود وهـو أن الـنبي ﷺ قال : «تعلمـوا الفـرائض وعلمـوها الناس فإني امـرؤ مقبـوض وإن هذا العلم سيقبض وتظهـر الفتن حتى يختلف الـرجـلان في الفـريضـة فلا يجـدان من يفصل بينهما» [صححه الحاكم وغيره]).

HOW TO WORK AN ESTATE DIVISION PROBLEM

كيفية حل مسائل المواريث

L4.1   (n: To work an estate division problem, one should:

(a)   determine the amount of the deceased's estate after deducting the L4.2–3 expenses;

(b)   make a list showing which of the deceased's heirs mentioned at L4.4 exist;

(c) eliminate from the list any heirs with preventives L5.1–4;

(d) on a sheet of paper, copy the parenthesized introductory paragraph ("N: summary of ——'s share,") for every eligible heir that exists, such as the deceased's:

(1) husband (dis: L6.3);

(2) wife (L6.4);

(3) father (L6.5);

(4) mother (L6.6);

(5) daughter (L6.7);

(as mentioned at L6.8, the shares of the above-named family members are not eliminated by anyone, though the shares of those named below may be eliminated by the existence of certain other heirs)

(6) son's daughter (L6.9);

(7) full sister (L6.10);

(8) half sister from the same father (L6.11);

(9) grandfather (father's father only) (L6.13);

(10) grandmother (L6.18);

(11) half brother or half sister from the same mother (L6.20);

(12) and then the others (sons and so forth) mentioned at L6.22;

(e) read section L7 and cross off the list of heirs those whose shares are eliminated by the other existent heirs;

(f) if any *universal heirs* (def: L10.5) exist, see which of them eliminates the shares of the other universal heirs, as at L10.6;

(g) make a table of the heirs remaining (after (e) and (f) above) like the tables shown at L6.6, where one writes the type of heir, the fraction each deserves (with the universal heir receiving the remainder, if any), and then at the top writes the total shares (this being the common denominator of the fractions), after which one calculates the shares that go to each;

(h) if the fractions (of those besides the universal heir) add up to more than one (i.e. the total estate), then one must adjust for this as shown at L8.2;

(i) but if the fractions add up to less than the total estate and there is no universal heir to inherit the rest, then one must redistribute the shares as described at L9.1–2.

One may practice and test one's skill at estate division by reading through the present section and doing the problems depicted in the tables, though to do all the problems one must have (or memorize) a full worksheet that contains all the information mentioned in (d), (h), and (i), above, plus the rules concerning universal heirs discussed at L10.1–4. Finally, it is best to check one's answers with an Islamic scholar, preferably a teacher from whom to take instruction, since this is a subject that is easier to acquire from its masters than from books.)

EXPENSES DEDUCTED FROM THE ESTATE PRIOR
TO ESTATE DIVISION

ما يؤخذ من تركه الميت قبل
الإرث

L4.2   The first thing (O: obligatorily) taken from X's property is the expense of preparing his body (O: such as the cost of the water to wash him, the washer's fee, cost of the shroud and perfume placed therein, pallbearers' fees, and so forth) and of burying him. These expenses are deducted before X's debts are paid, his bequests fulfilled, or his estate divided, unless there is a financial obligation due on the property itself, such as:

(1)   when there is zakat (A: due from any year X neglected to pay it before his death);

(2)   when some of the property has been put up as collateral (dis: k11.2);

(3)   or when X dies bankrupt with unpaid-for merchandise among his property (A: which must be returned to the seller before paying other expenses from X's property).

L4.2   يُبْدأ مِنْ تركة الميت (وجوباً) بمـؤنـة نجهيزه (من ثمن ماء غسله وأجرة مغسله وكفنـه وثمن حنـوط يوضـع في الكفن وأجـرة الحامـل وغير ذلك) ودفنه قبـل الـديـون والـوصايا والإرث، إلّا أن يَتَعَلَّقَ بعين التـركـة حقّ كالـزكـاة والرهن [والجـاني] والمبيـع إذا مَات المشتري مفلسـاً. فإنّ حقوق هؤلاء تُقَدَّم على مؤنة التجهيز والدفن.

L4.3   After the above are paid, the following measures are taken (A: and the sequence given is obligatory):

(1)   X's debts are paid (N: though if a government takes non-Islamic estate taxes, these are deducted from the main part of the estate (A: before debts or bequests, as any other loss would be));

(2)   then X's bequests (def: L1–3) are carried out (O: from a third of what remains after debts);

(3)   and then X's remaining property is divided between his estate division heirs.

L4.3   ثمَّ بعـد ذلـك تُقْضَى ديونُه ثمَّ تُنَفَّذُ وصاياه (من ثلث ما بقي بعد الدين) ثمَّ تُقَسَّم تركتُهُ بينَ ورثتِهِ.

HEIRS

L4.4   X's male heirs consist of:

(1)   X's son;

L4.4   والـوارثـونَ مِنَ الـرجـالِ [عشرةٌ] الابنُ وابنُهُ وإنْ سَفَل والأبُ وأبوهُ

(2) X's son's son, son's son's son, and on down;

(3) X's father;

(4) X's father's father (A: the term *grandfather* throughout the book of inheritance refers only to this paternal grandfather), father's father's father, and on up;

(5) X's full brother, or half brother from X's father or mother;

(6) the son of X's full brother, or son of X's half brother from the same father;

(7) X's father's full brother, or father's half brother from the same father;

(8) the son of X's father's full brother or father's half brother from the same father;

(9) and X's husband.

X's female heirs are:

(1) X's daughter;

(2) X's son's daughter, son's son's daughter, son's son's son's daughter, and on down;

(3) X's mother;

(4) X's grandmother (whether she is the mother of X's father or mother), great-grandmother, and on up;

(5) X's full sister, or half sister from the same father or mother;

(6) and X's wife.

EXTENDED FAMILY MEMBERS WHO DO NOT NORMALLY INHERIT

L4.5   The following extended family members may not inherit from X's estate (except under the conditions discussed at L10.8):

وإنْ عَلا والأخُ شقيقـاً كانَ أوْ لأبٍ أوْ لأُم وابنُ الأخِ الشقيقِ أوْ لأبٍ والعمُّ الشقيقُ أوْ لأبٍ وابنُـهُمـا والـزوجُ [والمعتقُ]. والـوارثاتُ منَ النساءِ [سبعٌ] البنتُ وبنتُ الابنِ وإنْ سَفَلَ والأمُ والجـدةُ أمُ الأمِ وأمُّ الأبِ وإنْ عَلَتْ والأختُ شقيقـةً كانَتْ أوْ لأبٍ أوْ لأُم والزوجةُ [والمعتقةُ].

ذوو الأرحــام الـذيـن لا يرثــون بطريق الأصالة

L4.5   وأمّـا ذُوو الأرحامِ وهمُ أولادُ

(1) X's daughter's children (O: male or female);

(2) X's mother's brother's sons;

(3) X's sister's children, the sons or daughters of X's daughter's children, or the sons or daughters of X's sister's children;

(4) X's brother's (O: whether full brother's, or half brother's from either parent) daughters;

(5) X's father's brother's (O: whether full brother's, or half brother's from the same father) daughters;

(6) X's father's half brother from the same mother;

(7) X's mother's father;

(8) X's mother's brother or sister;

(9) X's father's sister;

(10) or anyone related to X through one of the above.

*

البنـات (ذكوراً كانوا أو إناثاً) وبنوُ الإخوة للأمّ وأولادُ الأخـوات وبنوهُنَّ (وبنو أولاد البنات وبنو أولاد الأخوات) وبناتُهُنَّ (أي بنات أولاد البنات وبنات أولاد الأخوات) وبناتُ الإخوة (مطلقاً أي أشقاء أو لأب أو لأمّ) وبنـاتُ الأعمـام (سواء كان الأعمام أشقـاء أو لأب) والعمُّ للأمّ أي أخُـو الأب لأمه وأبُو الأمّ والخالُ والخالةُ والعمةُ ومَنْ أَدْلَى بهمْ فلا يَرِثُونَ عندَنا بطريق الأصالة بلْ (يرثون) إذا فَسَدَ بيتُ المالِ كَمَا سَيَأتِي.

L5.0 THE FOUR PREVENTIVES OF INHERITING AN ESTATE DIVISION SHARE

(O: Preventive means that if someone is an estate division heir (def: L4.4) but one of the following characteristics exists in him, then he may not inherit.) (A: In calculating the estate division, an heir who is made ineligible by a preventive is considered nonexistent. Such a person is a nonheir, and as such is eligible for a bequest (def: L1.0) if X wills him one.)
(n: Given X, the deceased; and Z, his heir.)

L5.0 وموانعُ الإرثِ أربعةٌ :

(والمراد أنه إذا وجد شخص فيه سبب الإرث لكنه اتصف بوصف مانع منه فلا يرث).

L5.1 The first preventive is killing. Whoever kills X may not inherit from him, no matter whether the killing was:

L5.1 الأولُ القتـلُ فمَنْ قَتَـلَ مُوَرِّثَهُ لمْ يَرِثْهُ سواءٌ قَتَلَهُ بحقٍّ كالقصاص أوْ في

(1) lawful, as in retaliation (def: o3) or imposing a criminal penalty;

(2) without lawful right;

(3) accidental;

(4) intentional;

(5) direct (O: such as Z shooting while hunting, and the shot hitting X);

(6) or when Z is a causal factor in X's death, such as testifying to an act of X's that calls for retaliation against X, or such as digging a well into which X falls.

To summarize, whoever has a hand in X's death, no matter how, cannot inherit from him.

الحدّ أوْ بغيرِه خَطأً كَانَ أوعمداً مباشرةً كَانَ (كأن رمى صيـداً فأصـاب مورثـه) أوْ سبباً مثـل أنْ يَشْهَ ـَ عليـه بمَـا يُوجـبُ القصـاص أوْ حَفَـر بئـراً فوَقَـع فيهَا . والحـاصلُ أنَّـهُ لا يرثُهُ مَتَى كَانَ لهُ مَدْخَلٌ في قتلِهِ بأيّ طريقٍ كَانَ .

L5.2   The second preventive is being non-Muslim: a Muslim may not inherit from a non-Muslim, and a non-Muslim may not inherit from a Muslim (dis: L1.0).

L5.2   الثـاني الكفرُ فلا يرثُ مسلمٌ مِن كافـرٍ ولا كافـرٌ مِن مسلمٍ [ولا يَرثُ الكافرُ الحَربيُّ إلّا مِنَ الحَربيِّ وأمَّا الذميُّ والمعـاهدُ والمستأمَنُ فيَتَوارثُونَ بعضُهُمْ مِن بعضٍ وإنِ اخْتَلَفَتْ مللُهُمْ ودارُهُمْ . وأمَّا المرتدُّ فَلا يَرثُ وَلاَ يُورَثُ].

L5.3   The third preventive is slavery.

L5.3   الثـالثُ الرقُّ [فالرقيقُ لا يَرثُ ولا يُورَثُ ومَنْ بعضُـهُ حرٌّ لا يَرثُ لكنْ يُوَرَثُ بمَا جَمَعَهُ ببعضِهِ الحرِّ].

L5.4   The fourth is uncertainty as to who died first, such as when X and Z both drown or both die in the collapse of a building, and it is not known who died before the other. In such a case neither may inherit from the other.

L5.4   الرابعُ استيهامُ وقتِ الموتِ فإذا مَاتَ متـوارثـانِ بغـرقٍ أوْ تحتَ هدمٍ ولمْ يُعْلَمْ السـابقُ منهُمَا لمْ يَرثْ أحدُهُمَا مِنَ الآخرِ .

*

L6.0   THE ESTATE DIVISION SHARES

L6.0   ميراث أهل الفروض

L6.1   The six obligatory shares mentioned in the

L6.1   [أعْنِي] الفـروضُ الستـةَ

Koran (Koran 4:11–12) are one-half, one-fourth, one-eighth, two-thirds, one-third, and one-sixth.

المــذكــورةُ في القــرآنِ [و] هيَ النصفُ والربعُ والثمنُ والثلثانِ والثلثُ والسدسُ .

L6.2 They go to ten categories:

وهيَ لعشــرةِ الــزوجانِ [(هما الــزوج والــزوجة)] والأبوانِ [(هما الأب والأم)] والبنـاتُ وبناتُ الابن (وإن نزل) والأخــواتُ والجــدُ والجـداتُ والإخوةُ والأخواتُ مِنَ الأمِّ .

   (1) X's husband;

   (2) X's wife;

   (3) X's father;

   (4) X's mother;

   (5) X's daughters;

   (6) X's son's daughters, or the daughters of X's son's son, son's son's son, and on down;

   (7) X's sisters;

   (8) X's father's father;

   (9) X's mother's or father's mother;

   (10) X's half brothers or half sisters from the same mother.

L6.3 (N: A summary of X's husband's share:
—1/2 if there is no inheriting descendant.
—1/4 if there is an inheriting descendant.
—The husband's share is not eliminated by anyone.)

(ح): وفرض الزوج بشكل مختصر :
- ٢ / ١ إذا لم يكن معه فرع وارث .
- ١ / ٤ إذا كان معه فرع وارث .
- ولا يحرمه من الميراث أحد .
فأمَّا الزوجُ فلَهُ النصفُ مَعَ عدم الولدِ (لزوجته ولو من غيره) (ح : والولد يشمل الــذكر والأنثى) أوْولدِ ابن وارث (قيـد فيهمـا) ولـهُ (أي للزوج) الــربعُ مَعَ الولدِ (سـواء كان منه أو من غيـره ذكراً كان أو أنثى) أوْ ولدِ الابن .

X's husband:

   (1) receives one-half the estate when X has no child who may inherit (O: even if the child is from a different husband) (N: the word *child* (Ar. walad) including both males and females (A: of all ages)), and X's son has no child who may inherit;

   (2) but receives one-fourth the estate when X has a child who may inherit (O: whether from X by this husband or a different husband, and whether male or female), or when X's son has a child who may inherit.

L6.4 (N: A summary of X's wife's share:
—1/4 if there is no inheriting descendant.
—1/8 if there is an inheriting descendant.
—The wife's share is not eliminated by anyone.)

X's wife:

(1) receives one-fourth the estate when X has no child to inherit (O: even if by a different wife) and X's son has no child to inherit;

(2) but receives one-eighth the estate when X has a child to inherit, or X's son has a child to inherit (O: whether X's son is from her or from another wife).

If there are two, three, or four wives, they jointly receive the one-fourth or one-eighth (O: meaning that the share apportioned to one wife is given to two or more (A: to divide up between them)).

L6.5 (N: A summary of X's father's share:
—1/6 if there is an inheriting descendent.
—*Universal heir* (def: L10.5) if there is no male inheriting descendant.
—The father's share is not eliminated by anyone.)

X's father:

(1) receives one-sixth of the estate when X has a son to inherit, or when X's son has a son to inherit (O: or when X has a daughter or X's son has a daughter, who may inherit (N: though in such a case, the father takes (A: the sixth plus) the remainder of the estate as universal heir (n: as discussed next)));

(2) but is universal heir (O: by himself, meaning he takes the whole estate if there are no others who have an obligatory share coming; or if there are such others, he receives the remainder of the estate after they have received their shares) when X has no son to inherit and X's son has no son to inherit.

L6.6 (N: A summary of X's mother's share:
—1/6 if there is an inheriting descendant, or if

L6.4 (ح) : وفرض الزوجة بشكل مختصر :

ـ ٤/١ إذا لم يكن معها فرع وارث .

ـ ٨/١ إذا كان معها فرع وارث .

ـ ولا يحرمها من الميراث أحد .

وأمّا الزوجةُ فلهَا الربعُ مَعَ عدمِ الولدِ (للزوج ولو من غيرهـا) أوْ ولد ابنٍ (أي للزوج) وارثٍ ولهَـا الثمنُ مَعَ (وجـود) الولدِ أوْ (مع وجود) ولدِ الابن (سواء كان منهـا أو من غيرهـا) وللزوجتين والثلاثِ والأربعِ ما للواحـدةِ منَ الـربعِ والثمنِ (والمعنى أن ما ثبت للزوجـة الـواحـدة ثابت للزوجتين فأكثر) .

L6.5 وفرض الأب بشكل مختصر :

ـ ٦/١ مع الفرع الوارث .

ـ عصبة إن لم يكن فرع وارث ذكر .

ـ ولا يحرمه من الميراث أحد .

وأمَّـا الأبُ فلهُ السدسُ مَعَ (وجـود) الابن وابنِ الابن (والواو بمعنى أو، وكذا يستحقه مع وجود البنت وبنت الابن (ح : لكنـه يأخـذ البـاقي تعصيباً)) فإنْ لمْ يَكُنْ معهُ ابنٌ ولا ابنُ ابنٍ فهوَ (أي الأب) حينئذٍ عصبةٌ (أي بنفسه فقط فيأخذ جميع المال إذا انـفـرد أو ما بقي بعـد أصحـاب الفروض) [كما سَيَأتي] .

L6.6 (ح) : وفرض الأم بشكل مختصر :

there are two or more of X's brothers or sisters.

—1/3 of the remainder after deducting the share of X's husband or wife in cases where the heirs include both X's father and the husband or wife, but no inheriting descendant.

—1/3 of the estate when none of the above-mentioned heirs exists.

—The mother's share is not eliminated by any-one.)

X's mother:

(1) receives one-third of the estate when all three of the following are the case:

(a) X has no child (male or female) who may inherit, nor does X's son;

(b) X does not have two or more brothers or sisters, whether full brothers or sisters, or half brothers or sisters from either parent;

(c) and the heirs do not include X's husband and X's two parents, or X's wife and two parents (A: of which X's mother is one);

(2) she receives one-sixth of the estate when (non-(a) above) X has a child who may inherit, or when (non-(b)) X has two or more brothers or sisters;

(3) and she receives one-third of the remainder after deducting the share of X's husband or wife when:

—(non-(c) above) the heirs include X's husband and two parents, in which case she receives one-third of the remainder after X's husband receives his share of one-half, meaning she receives a sixth of the estate, as that is a third of the remainder, and X's father receives the rest:

	shares:	*6
husband	1/2	3
mother	1/6	1
father	universal heir	2

(*common denominator of 1/2 and 1/6)

١ / ٦ - مع الفرع الـوارث، وكـذا مع عدد من الإخوة والأخوات .

١ / ٣ - البـاقي بعـد حصة الـزوج أو الـزوجة إن كان معها أحد الزوجين وأب بلا فرع وارث .

١ / ٣. - مع عدم المذكورين أعلاه .

- ولا يحرمها من الميراث أحد) .

وأمَّـا الأُمُّ فلهـا الثلثُ إذا لـمْ يكُنْ مَعَهَا ولدُ ولا ولدُ ابنٍ ذكراً كَانَ أَوْ أُنثَىٰ ولا اثنانِ (فأكثرُ) مِنَ الإخوة والأخواتِ سواءٌ كَانُوا أشقَّـاءَ أَوْ لأبٍ أَوْ لأَمٍّ، ولمْ تَكُنْ في مسألةِ زوجٍ وأبَـوينِ ولا (في مسألـةِ) زوجةٍ وأبوينِ . فإنْ كَانَ معهَا ولدُ أَوْ ولدُ ابنٍ، أو اثنانِ (فأكثرُ) مِنَ الإخوة والأخواتِ فلهَا السدسُ (في هذه الصور كلها) وإنْ كَانَتْ في مسألـةِ زوجٍ (والميت فيهـا الـزوجة) وأبَـوينِ أَوْ زوجةٍ (والميت فيهـا الـزوج وهي المسألـة الثانية) وأبوين فلهَا ثلثُ مَا بقِيَ بعد فرض الزوج أو الزوجة والباقي للأبِ . فَيَـأْخُذُ الزوجُ في الأُولىٰ النصفَ

—or (non-(c) above) when the heirs include X's wife and two parents, in which case she receives one-third of the remainder after X's wife receives her share of one-fourth, meaning that the mother receives one-fourth of the estate, as that is a third of the remainder, and the father receives the rest:

ولهـا السـدسُ لأنـهُ ثلثُ ما بَقِيَ والبـاقي للأَب. وفي الثـانيـةِ تأخـذُ الزوجةُ الربَع والأُمُّ الربَعَ لأنَّهُ ثلثُ مَا بَقِيَ والبـاقي للأَب.

		shares:	4
wife	1/4		1
mother	1/4		1
father	universal heir		2

L6.7   (N: A summary of X's daughter's share:
—1/2 if there are no other of X's sons or daughters (n: whether full or half brothers or sisters to her).
—2/3 for her to share equally (if there are no sons) with other daughters, if any.
—She is *co-universal heir* (def: L10.3) with X's son(s) if existent, meaning that they jointly constitute the universal heir, dividing this share so that each male receives twice the amount of each female (A: since men are obliged to support women in Islam (dis: m11) and not vice versa).
—The daughter's share is not eliminated by anyone.)

L6.7   (ح: وفرض البنت بشكل مختصر:
ـ ٢/١ إذا لم يكن معها بنت ولا ابن.
ـ ٢/٣ لها ولمن معها من البنات (عند عدم الابن) يقسم بالتساوي.
ـ وهي عصبة بالابن فأكثر للذكر كالأنثيين.
ـ ولا يحرمها من الميراث أحد).
وأمّـا البنتُ المنفـردةُ (عمن يعصبهـا كأخيهـا وعمن في درجتهـا كأختهـا) فلَها النصفُ وللبتين فَصَاعداً الثلثان.

(1) X's sole daughter (O: who is without a co-universal heir such as her brother, and without someone else on her own level, such as her sister) receives half of the estate.

(2) Two or more daughters jointly receive two-thirds.

L6.8   (N: It is important to remember for the persons named in the following rulings that the share of any of them who is related to X through an inheriting heir is *eliminated* by the existence of that heir (dis: L7.4–6), except for X's half brother from the same mother, whose share is not eliminated by the mother's existence.)

L6.8   (ح: ومن المهم أن يذكر فيما يتعلق بالأحكام التالية أن كل من أدلى إلى الميت بوارث، يحجبـه ذلـك الـوارث حجبَ حرمانٍ إلّا الأخ لأم فلا تحجبه الأم بل يرث نصيبه مع وجودها).

L6.9   (N: A summary of the share of X's son's daughter:
—Her share is eliminated if X's son exists (n: an

L6.9   (ح: وفرض بنت الابن بشكل مختصر:
ـ تحرم مع الابن.

example of the above rule).

—1/2 if X has no daughter, son's son, or any other daughter of a son.

—2/3 for her to share equally with the other daughters of X's son(s), if X has no daughter(s) or son's son(s).

—1/6 when there is a sole daughter (def: L6.7(1)).

—She is co-universal heir (def: L10.3) with X's son's son(s) (A: in the absence of X's daughter, dividing this share so that each male receives twice the share of each female).

—Her share is eliminated when X has two or more daughters.)

When X's sole daughter (def: L6.7(1)) exists, X's son's daughter(s) (A: if there are more than one, they share) receives one-sixth of the estate, which with the sole daughter's share of one-half, makes two-thirds (N: which is the maximum that may go to the category of daughters).

L6.10   (N: A summary of the share of X's full sister:

—1/2 if there are no other full brothers or sisters.

—2/3 for her to share equally with other full sisters.

—She is co-universal heir (def: L10.3) with full brother(s) if any, each male receiving twice the share of each female.

—She is *universal heir through* X's daughter(s) (def: L10.4).

—Her share is eliminated if X's father or X's son exists.)

(1)   X's sole full sister (N: meaning no other full brothers or sisters exist) receives one-half of the estate.

(2)   Two or more such sisters (N: when there are no full brothers) jointly receive two-thirds.

(n: L6.12 discusses X's full sister(s) with X's daughters.)

L6.11   (N: A summary of the share of X's half sister from the same father:

—1/2 in the absence of X's full brother, full sister,

ـ ٢/١ إذا لم يكن معها بنت ولا بنت ابن ولا ابن ابن.

ـ ٣/٢ إذا كان معها بنت ابن ولا توجد بنت ولا ابن ابن.

ـ ٦/١ [(تكـمـلـة الثلثين)] إذا كانت معها بنت.

ـ عصبة بابن ابن.

ـ تحرم مع بنتين فصاعداً.

ولبنتِ الابن فصاعداً مَعَ بنتِ الصلب الفـردة السـدسُ تكملةُ الثلثين (ح : لأنَّ جنس البنات غايةُ فرضه الثلثان).

L6.10   (ح : وفـرض الأخت الشقيقـة بشكل مختصر :

ـ ٢/١ إذا لم يكن معهـا أخ شـقيق ولا أخت شقيقة.

ـ ٣/٢ لهـا ولأختهـا إذا كانت معهـا أخت شقيقة فأكثر.

ـ عصبة بالشقيق.

ـ عصبة مع البنات.

ـ تحرم مع الأب أو الابن).

وأمّـا الأخـتُ الفـردةُ الشقيقـةُ فلهـا النصفُ ولأثنتين فصاعداً الثلثانِ.

L6.11   (ح : وفـرض الأخـت لأب بشكل مختصر :

ـ ٢/١ مع عدم الـشـقـيـق والشقيقـة

other half sister from the same father, and half brother from the same father.
—2/3 for her to share equally with other half sister(s) from the same father, when there are no full brothers or sisters, and no half brothers from the same father.
—1/6 when there is X's sole full sister.
—She is universal heir through X's daughters or X's son's daughters (def: L10.4), provided there are no full brothers or sisters, or half brothers from the same father.
—She is co-universal heir (def: L10.3) with X's half brother(s) from the same father, the male receiving twice the share of each female.
—Her share is eliminated if X's father or son exists.)

(1) X's sole half sister from the same father receives one-half of the estate.

(2) Two or more such paternal half sisters jointly receive two-thirds.

(3) When such a half sister, or two or more, exists with X's sole full sister, then the half sister(s) (A: jointly, if more than one) receives one-sixth, which, with the half that goes to the full sister, makes two-thirds.

L6.12   X's full sister(s) is universal heir through X's daughter(s) (def: L10.4). If X has no full sisters, X's half sisters by the same father are the estate's universal heirs through X's daughter(s) (L10.4).

An example of the former is when the heirs are X's daughter and full sister. The daughter receives one-half (dis: L6.7(1)), and the sister receives the rest (A: as universal heir):

		shares: 2
daughter	1/2	1
full sister	universal heir	1

Another example is when there are X's two daughters, a full sister, and a paternal half sister, in which case the two daughters jointly receive two-thirds (dis: L6.7(2)), and the full sister receives the rest (A: as universal heir), while the

والأخت لأب والأخ لأب .
ـ ٢/٣ لها ولأختها من الأب مَعَ عدم الشقيق والشقيقة والأخ لأب .
ـ ١/٦ مع الشقيقة [(تكملة الثلثين)] .
ـ عصبـة مع البنـات أو بنات الابن إذا لم يكن شقيق ولا شقيقة ولا أخ لأب .
ـ عصبة بالأخ لأب .
ـ تحرم مع الأب أو الابن .
وإنْ كَانَتْ (ح : الأخت الفـردة) مِنَ الأب فلهَا النصفُ ولاثنتين فصـاعـداً الثلثـان وللأختِ مِنَ الأب فصاعداً مَعَ الشقيقةِ الفردةِ السدسُ تكملةُ الثلثين .

L6.12 والأخــواتُ الـشـقيقـاتُ مَعَ البنـاتِ عصبةٌ . فإنْ فُقِدْنَ (أي الأخوات الشقيقـات) فالأخـواتُ مِنَ الأب [(يقمن مقـامـهـن في التعصيب)] مثـالُـهُ بنتٌ وأختٌ : للبنتِ النصفُ والباقي للأختِ ؛ بنتـانِ وأختٌ شقيقة وأختٌ لأب : للبنتين الثلثان والباقي للشقيقةِ ولا شيءَ للأخرى

paternal half sister's share is eliminated (A: by the full sister's universal heirship):

[(ح: أي للأخت لأب)].

	shares:	3
2 daughters	2/3	2
full sister	universal heir	1
half sister	eliminated	0

L6.13 (N: summary of X's grandfather's (father's father's) share:
—His share is eliminated if X's father exists.
—1/6 if X has an inheriting male descendant.
—He is universal heir in the absence of both X's father and any inheriting male descendant.
—If X's brother(s) or sister(s) exists, then:

(1) when there is no other heir who has an obligatory share coming, then the grandfather receives whichever of the following two alternatives yields the maximum:

— 1/3 of the estate;

— or dividing the estate with X's brother(s) or sister(s) as if he were one of them, the male receiving twice the share of the female. If only X's sister(s) exists, then she becomes co-universal heir (def: L10.3) with him;

(2) but when there are one or more other heirs who have an obligatory share coming besides the brother(s) or sister(s), then the grandfather receives whichever of the following three alternatives yields the maximum:

—1/6 of the estate;

—1/3 of the remainder after the (non-brother/sister) heir(s) receives their share;

—or dividing the estate with X's brother(s) or sister(s) as if he were one of them, the male receiving twice the share of the female. If only X's sister(s) exists, then she becomes co-universal heir (L10.3) with him.)

As for the grandfather, sometimes X's brothers or sisters exist with him and sometimes they do not.

L6.13 (ح: وفرض الجد بشكل مختصر:
- يحرم مع الأب .
- ١/٦ مع فرع وارث ذكر .
- عصبة مع عدم الأب وفرع وارث ذكر .
- وإذا كان معه إخوة وأخوات :
(١) فإن لم يكن صاحب فرض فللجد الأوفر من شيئين :
أ: الثلث .
ب: المقاسمة مع الإخوة والأخوات كواحد منهم للذكر كالأنثيين ويعصّب الأخوات .
(٢) وإنْ كان هنالك صاحب فرض فللجد الأوفر من ثلاثة أشياء :
أ: ١/٦ .
ب: ٣/١ الباقي بعد حصة صاحب الفرض .
ج: المقاسمة مع الإخوة والأخوات كما تقدم ويعصّب الأخوات) .
وأمَّا الجدُّ فتارةً يكونُ مَعَهُ إخوةٌ وأخـواتٌ وتارةً لا . فإنْ لمْ يَكُونُوا مَعَهُ فلَهُ

When they do not, then the grandfather receives one-sixth of the estate if X's son or son's son (O: or X's daughters or son's daughters) exist (N: but in such a case he takes the sixth plus the rest as universal heir); while the grandfather is the universal heir (def: L10.5) in the absence of X's son or son's son (N: or daughter or son's daughter).

When X's (full or paternal half) brothers or sisters exist, then sometimes there are other inheriting heirs (dis: L6.15) and sometimes not (L6.14).

السـدسُ مَعَ الابن أو ابن الابن (ومثـل الــذكر في ذلك الأنثى مع البنت وبنت الابن (ح : ولكنـه يأخذ الباقي تعصيباً)) . ومَـع عدمِهمَـا (أي الابن وابن الابن) هو عصبـةٌ كَمَـا سَيَأتي . وإنْ كانَ مَعَهُ إخوةٌ وأخواتٌ أشقاءُ أوْ لأبٍ فتارةً يَكُونُ مَعَهُ ذُو فرضٍ وتارةً لا .

L6.14   When (besides X's brother(s) or sister(s)) the grandfather's cosurvivors do not include other inheriting heirs, the grandfather divides the estate with the brothers (A: and sisters) as if he were one of them, and (if there are only sisters) is co-universal heir (def: L10.3) with the sisters.

But such a division is only effected when it does not result in less than one-third of the estate going to the grandfather. If it would result in less than a third for him, then his obligatory share is one-third of the estate, and the brothers or sisters divide the rest between them, the males receiving the share of two females. This is illustrated by the following examples (A: in each of which the grandfather receives at least a third):

L6.14   فإنْ لَمْ يَكُـنْ مَعَـهُمْ ذُو فرضٍ قاسَم الجدُّ الإخـوة وعَصَّبَ إناثَهُمْ ما لمْ يَنْقُصْ ما يَخُصُّـهُ بالمقـاسمـةِ عنْ ثلثِ جميـع المـالِ . فإنْ نَقَصَ فإنَّهُ يُفْرَضُ لهُ الثلثُ ويُجْعَلُ البـاقي للإخوة والأخواتِ للذكر مثلُ حظِّ الأنثيين مثالُهُ :

(1)   X's grandfather and one sister:

	shares:	3
grandfather		2
sister		1

(١) جدُّ وأختُ .

(2)   grandfather and two sisters:

	shares:	4
grandfather		2
sister		1
sister		1

(٢) أوْ أختينِ .

(3)   grandfather and three sisters:

	shares:	5
grandfather		2
sister		1
sister		1
sister		1

(٣) أوْ ثلاثٌ .

(4) grandfather and four sisters:

	shares: 6
grandfather	2
sister	1
sister	1
sister	1
sister	1

(٤) أوْ أربعٌ .

(5) grandfather and one brother:

	shares: 2
grandfather	1
brother	1

(٥) أوْ جدٌ وأخٌ .

(6) grandfather and two brothers:

	shares: 3
grandfather	1
brother	1
brother	1

(٦) أوْ أخَوانِ .

(7) grandfather, brother, and sister:

	shares: 5
grandfather	2
brother	2
sister	1

(٧) أوْ أخٌ وأختٌ .

(8) grandfather, brother, and two sisters:

	shares: 6
grandfather	2
brother	2
sister	1
sister	1

(٨) أوْ أخٌ وأختانِ .

In each of the above examples, the grandfather divides the estate with them, the male receiving the share of two females.

فَيُقَاسِمُ في هذهِ الصورِ للذكرِ مثلُ حظِّ الأنثيين .

L6.15 When (besides X's brothers or sisters) the grandfather's cosurvivors include another inheriting heir, then the heir is given his share, and the grandfather receives the maximal amount of three possibilities:

L6.15 وإنْ كَانَ مَعَهُ ذُو فرضٍ فُرِضَ لِذي الفـرضِ فرضُـهُ ثُمَّ يُعْطَى الجـدُّ مِنَ البـاقي الأوفـرَ لَهُ مِنْ ثلاثـةِ أشيـاءَ إمَّـا الـمقـاسـمـةُ أو ثلثُ ما يَبْقَى أوْ سدسُ

(a) division (A: meaning to divide it with the brothers or sisters as in the above examples);

(b) a third of the remainder (A: taking a third of what remains after the (non-brother/sister) heir has taken his share);

(c) or one-sixth of the estate (A: as the estate stands before the above-mentioned heir has received his share).

جميع المال .
مثالُهُ :

This ruling may be illustrated by (n: the following four examples):

(1) X's husband, grandfather, and brother, where division is better for the grandfather. (n: To show why division ((a) above) is better, we may compare the three possibilities ((a), (b), and (c)) for this example:

(١) زوجٌ وجدٌّ وأخٌ : المقاسمةُ خيرٌ لَهُ .

(a) division:

		shares:	4
husband	1/2 (dis: L6.3(1))		2
grandfather			1
brother	division		1

(b) third of remainder (after the husband's share):

		shares:	6
husband	1/2		3
grandfather	1/3 remainder		1
brother	universal		2

(c) sixth of estate:

		shares:	6
husband	1/2		3
grandfather	1/6 estate		1
brother	universal		2

The comparison reveals that division, giving the grandfather 1/4, is better than the other alternatives, which only give him 1/6, and so division is the alternative that must be implemented.)

(2) X's two daughters, two brothers, and grandfather, where a sixth of the estate is better for him. (n: Comparison:

(٢) بنتـانِ وأخـوانِ وجـدٌّ : سدسُ جميع المـال خيرُ لَهُ .

(a) division:

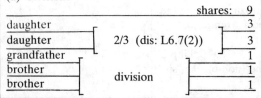

		shares:	9
daughter			3
daughter	2/3 (dis: L6.7(2))		3
grandfather			1
brother			1
brother	division		1

(b) third of remainder (after the daughters' share):

		shares:	9
daughter			3
daughter	2/3		3
grandfather	1/3 remainder		1
brother			1
brother	universal		1

(c) sixth of estate:

		shares:	12
daughter			4
daughter	2/3		4
grandfather	1/6 estate		2
brother			1
brother	universal		1

The comparison reveals that a sixth of the estate is better than the other alternatives, which only give him 1/9, and so the former is the alternative that must be implemented.)

(3) X's wife, three brothers, and grandfather, where a third of the remainder is better for him. (n: Comparison:

(a) division:

		shares:	16
wife	1/4 (dis: L6.4(1))		4
grandfather			3
brother			3
brother	division		3
brother			3

(b) third of remainder (after the wife's share):

		shares:	12
wife	1/4		3
grandfather	1/3 remainder		3
brother			2
brother	universal		2
brother			2

(c) sixth of estate:

		shares:	36
wife	1/4		9
grandfather	1/6 estate		6
brother			7
brother	universal		7
brother			7

(٣) زوجةٌ وثـلاثةُ إخوةٍ وجدٌّ : ثلثُ الباقي خيرٌ له .

487

The comparison reveals that a third of the remainder, which gives the grandfather 1/4, is better for him than division with the brothers (which gives him 3/16), or a sixth of the estate, so he must receive a third of the remainder.)

(4) X's two daughters, mother, grandfather, and brothers, where a sixth of the estate is better for him. (n: Comparision:

(٤) بنتـــانِ وأُمٌّ وجـدٌّ وإخـوةٌ: للبـنتين الثلثـان وللأُمِّ الســدسُ وللجـدِّ الســدسُ وتَسْقُطُ الإخوةُ.

(a) division:

		shares:	6
daughter			2
daughter	2/3 (dis: L6.7(2))		2
mother	1/6 (dis: L6.6(2))		1
grandfather			
brothers	division		1

(b) third of remainder (after the shares of the daughters and mother):

		shares:	18
daughter			6
daughter	2/3		6
mother	1/6		3
grandfather	1/3 remainder		1
brothers	universal		2

(c) sixth of estate:

		shares:	6
daughter			2
daughter	2/3		2
mother	1/6		1
grandfather	1/6		1

(In this case, there is no one who can eliminate the shares of the inheriting heirs above, who have used up the estate so that there is nothing left for the universal heir (the brothers) to inherit (dis: L10.5):)

brothers	eliminated		0

The comparison shows that a sixth of the estate is better for the grandfather than a third of the remainder, which would give him 1/16, or division with the brothers, which would give him 1/12 or less, and so he must receive a sixth of the estate.)

L6.16 If both X's brothers and half brothers from the same father exist with the grandfather, the brothers add the number of the half brothers' shares with their own shares in calculating their own versus the grandfather's, but then the brothers receive both their own shares and the half brothers' shares. (A: The latter are eliminated (dis: L7.3) by the brothers, but are initially reckoned in as a dispensation for the brothers.)

This may by illustrated by the following example, in which there is X's grandfather, brother, and half brother from the same father.

(initial division)		shares:	3
grandfather			1
brother	division		1
half brother			1

but then, because the brother eliminates the half brother's share,

		shares:	3
grandfather			1
brother			2
half brother	eliminated		0

and this is the actual division.

In a second, similar case, if there is a sister, half brother from the same father, and grandfather, then (A: the half brother's share is reckoned with the sister's share versus that of the grandfather, and) her portion of the estate is brought up to one-half (A: which is the maximum she may receive, as at L6.10(1)) from the (n: additive) amount, and the rest goes to the half brother (A: since the grandfather already has his share, and she may receive no more than her obligatory share of one-half). (n: To illustrate, first we make a plain division, the males receiving the share of two females:

		shares:	5
grandfather			2
sister	division		1
half brother			2

Then, as in the **previous case**, we give the half brother's share to **the sister**, since there is none to eliminate her **full** share of one-half (dis: L6.10(1)).

L6.16 وإنِ اجْتَمَعَ مَعَهُ الإخْوَةُ الأشِقّاءُ والإخوةُ للأبِ فإنَّ الأشِقاءَ عندَ المقاسمةِ يَعُدُّونَ على الجدِّ الإخوةَ مِنَ الأبِ ثُمَّ يَأْخُذُونَ نصيبَهُمْ . مثالُهُ جدٌّ وأخٌ شقيقٌ وأخٌ لأبٍ : للجـدِّ الثلثُ والثلثـانِ للأخ الـشـقـيـق : الثلثُ الـذي خَصَّـهُ بالقسمة والثلثُ الذي هُوَ نصيبُ الأخِ مِنَ الأبِ لأنَّ الشقيقَ يَحْجُبُهُ فيَعُودُ نَفْعُهُ إليْهِ . فإنْ كانَ الشقيقُ أختـاً فردةً كَمَـلَ لَهَا الأخُ مِنَ الأبِ النصفَ والباقِي لَهُ .

	shares:	5
grandfather		2
sister		3
half brother		0

But since this gives the sister more than her maximal share of one-half, the surplus is returned to the half brother, and this is the final division. Here, for convenient redivision, we multiply the case's shares by two:

(2 × 5 =)	shares:	10
grandfather		4
sister		5
half brother		1

which is the actual division.)

L6.17 When there is a sister (O: full sister or half sister from the same father) and grandfather, the sister does not normally receive a particular obligatory share (O: since she is co-universal heir (def: L10.3) with the grandfather), except in the following case (Ar. al-akdariyya, lit. "the murkiest") in which there is X's husband, mother, grandfather, and sister.

		shares:	6
husband	1/2 (dis: L6.3(1))		3
mother	1/3 (dis: L6.6(1))		2
grandfather	1/6 (dis: L6.15(c))		1

But at this point, the estate has been used up, despite the fact that the sister deserves her share of one-half, and no one can eliminate it:

sister	1/2 (dis: L6.10(1))	3

so we redivide the estate by adding the three shares that the sister deserves to the initial division's six shares, which become nine (A: this procedure being an *adjustment* ('awl, def: L8.1) for not being able to give everyone full shares, one which proportionately distributes the deficit to all recipients).

(6 + 3 =)	shares:	9
husband		3
mother		2
grandfather		1
sister		3

L6.17 ولا يُفْرَضُ للأختِ ([لغير أم] وهي الأخت الشقيقة والأخت للأب) مَعَ الجــدَّ (وإنمـا لم يفـرض لهـا معـه لأنـه يعصبها) إلَّا في الأكـدرية وهي زوجٌ وأُمٌّ وجـدٌّ وأخـتٌ شقيقـةٌ فللزوج النصفُ وللأُمِّ الثلثُ وللجـدِّ السـدسُ اسْتُغْرِقَ المـالُ وليَس هنـا مَنْ يَحْجُبُ الأخْتَ عن فرْضِهـا فتَعُـولُ المسألـةُ بنصيب الأخت فَتُقْسَمُ من تسعةٍ للزوجة ثلاثةٌ من التسعة وللأُمِّ اثنــانِ يَبْقَى أربعـةً وهي نصيبُ الأختِ والجـدِّ وتُجْمَعُ وتُقْسَمُ بينَها وبينَه

But this results in the grandfather receiving less than if he were to divide the remaining estate with the sister (n: which is impermissible because of ruling L6.15), and so the grandfather and sister add their shares to together (equalling four) and divide them, the male receiving the portion of two females. (n: Here, for convenient redivision, we multiply the case's shares by three:

(3 × 9 =)		shares:	27
husband			9
mother			6
grandfather			8
sister	division		4

للذكرِ مثلُ حظّ الأنثيين.

and this is the actual division.)

L6.18   (N: A summary of the share of X's grandmother (whether she is X's father's mother or mother's mother, or, if both exist, they share the portion):
—1/6 if X's mother does not exist.
—Her share is eliminated if X's mother exists.
—Her share is eliminated by the existence of X's father if X is descended from her through the father.)

(ح: وفـرض الجـدّةِ (أي أم L6.18 الأب أو أم الأم، وإن كانتـا معـاً فالحصـة لهما) بشكل مختصر:
- ١/٦ مع عدم الأم.
- تحرم مع الأم.
- تحرم مع الأب إن كَانت من جهته).
وأمَّا الجدةُ فإنْ كَانَتْ أمَّ الأمّ وأمَّ الأمَّ وهكَذا أوْ أمَّ الأبِ أو أمَّ أمَّ الأبِ وهكذا أوْ أمَّ أبي الأبِ وهكـذا فلَهَا السـدسُ. وإنْ

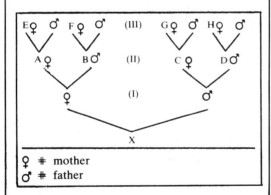

(1) X's grandmother (or great-grandmother) gets one-sixth of the estate when:
—she is A, E, and so on, up that line (n: on the chart above);
—she is C, G, and so on, up that line;
—or when she is H, and so on, up that line.

(2) If there are two grandmothers/great-grandmothers on the same level (A: level II, for example), they jointly get one-sixth to share between them, such as when both C and A exist, or when both G and H exist.

(3) If one of two surviving grandmothers/great-grandmothers is closer (A: on a closer level) to X, then:

(a) if the closer of the two is on X's mother's side (n: the left of the chart) then she eliminates the share of the farther of the two. For example, the existence of A eliminates G's share;

(b) but if the closer of the two is on the father's side (n: the right of the chart), she does not eliminate the share of the one on the mother's side who is farther from X. Rather, both jointly receive the sixth to divide between them. For example, C does not eliminate E.

L6.19 As for great-grandmother F, she does not inherit, as she is an extended family member who may not inherit (A: being related to X through B, who may not inherit (dis: L4.5(7,10))).

L6.20 (N: A summary of the share of X's half brother or sister from the same mother:
—1/6 if there is just one of them, when none of X's inheriting male ancestors (A: father on up) exists, nor any inheriting descendants.
—1/3 if there are two or more of them, to share between them, but which is divided so that males and females receive equal shares.
—Their share is eliminated by the existence of any of X's inheriting male ancestors or inheriting descendants.)

(1) X's half brother or sister from the same mother receives one-sixth if alone.

(2) When there are two or more of them, they jointly receive one-third. This amount is divided with equal shares going to male and female alike.

اجْتَمَعَتْ جدّتانِ في درجةٍ فلهُمَا السدسُ مثلَ أمّ أب وأمّ أمّ أوْ أمّ أمّ أب وأمّ أبي أب . وإنْ كَانَتْ إحدَاهُمَا أقربَ فإنْ كَانَت القربى منْ جهةِ الأمّ أسْقَطَتِ البُعْدَى مثلَ أمّ أمّ وأمّ أمّ أب وإنْ كَانَتْ منْ جهةِ الأب لمْ تُسْقِطِ البُعْدَى بلْ تَشْتَـركانِ في السدسِ مثلَ أمّ أب وأمّ أمّ أمّ .

L6.19 وأمّـا الجـدّةُ التي هِيَ أمُّ أبي الأمّ فَلا تَرثُ بَلْ هِيَ منْ ذَوي الأرحـامِ [كَمَا سَبَقَ] .

L6.20 (ح: وفـرض الأخ لأمّ أو الأخت لأمّ بشكل مختصر :
- ١ / ٦ للواحد إذا لم يكن معـه أصل وارث ذكر ولا فرع وارث .
- ١ / ٣ للاثنين فأكثـر من الإخوة لأمّ (للذكر كالأنثى) .
- يحرم بأصل ذكر وارث وفرع وارث .)
وأمّـا الإخـوةُ والأخـواتِ مِنَ الأمّ فللواحـد منهُمُ السدسُ وللاثنين فصاعداً الثلثُ ذكورُهُمْ وإناثُهُمْ فيهِ سواءٌ .

L6.21   To summarize all of the foregoing:

(1)   One-half of the estate is the obligatory share of five types of heir:
—X's husband, under certain circumstances (dis: L6.3(1));
—X's (sole) daughter (L6.7(1));
—X's son's daughter (L6.9(N:));
—X's (sole) full sister (L6.10(1));
—and X's (sole) half sister from the same father (L6.11(1)).

(2)   One-fourth of the estate is the obligatory share of two types of heir:
—X's husband, under certain circumstances (L6.3(2));
—and X's wife (L6.4(1)).

(3)   One-eighth of the estate is the obligatory share of X's wife, under certain circumstances (L6.4(2)).

(4)   Two-thirds of the estate is the obligatory share of four types of heir:
—two or more of X's daughters (L6.7(2));
—two or more of X's son's daughters (L6.9(N:));
—two or more of X's full sisters (L6.10(2));
—and two or more or X's half sisters from the same father (L6.11(2)).

(5)   One-third of the estate is the obligatory share of:
—X's mother, under certain circumstances (L6.6(1));
—two or more of X's half brothers or sisters from the same mother (L6.20(2));
—and it may be the share of the grandfather when X's brothers exist (L6.14, second par.).

(6)   One-sixth of the estate is the obligatory share of seven types of heir:
—X's father (L6.5(1));
—X's grandfather (L6.13(N:) and L6.15(c));
—X's mother (L6.6(N:));
—X's grandmother (L6.18(1));
—one or more daughters of X's son when X's daughter also exists (L6.9);
—one or more of X's half sisters from the same

L6.21 فَنَلَخَّصَ مِنْ ذلكَ أنَّ النصفَ فرضُ خمسةٍ :

الــزوجُ في حالةٍ والبنتُ وبنتُ الابنِ والأختُ الشقيقةُ أوْ لأبٍ . والـربعُ فرضُ اثنين الــزوجُ في حالةٍ والزوجةُ في حالةٍ . والثمنَ فرضٌ للزوجةِ في حالةٍ . والثلثان فرضُ أربعةٍ البنتـانِ فصاعداً أوْ بنتا الابنِ فصاعـداً والأختان فصاعداً الشقيقتان أوْ للأبِ . والثلثُ فرضُ اثنين الأمُّ في حالـةٍ واثنانِ فأكثرَ مِنْ ولد الأمِّ وقدْ يُفْرَضُ للجدِّ مَعَ الإخـوةِ . والسدسُ فرضُ سبعةٍ الأبُ في حالـةٍ والجدُّ في حالـةٍ والأمُّ في حالةٍ والجدةُ في حالةٍ ولبنتِ الابنِ فصاعداً مَعَ بنتِ الصلبِ ولأختٍ أوْ أخـواتٍ لأبٍ مَعَ

father when X's sole full sister also exists
(L6.11(3));
—and X's sole half brother from the same mother
(L6.20(1)).

شقيقةٍ فردةٍ ولواحدٍ من الإخوةِ للأم.

L6.22   (N: A summary of the other heirs' shares:

(1) X's son is universal heir.

(2) X's son's son:
—is eliminated by X's son;
—and is universal heir in the absence of X's son.

(3) X's full brother:
—is eliminated by the existence of an inheriting
male descendant;
—is eliminated by X's father;
—and is universal heir in the absence of both an
inheriting male descendant and father.

(4) X's half brother by the same father:
—is eliminated by any inheriting male descendant;
—is eliminated by X's father;
—is eliminated by X's full brother;
—and is universal heir in the absence of all these.

(5) The son of X's full brother is the same as
X's full brother ((3) above), but eliminated by
him.

(6) The son of X's half brother by the same
father is the same as (5) above, but eliminated by
him.

(7) The brother of X's father:
—is eliminated by any of the following: X's father,
grandfather, brothers, and their sons;
—and is universal heir in the absence of all of
these.

(8) The son of the brother of X's father is the
same as (7) above, but eliminated by him.)

ح : وفــروض الــوارثيـــن   L6.22
الآخرين بشكل مختصر :
الابن :
- عصبة .
ابن الابن :
- يحرم مع الابن .
- عصبة مع عدم الابن .
الأخ الشقيق :
- يحرم بالفرع الوارث الذكر .
- يحرم بالأب .
- عصبة مع عدم فرع وارث ذكر وأب .
الأخ لأب :
- يحرم بالفرع الوارث الذكر .
- يحرم بالأب .
- يحرم بالشقيق .
- عصبة مع عدم المذكورين أعلاه .
ابن الأخ الشقيق :
- كالأخ الشقيق لكن يحرم معه .
ابن الأخ لأب :
- كابن الأخ الشقيق لكن يحرم معه .
العم :
- يحرم بالأب والجد والإخوة
وأبنائهم .
- عصبة مع عدم المذكورين .
ابن العم :
- كالعم لكن يحرم معه .)

*

L7.0 THOSE WHOSE SHARES ARE ELIMINATED BY OTHERS (HAJB)	**L7.0 الحجب**
L7.1 The share of X's half brother from the same mother is eliminated by the existence of four types of heir: —X's inheriting descendant (male or female); —the descendant (male or female) of X's son; —X's father; —or X's grandfather.	**L7.1** لا يَرِثُ الأخُ مِنَ الأُمِّ مَعَ أربعةٍ: الولدُ وولدُ الابنِ ذكراً كانَ أوْ أُنثَى والأبُ والجدُّ.
L7.2 The share of X's full brother is eliminated by three: —X's son; —X's son's son; —or X's father.	**L7.2** ولا يَرِثُ الأخُ الشقيقُ مَعَ ثلاثةٍ: الابنُ وابنُ الابنِ والأبُ.
L7.3 The share of X's half brother from the same father is eliminated by four: —X's son; —X's son's son; —X's father; —or X's full brother.	**L7.3** ولا يَرِثُ الأخُ مِنَ الأبِ مَعَ أربعةٍ: هؤلاءِ الثلاثةِ والأخُ الشقيقُ.
L7.4 The share of the son of X's son is eliminated by X's son, and likewise the son of the son of X's son, and on down: each is eliminated by the existence of a son closer to X (A: meaning fewer generations from X, even if the one who is closer is from a different one of X's sons).	**L7.4** ولا يَرِثُ ابنُ الابنِ فسافلاً مَعَ الابنِ ولا مَعَ ابنِ ابنٍ أقربَ منهُ.
L7.5 X's grandmother or great-grandmother does not inherit if X's mother exists.	**L7.5** ولا الجداتُ كلُّهُنَّ مِنْ أيِّ جهةٍ كُنَّ مَعَ الأُمِّ.
L7.6 Neither X's grandfather (A: i.e. father's father) nor grandmother or great-grandmother on the father's side may inherit when X's father exists.	**L7.6** ولا الجدُّ والجدةُ التي مِنْ جهةِ الأبِ مَعَ الأبِ.
L7.7 When X's daughters receive a full two-thirds of the estate (dis: L6.7(2)), then the daughters of X's son do not inherit, unless they are	**L7.7** وإذا اسْتَكْمَلَت البناتُ الثلثين لَمْ تَرِثْ بناتُ الابنِ إلّا أنْ يَكُونَ في

made co-universal heirs (def: L10.3) by the existence of a male who is at the same distance (A: number of generations) from X as they are, or by one who is farther from X than they. When they are co-universal heirs, the male receives the share of two females.

For example, if there are two daughters and a daughter of X's son, the two daughters take two-thirds and the son's daughter receives nothing. But if there also exists with her X's son's son, or son's son's son, then she (A: as co-universal heir (def: L10.3) with him) gets the rest of the estate with him, the male receiving the share of two females (N: and such a male is nicknamed her *blessed brother* (akh mubarak)).

L7.8   Similarly, when X's full sisters receive two-thirds of the estate (dis: L6.10(2)), then X's half sisters from the same father do not inherit, unless they have a brother to make them co-universal heirs, the male receiving the share of two females.

L7.9   Someone who does not inherit to begin with (N: due to the existence of a preventive (def: L5)) cannot eliminate the share of anyone (A: such a person being as if nonexistent in figuring the estate division).

L7.10   Someone who may inherit, but whose share has been eliminated by another, can not eliminate the share of anyone, although such a person's existence may diminish the share of someone, as when there exist X's half brothers from the same mother, and X's father and mother. In such a case, the half brothers do not inherit (dis: L6.20(N:)), but their existence diminishes the mother's share from a third to a sixth (dis: L6.6(2)).

درجتِهِنَّ أَوْ أَسْفَلَ مِنْهُنَّ ذكرٌ يُعَصِّبُهُنَّ للذكرِ مثلُ حظِّ الأنثيينِ . مثالُهُ بنتانِ وبنتُ ابنٍ : للبنتينِ الثلثانِ ولا شيءَ لبنتِ الابنِ . فلوْ كانَ مَعَهَا ابنُ ابنٍ أو ابنُ ابنِ ابنٍ كانَ الباقي لَهَا ولَهُ ، للذكرِ مثلُ حظّ الأنثيينِ .

L7.8   وإذا اسْتَكْمَلَتِ الأخـواتُ الشقيقـاتُ الثلثينِ لمْ تَرثِ الأخـواتُ مِنَ الأبِ إلّا أنْ يَكـونَ مَعَـهُـنُّ أخٌ لهـنَّ فيُعَصِّبُهُنَّ للذكرِ مثلُ حظِّ الأنثيينِ .

L7.9   ومَنْ لا يَرثُ أصلًا لا يَحْجُبُ أحداً .

L7.10   ومَنْ يَرثُ ولكنـهُ محجـوبٌ لا يَحْجُبُ أيضـاً حَجْبَ حرمـانٍ لكنهُ قَدْ يَحْجُبُ حجبَ تنقيص مثلَ الإخوةِ مِنَ الأمِّ مَعَ الأبِ والأمِّ لا يَرثُونَ ويَحْجُبُونَ الأمَّ مِنَ الثلثِ إلى السدسِ .

*

L8.0 ADJUSTMENT WHEN THE SHARES EXCEED THE TOTAL ESTATE ('AWL)

L8.0 العول

L8.1 (A: *Adjustment* ('awl) is used in cases where the estate is not enough to give everyone their full shares, and proportionately distributes the deficit to all the heirs in an equitable way.)

L8.2 Whenever the shares deserved by heirs exceed the number of available shares, the number of shares is additively increased to the number needed.

An example is the case (al-mubahala) in which there are X's husband, mother, and full sister:

		shares: 6
husband	1/2 (dis: L6.3(1))	3
sister	1/2 (dis: L6.10(1))	3

but at this point, the estate has been used up despite the fact that the mother deserves her share of one-third, and no one can eliminate it:

mother	1/3 (dis: L6.6(1))	2

so we redivide the estate by adding the mother's portion (n: two shares) as an adjustment:

(6 + 2 =)	shares: 8
husband	3
sister	3
mother	2

and this is the actual division. (n: L6.17 furnishes another example of adjustment.)

L8.2 ومـتـى زادَتِ الفـروضُ على السهام أُعيلَتْ بالجـزء الزائد مثلُ مسألة المبـاهلةِ وهيَ زوجٌ وأمُ وأختٌ شقيقـةٌ فللزوج النصفُ وللأخـتِ النـصفُ استُغـرِقَ المالُ والأمُ لا تُحْجَبُ فيُفْـرَضُ لَهَا الثلثُ فتُعَـالُ بفرض الأمِّ فَتَنقَسِمُ مِنْ ثمانيةٍ للزوج ثلاثةٌ وللأختِ ثلاثةٌ وللأمِّ اثنانِ.

*

L9.0 REDISTRIBUTION WHEN THE SHARES ARE LESS THAN THE ESTATE (RADD)

(n: This section has been moved here from its original place after L10.7 below.)

L9.0 الرد

(ت: قد نُقل هذا الباب هنا من مكانه الأصلي بعـد ترتيب عصبـات الـولاء في باب العصبات).

L9.1　If X has no (A: universal heir) relatives (def: L10.5), then (A: the remainder of) his estate goes to the Muslim common fund (bayt al-mal) as an inheritance to the Muslims, provided the Islamic ruler is just.

If the Islamic ruler is not just (A: or not existent), then it (A: the excess) is *redistributed* among the inheriting heirs in proportion to their relative shares, except for X's husband or wife, who may not receive any of the redistributed amount.

L9.1　فإذا لمْ يَكُـنْ للمـيتِ أقـاربُ [ولا ولاءَ عليْهِ] انْتَقَلَ مالُهُ إلى بيتِ المالِ إرثاً للمسلمينَ إنْ كَانَ السلطانُ عادلاً . فإنْ لمْ يَكُـنْ عادلاً رُدَّ على ذَوي الفـروضِ منْ غيـرِ الـزوجينِ على قدرِ فروضِهِمْ [إنْ كَانَ ثَمَّ ذُو فرضٍ] .

L9.2　(N: Three illustrations of redistribution follow:

(1) X's sister and grandmother:

		shares:	6
sister	1/2 (dis: L6.10(1))		3
grandmother	1/6 (dis: L6.18(1))		1

But at this point, the obligatory shares are less than the estate, so we redistribute the excess estate in proportion to the heirs' respective shares by reducing the shares of the case to four, which is the number of the existing heirs' shares:

(3 + 1 =)	shares:	4
sister		3
grandmother		1

and this is the solution, and is how we redistribute in cases that require it, when there is neither a husband nor wife among the heirs. As for when there is a husband or wife, the examples below furnish illustrations of the division.

(2) X's wife, half brother from the same mother, and grandmother:

		shares:	12
wife	1/4 (dis: L6.4(1))		3
half brother	1/6 (dis: L6.20(1))		2
grandmother	1/6 (dis: L6.18(1))		2

But here, the obligatory shares are still less than the estate, in which there are five remaining shares:

excess	5

So, excluding the wife as mentioned above (L9.1 (end)), we divide the excess between the half brother and grandmother in proportion to their respective shares, namely two-to-two, which means a half-and-half division of the excess five shares. For convenient division of these five shares, we first multiply the case's total shares by two:

(12 × 2 =)	shares:	24
wife		6
half brother		4
grandmother		4
excess		10

and then we divide the ten excess shares between the half brother and grand-mother, while the wife gets only her original share (dis: L9.1 (end)):

		shares:	24
wife			6
half brother	(5 + 4 =)		9
grandmother	(5 + 4 =)		9

and this is the solution.

(3) X's wife, mother, and half brother from the same mother:

		shares:	12
wife	1/4 (dis: L6.4(1))		3
mother	1/3 (dis: L6.6(1))		4
half brother	1/6 (dis: L6.20(1))		2

But the obligatory shares are still less than the estate, in which there are three remaining shares:

excess	3

So, excluding the wife, as before, we divide the excess between the mother and half brother in proportion to their respective shares, namely four-to-two, which means a two-to-one division of the three excess shares:

		shares:	12
wife			3
mother	(2 + 4 =)		6
half brother	(1 + 2 =)		3

and this is the solution.)

*

L10.0 UNIVERSAL HEIR ('ASABA)

العصبات L10.0

L10.1 (A: A universal heir ('asaba) is someone who takes the remaining estate, if any, after heirs deserving obligatory shares have taken them. When there are no such heirs, the universal heir takes all. There are three types of universal heir:

(1) universal heir by oneself ('asaba bi nafsihi);

(2) co-universal heir ('asaba bi ghayrihi);

(3) and universal heir through the existence of another ('asaba ma'a ghayrihi).)

(n: The following three definitional entries have been added to this section by the translator.)

UNIVERSAL HEIR BY ONESELF

العصبة بنفسه

L10.2 (Hasanayn Muhammad Makhluf:) The *universal heir by oneself* is X's male relative who is not related to X through a female, whether this be because:

(1) there is no one between him and X, as is the case with X's father or son;

(2) or whether because there is someone between him and X, but not a female, such as X's grandfather (the father of X's father), X's son's son, X's full brother, or X's half brother from the same father.

L10.2 (حسنين محمد مخلوف:)
العـاصب بنفسه : هو القريب الذكر الذي
لا يدخل في نسبته إلى الميت أنثى بأن لم
يكن بينه وبين الميت واسطة أصلاً كالأب
والابن ، أو كانت بينهمـا واسطـة غير أنثى
كالجد أبي الأب وابن الابن والأخ لأبوين
أو لأب .

CO-UNIVERSAL HEIR

العصبة بغيره

L10.3 The *co-universal heir* is any female deserving an obligatory share who requires someone else in order to become a universal heir, and with whom she participates in this universal share.

It is a class confined to four types of women, those whose share if alone is one-half, and if there are more than one is two-thirds. They are:

(1) X's daughter;

(2) X's son's daughter;

(3) X's full sister;

(4) and X's half sister from the same father.

Whenever a male exists with one of these four who

L10.3 العصبة بغيره : كل أنثى
صاحبة فرض احتاجت في عصوبتها إلى
الغير وشــاركتـه في تلك العصوبـة .
وتنحصر في أربع من النساء فرضهن
النصف للواحدة والثلثان للأكثر من
الواحدة وهن :
ـ البنت الصلبية .
ـ وبنت الابن .
ـ والأخت الشقيقة .
ـ والأخت لأب .
ـ فإذا وُجـد مع كل واحـدة منـهــن

is universal heir by himself (def: L10.2), of the same generation as her and of the same strength (N: i.e. both are full or half siblings), she becomes co-universal heir with him and inherits by the universal share, not her obligatory share. They divide the universal share so the male receives the portion of two females.

عاصب بنفسه في درجتها وقوتها صارت عصبـة به فتـرث معـه بالـتـعصيب لا بالفرض، ويرثان معاً للذكر مثل حظ الأنثيين.

UNIVERSAL HEIR THROUGH THE EXISTENCE OF ANOTHER

العصبة مع غيره

L10.4   The *universal heir through the existence of another* is any female deserving an obligatory share who requires someone else to become a universal heir, but with whom she does not share this universal share.

L10.4   الـعصبـة مع غيــره كل أنثى صاحبة فرض احتاجت في عصوبتها إلى الغير ولم يشاركها ذلك الغير في العصوبة.

These are only two people from among those who deserve obligatory shares:

وهما اثنتان فقط من أصحاب الفروض:

(1) X's full sister;

- الأخت الشقيقة.

(2) and X's half sister from the same father;

- والأخت لأب.

provided that X's brother, who would form a co-universal heir (def: L10.3) with them (A: in which case they would not be a *universal heir through another*) does not exist, and provided that either of the above two females exists with X's daughter(s) or son's daughter(s), and on down (A: these being the someone else needed to make them a universal heir through another) (*al-Mawarith fi al-shari'a al-Islamiyya* (y80), 99, 102, 103).

إذا لم يكن مع الـواحـدة منهمـا أخ معصّب، ووُجـدت مع بنت صلبيـة أو أكثـر، أو بنت ابن وإن نزل [محـرّر من كتاب المواريث في الشريعة الإسلامية].

L10.5   The *universal heir* is a person who takes the whole estate if there is no other heir, or takes any of it that is in excess of the obligatory portions which are given to heirs, when they also exist. If there is nothing in excess of the heirs' obligatory shares, then the universal heir does not receive anything.

L10.5   والعصبـة مَن يَأْخُـذُ جميـعَ المال إذَا انْفَـرَدَ أوْ ما يَفْضُلُ عنْ صاحب الفرض إذا اجْتَمَعَ مَعَهُ. فإنْ لمْ يَفْضُلْ عنْ صاحب الفرضِ شيءٌ سَقَطَتِ العصباتُ.

L10.6   Their order (A: these being the *universal heirs by themselves* (def: L10.2)) in closeness to X (A: such that the existence of someone at the first of the list eliminates the universal heirship of anyone following him) is:

L10.6   وأقـربُهُمُ الابنُ ثُمَّ ابنُ الابن

(1) X's son;

(2) X's son's son;

(3) X's son's son's son, and on down, no matter how many generations;

(4) X's father;

(5) X's father's father;

(6) X's father's father's father, and on up, no matter how many generations;

(7) X's full brother;

(8) X's half brother from the same father;

(9) the son of X's full brother;

(10) the son of X's half brother from the same father;

(11) the brother of X's father;

(12) the son of the brother of X's father, this son's son, and on down;

(13) the brother of X's father's father;

(14) and then (13)'s son, this son's son, and on down.

وإنْ سَفَـلَ ثمَّ الأبُ ثمَّ الـجـدُّ وإنْ عَلا والأخُ للأبـويـن ثمَّ للأب ثمَّ ابـنُ الأخ للأبـويـن ثمَّ ابنُ الأخ للأب ثمَّ العمُّ ثمَّ ابنُهُ وإنْ سَفَلَ ثمَّ عمُّ الأب ثمَّ ابنُهُ وهكذا.

L10.7 [فإنْ لمْ يكُنْ لَهُ عصباتُ نسب فعصباتُ الولاء . فمَنْ عَتَقَ عليْهِ عبدٌ إمّا بإعتاقٍ أوْ تدبيرٍ أو كتابةٍ أو استيلادٍ أوْ غير ذلك فولاؤُهُ لهُ . فإذَا ماتَ هذَا العتيقُ وليْسَ لهُ وارثٌ ذُو فرضٍ ولا عصبةٌ وَرِثَهُ المُعْتِقُ بالولاءِ . فإنْ كانَ المعتِقُ ميتاً انْتَقَلَ الولاءُ إلى عصباتِهِ دونَ سائرِ الورثةِ يُقَدَّمُ الأقرَبُ فالأقربُ على الترتيبِ المتقدِّم إلاّ أنَّ الأخَ يُشارِكَ الجدَّ وهنا الأخُ مقدَّمٌ على الجدِّ . فإنْ لمْ يكُنْ للمعتِقِ عصبةُ نسب انْتَقَلَ إلى مُعْتِقِ المعتِقِ ثمَّ إلى عصبتِهِ وللمعتِقِ أيضاً الولاءُ على أولادِ العتيقِ فيُقَدَّمُ معتِقُ الأب على معتِقِ الأمّ . فلوْ تزَوَّجَ عبدٌ بمعتقةٍ فأَتَتْ بولدٍ فولاؤُهُ لمعتِقِ الأمّ، فلوْ عَتَقَ أبوهُ بعدَ ذلك انْجَرَّ الولاءُ مِنْ معتِقِ الأمّ إلى معتِقِ الأب . ولا تَرِثُ المرأةُ بالولاءِ إلاّ مِنْ عتيقِها وأولادِه وعتقائِه].

L10.8 When there is no universal heir, and no heir inheriting an obligatory portion that the excess estate could be redistributed to (dis: L9.1), then the estate is divided between the extended family members (def: L4.5) such that each of them

L10.8 وإلا [(ت): أي وإن لم يكـن للميت صاحبُ فرضٍ ولا أقاربُ عصبةٍ)] فيُصرَفُ إلى ذوي الأرحامِ فيُقام كلُ واحدٍ

takes the place of the person through whom they are related to X. For example:

(1) X's daughter's child takes the share of X's daughter;

(2) X's sister's child takes the share of X's sister;

(3) X's brothers' daughters take the share of the brothers;

(4) the daughters of X's father's brother take the latter's share;

(5) X's mother's father takes her share;

(6) X's mother's brother or sister takes her share;

(7) and X's father's half brother or sister from the same mother takes the father's share.

منهُمْ مقـامَ مَنْ يُدلي به فَيُجْعَــلُ ولــدُ البنــاتِ والأخــواتِ كأمهــاتِهم وبنــاتُ الإخــوة والأعمــام كآبــائِهم وأبــو الأمّ والــخــال والخــالــةِ كالأمّ، والعمُّ للأمّ والعمةُ كالأبِ.

L10.9 No universal heir may inherit (A: a universal share) when there is a universal heir who is closer to X than he is.

L10.9 ولا يَرِثُ أحدٌ بالتعصيب وثَمَّ أقربُ منهُ.

L10.10 No one constitutes a co-universal heir (def: L10.3) with his sister except:

(1) X's son (N: with X's daughter);

(2) X's son's son (N: with X's son's daughter);

(3) and X's brother (A: with X's sister).

Each of them constitutes a co-universal heir with his sister, the male receiving the portion of two females.

L10.10 ولا يُعَصِّبُ أحــدٌ أختَــهُ إلّا الابنُ وابنُ الابن والأخُ فإنهُمْ يُعَصِّبُــونَ أخواتِهم للذكر مثلُ حظّ الأنثيين.

L10.11 (N: In addition to being co-universal heir with X's son's daughter ((2) above),) X's son's son (N: or son's son's son, and on down) is (n: also) co-universal heir with the daughters of his father's brother who are of the same generation as he, and

L10.11 ويُعَصِّبُ ابنُ الابن مَنْ يُحَاذِيه

those of his father's sisters and the daughters of his father's father's brother(s) who are above him (N: of a closer generation to X), provided they (A: those closer to X than he) have no obligatory shares coming. (N: Because if they do, then they take their share and are not co-universal heirs with him. This may be illustrated by the following example:

بِنْ بناتِ عمّهِ وَيُعَصِّبُ مَنْ فوقَهُ من عماتِه وبناتِ عمِّ أبيه إذا لـم يَكُنْ لَهُنَّ فرضٌ.

(1) X's husband, daughter, son's daughter, son's son's daughter, and son's son's son:

		shares:	12
husband	1/4 (dis: L6.3(2))		3
daughter	1/2 (dis: L6.7(1))		6
son's daughter	1/6 (dis: L6.9)		2
son's son's daughter			
son's son's son	universal		1

But if there were two of X's daughters in the above case, we would have to divide the estate as follows:

		shares:	12
husband			3
2 daughters	2/3 (dis: L6.7(2))		8

Here, the son's daughter does not have an obligatory share coming, since the two daughters have taken the full two-thirds, and so the son's daughter (dis: text above) is co-universal heir with the son's son's daughter and son's son's son:

son's daughter			
son's son's daughter	universal		1
son's son's son			

L10.12 A person who is a universal heir does not participate in the share of someone who has an obligatory share coming, except in the following case (al-musharraka):

L10.12 ولا يُشـاركُ عاصبٌ ذا فرضٍ إلَّا الـمـشـــركَـة وهِي : زوجٌ وأُمّ أوْجدةٌ واثنانِ [فأكثرُ] مِنَ الإخوة للأُمّ وأخٌ شقيقٌ [فأكـثـرُ ،] للزوج الـنـصـفُ وللأُمِّ [أوِ الجـدةِ] السـدسُ وللإخـوة للأُمّ الثلُثُ

Given X's husband, mother (or grandmother, for the result is the same), two half brothers from the same mother, and a full brother:

		shares:	6
husband	1/2 (dis: L6.3(1))		3
mother	1/6 (dis: L6.6(2))		1
2 half brothers	1/3 (dis: L6.20(2))		2

in which case the estate has been used up and nothing remains for the brother:

full brother	universal	0

يشاركُهُمْ فيه الشقيقُ.

(N: But the full brother is closer to X than the half brothers, and should not be eliminated by their share, so an exception is made and the half brothers and full brother are made co-universal heirs:)

	shares:	6
husband		3
mother		1

2 half brothers		
full brother	universal	2

(N: It is important to remember in such cases that the universal share is divided so the males and females receive *equal* shares (dis: L6.20(2)).)

L10.13 When a person both deserves an obligatory share and is a universal heir, then he inherits both of these.

An example is when the son of X's father's brother (A: who is universal heir (dis: L6.22(8))) is also X's husband (A: deserving a husband's share (dis: L6.3)); or when the son of X's father's brother is also X's half brother from the same mother.

L10.13 ومَتَى وُجِدَ في شخصٍ جهتا فرضٍ وتعصيب وَرِثَ بهِمَا كابنِ عمٍّ هو زوجُ أو ابنِ عمٍّ هوَ أخٌ لأُمٍّ.

*

BOOK M

MARRIAGE

CONTENTS:

---

m1.0   WHO SHOULD MARRY

(O: The legal basis for marriage, prior to scholarly consensus (ijma‘), is such Koranic

m1.0 مَنْ يُنْدَبُ لَهُ النِّكَاحُ

(والأصل فيه قبل الإجماع آيات كقوله

verses as,

"Marry such women as seem good to you"
(Koran 4:3),

and hadiths such as,

"Marry one another, that you may increase,"

which was related by Shafi'i.)

m1.1   A man who needs to marry (O: because of
desire for sexual intercourse) and has enough
money (O: for the brides's marriage payment
(mahr, def: m8), for clothing for the season of the
year in which he marries, and the expenditures of
one day) is recommended to do so (O: to protect
his religion, no matter whether he is occupied with
religious devotions or not). One who needs to
marry but does not have enough to pay for these
expenses is recommended not to marry, but rather
to suppress his sexual desire by fasting (O: and if
it is not suppressed by fasting, then he should
marry, borrowing the money to pay the bride's
marriage payment if she will not accept his owing
it to her).

m1.2   It is offensive for someone who does not
need marriage (O: being undesirous of it because
of a physical defect or other reason) to marry
when he does not have enough money to cover the
expenses. Marriage is not offensive for a man who
has enough money, even when there is something
that might prevent him from doing so such as old
age or a chronic illness, though it is superior for
him to devote himself to worship instead. If he
does not devote himself to worship (O: being
occupied with enjoyments and not thinking of
worship at all) then marriage is better (O: since
someone whose lack of sexual desire is not due to
a physical defect may later have such desire, as
opposed to someone whose lack of desire is
because of such a defect, to whom this will not
happen).

m1.3   As for a woman, if she needs to marry, it is
recommended for her to do so, though if she does

تعـالى : ﴿فَـانْكِحُـوا مَا طَابَ لَكُمْ مِنَ
النِّسَاءِ﴾ [النساء : ٣]، وأخبار كخبر :
«تناكحوا تكثروا» رواه الشافعي) .

m1.1   مَنِ احْتَاجَ إلى النكاحِ (بتوقانه
للوطء) مِنَ الـرجالِ ووَجَدَ أهبةً (من مهر
وكسوة فصل التمكين ونفقة يومه) نُدِبَ لَهُ
(أي [لمن احتـاجَ] تحصيناً لدينه سواء
كان مشتغلاً بالعبادة أم لا) .
ومَنِ احْتَاجَ وفَقَدَ الأهبةَ نُدِبَ تركُهُ،
ويَكْسِـرُ شهوتَهُ بالصوم (فإن لم ينكسر
بالصوم يتزوج ويكلف اقتراض المهر إن
لم ترض بذمته) .

m1.2   ومَنْ لَمْ يَحْتَـجْ إلى النكـاحِ
(بأن كان غيـر تائق إليه لعلة أو غيرهـا)
وفَقَدَ الأهبةَ كُرِهَ لَهُ .
ومَنْ وَجَدَهـا (أي الأهبة) ووُجِدَ مانعٌ
به مِنْ هرمٍ ومرضٍ دائمٍ لَمْ يُكْـرَهْ لكنِ
الاشتغالُ بالعبادة أفضلُ .
فإنْ لَمْ يَتَعَبَّدْ (بأن كان مشتـغـلاً
باللذات ولم يلتفت إلى العبـادة أصـلاً)
فالنكـاحُ أفضلُ (لأن غير التائق لا لعلة
ربما حصل له التوقان بعد ذلك، بخلاف
غير التائق لعلة لا يحصل له ذلك) .

m1.3   وأمَّـا المـرأةُ فإنِ احْتَاجَتْ إلى
النكاحِ نُدِبَ لَهَا . وإلَّا (بأن كانت نفسها

not, (O: not feeling any sexual desire within herself, and she is engaged in worship,) then it is offensive for her to do so. (N: Though such a woman needs a husband or unmarriageable relative to travel and so forth (dis: m10.3).)

غير تائقة وهي مشتغلة بالعبادة) فَيُكْرَهُ.

DESIRABLE CHARACTERISTICS IN A BRIDE

الصفات المحمودة شرعاً في المخطوبة

m1.4   It is recommended for a man to marry a virgin (O: unless there is a reason not to, such as sexual incapacity or needing someone to take care of his children) (A: though it is permissible to marry a nonvirgin even if she has not previously married (dis: p12.1(3(n:)))) who is fertile (O: which in a virgin is inferable from her relatives), attractive, intelligent, religious, of a good family, and not a close relative. (O: In *Sharh al-Minhaj*, Ibn Hajar notes that when one must choose between the above characteristics, the order of preference should be:

m1.4   وَيُنْدَبُ أَنْ يَتَزَوَّجَ بِكْرٍ (إن لم يقم به عذر [كضعف الآلة أو] احتيـاجـه لمن يقـوم على عياله) ولودٍ (ويعرف كون البكـر ولـوداً بأقـاربهـا) جميلةٍ عاقلةٍ دَيِّنَةٍ نسيبةٍ (أي طيبة النسب) لَيْسَتْ ذاتَ قرابةٍ قريبـةٍ (قـال الشيـخ ابن حجر في شرح المنهـاج ولو تعارضت عليه تلك الصفات [فالذي يظهر أنه] تقدم ذات الدين مطلقاً ثم العقـل وحسن الخلق ثم السـولادة ثم النـسـب ثم البكـارة ثم الجمـال ثم ما المصلحة فيه).

(1) religiousness, which takes precedence over anything else;

(2) intelligence;

(3) a good character and disposition;

(4) fertility;

(5) a good family;

(6) virginity;

(7) beauty;

(8) and then that which fulfills some other relevant interest.)

*

m2.0   ENGAGEMENT AND LOOKING AT THE OPPOSITE SEX

m2.0   آداب الـخطبـة وأحكام النظر إلى غير محرم

SUNNAS OF ENGAGEMENT

مندوبات تتعلق بالنكاح

m2.1   (O: It is recommended for a guardian to offer his marriageable female charges in marriage to righteous men. It is sunna:

(1) to intend by one's marriage to fulfill the sunna and protect one's religion, since one is only rewarded for it if one intends some form of obedience to Allah, such as remaining chaste or having a pious son;

(2) for the marriage contract to be made in a mosque;

(3) and for it to take place on Friday, at the first of the day, and in the month of Shawwal.)

LOOKING AT ONE'S PROSPECTIVE BRIDE

m2.2   The sunna when one wants to marry a woman is to look at her face and hands (O: as the face indicates her beauty, and the hands her robustness of body. Tirmidhi reports from al-Mughira that when he got engaged to a woman, the Prophet (Allah bless him and give him peace) said,

"Look at her, for it is likelier to last between you,"

meaning that love is likelier to last, and tenderness) before getting engaged to her, even if the woman does not give her permission to do so (O: since the Lawgiver's permission is sufficient). Such a person is entitled to repeat looking at her (A: as many times as he wishes) (O: when he needs to make sure of how she looks, so he does not come to have regrets after getting married. And she is entitled to do the same) but he may not look at other than her face and hands. (O: If unable to go see her, he should send a reliable woman to go see her for him, as such a woman would be likely to notice more than he, and she may describe her to him, this being an exception to the unlawfulness of describing a woman to a man who is not one of her unmarriageable kin.)

م2.1   (يـنـدب للولي عرض موليتـه على ذوي الـصـلاح. ويـسـن أن يـنـوي بالنكـاح السنة وصـون دينه وإنما يثاب عليـه إن قصـد به طاعة من نحو عفة وولد صالح وأن يكون العقد في المسجد ويوم الجمعة وأول النهار وفي شوال).

حكم النظر إلى المخطوبة

م2.2   فإذا عَزَمَ على نكـاح امـرأةٍ فالسنةُ أنْ يَنْظُرَ إلى وجهها وكَفَّيْهَا (لأن الـوجـه يدل على الجمـال واليـدين على خصب البدن وروى الترمذي عن المغيرة أنه خطب امرأة فقال له النبي ﷺ: «انظر إليها فإنه أحرى أن يؤدم بينكما» أي تدوم بينكم المودة والألفة) قبلَ أنْ يَخْطِبَهَا وإنْ لمْ تأْذَنْ في ذلـكَ (اكتفـاء بإذن الشـارع) ولـهُ تكـريـرُ النظـرِ (إليها عند حاجته إليه ليتبين هيئة منظوره فلا يندم بعد نكاحه ولهـا مثله) ولا يَنْظُرُ غيرَ الوجهِ والكفين. (وإن لم يتيسر له النظر فيبعث امرأة أمينة تنظرها له وهي ترى منها أكثر مما يرى هو ولهـا أن تصفهـا له ويكـون مستثنى من النهي عن وصف الأجنبية للأجنبي).

أحكام نظر الرجال إلى النساء

m2.3   It is unlawful for a man to look at a woman who is not his wife or one of his unmarriageable kin (def: m6.1) (O: there being no difference in this between the face and hands or some other part of a woman (N: if it is uncovered), though *part* excludes her voice, which is not unlawful to listen to as long as temptation is unlikely. Allah Most High says,

"Tell believers to lower their gaze" (Koran 24:30).

A majority of scholars (n: with the exception of some Hanafis, as at m2.8 below) have been recorded as holding that it is unlawful for women to leave the house with faces unveiled, whether or not there is likelihood of temptation. When there *is* likelihood of temptation, scholars unanimously concur that it is unlawful, *temptation* meaning anything that leads to sexual intercourse or its usual preliminaries. As for when there is real need (dis: m2.11), looking is not unlawful, provided temptation is unlikely).
(A: Being alone with a woman who is not one's wife or unmarriageable kin is absolutely unlawful, though if there are two women and a man, the man and the woman are no longer considered *alone*.)

m2.4   A man may look at his wife (N: or vice versa) including her nakedness (def: f5.3), though it is offensive for either husband or wife to look at the other's genitals.

m2.5   A man may look at his unmarriageable female relatives (def: m6.1), and a woman look at her unmarriageable male relatives (m6.2), viewing any part of the body (N: that shows e.g. while they are working) except what is between the navel and knees.

m2.6   As for a woman looking at (O: a man) other than her husband or unmarriageable male

m2.3   ويَحْرُمُ أَنْ يَنْظُرَ الرجلُ إلى شيءٍ من الأجنبيـة (ولا فرق في الشيء المـذكـور بين الـوجـه والكفين أو غيرهما [كـالشعـر] [والمراد بالشيء ما كان جزءاً منها] وليس الصوت منها فلا يحرم سماعه ما لم يخف منه فتنة . قال تعـالى : ﴿قُلْ لِلْمُؤْمِنِينَ يَغُضُّوا مِنْ أَبْصَارِهِمْ﴾ وقد نقل الاتفـاق على منـع النسـاء من الخروج سافرات الوجوه ولا فرق بين خوف الفتنة وعدمها وهـو عنـد خوفهـا مجمـع عليه والمـراد من خوف الفتنـة ما يدعـو إلى الجماع ومقـدمـاتهـا وأما مع الحاجة فلا يحرم إن لم يخف فتنة) [حرةً كَانَتْ أَوْ أَمَّةً أو الأمرد الحسن بلا شهوة مَعَ أمن الفتنة وقيـلَ يَجُـوزُ أَنْ يَنْظُرَ منَ الأمـةِ مَا عَدَا عورتَهَا عندَ الأمن].

m2.4   ويَنْظُرُ إلى زوجتـه [وأَمتِه] حَتَّى العـورة لكنْ يُكْـرَهُ نظـرُ كلّ منَ الزوجين إلى فرج الآخر.

m2.5   ويَنْظُرُ [العبـد إلى سيـدتِه والممسـوح إلى الأجنبية و] الـرجلَ إلى محارمه (ح : إلى ما يبـدو عنـد المهنـة) والمـرأة إلى محـرمهـا فيمـا عَدَا ما بين السرة والركبة.

m2.6   وأمّـا نظرُهَا إلى (رجل) غير زوجهـا ومحرمهـا فحرامٌ كنظـرِه إليهـا

relatives, it is unlawful, just as a man's looking at her is.

[وقيل يَحلُّ أنْ تَنْظُرَ منهُ ما عَدا عورتَهُ عند الأمن].

m2.7   It is unlawful for a woman to show any part of her body to an adolescent boy or a non-Muslim woman (n: unless the latter is her kinswoman (def: m6.1(1–12)), in which case it is permissible (*Mughni al-muhtaj ila ma'rifa ma'ani alfaz al-Minhaj* (y73), 3.132)).

m2.7   ويَحْرُمُ عليْها كَشفُ شيء من بدنِها لمراهقٍ أو لامرأةٍ كافرةٍ [فَلْيَحْذَر النساءُ في الحماماتِ من ذلكَ].

m2.8   (n: The following rulings from the Hanafi school have been added here as a dispensation (dis: c6.3).)
(Ahmad Quduri:)

(1)   It is not permissible for a man to look at a woman who is not his wife or unmarriageable relative except for her face and hands ((Maydani:) because of the necessity of her need to deal with men in giving and taking and the like). If a man is not safe from lust, he may not look at her face except when it is demanded by necessity.

(2)   A man may look at the whole body of another man except for what is between the navel and (A: including) the knees (A: as the knees are considered nakedness by Hanafis, though not by Shafi'is).

(3)   A woman may look at the parts of a man that another man is permitted to look at.

(4)   A woman may look at the parts of another woman that a man is permitted to look at of another man.

(*al-Lubab fi sharh al-Kitab* (y88), 4.162–63)

m2.8   (ت: قد نقل المترجم الأحكام التالية هنا من المذهب الحنفي على سبيل الرخصة).
(أحمد القدوري:)

ـ لا يَجُوزُ أنْ يَنْظُرَ الرجلُ من الأجنبية إلّا إلى وجهها وكَفَّيْها (ضرورةَ احتياجها إلى المعاملة مع الرجال أخذاً وإعطاءً وغيرِ ذلك). وإنْ كانَ لا يأمَنُ الشهوةَ لا يَنْظُرُ إلى وجهها إلّا لحاجةٍ [(ضرورية)].

ـ ويَنْظُرُ الرجلُ من الرجل إلى جميع بدنِهِ إلّا ما بينَ سُرَّتهِ إلى ركبتهِ.

ـ ويَجُوزُ للمرأةِ أنْ تَنْظُرَ من الرجل إلى ما يَنْظُرُ الرجلُ إليه منهُ.

ـ وتَنْظُرُ المرأةُ من المرأةِ ما يَجُوزُ للرجل أنْ يَنْظُرَ إليه من الرجل.

[محرّر من اللباب في شرح الكتاب: ١٦٢/٤ - ١٦٣].

m2.9   Whenever looking is unlawful, so is touching (O: *whenever* meaning the *part;* i.e. whatever is unlawful to look at is also unlawful to touch). (N: And any permissible looking that leads to temptation is unlawful.) (A: Ordinary people sometimes mistakenly assume that the Hanafi position that touching a woman does not nullify one's ablution (wudu) means they permit men shaking

m2.9   ومَتَى (والمعنى على المكان أي في كل جزء حرم نظرُه حرم مسُّه) حُرُمَ النظرُ حُرُمَ اللمسُ (ح: وكل نظر مباح أدى إلى فتنةٍ يمنعُ). (ع: قد يتوهم العوام بأن عدم نقض الوضوء بلمس المرأة عند الحنفية يعني أنهم يجيزون

hands with women who are not wives or unmarriageable relatives, something which is unlawful, and which neither the Hanafi school nor any other holds to be permissible.)

للرجـل مصافحـة غير محارمـه من النسـاء، وهي حرام عندهم وعند غيرهم من المذاهب).

DOCTORS TREATING PATIENTS OF THE OPPOSITE SEX

أحكام معالجة الرجل والمرأة

m2.10 Both (O: looking and touching) are permissible for medicinal bloodletting, cupping, and medical treatment (N: when there is real need. A Muslim woman needing medical attention must be treated by a Muslim woman doctor, or if there is none, then by a non-Muslim woman doctor. If there is none, then a male Muslim doctor may treat her, while if none of the above are available, then a male non-Muslim doctor. If the doctor is of the opposite sex, her husband or an unmarriageable male relative (def: m6.2) must be present. It is obligatory to observe this order in selecting a doctor). (A: The same rules apply to Muslim men with regard to having a doctor of the same sex and religion: the same sex takes precedence over the same religion.)

(O: Necessary treatment of her face or hands permits looking at either. As for other parts of the body, the criterion for permissibility is the severity of the need for treatment, meaning that there must be an ailment as severe as those permitting dry ablution (def: e12.9), and if the part concerned is the genitals, the need must be even more acute (N: though it includes gynecological examinations for women with fertility problems, which are permissible).

m2.10 وَيُبَاحَانِ (أي النظر والمس) لفصدٍ وحجامةٍ ومداواةٍ. (ح: أي: عنـد الحـاجـة المـؤكـدة. والمسلمـة المحتـاجـة إلى معـالجة طبية تتعـالـج وجوبـاً عنـد طبيبـة مسلمة، فإن فُقـدت فطبيبـة كافرة، فإن فقدت فطبيب مسلم، فإن فُقـدوا جميعـاً فطبيب كافـر. وإن تعين طبيب ذكـر فلا بد من حضـور زوجهـا أو محرمهـا الذكر. ومراعاة هذا الترتيب واجب). (ع: والترتيب المذكور ينطبق على الـرجـل المسلم المحتاج إلى معـالجة، بحيث وحدة الجنس تقدم على وحدة الأديان).

(والمعـالجة في الوجه والكفين يكفي فيهما الحاجة المحجوزة للنظر ويعتبر في غيـرهمـا تأكـدها وهو ما يبيح التيمم وفي الفرج مزيد تأكدها).

PERMISSIBLE LOOKING AT A MARRIAGEABLE MEMBER OF THE OPPOSITE SEX

ما يبيح النظر إلى غير المحارم

m2.11 Looking at a woman is permissible for testimony in court, for commercial dealings (O: with a marriageable man, or noncommercial dealings, as when he wishes to marry her), and so forth (O: such as obligatory or recommended learning (def: a4, a6)), in which cases looking is permissible to the degree required. (O: It is not permissible to

m2.11 وَيُبَاحُ النظرُ لشهادةٍ ومعاملةٍ (الأجنبي لها وغير ذلك كأن يريد نكاحها) ونحـوهمَـا (كتعليم واجب أو منـدوب) بقـدر الحـاجةِ. (فلا يجوز مجاوزتها كأن

exceed the degree required, as when looking at part of the face is sufficient, in which case looking at the rest of it is not permissible, as it exceeds the amount required.)

يكتفي في النظر للوجه ببعضه فلا يجوز حينئذ النظر إلى باقيه لأنه زائد على قدر الحاجة) .

RULES FOR PROPOSING MARRIAGE OR ACCEPTING A PROPOSAL

متى تجوز خطبة المرأة

m2.12 It is unlawful to propose marriage, openly or allusively, to another's wife when she is in the waiting period of an unfinalized (A: i.e. less than threefold (dis: n9.0(N:))) divorce (O: because she is still considered as a wife is).

m2.12 ويَحْرُمُ أَنْ يُصَرِّحَ أَوْ يُعَرِّضَ بخطبة المعتدة مِنْ غيره إذا كانَتْ رجعية (لأنها حينئذ في معنى الزوجة) .

m2.13 As for a woman who is in any of the following types of waiting period (def: n9), it is unlawful for a suitor to propose openly to her, though not for him to hint at it:

(1) the waiting period of a finalized (threefold) divorce;

(2) the waiting period after having had her husband release her for payment (def: n5);

(3) or the waiting period to remarry after her husband's death (def: n9.11).

(O: Proposing allusively is only permissible in such cases because of the husband's lack of authority over her. To propose *openly* means to decisively indicate one's desire to wed, such as by saying, "I want to marry you," while to propose *allusively* means to employ words that could indicate a desire to marry or something else, such as "I am desirous of you," or "You are beautiful," for these do not necessarily imply a desire for marriage.)

m2.13 وأمَّا المعتـدةُ البائنُ بثلاثٍ أوْ خلعٍ أوْ عنِ الـوفـاةِ فَيَحْرُمُ التصريحُ دونَ التعريض (وإنما حلت في البـائن وما بعـدهـا لعـدم سلطـة الـزوج عليها والتصريـح ما يقطع بالـرغبة في النكاح كأريـد أن أنكحـك والتعريض ما يحتمل الـرغبة في النكاح وغيرها نحو: أنا راغب فيـك، وأنت جميلة، فهـذه الألفـاظ لا تستلزم الرغبة في النكاح) .

m2.14 (O: The rulings regarding the lawfulness or unlawfulness of a woman's *accepting* a marriage proposal are the same as those for proposing to her (def: m2.12–13).)

m2.14 (وحكم جواب الخطبـة حكم الخطبة حلًا وحرماً) .

m2.15 It is unlawful to propose marriage to a woman to whom another has already done so, if the first proposal has been openly accepted, unless the first suitor gives his permission. (O: And like his permission in the legality of another proposing to her is when the first suitor has shown himself disinclined, such as by having given up, or when enough time has elapsed to give others the impression that he no longer wants to marry, or when the woman's guardian (def: m3.4) becomes averse to him.) But if the first suitor's proposal was not openly accepted, then a second suitor may propose to her. (O: It is also permissible for one to take the initiative and propose to a woman when one does not know whether or not she is engaged, or whether the first proposal was plainly accepted or not.)

m2.16 Whoever is asked about what kind of person a prospective groom is should truthfully mention his failings (O: meaning his defects and mistakes. This is obligatory (N: but only to the degree necessary (A: to protect the person who is asking)), as Nawawi has stated in *al-Adhkar* (dis: r2.20(2))).

m2.17 It is recommended to give a short address when (O: i.e. before) making a marriage proposal (O: *address* meaning words begun by praising Allah and concluded with a supplication and moral exhortation. If one wants to be brief, one may simply say, "Praise be to Allah, and blessings and peace upon the Messenger of Allah (Allah bless him and give him peace). I enjoin you to fear Allah. I have come to you to engage your noblest [A: mentioning her name]." Then her guardian gives a similar address).

It is also recommended to give another brief address when (O: i.e. just before) the marriage contract is made, saying (O: i.e. it is recommended for the guardian to say, before the contract is formally effected), "I marry her to you according to the command of Allah Most High, to kindly retain or graciously release."

م2.15 وتَحْـرُمُ الخِطْبَةُ على خِطْبةِ الغيـرِ إذا صُرِّحَ لهُ إلَّا بإذنـهِ (ومثـل الإذن في جواز خطبـة الثاني إعـراض الخاطب الأول، وفي معناه ما لو ترك الأول أو طال الزمان بعد إجابته بحيث يعدونه معرضاً، أو إعـراض الـولي عن الخـاطب) فإنْ لَمْ يُصَرَّحْ بإجابتهِ جازَ. (ويجـوز الهجوم على الخطبـة لمن لم يدر أخطبت المـرأة وأجيب الخاطب أم لا).

م2.16 ومَنِ اسْتُشِيرَ في خاطب فَلْيَـذْكُرْ مساويهُ (بمعنى العيوب والزلات وظـاهـر الأمر الوجوب كما عبر به النووي في الأذكار) بصدقٍ.

م2.17 ويُنْـدَبُ أنْ يَخْطُبَ عنـدَ الخِطْبَةِ (أي قبلها وهي كلام مفتح بحمد الله مختـتم بدعـاء ووعـظ، فإن أراد اختصـارهـا فيقول الحمـدُ لله والصلاةُ والسـلامُ على رسـول الله ﷺ أُوصِيكُمْ بتقـوى اللهِ جِئْتُكُمْ خَاطِباً كريمتكُمْ فلانة فيخطب الولي كذلك).

و(ينـدب خطبة أخرى) عندَ (أي قبل) العقـد ويَقُولَ (أي الـولي قبـل العقـد): أُزَوِّجُـكَ على ما أمَـرَ اللهُ تعـالى بهِ مِنْ إمسـاكٍ بمعـروفٍ أوْ تسـريـحٍ بإحسانٍ. [ولـوْ خَطَبَ الـوليُ عنـدَ الإيجـاب فقـالَ الـزوجُ الحمـدُ لله والصلاةُ على رسـولِ اللهِ قَبِلْتُ صَحَّ ولكنَّهُ لا يُنْدَبُ وَقِيلَ يُنْدَبُ].

*

| m3.0 THE INTEGRALS OF A MARRIAGE AGREEMENT | أركان النكاح   m3.0 |

m3.1 Marriage has integrals (A: which are five in number:

    (a) the spoken form;

    (b) the witnesses;

    (c) the bride's guardian;

    (d) the groom;

    (e) and the bride).

m3.1 وللنكاح أركانٌ (ع): خمسة، هي: الـصيغـة، والشهـود، والـولي، والزوج، والمرأة).

THE SPOKEN FORM

الصيغة

m3.2 The first integral is the explicitly stated spoken form (O: comprising a spoken offer by the guardian and its acceptance by the groom, like other, nonmarital transactions. Its necessary conditions are the same as those of valid sale (def: k1.1(a,b,c,d,e))), the form being valid in languages other than Arabic even when one is able to speak Arabic.

    The spoken form is not valid if allusive. Nor is it valid without:

    (a) a statement (N: from the guardian) that effects it, namely "I marry you" (n: i.e. *to her,* the Arabic *zawwaja* meaning to marry someone to another);

    (b) and an immediate spoken acceptance (A: by the groom), namely "I marry her," or "I accept her marriage."

    (N: The spoken form, when the other integrals exist, is what is meant by the term *marriage contract,* not an actual written document, though it is sunna to write it. Extraneous conditions added to the marriage contract, such as that the husband observe monogamy or the like, are not binding, being meaningless, though they do not invalidate the marriage agreement, which remains effective.)

m3.2 الأولُ الصيغـةُ الصـريحـةُ (المشـتـملة على الإيجـاب من الـولي والقبـول من الـزوج كغيـر النكـاح من المعـامـلات وشرط فيه ما شرط في صيغة البيع) ولـوْ بالعجمية لِمَنْ يُحْسِنُ العربية لا بالكنـاية، فلا يَصِحُّ إلّا بإيجاب منجز وهـوَ: زَوَّجْتُكَ؛ [أَوْ: أَنكحْتُـكَ؛ فقطْ] وقبـول على الفور وهوَ: تَزَوَّجْتُهَا؛ [أَوْ: نَكَـحْتُـهَـا؛] أَوْ: قَبِلْتُ نكـاحَهـا [أو تزويـجهَـا. فلواقْـتَصَـر على قَبِلْتُ لَمْ يَنْعقدْ. ولوْ قالَ زَوِّجْني فقَالَ زَوَّجْتُكَ صَحَّ].

THE WITNESSES

الشهود

m3.3   The second integral is that the marriage have witnesses, it not being valid unless two witnesses are present who are:

(a) male (O: since a marriage witnessed by a man and two women would not be valid (A: though it would be valid in the Hanafi school));

(b) sound of hearing;

(c) sound of eyesight;

(d) familiar with the language of the two contracting parties;

(e) Muslims;

(f) and upright (def: o24.4) witnesses, even if their uprightness is merely apparent (O: since marriages take place among average, common people, and if they were made responsible to know the inward uprightness of witnesses, it would cause delays and difficulties. *Apparent uprightness* means the person is outwardly known to be upright, even if he is inwardly unknown).

m3.3   الثــاني الشهـودُ فلا يَصِحُّ إلّا بحضرةِ شاهدينِ ذكرينِ (فلا ينعقد برجل وامـرأتين) [حـــرين] سميعينِ بصيرينِ عارفين بلسانِ المتعاقدينِ مسلمين عدلينِ ولوْ مستورَيِ العدالةِ (لأن النكاح يجري بين أوساط الناس والعوام ولو كلفوا معرفة العـدالة الباطنة لطال الأمر وشق عليهم ، فالمستور هو من عرف بالعدالة ظاهراً لا باطناً) .

THE BRIDE'S GUARDIAN

الولي

m3.4   The third integral is the (A: bride's) guardian (O: since a woman may not conduct her own marriage. Ibn Majah relates that the Prophet (Allah bless him and give him peace) said,

"Let no woman marry a woman to another or marry herself to another."

Daraqutni related this hadith with a chain of transmission meeting the standards of Bukhari and Muslim). The marriage agreement is not valid without a guardian who is:

(a) male;

m3.4   الثالثُ الوليُّ (فلا تعقد المرأة النكـاح وروى ابن ماجـه خبـر «لا تزوج المـرأة المرأة ولا المـرأة نفسها» أخرجه الــدارقطني بإسناد على شرط الشيخين) فَلَا يَصِـحُّ إلّا بوليٍ ذكـرٍ مكلَّفٍ [حـرٍّ]

(b) legally responsible (mukallaf, def: c8.1);

(c) Muslim;

(d) upright (def: o24.4);

(e) and of sound judgement.

The following may not be a bride's guardian:

(1) (non-(a) above) a woman;

(2) (non-(b)) a child or insane person;

(3) (non-(c)) a non-Muslim;

(4) (non-(d)) a corrupt person (def: o24.3) (O: though the opinion of most later scholars is that a corrupt person may be a guardian);

(5) or (non-(e)) someone whose judgement is unsound because of old age or weakmindedness (O: whether innate or acquired. *Old age* includes someone with severe pain or illnesses which distract him from realizing what is most advantageous for his charge and her interests, since such a person would be incapable of learning how suitors really are and whether they are an appropriate match (def: m4) for the bride). It is of no consequence if the guardian is blind.

A non-Muslim responsible for a non-Muslim bride may be her guardian (O: provided he does not violate the rules of his own religion), though a Muslim may not.

مسلمٍ عدلٍ تامِّ النظرِ. فلا ولايةَ لامرأةٍ وصبيٍّ ومجنونٍ [ورقيقٍ] وكافرٍ وفاسقٍ (ولكن أفتى أكثـر المتأخـرين [لا سيمـا الخـراسانيون] بأنه يلي) [وسفيهٍ] ومختلِّ النظرِ بهرمٍ وخبلٍ (جبلي أو عارضي وفي معنى الهـرم كثرة الآلام والأسقام الشاغلة عن العلم بمـواضع الحظ والمصلحة أي فيكـون عاجـزاً عن البحث عن أحـوال الأزواج ومعرفة الكفء منهم). ولا يَضُرُّ العَمَى. ويَلي الكـافـرُ موليَّتَهُ الكـافـرة (بشرطِ أن لا يرتكب محظوراً في دينه). ولا يَلِيها (أي الكافرة) المسلمُ.

m3.5 [إلَّا السيدُ في أمتِهِ والسلطانُ في نسـاءِ أهـلِ الذمةِ فيُزَوِّجُهَا السيدُ ولوْ فاسقاً. فإنْ كَانَتْ لامرأةٍ زوَّجَهَا مَنْ يُزَوِّجُ السيدة بإذنِ السيدة. فإنْ كَانَتْ السيدةُ غيرَ رشيدةٍ زوَّجَهَا أبو السيدة أوْ جدُّهَا].

m3.6 (n: If the bride has no Muslim guardian and there is no Islamic magistrate to act as one, she may authorize a male Muslim who has the qualifications of an Islamic judge (def: o22.1)—or if there is none, then a male Muslim who is legally upright (def: o24.4)—to act as her guardian in marrying her to the groom (*Mughni al-muhtaj ila ma'rifa ma'ani alfaz al-Minhaj* (y73), 3.147).)

THE ORDER OF LAWFUL GUARDIANSHIP
AMONG THE BRIDE'S RELATIVES

أحق الأولياء بتزويج المرأة

m3.7   The male relatives of a free woman are the ones who may marry her to another, and the order (O: as to who has the right to be her guardian) is her:

(1) father;

(2) father's father (O: and on up);

(3) brother;

(4) brother's son;

(5) father's brother;

(6) her father's brother's son (O: and so on, in the same order as the universal heirs in estate division (def: L10.6(12–14));

(7) and then the Islamic magistrate (A: i.e. the judge (qadi)).

None of the above may marry her to someone when a family member higher on the list exists. If there are two of equal standing (A: two brothers, for example) and one is related to her through two parents while the other is related to her through the father alone, then the one related to her through both parents is the guardian. If both are equal in this respect, precedence is given to the oldest, most learned in Sacred Law, and most god-fearing. But if the other (A: less deserving of two would-be guardians who are of equal affiliation to her) marries her to the groom, the marriage is valid. If both insist on being the one, they draw lots to see who will do it, though if the loser marries her to the groom, the marriage is also legally valid.

m3.8   If a guardian does not have the right to be a guardian because of the existence of one of the above-mentioned preventives (dis: m3.4(1–5)), the guardianship devolves to the next family member in the m3.7 order of lawful guardians.

m3.7   وأمَّا الحرةُ فيُزَوِّجُهَا عصباتُها وأولادُهُمْ (أي أحقهم بالـولايـة) الأبُ ثمَّ الجدُّ (وإن علا) ثمَّ الأخُ ثمَّ ابنُهُ ثمَّ العمُّ ثمَّ ابنُهُ (وكـذا بقية عصبات النسب على ترتيب الإرث) [ثمَّ المعتقُ ثمَّ عصبتُهُ ثمَّ معتقُ المعتق ثمَّ عصبتُهُ] ثمَّ الحاكمُ.

ولا يُزَوِّجُ أحـدٌ منهُمْ وهنـاكَ مَنْ هو أقـربُ منـهُ. فإن اسْتَوَى اثنانِ في الدرجةِ وأحـدُهُمَا مَنْ يُدْلي بأبـوين والآخرُ بأبٍ فالـوليُّ مَنْ يُدْلي بأبـوين. فإن اسْتَـوَيَـا فالأولـى أنْ يُقـدَّمَ أسـنُّهُمَـا وأعلمُهُمَـا وأورعُهُمَا. فإنْ زَوَّجَ الآخـرُ صحَّ. وإنْ تَشَـاحَّا أُقْرِعَ. وإنْ زَوَّجَ غيرُ مَنْ خَرَجَتْ قرعتُهُ صحَّ أيضاً.

m3.8   وإنْ خَرَجَ الوليُّ عَنْ أنْ يكُونَ وليـاً بشيءٍ مِنَ المـوانِع المتقدمةِ انْتَقَلَت الولايةُ إلى مَنْ بعدَهُ مِنَ الأولياءِ.

THE BRIDE'S RIGHT TO MARRY A SUITABLE
MATCH OF HER CHOICE

حكم عضل الولي المرأة عن النكاح

m3.9   Whenever a free woman asks to marry a
suitor who is a suitable match (def: m4) (O: by
telling her guardian, "Marry me to him"), the
guardian must marry her to him (O: whether she is
a virgin or nonvirgin, and whether prepubescent
or not). The Islamic magistrate (A: i.e. judge)
marries her to such a groom if the guardian:

(1) in the presence of the magistrate refuses
to marry her to the groom;

(2) is on a journey farther than 81 km./50 mi.
from home;

(3) or is in a state of pilgrim sanctity (ihram)
(O: for hajj, 'umra, or both) (dis: j3.20).

In such cases, the guardianship does not devolve
to the next most eligible in the m3.7 order of lawful guardians. If (non-(2) above) the guardian is
on a journey of less than 81 km./50 mi. from home,
the bride may not be married to someone without
the guardian's leave.

m3.9   ومتى دَعَتِ الحـرةُ إلى كفءٍ
(بأن قالـت لوليهـا زوجني منــه) لَزِمَـهُ
تزويجُها (سواء كانت الطـالبة للتزويج
بكـراً أم ثيباً وكـلامه أيضـاً يشمـل غير
البـالغة) فإنْ عَضَلَهـا أيْ مَنَعَها بين يَدَيِ
الحـاكِم أوكَانَ (الـولي) غائبـاً في مسافة
القصر أوكَانَ مُحْرِماً (بحج فقط أو بعمرة
فقـط أو محرماً بهما) زَوَّجَها الحاكمُ ولا
تَنْتَقِلُ الـولايةُ إلى الأبعدِ. وإنْ غَابَ إلى
دون مسافة القصر لَمْ تُزَوَّجْ إلا بإذنِهِ.

COMMISSIONING ANOTHER TO EFFECT THE
MARRIAGE AGREEMENT

توكيل الولي غيره بعقد النكاح

m3.10 The guardian may commission another
(def: k17.5–6) to marry his charge to someone,
though it is not permissible to commission someone who himself lacks the requisite conditions
(m3.4(a,b,c,d,e)) to be a guardian.
      The groom too may commission someone to
accept the marriage agreement on his behalf, provided the person commissioned is someone who
would be legally entitled to accept such a marriage
for himself. (O: A child, for example, may not
accept a marriage for himself, let alone someone
else, nor may a woman be commissioned for this,
nor someone in a state of pilgrim sanctity
(ihram).)

m3.10 ويَـجُــوزُ للولـيِّ أنْ يُوَكِّـلَ
بتـزويجِهـا. ولا يَجُوزُ أنْ يُوَكَّلَ إلا مَنْ
يَجُوزُ أنْ يَكُونَ ولياً.
وللـزوج أنْ يُوَكِّـلَ في القَبـولِ مَنْ
يَجُوزُ أنْ يَقْبَلَ النكـاحَ لنفسِه (فلا يوكل
صبي لأنه لا يصح أن يقبل الصبي النكاح
لنفسه فلا يقبل لغيره بالأولى ولا امرأة ولا
محرماً [ولوْ عبداً].

m3.11 Neither the guardian of the bride nor his agent may state the marriage offer (def: m3.2(a)) for the guardian's own marriage (A: to her). If her guardian wants to marry her, as when, for example, he is the son of her father's brother, then he lets a different son of the father's brother stand in as guardian. If there is no one in his own degree (A: of relation to her), then the Islamic judge stands in as guardian.

m3.12 No one may state both the proposal and its acceptance (def: m3.2(a,b)) for one marriage, except the bride's grandfather when marrying his son's daughter to his (A: other) son's son.

GUARDIANS WHO MAY MARRY A VIRGIN
TO A MAN WITHOUT HER CONSENT

m3.13 Guardians are of two types, those who may compel their female charges to marry someone, and those who may not.

(1) The only guardians who may compel their charge to marry are a virgin bride's father or father's father, *compel* meaning to marry her to a suitable match (def: m4) without her consent.

(2) Those who may not compel her are not entitled to marry her to someone unless she accepts and gives her permission.

Whenever the bride is a virgin, the father or father's father may marry her to someone without her permission, though it is recommended to ask her permission if she has reached puberty. A virgin's silence is considered as permission.
As for the nonvirgin of sound mind, no one may marry her to another after she has reached puberty without her express permission, no matter whether the guardian is the father, father's father, or someone else.

m3.11 وليسَ للوليِّ ولا للوكيـل أَنْ يُوجِبَ النكـاحَ لنفسِهِ . فَلَوْ أرادَ وليُّها أَنْ يَتَـزَّوجَهـا كابنِ العمِّ فَوَّضَ العقدَ إلى ابنِ عمٍّ في درجتِهِ . فإِنْ فُقِدَ فالقاضِي .

m3.12 وليـسَ لأحـدٍ أَنْ يَتَـوَلَّـى الإيجـابَ والقبـولَ في نكـاحٍ واحدٍ إلاَّ الجدُّ في تزويجِ بنتِ ابنِهِ بابنِ ابنِهِ .

الولي المجبر

m3.13 ثمَّ الـوليُّ على قسمينِ مجبـرٌ وغيـرُ مجبـرٍ . فالمجبـرُ هوَ الأبُ والجدُّ خاصةً في تزويجِ البكرِ فقط [وكَذا السيدُ في أَمتِهِ مطلقـاً] ومعنى المجبرِ أنَّ لهُ أَنْ يُزَوَّجَهـا مِنْ كفءٍ بغيـرِ رضـاهـا . وغيـرُ المجبرِ لا يُزَوِّجُ إلاَّ برضاهـا وإذنِها . فمتَى كَانَتْ بكـراً جَازَ للأبِ أو الجدَّ تزويجُها بغيرِ إذنِها لكِنْ يُنْدَبُ استئذانُ البالغةِ ، وإذنُهَا السكوتُ . وأمَّا الثيبُ العاقلةُ فلا يُزَوِّجُها أحدٌ إلاَّ بإذنِهَـا بعـدَ البلوغِ باللفـظِ سواءُ الأبُ والجدُّ وغيرُهُمَا .

m3.14 [وأمَّا قبـلَ البلوغِ فلا تُزَوَّجُ (الثيب) أصلاً . وإنْ كَانَتْ (الثيب) مجنـونـةً صغيرةً زوَّجَها الأبُ أو الجدُّ . أَوْ كبيرةً زوَّجَها الأبُ أو الجدُّ أو الحاكمُ ، لكنِ الحاكمُ يُزَوِّجُها للحاجةِ والأبُ والجدُّ يُزَوِّجُها للحاجةِ والمصلحةِ . ولا يَلْزَمُ السيدَ تزويجُ الأمةِ والمكاتبةِ وإنْ طلبتا] .

m3.15 No guardian may marry a woman to someone who is not a suitable match (def: m4) without her acceptance and the acceptance of all who can be guardians (def: m3.7). If the Islamic magistrate is her guardian, he may not under any circumstances marry her to someone who is not a suitable match for her.

If the bride selects a suitor who is not a suitable match for her, the guardian is not obliged to marry her to him. If she selects a suitable match but her guardian chooses a different suitor who is also a suitable match, then the man chosen by the guardian takes precedence if the guardian is one who may lawfully compel her to marry (def: m3.13(1)), while the one she selects takes precedence when the guardian may not lawfully compel her to marry (m3.13(2)).

*

m4.0 A SUITABLE MATCH (KAFA'A)

(N: The definition of a *suitable match* should not be misunderstood as a recommendation for whom to marry. It is merely a legal restriction to protect a woman's interests when the father or grandfather of a virgin marry her to someone without her consent (dis: m3.13,15). As for when she wishes to marry someone who is not a suitable match, and her guardian has no objection, there is nothing wrong or offensive in her doing so.)

m4.1 *Suitability* concerns lineage, religiousness, profession, and being free of defects that permit annulling the marriage contract (def: m7). (N: As for color, it is of no consideration in suitability.)

m4.2 The following are not suitable matches for one another:

(1) a non-Arab man for an Arab woman (O: because of the hadith that the Prophet (Allah bless him and give him peace) said,

"Allah has chosen the Arabs above others");

m3.15 ولا يُزَوِّجُ أحدٌ مِنَ الأولياءِ المرأةَ مِنْ غيرِ كفءٍ إلَّا برضاهـا ورضا سائرِ الأولياءِ فإنْ كانَ وليُّهَا الحاكمَ لمْ تُزَوَّجْ مِنْ غيرِ كفءٍ أصلًا وإنْ رَضِيَتْ. وإنْ دَعَتْ إلى غيرِ كفءٍ لمْ يَلْزم الـوليَّ تزويجُها. وإنْ عَيَّنَتْ كفئاً وعَيَّنَ الـوليُّ كفئـاً غيـرَهُ فمَنْ عَيَّنَـهُ الـوليُّ أولى إنْ كانَ مجبراً وإلَّا فَمَنْ عَيَّنَتْهُ أولى.

m4.0 الكفاءة

(ح: لا يُتوهم أن الكفـاءة إرشـاد للإنسان ليعرف الأفضل عند الزواج؛ بل إنما هي تقييد للولي لحفظ مصالح البكر التي يزوجها الأب أو الجد بغير إذنها. أما إذا أرادت [البالغة] أن تتزوج من غير كفء، ولا مانع عند الـولي، فلا حرمة حينئذ ولا كراهة).

m4.1 والكفـاءةُ في النسب والـدين [والحـريـة] والصنعة وسلامةِ العيـوب المثبتة للخيار (ح: وأما اللون فلا اعتبار له في الكفاءة).

m4.2 فلا يُكـافيءُ العجميُّ عربيـة (لمـا في الحـديث من قوله ﷺ «إن الله اصطفى العرب على غيـرهم») [ولا غيرُ قرشيٍّ ولا غيـرُ هاشميٍّ أوْمطلبيٍّ هاشميـةً

(2) a corrupt man (def: o24.3) for a virtuous woman (O: though it is sufficient for the would-be husband to have given up his wrongdoing);

(3) a man of a lowly profession for the daughter of someone with a higher profession, such as a tailor wanting to marry a merchant's daughter (A: though an Islamic scholar is a suitable match for any level whatever);

(4) or someone with a defect that permits annulling the marriage (def: m7) for someone without such defects.

Being wealthy has nothing to do with suitability (O: for money comes and goes, and those with self-respect and intelligence do not take pride in it), nor does being elderly.

m4.3 The marriage agreement is invalid whenever a guardian marries his charge to someone who is not a suitable match for her, if done without both her acceptance and the acceptance of all who are eligible as guardians (def: m3.7) and are on the guardian's level of relation to her (A: such as his brothers). But if both these parties agree, then the bride's relatives further from her than the guardian may not object.

m4.4 When the father or father's father see that the best advantage is to be served by marrying a young boy (or girl) to someone, they may do so, though they are not entitled to marry the child to someone with a physical defect (dis: m7) that legally permits annulment of the marriage.

m4.5 If a person is foolhardy (safih, def: k13.1(A:)) or continuously insane, but needs to marry, then his father, grandfather, or the Islamic magistrate may marry him to someone. If they grant permission to the foolhardy person to marry himself, his marriage is valid, though if he does so without their leave, it is invalid.

أوْ مطلبيــةٌ] ولا فاسقٌ عفيفـةً (ويكفي في الزوج خلوصه من الفسق) [ولا عبدٌ حرةً ولا الــعـتـيـقُ أوْ مَنْ مَسَّ آبـاءَهُ رقٌّ حرةَ الأصل] ولا ذُو حرفةٍ دنيئةٍ بنتَ ذِي حرفةٍ أرفعَ كخياطٍ بنتَ تاجرٍ، ولا معيبٌ بعيبٍ يُثْبِتُ الخيارَ سليمةً منهُ ولا اعتبارَ باليسارِ (لأن المال غادٍ ورائحٌ ولا يفتخر به أهل المروءات والبصائر) والشيخوخةِ .

m4.3 فمتَى زَوَّجَهَا بغيرِ كفءٍ بغيرِ رضـاهـا ورضَا الأولياءِ الـذينَ هُمْ في درجتِهِ فالنكاحُ باطلٌ . وإنْ رَضُوا أوْ رَضِيَتْ فليْسَ للأبعدِ اعتراضٌ .

m4.4 وإذا رأَى الأبُ أو الــجـدُّ المصلحـةَ في تزويجِ الصغيرِ والصغيرةِ زَوَّجَهُ وليْسَ لهُ أنْ يُزَوِّجَهُ [أمةً ولا] معيبةً .

m4.5 وإنْ كانَ سفيهــاً أوْ مجنونــاً مطبقاً واحْتاجَ إلى النكاحِ زَوَّجَهُ الأبُ أو الجدُ أو الحاكمُ . فإنْ أذِنُوا للسفيه لِيَعْقِدَ لنفسِهِ جازَ. وإنْ عَقَدَ بلا إذنٍ فباطلٌ .

m4.6 [وإنْ كانَ مطلاقاً تَسَرَّى جاريةً واحدةً. والعبدُ الصغيرُ يُزَوِّجُهُ السيدُ. والكبيرُ يَتَزَوَّجُ بإذنِهِ. وليْسَ للسيدِ إجبارُهُ على النكاحِ ولا للعبدِ إجبارُ السيدِ عليهِ].

m5.0 CONJUGAL RIGHTS	m5.0 الاستمتاع

THE WIFE'S MARITAL OBLIGATIONS

متى يجب تسليم المرأة للزوج

m5.1   It is obligatory for a woman to let her husband have sex with her immediately when:

(a) he asks her;

(b) at home (O: *home* meaning the place in which he is currently staying, even if being lent to him or rented);

(c) and she can physically endure it.

(d) (O: Another condition that should be added is that her marriage payment (mahr, def: m8) has been received or deferred to a term not yet expired.

As for when sex with her is not possible, such that having it would entail manifest harm to her, then she is not obliged to comply.)

If she asks him to wait, she is awaited, to a maximum of three days. (O: She does not ask to wait because of not having finished her period or postnatal bleeding, for there is no physical harm entailed in her complying as she is, though if she fears that such foreplay with him will lead to actual copulation (A: which is unlawful under such circumstances), then she may refuse, as that is not obligatory). (n: w45 discusses wives' other duties to husbands.)

m5.1   يَجِبُ تسليمُ المرأةِ على الفورِ إذا طَلَبَها في منزلِ الزوجِ (والمراد بالمنزل مكانه الذي هو مستقر فيه ولو بالعارية أو بالاستئجار) إنْ كانَتْ تطيقُ الاستمتاعَ (ويضاف إلى هذه الشروط المذكورة كون الصداق مقبوضاً أو مؤجلاً لم يحل. أما إذا لم يمكن الاستمتاع بها بحيث يحصل لها ضرر بيّن بالوطء فلا يجب تسليمُها) فإنْ سألَت الانتظارَ انتُظِرَت وأكثرُهُ ثلاثةُ أيامٍ (ولا تمهل لزوال الحيض أو النفاس إذ لا ضرر عليها في تسليمها كذلك نعم لو خافت من مضاجعته الوطء فلها الامتناع منها إذ لا يجب عليها ذلك) [فإنْ كانَتْ أمَةً لم يجبْ تسليمُها إلا بالليل وهيَ بالنهار عندَ السيدِ].

THE WIFE'S RIGHT TO INTERCOURSE

القول بوجوب تحصين الزوجة

m5.2   (Imam Ghazali:) One should make love to one's wife every four nights, as is fairest, since the number of wives one may have is four, and one may wait this long to do so, though one should make love to her more or less than this, according to the amount she needs to remain chaste and free of want for it (N: if one is able), since it is obligatory for a husband to enable her to keep chaste (*Ihya' 'ulum al-din* (y39), 2.46).

m5.2   (الإمام الغزالي:) وينبغي أن يأتيها في كل أربع ليال مرة إذ عدد النساء أربعة فجاز التأخير إلى هذا الحد نعم ينبغي أن يزيد أو ينقص بحسب حاجتها (ح: وقدرته) في التحصين فإن تحصينها واجب عليه [نقل من إحياء علوم الدين: ٢/ ٤٦].

THE WEDDING NIGHT

ما يقال أول ما يلقاها

m5.3   The first time they sleep together, it is recommended for the husband to grasp his bride's forelock and supplicate Allah for an increase in blessings (baraka) (O: such as by saying, "May Allah bless each of us in their partner").

m5.3   والمستحبُّ أَنْ يَأْخُـذَ الـزوجُ بناصيتِهَا أولَ ما يَلْقَـاهَـا ويَـدْعُوَ بالبركةِ (كأن يقول بارك الله لكل منا في صاحبه) .

THE HUSBAND'S RIGHTS

حق الزوج في الاستمتاع

m5.4   A husband possesses full right to enjoy his wife's person (A: from the top of her head to the bottoms of her feet, though anal intercourse (dis: p75.20) is absolutely unlawful) in what does not physically harm her.
    He is entitled to take her with him when he travels.

m5.4   ويَمْلِكُ الاستمتاعَ بِهَا مِنْ غيرِ إضرارٍ.
ولَهُ أَنْ يُسَافِرَ بِهَا [وإنْ كَانَتْ حرةً] .

CONTRACEPTION

العزل

m5.5   The husband is permitted to practice coitus interruptus (n: w46 discusses the relation of this to other methods of contraception) in lovemaking with his wife (O: meaning to make love to her until he feels an impending orgasm, when he withdraws to ejaculate outside the vagina) though it is better not to (O: it being considered offensive in our school (dis: w46.2) because it is a means to prevent reproduction).

m5.5   ولهُ أَنْ يَعْزِلَ عَنْهَا (بأن يجامع الـزوج حتى يقرب الإنـزال فينزع لينزل (خـارج الفـرج) [حرةً كَانَتْ أو أمةً] لكنِ الأولى أَنْ لا يَفْعَـلَ (والعزل مكروه عندنا لأنه طريق إلى قطع النسل) .

m5.6   The husband is entitled to insist that his wife undertake both the measures necessary for having sex with her such as the purificatory bath (ghusl) after her monthly period, and those necessary to full enjoyment of her such as the purificatory bath after major ritual impurity (janaba), shaving her private parts, and removing filth.

m5.6   ولـهُ أَنْ يُلزِمَهَـا بِمَا يَتَوَقَّفُ الاستمتـاعُ عليـهِ كالغسـلِ مِنَ الحيضِ وبِمَا يَتَوَقَّفُ عليه كمالُ اللذاتِ كالغسلِ مِنَ الجنابةِ والاستحدادِ وإزالةِ الأوساخِ .

*

m6.0 UNMARRIAGEABLE KIN (MAHRAM)

(N: It is unlawful for one to marry one's ancestors, descendants, parents' descendants, or the first generation of one's grandparent's offspring, meaning one's paternal or maternal aunts (n: or uncles, if one is female). One's *unmarriageable kin* (mahram) are those one is forbidden to marry forever.)

m6.1   It is unlawful (O: meaning both sinful and legally invalid) for a man to marry his:

(1) mother;

(2) grandmothers (O: from his mother's or father's side) and on up;

(3) daughters;

(4) daughters of his children, children's children, and on down;

(5) sisters;

(6) daughters of brothers or sisters, their children's daughters, and on down;

(7) mother's sisters, grandmother's sisters, and on up;

(8) father's sisters, father's father's sisters, and on up;

(9) wife's mother;

(10) wife's grandmother;

(11) the wives of his father, father's father, and on up;

(12) the wives of his children, children's children, and on down;

(all of whom ((9) through (12)) are unlawful for him to marry by the mere fact of marriage. As for a man's wife's daughter (N: from a different husband), she is not unlawful for him to marry until

المحارم   m6.0

(ح: يحـرم على الإنسـان أصـولـه وفـروعـه وفروع أبـويه والطبقة الأولى من فروع أجـداده وجداته (عمـاته وخالاته). والمحرم هي التي يحرم نكاحها على التأبيد).

m6.1 يَحْـرُمُ (بمعنى التأثيم وعـدم الصحة) نكـاحُ الأُمّ والجـدـات (من جهة الأم أو من جهة الأب) وإنْ عَلَوْنَ والبنـات وبنـاتِ الأولادِ وإنْ سَفَـلْنَ والأخـوـات وبنـاتِ الإخـوة والأخـواتِ وإنْ سَفَلْنَ والعمـاتِ والخـالاتِ وإنْ عَلَوْنَ وأمُّ الـزوجةِ وجدتِها وأزواج آبائِه وأولادِه: هؤلاء كلُهُنَّ يَحْـرُمْنَ بمجـرد العقدِ. وأمّا بنتُ زوجتِه فلا تَحْرُمُ إلّا بالدخولِ بالأُمّ.

527

he has had sexual intercourse with her mother. Were he to divorce the mother before intercourse, it would be permissible for him to marry the daughter)

(13) (n: and all those considered as unmarriageable kin to him through his having been breast-fed by a particular wet nurse in infancy, as at n12.2).

m6.2   (N: It is unlawful and invalid for a woman to marry her:

(1) father, grandfather, and on up;

(2) son, son's son, daughter's son, and on down;

(3) brother;

(4) father's brother, meaning the brother of any male ancestor;

(5) mother's brother, meaning the brother of any female ancestor;

(6) brother's son, sister's son, or any other descendants of brothers or sisters;

(7) the husband of her mother, grandmother, and on up;

(8) the husband of her daughter or other female descendant;

(9) her husband's father, grandfather, and on up, and husband's son and descendants;

(10) (n: and unmarriageable kin to her through her having been breast-fed by a particular wet nurse in infancy, as at n12.2).

m6.3   It is unlawful for a man to marry both:

(1) a woman and her sister;

(2) a woman and her father's sister;

فإنْ أبَانَ الأُمَّ قبلَ الـدخـول بهَا حَلَّتْ لَهُ بنتُهـا . [ويَحـرُمُ عليهِ مَنْ وَطِئَها أحدُ آبائِهِ (وإن علوا) أوْ أبنـائِـهِ (وإن سفلوا) بمِلكٍ أوْ شبهَةٍ ، وأمهـاتُ موطوأتِهِ هوَ بمِلكٍ أوْ شبهَةٍ ، وبناتُهَا ؛ كلُّ ذلكَ تحريماً مؤبداً] .

m6.2 (ح : يحـرُم ولا يصـحّ نكـاح المرأة محارمها وهم من الرجال ما يلي :
١ـ أبوها وجدها وإن علا .
٢ـ ابنها وابن ابنها وابن بنتها وإن سفل .
٣ـ أخوها .
٤ـ عمها ، وهو أخو كل رجل ولدها .
٥ـ خالها ، وهو أخو كل امرأة ولدتها .
٦ـ ابن أخيها وابن أختهـا ، وكـذا كل ذرية أخيها أو أختها .
٧ـ زوج أمها أو جدتها وإن علت .
٨ـ زوج ابنتها وكل امرأة من ذريتها .
٩ـ أبـو زوجهـا وجـدّه وإن علا ، وابن زوجها وذريته) .
١٠ـ (ت : ومحارمها بالرضاع) .

m6.3 ويَحـرُمُ أنْ يَجْمَعَ بينَ المـرأة وأخَتها أوْ عمَتِها أوْ خالتِها .

(3) or a woman and her mother's sister.

(N: But if a man is no longer married to one of the above and the waiting period (def: n9) has expired, then he may marry the other.)

(ح: لكن إن انتهى زواج الرجل بإحدى المذكورات وانقضت العدة فلا مانع من التزوج بأخرى).

[m6.4 وإنْ تَزَوَّجَ امرأةً ثم وَطِئَها أبوهُ أو ابنُهُ بشبهةٍ أو وَطِىءَ هو أمَّها أوْ بنتَها بشبهةٍ انْفَسَخَ نكاحُها (ح: وأما إن زنيا فلا ينفسخ لأن التحريم بالمصاهرة احترام للوطء الشرعي وأما الزنا فليس له احترام ولا يترتب عليه تحريم الأمهات والبنات ونحوهن)].

m6.5 The same categories of relatives who are unlawful for one to marry because of one's kinship relation to them are also unlawful to one by "foster relationship," through having been breast-fed by a particular wet nurse in infancy (dis: n12.2) (N: since someone nursed in infancy by a woman is prohibited to marry those whom her offspring and her husband's offspring are prohibited to marry).

m6.5 وما حَرُمَ مِنْ ذلك بالنسب حَرُمَ بالرضاع (ح: فمن رضع من امرأة حرم عليه ما يحرم على أبنائها وأبناء زوجها).

[m6.6 ومَنْ حَرُمَ نكاحُها ممَّنْ ذَكَرْناهُ حَرُمَ وطؤُها بملكِ اليمين ومَنْ وَطِىءَ أَمَتَهُ ثم تَزَوَّجَ أختَها أوْ عمتَها أوْ خالَتَها حَلَّتْ له المنكوحةُ وحَرُمَتِ المملوكةُ].

m6.7 It is unlawful for a Muslim man to marry:

(1) a Zoroastrian woman;

(2) an idol worshipper;

(3) an apostate from Islam (murtadd, def: o8);

(4) or a woman with one parent who is Jewish or Christian, while the other is Zoroastrian.

(5) (N: It is not lawful or valid for a Muslim man to be married to any woman who is not either a Muslim, Christian, or Jew; nor is it lawful or valid for a Muslim woman to be married to anyone besides a Muslim.)

m6.7 ويَحرُمُ على المسلم نكاحُ المجوسيةِ والوثنيةِ والمرتدةِ ومَنْ أحدُ أبويها كتابيٌّ والآخرُ مجوسيٌّ [والأمةِ الكتابيةِ وجاريةِ ابنِهِ وجاريةِ نفسِهِ ومالكتِهِ لكنْ يَجُوزُ وطءُ الأمةِ الكتابيةِ بملكِ اليمين].

m6.8 It is unlawful for a man who has divorced his wife by public imprecation (def: n11) to

m6.8 وتَحرُمُ الملاعنةُ على الملاعنِ (ح: لكنها ليست بمحرم له،

remarry her (N: though she is not considered his unmarriageable kin (mahram), and he may not look at or be alone with her).

فلا يجوز له النظر إليها ولا الخلوة بها) .

m6.9   It is unlawful to marry a woman who is in a state of pilgrim sanctity (ihram, def: j3) (N: for hajj or 'umra), or in her waiting period (def: n9) after marriage to another.

m6.9   ونكـاحُ المُحْرِمَةِ (ح: بحجٍ أو عمرةٍ) والمعتدةِ مِنْ غيرِهِ .

m6.10 It is unlawful for a free man to marry more than four women. It is fitter to confine oneself to just one.

m6.10   ويَحْرُمُ على الحرِّ أَنْ يَجْمَعَ بين أكثرَ مِن أربعٍ والأولى الاقتصارُ على واحدةٍ .

m6.11   [ولهُ أَنْ يطأَ بملكِ اليمينِ ما شاءَ. ويَحْرُمُ على العبدِ أكثرُ مِن اثنتينِ. ويَحْرُمُ على الحرِّ نكاحُ الأَمةِ المسلمةِ إلَّا أَنْ يَخافَ العنتَ وهوَ الوقوعُ في الزنا وليْسَ عندَهُ حرةٌ تَصْلُحُ للاستمتاعِ وعَجَزَ عَنْ صداقِ حرةٍ أو ثمنِ جاريةٍ تَصْلُحُ] .

m6.12 The following types of marriage are legally invalid:

(1) to marry by "trading daughters [or sisters]" (A: such that the marriage of each by the guardian of the other supposedly takes the place of the woman's marriage payment (mahr));

(2) to have a "temporary marriage" (mut'a), meaning to marry a woman for a stipulated period (O: whether specified, such as a month, or unknown, such as "until So-and-so comes");

(3) or to marry a woman after her threefold divorce solely to cohabit and thus permit her (dis: n7.7) to remarry her previous husband (A: which is an enormity (dis: p29)), though if the marriage agreement is made for this reason but does not expressly stipulate it, then it is legally valid (dis: c5.2).

m6.12   ولا يَصِـحُّ نكـاحُ الشغـارِ، ونكـاحُ المتعـةِ وهـوَ أَنْ يُنْكِحهـا إلى مدةٍ (معلومـةٍ كشهرٍ أو مجهولةٍ كقدومِ زيدٍ)، ولا نكـاحُ المـحلِّلِ، وهـوَ أَنْ يُنْكِحَهـا ليُحَلِّلَهـا للذي طلَّقَهـا ثلاثـاً . فإنْ عَقَـدَ لذلكَ ولمْ يَشْتَرِطْ صَحَّ .

*

m7.0 DEFECTS IN THE SPOUSE PERMITTING ANNULMENT OF MARRIAGE

m7.1 In any of the following circumstances, the husband or wife has the option to annul the marriage agreement immediately, if this is done in the presence of the Islamic magistrate (O: or a third party chosen to judge between them (dis: o21.4), provided that he is a *mujtahid* (def: o22.1(d)) and there is no Islamic judge), even when the partner annulling the marriage has the same defect whose existence in the spouse has motivated him or her to annul it (O: as when, for example, both are insane):

(1) one finds that the spouse is not sane, or has elephantiasis or leprosy;

(2) the husband finds that the wife's vagina is closed or nearly so because of an abnormal growth of flesh or bone;

(3) or the wife finds that the husband is impotent, or that his penis has been dissevered.

The agreement may also be annulled when the defect occurs after making the marriage agreement, except when a husband's impotence occurs after he has had sexual intercourse with his wife, in which case annulment is no longer possible. When a husband (N: impotent from the beginning) acknowledges his impotence, the magistrate postpones action on the case for one year from the day it is first submitted to his consideration. If the husband has intercourse with her during the year, then she is not entitled to annul the marriage, though if he does not, then she may annul it. In cases of impotence, her above-mentioned prerogative of annulling the marriage "immediately" means after this period of one year.

m7.2 When a marriage is annulled before sexual intercourse, the woman does not receive her marriage payment (mahr) (N: no matter whether the defect is in her or in him (A: as opposed to divorce before sexual intercourse, as discussed at m8.7)).

العيوب المثبتة m7.0
للخيار في فسخ النكاح

m7.1 إذا وَجَدَ أحدُهُمَا الآخرَ مجنوناً أوْ مجذوماً أوْ أبرص أوْ وَجَدَها رتقاءَ أوْ قرناءَ أوْ وَجَدَتْهُ عنيناً أوْ مجبوباً ثَبَتَ الخيارُ في فسخ النكاح على الفور عند الحاكم (ومثل القاضي في ذلك المحكم بشرطه وهو أن يكون مجتهداً ولا قاضي) سواءٌ كانَ به ذلك العيبُ (بأن اتحد عيبهما كجنون كل منهما) أمْ لاَ .

ولوْ حَدَثَ العيبُ (المثبت للخيار بعد العقد) ثَبَتَ الخيارُ أيضاً ، إلاّ أنْ تَحْدُثَ العُنَّةُ بعد أنْ يطأَها فلاَ خيارَ وإذا أقَرَّ (الزوج) بالعنة أجَّلَهُ الحاكم سنةً مِنْ يوم المـرافعـة إليـهِ (أي القاضي) . فإنْ جَامَعَ فيهَا فلاَ فسخَ لهَا . وإلَّا فلهَا الفسخُ . والمرادُ بالفور في العنة عَقيبَ السنة .

m7.2 ومتَى وقَعَ الفسخُ فإنْ كانَ قبلَ الدخول فلا مهرَ (ح: سواءَ كان العيب بها أم به) .

When a marriage is annulled after intercourse because of a defect that occurred after it, the full marriage payment stipulated by their agreement must be paid to her.

When a marriage is annulled (N: after sexual intercourse) because of a defect that occurred before intercourse (O: whether simultaneously with the marriage agreement or after it but before intercourse), then the bride is only given the amount typically received as marriage payment by similar brides (def: m8.8).

أَوْ بعدَهُ بعيبٍ حَدَثَ بعدَ الوطءِ وَجَبَ المسمَّى .

أَوْ (كان الفسخُ) بعيبٍ حَدَثَ قبلَهُ (أي قبـل الـدخولِ سواء كانَ مقـارناً للعقدِ أو حادثاً بعدَه وقبلَ الوطءِ) فمهرُ المثلِ .

m7.3   [وإنْ شَرَطَ أَنَّهـا حرَةٌ فَبَـانَتْ أمـةً وهـو ممَّنْ يُحلُّ لُه نكـاحُ الأمةِ تَخَيَّـرَ . وإنْ شَرَطَ أَنَّها أمةٌ فَبَانَتْ حرةً، أوْلَمْ يشرِطْ فَبَانَتْ أمةً أوْ كتابيةً فلا خيارَ . وإنْ تَزَوَّجَ عبدٌ بأمةٍ فأُعتِقَتْ فلَها أنْ تَفْسَخَ نكاحُه علَى الفورِ منْ غيرِ الحاكمِ] .

m7.4   If any of the following occurs before intercourse has taken place, then the marriage is immediately annulled:

(1)   one of a couple who are idolators becomes a Muslim;

(2)   one of a Zoroastrian couple becomes Muslim;

(3)   the wife of a Jew or Christian becomes a Muslim;

(4)   both husband and wife leave Islam;

(5)   or one of them does.

But when one of the above things happens after intercourse, then a waiting period (def: n9) must intervene before the marriage is annulled. If both husband and wife (A: are, or) become Muslim before the waiting period finishes, then their marriage continues. And if not, then the marriage is considered to have been over since the change of religion first took place.

m7.4   وإذا أَسْلَمَ أحـدُ الـزوجينِ الوثنيينِ أوْ المجـوسيينِ أوْ أَسْلَمَتِ المرأةُ والـزوجُ يهـوديٌّ أو نصـرانيٌّ أو ارْتَـدَّ الزوجـانِ المسلمانِ أوْ أحدُهُمَا فإنْ كانَ قبـلَ الـدخولِ تَعجَّلَتِ الفرقةُ . وإنْ كانَ بعـدَهُ تَوَقَّفَتْ علَى انقضـاءِ العـدةِ، فإنِ اجْتَمَعـا علَى الإسـلامِ قبـلَ انقضائِها دَامَ النكاحُ وإلَّا حُكِمَ بالفرقةِ منْ حينِ تبديلِ الدينِ .

m7.5   When a (A: non-Muslim) man who has more than four wives becomes Muslim, he is obliged to choose just four of them (A: and the others' marriages are annulled).

m7.5   وإنْ أَسْلَمَ علَى أكثرَ منْ أربعٍ اخْتَارَ أربعاً منهُنَّ .

m8.0   THE BRIDE'S MARRIAGE PAYMENT (MAHR)

(O: The marriage payment is the money or property a husband must pay a woman to marry her.)

m8.1   It is sunna to name the amount of the marriage payment in the marriage agreement (O: to prevent discord). If it is not mentioned, it does not hurt (O: the validity of the marriage, though if unmentioned in the agreement, it is considered to be the amount typically received as marriage payment by similar brides (def: m8.8). There is complete scholarly consensus on the validity of a contract that does not mention it, though it is offensive not to).

m8.2   A guardian may not marry his prepubescent daughter to someone for less than the amount typically received as marriage payment by similar brides, nor marry his prepubescent son to a female who is given more than the amount typically received. If he does either of these, the amount stipulated is void and the amount typically received is paid instead (O: in both these cases, as a necessary condition for the validity of the marriage contract).

m8.3   Nor may a foolhardy man (def: k13.1(A:)) marry a woman for more than the amount typically received as marriage payment by similar brides.

m8.4   Anything that may be lawfully used as a price (def: k2) may be given as marriage payment. It may be paid immediately or deferred, and may be an individual article ('ayn), a financial obligation (dayn), or the use or benefit of something.

m8.5   The bride possesses the marriage payment when it has been expressly stipulated (O: in the marriage agreement, whether validly stipulated or invalidly. If valid, she owns the amount stated, while if invalid, she owns the amount typically

م8.0   المهر

(والمهر هو اسم للمال الواجب للمرأة على الزوج بنكاح) .

م8.1   يُسَنُّ تسميتُهُ في العقد (لأنه أدفع للخصومة) فإنْ لمْ يُذكَرْ لمْ يَضُرَّ (أي في صحة النكاح فإذا خلا العقد عن تسميته فيرجع فيه إلى مهر المثل وإخلاؤه عنه جائز إجماعاً لكن مع الكراهة) .

م8.2   ولا يُزَوِّجُ ابنتَهُ الصغيرةَ بأقلَّ مِنْ مهر المثل ولا ابنَهُ الصغيرَ بأكثرَ مِنْ مهرِ المثلِ . فإنْ فَعَلَ بطَلَ المسمَّى ووَجَبَ مهرُ المثلِ (في الصورتين لصحة النكاح) .

م8.3   ولا يَتَزَوَّجُ السفيهُ [والعبدُ] بأكثرَ مِنْ مهرِ المثلِ .

م8.4   وكلُّ ما جازَ أنْ يَكُونَ ثمناً جازَ جعلُهُ صداقاً . ويَجُوزُ حالاً ومؤجلاً وعيناً وديناً ومنفعةً .

م8.5   وتَمْلِكُهُ بالتسمية (أي ذكره في صلب العقد سواء كانت صحيحة أو فاسدة ففي التسمية الصحيحة تملك المسمى بعينه وفي الفاسدة تملك مهر

533

received as marriage payment by similar brides (def: m8.8). She may dispose of it when she accepts it, and her ownership of it is finalized when her husband has sexual intercourse with her (O: after which none of it is refundable), or when one of them dies before they have had intercourse.

المثل). وتتصرَّفُ فيه بالقبض ويستقرُّ بالدخول (فلا يسقط حينئذ منه شيء) أو بموت أحدِهما قبلَ الدخول.

m8.6 If payable immediately, the bride may refuse to have sexual intercourse until her husband gives her the marriage payment, though if she allows him to have intercourse with her before she accepts the amount, she may no longer refuse to have intercourse (N: but may demand the amount).

m8.6 ولهـا أنْ تَمْتَنِـعَ مِن تَسْليم نفسِهـا حتَّى تَقْبِضَـهُ إنْ كَانَ حالاً. فإنْ سلَّمَتْ نفسَهـا إليـه فوَطِئَهـا قبلَ القبض سَقَطَ حقُّها من الامتناع (ح: وتطالب بالمهر).

m8.7 If the couple is separated (A: by having annulled the marriage (dis: m7.4)), before intercourse because of an act on the bride's part, as when she becomes a Muslim (O: and the husband remains non-Muslim), or she leaves Islam (O: and the husband remains Muslim), then she is not entitled to any of the marriage payment. But if it is because of an act on the husband's part, as when he becomes Muslim, leaves Islam, or divorces her, then she receives only half of the marriage payment; or the husband may ask for half of it back (O: if she has already accepted it), provided the article given as payment still exists. If it does not, he receives half of the lowest market value of similar articles between the time of the marriage agreement and when the article ceased to exist. If the article was diminished while in the bride's possession, the husband has a choice between taking it back in its defective condition, or accepting half of its value.

m8.7 وإنْ وَرَدَتْ فرقـةٌ مِنْ جهتِهَا قبلَ الدخول بأنْ أسْلَمَتْ (وبقي الزوج على الكفر) أو ارْتَدَّتْ (وبقي الزوج على الإسلام) سَقَطَ المهرُ. أوْ مِنْ جهتِه بأنْ أسْلَمَ أو ارْتَدَّ أوْ طَلَّقَ سَقَطَ نصفُهُ ويَرْجِعُ في نصفِهِ (إن قبضته) إنْ كَانَ باقياً بعينِه وإلاَّ فنصف قيمتِه أقلَّ مَا كَانَتْ مِنَ العقدِ إلى التلفِ. [فإنْ كَانَ زائداً زيادةً منفصلةً رجَعَ في النصفِ دون الزيادة. أوْ متصلةً تَخَيَّـرَتْ بيـنَ ردِه زائـداً وبيـنَ نصف قيمتِه]. وإنْ كَانَ ناقصاً تَخَيَّـرَ بين أخذِه ناقصاً وبينَ نصف قيمتِه.

THE AMOUNT TYPICALLY RECEIVED AS MARRIAGE PAYMENT BY SIMILAR BRIDES

مهر المثل

m8.8 The *amount typically received as marriage payment by similar brides* (mahr al-mithl) means that which would be desirable to a woman like her (O: a woman like the bride, under normal circumstances), *like her* meaning a woman of her

m8.8 ثمَ مهرُ المثل هوَ مايُرغَبُ به في مثلهـا (أي مثـل المتـزوجة عادة من النسـاء) فيُعْتَبـرُ بمَنْ يُسـاويهَا مِنْ نسـاء

relatives resembling her in such characteristics as age, intelligence, beauty, wealth, being virgin or nonvirgin, and in having the same hometown. (O: Her relatives living therein are taken as the standard, and not those living elsewhere, since the amount typically received varies in different towns. Rafi'i holds that if all of them live in another town, they are nevertheless more suitable to be taken as the standard than nonfamily women from the same town.) If the bride is superior to them (O: respecting the above characteristics) or inferior, then this is taken into consideration (O: meaning she deserves a marriage payment that suits how she is). If she has no female relatives related to her through her father, then those *like her* refers to her maternal relatives (O: i.e. the mother's relatives, such as the bride's grandmother or mother's sister). If none of the above exist, then the standard for comparison is the marriage payment of those women of the same town who resemble the bride.

WHEN A HUSBAND IS UNABLE TO PAY THE MARRIAGE PAYMENT

m8.9   When a husband proves financially unable to give his wife the marriage payment (A: if it has not been deferred) before the first time they have sexual intercourse, then the bride may annul the marriage, though if he proves unable afterwards, she may not.

 If husband and wife disagree (A: in court, when neither side has proof) as to whether he has given her (O: all, or part of) the marriage payment, then the wife's word is accepted over the husband's (dis: k8.2). But if they disagree as to whether they have had sexual intercourse, the husband's word is accepted over the wife's.

m8.10   A man is obliged to pay a woman the amount typically received as marriage payment by similar brides (def: m8.8) when the marriage was (N: consummated, but) invalid, or when a man forces a woman to fornicate with him. When a woman voluntarily fornicates with a man, she does not receive any marriage payment.

عصبـاتِهـا في السـنّ والعقـل والجمـالِ واليسـار والثيـوبـةِ والبكـارةِ والبلدِ (فيعتبر بمن فيهـا من نسـاء عصبـاتهـا دون غيرهـا لأن عادة البـلاد في المهـر مختلفـة . قال الـرافعي ولـو كان جميعهن في بلد أخرى فالاعـتبـار بهـن أولى من الاعتبـار بالأجنبيـات في تلك البلدة) فإن اخْتَصَّتْ (المـرأة عنهن) بمـزيـدٍ (من الصفـات المـذكـورة) أو نقص رُوعِـيَ ذلـك (والمعنى فرض لها مهر لائق بالحال) فإنْ لمْ يَكُنْ لَهَا عصبـاتٌ منَ النسـاء فبالأرحام (قرابـات الأمّ كالجـدة والخالة) وإلّا فبنسـاء بلدِها ومَنْ يُشْبِهُهَا .

إعسار الزوج بالمهر

m8.9   وإذا أَعْسَـرَ (الـزوج) بالمهر قبـل الـدخولِ فلهـا الفسخُ . أوْ بعدَهُ فَلا . فإن اخْتَلَفَـا في قبضِ الصـداقِ (كله أو بعضه) فالقولُ قولُهَا . أوْ في الوطءِ فقولُهُ .

m8.10   ومَنْ وطِىءَ امـرأةً [بشبهـةٍ أوْ] في نكـاحٍ فاسـدٍ أوْ زنـاً وهيَ مكرهةً لَزِمَهُ مهـرُ المثـل . وإنْ طَاوَعَتْـهُ علىَ الزنَا فَلا مهْرَ لَهَا .

AMENITY PAYMENT

m8.11 Whenever a woman is divorced (O: before having had intercourse) and the marriage payment is reduced to one-half (dis: m8.7), she does not receive an *amenity payment* (def: below). But she is entitled to one when the marriage payment is not reduced to one-half, such as when:

(1) she receives no marriage payment because of having allowed her guardian to choose a spouse for her and then having been divorced before intercourse and before any payment was stipulated;

(2) or when she receives the full marriage payment, as when she is divorced after intercourse.

An *amenity payment* is an amount (N: paid by the husband) determined by the Islamic judge through his own personal reasoning (O: it being obligatory that both the husband and wife agree to it, and sunna that it not be less than thirty dirhams (n: 88.94 grams of silver) or something worth that much, and that it amount to less than half the marriage payment), in view of the circumstances of both parties (O: such as how rich or poor the husband is, and the wife's lineage and other characteristics previously discussed).

تمتيع المطلقة

m8.11 وحيثُ طُلِّقَت (الزوجة قبل الدخول) وشُطِرَ المهرُ لا مُتْعَةَ لَها. وحيثُ لم يَتَشطَّر إمّا بأنْ لا يَجِبَ شيءٌ كالمفوَّضة إذا طُلِّقَت قبلَ الدخول والفرض، أو بأنْ يَجِبَ الكُلُّ كالطلاق بعدَ الدخول ؛ وَجَبَ لها المتعةُ .

وهيَ شيءٌ [(من المـال)] يُقـدِّرُهُ القـاضِي باجتهادِهِ (والواجب فيها ما يتراضى الزوجان عليه ويسن أن لا تنقص عن ثلاثين درهماً أو ما قيمته ذلك وأن لا تبلغ نصف المهر) ويُعْتَبَرُ فيـهِ حَالُ الزوجين (من يسار الزوج وإعساره ونسب المرأة وصفاتها السابقة) .

*

m9.0 THE WEDDING FEAST

m9.1 The wedding feast is a sunna (A: whose time never expires, though it is recommended to be after intercourse). The sunna is for the meal to consist of a sheep or goat (*shah*, def: h2.5), though it is permissible to serve whatever food is readily available.

THE OBLIGATION TO ATTEND

m9.2 It is obligatory for whoever is invited to attend (O: and whoever does not respond to the

m9.0 وليمة العرس

m9.1 وليمـةُ العرسِ سُنَّةٌ. والسُّنَّةُ أنْ يُولِم بشاةٍ ويَجوزُ ما تَيَسَّرَ منَ الطعامِ .

وجوب الحضور لمن دعي

m9.2 ومَنْ دُعِي إلَيْها لَزِمَتْهُ الإجابةُ (ومن لم يجب الدعوة فقد عصى الله

invitation has disobeyed Allah and His messenger (Allah bless him and give him peace)), whether fasting or not. If one attends, it is recommended to eat, though not obligatory. If one is performing a voluntary fast and attends, and it is not burdensome for the host, then it is best to complete one's fast, though if this would weigh on the host, it is better for one to eat. It is only obligatory to respond to such an invitation if the following conditions are met:

(a) that the host not have invited the rich to the exclusion of the poor;

(b) that the invitation be for the first day of the wedding feast, for if the host celebrates it for three days, it is not obligatory to respond if invited on the second day, and offensive to do so on the third;

(c) that the motive for attending not be fear of the host or desire for the prestige of having attended;

(d) that no one will be there who will hurt one, or whose company is unsuitable (O: because of their vileness, for example, such as people devoid of morals or character);

(e) and that there will be nothing blameworthy there such as flutes, wine, silk-covered sitting mats, or pictures of animate life (dis: p44) on the ceiling, walls, upright pillows (O: not those lying flat (dis: below)), or draperies; or clothing inscribed with something blameworthy, and so forth (O: since a person who attends in the presence of such things is as though accepting and acquiescing to what is condemnable). But if the blameworthy thing will be removed through one's attending, or if the above-mentioned pictures are on the ground, a carpet, or pillows people lean upon (N: or other humiliated deployment, which is lawful), or if the living figures are decapitated, or there are pictures of (n: vegetative life such as) trees, then one must attend.

m9.3 Strewing sweets and the like around at marriage agreements or picking them up is not offensive, but it is better not to.

ورسوله) صائماً كانَ أو مفطراً . فإذا حَضَرَ نُدِبَ لهُ الأكلُ ولا يجبُ . فإنْ كانَ صائماً تطـوعـاً ولمْ يَشُقَّ على صاحب الـوليـمة صومُهُ فإتمـام الصوم أفضلُ . وإنْ شَقَّ عليـه صومُهُ فالفطرُ أفضـلُ . ولـوجوب الإجابة شروطٌ : أنْ لا يَخُصَّ بها الأغنياءَ دونَ الفقراء، وأنْ يدعوهُ في اليوم الأول فإنْ أوْلَمَ ثلاثة أيام فدَعاهُ في اليوم الثاني لمْ تَجبْ أوفي الثـالثِ كُرهَتْ إجابتُهُ، وأنْ لا يَحْضُرَهُ لخوفٍ منـهُ أوْ طمعـاً في جاهِهِ، وأنْ لا يَكُونَ ثَمَ مَنْ يَتَأذَّى أوْ لا تَليقُ به مجالستُهُ (لقبحه مثلاً كالأراذل) ولا منكرٌ مِنْ زمرٍ وخمرٍ وفُرُشٍ حرير وصور حيـوانٍ على سقـفٍ أوْ جدارٍ أوْ وسادةٍ منصوبـةٍ (لا مطروحة) أوْ سترٍ أوْ ثوبٍ مكتـوبٍ عليـه منكرٌ وغير ذلك (لأنه بالحضور يصير كالراضي بالمنكر ومقرراً له) فإنْ كانَ المنكـرُ يَزُولُ بحضـورِه أوْ كانَتِ الصـورُ على الأرض في بسـاطٍ أوْ مخـدةٍ يتَّكىءُ عليها أوْ مقطوعة الرأس أو صُورَ الشجر فَليَحْضُرْ.

m9.3 ولا يُكرهُ نثرُ السُّكَّر ونحوِه في الإملاكات بَلْ هوَ خلافُ الأولى والتقاطُهُ أيضاً خلافُ الأولى .

| m10.0 RELATIONS BETWEEN A HUSBAND AND WIVES | m10.0 معاشرة الأزواج |

m10.1 It is obligatory for both husband and wife to treat each other well (O: since Allah Most High says,

"Women deserve the like of what they are obliged to give, in kindness" (Koran 2:228)),

and for each to give the other what they must (O: meaning that both spouses are required to, the husband giving her the expenditures he is obliged to (def: m11), and the wife giving herself to him and obeying him concerning his rights therein) without intentional delays or displaying resentment.

m10.1 يجبُ على كلِّ واحـدٍ منَ الـزوجين المعـاشرةُ بالمعروف (قـال تعـالى: ﴿وَلَهُنَّ مِثْـلُ الَّـذِي عَلَيْهِنَّ بِالمَعْرُوفِ﴾) وبـذلُ ما يَلْزَمُـهُ (أي يلزم كل من الزوجين بأن يبذل الزوج ما يجب عليـه من النفقـة وتسلم المـرأة نفسهـا له وتطيعه فيمـا يتعلق به من حقـه) مِنْ غيـر مَطْـلٍ [(والمطل مدافعة الحق مع القدرة على التأدية)] ولا إظهار كراهِةٍ.

m10.2 It is unlawful for a man to house two wives in the same lodgings unless they both agree.

m10.2 ويَحْرُمُ على الرجلِ أنْ يُسْكِنَ زوجتين في مسكنٍ واحدٍ إلَّا برضاهُمَا.

PERMITTING ONE'S WIFE TO LEAVE THE HOUSE

حكم خروج المرأة من بيتها

m10.3 (A: A husband may permit his wife to leave the house for a lesson in Sacred Law, for invocation of Allah (dhikr), to see her female friends, or to go to any place in the town. A woman may not leave the city without her husband or a member of her unmarriageable kin (def: m6.2) accompanying her, unless the journey is obligatory, like the hajj. It is unlawful for her to travel otherwise, and unlawful for her husband to allow her to.) (n: In the Hanafi school, it is not unlawful for her to travel beyond city limits without a husband or member of her unmarriageable kin unless the distance to her intended destination exceeds ca. 77 km./ 48 mi. (al-Lubab fi sharh al-Kitab (y88), 1.105).)

m10.4 The husband may forbid his wife to leave the home (O: because of the hadith related by Bayhaqi that the Prophet (Allah bless him and give him peace) said,

"It is not permissible for a woman who believes in Allah and the Last Day to allow someone into her husband's house if he is opposed, or to go out if he is averse").

But if one of her relatives dies, it is preferable to let her leave to visit them.

m10.4 ولهُ أن يَمْنَعَهـا منَ الخـروج منْ منـزلِـه (لمـا روى البيهقي من قوله ﷺ: «لا يحـل لامرأة تؤمن بالله واليوم الآخـر أن تأذن في بيت زوجهـا وهـو كاره ولا أن تخـرج وهـو كاره»). فإنْ مَاتَ لَهَا قريبٌ اسْتُحِبَّ أنْ يأذَنَ لَهَا في الخروج.

TAKING TURNS WITH WIVES

القسم بين الزوجات

m10.5 A husband with more than one wife is not obliged to spend his nights with them in turns but may keep away from them (A: all) without sin. But he may not begin spending the night with one of them unless he chooses her by drawing lots. Whenever he spends the night with one wife, he is obliged to spend nights with the others, giving equal time to each one. When a husband intends to begin staying with his wives (A: after an intermission or absence), the wife whose lot is drawn is the first with whom he spends the night. All are included in taking turns, whether a wife in her period or postnatal bleeding, one who is ill, or one who cannot have intercourse because of a vaginal birth defect.

The minimal amount of time for one turn is a night and day, whether the day comes before or after the night; while the maximum is three days (A: and nights. The minimal turn for the Hanafi and Maliki schools is whatever all can agree upon). It may not be more than three days (A: except by their leave). The basic *turn* of someone who makes their living by day is the night, with the day being an adjunct, while for someone who makes their living at night, such as a watchman, the basic turn is the day.

In staying the night, the husband is not obliged to have sexual intercourse with the wife, though it is recommended to have intercourse (and share all other marital enjoyments) with all one's wives on an equal basis.

m10.5 ومَنْ لهُ نساءٌ لا يَجِبُ عليهِ أنْ يَقْسِمَ لهُنَّ بلْ لهُ الإعـراضُ عنـهنَّ بلا إثمٍ . ولَيْسَ لهُ أنْ يَبْتَـدِىءَ المبيتَ عنـدَ إحداهُنَّ إلّا بالقرعةِ . فإنْ باتَ عندَ واحدةٍ منهُنَّ لَزِمَهُ المبيتُ عنـدَ الباقياتِ بقدرِهِ . فإذا أرادَ القسمَ أقْرَعَ فمَنْ خَرَجَتْ قرعتُها قَدَّمَـهـا . ويَقْسِمُ للحـائضِ والنفسـاءِ والمـريضـةِ والرتقاءِ . [فإنْ كانَ معهُ حرةٌ وأمةٌ قَسَمَ للحرةِ مثـلَ ما للأمةِ مرتينِ] . وأقـلُ القسمِ ليلةٌ ويَتْبَعُهـا يومُ قبلَهـا أوْ بعـدَهـا وأكثـرُهُ ثلاثـةُ أيامٍ ولا يُزادُ على ذلكَ . وعمادُ القسمِ الليلُ . والنهارُ تابعٌ لمَنْ معيشتُهُ بالنهـارِ . فإنْ كانَتْ معيشتُـهُ بالليلِ كالحـارسِ فعمادُ قسمِهِ بالنهارِ . ولا يَجِبُ عليهِ وطءٌ لكنْ تُنْـدَبُ التسويةُ بَيْنَهُنَّ فيهِ وفي سائرِ الاستمتاعاتِ .

m10.6 If the husband wants to take one of his wives on a journey with him, he may not do so unless he draws lots to see who it will be. If he draws lots (A: and takes the winner with him), then when he returns, he does not need to make up the turns which the other wives missed while he was on the journey. If he did not draw lots but just chose a wife to travel with him, this is a sin, and on his return he must give equal time to the other wives for the time they missed.

m10.6 وإنْ أرادَ أنْ يُسَافِرَ بامرأةٍ منهُنَّ لمْ يَجُـزْ إلّا بقـرعـةٍ . فإنْ سَافَـرَ بقرعةٍ لمْ يَقْضِ للمقيمةِ . وإنْ سَافَرَ بها بغيرِ قرعةٍ أثِمَ ولَزِمَهُ القضاءُ .

m10.7 It is permissible for one of the wives to give her turn to another wife, if the husband

m10.7 ومَنْ وَهَبَتْ حقَّهـا مِنَ القسـمِ لبعضِ ضرائرِها برضا الزوجِ جَازَ . وإنْ

agrees. If one of them gives him her turn, then he may give it to whomever he wants. If the wife later chooses to take her turn back, she returns to her usual place in the order of taking turns as it stands on the day she takes it back.

m10.8   It is not permissible for a husband to enter the quarters of a wife during another wife's turn without business there, though if he stops in during the day because of something he needs, or during the night because of something absolutely necessary (A: such as bringing her supper), then he may enter. Otherwise he may not.

If he prolongs such a visit, then he is obliged to make up the turn of the wife whose turn it originally was.

m10.9   If a man marries a new wife when he already has another, he interrupts the succession of turns to spend time with the new wife. If she is a virgin, then he stays with her seven days and need not make them up with the other wives. If she is a nonvirgin, then he may choose to either spend seven days with her and make up (O: to the others the number in excess of three days), or spend three days with her and not make up the time with the others. In such cases it is recommended to let the new wife choose the alternative she prefers. If the husband stays with her for seven days at her request, he must make up all seven days with the others, though if he stays seven days without her having requested it, he need only make up four with the others.

m10.10 The husband is entitled to leave home during the day to fulfill his needs and obligations.

DEALING WITH A REBELLIOUS WIFE

m10.12 When a husband notices *signs* of rebelliousness in his wife (nushuz, dis: p42) (O:

وَهَبَتْ للزوجِ جَعَلَهُ لِمَنْ شَاءَ مِنهنَّ . فإنْ رَجَعَتْ في الهبةِ عادَتْ إلى الدورِ مِنْ يوم الرجوعِ .

m10.8 ولا يَجُوزُ أَنْ يَدْخُلَ على امرأة في نوبةِ أخرَى بلا شُغْلٍ . فإنْ دَخَلَ بالنهارِ لحاجةٍ أوْ بالليل لضرورةٍ جَازَ . وإلّا فَلا . وإنْ أقامَ لَزِمَهُ القضاءُ .

m10.9 وإن تَزَوَّجَ جديــدةً وعــنــدَهُ غيـرَهَا قطَعَ الدورَ للجديدة . فإنْ كانَتْ بكراً أقامَ عندَها سبعاً ولمْ يَقْضِ . وإنْ كانَتْ ثيّباً فهوَ بالخيارِ بينَ أَنْ يُقيمَ عندَها سبعاً ويَقْضِي (للبــاقيــات ما زادَ على ثلاثٍ) وبيـنَ أَنْ يُقيمَ ثلاثاً ولا يَقْضِيَ . ويُنْدَبُ لهُ أَنْ يُخَيِّرَهَا بينَهُمَا . فإنْ أقامَ سبعاً بطلبِهَا قَضَى السبعَ . أوْ بدونِه قَضَى أربعاً فَقَطْ .

m10.10 ولـهُ الخـروجُ نهـاراً لقضـاءِ الحاجاتِ والحقوقِ .

m10.11 [ومَنْ مَلَكَ إماءً لمْ يَلْزَمْهُ أَنْ يَقْسِمَ لهنَّ . ويُنْدَبُ أنْ لا يُعَطِّلَهُنَّ مِنَ الوطءِ وأنْ يُسَاوِيَ بَيْنَهُنَّ فيه] .

معاملة الناشز

m10.12 وإذا رَأَى مِنَ المـرأةِ أمـاراتِ النشوزِ (قولاً كان النشوزُ كأن تجيبه بكلام

whether in words, as when she answers him coldly when she used to do so politely, or he asks her to come to bed and she refuses, contrary to her usual habit; or whether in acts, as when he finds her averse to him when she was previously kind and cheerful), he warns her in words (O: without keeping from her or hitting her, for it may be that she has an excuse. The warning could be to tell her, "Fear Allah concerning the rights you owe to me," or it could be to explain that rebelliousness nullifies his obligation to support her and give her a turn amongst other wives, or it could be to inform her, "Your obeying me [def: (3) below] is religiously obligatory"). If she *commits* rebelliousness, he keeps from sleeping (O: and having sex) with her without words, and may hit her, but not in a way that injures her, meaning he may not (A: bruise her,) break bones, wound her, or cause blood to flow. (O: It is unlawful to strike another's face.) He may hit her whether she is rebellious only once or whether more than once, though a weaker opinion holds that he may not hit her unless there is repeated rebelliousness.

(N: To clarify this paragraph, we mention the following rulings:

(1) Both man and wife are obliged to treat each other kindly and graciously.

(2) It is not lawful for a wife to leave the house except by the permission of her husband, though she may do so without permission when there is a pressing necessity. Nor may a wife permit anyone to enter her husband's home unless he agrees, even their unmarriageable kin. Nor may she be alone with a nonfamily-member male, under any circumstances.

(3) It is obligatory for a wife to obey her husband as is customary in allowing him full lawful sexual enjoyment of her person. It is obligatory for the husband to enable her to remain chaste and free of want for sex if he is able. It is not obligatory for the wife to serve her husband (dis: w45.1); if she does so, it is voluntary charity.

(4) If the wife does not fulfill one of the above-mentioned obligations, she is termed "rebellious" (nashiz), and the husband takes the

خشن بعد أن كان بليـن ، وإذا دعـاهـا إلى فراشـه لا تجيبـه بعـد أن كانت تجيبـه ؛ أو فعـلاً كأن يجـد منهـا إعراضاً وعبوساً بعد لطف وطـلاقـة وجه) وَعَظَهَا بالكلام (بلا هجر وضرب فلعلها أن تبدي عذراً ، كأن يقول لها : اتقي الله في الحق الواجب لي عليك ؛ ويبين لها أن النشـوز يسقط النفقة والقسم ، وكأن يقـول لهـا : طاعتي عليك فرض) وإنْ صَرَّحَتْ بالنشـوز هَجَرَها في الفراش (فلا يضـاجعهـا) دون الكـلام وضربَهَا ضرباً (وضرب الوجه لا يجوز) غيـر مُبَرِّح أي لا يكُسِرُ عظماً ولا يُجْرَحُ لحمـاً ولا يَنْهَرُ دمـاً سواءٌ نَشَزَتْ مرةً أوْ تَكَرَّرَ منْهـا . وقيلَ لا يَضْرِبُها إلا إذا تَكَرَّرَ نشورُهَا .

(ح : توضيحـاً لهـذه الفقـرة نذكر الأحكام التالية :

ـ يجب على كل من الـزوجين معـاملة صاحبه بالمعروف والإحسان .

ـ لا يجـوز للزوجـة أن تخرج من بيت الـزوجيـة إلا بإذن الزوج ، ويجوز لها أن تخـرج عند الضرورة بلا إذن . ولا يجوز للزوجـة أن تأذن لأحـد أن يدخـل بيت الـزوج إلا برضـاه حتى محـارمها . ولا تجوز الخلوة بالأجنبي على كل حال .

ـ يجب على الـزوجة طاعة الزوج في الاستـمتـاع الجـنـسـي المـشـروع بالمعروف ، وعلى الزوج أن يعف زوجته إن استطاع . ولا يجب على المرأة خدمة الزوج فإن فعلت فهي متبرعة .

ـ إذا لم تقم الـزوجة بمـا يجب عليها ممـا سبق سميت ناشـزاً ، وعنـدئـذ يتبـع

541

following steps to correct matters:

(a) admonition and advice, by explaining the unlawfulness of rebellion, its harmful effect on married life, and by listening to her viewpoint on the matter;

(b) if admonition is ineffectual, he keeps from her by not sleeping in bed with her, by which both learn the degree to which they need each other;

(c) if keeping from her is ineffectual, it is permissible for him to hit her if he believes that hitting her will bring her back to the right path, though if he does not think so, it is not permissible. His hitting her may not be in a way that injures her, and is his last recourse to save the family;

(d) if the disagreement does not end after all this, each partner chooses an arbitrator to solve the dispute by settlement, or divorce.)

*

m11.0 THE WIFE'S FINANCIAL SUPPORT

(O: *Support* means the financial rights of a wife.)

m11.1 (A: The rulings of this section are not recommendations for how much to spend, but rather define the minimum permissible, which a stingy husband may not lawfully spend less than. Extra spending on one's wife is charity.)

FOOD

m11.2 The husband is obliged to provide his wife's sustenance day by day. If affluent, he must daily furnish her with one liter of the grain that is the staple food of the town in which they live. (O: By the *grain that is the staple food* of the town, the author means *if people eat it.* If not, then whatever they eat, even if it is hardened, dried white cheese. If the wife asks for something other than the staple food of the town, the husband does not have to

الزوج الخطوات التالية للإصلاح :

(١) الوعظ والنصيحة فيبين لها حرمة النشوز وضرره على الحياة الزوجية ، ويسمع وجهة نظرها في الموضوع .

(٢) إن لم ينفع الوعظ هجرها فلا ينام معها في الفراش ، وبذلك يعرف كل منهما مدى حاجته لصاحبه .

(٣) إذا لم ينفع الهجر جاز له ضربها إن ظن أن الضرب يردها للصواب ، وإلا فلا ، ويكون الضرب غير مبرح ، وهو محاولة أخيرة لإنقاذ الأسرة .

(٤) إذا لم ينته الخلاف بعد كل هذا انتخب كل من الزوجين حكماً لحل الخلاف ، بالإصلاح أو الطلاق) .

m11.0 نفقة الزوجة

(والمراد ما يجب للزوجة من الحقوق المالية)

الطعام

m11.2 يَجِبُ على الزوجِ نفقةُ زوجتِهِ يوماً بيوم . فإنْ كَانَ موسراً لَزِمَهُ مَدّان مِنَ الحبِّ المقتـاتِ في البلدِ . (وقول المصنف من الحب المقتـات أي إن كانوا يقتاتونه ؛ وإلا فمما يقتاتونه . ولو أقطاً فلو طلبت غير ما يقتات في البلد لم تلزمه الإجابة . ولو بذل لها غيره لم يلزمها

provide it for her, and if he gives her something besides the staple, she need not accept it. The staple food is what is obligatory.) If he is not affluent, then he is obliged to provide 0.51 liters of grain a day for his wife; while if between affluence and nonaffluence, he must provide 0.77 liters per day.

He is also obliged to cover the expenses of grinding it into flour and baking it into bread (O: even when she is used to doing it herself, as there would otherwise be need for this expenditure), and to buy the foods that normally accompany bread to make it savory and agreeable, as much as is customary in the town of meat, oil, and so forth (O: such as dates, vinegar, and cheese. The obligatory measures differ with the seasons, it being necessary in each season to provide that which is proper to it. Fruits might predominate in one season, and thus be obligatory. As for the obligatory amount of meat, one sees how much is customarily consumed in town per week).

If husband and wife agree that he give her compensation in place of the above-mentioned (O: grain and other things she is entitled to, the compensation being in money or clothing), this is permissible.

ARTICLES FOR PERSONAL HYGIENE

m11.3 The wife in entitled to what she needs of oil for her hair, shampoo (lit. "sidr"), and a comb (O: to keep her hair clean, of the kind and amount that is customary in town, in order to prevent harm to herself. If oil scented with rose or violet is the custom of the town, it must be provided, though not things which are merely cosmetic and not for cleanliness, such as eyeliner or henna, which need not be provided, though the husband may provide them if he wishes. It is also obligatory for him to provide deodorant (lit. "litharge") or the like to stop underarm odor if water and soap will not suffice), and the price of water for her purificatory bath (ghusl) when the reason for it is sexual intercourse or the end of postnatal bleeding, though not if the reason is the end of her monthly period or something else (dis: m11.1).

القبـول بل يتعين ما يقتـاتـونه) . وإنْ كانَ معسـراً فمـدُ . وإنْ كانَ متـوسطـاً فمـدُ ونصفٌ . ويَلْزَمُـهُ مَعَ ذلـكَ أجـرةُ الطحن والخبز (وإن اعتادته بنفسها للحاجة لهذه الأجرة) والأدم علىٰ حسب عادة البلدِ مِنَ اللحم والدهن وغير ذلكَ (كالتمر والخل والجبن . ويختلف الـواجب بالفصـول فيجب في كل فصل ما يناسبه ، وقد تغلب الفـواكـه في أوقـاتهـا فتجب . وينظـر في اللحم إلىٰ عادة المحل من أسبوع أو غيره) .

فإنْ تَرَاضَيَـا علىٰ أخـذِ العـوضِ عـنْ ذلـكَ (المـذكور مما وجب لها من الحب ومـا بعـده . وذلك العـوض كالـدراهم والدنانير والثياب) جَازَ .

أدوات التنظيف

m11.3 ولَهَا ما تَحْتَاجُ إليهِ مِنَ الدهن للرأس والسـدر والمشـطِ (لتنظيفه علىٰ عادة البلد جنسـاً وقـدراً ، دفعـاً للضـرر . وإن جرت العـادة فيه باستعمـال الـدهن المطيب بنحـو الـورد والبنفسـج وجب بخـلاف ما لا يقصـد منـه التنظيف بل التـزين كالكحـل والخضـاب ، فإنـه لا يجب بل هو باختيار الـزوج . ويجب لها مرتك ونحوه لدفع الصنان إن لم يندفع بالمـاء و[التراب] (ت: أو في زمـاننـا الصابون) وثمن ماء الاغتسـال إنْ كانَ سببُهُ جماعاً أوْ نفاساً فإنْ كانَ سببُهُ حيضاً أوْ غير ذلك لَمْ يَلْزَمْهُ .

COSMETICS AND MEDICINE	الطيب والأدوية

m11.4 The husband is not obliged (N: but rather is recommended) to pay for his wife's cosmetics, doctor's fees, the purchase of medicine for her, and similar expenses (A: though he must pay for expenditures connected with childbirth).

m11.4 ولا يَلْزَمُهُ ثمنُ الطيب [(الذي يقصد للزينة)] ولا أجرةُ الطبيب ولا شراءُ الأدوية ونحوِ ذلك.

CLOTHING	الكسوة

m11.5 A wife is entitled to the kind of clothing that is customary in town for dressing oneself (O: and not just anything termed *clothing* will suffice. What is obligatory is the amount necessary for the woman, which varies according to whether she is tall or short, thin or fat, and with the hot or cold climate of various towns. In the summertime, it is obligatory to provide her with a head covering, shift, underdrawers, shoes, and a shawl, because of her need to go out; and the same in the wintertime, plus a cloak quilted with cotton to protect her against the cold. If she needs two cloaks because of the extreme cold, it is obligatory to provide them. If she needs fuel because of the severity of the winter, it is obligatory to buy the necessary wood and coal) and (O: he must also provide the amount customary in town of the) bedding, blankets, and pillows that are suitable for someone of his income. (O: She also deserves cooking implements, and utensils for eating and drinking).

m11.5 ويَجِبُ لها مِنَ الكسوة ما جَرَت به العادةُ في البلدِ مِنْ ثيابِ البدن (ولا يكفي ما ينطلق عليه اسم الكسوة بل تجب على قدر كفاية المرأة فتختلف بطولها وقصرها وهزالها وسمنها واختلاف البلد حرارة وبرودة. فيجب لها في الصيف خمار وقميص وسراويل وخف ورداء لحاجتها إلى الخروج وفي الشتاء مثل ذلك وتزاد جبة محشوة بقطن لدفع البرد. ولو احتاجت إلى جبتين لشدة البرد وجبتا. وإذا لم تستغن بالشتاء عن الوقود لشدة البرد فيجب لها من الحطب والفحم ما يندفع به الحاجة) ويجب لها أيضاً ما جرت به العادة في البلد من) الفرش والغطاء والوسادة على حسب ما يليقُ بيساره وإعساره (ويجب لها أيضاً عليه آلة الطبخ والأكل والشرب).

m11.6 It is obligatory for the husband to give his wife the expenditures for her support at the first of each day, and to provide her clothing at the first of each season (O: meaning the beginning of winter and summer).

m11.6 ويَجِبُ تسليمُ النفقةِ إليها مِنْ أولِ النهارِ وتسليمُ الكسوةِ مِنْ أولِ الفصل (أي أول فصل الشتاء وأول فصل الصيف).

m11.7 If he gives her clothing for a season, and it wears out before the end of the season, he is not obliged to furnish new clothing, though if it lasts beyond the season, he is nevertheless obliged to provide new clothing for each new season. The wife is entitled to dispose of the clothing as she

m11.7 فإنْ أعطاها كسوةَ مدةٍ فبَلِيَتْ قبلها لم يَلْزَمْهُ إبدالُها. وإنْ بَقِيَتْ بعدَ المدةِ لَزِمَهُ التجديدُ. ولها أنْ تَتَصَرَّفَ في كسوتها بالبيع

wishes, whether by selling it or other (O: means of disposal, such as giving it away, the reason being that it is her own property).

وغيره (من أنواع التصرفات كالهبة وهذا مبني على أنها تمليك) .

HOUSING AND SERVANTS

المسكن والخادم

m11.8 The wife is entitled to housing of the same quality as that of similar women. (O: The standard of housing depends on the wife herself, while the standard for her clothing and support takes the state of the husband into consideration. The difference is because the expenditures for her support and clothing become her own property and are not merely for her use, while housing is solely for use (N: meaning that while she can take compensation in place of food or clothing and buy some other kind, she cannot rent a different house). In any case, she is obliged to stay in the lodgings her husband arranges for her.)

m11.8 ويـجـب لَهـا سكنَى مثلِهـا (والسكنى تعتبر بالـزوجة بخلاف النفقة والكسوة فإنهمـا تعتبر بالزوج والفرق أن النفقة والكسوة تمليك لا إمتاع بخلاف السكنى فإنها إمتـاع (ح) : فتستطيع أن تشتري بدل الطعام والكساء ولا تستطيع أن تستأجـر بدل المسكن) وعلى كل حال يجب عليها ملازمة المسكن الذي أعده وهيأه الـزوج لها) . وإنْ كَانَتْ تُخْدَمُ في بيتِ أبيهـا لَزِمَـهُ إخْـدَامُهَـا [وتَلْزَمُـهُ نفقة الخادم إذا كَانَ مِلْكَها] .

If she had servants in her father's house, the husband is obliged to provide servants for her.

THE CONDITIONS THAT ENTITLE A WIFE TO SUPPORT

شروط لزوم النفقة

m11.9 The husband is only obliged to support his wife when she gives herself to him or offers to, meaning she allows him full enjoyment of her person and does not refuse him sex at any time of the night or day. She is not entitled to support from her husband when:

m11.9 وإنمـا تَلزَمُهُ النفقةُ إذا سَلَّمَتْ المـرأةُ نفسَهـا إليه أوْ عَرَضَتْ نفسَها عليْه [أوْ عَرَضَهـا وليُّهـا إنْ كَانَتْ صغيرةً سواءٌ كَانَ الـزوجُ كبيراً أوْ صغيـراً لا يَتأتَّى منـه الـوطءُ . إلَّا أنْ تُسَـلَّم وهيَ صغيرةً ولا يُمْكِنُ وطؤُهَـا فَلَا نفقةَ لَها] وشرطُ ذلك

(1) she is rebellious (nashiz, def: m10.12(N:)) (O: meaning when she does not obey him) even if for a moment;

أيضـاً أنْ تُمَكِّنَهُ التمكينَ التـامَّ بحيثُ لا تَمْتَنِعُ منـهُ في ليـلٍ أوْ نهـارٍ . فلوْ نَشَزَتْ (الـزوجـة أي خرجت عن طاعـة الزوج)

(2) she travels without his permission, or with his permission but for one of her own needs;

ولوْ في ساعـةٍ [أوْ لحظة من لحظات النهار أو الليل)] أوْ سَافَرَتْ بغير إذنِه أوْ

(3) she assumes ihram for hajj or 'umra (def: j3);

بإذنِه لحاجتِهـا أوْ أحْرَمَتْ أوْ صَامَتْ تطوعاً بغير إذنِـه (وفي صوم النفل إذا أقرها ولم

(4) or when she performs a voluntary fast without her husband's permission (O: though if he allows her to fast and does not ask her to break it, he must provide her support).

يأمرها بالإفطار فلا تسقـط نفقتهـا [أوْ كَانَتْ أمـةً فَسَلَّمَهَا السيدُ ليـلاً فقطْ] فَلَا نفقةَ لَها .

545

SUPPORT FOR A WOMAN IN HER
POSTMARITAL WAITING PERIOD

m11.10 As for a woman in her postmarital waiting period (def: n9), she is entitled to housing during it no matter if it is because of her husband's death, a divorce in which the husband may take her back, or a threefold, finalized divorce. As for her support (A: in terms of food) and clothing:

(1) it is not obligatory to provide her with it during the waiting period after (N: a threefold divorce, a release for payment (def: n5), or) her husband's death;

(2) it must be provided in the waiting period of a (A: not yet threefold) divorce in which her husband may take her back;

(3) and if a woman in the waiting period of a threefold divorce is pregnant, she is given support each day (A: until the child is born, after which she is entitled to support and wages for taking care of it), but if not pregnant, she is not entitled to support.

m11.11 If the husband and wife disagree (A: in court, when neither has proof (dis: k8.2)) about whether she received her support from him, her word is accepted over his. If they disagree as to whether she allowed him full enjoyment of her person, then his word is accepted over hers unless he admits that she first made herself available to him, but claims she then refused, in which case her word is accepted over his.

m11.12 Whenever the husband neglects to provide his wife's support for a period of time, the amount he should have paid remains a debt he owes to her.

m11.13 The wife is entitled to annul their marriage whenever the husband is unable to provide her with the support obligatory for a nonaffluent person to pay (def: m11.2) and provide clothing or

m11.10 وأمّا المعتدةُ فيجبُ لَهَا السكنى في مدة العدة سواءٌ كانَتْ العدةُ عدةَ وفاةٍ أوْ رجعيةٍ أوْ بائنٍ . وأمّا النفقةُ فلا تَجِبُ في عدة الوفاةِ وتَجِبُ للرجعيةِ مطلقاً وللبائنِ إنْ كانَتْ حاملاً يَدْفَعُ إليهَا يوماً بيومٍ وإنْ لمْ تَكُنْ البائنُ حاملاً فلا نفقةَ لَها . والكسوةُ كالنفقة .

m11.11 وإن اخْتَلَفَ الزوجانِ في قبض النفقةِ فالقولُ قولُهَا . وإن اخْتَلَفَ في التمكين فالقولُ قولُه إلّا أنْ يَعْتَرِفَ بأنهَا مَكَّنَتْ أولاً ثمَّ يَدَّعِي النشوزَ [(أي بعد التمكين)] فالقولُ قولُها .

m11.12 ومتَى تَرَكَ الإنفاقَ عليهَا مدةً صارتْ النفقةُ عليهِ ديناً .

m11.13 وإذا أغْسَرَ بنفقة المعسرينَ أوْ بالكسوةِ أوْ بالسكنى بَثَ لَهَا فسْخُ

housing for her.

If she wishes, she may choose to bear with him (O: supporting herself with her own money), and it (O: the amount the husband is unable to pay) remains a financial obligation that he owes her. (O: If she does not wish to tolerate his financial incapacity, she cannot annul the marriage by herself, but must establish her husband's inability to support her before the Islamic judge, who annuls the marriage or allows her to do so, since he is the one who judges the matter (A: and if there is no judge, she has two persons (def: o21.4) decide)).)

النكاح . فإنْ شَاءَتْ صَبَرَتْ (بأن أنفقت على نفسها من مالها) وبَقِيَ ذلكَ (أي ما أعسر به الزوج) لَهَا في ذمتِهِ (وإذا لم تصبر على الإعسار فلا تستقل بالفسخ بل لا بد من ثبوت الإعسار عند القاضي فيفسخه أو يأذن لها فيه لأنه مجتهد فيه) .

m11.14 The wife is not entitled to annul the marriage when the husband is unable to provide foods besides the staple food, support her servant, or provide the support that must be provided by an affluent person or person between affluence and nonaffluence (def: m11.2).

m11.14 وإنْ أَعْسَرَ بالأدم أوْ بنفقة الخادم أوْ بنفقة الموسرين أو المتوسطين فلا فسخَ لَهَا .

m11.15 [وإنْ كَانَ الزوجُ عبداً فالنفقةُ في كسبِهِ . وإلّا ففي يدِهِ إنْ كَانَ مأذوناً لهُ في التجارة . وإلّا فإنْ شَاءَتْ فَسَخَتْ وإنْ شَاءَت صَبَرَت إلى أنْ يَعْتِقَ فتأْخُذَ منْهُ] .

*

m12.0 SUPPORT OF ONE'S PARENTS AND CHILDREN

m12.0 وجوب الإنفاق على الأصول والفروع

m12.1 It is obligatory for one to support the persons listed below, whether one is male or female, when one has money in excess of one's own living expenses and (n: if male,) those of one's wife (O: meaning enough for a day and night, oneself taking priority over others, followed by one's wife, who takes precedence over other family members):

(1) one's father, father's father, and on up;

(2) one's mother, grandmothers (from either parent's side) and on up (O: it making no difference what their religion is (A: since the religion of

m12.1 يَجِبُ على الشخص ذكراً كانَ أوْ أنثى إذا فَضَلَ عنْ نفقتِهِ ونفقة زوجتِهِ (يومه وليلته ، فهو مقدم على غيره والزوجة مقدمة على القريب) أنْ يُنْفِقَ على الآباءِ والأمهاتِ وإنْ عَلَوْا مِنْ أيِّ جهةٍ كَانُوا (وإن اختلفت ملتهما) وعلى

the family members is of no consequence in any of the rulings of this section));

(3) and one's children, male and female, their children, and on down.

(O: Money *in excess* of one's own living expenses and those of one's wife means one is obliged to sell (A: if necessary to fulfill the obligation to support the above-mentioned persons) whatever must be sold when one has to pay debts, including real estate and other property.)

But supporting the above-mentioned persons is only obligatory when:

(a) there is poverty (O: a restriction applicable to both support of one's ancestors and one's descendants, meaning that it is necessary in order for it to be obligatory to support one's ancestor that the ancestor be poor, since if he has enough money, one need not support him);

(b) and incapacity (O: to earn a living) due to chronic illness, being a child, or to mental illness. (O: This condition is only applicable to support of one's offspring, not of one's ancestors. If an (A: impoverished) ancestor (A: such as one's father) were able to earn a living from a job suitable to him, it would nevertheless be obligatory for one to support him, and he would not be called upon to gain a livelihood, because of the extreme respect due to him, as opposed to one's descendant, whom one need not support if the descendant is able to earn his own living, but who rather is called upon to do so himself.

The upshot is that the support of whoever has enough money for their own support is not obligatory upon another family member, no matter whether the former is mentally ill or sane, a child or adult, chronically ill or well; because he does not deserve charity in such a condition—while a descendant able to earn an adequate living does not deserve support from his ancestors.)

m12.2 A child is obliged to support his father's wife (A: if the father cannot).

الأولادِ وأولادِهمْ وإنْ سَفَلُوا ذكوراً كانُوا أوْ إناثاً (ويفهم من اقتصار المصنف على الفاضل عن قوته وقوت زوجته أنه يباع في هذه النفقـة ما يبـاع في الـدين من عقـار وغيـره)، بشـرطِ الفقـر (وهـو معتبـر في الأصول والفروع. أي يشترط في وجوب نفقـة الأصل على الفرع أن يكون الأصل فقيـراً. فإن كان غنياً بمال فلا تجب نفقته على الفـرع) والعجـز (أي عن الكسب، شرط في الفـرع دون الأصل. ولـو قدر الأصل على كسب لائق به وجبت النفقة له ولا يكـلف الكـسب لعظم حرمتـه بخـلاف الفـرع إذا قدر على الكسب فلا تجـب نفقتـه على الأصـل بل يكلف الكسب) إمّـا بزمـانـةٍ أوْ طفـولـةٍ أوْ جنونٍ (والحـاصل أن من له ما يكفيـه لنفقته لم تجب نفقته على القريب، مجنوناً كان أو عاقـلاً، صغيـراً كان أو كبيـراً، زمناً أو صحيح البدن، إذ لم يكن أهلاً للمواساة في هذه الحـالـة ومن يكتسب ويغنيـه بالنسبة للفرع لا نفقة له على أصله).

m12.2 وتَجِبُ نفقةُ زوجةِ الأبِ (على الولد).

m12.3 When a person has both ancestors and children (A: deserving support) but does not have enough for all, then (O: after himself and then his wife) he gives precedence (A: in order) to:

(1) his mother;

(2) his father;

(3) his young son (O: or daughter);

(4) and then to his adult children (A: if they are unable to earn).

m12.4 The amount of such support must be enough to suffice, though (N: if this much is not paid) it does not become a debt owed by the person who should have given it. (O: It is no longer obligatory after its time has passed (A: but if the deserving person borrows money to support himself during this period, the person who should have supported him is obliged to pay the debt), even though the person who was obliged to give it has committed a sin by thus allowing the time to pass.)

m12.5 When a father who is poor needs to marry, then a son who is financially able must provide him with the means to keep chaste by finding him a wife (O: i.e. by giving her the marriage payment (mahr, def: m8). It is not permissible to marry him to a deformed or aged woman).

m12.6 Whoever owns an animal is obliged to pay for its maintenance.
(O: The restoration and maintenance of property without a living spirit, such as a canal or house, is not obligatory for its owner. Mutawalli explains this by the fact that such maintenance is an augmentation to the property and as such is not mandatory, as opposed to livestock, whose owner must feed them, since to neglect to do so would entail harm for them. Other scholars explain the difference in terms of the sacredness of animate life, which the author of al-Istiqsa' (n: 'Uthman ibn 'Isa Marani) says is the reason that it is wrong

m12.3 فإنْ كَانَ لَهُ آبـاءٌ وأولادُ ولـمْ يَقْـدِرْ على نفقةِ الكـلِّ قَدَّمَ (بعد نفسه ثم زوجتــه) الأُمَّ ثمَّ الأَبَ ثمَّ الابنَ الصغيـرَ (والبنت الصغيرة في معناه) ثمَّ الكبيرَ.

m12.4 وهـذِهِ النفقةُ مقـدَّرةٌ بالكفايةِ ولا تَسْتقِرُّ في الـذمةِ (بـل تسقط بمضي الزمان وإن أثم المنفق بهذا المضي).

m12.5 وإن احْتاجَ الوالدُ المعسرُ إلى النكـاحِ لَزِمَ الـولـدَ الموسرَ إعفافُهُ بالتـزويـجِ (بأن يسلمها مهرها ولا يجوز أن ينكحه شوهاء أو عجوزاً [أو التَّسري].

m12.6 ومَنْ مَلَكَ [رقيقـاً أوْ] دوابَّ لزِمَهُ النفقةُ [والكسوةُ فإنْ امْتَنَعَ ألْزَمَهُ الحاكمُ، فإنْ لـمْ يَكُنْ لهُ مالٌ أُكـرِيَ عليهِ إنْ أمْكَنَ، وإلّا بِيعَ عليهِ]. (وما لا روح له كقناةٍ ودارٍ لا تجب عمارتها على مالكها وعلله المتـولي بأن ذلك تنميـة للمال ولا تجب تنميته بخـلاف البهـائم يجبر على علفهـا لأن في تركـه إضـراراً بهـا. وفرق غيره بحرمة الروح. قال في الاستقصاء:

for someone to prevent living things from drinking surplus water (dis: p69), while it is not a sin to neglect watering crops.)

ولهذا يأثم بمنعه فضل الماء عن الحيوان ولا يأثم بمنعه عن الزرع).

*

m13.0 CHILD CARE AND CUSTODY

(O: The meaning of *child care* in Sacred Law is the protection of someone who does not possess discernment and cannot manage for himself, whether a child or a mentally ill adult, by seeing to his interests through such things as bathing him, washing his clothes, or grooming him; or securing an infant in the cradle, turning him over to sleep, and protecting him from death or harm. It entails a kind of authority and control and may be possessed by either men or women, though women have a better right to it, since they are tenderer towards children, more patient in carrying out the demands of the task, more discerning in raising children, and more steadfast in staying with them. The following discussion first centers on who best deserves the custody of a child, in order of precedence, and then treats the characteristics of the guardian and ward.)

m13.0 الحضانة

(وحقيقتها شرعاً القيام بحفظ من لا يميز ولا يستقل بأمر نفسه طفلاً كان أو مجنوناً كبيراً وتربيته بما يصلحه كأن يتعهده بغسل جسده وثيابه ودهنه وكحله وربط الصغير في المهد وتحريكه لينام ووقايته عما يهلكه ويضره . وفيها نوع ولاية وسلطنة وتثبت لكل من الرجال والنساء لكن النساء بها أليق لأنهن بالمحضون أشفق وعلى القيام بها أصبر وبأمر التربية أبصر وأشد ملازمة للأطفال . والكلام أولاً في مستحق الحضانة وترتيبهم ، ثم في صفات الحاضن والمحضون).

m13.1 The person with best right to custody of a child (A: in order) (O: when there is a dispute concerning who should have it) is:

(1) the mother;

(2) the mother's mother, mother's mother's mother, and on up, such that the one of the generation closest to the child takes precedence;

(3) the father;

(4) the father's mother, father's mother's mother, and on up, where again, the one of the generation closest to the child takes precedence;

(5) the father's father;

(6) the father's father's mother, her mother, and on up, where the one of the generation that is closest takes precedence;

m13.1 أحقُّ الناس بحضانة الطفل (عند التنازع في طلبها) الأُمُّ ثمَّ أمهاتُها المدلياتُ بإناثٍ تُقَدَّمُ القربَى فالقربى ثمَّ الأبُ ثمَّ أمهاتُهُ كذلك ثمَّ أبوهُ ثمَّ أمهاتُهُ

(7) full sister;

(8) full brother (O: though when the siblings are all male or all female and there is a disagreement over who should have custody, they draw lots to see who will get it. When both males and females exist, females take precedence);

(9) the child's half brothers or sisters from the same father;

(10) the half brothers or sisters from the same mother;

(11) the mother's sister;

(12) the daughters of the full brothers;

(13) the sons of the full brothers;

(14) the daughters of the half brothers from the same father;

(15) the sons of the half brothers from the same father;

(16) the daughters of the half brothers from the same mother;

(17) the sons of the half brothers from the same mother;

(18) the father's sister;

(19) the father's brother;

(20) the daughters of the mother's sister;

(21) the daughters of the father's brother;

(22) and then the son of the father's brother.

m13.2 The necessary conditions for a person to have custody of a child are:

(a) uprightness (def: o24.4) (O: a corrupt person may not be a guardian, because child care is a position of authority, and the corrupt are

كذلكَ ثمَّ الأختُ الشقيقةُ ثمَّ الأخ الشقيقُ (وعند الاتحاد في الذكورة فقط أو الأنوثة فقط يقرع بينهم أو بينهن عند التنازع و[تقدم قريباً أن] الأنثى أليق من الـذكر عنـد الاختلاف بينهما) ثمَّ للأب ثمَّ للأمّ ثمَّ الخالـةُ ثمَّ بنـاتُ الإخـوة للأبوينِ ثمَّ بنـوهُمْ ثمَّ للأب ثمَّ بنـوهُمْ ثمَّ للأمّ ثمَّ بنوهُمْ ثمَّ العمـةُ ثمَّ العمُ ثمَّ بناتُ الخالة ثمَّ بناتُ العمِّ ثمَّ ابنُ العمِّ .

m13.2 وشـرطُ الحاضنِ العدالةُ (فلا يكـون الفاسق حاضناً لأن الحضانة ولاية والفـاسق ليس من أهلها . وقال الماوردي

unqualified for it. Mawardi and Ruyani hold that outward uprightness (def: m3.3(f)) is sufficient unless there is open wrongdoing. If the corruptness of a child's mother consists of her not performing the prayer (salat), she has no right to custody of the child, who might grow up to be like her, ending up in the same vile condition of not praying, for keeping another's company has its effects);

(b) sanity (O: since a mother uninterruptedly insane has no right to custody, though if her insanity is slight, such as a single day per year, her right to custody is not vitiated by it);

(c) and if the child is Muslim, it is a necessary condition that the person with custody be a Muslim (O: because it is a position of authority, and a non-Muslim has no right to authority and hence no right to raise a Muslim. If a non-Muslim were given charge of the custody and upbringing of the child, the child might acquire the character traits of unbelief (kufr)).

والروياني إنه تكفي العدالة الظاهرة حتى يتبين الفسق . ولو كانت الأم فاسقة بترك الصلاة فلا حضانة لها لأن المحضون ربما يشب على طريقتها فيتربى عندها على حالة قبيحة من ترك الصلاة لأن الصحبة تؤثر) والعقل (فلا حضانة لمجنونة أطبق جنونها فإن قل جنونها كيوم في سنة لم يبطل حق الحضانة بذلك) [والحرية] .

وكذا الإسلام إنْ كانَ الطفلُ مسلماً (لأنها ولاية والكافر ليس من أهلها ولا حق له في تربية المسلم لأنه لو ثبت له الحضانة عليه والتربية له لشب الولد على خصال الكفر) .

m13.3 (A: It is offensive to send one's children to a day-care center run by non-Muslims. It is unlawful to send Muslim children to Christian schools, or those which are designedly atheist, though it is not unlawful to send them to public schools in which religion is not mentioned (N: in a way that threatens the students' belief in Islam).)

m13.4   A woman has no right to custody (A: of her child from a previous marriage) when she remarries (O: because married life will occupy her with fulfilling the rights of her husband and prevent her from tending the child. It makes no difference in such cases if the (A: new) husband agrees or not (N: since the child's custody in such a case automatically devolves to the next most eligible on the list (dis: m13.1)), unless the person she marries is someone (A: on the list) who is entitled to the child's custody anyway (O: as opposed to someone unrelated to the child, since such a person, even if willing, does not deserve custody because he lacks the tenderness for the child that a relative would have).

m13.4   ولا حقَّ للمرأة إذا نُكِحَتْ (لأن النكاح يشغلها بحق الزوج ويمنعها من القيام بخدمة المحضون ولا أثر لرضا الزوج (ح : وعندئذ ينتقل حق الحضانة لمن بعدها)) إلا أنْ تَنْكِحَ مَنْ لهُ حضانتُهُ (على الولد بخلاف الأجنبي فلا حق له في الحضانة ولو رضي بها لأنه لا شفقة له كشفقة القريب) .

m13.5 When a child reaches the age of discrimination (O: which generally occurs around seven or eight years of age) he is given a choice as to which of his parents he wants to stay with (O: since the Prophet (Allah bless him and give him peace) gave a young boy the choice between his father and his mother. The child is only given such a choice when the necessary conditions for child custody (def: m13.2) exist in both parents. If one of them lacks a single condition, then the child is not given a choice, because someone lacking one of the conditions is as though nonexistent).

If the child chooses one of the parents, he is given to the care of that one, though if a son chooses his mother, he is left with his father during the day so the father can teach him and train him. (O: Other possible outcomes of such a choice are when the child chooses both parents, in which case they draw lots to see who receives custody of him; or when he chooses neither, in which case the mother takes precedence since the custody is hers, and the child has not chosen someone else.) If the child subsequently chooses the other parent, he is given to the care of them (O: for he might want to stay with one of them at one time and with the other at another, just as one desires food at one time but not another. Or the child's intention might be to maintain good relations with both sides. The author restricts the permissibility of such cases of transferring the child's custody from one to another by saying:) unless it is apparent that the child is merely enamored with going back and forth or is weakminded (O: indicating his lack of discernment. In such cases his choice is not followed, and he remains with whomever he was with before reaching the age of discernment).

m13.5 وإذا بَلَغَ الصغيرُ حَدّاً يُمَيِّزُ فيه (وهـو يحصـل غالبـاً سـن السبع أو الثمان من السنين) خُيِّرَ بين أبـوَيْه (لتخييره ﷺ غلامـاً بين أبيـه وأمـه [حسنـه الترمذي]. وإنمـا يخيـر بين الأبـوين إذا اجتمعت شـروط الحضـانـة فيهمـا فإذا فقـدت الشـروط كلهـا أو بعضها من أحدهما فلا تخيير لأن من فقدت فيه الشروط كالعدم) فإن اخْتَارَ أحَدَهُمَا سُلِّمَ إليه لكنْ إن اخْتَارَ الابنُ أمَّـهُ كَانَ عنـد أبيـه بالنهـار لِيُعَلِّمَـهُ ويُـؤَدِّبَـهُ. (قد بقي من صور الاختيار ما لو اختارهما فحينئذ يقرع بينهما ويسلم لمن خرجت له القرعة منهما. وما لو لم يختر واحداً منهما فالأم أولى لأن الحضانة لها ولم يختـر غيرها). فإنْ عَادَ واخْتَارَ الآخَر دُفِـعَ إليـه فإنْ عاد واخْتَـارَ الأولَ أعيدَ إليه (فقد يشتهي المقام عند أحدهما في وقت وعنـد الآخـر في وقت كما يشتهي الطعام في وقـت ويـزهـد فيـه في وقت آخر. وقد يقصد مراعـاة الجـانبين وقيـد المصنف جواز تنقله من واحـد إلى واحد بقـولـه) وهكـذا إلى أنْ يَظْهَـرَ منـهُ بهذا وَلَعٌ وخَبلٌ (يدل ذلك على قلة تمييزه فلا يتبع اختياره بل يترك عند من كان عنده قبل التمييز).

*

BOOK N

DIVORCE

CONTENTS:

n1.0   WHO MAY EFFECT A DIVORCE

(O: The legal basis for the permissibility of divorce is the Koran, sunna, and consensus of Muslims. As for the Koran, Allah Most High says,

"Divorce is two times ..." (Koran 2:229).

And as for the sunna, there is the rigorously authenticated (sahih) hadith,

"No permissible thing is more detested by Allah than divorce."

Our sheikh, Bajuri, says the meaning of *permissible* in the hadith is *offensive,* since it is permissible, meaning lawful, though detested by Allah.
    Its integrals are five:

(a) the spoken form;

(b) the wife;

(c) the authority to effect it;

(d) the intention;

(e) and the person who effects it (A: i.e. the husband).)

n1.1   Divorce is valid from any:

(a) husband;

(b) who is sane;

(c) has reached puberty;

(d) and who voluntarily effects it.

n1.0   ممن يصح الطلاق

(والأصـل في الطـلاق الكتاب والسنة وإجمـاع الأمـة . أما الكتاب فقد قال الله تعـالى فيه : ﴿الطَّلاقُ مَرَّتَانِ﴾ وأما السنة فللخبـر الصحيح «ليس شيء من الحلال أبغض إلى الله من الطلاق» . وقال شيخنا العـلامة البـاجوري والمراد بالحلال في هذا الحــديث الشـريف المكروه فإنـه حلال بمعنى جائـز لكنـه مبغـوض لله . وأركانه خمسة : صيغة ومحل وولاية عليه وقصد ومطلق) .

n1.1   يَصِـحُّ الطـلاقُ مِنْ كلِّ زوج
عاقلٍ بالغٍ مختارٍ .

A divorce is not valid from:

    (1) (non-(c) above) a child;

    (2) (non-(b)) someone insane;

    (3) or (non-(d)) someone who is wrongfully coerced to do it, as when one is threatened with death, dismemberment, being severely beaten, or even mere verbal abuse or a slight beating if the person being coerced is someone whose public image is important and would thereby suffer. (O: Someone being forced should use words that give a misleading impression (def: r10.2) for his ostensible "divorce.")

فلا يَصِحّ طلاقُ صبيٍّ ومجنونٍ ومكرَهٍ بغير حقٍّ مثل أَنْ هُدِّدَ بقتل أَوْ قطع عضوٍ أَوْ ضربٍ مُبَرِّحٍ ، وكَذا شتم أَوْ ضربٍ يسيرٍ و(المهدَّد) هو مِنْ ذوي المـرواتِ والأقدارِ . (وينبغي للمكرَه أن يوري) .

n1.2   A statement of divorce is legally effective when pronounced by a person whose mental faculties are lacking because of something inexcusable such as having become intoxicated or having needlessly taken some mind-altering drug (O: though someone who takes such a drug out of need for medical treatment is considered as an insane person, in that his statement of divorce is not legally effective).

n1.2   ومَنْ زَالَ عقلُهُ بسبب لَا يُعْـذَرُ فيه كالسكرانِ ومَنْ شرِبَ دواءً يُزيلُ العقلَ بلا حاجةٍ يَقَعُ طلاقُهُ (ومن شرب ما يزيل عقله لحاجة التداوي فهو كالمجنون فلا يقع طلاقه) .

n1.3   The person conducting the divorce may effect it himself or commission another (def: k17.5–6) to do so, even if the person commissioned is a woman.

    The person commissioned may effect the divorce at any time (O: provided the one who commissions him does not cancel the commission before the divorce takes place (dis: k17.16)), though when a husband tells his wife, "Divorce yourself," then if she immediately says, "I divorce myself," she is divorced, but if she delays, she is not divorced unless the husband has said, "Divorce yourself whenever you wish."

n1.3   ولَـهُ أَنْ يُطَلِّقَ بنفسِـهِ ولَـهُ أَنْ يُوكِّلَ ولو امرأةً .
وللوكيـلِ أَنْ يُطَلِّقَ مَتَى شَاءَ (مـا لم يعـزلـه الموكل قبل إيقاع الطلاق الموكل فيه) لكنْ إذَا قَالَ لزوجتِهِ : طَلِّقي نفسَكِ ؛ فَقَـالَـتْ على الفـورِ : طَلَّقْـتُ نفسي ؛ طَلُقَتْ . وإنْ أَخَّرَتْ فلا . إلَّا أَنْ يَقُـولَ : طَلِّقي نفسَكِ مَتَى شِئْتِ .

*

n2.0   GENERAL PROVISIONS CONCERNING DIVORCE

n2.1   A free man has three pronouncements of divorce (O: because of the word of Allah Most High,

"Divorce is two times, then retain with kindness or graciously release" (Koran 2:229),

and when the Prophet (Allah bless him and give him peace) was asked about the third time, he said,

"It is Allah's having said, 'or graciously release' ").

n2.2   It is offensive to make a pronouncement of divorce when there is no need (O: *need* including when the wife has displeasing qualities or morals), to make three pronouncements (N: even if separate) being more offensive, and combining them in one interval of purity between menstruations even more offensive.

n2.3   There are various categories of divorce: sunna, unlawful innovation, and that which is neither sunna nor unlawful innovation.
    The *sunna* is to make a pronouncement of divorce in an interval between menstruations in which no sexual intercourse with the wife has taken place.
    Unlawful innovation consists of either making a pronouncement of divorce during the woman's menstrual period when this is not for payment (O: from the wife in exchange for the husband's releasing her from marriage (def: n5), though if the divorce *is* in exchange for a sum paid by the wife, it is not unlawful innovation because it implies that she accepts that the waiting period should be thus prolonged (dis: n9.7))—or else making the pronouncement during an interval between menstruations in which they have had sexual intercourse. If one effects such a divorce, it is recommended to take the wife back (O: if one did not pronounce it the full number of (n: three)

n2.0   أحكام عامة تتعلق بالطلاق

n2.1   ويَمْلِكُ الحرُّ ثلاثَ تطليقاتٍ (لقوله تعالى: ﴿الطَّلاَقُ مَرَّتَانِ فَإِمْسَاكٌ بِمَعْرُوفٍ أَوْ تَسْرِيحٌ بِإِحْسَانٍ﴾ وقد قال ﷺ [كما صححه ابن القطان] حين سئل عن الثالثة «هو قوله أو تسريح بإحسان») [والعبدُ طلقتين].

n2.2   ويُكْرَهُ الطلاقُ من غير حاجةٍ (ومن الحاجة أن لا تكون الزوجة مرضية الصفات والأخلاق) والثلاثُ (ح: ولو مفرقة) أشدُّ وجمعُها في طهرٍ واحدٍ أشدُّ.

n2.3   ثمَّ الطلاقُ على أقسامٍ سنيٍّ وبدعيٍّ محرم وخالٍ عن السنة والبدعة. فأمَّا السنيُّ فهـوَ أنْ يُطَلَّقَ في طهـرٍ لمْ يُجَامِعْ فيه.
    والبـدعيُّ المـحـرمُ أنْ يُطَلَّقَ في الحيض بلا عوضٍ (أي من غيـر عوض تدفعه الزوجة في مقابلة الطلاق فإن كان الطلاق في مقابلة ما دفعته الزوجة له فلا يكون بدعياً لأنها راضية بتطويل العدة) أو في طهرٍ جامَعَهَا فيهِ. فإذَا فَعَلَ [أي طلق الزوجة طلاقاً بدعياً] نُدِبَ لهُ أنْ يُرَاجِعَهَا (إن لم يستـوف عدد الطـلاق. وأمَّـا

times).

Neither sunna nor unlawful innovation means the divorce of a wife who is prepubescent, post-menopausal, pregnant, or one with whom one has not yet had sexual intercourse.

الخـالي عنهمـا فطـلاق الصغيرة والآيسة من الحيض والحامل وغير المدخول بها .

*

n3.0 THE WORDS THAT EFFECT A DIVORCE

n3.0 الألفاظ التي يقع بها الطلاق

n3.1 The words that effect a divorce may be plain or allusive. Plain words effect the divorce whether one intends divorce by them or not, while allusive words do not effect it unless one intends divorce by them.

n3.1 الألفاظُ التي يَقَعُ بها الطلاقُ صريحٌ وكنـايةٌ . فالصـريحُ يَقَعُ به سواءٌ نَوَى به الطلاقَ أمْ لا ، ولا يَقَعُ بالكنايةِ إلاّ أنْ يَنْوِيَ به الطلاق .

n3.2 Using *plain words* to effect a divorce means expressly pronouncing the word *divorce* (O: or words derived from it). When the husband says, "I divorce you," or "You are divorced," the wife is divorced whether he has made the intention or not.

(A: Here and in the rulings below, expressions such as "The wife is divorced," or "The divorce is effected," mean just one of the three times (def: n9.0(N:)) necessary to finalize it, unless the husband thereby intends a two- or threefold divorce (dis: n3.5) or repeats the words three times.)

n3.2 فالصـريحُ لفـظُ الطلاقِ (أي المشتق منه) [والفـراق والسـراح] . فإذا قال طَلَّقْتـكِ [أوْ فَارَقْتُكِ أوْ سَرَّحْتُكِ] أوْ أنتِ طالقٌ [أوْ مطلَّقةٌ أوْ مفارقةٌ أوْ مسرحةٌ] طُلَّقَتْ سواءٌ نَوَى به الطلاقَ أمْ لا .

n3.3 Using *allusive words* to effect a divorce includes:

(1) the husband's saying, "You are now alone," "You are free," "You are separated," "You are parted," "You are no longer lawful to me," "Rejoin your kin," "You are footloose," and the like;

(2) his saying, "I am divorced from you";

(3) or when he commissions the wife to pronounce the divorce, and she says, "You are divorced";

n3.3 والكنـايةُ قولُـهُ : أنتِ خليةٌ أوْ بريـةٌ أوْ بتَّـةٌ أوْ بائنٌ وحـرامٌ [وآعْتَـدِّي وآسْتَبْـرِئي وتَقَنَّعِي] وألْحقي بأهلِكِ وحبلُكِ على غاربِكِ ونحو ذلكَ؟ أوْ قَالَ : أنـا منْكِ طالقٌ ؛ أوْ فَوَّض الطـلاقَ إلَيْهـا فقَالَتْ : أنتِ طالقٌ أوْ قِيلَ أَلكَ زوجةٌ؟

(4) when someone asks, "Do you have a wife?" and he says "No"

(5) or when the husband writes words that effect the divorce (O: no matter whether able or unable to speak at the time of writing, or whether he is present or absent, or whether he writes in plain or allusive words).

When one intends divorce by any of the above, the words effect it, but if one does not, they do not.

n3.4   When a husband is asked, "Have you divorced your wife?" and he says "Yes," then she is divorced (O: even if he does not intend).

n3.5   If the husband says, "You are divorced," and thereby intends a two- or threefold pronouncement, then whatever number he intends is effected, this rule holding for all words that effect divorce, whether plain or allusive. (O: The proof that a single pronouncement can validly effect a threefold divorce is the hadith classified as rigorously authenticated (sahih) by Ibn Hibban that the Prophet (Allah bless him and give him peace), when Rukana divorced his wife and then said, "I did not intend it except as one time," made him swear an oath to that effect, and then returned her to him. If a single pronouncement could not effect a threefold divorce, there would not have been any point in the Prophet's making him swear the oath (Allah bless him and give him peace).)

n3.7   If a husband tells his wife, "You are divorced *in sha' Allah* [if Allah wills]," or "if Allah does not will," or "unless Allah wills," then the divorce is not effected.

فَقَالَ لا ؛ أَوْكَتَبَ لفظَ الطلاقِ (سواء كان وقت الكتـابةِ أخـرس أو ناطقاً حاضراً أو غائباً وسـواء كتب لفـظ الصـريح أو لفظ الكنـايةِ) . فإذا نَوَى بجميعِ ذلكَ الطلاقَ وَقَعَ وإنْ لَمْ يَنْوِ لَمْ يَقَعْ .

n3.4   وإذا قِيلَ لَهُ : طَلَّقْتَ امرأتَك؟ فقال : نَعَمْ ؛ طُلِّقَتْ (وإن لم ينو) .

n3.5   وإذا قَالَ : أنتِ طالقٌ ؛ ونَوَى بِه إيقاعُ طلقتين أوْ ثلاثاً وَقَعَ ما نَوَى وكَذَا سائرُ ألفاظِ الطلاقِ صريحِها وكنايتها . (والـدلـيـل على وقوع الثلاث ما رواه ابن حبـان وصححـه أنه ﷺ حلف ركانة حين طلق زوجتـه ألبتـة ثم قال ما أردت إلا واحـدة فحلفـه ﷺ على ذلك وردها عليه ولو لم تقع الثلاث لم يكن في الحلف فائدة) .

n3.6   [وإذا أَضَافَ الطلاقَ إلى بعضٍ مِنْ أبعاضِها مثـلَ أنْ قَالَ : نصفُكِ طالقٌ طُلِّقَتْ طلقةً واحدةً. وكذا إذا قَالَ : أنتِ طالقٌ نصف طلقةٍ ، أوْ ربعِ طلقةٍ طُلِّقَتْ طلقةً. وإذا قَالَ : أنتِ طالقٌ ثلاثاً إلّا طلقةً طُلِّقَتْ طلقتين ؛ أوْ ثلاثاً إلّا طلقتين طُلِّقَتْ طلقةً ، أو ثلاثاً إلّا ثلاثاً طُلِّقَتْ ثلاثاً] .

n3.7   وإنْ قَالَ : أنتِ طالـقٌ إنْ شَاء اللهُ أوْ إنْ لمْ يَشـإ اللهُ وكَـذا إلّا أنْ يَشـاءَ اللهُ لمْ تُطَلَّقْ .

*

n4.0 CONDITIONAL EXPRESSIONS THAT EFFECT DIVORCE	**n4.0 تعليق الطلاق على شرط**
n4.1 It is permissible to make the efficacy of a divorce conditional. If the husband makes the divorce conditional on something, and the event occurs, then the wife is divorced. If he says, "If your monthly period begins, you are divorced," then she is divorced when her menstrual flow appears.	n4.1 ويَجُوزُ تعليقُ الطلاقِ على شرطٍ. وإنْ عَلَّقَهُ على شرطٍ ووُجِدَ ذلكَ الشرطُ طُلِّقَتْ. فإذا قالَ: إنْ حِضْتِ فأنتِ طالقٌ طُلِّقَتْ بمجرد رؤية الدم.
	n4.2 [فـإذا قَالَتْ حِضْتُ فكَـذَّبها فالقـولُ قولُها مَعَ يمينها. وإنْ قال: إنْ حِضْتِ فضرتُكِ طالقٌ فقَالَتْ: حِضْتُ: فكَذَّبها فالقولُ قولُهُ ولمْ تُطَلَّقْ الضرةُ].
n4.3 If the husband says, "If you leave the house without my permission, you are divorced," then gives her permission to go out, and she does but then goes out a second time without permission, she is not divorced.	n4.3 وإنْ قَالَ: إنْ خَرَجْـتِ إلَّا بإذنـي فأنـتِ طـالـقٌ؛ ثمَّ أذِنَ لَهـا في الخروج مرةً فخَرَجَتْ ثمَّ خَرَجَتْ بعدَ ذلـكَ بلا إذنٍ لمْ تُطَلَّقْ. وإنْ قَال: كلَّمـا
If he says, "Anytime you go out without my permission you are divorced," then if she leaves at anytime without permission, she is divorced.	خَرَجْتِ إلَّا بإذنـي فأنتِ طالقٌ؛ فبأيِّ مرةٍ خَرَجَتْ بغير إذنه طُلِّقَتْ.
	n4.4 [وإنْ قَالَ: مَتَى وَقَعَ عليكِ طلاقي فأنتِ طالقٌ قبلَهُ ثلاثاً ثمَّ قَالَ بَعْدَ ذلك أنتِ طالقٌ طُلِّقَتْ المنجزُ فقطْ].
n4.5 When a husband makes a divorce conditional on one of his own acts but then does the act not remembering that he made it a condition, or does the act because he is forced to, the wife is not divorced.	n4.5 ومَنْ عَلَّقَ بفعـلِ نفسِهِ ففَعَلَ ناسياً أوْ مكرَهاً لمْ يَقَعْ.
n4.6 When the husband makes a divorce conditional on another person's act, such as by saying, "If So-and-so enters the house, you are divorced," and the person enters before or after he knows it is a condition, whether remembering it or not, then if the person named is not someone who would mind if they were divorced (O: meaning it is no problem for him if it happens, and he would not be saddened if it did, because of lack of friendship for them), then the wife is divorced. But if the person knows it is a condition and enters forgetfully, then if he is someone who would mind	n4.6 وإنْ عَلَّقَ بفعـلِ غيرِه مثلَ: إنْ دَخَلَ زيدُ الدارَ فأنتِ طالقٌ؛ فدَخَلَها قبـلَ علمِـهِ بالتعليقِ أوْ بعدَهُ ذاكـراً لهُ أوْ ناسياً وكَـانَ غيـرَ مبالٍ بحنثِه (يعني أنه لا يشقُ عليـه حنثه ولا يحـزَن عليـه لعـدم صداقة بينهما) طُلِّقَتْ. وإنْ علِمَ بالتعليقِ فدَخَـلَ ناسياً وهـوَ ممِّنْ يُبَالي بحنثِهِ لمْ

if they were divorced, the wife is not divorced.

If the husband, tells his wife, "If you enter that house, you are divorced," and she is subsequently divorced from him with a finalized divorce, after which he remarries her, and she then enters the house, then she is not divorced.

*

n5.0 A RELEASE FOR PAYMENT FROM THE WIFE (KHUL')

(O: A *release for payment* means a separation in return for remuneration given to the husband (A: which is a finalized cancellation of the marriage agreement, differing from a threefold divorce by the fact that they may remarry in such a case without her marrying another husband first (dis: n7.7)).)

n5.1 A release for payment is valid from any person whose divorce is valid (def: n1.1).

n5.2 Release is offensive except when:

(1) the husband or wife fear they will not be able to keep within Allah's limits (O: i.e. those that Allah Most High has made obligatory upon them (dis: m10.1)) while the marriage lasts;

(2) or when the husband swears that a threefold divorce is incumbent upon him if he performs some action, but then finds he needs to do it (O: since he cannot clear himself from the oath without giving her a release), so he releases her, marries her (O: with a new agreement, a new marriage payment (mahr), and upright witnesses), and then does the act on which the divorce was conditional (O: though it is fitter to do it before the new marriage, as the oath is nullified as soon as they are unmarried), for then its performance does not necessitate a threefold divorce.

n5.3 If the husband is foolhardy (A: meaning suspended by the court from dealing in his own

---

تُطَلَّقْ . وإنْ قَالَ : إنْ دَخَلْتِ الـدَّارَ فأنتِ طالقٌ ثمَّ بَانَتْ منهُ [إمَّا بطلقةٍ أوْ بثلاثٍ] ثمَّ تَزَوَّجَها ثمَّ دَخَلتِ الدارَ لمْ تُطَلَّقْ .

n5.0 الخلع
(وهو فرقة على عوض يرجع إلى الزوج) .
(ع : وهـو طلاق بائن ، يختلف عن الطلاق الثلاثي البـائن بجواز عقد نكاح جديد بينهما بدون محلّل) .

n5.1 يَصِحُّ الخلعُ مِمَّنْ يَصِحُّ طلاقُهُ

n5.2 ويُكْرَهُ إلَّا في حالين : أحدُهُما أنْ يَخافا أوْ أحدُهُما أنْ لا يُقِيمَا حدودَ اللهِ (أي ما افترضه تعالى عليهما) ما دَامَا على الـزوجيةِ . والثـاني أنْ يَحْلِفَ بالطلاقِ الثلاثِ على تركِ فعلٍ شيءٍ ثمَّ يَحْتَاجُ إلى فعلهِ (فـلا يتـخلص من اليمين إلا بالخلع فحينئذ) فيُخَالِعُهَا ثمَّ يَتَزَوَّجُهَا (بعقد جديد ومهر جديد وشهود عدول) ثمَّ يَفْعَـلُ المحلوفَ عليـهِ (وفعله قبـلَ الـزوج أولى لانحـلال اليمين في حال البيـنونة) فإنَّهُ لا يَقَعُ عليه الطلاقُ الثالثُ [كَما سَبَقَ] .

n5.3 وإنْ كَانَ الـزوج سفيهاً صَحَّ

money because of chronic carelessness (dis: k13.1(A:))). his granting a release is valid, though his guardian accepts the compensation.

A release for compensation is not legally valid from a wife who is foolhardy.

خُلْعُهُ ويدْفَعُ العوضَ إلى ولِيّهِ. ولا يصحُّ خُلْعُ سفيهةٍ. [وليسَ للوليِّ أنْ يُخالِعَ امرأةَ الطفلِ. ولا أنْ يُخالِعَ الطفلَ بمالِها ويَصِحُّ بمال الوليِّ].

n5.4   A release is validly effected by both the words for divorce and the words for release, such as "You are divorced for a thousand," or "I release you for a thousand," and if the wife says "I accept," then she is separated from him and she owes him the thousand. She is also released when the husband says, "If you give me a thousand, you are divorced," and then she gives him it, or when she says, "Divorce me for a thousand," and he says, "You are divorced," in which case she is released and owes him the thousand.

n5.4   ويصحُّ بلفظ الطلاق ولفظِ الخلع مثـلُ : أنتِ طالقٌ على ألفٍ، أو خالعتُـكِ على ألفٍ. فإنْ قالَتْ : قَبِلْتُ، بانَتْ ولزِمَها الألفُ. وكذلكَ إنْ قال : إنْ أعْطَيْتِني ألفاً فأنْتِ طالقٌ ، فأعْطَتْهُ بانَتْ. وكـذلـكَ إذا قالَتْ : طَلِّقْـني على ألفٍ فقال : أنتِ طالقٌ ؛ بانَتْ ولزِمَها الألفُ.

n5.5   Anything that may be used as a marriage payment (def: m8.4) may be used as recompense for a release. If a husband releases his wife for something not determinately known (non-k2.1(e)) or without lawful value (non-k2.3) such as wine, then she is released in exchange for the amount typically received as marriage payment by women like her (def: m8.8).

n5.5   وما جَازَ أنْ يَكُونَ صداقاً جَازَ أنْ يَكُونَ عوضاً في الخلعِ. فلَوْ خَالَعَ بمجهولٍ أوْ غيرِ متمولٍ كالخمرِ بانَتْ بمهرِ المثلِ.

n5.6   A release enacted by words that effect it is a divorce in plain words (A: in not needing the intention (dis: n3.2), (N: in having a waiting period (def: n9),) and in being a finalized cancellation of the marriage, though as previously mentioned (n5.0(A:)), the partners may remarry each other (N: even if before the end of the waiting period) without the wife first having to marry another).

n5.6   وهوَ بلفظِ الخلع طلاقٌ صريحٌ (ع) : في عدم احتياجـه إلى النيـة (ح) : وفي أن له عدة) وفي أنه طلاق بائن ، ولكن للزوجين أن يعقـدا عقـداً جديـداً (ح) : ولـو قبل انقضاء العدة) بلا محلّلٍ ، كما سبق).

*

n6.0   DOUBTS ABOUT THE FACT OF HAVING DIVORCED
(A: *Doubt* means that one does not remember exactly what one said or did. As for when one is ignorant of rulings about divorce or

n6.0   الشك في الطلاق
(ع) : ومعنى الشـك في الطـلاق أن الـزوج لا يذكر بدقة ماذا قد قال أو فعل أما من جهل أحكـام الطلاق أو ما يترتب

على فعله ، فليس بعذر ويلزمه سؤال أهل العلم) .

the consequences of one's actions, it is not an excuse, and one must ask those who know.)

n6.1   Whoever does not know whether he has divorced his wife or not has not divorced her. It is more godfearing in such a case to take the wife back.

n6.1   مَنْ شَكَّ هَلْ طَلَّقَ أَمْ لا لَمْ تُطَلِّقْ . والورعُ أَنْ يُرَاجِعَ .

n6.2   If one does not know whether one has divorced one's wife once or whether more than once, then one has divorced her the least number one is certain of.

n6.2   وإِنْ شَكَّ هَلْ طَلَّقَ طلقـةً أَوْ أكثرَ وَقَعَ الأقَلُّ .

n6.3   When a husband divorces his wife with a threefold divorce during his deathbed illness (def: L3.6(1–4)), she does not inherit (A: a wife's estate division share (def: L6.4)) from the division of his estate (A: though if it is less than a threefold divorce, she inherits).

n6.3   ومَـنْ طَلَّقَ ثلاثـاً في مرض موتهِ لمْ تَرِثْهُ المطلّقةُ .

*

n7.0   TAKING BACK A DIVORCED WIFE (RAJ‘A)
   (O: Lexically, to take back means returning, and in Sacred Law it means the return of a woman who is in her waiting period (def: n9) from an unfinalized, non-threefold divorce to the state of marriage.)

n7.0   الرجعة
(وهـو لغة المرة من الرجوع وشرعاً رد المرأة إلى النكاح من طلاق غير بائن في العدة) .

n7.1   When a free man pronounces divorce upon his wife once or twice after previously having had sexual intercourse with her, then if the divorce is not (A: a release) for compensation (def: n5), he may take her back at any time before the end of her waiting period (def: n9), whether she wishes to return or not. Or he may finalize the divorce during this period (A: by pronouncing it a third time).

n7.1   وإِذا طَلَّقَ الـحـرُّ طلقـةً أَوْ طلقتيـنِ [أَو طَلَّقَ العبـدُ طلقـةً] بعـد الـدخـولِ بلا عوض فلَهُ قبلَ أَنْ تَنْقَضِيَ العـدةُ أَنْ يُراجِعَ سواءً رَضِيَتْ أَمْ لا . ولَهُ أَنْ يُطَلِّقَهَا .

n7.2   If the husband or wife dies (A: during the waiting period (N: of an unfinalized, non-

n7.2   وإِنْ مَاتَ أحدُهُمَا وَرِثَهُ الآخرُ

threefold divorce)), then the spouse inherits his or her obligatory share from the deceased's estate division (dis: L6), though it is not permissible for the husband to have sexual intercourse with, look at, or physically enjoy the wife before he takes her back.

لكنْ لا يَحِلُّ لَهُ وطؤُها ولا النظرُ إلَيْها ولا الاستمتاعُ بها قبلَ المراجعة.

n7.3   When a divorce occurs before the husband has made love to the wife, or afterwards (A: in a release) for compensation from her, then he may not take her back (A: without remarrying her).

n7.3 وإنْ كَانَ الطـلاقُ قبـلَ الدخولِ أوْ بعدَهُ بعوضٍ فلا رجعةَ لهُ.

n7.4   Returning the wife to marriage is only valid by explicitly stating it, such as by saying, "I return her," "I take her back," or, "I retain her." (N: The Hanafis consider the husband's touching her with desire, such as kissing her, to be a valid return to marriage.)

n7.4 ولا تَصِحُّ الـرجعةُ إلّا باللفظِ فقـطْ فيَقُـولُ: رَاجَعْتُهـا أوْ رَدَدْتُهـا أوْ أسكتُهـا. (ح: وعنـد الحنفيـة تعتبـر المباشرة بشهوة كالتقبيل مراجعة).

n7.5   It is not a necessary condition (O: but is sunna) to have the return attested to by witnesses.

n7.5 ولا يُشْتَرَطُ الإشهادُ (بل يسن).

n7.6   When a husband takes a wife back, she returns with whatever number (A: of times of saying "I divorce you") remains to complete a threefold divorce. (A: If, for example, he has said it twice, then she only has one time left.)

n7.6 وإذا رَاجَعَهـا عَادَتْ إليـهِ بمَا بَقِيَ مِنْ عدد الطلاق.

n7.7   When a free man has pronounced a threefold divorce, the divorced wife is unlawful for him to remarry until she has married another husband in a valid marriage and the new husband has copulated (dis: p29) with her, which at minimum means that the head of his erect penis fully enters her vagina.

n7.7 أمّـا إذا طَلَّقَ الحـرُّ ثلاثـاً [أو العبـدُ طلقتين] حُرِمَتْ عليْـهِ حتّى تَنْكِحَ زوجاً غيرَهُ نكـاحـاً صحيحاً ويَطأها في الفـرجِ وأدنـاهُ تغيبُ الحشفةِ بشـرطِ انتشارِ الذكرِ.

*

n8.0   FORSWEARING ONE'S WIFE MORE THAN FOUR MONTHS
     (O: In Sacred Law, *forswearing* means that the husband swears he will not have sexual inter-

n8.0 الإيلاء
(وهـو شرعاً حلف زوج على الامتناع

course with his wife, either for an unrestricted period or for more than four months.)

من وطء زوجته مطلقاً أو أكثر من أربعة أشهر).

n8.1   Forswearing one's wife is unlawful. It consists in the husband swearing an oath by Allah (def: o18) that for more that four months (O: *more than four months* including oaths in which no time period is stipulated) he will not have sexual intercourse with his wife, or swears that if he does, then he is obliged to divorce her, fast, pray, or something else.

n8.1   الإيـلاءُ حرامٌ وهـوَ أَنْ يَحْلِفَ الـزوجُ بالله أَوْ بالطلاقِ [أَوْ بالعتق] أَوْ بالتـزام صوم أَوْ صلاةٍ أَوْ غيـرِ ذلكَ يميناً يَمْنَعُ الجماعَ في الفـرجِ أَكثَرَ مِنْ أربعةِ أشهر (ودخل في قوله أربعة أشهر ما لو أطلق الامتناع).

n8.2   [فـإذا حَلَفَ كذلكَ صَارَ موليـاً فَيُضْـرَبُ (أي تقـدر) لهُ مدةُ أربعـةِ أشهر (وجـوباً ولو بلا قاض وابتداؤها من الإيلاء) فإذا انْقَضَتْ ولمْ يُجامِعْ فيها ولا مانعَ مِنْ جهتِها فلها عَقِبَ المدة إمّا بالطلاق أَوْ بالوطء إذا لَمْ يكنْ بِه مانعٌ يَمْنَعُه مِنَ الوطء. فإنْ جَامَعَ فذاكَ، وإلّا (أي وإن لم يجامع ولم يطلق) طَلَّقَ عليه الحاكمُ (طلقة واحدة)].

n8.3   A husband is not considered to have forsworn his wife (A: in the above unlawful sense) when he forswears sexual intercourse for four months or less, or when he is impotent.

n8.3   ومتى حَلَفَ عَلى أربعةِ أشهر فَما دونَها أَوْ كَانَ الزوجُ عنيناً [أَوْ مجبوباً] فَلَيْسَ موليـاً.

n8.4   [(الظهارُ) الظهـارُ هوَ أَنْ يُشَبِّهَ امرأتَهُ بظهرِ أمِّهِ أَوْ غيرِها مِنْ محارِمِهِ أَوْ بعضوٍ مِنْ أعضائها فَيَقُولَ: أنتِ عليَّ كظهرِ أمّي أَوْ كفرجِها أَوْ كيدِها. فإذا قَالَ ذلكَ ووُجِدَ العودُ لزمَتْهُ الكفارةُ وحَرُمَ وطؤُها حَتّى يُكَفِّرَ. والعودُ هوَ أَنْ يُمْسِكُها بعدَ الظهارِ زمناً يُمْكِنُهُ أَنْ يَقُولَ لَهَا فيه: أنتِ طالقٌ؛ فلمْ يَقُلْ. فإنْ عَقَبَ الظهارَ بالطلاقِ على الفورِ طَلَّقَتْ ولا كفارةَ. والكفارةُ عتقُ رقبةٍ مؤمنةٍ سليمةٍ مِنَ العيـوبِ التي تَضُرُّ بالعملِ فإنْ لَمْ يَجِدْ فصيامُ شهرينِ متتابعين. فإنْ لَمْ يَسْتَطِعْ فإطعامُ ستينَ مسكيناً كلَّ مسكينٍ مداً مِنْ قوتِ البلدِ حباً بالنية].

*

n9.0   A WOMAN'S POSTMARITAL WAITING PERIOD ('IDDA)

(O: Meaning the period in which a woman waits (N: before she may remarry) to verify that she is not pregnant, or out of mourning for her deceased husband.)

n9.0   العدة
(وهي مدة تتربص فيها المرأة لمعرفة براءة رحمها [أو للتعبد] أو لتفجعها على زوج).

(N: If the waiting period finishes after a once- or twice-pronounced divorce, the wife is free to marry another man or to remarry the husband with a new contract—returning to the latter with the number of times left (one or two) needed to enact a threefold, finalized divorce (dis: n7.7); while if the waiting period of a less-than-thrice-pronounced divorce has not yet expired, the husband may take her back (def: n7) without a new contract.)

(n: The husband's obligation to support her during the waiting period is discussed at m11.10 above.)

n9.1 There is no waiting period for a woman divorced before having had sexual intercourse with her husband.

n9.2 A waiting period is obligatory for a woman divorced after intercourse, whether the husband and wife are prepubescent, have reached puberty, or one has and the other has not.

Intercourse means copulation (def: n7.7). If the husband was alone with her but did not copulate with her, and then divorced her, there is no waiting period.

n9.3 When a waiting period is obligatory (O: upon a woman, because of divorce or annulment of marriage), then if she is pregnant, the waiting period ends when she gives birth, provided two conditions are met:

(a) The first is that she has given birth to all she was carrying. If carrying two or more children, it is necessary that she have given birth to all, whether live or stillborn, and whether fully developed or an undeveloped fetus which midwives (O: two or more) swear is the beginning of a human form. Whenever there is less than six months between two births, the babies are considered twins. There is no maximal number that may be born, as it is possible for a woman to give birth to four or more babies from one pregnancy.

(b) The second condition is that the child is from the husband whom the waiting period is for. If the woman is pregnant from committing adultery (def: n11.2(O:)) (O: or from a marriage which was invalid, after which the husband divorced her), the waiting period does not end when she gives birth, but rather (N: after giving birth), she completes the waiting period of a woman who has been divorced (def: n9.6).

n9.1 مَنْ طَلَّقَ امرأتَهُ قبلَ الدخولِ فلا عدةَ عليها.

n9.2 وإنْ طَلَّقَ بعـدَهُ لزِمَتْهـا العـدةُ سواءٌ كانَ الـزوجانِ صغيرينِ أوْ بالغينِ أوْ أحدُهُمَا بالغاً والآخرُ صغيراً. والمرادُ بالدخولِ الوطءُ فلوْ خَلا بها ولمْ يَطأها ثم طَلَّقَ فلا عِدَّةَ.

n9.3 وإذا وَجَبَتِ العدةُ (على المرأةِ بطلاقٍ أوْ فسخٍ) فإنْ كَانَتْ حاملاً انْقَضَتْ بوضعِهِ بشرطَيْنِ:

أحدُهُمَا: أنْ يَنْفَصِلَ جميعُ الحملِ حتى لوْ كَانَ ولدَيْنِ أوْ أكثرَ اشْتُرِطَ انْفِصَالُ الجميعِ حياً أوْ ميتاً كاملَ الخِلْقةِ أوْ مضغةً لمْ يَتَصَوَّرْ وشهدَ القوابلُ (اثنتانِ فأكثرُ) أنَّهُ مَبْدأُ خلقٍ آدميٍّ. ومتى كَانَ بينَ الـولدينِ ستةُ أشهرٍ فهمَا توأمانِ. ولا حَدَّ لعـددِ الحملِ فيَجُوزُ أنْ تَضَعَ في حملٍ واحدٍ أربعةَ أولادٍ أوْ أكثرَ مِنْ ذلك.

الثاني: أنْ يَكُونَ الولدُ منسوباً إلى مَنْ لهُ العـدةُ. فلوْ حَمَلَتْ من زنـاً [أوْ وطءِ شبهةٍ] (أو حملت في نكـاحٍ فاسـدٍ ثم طلقها الزوجُ) لمْ تَنْقَضِ عدةُ المطلِّقِ به بلْ [في حملِ وطءِ الشبهةِ] تَسْتَقْبِلُ عدةَ المطلِّقِ بعدَ الوضعِ.

n9.4 [وكذا في حملِ الزنَا (لكنْ هذه الصورة ضعيفة، والمعتمد فيها أنها تكمل عدة الطلاق ولا نظر لحمل الزنا) إنْ لمْ تَحِضْ على الحملِ. فإنْ حَاضَتْ على الحملِ انْقَضَتْ بثلاثةِ أطهارٍ (محسوباً منهُ (أي من الحيض المفهوم من الفعل)].

n9.5   The minimal duration of a pregnancy (A: from which a live child is born) is six months, while the maximum is four years.

n9.6   If a woman is not pregnant and has menstrual periods, her waiting period ends when three intervals between menstruations have finished. A part of an interval between menstruations is considered the same as a whole interval. Thus, if the woman's husband divorced her and her menses began an instant later, her waiting period would end after two more intervals between menstruations had finished and a third menstruation begun.

n9.7   If a woman is divorced during her menstrual period, she must wait until the end of three intervals between menstruations. When her fourth menstruation begins, her waiting period is over.

n9.8   There is no difference in respect to the above rulings (n9.6–7) whether a woman's menstrual periods are close together or far apart, *close together,* for example, meaning a woman whose period lasts a single day and night, and who has fifteen days between periods. Were such a woman divorced just before the end of an interval between menses (A: by a single moment), then her waiting period would finish in thirty-two days and two moments (O: one of which would be part of the waiting period, i.e. the one in which the divorce occurred, and the second of which would not be part of it, namely, that in which it became evident that the waiting period was over by the onset of a subsequent menstruation). If such a woman were divorced at the end of a menstrual period, her waiting period would be forty-seven days plus a moment. These are the shortest possible waiting periods.

An example of a woman whose periods are *far apart* is one whose menstruation lasts fifteen days, and whose intervals between menses last, for example, a year or more. Such a woman must wait for three intervals between menstruations, even if it takes years (N: though medicine may be taken to induce or regulate menstruations).

n9.5   وأقـلُّ مدة الحمـلِ ستةُ أشهرٍ وأكثرُهُ أربعُ سنينَ.

n9.6   وإنْ لمْ تَكُنْ حامـلاً فإنْ كانَتْ مِمَّنْ تحيضُ اعتـدَّتْ بثـلاثـةِ قروءٍ. «القروءُ الأطهارُ».
ويُحسَبُ لَهـا بعضُ الطهـرِ طهـراً كامـلاً. فإنْ طلَّقَهَا فحَاضَتْ بعدَ لحظةٍ انقضَتْ بمُضيِّ طهرين آخرين والشروع في الحيضةِ الثالثةِ.

n9.7   وإنْ طلَّقَ في الـحيضِ فلا بدَّ مِنْ ثلاثةِ أطهارٍ كواملَ. فإذا شَرَعَتْ في الحيضةِ الرابعةِ انْقَضَتْ.

n9.8   ولا فرقَ بيـنَ أنْ يَتَـقَـارَبَ حيضُهـا أوْ يَتبَاعَـدَ فمثـالُ التقاربِ أنْ تحيضَ يوماً وليلةً وتطْهُرَ خمسةَ عشرَ يوماً. فإذا طُلِّقَتْ في آخرِ الطهرِ انْقَضَتْ عدتُـهَـا باثنين وثلاثين يومـاً ولحظتين (إحـداهمـا محسوبـة من العـدة وهي اللحظـة التي وقع الطلاقُ فيها والثانية ليست منهـا بل يتبين بها انقضـاء العـدة بالشروع فيها). أوْ في آخرِ حيضٍ فسبعةٍ وأربعين يوماً ولحظـةٍ وهـوَ أقلُّ الممكنِ [في الحـرة] ومثـالُ التبـاعُـدِ أنْ تحيض خمسةَ عشرَ يوماً وتطْهُرَ سنةً مثلاً أوْ أكثرَ. فلا بدَّ مِنَ الأطهارِ الثلاثةِ ولوْ أقَامَتْ سنينَ.

n9.9   The waiting period for a woman who does not menstruate, whether prepubescent or postmenopausal, is three months.

If a woman normally menstruates, but her periods have stopped for some reason such as breastfeeding or the like, or without apparent reason, then she must wait until the age of menopause, after which her waiting period is three months. (N: In the Maliki school, such a woman must wait nine months, and if neither pregnancy nor menses appear, she is considered to be as if menopausal, and her waiting period is three more months, making a total of one entire year in which there is no menstrual flow.)

n9.10   All of the above rulings apply to the waiting period for divorce (N: or release (def: n5)).

THE WAITING PERIOD FOR A DECEASED HUSBAND

n9.11   If a woman's husband dies, even if during the waiting period of a nonfinalized divorce, then if she is pregnant, her waiting period ends when she gives birth, as previously mentioned (n9.3). But if not (O: i.e. if the deceased's wife is not pregnant from him), her waiting period is four months and ten days, no matter whether she normally menstruates or not (N: and no matter whether the husband has had sexual intercourse with her or not).

THE LODGINGS OF A WOMAN IN HER WAITING PERIOD

n9.13   A woman in her waiting period is obliged to remain in the home (O: and neither the husband nor his family may force her out; nor may she leave. If the husband agrees to allow her to leave when there is no necessity, it is still not permissible).

n9.9 وإنْ كَانَتْ مِمَّنْ لا تَحِيضُ لِصِغَرٍ أوْ إياسٍ اعْتَدَّتْ بِثلاثةِ أشهُرٍ.

وإنْ كَانَتْ مِمَّنْ تَحِيضُ فانْقَطَعَ دمُها لعارِضٍ كرِضاعٍ ونحوِهِ أوْ بِلا عارِضٍ ظاهِرٍ صَبَرَتْ (وجوباً) إلى سِنِّ اليأسِ مِنَ الحيضِ ثمَّ تَعْتَدُّ بِثلاثةِ أشهُرٍ. (ح: وفي مذهبِ المالكيةِ تنتظر تسعة أشهر فإن لم يظهر حمل ولا وجد حيض اعتبرت آيسة فتعتد بثلاثة أشهر ويكون المجموع سنة بيضاء، أي لا دم فيها).

n9.10 هٰذا كلُّهُ في عِدةِ الطلاقِ.

عِدة الوفاة

n9.11 فإنْ تُوُفِّي عنْها زوجُها ولوْ في خلالِ عدةِ الرجعيةِ فإنْ كانَتْ حامِلاً اعْتَدَّتْ بالوضعِ كَما تَقَدَّمَ. وإلّا (أي وإن لم تكن المتوفى عنها زوجها حاملاً منه) فبأربعةِ أشهرٍ وعشرةِ أيامٍ سواءٌ كانَتْ مِمَّنْ تَحِيضُ أمْ لا (ح: وسواء دخل بها الزوج أم لا).

n9.12 [هٰذا كلُّهُ في الحرةِ. أمَّا إذا كانَتْ زوجتُهُ أمةً أوْ مبعضةً فالحامِلُ بالوضعِ وغيرُها مِمَّنْ تَحِيضُ بطهرينِ، ومَنْ لا تَحِيضُ بشهرٍ ونصفٍ وفي الوفاةِ بشهرينِ وخمسةِ أيامٍ. ومَنْ وُطِئَتْ بشبهةٍ تَعْتَدُّ مِنَ الوطءِ كالمطلقةِ].

سكنى المعتدة

n9.13 ويَلْزَمُ المعتدةَ ملازمةُ المنزلِ (فليس للزوج ولا لأهلِه إخراجها منه. ولا لها أن تخرج. ولو وافقها الزوج على خروجها منه بغير حاجة لم يجز). فأمَّا

A woman in the waiting period of an unfinalized, less than threefold divorce is under the husband's authority and may not leave without his permission. If in the waiting period of a finalized divorce (N: or release (def: n5)) (O: or annulment,) or after her husband's death, a woman may leave home during the day to fulfill her needs (N: including work, if she has no means of support) and obligations.

الـرجعيةُ ففي حكمِ الزوج لا تَخْرُجُ إلَّا بإذنِهِ ويَجُوزُ للبـائن (بطلاق أو فسخ) وللمتوفَّى عنْهـا زوجُهـا أنْ تَخْرُجَ بالنهار لقضاءِ حاجيها وأداءِ الحقوقِ.

n9.14   The waiting period must take place in the same lodgings where the divorce occurred, and the woman may not be moved to other quarters unless there is a real necessity, such as fear (O: for her person or property), or when the landlord objects (O: such as when the house in question was on loan to the husband and its time has expired), or because of considerable annoyance to the woman from neighbors or the husband's relatives, or annoyance to them from her—in all of which cases she may move to the nearest available housing.

n9.14   وتَجبُ العـدةُ في المسكنِ الـذي طَلَّقَهَـا فيهِ. ولا يَجُوزُ نقلُهَـا إلَّا لضـرورةٍ: إمَّا الخـوفُ (على نفسهـا أو مالهـا) أوْ منعُ مالِكِهِ (أي المنزل الذي هو محل الفراق بأن كان معـاراً للزوج وقـد فرغـت مدةِ العـاريـةِ) أوْ كثـرةُ تأذيهَـا بجيـرانِهَـا أوْ أقاربِ زوجها أوْ تأذيهِمْ بهَا فَتَنْتَقِلُ إلى أقربِ مسكنٍ إليهِ.

n9.15   It is unlawful for the husband of a woman in her waiting period to be alone with her or share the same housing (N: i.e. he must move out) unless she is in a (O: separate) wing of the house (O: with its own kitchen, restroom, cistern, and stairs to the roof, in which case it is permissible to share the housing, which is as if it were two neighboring houses).

n9.15   ويَحْـرُمُ على المطلِّقِ الخلوةُ بهَا في العدةِ أوْ مساكنتُها إلَّا أنْ يكونَ كلُّ منْهُمـا في بيتٍ (منفرد) بمـرافقِهِ (من المطبخِ والمستراحِ (ح: أي المرحاض) والبئـرِ والمصعدِ إلى السطحِ. فيجوز لأنهما كدارين متجاورتين).

AVOIDING ADORNMENT AFTER A HUSBAND'S DEATH OR A FINALIZED DIVORCE

الإحداد

n9.16   It is obligatory for a woman whose husband has died (N: while she was his wife, or died while she was in the waiting period of an unfinalized divorce from him) to avoid adornment during the subsequent waiting period. It is recommended for a woman to do so during the waiting period of a finalized divorce. It is unlawful for a woman to avoid adornment longer than three days for the death of anyone besides her husband. *Avoiding adornment* means not to enhance her

n9.16   ويجبُ (ح: على الـزوجـة والرجعية) الإحدادُ في عدةِ الوفاة. ويُنْدَبُ في البائنِ. ويَحْرُمُ على ميتٍ غيرِ الزوج أكثرَ منْ ثلاثةِ أيامٍ. وهوَ أنْ تتـرُكَ الزينةَ ولا تَلْبَسَ الحلِيَّ

beauty, wear jewelry or cosmetics, and so forth. A woman avoiding adornment should not wear solid colors (N: if intended to beautify) such as blues, greens, reds, or yellows; or style her hair or use cosmetics for body, clothes, or food (A: such as saffron in rice). She may wear silk, wash her hair (N: or comb it, or bathe) for cleanliness, or pare her nails during this period.

ولا تَخْتَضِبَ ولا تَكْتَحِـلَ بإثمِـدٍ ونحـوه [فإنْ احْتَاجَتْ إلى الكحل (لرمد ونحوه) فبالليل وتزيلُهُ بالنهار] ولاَ تَلْبَسُ الصافيَ مِنْ أزرقَ وأخضـرَ وأحمـرَ وأصفـرَ ولا تُرَجِّلُ الشعرَ ولا تَسْتَعْمِـلُ طيباً في بدنٍ وثـوبٍ ومأكـولٍ ولهَا لبسُ الإبـريسِم وغسـلُ الرأسِ للتنظيفِ (ح : والامتشاط والحمام) وتقليم الأظفار .

THE END OF THE WAITING PERIOD

أحكام متفرقة في انقضاء العدة

n9.17   If the husband of a woman in her waiting period takes her back but divorces her again before having had sexual intercourse with her, then a new waiting period starts over from the beginning (N: though it is unlawful for him to do this merely to prolong her waiting period).

If a husband releases his wife for payment (def: n5), remarries her during the release's waiting period, but divorces her before having had sexual intercourse, then she merely finishes the remainder of the release's waiting period.

n9.17   وإذا رَاجَـعَ المعتدة ثُمَّ طَلَّقَهَا قبـلَ الـدخول تَسْتَأْنِفُ عدةً جديدةً (ح : ويحرم عليه أن يفعل هذا ليطيل عدتها) . وإنْ تَزوَّجَ مَنْ خَالَعَهَـا في عدتـهِ ثُمَّ طَلَّقَهَا قبلَ الدخولِ بَنَتْ على العدةِ الأولى .

n9.18   When a woman claims that her waiting period has expired (O: if it does not comprise a particular number of months, but rather consists of a number of intervals between menstruations, or of giving birth) within an amount of time in which it could have possibly ended, then her word is accepted (dis: k8.2).

n9.18   ومتى ادَّعَتِ المـرأةُ انقضـاءَ العـدةِ (بغيرِ الأشهر سواء كان بالأقراء أو بوضـعِ الحمل) في زمنٍ يُمْكِنُ انْقضاؤُهَا فيه قُبلَ قولُها .

n9.19   If news of a husband's death reaches a woman after his death by four months and ten days, her waiting period is already over (O: since her knowledge of his death is not a condition for the waiting period).

n9.19   وإذا بَلَغَهَا خبرُ موتِه بعدَ أربعةِ أشهرٍ وعشرةِ أيامٍ فقَدِ انْقَضَتِ العدةُ (لأن علمها بموته ليس شرطاً في انقضاء العدة) .

n9.20   [مَنْ مَلَكَ أمةً حَرُمَ عليهِ وطؤُهَا والاستمتاعُ بها حتَّى يَسْتَبْرِئَهَا بعدَ قبضِهَا بالوضع إنْ كانَتْ حاملاً وبحيضةٍ إنْ كانَتْ حائلاً تحيضُ . وإلاَّ فبشهرٍ . وإنْ كانَتْ زوجتَهُ فأشْتَراهَا انْفَسَخَ النكاحُ وحَلَّتْ لَه بملكِ اليمينِ مِنْ غيرِ استبراءٍ . ومَنْ زَوَّجَ أمتَهُ أوْ كَاتَبَهَا ثُمَّ زَالَ النكاحُ والكتابةُ لمْ يَطأْها حتَّى يَسْتَبْرِئَهَا . ولهُ الاستمتاعُ بالمسبية في مدة الاستبراء بغير الجماع . ومَنْ وطىءَ أمتَهُ حَرُمَ عليه أنْ يُزَوِّجَهَا حتَّى يَسْتَبْرِئَهَا] .

571

n10.0 ESTABLISHING PATERNITY	n10.0 ثبوت نسب الولد

n10.1 [وَمَنْ أَتَتْ أَمَتُهُ بِوَلَدٍ فَإِنْ ثَبَتَ أَنَّهُ وَطِئَهَا لَحِقَهُ سواءٌ كَانَ يَعْزِلُ مِنِّهُ عَنْهَا أَمْ لا . وإِن لَمْ يَكُنْ وَطِئَهَا لَمْ يَلْحَقْهُ] .

n10.2 The husband of a woman who bears a child (O: no matter whether his marriage to her is valid or invalid) is considered to be the child's father whenever it is (N: legally) possible that the child could be his, meaning that:

n10.2 وَمَنْ أَتَتْ زوجتُهُ (سـواء تزوجها بعقد صحيح أو فاسد) بوَلَدٍ لَحِقَهُ نَسَبُهُ إِنْ أَمْكَنَ أَنْ يَكُـونَ مِنـهُ بأَنْ تَأْتِيَ بِه بعـدَ ستـةِ أَشهـرٍ ولحظـةٍ مِنْ حِينِ العَقـدِ ودونَ أَربـعِ سنيـنَ مِنْ حِيـنِ إِمكـانِ الاجتمـاعِ مَعَها إِذا أَمْكَنَ وطؤُهَا ولَوْ على

(a) the woman gave birth to the child six months plus a moment after the marriage agreement;

بعدٍ، وإِنْ لَمْ يَعْلَمْ أَنهُ وَطِئَ [بخلافِ ما سَبَقَ في أَمتِهِ] بشـرطِ أَنْ يَكُـونَ للزوجِ تسعُ سنينَ ونصفٌ [ولحظةٌ تَسَعُ الوطءَ] .

(b) she gave birth to it less than four years from when she and her husband could last have possibly met and had sexual intercourse, even if they were living at a distance from one another, and even if the husband does not know whether he had sexual intercourse with her. (A: These conditions are for the child's protection against being disowned, and only concern what can be established in court. Hence, if the husband and wife were living apart at a distance at which they could possibly have travelled and met, for the child's sake the court presumes the child to be the husband's);

(c) and the husband is at least nine and a half years old.

n10.3 The husband is not legally considered the child's father when the child could not possibly be his, such as when:

n10.3 فإِنْ لَمْ يُمْكِنْ أَنْ يَكُونَ مِنهُ بأَنْ أَتَتْ بِه لدونِ ستةِ أَشهرٍ أَوْ لأَكثَرَ مِنْ أَربعِ سنينَ أَوْ مَعَ القطـعِ بأَنـهُ لمْ يَطَأْها أَوْ كَانَ للزوجِ مِن السِّـنِّ دونَ ما تَقـدَّمَ أَوْ كَانَ مقطوعَ الذكرِ والأَنثيين جميعاً لمْ يَلْحَقْهُ] .

(1) (non-(a) and (b) above) the wife gave birth to the child in less than six months or more than four years since intercourse;

(2) (non-(b)) the husband is absolutely certain he did not have sexual intercourse with her;

(3) (non-(c)) the husband is under the above-mentioned age;

(4) or the husband's genitals have been dissevered.

n10.4   Whenever a husband is absolutely certain that a child which is legally considered his (def: n10.2) is not his, by knowing that he never had intercourse with the wife at all (O: or did, but less than six months or more than four years before the birth), then he is obliged to deny paternity by public imprecation (li'an, def: n11.3) (O: immediately, because denying paternity of a child immediately is like the return of defective merchandise (dis: k5.7). He does so by going to the Islamic judge and saying, "This child is not mine." If he delays, his denial is no longer valid. As for the public imprecation itself, he may perform it at any time thereafter. If he claims that he was ignorant of the necessity of denying paternity, or the obligatory character of its immediacy, and he is someone who might well be ignorant of it, then his claim (A: of ignorance) is accepted when he swears an oath to that effect. Denial of paternity likewise entails charging the wife with adultery, and this too is obligatory immediately).

n10.5   If a husband is not absolutely sure that the child is from someone else, it is unlawful for him to deny paternity (O: as mere doubts that have arisen in his mind are of no consequence) and unlawful to charge his wife with adultery. (O: It is also unlawful for him to publicly imprecate (def: n11.3) against her in such a case, even when he knows she has committed adultery, because the child would suffer harm through his mother being charged with adultery and its being established against her by public imprecation, the child being disgraced by this and gossip circulated about him. The child need not endure this harm merely to satisfy the husband's revenge, who may separate from her by divorce.)

n10.6   When a child is legally considered (def: n10.2) to be from a husband who is entitled to deny paternity but delays doing so without excuse and subsequently wants to deny it by public imprecation, we (O: i.e. the judge) do not allow him to do so (O: because denial of paternity must take place immediately, as mentioned above (n10.4), and his delay obviates the possibility of denial). But if the husband intends to deny paternity immediately, we implement his intention.

n10.4   ومتَى تَحَقَّقَ الزوجُ أنَّ الوَلدَ الذي أَلحَقَهُ الشرعُ به لَيْسَ منهُ بأنْ عَلِمَ هوَ أنـهُ لم يَطَأهَـا أبـداً (أو وطئها ولكن ولـدتـه لدون ستة أشهر من وطئه أو لفوق أربع سنين منـه) لَزِمَهُ نَفْيُهُ باللعان (فوراً لأن نفي الولـد على الفور كالرد بالعيب بأن يأتي القاضي ويقول له : إن هذا الولد ليس مني . فإن أخر ذلك لم يصح نفيه بعـد . وأمـا اللعـان فهو على التراخي بعد ذلـك ولـو ادعى جهـل النفي أو الفـوريـة وكـان ممن يخفى عليه ذلك صدق بيمينه ويلزم من نفي الولـد قذف الزوجـة وهو واجب حينئذ فوراً).

n10.5   وإنْ لم يَتَحَقَّقْ أنـهُ منْ غيرِه حَرُمَ عليـه نفيُهُ (ولا عبرة بريبة يجدها في نفسه) وقذفُهَا (وكذلك يحرم عليه لعانها وإن علم زناها لأن الولد يتضرر بنسبة أمه إلى الزنـا وإثباتـه عليها باللعان لأنه يعير بذلـك وتطلق فيـه الألسنة فلا يحتمل هذا الضرر لغرض الانتقـام والفـراق ممكن بالطلاق) [وإنْ كَانَ الولدُ أسودَ وهوَ أبيضُ أوْ غيرَ ذلكَ].

n10.6   ومَنْ لَحِقَهُ نسبٌ فأَخَّرَ نفيَهُ بلا عذرٍ ثمَّ أرادَ أنْ يَنْفِيَهُ باللعان لم نُجِبْهُ إلى ذلكَ (والمعنى أن القاضي لم يجاوبه فيه لأن نفي الولـد يكـون على الفور كما مر والتأخير يسقط نفيه عنه [كالرد بالعيب]) وإنْ أَرَادَ نفيَهُ على الفور أَجَبْنَاهُ إليهِ .

n11.0 CHARGING ONE'S WIFE WITH ADULTERY	**n11.0 قذف الزوجة بالزنا**

n11.1 Anyone who charges his wife with adultery (O: in plain words, as when he says, "You adulteress," or allusively, as when he says, "I did not find you a virgin,") and who is thereby liable to be punished for accusing another of adultery without witnesses (dis: o13.1), may prevent the punishment by public imprecation against her (li'an, def: n11.3), provided he:

(a) has reached puberty;

(b) is sane;

(c) does so voluntarily;

and provided his wife:

(d) is legally innocent of adultery (A: meaning there is neither a confession from her nor four eyewitnesses (dis: n11.2(O:)));

(e) and that she is capable of sexual intercourse.

n11.1 مَنْ قَذَفَ زوجَتَـهُ بالـزنـا (صـريحاً كقوله : يا زانية أو كناية كقوله : لم أجدك عذراء) فَطُولِبَ بحدِّ القذف فلَهُ أنْ يُسْقِطَهُ باللعانِ بشرطِ أنْ يَكُونَ الزوجُ بالغـاً عاقـلاً مختـاراً وأنْ تَكـونَ الـزوجة عفيفةً يُمْكِنُ أنْ تُوطَأ .

n11.2 A husband who accuses his wife of adultery is disciplined (ta'zir, def: o17) by the magistrate and not allowed to imprecate against her when her adultery is already legally established (O: whether by her own admission, or by proof, meaning that four upright witnesses (o24.4) have looked at her when she was copulating and seen the adulterer's penis in her vagina), or when (N: adultery is impossible, such as when) the person accused is a mere infant.

n11.2 فلَوْ قَذَفَ مَنْ ثَبَتَ زنَاهَا (إمَّا بإقـرارهـا أو بالبينة وهي أربعة من الرجال العـدول بأن نظروا إليها وقت زناها ورأوا ذكـر الـزاني في فرجهـا) أوْ طفلةً [كبنت شهرٍ] عُزِّرَ ولـمْ يُلاعِنْ .

n11.3 Public imprecation consists of the Islamic magistrate (O: or his equivalent) telling the husband to repeat four times, "I testify by Allah that I am truthful in charging her with adultery" (O: and it is necessary to identify her by her first and family name, though if she is present he says, "this

اللعان

n11.3 واللعـانُ أنْ يَأْمـرَهُ الحاكمُ (أو من يقـوم مقـامـه) أنْ يَقُـولَ أربَعَ مراتٍ : أَشْهـدُ بالله إنِّي مِنَ الصـادقينَ فيمَا رَمَيْتُهـا به مِنَ الـزنـا (ولا بد أن يميـزهـا باسمهـا ويـرفـع نسبهـا . وإن كانت حاضرة قال

wife of mine." and points to her); and if there is a child, "and that this child [O: or if absent, "the child she gave birth to from adultery"] is not from me." The fifth time, after the magistrate warns him, enjoins him to fear Allah (O: reminding him that the punishment of the hereafter is worse than punishment in the present life), and after he has put his hand in front of the husband's mouth, the husband adds, "And may the curse of Allah be upon me if I am lying."

زوجتي هذه وأشار إليها) وأنَّ هذا الـولد (وإن كان غائباً قال وإن الولد الذي ولدته من الـزنـا) لَيْسَ مِنِّي إنْ كان هناك ولدٌ ثُمَّ يَقُولُ في الخـامسة بعدَ أنْ يَعِظَهُ الحاكمُ ويُخَـوِّفُهُ (بالله تعالى ويذكره بأن عذاب الآخـرة أشد من عذاب الدنيا) ويَضَع يَدَهُ على فيه : وعلَيَّ لعنةُ الله إنْ كُنْتُ من الكاذبينَ .

n11.4 When the husband has done this, he is no longer liable to be punished for accusing another of adultery without witnesses, he has denied paternity of the child, and his wife is divorced from him and unlawful for him to marry, be alone with, or look at, forever. She is now liable to be punished for adultery.

n11.4 فإذا فَعَـلَ ذلـك سَقَط عنهُ حدُّ القـذف وانْتَفَى عنهُ نسبُ الولد وبَانَتْ منهُ وحَرُمَتْ على التأبيد ولَزِمَها حدُّ الزنَا .

n11.5 The wife in such a case may avoid being punished for adultery by public imprecation against the husband. Upon being ordered by the magistrate, she says four times, "I testify by Allah that he is lying about what he has charged me with." The fifth time, after being warned by the magistrate of the severity of the consequences, as described above, she says, "And may the wrath of Allah be upon me if he is telling the truth." When she has done this, she is no longer liable to be punished for adultery.

n11.5 ولَهَا أنْ تُسْقِطَـهُ عَنْ نفسهَا باللعـانِ فتَقُولَ بأمر الحاكم أربعَ مراتٍ : أشْهَـدُ بالله إنـهُ لمِنَ الكاذبينَ فيمَا رَمَانِي بـه ؛ ثُمَّ تَقُولُ في الخامسة بعدَ الوعظ كَمَا سَبَـقَ : وعـلَيَّ غضـبُ الـله إنْ كان من الصادقينَ . فإذا فَعَلَتْ هذِه سَقَط عنها حدُّ الزنَا .

n11.6 (O: Public imprecation is legally valid in a non-Arabic language even when the speaker knows Arabic, because the imprecation is a kind of oath or attestation, either of which may be given in any language.)

n11.6 (وصح اللعان بغير عربية وإن عرفها لأن اللعان يمين أو شهادة وهما في اللغات) .

*

n12.0 BECOMING UNMARRIAGEABLE KIN BY SUCKLING (RIDA')

n12.0 الرضاع

n12.1 An infant becomes the "child" of the female who breast-feeds him (A: in respect to

n12.1 إذا ثَارَ (أي ظهـر) لبِنتِ تسـع

being unable to marry her, to the permissibility of looking at her and being alone with her, and in his ablution (wudu) not being nullified by touching her) when:

(a) the milk comes from a female at least nine years old, whether it is occasioned by sexual intercourse or something else;

(b) and she breast-feeds a child who is less than two full years old;

(c) in at least five separate breast-feedings (O: a restriction that excludes anything less than five, which is of no consequence. *Separate* breast-feedings means whatever is commonly acknowledged (def: f4.5) to be separate).

n12.2   In such a case:

(1) it is unlawful for the wet nurse to marry the child and its subsequent descendants (O: by familial relation or by suckling) exclusively (O: *exclusively* meaning that only the child's descendants become unlawful for her to marry, not the child's ancestors (N: or brothers));

(2) she becomes the child's "mother," and it is unlawful for the child to marry her, her ancestors (O: by familial relation or by suckling), her descendants (O: who become as if they were the child's brothers and sisters), or her brothers and sisters (O: though the child is not forbidden to marry the latters' children).

n12.3   If the wet nurse's milk was occasioned by a pregnancy from her husband, then:

(1) the child she nurses becomes the husband's "child," and the husband may not marry the child or its descendants (O: by familial relation or by suckling, since they are now as if his grandchildren) exclusively;

(2) and the husband becomes the child's "father," and it is unlawful for the child to marry him, his ancestors, his descendants, or his brothers and sisters.

سنينَ لبنٌ مِنْ وطءٍ أَوْ مِنْ غيـره فأرْضَعَتْ طفـلاً لـهُ دونَ الحوليـنِ خمسَ رضعـاتٍ متفـرقـاتٍ (فخـرج به ما إذا كان أقل منها فلا يؤثر. والتفرق مرجعه العرف) صَارَ ابنَهَا.

n12.2   فيَحْرُمُ عليْهَا هو وفروعُهُ (من النسب والـرضاع) فقَطْ (ومـراده به أن التحـريم خاص بفـروعـه ولا يسـري إلى أصـولـه (ح : وحواشيـه)). وصَارَتْ أمُّهُ فتَحْـرُمُ عليـهِ هيَ وأصولُهَـا (من النسب والرضاع) وفروعُهَا (فيصير أولادها إخوته وأخواته) وإخوتُهَـا وأخواتُهَا (ولا تثبت الحرمـة بين الـرضيـع وبين أولاد إخوة المرضعة وأخواتها).

n12.3   وإنْ ثَارَ الـلبنُ من حمـلٍ من زوجٍ صَارَ الـرضيعُ ابناً للزوج فيَحْرُمُ عليـه الـرضيـعُ وفروعُهُ (من النسب والرضاع لأنهم أحفاده) فقطْ وصَار الزوج أبـاهُ. فيَحْـرُمُ على الـرضيـعِ هوَ وأصولُهُ وفروعُهُ وإخوتُهُ وأخواتُهُ.

n12.4 Upon becoming unmarriageable kin through suckling, marriage between the above-mentioned persons is prohibited, and it is permissible for the respective members of the opposite sex to look at each other as they do with their familial unmarriageable relatives (dis: m2.5), and to be alone with them (O: though other kinds of rulings applicable to natural relatives, such as inheritance (def: L4–6) or having to support them (m12) are not applicable to unmarriageable kin by suckling).

n12.4 فَيَحْرُمُ النكِاحُ ويَحِلُّ النظرُ والخلوةُ كالنسبِ (دون سائـر أحكـامـه كالميراث والنفقة).

*

BOOK O

JUSTICE

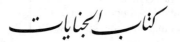

CONTENTS:

o1.0   WHO IS SUBJECT TO RETALIATION FOR INJURIOUS CRIMES

(O: *Injurious crimes* includes not only those

o1.0 على من يجب القصاص في الجنايات

(والجنايات شاملة للجناية بالجارح)

committed with injurious weapons, but those inflicted otherwise as well, such as with sorcery (def: x136). Killing without right is, after unbelief, one of the very worst enormities, as Shafi'i explicitly states in (n: Muzani's) *The Epitome*. The Prophet (Allah bless him and give him peace) said:

"The blood of a Muslim man who testifies that there is no god but Allah and that I am the Messenger of Allah is not lawful to shed unless he be one of three: a married adulterer, someone killed in retaliation for killing another, or someone who abandons his religion and the Muslim community,"

and in another hadith,

"The killing of a believer is more heinous in Allah's sight that doing away with all of this world."

Allah Most High says:

"... and not to slay the soul that Allah has forbidden, except with right" (Koran 6:151),

and,

"O you who believe, retaliation is prescribed for you regarding the slain..." (Koran 2:178).)

و بغيره كسحر . والقتل بغير حق من أكبر الكبائر بعد الكفر نص عليه الشافعي في المختصر . قال ﷺ : «لا يَحِلُّ دم امرىء مسلم يشهد أن لا إله إلا الله وأني رسول الله إلا بإحدى ثلاث الشَّيِّبُ الزاني والنفس بالنفس والتارك لدينه المفارق للجماعة» ؛ وفي الحديث : «لَقَتْلُ مؤمن عند الله أعظم من زوال الدنيا» . قال تعالى : ﴿وَلَا تَقْتُلُوا النَّفْسَ الَّتِي حَرَّمَ اللَّهُ إِلَّا بِالْحَقِّ﴾ [الأنعام : ١٥١]؛ وقال تعالى : ﴿يَا أَيُّهَا الَّذِينَ آمَنُوا كُتِبَ عَلَيْكُمُ القِصَاصُ﴾ [البقرة : ١٧٨]) .

o1.1 Retaliation is obligatory (A: if the person entitled wishes to take it (dis: o3.8)) against anyone who kills a human being purely intentionally and without right. (O: *Intentionally* is a first restriction and excludes killing someone through an honest mistake, while *purely* excludes a mistake made in a deliberate injury (def: o2.3), and *without right* excludes cases of justifiable homicide such as lawful retaliation.)

o1.1 يَجِبُ القِصَاصُ على مَنْ قَتَلَ إنساناً عمداً محضاً عدواناً . (فالعمد قيد أول خرج به الخطأ وبالمحض عمد الخطأ وبالعدوان ما لو قتله بحق كالقصاص) .

o1.2 The following are not subject to retaliation:

(1) a child or insane person, under any circumstances (O: whether Muslim or non-Muslim.

o1.2 لكِنْ لا يَجِبُ على صبيٍّ ومجنونٍ مطلقاً (سواء كانا مسلمين أو

The ruling for a person intermittently insane is that he is considered as a sane person when in his right mind, and as if someone continuously insane when in an interval of insanity. If someone against whom retaliation is obligatory subsequently becomes insane, the full penalty is nevertheless exacted. A homicide committed by someone who is drunk is (A: considered the same as that of a sane person,) like his pronouncing divorce (dis: n1.2));

(2) a Muslim for killing a non-Muslim;

(3) a Jewish or Christian subject of the Islamic state for killing an apostate from Islam (O: because a subject of the state is under its protection, while killing an apostate from Islam is without consequences);

(4) a father or mother (or their fathers or mothers) for killing their offspring, or offspring's offspring;

(5) nor is retaliation permissible to a descendant for (A: his ancestor's) killing someone whose death would otherwise entitle the descendant to retaliate, such as when his father kills his mother.

*

o2.0 INTENTIONALITY IN INJURIOUS CRIMES

o2.1 Injurious crimes (O: of all types, whether killing or something less) are of three types:

(1) an honest mistake;

(2) a mistake made in a deliberate injury;

(3) or purely intentional.

o2.2 An *honest mistake* is an act such as shooting an arrow at a wall and hitting a person (O: or shooting at a person and hitting someone else), or

كافرين . والـذي جنونه منقطع فهـو كالعـاقـل في وقت إفـاقتـه وكـالمطبق في وقت جنونه . ومن وجب عليه القصاص وقد جن من بعد الوجوب استوفي منه في حال جنـونه . وقتل السكران كطلاقه) ولا على مسلم بقتل كافر [ولا على حرٌ بقتل عبدٍ] ولا على ذميٍّ بقتـل مرتـدٍ (لأن الـذمي معصوم والمـرتـد مهـدر) ولا على الأب والأمِّ وآبـائهمَا وأمهاتهمَا بقتل الولدِ وولدِ الـولدِ ولا بقتـل مَنْ يَثْبُتُ القصـاصُ فيه للولدِ مثلُ أنْ يَقْتُلَ الأبُ الأمَّ .

o2.0 أقسام الجنايات

o2.1 ثمَّ الجنـايـاتُ (من حيث هي سواء كانت على النفس أو على ما دونهـا) ثلاثـةٌ : خطأ ؛ وعمـدُ خطـإٍ ؛ وعمـدٌ محضٌ .

o2.2 فالـخطـأُ مثـلُ أنْ يَرْميَ إلى حائـطٍ فَيُصيبَ إنساناً (وكذا لو رمى إنساناً

slipping from a height and falling on someone. The criterion for it is that the act is intended but not the person, or neither the act nor the person is intended.

فأصـاب غيره) أوْ يَزْلقَ مِنْ شاهقٍ فيَقـعَ على إنسانٍ وضـابطُهُ أنْ يَقْصِدَ الفعلَ ولا يَقْصِدَ الشخصَ أوْ لا يَقْصِدَهُما. ·

o2.3   A *mistake made in a deliberate injury* is when one intends an injury that is not generally fatal, such as hitting someone with a light stick in a nonvital spot (A: from which the person dies) and the like.

o2.3   وعمدُ الخطأ أنْ يَقْصِدَ الجنايةَ بما لا يَقْتُـلَ غالباً مثـلَ أنْ يَضْـربَهُ بعصاً خفيفةٍ في غيرِ مَقْتَلٍ ونحوِ ذلكَ.

o2.4   *Purely intentional* means to intend an injury of the type that is generally fatal, whether with a blunt instrument or a sharp one.

o2.4   والعمدُ أنْ يَقْصِدَ الجنايةَ بما يَقْتُلُ غالباً سواءٌ كانَ مثقَّلاً أوْ محدَّداً.

*

o3.0   RETALIATION FOR BODILY INJURY OR DEATH (QISAS)

o3.0 أحكام العمد في الجنايات

o3.1   Retaliation is obligatory (A: if those entitled wish to take it (dis: o3.8)) when there is a (N: purely) intentional injury (def: o2.4) against life or limb.

o3.1   فإنْ كانَتِ الجنايةُ عمداً (ح: محضاً) على النفسِ أو الأطرافِ وَجَبَ القصاصُ.

o3.2   Retaliation is obligatory in return for injuries (A: part for commensurate part) whenever the retaliatory injury can be (O: fully) inflicted without exceeding the extent of the original injury, such as (A: when the retaliatory injury is on) an eye, eyelid, the soft part of the nose, the ear, tooth, lip, hand, foot, finger, fingertip, penis, testicles, vulva, and the like; provided that the retaliatory injury is like the original, meaning that a right member is not taken for a left, an upper one for a lower, nor a functional member for a paralyzed one. (N: Nor is there retaliation for nonfatal bullet wounds in the stomach or chest, for example, because such injuries cannot be reproduced without risk of greater damage than the original, for which reason they call for an indemnity (dis: o4.15) alone.) There is no retaliation for (O: breaking) a bone (A: though payment is due to cover the cost of treatment and so forth).

o3.2   فيَجـبُ في الأعضـاءِ حيثُ أمْكَنَ (استيعـاب القصـاص فيها) مِنْ غيرِ حَيْفٍ [(بأن لا يزيـد على أخذ الواجب)] كالعين والجفنِ ومارنِ الأنفِ [وهوَ ما لانَ منهُ] والأذنِ والسنِّ والشفةِ واليدِ والرِّجلِ والأصابـع والأنـامـل والـذكرِ والأنثيينِ والفرجِ ونحوِ ذلكَ بشرطِ المماثلة. فلا تؤخَـذُ يمينٌ بيسـارٍ ولا أعلى بأسفَـلَ [وبـالعكسِ] ولا صحيـحٌ بأشلَّ. ولا قصاصَ في (كسر) عظمٍ. [فلوْ قَطَعَ اليدَ مِنْ وَسَـطِ الـذراعِ اقْتُصَّ مِنَ الكفِّ وفي البـاقي حكـومةٌ (وهي جزء مقدر من الدية لتعذر القصاص)].

o3.3   Females are entitled to retaliate against males, children against adults, and lower class people against upper class; whether the retaliation is a life for a life, or limb for a limb.

o3.3 وُيُقْتَصُّ للأنثى مِنَ الـذكـر وللطفـل مِنَ الكبيـر وللوضيـع مِنَ الشريفِ في النفسِ والأعضاءِ.

o3.4   It is not permissible to exact retaliation against someone without the presence of the caliph (def: o25) or his representative (O: meaning that it is necessary to have the permission of one of them because of the danger and lack of knowledge involved in exacting retaliation oneself, as it requires the judgement and personal reasoning of a ruler. If someone takes retaliation without the caliph's permission, then it is valid (A: i.e. suffices the demand for it) but the person who took it is disciplined (def: o17) for arrogating the caliph's prerogative, since administering retaliation is one of his functions, and to encroach upon it is wrong).
     If a person who is entitled to retaliate is able to do so proficiently (O: being a strong man who knows how to do it), he is allowed to. If not, he is ordered (N: by the ruler or his representative) to have another do it.

o3.4 ولا يَجُوزُ أنْ يُسْتَـوْفَـى القصـاص إلّا بحضـرة السلطان أوْ نائبِه. (أي أنـه يتـوقف على إذن أحدهما لما في استيفائـه بنفسه مِن الخطر وعدم المعرفة فيحتـاج فيه إلى نظر الحاكم واجتهاده فلو استـوفـاه بغيـر إذنـه وقـع المـوقـع وعزر لافتيـاتـه على السلطان لأن القصاص مِن وظيفتـه والمخالفة فيه لا تليق). فإنْ كَانَ مَن لَهُ القصـاصُ يُحْسِنُـه (بأن كان رجـلاً قويـاً عارفـاً بكيفيتـه) مَكّنَـهُ منهُ وإلّا أمَرَهُ بالتوكيل (ح: أي أمره الحاكم أو نائبه).

o3.5   If two (O: or more) people are entitled to exact retaliation against the offender, it is not permissible for just one of them to insist on doing so (O: though if they choose one of themselves to exact it, this is permissible, and the one chosen is considered as the other's commissioned agent. The two may not take retaliation together, as this amounts to torturing the person being retaliated against). If each insists that he be the one, they draw lots to see who will do it.

o3.5 وإنْ كَانَ القصـاصُ لاثنين (أو أكثر) لَمْ يَجُزْ لأحدِهِمَا أنْ يَنْفَرِدَ بِه (وإن اتفقـا على أن أحـدهما يستوفي القصاص جازَ وكان وكيلاً عن الآخر. ولا يستوفيانه معـاً لأن فيه تعذيباً للمقتص منه). فإنْ تَشَاحّا فيمَنْ يَسْتَوْفِيه أقْرِعَ بينَهُمَا.

o3.6   There is no retaliation against a pregnant woman until she has given birth and the infant is able to suffice with another's milk.

o3.6 ولا يُقْتَصُّ مِنْ حامـلٍ حتّى تَضَعَ ويَسْتَغْنِيَ الولدَ بلبن غيرِها.

o3.7 [ومَنْ قَطَعَ اليدَ ثمَّ قَتَلَ تُقْطَعُ يدُهُ ثمَّ يُقْتَلُ. فإنْ قَطَعَ اليدَ فَمَاتَ مِنْ ذلكَ قُطِعَتْ يدُهُ. فإنْ مَاتَ فَهُوَ. وإلَّا قُتِلَ].

o3.8   Whenever someone who is entitled to exact retaliation decides instead to forgive the

o3.8 ومتَى عَفَا مستحقُّ القصاص (عنه) على الدية سَقَطَ القصاصُ ووَجَبَتْ

offender and take an indemnity (def: o4) from him, then retaliation is no longer called for, and the deserving person is entitled to the indemnity. If some of a group of people who are entitled to retaliaton agree to forgo it, as when a murder victim has children and one of them forgives the murderer, then retaliation is no longer obligatory, and the group deserves an indemnity from the offender. (A: Or the indemnity may also be waived.)

الـديةُ. بلْ لَوْ عَفَا بعضُ المستحقينَ مثلُ إنْ كَانَ للمقتــول أولادٌ فيَعْفـو أحـدُهُم سَقَطَ القصاصُ ووَجَبَتِ الديةُ.

o3.9   When someone kills a group of people or maims them one after another, retaliation is exacted for the first individual attacked, and the other deserving parties receive an indemnity. If the offender injures them all at once, then those entitled to retaliate against him draw lots to determine who will do so.

o3.9   ومَنْ قَتَلَ جماعةً أوْ قَطَعَ عضواً مِنْ جماعةٍ واحداً بعـد واحدٍ اقْتُصَّ منهُ للأولِ وللبـاقينَ الـديةُ. فإنْ جَنى عليهِمْ دفعةً أُقْرِعَ.

o3.10   When a group of people together murder a single person, they are all killed in retaliation, no matter whether the amount of injury inflicted by each upon the victim is the same or whether it differs.

o3.10   فإنِ اشْتَـرَكَ جمـاعـةٌ في قتلِ واحدٍ قُتِلُوا به سواءٌ اسْتَوَتْ جناياتُهُمْ أوْ تَفاوَتَتْ.

o3.11   [حتَّى لوْ جَرَحَهُ واحدٌ جراحةً وآخرُ مائةَ جراحةٍ ومَاتَ وكانَتْ تلكَ الجراحةُ المنفردةُ أوْ تلكَ الجراحاتُ ممَّا لو انْفَرَدَتْ لقَتَلَتْ لزمَهُمَا القصاصُ. اللهمَّ إلاَّ إنْ يَقْطَعَ الثاني جنايةَ الأولِ بأنْ يَقْطَعَ الأولُ يدَهُ ونحوَهَا ويقْطَعَ الثاني رقبتَهُ أوْ يقُدَّهُ نصفينِ، فالأولُ جارحٌ والثاني قاتلٌ].

o3.12   There is no retaliation against anyone for an injury or death caused by someone who did so intentionally but in conjunction with someone who did so by mistake.

When an injurious crime is caused by a nonfamily member in cooperation with the victim's father, retaliation is only taken against the nonfamily member (dis: o1.2(4)).

o3.12   ولوْ شَارَكَ العامـدُ مخطئاً فلا قصاصَ على أحدٍ.

ولوْ شَارَكَ الأجنبيُّ أبًا اقْتُصَّ مِنَ الأجنبيِّ.

o3.13   Retaliation is also obligatory (dis: o3.8) for every wound that cuts to the bone, such as a cut on the head or face that reaches the skull, or a cut to the bone in the upper arm, lower leg, or thigh. *To the bone* means that it is known that a knife or

o3.13   ويَجِبُ القصاصُ أيضاً في كلِّ جرحٍ انْتَهَى إلى عظمٍ كالمـوضحةِ في الـرأسِ والـوجهِ وجرحِ العضدِ والساقِ والفخـذِ إذا انْتَهَى الجرحُ إلى العظمِ. والمـرادُ بالمـوضحةِ وبانتهاءِ الجرحِ إلى الـعظمِ أنْ يُعْلَمَ وصـولُ السـكينِ أو

a needle, for example, has reached the bone, not that the wound actually exposes the bone to view.

المسلةِ مثلًا إلى العظم ولا يُشْتَرَطُ ظهورُ العظم ورؤيتُهُ.

*

o4.0   INDEMNITY (DIYA)

(A: The rulings below concern the maximum that the victim or victim's family may demand. If both sides agree on an indemnity of lesser amount, or nothing at all, this is legally valid and binding.)

o4.0   الدية

(ع : ما يأتي من الأحكـام يبين أكثـر ما يمكن أن يطلبه المجني عليه أو عائلته . فإن صالحوا على أقل منه أو عفوا فصحيح لازم).

o4.1   An indemnity is obligatory (N: though it may by waived by deserving recipients, like retaliation) in cases of death caused:

(1) by an honest mistake (def: o2.2);

(2) by a mistake made in a deliberate injury (o2.3);

(3) or intentionally, if those entitled to retaliate agree to forgo retaliation (dis: o3.8).

o4.1   إذا كَانَ القتـلُ خطأً أوْ عمدَ خطـأ أوْ آلَ الأمـرُ في العمـدِ بالعفـو إلى الديةِ وَجَبَت الديةُ .

o4.2   The indemnity for killing a male Muslim is 100 camels.

(N: Shafi'i scholars early converted the pastoral equivalents to gold dinars (n: one dinar equalling 4.235 grams of gold (dis: w15)), the amount due in the rulings below being the *weight* of the gold, regardless of its current market value.) (A: The stronger position in the Shafi'i school is that indemnities should be reckoned in camels, after which both parties may agree on a lesser amount or another form of payment.)

o4.2   وديةُ [الحرِّ] المسلم الـذكرِ مائةُ مِنَ الإبلِ .

(ح : قد قدّر العلمـاء ـ من زمن بعيد ـ الـدية بالإبل بدنانير ذهبية، والاعتبار في الأحكـام التـالية بالـوزن لا بالقيمة في السـوق (ع : والراجح في المذهب تقدير الـدية بالإبل، وبعده، فللطرفين أن يتفقا على أقل من المسمّى أو على غير الإبل)).

THE INDEMNITY FOR A PURELY INTENTIONAL KILLING

دية العمد المغلظة

o4.3   The indemnity for cases of purely intentional homicide (def: o2.4) is made severe in three ways:

o4.3   فإنْ كان عمداً فهيَ مغلَّظة مِنْ ثلاثةِ أوجهٍ : كونُها حالَّةً وعلى الجاني

(a) it must be paid immediately;

(b) it is due from the offender himself;

(c) and the amount paid is (N: 1,333.3 gold dinars (n: 5,646.6 grams of gold) or else:) 30 she-camels in their fourth year, 30 she-camels in their fifth year, and 40 pregnant she-camels.

ومثلثــةً : ثلاثينَ حقّــةً وثــلاثينَ جذعـة وأربعينَ خَلِفةً أي حوامِل في بطونِها أولادُها .

THE INDEMNITY FOR DEATH BY MISTAKE IN A DELIBERATE INJURY

تغليظ دية عمد الخطأ

o4.4   When the killing is a mistake made in a deliberate injury (def: o2.3), the indemnity is only made severe in one respect, namely that the payment consists of the three types of camel mentioned above (n: or 5,646.6 grams of gold), while it is less severe in that:

(a) payment is deferred (def: o4.11);

(b) and is due (N: not from the offender, but) from those of the offender's extended family who are required to pay ('aqila, def: o4.10).

o4.4   وإنْ كَانَ عمــدَ خطأٍ فهِــيَ مغلظـةٌ منْ وجهٍ واحدٍ، كونُهـا مثلثـةً ؛ مخففةٌ مـنْ وجهينِ كونُها مؤجّلَةً وعلى العاقلة .

THE INDEMNITY FOR A DEATH CAUSED BY AN HONEST MISTAKE

دية الخطأ المخففة

o4.5   When the killing occurred through an honest mistake (def: o2.2), the indemnity is less severe in three ways:

(a) payment is deferred;

(b) it is due from those of the offender's extended family who are required to pay (def: o4.10);

(c) and the amount paid is (N: 1,000 gold dinars (n: 4,235.0 grams of gold) or:) 20 she-camels in their second year, 20 she-camels and 20 he-camels in their third year, 20 she-camels in their fourth year, and 20 she-camels in their fifth year.

o4.5   وإنْ كَانَ خطأ، فهيَ مخفَّفةٌ منْ ثلاثـةِ أوجهٍ : كونُهـا مؤجّلَةً وعلى العاقلة ومخمَّسَـةً عشرينَ بنتَ مخاضٍ وعشرينَ بنتَ لبونٍ وعشـرينَ ابنَ لبـونٍ وعشرينَ حقةً وعشرينَ جذعةً .

o4.6   But no matter whether the killing was a mistake or intentional, the three-types-of-camel-indemnity (def: o4.3(c)) must be paid if the person killed was:

(1) an *unmarriageable kin by birth* relative of the killer (def: m6.1(1–8) and m6.2(1–6));

(2) slain in the Sacred Precinct in Mecca;

(3) or killed during one of the sacrosanct months of Dhul Qa'da, Dhul Hijja, Muharram, or Rajab.

o4.7   Defective animals may not constitute payment.

o4.8   It is permissible for deserving recipients to accept payment other than camels if both parties agree.

o4.9   (A: For the rulings below, one multiplies the fraction named by the indemnity appropriate to the death or injury's type of intentionality and other relevant circumstances that determine the amount of a male Muslim's indemnity (def: o4.2–6 and o4.13).)

The indemnity for the death or injury of a woman is one-half the indemnity paid for a man.

The indemnity paid for a Jew or Christian is one-third of the indemnity paid for a Muslim. The indemnity paid for a Zoroastrian is one-fifteenth of that of a Muslim.

When a miscarriage results from someone having struck the stomach of a pregnant woman (O: or other part of her, or when someone frightens her, resulting in a miscarriage), the indemnity for the fetus is a male or female slave worth one-twentieth of the indemnity payable for killing the fetus's father, or one-tenth that of its mother. (A: The indemnity is whatever they agree upon.)

o4.10   The members of the offender's extended family who are liable for certain kinds of in-

عربي:

o4.6   اللهُمَّ إلّا أنْ يُقْتَلَ ذا رحمٍ محرمٍ أوْ في الحرمِ أوْ في الأشهرِ الحُرُمِ وهِيَ ذو القعـدةِ وذو الحجـةِ والمحـرمُ ورجبٌ فإنّها تَكُونُ مثلثةً خطأً كَانَ أوْ عمداً.

o4.7   ولا يُؤْخَذُ في الإبلِ معيبٌ.

o4.8   فإنْ تَرَاضَوا على العوضِ عن الإبلِ جَازَ.

o4.9   وديةُ المرأةِ في النفسِ وغيرِها نصفُ ديةِ الرجلِ.

وديةُ اليهوديِّ والنصرانيِّ ثلثُ ديةِ المسلمِ.

وديةُ المجوسيِّ ثلثا عُشْرِ ديةِ المسلمِ [وديةُ العبدِ قيمتُهُ وأعضاؤُهُ وجراحاتُهُ ما نَقَصَ منْهَا].

وفيـمَـا إذا ضَرَبَ بطْنَهَـا (أوْ ضربَ غيرهـا من أعضائها أوْ أخافها بلا ضَربٍ) فألْقَتْ جنينـاً ميتـاً غرةً وهيَ عبـدٌ أوْ أمةٌ [سليمٌ] بقيمـةِ نصفِ عُشْـرِ ديةِ الأبِ أوْ عُشْرِ ديةِ الأمِّ.

o4.10   والعـاقلةُ هِيَ العصباتُ ما عَدَا

demnities consist of the offender's universal heirs, excluding his father, father's father (O: and on up), his son, son's son (O: and on down). (A: Meaning that they consist of those mentioned at L10.6(7–14).) Those of the extended family who are poor (A: *poor* meaning someone who has enough for himself but no more), prepubescent, or insane are not obliged to pay (N: anything in conjunction with the other members). If the offender is Muslim, then his non-Muslim relatives are not obliged to pay, as is also the case if the offender is non-Muslim and his relatives are Muslim.

الأبَ والجدَّ (وإن علا) والابنَ وابنَ الابن (وإن سفل) ولا يَعْقِلُ الفقيرُ (ح): أي لا يجب عليه دفع شيء من الـدية مشاركةً للعاقلة) ولا صبيٌّ ولا مجنونٌ ولا كافرٌ عنْ مسلم، وعكسُه.

o4.11   When the extended family is obliged to, they must pay the entire indemnity of 100 camels (N: or the gold equivalents) within three years. Every required extended family member who is well-off is obliged to pay one-half dinar (n: 2.1175 grams of gold) at the end of each year, while every member who is between affluence and poverty is obliged to pay a quarter dinar (n: 1.05875 grams of gold). If any of the indemnity remains to be paid after three years (N: or if the offender has no family to pay it), it is paid by the Muslim common fund (bayt al-mal). If there is none, the offender himself must pay.

o4.11   فيجبُ عليهمْ ديةُ النفس الكاملةِ أعْني المائةَ منَ الإبل في ثلاثِ سنينَ. فيجبُ على كلِّ غنيٍّ عندَ الحولِ في كلِّ سنةٍ نصفُ دينارٍ وعلى كلِّ متوسطٍ ربعُ دينارٍ. فإذا بقيَ شيءٌ أُخذَ منْ بيت المالِ. وإلَّا فمنَ الجاني.

o4.12   When the indemnity due is less than a full indemnity (A: *full* meaning that which is due for a Muslim male (def: o4.2–6)), as when it is for a wound, miscarriage, female, or a Jewish or Christian subject of the Islamic state, then:

o4.12   وإنْ كانَ الـواجبُ أقلَّ منْ دية النفس الكاملةِ كواجبِ الجراحاتِ ودية الجنين والمرأةِ والذميِّ فمَا كانَ قدرَ ثلثِ الكاملةِ أوْ أقلَّ ففي سنةٍ. وإنْ كانَ الثلثينِ أوْ أقلَّ فالثلثُ في سنةٍ والباقي في الثانية. فإنْ زادَ على الثلثين فالثلثـانِ في السنتينِ والباقي في الثالثة.

(1)   if it consists of one-third or less of a full indemnity, it must be paid within one year;

(2)   if it consists of two-thirds or less of a full indemnity, then one of the thirds must be paid in the first year, and the rest in the second year;

(3)   and if it amounts to more than two-thirds of a full indemnity, then the two-thirds must be paid within two years and the rest in the third year.

THE INDEMNITY FOR BODILY INJURIES

ديةُ الأعضاء

o4.13 If a nonpaired body part of aesthetic value and utility (A: a tongue, for example) is dissevered, then a full indemnity is paid, meaning the indemnity due if the member's owner were killed (def: o4.2–6, o4.9).

The same is due for each pair of limbs: if both are cut off, a full indemnity is paid, while if only one is cut off, then half the full indemnity. The same is true for the faculties of sense (A: such as hearing): for each faculty the injury eliminates, there is a full indemnity. Thus, a full indemnity is paid for cutting off two ears, and a half indemnity for one. This also holds for a pair of eyes, lips, jaws, hands, feet, buttocks, testicles, eyelids, the nipples of a female, vulval labia, the soft part of the nose, the tongue, head of the penis, or whole penis. A full indemnity is also paid for injuries which paralyze these members, or for injuring the peritioneal wall between vagina and rectum so they become one aperture, or for flaying a person, breaking his back, or eliminating the use of his mind, hearing, vision, speech, sense of smell, or taste.

o4.13 وكلُّ عضوٍ مفردٍ فيه جمالٌ ومنفعةٌ إذا قُطِعَ وَجَبَتْ فيه ديةٌ كاملةٌ مثلُ ديةِ صاحبِ العضوِ لوْ قَتَلَهُ. وكَذَا كلُّ عضوين منْ جنسٍ : فإنْ قطَعَهُمَا ففيهمَا الديةُ وفي أحدِهمَا نصفُهَا. وكذا المعاني واللطائفُ ففي كلِّ معنًى مِنْهُمَا الديةُ. ففي قطعِ الأذنين الديةُ وفي أحدِهمَا نصفُهَا. ومثلُهُمَا العينانِ والشفتانِ واللحيانِ والكفانِ والقدمانِ بأصابعهمَا والأليتانِ والأنثيانِ والأجفانِ وحلمتَا المرأة وشفرَاهَا ومارنُ الأنف واللسانُ والحشفةُ وجميعُ الذكرِ. وكَذا في شللِ هذه الأعضاء والإفضاء وسَلْخِ الجلدِ وكسرِ الصلبِ وإذهابِ العقلِ والسمعِ أو الضوءِ أو النطقِ أو الشمِّ أو الذوقِ.

o4.14 The indemnity for each finger is ten camels, and five for each tooth (N: or 10 and 5 percent respectively of the equivalent gold values (def: o4.3–5), depending on the relevant circumstances (dis: o4.9(A:))).

o4.14 وفي كلِّ أصبعٍ عشرٌ منَ الإبلِ وفي كل سنٍ خمسٌ.

o4.15 As for wounds on the body, their indemnity consists of a fraction of the full indemnity proportionate (A: by the calculation of the Islamic magistrate) to the extent of the damage.

o4.15 وأمَّا الجراحاتُ في البدنِ فالحكومةُ.

o4.16 The indemnity for wounds on the head or face, when not to the bone, is also such a proportionate fraction, though if such wounds are to the bone, as mentioned above (o3.13), the indemnity is five camels (dis: o4.14(N:)).

There are other injuries which I prefer to omit for the sake of brevity.

o4.16 وفي الرأسِ والوجهِ فمَا دونَ الموضحةِ فيه الحكومةُ. وأمَّا الموضحةُ [وهيَ ما أوْضَحتِ العظمَ] كمَا تَقدَّمَ ففيها خمسٌ منَ الإبلِ. وبقيَتْ جناياتٌ أخَرَ آثَرْتُ تركَهَا لئلّا يطُولَ الكلامُ.

o4.17   There is no indemnity obligatory for killing a non-Muslim at war with Muslims (harbi), someone who has left Islam, someone sentenced to death by stoning (A: for adultery (def: o12)) by virtue of having been convicted in court, or those it is obligatory to kill by military action (N: such as a band of highwaymen).

o4.17   ولا تَجِبُ الديةُ بقتل الحربيِّ والمـرتدّ ومَنْ وَجَبَ رجمُهُ بالبينة أوْ تَحَتَّمَ قتلُهُ في المحاربة [ولا على السيد بقتل عبده] .

*

o5.0   THE EXPIATION TO ALLAH FOR TAKING A HUMAN LIFE

o5.0   كفــارة القتــل لحق الله تعالى

o5.1   An expiation is due to Allah Most High from anyone who kills someone unlawful to kill, whether the killing is through a mistake or is intentional, and no matter whether retaliation (def: o3) or an indemnity (o4) is obligatory or not.

o5.1   تَجِبُ الكفارةُ على مَنْ قَتَلَ مَنْ يَحْـرُمُ قتلُهُ لحقِّ اللهِ تعـالى خطأً كانَ أوْ عمداً سواءً لَزِمَهُ قصاصٌ أوْ ديةٌ أوْ لمْ يلْزَمْهُ شيءٌ مِنْهُمَا .

o5.2   The expiation consists of freeing a slave (def: k32), or if one cannot, then two consecutive months of fasting. (O: There is no difference in this precedence order whether the killer is legally accountable or not, as when he is a child or insane, in which case the guardian must free a slave on his behalf. (A: Though if a child fasts, it fulfills the expiation.))

o5.2   وهـوَ عتقُ رقبةٍ فإنْ لمْ يَجِدْ فصيامُ شهـرين متتابعين (ولا فرق في التـرتيب بين المكلف وغيـره كالصبي والمجنون فيعتق عنهما وليهما) (ع : فإن صام الصبي أجزأه) .

o5.3   [فلوْ قَتَلَ نساءَ أهلِ الحربِ وأولادَهُمْ فلَا كفارةَ لأنَّهُمْ وإنْ حَرُمَ قتلُهم لحقِّ اللهِ تعالى بلْ لحقِّ الغانمينَ] .

o5.4   (O: There is no expiation for killing someone who has left Islam, a highwayman (def: o15), or a convicted married adulterer, even when someone besides the caliph kills him.)

o5.4   (وكـذا لا كفارة بقتل المرتد وقـاطـع الطريق والـزاني المحصن إذا قتلهم غير الإمام) .

*

o6.0   FIGHTING THOSE WHO REBEL AGAINST THE CALIPH

o6.0   قتال البغاة

o6.1   When a group of Muslims rebel against the caliph (khalifa, def: o25) and want to over-

o6.1   إذا خَرَجَ على الإمــام طائفـةٌ منَ المسلمين ورامُوا خلعَهُ أوْ مَنَعُوا حقاً

throw him, or refuse to fulfill an obligation imposed by Sacred Law such as zakat, and rise in armed insurrection, he sends someone to them and redresses their grievances if possible.

If they obdurately refuse to obey him (O: no matter whether he is just or unjust, as Nawawi mentions in his commentary on *Sahih Muslim*, citing the consensus of Muslims (ijma', def: b7) that it is unlawful to revolt against caliphs and fight them, even if they are corrupt), he fights them with (O: military) weaponry that does not cause general destruction, as do fire and mangonel (O: for the aim is to suppress them, not destroy them), and does not pursue those who retreat, or kill the wounded.

شرعـاً كالـزكـاة وَامْتَنَعُـوا بالحرب بَعَثَ إليهِم وأزالَ علَّتَهُمْ إنْ أمْكَنَ.

فإنْ أبَوا (عـادلاً كان أو جائـراً كما في شرح مسلم للنـووي من حكـايـة إجماع المسلمين على حرمـة الخـروج عليهم وقتـالهم وإن كانـوا فسقـة) فَقَاتَلَهُمْ بِمَـا لا يَعُمُّ شرُّهُ (من آلات الـحـرب) كالنـار والـمنجـنيـق (لأن القـصـد كفهم لا إهلاكهم) ولا يَتْبَعُ مُدْبرَهُمْ ولا يَقْتُل جريحَهُمْ.

o6.2   There is no financial responsibility for what they destroy of ours nor what we destroy of theirs in such military action.

o6.2   ومـا أَتْلَفُـوهُ علَيْنَـا أو أتْلَفْنَـاهُ عليهِمْ في الحربِ لا ضمانَ فيه.

o6.3   They are subject to Islamic laws (O: because they have not committed an act that puts them outside of Islam that they should be considered non-Muslims. Nor are they considered morally corrupt, for *rebels* is not a pejorative term, but rather they merely have a mistaken understanding), and the decisions of their Islamic judge are considered legally effective (O: provided he does not declare the lives of upright Muslims (def: o24.4) to be justly forfeitable) if they are such as would be effective if made by our own judge.

o6.3   وأحكـامُ الإسـلام جاريـةٌ عليهِمْ (فـإنهم لم يرتكبـوا مكفـراً حتى يحكم عليهم بالكفر وليسـوا بفسقـة بل البغي ليس باسم لهم لكنهم مخطئـون في تأويـلهم) ويُنَفَّـذُ منْ حكم قاضيهِمْ (إن لم يستحـل دمـاء أهل العدل) ما يُنَفَّذُ منْ حكمِ قاضينَا.

o6.4   If they do not rebel by war, the caliph may not fight them.

o6.4   وإنْ لمْ يَمْتَنعُوا بالحرب لمْ يُقَاتِلْهُمْ.

*

o7.0   WARDING OFF AGGRESSORS

o7.0   الصيال

o7.1   Someone whom a Muslim is trying to kill is entitled to kill the Muslim, though it is not obligatory to. Someone whom a non-Muslim or animal is trying to kill is obliged to defend himself.

o7.1   ومَنْ قَصَدَهُ مسلمٌ يُريـدُ قتلَهُ جازَ لهُ قتلُهُ ولا يَجبُ.
وإنْ قَصَدَهُ كافرٌ أوْ بهيمةٌ وَجَبَ دفعُهُ.

o7.2 If an aggressor is trying to take one's money or property, it is permissible to defend it but not obligatory. If the aggressor intends one's womenfolk (O: such as one's wife or son's wife), it is obligatory to defend them.

o7.3 To *defend* means to use the minimum amount of force required. If one knows that shouting will repel the aggressor, one may not strike him. If a hand is enough, a stick may not be employed. If a stick will do, a sword may not be used. If cutting the other's hand will suffice, one may not kill him. (O: Mawardi states that this precedence order is for crimes that are not indecencies. As for when an aggressor is raping someone whom it is unlawful for him to have sexual intercourse with, it is permissible to kill him forthwith.) Someone who knows (O: i.e. believes) that an aggressor cannot be dissuaded by anything short of killing him may kill him and is not accountable for it.

o7.4 When one has warded off an aggressor, it is unlawful to take further measures against him.

*

o8.0 APOSTASY FROM ISLAM (RIDDA)

(O: Leaving Islam is the ugliest form of unbelief (kufr) and the worst. It may come about through sarcasm, as when someone is told, "Trim your nails, it is sunna," and he replies, "I would not do it even if it were," as opposed to when some circumstance exists which exonerates him of having committed apostasy, such as when his tongue runs away with him, or when he is quoting someone, or says it out of fear.)

o8.1 When a person who has reached puberty and is sane voluntarily apostatizes from Islam, he deserves to be killed.

o8.2 In such a case, it is obligatory for the caliph (A: or his representative) to ask him to

٧.٢ وإنْ قَصَدَ مالَهُ جازَ الدفعُ ولا يَجِبُ.

وإنْ قَصَدَ حريمَهُ (كزوجته وزوجة ولده) وَجَبَ الدفعُ.

٧.٣ ويُدفَعُ بالأسهل فالأسهل. فإنْ عَرَفَ أنهُ يَندَفِعُ بالصياحِ فليْسَ لهُ ضربُهُ. أوْ باليدِ فليْسَ لهُ بالعصا. أوْ بالعصا فليْسَ لهُ السيفُ. أوْ بقطعِ اليدِ فليْسَ له قتلُهُ. (وقالَ الماوردي هذا التدريج في غير الفاحشة أما من أولج في الفرج المحرم فيجوز أن يبدأ بالقتل) فإنْ تَحَقَّقَ أنهُ لا يَندَفِعُ إلّا بقتلِهِ فلهُ قتلُهُ ولا شيءَ عليْهِ (والمراد بالتحقق غلبة الظن).

٧.٤ وإذا اندَفَعَ حَرُمَ التعرضُ لَهُ.

٨.٠ الردة

(وهي أقبح أنواع الكفر وأغلظها. فقد يكون استهزاء كأن قيل له: قص أظفارك فإنه سنة؛ فقال: لا أفعله وإن كان سنة؛ بخلاف ما لو اقترن به ما يخرجه عن الردة كسبق اللسان أو حكاية أو خوف).

٨.١ مَن ارتَدَّ عن الإسلام وهوَ بالغٌ عاقلٌ مختارٌ استَحَقَّ القتلَ.

٨.٢ ويَجبُ على الإمامِ استتابتُهُ

repent and return to Islam. If he does, it is accepted from him, but if he refuses, he is immediately killed.

فإنْ رَجَعَ إلى الإسلام قُبِلَ منهُ وإنْ أَبَى قُتِلَ في الحالِ.

o8.3   If he is a freeman, no one besides the caliph or his representative may kill him. If someone else kills him, the killer is disciplined (def: o17) (O: for arrogating the caliph's prerogative and encroaching upon his rights, as this is one of his duties).

o8.3   فإنْ كانَ حراً لمْ يَقْتُلْهُ إلاَّ الإمامُ أوْ نائبُهُ. فإنْ قَتَلَهُ غيرُهُ عُزِّرَ (لافتياتِه وتعديه على السلطان لأن هذا من وظيفته).

o8.4   There is no indemnity for killing an apostate (O: or any expiation, since it is killing someone who deserves to die).

o8.4   ولا ديةَ عليهِ (ولا كفارة أيضاً لأنه قتل مستحق) [وإنْ كانَ عبداً فللسيد قتلُهُ].

o8.5   If he apostatizes from Islam and returns several times, it (O: i.e. his return to Islam, which occurs when he states the two Testifications of Faith (def: o8.7(12))) is accepted from him, though he is disciplined (o17).

o8.5   وإنْ تَكَرَّرَتْ ردَّتُهُ وإسلامُهُ قُبِلَ منهُ (الرجوع إلى الإسلام ويكون حاصلاً بالنطق بالشهادتين) ويُعزَّرُ.

o8.6   (A: If a spouse in a consummated marriage apostatizes from Islam, the couple are separated for a waiting period consisting of three intervals between menstruations. If the spouse returns to Islam before the waiting period ends, the marriage is not annulled but is considered to have continued the whole time (dis: m7.4).)

ACTS THAT ENTAIL LEAVING ISLAM

الأمور التي تحصل بها الردة

o8.7   (O: Among the things that entail apostasy from Islam (may Allah protect us from them) are:

o8.7   ((تنبيه)) في أمور تحصل بها الردة والعياذ بالله منها:) السجود لصنم سواء كان على جهة الاستهزاء أو العناد أو الاعتقاد كمن اعتقد حدوث الصانع. ومثل الصنم الشمس والقمر ومثل السجود الركوع لغير الله فيكفر به إن قصد تعظيمه كتعظيم الله. ومنها نية الكفر ولو في المستقبل ومثل نية الكفر

(1)   to prostrate to an idol, whether sarcastically, out of mere contrariness, or in actual conviction, like that of someone who believes the Creator to be something that has originated in time. Like idols in this respect are the sun or moon, and like prostration is bowing to other than Allah, if one intends reverence towards it like the reverence due to Allah;

(2)   to intend to commit unbelief, even if in the future. And like this intention is hesitating

whether to do so or not: one thereby immediately commits unbelief;

(3) to speak words that imply unbelief such as "Allah is the third of three," or "I am Allah"— unless one's tongue has run away with one, or one is quoting another, or is one of the friends of Allah Most High (wali, def: w33) in a spiritually intoxicated state of total oblivion (A: friend of Allah or not, someone totally oblivious is as if insane, and is not held legally responsible (dis: k13.1(O:))), for these latter do not entail unbelief;

(4) to revile Allah or His messenger (Allah bless him and give him peace);

(5) to deny the existence of Allah, His beginningless eternality, His endless eternality, or to deny any of His attributes which the consensus of Muslims ascribes to Him (dis: v1);

(6) to be sarcastic about Allah's name, His command, His interdiction, His promise, or His threat;

(7) to deny any verse of the Koran or anything which by scholarly consensus (def: b7) belongs to it, or to add a verse that does not belong to it;

(8) to mockingly say, "I don't know what faith is";

(9) to reply to someone who says, "There is no power or strength save through Allah": "Your saying 'There's no power or strength, etc.' won't save you from hunger";

(10) for a tyrant, after an oppressed person says, "This is through the decree of Allah," to reply, "I act without the decree of Allah";

(11) to say that a Muslim is an unbeliever (kafir) (dis: w47) in words that are uninterpretable as merely meaning he is an *ingrate* towards Allah for divinely given blessings (n: in Arabic, also "kafir");

التردد فيه فيكفر به أيضاً . ومنها القول المكفر بأن يقول الله ثالث الثلاثة أو يقول أنا الله ما لم يسبق إليه لسانه أو يقوله حكاية عن غيره أو يقوله الولي في غيبته ، فلا يكفر . ومنها مسبة الله ورسوله . ومنها إنكار وجود الله أو قدمه أو بقائه ؛ وكذلك إنكار الصفات المجمع عليها . ومنها الاستخفاف باسم الله أو أمره أو نهيه أو وعده أو وعيده أو جحد آية من القرآن ومجمعاً على ثبوتها أو زاد فيه آية ليست منه . ومنها ما لو قال لا أدري ما الإيمان احتقاراً ؛ أو قال لمن حوقل لا حول لا تغني من جوع ؛ أو قال الظالم بعد قول المظلوم هذا بتقدير الله : أنا أفعل بغير تقدير الله . ومنها ما لو كفّر مسلماً من غير تأويل بكفر النعمة . ومنها

(12) when someone asks to be taught the Testification of Faith (Ar. Shahada, the words, "La ilaha ill Allahu Muhammadun rasulu Llah" (There is no god but Allah, Muhammad is the Messenger of Allah)), and a Muslim refuses to teach him it;

(13) to describe a Muslim or someone who wants to become a Muslim in terms of *unbelief* (kufr);

(14) to deny the obligatory character of something which by the consensus of Muslims (ijma', def: b7) is part of Islam, when it is well known as such, like the prayer (salat) or even one rak'a from one of the five obligatory prayers, if there is no excuse (def: u2.4);

(15) to hold that any of Allah's messengers or prophets are liars, or to deny their being sent;

(n: 'Ala' al-Din 'Abidin adds the following:

(16) to revile the religion of Islam;

(17) to believe that things in themselves or by their own nature have any causal influence independent of the will of Allah;

(18) to deny the existence of angels or jinn (def: w22), or the heavens;

(19) to be sarcastic about any ruling of the Sacred Law;

(20) or to deny that Allah intended the Prophet's message (Allah bless him and give him peace) to be the religion followed by the entire world (dis: w4.3–4) (*al-Hadiyya al-'Ala'iyya* (y4), 423–24).)

There are others, for the subject is nearly limitless. May Allah Most High save us and all Muslims from it.)

*

ما لو طلب شخص تلقين الشهادتين من شخص فلم يلقنه . ومنها ما لو أشار بالكفر على مسلم أو كافر أراد الإسلام . ومنها ما لو جحد مجمعاً عليه معلوماً من الدين بالضرورة بلا عذر كصلاة أو ركعة من الصلوات الخمس . ومنها ما لو كذّب رسولاً من رسل الله أو نبياً من أنبيائه أو أنكر رسالته بأن قال لم يرسله) .

(ت : وقال الشيخ علاء الدين عابدين : «ومن الكفر ما إذا سب دين الإسلام؛ أو اعتقد بتأثير الأشياء بنفسها وطبعها بدون إرادة الله ؛ أو أنكر وجود الملائكة أو الجن أو السموات ؛ أو استخف بحكم من أحكام الشريعة ؛ أو أنكر عموم رسالته ﷺ) [نقل من الهدية العلائية : ٤٢٣ ـ ٤٢٤ ،] (ومنها غير ذلك وهذا باب لا ساحل له نجانا الله تعالى وجميع المسلمين منه) .

o9.0   JIHAD

(O: *Jihad* means to war against non-Muslims, and is etymologically derived from the word *mujahada,* signifying warfare to establish the religion. And it is the lesser jihad. As for the greater jihad, it is spiritual warfare against the lower self (nafs), which is why the Prophet (Allah bless him and give him peace) said as he was returning from jihad,

"We have returned from the lesser jihad to the greater jihad."

The scriptural basis for jihad, prior to scholarly consensus (def: b7) is such Koranic verses as:

(1) "Fighting is prescribed for you" (Koran 2:216);

(2) "Slay them wherever you find them" (Koran 4:89);

(3) "Fight the idolators utterly" (Koran 9:36);

and such hadiths as the one related by Bukhari and Muslim that the Prophet (Allah bless him and give him peace) said:

"I have been commanded to fight people until they testify that there is no god but Allah and that Muhammad is the Messenger of Allah, and perform the prayer, and pay zakat. If they say it, they have saved their blood and possessions from me, except for the rights of Islam over them. And their final reckoning is with Allah";

and the hadith reported by Muslim,

"To go forth in the morning or evening to fight in the path of Allah is better than the whole world and everything in it."

Details concerning jihad are found in the accounts of the military expeditions of the Prophet (Allah bless him and give him peace), including his own martial forays and those on which he dispatched others. The former consist of

o9.0 الجهاد

(وهو قتال الكفار. والجهاد مأخوذ من المجاهدة وهي المقاتلة لإقامة الدين وهـذا هو الجهاد الأصغر وأمـا الجهاد الأكبر فهو مجاهدة النفس. فلذلك كان ﷺ يقول إذا رجع من الجهاد: «رجعنا من الجهاد الأصغر إلى الجهاد الأكبر». والأصل فيه قبل الإجماع آيات كقوله تعالى: ﴿كُتِبَ عَلَيْكُمُ القِتَالُ﴾ وقوله تعالى: ﴿وَاقْتُلُوهُمْ حَيْثُ وَجَدْتُمُوهُمْ﴾ وقوله تعالى: ﴿قَاتِلُوا المُشْرِكِينَ كَافَّةً﴾.

وأخبار كخبر الصحيحين أنه ﷺ قال: «أُمِرْتُ أن أُقاتل الناس حتى يشهدوا أن لا إله إلا الله وأن محمداً رسول الله ويقيموا الصلاة ويؤتوا الزكاة فإذا قالوها عصموا مني دماءهم وأموالهم إلا بحق الإسلام وحسابهم على الله».

وخبر مسلم «لغدوة أو روحة في سبيل الله خير من الدنيا وما فيها».

وتـفصيله متلقى من سيـره ﷺ في غزواتـه وبعوثـه. فالأولى ما خرج فيها بنفسـه الشـريفة وكـانت سبعـاً وعشرين

the ones he personally attended, some twenty-seven (others say twenty-nine) of them. He fought in eight of them, and killed only one person with his noble hand, Ubayy ibn Khalaf, at the battle of Uhud. On the latter expeditions he sent others to fight, himself remaining at Medina, and these were forty-seven in number.)

وقيل تسعاً وعشرين . ولم يقاتل بنفسه إلا في ثمانية : ولم يقتـل بيـده الكريمة إلا واحداً وهو أبي بـن خلف في غزوة أحد . والثـانية لم يخرج فيها بنفسه بل بعث من يقاتل مع بقائه في المدينة وكانت سبعاً وأربعين].

THE OBLIGATORY CHARACTER OF JIHAD

وجوب الجهاد

o9.1   Jihad is a communal obligation (def: c3.2). When enough people perform it to successfully accomplish it, it is no longer obligatory upon others (O: the evidence for which is the Prophet's saying (Allah bless him and give him peace),

"He who provides the equipment for a soldier in jihad has himself performed jihad,"

and Allah Most High having said:

"Those of the believers who are unhurt but sit behind are not equal to those who fight in Allah's path with their property and lives. Allah has preferred those who fight with their property and lives a whole degree above those who sit behind. And to each, Allah has promised great good" (Koran 4:95).

If none of those concerned perform jihad, and it does not happen at all, then everyone who is aware that it is obligatory is guilty of sin, if there was a possibility of having performed it. In the time of the Prophet (Allah bless him and give him peace) jihad was a communal obligation after his emigration (hijra) to Medina. As for subsequent times, there are two possible states in respect to non-Muslims.

The first is when they are in their own countries, in which case jihad (def: o9.8) is a communal obligation, and this is what our author is speaking of when he says, "Jihad is a communal obligation," meaning upon the Muslims each year.

The second state is when non-Muslims invade a Muslim country or near to one, in which case jihad is personally obligatory (def: c3.2) upon the inhabitants of that country, who must repel the non-Muslims with whatever they can).

o9.1   الجهادُ فرضُ كفايةٍ : إذا قَامَ بِهِ مَنْ فيهِ الكفـايـةُ سَقَطَ عن الباقينَ (لقوله ﷺ : «من جهز غازيـاً في سبيل الله فقد غزا» . وقـد قال الله تعـالى : ﴿لَا يَسْتَوِي القَـاعِدُونَ مِنَ المُؤْمِنِينَ غَيْرُ أُولِي الضَّرَرِ وَالمُجَـاهِـدُونَ في سَبِيـلِ اللَّهِ بِأَمْوَالِهِمْ وَأَنْفُسِهِمْ فَضَّلَ اللَّهُ المُجَاهِدِينَ بِأَمْوَالِهِمْ وَأَنْفُسِهِمْ عَلَى القَـاعِـدِينَ دَرَجَةً وَكُلًّا وَعَدَ اللَّهُ الحُسْنَى﴾ [النساء : ٩٤].

فإن لم يقـم به من ذكـر ولم يحصل أصلاً أثم كل من علم بفرضيته مع القدرة على القيـام بـه . وكـان الأمـر بـه في عهد رسـول الله ﷺ فرض كفاية بعد الهجرة . وأمـا بعـده فللكفـار حالان أحـدهمـا أن يكونوا بـبلادهم فالجهاد فرض كفاية وهذا هو المـراد بقـول المصنف سابقـاً الجهاد فرض كفـايـة أي على المسلمين في كل سنة . والحال الثاني أن يدخل الكفار بلادهم من بلاد المسلمين أو ينـزلـوا قريبـاً منهـا ؛ فالجهـاد حينئـذ فرض عين عليهم فيلزم أهل ذلك البلد دفع الكفار بما يمكن منهم) .

o9.2   Jihad is personally obligatory upon all those present in the battle lines (A: and to flee is an enormity (dis: p11)) (O: provided one is able to fight. If unable, because of illness or the death of one's mount when not able to fight on foot, or because one no longer has a weapon, then one may leave. One may also leave if the opposing non-Muslim army is more than twice the size of the Muslim force).

o9.3   Jihad is also (O: personally) obligatory for everyone (O: able to perform it, male or female, old or young) when the enemy has surrounded the Muslims (O: on every side, having entered our territory, even if the land consists of ruins, wilderness, or mountains, for non-Muslim forces entering Muslim lands is a weighty matter that cannot be ignored, but must be met with effort and struggle to repel them by every possible means. All of which is if conditions permit gathering (A: the above-mentioned) people, provisioning them, and readying them for war. If conditions do not permit this, as when the enemy has overrun the Muslims such that they are unable to provision or prepare themselves for war, then whoever is found by a non-Muslim and knows he will be killed if captured is obliged to defend himself in whatever way possible. But if not certain that he will be killed, meaning that he might or might not be, as when he might merely be taken captive, and he knows he will be killed if he does not surrender, then he may either surrender or fight. A woman too has a choice between fighting or surrendering if she is certain that she will not be subjected to an indecent act if captured. If uncertain that she will be safe from such an act, she is obliged to fight, and surrender is not permissible).

WHO IS OBLIGED TO FIGHT IN JIHAD

o9.4   Those called upon (O: to perform jihad when it is a communal obligation) are every able-bodied man who has reached puberty and is sane.

o9.2   وَيَتَعَيَّنُ على مَنْ حَضَرَ الصفَّ (ومحـل ذلك مع القدرة على القتال. فإن عجز عن القتال لمرض أو لموت فرسه ولا يستطيع القتال راجلًا أو لم يبق معه سلاح فله الانصراف. وأمـا إذا زاد الكفار على الضعف جاز الانصراف).

o9.3   وكَـذا (يتعين) على كلِّ أحـدٍ (سواء كان الأحـد ذكراً أو أنثى كبيراً أو صغيـراً مطيقـاً له) إذا أَحَـاطَ بالمسلمين عدوٌ (من كل جانب وقد دخلوا أرضنا ولو كان خراباً أو بريـة أو جبلاً لأن دخـول الكفـار دار الإسلام أمـر عظيم لا يمكن إهماله فلا بد من الجد والاجتهاد في دفعه بكـل ما يمكن. هذا إذا احتمـل الحـال اجتمـاعـهـم وتأهبهم واستعـدادهم للحرب. وإن لم يحتمل الحال ذلك بأن غشيهم العـدو بحيث لم يتمكنـوا من التأهب والاستعداد للحرب، فمن وقع عليه كافر وعلم أنه يقتل إن أخذه فعليه أن يمنع عن نفسه بما أمكن. وإن لم يعلم ما تقـدم بأن كان يجـوز أنـه إن أخـذ قـتـل ويجـوز أنه لا يقتل بأن يؤسر وعلم أنه إن امتنـع من الاستسـلام قتـل فله استسلام وقتل. وإن أمنت المرأة فاحشة إن أخذت فلها استسلام وقتـل أيضاً. فإن لـم تأمن المـرأة فاحشة إن أخذت تعين الجهاد ولا يجوز الاستسلام).

المكلفون بالجهاد

o9.4   ويُخَـاطَبُ بـه (أي بالجهـاد حيث كان فرض كفاية) كلُّ ذكرٍ حرٍّ بالغٍ عاقلٍ مستطيعٍ.

o9.5   The following may not fight in jihad:

(1)   someone in debt, unless his creditor gives him leave;

(2)   or someone with at least one Muslim parent, until they give their permission;

unless the Muslims are surrounded by the enemy, in which case it is permissible for them to fight without permission.

o9.6   It is offensive to conduct a military expedition against hostile non-Muslims without the caliph's permission (A: though if there is no caliph (def: o25), no permission is required).

o9.7   Muslims may not seek help from non-Muslim allies unless the Muslims are considerably outnumbered and the allies are of goodwill towards the Muslims.

THE OBJECTIVES OF JIHAD

o9.8   The caliph (o25) makes war upon Jews, Christians, and Zoroastrians (N: provided he has first invited them to enter Islam in faith and practice, and if they will not, then invited them to enter the social *order* of Islam by paying the non-Muslim poll tax (jizya, def: o11.4)—which is the significance of their paying it, not the money itself—while remaining in their ancestral religions) (O: and the war continues) until they become Muslim or else pay the non-Muslim poll tax (O: in accordance with the word of Allah Most High,

"Fight those who do not believe in Allah and the Last Day and who forbid not what Allah and His messenger have forbidden—who do not practice the religion of truth, being of those who have been given the Book—until they pay the poll tax out of hand and are humbled" (Koran 9:29),

the time and place for which is before the final descent of Jesus (upon whom be peace). After his

o9.5   ولا يُجَاهِدُ المديونُ إلَّا بإذنِ غريمِهِ [ولا العبـدُ إلَّا بإذنِ سيدِهِ] ولا مَنْ أحـدُ أبـوَيْـه مسلمٌ إلَّا بإذنِـه إلَّا إذا أَحَاطَ العدوُّ فَيَجُوزُ بلا إذنٍ.

o9.6   وَيُكْرَهُ الغزوُ دونَ إذنِ الإمامِ.

o9.7   ولا يستعينُ بمشـركٍ إلَّا أنْ يَقِلَّ المسلمونَ وتكُونَ نِيتُـهُ حسنَةً للمسلمينَ.

غايات الجهاد

o9.8   وَيُقَـاتِـلُ (الإمـامُ) اليهـودَ والنصارَى والمجوسَ (ويستمر ذلك) إلَّا أنْ يُسْلِمُـوا أوْ يَبْـذُلُوا الجزيةَ (عملاً بقوله تعالى: ﴿فَاتِلُوا الَّذِينَ لَا يُؤْمِنُونَ بِاللَّهِ وَلَا بِالْيَـوْمِ الآخِرِ وَلَا يُحَرِّمُونَ مَا حَرَّمَ اللَّهُ وَرَسُولُـهُ وَلَا يَدِينُونَ دِينَ الْحَقِّ مِنَ الَّذِينَ أُوتُـوا الكِتَابَ حَتَّى يُعْطُوا الجِزْيَةَ عَنْ يَدٍ وَهُمْ صَاغِرُونَ﴾ ومحـل هذا قبـل نزول عيسى عليه السلام أما بعد فلا يقبل منهم

final coming, nothing but Islam will be accepted from them, for taking the poll tax is only effective until Jesus' descent (upon him and our Prophet be peace), which is the divinely revealed law of Muhammad. The coming of Jesus does not entail a separate divinely revealed law, for he will rule by the law of Muhammad. As for the Prophet's saying (Allah bless him and give him peace),

"I am the last, there will be no prophet after me,"

this does not contradict the final coming of Jesus (upon whom be peace), since he will not rule according to the Evangel, but as a follower of our Prophet (Allah bless him and give him peace)).

o9.9   The caliph fights all other peoples until they become Muslim (O: because they are not a people with a Book, nor honored as such, and are not permitted to settle with paying the poll tax (jizya)) (n: though according to the Hanafi school, peoples of all other religions, even idol worshippers, are permitted to live under the protection of the Islamic state if they either become Muslim or agree to pay the poll tax, the sole exceptions to which are apostates from Islam and idol worshippers who are Arabs, neither of whom has any choice but becoming Muslim (al-Hidaya sharh Bidaya al-mubtadi' (y21), 6.48–49)).

THE RULES OF WARFARE

o9.10   It is not permissible (A: in jihad) to kill women or children unless they are fighting against the Muslims. Nor is it permissible to kill animals, unless they are being ridden into battle against the Muslims, or if killing them will help defeat the enemy. It is permissible to kill old men (O: *old man* (shaykh) meaning someone more than forty years of age) and monks.

o9.11   It is unlawful to kill a non-Muslim to whom a Muslim has given his guarantee of protection (O: whether the non-Muslim is one or more

إلا الإسلام لأن أخذ الجزية منهم مغياً إلى نزول عيسى عليه وعلى نبينا أفضل الصلاة والسلام وهذا هو شرعه ﷺ . فنزول عيسى عليه السلام ليس بشرع مستقل بل حاكم بشرعه ﷺ . وأما قوله ﷺ : «أنا العاقب لا نبي بعدي» فلا ينافي نزول عيسى عليه السلام لأنه لا يحكم بالإنجيل بل هو تابع له ﷺ) .

o9.9   ويُقَاتِلُ مَنْ سِوَاهُمْ إلَّا أَنْ يُسْلِمُوا (لعدم كتاب لهم فليسوا محترمين ولا يقرروا بالجزية) . (ت: وعند الحنفية يقر مَن سواهم بالجزية - حتى عبدة الأوثان من العجم، فلهم أن يسلموا أو أن يدفعوا الجزية، وعندئذ يعيشون تحت حفظ دولة الإسلام - بخلاف المرتدين وعبدة الأوثان من العرب، فلا يقبل منهم إلا الإسلام [الهداية ٦/ ٤٨ - ٤٩]) .

أحكام في القتال

o9.10   ولا يَجُوزُ قتلُ النساء والصبيان إلَّا أَنْ يُقَاتِلُوا . ولا الدوابّ إلَّا أَنْ يُقَاتِلُوا عَلَيْهَا أَوْ نَسْتَعِينَ بقتلهَا عليهِمْ . ويَجُوزُ قتلُ الشيوخ (وهو من جاوز الأربعين) والرهبان .

o9.11   ومَنْ أَمَّنَهُ مِنَ الكفَّار مسلمٌ بالغٌ عاقلٌ مختارٌ (غير أسير ونحو

than one, provided the number is limited, and the Muslim's protecting them does not harm the Muslims, as when they are spies) provided the protecting Muslim has reached puberty, is sane, and does so voluntarily (O: and is not a prisoner of them or a spy).

جاسوس) [ولوْ عبداً] حَرُمَ قتلُهُ (سواء كان واحداً أو أكثر بشرط أن يكون عدداً محصوراً وأن لا يكون في تأمينه ضرر على المسلمين كالجاسوس) .

o9.12   Whoever enters Islam before being captured may not be killed or his property confiscated, or his young children taken captive.

o9.12 ومَنْ أَسلَم منْهُمْ قبلَ الأسر حُقِنَ دمُهُ ومالُهُ وصغارُ أولادِه عن السبي .

o9.13   When a child or a woman is taken captive, they become slaves by the fact of capture, and the woman's previous marriage is immediately annulled.

o9.13 ومتَى أُسِرَ منْهُمْ صبيٌّ أو امرأةٌ أُرِقَّ بنفس الأسر وينفسخُ نكاحُها .

o9.14   When an adult male is taken captive, the caliph (def: o25) considers the interests (O: of Islam and the Muslims) and decides between the prisoner's death, slavery, release without paying anything, or ransoming himself in exchange for money or for a Muslim captive held by the enemy.

If the prisoner becomes a Muslim (O: before the caliph chooses any of the four alternatives) then he may not be killed, and one of the other three alternatives is chosen.

o9.14 أوْ بالغٌ تخيَّر الإمامُ بالمصلحةِ (للإسلام والمسلمين) بين القتل والاسترقاق والمنّ والفداء بمالٍ أوْ بأسير مسلم . فإنْ أَسلَمَ (قبل أن يختار الإمام فيه شيئاً من الخصال المذكورة) سَقطَ قتلُهُ ويُخَيَّرُ بين الثلاثِ الباقيةِ .

o9.15   It is permissible in jihad to cut down the enemy's trees and destroy their dwellings.

o9.15 ويَجُوزُ قطعُ أشجارِهِمْ وتخريبُ ديارِهِمْ .

TRUCES

الهدنة

o9.16   (O: As for truces, the author does not mention them. In Sacred Law truce means a peace treaty with those hostile to Islam, involving a cessation of fighting for a specified period, whether for payment or something else. The scriptural basis for them includes such Koranic verses as:

(1) "An acquittal from Allah and His messenger..." (Koran 9:1);

(2) "If they incline towards peace, then incline towards it also" (Koran 8:61);

o9.16 (وأمَّا ما يتعلق بالهدنة فلم يذكره المصنف . وهي شرعاً مصالحة أهل الحرب على ترك القتال مدة معينة بعوضٍ أو غيره . والأصل فيها قوله تعالى : ﴿بَرَاءَةٌ مِنَ اللَّهِ وَرَسُولِهِ﴾ الآية ؛ وقوله : ﴿وَإِنْ جَنَحُوا لِلسَّلْمِ فَاجْنَحْ لَهَا﴾ ؛

as well as the truce which the Prophet (Allah bless him and give him peace) made with Quraysh in the year of Hudaybiya, as related by Bukhari and Muslim.

Truces are permissible, not obligatory. The only one who may effect a truce is the Muslim ruler of a region (or his representative) with a segment of the non-Muslims of the region, or the caliph (o25) (or his representative). When made with other than a *portion* of the non-Muslims, or when made with all of them, or with all in a particular region such as India or Asia Minor, then only the caliph (or his representative) may effect it, for it is a matter of the gravest consequence because it entails the nonperformance of jihad, whether globally or in a given locality, and our interests must be looked after therein, which is why it is best left to the caliph under any circumstances, or to someone he delegates to see to the interests of the various regions.

There must be some interest served in making a truce other than mere preservation of the status quo. Allah Most High says,

"So do not be fainthearted and call for peace, when it is you who are the uppermost" (Koran 47:35).

Interests that justify making a truce are such things as Muslim weakness because of lack of numbers or materiel, or the hope of an enemy becoming Muslim, for the Prophet (Allah bless him and give him peace) made a truce in the year Mecca was liberated with Safwan ibn Umayya for four months in hope that he would become Muslim, and he entered Islam before its time was up. If the Muslims are weak, a truce may be made for ten years if necessary, for the Prophet (Allah bless him and give him peace) made a truce with Quraysh for that long, as is related by Abu Dawud. It is not permissible to stipulate longer than that, save by means of new truces, each of which does not exceed ten years.

The rulings of such a truce are inferable from those of the non-Muslim poll tax (def: o11); namely, that when a valid truce has been effected, no harm may be done to non-Muslims until it expires.)

ومهادنته ﷺ قريشاً عام الحديبية كما رواه الشيخان . وهي جائزة لا واجبة . وإنما يعقدها لبعض كفار إقليم واليه ولو بنائبه ، أو إمامٌ ولو بنائبه ، ولغيره من الكفار كلهم وكفار إقليم كالهند والروم إمامٌ ولو بنائبه لأنها من الأمور العظام لما فيها من ترك الجهاد مطلقاً أو في جهة لأنه لا بد فيه من رعاية مصلحتنا فاللائق تفويضها للإمام مطلقاً أو من فوض إليه الإمام مصلحة الأقاليم . ولا بد من المصلحة في المهادنة فلا يكفي انتفاء المفسدة . قال تعالى : ﴿فَلَا تَهِنُوا وَتَدْعُوا إِلَى السَّلْمِ وَأَنْتُمُ الْأَعْلَوْنَ﴾ . والمصلحة التي تكون سبباً في الهدنة كضعفنا بقلة عدد أو أهبة أو رجاء إسلام ، لأنه ﷺ هادن صفوان بن أمية أربعة أشهر عام الفتح رجاء إسلامه فأسلم قبل مضيها . وإن كان بنا ضعف فإلى عشر سنين لحاجة ، ولأنه ﷺ هادن قريشاً هذه المدة رواه أبو داود . فلا يجوز أكثر منها إلا في عقود متفرقة . وشرط في كل عقد أن لا يزيد على عشر . وحكمها معلوم من عقد الجزية ، وهو أنه يلزمنا عند عقدها الصحيح الكف عنهم حتى تنقضي مدتها) .

o10.0 THE SPOILS OF BATTLE

o10.0 الغنيمة

o10.1   A free male Muslim who has reached puberty and is sane is entitled to the spoils of battle when he has participated in a battle to the end of it.

After personal booty (def: o10.2), the collective spoils of the battle are divided into five parts. The first fifth is set aside (dis: o10.3), and the remaining four are distributed, one share to each infantryman and three shares to each cavalryman. From these latter four fifths also, a token payment is given at the leader's discretion to women, children, and non-Muslim participants on the Muslim side.

A combatant only takes possession of his share of the spoils at the official division. (A: Or he may choose to waive his right to it.)

o10.1 الغنيمةُ لمَنْ حضَرَ الوقعةَ إلى آخرِها. فتُقْسَم بينَهُمْ بَعْدَ إخراج السلبِ وخمسِها؛ للراجل سهمٌ وللفارس ثلاثةُ أسهم إذا كانَ ذكراً حراً بالغاً مسلماً عاقلاً. ويُرْضَخ للمرأة [والعبد] والصبيّ والكافر إنْ حضَرُوا بإذنِ الإمام مِنْ أربعةِ أخماسِها.

وإنّما تُمْلَكُ الغنيمةُ بالقسمةِ [أو اختيارِ التَمَلُّكِ].

o10.2   As for personal booty, anyone who, despite resistance, kills one of the enemy or effectively incapacitates him, risking his own life thereby, is entitled to whatever he can take from the enemy, meaning as much as he can take away with him in the battle, such as a mount, clothes, weaponry, money, or other.

o10.2 وأما السلبُ فمَنْ قتَلَ قتيلاً أو كفى شرَّه وكانَ المقتولُ ممتنعاً وغرَّرَ القاتلُ بنفسِهِ في قتلِه اسْتَحَقَّ سلبَهُ. وهوَ ما احْتَوَتْ يدُهُ عليهِ في الوقعةِ مِنْ فرسٍ وثيابٍ وسلاحٍ ونفقةٍ وغيرِ ذلكَ.

o10.3   As for the first fifth that is taken from the spoils, it is divided in turn into five parts, a share each going to:

(1) the Prophet (Allah bless him and give him peace), and after his death, to such Islamic interests as fortifying defenses on the frontiers, salaries for Islamic judges, muezzins, and the like;

(2) relatives of the Prophet (Allah bless him and give him peace) of the Bani Hashim and Bani Muttalib clans, each male receiving the share of two females;

(3) orphans who are poor;

(4) those short of money (def: h8.11);

(5) and travellers needing money (h8.18).

o10.3 فأمَّا الخمسُ فيُقْسَمُ على خمسةٍ أيضاً: سهمٌ للنبيِّ ﷺ فيُصْرَفُ بعدَهُ في المصالح مِنْ سدِّ الثغورِ وأرزاقِ القضاةِ والمؤذنينَ ونحوِهم؛ وسهمٌ لذوي القربى مِنْ بني هاشمٍ وبني المطلب للذكر مثلُ حظّ الأنثيين؛ وسهمٌ لليتامَى الفقراءِ؛ وسهمٌ للمساكينِ؛ وسهمٌ لابن السبيلِ.

o11.0 NON-MUSLIM SUBJECTS OF THE ISLAMIC STATE (AHL AL-DHIMMA)

o11.1   A formal agreement of protection is made with citizens who are:

(1) Jews;

(2) Christians;

(3) Zoroastrians;

(4) Samarians and Sabians, if their religions do not respectively contradict the fundamental bases of Judaism and Christianity;

(5) and those who adhere to the religion of Abraham or one of the other prophets (upon whom be blessings and peace).

o11.2   Such an agreement may not be effected with those who are idol worshippers (dis: o9.9(n:)), or those who do not have a Sacred Book or something that could have been a Book.

(A: *Something that could have been a Book* refers to those like the Zoroastrians, who have remnants resembling an ancient Book. As for the psuedoscriptures of cults that have appeared since Islam (n: such as the Sikhs, Baha'is, Mormons, Qadianis, etc.), they neither are nor could be a Book, since the Koran is the final revelation (dis: w4).)

o11.3   Such an agreement is only valid when the subject peoples:

(a) follow the rules of Islam (A: those mentioned below (o11.5) and those involving public behavior and dress, though in acts of worship and their private lives, the subject communities have their own laws, judges, and courts, enforcing the rules of their own religion among themselves);

(b) and pay the non-Muslim poll tax (jizya).

أهل الذمة   o11.0

o11.1   تُعْقَدُ الذمةُ لليهود والنصارَى والمجوس [ولمنْ دَخَلَ في دين اليهود والنصارَى قبل النسخِ والتبديل] والسامرة والصابئة إنْ وَافَقوهُمْ في أصل دينِهِمْ ولمنْ تَمَسّكَ بدين إبراهيمَ أوْ غيرهِ منَ الأنبياء عليهِمْ الصلاةُ والسلامُ.

o11.2   ولا يُعْقَدُ لوثنيٍّ ومنْ لا كتابَ لهُ ولا شبهةَ كتابٍ.

(ع: والمـراد بشبهـة كتـاب من كان كالمجوس فلهم بقـايا تشبه كتاباً قديماً. أما الكتب البـاطلة لدى فرق ظهرت بعد الإسـلام (ت: كالسـيخ والبـهائيين والمورمونيين والقاديانيين) فليست كتباً ولا شبهة كتب، لأن القرآن خاتمة الوحي).

o11.3   ولا يَصِحُّ إلّا بشرطَيْن: التزامُ أحكامِ الإسلام وبذلُ الجزية.

THE NON-MUSLIM POLL TAX

الجزية

o11.4 The minimum non-Muslim poll tax is one dinar (n: 4.235 grams of gold) per person (A: per year). The maximum is whatever both sides agree upon.

It is collected with leniency and politeness, as are all debts, and is not levied on women, children, or the insane.

o11.4   وأقلّها دينارٌ مِنْ كلِّ شخصٍ وأكثرُها ما تَرَاضَوا عليهِ. وتُؤخَذُ منهُمْ برفقٍ كسائرِ الدُّيونِ ولا تُؤخَذُ مِنْ امرأةٍ وصبيٍّ ومجنونٍ [وعبدٍ].

o11.5 Such non-Muslim subjects are obliged to comply with Islamic rules that pertain to the safety and indemnity of life, reputation, and property. In addition, they:

(1) are penalized for committing adultery or theft, though not for drunkenness;

(2) are distinguished from Muslims in dress, wearing a wide cloth belt (zunnar);

(3) are not greeted with "as-Salamu 'alaykum";

(4) must keep to the side of the street;

(5) may not build higher than or as high as the Muslims' buildings, though if they acquire a tall house, it is not razed;

(6) are forbidden to openly display wine or pork, (A: to ring church bells or display crosses,) recite the Torah or Evangel aloud, or make public display of their funerals and feastdays;

(7) and are forbidden to build new churches.

o11.5   ويُلزمُونَ بأحْكامِنا مِنْ ضمانِ النفسِ والعِرضِ والمالِ ويُحَدُّونَ للزِنَا والسِّرقةِ لا للسكرِ. ويَتَمَيَّزُونَ في اللباسِ والزنانيرِ [ويَكونُ في رقابِهم جرسٌ في الحمامِ ولا يَركَبُونَ فرساً بلْ بغالاً أو حماراً عرضاً] ولا يُبْدَءُونَ بسلامٍ ويُلْجَؤُونَ إلى أضيقِ الطريقِ ولا يَعْلُونَ على المسلمين في البناءِ ولا يُساوُونَهُمْ فإنْ تَمَلَّكُوا داراً عاليةً لمْ تُهْدَمْ ويُمنَعُونَ مِنْ إظهارِ خمرٍ وخنزيرٍ [وناقوسٍ] وجهرِ التوراةِ والإنجيلِ وجنائزِهِمْ وأعيادِهِمْ ومِنْ إحداثِ كنيسةٍ [فلَوْ صُولحُوا في بلدانِهم على الجزيةِ لمْ يُمنَعُوا مِنْ ذلكَ].

o11.6 They are forbidden to reside in the Hijaz, meaning the area and towns around Mecca, Medina, and Yamama, for more than three days (when the caliph allows them to enter there for something they need).

o11.6   ويُمنَعُونَ مِنَ المقامِ بالحجازِ وهيَ مكةُ والمدينةُ واليمامةُ وقراها أكثرَ مِنْ ثلاثةِ أيامٍ إذا أذنَ لَهُمْ الإمامُ في الدخولِ لحاجةٍ.

o11.7 A non-Muslim may not enter the Meccan Sacred Precinct (Haram) under any cir-

o11.7   ولا يُمَكَّنُ مشركٌ مِنَ الحرمِ

cumstances, or enter any other mosque without permission (A: nor may Muslims enter churches without their permission).

بِحالٍ. ولا يَدْخُلُونَ مسجداً إلاَّ بإذنٍ.

o11.8   It is obligatory for the caliph (def: o25) to protect those of them who are in Muslim lands just as he would Muslims, and to seek the release of those of them who are captured.

o11.8   وعلى الإمـامِ حفظُ مَنْ كَانَ منهُمْ في دارِنـا كَمَـا يَحْفَـظُ المسلمين واستنقاذُ مَنْ أسِرَ منهُمْ.

o11.9   If non-Muslim subjects of the Islamic state refuse to conform to the rules of Islam, or to pay the non-Muslim poll tax, then their agreement with the state has been violated (dis: o11.11) (A: though if only one of them disobeys, it concerns him alone).

o11.9   فإنِ امْتَنَعُوا مِنَ التزام أحكام الملة وأداءِ الجزية اُنْتَقَضَ عهدُهُمْ مطلقاً.

o11.10 The agreement is also violated (A: with respect to the offender alone) if the state has stipulated that any of the following things break it, and one of the subjects does so anyway, though if the state has not stipulated that these break the agreement, then they do not; namely, if one of the subject people:

o11.10 وإنْ زَنَى أحدٌ منهُمْ بمسلمةٍ أوْ أصابَهـا بنكاحٍ أوْ آوَى عيناً أوْ فَتَنَ مسلماً عنْ دينهِ أوْ قَتَلَهُ أوْ ذَكَرَ اللهَ أوْ رسولَهُ أوْ دينَـهُ بِمَـا لا يَجُـوزُ فإنْ شَرَطَ عليهِـمْ الانتقاضَ بذلكَ انْتَقَضَ. وإلاَّ فَلا.

(1) commits adultery with a Muslim woman or marries her;

(2) conceals spies of hostile forces;

(3) leads a Muslim away from Islam;

(4) kills a Muslim;

(5) or mentions something impermissible about Allah, the Prophet (Allah bless him and give him peace), or Islam.

o11.11 When a subject's agreement with the state has been violated, the caliph chooses between the four alternatives mentioned above in connection with prisoners of war (o9.14).

o11.11 ومَنْ انْتَقَضَ عهدُهُ تَخَيَّرَ الإمامُ فيه بين الخصالِ الأربعِ في الأسيرِ.

*

o12.0 THE PENALTY FOR FORNICATION OR SODOMY

o12.1 The legal penalty is obligatorily imposed upon anyone who fornicates or commits sodomy (A: provided it is legally established (def: n11.2(O:))) when they:

(a) have reached puberty;

(b) are sane;

(c) and commit the act voluntarily;

no matter whether the person is a Muslim, non-Muslim subject of the Islamic state, or someone who has left Islam.

o12.2 If the offender is someone with the capacity to remain chaste, then he or she is stoned to death (def: o12.6), *someone with the capacity to remain chaste* meaning anyone who has had sexual intercourse (A: at least once) with their spouse in a valid marriage, and is free, of age, and sane. A person is not considered to have the capacity to remain chaste if he or she has only had intercourse in a marriage that is invalid, or is prepubescent at the time of marital intercourse, or is someone insane at the time of marital intercourse who subsequently regains their sanity prior to committing adultery.

If the offender is not someone with the capacity to remain chaste, then the penalty consists of being scourged (def: o12.5) one hundred stripes and banished to a distance of at least 81 km./50 mi. for one year.

o12.4 Someone who commits fornication is not punished if he says that he did not know it was unlawful, provided he is a new Muslim or grew up in a remote (O: from Islamic scholars) wilderness,

حد الزنا واللواط   o12.0

o12.1   إذا زَنَى أولاطَ البـالـغُ العاقلُ المختـارُ مسلماً كانَ أوْ ذمياً أوْ مرتداً [حراً كانَ أوْ عبداً] وَجَبَ عليهِ الحدُّ.

o12.2   فإنْ كانَ محصناً رُجِمَ حَتَّى يَمُوت. والمحصنُ مَنْ وَطِىءَ في القبل في نكـاح صحيح وهـوَ حرٌّ بالغٌ عاقلُ فلَوْ وَطِىءَ زوجتَهُ [في الدبر أوْ جاريتَهُ في القبـل أوْ] في نكـاح فاسـدٍ أوْ وَطِىءَ زوجتَـهُ وهـوَ [عبـدُ ثمَّ عَتَقَ أوْ] صبيُّ أوْ مجنونُ ثمَّ أفاق ورَنَى فَلَيْسَ بمحصنٍ. وغيـرُ المحصنِ [إنْ كانَ حراً] جُلِدَ مائةَ جلدةٍ وغُـرِّبَ سنةً إلى مسافة القصر [وإنْ كانَ عبـداً جُلِدَ خمسـينَ وغُـرِّبَ نصفَ سنةٍ].

o12.3   [ومَنْ وَطِىءَ بهيمـةً أو امـرأةً ميتـةً أوْ حيةً فيمَا دونَ الفرج أوْ جاريةً يَمْلِكُ بعضَها أوْ أختَهُ المملوكةَ لَهُ أوْ وَطِىءَ زوجتَهُ في الحيض أوْ الدبر أو اسْتَمْنَى بيدِهِ أوْ أتَتِ المرأةُ المرأةَ لا حدَّ عليه ويُعَزَّرُ].

o12.4   ومَنْ زَنَى وقـالَ: لا أعـلَمُ تحريمَ الزنا وكانَ قريبَ عهدٍ بالإسلام أوْ نَشَـأ بباديةٍ بعيدةٍ (عن العلماء) لَمْ يُحَدَّ

though if neither of these is the case, such a person is punished.

وإنْ لَمْ يَكُنْ كذلكَ حُدَّ.

o12.5   An offender is not scourged in intense heat or bitter cold, or when he is ill and recovery is expected (until he recovers), or in a mosque, or when the offender is a woman who is pregnant, until she gives birth and has recovered from childbed pains. The whip used should be neither new nor old and worn-out, but something in between. The offender is not stretched out when scourged, or bound (O: as his hands are left loose to fend off blows), or undressed (O: but rather an ankle-length shirt is left upon him or her), and the scourger does not lay the stripes on hard (O: by raising his arm, such that he draws blood). The scourger distributes the blows over various parts of the body, avoiding the vital points and the face. A man is scourged standing; a woman, sitting and covered (O: by a garment wrapped around her). If the offender is emaciated, or sick from an illness not expected to improve, then he or she is scourged with a single date palm frond (O: upon which there are a hundred strips, or fifty. If a hundred, such an offender is struck once with it, and if fifty, then twice), or with the edge of a garment.

o12.5   ولا يُجْـلَدُ في حَرٍّ وبـردٍ شديـدين ومـرض يُرْجَى بـرؤُهُ حتَّى يبْرأ ولا في المسجدِ ولا المرأةُ في الحبلِ حتَّى تَضعَ ويزولَ ألمُ الولادة . ولا يُجْلَدُ بسـوطٍ جديـدٍ ولا بالٍ بلْ بسـوطٍ بين السـوطين . ولا يُمَدُّ (المجلودُ) ولا يُمَدُّ (بـلْ تتـرك يداه مطلقتين يتقي بهمـا) ولا يُجَرَّدُ (من ثيابه بل يترك عليه قميصه رجلاً كان أو امرأة) ولا يُبَالِغُ في الضرب (برفع يده بحيث ينهر الدم) ويُفَرَّقَهُ على أعضائِه ويَتَـوقَّى المقاتِلَ والوجهَ ويُضْرَبُ الرجلُ قائمـاً والمـرأةُ جالسـةً مستـورةً (بثـوب ملفوف عليها) فإنْ كان نحيفاً أوْ مريضاً لا يُرْجَى بـرؤُهُ جُلِدَ بعثكـالِ النخـلِ (أي عرجـون عليه مائة غصن أو خمسون ففي المـائـةِ يضرب ضربـة واحـدة وفي الخمسين يضرب مرتين) وأطراف الثياب .

o12.6   If the penalty is stoning, the offender is stoned even in severe heat or cold, and even if he has an illness from which he is expected to recover. A pregnant woman is not stoned until she gives birth and the child can suffice with the milk of another.

o12.6   وإنْ كَانَ الحدُّ رجماً رُجِمَ ولوْ في حَرٍّ أوْ بردٍ أوْ مرضٍ مرجوٌّ الزوالِ ولا تُرْجَمُ الحامـلُ حتَّى تَضعَ ويسْتَغْنِيَ الولدُ بلبن غيرها [وللسيدِ أنْ يقيم الحدَّ على رقيقِه].

*

o13.0   THE PENALTY FOR ACCUSING A PERSON OF ADULTERY WITHOUT PROOF

o13.0   حد القذف

o13.1   When a person (who has reached puberty and is sane) voluntarily:

o13.1   إذا قَذَفَ البـالِـغُ العـاقِـلُ المختـارُ وهـو مسلم أوْ ذميٌّ أوْ مرتدٌّ أوْ

(a)   accuses another person of adultery or

sodomy, whether the accusation is in plain words or allusive words intended as an accusation;

(b) and the accused is someone who could be chaste (def: o13.2) and is not the offspring of the accuser;

then the accuser is subject to the penalty for accusing a person of adultery without four witnesses (A: which, if it concerns his spouse, he may obviate by public imprecation (dis: n11.1)), no matter whether he is a Muslim, non-Muslim subject of the Islamic state, someone who has left Islam, or is of a group that has a truce with Muslims.

مســتأمـنٌ محـصنـاً لَيْسَ بولـدِ لَهُ (أي للقـاذف) بالـزنـا أو اللواطِ بالصـريـحِ أوْ بالكنايةِ مَعَ النيةِ لَزِمَهُ الحدُّ.

o13.2 *Someone who could be chaste* in this context means someone who has reached puberty, is sane, free, Muslim, and has not committed an act of fornication (O: that is punishable) (A: meaning it has not been legally established (def: n11.2(O:))).

o13.2 والمحصنُ هُنَـا هوَ البـالـغُ العـاقـلُ الحرُّ المسلمُ العفيفُ (عن وطء يحد به).

o13.3 · The penalty for making such an accusation without witnesses is to be scourged (def: o12.5) eighty lashes.

o13.3 فَيُجْلَدُ [الحرُّ] ثمانين [والعبدُ أربعينَ].

o13.4 Accusations in *plain words* include such expressions as "You have committed fornication," and the like, while *allusive words* means such expressions as "You lecher," or "You wretch." If the latter terms are accompanied by the intention to accuse, they amount to an accusation, though if not, they do not. The accuser is the one whose word is accepted (A: when there is no proof, if he swears an oath) as to what he intended by such allusive words.

o13.4 فالصـريـحُ: زَنَيْتَ [أوْ لُطْتَ أوْ: زَنَى فرجُكَ] ونحوِه. والكنـايةُ نحوُ: يا فاجرُ يا خبيثُ. فإنْ نَوَى بِه القـذفَ حُدَّ. وإلّا فلا. والقـولُ قولُ القـاذفِ في النيةِ [وإنْ قَالَ: أنتَ أزنَى النـاسِ أوْ أزنَى مِنْ فلانٍ؛ فهـوَ كنايةٌ. أوْ: فلانٌ زانٍ وأنتَ أزنَى منهُ فصريحٌ].

o13.5 If someone accuses a whole group of people of adultery who could not possibly all be guilty, such as saying, "All the people in Egypt are adulterers," he is disciplined (def: o17). But when his accusation is not impossible, such as saying, "The So-and-so clan are adulterers," then he must bear a separate penalty for every single person in the group.

o13.5 وإنْ قَذَفَ جمـاعـةً يَمْتَنِعُ أنْ يَكُونُوا كُلُهُمْ زناةً كقولِه: أهلُ مصرَ كلُّهُمْ زناةٌ عُزِّرَ. وإنْ لم يَمْتَنِعْ كقولِه: بنُو فلانٍ زناةٌ لَزِمَهُ لكلِّ واحدٍ حدٌّ.

o13.6 Someone who twice accuses someone of adultery without witnesses is punished only once. Someone who accuses a person of adultery and is punished for the accusation, but then again accuses the person of the same act of fornication is merely disciplined (def: o17).

o13.6 ولوْ قَذَفَهُ بِزِنْيَتَيْنِ لَزِمَهُ حَدٌّ واحِدٌ.

وإنْ قَذَفَهُ فَحُدَّ ثمَّ قَذَفَهُ ثانياً بذلكَ الزنَا أوْ بغيرِه عُزِّرَ فَقطْ.

o13.7 When someone accuses a person who could possibly be chaste (def: o13.2) of adultery, but the accuser has not yet been punished at the time the accused subsequently commits an act of fornication, then the accuser is not punished.

o13.7 ولـوْ قَذَفَ محصناً فلَمْ يُحَدَّ حتَّى زَنَى المحصنُ سَقطَ الحدُّ.

o13.8 The penalty for accusing a person of adultery without witnesses is only carried out when the Islamic magistrate is present, and the accused requests that it be carried out. If the accused forgives the offender, there is no punishment.

o13.8 ولا يُسْتَـوْفَى إلَّا بحضـرة الحاكم وبمطالبة المقذوف. فإنْ عَفَا سَقطَ.

o13.9 When an accusation has been made, if the accused dies (A: before the accuser has been punished), then his right (A: to demand that the punishment be carried out) is given to his heirs.

o13.9 وإنْ مَاتَ (المقـذوف) انْتَقـلَ حقُّهُ لوارثِه.

o13.10 [ولـوْ قَالَ لرجـلٍ : اقْـذِفْني؛ فَقَـذَفَهُ لمْ يُحَدَّ (كما لا يجب على الشخص قصاص إذا أمره شخص بقتل نفسه فقتله لأنه بأمره). ولوْ قَذَفَ عبداً ثَبَتَ لهُ التعزيزُ].

*

o14.0 THE PENALTY FOR THEFT

o14.0 حد السرقة

o14.1 A person's right hand is amputated, whether he is a Muslim, non-Muslim subject of the Islamic state, or someone who has left Islam, when he:

o14.1 إذا سَرَقَ البـالِـغُ العـاقـلُ المختـارُ وهو مسلمٌ أوْ ذميٌ أوْ مرتدٌ نصاباً

(a) has reached puberty;

(b) is sane;

(c) is acting voluntarily;

(d) and steals at least a quarter of a dinar (n: 1.058 grams of gold) or goods worth that much (A: at the market prices current) at the time of the theft;

(e) from a place meeting the security requirements normal (A: in that locality and time) for safeguarding similar articles (def: o14.3);

(f) provided there is no possible confusion (dis: o14.2(3)) as to whether he took it by way of theft or for some other reason.

If a person steals a second time, his left foot is amputated; if a third time, then his left hand; and if he steals again, then his right foot. If he steals a fifth time, he is disciplined (def: o17). If he does not have a right hand (N: at the first offense), then his left foot is amputated. If he has a right hand but loses it after the theft (O: by an act of God) but before he has been punished for it, then nothing is amputated. After amputation, the limb is cauterized with hot oil (A: which in previous times was the means to stop the bleeding and save the criminal's life).

o14.2   A person's hand is not amputated when:

(1) (non-(d) above) he steals less than the equivalent of 1.058 grams of gold;

(2) (non-(e)) he steals the article from a place the does not meet normal requirements for safeguarding similar articles (dis: below);

(3) or (non-(f)) when there is a possible confusion as to why he took it, as when it was taken from the Muslim common fund (bayt al-mal) (O: provided the person is Muslim, since he might have intended to use it to build mosques, bridges, or hospices), or when it belongs to his son or father.

o14.3   A *place that meets normal security requirements for safeguarding similar articles* means a place appropriate for keeping the thing, this varying with the type of article, the different countries,

مِنَ المَالِ وهوَ رُبعُ دينارٍ أوْ ما قيمتُهُ ربعُ دينارٍ حالَ السرقةِ مِنْ حرزِ مثلِهِ ولا شبهةَ لهُ فيهِ قُطِعَتْ يدُهُ اليمنَى.

فإنْ سَرَقَ ثانياً قُطِعَتْ رجلُهُ اليسرَى. فإنْ عادَ قُطِعَتْ يدُهُ اليسرَى. فإنْ عادَ قُطِعَتْ رجلُهُ اليمنَى فإنْ عادَ عُزِّرَ. فإنْ لمْ يكُنْ لهُ يمينٌ قُطِعَتْ رجلُهُ اليسرَى. وإنْ كانَتْ فلَمْ تُقطَعْ حتَّى ذَهَبَتْ (بآفةٍ سماويةٍ) سَقَطَ القطعُ. وإذَا قُطِعَ غُمِسَ المقطعُ بالزيتِ الحارِّ.

o14.2   فإنْ سَرَقَ دونَ النصابِ أوْ مِنْ غيرِ حرزٍ أوْ ما لهُ شبهةٌ كمالِ بيتِ المالِ (إذَا كانَ السارقُ له مسلماً، لأنـه قد يصرف في عمارةِ المسـاجـدِ والقنـاطيرِ والـربـاطاتِ) أوْ مالِ ابنِهِ أوْ أبيهِ [أوْ مالِ مالكِهِ] لمْ يُقطَعْ.

o14.3   وحـرزُ كلِّ شيءٍ بحـسـبِـهِ ويَختلِفُ باختـلافِ المالِ والبلادِ وعدلِ

and with the justness of the ruler or lack of it, as well as the ruler's relative strength or weakness. A suitable place for safeguarding fine clothes, money, jewels, and jewelry, for example, is a locked box; the place for trade goods, a locked warehouse with guards; the place for livestock, a stable; the place for pallets and bedding, a shelf in the house; and the place for a shroud, the grave.

السلطانِ وجورِه وقـوتِه وضعفِهِ . فحرزُ
الـثيـاب والنقـودِ والجـواهـرِ والحلِّي
الصنـدوقُ المقفَـلُ . وحـرزُ الأمتعـةِ
الـدكـاكِينُ المقفلةُ ثمَّ حارسٌ . والدوابِّ
الاصطبلُ . والأثاثُ صفةُ البيتِ [بحسب
العادةِ] . وحرزُ الكفنِ القبرُ .

o14.4   If two persons jointly steal the equivalent of 1.058 grams of gold, then neither's hand is amputated.

o14.4   ولـو اشْتَـرَكَ اثنانِ في إخراج
النصابِ فقطْ لمْ يُقطَعْ واحدٌ منهُمَا .

o14.5   A freeman's hand may not be amputated by anyone besides the caliph or his representative (def: o25).

o14.5   ولا يَقطَعُ الحـرَّ إلَّا الإمـامُ أوْ
نائبُهُ [ويَقطَعُ العبدَ سيدُهُ] .

o14.6   There is no amputation for forcible seizure (O: meaning someone relying on force (N: to take people's money, who has a gang nearby to abet him in this)), snatching (O: meaning someone who depends on running away and is unarmed), or betraying a trust (O: of something entrusted to him, such as a deposit for safekeeping), or appropriating something by disavowal (A: i.e. denying that the victim loaned or entrusted him with such and such a thing), (O: because of the Prophet's (Allah bless him and give him peace) saying,

"There is no amputation for someone who seizes by force, snatches and runs, or betrays a trust,"

a hadith Tirmidhi classified as rigorously authenticated (sahih)). (A: But if one of the above-mentioned persons is a repeated offender whom it is in the interests of society to kill, the caliph may kill him.)

o14.6   ولا قَطعَ على مَن انْتَهَبَ (وهو
الذي يعتمد القوة (ح : في أخذ مالِ الناس
ولـه جمـاعـةٌ قريبـون يتقـوى بهم على
ذلك)) أوْ اخْتَلَسَ (والمختلِس هو الـذي
يعتمـد الهرب وليس له شوكة) أوْ خَانَ
(فيما استؤمن عليه من وديعة ونحوها كأن
أكلهـا) أوْ جَحَـدَ . (قـال ﷺ «ليس على
الـمنتهبِ والمختلِسِ والخـائنِ قطعٌ»
صححه الترمذي) .

*

o15.0 THE PENALTY FOR HIGHWAY ROBBERY

o15.0 حد قطع الطريق

o15.1 The caliph is obliged to summon whoever uses a weapon (O: though force suffices to be considered a *weapon,* or taking money by dint of one's fists) and makes people afraid to use the road (O: no matter whether in the wilderness, a village, or in the country; meaning he frightens those who pass along the way by means of his strength or weapons). If the highwayman responds to the summons before he has injured anyone, then he is only disciplined (def: o17).

If he steals the equivalent of 1.058 grams of gold under the previously mentioned conditions (o14.1), both his right hand and left foot are amputated.

(A: The difference between a highwayman and someone who takes by forcible seizure (dis: o14.6) is that the latter does so within earshot of help, while the offense of the highwayman is far greater because he menaces the lifeline of the community, its trade routes.)

o15.1 مَنْ شَهَرَ السِّلاحَ (ويكفي القهر وأخذ المال بالوكز والضرب بجمع الكف) وأَخافَ السبيلَ (سواء في برية أو في قرية أو بلد والمراد أخاف من يمر في الطريق لقوته وشوكته) وَجَبَ على الإمام طلبُهُ.

فإنْ وَقَعَ قبلَ جنايةٍ عُزِّرَ. وإنْ سَرَقَ نصاباً بشرطِهِ قُطِعَتْ يدُهُ اليمنى ورجلُهُ اليسرى.

o15.2 If a highwayman kills someone, he must be executed, even when the person entitled to retaliation (def: o3) agrees to forgo it. If the highwayman robs and kills, he is killed and then left crucified for three days. If he wounds or maims someone, retaliation is taken against him, though it may be waived by those entitled to take it.

o15.2 وإنْ قَتَلَ قُتِلَ حتماً وإنْ عَفَا وليُّ الدم. وإنْ سَرَقَ وقَتَلَ قُتِلَ ثمَّ صُلِبَ ثلاثةَ أيام. وإنْ جَرَحَ أوْ قَطَعَ طرفاً اقْتُصَّ منهُ مِنْ غيرِ تَحَتُّمٍ.

o15.3 (N: The penalty for highway robbery, such as mandatory execution, crucifixion, and amputating the hand and foot, is cancelled if the highwayman repents (A: desists, and gives himself up) before he has been apprehended, though he is still liable to retaliation (def: o3) by parties entitled to it (A: for injuries or deaths he caused to victims) and is financially responsible for restoring the money he has taken.)

o15.3 (ح): وتسقط بتوبته عن قطع الطريق قبل القدرة عليه العقوبة الخاصة بقطع الطريق كتحتم القتل والصلب وقطع اليد والرجل، ويكون أمر القصاص لولي الدم، ويضمن ما أخذ من مال).

*

o16.0 THE PENALTY FOR DRINKING

o16.0 حد الشرب

o16.1 Any beverage that intoxicates when taken in large quantities is unlawful both in small and large quantities, whether it is wine, (A: fermented) raisin drink, or something else.

o16.1 كلُّ شراب أَسْكَـرَ كثيرُهُ حُرُمَ قليلُهُ وكثيرُهُ خمراً كانَ أَوْ نبيذاً أَوْ غيرُهُمَا.

o16.2 The penalty for drinking is obligatorily enforced against anyone who:

(a) drinks;

(b) has reached puberty;

(c) is sane;

(d) is Muslim;

(e) does so voluntarily;

(f) and knows it is unlawful (A: the restrictions mentioned above (o12.4) about the ignorance of the prohibition of adultery also applying here).

o16.2 فَمَنْ شَرِب وهــوَ بالغٌ عاقلٌ مسلمٌ مختارٌ عالمٌ بِه وبتحريمِه لَزِمَهُ الحدُّ.

o16.3 The penalty for drinking is to be scourged forty stripes, with hands, sandals, and ends of clothes. It may be administered with a whip, but if the offender dies, an indemnity (def: o4.4) is due (A: from the scourger) for his death. If the caliph (def: o25) increases the penalty to eighty stripes, it is legally valid, but if the offender dies from the increase, the caliph must pay an adjusted indemnity, such that if he is given forty-one stripes and dies, the caliph must pay 1/41 of a full indemnity.

o16.3 وهــوَ أربعــونَ جلدةً [للحرِّ وعشــرونَ للعبــدِ] بالأيــدي والنعــال وأطرافِ الثيابِ. ويَجوزُ بالسوطِ لكنْ إنْ مَاتَ بالسياطِ وجَبَتْ ديتُهُ.

فإنْ رأى (الإمــام) أنْ يَزيدَ [في الحرِّ] إلى ثمانينَ [وفي العبدِ إلى أربعينَ] جازَ لكنْ لوْ مَاتَ منَ الـزيـادة ضَمِنَ (الإمام ديتَه) بالقسطِ. فلوْ ضَرَبَهُ إحدَى وأربعينَ فمَـاتَ ضَمِـنَ جزءاً مِنْ واحـدٍ وأربعينَ جزءاً مِنْ ديتِه.

o16.4 Someone who commits adultery several times (O: or drinks several times, or steals several times) before being punished is only punished once for each type of crime.

o16.4 ومَنْ زَنَى دفعـاتٍ (أوشرب دفعـات أو سرق كذلك) ولمْ يُحَدَّ أجْزَأَهُ لكلِّ جنسٍ حدٌّ واحدٌ.

o16.5 The penalty for a crime is not obviated by the offender's having repented for it, with the sole

o16.5 ومَنْ وَجَب عَلَيْهِ حدٌّ وتَابَ مِنهُ

exception of the highwayman, who is not penalized at all (dis: o15.3) if he repents before he is caught.

لَمْ يَسْقُطْ إلَّا حَدَّ قاطِعِ الطريقِ إذَا تَابَ قبلَ القدرة (عليه) فَيَسْقُطُ جميعُ حدِّه .

o16.6   It is not permissible to drink an intoxicant under any circumstances, whether for medicine (O: or in bread, or to cook meat with it,) or out of extreme thirst, with the sole exception of when one is choking on a piece of food and there is no other means of clearing it from one's throat save by drinking the intoxicant, in which case it is obligatory. (O: Sheikh al-Islam (A: Zakariyya Ansari) states, "It may not be used for medicine or extreme thirst, though there is no prescribed penalty for doing so, even when something besides it is available." The prohibition of using it for medicine or extreme thirst refers to when it is unadmixed, as opposed to when it is compounded with something else that renders it completely indistinguishable, such that no taste, color, or odor of it remains, in which case it is permissible.)

o16.6   ولا يَجُوزُ شربُ المسكرِ في حالٍ مِنَ الأحوالِ لا للتداوي (ولا أكله بالخبزِ وطبخِ اللحم به) ولا للعطشِ إلَّا أنْ يُغَصَّ بلقمةٍ ولا يَجِدَ ما يُسيغُها به فيَجبُ . (وعبارةُ شيـخِ الإسـلام : «لا يتناوله لتداو وعطش ولا يحد به وإن وجد غيـره». وما ذكـر من منعِ التـداوي أو الشـرب للعطش محله في صرفها بخلاف ما إذا خلطت بغيرها واستهلكت بحيث لم يبق لهـا طعم ولا لون ولا ريـح فإنهـا تجوز حينئذ) .

NONALCOHOLIC INTOXICANTS

المخدرات

o16.7   (Muhammad Shirbini Khatib:) The term *beverage* (dis: o16.1) excludes plants, such as hashish, which hashish users eat. The two sheikhs (A: Rafi'i and Nawawi) report in their section on foods the position of Ruyani that eating it is unlawful, though no legal penalty is fixed for it (*Mughni al-muhtaj ila ma'rifa ma'ani alfaz al-Minhaj* (y73), 4.187).

(al-Mawsu'a al-fiqhiyya:) Just as any beverage that intoxicates when taken in large quantities is also unlawful in small quantities, so too it is absolutely unlawful to use any solid substance detrimental to mind or body which produces languor or has a narcotic effect, this prohibition applying to the amount that is deleterious of it, not to the minute, beneficial amounts prescribed to treat illnesses, for such substances are not unlawful in themselves, but unlawful because they are deleterious (*Mawdu' al-ashriba.* Tab'a tamhidiyya li mawdu'at al-Mawsu'a al-fiqhiyya, no. 1 (y134), 49).

o16.7   (محمد الشربيني الخطيب :) وخـرج بالـشـراب النبـات . [قـال الـدميـري :] كالحشيشة التي تأكلها الخـرافيش . ونقل الشيخـان في باب الأطعمـة عن الـروياني أن أكله حرام ولا حد فيه [نقل من مغني المحتاج إلى معرفة ألفاظ المنهاج : ١٨٧/٤] .

«كمـا أن ما أسكر كثيره حرم قليله من المائعـات كذلـك يحرم مطلقـاً ما يُفتَّرُ ويُخَـدِّرُ من الأشيـاء الجامـدة المضرة بالعقل أو غيره من أعضاء الجسد . وذلك إذا تنـاول قدراً مضراً منهـا دون القليـل النـافع من أجـل التـداوي لأن حرمتهـا ليست لعينها بل لضررها [نقل من طبعة تمهيدية لموضوعات الموسوعة الفقهية] .

o17.0   DISCIPLINARY ACTION (TA'ZIR)

o17.0   التعزير

o17.1   Someone who commits an act of disobedience to Allah Most High that entails neither a prescribed legal penalty nor expiation, such as bearing false witness, is disciplined to the extent the caliph (def: o25) deems appropriate. (O: He exercises his own legal reasoning (ijtihad) and does what he thinks should be done, whether imprisonment and beating, either one separately, or mere verbal reprimand. He may not administer a more severe degree of punishment than what he feels is strictly necessary.)

o17.1   مَنْ أَتَى معصيةً لا حدَّ فيهَا ولا كفارةً ومنهُ شهادةُ الزورِ عُزِّرَ على حسب ما يَرَاهُ الحاكمُ. (فيجتهد الإمام ويفعل ما يراه من الجمع بين الحبس والضرب أو اقتصر على أحدهما وله الاقتصار على أحدهما وله الاقتصار على التوبيخ باللسان. فلا يرقى إلى مرتبة وهو يرى ما دونه كافياً).

o17.2   Disciplinary action may not reach the amount of the least prescribed legal penalty. For example, a freeman (O: if scourged) may not receive forty stripes.

o17.2   ولا يَبْلُغُ بِه أدنَى الحدودِ. فلا يَبْلُغُ بتعزيرِ الحرِّ (إذا جلده) إلى أربعينَ [ولا بتعزيرِ العبدِ عشرينَ].

o17.3   If the caliph sees fit not to take any disciplinary action, this is also permissible (O: when it concerns a right owed to Allah Most High, for the ruler is entrusted with using his own legal reasoning. But if it concerns a right owed to a fellow human being who has demanded that it be fulfilled (A: such as when someone has been cheated) it is impermissible to do nothing. If a person is entitled to have another disciplined, but instead forgives him, the ruler may nevertheless discipline him).

o17.3   وإذا رَأَى تركَـهُ جازَ (إذا كان لحق الله تعالى فإنه موكول إلى اجتهاده. أما إذا كان لحق الآدمي وقـد طلبه فلا يجـوز له تركـه. وإذا عفا الـمستحق للتعزير عنه جاز للحاكم أن يعزر).

o17.4   (O: A father or grandfather (and on up) is entitled to discipline those under his care when they commit an act that is unbecoming. And so may a mother with her child. A husband is entitled to discipline his wife for not giving him his rights (def: m5.1). A teacher may discipline a student. (A: Spanking a student, for example, is permissible if there is a valid lawful purpose to be served thereby, and the student's guardian has given the teacher permission.))

o17.4   (وللأب وإن علا تعزير موليه بارتكابـه ما لا يليق. ويشبه أن يكون كذلـك للأم مع صبي. وللزوج تعزير زوجته لحقه. وللمعلم تعزير المتعلم منه).

*

o18.0 OATHS (YAMIN)
(A: An oath is a solemn statement to do or refrain from something, or that something is true, such that if things turn out otherwise, the swearer must make an expiation (def: o20.2).)

o18.0 الأيمان

o18.1 An oath is only valid from a person (O: whether Muslim or non-Muslim) who:

(a) has reached puberty;

(b) is sane;

(c) makes the oath voluntarily;

(d) and intends an oath thereby.

o18.1 إنَّــمــا يَصِـحُّ اليمينُ مِن بالـغٍ عاقـلٍ مختـارٍ قاصـدٍ إلى اليمين (مسلماً كان أو كافراً).

o18.2 The oath of someone whose tongue runs away with him and who unthinkingly swears an oath, or someone who intends a particular oath but unintentionally swears something else, does not count and is an *unintentional oath* (A: which is mentioned in the Holy Koran (n: at 5:89)).

o18.2 فَمَنْ سَبَقَ لسانُهُ إليهَا أوْ قَصَدَ الحلفَ على شيءٍ فَسَبَقَ لسـانُهُ إلى غيرِه لمْ يَنْعَقِدْ. وذلكَ مِنْ لغو اليمين.

o18.3 An oath is only validly effected if sworn by a name of Allah Most High, or an attribute of His entity (dhat).
(N: It is offensive to swear an oath by other than Allah if one merely intends it as an asseveration of one's statement, though it is unlawful to do so if one intends reverence to the thing sworn by.)

o18.3 ولا تَنْعَقِدُ إلَّا باسمٍ مِنْ أسماءِ اللهِ تعالى أوْ صفةٍ مِنْ صفاتِ ذاتِهِ.
(ح: ويكره الحلف بغير الله إن نوى مجـرّد تأكيـد لكـلامـه. ويحـرم إن نوى تعظيماً لما يحلف به).

o18.4 There are some names of Allah Most High that are applied to no one but Him, such as *Allah, the All-merciful, the All-vigilant,* and *Knower of the Unseen.* An oath sworn by any of these is valid without restriction.

o18.4 ثمَّ مِنْ أسمـاءِ اللهِ تعالى ما لا يَتَسَمَّى بِه غيرُهُ كاللهِ والرحمن والمهيمن وعلَّامِ الغيوبِ. فيَنْعَقِدُ بها اليمينُ مطلقاً.

o18.5 Other names of Allah may be conditionally applied to other than Him, such as *Lord* (Rabb) (n: *rabb bayt* meaning, for example, *home owner*), *the All-compassionate* (al-Rahim) (n: *rahim al-qalb* meaning *softhearted*), or *the Omnipotent* (al-Qadir) (n: *qadir 'alayhi* meaning

o18.5 ومنهـا ما يَتَسَمَّى بِه غيرُهُ مَع التقييدِ كالربِّ والرحيمِ والقادرِ. فتَنْعَقِدُ

capable of it; the second term of each of these examples indicating that Allah is not meant). An oath sworn by such names is validly effected unless the swearer specifically intends something else.

بها اليمين، إلَّا أَنْ يَنْويَ غيرَ اليمينِ.

o18.6 Other of Allah's names are applied to both Him and His creatures, such as *the Living* (al-Hayy), *the Existent* (al-Mawjud), or *the Seeing* (al-Basir). An oath sworn by such names is not validly effected unless the swearer specifically intends it as an oath.

o18.6 ومنهـا ما هوَ مُشْـتَـرَكٌ كالحيِّ والمـوجـود والبصيـر. فلا تَنْعَقـدُ بهَـا اليمينُ، إلَّا أَنْ يَنْويَ بهَا اليمينَ.

o18.7 An oath sworn by the attributes of Allah that are inapplicable to creatures, such as *Allah's glory, His exaltedness, His endless eternality,* or *the Koran,* is validly effected without restriction.

o18.7 وصفـاتُـهُ إنْ لَمْ تُسْتَعْمَـلْ في مخلوقٍ نحوَ عزة الله وكبريـائِه وبقائِه والقرآنَ فَتَنْعَقدُ بها اليمينُ مطلقاً.

o18.8 An oath sworn by divine attributes that are sometimes used to allude to creatures, such as *Allah's knowledge, His power,* or *His right,* is validly effected unless the swearer intends something else by them, such as meaning by *knowledge* the things known, by *power* the things under its sway, or by *right* (n: the) acts of worship (n: that are His right), in which cases an oath has not been validly effected.

o18.8 وإنْ كانت قدْ تُسْتَعْمَلُ في مخلوقٍ نحوَ علمِ اللهِ وقـدرتـه وحقِّه فَيَنْعَقـدُ بهَـا اليمينُ، إلَّا أَنْ يَنْويَ بالعلمِ المعلومَ وبـالقـدرةِ المقـدورَ وبـالحقِّ العبادةَ فلَا.

o18.9 An oath is validly effected when a person says, "I swear by Allah that...," or "I've sworn by Allah that...," unless the person merely intends to inform.

o18.9 ولوْ قَالَ: أُقْسِمُ باللهِ وأَقْسَمْتُ باللهِ انْعَقَدَتْ، إلَّا أَنْ يَنْويَ بهَا الإخبارَ.

o18.10 Unless one particularly intends it as an oath, an oath is not validly effected when the following expressions are used: "I will not do such and such, by the life of Allah," or "I resolve by Allah," or "by the covenant of Allah," "His guarantee," "His trust," "His sufficiency," or "I ask you by Allah," or "I swear by Allah that you must do such and such."

o18.10 ولـوْ قَالَ: لعمـرُ اللهِ وأشْهَـدُ باللهِ أوْ أُعْزِمُ باللهِ أوْ عليَّ عهدُ اللهِ أوْ ذمّتُهُ أوْ أمـانتُـهُ أوْ كفايتُهُ لا أفْعَلُ كذَا أوْ أسْألُكَ باللهِ أوْ أقْسَمْتُ عليكَ باللهِ لَمْ تَنْعَقِدْ، إلَّا أَنْ يَنْويَ بِه اليمينَ.

*

o19.0 EXAMPLES OF BREAKING AND NOT BREAKING OATHS

o19.1 If one swears, "I will not eat this wheat," but then makes it into flour or bread (A: and eats it), one has not broken one's oath.

If one swears, "I will not drink from this river," but then drinks its water from a jug, one has broken one's oath.

If one swears, "I will not eat meat," but then eats fat, kidneys, tripe, liver, heart, spleen, fish, or locusts, one has not broken one's oath.

o19.3 If one swears, "I will not enter the house," but then does so absentmindedly, in ignorance of its being the house, under compulsion, or by being carried in, then one's oath is not broken and is still in effect.

o19.5 When a person swearing an oath about something (O: in the future, affirming or denying that it will occur) includes the expression *in sha' Allah* ("if Allah wills") before finishing the oath, then the oath is not broken in any event if he thereby intends to provide for exceptions. But if he merely says it out of habit, not intending to make an exception to his oath, or if he says it after having finished swearing the oath, then the exception is not valid (O: because when an oath has

ما يقتضي الحنث o19.0

o19.1 ومَن حَلَفَ [لا أَدْخُلُ بيتـاً فدَخَـلَ بيتَ شعرٍ حَنِثَ وإنْ كانَ حضرياً وإنْ دَخَـلَ مسجداً فلاَ أوْ] لا آكُلُ هذِه الحنطةَ فجَعَلَهَا دقيقاً أوْ خبزاً لَمْ يَحْنَثْ [أوْ لا آكُلُ سمناً فأكَلهُ في عصيدةٍ ونحوِها وهو ظاهِرٌ فيها] أوْ لا أَشْرَبُ مِنْ هذا النهر فشَرِبَ ماءهُ في كوزٍ حَنِثَ. أوْ لا آكُلُ لحماً فأكَلَ شحماً أوْ كليةً أوْ كرشاً أوْ كبِداً أوْ قلباً أوْ طحالاً أوْ [أليـةً أوْ] سمكـاً أوْ جراداً فلا حنث.

o19.2 [أوْ لا أَلْبَسُ لزيدٍ ثوباً فوَهَبَهُ لهُ أو اشْتَراهُ له فلا. أوْ لا أَهَبُهُ فتَصَدَّقَ عليهِ حَنِثَ. أوْ لا أَعارَهُ أوْ وَهَبَهُ فلَمْ يَقْبَلْ، أوْ قبلَ ولمْ يَقْبِضْ فلا. أوْ لا أَتَكَلَّمُ فَقَرَأَ القرآنَ، أوْ لا أُكَلِّمُ فلاناً فَراسَلَهُ أوْ كاتَبَهُ أوْ أَشارَ إليهِ، أوْ لا أَسْتَخْدِمُهُ فخَدَمَهُ وهو ساكتٌ أوْ لا أَتَزَوَّجُ أوْ لا أُطَلِّقُ أوْ لا أَبيعُ فوَكَّلَ غيرَهُ فَفَعَلَ، أوْ لا آكُلُ هذِه التمرةَ فَاخْتَلَطَتْ بتمرٍ كثيرٍ فأكَلَ إلاَّ تمرةً لا يَعْلَمُها، أوْ لا أَشْرَبُ ماء النهر فشَرِبَ بعضَهُ: لَمْ يَحْنَثْ. أوْ لا آكُلُهُ زماناً أوْ حيناً بَرَّ بأدنَى زمنٍ].

o19.3 أوْ لا أَدْخُلُ الدارَ مثلاً فدَخَلَها ناسياً أوْ جاهلاً أوْ مكرهاً أوْ محمولاً لَمْ يَحْنَثْ واليمينُ باقيةٌ لَمْ تَنْحَلَّ.

o19.4 [أوْ لَيَأْكُلَنَّ هذا غداً فأكَلَهُ في يومهِ أوْ أَتْلَفَهُ أوْ تَلِفَ مِنَ الغدِ بعدَ إمكانِ أكلِهِ حَنِثَ. وإنْ تَلِفَ في يومهِ فلاَ. أوْ لا أَسْكُنُ هذِه الدارَ فخَرَجَ منها بنيةِ التحويلِ ثمَّ دخَلَ لنقلِ القماشِ لَمْ يَحْنَثْ. أوْ لا أُساكِنُ زيداً فسَكَنَ كلَّ واحدٍ منهمَا في بيتٍ مِنْ دارٍ كبيرةٍ وانْفَرَدَ ببابٍ ومِرافقٍ لَمْ يَحْنَثْ. أوْ لا أَلْبَسُ هذا الثوبَ وهو لابِسُهُ، أوْ لا أَرْكَبُ هذا وهو راكِبُهُ، أوْ لا أَدْخُلُ هذِه الدارَ وهو فيها فَاسْتَدامَ حَنِثَ. أوْ لا أَتَزَوَّجُ وهو متزوجٌ، أوْ لا أَتَطَيَّبُ وهو متطيّبٌ أوْ لا أَتَطَهَّرُ وهو متطهِّرٌ فَاسْتَدامَ فلا. أوْ لا أَدْخُلُ هذِه الدارَ فصَعَدَ سطحَها مِنْ خارجِها أوْ صارَتْ عرصةً فدَخَلَها لَمْ يَحْنَثْ. أوْ لا أَدْخُلُ دارَ زيدٍ فدَخَلَ مسكَنَهُ بكراءٍ أوْ عاريةٍ لَمْ يَحْنَثْ إلاَّ أنْ يَنْويَ ما يَسْكُنُهُ].

o19.5 وإذا حَلَفَ على شيءٍ (مستقبلٍ إثباتاً كانَ أوْ نفياً) فقَالَ إنْ شَاءَ اللهُ تعـالى مُتَّصِلاً باليمينِ وكانَ قَصَدَ الاسـتِثـناءَ قبـلَ فراغِـهِ مِنَ اليمينِ لَمْ يَحْنَثْ. وإنْ جَرَى الاستثناءُ على لسانِهِ على عادتِهِ ولمْ يَقصِدْ بهِ رفعَ اليمينِ أو بَدَا لهُ الاستثناءُ بعـدَ الفراغِ مِنَ اليمينِ لَمْ يَصِحَّ الاستثناءُ (لأن اليمينَ بعدَ تمامِه

been completed, its efficacy is established and not eradicable by a statement of exception).

يثبت حكمه فلا يرتفع بالاستثناء).

*

o20.0 THE EXPIATION FOR A BROKEN OATH

o20.0 كفارة اليمين

o20.1 An expiation is obligatory for someone who swears and breaks an oath. If the swearer is entitled to expiate by the expenditure of property (def: o20.2(1–3)), it is permissible for him to do so before or after breaking the oath. But if it consists of fasting, then he may only do so after breaking the oath.

o20.1 إذا حَلَفَ وحَنِثْتَ لَزِمَتْهُ الكَفَّارَةُ. فإنْ كانَ يُكَفِّرُ بالمالِ جازَ قبل الحنثِ وبعدَهُ. وإنْ كانَ بالصومِ لمْ يَجُزْ إلّا بعدَهُ.

o20.2 The expiation consists of (N: a choice of any) one of the following:

(1) to free a sound Muslim slave;

(2) to feed ten people who are (N: poor or) short of money (def: h8.8–11) each 0.51 liters of grain (O: though it is not a condition that it be grain, but rather the type of food payable for the zakat of 'Eid al-Fitr (def: h7.6), even if not grain (A: and the Hanafi school permits giving its value in money));

(3) or to provide clothing of any kind for ten such persons, even if it consists of a wraparound or clothing previously washed, though not if ragged.

If one is unable to do any of the above, one must fast for three days. It is better to fast them consecutively, though permissible to do so non-consecutively.

o20.2 وهيَ عِتقُ رقبةٍ [صفتُها كرقبةِ الظهارِ]، أوْ إطعامُ عشرةِ مساكينَ كلَّ مسكينٍ رطلٍ وثلثَ رطلٍ بالبغدادي حباً (وهو ليس بقيدٍ بل المدارُ على ما يكفي في الفطرة ويجزِىء فيها وإن لم يكن حباً) [منْ قوتِ البلدِ]، أوْ كسوتُهُم بما يَنْطَلِقُ عليهِ اسمُ الكسوةِ ولوْ مئزراً (وهو الإزارُ) ومغسولاً لا خَلقاً. ويُخَيَّرُ بينَ الأنواعِ الثلاثةِ.

فإنْ عَجَزَ عنْ أحدِ الأنواعِ الثلاثةِ صامَ ثلاثةَ أيامٍ. والأفضلُ تَوَاليها. ويَجُوزُ متفرقةً.

o20.3 [والعبدُ لا يُكَفِّرُ بالمالِ وإنْ أَذِنَ لهُ السيدُ، بلْ بالصومِ. ومَنْ بعضُهُ حرٌّ يُكَفِّرُ بالطعامِ والكسوةِ دونَ العتقِ].

o20.4 (O: Someone eligible to receive zakat funds or expiations because of being poor (def:

o20.4 (ومــن كان له أن يأخـذ من سهمِ الفقراءِ والمساكينِ في الــزكــاة

623

| h8.8) or short of money (def: h8.11) may expiate broken oaths by fasting.) | والكفارات فله أن يكفر بالصوم) . |

*

o21.0   THE JUDGESHIP

o21.0   القضاء

o21.1   To undertake the Islamic judgeship is a communal obligation (def: c3.2) (O: for those capable of performing it in a particular area). If only one competent person exists who can perform it, then it is personally obligatory for him to do so. If he refuses, he is compelled to accept (O: though he is only obliged to accept the judgeship when it is in his own home area, not when it is elsewhere, for this would be like a punishment, involving as it does wholly leaving one's home). Such an individual person may not take a salary for it—(N: because in respect to him it has become personally obligatory, and it is not permissible to take a wage for something personally obligatory, as opposed to something that is a communal obligation (A: for which accepting a wage is permissible))—unless he is needy (O: in which case the Muslim common fund gives him enough to cover his expenses and those of his dependents, without wastefulness or penury. But if he agrees to judge without being paid (N: i.e. in expectation of the reward from Allah), it is better for him).

o21.1   ولايةُ القضاء فرضُ كفايةٍ (في حق الصالحين له في الناحية (ح : أي الإقليم)) . فإنْ لَمْ يَكُنْ مَنْ يَصْلُحُ إلَّا واحدٌ تَعَيَّنَ عليهِ . فإن امْتَنَعَ أُجْبِرَ . (وإنما يلزمه القبول والطلب في ناحيته فلا يلزمانه في غيرها لأن ذلك تعذيب لما فيه من ترك الوطن بالكلية) . ولَيْسَ لهذا أنْ يَأْخُذُ عليهِ رزقاً (ح : لأنه صار في حقه فرض عين ولا يجوز أخذ الأجر على فروض العين بخلاف فرض الكفاية) إلَّا أنْ يَكُونَ محتاجاً (فيجعل له بيت المال ما يكفيه لنفقته ونفقة عياله من غير إسراف ولا تقتير ، وإن احتسب (ح : أي عمل احتساباً لوجه الله) فهو أفضل) .

o21.2   It is permissible to have two or more judges in the same town.

o21.2   ويَجُوزُ في بلدٍ قاضيانِ فأكثرُ .

o21.3   It is not valid for anyone besides the caliph (def: o25) or his representative to appoint someone as judge.

o21.3   ولا يَصِحُّ إلَّا بتولية الإمام لُ أوْ نائبِه .

o21.4   It is permissible for two parties to select a third party to judge between them if he is competent for the judgeship (def: o22.1) (O: provided the case does not concern Allah's prescribed penalties, (A: and they may select such a person) even when a judge exists). It is obligatory for them

o21.4   وإنْ حَكَّمَ الخصمانِ رجلًا يصْلُحُ للقضاءِ جازَ (وهـذا في غير حدود الله تعـالى ، ولـو مع وجـود قاض) ولـزم

to accept his decision on their case, though if either litigant withdraws his nomination before the third party gives his judgement, the latter may not judge.

حكمُهُ [وإنْ لَمْ يَتَراضيَا بهِ بعدَ الحكم]. لكـنْ إنْ رَجَـعَ فيـهِ (أي في التـحكيم) أحدُهُمَا قبلَ أَنْ يَحْكُمَ امْتَنَعَ الحكمُ.

*

o22.0 THE JUDGE AND THE COURT

o22.0 شروط الـقـاضي وصفة المحكمة

o22.1 The necessary qualifications for being an Islamic judge (qadi) are:

(a) to be a male freeman;

(b) to have full capacity for moral answerability (taklif, def: c8.1);

(c) to be upright (o24.4);

(d) to possess knowledge (O: of the rulings of Sacred Law, meaning by way of personal legal reasoning (ijtihad) (A: from primary texts), not merely by following a particular qualified scholar (taqlid) (A: i.e. if he follows qualified scholarship, he must know and agree with how the rulings are derived, not merely report them). Being qualified to perform legal reasoning (ijtihad) requires knowledge of the rules and principles of the Koran, the sunna (A: in this context meaning the *hadith*, not the *sunna* as opposed to the *obligatory*), (N: as well as knowledge of scholarly consensus (ijma', def: b7)), and analogy (def: III below), together with knowing the types of each of these. (A: The knowledge of each "type" below implies familiarity with subtypes and kinds, but the commentator has deemed the mention of the category as a whole sufficient to give readers a general idea.)

(I) The types of Koranic rules include, for example:

(1) those ('amm) of general applicability to different types of legal rulings;

o22.1 وَيُشْتَرَطُ في القاضي الذكورةُ والحـريـةُ والتكليفُ والعـدالـةُ والعلمُ (بالأحكـام الشرعيـة بطريق الاجتهاد لا بالتقليـد، وأهليـة الاجتهـاد تتـوقف على معـرفـة أحكـام القـرآن والسنة (ح: والإجمـاع) والقيـاس مع معرفة أنواعها. فمن أنـواع القـرآن: العـام، والخـاص،

(2) those (khass) applicable to only one particular ruling or type of ruling;

(3) those (mujmal) which require details and explanation in order to be properly understood;

(4) those (mubayyan) which are plain without added details;

(5) those (mutlaq) applicable without restriction;

(6) those (muqayyad) which have restrictions;

(7) those (nass) which unequivocally decide a particular legal question;

(8) those (zahir) with a probable legal signification, but which may also bear an alternative interpretation;

(9) those (nasikh) which supersede previously revealed Koranic verses;

(10) and those (mansukh) which are superseded by later verses.

(II) The types of sunna (A: i.e. hadith) include:

(1) hadiths (mutawatir) related by whole groups of individuals from whole groups, in multiple contiguous channels of transmission leading back to the Prophet himself (Allah bless him and give him peace), such that the sheer number of separate channels at each stage of transmission is too many for it to be possible for all to have conspired to fabricate the hadith (A: which is thereby obligatory to believe in, and denial of which is unbelief (kufr));

(2) hadiths (ahad) related by fewer than the above-mentioned group at one or more stages of the transmission, though traced through contiguous successive narrators back to the Prophet (Allah bless him and give him peace). (n: If a hadith is transmitted through just one individual at any point in the history of its transmission, the

والـمـجـمـل، والـمـبـيـن، والمطلق، والمقيـد، والنص، والظـاهـر، والناسخ، والمنسـوخ. ومن أنواع السنة: المتواتر، والآحاد، [والمتصل]، وغيره. (ت: قال

hadith is termed *singular* (gharib). If it is transmitted through just *two* people at any stage of its transmission, it is termed *rare* (`aziz). If its channels of transmission come through only three people at any point of its history, it is termed *well-known* (mashhur). These designations do not directly influence the authenticity rating of the hadith, since a *singular* hadith, for example, might be *rigorously authenticated* (sahih), well authenticated (hasan) (N: hadiths of both types being obligatory for a Muslim to believe in, though someone who denies them is merely considered corrupt (fasiq), not an unbeliever (kafir)), or *not well authenticated* (da'if), depending on the reliability ratings of the narrators and other factors weighed and judged by hadith specialists);

(3) and other kinds. (n: Yusuf Ardabili mentions the following in his list of qualifications for performing legal reasoning (ijtihad):)

(4) hadiths (mursal) from one of those (tabi'i) who had personally met (N: not only met, but actually studied under) one or more of the prophetic Companions (Sahaba) but not the Prophet himself (Allah bless him and give him peace) (n: hadiths reported in the form, "The Prophet said [or did] such and such," without mentioning the Companion who related it directly from the Prophet);

(5) hadiths (musnad) related through a contiguous series of transmitters back to the Prophet (Allah bless him and give him peace);

(6) hadiths (muttasil) related through a contiguous series of transmitters (n: either from the Prophet (Allah bless him and give him peace), such a hadith being termed *ascribed* (marfu'), or else only from one of the Companions, such a hadith being termed *arrested* (mawquf));

(7) hadiths (munqata') related through a chain of transmitters of whom one is unknown (n: though if two or more are unknown, it is not considered merely *incontiguous* (munqata'), but rather *problematic* (mu'dal));

(8) the positive and negative personal factors (jarh wa ta'dil) determining the reliability ratings

يوسف أردبيلي: والمـرسـل، والمسند، والمتصـل، والمنقطـع، وحـال الـرواة جرحاً وتعـديلاً، [الثالث] أقاويل علماء

of the individual narrators of a hadith's channel of transmission;

(9) the positions held by the most learned of the Companions (Sahaba) on legal questions, and those of the scholars who came after them;

(10) and on which of these positions there is scholarly consensus (def: b7), and which are differed upon (*Kitab al-anwar li a'mal al-abrar fi fiqh al-Imam al-Shafi'i* (y11), 2.391).

(n: The English glosses and remarks on the meanings of the above hadith terminology are from notes taken by the translator at a lesson with hadith specialist Sheikh Shu'ayb Arna'ut.)

(III) Types of **analogical reasoning** (qiyas) include:

(1) making an *a fortiori* analogy between acts p and q, where if p takes a ruling, q is even likelier to take the same ruling. For example, if saying "Uff!" to one's parents is unlawful (n: as at Koran 17:23), one may analogically infer that beating them must also be unlawful;

(2) making an analogy between acts p and q, where if p takes a ruling, one may infer that q is equally likely to take the same ruling. For example, if it is unlawful to wrongfully consume an orphan's property, then it must also be unlawful to destroy his property by burning it up;

(3) and making an analogy between acts p and q, where if p takes a ruling, one may infer that it is likely, though less certain, that q takes the same ruling (A: because of a common feature in the two acts which functions as the basis ('illa) for the analogy). For example, if usurious gain (riba) is unlawful in selling wheat (dis: k3.1), then it is also unlawful in selling apples, the basis for the analogy being that both are *food*.

The meaning of *knowledge* of the above matters is (A: for a judge) to know part of what is connected with the Koran, sunna (A: i.e. hadith), and

الصحـابـة فمن بعـدهم إجماعاً واختلافاً [نقـل من كتاب الأنوار لأعمال الأبرار في فقه الإمام الشافعي: ٢/ ٣٩١].

ومن أنـواع القيـاس: الأولوي كقيـاس ضرب الوالدين على التأفيف، والمساوي كقيـاس إحـراق مال اليتيم على أكله في التحـريم فيهمـا، والأدون كقياس التفاح على البر في باب الربا بجامع الطعام. والمـراد بعض ما يتعلق بالقرآن والسنة

analogy, not complete knowledge of the Book of
Allah, total familiarity with the rules of the sunna,
or comprehensive mastery of the rules of analogical reasoning, but rather that which is pertinent to
giving judgements in court (A: though an *absolute*
expert in Islamic legal reasoning (mujtahid mutlaq) such as Abu Hanifa, Malik, Shafi'i, or
Ahmad, is obliged to know what relates to every
subject matter in Sacred Law). He must know the
reliability ratings of hadith narrators in strength
and weakness. When two primary texts seem to
contend, he gives precedence to:

(1) those of particular applicability (khass)
over those of general applicability ('amm);

(2) those that take restrictions (muqayyad)
over those that do not (mutlaq);

(3) those which unequivocally settle a particular question (nass) over those of merely probabilistic legal significance (zahir);

(4) those which are literal (muhkam) over
those which are figurative (mutashabih);

(5) and those which supersede previous rulings, those with a contiguous channel of transmission, and those with a well-authenticated channel
of transmission, over their respective opposites.

He must also have knowledge of the Arabic
language, its lexicon, grammar, word morphol-
ogy, and rhetoric.

He must likewise know the positions of the
scholars of Sacred Law regarding their consensus
and differences, and not contradict their consensus (A: which is unlawful (dis: b7.2)) with his own
reasoning.

If no one possesses the above-mentioned
qualifications, and a strong ruler appoints an unfit
Muslim to the bench, such as someone who is
immoral, or who (A: is incapable of independent
legal reasoning (ijtihad) and) merely follows
other qualified scholars (taqlid), or a child, or a
woman, then the appointee's decisions are
implemented because of necessity, so as not to vitiate people's concerns and interests (A: and this
is what exists in our day, when the conditions for

والقيــاس لا جميــع معـرفـة كتـاب الله
وجميــع أحكــام السنـة وجميـع أحكـام
القياس. بل ما يتعلق بالقضاء. ولا بد له
من معـرفة حال الـرواة قوة وضعفاً فيقدم
عنــد التعــارض: الخـــاص على العــام
والمقيد على المطلق والنص على الظاهر
والـمحكم على المتشــابـه والنـــاســخ
والمتصل والقـوي على مقـابلها. ولا بد
من معـرفة لسان العرب لغة ونحواً وصرفاً
وبلاغة، وأقوال العلماء إجماعاً واختلافاً
فلا يخالفهم في اجتهاده. فإن فقد الشرط
المــذكـور فولى سلطـان ذو شوكـة مسلماً
غيـر أهل كفاسق ومقلد وصبي وامرأة نفذ
حكمـــه وقضـاؤه للضـرورة لئـلا تتعطل

an Islamic judge are seldom met with));

    (e) sound hearing;

    (f) sound eyesight;

    (g) and the faculty of speech.

    (O: The author did not mention the necessary condition of being a Muslim, evidently feeling that *uprightness* ((c) above) was sufficient to imply it.)

مصـالـح الناس) والسمعُ والبصرُ والنطقُ (ولم ينبـه المصنف على شرط الإسـلام والظاهر أنه اكتفى بوصف العدالة عنه) .

o22.2   It is recommended that the judge be stern without harshness, and flexible without weakness (O: so the litigants do not despise or disdain him, for otherwise, people entitled to rights would not be able to obtain them).

o22.2   ويُنْدَبُ أَنْ يَكـونَ شديداً بلا عنفٍ لينـاً بلا ضعفٍ (حتى لا تحتقـره وتستخفـه الخصـوم. وإذا كان كذلك تضيع الحقوق على أربابها) .

o22.3   If the judge needs to appoint another person to handle a part of his caseload because it is too heavy for him, then he may assign someone to deal with the extra cases if the person himself is qualified to be a judge. If the judge does not need to, he may not appoint such a person without special permission (A: from the regional ruler).

o22.3   وإنِ احْتَـاجَ أَنْ يَسْتَخْلِفَ في (بعض) أعمـالِـه (وأحكـامـه) لكـثـرتهَـا اسْتَخْلَفَ مَنْ يَصْلُحُ. وإنْ لَمْ يَحْتَجْ فلا، إلَّا أَنْ يُؤْذَنَ لُه .

o22.4   If the judge needs a court secretary, he must be Muslim, upright (def: o24.4), sane, and learned (O: meaning familiar with writing up plaintiffs' cases, recording what is done in each case and the judge's decisions, and must be able to distinguish between writing it correctly and incorrectly. The above four conditions are obligatory, there only remaining to be mentioned that the secretary must be male and free).

o22.4   وإنِ احْتَـاجَ إلى كاتبٍ فَلْيَكُنْ مسلماً عدلاً عاقلاً فقيهاً (والمراد من كونه فقيهـاً أن يكـون عارفـاً بكتـابـة محاضـر وسجـلات وكتب حكمية ليعلم صحة ما يكتبـه من فساده وهذه الأربعة لا بد منها وبقي من شروط الكاتب كونه ذكراً حراً) .

o22.5   The judge should not have a doorkeeper (O: if there is no crowd), though if he needs one, the doorkeeper must be sane, reliable, and unbribable.

o22.5   ولا يَتَّخِـذُ حاجبـاً (إن لم يَكن ثم زحمـة) فإنِ احْتَـاجَ فَلْيَكُنْ عاقـلاً أميناً بعيداً مِنَ الطمعِ .

o22.6   When not in the area of his jurisdiction, the judge may not give legal decisions, appoint others, or hear evidence (O: or claims).

o22.6   ولا يَحْكُمُ (القاضي) ولا يُوَلِّي ولا يَسْمَعُ البينَة (بل ولا الدعوى) في غير عملِهِ . [ح : أي غير منطقة عمله)] .

o22.7 He may not accept gifts except from someone who customarily gave him gifts before he became judge, who is not a plaintiff, and whose gifts are not more lavish than those given before the judge's appointment. (O: The same is true for entertaining the judge as a guest, as well as lending articles to him which are of rentable value, such as lending him lodgings.) It is better for a judge not to accept any gifts. (O: And whenever gifts are not lawful to accept, he does not legally own them but must return them.)

o22.8 A judge may not decide cases involving his son (O: son's son, and on down) or his father (O: father's father, and on up, or cases involving his partner in a shared enterprise).

o22.9 He should not decide cases when angry, hungry, thirsty, overwrought, exultant, ill, tired, flatulent, annoyed, or when the weather is irritatingly hot or cold (O: it being offensive for a judge to decide a case in any state that affects his temperament for the worse), though if he does, his decision is implemented.

o22.10 The judge should not sit in a mosque to decide cases (O: lest voices be raised therein, and because he might need to bring in the insane, children, a woman in her period, or non-Muslims; for which reasons sitting in a mosque to decide cases is offensive). But if his sitting in the mosque (O: in prayer, spiritual retreat (i'tikaf), or awaiting group prayer) happens to coincide with the coming of two litigants, then he may judge between them (O: without it being offensive).

o22.11 The judge should sit with tranquility and gravity (O: as it creates greater respect for him and makes it likelier that he will be obeyed). He should have witnesses present and scholars of jurisprudence to consult with on points of difficulty. If a case is not clear, he should postpone giving a decision on it. He may not merely imitate another's decision on a case (A: but must be capable of expert legal reasoning (ijtihad) himself).

٧. ٢٢ه ولاَ يَقْبَلُ هديةً إلّا ممَّنْ كَانَ يُهَادِيهِ قبلَ الـوِلايةِ ولمْ تكنْ لهُ خصومةٌ ولمْ تَزِدْ هديتُهُ بعدَ التوليةِ (على هديته قبلها ومثل الهدية في هذا الحكم الضيافة والعـاريـة إن كانت لمنفعة تقـابـل بأجرة كسكنى دار). ومَعَ هٰذا فالأفضلُ أنْ لا يَقْبَلَهَا. (وحيـث حرمت لا يملكهـا المهدى إليه فيجب ردها).

٨. ٢٢ه ولا يَحْكُمُ لِولـدِهِ (وإن سفل) ولا لوالـدِهِ (وإن علا) [ولا لرقيقـهِ] (ولا يقضي لشريكه في الأمر المشترك).

٩. ٢٢ه ولا يَقْضِي وهـوَ غضبـانُ ولا جائعٌ ولا عطشـانُ ولا مهمـومٌ ولا فرحانُ ولا مريضٌ ولا نعـسـانُ ولا حاقـنٌ ولا ضجرانُ ولا في حرٍّ مزعجٍ وبـردٍ مؤلمٍ ((والضابط الجامع لما تقدم وغيره أنه] يكره للقاضي القضاء في كل حال يسوء فيه خلقه) فإنْ فَعَلَ نَفَذَ حكمُهُ.

١٠. ٢٢ه ولا يَجْـلِسُ في الـمـسجـد للحكم (صونـاً له عن ارتفاع الأصوات ولأنـه قد يحتـاج إلى إحضار المجانين والصبيان ومن كانت حائضة والكفار فالجلوس في المسجـد لأجـل الحكم مكروه). فإنْ اتَّفَقَ جلوسُهُ فيهِ (لصلاة واعتكـاف وانتظـار جمـاعـة) وحَضَرَ خصمانِ حكمَ بينهُمَا (من غير كراهة).

١١. ٢٢ه ويَجْلِسُ بسكينةٍ ووقارٍ (لأنه أعظم لهيبتـه وأدعى لطـاعتـه). ويُحْضِرُ الشهودَ والفقهاءَ ويُشاوِرُهُمْ فيمَا يُشْكِلُ وإنْ لمْ يَتَّضِحْ أخَّرَهُ. ولمْ يُقَلِّدْ غيرَهُ في الحكم.

o22.12 The judge handles the cases on a first-come-first-served basis, one case per turn. If two arrive at the same time, they draw lots to see whose case will be heard first.

The judge (O: obligatorily) treats two litigants impartially, seating both in places of equal honor, attending to each, and so forth, unless one is a non-Muslim, in which case he gives the Muslim a better seat. He may not treat either litigant rudely, nor prompt one (O: as to how to state his case).

o22.13 The judge may intercede with one of them on behalf of the other (O: meaning to ask the two parties to settle their differences, which is what a judge's "intercession" is. It does not take place until after the truth has been established, which obviates his unfairly inclining to either one) and he may also pay one litigant what the other owes him.

o22.14 (N: When assigned to a new jurisdiction,) the judge first looks into the cases of the imprisoned, then orphans, and then of lost and found items.

*

o23.0   COURT CLAIMS

o23.1   If a plaintiff makes a claim that is not true, the judge considers it as if he had not heard it (O: and need not ask the defendant about it).

When a claim is true, the judge asks the defendant, "What do you say?" If the defendant admits the claim is true, the judge does not give a decision on the case (A: there being no need to) unless the plaintiff asks him to. But if the defendant denies the claim, then if the plaintiff has no proof, the defendant's word is accepted if he swears an oath to that effect. (O: This is when the claim does not involve blood (A: i.e. retaliation (def: o3) or indemnity (o4)). If it does, then if there is obscurity in the matter, the plaintiff's

٠٢٢.١٢ وَيَبْدَأُ بِالْخُصُومِ بِالْأَوَّلِ فَالأَوَّلِ فِي خُصُومَةٍ (واحدةٍ) فَقَطْ. فإِنِ اسْتَوَوْا (أَيِ الخصومُ في المَجيءِ بأنْ جَاءُوا معاً) أُقْرِعَ.

وَيُسَوِّي (القاضِي وجوباً) بَيْنَهُمَا في المجلسِ والإقبالِ وغيرِ ذلكَ إلَّا أَنْ يَكُونَ أحَدُهُمَا كافراً فيُقَدَّمُ المُسلمُ عليه في المجلسِ. ولا يُعَنِّفُ أحَدَهُمَا، ولا يُلَقِّنُهُ (حجةً).

٠٢٢.١٣ ولهُ أَنْ يَشْفَعَ (إلى خصمِه أي أَنْ يَطْلُبَ مِنَ الخَصمينِ أَنْ يَصطلِحا وهذا هو معنى شَفاعَةِ القاضِي وهي لا تكونُ إلَّا بعدَ ثُبوتِ الحقِّ وحينئذٍ يَنتفِي الميلُ إليه) وَيُؤَدِّيَ عَنْ أحَدِهِمَا ما لَزِمَهُ.

٠٢٢.١٤ وَيَنْظُرُ أوَّلَ شيءٍ (ح: عندَ تولِيهِ القضاءَ في مركزِ عملهِ الجديدِ) في المحبوسِينَ ثُمَّ في الأيتامِ ثُمَّ في اللقطةِ.

٠٢٣.٠   أُصولُ المُحاكماتِ

٠٢٣.١   إذَا ادَّعَى الخصمُ دَعْوَى غيرَ صحيحةٍ لَمْ يَسْمَعْها (القاضِي فلا يَترتبُ عليه سؤالُ الخصمِ الذي هو المدعِي عليه).

وإنْ كَانَتْ صحيحةً قَالَ للآخَرِ: ما تَقولُ؟ فإذا أَقَرَّ لَمْ يَحْكُمْ عليه إلَّا بطلَبِ المدعِي.

وإذَا أَنْكَرَ فإنْ لَمْ يَكُنْ للمُدَّعِي بينةٌ فالقولُ قولُ المُدَّعَى عليه بيمينِه (في غيرِ دعوى الدمِ أما في الدمِ حيث ظهرَ لوثٌ

word is accepted (N: provided fifty separate oaths are sworn by and distributed over all those entitled to take retaliation).) The judge does not have the defendant swear an oath unless the plaintiff requests it. If the defendant refuses to swear, then the judge has the plaintiff swear (A: that his claim is true), and when he does, he is entitled (O: to what he has claimed) (A: from the defendant). But if the plaintiff also refuses to swear, the judge dismisses both of them (O: from his presence). If the defendant is silent (O: not responding to the claim against him) then the judge should say, "Would that you would answer, for unless you do, I'll give the plaintiff the opportunity to swear an oath." If the defendant does not, then the plaintiff may swear an oath, and if he does, he is entitled to his claim.

o23.2 If the judge knows the truth of the claim (O: against the defendant), and it concerns one of the prescribed penalties of Allah Most High, meaning for fornication, theft, rebellion, or drinking, then he may not sentence the defendant on that basis alone (O: on the basis of his knowledge of one of the above crimes. It is related of Abu Bakr Siddiq (Allah be well pleased with him) that he said,

"Were I to see someone who deserved a prescribed legal penalty, I would not punish him unless two witnesses attested to his deserving it in front of me.")

But when the judge knows the truth about something other than prescribed legal penalties, he must judge accordingly (O: the necessary condition for which is that he plainly state that he knows, such as by saying, "I know what he claims against you to be true, and have judged you according to my knowledge").

o23.3 When the judge does not know the language of the litigants, then he refers to upright (def: o24.4) persons familiar with it, provided they are a number (O: two or more) sufficient to substantiate the claim (def: o24.7–10).

فالـقـول قـول الـمـدعي (ح: مع حلف خمسين يميناً توزع على أولياء الدم)).

ولا يُحَلِّفُهُ إلّا بطلب المدعي. فإن امْتَنَعَ مِنَ اليمين ردّها على المدّعي. فإنْ حَلَفَ اسْتَحَقَّ (الـمـدعي به). وإن امْتَنَعَ صَرَفَهُمَا (القاضي عن مجلسه). وإنْ سَكَتَ الـمـدعـى عليـه (عـن جواب الدعوى) فَلْيَقُلْ لهُ: إنْ أَجَبْتَ وإلّا رَدَدْتُ اليمينَ عليـه. فإن لمْ يُجِبْ رُدَّتِ اليمينُ على المدعي فيَحْلِفُ ويَسْتَحِقُّ.

o23.2 وإنْ كَانَ القاضي يَعْلَمُ وجوبَ الحقِّ (على المـدعى عليـه) فإنْ كَانَ في حدودِ اللهِ تعـالى وهـوَ الـزنـا والسـرقـةُ والمحاربـةُ والشـربُ لمْ يَحْكُمْ به (أي بعلمه بما ذكر وقـد روي عن أبي بكر الصديق رضي الله عنه أنه قال: «لو رأيت رجلاً عليه حد لم أحده حتى يشهد عندي شاهدان») وإنْ كَانَ غيـرَ ذلكَ حَكَمَ بهِ. (وشـرط الحكم به أن يصرح بمستنـده فيقـول: علمتُ أن له عليـك ما ادعـاه وحكمت عليك بعلمي).

o23.3 وإذا لمْ يَعْرِفْ لسانَ الخصمِ رَجَعَ فيه إلى عدل يَعْرِفُ بشرطِ أنْ يَكُونَ عدداً (اثنين فأكثر) يَثْبُتُ فيه ذلك الحقُّ.

o23.4 If a judge gives a decision on a case but then learns of an unequivocal text relating to it (O: from the Koran or *mutawatir* hadith (def: o22.1(d(II)))), a consensus of scholars, or an *a fortiori* analogy (o22.1(d(III))), that controverts his decision, then he reverses it..

o23.5 A court claim is not valid except from a plaintiff possessing full right to deal with his own property.

o23.6 It is not valid to litigate over something that is not determinately known (def: k2.1(e)), though some exceptions to this exist, such as claiming a bequest.

If the plaintiff is claiming a financial obligation (dayn), he must mention its type, amount, and description.

If he is claiming some particular article ('ayn) (O: such as a house), he must identify it. If he is unable to (O: as when the article is portable, and out of town), then he must describe it (O: with a description that would be valid for buying in advance (def: k9.2(d,g))).

o23.7 If a defendant denies a claim against him (A: and the plaintiff has no proof) then his denial is accepted (A: provided he swears on oath), as also when he says, "I owe him nothing."

o23.8 If the claim is for a particular article that is currently in the possession of one of the litigants, then the word of the person who *has* it is accepted when he swears an oath that it is his. If the article is in the possession of both litigants (O: together, and there is no proof as to whose it is; or when it is in the possession of neither, such as when a third party has it), then each swears an oath (O: that it does not belong to the other) and half the article is given to each of them.

o23.9 When another person owes one something, but denies it, then one may take it from his property without his leave (O: whether one has

o23.4 وإذا حَكَمَ بِشيءٍ فوَجَدَ النصَّ (من الكتـــاب أو السنـــة المتـــواتـــرة) أو الإجماعَ أوِ القياسَ الجليَّ بخلافِهِ نَقَضَهُ.

o23.5 ولا تَصِـــحُّ الـــدَّعَـوى إلّا مِنْ مطلقِ التصرفِ.

o23.6 ولا تَصِـحُّ دعـوَى المجهـولِ إلّا في مسـائلَ. منهَا الوصيةُ. فإنِ ادَّعَى ديناً ذَكَرَ الجنسَ والقـدرَ والصفةَ أوْ عيناً يُمْكِنُ تعيينُهـا (كأن كانت داراً) عَيَّنَهـا. وإلَّا (بأن تكـون العيـن منقـولة وهي غائبة عنِ البلدِ) ذَكَرَ صفتَهـا (المعتبرة في بابِ السلمِ).

o23.7 فإنْ أَنْكَـرَ المـدعَى عليه ما ادّعَـاهُ صَحَّ الجـوابُ. وكَـذا إنْ قال: لا يَسْتحقُّ عليَّ شيئاً.

o23.8 فإنْ كانَ المدّعَى بِهِ عيناً في يدِ أحـدِهمَـا فالقـولُ قولُـهُ (أي قول من هي بيده) بيمينِه. فإنْ كانَ في يدِهمَا (معاً ولا بينـة أو لم يكن في يدِ أحدٍ منهما بأن كان في يدِ ثالثٍ) حَلَفَـا (أي حلف كل واحد يميناً على نفي كونه للآخر) وجُعِلَ بينَهُمَا نصفينِ.

o23.9 ومَن لهُ حقٌّ على منكِـرٍ فلهُ أنْ يأخذَهُ مِنْ مالِـهِ بغيرِ إذنِهِ (سواء كانت له

proof of it or not). But if the person acknowledges that he owes it to one, one may not simply take it from him (O: because a debtor may pay back a debt from whatever part of his property he wishes).

بذلـك الحق بينــة أم لا). فإنْ كَانَ (من عليــه الحق) مقراً فلا (لأن للمـديون أن يؤديه من حيث شاء).

*

o24.0 WITNESSING AND TESTIFYING

o24.0 الشهادة

o24.1 It is a communal obligation (def: c3.2) to both witness (A: i.e. observe) legal events and to testify to having witnessed them. If there is only one person to do so, then it is personally obligatory upon him, in which case he may not accept payment for it, though if it is not personally obligatory, he may accept a fee.

o24.1 تحمُّلهَا وأداؤُهَا فرضُ كفايةٍ. فإنْ لمْ يكُنْ إلَّا هوَ تَعَيَّن عليـه. ولا يَجوزُ أنْ يَأْخذَ أجرةً حينئذٍ. فإنْ لمْ يَتَعَيَّنْ فلهُ الأخذُ.

o24.2 Legal testimony is only acceptable from a witness who:

(a) is free;

(b) is fully legally responsible (mukallaf, def: c8.1) (O: as testimony is not accepted from a child or insane person, even when the child's testimony regards injuries among children that occurred at play);

(c) is able to speak;

(d) is mentally awake;

(e) is religious (O: meaning upright (o24.4) (A: and Muslim), for Allah Most High says,

"Let those of rectitude among you testify" (Koran 65:2),

and unbelief is the vilest form of corruption, as goes without saying);

(f) and who is outwardly respectable (O: *respectability* (muru'a) meaning to have the positive traits which one's peers possess in one's par-

o24.2 ولا تُقْبَـلُ إلَّا مِنْ حرٍّ مكـلفٍ (فـلا تقبـل من صبي ولا مجنـون ولـو في الجـراحـات الـواقعـة بين الصبيـان في اللعب) ناطقٍ مستيقظٍ حسن الديانة (فإن المـراد به العدل لقوله تعالى: ﴿وَأَشْهِدُوا ذَوَيْ عَدْلٍ مِنْكُمْ﴾ والكفـر أشـد أنـواع الفسق فلا حاجـة إلى التصـريح به) ظاهر الـمـروءَةِ (والمـروءة هي التخلق بخلق أمثـاله في زمـانـه ومكـانـه وعبـارة شيخ

ticular time and place. Sheikh al-Islam (A: Zakariyya Ansari) says, "Respectability is refraining from conduct that is unseemly according to standards commonly acknowledged among those who observe the precepts and rules of the Sacred Law." It is according to *standards commonly acknowledged* (def: f4.5) because there are no absolute standards for it, but rather it varies with different persons, conditions, and places. Such things as eating and drinking (A: in the marketplace) or wearing nothing on one's head may vitiate it (A: though the latter is of no consequence in our times), as may a religious scholar's wearing a robe or cap in places where it is not customary for him to do so).

The testimony of an absentminded person (O: meaning someone who often makes mistakes and forgets) is not acceptable (O: because he is unreliable).

o24.3 Nor is testimony acceptable from someone who:

(1) has committed an *enormity* (O: meaning something severely threatened against in an unequivocal text from the Koran or hadith (dis: book p) (N: though if someone who commits such an act then repents (def: p77) and is felt to be sincere in this, he regains his legal uprightness and his testimony is accepted, provided he is tested after his repentance long enough to believe in its genuineness);

(2) persists in a lesser sin (O: because it then becomes an enormity, as opposed to when one does not persist therein. A *lesser sin* is one that has not been severely threatened against in an unequivocal text);

(3) or is without respectability (def: o24.2(f)), such as a street-sweeper, bathhouse attendant, and the like.

(A: A legally *corrupt* or *immoral* person (fasiq) is someone guilty of (1) or (2) above.)

الإسلام «والمروءة توقي الأدناس عرفاً ممن يراعي مناهج الشرع وآدابه» وهي توقي الأدناس عرفاً لأنها لا تنضبط بل تختلف باختلاف الأشخاص والأحوال والأماكن فيسقطها أكل وشرب وكشف رأس ولبس فقيه قباء أو قلنسوة بمكان لا عادة له أن يفعلها فيه).

ولا تُقْبَلُ مِنْ مُغَفَّل (وهو من كثر غلطه ونسيانه؛ لعدم الوثوق به).

o24.3 ولا مِنْ صاحب كبيرة (والكبيرة هي ما ورد فيها وعيد شديد بنص كتاب أو سنة) (ح: لكن إن تاب الفاسق توبة صادقة عادت إليه عدالته وتقبل شهادته بشرط اختباره بعد التوبة مدة يظن صدق توبته) ولا مِن مُدْمِن على صغيرة (لأنها صارت ملحقة بالكبيرة بخلاف ما إذا لم يصر عليها، والصغيرة هي التي لم يرد فيها وعيد شديد) ولا مِمَّنْ لا مروءةَ لَهُ ككنّاس وقيّم حمام ونحو ذلك.

o24.4   (A: Normal *uprightness* ('adala) for purposes other than giving testimony in court means that one avoids (1) and (2) above, while (3) concerns court testimony alone (N: i.e. *uprightness* for testimony in court means a person is none of the above).)

o24.5   The testimony of a blind person is accepted about events witnessed before he became blind, though not events witnessed after, unless they are public events that are discussed among people, or when someone says something the blind person hears (O: such as a divorce, for example), and he takes the speaker by the hand and conducts him to the judge and testifies as to what he has said.

o24.5 وتُقْبَلُ شهادةُ الأعمى فيما تَحَمَّلَ قبلَ العمى . ولا تُقْبَلُ فيما تَحَمَّلَ بعدَهُ إلَّا بالاستفاضةِ أوْ أنْ يُقَالَ في أذنِهِ شيءٌ (كطلاقٍ) فيُمْسِكُ القائلَ ويَحْمِلُهُ إلى القاضي ويَشْهَدُ بِمَا قَالَ هذا لَهُ .

o24.6   The testimony of any of the following is unacceptable:

(1)   a person testifying for his son (O: son's son, and on down) or his father (O: father's father, and on up);

(2)   a person who stands to benefit (O: by his own testimony);

(3)   a person who stands to avoid loss to himself through his testimony;

(4)   a person testifying about his enemy;

(5)   or a person testifying about his own act.

o24.6 ولا تُقْبَلُ شهادةُ الشخص لولدِهِ (وإن سفل) ووالدِهِ (وإن علا) ولا شهادةُ مَنْ يَجُرُّ لنفسِهِ (بشهادتهِ) نفعاً ولا مَنْ يَدْفَعُ عنْها ضرراً ولا شهادةُ العدوِّ على عدوِّهِ ولا شهادةُ الشخصِ على فعلِ نفسِهِ .

o24.7   The testimony of the following is legally acceptable when it concerns cases involving property, or transactions dealing with property, such as sales:

(1)   two men;

(2)   two women and a man;

(3)   or a male witness together with the oath of the plaintiff.

o24.7 فَيُقْبَلُ في المالِ وما يُقْصَدُ منهُ المالُ كالبيعِ رجلانِ أوْ رجلٌ وامرأتانِ أوْ شاهدٌ مَعَ يمينِ المدَّعِي .

o24.8   If testimony does not concern property, such as a marriage or prescribed legal penalties,

o24.8 ومــا لا يُقْصَـدُ منــهُ المـالُ كالنكــاح والحــدودِ لم يُقْبَلْ فيـهِ إلَّا

then only two male witnesses may testify (A: though the Hanafi school holds that two women and a man may testify for marriage).

شاهدانِ ذكرانِ.

o24.9 If testimony concerns fornication or sodomy, then it requires four male witnesses (O: who testify, in the case of fornication, that they have seen the offender insert the head of his penis into her vagina).

o24.9 ولا يُقْبَـلُ في الـزنَـا واللواطِ [وإتيــانِ البهيمـة] إلّا أربعـةُ ذكـورٍ (يشهـدون أنهم رأوه أدخـل حشفتـه في فرجها بالزنا).

o24.10 If testimony concerns things which men do not typically see (O: but women do), such as childbirth, then it is sufficient to have two male witnesses, a man and two women, or four women.

o24.10 ويُقْبَـلُ فيمَـا لا يَطَّلِعُ عليـهِ الـرجالُ (ويطلع عليه النساء) كالولادةِ رجلانِ أوْ رجلٌ وامرأتانِ أوْ أربعُ نسوةٍ.

*

o25.0   THE CALIPHATE

(n: This section has been added here by the translator because the caliphate is both obligatory in itself and the necessary precondition for hundreds of rulings (books k through o) established by Allah Most High to govern and guide Islamic community life. What follows has been edited from *al-Ahkam al-sultaniyya wa al-wilayat al-diniyya* by Imam Abul Hasan Mawardi, together with three principal commentaries on Imam Nawawi's *Minhaj al-talibin*, extracts from which are indicated by parentheses and the initial of the commentator, Ibn Hajar Haytami (H:), Muhammad Shirbini Khatib (K:), or 'Abd al-Hamid Sharwani (S:).)

o25.0   الخلافة

THE OBLIGATORY CHARACTER OF
THE CALIPHATE

وجوب الخلافة

o25.1 (Mawardi:) The reason the office of supreme leadership has been established in Sacred Law is to fulfill the caliphal successorship to prophethood in preserving the religion and managing this-worldly affairs. The investiture of someone from the Islamic Community (Umma) able to fulfill the duties of the caliphate is obligatory by scholarly consensus (def: b7), though scholars differ as to whether its obligatory character is established through reason or through Revealed Law. Some say that it is obligatory by human reason, because of the agreement of rational individuals to have a leader to prevent

o25.1 (المـاوردي:) الإمـامـة موضوعـة لخلافة النبوة في حراسة الدين وسيـاسة الدنيا. وعقدها لمن يقوم بها في الأمـة واجب بالإجمـاع [وإن شذ عنهم الأصم]. واختلف في وجوبها هل وجبت بالعقل أو بالشرع؟ فقالت طائفة وجبت بالعقل لمـا في طباع العقلاء من التسليم لزعيم يمنعهم من التظالم ويفصل بينهم في التنـازع والتخـاصم. ولـولا الـولاة لكـانـوا فوضى مهملين وهمج مضاعين. وقـالت طائفة أخرى: بل وجبت بالشرع

them from wronging one another and to come between them when conflict and arguments arise. Without authorities, there would be a chaos of neglected people and a disorderly mob. Others hold that it is obligatory not through reason, but rather through Sacred Law, for the caliph performs functions that human reason might not otherwise deem ethically imperative, and which are not entailed by reason alone, for reason merely requires that rational beings refrain from reciprocal oppression and strife, such that each individual conform with the demands of fairness in behaving towards others with justice and social cohesion, each evaluating their course with their own mind, not anyone else's, whereas Sacred Law stipulates that human concerns be consigned to the person religiously responsible for them. Allah Mighty and Majestic says,

"You who believe, obey Allah and obey the Prophet and those of authority among you" (Koran 4:59),

thereby obliging us to obey those in command, namely the leader with authority over us. Abu Hurayra relates that the Prophet (Allah bless him and give him peace) said,

"Leaders shall rule you after me, the godfearing of them ruling you with godfearingness and the profligate ruling you with wickedness. So listen to them and obey them in everything that is right; for if they do well, it will count for you and for them, and if they do badly, it will count for you and against them."

(al-Ahkam al-sultaniyya wa al-wilayat al-diniyya (y87), 5–6)

o25.2 (H: The caliphate is a communal obligation (def: c3.2) just as the judgeship is (S: because the Islamic community needs a ruler to uphold the religion, defend the sunna, succor the oppressed from oppressors, fulfill rights, and restore them to whom they belong).)

دون العقل لأن الإمام يقوم بأمور شرعية قد كان مجوزاً في العقل أن لا يرد التعبد بها، فلم يكن العقل موجباً لها، وإنما أوجب العقل أن يمنع كل واحد من نفسه من العقلاء عن التظالم والتقاطع، ويأخذ بمقتضى العدل في التناصف والتواصل، فيتدبر بعقله لا بعقل غيره. ولكن جاء الشرع بتفويض الأمور إلى وليه في الدين. قال الله عز وجل:

﴿يَا أَيُّهَا الَّذِينَ آمَنُوا أَطِيعُوا اللَّهَ وَأَطِيعُوا الرَّسُولَ وَأُولِي الْأَمْرِ مِنْكُمْ﴾ [سورة النساء: ٥٦]، ففرض علينا طاعة أولي الأمر فينا وهم الأئمة المتأمرين علينا و[روى هشام بن عروة عن أبي صالح] عن أبي هريرة أن رسول الله ﷺ قال:

«سيليكم بعدي ولاة فيليكم البر ببره ويليكم الفاجر بفجوره فاسمعوا لهم وأطيعوا في كل ما وافق الحق. فإن أحسنوا فلكم ولهم، وإن أساءوا فلكم وعليهم» [محرر من الأحكام السلطانية والولايات الدينية ٥ ـ ٦].

[ت: تنبيه: النص التالي منقول من منهاج الطالبين للإمام النووي، فصل شروط الإمام الأعظم. وأثبتنا في ثنايا المتن تعليقات من ثلاثة شروح مشهورة قد ميزناها من الأصل بوضعها بين القوسين وبكونها مشاراً إليها بحروف من أسماء أصحابها. فالتعليقات من كتاب تحفة المحتاج للإمام ابن حجر الهيتمي مشار إليها بالحرف «هـ»، والتعليقات للشيخ عبد الحميد الشرواني من حاشيته على التحفة قد أشرنا إليها بالحرف «ش» وأما التعليقات من كتاب مغني المحتاج للإمام محمد الشربيني الخطيب فمشار إليه بالحرف «ب». وبالله التوفيق].

o25.2 (هـ: الإمامة هي فرض كفاية كالقضاء (ش: إذ لا بد للأمة من إمام يقيم الدين وينصر السنة وينصف المظلوم من الظالم ويستوفي الحقوق ويضعها مواضعها)).

THE QUALIFICATIONS OF A CALIPH

شروط الإمام الأعظم

o25.3　(Nawawi:) Among the qualifications of the caliph are that he be:

(a) Muslim (H: so that he may see to the best interests of Islam and the Muslims (K: it being invalid to appoint a non-Muslim (kafir) to authority, even to rule non-Muslims.) (S: Qadi 'Iyad states that there is scholarly consensus (def: b7) that it is not legally valid to invest a non-Muslim as caliph, and that if a caliph becomes a non-Muslim (dis: o8.7) he is no longer caliph, as also when he does not maintain the prescribed prayers (A: meaning to both perform them himself and order Muslims to) and summon the people to them, and likewise (according to the majority of scholars) if he makes reprehensible innovations (bid'a, def: w29.3) (A: by imposing an innovation on people that is offensive or unlawful). If the caliph becomes a non-Muslim, alters the Sacred Law—(N: such alteration being of two types, one of which consists of his changing the Law by legislating something which contravenes it while believing in the validity of the provisions of the Sacred Law, this being an *injustice* that does not permit rebellion against him, while the other consists of imposing rules that contravene the provisions of the religion while believing in the validity of the rules he has imposed, this being unbelief (kufr) (A: it is questionable whether anyone would impose such rules without believing in their validity))—or imposes reprehensible innovations while in office, then he loses his authority and need no longer be obeyed, and it is obligatory for Muslims to rise against him if possible, remove him from office, and install an upright leader in his place. If only some are able, they are obliged to rise up and remove the unbeliever (A: whether they believe they will succeed or fail), though it is not obligatory to try to remove a leader who imposes reprehensible innovations unless they believe it possible. If they are certain that they are unable to (A: remove an innovator), they are not obliged to rise against him. Rather, a Muslim in such a case should emigrate from his country (N: if he can find a better one), fleeing with his religion (A: which is obligatory if he is prevented in

o25.3　(النووي:) شرطُ الإمام كونُه مسلماً (هـ: ليراعي مصلحة الإسلام والمسلمين) (ب: فلا تصح تولية كافر ولو على كافر) (ش: قال القاضي عياض: أجمع العلماء على أن الإمامة لا تنعقد لكافر وعلى أنه لو طرأ عليه الكفر انعزل، وكذا لو ترك إقامة الصلوات والدعاء إليها. قال: وكذلك عند جمهورهم البدعة (ح: المكفرة) [...]. فلو طرأ عليه كفر وتغيير الشرع (ح: وتغيير الشرع على نوعين: تغيير الشرع بمعنى أن يأمر بما يخالف به الشرع معتقداً صحة ما ورد في الشرع، وهذا ظلم لا يبيح الخروج عليه. وأما إذا أتى بأحكام تخالف أحكام الدين معتقداً أن هذه هي الأحكام الصحيحة، فهذا كفر) أو بدعة خرج عن حكم الولاية وسقطت طاعته ووجب على المسلمين القيام عليه وخلعه ونصب إمام عدل إن أمكنهم ذلك. فإن لم يقع ذلك إلا لطائفة، وجب عليهم القيام بخلع الكافر ولا يجب في المبتدع إلا إذا ظنوا القدرة عليه فإن تحققوا العجز لم يجب القيام. ويهاجر المسلم عن أرضه إلى غيرها ويفر بدينه (ح: إن وجد بلداً أفضل)) مكلفاً

his home country from openly performing acts of worship)));

(b) possessed of legal responsibility (def: c8.1) (K: so as to command the people, it being invalid for a child or insane person to lead);

(c) free (K: so that others may consider him competent and worthy of respect);

(d) male (K: to be able to devote himself full-time to the task, and to mix with men, the leadership of a woman being invalid because of the rigorously authenticated (sahih) hadith,

"A people that leaves its leadership to a woman will never succeed");

(e) of the Quraysh tribe (K: because of the (H: well-authenticated (hasan)) hadith related by Nasa'i,

"The Imams are of the Quraysh,"

a hadith adhered to by the Companions of the Prophet (Allah bless him and give him peace) and those after them, this qualification being obligatory when there is a member of Quraysh available who meets the other conditions) (H: though when there is not, then the next most eligible is a qualified member of the Kinana tribe, then of the Arabs, then of the non-Arabs);

(f) capable of expert legal reasoning (ijtihad) (H: as a judge must be (def: o22.1(d))) and with even greater need (K: so as to know the rulings of Sacred Law, teach people, and not need to seek the legal opinion of others concerning uprecedented events), scholarly consensus (def: b7) having been related concerning this condition, which is not contradicted by the statement of the Qadi (A: 'Iyad) that "an ignorant upright person is fitter than a knowledgeable corrupt one," since the former would be able to refer matters requiring expert legal reasoning to qualified scholars, and moreover the remark applies to when the available leaders are not capable of legal reasoning (S: while possessing the other qualifications for leadership));

(ب: لِيَلِي أَمْرَ النَّاسِ، فلا تصحّ إمامة صبي ومجنون [بـإجمـاع]) حراً (ب: لِيكمـل ويهـاب) ذكـراً (ب: لِيتفـرغ ويتمكن من مخـالطـة الرجال. فلا تصح ولايـة امرأة لمـا في الصحيح: «لن يفلح قوم ولـوا أمرهم امرأة») قُرَشِياً (ب: لخبر النسائي (هـ: إسناده جيد): «الأئمة من قريش» وبـه أخذ الصحابة فمن بعدهم. هذا عنـد تيسـر قرشي جامـع للشـروط (هـ: فإن فقـد قرشي جامـع للشـروط فكنـاني فرجـل من ولـد إسماعيل [صلى الله على نبينـا وعليه وسلم]. ومر في ذلك كلام في الـفيء والـكفـاءة] فعـجمي) مجتهـداً (هـ: كالقـاضي بل أولى (ب: لِيعـرف الأحكام ويعلم النـاس ولا يحتاج إلى استفتـاء غيره في الحوادث) بل حكي فيه الإجماع ولا ينافيه قول القاضي «عدل جاهـل أولـى من فاسق عالم» لأن الأول يمكنـه التفـويض للعلمـاء فيمـا يفتقـر للاجتهـاد لأن محله عنـد فقد المجتهدين (ش: المتصفين ببقية شروط الإمامة))

(g) courageous (K: meaning undaunted by danger, that he may stand alone, direct troops, and vanquish foes);

(h) possessed of discernment (H: in order to lead followers and see to their best interests, religious or this-worldly, *discernment* meaning at minimum to know the various capacities of people), sound hearing and eyesight, and the faculty of speech (K: so as to decisively arbitrate matters);

(i) (H: and be upright (def: o24.4) as a judge must be, and with even greater need. But it is valid, if forced to, to resort to the leadership of a corrupt person, which is why Ibn 'Abd al-Salam says, "If there are no upright leaders or rulers available, then the least corrupt is given precedence").

THE THREE WAYS A CALIPH MAY BE INVESTED WITH OFFICE

o25.4   The caliphate may legally be effected (K: through three means, the first of which is):

(1) by an oath of fealty (H: like the one sworn by the prophetic Companions to Abu Bakr (Allah be well pleased with them)) which, according to the soundest position, is (H: legally binding if it is) the oath of *those with discretionary power to enact or disolve a pact* (ahl al-hall wa al-'aqd) of the scholars, leaders, and notables able to attend (K: since the matter is accomplished through them, and all the people follow them. It is not a condition that all those with discretionary power to enact or dissolve a pact be present from every remote region, or that there be a particular number present, as the author's words seem to imply, but rather, if discretionary power to enact or dissolve a pact exists in a single individual who is obeyed, his oath of fealty is sufficient.) (H: As for an oath of fealty from common people without discretionary power to enact or dissolve a pact, it is of no consequence) and they (H: those pledging fealty) must possess the qualifications necessary to be a witness (K: such as uprightness and so forth

شجَاعـاً (ب: والشجاعة قوة القلب عند البأس، لينفرد بنفسه ويـدبر الجيوش ويقهر الأعـداء) ذا رأيٍ (هـ: يسوس به [ش: أي يحكم به)] الـرعيـة ويـدبر مصـالحهم الـدينيـة والـدنيـوية [قـال الهروي:] وأدناه أن يعرف أقدار الناس) وَسمـعٍ وبصـرٍ ونطقٍ (ب: ليتأتى منه فصلُ الأمورِ) (هـ: وعدلاً كالقاضي بل أولى. فلو اضطر لولاية فاسق جاز. ومن ثم قال ابن عبـد السـلام: لو تعـذرت العدالة في الأئمة والحكام قدمنا أقلهم فسقاً).

ثلاث طرق لانعقاد الإمامة

o25.4   وتَنْعَقِـدُ الإمـامـةُ (ب: بثلاثة طرق أحدها:)

(١) بالبَيْعَة (هـ: كما بايع الصحابة أبا بكـر رضي الله عنهم) والأصَـحُّ (هـ: أن المعتبـر هو ببيعـة أهل الحل والعقد من العلمـاء والـرؤسـاء ووجـوه الناس الذين يتيسـر اجتمـاعهم (ب: لأن الأمر ينتظم بهم ويتبعهم سائـر النـاس. ولا يشترط اتفـاق أهل الحل والعقد من سائر الأقطار البعيدة ولا يشترط عدد كما يوهمه كلامه، بل لو تعلق الحل والعقـد بواحـد مطاع كفت بيعتـه .) (هـ: وأمـا بيعـة غير أهل الحل والعقد من العـوام فلا عبـرة بها) وَشَـرْطُهُمْ (هـ: أي المتبـايعين) صِفَـةُ الشهود (ب: من العدالة وغيرها) [محرّر

(def: o24.2)) (*Mughni al-muhtaj ila ma'rifa ma'ani alfaz al-Minhaj* (y73), 4.129–31, and *Hawashi al-Shaykh 'Abd al-Hamid al-Sharwani wa al-Shaykh Ahmad ibn Qasim al-'Abbadi 'ala Tuhfa al-muhtaj bi sharh al-Minhaj* (y2), 9.74–76).

(Mawardi:) When those with power to enact or dissolve a pact meet to select the caliph, they examine the state of the available qualified candidates, giving precedence to the best of them and most fully qualified, whose leadership the public will readily accept and whose investiture people will not hesitate to recognise. When there is only one person whom the examiners' reasoning leads them to select, they offer him the position. If he accepts, they swear an oath of fealty to him and the supreme leadership is thereby invested in him, the entire Islamic Community (Umma) being compelled to acknowledge fealty to him and submit in obedience to him. But if he refuses the caliphal office, not responding to their offer, he is not forced to comply—as investiture comes of acceptance and free choice, not compulsion and constraint—and they turn to another qualified candidate (*al-Ahkam al-sultaniyya wa al-wilayat al-diniyya* (y87), 7–8);

(2) (Nawawi:) and (H: the second means (K: through which it may be effected is)) by the caliph appointing a successor (H: meaning someone after him, even if it be his descendant or ancestor, for Abu Bakr appointed 'Umar (Allah be well pleased with them) as his successor, and scholarly consensus (def: b7) was effected in recognizing its legal validity. This type of investiture consists of the caliph appointing a successor while still alive, to succeed him after death. Though actually his successor during his life, the successor's disposal of affairs is suspended until the caliph dies).

If the caliph appoints a group to select a successor from among themselves, it is as if he had appointed a successor (K: though the successor is not yet identified) (H: resembling an appointment in it being legally binding and obligatory to accept the outcome of their choice) and they choose one of their number (K: after the caliph's death, investing the person they select with the caliphate) (H: because 'Umar appointed a committee of six to choose his successor from among themselves: 'Ali, 'Uthman, Zubayr, 'Abd al-Rahman ibn 'Awf, Sa'd ibn Abi Waqqas, and Talha, and after

من مغني المحتـاج إلى معـرفـة ألفـاظ المنهاج : ٤/ ١٢٩ ـ ١٣١، ومن حواشي الشيخ عبـد الحميـد الشـرواني والشيخ أحمـد بن قاسم العبـادي على تحفة المحتاج بشرح المنهاج : ٩/ ٧٤ ـ [٧٦]. (المـاوردي :) فإذا اجتمع أهـل العقـد والحل للاختيـار وتصفحـوا أحـوال أهل الإمـامة المـوجودة فيهم شروطها فقدموا للبيعة منهم أكثـرهم فضـلاً وأكملهم شروطـاً ومن يسرع الناس إلى طاعته ولا يتـوقفـون عن بيعته. فإذا تعين لهم من أداهم الاجتهـاد إلى اختياره عرضـوهـا عليـه . فإن أجـاب إليهـا بايعـوه عليهـا وانعقدت ببيعتيه له الإمـامة فلزم كافة الأمـة الدخول في بيعته والانقياد لطاعته. وإن امتنـع من الإمـامة ولم يُجِبْ إليها لم يجبر عليها لأنها عقد مراضاة واختيار ولا يدخله إكراه ولا إجبار، وعدل عنه إلى من سواه من مستحقيهـا [نقـل من الأحكـام السلطانية والولايات الدينية : ٧ ـ ٨].

(٢) وَهـ: ثانيهـا (ب: ينعقـد)) بآسْتِخْلافِ الإمام (هـ: واحداً بعده ولو فرعه أو أصله [ويعبر عنه بعهده إليه] كما عهـد أبـو بكر إلى عمر رضي الله عنهما، وانعقد الإجمـاع على الاعتداد بذلك. وصورته أن يعقـد له الخـلافة في حياته ليكون هو الخليفة بعـده، فهو وإن كان خليفته في حياته لكن تصرفه موقوف على موتـه). فَلَوْ جَعَـلَ (هـ: الإمـام) الأمْـرَ شورى بين جمعٍ فكَاسْتِخْلافٍ (هـ: في الاعتـداد به ووجـوب العمـل بقضيتـه) (ب: إلا أن المستخلف غيـر معين) فَيَرْضَـوْنَ أَحَدَهُمْ (ب: بعد موت الإمام فيعينونه للخلافة) (هـ: لأن عمر جعل الأمـر شورى بين ستـة: علي وعثمـان والـزبير وعبد الرحمن بن عوف وسعد بن أبي وقاص وطلحة، فاتفقوا بعد موته على

his death they agreed upon 'Uthman, (Allah be well pleased with them));

(3) and (H: the third means is) through seizure of power by an individual possessing the qualifications of a caliph (H: meaning by force, since the interests of the whole might be realized through such a takeover, this being if the caliph has died, or has himself obtained office through seizure of power, i.e. when he lacks some of the necessary qualifications.) (S: As for when the office is wrested from a living caliph, then if he himself became caliph through seizure of power, the caliphate of his deposer is legally valid. But if he became caliph through an oath of fealty (def: o25.4(1)) or having been appointed as the previous caliph's successor (def: o25.4(2)), then the deposer's caliphate is not legally valid). A takeover is also legally valid, according to the soundest position, by someone lacking moral rectitude (dis: o25.3(i)) or knowledge of Sacred Law (o25.3(f)) (K: meaning the caliphate of a person lacking either condition is legally valid when the other conditions exist) (H: as is the takeover of someone lacking other qualifications, even if he does not possess any of them (S: besides Islam, for if a non-Muslim seizes the caliphate, it is not legally binding, and so too, according to most scholars, with someone who makes reprehensible innovations, as previously mentioned (dis: o25.3(a))). The caliphate of someone who seizes power is considered valid, even though his act of usurpation is disobedience, in view of the danger from the anarchy and strife that would otherwise ensue).

THE OBLIGATORY CHARACTER OF OBEDIENCE TO THE CALIPH

o25.5   (K: It is obligatory to obey the commands and interdictions of the caliph (N: or his representative (def: o25.7–10)) in everything that is lawful (A: meaning it is obligatory to obey him in everything that is not unlawful, offensive, or merely in his own personal interests), even if he is unjust, because of the hadith,

"Hear and obey, even if the ruler placed over

عثمان رضي الله عنهم).

(٣) و(هـ: ثالثها) بِاسْتِيلَاءِ جامعِ الشروط (هـ: بالشوكة لانتظام الشمل به. هذا إن مات الإمام أو كان متغلباً، أي ولم يجمع الشروط). (ش: أما الاستيلاء على الحي فإن كان الحي متغلباً انعقدت إمامة المتغلب عليه، وإن كان إماماً ببيعة أو عهد لم تنعقد إمامة المتغلب عليه) وكَذَا فاسقٌ جاهلٌ (ب: تنعقد إمامة كل منهما مع وجود بقية الشروط (هـ: وغيرهما وإن اختلت فيه الشروط كلها (ش: أي إلا الإسلام. أما لو استولى كافر على الإمامة فلا تنعقد وتقدم [عن شرح صحيح مسلم] أن المبتدع كالكافر هنا عند الجمهور)) في الأصَحّ (هـ: وإن عصى بما فعل، حذراً من تشتت الأمر وثوران الفتن).

وجوب طاعة الإمام

o25.5   (ب: تجب طاعة الإمام (ح: ونائبه) وإن كان جائزاً فيما يجوز من أمره ونهيه لخبر: «اسمعوا وأطيعوا وإن أُمّر

you is an Ethiopian slave with amputated extremities,"

and because the purpose of his authority is Islamic unity, which could not be realized if obeying him were not obligatory. It is also obligatory for him to give sincere counsel to those under him to the extent that it is possible.)

عليكم عبد حبشي مجدع الأطراف» ولأن المقصود من نصبه اتحاد الكلمة ، ولا يحصل ذلك إلا بوجوب الطاعة، وتجب نصيحته للرعية بحسب قدرته) .

THE INVALIDITY OF A PLURALITY OF CALIPHS

عدم صحة عقد الإمامة لإثنين فأكثر

o25.6 (K: It is not permissible for two or more individuals to be invested with the caliphate (H: at one time), even when they are in different regions, or remote from one another, because of the disunity of purpose and political dissolution it entails. If two are simultaneously invested as caliph, neither's caliphate is valid. If invested serially, the caliphate of the first of them is legally valid and the second is disciplined (def: o17) for committing an unlawful act, together with those who swear fealty to him, if they are aware of the first's investiture as caliph) (*Mughni al-muhtaj ila ma'rifa ma'ani alfaz al-Minhaj* (y73), 4.132, and *Hawashi al-Shaykh 'Abd al-Hamid al-Sharwani wa al-Shaykh Ahmad ibn Qasim al-'Abbadi 'ala Tuhfa al-muhtaj bi sharh al-Minhaj* (y2), 9.77–78).

o25.6 (ب) ولا يجوز عقدها لإمامين (هـ: في وقت واحد) فأكثر ولو بأقاليم ولو تباعدت لما في ذلك من اختلال الرأي وتفرق الشمل . فإن عقدت لاثنين معاً بطلتا ، أو مرتباً انعقدت للسابق [كما في النكاح على امرأة] ويعزر الثاني ومبايعوه إن علموا ببيعة السابق لارتكابهم محرماً [محرّر من مغني المحتاج إلى معرفة معاني ألفاظ المنهاج : ٤ / ١٣٢ ؛ ومن حواشي الشيخ عبد الحميد الشرواني والشيخ أحمد بن قاسم العبادي على تحفة المحتاج بشرح المنهاج : ٩ / ٧٧ ـ ٧٨] .

DELEGATING AUTHORITY TO THOSE UNDER THE CALIPH

تقليد الوزارة

o25.7 (Mawardi:) The authority delegated to a minister of state may be of two kinds, full or limitary.

(1) *Full* ministerial authority is when the caliph appoints as minister an individual who is entrusted with independently managing matters through his own judgement and implementing them according to his own personal reasoning (ijtihad).
Appointing such an individual is not legally invalid, for Allah Most High says, quoting His prophet Moses (Allah bless him and give him peace),

o25.7 (الماوردي:) الوزارة على ضربين : وزارة تفويض ووزارة تنفيذ .

(١) فأما وزارة التفويض فهو أن يستوزر الإمام من يفوض إليه تدبير الأمور برأيه وإمضاءها على اجتهاده . وليس يمتنع جواز هذه الوزارة . قال الله تعالى حكاية عن نبيه موسى عليه الصلاة والسلام :

"And appoint for me a minister from my family, Aaron my brother; fortify me through him and have him share my task" (Koran 20:29–32),

and if valid respecting the task of prophethood, it is valid *a fortiori* regarding the function of the caliphate. Another reason is that the direction of the Islamic Community (Umma), which is the caliph's duty, cannot be fully conducted alone without delegating responsibility; for him to appoint a minister to participate therein is sounder than attempting to manage everything himself, a minister to help keep him from following mere personal caprice, that he may thus be further from error and safer from mistakes.

The conditions necessary for such a minister are the same as those for a caliph, excepting lineage alone (dis: o25.3(e)), for the minister must implement his views and execute his judgements, and must accordingly be capable of expert legal reasoning (ijtihad). He must also possess an additional qualification to those required for the caliphate, namely, by being specially qualified to perform the function he is appointed to.

(2) *Limitary* ministerial authority is a lesser responsibility and has fewer conditions, since the role of personal judgement therein is confined to the views of the caliph and their implementation, this minister being, as it were, an intermediary between the caliph, his subjects, and their appointed rulers; delivering orders, performing directives, implementing judgements, informing of official appointments, mustering armies, and informing the caliph in turn of important events, that the minister may deal with them as the caliph orders. He is an assistant in carrying out matters and is not appointed to command them or have authority over them. Such a ministry does not require an appointment but only the caliph's permission.

o25.8   When the caliph appoints a ruler over a region or city, the ruler's authority may be of two kinds, general or specific. The general may in turn be of two types, authority in view of merit, which is invested voluntarily; and authority in view of siezure of power, invested out of necessity.

﴿وَاجْعَل لِّي وَزِيراً مِنْ أَهْلِي هَارُونَ أَخِي اشْدُدْ بِهِ أَزْرِي وَأَشْرِكْهُ فِي أَمْرِي﴾ [سورة طه : ٢٩] .

فإذا جاز ذلك في النبوة كان في الإمامة أجوز ، ولأن ما وُكل للإمام من تدبير الأمة لا يقدر على مباشرة جميعه إلا باستنابة ، ونيابة الوزير المشارك له في تدبير أصح في تنفيذ الأمور من تفرده بها ، ليستظهر به على نفسه ، وبها يكون أبعد من الزلل وأمنع من الخلل .

ويعتبر في تقليد هذه الوزارة شروط الإمامة إلا النسب وحده لأنه ممضي الآراء ومنفذ الاجتهاد فاقتضى أن يكون على صفات المجتهدين . ويُحتاج فيها إلى شرط زائد على شروط الإمامة وهو أن يكون من أهل الكفاية فيما وكل إليه [. . .] .

(٢) وأما وزارة التنفيذ فحكمها أضعف وشروطها أقل ، لأن النظر فيها مقصور على رأي الإمام وتدبيره ، وهذا الوزير وسط بينه وبين الرعايا والولاة يؤدي عنه ما أمر وينفذ عنه ما ذكر ويمضي ما حكم ويخبر بتقليد الولاة وتجهيز الجيوش ويعرض عليه ما ورد من مهم وتجدد من حدث ملم ليعمل فيه ما يؤمر به . فهو معين في تنفيذ الأمور وليس بوال عليها ولا متقلداً لها [. . .] وليس تفتقر هذه الوزارة إلى تقليد ، وإنما يراعى فيها مجرد الإذن .

o25.8   وإذا قلد الخليفة أميراً على إقليم أو بلد كانت إمارته على ضربين عامة وخاصة . فأما العامة فعلى ضربين : إمارة استكفاء بعقد عن اختيار ، وإمارة استيلاء بعقد عن اضطرار .

o25.9 *Authority in view of merit* is that which is freely invested by the caliph through his own choice, and entails delegating a given limitary function and the use of judgement within a range of familiar alternatives. This investiture consists of the caliph appointing an individual to independently govern a city or region with authority over all its inhabitants and discretion in familiar affairs for all matters of government, including seven functions:

(1) raising and deploying armies on the frontiers and fixing their salaries, if the caliph has not already done so;

(2) reviewing laws and appointing judges and magistrates;

(3) collecting the annual rate (khiraj) from those allowed to remain on land taken by Islamic conquests, gathering zakat from those obliged to pay, appointing workers to handle it, and distributing it to eligible recipients;

(4) protecting the religion and the sacrosanct, preserving the religion from alteration and substitution;

(5) enforcing the prescribed legal meaures connected with the rights of Allah and men;

(6) leading Muslims at group and Friday prayers, whether personally or by representative;

(7) facilitating travel to the hajj for both pilgrims from the region itself and those passing through from elsewhere, that they may proceed to the pilgrimage with all necessary help;

(8) and if the area has a border adjacent to enemy lands, an eighth duty arises, namely to undertake jihad against enemies, dividing the spoils of battle among combatants, and setting aside a fifth (def: o10.3) for deserving recipients.

o25.10 *Authority in view of seizure of power*, invested out of necessity, is when a leader forcibly takes power in an area over which the caliph sub-

o25.9 فإمارة الاستكفاء التي تنعقد عن اختياره فتشتمل على عمل محدود ونظر معهود، والتقليد فيها أن يفوض إليه الخليفة إمارة بلد أو إقليم ولايةً على جميع أهله ونظراً في المعهود من سائر أعماله [فيصير عام النظر فيما كان محدوداً من عمل ومعهوداً من نظر] فيشتمل نظره فيه على سبعة أمور: أحدها النظر في تدبير الجيوش وترتيبهم في النواحي وتقدير أرزاقهم إلا أن يكون الخليفة قدرها عليهم . . . والثاني النظر في الأحكام وتقليد القضاة والحكام. والثالث جباية الخراج وقبض الصدقات وتقليد العمال فيهما وتفريق ما استُحِقَ منها . والرابع حماية الدين والذب عن الحريم ومراعاة الدين من تغيير أو تبديل . والخامس إقامة الحدود في حق الله وحقوق الآدميين. والسادس الإمامة في الجمع والجماعات حتى يؤم بها أو يستخلف عليها . والسابع تسيير الحجيج من عمله ومن سلكه من غير أهله حتى يتوجهوا معانين عليه . فإن كان هذا الإقليم ثغراً متاخماً للعدو اقترن بها ثامن وهو جهاد من يليه من الأعداء وقسم غنائمهم في المقاتلة وأخذ خمسها لأهل الخمس [. . .] .

o25.10 وأما إمارة الاستيلاء التي تنعقد عن اضطرار فهي أن يستولي الأمير بالقوة على بلاد يقلده الخليفة إمارتها ويفوض

sequently confirms his authority and invests him with its management and rule. Such a leader attains political authority and management by takeover, while the caliph, by giving him authorization, is enabled to enforce the rules of the religion so that the matter may be brought from invalidity to validity and from unlawfulness to legitimacy. And if this process is beyond what is normally recognized as true investiture of authority with its conditions and rules, it yet preserves the ordinances of the Sacred Law and rules of the religion that may not be left vitiated and compromised (*al-Ahkam al-sultaniyya wa al-wilayat al-diniyya* (y87), 25–39).

*

o26.0   THE CONCLUSION OF 'UMDAT AL-SALIK

o26.1   And Allah Most High and Glorious knows best what is correct (O: meaning that He knows best what actually corresponds to the truth, in word and deed, the author thereby denying the claim to know better. There is scholarly disagreement as to whether the truth (A: about the rule of Allah for a particular ruling) is really one or multiple (A: many scholars holding that *all* positions of qualified *mujtahid*s on a question are correct). In fact, it is one, the Imam who is right about it (Allah be well pleased with them all) receiving two rewards, one for his attempt and one for being correct, while the one who is not is mistaken, receiving a reward for his effort and being excused for his mistake. All of which applies to particular rulings of Sacred Law (furu'), as opposed to fundamentals of Islamic faith (usul, def: books u and v), in which the person wrong about them is guilty of serious sin, as is anyone who contradicts the tenets of the orthodox Sunni Community (Ahl al-Sunna wa al-Jama'a)).

*

إليـه تدبيـرهـا وسياستهـا، فيكون الأمير باستيـلائـه مستبـداً بالسيـاسـة والتـدبير، والخليفـة بإذنـه منفـذاً لأحكـام الـدين ليـخـرج من الفسـاد إلى الصحـة ومن الحظر إلى الإباحة. وهذا وإن خرج عن عرف التـقليـد المـطـلـق في شروطـه وأحكـامه ففيه من حفظ القوانين الشرعية وحراسـة الأحكـام الدينية ما لا يجوز أن يتـرك مختـلًا مدخـولًا . . . [محرر من الأحكام السلطانية والولايات الدينية ٢٥ ـ ٣٩].

o26.0   خاتمـة كتـاب عمدة السالك وعدة الناسك

o26.1   واللهُ سبحـانـهُ وتعـالى أعلم بالصـواب (أي بما يوافق الحق في الواقع من القـول والفعل. وكان المصنف قصد بذلك التبـري من دعوى الأعلمية. وهل الحق في الـواقـع واحـد أو متعـدد؟ فيـه خلاف. والحق أنه واحـد فمن وافقه من الأئمة رضي الله عنهم فهو المصيب وله أجـران أجـر على اجتهـاده وأجـر على إصـابتـه. ومن لم يوافقه فهو مخطىء وله أجر على اجتهـاده وهـو معذور في خطئه وهـذا في الفـروع، وأمـا في الأصـول فالمخطىء آثم كـ [المعتـزلـة و] كل من خالف أهل السنة والجماعة).

*

BOOK P

ENORMITIES

كتاب الكبائر

CONTENTS:

The Engulfing Oath   p23.0
The Inveterate Liar   p24.0
Suicide   p25.0
The Bad Judge   p26.0
Permitting One's Wife to Fornicate   p27.0
Masculine Women and Effeminate Men   p28.0
Marrying Solely to Return to the Previous Husband   p29.0
Eating Unslaughtered Meat, Blood, or Pork   p30.0
Not Freeing Oneself of All Traces of Urine   p31.0
Collecting Taxes   p32.0
      Those Who Accept Tax Moneys   p32.3
Showing Off in Good Works   p33.0
Breach of Faith   p34.0
Learning Sacred Knowledge for the Sake of This World   p35.0
Reminding Recipients of One's Charity to Them   p36.0
Disbelieving in Destiny (Qadr)   p37.0
Listening to People's Private Conversations   p38.0
Cursing Others   p39.0
Leaving One's Leader   p40.0
Believing in Fortune-Tellers or Astrologers   p41.0
A Wife's Rebelling Against Her Husband   p42.0
      Conditions for Permissibility of Leaving Home   p42.2(4)
Severing Ties of Kinship   p43.0
      Meaning of *Maintaining the Bonds of Kinship* p43.0(A:)
Making Pictures   p44.0
The Talebearer Who Stirs Up Enmity Between People   p45.0
Loudly Lamenting the Dead   p46.0
Attacking Another's Ancestry   p47.0
Excesses Against Others   p48.0
Armed Insurrection and Considering Muslims Unbelievers   p49.0
Hurting or Reviling Muslims   p50.0
Harming the Friends (Awliya') of Allah Most High   p51.0
Dragging the Hem of One's Garment out of Conceit   p52.0
Men Wearing Silk or Gold   p53.0
Slaughtering in Other Than Allah's Name   p54.0
Surreptitiously Changing Property-Line Markers   p55.0
Disparaging the Prophetic Companions (Sahaba)   p56.0
Disparaging the Medinan Helpers (Ansar)   p57.0
Inaugurating a Reprehensible Innovation   (Bid'a)   p58.0
Women Wearing False Hair and the Like   p59.0
Pointing a Blade at One's Brother   p60.0
Falsely Claiming Someone Is One's Father   p61.0
Believing That Something Portends Bad Luck   p62.0
Drinking from Gold or Silver Vessels   p63.0
Arguing, Picking Apart Another's Words, and Quarrelling   p64.0
Stinting When Weighing or Measuring Out Goods   p65.0
Feeling Secure from Allah's Devising   p66.0
Despairing of the Mercy of Allah and Loss of Hope   p67.0
Ingratitude to Someone Who Does One a Kindness   p68.0

p0.0   THE AUTHOR'S INTRODUCTION   مقــدمــة المـــؤلف   p0.0
(n: The first of the books translated as appendices to our basic text *'Umdat al-salik* concerns the *enormities* alluded to above in the context of court testimony

(dis: o24.3), and has been edited from the *Kitab al-kaba'ir* [Book of enormities] of Imam Dhahabi, who defines an *enormity* as any sin entailing either a threat of punishment in the hereafter explicitly mentioned by the Koran or hadith, a prescribed legal penalty (hadd), or being accursed by Allah or His messenger (Allah bless him and give him peace).)

p0.1   In the name of Allah, Most Merciful and Compassionate.

O Lord, facilitate and help. The sheikh, Imam, and hadith master (hafiz, def: w48.2(end)) Shams al-Din Muhammad ibn Ahmad ibn ‘Uthman Dhahabi (may Allah forgive him) said: Praise be to Allah for true faith in Him, His books, messengers, angels, and decrees. Allah bless our prophet Muhammad, his folk, and those who support him, with a lasting blessing that will grant us the Abode of Permanence near to Him.

This is a book useful in knowing the enormities, both in general and in detail. May Allah by His mercy enable us to avoid them. Allah Most High says,

"If you avoid the enormities of what you have been forbidden, We shall acquit you of your wrongdoings and admit you to a generous place to enter" (Koran 4:31).

In this text, Allah Most High promises whoever avoids the enormities to admit him to paradise. The Prophet (Allah bless him and give him peace) said,

"The five prescribed prayers, and from one Friday prayer to another entail forgiveness for what is between them as long as you do not commit the enormities."

So we are obliged to learn what they are, that the Muslim may avoid them.

*

p1.0   ASCRIBING ASSOCIATES TO ALLAH MOST HIGH (SHIRK)

p1.1   *Ascribing associates to Allah Most High* means to hold that Allah has an equal, whereas

بسم الله الرحمن الرحيم . p0.1
ربِّ يسر وأعن . قال الشيخ الإمام الحافظ شمس الـدين محمد بن أحمد بن عثمان الذهبي غفر الله له :
الحمـد لله على الإيمـان به وبكتبه ورسله ومـلائكتـه وأقـداره ، وصلى الله على نبينا محمد وآله وأنصاره صلاةً دائمة تحلنا دار القرار في جواره .
هذا كتـاب نافـع في معـرفة الكبـائر إجمالاً وتفصيلاً رزقنا الله اجتنابها برحمته .
قال الله تعـالى : ﴿إِنْ تَجْتَنِبُوا كَبَائِرَ مَا تُنْهَوْنَ عَنْهُ نُكَفِّرْ عَنْكُمْ سَيِّئَاتِكُمْ وَنُدْخِلْكُمْ مُدْخَـلاً كَرِيمًا﴾ [النسـاء : ٣١]. فقـد تكفـل الله تعالى بهذا النص لمن اجتنب الكبائر بأن يدخله الجنة .
وقال النبي ﷺ :
«الـصلوات الخمس ، والجمعـة إلى الـجمعـة كفـارة لمـا بينهن ما لم تغشَ الكبائر» [رواه مسلم].
فتعين علينا الفحص عن الكبائر ما هي لكي يجتنبها المسلم .

الشرك بالله تعالى   p1.0

وهـو أن تجعـل لله نداً وهـو   p1.1

He has created you, and to worship another with Him, whether it be a stone, human, sun, moon, prophet, sheikh, jinn, star, angel, or other.

خلقك، وتعبد معه غيره من حجر أو بشر أو شمس أو قمر، أو نبي أو شيخ أو جني أو نجم أو ملك أو غير ذلك.

p1.2   Allah Most High says:

p1.2   قال الله تعالى:

(1) "Allah does not forgive that any should be associated with Him, but forgives what is other than that to whomever He wills" (Koran 4:48).

﴿إِنَّ اللَّهَ لَا يَغْفِرُ أَنْ يُشْرَكَ بِهِ وَيَغْفِرُ مَا دُونَ ذَلِكَ لِمَنْ يَشَاءُ﴾ [النساء: ٤٧].

(2) "Surely, whoever ascribes associates to Allah, Allah has forbidden him paradise, and his refuge is hell" (Koran 5:72).

وقال: ﴿إِنَّـهُ مَنْ يُشْرِكْ بِاللَّهِ فَقَدْ حَرَّمَ اللَّهُ عَلَيْهِ الْجَنَّةَ وَمَأْوَاهُ النَّارُ﴾ [المائدة: ٧٢].

(3) "Of a certainty, worshipping others with Allah is a tremendous injustice" (Koran 31:13).

وقال: ﴿إِنَّ الشِّـرْكَ لَظُلْمٌ عَظِيمٌ﴾ [لقمان: ١٣].

p1.3   The Koranic verses concerning this are very numerous, it being absolutely certain that whoever ascribes associates to Allah and dies in such a state is one of hell's inhabitants, just as whoever believes in Allah and dies as a believer is one of the inhabitants of paradise, even if he should be punished first.

p1.3   والآيات في ذلك كثيرة فمن أشرك بالله ثم مات مشركاً فهو من أصحاب النار قطعاً، كما أن من آمن بالله ومات مؤمناً فهو من أصحاب الجنة وإن عذب.

*

p2.0   KILLING A HUMAN BEING

p2.0   قتل النفس

p2.1   Allah Most High says:

p2.1   قال الله تعالى: ﴿وَمَنْ يَقْتُلْ

(1) "Whoever intentionally kills a believer, his recompense shall be hell, abiding therein forever, and Allah shall be wroth with him, damn him, and ready for him a painful torment" (Koran 4:93).

مُؤْمِناً مُتَعَمِّداً فَجَزَاؤُهُ جَهَنَّمُ خَالِداً فِيهَا وَغَضِبَ اللَّهُ عَلَيْهِ وَلَعَنَهُ وَأَعَدَّ لَهُ عَذَاباً عَظِيماً﴾ [النساء: ٩٣].

(2) "Whoever takes a life other than to retaliate for a killing or for corruption in the land is as if he had slain all mankind" (Koran 5:32).

وقال تعالى: ﴿مَنْ قَتَلَ نَفْساً بِغَيْرِ نَفْسٍ أَوْ فَسَادٍ فِي الْأَرْضِ فَكَأَنَّمَا قَتَلَ النَّاسَ جَمِيعاً﴾ [المائدة: ٣٢].

p2.2   The Prophet (Allah bless him and give him peace) said:

p2.2   وقال عليه الصلاة والسلام:

"When two Muslims meet with drawn swords, both the slayer and the slain go to hell." Someone said, "O Messenger of Allah, that is for the slayer. But why the slain?" And he replied, "Because he meant to kill the other."

«إذا التقى المسلمانِ بسيفَيْهما فالقاتـلُ والمقتول في النار. قيل يا رسولَ اللهِ هذا للقاتـلِ فمـا بال المقتـول؟ قال: إنه كان حريصاً على قتل صاحبه» [رواه البخاري].

*

p3.0   SORCERY

السحر   p3.0

p3.1   Sorcery is an enormity because the sorcerer must necessarily disbelieve (dis: x136), and the accursed Devil has no other motive for teaching a person witchcraft than that he might thereby ascribe associates to Allah (shirk).

p3.1   لأن الساحـر لا بد وأن يكفـر، ومـا للشيطان الملعون غرض في تعليمه الإنسان السحر إلا ليشرك به.

p3.2   Allah Most High says:

(1) "A sorcerer will never prosper wherever he goes" (Koran 20:69).

(2) "… But the devils disbelieved, teaching people sorcery" (Koran 2:102).

And Allah Most High says, concerning Harut and Marut,

(3) "The two do not teach anyone before telling them, 'We are only a temptation, so be not unbelievers,' but they learn from these two that which they use to separate a man from his wife" (Koran 2:102).

p3.2   قال الله تعالى:
﴿وَلاَ يُفْلِحُ السَّاحِـرُ حَيْثُ أَتَى﴾ [طه: ٦٩].
وقـال الله تعـالى: ﴿وَلَكِنَّ الشَّيَاطِينَ كَفَرُوا يُعَلِّمُونَ النَّاسَ السِّحْرَ﴾ [البقرة: ١٠٢].
وقال الله تعالى عن هاروت وماروت:
﴿وَمَا يُعَلِّمَانِ مِنْ أَحَدٍ حَتَّى يَقُـولاَ إِنَّمَا نَحْنُ فِتْنَةٌ فَلاَ تَكْفُـرْ فَيَتَعَلَّمُـونَ مِنْهُمَا مَا يُفَـرِّقُـونَ بِهِ بَيْنَ المَـرْءِ وَزَوْجِهِ . . .﴾ [البقرة: ١٠٢].

*

p4.0   NOT PERFORMING THE PRAYER

ترك الصلاة   p4.0

p4.1   Allah Most High says:

(1) But a generation followed them who dissipated the prayer and pursued [their] lusts, and they shall find Ghayy [n: a "valley in hell" (Tafsir

p4.1   قال الله تعالى: ﴿فَخَلَفَ مِنْ بَعْدِهِمْ خَلْفٌ أَضَاعُـوا الصَّلاةَ وَاتَّبَعُوا الشَّهَـوَاتِ فَسَـوْفَ يَلْقَوْنَ غَيّاً . إِلّا مَنْ

al-Jalalayn (y77), 402], save he who repents..."
(Koran 19:59–60).

(2) "Woe to those who pray, unmindful of their prayers" (Koran 107:4–5).

(3) " 'What has brought you to hell?' And they shall say, 'We were not of those who prayed' " (Koran 74:42–43).

p4.2   The Prophet (Allah bless him and give him peace) said,

"The agreement that is between us and them is the prayer: whoever leaves it has disbelieved [dis: w18.2–5]."

*

p5.0   NOT PAYING ZAKAT

p5.1   Allah Most High says:

(1) "Woe unto polytheists, who do not pay zakat and are disbelievers in the hereafter" (Koran 41:6–7).

(2) "Those who hoard gold and silver, spending it not in the way of Allah, give them glad tidings of a painful torment, the day they are roasted upon it in the fire of hell" (Koran 9:34–35).

*

p6.0   SHOWING DISRESPECT TO ONE'S PARENTS

p6.1   Allah Most High says:

(1) "Your Lord decrees that you shall worship none but Him and treat your parents well,

تَابَ ... ﴾ [مريم : ٥٩ ـ ٦٠].

وقال تعالى : ﴿فَوَيْلٌ لِلْمُصَلِّينَ الَّذِينَ هُمْ عَنْ صَلاتِهِمْ سَاهُونَ﴾ [الماعون : ٤ ـ ٥].

وقال تعالى : ﴿مَا سَلَكَكُمْ فِي سَقَرَ قَالُوا لَمْ نَكُ مِنَ الْمُصَلِّينَ ... ﴾ [المدثر : ٤٢ ـ ٤٣].

p4.2   وقال عليه الصلاة والسلام : «العهدُ الذي بيننا وبينهم الصلاة فمن تركها فقد كفر» [رواه الترمذي والنسائي وأحمد وابن ماجه والحاكم].

p5.0   منع الزكاة

p5.1   قال الله تعالى : ﴿وَوَيْلٌ لِلْمُشْرِكِينَ، الَّذِينَ لا يُؤْتُونَ الزَّكاةَ وَهُمْ بِالآخِرَةِ هُمْ كَافِرُونَ﴾ [فصلت : ٦ـ٧].

وقال : ﴿وَالَّذِينَ يَكْنِزُونَ الذَّهَبَ وَالفِضَّةَ وَلا يُنْفِقُونَهَا فِي سَبِيلِ اللهِ فَبَشِّرْهُمْ بِعَذَابٍ أَلِيمٍ ، يَوْمَ يُحْمَى عَلَيْهَا فِي نَارِ جَهَنَّمَ ... ﴾ [التوبة : ٣٤ ـ ٣٥].

p6.0   عقوق الوالدين

p6.1   قال الله عزّ وجلّ : ﴿وَقَضَى رَبُّكَ أَلّا تَعْبُدُوا إِلّا إِيّاهُ وَبِالوَالِدَيْنِ

and if one or both of them reach old age with you, say not 'Uff!' to them nor upbraid them, but speak noble words and lower the wing of humility to them out of mercy'' (Koran 17:23–24).

(2) ''And We enjoin man to be good to his parents'' (Koran 29:8).

p6.2   The Prophet (Allah bless him and give him peace) said,

''Shall I not tell you of the worst of the enormities? ...''

and one of those he mentioned was undutiful behavior to one's parents.

*

p7.0   ACCEPTING USURIOUS GAIN (RIBA) (def: k3)

p7.1   Allah Most High says:

''O you who believe: fear Allah and forgo what remains of usurious gain if you are believers. If you will not, then know of a declaration of war [against you] from Allah and His messenger'' (Koran 2:278–79).

p7.2   The Prophet (Allah bless him and give him peace) said,

''May Allah curse him who eats of usurious gain (riba) or feeds it to another [A: curse (la'n) meaning to put someone far from the divine mercy].''

*

إِحْسَاناً، إِمَّا يَبْلُغَنَّ عِنْدَكَ الكِبَرَ أَحَدُهُمَا أَوْ كِلاَهُمَا فَلا تَقُلْ لَهُمَا أُفَّ وَلاَ تَنْهَرْهُمَا وَقُلْ لَهُمَا قَوْلاً كَرِيماً. وَاخْفِضْ لَهُمَا جَنَاحَ الذُّلِّ مِنَ الرَّحْمَةِ . . .﴾ [الإسراء: ٢٣ – ٢٤].

وقــال تعــالى: ﴿وَوَصَّيْنَا الإِنْسَانَ بِوَالِدَيْهِ حُسْناً . . .﴾ [العنكبوت: ٨].

p6.2   وقــال النبي ﷺ: «ألا أنْبِّئكم بِأكِبر الكَبائر؟ . . .» فذكـر منها عقوق الوالدينِ [متفق عليه].

p7.0   أكل الربا

p7.1   قال الله تعــالى: ﴿يَــا أَيُّهَــا الَّــذِينَ آمَنُــوا اتَّقُــوا اللَّهَ وَذَرُوا مَا بَقِيَ مِنْ الرِّبَا إِنْ كُنْتُمْ مُؤْمِنِينَ فَإِنْ لَمْ تَفْعَلُوا فَأْذَنُوا بِحَرْبٍ مِنَ اللَّهِ وَرَسُولِهِ . . .﴾ [البقرة: ٢٧٨ – ٢٧٩].

p7.2   وقــال ﷺ: «لـعنَ اللَّهُ آكِــلَ الرِّبَا وموكلَهُ» [رواه مسلم].

p8.0   WRONGFULLY CONSUMING AN ORPHAN'S PROPERTY

أكل مال اليتيم ظلماً   p8.0

p8.1   Allah Most High says:

(1) "Verily, those who wrongfully eat the property of orphans but fill their bellies with fire, and shall roast in a blaze" (Koran 4:10).

(2) "Approach not the orphan's property, save in exchange for that which is better" (Koran 6:152).

p8.1   قال الله تعـالى: ﴿إِنَّ الَّـذِينَ يَأْكُلُونَ أَموالَ اليَتَامَى ظُلْمـاً إِنَّمَا يَأْكُلُونَ فِي بُطُـونِهِـمْ نَاراً وَسَيَصْلَوْنَ سَعِـيراً﴾ [النساء: ١٠].
وقـال تعـالى: ﴿وَلَا تَقْرَبُوا مَالَ اليَتِيم إِلَّا بِالَّتِي هِيَ أَحْسَنُ...﴾ [الأنعام: ١٥٢].

p8.2   If the orphan's guardian is poor and consumes some of his charge's property without exceeding what is permissible, there is no harm in it (A: *no harm* (la ba's) being a technical term in Sacred Law meaning that it is better not to). What is in excess of the permissible is absolutely unlawful. (N: Scholars say that the guardian may lawfully only take whichever is less: the amount he needs, or else the wage typically received for work comparable to that performed for the orphan.) The criterion of the *permissible* is what is customary among people who are true believers free from base, ulterior motives.

p8.2   وكل ولِيّ ليتيم كان فقيراً فأكل بالمعـروف فلا بأس عليـه، ومـا زاد على المعروف فسحت حرام (ح: قال العلماء يأكل الأقل من حاجته وأجرة مثل ما عمل به لليتيم) والمعروف يُرجع فيه إلى عرف الناس المؤمنين الخالين من الأغراض الخبيثة.

*

p9.0   LYING ABOUT THE PROPHET (ALLAH BLESS HIM AND GIVE HIM PEACE)

الكذب على النبي ﷺ   p9.0

p9.1   Some scholars hold that lying about the Prophet (Allah bless him and give him peace) is unbelief (kufr) that puts one beyond the pale of Islam. There is no doubt that a premeditated lie against Allah and His messenger that declares something which is unlawful to be permissible or something permissible to be unlawful is pure unbelief. The question (A: as to when it is an enormity rather than outright unbelief) only concerns lies about other than that.

p9.1   قد ذهب طائفـة من العلمـاء إلى أن الكـذب على رسول الله ﷺ كفر ينقـل عن المـلة، ولا ريب أن تعمـد الكذب على الله ورسوله في تحليل حرام أو تحريم حلال كفر محض؛ وإنما الشأن في الكذب عليه في سوى ذلك.

p9.2   The Prophet (Allah bless him and give him peace) said:

(1) "A lie about me is not the same as a lie about someone else: whoever intentionally lies about me shall take a place for himself in hell."

(2) "Whoever relates words purportedly from me, thinking it is a lie, is a liar."

p9.3   It is clear from this that narrating a forged (mawdu') hadith is not permissible.

p9.4   (Ibn Kathir:) As for detecting forged hadiths, there are many signs that enable one to do so, such as internal evidence of forgery in wording or content, including poor grammar, corrupt meaning, the mention of incredible rewards for inconsiderable efforts, or inconsistency with what is established in the Koran and rigorously authenticated (sahih) hadith. It is not permissible for anyone to relate such a hadith except by way of condemning it, to warn one of the ignorant public or common people who might be deceived by it. There are many types of individuals who forge hadiths, including those with corrupt convictions about basic tenets of Islamic faith, as well as devotees who believe they are doing good by making up hadith-like stories that encourage others to do good, avoid bad, or perform meritorious acts, that such stories may be acted upon (al-Bahith al-hathith sharh Ikhtisar 'ulum al-hadith (y61), 78).

قال النبي ﷺ : «إنَّ كذباً عليَّ ليس كَكذبٍ على غيري : مَن كذب عليَّ عامداً فليتبوأ مقعدَهُ من النار» [رواه البخاري].

وقال : «مَن رَوَى عنّي حديثاً وهو يرى أنه كذبٌ فهو أحد الكاذبين» [رواه مسلم].

p9.3   فلاحَ بهذا أنّ رواية الموضوع لا تحلُّ.

p9.4   (ابن كثير:) أمـا معـرفـة المـوضوع المختلق المصنوع فعلى ذلك شواهد كثيرة: منها إقرار وضعه على نفسـه، قالاً أو حالاً، ومن ذلك ركاكةُ ألفاظه، وفساد معناه، أو مجازفة فاحشة، أو مخـالفة لمـا ثبت في الكتـاب والسنة الصحيحـة. فلا تجـوز روايتـه لأحد من النـاس، إلا على سبيـل القـدحِ فيه، ليحـذره من يغترّ به من الجهلة والعوام والرعاع. والواضعون أقسام كثيرة: منهم زنـادقة، ومنهم متعبـدون يحسبون أنهم يحسنـون صنعـاً، يضعون أحاديث فيها ترغيب وتـرهيب، وفي فضائـل الأعمال ليُعْمَـل بهـا [نقل من البـاحث الحثيث شرح اختصار علوم الحديث: ٧٨].

p9.5   (n: Having discussed lies and forgeries, we must strictly distinguish them from the hadith category called *not well authenticated* (da'if, lit. "weak"), so-termed because of such factors as having a channel of transmission containing a narrator whose memory was poor, one who was unreliable, unidentified by name, or for other reasons. Such hadiths legally differ from forgeries in the permissibility of ascribing them to the Prophet (Allah bless him and give him peace) and in other ways discussed at w48 below.)

*

p10.0 BREAKING ONE'S FAST DURING RAMADAN

p10.1 The Prophet (Allah bless him and give him peace) said:

(1) "Whoever breaks a fast-day of Ramadan without an excuse or dispensation could not requite it by fasting a lifetime, were he to do so [A: meaning that making up that day, while obligatory, does not remove the sin, though repentance does]."

The above hadith is not well authenticated.

(2) "The five prescribed prayers, and from one Friday prayer to another or from Ramadan to Ramadan, expiate the sins between them as long as the enormities are avoided."

(3) "Islam is based on five things: testifying that there is no god but Allah and that Muhammad is the Messenger of Allah, performing the prayer, giving zakat, fasting Ramadan, and the pilgrimage to the House (Kaaba)."

*

p11.0 FLEEING FROM COMBAT IN JIHAD

p11.1 Allah Most High says,

"On that day, whoever turns his back to them, unless pretending flight in order to reattack, or separating to join another unit, will bear the wrath of Allah and his refuge will be hell, a terrible end" (Koran 8:16).

*

p10.0 إفطـار رمضـان

p10.1 قال النبي ﷺ: «من أفطر يوماً من رمضـان من غيـر عذر ولا رخصـة لم يقضِه صيامُ الدهر وإن صامَهُ» [رواه الترمذي].

هذا لم يثبت.

وقـال عليـه الـصـلاة والـسـلام: «الـصلوات الـخمس، والجمعة إلى الجمعة ورمضان إلى رمضان كفارات لما بينهن ما اجْتُنِبَتِ الكبائر» [رواه مسلم].

وقـال عليـه الصلاة والسلام: «بُني الإسلام على خمس: شهادة أن لا إله إلا الـلـه وأنَّ محمـداً رسـول الله، وإقـام الصلاة وإيتاء الزكاة، وصوم رمضان وحج البيت» [متفق عليه].

p11.0 الفرار من الزحف

p11.1 قال الله تعـالى: ﴿وَمَنْ يُوَلِّهِمْ يَوْمَئِذٍ دُبُرَهُ إلَّا مُتَحَرِّفاً لِقِتالٍ أوْ مُتَحَيِّزاً إلى فِئَةٍ فَقَدْ باءَ بِغَضَبٍ مِنَ اللَّهِ وَمَأْوَاهُ جَهَنَّمُ وَبِئْسَ المَصِيرُ﴾ [الأنفال: ١٦].

p12.0 FORNICATION

p12.1 Allah Most High says:

(1) "Approach not fornication, it is surely an indecency and evil as a way" (Koran 17:32).

(2) "The fornicator and fornicatress, scourge them each a hundred stripes and let not pity for them take you" (Koran 24:2).

(3) "The fornicator shall not wed other than a fornicatress or idolatress. The fornicatress, none shall wed her but a fornicator or idolator. That is unlawful for believers" (Koran 24:3).

(n: The latter verse "was revealed when some poor Muslim emigrants in Medina were considering marrying the polytheists' prostitutes, who were wealthy, so that the prostitutes could provide for them. One opinion is that the Koranic prohibition concerned these people alone. A second position is that it was a general prohibition, but was superseded by the revelation of the subsequent verse,

'And marry those of you who are without spouses' (Koran 24:32)."

(*Tafsir al-Jalalayn* (y77), 457))

p12.2 The Prophet (Allah bless him and give him peace) said,

"Whoever fornicates or drinks wine, Allah takes his faith from him as a man takes a shirt off over his head."

*

p13.0 THE LEADER WHO MISLEADS HIS FOLLOWING, THE TYRANT AND OPPRESSOR

p13.1 Allah Most High says:

(1) "The dispute [lit. "way against"] is only

الزنا p12.0

p12.1 قال الله تعالى: ﴿وَلاَ تَقْرَبُوا الزِّنَا إِنَّهُ كَانَ فَاحِشَةً وَسَاءَ سَبِيلاً﴾ [الإسراء: ٣٢].

وقال تعالى: ﴿الزَّانِيَةُ وَالزَّانِي فَاجْلِدُوا كُلَّ وَاحِدٍ مِنْهُمَا مائةَ جَلْدَةٍ وَلاَ تَأْخُذْكُمْ بِهِمَا رَأْفَةٌ . . .﴾ [النور: ٢].

وقـال: ﴿الزَّانِي لَا يَنْكِحُ إِلَّا زَانِيَةً أَوْ مُشْرِكَةً وَالزَّانِيَةُ لَا يَنْكِحُهَا إِلَّا زَانٍ أَوْ مُشْرِكٍ وَحُرِّمَ ذَلِكَ عَلَى المُؤْمِنِينَ﴾ [النور: ٣].

(نزل ذلك لما همّ فقراء المهاجرين أن يتزوجوا بغايا المشركين وهن موسرات لينفقن عليهم. فقيل التحريم خاص بهم، وقيل عام ونُسخ بقوله تعالى: ﴿وَأَنْكِحُوا الأَيَامَى مِنْكُمْ﴾ [النور: ٣٢].» [نقل من تفسير الجلالين، ٤٥٧].

p12.2 وروي عن النبي ﷺ قال: «من زنى أو شربَ الخمر نزع الله منه الإيمان كما يخلع الإنسان القميص من رأسه» [رواه الحاكم].

p13.0 الإمامُ الغاشُّ لرعيته الظالم الجبار

p13.1 قال الله تعالى: ﴿إِنَّمَا السَّبِيلُ

with those who oppress people and wrongfully commit aggression in the land: these will have a painful torment" (Koran 42:42).

(2) "They did not forbid each other the evil that they did, and how wicked was what they would do" (Koran 5:79).

p13.2 The Prophet (Allah bless him and give him peace) said:

(1) "All of you are trustees, and each is responsible for those entrusted to his care."

(2) "Any superior who misrules his followers shall go to hell."

(3) "There will come corrupt, tyrannous rulers: whoever confirms their lies and assists them in their oppression is not of me, nor I of him, and shall not meet me at my watering place in paradise."

(4) "He who shows no mercy will not be shown any."

(5) "The worst of your rulers shall be those whom you detest and who detest you, whom you curse and who curse you." They said, "O Messenger of Allah, can we not throw them out?" And he replied, "No, not as long as they maintain the prescribed prayer [dis: o25.3(a(A:))] among you."

(6) "You'll be anxious to lead, and this will be a source of remorse to you on the Day of Judgement."

*

p14.0 DRINKING

p14.1 Allah Most High says:

(1) "They will ask you about wine and gambling. Say: 'There is great sin therein' " (Koran 2:219).

علَى الَّذينَ يَظْلِمُونَ النَّاسَ وَيَبْغُونَ فِي الأَرْضِ بِغَيْرِ الحَقِّ أُولئِكَ لَهُمْ عَذابٌ أَليمٌ﴾ [الشورى: ٤٢].

وقال تعالى: ﴿كَانُوا لاَ يَتَناهَوْنَ عَنْ مُنْكَرٍ فَعَلُوهُ لَبِئْسَ مَا كَانُوا يَفْعَلُونَ﴾ [المائدة: ٧٩].

p13.2 وقال النبي ﷺ: «كلكم راعٍ وكلكم مسؤولٌ عن رعيته...» [رواه البخاري].

وقال: «أيما راعٍ غش رعيته فهو في النار» [رواه الطبراني].

وقال: سيكون أمراء فسقة جورة؛ فمن صدقهم بكـذبهم، وأعـانهم على ظلمـهم فليس مني ولستُ منـه ولن يرد عليّ الحوض» [رواه الحاكم].

وقال عليه الصلاة والسلام: «من لا يَرْحم لا يُرْحم» [رواه البخاري].

وقال: «شـرار أئمـتكـم الـذين تبـغـضـونهم ويبغضـونكم وتلعنـونهم ويلعنـونكم. قالـوا يا رسـول الله، أفـلا نـنابـذهم؟ قال لا ما أقاموا فيكم الصلاة» [رواه مسلم].

وقال النبي ﷺ: «ستحـرصـون على الإمارة وستكون ندامةً يوم القيامة» [رواه البخاري].

p14.0 شرب الخمـر

p14.1 قال الله تعـالى: ﴿يَسْـأَلُونَكَ عَنِ الخَـمْـرِ والـمَـيْسِـرِ قُلْ فِيهِمَا إِثْمٌ كَبِيرٌ...﴾ [البقرة: ٢١٩].

(2) " O you believe: wine, gambling, idols, and fortune-telling arrows are but filth of the Devil's handiwork, so shun them..." (Koran 5:90).

p14.2 The Prophet (Allah bless him and give him peace) said:

(1) "Scourge whoever drinks wine. If he drinks it again, scourge him again. If he drinks it again, scourge him again. If he drinks it a fourth time, kill him." (N: The ruling of this hadith was later superseded, for the Prophet (Allah bless him and give him peace) was brought a drunkard for a fourth time, but did not kill him, showing that execution had been superseded, though the hadith remains a proof that the crime of drunkenness is an enormity.)

(2) "Allah has cursed wine, and whoever drinks it, pours it, sells it, buys it, presses it for another, presses it for himself, carries it, accepts its delivery, or eats its price."

(3) "Whoever drinks wine in this world shall be forbidden it in the next."

*

p15.0 ARROGANCE, PRIDE, CONCEIT, VANITY, AND HAUGHTINESS

p15.1 Allah Most High says:

(1) "Moses said, 'I surely seek refuge in my Lord and yours from every arrogant person who disbelieves in the Day of Reckoning' " (Koran 40:27).

(2) "Assuredly, Allah loves not those who hold aloof out of pride" (Koran 16:23).

(3) "Such is the Final Abode. We grant it to those who seek not exaltation in the land, nor corruption" (Koran 28:83).

وقال: ﴿يَا أَيُّهَا الَّذِينَ آمَنُوا إِنَّمَا الْخَمْرُ وَالْمَيْسِرُ وَالْأَنْصَابُ وَالْأَزْلَامُ رِجْسٌ مِنْ عَمَلِ الشَّيْطَانِ فَاجْتَنِبُوهُ...﴾ [المائدة: ٩٠ ـ ٩١].

p14.2 وقال ﷺ: «من شرب الخمر فاجلدوه، فإن عاد فاجلدوه، فإن شربها فاجلدوه، فإن شربها الرابعة فاقتلوه» [رواه الترمذي] (ح: وهذا الحديث منسوخ لأن النبي ﷺ أُتِيَ إليه بالسكير في المرة الرابعة فلم يقتله فدل على نسخ القتل، لكن الدلالة على عظم جريمة السكر باقية).

ـ «لعن الله الخمر وشاربها وساقيها وبائعها ومبتاعها وعاصرها ومعتصرها، وحاملها والمحمولة إليه وآكل ثمنها» [رواه أبو داود والحاكم؛ أضافه هنا المترجم من الجامع الصغير للسيوطي: حديث رقم ٧٢٥٣].

وقال عليه الصلاة والسلام: «من شرب الخمر في الدنيا حرمها في الآخرة» [متفق عليه].

p15.0 الكبر والفخر والخيلاء والعجب والتيه

p15.1 قال الله تعالى: ﴿وَقَالَ مُوسَى إِنِّي عُذْتُ بِرَبِّي وَرَبِّكُمْ مِنْ كُلِّ مُتَكَبِّرٍ لَا يُؤْمِنُ بِيَوْمِ الْحِسَابِ﴾ [غافر: ٢٧].

ـ وقال تعالى: ﴿إِنَّهُ لَا يُحِبُّ الْمُسْتَكْبِرِينَ﴾ [النحل: ٢٣].

ـ قال الله تعالى: ﴿تِلْكَ الدَّارُ الْآخِرَةُ نَجْعَلُهَا لِلَّذِينَ لَا يُرِيدُونَ عُلُوّاً فِي الْأَرْضِ وَلَا فَسَاداً﴾ [القصص: ٨٣].

(4) "Turn not your cheek from people out of pride, nor walk haughtily through the land, for Allah loves no one who is conceited and boastful" (Koran 31:18).

ـ وقـال تعـالى : ﴿وَلاَ تُصَعِّـرْ خَدَّكَ لِلنَّـاسِ وَلاَ تَمْشِ فِي الْأَرْضِ مَرَحَاً إِنَّ اللَّـهَ لاَ يُحِـبُّ كُلَّ مُخْتَـالٍ فَخُورٍ﴾ [لقمان : ١٨].

p15.2 The Prophet (Allah bless him and give him peace) said:

p15.2 وقـال ﷺ : «يُحشر الجبّارون رالمتكبــرون يوم القيـامـة أمثـال الـذر، يطؤهم الناس» [رواه الترمذي].

(1) "Tyrants and the arrogant will be raised on the Last Day as grain strewn underfoot that people will walk upon."

وقال : «لا يدخـل الجنـة مَن كان في قلبه مثقال ذرة من الكبر» فقال رجلٌ : «إن الـرجـل يحب أن يكون ثوبه حسناً ونعله حسنـة» فقـال : «إن الله جميـل يحب الجمـال، الكبر بطر الحق وغمط الناس» [رواه مسلم].

(2) "No one with the slightest particle of arrogance in his heart will enter paradise." A man remarked, "But a man likes his clothes to be nice and his sandals good." The Prophet (Allah bless him and give him peace) said, "Verily, Allah is beautiful and loves beauty. Arrogance is refusing to acknowledge what is right and considering others beneath one."

وقال ﷺ : «يقول الله تعالى : العظمة إزاري والكبرياء ردائي فمن نازعني فيهما ألقيته في النار» [رواه مسلم].

(3) Allah Most High says, "Greatness is My garment and haughtiness My mantle: whoever vies with Me for them I will throw into hell."

وقال سلمة بن الأكوع : أكل رجل عند النبي ﷺ بشماله فقال : كلْ بيمينك قال : لا أستطيـعُ . ما منعه إلا الكبر . قال : «لا استطعتَ» فما رفعها إلى فيه بعد [رواه مسلم].

(4) Salama ibn al-Akwa' recounts that a man was eating with his left hand in the presence of the Prophet (Allah bless him and give him peace). The Prophet told him, "Eat with your right," to which the man replied, "I cannot," though nothing stopped him but arrogance. The Prophet said, "May you not be able to." And the man could never lift his right hand to his mouth again.

p15.3 The wickedest arrogance is that of someone who exalts himself over people because of his learning and gloats to himself about his superiority. The knowledge of such a person is of absolutely no benefit to him. Whoever learns Sacred Knowledge for the sake of the next world is unsettled by his learning, his heart is humbled and his ego lowered. Such a person lies in wait for his selfishness and never gives it free rein. He constantly takes his ego to task and corrects it. Were he to neglect it, it would diverge from the right path and destroy him. The person who seeks knowledge to take pride in it or to gain a position of leadership,

p15.3 [قلت :] وأشرُّ الكبر من تكبر على العبـاد بعلمـه، وتعـاظم في نفسه بفضيلته . فإن هذا لم ينفعه علمـه، فإن من طلب الـعلم للآخـرة كسـره علمُـه وخشع قلبه واستكانت نفسه، وكان على نفسـه بالمرصاد، فلم يفتـر عنهـا، بل يحـاسبهـا كل وقت ويثقفهـا ؛ فإن غفل عنهـا جمـحت عن الطـريق المستقيم وأهـلكتـه . ومن طلب الـعلم للفخـر والـريـاسة، ونظر إلى المسلمين شزراً

looking disdainfully at other Muslims, thinking them fools and making light of them—all this is the most enormous arrogance, and "no one with the slightest particle of arrogance in his heart will enter paradise."

وتحـامق عليهم، وازدرى بهم؛ فهذا من أكبـر الكبـر، ولا يدخل الجنة من في قلبه مثقال ذرة من كبر.

*

p16.0   BEARING FALSE WITNESS

شهادة الزور   p16.0

p16.1   Allah Most High says,

"Shun the abomination of idols, and shun false testimony" (Koran 22:30).

p16.1   قال الله تعـالى: ﴿فَاجْتَنِبُوا الرِّجْسَ مِنَ الأَوْثَانِ وَاجْتَنِبُوا قَوْلَ الزُّورِ﴾ [الحج: ٣٠].

p16.2   The Prophet (Allah bless him and give him peace) said:

(1) "On the Day of Judgement, the feet of the person who bore false witness will not stir from their place before their owner is condemned to hell."

(2) "Shall I tell you of the worst enormities?—worshipping others with Allah, showing disrespect to parents, giving a false statement, and testifying to the truth of a falsehood." And he kept repeating it until we were telling ourselves [N: out of sympathy for him because of the strain of repeating it], "If only he would be silent."

p16.2   وفي الحديث: «لا تزول قدما شاهـدِ الـزور يوم القيـامـة حتى تجب له النار» [رواه الحاكم].
وقـال ﷺ: «ألا أنبّئكم بأكبر الكبائر: الإشـراك بالله، وعقوق الوالدين، وقول الـزور، وشهادة الزور». فمازال يكرّرها حتى قلنـا: ليتـه سكت (ح: اشفاقاً عليه لمـا لحقـه من التعب بتكـرارهـا) [رواه البخاري ومسلم].

*

p17.0   SODOMY AND LESBIANISM

اللواط   p17.0

p17.1   In more than one place in the Holy Koran, Allah recounts to us the story of Lot's people, and how He destroyed them for their wicked practice. There is consensus among both Muslims and the followers of all other religions that sodomy is an enormity. It is even viler and uglier than adultery.

p17.1   قد قصّ الله علينـا قصـة قوم لوط في غير ما موضع من كتابه العزيز وأنه أهلكـهـم بفـعـلهـم الخبيث. وأجمـع المسلمـون وأهـل الملل أن التلوط من الكبائر. واللواط أفحش من الزنا وأقبح.

p17.2   Allah Most High says:

"Do you approach the males of humanity, leaving the wives Allah has created for you? But you are a people who transgress" (Koran 26:165–66).

p17.3   The Prophet (Allah bless him and give him peace) said:

(1) "Kill the one who sodomizes and the one who lets it be done to him."

(2) "May Allah curse him who does what Lot's people did."

(3) "Lesbianism by women is adultery between them."

*

p18.0 CHARGING A WOMAN WHO COULD BE CHASTE (def: o13.2) WITH ADULTERY

p18.1   Allah Most High says:

(1) "Those who accuse believing women, unmindful though innocent, are cursed in this world and the next and shall receive a painful torment" (Koran 24:23).

(2) "Those who accuse innocent women without producing four witnesses, scourge them eighty stripes" (Koran 24:4).

p18.2   The Prophet (Allah bless him and give him peace) said,

"Avoid the seven heinous sins..."

and he mentioned charging believing women, unmindful though innocent, with adultery.

p17.2   قال الله تعالى: ﴿أَتَأْتُونَ الذُّكْرَانَ مِنَ الْعَالَمِينَ وَتَذَرُونَ مَا خَلَقَ لَكُمْ رَبُّكُمْ مِنْ أَزْوَاجِكُمْ بَلْ أَنْتُمْ قَوْمٌ عَادُونَ﴾ [الشعراء: ١٦٥ ـ ١٦٦].

p17.3   قال النبي ﷺ: «اقتلوا الفاعلَ والمفعولَ به» [رواه الترمذي].
وعنه ﷺ قال: «لعن الله من عَمِلَ عملَ قوم لوطٍ» [رواه ابن حبان].
ويُروى عن النبي ﷺ أنه قال: «سحاق النساء زناً بينهن» [رواه الطبراني].

p18.0 قذف المحصنات

p18.1   قال الله تعالى: ﴿إِنَّ الَّذِينَ يَرْمُونَ الْمُحْصَنَاتِ الْغَافِلَاتِ الْمُؤْمِنَاتِ لُعِنُوا فِي الدُّنْيَا وَالْآخِرَةِ وَلَهُمْ عَذَابٌ عَظِيمٌ﴾ [النور: ٢٣].
وقال: ﴿وَالَّذِينَ يَرْمُونَ الْمُحْصَنَاتِ ثُمَّ لَمْ يَأْتُوا بِأَرْبَعَةِ شُهَدَاءَ فَاجْلِدُوهُمْ ثَمَانِينَ جَلْدَةً...﴾ [النور: ٤].

p18.2   وقال ﷺ: «اجتنبوا السبعَ الموبقات...» فذكر منها قذف المحصناتِ الغافلات المؤمنات.

p18.3   As for someone who accuses the Mother of the Faithful 'A'isha of adultery after the revelation from heaven of her innocence (Koran 24:11–12), such a person is an unbeliever (kafir) denying the Koran and must be killed.

p18.3   أمــا من قذف أم الـمــؤمنين عائشــة رضي الله عنهـا بعد نزول براءتها من السماء فهو كافر مكذب للقرآن فيُقْتَل .

*

p19.0   MISAPPROPRIATING SPOILS OF WAR, MUSLIM FUNDS, OR ZAKAT

p19.0   الغلول من الغنيمــة ومن بيت المال والزكاة

p19.1   Allah Most High says:

"No prophet has been given to misappropriate wealth. Whoever does so shall bring what they have taken on the Day of Judgement" (Koran 3:161).

p19.1   قال الله تعــالى : ﴿وَمَـا كَانَ لِنَبِيٍّ أَنْ يَغُلَّ ، وَمَنْ يَغْلُلْ يَأْتِ بِمَا غَلَّ يَوْمَ القِيَامَةِ﴾ [آل عمران : ١٦١].

p19.2   The Prophet (Allah bless him and give him peace) said:

"... By Allah, none of you shall wrongfully take something save that he will meet Allah carrying it on Judgement Day, and I swear I will not recognize any of you who is carrying a grunting camel, lowing cow, or bleating sheep when you meet Allah." Then he lifted his hands and said, "O Allah, have I told them?"

p19.2   قال النبي ﷺ : « . . . واللهِ لا يأخذ أحدٌ منكم شيئاً بغير حق إلّا لقيَ اللهَ يحملُهُ يومَ القيـامةِ. [فلأعرفنَّ (ت : وفي رواية مشهورة :] فَلَا أعرفنَّ رجلاً منكم لقي اللهَ يحمل بعيراً له رغاء، أو بقرة لها خوار، أو شاة تَيْعـر». ثم رفع يديه فقال : «اللهم هل بلغت» [رواه البخاري].

*

p20.0   TAKING PEOPLE'S PROPERTY THROUGH FALSEHOOD

p20.0   الظلــم بأخـــذ أمـوال الناس بالباطل

p20.1   Allah Most High says,

"Consume not one another's property through falsehood, nor proffer it to those who judge [between you]..." (Koran 2:188).

p20.1   قال الله تعــالى : ﴿وَلَا تَأْكُلُوا أَمْوَالَكُمْ بَيْنَكُمْ بِالْبَاطِلِ وَتُـدْلُوا بِهَا إِلَى الْحُكَّامِ . . .﴾ [البقرة : ١٨٨].

p20.2   The category of taking other's property through falsehood includes such people as those who impose non-Islamic taxes (def: p32), the highwayman who blocks the road, the thief, the idler, the betrayer of a trust, the cheater or adulterator of trade goods, the borrower who denies having borrowed something, the person who stints when weighing or measuring out goods, the person who picks up lost and found property and does not give notice of having found it, the person who sells merchandise with a hidden defect, the gambler, and the merchant who tells the buyer that the merchandise cost more than it did.

p20.3   The Prophet (Allah bless him and give him peace) said:

(1)   "Whoever appropriates a handsbreadth of land through falsehood shall be made to carry it, as thick as seven earths, around his neck on Judgement Day."

(2)   "For someone to put off repayment of a debt when able to pay is an injustice."

(3)   A man said, "O Messenger of Allah, will my mistakes be forgiven me if I am killed, in steadfastness and anticipating Allah's reward, advancing and not retreating?" He replied, "Yes, except for debts."

(4)   "Flesh nurtured on ill-gotten wealth will not enter paradise. The hellfire has a better right to it."

(5)   "There is a record that Allah will not ignore the slightest bit of. It is the oppression of Allah's servants."

p20.4   Oppression is of three types. The first is consuming property through falsehood; the second, oppressing Allah's servants by killing, hitting, breaking bones or causing wounds; and the third, oppressing them through spoken abuse, cursing, reviling, or accusing them of adultery or sodomy without proof. The Prophet (Allah bless him and give him peace) said in an address to the people at Mina,

p20.2   ويــدخــل في هذا البــاب : المكاس وقاطع الطريق والسارق والبطّال والخــائن والــزغلي ومن استعــار شيئــاً فجحــده ، ومَن طفّف الــوزن والكيــل ، ومن التقط مالاً فلم يعرفه ، ومن باع شيئاً فيه عيب فغطّــاه ، والمقــامــر ، ومخبر المشتري بالزائد .

p20.3   وقال ﷺ : «من ظلم شبراً من الأرض طُوّقَهُ إلى سبع أرضين يوم القيامة» [رواه البخاري] .

وقــال عليه الصـلاة والسـلام : «مطلُ الغنيّ ظلمٌ» [رواه البخاري] .

وقــال رجل : يا رسـول الله إن قُتِلْتُ صابراً محتسباً مقبــلاً غيــر مدبِر ، أتكفَّرُ عني خطاياي؟ قال نعم ، إلا الدين» [رواه مسلم] .

[وعن جابــر رضي الله عنه أن النبي قال لكعب بن عجرة :] «لا يدخــل الجنة لحــم نبت من سحتٍ ، النــار أولى به» [رواه الحاكم] .

وفي الحديث : «وديوان لا يترك الله منه شيئاً وهو ظلم العباد» [رواه أحمد] .

p20.4   والظلم على ثلاثــة أقســام : أحــدهـا : أكل المـال بالباطل . وثانيها : ظلم العباد بالقتل والضـرب والكسـر والجراح . وثالثها : ظلم العبــاد بالشتم واللعن والسب والقــذف . وقــد خطب النـبي ﷺ النـاس بمنى فقـال : «إن

"Verily, your blood, property, and reputations are as inviolable to one another as the inviolability of this day, this month, and this city of yours."

دمـاءكم وأمـوالكم وأعـراضكم عليكم حرام كحرمة يومكم هذا في شهركم هذا في بلدكم هذا» [متفق عليه].

*

p21.0   THEFT

p21.0   السرقة

p21.1   Allah Most High says:

"Thieves, male or female—cut off their hands in retribution for what they have earned, as an exemplary punishment from Allah. Allah is Almighty and Wise" (Koran 5:38).

p21.1   قال الله تعـالى: ﴿وَالسَّارِقُ وَالسَّارِقَةُ فَاقْطَعُوا أَيْدِيَهُمَا جَزَاءً بِمَا كَسَبَا نَكَالاً مِنَ اللَّهِ وَاللَّهُ عَزِيــزٌ حَكِـيـمٌ﴾ [المائدة: ٣٨].

p21.2   The Prophet (Allah bless him and give him peace) said:

(1) "Allah curse the thief whose hand is cut for stealing a rope."

(2) "If Muhammad's daughter Fatima stole, I would cut off her hand."

p21.2   وقــال النـبي ﷺ: «لعن اللهُ السارقَ يسرق الحبلَ فَتُقْطَعُ يدُه» [رواه البخاري].
«لــو أنَّ فاطمــة بنتَ محمــدٍ سَرَقَتْ لَقَطَعْتُ يدها» [رواه البخاري].

p21.3   A thief's repentance is of no benefit to him until he returns whatever he stole (dis: p77.3). If moneyless, he must have the victim absolve him of financial responsibility.

p21.3   [قلت:] ولا تنفــع الســارق توبته إلا بأن يرد ما سرقه. فإن كان مفلساً تحلَّل من صاحب المال.

*

p22.0   HIGHWAYMEN WHO MENACE THE ROAD

(A: The amount of money they ask makes no difference, and like this, in being money taken through falsehood, are all measures imposed upon travellers without their free choice, such as tariffs, mandatory currency exchange, visa fees, and so forth.)

p22.0   قطع الطريق

p22.1   Allah Most High says:

"The recompense of those at war with Allah

p22.1   قال الله تعـالى: ﴿إِنَّمَا جَزَاءُ الَّذِينَ يُحَارِبُونَ اللَّهَ وَرَسُولَهُ وَيَسْعَوْنَ فِي

and His messenger and who strive for corruption in the land is that they be killed or crucified, or a hand and foot cut off from opposite sides, or banished from the land. That is their humiliation in this world, and an immense torment awaits them in the next" (Koran 5:33).

الأَرْضِ فَسَاداً أَنْ يُقَتَّلُوا أَوْيُصَلَّبُوا أَوْ تُقَطَّعَ أَيْدِيهِمْ وَأَرْجُلُهُمْ مِنْ خِلافٍ أَوْ يُنْفَوْا مِنَ الأَرْضِ ذلِكَ لَهُمْ خِزْيٌ فِي الدُّنْيَا وَلَـهُـمْ فِي الآخِـرَةِ عَذَابٌ عَظِـيـمٌ﴾ [المائدة : ٣٣].

p22.2   Merely making people feel that the way is unsafe is to commit an enormity, so how then if such a person should take money?

p22.2 فمجـرد إخـافتـه السبيـل هو مرتكب الكبيرة، فكيف إذا أخذ المال؟

*

p23.0   THE ENGULFING OATH

p23.0 اليمين الغموس

p23.1   An engulfing oath is one in which there is premeditated lying. It is termed *engulfing* because it whelms its swearer in sin.

p23.1 واليمين الغموس : التي يتعمد فيها الكذب . سُميت غموساً لأنها تغمس الحالف في الإثم .

p23.2   The Prophet (Allah bless him and give him peace) said:

(1) "The enormities are worshipping others with Allah, showing disrespect to parents, killing a human being, and the engulfing oath."

(2) "A man once said, 'By Allah, Allah will not forgive So-and-so.' Allah said, 'Who is it that swears I must not forgive So-and-so? I forgive him and annul all your works.' "

p23.2 قال النبي ﷺ : «الكبـائـر الإشـراك بالله ، وعقوق الوالدين ، وقتل النفس ، واليمين الغموس» [رواه البخاري].
«قال رجل : والله لا يغفر اللهُ لفلانٍ . فقـال الله تعـالى : من ذا الذي يتألَّى عليّ أني لا أغفر لفلانٍ ، قد غفرتُ له وأحبطتُ عملك» [رواه مسلم].

*

p24.0   THE INVETERATE LIAR

p24.0 الكذّاب في غالب أقواله

p24.1   Allah Most High says:

(1)   Allah guides not the profligate liar" (Koran 40:28).

(2)   "May liars perish" (Koran 51:10).

p24.1 قال الله تعـالى : ﴿إنَّ اللَّهَ لاَ يَهْدِي مَنْ هُوَ مُسْرِفٌ كَذَّابٌ﴾ [غافر : ٢٨].
ـ وقـال : ﴿قُتِـلَ الـخـرَّاصُـونَ﴾ [الذاريات : ١٠].

p24.2 The Prophet (Allah bless him and give him peace) said:

(1) "Lying leads one to wickedness and wickedness leads one to hell. A man keeps lying until Allah records that he is an inveterate liar."

(2) "The marks of a hypocrite are three: when he speaks he lies, when he makes a promise he breaks it, and when entrusted with something he betrays the trust."

(3) "A believer's natural disposition might comprise any trait other than treachery and untruthfulness."

*

p25.0 SUICIDE

p25.1 Allah Most High says:

"Do not kill yourselves, for Allah is compassionate towards you. Whoever does so, in transgression and wrongfully, We shall roast in a fire, and that is an easy matter for Allah" (Koran 4:29–30).

p25.2 The Prophet (Allah bless him and give him peace) said:

(1) "Of those before you, there was once a wounded man who could not bear it, so he took a knife and cut his arm, and bled until he died. Allah Most High said, 'My slave has taken his life before I have, so I forbid him paradise.' "

(2) "Whoever kills himself with a knife will abide forever in the fire of hell, perpetually stabbing his belly with it. Whoever kills himself with poison will abide forever in the fire of hell, poison in hand, perpetually drinking of it."

*

p24.2 قال النبي ﷺ: «إن الكذب يهدي إلى الفجور وإن الفجور يهدي إلى النار. ولا يزال الرجل يكذب حتى يكتب عند الله كذاباً» [رواه البخاري].

وقال ﷺ: «آية المنافق ثلاث: إذا حدّث كذب، وإذا وعد أخلف، وإذا ائتمن خان» [رواه البخاري].

وعنه ﷺ: «يُطبع المؤمنُ على كل شيءٍ ليس الخيانة والكذب» [رواه أحمد].

p25.0 قاتل نفسه

p25.1 قال الله تعالى: ﴿وَلَا تَقْتُلُوا أَنْفُسَكُمْ إِنَّ اللَّهَ كَانَ بِكُمْ رَحِيمًا. وَمَنْ يَفْعَلْ ذَلِكَ عُدْوَانًا وَظُلْمًا فَسَوْفَ نُصْلِيهِ نَارًا وَكَانَ ذَلِكَ عَلَى اللَّهِ يَسِيرًا﴾ [النساء: ٢٩].

p25.2 وعن النبي ﷺ قال: «كان ممن كان قبلكم رجلٌ به جرح فجزع، فأخذ سكيناً فحزّ بها يده فما رقأ الدمُ حتى مات. قال الله تعالى: بادرني عبدي بنفسه، حرمت عليه الجنة» [متفق عليه].

وقال رسول الله ﷺ من قتل نفسه بحديدةٍ فحديدته في يده يتوجّأ بها في بطنه في نار جهنم خالداً مخلداً فيها أبداً ومن قتل نفسه بسُمٍّ فسمُّه في يده يتحسّاهُ في نار جهنم خالداً مخلداً فيها أبداً» [متفق عليه].

*

p26.0 THE BAD JUDGE

p26.1 Allah Most High says:

(1) "Whoso does not judge by what Allah has revealed, those are the unbelievers" (Koran 5:44).

(2) "Those who conceal the clear explanations and guidance We have revealed, after We have explained it in the Book to people, are cursed by Allah and those who curse" (Koran 2:159).

p26.2 The Prophet (Allah bless him and give him peace) said:

(1) "One judge shall go to paradise, and two to hell. The judge who knows what is right and judges accordingly shall be in paradise. The one who knows what is right but intentionally judges unjustly will go to hell, and so will the judge who judges without knowledge."

Anyone who judges without knowledge or evidence from Allah and His messenger regarding the matter he gives an opinion on is subject to this threat.

(2) "Whoever is appointed to judge between people is as though slaughtered without a knife."

p26.3 It is unlawful for a judge to rule on a case when angry, especially at a litigant. When a judge's qualities combine an insufficiency of Sacred Knowledge, unworthy intention, bad disposition, and lack of godfearingness, then his destruction is complete and he must resign and hasten to save himself from hell.

*

p26.0 القاضي السوء

p26.1 قال الله تعـالى: ﴿وَمَنْ لَمْ يَحْكُمْ بِمَا أَنْزَلَ اللَّهُ فَأُولَئِكَ هُمُ الكَافِرُونَ﴾ [المائدة: ٤٤].
وقال تعالى: ﴿إِنَّ الَّذِينَ يَكْتُمُونَ مَا أَنْزَلْنَا مِنَ البَيِّنَاتِ وَالهُدَى مِنْ بَعْدِ مَا بَيَّنَّاهُ لِلنَّاسِ فِي الكِتَابِ أُولَئِكَ يَلْعَنُهُمُ اللَّهُ وَيَلْعَنُهُمُ اللَّاعِنُونَ﴾ [البقرة: ١٥٩].

p26.2 وعن النبي ﷺ قال: «قاضٍ في الجنّة وقاضيانِ في النار؛ قاضٍ عرف الحق فقضى به فهو في الجنة، وقاضٍ عرف الحق فجار متعمداً فهو في النار، وقاضٍ قضى بغير علم فهو في النار» [رواه الحاكم]. [قلت:] فكل من قضى بغير علم ولا بينة من الله ورسوله على ما يقضي فهو داخل في هذا الوعيد.
وعن النبي ﷺ أنه قال: «مَنْ جُعِلَ قاضياً بين الناس فكأنما ذُبِحَ بغير سكين» [رواه أبو داود].

p26.3 ويحرم على القاضي أن يحكم وهو غضبان، لا سيما من الخصم. وإذا اجتمع في القاضي قلة علم، وسوء قصد، وأخلاق زعرة، وقلة الورع؛ فقد تمت خسارته ووجب عليه أن يعزل نفسه ويبادر بالخلاص من النار.

p27.0   PERMITTING ONE'S WIFE TO FORNICATE

p27.1   Allah Most High says:

"None shall wed a fornicatress but a fornicator or idolator. That is unlawful for believers" (Koran 24:3).

p27.2   The Prophet (Allah bless him and give him peace) said,

"Three will not enter paradise: he who is disrespectful to his parents, he who lets his wife fornicate with another, and women who affect masculinity."

p27.3   Someone who suspects his wife of indecency but pretends not to know because he loves her is not as bad as someone who actually pimps for her. There is no good in a man without jealousy for his rights.

*

p28.0   MASCULINE WOMEN AND EFFEMINATE MEN

p28.1   The Prophet (Allah bless him and give him peace) said,

(1) "Men are already destroyed when they obey women."

(2) The Prophet (Allah bless him and give him peace) cursed effeminate men and masculine women.

(3) The Prophet (Allah bless him and give him peace) cursed men who wear women's clothing and women who wear men's.

p27.0 القـــواد المـستحسن على أهله

p27.1   قال الله تعالى :
﴿وَالزَّانِيَةُ لاَ يَنْكِحُهَا إِلاَّ زَانٍ أَوْ مُشْرِكٍ وَحُرِّمَ ذَلِكَ عَلَى الْمُؤْمِنِينَ﴾ [النور: ٣].

p27.2   وعن النبي ﷺ أنه قال : «ثلاثة لا يدخلون الجنـة العاق لوالديْه والدَّيُّوثُ ورجلةُ النساء» [رواه الحاكم].

p27.3   فمن كان يظن بأهله الفـاحشة ويتغـافل لمحبته فيها فهو دون من يعرِّس عليها . ولا خير فيمن لا غيرة له .

p28.0   الـــرجلة من النسـاء والمخنث من الرجال

p28.1   قال ﷺ : «الآن هلك الـرجال حين أطاعوا النساء» [رواه أحمد].
[قـال ابن عبـاس :] «لَعَنَ رسول الله ﷺ المخنثين من الـرجـال والمترجلات من النسـاء» [رواه البخـاري]. [وقال أبو هريــرة :] «لَعَنَ رسـول الله ﷺ الرجـل يلبس لبسـة المـرأة والمـرأة تلبس لبسـة الرجل» [رواه أبو داود].

p29.0 MARRYING SOLELY TO RETURN TO THE PREVIOUS HUSBAND

p29.0 المحلِّل والمحلَّل له

p29.1 The Prophet (Allah bless him and give him peace) cursed the man who marries a woman after her divorce solely to permit her first husband to remarry her (dis: n7.7) and cursed the first husband.

p29.1 [صحّ من حديث ابن مسعود رضي الله عنــه أن] رسـول الله ﷺ لعن المحلِّل والمحلَّل له» [رواه النسائي].

*

p30.0 EATING UNSLAUGHTERED MEAT, BLOOD, OR PORK

p30.0 أكــل الميتـة والـدم ولحم الخنزير

p30.1 Allah Most High says,

"Say: 'I find nothing in what has been revealed to me that is unlawful for a person to eat except unslaughtered meat, blood outpoured, or the flesh of swine, for all this is filth' " (Koran 6:145).

p30.1 قال الله تعالى:
﴿قُلْ لَا أَجِدُ فِيمَا أُوحِيَ إِلَيَّ مُحَرَّمًا عَلَى طَاعِمٍ يَطْعَمُهُ إِلَّا أَنْ يَكُونَ مَيْتَةً أَوْ دَمًا مَسْفُوحًا أَوْ لَحْمَ خِنْــزِيــرٍ فَإِنَّهُ رِجْسٌ...﴾ [الأنعام: ١٤٥].

p30.2 Whoever premeditatedly eats these when not forced by necessity is a criminal.

p30.2 فمن تعمــد أكـل ذلـك لغير ضرورة فهو من المجرمين.

*

p31.0 NOT FREEING ONESELF OF ALL TRACES OF URINE

p31.0 عدم التنـزه من البول

p31.1 Allah Most High says,

"And your raiment purify" (Koran 74:4).

p31.1 قال الله تعالى:
﴿وَثِيَابَكَ فَطَهِّرْ﴾ [المدثر: ٤].

p31.2 The Prophet (Allah bless him and give him peace):

(1) passed by two graves and said, "The two are being tormented, and not for anything excessive: one of them did not free himself of traces of urine, while the other was a talebearer [def: r3]."

p31.2 وقال النبي ﷺ، ومرَّ بقبرين: «إنهمـا يُعَـذَّبـانِ وما يعذَّبانِ في كبير، أما أحـدُهمـا فكـان لا يستنـزه من بوله، وأما الآخرُ فكان يمشي بالنميمة» [متفق عليه].

(2) And he said, "Take care to remove all vestiges of urine from your persons, because it is the main reason for torment in one's grave."

Moreover, the prayer of someone who does not protect his person and clothing from urine is not acceptable (A: which is how scholars interpret the above hadiths, as applying to those who are negligent in removing all traces of urine before they pray).

*

وعن النبي ﷺ أنه قال: «تنـزهـوا من البول فإن عامة عذاب القبر منه» [رواه الدارقطني].

ثم إن من لم يحترز من البول في بدنه وثيابه فصلاته غير مقبولة.

p32.0 COLLECTING TAXES

(A: Meaning to take revenues other than those which are countenanced by Sacred Law such as zakat or the non-Muslim poll tax (jizya) (N: though the state may take taxes to the extent necessary to prevent the general detriment).)

المكّاس p32.0

(ع: والمـراد جبـايـة غير ما ورد أخذه بالشرع كالـزكـاة والجـزية [والخمس] ح: ويجوز للدولة فرض الضرائب بقدر ما يندفع به الضرر العام)).

p32.1 Such people are among those meant by the words of Allah Most High,

"The dispute is only with those who oppress people, and wrongfully exceed proper bounds in the land: these will have a painful torment" (Koran 42:42).

p32.1 وهـو داخـل في قوله تعـالى: ﴿إنَّمَا السَّبِيلُ عَلَى الَّذِينَ يَظْلِمُونَ النَّاسَ وَيَبْغُـونَ فِي الأَرْضِ بِغَيْـرِ الحَقِّ أُوْلِئكَ لَهُمْ عَذَابٌ أَلِيمٌ﴾ [الشورى: ٤٢].

p32.2 And in the hadith of the adulteress who purified herself by voluntarily being stoned to death, there is the Prophet's remark (Allah bless him and give him peace),

"She has made a repentance so sincere that if even a tax taker repented with the like of it, he would be forgiven."

p32.2 وفي الحـديـث في الزانية التي طهّرت نفسها بالرجم: «لقدْ تابتْ توبةً لو تابها صاحب مكس لغفر له» [رواه مسلم].

p32.3 He who imposes taxes resembles a highwayman, and is worse than a thief. But one who burdens the people, imposing over new levies on them, is more tyrannous and oppressive than someone more equitable therein who treats those under him more kindly. Those who gather taxes, who do the clerical work, or who accept the proceeds, such as a soldier, sheikh, or head of a Sufi

p32.3 والمكّاس فيـه شبـه من قاطع الطـريـق، وهـو شر من اللص. فإن مَن عسف النـاس وجـدد عليهم ضـرائب، فهـو أظلم وأغشم ممن أنصف في مكسه ورفق برعيتـه. وجابي المكس وكاتبه وآخـذه من جنـدي وشيخ وصاحب زاوية

center (zawiya)—all bear the sin, and are eating of ill-gotten wealth (dis: w49).

*

p33.0 SHOWING OFF IN GOOD WORKS

p33.0 الرياء

p33.1   Allah Most High says:

(1) "The hypocrites are trying to fool Allah, while it is He who is outwitting them. And when they stand to pray they do so lazily, showing off to people, remembering Allah but little" (Koran 4:142).

(2) "O you who believe: do not nullify your charity by reminding recipients of having given it and by offending them, like someone who spends his money as a show for people" (Koran 2:264).

p33.2   The Prophet (Allah bless him and give him peace) said:

(1) "The first person judged on Resurrection Day will be a man martyred in battle.
"He will be brought forth, Allah will reacquaint him with His blessings upon him and the man will acknowledge them, whereupon Allah will say, 'What have you done with them?' to which the man will respond, 'I fought to the death for You.'
"Allah will reply, 'You lie. You fought in order to be called a hero, and it has already been said.' Then he will be sentenced and dragged away on his face to be flung into the fire.
"Then a man will be brought forward who learned Sacred Knowledge, taught it to others, and who recited the Koran. Allah will remind him of His gifts to him and the man will acknowledge them, and then Allah will say, 'What have you done with them?' The man will answer, 'I acquired Sacred Knowledge, taught it, and recited the Koran, for Your sake.'
"Allah will say, 'You lie. You learned so as to be called a scholar, and read the Koran so as to be

called a reciter, and it has already been said.' Then the man will be sentenced and dragged away on his face to be flung into the fire.

"Then a man will be brought forward whom Allah expansively provided for, lavishing varieties of property upon him, and Allah will recall to him the benefits bestowed, and the man will acknowledge them, to which Allah will say, 'And what have you done with them?' The man will answer, 'I have not left a single kind of expenditure You love to see made in Your cause, save that I have spent on it for Your sake.'

"Allah will say, 'You lie. You did it so as to be called generous, and it has already been said.' Then he will be sentenced and dragged away on his face to be flung into the fire.''

(2) "The slightest bit of showing off in good works is as if worshipping others with Allah."

قارىءٌ، فقد قيل. ثم أمر به فسُحب على وجهـه حتى ألقي في النـار. ورجـل وسّع اللهُ عليه وأعطاهُ من أصناف المال فأتي به فعـرّفه نعمَـه فعـرفهـا، فقال: ما عملتَ فيهـا؟ قال: ما تركتُ من سبيـل تحب أن يُنْفَقَ فيه إلا أنفقتُ فيه لك. قال: كذبتَ ولكنك فعلتَ ليقالَ هو جوادٌ فقد قيل. ثمّ أمـر به فسُحب على وجهـه حتى ألقي في النار» [رواه مسلم].

وقال: «اليسير من الرياء شركٌ» [رواه الحاكم].

p33.3   (A: When there is an act of obedience the servant intends to conceal but Allah reveals, then it is merely gratitude for His blessings to admit it to others and thank Him for it. When asked if one is fasting, for example, and one is, then one should say "Praise be to Allah" (al-Hamdu lillah).)

*

p34.0   BREACH OF FAITH

p34.0   الخيانة

p34.1   Allah Most High says,

"Do not betray Allah and His messenger, nor knowingly betray your trusts" (Koran 8:27).

p34.1   قال الله تعالى:
﴿لاَ تَخُونُوا اللَّهَ وَالرَّسُولَ وَتَخُونُوا أَمَانَاتِكُمْ وَأَنتُمْ تَعْلَمُونَ﴾ [الأنفال: ٢٧].

p34.2   The Prophet (Allah bless him and give him peace) said:

"Someone who cannot keep a trust is devoid of faith. Someone who cannot keep an agreement is devoid of religion."

p34.2   وقـال النبي ﷺ: «لا إيمـان لمن لا أمانة له، ولا دين لمن لا عهد له» [رواه أحمد].

p34.3   A breach of faith in anything is very ugly, but in some matters is worse than others. A person

p34.3   والخيانـة في كل شيء قبيحة وبعضهـا شرّ من بعض. وليس مَن خانك

who cheats one for a pittance is not like a person who betrays one concerning one's wife and money, perpetrating outrages.

في فلسٍ كمن خانك في أهلك ومالك وارتكب العظائم .

*

p35.0 LEARNING SACRED KNOWLEDGE FOR THE SAKE OF THIS WORLD, OR CONCEALING IT

(A: Learning Sacred Knowledge for the sake of this world means that if not for this-worldly reasons, a person would not have bothered to learn (dis: a3.1).)

p35.0 التعلم للدنيا وكتمان العلم

(ع : والتعلم للدنيا معناه : لولا أسباب دنيوية لما تعلم [ح : العلم الشرعي]).

p35.1 Allah Most High says:

(1) "Only the knowledgeable of His slaves fear Allah" (Koran 35:28).

(2) "Those who conceal what Allah has revealed of the Book and purchase a trifling price thereby, these but fill their bellies with hellfire" (Koran 2:174).

(3) "And Allah made a covenant with those given the Book to explain it to people and not keep it from them. But they flung it behind their backs" (Koran 3:187).

p35.1 قال الله تعالى :
﴿إِنَّمَا يَخْشَى اللَّهَ مِنْ عِبَادِهِ العُلَمَاءُ﴾
[فاطر : ٢٨].
وقال تعالى : ﴿إِنَّ الَّذِينَ يَكْتُمُونَ مَا أَنْزَلَ اللَّهُ مِنَ الكِتَابِ وَيَشْتَرُونَ بِهِ ثَمَنًا قَلِيلًا أُولَئِكَ مَا يَأْكُلُونَ فِي بُطُونِهِمْ إِلَّا النَّارَ﴾ [البقرة : ١٧٤].
وقال : ﴿وَإِذْ أَخَذَ اللَّهُ مِيثَاقَ الَّذِينَ أُوتُوا الكِتَابَ لَتُبَيِّنُنَّهُ لِلنَّاسِ وَلَا تَكْتُمُونَهُ فَنَبَذُوهُ وَرَاءَ ظُهُورِهِمْ [. . .]﴾ [آل عمران : ١٨٧].

p35.2 The Prophet (Allah bless him and give him peace) said,

"Anyone who seeks Sacred Knowledge to vie with scholars, argue with fools, or win people's hearts will go to hell."

p35.2 وقال النبي ﷺ : «مَن ابتغَى العلم ليباهي به العلماء أو يماري به السفهاء أو تقبل أفئدة الناس إليه فإلى النار» [رواه الترمذي].

p35.3 Hilal ibn al-'Ala' said, "Seeking Sacred Knowledge is arduous, learning it is harder than seeking it, applying it is harder than learning it, and remaining safe from it is even harder than applying it."

p35.3 وقال هلال بن العلاء : طلب العلم شديد وحفظه أشدُ من طلبه والعمل به أشد من حفظه ، والسلامة منه أشد من العمل به .

*

p36.0   REMINDING RECIPIENTS OF ONE'S CHARITY TO THEM

p36.1   Allah Most High says,

"O you believe: do not nullify your charity by reminding recipients of having given it and by offending them" (Koran 2:264).

p36.2   The Prophet (Allah bless him and give him peace) said,

"There are three people whom Allah will not speak to, look at, or exonerate on the Day of Judgement, and who will have a painful torment: he who wears the hem of his garment low [A: out of pride], he who reminds recipients of his charity to them, and he who sells merchandise swearing that he paid more for it than he actually did."

*

p37.0   DISBELIEVING IN DESTINY (QADR)

p37.1   Allah Most High says:

(1)   "Verily, We have created everything in a determined measure" (Koran 54:49).

(2)   "Allah has created you and what you do" (Koran 37:96).

(3)   "Whomever Allah leads astray has no guide" (Koran 7:186).

(4)   "And Allah knowingly led him astray" (Koran 45:23).

(5)   "But you will not want to unless Allah wants" (Koran 76:30).

(6)   "And He inspired it [A: the human soul] its evil and its godfearingness" (Koran 91:8).

المنّان   p36.0

p36.1   قال الله تعالى:
﴿يَا أَيُّهَا الَّذِينَ آمَنُوا لَا تُبْطِلُوا صَدَقَاتِكُمْ بِالْمَنِّ وَالأَذَىٰ﴾ [البقرة: ٢٦٤].

p36.2   وفي الحديث الصحيح: «ثلاثة لا يكلمهم اللهُ ولا ينظر إليهم يوم القيامة ولا يزكّيهم ولهم عذابٌ أليمٌ: المسبل إزاره، والمنان، والمنفق سلعته بالحلف الكاذب».

المكذِّبُ بالقدر   p37.0

p37.1   قال الله تعالى:
﴿إِنَّا كُلَّ شَيْءٍ خَلَقْنَاهُ بِقَدَرٍ﴾ [القمر: ٤٩].
وقال تعالى: ﴿وَاللَّهُ خَلَقَكُمْ وَمَا تَعْمَلُونَ﴾ [الصافات: ٩٦].
وقال تعالى: ﴿وَمَنْ يُضْلِلِ اللَّهُ فَلَا هَادِيَ لَهُ﴾ [الأعراف: ١٨٦].
وقال: ﴿وَأَضَلَّهُ اللَّهُ عَلَىٰ عِلْمٍ﴾ [الجاثية: ٢٣].
وقال: ﴿وَمَا تَشَاؤُونَ إِلَّا أَنْ يَشَاءَ اللَّهُ﴾ [الإنسان: ٣٠].
وقال: ﴿فَأَلْهَمَهَا فُجُورَهَا وَتَقْوَاهَا﴾ [الشمس: ٨].

p37.2 The Prophet (Allah bless him and give him peace):

(1) "O Messenger of Allah, what is faith?" And he replied, "To believe in Allah, His angels, His messengers, the resurrection after death, and in destiny (qadr, def: u3.7–8), its good and evil."

(2) "There are six whom I curse, Allah curses, and who are cursed by every prophet whose supplications are answered: he who denies Allah's destiny, he who adds anything to Allah's book, he who rules arrogantly, he who considers what Allah has prohibited to be lawful, he who deems it permissible to treat my family in ways Allah has forbidden [A: such as insulting or reviling them], and he who abandons my sunna [A: out of disdain for it]."

*

p38.0 LISTENING TO PEOPLE'S PRIVATE CONVERSATIONS

p38.1 Allah Most High says,

"Do not spy" (Koran 49:12).

p38.2 The Prophet (Allah bless him and give him peace) said,

"Whoever listens to people who are averse to his listening shall have molten lead poured into his ears on the Day of Judgement."

p38.3 This may not be an enormity (A: in some cases (dis: r6.4)).

*

p39.0 CURSING OTHERS (dis: r38)

p39.1 The Prophet (Allah bless him and give him peace) said:

p37.2 «يا رسول الله، ما الإيمانُ؟»
قال: «أن تؤمن بالله وملائكته وكتبه ورسله والبعث بعد الموت والقدر خيره وشرّه» [رواه البخاري].

قال رسول الله ﷺ: «ستة لَعَنتُهم، ولعنهم اللهُ، وكلُّ نبيٍّ مجاب: المكذب بقدر الله، والزائد في كتاب الله، والمتسلط بالجبروت، والمستحل حرم الله، والمستحل من عترتي ما حرّم الله، والتارك لسنتي» [رواه الترمذي].

p38.0 المستمع على الناس ما يسرون

p38.1 قال الله تعالى:
﴿وَلَا تَجَسَّسُوا﴾ [الحجرات: ١٢].

p38.2 وقال النبي ﷺ: «مَن استمع إلى حديث قوم وهم له كارهون صُبَّ في أذنيه الآنُك يوم القيامة [...]» [رواه البخاري].

p38.3 ولعلها ليست بكبيرة.

p39.0 اللّعان

p39.1 قال النبي ﷺ: «لعن المؤمن

(1) "Cursing a believer is like killing him."

(2) "When a servant curses something, the curse rises up to the sky, where the doors of the sky shut it out, and then it falls back to earth, where the doors of the earth shut it out. Then it searches right and left and when it does not find anywhere to go it comes back to the thing which was cursed, should it deserve it. If not, it returns upon the person who uttered it."

(3) While the Prophet (Allah bless him and give him peace) was on a journey, there was a woman of the Medinan Helpers (Ansar) riding a camel which annoyed her, whereupon she cursed it. The Prophet heard this and said, "Take off what is on its back and release it, for it has been cursed." And it is as if I can still see it now, walking along among the people, no one stopping it.

*

p40.0   LEAVING ONE'S LEADER

p40.1   Allah Most High says,

"Fulfill covenants, for surely convenants will be asked about" (Koran 17:34).

p40.2   The Prophet (Allah bless him and give him peace) said:

"He who obeys me obeys Allah, and he who disobeys me disobeys Allah. He who obeys the leader obeys me, and he who disobeys the leader disobeys me."

(A: The *leader* referred to in the hadith is the caliph of the Muslims or his authorized representative (dis: o25.5). Whenever there is a group of three or more Muslims, it is sunna for a leader (amir) to be chosen. It is sunna to obey such a leader, and leaving him or not obeying him contravenes what is recommended, but is not unlawful.)

كقتله» [رواه البخاري].

وعنه ﷺ أنه قال: «إن العبد إذا لعن شيئاً صَعِدَتْ اللعنة إلى السماء، فتُغْلَقُ أبواب السماء دونها، ثم تهبط إلى الأرض فتغلق أبوابها دونها، ثم تأخذ يميناً وشمالاً، فإذا لم تجد مساغاً رجعت إلى الذي لُعِنَ إن كان أهلاً لذلك، وإلا رجعت إلى قائلها» [رواه أبو داود].

«بينما رسول الله ﷺ في بعض أسفاره، وامرأةٌ من الأنصار على ناقةٍ، فضَجِرَتْ فلعنتها، فسمع ذلك رسول الله ﷺ، فقال: «خذوا ما عليها ودَعُوها فإنها ملعونةٌ» [قال عمرانُ] فكأني أنظر إليها الآن تمشي في الناس ما يعرِضُ لها أحدٌ» [رواه مسلم].

الغادر بأميره   p40.0

قال الله تعالى: p40.1
﴿وَأَوْفُوا بِالعَهْدِ إنَّ العَهْدَ كَانَ مَسْؤُولاً﴾ [الإسراء: ٣٤].

وقال ﷺ: «من أطاعني فقد   p40.2
أطاع اللهَ، ومَن عصاني فقد عصَى اللهَ ومن يُطِع الأميرَ فقد أطاعني، ومَن يَعْصِ الأمير فقد عصاني» [رواه البخاري].

(ع: الأمير المذكور في الحديث هو خليفة المسلمين أو نائبه. وأما إذا اجتمع ثلاثة مسلمين فأكثر فالسنة أن يختاروا أميراً لهم، ويسن طاعته. ومغادرته أو عدم إطاعته تخالف المسنون لكن لا يحرم).

p41.0 BELIEVING IN FORTUNE-TELLERS OR ASTROLOGERS

p41.1   Allah Most High says:

(1) "Pursue not that which you have no knowledge of" (Koran 17:36).

(2) "[He is] the Knower of the Unseen, and discloses not His unseen to anyone [dis: w60.1], except to a messenger with whom He is pleased" (Koran 72:26–27).

p41.2   The Prophet (Allah bless him and give him peace) said:

(1) "Whoever goes to a 'psychic' ('arraf) or fortune-teller and believes what he says has disbelieved in what has been revealed to Muhammad."

(2) "Allah Most High says, 'One of My servants reaches daybreak a believer, another an unbeliever. He who says, "We have received rain by Allah's grace," is a believer in Me and a disbeliever in the planets. But he who says, "We have received rain by the effects of such and such a mansion of the moon," is an unbeliever in Me and a believer in planets [A: if he thinks they have a causal influence independent of the will of Allah (dis: o8.7(17))].' "

(3) "Whoever goes to a 'psychic,' asks him about something, and believes him, will not have his prayer accepted for forty days."

*

p42.0 A WIFE'S REBELLING AGAINST HER HUSBAND (def: m10.12)

p42.1   Allah Most High says:

"Men are the guardians of women, since Allah has been more generous to one than the

p41.0 تصديق الكاهن والمنجم

p41.1 قال الله تعالى:
﴿وَلاَ تَقْفُ مَا لَيْسَ لَكَ بِهِ عِلْمُ [. . .]﴾ [الإسراء: ٣٦].
وقـال تعالى: ﴿عَالِمُ الغَيْبِ فَلاَ يُظْهِرُ عَلَى غَيْبِهِ أَحَداً إِلاَّ مَنِ ارْتَضَىٰ مِنْ رَسُولٍ﴾ [الجن: ٢٦ ـ ٢٧].

p41.2 وقال ﷺ: «من أتى عرافاً أو كاهناً فصدقه بما يقول فقد كفر بما أنزل على محمد ﷺ» [رواه أبو داود].
وقال ﷺ [صبيحة ليلة مطيرة]: «يقول اللـه تعـالى: أصبـح من عبـادي مؤمنٌ وكافرٌ، فمن قال مُطرنا بفضل الله فذلك مؤمنٌ بي كافرٌ بالكوكب. ومن قال مُطرنا بنوءِ كذا فذلك كافرٌ بي مؤمنٌ بالكوكب» [رواه البخاري ومسلم].
وقـال ﷺ: «من أتى عرّافاً فسأله عن شيءٍ فَصَـدَّقَـهُ لم تُقبـل له صلاةُ أربعين يوماً» [رواه مسلم].

p42.0 نشوز المرأة

p42.1 قال الله تعـالى: ﴿الـرِّجَالُ قَوَّامُونَ عَلَى النِّسَاءِ بِمَا فَضَّلَ اللَّهُ بَعْضَهُمْ

other, and because of what they [men] spend from their wealth. So righteous women will be obedient, and in absence watchful, for Allah is watchful. And if you fear their intractability, warn them, send them from bed, or hit them. But if they obey you, seek no way to blame them" (Koran 4:34).

عَلَى بَعْضٍ وَبِمَا أَنْفَقُوا مِنْ أَمْوَالِهِمْ فَالصَّالِحَاتُ قَانِتَاتٌ حَافِظَاتٌ لِلْغَيْبِ بِمَا حَفِظَ اللَّهُ، وَاللَّاتِي تَخَافُونَ نُشُوزَهُنَّ فَعِظُوهُنَّ وَاهْجُرُوهُنَّ فِي المَضَاجِعِ وَاضْرِبُوهُنَّ فَإِنْ أَطَعْنَكُمْ فَلَا تَبْغُوا عَلَيْهِنَّ سَبِيلًا﴾ [النساء: ٣٤].

p42.2 The Prophet (Allah bless him and give him peace) said:

(1) "Allah will not look at a woman who is ungrateful to her husband, while unable to do without him."

(2) "When a man calls his wife to his bed and she will not come, and he spends the night angry with her, the angels curse her until morning."

(3) "It is not lawful for a woman to fast when her husband is present, save by his leave. Nor to permit anyone into his house except with his permission."

(4) "Whoever leaves her husband's house [A: without his permission], the angels curse her until she returns or repents."

(Khalil Nahlawi:) It is a condition for the permissibility of her going out (dis: m10.3–4) that she take no measures to enhance her beauty, and that her figure is concealed or altered to a form unlikely to draw looks from men or attract them. Allah Most High says,

"Remain in your homes and do not display your beauty as women did in the pre-Islamic period of ignorance" (Koran 33:33).

(*al-Durar al-mubaha* (y99), 160)

p42.2   قال رسول الله ﷺ: «لا ينظر الله إلى امرأةٍ لا تشكر لزوجها وهي لا تستغني عنه» [رواه النسائي].

وقال النبي ﷺ: «إذا دعا الرجلُ امرأته إلى فراشه فلم تأت فبات غضبان عليها لعنتها الملائكة حتى تصبح» [رواه البخاري].

وقال ﷺ: «لا يحل لامرأةٍ أن تصوم وزوجها شاهدٌ إلا بإذنه، ولا تأذن في بيته إلا بإذنه» [رواه البخاري].

ويُروى عن النبي ﷺ أنه قال: «مَن خرجتْ من بيت زوجها لعنتها الملائكة حتى ترجع أو تتوب» [رواه الطبراني].

(خليل النحلاوي:) وحيث أبحنا الخروج فإنما يباح بشرط عدم الزينة وتغيير الهيئة إلى ما لا يكون داعيةً لنظر الرجال واستمالة. قال الله تعالى: ﴿وَقَرْنَ فِي بُيُوتِكُنَّ وَلَا تَبَرَّجْنَ تَبَرُّجَ الجَاهِلِيَّةِ الأُولَى﴾ [الأحزاب: ٣٣]. [نقل من الدرر المباحة في الحظر والإباحة: ١٧٢ - ١٧٣].

*

p43.0 SEVERING TIES OF KINSHIP

(A: The opposite, *maintaining the bonds of kinship* (silat al-rahim), means politeness, kind

p43.0   قاطع الرحم

(ع: وعكس قطع الرحم هو صلة الرحم ومعناها معاملتهم بالأدب

treament, and concern for all one's relatives, even if distantly related, corrupt, non-Muslim, or unappreciative.)

والمعروف والاعتناء بجميعهم ، بُعداء كانوا أو فساقاً أو كفاراً أو غير شاكرين) .

p43.1 Allah Most High says:

"If you turn back, would you then cause corruption in the land, severing your family ties? Those are the ones whom Allah has cursed and deafened, and blinded their sight" (Koran 47:22–23).

p43.1 قال الله تعالى : ﴿فَهَلْ عَسَيْتُمْ إِنْ تَوَلَّيْتُمْ أَنْ تُفْسِدُوا فِي الْأَرْضِ وَتُقَطِّعُوا أَرْحَامَكُمْ . أُولَئِكَ الَّذِينَ لَعَنَهُمُ اللَّهُ فَأَصَمَّهُمْ وَأَعْمَى أَبْصَارَهُمْ﴾ [محمد : ٢٢ ـ ٢٤] .

p43.2 The Prophet (Allah bless him and give him peace) said:

(1) "He who severs his family ties will not enter paradise."

(2) "Whoever believes in Allah and the Last Day, let him maintain the bonds of kinship."

p43.2 قال النبي ﷺ : «لا يدخل الجنة قاطعُ رحمٍ﴾ [رواه البخاري] . وقال ﷺ : «مَن كان يؤمن بالله واليوم الآخر فليصل رحمه» [رواه البخاري] .

*

p44.0 MAKING PICTURES

p44.0 المصوِّر

p44.1 The Prophet (Allah bless him and give him peace) said:

(1) "Every maker of pictures will go to the fire, where a being will be set upon him for each picture he made, to torment him in hell."

(2) "Whoever makes an image shall be required [on the Last Day] to breathe a spirit into it, but will never be able to do so."

(n: Other hadith evidence appears at w50, which discusses legal questions relating to the artistic, photographic, and televisual depiction of animate life.)

p44.1 قال النبي ﷺ : «كلُّ مصوِّرٍ في النار يجعل له بكل صورةٍ صوّرها نَفْساً فيعذبه في جهنم» [رواه البخاري] . وقال النبي ﷺ : «من صوّر صورةً كُلِّفَ أن ينفخ فيها الروح (يوم القيامة) وليس بنافخ» [رواه البخاري] .

*

p45.0 THE TALEBEARER WHO STIRS UP ENMITY BETWEEN PEOPLE (dis: r3)

p45.1 Allah Most High says,

"Obey not every wretched swearer; slanderer, going about with tales" (Koran 68:10–11).

p45.2 The Prophet (Allah bless him and give him peace) said:

(1) "He who stirs up enmity among people by quoting their words to each other will not enter paradise."

(2) "You find that among the worst people is someone who is two-faced, showing one face to some and another face to others."

(3) "Do not tell me anything about my Companions, for I want to meet them without disquiet in my heart."

*

p46.0 LOUDLY LAMENTING THE DEAD

p46.1 The Prophet (Allah bless him and give him peace) said,

"He who slaps his cheeks, rips his pockets, or calls out the cries of the pre-Islamic period of ignorance is not of us."

*

p47.0 ATTACKING ANOTHER'S ANCESTRY

p47.1 The Prophet (Allah bless him and give him peace) said,

النمام p45.0

p45.1 قال الله تعالى:
﴿وَلاَ تُطِعْ كُلَّ حَلاَّفٍ مَهِينٍ هَمَّازٍ مَشَّاءٍ بِنَمِيمٍ﴾ [القلم: ١٠ - ١١].

p45.2 وقــال النبي ﷺ: «لا يدخـل الجنة نَمَّام» [رواه البخاري].
وقال النبي ﷺ: «تجد من شرار الناس ذا الـوجهين: هو الـذي يأتي هؤلاء بوجهٍ وهؤلاء بوجهٍ» [رواه البخاري].
وعن النبي ﷺ قال: «لا يُبلغني أحـدٌ عن أصحـابي شيئاً فإني أحب أن أخـرج إليهم وأنا سليم الصدر» [رواه أبو داود].

النياحة واللطم p46.0

p46.1 قال ﷺ: «ليس منا من ضرب الخــدود وشق الجيــوب ودعـا بدعـوى الجاهلية» [رواه البخاري].

الطعن في الأنساب p47.0

p47.1 قال النبي ﷺ: «اثنتـان هما

"Two qualities in people are unbelief: attacking another's ancestry, and wailing over the dead."

(N: The hadith does not mean that these things put one beyond the pale of Islam, but that they are the actions of the unbelievers.)

*

p48.0 EXCESSES AGAINST OTHERS

p48.1   Allah Most High says,

"The dispute is only with those who oppress people and wrongfully commit aggression in the land: these will have a painful torment" (Koran 42:42).

p48.2   The Prophet (Allah bless him and give him peace) said,

(1) "Allah has inspired to me that you are all to be humble towards each other, such that no one transgresses against or exalts himself above another."

(2) Malik Rahawi said: "O Messenger of Allah, I have been given of beauty that which you see, and I do not like anyone to wear better sandals than I. Is this of presumptuous pride?" He answered, "This is not of presumptuousness, which rather consists of refusing to admit the truth and considering people inferior."

(3) "A woman was tortured for a cat she imprisoned until it died. She went to hell because of it, having neither fed nor watered it, for she confined it; nor yet having let it go to forage on the small creatures of the earth."

(4) "Allah will certainly torture those who torture people in this world."

بالناس كفرٌ: الطعن في النسب، والنياحة على الميت» [رواه مسلم].

(ح): وليس معنى الحديث أنهما يخرجان عن الملة، ولكنهما من أفعال الكفار).

p48.0 البغي

p48.1   قال الله تعالى:

﴿إِنَّمَا السَّبِيلُ عَلَى الَّذِينَ يَظْلِمُونَ النَّاسَ وَيَبْغُونَ فِي الأَرْضِ بِغَيْرِ الحَقِّ أُولَئِكَ لَهُمْ عَذَابٌ أَلِيمٌ﴾ [الشورى: ٤٢].

p48.2   قال النبي ﷺ: «إن الله أوحى إليَّ أن تواضعوا حتى لا يبغي أحد على أحد ولا يفخر أحد على أحد» [رواه مسلم].

قال مالك الرهاوي: «يا رسول الله، قد أُعطيتُ من الجمال ما ترى، وما أحبُّ أنَّ أحداً يفوقني بشِراك (نعلي)، أفذاك من البغي؟» ـ قال: «ليس ذلك من البغي، ولكن البغيَ بطرُ الحق [أو قال سفهُ الحق] وغمط الناس» [رواه الحاكم].

وقال النبي ﷺ: «عُذِّبَت امرأةٌ في هرةٍ سجنتها حتى ماتت، فدخلت فيها النار، لا هي أطعمتها وسقتها، إذ حبستها؛ ولا هي تركتها تأكل من خشاش الأرض» [رواه البخاري].

وقال النبي ﷺ: «إن الله يعذِّب الذين يعذبون الناس في الدنيا» [رواه مسلم].

p49.0 ARMED INSURRECTION AND CONSIDERING MUSLIMS UNBELIEVERS

(A: The early *Kharijite* sect committed these transgressions.)

p49.1   Allah Most High says:

(1) "Do not commit transgressions; surely Allah loves not the transgressors" (Koran 2:190).

(2) "Whoever disobeys Allah and His messenger has gone manifestly astray" (Koran 33:36).

p49.2   The Prophet (Allah bless him and give him peace) said,

"If someone says to his Muslim brother, 'You unbeliever,' one of them deserves the name."

*

p50.0 HURTING OR REVILING MUSLIMS

p50.1   Allah Most High says:

(1) "Those who hurt believing men and women who have done nothing to deserve it shall bear the burden of calumny and open sin" (Koran 33:58).

(2) "Do not spy and do not slander one another" (Koran 49:12).

(3) "Woe to whoever disparages others behind their back or to their face" (Koran: 104:1).

(4) "Those who love that scandal should be spread concerning the believers shall have a painful torment in this world and the next" (Koran 24:19).

p50.2   The Prophet (Allah bless him and give him peace) said:

(ع : ارتكبهما فرقة الخوارج قديماً) .

p49.1 قال الله تعالى :

﴿وَلاَ تَعْتَـدُوا إِنَّ اللَّـهَ لاَ يُحِـبُّ الْمُعْتَدِينَ﴾ [البقرة : ١٩٠] .

وقال تعالى :

﴿وَمَنْ يَعْص اللَّهَ وَرَسُولَهُ فَقَـدْ ضَلَّ ضَلاَلاً مُبِيناً﴾ [الأحزاب : ٣٦] .

p49.2 وقـال الـنبـي ﷺ : «من قال لأخيه المسلم يا كافر فقد باء بها أحدهما» [رواه البخاري] .

p50.0 أذية المسلمين وشتمهم

قال الله تعالى :

p50.1 ﴿وَالَّذِينَ يُؤْذُونَ الْمُؤْمِنِينَ والْمُؤْمِنَات بِغَيرِ مَا اكْتَسَبُوا فَقَدْ احْتَمَلُوا بُهْتَاناً وَإِثْماً مُبِيناً﴾ [الأحزاب : ٥٨] .

وقال تعالى : ﴿وَلاَ تَجَسَّسُوا وَلاَ يَغْتَب بَعْضُكُمْ بَعْضاً﴾ [الحجرات : ١٢] .

وقال تعالى : ﴿وَيْلٌ لِكُلِّ هُمَزَةٍ لُمَزَةٍ﴾ [الهمزة : ١] .

وقـال الله تعـالـى : ﴿إِنَّ الَّذِينَ يُحِبُّونَ أَنْ تَشِيعَ الْفَاحِشَـةُ فِي الَّذِينَ آمَنُـوا لَهُمْ عَذَابٌ أَلِيمٌ فِي الدُّنْيَا وَالآخِرَةِ﴾ [النور : ١٩] .

p50.2 قال ﷺ : «الـمـسـلم أخـو

(1) "The Muslim is the brother of the Muslim. He does not oppress him, hang back from coming to his aid, or belittle him. It is sufficiently wicked for someone to demean his fellow Muslim."

(2) "By Allah, he does not believe. By Allah, he does not believe. By Allah, he does not believe." Someone asked, "Who, O Messenger of Allah?" And he said, "He whose neighbor is not safe from his evil conduct."

(3) Someone said, "O Messenger of Allah, So-and-so spends her nights praying and her days fasting, but there is something in her tongue that maliciously injures her neighbors." He replied, "There is no good in her, she will go to hell."

(4) "When I was taken up in the Ascent (Mi'raj), I passed by people with fingernails of copper who were raking their faces and chests with them. I asked, 'Who are they, Gabriel?' and he said, 'They are those who slandered others [lit. "ate people's flesh"] and attacked their reputations.'"

(5) "No man charges another with corruption or unbelief, save that the charge returns against himself if the other is not as he said."

(6) "Do not revile the dead, for they have gone on to what they have sent ahead."

*

المسلم، لا يظلمه ولا يخذله ولا يحقره، بحسب امرىءٍ من الشـرِّ أن يحقر أخـاه المسلم» [رواه مسلم].

وقال: «واللهِ لا يؤمن، واللهِ لا يؤمن، والله لا يؤمن! قيـل مَن يا رسـول الله؟ قال: الذي لا يأمن جاره بوائقه» [رواه البخاري].

قيـل: «يا رسول الله، إن فلانة تصلّي الليـل وتصـوم النهـار، وفي لسـانها شيءٌ يؤذي جيرانها، سليطةٌ». فقال: «لا خير فيها هي في النار» [رواه الحاكم].

قال رسـول الله ﷺ: «لمـا عُرِجَ بي مررتُ بقـومٍ لهم أظفارٌ من نحـاسٍ يخمشـون وجوههم وصدورهم. فقلتُ: مَن هؤلاء يا جبريلُ؟ فقال: الذين يأكلون لحـوم النـاس ويقعـون في أعـراضهم» [رواه أبو داود].

وقـال ﷺ: «لا يرمي رجـلٌ رجـلاً بالفسوق والكفر إلا ارتدَّ عليه إن لم يكن صاحبه كذلك» [رواه البخاري].

وقال ﷺ: «لا تسبوا الأموات فإنهم قد أفضَوْا إلى ما قدّموا» [رواه البخاري].

p51.0 HARMING THE FRIENDS (AWLIYA') OF ALLAH MOST HIGH

p51.1 Allah Most High says,

"Verily, those who offend Allah and His messenger are cursed by Allah in this world and the next, and He has prepared for them a humiliating torment" (Koran 33:57).

p51.0 أذية أولياء الله تعالى

p51.1 قال الله تعالى:
﴿إِنَّ الَّذِينَ يُؤْذُونَ اللَّهَ وَرَسُولَهُ لَعَنَهُمُ اللَّهُ فِي الدُّنْيَا وَالْآخِرَةِ وَأَعَدَّ لَهُمْ عَذَابًا مُهِينًا﴾ [الأحزاب: ٥٧].

p51.2   The Prophet (Allah bless him and give him peace) said:

(1) "Abu Bakr, if you anger them [some of the poorer Emigrants], you anger your Lord."

(2) "Allah Most High says: 'He who is hostile to a friend (wali) of Mine I declare war against. My slave approaches Me with nothing more beloved to Me than what I have made obligatory for him, and My slave keeps drawing nearer to Me with voluntary works until I love him. And when I love him, I am his hearing with which he hears, his sight with which he sees, his hand with which he seizes, and his foot with which he walks. If he asks Me, I will surely give to him, and if he seeks refuge in Me, I will surely protect him.' "

(n: This hadith is explained in detail at w33, which discusses the friends (awliya') of Allah Most High.)

*

p52.0 DRAGGING THE HEM OF ONE'S GARMENT OUT OF CONCEIT

p52.1   Allah Most High says,

"... Nor walk haughtily through the land" (Koran 31:18).

p52.2   The Prophet (Allah bless him and give him peace) said:

(1) "The caftan of the Muslim comes down to midcalf, there being no harm in what is between this and the anklebones, though any of it below the anklebones is in hell. Whoever lets the hem of his garment drag on the ground out of pride, Allah will not look at him."

(2) "While a man was walking along in a new set of clothes, with a swagger to his step, pleased with himself, and his hair combed down, Allah

---

p51.2   وفي الحديث: «يا أبا بكر! إن كنتَ أغضبتَهم لقد أغضبتَ ربَّكَ» (يعني بعض فقراء المهاجرين) [رواه مسلم].

قال رسـول الله ﷺ: «إن الله تعـالى قال: مَن عَادَىٰ لي ولـيـاً فقـد آذنـتُه بالحرب. وما تقرب إليَّ عبدي بشيءٍ أحبَّ إليَّ ممـا افترضتُ عليـه مما يزال عبـدي يتقرب إليَّ بالنـوافـل حتى أحبه، فإذا أحببتُـه كنتُ سمعَـه الـذي يسمَعُ به وبصرَه الذي يُبْصِرُ به ويدَه التي يبطش بها ورجلَه الـتي يمـشي بهـا، وإنْ سألني أعطيتُه ولئِن استعاذني لأعيذنَّه» [رواه البخاري].

---

p52.0   إسبال الإزار تعزُّراً

p52.1   قال الله تعـالى: ﴿ولَا تَمْشِ في الأَرْضِ مَرَحَاً﴾ [لقمان: ١٨].

p52.2   قال النبي ﷺ: «أزرة المسلم إلى نصف السـاق ولا حرج [أو لا جناح] فيمـا بينه وبين الكعبين؛ ومـا كان أسفل من الكعبين فهـو في النـار. ومَن جر إزاره بطراً لم ينظر الله إليه» [رواه أبو داود].

وقال النبي ﷺ: «بينما رجلٌ يمشي في حلة تعجبه نفسه، مرجِّلٌ رأسه يختال في مشيتـه؛ إذ خسف الله به الأرض فهـو

caused the earth to swallow him, and he will keep sinking until the Last Day."	يتجلجل فيها إلى يوم القيامة» [رواه البخاري].

*

p53.0   MEN WEARING SILK OR GOLD

p53.1   Allah Most High says,

"And the raiment of godfearingness is better" (Koran 7:26).

p53.2   The Prophet (Allah bless him and give him peace) said:

(1) "Only those with no share in the next world wear silk in this one."

(2) "Wearing gold and silk has been made unlawful for the men of my Community but permissible for its women."

p53.0 لبـــاس الـحـــريـــر والذهب للرجل

p53.1 قال الله تعـــالى : ﴿وَلِبَاسُ التَّقْوَى ذَلِكَ خَيْرٌ﴾ [الأعراف: ٢٦].

p53.2 وقال ﷺ : «إنما يلبس الحرير (في الـدنيا) من لا خلاق له في الآخرة» [رواه البخاري].

وقـال ﷺ : «حُـرّم لبـــاس الـــذهب والحـريـر على ذكور أمتي وأحل لإنائهم» [رواه الترمذي].

*

p54.0   SLAUGHTERING IN OTHER THAN ALLAH'S NAME

p54.1   Allah Most High says,

"Eat not of what the name of Allah has not been mentioned over; verily it is disobedience" (Koran 6:121).

p54.2   The Prophet (Allah bless him and give him peace) said,

"May Allah curse whoever slaughters in other than Allah's name."

p54.0 من ذبـح لغيــر الله

p54.1 قال الله تعـــالى : ﴿وَلاَ تَأْكُلُوا مِمَّـا لَمْ يُذْكَـرِ اسْـمُ الـلَّهِ عَلَيْـهِ وَإِنَّـهُ لَفِسْقٌ . . .﴾ [الأنعام: ١٢١].

p54.2 وقال ﷺ : «لعن الله من ذبح لغير الله» [رواه أحمد].

*

p55.0 SURREPTITIOUSLY CHANGING PROPERTY-LINE MARKERS	p55.0 من غيّر منار الأرض
p55.1 The Prophet (Allah bless him and give him peace) said,

"May Allah curse whoever changes the land's property-line markers." | p55.1 قال رسـول الله ﷺ : « . . . لعن الله من غيّــرَ تخــومَ الأرض . . . » [رواه أحمد] . |

*

p56.0 DISPARAGING THE PROPHETIC COMPANIONS (SAHABA)	p56.0 سبّ الصحابة رضي الله عنهم أجمعين
p56.1 The Prophet (Allah bless him and give him peace) said,

"The curse of Allah is upon whoever reviles my Companions." | p56.1 عن الـنبي ﷺ : «مـن سبّ أصحابي فعليه لعنـة الله» [رواه ابن أبي عاصم] . |
| p56.2 'Ali ibn Abi Talib (Allah be well pleased with him) said,

"By Him who cleaves the seed and creates the soul, it is the solemn word of the Illiterate Prophet to me that none shall love me except a believer, and none hate me except a hypocrite." | p56.2 وقــال علي رضي الله عنــه : «والذي فلق الحبة وبرأ النسمة ، إنه لعهدُ الـنبي الأمي إليَّ : لا يحبني إلا مؤمن ولا يبغضني إلا منافقٌ» [رواه مسلم] . |

*

p57.0 DISPARAGING THE MEDINAN HELPERS (ANSAR)	p57.0 سبّ الأنصار
p57.1 The Prophet (Allah bless him and give him peace) said,

"The sign of faith is love of the Helpers (Ansar), and the sign of hypocrisy is hatred of the Helpers." | p57.1 قال النبي ﷺ : «آيـة الإيمـان حب الأنصـار وآيـة النفاق بغض الأنصار» [رواه البخاري] . |

p58.0 HE WHO INAUGURATES
A REPREHENSIBLE INNOVATION
(BID'A) (def: w29.3)

p58.1 The Prophet (Allah bless him and give him peace) said:

(1) "He who calls others to misguidance is guilty of a sin equal to the sins of all who follow him therein without this diminishing their own sins in the slightest."

(2) "He who inaugurates a good sunna [custom] in Islam earns the reward of it and of all who perform it after him without diminishing their own rewards in the slightest. And he who introduces a bad sunna is guilty of the sin of it and of all who perform it after him without diminishing their own sins in the slightest."

*

p59.0 WOMEN WEARING FALSE
HAIR AND THE LIKE

p59.1 The Prophet (Allah bless him and give him peace) said,

"Allah curse women who wear false hair or arrange it for others, who tattoo or have themselves tattooed, who pluck facial hair or eyebrows or have them plucked, and women who separate their front teeth for beauty, altering what Allah has created."

(n: w51 discusses women removing facial hair.)

*

p60.0 POINTING A BLADE AT ONE'S
BROTHER

p60.1 The Prophet (Allah bless him and give him peace) said:

p58.0 مَن [دعا إلى ضلالة
أو] سنَّ سنةً سيئة

p58.1 قال النبي ﷺ: «مَن دعا إلى ضلالة كان عليه من الإثم مثـلُ آثـام مَن تبعه لا ينقص ذلك من آثامهم شيئاً» [رواه مسلم].

قال رسـول اللـه ﷺ: «مـن سنَّ في الإسلام سنَّةً حسنةً فله أجرها وأجر من عمـل بهـا من بعـده من غير أن ينقص من أجـورهم شيئـاً ومن سنّ سنَّةً سيئـةً كان عليه وزرُها ووزرُ من عَمِلَ بها من بعده من غيـر أن ينقص من أوزارهـم شيئـاً» [رواه مسلم].

p59.0 الـواصلة في شعـرها
[والمتفلجة والواشمة]

p59.1 قال النـبي ﷺ: «لـعـن اللهُ الـواصلـة والمستـوصلة، والـواشمـة والمستـوشمة، والنـامصة والمتنمصة، والمتفلجـات للحسن المغيـرات خلقَ الله» [رواه البخاري].

p60.0 مَن أشار إلى أخيه
بحديدة

p60.1 قال النبي ﷺ: «من أشـار إلى

"The angels curse whoever points a blade [A: or other weapon] at his brother [until he ceases], even if it be his brother from his mother and father."

أخيه بحديدة، فإن الملائكة تلعنُه (حتى ينتهي) وإن كان أخاه من أمه وأبيه» [رواه مسلم].

*

p61.0 FALSELY CLAIMING SOMEONE IS ONE'S FATHER

p61.1 The Prophet (Allah bless him and give him peace) said:

(1) "Paradise is forbidden to whoever falsely claims someone is his father, knowing he is not."

(2) "Do not wish for fathers other than your own. For someone to wish for a different father is unbelief."

p61.0 **من ادعى إلى غير أبيه**

p61.1 قـال رسـول الله ﷺ: «مَن ادعى إلى غيـر أبيـه وهـو يعلم أنه غيرُ أبيه فالجنة عليه حرامٌ» [رواه البخاري].
وعـن النبي ﷺ قال: «لا ترغبـوا عن آبـائكم، فمن رَغبَ عن أبيـه فهـو كفرٌ» [رواه البخاري].

*

p62.0 BELIEVING THAT SOMETHING PORTENDS BAD LUCK

p62.1 The Prophet (Allah bless him and give him peace) said,

"Belief in a bad omen is polytheism (shirk)."

p62.0 **الطيرة**

p62.1 قال رسـول الله ﷺ: «الطِّيَرَةُ شركٌ» [رواه الترمذي].

*

p63.0 DRINKING FROM GOLD OR SILVER VESSELS

p63.1 The Prophet (Allah bless him and give him peace) said:

(1) "Do not wear silk or brocade. Do not drink from vessels of gold or silver or eat from

p63.0 **الشرب في الذهب والفضة**

p63.1 قال النـبي ﷺ: «لا تلبسـوا الحريـر ولا الديباج، ولا تشربوا في آنية الـذهب والفضـة ولا تأكلوا في صحافها

dishes made of them: these are for others [A: i.e. non-Muslims] in this world, and for you in the next."

(2) "He who eats or drinks from vessels of gold or silver but swallows hellfire into his belly."

*

p64.0 ARGUING, PICKING APART ANOTHER'S WORDS, AND QUARRELLING

p64.1   Allah Most High says:

(1) "They did not mention him [Jesus] to you as an example except for argument. Rather, they are quarrelsome people" (Koran 43:58).

(2) "Those who argue about the signs of Allah without authority having been given to them have nothing in their hearts but pride, to which they will never attain" (Koran 40:56).

p64.2   The Prophet (Allah bless him and give him peace) said:

(1) "The man most hated by Allah is the obstinate arguer."

(2) "No people went astray after having been guided save that they were afflicted with arguing."

(3) "Arguing over the Koran is unbelief."

(4) "He who presses for something he knows is false remains under the hatred of Allah until he gives it up."

(5) "The thing I fear most for my Community is the eloquent hypocrite."

(6) "Modesty and being at a loss for words are two components of true faith, while vulgarity

فإنها لهم في الدنيا ولكم في الآخرة [رواه البخاري].

وقال ﷺ: «إن الذي يأكل أو يشرب في إناء الذهب والفضة إنما يجرجر في بطنه نار جهنم» [رواه مسلم].

p64.0   الجدال والمراء واللدد

p64.1   قال الله تعالى:
﴿مَا ضَرَبُوهُ لَكَ إِلَّا جَدَلاً . بَلْ هُمْ قَوْمٌ خَصِمُونَ﴾ [الزخرف: ٥٨].

وقال تعالى: ﴿إِنَّ الَّذِينَ يُجَادِلُونَ فِي آيَاتِ اللّهِ بِغَيْرِ سُلْطَانٍ أَتَاهُمْ إِنْ فِي صُدُورِهِمْ إِلَّا كِبْرٌ مَا هُم بِبَالِغِيهِ﴾ [غافر: ٥٦].

p64.2   وقال النبي ﷺ: «إنَّ أبغض الرجال إلى الله تعالى الألدُّ الخَصِمُ» [رواه البخاري].

وقال: «ما ضلَّ قومٌ بعد هدىً كانوا عليه إلا أوتوا الجدلَ...» [رواه الترمذي].

وقال: «المراء في القرآن كفرٌ» [رواه أبو داود].

وقال: «من خاصم في باطل ـ وهو يعلم ـ لم يزل في سخط الله حتى ينزع» [رواه أبو داود].

وقال: «أخوَفُ ما أخافُ على أمتي كل منافق عليم اللسان» [رواه أحمد].

وقال: «الحياءُ والعَيُّ شعبتانِ من

693

and long-windedness are two components of hypocrisy."

الإيمـان والبـذاءُ والبيـانُ شعبتـان من النفاق» [رواه الترمذي].

*

p65.0 STINTING WHEN WEIGHING OR MEASURING OUT GOODS

p65.0 المطفِّف في وزنه وكيله

p65.1   Allah Most High says:

p65.1   قال الله تعالى:

"Woe to stinters who take their full share when measuring goods from people but skimp when measuring or weighing out for them. Do these not believe they will be raised to a momentous day, a day when people will stand before the Lord of the Worlds?" (Koran 83:1–6).

﴿وَيْـلٌ لِلْمُطَفِّفِينَ الَّـذِينَ إِذَا اكْتَـالُـوا عَلَى النَّاسِ يَسْتَوْفُـونَ، وَإِذَا كَالُوهُمْ أَوْ وَزَنُوهُمْ يُخْسِـرُونَ. أَلَا يَظُنُّ أُولَئِكَ أَنَّهُم مَبْعُـوثُـونَ لِيَوْمٍ عَظِيمٍ. يَوْمَ يَقُومُ النَّاسُ لِرَبِّ العَالَمِينَ﴾ [المطففين: ١ - ٦].

p65.2   This is a type of theft, a breach of faith, and consuming others' property through falsehood.

p65.2   وذلـك ضرب من السـرقـة والخيانة، وأكل المال بالباطل.

*

p66.0 FEELING SECURE FROM ALLAH'S DEVISING

p66.0 الأمن من مكر الله تعالى

p66.1   Allah Most High says:

p66.1   قال الله تعالى:

(1) "None feels safe from Allah's devising except people who are ruined" (Koran 7:99).

﴿فَـلَا يَأْمَـنُ مَكْـرَ اللَّـهِ إِلَّا الـقَـوْمُ الخَاسِرُونَ﴾ [الأعراف: ٩٩].

(2) "... until, when they were exulting in what they had been given, We suddenly seized them" (Koran 6:44).

وقـال تعـالى: ﴿حَتَّى إِذَا فَرِحُـوا بِمَا أُوتُوا أَخَذْنَاهُمْ بَغْتَةً﴾ [الأنعام: ٤٤].

(3) "Verily, those who do not hope to meet Us, who enjoy this world and feel at ease with it, and those who are oblivious to Our signs: their refuge is hell for what they have earned" (Koran 10:7–8).

وقـال تعـالى: ﴿إِنَّ الَّـذِينَ لَا يَرْجُـونَ لِقَـاءَنَا وَرَضُوا بِالحَياةِ الدُّنْيَا وَاطْمَأَنُّوا بِهَا وَالَّـذِينَ هُمْ عَنْ آيَـاتِنَـا غَافِلُونَ أُولَئِكَ مَأْوَاهُمُ النَّارُ بِمَا كَانُوا يَكْسِبُونَ﴾ [يونس: ٧ - ٨]

*

p67.0 DESPAIRING OF THE MERCY OF ALLAH AND LOSS OF HOPE

p67.1 Allah Most High says:

(1) "None despairs of the mercy of Allah except people who disbelieve" (Koran 12:87).

(2) "It is He who sends down the rain after they have lost hope" (Koran 42:28).

(3) "Say: 'O My slaves who have been prodigal against yourselves, do not despair of the mercy of Allah' " (Koran 39:53).

p67.2 The Prophet (Allah bless him and give him peace) said,

"Let none of you die except thinking the best of Allah."

*

p68.0 INGRATITUDE TO SOMEONE WHO DOES ONE A KINDNESS

p68.1 Allah Most High says:

"... to show thanks to Me, and to your parents ..." (Koran 31:14).

p68.2 The Prophet (Allah bless him and give him peace) said,

"He who does not thank people is unthankful to Allah."

p68.3 One of the early Muslims said: "Ingratitude for a kindness is one of the enormities. *Gratitude* consists of reciprocating it or supplicating for the person."

p67.0 الإياس من رَوْح الله [تعالى] والقنوط

p67.1 قال الله تعالى :
﴿إِنَّهُ لَا يَيْأَسُ مِنْ رَوْحِ اللَّهِ إِلَّا القَوْمُ الكَافِرُونَ﴾ [يوسف : ٨٧].
وقـال تعالى : ﴿وَهُوَ الَّذِي يُنَزِّلُ الغَيْثَ مِنْ بَعْدِ مَا قَنَطُوا﴾ [الشورى : ٢٨].
وقـال تعـالى : ﴿قُـلْ يَا عِبَـادِيَ الَّذِينَ أَسْـرَفُـوا عَلَى أَنْفُسِهِمْ لَا تَقْنَطُوا مِنْ رَحْمَةِ اللَّهِ﴾ [الزمر : ٥٣].

p67.2 وقـال النبي ﷺ : «لا يمـوتَنَّ أحدُكم إلا وهو حَسَنُ الظن بالله» [رواه مسلم].

p68.0 كفران نعمة المحسن

p68.1 قال الله تعالى :
﴿ . . . أَنِ اشْكُرْ لِي وَلِوَالِدَيْكَ . . . ﴾ [لقمان : ١٤].

p68.2 قال النبي ﷺ : «لا يشكر الله من لا يشكر الناس» [رواه أبو داود].

p68.3 وقـال بعض السلف «كفـران النعمة من الكبائر، وشكرها بالمجازاة أو بالدعاء».

p69.0 WITHHOLDING EXCESS WATER FROM OTHERS

منع فضل الماء p69.0

p69.1 The Prophet (Allah bless him and give him peace) said:

(1) "Whoever denies others his surplus water or pasturage, Allah shall deny him His blessing on the Day of Judgement."

(2) "Do not sell surplus water."

p69.1 عن النبي ﷺ قال: «مَن منع فضل الماء أو فضل كلئه منعه الله فضله يوم القيامة» [رواه أحمد].

وقـال ﷺ: «لا تبيعـوا فضـل المـاء» [رواه البخاري].

*

p70.0 BRANDING AN ANIMAL'S FACE

مَن وسم دابة في الوجه p70.0

p70.1 The Prophet (Allah bless him and give him peace) passed by a donkey whose face had been branded and said,

"Haven't you heard that I have cursed whoever brands or strikes the faces of livestock?"

—and he forbade it.

p70.1 [عن جابر رضي الله عنه] أن النبي ﷺ مرّ بحمـار قد وسم في وجهـه فقـال: «أمـا بلغكم أني لعنتُ مَن وسم البـهـيـمـة في وجههـا، أو ضربهـا في وجهها؟» ونهى عن ذلك [رواه أبو داود].

p70.2 The words of the Prophet (Allah bless him and give him peace) "Haven't you heard that I have cursed..." imply that he who has not heard the warning against an act is not guilty of sin by committing it, though whoever has heard and knows is included in the curse. We hold that it is likewise with all these enormities, except those which are necessarily known as being of the religion (def: f1.3(N:)).

p70.2 فقـولـه ﷺ: «أمـا بلغكم أني لعنتُ» يفهم منه أن مَن لم يبلغـه الـزجـر غيـر آثم، وأن مَن بلغـه وعرف فهو داخل في اللعنـة، وكـذا نقـول في عامـة هذه الكبائر إلا ما علم منها بالاضطرار من الدين.

*

p71.0 GAMBLING

القمار p71.0

p71.1 Allah Most High says:

"Wine, gambling, idols, and fortune-telling

p71.1 قال الله تعالى: ﴿إنَّمَا الخَمْرُ وَالمَيْسِرُ وَالأَنْصَابُ

arrows are but filth of the Devil's handiwork, so shun it, that you may succeed. The Devil only wants to create enmity and hatred between you over wine and gambling, and to prevent you from remembering Allah and from prayer. Will you not then desist?'' (Koran 5:90–91).

p71.2   The Prophet (Allah bless him and give him peace) said,

"Whoever says to his companion, 'Come, I will play you for stakes,' must expiate by giving charity,''

If merely saying this is a sin that calls for charity in expiation, what must one suppose about actually doing it? It is a form of consuming others' wealth through falsehood.

*

p72.0 VIOLATING THE MECCAN SACRED PRECINCT (HARAM)

p72.1   Allah Most High says:

"... and al-Masjid al-Haram which We have appointed equally for all people, he who stays therein as well as the desert dweller. Whoever intends to violate it out of wrongdoing, We shall make him taste a painful torment'' (Koran 22:25).

(n: The words *out of wrongdoing* in the above verse mean "by reason of doing wrong through committing an act that is forbidden therein, even if it merely consists of reviling one of the caretakers'' (*Tafsir al-Jalalayn* (y77), 436).)

p72.2   The Prophet (Allah bless him and give him peace) said,

"Of all people, the greatest in outrage against Allah is he who kills in the Meccan Sacred Precinct, who kills someone who is not trying to kill

وَالأَزْلاَمُ رِجْسٌ مِنْ عَمَلِ الـشَّـيْطَـانِ فَاجْتَنِبُوهُ لَعَلَّكُمْ تُفْلِحُونَ . إِنَّمَا يُرِيدُ الشَّيْطَانُ أَنْ يُوقِعَ بَيْنَكُمُ العَدَاوَةَ وَالبَغْضَاءَ فِي الخَمْرِ وَالمَيْسِرِ وَيَصُدَّكُمْ عَنْ ذِكْرِ اللَّهِ وَعَنِ الـصَّـلاةِ فَهَـلْ أَنْـتُـمْ مُنْتَهُونَ﴾. [المائدة: ٩٠ ـ ٩١].

p71.2   وقـال الـنبي ﷺ: «مَن قال لصاحبه تعالَ أقامِرْكَ فليتصدّق» [رواه البخاري ومسلم].
فإذا كان مجرد القـول معصيـة موجبة للصدقة المكفرة، فما ظنك بالفعل؟ وهو داخل في أكل المال بالباطل .

p72.0 الإلحاد في الحرم

p72.1   قال الله تعالى:
﴿... وَالـمَسْجِـدِ الحَـرَامِ الَّـذِي جَعَلْنَاهُ لِلنَّاسِ سَوَاءً العَاكِفُ فِيهِ وَالبَادِ، وَمَنْ يُرِدْ فِيهِ بِإِلْحَادٍ بِظُلْمٍ نُذِقْهُ مِنْ عَذَابٍ أَلِيمٍ﴾ [الحج: ٢٥].
(ت: أمـا معنى كلمة «بظلم» في الآية الكريمة، فقد قال في تفسير الجلالين: «أي بسببه بأن ارتكب منهيـاً ولـو شتم الخادم». [نقل من تفسير الجلالين: ٤٣٦]).

p72.2   وعن النبي ﷺ قال: «إنّ أعتى الناس على الله من قتـل في الحرم، أو

him, or who kills because of the feuds of pre-Islamic times."

قتل غير قاتله ، أو قتل بذ حول الجاهلية»
[رواه أحمد] .

*

p73.0 FORGOING THE FRIDAY PRAYER TO PRAY ALONE

p73.0 تارك الجمعة ليصلي وحده

p73.1 The Prophet (Allah bless him and give him peace) said:

(1) "I've considered having a man lead people at prayer and going myself to those who hang back from attending the Friday prayer to burn their houses down upon them."

(2) "Going to the Friday prayer is obligatory for every male who has reached puberty."

p73.1 عن النبي ﷺ : «لقـد هممتُ أنْ آمـر رجلاً يصلي بالنـاس ، ثم أحـرّق على رجالٍ يتخلّفون عن الجمعة بيوتَهم»
[رواه مسلم] .
وعن النبي ﷺ قال : «رواحُ الجمعـة واجبٌ على كل محتلم» [رواه النسائي] .

*

p74.0 SPYING ON THE MUSLIMS AND REVEALING THEIR WEAKNESSES

p74.0 من جسَّ على المسلمين ودل على عوراتهم

p74.1 Included in this subject is the hadith of Hatib ibn Abi Balta'a (A: who sent a secret letter telling of the Muslims' military plans to his relatives in Mecca in hopes that they would not get hurt) whom 'Umar (Allah be well pleased with him) wanted to kill for what he had done, but the Prophet (Allah bless him and give him peace) forbade 'Umar to, as Hatib had fought at Badr (A: and by accepting Hatib's excuse, left nothing for any Muslim to criticize (dis: p75.3)).

If someone's spying entails undermining Islam and its people, or the killing, captivity, enslavement, or plundering of the Muslims, or anything of the like, then he is one of those who strive for corruption in the land, destroying tillage and offspring, and he is subject to death, and deserves the torment (A: of hellfire), may Allah save us from it. Anyone who spies necessarily

p74.1 في البـاب حديث حاطب بن أبي بلتعة وأن عمر رضي الله عنه أراد قتله بمـا فعل ، فمنعه النبي ﷺ من قتله لكونه شهد بدراً .
فإن ترتـب على جسِّـه وهـن على الإسـلام وأهله ، وقتـل المسلمين وسبي وأسـر ونهب ، أو شيء من ذلـك ؛ فهـذا ممـن سـعـى في الأرض فسـاداً وأهلك الحرث والنسل ، وتعين قتله ، وحق عليه العذاب ، نسأل الله العافية .
وبـالضـرورة يدري كل ذي جسَّ أن

knows that if ordinary talebearing is an enormity (dis: p45), a spy's carrying information is far more abominable and heinous.

*

p75.0 PROBABLE ENORMITIES

(n: Commentaries by Imam Nawawi and 'Abd al-Ra'uf Munawi have been added by the translator to some of the following hadiths.)

ENVY

p75.1 The Prophet (Allah bless him and give him peace) said:

(1) "Beware of envy, for envy consumes good works as fire consumes wood."

(2) "None of you believes until he loves for his brother what he loves for himself."

(Nawawi:) It is fitter to interpret this hadith as referring to universal brotherhood, including both Muslims and non-Muslims, such that one loves for one's non-Muslim brother what one loves for oneself, i.e. to enter Islam, just as one loves one's Muslim brother to remain in Islam, this being why it is desirable (mustahabb) to pray for the guidance of non-Muslims. The hadith is understood as denying that someone who does not love for his brother what he loves for himself has perfect faith, *love* meaning to want what is good and advantageous for him, referring to religious love, not individual human love. For one's human nature might well dislike another's attaining the good, or surpassing oneself therein, though it is obligatory for one to resist this human tendency and pray for one's brother and desire for him what one desires for oneself. Someone who does not love for his brother what he loves for himself is *envious*, and envy, as Ghazali notes, is of three types (A: all of them unlawful). The first is to wish that another person cease to have something good in order to obtain it oneself. The second is to wish that

p75.0 ما يحتمل أنه من الكبائر

الحسد

p75.1 قال النبي ﷺ: «إياكم والحسد، فإن الحسد يأكل الحسنات كما تأكل النار الحطب» [رواه أبو داود]. وقال ﷺ: «لا يؤمن أحدكم حتى يحب لأخيه ما يحب لنفسه» [رواه البخاري].

(النووي:) الأولى أن يحمل ذلك على عموم الأخوة حتى يشمل الكافر والمسلم، فيحب لأخيه الكافر ما يحب لنفسه من دخوله في الإسلام، كما يحب لأخيه المسلم دوامه على الإسلام. ولهذا كان الدعاء بالهداية للكافر مستحباً.

والحديث محمول على نفي الإيمان الكامل عمن لم يحب لأخيه ما يحب لنفسه. والمراد بالمحبة إرادة الخير والمنفعة، ثم المراد المحبة الدينية لا المحبة البشرية. فإن الطباع البشرية قد تكره حصول الخير وتمييز غيرها عليها، والإنسان يجب عليه أن يخالف الطباع البشرية ويدعو لأخيه ويتمنى له ما يحب لنفسه. والشخص متى لم يحب لأخيه ما يحب لنفسه كان حسوداً، والحسد ـ كما قال الغزالي ـ ينقسم إلى ثلاثة أقسام: الأول أن يتمنى زوال نعمة الغير وحصولها لنفسه. الثاني أن يتمنى زوال

another lose something good, even if one does not obtain it, as when one already has another like it, or does not want it, this being worse than the previous type. The third is when one does not wish that the other cease to have something good, but resents his having surpassed one in attainment or position, accepting his parity with one but not his superiority. And this is unlawful as well, because one thereby objects to Allah's division of His favor among His servants. Allah Most High says:

"Are they the ones who apportion the mercy of your Lord? It is We who have divided their livelihoods between them in this life, and raised some of them in degrees above others" (Koran 43:32).

So whoever does not accept this division opposes Allah Most High in His apportionment and His wisdom. One must remedy one's human nature, make it accept destiny, and resist it by praying that one's enemy be given what one's self-interest might prefer him not to have (al-Arba'un al-Nawawiyya wa sharhuha (y103), 40).

NOT LOVING THE PROPHET (ALLAH BLESS HIM AND GIVE HIM PEACE) MORE THAN ALL PEOPLE

p75.2 The Prophet (Allah bless him and give him peace) said,

"None of you believes until I am more beloved to him than his wife, child, self, and all people."

(Munawi:) Kirmani says, "*Love of the Prophet* (Allah bless him and give him peace) means the will to obey him and not disobey him, this being one of the obligations of Islam" (*Fayd al-Qadir sharh al-Jami' al-saghir* (y91), 6.441).

CONTENDING WITH WHAT THE PROPHET (ALLAH BLESS HIM AND GIVE HIM PEACE) HAS BROUGHT

p75.3 The Prophet (Allah bless him and give

نعمة الغير وإنْ لم تحصل له، كما إذا كان عنده مثلها أو لم يكن يحبها وهذا شرّ من الأول.

والثالث أن لا يتمنى زوال النعمة عن الغير لكن يكره ارتفاعه عليه في الحظ والمنزلة ويرضى بالمساواة ولا يرضى بالزيادة. وهذا أيضاً محرّم، لأنه لم يرض بقسمة الله تعالى. قال الله تعالى:

﴿أَهُمْ يَقْسِمُونَ رَحْمَةَ رَبِّكَ؟ نَحْنُ قَسَمْنَا بَيْنَهُمْ مَعِيشَتَهُمْ فِي الْحَيَاةِ الدُّنْيَا وَرَفَعْنَا بَعْضَهُمْ فَوْقَ بَعْضٍ دَرَجَاتٍ﴾ [الزخرف: ٣٢].

فمن لم يرض بالقسمة فقد عارض الله تعالى في قسمه وحكمته، وعلى الإنسان أن يعالج نفسه ويحملها على الرضا بالقضاء، ويخالفها بالدعاء لعدوه بما يخالف النفس [نقل من الأربعين النووية وشرحها: ٤٠].

أن يحب المرء أحداً أكثر من رسول الله ﷺ

p75.2 قال النبي ﷺ: «لا يؤمنُ أحدكم حتى أكون أحبَّ إليه من أهله وولده ونفسه والناس أجمعين» [رواه البخاري].

(المناوي:) قال الكرماني: «ومحبة الرسول ﷺ إرادة طاعته وترك مخالفته وهو من واجبات الإسلام» [نقل من فيض القدير شرح الجامع الصغير: ٦/ ٤٤١].

عدم التسليم بما جاء به الرسول ﷺ

p75.3 قال النبي ﷺ: «لا يؤمن

him peace) said,

"None of you believes until his inclinations conform to what I have brought."

(Nawawi:) This means a person must examine his acts in light of the Koran and sunna, suspending his own inclinations and following what the Prophet (Allah bless him and give him peace) has brought. The hadith resembles the word of Allah Most High,

"When Allah and His messenger have decided a matter, no believer, male or female, has a choice in their affair" (Koran 33:36).

(al-Arba'un al-Nawawiyya wa sharhuha (y103), 74)

ACQUIESCING TO DISOBEDIENCE

p75.4 The Prophet (Allah bless him and give him peace) said:

(1) "Whoever of you sees something wrong, let him change it with his hand (dis: book q). If unable, then let him change it with his tongue. If unable, then with his heart. And that is the weakest degree of faith."

And in the hadith related by Muslim concerning oppressors:

(2) "Whoever fights them with his hand is a believer, whoever fights them with his tongue is a believer, whoever fights them in his heart is a believer, Beyond that, there is not a mustard grain of faith."

This hadith proves that whoever does not condemn acts of disobedience in his heart or wish they would cease is devoid of faith. Fighting with the heart includes asking Allah Most High to annihilate the falsehood and its perpetrators, or improve them.

(3) "Leaders will be placed over you that some of you will accept and some of you condemn.

أحدُكم حتى يكون هواه تبعاً لما جئت به»
[رواه الديلمي].

(النووي:) يعني الشخص يجب عليه أن يعــرض عمله على الكتــاب والسنـة ويخالف هواه ويتبع ما جاء به ﷺ. وهذا نظيـر قولـه تعـالى: ﴿وَمَا كَانَ لِمُؤْمِنٍ وَلَا مُؤْمِنَةٍ إِذَا قَضَى اللَّهُ وَرَسُولُهُ أَمْراً أَنْ يَكُونَ لَهُمُ الْخِيَرَةُ مِنْ أَمْرِهِمْ﴾ [الأحزاب: ٣٦].
[نقل من الأربعين النووية وشرحها: ٧٤].

الرضى بمنكر

p75.4 قال الـنـبـي ﷺ: «مـن رأى منكم منكراً فليغيره بيده، فإن لم يستطع فبلسـانـه، فإن لم يستطع فبقلبه وذلك أضعف الإيمان» [رواه مسلم].

وفي حديث لمسلم في الظلمة: «فمن جاهـدهم بيده فهو مؤمنٌ، ومن جاهدهم بلسـانـه فهـو مؤمنٌ، ومَن جاهدهم بقلبه فهـو مؤمنٌ، ليس وراء ذلك من الإيمان حبة خردل» [رواه مسلم].

وفيـه دلـيـل على أن من لم يـنكــر المعاصي بقلبه ولا يود زوالها فإنه عديم الإيمان. ومِن جهاد القلب التـوجه إلى الله تعالى أن يمحق الباطل وأهله أو أن يصلحهم.

وقـال ﷺ: «إنه يُستعمل عليكم أمراء فتعرفون وتنكرون: فمن كره فقد بَرِىءَ،

Whoever dislikes what they do is innocent. Whoever condemns what they do is secure. But not whoever accepts and follows them." Someone said, "Shouldn't we fight them?" And he replied, "No, not as long as they maintain the prayer [dis: o25.3(a(A:))] among you."

ومـن أنكـر فقـد سَلِمَ، ولكنْ مَن رضي وتـابعَ». قيل: أفلا نقاتلهم؟ قال: «لا ما أقاموا فيكم الصلاة». [رواه مسلم].

HELPING ANOTHER TO WRONGFULLY DISPUTE

الإعانة على خصومة بغير حق

p75.5 The Prophet (Allah bless him and give him peace) said,

"He who helps another to argue without right remains under the hatred of Allah until he gives up."

p75.5   قال النبي ﷺ: «مَن أعان على خصومةٍ بغير حقٍّ كان في سخط الله حتى ينزَعَ» [رواه الحاكم].

UNDERHANDEDNESS

الخديعة [في غير الجهاد]

p75.6 The Prophet (Allah bless him and give him peace) said,

"Plotting and duplicity are in the hellfire."

p75.6   قال النبي ﷺ: «المكر والخديعة في النار» [رواه البيهقي].

DISAFFECTING A PERSON'S SPOUSE OR SERVANT FROM HIM

من خبب على امرىء زوجته أو مملوكه

p75.7 The Prophet (Allah bless him and give him peace) said,

"He who disaffects a person's wife or servant from him is not of us."

p75.7   قال الـنبي ﷺ: «مَن خَبَّبَ على امـرىءٍ زوجته أو مملوكه فليس منا» [رواه أبو داود].

VULGARITY

البذاء في القول

p75.8 The Prophet (Allah bless him and give him peace) said:

(1) "Modesty is of faith, and faith is in paradise. Vulgarity is of rudeness, and rudeness is in hell."

p75.8   قال الـنبي ﷺ: «الحيـاءُ من الإيمـان والإيمـان في الجنة، والبذاءُ من الجفاء والجفاءُ في النار» [رواه الحاكم].

(2) "Allah detests the foulmouthed, vulgar person."

وقـال ﷺ: «إن الله يبغض الفـاحش البذيء» [رواه أبو داود].

BEING LEADERLESS

من خرج على الإمام الحق

p75.9 The Prophet (Allah bless him and give him peace) said,

"The death of someone who dies without the leader of a group over him is as if he had died in the pre-Islamic period of ignorance [A: *leader* meaning the caliph (def: o25) or his representative, if they exist (dis: p40.2(A:)]."

p75.9 قال الـنبي ﷺ: «مَن مات وليس عليه إمـامُ جمـاعـة فإنّ موتته موتةٌ جاهليةٌ» [رواه الحاكم].

BENEFITING AT A MUSLIM'S EXPENSE

من أراد حظـاً دنيـويـاً بالطعن في مسلم بغير حق

p75.10 The Prophet (Allah bless him and give him peace) said:

"Whoever eats food obtained at the expense of a Muslim, Allah will feed him hellfire on Judgement Day. He who gains a prestigious reputation at the expense of a Muslim, Allah will reduce him to the position of the show-offs and boasters (def: p33.2) on Judgement Day. He who wears a garment acquired at the expense of a Muslim, Allah will dress him in a garment of fire on Judgement Day."

p75.10 قال الـنبي ﷺ: «مـن أكـل بمسلم أكلة أطعمه الله بها أكلةً من النار يوم القيـامـة، ومن أقـام بمسلم مقـام سمعةٍ، أقـامـه الله يوم القيـامـة مقام رياءٍ وسمعةٍ، ومن اكتسى بمسلم ثوباً كساه الله ثوباً من نارٍ يوم القيامة» [رواه الحاكم].

SHUNNING A MUSLIM WITHOUT RIGHT

هجر المسلم بغير حق

p75.11 The Prophet (Allah bless him and give him peace) said,

"Whoever shuns his brother for a year is as though he had spilled his blood."

(Munawi:) This means that avoiding him for a year deserves punishment in the hereafter just as spilling his blood does, and that both the person who shuns someone and he who kills someone are involved in sin, though not on the same level, for the use of a simile does not imply the parity of the

p75.11 قال النبي ﷺ: «من هجر أخاه سنةً فهو كسفك دمِه» [رواه الحاكم].
(المناوي:) [«من هجر أخاه» (في الإسلام) «سنة» (أي بغيـر عذر شرعي) «فهو كسفك دمه» [] أي مهـاجرته سنة توجب العقوبة كما أن سفك دمه يوجبها، والمراد اشتراك الهاجر والقاتل في الإثم، لا في قدره، ولا يلزم التساوي بين المشبه

simile's subject to the thing with which it has been compared. Shafi'i holds it is unlawful to shun a Muslim for three days unless there is a valid reason such as the religious improvement of the person avoiding the other or person being avoided, or when the latter is morally corrupt or involved in reprehensible innovation (bid'a, def: w29.3) (*Fayd al-Qadir sharh al-Jami' al-saghir* (y91), 6.234).

INTERCEDING FOR THE GUILTY

p75.12 The Prophet (Allah bless him and give him peace) said,

"He whose intercession comes between a criminal and one of Allah's prescribed penalties has defied Allah in His command."

SAYING SOMETHING THAT ALLAH DETESTS

p75.13 The Prophet (Allah bless him and give him peace) said:

(1) "A man says something Allah detests that he does not think twice about, for which he plunges into hell [dis: r1]."

(2) "A man says something pleasing to Allah, not imagining it amounts to what it does, for which Allah records His pleasure in him until Judgement Day. And a man says something that angers Allah, not imagining it amounts to what it does, for which Allah records His wrath against him until the day he meets Him."

SAYING "MASTER" (SAYYID) TO A HYPOCRITE

p75.14 The Prophet (Allah bless him and give him peace) said,

"Do not say "master" to a hypocrite, for if he is a master, you have angered your Lord Mighty and Majestic."

والمشبه به.

ومــذهب الشـافعي أن هجر المسلم فوق ثلاث حرام إلا لمصلحــة كإصــلاح دين الهــاجر أو المهجور أو لنحو فسقه أو بدعته [نقل من فيض القدير شرح الجامع الصغير: ٦/ ٢٣٤].

الشفاعة في الحدود

p75.12 قال الـنبي ﷺ: «مَن حالت شفـاعته دون حدِ من حدود الله فقد ضَادَّ اللهَ في أمره» [رواه أبو داود].

التكلم بما يسخط الله

p75.13 قال النبي ﷺ: «إنَّ الـرجـلَ ليتكلم بالكلمة من سخط الله لا يلقي لها بالاً يهوي بها في جهنم» [رواه البخاري].

وقال ﷺ: «إن الرجل ليتكلم بالكلمة من رضوان الله ما (كان) يظن أن تبلغ ما بلغت يكتب الله له بهـا رضـوانـه إلى يوم القيـامـة. وإن الرجل ليتكلم بالكلمة من سخـط الله ما كان يظن أن تبلغ ما بلغت يكتب الله له بهـا سخطـه إلى يوم يلقـاه» [رواه الترمذي].

أن يقول لمنافق يا سيد

p75.14 قال الـنبي ﷺ: «لا تقـولـوا للمنــافق سيدٌ، فإنـه إنْ يَكُ سيداً فقـد أسخطتم ربَّكم عز وجل» [رواه أبو داود].

BREAKING A PROMISE	إخلاف الوعد

p75.15 The Prophet (Allah bless him and give him peace) said,

"The signs of a hypocrite are three: when he speaks he lies, when he promises he breaks it, and when entrusted he betrays his trust."

(A: If one makes an ordinary promise to another person, it is sunna to keep the promise, though it is strictly unlawful to make a promise that one has no intention to keep, this being how scholars interpret the above hadith.)

Lying and betraying a trust have been mentioned before, while here we are discussing promise breaking. Allah Most High says,

"Of them, there is one who promised Allah, 'If He bestows of His generosity on us, we shall certainly give charity and be of the righteous' " (Koran 9:75).

(n: Suyuti notes that the person referred to above "is Tha'laba ibn Hatib, who asked the Prophet (Allah bless him and give him peace) to pray that Allah would enrich him, so that he might give everyone their just due. So the Prophet supplicated for him and he became wealthy, but then he stopped coming to the Friday prayer, withdrew from the community, and refused to pay zakat, as Allah Most High says:

"'But when He gave to them of His generosity, they hoarded it and turned away in aversion. So He punished them by putting hypocrisy into their hearts until the day they meet Him, because they broke their promise to Allah and lied' (Koran 9:76–77).

Some time after this, he brought the Prophet (Allah bless him and give him peace) his zakat, but the Prophet told him, 'Allah forbids me to accept it from you,' at which Tha'laba threw handfuls of dust upon his own head. He later [A: in the time of the subsequent caliphate] took his zakat to Abu Bakr, but he would not accept it. Then to 'Umar, but he would not accept it. Then he took it to 'Uthman, but he would not accept it either, and he died in the reign of 'Uthman" (Tafsir al-Jalalayn (y77), 253).)

p75.15 قال النبي ﷺ : «آية المنافق ثلاث : إذا حدّث كذب ، وإذا وعـد أخلف ، وإذا اؤتمن خان» [متفق عليه] .

فأمـا الكـذب والخيـانـة فقـد مرّا وأما خلف الـوعـد فهـو المقصـود بالـذكر هنا ، وقد قال الله تعالى :

﴿وَمِنْهُمْ مَنْ عَاهَدَ اللَّهَ لَئِنْ آتَانَا مِنْ فَضْلِهِ لَنَصَّدَّقَنَّ وَلَنَكُونَنَّ مِنَ الصَّالِحِينَ﴾ [التوبة : ٧٥] . (ت : قال السيوطي : وهو ثعلبة بن حاطب سأل النبي ﷺ أن يدعوله أن يرزقه الله مالاً ويؤدي منه كل ذي حق حقـه فدعـا له فوسـع عليـه فانقطـع عن الجمعة والجماعة ومنع الزكاة كما قال تعالى :)

﴿فَلَمَّا آتَاهُمْ مِنْ فَضْلِهِ بَخِلُوا بِهِ وَتَوَلَّوا وَهُمْ مُعْرِضُونَ . فَأَعْقَبَهُمْ نِفَاقاً فِي قُلُوبِهِمْ إِلَى يَوْمِ يَلْقَوْنَهُ بِمَا أَخْلَفُوا اللَّهَ مَا وَعَدُوهُ وَبِمَا كَانُوا يَكْذِبُونَ﴾ . [التوبة : ٧٦ - ٧٧]

فجاء بعـد ذلـك إلى النبي ﷺ بزكاته فقـال : «إن الله منعني أن أقبـل منـك» ؛ فجعل يحثو التراب على رأسه ثم جاء بها إلى أبي بكـر فلم يقبلهـا ثم إلى عمـر فلم يقبلها ثم إلى عثمان فلم يقبلها ومات في زمانه [نقل من تفسير الجلالين : ٢٥٣] .

NOT TRIMMING ONE'S MUSTACHE	عدم قص الشــارب إذا كان يغطي الشفة العليا
p75.16 The Prophet (Allah bless him and give him peace) said:	p75.16 قال النبي ﷺ: «من لم يأخـذ (من) شاربه فليس منا» [رواه الترمذي].
(1) "He who does not trim his mustache [def: e4.1(2)] is not one of us."	وقـال ﷺ: «خالِفُوا المجوس: وفّروا اللحى وأحفوا الشوارب» [رواه البخاري].
(2) "Be different from the Zoroastrians: grow your beards and trim your mustaches."	
NOT PERFORMING THE HAJJ WHEN ABLE TO	عدم الحج مع الاستطاعة
p75.17 'Umar ibn Khattab (Allah be well pleased with him) said:	p75.17 قال عمـر بن الخطـاب رضي الله عنه: «لقـد هممت أن أبعث رجـالاً إلى هذه الأمـصـار فينظـروا كل من لم يحـج؛ فمن كانـت له جدة ولـم يحـج فيضـربـوا عليهم الجـزيـة، ما هم بمسلمين. ما هم بمسلمين» [رواه سعيد ابن منصور].
"I've considered sending men to these cities to see who has not made the pilgrimage, and collect the non-Muslim poll tax (jizya, def: o11.4) from everyone possessing the means who has not performed it [def: j1.5–10]. They are not Muslims. They are not Muslims."	
KEEPING AN INHERITANCE FROM AN HEIR	من احتال فحرم وارثه من الميراث
p75.18 The Prophet (Allah bless him and give him peace) said,	p75.18 قال الـنـبـي ﷺ: مَن فرَّ مِن ميراث وارثه قطـع اللهُ ميراثه من الجنة» [رواه ابن ماجه].
"Whoever prevents his heirs from receiving their inheritance [dis: w52.1(234–36)], Allah will prevent his inheriting paradise."	
TALKING ABOUT HOW ONE'S WIFE MAKES LOVE	إفشـاء سر ما يجري بين الـرجـل وزوجته في الجماع
p75.19 The Prophet (Allah bless him and give him peace) said,	p75.19 قال الـنـبـي ﷺ: «إنَّ من شرّ الناس عند الله منـزلـةً يوم القيامة رجلٌ يُفضي إلى امـرأتـه وتُفضي إليه، ثم ينشر سِرَّها» [رواه مسلم].
"Among the worst people in Allah's sight on Judgement Day will be the man who makes love to his wife and she to him, and he divulges her secret."	

SODOMIZING ONE'S WIFE

اتيان المرأة في دبرها

p75.20 The Prophet (Allah Bless him and give him peace) said,

"He who sodomizes a woman is accursed."

p75.20 قال رسول الله ﷺ: «ملعونٌ من أتى امرأةً في دبرها» [رواه أحمد].

INTERCOURSE WITH ONE'S WIFE DURING MENSTRUATION

مجامعة الحائض

p75.21 The Prophet (Allah bless him and give him peace) said,

"Whoever has intercourse with a woman during her period, or sodomizes a woman, or who goes to a fortune-teller and believes him, has committed unbelief [A: if he considers any of these permissible]."

p75.21 وعن النبي ﷺ: «مَن أتى حائضاً (في فرجها) أو امرأةً في دبرها، أو كاهناً فصدّقه فقد كفرَ» [رواه أبو داود].

LOOKING INTO ANOTHER'S HOUSE WITHOUT LEAVE

النظر في بيت الغير بغير إذنه

p75.22 The Prophet (Allah bless him and give him peace) said:

(1) "Were a man to look at you without permission and you threw a rock at him and knocked out his eye, you would not have committed any offense."

(2) "Whoever peeps into a house without its people's leave, they may put out his eye."

p75.22 قال النبي ﷺ: «لو أن رجلاً اطلع عليك بغير إذن فحذفته بحصاة ففقأت عينه، ما كان عليك جناح» [رواه البخاري ومسلم].
وقال ﷺ: «مَن اطّلع في بيت قومٍ بغير إذنهم فقد حل لهم أنْ يفقؤوا عينَهُ» [أخرجه مسلم].

EXCESSIVENESS IN RELIGION

الغلو في الدين

p75.23 Allah Most High says,

"Say: 'O people of the Book, do not be excessive in your religion'" (Koran 4:171).

(Qurtubi:) According to exegetes, this refers to the extremism of the Jews concerning

p75.23 قال الله تعالى: ﴿قُلْ يَا أَهْلَ الكِتَابِ لاَ تَغْلُوا في دِينِكُم. . .﴾ [النساء: ١٧١].
(القرطبي:) يعني بذلك فيما ذكره المفسرون غلوّ اليهود في عيسى حتى

Jesus in accusing Mary of fornication, and the extremism of the Christians in considering him a god. For both excessiveness and remissness are evil, and both may be unbelief (*al-Jami' li ahkam al-Qur'an* (y117), 6.21).

The Prophet (Allah bless him and give him peace) said,

"Beware of going to extremes [in religion], for those before you were only destroyed through excessiveness."

(Munawi:) Ibn Taymiya says, "His saying 'Beware of going to extremes in religion' is a general prohibition applying to all types of extremes, whether in beliefs or works" (*Fayd al-Qadir sharh al-Jami' al-saghir* (y91), 3.126).

NOT ACCEPTING A SWORN STATEMENT

p75.24 The Prophet (Allah bless him and give him peace) said,

"Whoever is sworn to in Allah's name, let him accept it, for whoever does not has nothing to do with Allah in anything."

STINGINESS

p75.25 Allah Most High says:

(1) "Whoever is watchful against the stinginess of his own soul, those are the successful" (Koran 59:9).

(2) "Here you are, called upon to spend in the Way of Allah, and some of you are being stingy, while whoever is stingy is only ungenerous towards himself. It is Allah who is rich and you who are the poor" (Koran 47:38).

The Prophet (Allah bless him and give him peace) said:

قذفــوا مريم وغلّو النصــارى فيـــه حتى جعلوه رباً. فالإفراط والتفريط كله سيئةٌ وكفرٌ [نقـل من الجامع لأحكام القرآن: ٦/ ٢١].

قال رسـول الله ﷺ: «إيـاكم والغلوّ (في الـدين): فإنمـا هلك من كان قبلكم بالغلوّ (في الدين)» [رواه النسائي].

(المناوي:) قال ابن تيمية: «قـوله إيـاكم والغلّو في الـدين عامٌ في جميع أنـواع الغلوّ في الاعتقـادات والأعمـال» [نقـل من فيض القـدير شرح الجامـع الصغير: ٣/ ١٢٦].

عدم الرضا بيمين المسلم الصالح

p75.24 عن النبي ﷺ قال: «مَن حُلِف له بـاللـه فليـرضَ ومن لم يرض فليس من الله في شيء» [رواه ابن ماجه].

الشح

p75.25 قال تعالى: ﴿وَمَنْ يُوقَ شُحَّ نَفْسِهِ فَأُولَئِكَ هُمُ المُفْلِحُونَ﴾ [الحشر: ٩].

وقـال تعـالى: ﴿هَا أَنْتُمْ هَؤُلَاءِ تُدْعَوْنَ لِتُنْفِقُوا فِي سَبِيلِ اللَّهِ فَمِنْكُمْ مَنْ يَبْخَلُ، وَمَنْ يَبْخَلْ فَإِنَّمَا يَبْخَلُ عَنْ نَفْسِهِ وَاللَّهُ الغَنِيُّ وَأَنْتُمُ الفُقَرَاءُ﴾ [محمد: ٣٨].

وقال ﷺ: «وأيُّ داءٍ أدوَى من البخل»

(1) "What disease is worse than stinginess?"

(2) "Three things are deadly: avarice obeyed, caprice yielded to, and opinionated people's pride in their opinions."

[رواه البخاري].

وفي الحديث: «ثلاثٌ مهلكات: شُحٌ مطاع، وهوىً متبَع، وإعجابُ كل ذي رأي برأيه» [رواه البزار والبيهقي وغيرهما].

SITTING IN THE CENTER OF A CIRCLE

الجلوس في وسط الحلقة

p75.26 The Prophet (Allah bless him and give him peace) cursed whoever sits in the middle of a circle of people (A: because such a person sees himself as better than they are).

p75.26 [وصحح الترمذي أنَّ] النبي ﷺ لعن الجالس وسطَ الحلقة.

PASSING IN FRONT OF SOMEONE PERFORMING THE PRAYER

المرور بين يدي المصلي

p75.27 The Prophet (Allah bless him and give him peace) said,

"If someone passing in front of a person performing the prayer knew of the penalty for it, it would be better for him to wait for forty [n: a variant has, "a hundred years"]."

(A: *In front* means within the length of the person's prostration, or the distance to the barrier he is using (def: f7) if it is not far.)

(Munawi:) Ibn Daqiq al-'Eid says: "A Maliki scholar has distinguished four situations respecting the sin of the person praying and the person who passes in front of him [n: given P, the person praying, and Q, the person passing in front of him]:

(1) Q sins but not P when P is praying behind a barrier in a place that is not a commonly used walkway and Q passes in front of him when there is another alternative (A: meaning another route, since to stop and wait is not considered an alternative, though it is superior);

(2) P sins but not Q when P is praying in a commonly used walkway without a barrier, or at a considerable distance from one, and Q has no other alternative but to pass in front of him;

p75.27 وقال ﷺ: «لو يعلم المارُّ بين يدي المصلي ماذا عليـه لكــان أن يقف أربعين (ت: وفي رواية: «مائـة عام») خيراً له» [رواه البخاري].

(المنـاوي:) قال ابن دقيق العيـد: قسم بعض المـالكيـة أحـوال المـار والمصلي في الإثم وعدمه أربعة أقسام: [يأثم المـار دون المصلي وعكسـه ويأثمان معاً وعكسه].

والأولى: أن يصلي إلى سترة في غير مشرع وللمار مندوحة فيأثم المار دون المصلي.

والثانيـة أن يصلي في مشـرع مسلوك بغيـر سترة أو مباعداً عنها ولا يجد المار مندوحة فيأثم المصلِّي دون المارّ.

(3) both P and Q sin when P is praying in circumstances like (2) above, if Q has an alternative route but passes in front of P anyway;

(4) and neither P nor Q sin when P is praying in circumstances like (1) above, if Q has no alternative and passes in front of P.''

(*Fayd al-Qadir sharh al-Jami' al-saghir* (y91), 5.338)

والثــالثــة كالثــانيـة لكن يجـد المـار مندوحة ، فيأثمان .

والـرابعـة كالأولى لكن يجـد المـار منـدوحة فلا يأثمـان [نقل من فيض القدير شرح الجامع الصغير: ٥/ ٣٣٨] .

NOT LOVING ONE'S FELLOW MUSLIMS

عدم محبة المسلمين

p75.28 The Prophet (Allah bless him and give him peace) said:

"By Him in whose hand is my soul, none of you will enter paradise until you believe, and none of you will believe until you love each other. Shall I not tell you of something which if you do it will create love among you? Increase the custom of greeting each other with 'as-Salamu 'alaykum.' "

(*Kitab al-kaba'ir wa tabyin al-maharim* (y36), 35–181)

p75.28 قال رسـول الله ﷺ : «والذي نفسي بيـده لا تدخلون الجنـة حتى تؤمنوا ولا تؤمنـوا حتى تحـابّـوا ، ألا أدلكم على شيء إذا فعلتمـوه تحـاببتم؟ أفشوا السلام بينكم» [رواه مسلم] .

[محـرّر من كتـاب الكبـائـر وتبيين المحارم: ٣٥ ـ ١٨١] .

*

p76.0 (n: Most of the above enormities are agreed upon by all four schools of jurisprudence. A more comprehensive list by Ibn Hajar Haytami is given below at w52.)

*

p77.0 THE CONDITIONS OF A VALID REPENTANCE

p77.0 شروط التوبة

p77.1 (Nawawi: (n: with commentary by Muhammad ibn 'Allan Bakri (B:))) Scholars state that repentance is obligatory for every sin (B: there being scholarly consensus (def: b7) that it is obligatory for both lesser sins and enormities, and for both outward acts and inward ones such as malice or envy).

p77.1 (النـووي (ت: بشرح محمد بن علان البـكـري (ب:)) :) قال العلماء: التوبة واجبة من كل ذنب (ب : ووجـوبهـا مجمـع عليـه، لا فرق بين الصغـائـر والكبـائـر، الظـاهـرة والباطنة كالحقد والحسد) .

p77.2 When a person's disobedience is solely between him and Allah Most High, unconnected with another human being's rights, his repentance has three conditions:

(a) to desist from the sin;

(b) to regret having done it (B: because of its being disobedience, since regretting it for some other reason is of no consequence);

(c) and to resolve never to commit it again.

(B: Some hold that after having repented of it, it is also a condition that one abandon the company of whoever committed the act with one, and also that one's repentance be purely for the sake of Allah, a restriction that Ibn Hajar Haytami embeds in the first condition above by saying, "to desist from the sin solely for the sake of Allah, since abandoning it out of fear, ostentation, or other motive besides Allah Most High is not considered desisting.") If any of these conditions is lacking, one's repentance is not valid.

p77.3 If the act of disobedience is connected with the rights of another human being, repentance for it has four conditions: the three mentioned above, plus clearing oneself of the obligation owed to the other person. If this obligation is property or the like, one must return it (A: by any means, secretly or openly, even as an ostensible gift) to him (B: i.e. to its owner, meaning to return the article itself if it still exists, or if it does not, then a substitute, whether this be its value or an equal amount of it). (N: Becoming a Muslim eliminates all previous sins except those involving rights or property owed to other people. Allah does not pardon these until they are restored or forgiven.)

If the right in question is the penalty for charging someone with adultery when there are not four witnesses (def: o13) or the like (B: such as a victim's right to retaliate (o3) for a homicide or injury) then one must give oneself up to him (B: to permit him to inflict the penalty due) or else ask him to forgive it. (B: The author's words seem to imply that the validity of repentance depends on

p77.2 فإن كانت المعصية بين العبد وبين الله تعالى لا تتعلق بحق آدمي فلها ثلاثة شروط: أحدها أن يقلع عن المعصية، والثاني أن يندم على فعلها (ب: من حيث أنها معصية، فلو ندم عليها لا من هذه الحيثية لم يعتد بندمه)، والثالث أن يعزم أن لا يعود إليها [(ب: أي إلى مثلها)] أبداً (هذا وزاد بعضهم اشتراط عدم صحبة من ارتكب معه المعصية بعد التوبة وأن تكون التوبة لله تعالى خاصة. وأدرج ابن حجر الهيتمي هذا القيد في الشرط الأول [وهو الإقلاع] فقال: ترك الذنب لله تعالى فلو تركه لخوفٍ أو رياء أو غير ذلك من الأغراض التي لغير الله تعالى لم يعتد بتركه.) فإن فقد أحد هذه الثلاثة، لم تصح توبته.

p77.3 وإن كانت المعصية تتعلق بآدمي فشروطها أربعة: هذه الثلاثة وأن يبرأ من حق صاحبها. فإن كانت مالاً أو نحوه رده إليه (ب: أي إلى صاحبه بعينه إن كان موجوداً وبدله عند تلفه من قيمة أو مثل) وإن كان حد القذف ونحوه (ب: أي نحو القذف كالقتل والقطع قصاصاً) مكّنه (ب: أي صاحب الحق) منه (ب: أي من الحد أي استيفائه منه) أو طلب عفوه (ب: وظاهر كلامه توقف صحة التوبة على ما ذكر من الرد والتمكين أي

performing the above, of returning the property or giving oneself up—i.e. when possible, for otherwise one intends to do so when possible, or asks the victim for amnesty—but the position of the Imam (A: Juwayni), which 'Izz ibn 'Abd al-Salam and our author (n: Nawawi) also follow, is that one's repentance is valid regarding the rights of Allah Most High (N: through merely repenting), while the other person's right is an obligation that remains upon one (dis: w53), as does the sin of not discharging it).

If the wrong done to another consists of slander (def: r2), then one must have him pardon it (B: by informing him so he can forgive one, though informing him is only a necessary condition when doing so will not cause even greater harm, though if it will, as when one fears the other will kill one, informing him is not obligatory. Both asking for the person's forgiveness and informing him of what one said are only obligatory when he has heard that he has been slandered. If he has not, then asking Allah's forgiveness is sufficient) (*Riyad al-salihin* (y107), 10–11, and *Dalil al-falihin li turuq Riyad al-salihin* (y25), 1.88–91).

إن أمكنه ذلك وإلا نوى ذلك إذا قدر أو طلب العفو، لكن ذهب الإمام ـ وتبعه العز بن عبد السلام وأقره المصنف ـ إلى صحة توبته وإن لم يسلم نفسه بالنسبة لحق الله تعالى ويبقى عليه حق الآدمي وإثم الامتناع).

وإن كانت غيبة استحله منها (ب: أي بأن يخبره بما قاله حتى يصح تحليله لكن محل تعين الإخبار ما لم يترتب عليه ضرر أعظم، وإلا كأن يخشى قتله بذلك مثلاً فلا، ومحل تعين الإخبار والاستحلال إن بلغه الاغتياب، وإلا كفى الاستغفار) [نقل من رياض الصالحين: ١٠ ـ ١١؛ ومحرر من كتاب دليل الفالحين لطرق رياض الصالحين: ١/ ٨٨ ـ ٩٠].

*

BOOK Q

COMMANDING THE RIGHT AND FORBIDDING THE WRONG

كتاب الأمر بالمعروف والنهي عن المنكر

CONTENTS:

| q0.0   INTRODUCTION | المقدمة   q0.0 |

q0.1   (n: The discussion and analysis that follow are Imam Ghazali's, edited by the Hanbali scholar Ibn Qudama Maqdisi from an earlier abridgement of Ghazali's *Ihya' 'ulum al-din* by 'Abd al-Rahman ibn Jawzi, which Maqdisi shortened to a single volume whose conciseness, if less vivid than the *Ihya'*, better lends itself to the purpose of the present section, which is to discuss the practical implications of an important aspect of Sacred Law.)

q0.2   (Ibn Qudama Maqdisi:) One should know that commanding the right and forbidding the wrong is the most important fundamental of the religion, and is the mission that Allah sent the prophets to fulfill. If it were folded up and put away, religion itself would vanish, dissolution appear, and whole lands come to ruin.

q0.2   (ابن قدامة المقدسي:) اعلم أن الأمر بالمعروف والنهي عن المنكر هو القطب الأعظم في الــدين، وهــو المهم الــذي بعــث الــله به النبيين، ولــو طوي بســاطــه، لاضمحلت الــديانة وظهـر الفساد، وخربت البلاد.

*

q1.0   THE OBLIGATION TO COMMAND THE RIGHT

q1.0   وجوب الأمر بالمعروف

q1.1   Allah Most High says,

"Let there be a group of you who call to good, commanding the right and forbidding the wrong, for those are the successful" (Koran 3:104).

This verse explains that commanding the right and forbidding the wrong are a *communal* rather than a personal obligation (dis: c3.2), for He says, "Let there be a group of you..." and not, "All of you command the right." So if enough people do it (A: meaning that whenever a wrong is seen, one of those who see it corrects it), the responsibility is lifted from the rest, those who perform it being expressly mentioned as the successful. There are many verses in the Holy Koran about commanding the right and forbidding the wrong.

q1.1   قال الله تعالى: ﴿وَلْتَكُنْ مِنْكُمْ أُمَّةٌ يَدْعُــونَ إِلَى الخَيْرِ وَيَــأْمُرُونَ بِالمَعْرُوفِ وَيَنْهَوْنَ عَنِ المُنْكَرِ وَأُولئِكَ هُمُ المُفْلِحُونَ﴾ [آل عمران: ١٠٤].

وفي هذه الآيــة بيــان أنـه فرض على الكفــايـة لا فرض عين لأنه قال: ﴿وَلْتَكُنْ مِنْكُمْ أُمَّةٌ﴾ ولم يقل: كونوا كلكم آمرين بالمعــروف؛ فإذا قام به من يكفي سقط عن البــاقين، واختص الفــلاح بالقــائمين المبــاشرين له. وفي القرآن العظيم آيات كثيرة في الأمر بالمعروف والنهي عن المنكر.

q1.2   The Prophet (Allah bless him and give him peace) said:

q1.2   [وعن النعمــان بن بشير رضي الله عنــه قال: سمعت] رسول الله ﷺ

(1) "Those who keep within Allah's limits and those who transgress them or allow them to be compromised may be compared to people on a ship, some of whom must stay below deck in the hardest and worst place, while others get passage above. When those below need water, they pass through those on the upper deck, injuring and annoying them until those below reflect, 'If we were to stave a hole in the hull we could get water without troubling those above.' Were those above deck to leave those below to themselves, all would be destroyed, while if they were to help them, all would be saved."

(2) "Whoever of you sees something wrong, let him change it with his hand. If unable to, then let him change it with his tongue. If unable, then with his heart. And that is the weakest degree of faith."

(3) "The best jihad is speaking the truth to an unjust ruler."

(4) "When you see my Community too intimidated by an oppressor to tell him, 'You are a tyrant,' then you may as well say goodbye to them."

(5) "Command the right and forbid the wrong, or Allah will put the worst of you in charge of the best of you, and the best will supplicate Allah and be left unanswered."

q1.3   Abu Bakr (Allah be well pleased with him) rose from his place, and after having praised Allah Most High, said, "O people: you recite the verse,

" 'O you who believe: you are responsible for yourselves; those who go astray will not harm you if you are guided' (Koran 5:105),

"while we have heard the Messenger of Allah (Allah bless him and give him peace) say,

" 'People who do not change something wrong when they see it are on the verge of a sweeping punishment from Allah.' "

يقـول: «مثـل القـائم على حدود الله والواقـع فيهـا والمـداهن فيهـا، مثل قوم ركبـوا سفينـة فأصـاب بعضهم أسفلهـا وأوعـرهـا وشـرهـا، وأصـاب بعضهم أعـلاهـا؛ فكـان الـذين في أسفلهـا إذا استقـوا المـاء مروا على من فوقهـم فآذوهم، فقالوا: لو خرقنا في نصيبنا خرقاً فاستقينـا منـه ولم نؤذ من فوقنـا؛ فإن تركـوهم وأمـرهم هلكوا جميعـاً، وإن أخـذوا على أيـديهم نجـوا جميعاً» [رواه البخاري] [...].

فقد جاء في الحديث [المشهـور من رواية مسلم] أن النبي ﷺ قال: «من رأى منكم منكراً فليغيره بيده، فإن لم يستطع فبلسـانه، فإن لم يستطـع فبقلبه، وذلك أضعف الإيمان».

وفي حديث آخـر: «أفضـل الجهـاد كلمة حق عند سلطان جائر» [رواه أحمد].

وفي حديـث آخـر: «إذا رأيـت أمتي تهـاب الظالم أن تقـول له: أنت ظالم، فقد تودّع منهم» [...].

وعنه ﷺ أنه قال: «لتأمرن بالمعروف ولتنهـون عن المنكـر أو ليسلطن الله شراركم على خيـاركم فيدعو خيـاركم فلا يستجاب لهم».

q1.3   وقـام أبـو بكر رضي الله عنه، فحمـد الله تعـالى وأثنى عليـه، ثم قال: أيها الناس إنكم تقرؤون هذه الآية: ﴿يَا أَيُّهَا الَّذِينَ آمَنُوا عَلَيْكُمْ أَنْفُسَكُمْ لَا يَضُرُّكُمْ مَنْ ضَلَّ إِذَا اهْتَدَيْتُمْ﴾ [المائدة: ١٠٥].

وإنّا سمعنا رسول الله ﷺ يقول: «إن النـاس إذا رأوا المنكر فلم يغيروه أوشك أن يعمهم الله بعذاب».

q2.0 WHO MAY COMMAND THE RIGHT AND FORBID THE WRONG

q2.0 شروط الأمــر بالمعروف والناهي عن المنكر

LEGAL RESPONSIBILITY

التكليف

q2.1   There are four integrals (def: q2–5) in commanding the right and forbidding the wrong, the first of which is that the person doing so be legally responsible (def: c8.1), Muslim, and able to, these being the conditions for it to be obligatory, though a child of the age of discrimination (def: f1.2) who condemns something dishonorable is rewarded for doing so, even if it is not obligatory for him to.

q2.1   [اعـلم أن] أركــان الأمــر بالمعــروف والنهي عن المنكر أربعـة: أحـدها أن يكــون المنكــر مكلفــاً مسلماً قادراً، وهـذا شرط لوجوب الإنكار. فإن الصبي المميـز له إنكار المنكر، ويثاب على ذلك لكن لا يجب عليه.

MORAL RECTITUDE IS NOT A CONDITION

لا تشترط العدالة

q2.2   As for requirements of moral rectitude in the person giving the reprimand, some scholars take this into consideration and say that a corrupt person is not entitled to censure, a position for which they adduce the word of Allah Most High,

"Do you enjoin piety to others and forget yourselves?" (Koran 2:44),

but there are no grounds in the verse for such an inference.

q2.2   وأمـا عدالة المنكِر فاعتبرها قوم وقالـوا: ليس للفـاسق أن يحتسب، وإنمـا استـدلـوا بقوله تعالى: ﴿أَتَأْمُرُونَ النَّاسَ بِالْبِرِّ وَتَنْسَوْنَ أَنْفُسَكُمْ﴾ [البقرة: ٤٤] وليس لهم في ذلك حجة.

HAVING THE CALIPH'S PERMISSION

حكم إذن الإمام

q2.3   Some scholars stipulate that the person delivering the censure must have permission to do so from the caliph (def: o25) or his regional appointee, and do not grant that private individuals may censure others. This is untrue, for the Koranic verses and hadiths all indicate that whoever sees something wrong and does nothing has sinned. Stipulating that there must be permission from the caliph is mere arbitrary opinion. One should realize that there are five levels of censure: explaining the wrong nature of the act, admonish-

q2.3   واشتــرط قوم كون الـمنكـر مأذوناً فيـه من جهة الإمام أو الوالي، ولم يجيزوا لآحاد الرعية الحسبة وهذا فاسد، لأن الآيات والأخبار عامة تدل على أن كل من رأى منكـراً فسكـت عنـه عصى، فالتخصيص بإذن الإمام تحكم. [...و] اعـلم أن الـحسبة لهـا خمس مراتب: التعـريف، والـوعظ بالكـلام اللطيف، و[الثـالـثـة:] الـسب والتـعنيف،

ing the person politely, reviling him and harshness, forcibly stopping the act (such as by breaking musical instruments or pouring out wine), and finally, intimidation and threatening to strike the person or actually hitting him to stop what he is doing. It is the latter level, not the first four, that requires the caliph, because it may lead to civil disorder. The early Muslims' invariable practice of reprimanding those in authority decisively proves by their consensus (def: b7) that there is no need for a superior's authorization. If it be wondered whether a child is entitled to reprove his father, or a wife her husband, or for private citizens to reprove their ruler, the answer is that *all* are fundamentally entitled to. We have distinguished the five levels: the child is entitled to explain the nature of the act, to admonish and advise his parents politely, and finally may censure at the fourth level by such things as breaking a lute, pouring out wine, and so forth. This is also the sequence that should be observed by a wife. As for private citizens with their ruler, the matter is much graver than a child's reproving his father, and citizens are only entitled to explain the matter and advise.

BEING ABLE TO CENSURE

q2.4   It is a necessary condition that the person condemning something wrong be *able* to do so. Someone who is unable is not obliged to condemn it except in his heart. The obligation is not only lifted when physically unable, but also when one fears that problems (def: q2.7) will result for one, which also comes under the heading of inability. The obligation to censure the wrong is likewise lifted when one knows that the reproach will be ineffective. Four situations may be distinguished with respect to this.

(1)   When one knows (def: q2.6) the wrong will be eliminated by speaking or acting without this entailing problems for oneself, one is obliged to censure it.

(2)   When one knows that speaking will be ineffective and one will be beaten if one does, one is not obliged to.

و[الرابعة :] المنع والقهر ككسر الملاهي وإراقة الخمر و[الخامس :] التخويف والتهديد بالضرب ، أو مباشرة الضرب له حتى يمتنع عما هو عليه ، فهذه المرتبة تحتاج إلى الإمام دون ما قبلها لأنه ربما جر إلى فتنة .

واستمرار عادات السلف على الحسبة على الـولاة قاطـع بإجـمـاعـهـم على الاستغناء عن التفويض .

فإن قيـل : هل تثبت الحسبة للولد [...] والـزوجة على الـزوج ، والرعية على الوالي؟ قلنا : أصل الولاية ثابت للكل .

وقـد رتبنـا للحسبة خمس مراتب : فللولد من ذلك الحسبة بالتعريف ، ثم بالـوعـظ والنصح باللطف ، وله من الرتبة الـرابعـة أن يكسر العود ، ويريق الخمر ، ونحو ذلك وهذا الترتيب ينبغي أن يجري في [العبد] والـزوجة . وأما الـرعية مع السلطان ، فالأمر فيه أشد من الـولد ، فليس معه إلا التعريف والنصح .

القدرة على الإنكار

q2.4   ويشتـرط كون المنكـر قادراً على الإنكار ، فأمـا العـاجـز فليس عليه إنكار إلا بقلبه ، ولا يقف سقوط الوجوب على العجز الحسّي ، بل يلتحق به خوف مكروه يناله ، فذلك في معنى العجز .

وكذلك إذا علم أن إنكاره لا ينفع ، فينقسم إلى أربعة أحوال :

أحدها أن يعلم أن المنكر يزول بقوله أو فعله من غير مكروه يلحقه فيجب عليه الإنكار .

الحالة الثانية أن يعلم أن كلامه لا ينفع وأنه إن تكلم ضرب ، فيرتفع الوجوب .

(3) When one knows that one's censure will be ineffective but it does not entail problems for one, it is not obligatory, because of its ineffectiveness, though one is still recommended to censure the act is order to manifest the standards of Islam and remind people of their religion.

(A: Hadiths that seem to show the nonobligatoriness of commanding the right and forbidding the wrong are understood by Islamic scholars as referring to specific situations in which censure is ineffectual, and are not global statements about this obligation's inapplicability to a certain era of history, such as our own or some future time. Commanding the right and forbidding the wrong will be obligatory until the Day of Judgement.)

(4) And when one knows that it will cause problems for one but the wrong will be eliminated by censuring it, such as with breaking a lute or dumping out wine when one knows one will be beaten for it, then one is not obliged but rather *recommended* to, as is evident from the hadith,

"The best jihad is speaking the truth to an unjust ruler."

There is no disagreement among scholars that it is permissible for a single Muslim to attack battle-lines of unbelievers headlong and fight them even if he knows he will be killed. But if one knows it will not hurt them at all, such as if a blind man were to hurl himself against them, then it is unlawful. Likewise, if someone who is alone sees a corrupt person with a bottle of wine beside him and a sword in his hand, and he knows that the person will chop his neck if he censures him for drinking, it is not permissible for him to do so, as it would not entail any religious advantage worth giving one's life for. Such censure is only praiseworthy when one is able to eliminate the wrong and one's action will produce some benefit.

q2.5   If one wants to censure something but knows it will result in one's companions also being beaten with one, it is not permissible for one to do so, because one is incapable of removing one blameworthy thing without its leading to another.

الحـالـة الثـالـثة أن يعلم أن إنكـاره لا يفيـد لكنـه لا يخـاف مكروهاً، فلا يجب عليه الأمـر لعـدم الفائدة، لكن يستحب لإظهار شعائر الإسلام والتذكير بالدين.

الحـالـة الرابـعة أن يعلم أنـه يصاب بمكروه ولكن يبطل المنكر بفعله مثل أن يكسـر العـود ويريق الخمـر ويعلم أنـه يضرب عقيب ذلك، فيرتفع الوجوب عنه ويبقى مستحبـاً لقـولـه في الحـديـث: «أفضل الجهاد كلمة حق عند سلطان جائر».

ولا خلاف أنـه يجـوز للمسلم الواحد أن يهجم على صفـوف الكفـار ويقـاتل، وإن علم أنه يقتل.

لكـن إن علم أنـه لا نكـايـة له في الكفـار، كالأعمى يطـرح نفسـه على الصف، حرم ذلك.

وكـذلـك لو رأى فاسقـاً وحـده وعنده قدح خمر وبيده سيف، وعلم أنه لو أنكر عليه لشرب الخمر لضرب عنقه، لـم يجز له الإقـدام على ذلـك لأن هذا لا يؤثـر في الدين أثـراً يفديـه بنفسه، وإنما يستحب له الإنكـار إذا قدر على إبطـال المنكر وظهر لفعله فائدة [كمن يحمل في صف الكفار ونحوه].

q2.5   وإن علم المنكـر أنـه يضرب معـه غيـره من أصحابه لم تجز له الحسبة لأنه عجز عن دفع المنكر إلا بإفضائه إلى منكر آخر [...].

(N: It is not lawful to censure anything reprehensible when doing so will lead to a thing or state that is *more* reprehensible.)

(ح: ولا يجوز النهي عن المنكر إذا أدى ذلك إلى منكر أعظم).

q2.6   *Know* only means what one believes will probably result. Someone who thinks that it will create problems for him is not obligated to censure, though someone who does not believe that problems will result is obliged to.

Cowardice does not enter into consideration here, nor foolhardy courage, but rather the normal temperament of someone with a sound disposition.

q2.6   ولسنا نعني بالعلم في هذه المواضيع إلا غلبة الظن فمن غلب على ظنه أنه يصيبه مكروه، لم يجب عليه الإنكار، وإن غلب على ظنه أنه لا يصيبه وجَبَ.

ولا اعتبار بحالة الجبان، ولا بالشجاع المتهور، بل الاعتبار بالمعتدل الطبع، السليم المزاج.

q2.7   *Problems* means being beaten, killed, robbed, or acquiring a bad name in town. As for being reviled and disparaged, it is not an excuse to remain silent, for someone who commands what is right generally meets with it.

q2.7   ونعني بالمكروه الضرب أو القتل، وكذلك نهب المال والإشهار في البلد مع تسويد الوجه. فأما السب والشتم فليس بعذر في السكوت، لأن الأمر بالمعروف يلقى ذلك في الغالب.

*

q3.0   WHAT MAY BE CENSURED

q3.0   ما فيه الحسبة

q3.1   The second integral of commanding the right and forbidding the wrong is that the thing censured is something blameworthy that exists at present and is apparent.

Blameworthy means that its occurrence is prohibited by Sacred Law, this being of wider scope than mere disobedience, for someone who sees a child or insane person drinking wine (A: which is not a sin in relation to them) is obliged to pour it out and forbid them.

That exists at present excludes someone who has drunk wine and is now finished, and so forth. It also excludes something which will take place later, as when there is evidence that a person intends to go drinking that night. There is no censure in such cases other than to appeal to the person's conscience.

Apparent excludes someone who conceals his disobedience at home and locks his door. It is not permissible to spy on him. An exception is if

q3.1   الركن الثاني أن يكون ما فيه الحسبة منكراً موجوداً في الحال ظاهراً.
فمعنى كونه منكراً أن يكون محظور الوقوع في الشرع.
والمنكر أعم من المعصية إذ من رأى صبياً أو مجنوناً يشرب الخمر، فعليه أن يريق خمره ويمنعه.
وقولنا موجوداً في الحال احتراز ممن شرب الخمر وفرغ من شربها، ونحو ذلك [...].
وفيه أيضاً احتراز عما سيوجد في ثاني الحال، كمن يعلم بقرينة حاله أنه عازم على الشرب الليلة، فلا حسبة عليه إلا بالوعظ.
وقولنا ظاهراً احتراز ممن تستر بالمعصية في داره وأغلق بابه فإنه لا يجوز أن يتجسس عليه إلا أن يظهر ما يعرفه من

something is manifest to another outside the house, such as the sound of pipes and lutes. Someone who hears them may enter and break the instruments. If one smells the odor of wine outside the house, the sounder opinion is that it is permissible to enter and condemn it.

ONE MAY NOT CONDEMN ANOTHER FOR QUESTIONS INVOLVING DIFFERENCES AMONG SCHOOLS OF JURISPRUDENCE

q3.2   It is a necessary condition that the thing censured be something whose blameworthiness is not merely established by *ijtihad* (n: the independent legal reasoning of a particular Imam). Any question in which there is *ijtihad* may not be a cause for censure. A Hanafi, for example, may not condemn a Shafi‘i for eating something slaughtered without the Basmala (dis: j17.5(4)), nor a Shafi‘i condemn a Hanafi for drinking some nonintoxicating raisin drink (N: nor a Muslim condemn a non-Muslim for drinking wine (dis: o11.5(1))). (A: But if two individuals follow the same school of Sacred Law and one commits an act that is unlawful or offensive in that school or in each of the two's respective schools, it is obligatory for the other person to condemn the act even when it involves the *ijtihad* of their Imam. And the Shafi‘i must condemn the Hanafi for eating something slaughtered without the Basmala, as the Hanafi is doing something he believes to be wrong.)

*

q4.0   THE PERSON DOING THE WRONG

q4.1   The third integral of commanding the right and forbidding the wrong is the person being reprimanded. It is sufficient that he be a person, and is not necessary that he be legally responsible, as we have previously mentioned (q3.1) in respect to censuring a child or insane person.

هو خارج الـدار، كأصـوات المـزامير والعيـدان، فلمن سمـع ذلـك أن يدخـل ويكسـر المـلاهي، فإن فاحت رائحـة الخمر فالأظهر جواز الإنكار.

لا يجـوز الإنكـار فيمـا يتعلق بالمسائل الخلافية بين المذاهب

q3.2   ويشتـرط في إنكـار المنكر أن يكـون معلومـاً كونـه منكـراً بغير اجتهاد. فكـل ما هو في محـل الاجتهاد فلا حسبة فيه. فليس للحنفي أن ينكر على الشافعي أكله متـروك التسمية، ولا للشـافعي أن ينكر على الحنفي شربه يسير النبيذ الذي ليس بمسكر.

q4.0   المنكر عليه

q4.1   الـركن الثالث في المنكر عليه ويكفي في صفتـه أن يكـون إنسـاناً ولا يشترط كونـه مكلفاً كمـا بينا قبله من أنه ينكر على الصبي والمجنون.

q5.0 THE ACT OF CENSURING	q5.0 الاحتساب

q5.1 The fourth integral is the censure itself, which has various degrees of severity and has rules.

q5.1   الركن الرابع نفس الاحتساب، وله درجات وآداب .

KNOWLEDGE OF THE WRONG ACT

الاطلاع على المنكر

q5.2 The first degree consists of knowing the wrong act. One should not eavesdrop at another's house in order to hear the sounds of musical instruments, or try to catch the scent of wine, or feel for an object concealed beneath someone's shirt to see if it is a flute, or ask a person's neighbors to see what he is doing. But if two upright witnesses (def: o24.4) come and inform one that someone is drinking, one may enter his house and take him to task.

q5.2   الدرجة الأولى أن يعرف المنكر .
فلا ينبغي له أن يسترق السمع على دار غيره ليسمع صوت الأوتار، ولا يتعرض للشم ليدرك رائحة الخمر، ولا أن يمس ما قد ستر بثوب ليعرف شكل المزمار، ولا أن يستخبر جيرانه ليخبروه بما يجري . بل لو أخبره عدلان ابتداءً أن فلاناً يشرب الخمر، فله إذ ذاك أن يدخل وينكر .

EXPLAINING THAT SOMETHING IS WRONG

بيان الحكم لمرتكب المنكر

q5.3 The second degree consists of explaining that an act is wrong, since an ignorant person will often do something he does not know is blameworthy, but will stop when he finds out. So one must explain it politely, saying, for example: "People are not born scholars; we were unfamiliar with many things in Sacred Law until scholars mentioned them to us. Perhaps there are not many in your hometown," and thus lead up to it diplomatically so the person understands without being offended. To avoid the evil of remaining silent when there is something wrong, only to commit the evil of offending a Muslim when able not to, is like washing away blood with urine.

q5.3   الدرجة الثانية التعريف، فإن الجاهل يقدم على الشيء لا يظنه منكراً فإذا عرف أقلع عنه .
فيجب تعريفه باللطف فيقال له إن الإنسان لا يولد عالماً ولقد كنا جاهلين بأمور الشرع حتى علمنا العلماء، فلعل قريتك خالية من أهل العلم، فهكذا يتلطف به ليحصل التعريف من غير إيذاء . ومن اجتنب محظور السكوت عن المنكر واستبدل عنه محظور الإيذاء للمسلم مع الاستغناء عنه، فقد غسل الدم بالبول .

FORBIDDING THE ACT VERBALLY

النهي بالوعظ والنصح

q5.4 The third degree of severity is to prohibit the act by admonition, advice, and making the other fear Allah, mentioning the hadiths of divine

q5.4   الدرجة الثالثة النهي بالوعظ والنصح والتخويف بالله، ويورد عليه الأخبار الواردة بالوعيد ويحكي له سيرة

punishment for it and reminding the person how the early Muslims behaved, all of which should be done with sympathy and kindness, not harshness or anger. The great danger here which one must beware of is that a learned person explaining that something is wrong may be proud of his know-ledge and gloat over the lowliness of the other's ignorance, which is like saving someone from a fire by casting oneself into it. It is ignorant in the extreme, a deep disgrace, and a delusion from the Devil. The touchstone and test for this is to ask oneself whether one would prefer the censured person to stop at his own or another's behest, or whether one would prefer to forbid him oneself. If reproving him is difficult and weighs upon one, and one would prefer that someone else do it, then one should proceed, for religion is the motive. But if it is otherwise, then one is following mere personal caprice and using the censuring of others as a means to display one's merit, and one should fear Allah and censure oneself first.

CENSURING WITH HARSH WORDS

السلف ويكون ذلك بشفقة ولطف من غير عنف وغضب . وهنا هنا آفة عظيمة ينبغي أن يتوقاها ، وهو أن العالم يرى عند التعريف عن نفسه بالعلم وذل غيره بالجهل ، ومثال ذلك مثال من يخلص غيره من النار بإحراق نفسه ، وهو غاية الجهل ومذلة عظيمة وغرور من الشيطان . ولذلك محك ومعيار فينبغي أن يمتحن به المحتسب نفسه ، وهو أن يكون امتناع ذلك الإنسان عن المنكر بنفسه أو باحتساب غيره عليه أحب إليه من امتناعه عنه باحتسابه فإن كانت الحسبة شاقة عليه ثقيلة على نفسه ، وهو يود أن يكفى بغيره فليحتسب فإنّ باعثه هو الدين ، وإن كان الأمر بالعكس فهو متبع هوى نفسه ، متوسل إلى إظهار جاهه بواسطة إنكاره فليتق الله وليحتسب أولاً على نفسه [. . .] .

التغيير باللسان

q5.5   The fourth degree of severity consists of reviling the person and bearing down on him with sharp, harsh words. One does not resort to this degree unless one is unable to prevent the person by politeness, and he shows he wants to persist or mocks one's admonitions and advice. *Reviling him* does not mean vulgarity and lies, but rather saying "You degenerate," "You idiot," "You ignoramus," "Do you not fear Allah?" and so forth. Allah Most High quotes Ibrahim (upon whom be peace) saying:

"Fie on you and what you worship apart from Allah! Can you not think?" (Koran 21:67).

q5.5   الدرجة الرابعة السب والتعنيف بالقول الغليظ الخشن . وإنما يعدل إلى هذا عند العجز عن المنع باللطف وظهور مبادئ الإصرار والاستهزاء بالوعظ والنصح .
ولسنا نعني بالسب الفحش والكذب ، بل نقول له : يا فاسق ، يا أحمق ، يا جاهل ، ألا تخاف الله؟ قال الله تعالى حكاية عن إبراهيم عليه السلام :
﴿أُفٍّ لَكُمْ وَلِمَا تَعْبُدُونَ مِنْ دُونِ اللَّهِ أَفَلَا تَعْقِلُونَ﴾ [الأنبياء : ٦٧].

RIGHTING THE WRONG BY HAND

التغيير باليد

q5.6   The fifth degree consists of changing the blameworthy thing with one's hand, such as by breaking musical instruments, pouring out wine,

q5.6   الدرجة الخامسة التغيير باليد ، كـكسـر الملاهي ، وإراقة الخمر ،

or turning someone out of a house wrongfully appropriated. There are two rules for this degree:

(1) not to do so when one can get the person to do it himself, i.e. if one can get someone to leave the land he has unjustly taken, one should not drag or push him from it;

(2) and to break the instruments, for example, just enough to obviate their being used for disobedience and no more, or to be careful not to break the bottles when pouring out wine. If one cannot manage except by throwing rocks at the bottles or the like, then one may do so and is not obliged to cover the damages.

If it be wondered whether one may break the bottles or drag someone by the foot out of a wrongfully appropriated house to create fear, as an object lesson to others, the answer is that this is for leaders alone and is not permissible for private individuals because of the obscurity of the decision-making criteria in the matter.

INTIMIDATION

q5.7   The sixth degree is threatening and intimidation, such as by saying, "Stop this or I'll—"; and when possible this should precede actually hitting the person. The rule for this level is not to make a threat that one cannot carry out, such as saying "or I'll seize your house," or "take your wife hostage," because if one says this seriously, it is unlawful, and if not serious, then one is lying.

ASSAULT

q5.8   The seventh degree is to directly hit or kick the person, or similar measures that do not involve weapons. This is permissible for private individuals provided it is necessary, and that one confines oneself to the minimum needed to stop the reprehensible action and nothing more. When

وإخراجه من الدار المغصوبة

وفي هذه الدرجة أدبان :

أحدهما أن لا يباشر التغيير ما لم يعجز عن تكليف المنكر عليه ذلك . فإذا أمكنه أن يكلفه الخروج عن الأرض المغصوبة فلا ينبغي أن يجره ولا يدفعه .

والثاني أن يكسر الملاهي كسراً يبطل صلاحيتها للفساد ، ولا يزيد على ذلك ويتوقى في إراقة الخمور كسر الأواني إن وجد إليـه سبيلاً . وإن لم يقدر إلا بأن يرمي ظروفها بحجر أو نحوه ، فله ذلك ، وتسقط قيمة الظروف .

فإن قيــل هلا يجـــوز الكسـر زجراً ، وكذلك الجر بالرجل في الإخراج من الـدار المغصوبة زجراً؟ قلنا : إنما يجوز مثل ذلك للولاة ، ولا يجوز لآحاد الرعية ، لخفاء وجه الاجتهاد فيه .

التهديد والتخويف

q5.7   الدرجــة السـادسـة التهـديد والتخـويف كقولـه : دع عنك هذا وإلا فعلت بك كذا وكـذا ؛ وينبغي أن يقــدم هذا على تحقيق الضرب إذا أمكن تقديمه .

والأدب في هذه الـرتبــة أن لا يهـدد بوعيد لا يجـوز تحقيقـه كقولـه : لأهين دارك ؛ ولأسبين زوجتــك ؛ لأنــه إن قال ذلك عـن عزم فهـو حرام ، وإن قاله عن غير عزم فهو كذب .

مباشرة الضرب

q5.8   الــدرجــة السـابعــة مباشـرة الضرب باليد والرجل وغير ذلك مما ليس فيه إشهار سلاح .

وذلك جائـز للآحاد بشرط الضرورة والاقتصـار على قدر الحـاجة . فإذا اندفع

the action has been stopped, one refrains from doing anything further.

المنكر فينبغي أن يكف .

FORCE OF ARMS

شهر السلاح

q5.9   The eighth degree is when one is unable to censure the act by oneself and requires the armed assistance of others. Sometimes the person being reproved may also get people to assist him, and a skirmish may ensue, so the soundest legal opinion is that this degree requires authorization from the caliph (def: o25), since it leads to strife and the outbreak of civil discord. Another view is that there is no need for the caliph's permission.

q5.9   الدرجة الثامنة أن لا يقدر على الإنكـار بنفسـه ويحتـاج إلى أعـوان يشهـرون السـلاح . فإنـه ربمـا يستمـد الفـاسق أيضاً بأعوانه ويؤدي إلى القتال ، فالصحيـح أن ذلـك يحتاج إلى إذن الإمام لأنه يؤدي إلى الفتن وهيجان الفساد . وقيل لا يشترط في ذلك إذن الإمام .

*

q6.0   THE ATTRIBUTES OF THE PERSON CENSURING

q6.0   صفات المحتسب

q6.1   Having presented in detail the rules for someone condemning the wrong, they may be summarized in three traits needed by the person giving the reprimand:

(1) knowledge of the (A: above-mentioned) appropriate circumstances for censure and their definitions, so as to keep within lawful bounds;

(2) godfearingness, without which one might know something but not apply it because of some personal interest;

(3) and good character, the prime prerequisite for being able to control oneself, for when anger is aroused, mere knowledge and piousness are seldom sufficient to suppress it if character is lacking.

q6.1   وقـد ذكرنـا آداب المحتسب مفصلة ، وجملتها ثلاث صفات في المحتسب :
ـ العلم بمـواقـع الحسبة وحـدودهـا
[. . .] ليقتصر على حد الشرع .
ـ والثـاني : الـورع فإنـه قد يعلم شيئاً ولا يعمل به لغرض من الأغراض .
ـ والثـالـث : حسن الخلق وهـو أصـل ليـتـمـكن من الكف فإن الغضب إذا هاج لم يَكُفِ مجرد العلم والورع في قمعه ما لم يكن في الطبع خلق حسن .

REDUCING ONE'S DEPENDENCE ON OTHERS

تقليل العلائق وقطع الطمع عن الخلق

q6.2   Among the rules for commanding the right and forbidding the wrong is to depend less on

q6.2   ومن الآداب تقليـل العلائق ،

others and eliminate desire for what they have, so as not to have to compromise one's principles. A story is told about one of the early Muslims who used to get offal each day from the neighborhood butcher for his cat. He noticed something blameworthy about the butcher, so he returned home and turned out the cat before returning to reprimand the man, who retorted, "From now on, I'm not giving you a thing for your cat," to which he replied, "I did not censure you till I gave up both the cat and any desire for what you have." And this is the fact of the matter. One cannot reprimand others as long as one is anxious for two things: the things people give one, and their approval and praise of one.

وقطع الطمع عن الخلق لتزول المداهنة .

فقد حُكي عن بعض السلف أنه كان له سنور وكان يأخذ لسنوره في كل يوم من قصاب في جواره شيئاً من الغدد . فرأى على القصاب منكراً ، فدخل الدار فأخرج السنور ، ثم جاءه فأنكر على القصاب ، فقال : لا أعطيك بعد هذا شيئاً لسنورك ، فقال : ما أنكرت عليك إلا بعد إخراج السنور وقطع الطمع منك . وهذا صحيح . فإن لم يقطع الطمع من الناس من شيئين لم يقدر على الإنكار عليهم : أحدهما من لطف ينالونه به ، والثاني من رضاهم عنه وثنائهم عليه .

q6.3   As for politeness in commanding the right and forbidding the wrong, it is obligatory. Allah Most High says,

"Speak unto him gentle words" (Koran 20:44)

(A: this being to Pharaoh, the enemy of Allah, so how then with one's fellow Muslims?) (*Mukhtasar Minhaj al-qasidin* (y62), 123–30).

q6.3   وأما الرفق في الأمر بالمعروف والنهي عن المنكر فمتعيّن . قال الله تعالى :

﴿فَقُولَا لَهُ قَوْلًا لَيِّنًا﴾ [طه : ٤٤] .

(ع : هذا في فرعون عدو الله ، فكيف بالمسلم في أخيه المسلم؟) .

[محرّر من مختصر منهاج القاصدين : ١٢٣ ـ ١٣٠] .

*

BOOK R

HOLDING ONE'S TONGUE

CONTENTS:

r0.0 INTRODUCTION	المقدمة r0.0

r0.1   (n: Book r has been edited from Nawawi's *al-Adhkar al-muntakhaba min kalam Sayyid al-Abrar* and from *al-Durar al-mubaha fi al-hazr wa al-ibaha*, a work on the lawful and unlawful by the Hanafi scholar Khalil Nahlawi.)

r0.2   (Nawawi:) Having previously discussed what Allah Most Glorious and Exalted has facilitated of recommended invocation (dhikr) and the like, I wish to add here the expressions which are offensive or unlawful, that the book might fully encompass the rulings on words and explain their categories, mentioning the objects thereof that every religious person needs to know (*al-Adhkar* (y102), 450).

r0.2   (النووي:) وقد ذكرت ما يسر الله سبحانه وتعالى من الأذكار المستحبة ونحوها فيما سبق، وأردت أن أضم إليها ما يكـره أو يحـرم من الألفـاظ ليكـون الكتـاب جامعاً لأحكـام الألفـاظ، ومبيناً أقسـامهـا، فأذكر من ذلك مقاصد يحتاج إلى معرفتهـا كلّ متدين [نقل من الأذكار المنتخبة من كلام سيد الأبرار: ٤٥٠].

r1.0 THE IMPORTANCE OF HOLDING ONE'S TONGUE

r1.1 (Nawawi:) Every legally responsible person should refrain from saying anything except when there is a clear advantage to speaking. Whenever speaking and not speaking are of equal benefit, it is sunna to remain silent, for permissible speech easily leads to that which is unlawful or offensive, as actually happens much or even most of the time—and there is no substitute for safety. The Prophet (Allah) bless him and give him peace) said,

"Whoever believes in Allah and the Last Day, let him say what is good or remain silent."

This hadith, whose authenticity Bukhari and Muslim concur upon, is an explicit legal text indicating that a person should not speak unless what he intends to say is good, meaning that the benefit of it is apparent to him. Whenever one doubts that there is a clear advantage, one should not speak. Imam Shafi'i (Allah have mercy on him) said, "When one wishes to speak, one must first reflect, and if there is a clear interest to be served by speaking, one speaks, while if one doubts it, one remains silent until the advantage becomes apparent."

r1.2 The Prophet (Allah bless him and give him peace):

(1) "O Messenger of Allah, which of the Muslims is best?" And he said, "He who the Muslims are safe from his tongue and his hand."

(2) "A servant unthinkingly says something pleasing to Allah Most High for which Allah raises him whole degrees. And a servant unthinkingly says something detested by Allah Most High for which he plunges into hell."

(3) "The excellence of a person's Islam includes leaving what does not concern him [def: w54]."

---

r1.0 أهمية حفظ اللسان

r1.1 (النووي:) [اعلم أنه] ينبغي لكل مكلف أن يحفظ لسانه عن جميع الكلام إلا كلاماً تظهر المصلحة فيه. ومتى استوى الكلام وتركه في المصلحة فالسنة الإمساك عنه، لأنه قد ينجرّ الكلام المباح إلى حرام أو مكروه، بل هذا كثير أو غالب في العادة، والسلامة لا يعدلها شيء. [روينا في صحيحي البخاري ومسلم عن أبي هريرة رضي الله عنه] عن النبي ﷺ قال: «مَن كان يؤمن بالله واليوم الآخر فليقل خيراً أو ليصمت».

قلت: فهذا الحديث المتفق على صحته نص صريح في أنه لا ينبغي أن يتكلم إلا إذا كان الكلام خيراً، وهو الذي ظهرت له مصلحته. ومتى شك في ظهور المصلحة فلا يتكلم. وقد قال الإمام الشافعي رحمه الله: إذا أراد الكلام فعليه أن يفكر قبل كلامه، فإن ظهرت المصلحة تكلم. وإن شك لم يتكلم حتى تظهر.

r1.2 [وروينا في صحيحيهما عن أبي موسى الأشعري قال: قلت] يا رسول الله أي المسلمين أفضل؟ قال: «مَن سَلِمَ المسلمون من لسانِه ويدِه».

- [وروينا في صحيح البخاري عن أبي هريرة عن النبي ﷺ قال:] «إن العبد ليتكلم بالكلمة من رضوان الله تعالى ما يُلقي لها بالاً يرفع اللهُ تعالى بها درجاتٍ. وإن العبد ليتكلم بالكلمة من سخط الله تعالى لا يُلقي لها بالاً يهوي بها في جهنم».

- [وروينا في كتاب الترمذي وابن ماجه عن أبي هريرة عن النبي ﷺ قال:] «مِن حسن إسلام المرء تركه ما لا يعنيه». [حديث حسن].

(4) "Do not speak much without mentioning Allah (dhikr), for too much speech without mentioning Allah hardens the heart, and the hard-hearted are the farthest of all people from Allah Most High."

(5) "All of a human being's words count against him and not for him, except commanding the right, forbidding the wrong, and the mention of Allah Most High (dhikr)."

r1.3   The Master Abul Qasim Qushayri (Allah have mercy on him) said, "Safety lies in remaining silent, which should be one's basis. Silence at the appropriate time is the mark of men, just as speech at the appropriate time is one of the finest qualities. I have heard Abu 'Ali Daqqaq (Allah be well pleased with him) say, 'He who is silent when something should be said is a tongueless villain' " (ibid., 450–55).

*

r2.0   SLANDER (GHIBA)

r2.1   (Nawawi:) Slander and talebearing are two of the ugliest and most frequently met with qualities among men, few people being safe from them. I have begun with them because of the widespread need to warn people of them.

SLANDER

r2.2   *Slander* (ghiba) means to mention anything concerning a person that he would dislike, whether about his body, religion, everyday life, self, disposition, property, son, father, wife, servant, turban, garment, gait, movements, smiling, dissoluteness, frowning, cheerfulness, or anything else connected with him.

- [وروينا في كتاب الترمذي عن ابن عمر رضي الله عنهما قال : قال رسول الله ﷺ :] «لاَ تُكْثِرُوا الكلام بغير ذكر الله فإن كثرة الكلام بغير ذكر الله تعالى قسوةٌ للقلب وإن أبعد الناس من الله تعالى القلب القاسي».

- [وروينا في كتاب الترمذي وابن ماجه عن أم حبيبة رضي الله عنها عن النبي ﷺ :] «كل كلام ابن آدم عليه لا له إلا أمراً بمعروف ونهياً عن منكر أو ذكراً لله تعالى».

r1.3   [وروينا] عن الأستاذ أبي القاسم القشيري رحمه الله [في رسالته المشهورة] : قال : الصمت السلامة وهو الأصل ، والسكوت في وقته صفة الرجال كما أن النطق في موضعه أشرف الخصال . قال : سمعت أبا علي الدقاق رضي الله عنه يقول : من سكت عن الحق فهو شيطان أخرس [محرر من المرجع المذكور : ٤٥٠ ـ ٤٥٥].

r2.0   الغيبة [والنميمة]

r2.1   (النووي:) [اعلم أن] هاتين الخصلتين من أقبح القبائح وأكثرها انتشاراً في الناس، حتى ما يسلم منهما إلا القليل من الناس . فلعموم الحاجة إلى التحذير منهما بدأت بهما .

الغيبة

r2.2   فأمّا الغيبة فهي ذكرك الإنسان بما فيه مما يكره، سواء كان في بدنه أو دينه أو دنياه أو نفسه أو خُلقه أو ماله أو ولده أو والده أو زوجه أو خادمه [. . .] أو عمامته أو ثوبه أو مشيته وحركته وبشاشته وخلاعته وعبوسه وطلاقته أو غير ذلك مما

Mention means by word, writing, sign, or indicating him with one's eye, hand, head, and so forth.

Body refers to saying such things as that someone is blind, lame, bleary-eyed, bald, short, tall, dark, or pale.

Religion includes saying that he is corrupt, a thief, cannot be trusted, is a tyrant, does not care about the prayer, does not watch to avoid filth, does not honor his father, does not spend zakat on what it should be spent on, or does not avoid slandering others.

Everyday life includes saying that his manners are poor; he does not care about others; does not think he owes anyone anything; that he talks, eats, or sleeps too much; or sleeps or sits when he should not.

Father refers to saying such things as that his father is corrupt, his father is an Indian, Nabatean, African, cobbler, draper, carpenter, blacksmith, or weaver (N: if mentioned derogatorily).

Disposition includes saying that he has bad character, is arrogant, a show-off, overhasty, domineering, incapable, fainthearted, irresponsible, gloomy, dissolute, and so forth.

Clothing means saying such things as that his sleeves are too loose, his garment hangs too low, is dirty, or the like. Other remarks can be judged by the above examples. The determining factor is mentioning about a person what he would not like.

r2.3   As for talebearing (namima), it consists of quoting someone's words to another in a way that worsens relations between them.

THE EVIDENCE THAT SLANDER
AND TALEBEARING ARE UNLAWFUL

r2.4   The above define slander and talebearing. As for the ruling on them, it is that they are unlawful, by the consensus (def: b7) of Muslims. There is much explicit and intersubstantiative evidence that they are unlawful from the Koran, sunna, and consensus of the Muslim Community.

يتعلق به ، سواء ذكرته بلفظك أو كتابك ، أو رمزت أو أشرت إليه بعينك أو يدك أو رأسك أو نحو ذلك .

أما البدن فكقولك : أعمى أعرج أعمش أقرع قصير طويل أسود أصفر .

وأما الدين فكقولك : فاسق سارق خائن ظالم متهاون بالصلاة ، متساهل في النجاسات ، ليس باراً بوالده ، لا يضع الزكاة مواضعها ، لا يجتنب الغيبة .

وأما الدنيا : فقليل الأدب يتهاون بالناس ، لا يرى لأحد عليه حقاً ، كثير الكلام كثير الأكل والنوم ، ينام في غير وقته ، يجلس في غير موضعه .

وأما المتعلق بوالده فكقوله : أبوه فاسق أو هندي أو نبطي أو زنجي ، إسكاف بزاز [. . .] نجار حداد حائك .

وأما الخلق فكقوله : سيء الخلق ، متكبر مراء عجول جبار عاجز ، ضعيف القلب ، متهور عبوس خليع ونحوه .

وأما الثوب : فواسع الكم ، طويل الذيل ، وسخ الثوب ونحو ذلك . ويقاس الباقي بما ذكرناه . وضابطه ذكره بما يكره .

r2.3   وأما النميمة فهي نقل كلام الناس بعضهم إلى بعض على جهة الإفساد .

الأدلة على تحريم الغيبة والنميمة

r2.4   هذا بيانهما . وأما حكمهما فهما حرام بإجماع المسلمين . وقد تظاهرت على تحريمها الدلائل الصريحة من الكتاب والسنة وإجماع المسلمين .

731

r2.5   Allah Most High says:

(1) "Do not slander one another" (Koran 49:12).

(2) "Woe to whomever disparages others behind their back or to their face" (Koran 104:1).

(3) "... slanderer, going about with tales" (Koran 68:11).

r2.6   The Prophet (Allah bless him and give him peace) said:

(1) "The talebearer will not enter paradise."

(2) "Do you know what slander is?" They answered, "Allah and His messenger know best." He said, "It is to mention of your brother that which he would dislike." Someone asked, "What if he is as I say?" And he replied, "If he is as you say, you have slandered him, and if not, you have calumniated him."

(3) "The Muslim is the brother of the Muslim. He does not betray him, lie to him, or hang back from coming to his aid. All of the Muslim is inviolable to his fellow Muslim: his reputation, his property, his blood. Godfearingness is here [N: pointing to his heart]. It is sufficiently wicked for someone to belittle his fellow Muslim."

MIMICKING ANOTHER'S IDIOSYNCRACIES

r2.7   We have mentioned above that slander is saying anything about a person that he would dislike, whether aloud, in writing, by a sign, or a gesture. Anything by which one conveys a Muslim's (A: or non-Muslim's) shortcomings to another is slander, and unlawful. It includes doing imitations of someone, such as by walking with a limp, with

قال الله تعالى :   r2.5

﴿وَلاَ يَغْتَبْ بَعْضُكُمْ بَعْضَاً﴾

[الحجرات : ١٢] .

وقال تعالى :

﴿وَيْلٌ لِكُلِّ هُمَزَةٍ لُمَزَةٍ﴾ [الهمزة :

١] .

وقال تعالى :

﴿هَمَّازٍ مَشَّاءٍ بِنَمِيمٍ﴾ [القلم : ١١] .

[وروينا في صحيحي   r2.6

البخاري ومسلم عن حذيفة رضي الله

عنه] النبي ﷺ قال : «لا يدخل الجنة

نمامٌ» .

- [وروينا في صحيح مسلم وسنن أبي

داود والترمذي والنسائي عن أبي هريرة

رضي الله عنه أن رسول الله ﷺ قال :]

«أتدرون ما الغيبة؟ قالوا : الله ورسوله

أعلم . قال : ذكرك أخاك بما يكرهُ؛ قيل

أفرأيت إن كان في أخي ما أقول؟ قال :

إن كان فيه ما تقول فقد اغتبته، وإن لم

يكن فيه ما تقول فقد بهتَّهُ» [قال الترمذي

حديث حسن صحيح] .

- [وروينا في كتاب الترمذي عن أبي

هريرة رضي الله عنه قال : قال رسول الله

ﷺ :] «المسلم أخو المسلم لا يخونُه ولا

يكــذبُـه ولا يخـذُلُه . كل المسلم على

المسلم حرامٌ : عرضـه ومـالـه ودمه ،

التقوى ههنا . بحسب امرىءٍ من الشر أن

يحقـر أخـاه المسلم» [قـال الترمـذي :

حديث حسن] .

المحاكاة

قد ذكرنا في الباب السابق أن   r2.7

الغيبة ذكرك الإنسان بما يكره ، سواء

ذكرته بلفظك أو في كتابك ، أو رمزت أو

أشـرت إليه [بعينك أو يدك أو رأسك]

وضابطه : كل ما أفهمت به غيرك نقصان

مسلم فهـو غيبـة محـرمة . ومن ذلك

المحاكاة بأن يمشي متعرجاً أو متطأطئاً أو

a stoop, or similar posture, intending to mimic the person with such a deficiency. Anything of this sort is unquestionably unlawful.

على غير ذلك من الهيئات مريداً حكاية هيئة من ينتقصه بذلك ، فكل ذلك حرام بلا خلاف .

SLANDER IN PUBLISHED WORKS

الغيبة في المؤلفات

r2.8   Slander also includes the author of a book mentioning a specific person in his work by saying, "So-and-so says such and such," which is unlawful if he thereby intends to demean him. But if he wants to clarify the person's mistake so that others will not follow him, or expose the weakness of his scholarship so others will not be deceived and accept what he says, it is not slander, but rather advice that is obligatory, and is rewarded by Allah for the person who intends it as such.

Nor is it slander for a writer or other person to say, "There are those [or "a certain group"] who say such and such, which is a mistake, error, ignorance, and folly," and so forth, which is not slander because slander entails mentioning a particular person or a group of specific individuals.

r2.8   ومن ذلك إذا ذكر مصنف كتاب شخصاً بعينه في كتابه قائلاً : قال فلان كذا ؛ مريداً تنقصه [والشناعة عليه] فهو حرام .

فإن أراد بيان غلطه لئلا يقلد أو بيان ضعفه في العلم لئلا يغتر به ويقبل قوله ، فهذا ليس غيبة بل نصيحة واجبة يثاب عليه إذا أراد ذلك .

وكذا إذا قال المصنف أو غيره : قال قوم أو جماعة كذا ، وهذا غلط أو خطأ أو جهالة وغفلة ونحو ذلك ؛ فليس غيبة ، إنما الغيبة ذكر الإنسان بعينه أو جماعة معينين .

SLANDER BY ALLUSION AND INNUENDO

الغيبة بالتعريض

r2.9   When the person being spoken to understands whom one is referring to, it is slander and unlawful to say, for example, "A certain person did such and such," or "A certain scholar," "Someone with pretensions to knowledge," "A certain mufti," "A certain person regarded as good," "Someone who claims to be an ascetic," "One of those who passed by us today," or "One of the people we saw." This includes the slander of some would-be scholars and devotees, who make slanderous innuendoes that are as clearly understood as if they were plainly stated. When one of them is asked, for example, how So-and-so is, he replies, "May Allah improve us," "May Allah forgive us," "May Allah improve him," "We ask Allah's forbearance," "Praise be to Allah who has not afflicted us with visiting oppressors," "We take refuge in Allah from evil," "May Allah forgive us for lack of modesty," "May Allah relent towards us," and the like, from which the listener

r2.9   ومن الغيبة المحرمة قولك : فعل كذا بعض الناس أو بعض الفقهاء ، أو بعض من يدّعي العلم ، أو بعض المفتين ، أو بعض من ينسب إلى الصلاح أو يدّعي الزهد ، أو بعض من مرّ بنا اليوم ، أو بعض من رأيناه ، أو نحو ذلك ؛ إذا كان المخاطب يفهمه بعينه لحصول التفهيم . ومن ذلك غيبة المتفقهين والمتعبدين ، فإنهم يعرضون بالغيبة تعريضاً يفهم به كما يفهم بالصريح . فيقال لأحدهم : كيف حال فلان؟ فيقول : الله يصلحنا ، الله يغفر لنا ، الله يصلحه ، نسأل الله العافية ، نحمد الله الذي لم يبتلنا بالدخول على الظلمة ، نعوذ بالله من الشرّ ، الله يعافينا من قلة الحياء ، الله يتوب علينا ، وما أشبه ذلك مما يفهم منه

understands the person's shortcomings. All of this is slander and is unlawful, just as when one says, "So-and-so is afflicted with what we all are," or "There's no way he can manage this," or "We all do it."

تنقصه ؛ فكل ذلك غيبة محرمة .
وكذلك إذا قال فلان ابتلى بما ابتلينا به كلنا ، أو ماله حيلة في هذا ، كلنا نفعله .

r2.10   The above are but examples. Otherwise, as previously mentioned, the criterion for slander is that one gives the person being addressed to understand another's faults.

r2.10   وهذه أمثلة وإلا فضابط الغيبة : تفهيمك المخاطب نقص إنسان .

LISTING TO SLANDER

حرمة استماع الغيبة

r2.11   Just as slander is unlawful for the one who says it, it is also unlawful for the person hearing it to listen and acquiesce to. It is obligatory whenever one hears someone begin to slander another to tell him to stop if this does not entail manifest harm to one. If it does, then one is obliged to condemn it in one's heart and to leave the company if able. When the person who hears it is able to condemn it in words or change the subject, then he must. It is a sin for him not to. But if the hearer tells the slanderer to be silent while desiring him in his heart to continue, this, as Ghazali notes, is hypocrisy that does not lift the sin from him, for one must dislike it in one's heart.

r2.11   [اعلم أن] الغيبة كما يحرم على المغتاب ذكرها يحرم على السامع استماعها وإقرارها . فيجب على من سمع إنساناً يبتدىء بغيبة محرمة أن ينهاه إن لم يخف ضرراً ظاهراً ، فإن خافه وجب عليه الإنكار بقلبه ومفارقة ذلك المجلس إن تمكن من مفارقته . فإن قدر على الإنكار بلسانه أو على قطع الغيبة بكلام آخر لزمه ذلك ، فإن لم يفعل عصى . فإن قال بلسانه : اسكت ؛ وهو يشتهي بقلبه استمراره فقال [أبو حامد] الغزالي : ذلك نفاق لا يخرجه عن الإثم ، ولا بدّ من كراهته بقلبه .

r2.12   Whenever one is forced to remain at a gathering where there is slander and one is unable to condemn it, or one's condemnation goes unheeded and one cannot leave, it is nevertheless unlawful to listen or pay attention to. What one should do is invoke Allah (dhikr) with the tongue and heart, or heart alone, or think about something else to distract one from listening to it. When this is done, whatever one hears under such circumstances does not harm one as long as one does not listen to or heed the conversation. And if afterwards one is able to leave the assembly and the people are persisting in slander and the like, then one must leave. Allah Most High says:

"When you see those engaged in idle discussion about Our signs, keep apart from them until

r2.12   ومتى اضطرّ إلى المقام في ذلك المجلس الذي فيه الغيبة وعجز عن الإنكار أو أنكر فلم يقبل منه ولم يمكنه المفارقة بطريق ، حرم عليه الاستماع والإصغاء للغيبة .
بل طريقه أن يذكر الله تعالى بلسانه وقلبه ، أو بقلبه ، أو يفكر في أمر آخر ليشتغل عن استماعها . ولا يضره بعد ذلك السماع من غير استماع وإصغاء في هذه الحالة المذكورة . فإن تمكن بعد ذلك من المفارقة وهم مستمرون في الغيبة ونحوها وجب عليه المفارقة . قال الله تعالى :
﴿وَإِذَا رَأَيْتَ الَّذِينَ يَخُوضُونَ فِي آيَاتِنَا

they speak of other things. And if the Devil makes you forget, then do not sit with wrong-doing people after being reminded" (Koran 6:68).

r2.13 Ibrahim ibn Adham (Allah be well pleased with him) answered an invitation to come to a wedding feast, where some of those present mentioned that a certain person who did not attend was "unpleasant." Ibrahim said, "I myself have done this by coming to a place where others are slandered," and he left and would not eat for three days.

SLANDERING ANOTHER IN ONE'S HEART

r2.14 Entertaining bad thoughts about others (su' al-zann) is as unlawful as expressing them. Just as it is unlawful to tell another of the failings of a person, so too it is unlawful to speak to oneself of them and think badly of him. Allah Most High says,

"Shun much of surmise" (Koran 49:12).

The Prophet (Allah bless him and give him peace) said,

"Beware of suspicions, for they are the most lying of words."

There are many hadiths which say the same, and they refer to an established conviction or judgement in the heart that another is bad. As for passing thoughts and fancies that do not last, when the person having them does not persist in them, scholars concur that they are excusable, since their occurrence is involuntary and there is no way to avoid them. The Prophet (Allah bless him and give him peace) said,

"For those of my Community, Allah over-looks the thoughts that come to mind as long as they are not uttered or acted upon."

Scholars say this refers to passing thoughts that do not abide, whether of slander, unbelief (kufr), or

فَأَعْرِضْ عَنْهُمْ حَتَّى يَخُوضُوا فِي حَدِيثٍ غَيْرِهِ وَإِمَّا يُنْسِيَنَّكَ الشَّيْطَانُ فَلَا تَقْعُدْ بَعْدَ الذِّكْرَى مَعَ الْقَوْمِ الظَّالِمِينَ﴾ [الأنعام: ٦٨].

r2.13 [وروينا عن] إبراهيم بن أدهم رضي الله عنه [أنه] دعي إلى وليمة، فحضر، فذكروا رجلاً لم يأتهم، فقالوا إنه ثقيل.

فقال إبراهيم: أنا فعلت هذا بنفسي حيث حضرت موضعاً يغتاب فيه الناس، فخرج ولم يأكل ثلاثة أيام.

الغيبة بالقلب

r2.14 [اعلم أن] سوء الظن حرام مثل القول. فكما يحرم أن تحدث غيرك بمساوي إنسان يحرم أن تحدث نفسك بذلك وتسيء الظن به. قال الله تعالى: ﴿اجْتَنِبُوا كَثِيراً مِنَ الظَّنِّ﴾ [الحجرات: ١٢].

[وروينا في صحيحي البخاري ومسلم عن أبي هريرة رضي الله عنه أن] رسول الله ﷺ قال: «إياكم والظن فإن الظن أكذب الحديث».

والأحاديث بمعنى ما ذكرته كثيرة والمراد بذلك عقد القلب وحكمه على غيرك بالسوء. فأما الخواطر وحديث النفس إذا لم يستقر ويستمر عليه صاحبه فمعفو عنه باتفاق العلماء، لأنه لا اختيار له في وقوعه، ولا طريق له إلى الانفكاك عنه. و[في الصحيح عن] رسول الله ﷺ [أنه] قال: إنّ الله تجاوز لأمتي ما حدثت به أنفسها ما لم تتكلم به أو تعمل».

قال العلماء المراد به الخواطر التي لا تستقر. قالوا وسواء كان ذلك الخاطر غيبة أو كفراً أو غيرهما. فمن خطر له الكفر

something else. Whoever entertains a passing notion of unbelief that is a mere fancy whose occurrence is unintentional and immediately dismissed is not an unbeliever and is not to blame. The reason such things are excusable is that there is no way to take precaution against them. One can only avoid continuing therein, which is why persistence in them and the established conviction of them in one's heart is unlawful.

Whenever one has a passing thought of slander, one is obliged to reject it and summon to mind extenuating circumstances which explain away the appearances that seem to imply the bad opinion. Imam Abu Hamid Ghazali says in the *Ihya'*: "A bad thought about someone that occurs in one's heart is a notion suggested by the Devil, and one should dismiss it, for the Devil is the most corrupt of the corrupt, and Allah Most High says,

" 'If a corrupt person brings you news, verify it, lest you hurt others out of ignorance and then regret what you have done' (Koran 49:6).

It is not permissible to believe Satan, and if the appearance of wrongdoing can possibly be interpreted otherwise, it is not lawful to think badly of another. The Devil may enter the heart at the slightest impression of others' mistakes, suggesting that one only noticed it because of one's superior intelligence and discernment, and that "the believer sees with the light of Allah," which upon examination often amounts to nothing more than repeating the Devil's deceit and obscurities. If a reliable witness informs one of something bad about another, one should neither believe it nor disbelieve it, in order to avoid thinking badly of either of them. And whenever one has a bad thought about a Muslim one should increase one's concern and respect for him, as this will madden the Devil and put him off, and he will not suggest the like of it to one again for fear that one will occupy oneself with prayer for the person.

"If one learns of a Muslim's mistake by undeniable proof, one should advise him about it in private and not let the Devil delude one into slandering him. And when admonishing him, one should not gloat over his shortcoming and the fact that he is regarding one with respect while one is regarding him with disdain, but one's intention should

مجرد خطران من غير تعمد لتحصيله ثم صرفه في الحال فليس بكافر ولا شيء عليه . وسبب العفو ما ذكرناه من تعذر اجتنابه . وإنما الممكن اجتناب الاستمرار عليه فلهذا كان الاستمرار وعقد القلب حراماً .

ومهما عرض لك هذا الخاطر بالغيبة [وغيرها من المعاصي] وجب عليك دفعه بالإعراض عنه وذكر التأويلات الصارفة له عن ظاهره . قال الإمام أبو حامد الغزالي في الإحياء : إذا وقع في قلبك ظن السوء فهو من وسوسة الشيطان يلقيه إليك فينبغي أن تكذبه فإنه أفسق الفساق ، وقد قال الله تعالى :

﴿إِنْ جَاءَكُمْ فَاسِقٌ بِنَبَأٍ فَتَبَيَّنُوا أَنْ تُصِيبُوا قَوْماً بِجَهَالَةٍ فَتُصْبِحُوا عَلَى مَا فَعَلْتُمْ نَادِمِينَ﴾ [الحجرات : ٧].

فلا يجوز تصديق إبليس . فإن كان هناك قرينة تدل على فساد واحتمل خلافه لم تجز إساءة الظن . [. . .] فإن الشيطان قد يقرب إلى القلب بأدنى خيال مساوىء الناس ، ويلقي إليه أن هذا من فطنتك وذكائك وسرعة تنبهك ، وأن المؤمن ينظر بنور الله ؛ وإنما هو على التحقيق ناطق بغرور الشيطان وظلمته .

وإن أخبرك عدل بذلك فلا تصدقه ولا تكذبه لئلا تسيء الظن بأحدهما .

ومهما خطر لك سوء في مسلم فزد في مراعاته وإكرامه . فإن ذلك يغيظ الشيطان ويدفعه عنك فلا يلقي إليك مثله خيفة من اشتغالك بالدعاء له .

ومهما عرفت هفوة مسلم بحجة لا شك فيها فانصحه في السر ولا يخدعنك الشيطان فيدعوك إلى اغتيابه . وإذا وعظته فلا تعظه وأنت مسرور باطلاعك على نقصه فينظر إليك بعين التعظيم وتنظر إليه بالاستصغار ، ولكن اقصد تخليصه من

rather be to help him disengage from the act of dis-obedience, over which one is as sad as if one had committed it oneself. One should be happier if he desists from it without being admonished than if he desists because of one's admonishment." These are Ghazali's words.

الإثم وأنت حزين كما تحزن على نفسك إذا دخلك نقص.

وينبغي أن يكون تركه لذلك النقص بغير وعظك وعظك أحب إليك من تركه بوعظك. ـ هذا كلام الغزالي ـ.

r2.15 We have mentioned that it is obligatory for a person with a passing ill thought of another to dispell it, this being when no interest recongnised by Sacred Law conduces one to reflect upon it, for if there is such an interest, it is permissible to weigh and consider the individual's deficiency and warn others of it, as when evaluating the reliability of court witnesses or hadith transmitters, and in other cases we will mention below in the section on permissible slander.

r2.15 قد ذكرنا أنه يجب عليه إذا عرض له خاطر بسوء الظن أن يقطعه. وهذا إذا لم تدع إلى الفكر في ذلك مصلحة شرعية؛ فإن دعت جاز الفكر في نقيصته والترغيب عنها كما في جرح الشهود والرواة وغير ذلك مما ذكرنا في باب ما يباح من الغيبة.

PERMISSIBLE SLANDER

ما يباح من الغيبة

r2.16 Slander, though unlawful, is sometimes permissible for a lawful purpose, the legitimating factor being that there is some aim countenanced by Sacred Law that is unattainable by other means. This may be for one of six reasons.

r2.16 [اعلم أن] الغيبة وإن كانت محرمة فإنها تباح في أحوال للمصلحة. والمجوز لهذا غرض صحيح شرعي لا يمكن الوصول إليه إلا بها، وهو أحد ستة أسباب.

REDRESSING GRIEVANCES

التظلم

r2.17 The first is the redress of grievances. Someone wronged may seek redress from the Islamic ruler, judge, or others with the authority or power to help one against the person who has wronged one. One may say, "So-and-so has wronged me," "done such and such to me," "took such and such of mine," and similar remarks.

r2.17 الأول التظلم. فيجوز للمظلوم أن يتظلم إلى السلطان والقاضي وغيرهما ممن له ولاية أو له قدرة على إنصافه من ظالمه. فيذكر أن: فلاناً ظلمني، وفعل بي كذا، وأخذ لي كذا؛ ونحو ذلك.

ELIMINATING WRONGDOING

إزالة المنكر

r2.18 The second is seeking aid in righting a wrong or correcting a wrongdoer, such as by say-ing to someone expected to be able to set things

r2.18 الثاني الاستعانة على تغيير المنكر ورد العاصي إلى الصواب. فيقول لمن يرجو قدرته على إزالة المنكر: فلان

right, "So-and-so is doing such and such, so warn him not to continue," and the like. The intention in such a case must be to take the measures necessary to eliminate the wrong, for if this is not one's purpose, it is unlawful.

يعمل كذا فازجره عنه ونحو ذلك . ويكون مقصوده التوسل إلى إزالة المنكر . فإن لم يقصد ذلك كان حراماً .

ASKING FOR A LEGAL OPINION

الاستفتاء

r2.19   The third is asking for a legal opinion, such as by saying to the mufti, "My father [or "brother," or "So-and-so,"] has wronged me by doing such and such. May he do so or not?" "How can I be rid of him," "get what is coming to me," "stop the injustice," and so forth. Or such as saying, "My wife does such and such to me," "My husband does such and such," and the like. This is permissible when necessary, but to be on the safe side it is best to say, "What do you think of a man whose case is such and such," or " a husband [or "wife"] who does such and such," and so on, since this accomplishes one's aim without referring to particular people. But it is nevertheless permissible to identify a particular person, as is attested to by the hadith in which Hind said,

r2.19   الثالث الاستفتاء بأن يقول للمفتي : ظلمني أبي أو أخي أو فلان بكذا ، فهل له ذلك أم لا؟ وما طريقي في الخلاص منه وتحصيل حقي ودفع الظلم عني؟ ونحو ذلك . وكذلك قوله : زوجتي تفعل معي كذا ؛ أو زوجي يفعل كذا ؛ ونحو ذلك . فهذا جائز للحاجة . ولكن الأحوط أن يقول : ما تقول في رجل كان من أمره كذا ؛ أو في زوج أو زوجة تفعل كذا ؛ ونحو ذلك ، فإنه يحصل به الغرض من غير تعيين . ومع ذلك فالتعيين جائز لحديث هند [الذي سنذكره إن شاء الله تعالى وقولها] «يا رسول الله إن أبا سفيان رجل شحيح» الحديث . ولم ينهها رسول الله ﷺ .

"O Messenger of Allah, Abu Sufyan is a stingy man..."

and the Prophet (Allah bless him and give him peace) did not forbid her.

WARNING MUSLIMS OF EVIL

تحذير المسلمين من الشر

r2.20   The fourth reason is to warn Muslims of evil and advise them, which may take several forms, including:

(1) Impugning unreliable hadith transmitters or court witnesses, which is permissible by consensus of all Muslims, even obligatory, because of the need for it.

(2) When a person seeks one's advice about marrying into a certain family, entering into a partnership with someone, depositing something

r2.20   الرابع تحذير المسلمين من الشر ونصيحتهم وذلك من وجوه : منها جرح المجروحين من الرواة للحديث والشهود . وذلك جائز بإجماع المسلمين ، بل واجب للحاجة . ومنها إذا استشارك إنسان في مصاهرته أو مشاركته أو إيداعه أو الإيداع عنده أو

for safekeeping with him, accepting such a deposit, or some other transaction with him, it is obligatory for one to tell the person asking what one knows about the other by way of advising him. If one can accomplish this by merely saying, "Dealing with him is of no advantage to you," "Marrying into the family is not in your interests," "Do not do it," and similar expressions, then one may not elaborate on the individual's shortcomings. But if it cannot be accomplished without explicitly mentioning the individual, one may do so.

(3) When one notices a student of Sacred Law going to learn from a teacher who is guilty of reprehensible innovations in religious matters (bid'a, def: w29.3) or who is corrupt, and one apprehends harm to the student thereby, one must advise him and explain how the teacher really is. It is necessary in such a case that one intend to give sincere counsel. Mistakes are sometimes made in this, as the person warning another may be motivated by envy, which the Devil has duped him into believing is heartfelt advice and compassion, so one must beware of this.

(4) And when there is someone in a position of responsibility who is not doing the job as it should be done, because of being unfit for it, corrupt, inattentive, or the like, one must mention this to the person with authority over him so he can remove him and find another to do the job properly, or be aware of how he is so as to deal with him as he should be dealt with and not be deluded by him, to urge him to either improve or else be replaced.

SOMEONE UNCONCERNED WITH CONCEALING THEIR DISOBEDIENCE

r2.21   A fifth reason that permits slander is when the person is making no effort to conceal his corruption or involvement in reprehensible innovation (bid'a), such as someone who openly drinks wine, confiscates others' property, gathers taxes uncountenanced by Sacred Law, collects money wrongfully, or perpetrates other falsehoods, in

معاملته بغير ذلك ، وجب عليك أن تذكر له ما تعلمه منه على جهة النصيحة . فإن حصل الغرض بمجرد قولك : لا تصلح لك معاملته أو مصاهرته أو لا تفعل هذا أو نحو ذلك ، لم تجز الزيادة بذكر المساوي .

وإن لم يحصل الغرض إلا بالتصريح بعينه فاذكره بصريحه .

ومنها إذا رأيت متفقهاً يتردد إلى مبتدع أو فاسق يأخذ عنه العلم خفت أن يتضرر المتفقه بذلك ، فعليك نصيحته ببيان حاله . ويشترط أن تقصد النصيحة . وهذا مما يغلط فيه ، وقد يحمل المتكلم بذلك الحسد ، ويلبس الشيطان عليه ذلك ويخيل إليه أنه نصيحة وشفقة ، فليتفطن لذلك .

ومنها أن يكون له ولاية لا يقوم بها على وجهها ، إما بأن لا يكون صالحاً لها ، وإما بأن يكون فاسقاً أو مغفلاً ونحو ذلك .

فيجب ذكر ذلك لمن له عليه ولاية عامة ليزيله ويولي من يصلح ، أو يعلم ذلك منه ليعامله بمقتضى حاله ولا يغتر به وأن يسعى في أن يحثه على الاستقامة أو يستبدل به .

المجاهرة بالفسق

r2.21   الخامس أن يكون مجاهراً بفسقه أو بدعته كالمجاهر بشرب الخمر أو مصادرة الناس وأخذ المكس وجباية الأموال ظلماً وتولي الأمور الباطلة .

which cases it is permissible to speak about what he is unconcerned to conceal, but unlawful to mention his other faults unless there is some other valid reason that permits it, of those we have discussed.

فيجوز ذكره بما يجاهر به ويحرم ذكره بغيره من العيوب إلا أن يكون لجوازه سبب آخر مما ذكرناه.

IDENTIFICATION

التعريف

r2.22   The sixth reason is to identify someone. When a person is known by a nickname such as "the Bleary-eyed," "the Lame," "the Deaf," "the Blind," "the Cross-eyed," or similar, it is permissible to refer to him by that name if one's intention is to identify him. It is unlawful to do so by way of pointing out his deficiencies. And if one can identify him by some other means, it is better.

r2.22   السادس التعريف فإذا كان الإنسان معروفاً بلقب كالأعمش والأعرج والأصم والأعمى والأحول وغيرهم جاز تعريفه بذلك بنية التعريف، ويحرم إطلاقه على جهة النقص. ولو أمكن التعريف بغيره كان أولى.

r2.23   These then, are six reasons Islamic scholars mention that permit slander in the above cases (al-Adhkar (y102), 455–69).

r2.23   فهذه ستة أسباب ذكرها العلماء مما تباح بها الغيبة على ما ذكرناه. [محرر من الأذكار: ٤٥٥ ـ ٤٦٩ بتقديم وتأخير].

*

r3.0   TALEBEARING (NAMIMA)

r3.0   تحريم النميمة

r3.1   (Nawawi:) Having summarily mentioned that talebearing (namima) is unlawful, with the evidence for this and a description of its nature, we now want to add a fuller explanation of it. Imam Abu Hamid Ghazali says, "Talebearing is a term that is usually applied only to someone who conveys to a person what another has said about him, such as by saying, 'So-and-so says such and such about you.' In fact, talebearing is not limited to that, but rather consists of revealing anything whose disclosure is resented, whether resented by the person who originally said it, the person to whom it is disclosed, or by a third party. It makes no difference whether the disclosure is in word, writing, a sign, nodding, or other; whether it concerns word or deed; or whether it concerns something bad or otherwise. The reality of talebearing

r3.1   (النووي:) قد ذكرنا تحريمها ودلائلها وما جاء في الوعيد عليها وذكرنا بيان حقيقتها ولكنه مختصر، ونزيد الآن في شرحه. قال الإمام أبو حامد الغزالي [رحمه الله]: النميمة إنما تطلق في الغالب على من ينم قول الغير إلى المقول فيه كقوله: فلان يقول فيك كذا. وليست النميمة مخصوصة بذلك؛ بل حدها كشف ما يكره كشفه سواء كرهه المنقول عنه أو المنقول إليه، أو ثالث، وسواء كان الكشف بالقول أو الكتابة أو الرمز أو الإيماء أو نحوها؛ وسواء كان المنقول من الأقوال أو الأعمال؛ وسواء كان عيباً أو غيره. فحقيقة النميمة إفشاء

lies in divulging a secret, in revealing something confidential whose disclosure is resented. A person should not speak of anything he notices about people besides that which benefits a Muslim to relate or prevents disobedience. Anyone approached with a story, who is told, 'So-and-so says such and such about you,' must do six things:

(1) disbelieve it, for talebearers are corrupt, and their information unacceptable;

(2) tell the talebearer to stop, admonish him about it, and condemn the shamefulness of what he has done;

(3) hate him for the sake of Allah Most High, for he is detestable in Allah's sight, and hating for the sake of Allah Most High is obligatory;

(4) not think badly of the person whom the words are supposedly from, for Allah Most High says,

'Shun much of surmise' (Koran 49:12);

(5) not let what has been said prompt him to spy or investigate whether it is true, for Allah Most High says,

'Do not spy' (Koran 49:12);

(6) and not to do himself what he has forbidden the talebearer to do, by relating it to others."

(Ibid., 471–72)

*

r4.0   SAYING "THE PEOPLE HAVE GONE TO RUIN"

r4.1   The Prophet (Allah bless him and give him peace) said,

"When a man says, 'The people have gone to ruin,' he is the most ruined of all."

السر وهتك الستر عما يكره كشفه .

وينبغي للإنسان أن يسكت عن كل ما رآه من أحوال الناس إلا ما في حكايته فائدة لمسلم أو دفع معصية .

وكل من حُمِلت إليه نميمة وقيل له : قال فيك فلان كذا ؛ لزمه ستة أمور :

ـ الأول أن لا يصدقه لأن النمام فاسق وهو مردود الخبر .

ـ الثاني أن ينهاه عن ذلك وينصحه ويقبح فعله .

ـ الثالث أن يبغضه في الله تعالى فإنه بغيض عند الله تعالى والبغض في الله تعالى واجب .

ـ الرابع أن لا يظن بالمنقول عنه السوء لقول الله تعالى :

﴿اجْتَنِبُوا كَثِيراً مِنَ الظَّنِّ﴾ .

ـ الخامس أن لا يحملك ما حكي لك على التجسُّس والبحث عن تحقيق ذلك ، قال الله تعالى :

﴿وَلَا تَجَسَّسُوا﴾ .

ـ السادس أن لا يرضى لنفسه ما نهى النمام عنه فلا يحكي نميمته [نقل من المرجع المذكور : ٤٧١ ـ ٤٧٢] .

r4.0   النهي عن قول «هلك الناس»

r4.1   [عن أبي هريرة أن] رسول الله ﷺ قال : «إذا قال الرجلُ : هلك الناسُ ؛ فهو أهلكُهُمْ» [قال أبو إسحاق لا أدري أهلكَهُمْ بالنصب أو أهلكُهُمْ بالرفع] . [رواه مسلم] .

r4.2   (Nawawi:) Khattabi says the hadith means that a person who continually finds fault with people and mentions their failings is the most ruined of all, i.e. he becomes worse than they are because of the sin he commits in disparaging and attacking them, which may also lead to conceitedness and seeing himself as better than they.

Scholars concur that the condemnation only applies to someone who says the like of this out of contempt for people, considering them inferior and himself superior, despising the way they are because of his ignorance of the divine wisdom in Allah's creating them. But if one says it out of sadness at seeing one's own religious failings and those of others, there is no harm in it, just as there is no blame in saying, "For all I know, every one of the Prophet's Community (Allah bless him and give him peace) performs the prayer." This is how Imam Malik explained the hadith, and others have followed him therein (*Sahih Muslim bi Sharh al-Nawawi* (y93), 16.175–76).

*

r5.0   INFORMING ON ANOTHER

r5.1   The Prophet (Allah bless him and give him peace) said,

"Let none of my Companions inform me of anything another of them has said, for I wish to come out to you without disquiet in my heart."

(*al-Adhkar* (y102), 473)

*

r6.0   TWO PEOPLE CONVERSING SO A THIRD CANNOT HEAR

r6.1   The Prophet (Allah bless him and give him peace) said,

r4.2   وقـال الخطـابي معنـاه لا يزال الـرجل يعيب النـاس ويـذكر مساويهم ويقول فسد الناس وهلكوا ونحو ذلك فإذا فعل ذلك فهو أهلكهم أي أسوأ حالاً منهم بما يلحقه من الإثم في عيبهم والـوقيعة فيهم وربما أداه ذلك إلى العجب بنفسه ورؤيته أنه خير منهم [. . .].

واتفق العلمـاء علـى أن هذا الـذم إنما هو فيمن قالـه علـى سبيـل الإزراء على النـاس واحتقـارهم وتفضيل نفسه عليهم وتقبيح أحوالهم لأنه لا يعلم سرّ الله في خلقه.

قالـوا فأما من قال ذلك تحزناً لما يرى في نفسه وفي النـاس من النقص في أمر الـديـن فلا بأس عليـه كمـا إذا قال : لا أعـرف من أمة النبي ﷺ إلا أنهم يصلون جميعـاً. هكـذا فسره الإمام مالك وتابعه النـاس عليـه [محـرّر من صحيح مسلم بشـرح النـووي : ١٦/ ١٧٥ ـ ١٧٦ بتقديم وتأخير].

r5.0   النـهي عن نقـل الحديث إلى ولاة الأمور

r5.1   [روينـا في كتـابي أبي داود والتـرمـذي عن ابن مسعود رضي الله عنه قال :] قال رسـول الـله ﷺ : «لا يبلّغْني أحدٌ من أصحابي عن أحد شيئاً، فإني أحب أن أخرج إليكم وأنا سليم الصدر» [نقل من الأذكار : ٤٧٣].

*

r6.0   تناجي اثنين عند ثالث

r6.1   [عن ابن مسعـود رضي الله عنـه أن] رسـول الله ﷺ قال : «إذا كنتم

"When there are only three of you, two of you may not speak together apart from the third unless you join a group of others, lest your doing so sadden him."

ثلاثة فلا يتناجى رجلان دون الآخر حتى تختلطوا بالناس ، فإن ذلك يحزنه» [رواه أحمد].

r6.2   (Nahlawi:) Nawawi (Allah have mercy on him) says this hadith prohibits two individuals conversing privately when a third is present, and likewise prohibits three or more people from doing so when there is a single person apart from them. The prohibition indicates its unlawfulness, it being impermissible for a group to converse apart from a single individual unless he gives his permission. Imam Malik (Allah have mercy on him), our colleagues, and the majority of scholars hold that the prohibition is applicable at all times, whether one is at home or travelling, though some (A: Hanafi) scholars say that such converse is forbidden only while travelling, not when at home, for when travelling it may portend danger.

r6.2   (النحلاوي :) قال النووي رحمه الله تعالى : وفي الحديث النهي عن تناجي اثنين بحضرة ثالث وكذا ثلاثة وأكثر بحضرة واحد ، وهو نهي تحريم . فيحرم على الجماعة المناجاة دون واحد منهم إلا أن يأذن . ومذهب مالك رحمه الله تعالى وأصحابنا وجماهير العلماء أن النهي عامٌّ في كل الأزمان وفي الحضر والسفر . وقال بعض العلماء إنما المنهي عنه المناجاة في السفر دون الحضر لأن السفر مظنة الخوف .

r6.3   As for when there are four people and two of them speak privately in low tones apart from the other two, scholars agree that there is no harm in this.

r6.3   وأما إذا كانوا أربعة فتناجى اثنان دون اثنين فلا بأس بالإجماع .

r6.4   The prohibition of listening to the conversation of people who are averse to one's listening likewise means it is unlawful, though only when the conversation does not entail harm to the listener, for if it does, one may listen to protect oneself from them (*al-Durar al-mubaha* (y99), 159).

r6.4   وكذا النهي عن استماع حديث قوم يكرهون استماعه له ، إلا أن يكون ذلك الحديث منهم في قصد إضرار المستمع فيستمع ليحترز منهم [نقل من الدرر المباحة في الحظر والإباحة : ١٥٩].

*

r7.0   GIVING DIRECTIONS TO SOMEONE WHO WANTS TO DO WRONG

r7.0   الدلالة على الطريق لمن يريد المعصية

r7.1   (Nahlawi:) It is not permissible to give directions and the like to someone intending to perpetrate a sin, because it is helping another to commit disobedience. Allah Most High says,

r7.1   (النحلاوي :) وأما الدلالة على الطريق ونحوه لمن يريد المعصية ، فإنها لا تجوز ، لأنها إعانة على المعصية . قال الله تعالى :

"Do not assist one another in sin and aggression" (Koran 5:2).

Giving directions to wrongdoers includes:

(1) showing the way to policemen and tyrants when they are going to commit injustice and corruption;

(2) teaching questions of Sacred Law to those learning it in bad faith (N: i.e. who do not want the knowledge to apply it in their lives, but for some unworthy purpose);

(3) teaching positions in Sacred Law that are rejected (A: meaning those that are not accepted by any of the four schools of jurisprudence (dis: b7.6)) or weak (dis: w12.2), or anything else that informs people of how to commit disobedience to Allah Most High;

(4) and permitting or authorizing a person to do something that entails disobedience, for acceptance of disobedience is disobedience.

(Ibid., 159–60)

*

r8.0   LYING

r8.1   (Nawawi:) Primary texts from the Koran and sunna that it is unlawful to lie (dis: p24) are both numerous and intersubstantiative, it being among the ugliest sins and most disgusting faults. Because of the scholarly consensus of the Community (Umma) that it is prohibited and the unanimity and amount of the primary textual evidence, there is little need to cite particular examples thereof, our only concern here being to explain the exceptions to what is considered lying, and apprise of the details.

PERMISSIBLE LYING

r8.2   The Prophet (Allah bless him and give

﴿وَلاَ تَعَاوَنُوا عَلَى الإِثْمِ وَالعُدْوَانِ﴾ .
ومنها الدالة للشرطي والظلمة إذا ذهبوا إلى الظلم والفسق . ومنها تعليم المسائل للمبطل (ح : وهو الذي لا يريد العلم للعمل به بل يريده لمقصد فاسد) وتعليم الأقوال المهجورة والضعيفة ونحو ذلك من كل ما فيه دلالة على معصية من معاصي الله تعالى . ومنها الإذن والإجازة فيما هو معصية ، فإن الرضا بالمعصية معصية . [محرر من المرجع المذكور: [١٥٩] .

r8.0   الكذب

r8.1   (النووي :) قد تظاهرت نصوص الكتاب والسنة على تحريم الكذب [في الجملة]، وهو من قبائح الذنوب وفواحش العيوب .
وإجماع الأمة منعقد على تحريمه مع النصوص المتظاهرة فلا ضرورة إلى نقل أفرادها .
وإنما المهم بيان ما يستثنى منه والتنبيه على دقائقه .

ما يباح من الكذب

r8.2   [وعن أم كلثوم رضي الله عنها

him peace) said,

"He who settles disagreements between people to bring about good or says something commendable is not a liar."

This much is related by both Bukhari and Muslim, with Muslim's version recording that Umm Kulthum added,

"I did not hear him permit untruth in anything people say, except for three things: war, settling disagreements, and a man talking with his wife or she with him (A: in smoothing over differences)."

This is an explicit statement that lying is sometimes permissible for a given interest, scholars having established criteria defining what types of it are lawful. The best analysis of it I have seen is by Imam Abu Hamid Ghazali, who says: "Speaking is a means to achieve objectives. If a praiseworthy aim is attainable through both telling the truth and lying, it is unlawful to accomplish through lying because there is no need for it. When it is possible to achieve such an aim by lying but not by telling the truth, it is permissible to lie if attaining the goal is permissible (N: i.e. when the purpose of lying is to circumvent someone who is preventing one from doing something permissible), and obligatory to lie if the goal is obligatory. When, for example, one is concealing a Muslim from an oppressor who asks where he is, it is obligatory to lie about his being hidden. Or when a person deposits an article with one for safekeeping and an oppressor wanting to appropriate it inquires about it, it is obligatory to lie about having concealed it, for if one informs him about the article and he then siezes it, one is financially liable (A: to the owner) to cover the article's cost. Whether the purpose is war, settling a disagreement, or gaining the sympathy of a victim legally entitled to retaliate against one so that he will forbear to do so; it is not unlawful to lie when any of these aims can only be attained through lying. But it is religiously more precautionary (def: c6.5) in all such cases to employ words that give a misleading impression, meaning to intend by one's words something that is literally true, in respect to

أنها سمعت] رسول الله ﷺ يقول:
«ليس الكذاب الذي يُصْلِحُ بين الناس فينمي خيراً أو يقولُ خيراً». هذا القدر في صحيحهما، وزاد مسلم في رواية له: «قالت أم كلثوم: ولم أسمعه يرخص في شيءٍ مما يقول الناس إلا في ثلاث: يعني الحرب والإصلاح بين الناس وحديث الرجل امرأته والمرأة زوجها».

فهذا حديث صريح في إباحة بعض الكذب للمصلحة وقد ضبط العلماء ما يباح منه. وأحسن ما رأيته في ضبطه، ما ذكره الإمام أبو حامد الغزالي فقال: الكلام وسيلة إلى المقاصد، فكل مقصود محمود يمكن التوصل إليه بالصدق والكذب جميعاً، فالكذب فيه حرام لعدم الحاجة إليه، وإن أمكن التوصل إليه بالكذب ولم يمكن بالصدق فالكذب فيه مباح إن كان تحصيل ذلك المقصود مباحاً (ح: أي إن كان الكذب لدفع من يريد منعه من فعل مباح) وواجب إن كان المقصود واجباً.

فإذا اختفى مسلم من ظالم وسأل عنه وجب الكذب بإخفائه.

وكذا لو كان عنده [أو عند غيره] وديعة وسأل عنها ظالم يريد أخذها وجب عليه الكذب بإخفائها، حتى لو أخبره بوديعة عنده فأخذها الظالم قهراً، وجب ضمانها على المودع المخبر.

وكذلك لو كان مقصود حرب أو إصلاح ذات البين أو استمالة قلب المجني عليه في العفو عن الجناية لا يحصل إلا بالكذب، فالكذب ليس بحرام، وهذا إذا لم يحصل الغرض إلا بالكذب.

والاحتياط في هذا كله أن يورّي؛ ومعنى التورية أن يقصد بعبارته مقصوداً صحيحاً ليس هو كاذباً بالنسبة إليه، وإن

which one is not lying (def: r10.2), while the outward purport of the words deceives the hearer, though even if one does not have such an intention and merely lies without intending anything else, it is not unlawful in the above circumstances.

كان كاذباً في ظاهر اللفظ .

ولـو لم يقصـد هذا بل أطلق عبـارة الكذب بحرام في هذا الموضع .

"This is true of every expression connected with a legitimating desired end, whether one's own or another's. An example of a legitimating end of one's own is when an oppressor intending to appropriate one's property inquires about it, in which case one may deny it. Or if a ruler asks one about a wicked act one has committed that is solely between oneself and Allah Most High (N: i.e. it does not concern the rights of another), in which case one is entitled to disclaim it, such as by saying, 'I did not commit fornication,' or 'I did not drink.' There are many well known hadiths in which those who admitted they deserved punishment were given prompting (A: by the Prophet (Allah bless him and give him peace)) to retract their confessions. An example of a legitimating desired end of another is when one is asked about another's secret and one disacknowledges it. And so on. One should compare the bad consequences entailed by lying to those entailed by telling the truth, and if the consequences of telling the truth are more damaging, one is entitled to lie, though if the reverse is true or if one does not know which entails more damage, then lying is unlawful. Whenever lying is permissible, if the factor which permits it is a desired end of one's own, it is recommended not to lie, but when the factor that permits it is the desired end of another, it is not lawful to infringe upon his rights. Strictness (A: as opposed to the above dispensations (rukhsa, def: c6.2)) is to forgo lying in every case where it is not legally obligatory."

[قال أبو حامد الغزالي :] وكذلك كل ما ارتبط به غرض مقصود صحيح له أو لغيره .

فالـذي له مثـل أن يأخذه ظالم ويسأله عن ماله ليأخـذه فله أن ينكـره ، أو يسأله السلطان عن فاحشة بينه وبين الله تعالى ارتكبهـا ؛ فله أن ينكـرهـا ويقـول : ما زنيت ، أو ما شربت مثـلاً . وقـد اشتهرت الأحاديث بتلقين الـذين أقـروا بالحـدود الرجوع عن الإقرار .

وأما غرض غيره فمثـل أن يسأل عن سرّ أخيه فينكره ونحو ذلك .

وينبغي أن يقابـل بين مفسدة الكذب والمفسـدة المترتبـة على الصـدق ؛ فإن كانت المفسدة في الصدق أشد ضرراً من الكـذب ، وإن كان عكسه ، أو شك حرم عليه الكذب .

ومتى جاز الكـذب فإن كان المبيـح غرضـاً يتعـلق بنفسـه فيستحب أن لا يكـذب . ومتى كان متعلقـاً بغيـره لم تجز المسامحة بحق غيره .

والحزم تركه في كل موضع أبيح إلا إذا كان واجباً .

r8.3   The position of Ahl al-Sunna is that *lying* means to inform another that something is otherwise than it really is, whether intentionally or out of ignorance. One is not culpable if ignorant of it, but only if one lies intentionally, the evidence for which is that the Prophet (Allah bless him and give him peace) made intentionality a condition when he said,

r8.3   [واعلم أن] مذهب أهل السنة أن الكذب هو الإخبار عن الشيء بخلاف ما هو ، سواء تعمدت ذلك أم جهلته لكن لا يأثم في الجهل وإنما يأثم في العمد .

ودليل أصحابنا تقييد النبي ﷺ : «من كذب عليّ متعمـداً فليتبـوّأ مقعـدَهُ من

"Whoever lies about me intentionally shall

take a place for himself in hell.''

(al-Adhkar (y102), 510–12)

النـار». [محـرّر من الأذكار المتخبة من كلام سيد الأبرار: ٥١٠ ـ ٥١٢].

*

r9.0   EXAGGERATION

r9.0   المبالغة في الكلام

r9.1   (Nawawi:) Ghazali says: "Among the forms of lying that are unlawful but not serious enough to stigmatize their perpetrator as legally corrupt (dis: o24.3) is the customary exaggeration of saying, 'I've told you a hundred times,' or 'asked after you a hundred times,' and so forth, since one does not thereby intend to inform the other how many times it has been, but only to indicate that it has been too many. In such cases, if the speaker in fact has only asked after the other but once, he is lying, though if he has asked after him a number of times considerably more than what is generally accepted, he is not committing a sin by saying it, even if it has not been 'a hundred times.' There are intermediate degrees between these two at which the exaggerator becomes a liar."

r9.1   (النـووي:) قال الغـزالي: ومن الكـذب المحـرم الـذي لا يوجب الفسق ما جرت به العـادة في المبـالغة كقـولـه: قلت لك مائة مرة، وطلبتك مائة مرة ونحوه فإنه لا يراد به تفهيم المرات بل تفهيم المبالغة، فإن لم يكن طلبه إلا مرة واحـدة كان كاذبـاً. وإن طلبـه مرات لا يعتـاد مثلها في الكثـرة لم يأثم، وإن لم يبلغ مائة مرة.

وبينهمـا درجـات يتعرض المبـالغ للكذب فيها.

r9.2   The proof that exaggeration is sometimes permissible and not considered lying is the hadith related by Bukhari and Muslim that the Prophet (Allah bless him and give him peace) said,

"... As for Abul Jahm, his stick never leaves his shoulder, while Mu'awiya does not own a thing,"

it being understood that the latter owned the garment he was wearing, and the former set his stick aside when he slept and at other times. And Allah alone gives success (ibid., 515–16).

r9.2   [قلت:] دليل جواز المبالغة وأنـه لا يعـدّ كذبـاً ما [رويـنـاه] في الصحيحين أن النبي ﷺ قال: «أمـا أبـو الجهم فلا يضع العصا عن عاتقـه، وأما معاوية فلا مال له» ومعلوم أنه كان له ثوبٌ يلبسه، وأنه كان يضع العصا في وقت النـوم وغيـره. وبـالله التـوفيق [نقـل من المرجع المذكور: ٥١٥ ـ ٥١٦].

*

r10.0 GIVING A MISLEADING IMPRESSION

r10.0   التعريض والتورية

r10.1   (Nawawi:) Giving a misleading impression is among the most important topics, being frequently met with and often abused. It befits us to examine the matter closely, and whoever learns of it should reflect upon it and apply it. Having previously mentioned that lying is severely prohibited, and the danger that exists in saying something without any particular intention, what follows below shows a safe alternative to these.

r10.1   (النـووي:) [اعلم أن] هذا الباب من أهم الأبواب، فإنه ممـا يكثر استعمالـه وتعمّ به البلوى. فينبغي لنا أن نعتني بتحقيقـه، وينبغي للواقف عليـه أن يتأملـه ويعمل به. وقد قدمنا ما في الكذب من التحـريم الغليـظ، ومـا في إطلاق اللسـان من الخطر، وهـذا الباب طريق إلى السلامة من ذلك.

r10.2   *Giving a misleading impression* means to utter an expression that ostensibly implies one meaning, while intending a different meaning the expression may also have, one that contradicts the ostensive purport. It is a kind of deception.

(A: It often takes the form of the speaker intending a specific referent while the hearer understands a more general one, as when a person asks a householder, "Is So-and-so here?" to which the householder, intending the space between himself and the questioner rather than the space inside the house, replies, "He is not here.")

r10.2   [واعلـم أن] التـوريـة والتعـريض معنـاهمـا: أن تطلق لفظاً هو ظاهـر في معنى وتريد به معنى آخر يتناوله ذلك اللفظ، لكنه خلاف ظاهره، وهذا ضرب من التغرير والخداع.

r10.3   Scholars say that there is no harm (def: p8.2(A:)) in giving a misleading impression if required by an interest countenanced by Sacred Law that is more important than *not* misleading the person being addressed, or if there is a pressing need which could not otherwise be fulfilled except through lying. When neither of these is the case, giving a misleading impression is offensive though not unlawful unless used as a means for wrongful gain or suppressing another's right, in which case it becomes unlawful. The above determine its permissibility. As for the hadith evidence, some of which permits it and some of which does not, it is to be interpreted in the light of the above criteria (*al-Adhkar* (y102), 514).

r10.3   قال العلمـاء: فإن دعت إلى ذلك مصلحة شرعية راجحة على خداع المخـاطب أو حاجـة لا منـدوحة عنها إلا بالكـذب فلا بأس بالتعـريض. وإن لم يكن شيء من ذلـك فهـو مكـروه وليس بحـرام إلا أن يتـوصل به إلى أخذ باطل أو دفـع حقّ فيصير حينئذ حراماً، هذا ضابط الباب. فأما الآثار الواردة فيه فقد جاء من الآثار ما يبيحه وما لا يبيحه وهي محمولة على هذا التفصيـل الذي ذكرناه [نقل من الأذكار: ٥١٤].

*

r11.0 VERIFYING ONE'S WORDS BEFORE SPEAKING

r11.1 Allah Most High says:

(1) "Pursue not that of which you have no knowledge. The hearing, the eyesight, the heart: all will be asked about" (Koran 17:36).

(2) "He utters not a word save that an observer is present beside him" (Koran 50:18).

r11.2 The Prophet (Allah bless him and give him peace) said,

"It is lying enough for a man to repeat everything he hears."

(Ibid., 512–13)

*

r12.0 SPEAKING OF TAXES AS "THE RULER'S RIGHT"

r12.1 (Nawawi:) One of the things most sternly prohibited and needful to warn people against is what the common people say about sales tax and the like (dis: p32), namely that "this is the ruler's right," or "you have to pay the ruler's due," and so forth, of references to "right," "obligation," and so on. This is one of the most objectionable practices and ugliest of reprehensible innovations. Some scholars even hold that anyone who calls these taxes a right thereby becomes an unbeliever, beyond the pale of Islam. But in fact, such a person does not become an unbeliever unless he actually considers it right while knowing it is unjust. The proper way to mention these is to say "the ruler's tax," "revenue," or similar words. And Allah alone gives success (ibid., 499–500).

*

r11.0 الـحـث على التثبت
فيما يحكيه الإنسان

r11.1 قال الله تعالى:
﴿وَلاَ تَقْـفُ مَا لَيْسَ لَكَ بِهِ عِلْمٌ إِنَّ السَّمْعَ وَالبَصَرَ وَالفُؤَادَ كُلُّ أُولَئِكَ كَانَ عَنْهُ مَسْؤُولاً﴾ [الإسراء: ٣٦].
وقال تعالى:
﴿مَا يَلْفِظُ مِنْ قَوْلٍ إِلاَّ لَدَيْهِ رَقِيبٌ عَتِيدٌ﴾ [ق: ١٨].

r11.2 [وروينا في صحيح مسلم عن حفص بن عاصم التابعي الجليل عن أبي هريرة رضي الله عنه أن] النبي ﷺ قال: «كفى بالمرء كذباً أن يحدث بكل ما سمع». [نقل من المرجع المذكور: ٥١٢ ـ ٥١٣].

r12.0 تسمية المكوس حقاً

r12.1 (النووي:) مما يتأكد النهي عنه والتحذير منه ما يقوله العوام وأشباههم في هذه المكوس التي تؤخذ ممن يبيع ويشتري ونحوهما، فإنهم يقولون: هذا حق السلطان؛ أو: عليك حق السلطان ونحو ذلك من العبارات المشتملة على تسميته حقاً أو لازماً ونحو ذلك، وهذا من أشد المنكرات وأشنع المستحدثات. حتى قال بعض العلماء: من سمى هذا حقاً فهو كافر خارج عن ملة الإسلام. والصحيح أنه لا يكفر إلا إذا اعتقده حقاً مع علمه بأنه ظلم. فالصواب أن يقال فيه: المكس أو ضريبة السلطان أو نحو ذلك من العبارات. وبالله التوفيق [نقل من المرجع المذكور: ٤٩٩ ـ ٥٠٠].

r13.0 CONVERSING ABOUT WHAT IS USELESS OR IMMORAL

r13.0 الخوض في الباطل

r13.1 (Nahlawi:) Conversing about what is useless or immoral means discussing acts of disobedience, such as stories about drinking sessions and fornicators when there is no legitimate purpose connected with the conversation, which is unlawful because it manifests one's own disobedience or another's without there being any need to. Ibn Mas'ud (Allah be well pleased with him) said,

"The greatest in sins on the Judgement Day will be the one most given to speaking about the useless and immoral."

r13.1 (النحـلاوي:) الخـوض في الباطل هو الكلام في المعاصي كحكايات مجـالس الخمـر، والـزناة، والزواني من غيـر أن يتعلق بها غرض صحيح، وهذا حرام، لأنه إظهار لمعصية نفسه أو غيره من غيـر حاجـة داعية إلى ذلك. وعن ابن مسعـود رضي الله عنـه موقـوفاً أنه قال: «أعظم النـاس خطـايا يوم القيامة أكثرهم خوضاً في الباطل» [رواه ابن أبي الدنيا].

SPEAKING ABOUT WHAT DOES NOT CONCERN ONE

الخوض فيما لا يعني

r13.2 As for speaking about what does not concern one, such as the story of one's travels, and the mountains, rivers, food, and clothes one saw while on them; when it does not contain lies, slander, ostentation, or other things that are unlawful, it is not in itself prohibited. Rather, it may be recommended, as when inspired by a good intention such as preventing others of accusing one of being arrogant or proud of not speaking, allaying another's timorousness, cheering up someone sad or ill, amusing or getting along well with the womenfolk, showing kindness to children, or similar motives. With these intentions it is not considered to be what does not concern one.

r13.2 وأمـا الكلام فيما لا يعني مثل حكـاية أسفـارك وما رأيت فيها من جبال وأنهار وأطعمة وثياب، فهذا ـ إذا خلا عن الكـذب والغيبة والـرياء ونحوهـا من المحرمات ـ لا يحرم، بل قد يُستحب إذا قارنـه نية صالحـة مثـل دفع التهمة بالكبر والعجب بعـدم التكلم، أو دفـع المهابة، أو دفع الحزن عن المحزون والمصاب، وتسليـة النساء، وحسن المعاشرة معهن، أو التلطف بالصبيـان، وبهـذه النيـات يخرج عن حد ما لا يعني.

r13.3 It is recommended and praiseworthy to leave anything that does not concern one (def: w54) because one squanders one's life by involvement in it and in mere amusement. The Prophet (Allah bless him and give him peace) said,

"The excellence of a person's Islam includes leaving what does not concern him,"

including excess verbiage, meaning to elaborate more than necessary about matters which do con-

r13.3 فكـل ما لا يعني يستحب تركه، لتضييع العمر فيه واللهـو. قال ﷺ: «من حسن إسـلام المرء: تركه ما لا يعنيه». ومنه فضول الكلام وهو الزيادة فيما يعني على قدر الحاجة. ومنه السؤال

cern one, or to ask about things which are of no importance; though it does not include clarifying the details of difficult legal questions, especially to those of limited understanding, or the need to repeat an exhortation, reminder, instruction, or the like, since it might be necessary. But when it is unnecessary to add details, one should express oneself succinctly and with brevity. The Prophet (Allah bless him and give him peace) said,

"Good tidings to him who avoids the excess in his speech and spends the excess of his money."

'Ali (Allah ennoble his countenance) said,

"The best discourse is expressive, great, brief, and interesting."

(al-Durar al-mubaha (y99), 135–36)

*

r14.0   EXPLAINING THE KORAN BY PERSONAL OPINION

r14.1 The Prophet (Allah bless him and give him peace) said,

"Whoever speaks of the Book of Allah from his own opinion is in error."

r14.2 (Nahlawi:) The jurist Abul Layth says in *Bustan al-'arifin,* "The [above] prohibition only applies to the allegorical parts of it (dis: w6), not to all of it, since Allah Most High says,

" 'As for those with deviance in their hearts, they pursue the allegorical of it' (Koran 3:7).

"The Koran came as a proof of moral answerability against all mankind and jinn, while if interpreting it were not permissible, it could not be a decisive proof. Since it is decisive, it is permissible for someone acquainted with the dialects of the Arabs and the circumstances under which various verses were revealed to interpret it. As for

عمـا لا يهم ، وليس منـه التفصيـل في المسـائـل المشكلة ، خصـوصـاً للأفهام القـاصـرة ، والتكـرار في العظـة والتذكير والتعليم ونحوها ، لأنه للحاجة . وفيمـا لا حاجة فيـه يستحب الإيجاز والاختصـار . قال ﷺ : «طـوبى لمن أمسك الفضل من كلامه وأنفق الفضل من ماله» .

وقال علي كرم الله وجهه : خير الكلام ما دلّ وجـلّ وقـلّ ولم يُمـلّ [محـرر من الدرر المباحة في الحظر والإباحة : ١٣٥ ـ [١٣٦] .

r14.0   تفسير القرآن بالرأي

r14.1 [عن جندب رضي الله عنه أنه قال :] قال رسـول الله ﷺ : «من قال في كتاب الله برأيه فقد أخطأ» [رواه أبو داود والترمذي] .

r14.2 (النحـلاوي :) قال الفقيـه أبو الليث في بستان العـارفين : النهي إنما ورد في المتشـابه منه ، لا في جميعه ، كما قال تعالى :

﴿فَـأَمَّا الَّذِينَ في قُلُوبِهِمْ زَيْغٌ فَيَتَّبِعُونَ مَا تَشَـابَـهَ مِنْهُ﴾ [آل عمـران : ٧] ، إنَّ القرآن إنمـا أنزل حجةً على الخلق ، فلو لم يجـز التفسيـر ، لا يكـون حجةً بالغةً ، فإذا كان كذلك جاز ـ لمن يعـرف لغـات العرب ، وعرف شأن النزول ـ أن يفسره . وأمـا من كان من المتكلفين ، ولم يعـرف

751

would-be exegetes who do not know the dimensions of Arabic, the figurative, literal, and the types of metaphor, it is not permissible for them to explain it beyond what they have heard, by way of reporting and not actual interpretation."

The generality of the prohibition also entails that whoever does not know which verses abrogate others and which are abrogated, the points upon which there is scholarly consensus (def: b7), and the tenets of faith of Ahl al-Sunna, is not safe from error if he interprets the Koran with nothing beyond the implications of the Arabic. Mere linguistic familiarity with the language is insufficient, and one must also know what we have just mentioned. When one knows both, one may interpret the Koran, and is not doing so by mere opinion (ibid., 158).

وجوهَ العربية ـ من المجاز والحقيقة ، وأنـواع الاستعـارات ـ فلا يجـوز لـه أن يفسّره، إلا مقدار ما سمع ، فيكون ذلك على وجه الحكاية لا على سبيل التفسير . اهـ.

ومـن جملة محمـل الـنهي : مَنْ لا يعـرف النـاسخ والمنسوخ ومـواضـع الإجمـاع وعقائد أهل السنة ، فيفسر على مقتضى العربية فلا يأمن من الخطأ . فلا يفيد مجـرد معـرفة وجوه اللغة ، بل لا بد معهـا من معـرفة ما ذكرناه . فإذا حصل له هاتـان المعـرفتـان ، فله أن يفسـر ، ولا يكـون تفسيـره بالـرأي [. . .] [نقل من المرجع المذكور: ١٥٨].

r14.3   (A: The above is equally true of hadith. Koran and hadith commentaries are of tremendous importance to teachers, speakers, writers, and translators who are preparing materials to present to Muslim audiences. The dictionary is not enough.)

*

r15.0   ASKING ABOUT THE NATURE OF ALLAH MOST HIGH

r15.0 السؤال عن كنه ذات الله تعالى

r15.1   The Prophet (Allah bless him and give him peace) said:

"People will keep wondering and asking each other until it is said, 'This is Allah's creation, but who created Allah?' Whoever finds anything like this, let him say, 'I believe in Allah and His messengers.'"

(Ibid., 140)

r15.1   قال رسـول الله ﷺ : «لا يزال النـاس يتسـاءلون ، حتى يقال : هذا خلق الله فمنْ خلق الله؟ فمن وجـد من ذلـك شيئـاً فليقـل : آمنت بالله ورسله» [متفق عليه] [نقل من المرجع المذكور: ١٤٠].

*

r16.0   HYPOCRISY

r16.1   (Nahlawi:) Hypocrisy is when a person's outward does not correspond to his inward, or his words to his deeds. It is of two kinds, hypocrisy in belief and hypocrisy in acts. Hypocrisy in belief is another name for concealed unbelief while outwardly professing Islam. It is the very worst form of unbelief. Allah Mighty and Majestic says,

"Verily the hypocrites shall be in the lowest abyss of hell" (Koran 4:145).

And this type consigns its perpetrator to hell forever. As for hypocrisy in act, it is that which does not concern one's faith. It is also termed spoken hypocrisy, and consists of saying what contradicts one's true state. It is one of the greatest of sins. It includes being two-faced, like the person who, when two people are at odds, speaks words to each that confirm their respective sides, or tells each what the other has said, or endorses the enmity of each, praises each, and promises each to help against the other. This is hypocrisy and more. But its blameworthiness applies only to worsening relations between people, for if done to settle their differences, it is praiseworthy.

It is seldom that a person who visits leaders and important people is free of spoken hypocrisy. Someone told Ibn 'Umar (Allah be well pleased with father and son), "We visit our leaders and speak, but when we leave, we say something else." He replied, "In the days of the Messenger of Allah (Allah bless him and give him peace) we considered this hypocrisy."

r16.2   As for assuaging those from whom one apprehends harm (mudara), it is permissible, being done to obviate the damage and evil anticipated from certain people, whether it be a ruler or someone else one has reason to fear (al-Durar al-mubaha (y99), 116–18).

---

r16.0   النفاق

r16.1   (النحلاوي:) النفاق هو عدم موافقة الظاهر للباطن والقول للفعل. وهو على قسمين: اعتقادي وعملي. أما النفاق الاعتقادي فهو عبارة عن إبطان الكفر وإظهار الإسلام، وهو أشد أنواع الكفر ولذلك قال الله عز وجل:

﴿إِنَّ الْمُنَافِقِينَ فِي الدَّرْكِ الْأَسْفَلِ مِنَ النَّارِ﴾ [النساء: ١٤٥].

وهذا يخلد صاحبه في النار. [...] وأما النفاق العملي فهو ما لا يكون في الاعتقاد ويقال له النفاق القولي وهو مخالفة القول الباطن، وهو من أكبر الذنوب. ومنه كلام ذي اللسانين وهو الذي يتكلم بين المتعاديين عند كل واحد منهما بكلام يوافقه، أو ينقل كلام كل واحد إلى الآخر، أو كان يحسّن لكل واحد منهما ما هو عليه من المعاداة ويثني عليه أو يَعِد كل واحد منهما أن ينصره، وهو يتضمن النفاق ويزيد عليه. وهذا كله إذا كان على وجه الإفساد. وأما إذا كان على وجه الإصلاح فمحمود.

وقلما يخلو عن هذا النفاق القولي المذكور من يدخل على الأمراء والكبراء.

قيل لابن عمر رضي الله عنهما: إنا ندخل على أمرائنا فنقول القول فإذا خرجنا قلنا غيره. قال: كنا نعدّ ذلك نفاقاً على عهد رسول الله ﷺ [رواه الطبراني].

r16.2   وأما المداراة فتجوز وهي ما يكون لدرء الضرر والشر المتوقع من بعض الناس حاكماً كان أو غيره ممن يخاف منه [محرر من الدرر المباحة: ١١٦ - ١١٨].

*

r17.0   COMPROMISING ONE'S PRINCIPLES

r17.1   (Nahlawi:) *Compromising one's principles* means religious lassitude and weakness, such as by saying nothing upon seeing acts of disobedience or unlawful things when able to change them without suffering harm. Such silence is unlawful. Its opposite is firmness in religion. Allah Most High says,

"They fight in the path of Allah and fear not the blame of whoever may blame them" (Koran 5:54).

And the Prophet (Allah bless him and give him peace) said,

"Speak the truth, even if bitter."

But when one's silence is to prevent damage to oneself or others, it is a permissible form of assuaging those from whom one apprehends harm (mudara), and even recommended in some cases, as when it results in being saved from injustice, or is a means to fulfill a right recognized by Sacred Law (ibid., 112–13).

*

r18.0   RIDICULE AND SARCASM

r18.1   (Nahlawi:) Ridicule entails showing disdain, sarcasm, or contempt for another in a way that causes laughter, whether by mimicking another's words or actions, by a gesture or by allusion. It is unlawful. Allah Most High says:

(1) "Those who demean believers who voluntarily give charity— ridiculing those who find nothing to give but their own effort—it is Allah who is ridiculing them, and they shall suffer a painful torment" (Koran 9:79).

(2) "O you who believe: let not some men deride others who might well be better than they;

المداهنة   r17.0

r17.1   (النحــلاوي:) المداهنة هي الفتــور والضــعف في أمــر الــدين كالسكــوت عنــد مشــاهــدة المعـاصي والمنـاهي ، مع القـدرة على التغييـر بلا ضــرر فهـذا السكــوت حرام . وضـده الصلاة في الدين . قال الله تعالى :
﴿يُجَـاهِـدُونَ فِي سَبِيــلِ اللَّهِ وَلَا يَخَافُونَ لَوْمَةَ لَائِمٍ﴾ [المائدة : ٥٤].
وقال النبي ﷺ :
«قل الحق وإن كان مُرّاً».
فإن كان سكـوتـه لدرء ضـرر عن نفسه أو غيره فهو مداراة جائزة، بل مستحبة في بعض المـواضع ، إذا توصل بها إلى إنقاذ أحـد من ظلم أو إيصـال إلى استيفاء حق شرعي [محرر من المـرجـع المـذكور : ١١٢ ـ ١١٣].

السخرية   r18.0
والاستخفاف

r18.1   (النحــلاوي:) السخريــة تتضمن الاستصغار والاستخفـاف بالغير والاستهانة به على وجه يضحك منه . وقد يكون ذلك بالمحاكاة في القول، والفعـل ، وقـد يكــون بالإشارة والإيماء، وهي حرام . قال الله تعالى :
﴿الَّـذِينَ يَلْمِـزُونَ المُطَّـوِّعِينَ مِنَ المُؤْمِنِينَ فِي الصَّدَقَاتِ وَالَّذِينَ لَا يَجِدُونَ إِلَّا جُهْـدَهُمْ فَيَسْخَـرُونَ مِنْهُمْ سَخِـرَ اللَّهُ مِنْهُمْ وَلَهُمْ عَذَابٌ أَلِيمٌ﴾ [التوبة : ٧٩].
وقال تعالى :
﴿يَا أَيُّهَـا الَّذِينَ آمَنُوا لَا يَسْخَرْ قَوْمٌ مِنْ

and let not some women ridicule others who might well be better than they. Do not belittle one another or insult one another with nicknames" (Koran 49:11).

The Prophet (Allah bless him and give him peace) said:

"A gate in paradise will open to one of those who mock people and a cry will be heard, 'Come here, come here,' and he will come forward in concern and anxiety, but when he reaches it, it will close in front of him. And this will happen again and again, until the gate will open and the cry 'Come here, come here' will be heard as before, but he will not approach because he knows it will only close in front of him."

r18.2   Ridicule is only unlawful when it hurts others' feelings. As for someone who purposely makes himself a laughingstock, perhaps such a person enjoys it, and jokes about him are considered mere humor. What is unlawful is the sarcasm that offends the person ridiculed, because of the insult and disdain involved, such as by laughing at his way of speaking, what he does, how he looks, or his physique because of a defect therein. To laugh at any of these is to commit ridicule that is unlawful (ibid., 126–27).

*

r19.0   JOKING

r19.1   (Nahlawi:) The necessary condition for the permissibility of joking is that it does not contain lies or occasion fright to a Muslim or a non-Muslim citizen, because this hurts others, and we are forbidden to do so.

r19.2   Excessive joking is blameworthy and forbidden, since it eliminates one's dignity and reserve, and creates resentment in certain situations and people. It also causes immoderate laughter, which kills the heart. The Prophet (Allah bless him and give him peace) said to his Companions,

"Who will take these words and apply them, or knows someone who will?" Abu Hurayra answered, "I will, O Messenger of Allah," whereupon the Prophet (Allah bless him and give him peace) took his hand and enumerated five things, saying:

"Avoid the unlawful and you will be the most religious of people."

"Be satisfied with what Allah has alotted you and you will be the richest of people."

"Treat your neighbor well and you will be a believer."

"Love for others what you love for yourself and you will be a Muslim."

"Avoid excessive laughter, for too much laughter kills the heart."

(*al-Durar al-mubaha* (y99), 127–28)

*

r20.0   PICKING APART ANOTHER'S WORDS

r20.1   (Nahlawi:) *Picking apart another's words* consists of attacking another's speech by revealing the mistakes in it, whether its weak Arabic, meaning, or the intention of the speaker, as when one says, "This is true, but you do not intend the truth by it," when such an attack involves no other motive than contempt for the other and displaying one's cleverness. It is unlawful. The Prophet (Allah bless him and give him peace) said:

"Whoever forgoes to cavil when he is in the wrong will have a home built for him on the edge

وتـورث الـضغينـة في بعض الأحـوال والأشخاص، وتورث أيضاً كثرة الضحك المميت للقلب . روى الـتـرمـذي عن أبي هريرة رضي الله عنه أنه قال : قال رسول الله ﷺ لأصحـابـه : «مَن يأخـذ هؤلاء الكلمـات فيعمـل بهن أو يعلم من يعمـل بهن؟» قال أبـو هريرة : أنا يا رسول الله ، فأخذ بيدي فعدّ خمساً فقال :

«اتق المحارم تكن أعبد الناس .

وارض بما قسم الله لك تكن أغنى الناس .

وأحسن إلى جارك تكن مؤمناً .

وأحب للناس ما تحب لنفسك تكن مسلماً .

ولا تكثر الضحك فإن كثرة الضحك تميت القلب» [رواه أحمـد] [نقـل من الدرر المباحة : ١٢٧ ـ ١٢٨].

r20.0   المراء

r20.1   (النحلاوي :) المراء هو طعن في كلام الغير بإظهار خلل فيه ، إما باللفظ من جهة العربية ، أو في المعنى ، أو في قصـد المتكلم بأن يقـول : هذا الكلام حق ، ولكن ليس قصدك منـه الحق ؛ من غيـر أن يرتبـط به غرض سوى تحقيـر الغيـر ، وإظهار مزيـة الكيـاسـة ، وهـذا حرام . [عن أبي أمامة رضي الله عنه ، أنه قال :] قال رسـول اللـه ﷺ : «مَـن ترك المراء ـ وهو مُبطل ـ بني له بيت في ربض

of paradise. Whoever forgoes it when in the right will have a home built for him in the middle of paradise. And whoever improves his own character, a home will be built for him in the highest part of paradise.''

When a believer hears something true, it befits him to accept it. If it is not true, but is unconnected with religious matters, he should remain silent, though if connected with religious matters, he is obliged to show that it is false and to condemn it if there is a chance that anyone will believe him, because this is forbidding the wrong.

GIVING A POSITIVE INTERPRETATION TO OTHERS' SEEMING MISTAKES

r20.2   Nawawi (Allah Most High have mercy on him) mentions, in the section of the introduction of *Sharh al-Muhadhdhab* about the behavior of teacher and student, that "it is obligatory for a student to give a positive interpretation to every utterance of his brothers that seems to be wrong until he has exhausted seventy excuses. No one is incapable of this except a failure.''

READING WORKS THAT ARE BEYOND ONE'S UNDERSTANDING OR CAPACITY

r20.3   The Sheikh al-Akbar (A: Muhyiddin ibn al-'Arabi), Allah Most High sanctify his inmost being, writes in his letter about the spiritual station of annihilation in gnostic vision: "When a book falls into a person's hands concerning a subject he knows nothing about [A: *knows* meaning through having studied it with sheikhs who are masters of it] and has not learned by engaging in it at first hand, he should do absolutely nothing with the book, but rather return it to those whom it concerns. He should not believe, disbelieve, or discuss it at all'' (ibid., 131–32).

الجنة ، ومن تركه ـ وهو محق ـ بني له في وسطها ومن حسّن خلقه ، بُني له في أعلاها» [رواه الترمذي] .

والذي ينبغي للمؤمن إذا سمع كلاماً ، إن كان حقاً أن يصدقه ، وإن كان باطلاً ، ولم يكن متعلقاً بأمور الدين أن يسكت عنه ، وإن كان متعلقاً بها يجب إظهار البطلان ، والإنكار إن رجا القبول ، لأنه نهي عن المنكر .

وجوب حمل كلام الغير على المحامل الحسنة

r20.2   وذكر النووي رحمه الله تعالى في أدب العالم والمتعلم من مقدمة شرح المهذب ، أنـه يجب على الطـالب أن يحمل إخوانه على المحامل الحسنة ، في كل كلام يفهم منه نقص ، إلى سبعين محملاً ، ثم قال : ولا يعجـز عن ذلك إلا كل قليل التوفيق .

عدم الاعتراض بغير علم

r20.3   وقال الشيخ الأكبر ـ قدس الله تعالى سره ـ في رسالته التي صنفها في تحقيق مقـام الفنـاء في الشهـود : فينبغي لمن وقـع في يده كتـاب في علم لا يعرفه ولا سلك طريقه ، أن لا يبدى ولا يعيد ، وأن يرده على أهـله ولا يؤمـن به ، ولا يكفر ، ولا يخوض فيـه البتة» [نقل من المرجع المذكور : ١٣١ ـ ١٣٢] .

*

r21.0   LEARNED DISPUTATION

r21.1   (Nahlawi:) Disputation is what relates to clarifying various legal positions and making a case for them. When the intention behind this is to embarrass one's opponent or display one's superiority, it is unlawful or even unbelief according to some scholars. But when disputation is intended to reveal the truth, as is rare, then it is permissible or even recommended. Allah Most High says,

"Dispute with them with that which is better" (Koran 16:125),

meaning, as Baydawi notes, by the best means of disputation, gently and affably, using the simplest approach and most familiar premises, since this more effectively cools opponents' vehemence and exposes their contentiousness (ibid., 132).

*

r22.0   ARGUING

r22.1   (Nawawi:) Arguing is importunateness in speech to gain one's end, whether monetary or other. It may be intitiated by oneself or in response to another. If one objects that a person must argue to obtain his rights, the reply is that the stern condemnation of it applies to those who argue without right or knowledge, or someone who adds abuse to his speech that is not necessary to secure his rights, or is motivated to argue by nothing besides an obstinate desire to win and to finish his opponent. As for someone who has been wronged and makes his case in a way compatible with the Sacred Law, without belligerence, excessiveness, or importunateness, and not intending mere obstinacy and abuse, it is not unlawful, though it is better to avoid it if there is any way to do so, for keeping one's tongue within the limits of fair play during the course of an argument is virtually impossible. Moreover, arguing produces rancor in hearts and causes animosity that can lead to

 r21.0   الجدال

r21.1   (النحلاوي:) الجدال هو ما يتعلق بإظهار المذاهب، وتقريرها.

فإن قصـد تخجيـل الخصم وإظهار فضـله فحـرام، بل كفـر عنـد بعض العلمـاء. وإن قصـد إظهـار الحق، وهو نادر، فجائزٌ بل مندوب إليه. قال الله تعالى:

﴿وَجَـادِلْـهُـمْ بِالَّـتِي هِيَ أَحْـسَـنْ﴾ [النحـل: ١٢٥]، أي بالطريقة التي هي أحسن طرق المجـادلـة من الـرفق واللين وإيثـار الوجه الأيسر والمقدمات التي هي أشهـر، فإن ذلـك أنفع في تسكين لهبهم وتبيين شغبهم. ذكره البيضـاوي [محرر من المرجع المذكور: ١٣٢].

r22.0   الخصومة

r22.1   (النووي:) [قـال الغزالي:] أمـا الخصـومة فلجاج في الكلام ليستوفي به مقصـوده من مال أو غيـره. وتارة يكون ابتداء وتارة يكون اعتراضاً. فإن قلت: لا بد للإنـسـان من الخصـومـة لاستيفـاء حقوقه؛ فالجواب [مـا أجاب به الإمام الغزالي] أن الـذم المتأكـد إنمـا هو لمن خاصم بالبـاطـل وبغيـر علم [...] وكذلك من خلط بالخصومة كلمات تؤذي وليس له إليهـا حاجـة في تحصيل حقه، وكذلك من يحمله على الخصومة محض العنـاد لقهـر الخصم وكسـره [فهـذا هو المـذمـوم]. وأمـا المظلوم الـذي ينصـر حجته بطريق الشرع من غير لدد وإسراف وزيادة لجاج [على الحاجة] من غير قصد عنـاد ولا إيـذاء، ففعلُه هذا ليس حراماً ولكن الأولى تركه ما وجد إليه سبيلاً لأن

actual hatred between two people, until each comes to be pleased when harm befalls the other and to be displeased at the good, and unleashes his tongue against the other's reputation. Whoever argues runs the risk of these calamities. At minimum, a quarrel comes to preoccupy one's heart so that during the prayer one's thoughts turn to debating and arguing, and one does not remain as one should.

ضبط اللسان في الخصومة على حد الاعتدال متعذر، والخصومة توغر الصدور وتهيج الغضب، وإذا هاج الغضب حصل الحقد بينهما حتى يفرح كل واحد بمساءة الآخر ويحزن بمسرته ويطلق اللسان في عرضه. فمن خاصم فقد تعرض لهذه الآفات. وأقل ما فيه اشتغال القلب حتى أنه يكون في صلاته وخاطره معلق بالمحاجة والخصومة فلا يبقى حاله على الاستقامة.

r22.2 A certain person remarked, "I have not seen anything that impairs one's religion, diminishes one's respectability, ends one's happiness, or preoccupies one's heart like arguing" (al-Adhkar (y102), 502–3).

r22.2 قال بعضهم: ما رأيت شيئاً أذهب للدين ولا أنقص للمروءة ولا أضيع للذة ولا أشغل للقلب من الخصومة [محرر من الأذكار: ٥٠٢ ـ ٥٠٣؛ بتقديم وتأخير].

*

r23.0 ASKING ABOUT ANOTHER'S MISTAKES

r23.0 السؤال عن المشكلات

r23.1 (Nahlawi:) It is forbidden to ask about another's errors and blunders in order to tell them they have made a mistake or to embarrass them, being unlawful because it entails injury to another and belittling him in front of people. But when one's asking about mistakes is to learn or teach, or to test or sharpen students' minds or make them reflect, then it is recommended and desirable, because it facilitates the comprehension of religious knowledge (al-Durar al-mubaha (y99), 140).

r23.1 يحرم السؤال عن المشكلات ومواضع الغلط للتغليط والتخجيل، وهو حرام لأنه يترتب عليه إيذاء الغير واحتقاره بين الناس [...] بخلاف السؤال عنها للتعلم أو التعليم واختبار أذهان الطلبة أو تشحيذها أو حثهم على التأمل فإنه مستحب لما فيه من الإعانة على فهم العلم [محرر من الدرر المباحة: ١٤٠].

*

r24.0 SEARCHING OUT A PERSON'S FAULTS

r24.0 التفتيش عن عيوب الناس

r24.1 (Nahlawi:) Asking about and searching out the faults of others is spying, which Allah Most High has forbidden by saying,

r24.1 (النحلاوي:) السؤال والتفتيش عن عيوب الناس هو التجسس الذي نهى الله تعالى عنه بقوله سبحانه:

"Do not spy" (Koran 49:12),

meaning to look for the shameful points of Muslims. The Prophet (Allah bless him and give him peace) said:

(1) "If you search for people's shameful points, you corrupt them..."

(2) "O you who have entered Islam with your tongues but whose hearts faith has not entered: do not slander people, and do not ferret out people's shameful points. Whoever searches out the shameful points of his brother, Allah will search out his own shameful points, and if Allah searches out a person's shameful points, be sure that He will disgrace him even if he should remain in the middle of his house."

(Ibid., 145)

*

r25.0   DISPLAYING SATISFACTION AT A MUSLIM'S TROUBLES

r25.1   The Prophet (Allah bless him and give him peace) said,

"Do not show joy at the misfortune of your brother, lest Allah have mercy on him and afflict you with misfortune."

(*al-Adhkar* (y102), 474)

*

r26.0   OBSCENITY

r26.1   The Prophet (Allah bless him and give him peace) said:

(1) "A believer is not given to reviling, cursing, obscenity, or vulgarity."

﴿وَلَا تَجَسَّسُوا﴾ [الحجرات: ١٢].

ومعناه تتبع عورات المسلمين. وجاء في الحديث الصحيح: «إنك إن تتبعت عورات الناس أفسدتهم...».

- [وعن أبي برزة رضي الله عنه أنه قال:] قال رسول الله ﷺ: «يا معشر من أسلم بلسانه، ولم يدخل الإيمان في قلبه، لا تغتابوا الناس ولا تتبعوا عوراتهم، فإنه من تتبع عورة أخيه، تتبع الله عورته، ومن تتبع الله عورته يفضحه ولو كان في جوف بيته» [رواه أبو داود] [نقل من المرجع المذكور: ١٤٥].

r25.0   إظهار الشماتة بالمسلم

r25.1   [روينا في كتاب الترمذي عن واثلة بن الأسقع رضي الله عنه قال:] قال رسول الله ﷺ: «لا تظهر الشماتة لأخيك فيرحمه الله ويبتليك» [قال الترمذي: حديث حسن] [نقل من الأذكار: ٤٧٤].

r26.0   الفحش في القول

r26.1   [روينا في كتاب الترمذي عن عبد الله بن مسعود رضي الله عنه قال:] قال رسول الله ﷺ: «ليس المؤمن بالطعان ولا اللعان ولا الفاحش ولا

(2) "Whatever contains vulgarity is made ugly by it, and whatever contains modesty is made beautiful by it."

r26.2 (Nawawi:) Obscenity and vulgarity are forbidden, as is attested to by many well-known and rigorously authenticated (sahih) hadiths, *obscenity* meaning to express ugly or vulgar matters in plain words, even if they are true and the speaker is being honest. One should instead express such things by alluding to them in a polite way that nevertheless conveys what is meant, as is done by the Holy Koran and authentic noble hadiths. Allah Most High says:

(1) "It is permitted to you on the nights of the fast to enter unto your wives" (Koran 2:187).

(2) "How can you take it [the marriage payment] back when you have entered unto one another?" (Koran 4:21).

(3) "But if you divorce them before you have touched them..." (Koran 2:237).

There are many Koranic verses and authentic hadiths that employ similar words. Scholars say that comprehensible allusions should be used for these and other matters one is hesitant to mention by name. One alludes, for example, to sexual intercourse with a woman as "going unto," "lovemaking," "sleeping with," and so forth, and does not use explicit words such as *copulate* or the like; and similarly alludes to urinating and voiding excrement as "answering the call of nature," or "going to the bathroom," and does not simply say "defecate," "urinate," and so forth. The same is true of mentioning personal blemishes such as leprosy, halitosis, underarm odor, and the like, which one should refer to by polite words that indicate what is meant. Other matters should be dealt with as in the above-mentioned examples— all of which applies to cases in which there is no need to plainly refer to these things by name. When the need arises to explain or teach, and one

البذيء» [قال الترمذي : حديث حسن .
ورويـنـا في كتاب الترمذي وابن ماجه عن
أنس رضي الله عنـه قال : قال رسول الله
ﷺ :] «مـا كان الـفـحـش في شيء إلا
شانـه ، ومـا كان الحياء في شيء إلا زانه»
[قال الترمذي : حديث حسن] .

r26.2　（النـووي :) وممـا ينهى عنـه
الفحش وبـذاءة اللسـان ، والأحـاديث
الصحيحـة فيه كثيرة معـروفة ، ومعنـاه
التعبيـر عن الأمـور المستقبحة بعبارة
صريحة ، وإن كانت صحيحة والمتكلم
بهـا صادق . وينبغي أن يستعمل في ذلك
الكنـايات ويعبر عنها بعبارة جميلة يفهم
بهـا الغـرض ، وبهـذا جاء القـرآن العزيز
والسنن الصحيحة المكرمة .

قال الله تعالى :
﴿أُحِلَّ لَكُمْ لَيْلَةَ الصِّيَامِ الرَّفَثُ إِلَى
نِسَائِكُمْ﴾ [البقرة : ١٨٧] .

وقال تعالى :
﴿وَكَيْفَ تَأْخُذُونَهُ وَقَدْ أَفْضَى بَعْضُكُمْ
إِلَى بَعْضٍ﴾ [النساء : ٢١] .

وقال تعالى :
﴿وَإِنْ طَلَّقْتُمُوهُنَّ مِنْ قَبْلِ أَنْ
تَمَسُّوهُنَّ﴾ [البقرة : ٢٣٧] .

والآيـات والأحـاديث الصحيحـة في
ذلك كثيرة .

قال العلمـاء : فينبغي أن يستعمـل في
هذا وما أشبهه من العبارات التي يستحى
من ذكرها بصريح اسمها الكنايات
المفهمة .

فيكنى عن جمـاع المـرأة بالإفضـاء
والـدخول والمعاشرة والوقاع ونحوها ولا
يصرّح بالنيك والجماع ونحوهما .

وكـذلـك يكنى عن البـول والتغـوط
بقضاء الحاجة والذهاب إلى الخلاء ، ولا
يصرّح بالخراءة والبول ونحوهما .

وكـذلـك ذكر العيوب كالبرص والبخر
والصنان وغيرها يعبر عنها بعبارات جميلة
يفهم منها الغرض .

ويلحق بما ذكرنا من الأمثلة ما سواه .
و[اعـلـم أن] هذا كله إذا لم تدع

fears that the listener may not grasp one's allusion or may misunderstand the meaning, one should plainly say the thing's name so that the real meaning is understood. And this is how one should interpret the hadiths that have reached us which contain such straightforward expressions, as arising from the needs we have mentioned, for communicating clearly is more important than mere decorum. And Allah alone gives success (ibid.. (y102), 508–9).

الحاجة إلى التصريح بصريح اسمه ، فإن دعت حاجة لغرض البيان والتعليم وخيف أن المخاطب لا يفهم المجاز، أو يفهم غير المراد صرّح حينئذ باسمه الصريح ليحصل الإفهام الحقيقي .

وعلى هذا يحمل ما جاء في الأحاديث من التصريح بمثل هذا، فإن ذلك محمول على الحاجة كما ذكرنا، فإن تحصيل الإفهام في هذا أولى من مراعاة مجرد الأدب ، وبالله التوفيق [محرر من المرجع المذكور: ٥٠٨ ـ ٥٠٩ بتقديم وتأخير] .

*

r27.0   SEVERITY IN SPEECH AND HARSHNESS

r27.1   (Nahlawi:) Severity in speech and harshness are blameworthy when out of place, their proper place being in forbidding the wrong, if gentleness and affability prove ineffective (dis: q5.5), as well as in imposing prescribed legal penalties, and in reprimanding or disciplining those who require it. Allah Most High says:

(1) "... And be harsh with them" (Koran 9:73).

(2) "Let them find severity in you" (Koran 9:123).

(3) "Let not pity for them seize you concerning the religion of Allah" (Koran 24:2).

r27.2   Other than in the above-mentioned cases, it is praiseworthy for one to use amiable words, have a cheerful expression, and to smile. The Prophet (Allah bless him and give him peace) said:

"There is a dwelling in paradise whose outside can be seen from inside [A: from its lucidness

r27.0   غلظة الكلام والعنف

r27.1   (النحلاوي :) غلظة الكلام والعنف مذمومان ، وهذا إذا كان في غير محله ، ومحلّه النهي عن المنكر إذا لم ينجح الرفق واللين .

ومحلّه أيضاً إقامة الحدود والتعزير والتأديب لمن يستوجب ذلك . قال الله تعالى :

﴿وَٱغْلُظْ عَلَيْهِمْ﴾ [التوبة : ٧٣] .

وقال تعالى :

﴿وَلْيَجِدُوا فِيكُمْ غِلْظَةً﴾ [التوبة : ١٢٣] .

وقال تعالى :

﴿وَلَا تَأْخُذْكُم بِهِمَا رَأْفَةٌ فِي دِينِ اللَّهِ﴾ [النور : ٢] .

r27.2   وفيما عداها يُستحب للإنسان طيب الكلام، وطلاقة الوجه والتبسم . [عن عبد الله بن عمر رضي الله عنهما، أن] النبي ﷺ قال : «في الجنة غرفة يُرى ظاهرها من باطنها» ، فقال أبو مالك

and purity]." Abu Malik Ash'ari asked, "Whose shall it be, O Messenger of Allah?" And he said, "He whose speech is fair, who feeds others, and who spends the night standing in prayer when people sleep."

(*al-Durar al-mubaha* (y99), 144–45)

الأشعري : لمن هي يا رسول الله؟ قال : لمن أطاب الكلام وأطعم الطعام وبات قائماً والناس نيام» [رواه الطبراني في الكبير] [نقل من الدرر المباحة : ١٤٤ ـ ١٤٥].

*

r28.0   FRIGHTENING OR COERCING A BELIEVER

r28.0 إخـافـة المؤمن [من غيـر ذنب] وإكراهه [على ما. لا يريده]

r28.1   (Nahlawi:) To make a believer fear other than disobedience or coerce him to do something he is averse to, such as giving a gift, marrying, or selling something—all this is hurting him, and hurting a believer is unlawful. The Prophet (Allah bless him and give him peace) said,

"Whoever frightens a believer, it is incumbent that Allah not protect him from the terrors of Judgement Day as a fitting recompense."

Najm al-Ghazzi says in *Husn al-tanabbuh*, "Among the works of the Devil is frightening, annoying, or alarming a believer, all of which is unlawful" (ibid., 157–58).

r28.1   (النحلاوي :) إخافة المؤمن من غيـر ذنب، وإكراهه على ما لا يريده ـ كالهبة والنكاح والبيع ـ فإن ذلك إيذاء له وإيذاء المؤمن حرام. [عن عمر رضي الله عنه أنه قال : سمعت] رسول الله ﷺ يقـول : «من أخـاف مؤمناً، كان حقاً على الله تعـالى أن لا يؤمنـه من الأفـزاع يوم القيامة، جزاءً وفاقاً [رواه الطبراني في الكبيـر بإسناد ضعيف]. وفي حسن التنبه للنجم الغـزي : ومن أعمـال الشيطـان تخويف المـؤمن وإزعاجه، وترويعه، وكـل ذلـك حرام [نقـل من المـرجع المذكور : ١٥٧ ـ ١٥٨].

*

r29.0   REJECTING A BROTHER'S EXCUSE

r29.0   رد عذر أخيه

r29.1   The Prophet (Allah bless him and give him) said,

"When someone offers an excuse to his fellow Muslim and the latter does not accept it, his sin is like the crime of imposing taxes [dis: p32]."

(Ibid., 157)

r29.1   [عن جودان رضي الله عنه أنه قال :] قال رسـول الله ﷺ : «من اعتـذر إلى أخيه المسلم فلم يقبل منه، كان عليه مثل خطيئة مكس» [رواه ابن ماجه] [نقل من المرجع المذكور : ١٥٧].

r30.0   DRIVING AWAY THE POOR, THE WEAK, THE ORPHAN, OR THE BEGGAR

r30.1   Allah Most High says:

(1) "As for the orphan, do not oppress him; and as for the beggar [dis: r39], turn him not away" (Koran 93:9–10).

(2) "Do not drive away those who call upon their Lord morning and evening, seeking His countenance: you are not responsible for anything of their account, nor they for anything of yours, that you should drive them away and thus become of the wrongdoers" (Koran 6:52).

(3) "Lower your wing unto the believers" (Koran 15:88).

(*al-Adhkar* (y102), 481–82)

*

r31.0   PUTTING OFF ONE'S FATHER OR MOTHER

r31.1   (Nawawi:) It is very sternly prohibited to put off one's father or mother. Allah Most High says:

"Your Lord decrees that you shall worship none but Him and treat your parents well. If one or both of them reach old age while with you, do not say 'Uff' to them or put them off, but speak respectfully to them. Lower for them the wing of humbleness, out of mercy, and say, 'O Lord, have mercy on them, as they raised me when I was young' " (Koran 17.24–25).

(Ibid., 509)

*

r30.0 طرد الـفـقـيـر والضعيف واليتيم والسائل

r30.1   قال الله تعالى :
﴿فَأَمَّا الْيَتِيمَ فَلاَ تَقْهَرْ، وَأَمَّا السَّائِلَ فَلاَ تَنْهَرْ﴾ [الضحى : ٩ - ١٠] .
وقال : ﴿وَلاَ تَطْرُدِ الَّذِينَ يَدْعُونَ رَبَّهُمْ بِالْغَدَاةِ وَالْعَشِيِّ يُرِيدُونَ وَجْهَهُ مَا عَلَيْكَ مِنْ حِسَابِهِمْ مِنْ شَيْءٍ وَمَا مِنْ حِسَابِكَ عَلَيْهِمْ مِنْ شَيْءٍ فَتَطْرُدَهُمْ فَتَكُونَ مِنَ الظَّالِمِينَ﴾ [الأنعام : ٥٢] .
وقال تعالى :
﴿وَاخْفِضْ جَنَاحَكَ لِلْمُؤْمِنِينَ﴾ [الحجر : ٨٨] . [محرر من الأذكار : ٤٨١ - ٤٨٢] .

r31.0   انتهار الوالد والوالدة

r31.1   (النووي :) يحرم انتهار الوالد والوالدة [وشبههما] تحريماً غليظاً . قال الله تعالى :
﴿وَقَضَى رَبُّكَ أَلاَّ تَعْبُدُوا إِلاَّ إِيَّاهُ وَبِالْوَالِدَيْنِ إِحْسَاناً إِمَّا يَبْلُغَنَّ عِنْدَكَ الْكِبَرَ أَحَدُهُمَا أَوْ كِلاَهُمَا فَلاَ تَقُلْ لَهُمَا أُفٍّ وَلاَ تَنْهَرْهُمَا وَقُلْ لَهُمَا قَوْلاً كَرِيماً . وَاخْفِضْ لَهُمَا جَنَاحَ الذُّلِّ مِنَ الرَّحْمَةِ وَقُلْ رَبِّ ارْحَمْهُمَا كَمَا رَبَّيَانِي صَغِيراً﴾ [الإسراء : ٢٤ - ٢٥] . [محرر من الـمـرجـع المذكور : ٥٠٩] .

r32.0 CIRCUMSTANCES IN WHICH CONVERSATION IS OFFENSIVE

(N: *Offensive*, when used without further qualification by Hanafis (A: in their books on the lawful and unlawful (al-hazr wa al-ibaha)) means *unlawfully offensive* (makruh tahriman), and its ruling is the same as the unlawful (A: is in the Shafi'i school).)

INTERRUPTING ONESELF OR OTHERS

r32.1 (Nahlawi:) It is offensive to interrupt someone else's words with one's own when the former consist of teaching Sacred Knowledge. Some scholars hold that to greet a group with "as-Salamu 'alaykum" when they are learning religious knowledge is a sin. It is also offensive to interrupt one's own words with speech of a different kind when reciting Koran, supplicating, explaining the Koran, teaching hadith, or addressing people, and while doing this, for example, one turns to someone and tells him to go buy some things needed at home.

Conversation is offensive for anyone seated listening to a pious exhortation, or instruction, or in the presence of someone above his own level. It is also offensive for such a person merely to turn to look at something else, or to stir when there is no need, all of which is poor manners, levity, precipitateness, and thoughtlessness. Rather, the one speaking should set forth what he means to say without irrelevant asides until finished, and the person addressed should heed the speaker, paying attention to him and listening until he finishes, without looking around, stirring, or talking; especially if the speaker is explaining the words of Allah Most High or His messenger (Allah bless him and give him peace). But one is excused if a pressing physical or religious need arises that there is no alternative but to fulfill, since necessity excuses one from any rule whatever (A: but only to the degree demanded by necessity).

DISRESPECT TO THOSE WITH AUTHORITY OVER ONE

r32.2 It is offensive to contend against the words of anyone with authority over one (A: counte-

---

r32.0 المواضع التي يكره فيها الكلام

(ح : والكراهة إذا أطلقت (ع : في باب الحظر والإباحة) عند الحنفية فالمراد كراهة التحريم وحكمه حكم الحرام).

قطع كلام غيره أو نفسه

r32.1 (النحلاوي : منها قطع كلام الغير وحديثه بكلامه من غير ضرورة ، خصوصاً إذا كان في مذاكرة العلم ، وقد قالوا إن السلام على الجالس لمذاكرة العلم إثم . وكذا قطع كلام نفسه بخلاف جنسه كمن يقرأ أو يدعو أو يفسر أو يحدّث أو يخطب للناس ، ويلتفت في أثنائه إلى شخص فيأمره ببعض حوائج بيته أو نحوه .

وكذا تكلّم من هو في مجلس عِظة أو تدريس أو في مجلس من هو فوقه ، وكذا مجرد التفاته وتحركه من غير حاجة ، وكل هذا سوء أدب ، وخفة ، وعجلة ، وسفه . بل على المتكلم أن يسرد كلامه إلى أن ينتهي من غير تخلل كلام أجنبي ، وعلى المخاطب التوجُّه إليه والإنصات والاستماع إلى أن ينتهي كلامه بلا التفات ولا تحرك ولا تكلم ، خصوصاً إذا كان المتكلم في تفسير كلام الله تعالى ، أو كلام رسول الله ﷺ ؛ إلا أن تبدو حاجة داعية طبعاً أو شرعاً ، فلا يجد بداً من بعد ما ذكر . فإن الضرورة مستثناة من الأحكام المطلقة .

رد التابع كلام متبوعه

r32.2 ومنها رد التابع كلام متبوعه ،

nanced by Sacred Law), or talk back, oppose, rebut, or disobey such a person in anything lawful (A: meaning not unlawful or offensive), the prohibition applying to such people as a follower with his leader, son with his parents, student with his teacher, wife with her husband, or unlearned person with a scholar. All of this is very ugly behavior and deserves disciplinary action (def: o17), since each of these is obliged to obey the one over them.

ومقـابلتـه، ومخـالفتـه وعدم قبوله، وعدم إطـاعتـه في أمر مشروع ـ كالرعية للأمير، والولد لوالديه، والتلميذ لأستاذه، والمرأة لزوجهـا، والجـاهـل للعالم ـ وهذا قبيح جداً يَستحق به التعـزير، لأن طاعة هؤلاء واجبة عليهم.

THIS-WORLDLY WORDS IN A MOSQUE

كلام الدنيا في المسجد

r32.3   It is offensive to speak about this-worldly matters, meaning words that would otherwise be permissible, in a mosque when there is no excuse (A: if one makes a habit of it). (N: The more reliable position is that it is not offensive, but merely better not to (khilaf al-awla).)

r32.3   ومـنهـا كلام الـدنيـا في المسـاجد، أي الكلام المباح، بلا عذر؛ فإنه مكروه.

SPEAKING DURING THE SERMON
OF THE FRIDAY PRAYER

الكلام في حال الخطبة

r32.4   It is offensive to speak during the sermon on Friday, whether it be to say "Subhan Allah," the Blessings on the Prophet (Allah bless him and give him peace), or to command the right or forbid the wrong, the reason for the prohibition being that listening to the Friday prayer sermon is obligatory, as it takes the place of two of the rak'as of the noon prayer, so that things offensive during the prayer are offensive while listening to the sermon. The Prophet (Allah bless him and give him peace) said,

"When the imam is giving the sermon on Friday, and you tell your companion 'Listen,' you have made an impertinent remark."

r32.4   ومـنهـا: الكـلام في حال الخطبـة ـ ولـو تسبيحـاً، أو تصلية أو أمراً بالمعروف، ونهياً عن المنكر ـ وأصله أن استمـاع الخطبـة ـ في الجمعـة ـ فرضٌ لتنـزيلهـا منـزلـة ركعتي الظهـر، فيكره لمستمع الخطبة ما يكره في الصلاة. قال ﷺ: «إذا قلت لصاحبك يوم الجمعة: أنصت ـ والإمـام يخطب ـ فقـد لغـوت» [رواه البخاري ومسلم].

SPEAKING WHEN THE KORAN IS
BEING RECITED

الكلام عند قراءة القرآن

r32.5   It is offensive to speak when the Koran is being recited, for listening to it and heeding it are

r32.5   ومنهـا: الكـلام عنـد قراءة القـرآن. والإنصاتُ عند قراءته واستماعُهُ

absolutely obligatory, whether one is performing the prayer or not, and whether one comprehends it or not (A: but only if its words are distinctly audible to one). Allah Most High says,

"When the Koran is recited, listen and pay heed to it" (Koran 7:204).

SPEAKING WITHOUT NEED TO A MEMBER OF THE OPPOSITE SEX

r32.6 It is offensive for a male to speak without need to a young woman who is not a member of his unmarriageable kin (def: m6.1). He should not say "Arhamkum Allah" (Allah have mercy on you) if she sneezes, greet her with "as-Salamu 'alaykum" (A: which is unlawful in the Shafi'i school) nor return her Salams if she says them (A: which is offensive for Shafi'is). He should not say these aloud, but to himself, all of which likewise holds for a young woman's speaking to a man who is not a member of her unmarriageable kin (m6.2). The prohibition of these is due to the Prophet's having said (Allah bless him and give him peace),

"The adultery of the tongue is speech."

SPEAKING WHEN LOVEMAKING OR IN THE LAVATORY

r32.7 It is offensive to speak while lovemaking, or when in the lavatory or relieving oneself.
    It is offensive to laugh in circumstances in which speaking is offensive.

SPEAKING AFTER THE COMING OF DAWN BEFORE PERFORMING THE DAWN PRAYER

r32.8 It is offensive to speak of this-worldly things between dawn and performing the dawn prayer (subh). Some hold this extends until sunrise (al-Durar al-mubaha (y99), 145–49).

واجبٌ مطلقاً سواء كان في الصلاة أو خارجها، فاهماً للمعاني أو غير فاهم. قال الله تعالى:

﴿وَإِذَا قُرِىءَ الْقُرْآنُ فَاسْتَمِعُوا لَهُ وَأَنْصِتُوا﴾ [الأعراف: ٢٠٤].

الكلام مع غير محرم بلا حاجة

r32.6 ومنها: الكلام مع الشابة الأجنبية بلا حاجة حتى لا يشمتها إذا عطست، ولا يسلّم عليها، ولا يرد سلامها جهراً بل في نفسه، وكذا العكس لقوله ﷺ: «واللسان زناه الكلام» [ت: من حديث رواه مسلم].

الكلام عند الجماع وعند قضاء الحاجة

r32.7 ومنها الكلام عند الجماع، ومنها الكلام في الخلاء وعند قضاء الحاجة.
    وكذا يكره الضحك في المواضع التي يكره فيها الكلام.

الكلام بعد طلوع الفجر إلى الصلاة

r32.8 ومنها كلام الدنيا بعد طلوع الفجر إلى الصلاة، وقيل إلى طلوع الشمس [محرر من الدرر المباحة: ١٤٥ ـ ١٤٩؛ بتقديم وتأخير].

CONVERSATION AFTER PERFORMING
THE NIGHTFALL PRAYER ('ISHA)

r32.9   (Nawawi:) It is offensive for someone who
has prayed the nightfall prayer ('isha) to converse
about things permitted at other times, meaning
permissible words which would otherwise be the
same to say or not to. Discourse that is unlawful or
offensive at other times is even more sternly prohibited or offensive at this time. As for conversation about what is good, such as teaching Sacred
Knowledge, relating the words of the pious,
describing noble qualities, or speaking to one's
guest, none of these is offensive, but rather they
are commendable (al-Adhkar (y102), 504).

r32.9   (النووي:) ويكره لمن صلى
العشاء الآخرة أن يتحدث بالحديث
المباح في غير هذا الوقت وأعني بالمباح
الذي استوى فعله وتركه . فأما الحديث
المحرم في غير هذا الوقت أو المكروه
فهو في هذا الوقت أشد تحريماً وكراهةً .
وأما الحديث في الخير كمذاكرة العلم
وحكايات الصالحين ومكارم الأخلاق
والحديث مع الضيف فلا كراهة فيه بل
هو مستحب [نقل من الأذكار المنتخبة من
كلام سيد الأبرار : ٥٠٤].

*

r33.0   PEOPLE OFFENSIVE TO GREET
WITH SALAMS

r33.0   المواضع التي يكره
فيها السلام

r33.1   (Nahlawi:) It is offensive (def: r32.0) to
greet with "as-Salamu 'alaykum" anyone who is:

(1)   performing the prayer, reciting the
Koran, invoking Allah (dhikr), reading hadith to
others, giving the Friday prayer sermon (khutba),
or listening to any of these;

(2)   a student of jurisprudence repeating a
lesson over to himself to facilitate memorizing it,
someone informing ordinary people of legal rulings, or anyone engaged in a lesson of Sacred
Knowledge;

(3)   giving the call to prayer or call to commence (iqama);

(4)   teaching;

(5)   seated waiting for the prayer, or saying
"Subhan Allah";

(6)   eating;

r33.1   (النحلاوي:) من المواضع
التي يكره فيها السلام : السلام على
مصلٍ ، وقارئٍ ، وذاكرٍ ، ومحدّثٍ ،
وخطيب ومن يصغي إليهم ، ومكرر فقه ،
ومن يفصل الأحكام بين الناس ، ومن هو
في حال مذاكرة العلم الشرعي ، ومؤذن ،
ومقيم ، ومدرّس ، ومن جلس للصلاة ،
والتسبيح ، والمشغول بالأكل ، والفاسق

(7) a corrupt person who does not conceal his acts of disobedience;

(8) a young lady who is not a member of one's unmarriageable kin (dis: r32.6);

(9) someone who plays games that are not permissible (dis: k29.5), slanders others, sings, is an old wag, a chronic liar, addicted to profitless conversation, reviles others, or looks at women's faces, all of whom are offensive to greet unless their repentance from these things is known;

(10) someone who is enjoying his wife, whose nakedness is exposed, who is relieving himself, drowsy, asleep, or someone who is in a bathhouse.

RESPONDING TO SALAMS

r33.2   It is not obligatory to respond to someone's Salams in circumstances where greeting him is uncalled-for, except for a corrupt person ((7) above), whose Salams it is obligatory to return. It is not obligatory to answer the Salams of someone who is a child, intoxicated, or insane. Nawawi (Allah Most High have mercy on him) says in his commentary on *Sahih Muslim,* "Scholars disagree about greeting non-Muslims with 'as-Salamu 'alaykum' or returning their Salams. We hold that it is unlawful to say it to them first, though is obligatory to return their greetings by saying 'Wa 'alaykum' (and upon you), or simply, ''Alaykum.' Other scholars hold it is permissible to greet them first with 'as-Salamu 'alaykum' '' (*al-Durar al-mubaha* (y99), 150–51).

*

r34.0   BOASTING

r34.1   Allah Most High says,

"Do not praise yourselves: He knows best who is godfearing" (Koran 53:32).

لو معلناً، والأجنبيات الفتيات، وعلى من يلعب لعباً غير مباح، ومن يغتاب الناس، وعلى من يغني، وعلى الشيخ الممازح، والكــذاب، والــلاغي، وعلى من يسب الناس، أو ينظر وجوه الأجنبيات، ما لم تُعرف توبتُهم، وعلى من يتمتع مع أهله، ومـكـشـوف عورة، ومـن هو في حال التغـوط، أو البـول، أو ناعس أو نائم، أو في الحمام.

رد السلام

r33.2   لا يجب الـرد في كل محـلٍّ لا يُشـرع فيـه الســلام، إلا في الفـاسـق، فينبغي وجوب الـرد عليـه. ولا يجب رد سلام الطفل، والسكران والمجنون [ولا مَن يقـول: سلامْ عليكـم؛ بسكــون الميم]. وقـال النـووي رحمه الله تعالى في شرح مسلم اختلف العلمــاء في رد السـلام على الكفار وابتدائهم به فمذهبنا تحريم ابتدائه ووجوب رده عليهم بأن يقـول: وعليكم؛ أو: عليكم؛ فقـط. وذهب طائفـة إلى جواز ابتـدائنـا لهم بالسلام [محرر من الدرر المباحة: ١٥٠ ـ ١٥١؛ بتقديم وتأخير].

r34.0   الافتخار

r34.1   قال الله تعالى:
﴿فـلَا تُزَكُّـوا أَنْفُسَكُمْ هُوَ أَعْلَمُ بِمَنِ اتَّقَى﴾ [النجم: ٣٢].

r34.2   The Prophet (Allah bless him and give him peace) said,

"Allah has inspired to me that you are all to be humble towards each other such that no one transgresses against or exalts himself above another."

(al-Adhkar (y102), 473–74)

*

r35.0   REVEALING ONE'S SINS TO OTHERS

r35.1   The Prophet (Allah bless him and give him peace) said:

"All of my Community shall be pardoned, save those who commit sins openly. Committing them *openly* includes a man who does something shameful at night, and when morning comes, Allah having hidden his act, he says, 'O So-and-so, last night I did such and such'; his Lord having concealed it for him at night, while in the morning he pulls away the cover with which Allah had concealed it for him."

r35.2   (Nawawi:) It is offensive for a person who has been afflicted with an act of disobedience or the like to inform another of it. Rather, one should repent to Allah Most High by desisting from it at once, regretting what one has done, and firmly resolving never to do the like of it again. These three things are the integrals of repentance, which is not valid without them. There is no harm in telling about a sin to one's sheikh or other person who may be expected to teach one how to desist from the act or refrain from similar acts, or apprise one of the causes that led to it, or pray for one, and so forth. If such is the case, informing him is commendable. It is only offensive to do so when no such interest can be served (ibid., 498).

r34.2 [وروينــا فـي صحيــح مسلم وسنن أبي داود وغيـرهمـا عن عيـاض بن حمار الصحابي رضي الله عنه قال:] قال رسول الله ﷺ: «إنَّ الله تعالى أوحى إليّ أن تواضعـوا حتى لا يبغي أحـدٌ على أحد ولا يفخــر أحــد على أحــد» [نقـل من الأذكار: ٤٧٣ ـ ٤٧٤].

r35.0   إخبار الإنسـان غيره بمعصية نفسه

r35.1 [روينا في صحيحي البخاري ومسلم عن أبي هريــرة رضي الله عنـه قال: سمعت] رسـول الله ﷺ يقـول: «كـل أمتي معـافى إلا المجاهرين، وإنّ من المجــاهرة أن يعمل الـرجـل بالليل عمـلًا ثم يصبح وقد سَتَرَهُ الله تعالى عليه فيقـول: يا فلان عملتُ البـارحـة كذا وكـذا، وقـد بات يستـره ربـه، ويُصبح يكشف ستر الله عليه».

r35.2   (النــووي:) يكره للإنسان إذا ابتلي بمعصية أو نحـوهـا أن يخبـر غيـره بذلك. بل ينبغي أن يتوب إلى الله تعالى فيقلع عنهـا في الحـال ويندم على ما فعل ويعـزم أن لا يعـود إلى مثلهـا أبـداً؛ فهذه الثـلاثة هي أركـان التـوبة لا تصـح إلا باجتماعهـا. فإن أخبر بمعصيته شيخه أو شبهه ممن يرجو بإخبـاره أن يعلمه مخرجـاً من معصيتـه، أو ليعلمـه ما يسلم به من الـوقـوع في مثلهـا، أو يعرف السبب الذي أوقعـه فيهـا، أو يدعـو له أو نحو ذلك فلا بأس به، بل هو حسن، وإنمـا يكـره إذا انتفت هذه المصلحة [محرر من المرجع المذكور: ٤٩٨، بتقديم وتأخير].

r36.0   REVEALING A SECRET

r36.1   The Prophet (Allah bless him and give him peace) said,

"When a man says something, then glances left or right, his words are a confidence to be kept."

(Ibid., 507)

r36.1 [وروينــا في سنن أبي داود والتـرمذي عن جابر رضي الله عنه قال:] قال رسـول الله ﷺ: «إذا حدّث الرجـل بالحـديث ثم التفت فهي أمـانة» [(قال الترمذي: حديث حسن) نقل من المرجع المذكور: ٥٠٧].

r36.2   (Nahlawi:) *Telling a secret* means to inform others of a remark, action, or state which one learns of from someone who wants it to remain hidden, whether it be good or bad. This is hurting him, and hurting others is unlawful.

Whenever people meet, it is obligatory to keep secret any act that occurs, any word spoken, or any state attributable to someone, when these concern something one would normally wish to remain confidential, while not being unlawful. If unlawful, then:

(1) If it is against Allah Most High alone and does not involve legal measures such as prescribed legal penalties or disciplinary action (def: o17), then it must be kept secret.

(2) If it involves legal measures, as do fornication (dis: o12) and drinking (o16), then one has a choice between revealing it or not, though it is superior to conceal it.

(3) If it involves another person's rights, then if concealing it entails harm to anyone, or if it concerns prescribed legal measures such as retaliation for an injury or death (def: o3), or covering the cost of an article destroyed through negligence, then if the person whose rights have been infringed is ignorant of it, one is obliged to make the matter known, and must testify to it if asked to.

(4) If it involves another's rights, but concealing it does not entail harm to anyone and it does not concern prescribed legal measures, or it entails one of these two, but the person concerned

r36.2   (النحلاوي:) إفشاء السر هو نشرُ [وإظهارُ] القول أو الفعل أو الحال الـذي يعلمه الإنسان من غـيره، عند الناس، حيث لا يريـد ذلك الغير اطلاع أحدٍ عليه، من خير أو شر. فإن فيه إيذاء ذلك الغير، والإيذاء حرام.

[واعلم أن] كل ما وقع من الأعمال، أو قيل من الكلام، أو اتصف به متصف من الأحوال في مجلس من المجـالس، ممـا يكره إفشاؤه: إن لم يخالف الشرع، يلزم كتمانه. وإن خالف الشرع:

ـ فإن كان حق الله تعالى ولم يتعلق به حكم شرعي كالحد والتعزير فكذلك.

ـ وإن تعــلق بحكــم شرعــي فلك الخيار، والستر أفضل كالزنى وشرب الخمر.

ـ وإن كان حق العـبـد: فإن تعلق به ضررُ لأحدٍ، أو حكم شرعي كالقصاص والتضمين، فعليك الإعلامُ إن جهل ذلك الأمر، والشهادةُ إن طُلب منك.

ـ وإلا، بأن كان لم يتــعــلــق به ضررٌ لأحد، ولا تعلق به حكمٌ شرعي، أو تعلق به حكمٌ شرعي، أو تعلق به ذلــك ولكنـه

already knows of it through another and one has not been asked to testify about it, then one is obliged to conceal the matter.

(al-Durar al-mubaha (y99), 134)

*

r37.0 DISAFFECTING A PERSON'S FAMILY FROM HIM

r37.1 (Nawawi:) It is unlawful for a person to mention anything to another's servant, wife, son, and so forth that could disaffect them from him, unless one is commanding the right or forbidding the wrong. The Prophet (Allah bless him and give him peace) said,

"He who disaffects a person's wife or servant from him is not of us."

(al-Adhkar (y102), 498)

*

r38.0 CURSING

THE PROHIBITON OF CURSING OTHERS

r38.1 (Nawawi:) Cursing an upright Muslim is unlawful by unanimous consensus of all Muslims. The Prophet (Allah bless him and give him peace) said,

"Cursing a believer is like killing him."

THE PERMISSIBILITY OF CURSING THOSE WHO COMMIT DISOBEDIENCE WHEN THEY ARE NOT PERSONALLY IDENTIFIED OR KNOWN

r38.2 It is permissible (A: but not rewarded by Allah) to curse those who possess blameworthy

عُلِمَ من غيرك ولم يجهل ولم تطلب منك الشهادة به، فالكتم واجب عليك حينئذٍ [محرّر من الدرر المباحة: ١٣٤].

r37.0 إفساد أهل الإنسان عليه

r37.1 (النـووي:) يحـرم على الـمكلف أن يحـدّث عبـد الإنسـان أو زوجته أو ابنه ونحـوهم بمـا يفسدهم به عليـه إذا لم يكـن ما يحـدثهم به أمـراً بالمعروف أو نهياً عن منكر. [وروينا في كتـابي أبي داود والنسـائي عن أبي هريرة رضي الله عنـه قال:] قال رسـول الله ﷺ: «مَن خَبَّبَ زوجةَ امرىءٍ أو مملوكَهُ فليس منا» [محرر من الأذكار: ٤٩٨].

r38.0 اللعن

النهي عن لعن الغير

r38.1 (النـووي:)[...] لعـن المسلم المصون حرام بإجماع المسلمين [...] روينـا في صحيحي البخـاري ومسلم عن ثابت بن الضحـاك رضي الله عنه وكان من أصحاب الشجرة قال:] قال رسول الله ﷺ: «لعن المؤمن كقتله».

جواز لعن أصحاب المعاصي غير المعينين أو المعروفين

r38.2 ويجـوز لعـن أصحـاب الأوصـاف المـذمـومـة كقولك: لعن الله

characteristics, such as by saying, "Allah curse oppressors," "Allah curse the corrupt," "Allah curse picture makers," and so forth. Well-known and rigorously authenticated (sahih) hadiths verify that the Prophet (Allah bless him and give him peace) said:

(1) "Allah curse her who wears false hair and her who arranges it for another";

(2) "Allah curse him who eats usurious gain (riba)";

(3) "Allah curse those who make pictures";

(4) "Allah curse him who surreptitiously changes property-line markers";

all of these being found in Bukhari, Muslim, or both.

As for cursing a particular person who commits some act of disobedience, such as an oppressor, adulterer, maker of pictures, thief, or one who consumes usurious gain; the hadith evidence seems to suggest it is not unlawful, though Ghazali indicates (A: and it is the most reliable opinion) that it *is* unlawful unless the person cursed is someone we know has died in a state of unbelief, such as Abu Lahab, Abu Jahl, Pharaoh, Haman, and their likes. This, as Ghazali notes, is "because *to curse* means to distance another from the mercy of Allah Most High, while we do not know how the particular corrupt person or non-Muslim will end his life. As for those the Prophet (Allah bless him and give him peace) personally cursed, perhaps it was because he knew they would die in unbelief. Praying that evil befalls a person is similar to cursing, even when against a tyrant, such as saying, 'May Allah not heal him,' 'May Allah not keep him safe,' and similar remarks, all of which are blameworthy [A: being unlawful, if of a Muslim]. And likewise for cursing any animals or inanimate objects whatever—all this is objectionable [A: meaning offensive]" (*al-Adhkar* (y102), 476–80).

الظـالمين [. . .] لعن الله الفـاسقين ، لعن الله المصورين ، ونحـو ذلـك [كما تقدم في الفصل السابق . . .]. وثبت في الأحاديث الصحيحة المشهورة أن رسول اللـه ﷺ قال : «لـعـن الله الـواصـلة والمستـوصلة» [الحـديث ، وأنـه قال :] «لعن الله آكـل الـربا» [الحديث] ، [وأنه قال :] «لـعـن الله المصـوريـن» ، [وأنـه قال :] «لعن الله مَن غَيَّرَ منار الأرض» ، وجـمـيـع هذه الألـفـاظ في صحيحي البخاري ومسلم بعضها فيهما وبعضها في أحدهما .

وأمـا لعن الإنسـان بعينه ممن اتصف بشيء من المعـاصي كـ[. . .] ظالم أو زان أو مصوّر أو سارق أو آكل ربا فظواهر الأحاديث أنه ليس بحرام .

وأشار الغزالي إلى تحريمه إلا في حق مَن علمنا أنه مات على الكفر كأبي لهب وأبي جهل وفرعون وهامان وأشباههم . قال : لأن اللعن هو الإبعاد عن رحمة الله تعالى ، وما ندري ما يختم به لهذا الفاسق أو الكـافـر . [قـال :] وأمـا الـذين لعنهم رسول الله ﷺ بأعيـانهم فيجـوز أنه ﷺ علم موتهم على الكفر . [قال :] ويقرب من اللعن الدعاء على الإنسان بالشر حتى الـدعـاء على الظالم كقـول الإنسان : لا أصـح الله جسمه ولا سلمه الله ، وما جرى مجراه ، وكل ذلك مذموم ، وكذلك لعن جمـيـع الحيوانـات والجمـاد فكله مذموم [محرر من الأذكار : ٤٧٦ ـ ٤٨٠ ؛ بتقديم وتأخير] .

*

r39.0 BEGGING	r39.0 التسول

r39.1 (Nahlawi:) It is unlawful to ask for money or other worldly advantage from someone one has no right to ask, unless there is a necessity to. The Prophet (Allah bless him and give him peace) said,

"One of you keeps begging until when he meets Allah Most High, there is not a piece of flesh left on his face,"

which is interpreted as referring to anyone who asks when it is not permissible to do so. The degree of necessity that permits begging is when one is unable to earn a living due to illness or weakness and does not have enough food to last one day (*al-Durar al-mubaha* (y99), 139).

r39.1 (النحـــلاوي :) سؤال المـال والمنفعــة الـدنيـويـة ممن لا حق له فيـه حرام، إلا عنـد الضـرورة الـداعية إليه . [عن ابن عمـر رضي الله عنهما أن] النبي ﷺ قال: «لا تزال المسألـة بأحدكم حتى يلقى الله تعـــالى وليس في وجهــه مزعـة لحم» [رواه البخـاري]. وهـذا محمول على كل من سأل سؤالاً لا يجــوز له . [. . .] والضـرورة التي تبيح السؤال : أن لا يقـدر على الكسب للمرض أو الضعف وأن لا يكون عنـده قوت يوم [محرر من الدرر المباحة : ١٣٩].

*

r40.0 MUSIC, SONG, AND DANCE	r40.0 الملاهي والغناء والرقص

MUSICAL INSTRUMENTS

الملاهي

r40.1 (Ibn Hajar Haytami:) As for the condemnation of musical instruments, flutes, strings, and the like by the Truthful and Trustworthy (Allah bless him and give him peace), who

"does not speak from personal caprice: it is nothing besides a revelation inspired" (Koran 53:3–4),

let those who refuse to obey him beware lest calamity strike them, or a painful torment. The Prophet (Allah bless him and give him peace) said:

(1) "Allah Mighty and Majestic sent me as a guidance and mercy to believers and commanded me to do away with musical instruments, flutes, strings, crucifixes, and the affair of the pre-Islamic period of ignorance."

r40.1 (ابن حجر الهيتمي :) أمـا ذم المعـازف والمـزامير والأوتار ونحوها مما جاء عن الصـادق المصـدوق الـذي لا ﴿ينطق عن الهوى إن هو إلا وحي يوحى﴾ فليحـذر الـذين يخـالفـون عن أمـره أن تصيبهم فتنة أو يصيبهم عذاب أليم . ـ [عن أبي أمامة رضي الله عنه قال :] قال رسـول الله ﷺ : «إن الله عز وجـل بعثني هدىً ورحمـةً للمـؤمنين وأمرني بمحق المعـازف والمـزامير والأوتـار والصليب وأمر الجاهلية . . . » [رواه أبو داود] . ـ [وعن أنس رضي الله عنه أن رسول الله ﷺ قال :] «من قعـد إلى قينـة يستمع منها صب الله في أذنيه الآنك يوم القيامة»

(2) "On the Day of Resurrection, Allah will pour molten lead into the ears of whoever sits listening to a songstress."

(3) "Song makes hypocrisy grow in the heart as water does herbage."

(4) "This Community will experience the swallowing up of some people by the earth, metamorphosis of some into animals, and being rained upon with stones." Someone asked, "When will this be, O Messenger of Allah?" and he said, "When songstresses and musical instruments appear and wine is held to be lawful."

(5) "There will be peoples of my Community who will hold fornication, silk, wine, and musical instruments to be lawful...."

All of this is explicit and compelling textual evidence that musical instruments of all types are unlawful (*Kaff al-ra'a' 'an muharramat al-lahw wa al-sama'* (y49), 2.269–70).

r40.2 (Nawawi:) It is unlawful to use musical instruments—such as those which drinkers are known for, like the mandolin, lute, cymbals, and flute—or to listen to them. It is permissible to play the tambourine at weddings, circumcisions, and other times, even if it has bells on its sides. Beating the kuba, a long drum with a narrow middle, is unlawful (*Mughni al-muhtaj ila ma'rifa ma'ani alfaz al-Minhaj* (y73), 4.429–30).

SINGING UNACCOMPANIED BY MUSICAL INSTRUMENTS

r40.3 (Ibn Hajar Haytami:) As for listening to singing that is not accompanied by instruments,

[رواه ابن صصرى في أماليه وابن عساكر في تاريخه].

ـ [وعن ابن مسعود رضي الله عنه أن النبي ﷺ قال:] «الغناء ينبت النفاق في القلب كما ينبت الماء البقـل» [رواه البيهقي وابن أبي الدنيا].

ـ [وعـن سهـل بن سعـد قال: قال رسول الله ﷺ:] «يكون في هذه الأمة خسف ومسخ وقذف. قيل: ومتى ذلك يا رسـول الله؟ قال: إذا ظهـرت القينـات والمعازف واستحلت الخمر» [رواه عبد بن حميد واللفظ له وابن ماجه مختصراً، ومدار مسانيدها على عبد الرحمن بن زيد بن أسلم وهـو ضعيف. وصح من طرق خلافاً لما وَهَم فيه ابن حزم فقد علقه البخـاري ووصله الإسمـاعيلي وأحمـد وابن ماجه وأبو نعيم وأبو داود بأسانيد صحيحة لا مطعن فيها، وصححه جماعة آخرون من الأئمة كما قاله بعض الحفاظ أنـه ﷺ قال:] «ليكـونن في أمتي أقوام يستحلون الحر والحرير والخمر والمعازف» .

وهـذا صريح ظاهر في تحريم جميع آلات اللهـو المطربـة [محـرر من كف الرعاع عن محرمات اللهو والسماع: ٢/ ٢٦٩ ـ ٢٧٠].

r40.2 (النـووي:) ويحرم استعمال آلـة من شعار الشربة كطنبور وعود وصنج ومزمار [عراقي] واستماعها. ويجوز دفّ لعرس وختان، وكذا غيرهما [في الأصح] وإن كان فيـه جلاجـل. ويحرم ضرب الكـوبة وهي طبل طويـل ضيق الـوسط [نقل من مغني المحتاج إلى معرفة معاني ألفاظ المنهاج: ٤/ ٤٢٩ ـ ٤٣٠].

حكم الغناء من غير آلة

r40.3 (ابن حجر الهيتمي:) (أمـا) سماع مجرد الغناء من غير آلة: اعلم [أن

one should know that singing or listening to singing is offensive except under the circumstances to be mentioned in what follows. Some scholars hold that singing is sunna at weddings and the like, and of our Imams, Ghazali and 'Izz ibn 'Abd al-Salam say that it is sunna if it moves one to a noble state of mind that makes one remember the hereafter. It is clear from this that all poetry which encourages good deeds, wisdom, noble qualities, abstinence from this-worldly things, or similar pious traits such as urging one to obey Allah, follow the sunna, or shun disobedience, is sunna to write, sing, or listen to, as more than one of our Imams have stated is obvious, since using a means to do good is itself doing good (*Kaff al-ra'a' 'an muharramat al-lahw wa al-sama'* (y49), 2.273).

مذهبنا] أنه يكره الغناء وسماعه إلا أن يقترن به ما يأتي . وقال بعض العلماء أنه سنة في العرس ونحوه . وقـال الغـزالي وابن عبـد السـلام من أئمتنـا أنـه سنة إن حرك لحـال سني مذكـر للآخرة اهـ . وبه يعلم أن كل شعر فيه الأمر بالطاعة أوكان حكمة أوكان في مكارم الأخلاق أو الزهد ونحـو ذلـك من خصـال البـر كحث على طاعة أو سنة أو اجتناب معصية يكون كل من إنشـائـه وإنشـاده وسمـاعـه سنة كما صرح به غير واحد من أئمتنا هو ظاهر ، إذ وسيلة الطـاعة طاعة [نقل من كف الرعاع عن محرمات اللهو والسماع : ٢/ ٢٧٣].

DANCING

الرقص

r40.4 (Nawawi: (n: with commentary by Muhammad Shirbini Khatib)) It is not prohibited to dance ((Shirbini:) which is not unlawful because it is only motions made while standing or bowing. Furani and others have expressly stated that neither is it offensive, but rather is permissible, as is attested to by the hadith related in the *Sahih*s of Bukhari and Muslim that the Prophet (Allah bless him and give him peace) stood before 'A'isha (Allah be well pleased with her) to screen her from view so that she could observe the Abyssinians sporting and dancing)—unless it is languid, like the movements of the effeminate (*Mughni al-muhtaj ila ma'rifa ma'ani alfaz al-Minhaj* (y73), 4.430).

r40.4 (النـووي (ت : بشرح محمد الشـربيني الخطيب) :) [ويَحْرُمُ ضربُ الكـوبـة] لَا الرقصُ (فلا يحرم لأنه مجرد حركات على استقامة أو اعوجاج ولا يكره كمـا صرّح به الفـوراني وغيـره بل يبـاح لخبـر الصحيحين : «أنه ﷺ وقف لعائشة رضي الله عنهـا يسترهـا حتى تنظر إلى الحبشـة وهم يلعبـون ويـزفنون» إلّا أنْ يَكُـونَ فيـهِ تكَسُّرٌ كفعل المخنثِ [محرر من مغني المحتاج إلى معرفة معاني ألفاظ المنهاج : ٤/ ٤٣٠].

*

BOOK S

DELUSIONS

CONTENTS:

s1.0 THOSE DELUDED BY THIS WORLD, ALLAH'S FORGIVENESS, OR THEIR OWN WORKS

s1.1 (Ibn Qudama Maqdisi (dis: q0.1):) There are people misled by this world, saying, "Cash is better than credit: this world is cash while the next world is credit." And it is a point of deception, for cash cannot be better than credit unless the amount of each is equal. Now a person's life, when compared to the hereafter, obviously does not amount to even a thousandth part before he breathes his last, while someone who says that "cash is better than credit" means "provided the credit equals the cash." And this is the delusion of unbelievers. As for those immersed by sin while their faith in eternal truths remains sound, they share this delusion with unbelievers, by preferring the present life to the hereafter, but their lot is easier than the unbelievers' in that their basic faith will keep them from unending punishment.

THOSE DELUDED BY ALLAH'S FORGIVENESS

s1.2 Other sinners delude themselves by saying, "Allah is generous, we but rely on His forgiveness," while the learned tell us that if one longs for something one pursues it, and if one fears something one shuns it. Whoever hopes for forgiveness while persisting in wrongdoing is

s1.0 من يغتــر بالــدنيــا أو بعفو الله أو بالعمل الصالح

s1.1 (ابن قدامة:) من النــاس من غرّه الــدنيا فقال: النقد خير من النسيئة والــدنيــا نقــد والآخرة نسيئة. وهذا محل التلبيس، فإن النقــد لا يكــون خيــر من النسيئة إلا إذا كان مثل النسيئة. ومعلوم أن عمر الإنسان بالإضافة إلى مدة الآخرة ليس بجــزء من ألف جزء إلى أن ينقطــع النفس، وإنمــا أراد من قال النقد خير من النسيئة إذا كانت النسيئة مثل النقد. وهذا غرور الكفار. فأما ملابسو المعاصي مع سلامة عقائدهم، فإنهم قد شاركوا الكفار في هذا الغرور، لأنهم آثروا الدنيا على الآخــرة، إلا أن أمــرهم أسهل من أمر الكفار، من جهة أن أصل الإيمان يمنعهم من عقاب الأبد.

من يغتر بعفو الله

s1.2 ومن العصاة من يغتر فيقول: إن الله كريم، وإنمــا نتكــل على عفوه [وربمــا اغترّوا بصلاح آبائهم] وقد قال العلمــاء: من رجــا شيئاً طلبه، ومن خاف شيئــاً هرب منه، ومن رجا الغفــران مع

deluded. One must know that Allah Most High, with His vast mercy, is terrible in retribution, having decreed that unbelievers shall abide in hell forever (dis: w55) even though their unbelief does not hurt Him in the slightest. He has made some of His servants prey to infirmities and trials in this world, though He, Glorious and Exalted, is quite able to eliminate them. Moreover, He has made us fear His punishment. How can we not be afraid? Fear and hope drive and arouse one to action. That which does not spur one to works is deception, as is clear from the fact that the "hope" of most people makes them do nothing at all or prefer disobedience. It is odd that early Muslims both worked and feared, while nowadays, though falling far short, people feel secure and tranquil as though they knew more about the generosity of Allah Most High than the prophets and the righteous. If it could be had by wishing, why did the latter fatigue themselves and weep so much? Does Allah condemn the Jews and Christians for anything besides being this way when He says,

"They grasp at the paltry things of this low life and say, 'We shall be forgiven' " (Koran 7:169).

This delusion resembles that of people who do both good and evil, but more of evil, while imagining their good to be greater. One might see them give a dirham as charity while having wrongfully appropriated many times that amount, or maybe even giving as charity something wrongfully acquired, relying on such a donation, which is like someone putting a dirham in one scalepan, a thousand in the other, and hoping the scale will balance. Or another of them who thinks his good acts are more than his evil ones, the reason for which is that he keeps track of the number of good deeds, but does not take himself to task for the bad ones, nor consider his sins. For example, he says, "Astaghfir Allah" (May Allah forgive me) and "Subhan Allah" (Glory be to Allah) a hundred times a day, but then spends the rest of his day slandering Muslims and making ugly remarks, seeing the virtue of saying "Subhan Allah" and "Astighfir Allah," but not the punishment for slander and forbidden speech.

الإصـرار فهـو مغـرور . وليعلم أن الله تعالى مع سعة رحمته شديد العقاب ، وقد قضى بتخليـد الكفار في النار ، مع أنه لا يضـره كفـرهم ، وقـد سلط الأمـراض والمحن على خلق من عباده في الـدنيا ، وهـو سبحانه قادر على إزالتها ، ثم خوفنا من عقـابه فكيف لا نخاف؟ فالخـوف والـرجـاء سائقان يبعثان على العمل ، وما لا يبعث على العمل فهـو غرور . يوضح هذا أن رجـاء أكثـر الخلق يحملهم على البطالة وإيثار المعاصي . والعجب أن القرن الأول عملوا وخافوا ، ثم أهل هذا الـزمـان أمنوا مع التقصير واطمأنـوا ، أتـراهم عرفوا من كرم الله ما لم يعرف الأنبياء والصالحون؟ ولو كان هذا الأمر يدرك بالمـنى ، فلمَ تعب أولئـك وكثـر بكاؤهم؟ وهل ذم أهل الكتاب بقوله :

﴿يَأْخُذُونَ عَرَضَ هذا الأَدْنَى وَيَقُولُونَ سَيُغْفَرُ لَنَا﴾ [الأعراف : ١٦٩]إلا لمثل هذا الحال؟

[. . .] ويقرب من هذا الغرور غرور أقـوام لهـم طاعـات ومعـاصي ، إلا أن معاصيهم أكثـر ، وهم يظنون أن حسناتهم ترجـح ، فتـرى الـواحـد منهم يتصدق بدرهـم ويكـون قد تنـاول من الغصب أضعاف ذلك ، ولعل الذي تصدق به من المغصوب ، ويتكل على تلك الصدقة ، وما هو إلا كمن وضع درهماً في كفة وألفاً في أخـرى ، ثم رجا أن يرجح الـدرهم بألف . ومنهم من يظن أن طاعاته أكثر من معـاصيـه وسبب ذلـك أنه يحفظ عدد حسنـاته ولا يحاسب نفسه على سيئاته ، ولا يتفقـد ذنـوبـه ، كالـذي يستغفر الله ويسبحه مائة مرة في اليوم ثم يظل طول نهـاره يغتاب المسلمين ، ويتكلم بمـا لا يُرْضَى ، فهـو ينظر في فضائـل التسبيح والاستغفار ، ولا ينظـر في عقـوبـة الغية والكلام المنهي عنه .

s1.3   Delusions generally occur among four kinds of people: Islamic scholars, devotees, would-be Sufis, and the wealthy.

s1.3 ويقـع الاغترار في الأغلب في حَق أربعـة أصنـاف: العلمـاء، والعبّـاد والمتصوفة، والأغنياء.

*

s2.0   THE DELUSIONS OF ISLAMIC SCHOLARS

s2.0   غرور أهل العلم

THOSE REMISS IN OUTWARD CONDUCT

من أهمل الطاعة الظاهرة

s2.1   As for religious scholars, some master the legal and rational sciences but neglect to examine their outward habits and practices, not keeping their external self from sin or making it faithful in obedience. They are deluded by their learning and feel sure they rate high with Allah. If they were to look with the eye of insight, they would see that the whole point of knowing about religious practice is to apply it. Without works, it is useless. Allah Most High says,

"He who purifies it [the soul] has succeeded" (Koran 91:9),

not, "He who knows how to purify it has succeeded." If the Devil reminds such a person of the virtues of learned people, let the person for his part remember what has reached us about corrupt scholars, such as Allah's saying,

"... like a donkey laden with books" (Koran 62:5).

s2.1   فأمـا أهل العلم [...] منهم فـرق أحـكمـوا العلوم الشـرعيـة والعقلية، وأهملوا تفقـد الجـوارح وحفظهـا عن المعـاصي، وإلزامها الطاعات، واغتروا بعلمهم، وظنوا أنهم من الله بمكان. ولو نظـر هؤلاء بعين البصيرة علمـوا أن علم المعـاملة لا يراد به إلا العمـل، ولـولا العمل لم يكن له قدر. قال الله تعالى: ﴿قَـدْ أَفْلَحَ مَنْ زَكَّاهَا﴾ [الشمس: ٩] ولم يقـل قد أفلح من تعلم كيف يزكيهـا. فإن تلا عليـه الشيطـان فضائل أهل العلم فليـذكـر ما ورد في العالم الفاجر [...] كقوله تعالى: ﴿كَمَثَـلِ الحِمَـارِ يَحْمِـلُ أَسْفَـاراً﴾ [الجمعة: ٥].

THOSE WHO NEGLECT THEIR INWARD FAULTS

من أهمل العيوب الباطنة

s2.2   Others master religious learning and its outward performance, but do not examine their hearts to eliminate the blameworthy traits therein such as pride, envy, ostentation, and seeking exaltation or fame. These have made their exterior seemly while neglecting their interior, forgetting the words of the Prophet (Allah bless him and give him peace),

s2.2   ومنهم فرقـة أخـرى أحكمـوا العلم والعمـل الظـاهـر، ولم يتفقـدوا قلوبهم ليمحوا الصفات المذمومة منها، كالكبـر والحسـد والـريـاء وطلب العلو وطلب الشهرة، فهـؤلاء زينـوا ظاهرهم وأهملوا بواطنهم، ونسوا قوله ﷺ:

"Allah does not look at your appearance or property, but only at your hearts and works."

Such people apply themselves to works but do not apply themselves to hearts, though the heart is the real foundation, since no one is saved

"except he who comes to Allah with a pure heart" (Koran 26:89).

They resemble someone who sows grain that comes up with weeds choking it out, but when ordered to weed it, merely trims away the weeds' twigs and stems, neglecting the roots, which take stronger hold.

Another segment of scholars know that these inner qualities are condemnable, but out of self-satisfaction feel they are above them, and that they are too good as far as Allah is concerned for Him to afflict them with such traits, that only common people have them and not people at their own level of learning. When symptoms of arrogance or avidness for leadership appear in such people, one of them may say, "This is not arrogance, but only seeking to exalt Islam, display the nobility of religious learning, and to spite those given to reprehensible innovations. Were I to wear clothes less fine or sit with a lower class of people, the enemies of religion would smirk, and gloat at my humiliation, which amounts to humiliating Islam." And he forgets about delusion, and that it is Satan who has seduced him with this, which is plain from the fact that the Prophet (Allah bless him and give him peace) and his Companions were humble in manner and preferred the way of poverty and lowliness.

Still other scholars have acquired religious knowledge, purified their exterior actions, making them seemly with obedience, and examined their hearts, purifying them of ostentation, envy, pride, and the like, and yet there remain snares of the Devil and tricks of the ego hidden in the recesses of their hearts which they have failed to notice and thus neglected. You might see one of them spending the night and day in learning various religious sciences, organizing them, and polishing up their terminology, such a person thinking his motive is the desire to manifest the religion of Allah Most High, while the real motive

«إن اللــه لا ينظــر إلـى صوركــم وأموالكم، وإنما ينظر إلى قلوبكم وأعمالكم».

فتعاهــدوا الأعمــال، ولم يتعــاهــدوا القلوب، والقلب هو الأصـل، إذ لا ينجو ﴿إلَّا مَنْ أَتَى اللَّهَ بِقَلْبٍ سَلِيمٍ﴾ [الشعراء: ٨٩].

ومثال هؤلاء كمثـل رجـل زرع زرعاً فنبت ونبت معـه حشيش يفسـده، فأمر بقلعه، فأخذ يجز رؤوسه وأطرافه ويترك أصوله، فلم تزل أصوله تقوى.

وفرقة أخرى علموا أن هذه الأخلاق الباطنة مذمومة إلا أنهم بعجبهم بأنفسهم يظنون أنهم منفكون عنهـا، وأنهم أرفع عنـد الله من أن يبتليهم بذلـك، وإنمـا يبتلي بذلـك العوام دون من بلغ مبلغهم من العلم، فإذا ظهر عليهم مخايل الكبر والـريـاسـة قال أحدهم: ما هذا بكبـر، وإنما هو طلب عز الدين، وإظهار شرف العـلم، وإرغام المبتـدعين، فإني لو لبست الـدون من الثياب، وجلست في الـدون من المجـالس شمتت بي أعـداء الـديـن وفرحـوا بذلِـي، وفي ذلي ذل الإسـلام، وينسى الغـرور وأن إبليس هو الـذي سول له هذا بدليـل أن النبي ﷺ وأصحابه كانوا يتواضعون ويؤثرون الفقر والمسكنة [. . .].

وفرقة أخرى أحكموا العلم، وطهروا جوارحهم وزيَّنـوهـا بالطاعات، وتفقدوا قلوبهم بتصفيتهـا من الـريـاء والحسد والكبـر ونحـو ذلك ولكن بقيت في زوايا القلب خفايا مـن مكـائد الشيطان وخدع النفس لم يفطنـوا لهـا وأهملوهـا، فتـرى أحدهم يَسهر ليله ويُنصب نهاره في جمع العلوم وتـرتيبهـا وتحسين ألفاظها، ويرى أن باعثه على ذلك الحرص على إظهار دين الله تعالى، وربما كان الباعث لذلك

might be to make a name for himself and enhance his prestige. Perhaps too, his published work is not entirely free of self-praise, whether overtly, by wide, sweeping claims, or covertly, by attacks on others, to show by attacking them that he is better than they are and more knowledgeable. Such kinds of behavior and similar ones are hidden faults which few discern but the wisest and strongest. Those as weak as we are have little hope of doing so, but at least a person should be aware of his own defects and wish they were corrected. There is hope for someone whose good acts make him happy and wicked ones make him sad, unlike someone who applauds himself and thinks himself the best of men.

s2.3   The above are the delusions of those who master important branches of Sacred Knowledge. How then for those who content themselves with studying fields not essential to them, neglecting the important ones?

THEOLOGICAL POLEMICISTS

s2.4   Among them are those who busy themselves with theological polemics against heretical beliefs, and refuting the unorthodox. Scholars engaged in this are of two types, those in the wrong and those in the right, the former advocating something other than the sunna, the latter advocating the sunna. Both are deluded. The misguidedness of those in the wrong is obvious (A: since they have left the Koran and sunna which are divinely protected). As for those in the right, their delusion is in believing that arguing is the most important activity and greatest spiritual work in the religion of Allah Most High. They maintain that one's religion is not complete until one has made lengthy investigations into one's beliefs, and that someone who simply believes in Allah and His messenger without preparing a case for it is deficient in faith. Because of this mistaken presumption, they spend their lives learning how to dispute, conducting in-depth studies of statements of theological controversies until their spiritual insight eventually goes blind. They do not pause

طلب الــذكـر وانتشار الصيت . ولعله لا يخلو في تصنيفه من الثناء على نفسه إما صريحاً بالـدعـاوي الطـويلة العريضة ، وإما ضمناً بالطعن في غيره ليبين في طعنه في غيـره أنـه أفضل من ذلك الغير وأعظم منـه علماً . فهذا وأمثاله من خفايا العيوب التي لا يفطن لها إلا الأكياس الأقوياء ولا مطمـع فيـه لأمثالـنـا من الضعفاء ، إلا أن أقل الـدرجـات أن يعرف الإنسان عيوب نفسه ويحرص على صلاحها . ومن سرته حسنته وساءته سيئته ، فهو مرجو أمره ، بخلاف من يزكي نفسه ويظن أنه من خيار الخلق .

s2.3   فهـذا غرور الــذيـن حصلوا العلوم المهمة ، فكيف بالـذين قنعوا من العلوم بما لا يهمهم وتركوا المهم .

غرور أهل الكلام والمجادلة

s2.4   فمنهم [. . .] فرقـة [. . .] اشتغلوا بعلم الكـلام والمجـادلـة في الأهـواء والرد على المخالفين . ثم هؤلاء طائفتـان : ضالـة ومحقة ، فالضالة التي تدعو إلى غير السنة ، والمحقة التي تدعو إلى السنة ، والغرور شامل لجميعهم . أما الضالة فاغترارهـا ظاهـر . وأما المحقة فاغتـرارها من حيث أنها ظنت أن الجدال أهم الأمور ، وأفضل القربـات في دين الله تعالى ، وزعمت أنه لا يتم لأحد دينه ما لم يبحث ، وأن من صدق الله ورسوله من غيـر تحـرير دليـل ، فليس بكـامـل الإيمـان ، فلهذا الظن الفـاسـد قطعـوا أعمـارهم في تعلم الجـدل والبحث عن المقـالات ، وعميت بصائرهم فلم يلتفتوا

to consider that the early Muslims, whom the Prophet (Allah bless him and give him peace) testified were the very best of mankind, and who lived to see many a reprehensible innovation (bid'a) and deviant belief, did not expose themselves and their religion to quarrels and disputation, or busy themselves therein at the expense of their hearts and works. They did not talk about it at all, except under necessity to refute misguidance. And if they saw someone persisting in blameworthy innovation, they had nothing more to do with him, without further debate or argument. The hadith has reached us,

"No people went astray after having been guided save that they were afflicted with arguing."

SERMONIZERS

s2.5   Others spend their time in homilies to people, the highest class of whom speak about traits of the self and qualities of the heart such as fear, hope, patience, gratitude, reliance on Allah, abstinence, certainty, and sincerity; thinking that by merely speaking of them, even if they do not have them, they acquire them. Such people call to Allah while they themselves flee from Him. They are among the most deluded. And some of them turn from the proper way of exhorting others to relating baseless tales, adding words that are neither acceptable to Sacred Law nor to human intelligence, in an attempt to say something novel.

LEARNING HADITH FOR THE SAKE
OF MAKING A REPUTATION

s2.6   Others spend their time in listening to hadiths, gathering variants and rare chains of transmission or chains remarkable for having come through but few transmitters of advanced years. The concern of one of them is to go from city to city, seeing sheikhs in order to drop names, saying, "I relate from So-and-so," "I've met So-and-so," or "I know chains of transmission no one else does."

إلى القــرن الأول ، وأن النبي ﷺ شهــد لهم بأنهم خيـر الخلق ، وأنهم قد أدركـوا كثيــراً من البــدع والهـوى ، فلم يجعلوا أعمــارهم ودينهم غرضــاً للخصومـات والمجــادلات ، ولم يشتغلوا بذلـك عن تفقـد قلوبهم وجوارحهم ، بل لم يتكلموا فيــه إلا لضــرورة رد الضــلال ، فإن رأوا مصراً على بدعته هجروه من غير ممــاراة ولا جدل . وقـد روي في الحـديث : «مـا ضل قوم بعد هُدىً إلا أوتوا الجدل» .

غرور الوعاظ

s2.5   وفرقة أخرى اشتغلوا بالوعظ وأعلاهم رتبة من يتكلم في أخلاق النفس وصفــات القلب من الخــوف والـرجــاء والصبر والشكـر والتوكل والزهد واليقين والإخلاص ، وهم يظنون أنهم إذا تكلموا بهذه الصفات وهم منفكون عنها أنهم من أهلهــا ، فهــؤلاء يدعــون إلى الله وهم هاربــون منـه ، فهم أعظم النـاس غرة . ومن هؤلاء من يعدل عن المنهاج الواجب في الوعظ إلى الشطح وتلفيق كلام خارج عن قانون الشرع والعقل طلباً للإغراب .

غرور أهل الحديث

s2.6   [. . .] ومنهم فرقـة استغرقوا أوقـاتهم في سمــاع الحـديث ، وجمـع روايـاته ، وأسانيده الغريبة والعالية ، فهَمُّ أحدهم أن يدور البــلاد ، ويرى الشيوخ ليقــول : أنــا أروي عن فلان ، ولـقيت فلاناً ، ولي من الأسناد ما ليس لغيري .

غرور علماء اللغة

s2.7   Others devote their time to advanced studies in Arabic grammar, lexicography, and poetry, claiming they are the scholars of the Islamic Community, dissipating their lives in subtleties of grammar and diction. If they stopped to think, they would realize that someone who wastes his lifetime in the knowledge of the language of the Arabs is like someone who wastes it in knowledge of the language of the Turks. Arabic is only distinguished above the latter in that the Sacred Law has come in it. As for lexicology, there are only two areas in which it is necessary for one to gain an understanding of rare words: those of the Koran, and those of the hadith. As for grammar, one but needs enough to use the language properly.

s2.7   ومنهم فرقة اشتغلوا بعلم النحو واللغة والشعر، وزعموا أنهم علماء الأمة، وأذهبوا أعمارهم في دقائق النحو واللغة، ولو عقلوا لعلموا أن مضيّع عمره في معرفة لغة العرب كالمضيّع عمره في معرفة لغة الترك وإنما فارقتها لغة العرب لأجل ورود الشريعة بها، فيكفي من اللغة علم الغريبين: غريب القرآن، والحديث، ومن النحو ما يقوّم به اللسان [. . .].

s2.8   The really fortunate person is he who takes of each thing the amount that is critical to him and then goes on to apply it, putting his effort behind it and purifying it of imperfection. And this is the real aim.

s2.8   والسعيد من أخذ من كل شيء من هذا حاجته المهمة لا غير، وتجاوز إلى العمل، واجتهد فيه وفي تصفيته من الشوائب فهذا هو المقصود [. . .].

*

s3.0   THE DELUSIONS OF DEVOTEES

s3.0   غرور أرباب التعبد

s3.1   Devotees are of various types, including those remiss about obligatory acts while engaging in extra devotions and supererogatory works.

s3.1   وهم فرق. فرقة أهملوا الفرائض واشتغلوا بالنوافل والفضائل.

s3.2   Sometimes they are so worried about using water for purification that it reaches the level of obsessive doubt (waswasa) about the validity of their ablution. You might see one of them unsatisfied with water the Sacred Law deems fit for ablution, imagining remote possibilities that it could be affected with something unclean, while not having such concern for the lawfulness of the source of the food he eats. Were he to reverse these two, applying the care he takes for the water

s3.2   وربما تعمقوا في استعمال الماء حتى خرجوا إلى الوسوسة في الوضوء، فترى أحدهم لا يرضى بالماء المحكوم له بالطهارة شرعاً، بل يقدر له الاحتمالات البعيدة في التنجس، ولا يقدر ذلك في مطعمه. فلو انقلب هذا الاحتياط من الماء إلى المطعم لكان أشبه

instead to his food, he would be closer to the practice of the early Muslims. 'Umar (Allah be well pleased with him) performed ablution from the water jar of a Christian despite signs that it might well be unclean, while he used to refrain from many kinds of permissible things for fear of falling into the unlawful.

بسيـر السلف ، فإن عمـر رضي الله عنـه توضأ من جرة نصرانية مع ظهور احتمال النجاسـة ، وكـان مع هذا يدع أنواعاً من الحلال خوفاً من الوقوع في الحرام [. . .] .

s3.3   Others are so bedeviled by inner misgivings at their initial Allahu Akbar in the prayer that they may miss a rak'a with the imam. And like them are those with obsessive doubts about the proper pronunciation of the letters of the Fatiha and other spoken elements of the prayer. One of them may take precaution upon precaution in doubling the doubled letters, distinguishing ض from ظ,   and so forth, beyond the necessary, until he is finally so concerned about it that he does not think about anything else, neglecting the meaning of the Koran and the lessons he should be taking from it. And this is among the ugliest forms of delusion, for people are not required to pronounce the letters when reciting the Koran with more precision than that with which classical Arabic is normally spoken. Such people are as if delivering a message to a ruler, the messenger fastidiously pronouncing each letter and repeating those he is unsatisfied with, having quite forgotten the purpose of the message and the dignity of the assembly before whom he is delivering it. How richly such a person deserves to be thrown out and taught a lesson.

s3.3   ومنهـم من غلبـت عليـه الـوسوسة في تكبيرة الإحرام في الصلاة ، حتى ربما فاتتـه ركعـة مع الإمام . ومنهم من يتوسوس في إخراج حروف الفاتحة وسائر الأذكار من مخـارجها ، فلا يزال يحتـاط في التشديدات والفرق بين الضاد والظاء فوق الحـاجة ، ونحو ذلك بحيث يهتم بذلـك حتى لا يتفكـر فيمـا سواه ، ويـذهل عن معنى القرآن والاتعـاظ به . وهذا من أقبح أنواع الغرور فإن الخلق لم يتكلفـوا من تحقيق مخـارج الحروف في تلاوة القرآن إلا ما جرت به العادة في الكلام .
ومثـال هؤلاء مثـال من حمل رسالة إلى سلطـان ، فأخـذ يؤدي الرسالة بالتأنق في مخارج الحروف وتكراره ، وهو غافل عن مقصود الرسالة ومراعاة حرمة المجلس ، فما أحراه بالطرد والتأديب .

s3.4   A third group is deluded by reciting the Koran, which they rush through, perhaps finishing twice a day, the tongue of one of them being occupied therein while his heart is wandering through the valleys of daydream, not reflecting on its meanings, heeding its exhortations, or obeying its ordinances and prohibitions. Such a person is misled, believing the Koran is only intended for reciting. He is like someone to whom his master has written a letter charging him with certain matters and forbidding him others, while the servant does not bother the understand it or carry it out but simply memorizes it and repeats it, thinking that this is the purport of it, while violating the

s3.4   وفرقـة أخـرى اغتـروا بقـراءة القرآن ، فهم يهـذُّونه هذاً ، وربما ختموا في اليوم مرتين ، فلسان أحدهم يجري به وقلبـه يتـردد في أودية الأماني ، ولا يتفكر في معـاني القرآن ولا يتعظ بمواعظه ، ولا يقف عند أوامره ونواهيه فهذا مغرو يظن أن المقصـود من القـرآن التـلاوة فقط . ومثـال ذلك ، مثـال عبـد كتب إليه مولاه كتابـاً يأمره فيه وينهاه ، فلم يصرف عنايته إلى فهمـه والعمـل به ، بل اقتصـر على حفظه وتكراره ، ظاناً أن ذلك هو المراد منـه ، مع مخالفته أمر مولاه ونهيه . ومنهم

master's commands and prohibitions. Others relish the sound of their own voice in reciting the Koran, disregarding its significance. One should examine one's heart as to whether one is enjoying the meter, the sound, or the meaning (A: though it is not blameworthy to enjoy the meter or sound, unless one is unconcerned with the meaning).

من يلتـذ بصـوتـه بالقـرآن ، معـرضـاً عن معـانيه ، فينبغي أن يتفقد قلبه فيعرف هل التذاذه بالنظم ، أو بالصوت ، أو بالمعاني .

s3.5   Others are deceived by fasting, and frequently practice it, but do not restrain their tongue from slander and useless words, keep their belly from ill-gotten or unlawful food with which to break their fast, or free their heart from ostentation.

s3.5   وفـرقـة أخـرى اغترّوا بالصوم وأكثروا منـه ، وهم لا يحفظـون ألسنتهم عن الغيبـة والفضـول ، ولا بطـونهم من الحرام عند الإفطار ، ولا خواطرهم عن الرياء .

s3.6   Others are deluded by going on pilgrimage, departing for it without restoring the rights of people they have wronged (dis: p77.3), meeting their financial obligations, asking the permission of their parents, or obtaining lawfully gotten provision. And this may be after having fulfilled the obligatory hajj, while they neglect obligatory acts of worship enroute, are unable to purify their garments and person, and do not refrain from unpermitted sex or getting into arguments, despite which they think all is well with them, being self-deceived.

s3.6   ومنهـم من اغتـر بالحـج ، فيخرج إليه من غير خروج عن المظالم ، وقضـاء الـديـون واستـرضـاء الـوالدين ، وطلب الـزاد الحـلال ، وقد يفعلون ذلك بعـد سقوط فرض الحج ويضيعـون في الطـريق [العبـادة و] الفرائض ويعجـزون عن طهـارة الثوب والبدن ، ولا يحترزون من الـرفث والخصـام ، وهم مع ذلـك يظنون أنهم على خير وهم مغرورون .

s3.7   Others command the right and forbid the wrong, while forgetting themselves.

s3.7   وفـرقـة أخـرى أخذوا في الأمر بالمعروف والنهي عن المنكر ، ونسوا أنفسهم .

s3.8   Others include the imam who leads the group prayer at the mosque, but when someone more godfearing or knowledgeable is allowed to lead in his stead, it weighs heavily on him. Or the muezzin who calls to the prayer, believing he is doing it for the sake of Allah, but when someone else gives the call in his absence, it annoys him and he says, "He has infringed on my position."

s3.8   ومنهم من يؤم في مسجـد ولو تقدم عليه أورع منه وأعلم ثقل عليه . ومنهم من يؤذن ويظن أن ذلـك لله ، ولـو أذن غيـره في غيبـته ، اشتد عليه ذلك وقال : قد زاحمني في مرتبتي [. . .] .

s3.9   Others eschew material possessions, content with poor clothes and food and with living in mosques, thinking that they have reached the rank of the abstinent (zuhhad), while they are avid

s3.9   وفـرقـة أخـرى زهـدت في الـمـال ، وقـنعت بالـدون من اللبـاس والطـعـام ، وقـنـعـت من الـمـسكـن

for leadership and prestige. In fact, they have given up the lesser of two matters while getting involved in the more deadly.

s3.10   Still others enthusiastically perform supererogatory acts while not being concerned for the obligatory ones. You may see one of them savoring the midmorning or night vigil prayer, but finding no satisfaction in the prescribed prayer, nor hastening to pray it at the first of its time. Such a person has forgotten the Prophet's words (Allah bless him and give him peace) relating that Allah Mighty and Majestic said,

"Those near to Me do not approach Me with anything like that which I have made obligatory upon them."

s3.11   There is no spiritual labor without its dangers, and those who do not know them fall prey to them. Whoever wishes to learn them should study the dangers of ostentation that exist in acts of worship, from fasting and prayer to all the rest, in the chapters set forth in this book (A: i.e. Ibn Qudama's source here, Ghazali's *Ihya' 'ulum al-din*).

*

s4.0   THE DELUSIONS OF WOULD-BE SUFIS

s4.1   The deluded among them are of various types. Some are deluded by the dress, terminology, or demeanor of the Sufis. They imitate the sincere Sufis (dis: w9) externally, but do not tax themselves with spiritual struggle or self-discipline. Rather, they pounce upon and quarrel over wealth that is unlawful, doubtful, or from rulers (dis: p32.3), rending each other's honor whenever they are at cross-purposes. The delusion of these is obvious. They are like an old woman who hears that the names of courageous, valiant soldiers are

بالمســاجـد، فظنت أنهــا أدركت رتبـة الـزهاد، وهم مع هذا شديدو الرغبة في الرياسة والجاه، فقد تركوا أهون الأمرين وباؤوا بأعظم المهلكين.

s3.10   وفرقـة أخرى حرصت على النـوافـل ولم تعتن بالفـرائض، فتـرى أحـدهم يفرح بصلاة الضحى وصلاة الليل، ولا يجد للفريضة لذة ولا يحرص على المبـادرة إليهـا في أول الـوقت، وينسى قوله ﷺ فيما يرويه عن ربه عز وجل:

«ما تقرّب المتقربون إليَّ بمثل أداء ما افترضت عليهم» [. . .].

s3.11   ومـا من عمـل إلا وفيـه آفـات فمن لم يعرفها وقع فيها، ومن أراد أن يعرفها، [فلينظـر في كتابنا هذا]، فينظر في آفات الرياء الحاصل في العبادات من الصـوم والصـلاة وفي جميع القربات في الأبواب المرتبة في هذا الكتاب.

s4.0   غرور المتصوفة

s4.1   والمغـرورون منهم فرق. فرقـة منهم اغتروا بالزي والنطق والهيئة، فتشبهوا بالصادقين من الصوفية بالظاهر، ولـم يتـعبـوا أنفسهم في المجـاهـدة والـرياضة. ثم هم يتكالبون على الحرام والشبهـات وأمـوال السـلاطين ويمـزق بعضهم أعـراض بعض إذا اختلفـوا في غرض، وهؤلاء غرورهم ظاهر. ومثالهم مثـال عجـوز سمعـت أن الـشجعـان

inscribed in the official roster and they are ceded whole tracts of land. Feeling a longing within herself, she dons hauberk and helmet, learns a few heroic stanzas and the details of their apparel and characteristics, and then sets out for the camp. Her name is duly entered in the lists, but when she reports for inspection, she is ordered to take off the helmet and armor to see what is underneath, and to be tried in combat. When she complies, it turns out that she is a feeble old crone, and she is told, "You only came to mock the king and his court!—Take her away and throw her under the elephant's feet." And she is flung under it to be trampled.

Thus will be the state of pretenders to Sufism on the Day of Judgement, when they stand revealed and are brought before the Supreme Judge, who looks at hearts, not patched clothes or Sufi dress.

والأبطال من المقاتلين تثبت أسماؤهم في الديوان، ويقطع كل واحد منهم قطراً من أقطار الأرض، فاشتاقت نفسها إلى ذلك فلبست درعاً ووضعت على رأسها مغفراً، وتعلمت من رَجَز الأبطال أبياتاً، وتعلمت زيهم وجمع شمائلهم، ثم توجهت إلى العسكر، فكتب اسمها في ديوان الشجعان، فلما حضرت في ديوان العرض، أمرت بتجريد المغفر والدرع لينظر ما تحته وتمتحن بالمبارزة. فلما جردت إذا هي عجوز ضعيفة زمنة، فقيل لها: جئت تستهزئين بالملك وأهل حضرته، خذوها وألقوها بين يدي الفيل، فألقيت إليه.

فهكذا يكون حال المدعين التصوف في القيامة إذا كشف عنهم الغطاء، وعرضوا على الحاكم الأكبر الذي ينظر إلى القلب لا إلى المرقعات والزي.

s4.2   Others claim to have attained to gnosis and contemplative knowledge of the Divine, to have passed through spiritual stations and states, and to have reached nearness to Allah, while they know nothing of any of this except the words. You might see one of them reiterating these terms, thinking it above the combined learning of the first and last, and looking with condescension upon the scholars of Sacred Law, hadith, and other disciplines, to say nothing of ordinary Muslims. Sometimes a common person will keep their company for many days, picking up these artificial phrases and parroting them as if he were speaking divine revelation, with sneering contempt for scholars and worshippers, saying that they are veiled from Allah (A: which could be true, though saying it by way of self-praise is very wrong) while he has attained to the Truth, and that he is one of those brought near to Allah—while Allah considers him a debauched hypocrite, and the transformed ones know him to be an ignorant fool who has not acquired sound knowledge, perfected his character, or kept watch over his heart, but merely pursued his own fancy and memorized a lot of gibberish.

s4.2   وفرقة أخرى ادعت علم المعرفة، ومشاهدة الحق، ومجاوزة المقامات والأحوال، والوصول إلى القرب، ولا يعرفون من تلك الأمور إلا الأسماء. فترى أحدهم يرددها ويظن أن ذلك أعلى من علم الأولين والآخرين، فهو ينظر إلى الفقهاء والمحدثين وأصناف العلماء بعين الازدراء، فضلاً عن العوام. حتى إن بعض العامة يلازمهم الأيام الكثيرة، ويتلقف منهم تلك الكلمات المزيفة، ويرددها كأنه يتكلم عن الوحي، ويحتقر في ذلك جميع العلماء والعباد، ويقول: إنهم محجوبون عن الله وإنه هو الواصل إلى الحق، وإنه من المقربين، وهو عند الله من الفجار المنافقين، وعند أرباب القلوب من الحمقى الجاهلين، لم يُحكم علماً ولم يهذّب خلقاً، ولم يراقب قلباً سوى اتباع الهوى وحفظ الهذيان.

s4.3   Others roll up and put away the carpet of the Sacred Law, rejecting its rulings and considering the unlawful and the lawful to be equal, saying, "Allah does not need my works, so why should I bother?" One of them may say, "Outward devotions have no value, only hearts mean anything. Our hearts are aflame with the love of Allah Most High, and we have attained to gnosis of Him. If we are bodily immersed in this world, yet our hearts are in worshipful seclusion in the presence of the Divine. Outwardly we may give in to our desires, but not in our hearts." They claim to have surpassed the rank of the common people, beyond the need to school the lower self with physical devotions, and that gratifying bodily lusts does not divert them from the path of Allah Most High because of their firmness therein. They exalt themselves above the level of the prophets (upon whom be peace) who used to weep for years over a single mistake.

s4.3 وفرقة منهم طووا بساط الشرع، ورفضوا الأحكام، وسووا بين الحلال والحرام، وبعضهم يقول: إن الله مستغن عن عملي فلِمَ أتعب نفسي؟ وبعضهم يقول: لا قدر للأعمال بالجوارح، وإنما النظر إلى القلوب، وقلوبنا والهمة بحب الله تعالى، وواصلة إلى معرفته، فنحن مع الشهوات بالظواهر لا بالقلوب، ويزعمون أنهم قد ترقوا عن رتبة العوام، واستغنوا عن تهذيب النفس بالأعمال البدنية، وأن الشهوات لا تصدهم عن طريق الله تعالى لقوتهم فيها ويرفعون أنفسهم عن درجة الأنبياء، لأن الأنبياء عليهم السلام كانوا يكون على خطيئة واحدة سنين.

s4.4   (n: As no age is without pretenders to Sufism, the following texts will hopefully be useful in letting some principal Sufis describe in their own words the delusions of those who consider themselves "above the Sacred Law.")

s4.5   (Ibn 'Ajiba:) Someone said to Junayd, "There is a group who claim they arrive to a state in which legal responsibility no longer applies to them." "They have arrived," he replied, "but to hell" (*Iqaz al-himam fi sharh al-Hikam* (y54), 210).

s4.5   (ابن عجيبة:) الجنيد [رضي الله عنه . . .] قيل له إن جماعة يزعمون أنهم يصلون إلى حالة يسقط عنهم التكليف. قال: وصلوا ولكن إلى سقر [محرر من إيقاظ الهمم في شرح الحكم: ٢١٠].

s4.6   (Ghazali:) When anyone claims there is a state between him and Allah relieving him of the need to obey the Sacred Law such that the prayer, fasting, and so forth are not obligatory for him, or that drinking wine and taking other people's money are permissible for him—as some pretenders to Sufism, namely those "above the Sacred Law" (ibahiyyun) have claimed—there is no doubt that the imam of the Muslims or his representative is obliged to kill him. Some hold that executing such a person is better in Allah's sight than killing a hundred unbelievers in the path of Allah Most High (*Hashiya al-Shaykh Ibrahim al-Bajuri* (y5), 2.267).

s4.6   (الإمام الغزالي:) لو زعم زاعم أن بينه وبين الله حالة أسقطت عنه التكليف بحيث لا يجب عليه الصلاة ولا الصوم ونحوهما وأحلت له شرب الخمر وأكل أموال الناس، كما زعمه بعض من يدعي التصوف وهم الإباحيون فلا شك في وجوب قتله على الإمام أو نائبه بل قال بعضهم قتل واحد منهم أفضل عند الله من قتل مائة حربي في سبيل الله تعالى [نقل من حاشية الباجوري على ابن قاسم: ٢/ ٢٦٧].

s4.7   (Muhyiddin ibn al-'Arabi:) When we see someone in this Community who claims to be able to guide others to Allah, but is remiss in but one rule of the Sacred Law—even if he manifests miracles that stagger the mind—asserting that his shortcoming is a special dispensation for him, we do not even turn to look at him, for such a person is not a sheikh, nor is he speaking the truth, for no one is entrusted with the secrets of Allah Most High save one in whom the ordinances of the Sacred Law are preserved (*Jami' karamat al-awliya* (y95), 1.3).

s4.8   (Sheikh Ahmad al-'Alawi:) The friend of Allah (wali) is not divinely protected from error, for which reason he is to be feared for and his word is not to be relied upon when it exceeds what has been conveyed by the sunna concerning matters of the afterlife, because he is suspended from making any new provisions in the Sacred Law, and in respect to the prophets (upon whom be peace) he is not a guide. He is only entitled to believe what the Lawgiver has informed of.

"Today I have perfected your religion for you and completed My favor upon you, and I please that Islam be your religion" (Koran 5:3).

The gnostic in the first of his states is strongly affected by the initial impact, and will sometimes try to take on a discussion of the affairs of the afterlife, as opposed to the final state, in which he may be so quiescent that an unknowing observer might assume its strength had waned, though this is rather the result of his perfection and firmness in his station. It has been said that the way begins in madness, proceeds to arts, and ends in quietude. So one is obliged, whenever one's rapture subsides, to return to what the Lawgiver has stated, without personal figurative interpretations. This is why our author says, "Faith is incisive," meaning that one cuts the self short whenever it wants eminence and elevation. The gnostic's spiritual will, exalted above all else, must carry him beyond what we have just mentioned. For he is outside our phenomenal frame of reference and all it contains, and whenever he wants to speak about things of the afterlife his words are high, unintel-

س4.7   (محيي الدين بن العربي:) إذا رأينا مَن يدعي في هذه الأمة مقام الدعاء إلى الله تعالى على بصيرة ويخل بأدب من آداب الشريعة ولو ظهر عليه من خرق العوائد ما يبهر العقول ويقول إن ذلك أدب يخصه لا نلتفت إليه وليس بشيخ ولا محق فإنه لا يؤمن على أسرار الله تعالى إلا من يحفظ عليه آداب الشريعة [نقل من جامع كرامات الأولياء : ١ / ٣].

س4.8   (الشيخ أحمد العلوي:) والولي ليس بمعصوم فلهذا يخاف عليه ولا يعمل بمقاله أي فيما زاد على السنة من أحوال الآخرة لأنه محجور عليه في التشريع فهو غير مرشد بالنسبة للمرسلين عليهم السلام وليس له إلا الإيمان بما أخبر به الشارع .

﴿الْيَوْمَ أَكْمَلْتُ لَكُمْ دِينَكُمْ وَأَتْمَمْتُ عَلَيْكُمْ نِعْمَتِي وَرَضِيتُ لَكُمُ الْإِسْلَامَ دِينًا﴾ .

لأن العارف في ابتداء حاله تطرأ عليه قوة الابتداء حتى ربما يمد يده في أمور الآخرة بخلاف حالة الانتهاء فقد يسكن سكونًا تامًا حتى يظن الجاهل أنه نقص من حاله وكل ذلك من كماله ورسوخه في مقامه قد قيل إن الطريقة أولها جنون ووسطها فنون وآخرها سكون وعليه كلما سكنت روعته وجب عليه الرجوع فيما أخبر به الشارع بدون تأويل منه ولهذا قال الناظم الإيمان جزم أي يقطع نفسه كلما أرادت العلو والارتفاع لأن العارف يحمله عما ذكرنا علو همته عن الكل إذ هو خارج عن المظهر وما فيه وكلما أراد أن يتكلم بأحوال الآخرة يتكلم بكلام عال

ligible, and a source of trouble to both those who believe him and those who do not, which is why he is forbidden speech about it, and as much as he increasingly forgoes it, he increases in nearness to Allah and in safety. Sufis call this station *subsistence* (baqa'). Before a disciple is firmly established therein, it is to be feared that he will be overtaken by misfortune because of his lack of a foothold in the state of subsistence, a juncture that has been called "from annihilation to subsistence, or annihilation to perdition" (*al-Minah al-quddusiyya fi sharh al-Murshid al-mu'in bi tariq al-Sufiyya* (y8), 67–68).

غير معقـول فيكـون فتنة على من صدقه وعلى من لم يصدقه فلهذا منع من الكلام وكلمـا تنازل وازداد في التنازل ازداد قرباً من الله وأمناً وهـذا المقام هو المسمى عنــد القـوم بمقـام البقاء ويخاف على المـريد قبـل رسـوخه فيه أن يغلب عليه الشقاء لعـدم تمكنه من البقاء ولهذا يقال من الفناء للبقاء أو من الفناء للشقاء [نقل من المنح القـدوسية في شرح المـرشد المعين بطريق الصوفية : ٦٧ ـ ٦٨].

s4.9   ('Abd al-Karim Jili:) My brother, Allah have mercy on you, I have travelled to the remotest cities and dealt with all types of people, but never has my eye seen, nor ear heard of, nor is there any uglier or farther from the presence of Allah Most High than a certain group who pretend they are accomplished Sufis, claiming for themselves a lineal spiritual tradition from the perfected ones and appearing in their guise, while they do not believe in Allah, His messengers, or the Last Day, and do not comply with the responsibilities of the Sacred Law, depicting the states of the prophets and their messages in a manner that no one with a particle of faith in his heart can accept, let alone someone who has reached the level of those to whom the unseen is disclosed and who have gnostic insight. We have seen a great number of their luminaries in cities in Azerbaijan, Shirwan, Jilan, and Khurasan, may Allah curse them all (*Idah al-maqsud min wahdat al-wujud* (y98), 17–18).

s4.9   (عبـد الكـريم الجيلي :) يا أخي رحمـك الله قد سافـرت إلى أقصى البـلاد ، وعاشـرت أصناف العباد ، فما رأت عيني ولا سمعت أذني ، ولا أقبح ولا أبعـد عن جنـاب الله تعـالى من طائفة تدعي أنهـا من كُمَّل الصوفيـة وتنسب نفسها إلى الكُمَّل وتظهر بصورتهم ، ومع هذا لا تؤمـن باللـه ورسـله ولا باليـوم الآخـر ، ولا تتقيد بالتكـاليف الشرعيـة وتقرر أحوال الرسل وما جاءوا به بوجه لا يرتضيـه من في قلبـه مثقـال ذرة من الإيمـان ، فكيف من وصـل إلى مراتب أهـل الكـشف والعيـان ، ورأينـا منهم جمـاعـة كثيـرة من أكـابرهم في بلاد أذربيجان وشيروان وجيلان وخراسان ، لعـن اللـه جميعهم [نقـل من إيضـاح المقصود من وحدة الوجود : ١٧ ـ ١٨].

s4.10   The delusions of those "above the Sacred Law" are beyond number, all of it mistakes and inner suggestions with which the Devil has tricked them because of their having taken up spiritual struggle before they mastered the rules of the Sacred Law, and they did not connect themselves with a sheikh of learning and religion worthy of being followed (dis: w9.5–9).

s4.10   وأصنـاف غرور أهل الإباحة لا تحصى ، وكل ذلك أغاليط ووسـاوس خدعـهم الشـيطان بهـا لاشتغـالهم بالمجاهـدة قبل إحكام العلم ، من غير اقتـداء بشيخ صاحب علم ودين صالح للاقتداء به .

s4.11   Other students of Sufism proceed on the right path, engage in spiritual struggle, begin to

s4.11   ومنهم فرقـة أخـرى جاوزوا هذه الطـريـق ، واشتغلوا بالمجاهـدة

actually travel in the way, and the door of gnosis, contemplative knowledge of the Divine, opens to them. But when they sniff the first traces of this knowledge, it surprises them and they exult in it and are pleased by the strangeness of it, until their hearts become fettered with turning to it and thinking about it, and how it was disclosed to them but not others. And all of this is delusion, for the wonders met with in the path of Allah Glorious and Exalted are endless. If one stops with a particular marvel and becomes enamored with it, one's progress falters and one fails to reach the goal. Such a person is like someone going to see a king, who notices a garden at the palace gate with flowers in it, the like of which he has never seen, and who stops to look at them until there is no longer time to meet the king.

*

s5.0   THE DELUSIONS OF THE WEALTHY

s5.1   The deluded among the wealthy are of various types. Some of them eagerly build mosques, schools, hospices, aqueducts, whatever people can see, and write their names upon them to perpetuate their memory and keep it alive after their death, while if one of them were called upon to spend a single dinar on something that did not have his name on it, it would be a burden for him. If not for the fact that his aim is other people and not Allah Himself, this would not be so hard for him, as Allah is looking at him whether he writes his name or not.

Others spend money embellishing mosques with ornamentation and bas-reliefs, which are prohibited by Sacred Law and distracting to the people praying in them. The aim in prayer is humble awe and an attentive heart, while this ornamentation spoils the hearts of those praying. And if the money spent on such things is from an unlawful source to begin with, so much greater the delusion. Malik ibn Dinar (Allah have mercy on him) said, "A man came to a mosque, stopped at the entrance, and said, 'Someone like me does not

وابتـدؤوا بسلوك الطريق وانفتح لهـم بـاب المعـرفة، فلمـا استنشقـوا مبـادىء ريح المغـرفـة، تعجبـوا منهـا وفرحـوا بهـا وأعـجبهـم غريبهـا، فتقيـدت قلوبهم بالالتفـات إليهـا والتفكـر فيهـا، وكيفيـة انفتـاح بابهـا عليهم وانسـدادهـا عن غيـرهم، وكل ذلـك غرور لأن عجائـب طريق الله سبحـانـه وتعـالى، ليس لهـا نهـايـة. ولـو وقف مع كل أعجوبة وتقيد بهـا، قصرت خطـاه وأخرّه عن الوصول إلى القصـد وكـان مثـالـه مثـال من قصد ملكـاً، فرأى على بابه روضة فيها أزهار لم يكن رأى مثلها، فوقف ينظر إليها حتى فاته الوقت الذي يمكن فيه لقاء الملك.

s5.0   غرور أرباب الأموال

s5.1   وهـم فـرق. ففـرقـة منهـم يحرصون على بناء المساجد والمدارس والـربـاطـات والقنـاطـر وما يظهر للناس ويكتبون أسماءهم عليها ليتخلد ذكرهم، ويبقى بعـد المـوت أثـرهم، ولـو كلف أحدهم أن ينفق ديناراً ولا يكتب اسمه في المـوضـع الـذي أنفق عليـه لشق عليـه، ولولا أنه يريد وجه الناس لا وجه الله لما شق عليـه ذلـك، فإن الله يطلع عليـه، سواء كتب اسمه أو لم يكتبه.

وبعضهم يصـرف المـال في زخرفـة المسجـد وتزيينه بالنقوش التي هي منهي عنها وشاغلة للمصلين، فإن المقصود من الصـلاة الخشـوع وحضور القلب، وذلك يفسد قلوب المصلين. فأمّا إن كان المال الـذي صرفه في ذلك حراماً كان أشد في الغـرور. قال مالك بن دينار رحمه الله: أتى رجـل مسجـداً فوقف على البـاب وقـال، مثلي لا يدخـل بيت الله، فكتب

enter a house of Allah'—for which he was accorded the rank of those with perfect faith (siddiq)." And this is how we should revere mosques, by seeing them as defiled by our entering them with our self as bad as it is, an affront to them; not by seeing to their defilement with the unlawful and with this-worldly embellishment, trying to outdo Allah Most High. The delusion of someone who does this is in thinking the wrong to be right.

في مكـانـه صديقاً. فبهذا ينبغي أن تعظم المسـاجد، وهو أن يرى تلويث المسجد بدخوله فيه بنفسه جناية على المسجد، لا أن يرى تلويـث المسجـد بالحـرام، أو بزخرف الدنيا منه على الله تعالى، فغرور هذا من حيث أنه يرى المنكر معروفاً.

s5.2   Others protect their money, holding fast to it with the tight fist of greed, and then occupy themselves with bodily works of worship that do not cost much, like fasting, prayer, or reciting the whole Koran. They are deluded, for stinginess is deadly (dis: p75.25) and has taken over their heart. They need to rid themselves of it by spending of their wealth, but are too busy with supererogatory works to do so. They are like someone who, when a snake has entered his clothes, sets about cooking up a syrup of vinegar and honey to reduce his bile.

s5.2   وفرقة أخرى يحفظون الأموال ويـمسـكـونهـا بخـلاً، ثم يشتغلون بالعبـادات البدنية التي لا تحتاج إلى نفقة المـال، كالصيام والصـلاة وختم القرآن وهم مغرورون لأن البخـل مهلك، وقد استولى على قلوبهم، فهم محتاجون إلى قمعه بإخراج المـال، فقـد اشتغلوا عنه بفضائـل لا تجب عليهم. ومثـالهم مثال من دخلت في ثوبه حيّة، فاشتغـل عنها بطبخ السكنجبين لتسكن به الصفراء.

s5.3   There are others whose selfishness will not let them give anything but zakat. One of them may pay out the worst property he has, or give it to those of the poor who are useful to him, vacillating between which of his ulterior motives can best be served, or as to whom he may have use for in the future or is "good for something" in particular. Another may deliver his zakat to a prominent public figure so he will consider him to be someone and later fulfill his needs. And all of this invalidates the intention, the person who does it being deluded by wanting recompense from others for worshipping Allah Most High.

s5.3   ومنهم من لا تسمـح نفسـه إلا بأداء الـزكـاة فقـط، فيخـرج الـرديء من المـال، أو يعطي من الفقراء من يخدمه، ويتـردد في حاجاته، أو من يحتاج إليه في المستقبل أو من فيه غرض. ومنهم من يسلم من ذلـك إلى بعض الأكابر ليفرفه، لينال بذلـك عنده منزلة ويقوم بحوائجه، وكل ذلك مفسد للنية وصاحبه مغرور لأنه يطلب بعبادة الله تعالى عوضاً عن غيره.

s5.4   Some wealthy people and others are deluded by frequenting circles of *dhikr* (remembrance of Allah), thinking that merely attending them will take the place of works and of a sober look at the afterlife, though it is not so, for circles of *dhikr* are only commendable in that they motivate one to do good. And anything that is a means to something else is pointless if it does not achieve

s5.4   وفـرقـة أخرى من أربـاب الأمـوال وغيـرهم، اغتـروا بحضـور مجـالس الذكر، وظنوا أن نفس الحضور يغنـيهم عن العمـل والاتعـاظ، وليس كذلك لأن مجلس الذكر إنما فُضّل لكونه مرغباً في الخير، وكل ما يراد لغيره إذا لم

it. When one of them hears something that creates fear of divine punishment, he says nothing more than, "O Protector, keep us safe," or "I take refuge in Allah," thinking he has done all that is necessary. He is like a sick person who comes to a group of doctors to hear what is happening. Or a hungry person who visits someone who can describe delicious food to him, and then leaves. It does not do him much good. And likewise with hearing acts of obedience described without applying them: every admonition that does not change something within one that affects one's actions is a case against one.

*

s6.0   REMEDYING DELUSIONS

s6.1   If it be objected that I have not mentioned a single action which is free of delusion, the reply is that the matter of the afterlife hinges upon one thing alone: straightening out one's heart. And no one is incapable of it except someone whose intention is insincere. If a person were as concerned about the next world as this one, he would certainly achieve it. The early Muslims did so, and so have those who have followed them in excellence.

Three things can be used to help rid oneself of delusions:

(1) intelligence, the real light by which a person sees things as they are;

(2) knowledge, through which a person knows himself, his Lord, his this-worldly life, and the life to come;

(3) and learning, by which we mean learning how to travel the way to Allah Most High, the pitfalls therein, and learning what will bring one nearer and guide one, all of which may be found in this book (dis: s3.11(A:)).

When a person has done all this, he should be wary lest the Devil beguile him and make him desirous for leadership, or lest he feel secure from

يوصـل إلى ذلك الغير فلا وقع له . وربما سمـع أحـدهم التخويف، فلا يزيد على قولـه : يا سلام سلم ؛ أو: أعـوذ بالله ؛ ويظن أنـه قد أتى بالمقصـود . ومثال هذا كمثـل مريض يحضـر عند الأطباء فيسمع ما يجري، أو الجـائـع يحضـر عنـد من يصف له الأطعمة اللذيذة ثم ينصرف فلا يغني ذلك عنـه . فكـذلك سماع وصف الطـاعات دون العمل بها، فكل وعظ لم يغير منك صفة تتغير بها أفعالك فهو حجة عليك .

s6.0   معالجة الغرور

s6.1   فإن قيـل : فمـا ذكـرت من مداخـل الغرور أمراً لا يكاد يخلص منه ؛ فالجواب : أن مدار أمر الآخرة على معنى واحـد، وهو تقويم القلب، ولا يعجز عن ذلك إلا من لم تصدق نيته، فإن الإنسان لو اهتم بأمـر الآخرة كما اهتم بأمر الدنيا لـنالهـا . وقـد فعل ذلك السلف الصالح ومن تبعهم بإحسان .

ويستعـان على التخلص من الغرور بثلاثة أشياء :

ـ العقل وهو النور الأصلي الذي يدرك به الإنسان حقائق الأشياء .

ـ المعرفة التي يعرف بها الإنسان نفسه وربه ودنياه وآخرته .

[. . .] ـ والـعـلم، نعـني به الـعـلم بكيفيـة سلوك الطـريـق إلى الله تعـالى وآفـاتهـا، والعلم بمـا يقربه منه ويهديه، وجميع ذلك في كتابنا هذا .

[. . .] وإذا فعل جميع ذلك ينبغي أن يكون خائفاً أن يخدعه الشيطان، ويدعوه إلى الـرياسة ويخاف عليه أيضاً من الأمن

Allah's devising (def: p66). Fear should never be absent from the hearts of the friends (awliya') of Allah. We ask Allah to protect us from delusion and that we may end our lives well. Truly, He is near and answers supplications (*Mukhtasar Minhaj al-qasidin* (y62), 237–50).

من مكر الله تعالى . [. . .] فلا ينبغي أن يفـارق الخوف قلوب الأولياء أبداً . نسأل الله تعـالى السـلامة من الغرور، وحسن الخـاتمـة، إنـه قريب مجيب [محرّر من مختصر منهاج القاصدين: ٢٣٧ – ٢٥٠].

*

BOOK T

A PURE HEART

كتاب القلب السليم

CONTENTS:

---

t1.0 INTENTION, SINCERITY, AND BEING TRUE

INTENTION

t1.1 (Nawawi:) Allah Most High says,

"Whoever leaves home to emigrate to Allah and His messenger but whom death overtakes: paying his recompense falls to Allah" (Koran 4:100).

The Prophet (Allah bless him and give him peace) said:

t1.0 النية والإخلاص والصدق

النية

t1.1 (النووي:) قال الله تعالى:
﴿وَمَنْ يَخْرُجْ مِنْ بَيْتِهِ مُهَاجِراً إِلَى اللّٰهِ وَرَسُولِهِ ثُمَّ يُدْرِكْهُ المَوْتُ فَقَدْ وَقَعَ أَجْرُهُ عَلَى اللّٰهِ﴾ [النساء: ١٠٠].
[وروينا عن أمير المؤمنين عمر بن الخطاب رضي الله عنه قال: سمعت] رسول الله ﷺ يقول: «إِنَّما الأعمال

"Works are only according to intentions, and a man only receives what he intends. Whoever's emigration was to Allah and His messenger has truly emigrated to Allah and His messenger; and whoever's emigration was for worldly gain or to wed a woman, his is for that to which he emigrated."

This is a hadith whose authenticity Bukhari and Muslim agree upon, and there is complete scholarly consensus on the greatness of its rank and majesty. It is one of the cornerstones, fundamental supports, and most important integrals of faith. Imam Shafi'i (Allah have mercy on him) said it enters into seventy chapters of jurisprudence. He also said it constitutes one-third of Sacred Knowledge.

SINCERITY (IKHLAS)

t1.2   Allah Most High says:

(1) "Nor were they commanded save to worship Him, sincere to Him in their religion" (Koran 98:5).

(2) "So worship Allah with sincerity" (Koran 39:2).

t1.3   The Master Abul Qasim Qushayri (Allah have mercy on him) said: "Sincerity is to make Allah one's sole aim in acts of obedience, meaning to intend by one's obedience to draw nearer to Allah Most High and nothing else, whether hypocrisy before others, acquiring esteem in their eyes, love of their praise, or anything besides drawing nearer to Allah. One could say that sincerity is purifying the mind from paying attention to one's fellow creatures."

t1.4   Abu 'Uthman (Allah have mercy on him) said, "Sincerity it to forget to regard men by continuously regarding their Maker." He also said, "The sincerity of ordinary people is that which is

بالنِّيَّات وإِنَّما لكـل امرىء ما نوى فمن كانت هجرته إلى الله ورسوله فهجرته إلى الله ورسولـه ومن كانت هجرتـه لدنـيا يُصيبها أو امـرأة ينكحها فهجـرته إلى ما هاجر إليه».

وهـو حديث صحيح متفق على صحته مجمـع على عظم موقعـه وجـلالتـه وهـو إحـدى قواعـد الإيمان وأول دعائمه وآكد الأركـان. قال الشـافعي رحمه الله يدخل هذا الحـديث في سبعين بابـاً من الفقـه: وقال أيضاً هو ثلث العلم.

الإخلاص

t1.2   قال الله تعالى:
﴿وَمَا أُمِرُوا إِلَّا لِيَعْبُدُوا اللَّهَ مُخْلِصِينَ لَهُ الدِّينَ﴾ [البينة: ٥].
وقال تعالى:
﴿فَاعْبُدِ اللَّهَ مُخْلِصاً﴾ [الزمر: ٢].
.[...]

t1.3   وعن الأسـتـاذ أبي القـاسم القـشيـري رحمـه الله [في رسـالتـه المشهـورة] قال: الإخـلاص إفراد الحق في الطاعـة بالقصـد وهو أن يريد بطاعته التقرب إلى الله تعالى دون شيء آخر من تصنـع لمخلوق أو اكتسـاب محمدة عند النـاس أو محبة مدح من الخلق أو شيء سوى التقرب إلى الله تعالى قال ويصح أن يقـال الإخـلاص تصفيـة العقـل عن ملاحظة المخلوقين. [...].

t1.4   وعن أبي عثمـان رحمـه الله قال: الإخلاص نسيان رؤية الخلق بدوام النظـر إلى الخـالـق. [...] وعن أبي

free of self-interest, while the sincerity of the elect is that which comes over them, not from them, for acts of worship appear in them from which they are at a remove, and neither observe nor consider" (*al-Majmu'* (y108), 1.16–17).

t1.5 (Nawawi:) Abu Yazid (Allah Most High be well pleased with him) said:

"For twelve years I was the blacksmith of my soul; for five, the mirror of my heart; for one year I observed what was between them, and, lo, around my waist I found the girdle of unbelief (zunnar) in plain view. So I worked for five years at cutting it, seeking a way to dissever it, until at length this was revealed to me and looking at mankind, I saw them as dead and prayed a fourfold Allahu Akbar over them."

Sufficient to show the subtlety of the hiddenness of ostentation is the difficulty with which this master recognized it, who had few equals in this path. As for his remark "I saw them as dead," it is of the greatest worth and excellence, words that express this meaning being seldom met with outside those of the Prophet (Allah bless him and give him peace). What it signifies is that when he underwent this spiritual struggle and his lower self became trained and his heart enlightened, when he had mastered the self, subdued it, taken full possession of it, and made it submit in everything, he looked at all creatures and found them as if dead, without discoverable trait. They could not harm or benefit, bestow or keep back, give life or death, join or separate, bring close or make far, save or damn, give sustenance or withhold it; they possessed neither benefit nor harm to themselves, neither life nor death, nor resurrection. Now, the dead are dealt with, regarding these things, as deceased, and they are not feared, nor are hopes placed in them, nor does desire arise for what they have. We do not do anything for their sake, refrain from anything for their sake, or forgo any act of obedience to Allah for their sake, any more than we would to win the praise of the dead. They are not shown-off in front of, their favor is not

عثمـان قال : إخـلاص العوام ما لا يكون للنفس فيـه حظ وإخـلاص الخـواص ما يجري عليهم لا بهم فتبدو منهم الطاعات وهم عنها بمعزل ولا يقع لهم عليها روية ولا بها اعتداد [محرر من المجموع : ١/ ١٦ ـ ١٧ ؛ بتقديم وتأخير] .

t1.5 (النـووي :) قال أبـو يزيـد رضي الله تعـالى عنـه : كنت ثنتي عشـرة سنـة حداد نفسـي ، وخمس سنين كنت مرآة قلبي ، وسنةً أنظر فيما بينهما فإذا في وسطي زنـار ظاهـر . فعملت في قطعـه خمس سنين أنظـر كيف أقطـع ، فكُشِفَ لي فنظـرت إلى الـخلق فرأيتهم موتى ، فكبرت عليهم أربع تكبيرات [...].

[قلت :] يكفي في شدة خفـاء الريـاء اشتبـاهه هذا الاشتبـاه على هذا السيـد الـذي عز نظيـره في هذا الطريق . وأمـا قوله : فرأيتهم موتى ؛ فهـو في غـاية من النفـاسة والحسن قل ما يوجـد في غـير كلام النـبي ﷺ كلام يحصـل معنـاه [...]. فمعنـاه أنـه لمـا جاهـد هذه المجـاهـدة ، وتهـذبت نفسه ، واستنـار قلبـه ، واستـولى على نفسه وقهـرهـا ، وملكها ملكـاً تامـاً ، وانقـادت له انقيـاداً خالـصـاً ، نظـر إلى جميـع المخلوقين فوجدهم موتى لا حكَمَ لهم . فلا يضرون ولا ينفعون ، ولا يعطون ولا يمنعون ، ولا يحيـون ولا يميتـون ، ولا يَصِلون ولا يقطعـون ، ولا يقـربون ولا يبعدون ، ولا يسعـدون ولا يشقـون ، ولا يرزقـون ولا يحرمون ، ولا يملكون لأنفسهم نفعاً ولا ضراً ، ولا يملكـون موتـاً ولا حيـاة ولا نشـوراً . وهـذا صفـة الأموات أن يعاملوا معاملة الموتى في هذه الأمور المذكورة ، وأن لا يُخافـوا ولا يُرجَـوا ولا يطمع فيما عنـدهم [...] ، ولا نفعل شيئاً لهم ، أو نتركه لهم ، ولا نمتنع من القيام بشيء من طاعات الله بسببهم ولا نمتنع من ذلك بسبب الميت فنكترث بمدحهم [...]. ولا يراءوا ولا يداهنـوا ، أو يُشتغـل بهم ،

sought through flattery or compromise of principles, and they do not occupy one's attention. They are not held in contempt or disparaged; their defects are unmentioned, their shameful points unsought out, their mistakes uncriticized; though if penalties prescribed by Sacred Law are incurred, we enforce them. In short, they are as though nonexistent in everything we have mentioned, the decisions of Allah Most High holding sway over them. Whoever deals with them accordingly has attained to the good of this world and the next. May Allah Most Generous give us success in realizing it (*Bustan al-'arifin* (y104), 131–34).

ولا يحتقروا ولا ينتقصوا، ولا تُذكر عيوبهم، ولا تُتبع عثراتهم، ولا ينقب عن زلاتهم [. . .] مع أنا نقيم عليهم ما جاء الشرع به من الحدود [. . .] فالحاصل أنهم كالعدم في جميع ما ذكرناه [فهم مدبّرون] تجري فيهم أحكام الله تعالى. فمن عاملهم هذه المعاملة جمع خير الآخرة والدنيا. نسأل الله الكريم التوفيق لذلك [محرّر من بستان العارفين: ١٣١ ـ ١٣٤؛ بتقديم وتأخير].

BEING TRUE (SIDQ)

الصدق

t1.6   (Nawawi:) As for being true, Allah Most High says,

t1.6   (النووي:) وأما الصدق فقال الله تعالى:

"O you who believe, fear Allah, and be with those who are true" (Koran 9:119).

﴿يَا أَيُّهَا الَّذِينَ آمَنُوا اتَّقُوا اللَّهَ وَكُونُوا مَعَ الصَّادِقِينَ﴾ [التوبة: ١١٩].

t1.7   Sahl ibn 'Abdullah Tustari said, "The servant who compromises his principles, for himself or another, will never catch even a scent of being true."

t1.7   [وروينا عن] سهل بن عبد الله التستري قال: لا يشم رائحة الصدق عبد داهن نفسه أو غيره. [. . .].

t1.8   It is related that Harith al-Muhasibi (Allah have mercy on him) said: "A person who is true would not care if his whole value vanished from the hearts of men for the sake of bettering his heart. He does not like people seeing the smallest bit of his good acts, and does not mind their noticing the worst of them, for to be otherwise would show he wants to be more in their eyes, and this is out of character for those of great faith (siddiqin)."

t1.8   وعن الحارث [بن أسد] المحاسبي [بضم الميم] رحمه الله قال: الصادق هو الذي لو خرج كل قدر له في قلوب الخلق من أجل صلاح قلبه ولا يحب اطلاع الناس على مثاقيل الذر من حسن عمله ولا يكره اطلاعهم على السيء من عمله لأن كراهته ذلك دليل على أنه يحب الزيادة عندهم وليس هذا من أخلاق الصديقين. [. . .].

t1.9   Dhul Nun al-Misri (Allah have mercy on him) said: "Truth is the sword of Allah. Whatever it is put to, it cuts" (*al-Majmu'* (y108), 1.17).

t1.9   وعن ذي النون رحمه الله قال: الصدق سيف الله ما وضع على شيء إلا قطعه [محرر من المجموع: ١/ ١٧؛ بتقديم وتأخير].

*

| t2.0 A LETTER TO ONE OF THE BRETHREN | t2.0 كتاب لبعض الإخوان |

t2.1   (Ibn 'Ata' Illah:) I know of nothing more useful to you than four matters: surrender to Allah, to humbly entreat Him, to think the best of Him, and to perpetually renew your repentance to Him, even if you should repeat a sin seventy times in a day.

t2.1   (ابن عطاء الله :) وبعد، فلا أرى شيئاً أنفع لك من أمور أربعة : الاستسلام إلى الله، والتضرع إليه، وحسن الظن به، وتجديد التوبة إليه ولو عدت إلى الذنب في اليوم سبعين مرة .

SURRENDER TO ALLAH

الاستسلام لله تعالى

t2.2   Surrender to Him gives you relief in the present life from having to plan while He does, triumph in the next life through the supreme favor, and safety from the idolatry of contention, for how should you contend with Him for something you do not own with Him? Cast yourself amidst His kingdom, meager in its plentitude and insignificant in its vastness, and He will plan for you as He does for it. Do not leave the slavehood that is yours for claims to a lordship that you have no claim to. To plan and choose for oneself are enormities with respect to hearts and inmost souls, as you find it the Book of Allah Most High where Allah says:

t2.2   ففي الاستسلام إليه الراحةُ من التدبير معه عاجلاً والظفر بالمنة العظمى آجلاً، والسلامةُ من الشرك بالمنازعة، ومن أين لك أن تنازعه فيما لا تملك معه، وألق نفسك في مملكته فإنك قليل في كثيرها، وصغير في كبيرها، يدبّرك كما يدبّرها . فلا تخرج عما هو لك من العبودية إلى ما ليس لك من ادعاء وصف الربوبية . فإن التدبير والاختيار من كبائر القلوب والأسرار وتجد ذلك في كتاب الله تعالى، قال الله تعالى :

"Your Lord creates whatever He wills and chooses, and they do not have a choice. Glory be to Allah above what they associate with Him" (Koran 28:68).

﴿وَرَبُّكَ يَخْلُقُ مَا يَشَاءُ وَيَخْتَارُ مَا كَانَ لَهُمُ الْخِيَرَةُ سُبْحَانَهُ وَتَعَالَى عَمَّا يُشْرِكُونَ﴾ [القصص : ٦٨] .

EARNESTLY ENTREATING ALLAH

التضرع إلى الله تعالى

t2.3   As for earnestly entreating Allah, in it lies the coming of increase, lifting of hardships, enwrapment in mantles of divine gifts, and safety from affliction. One is repaid for it in times of hardship by the Master's undertaking one's protection, and in times of ease by His seeing to one's gain. It is the greatest threshold and straightest way. It is effectual despite unbelief, so how could it be ineffectual with faith? Have you not heard the words of Allah Most High:

t2.3   وأما التضرع إلى الله تعالى ففيه نزولُ الزوائد، ورفعُ الشدائد، والانطواءُ في أردية المنن والسلامة من المحن، فتُعَوَّضُ جزاءَ ذلك أن يتولَّى مولاك الدفع عن نفسك في المضار والجلب لك في المسار . وهو الباب لك في المسار . وهو الباب الأعظم، والسبيل الأقوم، تؤثر مع الكفران، فكيف لا يؤثر مع الإيمان؟ ألم تسمع قوله تعالى :

"And when you are touched by affliction at sea, those to whom you pray besides Him are lost, but when He delivers you to shore, you turn away. Surely man is an ingrate" (Koran 17:67)

﴿وَإِذَا مَسَّكُمُ الضُّرُّ فِي الْبَحْرِ ضَلَّ مَنْ تَدْعُونَ إِلاَّ إِيَّاهُ فَلَمَّا نَجَّاكُمْ إِلَى الْبَرِّ أَعْرَضْتُمْ وَكَانَ الإِنْسَانُ كَفُوراً﴾ [الإسراء: ٦٧].

—meaning that He answers you. Earnest entreaty is the door Allah Most High has placed between Himself and His servants. Gifts come to whomever betakes himself to it, and spiritual favors unceasingly reach whoever stands before it. Whoever enters unto Him by it attains to the reality of divine assistance. And whenever He releases unto you through it, He bestows of every good thing in the most lavish gift giving, as is found in the Book of Allah Most High where Allah says,

أي فأجابكم. وهو الباب الذي جعله الله تعالى بينه وبين عباده. تَرِدُ وارداتُ الألطاف على من توجّه إليه، وتتوالى المنن على من وقف به عليه. ويصل إلى حقيقة العناية من دخل منه إليه. ومتى فتح عليك به فتح عليك من كل خيراته وأوسع هباته، وتجد ذلك في كتاب الله تعالى قال الله تعالى:

"If only they had earnestly entreated Us when Our vengeance reached them" (Koran 6:43).

﴿فَلَوْلاَ إِذْ جَاءَهُمْ بَأْسُنَا تَضَرَّعُوا﴾ [الأنعام: ٤٣].

THINKING THE BEST OF ALLAH

حسن الظن بالله عز وجل

t2.4   As for thinking the best of Allah, how tremendous it is for whomever Allah has blessed with it. Whoever has it does not lack the slightest bit of good, and whoever lacks it will never find any. You will never have a better excuse to Allah than it, or one more profitable. Nor anything that better leads you to Allah or is more guidance giving. It informs one what Allah will make of one and gives good tidings the like of whose words no eye has ever read nor tongue given utterance to. This is found in the sunna of the Prophet (Allah bless him and give him peace), where he says, quoting Allah,

t2.4   وأما حسنُ الظن بالله فيخٍ بخٍ لمن منّ اللهُ عليه بها. فمن وجدها لم يفقد من الخير شيئاً، ومن فقدها لم يجد منه شيئاً. لا تجد لك عذراً عند الله أنفع لك منها ولا أجدَى. ولا تجدُ أدلَّ على الله منها ولا أهدى. تُعلمك عن الله بما يريد أن يصنعه معك، وتبشّرك بيشائرَ لا تقرأ سطورها العينان، ولا يترجم عنها اللسان. وتجد ذلك في سنة رسول الله ﷺ حاكياً عن الله: «أنا عند ظن عبدي بي».

"I am nigh to what My servant expects of Me."

CONTINUALLY RENEWED REPENTANCE

تجديد التوبة

t2.5   As for continually renewing one's repentance to Allah, it is the wellspring of every spiritual rank and station from first to last, inwardly and outwardly. There is no excellence in

t2.5   وأما تجديد التوبة إليه فهي عين كل رتبةٍ ومقام أوله وآخره، باطنه وظاهره، لا مزية لمن فقدها، ولا فقدَ

one who lacks it, and nothing lacking in one who has it. It is the key to every good, outwardly and inwardly, the very soul of stations of wisdom, and the reason men are made friends of Allah (awliya'). If the repentance of the Axis of the World (Qutb) were like that of the ordinary righteous person because of equality in station, the higher of them would not surpass the other for his exaltedness of rank and tremendousness of spiritual certainty. Allah Most Glorious and Exalted has not made any rank below it except that of wrongdoing, as Allah Most High says,

"Whoever does not repent, they are the wrongdoers" (Koran 49:11),

it being required from every messenger and prophet, every great-faithed one (siddiq) and friend of Allah (wali), every godfearing pious person, misguided profligate, and every doomed unbeliever. You may find this in the Book of Allah Most High where Allah Glorious and Exalted says,

"O people: fear your Lord" (Koran 4:1),

godfearingness being through repentance to Him and regret before Him. The repentance of those who do evil lies in abandoning it, while the repentance of those who do good lies in not halting with their good, whether it consists of spiritual effort or its rewards. The repentance of both is the same: not to stop at it.

"... the faith of your father Ibrahim. He has named you Muslims" (Koran 22:78).

It was of Ibrahim's faith not to halt with what passes away, or fix his regard on existent things. In quoting him to us, Allah Most High says,

"I love not things which pass away" (Koran 6:76).

t2.6 In general, someone who cannot benefit from a little will not benefit from a lot (A: since a lot of work does not avail without sincerity), and someone who cannot profit from a hint will not

لمن وجـدهـا ، مفتـاحُ كل خيرٍ ظاهرٍ وبـاطـن ، روحُ الـمـقـامـات وسبـبُ الـولايـات . ولـو استـوت تـوبـة القطب والصـالـح لاستـواء مقامهما لم يرتفع عنه رفيع المقام لرفعة شأنه ولعظيم إيقانه . لم يجعل الحق سبحانه وتعالى رتبة دونها إلا الظلمَ فقال سبحانه وتعالى :

﴿وَمَنْ لَمْ يَتُبْ فَأُولَئِكَ هُمُ الظَّالِمُونَ﴾ [الحجرات : ١١] .

فهـي مطـلـوبـة من كل رسـول ونبي وصـدّيق وولي وبـارٍ تقيّ ، وفاجر غويّ ، وكـافرٍ شقيّ ، وتجـد ذلك في كتاب الله تعالى ، قال الله سبحانه وتعالى :

﴿يَا أَيُّهَا النَّاسُ اتَّقُوا رَبَّكُمْ﴾ [النساء : ١] .

فتقـواه بالتـوبـة إليـه والندم بين يديه . فأهـل الـشـرور توبتهم بالخـروج من شرورهم ، وأهـل الخيـور توبتهم بعـدم الوقوف مع خيورهم ورْداً كانت أو واردا . كلاهما مع عدم الوقوف معهما واحدٌ .

«مِلَّةَ أَبِيكُمْ إِبْرَاهِيمَ هُوَ سَمَّاكُمُ الْمُسْلِمِينَ﴾ [الحج : ٧٨] .

وإن من ملة إبراهيم عدم الـوقوف مع الفـانيـات والانقطاع عن نظر الكائنات ، قال الله سبحانه وتعالى مخبراً عنه :

﴿لَا أُحِبُّ الْآفِلِينَ﴾ [الأنعام : ٧٦] .

t2.6 وبالجملة من لم ينفعه القليل لم ينفعـه الكثير ومن لم تنفعه الإشارة لم

profit from a plain remark. When Allah gives you understanding, your hearing will not cease nor your benefiting be restricted to a certain time. May Allah give us and you to understand Him, give us and you to hear Him, dissever us from everything besides Him, enter us into His shade and protection, and make us of those to whom He has given spiritual insight, guidance, and a yearning for His nearness. May He not scatter the intention of our hearts but rather center our purpose on Him, and remove our cares by bringing us to our destination. Ameen.

May there be safety for the whole group, and blessings and peace upon the Best of Messengers (*al-Hikam al-'Ata'iyya wa al-munajat al-ilahiyya* (y56), 103–9).

*

t3.0 COUNSELS AND MAXIMS

t3.1 (Muhammad Sa'id Burhani:) Do not limit yourself to deep words and profound spiritual allusions but make provision for the afterlife before death comes, when fine words will be lost and the rak'as you prayed by night or day will remain.

t3.2 Give voluntary charity as much as possible, for you owe more than merely the zakat obligatory. Make provision for the afterlife by giving while you have health and want to cling to your money out of fear of poverty, seeing life before you. Allah Most High says,

"Whoever is watchful against the stinginess of his own soul, those shall be the successful" (Koran 59:9),

meaning they shall be saved.

t3.3 Never obey anyone of Allah's servants, even father or mother, in an act of disobedience to Allah, for there is no obedience to a creature in disobedience to the Creator.

تنفـع فيـه العبـارة . وإذا أفهمك الله لم ينقطـع سمـاعُك ولم يتحيّن انتفـاعك . فهّمنـا اللهُ وإيّـاك عنه وأسمعنا وإيّاك منه وقطَعَنـا عن كل شيء سواه ، وأدخلنـا في كنفه وحماه ، وجعلنا ممن بَصّرَهُ وهداه ، وإلى كنفه آواه ، ولا شَتَّتَ قلوبنا ، وجمع عليه همـومنـا ، وأزال بالـوصول كروبنـا آمين . والسلامة على الجماعة أجمعين والصّـلاة والسلام على سيد المرسلين [نقـل من الحكم العطائيـة والمنـاجـاة الإلهية : ١٠٣ ـ ١٠٩].

t3.0 النصائح والوصايا

t3.1 (محمـد سعيـد البرهاني :) لا تقتصر على العبارات ولا على الإشارات بل تزوّد لآخرتـك قبـل حلول المنـون ، حيث تذهب العبـارات والإشـارات ولا يبقى إلا ركعات ركعتها في ليل أو نهار .

t3.2 عليك بالإكثـار من الصدقـة النافلة فإنّ عليك في مالك حقاً زائداً على الـزكـاة المفروضة . فتـزود لآخرتـك وتصدق وأنت صحيح شحيح تخاف الفقر وتأمل الحياة . قال تعالى :
﴿وَمَنْ يُوقَ شُحَّ نَفْسِهِ فَأُولئِكَ هُمُ الْمُفْلِحُونَ﴾ .
أي الناجون .

t3.3 لا تطـع أحداً من عباد الله ولو كان أبـاً أو أمـاً في معصية الله إذ لا طاعة لمخلوق في معصية الخالق .

t3.4   Do not wrong another person, for wrongs done to others are clouds of darkness on the Day of Judgement. Wronging others includes not doing what Allah has obliged you to do for them.

t3.5   Beware of enmity against anyone who has said, "La ilaha ill Allah" (There is no god but Allah), for Allah has honored them with faith, and particularly the righteous of them, for Allah Most High says in a rigorously authenticated (sahih) hadith,

"He who makes an enemy of a friend of Mine, I declare war against."

t3.6   Tell the truth when you speak. It is one of the worst betrayals to tell your brother something he thinks you are being honest about when the matter is otherwise.

t3.7   Be honest in your clothes and dress. It is an outrage against Allah to appear to His servants in the guise of the righteous while secretly contradicting it with the works of the wicked.

t3.8   Recite the Koran and contemplate its meanings. Reflect while reading it on the qualities Allah has praised, with which He describes the people He loves. Acquire these qualities yourself and shun those Allah has condemned. Do your utmost to memorize the Holy Koran by acts as you do by words.

t3.9   Never explain a verse of the Holy Koran by your own opinion, but check as to how it has been understood by the scholars of Sacred Law and men of wisdom who came before you. If you comprehend something else by it and what you have understood contradicts the Sacred Law, forsake your wretched opinion and fling it against the wall.

t3.10   Beware lest you ever say anything that does not conform to the Sacred Law. Know that

t3.4   إيـاك والظـلم فإن الظـلم ظلمـات يوم القيامة . ومن ظلم العباد أن تمنعهم حقوقاً أوجب الله عليك أداءها إليهم .

t3.5   إيـاك ومعـاداة أهـل لا إلـه إلا الله ، فإن الله أكـرمهم بنعمـة الإيمـان خصوصـاً الصـالحين منهم . يقـول الله تعالى في الحديث الصحيح : «من عادى لي ولياً فقد آذنته بالحرب» .

t3.6   عليـك بصـدق الكـلام إذ من أعظم الخيانة أن تحدّث أخاك حديثاً يرى أنك صادق فيه وأنت على غير ذلك .

t3.7   عليـك بالصدق في قيـافتـك ولباسك لأنه من شدة الجراءة على الله أن تظهـر أمـام عبـاد الله بثيـاب الصـالحين وتبارزه سراً بأعمال الفاسقين .

t3.8   عليـك بتـلاوة القرآن وتدبّره . وانظر أثنـاء تلاوتـك إلى ما حمد الله من الصفـات التي وصف بهـا أحبابه فاتصف أنت بهـا ومـا ذمّ من الصفـات فاجتنبهـا . واجتهـد أن تحفظ القرآن الكريم بالعمل كما تحفظه بالتلاوة .

t3.9   لا تفسّر آية من القرآن الكريم برأيك بل ارجع إلى ما فهم منها سلفك من علمـاء شرعيين وعـارفين وإن فهمت خلاف ذلـك وصـادم ما فهمت الشـرع المطهّر فاتـرك فهمك السقيم واضرب به عرض الحائط .

t3.10   الله الله أن تنطق بلسـانك إلا بمـا يوافق الشـرع المطهّر . واعلم بأن

the highest stage of the perfected ones (rijal) is the Sacred Law of Muhammad (Allah bless him and give him peace). And know that the esoteric that contravenes the exoteric is a fraud.

t3.11   Take care to eat lawful food bought with a lawful income, for the entire body of someone who eats what is lawful, his hearing, eyesight, hands, and feet, are disposed to obey Allah whether he wishes to or not; while the whole body of someone who eats the unlawful is disposed to do wrong whether he wants to or not.

t3.12   Keep the thought of Allah Mighty and Majestic ever before you with respect to what He takes from you and what He gives. He takes away nothing except that you may show patience and win His love, for He loves the patient, and when He loves you, He will treat you as a lover does his beloved. And so too, when He gives to you, He bestows blessings upon you that you may give thanks, for He loves the thankful.

t3.13   Do not walk a step, take a bite, or make a move without intending thereby to draw nearer to Allah.

t3.14   Perform the remembrance of Allah (dhikr) silently and aloud, in a group and when alone, for Allah Most High says,

"Remember Me: I will remember you" (Koran 2:152).

It is sufficient as to its worth that Allah is remembering you as long as you are remembering Him.

t3.15   Give frequent utterance to the axiom of Islam "La ilaha ill Allah" (There is no god but Allah), for it is the greatest invocation (dhikr), as is mentioned in the hadith,

"The best thing I or any of the prophets before me have said is 'La ilaha ill Allah.' "

نهـاية سير الـرجال الشرع المحمدي. وكل باطن خالف الظاهر فهو باطل.

t3.11   عليـك بأكل الحلال، لأن من أكل الحلال انصرفت أعضاؤه ـ من سمع وبصـر ويد ورجل ـ إلى طاعة الله شاء أو أبى. ومن أكل الحـرام انصرفت أعضاؤه إلى المعاصي شاء أو أبى.

t3.12   عليـك بمـراقبة الله عز وجل فيمـا أخـذ منك وفيما أعطاك. فإنه تعالى ما أخـذ منك إلا لتصبر فيحبك لأنه يحب الصابـرين، وإذا أحبـك عاملك معاملة المحب لمحبوبـه. وكـذلك إذا أعطاك فإنه أنعم عليك لتشكر وإنه تعالى يحب الشاكرين.

t3.13   إياك أن تخطو خطوة أو تأكل لقمـة أو تتحـرك حركة إلا وأنت تنوي بها قربة إلى الله.

t3.14   عليـك بذكـر الله في السـر والـعـلن وفي الملأ وفي نفسـك فإن الله تعالى يقول:
﴿فَاذْكُرُونِي أَذْكُرْكُمْ﴾ فكفى بك قدراً إذا كان الله لك ذاكراً ما دمت له ذاكراً.

t3.15   أكثر من ذكر كلمة الإسلام «لا إله إلا الله» فإنها أفضل الأذكار لحديث: «أفضـل ما قلته أنا والنبيون من قبلي: لا إله إلا الله»، وفي الحديث القدسي:

And in a hadith qudsi,

«لو أن السموات السبع والأرضين السبع في كفة ولا إله إلا الله في كفة مالت بهن لا إله إلا الله».

> "Were the seven heavens and seven earths placed on one side of a balance scale and 'La ilaha ill Allah' placed on the other, the latter would outweigh them all."

t3.16   Train your children in points of Islamic behavior so they grow up to be Muslims who love Islam and respect the religion of Islam.

t3.16   أدّب أولادك بآداب إسلامية ليكونوا في كبرهم مسلمين يحبون الإسلام ويحترمون دين الإسلام.

t3.17   Do not seek exaltation on earth, but have humility in whatever degree Allah has raised you to. For Allah has brought you forth from the earth, your mother, and it is unseemly to exalt yourself above her. As a hadith says,

t3.17   احذر يا أخي أن تريد علواً في الأرض وعليك بالتواضع مهما أعلى الله منصبك. لأنه تعالى إنما أنشأك من الأرض وهي أمك فلا يليق بك أن تعلو عليها. وفي الأثر:

> "Allah has charged Himself to raise nothing in this world, save that He will lower it again."

«إن حقاً على الله أن لا يرفع شيئاً من الدنيا إلا وضعه». فإن كنت ذلك الشيء فانتظر وضع الله إياك.

So if you are such a thing, you may expect to be lowered by Allah.

t3.18   Always visit those who are ill, as it helps one reflect and take admonition, for someone ill is close to Allah. One has only to consider that the sick person has no one to call upon but Allah, nothing to reflect on but Allah, and his condition reminds one of the blessing of health (al-Hall al-sadid li ma astashkalahu al-murid (y46), 29–32).

t3.18   عليك بعيادة المرضى لما فيها من الاعتبار والذكرى، فإن المريض قريب من الله. ألا ترى أن المريض ما له استغاثة إلا بالله ولا ذكر إلا لله، وهيئته تذكرك نعمة العافية [محرر من الحل السديد لما استشكله المريد: ٢٩ ـ ٣٢؛ بتقديم وتأخير].

*

BOOK U

THE GABRIEL HADITH

CONTENTS:

---

u1.0   THE HADITH TEXT

متن الحديث   u1.0

u1.1   'Umar ibn Khattab (Allah be well pleased with him) said:

    "As we sat one day with the Messenger of Allah (Allah bless him and give him peace), a man with pure white clothing and jet black hair came to

u1.1   [. . .] حدثني أبي] عمــر بن الخطاب قال : بينما نحن عند رسول الله ﷺ ذات يوم إذ طلع علينا رجلٌ شديد بيـاض الثيـاب شديد سواد الشعر لا يُرى

us, without a trace of travelling upon him, though none of us knew him. He sat down before the Prophet (Allah bless him and give him peace) bracing his knees against his, and resting his hands on his legs, said: 'Muhammad, tell me about Islam.' The Messenger of Allah (Allah bless him and give him peace) said: 'Islam is to testify there is no god but Allah and that Muhammad is the Messenger of Allah, and to perform the prayer, give zakat, fast in Ramadan, and perform the pilgrimage to the House if you can find a way.' He said: 'You have spoken the truth,' and we were surprised that he should ask and then confirm the answer. Then he said: 'Tell me about true faith (iman),' and the Prophet (Allah bless him and give him peace) answered: 'It is to believe in Allah, His angels, His inspired Books, His messengers, the Last Day, and in destiny, its good and evil.' 'You have spoken the truth,' he said, 'Now tell me about the perfection of faith (ihsan),' and the Prophet (Allah bless him and give him peace) answered: 'It is to adore Allah as if you see Him, and if you see Him not, He nevertheless sees you.' 'Tell me of the Hour,' said the visitor, and he was told: 'The one questioned knows no more about it than the questioner.' 'Then tell me of its portents,' he said, and the Prophet (Allah bless him and give him peace) replied: 'That the slave woman shall give birth to her mistress, and that you shall see barefoot, naked, penniless shepherds vying in constructing high buildings.' Then the visitor left. I waited a while, and the Prophet (Allah bless him and give him peace) said to me, 'Do you know, 'Umar, who was the questioner?' and I replied, 'Allah and His messenger know best.' He said, 'It was Gabriel, who came to you to teach you your religion' " (*Sahih Muslim* (y92), 1.37–38).

عليـه أثـر السفر ولا يعـرفه منا أحدٌ حتى جلس إلـى النبي ﷺ فأسنـد ركبتيـه إلى ركبتيـه ووضـع كفيه على فخذيه وقال : يا محمد أخبرني عن الإسلام فقال رسول الله ﷺ : «الإسلام أن تشهد أن لا إله إلا الله وأنّ محمداً رسول الله وتقيم الصلاة وتـؤتي الزكاة وتصوم رمضان وتحج البيت إن استطعت إليه سبيلاً». قال : صدقت ؛ قال : فعجبنا له يسألـه ويصدقـه . قال : فأخبـرني عن الإيمـان . قال : «أن تؤمن بالله وملائكتـه وكتبه ورسله واليوم الآخر وتـؤمن بالقـدر خيـره وشـره». قال : صدقت ؛ قال : فأخبرني عن الإحسـان . قال : «أن تعبد الله كأنك تراه فإن لـم تكن تراه فإنـه يراك». قال : فأخبـرني عن السـاعة ، قال : «ما المسؤول عنها بأعلم من السائل». قال : فأخبرني عن أمارتها، قال : «أن تلد الأمة ربتها وأن ترى الحفاة العراة العالة رعاء الشاء يتطاولون في البنيان». قال : ثم انطلق فلبثتُ مليأ ثم قال لي : «يـا عمـر أتـدري من السـائل؟» قلت : الله ورسـولـه أعلم قال : «فإنـه جبريـل أتـاكم يعلّمكم دينكم» [نقل من صحيح مسلم : ١ / ٣٧ ـ ٣٨].

*

u2.0   ISLAM

u2.1   "Islam is to testify there is no god but Allah and that Muhammad is the Messenger of Allah, and to perform the prayer, give zakat, fast in Ramadan, and perform the pilgrimage to the House if you can find a way."

الإسلام   u2.0

«الإسلام أن تشهـد أن لا إلـه   **u2.1**
إلا الـله وأنّ محمـداً رسـول الله وتقيم الصلاة وتؤتي الزكاة وتصوم رمضان وتحج البيت إن استطعت إليه سبيلاً».

u2.2   (Nawawi:) The sheikh and Imam Ibn Salah (Allah have mercy on him) said: "Being a Muslim is outwardly established by one's saying the two Testifications of Faith (Shahadatayn) (N: even if they are not spoken in Arabic). The Prophet (Allah bless him and give him peace) only added the prayer, zakat, the pilgrimage, and the fast because they are the most patent and greatest of Islamic observances. One's submission (istis-lam) is perfected through performing them, and neglecting them suggests that one has dissolved or vitiated the terms of one's compliance. Moreover the term *faith* (iman) encompasses all of the things by which Islam is explained in this hadith, and indeed, all acts of obedience, for they are the fruits of the inner conviction that is the underlying basis of faith, and are what strengthen, complete, and preserve it."

u2.3   The position of Muslim orthodoxy is that no Muslim becomes a non-Muslim through sin. Muslims of heretical sectarian groups and those of reprehensible innovations (bid'a) are not thereby non-Muslims (dis: w47.2).

u2.4   Any Muslim who denies something that is necessarily known (def: f1.3(N:)) to be of the religion of Islam is adjudged a renegade and an unbeliever unless he is a recent convert or was born and raised in the wilderness or for some similar reason has been unable to learn his religion properly. Muslims in such a condition should be informed about the truth, and if they then continue as before, they are adjudged non-Muslims, as is also the case with any Muslim who believes it permissible to commit adultery, drink wine, kill without right, or do other acts that are necessarily known to be unlawful (*Sahih Muslim bi sharh al-Nawawi* (y93), 1.147–50).

*

u3.0   TRUE FAITH (IMAN)

u3.1   "[True faith] is to believe in Allah, His

---

u2.2   (النووي :) قال الشيخ الإمام [أبـو عمـرو] بن الصـلاح رحمه الله : [. . .] وحكم الإسلام في الظـاهـر ثبت بالشهـادتين وإنمـا أضاف إليهما الصلاة والزكاة والحج والصوم لكونها أظهر شعائر الإسـلام وأعظمهـا وبقيـامـه بهـا يتم استسـلامه وتـركه لها يشعر بانحلال قيد انقيـاده أو اختـلالـه . ثم أن اسم الإيمان يتناول ما فسّر به الإسلام في هذا الحديث وسـائر الطاعات لكونها ثمرات للتصديق البـاطن الـذي هو أصل الإيمان ومقويات ومتممات وحافظات له . [. . .] .

u2.3   [النـووي :] واعـلم أن مذهب أهل الحق أنـه لا يكفـر أحـد من أهل القبلة بذنب ولا يكفر أهل الأهواء والبدع .

u2.4   وأن من جحد ما يعلم من دين الإسلام ضرورة حكم بردته وكفره إلا أن يكـون قريب عهـد بالإسلام أو نشأ بيادية بعيـدة ونحوه ممن يخفى عليـه . فيعرف ذلك فإن استمر حكم بكفره وكذا حكم من استحل الزنا أو الخمر أو القتل أو غير ذلك من المحرمات التي يعلم تحريمها ضرورة [محرر من صحيح مسلم بشرح النووي : ١/ ١٤٧ ـ ١٥٠] .

u3.0   الإيمان

u3.1   [قـال]: «أن تؤمـن بالـله

angels, His inspired Books, His messengers, the Last Day, and in destiny, its good and evil.''

وملائكته وكتبه ورسله واليوم الآخر وتؤمن بالقدر خيره وشره» .

BELIEF IN ALLAH

الإيمان بالله

u3.2   (Muhammad Jurdani:)To believe in *Allah* means in His existence, His sole godhood (rububiyya, that no one else participates in His attribute of divinity or in the rights He has over His creatures), His oneness and uniqueness (wahdaniyya), and that He is characterized by every perfection and exalted above any imperfection or impossibility (dis: v1).

u3.2   (محمد الجرداني :) «الإيمان هو أن تؤمن» (أي تصدق) «بـالله» (أي بوجـوده وربوبيته ووحدانيته وأنه متصف بكل كمال ومنزه عن كل نقص ومحال) .

BELIEF IN ANGELS

الإيمان بالملائكة

u3.3   To believe in *His angels* means in beings with bodies of light who are capable of changing form to assume various appearances. *Believe* means to be convinced that they exist, and are honored servants who do not disobey what Allah orders them to do, but do whatever they are commanded. Only Allah Most High knows how many there are, but a hadith relates that there is not a foot of space in the seven heavens that does not contain an angel standing in prayer, bowing, or prostrating. We are obliged to know ten individual angels:

u3.3   «ومـلائكتـه» (أي أن تؤمن بمـلائكته وهم أجسـام نورانيـة قادرون على التشكـل بأشكـال مختلفة . ومعنى الإيمـان بهم التصـديق بوجـودهم وأنهم عبـاد مكـرمـون لا يعصون الله ما أمرهم ويفعلون ما يؤمـرون . وهم بالغـون في الكثـرة ما لا يعلمه إلا الله تعالى وقد ورد مرفوعـاً : ما في السمـوات السبع موضع قدم [ولا شبر ولا كف] إلا وفيه ملك قائم أو راكع أو ساجد .

يجب علينا معرفة عشرة من الملائكة تفصيـلاً وهم جبريل وميكائيل وإسرافيل وعـزرائيـل ومنكر ونكير ورضوان ومالك

(1) Jibril (Gabriel);

(2) Mika'il;

(3) Israfil;

(4) 'Azra'il;

(5) Munkar;

(6) Nakir;

(7) Ridwan;

(8) Malik;

(9 and 10) and the two scribes who record one's good and bad deeds, each of whom is called a "present observer."

وكاتبا الحسنات والسيئات ويسمى كل منهما رقيباً عتيداً) .

BELIEF IN ALLAH'S INSPIRED BOOKS

الإيمان بكتب الله المنزلة

u3.4   To believe in *His inspired Books* means those which He revealed to His messengers, *believe* meaning to be convinced that they are the word of Allah Most High, and all they contain is the truth.

(A: The obligation of belief applies to the original revelations, not the various scriptures in the hands of non-Muslims, which are textually corrupt in their present form.)

Scholars differ as to how many Books there are. Some hold they number 104, and some say otherwise. One is obliged to know four particular Books:

(1) the Tawrah (Torah), revealed to our liegelord Musa (Moses);

(2) the Injil (Evangel), revealed to our liegelord 'Isa (Jesus);

(3) the Zabur (Psalms), revealed to our liegelord Dawud (David);

(4) and the Qur'an (Koran), revealed to our liegelord Muhammad (Allah bless them all and give them peace).

u3.4   «وكتبه» (أي وأن تؤمن بكتبه التي أنزلها على رسله . ومعنى الإيمان بها التصديق بأنها كلام الله تعالى وأن جميع ما تضمنته حق .

واختلف في عددها فقيل إنها مائة وأربعة وقيل غير ذلك . ويجب معرفة أربعة منها تفصيلاً وهي التوراة لسيدنا موسى والإنجيل لسيدنا عيسى والزبور لسيدنا داود والقرآن لسيدنا محمد ﷺ وعليهم أجمعين) .

BELIEF IN ALLAH'S MESSENGERS

الإيمان برسل الله

u3.5   To believe in *His messengers* means to be convinced that Allah Most High sent them to men and jinn (khalq) to guide them to the path of the Truth, and that they have told the truth about everything they have conveyed from Allah Most High. It is obligatory to know twenty-five particular messengers:

(1) Adam;

u3.5   «ورسله» أي وأن تؤمن برسله بأن تصدق بأن الله تعالى أرسلهم إلى الخلق لهدايتهم إلى طريق الحق وأنهم صادقون في جميع ما جاؤوا به عن الله تعالى . و[تقدم أنه] يجب معرفة خمسة وعشرين وهم آدم وإدريس ، ونوح ،

(2) Idris (Enoch);	وهــود، وصــالح، ولـوط، وإبـراهيم، وإسمــاعيــل، وإسحــاق، ويعقـوب، ويـوسف، وشعيب، وهارون، وموسى، وداود، وسليمـان، وأيـوب، وذو الكفـل، ويـونس، وإلـيـاس واليسـع، وزكـريـا، ويحيى وعيسى ومحمد ﷺ وعليهم أجمعين).
(3) Nuh (Noah);	
(4) Hud;	
(5) Salih;	
(6) Lut (Lot);	
(7) Ibrahim (Abraham);	
(8) Isma'il (Ishmael);	
(9) Ishaq (Isaac);	
(10) Ya'qub (Jacob);	
(11) Yusuf (Joseph);	
(12) Shu'ayb;	
(13) Harun (Aaron);	
(14) Musa (Moses);	
(15) Dawud (David);	
(16) Sulayman (Soloman);	
(17) Ayyub (Job);	
(18) Dhul Kifl (Ezekiel);	
(19) Yunus (Jonah);	
(20) Ilyas (Elias);	
(21) al-Yasa' (Elisha);	
(22) Zakariyya (Zacharias);	
(23) Yahya (John);	
(24) 'Isa (Jesus);	
(25) and Muhammad (Allah bless them all and give them peace).	

BELIEF IN THE LAST DAY	الإيمان باليوم الآخر

u3.6   To believe in *the Last Day* means the Day of Resurrection, called the *last* because it is not followed by night. *Believe* means to be convinced that it will come to pass with all it implies, including the resurrection of the dead, their reckoning, the weighing of their good deeds against their bad ones, their passing over the high, narrow bridge that spans the hellfire (sirat), and that some will be put in hell out of justice, and some in paradise out of Allah's pure generosity. (n: The eternality of paradise and hell is discussed at w55.)

u3.6   «واليوم الآخر» (أي وأن تؤمن باليوم الآخر وهو يوم القيامة وسمي آخر لأنه لا ليل بعده. ومعنى الإيمان به التصديق بوجوده وبجميع ما اشتمل عليه من بعث المخلوقات وحسابهم ووزن أعمالهم ومرورهم على الصراط وإدخال بعضهم النار بالعدل وبعضهم الجنة بالفضل).

BELIEF IN DESTINY, ITS GOOD AND EVIL	الإيمان بالقدر خيره وشره

u3.7   To believe in *destiny, its good and evil* means to be convinced that Allah Most High has ordained both good and evil before creating creation, and that all that has been and all that will be only exists through Allah's decree, foreordinance, and will. Early Muslims used to answer whoever asked about destiny by saying, "It is knowing that what hits you was not going to miss, and what misses you was not going to hit" (*al-Jawahir al-lu'lu'iyya fi sharh al-Arba'in al-Nawawiyya* (y68), 35–37).

u3.7   «وتؤمن بالقدر خيره وشره» (أي بأن تعتقد وتصدق بأن الله تعالى قدر الخير والشر قبل خلق الخلق وأن جميع ما كان وما يكون بقضاء الله تعالى وقدره وإرادته [. . .] كان السلف الصالح يجيبون من سألهم عن القضاء والقدر بقولهم : أن تعلم أن ما أصابك لم يكن ليخطئك وما أخطأك لم يكن ليصيبك [محرر من الجواهر اللؤلؤية في شرح الأربعين النووية : ٣٥ ـ ٣٧].

u3.8   (N:) As for Allah's creating acts, we believe that the real doer of everything is Allah. He is the one who burns, not the fire or the person who lighted the fire; He is the one who cuts, not the knife or the person holding the knife; He is the one who drowns a man, not the water or the person who threw him in, and so forth. Here, people always raise the question that if Allah Most High is the real doer, why are people held responsible? The answer is that Allah Most High does not hold people responsible for creating the act, but rather for choosing the act. One proof of this is that a person who cannot choose is not held responsible, such as someone asleep, insane, a child, forced, unremembering, or someone who makes an honest mistake. The legal responsibility of such people is lifted because they lack full voluntary

u3.8   (ح: [. . .]و) أما خلق الأفعال فنحن نعتقد بأن الفاعل الحقيقي لكل شيء هو الله فهو الذي يحرق وليس النار ولا من أشعل النار، وهو الذي يقطع وليس السكين ولا من حمل السكين، وهو الذي يغرق وليس الماء ولا من ألقى في الماء وهكذا.
وهنا يثور سؤال عند الناس دائماً : إذا كان الله تعالى هو الفاعل الحقيقي فلماذا يحاسب العباد؟
والجواب أن الله تعالى لا يحاسبهم على خلق الفعل بل على اختيار الفعل. ودليل ذلك أن من ليس له اختيار ليس عليه حساب كالنائم، والمجنون،

choice. Another proof is that Nimrod sinned for choosing to burn Ibrahim (upon whom be peace) even though Ibrahim did not burn (Koran 21:69); and that Ibrahim (upon whom be peace) became the Friend of the All-merciful for choosing to sacrifice his son out of obedience to Allah, even though his knife did not cut and his son was not sacrificed (Koran 37:105), all of this showing that the servant is held responsible for his choice, which scholars of the divine unity (tawhid) term the servant's *acquisition* (kasb).

As for Allah's eternally preexistent knowledge, we believe that Allah knows everything before, during, and after it is, and knows how it is when it occurs. But does the servant have access to this knowledge? Not at all. So the servant chooses to do acts on the basis of a desire within himself, not because he knows Allah's knowledge, and he is held responsible for his choice even though it corresponds with Allah's eternally preexistent knowledge.

It is clear from the above that *belief in destiny* means that Muslims believe Allah has destined and ordained matters in past eternity, and that nothing in existence lies outside of His eternal will, and He is the Creator of everything, while the servant is only held responsible for his own choices (*Mudhakkirat fi al-tawhid* (y113), 41–42).

*

u4.0   THE PERFECTION OF FAITH (IHSAN)

u4.1 "[The perfection of faith] is to adore Allah as if you see Him, and if you see Him not, He nevertheless sees you."

u4.2 (Muhammad Jurdani:) *To adore Allah as if you see Him* means to obey Him while sincere in

---

والصبي، والمكره، والناسي، والمخطىء. فهؤلاء لما سلب اختيارهم الكامل سقط عنهم التكليف. وبدليل أن النمرود أثم لأنه اختار حرق إبراهيم عليه السلام وإن لم يحترق إبراهيم. وإبراهيم عليه السلام صار خليل الرحمن لأنه اختار ذبح ولده طاعة لله وإن كانت سكينه لم تقطع وولده لم يذبح. فدل هذا كله على أن العبد يحاسب على اختياره وهذا ما يسميه علماء التوحيد «الكسب» [. . .].

وأما علم الله القديم: فنحن نعتقد أن الله تعالى يعلم كل شيء قبل أن يكون وعندما يكون وبعد أن يكون وكيف يكون إذا كان. لكن هل يطلع العبد على هذا العلم؟ اللهم لا.

إذن فالعبد يختار الأفعال لهوى في نفسه لا بسبب اطلاعه على علم الله، ولذا كان محاسباً على اختياره وإن كان هذا الاختيار قد وافق ما في علم الله القديم. [. . .].

فتبين من هذا أن الإيمان بالقضاء والقدر معناه أن يعتقد المسلم بأن الله تعالى قد قضى الأمور وقدرها في سابق الأزل وأنه عز وجل لا يخرج عن إرادته شيء في الوجود وهو الخالق لكل شيء وأن العبد إنما يحاسب على اختياره فقط [محرر من مذكرات في التوحيد: ٤١ ـ ٤٢].

الإحسان   u4.0

u4.1 «أن تعبد الله كأنك تراه فإن لم تكن تراه فإنه يراك».

u4.2 (محمد الجرداني:) «أن تعبد الله كأنك تراه» (أي أن تطيعه وأنت

worship, humble, lowly, and fearful, as though one beholds Him. *And if you see Him not, He nevertheless sees you* means that if one is not as if beholding Him in worship, but oblivious to this contemplation, one should nevertheless persist in excellence of performance and imagine oneself before Allah Most High and that He is looking at one's inmost being and outward self, to thereby attain to the basis of perfection. Scholars mention that there are three spiritual stations a servant may have in his worship:

(1) to worship in a way that fulfills its obligations, by observing all its conditions and integrals;

(2) to do this while immersed in the sea of gnostic inspiration (mukashafa) until it is as if the worshipper actually beholds Allah Most High, this being the station of contemplative spiritual vision (mushahada);

(3) and to worship as mentioned above, though mainly aware that Allah sees one, this being the station of vigilance (muraqaba).

All three of these are of the perfection of faith (ihsan), but the perfection required for the validity of worship is only the first, while perfection in the latter senses is the mark of the elect, and not possible for many (*al-Jawahir al-lu'lu'iyya fi sharh al-Arba'in al-Nawawiyya* (y68), 37–38).

مخلص له في العبادة خاضع ذليل خاشع كأنك تعاينه).

«فإن لم تكن تراه فإنه يراك» (أي فإن لم تكن في عبادته كأنك تراه بأن غفلت عن تلك المشاهدة فاستمر على إحسان العبادة واستحضر أنك بين يدي الله تعالى وأنه مطلع على سرك وعلانيتك ليحصل لك أصل الكمال.

وقد ذكر العلماء أن للعبد في عبادته ثلاثة مقامات:

ـ الأول أن يفعلها على الوجه الذي يسقط معه الطلب بأن تكون مستوفية للشروط والأركان.

ـ الثاني أن يفعلها كذلك وقد استغرق في بحر المكاشفة حتى كأنه يرى الله تعالى وهذا مقام المشاهدة.

ـ الثالث أن يفعلها كذلك وقد غلب عليه أن الله تعالى يشاهده وهذا مقام المراقبة.

وكل من المقامات الثلاثة إحسان إلا أن الإحسان المشروط في صحة العبادة إنما هو الأول وأما الإحسان بالمعنيين الأخيرين فهو من صفة الخواص ومتعذر من كثيرين [نقل من الجواهر اللؤلؤية في شرح الأربعين النووية: ٣٧ ـ ٣٨].

*

BOOK V

ALLAH AND HIS MESSENGER

كتاب الاعتقاد في الله ورسوله

CONTENTS:

---

v1.0   ALLAH

الله   v1.0

v1.1   (Ghazali:) Praise be to Allah, who originates all and returns it, who does as He wills, He

v1.1 (الـغـزالـي:) الـحـمـد لله المبــدىء المعيـد الفعـال لمـا يريـد ذي

of the noble Throne and overwhelming force, the Guide of His elect servants to the wisest path and straightest way, who has blessed them, after having had them attest to His oneness, by preserving the tenets of their religion from the darknesses of doubt and misgivings, bringing them through His providence and guidance to follow His chosen Messenger and the example of his noble and honored Companions; He who manifests Himself and His acts to His servants through His sublime attributes, of which none possess knowledge save those who give heed with a present mind.

العرش المجيد والبطش الشديد الهادي صفوة العبيد إلى المنهج الرشيد والمسلك السديد، المنعم عليهم بعد شهادة التوحيد بحراسة عقائدهم عن ظلمات التشكيك والترديد، السالك بهم إلى اتباع رسوله المصطفى واقتفاء آثار صحبه الأكرمين المكرمين بالتأييد والتسديد، المتجلي لهم في ذاته وأفعاله بمحاسن أوصافه التي لا يدركها إلا من ألقى السمع وهو شهيد [المعرف إياهم :] .

HIS ONENESS

الوحدانية

v1.2   He is one in being without partner, unique without peer, ultimate without opposite, alone without equal. He is one, preeternal, beginninglessly uncreate, everlastingly abiding, unceasingly existent, eternally limitless, the ever self-subsisting through whom all else subsists, ever enduring, without end. He is, was, and ever will be possessed of all attributes of majesty, unannihilated by dissolution or separation through the passage of eons or terminus of interims. He is the First and Last, the Outward and Inward, and He has knowledge of everything.

v1.2   أنه في ذاته واحد لا شريك له، فرد لا مثل له، صمد لا ضد له، منفرد لا ند له، وأنه واحد قديم لا أول له، أزلي لا بداية له، مستمر الوجود لا آخر له، أبدي لا نهاية له، قيوم لا انقطاع له، دائم لا انصرام له، لم يزل ولا يزال موصوفاً بنعوت الجلال لا يقضى عليه بالانقضاء والانفصال بتصرم الآباد وانقراض الآجال، بل هو الأول والآخر والظاهر والباطن وهو بكل شيء عليم .

HIS TRANSCENDENCE

التنزيه

v1.3   He is not a body with a form, or a limitary, quantitative substance, not resembling bodies in quantifiability or divisibility, or in being a substance or qualified by substance, or being an accident or qualified by accidents. He does not resemble anything that exists, nor anything that exists resemble Him. There is nothing whatsoever like unto Him, nor is He like unto anything. He is not delimited by magnitude, contained by places, encompassed by directions, or bounded by heavens or earth. He is 'established on the Throne' (mustawin, Koran 20:5) in the way He says and the meaning He intends, 'established' in a manner transcending contact, settledness, fixity, indwelling, or movement. The Throne does not

v1.3   وأنه ليس بجسم مصور ولا جوهر محدود مقدر، وأنه لا يماثل الأجسام لا في التقدير ولا في قبول الانقسام، وأنه ليس بجوهر ولا تحله الجواهر ولا بعرض ولا تحله الأعراض، بل لا يماثل موجوداً ولا يماثله موجود، ليس كمثله شيء ولا هو مثل شيء، وأنه لا يحده المقدار ولا تحويه الأقطار ولا تحيط به الجهات ولا تكتنفه الأرضون ولا السموات، وأنه مستو على العرش على الوجه الذي قاله وبالمعنى الذي أراده استواء منزهاً عن المماسة والاستقرار والتمكن والحلول والانتقال، لا يحمله

bear Him up, but is borne up by the subtlety of His infinite power, as are the angels who carry it, and all are powerless in His grasp. He is above the Throne, the heavens, and all else to the farthest reaches of the stars, with an aboveness that does not increase His nearness to the Throne or heavens, or His distance from the earth and what lies beneath it. He is as exalted in degree above the Throne and the heavens as He is above the earth and its depths, though He is near to everything in existence, nearer to a servant than his own jugular vein, and is witness to everything. His nearness no more resembles the nearness of objects to one another than His entity resembles the entities of objects. He does not indwell in anything, nor anything indwell in Him. He is as exalted above containment in space as He is above confinement in time. He was, before creating time and space, and is now even as He was. He is distinguished from His creation by His attributes. There is nothing in His entity other than Him, nor is His entity in what is other than Him. He is beyond change and motion: events neither occur within Him nor changes befall Him. He remains in His attributes of majesty exalted above change, and in the attributes of His perfection beyond needing any increase in perfection. The existence of His entity is known by human reason, and in the afterlife is beheld by the eyesight of the righteous as a beatitude and favor, to consummate their perfect joy with the sight of His Noble Countenance.

HIS LIFE AND ALMIGHTY POWER

v1.4   He Most High is living, almighty, overmastering, triumphant, unaffected by inability or weakness; unsusceptible to drowsiness, sleep, annihilation, or death; possessed of absolute sovereignty and might, of irresistible power and force. His is the majesty and sway, the creation and command. The heavens are enfolded in His right hand and all beings are powerless in His grasp. He alone creates, begins, gives existence, and originates. He creates all beings and their acts, ordains their sustenance and terms. Nothing possible is out of His grasp, the disposal of no matter is beyond His power. The number of things

العرش بل العرش وحملته محمولون بلطف قدرته ومقهورون في قبضته وهو فوق العرش والسماء وفوق كل شيء إلى تخوم الثرى فوقية لا تزيده قرباً إلى العرش والسماء كما لا تزيده بعداً عن الأرض والثرى؛ بل هو رفيع الدرجات عن العرش والسماء كما أنه رفيع الدرجات عن الأرض والثرى، وهو مع ذلك قريب من كل موجود وهو أقرب إلى العبد من حبل الوريد، وهو على كل شيء شهيد، إذ لا يماثل قربه قرب الأجسام كما لا تماثل ذاته ذات الأجسام؛ وأنه لا يحل في شيء ولا يحل فيه شيء؛ تعالى عن أن يحويه مكان كما تقدس أن يحده زمان؛ بل كان قبل أن خلق الزمان والمكان وهو الآن على ما عليه كان؛ وأنه بائن عن خلقه بصفاته، ليس في ذاته سواه ولا في سواه ذاته؛ وأنه مقدس عن التغير والانتقال ولا تحله الحوادث ولا تعتريه العوارض، بل لا يزال في نعوت جلاله منزهاً عن الزوال وفي صفات كماله مستغنياً عن زيادة الاستكمال وأنه في ذاته معلوم الوجود بالعقول مرئيّ الذات بالأبصار نعمة منه ولطفاً بالأبرار في دار القرار وإتماماً منه للنعيم بالنظر إلى وجهه الكريم.

الحياة والقدرة

v1.4   وأنه تعالى حي قادر جبار قاهر لا يعتريه قصور ولا عجز ولا تأخذه سنة ولا نوم ولا يعارضه فناء ولا موت وأنه ذو الملك والملكوت والعزة والجبروت، له السلطان والقهر والخلق والأمر؛ والسموات مطويات بيمينه والخلائق مقهورون في قبضته؛ وأنه المنفرد بالخلق والاختراع المتوحد بالإيجاد والإبداع. خلق الخلق وأعمالهم وقدّر أرزاقهم وآجالهم. لا يشذ عن قبضته مقدور ولا يعزب عن قدرته تصاريف

He can do is limitless, the amount He knows is infinite.

HIS KNOWLEDGE

v1.5 He knows all things knowable, encompassing all that takes place from the depths of the earth to the highest heaven. He knows without an atom's weight in the earth or heavens escaping His knowledge. He knows the creeping of a black ant across a great stone on a lightless night, and the motion in the air of a particle of dust on a windy day. He knows the concealed and the yet more hidden, the buried recesses of hearts, the movement of thought, and the opacities of the inmost soul; with preeternal, beginningless knowledge that He has always possessed from the limitless reaches of past eternity, not with awareness originating within Him through being imparted or conveyed.

HIS WILL

v1.6 He Most High wills all that exists and directs all events. Nothing occurs in the physical or spiritual world, be it meager or much, little or great, good or evil, of benefit or detriment, faith or unbelief, knowledge or ignorance, triumph or ruin, increase or decrease, obedience or sin; save through His ordinance, apportionment, wisdom, and decision. What He wills is, and what He does not will is not. Neither sidelong glance nor passing thought is beyond His design. He originates all and returns it, does what He wills, and none can repulse His command. There is no rescinding His destiny, no flight for a servant from disobeying Him except through divinely given success therein and mercy, and no strength to obey Him save through His choice and decree. If all mankind, jinn, angels, and devils combined their efforts to move or to still a single particle of the universe without His will and choice, they would be unable to. His will, like His other attributes, exists in His entity and He ever possesses it. He has willed from preeternity the existence of all things at the times

الأمور. لا تحصى مقدوراته ولا تتناهى معلوماته.

العلم

v1.5 وأنه عالم بجميع المعلومات محيط بما يجري من تخوم الأرضين إلى أعلى السموات. وأنه عالم لا يعزب عن علمه مثقـال ذرة في الأرض ولا في السمـاء. بل يعلم دبيب النملة السـوداء على الصخرة الصماء في الليلة الظلماء ويدرك حركة الذر في جو الهواء. ويعلم السـر وأخفـى ويطلع على هواجس الضمائر وحركـات الخواطر وخفيات السرائر، بعلم قديم أزلي لم يزل موصوفاً به في أزل الآزال، لا بعلم متجدد حاصل في ذاته بالحلول والانتقال.

الإرادة

v1.6 وأنه تعالى مريـد للكـائنات مدبر للحـادثـات. فلا يجري في الملك والملكـوت قليل أوكثير، صغير أوكبير، خيـر أو شر، نفـع أو ضر، إيمان أوكفر، عرفـان أو نكـر، فوز أو خسران، زيادة أو نقصـان، طاعة أو عصيان، إلا بقضائه وقدره وحكمته ومشيئته. فما شاء كان وما لم يشأ لم يكن. لا يخرج عن مشيئته لفتة ناظـر ولا فلتـة خاطـر. بل هو المبـدىء المعيد الفعال لما يريد لا رادّ لأمره، ولا معقب لقضـائـه ولا مهـرب لعبـد عن معصيته إلا بتوفيقه ورحمته، ولا قوة على طاعتـه إلا بمشيئتـه وإرادتـه. فلو اجتمع الإنس والجن والمـلائكة والشياطين على أن يحركوا في العالم ذرة أو يسكنوها دون إرادته ومشيئته لعجـزوا عن ذلـك. وأن إرادته قائمة بذاته في جملة صفاته لم يزل كذلك موصوفاً بها مريداً في أزله لوجود الأشياء في أوقاتها التي قدرها فوجدت في

He has chosen. They occur at the times which He has destined from beginningless eternity, occurring neither before nor after, but taking place in accordance with His knowledge and will, without substitution or alteration. He directs events without successive thoughts or waiting for time to elapse, which is why nothing diverts Him from anything else.

HIS HEARING AND SIGHT

أوقاتها كما أراده في أزله من غير تقدم ولا تأخر بل وقعت على وفق علمه وإرادته من غير تبدل ولا تغير . دبر الأمور لا بترتيب أفكار ولا تربص زمان فلذلك لم يشغله شأن عن شأن .

السمع والبصر

v1.7   He Most High is all-hearing and all-seeing. He hears and sees, no sound however slight eluding His hearing, and no sight however minute escaping His vision. Distance does not obscure His hearing nor darkness hinder His vision. He sees without pupil or eyelids, and hears without ear canal or ears, just as He knows without a heart, seizes without limb, and creates without implement. His attributes no more resemble the attributes of His creatures than His entity resembles the entity of His creatures.

v1.7   وأنه تعالى سميع بصير . يسمع ويرى لا يعزب عن سمعه مسموع وإن خفي ولا يغب عن رؤيته مرئي وإن دق . ولا يحجب سمعه بعد ولا يدفع رؤيته ظلام . يرى من غير حدقة وأجفان ويسمع من غير أصمخة وآذان ، كما يعلم بغير قلب ويبطش بغير جارحة ويخلق بغير آلة . إذ لا تشبه صفاته صفات الخلق كما لا تشبه ذاته ذوات الخلق .

HIS SPEECH

الكلام

v1.8   He Most High speaks, commands, forbids, promises, and warns, with beginninglessly eternal speech that is an attribute of His entity, not resembling the speech of creatures in being a sound generated by the passage of air or impact of bodies, nor in letters articulated by compressing the lips or moving the tongue. The Koran, Torah, Evangel, and Psalms are His Books, revealed to His messengers (upon whom be peace). The Koran is recited with tongues, written in books, and memorized in hearts despite being beginninglessly eternal, an attribute of the entity of Allah Most High, unsubject to disseverance and separation by conveyance to hearts or pages. Moses (Allah bless him and give him peace) heard the speech of Allah without sound or letter, just as the righteous see the entity of Allah Most High in the afterlife without substance or accident.

Since Allah possesses all of the above attributes, He is living, knowing, omnipotent, willing,

v1.8   وأنه تعالى متكلم آمر ناهٍ واعد متوعد بكلام أزلي قديم قائم بذاته فليس بصوت يحدث من إنسلال هواء أو اصطكاك أجرام ، ولا بحرف ينقطع بإطباق شفة أو تحريك لسان . وأن القرآن والتوراة والإنجيل والزبور كتبه المنزلة على رسله عليهم السلام . وأن القرآن مقروء بالألسنة مكتوب في المصاحف محفوظ في القلوب وأنه مع ذلك قديم قائم بذات الله تعالى لا يقبل الانفصال والافتراق بالانتقال إلى القلوب والأوراق . وأن موسى ﷺ سمع كلام الله بغير صوت ولا حرف كما يرى الأبرار ذات الله تعالى في الآخرة من غير جوهر ولا عرض .

وإذا كانت له هذه الصفات ، كان حياً عالماً قادراً مريداً سميعاً بصيراً متكلماً

hearing, seeing, and speaking by virtue of His life, power, knowledge, will, hearing, sight, and speech, not merely by virtue of His entity.

HIS ACTS

v1.9 Everything besides Him Glorious and Exalted exists through His action, proceeding from His justice in the best, fullest, most perfect and equitable way. He is wise in His acts and just in His decrees. His justice is not comparable to the justice of His servants, since injustice may only be imagined from a servant through his disposal of what belongs to another, while this is inconceivable from Allah Most High, since nothing belongs to anyone besides Him that He should unjustly dispose of it. Everything besides Him, be it human, jinn, angel, devil, heaven, earth, animal, vegetable, mineral, substance, accident, intelligible, or sensory, is contingent, and was brought into existence through His power after not being, created by Him after it was nothing. He alone existed in preeternity, and nothing else. He then originated creation, that His omnipotence might be manifest, His prior decree effected, and His eternal word realized; not from needing or requiring anything in creation. Our origination, beginning, and responsibility are of Allah's generosity, not because of their being obligatory for Him, and His blessings and benefaction exist because of His favor, not because of being due from Him. Everything that exists is indebted to Him for His generosity and goodness, His blessings and benevolence; for He is well able to pour all manner of torments upon His servants and try them with every variety of suffering and illness, and were He to do so, it would be just on His part and not wicked or unfair. He Mighty and Majestic rewards His servants, the believers, for their acts of obedience because of His generosity and in fulfillment of His word, not because of their deserving it or His owing it to them. He is not obliged to anyone to do anything, nor is injustice on His part conceivable, for He does not owe any rights to anyone. The obligation of men and jinn to perform acts of obedience is established by His having informed them of it upon the tongues of the

بالحياة والقدرة والعلم والإرادة والسمع والبصر والكلام لا بمجرد الذات .

الأفعال

v1.9 وأنه سبحانه وتعالى لا موجود سواه إلا وهو حادث بفعله وفائض من عدله على أحسن الوجوه وأكملها وأتمها وأعدلها . وأنه حكيم في أفعاله عادل في أقضيته . لا يقاس عدله بعدل العباد إذ العبد يتصور منه الظلم بتصرفه في ملك غيره ولا يتصور الظلم من الله تعالى فإنه لا يصادف لغيره ملكاً حتى يكون تصرفه فيه ظلماً فكل ما سواه من إنس وجن وملك وشيطان وسماء وأرض وحيوان ونبات وجماد وجوهر وعرض ومدرك ومحسوس حادث اخترعه بقدرته بعد العدم اختراعاً وأنشأه انشاءً بعد أن لم يكن شيئاً . إذ كان في الأزل موجوداً وحده ولم يكن معه غيره . فأحدث الخلق بعد ذلك إظهاراً لقدرته وتحقيقاً لما سبق من إرادته ولما حق في الأزل من كلمته ، لا لافتقاره إليه وحاجته . وأنه متفضل بالخلق والاختراع والتكليف لا عن وجوب ومتطول بالإنعام والإصلاح لا عن لزوم . فله الفضل والإحسان والنعمة والامتنان إذ كان قادراً على أن يصب على عباده أنواع العذاب ويبتليهم بضروب الآلام والأوصاب ، ولو فعل ذلك لكان منه عدلاً ولم يكن منه قبيحاً ولا ظلماً . وأنه عز وجل يثيب عباده المؤمنين على الطاعات بحكم الكرم والوعد لا بحكم الاستحقاق واللزوم له . إذ لا يجب عليه لأحد فعل ولا يتصور منه ظلم ولا يجب لأحد عليه حق . وأن حقه في الطاعات وجب على الخلق بإيجابه على ألسنة

prophets (upon whom be peace), and not by unaided human reason. He sent the prophets and manifested the truth of their messages by unmistakable, inimitable miracles. They have communicated His commands, prohibitions, promises, and warnings, and it is obligatory for mankind and jinn to believe in what they have conveyed.

أنبيائه عليهم السلام، لا بمجرد العقل . ولكنــه بعث الــرســل وأظهــر صدقهم بالمعجـزات الظاهـرة فبلّغـوا أمره ونهيه ووعـده ووعيـده، فوجب على الخلق تصديقهم فيما جاؤوا به .

*

v2.0   HIS MESSENGER

v2.0   الرسول

v2.1   Allah Most High sent Muhammad (Allah bless him and give him peace), the Qurayshite unlettered prophet, to deliver His inspired message to the entire world, Arabs and non-Arabs, jinn and mankind, superseding and abrogating all previous religious systems with the Prophet's Sacred Law, except for the provisions of them that the new revelation explicitly reconfirmed. Allah has favored him above all the other prophets and made him the highest of mankind, rejecting anyone's attesting to the divine oneness by saying "There is no god but Allah," unless they also attest to the Prophet by saying "Muhammad is the Messenger of Allah." He has obliged men and jinn to believe everything the Prophet (Allah bless him and give him peace) has informed us concerning this world and the next, and does not accept anyone's faith unless they believe in what he has told us will happen after death.

v2.1   [معنى الكلمــة الثـانيـة وهي الشهادة للرسل بالرسالة و] أنه بعث النبي الأمي القرشي محمداً ﷺ برسالتـه إلى كافـة الــعــرب والــعجم والجن والإنس فنسـخ بشريعته الشرائع إلا ما قرره منها . وفضّله على سائـر الأنبيــاء وجعله سيد البشـر ومنع كمال الإيمان بشهادة التوحيد وهـو قول لا إلـه إلا الله ما لم تقتـرن بهـا شهـادة الرسـول وهو قولك محمد رسول الله . وألـزم الخلق تصـديقه في جميع ما أخبر عنه من أمور الدنيا والآخرة . وأنه لا يتقبـل إيمـان عبـد حتى يؤمن بما أخبر به بعد الموت .

THE TRIAL OF THE GRAVE

فتنة القبر

v2.2   The first of these matters is the questioning of Munkar and Nakir, two tremendous, awe-inspiring personages who sit a servant upright in his grave, body and soul, and ask him about the unity of Allah and the messengerhood of the Prophet (Allah bless him and give him peace), saying, "Who is your Lord, what is your religion, and who is your prophet?" It is they who try people in the grave, their questioning being the

v2.2   وأولـه سؤال منكر ونكير وهما ملكـان مهيبـان هائـلان يقعدان العبد في قبـره سويـاً ذا روح وجسـد فيسألانـه عن التـوحيد والرسالة ويقولان له : من ربك وما دينـك ومن نبيـك؟ وهمـا فتـانا القبر وسؤالهما أول فتنة بعد الموت . وأن يؤمن

first ordeal after death. It is also obligatory to believe in the torment of the grave, that it is a fact, is just, and affects both body and soul, in the way Allah wills.

بعـذاب القبـر وأنه حق وحكمه عدل على الجسم والروح على ما شاء الله .

THE SCALE

الميزان

v2.3   It is obligatory to believe in the scale, which consists of two scalepans and a balance indicator between them and is as great in size as the thickness of the heavens and earth. It weighs a servant's deeds through the power of Allah Most High, and the weights placed on it are as fine as an atom or mustard seed, that justice may be perfectly done. The pages recording one's good deeds will be placed in a form pleasing to behold on the side of the scale for Light, weighing it down according to their rank with Allah, through His generosity, while the pages recording one's bad deeds will be placed in an ugly form on the side of Darkness, diminishing the weight of the opposite side through Allah's justice.

v2.3   وأن يؤمـن بالــميــزان ذي الكفتين واللسـان وصفتـه في العِظم أنـه مثل طبقـات السمـوات والأرض . توزن فيـه الأعمـال بقـدرة الله تعالى . والصنج يومئـذ مثـاقيل الذر والخردل تحقيقاً لتمام العـدل . وتـوضع صحائف الحسنات في صورة حسنة في كفـة النـور فيثقـل بها الميزان على قدر درجاتها عند الله بفضل الله ، وتطـرح صحـائف السيئـات في صورة قبيحـة في كفة الظلمـة فيخف بها الميزان بعدل الله .

THE BRIDGE OVER HELL

الصراط

v2.4   It is obligatory to believe in the bridge over hell (sirat), a bridge spanning the breadth of hell, sharper than a sword and finer than a hair, which unbelievers' feet shall slip from by Allah's decree and plunge them into hell, and the feet of believers shall be made fast upon by Allah's generosity, and from thence they shall be conducted to the Final Abode.

v2.4   وأن يؤمن بأن الصــراط حق ، وهو جسر ممدود على متن جهنم أحدّ من السيف وأدق من الشعـرة تزل عليـه أقدام الكـافرين بحكم الله سبحانه فتهوي بهم إلى النـار وتثبت عليـه أقـدام المـؤمنين بفضل الله فيساقون إلى دار القرار .

THE WATERING PLACE

الحوض

v2.5   It is obligatory to believe in a watering place people will come to, the watering place of Muhammad (Allah bless him and give him peace), which believers will drink from before entering paradise, after having crossed the bridge over hell. Whoever drinks from it will never thirst again. Its width is a month's journey across, its

v2.5   وأن يؤمن بالحـوض المـورود حوض محمـد ﷺ يشـرب منه المؤمنون قبـل دخـول الجنـة وبعد جواز الصراط . من شرب منه شربة لم يظمأ بعدها أبداً . عرضـه مسيـرة شهر ماؤه أشـد بياضـاً من

water whiter than milk and sweeter than honey, and there are as many pitchers around it as stars in the sky. Two aqueducts pour into it from Kawthar, a spring in paradise.

اللبن وأحلى من العسل حوله أباريق عددها بعدد نجوم السماء. فيه ميزابان يصبان فيه من الكوثر.

THE FINAL RECKONING

الحساب

v2.6   It is obligatory to believe in the Final Reckoning and the disparity in the way various people are dealt with therein, some made to answer, others pardoned, and some admitted to paradise without reckoning, being the intimates of Allah (muqarrabun). Allah Most High shall ask whomever He wills of the prophets if they have conveyed their message, ask unbelievers why they denied the messengers, ask those of reprehensible innovation (bid'a) about the sunna, and ask Muslims about their works.

v2.6   وأن يؤمن بالحساب وتفاوت الناس فيه إلى مناقش في الحساب وإلى مسامح فيه وإلى من يدخل الجنة بغير حساب وهم المقربون. فيسأل الله تعالى من شاء من الأنبياء عن تبليغ الرسالة ومن شاء من الكفار عن تكذيب المرسلين ويسأل المبتدعة عن السنة ويسأل المسلمين عن الأعمال.

BELIEVERS SHALL DEPART FROM HELL

خروج الموحدين من النار

v2.7   It is obligatory to hold that true believers in the oneness of Allah (N: who follow the prophet of their age (dis: w4.4)) will be taken out of hell after having paid for their sins, through the generosity of Allah Mighty and Majestic. No one who is a true monotheist will abide in the fire forever.

v2.7   وأن يؤمن بإخراج الموحدين من النار بعد الانتقام [حتى لا يبقى في جهنم موحد] بفضل الله تعالى فلا يخلد في النار موحد.

THE INTERCESSION OF THE PROPHETS AND RIGHTEOUS

شفاعة الأنبياء والصالحين

v2.8   It is obligatory to believe in the intercession of first the prophets, then religious scholars, then martyrs, then other believers, the intercession of each one commensurate with his rank and position with Allah Most High. Any believer remaining in hell without intercessor shall be taken out of it by the favor of Allah, no one who believes remaining in it forever, and anyone with an atom's weight of faith in his heart will eventually depart from it.

v2.8   وأن يؤمن بشفاعة الأنبياء ثم العلماء ثم الشهداء ثم سائر المؤمنين على حسب جاهه ومنزلته عند الله تعالى. ومن بقي من المؤمنين ولم يكن له شفيع أخرج بفضل الله عز وجل فلا يخلد في النار مؤمن بل يخرج منها من كان في قلبه مثقال ذرة من الإيمان.

THE EXCELLENCE OF THE
PROPHETIC COMPANIONS (SAHABA)

فضل الصحابة

v2.9   It is obligatory to believe in the excellence
(dis: w56) of the prophetic Companions (Allah be
well pleased with them). One must think the best
of all of the Companions of the Prophet (Allah
bless him and give him peace), and praise them
just as Allah Mighty and Majestic (n: e.g., at
Koran 3:110) and His messenger have praised
them (Allah bless them all and give them peace).

v2.9   وأن يعتقــد فضـل الصحـابـة
رضي الله عنهم [. . .] وأن يحسن الظن
بجميـع الصحـابة ويثني عليهم كما أثنى
الله عز وجل عليهم ورسوله ﷺ وعليهم
أجمعين .

*

v3.0   CONCLUSION

v3.0   الخاتمة

v3.1   All of the foregoing has been conveyed by
prophetic hadith and attested to by the words of
the early Muslims. Whoever believes it with deep
conviction belongs to those of the truth, who follow the sunna, and distinguishes himself from the
faction who have strayed, the sect adhering to reprehensible innovation (bid'a). We ask Allah
through His mercy for perfect certainty and steadfastness in religion, for ourselves and all Muslims;
He is the Most Merciful of the Merciful. May
Allah bless our liegelord Muhammad, and every
chosen servant (Ihya' 'ulum al-din (y39), 1.79–
83).

v3.1   فكــل ذلـك ممــا وردت به
الأخبار وشهدت به الآثـار . فمن اعتقد
جميـع ذلـك موقنـاً به كان من أهل الحق
وعصـابـة السنة ، وفـارق رهـط الضلال
وحـزب البـدعة . فنسأل الله كمال اليقين
وحسن الثبــات في الـدين لنــا ولكـافة
المسلمين برحمته ، إنه أرحم الراحمين .
وصلى الله على سيدنـا محمد وعلى كل
عبد مصطفى [نقل من إحياء علوم الدين
١ / ٧٩ - ٨٣] .

*

825

BOOK W

NOTES AND APPENDICES

تَعْلِيقَاتٌ وَمَلَاحِق

CONTENTS:

Contents

---

w1.0   TRANSLITERATION OF *DHIKR* AND SUPPLICATIONS

w1.0 الأذكــار والأدعيـة حسب نطقها بالعربية

w1.1   (n:) This section uses a system of transliteration like that of Martin Lings's *Muhammad*, with a few changes such as symbolizing the letter ظ as ḍh instead of ẓ, to better represent the classical pronunciation, and the use of parentheses at the end of words for letters not pronounced when one pauses after them, and at the beginning of words for letters not pronounced when the final vowel of the previous word is elided with what follows it. The letters are:

Arabic	English	Arabic	English	Arabic	English
ء	’	ز	z	ق	q
ب	b	س	s	ك	k
ت	t	ش	sh	ل	l
ث	th	ص	ṣ	م	m
ج	j	ض	ḍ	ن	n
ح	ḥ	ط	ṭ	و	w
خ	kh	ظ	ḍh	ه	h
د	d	ع	‘	ة	t
ذ	dh	غ	gh	ي	y
ر	r	ف	f		

(short vowels)		(long vowels)		(dipthongs)	
´	a	ا ,	ā	ْو	— aw
,	u	و ,	ū	ﹾيْ	— ay
—	i	ي ,	ī	ﹾيّ	— iyy
				ّو ,	— uww

w1.2   (Martin Lings:) The Arabs sometimes call themselves "the people of
Ḍād" because they claim that they alone possess the letter *ḍād*, which sounds like
a heavy "d" pronounced far back in the mouth. It is normally transcribed, as here,
by *ḍ*. Analogously, *ṣ*, *ṭ*, and *z* (n: *dh* below) stand for other characteristic heavy
back consonants, whereas *d, s, t,* and *z* stand for the corresponding front consonants, which are pronounced more or less as in English. The letter *ḥ* is a tensely
breathed *h* sound; *q* is a guttural k sound; *th* is to be pronounced as these letters
in *think*, *dh* as they are in *this*, *gh* like a French *r*, *kh* like *ch* in Scottish *loch*. The
asper ʿ denotes the letter *ʿayn*, which is produced by narrowing the passage in the
depth of the throat and then forcing the breath through it. The apostrophe ʾ
denotes the "*hamzah* of discontinuity," which means a slight catch in the breath.
Since in English initial vowel sounds are regularly preceded by this catch, the initial *hamzah* has not been transcribed here, e.g. *Aḥmad*, not *ʾAḥmad*. The "*hamzah* of continuity" indicates the running of two words into one by the elision, at
the beginning of the second word, of the first letter of the definite article *al-*, the
a of which is always elided except at the beginning of a sentence. This elision is
shown here simply by the omission of the letter in question, e.g. *Abu l-ʿĀṣ*, not
Abu al-ʿĀṣ; the continuity has the effect of shortening any long vowel which
immediately precedes this *hamzah*. The first letter of the Divine Name *Allāh* is
also elided except except at the beginning of a sentence or when it stands alone,
e.g. *bismi Llāh* ...

   The short vowels *a, i, u* are like the vowel sounds of *sat* [n: like the vowel
sound of *set* in American pronunciation], *sit, soot; ā* ... is like the vowel sound of
bare [n: like that of *flat* for Americans], but back consonants next to it attract it
to that of *bar; ī* and *ū* are like the vowel sounds of *seen* and *soon; ay* is between
those of *sign* and *sane; aw* is like that of *cow* (*Muhammad* (y75), 348).

PURIFICATION

w1.3   (e5.5) Before ablution (wudu): "Bismi Llāh(i)," or optimally, "Bismi
Llāhi r-Raḥmāni r-Raḥīm.
   Prior to this, it is sunna to say, "Aʿūdhu bi Llāhi mina sh-shayṭāni r-Rajīm,"
and to add, after the Basmala, "Al-ḥamdu li Llāhi ʿala l-Islāmi wa niʿmatih(i), al-
ḥamdu li Llāhi lladhī jaʿala l-māʾa ṭahūran wa l-Islāma nūra(n). Rabbi aʿūdhu bika
min hamazāti ah-shayāṭīna wa aʿūdhu bika Rabbi an yaḥdurūn."
   If one neglects to say the Basmala at the first of ablution, one pronounces it
during ablution, saying, "Bismi Llāhi awwalahu wa ākhirah."

w1.4   (e5.18) After ablution (wudu): "Ash-hadu an lā ilāha illa Llāhu waḥdahu
lā sharīka lah(u), wa ash-hadu anna Muḥammadan 'abduhu wa rasūluh(u);
Allāhumma j'alnī mina t-tawwābīn(a), wa j'alnī mina l-mutaṭahhirīn(a), wa j'alnī
min 'ibādika ṣ-ṣāliḥīn(a); subḥānaka Llāhumma wa bi ḥamdik(a), ash-hadu an lā
ilāha illā ant(a), astaghfiruka wa atūbu ilayk."

w1.5   (e9.1(5)) Before entering the lavatory: "Bismi Llāh(i), Allāhumma innī
a'ūdhu bika mina l-khubuthi wa l-khabā'ith"; and after leaving: "Ghufrānak(a),
al-ḥamdu li Llāhi lladhī adh-haba 'anniya l-adha wa 'āfānī."

w1.6   (e11.1(1)) Before the purificatory bath (ghusl): "Bismi Llāhi r-Raḥmāni
r-Raḥīm."

w1.7   (e12.17(1)) Before dry ablution (tayammum): "Bismi Llāhi r-Raḥmāni r-
Raḥīm."

THE CALL TO PRAYER

w1.8   (f3.6) The call to prayer (adhan) is: "Allāhu akbaru Llāhu akbar, Allāhu
akbaru Llāhu akbar, ash-hadu an lā ilāha illa Llāh, ash-hadu an lā ilāha illa Llāh,
ash-hadu anna Muḥammadan rasūlu Llāh, ash-hadu anna Muḥammadan rasūlu
Llāh; ḥayya 'ala ṣ-ṣalāh; ḥayya 'ala ṣ-ṣalāh; ḥayya 'ala l-falāḥ, ḥayya 'ala l-falāḥ;
[and here, before the dawn prayer only: "Aṣ-ṣalātu khayrun mina n-nawm, aṣ-
ṣalātu khayrun mina n-nawm";] Allāhu akbaru Llāhu akbar, lā ilāha illa Llāh."
(See note f3.9(3(A:)) about the pauses between the sentences.)

w1.9   (f3.6) The call to commence (iqama) is: "Allāhu akbaru Llāhu akbar, ash-
hadu an lā ilāha illa Llāh, ash-hadu anna Muḥammadan rasūlu Llāh, ḥayya 'ala ṣ-
ṣalā(ti) ḥayya 'ala l-falāḥ, qadi qāmati ṣ-ṣalā(tu) qadi qāmati ṣ-ṣalāh, Allāhu
akbaru Llāhu akbar, lā ilāha illa Llāh."

w1.10   (f3.11, second par.) The reply to "Come to the prayer" (ḥayya 'ala ṣ-
ṣalāh) and "Come to success" (ḥayya 'ala l-falāḥ) is: "Lā ḥawla wa lā quwwata illā
bi Llāh."

w1.11   (f3.11, second par.) The reply to "The prayer is better than sleep" (aṣ-
ṣalātu khayrun mina n-nawm) in the call to the dawn prayer is: "Ṣadaqt(a) wa
barirt."

w1.12   (f3.11, third par.) The reply to "The prayer is commencing" (qadi qāmati ṣ-ṣalāh) is: "Aqāmaha Llāhu wa adāmahā mā dāmati s-samāwātu wa l-arḍ(u) wa ja'alanī min ṣālihī ahlihā.''

w1.13 (f3.12) After blessing the Prophet (Allah bless him and give him peace) subsequently to the call to prayer or call to commence, one adds: "Allāhumma Rabba hādhihi d-da'wati t-tāmmati wa ṣ-ṣalāti l-qā'ima(ti), āti Sayyidanā Muḥammadani l-wasīlata wa l-faḍīlata wa d-darajata r-rafī'a(ta), wa b'ath-hu maqāman maḥmūdani lladhī wa'adtah.''

DESCRIPTION OF THE PRAYER

w1.14 (f8.13) The Opening Supplication (Istiftah): "Wajjahtu wajhī li lladhī faṭara s-samāwāti wa l-arḍa ḥanīfan Musliman wa mā ana mina l-mushrikīn; inna ṣalātī wa nusukī wa maḥyāya wa mamātī li Llāhi Rabbi l-'Ālamīna lā sharīka lah(u), wa bi dhālika umirtu wa ana mina l-Muslimīn.''

w1.15 (f8.16) Saying, "I take refuge, etc." (ta'awwudh): "A'ūdhu bi Llāhi mina sh-Shayṭāni r-rajīm.''

w1.16 (f8.17) The Fatiha:

"In the name of Allah, Most Merciful and Compassionate. All praise be to Allah, Lord of the Worlds, Most Merciful and Compassionate, Master of the Day of Reckoning. You alone we worship, in You alone we seek help. Guide us in the straight way, the way of those You have blessed, not of those whom wrath is upon or those who are lost" (Koran 1:1–7).

الفاتحة w1.16

بِسْمِ اللَّهِ الرَّحْمَنِ الرَّحِيمِ ، الحَمْدُ لِلَّهِ رَبِّ العَالَمِينَ ، الرَّحْمَنِ الرَّحِيمِ ، مَلكِ يَوْمِ الدِّينِ ، إِيَّاكَ نَعْبُدُ وَإِيَّاكَ نَسْتَعِينُ آهْدِنَا الصِّرَاطَ المُسْتَقِيمَ ، صِرَاطَ الَّذِينَ أَنْعَمْتَ عَلَيْهِمْ غَيْرِ المَغْضُوبِ عَلَيْهِمْ وَلَا الضَّالِينَ .

w1.17 (f8.19) After the Fatiha: "Āmīn.''

w1.18 (f8.30, fourth par.) The minimal *dhikr* when bowing: "Subḥāna Rabbiya l-'Adhīm.''
(f8.30, fifth par.) The optimal *dhikr* when bowing, after having said the above: "Allāhumma laka raka'tu wa bika āmantu wa laka aslamt(u); khasha'a laka sam'ī wa baṣarī wa mukhkhī wa 'adhamī wa ma staqallat bihi qadamī.''

w1.19 (f8.32) The minimal *dhikr* when straightening back up from bowing: "Sami'a Llāhu li man ḥamidah," and when one reaches the upright position, "Rabbanā laka l-ḥamd(u), mil'a s-samāwāti wa mil'a l-arḍi wa mil'a mā shi'ta min shay'in ba'd.''

(f8.32) It is optimal, after having said the above, to add: "Ahla th-thanā'i wa l-majd(i), aḥaqqu mā qāla l-'abd(u), wa kullunā laka 'abd(un), lā māni'a li mā a'ṭayta wa lā mu'ṭiya li mā mana't(a), wa lā yanfa'u dha l-jaddi minka l-jadd."

w1.20   (f8.35(5)) The minimal *dhikr* when prostrating: "Subḥāna Rabbiya l-A'lā."

(f8.35(5), second par.) It is optimal, after having said the above, to add: "Allāhumma laka sajadtu wa bika āmantu wa laka aslamt(u), sajada wajhī li lladhī khalaqahu wa ṣawwarahu wa shaqqa sam'ahu wa baṣarahu bi ḥawlihi wa quw-watih(i), tabāraka Llāhu Aḥsanu l-Khāliqīn."

w1.21   (f8.37(4)) When sitting back between prostrations: "Allāhumma ghfir lī wa rḥamnī wa 'āfinī wa jburnī wa hdinī wa rzuqnī."

w1.22   (f8.45) The minimal Testification of Faith (Tashahhud): "At-taḥiyyātu li Llāh(i), salāmun 'alayka ayyuha n-Nabiyyu wa raḥmatu Llāhi wa barakātuh, salāmun 'alaynā wa 'alā 'ibādi Llāhi ṣ-ṣāliḥīn, ash-hadu an lā ilāha illa Llāhu wa anna Muḥammadan rasūlu Llāh."

(f8.45, second par.) The optimal Testification of Faith: "At-taḥiyyātu l-mubārakātu ṣ-ṣalawātu ṭ-ṭayyibātu li Llāh, as-salāmu 'alayka ayyuha n-Nabiyyu wa raḥmatu Llāhi wa barakātuh, as-salāmu 'alaynā wa 'alā 'ibādi Llāhi ṣ-ṣāliḥīn, ash-hadu an lā ilāha illa Llāh(u), wa ash-hadu anna Muḥammadan rasūlu Llāh."

w1.23   (f8.45, fifth par.) The minimal Blessings on the Prophet (Allah bless him and give him peace) in the Testification of Faith (Tashahhud): "Allāhumma ṣalli 'alā Muḥammad."

(f8.45, sixth par.) The optimal Blessings on the Prophet (Allah bless him and give him peace) in the Testification of Faith (Tashahhud): "Allāhumma ṣalli 'alā Muḥammadin wa 'alā āli Muḥammadin kamā ṣallayta 'alā Ibrāhīma wa 'alā āli Ibrāhīm(a), wa bārik 'alā Muḥammadin wa 'alā āli Muḥammadin kamā bārakta 'alā Ibrāhīma wa 'alā āli Ibrāhīm(a), fi l-'ālamīna innaka ḥamīdun majīd." It is desirable to add the word *sayyidinā* (our liegelord) before each mention of the names *Muhammad* and *Ibrahim,* saying, "Allāhumma ṣalli 'alā Sayyidinā Muḥammadin wa 'alā āli Sayyidinā Muḥammadin kamā ṣallayta 'alā Sayyidinā Ibrāhīma ..." etc.

w1.24   (f8.46) The supplication after the Testification of Faith (Tashahhud): "Allāhumma ghfir lī mā qaddamtu wa mā akhkhartu wa mā asrartu wa mā a'lantu wa mā asraftu wa mā anta a'lamu bihi minnī, anta l-Muqaddimu wa anta l-Mu'akhkhir(u), lā ilāha illā ant."

w1.25   (f8.47) The minimal Salams to close the prayer: "As-Salāmu 'alaykum."

(f8.47, second par.) The optimal Salams to close the prayer: "As-salāmu 'alaykum wa raḥmatu Llāh."

w1.26   (f8.50) Post-prayer *dhikr:*

(1)   ﴿اللهُ لاإِلَهَ إِلَّا هُوَ الحَيُّ القَيُّومُ لا تَأْخُذُهُ سِنَةٌ ولا نَوْمٌ لَهُ ما في السَّمواتِ وما في الأرضِ مَنْ ذا الَّذي يَشْفَعُ عِنْدَهُ إلَّا بِإذْنِهِ يَعْلَمُ ما بَيْنَ أَيْدِيهِمْ وما خَلْفَهُمْ وَلا يُحيطونَ بِشَيْءٍ مِنْ عِلْمِهِ إلَّا بِما شاءَ وَسِعَ كُرْسِيُّهُ السَّمواتِ والأرْضَ وَلا يَؤُودُهُ حِفْظُهُما وهُوَ العَلِيُّ العَظِيمُ﴾ .

(2)   ﴿بِسْمِ اللهِ الرَّحْمَنِ الرَّحيمِ قُلْ هُوَ اللهُ أَحَدٌ اللهُ الصَّمَدُ لَمْ يَلِدْ ولَمْ يُولَدْ ولَمْ يَكُنْ لَهُ كُفُواً أَحَدٌ﴾ ,

(3)   ﴿بِسْمِ اللهِ الرَّحْمَنِ الرَّحيمِ قُلْ أَعُوذُ بِرَبِّ الفَلَقِ مِنْ شَرِّ ما خَلَقَ ومِنْ شَرِّ غاسِقٍ إذا وَقَبَ ومِنْ شَرِّ النَّفّاثاتِ في العُقَدِ ومِنْ شَرِّ حاسِدٍ إذا حَسَدَ﴾ .

(4)   ﴿بِسْمِ اللهِ الرَّحْمَنِ الرَّحيمِ قُلْ أَعُوذُ بِرَبِّ النّاسِ مَلِكِ النّاسِ إلهِ النّاسِ مِنْ شَرِّ الوَسْواسِ الخَنّاسِ الَّذي يُوَسْوِسُ في صُدُورِ النّاسِ مِنَ الجِنَّةِ والنّاسِ﴾ .

(5)   "Astaghfiru Llāh(a)."

(6)   "Allāhumma anta s-Salāmu wa minka s-salām(u), tabārakta yā Dha l-Jalāli wa l-Ikrām."

(7)   "Allāhumma lā māni'a li mā a'tayt(a), wa lā mu'tiya li mā mana't(a), wa lā yanfa'u dha l-jaddi minka l-jadd."

(8)   "Subḥāna Llāh(i)."

(9)   "Al-ḥamdu li Llāh(i)."

(10)   "Allāhu akbar(u)."

(11)   "Lā ilāha illa Llāhu waḥdahu lā sharīka lah(u), lahu l-mulku wa lahu l-ḥamdu wa huwa 'alā kulli shay'in qadīr."

w1.27   (f8.53) The supplication (qunut) in the dawn prayer after straightening up from bowing in the second rak'a, where, if praying alone, one uses the *ī* wherever it is italicized below, while if leading a group, one substitutes *ā* for each italicized *ī:* "Allāhumma hdinī fī man hadayt(a), wa 'āfinī fī man 'āfayt(a), wa tawallanī fī man tawallayt(a), wa bārik *lī* [*lanā* if leading a group] fī mā a'tayt(a), wa qinī sharra mā qaḍayt(a), fa innaka taqdī wa lā yuqḍā 'alayk(a), wa innahu lā yaḍillu man wālayt(a), tabārakta Rabbanā wa ta'ālayt." It is commendable to add "wa lā ya'izzu man 'ādayt(a)," before the word *tabārakta* in the last sentence.

SUPEREROGATORY PRAYERS

w1.28   (f10.5, second par.) When praying *witr* after *tarawih*, one adds the following to the above supplication (qunut): "Allāhumma innā nasta'īnuka wa nastaghfiruka wa nastahdīka wa nu'minu bika wa natawakkalu 'alayka wa nuthnī 'alayka l-khayra kullah(u), nashkuruka a lā nakfiruk(a), wa nakhla'u wa natruku man yafjuruk(a), Allāhumma iyyāka na'budu wa laka nusallī wa nasjudu illayka wa nas'ā wa naḥfid(u), narjū raḥmataka wa nakhshā 'adhābaka inna 'adhābaka l-jidda bi l-kuffāri mulḥiq."

w1.29 (f10.10, second par.) A substitute for two rak'as of greeting the mosque: "Subḥāna Llāhi wa l-ḥamdu li Llāhi wa lā ilāha illa Llāhu, wa Llāhu akbar."

w1.30 (f10.12, third par.) The supplication of the prayer for guidance (istikhara): "Allāhumma innī astakhīruka bi 'ilmika wa staqdiruka bi qudratika wa as'aluka min faḍlika l-'aḍīm, fa'innaka taqdiru wa lā aqdir(u), wa ta'lamu wa lā a'lam(u), wa anta 'Allāmu l-Ghuyūb(i), Allāhumma in kunta ta'lamu anna hādha l-amra khayrun lī fī *dīnī wa ma'āshī wa 'āqibati amrī* [a variant has " 'ājili amrī wa ājilih(i)" in place of the italicized] fa qdurhu lī wa yassirhu lī thumma bārik lī fīh(i), wa in kunta ta'lamu anna hādha l-amra sharrun lī fī *dīni wa ma'āshī wa 'āqibati amrī* [the variant has " 'ājili amrī wa ājilih(i)" as before] fa ṣrifhu 'annī wa ṣrifnī 'anhu wa qdur liya l-khayra haythu kāna thumma raddinī bih(i)," then one mentions the matter at hand.

THE FRIDAY PRAYER

w1.31 (f18.9(e) third par.) Minimal sermon (khutba) for the Friday prayer: "Inna l-ḥamda li Llāh, naḥmaduhu wa nasta'īnuhu wa nastaghfiruh(u), na'ūdhu bi Llāhi min shurūri anfusinā wa min sayyi'āti a'mālinā, man yahdi Llāhu fa lā mudilla lah(u), wa man yudlil fa lā hādiya lah(u), wa ash-hadu an lā ilāha illa Llāhu waḥdahu lā sharīka lah(u), wa ash-hadu anna Muḥammadan 'abduhu wa rasūluh(u), ṣalla Llāhu 'alayhi wa sallama wa 'alā ālihi wa aṣ-ḥābih(i), yā ayyuha lladhīna āmanu ttaqu Llāha ḥaqqa tuqātih(i), wa lā tamutunna illā wa antum Muslimūn(a). 'Yā ayyuha n-nāsu ttaqū Rabbakumu lladhī khalaqakum min nafsin wāḥidatin wa khalaqa minhā zawjahā wa baththa minhumā rijālan kathīran wa nisā'a(n), wa ttaqu Llāha lladhī tasā'alūna bihi wa l-arḥām(a), inna Llāha kāna 'alaykum raqība(n).' "

THE PRAYER ON THE TWO 'EIDS

w1.32 (f19.8, last par.) The Allahu Akbars and additional *dhikr* of 'Eid al-Adha: "Allahu akbaru Llāhu akbaru Llāhu akbar, lā ilāha illa Llāh, Allāhu akbaru Llāhu akbar(u), wa li Llāhi l-ḥamd." It is commendable to add to this: "Allāhu akbaru kabīra(n), wa l-ḥamdu li Llāhi kathīra(n), wa subḥāna Llāhi bukratan wa aṣīla(n), lā ilāha illa Llāhu wa lā na'budu illā iyyāh(u), mukhliṣīna lahu d -dīn(a), wa law kariha l-kāfirūn. Lā ilāha illa Llāhu waḥdah(u), ṣadaqa wa'dah(u), wa naṣara 'abdah(u), wa a'azza jundah(u), wa hazama l-aḥzāba waḥdah(u), lā ilāha illa Llāhu wa Llāhu akbar."

THE DROUGHT PRAYER

w1.33 (f21.3, second par.) In the drought prayer, the imam says the following nine times before the first sermon (khutba) and seven times before the second: "Astaghfiru Llāha l-'Adhīma lladhī lā ilāha illā huwa l-Ḥayya l-Qayyūma wa atūbu ilayh."

(f21.3, fourth par.) He frequently says "Astaghfiru Llāh," the Blessings on the Prophet (Allah bless him and give him peace), and supplicates Allah with the following Koranic verses: "Istaghfirū Rabbakum innahu kāna ghaffāra(n), yursili s-samā'a 'alaykum midrāra(n), wa yumdidkum bi amwālin wa banīna wa yaj'al lakum jannātin wa yaj'al lakum anhāra."

(f21.3, seventh par.) The drought prayer supplication: "Allāhumma sqinā ghaythan mughīthan hanī'an marī'an sahhan 'āmman ghadaqan ṭabaqan mujalli-lan dā'iman ilā yawmi d-dīn. Allāhumma inna bi l-'ibādi wa l-bilādi min al-jahdi wa l-jū'i wa d-danki mā lā nashkū illā ilayk(a), Allāhumma anbit lanā z-zar'a wa adirra lana ḍ-ḍar'a wa anzil 'alaynā min barakāti s-samā'(i), wa anbit lanā min barakāti l-arḍi wa kshif 'annā mina l-balā'i mā lā yakshifuhu ghayruk."

w1.34 (f21.6) When thunder is heard: "Subḥāna lladhī yusabbiḥu r-ra'du bi ḥamdihi wa l-malā'ikatu min khīfatih."

When lightning is seen: "Subḥana man yurīkumu l-barqa khawfan wa ṭama'a(n)."

w1.35 (f21.7) Supplication against too much rain: "Allāhuma hawalaynā wa lā 'alaynā; Allāhumma 'ala ḍh-ḍhirābi wa l-ākāmi wa buṭūni l-awdiyati wa manābiti sh-shajar."

VISITING THE SICK

w1.36 (g1.4) Supplication for Allah to heal a sick person: "Allāhumma Rabba n-Nāsi adh-hibi l-ba'sa wa shfi wa anta sh-Shāfi lā shāfiya illā anta shifā'an lā yughādiru alaman wa lā saqama(n)."

THE FUNERAL PRAYER (JANAZA)

w1.37 (g4.10) Supplication after the third Allahu Akbar of the funeral prayer: "Allāhumma hādhā 'abduka wa bnu 'abdik(a), kharaja min rawḥi d-dunyā wa sa'atihā, wa maḥbubūhu wa aḥibbā'uhu fīhā, ilā ḍhulmati l-qabri wa mā huwa lāqīh(i), kāna yash-hadu an lā ilāha illā anta waḥdaka lā sharīka lak(a), wa anna Muḥammadan 'abduka wa rasūluk(a), wa anta a'lamu bihi minnā. Allāhumma innahu nazala bika wa anta ghaniyyun 'an 'adhābihi wa qad ji'nāka rāghibīna ilayka shufa'ā'a lah(u). Allāhumma, in kāna muḥsinan fa zid fī iḥsānih(i), wa in kāna musī'an fa tajāwaz 'anhu wa laqqihi bi raḥmatika riḍāk(a), wa qihi fitnata l-qabri wa 'adhabāhu wa fsaḥ lahu fī qabrihi wa jāfi l-arḍa 'an janbayhi wa laqqihi bi raḥmatika l-amna min 'adhābika ḥattā tab'athahu āminan ilā jannatika yā Arḥama r-Rāhimīn."

(g4.11) One may add the following, before the above supplication: "Allāhumma ghfir li ḥayyinā wa mayyitinā wa shāhidinā wa ghā'ibinā wa saghīrinā wa kabīrinā wa dhakarinā wa unthānā. Allāhumma man aḥyaytahu minnā fa ḥyihi 'ala l-Islām, wa man tawaffaytahu minnā fa tawaffihi 'ala l-Īmān."

(g4.11, second par.) If the deceased is a child, one may say, with the above addition: "Allāhumma j'alhu faraṭan li abuwayhi wa salafan wa dhukhran wa 'idhatan wa 'tibāran wa shāfi'a(n), wa thaqqil bihi mawāzīnahumā wa frighi ṣ-ṣabra 'alā qulūbihimā."

w1.38 (g4.12) After the fourth Allahu Akbar of the funeral prayer: "Allāhumma lā taḥrimnā ajrahu wa lā taftinnā ba'dahu wa ghfir lanā wa lah(u)."

w1.39 (g4.13(f)) The minimal supplication after the third Allahu Akbar of the funeral prayer: "Allāhumma ghfir li hādha l-mayyit."

BURIAL

w1.40 (g5.4(1) When putting the deceased in the grave: "Bismi Llāhi wa 'alā millati rasūli Llāhi ṣalla Llāhu 'alayhi wa sallam."

w1.41 (g5.6) With the first handfuls of earth in burying the dead:
First handful: "Minhā khalaqnākum."
Second handful: "Wa fīhā nu'īdukum."
Third handful: "Wa minhā nukhrijukum tāratan ukhrā."

w1.42 (g5.6(2) Supplication for the person buried: "Allāhumma thabbit-hu, Allāhumma laqqinhu ḥujjatah(u)."

w1.43 (g5.8, second par.) Greeting to buried believers: "Salāmun 'alaykum dāra qawmin mu'minīn(a), wa innā in shā' Allāhu bikum lāḥiqūn."

w1.44 (g6.2(1–3)) Condolences:
To a Muslim who's lost a Muslim: "A'dhama Llāhu ajraka wa aḥsana 'azā'aka wa ghafara li mayyitik(a)."
To a Muslim who's lost a non-Muslim: "A'dhama Llāhu ajraka wa aḥsana 'azā'ak(a)."
To a non-Muslim who's lost a Muslim: "Aḥsana Llāhu 'azā'aka wa ghafara li mayyitik(a)."

ZAKAT

w1.45 (h8.4) Supplication by the zakat recipient for the zakat giver: "Ājaraka Llāhu fīmā a'ṭayt(a), wa bāraka laka fīmā abqayt(a), wa ja'alahu laka ṭahūra(n)."

FASTING RAMADAN

w1.46 (i1.25) *Dhikr* upon breaking one's fast: "Allāhumma laka ṣumtu wa 'alā rizqika afṭart."

w1.47 (i3.2, last par.) Supplication for Laylat al-Qadr: "Allāhumma innaka 'afuwwun tuḥibbu l-'afwa fa 'fu 'annī."

THE PILGRIMAGE

w1.48 (j3.4) The pilgrim chant of "Labbayk": "Labbayka Llāhumma labbayk, labbayka lā sharīka laka labbayk, inna l-ḥamda wa n-ni'mata laka wa l-mulk, lā sharīka lak." (Thrice.)
Then one says the Blessings on the Prophet (Allah bless him and give him peace), and then asks Allah for paradise and seeks refuge in Him from hell by saying: "Allāhumma innī as'aluka l-jannata wa na'īmahā wa riḍwānak(a), wa a'ūdhu bika min sakhaṭika wa n-nār."
(j3.4, last par.) If one sees something pleasing (or offensive) while in ihram, one says: "Labbayka inna l-'aysha 'ayshu l-ākhira."

w1.49 (j4.2) Supplication upon first seeing the Kaaba: "Allāhumma zid hādha l-bayta tashrīfan wa takrīman wa ta'ḍhīman wa muhāba(tan), wa zid man sharrafahu wa 'aḍhḍhamahu mimman hajjahu wa 'tamarahu tashrīfan wa takrīman wa ta'ḍhīman wa birra(n), Allāhumma anta s-Salāmu wa minka s-salāmu fa ḥayyinā Rabbanā bi s-salām."

w1.50 (j5.3(2–3)) When kissing the Black Stone: "Allāhu akbaru Llāhu akbaru Llāhu akbar(u), Allāhumma īmānan bika wa taṣdīqan bi kitābika wa wafā'an bi 'ahdika wa ttibā'an li sunnati nabiyyika ṣalla Llāhu 'alayhi wa sallam."
(j5.5) When passing the Kaaba's door in circumambulation: "Allāhumma inna hādha l-bayta baytuka wa l-ḥarama ḥaramuka wa l-amna amnuk(a), wa hādhā maqāmu l-'ā'idhi bika mina n-nār."
(j5.6) When passing the corner by Hijr Isma'il: "Allāhumma innī a'ūdhu bika mina sh-shakki wa sh-shirki wa sh-shiqāqi wa n-nifāqi wa sū'i l-akhlāq(i), wa sū'i l-munqalabi fi l-māli wa l-ahli wa l-walad."
(j5.7) When passing the rainspout at the top of the Kaaba (Mizab al-Rahma):

"Allāhumma adhillanī fī dhillika yawma lā dhilla illā dhilluk(a), wa sqinī bi ka'si nabiyyika Muhammadin salla Llāhu 'alayhi wa sallama mashraban hanī'an lā adhma'u ba'dahu abada(n)."

(j5.8) When between the third corner and the Yamani corner: "Allāhumma j'alhu hajjan mabrūran wa sa'yan mashkūran wa 'amalan maqbūlan wa tijāratan lan tabūr(a), yā 'Azīzu yā Ghafūr."

w1.51   (j5.13, fourth par.) When trotting in first three rounds of circumambulation: "Allāhumma j'alhu hajjan mabrūran wa sa'yan mashkūran wa dhanban maghfūra(n)."

(j5.13, fifth par.) When performing the last four rounds of circumambulation: "Rabbi ghfir wa rham wa 'fu 'ammā ta'lam(u), innaka anta l-A'azzu l-Akram(u), Rabbanā ātinā fi d-dunyā hasanatan wa fi l-ākhirati hasanatan wa qinā 'adhāba n-nār."

w1.52   (j5.18, second par.) Supplication after two rak'as at the Station of Ibrahim: "Allāhumma hādhā baladuka wa l-masjidu l-harāmu wa baytuka l-haram(u), wa ana 'abduka bnu 'abdika wa bnu amatik(a), ataytuka bi dhūnubin kathīratin wa khatāyā jammatin wa a'mālin sayyi'a(tin), wa hādhā maqāmu l-'ā'idhi bika mina n-nār; fa ghfir lī, innaka anta l-Ghafūru r-Rahīm. Allāhumma innaka da'awta 'ibādaka ilā baytika l-harām wa qad ji'tu tāliban rahmataka muttabi'an mardātika wa anta muthīb(un), fa ghfir lī wa rhamnī, innaka 'alā kulli shay'in qadīr."

w1.53   (j6.2(2)) *Dhikr* on Safa: "Lā ilāha illa Llāhu wahdahu lā sharīka lah(u), lahu l-mulku wa lahu l-hamdu yuhyī wa yumīt(u), bi yadihi l-khayru wa huwa 'alā kulli shay'in qadīr. Lā ilāha illa Llāhu wahdahu lā sharīka lah(u), anjaza wa'dah(u), wa nasara 'abdah(u), wa hazama l-ahzāba wahdah(u), lā ilāha illa Llāhu wa lā na'budu illā iyyāhu mukhlisīna lahu d-dīna wa law kariha l-kāfirūn."

w1.54   (j6.5) Supplication between Safa and Marwa: "Rabbi ghfir wa rham wa tajāwaz 'ammā ta'lamu innaka anta l-A'azzu l-Akram(u), Allāhumma Rabbanā ātinā fi d-dunyā hasanatan wa fi l-ākhirati hasanatan wa qinā 'adhāba n-nār."

w1.55   (j7.3) On the way to 'Arafa: "Allāhumma ilayka tawajjaht(u), wa li wajhika l-karīmi aradt(u), fa j'al dhanbī maghfūran wa hajjī mabrūran wa rhamnī wa lā tukhayyibnī."

w1.56   (j8.2, second par.) When standing at 'Arafa: "Lā ilāha illa Llāhu wahdahu lā sharīka lah(u), lahu l-mulku wa lahu l-hamdu wa huwa 'alā kulli shay'in qadīr."

w1.57   (j9.2) When standing at al-Mash'ar al-Haram: "Allāhumma kamā awqaftanā fīhi wa araytanā iyyāh(u), fa waffiqnā li dhikrika kamā hadaytanā, wa ghfir lanā wa rhamnā kamā wa'adtanā bi qawlika wa qawluka l-ḥaqq(u): Fa idhā afaḍ-tum min 'Arafātin fa dhkuru Llāha 'inda l-Mash'ari l-Ḥarām(i), wa dhkurūhu kamā hādākum wa in kuntum min qablihi la mina ḍ-ḍāllīn(a), thumma afīḍū min ḥaythu afāḍa n-nās(u), wa staghfiru Llāha inna Llāha ghafūrun raḥīm. Rabbanā ātinā fi d-dunyā ḥasantan wa fi l-ākhirati ḥasanatan wa qinā 'adhāba n-nār."

w1.58 (j9.8(2)) Supplication after cutting one's hair: "Allāhu akbaru Llāhu akbaru Llāhu akbar(u), wa li Llāhi l-ḥamd."

w1.59 (j11.3) Supplication after farewell circumambulation: "Allāhumma inna l-bayta baytuka wa l-'abda 'abduka wa bnu 'abdayk(a), ḥamaltanī 'alā mā sakhkharta lī min khalqika ḥattā ṣayyartanī fī bilādika wa ballaghtanī bi ni'matika ḥatta a'antanī 'alā qadā'i manāsikik(a), fa in kunta raḍīta 'annī fa zdad 'annī riḍā(n), wa illā fa munna l-'āna qabla an tan'ā 'an baytika dārī wa yab'uda 'anhu mazārī, hādhā awānu nṣirāfī in adhinta lī, ghayra mustabdilin bika wa lā bi baytika wa lā rāghibin 'anka wa lā 'an baytik(a), Allāhumma fa aṣ-ḥibniya l-'āfiyata fī badanī wa l-'iṣmata fī dīnī wa aḥsin munqalabī wa rzuqni l-'amal bi ṭā'atika mā abqaytanī wa jma' lī khayrayi d-dunyā wa l-ākhira(ti), innaka 'alā kulli shay'in qadīr." Then one blesses the Prophet (Allah bless him and give him peace).

w1.60 (j13.1) Supplication when entering a mosque: "Bismi Llāhi wa l-ḥamdu li Llāh(i), Allāhumma ṣalli 'alā Sayyidinā Muḥammadin wa 'alā ālihi wa aṣ-ḥābihi wa sallim. Allāhumma ftaḥ lī abwāba raḥmatik."

w1.61 (j13.2) Greeting the Prophet (Allah bless him and give him peace): "As-salāmu 'alayka yā Rasūla Llāh(i), as-salāmu 'alayka yā Nabiyya Llāh(i), as-salāmu 'alayka yā Khīrata Llāh(i), as-salāmu 'alayka yā Khayra Khalqi Llāh(i), as-salāmu 'alayka yā Ḥabība Llāh."

MARRIAGE

w1.62 (m2.17) Sunna address (khutba) before making a marriage proposal: "Al-ḥamdu li Llāh(i), wa ṣ-ṣalātu wa s-salāmu 'alā rasūli Llāh(i) ṣalla Llāhu 'alayhi wa sallam(a), ūṣīkum bi taqwa Llāh(i), ji'tukum khāṭiban karīmatakum [and here one mentions her name]."

(m2.17, second par.) Sunna address before marrying: "Uzawwijuka 'alā mā amara Llāhu Ta'āla bihi min imsākin bi ma'rūf(in), aw tasrīḥin bi iḥsān(in)."

w1.63 (m3.2(a)) Words that effect a marriage: "Zawwajtuka," or "An-kaḥtuka."

(m3.2(b)) The spoken acceptance: "Tazawwajtuhā," or "Qabiltu nikāḥahā."

w1.64   (m5.3) Supplication for the wedding night: "Bāraka Llāhu li kullin minnā fī ṣāḥibih."

AMULETS AND PROTECTIVE WORDS

w1.65   (w17.2, second par.) Supplication for fearful situations: "A'ūdhu bi kalimāti Llāhi t-tāmmati min ghaḍabihi wa min hamazāti sh-shayāṭīna an yaḥḍūrun."

SUPPLICATING ALLAH (TAWASSUL) THROUGH THE PROPHET (ALLAH BLESS HIM AND GIVE HIM PEACE) IN THE PRAYER OF NEED

w1.66   (w40.3, second par.) Supplicating Allah through the Prophet (Allah bless him and give him peace): "Allāhumma innī as'aluka wa atawajjahu ilayka bi nabiyyī Muḥammad(in), Nabiyyi r-Raḥma(ti), yā Muḥammadu innī astashfaʻu bika ʻalā Rabbī fī ḥājatī li tuqḍā lī, Allāhumma shaffiʻhu fiyya."
(w40.4, second par.) Another form: "Allāhumma innī as'aluka wa atawaj-jahu ilayka bi nabiyyinā Muḥammad(in), Nabiyyi r-Raḥma(ti), yā Muḥammadu innī atawajjahu bika ilā Rabbī fa yaqḍiya ḥājatī," and one mentions one's need.

*

w2.0   INDEX FOR TAPE-RECORDING *DHIKR* AND SUPPLICATIONS

w2.0 دليل مواضع الأذكار والأدعية

w2.1   (n:) Those who want to tape-record a native speaker of Arabic reciting the *dhikr* of this volume—an easier way to learn than using only the transliterations provided above—may wish to use the following index as a taping sequence:

(e5.5) Before ablution (wudu)
(e5.18) After ablution
(e9.1(5)) Before and after using the lavatory
(e11.1(1)) Before the purificatory bath (ghusl)
(e12.17(1)) Before dry ablution (tayammum)
(f3.6) The call to prayer (adhan)
(f3.6) The call to commence (iqama)
(f3.11, second par.) Replies to "Come to the prayer" and "Come to success" in the call to prayer
(f3.11, second par.) Reply to "Prayer is better than sleep" in the call to the dawn prayer
(f3.11, third par.) Reply to "The prayer is commencing" in the call to commence
(f3.12) After blessing the Prophet (Allah bless him and give him peace) sub-

sequent to the call to prayer

(f8.13) The Opening Supplication of the prayer (Istiftah)

(f8.16) "I take refuge, etc." (ta'awwudh)

(f8.17) The Fatiha

(f8.19) After the Fatiha

(f8.30, fourth par.) The minimal *dhikr* when when bowing

(f8.30, fifth par.) The optimal *dhikr* when bowing

(f8.32) The minimal *dhikr* when straightening up

(f8.32) The optimal *dhikr* when straightening up

(f8.35(5)) Minimal *dhikr* when prostrating

(f8.35(5), second par.) Optimal addition to this

(f8.37(4)) When sitting back between prostrations

(f8.45) Minimal Testification of Faith (Tashahhud)

(f8.45, second par.) Optimal Testification of Faith

(f8.45, fifth par.) Minimal Blessings on the Prophet (Allah bless him and give him peace) after the Testification of Faith

(f8.45, sixth par.) Optimal Blessings on the Prophet (Allah bless him and give him peace) after the Testification of Faith

(f8.46) Supplication after the Testification of Faith

(f8.47) Minimal Salams to close the prayer

(f8.47, second par.) Optimal Salams to close the prayer

(f8.50) Post-prayer *dhikr*

(f8.53) Supplication (qunut) in the dawn prayer after straightening up from bowing in the second rak'a

(f10.5, second par.) Addition to the above supplication (qunut) when praying *witr* after *tarawih*

(f10.10, second par.) Substitute for two rak'as of greeting the mosque

(f10.12, third par.) Supplication of the prayer for guidance (istikhara)

(f18.9(e)) Minimal sermon (khutba) for the Friday prayer

(f19.8, last par.) The Allahu Akbars and additional *dhikr* of 'Eid al-Adha

(f21.3, second par.) *Dhikr* said by the imam in drought prayer before sermon (khutba)

(f21.3, fourth par.) Koranic supplication used during the drought prayer

(f21.3, seventh par.) The drought prayer supplication

(f21.6) *Dhikr* for thunder and lightning

(f21.7) Supplication against too much rain

(g1.4) Supplication for Allah to heal a sick person

(g4.10) Supplication after the third Allahu Akbar of the funeral prayer

(g4.11) Addition said prior to the above supplication

(g4.11, second par.) Supplication said with the latter addition if the deceased is a child

(g4.12) After the fourth Allahu Akbar of the funeral prayer

(g4.13(f)) Minimal supplication after the third Allahu Akbar of the funeral prayer

(g5.4(1) When putting the deceased in the grave

(g5.6) With the first handfuls of earth in burying the dead

(g5.6(2)) Supplication for the person buried

(g5.8, second par.) Greeting to buried believers

(g6.2(1–3)) Condolences to those who have lost next of kin

(h8.4) Supplication by the zakat recipient for the giver

(i1.25) *Dhikr* upon breaking one's fast

(i3.2, last par.) Supplication for Laylat al-Qadr

(j3.4) The pilgrim chant of "Labbayk"

(j3.4, last par.) If one sees something pleasing (or offensive) while in ihram

(j4.2) Supplication upon first seeing the Kaaba

(j5.3)2–3)) When kissing the Black Stone

(j5.5) When passing the Kaaba's door in circumambulation

(j5.6) When passing the corner by Hijr Isma'il

(j5.7) When passing the rainspout at the top of the Kaaba (Mizab al-Rahma)

(j5.8) When between the third corner and the Yamani corner

(j5.13, fourth par.) When trotting in the first three rounds of circumambulation

(j5.13, fifth par.) When performing the last four rounds

(j5.18, second par.) Supplication after two rak'as at the Station of Ibrahim

(j6.2(2)) *Dhikr* at Safa

(j6.5) Supplication between Safa and Marwa

(j7.3) On the way to 'Arafa

(j8.2, second par.) When standing at 'Arafa

(j9.2) When standing at al-Mash'ar al-Haram

(j9.8(2)) Supplication after cutting one's hair

(j11.3) Supplication after the farewell circumambulation

(j13.1) Supplication when entering a mosque

(j13.2) Greeting the Prophet (Allah bless him and give him peace)

(m2.17) Address (khutba) before making a marriage proposal

(m2.17, second par.) Address before marrying

(m3.2(a)) Words that effect a marriage

(m3.2(b)) The spoken acceptance

(m5.3) Supplication for the wedding night

(w17.2, second par.) Supplication for fearful situations

(w40.3, second par.) Supplicating Allah (tawassul) through the Prophet

*

w3.0   REASON AND SACRED LAW (from a1.4)

w3.0   العقل والشرع

w3.1   (Ghazali:) The way that the medicines of acts of worship work, their limits and amounts being specified and determined by the prophets, cannot be comprehended by the apparatus of intellectuals' "intelligence." Rather, it is necessary to follow the example of the prophets, to whom these properties are perceived through prophetic light, not the apparatus of the mind.

If a philosopher denies the possibility of such properties, in the numbers of the rak'as of the prayer, stoning the pillars at Mina, the number of hajj integrals, or any of the acts of worship in Sac-

w3.1   (الغــزالي:) [. . .] وأدوية العبـادات بحـدودها ومقاديرها المحدودة المقـدرة من جهـة الأنبياء، لا يدرك وجه تأثيرهـا ببضاعة عقل العقلاء، بل يجب فيهـا تقليـد الأنبيـاء الـذين أدركـوا تلك الخواص بنور النبوة لا ببضاعة العقل.

[. . .] فإن أنكـر فلسفي إمكـان هذه الخــواص في أعــداد الـركعـات ورمي الجمـار وعدد أركان الحج وسائر تعبدات

red Law, he will not find any difference in principle between such properties and those of the various medicines, for example, or the stars. If he says, "I have tested something of both astronomy and medicine, and found them to be correct, so that my heart has accepted them and I no longer think them farfetched or reject them; while I have not tried this, so how can I know it exists, or investigate it, should I acknowledge its possibility?"—I would answer, "But you do not always confine your acceptance to what you have personally tried. Rather, you accept information from others who have, and you follow them. Let us imagine a man who reaches physical and mental maturity without ever experiencing a disease, but who then falls ill. He has a concerned father with skill in medicine, whose claims to medical knowledge he has heard as long as he can remember, and his father now compounds some medicine and says, 'This is appropriate for your disease and will cure it.' How much will the patient's intellect demand, even if the medicine is bitter and tastes unpleasant? Will he take it, or will he call the doctor a liar, saying, 'I do not see the suitability of this medicine for effecting a cure, since I've never tried it.' You would doubtless consider him a fool for this. And just so do the knowledgeable who possess spiritual insight consider your reservations."

If such a person says: "But how can I be certain of the sincerity of the Prophet's concern (Allah bless him and give him peace), and his knowledge of this medicine?" I reply, "How did you learn of your father's concern when it was not something physically perceptible? You acquired incontestably certain knowledge of it by the evidence of how he has always behaved and by observing his actions, their causes and results. So too, whoever examines what the Prophet said (Allah bless him and give him peace) and the accounts in hadiths of his concern for guiding others and his kindly way of urging them with graciousness and tact to improve their character and forget their differences—in a word, urging them to accept the only means capable of improving their religious and this-worldly concerns—whoever examines these will gain complete certainty that the Prophet's concern towards his Community was greater than a father's for his son. When one considers the wondrous deeds that appeared

الشـرع، لم يجـد بينهـا وبين خواص الأدويـة والنجـوم فرقاً أصلاً . فإن قال قد جربت شيئاً من النجوم وشيئاً من الطب، فوجـدت بعضه صادقاً، فانقدح في نفسي تصديقه وسقط من قلبي استبعاده ونفرته ؛ وهـذا لم أجـربـه، فبم أعلم وجـوده وتحقيقه إن أقررت بإمكانه ؛ فأقول : إنك لا تقتصـر على تصـديق ما جربتـه، بل سمعت أخبار المجربين وقلدتهم [...] فإنـا لو فرضنا رجلاً بلغ وعقل ولم يجرب المـرض فمـرض ولـه والـد مشفق حاذق بالطب يسمع دعواه في معرفة الطب منذ عقل فعجن له والده دواء فقال هذا يصلح لمـرضـك، ويشفيك من سقمـك فمـاذا يقتضيه عقله، وإن كان الـدواء مراً كريه المذاق، أيتناول أو يكذّب ويقول : أنا لا أعقـل مناسبـة هذا الـدواء لتحصيل الشفـاء، ولم أجـربـه . فلا شك أنـك تستحمقه إن فعـل ذلـك، وكــذلك يستحمقك أهل البصائر في توقفك . فإن قلت فبم أعرف شفقة النبي عليه السلام ومعـرفته بهذا الطب؟ فأقول : وبم عرفت شفقة أبيك وليس ذلك أمراً محسوساً، بل عرفتها بقرائن أحواله وشواهد أعماله في مصادره وموارده علماً ضروريـاً لا تمـاري فيـه، ومن نظر في أقوال رسول الله عليه الصـلاة والسـلام ومـا ورد من الأخبار في اهتمـامه بإرشـاد الخلق وتلطفه في جر النـاس بأنـواع الرفق واللطف إلى تحسين الأخـلاق وإصلاح ذات البين، وبالجملة إلى مـا لا يصلح إلا به من دينهم ودنيـاهم، حصـل لـه علم ضروري بأن شفقتـه على أمتـه أعظم من شفقـة الـوالـد على ولده . وإذا نظر إلى عجـائب مـا ظهـر عليـه من

at his hands (Allah bless him and give him peace), the wonders of the unseen imparted by the Koran through his tongue and conveyed by prophetic hadith, when one looks at what he said about the latter days which has come to pass as he foretold; one gains absolute certainty that he reached the sphere which lies above and beyond the mind, and that the eye which opens onto the unseen that none but the elect know, of matters unfathomable to intellects, was opened for him (*al-Munqidh min al-dalal* (y41), 58, 67–69).

الأفعال، وإلى عجائب الغيب الذي أخبر عنه القرآن على لسانه وفي الأخبار، وإلى ما ذكره في آخر الـزمـان فظهر ذلك كما ذكره، علم علمـاً ضرورياً أنه بلغ الطور الـذي وراء العقل وانفتحت له العين التي يتكشف منهـا الغيب، الـذي لا يدركه إلا الخـواص والأمور التي لا تدركها العقول [محرر من المنقذ من الضلال: ٥٨، ٦٧ ـ ٦٩].

*

w4.0   THE FINALITY OF THE PROPHET'S MESSAGE (from a1.5)

w4.0   اكتمال الإسلام

w4.1   (n:) This section has been translated to clarify some possible confusions among Muslims as to Islam's place among world religions. The discussion centers on three points:

(1) Muhammad (Allah bless him and give him peace) is the last prophet and messenger. Anyone claiming to be a prophet or messenger of Allah after him or to found a new religion is a fraud, misled and misleading.

(2) Previously revealed religions were valid in their own eras, as is attested to by many verses of the Holy Koran, but were abrogated by the universal message of Islam, as is equally attested to by many verses of the Koran. Both points are worthy of attention from English-speaking Muslims, who are occasionally exposed to erroneous theories advanced by some teachers and Koran translators affirming these religions' validity but denying or not mentioning their abrogation, or that it is unbelief (kufr) to hold that the remnant cults now bearing the names of formerly valid religions, such as "Christianity" or "Judaism," are acceptable to Allah Most High after He has sent the final Messenger (Allah bless him give him peace) to the entire world (dis: o8.7(20)). This is a matter over which there is no disagreement among Islamic scholars, and if English-speaking Muslims at times discuss it as if there were some question about it, the only reason can be that no one has yet offered them a translation of a scholarly Koranic exegesis (tafsir) to explain the accord between the various Koranic verses, and their agreement with the sunna. The few passages translated below will hopefully be of use until this has been done.

(3) Islam is the final religion that Allah Most High will never lessen or abrogate until the Last Day. A hadith that seems to imply that "a tenth of Islam" will be enough for Muslims in the latter days is discussed at the end of the section.

MUHAMMAD IS THE LAST PROPHET
AND MESSENGER (ALLAH BLESS
HIM AND GIVE HIM PEACE)

لا رسول بعد محمد ﷺ ، ولا نبي

w4.2   (Ibn Kathir:) Allah Most High says:

"Muhammad is not the father of any man
among you, but the Messenger of Allah and the
Last of the Prophets. And Allah has knowledge of
everything" (Koran 33:40).

This Koranic verse is an unequivocally decisive
primary text establishing that there will be no
prophet after him. And since there will be no
prophet (nabi), it follows *a fortiori* that there will
be no prophetic messenger (rasul). The Prophet
(Allah bless him and give him peace) said:

(1) "Messengerhood and prophethood have
ceased. There will be no messenger or prophet
after me."

(2) "My likeness among the prophets is as a
man who, having built a house and put the finishing touches on it and made it seemly, yet left one
place without a brick. When anyone entered it and
saw this, he would exclaim, 'How excellent it is,
but for the place of this brick.' Now, I am the place
of that brick: through me the line of the prophets
(Allah bless them and give them peace) has been
brought to completion."

(3) "I have been favored above the prophets
in six things: I have been endowed with consummate succinctness of speech, made triumphant
through dread, war booty has been made lawful
for me, the whole earth has been made a purified
place of worship for me, I have been sent to all
created beings, and the succession of prophets has
been completed in me."

Allah Most Blessed and Exalted has stated in
His Book, as has His messenger (Allah bless him
and give him peace) in hadiths of numerous
channels of transmission (mutawatir, def:
o22.1(d(II))) that there will be no prophet after
him, so that everyone may know that whoever

w4.2   (ابن كثير:) قال الله تعالى :
﴿مَا كَانَ مُحَمَّدٌ أَبَا أَحَدٍ مِنْ رِجالِكُمْ
وَلَكِنْ رَسُولَ اللَّهِ وَخَاتَمَ النَّبِيِّينَ وَكَانَ اللَّهُ
بِكُلِّ شَيْءٍ عَلِيماً﴾ [الأحزاب: ٤٠].
فهذه الآية نص في أنه لا نبي بعده وإذا
كان لا نبي بعده فلا رسول بالطريق
الأولى والأخرى. قال رسول الله ﷺ :
ـ «إن الرسالة والنبوة قد انقطعت فلا
رسول بعدي ولا نبي» [...] [رواه
أحمد].

ـ [قال رسول الله ﷺ :] «مثلي ومثل
الأنبياء كمثل رجل بنى داراً فأكملها
وأحسنها إلا موضع لبنة ، فكان من دخلها
فنظر إليها قال: ما أحسنها إلا موضع هذه
اللبنة فأنا موضع اللبنة ، ختم بي الأنبياء
عليهم الصلاة والسلام» [رواه
البخاري].

[عن أبي هريرة رضي الله عنه أن
رسول الله ﷺ قال:] «فُضِّلتُ على
الأنبياء بست: أعطيت جوامع الكلم ،
ونصرت بالرعب ، وأحلت لي الغنائم ،
وجعلت لي الأرض مسجداً وطهوراً ،
وأرسلت إلى الخلق كافة ، وختم بي
النبيون» [رواه الترمذي وابن ماجه].

[...] وقد أخبر الله تبارك وتعالى في
كتابه ورسوله ﷺ في السنة المتواترة عنه
أنه لا نبي بعده ليعلموا أن كل من ادعى
هذا المقام بعده فهو كذاب أفاك دجال.

claims this rank thereafter is a lying pretender, misled and misleading, even if he should stage miracles and exhibit all kinds of magic, talismans, and spells (*Tafsir al-Qur'an al-'Azim* (y60), 3.493–94).

THE ABROGATION OF
PREVIOUSLY REVEALED RELIGIONS

w4.3   (Imam Baghawi:) The Prophet (Allah bless him and give him peace) said:

"By Him in whose hand is the soul of Muhammad, any person of this Community, any Jew, or any Christian who hears of me and dies without believing in what I have been sent with will be an inhabitant of hell."

This is a rigorously authenticated (sahih) hadith that was recorded by Muslim (*Sharh al-sunna* (y22), 1.104–5).

w4.4   (Ibn Kathir:) Allah Most High says:

"Surely those who believe, those of Jewry, the Christians, and the Sabaeans—whoever has faith in Allah and the Last Day, and works righteousness, their wage awaits them with their Lord, and no fear shall be upon them, and neither shall they sorrow" (Koran 2:62).

Suddi states that the verse "Surely those who believe, etc." was revealed about the former companions of Salman the Persian when he mentioned them to the Prophet (Allah bless him and give him peace), relating how they had been, saying, "They used to pray, fast, and believe in you, and testify that you would be sent as a prophet." When he had finished praising them, the Prophet (Allah bless him and give him peace) replied, "Salman, they are the denizens of hell," which came to discomfit Salman greatly, and so Allah revealed this verse.

The *faith* of the Jews was that of whoever adhered to the Torah and the sunna of Moses (upon whom be peace) until the coming of Jesus.

ضال مضـل ، ولـو تخـرق [وشعبذ] وأتى بأنـواع السحر والطـلاسم والنيـر نجيات [محـــرر من تفسيــر القـرآن العظيم : ٣/ ٤٩٣ - ٤٩٤].

نسخ الأديان التي سبقت الإسلام

w4.3   (الإمــام البغـوي :) [... .]
قال :] قال رسول الله ﷺ : «والذي نفس محمـد في يده لا يسمـع بي أحدٌ من هذه الأمة ، ولا يهوديٌ ، ولا نصرانيٌ ، ومات ولـم يؤمـن بالـذي أرسلتُ به إلا كان من أصحاب النار» .
هذا حديث صحيـح [ت : من روايـة عبـد الـرزاق] أخرجـه مسلم [(ت : بخلاف يسير في اللفظ) من وجه آخر عن أبي هريـرة] [نقـل من شرح السنـة : ١/ ١٠٤ - ١٠٥].

w4.4   (ابن كثير :) قال الله تعالى :
﴿إنَّ الـذيـن آمَنُـوا والـذينَ هَادوا والنَّصَارى والصَّابئينَ ، مَنْ آمَنَ باللَّهِ واليَوْمِ الآخرِ وعَمِلَ صَالحاً فَلَهُمْ أجْرُهُمْ عنْـدَ رَبِّـهـمْ وَلا خَوْفُ عَلَيْـهـمْ وَلا هُمْ يَحْزَنُونَ﴾ [البقرة: ٦٢].
قال السدي : ﴿إن الذين آمنوا [والذين هادوا والنصارى والصابئين من آمن بالله واليـوم الآخر وعمل صالحاً]﴾الآية نزلت في أصحاب سلمـان الفـارسي بينا هو يحـدّث النبي ﷺ إذ ذكر أصحابه فأخبره خبـرهم فقـال كانوا يصلون ويصـومـون ويـؤمنون بك ويشهدون أنك ستبعث نبياً فلمـا فرغ سلمان من ثنائه عليهم قال له نبي الله ﷺ «يا سلمان هم من أهل النار» فاشتد ذلك على سلمان فأنزل الله هذه الآية . فكـان إيمان اليهود أنه من تمسك بالتـوراة وسنة موسى عليـه السـلام حتى جاء عيـسى فلمـا جاء عيـسى كان من

When Jesus came, whoever held fast to the Torah and the sunna of Moses without giving them up and following Jesus was lost.

The *faith* of the Christians was that whoever adhered to the Evangel and precepts of Jesus, their faith was valid and acceptable until the coming of Muhammad (Allah bless him and give him peace). Those of them who did not then follow Muhammad (Allah bless him and give him peace) and give up the sunna of Jesus and the Evangel were lost.

The foregoing is not contradicted by the hadith relating that the verse,

"Surely those who believe, those of Jewry, the Christians, and the Sabaeans—whoever has faith in Allah and the Last Day..."

was followed by Allah revealing,

"Whoever seeks a religion other than Islam will never have it accepted of him, and he will be of those who have truly failed in the hereafter" (Koran 3:85),

for the hadith merely confirms that no one's way or spiritual works are acceptable unless they conform to the Sacred Law of Muhammad (Allah bless him and give him peace) now that he has been sent with it. As for people prior to this, anyone who followed the messenger of his own time was guided, on the right path, and was saved (*Tafsir al-Qur'an al-'Azim* (y60), 1.103).

ISLAM IS THE FINAL RELIGION THAT
ALLAH WILL NEVER ABROGATE UNTIL THE
LAST DAY

w4.5   (Ibn Kathir:) Allah Most High says,

"Today I have perfected your religion for you and completed My favor upon you, and I please that your religion be Islam" (Koran 5:3),

meaning, "So accept it for yourselves, for it is the religion Allah loves and accepts, with which He

تمسك بالتوراة وأخذ بسنة موسى فلم يدعها ولم يتبع عيسى كان هالكاً. وإيمان النصارى أن من كان تمسك بالإنجيل منهم وشرائع عيسى كان مؤمناً مقبولاً منه حتى جاء محمد ﷺ فمن لم يتبع محمداً ﷺ منهم ويدع ما كان عليه من سنة عيسى والإنجيل كان هالكاً. [قلت:] هذا لا ينافي ما روى [علي بن أبي طلحة عن ابن عباس]: إن الذين آمنوا والذين هادوا والنصارى والصابئين من آمن بالله واليوم الآخر] [قال:] فأنزل الله بعد ذلك ﴿وَمَنْ يَبْتَغِ غَيْرَ الإِسْلَامِ دِيناً فَلَنْ يُقْبَلَ مِنْهُ وَهُوَ فِي الآخِرَةِ مِنَ الخَاسِرِينَ﴾. فإن هذا [الذي قاله ابن عباس] إخبار عن أنه لا يقبل من أحد طريقة ولا عمل إلا ما كان موافقاً لشريعة محمد ﷺ بعد أن بعثه به. فأما قبل ذلك فكل من اتبع الرسول في زمانه فهو على هدى وسبيل ونجاة [محرر من تفسير القرآن العظيم: ١٠٣/١].

الإسلام خاتم الأديان الذي لا ينسخه شيء

w4.5   (ابن كثير:) قال الله تعالى: ﴿اليَوْمَ أَكْمَلْتُ لَكُمْ دِينَكُمْ وَأَتْمَمْتُ عَلَيْكُمْ نِعْمَتِي وَرَضِيتُ لَكُمُ الإِسْلامَ دِيناً﴾ [المائدة: ٣].
أي: فارضوه أنتم لأنفسكم فإنه الدين الذي أحبه الله ورضيه وبعث به أفضل الرسل الكرام، وأنزل به أشرف كتبه.

has sent the best of noble messengers and has revealed in the most sublime of His Books." 'Ali ibn Abi Talha relates from Ibn 'Abbas that

"Today I have perfected your religion for you...

means Islam, Allah thereby informing His prophet (Allah bless him and give him peace) and the believers that He has perfected their faith for them, so they will never require anything more. He has completed it and will never diminish it, is pleased with it and will never detest it (ibid., 2.12).

وقـال علي بن أبي طلحة عن ابن عباس قولـه: ﴿الْيَوْمَ أَكْمَلْتُ لَكُمْ دِينَكُمْ﴾ وهو الإسلام، أخبر الله نبيه ﷺ والمؤمنين أنه أكمــل لهم الإيمـان فلا يحتاجـون إلى زيادة أبداً، وقد أتمه الله فلا ينقصه أبداً، وقـد رضيه الله فلا يسخطه أبداً [نقل من تفسير القرآن الكريم: ٢/ ١٢].

w4.6　(Qurtubi:) It is likely that by

"... I please that your religion be Islam" (Koran 5:3),

Allah means, "I am pleased with your Islam that you follow today as a religion that will endure in its perfection until the end of time, and I will cause nothing of it to be abrogated" (al-Jami' li ahkam al-Qur'an (y117), 6.63).

w4.6　(القرطبي:) ويحتمل أن يريد ﴿رَضِيتُ لَكُمُ الإسْلامَ دِيناً﴾ أي رضيت إسـلامكم الـذي أنتم عليـه اليوم ديناً باقياً بكمالـه إلى آخر الأبـد لا أنسخ منه شيئاً [نقل من الجامع لأحكام القرآن: ٦/ ٦٣].

w4.7　(n: The following hadith has been represented by some contemporary Muslims as meaning that a tenth of Islam will be enough for Muslims in the latter days, a misunderstanding felt to merit the explanation provided by the commentary below.)

The Prophet (Allah bless him and give him peace) said:

"Verily you are in a time when whoever of you abandons a tenth of what he has been commanded shall be lost. There will come a time when whoever practices a tenth of what he has been commanded will find salvation."

Verily you
('Abd al-Ra'uf Munawi:) O Companions of the Prophet
are in a time
characterized by safety, and the glory of Islam
when whoever of you abandons a tenth of

w4.7　قال النـبي ﷺ: «إنكم في زمان من ترك منكم عُشرَ ما أمر به هلك، ثم يأتي زمان من عمل منهم بعُشر ما أمر به نجا» [رواه الترمذي].
(عبـد الـرؤوف المناوي:) «إنكم» (أيها الصحب).
«في زمان» (متصف بالأمن وعزة الإسلام).
«من ترك منكم» (فيه)
«عشـر ما أمر به» (من الأمر بالمعروف

what he has been commanded

meaning of the obligation to command the right and forbid the wrong (def: q1), for it is not permissible to interpret this utterance as applicable to all that has been commanded, it being understood that a Muslim has no excuse for neglecting things which are personally obligatory

will be lost

to destruction, since the religion of Islam is now strong and there are many who aid it, so that your abandoning it is a shortcoming for which no one is excused under such circumstances.

There will come a time

in which Islam will weaken, tyrants multiply, corruption spread, lying pretenders grow numerous, and those helping the religion grow few, so that Muslims will be excused for leaving some things out of sheer incapacity, without being guilty of remissness

when whoever

of the people of that time which contains trials and afflictions

practices a tenth of what he has been commanded will find salvation

because he is under duress, and Allah charges no soul with more than it is capable of, as He says,

"Fear Allah as much as you are able to" (Koran 64:16).

Tirmidhi recorded this hadith, which he termed *singular* (gharib), while Ibn Jawzi listed it in his work on hadith forgeries, mentioning that Nasa'i said it was unacknowledgeable, having been conveyed through Nuʿaym ibn Hammad, an unreliable transmitter (*Fayd al-Qadir sharh al-Jamiʿ al-saghir* (y91), 2.556).

*

w5.0 IN WHAT SENSE "THIS WORLD IS ACCURSED" (from a2.2(8))

w5.1 The Prophet (Allah bless him and give him peace) said:

والنهي عن المنكر إذ لا يجوز صرف هذا القـول إلى عموم المأمورات لما عرف أن المسلم لا يعذر فيما يهمل من فرض عيني).

«هـلك» (أي في ورطـات الهلاك لأن الـدين عزيـز وفي أنصاره كثرة فالترك تقصير منكم فلا عذر لأحد في التهاون حالتئذ).

«ثم يأتي زمان» (يضعف فيه الإسلام وتكثـر الظـلمـة ويعم الفسق ويكثـر الـدجـالـون وتقل أنصـار الـدين فيعـذر المسلمـون في الترك إذ ذاك لعدم القدرة وفقد التقصير وحينئذ:)

«من عمـل منهم» (أي من أهل ذلك الزمن المحتوي على المحن والفتن).

«بُعْشـر ما أمر به نجا» (لأنه مقدور ولا يكلف الله نفساً إلا وسعها:

﴿فَاتَّقُوا اللَّهَ مَا اسْتَطَعْتُمْ﴾ [التغابن: ١٦].

رواه الترمذي [في آخر الفتن عن أبي هريـرة] وقـال غريـب. وأورده ابـن الجـوزي في الـواهيـات وقـال: قال النسائي: حديث منكـر، رواه نعيم بن حمـاد وليس بثقة [محرر من فيض القدير شرح الجامع الصغير ٢/ ٥٥٦].

w5.0 معنى «الدنيا ملعونة»

w5.1 [عن أبي هريرة رضي الله عنه قال: سمعت] رسول الله ﷺ يقول:

"This world and all it contains are accursed, except for the remembrance of Allah Most High, that which He loves, someone with Sacred Knowledge, or someone learning it."

This world and all it contains are accursed
(Muhammad Ibn 'Allan Bakri:) meaning remote from Allah,
except for the remembrance of Allah Most High,. that which He loves, someone with Sacred Knowledge, or someone learning it.
Acts of obedience are not of *this world,* nor are the purified ones, of the prophets and friends of Allah (awliya', def: w33). The agreement between the primary texts that condemn this world and those that praise it lies in understanding the former as referring to what distances one from Allah Most High, while the latter refer to what brings one closer to Him (*Dalil al-falihin li turuq Riyad al-salihin* (y25), 7.197).

*

w6.0   FIGURATIVE INTERPRETATION (TA'WIL) OF THE KORAN AND HADITH (from a4.3)

w6.1   (Ghazali:) Those who are profligate in disregarding the literal meaning of texts go so far as to alter most or all scriptural evidences and proofs, metaphorically interpreting even the words of Allah Most High,

"Their hands shall speak to us and their feet shall testify" (Koran 36:65),

and,

"They will say to their skins, 'Why have you testified against us,' and they will reply, 'Allah has made us speak, as He has made all to speak' " (Koran 41:21),

likewise explaining away the questions of Munkar and Nakir (def: v2.2), the scale (v2.3), the bridge over hell (v2.4), the final reckoning (v2.6), and

«الـدنـيا ملعونة ملعون ما فيها إلا فيها ذكر الله تعـالى ومـا والاه وعـالمـاً ومتعلمـاً [رواه الترمذي وقال حديث حسن].

«محمـد بن علان البكـري:) «الـدنيا ملعـونـة» (أي بعيـدة عن الله) «ملعـون» (أي بعيد) «ما فيها» (. . .) «إلا ذكر الله ومـا والاه وعـالمـاً ومتعلمـاً» (وليس من الـدنيا الطاعات ولا الأصفياء من الأنبياء والأولياء . و[تقدم] الجمع بين الوارد في ذم الـدنيا والوارد في مدحها بحمل الأول على ما يبعد عن الله تعالى والثاني على ما يقرب إليه [. . .] [محرر من كتاب دليل الفالحين لطرق رياض الصالحين: ٧/ ١٩٧].

w6.0   درجات التأويل

w6.1   (الـغــزالي:) [. . .] فمـن مسـرف، في رفع الظواهر انتهى إلى تغيير جميع الظواهر والبراهين أو أكثرها حتى حملوا قولـه تعـالى: ﴿وَتُكَلِّمُنَا أَيْدِيهِمْ وَتَشْهَدُ أَرْجُلُهُمْ﴾ وقوله تعالى: ﴿وَقَالُوا لِجُلُودِهِمْ لِمَ شَهِدْتُمْ عَلَيْنَا قَالُوا أَنْطَقَنَا اللَّهُ الَّذِي أَنْطَقَ كَلَّ شَيْءٍ﴾ وكـذلـك المخـاطبـات التي تجري من منكر ونكير وفي الـمـيـزان والصـراط والحسـاب

the words of the people of hell to the people of paradise,

"Pour water upon us, or of that which Allah has provided you" (Koran 7:50),

claiming that all this is "what their state would say if it could speak."

w6.2   Others have gone to the opposite extreme of barring *all* figurative interpretation, among them Ahmad ibn Hanbal (Allah be well pleased with him), who even forbade metaphorical interpretation of Allah's words,

" 'Be!' and it is" (Koran 36:82),

some of his school claiming that this is an actual utterance of articulated letters and a voice, proceeding from Allah Most High at every moment, commensurate in number with every existent being. I have heard some members of his school say that he forbade metaphorical interpretation of all but three expressions, namely the Prophet's having said (Allah bless him and give him peace):

(1) "The Black Stone is the right hand of Allah in His earth";

(2) "The heart of the believer is between two of the fingers of the All-merciful";

and,

(3) "Verily, I find the breath of the All-merciful from the direction of Yemen."

Literalists have shown an inclination towards prohibiting all figurative interpretation, while what one should believe of Ahmad ibn Hanbal (Allah be well pleased with him) is that he knew that Allah's 'establishment on the Throne' did not consist of being at rest, any more than His 'coming down' consisted of physical motion, but rather he forbade figurative interpretation in order to close the discussion in the interests of the people, for once the door is opened, the rift widens and the matter gets out of control, exceeding the bounds

ومنــاظـرات أهـل النـار وأهـل الجنــة في
قولهـم: ﴿أَفِيضُوا عَلَيْنَا مِنَ المَاءِ أَوْمِمَّا
رَزَقَكُمُ اللَّهُ﴾ زعموا أن ذلك كله بلسان
الحال.

w6.2   وغـلا آخرون في حسم الباب
منهم أحمـد بن حنبل رضي الله عنه حتى
منع تأويل قوله: ﴿كُنْ فَيَكُونُ﴾ وزعموا
أن ذلك خطاب بحرف وصوت يوجد من
الله تعـالى في كل لحظـة بعـدد كون كل
مكـوّن. حتى سمعت بعض أصحــابـه
يقول إنه حسم باب التأويـل إلا لثـلاثـة
ألفاظ، قوله ﷺ:
«الحجر الأسـود يمين الله في أرضه»
[(ت: رواه الحـاكم وصححه من حديث
عبد الله بن عمـرو)]؛ وقوله ﷺ: «قلب
المؤمن بين إصبعين من أصابع الرحمن»
[(ت: رواه أحمـد)] وقـوله ﷺ: «إني
أجـد نفس الـرحمن من جانب اليمن».
ومال إلى حسم الباب أرباب الظواهر.
والظن بأحمد بن حنبل رضي الله عنه
أنـه علم أن الاستـواء ليس هو الاستقرار
والنـزول ليس هو الانتقـال ولكنـه منع
التأويـل حسمـاً للبـاب ورعـايـة لصـالح
الخلق، فإنـه إذا فتح الباب اتسع الخرق
وخــرج الأمـر عن الضبـط وجـاوز حد

of moderation. And since what is beyond the moderate is without limits, there is no harm in sternly warning against figurative interpretation, a position that is attested to by the behavior of the early Muslims, who used to say, "Accept such things as they have come." When asked about Allah's 'establishment on the Throne', Imam Malik (Allah have mercy on him) said, " 'Establishment' is known, the how of it is unknown, belief in it is obligatory, and questions about it are reprehensible innovation (bid'a)."

w6.3   Another group of scholars have taken a moderate position, admitting figurative interpretation of all matters connected with the attributes of Allah Most Glorious (n: i.e. by explaining anthropomorphic words in a way befitting the divine attributes (def: v1), interpreting His 'hand', for example, as an allusion to His omnipotence), while leaving all matters connected with the afterlife to their outward literal purport, prohibiting any metaphorical interpretation of them. These are the Ash'aris (dis: w57).

w6.4   The Mu'tazilites (N: a philosophical school that subjected the fundamentals of Islam to rationalistic theories) went further, metaphorically explaining the inhabitants of paradise's seeing of Allah Most High (v1.3, end), His hearing, His sight, and the nocturnal ascent (mi'raj) of the Prophet (Allah bless him and give him peace), claiming that it was not in the body. They also explained away the torment of the grave, the scale, the bridge over hell, and a number of the matters of the afterlife, though they acknowledged the bodily resurrection and judgement, the reality of paradise with the physical pleasures its inhabitants will enjoy of foods, scents, and lovemaking; and the reality of the hellfire as something that incinerates skin and melts fat.

The philosophers went even further than the extremes reached by the Mu'tazilites, explaining *everything* that has reached us about the afterlife as being metaphorical, reducing it to intellectual or spiritual states of pain and mental enjoyments, denying the bodily resurrection and judgement, saying that souls subsist forever and will be

الاقتصاد ، إذ حد ما جاوز الاقتصاد لا ينضبط ؛ فلا بأس بهذا الزجر ويشهد له سيرة السلف ، فإنهم كانوا يقولون : أمرّوها كما جاءت . حتى قال مالك رحمه الله لما سئل عن الاستواء : الاستواء معلوم والكيفية مجهولة والإيمان به واجب والسؤال عنه بدعة .

w6.3   وذهبت طائفة إلى الاقتصاد وفتحوا باب التأويل في كل ما يتعلق بصفات الله سبحانه ، وتركوا ما يتعلق بالآخرة على ظواهرها ومنعوا التأويل فيه وهم الأشعرية .

w6.4   وزاد المعتزلة عليهم حتى أولوا من صفاته تعالى الرؤية وأوّلوا كونه سميعاً بصيراً وأوّلوا المعراج وزعموا أنه لم يكن بالجسد وأوّلوا عذاب القبر والميزان والصراط وجملة من أحكام الآخرة ولكن أقروا بحشر الأجساد وبالجنة واشتمالها على المأكولات والمشمومات والمنكوحات والملاذ المحسوسة وبالنار واشتمالها على جسم محسوس محرق يحرق الجلود ويذيب الشحوم .

ومن ترقيهم إلى هذا الحد زاد الفلاسفة فأوّلوا كل ما ورد في الآخرة وردوه إلى آلام عقلية وروحانية ولذات عقلية وأنكروا حشر الأجساد وقالوا ببقاء النفوس وأنها تكون إما معذبة وإما منعمة

punished or rewarded with torment and pleasure undetectable by the senses. It is these who are the real profligates.

بعذاب ونعيم لا يدرك بالحس . وهؤلاء هم المسرفون .

w6.5   The way of moderation between all this dissolution on the one hand, and the rigidity of the Hanbalis on the other, is a very fine line and difficult to perceive, one which few people know except the successful. (n: Sections v1–v2 describe Ghazali's ''way of moderation'' in detail.) (*Ihya' 'ulum al-din* (y39), 1.92)

w6.5   وحــد الاقـتـصــاد بيــن هذا الانحـلال كله وبين جمـود الحنابلة دقيق غامض لا يطـلع عليـه إلا الـمــوفقــون [...] [نقل من إحياء علوم الدين: .[٩٢/١]

*

w7.0   ON DIVINE INDWELLING (HULUL) AND ''UNION WITH GOD'' (ITTIHAD) (from a4.3)

w7.0   استحالة الحلول والاتحاد

DIVINE INDWELLING (HULUL)

الحلول

w7.1   (Ghazali:) The concept of divine indwelling (n: e.g. ''God incarnate'' in a human being) may mean one of only two things:

(1) The first is the relation between an object and the place it occupies, which can only exist between two spatially extended things, and is clearly impossible for the One who is beyond all corporeality (dis: v1.3).

(2) The second is the relation between a substance and accident, for an accident exists *by means of* a substance (n: the accident of 'redness', for example, being incapable of subsisting independently of particular red things), a relation which can be expressed as its subsisting *through* the substance. But this is impossible for anything that is already self-subsistent, and one cannot mention Allah Most High in such a connection, for it is impossible that something *self-subsistent* should subsist through *another* self-subsistent; there remaining only the mode of corporeal bodies physically adjacent, where 'indwelling' cannot even be conceived between two servants,

w7.1   (الـغــزالـي :) المفهــوم من الحلول أمران أحدهمـا النسبة التي بين الجسم وبين مكانه الذي يكون فيه وذلك لا يكـون إلا بين جسمين فالبـري ء عن معنى الجسمية يستحيـل في حقه ذلك ، والثـاني النسبة التي بين العرض والجوهر فإن العرض يكون قوامه بالجوهر فقد يعبر عنه بأنه حال فيه وذلك محال على كل ما قوامه بنفسه فدع عنـك ذكر الرب تعالى في هذا المعرض فإن كل ما قوامه بنفسه يستحيـل أن يحـل فيمـا قوامه بنفسه ، إلا بطريق المجاورة الواقعة بين الأجسام فلا يتصور الحلول بين عبدين فكيف يتصور

855

let alone between the servant and the Lord Most High.

بين العبد والرب تعالى .

"UNION WITH GOD" (ITTIHAD)

الاتحاد

w7.2   "Union with God" is even more patently false, since saying "The slave has become the Lord" is self-contradictory, it befitting the Lord Most Glorious to be held above speaking absurdities of Him, while it can be categorically affirmed that any statement claiming that one thing has become another concurrently existing thing is impossible, for if the existence of *both* Zayd and 'Amr, for example, is acknowledged, and someone asserts that Zayd has *become* 'Amr and united with *him*, then this unification must entail one of four **things**, beyond which there is no other possibility:

w7.2   وأما الاتحاد فذلك أيضاً أظهر بطلاناً لأن قول القائل إن العبد صار هو الرب كلام متناقض في نفسه ، بل ينبغي أن ينزه الرب سبحانه عن أن يجري اللسان في حقه بأمثال هذه المحاولات ويقول قولاً مطلقاً ، إن قول القائل إن شيئاً صار شيئاً آخر محال على الإطلاق لأنا نقول إذا عقل زيد وحده وعمرو وحده ثم قيل إن زيداً صار عمرواً واتحد به فلا يخلو عند الاتحاد إما أن يكون كلاهما موجودين أو كلاهما معدومين أو زيد موجوداً وعمرو معدوماً أو بالعكس ولا يمكن قسم وراء هذه الأربعة .

(1) that both exist;

(2) that neither exists;

(3) that Zayd exists but 'Amr does not;

(4) or that 'Amr exists but Zayd does not.

Now if both exist, neither has become the other, but rather each exists. At the very most, they might occupy the same locus, which does not necessarily entail unification, since qualities such as knowledge, will, and power, for example, might exist together in one individual without each requiring a separate locus, while it is plain that power is not knowledge or will, and they have not "unified."

فإن كانا موجودين فلم يصر أحدهما عين الآخر . بل عين كل واحد منهما موجود وإنما الغاية أن يتحد مكانهما وذلك لا يوجب الاتحاد ، فإن العلم والإرادة والقدرة قد تجتمع في ذات واحدة ولا يتباين محلها ولا تكون القدرة هي العلم ولا الإرادة ، ولا يكون قد اتحد البعض بالبعض . وإن كانا معدومين فما اتحدا بل عدما ولعل الحادث شيء ثالث . وإن كان أحدهما معدوماً والآخر موجوداً فلا اتحاد إذ لا يتحد موجود بمعدوم فالاتحاد بين الشيئين مطلقاً محال وهذا جار في الذوات المتماثلة فضلاً عن المختلفة .

If neither exists ((2) above), they have not unified but have both ceased to exist, with the result perhaps of a third thing.

And if one of them exists but the other does not, then they cannot have unified, for an existent thing cannot "be one" with a nonexistent thing.

So union between two concurrent things is absolutely impossible, even if they are alike, let alone if they are different.

"UNION" IN POETIC LICENSE

w7.3   Whenever *union* is mentioned and it is said that "he is *him*," it is only by way of figurative extension and poetic license, conformable with the usage of Sufis and poets, who employ metaphorical means to enhance their words' effect upon listeners' understanding, as when a poet says, "I am my beloved and my beloved is me," which is a metaphor on the part of the poet, who does not mean that in fact he *is* him, but only that it is as though he were him, for his concern is now wholly absorbed in him, just as his concern *was* absorbed in himself, and so he expresses this condition as *union*, by way of poetic license. And this is how one should interpret the words of Abu Yazid, "I sloughed off my ego as a snake sheds its skin, and looked, and I was Him," meaning that whoever sloughs off the desires, caprices, and concerns of their ego no longer has any capacity or concern save for Allah Most High, and when nothing enters a servant's heart besides the Majesty and Beauty of Allah and he becomes wholly immersed therein, he is "as though he were Him," not that he actually *is* Him. There is a difference between saying "as though he were him" and saying "he is him," though "as though he were him" may be expressed by saying "he is him," just as poets sometimes say, "It is as though I were my beloved," and at other times, "I am my beloved."

And this can occasion a misstep, for someone without a firm footing in rational knowledge might not distinguish between one sense and the other, and looking at his own perfection, embellished with the dazzling raiment of the Truth, think that he is Him, saying, "I am the Truth," while he has made the mistake of the Christians who saw this in the person of Jesus (on whom be peace) and said that he was the Divinity. For that matter, the person errors who looks in a mirror reflecting a colored image and thinks it is the image of the mirror and the color is the color of the mirror, while this can never be, for the mirror is colorless in itself, and its nature is to reflect colored images in a way that makes those observing mere appearances think they are the appearance of the mirror itself, just as a child, when he sees

w7.3   وحيث يطلق الاتحاد ويقال هو وهو لا يكون إلا بطريق التوسع والتجوز اللائق بعادة الصوفية والشعراء فإنهم لأجل تحسين موقع الكلام من الأفهام يسلكون سبيل الاستعارة كما يقول الشاعر: أنا من أهوى ومن أهوى أنا؛ وذلك مؤول عند الشاعر فإنه لا يعني به أنه هو تحقيقاً بل كأنه هو، فإنه مستغرق الهم به كما يكون هو مستغرق الهم بنفسه فيعبر عن هذه الحالة بالاتحاد على سبيل التجوز. وعليه ينبغي أن يحمل قول أبي يزيد حيث قال: انسلخت من نفسي كما تنسلخ الحية من جلدها فنظرت فإذا أنا هو. ويكون معناه أن من ينسلخ من شهوات نفسه وهواها وهمها فلا يبقى فيه متسع لغير الله ولا يكون له هم سوى الله تعالى فإذا لم يحل في القلب إلا جلال الله وجماله حتى صار مستغرقاً به يصير كأنه هو لا أنه هو تحقيقاً. وفرق بين قولنا هو وبين قولنا هو لكن قد يعبر بقولنا هو وهو عن قولنا كأنه هو كما أن الشاعر تارة يقول كأني من أهوى وتارة يقول أنا من أهوى. وهذه مزلة قدم فإن من ليس له قدم راسخ في المعقولات ربما لم يتميز له أحدهما عن الآخر فينظر إلى كمال ذاته وقد تزين بما تلألأ فيه من حلية الحق فيظن أنه هو فيقول أنا الحق وهو غالط غلط النصارى حيث رأوا ذلك في ذات عيسى عليه السلام فقالوا هو الإله. بل غلط من ينظر إلى مرآة قد انطبع فيها صورة متلونة فيظن أن تلك الصورة هي صورة المرآة وإن ذلك اللون لون المرآة وهيهات بل المرآة في ذاتها لا لون لها وشأنها قبول صور الألوان على وجه يتخايل إلى الناظرين إلى ظاهر الأمور أن ذلك هي صورة المرآة، حتى أن الصبي إذ رأى إنساناً في

someone in a mirror, may think the person is actually *in* the mirror. So too, the heart in itself is without form or configuration, and its own structure is merely to conform to intellectual impressions of figures, forms and realities, such that whatever enters it is as if in union with it, not that it is in actual fact truly united with it. When someone who does not know of glasses or wine sees a glass of wine, he may not realize the difference between them, and will sometimes say there is no wine, and sometimes that there is no glass.

The words "I am the Truth" either mean the same as the poet's saying "I am my beloved and my beloved is me," or else the speaker has made the same mistake as the Christians in believing in the union of divinity and humanity. If it is true he actually said it, Abu Yazid's utterance, "Glory be to me, how great is my state" either passed his lips by way of quoting Allah Most High, just as, if he had heard and repeated,

"There is no god but Me, so worship Me" (Koran 20:14),

it would be interpreted as a quote—or else he was attesting to the fullness of the share of inner purity he beheld within himself, and spoke of the purity of his soul by saying "Glory be to me," seeing the greatness of his state in relation to the state of most of humanity, and saying, "How great is my state," while knowing his purity and the magnitude of his state were in comparison to other *people,* not the sacred purity of the Lord Most High or His greatness, this utterance passing his lips while in a state of spiritual intoxication and being overcome by a state, since the return to sobriety obliges one to hold one's tongue from words that mislead, and while intoxicated perhaps he was unable to do this. If one goes beyond both these two interpretations to actual "union with God," it is manifestly absurd, and one should not so esteem people's rank that one accepts the absurd. One should know men by their having spoken the truth, not that it is the truth by certain men having spoken it (*al-Maqsad al-asna sharh asma' Allah al-husna* (y40), 146–50).

الـمـرآة ظن أن الإنـسـان في المـرآة . فكذلك القلب خال عن الصورة في نفسه وعن الهيئات ، وإنمـا هيئتـه قبول معاني الهيئـات والصـور والحقـائق فمـا يحله يكـون كالمتحد به لا أنه متحد به تحقيقاً . ومن لا يعـرف الـزجـاج والخمـر إذا رأى زجاجة فيها الخمر لم يدرك تباينهـا فتارة يقول لا خمر وتارة يقول لا زجاجة [. . .] .

وقــول من قال منهم أنا الحق فإمـا أن يكـون معنـاه معنى قول الشـاعـر : أنا من أهوى ومن أهـوى أنا ، وإما أن يكون قد غلط في ذلك كمـا غلطت النصارى في ظنهم اتحاد اللاهوت بالناسوت .

وقول أبي يزيد إن صح عنه : سبحاني ما أعظم شأني : إمـا أن يكون ذلك جارياً على لسانه في معرض الحكاية عن الله تعـالى كمـا لو سمع وهو يقول : لا إله إلا أنا فاعبدني ، لكان يحمل على الحكاية ؛ وإمـا أن يكـون قد شاهـد كمال حظه من صفة القـدس [على ما ذكرنـا في الترقي بالمعـرفة عن الموهومات والمحسوسات وبـالهمـة عن الحظوظ والشهوات] فأخبر عن قدس نفسه فقـال : سبحـاني ، ورأى عظم شأنـه بالإضـافـة إلى شأن عمـوم الخلق فقـال : ما أعظم شأني ، وهـو مع ذلك يعلم أن قدسه وعظم شأنه بالإضافة إلى الخلق لا نسبة إلى قدس الرب تعالى وعظم شأنه ويكون قد جرى هذا اللفظ على لسـانـه في سكر وغلبة حال ، فإن الـرجـوع إلى الصحو واعتـدال الحـال يوجب حفظ اللسان عن الألفاظ الموهمة وحـال السكر ربما يخل لا يحتمل ذلك . فإن جاوزت هذين التأويلين إلى الاتحـاد فذلك محـال قطعاً فلا تنظر إلى مناصب الرجال حتى تصدق بالمحال بل ينبغي أن تعـرف الـرجـال بالحق لا الحق بالـرجال [محـرر من المقصد الأسنى في شرح أسماء الله الحسنى : ١٤٦ ـ ١٥٠] .

w7.4   (n:) Among the disservices done to Islam by some Western scholars is their tireless insistence that the Sufi term *wusul* ("to arrive") be translated as if it meant *ittihad* ("to unify") with the result that their translations of Sufi works are filled with talk of "union with God," a rendering that has come to be traditional and authoritative among them, while it is a fallacious conception that the masters of Sufism from every age have taken pains to dissociate themselves, their method, and their students from. So it is perhaps fitting to conclude this section with two of the aphorisms of the great Shadhili master Ibn 'Ata' Illah, who said:

"Your **reaching Allah** is your reaching the *knowledge* of Him, for other than that, Our Lord is too exalted for anything to be joined with Him or for Him to be joined with anything";

and said,

"The affirmation of electhood does not necessitate a negation of the fact of being human. Election is merely like the rise of the daylight's sun: it appears on the horizon without being part of it. Sometimes He takes it from you and returns you to your own bounds. For daylight is not from you to yourself. It comes over you."

(*al-Hikam al-'Ata'iyya wa al-munajat al-ilahiyya* (y56), 59, 66, aphorisms 213 and 249)

ـ وصولُكَ إلى الله وصولُكَ إلى العلم
به ، وإلا فجَلَّ رَبُّنـا أن يتصل به شيء أو
يتصل هو بشيء .

ـ لا يَلْزَمُ من ثبـوت الخصوصيـة عدمُ
وصفِ البشـريـة ، إنمـا مَثَلُ الخصوصية
كإشـراق شمس النهار : ظهرت في الأفق
وليست منه . تارة يَقْبِضُ ذلك عنك فيردك
إلى حدودك . فالنهـار ليس منك وإليك ،
ولكـنـه واردٌ عليـك [نقـل من الحكم
العطائية والمناجاة الإلهية : ٥٩ ، ٦٦] .

*

w8.0   ALLAH IS EXALTED
ABOVE NEEDING SPACE
OR TIME (from a4.3)

w8.0   تنـزيه الله تعالى عن
المكان والزمان

w8.1   (Muhammad Hamid:) What is obligatory for a human being to know is that Allah the Creator, glory be to Him, is absolutely free of need (al-Ghani) of anything He has created, and free of need for the heavens or the earth. He is transcendently beyond "being in the sky" or "being on earth" in the manner that things are in things, created beings in created beings, or things in circumstances are encompassed by their circumstances, for it is He who

"There is nothing whatsoever like unto Him, and He is the All-hearing, the All-seeing" (Koran 42:11),

w8.1   (محمد الحامد :) الذي يجب
على الإنسـان أن يعلمه أن الله الخـالق
سبـحـانـه له الـغنى المطلق عن كل ما
خلق ، وعـن السـمـاء والأرض أيضـاً ،
سبـحـان الله أن يكـون في السماء أو في
الأرض كمـا يكون الحادث في الحادث ،
والمخلوق في المخلوق ، والمظروف في
الظرف ، وهو الذي :
﴿لَيْسَ كَمِثْلِهِ شَيْءٌ وَهُوَ السَّمِيعُ
البَصِيرُ﴾ .

and,

"He did not give birth, nor was He born, and there is none who is His equal" (Koran 112:3–4).

Aside from all the proofs from the Koran and sunna, the rational evidence is decisive that Allah Most High is absolutely beyond any resemblance to created things, in His entity, attributes, and acts. The noble Koranic verse,

"He is Allah in the heavens and the earth; He knows your secrets and what you reveal, and knows what you are earning" (Koran 6:3),

means that He Most Glorious is the one who is rightfully worshipped in both the heavens and earth, who alone possesses the attribute of divinity in both; and the inhabitants of the heavens know He is the True God, just as the inhabitants of the earth know it, and the former worship him just as the latter do (*Rudud 'ala abatil wa rasa'il al-Shaykh Muhammad al-Hamid* (y44), 2.20–21).

w8.2   (Qurtubi:) Allah Most High says,

"Do you feel secure that He who is in the heavens will not make the earth swallow you while it quakes?" (Koran 67:16),

which may mean, "Do you feel secure that He who is the Creator of whomever is in the heavens will not make the earth swallow you, as He did Korah?" The more exacting hold that it (n: i.e. *in* the heavens) signifies, "Do you feel secure from Him who is *over* the heavens," just as Allah says,

"Journey *in* the earth" (Koran 9:2),

meaning *over* it; not over it by way of physical contact or spatialization, but by way of omnipotent power and control. Another position is that it means, "Do you feel secure from Him who is *over* ('ala) the heavens," i.e. just as it is said, "So-and-so is over Iraq and the Hijaz," meaning that he is the governor and commander of them. The hadiths on this subject are numerous, rigorously authenticated (sahih), and widely known, and

﴿لَمْ يَلِدْ وَلَمْ يُولَدْ وَلَمْ يَكُنْ لَهُ كُفُواً أَحَدٌ﴾.

وإن البرهان العقلي ـ إلى جانب البرهان النقلي ـ جازم بتنزهه تعالى عن مشابهة المخلوقات مطلقاً، ذاتاً وصفاً وفعلاً، والآية الكريمة:

﴿وَهُوَ اللَّهُ فِي السَّمٰوٰاتِ وَفِي الأَرْضِ يَعْلَمُ سِرَّكُمْ وَجَهْرَكُمْ وَيَعْلَمُ ما تَكْسِبُونَ﴾

تعني أنه سبحانه المعبود بحق فيهما، والموصوف بالألوهية فيهما، ويعرفه أهل السماء بأنه الإله الحق كما يعرفه أهل الأرض ويعبدونه كما يعبدونه [نقل من ردود على أباطيل ورسائل الشيخ محمد الحامد : ٢/ ٢٠ ـ ٢١].

w8.2   (القرطبي :) قوله تعالى : ﴿أَأَمِنْتُمْ مَنْ فِي السَّمَاءِ أَنْ يَخْسِفَ بِكُمُ الأَرْضَ فَإِذَا هِيَ تَمُورُ﴾ [الملك : ١٦].

[. . . قلت :] ويحتمل أن يكون المعنى : أأمنتم خالق مَن في السماء أن يخسف بكم الأرض كما خسفها بقارون [. . .].

وقال المحققون : أمنتم مَن فوق السماء ؛ كقوله : ﴿فَسِيحُوا فِي الأَرْضِ﴾ أي فوقها لا بالمماسّة والتحيز لكن بالقهر والتدبير. وقيل : معناه أمنتم من على السماء ؛ [كقوله تعالى : ﴿وَلأُصَلِّبَنَّكُمْ فِي جُذُوعِ النَّخْلِ﴾ أي عليها . ومعناه أنه مديرها ومالكها ؛] كما يقال : فلان على العراق والحجاز ؛ أي واليها وأميرها . والأخبار في هذا الباب كثيرة صحيحة

indicate the exaltedness of Allah, being undeniable by anyone save an atheist or obstinate ignoramus. Their meaning is to dignify Allah and exalt Him above what is base and low, to characterize Him by exaltedness and grandeur, not by being in places, particular directions, or within limits, for these are the qualities of physical bodies. The hands are only raised skyward when one supplicates because the sky is from whence divine revelation descends and rains fall, the place of purity and the wellspring of the purified ones of the angels, and that servants' works are raised to it and over it are the Throne and His paradise—just as Allah has made the Kaaba the direction of supplication and the prayer. He created all places and has no need of them. He was without space or time in His beginningless eternity before creating space and time, and is now as He ever has been (al-Jami' li ahkam al-Qur'an (y117), 18.216).

منتشـرة، مشيرة إلى العلو، لا يدفعها إلا ملحدٌ أو جاهل معاند. والمراد بها توقيره وتنـزيهـه عن السفـل والتحت. ووصفه بالعلو والعظمـة لا بالأمـاكن والجهـات والحدود لأنها صفات الأجسام.

وإنما ترفع الأيدي بالدعاء إلى السماء لأن السمـاء مهبط الوحي، ومنزل القطر، ومحـل القُـدس، ومعـدن المطهـرين من المـلائكـة وإليهـا ترفع أعمـال العبـاد، وفـوقهـا عرشـه وجنتـه؛ كمـا جعـل الله الكعبة قبلةً للدعـاء والصلاة، ولأنه خلق الأمكنة وهو غير محتاج إليها.

وكـان في أزلـه قبـل خلق المكـان والـزمان ولا مكان ولا زمان. وهو الآن على ما عليـه كان [محـرر من الجامـع لأحكام القرآن: ١٨/ ٢١٦].

*

w9.0   SUFISM (from a4.7)

w9.0   التصوف

w9.1   (Muhammad Amin Kurdi:) *Sufism* is a knowledge through which one knows the states of the human soul, praiseworthy or blameworthy, how to purify it from the blameworthy and ennoble it by acquiring the praiseworthy, and to journey and proceed to Allah Most High, fleeing unto Him. Its fruits are the heart's development, knowledge of God through direct experience and ecstasy, salvation in the next world, triumph through gaining Allah's pleasure, the attainment of eternal happiness, and illuminating and purifying the heart so that noble matters disclose themselves, extraordinary states are revealed, and one perceives what the insight of others is blind to (*Tanwir al-qulub fi mu'amala 'Allam al-Ghuyub* (y74), 406).

w9.1   (محمـد أمين الكـردي:) [فحد] التصوف هو علم يعرف به أحوال النفس محمـودهـا ومـذمـومهـا وكيفيـة تطهيـرهـا من المـذمـوم منهـا وتحليتهـا بالاتصـاف بمحمـودهـا وكيفيـة السلوك والسير إلى الله تعالى والفرار إليه [...] وثمـرتـه تهذيب القلوب ومعـرفـة علام الغيـوب ذوقـاً ووجـدانـاً، والنجـاة في الآخـرة، والفـوز برضـا الله تعالى، ونيل السعـادة الأبـديـة، وتنوير القلب وصفاؤه بحيث ينكشف له أمـور جليلة ويشهـد أحوالاً عجيبة ويعاين ما عميت عنه بصيرة غيـره [محرر من تنوير القلوب في معاملة علام الغيوب: ٤٠٦].

w9.2   (Nawawi:) The way of Sufism is based on five principles: having godfearingness privately and publicly, living according to the sunna in word and deed, indifference to whether others accept or reject one, satisfaction with Allah Most High in

w9.2   (النووي:) [المقصد السابع في] أصـول طريق التصوف هي خمسة: تقـوى الله في السر والعـلانيـة، واتبـاع السنـة في الأقـوال والأفعـال، والإعراض عن الخلق في الإقبـال والإدبار، والرضا

dearth and plenty, and returning to Allah in happiness or affliction. The principles of treating the illnesses of the soul are also five: lightening the stomach by diminishing one's food and drink, taking refuge in Allah Most High from the unforeseen when it befalls, shunning situations involving what one fears to fall victim to, continually asking for Allah's forgiveness and His blessings upon the Prophet (Allah bless him and give him peace) night and day with full presence of mind, and keeping the company of him who guides one to Allah (*al-Maqasid fi bayan ma yajibu ma'rifatuhu min al-din* (y106), 83–84, 87).

w9.3   (Ahmad Zarruq:) Aspects of Sufism, defined, delineated, and explained, amount to nearly two thousand, all of them reducible to sincerity in turning to Allah Most High, something of which they are only facets, and Allah knows best. The necessary condition of sincerity of approach is that it be what the Truth Most High accepts, and by the means He accepts. Now, something lacking its necessary condition cannot exist,

"And He does not accept unbelief for His servants" (Koran 39:7),

so one must realize true faith (iman),

"and if you show gratitude, He will accept it of you" (Koran 39:7),

which entails applying Islam. So there is no Sufism except through comprehension of Sacred Law, for the outward rules of Allah Most High are not known save through it, and there is no comprehension of Sacred Law without Sufism, for works are nothing without sincerity of approach, as expressed by the words of Imam Malik (Allah have mercy on him):

"He who practices Sufism without learning Sacred Law corrupts his faith, while he who learns Sacred Law without practicing Sufism corrupts himself. Only he who combines the two proves true."

(*Iqaz al-himam fi sharh al-Hikam* (y54), 5–6)

عن الله تعـالى في القليـل والكثيـر، والـرجـوع إلـى اللـه في السـراء والضـراء . . . وأصـول ما تداوى به علل النـفس خمسـة : تخفيف المعـدة بقلة الطعـام والشـراب، والالتجـاء إلى الله تعـالى ممـا يعرض عند عروضه، والفرار من مواقف ما يُخشى الـوقـوع فيه، ودوام الاستغفـار مع الصـلاة على النبي ﷺ آناء الليل وأطراف النهار باجتماع الخاطر، وصحبة من يدلـك على الله [محرّر من المقـاصـد في بيـان ما يجب معـرفتـه من الدين : ٨٣ ـ ٨٤، ٨٧].

w9.3   (أحمـد زروق:) قد حد التصوف ورسم وفسر بوجـوه تبلغ نحو ألفين ترجع كلهـا لصدق التوجه إلى الله تعـالى، وإنمـا هي وجـوه فيـه والله أعلم [. . .] ولـ[. . .] صدق التـوجـه مشروط بكـونـه من حيث يرضاه الحق تعالى، ولا يصـح مشروط بدون شرطه ـ﴿ولا يرضى لعبـاده الكفـر﴾ـ. فلزم تحقيق الإيمـان، ـ﴿وإن تشكروا يرضه لكم﴾ـ. فلزم العمل بالإسلام فلا تصوف إلا بفقه، إذ لا تُعرف أحكام الله تعالى الظاهرة إلا منه، ولا فقه إلا بتصـوف، إذ لا عمـل إلا بصدق توجه [. . .] ومنه قول مالك رحمه الله : «من تصـوف ولم يتفقـه فقـد تزندق، ومن تفقه ولم يتصـوف فقد تفسق، ومن جمع بينهما فقد تحقق» [محرر من إيقاظ الهـمم في شرح الحكم : ٥ ـ ٦].

w9.4 (n:) As for the meaning of *proving true,* its sheikhs say that Sufism is not a fixity on a particular type of worship, but rather the attachment of the heart to Allah Most High, mere honesty therein demanding that whenever something is preferred by the standards of the Sacred Law for someone in one's circumstances, one does it. This is why we find that Sufis have served Islam in a wide variety of capacities. Many of the scholars cited throughout the present volume, for example, also had the higher education of Sufism, among them Imam Muhammad Amin Ibn 'Abidin, Sheikh al-Islam Zakariyya Ansari, Muhammad Abul Mawahib, Sheikh Ibrahim Bajuri, Muhammad Sa'id Burhani, 'Abd al-Wakil Durubi, Imam Ghazali, Muhammad Hamid, Imam Abu Hanifa, Sheikh Muhammad Hashimi, Imam Ibn Hajar Haytami, Ibn 'Ajiba, Ibn 'Ata' Illah, Imam 'Izz ibn 'Abd al-Salam, the author of our basic text Ahmad ibn Naqib al-Misri, Muhammad 'Abdullah Jurdani, Muhammad Amin Kurdi, Imam Malik, 'Abd al-Ra'uf Munawi, Zayn al-Din Mallibari, Yusuf Nabahani, 'Abd al-Ghani Nabulsi, Khalil Nahlawi, Imam Nawawi, 'Abd al-Wahhab Sha'rani, Imam Taqi al-Din Subki, Jalal al-Din Suyuti, Hakim Tirmidhi, and others.

Among the Sufis who aided Islam with sword as well as pen, according to B.G. Martin's *Muslim Brotherhoods in Nineteenth Century Africa* (y86), are such men as the Naqshbandi sheikh Shamil Daghestani, who fought a prolonged war against the Russians in the Caucasus in the nineteenth century; Sayyid Muhammad 'Abdullah al-Somali, a sheikh of the Salihiyya order who led Muslims against the British and Italians in Somalia from 1899 to 1920; the Qadiri sheikh 'Uthman ibn Fodi, who led jihad in Northern Nigeria from 1804 to 1808 to establish Islamic rule; the Qadiri sheikh 'Abd al-Qadir al-Jaza'iri, who led the Algerians against the French from 1832 to 1847; the Darqawi faqir al-Hajj Muhammad al-Ahrash, who fought the French in Egypt in 1799; the Tijani sheikh al-Hajj 'Umar Tal, who led Islamic jihad in Guinea, Senegal, and Mali from 1852 to 1864; and the Qadiri sheikh Ma' al-'Aynayn al-Qalqami, who helped marshal Muslim resistance to the French in northern Mauritania and southern Morocco from 1905 to 1909.

Among the Sufis whose missionary work Islamized entire regions are such men as the founder of the Sanusiyya order, Muhammad 'Ali Sanusi, whose efforts and jihad from 1807 to 1859 consolidated Islam as the religion of peoples from the Libyan Desert to sub-Saharan Africa; the Shadhili sheikh Muhammad Ma'ruf and Qadiri sheikh Uways al-Barawi, whose efforts spread Islam westward and inland from the East African Coast; and the hundreds of anonymous Naqshbandi sheikhs who taught and preserved Islam among the peoples of what is now the southern Soviet Union and who still serve the religion there despite official pressure. It is plain from the example of these and similar men that the attachment of the heart to Allah, which is the main emphasis of Sufism, does not hinder spiritual works of any kind, but may rather provide a real basis for them. And Allah alone gives success.

w9.5 ('Abd al-Wahhab Sha'rani:) The path of the Sufis is built of the Koran and sunna, and is based upon living according to the morals of the prophets and purified ones. It may not be blamed unless it violates an explicit statement from the

w9.5 (عبد الوهاب الشعراني:) إن طريق القوم مشيدة بالكتاب والسنة، ومبنية على سلوك أخلاق الأنبياء والأصفياء، وهي لا تكون مذمومة إلا إن

Koran, sunna, or scholarly consensus (def: b7), exclusively. If it does not contravene one of these, the very most that one may say of it is that it is an understanding a Muslim man has been given, so let whoever wishes act upon it, and whoever does not refrain, this being as true of works as of understanding. So no pretext remains for condemning it except one's own low opinion of others (dis: r2.14), or interpreting what they do as ostentation, which is unlawful.

Whoever carefully examines the branches of knowledge of the Folk of Allah Most High will find that none of them are beyond the pale of the Sacred Law. How should they lie beyond the pale of the Sacred Law when it is the law that connects the Sufis to Allah at every moment? Rather, the reason for the doubts of someone unfamiliar with the way of the Sufis that it is of the very essence of the Sacred Law is the fact that such a person has not thoroughly mastered the knowledge of the law. This is why Junayd (Allah Most High have mercy on him) said, "This knowledge of ours is built of the Koran and sunna," in reply to those of his time or any other who imagine that it is beyond the pale of the Koran and sunna.

The Folk unanimously concur that none is fit to teach in the path of Allah Mighty and Majestic save someone with comprehensive mastery of the Sacred Law, who knows its explicit and implicit rulings, which of them are of general applicability and which are particular, which supersede others and which are superseded. He must also have a thorough grounding in Arabic, be familiar with its figurative modes and similes, and so forth. So every true Sufi is a scholar is Sacred Law, though the reverse is not necessarily true.

To summarize, no one denies the states of the Sufis except someone ignorant of the way they are. Qushayri says, "No era of the Islamic period has had a true sheikh of this group, save that the Imams of the scholars of that time deferred to him, showed humility towards him, and visited him for the benefit of his spiritual grace (baraka). If the Folk had no superiority or election, the matter would have been the other way around" (*al-Tabaqat al-kubra al-musamma bi Lawaqih al-anwar fi tabaqat al-akhyar* (y124), 1.4).

خالفت صريح القرآن أو السنة أو الإجماع لا غير ، وأما إذا لم تخالف فغاية الكلام أنه فهم أوتيه رجل مسلم فمن شاء فليعمل به ومن شاء تركه ، ونظير الفهم في ذلك الأفعال وما بقي باب للإنكار إلا سوء الظن بهم وحملهم على الرياء وذلك لا يجوز شرعاً . [. . .] فمن دقق النظر علم أنه لا يخرج شيء من علوم أهل الله تعالى عن الشريعة وكيف تخرج علومهم عن الشريعة والشريعة هي التي تصلهم إلى الله عز وجل في كل لحظة ولكن أصل استغراب من لا إلمام له بأهل الطريق أن علم التصوف من عين الشريعة كونه لم يتبحر في علم الشريعة ولذلك قال الجنيد رحمه الله تعالى علمنا هذا مشيد بالكتاب والسنة رداً على من توهم خروجه عنهما في ذلك الزمان أو غيره . وقد أجمع القوم على أنه لا يصلح للتصدر في طريق الله عز وجل إلا من تبحر في علم الشريعة وعلم منطوقها ومفهومها وخاصها وعامها وناسخها ومنسوخها وتبحر في لغة العرب حتى عرف مجازاتها واستعاراتها وغير ذلك فكل صوفي فقيه ولا عكس .

وبالجملة فما أنكر أحوال الصوفية إلا من جهل حالهم . وقال القشيري : لم يكن عصر في مدة الإسلام وفيه شيخ من هذه الطائفة إلا وأئمة ذلك الوقت من العلماء قد استسلموا لذلك الشيخ وتواضعوا له وتبركوا به . ولولا مزية وخصوصية للقوم لكان الأمر بالعكس [انتهى] [محرر من الطبقات الكبرى المسماة بلواقح الأنوار في طبقات الأخيار: ١ / ٤] .

*

SUFI SHEIKHS

الشيخ الصوفي

w9.6   (Ahmad Zarruq:) The conditions of a sheikh to whom a disciple may entrust himself are five:

(a) sound religious knowledge;

(b) true experience of the Divine;

(c) exalted purpose and will;

(d) a praiseworthy nature;

(e) and penetrating insight.

Someone with all five of the following is not fit to be a sheikh:

(1) ignorance of the religion;

(2) disparaging the honor of the Muslims;

(3) involvement in what does not concern him;

(4) following caprice in everything;

(5) and showing bad character without a second thought.

If there is no sheikh who is a true guide (murshid, def: w9.7), or there is one, but he lacks one of the five conditions, then the disciple should rely on those of his qualities that are perfected in him, and deal with him as a brother (A: meaning the sheikh and disciple advise one another) regarding the rest (*Kitab qawanin hukm al-ishraq ila kaffa al-Sufiyya fi jami' al-afaq* (y121), 119).

w9.6   (أحـمـد زروق:) [. . .]
وشـروط الشيخ الـذي يلقي إليـه المريد نفـسـه خمسـة : علم صحيـح ، وذوق صريـح ، وهمـة عاليـة ، وحـالة مرضية ، وبصيرة نافذة .
ومن فيـه خمس لا تصـح مشيختـه : الـجـهـل بالـديـن ، وإسقـاط حرمـة المسلمين ، ودخـول فيما لا يعني ، واتباع الهـوى في كل شيء ، وسـوء الخلق من غير مبالاة [. . .] .
وإن لم يكن شيـخ مرشـد وإن وجد ناقصـاً عن شروطه الخمس ، اعتمد على ما كـمـل فيـه وعـومـل بالأخـوة في الباقي [محـر ر من كتـاب قوانين حكم الإشراق إلى كافة الصوفية في جميع الآفاق : ١١٩] .

THE PURPOSE OF TAKING
A SHEIKH AND A PATH

المقصود من اتخاذ شيخ وطريق

w9.7   (Muhammad Hashimi:) As for when the path is merely "for the blessing of it" and the sheikh lacks some of the conditions of a true

w9.7   (محمـد الهـاشمي :) [. . .]
وأما إذا كانت الطريق طريق تبرُّك والشيخ بنقصـه بعض شروط الإرشـاد ، أو تعـدد

guide, or when the disciple is seeking several different aims from it at once, or the disciple's intention is contrary to the spiritual will of the sheikh, or the time required is unduly prolonged, or he is separated from his sheikh by the latter's death or the exigencies of the times and has not yet completed his journey to Allah on the path or attained his goal from it—then it is obligatory for him to go and associate with someone who can complete his journey for him and convey him to what he seeks from the path, as it is not permissible for him to remain bound to the first sheikh his whole life if it is only to die in ignorance of his Lord, claiming that this is the purpose of the path. By no means is this the purpose. The purpose of the path is to reach the goal, and a path that does not reach it is a means without an end. The path was made for travel on it with the intention of reaching one's goal, not for remaining and residing in even if this leads to dying in ignorance of one's Lord. The meaning of a true disciple is one who forthrightly submits himself to a living sheikh who is a guide (murshid) during the days of his journey to Allah Most High so that the sheikh may put him through the stages of the journey until he can say to him, "Here you are, and here is your Lord" (al-Hall al-sadid li ma astashkalahu al-murid (y46), 7).

مطلوب المريد أو خالفت نيةُ المريد همةَ الشيخ وتعدد الزمان ، أو فارق شيخه بموت أو غيره من حوادث الزمان وكان لم يتمم سيره إلى الله في الطريق ولم يحصّـل مقصوده من الطريق على يده فيجب عليـه صحبـة من يتمم له سلوكـه ويـوصله إلى مطلوبه من الطريق ، ولا يجوز أن يبقى مربوطاً بالأول طول عمره ولو أدى ذلك إلى موته جاهلاً بربه ويزعم أن ذلك هو المقصود من الطريق . كلّا . فإن المقصود من الطريق الـوصول إلى المطلوب ، فطريق بلا وصول وسيلة بلا غاية . والطريق جعلت للسير فيها بقصد الـوصول إلى مطلوبه لا للمكث والإقامة فيها ولو أدى ذلك إلى موته جاهلاً بربه . والمـراد بالمـريد الحقيقي هو الذي سلم نفسه مباشرة بالفعل للشيخ المرشد الحي في أيـام السير إلى الله تعالى ليسلك به الطريق إلى أن يقول له : ها أنت وربك [نقل من الحـل السـديد لمـا استشكله المريد : ٦ ـ ٧] .

---

w9.8   (n:) Muhammad Hashimi's above words about submitting oneself to a living sheikh refer to matters within the range of the *permissible* or *recommended*, not what contradicts the Sacred Law or beliefs of Islam (def: v1–v2), **for no true sheikh would ever countenance such a contravention (dis: s4.7), let alone have a disciple do so, a fact that furnishes the subject of the remaining articles of this section.**

---

w9.9   ('Izz ibn 'Abd al-Salam:) The Sacred Law is the scale upon which men are weighed and profit is distinguished from loss. He who weighs heavily on the scales of the Sacred Law is of the friends (awliya') of Allah, among whom there is disparity of degree. And he who comes up short in the scales of the Sacred Law is of the people of ruin, among whom there is also disparity of degree. If one sees someone who can fly through the air, walk on water, or inform one of the unseen, but who contravenes the Sacred Law by committing

w9.9   (العـز بن عبـد السـلام :) إن الشـرع ميزان يوزن به الرجال وبه يتيقن الربح من الخسران . فمن رجح في ميزان الـشـرع كان من أوليـاء الله ، وتختلف مراتب الـرجحـان . ومن نقص في ميزان الشرع فأولئك أهل الخسران ، وتفاوت خفتـهـم في الميـزان [. . .] فإذا رأيت إنساناً يطير في الهواء ويمشي على الماء ، أو يخبر بالمغيبـات ، ويخـالف الشرع

an unlawful act without an extenuating circumstance that legally excuses it, or who neglects an obligatory act without lawful reason, one may know that such a person is a devil Allah has placed there as a temptation to the ignorant. Nor is it far-fetched that such a person should be one of the means by which Allah chooses to lead men astray, for the Antichrist will bring the dead to life and make the living die, all as a temptation and affliction to those who would be misled (*al-Imam al-'Izz ibn 'Abd al-Salam wa atharuhu fi al-fiqh al-Islami* (y38), 1.137).

بارتكـاب المحـرمات بغير سبب محلل، أو يتـرك الـواجبـات بغيـر سبب مجـوز، فاعلم أنه شيطان نصبه الله فتنة للجهلة، وليس ذلـك ببعيـد من الأسبـاب التي وضعهـا الله للضـلال فإن الـدجال يحيي ويميت، فتنـة لأهل الضلال [محرّر من الإمـام العز بن عبد السلام وأثره في الفقه الإسلامي : ١/ ١٣٧].

THE STORY OF KHIDR AND MOSES

قصة الخضر وموسى عليهما السلام

w9.10 (A:) There is sometimes discussion as to whether the story of Khidr and Moses (Koran 18:65–82) does not show that exceptions to Islamic Law are possible. In fact, the verses give no grounds for such an inference, for two reasons. The first is that the context of the story is the age of Moses, not the age of Muhammad (Allah bless him and give him peace), whose Sacred Law is distinguished above that of any of the previous prophets by being final and inabrogable (dis: w4.2–7). The second reason is that Khidr, as the vast majority of scholars affirm, was himself a prophet and his actions were given to him to perform by divine revelation (wahy), this invalidating any comparison between Khidr's exceptionality to the law of Moses and that of any individual born in our own times, for there is no prophet born after the time of Muhammad (Allah bless him and give him peace).

It might be wondered why Allah Most High mentions the story of Khidr and Moses in the Koran at all, if the exceptionality of Khidr was restricted to the time of Moses. The answer is that there is much wisdom in the story, such as that some particular excellence not found in the superior of two things or people may well be found in the inferior of them, for Moses was a prophetic messenger (rasul) while Khidr was only a prophet (nabi); that there are secrets given to certain of Allah's servants which not everyone in the Community (Umma) is responsible to know; that one should learn wisdom wherever one can; and that no matter how much one knows, one should not claim to have knowledge. And Allah knows best.

SUFISM AND ORTHODOXY

براءة التصوف من أهل الأهواء

w9.11 ('Abd al-Qahir Baghdadi:) The book *Tarikh al-Sufiyya* [The history of the Sufis] by Abu 'Abd al-Rahman Sulami, comprises the biographies of nearly a thousand sheikhs of the Sufis, none of whom belonged to heretical sects and all

w9.11 (عبد القاهر البغدادي :) وقد اشتمـل كتاب تاريـخ الصـوفية لأبي عبد الرحمن السلمي على زهاء ألف شيخ من الصـوفية ما فيهم واحد من أهل الأهواء .

of whom were of the Sunni community, with the exception of only three of them: Abu Hilman of Damascus, who pretended to be of the Sufis but actually believed in incarnationism (hulul, def: w7.1); Husayn ibn Mansur al-Hallaj, whose case remains problematic, though Ibn 'Ata', Ibn Khafif, and Abul Qasim al-Nasrabadhi approved of him; and al-Qannad, whom the Sufis accused of being a Mu'tazilite (def: w6.4) and rejected, for the good does not accept the wicked (*Usul al-din* (y23), 315–16).

بل كلهم من أهـل السنـة سوى ثلاثـة منهم: أحـدهم أبـو حلمان الدمشقي فإنه تستر بالصوفية وكان من الحلولية. والثاني الـحـسـين بن منصـور الحـلاج وشأنـه مشكل. وقد رضيه ابن عطاء وابن خفيف وأبـو القـاسم النصرآباذي. والثالث القناد اتهمتـه الصـوفيـة بالاعتـزال فطـردوه لأن الطيب لا يقبـل الخبيث [نقـل من أصول الدين: ٣١٥ ـ ٣١٦].

*

w10.0 IN WHAT SENSE PHILOSOPHY IS UNLAWFUL
(from a7.2(2))

w10.0 معنى القول بحرمة الفلسفة

w10.1 (n:) Anyone who has made a serious study of "philosophy" must acknowledge that the term has been applied to a great many widely varying procedures and styles of thought throughout its long history, and that there is little substantial agreement among philosophers as to what philosophy is or should be. What Nawawi and other Islamic scholars seem to have in mind when they speak of the unlawful character of philosophy is not the efforts at a logical critique of the methodology of the sciences which have been seen particularly in this century, but rather cosmological theories and all-too-human attempts to solve ultimate questions about man, God, life after death, and so forth, without the divinely revealed guidance of the Koran and sunna: Any opinion that contradicts a well-known tenet of Islamic belief that there is scholarly consensus upon (ijma', def: b7) is unbelief (kufr), and is unlawful to learn or teach, except by way of explaining that it is unlawful. And Allah knows best.

*

w11.0 THE UNLAWFULNESS OF THE SCIENCES OF THE MATERIALISTS
(from a7.2(5))

w11.0 معنى القـول بحـرمة علوم الطبائعيين

w11.1 (N:) The unlawfulness of the "sciences of the materialists" refers to the conviction of materialists that things *in themselves* or *by their own nature* have a causal influence independent of the will of Allah. To believe this is unbelief (dis: o8.7(17)) that puts one beyond the pale of Islam. Muslims working in the sciences must remember that they are dealing with figurative causes (asbab majaziyya), not real ones, for Allah alone is the real cause.

w12.0 THE REASON FOR VARIOUS POSITIONS WITHIN ONE SCHOOL (from b1.2)

w12.0 سبب الخلاف في المذهب الواحد

LEVELS OF SCHOLARS

طبقات علماء المذهب

w12.1 (Salih Mu'adhdhin:) To clarify the reason for scholarly disagreement within one legal school, we may say that scholars divide each school into various levels, the most important of which (N: after the Imam) may be characterized as follows:

(1) the first level, composed of those qualified to do *ijtihad* (independent legal reasoning) within the school, deploying it according to the general methodological principles established by their Imams, and who transmit the words of the Imam, such scholars being called *colleagues*, including men like Muzani;

(2) the second level, composed of those qualified to do *ijtihad* on particular legal questions that were not discussed by the Imam of the school, including such scholars as Imam Ghazali;

(3) the third level, composed of those qualified to do textual exegesis, and who because of their comprehensive mastery of the works of the school, specialize in interpreting the positions of their Imams that require details and explanation to be properly understood, and in specifying the precise meaning of rulings which might otherwise be understood equivocally; including such scholars as the Imam of the Two Sanctuaries, Juwayni;

(4) and the fourth level, which is composed of those qualified to weigh various scholarly positions and judge which is the soundest, evaluating their Imams' positions in terms of the reliability of the narrators of the channels of transmission of the opinion from the Imam, or in terms of the understanding shown in treating particular legal questions; and who may then say which is the stronger or more suitable position; this level including such men as the Two Sheikhs, Rafi'i and Nawawi.

w12.1 (صالح مؤذن:) لتوضيح سبب الخلاف في المذهب الواحد نقول: قسم العلماء كل مذهب إلى طبقات أهمها:

الطبقة الأولى: أهل الاجتهاد في المذهب وهؤلاء يجتهدون ضمن أصول الاجتهاد التي وضعها أئمتهم وينقلون كلام الإمام وهم الأصحاب كالمزني.

الطبقة الثانية: أهل الاجتهاد في المسائل التي لم ترد على إمام المذهب كالإمام الغزالي.

الطبقة الثالثة: أهل التخريج وهؤلاء لإحاطتهم بالمذهب يقتصرون على تفسير قول مجمل من أقوال أئمتهم أو تعيين وجه معين لحكم يحتمل وجهين كإمام الحرمين الجويني.

الطبقة الرابعة: أهل الترجيح وهؤلاء يرجحون ما روي عن أئمتهم من جهة الرواية أو من جهة الدراية فيقول هذا أصح أو أولى ومن هؤلاء الشيخان الرافعي والنووي.

It is apparent from the foregoing that scholarly differences may occur at each of the levels: in the deductions of the colleagues and their *ijtihad* within the general methodological principles of the school, in judging one position of the Imam of the school to be sounder than another of his positions, or in judging one position's channel of transmission to be sounder than another's; all of which take place according to the evidence available to the particular scholar and his understanding of the Imam's words (*'Umdat al-salik* (y90), 18).

وهكذا نرى أنه في كل طبقة يمكن أن يحصل الخلاف في استنباط الأصحاب واجتهادهم ضمن أصول المذهب أو في ترجيح قول على قول من أقوال إمام المذهب أو ترجيح رواية على أخرى كل ذلك حسب ما يتوافر لدى كل واحد منهم من الأدلة وبحسب فهمه لكلام الإمام [نقل من تعليق لصالح مؤذن على هامش عمدة السالك وعدة الناسك : ١٨] .

IT IS OBLIGATORY TO JUDGE ACCORDING
TO THE STRONGEST POSITION IN A SCHOOL

وجوب الحكم بالراجح في المذهب

w12.2 (Zayn al-Din Mallibari:) Al-'Iraqi and Ibn Salah have recorded scholarly consensus (def: b7) that it is not permissible to judge by other than the strongest legal position in a school, as Subki has explicitly stated at length in several places in his *Fatawi*, considering it to be "judging by other than what Allah has revealed," since Allah Most High has made it obligatory for *mujtahids* (def: o22.1(d)) to adopt the position for which the evidence is strongest, and has made it obligatory for non-*mujtahids* to follow the *ijtihad* of *mujtahids* in all works that are personally obligatory (dis: b2.1).

w12.2 (زين الدين المليباري :) نقل العراقي وابن الصلاح الإجماع على أنه لا يجوز الحكم بخلاف الراجح في المذهب وصرح السبكي بذلك في مواضع من فتاويه وأطال وجعل ذلك من الحكم بخلاف ما أنزل الله لأن الله تعالى أوجب على المجتهدين أن يأخذوا بالراجح وأوجب على غيرهم تقليدهم فيما يجب عليهم العمل به .

THE STRONGEST POSITION
IN THE SHAFI'I SCHOOL

المعتمد في المذهب الشافعي

w12.3 Jalal Bulqini relates from his father (A: Siraj al-Din) that "the soundest position in the [A: Shafi'i] school for court rulings and formal legal opinions (fatwa) [n: in order of which must be accepted first when available] is what Nawawi and Rafi'i agree upon; then Nawawi's position; then Rafi'i's; then what has been judged strongest by the majority of scholars; then by the most knowledgeable; then by the most godfearing." Our sheikh (A: Ibn Hajar Haytami) states that this is what has been agreed upon by the most exacting of the later scholars, and is the position our sheikhs have enjoined us to rely on (*Kitab fath al-*

w12.3 ونقل الجلال البلقيني عن والده [. . .] أن المعتمد في المذهب للحكم والفتوى ما اتفق عليه الشيخان فما جزم به النووي فالرافعي فما رجحه الأكثر فالأعلم فالأورع . قال شيخنا هذا ما أطبق عليه محققو المتأخرين والذي أوصى باعتماده مشايخنا [محرر من كتاب

Mu'in bi sharh Qurra al-'ayn bi muhimmat al-din (y85), 348).	فتح المعين بشرح قرة العين : ٣٤٨].

*

w13.0 SLAVERY IN ISLAM (from c3.4) (see also k32)

w13.0 الرق في الإسلام

w13.1 (Titus Burckhardt:) Slavery within Islamic culture is not to be confused with Roman slavery or with the American variety of the nineteenth century; in Islam the slave was never a mere "thing." If his master treated him badly, he could appeal to a judge and procure his freedom. His dignity as a Muslim was inviolable. Originally the status of slave was simply the outcome of having been taken as a prisoner of war. A captive who could not buy his own freedom by means of ransom remained in the possession of the captor until he had earned his freedom by work or until he was granted liberty by his master (*Moorish Culture in Spain* (y32), 30).

*

w14.0 FOLLOWING ANOTHER IMAM IN LEGAL RULINGS (from c6.4, end)

w14.0 من قلد غير إمامه

w14.1 (Ibn Hajar Haytami:) There are a number of states one may have in following the legal position of an Imam other than one's own, among them:

(1) to believe that the other Imam's position on the particular question is stronger, in which case it is permissible to follow him in deference to what one believes to be the sounder position;

(2) to believe that the position of one's own Imam is stronger, or not to know which Imam has the stronger position on the question, in both of which cases it is permissible to follow the position of the other Imam whether or not one thereby intends to take the way that is religiously more precautionary (dis: c6.5), in which case it is not offensive, though if it is a mere stratagem that is not intended as such (N: i.e. not intended as being religiously more precautionary) it is offensive;

w14.1 (ابن حجر الهيتمي): [...] لمقلد غير إمامه أحوال [ذكرها السبكي أخذاً من كلامهم (ح: أي كلام الأصوليين)]:

ـ أحدها: أن يعتقد رجحان مذهب الغير في تلك المسألة فيجوز اتباعاً للراجح في ظنه.

ـ الثانية: أن يعتقد رجحان مذهب إمامه أو لا يعتقد رجحان واحد منهما، فيجوز أيضاً سواء قصد الاحتياط لدينه [...] ولا كراهة حينئذ بخلاف الحيلة على غير هذا الوجه (ح: أي غير وجه الاحتياط) فإنها مكروهة.

(3) to intend by following the other Imam to take a dispensation when there is a need for it (N: such as a Shafi'i circumambulating the Kaaba at a crowded hajj (dis: j5.16(b)) who follows the position of Abu Hanifa that touching a woman does not nullify one's ablution), in which case it is permissible to follow the other Imam, unless one believes both that the position of one's own Imam is stronger, and that it is obligatory to follow the more knowledgeable of the two;

(4) to intend merely following the easier way of taking a dispensation when (N: neither (2) nor (3) above is the case, and) one does not believe that it is the stronger position, in which case following it is not permissible, as Subki says, "because one is then merely pursuing one's own caprice, and it is not for the sake of religion";

(5) to do this frequently, so as to become one of those who seek out dispensations (dis: c6.4), taking the easiest ruling from every school, which is also forbidden, as it connotes a dissolution of the limits of legal responsibility;

(6) to assemble by such a procedure a single composite act that is unacceptable by the consensus of scholars (def: b7), which is impermissible, such as when a Shafi'i follows Imam Malik in considering dogs to be physically pure, but only wipes part of his head when performing ablution (wudu), for in such a case his prayer is not considered valid by Malik, because he has not wiped his whole head, nor yet by Shafi'i, because of the physical impurity of dogs (N: though it is unobjectionable to piece together such a composite act by way of following the scholarly evidences supporting each part, if one is qualified to appreciate them (def: o22.1(d)), since then one has become a *mujtahid* on the question);

(7) or to follow one's original Imam in doing an act whose consequences are still in effect when one subsequently intends to follow another Imam, despite the continued existence of the first act's consequences; such as a Hanafi who, by right of being a neighbor, acquires a piece of land by preempting a neighbor's sale of it to another (shuf'a, def: k21) (N: since one of the purposes

ـ الثالثة : أن يقصد بتقليده الرخصة فيما دعت حاجته إليه (ح : كتقليد شافعي مذهب أبي حنيفة في عدم نقض الوضوء بلمس المرأة عند طوافه للحج مع الازدحام) فيجوز أيضاً ، إلا أن يكون يعتقد رجحان مذهب إمامه وأنه يجب تقليد الأعلم .

ـ الرابعة أن يقصد مجرد الترخص (ح : مع عدم وجود الحال الثاني ولا الثالث) من غير أن يغلب على ظنه رجحانه فيمتنع كما قاله السبكي . قال : إنه حينئذ متبع لهواه لا للدين .

ـ الخامسة : أن يكثر من ذلك بحيث يصير متتبعاً للرخص بأن يأخذ من كل مذهب بالأسهل منه ، فيمتنع أيضاً لأنه يشعر بانحلال ربقة التكليف .

ـ السادسة : أن يجتمع من ذلك حقيقة مركبة ممتنعة بالإجماع ، فيمتنع كأن يقلد شافعي مالكاً في طهارة الكلب ويمسح بعض رأسه لأن صلاته حينئذ لا يقول بها مالك لعدم مسح كل الرأس ولا الشافعي لنجاسة الكلب [. . .] . (ح : لكن إن لفق بدليل فلا بأس عليه إن كان فيه أهلية معرفة الدليل فإذاً صار مجتهداً فيه) .

ـ السابعة : أن يعمل بتقليده الأول ويستمر على آثاره ثم يريد أن يقلد غير إمامه مع بقاء تلك الآثار كحنفي أخذ بشفعة الجوار [عملاً بمذهبه] (ح : لأن

that permit preemption in the Hanafi school is to prevent property adjacent to one's own from being acquired by an objectionable neighbor (n: though the Shafi'i school does not allow preemption for such a reason (dis: k21.0(N:))))—but when a second neighbor for the same reason preempts the Hanafi's taking possession of the land, the Hanafi refuses to allow the second preemption on the pretext that he now follows the Shafi'i school on the question, which is not permissible because it confirms that he is mistaken, either by following the first opinion or by following the second, while he is but a single responsible individual.

(*al-Fatawa al-hadithiyya* (y48), 113–14)

دفع جار السـوء سبب من أسباب الشفعة عنـد الحنفية [فقالوا بالشفعة للجوار]) ثم تستحق عليـه فيـريـد العمـل بمـذهب الشـافعي فلا يجـوز لتحقق خطئه إما في الأول أو الثاني مع أنه شخص واحد مكلف .

[محرّر من الفتاوى الحديثية: ١١٣ ـ ١١٤].

*

w15.0 METRIC EQUIVALENTS OF ISLAMIC WEIGHTS AND MEASURES (from e1.11)

w15.0 ما يعـادل المكـايـيـل والأوزان الإسـلامـيـة في النظام المتري

w15.1 (n:) The metric equivalents of the Islamic weights and measures mentioned in the present work are as follows:

1 *mithqal* = 4.235 grams
1 dinar = 1 *mithqal* = 4.235 grams
1 dirham = 2.9645 grams
1 *ritl* = 381.15 grams
1 *mudd* = 0.51 liters
1 *sa'* = 2.03 liters
5 *awsuq* = 609.84 kilograms
Qullatayn = 216 liters
1 *dhira'* = 48 centimeters
The distance permitting shortening prayers = 81 km./ 50 mi.

HOW THE EQUIVALENTS WERE ARRIVED AT

w15.2 The weight of the classic Islamic gold dinar, one *mithqal*, is the basis for virtually all the other weights and measures mentioned above. The present volume's estimate of this all-important criterion is based on numismatic studies of ancient glass disc *mithqal*-weights, most of them dating back to A.H. 164/A.D. 780, which were originally produced as the standard to gauge the weight of the Islamic dinar, the difference in the weight of all such discs discovered up to the present time not exceeding a third of a milligram. Particularly impressive for accuracy is a study by P. Casanova, who conducted weight tests of several hundred intact specimens of such glass discs, each 18 *mithqal*s, and found them to weigh 76.23 grams, from which one may infer a *mithqal* value of 4.235 grams, a result that is especially reliable because it is not possible for the error factor therein to exceed 1/18 per *mithqal* (*al-Makayil wa al-awzan al-Islamiyya* (y50), 9–10). This study furnished the estimate used by the present volume.

The weight of the dirham is 7/10 of the weight of the *mithqal* (*Mughni al-muhtaj ila ma'rifa ma'ani alfaz al-Minhaj* (y73), 1.389), or 2.9645 grams.

The weight of the *ritl* has been estimated by Nawawi as 128 and 4/7 dirhams (*Fayd al-Ilah al-Malik* (y27), 1.15), equalling 128.5714285 dirhams, or 381.15 grams.

The *mudd* is a volume measure that in the Arabic of e5.25 is estimated in terms of a weight, 1 1/3 *ritl*, the weight of water being understood to furnish the basis for conversion to volume, just as it is at e1.11, where *qullatayn* is defined in terms of both. One and one-third *ritl* is 508.1999 grams, giving us a *mudd* of 0.5081999 liters, rounded off to 0.51 liters in the translation.

The *sa'* is 5 1/3 *ritl*s (dis: Ar. e5.25) or four *mudd*s, equalling 2.0327996 liters, rounded off to 2.03 liters in the translation.

Five *awsuq* amounts to 1600 *ritl*s (dis: Ar. h3.4), considered as a weight (*Fayd al-Ilah al-Malik* (y27), 1.248), equalling 609.84 kilograms.

Qullatayn is estimated at e1.11 as about 500 *ritl*s (190.575 liters), or 1 1/4 *dhira'*, (lit. *cubit*, meaning the Shafi'i *dhira'*, for otherwise the term has been applied to a wide variety of measures) in height, width, and length, from which one may infer that the *dhira'* is 46.03 centimeters. The translator found both these metric equivalents satisfactory, but in deference to the *ijtihad* of Sheikh Muhammad Amin Kurdi in *Tanwir al-qulub fi mu'amala 'Allam al-Ghuyub* (y74), 172, and Sheikh Ridwan al-'Adal Baybars in *Kitab rawda al-muhtajin li ma'rifa qawa'id al-din* (y29), 186, who both estimate the *dhira'* at 48 centimeters, the latter figure has been adopted, and it yields an estimated *qullatayn* volume of 216 liters (a cube of 60 centimeters on each side) which may be considered religiously more precautionary than the above *qullatayn* estimate, since the greater estimate fulfills the legal requirements of the lesser estimate, though not vice versa.

Adopting a *dhira'* estimate of 48 centimeters rather than 46.03 centimeters yields a distance permitting shortening prayers (masafa al-qasr) of 80.640 kilometers (*Tanwir al-qulub fi mu'amala 'Allam al-Ghuyub* (y74), 172), rather than the 77.3304 kilometers inferable from the lesser estimate; and the greater estimate has been preferred here as well, since it enters into a great many rulings and is religiously more precautionary in the sense explained above. It has been rounded off in the translation to 81 km./ 50 mi.

*

w16.0 PROPER MANNERS TOWARDS THE HOLY KORAN (from e8.1, end)

w16.1 (Qurtubi:) It is of the inviolability of the Koran:

(1) not to touch it except in a state of ritual purity (dis: w16.2), and to recite it when in a state of ritual purity;

(2) to brush one's teeth with a toothstick (def: e3), remove food particles from between them, and freshen one's mouth before reciting, since it is the way through which the Koran passes;

(3) to sit up straight if not in prayer, and not lean back;

(4) to dress for reciting it as if intending to visit a prince, for the reciter is engaged in intimate discourse;

(5) to face the direction of prayer (qibla) to recite;

(6) to rinse the mouth out with water if one expectorates mucus or phlegm;

(7) to stop reciting when one yawns, for when reciting, one is addressing one's Lord in intimate conversation, while yawning is from the Devil;

(8) when beginning to recite, to take refuge in Allah from the accursed Devil (def: w1.15) and say the Basmala (w1.6), whether one has begun at the first of the sura or some other part one has reached;

(9) once one has begun, not to interrupt one's recital from moment to moment with human words, unless absolutely necessary;

(10) to be alone when reciting it, so that no one interrupts one, forcing one to mix the words of the Koran with replying, for this nullifies the effectiveness of having taken refuge in Allah from the Devil at the beginning;

w16.0 التأدب مع القرآن الكريم

w16.1 (الإمام القرطبي:) [قال الترمذي الحكيم أبو عبد الله في نوادر الأصول:]

فمن حرمة القرآن ألا يمسه إلا طاهراً.

ومن حرمته أن يقرأه وهو على طهارة.

ومن حرمته أن يستاك ويتخلل فيطيب فاه، إذ هو طريقه [...] [ت: وقال الترمذي في المرجع المذكور، ص٣٣٣:] وأن تستوي قاعداً إن كنت في غير الصلاة ولا تكون متكئاً).

ومن حرمته أن يتلبس كما يتلبس للدخول على الأمير لأنه مناج.

ومن حرمته أن يستقبل القبلة لقراءته [...].

ومن حرمته أن يتمضمض كلما تنخع [...].

ومن حرمته إذا تثاءب أن يمسك عن القراءة لأنه إذا قرأ فهو مخاطب ربه مناج، والتثاؤب من الشيطان [...].

ومن حرمته أن يستعيذ بالله عند ابتدائه للقراءة من الشيطان الرجيم، ويقرأ بسم الله الرحمن الرحيم إن كان ابتدأ قراءته من أول السورة أو من حيث بلغ.

ومن حرمته إذا أخذ في القراءة لم يقطعها ساعة فساعة بكلام الآدميين من غير ضرورة.

ومن حرمته أن يخلو بقراءته حتى لا يقطع عليه أحد بكلام فيخلطه بجوابه لأنه إذا فعل ذلك زال عنه سلطان الاستعاذة الذي استعاذ في البدء.

(11) to recite it leisurely and without haste, distinctly pronouncing each letter;

(12) to use one's mind and understanding in order to comprehend what is being said to one;

(13) to pause at verses that promise Allah's favor, to long for Allah Most High and ask of His bounty; and at verses that warn of His punishment to ask Him to save one from it;

(14) to pause at the accounts of bygone peoples and individuals to heed and benefit from their example;

(15) to find out the meanings of the Koran's unusual lexical usages;

(16) to give each letter its due so as to clearly and fully pronounce every word, for each letter counts as ten good deeds;

(17) whenever one finishes reciting, to attest to the veracity of one's Lord, and that His messenger (Allah bless him and give him peace) has delivered his message, and to testify to this, saying: "Our Lord, You have spoken the truth, Your messengers have delivered their tidings, and we are witnesses to this. O Allah, make us of those who bear witness to the truth and who act with justice"; after which one supplicates Allah with prayers;

(18) not to select certain verses from each sura to recite, but rather recite the whole sura;

(19) if one puts the Koran down, not to leave it open;

(20) not to place other books upon the Koran, which should always be higher than all other books (N: though the books of each shelf of a bookcase, for example, are considered separately in this), whether they are books of Sacred Knowledge or something else;

(21) to place the Koran on one's lap when reading, or on something in front of one, not on the floor;

ومن حرمته أن يقرأه على تؤدة وترسيل وترتيل .

ومن حرمتـه أن يستعمـل فيـه ذهنـه وفهمه حتى يعقل ما يخاطب به .

ومن حرمتـه أن يقف على آيـة الـوعـد فيرغب إلى الله تعالى ويسأله من فضله ، وأن يقف على آيـة الـوعـيـد فيستجير بالله منـه ، ومن حرمتـه أن يقف على أمثـالـه فيمتثلها ، ومن حرمته أن يلتمس غرائبه .

ومن حرمته أن يؤدي لكـل حرف حقه من الأداء حتى يُبرز الكلام باللفظ تماماً ، فإن بكل حرف عشر حسنات .

ومن حرمته إذا انتهت قراءته أن يصدق ربـه ويشهـد بالبلاغ لرسوله ﷺ ، ويشهد على ذلـك أنه حق ، فيقول : صدقتَ ربّنا وبلّغتْ رسلـك ونـحن على ذلـك من الشاهدين اللهم اجعلنا من شهداء الحق القائمين بالقسط ؛ ثم يدعو بدعوات .

ومن حرمته إذا قرأه ألا يلتقط الآي من كل سورة فيقـرأها [. . .] (ت : بل)[يقرأ السورة كلها [. . .] .

ومن حرمتـه إذا وضـع المصحف ألا يتركـه منشـوراً ، وألا يضع فوقه شيئاً من الكتب حتى يكون أبداً عالياً لسائر الكتب علماً كان أو غيره .

ومن حرمتـه أن يضعـه في حجـره إذا قرأه أو على شيء بين يديه ولا يضعه بالأرض .

(22) not to wipe it from a slate with spittle, but rather wash it off with water; and if one washes it off with water, to avoid putting the water where there are unclean substances (najasa) or where people walk. Such water has its own inviolability, and there were those of the early Muslims before us who used water that washed away Koran to effect cures;

(23) not to use sheets upon which it has been written as bookcovers, which is extremely rude, but rather to erase the Koran from them with water;

(24) not to let a day go by without looking at least once at the pages of the Koran;

(25) to give one's eyes their share of looking at it, for the eyes lead to the soul (nafs), whereas there is a veil between the breast (N: i.e. the place where it is remembered) and the soul, and the Koran is in the breast. When one recites it from memory, only one's ears hear and convey it to the soul; while if one is looking at the words, both eye and ear participate in the performance, discharging it more completely, and the eyes as well as the ears are given their due;

(26) not to trivially quote the Koran at the occurrence of everyday events, as by saying, for example, when someone comes,

"You have come hither according to a decree, O Moses" (Koran 20:40),

or,

"Eat and drink heartily for what you have done aforetimes, in days gone by" (Koran 69:24),

when food is brought out, and so forth;

(27) not to recite it to song tunes like those of the corrupt, or with the tremulous tones of Christians or the plaintiveness of monkery, all of which is misguidance;

(28) when writing the Koran to do so in a clear, elegant hand;

ومن حرمتـه ألا يمحـوه من اللوح بالبصاق ولكن يغسله بالماء. ومن حرمته إذا غسله بالمـاء أن يتـوقى النجاسات من المـواضـع، والمـواقـع التي توطأ، فإن لتلك الغسـالـة حرمـة، وكان مَن قبلنا من السلف منهم من يستشفي بغسالته.

ومن حرمتـه ألا يتخـذ الصحيفة [إذا بليت ودرست] وقايـة للكتب، فإن ذلك جفاء عظيم، ولكن يمحوها بالماء.

ومن حرمته ألا يُخلي يوماً من أيامه من النظـر في المصحف مرة [...]، ومن حرمتـه أن يعطي عينيـه حظهمـا منه، فإن العيـن تؤدي إلى النفس، وبين النفس والصـدر حجـاب، والقرآن في الصدر؛ فإذا قرأه عن ظهر قلب فإنمـا يسمـع أذنه فتـؤدي إلى النفس، فإذا نظر في الخط كانت العين والأذن قد اشتركتا في الأداء، وذلك أوفر للأداء، وكان قد أخذت العين حظها كالأذن، [...].

ومن حرمته ألا يتأوله عندما يعرض له شيء من أمر الـدنيا، [...] ـ والتأويل مثل قولك للرجل إذا جاءك: «جئت على قدر يا موسى» ومثل قولـه تعالى: ﴿كُلُوا وَاشْـرَبُـوا هَنِيئًا بِمَـا أَسْلَفْتُمْ فِي الأَيَّامِ الخَالِيَةِ﴾ [هذا] عند حضـور الطعـام وأشبـاه هذا، [...].

ومن حرمتـه ألا يقرأه بألحـان الغنـاء كلحـون أهـل الـفسق، ولا بتـرجيـع النصارى ولا نوح الـرهبـانية، فإن ذلك كله زيغ [وقد تقدم].

ومـن حرمتـه أن يجلّل تخطيطـه إذا خطه، [...].

(29) not to recite it aloud over another's reciting of it, so as to spoil it for him and make him resent what he hears, making it as if it were some kind of competition;

(30) not to recite it in marketplaces, places of clamor and frivolity, or where fools gather;

(31) not to use the Koran as pillow, or lean upon it;

(32) not to toss it when one wants to hand it to another;

(33) not to miniaturize the Koran, mix into it what is not of it, or mingle this-worldly adornment with it by embellishing or writing it with gold;

(34) not to write it on the ground or on walls, as is done in some new mosques;

(35) not to write an amulet (def: w17) with it and enter the lavatory, unless it is encased in leather, silver, or other, for then it is as if kept in the heart;

(36) if one writes it (N: with saffron, for example on the inside of a dish) and then (N: dissolves the writing into water and) drinks it (N: for a cure or other purpose), one should say the Basmala (def: w1.6) at every breath and make a noble and worthy intention, for Allah only gives to one according to one's intention;

(37) and if one finishes reciting the entire Koran, to begin it anew, that it may not resemble something that has been abandoned.

(al-Jami' li ahkam al-Qur'an (y117), 1.27–31)

w16.2 (Imam Baghawi:) 'Abdullah ibn Abu Bakr ibn Muhammad ibn 'Amr ibn Hazm reported that the letter that the Prophet (Allah bless him and give him peace) wrote (N: i.e. dictated and had sent) to 'Amr ibn Hazm contained the injunction that

"none may touch the Koran but someone in a state of ritual purity."

ومن حرمته ألا يجهر بعض على بعض في القراءة فيفسد عليه حتى يبغض إليه ما يسمع ويكون كهيئة المغالبة، [...].
ومن حرمته ألا يقرأ في الأسواق ولا في مواطن اللغط واللغو ومجمع السفهاء [...].
ومن حرمته ألا يتوسد المصحف ولا يعتمد عليه، ولا يرمي به إلى صاحبه إذا أراد أن يناوله، ومن حرمته ألا يصغر المصحف [...]. قلت: وروي عن عمر بن الخطاب رضي الله عنه أنه رأى مصحفاً صغيراً في يد رجل فقال: من كتبه؟ قال: أنا؛ فضربه بالدرة، وقال: عظموا القرآن [...].
ومن حرمته ألا يخلط فيه ما ليس منه، ومن حرمته ألا يحلى بالذهب ولا يكتب بالذهب فتخلط به زينة الدنيا [...]، ومن حرمته ألا يكتب على الأرض ولا على حائط كما يفعل به في المساجد المحدثة [...].
ومن حرمته أن لا يكتب التعاويذ منه ثم يدخل به في الخلاء إلا أن يكون في غلاف من أدم أو فضة أو غيره فيكون كأنه في صدرك.
ومن حرمته إذا كتبه وشرب به سمّى الله على كل نفس وعظّم النية فيه فإن الله يؤتيه على قدر نيته [...]، ومن حرمته أن يفتتحه كلما ختمه حتى لا يكون كهيئة المهجور [...] [محرّر من الجامع لأحكام القرآن: ١/ ٢٧ ـ ٣١ بتقديم وتأخير].

w16.2 (الإمام البغوي:) [...] [عن عبد الله بن أبي بكر بن محمد بن عمرو بن حزم أنّ الكتاب الذي كتبه رسول الله ﷺ لعمرو بن حزم: «أنّ لا يمسّ القرآن إلا طاهرٌ».

(Shu'ayb Arna'ut:) This is a rigorously authenticated (sahih) hadith, and was related in *al-Muwatta'* (y82), 1.199, in the section on the Koran, the chapter of "The Demand to Perform Ablution for Whoever Touches the Koran." Abu 'Umar states, "There is no disagreement reported from Malik that this hadith is *mursal* [def: o22.1(d(II(4)))], though it has also been related through a good channel with a contiguous series of transmitters (musnad) from the Prophet (Allah bless him and give him peace), the letter itself being well known to specialists in the field of prophetic biography and so famous among scholars that its renown suffices it from the need for a pedigree [dis: w48.3]." The hadith has various other channels of transmission and corroboratory evidences that strengthen it and raise it to the degree of rigorously authenticated (sahih). See them in *Nasb al-raya* (y135), 1.196–99 (*Sharh al-sunna* (y22), 2.47–48).

*

w17.0 PROTECTIVE OR HEALING WORDS (RUQYA) AND AMULETS (from e8.2)

w17.1 (Mansur 'Ali Nasif:) Protective or healing words are permitted by Sacred Law and are called for when there is need for them, provided three conditions are met:

(a) that they consist of the word of Allah Most High, His names, or His attributes (n: the hadiths prohibiting amulets being interpreted as referring to the beads and so forth that were used in the pre-Islamic period of ignorance (dis: w17.3));

(b) that they be in Arabic;

(c) and that the user not believe the words have any effect in themselves (n: which is unbelief, as at o8.7(17)), but are rather empowered to do so by Allah Most High.

(شعيب الأرنـؤوط:) (هـو) حديث صحيـح، وهـو في «الموطأ» ١/ ١٩٩ في القـرآن: باب الأمـر بالـوضـوء لمن مس القـرآن، قال أبـو عمـر: لا خلاف عن مالك في إرسال هذا الحديث، وقد روي مسنداً من وجه صالح، وهو كتاب مشهور عنـد أهل السير، معـروف عند أهل العلم معـرفـة يستغنى بهـا في شهـرتهـا عن الإسنـاد؛ [قـلت:] وللحـديث طرق وشـواهد يتقوى بها، ويصح، انظرها في «نصب الراية» ١/ ١٩٦ ـ ١٩٩ [نقل من شرح السنة: ٢/ ٤٧ ـ ٤٨].

w17.0 جواز الرقى والتمائم

w17.1 (مـنصـور علي ناصف:) [. . .] فالـرقـية مشـروعة ومطلوبة عند الحـاجة بشرط أن تكون بكلام الله تعالى أو بأسمـائـه أو صفاته، وأن تكون باللفظ العـربـي، وأن يعتقد أن الـرقـية لا تؤثر بنفسهـا بل بتقـديـر الله تعـالى. والتميمة

Amulets are like protective or healing words (ruqya) in the need for these conditions. And Allah knows best (al-Taj al-jami' li al-usul fi ahadith al-Rasul (y100), 3.219).

w17.2 (Nawawi:) One may adduce as evidence for their permissibility the hadith of 'Amr ibn Shu'ayb, from his father, from his grandfather, that the Messenger of Allah (Allah bless him and give him peace) used to teach them for fearful situations the words,

"I seek refuge in Allah's perfect words from His wrath, the evil of His servants, the whispered insinuations of devils, and lest they come to me."

'Abdullah ibn 'Amr used to teach these words to those of his sons who had reached the age of reason, and used to write them and hang them upon those who had not (al-Majmu' (y108), 2.71).

w17.3 (Ibn Hajar Haytami:) A group of ten riders came to the Prophet (Allah bless him and give him peace), who had nine of them swear a covenant with him, but would not let the tenth do so. They asked, "What is the matter with him?" and the Prophet (Allah bless him and give him peace) replied that there was an amulet on his upper arm, so the man cut it off, and the Prophet let him swear his covenant, after which the Prophet (Allah bless him and give him peace) said,

"Whoever hangs one has ascribed associates (shirk) to Allah."

It is obligatory to interpret the above as referring to what they used to do of hanging a bead on themselves and calling it an "amulet" (tamima), and the like, believing it would protect them from calamities. Without a doubt, to believe this is ignorance and misguidance, and one of the worst enormities, since if it is not associating others with Allah (shirk), it leads to it, for nothing can benefit or harm one, prevent or turn aside, except for Allah Most High (al-Zawajir 'an iqtiraf al-kaba'ir (y49), 1.166).

كالرقية في هذا والله أعلم [نقل من كتاب التاج الجامع للأصول في أحاديث الرسول ﷺ: ٣/ ٢١٩].

w17.2 (النـووي:) [. . .] وقـد يستـدل للإباحة بحديث عمرو بن شعيب عن أبيه عن جده أن رسول الله ﷺ «كان يعـلمـهـم من الفـزع كلمـات: أعـوذ بكلمـات الله التـامة من غضبه وشر عباده ومن همـزات الشياطين وأن يحضرون». قال: وكان عبد الله بن عمرو يعلمهن من عقل من بنيه ومن لم يعقل كتبه فأعلقه عليـه» [رواه أبـو داود والتـرمـذي وقـال حديث حسن] [نقل من المجموع: ٢/ ٧١].

w17.3 (ابن حجر الهيتمي:) [. . .] جاء في ركب عشـرة إلى رسول الله ﷺ فبـايـع تسعـة وأمسـك عن رجـل منهم فقالـوا: ما شأنـه؟ فقـال: إن في عضده تميمة، فقطع الرجل التميمة فبايعه النبي ﷺ ثم قال: «من علق فقد أشرك». [. . .] يتعـين حمله على ما كانـوا بفعلونه من تعليق خرزة يسمونها تميمة أو نحوها يرون أنها تدفع عنهم الآفات، ولا شك أن اعتقاد هذا جهل وضلال وأنه من أكبر الكبائر لأنـه إن لم يكن شركـا فهو يؤدي إليه إذ لا ينفع ويضر ويمنع ويدفع إلا الله تعالى [محرر من الـزواجر عن اقتراف الكبائر: ١/ ١٦٦].

w18.0 MAKING UP MISSED PRAYERS IS OBLIGATORY (from f1.1)

w18.0 وجـــوب قضـــاء الصلوات الفائتة

w18.1 (n:) This section discusses the view of some contemporary Muslims that someone who purposely misses one or more prescribed prayers need not make them up, which some say is because whoever intentionally neglects an obligatory prayer thereby becomes an unbeliever (kafir), and unbelievers are not obliged to pray. Besides being a weak position that contravenes all four schools of jurisprudence, those who miss prayers and neglect to make them up because of adopting this view will meet their Lord without having performed the first thing they shall be asked about on the Day of Judgement, their obligatory prayers. The following discussion, in explaining why the overwhelming majority of Islamic scholars hold that making up missed prescribed prayers is obligatory, centers on two points:

(1) that a Muslim who misses a prayer out of unconcern cannot by that fact alone be considered an unbeliever;

(2) and that the view that a prayer purposely missed cannot be made up is incorrect.

A MUSLIM WHO NEGLECTS A PRAYER DOES NOT THEREBY BECOME AN UNBELIEVER

المسلم التارك للصلاة لا يكفر

w18.2 (N:) The Hanafis, Malikis, and Shafi'is all hold that someone who misses the prayer out of laziness is a Muslim, and that missing the prayer does not entail his being an unbeliever. Nawawi says, "This is what the vast majority of early and later scholars have held" (al-Majmu' (y108), 3.16). As for the Hanbalis, they have two views, the first being that such a person becomes an unbeliever and is dealt with as a renegade from Islam (def: o8.2), while the second view is that he does not become an unbeliever, and this is what Ibn Qudama, in al-Mughni (y63), 2.329, has declared to be the soundest position. The opinion that such a person becomes an unbeliever has been ascribed to 'Ali ibn Abi Talib (Allah ennoble his countenance), Ibn al-Mubarak, Ishaq ibn Rahawayh, and some Shafi'is.

w18.2 (ح) : ذهب الحنفيـة والمالكية والشـــافعيـة إلى أن تارك الصـــلاة كســلا مسلم ، وإن ترك الصلاة لا يوجب الحكم بالكفر . قال النووي : «وبه قال الأكثرون من السلف والخلف».

وأمــا الحنابلة فلهم في ذلـك رأيــان : الأول أنـه يكفر ويعامل كالمرتد ، والثاني أنـه لا يكفر ، وقـد رجح ابن قدامة في المغني عدم كفــره . وقــد روي القــول بكفــره عن علي بن أبي طالـب ، وابن المبارك ، وإسحق بن راهويه وبعض الشافعية .

THE EVIDENCE THAT SOMEONE WHO NEGLECTS THE PRAYER IS AN UNBELIEVER

حجة من قال بكفر تارك الصلاة

w18.3 Those who hold that whoever misses a prayer becomes an unbeliever adduce the following evidence:

(1) The hadith of Jabir (Allah be well pleased with him) that he heard the Messenger of Allah (Allah bless him and give him peace) say,

"Between a man between polytheism and unbelief is the nonperformance of the prayer,"

which was related by Muslim.

(2) The hadith of Burayda (Allah be well pleased with him) that the Prophet (Allah bless him and give him peace) said,

"The covenant between us and them consists of the prayer: whoever leaves it has disbelieved,"

a hadith related by Tirmidhi and Nasa'i, the former saying that it was well authenticated (hasan).

(3) The words of 'Abdullah ibn Shaqiq 'Uqayli, one of those (tabi'i) who met and studied under some of the Companions, and someone whose eminence is agreed upon,

"The Companions of Muhammad (Allah bless him and give him peace) did not view the nonperformance of anything as unbelief besides the prayer,"

which was related by Tirmidhi in the Book of Faith with a rigorously authenticated (sahih) channel of transmission.

(4) And the Prophet's saying (Allah bless him and give him peace):

"The first thing you lose from your religion is keeping trusts, and the last thing you lose is the prayer,"

Imam Ahmad commenting that nothing remains of whatever the last has gone.

w18.3 من قال بكفره احتج بما يلي:

١ـ عن جابــر رضي الـله عنـه قال: سمعت رسول الله ﷺ يقول: «إن بين الـرجـل وبين الشـرك والكفر ترك الصلاة».

رواه مسلم.

٢ـ عن بريدة رضي الله عنه عن النبي ﷺ قال: «العهد الذي بيننا وبينهم الصلاة فمن تركها فقد كفر».

رواه التـرمـذي والنسـائي وقـال الترمذي حديث حسن.

٣ـ وعـن عبـد الله بن شقيق العقيلي التابعي المتفق على جلالته قال: «كـان أصحاب محمـد ﷺ لا يرون شيئاً من الأعمال تركه كفر غير الصلاة».

رواه الترمذي في كتاب الإيمان بإسناد صحيح.

٤ـ قول النبي ﷺ: «أول ما تفقـدون من دينكم الأمـانة وآخر ما تفقدون الصلاة».

قال الإمـام أحمد كل شيء ذهب آخره لم يبق منه شيء.

THE EVIDENCE THAT SOMEONE
WHO NEGLECTS THE PRAYER
IS NOT AN UNBELIEVER

حجة من قال بعدم كفر تارك الصلاة

w18.4 Those who hold that whoever neglects a prayer does not thereby become an unbeliever adduce the following evidence:

(1) The hadith of 'Ubada ibn Samit (Allah be well pleased with him) that he heard the Prophet (Allah bless him and give him peace) say:

"Allah has made five prayers obligatory: whoever performs their ablution well and prays them in their time, completing the bowing, the humility, and the awe that is due in them, has entered a solemn pact with Allah to forgive him. And whoever does not, has no pact with Allah: should He want, He will forgive him, and should He want, He will torment him,"

which is a rigorously authenticated (sahih) hadith related by Abu Dawud and others through multiple authentic channels of transmission. The evidence of the hadith is that the case of someone who does not pray is up to Allah's considered choice, meaning that Allah could choose *not* to torment him, while it is necessarily established that unbelievers will be tormented and enter hell (n: *necessarily* established in that the words of the Koran will necessarily be realized against them, just as Allah has stated (dis: w55.3(2)))—a consideration which with the above hadith indicates that someone who neglects to pray is not an unbeliever.

(2) The words of the Prophet (Allah bless him and give him peace),

"Whoever dies knowing that there is no god but Allah shall enter paradise,"

a hadith related by Muslim that in its generality implies that someone who does not perform the prayer but believes that there is no god but Allah, will enter paradise, whereas if he were an unbeliever, he would not enter it. There are many similar hadiths that imply this in their generality.

w18.4 واستـدل من قال بعـدم كفـر تارك الصلاة كسلاً بما يلي :

١ـ عن عبـادة بن الصـامت رضي الله عنه قال : سمعت رسول الله ﷺ يقول : «خمس صلوات افتـرضهن الله ، من أحسن وضـوءهن وصـلاهن لوقتهن وأتم ركوعهن وخشوعهن كان له على الله عهد أن يغفر له ، ومن لم يفعل ، فليس له على الله عهد إن شاء غفر وإن شاء عذبه» . حديث صحيح رواه أبـو داود وغيـره بأسانيـد صحيحـة . ووجـه الـدلالـة في الحـديث أن من لم يصـل داخـل تحت المشيئة وقـد يشاء الله أن لا يعذبه مع أن الكفار مقطوع بعـذابهم ودخـولهم النار فدل على أن تارك الصلاة ليس من الكفار .

٢ـ قوله ﷺ :
«من مات وهـو يعلم أن لا إلـه إلا الله دخل الجنة» .

رواه مسلم . وهـذا يفيـد بعمومه أن تارك الصلاة المعتقـد بأنه لا إله إلا الله يدخل الجنة ، ولو كان كافراً لم يدخلها . ومثـل هذه الأحـاديث كثيـر وعمـومها يفيد ذلك .

(3)   That Muslims from earliest times to the present have considered the Muslim who misses the prayer to be entitled to inherit by way of estate division and be inherited from. If in their view he were an unbeliever, he would not inherit or be inherited from (dis: L5.2).

(4)   And the consensus of Muslims that the body of someone who neglects the prayer must be washed and prayed over. Were he an unbeliever in their view, they would not wash, shroud, or pray over him.

A DISCUSSION OF THE EVIDENCE

w18.5 Scholars reply as follows to the hadiths adduced by those who claim that whoever misses the prayer is an unbeliever:

(1)   The point of the hadiths is to emphasize the enormity of the crime of whoever misses the prayer and to liken him to unbelievers, not that it is actual **unbelief**. Other hadiths make their point in this way, such as the words of the Prophet (Allah bless him and give him peace),

"Reviling a Muslim is corruption and fighting him is unbelief,"

and similar ones.

(2)   Their meaning is that the person who misses the prayer is like unbelievers in certain respects, such as that he is obligatorily executed (dis: f1.4). Scholars have had recourse to this interpretation in order to reach an accord between these texts of the Sacred Law and its basic principles, since a Muslim, of course, may not be judged an unbeliever unless there is absolute certainty of it, or be considered an unbeliever for something without unquestionable evidence that his act, statement, or belief is in fact unbelief (kufr). It thus appears that the strongest position is that someone who misses the prayer out of neglect is not an unbeliever, for besides the texts that imply his unbelief, others imply the contrary, and the former can bear an alternate interpretation.

٣ـ أن المسلمين سلفاً وخلفاً مازالوا يورّثون تارك الصلاة ويرثون عنه ولو كان كافراً في نظرهم لما ورث ولا ورث عنه .

٤ـ اتفاق المسلمين على غسل تارك الصلاة والصلاة عليه . ولو كان كافراً في نظرهم لما غسلوه ولا كفنوه ولا صلوا عليه .

مناقشة الأدلة

w18.5 [. . .] يجيبون عما ورد في الأحاديث التي احتج بها من قال بكفره بما يلي :

١ـ أن المراد بهذه الأحاديث التغليظ على تارك الصلاة وتشبيهه بالكفار لا حقيقة الكفر كقول النبي ﷺ : «سباب المسلم فسوق وقتاله كفر» [رواه البخاري] [. . .] وأشباه ذلك .

٢ـ [وقالوا إن] المراد أن تارك الصلاة مشارك للكافر في بعض أحكامه وهو وجوب القتل .

وإنما لجأوا إلى هذا التأويل للجمع بين نصوص الشرع وقواعده [التي ذكرناها]، ومن المعلوم أنه لا يحكم بكفر المسلم إلا بيقين ولا يكفر بشيء إلا إذا وجد دليل قاطع على أن هذا العمل أو القول أو العقيدة كفر .

ولهذا يبدو [لي] رجحان القول بعدم كفر تارك الصلاة كسلاً لأن النصوص الواردة بكفره يوجد ما يعارضها وهي قابلة للتأويل .

MAKING UP MISSED PRAYERS

w18.6 As to whether it is obligatory to make up prayers missed without an excuse, this is a question raised nowadays by some students of jurisprudence, in an era when deliberate nonperformance of obligatory prayer and fasting has become frequent. They believe that the position well known to both scholars and ordinary people that it is obligatory to make up missed prayers and fast-days might be a deterrent from repentance, and they look to eliminate it by adopting the opinions of certain scholars, advancing the position of Ibn Hazm, Ibn Taymiya, and others, while what is obligatory is to defer to the Koran and sunna for the final decision, as the Prophet (Allah bless him and give him peace) has said,

"None of you believes until his inclinations conform to what I have brought,"

and it is obligatory to know what the evidence bears out, since one should, as has been said, "know men by their having spoken the truth, not that it is the truth by certain men having spoken it." So we will expound the question with its evidence, and then see what the evidence shows.

w18.7 The vast majority of scholars, including those of the four main schools of jurisprudence, have concluded that it is obligatory to make up deliberately missed prayers and fast-days, and have even reported scholarly consensus (def: b7) on the obligatory character of making them up, as is mentioned in (n: the Hanbali) *al-Mughni* (y63), 2.332; (n: the Hanafi) *Sharh al-'inaya 'ala al-Hidaya* (y21), 1.485; and in (n: the Shafi'i) *al-Majmu'* (y108), 3.71; while Ibn Hazm, Ibn Taymiya, and Ibn al-Qayyim conclude that someone who deliberately does not perform the prayer until its time is finished can never make it up, but should do as much good and perform as many supererogatory prayers as possible in order to tip the balance in his favor on the Day of Judgement, and repent and ask forgiveness of Allah Mighty and Majestic.

قضاء ما فات من الصلوات بلا عذر

w18.6 وهل يجب قضاء ما فات من الصلاة بلا عذر؟ هذه المسألة مما يثيره بعض المتفقهين هذه الأيام بعد أن كثر ترك الصلاة والصوم عمداً، ويرون أن القول بوجوب قضاء ما فات من الصلاة أو الصيام كما هو معروف بين العلماء والعامة قد يكون مانعاً من التوبة، ويلتمسون لإسقاط القضاء سنداً من أقوال بعض العلماء، فيحتجون بقول ابن حزم وابن تيمية وغيرهما، والواجب أن نحتكم إلى الكتاب والسنة. قال رسول الله ﷺ:

«لا يؤمن أحدكم حتى يكون هواه تبعاً لما جئت به» [رواه الأصفهاني في كتاب الحجة].

والواجب معرفة ما يؤدي إليه الدليل، فقد قيل اعرف الرجال بالحق ولا تعرف الحق بالرجال، ونحن نعرض هذه المسألة بأدلتها ثم نرى ما الذي يؤيده الدليل.

w18.7 ذهب جمهور الفقهاء ومنهم أصحاب المذاهب الأربعة المشهورة إلى وجوب قضاء ما فات من الصلاة أو الصيام عمداً. بل قالوا إن وجوب القضاء إجماع كما ذكر في المغني، وشرح العناية على الهداية [...] والمجموع [...] وذهب ابن حزم وابن تيمية وابن القيم إلى أن من تعمد ترك الصلاة حتى خرج وقتها لا يقدر على قضائها أبداً، فليكثر من فعل الخير وصلاة التطوع ليثقل ميزانه يوم القيامة وليتب وليستغفر الله عز وجل.

THE EVIDENCE THAT SOMEONE WHO
MISSES A PRAYER MUST MAKE IT UP

w18.8 The scholarly majority adduce the following evidence:

(1) The words of the Prophet (Allah bless him and give him peace),

"When any of you sleeps through the prayer or forgets it, then let him pray it when he remembers, for Allah Mighty and Majestic says,

" 'Perform the prayer for My remembrance' (Koran 20:14),"

a hadith related by Muslim. The evidence therein is that despite sleep and forgetfulness being lawful excuses, the obligation to perform the prayer is not eliminated by its time having passed, and the person who has slept or forgotten is required to make it up. So the prayer of someone who has missed it without excuse *a fortiori* remains still obligatory for him to pray, and is *a fortiori* mandatory to make up. The hadith moreover shows that obligatory acts of worship, just as they may initially occur at their specific time, may also validly occur after this time. The delay being a *sin* is a separate issue: if one excusably delays the prayer, there is no sin, while if one delays it without excuse, the sin occurs—but the hadith shows that a prayer's relationship to its specific time is not an intrinsic relationship entailed by its very nature, such that an obligatory prayer cannot be called an obligatory prayer unless it occurs within its proper time. Rather, it may occur after its time and still be termed an obligatory prayer.

(2) The words of the Prophet (Allah bless him and give him peace),

"A debt to Allah has better right to be fulfilled,"

a hadith related by Bukhari and Muslim. The hadith's context is that of making up another person's hajj (dis: j1.9), and the Prophet (Allah bless him and give him peace) likened the missed wor-

استدلال من قال بوجوب القضاء

w18.8   استدل الجمهور لمذهبهم بما يلي :

١ـ قول النبي ﷺ :

«إذا رقـد أحـدكم عن الصلاة أو غفل عنها فليصلها إذا ذكرها فإن الله عز وجل يقول : أقم الصلاة لذكري» رواه مسلم . ووجه الـدلالـة أن النوم والنسيان من الأعذار الشرعية ومع ذلك لم يسقط بهما وجوب الصلاة بعد خروج وقتها وطولب النـائم والنـاسي بالقضـاء ، فمن فاتته الصلاة بلا عذر أولى بعدم السقوط وأولى بوجوب القضاء .

ثم إن الحـديث قد أفـاد أن الفـرائض كمـا تقع في وقتهـا المحـدد لهـا ابتـداء يمكن إيقـاعهـا بعد الوقت [إلا ما استثناه الـدليـل كالحـج]. وكون التأخير إثماً أمر آخـر ، فإن أخـرت بعـذر فلا إثم ، وإن أخـرت بلا عذر فالإثـم حاصـل . لكن الحـديث أفـاد أن الارتبـاط بالـوقت ليس كارتبـاط الصفة بالمـوصوف بحيث لا تسمى الفـريضة باسمها إلا إذا وقعت في وقتهـا بل يمكن أن تقع بعد الوقت ويكون لها نفس الاسم [...].

٢ـ قول النبي ﷺ :

«دَيْـنُ اللـه أحـق أن يقـضى» رواه البخاري ومسلم .

والحديث وارد في الحج عن الغير وقد شبه العبـادة الفائتة بالدين وورد مثله في الصوم فدل ذلك على أن العبادة إذا فاتت

ship to a debt, similar hadiths existing about fasting, proving that acts of worship, when missed, regardless of the reason, become a debt that must be repaid just as other debts are, and with even better right. We say "regardless of the reason" because the Prophet (Allah bless him and give him peace) did not ask the questioner about the reason for its having been missed. And if this is established in relation to making up the worship of another, it holds with still better right for making up one's *own* missed acts of worship.

(3) It is rigorously authenticated that the Prophet (Allah bless him and give him peace) was prevented from performing the midafternoon prayer ('asr) until the sun had set because of fighting unbelievers at the Battle of the Confederates, when the prayer of peril (def: f16) had not yet been legislated, and he said,

"May Allah fill their graves and houses with fire, as they have occupied us from performing the midmost prayer until the sun set,"

a hadith related by Bukhari and Muslim. The evidence therein is that missing the prayer was excused here, whether because of forgetfulness or absentmindedness in view of the fighting, or because delaying the prayer was permissible under such circumstances before the prayer of peril had been legislated—but in either case it shows that a prayer may be validly performed after its time has finished.

(4) The words of the Prophet (Allah bless him and give him peace),

"Someone fasting who unintentionally vomits is not obliged to make up his fast, but whoever causes himself to vomit must make it up,"

the evidence therein being that it mentions two situations in which the fast is broken, the first being when it is excusably broken, namely, by someone overcome by vomiting, which does not legally vitiate his fast and which he is therefore not obliged to make up; and the second being when it is inexcusably broken, where, by consensus of all scholars, the person has committed a sin by break-

ـ بصرف النظر عن سبب فواتها ـ صارت ديناً يقضى كما تقضى الـديـون وأولى [...] وأقول: «بصرف النظر عن سبب الفـوات» لأن النبي ﷺ لم يستفسر من السائل عن سبب الفوات، فإذا ثبت هذا في القضاء عن الغير فالقضاء عن النفس أولى.

٣ـ ثبت أن النبي ﷺ قد شغـل عن صلاة الـعصر بقتـال الكفـار في غـزوة الأحـزاب ولـم تكن قد شرعـت صلاة الخوف حتى غابت الشمس وقال: «ملأ الله قبـورهم وبيـوتهم ناراً كمـا شغلونـا عن الصلاة الوسطى حتى غابت الشمس» متفق عليه.

ووجه الـدلالـة أن الفـوات هنـا كان بعـذر، إمـا للنسيـان والسهـو نظراً لحال القتـال، أو أنـه كان من الجـائـز تأخيـر الصلاة في مثل هذه الحالة قبل أن تشرع صلاة الخوف [ولم يكن تأخيرها معصية قطعاً لأن الأنبياء معصومون ومن قال ذلك يكفر]، لكن محل الشـاهـد أن الصلاة يمكن إيقاعها بعد خروج وقتها.

٤ـ قول النبي ﷺ: «مـن ذرعـه القيء وهـو صائم فليس عليه قضاء ومن استقاء فليقض» [رواه ابن ماجه].

ووجه الدلالة أن الحديث ذكر حالتين للإفطار، الأولى حالة المعـذور وهو من غلبـه القيء، وهـذا لا يفسـد صومه ولا قضاء عليـه. والثـانية حالة غير المعذور الآثم بإفطـاره بالاتفـاق وهـذا قد أوجب

ing it and the very words of the hadith oblige him to make it up. And this is the significant point, that the Prophet (Allah bless him and give him peace) declared it obligatory for whoever breaks the fast without excuse to make it up, which proves that an act of worship missed without excuse is obligatory to make up afterwards, even if the person who delays it past its time has committed a sin by doing so.

REPLIES TO THE OBJECTIONS OF IBN HAZM CONCERNING THE VALIDITY OF MAKING UP MISSED PRAYERS

w18.9　Ibn Hazm and those who agree with him adduce the following evidence:

(1)　The word of Allah Most High,

"Woe to those who pray, unmindful of their prayers" (Koran 107:4–5),

and His word, Mighty and Majestic,

"But a generation followed them who dissipated the prayer and pursued [their] lusts, and they shall find *Ghayy* [n: a "valley in hell" (*Tafsir al-Jalalayn* (y77), 402)]" (Koran 19:59),

the evidence therein being that if the person who intentionally missed the prayer could perform it after its time, there would not be any woe to him, nor would he find *Ghayy*.

(Reply:) Both these verses refer to those who do not repent. There is no disagreement about this, as is attested to by the rest of the second verse,

"... save he who repents, believes, and does good" (Koran 19:60),

there being no disagreement about the validity of the meaning, though there is about the means of repentance. Does someone who has repented make the prayers up, or does he perform supererogatory prayers (dis: w18.9(8)) in their

عليه الحديث القضاء.

وهـذا موضع الشـاهد : أن النبي ﷺ أوجب القضاء على من أفطر بلا عذر فدل على أن الـعبـادة إذا فاتت بلا عذر وجب قضـاؤهـا بعـد الوقت ولو كان المؤخر لها عن وقتها آثماً بتأخيرها [. . .].

ردود على ما احتــج به ابـن حزم لعدم صحة القضاء

w18.9　وقـد استــدل ابن حزم ومن وافقه بما يلي :

١ ـ قول الله تعالى :

«فَـوَيْـلٌ لِلْمُصَلِّينَ الَّـذِينَ هُمْ عَنْ صَلَاتِهِمْ سَاهُونَ» [الماعون : ٤ ـ ٥].

وقوله عز وجل :

«فَخَلَفَ مِنْ بَعْدِهِمْ خَلْفٌ أَضَـاعُـوا الصَّـلاةَ وَاتَّبَعُـوا الشَّهَـوَاتِ فَسَوْفَ يَلْقَوْنَ غَيًّا» [مريم : ٥٩].

ووجه الـدلالة أنه لو كان العامد لترك الصـلاة مدركـاً لها بعد الوقت لما كان له الويل ولا لقي الغي.

(قلت :) هما فيمن لم يتب ، وهذا لا خلاف فيه بدليـل تمـام الآيـة الثانية وهو قوله تعالى :

«إِلَّا مَنْ تَابَ وَآمَنَ وَعَمِلَ صَالِحًا . . . ».

وهـذا المعنى لا خلاف في صحتـه ، لكن الخــلاف في طريقـة التـوبـة : هل يقـضي أم يصـلي نافلة؟ والجمهــور لم

stead? The scholarly majority do not claim that he who makes them up has properly performed them.

(2) The prayer has a set time, there being no difference between someone who prays it before its time and someone who prays it after. Because both have prayed it in other than its time, both have transgressed against Allah's limits, and Allah has said,

"Whoever transgresses against Allah's limits has wronged himself" (Koran 65:1).

Otherwise, defining the time would be pointless. Scholars agree that the prayer of whoever prays before the prayer's time does not suffice, and so too must be the prayer of whoever prays after it.

(Reply:) As for the prayer having a definite time, the scholarly majority do not disagree about this, and the suggestion that they do not distinguish between someone who prays during the time and someone who prays after it is not true. It is regrettable to accuse them of this when it is baseless.

(3) Making up missed prayers requires an evidential basis, and there is not any (since in Ibn Hazm's opinion, analogical reasoning (qiyas, def: o22.1(d(III)))) is not an acceptable form of legal evidence, which for him can only consist of the Koran, sunna, and scholarly consensus): if it were obligatory, Allah Most High or His messenger (Allah bless him and give him peace) would have explained it.

(Reply:) As for the statement that making up a missed prayer requires an evidential basis, and there is not any; the evidence exists, and we have presented it (dis: w18.8) and shall clarify it further.

(4) It is invalid to make an analogy between someone who intentionally misses a prayer and someone who forgets it and the like, for intentionality is the opposite of forgetfulness. Someone who intentionally misses a prayer is disobedient, while someone who forgets is not.

يقولوا : من قضاها فقد أدركها .

٢ ـ أن الصلاة لها وقت محدد ولا فرق بين من صلاها قبل وقتها ومن صلاها بعد وقتها لأن كليهما صلى في غير الوقت ، وكليهما تعدى حدود الله وقد قال الله تعالى :

﴿ وَمَن يَتَعَدَّ حُدُودَ اللَّهِ فَقَدْ ظَلَمَ نَفْسَهُ ﴾ [الطلاق : ١] .

وإلا لما كان لتحديد الوقت فائدة ، ومن صلى قبل الوقت فصلاته غير مجزية باتفاق ؛ فيكون من صلى بعد الوقت مثله .

(قلت :) أما أن الصلاة لها وقت محدد ، فالجمهور لا يخالفون في ذلك ، والقول بعدم تفريقهم بين من صلى في الوقت ومن صلى بعده ليس صواباً ، ومن المؤسف أن ينسب هذا إليهم وليس له أصل .

٣ ـ القضاء يحتاج إلى دليل ولا دليل ـ وليس القياس دليلاً عنده ، بل الدليل الكتاب والسنة والإجماع فقط ـ ولو كان واجباً لبينه الله تعالى أو بينه رسوله عليه الصلاة والسلام .

(قلت :) أما أن القضاء لا دليل عليه ، فالدليل موجود وقد قدمنا أدلة الجمهور وسنزيدها إيضاحاً .

٤ ـ لا يصح قياس العامد على الناسي ونحوه ، لأن العامد ضد الناسي والأول عاص والثاني غير عاص .

(Reply:) The validity of the analogy between the person who intentionally misses it and the person who unintentionally misses it has been previously discussed in the evidence of the scholarly majority (w18.8(4)).

(5) Narrations from the prophetic Companions attest to the fact that delaying the prayer past its time is unlawful. If making up a prayer could suffice in its stead, these would have no meaning.

(Reply:) The unlawfulness of delaying the prayer past its time is agreed upon, and no one says that it is permissible.

(6) The prayer of peril (def: f16) is evidence that it is not possible to delay a prayer past its time, and so is the prayer of the sick person (f14).

(Reply:) As for the prayers of peril and illness, the scholarly majority acknowledge them and do not permit delaying the prayer because of peril or illness. The prayers of the imperilled or sick person, which do not require many of the integrals and conditions required by a normal prayer, attest to the position of the majority that the Sacred Law does not lift the obligation of the prayer from such people as it does from a woman in her menstrual period. Rather, because it is impossible for the imperilled and sick person to currently perform the prayer while observing all its conditions and integrals, their only alternative is to either make it up later or perform it while desregarding some of them, so the latter is permitted for them in order to obviate an accumulation of unperformed prayers, and Allah knows best.

And if the responsibility for performing the obligatory prayer is not lifted from the imperilled or sick person, how should it be lifted from the person who *intentionally* misses it?

(7) It is inadmissible to adduce the hadith of the delayed prayer at the Battle of the Confederates (dis: w18.8(3)) because the discussion here centers on the person who commits disobedience by delaying it, while the Prophet (Allah bless him and give him peace) was not disobedient therein, and whoever ascribes disobedience to the Prophet (Allah bless him and give him peace) has committed unbelief (kufr).

(قلت :) أما وجه قياس العامد على الناسي فقد تقدم في حجة الجمهور .

٥ ـ استشهد بآثار عن الصحابة في تحريم تأخير الصلاة عن وقتها ، فلو كان القضاء يغني لما كان لهذا معنى .

(قلت :) تحريم تأخير الصلاة عن وقتها متفق عليه ولا قائل بجواز التأخير .

٦ ـ صلاة الخوف دليل على عدم إمكان التأخير عن الوقت ، وكذلك صلاة المريض .

(قلت :) أما صلاة الخوف والمرض فالجمهور يقولون بهما ولا يجيزون التأخير بسبب الخوف أو المرض وصلاة المريض وصلاة الخائف ـ مع ما فيهما من تجاوز عن كثير من أركان الصلاة وشروطها ـ تشهدان لمذهب الجمهور لأن الشرع لم يسقط الصلاة عنهما كالحائض ، والأداء مع مراعاة الشروط والأركان متعذر ، فلم يبق إلا القضاء أو الأداء مع التجاوز ، فأبيح الأداء مع التجاوز حتى لا تتراكم الفوائت والله أعلم . وإذا لم تسقط عنهم الفريضة فكيف تسقط عن العامد؟

٧ـ لا يجوز الاحتجاج بحديث تأخير الصلاة يوم الخندق لأن الكلام هنا عن العاصي بالتأخير والنبي ﷺ لم يكن عاصياً بذلك [كما تقدم] ومن نسب العصيان للرسول ﷺ فقد كفر .

(Reply:) Adducing this hadith is not inadmissible as he claims, but is like adducing the cases of the sleeper or forgetful person, in illustrating the conceivability of the existence of an obligation after its original time has ended.

(8) As for the obligatory character of repentance and doing as many supererogatory acts of worship as possible (n: in place of the missed one), the evidence is the word of Allah Most High,

"But a generation followed them who dissipated the prayer and pursued [their] lusts, and they shall find *Ghayy,* save he who repents, believes, and does good, for those shall enter paradise" (Koran 19:59–60),

and many similar verses in the Book of Allah Most High. Another proof is the words of the Prophet (Allah bless him and give him peace):

"The first of people's works that they shall be called to account for on the Day of Judgement is the prayer. Our Lord Holy and Exalted will say to His angels, while knowing better than they, 'Look at the prayer of My servant: did he perform it in full, or fall short of it?' If it is complete, it will be inscribed as complete, while if anything is missing from it, He will say, 'Look to see if My servant has any supererogatory worship,' and if he has, Allah will say, 'Complete My servant's obligatory prayers for him from his supererogatory ones.' And he will be dealt with likewise in his other works."

(Reply:) Whoever reflects on the evidence of both sides will notice the following:

(a) The difference of opinion is less at the practical level than at the theoretical, for Ibn Hazm requires the person who intentionally misses the prayer to perform as many supererogatory prayers as the missed obligatory one and more, so as to be counted for his obligatory prayer on the Day of Judgement. We say "and more" because he states in *al-Muhalla* that "there is a certain amount of good in the obligatory prayer and a cer-

(قلت:) الاحتجاج بقصة صلاة الخندق ليس كما يقول بل هو كالاحتجاج بقضاء النائم والناسي، أي من حيث تصور وجود الفرض بعد فوات وقته الأصلي.

٨ـ أما وجوب التوبة والإكثار من التطوع، فالدليل عليه قول الله تعالى: ﴿فَخَلَفَ مِنْ بَعْدِهِمْ خَلْفٌ أَضَاعُوا الصَّلَاةَ وَاتَّبَعُوا الشَّهَوَاتِ فَسَوْفَ يَلْقَوْنَ غَيًّا، إِلَّا مَنْ تَابَ وَآمَنَ وَعَمِلَ صَالِحًا فَأُولَئِكَ يَدْخُلُونَ الجَنَّةَ﴾ [مريم: ٥٩ ـ ٦٠].

ومثل هذه الآية كثير في كتاب الله تعالى.

ولقول النبي ﷺ: «أول ما يحاسب الناس به يوم القيامة من أعمالهم الصلاة، يقول ربنا تبارك وتعالى لملائكته وهو أعلم: انظروا في صلاة عبدي أتمها أو نقصها؛ فإن كانت تامة كتبت تامة، وإن كان انتقص منها شيئاً قال انظروا هل لعبدي من تطوع فإن كان له تطوع قال: أتموا لعبدي فريضته من تطوعه ثم تؤخذ الأعمال على ذلك» [رواه النسائي].

(قلت:) من تأمل رأي الطرفين يبدو له ما يأتي:

١ـ أن الخلاف ليس عملياً بل هو نظري لأن ابن حزم يطالب تارك الصلاة عمداً بصلاة نوافل تعادل الفريضة الفائتة وزيادة لكي تحسب له عن الفريضة يوم القيامة، وإنما قلت: وزيادة لأنه يقول في المحلّى: «الفريضة فيها جزء من الخير، والنافلة فيها جزء من الخير، فلا

tain amount in the supererogatory, so the cumulative amount of good when many supererogatory prayers are performed must equal some fraction or more of the amount in the obligatory prayer" (al-Muhalla (y58), 2.332), whereas the scholarly majority require the person, for each missed obligatory prayer, to pray one like it, termed a *makeup*. So the difference of opinion goes back to the intention and the name of such a prayer. Do we call it *supererogatory* or a *makeup,* and does the person praying it intend an unconditional supererogatory prayer to take the place of the missed obligatory prayer, or intend the missed obligatory prayer? The difference, as we said, is mainly theoretical.

It is clear from the foregoing that Ibn Hazm is not opening a way out of performing obligatory prayers for those who miss them. Rather, he is severer on them, requiring that they perform *more* supererogatory prayers than the obligatory ones they missed. To further clarify, we note that Ibn Hazm and the others who hold that it is invalid to make up missed prayers only say this to make it harder on the person who does not pray, because they feel that making up missed prayers has been legislated as a mercy to someone who has slept through the prayer or forgotten it, or to others with lawful excuses. As for the person who sins by deliberately not performing it, he does not deserve this mercy, and they feel that his sin is too enormous to be expiated by making it up. This is a point that deserves attention, because it is the opposite of what most of those who advocate this view understand.

(b) It will be noticed from Ibn Hazm's evidence that he thinks the scholarly majority consider the makeup of the person who has slept through the prayer and the makeup of the person who has deliberately missed it to be equivalent in every respect, and that they likewise consider the makeup of the person who has sinned by missing the prayer to be equivalent to performing it in its proper time. He says, "From whence does he who permits its intentional nonperformance until its time is up derive this permissibility, ordering the person to pray it after its time, and informing him that it fulfills his obligation—without Koran, a sound or even weak hadith, a statement from a

بد أن يجتمع من جزء التطوع إذا كثر ما يوازي جزء الفريضة ويزيد عليه» . والجمهور يطالبه أن يصلي عن كل فريضة مثلها باسم القضاء، فرجع الخلاف إلى النية والاسم: هل نسميها نافلة أو قضاء؟ وهل ينوي بصلاتها النافلة المطلقة لتسد مسد الفريضة الفائتة أم ينوي الفريضة الفائتة؟ وهذا خلاف نظري كما قلت .

ومن النقطة السابقة يظهر أن ابن حزم لا يفتح لتاركي الصلاة باب التهرب من الفرائض بل يشدد عليهم ويطالبهم بنوافل تزيد على ما تركوا من فرائض.

وأزيد هذه النقطة إيضاحاً فأقول: إن ابن حزم وغيره ممن قال بعدم صحة القضاء إنما قالوا ذلك من باب التشديد على تارك الصلاة لأنهم رأوا أن القضاء شرع رحمة بالنائم والناسي وأصحاب الأعذار، أما العامد الآثم بتركها فلا يستحق هذه الرحمة، فهم يرون أن ذنبه أكبر من أن يكفر بالقضاء.

وهذه النقطة جديرة بالاهتمام لأنها عكس ما يفهمه الكثيرون من الذين ينادون بهذا الرأي.

ـ ويلاحظ من أدلة ابن حزم أنه يرى أن الجمهور يساوون بين قضاء النائم ونحوه وبين قضاء العامد من كل وجه، ويساوون بين قضاء الآثم بالترك وبين الأداء. ففي المحلى هو يقول: فمن أين أجاز من أجاز تعمد تركها حتى يخرج وقتها، ثم أمره بأن يصليها بعد الوقت، وأخبره بأنها تجزئه كذلك من غير قرآن ولا سنة صحيحة ولا سقيمة ولا قول

prophetic Companion, or analogy?" (*al-Muhalla* (y58), 2.330). Glory be to Allah! Whoever said that it is permissible to intentionally miss the prayer? As we have previously mentioned, the scholarly majority hold that the person who intentionally misses it should be killed (dis: f1.4). Is he executed for doing something permissible? May Allah have mercy on Ibn Hazm, who was not accurate in this, and to say otherwise would have been more proper for him.

w18.10 Is the person who misses the prayer without excuse like someone who has an excuse, in being able to validly perform the obligatory prayer after its time in the name of an obligatory prayer, even if all scholars agree he has committed a sin by thus delaying it? This is the area of disagreement. The scholarly majority, adducing the foregoing evidence, hold that he may validly do so, while Ibn Hazm says this is invalid, because an unexcused person is not like an excused one.

But Ibn Hazm agrees with the majority that someone who intentionally vomits while fasting Ramadan (dis: w18.8(4)) has committed a sin—i.e. is unexcused—and yet is obliged to make up the fast. This fact establishes the rule for the scholarly majority, if not for Ibn Hazm, because such an individual is an unexcused person who has deliberately vitiated his time-restricted act of worship, and the Lawgiver has made it obligatory for him to make it up—so why should it not be obligatory for other unexcused persons to make up similar acts of worship? This demonstrates that the scholarly majority's opinion is correct. And if Ibn Hazm may be excused because he does not accept analogical reasoning (qiyas), what excuse is there for those who employ analogical reasoning as evidence, and yet accept his opinion?

Nawawi says: "There is consensus among all scholars who matter that whoever deliberately misses the prayer is obliged to make it up. Abu Muhammad 'Ali Ibn Hazm contravened them in this, saying that such a person can never make up the prayer and that doing so can never be valid. What he has said, besides being a violation of scholarly consensus (dis: b7.2), is untrue from the standpoint of evidence, and despite a prolonged discourse to prove his contention, what he men-

لصاحب ولا قياس؟

وسبحان الله من الذي يقول بجواز تعمد ترك الصلاة؟ لقد قدمنا أنهم يقولون بقتل تارك الصلاة ، فهل يقتل فيما يجوز فعله؟ رحم الله ابن حزم لقد كان غير دقيق في هذا ، وغير هذا أولى به .

w18.10 [. . .] هل غير المعذور كالمعذور ، يصح أن يؤدي الفريضة بعد وقتها باسم الفريضة؟ مع الاتفاق على كونه آثماً بالتأخير؟ وهنا موطن الخلاف : أما الجمهور فيقولون نعم يصح منه ذلك استناداً لما تقدم من أدلة ، وابن حزم يقول لا يصح لأن غير المعذور ليس كالمعذور . لكن ابن حزم يوافق الجمهور على أن من استقاء وهو صائم في رمضان فهو آثم ـ أي غير معذور ـ وعليه القضاء . وهكذا اطردت القاعدة عند الجمهور ولم تطرد عند ابن حزم ، فهذا غير معذور أبطل عبادته المؤقتة عمداً فأوجب عليه الشارع القضاء فلماذا لا يطالب بالقضاء أمثاله من غير المعذورين؟ فظهر أن الحق مع الجمهور .

وإذا كان لابن حزم عذره ، لأنه لا يأخذ بالقياس فما عذر الذين يحتجون بالقياس ثم يتبعون رأيه؟

قال النووي : «أجمع العلماء الذين يعتد بهم على أن من ترك صلاة عمداً لزمه قضاؤها . وخالفهم أبو محمد علي بن حزم فقال إنه لا يقدر على قضائها أبداً ولا يصح فعلها أبداً [. . .] وهذا الذي قاله مع أنه مخالف للإجماع باطل من جهة الدليل ، وبسط هو الكلام في الاستدلال وليس فيما ذكر دلالة أصلاً» .

tions is devoid of anything that bears it out" (*al-Majmu'* (y108), 3.71).

(*Qada' al-'ibadat wa al-niyaba fiha* (y114), 198–211)

*

w19.0 FASTING AND PRAYING AT NORTHERLY LATITUDES
(from f2.1, end)

FASTING

w19.1 (n: The Egyptian mufti Hasanayn Muhammad Makhluf was asked for a formal legal opinion (fatwa) concerning the ruling for fasting Ramadan by Muslims living in northern Europe, where the period of fasting during the day may reach 19 hours, 22 hours, or even more. What follows has been translated from the answer he gave.)

(Hasanayn Muhammad Makhluf:) Fasting, as defined by Sacred Law, begins at the coming of dawn and ends at sunset of each day, its time span varying with the different situations of various countries. No matter how long this period is, its mere length is not considered a legitimate excuse permitting one not to fast. It is only permissible not to fast (N: a day or more of Ramadan, making up the missed fast-day by fasting a day in its place later in the year) if one believes it probable that fasting the whole day will lead to illness or exhaustion that will harm one (dis: c7.2) (N: for example, such that one cannot continue working), whether this belief is because of:

(1) a symptom that appears;

(2) having previously tried to fast this long (N: until unable to do so because of weakness, dizziness, etc., and then having eaten);

(3) or being informed by a competent physician.

[محـرر بالتصرف من قضاء العبـادات والنيـابـة فيهـا: ١٩٨ ـ ٢١١ بتقـديم وتأخير، وقد راجعه المؤلف حفظه الله].

w19.0 الصيام والصلاة في المناطق الشمالية

الصيام

w19.1 (ت: استُفتـي المفتـي المصري حسنين محمد مخلوف في صوم رمضان عند مسلمي شمال أوروبا، حيث تصـل ساعـات النهار تسع عشر ساعة أو اثنين وعشـرين ساعـة أو أكثـر. فالنص التالي من جوابه).

(حـسنـين محـمـد مخلوف:) [...] والصـوم الشرعي يبتدىء من طلوع الفجر ويـنـتـهـي بغـروب الـشـمـس كل يوم، فتختلف مدته باختلاف عروض البلاد، وكيفمـا كانت المـدة فإن مجـرد طولها لا يعـدُّ عذراً شرعيـاً يبيح الفطر، وإنما يباح الفطر إذا غلب على ظن الإنسـان بأمـارة ظهـرت أو تجربة وقعت أو بإخبار طبيب حاذق أن صومـه هذه المـدة يفضي إلى مرضه أو إلى إعبـاء شديـد يضـره، [كما صرح به أئمـة الحنفيـة،] فيكـون حكمه

The ruling in such a case is like that of someone who is ill and fears destruction, an increase in his ailment, or a delay in his recovery were he to fast. This is the general basis of the dispensation not to fast and of leniency for those responsible for the obligations of Sacred Law. Everyone who knows himself and is aware of the reality of his case will know whether it is lawful or unlawful for him not to fast. When one's fasting the long period will lead to illness, debility, or exhaustion, whether these are certainly established or whether considered likely because of one of the above-mentioned means of knowledge, it is permissible for one to take the dispensation not to fast; and when fasting will not lead to this, it is unlawful for one not to fast. People differ in this respect, and for the condition of each there is a particular ruling (*Fatawa shar'iyya wa buhuth Islamiyya* (y79), 1.271–73).

حكم المريض الذي يخشى التلف أو أن يزيد مرضه أو يبطىء شفاؤه إذا صام . هذا هو المبدأ العام في رخصة الفطر وفي التيسير على المكلفين . وكل امرىء بصير بنفسه ، عليم بحقيقة أمره ، يعرف مكانها من حلّ الفطر وحرمته . فإذا كان صومه المدة الطويلة يؤدي إلى إصابته بمرض أو ضعف أو إعياء ، يقيناً أو في غالب الظن بإحدى الوسائل العلمية التي أومأنا إليها ، حل له الترخص بالفطر ، وإذا كان لا يؤدي إلى ذلك حرم عليه الفطر . والناس في ذلك مختلفون ولكل حالة حكمها [. . .] [نقل من فتاوى شرعية وبحوث إسلامية : ١ / ٢٧١ – ٢٧٣] .

PRAYING

الصلاة

w19.2 (A: If one's location does not have one or more of the prayer times (n: such as true dawn (def: f2.1(4(n:))), sunrise, etc., due to the extreme northerly latitude), then one should pray at the same time as the closest city that has the true times (n: though for each degree of longitude that this closest city lies to the east of one's location, the prayer time of the city will arrive earlier than at one's own position by four minutes, and one may wish to compensate for this error factor by the appropriate calculations, i.e. not praying simultaneously with that city's times, but rather after its time by four minutes for each degree of longitude it lies to the east, or before its time by four minutes for each degree of longitude it lies to the west. In any case, as pointed out at f2.12, if one's prayer times for a number of days are later found to have been mistaken, one only needs to make up one day's prayers. As for learning the time of the closest city having the true times, the best means as of this writing is the pocket-size computer designed by a Syrian engineer and marketed under the name of "Prayer Minder," that is based on precise astronomical data, programmed for fifty years, and when given various cities' geographical coordinates supplied in the accompanying booklet, provides the prayer times of most major cities in the world).)

(N: For both the dawn prayer (subh) and the *dawn* that marks the beginning of fast-days of Ramadan, if there is sunset and sunrise at one's location but not true dawn because of the persistence of twilight all night, one copies the nearest city that has the true times in terms of the amount of time by which dawn in that city precedes sunrise there. Thus if dawn in this nearest city precedes sunrise by 90 minutes, one's own "dawn" occurs 90 minutes before the sunrise in one's own city. And similarly for the amount of time by which nightfall ('isha) follows the sunset prayer (maghrib).)

w20.0 THE MERIT OF *WIRD*S
(from f2.5)

w20.0 فضيلة الأوراد

w20.1 (Ibn Hajar Haytami:) The *wird*s (n: a particular amount of daily *dhikr* or Koran recital) Sufis customarily recite after prayers, according to their degree of spiritual advancement, have an authentic legal basis in the hadith related by Bayhaqi that the Prophet (Allah bless him and give him peace) said,

> "To invoke Allah Most High (dhikr) with people after the dawn prayer until sunrise is more beloved to me than this world and all it contains, and to invoke Allah Most High with people after the midafternoon prayer until sunset is more beloved to me than this world and all it contains."

Because the Sufis' practice of joining to recite *wird*s and *dhikr* after the dawn prayer and at other times has a rigorously authenticated (sahih) basis in the sunna, namely the above-mentioned hadith, there can be no objection to their doing so (*al-Fatawa al-hadithiyya* (y48), 76).

w20.1 (ابن حجر الهيتمي:) وأوراد الصوفية التي يقرؤونها بعد الصلوات على حسب عاداتهم في سلوكهم لها أصل أصيل، فقد روى البيهقي [عن أنس رضي الله عنه] أن النبي ﷺ قال:

«لأن أذكر الله تعالى مع قوم بعد صلاة الفجر إلى طلوع الشمس أحب إليّ من الدنيا وما فيها، ولأن أذكر الله تعالى مع قوم بعد صلاة العصر إلى أن تغيب الشمس أحب إليّ من الدنيا وما فيها». [...].

وإذا ثبت أن لما يعتاده الصوفية من اجتماعهم على الأذكار والأوراد بعد الصبح وغيره أصلاً صحيحاً من السنة وهو ما ذكرناه، فلا اعتراض عليهم في ذلك [محرر من الفتاوى الحديثية: [٧٦.

*

w21.0 PRAYING TOWARDS TOMBS (from f4.14)

w21.0 الصلاة عند القبور واتخاذ مساجد عندها

w21.1 (Ibn Hajar Haytami:) Ahmad, Bukhari, Muslim, and Nasa'i relate that the Prophet (Allah bless him and give him peace) said,

> "May Allah curse the Jews and Christians; they have taken the tombs of their prophets as places of worship,"

and Ahmad, Bukhari, Muslim, and Nasa'i also relate the hadith,

> "They are the ones who, when a righteous man among them died, would build a place of worship upon his grave and paint those icons in it. They will be the wickedest of creation in Allah's sight on the Day of Judgement."

w21.1 (ابن حجر الهيتمي:) أخرج [أحمد عن أسامة و] أحمد والشيخان والنسائي [عن عائشة وابن عباس ومسلم عن أبي هريرة]: «لعن الله اليهود والنصارى اتخذوا قبور أنبيائهم مساجد».

وأحمد والشيخان والنسائي: «أولئك إذا كان فيهم الرجل الصالح فمات بنوا على قبره مسجداً وصوروا تلك الصور، أولئك شرار الخلق عند الله يوم القيامة». [...].

The reason for considering it an enormity to take a grave as a place of worship is obvious, for the Prophet (Allah bless him and give him peace) cursed those who did this with the graves of their prophets, and considered those who did it with the graves of the righteous to be "the wickedest of creation in Allah's sight on the Day of Judgement."

Taking a grave as a place of worship means to pray *on* the grave or *towards* it. The prohibition, moreover, applies exclusively to the grave of someone venerated, whether a prophet or friend of Allah (wali, def: w33), as is shown by the hadith's wording "when there was a righteous man among them"; for which reason our colleagues say that it is unlawful to perform the prayer towards the graves of the prophets or friends of Allah "for the blessing of it" (tabarruk, dis: w31) or out of reverence for it, that is, under two conditions:

(a) that the grave is of someone who is honored and venerated;

(b) and that the prayer is performed towards or on the grave with the intention of gaining the blessing of it, or out of reverence for it.

That such an action is an enormity is clear from the above hadiths (A: though if either condition is lacking, performing the prayer near a grave is unobjectionable) (al-Zawajir 'an iqtiraf al-kaba'ir (y49), 1.148–49).

*

w22.0 THE JINN (from f5.1)

BELIEF IN THE JINN

w22.1 ('Ala' al-Din 'Abidin:) Our prophet Muhammad (Allah bless him and give him peace), who was truthful in all that he did and said, has informed us of matters that are mandatory—personally obligatory for each of us—to believe, accept, and not doubt or be sarcastic about the

---

عدُّ هذه [الستة] من الكبائر [وقع في كلام بعض الشافعية ووجه أخذ اتخاذ القبر مسجداً منها] واضح لأنه لعن من فعل ذلك بقبور أنبيائه وجعل من فعل ذلك بقبور صلحائه شر الخلق عند الله يوم القيامة [. . .] واتخاذ القبر مسجداً معناه الصلاة عليه أو إليه [. . .] وإنما يتجه هذا الأخذ إن كان القبر قبر معظم من نبي أو ولي كما أشارت إليه رواية: «إذا كان فيهم الرجل الصالح» ومن ثم قال أصحابنا: «تحرم الصلاة إلى قبور الأنبياء والأولياء تبركاً وإعظاماً» فاشترطوا شيئين أن يكون قبر معظم وأن يقصد بالصلاة إليه ومثلها الصلاة عليه التبرك والإعظام، وكون هذا الفعل كبير ظاهر من الأحاديث المذكورة [. . .] [محرر من الزواجر عن اقتراف الكبائر: ١/ ١٤٨ - ١٤٩].

w22.0   الجن

وجوب الإيمان بوجود الجن

w22.1   (علاء الدين عابدين:) [. . .] ﷺ فاعلم أن نبينا [ورسولنا] محمداً الصادق في جميع أحواله وأقواله، قد جاءنا بأشياء يفترض علينا ـ فرضاً عينياً ـ أن نؤمن بها ونصدقه فيها لا نرتاب في

slightest bit of. Among the things of which he informed us is that Allah Most High has created angels (def: u3.3) that are pure spirits, neither masculine nor feminine, and created jinn, fiery beings that can assume various forms. The good jinn are Muslims and believers, and will be with us in paradise, where we will see them but they will not see us—the opposite of this world—while the immoral and wicked of them are called *devils,* being of the offspring of Satan, who used to be in paradise, but disobeyed the command of his Lord, and is now

"of those reprieved till the day of a known time" (Koran 15:37–38).

(*al-Hadiyya al-'Ala'iyya* (y4), 460–63)

THE DIFFERENCE BETWEEN JINN AND ANGELS

w22.2 (Muhammad Sa'id Burhani:) The difference between jinn and angels is that angels are created of light, while jinn are created of fire. Angels (upon whom be peace) do not reproduce, while jinn do. Angels do not commit disobedience, while jinn include both the obedient and the disobedient, both believer and unbeliever, the rebellious of them being called devils. Jinn assume various forms, both noble and base, such as that of a snake and the like, while the angels (upon whom be peace) only assume noble forms, like that of a human being. Angels live in the heavens and earth, while jinn live only on earth. Angels are not called to account on the Day of Judgement, but rather enter paradise, and whoever disparages one of them has committed unbelief. Angels like circles of religious learning and *dhikr,* and supplicate Allah to bless our Prophet (Allah bless him and give him peace) and us, and they ask forgiveness for those on earth. They rejoice at whoever visits the ill or seeks religious knowledge, out of pleasure with what he is doing (ibid., 463).

*

شيء من ذلـك ولا نسـتخف به [. . .] وممـا جاء به [ﷺ] : أن الله تعـالى خلق ملائكـة هم أرواح مجـردة لا توصف بذكورة ولا أنوثة [. . .] وخلق جناً، وهم أجساد نارية قابلة للتشكل. الصالح منهم مسلم مؤمن، يكـون معنا في الجنة، نراه ولا يرانا، عكس حالـة الـدنيـا، والفاجر الخبيث منهم يقـال له : الشيطـان، من نسل إبليس، الذي كان في الجنة، ففسق عن أمـر ربـه، والـذي هو الآن من المنظرين إلى يوم الوقت المعلوم.

الفرق بين الجن والملائكة

w22.2 (محمـد سعيد البـرهاني :) الفرق بين الجن والملائكة : أن الملائكة مخـلوقـة من نور والـجـن من نار، ـ والمـلائكة عليهم السـلام لا يتـوالـدون والجن يتـوالـدون، ـ والملائكـة لا تقع منهم المعصيـة، والجن منهم الطـائـع والعاصي، ومنهم المؤمن ومنهم الكافر، والمتمـرد منهم يقـال له شيطـان، والجن يتشكلون بأشكـال مختلفة، شريفة وغير شريفة، كحية ونحوها، والملائكة عليهم السـلام لا يتشكلون إلا بأشكـال شريفة كإنسـان، ـ والمـلائكـة مسكنهم السماء والأرض، والـجـن في الأرض، ـ والملائكة لا يحاسبون يوم القيـامـة، ويـدخلون الجنة، ومن سب واحداً منهم يكفر، ـ والملائكة يألفون مجالس العلم والـذكـر ويصلون على نبينا، وعلينـا، ويستغفرون لمن في الأرض، ويفرحون بزائـر المريض، وبطالب العلم رضـا بما يصنع، [إلى غيـر ما هنالك] [محرر من الهدية العلائية : ٤٦٠ ـ ٤٦٣].

w23.0 WOMEN'S OBLIGATORY CLOTHING (from f5.3)

w23.0 عورة المرأة

w23.1 (A:) The *nakedness* ('awra) of a woman that she is forbidden to reveal differs in the Shafi'i school according to different circumstances. In the privacy of the home, her nakedness is that which is between the navel and knees. In the prayer (n: or hajj, as at j3.24) it means everything besides the face and hands. And when outside the home on the street, it refers to the entire body (N: or for Hanafis, all but the face and hands (dis: m2.8), just as in prayer).

*

w24.0 PERFORMING THE OBLIGATORY PRAYER IN A VEHICLE (from f6.2)

w24.0 لزوم الاستقبال عند الصلاة المكتوبة في وسائط النقل

w24.1 (N:) All four schools of jurisprudence agree that it is obligatory for a traveller in a vehicle to stand and to face the direction of prayer (qibla) (n: and perform the prayer's other physical integrals) when performing a prescribed prayer. If it is impossible to stand or to face the direction of prayer (A: or according to Hanafis, if it poses a hardship (dis: below)), and one cannot stop and pray on the ground, then one prays as best one can in the vehicle. According to Hanafis and Malikis, such a prayer does not have to be made up when one is again able to perform it properly. though for Shafi'is, one must make it up.

w24.2 (A:) In the Hanafi school, if one is travelling in a bus or the like where facing the direction of prayer (qibla) poses a hardship (n: and one does not expect the vehicle to stop before the time for prayer has finished (dis: below, end)), one may validly perform the obligatory prayer in one's seat facing the direction of travel. Tahtawi writes:

"... The words of *al-Durar* allude to what we have mentioned, where the author says, '... because such a person is able to face the direction of prayer (qibla) without hardship...' the implication being that when it is not possible to face the direction of prayer, or when there is hardship in doing so, one is not obliged to face the direction of prayer; and the implications of legal texts are evidence, as will not be lost on anyone. As for the words of *Majma' al-riwayat* that 'if one is unable to [A: face the direction of prayer], one refrains from praying,' they are interpretable as referring to when one expects the excuse [A: for

« . . . وإلى ما ذكرنا يشير كلام الدرر حيث قال : «لأنه يمكنه الاستقبال من غير مشقة» إذ مفهومه أنه عند عدم الإمكان وعند المشقة لا يلزمه الاستقبال ومفاهيم الكتب حجة كما لا يخفى وما في مجمع الروايات أنه إن عجز يمسك عن الصلاة يمكن حمله على حالة الرجاء اهـ. أي

not facing it] to pass before the prayer's time is over" (*Hashiya 'ala Maraqi al-falah sharh Nur al-idah* (y127), 269).

(n: The Hanafi school does not permit joining two prayers in the time of one of them because of travelling (def: f15.9), so one may not do so when taking the above-mentioned dispensation (dis: c6.4, last par.).)

*

w25.0　DOUBTS ABOUT THE INTENTION OF PRAYER (from f8.3)

w25.1 ('Abd al-Wahhab Sha'rani:) I have heard Sheikh al-Islam Futuhi al-Hanbali (Allah have mercy on him) say: "Those with neurotic misgivings burden themselves with the 'words of the intention' they have made up and busy themselves in uttering, while none of this is authenticated as being from the Prophet (Allah bless him and give him peace), who only used to intend with his heart, as did his Companions. Neither he nor the Companions were ever heard to say other than 'Allahu akbar.' Were it conceivable that Allah Most High might require a rational person to pray 'without an intention,' it would be like a command that could not be carried out. Consider the person who goes to the washroom to perform ablution. Ask him where he is going and he will say, 'To perform ablution.' And ask him when he goes to the mosque, 'Where to?' and he will say, 'To pray.' How can a sane man with such a purpose in view doubt that he is intending ablution or prayer? It's a kind of madness" (*Lata'if al-minan wa al-akhlaq* (y122), 2.66–67).

*

w26.0　PRESENCE OF MIND IN PRAYER (from f8.21)

w26.1 (Ghazali:) Prayer is composed of invocation (dhikr), Koran recital, bowing, prostration, standing, and sitting. Without a doubt, the point

رجاء زوال العذر قبل الوقت [فتأمل اهـ. بتصـرف] [نقل من حاشيـة على مراقي الفلاح شرح نور الإيضاح : ٢٦٩].

w25.0 الاحــتــراز عن الوسوسة في نية الصلاة

w25.1 (عبـد الـوهـاب الشعراني :) [. . . و] سمعت شيـخ الإسـلام الفتوحي الحنبلي رحمـه الله تعـالى يقـول : «قـد أتعب الموسوسون أنفسهم في ألفاظ النية التي أحـدثـوها واشتغلوا بمخارج حروفها ولم يصح عنه ﷺ في ذلك شيء . إنما كان ينوي بقلبه فقـط وكـذلك أصحابه وكان لا يسمع منه ولا من أصحابه إلا لفظ «الله أكبر» لا غير . . . حتى لو قدر أن الله تعالى كلف العاقل بأن يصلي بلا نية لكان ذلـك كالتكليف بمـا لا يطـاق . وتأمل الإنسـان إذا ذهب إلى الميضأة يتـوضأ تقول له : إلى أين ؟ فيقول : لأتوضأ ؛ وإذا ذهب إلى المسجـد تقول له : إلى أين ؟ فيقـول : لأصلي ؛ فكيف يشك عاقل مع قصـده هذا أنـه غير ناوٍ للوضوء والصلاة ؟ هذا نوع جنـون [نقـل من لطـائف المنن والأخلاق : ٢ / ٦٦ ـ ٦٧].

w26.0 إحضار القلب في الصلاة

w26.1 (الغـزالي :) أما الصلاة فليس فيهـا إلا ذكر وقراءة وركوع وسجود وقيام وقعـود [. . .] ولا شك في أن المقصود

of reciting the Koran and *dhikr* is to glorify and praise, to humbly entreat and supplicate, while the one being addressed is Allah Mighty and Majestic. He whose heart is veiled by inattention is veiled from Allah, not apprehending or contemplating Him, but oblivious of whom he is speaking to, merely moving his tongue out of habit. How far this is from what is meant by prayer, which has been established to polish the heart, renew one's remembrance of Allah Mighty and Majestic, and to deepen the ties of faith in Him. As for bowing and prostrating, the point of them is certainly veneration, for if not, nothing remains but movements of the spine and head.

Hasan al-Basri said, "Every prayer performed without presence of heart is closer to deserving punishment," while it is related from Mu'adh ibn Jabal that "whoever knows who is on his right or left intentionally while at prayer has no prayer." And the Prophet (Allah bless him and give him peace) said,

"Truly, a servant performs the prayer without a sixth of it being recorded for him or a tenth, but only as much as he comprehends."

Had these words come from anyone else, they would have been adopted as "a school of thought." How then can we not go by them? 'Abd al-Wahid ibn Zayd said, "Scholars concur that none of a servant's prayer counts for him except what he comprehends," a position he considered established by scholarly consensus (ijma'). Innumerable statements of similar purport have reached us from godfearing scholars and those knowledgeable in the way of the hereafter. But while the truth lies in returning to the evidence of primary texts and hadiths, and the evidence is compelling that presence of mind is a condition for prayer, the context in which formal legal opinion can define outward moral responsibility is limited by the extent of people's shortcomings, and it is not possible to require them to have full presence of mind throughout the prayer, which hardly anyone can do except for very few (*Ihya' 'ulum al-din* (y39), 1.143–44).

من القـراءة والأذكـار الحمـد والثنـاء والتضـرع والـدعاء، والمخاطب هو الله عز وجل و(ت:) من كان) قلبه بحجاب الغفلة محجوب عنه فلا يراه ولا يشاهده بل هو غافل عن المخاطب ولسانه يتحرك بحكم العـادة فمـا أبعد هذا عن المقصود بالصــلاة التي شرعت لتصقيـل القلب وتجـديـد ذكـر الله عز وجل ورسوخ عقد الإيمـان به [...] وأمـا الركوع والسجود فالمقصـود بهمـا التعظيم قطعـاً [...] وإذا خرج عن كونـه تعظيمـاً لم يبق إلا مجرد حركـة الظهر والرأس [...].

وروي عن الحسن أنه قال: كل صلاة لا يحضر فيها القلب فهي إلى العقوبـة أسرع وعن معـاذ بن جبل: من عرف من على يمينه وشماله متعمداً وهو في الصلاة فلا صلاة له و[روي أيضـاً مسنـداً] قال رسول ﷺ: «إن العبد ليصلي الصلاة لا يكتب له سدسها ولا عشرها وإنما يكتب للعبد من صلاته ما عقل منها» [ت: قال الحافظ العراقي رواه أبو داود والنسائي وابن حبان من حديث عمـار بن يسـار بنحوه]. وهذا لو نقـل عن غيـره لجعـل مذهبـاً فكيف لا نتمسـك به؟ وقال عبـد الواحد بن زيد: أجمعت العلماء على أنه ليس للعبـد من صلاتـه إلا ما عقل منها؛ فجعله إجماعاً. وما نقل من هذا الجنس عن الفقهاء المتورعين وعن علماء الآخرة أكثر من أن يحصى. والحق الرجوع إلى أدلة الشـرع؛ والأخبار والآثار ظاهرة في هذا الشـرط إلا أن مقـام الـفتـوى في التكليف الظـاهـر يتقـدر بقـدر قصـور الخلق، فلا يمكن أن يشترط على الناس إحضار القلب في جميع الصلاة فإن ذلك يعجز عنه كل البشر إلا الأقلين [محرر من إحياء علوم الدين: ١/ ١٤٣ - ١٤٤].

*

w27.0 ROSARIES (from f9.8)

w27.0 مشروعية السبحة

w27.1 (Jalal al-Din Suyuti:) Having long heard questions concerning the rosary (subha) as to whether there is a basis for it in the sunna, I have compiled in this section the hadiths and accounts of early Muslims that relate to it.

Ibn 'Amr said, "I saw the Prophet (Allah bless him and give him peace) count the times he said 'Subhan Allah' on his hand."

Safiyya said, "The Prophet (Allah bless him and give him peace) entered the room where I sat with four thousand date stones in front of me and he asked, 'What is this, O daughter of Huyay?' I said, 'I am saying "Subhan Allah" with them.' He replied, 'I've said "Subhan Allah" more times than this since you've begun,' and I said, 'Show me how, O Messenger of Allah.' He said, 'Say, "Subhan Allah the number of everything He has created." ' "

w27.1 (جــلال الــدين السيوطي:)
[. . . وبــعــد] فقــد طال الســؤال عن
السبحة هل لها أصل في السنة؟ فجمعت
في هذا الجـزء متتبعاً فيـه ما ورد فيها من
الأحاديث والآثار. [. . . أخرج ابن أبي
شيبــة وأبــو داود والتــرمــذي والنسائي
والحـاكم وصححه] عن ابن عمرو قال:
«رأيت النبي ﷺ يعقـد التسبيح بيـده».
[. . . وأخـرج التــرمــذي والحــاكم
والطبراني] عن صفية قالت: «دخل عليَّ
رسول الله ﷺ وبين يدي أربعة آلاف نواة
أسبـح بهن فقـال: ما هذا يا بنت حيي؟
قلت: أسبح بهن؛ قال: قد سبحت منـذ
قمت على رأسـك أكثر من هذا، قلت:
علمني يا رسول الله؛ قال: قولي سبحان
الله عدد ما خلق من شيء» [صحيح
أيضاً].

w27.2 As one scholar has said, "Counting the times one says 'Subhan Allah' on one's fingers is superior to doing so on a rosary because of the hadith of Ibn 'Amr, though it has been said that if the person saying it is safe from mistakes in counting, his fingers are better, while if not, then saying it on a rosary is more suitable. Some of the most renowned Muslims have used rosaries, those from whom the religion is taken and who are relied upon, such as Abu Hurayra (Allah be well pleased with him), who had a string with two thousand knots in it, and did not use to go to sleep before saying 'Subhan Allah' with it twelve thousand times."

'Umar al-Maliki said, "I saw my teacher Hasan al-Basri with a rosary in his hand and said, 'Teacher, with your great eminence and the excellence of your worship, do you still use a rosary?' and he replied, 'Something we have used at the beginning we are not wont to leave at the end. I love to remember Allah with my heart, my hand, and my tongue.' " And how should it be otherwise, when the rosary reminds one of Allah Most High, and a person seldom sees one save that he

w27.2 [. . . قال بعض العلمــاء:]
عقـد التسبيح بالأنامل أفضل من السبحة
لحديث ابن عمرو ولكن يقال أن المسبح
إن أمن من الغلط كان عقـده بالأنــامـل
أفضل وإلا فالسبحـة أولى. وقـد اتخـذ
السبحة سادات يشار إليهم ويؤخذ عنهم
ويعتمد عليهم كأبي هريرة رضي الله عنه
كان لـه خيـط فيـه ألفـا عقدة فكان لا ينام
حتى يسبـح بـه ثنتي عشـرة ألف تسبيحة
[قـالـه عكرمـة، . . .]. [« . . . كذلك
رأيت أستاذي] عمـر المـالكي [وفي يده
سبحة فسألتـه عمـا سألتني عنه ف] قال:
[كذلك] رأيت أستاذي الحسن البصري
وفي يده سبحة فقلت: يا أستاذ مع عظم
شأنـك وحسن عبادتك وأنت إلى الآن مع
السبحة؟ فقال لي: شيء كنا نستعمله في
البدايات ما كنا نتركه في النهايات، أحب
أن أذكـر الله بقلبي وفي يدي ولسـاني»
[. . .] فكيف بها وهي مذكرة بالله تعالى
لأن الإنسـان قل أن يراهـا إلا ويـذكر الله

remembers Allah, this being among the greatest of its benefits (*al-Hawi li al-fatawi* (y130), 2.2–5).

وهــذا من أعظم فوائـدها [. . .] [محرر من الحـاوي للفتـاوي في الفقــه وعلوم التفسير والحــديث والأصــول والنحو والإعراب وسائر الفنون: ٢/ ٢ - ٥].

*

w28.0 THE SUNNAS BEFORE THE FRIDAY PRAYER (from f10.2)

w28.0 سنن قبل صلاة الجمعة

SUNNA RAK'AS BEFORE THE PRAYER

سنة الجمعة القبلية

w28.1 (Hasan Saqqaf:) As for the sunna rak'as prayed before the Friday prayer, there are hadiths about them, such as the following:

(1) "The Messenger of Allah (Allah bless him and give him peace) used to pray four rak'as before the Friday prayer and four after it."

The hadith master (hafiz, def: w48.2(end)) Wali al-Din al-'Iraqi states that its channel of transmission is good, the hadith containing an explicit reference to the sunna rak'as before the Friday prayer.

(2) Ibn Majah relates, with a rigorously authenticated (sahih) channel of transmission, that Abu Hurayra (Allah be well pleased with him) said, "Sulayk Ghatafani arrived while the Messenger of Allah (Allah bless him and give him peace) was giving the Friday prayer sermon (khutba), and the Messenger of Allah said to him, 'Did you pray before you came?' and he said no, to which the Prophet replied, 'Then pray two rak'as, keeping them brief.'"

The words of the Prophet (Allah bless him and give him peace) "before you came" furnish explicit proof of the sunna rak'as before the Friday prayer, for the rak'as of greeting the mosque (def: f10.10) are not performed before one arrives. Apparently Sulayk lived near the mosque, so the Prophet (Allah bless him and give him peace) thought that he had prayed before

w28.1 (حسن السقــاف:) [. . .] فأمـا سنة الجمعة القبلية فجـاءت فيها أحاديث منهـا: [روى الإمام الحافظ أبو الحسن الخلعي في فوائده بإسناد جيد من طريق أبي إسحــاق عن عاصم بن ضمـرة عن علي رضي الله عنه:] «كــان رســول الله ﷺ يصلي قبل الجمعة أربعاً وبعدها أربعاً.» قال الحـافظ ولي الدين العراقي [في طرح التثريب] إسناده جيد [وكذلك نص عليه . . . المناوي في فيض القدير: ٥/ ٢١٦] ففي هذا الحــديث تصـريح بسنة الجمعة القبلية.

وروى ابن ماجه بإسنـاد صحيـح عن أبي هريرة رضي الله عنه قال: جاء سُلَيك الغطفاني ورسول الله ﷺ يخطب، فقال له رســول اللـه ﷺ: «أصـليت قبــل أن تجيء؟ قال: لا، قال فصــلّ ركـعتين وتجوّز فيهمـا. [. . . وقـال الحـافظ الــعراقي في شرح الترمـذي إسنـاده صحيح. نقـل ذلك الحـافظ ولي الدين العـراقي في طرح التثريب: ٤/ ٢٤.] فقــوله ﷺ: قبل أن تجيء، دليل صريح على سنة الجمعة القبلية، لأن تحية المسجد لا تفعل قبل المجيء. [. . .] والظاهر أن سليك كان بقرب المسجد فظنـه النبي قد صلى قبـل مجيئــه إلى

coming, and when he informed him that he had not, he ordered him to pray them.

(3) Nafi‘ relates that "Ibn ‘Umar used to pray at length before the Friday prayer, performing two rak‘as in his home, saying that the Messenger of Allah (Allah bless him and give him peace) used to do this,"

a hadith related by Abu Dawud, and by Ibn Hibban in his *Sahih*.

It is thus very plain and clear that the sunna rak‘as before the Friday prayer are rigorously authenticated as being the practice of the Prophet (Allah bless him and give him peace), his Companions, and the early Muslims, and have been accepted as such by Islamic scholars.

THE SECOND CALL (ADHAN)
TO FRIDAY PRAYER

w28.2 The sunnas before the Friday prayer, meaning the two or four rak‘as before it, are a confirmed sunna (def: c4.1). The Prophet (Allah bless him and give him peace) used to pray four rak‘as in his house, which adjoined the mosque, after the beginning of the noon prayer's time. Then he would enter the mosque and ascend the pulpit (minbar), whereupon the muezzin would give the call to prayer (adhan) and the Prophet would rise for the sermon. The call to prayer thus took place after the prayer's time had begun and after praying four rak‘as. People only used to know when the prayer's time had initially come through their own intuition, and it was thus that the matter remained during the caliphates of our liegelord Abu Bakr and our liegelord ‘Umar (Allah be well pleased with them). Then our liegelord ‘Uthman (Allah be well pleased with him) established the sunna of a second call to prayer, this second one being the first in order of occurrence; which is to say, the *second call to prayer* that was established as a sunna by our liegelord ‘Uthman is the one that is *before* the call to prayer that occurs after the imam ascends the pulpit. So he made this second call to prayer—

المسجد فلما أخبره بأنه لم يصل أمره بصلاتهما.

وعن نافع قال: كان ابن عمر يطيل الصلاة قبل الجمعة ويصلي ركعتين في بيته ويحدث أن رسول الله ﷺ كان يفعل ذلك. رواه أبو داود وابن حبان في صحيحه [...].

[...] فتبين واتضح وضوحاً جلياً أن سنة الجمعة القبلية ثابتة عن رسول الله ﷺ وعن الصحابة وعن السلف، وقد قال بها العلماء.

سنية الأذان الثاني لصلاة الجمعة

w28.2 [...] سنة الجمعة القبلية أعني ركعتين أو أربعاً قبلها من السنن المؤكدات، وقد كان رسول الله ﷺ بعد أن [تزول الشمس ـ أي تميل عن وسط السماء و] يدخل وقت الظهر ـ يصلي أربع ركعات سنة للجمعة قبلها، في بيته وكان بيته في مسجده ﷺ [كما هو معلوم]، ثم يخرج إلى المسجد فيصعد على المنبر، فيؤذن المؤذن فيقوم للخطبة. فالأذان كان بعد دخول الوقت، وبعد أن يصلي الركعات الأربع. وإنما كانوا يعرفون زوالها سليقة وبقي الأمر هكذا في زمن سيدنا أبي بكر وكذا في زمن سيدنا عمر رضي الله عنهما. ثم سنَّ سيدنا عثمان رضي الله عنه الأذان الثاني، والأذان الثاني هو الأول توقيتاً بمعنى أن الأذان الثاني الـذي سَنَّهُ سيدنا عثمان قبل الذي يكون بعد صعود الإمام على المنبر. فجعل هذا الأذان الثاني

which is the first of the two to occur—a means of announcing to people that the prayer's time had come; namely, the noon prayer's time, when the sun has just passed its highest point in the sky for that day. As for the first call to prayer that existed in the time of the Prophet (Allah bless him and give him peace), it remained in its place, which was after the imam had ascended the pulpit, it being the second in order of occurrence but the first to be legally established.

Our liegelord 'Uthman's doing this was a good act that was confirmed by the consensus (ijma') of the prophetic Companions, not a single one of whom criticized him for it or opposed it; nor did any of those who came after them. Moreover, it is established that the Prophet (Allah bless him and give him peace) said,

"Hold fast to my sunna and the sunna of the Rightly Guided Caliphs; clamp your [very] teeth upon it,"

a rigorously authenticated (sahih) hadith related by Abu Dawud, Tirmidhi, Ibn Majah, Imam Ahmad, and Hakim. If someone objects that 'Uthman *innovated* this call to prayer, controverting the sunna that existed in the time of the Prophet (Allah bless him and give him peace), the answer is that such a person is in the wrong and mistaken for a number of reasons, among them:

(1) that he is accusing our liegelord 'Uthman of violating the sunna and inaugurating a reprehensible innovation (bid'a), an accusation such a person has no right to make (dis: w56.1);

(2) that he is charging the prophetic Companions who confirmed the correctness of our liegelord 'Uthman's act with confirming him upon a falsehood (batil), disregarding the Companions' consensus. Islamic scholars and specialists in fundamentals of Sacred Law state that the opinion and position of a Companion, when it becomes widely acted upon and no one is known to object to it, is considered to have become a scholarly consensus (ijma', def: b7) and is thus a decisive proof, Imam Nawawi being among those who explicitly record this, in his commentary on *Sahih Muslim* ((y93), 1.31);

(وهــو الأول زمناً) إعلاماً على دخـول الـوقت، أي وقت الظهـر وزوال الشمس عن كبـد السماء . وأما الأذان الأول الذي كان على عهد النبي ﷺ ، فبقي على محله وهو بعد صعود الإمام على المنبر ، فيكون الثاني زمناً والأول تشريعاً .

وفعـل سيـدنا عثمان لذلك فعل حسن أجمع عليـه الصحابة ولم يُعلَمْ أن أحداً أنكر عليـه من الصحابة ومن بعدهم أو خالفه . وقد ثبت أن النبي ﷺ قال :

«عليـكم بسنتي وسنـة الخلفـاء الراشدين المهـديين، عضّوا عليها بالنواجذ» .

وهـو حديث صحيـح رواه أبـو داود والترمذي وابن ماجه [والدارمي] والإمام أحمـد والحـاكم [وقال حديث صحيح ليس له علة، وأقره الذهبي] .

فمن تنطع قائلاً : لقـد ابتـدع عثمان هذا الأذان وخالف السنة التي كانت على عهـد رسـول الله ﷺ ، قلنـا له : أسأت وأخطأت من أوجه :

(الأول) : نسبت إلى سيـدنـا عثمان مخالفة السنـة ورميته بالابتداع وليس لك ذلك .

(الثاني) : نسبت إلى الصحابة الذين أقـروا سيـدنـا عثمان على هذا الفعل الإقـرار على البـاطل ولم تعتبر إجماعهم وقـد نص العلمـاء وأهل الأصول على أن قول الصحابي ومذهبه إذا انتشر ولم يُعلم له مخالف صار إجماعاً وهو حجة ، ممّن نص على ذلك الإمـام النووي في مقدمة شرحه على صحيح مسلم .

(3) and that the Prophet (Allah bless him and give him peace) gave us an order, saying,

"Hold fast to my sunna and the sunna of the Rightly Guided Caliphs..."

so that our liegelord 'Uthman's act is a sunna that the Prophet (Allah bless him and give him peace) clearly enjoins us to adhere to in this straightforward hadith.

It is thus plain that whoever seeks to eliminate or annul the second call to Friday prayer is striving to effect a blameworthy innovation and is in reality contravening the sunna, for he has abandoned the injunction that the Prophet (Allah bless him and give him peace) commanded us to obey ("al-Adilla al-jaliyya li sunna al-jumu'a al-qabliyya" (y120), 2–4).

(الثالث): أن النبي ﷺ وصّى وصيةً فقال:

«عليكم بسنتي وسنة الخلفاء الراشدين المهديين . . . » الحديث، فيكون ما فعله سيدنا عثمان سنة أوصى بالتمسك بها سيدنا رسول الله ﷺ في حديثه الصحيح الصريح هذا.

فيتضح ساعتئذ أن من سعى في إلغاء الأذان الثاني لصلاة الجمعة ساعٍ في بدعة مذمومة ومخالف للسنة حقيقة لأنه ترك وصية النبي ﷺ التي أمر بها [. . .] [محرر من رسالة الأدلة الجلية لسنة الجمعة القبلية: ٢ ــ ٤]. .

*

w29.0 INNOVATION (BID'A)
(from f10.15)

w29.0 معنى البدعة شرعاً

(n:) This section has been translated to clarify some possible misunderstandings of the concept of *innovation* (bid'a) in Islam, in light of the prophetic hadith,

"... Beware of matters newly begun, for every matter newly begun is innovation, every innovation is misguidance, and every misguidance is in hell."

« . . . وإياكم ومحدثات الأمور فإن كل محدث بدعة وكل بدعة ضلالة وكل ضلالة في النار».

The discussion centers on three points:

(1) Scholars say that the above hadith does not refer to all new things without restriction, but only to those which nothing in Sacred Law attests to the validity of. The use of the word *every* in the hadith does not indicate an absolute generalization, for there are many examples of similar generalizations in the Koran and sunna that are not applicable without restriction, but rather are qualified by restrictions found in other primary textual evidence.

(2) The sunna and way of the Prophet (Allah bless him and give him peace) was to accept new acts initiated in Islam that were of the good and did not conflict with established principles of Sacred Law, and to reject things that were otherwise.

(3) New matters in Islam may not be rejected merely because they did not exist in the first century, but must be evaluated and judged according to the com-

prehensive methodology of Sacred Law, by virtue of which it is and remains the final and universal moral code for all peoples until the end of time.

THE GENERALIZABILITY OF
THE HADITH "EVERY
INNOVATION IS MISGUIDANCE"

حديث «كل بدعة ضلالة» مخصوص

w29.1 (‘Abdullah Mahfuz Ba‘alawi:) There are many generalities in the Koran and sunna, all of them admitting of some qualification, such as the word of Allah Most High,

w29.1 (عبـد الله محفوظ باعلوي:) [. . . و] العمومـات في الكتـاب والسنة كثيـرة وكلهـا دخلهـا التخصيص [. . .] كقوله تعالى:

(1) "... And that a man can have nothing, except what he strives for" (Koran 53:39),

﴿وَأَنْ لَيْسَ لِلْإِنْسَانِ إِلَّا مَا سَعَى﴾.

despite there being an overwhelming amount of evidence that a Muslim benefits from the spiritual works of others (dis: w35.2), from his fellow Muslims, the prayers of angels for him, the funeral prayer over him, charity given by others in his name, and the supplications of believers for him;

ـ مع أن هناك من الأدلة ما يبلغ التواتر في أن الـمسلم ينتفـع بعمـل غيـره من إخوانه المسلمين ودعاء الملائكة [. . .] (و) صلاة الجنازة والصدقة عن الميت ثم دعاء المؤمنين [. . .].
وكذلك قوله تعالى:

(2) "Verily you and what you worship apart from Allah are the fuel of hell" (Koran 21:98),

﴿إِنَّكُمْ وَمَا تَعْبُـدُونَ مِنْ دُونِ اللَّهِ حَصَبُ جَهَنَّمَ﴾.

"what you worship" being a general expression, while there is no doubt that Jesus, his mother, and the angels were all worshipped apart from Allah, but are not what is meant by the verse;

ـ واسم المـوصول من صيغ العموم، ولكن ممـا لا شك فيـه أن عيسى عليـه السـلام وأمـه والملائكة وكلهم عبدوا من دون اللـه غيـر مرادين في الآيـة [. . .] وكقوله تعالى:]

(3) "But when they forgot what they had been reminded of, We opened unto them the doors of everything" (Koran 6:44),

﴿فَلَمَّا نَسُـوا مَا ذُكِّرُوا بِهِ فَتَحْنَا عَلَيْهِمْ أَبْوَابَ كُلِّ شَيْءٍ﴾.

though the doors of mercy were not opened unto them;

ـ مع أن أبواب الرحمة لم تفتح عليهم.

(4) and the hadith related by Muslim that the Prophet (Allah bless him and give him peace) said,

ومن ذلـك حديـث مسلم: سمعت رسول الله ﷺ يقول: «لن يلج النار أحد صلى قبـل طلوع الشمس وقبـل غروبها» وهـو من صيغ العمـوم قطعاً ليس على عمـومـه فإن من صلى هاتين الصلاتين

"No one who prays before sunrise and before sunset will enter hell,"

which is a generalized expression that definitely does not mean what its outward generality implies, for someone who prays the dawn and midafternoon prayers and neglects all other prayers and obligatory works is certainly not meant. It is rather a generalization whose intended referent is particular, or a generalization that is qualified by other texts, for when there are fully authenticated hadiths, it is obligatory to reach an accord between them, because they are in reality as a single hadith, the statements that appear without further qualification being qualified by those that furnish the qualification, that the combined implications of *all* of them may be utilized.

INNOVATION (BID'A) IN THE LIGHT
OF THE SUNNA OF THE PROPHET
CONCERNING NEW MATTERS

w29.2 *Sunna* and *innovation* (bid'a) are two opposed terms in the language of the Lawgiver (Allah bless him and give him peace), such that neither can be defined without reference to the other, meaning that they are opposites, and "things are made clear by their opposites." Many writers have sought to define innovation (bid'a) without defining the sunna, while it is primary, and have thus fallen into inextricable difficulties and conflicts with the primary textual evidence that contradicts their definition of innovation, whereas if they had first defined the sunna, they would have produced a criterion free of shortcomings.

    Sunna, in both the language of the Arabs and the Sacred Law, means *way,* as is illustrated by the words of the Prophet (Allah bless him and give him peace),

    "He who inaugurates a good sunna in Islam [dis: p58.1(2)] ... And he who introduces a bad sunna in Islam...,"

sunna meaning way or custom. The *way* of the Prophet (Allah bless him and give him peace) in giving guidance, accepting, and rejecting: this is the sunna. For "good sunna" and "bad sunna" mean a good way or bad way, and cannot possibly mean anything else. Thus, the meaning of *sunna* is not what most students, let alone ordinary people,

الفجـر والعصـر وتـرك ما عداهمـا من الصلوات والواجبات ليس مراداً قطعاً فهو من العـام الـذي أريد به الخصوص أو من العـام المخصـوص بالنصـوص . [قال الطيبي كمـا نقله عنه الحـافظ ابن حجر وأقـره] إن الأحـاديث إذا ثبتت وجب ضم بعضهـا إلى بعض فإنها في حكم الحديث الـواحد فيحمل مطلقهـا على مقيـدها ليحصل العمل بجميع ما في مضمونها .

مفهـوم البـدعـة في ضوء سنـة الرسول وطريقته ﷺ فيما يحدث

w29.2   السنة والبدعة أمران متقابلان في كلام صاحب الشـرع ﷺ فلا يتحدد أحدهمـا إلا بتحديد الآخر بمعنى أنهما ضدان (وبضـدهـا تبين الأشياء) وقـد جرى كثير من المـؤلفين إلى تحديـد البدعة دون أن يقوموا بتحديد السنة أولاً لأنهـا الأصـل ، فوقعـوا في ضيق لم يستطيعـوا الخروج عنه واصطدموا بأدلة تنـاقض تحديدهم للبدعة ولو أنهم سبقوا إلى تحديـد السنة لخرجوا بضـابط لا يتخلف [...] .

السنـة في لغة العـرب والشـرع هي الطريقة [...] كقول الرسول ﷺ : «مَن سنَّ في الإسلام سنَّة حسنـة» إلى قوله : «ومَن سنَّ في الإسـلام سنَّة سيئـة» ، أي طريقة [كما سبق] . فطريقة الرسول ﷺ في هديه وقبولـه ورده هي السنة [...] وسنة حسنة وسنة سيئة يعني طريقة حسنة أو طريقة سيئة ولا يحتمل غيـر ذلك . فليس المـراد إذاً ما يفهمـه عامة الطلاب فضلاً عن العـوام أنها الحديث النبوي أو

understand; namely, that it is the prophetic *hadith* (n: as when *sunna* is contrasted with *Kitab*, i.e. Koran, in distinguishing textual sources), or the opposite of the obligatory (n: as when *sunna*, i.e. recommended, is contrasted with *obligatory* in legal contexts), since the former is a technical usage coined by hadith scholars, while the latter is a technical usage coined by legal scholars and specialists in fundamentals of jurisprudence. Both of these are usages of later origin that are not what is meant by *sunna* here. Rather, the sunna of the Prophet (Allah bless him and give him peace) is his way of acting, ordering, accepting, and rejecting, and the way of his Rightly Guided Caliphs who followed his way of acting, ordering, accepting, and rejecting. So practices that are newly begun must be examined in light of the sunna of the Prophet (Allah bless him and give him peace) and his way and path in acceptance or rejection.

Now, there are great number of hadiths, most of them in the rigorously authenticated (sahih) collections, showing that many of the prophetic Companions initiated new acts, forms of invocation (dhikr), supplications (du‘a’), and so on, that the Prophet (Allah bless him and give him peace) had never previously done or ordered to be done. Rather, the Companions did them because of their inference and conviction that such acts were of the good that Islam and the Prophet of Islam came with and in general terms urged the like of be done, in accordance with the word of Allah Most High,

"And do the good, that haply you may succeed" (Koran 22:77),

and the hadith of the Prophet (Allah bless him and give him peace),

"He who inaugurates a good sunna in Islam earns the reward of it and of all who perform it after him without diminishing their own rewards in the slightest."

Though the original context of the hadith was giving charity, the interpretive principle established by the scholarly consensus (def: b7) of specialists in fundamentals of Sacred Law is that the point of

ما يقابـل الفـريضـة فإن الأول مصطلح المحـدثين والثـاني مصطلح الفقهـاء والأصوليين وكلاهما محدث ليس مراداً هنـا. فسنـة الرسـول ﷺ هي طريقته في الفعل والأمر والقبـول والرد وهي طريقة خلفـائـه الـذين سلكوا طريقته في الفعل والأمـر والقبـول والرد. إذاً فما أحدث لا بد من عرضه على سنـة الرسول وطريقته ﷺ في القبول والرد [. . .].

[اعلم . . .] أن هنـاك أحـاديث جمة جلها في الصحيح [أو من الصحيح] تثبت أن عدداً من الصحـابـة أحـدثـوا أعمـالاً وأذكـاراً وأدعيـة ونحـو ذلـك لـم يسبق للرسـول ﷺ فعلها أو الأمـر بها ولكنهم فعلوهـا استنبـاطـاً واعتقاداً أنها من الخير الذي جاء به الإسلام ورسول الإسلام ﷺ وحث على مثله عمومـاً تحت مظلة قوله تعالى:

﴿وَافْعَلُوا الْخَيْرَ لَعَلَّكُمْ تُفْلِحُونَ﴾.

ـ وقـول الرسـول ﷺ: «من سنَّ في الإسلام سنـة حسنة فله أجرها وأجر من عمـل بهـا بعـده من غيـر أن ينقص من أجـورهـم شيء» [كمـا سبـق] وهـذا الحديث وإن ورد في الصدقة فإن القاعدة الأصولية المجمع عليها: أن العبرة بعموم

primary texts lies in the *generality of their lexical significance,* not the *specificity of their historical context,* without this implying that just anyone may make provisions in the Sacred Law, for Islam is defined by principles and criteria, such that whatever one initiates as a sunna must be subject to its rules, strictures, and primary textual evidence.

From this investigative point of departure, one may observe that many of the prophetic Companions performed various acts through their own personal reasoning (ijtihad), and that the sunna and way of the Prophet (Allah bless him and give him peace) was both to accept those that were acts of worship and good deeds conformable with what the Sacred Law had established and not in conflict with it; and to reject those which were otherwise. This was his sunna and way, upon which his caliphal successors and Companions proceeded, and from which Islamic scholars (Allah be well pleased with them) have established the rule that any new matter must be judged according to the principles and primary texts of Sacred Law: whatever is attested to by the law as being good is acknowledged as good, and whatever is attested to by the law as being a contravention and bad is rejected as a blameworthy innovation (bid‘a). They sometimes term the former a *good innovation* (bid‘a hasana) in view of it lexically being termed an *innovation,* but legally speaking it is not really an innovation but rather an *inferable sunna* as long as the primary texts of the Sacred Law attest to its being acceptable.

We now turn to the primary textual evidence previously alluded to concerning the acts of the Companions and how the Prophet (Allah bless him and give him peace) responded to them:

(1) Bukhari and Muslim relate from Abu Hurayra (Allah be well pleased with him) that at the dawn prayer the Prophet (Allah bless him and give him peace) said to Bilal, "Bilal, tell me which of your acts in Islam you are most hopeful about, for I have heard the footfall of your sandals in paradise," and he replied, "I have done nothing I am more hopeful about than the fact that I do not perform ablution at any time of the night or day without praying with that ablution whatever has been destined for me to pray."

اللفظ لا بخصوص السبب . وليس معنى ذلك أن لكل أحد أن يشرع فإن الإسلام محدود القواعد والضوابط فلا بد أن يكون ما يسنه محفوظاً بقواعده وضوابطه وشواهده . من هذا المنطلق فعل كثير من الصحابة باجتهاداتهم أموراً فكانت سنة الرسول ﷺ وطريقته قبول ما كان من العبادة والخير ويتفق مع المشروع ولا يخالفه ، وردّ ما كان مخالفاً لذلك . فهذه سنته وطريقته التي سار عليها خلفاؤه وصحابته واقتبس منها العلماء رضوان الله عليهم قولهم إن ما يحدث يجب أن يعرض على قواعد الشريعة ونصوصها فما شهدت له الشريعة بالحسن فهو حسن مقبول وما شهدت له الشريعة بالمخالفة والقبح فهو المردود وهو البدعة المذمومة . وقد يسمون الأول «بدعة حسنة» من حيث اللغة باعتباره محدث وإلا فهو في الواقع ليس ببدعة شرعية بل هو «سنة مستنبطة» مادامت شواهد الشريعة تشهد لها بالقبول . [. . .] و[لنترك هذا الآن لـ] نورد الشواهد التي أشرنا إليها من عمل الصحابة وتصرف الرسول ﷺ معهم [. . .] .

(١) الحديث الأول ما رواه البخاري ومسلم [والإمام أحمد] عن أبي هريرة رضي الله عنه أن نبي الله ﷺ قال لبلال عند صلاة الفجر : يا بلال حدثني بأرجى عمل عملته في الإسلام، فإني سمعت دف نعليك في الجنة ؛ قال : ما عملت عملاً أرجى عندي من أني لم أتطهر طهوراً في ساعة من ليل أو نهار إلا صليت بذلك الطهور ما كتب لي .

Ibn Hajar ‘Asqalani says in *Fath al-Bari* that "the hadith shows it is permissible to use personal reasoning (ijtihad) in choosing times for acts of worship, for Bilal reached the conclusions he mentioned by his own inference, and the Prophet (Allah bless him and give him peace) confirmed him therein." Similar to this is the hadith in Bukhari about Khubayb (A: who asked to pray two rak‘as before being executed by idolators in Mecca), who was the first to establish the sunna of two rak‘as for those who are steadfast in going to their death. These hadiths are explicit evidence that Bilal and Khubayb used their own personal reasoning (ijtihad) in choosing the times of acts of worship, without any previous command or precedent from the Prophet (Allah bless him and give him peace) other than the general demand to perform the prayer.

(2) Bukhari and Muslim relate that Rifa‘a ibn Rafi‘ said, "When we were praying behind the Prophet (Allah bless him and give him peace) and he raised his head from bowing and said, 'Allah hears whoever praises Him,' a man behind him said, 'Our Lord, Yours is the praise, abundantly, wholesomely, and blessedly therein.' When he rose to leave, the Prophet (Allah bless him and give him peace) asked who said it, and when the man replied that it was he, the Prophet (Allah bless him and give him peace) said, 'I saw thirty-odd angels each striving to be the one to write it.'"

Ibn Hajar says in *Fath al-Bari* that the hadith "indicates the permissibility of initiating new expressions of *dhikr* in the prayer other than the ones related through hadith texts, as long as they do not contradict those conveyed by the hadith [n: since the above words were a mere enhancement and addendum to the known, sunna *dhikr*]."

(3) Bukhari relates from ‘A’isha (Allah be well pleased with her) that "the Prophet (Allah bless him and give him peace) dispatched a man at the head of a military expedition who recited the Koran for his companions at prayer, finishing each recital with al-Ikhlas (Koran 112). When they returned, they mentioned this to the Prophet (Allah bless him and give him peace), who told them, 'Ask him why he does this,' and when they

[. . .] قال الحـافظ ابن حجر في الفتـح : يستفـاد منه جواز الاجتهاد في توقيت العبادة لأن بلالاً توصل إلى ما ذكره بالاستنباط فصوبه الرسول ﷺ .

ومثل هذا حديث خبيب في البخاري وفيه وهو أول من سن الصلاة لكل مقتول صبراً ركعتين . فهـذه الأحاديث صريحة في أن بلالاً وخبيبـاً اجتهـدا في توقيت العبـادة ولم يسبق من الرسول ﷺ أمر ولا فعل إلا الطلب العام . [. . .] .

(٢) ما رواه البـخـاري ومـسـلم [وغيرهمـا في كتاب الصلاة في باب ربنا لك الحمد] عن رفاعة بن رافع قال : كنا نصلي وراء النبي ﷺ فلما رفع رأسه من الـركعة قال : سمع الله لمن حمده قال رجل وراءه : ربنا لك الحمد حمداً كثيراً طيباً مبـاركـاً فيه . فلما انصرف قال : من المتكلم ؟ قال : أنـا ؛ قال : رأيت بضعة وثلاثين ملكاً يبتدرونها أيهم يكتبها .

قال الحافظ في الفتح : يستدل به على جواز إحداث ذكر في الصلاة غير مأثور إذا كان غيـر مخالف للمأثور [وعلى جواز رفع الصوت بالذكر ما لم يشوش] . [. . .] .

(٣) روى البـخـاري [مـن كتـاب التـوحيد] عن عائشة رضي الله عنها أن النبي ﷺ بعث رجلاً على سرية وكان يقرأ لأصحـابـه في صلاته فيختم بقل هو الله أحد . فلما رجعوا ذكروا ذلك للنبي ﷺ فقـال : سلوه لأي شيء يصنـع ذلـك ؛

asked him, the man replied, 'Because it describes the All-merciful, and I love to recite it.' The Prophet (Allah bless him and give him peace) said to them, 'Tell him Allah loves him.' "

In spite of this, we do not know of any scholar who holds that doing the above is recommended, for the acts the Prophet (Allah bless him and give him peace) used to do regularly are superior, though his confirming the like of this illustrates his sunna regarding his acceptance of various forms of obedience and acts of worship, and shows he did not consider the like of this to be a reprehensible innovation (bid'a), as do the bigots who vie with each other to be the first to brand acts as innovation and misguidance. Further, it will be noticed that all the preceding hadiths are about the *prayer*, which is the most important of bodily acts of worship, and of which the Prophet (Allah bless him and give him peace) said,

"Pray as you have seen me pray,"

despite which he accepted the above examples of personal reasoning because they did not depart from the form defined by the Lawgiver, for every limit must be observed, while there is latitude in everything besides, as long as it is within the general category of being called for by Sacred Law. This is the sunna of the Prophet and his way (Allah bless him and give him peace) and is as clear as can be. Islamic scholars infer from it that every act for which there is evidence in Sacred Law that it is called for and which does not oppose an unequivocal primary text or entail harmful consequences is not included in the category of reprehensible innovation (bid'a), but rather is of the sunna, even if there should exist something whose performance is superior to it.

(4) Bukhari relates from Abu Sa'id al-Khudri that a band of the Companions of the Prophet (Allah bless him and give him peace) departed on one of their journeys, alighting at the encampment of some desert Arabs whom they asked to be their hosts, but who refused to have them as guests. The leader of the encampment was stung by a scorpian, and his followers tried everything to cure him, and when all had failed,

فسألوه فقال : لأنها صفة الرحمن وأنا أحب أن أقرأ بها . فقال النبي ﷺ : أخبروه أن الله يحبه .

[...] ومع كل هذا فلم نعلم أن أحداً من العلماء قال باستحباب ذلك ... لأن ما واظب عليه الرسول ﷺ هو الأفضل ولكن إقراره لمثل هذا يوضح سنته ﷺ في قبول ما كان مثل ذلك من أوجه الطاعات والعبادات ولا يعتبر مثله حدثاً مذموماً كما يتسابق المتشددون إلى التبديع والتضليل في الأفعال ... والأحاديث التي مرت كلها في الصلاة كما ترى وهي أهم أعمال العبادات البدنية وفيها قول الرسول ﷺ : «صلوا كما رأيتموني أصلي» ومع ذلك قبل هذه الاجتهادات لأنها لا تخرج عن الهيئة التي حددها الشارع . فكل حد لا بد من الالتزام به ، وما عدا ذلك فالأمر متسع مادام داخلاً في الأصل المطلوب . هذه هي سنة الرسول وطريقته وهذا في غاية الوضوح ويؤخذ منها ما أصله العلماء أن كل عمل يشهد له الشرع من الطلب ولم يصادم نصاً تترتب عليه مفسدة فليس داخلاً في حدود البدعة بل هو من السنة وإن كان غيره أفضل .

(٤) [حديث الرقية وقد] رواه البخاري [في أكثر من موضع من صحيحه وهذا نصه في باب النفث في الرقية :] عن أبي سعيد الخدري رضي الله عنه أن رهطاً من أصحاب النبي ﷺ انطلقوا في سفرة سافروها حتى نزلوا على حي من أحياء العرب فاستضافوهم فأبوا أن يضيفوهم فلُدِغَ سيد ذلك الحي [ت : أي لدغته عقرب ، كما في رواية الترمذي] فسعوا له بكل شيء فلم ينفعه

one said, "If you'd approach the group camped near you, one of them might have something." So they came to them and said, "O band of men, our leader has been stung and we've tried everything. Do any of you have something for it?" and one of them replied, "Yes, by Allah, I recite healing words [ruqya, def: w17] over people, but by Allah, we asked you to be our hosts and you refused, so I will not recite anything unless you give us a fee." They then agreed upon a herd of sheep, so the man went and began spitting and reciting the Fatiha over the victim until he got up and walked as if he were a camel released from its hobble, nothing the matter with him. They paid the agreed upon fee, which some of the Companions wanted to divide up, but the man who had done the reciting told them, "Do not do so until we reach the Prophet (Allah bless him and give him peace) and tell him what has happened, to see what he may order us to do." They came to the Prophet (Allah bless him and give him peace) and told him what had occurred, and he said, "How did you know it was of the words which heal? You were right. Divide up the herd and give me a share."

The hadith is explicit that the Companion had no previous knowledge that reciting the Fatiha to heal (ruqya) was countenanced by Sacred Law, but rather did so because of his own personal reasoning (ijtihad), and since it did not contravene anything that had been legislated, the Prophet (Allah bless him and give him peace) confirmed him therein because it was of his sunna and way to accept and confirm what contained good and did not entail harm, even if it did not proceed from the acts of the Prophet himself (Allah bless him and give him peace) as a definitive precedent.

(5) Bukhari relates from Abu Sa'id al-Khudri that one man heard another reciting al-Ikhlas (Koran 112) over and over again, so when morning came he went to the Prophet (Allah bless him and give him peace) and sarcastically mentioned it to him. The Prophet (Allah bless him and give him peace) said, "By Him in whose hand is my soul, it equals one-third of the Koran." Daraqutni recorded another version of this hadith in which the man said, "I have a neighbor who

شيء، فقال بعضهم : لو أتيتم هؤلاء الرهط الذي نزل بكم لعله يكون عند بعضهم شيء؛ فأتوهم فقالوا : يا أيها الرهط إن سيدنا لدغ فسعينا له بكل شيء فهل عند أحدمنكم شيء؟ فقال بعضهم : نعم والله إني لراق ولكن والله لقد استضفناكم فلم تضيفونا فما أنا براق لكم حتى تجعلوا لنا جعلاً . فصالحوهم على قطيع من الغنم فانطلق فجعل يتفل ويقرأ الحمد لله رب العالمين حتى لكأنما نشط من عقال فانطلق يمشي ما به قلبة فأوفوهم جعلهم الذي صالحوهم عليه فقال بعضهم : اقسموا، وقال الذي رقى : لا تفعلوا حتى نأتي رسول الله ﷺ فنذكر له الذي كان فننظر ما يأمرنا به ؛ فقدموا على رسول الله ﷺ فذكروا له فقال : وما يدريك أنها رقية أصبتم، اقسموا وأضربوا لي معكم بسهم .

[. . .] وهذا صريح في أن الصحابي لم يكن عنده علم متقدم بمشروعية الرقي بالفاتحة، ولكنه شيء فعله باجتهاده ولما لم يكن فيه مخالفة للمشروع أقره الرسول ﷺ لأن هذه سنته وطريقته في إقرار ما كان من الخير ولا تترتب عليه مفسدة وإن لم يكن من عمل الرسول ﷺ نصاً .

(٥) في البخاري [في فضائل قل هو الله أحد] عن أبي سعيد الخدري أن رجلاً سمع رجلاً يقرأ بقل هو الله أحد يرددها فلما أصبح جاء إلى النبي ﷺ وآله وسلم فذكر له ذلك وكان الرجل يتقالها فقال ﷺ : والذي نفسي بيده إنها لتعدل ثلث القرآن .

[. . .] وقد خرّج الدارقطني [. . .] هذا الحديث بلفظ : إن لي جاراً يقوم

prays at night and does not recite anything but al-Ikhlas."

The hadith shows that the Prophet (Allah bless him and give him peace) confirmed the person's restricting himself to this sura while praying at night, despite its not being what the Prophet himself did (Allah bless him and give him peace), for though the Prophet's practice of reciting from the whole Koran was superior, the man's act was within the general parameters of the sunna and there was nothing blameworthy about it in any case.

(6) Ahmad and Ibn Hibban relate from 'Abdullah ibn Burayda that his father said, "I entered the mosque with the Prophet (Allah bless him and give him peace), where a man was at prayer, supplicating: 'O Allah, I ask You by the fact that I testify You are Allah, there is no god but You, the One, the Ultimate, who did not beget and was not begotten, and to whom none is equal,' and the Prophet (Allah bless him and give him peace) said, 'By Him in whose hand is my soul, he has asked Allah by His greatest name, which if He is asked by it He gives, and if supplicated He answers.'"

It is plain that this supplication came spontaneously from the Companion, and since it conformed to what the Sacred Law calls for, the Prophet (Allah bless him and give him peace) confirmed it with the highest degree of approbation and acceptance, while it is not known that the Prophet (Allah bless him and give him peace) had ever taught it to him (*Adilla Ahl al-Sunna wa al-Jama'a* (y119), 119–33).

COMMENTARY ON THE HADITH
"EVERY INNOVATION IS MISGUIDANCE"

w29.3 The Prophet (Allah bless him and give him peace) said,

"... Beware of matters newly begun, for every innovation is misguidance."

بالليل فما يقرأ إلا بقل هو الله أحد اهـ.

وفي الحديث إقرار الرسول ﷺ على هذا التخصيص والاقتصار على هذه السورة في قيام الليل مع ما فيه من التخصيص الذي لم يكن من عمله ﷺ. [. . .] وما كان عليه عمل الرسول من القراءة بالقرآن كله أفضل من ذلك ولكن عمله وما يشبهه داخل في نطاق السنة وليس ما يذم بل هو محمود على كل حال.

(٦) روى [أصحاب السنن و] أحمد وابن حبان [في صحيحه] عن عبد بن بريدة عن أبيه قال: دخلت مع رسول الله ﷺ المسجد فإذا رجل يصلي يدعو: اللَّهُمَّ إِنِّي أَسْأَلُكَ بِأَنِّي أَشْهَدُ أَنَّكَ أَنْتَ اللَّهُ لَا إِلَهَ إِلَّا أَنْتَ الْأَحَدُ الصَّمَدُ الَّذِي لَمْ يَلِدْ وَلَمْ يُولَدْ وَلَمْ يَكُنْ لَهُ كُفُوًا أَحَدٌ؛ فقال النبي ﷺ: والذي نفسي بيده لقد سأل الله باسمه الأعظم الذي إذا سئل به أعطى وإذا دعي به أجاب اهـ.

وهذا دعاء أنشأه الصحابي فيما يظهر ولما كان مطابقاً للمطلوب أقره ﷺ بأعلى درجات الإقرار والرضاء ولم يعلم أن الرسول ﷺ علمه إياه [محرر من أدلة أهل السنة والجماعة: ١٢٣ ـ ١٣٣؛ بتقديم وتأخير].

شرح حديث «كل بدعة ضلالة»

w29.3 قال النبي ﷺ: «. . . . وإياكم ومحدثات الأمور، فإن كل بدعة ضلالة» [من حديث رواه أبو داود والترمذي وقال: حديث حسن صحيح].

Beware of matters newly begun

(Muhammad Jurdani:) meaning, "Distance yourselves and be wary of matters newly innovated that did not previously exist," i.e. things invented in Islam that contravene the Sacred Law,

for every innovation is misguidance

meaning that every innovation is the opposite of the truth, i.e. falsehood, a hadith that has been related elsewhere as:

for every newly begun matter is innovation, every innovation is misguidance, and every misguidance is in hell

meaning that everyone who is misguided, whether through himself or by following another, is in hell, the hadith referring to matters that are not good innovations with a basis in Sacred Law. It has been stated (A: by 'Izz ibn 'Abd al-Salam) that innovations (bid'a) fall under the five headings of the Sacred Law (n: i.e. the obligatory, unlawful, recommended, offensive, and permissible):

(1) The first category comprises innovations that are *obligatory,* such as recording the Koran and laws of Islam in writing when it was feared that something might be lost from them; the study of the disciplines of Arabic that are necessary to understand the Koran and sunna such as grammar, word declension, and lexicography; hadith classification to distinguish between genuine and spurious prophetic traditions; and the philosophical refutations of arguments advanced by the Mu'tazilites (def: w6.4) and the like.

(2) The second category is that of *unlawful* innovations such as non-Islamic taxes and levies (dis: p32), giving positions of authority in Sacred Law to those unfit for them, and devoting one's time to learning the beliefs of heretical sects that contravene the tenets of faith (def: v1–2) of Ahl al-Sunna.

(3) The third category consists of *recommended* innovations such as building hostels and schools of Sacred Law, recording the research of Islamic schools of legal thought, writing books on beneficial subjects, extensive research into fundamentals and particular applications of Sacred Law, in-depth studies of Arabic linguistics, the

(محمد الجرداني:) [...] [...] «...»
وإياكم ومحدثات» ([كلاهما منصوب بفعل مضمر، والتقدير:] باعدوا أنفسكم واحذروا محدثات» «الأمور» (أي الأمور المحدثة أي المخترعة في الدين المخالفة للشريعة) «فإن كل بدعة ضلالة» (أي خلاف الحق أي باطل وجاء في بعض روايات هذا الحديث:)
«فإن كل محدث بدعة وكل بدعة ضلالة وكل ضلالة في النار» (يعني صاحبها، من فاعل ومتبع. وهذا في غير البدعة الحسنة التي ترجع إلى أصل شرعي.
وقد قيل إن البدعة تنقسم إلى الأحكام الخمسة (ت: أي الواجب، والحرام، والمندوب، والمكروه، والمباح):
الأولى واجبة كتدوين القرآن والشرائع إذا خيف عليها الضياع وكالاشتغال بالعلوم العربية المتوقف عليها فهمُ الكتاب والسنة كالنحو والصرف واللغة وكتمييز صحيح الأحاديث من سقيمها والرد على نحو المعتزلة.
الثانية محرمة كالمكوس والمظالم وتولية المناصب الشرعية من لا يصلح لها والاشتغال بمذاهب أهل الضلال المخالفين لما عليه أهل السنة.
الثالثة المندوبة كبناء الربط ومدارس العلم الشرعي وتدوين المذاهب وتصنيف العلوم المستحسنة شرعاً وتقرير القواعد وكثرة التفريع وتتبع كلام العرب

reciting of *wirds* (def: w20) by those with a Sufi path (A: or circles of *dhikr* in which the movement of the participants increases their remembrance of Allah), and commemorating the birth (mawlid, dis: w58) of the prophet Muhammad (Allah bless him and give him peace) and wearing one's best and rejoicing at it.

(4) The fourth category includes innovations that are *offensive,* such as embellishing mosques, decorating the Koran, and having a backup man (muballigh) loudly repeat the spoken Allahu Akbar of the imam when the latter's voice is already clearly audible to those praying behind him.

(5) The fifth category is that of innovations that are *permissible,* such as sifting flour, using spoons, and having more enjoyable food, drink, and housing.

(*al-Jawahir al-lu'lu'iyya fi sharh al-Arba'in al-Nawawiyya* (y68), 220–21)

w29.4 ('Abdullah Muhammad Ghimari:) In his *al-Qawa'id al-kubra,* 'Izz ibn 'Abd al-Salam classifies innovations (bid'a), according to their benefit, harm, or indifference, into the five categories of rulings: the obligatory, recommended, unlawful, offensive, and permissible; giving examples of each and mentioning the principles of Sacred Law that verify his classification. His words on the subject display his keen insight and comprehensive knowledge of both the principles of jurisprudence and the human advantages and disadvantages in view of which the Lawgiver has established the rulings of Sacred Law.

Because his classification of innovation (bid'a) was established on a firm basis in Islamic jurisprudence and legal principles, it was confirmed by Imam Nawawi, Ibn Hajar 'Asqalani, and the vast majority of Islamic scholars, who received his words with acceptance and viewed it obligatory to apply them to the new events and contingencies that occur with the changing times and the peoples who live in them. One may not support the denial of his classification by clinging to the hadith "Every innovation is misguidance,"

وأوراد أهـل الطـريـق ، واصطنـاع مولـد المصطفى ﷺ وإظهـار الـزينـة والسرور به .

الـرابعـة المكـروهة كزخرفة المسـاجد وتـزويق المصـاحف والتبليـغ حيث بلغ المأمومين صوت الإمام .

الخـامسـة المبـاحـة كاتخاذ المنـاخل والمـلاعق والتـوسعـة في لذيـذ المـآكل والمشـارب والمسـاكن [نقل من الجواهر اللـؤلـؤيـة في شرح الأربعين النـوويـة : ٢٢٠ - ٢٢١].

w29.4 (عبد الله محمد الغماري:) قسم عز [الـديـن] بن عبـد السـلام في قواعـده الكبرى البـدعة باعتبار اشتمالها على المصلحة والمفسدة أو خلوها عنهما إلى أقسـام الحكم الخمسـة : الـوجوب والنـدب والحـرمـة والكـراهة والإبـاحة ، ومثـل لكل قسم منها وذكر ما يشهد له من قواعد الشـريعـة . وكلامه في ذلك كلام ناقد بصير أحاط خبراً بالقواعد الفقهية وعـرف المصـالح والمفاسد التي اعتبرها الشـارع في ترتيب الأحكـام على وفقها . [ومن مثـل سلطـان العلمـاء في معـرفـة ذلك؟] فجاء تقسيمه للبدعة مؤسساً على أساس من الفقه وقـواعـده متين ، ولـذا وافقه عليه الإمـام النووي والحافظ ابن حجـر وجمهور العلمـاء وتلقـوا كلامـه بالقبـول ، ورأوا أن العمـل به متعين في النـوازل والـوقـائـع التي تحدث مع تطور الـزمـان وأهـله [. . .] ولا يمكـن أن يتمسـك لإنكـاره بحديث «كـل بدعـة

because the only form of innovation that is without exception misguidance is that concerning tenets of faith, like the innovations of the Mu'tazilites, Qadarites, Murji'ites, and so on, that contradicted the beliefs of the early Muslims. This is the innovation of misguidance because it is harmful and devoid of benefit. As for innovation in works, meaning the occurrence of an act connected with worship or something else that did not exist in the first century of Islam, it must necessarily be judged according to the five categories mentioned by 'Izz ibn 'Abd al-Salam. To claim that such innovation is misguidance without further qualification is simply not applicable to it, for new things are among the exigencies brought into being by the passage of time and generations, and nothing that is new lacks a ruling of Allah Most High that is applicable to it, whether explicitly mentioned in primary texts, or inferable from them in some way. The only reason that Islamic law can be valid for every time and place and be the consummate and most perfect of all divine laws is because it comprises general methodological principles and universal criteria, together with the ability its scholars have been endowed with to understand its primary texts, the knowledge of types of analogy and parallelism, and the other excellences that characterize it. Were we to rule that every new act that has come into being after the first century of Islam is an innovation of misguidance without considering whether it entails benefit or harm, it would invalidate a large share of the fundamental bases of Sacred Law as well as those rulings established by analogical reasoning, and would narrow and limit the Sacred Law's vast and comprehensive scope (*Adilla Ahl al-Sunna wa al-Jama'a* (y119), 145–47).

*

w30.0 MIRACLES (KARAMAT)
(from f15.2)

w30.1 (Nawawi:) Muslim orthodoxy affirms the existence of miracles vouchsafed to the friends of Allah (awliya', def: w33), and that they occur and

ضلالة» لأن البدعـة التي هي ضلالة من غير استثناء هي البدعـة الاعتقادية كالمعتقـدات التي أحـدثهـا المعتـزلـة والقـدرية والمرجئة ونحوهم على خلاف ما كان يعتقـده السلف الصالح فهذه هي البـدعـة التي هي ضلالة لأنهـا مفسدة لا مصلحة فيهـا . أما البدعة العملية بمعنى حدوث عمل له تعلق بالعبـادة أو غيرهـا ولم يكن في الـزمن الأول فهـذا لا بد فيه من التقسيم الـذي ذكره عز [الـدين] ابن عبد السلام ولا يتأتى فيه القول بأنه ضلالة على الإطـلاق ، لأنه من باب الوقائع التي تحـدث على مـر الزمان والأجيال ، وكل واقعـة لا تخلو عن حكم لله تعـالى إمـا منصـوص عليـه أو مستنبط بوجه من وجوه الاستنباط ، والشريعة إنما صلحت لكل زمـان ومكان وكانت خاتمة الشرائع الإلهيـة وأكملها بما حوته من قواعد عامة وضـوابط كليـة ، مع ما أوتيه علماؤها من قوة الفهم في نصـوصهـا ومعرفة بالقياس والاستصحـاب وأنـواعهمـا إلى غير ذلك مما خصت به شريعتنا الغراء ، ولو [اتبعنا طريقـة الشاطبي و] حكمنا على كل عمل حدث بعد العصر الأول بأنه بدعة ضلالة من غيـر أن نعتبـر ما فيـه من مصلحة أو مفسـدة لزم ذلك إهـدار جانب كبيـر من قواعد الشريعة وقياساتها وتضييق لدائرتها الـواسعة [محرر من أدلة أهـل السنة والجماعة : ١٤٥ ـ ١٤٧].

w30.0 ثبوت الكرامات

w30.1 (النووي :) [اعلم أن] مذهب أهل الحق إثبات كرامـات الأولياء وأنها

917

exist throughout all eras of history, as is attested to by both rational evidence and the explicit texts of verses of the Holy Koran and numerous prophetic hadiths. As for the Koranic verses, they include:

(1) the word of Allah Most High in the story of Maryam,

" 'Shake the trunk of the palm tree towards you, and it will let fall fresh ripe dates upon you' " (Koran 19:25),

while Maryam, by scholarly consensus, was not a prophet (n: Qurtubi says, "By the word 'shake,' Allah ordered her to jar the withered palm trunk, that she might behold another of His miracles in reviving the lifeless tree" (al-Jami' li ahkam al-Qur'an (y117), 11.94));

(2) "Every time Zakariyya entered the Sanctuary, he found provision with her. He said, 'O Maryam, from whence has this come to you?' And she said, 'It is from Allah' " (Koran 3:37)

(n: Qurtubi says, "When Zakariyya used to enter where she was, he would find the fruits of wintertime with her in summer, and the fruits of summertime in winter, so he asked her, 'O Maryam, from whence has this come to you?' And she said, 'It is from Allah' " (al-Jami' li ahkam al-Qur'an (y117), 4.71));

(3) from the story of Sulayman's companion (N: who "possessed knowledge of the Book," and instantly brought from afar the throne of the Queen of Sheba to Sulayman (upon whom be peace)),

"... 'I will bring it to you before your glance returns to yourself' " (Koran 27:40)

(n: Qurtubi says, "According to most Koranic commentators, 'he who possessed knowledge of the Book' was Asuf ibn Barkhiya of the Israelites, a siddiq (lit. "one of great faith") who knew the greatest name of Allah, which if He is asked by it He gives, and if supplicated He answers (al-Jami' li ahkam al-Qur'an (y117), 13.204));

واقعـة موجـودة مستمـرة في الأعصـار. ويـدل عليـه دلائـل العقـول وصرائـح النقـول. [...].

وأمـا النقـول فآيات في القرآن العظيم وأحاديث مستفيضة أمـا الآيـات فقولـه تعالى في قصة مريم:

﴿وَهُزِّي إِلَيْكِ بِجِذْعِ النَّخْلَةِ تُسَاقِطْ عَلَيْكِ رُطَبَاً جَنِيَّاً﴾ [مريم: ٢٥].

(ت: قال القـرطبي: قولـه تعالـى: ﴿وَهُزِّي﴾ أمرها بهز الجذع اليابس لترى آيـة أخرى في إحيـاء موات الجذع [نقل من الجامـع لأحكـام القـرآن: ١١/ ٩٤].)، [...] ولم تكـن مريـم نبيـة بإجماع العلماء [...].

(٢) وقـوله تعالى: ﴿كُلَّمَا دَخَلَ عَلَيْهَا زَكَرِيَّا الـمِحْرَابَ وَجَدَ عِنْدَهَا رِزْقَاً، قَالَ يَا مَرْيَـمُ أَنَّـى لَكِ هذا، قَالَـتْ هُوَمِنْ عِنْـدِ اللّهِ﴾ [آل عمران: ٣٧].

(ت: قال القـرطبي: كان زكـريـا إذا دخـل عليهـا يجد عندها فاكهة الشتاء في القيـظ وفـاكهـة القيظ في الشتاء فقال: يا مريم أنَّى لَكِ هذا؟ فقالـت: هو من عند الله [نقل من الجامع لأحكام القرآن: ٤/ ٧١].)

(٣) ومن ذلك قصة صاحب سلمـان عليه السلام حيث قال:

﴿أَنَا آتِيـكَ بِه قَبْـلَ أَنْ يَرْتَـدَّ إِلَيْـكَ طَرْفُكَ﴾ [النمل: ٤٠].

(ت: قال القـرطبي: أكثر المفسرين على أن الـذي عنـده علم الكتاب آصف بن برخيـا وهو من بني إسرائيـل وكان صدِّيقـاً يحفظ اسم الله الأعظم الذي إذا سئـل بـه أعطـى، وإذا دعـي بـه أجاب [نقل من الجامع لأحكام القرآن: ١٣/ ٢٠٤].)

(4) and finally, all the miraculous events that took place in the story of the People of the Cave (Koran 18), who by scholarly consensus were not prophets.

As for hadiths that furnish evidence of miracles, there are many, such as:

(1) the hadith of the three people who took shelter in a cave, and when a great stone sealed off its entrance, each in turn made supplication to Allah, and the stone was moved aside for them, a hadith recorded in the *Sahih*s of Bukhari and Muslim;

(2) and the famous hadith recorded by Bukhari and others about the story of Khubayb al-Ansari (Allah be well pleased with him), a Companion of the Prophet (Allah bless him and give him peace), of whom Bint Harith said: "By Allah, I never saw a better prisoner than Khubayb. By Allah, one day I found him eating from a bunch of grapes in his hand, though he was manacled in irons and there was no fruit in all of Mecca."

The hadiths, narratives of the Companions, and accounts of the early and later Muslims on this subject are beyond number, and there is a sufficiency in those we have just mentioned (*Bustan al-'arifin* (y104), 142–54).

KINDS OF MIRACLES

w30.2 (Ibrahim Bajuri:) An inimitable prophetic miracle (mu'jiza) is an event contravening natural laws that appears at the hands of someone who claims to be a prophet and is challenged by those who deny this, such that the deniers are unable to perform the like of it. Such inimitable miracles are distinguished from:

(1) miracles of divine favor (karamat) which appear at the hands of servants of manifest righteousness (N: who are not prophets, as opposed to the above);

(2) miracles of provender (ma'una) (N: such as food being miraculously increased to feed a

وأما الأحاديث، فكثيرة:

(١) [...و] منها حديث أصحاب الغار الثلاثة الذين أووا إلى الغار فأطبقت صخرة عليهم بابه، فدعا كل واحد منهم بدعوة فانفرجت عنهم الصخرة، وهو مخرج في صحيحي البخاري ومسلم.

(٢) [...] ومنها الحديث المشهور في صحيح البخاري وغيره في قصة خبيب الأنصاري [بضم الخاء المعجمة] رضي الله تعالى عنه صاحب رسول الله ﷺ، وقول بنت الحارث: والله ما رأيت أسيراً قط خيراً من خبيب، والله لقد وجدته يوماً يأكل من قطف عنب في يده وأنه لموثق في الحديد وما بمكة من ثمر.

[...] والأحاديث والآثار وأقوال السلف والخلف في هذا الباب أكثر من أن تحصر، فيُكتفى بما أشرنا إليه [محرر من بستان العارفين: ١٤٢ - ١٥٤].

أنواع خوارق العادات

w30.2 (إبراهيم الباجوري:) [واعلم أن] المعجزة [...] هي أمر يظهر بخلاف العادة على يد مدعي النبوة عند تحدّي المنكرين على وجه يعجز المنكرين عن الإتيان بمثله. [...] وخرج بذلك:

(١) الكرامة وهي ما يظهر على يد عبد ظاهر الصلاح.

(٢) والمعونة وهي ما يظهر على يد

multitude), which appear at the hands of ordinary people to save them from hardship;

(3) miracles of delusion (istidraj), which consist of supernatural events that appear at the hands of an unrighteous person as a manifestation of Allah's intention to deceive him and lead him further astray;

(4) miracles of humiliation (ihana), which are supernatural events that appear at the hands of someone to show the falsity of his claims, as happened to (N: the false prophet) Musaylima the Liar, who spat in the eye of a one-eyed man to restore his sight, and the man's good eye went blind;

(5) miracles portending a prophetic mission (irhas), which occur before prophethood or messengerhood to establish the way for it, such as the cloud that gave shade to the Prophet (Allah bless him and give him peace) (N: in his youth, moving as he did and stopping as he did, while he was journeying with a caravan to Syria) before his prophetic mission;

(6) and sorcery (sihr) and also stage magic (sha'badha), which is accomplished by sleight of hand, making the illusory seem real.

(*Sharh Jawhara al-tawhid al-musamma Tuhfa al-murid* (y24), 133)

العوام تخليصاً لهم من شدة.

(٣) والاستدارج وهو ما يظهر على يد فاسق خديعةً ومكراً به.

(٤) والإهانـة وهي ما يظهر على يده تكذيباً له كما وقع لمسيلمة الكذاب، فإنه تفل في عين أعور لتبرأ فعميت الصحيحة [. . .].

(٥) و[خـرج بذلك] الإرهاص وهو ما كان قبـل النبـوة والـرسـالـة تأسيـساً لهـا كإظلال الغمام له ﷺ قبل البعثة [. . .].

(٦) و[خـرج بذلـك] السحـر ومنـه الشعبـذة وهي خفة في اليـد يرى أن لهـا حقيقة ولا حقيقة لها [. . .] [محرر من شـرح جوهـرة التـوحيـد المسمـاة تحفـة المريد: ١٣٣].

*

w31.0 OBTAINING BLESSINGS (TABARRUK) THROUGH THE RIGHTEOUS (from g3.9)

w31.0 التبرك بالصالحين
وآثارهم

w31.1 (A:) To hold that things have properties that cause benefit or harm independently of the will of Allah is unbelief (kufr), whether such properties are considered natural or supernatural. But the contention of certain people that showing veneration (ta'zim) for the righteous or that obtaining blessings (tabarruk) through them or their effects constitutes *worship* of them or associating others with Allah (shirk) is not supportable by the prophetic sunna, which attests to the contrary, as may be seen from the following hadiths:

(1) Bukhari relates that 'Uthman ibn 'Abdullah said: "My wife sent me to Umm Salama with a cup of water [here the subnarrator Isra'il closed three fingers to show its size] in which to dip a lock containing some of the Prophet's hair (Allah bless him and give him peace). Whenever a person was suffering from the evil eye or an illness, they would send her a vessel of water [A: which Umm Salama would dip the hair in, for treating the ill by their drinking it or washing with it]. I looked into the metal bell [N: holding the lock of hair] and saw some red hairs."

(2) Bukhari relates from Abu Musa that "the Prophet (Allah bless him and give him peace) called for a vessel of water, washed his hands and face in it, spat a mouthful of water back into it and then said to Abu Musa and Bilal, 'Drink from it and pour the rest over your faces and chests.'"

(3) Bukhari relates from Mahmud ibn Rabi' that "when the Prophet (Allah bless him and give him peace) performed his ablution, the Companions almost fought over the excess water."

The Prophet (Allah bless him and give him peace) would never have permitted the like of this if there were any suspicion of associating partners with Allah (shirk) in it. In each of the above hadiths and others, there is a clear basis for the legal validity of obtaining blessings through the effects of the righteous (tabarruk), as it was done with the Prophet's consent and wish by the Companions, this being the reason that Muslims after them have also done so. And Allah knows best.

*

w32.0 INSTRUCTING THE DECEASED (TALQIN) (from g5.6(1))

تلقين الميت w32.0

w32.1 (N:) *Instructing the deceased* (talqin) is when a Muslim sits beside the grave of his fellow Muslim after burial to speak to him, reminding him of the Testification of Faith "There is no god but Allah, Muhammad is the Messenger of Allah," and certain other matters of belief, such as that death is real, paradise is real, hell is real, and that Allah shall raise up those who are in their

(١) روى البخاري [في كتاب اللباس باب ما يذكر في الشيب] عن عثمان بن عبد الله [بن موهب] قال : أرسلني أهلي إلى أم سلمة بقدح من ماء (وقبض إسرائيل ثلاث أصابع) من قصةٍ فيها شعر من شعر النبي ﷺ . وكان إذا أصاب الإنسان عين أو شيء بعث إليها مخضبة . فاطلعتُ في الجلجل فرأيت شعرات حمراء .

(٢) وروى البخاري [في كتاب الوضوء باب استعمال فضل وضوء الناس من حديث أبي جحيفة] قال أبو موسى : دعا النبي ﷺ بقدح فيه ماء فغسل يديه ووجهه فيه ومجّ فيه ثم قال لهما ([ت : أي] أبي موسى وبلال) : «اشربا منه وأفرغا على وجوهكما ونحوركما» .

(٣) وروى البخاري [في نفس الباب من حديث ابن شهاب قال :] أخبرني محمود بن الربيع . . . «إذا توضأ النبي ﷺ كادوا يقتتلون على وضوئه» .

w32.1 (ح :) أما تلقين الميت فهو أن يجلس المسلم عند قبر أخيه المسلم بعد دفنه ليخاطبه مذكراً إياه بشهادة أن لا إله إلا الله وأن محمداً رسول الله . وبعض قواعد العقيدة الإسلامية من أن الموت حق والجنة حق والنار حق وأن الله يبعث

graves—and praying that the deceased will prove steadfast when the two angels question him. It does not have a particular form, but rather anything that accomplishes the above is called "instructing the deceased." The following evidence may be adduced for its validity in Sacred Law:

(1) The rigorously authenticated (sahih) hadith that the Prophet (Allah bless him and give him peace) ordered that the bodies of the idolators slain on the day of Badr be thrown into a well whose interior was uncased with stones, then he approached the well and began calling the unbelievers by their names and fathers' names, saying: "O So-and-so son of So-and-so, and So-and-so son of So-and-so: it would have been easier had you obeyed Allah and His messenger. We have found what our Lord promised to be true; have you found what your Lord promised to be true?" To which 'Umar said, "O Messenger of Allah, why speak to lifeless bodies?" And he replied, "By Him in whose hand is the soul of Muhammad, you do not hear my words better than they do."

(2) The Prophet (Allah bless him and give him peace) said:

"When a servant is laid in his grave and his friends have turned from him and he hears the footfalls of their sandals, two angels come to him, sit him upright, and ask him, 'What were you wont to say of this man Muhammad (Allah bless him and give him peace)?' The believer will answer, 'I testify that he is the slave of Allah and His messenger,' and it will be said, 'Look at your place in hell, Allah has changed it for a place in paradise,' and the man will behold both of them...."

(3) 'Uthman ibn 'Affan (Allah be well pleased with him) relates that when the Prophet (Allah bless him and give him peace) used to finish burying someone, he would stand by the grave and say, "All of you, ask Allah to forgive your brother and make him steadfast, for he is now being asked."

(4) Abu Umama said, "When I die, do with me as the Prophet (Allah bless him and give him

من في القبور. ويدعـو له بالتثبيت عند سؤال الـملكين. وليس للتلقين صيغة معيـنـة بل كل ما يؤدي إلى هذا المعنى يسمى تلقيناً. وقد يستدل لمشروعيته بما يلي:

(١) ورد في الحـديث الصحيـح أن رسول الله ﷺ أمر بقتلى المشركين يوم بدر فألقوا في قليب ثم جاء القليب فجعل ينادي الكفار بأسمائهم وأسماء آبائهم: يا فلان بن فلان ويـا فلان بن فلان أيسـركم أنكم أطعتم الله ورسـوله. فإنا قد وجدنا ما وعـدنـا ربنـا حقـاً فهل وجدتم ما وعد ربكم حقـاً؟ فقال عمر: يا رسول الله ما تكلم من أجسـاد لا أرواح لهـا؛ فقال: والذي نفس محمد بيده ما أنتم بأسمع لما أقول منهم [رواه البخاري].

(٢) [عـن أنس بن مالـك رضي الله عنـه] عن الـنبي ﷺ قال: إن العبـد إذا وضع في قبره وتولى عنه أصحابه وأنه ليسـمع قرع نعـالهم أتـاه ملكان فيقعدانه فيقـولان: ما كنت تقول في هذا الـرجل محمد ﷺ، فأمـا المؤمن فيقول: أشهد أنه عبـد الله ورسـوله، فيقال: انظر إلى مقعـدك من النـار قد أبدلك الله به مقعـداً من الجنة فيراهما جميعاً [الحديث رواه البخاري ومسلم وغيرهما].

(٣) وعن عثمـان بن عفـان رضي الله عنـه قال: كان النبي ﷺ إذا فرغ من دفن الميت وقف عليـه فقـال: «استغفـروا لأخيكم واسألوا له التثبيت فإنه الآن يسأل [رواه أبو داود].

(٤) وروي عن أبي أمامة قال: إذا أنا مت فاصنعوا بي كما أمرنا النبي ﷺ قال:

peace) ordered us, saying, 'When one of your brothers dies and you have smoothed over the earth upon his grave, let one of you stand at the head of the grave and say, "O So-and-so son of So-and-so [n: the latter "So-and-so" is feminine, naming the deceased's mother]"—for he will hear, though he cannot reply—and then say, "O So-and-so son of So-and-so," and he will sit upright; and then say, "O So-and-so son of So-and-so," and he will say, "Direct me, Allah have mercy on you," though you will not hear it, but should say, "Remember the creed upon which you departed from this world, the testification that there is no god but Allah, and Muhammad is His slave and messenger, and that you accepted Allah as your Lord, Islam as your religion, Muhammad as your prophet, and the Koran as your exemplar." For then the two angels Munkar and Nakir will take each other's hand and say, "Let us go, what is there to keep us beside someone who has been instructed how to make his plea?" '

"A man said, 'O Messenger of Allah, what if one does not know the name of his mother?' and he answered, 'Then one should mention his descent from his mother Eve, saying, "O So-and-so son of Eve..." ' "

Tabarani related this hadith in his *al-Muʿjam al-kabir*, and Ibn Hajar ʿAsqalani has said that "its chain of transmission is sound" (*Talkhis al-habir fi takhrij ahadith al-Rafiʿi al-kabir* (y15), 2.143). Some scholars have said that this hadith is not well authenticated (daʿif), while others have gone to the extreme of calling it a forgery.

DISCUSSION OF THE EVIDENCE

w32.2 The first three of the above hadiths, all of them rigorously authenticated (sahih), show that:

(1) a dead person hears the words of a living person speaking to him and even the sounds of movement around him;

(2) the dead are questioned in their graves;

إذا مات أحد من إخوانكم فسويتم التراب على قبره فليقم أحدكم على رأس قبره ثم ليقل : يا فلان بن فلانة ، فإنه يسمعه ولا يجيب ، ثم يقول : يا فلان بن فلانة ، فإنه يستوي قاعداً ثم يقول يا فلان بن فلانة ، فيقول : أرشدنا يرحمك الله ، ولكن لا تشعرون فليقل : اذكر ما خرجت عليه من الدنيا شهادة أن لا إله إلا الله ، وأن محمداً عبده ورسوله ، وأنك رضيت بالله رباً وبالإسلام ديناً وبمحمد نبياً وبالقرآن إماماً فإن منكراً ونكيراً يأخذ كل واحد بيد صاحبه ويقول : انطلق بنا ما يقعدنا عند من لقن حجته؟

فقال رجل : يا رسول الله فإن لم يعرف أمه قال : ينسبه إلى أمه حواء : يا فلان بن حواء .

هذا الحديث رواه الطبراني في معجمه الكبير وقال الحافظ ابن حجر : إسناده صالح ، وبعض العلماء يضعف هذا الحديث وبعضهم يبالغ فيجعله موضوعاً .

مناقشة الأدلة

w32.2 [. . . نستخلص من هذا أن] الأحاديث الثلاثة الأولى وهي أحاديث صحيحة تفيد ما يلي :

(١) أن الميت يسمع كلام الحي إذا خاطبه بل يسمع حركته من حوله .

(٢) أن الميت يسأل في قبره .

(3) and that it is legally valid after burial for a living person to ask Allah to forgive the deceased and make him steadfast for the questioning of the two angels.

As for the fourth hadith, scholars have felt comfortable with it, saying that if the deceased can hear, we should let him hear these words which he is in the direst need of in such circumstances, and even if the hadith that has conveyed them is not well authenticated, its content is valid and true.

The foregoing is what has been said about instructing the deceased (talqin), so whoever does it cannot be blamed, since they have something of a case for it; and whoever does not cannot be blamed, because they do not consider the case sufficient. In any event, we should be anxious to promote love and brotherhood between Muslims, and not divide the ranks with questions like this, for the important thing is our belief in the oneness of Allah, and the unity of the Islamic Community.

(٣) أن من المشروع أن يستغفر الحي للميت بعد دفنه ويطلب له التثبيت عند سؤال الملكين.

أما الحديث الرابع فقد استأنس به العلماء وقالوا إذا كان الميت يسمع فلنسمعه هذه الكلمات التي هو بأمس الحاجة إليها في هذا الموقف وإن كان الحديث الذي ورد بها ليس قوياً لكن مضمونة كلام حق صحيح [. . .]. هذا ما قيل في الموضوع ، وبناء عليه فمن فعله لا ننكر عليه لأن له حجة ما، ومن تركه لا ننكر عليه لأنه لا يرى هذا حجة . [. . .] واحرص على محبة المسلمين وأخوتهم ولا تفرق الصفوف بمثل هذه المسائل ، فأهم شيء توحيد الله ووحدة الأمة [محرر بالتصرف من فتوى للشيخ نوح علي سلمان وقد راجعه المؤلف حفظه الله تعالى].

*

w33.0 THE FRIENDS OF ALLAH (AWLIYA') (from g5.7(4))

w33.0 أولياء الله تعالى

w33.1　Allah Most High says:

"Verily the friends of Allah, no fear shall be upon them, nor shall they sorrow, those who believe and are godfearing. Great tidings are theirs in this life and the world to come. There is no changing the words of Allah, that is the supreme triumph" (Koran 10:62–64).

w33.1 قال الله تعالى :
﴿أَلَا إِنَّ أَوْلِيَاءَ اللَّهِ لَا خَوْفٌ عَلَيْهِمْ وَلَا هُمْ يَحْزَنُونَ، الَّذِينَ آمَنُوا وَكَانُوا يَتَّقُونَ، لَهُمُ الْبُشْرَى فِي الْحَيَاةِ الدُّنْيَا وَفِي الْآخِرَةِ لَا تَبْدِيلَ لِكَلِمَاتِ اللَّهِ ذَلِكَ هُوَ الْفَوْزُ الْعَظِيمُ﴾ [يونس : ٦٢ - ٦٤].

w33.2 (n:) The following rigorously authenticated (sahih) hadith has been translated below with two commentaries, one by 'Abd al-Ra'uf Munawi (M:) and the other by Muhammad ibn 'Allan Bakri (B:).
The Prophet (Allah bless him and give him peace) said:

"Allah Most High says: 'He who is hostile to a friend (wali) of Mine I declare war against. My

w33.2 (ت : قد ترجم الحديث الصحيح التالي بشرحين : أحدهما لعبد الرؤوف المناوي وشرحه مشار إليه بحرف «م»؛ والثاني لمحمد بن علان البكري وشرحه مشار إليه بحرف «ب»).
قال رسول الله ﷺ : «إن الله تعالى قال : من عادى لي ولياً فقد آذنتُهُ بالحرب ، وما تقرب إليَّ عبدي بشيء

slave approaches Me with nothing more beloved to Me than what I have made obligatory for him, and My slave keeps drawing nearer to Me with voluntary works until I love him. And when I love him, I am his hearing with which he hears, his sight with which he sees, his hand with which he seizes, and his foot with which he walks. If he asks Me, I will surely give to him, and if he seeks refuge in Me, I will surely protect him.' "

He who is hostile to a friend (wali) of Mine
(M: *friend* meaning the knower of Allah ('arif billah) who is constant in obedience to Him and sincere in his acts of worship)
(B: that is, he who is close to Allah by his devotion to Him through obeying His commands and shunning the acts He has forbidden)
I declare war against
(M: I inform him that I shall make war upon him, meaning that Allah will deal with him as one at war does, namely, with theophanies against him of manifestations of omnipotent force and majesty, this being the ultimate threat. The words *hostile to a friend (wali)* mean hostile to him for being a friend (wali), not just any hostility whatever. It excludes such things as taking him to court to have him fulfill an obligation. Rather, hostility to him for being a friend of Allah is to deny it out of mere obstinacy or envy, or to disparage or abuse him, and similar kinds of ill-treatment. And when the peril of being hostile toward such a person is appreciated, the reward for friendship with him may likewise be inferred)
(B: *I declare war against* means *I shall fight this enemy for him,* i.e. destroy him. And this is a very severe threat for opposing or having enmity towards someone Allah loves. Too, the affirmation of Allah's fighting the enemies of His friends entails the affirmation of His friendship for those who befriend them).
My slave approaches Me with nothing more beloved to Me than what I have made obligatory for him
(B: meaning the performance of what I have made obligatory for him, whether individually or communally. The obligatory is more beloved to Allah than voluntary devotions because it is more perfect, since the command to do it is absolute, implying a reward for its performance and punish-

أحبّ إليَّ ممـا افترضتُ عليـه ومـا يزال عبدي يتقرب إليَّ بالنـوافـل حتى أحبه ، فإذا أحببتُـهُ كنتُ سمعَـهُ الذي يسمعُ به ، وبصرَهُ الذي يُبصِرُ به ، ويدَهُ التي يبطش بهـا ورجلَهُ التي يمشي بهـا ، وإنْ سألني أعطيتُهُ ولئِنْ استعاذني لأعيذنَّهُ» [رواه البخاري] .

«. . . من عادى لي وليّاً» (م: والمراد بالولي العارف بالله المواظب على طاعته المخلص في عبادته) .

(ب: وهـو القريب من الله لتقربه إليه بامتثال أمره واجتناب نواهيه) .

«فقد آذنته بالحرب» .

(م: أي أعلمته بأني سأحاربه أي أن الله سيعامله معاملة المحارب من التجلي عليه بمظاهـر القهر والجـلال وهذا في الغـايـة القصوى من التهديـد . والمراد عاديّ وليّـاً لأجل ولايتـه لا مطلقاً فخرج نحو محاكمته لخـلاص حق . ومعاداته لولايته إما بإنكارها عناداً أو حسداً أو بسبِّ أو شتمه ونحو ذلك من ضروب الإيذاء . وإذا عُلم ما في معاداته من الوعيد علم ما في موالاته من الثواب) .

(ب: أي إنـي محـارب له عنـه أي مهلكه . وهـذا وعيـد شديـد لمعـانـدتـه ومعاداته مَن أحبه الله تعـالى ويلزم من ثبـوت محاربته تعالى لأعداء أوليائه ثبوت موالاته لمن والاهم) .

«وما تقرّب إليَّ عبدي بشيءٍ أحب إليَّ مما افترضتُ عليه» .

(ب: أي من أداء ما افتـرضتُ عليــه عيناً كان أو كفايةً وإنما كان أحب إليه من النفـل لأنـه أكمـل من حيث أن الأمر به جازم متضمن للثواب على فعله والعقاب

ment for its nonperformance, as opposed to voluntary devotions, whose nonperformance is unpunished, and which, it is said, amount to but one-seventieth of the value of an obligatory act),

and My slave keeps drawing nearer to Me with voluntary works until I love him. And when I love him, I am his hearing

(B: the protector of his hearing)

with which he hears

(B: meaning He who keeps it from being used to hear what is not permissible to listen to, such as slander, talebearing, and the like),

his sight with which he sees

(B: safeguarding it from what is unlawful to look at),

his hand with which he seizes

(B: so that he takes only what is lawful),

and his foot with which he walks

(B: so that he walks only to what is permitted)

(M: in summary, whoever draws near to Allah through what is obligatory, and then through voluntary works, Allah draws him nearer and elevates him from the level of true faith (iman) to the level of the perfection of faith (ihsan, dis: u4) such that the knowledge in his heart becomes visible to the eye of his spiritual perception. To fill one's heart with knowledge of Allah effaces what is other than Him, so that one speaks not except of Him, moves not save at His behest, and if one looks, it is through Him, and if one seizes, it is through Him. And this is the consummate awareness of the oneness of Allah)

(B: the consequence of which is the preservation of the individual's whole person, so that he forsakes selfish desire and is wholly absorbed in obedience. Another interpretive possibility is that the hadith is a metaphor for Allah's help and assistance, as if Allah Most High, figuratively speaking, were to play the role of the senses with which the individual perceives and the limbs he relies on. A variant has the addendum:)

so that through Me he hears, through Me he sees, through Me he seizes, and through Me he walks

(M: concerning which, the sheikhs of the Sufis (Allah Most High be well pleased with them) have had disclosures of the hidden and experiential indications that would make crumbled bones quake. But these are of no use save to those who

على تركه بخلاف النفل فإن الأمر به غير جازم يثاب على فعله ولا يعاقب على تركه ولأنه كما قيل جزء من سبعين جزءاً من الفرض) .

«وما يزال عبدي يتقرب إليّ بالنوافل حتى أحبه فإذا أحببته كنت سمعه» .

(ب : أي حافظ سمعه) .

«الذي يسمع به» .

(ب : أي حافظه عن أن يسمع به ما لا يحل سماعه من غيبة ونميمة وما في معناهما) .

«وبصره الذي يبصر به» .

(ب : أي حافظه عما يحرم النظر إليه) .

«ويده التي يبطش بها» .

(ب : فلا يبطش إلا فيما يحل) .

«ورجله التي يمشي بها» .

(ب : فلا يمشي إلا فيما يحل) .

(م : والحاصل أن مَن تقرب إليه بالفرض ثم النفل قَرَّبَهُ فرقاه من درجة الإيمان إلى مقام الإحسان حتى يصير ما في قلبه من المعرفة يشاهده بعين بصيرته وامتلاء القلب بمعرفته يمحي كل ما سواه فلا ينطق إلا بذكره ولا يتحرك إلا بأمره فإن نظر فبه أو سمع فبه أو بطش فبه وهذا هو كمال التوحيد) .

(ب : وحاصل ذلك حفظ جوارحه وأعضائه حتى يقلع عن الشهوات ويستغرق في الطاعات [. . .] ويجوز أن يكون مجازاً عن نصره وتأييده فكأنه تعالى نزل نفسه منزلة جوارحه التي يدرك بها ويستعين بها تشبيهاً . وزيادةً :) .

«فبي يسمع وبي يبصر وبي يبطش وبي يمشي» .

(م : وللمشائخ الصوفية رضي الله تعالى عنهم في هذا الباب فتوحات غيبية وإشارات ذوقية تهتزّ بها العظام البالية لكنها لا تصلح إلا لمن سلك سبيلهم

tread their path and come to know the wellspring from which they drink, as opposed to those who do not, and are not safe from grave error and falling into the abyss of believing that Allah can indwell in created things (hulul, dis: w7.1), or that other than Him can unite with Him (ittihad, w7.2))

(B: this then, and those who fancy that other than Allah can unite with Him or that Allah can indwell in created things claim that the import of the hadith is not figurative but literal, and that Allah, far exalted above what they say, actually permeates or unifies with one, may Allah render them even viler).

If he asks Me, I will surely give to him

(M: what he asks, as happened to many of the early Muslims),

and if he seeks refuge in Me, I will surely protect him

(M: from what he fears, this being the way of a lover with his beloved. His unquestionable promise, solemnified by the form of the oath (n: in the words "I will surely"), entails that whoever draws near to Him through the above will not have his prayer (du‘a’) rejected).

(*Dalil al-falihin li turuq Riyad al-salihin* (y25), 3.344–46, and *Fayd al-Qadir sharh al-Jami‘ al-saghir* (y91), 2.240–41)

*

w34.0 VISITING GRAVES (from g5.8)

w34.1 (Nawawi:) The Prophet (Allah bless him and give him peace) said,

"I had forbidden you to visit graves, but now visit them...."

This is one of the hadiths that comprise both the ruling that supersedes a previously valid ruling and the one superseded. It explicitly states that the prohibition of men visiting graves has been lifted. Scholars unanimously concur that visiting them is sunna for men. As for women, there is dis-

فعلم مشربهم بخلاف غيرهم فلا يؤمن عليه من الغلط فيهوي في مهواة الحلول والاتحاد) .

(ب : هذا والاتحادية والحلولية قبحهم الله يزعمون أن هذا في حقيقته وأنه تعالى عما يقولون علواً كبيراً حال فيه ومتحد به) .

«وإن سألني أعطيته» .

(م : مسؤوله كما وقع لكثير من السلف) .

«ولئن استعاذني لأعيذنه» .

(م : مما يخاف وهذا حال المحب مع محبوبه وفي وعده المحقق المؤكد بالقسم إيذان بأن من تقرب بما مر لا يرد دعاؤه) .

[محرَّر من دليل الفالحين لطرق رياض الصالحين : ٣/ ٣٤٤ ـ ٣٤٦، ومحرر من فيض القدير شرح الجامع الصغير : ٢/ ٢٤٠ ـ ٢٤١ بتقديم وتأخير] .

w34.0 سنّية زيارة القبور

w34.1 (النـووي :) [عن ابن بريـدة عن أبيه قال :] قال رسول الله ﷺ : «نـهـيـتـكـم عن زيـارة الـقـبـور فزوروها. . .» [رواه مسلم] .

هذا من الأحاديث التي تجمع الناسخ والمنسـوخ وهـو صريـح في نسخ نهي الـرجـال عن زيـارتها . وأجمعوا على أن زيارتها سنة لهم . وأمـا النسـاء ففيهن خلاف لأصحابنا [قدمناه وقدمنا أن] من

agreement among our colleagues about them, those who hold that women may not visit them saying that women are not intended by an address to men (n: the Arabic male plural imperative *zuruha*) (N: though the sounder position in the Shafi'i school is that woman may visit graves as long as it does not entail blameworthy things such as displays of grief, mixing of men and women, and the like. The hadiths prohibiting women from visiting graves are interpreted by Shafi'i scholars as applicable to the time before the prohibition was lifted by the above hadith) (*Sahih Muslim bi Sharh al-Nawawi* (y93), 7.46–47).

*

w35.0 DONATING THE REWARD FOR KORAN RECITAL TO THE DECEASED (from g5.8, end)

w35.1 (Muhammad Makhluf:) As for reciting the Koran for the deceased, whether at his grave or far from it, scholars disagree as to whether the reward for it reaches him. The scholarly majority hold that it does reach him, and this is the truth, especially if the reciter afterwards donates the reward of what he has read to the deceased. In such a case the reciter also receives the reward for his recital without this diminishing anything from the reward of the deceased (*Fatawa shar'iyya wa buhuth Islamiyya* (y79), 2.303).

w35.2 (N:) The position of Hanafis and Hanbalis is that a Muslim is entitled to donate the reward of any kind of worship he performs to whomever he wishes of the Muslim dead. As for Shafi'is and Malikis, they distinguish between acts that are valid to perform in another's stead and those that are not, the former being valid to donate the reward of to the deceased, while the latter are not, though the later scholars of the Shafi'is and Malikis incline toward the validity of donating the reward for any kind of worship whatever to the dead. The Hanafis and Hanbalis adduce the following evidence to support their position:

منعهن قال النساء لا يدخلن في خطاب الـرجـال [. . .] (ح: والأصـح في المـذهب الشافعي جواز زيارة النساء للقبـور ما لم يترتب على ذلك مفسدة شرعيـة كإظهـارهن الحـزن الشـديد أو اختـلاطهن بالـرجـال الأجانب ونحوهما . وأمـا الأحاديث الواردة في نهي النساء عن زيارة القبور فمحمولة عند الشافعية على ما قبـل النسـخ المـذكـور في الحـديث أعـلاه) [محرر من صحيح مسلم بشرح النووي : ٧/ ٤٦ ـ ٤٧].

w35.0 هبـة ثواب قراءة القران وغيرها من القربات للميت

w35.1 (محمـد مخلوف:) وأما قراءة القـرآن للميت سواء أكـانت على القبر أم بعيداً منه ، فقد اختلف الفقهاء في وصول ثوابها إليه ، والجمهور على الوصول وهو الحق ، خصـوصـاً إذا وهب القارىء بعد القـراءة ثواب ما قرأه للميت . وللقـارىء أيضـاً ثواب لا ينقص من أجر الميت شيئاً [نقل من فتاوى شرعية وبحوث إسلامية : ٢ /٣٠٣].

w35.2 (ح:) ذهب الحنفية والحنابلة إلى أن كل قربة فعلها المسلم له أن يهب ثوابهـا لمن شاء من أمـوات المسلمين . [. . .] وأما الشافعية والمالكية فقد فرقوا بين ما تصح فيه النيابة وما لا تصح ، فما تصـح فيه النيابة بجواز التبـرع به عن الميت ومـا لا تصح فيه النيابة لا يصح التبـرع به ، ولكن متأخـريهم يميلون إلى جواز التبرع بالكل . [. . .].
استدل الحنفية والحنابلة بما يلي :

(1) Bukhari and Muslim relate that the Prophet (Allah bless him and give him peace) sacrificed two rams of predominately white color, one for himself and the other for his Community (Umma). The evidence therein is that the Prophet (Allah bless him and give him peace) offered sacrifice animals and donated the reward to his Community, which includes both the living and the dead, both those who existed at his time and those who came after.

(2) Anas relates that he said to the Prophet (Allah bless him and give him peace): "O Messenger of Allah, we give in charity, perform the pilgrimage, and supplicate for our dead. Does this reach them?" He replied, "Yes, indeed it reaches them, and they rejoice thereat just as one of you rejoices at the gift of a tray of food."

(3) The Prophet (Allah bless him and give him peace) said, "Whoever dies with an obligatory fast to perform, his responsible family member may fast it in his stead."

(4) The Prophet (Allah bless him and give him peace) said, "Recite Ya Sin [Koran 36] over your dead."

(5) Allah Mighty and Majestic has informed us that the angels ask forgiveness for believers, as He says,

"The angels glorify their Lord with praise and ask forgiveness for those on earth" (Koran 42:5),

and He praises believers who ask forgiveness for their brethren, by saying,

"... And those who come after them say, 'Lord, forgive us and our brethren who have preceded us in faith'" (Koran 59:10).

(6) And the Prophet (Allah bless him and give him peace) used to supplicate for those he performed the funeral prayer over—the evidence in all of the above being that supplications (du'a) are an act of worship, for the Prophet (Allah bless him and give him peace) said,

---

(١) أن النبي ﷺ ضحّى بكبشين أملحين أحدهما عن نفسه والآخر عن أمته، رواه البخاري ومسلم. [...]

[ت] وليس في رواية الصحيحين «أحدهما عن نفسه الخ» بل جاء في سنن ابن ماجه مكملاً ومفسراً له] ووجه الدلالة [...] أن النبي ﷺ تبرع بالأضحية وجعل ثوابها لأمته وهذا يشمل الحي والميت ومن كان في زمنه ومن جاء بعده. [...]

(٢) وعن أنس أنه سأل النبي ﷺ فقال: يا رسول الله إنا نتصدق عن موتانا ونحج عنهم وندعو لهم فهل يصل ذلك إليهم؟ قال: «نعم، إنه ليصل إليهم وإنهم ليفرحون به كما يفرح أحدكم بالطبق إذا أهدي إليه» [رواه أبو حفص الكبير العكبري، كما ذكر في فتح القدير: ٣/ ١٤٣].

(٣) وقال عليه الصلاة والسلام: «من مات وعليه صوم صام عنه وليه» [رواه البخاري ومسلم].

(٤) وعن النبي ﷺ أنه قال: «اقرؤوا على موتاكم يس» [رواه أبو داود]. [...]

(٥) وأخبر الله عز وجل أن الملائكة تستغفر للمؤمنين فقال: ﴿وَالمَلَائِكَةُ يُسَبِّحُونَ بِحَمْدِ رَبِّهِمْ وَيَسْتَغْفِرُونَ لِمَنْ فِي الأَرْضِ﴾ [الشورى: ٥].

وأثنى الله تعالى على المؤمنين الذين يستغفرون لإخوانهم فقال: ﴿وَالَّذِينَ جَاءُوا مِنْ بَعْدِهِمْ يَقُولُونَ رَبَّنَا اغْفِرْ لَنَا وَلِإِخْوَانِنَا الَّذِينَ سَبَقُونَا بِالإِيمَانِ﴾ [الحشر: ١٠].

(٦) وكان ﷺ يدعو لمن صلى عليه من الأموات [والأحاديث في هذا متعددة في كتب السنة] ووجه الدلالة في هذا كله أن الدعاء عبادة قال ﷺ: «الدعاء هو

"Supplication is worship,"

while the above texts clearly show that supplications benefit others besides the one who makes them, even when the other does not ask for the supplication to be made for him.

The foregoing provides evidence that the deceased benefits from all types of worship, whether monetary or physical, since fasting, pilgrimage, supplications, and asking forgiveness are all physical acts of worship, and Allah Most High conveys the benefit of them to the deceased—and so it must also be with other works (*Qada' al-'ibadat wa al-niyaba fiha* (y114), 400–403).

العبـــادة» [رواه أبـــو داود وغيـــره] وهــذه النصوص واضحة في أن الدعاء ينتفع به غير صاحبه ولو لم يكن له تسبب في هذا الدعاء [. . .] .

[. . .] وفيها دلالة على انتفاع الميت بسـائر القرب سواء منها المالية والبدنية لأن الصوم والحج والـدعـاء والاستغفار عبادات بدنية وقد أوصل الله تعالى نفعها إلى الميت فكـذلك سواها [محـر ر من قضاء العبادات والنيابة فيهـا : ٤٠٠ – ٤٠٣ ؛ بتقـديم وتأخيـر ، راجعـه المؤلف حفظه الله تعالى] .

*

w36.0 STUDENTS OF SACRED LAW ACCEPTING ZAKAT (from h8.8(2))

w36.0 جواز الزكاة لطلبة العلم

w36.1 (Ghazali:) If someone attaining knowledge of Sacred Law would be prevented from doing so if he were to engage in earning a living, he is considered "poor" (N: in respect to the permissibility of his accepting zakat), and his ability to earn is not taken into consideration. But if he is merely a devotee whose gaining a livelihood would busy him from his religious devotions and schedule of supererogatory worship, then he must go earn a living, for earning is more important than devotions.

.... The second category consists of those who are short of money (miskin), i.e. whose income does not cover their expenses. Someone might possess a thousand dirhams and be "short of money," while another might possess nothing but an axe and a rope and be self-sufficient. The modest lodgings one lives in and the clothes that cover one, to the degree required by one's condition, do not negate one's being short of money. Nor do household furnishings, meaning those which one needs and are suitable for one. Nor does possessing books of law negate one's being short of money (n: if one is a student of Sacred Law accepting zakat, as above), for if one owned nothing but

w36.1 (الغزالي :) [. . . و] إن كان متفقهـاً ويمنعـه الاشتغـال بالكسب عن التفقه فهو فقير ولا تعتبر قدرته . وإن كان متعبـداً يمنعـه الكسب من وظـائف العبادات وأوراد الأوقـات فليكتسب لأن الكسب أولى من ذلك .

[. . .] الـصنف الثـاني المسـاكين والمسكين هو الـذي لا يفي دخله بخرجه فقد يملك ألف درهم وهو مسكين وقد لا يملك إلا فأساً وحبلاً وهو غني . والدويرة التي يسكنها والثوب الذي يستره على قدر حاله لا يسلبه اسم المسكين . وكذا أثاث البيت أعني ما يحتاج إليه وذلك ما يليق به . وكـذا كتب الفقه لا تخـرجـه عن الـمسكنة وإذا لم يملك إلا الكتب فلا

books, one would not be obligated to pay the zakat of 'Eid al-Fitr (dis: h7.1), since books are legally considered as clothing and furnishings are, in that one needs them. One should, however, take the way of greater precaution in curbing one's need for books. Books are only needed for three purposes: teaching, personal benefit, and reading for entertainment. As for the need of reading for entertainment, it is not considered legally significant, such as with books of poetry, historical chronicles, and similar, which are of no benefit in the hereafter and no use in this life except reading and enjoyment. Such books must be sold to pay what is due when one owes an expiation (dis: o20.4) or the zakat of 'Eid al-Fitr, and someone possessing them is not considered short of money. As for the need to teach, if one needs a book to earn a living, as do trainers, teachers, or instructors who work for a salary, such books are the tools of their trade and are not sold to pay the zakat of 'Eid al-Fitr, nor are the tools of a tailor or any other professional. Nor are one's books sold if one teaches to fulfill the communal obligation (def: a5.1); possessing them does not negate one's being short of money, for this is an important need.

As for personal benefit and learning from books, such as keeping books of medicine to treat oneself or books of pious exhortations to read and take admonition from, if there is a doctor or an exhorter in town, one does not need them, while if there is not, one does. Further, one may not happen to need to read a book except after a time, in which case the period in which one needs it should be stipulated, the most reasonable criterion for which would seem to be that whatever one is not in need of during the course of a year one does not really need, for someone with food in excess of his needs for one day is obliged to pay the zakat of 'Eid al-Fitr, and if we stipulate the need for food as being that of one day, we should consider the need for furnishings and clothing as one year, summer clothing not being sold in winter, for example. Books, clothing, and furnishings would seem to be alike in this. Or someone might have two copies of a book and not need both, such that if he were to say that one is more accurate while the other is of finer quality, so both are needed, we would tell him to be satisfied with the

تلزمه صدقة الفطر وحكم الكتاب حكم الثوب وأثاث البيت فإنه محتاج إليه ولكن ينبغي أن يحتاط في قطع الحاجة بالكتاب . فالكتاب محتاج إليه لثلاثة أغراض : التعليم والاستفادة والتفرج بالمطالعة . أما حاجة التفرج فلا تعتبر كاقتناء كتب الأشعار وتواريخ الأخبار وأمثال ذلك مما لا ينفع في الآخرة ولا يجري في الدنيا إلا مجرى التفرج والاستئناس فهذا يباع في الكفارة وزكاة الفطر ويمنع اسم المسكنة . وأما حاجة التعليم إن كان لأجل الكسب كالمؤدب والمعلم والمدرس بأجرة فهذه آلته فلا تباع في الفطرة كأدوات الخياط وسائر المحترفين . وإن كان يدرس للقيام بفرض الكفاية فلا تباع ولا يسلبه ذلك اسم المسكين لأنها حاجة مهمة . وأما حاجة الاستفادة والتعلم من الكتاب كادخاره كتب طب ليعالج بها نفسه أو كتاب وعظ ليطالع فيه ويتعظ به فإن كان في البلد طبيب وواعظ فهذا مستغنى عنه وإن لم يكن فهو محتاج إليه . ثم ربما لا يحتاج إلى مطالعة الكتاب إلا بعد مدة فينبغي أن يضبط مدة الحاجة والأقرب أن يقال ما لا يحتاج إليه في السنة فهو مستغنى عنه فإن من فضل من قوت يومه شيء لزمته الفطرة فإذا قدرنا القوت باليوم فحاجة أثاث البيت وثياب البدن ينبغي أن يقدر بالسنة فلا تباع ثياب الصيف في الشتاء . والكتب بالثياب والأثاث أشبه . وقد يكون له من كتاب نسختان فلا حاجة إلى إحداهما فإن قال إحداهما أصح والأخرى أحسن فأنا محتاج إليهما قلنا

more accurate one and sell the finer, forgoing mere entertainment and luxury. If one has two books on a subject, one of which is comprehensive and the other abridged, then if personal benefit is the purpose, one should keep the more comprehensive, while if one needs them to teach, one may require both, since each possesses a virtue not found in the other. Similar examples are innumerable and the discipline of jurisprudence cannot cover them all. Rather, the above have been mentioned because of widespread abuse, and to apprise of the merit of the above criterion over others. For it is impossible to deal with all cases, which would entail estimating the amount, number, and kinds of household furnishings and clothes, the spaciousness of a house or lack of it, and so forth, there being no firm limits to such matters. But the legal scholar must use personal reasoning (ijtihad) with respect to them and approximate the criteria that seem likeliest to him, braving the danger of falling into things of doubtful legality, while a godfearing person will take the path that is religiously more precautionary, leaving what causes him doubt for what does not. There are many gray areas between the two clear-cut extremes, and nothing can save one from them except following the way of greater precaution (*Ihya' 'ulum al-din* (y39), 1.199).

اكتف بالأصح وبع الأحسن ودع التفرج والترفه . وإن كان نسختان من علم واحد إحداهما بسيطة والأخرى وجيزة فإن كان مقصوده الاستفادة فليكتف بالبسيط وإن كان قصده التدريس فيحتاج إليهما إذ في كل واحـدة فائـدة ليست في الأخرى . وأمثال هذه الصور لا تنحصر ولم يتعرض له في فن الفقه . وإنما أوردناه لعموم البلوى والتنبيـه بحسن هذا النظـر على غيـره . فإن استقصاء هذه الصـور غيـر ممكن إذ يتعـدى مثل هذا النظر في أثاث البيت في مقدارهـا وعـددها ونوعها وفي ثياب البـدن وفي الـدار وسعتهـا وضيقها وليس لهـذه الأمـور حدود محدودة ولكن الفقيه يجتهـد فيهـا برأيـه ويقـرب في التحـديـدات بما يراه ويقتحم فيـه خطر الشبهـات والمتـورع يأخـذ فيـه بالإحوط ويدع ما يريبه إلى ما لا يريبه . والدرجات المتـوسطـة المشكلة بين الأطـراف المتقابلة الجلية كثيرة ولا ينجي منها إلا الاحتيـاط [محرر من إحياء علوم الدين : ١ / ١٩٩] .

*

w37.0 THE UNLAWFULNESS OF MASTURBATION (from i1.18(9))

w37.0 تحريم الاستمناء

w37.1 (N:) Masturbation with one's own hand is unlawful. Imam Shafi'i (Allah be well pleased with him) was asked in connection with masturbation about the word of Allah Most High:

"... those who guard their private parts, save from their wives or [bondwomen] whom their right hands own, for these are not blameworthy. But whoever seeks beyond that, those are the transgressors" (Koran 23:5–7),

﴿ . . . وَالَّذِيـنَ هُمْ لِفُـرُوجِهِـمْ حَافِظُـونَ إلَّا عَلَى أَزْوَاجِهِمْ أَوْ مَا مَلَكَتْ أَيْمَـانُهُمْ فَإِنَّهُمْ غَيْـرُ مَلُومِينَ فَمَن ابْتَغَى وَرَاءَ ذَلـكَ فَأُولئـكَ هُمُ الـعَـادُونَ﴾ [المؤمنون : ٥ ـ ٧] .

and said that these Koranic verses restrict permissible sex to what is mentioned in them, since the last verse denies that anything besides this is lawful.

w38.0 KEEPING SILENT ALL DAY IS OFFENSIVE (from i1.32)

w38.1 (O:) It is offensive for anyone to keep silent the whole day until night when there is no need, as is attested to by the hadith related by Abu Dawud that 'Ali (Allah be well pleased with him) said, "I have memorized from the Messenger of Allah (Allah bless him and give him peace) that no one is considered an orphan after puberty and no one may remain silent until nightfall." And Bukhari relates that Abu Bakr Siddiq (Allah be well pleased with him) said to a woman on hajj who had resolved to keep silent, "Speak, for this is not permissible but is a practice of the pre-Islamic period of ignorance."

Rather, one should occupy the tongue with Koran, *dhikr*, or other acts of obedience performed with the tongue (*Fayd al-Ilah al-Malik* (y27), 1.284).

w38.0 كراهية الصوم عن الكلام

w38.1 (عمر بركات:) ويكره لكل أحد صمت يوم إلى الليل من غير حاجة لما روى أبو داود [بإسناد حسن] عن علي رضي الله عنه قال: حفظت من رسول الله ﷺ: لا يتم بعد احتلام ولا صمت إلى الليل؛ وروى البخاري عن أبي بكر الصديق رضي الله عنه أنه قال لامرأة حجت مصمتة: تكلمي فإن هذا لا يحل فإنه من عمل الجاهلية.

بل ينبغي أن يشغل لسانه بتلاوة قرآن أو ذكر أو غير ذلك من الطاعات المتعلقة باللسان [محرر من فيض الإله المالك في حل ألفاظ عمدة السالك وعدة الناسك: ١/ ٢٨٤].

*

w39.0 LAYLAT AL-QADR (from i3.2)

w39.1 (Muhyiddin ibn al-'Arabi:) Diligently perform the night vigil prayer (tahajjud, def: f10.8) every night of the year, and do not neglect to supplicate Allah each night, letting part of your supplication be for forgiveness and well-being in your religion, this-worldly concerns, and the hereafter, for you do not know which night of the year will coincide with Laylat al-Qadr (*al-Futuhat al-Makkiyya* (y55), 4.486).

w39.0 ليلة القدر

w39.1 (محيي الدين بن العربي:) [...] وحافظ في السنة كلها على القيام كل ليلة [ولو بما ذكرت لك] ولا تهمل الدعاء في كل ليلة واجعل من دعائك السؤال في العفو والعافية في الدين والدنيا والآخرة فإنك لا تدري متى تصادف ليلة القدر من سنتك [نقل من الفتوحات المكية: ٤/ ٤٨٦].

*

w40.0 SUPPLICATING ALLAH THROUGH AN INTERMEDIARY (TAWASSUL) (from j13.2)

w40.1 (n: Special vocabulary:

Tawassul: supplicating Allah by means of an intermediary, whether it be a

w40.0 التوسل

living person, dead person, a good deed, or a name or attribute of Allah Most High.)

w40.2   (Yusuf Rifa'i:) I here want to convey the position, attested to by compelling legal evidence, of the orthodox majority of Sunni Muslims on the subject of supplicating Allah through an intermediary (tawassul), and so I say (and Allah alone gives success) that since there is no disagreement among scholars that supplicating Allah through an intermediary is in principle legally valid, the discussion of its details merely concerns derived rulings that involve interschool differences, unrelated to questions of belief or unbelief, monotheism or associating partners with Allah (shirk); the sphere of the question being limited to permissibility or impermissibility, and its ruling being that it is either lawful or unlawful. There is no difference among groups of Muslims in their consensus on the permissibility of three types of supplicating Allah through an intermediary (tawassul):

(1)   tawassul through a living righteous person to Allah Most High, as in the hadith of the blind man with the Prophet (Allah bless him and give him peace) as we shall explain;

(2)   the tawassul of a living person to Allah Most High through his own good deeds, as in the hadith of the three people trapped in a cave by a great stone, a hadith related by Imam Bukhari in his Sahih;

(3)   and the tawassul of a person to Allah Most High through His entity (dhat), names, attributes (dis: w29.2(6)), and so forth.

Since the legality of these types is agreed upon, there is no reason to set forth the evidence for them. The only area of disagreement is supplicating Allah (tawassul) through a righteous dead person. The majority of the orthodox Sunni Community hold that it is lawful, and have supporting hadith evidence, of which we will content ourselves with the Hadith of the Blind Man, since it is the central pivot upon which the discussion turns.

w40.2   (يوسف الرفاعي:) [. . .]
هذا وأود أن أنقل فيما يلي رأي أهل السنة والجماعة المستند إلى الأدلة الشرعية المحكمة في موضوع التوسل فأقول وبالله التوفيق [. . .] فمن حيث أن أصل التوسل مشروع لا خلاف عليه، كان الكلام في فروعه من الخلافيات التي لا تتعلق بإيمان ولا كفر، ولا توحيد ولا شرك، وإنما محلها الجواز والمنع، فحكمها الحلال والحرام.

إنه لا خلاف بين طوائف المسلمين إجماعاً على ثلاثة أنواع من التوسل:

- النوع الأول: التوسل بالحي الصالح إلى الله تعالى، كما في حديث الضرير مع النبي ﷺ، الذي سوف يأتي بيانه.

- النوع الثاني: توسل الحي بالعمل الصالح إلى الله تعالى، كما في حديث «الثلاثة أصحاب الغار والصخرة» الذي أورده الإمام البخاري في صحيحه.

- النوع الثالث: التوسل إلى الله بذاته تعالى، وبأسمائه وصفاته ونحوها.

وبما أن هذه الأنواع متفق على مشروعيتها، فلا داعي لسرد الأدلة عليها. وإنما الخلاف هو في التوسل بالميت الصالح؛ وقد أجازه جمهور المسلمين من أهل السنة والجماعة، ولديهم عليه الأدلة النقلية المتعاضدة نكتفي هنا منها بـ «حديث الأعمى» من حيث أنه المحور الأكبر في هذا الباب وعليه يدور النقاش.

THE HADITH OF THE BLIND MAN

w40.3 Tirmidhi relates, through his chain of narrators from 'Uthman ibn Hunayf, that a blind man came to the Prophet (Allah bless him and give him peace) and said, "I've been afflicted in my eyesight, so please pray to Allah for me." The Prophet (Allah bless him and give him peace) said: "Go make ablution (wudu), perform two rak'as of prayer, and then say:

" 'O Allah, I ask You and turn to You through my prophet Muhammad, the Prophet of Mercy; O Muhammad, I seek your intercession with my Lord *for the return of my eyesight* [and in another version: "for my need, that it may be fulfilled. O Allah, grant him intercession for me"].' "

The Prophet (Allah bless him and give him peace) added, "And if there is some need, do the same."

Scholars of Sacred Law infer from this hadith the recommended character of the *prayer of need*, in which someone in need of something from Allah Most High performs such a prayer and then turns to Allah with this supplication together with other suitable supplications, traditional or otherwise, according to the need and how the person feels. The express content of the hadith proves the legal validity of *tawassul* through a living person (n: as the Prophet (Allah bless him and give him peace) was alive at the time). It implicitly proves the validity of *tawassul* through a deceased one as well, since *tawassul* through a living or dead person is not through a physical body or through a life or death, but rather through the positive meaning (ma'na tayyib) attached to the person in both life and death. The body is but the vehicle that carries that significance, which requires that the person be respected whether alive or dead; for the words "O Muhammad" are an address to someone physically absent—in which state the living and dead are alike—an address to the meaning, dear to Allah, that is connected with his spirit, a meaning that is the ground of *tawassul*, be it through a living or dead person.

حديث الأعمى

w40.3 روى الترمذي بسنده عن عثمان بن حنيف أن رجلاً أعمى أتى النبي ﷺ فقال: إني أصبت في بصري فادع الله لي، قال: اذهب فتوضأ، وصل ركعتين ثم قل: «اللهم إني أسألك وأتوجه إليك بنبيّي محمد، نبي الرحمة، يا محمد إني أستشفع بك على ربي في رد بصري» ـ وفي رواية «في حاجتي لتقضى لي، اللهم شفعه فيّ» (ثم قال ﷺ:) وإن كانت حاجة فافعل مثل ذلك.

[وفي بعض روايات الحديث خلاف يسير في الألفاظ ليس بذي بال)] من هذا الحديث أخذ الفقهاء مندوبية صلاة الحاجة، فمن كانت له إلى الله تعالى حاجة، صلى هذه الصلاة، وتوجه إلى الله بهذا الدعاء، مع ما يناسبه من الدعاء المأثور وغير المأثور، مما تمس إليه الحاجة وما يشعر به صاحبها.

ومنطوق الحديث حجة في صحة التوسل بالحي، ومفهومه حجة على صحة التوسل بالحي أو الميت ليس توسلاً بالجسم ولا بالحياة ولا بالموت، ولكن بالمعنى الطيب الملازم للإنسان في الموت والحياة، وما الجسم إلا حقيبة لصيانة هذا المعنى، فاستوجب بهذا تكريمه حياً كان أو ميتاً، على أن قوله «يا محمد» نداء للغائب الذي يستوي فيه الحي والميت، فهو موجه إلى المعنى الكريم على الله، والملازم للروح، والذي هو موضع التوسل بالحي أو الميت على حد سواء.

THE HADITH OF THE MAN IN NEED

w40.4   Moreover, Tabarani, in his *al-Mu'jam al-saghir*, reports a hadith from 'Uthman ibn Hunayf that a man repeatedly visited 'Uthman ibn 'Affan (Allah be well pleased with him) concerning something he needed, but 'Uthman paid no attention to him or his need. The man met Ibn Hunayf and complained to him about the matter—this being after the death of the Prophet (Allah bless him and give him peace) and after the caliphates of Abu Bakr and 'Umar—so 'Uthman ibn Hunayf, who was one of the Companions who collected hadiths and were learned in the religion of Allah, said: "Go to the place of ablution and perform ablution (wudu), then come to the mosque, perform two rak'as of prayer therein, and say,

" 'O Allah, I ask You and turn to You through our prophet Muhammad, the Prophet of Mercy; O Muhammad, I turn through you to my Lord, that He may fulfill my need,'

"and mention your need. Then come so that I can go with you [N: to the caliph 'Uthman]." So the man left and did as he had been told, then went to the door of 'Uthman ibn 'Affan (Allah be well pleased with him), and the doorman came, took him by the hand, brought him to 'Uthman ibn 'Affan and seated him next to him on a cushion. 'Uthman asked, "What do you need?" and the man mentioned what he wanted, and 'Uthman accomplished it for him and then said, "I hadn't remembered your need until just now," adding, "Whenever you need something, just mention it." Then the man departed, met 'Uthman ibn Hunayf, and said to him, "May Allah reward you! He didn't see to my need or pay any attention to me until you spoke with him." 'Uthman ibn Hunayf replied, "By Allah, I didn't speak to him, but I have seen a blind man come to the Messenger of Allah (Allah bless him and give him peace) and complain to him of the loss of his eyesight. The Prophet (Allah bless him and give him peace) said, 'Can you not bear it?' and the man replied, 'O Messenger of Allah, I do not have anyone to lead me around, and it is a great hardship for me.' The Prophet (Allah bless him

حديث صاحب الحاجة

w40.4   ومع هذا فقد أخرج الطبراني في معجمه الصغير، عن [أبي أمامة بن سهـل بن حنيف، عن عمـه] عثمان بن حنيف: أن رجلاً كان يختلف إلى عثمان بن عفـان رضي الله عنه في حاجـة له، فكان عثمان لا يلتفت إليه ولا ينظر في حاجته، فلقي ابن حنيف فشكا إليه ذلك (أي بعد وفاة النبي ﷺ، وبعد خلافه أبي بكر وعمر).

فقال له عثمان بن حنيف (وهـو الصحابي المحدث العالم بدين الله): ايت الميضأة فتوضأ، ثم ايت المسجد، فصل فيه ركعتين، ثم قل:

«اللهم إني أسألك وأتوجه إليك بنبينا محمد نبي الرحمة، يا محمد: إني أتوجه بك إلى ربي فيقضي حاجتي» قال وتـذكر حاجتك، ورح حتى أروح معك.

فانطلق الـرجل يصنع ما قال له، ثم أتى باب عثمان بن عفان رضي الله عنه، فجاء البـواب حتى أخذ بيده فأدخله على عثمـان بن عفـان فأجلسه معـه على الطنفسة [(الوسادة)] فقال: ما حاجتك؟ فذكر حاجته وقضاها له، ثم قال له: ما ذكرت حاجتك حتى كان الساعة. وقال: ما كانت لك من حاجة فاذكرها!

ثم أن الـرجل خرج من عنده، فلقي عثمـان بن حنيف. فقال له: جزاك الله خيراً، ما كان ينظر في حاجتي ولا يلتفت إليَّ حتى كلمتـه [(يـريـد أن ابن حنيف كلمه، أي توسط له عند عثمان ابن عفان)].

فقال عثمـان بن حنيف: والله ما كلمته. لكني شهدت رسول الله ﷺ وأتاه ضرير فشكا إليه ذهاب بصره، فقال له النبي ﷺ: أفتصبر؟ فقال: يا رسول الله إنه ليس لي قائد، وقد شق عليَّ.

فقال ﷺ: ايت الميضأة فتوضأ، ثم

936

and give him peace) told him, 'Go to the place of ablution and perform ablution (wudu), then pray two rak'as of prayer and make these supplications.'" Ibn Hunayf went on, "By Allah, we didn't part company or speak long before the man returned to us as if nothing had ever been wrong with him."

This is an explicit, unequivocal text from a prophetic Companion proving the legal validity of *tawassul* through the dead. The account has been classed as rigorously authenticated (sahih) by Bayhaqi, Mundhiri, and Haythami.

THE AUTHENTICITY OF THE HADITH OF THE BLIND MAN

w40.5 Tirmidhi has stated that the hadith of the blind man is "a hadith that is well or rigorously authenticated but singular, being unknown except through this chain of narrators, from the hadith of Abu Ja'far, who is not Abu Ja'far Khatmi," which means that the narrators of this hadith, despite Abu Ja'far being unknown to Tirmidhi, were acceptable to the degree of being well or rigorously authenticated in either case. But scholars before Tirmidhi established that Abu Ja'far, this person unknown to Tirmidhi, was Abu Ja'far Khatmi himself. Ibn Abi Khaythama said, "The name of this Abu Ja'far, whom Hammad ibn Salama relates from, is 'Umayr ibn Yazid, and he is the Abu Ja'far that Shu'ba relates from," and then he related the hadith by the channel of transmission of 'Uthman from Shu'ba from Abu Ja'far. Ibn Taymiya, after relating the hadith of Tirmidhi, said, "All scholars say that he is Abu Ja'far Khatmi, and this is correct." Reflect on this. The hadith master Ibn Hajar notes in *Taqrib al-tahdhib* that he is Khatmi, and that he is reliable (saduq). Ibn 'Abd al-Barr likewise says that he is Khatmi in *al-Isti'ab fi ma'rifa al-ashab*. Moreover, Bayhaqi related the hadith by way of Hakim and confirmed that it was rigorously authenticated (sahih), Hakim having related it by a chain of transmission meeting the standards of Bukhari and Muslim, which the hadith master Dhahabi confirmed, and Shawkani cited as evidence. Dhahabi and Shawkani, who are they? The meaning of this is that all the men of the hadith's chain

صل ركعتين ، ثم ادع بهذه الدعوات . قال ابن حنيف : فوالله ما تفرقنا وطال بنا الحديث حتى دخل علينا الرجل كأن لم يكن به ضر قط .

وهذا نص صحابي قطعي صريح في صحة التوسل بالموتى ، وقد صحح هذه القصة البيهقي والمنذري والهيثمي [...]

تحقيق صحة حديث الضرير

w40.5 [...] وقد] قال الترمذي عنه : حديث حسن صحيح غريب ، لا يعرف إلا من هذا الوجه ، من حديث أبي جعفر ، قال : وهو غير الخطمي [بفتح الخاء] ومعنى هذا : أن رواة هذا الحديث مع مجهولية أبي جعفر عند الترمذي مقبولون بدرجة الحسن والصحة على الوجهين . وعلماء الحديث الذين سبقوا الترمذي حققوا أن أبا جعفر (هذا المجهول عند الترمذي) هو الخطمي بعينه ، قال ابن أبي خيثمة : أبو جعفر هذا ، الذي حدث عنه حماد بن سلمة : اسمه عمير بن يزيد ، وهو أبو جعفر الذي يروي عنه شعبة ، ثم روى الحديث من طريق عثمان ، عن شعبة ، عن أبي جعفر .

قال ابن تيمية ، بعد أن روى حديث الترمذي :

«وسائر العلماء قالوا هو أبو جعفر الخطمي ، وهو الصواب» فتأمل .

قلنا : وفي (تقريب التهذيب) للحافظ ابن حجر : أنه الخطمي وأنه صدوق [من السادسة] وفي (الاستيعاب) لابن عبد البر : أنه الخطمي كذلك ، ثم أن الحديث كذلك رواه البيهقي من طريق الحاكم وأقر تصحيحه ، وقد رواه الحاكم بسند على شرط الشيخين ، وأقره الحافظ

of transmission are known to top Imams of hadith such as Dhahabi (and who is severer than he?), Ibn Hajar (and who is more precise, learned, or painstaking than he?), Hakim, Bayhaqi, Tabarani, Ibn 'Abd al-Barr, Shawkani, and even Ibn Taymiya. This hadith was recorded by Bukhari in his *al-Tarikh al-kabir*, by Ibn Majah in his *Sunan*, where he said it was rigorously authenticated (sahih), by Nasa'i in *'Amal al-yawm wa al-layla*, by Abu Nu'aym in *Ma'rifa al-Sahaba*, by Bayhaqi in *Dala'il al-nubuwwa*, by Mundhiri in *al-Targhib wa al-tarhib*, by Haythami in *Majma' al-zawa'id wa manba' al-fawa'id*, by Tabarani in *al-Mu'jam al-kabir*, by Ibn Khuzayma in his *Sahih*, and by others. Nearly fifteen hadith masters (huffaz, hadith authorities with more than 100,000 hadiths and their chains of transmission by memory) have explicitly stated that this hadith is rigorously authenticated (sahih). As mentioned above, it has come with a chain of transmission meeting the standards of Bukhari and Muslim, so there is nothing left for a critic to attack or slanderer to disparage concerning the authenticity of the hadith. Consequently, as for the permissibility of supplicating Allah (tawassul) through either a living or dead person, it follows by human reason, scholarship, and sentiment, that there is flexibility in the matter. Whoever wants to can either take *tawassul* or leave it, without causing trouble or making accusations, since it has been this thoroughly checked (*Adilla Ahl al-Sunna wa al-Jama'a* (y119), 79–83).

الـذهبي ، واستشهد به الشوكاني . وهما! من هما؟

ومعنى هذا : أن جميـع رجـال السنـد معـروفـون لكبـار أئمة الحديث كالذهبي (وهـو من هو تشدداً) وابن حجر (وهو من هو ضبطـاً وحفظـاً وتحقيقـاً) والحـاكم ، والبيهقي ، والطبراني ، وابن عبـد البـر ، والشوكاني ، حتى ابن تيمية [. . . الخ] . ثم أن هذا الحـديث أخرجه البخاري في (التـاريـخ الكبيـر) وابن ماجـه في (السنن) ونص على صحته ، والنسائي في (عمل اليوم والليلة) وأبو نعيم في (معرفة الصحابة) والبيهقي في (دلائـل النبـوة) والمنـذري في (الترغيب) والهيثمي في (المجمع) والطبراني في (الكبير) وابن خزيمة في صحيحه ، وآخرون .

وقد نص على صحته نحو خمسة عشر حافظـاً ، وهكـذا جاء الحـديث كما قدمنا على شرط الـصحـيـحيـن : البخـاري ومسلم ، فلم يبق بعد هذا مطعن لطاعن ، أو مغمز لمغتمز في صحة الحديث .

وبـالتـالي في جواز التوسل بالحي والـميت جميعـاً من طريق : العقـل ، والعلم ، والعـاطفة ، في الأمر سعة : من شاء توسـل ومن شاء ترك بلا فتنـة ولا تأثيـم ، بعـد كل هذا التحقيق الـدقيق [محرر من أدلة أهل السنة والجماعة : ٧٩ ـ ٨٣] .

w40.6   (n:) It is well to review some salient features of the above article, such as:

(1) that there are two hadiths, Tirmidhi's hadith of the *blind man* and Tabarani's hadith of the *man in need* to whom 'Uthman ibn Hunayf related the story of the blind man, teaching him the *tawassul* that the Prophet (Allah bless him and give him peace) had taught the blind man.

(2) Tirmidhi's hadith is rigorously authenticated (sahih), being the subject of the above investigation of its chain of narrators, the authenticity of which is established beyond a reasonable doubt and attested to by nearly fifteen of the foremost hadith specialists of Islam. The hadith explicitly proves the validity of supplicating Allah (tawassul) through a living intermediary, as the Prophet (Allah bless him and give him peace) was alive at the time. The author of the article holds that the hadith implicitly shows the validity of supplicating Allah (tawassul) through a deceased intermediary as well, since:

The Prophet (Allah bless him and give him peace) told the blind man to go perform ablution (wudu), pray two rak'as, and then make the supplication containing the words, "O Muhammad, I seek your intercession with my Lord for the return of my eyesight," which is a call upon someone physically absent, a state in which the living and the dead are alike.

Supplicating Allah (tawassul) through a living or deceased intermediary is, in the author's words, "not *tawassul* through a physical body, or through a life or death, but rather through the positive meaning attached to the person in both life and death, for the body is but the vehicle that carries that significance."

And perhaps the most telling reason, though the author does not mention it, is that everything the Prophet (Allah bless him and give him peace) ordered to be done during his lifetime was *legislation* valid for all generations until the end of time unless proven otherwise by a subsequent indication from the Prophet himself (Allah bless him and give him peace), the *tawassul* he taught during his lifetime not requiring anything else to be generalized to any time thereafter.

(3) The authenticity of Tabarani's hadith of the man in need during the caliphate of 'Uthman (Allah be well pleased with him) is not discussed by the article in detail, but deserves consideration, since the hadith explicitly proves the legal validity of supplicating Allah (tawassul) through the deceased, for 'Uthman ibn Hunayf and indeed all the prophetic Companions, by scholarly consensus (ijma'), were legally upright ('udul, dis: w56), and are above being impugned with teaching someone an act of disobedience, much less idolatry (shirk). The hadith is rigorously authenticated (sahih), as Tabarani explicitly states in his *al-Mu'jam al-saghir* (y131), 1.184. The translator, wishing to verify the matter further, took the hadith with its chain of transmitters to hadith specialist Sheikh Shu'ayb Arna'ut, who after examining it, agreed that it was rigorously authenticated (sahih) as Tabarani indicated, a judgement which was also confirmed to the translator by the Moroccan hadith specialist Sheikh 'Abdullah Muhammad Ghimari, who characterized the hadith as "very rigorously authenticated," and noted that hadith masters Haythami and Mundhiri had explicitly concurred with Tabarani on its being rigorously authenticated (sahih). The upshot is that the recommendedness of *tawassul* to Allah Most High—through the living or the dead—is the position of the Shafi'i school, which is why both our author Ibn Naqib at j13.2, and Imam Nawawi in his *al-Adhkar* (y102), 281–82, and *al-Majmu'* (y108), 8.274, explicitly record that *tawassul* through the Prophet (Allah bless him and give him peace) and asking his intercession are recommended. A final article below by a Hanafi scholar concludes the discussion.

CALLING UPON THE RIGHTEOUS

نداء الصالحين

w40.7   (Muhammad Hamid:) As for calling upon (nida') the righteous (n: when they are physically absent, as in the words "O Muhammad" in the above hadiths), *tawassul* to Allah Most High

w40.7   (محمد الحامد:) (ت: [

أما) نداء الصالحين فيجوز التوسل بهم

إلى الله تعــالى، والــدعـــاء يكــون لله

through them is permissible, the supplication (du'a') being to Allah Most Glorious, and there is much evidence for its permissibility. Those who call on them intending *tawassul* cannot be blamed. As for someone who believes that those called upon can cause effects, benefit, or harm, which they create or cause to exist as Allah does, such a person is an idolator who has left Islam (dis: o8.7(17))—Allah be our refuge! This then, and a certain person has written an article that *tawassul* to Allah Most High through the righteous is unlawful, while the overwhelming majority of scholars hold it is permissible, and the evidence the writer uses to corroborate his viewpoint is devoid of anything that demonstrates what he is trying to prove. In declaring *tawassul* permissible, we are not hovering on the brink of idolatry (shirk) or coming anywhere near it, for the conviction that Allah Most High alone has influence over anything, outwardly or inwardly, is a conviction that flows through us like our very lifeblood. If *tawassul* were idolatry (shirk), or if there were any suspicion of idolatry in it, the Prophet (Allah Most High bless him and give him peace) would not have taught it to the blind man when the latter asked him to supplicate Allah for him, though in fact he did teach him to make *tawassul* to Allah through him. And the notion that *tawassul* is permissible only during the lifetime of the person through whom it is done but not after his death is unsupported by any viable foundation from Sacred Law (*Rudud 'ala abatil wa rasa'il al-Shaykh Muhammad al-Hamid* (y44), 2.39).

سبحانه، والأدلة على ذلك كثيرة، ومن ناداهم بقصد التوسل بهم لا يلام. أما من اعتقـد فيهم التأثيـر والنفـع والضرر خلقاً وإيجاداً كالـذي يكون من الله تعالى فهو مشـرك مرتـد عن الإسـلام والعيـاذ بالله. هذا وقد كتب بعض الناس كتابة حرم فيها التـوسـل إلى الله تعـالى بالصـالحين في حين أن جمهـرة العلماء تجيزه، وما أسند إليـه في تصـويب وجهـة نظره لا دليل فيه على ما يريد، وإننا في إجازتنا التوسل لا نحـوم حول الشـرك ولا ندنـو منـه لأن الاعتقاد بأن الله تعـالى هو المـؤثر وحده في الأمـور باديها وخافيها، هذا الاعتقاد سالك منا مسلك الروح. ولوكان التوسل شركاً أو فيه شائبة الشرك ما علمه نبي الله ﷺ للأعمى حين سألـه أن يدعـو الله له، فقد علمه التوسل به.

وإجازة التوسل في حياة المتوسل به لا بعد مماته لا يعتمد أصلاً شرعياً [نقل من ردود على أباطيـل ورسائل الشيخ محمد الحامد: ٢/ ٣٩].

*

w41.0 SMOKING (from j16.5)

w41.0 تحريم التدخين

w41.1 (A:) Many contemporary scholars hold it is unlawful to buy, sell, use, or grow tobacco, because of the unlawfulness of consuming what has been proven to be harmful, which is attested to by the word of the Prophet (Allah bless him and give him peace),

Let there be no harming, nor reciprocating harm,''

«لا ضرر ولا ضرار».

a well-authenticated hadith (n: of which Muhammad Jurdani says, "The ostensive meaning of this hadith is the prohibition of all forms of harmfulness, great or small, since the grammatical indefinite [n: of the words "harming" and "reciprocating harm"] in a negative context indicates generality" (*al-Jawahir al-lu'lu'iyya fi sharh al-Arba'in al-Nawawiyya* (y68), 244).)

حديـث حسـن [رواه ابـن ماجـه والـدارقطني وغيرهما مسنداً]. (ت: قال الشـارح محمـد الجـرداني: وظـاهر هذا الحـديث تحريم سائر أنواع الضرر ما قل منهـا ومـا كثر لأن النكرة في سياق النفي تعم [نقـل من الجواهر اللؤلؤية في شرح الأربعين النووية: ٢٤٤].

EVIDENCE OF THE
HARMFULNESS OF SMOKING

إثبات ضرر التدخين

w41.2 (Richard Doll and R. Peto:) .... Particularly large and impressive studies have been carried out in the United States (by the American Cancer Society and the National Cancer Institute), in Japan (by Hirayama), and in Sweden, and all point to the conclusion that, in countries in which many cigarette smokers have been smoking regularly since early adult life, lung cancer is some 10 to 15 times commoner in regular cigarette smokers than in lifelong non-smokers and up to 40 times commoner in very heavy smokers....

These observations that smokers were at far greater risk of lung cancer than nonsmokers did not, in themselves, prove that smoke caused the disease, although it was difficult to think of any other way in which such a close quantitative relationship could have been produced; but *other observations effectively exclude any alternative* [n: emphasis the translator's]. These include the fact that the relative risk of lung cancer increased with decreasing age of starting to smoke and decreased with the number of years that smoking had been stopped; that the increase in incidence appeared at an appropriate time after the increase in cigarette sales (after due allowance is made for a spurious increase due to improved diagnosis) and with an appropriate lag in time between the increase among men (who started to smoke cigarettes early this century) and that among women (who started about a quarter of a century later); and that there is a general parallelism between the incidence of the disease in different countries and social and religious groups and the corresponding figures for the consumption of cigarettes. (Furthermore, it was found that when extracts of cigarette smoke were applied repeatedly to the skins of laboratory mice many tumours developed.) (*Oxford Textbook of Medicine* (y76), 4.61)

(n: The foregoing is a statement by competent medical authorities that smoking is harmful to the body.)

w41.3 (Sulayman Bujayrmi:) Whatever harms the body or mind is unlawful, from which the unlawfulness of the well-known tobacco (dukhan) is known (*Tuhfa al-habib 'ala Sharh al-Khatib al-musamma bi al-Iqna' fi hall alfaz Abi Shuja'* (y6), 4.276).

w41.3 (سليمان البجيرمي:) [...]
ويحرم ما يضر البدن أو العقل: ومنه يعلم حرمة الـدخـان المشهور [نقل من تحفة الحبيب على شرح الخطيب ٤/ ٢٧٦].

(A: This is an explicit text (nass) from a Shafi'i scholar that establishes the ruling for smoking in our school. As for the evidence that growing, buying, and selling tobacco is unlawful, it consists in the principle of Sacred Law that whatever leads to the unlawful is itself unlawful. A number of Islamic scholars have explicitly declared the total prohibition of tobacco, among them Hashim al-Khatib, 'Ali al-Daqar, Badr al-Din al-Hasani, Sheikh al-Qalyubi, and Muhammad Hamid. In past centuries, before the harmfulness of tobacco had been scientifically established, some formal legal opinions (fatwas) were given that smoking was merely offensive. In light of what we know today about the harm tobacco causes, such opinions are plainly no longer the reliable position for *fatwa*. If uneducated Muslims who follow these opinions may plead ignorance, Islamic scholars, for their part, should fear Allah and remember that there is scholarly consensus that it is not lawful to judge by other than the soundest and most reliable position (dis: w12.2). Someone with knowledge is obliged to teach people what is closer to Islam.)

*

w42.0 BUYING AND SELLING INSURANCE IS UNLAWFUL (from k2.1(e))

w42.0 تحريم عقد التأمين

w42.1 (A:) In addition to the fact that they are usurious (riba, def: k3), buying and selling insurance policies are unlawful because of the Prophet's prohibition (Allah bless him and give him peace) of sales in which there is chance or risk (gharar). Muslim relates from Abu Hurayra that

"The Messenger of Allah (Allah bless him and give him peace) prohibited sales of 'whatever a pebble thrown by the seller hits,' and sales in which there is chance or risk (gharar)."

عن أبي هريرة قال : نهى رسول الله ﷺ عن بيع الحصاة وعن بيع الغرر [رواه مسلم في كتاب البيوع ؛ باب : بطلان بيع الحصاة والبيع الذي فيه الغرر ؛ صحيح مسلم : ٣/ ١١٥٣].

w42.2 (Nasir al-Mutarrizi:) *Gharar* is chance or risk, meaning it is not known whether it will come to be or not, such as selling fish in the water or birds on the wing. It includes transactions of unknown things, the particulars of which are not fully comprehended by the buyer and seller (*al-Mughrib fi tartib al-Mu'rib* (y94), 2.100).

w42.2 (ناصر المطرزي:) الغرر [. . .] هو الخطر الذي لا يدرك أيكون أم لا ، كبيع السمك في الماء والطير في الهواء [. . . قال الأزهري :] وتدخل البيوع المجهولة التي لا يحيط بها المتبايعان [محرر من المغرب في ترتيب المعرب : ٢/ ١٠٠].

w42.3 (n:) Urging the permissibility of insurance, one Muslim modernist has written that the very precise statistical data possessed by insurance companies concerning the probabilities of various eventualities makes what they are selling determinately known (ma'lum). This argument fails when one realizes that statistical data from a group of events yields probability figures that, properly speaking, are a description of the group as a whole, and are only *analogically* applied to the individual events within it. When generalized to similar groups of events in the future, such probabilities yield commercially useful knowledge about the likelihood of a particular outcome for these future groups. But they cannot and do not tell what the outcome will be for any *particular* member of the group, in this case the particular insurance policy. Thus, a "17 percent probability" that circumstances will enable one to collect such and such an amount on a policy is a mere description of the whole group of previous policy holders in similar circumstances, which does not tell whether one will collect the amount or not. One may collect a certain amount or may not collect it, which is precisely the *gharar* that is unlawful.

w42.4 (A:) When one needs a car in a country whose laws force one to have car liability insurance, buying the insurance has effectively become a tax, and is the moral responsibility of the lawmakers, not the person forced to comply.

*

w43.0 DEALING IN INTEREST (RIBA) IN ENEMY LANDS (DAR AL-HARB) (from k3.0, end)

w43.1 (Muhammad Hamid:) A formal legal opinion (fatwa) given by the mufti of Dar al-'Ulum and his assistant in Deoband, India, states that dealing in interest (riba, def: k3.0(N:)) is permissible between Muslims and non-Muslims in enemy lands (dar al-harb), meaning areas in which the rules of Islam do not exist, such countries not holding its validity or believing in it. This *fatwa* states that it is permissible for a Muslim to both take interest (riba) and give it, and claims that India is an enemy land (dar al-harb), so there is no objection to dealing in interest there, and it lastly permits Muslims to put their money in the banks of non-Muslims and take interest from them, and likewise permits them to loan the state money for interest. That is a summary of the contents of the *fatwa*. It bases the permissibility of dealing in interest (riba) with non-Muslims in enemy lands (dar al-harb, def: w43.5) on the opinion of Imams Abu Hanifa and Muhammad ibn Hasan Shaybani, the colleague of Abu Hanifa (Allah Most High have mercy on them). Without a doubt, this is what the two Imams have explicitly stated, and is the position of the Hanafi school, as conveyed in both its main texts and their commentaries.

w43.0 التعامل بالربا في دار الحرب

w43.1 (محمد الحامد:) صدرت فتوى من مفتي دار العلوم بديوبانـد في الهنـد ومن مساعـده، تصـرح بجـواز التعامل بالربا بين المسلمين وبين الكفار في دار الـحـرب، وهي البـلاد التي لا تسـري فيهـا أحكام الإسلام، إذ لا يعتقد أهله صحته فهم به غير مؤمنين.

وقـد أجازت هذه الفتوى أخذ المسلم الربا وإعطاءه، وزعمت أن بلاد الهند دار حرب، فلا حرج في التعامل بالربا فيها. وسمحت آخراً بوضع المسلمين أموالهم في مصارف غيـر المسلمين، وبأخـذ الفائدة الربوية منها، كما سوّغت إقراض الدولة المال بفائدة أيضاً.

هذا ملخص ما جاء في الفتوى.

وقـد بنت جواز التعـامـل مع غيـر المـسلمين في دار الحـرب على قول الإمامين أبي حنيفة وصاحبه محمد بن الحسن الشيباني رحمهما الله تعالى. ولا شك أن هذا صريح قولهمـا، وهو منقول المذهب متوناً وشروحاً.

Imams Shafi'i and Abu Yusuf, the colleague of Abu Hanifa, (Allah Most High have mercy on them) contradict this opinion. What I, while unqualified to intervene in positions that are differed upon by *mujtahid* Imams (def: o22.1(d)), would nevertheless like to direct attention to is that the dissenting opinion of Shafi'i and Abu Yusuf is not a feeble viewpoint unsupported by evidence—by no means is that the case. Their position on an issue like this deserves to be given its due, so that one can fully live up to the demands of religion. Nothing actualizes one's innocence like taking reasonable precautions, and perhaps a look at the evidence will dictate doing so.

لكن خالفهما في قولهما هذا الإمامان الشافعي رحمه الله وأبو يوسف صاحب أبي حنيفة رحمهما الله تعالى . ونحن وإن لم نكن أهلاً للدخول فيما بين الأئمة المجتهدين في خلافاتهم لكن الذي أحب توجيه النظر إليه هو أن خلاف الشافعي وأبي يوسف ليس بالخلاف الهزيل الذي لا يستند إلى دليل . كلا . فإن قولهما في مثل هذا جدير بأن يحسب له حسابه ، استبراء من المرء لدينه ، ولا يحقق البراءة شيء كالاحتياط المعقول ، ولعل النظر في الدليل يملي الأخذ بالحيطة .

THE EVIDENCE OF ABU HANIFA AND IMAM MUHAMMAD

حجة أبي حنيفة والإمام محمد

w43.2   The evidence of Abu Hanifa and Muhammad for the permissibility of taking interest (riba) from non-Muslims in enemy lands (dar al-harb) is the Prophet (Allah bless him and give him peace) having said,

w43.2   استدل أبو حنيفة ومحمد لجواز أخذ الربا من الكافرين في دار الحرب بقول النبي ﷺ :

"There is no usury (riba) between the Muslim and the hostile non-Muslim in enemy lands (dar al-harb),"

«لا ربا بين المسلم والحربي في دار الحرب» .

such that their property is lawful to us in their own lands. It is permissible for a Muslim who is there under a safe-conduct to take it from them with their approval, unless it is by way of deceit, which is unlawful because it violates the safe-conduct agreement they have effected with him that permits him to enter their lands under stipulation that he honor it, it being unlawful for him to violate it. As for when one of them enters our lands under a safe-conduct, it is not permissible to deal in interest (riba) with him, for our safe-conduct agreement with him makes his property inviolable to us, except what he transacts in a lawful way free of sin or blame, for the lands are those of Islam.

بأن مالهم مباح لنا في دارهم ، فإذا أخذه المسلم المستأمن منهم فيها برضاهم جاز ، إلا ما كان بطريق الغدر ، فهو حرام ، لمنافاته عقد الأمان الذي عقدوه له ، إذ سمحوا له بدخول دارهم ، وشرطوا عليه الوفاء به فيحرم عليه تعديه . أما إذا دخل مستأمن منهم دارنا فلا تسويغ للربا معه لأن عقد أماننا له يحرّم علينا ما له إلا ما كان بطريق شرعي لا إثم فيه ولا ملام ، إذ الدار دار إسلام .

THE EVIDENCE OF SHAFI'I AND ABU YUSUF

حجة الشافعي وأبي يوسف

w43.3   Shafi'i and Abu Yusuf hold that hostile

w43.3   والشافعي وأبو يوسف يعتبران

non-Muslims in their own lands are like those of them with a safe-conduct agreement in our lands: just as dealing in interest (riba) with one of them in our lands is not lawful, neither is dealing in it with them in theirs. They say that the above-mentioned hadith is singular (gharib), meaning it has reached us through but one single narrator. Kamal ibn al-Humam states in *Fath al-Qadir* that Shafi'i relates from Abu Yusuf that Abu Hanifa only held this position because a certain sheikh related from Makhul that "the Prophet (Allah bless him and give him peace) said,

" 'There is no usury (riba) between enemy non-Muslims,'

"[N: Makhul adding,] and I think he said, 'and people who are Muslims.' " Bayhaqi reports that Shafi'i said, "This hadith is not authenticated and there is no evidence in it." The Hanafi Sarakhsi says in *al-Mabsut*, "This hadith is *mursal* [n: i.e. reported by one of those (tabi'i) who had personally met and studied under one or more of the prophetic Companions (Sahaba) but not the Prophet himself (Allah bless him and give him peace), hadiths reported in the form of quoting the Prophet (Allah bless him and give him peace) without mentioning the name of the Companion who related it directly from him], though Makhul [n: the *tabi'i* in this case] is a reliable narrator, and a *mursal* hadith from someone like him is acceptable as evidence...."

w43.4 (n: Several pages follow, discussing the evidence and *ijtihad* of Abu Hanifa and Imam Muhammad, as to why they allow:

(a) taking interest (riba), not giving it;

(b) from an enemy non-Muslim, not from a Muslim;

(c) when both parties are in enemy lands (dar al-harb), not when either party or both are in Muslim lands.)

.... Thus, what the *fatwa* of the mufti of Dar al-'Ulum of Deoband says about the permissibility

الكافر الحربي في دارهم كالمستأمن في دارنا، فكما لا يحل الربا مع هذا لا يحل مع ذاك. وقالا في الحديث إنه غريب ـ أي تفرد به راو واحد فقط ـ.

قال الكمال بن الهمام في فتح القدير [الـذي شرح به كتـاب الهدايـة]: قال الشـافعي: قال أبـو يوسف: إنمـا قال أبو حنيفة هذا لأن بعض المشيخة حدثنا عن مكحول عن رسول الله ﷺ أنه قال:

«لا ربا بين أهل الحرب» أظنه قال:

«وأهـل الإسـلام» قال الشـافعي: وهـذا الحديث ليس بثابت ولا حجة فيه. أسنده عنه البيهقي.

قال [ـ أي شمس الأئمـة] السـرخسي الحنفي في المبسـوط ـ: هذا مرسل، ومكحول ثقة، والمرسل من مثله مقبول. [....]

w43.4 (ت: ويلي ما سبق ذكره عدة صفحات يناقش المؤلف فيهـا أدلة أبي حنيفة ومحمد واجتهادهما في تجويز:

ـ أخذ الربا (دون إعطائه).

ـ بشـرط أن يكـون من الكافر الحربي (لا من المسلم).

ـ وإنما يكـون كل من الآخذ والمعطي في دار الحـرب، لا إن كان أحـدهمـا أو كلاهما في دار الإسلام).

... وعلى هذا فمـا في فتـوى مفتي دار العلوم بديـوبانـد من إجـازة إعطاء

of the Muslim giving interest (riba) to non-Muslims in enemy lands (dar al-harb) being like the permissibility of taking it from them, is wrong and unacceptable because it flatly contradicts the authoritatively transmitted position of the Hanafi school, as Imam Sarakhsi has explicitly stated in *al-Sayr al-kabir wa sharhuhu,* for the recorded position of the Hanafi school is for the permissibility of *taking* it from them only, not the permissibility of giving it to them....

This then, and it should be noted that Muslims in enemy lands (dar al-harb) dealing with each other in interest (riba) is not lawful, even though the above-mentioned *fatwa* does not direct itself to the question....

As for the *fatwa's* permitting Muslims to put their money in non-Muslims' banks for interest (riba), and to loan the state money for interest, this could only be done conformably with the opinion of Abu Hanifa and Imam Muhammad if the Muslim were in enemy lands (dar al-harb) and put his money in the enemy non-Muslims' bank there, and similarly with loaning the state money for interest. As for doing it in Muslim lands, it is not permissible, no matter whether the bank is located in Muslim lands or enemy lands, for the Muslim is forbidden to do such a thing in Muslim countries because Islam's rulings apply there, and scholars stipulate for the permissibility of his dealing in interest (riba) that firstly it be with non-Muslims, and secondly in enemy lands, so the prohibition applies in either case.

WHAT IS MEANT BY "ENEMY LANDS" (DAR AL-HARB)

w43.5   As for the *fatwa's* claim that India is an enemy land (dar al-harb), it is not in its generality true. Because areas where Muslims reside and there is a remnant of Islam's rules—even if this is limited to marriages and what pertains to them, for example—are considered *Muslim lands.* A Muslim land does not become an enemy land except under three conditions:

(a) that the security of Muslims through their

المسلم الربا للحربيين في دار الحرب كإجازة أخذه منهم، ممنوع لا يسلم له لمخالفته منقول المذهب الذي صرح به شمس الأئمة السرخسي في «السير الكبير وشرحه». فإن المنقول هو جواز الأخذ منهم فقط، لا جواز إعطائهم ...

هذا ومما ينبغي أن يعلم أن تعامل المسلمين في دار الحرب بالربا فيما بينهم غير جائز، وإن لم تتعرض الفتوى المذكورة له ...

وأما سماح الفتوى بوضع المسلمين أموالهم في مصارف غير المسلمين بالفائدة الربوية وتسويغهما لهم إقراض الدولة المال بها أيضاً، فهو إنما يتم في قول أبي حنيفة ومحمد إذا كان المسلم في دار الحرب ووضع ماله في مصرف الحربيين في دارهم، وكذا الحكم في إقراض ماله للدولة بالفائدة، أما إذا كان في دار الإسلام فلا؛ سواء كان المصرف فيها أو في دار الحرب لأنه ممنوع من هذا التصرف في بلاد المسلمين لسريان أحكام الإسلام فيها، والفقهاء قيدوا الجواز بأن يكون التعامل بالربا معهم في دارهم فالمنع شامل للصورتين.

ما هي دار الحرب؟

w43.5   وأما زعم الفتوى أن بلاد الهند دار حرب فإنه على عمومه غير صحيح. ذلك بأن المناطق التي يقطنها المسلمون منها، وفيها بقية من أحكام الإسلام ولو كانت قاصرة على الأنكحة وما إليها مثلاً، تعتبر دار إسلام. ولا تنقلب دار الإسلام إلى دار حرب إلا بشروط ثلاثة هي:

أولاً: أن يزول الأمان الأول الذي كان

leader no longer exists and the security of non-Muslims has taken its place;

(b) that they have been surrounded on all sides such that it is impossible for the aid of Muslims to reach them;

(c) and that not a single one of Islam's rules remains therein (N: which effectively means that none of the lands that Islam has spread to and in which something of it remains can be considered an enemy land. As for other countries, *enemy lands* (dar al-harb, lit, "abode of war") consist of those with whom the Muslim countries (dar al-Islam) are at a state of war) (n: in the light of which, it is clear that there is virtually no country on the face of the earth where a Muslim has an excuse to behave differently than he would in an Islamic country, whether in his commercial or other dealings).

(*Rudud 'ala abatil wa rasa'il al-Shaykh Muhammad al-Hamid* (y44), 2.267–79)

للمسلمين بإمامهم ويحل محله أمان الكافرين .

ثانياً : أن يحاط بهم من كل جوانبهم فلا يمكن وصول مدد المسلمين إليها .

ثالثاً : أن لا يبقى فيها حكم من أحكام الإسلام [محرر من ردود على أباطيل ورسائل الشيخ محمد الحامد : ٢ / ٢٦٧ ـ ٢٧٩] .

(ح) : فلا يعد من دار الحرب بلد انتشر فيها الإسلام وبقي فيها شيء منه . أما غيره من البلاد ، فدار الحرب هي ما بينها وبين دار الإسلام حالة حرب (ت) : وفي ضوء هذا فلا يكاد يكون على وجه الأرض بلد يعذر المسلم بأن يتصرف خلاف تصرفه في دار الإسلام ، سواء في ماله أو في غيره)) .

PROTECTING LENDERS FROM
LOSS DUE TO INFLATION

ماذا يجب في وفاء القرض عند هبوط سعر العملة الورقية .

w43.6 (n:) Muhammad Amin ibn 'Abidin records that if one borrows ten *fils* (a monetary unit) which then lose *all* their value (kasada), one is not obliged, according to Abu Hanifa, to repay anything but the same amount of them. Abu Yusuf and Imam Muhammad, however, hold that one is obliged to repay their value (A: as it stood at the time of the loan) in silver (A: and since it is a financial obligation, the lender is entitled to accept other than silver in its place, such as the silver's value in currency at the market prices current on the day of repayment) (*Hashiyat radd al-muhtar 'ala al-Durr al-mukhtar sharh Tanwir al-absar* (y47), 5.162). As for a lawful alternative to interest for protecting the lender from losing money because of simple *inflation* (which in contradistinction to the above is a mere *decrease* in the value of currency), the best means would seem to be to initially loan a specific amount of gold or silver, and then repay the loan with the same amount of gold or silver, or its value in currency at the market prices current on the day of repayment, if the lender will accept this in place of it, as in (A:) above.

*

w44.0 BEQUEATHING MORE THAN ONE-THIRD OF ONE'S PROPERTY (from L3.1(A:))

w44.0 جواز الوصية بأكثر من ثلث المال عند فقد الورثة عند الحنفية

w44.1 (Muhammad Amin ibn 'Abidin:)

(Question:) "So-and-so bequeathed [wasiyya, def: L1.0(A:)] all of his property to a nonfamily member and died insisting on this, and only a wife survived him. She did not agree to permit this bequest [N: by waiving her own estate division share of one-fourth]. What is the ruling on it?"

(Answer:) "Bequeathing more than a third of one's property is not lawful when there is an estate division heir [n: or more than one] who deserves the whole estate. As for when an heir does not deserve the whole estate, such as a husband [N: whose maximal estate division share is one-half (dis L6.3)] or wife [N: whose maximal share is one-fourth (dis: L6.4)] [A: or when there are no eligible estate division heirs at all], then it is permissible to bequeath more than a third of one's property" (al-'Uqud al-durriyya fi tanqih al-Fatawa al-Hamidiyya (y53), 2.310).

w44.1 (محمد أمين بن عابدين :)
(سئل) فيما إذا أوصى زيد بجميع ماله لأجنبي ومات مصراً على ذلك من زوجة لا غير ولم تجز الزوجةُ الوصيةَ فكيف الحكم؟
(الجواب) الوصية بما زاد على الثلث غير جائزة إذا كان هناك وارث يستحق جميع المال. أما إذا كان لا يستحق جميع الميراث كالزوج والزوجة فإنه يجوز أن يوصي بما زاد على الثلث [نقل من العقود الدرية في تنقيح الفتاوى الحامدية : ٢/ ٣١٠].

*

w45.0 A WIFE'S MARITAL OBLIGATIONS (from m5.1, end)

w45.0 واجبات الزوجة

A WIFE'S MARITAL OBLIGATIONS IN THE SHAFI'I SCHOOL

واجبات الزوجة عند الشافعية

w45.1 (Abu Ishaq Shirazi:) A woman is not obliged to serve her husband by baking, grinding flour, cooking, washing, or any other kind of service, because the marriage contract entails, for her part, only that she let him enjoy her sexually, and she is not obligated to do other than that. (A: Rather, it is considered sunna in our school for the wife to do the housework, and the husband (who is obliged to support her) to earn the living, since this is how the Prophet (Allah bless him and give him peace) divided the work between Fatima and

w45.1 (أبو إسحق الشيرازي :)
[. . . و] لا يجب عليها خدمته في الخبز والطحن والطبخ والغسل وغيرها من الخدم لأن المعقود عليه من جهتها هو الاستمتاع فلا يلزمها ما سواه [نقل من المهذب في فقه الإمام الشافعي : ٢/ ٦٨]. (ع : بل عندنا يسن لها خدمته ويسن للزوج التكسب ـ إذ نفقتها واجبة

'Ali (Allah be well pleased with them)) (*al-Muhadhdhab fi fiqh al-Imam al-Shafi'i* (y125), 2.68).

A WIFE'S MARITAL OBLIGATIONS
IN THE HANAFI SCHOOL

w45.2 (Nahlawi:) The wife's serving her husband at home—by cooking, cleaning, and baking bread—is religiously obligatory for her, and if she does not, she is committing a sin, though it is not something that she may be forced to do by the court (*al-Durar al-mubaha fi al-hazr wa al-ibaha* (y99), 172).

*

w46.0 THE PERMISSIBILITY OF
CONTRACEPTION (from m5.5)

w46.1 (Yusuf Qaradawi:) Islam has encouraged prolific reproduction and blessed children, male and female. But birth control has been made a dispensation for the Muslim when rational motives and real necessities call for it. The prevalent means people resorted to for preventing or diminishing births in the time of the Prophet (Allah bless him and give him peace) was coitus interruptus, placing the sperm outside the womb when ejaculation was felt imminent, and the prophetic Companions did this during the time of prophethood and divine inspiration. Bukhari and Muslim relate from Jabir, "We used to practice coitus interruptus in the time of the Messenger of Allah (Allah bless him and give him peace), while the Koran was being revealed." And in *Sahih Muslim:* "We used to practice coitus interruptus in the time of the Messenger of Allah (Allah bless him and give him peace). Word of this reached him and he did not prohibit it."

A man came to the Prophet (Allah bless him and give him peace) and said: "O Messenger of Allah, I have a bondwoman with whom I practice coitus interruptus. I do not want her to get

عليه ـ لأن النبي ﷺ قسم العمل بين فاطمة وعلي رضي الله عنهما هكذا.

واجبات الزوجة عند الحنفية

w45.2 (النحلاوي:) [. . . و] وعليها خدمته داخل البيت ديانةً، من الطبخ والغَسل والخبز، ولو لم تفعل أثمت، ولكن لا تجبر عليها قضاءً [نقل من الدرر المباحة في الحظر والإباحة: ١٧٢].

w46.0 جواز تنظيم النسل

w46.1 (يوسف القرضاوي:) [. . .] قد حبب الإسلام في كثرة النسل، وبارك الأولاد ذكوراً وإناثاً ولكنه رخص للمسلم في تنظيم النسل إذا دعت إلى ذلك دواع معقولة وضرورات معتبرة، وقد كانت الوسيلة الشائعة التي يلجأ إليها الناس لمنع النسل أو تقليله في عهد الرسول ﷺ ـ هي العزل (وهو قذف النطفة خارج الرحم عند الإحساس بنزولها) وقد كان الصحابة يفعلون ذلك في عهد النبوة والوحي كما روي في الصحيحين عن جابر: «كنا نعزل على عهد رسول الله ﷺ والقرآن ينزل».

وفي صحيح مسلم: «كنا نعزل على عهد رسول الله فبلغ ذلك رسول الله ﷺ فلم ينهنا».

وجاء رجل إلى النبي ﷺ فقال: «يا رسول الله، إن لي جارية وأنا أعزل

pregnant, but I want what men want. The Jews say that coitus interruptus is a lesser form of killing one's children." The Prophet (Allah bless him and give him peace) said:

"The Jews have lied. If Allah wanted to create it, you would not be able to prevent it."

(*al-Halal wa al-haram fi al-Islam* (y110), 191–92)

THE OFFENSIVENESS OF
CONTRACEPTION IN THE
SHAFI'I SCHOOL

w46.2 (Ghazali:) It is of the etiquette of inter-course not to practice coitus interruptus, there being disagreement among scholars as to the per-missibility or offensiveness of doing so, though the correct position in our opinion is that it is permis-sible. As for its offensiveness, *offensive* is a term applied to things whose prohibition is closer to the unlawful, things whose prohibition is closer to the permissible, and things involving merely the non-performance of something meritorious; and it (n: coitus interruptus) is offensive in this third sense, the nonperformance of a meritorious act, just as it is said, for example, that "it is offensive for some-one in a mosque to sit without invoking Allah (dhikr) or praying," or "it is offensive for some-one living in Mecca not to perform the hajj every year." The meaning of this offensiveness is merely that it is forgoing what is fitter and more praiseworthy, as we established earlier in explain-ing the virtue of having a child (*Ihya' 'ulum al-din* (y39), 2.47).

*

w47.0 A WARNING AGAINST
CARELESS ACCUSATIONS OF
UNBELIEF (from o8.7(11))

w47.1 (Muhammad 'Alawi Maliki:) Many people error, may Allah correct them, in under-

عنهـا، وإني أكـره أن تحمـل وأنا أريد ما يريـد الـرجـال . وإن اليهـود تحدث : أن العـزل الموءودة الصغـرى» فقـال عليـه السـلام: «كـذبت اليهـود. لو أراد الله أن يخلقـه ما استطعت أن تصـرفـه» [رواه التـرمـذي وأصحاب السـنن] [نقل من الحلال والحرام في الإسلام : ١٩١ - ١٩٢].

كراهة العزل في المذهب
الشافعي

w46.2 (الغزالي :) ومن الآداب أن لا يعـزل [. . .] فإن عزل فقـد اختـلف العلمـاء في إباحتـه وكـراهتـه [. . .] والصحيـح عنـدنـا أن ذلك مبـاح وأمـا الكراهية فإنها تطلق لنهي التحريم ولنهي التنـزيـه ولتـرك الفضيلة . فهـو مكـروه بالمعنى الثـالث، أي فيـه تـرك فضيلة كمـا يقـال يكـره للقـاعد في المسجد أن يقعد فارغـاً لا يشتغل بذكـر أو صلاة، ويكـره للحـاضر في مكة مقيمـاً بها أن لا يحج كل سنـة، والمـراد بهذه الكراهية تـرك الأولى والفضيلة فقـط وهـذا ثابت لمـا بينـاه من الفضيلة في الـولد [محرر من إحياء علوم الدين : ٢ / ٤٧].

w47.0 الـتـحـذيـر من
المجازفة بالتكفير

w47.1 (محمـد علوي المـالكي :) يخطىء كثيـر من الناس ـ أصلحهم الله ـ

standing the real reasons that put a person beyond the fold of Islam and necessitate that he be considered an unbeliever. One sees them rushing to judge Muslims as unbelievers for mere contraventions of Sacred Law, until there is hardly a Muslim on the face of the earth, save a handful. While we endeavor to excuse such people and give them the benefit of the doubt, saying that perhaps they have a good motive such as the intention to fulfill the obligation to command the right and forbid the wrong, what has escaped them is that performing the duty of commanding the right and forbidding the wrong requires wisdom and goodly exhortation, and if the matter requires argument, it must be with that which is better, as Allah Most High says,

"Call to the path of your Lord with wisdom and goodly exhortation, and argue with them with that which is better" (Koran 16:125),

for this is likelier to gain acceptance and achieve one's purpose, and to do otherwise is error and folly.

If one tries to convince a Muslim—who prays, fulfills the obligations of Allah, avoids what He has prohibited, invites people to His religion, maintains His mosques, and keeps His covenants—to accept something one feels is the truth, but he views the matter to be otherwise, and the opinion of Islamic scholars affirming and denying it has been divided since time immemorial, and he will not agree with one's point of view; then if one charges him with unbelief merely because he opposes one's opinion, one has committed an enormous wrong and a grievous sin that Allah has forbidden, having rather called us to criticize with wisdom and graciousness. There is scholarly consensus that it is unlawful to charge with unbelief anyone who faces Mecca to pray, unless he denies the Almighty Creator, Majestic and Exalted, commits open polytheism that cannot be explained away by extenuating circumstances, denies prophethood, or something which is necessarily known as being of the religion, or which is *mutawatir* (def: o22.1(d(II))) (N: whether the latter is of the Koran or hadith), or which there is scholarly consensus upon its being necessarily

في فهم حقيقة الأسباب التي تخرج صاحبها عن دائرة الإسلام وتوجب عليه الحكم بالكفر. فتراهم يسارعون إلى الحكم على المسلم بالكفر لمجرد المخالفة حتى لم يبق من المسلمين على وجه الأرض إلا القليل. ونحن نتلمس لهؤلاء العذر تحسيناً للظن، ونقول لعل نيتهم حسنة من دافع واجب الأمر بالمعروف والنهي عن المنكر ولكن فاتهم أن واجب الأمر بالمعروف والنهي عن المنكر لا بد في أدائه من الحكمة والموعظة الحسنة وإذا اقتضى الأمر المجادلة يجب أن تكون بالتي هي أحسن كما قال تعالى :

﴿ادْعُ إِلَى سَبِيلِ رَبِّكَ بِالحِكْمَةِ وَالمَوْعِظَةِ الحَسَنَةِ وَجَادِلْهُمْ بِالَّتِي هِيَ أَحْسَنُ﴾ [الحجر : ١٢٥].

وذلك أدعى إلى القبول وأقرب للحصول على المأمول ومخالفته خطأ وحماقة.

فإذا دعوت مسلماً يصلي، ويؤدي فرائض الله، ويجتنب محارمه وينشر دعوته، ويشيد مساجده، ويقيم معاهده، إلى أمر تراه حقاً ويراه هو على خلافك، والرأي فيه بين العلماء مختلف قديماً إقراراً وإنكاراً فلم يطاوعك في رأيك فرميته بالكفر لمجرد مخالفته لرأيك فقد قارفت عظيمة نكراء، وأتيت أمراً إداً نهاك عنه الله ودعاك إلى الأخذ فيه بالحكمة والحسنى. وقد انعقد الإجماع على منع تكفير أحد من أهل القبلة إلا بما فيه نفي الصانع القادر جل وعلا أو شرك جلي لا يحتمل التأويل أو إنكار النبوة أو إنكار ما علم من الدين بالضرورة أو إنكار متواتر أو مجمع عليه ضرورة من الدين. والمعلوم من الدين ضرورة كالتوحيد والنبوات وختم الرسالة بمحمد ﷺ.

known as part of the religion. *Necessarily known* means such things as the oneness of Allah, the attributes of prophethood, that prophetic messengerhood has ended with Muhammad (Allah bless him and give him peace), the resurrection on the Last Day, the Final Reckoning, the recompense, and paradise and hell—the denier of any of which is an unbeliever, and which no Muslim has an excuse for ignorance of, unless he is a new convert to Islam, who is excused until he can learn, but not afterwards.

To judge a Muslim to be an unbeliever for anything besides the above is a very dangerous thing, as has come in the hadith,

"If someone says to his fellow Muslim, 'You unbeliever,' one of them deserves the name."

It is not valid for such a judgement to proceed from anyone except someone who knows the things that involve unbelief from those that acquit one of it in the light of the Sacred Law, and the strict demarcation between faith and unbelief according to the standards of the Law of Islam. It is not permissible for any human being to rush onto the field and charge another with unbelief on the basis of opinions and imaginings without having checked and made sure, and without firm knowledge. Otherwise the torrent would flood the valley floor, and not a Muslim would remain on the face of the earth, except a few. The Imam of the Two Sanctuaries (n: Juwayni) has said, "If we were asked to distinguish the expressions that deserve to be considered unbelief from those that do not, we would reply that this is a wish for something pointless to wish for, being too distant a reach and too stony a path to tread, involving as it does the very bases of the science of divine unity; someone who does not attain to the furthest reaches of the facts cannot arrive at anything reliable to vindicate his criteria for unbelief."

Because of this, we urge the utmost caution, in other than the above-mentioned cases, against careless accusations of unbelief, for they are extremely dangerous. And Allah guides to the best of ways, and unto Him is the final destination (*Mafahim yajibu an tusahhaha* (y83), 5–7).

والبعث في اليـوم الآخـر والحسـاب والجـزاء والجنـة والنار، يكفر جاحده ولا يعـذر أحـد من المسلمين بالجهـل به إلا من كان حديث عهد في الإسلام فإنه يعذر إلى أن يتعلمه فإنه لا يعذر بعده. [...].

وإن الحكم على المسلم بالكفـر في غيـر هذه المـواطن التي بيناها أمر خطير، وفي الحـديث: «من قال لأخيه المسلم يا كافر فقد باء بها أحدهما» [رواه البخاري].

ولا يصح صدوره إلا ممن عرف بنور الشريعة مداخل الكفر ومخارجه والحدود الفـاصلة بين الكفر والإيمان في حكم الشـريعـة الغـراء. فلا يجـوز لأي إنسان الركض في هذا الميدان والتكفير بالأوهام والـمظـان دون تثبت ويقين وعلم متين. وإلا اختلط سيلها بالأبطح ولم يبق مسلم على وجه الأرض إلا القليـل. [...] وكان إمام الحرمين يقول: لو قيـل لنـا فصلوا ما يقتضي التكفير من العبارات مما لا يقتضي لقلنـا هذا طمـع في غير مطمع فإن هذا بعيـد المـدرك وعـر المسلك يستمـد من أصول التوحيد ومن لم يحظ بنهايـات الحقـائق لم يتحصل من دلائل التكفير على وثائق.

لذلك نحـذر كل تحذير من المجازفة بالتكفيـر في غير المـواطن السابق بيانها لأنه جد خطيـر. والله الهـادي إلى سواء السبيل وإليه المصير [محرر من مفاهيم يجب أن تصحح: ٥ ـ ٧].

DEVIATIONS AND ABERRATIONS
THAT ARE UNQUESTIONABLY INVALID

w47.2 (Muhammad Sa'id Buti:) We do not consider *deviations and aberrations* to include any position reflecting a disagreement between Islamic scholars resulting from their differences on derived rulings or particular applications of Sacred Law, for these all return to its basic methodology. Rather, we categorically affirm that this is a normal variance entailed by the very nature of the case (dis b6.2) and its methodological bases, though we subject these various viewpoints to an examination of which is the soundest, classifying them according to their relative strengths and weaknesses, each of us through his own reasoning (ijtihad) and judgement.

Nor do deviant and aberrant opinions necessarily entail the unbelief of the people who hold them, or being beyond the pale of Islam. Rather, there are some opinions so deviant that they reach the degree of negating what is necessarily known as being of the religion, leading to what the Prophet (Allah bless him and give him peace) termed *open unbelief;* others whose deviance reaches only the degree of being a violation of the methodological principles concurred upon by scholars of the Arabic language and hence by scholars of Islamic Law, entailing blameworthy innovation (bid'a), and perhaps corruption and turning from the truth without excuse; and still others whose deviance and aberrance wavers between reaching actual unbelief and merely falling within the bounds of corruption and blameworthy innovation, the honest and sincere investigator not finding any firm basis to consider them unbelief, yet not being able to accept with confidence that they are only a marginal deviance that does not compromise the person who holds them or put him outside of Islam. In dealing with this category of deviations and intellectual aberrances, we prefer to follow the way of greater precaution, which in this context consists of understanding people's states insofar as possible as if they were still within the fold of Islam and under its rubric. For the mistake of giving them the benefit of the doubt does not entail the losses entailed by making a mistake

ليس كل شذوذ في الرأي كفر

w47.2 (محمـد سعيـد البـوطي:) [. . . و] لا نعـد من الشذوذ أو الانحراف كل مذهب أو رأي انعكس الخـلاف بين العـلمـاء فيـه عن خلافهـم في تلك الجـزئيـات أو التطبيقـات العـائـدة إلى المنهج ، بل هو ، فيمـا نجزم به ، خلاف طبيعي اقتضاه الخلاف في جذور القضية وأصـولها المنهجية ، وإن كنا نُخضع هذه الآراء الـخـلافيـة لميـزان التـرجيـح والتصنيف بين درجـات القوة والضعف ، فيمـا قد يهديه اجتهاد كل منا ونظره . [. . .]

ثم إن [هـذه] الآراء الشاذة والمنحرفة [التي سنستعـرض نمـاذج منهـا] ليست بالضـرورة مستوجبـة لكفر أصحابهـا وخروجهم عن الملة . بل فيهـا ما يشتد الشـذوذ والانحراف فيه بحيث يبلغ درجة إنـكـار ما هو معـروف من الـديـن بالضـرورة ، فيجـر ذلـك إلى ما سمـاه رسول الله ﷺ بالكفر البـواح . وفيهـا ما يقف الشـذوذ والانحراف فيه عنـد حد الخروج عن قواعد المنهج المتفق عليها عنـد علمـاء الشريعة الإسلامية ، فيستلزم ابتـداعـاً وربمـا فسقـاً وجنوحاً عن الحق بدون عذر . . . وفيهـا ما قد يتردد الشذوذ والانحـراف فيه بين بلوغ درجة الكفر وحـدود الفسق والابتـداع ، فلا يجـد فيه البـاحـث الـمنصف معتمداً راسخـاً للتكفيـر ، كمـا لا يطمئن إلى أنه انحراف جزئي لم ينـد بصـاحبـه ولم يخرجه عن دائرة الإسلام . ونحن في مثل هذا النوع من الشـذوذات والضلالات الفكرية نؤثر اتبـاع الحيطـة . وإنما الحيطـة في هذا المقـام حمـل حال النـاس ما أمكن على أنهم لا يزالون داخلين في حظيرة الإسلام واقـفيـن تحت مظلتـه ، فإن الخطأ في تحسين الظن بهم لن يجر الـوبـال الذي يجـره الخطأ في إساءة الظن بهم بنسبتهم

by not giving them it and accusing them of unbelief and having left Islam. Despite which, we spare no effort to explain their corruption, and that they have innovated something Allah Mighty and Majestic has not given leave to; explaining their deviation from the methodology agreed upon by the scholars of this Community and warning people not to be misled by them or affected by their falsehoods (*al-Salafiyya marhala zamaniyya mubaraka la madhhab Islami* (y34), 109–10).

إلى الكفر والمروق عن الإسلام . هذا مع العلم بأنـا لا نألـو جهداً في بيـان فسقهم وابتـداعهم لمـا لم يأذن به الله عز وجـل وشـذوذهم عن المنهج الـذي اتفق عليه علمـاء هذه الأمـة ، وفي تحذير الناس من الاغتـرار بهم والتأثـر بزيغهم [محـرر من السلفية مرحلة زمنيـة مبـاركـة لا مذهب إسلامي : ١٠٩ ـ ١١٠].

*

w48.0   WEAK HADITHS (from p9.5)

w48.0 الاحتجاج بالحديث الضعيف

w48.1   (A:) *Weak* (da'if) is a term for any hadith with a chain of transmission containing a narrator whose memory was poor, one who was not trustworthy, not identified by name, or for other reasons. But *weak* cannot simply be equated with *false*. Were this the case, mere analysis of the transmitters would be the universal criterion for acceptance or rejection of particular rulings based on hadiths. While scholars do use this measure in upgrading the work of preceding generations of legal authorities, they have not employed it as a simplistic expedient to eliminate every piece of legal information that is connected with a weak hadith, because of various considerations.

MULTIPLE MEANS OF TRANSMISSION

كثرة الطرق

w48.2   One of these is that when a piece of information is received through a means of transmission that may or may not be trustworthy, we generally have doubts about it. But when one and the same piece of information reaches us through several completely different channels, even though each one may or may not be trustworthy, the logical probability of the information's falsity is much reduced. And if we receive the very same piece of information from ten such channels, the possibility of its falsity does not usually even come to mind.

This verificatory principle has two important implications, one being the obligatory nature of belief in hadiths that are *mutawatir* (def: o22.1(d(II))), and the second being the weight that hadith scholars give to multiple means of transmission, which can raise a hadith from well authenticated (hasan) to rigorously authenticated (sahih), or from weak (da'if) to well authenticated, as described in the following account of a hadith's reclassification by a major specialist in hadith forgeries.

('Ali Qari:) The hadith "I am the city of knowledge and 'Ali is its gate," was mentioned by Tirmidhi in his *Jami'*, where he said it was

(علي القـاري :) حديث «أنـا مدينـة العلم وعليٌّ بابهـا» رواه التـرمـذي في جامعه وقال إنه منكر .

unacknowledgeable. Bukhari also said this, and said that it was without legitimate claim to authenticity. Ibn Ma'in said that it was a baseless lie, as did Abu Hatim and Yahya ibn Sa'id. Ibn Jawzi recorded it in his book of hadith forgeries, and was confirmed by Dhahabi and others in this. Ibn Daqiq al-'Eid said, "This hadith is not confirmed by scholars, and is held by some to be spurious." Daraqutni stated that it was uncorroborated. Ibn Hajar 'Asqalani was asked about it and answered that it was well authenticated (hasan), not rigorously authenticated (sahih), as Hakim had said, but not a forgery (mawdu') as Ibn Jawzi had said. This was mentioned by Suyuti. The hadith master (hafiz) Abu Sa'id 'Ala'i said, "The truth is that the hadith is well authenticated (hasan), in view of its multiple means of transmission, being neither rigorously authenticated (sahih) nor weak (da'if), much less a forgery" (*Risala al-mawdu'at* (y112), 26).

وكـذا قال البخـاري وقـال إنه ليس له وجه صحيح . وقال ابن معين إنه كذب لا أصـل له وكـذا قال أبـو حاتم ويحيى بن سعـيـد . وأورده ابـن الـجـوزي في المـوضـوعات ووافقه الذهبي وغيره على ذلـك . وقال ابن دقيق العيد هذا الحديث لم يثبتوه وقيل إنه باطل . وقال الدارقطني غير ثابت .

وسئل عنه الحافظ العسقلاني فأجاب بأنـه حسن لا صحيح كما قال الحاكم ولا موضوع كما قال ابن الجوزي ذكره السيوطي .

وقـال الحـافـظ أبـو سعـيـد العـلائي الصواب أنه حسن باعتبـار كثرة طرقه لا صحيح ولا ضعيف فضلًا عن أن يكـون موضوعـا [على ما ذكره الزركشي] [نقل من رسالة الموضوعات : ٢٦] .

(A:) Thus, when the person who has related a hadith is an Islamic scholar of the first rank, it is not enough for a student or popular writer to find one chain of transmission for the hadith that is weak. There are a great many hadiths with several chains of transmission, and adequate scholarly treatment of how these affect a hadith's authenticity has been traditionally held to require a master (hafiz), those like Bukhari, Muslim, Dhahabi, Ibn Kathir, or Suyuti who have memorized at least 100,000 hadiths—their texts, chains of transmission, and significance—to undertake the comparative study of the hadith's various chains of transmission that cannot be accurately assessed without such knowledge. Today, when not one hadith master (hafiz) remains in the Muslim Community, we do not accept the judgement of any would-be reclassifiers of hadith, no matter how large their popular following, unless it is corroborated by the work of previous hadith masters.

w48.3 Another reason why *weak* cannot simply be equated with *false* is the fact that *weak* is an attribute of the hadith's chain of transmission, while *false* is an attribute of the hadith's text. These are two different things, and the relationship between their respective reliabilities is a probabilistic expectation (istinbat) that is neither strictly causal, nor yet a necessary logical implication (lazim), there being four logical possibilities for any hadith:

(1) a sound text and sound chain of transmission, as with well-authenticated (hasan) or rigorously authenticated (sahih) hadiths;

(2) a sound text and an unsound chain of transmitters, reflecting the possibility that a transmitter with a poor memory, or unknown to the person who recorded the hadith, or one not trustworthy, is in principle capable of relating the hadith correctly;

(3) an unsound text and unsound chain of transmitters, as with hadiths that are forged (mawdu');

(4) or an unsound text and a sound chain of transmitters, reflecting the possibility that one of those who classify the personalities and reliability of various hadith transmitters could in principle make an error in their *ijtihad* regarding a particular person.

Because of the distinction between text and transmission, forms of evidence other than the authenticity rating of the chain of narrators are sometimes admissible, as when there is a consensus of legal scholars who have received the hadith with acceptance, which is an acknowledged form of corroboration for hadiths of the second type mentioned above.

(Isma'il Ansari:) Ibn Hajar 'Asqalani says: "Among the characteristics that necessitate acceptance is for scholars of Sacred Law to have concurred on applying the implications of a hadith. Such a hadith is acceptable, even obligatory to apply, as a number of the Imams of fundamentals of Islam (usul) have explicitly stated. Shafi'i, for example, says, 'What I have said about water when its taste, odor, and color change, has been related from the Prophet (Allah bless him and give him peace) through a channel of transmission that hadith scholars do not confirm the like of, but it is the position of all scholars without a single dissenting voice I know of.' And he said of the hadith 'There is no bequest to an estate division heir'—'Scholars of hadith do not corroborate it, but all scholars receive it with acceptance and apply it.'"

Ibn al-Qayyim, in his *I'lam al-muwaqqi'in*, when discussing the hadith of Mu'adh about judgements (A: in which the Prophet (Allah bless him and give him peace) asked Mu'adh ibn Jabal when dispatching him to Yemen how he would judge, to which Mu'adh replied that he would judge first by the Koran, then by the sunna, and then by his own reasoning (ijtihad)), says, "Legal scholars accept it and employ it as evidence, from which we learn that they hold it to be rigorously authenticated (sahih), just as we learn of the authenticity of the Prophet's saying (Allah bless him and give him peace):

(1) " 'There is no bequest to an estate division heir.'

(إسماعيل الأنصاري:) [. . .] وقال الصنعاني في توضيح الأفكار:] قال [الحافظ يعني] ابن حجر: من جملة صفات القبول [التي لم يتعرض لها شيخنا ـ يريد زين الدين في منظومته وشرحها] أن يتفق العلماء على العمل بمدلول حديث فإنه يقبل، حتى يجب العمل به وقد صرح بذلك جماعة من أئمة الأصول ومن أمثلته قول الشافعي: وما قلت إنه إذا غيّر طعم الماء وريحه ولونه يروى عن النبي ﷺ من وجه لا يثبت أهل الحديث مثله ولكنه قول العامة لا أعلم خلافاً. وقال في حديث «لا وصية لوارث» لا يثبته أهل العلم بالحديث ولكن العامة تلقته بالقبول وعملت به. [. . .].

[. . .] قال ابن القيم في إعلام الموقعين في كلام على حديث معاذ في القضاء: إن أهل العلم تلقوه واحتجوا به فوقفنا بذلك على صحته عندهم كما وقفنا على صحة قول رسول الله ﷺ «لا وصية لوارث» وقوله في البحر «هو الطهور ماؤه»

956

(2) " '[The hadith about the sea,] Its water is purifying.'

(3) " 'When buyer and seller differ about the price they have agreed upon and the merchandise still exists, each swears [N: that his side of the story is correct] and [N: if they cannot agree] they cancel the sale.'

(4) " 'The killer's extended family is responsible for the indemnity.'

"Even if these hadiths are unauthenticated in their chains of transmission, since virtually all scholars have related them, the hadiths' authenticity, which they accept, eliminates their need to verify the channels of transmission, and so it is too with the hadith of Mu'adh: the fact that all scholars have adduced it as evidence eliminates the need for their checking its means of transmission."

And Ibn 'Abd al-Barr says in *al-Istidhkar*, concerning Tirmidhi's having related that Bukhari said of the hadith of the sea "Its water is purifying" that it was rigorously authenticated (sahih)— "Hadith scholars do not consider hadiths with the like of its chain of transmission to be rigorously authenticated (sahih), though I hold it to be so, because scholars have received it with acceptance" (*al-Isaba fi nusra al-Khulafa' al-Rashidin wa al-Sahaba* (y10), 11.8–9).

(A:) Among the primary textual evidence for the admissibility of such hadiths is the word of the Prophet (Allah bless him and give him peace):

"Allah will never make my Community concur upon misguidance, and Allah's hand is over the group."

So it is inadequate for someone who proposes to annul a ruling of Sacred Law to adduce that the hadith supporting it has a weak chain of transmission, unless he can also establish both that there are not a number of similar variants or alternate channels of transmission that strengthen it, confirming this by means of a text by a hadith master (hafiz); and that the meaning of the hadith has not been received with acceptance by the scholars of the Muslim Community.

وقـولـه «إذا اختلف المتبـايعان في الثمن والسلعـة قائمـة تحالفا وترادا البيع» وقوله «الـديـة على العـاقلة» وإن كانت هذه الأحاديث لا تثبت من جهة الإسناد ولكن لمـا بلغتهـا الكـافـة غنوا بصحتها عندهم عن طلب الإسناد لها فكذلك حديث معاذ لمـا احتجـوا به جميعاً غنـوا عن طلب الإسناد. [...].

قال ابن عبـد البـر في الاستـذكـار لما حكي عن التـرمـذي أن البخـاري صحح حديث البحر «هـو الطهـور ماؤه» : أهـل الحديث لا يصححون مثل إسناده ولكن الحـديث عندي صحيح لأن العلماء تلقوه بالقبـول. [محرر من الإصابة في نصرة الخلفـاء الراشدين والصحابة في تصحيح حديث ابن خصيفة في التراويح : ١١/ ٨ ـ ٩؛ بتقديم وتأخير].

«لا يجمـع الله أمتي على ضلالـة أبداً ويـد الله على الجمـاعـة» [رواه الحـاكم ١/ ١١٦ بسند صحيح].

*

957

w49.0 ACCEPTING THE PROCEEDS OF UN-ISLAMIC TAX REVENUES (from p32.3)

w49.0 حل قبـول الـراتب على عمـل مشروع من دولة غير إسلامية

w49.1 (A:) A Muslim may take wages for lawful work from a government whose main income is non-Islamic tax revenues on condition that at least some of the government's property is from lawful transactions such as the money taken from customers paying for postal services, etc.; the legal basis for which is the principle that "the legitimate in Sacred Law is that whose origin is unknown," meaning not established to be unlawful. Similarly, it is lawful to accept money from a merchant, for example, who deals in interest with a bank, since one is able to presume that the money one is accepting is from the lawful part of his wealth.

*

w50.0 THE PROHIBITION OF DEPICTING ANIMATE LIFE (from p44.1 (n:))

w50.0 تحريم التصوير

HADITH EVIDENCE OF THE PROHIBITION OF DEPICTING ANIMATE LIFE

أدلة تحريم التصوير من السنة

w50.1 ('Abd al-Ghaffar 'Uyun al-Sud:) One should realize that the prohibition of picture making is extremely severe, that it is counted among the enormities, and the threats against doing it are very emphatic. Bukhari and Muslim relate that a man came to Ibn 'Abbas (Allah be well pleased with him and his father) and said, "My livelihood comes solely from my hands, and I make these pictures. Can you give me a legal opinion about them?" Ibn 'Abbas told him, "Come closer," and the man did. "Closer," he said, and the man did, until he put his hand on the man's head and said: "Shall I tell you what I heard from the Messenger of Allah (Allah bless him and give him peace)? I heard the Messenger of Allah say,

" 'Every maker of pictures will go to the fire, where a being will be set upon him to torment him in hell for each picture he made.'

"So if you must, draw trees and things without animate life in them."

w50.1 (عبـد الغفـار عيـون السـود:) وليعلم أن التصـويـر حرام شديد التحريم وهـو من الكبـائـر ومتـوعـد عليـه بالوعيد الشـديـد. ففي الصحيحين أن رجلاً جاء إلى ابن عبـاس رضي الله عنهمـا فقـال: إنمـا معيشتي من صنعـة يدي وإني أصنع هذه التصـاويـر فافتني فيهـا. فقال له: ادن مني؛ فدنـا ثم قال: ادن مني؛ فدنـا حتى وضـع يده على رأسـه وقال له: ألا أنبئك بمـا سمعت من رسول الله ﷺ؟ سمعت رسـول الله ﷺ يقـول: «كـل مصـوّر في النـار يجعل له بكـل صورة صوّرها نفسـاً تعـذبه في جهنم»، قال ابن عباس: فإن كنت لا بد فاعـلاً فاصنـع الشجـر ومـا لا نفس له.

And Tirmidhi relates that the Prophet (Allah bless him and give him peace) said,

"On the Day of Judgement, part of the hellfire will come forth with two eyes with which to see, two ears with which to hear, and a tongue with which to speak, saying, 'I have been ordered to deal with three: he who holds there is another god besides Allah, with every arrogant tyrant, and with makers of pictures.' "

And Bukhari, Tirmidhi, and Nasa'i relate the prophetic hadith from Ibn 'Abbas,

"Whoever makes a picture, Allah shall torture him with it on the Day of Judgement until he can breathe life into it, and he will never be able to."

IMITATING THE CREATIVE ACT OF ALLAH

w50.2 The reason for the unlawfulness of pictorial representation is that it imitates the creative act of Allah Most High, as is indicated by the hadith related by Bukhari and Muslim that 'A'isha (Allah be well pleased with her) said, "The Prophet (Allah bless him and give him peace) returned from a trip, and I had draped a cloth with pictures on it over a small closet. When he saw it, he ripped it down, his face colored, and he said,

" ' 'A'isha, the people most severely tortured by Allah on the Day of Judgement will be those who try to imitate what Allah has created,' "

the representation in question consisting of winged horses, as is mentioned in Muslim's version. (A: If the sole basis for the prohibition of pictures was that they were worshipped in pre-Islamic times as gods, as has been claimed by certain contemporary scholars, there would have been no point in the Prophet (Allah bless him and give him peace) tearing the cloth down, since 'A'isha was not an idol worshipper or raised among idolators.)

وأخرج الترمذي [وصححه] عن النبي ﷺ قال: «يـخـرج عُنُقٌ (أي جانب) من النار يوم القيامة له عينان يبصر بهما وأذنان يسمعـان ولسـان ينطق به يقـول: وكلت بثلاثة، بمن جعل مع الله إلهاً آخر وبكل جبار عنيد وبالمصورين .

وأخرج البخـاري والترمذي والنسائي من حديث ابن عباس مرفوعاً «من صوّر صورة عذبه الله بها يوم القيامة حتى ينفخ فيها الروح وما هو بنافخ» .

مضاهاة خلق الله

w50.2 وعلة المنع من التصوير ما فيه من مضاهاة خلق الله تعالى كما يشير إليه ما في الصحيحين [وغيرهما] عن عائشة رضي الله عنها قالت: «قـدم رسول الله ﷺ من سفر وقد سترت سهوة لي بقرام فيه تمـاثيل فلما رآه هتكه وتلون وجهه وقال: «يـا عائشـة أشـد النـاس عذاباً يوم القيامة الـذين يضاهون بخلق الله» [أي يشبهون ما يصنعونه بما يصنعه الله . والسهوة بفتح السين المهملة وسكون الهـاء: الخـزانة الصغيرة والقرام بكسر القاف هو الستر] . وكـانت التمـاثيـل صور الخيل ذوات الأجنحة على ما صرحت به رواية مسلم عنهـا . (ع: ولـو كان التحريم لمجرد أن الصور تعبد من دون الله ـ كما زعم بعض المعـاصـرين ـ لمـا كان لهتكه ﷺ قرام عائشـة فائـدة، لأنها لم تكن من عبـدة الأوثان ولا تربت فيهم) .

PROCURING PICTURES

اتخاذ الصور حرام كصنعها

w50.3 The foregoing hadiths show that producing representations is unlawful under any circumstances, and just as making a picture is unlawful, so too is procuring one, because the threat that pertains to the maker pertains to the user, for pictures are only made to be used.

w50.3 فـاعـلـم من ذلـك أن صنـعـة التصـويـر حرام بكـل حال وكمـا يحرم التصـويـر يحرم اتخاذ الصورة لأن الوعيد إذا حصـل لصـانعهـا فهـو حاصـل لمستعملها لأنها لا تصنع إلا لتستعمل.

w50.4 (A:) The determining factor in the prohibition of procuring images is the purpose for which they are procured. For example, someone who buys cookies with the shape of animals is not doing wrong if his purpose is to eat, though the maker of them is doing wrong. And similarly with books containing pictures, if the buyer intends obtaining the text, then the presence of pictures is the fault of the printer, not the buyer. The same holds for photographs (dis: w50.9) required for official documents: the authorities are responsible for the sin, not the individual forced to comply. As for dolls, making them is unlawful, though using them is merely offensive. And with rugs, making pictures in them is unlawful, though using such rugs is permissible.

THREE-DIMENSIONAL IMAGES

الصور المجسمة

w50.5 Regarding the prohibition, it makes no difference whether the figure is three-dimensional (lit. "has a shadow") or not, meaning when it has a solid form; as opposed to when it is portrayed on paper, a garment, a wall, or something else. This position (N: of there being no difference between images that are three-dimensional or otherwise) was held by the majority of the Companions, those who came after them, and the following generation, as is mentioned by Nawawi. Some of the early Muslims held that two-dimensional images were permissible, a view for which they adduced the Abu Talha hadith related by Bukhari and others, in which an exception is made for images depicted on cloth. But Nawawi understands the exception as referring to the depiction of trees and similar objects without animate life, interpreting the hadith this way to reach an accord between it and the above hadith (w50.2) about the Prophet (Allah bless him and give him peace) tearing down the cloth with which 'A'isha had covered the small closet, for it consisted of mere drawn images without three dimensions. Nawawi says, "The view

w50.5 [. . .] وسواء في ذلك ما له ظل من الصور وما لا ظل له أعني ما إذا كانت مجسمة ذات جرم أو رقماً في ورق أو ثوب أو حائط أو غير ذلك. وعلى هذا جمهـور الصحـابة والتابعين فمن بعدهم كمـا أفاده النووي. وقال بعض السلف لا بأس بالصـور التي لا ظل لهـا مستـدلين بحـديث أبي طلحـة عنـد البخاري وغيره وفيـه استثناء ما كان رقماً في ثوب وحمله النـووي على رقم صورة الشجرة ونحوها ممـا ليس بذي روح جمعـاً بينـه وبين ما تقدم من هتك النبي ﷺ قرام عائشة الذي سترت به السهوة فإنـه كان مجرد رقم لا ظل له. وقـال النـووي إن القول بأن ما لا

that non-three-dimensional images are unobjectionable is a falsehood," declaring it invalid. But if not an outright falsehood, it is a position that the evidence is against. (A: This was the position of some of the later followers of Imam Malik. As for the Imam himself, he held that pictures were as unlawful as statues.)

IMAGES PREVENT ANGELS FROM
ENTERING A HOUSE

w50.6 Another reason pictures are unlawful is that they prevent angels from entering the house where they are found (N: meaning the angels of mercy, though protecting angels enter such houses), as is attested to by the hadith related by Bukhari that the Prophet (Allah bless him and give him peace) said,

"Angels do not enter a house in which there are pictures,"

house meaning any place a person is, whether it be a building, tent, or other. Qurtubi says, "Angels do not enter a house where there are pictures because the person who puts them there is imitating non-Muslims, who put pictures in their homes and honor them, the angels abandoning such a person for this."

Nasa'i relates that Abu Hurayra (Allah be well pleased with him) said, "Gabriel (upon whom be peace) asked the Prophet for permission to enter his house, and when the Prophet told him to come in, Gabriel replied, 'How can I come in when there is a curtain in your house with pictures on it? You should either remove their heads or make it a mat to walk on, for we angels do not enter a house in which there are pictures,'" which shows that the pictures that prevent angels from entering are those that retain their original form and are in an unhumiliated deployment. As for images that are abased and walked upon by feet, or those whose form has been altered, these do not bar the angels' entry, *altered* meaning the onlooker imagines it is not the form of a living being, as is clearly implied by the version of this hadith related in the *Sunan* as, "…. Order that the

ظل له لا بأس به مذهب باطل كذا أطلق عليه البطلان فإن لم يكن باطلاً كما قال فهو مذهب مرجوح (ع) : وهو مذهب بعض متأخري المالكية . أما الإمام مالك فالصور حرام عنده مثل التماثيل المجسمة) .

الصور تمنع الملائكة من دخول البيت

w50.6 [. . .] ولأنها تمنع من دخول الملائكة بيتاً هي فيه (ح) : والمقصود ملائكة الرحمة ، أما ملائكة الحفظ فيدخلون) لحديث البخاري عنه ﷺ قال : «إن البيت الذي فيه صور لا تدخله الملائكة» . والمراد بالبيت المكان الذي يستقر فيه الشخص سواء كان بناء أو خيمة أو غير ذلك .

قال القرطبي : إنما لا تدخل الملائكة البيت الذي فيه الصور لأن متخذها قد تشبه بالكفار لأنهم يتخذون الصور في بيوتهم ويعظمونها فلم تدخل الملائكة بيته هجراً له على ذلك .

وأخرج النسائي عن أبي هريرة رضي الله عنه قال : «استأذن جبريل عليه السلام على النبي ﷺ فقال : أدخل ؛ فقال : كيف أدخل وفي بيتك ستر فيه تصاوير فإما أن تقطع رؤوسها أو تجعل بساطاً يوطأ فإنا معشر الملائكة لا ندخل بيتاً فيه تصاوير» فعلم من هذا أن الصورة التي تمنع من دخول الملائكة هي الباقية على هيأتها غير الممتهنة . أما الممتهنة التي توطأ بالأقدام أو التي غيرت هيأتها فغير مانعة من دخول الملائكة والمراد بتغييرها أن تجعل بحيث يتخيل للناظر إليها أنها ليست بصورة حيوان بدليل ما جاء في رواية هذا الحديث في السنن

heads of the images be removed so they resemble the form of trees."

بلفظ «مر برأس التمثال يقطع فيصير كهيأة الشجرة».

PORTRAITS

صورة بعض الجسم

w50.7 Some people might think there is no harm in having portraits made today because they are not full length but are rather from the chest up, imagining this to be permissible from the words of the scholars that "if a picture lacks a portion without which the figure could not live, there is no harm in it." This is a mistake that should be abandoned, for by the expression *without which the figure could not live,* scholars mean that the beholder's mind does not register the figure is a living one but rather perceives it as dead. Now, someone looking at pictures of only the upper half does not apprehend the figure as dead, but rather as living, save only that the lower half is as though sunken in a place that conceals it, or covered by something, which is because the lower half is not met by the viewer's gaze, and the area in view is merely confined to the upper half. For this reason, some scholars prohibit portrayal of the head alone, and whoever reflects on Gabriel's words, "Order that the heads of the figures be removed so that they resemble trees," can plainly see the truth of what we have mentioned.

w50.7 قد يظن بعض النـاس أنـه لا بأس باتخاذ الصـور اليـوم من حيـث أنها ليست تامـة بل هي من الصـدر فمـا فوقـه يتـوهم ذلك من قول الفقهـاء إن الصورة إذا كانت ممحـوة عضـو لا حيـاة بدونه لا بأس بها.

وهذا غلط ينبغي الرجوع عنه فإن مراد الفقهاء بقـولهم لا حياة بدونه نفي الحياة في تخيل النـاظـر إلى الصـورة بحيث لا يراهـا صورة حيوان حي بل صورة حيوان ميت. والناظر إلى الصور التي يصور فيها النصف الأعلى فقـط لا يتخيـل إليـه أنهـا صورة حيوان ميت بل صورة حيوان حي غيـر أن نصفـه الأسفـل كأنـه في مكـان منخفض يستره أو مغطى بشيء وذلك لأن النصف الأسفل غير مقصود بالنظر وإنما العمدة في النظر النصف الأعلى فلذا منع بعض الفقهـاء اتخـاذ صورة الرأس وحده [كمـا نص عليـه في المحيط]. ومن تأمل قول جبريـل عليـه السـلام: «مـر برأس التمثال يقطع فيصير كهيأة الشجرة» ظهر له ما ذكرنا.

w50.8 Others suppose that the sole reason for prohibiting pictures is that they were worshipped as gods apart from Allah, and that today there is no longer any danger of it, so there is no harm in having them. And this is totally wrong, for the banning of images is not only because they were worshipped, but also because of their imitating the creative act of Allah Most High, and the emulation therein of non-Muslims.

To summarize, the use of pictures comes of weakness of faith and unconcern for religious matters. Whoever prefers what his Master wishes above what gratifies his own ego and what he would personally care for will stay as far from

w50.8 ومن النـاس من يتـوهم أن تحـريم الصورة إنمـا كان من حيث أنها كانت تعبد من دون الله، أمـا اليـوم فقد أمن ذلك فلا بأس بها وهـذا غلط بحت لأن تحـريم الصـورة لا من حيث أنهـا كانت تعبد فقط بل لمـا فيهـا من مضاهاة خلق الله تعالى ولما فيها من التشبه بالكفرة.

وبالجملة اتخاذ الصور هو من ضعف الإيمان وقلة الاهتمام بالأمور الدينية ومن كان يؤثـر ما يرضـى عنـه مولاه على ما تشتهيـه نفسـه ويهواه يتباعد عن ذلك كل

them as possible (*al-Riyad al-nadira fi tafsir suratayy al-Fatiha wa al-Baqara* (y133), 1.139–44).

البُعد [محرر من الـريـاض النضـرة في تفسـير سورتي الفاتحة والبقرة: ١ / ١٣٩ ـ ١٤٤ ؛ بتقديم وتأخير] .

PHOTOGRAPHS OF ANIMATE LIFE

تصوير ما له روح بالآلة الفوتوغرافية

w50.9 (n: Photography did not exist in previous eras of Islamic scholarship, and contemporary scholars are divided about it. Some, like Muhammad Bakhit Muti'i, contend that photography is not picture making, but merely "the retention of an object's shadow" (habs al-zill) and therefore permissible, while others, like the author of the passage below, have not accepted such reasoning. Because of scholarly disagreement concerning its permissibility, one is not entitled to condemn Muslims who use photographs, though one may still distinguish between this dispensation (rukhsa, def: c6.3) and what is the stronger position and more precautionary in religion, and to this end the following article has been translated.)

(Muhammad Hamid:) A factual question arises here, namely that the photographic device does not act except through an agent, who causes this "shadow" to be fixed and retained by aiming and focusing the camera at a particular object to permit this fixation and make this retention appear. But since this is really an aquisition and is precisely image making, and since the prohibition of making pictures by the hand alone is not merely because of the hand's motion but because of what it thereby produces, then if the result is the same, should not the ruling also be? Moreover, hand-made images do not give the picture the fidelity of the camera-made image, which delineates features, conveys reality, and reveals details so that nothing great or small escapes it, being thus *abler* than the unaided hand to achieve pictorial representation, because of which the prohibition of making pictures thereby applies to it with still better right, and can never be mitigated by the mere fact that it consists in pressing a button as long as what is forbidden is even more fully realized thereby, since matters are judged by their intended outcomes, in permissibility or being unlawful. Just as killing someone by pressing a particular button on a device is unlawful, so too making a picture by this pressure is unlawful in view of the effect and result. Nor does the fact that it is widespread among people justify it. It is no different than interest (riba), adultery, drinking, gambling, or other blameworthy acts whose night

[محمـد الحـامـد:) [. . . و] هنا يرد سؤال علمـي هو أن الآلـة (ت: الفـوتـوغـرافيـة) لا عمل لها إلا بعامل فهو الـذي قصـد إلى تثبيت هذا الظـل وحبسـه بتـوجيههـا وتـركيـزهـا على نحو معين كي يتسنى هذا التثبيت ويظهـر هذا الحبس . على أنـه في الحقيقة التقاط التصوير عينه فإن تحريم التصـويـر باليد المجردة ليس لمحض حركتهـا بل لمـا ينشأ عنهـا وإذا كانت النتيجـة واحـدة أفـلا يكـون الحكم واحداً؟ بل إن التصـويـر باليد لا يعطي الصـورة وضوحـاً كالتصوير بالآلة الفـوتـوغـرافيـة هذه التي تبسـط المعالم وتحكي الـواقـع وتبـرز الدقائق فلا يفوت شيء من الصـورة قل أو جل فهي أقـدر على تحقيق التصـوير من اليـد المجردة فتحريم التصوير بها يتناولها تناولاً أولوياً ولن يخفف منه أنـه ضغط زر معين مادام الشيء المنهي عنه متحققاً بها أتم تحقق (فالأمـور بمقاصدها) حلاً وحرمة ، وكما أن قتـل النفس بضغط زر معين في آلـة حرام فكـذا التصـوير بهذا الضغط حرام اعتباراً بالأثر والنتيجة .

وشيـوع هذا التصـويـر في النـاس لا يجعله مباحـاً فمـا هو إلا كالـربـا والـزنا والخمر والقمـار وسائر المنكرات التي

has overspread the people and darkness enveloped them. The commonness of something that is wrong never makes it permissible. And groping for support from Sacred Law for each new reprehensible practice that appears is a dangerous misstep that forebodes great evil. Allah Most High says,

"These are Allah's limits, so transgress them not, for whoever goes beyond Allah's limits, those are the wrongdoers" (Koran 2:229).

(*Rudud 'ala abatil wa rasa'il al-Shaykh Muhammad al-Hamid* (y44), 1.164–65)

غشي الناس قتامها وعمهم ظلامها . وما كان انتشار المنكر أن يبيحه ، والتماس تكأة من الشرع لكل منكر يجد ويحدث مزلق خطير يؤذن بشر مستطير ، والله تعالى قال :

﴿ تِلْكَ حُدُودُ اللَّهِ فَلَا تَعْتَدُوهَا وَمَنْ يَتَعَدَّ حُدُودَ اللَّهِ فَأُولَئِكَ هُمُ الظَّالِمُونَ ﴾

[البقرة : ٢٢٩] [نقل من ردود على أباطيل ورسائل الشيخ محمد الحامد :
١ / ١٦٤ - ١٦٥] .

TELEVISION   التلفزيون

w50.10 (n:) The Council of Islamic Scholars (Majlisul Ulama) of Port Elizabeth, South Africa, have published a booklet on Islam and television in which they list the factors present in television that are unlawful or offensive, the existence of any one of which is sufficient to make watching it a violation of Sacred Law, including:

(1) pictures of animate objects and picture making (dis: w50);

(2) music (r40.1);

(3) immorality, nudity, illicit sex, pornography, etc. (m2.3–8);

(4) obscene language (r26.2);

(5) incitement to fornication (p12);

(6) negation of modesty (haya', dis: r26.1(2));

(7) scenes of violence, sadism, and crime in general portrayed (r13.1);

(8) the addictive influence exercised by TV;

(9) it encourages the acceptance of aggression as a mode of behavior (p48.1);

(10) it encourages imitation of the crimes portrayed (r7.1(3,(end)));

(11) the brainwashing action of TV, especially on the young (t3.16);

(12) TV stunts intellectual growth (w41.3);

(13) it wastes time (r13.3);

(14) it interferes with one's religious duties and one's necessary and important worldly duties (k29.5(4));

(15) it diverts one's attention from the remembrance of Allah (r1.2(5));

(16) and it falls under the category described by Islam as *pointless amusement* (lahw, def: r13.3).

(Majlisul Ulama:) In the face of this formidable array of evil factors and harmful effects no one can have any doubt of the illegality of television in Islam. Television, as has been seen, is an embodiment of sin and immorality. Islam can never condone or permit an institution which plays havoc with the spiritual, mental, and moral development of mankind (*Islam and Television* (y78), 20–21).

*

w51.0 WOMEN REMOVING FACIAL HAIR (from p59.1)

w51.0 النماص

w51.1 The Prophet (Allah bless him and give him peace) said,

w51.1 قال النبي ﷺ:

"May Allah curse women who wear false hair or arrange it for others, who tattoo or have themselves tattooed, who pluck facial hair or eyebrows or have them plucked, and women who separate their front teeth for beauty, altering what Allah has created."

«لـعـن الله الـواصلة والمستـوصلة والـواشمـة والمستـوشمة والنـامصـة والمتـنـمصـة والمتفلجـات للحسن المغيـرات خلق الله» [رواه الـذهبي في الكبائر وقال: متفق عليه].

w51.2 (Ibn Hajar 'Asqalani:) Nawawi says that "an exception from the prohibition of plucking away facial hair is when a woman has a beard, mustache, or hair growing between her lower lip and chin, in which cases it is not unlawful for her to remove it, but rather is commendable (mustahabb)," the permissibility being on condition that her husband knows of it and gives his permission, though it is prohibited if he does not, because of the deception it entails (*Fath al-Bari* (y17), 10.378).

w51.2 (ابن حجـر العسقـلاني:) [. . .و] قال الـنـووي: يستـثـنى من النماص ما إذا نبت للمرأة لحية أو شارب أو عنفقـة فلا يحـرم عليهـا إزالتهـا بل يستحب. [قلت:] وإطـلاقـه مقيـد بإذن الـزوج وعلمـه، وإلا فمتى خلا عن ذلك منع للتدليس [نقل من فتح الباري بشرح صحيـح الإمام أبي عبـد الله محمـد بن إسماعيل البخاري: ١٠/ ٣٧٨].

*

w52.0 IBN HAJAR HAYTAMI'S LIST OF ENORMITIES (from p76)

w52.0 الكبـــائـــر عنـد ابن حجر الهيتمي

w52.1 (A:) Ibn Hajar's purpose in *al-Zawajir 'an iqtiraf al-kaba'ir* is to warn readers against any act that an Islamic scholar has classified as an enormity. Because of the wider scope of the work, he does not confine himself, as does Imam Dhahabi, to sins agreed upon by scholars as being enormities, but also records those which are differed about, mentioning them by way of furnishing a fuller definition of godfearingness (taqwa).

INWARD ENORMITIES

الكبائر الباطنة

(1) Associating others with Allah Most High (shirk);

(١) الشرك [الأكبر أعاذنا الله منه].

(2) the lesser form of associating others with Allah (shirk), which is showing off in good works;

(٢) الشرك الأصغر وهو الرياء.

(3) anger without right, malice, and envy;

(٣) الغضب بالباطل والحقد والحسد.

(4) arrogance, pride, and conceit;

(٤) الكبر والعجب والخيلاء.

(5) cheating others;

(٥) الغش.

(6) hypocrisy;

(٦) النفاق.

(7) excesses against others;

(٧) البغي.

(8) keeping aloof from others out of pride or contempt for them;

(٨) الإعـراض عن الخلق استكبـاراً واحتقاراً لهم.

(9) conversations about what does not concern one (def: w54);

(٩) الخوض فيما لا يعني.

(10) acquisitive greed;

(١٠) الطمع.

(11) fear of poverty;

(١١) خوف الفقر.

(12) resentment about what Allah Most High has destined;

(١٢) سخط المقدور.

(13) admiring the rich and honoring them for their wealth;

(١٣) النظر إلى الأغنياء وتعظيمهم لغناهم.

(14) sarcasm towards the poor because of their poverty;

(١٤) الاستهزاء بالفقراء لفقرهم.

(15) avarice in holding on to one's possessions;	(١٥) الحرص.
(16) vying with others for worldly gain and taking pride in it;	(١٦) التنافس في الدنيا والمباهاة بها.
(17) adorning oneself for the sake of one's fellow creatures with what is unlawful as adornment;	(١٧) التزين للمخلوقين بما يحرم التزين به.
(18) compromising one's principles (def: r17);	(١٨) المداهنة.
(19) enjoying being praised for what one does not do;	(١٩) حب المدح بما لا يفعله.
(20) being too occupied with others' faults to notice one's own;	(٢٠) الاشتغال بعيوب الخلق عن عيوب النفس.
(21) forgetting one's blessings;	(٢١) نسيان النعمة.
(22) zealotry for other than Allah's religion;	(٢٢) الحمية لغير دين الله.
(23) being unthankful;	(٢٣) ترك الشكر.
(24) not accepting fate (dis: w59);	(٢٤) عدم الرضا بالقضاء.
(25) for a person not to take the rights of Allah Most High and His commands seriously;	(٢٥) هوان حقوق الله تعالى وأوامره على الإنسان.
(26) sarcasm towards, looking down on, or having contempt for the servants of Allah Most High;	(٢٦) سخريته بعباد الله تعالى وازدراؤه لهم واحتقاره إياهم.
(27) following one's caprice and ignoring the truth;	(٢٧) اتباع الهوى والإعراض عن الحق.
(28) plotting and treachery;	(٢٨) المكر والخداع.
(29) wanting the life of this world (N: more than the next);	(٢٩) إرادة الحياة الدنيا.
(30) obstinately opposing the truth;	(٣٠) معاندة الحق.
(31) thinking badly of a Muslim or not giving him the benefit of the doubt;	(٣١) سوء الظن بالمسلم.
(32) not accepting the truth when it conflicts with one's own preference, or when it comes from someone one dislikes;	(٣٢) عدم قبول الحق إذا جاء بما لا تهواه النفس أو جاء على يد من تكرهه وتبغضه.

(33) exulting in disobedience;	(٣٣) فرح العبد بالمعصية .
(34) persisting in disobedience;	(٣٤) الإصرار على المعصية .
(35) loving to be praised for one's acts of obedience;	(٣٥) محبة أن يحمد بما يفعله من الطاعات .
(36) satisfaction with the life of this world and being contented with it;	(٣٦) الرضا بالحياة الدنيا والطمأنينة إليها .
(37) forgetting Allah Most High and the next world;	(٣٧) نسيان الله تعالى والدار الآخرة .
(38) anger for the sake of one's ego and vindicating or justifying oneself when in the wrong;	(٣٨) الغضب للنفس والانتصار لها بالباطل .
(39) feeling secure from Allah's intrigue by committing acts of disobedience while relying on His mercy;	(٣٩) الأمن من مكر الله بالاسترسال في المعاصي مع الاتكال على الرحمة .
(40) despairing of Allah's mercy;	(٤٠) اليأس من رحمة الله .
(41) thinking badly of Allah Most High;	(٤١) سوء الظن بالله تعالى .
(42) loss of all hope in Allah's mercy;	(٤٢) القنوط من رحمة الله .
(43) learning Sacred Knowledge for the sake of this world;	(٤٣) تعلم العلم للدنيا .
(44) concealing Sacred Knowledge;	(٤٤) كتم العلم .
(45) not applying what one knows (N: in matters that occur);	(٤٥) عدم العمل بالعلم .
(46) claims to knowledge, mastery of the Koran, or any act of worship, made out of pride and boastfulness;	(٤٦) الدعوى في العلم أو القرآن أو شيء من العبادات زهواً وافتخاراً .
(47) neglect that results in the loss of people such as Islamic scholars, or sarcasm towards them;	(٤٧) إضاعة نحو العلماء والاستخفاف بهم .
(48) intentionally lying about Allah Most High;	(٤٨) تعمد الكذب على الله تعالى .
(49) intentionally lying about the Messenger of Allah (Allah bless him and give him peace);	(٤٩) أو على رسوله ﷺ .
(50) inaugurating a reprehensible innovation;	(٥٠) من سن سنة سيئة .

(51) abandoning the sunna;

(٥١) ترك السنة .

(52) disbelief in destiny;

(٥٢) التكذيب بالقدر .

(53) not fulfilling the terms of an agreement (A: if one intends this from its outset);

(٥٣) عدم الوفاء بالعهد .

(54) love of oppressors or the immoral, no matter what the type of their immorality;

(٥٤) محبة الظلمة أو الفسقة بأي نوع كان فسقهم .

(55) hating the righteous (N: for their righteousness);

(٥٥) بغض الصالحين (ح: لصلاحهم) .

(56) harming the friends of Allah (awliya') and enmity towards them;

(٥٦) أذية أولياء الله ومعاداتهم .

(57) reviling destiny;

(٥٧) سب الدهر .

(58) saying something that causes great harm or extensive damage, something that angers Allah Most High but to which the speaker pays little attention;

(٥٨) الكلمة التي تعظم مفسدتها وينتشر ضررها مما يسخط الله تعالى ولا يلقي لها قائلها بالاً .

(59) being ungrateful to someone who does one a kindness;

(٥٩) كفران نعمة المحسن .

(60) neglecting to say the blessings on the Prophet (Allah bless him and give him peace) when one hears his name mentioned;

(٦٠) ترك الصلاة على النبي ﷺ عند سماع ذكره ﷺ .

(Yusuf Nabahani:) Ibn Salah says: "One should be diligent about writing Allah's blessings and peace on the Messenger of Allah (Allah bless him and give him peace) whenever he is mentioned, and not grow weary of repeating it as often as it occurs, for this is one of the greatest benefits attained by students of hadith and their copyists, while someone oblivious to it misses an enormous reward. The blessings thus recorded are a written prayer, not words being quoted, so they are not restricted to the written version of the text that is related or the words of the original.... One should avoid writing it in two defective styles, one of which is deficient in form, i.e. alluding to the blessings by two letters or the like, as certain lazy, ignorant, or unlearned people do, writing *pbuh* instead of 'Allah bless him and give him peace'; while the other is deficient in meaning, i.e. by not adding the words 'and give him peace' " (*Sa'ada al-darayn fi al-salat 'ala Sayyid al-Kawnayn* (y96), 189);

(يوسف النبهاني :) [. . . و] قال ابن الصلاح : وينبغي أن يحافظ على كتب الصلاة والتسليم على رسول الله ﷺ عند ذكره ولا يسأم من تكرير ذلك عند تكرره فإن ذلك من أكبر الفوائد التي يتعجلها طلبة الحديث وكتبتهم ومن أغفل ذلك حرم حظاً عظيماً . وما يكتبه من ذلك فهو دعاء يثبته لا كلام يرويه فلذلك لا يتقيد بالرواية ولا يقتصر فيه على ما في الأصل [وهكذا الأمر في الثناء على الله تعالى عند ذكر اسمه نحو عز وجل وتبارك وتعالى . ثم قال] وليجتنب في إثباتها نقصين : أن يكتبها منقوصة صورة رامزاً إليها بحرفين أو نحو ذلك كما يفعله بعض الكسالى والجهلة والعوام فيكتبون صورة «صلعم» بدلاً عن ﷺ ؛ والثاني أن يكتبها منقوصة معنى بأن لا يكتب فيها وسلم اهـ [نقل من سعادة الدارين في الصلاة على سيد الكونين : ١٨٩] .

(61) such hardheartedness as would prevent one from feeding a needy person, for example;

(٦١) قسوة القلب بحيث تحمل صاحبها على منع إطعام المضطر مثلاً.

(62) acquiescing to any enormity;

(٦٢) الرضا بكبيرة من الكبائر.

(63) aiding someone in committing an enormity;

(٦٣) الإعانة عليها بأي نوع كان.

(64) persisting in wickedness and obscenity until people fear one for one's evil;

(٦٤) ملازمة الشر والفحش حتى يخشاه الناس اتقاء شره.

(65–66) cutting minted coins (N: into segments of which some are smaller than others and cause loss to users, and because it is destruction of Muslim moneys); or minting it in a fraudulent way that if people knew of, they would not accept;

(٦٥ـ٦٦) كسر دراهم ودنانير ؛ (ح : أي تقسيمها إلى أجزاء يكون بعضها صغير فيدخل النقص على المتعامل بها، ولأنه إتلاف نقود المسلمين) ؛ وضرب نحو الدراهم والدنانير على كيفية من الغش لو اطلع عليها الناس لما قبلوها.

PURIFICATION

الطهارة

(67) eating or drinking from a gold or silver vessel;

(٦٧) الأكل أو الشرب في آنية الذهب أو الفضة.

(68) forgetting the Koran, any of its verses, or even a single letter (A: the prohibition of *forgetting the Koran* being taken literally by the Shafi'i school, according to whom repentance entails rememorizing what has been forgotten, though not for Malik and Abu Hanifa, who interpret *forgetting* as abandoning its implications);

(٦٨) نسيان القرآن أو آية منه بل أو حرف.

(69) disputation and picking apart another's words—meaning to argue with another seeking merely to win or defeat him—when discussing the Koran or religion;

(٦٩) الجدال والمراء وهو المخاصمة والمحاجّة وطلب القهر والغلبة في القرآن أو الدين.

(70) defecating on a path;

(٧٠) التغوط في الطريق.

(71) not eliminating all traces of urine from one's person or clothes;

(٧١) عدم التنزه من البول في البدن أو الثوب.

(72) omitting any of the integrals of ablution (wudu);

(٧٢) ترك شيء من واجبات الوضوء.

(73) omitting any of the integrals of the purificatory bath (ghusl);

(٧٣) ترك شيء من واجبات الغسل.

(74) disclosing one's nakedness when there is no need, including entering a (N: public) bathhouse without a covering;

(٧٤) كشف العـورة لغيـر ضرورة، ومنه دخول الحمام بغير مئزر ساتر لها.

(75) sexual intercourse with a woman during menstruation;

(٧٥) وطء الحائض.

THE PRAYER

الصلاة

(76) deliberately not performing the prescribed prayer;

(٧٦) تعمد ترك الصلاة.

(77) deliberately performing the prayer before or after its time without an excuse such as travel or similar;

(٧٧) تعمد تأخير الصلاة عن وقتها أو تقديمها عليه من غير عذر كسفر الخ.

(78) sleeping on a roof that lacks a wall around its edges;

(٧٨) النوم على سطح لا تحجير به.

(79) omitting an obligatory feature of the prayer;

(٧٩) ترك واجب من واجبات الصلاة.

(80) lengthening one's hair with false hair, or having it done;

(٨٠) الوصل وطلب عمله.

(81) tattooing, or having it done;

(٨١) الوشم وطلب عمله.

(82) sharpening the teeth or having it done;

(٨٢) وشـر الأسنان أي تحـديـدهـا وطلب عمله.

(83) plucking eyebrows or facial hair, or having it done;

(٨٣) التـنميص وطلب عمله [وهـو جرد الوجه].

(84) walking in front of someone at prayer who has placed a barrier before himself;

(٨٤) الـمـرور بين يدي المصلي إذا صلى لسترة بشرطها.

(85) the people of a village or town all hanging back from praying one of the five prescribed prayers in congregation when the conditions obliging them to perform it in a group exist;

(٨٥) إطباق أهل القـريـة أو البلد أو نحـوهمـا على ترك الجماعة في فرض من المكتـوبـات الخمس وقـد وجـدت فيهم شروط وجوب الجماعة.

(86) for an imam to lead a group of people who dislike him;

(٨٦) إمامة الإنسان لقوم وهم له كارهون.

(87) leaving a row of people at prayer incomplete;

(٨٧) قطع الصف.

(88) not straightening the row of people praying;

(٨٨) عدم تسويته.

(89) getting ahead of the imam in the actions of the prayer;

(٨٩) مسابقة الإمام.

(90) raising one's eyes to the sky during the prayer;

(٩٠) رفع البصر إلى السماء في الصلاة.

(91) turning (N: one's chest) to either side when performing the prayer;

(٩١) الالتفات في الصلاة (ح: أي بصدره).

(92) putting one's hands on the hips while at prayer;

(٩٢) الاختصار فيها.

(93–98) taking graves as places of worship (def: w21.1); lighting lamps over them; taking them as idols; circumambulating around them; putting one's hands on them; or performing the prayer towards them;

(٩٣-٩٨) اتخاذ القبور مساجد؛ إيقاد السرج عليها؛ اتخاذها أوثاناً؛ الطواف بها؛ استلامها؛ الصلاة إليها.

(99–100) travelling alone ((Ibn Hajar Haytami:).... The position of Ibn Khuzayma that this is disobedience is interpreted as referring to someone who knows that considerable harm would result from his travelling alone or with only one companion); or for a woman to travel alone where indecencies may occur (N: which is an enormity if this is likely, but merely unlawful if it is not);

(٩٩-١٠٠) سفر الإنسان وحده ((ابن حجر:) فليحمل قول ابن خزيمة بالعصيان على من علم حصول ضرر عظيم له بسفره وحده أو مع آخر فقط). سفر المرأة وحدها بطريق تخاف فيها على بضعها.

(101) cancelling a trip or returning from one because of a "bad omen";

(١٠١) ترك السفر أو الرجوع منه تطيراً.

(102) neglecting to pray the Friday prayer in congregation when there is no excuse, even if one says one is "performing the noon prayer (zuhr) alone";

(١٠٢) ترك صلاة الجمعة مع الجماعة من غير عذر وإن قال إنه يصليها ظهراً وحده.

(103) stepping over people seated in the mosque for the Friday prayer;

(١٠٣) تخطي الرقاب يوم الجمعة.

(104) sitting in the center of a circle of people;

(١٠٤) الجلوس وسط الحلقة.

UNLAWFUL DRESS

ما يحرم لبسه

(105) for an adult male to wear pure silk (or cloth whose weight is mostly silk, even if it does not show) without an excuse such as preventing lice or itching;

(١٠٥) لبس الذكر البالغ العاقل الحرير الصرف أو الذي أكثره حرير وزناً لا ظهوراً من غير عذر كدفع قمل أو حكة.

(106) a male wearing gold, such as a ring, or wearing silver other than rings;

(١٠٦) تحلي الـذكـر البـالـغ العـاقل بذهب كخاتم أو فضة غير خاتم .

(107) men imitating women in things usually considered characteristic of women's dress, speech, and so forth; or vice versa;

(١٠٧) تشبـه الرجـال بالنسـاء فيـما يختصصن به عرفاً غالباً من لباس أو كلام أو نحوها أو بالعكس .

(108) a woman wearing a thin garment that reveals her body contours, or her inclining (N: showing desire for others) and making others incline towards her;

(١٠٨) لبس المـرأة ثوبـاً رقيقاً يصف بشرتها وميلها وإمالتها .

(109) having one's wraparound, robe, sleeves, or turban ends overly long from conceit;

(١٠٩) طول الإزار أو الثـوب أو الكم أو العذبة خيلاء .

(110) having a strutting gait;

(١١٠) التبختر في المشي .

(111) dying the beard or hair black for other than jihad or the like;

(١١١) خضب نحـو اللحيـة بالسـواد لغير غرض نحو جهاد .

(112) for a person to say after it rains, "The coming of such and such a star has brought us rain," believing it to have an effect;

(١١٢) قول الإنسـان إثـر المطـر : مطرنا بنوء نجم كذا أي وقته معتقداً أن له تأثيراً .

THE FUNERAL PRAYER

الجنازة

(113) clawing or slapping one's cheeks and the like (N: out of grief);

(١١٣) خمش أو لطم نحو الخد .

(114) ripping one's collar;

(١١٤) شق [نحو] الجيب .

(115) cries of lamentation;

(١١٥) النياحة .

(116) listening to them;

(١١٦) سماعها .

(117) shaving off or pulling out one's hair;

(١١٧) حلق أو نتف الشعر .

(118) cries of "woe" or "disaster" in afflictions;

(١١٨) الدعاء بالويل والثبور عند المصيبة .

(119) breaking the bones of the dead (A: or autopsies);

(١١٩) كسر عظم الميت .

(120) sitting on graves;

(١٢٠) الجلوس على القبور .

(121) praying upon graves or lighting lamps over them;

(١٢١) اتخـاذ المسـاجـد أو السـرج على القبور .

(122) women visiting graves (dis: w34.1, end);	(١٢٢) زيارة النساء لها .
(123) women following funeral processions;	(١٢٣) تشييعهن الجنائز .
(124) healing or protective words (ruqya) (N: that violate the conditions of Sacred Law (dis: w17.1));	(١٢٤) الرقى .
(125) hanging on an amulet (dis: w17.3);	(١٢٥) تعليق التمائم .
(126) disliking to meet Allah Most High;	(١٢٦) كراهة لقاء الله تعالى .
ZAKAT	الزكاة
(127) not paying zakat;	(١٢٧) ترك الزكاة .
(128) delaying payment after it is due, without lawful excuse;	(١٢٨) تأخيرها بعد وجوبها لغير عذر شرعي .
(129) for a creditor who knows that his debtor cannot pay to show greed towards him by pestering him or detaining him;	(١٢٩) شح الدائن على مدينه المعسر مع علمه بإعساره بالملازمة أو الحبس .
(130) dishonesty in handling or taking charity;	(١٣٠) الخيانة في الصدقة .
(131) collecting un-Islamic taxes or getting involved with any of the proceeds thereof (dis: p32);	(١٣١) جباية المكوس والدخول في شيء من توابعها .
(132) someone asking for charity who is not in need of it because of either having money or being able to earn some, but who rather asks out of greed or acquisitiveness;	(١٣٢) سؤال الغني بمال أو كسب التصدق عليه طمعاً وتكثراً .
(133) asking for charity with irritating insistence that injures the person being asked;	(١٣٣) الإلحاح في السؤال المؤذي للمسؤول إيذاء شديداً .
(134) not giving a relative the charity he has been compelled to ask one for, when able to give it and there is no excuse not to;	(١٣٤) منع الإنسان لقريبه [أو مولاه] مما سأله فيه لاضطراره إليه مع قدرة المانع عليه وعدم عذر له في المنع .
(135) reminding recipients of one's charity to them;	(١٣٥) المن بالصدقة .
(136) not giving access to one's surplus water when the person asking it is in need of it;	(١٣٦) منع فضل الماء بشرط الاحتياج أو الاضطرار إليه .

(137) being ungrateful for Allah's creatures' kindness to one, which entails being ungrateful for Allah's kindness to one;	(١٣٧) كفـران نعمة الخلق المستلزم لكفران نعمة الحق .
(138) to ask for anything besides paradise with the words "for Allah's sake" (bi wajh Allah);	(١٣٨) أن يسأل السائل بوجه الله غير الجنة .
(139) not to give to someone who asks "for Allah's sake";	(١٣٩) أن يمنع المسؤول سائله بوجه الله .
FASTING	الصيام
(140) not fasting a day of Ramadan;	(١٤٠) ترك صوم يوم من أيام رمضان .
(141) breaking one's fast during it;	(١٤١) الإفطار فيه .
(142) delaying making up a fast-day of Ramadan missed without excuse;	(١٤٢) تأخير قضاء ما تعدى بفطره من رمضان .
(143) a woman fasting a day that is not obligatory for her to fast immediately, when her husband is present and without his consent;	(١٤٣) صوم المرأة غير ما وجب فوراً وزوجها حاضر بغير رضاه .
(144) fasting on the two 'Eids, or on the three days that follow 'Eid al-Adha (Ayam al-Tashriq);	(١٤٤) صوم العيدين وأيام التشريق .
(145–46) nonperformance of a period of spiritual retreat (i'tikaf) that one has vowed for a certain time; or vitiating it by something such as lovemaking;	(١٤٥-٤٦) ترك الاعتكاف المنذور المضيق ؛ إبطاله بنحو الجماع .
(147) lovemaking in a mosque, even if not in spiritual retreat (i'tikaf);	(١٤٧) الجماع في المسجد ولو من غير معتكف .
THE PILGRIMAGE	الحج
(148) nonperformance of the pilgrimage (hajj) until one's death, after having been able to perform it;	(١٤٨) ترك الحج مع القدرة عليه إلى الموت .
(149) lovemaking on hajj or 'umra before partial release from ihram (def: j9.13);	(١٤٩) الجماع في الحج أو العمرة قبل التحلل الأول .
(150) for someone in ihram for hajj or 'umra to kill a game animal;	(١٥٠) قتل المحرم بحج أو عمرة صيداً مأكولاً وحشياً .

(151) a woman entering ihram for a supererogatory hajj or 'umra without her spouse's permission;

(١٥١) إحرام الحليلة بتطوع حج أو عمرة من غير إذن الحليل .

(152) not considering the Kaaba sacrosanct (N: i.e. not respecting it as one should);

(١٥٢) استحلال البيت الحرام .

(153) violating the sanctity of the Meccan Sacred Precinct (Haram) (dis: p72);

(١٥٣) الإلحاد في حرم مكة .

(154–59) frightening the people of the Prophet's city of Medina (upon its overseer be the best of prayers and peace); intending evil towards them; inaugurating an innovation (bid'a) therein, meaning a sin (N: like the opening of banks), or sheltering whoever does such a thing; cutting the trees of Medina; or cutting its grass;

(١٥٤ـ٥٩) إخافة أهل المدينة النبوية على مشرفها أفضل الصلاة والسلام؛ وإرادتهم بسوء؛ وإحداث حدث أي إثم فيها؛ وإيواء محدث ذلك الإثم؛ وقطع شجرها؛ أو حشيشها .

(160) nonperformance of the 'Eid al-Adha sacrifice by someone (N: such as a Hanafi) who holds it to be obligatory and is able to perform it;

(١٦٠) ترك الأضحية مع القدرة عند من قال بوجوبها .

(161) selling the hide of an 'Eid al-Adha sacrifice animal;

(١٦١) بيع جلد الأضحية .

(162–65) mutilating an animal by cutting off part of its nose or ear or the like; branding an animal's face; taking an animal as a target; or killing one for other than food;

(١٦٢ـ٦٥) المثلة بالحيوان كقطع شيء من نحو أنفه أو أذنه؛ ووسمه في وجهه؛ واتخاذه غرضاً؛ وقتله لغير الأكل .

(166) not killing and slaughtering as quickly and painlessly as possible;

(١٦٦) عدم إحسان القتلة والذبح .

(167) slaughtering in the name of other than Allah (N: is an enormity) when it is not outright unbelief, as when one does not intend the reverence of worship to the person for whom it is slaughtered (N: in which case it is not unbelief);

(١٦٧) الذبح باسم غير الله على وجه لا يكفر به بأن لم يقصد تعظيم المذبوح له كنحو التعظيم بالعبادة [والسجود] .

(168) to release a camel to roam and pasture freely for the rest of its life unridden and unused, in fulfillment of a vow;

(١٦٨) تسييب السوائب .

(169) calling someone "the King of Kings";

(١٦٩) التسمية بملك الأملاك .

(170) to take an intoxicant such as hashish, opium, henbane, ambergris, and the like, of substances that are not ritually unclean (najis);

(١٧٠) أكل المسكر الطاهر كالحشيشة والأفيون والشيكران وهو البنج وكالعنبر .

(171–73) to eat blood outpoured; pork; or unslaughtered meat;	(١٧١-٧٣) أكـل الـدم المسفوح؛ أو لحم الخنزير؛ أو الميتة .
(174) to burn an animal with fire;	(١٧٤) إحراق الحيوان بالنار .
(175–77) to consume something unclean (najis); revolting; or harmful;	(١٧٥-٧٧) تنـاول النجس؛ تنـاول المستقذر؛ تناول المضر .
TRADE	البيع
(178) selling a freeman as a slave;	(١٧٨) بيع الحر .
(179–85) consuming usurious gain (riba, def: k3); feeding the proceeds to others; recording a transaction involving it in writing; being a witness to one; acting as a go-between for two parties dealing in it; abetting it; or taking it through a subterfuge by someone who holds the subterfuge to be unlawful;	(١٧٩-٨٥) أكـل الـربـا؛ وإطعـامه؛ وكتابته؛ وشهادته؛ والسعي فيه؛ والإعانة عليه؛ والحيل في الربا وغيره عند من قال بتحريمها .
(186) not lending one's stud animal for use;	(١٨٦) منع الفحل .
(187) consuming wealth gotten through invalid transactions, or any other unlawful earnings;	(١٨٧) أكل المال بالبيوعات الفاسدة وسائر وجوه الأكساب المحرمة .
(188) hoarding a commodity for later sale at a high price when it becomes scarce;	(١٨٨) الاحتكار .
(189–93) selling grapes, raisins, or similar to someone who will make wine out of them; or wood or the like to someone who will make a musical instrument; weapons to non-Muslims who will use them against us; wine to someone who will drink it (N: as opposed to selling it to a vinegar maker, for example); or hemp or similar to someone who will use it as a drug;	(١٨٩-٩٣) بيـع الـعـنب والـزبيب ونحوهمـا ممن علم أنـه يعصـره خمراً؛ والخشب ونحـوه ممن يتخـذه آلـة لهـو؛ والسـلاح للحـربيين ليستعينـوا به على قتـالنـا؛ والخمر ممن يعلم أنه يشربها؛ ونحو الحشيشة ممن يعلم أنه يستعملها .
(194) having someone "bid up" a price to fool another bidder;	(١٩٤) النجش .
(195–96) undercutting another's price or deal (def: k4.7);	(١٩٥-٩٦) البيـع على بيـع الغيـر؛ والشراء على شرائه؛
(197) cheating in sales or the like, such as by not milking a dairy animal for several days before the sale to give the impression she's a good milk producer;	(١٩٧) الـغش في البيـع وغيـره كالتصـريـة وهي منـع حلب ذات اللبن إيهاماً لكثرته .

(198) selling merchandise at a higher price by lyingly swearing that it was purchased for more than it was;	(١٩٨) إنفاق السلعة بالحلف الكاذب.
(199) plotting and deceit;	(١٩٩) المكر والخديعة.
(200) selling short-measure, short-weight, or short-footage;	(٢٠٠) بخس نحو الكيل أو الوزن أو الذرع.
(201) any loan made to benefit the lender;	(٢٠١) القرض الذي يجر نفعاً للمقرض.
(202) to borrow money with the intention not to repay;	(٢٠٢) الاستدانة مع نيته عدم الوفاء.
(203) to borrow money when one has no hope of repaying it, as when one does not urgently need it, there is no obvious source to get the money to repay, and the lender is ignorant of the borrower's condition;	(٢٠٣) الاستدانة مع عدم رجائه بأن لم يضطر ولا كان له جهة ظاهرة يفي منها والدائن جاهل بحاله.
(204) for a borrower who can afford to pay back a debt to delay doing so without excuse when asked to repay;	(٢٠٤) مطل الغني بعد مطالبته من غير عذر.
(205) consuming an orphan's property;	(٢٠٥) أكل مال اليتيم.
(206) spending money, no matter how little, on something that is unlawful, even if only a lesser sin;	(٢٠٦) إنفاق مال ولو فلساً في محرم ولو صغيرة.
(207) to annoy one's neighbor, even if a non-Muslim subject, by the likes of having a view overlooking his walls, or building something uncountenanced by Sacred Law that is a nuisance to him;	(٢٠٧) إيذاء الجار ولو ذمياً كأن يشرف على حرمه أو يبني ما يؤذيه مما لا يسوغ له شرعاً.
(208) to build higher than one needs to, out of pride;	(٢٠٨) البناء فوق الحاجة للخيلاء.
(209) surreptitiously changing property-line markers;	(٢٠٩) تغيير منار الأرض.
(210) misleading a blind person from the way;	(٢١٠) إضلال الأعمى عن الطريق.
(211–12) doing something to a dead-end path or street without the permission of the people living on it; or doing something to a street that results in considerable and unlawful annoyance to people passing along it;	(٢١١-١٢) التصرف في الطريق غير النافذ بغير إذن أهله؛ والتصرف في الشارع مما يضر المارة إضراراً بليغاً غير سائغ شرعاً.

(213) for someone (who holds that it is not permissible) to do something not customarily tolerated to a shared wall without the other owner's permission;

(214) for the guarantor of a debt to refuse to cover the debt that he has guaranteed with a guarantee he believes to be valid;

(215) for one member of a partnership to cheat the other;

(216) for a person commissioned as an agent to betray the trust of the person who commissioned him;

(217) for a person to make a formal acknowledgement that he owes one of his heirs or a non-heir a debt, or that he has property belonging to such a person in his possession, when this is not true (N: but is rather done to cheat his estate division heirs of their just due, by thus effectively "willing" (wasiyya, def: L1.0) more than the lawful one-third of his property to such a person, who would be able to collect it as if it were his own, after the former's death);

(218) for an ill person not to make a formal acknowledgement of his debts or the articles in his keeping that belong to others when no one else whose word is acceptable knows of them except his heirs;

(219–20) a lying acknowledgement or denial of being someone's son;

(221–23) to employ an article lent for use ('ariyya) in other than the employment authorized by its lender; for the borrower to relend it to a third party without the original lender's permission when the borrower holds that such relending is not permissible; or for the person to whom the article has been lent to use it beyond the time stipulated by the lender;

(224) wrongful appropriation, meaning unjustly taking another's property (N: or right);

(225) to delay paying someone his wages, or

(٢١٣) التصرف في الجدار المشترك بغير إذن شريكه بما لا يحتمل عادة عند من قال بحرمة ذلك .

(٢١٤) امتناع الضامن ضماناً صحيحاً في عقيدته من أداء ما ضمنه للمضمون له .

(٢١٥) خيانة أحد الشريكين لشريكه .

(٢١٦) خيانة الوكيل لموكله .

(٢١٧) الإقرار لأحد ورثته كذباً أو لأجنبي بدين أو عين .

(٢١٨) ترك إقرار المريض بما عليه من الـديـون أو عنـده من الأعيـان إذا لم يعلم به من غير الورثة من يثبت بقوله .

(٢١٩-٢٠) الإقـرار بنسب كذباً ؛ أو جحده كذلك .

(٢٢١-٢٣) استعمـال العارية في غير المنفعة التي استعارها لها ؛ وإعارتها من غيـر إذن مالكهـا عنـد من قال بمنعهـا ؛ واستعمالها بعد المدة المؤقتة بها .

(٢٢٤) الغصب وهو الاستيـلاء على مال الغير (ح : أو حق الغير) ظلماً .

(٢٢٥) تأخير أجرة الأجير أو منعه منها

not giving them to him after the work has been completed;

بعد فراغ عمله .

(226) for someone (who holds it is unlawful) to build at 'Arafa, Muzdelifa, or Mina;

(٢٢٦) البناء بعرفة أو مزدلفة أو منى عند من قال بتحريمه .

(227) to forbid people things that are permissible to them, both in general and in particular;

(٢٢٧) منع الناس من الأشياء المباحة لهم على العموم أو الخصوص .

(228) renting any part of the street to another and taking payment for it, even if it is within the confines of one's property or store;

(٢٢٨) إكراء شيء من الشارع وأخذ أجرته وإن كان حريم ملكه أو دكانه .

(229) taking over water that is free for all to use, or forbidding such water to travellers;

(٢٢٩) الاستيلاء على ماء مباح ومنعه ابن السبيل .

(230) violating the stipulations of the founder of a pious endowment (waqf);

(٢٣٠) مخالفة شرط الواقف .

(231–32) to use a lost and found article without having fulfilled the conditions of advertising it before taking possession of it (dis: k27); or concealing it from its true owner after one knows who he is;

(٢٣١-٣٢) أن يتصرف في اللقطة قبل استيفاء شرائط تعريفها وتملكها ؛ وكتمها من ربها بعد علمه به .

(233) not having witnesses attest to one's having found a foundling child;

(٢٣٣) ترك الإشهاد عند أخذ اللقيط .

INHERITANCE AND BEQUEST

الفرائض والوصايا

(234–36) harming heirs in bequests; willing more than a third of one's property in bequests (dis: L3.1); or to fraudulently affirm that part or all of one's property belongs to some non-heir, or that one owes a debt that does not really exist, when this is done to prevent the estate from going to one's rightful heirs; or to falsely affirm that a debt someone owes one has been paid off; or to sell something for a token price or buy something at an exorbitant sum when it is done to keep property from one's heirs, or to donate a third of one's property to a charity not for Allah's sake but rather to diminish the shares of the heirs—all this is included in "harming others in bequests";

(٢٣٤-٣٦) الإضرار في الوصية ؛ وأن يوصي بأكثر من الثلث ؛ أو يقر بكل ماله أو بعضه لأجنبي ، أو يقر على نفسه بدين لا حقيقة له دفعاً للميراث عن الورثة ، أو يقر بأن الدين الذي كان له على فلان استوفاه منه ، أو يبيع شيئاً بثمن رخيص ، ويشتري شيئاً بثمن غال كل ذلك لغرض أن لا يصل المال إلى الورثة أو يوصي بالثلث لا لوجه الله لكن لغرض تنقيص الورثة فهذا هو الإضرار في الوصية .

(237) betraying one's trusts, such as with respect to articles given to one for safekeeping, put up as collateral, rented to one, and so forth;

(٢٣٧) الخيانة في الأمانات كالوديعة والعين المرهونة أو المستأجرة وغير ذلك .

MARRIAGE	النكاح

(238–40) looking with lust at a woman who is not one's unmarriageable kin (mahram, def: m6.1) when temptation is apprehended (A: if there is no temptation, it is unlawful, but not an enormity); touching such a woman; or being alone with her when neither party has one of their unmarriageable kin present to remind them of the limits of decorum—even if only a female—and the woman has no husband present;

(٢٣٨-٤٠) نظـر الأجنبيــة بشهـوة مع خوف فتنة ولمسها كذلك وكذا الخلوة بها بأن لم يكن معهمـا محـرم لأحـدهمـا يحتشمه ـ ولو امـرأة كذلك ـ ولا زوج لتلك الأجنبية .

(241–42) slander (def: r2); or accepting and acquiescing to it by not objecting when it is heard;

(٢٤١-٤٢) الغيبة ؛ والسكوت عليها رضاً وتقريراً .

(243) giving one another disliked nicknames;

(٢٤٣) التنابز بالألقاب المكروهة .

(244) ridicule or mockery towards a Muslim;

(٢٤٤) السخرية والاستهزاء بالمسلم .

(245) talebearing (namima, def: r3);

(٢٤٥) النميمة .

(246) being two-faced with people (dis: r16.1), while devoid of honor in Allah's sight;

(٢٤٦) كلام ذي الـلـسـانين وهـو ذو الوجهين الذي لا يكون عند الله وجيهاً .

(247) calumny;

(٢٤٧) البهت .

(248) for a guardian to keep a woman under his guardianship from marrying;

(٢٤٨) عضل الولي موليته عن النكاح .

(249) proposing marriage to a woman whom someone has already proposed to, when the previous proposal was permissible, plainly stated, and explicitly accepted by those whose acceptance counts;

(٢٤٩) الخطبــة على خطبـة الغيـر الجائزة الصريحة إذا أجيب صريحاً إليها ممن تعتبر إجابته .

(250–51) turning a wife's heart against her husband; or a husband's against his wife;

(٢٥٠-٥١) تخـبـيب الـمـرأة على زوجها أي إفسادها عليه ؛ والزوج على زوجته .

(252) for a man to make a marriage contract with a woman who is his unmarriageable kin (mahram, def: m6.1), whether by birth, marriage, or suckling (n12), even if such a marriage is not consummated;

(٢٥٢) عقـد الـرجـل على محـرمـه بنسب أو رضاع أو مصاهرة وإن لم يطأ .

(253–55) for a man who has divorced his wife to accept that she should marry and have intercourse with another solely for the purpose of

(٢٥٣-٥٥) رضا المطلق بالتحليل ؛

remarrying her himself (dis: n7.7); for the wife to comply with this; or for the second husband to marry her for such a purpose;

وطواعية المرأة المطلقة عليه ؛ ورضا الزوج المحلل له .

(256–57) for a man to reveal his wife's secret by mentioning details of their sexual intercourse or other similar private matters; or for her to reveal his;

(٢٥٦ـ٥٧) إفشاء الرجل سرّ زوجته ، وهي سره بأن تذكر ما وقع بينهما من تفاصيل الجماع ونحوها مما يخفى .

(258) sodomizing one's wife;

(٢٥٨) إتيان الزوجة في دبرها .

(259) to make love to one's spouse in the presence of a third party, male or female;

(٢٥٩) أن يجامع حليلته بحضرة أجنبية أو رجل أجنبي .

(260) to marry a woman with the intention not to pay her the marriage payment (mahr, def: m8) if she asks for it;

(٢٦٠) أن يتزوج امرأة وفي عزمه أن لا يوفيها صداقها لو طلبته .

(261) to make a representation of an animate creature upon anything, in a respectful or humiliated deployment, on the ground or elsewhere;

(٢٦١) تصوير ذي روح على أي شيء كان من معظّم أو ممتهن بأرض أو غيرها .

(262) *sponging*, meaning to join another at his meal to eat from it without his permission or acceptance;

(٢٦٢) التطفل وهو الدخول على طعام الغير ليأكل منه من غير إذنه ولا رضاه .

(263) for a guest to eat more than he needs to be full when he does not know of his host's acceptance of this;

(٢٦٣) وأكل الضيف زائداً على الشبع من غير أن يعلم رضا المضيف بذلك .

(264–65) a person's eating copiously of his own money when he knows this will harm him considerably; or being lavish in food and drink out of greediness and vanity;

(٢٦٤ـ٦٥) وإكثار الإنسان الأكل من مال نفسه بحيث يعلم أنه يضره ضرراً بيناً ؛ والتوسع في المآكل والمشارب شرهاً وبطراً .

(266) oppressively and wrongfully favoring one wife over another;

(٢٦٦) ترجيح إحدى الزوجات على الأخرى ظلماً وعدواناً .

(267–68) a husband not giving his wife her rights; or she not giving him his;

(٢٦٧ـ٦٨) منع الزوج حقاً من حقوق زوجته الواجبة لها عليه ؛ ومنعها حقاً له عليها .

(269–71) to avoid meeting one's fellow Muslim longer than three days for other than a reason permitted by Sacred Law; to turn one's face from him when one meets him; or have a change in heart towards him that results in either of these;

(٢٦٩ـ٧١) التهاجر بأن يهجر أخاه المسلم فوق ثلاثة أيام لغير غرض شرعي ؛ والتدابر وهو إعراض عن المسلم بأن يلقاه فيعرض عنه بوجهه ؛ والتشاحن وهو تغير القلوب المؤدي إلى أحد ذينك .

(272) a woman leaving her house perfumed

(٢٧٢) خروج المرأة من بيتها متعطرة

and adorned, even with her husband's permission;	متزينة ولو بإذن الزوج .
(273) the rebelliousness of a woman towards her husband, such as by leaving home without his permission or acceptance for other than a reason countenanced by Sacred Law;	(٢٧٣) نشوز المرأة بنحو خروجها من منزلها بغير إذن زوجها ورضاه لغير ضرورة شرعية .
(274–75) failure to provide one's wife with her support and clothing without lawful excuse; or neglecting one's dependents such as young children;	(٢٧٤-٧٥) منع نفقة الزوجة أو كسوتها من غير مسوّغ شرعي ؛ وإضاعة عياله كأولاده الصغار .
(276) disrespect towards either or both of one's parents, grandparents, and on up;	(٢٧٦) عقوق الوالدين أو أحدهما وإن علا .
(277) severing the ties of kinship;	(٢٧٧) قطع الرحم .
(278–79) tormenting a servant or beast of burden; or goading animals to fight each other;	(٢٧٨-٧٩) وتعذيب القن أو الدابة ؛ والتحريش بين البهائم .
(280) for a woman to ask her husband for a divorce when she has not suffered any harm from him;	(٢٨٠) سؤال المرأة زوجها الطلاق من غير بأس .
(281) for a husband to accept being a cuckhold;	(٢٨١) الديائة .
(282) pimping between men and women;	(٢٨٢) القيادة بين الرجال والنساء .
(283) for someone (who believes it is unlawful (dis: n7.4(N:))) to have intercourse with his divorced wife before formally taking her back;	(٢٨٣) وطء الرجعية قبل ارتجاعها ممن يعتقد تحريمه .
(284) foreswearing one's wife by an oath not to have intercourse with her for more than four months;	(٢٨٤) الإيلاء من الزوجة بأن يحلف ليمتنعنّ من وطها أكثر من أربعة أشهر .
(285–86) accusing a man or woman who could be chaste (def: o13.2) of adultery or sodomy; or acquiescing to such a charge by not objecting to it when heard;	(٢٨٥-٨٦) قذف المحصن أو المحصنة بزنا أو لواط ؛ والسكوت على ذلك .
(287–88) vituperating a Muslim or attacking his honor; or being the cause of another's cursing or disparaging one's parents;	(٢٨٧-٨٨) سب المسلم والاستطالة في عرضه ؛ وتسبب الإنسان في لعن أو شتم والديه .
(289) cursing a Muslim;	(٢٨٩) لعنه مسلماً .
(290) attacking someone's ancestry;	(٢٩٠) الطعن في النسب .

(291) for a woman to falsely ascribe her child from adultery to a people it is not from;

(٢٩١) أن تدخل المرأة على قوم من ليس منهم بزنا [أو وطء شبهة].

(292) a divorced woman's deceit regarding the end of her postmarital waiting period ('idda, def: n9);

(٢٩٢) الخيانة في انقضاء العدة.

(293) for a divorced woman during her post-marital waiting period to leave the lodgings she is obliged to remain in until its end, when there is no lawful excuse to go out (dis: n9.13–14);

(٢٩٣) خروج المعتدة من المسكن الذي يلزمها ملازمته إلى انقضاء العدة بغير عذر شرعي.

(294) for a woman whose husband has died not to avoid adornment (def: n9.16) during her waiting period;

(٢٩٤) عدم إحداد المتوفى عنها زوجها.

JUSTICE

الجنايات

(295) killing a Muslim or a non-Muslim subject of the Islamic state intentionally or quasi-intentionally;

(٢٩٥) قتل المسلم أو الذمي المعصوم عمداً أو شبه عمد.

(296) suicide;

(٢٩٦) قتل الإنسان نفسه.

(297–98) aiding another in an unlawful killing or its preliminaries;

(٢٩٧ـ٩٨) الإعانة على القتل المحرم أو مقدمته.

(299) to strike a Muslim or non-Muslim subject of the Islamic state without a lawful excuse;

(٢٩٩) ضرب المسلم أو الذمي بغير مسوّغ شرعي.

(300–301) frightening a Muslim; or gesturing at him with a weapon or the like;

(٣٠٠ـ٣٠١) ترويع المسلم؛ والإشارة إليه بسلاح أو نحوه.

(302–16) sorcery that does not entail unbelief; teaching it; learning it; having it done; professing to foretell the future, to be "psychic," or know the unseen (dis: w60.1); considering something a bad omen; divination by pebbles or drawing lines in sand; astrology; taking auguries from birds; going to someone who claims to foretell the future; going to a "psychic," a diviner by pebbles or lines, an astrologer, or an augerer or omen-reader from birds;

(٣٠٢ـ١٦) السحر الذي لا كفر فيه؛ وتعليمه؛ وتعلمه؛ وطلب عمله؛ والكهانة؛ والعرافة؛ والطيرة؛ والطرق؛ والتنجيم؛ والعيافة؛ وإتيان كاهن، وإتيان عراف؛ وإتيان طارق؛ وإتيان منجم؛ وإتيان ذي طيرة ليتطير له أو ذي عيافة ليخط له.

(317–18) rebellion against the caliph, even if he is unjust, when there is no mitigating pretext or one that is patently false; or betraying one's fealty

(٣١٧ـ١٨) البغي أي الخروج على الإمام ولو جائراً بلا تأويل أو تأويل يقطع ببطلانه؛ ونكث بيعة الإمام لفوات غرض

to him because of some worldly disadvantage in remaining loyal;

(319–21) to assume the caliphate or other position of authority when one knows oneself likely to betray it, or one has the intention to; or to ask for such a position or spend money to gain it when one has this knowledge or intention;

(322) for an oppressor or immoral person to take over any of the Muslims' concerns;

(323) to discharge a righteous and competent person from office and appoint someone who is not;

(324) for a caliph, leader, or judge to be unjust;

(325–26) for a leader to cheat his followers; or neglect to fullfill, through himself or a representative, their pressing concerns that they are compelled to obtain;

(327) for rulers, leaders, judges, or others to wrong a Muslim or non-Muslim subject of the Islamic state;

(328) to leave the oppressed unaided;

(329–31) visiting unjust rulers; aiding them in wronging others; or stirring their hearts against people by telling them falsehoods;

(332) sheltering the guilty, meaning to protect them from those who want to obtain their rights from them, *guilty* meaning those who commit an offense that entails a consequence stipulated by Sacred Law;

(333) saying to a Muslim "O unbeliever," or "O enemy of Allah";

(334) interceding for someone, to obviate one of the prescribed penalties of Sacred Law (hadd, def: o12–o16);

(335) blackening a Muslim's name and searching out his shameful points so as to disgrace and humiliate him before others;

دنيوي.

(٣١٩-٢١) تولي الإمامة أو الإمارة مع علمه بخيانة نفسه أو عزمه عليها؛ وسؤال ذلك وبذل مال عليه مع العلم أو العزم المذكورين.

(٣٢٢) تولية جائر أو فاسق أمراً من أمور المسلمين.

(٣٢٣) عزل الصالح وتولية من هو دونه.

(٣٢٤) جور الإمام أو الأمير أو القاضي.

(٣٢٥-٢٦) غشه لرعيته؛ واحتجابه عن قضاء حوائجهم المهمة المضطرين إليها بنفسه أو نائبه.

(٣٢٧) ظلم السلاطين والأمراء والقضاة وغيرهم مسلماً أو ذمياً.

(٣٢٨) خذلان المظلوم.

(٣٢٩-٣١) الدخول على الظلمة؛ وإعانتهم على الظلم؛ والسعاية إليهم باطل.

(٣٣٢) إيواء المحدثين أي منعهم ممن يريد استيفاء الحق منهم، والمراد بهم من يتعاطى مفسدة يلزمه بسببها أمر شرعي.

(٣٣٣) قول إنسان لمسلم يا كافر، أو يا عدو الله.

(٣٣٤) الشفاعة في حد من حدود الله تعالى.

(٣٣٥) هتك المسلم وتتبع عوراته حتى يفضحه ويذله بها بين الناس.

(336) displaying the attire of the righteous in public while committing unlawful acts, even if only lesser ones, when alone;

(337) compromising any of the prescribed legal penalties;

(338–43) fornication; sodomy; bestiality; sodomizing a woman; lesbianism between women (meaning one woman doing with another that which resembles what a man would do with her); or for a husband to have intercourse with the body of a deceased wife;

(344–46) consummating a marriage contracted with neither guardian nor witnesses; consummating a "temporary marriage"; or having intercourse with a prostitute;

(347) for a woman to allow someone to fornicate with her;

(348) theft;

(349) to block the road, meaning to threaten passers upon it, even if one does not kill anyone or take any money;

(350–61) drinking wine in any form or other intoxicant, even if only a drop; pressing out the juice to make wine or other intoxicant; pressing it for another person; carrying it for purposes of drinking, or having it carried; serving it to others or having it served; selling it; buying it; having it bought or sold; consuming the proceeds from selling it; or keeping wine or other intoxicant;

(362–65) attacking anyone under the state's protection in order to kill him, rob him, rape his wife, terrorize or frighten him;

(366) peeping into another's house without his permission, such as into the women's quarters;

(367) listening to people who are averse to being overheard;

(368) not getting circumcised, even after having reached puberty;

(٣٣٦) إظهــار زي الصــالحين في الملأ وانتهاك المحارم ولو صغائر في الخلوة.

(٣٣٧) المداهنة في إقامة حد من الحدود.

(٣٣٨-٤٣) الـزنـا؛ واللواط؛ وإتيان البهيمـة؛ والمرأة [الأجنبية] في دبرها؛ ومساحقة النسـاء، وهـو أن تفعل المرأة بالمرأة مثل صورة ما يفعل بها الرجل؛ ووطء الزوج لزوجته الميتة.

(٣٤٤-٤٦) والـوطء في نكاح بلا ولي ولا شهود؛ وفي نكاح المتعة؛ ووطء المستأجرة.

(٣٤٧) وإمساك المرأة لمن يزني بها.

(٣٤٨) السرقة.

(٣٤٩) قطع الطريق أي إخافتها وإن لم يقتل نفساً ولا أخذ مالاً.

(٣٥٠-٦١) شرب الـخمــر مطلقــاً والمسكـر من غيرهـا ولـو قطرة؛ وعصر أحـدهمـا؛ واعتصاره؛ وحمله وطلب حمله لنحو شربه؛ وسقيه وطلب سقيه؛ وبيعـه؛ وشراؤه؛ وطلب أحدهما؛ وأكل ثمنه؛ وإمساك أحدهما.

(٣٦٢-٦٥) الـصيـال على معصـوم لإرادة نحـو قتله أو أخـذ ماله أو انتهـاك حرمة بضعه أو لإرادة ترويعه وتخويفه.

(٣٦٦) أن يطلع من نحـو ثقب ضيق في دار غيره بغير إذنه على حرمه.

(٣٦٧) الـتسـمــع إلـى حديـث قوم يكرهون الاطلاع عليه.

(٣٦٨) ترك الختان بعد البلوغ.

(369–70) not performing jihad when personally obliged to; or no one performing it at all;	(٣٦٩ـ٧٠) ترك الجهاد عند تعينه ؛ وترك الناس الجهاد من أصله .
(371) people of outlying provinces neglecting to protect border fortifications;	(٣٧١) وترك أهل الإقليم تحصين ثغورهم .
(372–73) not commanding the right or forbidding the wrong when able to;	(٣٧٢ـ٧٣) ترك الأمر بالمعروف والنهي عن المنكر مع القدرة .
(374) one's actions contradicting one's words;	(٣٧٤) ومخالفة القول الفعل .
(375) not returning someone's greetings of Salam (dis: r33.2):	(٣٧٥) ترك رد السلام .
(376) to like for others to rise from their seat for one, because of pride and arrogance;	(٣٧٦) محبة الإنسان أن يقوم الناس له افتخاراً أو تعاظماً .
(377) fleeing from combat with unbelievers, unless one is falling back to regroup or separating to join another unit to reinforce them;	(٣٧٧) الفرار من الزحف إلا لتحرف لقتال أو لتحيز إلى فئة يستنجد بها .
(378) fleeing from an outbreak of plague (N: in one's town);	(٣٧٨) الفرار من الطاعون .
(379–80) pilfering from the spoils of war; or concealing such pilfering;	(٣٧٩ـ٨٠) الغلول من الغنيمة ؛ والستر عليه .
(381–83) killing, treachery towards, or wronging anyone who is under a safe-conduct, is a subject of the Islamic state, or is under an agreement of protection;	(٣٨١ـ٨٣) قتل أو غدر أو ظلم من له أمان أو ذمة أو عهد ؛
(384) showing others the weak points of the Muslims;	(٣٨٤) الدلالة على عورات المسلمين .
(385–86) acquiring a horse out of pride, or for wagers or gambling; or engaging in contests of marksmanship for any of these reasons;	(٣٨٥ـ٨٦) اتخاذ نحو الخيل تكبراً أو للمسابقة عليها رهاناً أو مقامرة ؛ والمناضلة بالسهام كذلك .
(387) to neglect one's marksmanship after having learned it, out of aversion for it, such as might lead to being defeated by the enemy and their mocking the people of Islam;	(٣٨٧) وترك الرمي بعد تعلمه رغبة عنه بحيث يؤدي إلى غلبة العدو واستهانته بأهل الإسلام .
(388–90) to swear an engulfing oath (def: p23); a lying oath; or to frequently swear oaths, even if truthful;	(٣٨٨ـ٩٠) اليمين الغموس ؛ واليمين الكاذبة ؛ وكثرة الأيمان وإن كان صادقاً .

(391–94) swearing by *one's trust;* or by an idol, for example; or the words of reckless people who say, "If I do that, I'm an unbeliever" or "quit of Islam" or "of the Prophet"; or to swear, "then I'm of such and such a religion," lyingly;

(٣٩١-٩٤) الحلف بالأمانة أو بالصنم مثلاً وقول بعض المجازفين: إن فعلت كذا فأنا كافر؛ أو بريء من الإسلام؛ أو النبي؛ الحلف بملة غير الإسلام كاذباً.

(395) not fulfilling a vow, no matter whether it was to perform an act of worship or whether made in the heat of anger;

(٣٩٥) عدم الوفاء بالنذر سواء أكان نذر قربة أم نذر لجاج.

(396–98) appointing a person to the judgeship who knows he is dishonest, unjust, or the like; for such a person to accept the judgeship; or seek it;

(٣٩٦-٩٨) تولية القضاء لمن يعلم من نفسه الخيانة أو الجور أو نحوهما؛ وتوليه؛ وسؤاله.

(399) to judge when ignorant;

(٣٩٩) القضاء بجهل.

(400) to judge unjustly;

(٤٠٠) أو بالجور.

(401) aiding and abetting someone making a false claim in court;

(٤٠١) إعانة المبطل ومساعدته.

(402) for a judge (or anyone else) to please people with what Allah Most High detests;

(٤٠٢) إرضاء القاضي وغيره الناس بما يسخط الله تعالى.

(403–5) taking or giving a bribe for falsehood; or being an intermediary between the persons giving and accepting it;

(٤٠٣-٠٥) أخذ الرشوة وإعطاؤها بباطل؛ والسعي فيها بين الراشي والمرتشي.

(406–7) accepting money for appointing a judge; or a person who is not personally obliged to take the judgeship (N: because no one else is competent) paying to attain it when he could do so without paying;

(٤٠٦-٧) أخذ المال على تولية الحكم؛ ودفعه حيث لم يتعين عليه القضاء ولم يلزمه البذل.

(408) a judge accepting a gift for having interceded for one of the litigants;

(٤٠٨) قبول الهدية بسبب شفاعته.

(409–10) arguing for a falsehood; or arguing without knowledge of who is in the right, as a judge's deputy does;

(٤٠٩-١٠) الخصومة بباطل؛ أو بغير علم كوكلاء القاضي.

(411–13) seeking one's rights, but with vehemence and lies, so as to offend the other party and defeat him; arguing out of pure obstinacy to prevail over one's opponent and finish him; and the picking apart of another's words and disputation which are reprehensible;

(٤١١-١٣) طلب حق لكن مع إظهار لدد وكذب لإيذاء الخصم والتسلط عليه؛ والخصومة لمحض العناد بقصد قهر الخصم وكسره؛ والمراء والجدال المذموم.

(414–15) for a person distributing zakat to divide it unjustly between recipients; or for the person who estimates how much will be due on crops to assess them unjustly;

(٤١٤-١٥) جور القاسم في قسمته والمقوِّم في تقويمه .

(416–18) falsely testifying; knowingly accepting such false testimony; or not testifying to something that one has witnessed when there is no excuse not to;

(٤١٦-١٨) شهادة الزور؛ وقبولها؛ وكتم الشهادة بلا عذر؛

(419) lying, when it entails a prescribed legal penalty or harm;

(٤١٩) الكذب الذي فيه حد أو ضرر .

(420) a plaintiff litigating against another person for something he knows is not his;

(٤٢٠) دعوى الإنسان على غيره بما يعلم أنه ليس له .

(421) sitting with those who drink or other immoral people out of friendship for them;

(٤٢١) الجلوس مع الشربة وغيرهم من الفساق إيناساً لهم .

(422) Koran reciters or religious scholars sitting in the company of the corrupt;

(٤٢٢) مجالسة القراء والفقهاء الفسقة .

(423–25) gambling, whether by itself or connected with offensive games like chess or unlawful ones like backgammon; playing backgammon; or for someone (who holds it is unlawful) to play chess;

(٢٣-٢٥ ٤) القمار سواء كان مستقلاً أو مقترناً بلعب مكروه كالشطرنج أو محرم كالنرد؛ واللعب بالنرد؛ واللعب بالشطرنج عند من قال بتحريمه .

(426–31) playing stringed instruments; listening to them; playing reed instruments; listening to them; beating a long drum (kuba); or listening to it;

(٢٦-٣١ ٤) ضرب وتر؛ واستماعه؛ وزمر بمزمر؛ واستماعه؛ وضرب بكوبة؛ واستماعه .

(432–33) embellishing a poetic ode by mentioning a particular woman, even without indecency, or mentioning an unnamed woman indecently; or to sing such an ode;

(٣٢-٣٣ ٤) التشبيب بامرأة [أجنبية] معينة وإن لم يذكرها بفحش أو بامرأة مبهمة مع ذكرها بالفحش؛ وإنشاد هذا التشبيب .

(434–37) poetry that contains mockery of a Muslim, obscenity, or lying; or singing such poetry and spreading it;

(٣٤-٣٧ ٤) الشعر المشتمل على هجو المسلم أو على فحش أو كذب فاحش؛ وإنشاد هذا الهجو وإذاعته .

(438) composing panegyrics with poetic figures of speech that exceed normal bounds, earning one's living thereby and spending most of one's time at it;

(٤٣٨) الإطراء في الشعر بما لم تجر العادة به والتكسب به مع صرف أكثر وقته .

(439) becoming habituated to a lesser sin or sins such that one's disobedience becomes more than one's obedience;

(٤٣٩) إدمان صغيرة أو صغائر بحيث تغلب معصيته طاعته .

(440) not repenting from an enormity;	(٤٤٠) ترك التوبة من كبيرة .
(441–42) hatred of the Medinan Helpers (Ansar); or speaking badly of any of the prophetic Companions (Allah be well pleased with them all).	(٤٤١-٤٢) بغض الأنصار؛ وشتم واحد من الصحابة رضوان الله عليهم أجمعين .
(*al-Zawajir 'an iqtiraf al-kaba'ir* (y49), 1.27–266, 2.3–230)	[محرر من كتاب الزواجر عن اقتراف الكبائر؛ ١ / ٢٧ ـ ٢٤٠ ، ٢/ ٣ ـ ٢٣٠].

w52.2 (n:) Some twenty-five of the enormities listed by Ibn Hajar have been omitted above because of being repetitions or about matters that are rare. As stated in the preface, many scholars do not consider all of the foregoing to be enormities, among them Abu Talib Makki, who restricts them solely to sins explicitly designated as enormities by the primary texts.

w52.3 (Abu Talib Makki:) .... My own position, to join between the different views mentioned above, is that they are seventeen in number. Four of them are of the works of the heart: (1) associating others with Allah Most High (shirk); (2) persisting in disobedience to Allah Most High; (3) despairing of the mercy of Allah Most High; (4) and feeling secure from the design of Allah Most High (def: p66). Four are of the tongue: (5) testifying to the truth of a falsehood; (6) charging someone who could be chaste (def: o13.2) with adultery; (7) swearing an engulfing oath, meaning one which negates something true and affirms something false, termed *engulfing* because it engulfs its swearer in the wrath of Allah Most High, or in hellfire; (8) and sorcery, meaning words and acts that transmute substances, alter people (n: changing	w52.3 (أبو طالب المكي :) [. . .] والذي عندي في جملة ذلك مجتمعاً من المتفرق سبع عشرة [تفصيلها]: أربعة من أعمال القلوب وهن : الشرك بالله تعالى، والإصرار على معصية الله تعالى، والقنوط من رحمة الله تعالى، والأمن من مكر الله تعالى؛ وأربعة في اللسان وهن : شهادة الزور، وقذف المحصن [وهو الحر البالغ المسلم]، واليمين الغموس وهي التي تبطل بها حقاً وتحق بها باطلاً [وقيل هي التي يقطع بها مال مسلم ظلماً ولو سواكاً من أراك] وسميت غموساً لأنها تغمسه في غضب الله تعالى وقيل [لأنها تغمس صاحبها] في النار، والسحر وهو ما كان من كلام أو فعل يقلب الأعيان أو يغير الإنسان وينقل

one's love for someone to hate, for example), or remove meanings from the things for which they were created.

Three are of the stomach:

(9) drinking wine or other intoxicating beverages;

(10) wrongfully consuming an orphan's property;

(11) and knowingly consuming usurious gain (riba).

Two are of the genitals:

(12) adultery;

(13) and sodomy.

Two are of the hands:

(14) murder;

(15) and theft.

One is of the feet:

(16) fleeing from combat with unbelievers when one is not outnumbered by more than two to one, unless falling back to regroup or separating to join another unit, believing one will attack again.

And one is of the whole body:

(17) a person's undutiful treatment of his parents, meaning, in summary, that when they swear an oath for him to do something that is not blameworthy, he does not fulfill their oath; if they ask him for something they need, he does not give it to them; if they trust him, he betrays them; if they are hungry, he eats his fill and does not feed them; and if they revile him, he strikes them;

Other scholars hold that *any* sin that is deliberate is an enormity... but what we have mentioned of the above bodily traits is among the

المعاني عن موضوعات خلقها [والسحرة هم النفاثات في العقد الذين أمر الله تعالى بالاستعاذة منهم]؛ وثلاثة في البطن وهي شرب الخمر والمسكر من الأشربة، وأكل مال اليتيم ظلماً، وأكل الربا وهو يعلم؛ واثنتان في الفرج وهما الزنا، وأن يعمل عمل قوم لوط في الأدبار؛ واثنتان في اليدين وهما القتل، والسرقة؛ وواحدة في الرجلين وهي الفرار من الزحف الواحد من اثنين غير متحرف [. . .] (ح: للقتال) ولا متحيزاً إلى فئة ولا معتقد الكرة؛ وواحدة في جميع الجسد وهي عقوق الوالدين وتفسير العقوق جملة : أن يقسما عليه في حق فلا يبر قسمهما، وأن يسألاه في حاجة فلا يعطيهما، وأن يأمناه فيخونهما، وأن يجوعا فيشبع ولا يطعمهما، وأن يستباه فيضربهما [. . .].

وقالت طائفة : كل عمد فهو كبيرة . . . فالذي ذكرناه من الخصائل هو من أوسط

soundest and most equitable opinions, is what scholars agree upon, and is what is conveyed by a great number of primary texts. These, then, are the deadly enormities that if one avoids them, one's wrongs will be forgiven and one's supererogatory works that are like in kind to the five duties that are the pillars of Islam (N: i.e. the Testification of Faith "La ilaha ill Allah Muhammadun rasul Allah," the prayer, zakat, fasting Ramadan, and hajj)—are counted for one. The reason for this is because the pillars of Islam and these enormities are antipodal counterparts, antithetical to each other in magnitude and significance, the enormities being so great that avoiding them expiates the other, lesser sins, and if the five duties that are the pillars of Islam are fully performed, they too expiate other wrongdoings, the servant is rewarded for his supererogatory works, and his bad deeds are changed for good ones. Such a person attains to great favor, and paradise is to be hoped for him and the stations of those who strive, for he is of the outstrippers in good deeds. Allah Most High says,

"If you avoid the enormities of what you have been forbidden, We shall acquit you of your wrongdoings" (Koran 4:31),

and says, after mentioning the enormities,

"... save he who repents, believes, and works righteousness: those Allah will change their bad deeds for good" (Koran 25:70).

And the Prophet (Allah bless him and give him peace) said,

"The five prayers entail forgiveness for what is between them as long as the enormities are avoided."

When the enormities are committed, they annul (N: supererogatory) good deeds just as the five duties of Islam annul the bad deeds that occur between them other than the enormities, which are too great for them to annul (N: but rather require a sincere repentance in order to be forgiven). So with a servant's committing enormities, nothing can remain for him on Judgement Day of

الأقوال وأعدلها وهو ما اتفقوا عليه وكثرت الأخبار فيه. فهذه الكبائر الموبقات التي من اجتنبها كفرت عنه السيئات وثبتت له النوافل من الفرائض الخمس التي هي أبنية الإسلام. وذلك أن دعائم الإسلام وهذه الكبائر قرينان يعتلجان ويتقاومان في العظم والمعنى بالتضاد، فالكبائر كبرت فكفّر اجتنابها ما دونها من الصغائر، والفرائض الخمس التي هي أبنية الإسلام إذا تممت كفرت ما بعدها من السيئات وثبت للعبد نوافله وتبدل سيئاته حسنات. فيكون له فضل عظيم يرجى له الجنة ومنازل العاملين وهو السابق بالخيرات. قال الله تعالى:

﴿إِنْ تَجْتَنِبُوا كَبَائِرَ مَا تُنْهَوْنَ عَنْهُ نُكَفِّرْ عَنْكُمْ سَيِّئَاتِكُمْ﴾ [النساء: ٣١].

وقال من بعد ذكر الكبائر:

﴿إِلَّا مَنْ تَابَ وَآمَنَ وَعَمِلَ عَمَلًا صَالِحًا فَأُولَئِكَ يُبَدِّلُ اللَّهُ سَيِّئَاتِهِمْ حَسَنَاتٍ﴾ [الفرقان: ٧٠].

وقال رسول الله ﷺ: «الصلوات الخمس كفارات لما بينهن ما اجتنبت الكبائر».

... فإذا انتهكت الكبائر أحبطت الأعمال. والفرائض أحبطت ما بينها من السيئات إلا الكبائر فإنها كبرت فلا تكفرها. فلا يبقى للعبد يوم القيامة مع ارتكاب الكبائر من الأعمال إلا الفرائض

his good works except the five duties of Islam, the enormities having devoured all his supererogatory works: hell is to be feared for such a person, and the stations of the profligates, and he has truly wronged himself, which Allah Most High warns believers against by saying,

"O you who believe, obey Allah and obey the Prophet, and do not nullify your works" (Koran 47:33),

and,

"Nay, but whoever earns a wicked deed and is encompassed by his error, those are the inhabitants of hell" (Koran 2:81),

referring, it is said, to enormities that encompass one's good deeds and efface them (*Qut al-qulub* (y81), 2.148–49).

*

w53.0 REPENTANCE DOES NOT ELIMINATE OTHERS' RIGHTS
(from p77.3)

w53.1 (Shu'ayb Arna'ut:) Bukhari and Ahmad relate that Jabir ibn 'Abdullah said, "I heard of a hadith that a certain man had heard from the Messenger of Allah (Allah bless him and give him peace), so I bought a camel, cinched my saddle on it, and travelled for a month to reach him, coming upon him in Damascus, the man being 'Abdullah ibn Unays. I told the doorman, 'Tell him Jabir is at the door,' and the reply came, 'Ibn 'Abdullah?' and when I said yes, he rushed out, stepping on the hem of his garment. He embraced me and I returned his embrace and said, 'Tell me the hadith I am informed you heard from the Messenger of Allah (Allah bless him and give him peace) about retaliation. I have been afraid that you or I would die before I heard it.' He said, 'I heard the Messenger of Allah (Allah bless him and give him peace) say:

الخمس وقد أكل سائر نوافله ارتكاب الكبائر فيخاف عليه النار ومنازل المسرفين وهذا هو الظالم لنفسه وهو الذي حذر الله تعالى المؤمنين عنه قال : ﴿ يَا أَيُّهَا الَّذِينَ آمَنُوا أَطِيعُوا اللَّهَ وَأَطِيعُوا الرَّسُولَ وَلَا تُبْطِلُوا أَعْمَالَكُمْ ﴾ [محمد : ٣٣] .

ـ ومنه قول تعالى : ﴿ بَلَى مَنْ كَسَبَ سَيِّئَةً وَأَحَاطَتْ بِهِ خَطِيئَتُـهُ [(ت : وتمام الآية :] فَأُولَئِكَ أَصْحَابُ النَّارِ ﴾) [البقرة : ٨١] .

قيـل هي الكبائر أحاطت بجميع حسناته فمحقتها [محرر من قوت القلوب في معـاملة المـحبـوب ووصف طريق المريد إلى مقام التوحيد : ٢/ ١٤٨ ـ ١٤٩] .

w53.0 التوبة لا تبطل حق الغير

w53.1 (شعيب الأرنؤوط :) [. . .] أخرجـ[ـه] البخاري [في «الأدب المفرد» (٩٧٠)] وأحمد [في «المسند» ٣/ ٤٩٥] وغيرهما من طريق عبد الله بن محمد ابن عقيل أنه سمع] جابر بن عبد الله يقول : بلغني عن رجـل حديث سمعه من رسول الله ﷺ ، فاشتـريت بعيـراً ، ثم شددت عليه رحلي ، فسـرت إليـه شهـراً حتى قدمت عليـه الشـام ، فإذا عبـد الله بن أنيس ، فقلت للبواب : قل له جابر على البـاب ، فقال : ابن عبد الله؟ قلت نعم ، فخـرج يطأ ثوبـه ، فاعتنقني واعتنقته ، فقلت : حديثاً بلغني عنك أنك سمعته من رسول الله ﷺ في القصـاص ، فخشيت أن تمـوت أو أموت قبل أن أسمعه ، قال :

" ' "People shall be mustered on the Day of Judgement naked, uncircumcized, and possessionless, and a call will be made to them in a voice that those who are far shall hear as well as those who are near, saying: 'I am the King, I am He who gives recompense: it is not meet for any inhabitant of hell to enter it while any of the inhabitants of paradise owes him something until I exact it of them. And it is not meet for any inhabitant of paradise to enter it while he owes any of the inhabitants of hell something until I exact it from him, even if it be the requital of a single slap of the face.' " We asked the Prophet (Allah bless him and give him peace), "How will this be, when we will meet Allah Mighty and Majestic naked, uncircumcized, and without a thing?" And he said, "With good and bad deeds." ' '

(*Sharh al-sunna* (y22), 1.280–81)

سمعت رسول الله ﷺ يقـول: «يحشـر الناس يوم القيامة [أو قال: العباد: العباد،] عراة غرلاً بهماً [،]، قال: قلنا: وما بهماً؟ قال: ليس معهم شيءٌ]، ثم ينـاديهم بصوت يسمعه مَن بعد [أحسبه قال:] كما يسمعه مَن قرب: أنـا الملك، أنـا الـديان، لا ينبغي لأحد من أهل النار أن يدخل النار، وله عند أحد من أهـل الجنة حق حتى أقصه منه، ولا ينبغي لأحد من أهل الجنة أن يدخل الجنة ولأحد من أهل النار عنده حق حتى أقصه منه حتى اللطمة، [قال:] قلنا: كيف، وإنما نأتي الله عز وجل عراة غرلاً بهماً؟ قال: «بالحسنات والسيئات» [وحسنه الحافظ وصححه الحاكم: ٢/ ٤٣٧ ـ ٤٣٨ ووافقه الـذهبي] [نقل من شرح السنة: ١/ ٢٨٠ ـ ٢٨١].

*

w54.0 LEAVING WHAT DOES NOT CONCERN ONE (from r1.2(3))

w54.1 The Prophet (Allah bless him and give him peace) said,

"The excellence of a person's Islam includes leaving what does not concern him."

The excellence of a person's Islam
(Muhammad Jurdani:) Meaning the fullness and perfection of a person's Islam and his submission to its rules
includes leaving what does not concern him
meaning that which is not connected with what is important to one, be it in word or deed. The matters that concern a person are those connected with necessities of life in gaining a livelihood and having a safe return in the afterlife. These do not amount to much in comparison with what does not concern one (*al-Jawahir al-lu'lu'iyya fi sharh al-Arba'in al-Nawawiyya* (y68), 99).

w54.0 ترك ما لا يعني

w54.1 قال النبي ﷺ:
«من حسن إسـلام المـرء تركـه ما لا يعنيه» [رواه الترمذي وغيره].
﴿محـمـد الجـردانـي:﴾ «من حسن إسـلام المـرء» (يعني من كمـال إسلام المرء وتمامه والاستسلام لأحكامه) «تركه ما لا يعنيه» (أي ما لا تتعلق عنايته به قولاً كان أو فعـلاً. والذي يعني الإنسـان من الأمور ما يتعلق بضرورة حياته في معاشه وسلامته في معاده وذلك يسير بالنسبة إلى ما لا يعنيه [محرر من الجـواهـر اللؤلؤية في شرح الأربعين النووية: ٩٩].

w55.0 THE ETERNALITY OF
PARADISE AND HELL (from s1.2)

w55.0 بقاء الجنة والنار

w55.1   (n:) The view that the punishment of unbelievers in hell is not eternal has been misrepresented by some Muslim writers and Koran translators as if it were a matter over which there is scholarly disagreement, or as if the proof of it from the Koran, hadith, and consensus of Muslims (ijma', def: b7) were capable of bearing more than one interpretation. The present section, by two of the foremost Sunni scholars in tenets of Islamic belief (usul), has been translated to clarify the question.

w55.2   ('Abd al-Qahir Baghdadi:) The scholars of Ahl al-Sunna and all the previous righteous of the Muslim Community are in unanimous agreement (ijma') that paradise and hell are eternal, and that the bliss of the inhabitants of paradise and the torment of unbelievers in hell will endure forever (*Usul al-din* (y23), 238).

w55.2   (عبد القاهر البغدادي:) أجمع أهل السنة وكل مَن سَلَف من أخيار الأمة على دوام بقاء الجنة والنار وعلى دوام نعيم أهل الجنة ودوام عذاب الكفرة في النار [نقل من أصول الدين: ٢٣٨].

w55.3   (Taqi al-Din Subki:) The faith of Muslims is that paradise and hell do not perish, Abu Muhammad Ibn Hazm having transmitted scholarly consensus (ijma') on this point and on the fact that whoever denies it is an unbeliever (kafir) by scholarly consensus. And there is no doubt of this, for it is necessarily known (def: f1.3(N)) as part of the religion of Islam, and proof after proof bears it out. Allah Most High says:

(1) "Nay, but whoever earns a wicked deed and is encompassed by his error, those are the inhabitants of hell, abiding therein forever" (Koran 2:81).

(2) "Verily those who disbelieve and die as unbelievers; the curse of Allah, the angels, and people, one and all, is upon them, abiding therein forever; the torment shall not be lightened from them, nor shall they be respited" (Koran 2:161–62).

(3) "Whoever of you leaves his religion and dies as an unbeliever, those are they whose works have failed in this world and the next, and those are the inhabitants of hell, abiding therein forever" (Koran 2:217).

w55.3   (تقي الدين السبكي:) [...] وبعد] فإن اعتقاد المسلمين أن الجنة والنار لا تفنيان وقد نقل أبو محمد بن حزم الإجماع على ذلك وأن من خالفه كافر بإجماع، ولا شك في ذلك فإنه معلوم من الدين بالضرورة وتواردت الأدلة عليه؛ قال الله تعالى:

﴿بَلَى مَنْ كَسَبَ سَيِّئَةً وَأَحَاطَتْ بِهِ خَطِيئَتُهُ فَأُولَئِكَ أَصْحَابُ النَّارِ هُمْ فِيهَا خَالِدُونَ﴾ [البقرة: ٨١].

وقال تعالى:

﴿إِنَّ الَّذِينَ كَفَرُوا وَمَاتُوا وَهُمْ كُفَّارٌ أُولَئِكَ عَلَيْهِمْ لَعْنَةُ اللَّهِ وَالْمَلائِكَةِ وَالنَّاسِ أَجْمَعِينَ خَالِدِينَ فِيهَا لا يُخَفَّفُ عَنْهُمُ الْعَذَابُ وَلا هُمْ يُنْظَرُونَ﴾ [البقرة: ١٦١-١٦٢].

وقال تعالى:

﴿وَمَنْ يَرْتَدِدْ مِنْكُمْ عَنْ دِينِهِ فَيَمُتْ وَهُوَ كَافِرٌ فَأُولَئِكَ حَبِطَتْ أَعْمَالُهُمْ فِي الدُّنْيَا وَالآخِرَةِ وَأُولَئِكَ أَصْحَابُ النَّارِ هُمْ فِيهَا خَالِدُونَ﴾ [البقرة: ٢١٧].

وقال تعالى:

(4) "Those who disbelieve, their friends are the evil ones, who lead them from the light to darknesses. Those are the dwellers of hell, abiding in it forever (Koran 2:257).

﴿وَالَّذِينَ كَفَرُوا أَوْلِيَاؤُهُمُ الطَّاغُوتُ يُخْرِجُونَهُمْ مِنَ النُّورِ إِلَى الظُّلُمَاتِ أُولَئِكَ أَصْحَابُ النَّارِ هُمْ فِيهَا خَالِدُونَ﴾ [البقرة: ٢٥٧].

(n: There follow some fifty-six Koranic verses of similar purport which have been left untranslated for the sake of brevity:

2:162	23:103	2:167	35:36
3:116	32:14	2:102	17:97
4:14	25:69	3:22	40:49–50
4:93	33:64–65	4:56	42:45
4:168–69	39:72	4:121	69:36
6:128	41:28	5:37	78:30
7:36	43:74–75	11:8	87:13
9:63	47:15	11:16	90:20
9:68	59:17	14:21	82:16.)
10:27	64:10	14:29	
11:106–7	72:23	23:108	
13:5	98:6	29:23	
16:29	2:86	45:35	
21:99	32:20	22:22	

.... The other verses that mean the same thing are very many, a fact that eliminates the possibility of explaining them away figuratively and necessitates complete conviction of them; just as the verses proving bodily resurrection, because of their great numbers, eliminate any possibility of explaining them away figuratively. We adjudge whoever explains these verses as if they were figurative to have committed unbelief because of the knowledge which the evidence *en masse* affords. And so it is too with the very numerous and intersubstantiative hadiths about this, such as the Prophet's saying (Allah bless him and give him peace):

(1) "Whoever kills himself with a knife will abide in the fire of hell, perpetually stabbing his belly with it, undying therein forever. And whoever hurls himself from a mountain and kills himself shall abide in the fire of hell, perpetually falling to his death, undying therein forever."

(2) "As for the inhabitants of hell who are its people, they shall be undying therein and unliving."

. . . وغيرها من الآيات كثير في هذا المعنى جداً وذلك يمنع من احتمال التأويل ويوجب القطع بذلك، كما أن الآيات الدالة على البعث الجسماني لكثرتها يمتنع تأويلها، ومن أوّلها حكمنا بكفره بمقتضى العلم جملة وكذلك الأحاديث المتظاهرة جداً على ذلك كقوله ﷺ:

«من قتل نفسه بحديدة فحديدته في يده يتوجأ بها في بطنه في نار جهنم خالداً مخلَّداً فيها أبداً ومن تردى من جبل فقتل نفسه فهو يتردى في نار جهنم خالداً مخلَّداً فيها أبداً» [متفق عليه من حديث أبي سعيد].

وقوله ﷺ: «أما أهل النار الذين هم أهلها فإنهم لا يموتون فيها ولا يحيون» [صحيح من حديث أبي سعيد].

(3) "When the people of paradise go to paradise and the people of hell go to hell, Death shall be brought forward, placed between paradise and hell, and slaughtered. And a crier shall be heard, 'O people of paradise, there is no death; O people of hell, there is no death!' "

And there is the like of the above evidence concerning paradise, as Allah Most High says:

(1) "Those who believe and do good works, they are the dwellers of paradise, abiding therein forever (Koran 2:82).

(2) "Whoever obeys Allah and His messenger, He will admit them to gardens beneath which rivers flow, abiding therein forever. That is the mighty triumph" (Koran 4:13).

(n: Thirty-eight verses of similar purport follow, which have been left untranslated, as before, for brevity:

2:82	11:23	23:11	56:17
3:15	10:26	25:15	57:12
10:62	11:108	25:76	58:22
3:198	13:35	29:58	50:34
4:13	14:23	4:122	64:9
4:57	15:48	39:73	65:11
5:85	18:3	41:8	95:6
5:119	18:107	43:71	98:8.)
9:89	20:76	41:30	
9:100	21:102	48:5	

.... So these are the verses we can recall about the eternality of paradise and hell. We have mentioned hell first because we've come across a work about hell perishing by one of the people of the present era. We have quoted about one hundred Koranic verses, approximately sixty concerning hell, and forty on paradise. *Immortality* (khuld) or words derived from it are found in thirty-four of those dealing with hell and thirty-eight of those about paradise. *Everlastingness* (ta'bid) has been mentioned in conjunction with immortality in four of those dealing with hell, and mentioned eight times about paradise, seven of them in connection with immortality. *Never leaving* and so forth has been plainly stated in over thirty verses. The consequence of the concatenate and intersubstantia-

وقولـه عليـه السـلام: «إذا صار أهل الجنة إلى الجنة وأهل النار إلى النار جيء بالمـوت حتى يجعـل بين الجنـة والنار فيـذبـح فينـادي مناد يا أهل الجنة لا موت ويـا أهل النـار لا موت» [وفي روايـة صحيـحـة: «فـخلود فلا موت»]. وفي الجنة مثل ذلك، وقال تعالى: ﴿وَالَّذِينَ آمَنُوا وَعَمِلُوا الصَّالِحَاتِ أُولَئِكَ أَصْحَابُ الجَنَّةِ هُمْ فِيهَا خَالِدُونَ﴾ [البقرة: ٨٢]. [...].
وقال تعالى: ﴿وَمَنْ يُطِعِ اللَّهَ وَرَسُولَهُ يُدْخِلْهُ جَنَّاتٍ تَجْرِي مِنْ تَحْتِهَا الأَنْهَارُ خَالِـدِينَ فِيهَـا وَذَلِكَ الفَوْزُ العَظِيمُ﴾ [النساء: ١٣].

... فهـذه الآيات التي استحضرناها في بقـاء الجنة والنار. وبـدأنا بالنار لأنَّا وقفنـا على تصنيف لبعض أهل العصر في فنائها. وقد ذكرنا نحو مائة آية، منها نحو ستين في النـار ونحـو أربعين في الجنة، وقـد ذكر الخلد أو ما اشتق منـه في أربع وثلاثين في النار وثمان وثلاثين في الجنة وذكـر التأبيـد في أربع في النار مع الخلود وفي ثمان في الجنة منها سبع مع الخلود، وذكر التصريح بعدم الخروج أو معناه في أكثـر من ثلاثين. وتضافـر هذه الآيات

997

tive character of these and similar verses is absolute certainty that what Allah Most High thereby intends is their literal meaning and significance. It is not something in which the outward sense might be used to imply other than the plain purport, which is why Muslims unanimously concur upon faith in it, descendants having taken it from ancestors in unbroken succession from their Prophet (Allah bless him and give him peace). It is integrally embedded in the innate faith (fitra) of the Muslims, necessarily known as part of the religion of Islam, and even held by all non-Muslim sects. Whoever denies it is an unbeliever (kafir), and whoever explains it away figuratively is the same as someone who figuratively explains away Koranic verses about the bodily resurrection, meaning that he too is an unbeliever, because knowing the verses necessitates belief.

I have come upon the above-mentioned work, whose author notes three positions about paradise and hell perishing: that both end, which he declares none of the early Muslims have said; that neither ends; and that paradise remains but hell ends; the latter of which he inclines toward and adopts, saying that it is the position of the early Muslims (salaf). Allah be our refuge from this! I exonerate the early Muslims from it and do not believe a single one of of them said it. There are only some words that have been ascribed to certain individuals of them that are to be taken as all problematic utterances are, meaning they are construed and interpreted in light of other than their ostensive sense, for just as there occur expressions requiring such exegesis in Koranic verses and hadiths, so too words occur in the discourse of scholars that must be fittingly explained. Whoever takes words of early Muslims that were spoken to motivate people to do good or be afraid of doing evil and so forth, and interprets them literally, recording them as if they were a ''school of thought'' has misled himself and others. Nor is this scholarship, for the way of scholars is to uncover the *meaning* of words and what is intended by them. When we are certain that what has been ascribed to a speaker is his actual position on a matter and his belief, we attribute it to him. But unless we are certain, we do not attribute it to him, this being especially true of basic tenets of Islamic belief like the above, about which Muslims unani-

ونظــائـرهـا يفيـد القطـع بإرادة حقيقتها ومعنـاها، وأن ذلك ليس مما استعمل فيه الظـاهـر في غيـر المـراد بـه ولذلك أجمع المسلمـون على اعتقاد ذلك وتلقوه خلفاً عن سلف عن نبيهم ﷺ . وهو مركوز في فطـرة المسلمـيـن معلوم من الـديـن بالضرورة بل وسائر الملل غير المسلمين يعتقـدون ذلك . ومن رد ذلك فهـو كافر ومن تأولـه فهو كمن يؤول الآيات الواردة في البعث الجسمـاني وهـو كافـر أيضاً بمقتضى العلم .

وقـد وقفت على التصنيف المـذكـور وذكر فيه ثلاثة أقوال في فناء الجنة والنار : أحدها أنهما تفنيان وقال إنه لم يقل به أحد من السلف .

والثاني أنهما لا تفنيان .

والثالـث أن الجنة تبقى والنـار تفنى . ومـال إلى هذا واختـاره وقـال إنـه قول السلف . ومعـاذ الله ، وأنا أبرىء السلف عن ذلك ولا أعتقد أن أحداً منهم قاله ، وإنمـا روي عن بعضهم كلمـات تأول كمـا تأول المشكـلات التي تردّ وتحمل على غيـر ظاهـرهـا . فكمـا أن الآيـات والأحـاديـث يقـع فيهـا ما يجب تأويله كذلـك كلام العلمـاء يقـع فيـه ما يجب تأويله . ومن جاء إلى كلمـات تردّ عن السلف في ترغيب أو ترهيب أو غيـر ذلك فأخذ بظاهرها وأثبتها أقوالاً ضل وأضل . وليس ذلـك من دأب الـعـلمـاء ودأب العلماء التنقير عن معنى الكلام والمراد به ومـا انتهى إلينا عن قائله فإذا تحققنـا أن ذلك مذهب واعتقاده نسبناه إليه وأما بدون ذلـك فلا . ولا سيمـا في مثل هذه العقائد التي المسلمـون مطبقـون فيهـا على شيء

mously agree on one position. How can one proceed to the opposite of what they believe and then
attribute it to the greatest of Muslims and exemp-
lars of the believers, considering it a topic of
scholarly disagreement as if it were a question
about ablution (wudu)? How remote whoever
does this is from knowledge and guidance! This is
a reprehensible innovation (bid'a) of the most
ominous and ugliest sort, and Allah has knowingly
led whoever says it astray....

(n: Several pages follow, examining various objections to the eternality of
hell raised by the above-mentioned author, some of them citing statements
ascribed to early Muslims, which, as Subki points out, apply to disobedient Muslims who will one day leave the hellfire, not to unbelievers, polytheists, or the
likes of Pharaoh and Satan. Only a few of these objections could be translated
below because of their length.)

(Objection:) There is a hadith in the *Musnad*
of Ahmad that herbiage will one day grow on the
floor of hell.

(Reply:) It is not in the *Musnad* of Ahmad,
but in others, and is a weak hadith. If it were
rigorously authenticated (sahih), it would be
interpreted as referring to the level where disobedient Muslims ('usat) are.

(Objection:) Harb Kirmani said, "I asked
Ishaq about the word of Allah Most High,

" '... except as your Lord wills' (Koran
11:107),

"and he replied, 'This verse applies to every threat
of punishment in the Koran.' " And it is related
from Abu Nadra that one of the Companions of
the Prophet (Allah bless him and give him peace)
said, "This verse applies to the entire Koran
wherever the words 'Abiding therein forever' are
mentioned."

(Reply:) If authenticated, these statements
are interpreted as applying to disobedient Muslims, for the departure of Muslim sinners from hell
is not explicitly stated in the Koran, but only in the
sunna, and is through intercession (dis: v2.8). So
the meaning of these statements is to show the
agreement between the Koran and sunna on this,
for the early Muslims had great fear, and did not
find in the Koran that true monotheists would
leave hell, and were afraid of unending punishment.

(Objection:) Allah has informed us that His

كيف يعمد إلى خلاف ما هم عليه ينسبه
إلى جُلّة المسلمين وقدوة المؤمنين
ويجعلها مسألة خلاف كمسألة في باب
الوضوء؟ ما أبعد من صنع هذا عن العلم
والهدى . وهذه بدعة من أنحس البدع
وأقبحها أضل الله من قالها على علم .
. [...]

[...] فإن قلتَ : [...] في مسند
أحمد حديث ذكر فيه أنه ينبت فيها
الجرجير .
قلتُ : ليس في مسند أحمد ولكنه في
غيره وهو ضعيف ولو صح حمل على
طبقة العصاة .
فإن قلتَ : قال حرب الكرماني :
سألت إسحق عن قول الله تعالى :
﴿إلَّا مَا شَاءَ رَبُّكَ﴾ .
فقال : أتت هذه الآية على كل وعيد
في القرآن . وعن أبي نضرة عن بعض
أصحاب النبي ﷺ قال : هذه الآية تأتي
على القرآن كله حيث كان في القرآن
﴿خَالِدِينَ فِيهَا﴾ تأتي عليه .
قلتُ : إن صحت هذه الآثار حملت
على العصاة لأن القرآن لم يرد فيه خروج
العصاة من النار صريحاً ، إنما ورد في
السنة بالشفاعة فالمراد بهذه الآثار موافقة
القرآن للسنة في ذلك . فإن السلف كانوا
شديدي الخوف ولم يجدوا في القرآن
خروج الموحدين من النار وكانوا يخافون
الخلود [...] .
[...] فإن قلتَ : [...] إنه أخبر أن

mercy encompasses everything (Koran 7:156), and has said, "My mercy has outstripped My wrath" (*Sahih al-Bukhari* (y30), 9.411), while if one hypothesizes an unending torment, there is no mercy at all.

(Reply:) The hereafter is of two abodes, an abode of mercy unmixed with anything else, which is paradise; and an abode of torment unmixed with anything else, which is hell; this being a proof of Allah's omnipotence, while the present life is compounded of both. So if by saying, "If one hypothesizes an unending torment, there is no mercy at all," one means to absolutely deny that there is any mercy, it is not true, for there is the very perfection of mercy in paradise; while if one means there is no mercy in hell, we reply that even if one holds that mercy and torment are *things*, Allah Most High says (n: in the remainder of the verse "My mercy encompasses everything"),

"I shall inscribe it for those who are godfearing" (Koran 7:156).

(Objection:) It is established that Allah is all-wise and all-compassionate, and that wicked souls (who, if they were returned to this world, would go back to their wrongdoing) are unfit to dwell in the abode of peace. Now, if given a torment that would purge their souls of this evil, it would be tenable with respect to the divine wisdom, but as for creating souls who do evil in this world and for whom there is nothing but torment in the next, this is a contradiction than which few things are more inconsistent with wisdom and mercy. This is why Jahm denied that Allah is the Most Merciful of the Merciful, but rather said that He does whatever He wills, and those who follow Jahm's path, like Ash'ari and others, do not hold that He actually has wisdom or mercy. But since it is established that He is all-wise and all-compassionate, and the falsity of Jahm's position is realized, this necessitates that we affirm what wisdom and mercy entail—so the position of the Mu'tazilites concerning His wisdom and mercy, as well as that of the Qadarites, determinists, and deniers of the divine attributes, are equally false, and the most glaring of their errors is considering hell eternal. That is what their positions imply, while Allah has

رحمته وسعت كل شيء، وسبقت رحمتي غضبي، فإذا قُدِّر عذاب لا آخر له لم يكن هناك رحمة البتة.

قلتُ: الآخرة داران: دار رحمة لا يشوبها شيء وهي الجنة، ودار عذاب لا يشوبه شيء وهي النار، وذلك دليل على القدرة. والدنيا مختلطة بهذا وبهذا. فقوله: إذا قدر عذاب لا آخر له لم يكن هناك رحمة البتة، إن أراد نفي الرحمة مطلقاً فليس بصحيح لأن هناك كمال الرحمة في الجنة وإن أراد لم يكن في النار، قلنا له: وإن قال إنها شيء والعقاب شيء وقد قال تعالى:

﴿فَسَأَكْتُبُهَا لِلَّذِينَ يَتَّقُونَ﴾ [الأعراف: ١٥٦].

فإن قلتَ: قد ثبت أنه حكيم رحيم والنفوس الشريرة التي لو وردت إلى الدنيا لعادت لا تصلح أن تسكن دار السلام، فإذا عذبوا عذاباً تخلص نفوسهم من ذلك الشر كان هذا معقولاً في الحكمة. أما خلق نفوس تعمل الشر في الدنيا، وفي الآخرة لا تكون إلا في العذاب فهذا تناقض يظهر فيه من مناقضة الحكمة والرحمة ما لا يظهر في غيره. ولهذا كان جهم ينكر أن يكون الله تعالى أرحم الراحمين بل يفعل ما يشاء. والذين سلكوا طريقته كالأشعري وغيره ليس عندهم في الحقيقة له حكمة ولا رحمة. وإذا ثبت أنه حكيم رحيم وعلم بطلان قول جهم تعين إثبات ما تقتضيه الحكمة والرحمة. وما قاله المعتزلة أيضاً باطل، فقول القدرية والمجبرة والنفاة في حكمته ورحمته باطل ومن أعظم غلطهم اعتقادهم تأبيد جهنم. فإن ذلك مستلزم ما قالوا، وقد أخبر تعالى أن أهل الجنة

informed us that the inhabitants of paradise and hell will not die, so they must have some abode, and it is impossible that they should be tormented after entering paradise, so no alternative remains except the abode of happiness. A living being is never without either pleasure or pain, and if pain is excluded, this necessarily implies eternal pleasure.

(Reply:) Having openly said what he has said at the end of the above, this person implies that Satan, Pharaoh, Haman, and all unbelievers will end up in eternal bliss and perpetual enjoyment, something that no Muslim, Christian, Jew, polytheist, or even philosopher has ever said. Muslims believe that paradise and hell last forever, while a polytheist holds that there will be no resurrection, and a philosopher believes that wicked souls will be in a state of pain. So we do not know of anyone who has made the statement this man has, which entails leaving Islam, because of the knowledge afforded by the sheer amount of the evidence against it. Glory be to Allah Most High, who says,

"Those who disbelieve in the signs of Allah and in meeting Him, it is they who shall despair of My mercy" (Koran 29:23),

and says,

"Whenever it abates, We shall increase for them the blaze" (Koran 17:97).

Allah's prophet (Allah bless him and give him peace) has informed us that Death shall be slaughtered between paradise and hell, which without doubt could only be done to show the people of hell's despair and their certainty of living forever in torment. Were they to move on to pleasure and enjoyment, it would be a great hope for them, better than death, and they would be without despair. How can anyone who believes in these verses and hadiths say such a thing? What he said about wisdom is ignorance, and what he said about Ash'ari (Allah be well pleased with him) is a deliberate lie against him that we seek refuge in Allah Most High from.

(Objection:) One could hold that souls are

والنــار لا يمــوتــون فلا بد لهم من دار ، ومحــال أن يعذبوا بعد دخول الجنة ، فلم يبق إلا دار النــعيم . والحي لا يخلو من لذة أو ألم فإذا انتفى الألم تعينت اللذة الدائمة .

قلتُ : قد صرح بمــا صرح به في آخر كلامه فيقتضي أن إبليس وفرعون وهامان وسـائر الكفار يصيرون إلى النعيم المقيم واللذة الدائمة . وهذا ما قال به مسلم ولا نصراني ولا يهــودي ولا مشــرك ولا فيلسـوف . أما المسلمون فيعتقدون دوام الجنة والنار ، وأمـا المشرك فيعتقد عدم البــعث ، وأمـا الفيلسـوف فيعتقـد أن النفوس الشريرة في ألم . فهـذا القول الـذي قاله هذا الرجل ما نعرف أحداً قاله وهـو خروج عن الإسـلام بمقتضى العلم إجمالاً وسبحان الله إذا كان الله تعالى يقول :

﴿أُولَٰئِكَ الَّذِينَ يَئِسُوا مِنْ رَحْمَتِي﴾ [العنكبوت : ٢٣] .

وكذلك قوله تعالى :
﴿كُلَّمَا خَبَتْ زِدْنَاهُمْ سَعِيرًا﴾ [الإسراء : ٩٧] .

ونبيه ﷺ يخبر بذبح الموت بين الجنة والنـار ولا شك أن ذلك إنما يُفعل إشارة إلى إيـاسهم وتحققهم البقـاء الـدائم في العـذاب . فلو كانـوا ينتقلون إلى اللذة والنعيم لكان ذلك رجاءً عظيماً لهم وخيراً من المـوت ولم يحصل لهم إياس . فمن يصـدق بهـذه الآيـات والأحـاديث كيف يقـول هذا الكـلام ؟ ومـا قاله من مخالفة الحكمة جهل ومـا ينسب إلى الأشعري رضي الله عنه افتراء عليه نعوذ بالله تعالى منه .

فإن قلتَ : قد يقـول إنـه تخـلص

cleansed of wickedness by this torment and then become Muslims.

(Reply:) Allah be our refuge! Their becoming Muslims in the hereafter will be of no benefit to them, by unanimous consensus of Muslims, and by the word of Allah Most High,

"Its faith will not benefit any soul that did not believe before" (Koran 6:158).

(Objection:) What wisdom is there in creating such people?

(Reply:) The wisdom lies in making manifest the divine omnipotence so that believers may contemplate it and reflect upon the immensity of the majesty of Allah Most High, who has the power on the one hand to create the angels, the righteous, the prophets, and the Liegelord of Creation Muhammad (Allah bless him and give him peace); and the power on the other hand to create Pharaoh, Haman, Abu Jahl, the fiends of jinn and mankind, and Satan, the Chief of Misguidance; and who has the power to create the two final abodes, each pure and unadmixed: one for everlasting happiness, the other for agonizing torment, and yet a third abode, this world, compounded of both. Glory to Him whose omnipotence is such, and whose magnificence is so exalted! Allah Most Glorious is well able to create all people as obedient believers, but He Most Glorious has willed to manifest the thing and its opposite, those who know to know it, and those who are ignorant to be ignorant of it, knowledge being the origin of all felicity and that from which true faith and obedience grow, and ignorance being the origin of all damnation and that from which all unbelief and disobedience grow. I have not seen anything ruinous to the affairs of this world or the next save that it was the result of ignorance, which is truly the most baneful of all things. ...Whoever says that heaven or hell perish is an unbeliever (*al-Rasa'il al-Subkiyya* (y52), 196–208).

نفوسهم من الشرِّ بذلك العذاب فيسلمون.

قلتُ: معـاذ الله. أمـا إسـلامهم في الآخـرة فلا ينفعهم بإجمـاع المسلمين، وبقوله تعالى:

﴿لَا يَنْفَعُ نَفْسًا إِيمَانُهَا لَمْ تَكُنْ آمَنَتْ مِنْ قَبْلُ﴾ [الأنعام: ١٥٨]. [...].

فإن قلتَ: ما في خلق هؤلاء من الحكمة؟

قلت: إظهار القدرة واعتبار المؤمنين وفكرتهم في عظمة الله تعالى القادر على أن يخلق المـلائكة والبشر الصـالحين والأنبياء ومحمـداً ﷺ سيد الخلق وعلى أن يخـلق من الطـرف الآخـر فرعـون وهامان وأبا جهل وشياطين الجن والإنس وإبليس رأس الضـلال والقادر على خلق الدارين متمحضة كل واحدة منهما: هذه للنعيم المقيم وهـذه للعـذاب الأليم ودار ثالثة وهي الـدنيا ممتـزجة من النوعين. فسبحـان مَن هذه قدرتُه وجلَّت عظمتُه. وكان الله سبحانه قادراً أن يخلق الناس كلهم مؤمنين طائعين ولكن أراد سبحـانه أن يبين الشيء وضـده علمـه من علمه وجهله من جهله. والعلم منشأ السعـادة كلهـا نشأ عنـه الإيمان والطاعة، والجهل منشـأ الشقـاوة كلهـا نشأ عنـه الكفـر والمعصية. ومـا رأيت مفسـدة من أمـور الـدنيا والآخـرة تنشأ إلا عن الجهـل فهو أضر الأشياء. [...] من قال بفناء الجنة والنـار أو أحـدهما فهـو كافـر [محرر من الـرسائل السبكية في الرد على ابن تيمية وتلميذه ابن قيم الجوزية: ١٩٦ - ٢٠٨].

*

w56.0 THE EXCELLENCE OF THE PROPHETIC COMPANIONS (SAHABA) (from v2.9)

w56.1 (Nawawi: (n: with commentary by Jalal al-Din Suyuti)) The prophetic *Companions* (N: meaning anyone who personally met the Prophet (Allah bless him and give him peace) and died believing in Islam) are all legally upright ('adal, def: o24.4), both those of them who took part in conflicts (dis: w56.3) and those who did not, by unanimous consensus of all scholars whose opinion matters. ((Suyuti:)) Allah Most High says,

"Thus have We made you a justly balanced nation" (Koran 2:143),

meaning upright, and He says,

"You are the best nation ever brought forth for people" (Koran 3:110),

the address being to those who were alive at that time. And the Prophet (Allah bless him and give him peace) said,

"The best of people are those of my time."

(*Tadrib al-rawi fi sharh Taqrib al-Nawawi* (y109), 2.214))

w56.2 (Wasiyyullah 'Abbas:) Among the evidence of the legal uprightness ('adala) of the Companions is the word of Allah Most High:

(1) "Muhammad is the Messenger of Allah, and those with him are hard against the unbelievers, compassionate towards one another. You see them bowing and prostrating, seeking bounty from Allah and His good pleasure. Their mark is upon their faces from the effect of prostration—that is their likeness in the Torah; and their likeness in the Evangel is as a grain that sends forth its shoot, strengthens it, and it thickens and rises straight upon its stalk, pleasing the sowers, that through them He may enrage the unbelievers. Allah promises those who believe and do good

---

w56.0 فضيلة الصحابة

w56.1 (النووي (ت: بشرح جلال الدين السيوطي) :) [. . .] الصحابة كلهم عدول، من لابس الفتن وغيـرُهُم بإجماع من يعتد به : (قال تعالى :

﴿وَكَـذَلِـكَ جَعَلْنَـاكُمْ أُمَّـةً وَسَطاً﴾ [البقرة : ١٤٣] الآية .

أي عدولاً، وقال تعالى :

﴿كُنْتُمْ خَيْرَ أُمَّةٍ أُخْرِجَتْ لِلنَّاسِ ﴾ [آل عمران : ١١٠] .

والخطاب فيهـا للموجودين حينئذ . وقـال ﷺ : «خيـر النـاس قرني» [رواه الشيخان] . . .) [نقل من تدريب الراوي في شرح تقريب النواوي : ٢/ ٢١٤] .

w56.2 (وصي الله عباس :) [(ت :] من) أدلة عدالة الصحابة من كتاب الله عز وجل : قال تعالى :

ـ ﴿مُحَمَّدٌ رَسُولُ اللَّهِ، وَالَّذِينَ مَعَهُ أَشِـدَّاءُ عَلَى الكُفَّارِ رُحَمَـاءُ بِينَهُمْ تَرَاهُمْ رُكَّعَـاً سُجَّـدَاً يَبْتَغُـونَ فَضْـلاً مِنَ اللَّهِ وَرِضْـوَاناً، سِيمَاهُمْ فِي وُجُوهِهِمْ مِنْ أَثَرِ السُّجُودِ ذلِكَ مَثَلُهُمْ فِي التَّوْرَاةِ وَمَثَلُهُمْ فِي الإنجِيلِ كَزَرْعٍ أَخْرَجَ شَطْأَهُ فَآزَرَهُ فَاسْتَغْلَظَ فَاسْتَوَى عَلَى سُوقِـهِ يُعْجِبُ الـزُرَّاعَ لِيَغِيظَ بِهِمُ الكُفَّارَ وَعَدَ اللَّهُ الَّذِينَ

1003

works of them forgiveness and an immense reward" (Koran 48:29).

آمَنُوا وَعَمِلُوا الصَّالِحَاتِ مِنْهُمْ مَغْفِرَةً وَأَجْرًا عَظِيمًا﴾ [الفتح: ٢٩].

وقال تعالى:

(2) "... And the outstrippers, the first of the Emigrants and the Helpers, and those who followed them in excellence: Allah is pleased with them, and they are pleased with Him, and He has prepared for them gardens under which rivers flow, abiding therein forever. That is the mighty triumph" (Koran 9:100).

﴿وَالسَّابِقُونَ الأَوَّلُونَ مِنَ المُهَاجِرِينَ وَالأَنْصَارِ وَالَّذِينَ اتَّبَعُوهُمْ بِإِحْسَانٍ رَضِيَ اللَّهُ عَنْهُمْ وَرَضُوا عَنْهُ، وَأَعَدَّ لَهُمْ جَنَّاتٍ تَجْرِي تَحْتَهَا الأَنْهَارُ، خَالِدِينَ فِيهَا أَبَدًا ذَلِكَ الفَوْزُ العَظِيمُ﴾ [التوبة: ١٠٠].

وقال تعالى:

(3) "... it is for the poor Emigrants, who were forced out of their homes and possessions, seeking bounty from Allah and His pleasure, aiding Allah and His messenger: those are the ones who are true" (Koran 59:8).

ـ ﴿لِلْفُقَرَاءِ المُهَاجِرِينَ الَّذِينَ أُخْرِجُوا مِنْ دِيَارِهِمْ وَأَمْوَالِهِمْ يَبْتَغُونَ فَضْلًا مِنَ اللَّهِ وَرِضْوَانًا وَيَنْصُرُونَ اللَّهَ وَرَسُولَهُ، أُولَئِكَ هُمُ الصَّادِقُونَ﴾ [الحشر: ٨].

وقال تعالى:

(4) "Allah was pleased with the believers when they swore fealty to you under the tree, and He knew what was in their hearts, sent down tranquility upon them, and rewarded them with a nigh victory" (Koran 48:18).

ـ ﴿لَقَدْ رَضِيَ اللَّهُ عَنِ المُؤْمِنِينَ إِذْ يُبَايِعُونَكَ تَحْتَ الشَّجَرَةِ فَعَلِمَ مَا فِي قُلُوبِهِمْ فَأَنْزَلَ السَّكِينَةَ عَلَيْهِمْ، وَأَثَابَهُمْ فَتْحًا قَرِيبًا﴾ [الفتح: ١٨] [...].

And as for evidence from the prophetic sunna, the Prophet (Allah bless him and give him peace) said,

ومن السنة النبوية: قال النبي ﷺ:

"Do not revile my Companions, for by Him in whose hand is my soul, were one of you to spend gold equal to Mount Uhud, you would not attain the reward of the handsful of one of them or even half of it [N: because what they spent benefited Islam more]."

«لا تَسُبُّوا أصحابي، فوالذي نفسي بيده لو أن أحدكم أنفق مثل أُحُدٍ ذهبًا ما أدرك مُدَّ أحدهم ولا نصيفه» [إسناده صحيح].

(n: While there is no disagreement among scholars that merely being a Companion is itself an excellence and rank that cannot be reached by anyone who came after them, one may appreciate yet another facet of their position with Allah by considering the hadith,

"When a human being dies, his work comes to an end except for three things: ongoing charity, knowledge benefited from, or a pious son who prays for him,"

«إذا مات ابن آدم انقطع عمله إلا من ثلاث: صدقة جارية أو علم ينتفع به أو ولد صالح يدعو له» [رواه مسلم].

which scholars say shows that whenever a member of the Muslim Community benefits from religious knowledge transmitted by a Companion from the Prophet (Allah bless him and give him peace), the reward for it is counted among the Companion's works. To realize the station of 'Umar, for example (Allah be well pleased with him), one has only to reflect on the number of Muslims throughout the centuries who have benefited from the hadith,

| "Works are only according to intentions…" | «إنَّما الأعمال بالنيّات» [من حديث عمر رواه الشيخان]. |

which enters into the validity of virtually every act of worship in a Muslim's life (dis: t1.1), and which no one besides 'Umar (Allah be well pleased with him) related from the Prophet (Allah bless him and give him peace). Or consider the hadith,

| "He who inaugurates a good sunna [custom] in Islam earns the reward of it and of all who perform it after him without diminishing their own rewards in the slightest…" | «من سنَّ في الإسلام سنَّة حسنة فله أجرها وأجر من عمل بها من بعده من غير أن ينقص من أجورهم شيئاً» [من حديث رواه مسلم]. |

and reflect that 'Uthman (Allah be well pleased with him) ordered the Koran to be gathered into the single volume that innumerable Muslims have recited and studied from that century to this, 'Uthman's share therein being renewed, according to the above hadith, each time a Koran is opened. Nor is it difficult to imagine a similar rank for those whose efforts and jihad led to whole nations and their posterity becoming Muslims down to the present age, from which examples and similar ones we may understand the superiority of both our Prophet (Allah bless him and give him peace), who is the exemplar of all who worship Allah on the face of the earth until the end of time, and of the early Muslims in general over all those who came after them.)

There is scholarly consensus of the Sunni Community that all the Companions are legally upright. Khatib (N: Baghdadi) says: "There are many hadiths of this purport, every one of them in conformity with the explicit text of the Koran, all of which attests to the purity of the Companions and necessitates the conviction of their uprightness and faultless character. None of them requires the exoneration of other human beings alongside the declaration of their unimpeachability by Allah Most High, who is well aware of their inmost state. Thus are they characterized until one of them should prove to have deliberately committed an act unexplainable as anything besides intentional disobedience, uninterpretable by extenuating circumstances, that they should be considered to have lost their legal uprightness; but this Allah has declared them innocent of, and has raised their station in His sight. Had none of what we have mentioned reached us from Allah Mighty and Majestic or His messenger (Allah bless him and give him peace) concerning them, the mere way they were—their emigration, jihad, backing of Islam, spending of lifeblood and possessions, slaying of fathers and sons, sincere advice in religion, and strength of faith and certitude—would

وأجمع أهل السنة والجماعة على عدالتهم . قال الخطيب (ح : البغدادي) : «والأخبار في هذا المعنى تتسع ، وكلها مطابقة لما ورد في نص القرآن ، وجميع ذلك يقتضي طهارة الصحابة والقطع على تعديلهم ونزاهتهم ، فلا يحتاج أحد منهم مع تعديل الله تعالى لهم المطلع على بواطنهم إلى تعديل أحد من الخلق له . فهم على هذه الصفة إلى أن يثبت على أحد ارتكاب ما لا يحتمل إلا قصد المعصية والخروج من باب التأويل فيحكم بسقوط العدالة ، وقد برأهم الله من ذلك ورفع أقدارهم عنده . على أنه لو لم يرد من الله عز وجل ورسوله فيهم شيء مما ذكرنا لأوجبت الحال التي كانوا عليها من الهجرة والجهاد والنصرة وبذل المهج والأموال وقتل الآباء والأولاد والمناصحة في الدين وقوة الإيمان واليقين القطع على عدالتهم والاعتقاد

necessitate the conviction of their uprightness, the certainty of their blamelessness, and their superiority over any appraisers or vindicators coming after them until the end of time."

As for the beliefs of the Mu'tazilites, and those of the *Shiites* who reject the legitimacy of the first three caliphs (n: these being termed *Rawafid* (lit. "Rejectors")), including the Twelver Shiites, as opposed to the *Ghulat* ("Extremists") on the one hand, who may believe that 'Ali is God, or that Gabriel (upon whom be peace) made a mistake in delivering the Koran to Muhammad (Allah bless him and give him peace) instead of 'Ali, and because of such convictions are unquestionably unbelievers; and as opposed to, on the other hand, the *Mufaddila* ("Preferers"), such as the Zaydis, who believe that 'Ali had a better claim to the imamate than the first three caliphs, though the latters' caliphates were nevertheless legally valid—which distinctions are courtesy of Sheikh Yusuf Rifa'i—it is sufficient to mention the position of Ibn Kathir, who says: "All of the Companions are legally upright according to the People of the Sunna and Community (Ahl al-Sunna wa al-Jama'a). The view of the Mu'tazilites that all of the Companions are upright except those who fought against 'Ali (dis: w56.3) is untrue, base, and unacceptable. As for the various sects of Shiites (Rawafid), their ignorance, lack of intelligence, and their contention that the Companions all committed unbelief except for seventeen of them, whom they name, it is gibberish without any corroboration except the corrupt opinion of benighted minds and caprice blindly pursued, and which does not even deserve a rebuttal, so patent is the evidence to the contrary" (*Kitab fada'il al-Sahaba* (y3), 1.13–16).

w56.3 (Ghazali:) The true imam after the Messenger of Allah (Allah bless him and give him peace) was Abu Bakr, then 'Umar, then 'Uthman, and then 'Ali (Allah be well pleased with them). The Prophet (Allah bless him and give him peace) never explicitly appointed an imam at all, since if one had been designated, he would have been likelier to have been known than the individuals appointed to oversee various lesser commissions of authority, or those assigned to

لنـزاهتهم وأنهم أفضـل من المعـدلين والمزكين الذين يجيئون من بعدهم أبد الآبدين . اهـ.

وأمـا عقيـدة المعتـزلـة والـروافض فنكـتـفي فيهـا بذكـر قول ابن كثيـر : «والصحـابـة كلهم عدول عند أهل السنة والجمـاعـة، وقـول المعتـزلة : الصحابة عدول إلا من قاتل علياً قول باطل مرذول ومـردود . وأما طوائف الروافض وجهلهم وقلة عقلهم ودعاويهم أن الصحابة كفروا إلا سبعة عشـر صحابياً وسموهم فهو من الهـذيـان بلا دليل إلا مجرد الرأي الفاسد عن ذهن بارد وهـوى متبـع، وهو أقل من أن يرد والبرهان على خلافه أظهر» [محرر من كتاب فضائل الصحابة : ١/ ١١٣ - ١١٦].

w56.3 (الغـزالي :) [السـابـع أن] الإمـام الحق بعـد رسـول الله ﷺ أبو بكر ثم عمر ثم عثمان ثم علي رضي الله عنهم ولم يكن نص رسـول الله ﷺ على إمـام أصلًا إذ لو كان لكـان أولى بالظهـور من نصبه آحاد الولاة والأمراء على الجنود في

lead the armies in various countries, and the identity of these was not hidden from anyone, so how should the identity of an imam have been? And if it had been known, how should it have been lost so as not to have been conveyed to us? Abu Bakr was thus not installed as imam save through being chosen and sworn fealty to, and as for the hypothesis that the Prophet (Allah bless him and give him peace) explicitly appointed someone else, it amounts to an accusation against all the Companions of contravening the Messenger of Allah (Allah bless him and give him peace), which is a violation of scholarly consensus (ijma'), and something that no one has had the effrontery to invent except the Shiites (Rawafid). The People of the Sunna and Community (Ahl al-Sunna wa al-Jama'a) believe in the blamelessness of all the Companions, and praise them as Allah Most Glorious and Exalted has praised them, and as has His messenger (Allah bless him and give him peace). The events that occurred between Mu'awiya and 'Ali (Allah be well pleased with both of them) proceeded from the personal reasoning (ijtihad) of each, not from any avidness of Mu'awiya for the imamate. 'Ali (Allah be well pleased with him) believed that delivering up those responsible for the death of 'Uthman, because of the numerousness of their clans and their dispersal throughout the army, would lead to an upheaval in the matter of the supreme leadership at its very inception, and he felt that to postpone dealing with them would be fitter; while Mu'awiya believed that in view of the enormity of their crime, to delay their apprehension would incite people against the leadership and cause needless loss of life. Some of the most outstanding scholars of Sacred Law have held that both sides in a disagreement between those qualified to do independent legal reasoning (ijtihad) are correct, while others hold that only one side is; but no one of any scholarly competence has ever suggested that 'Ali was in error (Ihya' 'ulum al-din (y39), 1.102).

البـلاد ولم يخف ذلك فكيف خفي هذا؟ وإن ظهـر فكيف انـدرس حتى لم ينقل إلينـا؟ فلم يكن أبو بكر إماماً إلا بالاختيار والبيعة وأمـا تقـدير النص على غيره فهو نسبة الصحابة كلهم إلى مخالفة رسول الله ﷺ وخرق الإجماع، وذلك مما لا يستجرىء على اختراعه إلا الروافض. واعتقـاد أهـل السنـة [(ت :] والجماعة) تزكيـة جميـع الصحابة والثناء عليهم كما أثنى الله سبحانه وتعالى ورسوله ﷺ. وما جرى بين معـاوية وعلي رضي الله عنهما كان مبنيـاً على الاجتهـاد لا منـازعـة من معـاوية في الإمامة إذ ظن علي رضي الله عنـه أن تسليم قتلة عثمـان مع كثـرة عشـائرهم واختلاطهم بالعسكر يؤدي إلى اضطراب أمـر الإمـامـة في بدايتها فرأى التأخـير أصـوب، وظن معـاوية أن تأخير أمـرهم مع عظم جنـايتهم يوجب الإغراء بالأئمة ويعرّض الدماء للسفك. وقد قال أفـاضـل العلماء كل مجتهد مصيب وقال قائلون المصيب واحـد. ولم يذهب إلى تخطئة علي ذو تحصيل أصـلاً [نقل من إحياء علوم الدين : ١/ ١٠٢].

*

w57.0 THE ASH'ARI SCHOOL
(from w6.3)

حقيقة الأشاعرة w57.0

w57.1 (n:) In fundamentals of Islamic faith (usul), virtually all of the scholars quoted in the present volume are Ash'aris, whose school of thought has been presented for readers to examine themselves in sections u3, v1, v2, and w8. The school's position on figurative interpretation (ta'wil) of primary texts has also been discussed at a4.2 and w6.3, the latter of which explains that like all orthodox Muslims, the Ash'aris interpret matters of the afterlife—heaven, hell, and so on—as literal realities, while interpreting certain expressions referring to attributes of Allah Most High—His 'hand', 'eyes', and the like—as figurative, meaning as allusions to His power, omniscience, and so forth. Though many, like Imam Ash'ari himself and Imam Nawawi, consign the knowledge of the real meaning of such expressions to Allah (tafwid), others of the school, originally in reply to anthropomorphists of their time, have found figurative interpretations both more useful to Islam, and ultimately, more convincing. To support their position, they adduce that since words such as *hand* must be either figurative (majazi) or literal (haqiqi), and since the literal meaning of *hand* is a bodily limb, an attribute that is unbelief (kufr) to ascribe to Allah Most High, the only other possibility is that it is figurative. The Koran contains many examples of figures of speech, such as,

"Whoever was blind in this life shall be blind in the hereafter, and even further astray" (Koran 17:72),

«وَمَنْ كَانَ فِي هَذِهِ أَعْمَى فَهُوَ فِي الآخِرَةِ أَعْمَى وَأَضَلُّ سَبِيلاً» [الإسراء: ٧٢].

which does not refer to the physically blind in this life, but rather to those *blind*, figuratively speaking, to the signs of Allah and heedless of His warnings. Or the verse,

"Today We forget you, as you have forgotten this day of yours" (Koran 45:34),

﴿الْيَوْمَ نَنسَاكُمْ كَمَا نَسِيتُمْ لِقَاءَ يَوْمِكُمْ هَذَا...﴾ [الجاثية: ٣٤].

in which Allah's *forgetting* cannot be literally interpreted as a divine attribute, for Allah forgets nothing, but must rather be understood in its intended figurative sense as meaning that Allah will abandon unbelievers to their punishment. Like virtually all languages of mankind, the ancient classical Arabic in which the Holy Koran was revealed abounds in metaphors, metonyms, figures of speech, and rhetorical embellishments—indeed, a revelation devoid of such features would have had little claim to eloquence among the Arabs—and the figurative interpretations of the Ash'aris are in general supported by compellingly similar linguistic examples, parallels, and lexical precedents drawn from the language's long history. Despite which, because of the possibility that Allah intends something other by such expressions than the particular interpretations suggested by scholars, the best and safest path for a Muslim is consignment of the knowledge of such things to Allah (tafwid), unless forced to refute anthropomorphists, who do not in effect worship the transcendent deity of Islam but rather a *form* like themselves, something unquestionably rejected by the Koranic verse,

"There is nothing whatsoever like unto Him" (Koran 42:11).

﴿ لَـيْـسَ كَـمِـثْـلِهِ شَيْءٌ ... ﴾
[الشورى: ١١].

The Ash'ari school has naturally earned the criticism of misconceived contemporary efforts to revive anthropomorphism, the excesses of whose proponents have inspired the author of the section below to remind Muslims of the fundamentally orthodox character of the school that has represented the majority of Sunni Muslims for the greater part of Islam's history.

w57.2 (Muhammad 'Alawi Maliki:) Many sons of Muslims are ignorant of the Ash'ari school, whom it represents, and its positions on tenets of Islamic faith, and yet some of them are not god-fearing enough to refrain from accusing it of deviance, departure from the religion of Islam, and heresy about the attributes of Allah. This ignorance of the Ash'ari school is a cause of rending the unity of Ahl al-Sunna and dispersing its ranks. Some have gone so far as to consider the Ash'aris among the categories of heretical sects, though it is beyond me how believers can be linked with misbelievers, or how Sunni Muslims can be considered equal with the most extreme faction of the Mu'tazilites, the Jahmites.

"Shall We deal with Muslims as We do criminals? How is it that you judge?" (Koran 68:35–36).

The Ash'aris are the Imams of the distinguished figures of guidance among the scholars of the Muslims, whose knowledge has filled the world from east to west, and whom people have unanimously concurred upon their excellence, scholarship, and religiousness. They include the first rank of Sunni scholars and most brilliant of their luminaries, who stood in the face of the excesses committed by the Mu'tazilites (dis: w6.4), and who constitute whole sections of the foremost Imams of hadith, Sacred Law, and Koranic exegesis. Sheikh al-Islam Ahmad ibn Hajar 'Asqalani, the mentor of hadith scholars and author of the book *Fath al-Bari bi sharh Sahih al-Bukhari*, which not a single Islamic scholar can dispense with, was Ash'ari. The sheikh of scholars of Sunni Islam, Imam Nawawi, author of *Sharh Sahih Muslim* and many of other famous works, was Ash'ari. The master of Koranic exegetes,

w57.2 (محمـد علوي المـالكي :)
يجهـل كثيـر من أبناء المسلمين مذهب الأشاعرة ولا يعرفون من هم الأشاعرة ولا طريقتهم في أمـر العقيدة؛ ولا يتـورع البعض أن ينسبهم إلى الضلال أو يرميهم بالمـروق من الدين والإلحاد في صفات الله . وهذا الجهل بمذهب الأشـاعـرة سبب تمـزق وحدة أهـل السنة وتشتت شملهم حتى غدا البعض يسلك الأشاعرة ضمن طوائف أهـل الضـلال، ولست أدري كيف يقرن بين أهل الإيمان وأهل الضـلال؟ وكيف يساوي بين أهـل السنة وبين غلاة المعتزلة وهم الجهمية؟
﴿ أَفَنَجْعَلُ الْمُسْلِمِينَ كَالْمُجْرِمِينَ مَا لَكُمْ كَيْفَ تَحْكُمُونَ ﴾ [القلم : ٣٥ ـ ٣٦].
الأشـاعـرة هم أئمة أعلام الهدى من علماء المسلمين، الذين ملأ علمهم مشارق الأرض ومغاربها وأطبق الناس على فضلهم ودينهم . هم جهابذة علماء أهل السنة وأعلام علمائهم الأفاضل الذين وقفوا في وجه طغيان المعتزلة [. . .] إنهم طوائف المحدثين والفقهاء والمفسرين من الأئمة الأعلام . شيخ الإسلام أحمد بن حجر العسقلاني شيخ المحدثين بلا مراء صاحب كتـاب «فتـح البـاري على شرح البخـاري» أشعري المذهب وكتـابه لا يستغني عنه أحد من العلماء . وشيخ علماء أهل السنة الإمام النووي صاحب «شرح صحيح مسلم» وصاحب المصنفات الشهيرة أشعري المذهب . وشيخ المفسرين الإمام القرطبي صاحب تفسير «الجامع لأحكام

Imam Qurtubi author of *al-Jami' li ahkam al-Qur'an,* was Ash'ari. Sheikh al-Islam Ibn Hajar Haytami, who wrote *al-Zawajir 'an iqtiraf al-kaba'ir,* was Ash'ari. The sheikh of Sacred Law and hadith, the conclusively definitive Zakariyya Ansari, was Ash'ari. Imam Abu Bakr Baqillani; Imam 'Asqalani; Imam Nasafi; Imam Shirbini; Abu Hayyan Tawhidi, author of the Koranic commentary *al-Bahr al-muhit;* Imam Ibn Juzayy, author of *al-Tashil fi 'ulum al-Tanzil;* and others—all of these were Imams of the Ash'aris. If we wanted to name all of the top scholars of hadith, Koranic exegesis, and Sacred Law who were Imams of the Ash'aris, we would be hard put to do so and require volumes merely to list these illustrious figures whose wisdom has filled the earth from east to west. And it is incumbent upon us to give credit where credit is due, recognizing the merit of those of knowledge and virtue who have served the Sacred Law of the Greatest of Messengers (Allah bless him and give him peace). What good is to be hoped for us if we impugn our foremost scholars and righteous forebears with charges of aberrancy and misguidance? Or how should Allah give us the benefit of their scholarship if we believe it is deviance and a departure from the way of Islam? I ask you, is there a single Islamic scholar of the present day, among all the Ph.D.'s and geniuses, who has done what Ibn Hajar 'Asqalani or Imam Nawawi have, of the service rendered by these two noble Imams (Allah enfold them in His mercy and bliss) to the pure prophetic sunna? How should we charge them and all Ash'aris with aberrancy when it is we who are in need of their scholarship? Or how can we take knowledge from them if they were in error? For as Imam Zuhri (Allah have mercy on him) says, "This knowledge is religion, so look well to whom you are taking your religion from."

Is it not sufficient for someone opposed to the Ash'aris to say, "Allah have mercy on them, they used their reasoning (ijtihad) in figuratively interpreting the divine attributes, which it would have been fitter for them not to do"; instead of accusing them of deviance and misguidance, or displaying anger towards whoever considers them to be of the Sunni Community? If Imam Nawawi, 'Asqalani, Qurtubi, Baqillani, al-Fakhr al-Razi, Haytami, Zakariyya Ansari, and others were not

القرآن» أشعري المـذهب . وشيـخ الإسلام ابن حجر الهيتمي صاحب كتاب «الـزواجر عن اقتـراف الكبـائر» أشعري المـذهب . وشيـخ الفقه والحديث الإمام الحجة الثبت زكريا الأنصاري أشعري المـذهب . والإمام العسقلاني والإمام النسفي والإمام الشربيني ، وأبو حيان التـوحيـدي صاحب تفسيـر «البحـر المحيط» ، والإمام ابن جزي صاحب «التسهيل في علوم التنـزيل» الخ . كل هؤلاء من أئمة الأشاعـرة . ولـو أردنا أن نعـدد هؤلاء الأعـلام من المـحـدثين والمفسرين والفقهاء من أئمة الأشاعرة لضاق بنـا الحـال واحتجنا إلى مجلدات في سرد أولئك العلماء الأفـاضل الذين ملأ علمهم مشارق الأرض ومغاربها . إن من الواجب أن نرد الجميل لأصحابه وأن نعرف الفضل لأهل العلم والفضل الذين خدمـوا شريعـة سيد المرسلين ﷺ [من العلمـاء الأعلام] . وأي خير يرجى فينا إن رمينا علماءنا وأسلافنا الصالحين بالزيغ والضلال؟ وكيف يفتح الله علينا لنستفيد من علومهم إذا كنا نعتقد فيها الانحراف والزيغ عن طريق الإسلام؟ إنني أقول : هل يوجد بين علماء العصر من الدكاترة والعباقرة من يقوم بما قام به شيخ الإسلام ابن حجر العسقلاني والإمام النووي من خدمة السنة النبـوية المطهرة كما فعل هذان الإمامان الجليـلان تغمدهما الله بالـرحمة والـرضوان؟ فكيف نرميهمـا ـ وسـائر الأشـاعـرة ـ بالضـلال ونحن بحـاجـة إلى علومهم هؤلاء؟ وكيف نأخذ العلوم عنهم إذا كانوا على ضلال وقد قال الإمام الزهري رحمه الله : إن هذا العلم دين فانظروا عمن تأخذون دينكم .

أفمـا كان يكفي أن يقـول المعارض : إنـهم رحمهم الله اجتهـدوا فأخطأوا في تأويل الصفات وكان الأولى أن لا يسلكوا هذا المسلك ؛ بدل أن نرميهم بالـزيـغ والضـلال ونغضب على من عدهم من أهل السنة والجماعة؟ وإذا لم يكن الإمام النووي والعسقلاني والقرطبي والباقلاني

among the most brilliant scholars and illustrious geniuses, or of the Sunni Community, then who are the Sunnis?

I sincerely entreat all who call others to this religion or who work in the field of propagating Islam to fear Allah respecting the honor of the Community of Muhammad (Allah bless him and give him peace), especially its greatest sages and scholars in Sacred Law. For the Community of Muhammad (Allah bless him and give him peace) is possessed of goodness until the Final Hour, while we are bereft of any if we fail to acknowledge the worth and excellence of our learned (*Mafahim yajibu an tusahhaha* (y83), 38–40).

والفخـر الـرازي والهيتمي وزكريـا الأنصـاري وغيـرهم من جهابذة العلماء وفطـاحـل النبغـاء إذا لم يكونوا من أهل السنة والجماعة فمن هم أهل السنة إذن؟

إنني أدعـو مخلصـاً كل الـدعـاة وكل العـاملين في حقـل الـدعوة الإسلامية أن يتقـوا الله في أمة محمد ﷺ وبخاصة في أجلة علمائها وأخيار فقهائها . فأمة محمد ﷺ بخير إلى قيام الساعة ولا خير فينا إذا لم نعـرف لعـلمـائنـا قدرهم وفضلهم [محرر من مفاهيم يجب أن تصحح : ٣٨ – ٤٠] .

*

w58.0 COMMEMORATING THE BIRTH (MAWLID) OF THE PROPHET (ALLAH BLESS HIM AND GIVE HIM PEACE) (from w29.3(3))

w58.0 عمل المولد

w58.1 (Jalal al-Din Suyuti:) The Sheikh of Islam and hadith master of his age, Ahmad ibn Hajar (N: 'Asqalani) was asked about the practice of commemorating the birth of the Prophet (Allah bless him and give him peace), and gave the following written reply: "As for the origin of the practice of commemorating the Prophet's birth (Allah bless him and give him peace), it is an innovation (bid'a) that has not been conveyed to us from any of the pious early Muslims of the first three centuries, despite which it has included both features that are praiseworthy and features that are not. If one takes care to include in such a commemoration only things that are praiseworthy and avoids those that are otherwise, it is a praiseworthy innovation (dis: w29.2), while if one does not, it is not.

"An authentic primary textual basis from which its legal validity is inferable has occurred to me, namely the rigorously authenticated (sahih) hadith in the collections of Bukhari and Muslim that 'the Prophet (Allah bless him and give him peace) came to Medina and found the Jews fasting on the tenth of Muharram ('Ashura'), so he asked

w58.1 (جـلال الـدين السيـوطي :) [. . . و] قد سئل شيـخ الإسـلام حافظ العصر [أبـو فضل] أحمد بن حجر (ح : العسقلاني) عن عمل المولد فأجاب بما نصـه : أصـل عمل المولد بدعة لم تنقل عن أحـد من السلف الصـالح من القرون الثلاثة ، ولكنها مع ذلك قد اشتملت على محـاسن وضـدهـا فمن تحرى في عملها المحاسن وتجنب ضدها كان بدعة حسنة وإلا فلا .

[قال :] وقـد ظهـر لي تخريجها على أصـل ثابت وهـو ما ثبت في الصحيحين من أن النبي ﷺ قدم المدينة فوجد اليهود يصومون يوم عاشوراء فسألهم فقالوا : هو

them about it and they replied, "It is the day on which Allah drowned Pharaoh and rescued Moses, so we fast it in thanks to Allah Most High," ' which indicates the validity of giving thanks to Allah for the blessings He has bestowed on a particular day in providing a benefit or averting an affliction, repeating one's thanks on the anniversary of that day every year, *giving thanks to Allah* taking any of various forms of worship such as prostration, fasting, giving charity, or reciting the Koran. And what blessing is greater than the birth of the Prophet (Allah bless him and give him peace), the Prophet of Mercy, on this day? In light of which, one should take care to commemorate it on the day itself in order to conform to the above story of Moses and the tenth of Muharram, though those who do not view the matter thus do not mind commemorating it on any day of the month, while some have expanded its time to any day of the year, whatever exception may be taken at such a view.

"The foregoing is in regard to its legal basis. As for what is done therein, it should be confined to what expresses thanksgiving to Allah Most High, of the like of the above-mentioned practices such as reciting the Koran, feeding others, giving charity, and singing something of the odes that praise the Prophet (Allah bless him and give him peace) or encourage one to do with less of this-worldly things, inspiring the hearts of the listeners to do good and to work for the hereafter. As for what is added to this, of listening to singing, amusement, and so forth, what should be said of it is that the permissible therein that displays rejoicing over the day is of no harm if conjoined with it, while what is unlawful, offensive, or unpraiseworthy (khilaf al-awla) is forbidden" (*al-Hawi li al-fatawi* (y130), 1.196).

يوم أغـرق الله فيـه فرعـون ونجى موسى فنحن نصـومه شكراً لله تعالى ؛ فيستفاد منـه فعل الشكر لله على ما من به في يوم معين من إسـداء نعمـة أو دفع نقمة ويعاد ذلـك في نظير ذلـك اليـوم من كل سنة . والـشكـر لله يحصـل بأنـواع العبـادة كالسجـود والصيـام والصـدقـة والتلاوة . وأي نعمـة أعظم من النعمـة بـبـروز النبي ﷺ نبي الرحمة في ذلك اليوم؟ وعلى هذا فينبغي أن يتحرى اليوم بعينه حتى يطابق قصـة موسى في يوم عاشـوراء ومـن لـم يلاحظ ذلك لا يبالي بعمل المولد في أي يوم من الشهر بل توسع قوم فنقلوه إلى أي يوم من السنة وفيـه ما فيه ، فهذا ما يتعلق بأصل عمله . وأما ما يعمل فيه فينبغي أن يقتصر فيـه على ما يفهم الشكر لله تعالى من نحو ما تقدم ذكره من التلاوة والإطعام والصدقة وإنشاد شيء من المدائح النبوية والزهدية المحركة للقلوب إلى فعل الخير والعمل للآخرة ، وأمـا ما يتبـع ذلك من السمـاع واللهو وغير ذلك فينبغي أن يقال ما كان في ذلـك مبـاحـاً بحيث يقتضي السرور بذلك اليوم لا بأس بإلحاقه به وما كان حراماً أو مكروهاً فيمنع وكذا ما كان خلاف الأولى [انتهى] [نقـل من الحاوي للفتـاوي في الـفقـه وعـلوم التفسيـر والحديث والأصول والنحـو والإعراب وسائر الفنون : ١ / ١٩٦] .

*

w59.0   THE ACCEPTANCE OF FATE (from w52.1(24))

w59.0   الرضا بالقضاء

THINGS INCONSISTENT WITH THE ACCEPTANCE OF FATE

ما يناقض الرضا بالقضاء

w59.1 (Ghazali:) Complaining, no matter what the circumstances, is inconsistent with accepting fate. Criticizing food and finding fault with it is a rejection of what Allah Most High has destined, since blaming what is made is blaming the maker, and everything is Allah's work. For a person to say that "poverty is an affliction and trial," or "having a family to support is worry and fatigue," or "working for a living is a burden and hardship"—all this is inconsistent with accepting fate. One should rather leave the plan to its planner, the kingdom to its king, and say, as 'Umar did (Allah be well pleased with him), "I do not care whether I become rich or poor, for I don't know which is better for me."

THINGS THAT ARE NOT INCONSISTENT
WITH THE ACCEPTANCE OF FATE

w59.2   As for prayers (du'a'), Allah requires us to worship Him thereby, as is substantiated by the great many supplications made by the Messenger of Allah (Allah bless him and give him peace) and all the prophets (upon whom be peace). Praying for forgiveness, for Allah's protection of one from acts of disobedience, and indeed for all means that assist one to practice one's religion—none of these is inconsistent with accepting what Allah Most High has destined, for Allah demands the worship of supplications from His servants so that their prayers may bring forth the purity of His remembrance, the humility of soul, and the softening of earnest entreaty so as to polish the heart, open it to spiritual insight, and obtain the manifold blessings of His kindnesses—just as carrying a pitcher and drinking water are not inconsistent with the acceptance of Allah's having decreed thirst. As drinking water to eliminate thirst is merely to employ one of the means that the. Creator of means has arranged, so too is prayer an instrumental relation that Allah Most High has devised and ordered to be used. To employ such means, in conformity with the normal way Allah Most High deals with the world (sunna Allah), is not inconsistent with full confidence in divine providence (tawakkul). Nor is hating acts of disobedience, detesting their perpetrators and causes, or striving

w59.1 (الـغـزالـي:) [ ] [و] الشكـوى تنـاقـض الـرضـا بكـل حـال وذم الأطعمة وعيبها يناقض الرضا بقضاء الله تعـالـى لأن مذمـة الصنعـة مذمـة للصـانع والكـل من صنع الله تعالى وقول القائل : الـفـقـر بلاء ومحنـة والعيـال هـمّ وتعب والاحـتراف كد ومشقـة كل ذلك قـادح في الرضا ، بل ينبغي أن يسلم التدبير لمدبره والمملكة لمـالكهـا ويقـول ما قـاله عمر رضي الله عنه : لا أبالي أصبحت غنياً أو فقيراً فإني لا أدري أيهما خير لي [...].

ما لا يناقض الرضا

w59.2   فأمـا الـدعـاء فقـد تعبدنا به ، وكثـرة دعـوات رسـول الله ﷺ وسـائر الأنبيـاء عليهم السلام تدل عليه . [ ] والدعاء بالمغفرة والعصمة من المعاصي وسـائـر الأسبـاب المعينة على الدين غير مناقض للرضا بقضاء الله تعالى . فإن الله تعبد العباد بالدعاء ليستخرج الدعاء منهم صفاء الذكر وخشوع القلب ورقة التضرع ويكـون ذلـك جلاء للقلب ومفتـاحـاً للكشف وسبـباً لتواتر مزايا اللطف كما أن حمل الكـوز وشرب المـاء ليس مناقضاً للرضـا بقضاء الله تعـالى في العطش ، وشرب المـاء طلبـاً لإزالة العطش مباشرة سبب رتبه مسبب الأسباب فكذلك الدعاء سبب رتبه الله تعـالى وأمر به . وقد ذكرنا أن التمسك بالأسبـاب جرياً على سنة الله تعـالى لا يناقض التوكل . [...] وكذلك كراهة المعـاصي ومقت أهلهـا ومقت أسبـابهـا والسعي في إزالتهـا بالأمـر

to remove them by commanding the right and forbidding the wrong (q1); none of which is inconsistent with accepting fate, though some deluded good-for-nothings have erred in this, claiming that since acts of disobedience, wickedness, and unbelief are from the destiny and decree of Allah Mighty and Majestic, accepting them is obligatory—while this is rather from their lack of understanding and blindness to the deeper purposes of Sacred Law. For Allah requires that we worship Him by condemning acts of disobedience, hating them, and not acquiescing to them, and blames those who accept them by saying:

"They willingly accept a worldly life [dis: w5] and are contented with it" (Koran 10:7);

and,

"They accept to remain with the women who stay behind; Allah has set a seal upon their hearts" (Koran 9:87).

And in a famous hadith,

"Whoever sees something wrong and accepts it is as though he had committed it."

It might be objected that Koranic verses and hadiths exist about accepting what Allah Most High has destined, while it is impossible and inconsistent with the divine unity that acts of disobedience should not be through Allah's having decreed them, and yet if they are from the decree of Allah Most High, then hating and detesting them is hatred of the decree of Allah, so how can one reconcile these two seemingly contradictory aspects or join between the acceptance and hatred of one and the same thing? The answer to this is that acceptance and displeasure are only inconsistent when directed towards a single aspect of single object in a single respect. For it is not inconsistent to dislike something in one respect and accept it in another, as when one's enemy dies who was the enemy of another of one's enemies and was striving to destroy him, such that one dislikes his death insofar as the nemesis of one's enemy has died, yet accepts it in that at least one of them has died. And so too, disobedience has

بالمعـروف والنهي عن المنكـر لا يناقضه أيضاً . وقـد غلط في ذلك بعض البطالين المغتـرين وزعم أن المعـاصي والفجـور والكفـر من قضـاء الله وقـدره عز وجل فيجب الرضـا به وهـذا جهـل بالتأويل وغفلة عن أسـرار الشرع . [. . .] و[أما] إنكار المعاصي وكراهتها وعدم الرضا بها فقـد تعبد الله به عباده وذمهم على الرضا بها فقال :

﴿وَرَضُوا بِالْحَيَاةِ الدُّنْيَا وَاطْمَأَنُّوا بِهَا﴾ [يونس : ٧] .

وقال تعالى :

﴿رَضُوا بِأَنْ يَكُونُوا مَعَ الْخَوَالِفِ وَطَبَعَ اللَّهُ عَلَى قُلُوبِهِمْ﴾ [التوبة : ٨٧] .

وفي الخبر المشهور :

«من شهد منكراً فرضي به فكأنه قد فعله» .

فإن قلت : فقد وردت الآيات والأخبار بالرضـا بقضـاء الله تعـالى فإن كانت المعاصي بغير قضاء الله تعالى فهو محال وهـو قادح في التـوحيـد وإن كانت بقضاء الله تعـالى فكراهتها ومقتها كراهة لقضاء الله تعـالى . وكيف السبيـل إلى الجمـع وهو متناقض على هذا الوجه وكيف يمكن الجمـع بين الرضـا والكراهـة في شيء واحد؟ [. . .] بل نقول] الرضا والكراهة يتضـادان إذا تواردا على شيء واحد من جهـة واحدة على وجه واحد . فليس من التضاد في شيء واحد أن يكـره من وجه ويرضى به من وجه . إذ قد يموت عدوَك الـذي هو أيضاً عدوّ بعض أعدائك وساع في إهـلاكـه فتكره موته من حيث أنه مات عدوّ عدوّك وترضاه من حيث أنه مات عدوّك .

وكذلك المعاصي لها وجهان وجه إلى

two aspects, one regarding Allah Most High, since it is His effect, choice, and will, in which respect one accepts it out of deference to the Sovereign and His sovereignty, assenting to His disposal of the matter; and another aspect regarding the perpetrator, since it is his acquisition and attribute (dis: u3.8), the sign of his being detested and odious to Allah, who has afflicted him with the causes of remoteness and hatred, in respect to which he is condemnable and blameworthy. And this clarifies the Koranic verses and hadiths about hatred for the sake of Allah and love for the sake of Allah, being unyielding towards the unbelievers, hard against them, and detesting them, while accepting the destiny of Allah Most High insofar as it is the decree of Allah Mighty and Majestic (*Ihya' 'ulum al-din* (y39), 4.300–303).

الله تعالى من حيث أنه فعله واختياره وإرادته فيرضى به من هذا الوجه تسليماً للملك إلى مالك الملك والرضا بما يفعله فيه ، ووجه إلى العبد من حيث أنه كسبه ووصفه وعلامة كونه ممقوتاً عند الله وبغيضاً عنده حيث سلط عليه أسباب البعد والمقت فهو من هذا الوجه منكر ومذموم . [. . .] وبهذا يتقرر جميع ما وردت به الأخبار من البغض في الله والحب في الله والتشديد على الكفار والتغليظ عليهم والمبالغة في مقتهم مع الرضا بقضاء الله تعالى من حيث أنه قضاء الله عز وجل [محرر من إحياء علوم الدين : ٤/ ٣٠٠ - ٣٠٣؛ بتقديم وتأخير] .

*

w60.0 KNOWLEDGE OF THE UNSEEN (from w52.1(306))

w60.0 علم الغيب

w60.1 (Ibn Hajar Haytami:)

(Question:) "Is someone who says, 'A believer knows the unseen (al-ghayb),' thereby considered an unbeliever, because of Allah Most High having said:

" 'No one in the heavens or earth knows the unseen except Allah' (Koran 27:65),

"and,

" '[He is] the Knower of the Unseen, and discloses not His unseen to anyone...' (Koran 72:26),

"or is such a person asked to further explain himself, in view of the possibility of knowing some details of the unseen?"

(Answer:) "He is not unconditionally considered an unbeliever, because of the possibility of otherwise construing his words, for it is obligatory to ask whomever says something interpretable as either being or not being unbelief for further

w60.1 (ابن حجر الهيتمي :) سئل [. . .] من قال إن المؤمن يعلم الغيب ، هل يكفر لقوله تعالى :

﴿ قُـل لاَ يَعْـلَمُ مَنْ فِي السَّمَـوَاتِ وَالأَرْضِ الغَيْبَ إِلاَّ اللَّهُ ﴾ [النمل : ٦٥] .

و﴿ عَالِمُ الغَيْبِ فَلاَ يُظْهِرُ عَلَى غَيْبِهِ أَحَداً ﴾ [الجن : ٢٦] .

أو يستفصل لجواز العلم بجزئيات من الغيب ؟

(فأجاب [بقوله رحمه الله ونفعنا به آمين] :) لا يطلق القول بكفره لاحتمال كلامه ومن تكلم بما يحتمل الكفر وغيره

clarification, as has been stated in [n: Nawawi's] *al-Rawda* and elsewhere....

"If asked to explain and such a person answers: 'By saying, "A believer knows the unseen," I meant that Allah could impart certain details of the unseen to some of the friends of Allah (awliya')'—this is accepted from him, since it is something logically possible and its occurrence has been documented, it being among the countless miracles [karamat, dis: w30] that have taken place over the ages. The possibility of such knowledge is amply attested to by what the Koran informs us about Khidr (Allah bless him and give him peace), and the account related of Abu Bakr Siddiq (Allah Most High be well pleased with him) that he told of his wife being pregnant with a boy, and thus it proved; or of 'Umar (Allah Most High be well pleased with him), who miraculously perceived [n: the Muslim commander] Sariya and his army who were in Persia, and while on the pulpit in Medina giving the Friday sermon, he said, 'O Sariya, the mountain!' warning them of the enemy ambush intending to exterminate the Muslims. Or the rigorously authenticated (sahih) hadith that the Prophet (Allah bless him and give him peace) said of 'Umar (Allah Most High be well pleased with him),

" 'He is of those who are spoken to [i.e. preternaturally inspired].'

"....What we have mentioned about the above Koranic verse [n: on the unseen] has been explicitly stated by Nawawi in his *Fatawa*, where he says: 'It means that no one except Allah knows this independently and with full cognizance of all things knowable. As for [n: knowledge imparted through] inimitable prophetic miracles (mu'jizat) and divine favors (karamat) it is through Allah's giving them to know it that it is known; as is also the case with what is known through ordinary means' " (*al-Fatawa al-hadithiyya* (y48), 311–13).

w60.2 (Muhammad Hamid:) Allah Most Glorious is the All-knower of things unseen and their inmost secrets, with primal, intrinsic, supernatural knowledge whose basis no one else has a share in. If any besides Him has awareness or

وجب استفصاله كما في الروضة وغيرها . . .

ومتى استفصل فقال : أردت بقولي المؤمن يعلم الغيب أن بعض الأولياء قد يعلمه الله ببعض المغيبات ، قبل منه ذلك لأنه جائز عقلاً وواقع نقلاً إذ هو من جملة الكرامات الخارجة عن الحصر على ممر الأعصار [. . .] ويكفي بذلك ما أخبر به القرآن عن الخضر [. . .] ﷺ ، وما جاء عن أبي بكر الصديق رضي الله تعالى عنه أنه أخبر عن حمل امرأته أنه ذكر وكان كذلك . وعن عمر رضي الله تعالى عنه أنه كشف عن سارية وجيشه وهم بالعجم فقال على منبر المدينة وهو يخطب يوم الجمعة : يا سارية الجبل ؛ يحذره الكمين الذي أراد استئصال المسلمين ، وما صح عنه ﷺ أنه قال في عمر رضي الله تعالى عنه : «إنه من المحدَّثين» ، أي الملهمين .

. . . وما ذكرنا في الآية صرح به النووي رحمه الله في فتاواه فقال : معناها لا يعلم ذلك استقلالاً وعلم إحاطة بكل المعلومات إلا الله . وأما المعجزات والكرامات فبإعلام الله لهم علمت ، وكذا ما علم بإجراء العادة [انتهى كلامه] [محرر من الفتاوى الحديثية : ٣١١ ـ ٣١٣] .

w60.2 (محمد الحامد :) الله سبحانه العليم بالغيوب ومكنوناتها علماً لدنّياً ذاتياً أصلياً لا يشاركه أحد في هذه الأصالة ، ولئن كان لغيره اطّلاع ومعرفة

knowledge, it is through their being made aware or given knowledge by Him Magnificent and Exalted. They are unable—being servants without capacity—to transcend their sphere or go beyond their limit to draw aside the veils from things unseen, and if not for His pouring something of the knowledge of these things upon their hearts, they would know nothing of it, little or much. Yet this knowledge is disparate in degree, and some of it higher than other of it and more certainly established.

The divine inspiration of it to prophet messengers is beyond doubt and above question, like the rising sun in its certitude and clarity, of which the Koran says,

"[He is] the Knower of the Unseen, and discloses not His unseen to anyone, save a messenger He approves: for him He places protectors before and behind" (Koran 72:26–27),

protectors meaning guards from among the angels, so that nothing of it is leaked to devils when it is being delivered to the Messenger (Allah bless him and give him peace), to safeguard its inimitability and it remain a unique prophetic sign (mu'jiza).

The miraculous perceptions (kashf) of the friends of Allah (awliya') are a truth we do not deny, for Bukhari relates in his *Sahih* from Abu Hurayra (Allah Most High be well pleased with him) that the Prophet (Allah bless him and give him peace) said:

"In the nations before you were people who were spoken to [i.e. inspired] though they were not prophets. If there is anyone in my Community, it is 'Umar ibn Khattab."

and Muslim relates in his *Sahih* from 'A'isha (Allah Most High be well pleased with her) that the Prophet (Allah bless him and give him peace) said:

"There used to be in the nations before you those who were spoken to. If there are any in my Community, 'Umar ibn Khattab is one of them."

But this intuition (ilham) does not equal the divine inspiration (wahy) of the prophets in strength (n:

فبإطلاعه وتعريفه جل وعلا ، وما كان لهم ـ وهم عباد عاجزون ـ أن يتخطوا طورهم ويتعدوا حدهم فيكشفوا السجوف عن المغيبات . ولولا إفاضته سبحانه على قلوبهم المعرفة ببعض الغيب ما عرفوا منه قليلاً ولا كثيراً . لكن هذه المعرفة متفاوتة فبعضها أرقى من بعض وأرسخ ثبوتاً . فالوحي بها للمرسلين لا يتطرق إليه شك ولا يعتريه ريب وهو كالشمس المشرقة ثبوتاً ووضوحاً ، وعن هذا جاء القرآن يقول :

﴿عَـٰلِمُ الغَيْبِ فَلَا يُظْهِـرُ عَلَىٰ غَيْبِهِ أَحَـداً . إِلَّا مَنْ ارْتَضَىٰ مِنْ رَسُولٍ فَإِنَّـهُ يَسْلُكُ مِنْ بَيْنِ يَدَيْهِ وَمِنْ خَلْفِهِ رَصَداً﴾ [الجن : ٢٦ ـ ٢٧] .

أي حرساً من الملائكة حتى لا يتسرب شيء منه إلى الشياطين وقت إلقائه إلى الرسول عليه الصلاة والسلام فيبقى الإعجاز وتسلم المعجزة .

والكشف للأولياء حق لا ننكره فقد روى البخاري في صحيحه عن أبي هريرة رضي الله تعالى عنه قال : قال رسول الله ﷺ :

«لقد كان فيمن كان قبلكم من الأمم ناس محدَّثون» ـ أي ملهَمون ـ «من غير أن يكونوا أنبياء ، وإن يكن في أمتي أحد فإنه عمر بن الخطاب» .

[ت : قلت لم أجده في البخاري بهذا اللفظ بل وجدت حديثين هما : «لقد كان فيما قبلكم من الأمم محدَّثون فإن يك في أمتي أحد فإنه عمر» وآخر : «لقد كان فيمن كان قبلكم من بني إسرائيل رجال يكلَّمون من غيـر أن يكونوا أنبياء . فإن يكن من أمتي منهم أحد فعمر» . فلعل المؤلف رحمه الله جمع بين الروايتين أو روى بمعناهما] . ولمسلم في صحيحه عن عائشة رضي الله تعالى عنها عن النبي ﷺ أنه كان يقول : «قد كان يكون في الأمم قبلكم محدَّثون فإن يكن في أمتي منهم أحد فإن عمر بن الخطاب منهم» .

لكن هذا الإلهام لا يساوي وحي الأنبياء في القوة لجواز كون إخبار الولي

of certainty), because of the possibility that what is apprehended by the friend of Allah (wali) is merely the thoughts of his own mind. As it is sometimes admixed, and other things are mistaken for it, the possibility of error exists in it, and it cannot be a basis for establishing legal rulings or a criterion for works.

As for what astrologers and fortune-tellers say, there is no way it can be accepted, for soothsaying was annulled when the Prophet (Allah bless him and give him peace) was sent and the heavens were safeguarded by stars, after which devils no longer had access to the heavens as they had had before, to eavesdrop on what angels were saying about the events on earth that Allah Most Glorious informed the angels of before they happened (n: Koran 15:17–18 and 72:8–10). The Holy Koran is explicit that

"they [the devils] are prevented from hearing" (Koran 26:212),

and in a hadith,

"Whoever goes to a 'psychic' ('arraf) or fortune-teller and believes what he says has disbelieved in what has been revealed to Muhammad [Allah bless him and give him peace]."

The things that such people inform of that actually come to pass belong to the category of coincidence, which is not given the slightest value in Islam.

All of which is on the topic of the unseen generally. As for the Final Hour, Allah Most High has veiled the knowledge of the time it will occur from all creatures entirely, and no one, archangel or prophetic messenger, knows when it will be, the Koranic verses and hadiths being intersubstantiative and in full agreement on this. Were I to list them it would be a lengthy matter, and what I have mentioned is adequate and sufficient for whomever the divine assistance reaches (*Rudud 'ala abatil wa rasa'il al-Shaykh Muhammad al-Hamid* (y44), 2.61–63).

مجـرد حديث نفس ، ولتلونـه أحيـاناً والتبـاسه فللخطأ فيـه احتمـال فلا يكون مناط تشريع ولا دستور عمل .

أمـا ما يقولـه المنجمون والكهّان فلا سبيـل إلى قبـوله وتصـديقه من حيث إن الكهانة بطلت ببعث النبي ﷺ ، وحرست السمـاء بالنجـوم ، فلم يعـد للشياطين خلوص كالـذي كان لهم من قبـل إليهـا لاستراق السمع بما يتحدث به الملائكة عن الكـوائن في الأرض ممـا يخبرهم به الله سبحـانه من قبـل أن يقـع . والقرآن الكريم صريح في هذا :

﴿إِنَّهُمْ عَنِ السَّمْعِ لَمَعْزُولُونَ﴾ [الشعراء : ٢١٢] .

وفي الحديث الشريف :

«من أتى عرّافاً أوكاهناً فصـدقـه بما يقـول فقد كفر بما أنزل على محمد» ﷺ [رواه الإمـام أحمـد والحـاكم من حديث أبي هريــرة عن رسـول ا لله عليـه وآلـه الصـلاة والسـلام .] وما يقع مما يخبرون به فهـو من قبيل الصـدفة التي لا يقام لها وزن في الإسلام .

هذا كله في الغيب عمـوماً ، وأمـا أمر السـاعـة فإن الله تعـالى حجب علم وقت وقـوعهـا عن الخلق كلهم أجمعين فلا يعلم وقتها أحـد ، لا ملك مقرب ولا نبي مرسـل ، والآيات والأحـاديث متظـاهـرة على هذا متضافرة فيه . ولو ذهبت أسردها لامتـد بي القول وطـال وفيما ذكرت غنية وكفـاية لمن لاحظته عين العناية [نقل من ردود على أبـاطيل ورسائل الشيخ محمد الحامد : ٢ / ٦١ - ٦٣] .

*

BOOK X

BIOGRAPHICAL NOTES

تراجــــــمُ الأعلام

INTRODUCTION:

(n:) The persons mentioned below are listed alphabetically, first name first, exactly as spelled in the English texts of the present volume, though titles like *Sheikh, Imam, al-Hajj, Sheikh al-Islam,* etc. are not taken into alphabetical consideration, such that Imam Ahmad, for example, is listed in the A's as *(Imam) Ahmad.* Also disregarded for the purposes of alphabetizing are the diacritic ' ('ayn), the Arabic definite article *al-,* and the word *ibn,* unless the latter is capitalized in the texts, as with Ibn Majah, for example, who is listed under *Ibn.*

As for recording the full name of each person, the procedure has been to write the name: "So-and-so *ibn* [lit. "son of"] So-and-so ibn So-and-so"—back to several ancestors; then a comma followed by the agnomen (kunya) if known, "Abu [lit. "father of"] So-and-so," which Muslim men adopt upon the birth of a son or daughter; then the reputational epithet (shuhra) if any, by which famous scholars were often known to each other and the public, such as "Zayn al-Din," or "Jalal al-Din"; and finally the ascriptive name (nisba) which denoted their family origin or residence. Thus, a typical name might be like that of Imam Dhahabi, for example, who was Muhammad ibn Ahmad ibn 'Uthman ibn Qaymaz, Abu Abdullah Shams al-Din al-Dhahabi. The order of the last three elements occasionally varies in Muslim biographical literature, but the order used here is widely accepted.

The biographies themselves contain facts of the individuals' lives (occasionally eclectic in details the sources differ about) as well as inferences and judgements by the translator that were felt to be warranted by the accounts related, marked by the letter *n* at the end of the entries in which they figure. Information from oral sources such as the translator's sheikhs is designated, as in the rest of the present volume, by the letters *A, N,* or the informant's name. Where the words *hadith master (hafiz)* appear, they mean that the subject of the biography was one of the mnemones of Islam, those scholars who had memorized at least one hundred thousand hadiths with their chains of transmission. In stories of pre-Islamic figures like the ancient prophets (upon whom be peace), the narratives of Bani Isra'il (Isra'iliyyat) have been freely quoted from the Koranic commentaries indicated, as Muslim scholars concur that they are permissible to relate in matters that do not contradict the principles of Islam (dis: *Fath al-Bari* (y17), 6.498–99, hadith 3461), and Allah knows best as to their authenticity. Finally, where both Hijra and Christian dates are used, the Hijra date is mentioned first, followed by the Christian date.

---

x1   (A:) (*see* 'Abd al-Wakil Durubi, x19).

x2   Aaron (*see* Harun, x135)

x3   'Abbas (j13.4) is al-'Abbas ibn 'Abd al-Muttalib ibn Hashim, the paternal uncle of the Prophet (Allah bless him and give him peace), and born before him by two years. In the pre-Islamic period of ignorance he was responsible for the custodianship of the Sacred Precinct and giving water to its visitants. He entered Islam and emigrated to Medina before Mecca was conquered by the Muslims, and died in Medina in A.H. 32 (*al-Shifa* (y116), 1.181).

x4   'Abd al-Ghaffar 'Uyun al-Sud (w50.1) was a Hanafi author and Koranic exegete of the present century who was a member of a family of scholars from Homs, Syria. He completed his three-volume commentary on the first two suras of the Koran, *al-Riyad al-nadira fi tafsir suratayy al-Fatiha wa al-Baqara* [The verdant gardens: an exegesis of the suras al-Fatiha and al-Baqara], sometime before 1343/1924–25 (A).

x5   'Abd al-Ghani Nabulsi (w9.4) is 'Abd al-Ghani ibn Isma'il ibn 'Abd al-Ghani al-Nabulsi, born in Damascus in 1050/1641. He was a prolific Hanafi Imam, mufti, Sufi, and poet, the author of nearly five hundred books and treatises in the natural and religious sciences, among them *Idah al-maqsud min wahdat al-wujud* [Clarifying what is meant by the 'unity of being'], in which he explains that by the 'unity of being' Sufis do not mean that the created universe is God, for God's being is necessary (wajib al-wujud) while the universe's being is merely possible (ja'iz al-wujud), i.e. subject to nonbeing, beginning, and ending, and it is impossible that one of these two orders of being could in any sense *be* the other, but rather the created universe's act of being is derived and subsumed by the divine act of creation, from which it has no ontic independence, and hence *is* only through the being of its Creator, the one true Being. 'Abd al-Ghani travelled to Baghdad, Palestine, Lebanon, Egypt, and the Hijaz, returning to settle in Damascus, where he authored most of his works and died in 1143/1733 (*Idah al-maqsud min wahdat al-wujud* (y98), 30; Sheikh 'Abd al-Rahman Shaghouri; and n).

x6   'Abd al-Hamid Sharwani (o25.0) was a Shafi'i scholar who lived in Mecca and in 1289/1872 completed his major work, comprising the most reliable positions of the later Shafi'i school in a ten-volume exegesis of Ibn Hajar Haytami's interlineal commentary on Nawawi's *Minhaj al-talibin* [The seekers' road], (*Hawashi al-Shaykh 'Abd al-Hamid al-Sharwani* (y2), 10.432–33).

x7   'Abd al-Karim Jili (s4.9) is 'Abd al-Karim ibn Ibrahim al-Jili, the Qutb of

Jilan, born in 768/1365. A great-grandson of 'Abd al-Qadir al-Jilani, he was a Sufi, gnostic, and scholar of Sacred Law who authored many works, among the most famous of which is his *al-Insan al-kamil fi ma'rifa al-awakhir wa al-awa'il* [The perfected man: on the knowledge of last and first things]. He died in 832/ 1428 (*al-A'lam* (y136), 4.50).

x8   'Abd al-Qadir al-Jaza'iri (w9.4) is 'Abd al-Qadir ibn Muhyiddin ibn Mustafa al-Hasani al-Jaza'iri. Born in Qaytana, Algeria, in 1222/1807, he was a leader of men, fighter for Islam (mujahid), and the author of the three-volume Sufi classic *al-Mawaqif* [Standpoints] that attests to both his mastery of the traditional Islamic disciplines and adepthood in the mystic path. Originally educated in Oran, he later performed the pilgrimage to Mecca with his father, visiting Medina, Damascus, and Baghdad. In 1246/1830, when the French entered Algeria, his fellow countrymen swore fealty to him and made him their leader, and he stood in the face of the invasion, personally leading his army into battle against the enemy until 1263/1847, when the Sultan of the West 'Abd al-Rahman ibn Hisham made a peace with the French, and 'Abd al-Qadir was taken to Toulon. In 1281/1864–65 he was allowed to move to Damascus, where he died in 1300/1883 (ibid., 4.45–46).

x9   'Abd al-Qahir al-Baghdadi (w9.11) is 'Abd al-Qahir ibn Tahir ibn Muhammad ibn 'Abdullah al-Baghdadi, a Shafi'i scholar, Imam in fundamentals of Islam (usul), and heresiologist who was born and raised in Baghdad, later moving to Nishapur. He was a teacher who used to lecture in seventeen subjects to students, and was the author of *Usul al-din* [The fundamentals of the religion] and *al-Farq bayn al-firaq* [The distinction between heretical sects], both major works on the beliefs of Ahl al-Sunna. He died in Asfara'in in 429/1037 (ibid., 4.48; and *Tabaqat al-Shafi'iyya al-kubra* (y128), 5.136).

x10   'Abd al-Rahman ibn 'Awf (o25.4(2)) is 'Abd al-Rahman ibn 'Awf ibn 'Abd 'Awf al-Qurashi, among the ten Companions whom the Prophet (Allah bless him and give him peace) affirmed would enter paradise. An early convert to Islam, he emigrated twice in the path of Allah, first to Ethiopia and then to Medina, and was one of those who fought in the battle of Badr. He died in A.H. 31 in Medina and is buried in al-Baqi' cemetery there (*al-Shifa* (y116), 1.281).

x11   'Abd al-Rahman Ba'alawi (b7.6) is 'Abd al-Rahman ibn Muhammad ibn Husayn ibn 'Umar Ba'alawi, Shafi'i scholar and the mufti of Hadramawt, Yemen. He finished writing *Bughyat al-mustarshidin fi talkhis fatawa ba'd al-a'imma min al-muta'akhkhirin* [The goal of guidance-seekers: a summary of the formal legal opinions of certain later Imams] in 1251/1835 (*al-A'lam* (y136), 3.333).

x12   'Abd al-Rahman ibn Jawzi (q0.1) is 'Abd al-Rahman ibn 'Ali ibn Muhammad al-Jawzi, born in Baghdad in 508/1114. A Hanbali Imam and one of the greatest scholars of his age in history and hadith, he authored nearly three hundred works in the sciences of hadith, Arabic grammar, Koranic exegesis, history, Sufism, physiognomy, medicine, and biographies of famous Muslims. He is sometimes confused with Ibn Qayyim al-Jawziyya, whom he was not related to, though the former's name (lit. "son of the superintendent of the Jawziyya") was derived from the name of the Jawziyya School founded by a grandson of Ibn al-Jawzi in Damascus where Ibn Qayyim's father worked: Ibn al-Jawzi died in Baghdad in 597/1201 (ibid., 3.316; and Sheikh Shu'ayb Arna'ut).

x13   'Abd al-Rahman Jaziri (f15.18) is 'Abd al-Rahman ibn Muhammad 'Awad al-Jaziri, born in Gezira Shandawil, Egypt, in 1299/1882. Educated at al-Azhar University in Cairo, he later taught there and authored his well known five-volume work on comparative Islamic law, *al-Fiqh 'ala al-madhahib al-arba'a* [Jurisprudence according to the four schools]. He died in Helwan, Egypt, in 1360/1941 (*al-A'lam* (y136), 3.334–35).

x14   (Sheikh) 'Abd al-Rahman Shaghouri (Document 1) is 'Abd al-Rahman ibn 'Abd al-Rahman al-Shaghouri, born in Homs, Syria, in 1332/1914. A Shafi'i scholar, poet, and Sufi, he moved at a young age to Damascus, where he was educated in Arabic grammar and lexicology, Sacred Law, and the Islamic religious sciences by such sheikhs as Husni al-Baghghal, Muhammad Barakat, 'Ali al-Daqar, Isma'il al-Tibi, Lutfi al-Hanafi, and others, and in Sufism by Sheikh Muhammad Hashimi, with whom he associated more than twenty years as a disciple and as the leader of his chorus of singers of mystical poetry (munshidin) at public circles of *dhikr*. Originally a weaver, then mechanic of textile machinery, and later foreman of technicians at a fabrics plant, he was instrumental in unionizing workers in the present century in Damascus, and served on the executive committee that led the Syrian Textile Workers' Union in a successful forty-day strike for workmen's compensation. He represented Syria in the United Arab Workers' Union, and has since led an active public life in seeing to the needs of Muslims. A Sufi adept, he has composed a volume (diwan) of his own poetry similar in tone and content to that of Sheikh Ahmad al-'Alawi, whose *tariqa* he is the heir and sheikh of in Damascus. In lessons with students, he teaches not only from classic texts like those of Sha'rani, and Ibn al-'Arabi's *al-Futuhat al-Makkiyya* [Meccan Revelations], but from the poetry, usually sung as odes before it is exposited, of such masters as Ibn al-Farid, al-Ghawth Abu Madyan, 'Abd al-Ghani Nabulsi, Ahmad al-'Alawi, and himself, explaining that their words are "scientific texts" (mutun 'ilmiyya) that may be correctly or incorrectly understood, depending on whether one has the knowledge and depth of Islamic learning to recognise their profound accord with the Sacred Law and faith of Islam. For this reason his *tariqa* emphasizes not only the illumination of the heart through *dhikr*, particularly by the solitary retreat (khalwa) under his strict supervision, but also the mastery of the tenets of faith of Ahl al-Sunna from classic Ash'ari texts which provide the meanings that are only given life and seriously comprehended through the gnosis of those who remember Allah much and whom Allah remembers. Sheikh 'Abd al-Rahman currently works as a professor of Islamic faith ('ilm al-tawhid) and the sciences of Arabic at a religious academy in Damascus (n).

x15   'Abd al-Ra'uf Munawi (p75.0) is Muhammad 'Abd al-Ra'uf ibn Taj al-'Arifin ibn 'Ali ibn Zayn al-'Abidin al-Munawi, born in 952/1545. A major Shafi'i scholar in the religious and traditional sciences, he lived in Cairo, where he devoted himself to research and writing, producing nearly eighty works, of which perhaps the most signal contribution is his six-volume *Fayd al-Qadir sharh al-Jami' al-saghir* [The outpouring of the Omnipotent: an exegesis of "The minor compendium"], a commentary on a famous hadith collection by Suyuti. Towards the end of his life, he weakened himself through lack of food and sleep, became ill, and finally had to dictate his works to his son. He died in 1031/1622 (*al-A'lam* (y136), 6.204; and n).

x16   'Abd al-Wahhab Khallaf (a1.1) is 'Abd al-Wahhab ibn 'Abd al-Wahid Khallaf, a twentieth-century Arabist, scholar, and specialist in Islamic jurisprudence. Born in 1305/1888 in Kafr al-Ziyat, Egypt, he graduated from the school of Islamic judiciary in Cairo in 1912, and also served as an inspector of Islamic courts in Cairo and as a member of the Academy of the Arabic Language. He was appointed assistant professor of Islamic jurisprudence in the Faculty of Law at the University of Cairo in 1935 and became full professor in 1948, authoring several works on Sacred Law and Koranic exegesis, among them *'Ilm usul al-fiqh* [The science of the fundamentals of Islamic jurisprudence], which is widely used in universities throughout the Islamic world. He died in Cairo in 1375/1956 (*al-A'lam* (y136), 4.184).

x17   'Abd al-Wahhab Sha'rani (c6.5) is 'Abd al-Wahhab ibn Ahmad ibn 'Ali al-Hanafi al-Sha'rani, born in 898/1493 in Qalqanshada, Egypt. A Shafi'i scholar and prolific author of works in Sufism, Sacred Law, and tenets of faith, he is probably most famous in the legal sphere for his classic, *al-Mizan al-kubra* [The supreme scale], in which he comparatively studies the rulings of all four Sunni schools of Sacred Law as if they were a single school, treating their differences according to their difficulty as either strictness ('azima) or dispensation (rukhsa). He was also a sheikh and adept in Sufism, among its outstanding Arab spokesmen, showing the unity between law and way in works that have remained popular to this day, among them *Lata'if al-minan wa al-akhlaq* [Subtleties of gifts and character], *Lawaqih al-anwar al-qudsiyya* [The fecundating sacred illuminations], and *Kitab al-yawaqit wa al-jawahir fi bayan 'aqa'id al-akabir* [The book of rubies and jewels: an explanation of the tenets of faith of mystic luminaries]. He died in Cairo in 973/1565 (ibid., 4.180–81; and n).

x18   'Abd al-Wahid ibn Zayd (w26.1) was one of the pious early Muslims. He knew Hasan al-Basri and other spiritual figures of his time, and was among those given to praying at night, for forty years performing the dawn prayer (subh) with the ablution (wudu) he had made for the nighfall prayer ('isha) (*al-Tabaqat al-kubra* (y124), 1.46).

x19   (Sheikh) 'Abd al-Wakil Durubi (Introduction) is 'Abd al-Wakil ibn 'Abd al-Wahid ibn Sa'id al-Durubi, Shafi'i sheikh, Sufi, and imam of Jami' Darwish Pasha (al-Darwishiyya) Mosque in Damascus. Born in 1333/1914 in Homs, Syria, he moved at the age of eighteen to Zabadani, where he read various Shafi'i works with Sheikh Ibrahim Tayyib al-Ghazzi, teacher in the school of Islamic judiciary, and with Sheikh Muhammad Salim Taha, the mufti of Zabadani. He studied a number of Shafi'i legal classics with them during his eighteen-year residence there including *al-Iqna' fi hall alfaz Abi Shuja'* [The persuading: an explanation of the terms in "Abu Shuja'"] by Muhammad Shirbini Khatib, the *Hashiya* [Commentary] of Sheikh Ibrahim Bajuri, and others in Shafi'i law, as well as works on fundamentals of Islamic belief ('ilm al-tawhid), hadith, Koranic exegesis, and

Sufism, before moving in 1950 to Damascus, where he was appointed imam of the Darwishiyya. The translator can attest to both his remarkable memory, which holds a number of traditional works in the Islamic sciences (mutun) in their entirety, and to his deep comprehension of Sacred Law and its ancillary disciplines, enriched by over thirty-five years of reading and discussion in his library and bookshop off the courtyard of the mosque. He has published a number of the works of scholars and mystics, among them a volume of poetry by 'Abd al-Ghani Nabulsi entitled *Diwan al-haqa'iq wa majmu' al-raqa'iq* [The collected poems of higher spiritual realities and compendium of heartfelt subtleties], Sheikh Ahmad al-'Alawi's *Diwan* [Collected poems] and *al-Minah al-quddusiyya fi sharh al-Murshid al-mu'in bi tariq al-Sufiyya* [Sacred gifts: a Sufi exegesis of "The helping guide"], Abul Mawahib Shadhili's *Qawanin hukm al-ishraq* [The laws of the dawning of illumination], and others. *'Umdat al-salik* was chosen to be translated for the present volume at his suggestion. His first sheikh in Sufism was Sa'd al-Din al-Jabawi of the Sa'diyya tariqa in Homs, who sent him to Sheikh Muhammad Hashimi when he moved to Damascus. As someone who knows through firsthand experience, he emphasizes the need for students of the Islamic disciplines to have a spiritual path to train the heart and avoid the dangers of pride and unworthy intention inherent in acquiring and teaching such knowledge. If there are increasingly fewer scholars like Sheikh 'Abd al-Wakil left in the world, it may happen that Allah will make the present work endure as a testimony to future generations of Muslims as to the seriousness and depth with which men like him understood Sacred Law, for the spirit that imbues the book is his (n).

x20   'Abdullah ibn 'Amr (w17.2) is 'Abdullah ibn 'Amr ibn al-'As (Allah be well pleased with him), one of the most renowned Companions of the Prophet (Allah bless him and give him peace), an ascetic whose keen intelligence was reflected in his devotion to worshipping Allah Most High, which he did until the Prophet (Allah bless him and give him peace) had to remind him, "Verily, your body, your wife, and your eyes have rights upon you ...." Among the main transmitters of hadiths, he was literate before entering Islam. He participated in the Muslim's battles, and at the end of his life lost his eyesight, dying in 65/684 (*al-A'lam* (y136), 4.111).

x21   'Abdullah ibn Abu Bakr ibn Muhammad ibn 'Amr ibn Hazm (w16.2) was a reliable hadith transmitter (thiqa) whose hadiths are recorded in Bukhari, Muslim, and other main collections, and who lived and served as a judge in Medina. He died in A.H. 135 at seventy years of age (*Taqrib al-tahdhib* (y16), 297).

x22   'Abdullah ibn Burayda (w29.2(6)) is 'Abdullah ibn Burayda ibn al-Husayb al-Aslami. One of those who met and studied under the Companions, he was the judge of Merv (in present-day Turkmen S.S.R.) and a reliable hadith transmitter (thiqa) whose hadiths are recorded in all six main hadith collections. He died in A.H. 105 at one hundred years of age (ibid., 297; and n).

x23   (Sheikh) 'Abdullah Diraz (b4.1) edited the four-volume *al-Muwafiqat* [Correspondences] of al-Shatibi in fundamentals of Islamic jurisprudence, and was among the religious scholars of Dumyat, Egypt, at the turn of the present century (Sheikh Shu'ayb Arna'ut).

x24   'Abdullah Mahfuz Ba'alawi (w29.1) is 'Abdullah ibn Mahfuz ibn Muhammad al-Haddad al-Ba'alawi, a contemporary Shafi'i scholar who was born in al-
Deys, South Yemen, in 1923. He studied at religious academies in Hadramawt,
was appointed as a judge in 1946, as presiding head of the court of appeals in
Mukalla in 1960, and as head of the judiciary of Hadramawt in 1965, a position
from which he resigned in 1970. In 1976 he was appointed lecturer in 'Aden University (al-Sunna wa al-bid'a (y20), back cover).

x25   'Abdullah Muhammad Ghimari (w29.4) is 'Abdullah ibn Muhammad ibn
al-Siddiq ibn Ahmad al-Ghimari, born in Tangiers, Morocco, in 1328/1910, a
descendant of the Prophet (Allah bless him and give him peace) through Hasan,
the son of 'Ali and Fatima (Allah be well pleased with them), and on his mother's
side from the Moroccan Sufi Ibn 'Ajiba. A specialist in Maliki and Shafi'i jurisprudence, fundamentals of Islamic law and faith (usul), and Arabic lexicology, he is
among the foremost living hadith experts (muhaddithin) and scholars in Sacred
Law. He first studied the Islamic sciences under the traditional scholars of
Morocco of his day, among them his father, the hadith specialist Muhammad ibn
Siddiq Ghimari, and Sheikh 'Abbas Bannani, after which he attended the
Qarawiyyin Madrasa in Fez, and then al-Azhar, whose scholars took him as an
authority and reference in the sciences of hadith, and where he studied under such
sheikhs as the grand mufti of Egypt Muhammad Bakhit al-Muti'i before returning
to Morocco, where he deepened his knowledge of hadith under the tutelage of his
brother, the hadith master (hafiz) Ahmad ibn Muhammad ibn Siddiq. He has
authored nearly 150 books and treatises on the sciences of Islam, which amply
attest to his rank among contemporaries, among the most famous of which are his
Bida' al-tafasir [The blameworthy innovations of Koranic exegeses], and al-Radd
al-muhkam al-matin [The invincibly strong rebuttal], which explains in detail why
Sunni Islam rejects the innovations of the Wahhabi sect in faith and works. He is
the sheikh of the Siddiqiyya branch of the Shadhili tariqa, and presently lives and
teaches at the order's zawiya in Tangiers (Sheikh Hasan Saqqaf; and n).

x26   'Abdullah ibn Shaqiq al-'Uqayli (w18.3(3)), originally of Basra, was a
reliable transmitter (thiqa) who related hadiths from such narrators as 'Abdullah
ibn Suraqa and 'Abdullah ibn Abi Jadh'a (Allah be well pleased with them), and
whose hadiths appear in the collections of Bukhari, Muslim, and others. He died
in A.H. 108 (Siyar a'lam al-nubala' (y37), 1.6, 11.110; and Taqrib al-tahdhib (y16),
307).

x27   'Abdullah ibn Unays (w53.1) is 'Abdullah ibn Unays al-Juhani (Allah be
well pleased with him), a prophetic Companion who lived in Medina, swore fealty
to the Prophet (Allah bless him and give him peace) at 'Aqaba, and fought at the
battle of Uhud. He died in Damascus in A.H. 54 during the caliphate of Mu'awiya
(Taqrib al-tahdhib (y16), 296).

x28   Abraham (see Ibrahim, x180)

x29   Abu 'Abd al-Rahman Sulami (w9.11) is Muhammad ibn al-Husayn ibn
Musa, Abu 'Abd al-Rahman al-Sulami, born in Nishapur, Persia, in 325/936. A
Shafi'i scholar and one of the foremost historians and sheikhs of the Sufis, he

wrote over a hundred works, among the most widely read of them his *Tabaqat al-Sufiyya* [The successive generations of Sufis]. He died in Nishapur in 412/1021 (*al-A'lam* (y136), 6.99; and *Tabaqat al-Shafi'iyya al-kubra* (y128), 4.143).

x30   Abu 'Ali Daqqaq (r1.3) is al-Hasan ibn 'Ali ibn Muhammad ibn Ishaq, Abu 'Ali al-Daqqaq, the Imam of the Sufis of his time and sheikh of Abul Qasim Qushayri. Originally from Nishapur, he learned Arabic there and fundamentals of Islamic faith and law, after which he travelled to Merv, where he studied Shafi'i jurisprudence and became an outstanding scholar, and then took the way of Sufism, applying himself to living what he had learned. He died in A.H. 405 (*Tabaqat al-Shafi'iyya al-kubra* (y128), 4.329–30).

x31   Abu Bakr (j13.2) is 'Abdullah ibn 'Uthman ibn 'Amir, Ibn Abi Quhafa, Abu Bakr al-Siddiq (Allah be well pleased with him) one of the greatest Companions of the Prophet (Allah bless him and give him peace). Born fifty-one years before the Hijra (A.D. 573) in Mecca, he was a prominent and wealthy figure among the Quraysh, learned, noble, and brave, and became the first adult male to accept Islam from the Prophet (Allah bless him and give him peace) and the first of the four Rightly Guided Caliphs after him. He forbade himself wine in the pre-Islamic period and did not drink. A man who saw many remarkable events during the lifetime of the Prophet (Allah bless him and give him peace), he fought in the Muslims' battles, bore their hardships, and spent his wealth to establish Islam. 'Umar ibn Khattab (Allah be well pleased with him) once attested that if the faith of Abu Bakr were placed on one side of a scale and the faith of the entire Muslim Community (Umma) on the other, Abu Bakr's would outweigh it. An eloquent speaker who was clement and forbearing towards all, he nevertheless possessed a tremendous personal courage and presence of mind that saved the day after the Prophet's death (Allah bless him and give him peace) when the desert Arabs turned from Islam and attacked the Muslims. If not for Abu Bakr's valiant and decisive leadership of the swift, hard-fought campaign that ended the insurrection, Islam might well have been lost and Allah not worshipped on the face of the earth. During his caliphate, Syria and Palestine were added to the Islamic lands as well as much of 'Iraq. He died in Medina in 13/634 (*al-A'lam* (y136), 4.102; and n).

x32   (Imam) Abu Bakr Baqillani (w57.2) is Muhammad ibn al-Tayyib ibn Muhammad ibn Ja'far, Abu Bakr al-Baqillani. An Islamic judge who was born in Basra in 338/950, he became one of the foremost figures in Islamic scholastic theology ('ilm al-kalam), and because of his logical acumen and swift, unhesitating replies, the caliph 'Adud al-Dawla dispatched him as an envoy to the Byzantine court in Constantinople, and he debated with Christian scholars in the presence of their king. He lived most of his life in Baghdad, where he authored a number of works on tenets of Islamic belief, and died in 403/1013 (*al-A'lam* (y136), 6.176).

x33   Abu Bakr Siddiq (*see* Abu Bakr, x31)

w34   Abu Darda' (a2.4) is 'Uwaymir ibn Malik ibn Qays ibn Umayya, Abu Darda' al-Khazraji (Allah be well pleased with him), one of the Medinan Helpers

(Ansar) and Companion of the Prophet (Allah bless him and give him peace), as notable among his contemporaries for his superb horsemanship as for his piety and wisdom in giving legal judgements. Before the prophetic mission he was first a merchant in Medina, and then devoted himself exclusively to worship, though when he became a Muslim he gained renown for his considerable courage in fighting for Islam. He was one of those who memorized the entire Koran during the lifetime of the Prophet (Allah bless him and give him peace), and when Mu'awiya, then a regional governor, appointed him to the judiciary in Damascus at the behest of 'Umar, he became its first judge. He died in Damascus in 32/652 (*al-A'lam* (y136), 5.98).

x35   Abu Dawud (Introduction) is Sulayman ibn al-Ash'ab ibn Ishaq ibn Bashir al-Azadi al-Sijistani, born in 202/817 in Sijistan, Persia, a Shafi'i scholar who, through numerous journeys to gain knowledge of the prophetic traditions, became a hadith master (hafiz) and the Imam of the science in his time. Muhammad ibn Ishaq al-Saghani once remarked of him, "Hadith was made subject to Abu Dawud as iron was made subject to the prophet Dawud (upon whom be peace)." And hadith master Musa ibn Ibrahim said: "Abu Dawud was created in this world for hadith, and in the next world for paradise. I have never seen better than he." Hakim observed, "Abu Dawud was the undisputed Imam of the people of hadith in his age." He died in Basra in 275/889 (ibid., 3.122; *Tabaqat al-Shafi'iyya al-kubra* (y128), 2.293; and *al-Targhib wa al-tarhib* (y9), 1.20).

x36   (Imam) Abu Hamid Ghazali (*see* (Imam) Ghazali, x127)

x37   (Imam) Abu Hanifa (b1.2) is Abu Hanifa al-Nu'man ibn Thabit, the Greatest Imam, born in A.H. 80 in Kufa. He was the scholar of Iraq and the foremost representative and exemplar of the school of juridical opinion (ra'y). The Hanafi school, which he founded, has decided court cases in the majority of Islamic lands for the greater part of Islam's history, including the Abbasid and Ottoman periods, and maintains its preeminence in Islamic courts today. Abu Hanifa was the first to analyse Islamic jurisprudence, divide it into subjects, distinguish its issues, and determine the range and criteria for analogical reasoning (qiyas) therein. Shafi'i used to say of him, "In jurisprudence, all scholars are the children of Abu Hanifa." The Imam and his school have been misunderstood by some who have believed that the Imam's knowledge of hadith was largely limited to what was transmitted by the narrators of Kufa, especially through the Companion Ibn Mas'ud. In fact, the Imam was a hadith expert who had all the hadiths of the Companions of Mecca and Medina in addition to those of Kufa, and only lacked the relatively few channels of narrators who were in Damascus. His *Musnad* [Ascribed traditions] is comparable in size to the *Muwatta'* of Imam Malik and the *Musnad* of Shafi'i which the latter based their respective schools upon, and when one reads *Muwatta' al-Imam Muhammad,* Malik's work which Abu Hanifa's disciple Muhammad ibn Hasan al-Shaybani studied and annotated for three years under Malik at Medina, one gains complete conviction from Muhammad's notes that virtually every hadith therein was familiar to Abu Hanifa before he arrived at the positions of his school, all of which is a persuasive case against the suggestions of the unlearned that Abu Hanifa did not know hadith. Nevertheless, the Imam was of an age that was plagued by hadith forgers, and he was moved by his extreme piety to reject any hadith that he was not reasonably sure was authentic, for which reason he applied a relatively selective range of hadith evidence in Sacred Law. His school, for example, does not accept qualifications or modifications of any ruling established by a Koranic verse (takhsis ayah) when such qualification comes through a hadith with but one, even if rigorously authenticated (sahih), channel of transmission, but only if it comes through a hadith with three separate channels of transmission. So despite Abu Hanifa's being a hadith specialist, his school reflects a legacy of extensive use of analogy and deduction from specific rulings and general principles established by primary texts acceptable to the Imam's rigorous standards, as well as the use of inference and juridical opinion as to what conforms to the human interests in general protected and furthered by Sacred Law.

With his legal brilliance, he was equally well known for his piety and asceticism, and though he had wealth from a number of shops selling cloth, to which he made occasional rounds in superintending their managers, he devoted his fortune to helping students and researchers in Sacred Law, and many a scholar was to realize how much the Imam's financial help had meant when it was discontinued after his death. He shunned sleep at night, and some called him the Peg because of his perpetual standing for prayer therein, often reciting the entire Koran in his nightly rak'as. He performed the dawn prayer for forty years with the ablution (wudu) made for the nightfall prayer, would only sleep a short while between his noon and midafternoon prayers, and by the end of his life, had recited the Holy Koran seven thousand times in the place where he died. He would never sit in the shade of a wall belonging to someone he had loaned money, saying, "Every loan that brings benefit is usury." He died in Baghdad in A.H. 150 at seventy years of age, leaving an intellectual and spiritual legacy that few scholars have ever equalled (*al-Tabaqat al-kubra* (y124), 1.53–54; *al-Targhib wa al-tarhib* (y9), 1.13; Sheikh Shu'ayb Arna'ut; and n).

x38   Abu Hatim (w48.2) is Muhammad ibn Idris ibn al-Mundhir ibn Dawud, Abu Hatim al-Hanzali, born in Rayy, Persia, in 195/810. He was a Shafi'i hadith master (hafiz) who was a contemporary of Bukhari and Muslim. He travelled much during his lifetime, to Iraq, Syria, Egypt, and Anatolia, and wrote a number of works in the field of hadith. He died in Baghdad in 277/890 at eighty years of age (*al-A'lam* (y136), 6.27; and *Tabaqat al-Shafi'iyya al-kubra* (y128), 2.207).

x39   Abu Hayyan Tawhidi (w57.2) is 'Ali ibn Muhammad ibn 'Abbas, Abu Hayyan al-Tawhidi. Born in Shiraz, Persia, where he taught in A.H. 400, he was an Imam in Arabic grammar and lexicology, a scholar in Shafi'i jurisprudence, history, and Sufism. Though stigmatized by Ibn Jawzi and Dhahabi as having corrupt beliefs, Taj al-Din Subki studied his works and declared: "Nothing has been established to my satisfaction about Abu Hayyan that gives reason to vituperate him. I have examined a great deal of what he said, and found nothing except a few things indicating that he had a strong personality and disdained his contemporaries, which does not deserve the criticism he has received" (*Tabaqat al-Shafi'iyya al-kubra* (y128), 5.286–88).

x40   Abu Hilman (w9.11) is Abu Hilman al-Dimashqi. Of Persian origin, he first promulgated his heretical innovations in Damascus, where he taught that every human being endowed with beauty was infused with the spirit of the Deity. He is also related to have said that whoever held his beliefs had no obligation to obey the Sacred Law (Sheikh Hasan Saqqaf).

x41   Abu Hurayra (o25.1) is 'Abd al-Rahman ibn Sakhr al-Dawsi (Allah be well pleased with him), one of the Companions of the Prophet (Allah bless him and give him peace) and the greatest of them in memorizing and relating hadiths. He came to Medina when the Prophet (Allah bless him and give him peace) was at Khaybar, and he became a Muslim in A.H. 7. He oversaw affairs at Medina for a time, and in the caliphate of 'Umar was made governor of Bahrain, though 'Umar found him too lenient and devoted to worship, and removed him, and when he later wanted to reinstate him, Abu Hurayra refused. He lived most of his life in Medina and died there in 59/679 at seventy-seven years of age (al-A'lam (y136), 3.308).

x42   Abu Ishaq Shirazi (w45.1) is Ibrahim ibn 'Ali ibn Yusuf, Abu Ishaq al-Fayruzabadi al-Shirazi, a Shafi'i Imam, teacher, and debater. Born in Fayruzabad, Persia, in 393/1003, he studied in Shiraz and Basra before coming to Baghdad where he displayed his genius in Sacred Law, becoming the mufti of the Islamic Community (Umma) of his time, the sheikh of the Nizamiyya Academy which the vizier Nizam al-Mulk built in Baghdad to accomodate Abu Ishaq's students. He was known for the persuasiveness with which he could urge a case in discussions, and he authored many works, among the most famous of them his two-volume al-Muhadhdhab fi fiqh al-Imam al-Shafi'i [The rarefaction: on the jurisprudence of Imam Shafi'i] which took him fourteen years to produce, and which furnished the basic text for Nawawi's al-Majmu': Sharh al-Muhadhdhab [The compendium: an exegesis of "The rarefaction"]. He died in Baghdad in 476/1083 (ibid., 1.51; and n).

x43   Abu Isra'il (j18.1) (Allah be well pleased with him) was a Companion of the Prophet (Allah bless him and give him peace) of whom little else is known. No one else among the Companions had this agnomen, though scholars disagree as to his true name, whether it was Qushayr, Yusayr, Qaysar, or Qays. He was of the Quraysh, though some have mistakenly supposed that he was of the people of Medina (Fath al-Bari (y17), 11.590).

x44   Abu Ja'far Khatmi (w40.5) is 'Umayr ibn Yazid ibn 'Umayr ibn Habib al-Ansari, Abu Ja'far al-Khatmi, a reliable hadith transmitter (saduq) who was the contemporary of some of the generation who met the prophetic Companions, though it is not established that he himself met any of them. Hadiths related by him appear in the collections of Abu Dawud, Tirmidhi, Nasa'i, and Ibn Majah. Originally from Medina, he lived in Basra and died sometime after A.H. 100 (Taqrib al-tahdhib (y16), 432).

x45   Abu Jahl (r38.2) is 'Amr ibn Hisham ibn Mughira, Abu al-Hakam al-Makhzumi, a noble of the Quraysh in Mecca, and enemy of Allah and His prophet (Allah bless him and give him peace). He was slain at the battle of Badr in 2/624 (al-A'lam (y136), 5.87; and al-Shifa (y116), 1.270).

x46   Abu Lahab (r38.2) is 'Abd al-'Uzza ibn 'Abd al-Muttalib ibn Hashim, the paternal uncle of the Prophet (Allah bless him and give him peace). A noble of the Quraysh, he was among the greatest in enmity against the Muslims, a proud and wealthy man who would not follow a religion brought by his brother's son. Surat al-Masad (Koran 111) was revealed in connection with him. He died after the battle of Badr in 2/624 (*al-A'lam* (y136), 4.12).

x47   Abul Hasan Ash'ari (a1.3) is 'Ali ibn Isma'il ibn Ishaq, Abu al-Hasan al-Ash'ari, the Imam of Ahl al-Sunna in tenets of faith, born in Basra in 260/874. A descendant of the Companion Abu Musa al-Ash'ari, he was a Shafi'i scholar and the founder of the school of tenets of faith that bears his name and reflects his powerful intellect and profound knowledge of the Holy Koran and hadith. Imam Ibn Hajar Haytami has defined Sunni Muslims (Ahl al-Sunna wa al-Jama'a) as "those who follow Abul Hasan Ash'ari and Abu Mansur Maturidi, the Two Imams of Ahl al-Sunna." The substantive differences between the two Imams amount to about six questions, though because the scholars of the Maturidi school were mainly confined to the lands beyond the Oxus before the Mongol depredations, and decimated thereafter, the Ash'ari school has been the standard-bearer for the faith of Sunni Islam for most of its history. Originally educated in the school of the Mu'tazilites (dis: w6.4), Imam Ash'ari saw the Prophet (Allah bless him and give him peace) in a dream three times one Ramadan, who told him, "O 'Ali, support the positions that have been transmitted from me, for they are the truth," after which he abandoned the Mu'tazilites and became the champion of Islamic orthodoxy as embodied in the Koran and hadith, defending it alike from the danger of image-worship by interpreting the divine attributes anthropomorphically, and the danger of denying the positive significance of the attributes of Allah and the life of the hereafter by explaining them away. Imam Ash'ari did not give figurative interpretations (ta'wil, dis: w6.3, w57) to problematic expressions of divine attributes, but rather urged they be accepted as they have come without saying how they are meant, while affirming that Allah is absolutely beyond any likeness to created things; though later members of his school did give such interpretations in rebuttal of anthropomorphists, preserving the faith of Islam from their innovations in the same spirit and with the same dedication that the Imam had preserved it before them by his rebuttals of the Mu'tazilites. He authored nearly three hundred books and treatises on all aspects of the faith of Ahl al-Sunna, and died in Baghdad in 324/936 (ibid., 4.263; *al-Fatawa al-hadithiyya* (y48), 280; *Tabaqat al-Shafi'iyya al-kubra* (y128), 3.347–49; A; and n).

x48   (Imam) Abul Hasan Mawardi (o25.0) is 'Ali ibn Muhammad ibn Habib, Abu al-Hasan al-Mawardi, born in Basra in 364/974. The head of the judiciary under the Abbasid caliph al-Qa'im bi Amr Illah, he was one of the foremost Shafi'i scholars of his era, and published major works in Islamic jurisprudence, Koranic exegesis, principles of law, and literature, of which his work on the caliphal system of Islamic government *al-Ahkam al-sultaniyya wa al-wilayat al-diniyya* [The rules of power and positions of religious authority] is still among the most professional available. He was respected by the caliphs of his time, and occasionally interceded for someone with them. He died in Baghdad in 450/1058 at eighty-six years of age (*al-A'lam* (y136), 4.327; *Tabaqat al-Shafi'iyya al-kubra* (y128), 5.267; and n).

x49   Abul Jahm (r9.2) is 'Amir ibn Hudhayfa ibn Ghanim, Abu al-Jahm al-Qurashi al-'Adawi (Allah be well pleased with him), a Companion of the Prophet (Allah bless him and give him peace). Some commentators say that the Prophet's advice (Allah bless him and give him peace) to a woman not to marry him because "he never leaves his stick" was an allusion to his perpetual travels away from home, while others say it referred to his harshness towards women (*al-Futuhat al-rabbaniyya* (y26), 7.13).

x50   Abul Layth (r14.2) is Mudar ibn Muhammad, Abu al-Layth al-Samarqandi of Samarkand (in present-day Uzbek S.S.R.), called the Imam of Guidance, a principle Hanafi scholar who authored works in Sacred Law, Koranic exegesis, and Islamic ethics and character (akhlaq), among the most famous of which were his *Tanbih al-ghafilin* [The apprising of the heedless] and *Bustan al-'arifin* [The grove of the gnostics]. He died in A.H. 383 (*al-Shifa* (y116), 1.51).

x51   Abul Qasim al-Junayd (c2.6) is al-Junayd ibn Muhammad ibn al-Junayd, Abu al-Qasim al-Baghdadi. Imam of the Sufis, he comprehensively joined between law and way, outward and inward, one of the most renowned mystics of Islamic history and at the same time an outstanding scholar of Sacred Law in the school of Abu Thawr. The historian Ibn al-Athir described him as "the Imam of the World of his time." Junayd once defined Sufism as "dissociating the beginninglessly eternal from that which originates in time (ifrad al-qadim 'an al-hadith)," and on another occasion simply as "the experience (al-dhawq)," both of which are typical of his succinctness. Though he left few written works, his sayings are preserved among the Sufis, to whom he remains an important authority in the path. He died in Baghdad in 297/910 (*al-A'lam* (y136), 2.141; and n).

x52   Abul Qasim al-Nasrabadhi (w9.11) is Ibrahim ibn Muhammad ibn Ahmad ibn Mahmawayh, Abu al-Qasim al-Nasrabadhi al-Naysaburi, born in Nasrabad, Persia. He was the sheikh of the Sufis of Khurasan in his time, and a scholar in hadith who studied with Ibn Khuzayma and others. Among those who transmitted hadiths from him were Imam Hakim, Sulami, and Abu 'Ali Daqqaq. At the end of his life he went on pilgrimage and remained close to the Kaaba in Mecca until his death in A.H. 367 (*Siyar a'lam al-nubala'* (y37), 16.263–64; and *Tabaqat al-Sufiyya* (y129), 484).

x53   Abul Qasim Qushayri (r1.3) is 'Abd al-Karim ibn Hawazin ibn 'Abd al-Malik, Abu al-Qasim al-Qushayri, born in Khurasan in 376/986. He was a Shafi'i scholar, Koranic exegete, and Sufi master who lived in Nishapur and authored several works, of which his *al-Risala al-Qushayriyya* [The Qushayri letter] is perhaps the most famous. He died in Nishapur in 465/1072 (*al-A'lam* (y136), 4.57; and *Tabaqat al-Shafi'iyya al-kubra* (y128), 5.153).

x54   Abu Malik Ash'ari (r27.2) is one of two Companions of the Prophet (Allah bless him and give him peace) who were known by this name, the one referred to by the hadith of our text being al-Harith ibn Harith, Abu Malik al-Ash'ari (Allah be well pleased with him), who later settled in Syria. Hadiths from him have been recorded by Muslim, Tirmidhi, and Nasa'i (*Taqrib al-tahdhib* (y16), 145; and Sheikh Shu'ayb Arna'ut).

x55   Abu Muhammad 'Ali ibn Hazm (*see* Ibn Hazm, x161)

x56   Abu Musa (w31.1(2)) is 'Abdullah ibn Qays ibn Salim, Abu Musa al-Ash'ari (Allah be well pleased with him), one of the Companions of the Prophet (Allah bless him and give him peace) who conquered and ruled new lands for Islam. Born in Yemen twenty-one years before the Hijra (A.D. 602), it is related that he had the most beautiful voice of any of the Companions in reciting the Koran. He came to Mecca when Islam appeared and accepted it, and emigrated to Ethiopia, after which the Prophet (Allah bless him and give him peace) appointed him to govern Zabid and 'Aden in Yemen. In A.H. 17, 'Umar made him governor of Basra, from whence Abu Musa proceeded to conquer Ahvaz and Isfahan, which 'Uthman, in his caliphate, confirmed him as governor over but later removed him, whereupon Abu Musa went to Kufa, whose inhabitants asked 'Uthman to appoint him as governor over them, which he did. Upon 'Uthman's death, 'Ali confirmed his appointment, but when 'Ali asked the people of Kufa to aid him in the Battle of al-Jamal, Abu Musa ordered them not to participate, and 'Ali rescinded his confirmation. He died in Kufa in 44/665 (*al-A'lam* (y136), 4.114).

x57   Abu Nadra (w55.3) is al-Mundhir ibn Malik ibn Quta'a, Abu Nadra of Basra, a reliable hadith narrator (thiqa) of the generation who met and studied under the Companions. His hadiths appear in the collections Bukhari, Muslim, Tirmidhi, Nasa'i, and others. He died in A.H. 108 or 109 (*Taqrib al-tahdhib* (y16), 546).

x58   Abu Nu'aym (w40.5) is Ahmad ibn 'Abdullah ibn Ahmad, Abu Nu'aym al-Asbahani, born in Isfahan, Persia, in 336/948. He was a Shafi'i scholar, hadith master (hafiz), and historian, who was reliable in memory and transmission. He is perhaps most famous for his ten-volume *Hilya al-awliya'* [The adornment of the saints], in which he records the lives and sayings of the early Muslims and friends of Allah (awliya'). He died in Isfahan in 430/1038 (*al-A'lam* (y136), 1.157; and *Tabaqat al-Shafi'iyya al-kubra* (y128), 4.18).

x59   Abu Sa'id 'Ala'i (w48.2) is Khalil ibn Kaykaldi ibn 'Abdullah, Abu Sa'id Salah al-Din al-'Ala'i, born in Damascus in 694/1295. He was educated in Damascus and became a hadith specialist and Shafi'i scholar, authoring many works in both Sacred Law and hadith. After much travel, he settled in Jerusalem, where he took a post as a teacher in al-Salahiyya school in A.H. 731, and later died there in 761/1359 (*al-A'lam* (y136), 2.321).

x60   Abu Sa'id al-Khudri (w29.2(4)) is Sa'd ibn Malik ibn Sinan, Abu Sa'id al-Khudri al-Khazraji (Allah be well pleased with him) one of the Medinan Helpers (Ansar), a Companion of the Prophet (Allah bless him and give him peace) who was born ten years before the Hijra (A.D. 613). He constantly kept the company of the Prophet (Allah bless him and give him peace), and some 1,170 hadiths were related by him. He participated in twelve of the Muslims' battles, and died in Medina in 74/693 (ibid., 3.87).

x61   Abu Sufyan (r2.19) is Sakhr ibn Harb ibn Umayya ibn 'Abd al-Shams ibn

'Abd al-Manaf, Abu Sufyan (Allah be well pleased with him), born fifty-seven years before the Hijra (A.D. 567). One of the nobles of the Quraysh in the pre-Islamic period, he was a Companion of the Prophet (Allah bless him and give him peace) and the father of Mu'awiya, head of the Umayyad caliphate. He led the Meccan idolators against the Muslims in the battles of Uhud and the Confederates, and entered Islam the day Mecca was conquered by the Muslims. A redoubtable warrior, he lost one eye fighting for Islam in the battle of Ta'if, and the other in the battle of Yarmouk, becoming totally blind. He died in Medina in 31/652 (ibid., 3.201).

x62   Abu Talha (w50.5) is Zayd ibn Sahl ibn al-Aswad, Abu Talha (Allah be well pleased with him) a Companion of the Prophet (Allah bless him and give him peace) who was born thirty-six years before the Hijra (A.D. 585) in Medina. A superb and valiant archer, he was one of the most celebrated Medinan Helpers (Ansar), swearing fealty to the Prophet (Allah bless him and give him peace) at 'Aqaba, and fighting in the battles of Badr, Uhud, and the rest. He died in Medina in 34/654 (ibid., 3.58–59).

x63   Abu Talib Makki (w52.2) is Muhammad ibn 'Ali ibn 'Atiyya, Abu Talib al-Harithi al-Makki. Born in Iraq between Baghdad and Wasit, he waš a Sufi, preacher (wa'iz), ascetic, and scholar of Sacred Law. His most influential work is probably the two-volume *Qut al-qulub fi mu'amala al-Mahbub wa wasf tariq al-murid ila maqam al-tawhid* [The sustenance of hearts: on dealing with the Beloved, and a description of the way to seekers of the spiritual station of witnessing the divine unity], a direct ancestor in its arrangement and style to Ghazali's *Ihya' 'ulum al-din* [Giving life to the sciences of the religion]. He died in Baghdad in 386/996 (ibid., 6.274; and n).

x64   Abu Umama (w32.1(4)) is Sudayy ibn 'Ajlan ibn Wahb, Abu Umama al-Bahili (Allah be well pleased with him), a Companion of the Prophet (Allah bless him and give him peace). He was with 'Ali in the battle of Siffin, and later settled in Syria. Some 250 hadiths are related from him by Bukhari and Muslim. He died in Homs in 81/700, the last of the Companions to die in Syria (*al-A'lam* (y136), 3.203).

x65   Abu 'Umar (w16.2) (*see* Ibn 'Abd al-Barr, x150)

x66   Abu 'Uthman (t1.4) is Sa'id ibn Isma'il ibn Sa'id ibn Mansur, Abu 'Uthman al-Hiri, originally from Rayy, Persia. He was a Sufi who first kept the company of Yahya ibn Mu'adh and Shah al-Kirmani, and then travelled to Nishapur, where he met Hafs al-Haddad, who married his daughter to Abu 'Uthman and took the the way from him. At his hands the path of Sufism spread in Nishapur, where he died in A.H. 292 (*al-Tabaqat al-kubra* (y124), 1.86; and *Tabaqat al-Sufiyya* (y129), 170).

x67   Abu Ya'la al-Mawsuli (a4.1) is Ahmad ibn 'Ali ibn al-Muthanna al-Tamimi, Abu Ya'la al-Mawsuli. He was a hadith master (hafiz) who was known as the Hadith Scholar of Mosul (in northern Iraq), and people undertook journeys to learn from him. He composed several collections of hadith and was nearly one hundred years old when he died in Mosul in 307/919 (*al-A'lam* (y136), 1.171).

x68   Abu Yazid (t1.5) is Tayfur ibn 'Isa ibn Sarushan, Abu Yazid al-Bistami, the famous Sufi born in 188/804 in Bistam, a city between Khurasan and Iraq. His grandfather was a Zoroastrian who became a Muslim. Many miracles and ecstatic utterances are attributed to Abu Yazid, whom some consider to have been the first to speak of the 'unity of being' (wahdat al-wujud, dis: x5) in a direct way. Among his numerous sayings on Sufism is "When Allah loves a servant, He imbues him with three attributes as a proof of His love: generosity like that of the sea, beneficence like that of the sun, and humility like that of the earth." When a prominent scholar once asked him from whence he had acquired his knowledge, he replied that it was from applying the maxim, "Whoever applies what he knows, Allah bequeaths him knowledge of what he did not know." He died in Bistam in 261/875 at seventy-one years of age (ibid., 3.235; *al-Imam al-'Izz Ibn 'Abd al-Salam* (y38), 1.136; *al-Tabaqat al-kubra* (y124), 1.77; and *Tabaqat al-Sufiyya* (y129), 67).

x69   Abu Yusuf (k24.2) is Ya'qub ibn Ibrahim ibn Habib al-Ansari, Abu Yusuf al-Kufi al-Baghdadi, born in Kufa in 113/731. He was the companion and student of Abu Hanifa, and the first to propagate his school. A hadith master (hafiz) and one of the most brilliant judicial minds in Islamic history, he served as judge in Baghdad during the caliphates of al-Mahdi and al-Hadi, and as head of the judiciary under the caliph Harun al-Rashid, who made the rulings of the Hanafi school the official state code for the entire Abbasid period. He was the first to write works on the fundamentals of Hanafi jurisprudence, a *mujtahid* Imam with an extensive knowledge of Koranic exegesis who authored works in hadith in addition to his many books and treatises in Sacred Law. He died in Baghdad in 182/798 (*al-A'lam* (y136), 8.193; and n).

x70   Adam (u3.5) (upon whom be peace) was the first prophet of Allah Most High. Created by Allah without father or mother, commentators relate that he lived 960 years, the Father of Mankind whose story is mentioned in many places in the Holy Koran (*al-Futuhat al-ilahiyya* (y65), 1.39; and n).

x71   'Adil Yusuf Rayhan (Document 2) is 'Adil ibn Yusuf ibn 'Isa, Abu Muhammad Rayhan, born in Jarash, Jordan, in 1944. He is a Sufi of the Hashmi-Darqawi tariqa who first took the way in 1961 from Sheikh Muhammad Sa'id Kurdi, the successor in Jordan of Sheikh Muhammad Hashimi of Damascus. He served Kurdi until his death in 1972, and among the teachings he had from him are the words, "The remembrance of Allah is the charter of saintship (al-dhikr man-shur al-wilaya)". He read Shafi'i jurisprudence with his sheikh as well as with Sheikh Barakat, the late mufti of Irbid, Jordan, and he currently studies with Sheikh Yunus Hamdan in Amman, where he lives and has a grocery store (n).

x72   (Imam) Ahmad (b1.2) is Ahmad ibn Muhammad ibn Hanbal ibn Hilal ibn Asad, Abu 'Abdullah al-Shaybani, Imam of Ahl al-Sunna, born in 164/780 in Baghdad, where he grew up as an orphan. For sixteen years he travelled in pursuit of the knowledge of hadith, to Kufa, Basra, Mecca, Medina, Yemen, Damascus,

Morocco, Algeria, Persia, and Khurasan, memorizing one hundred thousand hadiths, thirty thousand of which he recorded in his *Musnad* [Ascribed traditions]. Imam Ahmad was among the most outstanding students of Shafi'i, who when he left Baghdad for Egypt, said, "In departing from Baghdad, I have left no one in it more godfearing, learned in Sacred Law, abstinent, pious, or knowledgeable than Ibn Hanbal."

Out of piety, Imam Ahmad never gave a formal legal opinion (fatwa) while Shafi'i was in Iraq, and when he later formulated his school of jurisprudence, he mainly drew on explicit texts from the Koran, hadith, and scholarly consensus, with relatively little expansion from analogical reasoning (qiyas). He was probably the most learned in the sciences of hadith of the four great Imams of Sacred Law, and his students included many of the foremost scholars of hadith. Abu Dawud said of him: "Ahmad's gatherings were gatherings of the afterlife: nothing of this world was mentioned. Never once did I hear him mention this-worldly things." And Abu Zur'a said: "Ahmad was even greater than Ishaq [Rahawayh] and more knowledgeable in jurisprudence. I never saw anyone more perfect than Ahmad." He never once missed praying in the night, and used to recite the entire Koran daily. He said, "I saw the Lord of Power in my sleep, and said, 'O Lord, what is the best act through which those near to You draw nearer?' and He answered, 'Through [reciting] My word, O Ahmad.' I asked, 'With understanding, or without?' and He answered, 'With understanding and without.' " Ibrahim al-Harbi noted of Ahmad, "It is as though Allah gathered in him the combined knowledge of the first and the last."

Ahmad was imprisoned and tortured for twenty-eight months under the Abbasid caliph al-Mu'tasim in an effort to force him to publicly espouse the Mu'tazilite position that the Holy Koran was created, but the Imam bore up unflinchingly under the persecution and refused to renounce the belief of Ahl al-Sunna that the Koran is the uncreated word of Allah, after which Allah delivered and vindicated him. When Ahmad died in 241/855, he was accompanied to his resting place by a funeral procession of eight hundred thousand men and sixty thousand women, marking the departure of the last of the four great *mujtahid* Imams of Islam (*al-A'lam* (y136), 1.203; *Siyar a'lam al-nubala'* (y37), 11.198–99; *al-Tabaqat al-kubra* (y124), 1.55; *al-Targhib wa al-tarhib* (y9), 1.17; and n).

x73   (Sheikh) Ahmad al-'Alawi (s4.8) is Ahmad ibn Mustafa ibn 'Aliwa, Abu al-'Abbas al-'Alawi, born in Mostaghanem, Algeria, in 1291/1874. He was a Sufi, Maliki scholar, Koranic exegete, poet, and the sheikh and renewer of the Shadhili tariqa, of which he founded the 'Alawi-Darqawi order that bears his name. His teaching stressed the threefold nature of the Muslim religion (din) as mentioned in the Gabriel hadith (dis: u1): Islam, represented by one's inward and outward submission to the rules of Sacred Law; true faith (iman), in the tenets of faith of Ahl al-Sunna; and the perfection of faith (ihsan), in the knowledge of Allah which the way of Sufism provides the means to. He authored works in each of these spheres, though his most important legacy lay in the spiritual way he founded, which emphasized knowledge of Allah (ma'rifa) through the practice of solitary retreat (khalwa) under the supervision of a sheikh, and the invocation (dhikr) of the Supreme Name.

Europeans visited the sheikh, but some who met him later wrote works that tried to assimilate him to a sort of perennialist philosophy that would consider all religious traditions as valid and acceptable reflections of but a single truth, substituting *traditional spirituality versus modern materialism* for *Islam versus unbelief*. The sheikh's own works emphatically deny their philosophy, and the reason Allah afflicted them with it would seem to be that they did not remain with the sheikh long enough to absorb his state or become as he was, a follower of the way of the prophets and purified ones, rather taking their affiliation with him as a means to legitimize opinions they had from the first and were unwilling to ever relinquish, remaking the master, as it were, in their own image. The true measure of a spiritual way, however, does not lie in books produced by writers, in the wrong or in the right, but in the hearts it opens to knowledge of divine realities conveyed by prophetic revelation, and in this Sheikh Ahmad al-'Alawi, whose order has spread to the farthest reaches of the Muslim world, certainly stands as one of the greatest Sufi masters of Islamic history. He died in Mostaghanem in 1353/1934 (*al-A'lam* (y136), 1.258; Sheikh 'Abd al-Rahman Shaghouri; and n).

x74   (Sheikh al-Islam) Ahmad Ibn Hajar 'Asqalani (*see* Ibn Hajar 'Asqalani, x159)

x75   Ahmad ibn Hanbal (*see* (Imam) Ahmad, x72)

x76   Ahmad ibn Naqib al-Misri (Title Page) is Ahmad ibn Lu'lu' ibn 'Abdullah al-Rumi, Shihab al-Din Ibn al-Naqib al-Misri. His father was a Christian convert to Islam from Antakya, Turkey, who was originally captured and made a slave by a Muslim prince who then educated him and set him free, whereupon he served the prince as a captain (naqib) and later became a Sufi in the Baybarsiyya of Cairo, where his son was born in 702/1302. Ahmad grew up among Islamic scholars, memorizing the Holy Koran in its seven canonical readings (qira'at), and at the age of twenty studied Sacred Law, which he pursued until he excelled at it. Among his sheikhs were the great Shafi'i *mujtahid* and hadith master (hafiz), Imam Taqi al-Din Subki in Islamic jurisprudence, the hadith master Ibn Mulaqqin in the sciences of hadith, and Abu Hayyan in Arabic grammar. A master of Koran recitation, Shafi'i law, Koranic exegesis, fundamentals of Islamic faith and law, Arabic, and Sufism, he memorized a great many hadiths, expecially those connected with *dhikr* and devotions, and worked at length correcting and refining Abu Ishaq Shirazi's *al-Muhadhdhab* [The rarefaction], condensing Shirazi's *al-Tanbih* [The notification], and annotating Nawawi's *Minhaj al-talibin* [The seekers' road], all of which are reflected in his most famous work, *'Umdat al-salik wa 'uddat al-nasik* [The reliance of the traveller and tools of the worshipper], the basic text of the present volume, which follows the order of Shirazi's *al-Muhadhdhab* and the conclusions of Nawawi's *Minhaj* in a work he seemingly designed and edited for practical application in life, avoiding rare and obscure legal questions, and presenting only the soundest positions of the school. He never gave formal legal opinions or accepted an official teaching position, but rather applied himself to worship, writing, and teaching a relatively small circle of students. Those who knew him described him as learned, humble, quiet, dignified, intelligent, polite, godfearing, and ascetic. Despite his rigorous self-discipline in worship, he had a good sense of humor and a talent for relating amusing anecdotes. Devoted like his father to Sufism, he performed the hajj several times, and stayed for extended periods near the Kaaba. He died of the plague in the middle of Ramadan at sixty-seven years of age in Cairo in 769/1368 (*al-A'lam* (y136), 1.200; *'Umdat al-salik wa 'uddat al-nasik* (y90), 7; and n).

x77   Ahmad Quduri (m2.8) is Ahmad ibn Muhammad ibn Ahmad ibn Ja'far ibn Hamdan, Abu al-Husayn al-Quduri, born in Baghdad in 362/973. He was a scholar in Sacred Law who became the Hanafi school's foremost representative in Iraq. His most famous work is *Kitab al-Quduri* [Quduri's book], which has remained a classic in the school for nearly a thousand years. He also authored the seven-volume *al-Tajrid* [The abstract] on differences between the Shafi'i and Hanafi schools, and died in Baghdad in 428/1037 (*al-A'lam* (y136), 1.212).

x78   Ahmad Zarruq (w9.3) is Ahmad ibn Ahmad ibn Muhammad ibn 'Isa, Abu al-'Abbas Zarruq al-Burnusi, born in Fez, Morocco, in 846/1442. He was a Sufi, Maliki scholar, and hadith specialist who studied Sacred Law in Fez, Cairo, and Medina. He then became dedicated to Sufism, withdrew from the world, and took to a wandering life. He was one of the most renowned sheikhs of the Shadhili tariqa and authored a number of works, well written and concise, that attest to their author's illumination in the spiritual way. He died in Takrin, Libya, in 899/1493 (ibid, 1.91; and n).

x79   'A'isha (b3.2) is 'A'isha bint Abu Bakr al-Siddiq 'Abdullah ibn 'Uthman (Allah be well pleased with her), the wife of the Prophet (Allah bless him and give him peace) and Mother of the Faithful, born of the Quraysh nine years before the Hijra (A.D. 613) in Mecca. She was the most knowledgeable of Muslim women in Sacred Law, religion, and Islamic behavior (adab), having married the Prophet (Allah bless him and give him peace) in the second year after the Hijra, becoming the dearest of his wives to him in Medina. She related 2,210 hadiths from the Prophet (Allah bless him and give him peace), and after his death, leading figures of the Companions would come and ask her for legal opinions, which she would supply. She died in Medina in 58/678 (*al-A'lam* (y136), 3.240).

x80   'Ala' al-Din 'Abidin (o8.7(16)) is Muhammad 'Ala' al-Din ibn Muhammad Amin ibn 'Umar ibn 'Abd al-'Aziz 'Abidin, born in Damascus in 1244/1828. The son of Imam Muhammad Amin Ibn 'Abidin, he was a first-rank Hanafi scholar in his own right who was appointed during his lifetime to many posts in the Islamic judiciary. He travelled to Istanbul and was one of the members of the panel of scholars who authored *al-Majalla* [The lawbook], among the most famous works on Islamic governmental law produced during the Ottoman period. Though he originally wrote his *al-Hadiyya al-'Ala'iyya* [The gift of 'Ala'] as a primer in Sacred Law for schoolchildren, it has become an important Hanafi legal reference for subsequent scholars. Appointed as a judge in Tripoli, Lebanon, in 1292/1875, he later returned to Damascus, where he died in 1306/1889 (ibid., 6.270; and n).

x81   'Ali (b3.2) is Imam 'Ali ibn Abi Talib ibn 'Abd al-Muttalib, Abu al-Hasan al-Hashimi al-Qurashi (Allah be well pleased with him), the Friend (Wali) of Allah, Commander of the Faithful, and fourth of the Rightly Guided Caliphs, born of noble lineage in Mecca twenty-three years before the Hijra (A.D. 600) and raised from the age of five by the Prophet (Allah bless him and give him peace), who was the son of 'Ali's paternal uncle and later married his own daughter Fatima to him. When the Prophet (Allah bless him and give him peace) paired off the Meccan Emigrants and Medinan Helpers as brothers, he told 'Ali, "You are my brother." Strong, young, and valiant, he bore the Muslims' standard into battle after battle, was a renowned swordsman, and at Khaybar the Prophet (Allah bless him and give him peace) attested to 'Ali's love of Allah and Allah's love of 'Ali. He was of the ten who were informed that they would enter paradise, and was the first male to accept Islam from the Prophet (Allah bless him and give him peace), as well as the first to pray behind him. When 'Ali became caliph in A.H. 35 after the death of 'Uthman, he made Kufa his capital and patiently bore up under the dissension and civil strife with which the Muslims were afflicted during his caliphate (dis: w56.3). Heroically courageous, a wise and fair judge, a speaker of surpassing eloquence, and a sea of spiritual wisdom, he was among the most learned of the Companions, and related hundreds of hadiths. His signet ring was engraved with the words, "Allah is the King" (Allah al-Malik). When he was assassinated while at prayer by a Kharijite at Kufa in 40/661, his last words were, "There is no god but Allah, Muhammad is the Messenger of Allah" (*al-A'lam* (y136), 4.295; *al-Tabaqat al-kubra* (y124), 1.20; and n).

x82   'Ali ibn Abi Talha (w4.5) is 'Ali ibn Salim, a client of the Bani al-'Abbas tribe. He lived in Homs, Syria, and was of the generation who were contemporaries with some of those who met the prophetic Companions, but it is not established that he himself met any of them. He was an honest hadith transmitter, but made occasional mistakes. He died in A.H. 143 (*Taqrib al-tahdhib* (y16), 402).

x83   'Ali ibn Abi Talib (*see* 'Ali, x81)

x84   'Ali al-Daqar (w41.3) is Muhammad 'Ali ibn 'Abd al-Ghani al-Daqar, born in Damascus in 1294/1877. He was a Shafi'i scholar known among his contemporaries for his learning, piety, and efforts in the cause of Islam. Of a wealthy family, he brought about a virtual renaissance of Islamic learning in Damascus by founding al-Jami'iyya al-Ghurra', an institution of more than eleven separate schools that provided food, clothing, housing, and traditional instruction to needy students, particularly those from outlying rural areas and the Horan Plain south of Damascus, who returned to their homes to teach a whole generation of Muslims the religion. During the French occupation he travelled the Syrian countryside to towns and villages with the hadith scholar Badr al-Din al-Hasani, explaining to people the obligatory character of armed jihad against the colonialists. He was a sheikh of the Tijani tariqa who had all his students take the way, and many considered him a friend (wali) of Allah Most High. An ascetic in his private life, he spent himself, his wealth, and his life in the service of Islam, and died in Damascus in 1362/1943 (*Tarikh 'ulama' Damashq* (y1), 2.586–90; Sheikh 'Abd al-Rahman Shaghouri; and n).

x85   'Ali Qari (w48.2) is 'Ali ibn Sultan Muhammad, Nur al-Din al-Mulla al-Qari, born in Herat, Afghanistan. One of the foremost Hanafi scholars of his time, he lived in Mecca, and it is related that he used to earn his income by writing out one copy of the Holy Koran each year embellished with marginal notes containing commentary and canonical readings (qira'at), and selling it to live on the

proceeds until the following year. He authored a number of works in Hanafi jurisprudence, fundamentals of Islamic faith, the sciences of hadith, Sufism, history,
Arabic lexicology, and Koranic exegesis, though the most frequently used of his
works may well be his litany *al-Hizb al-a'zam* [The supreme daily *dhikr*], in which
he gathered hundreds of supplications from prophetic hadiths and divided them
into seven parts, one to be read each day of the week—a litany that forms an integral part of Muhammad al-Juzuli's celebrated manual of *dhikr, Dala'il al-khayrat*
[Guides to blessings]. He died in Mecca in 1014/1606 (*al-A'lam* (y136), 5.12;
and n).

x86   Allah (*see* v1.1)

x87   al-Amidi (b3.3) is 'Ali ibn Muhammad ibn Salim al-Taghlibi, Abu al-
Hasan Sayf al-Din al-Amidi, a specialist in fundamentals of Islamic law and faith
who was born in 551/1156 in Amid (present-day Diyarbakir, Turkey). Originally
a Hanbali, he became a Shafi'i when he came to Baghdad to study hadith, after
which he travelled first to Damascus and then to Cairo, where he taught and
became widely known. Some scholars there later grew envious of his reputation
and accused him of heresy, forcing him to leave Cairo secretly and take refuge in
Hama, Syria, from whence he proceeded to Damascus. He wrote some twenty
works, the most famous of which is his four-volume *al-Ihkam fi usul al-ahkam*
[The proficiency: on fundamentals of legal rulings]. He died in 631/1233 (*al-A'lam*
(y136), 4.332; and *Tabaqat al-Shafi'iyya al-kubra* (y128), 8.306).

x88   'Amr ibn Hazm (w16.2) is 'Amr ibn Hazm ibn Zayd ibn Lawdhan (Allah
be well pleased with him), a Medinan Helper and Companion of the Prophet
(Allah bless him and give him peace). He participated in the Battle of the Confederates and in subsequent battles, and when the Prophet (Allah bless him and give
him peace) appointed him governor over Najran, he wrote him a lengthy letter of
covenant containing legislation and instruction. He died in 53/673 (*al-A'lam*
(y136), 5.76).

x89   'Amr ibn Shu'ayb (w17.2) is 'Amr ibn Shu'ayb ibn Muhammad ibn 'Abdullah ibn 'Amr ibn al-'As, a reliable hadith narrator (saduq) of the generation of
whom some met the Companions. His hadiths were related by Abu Dawud, Tirmidhi, Nasa'i, and Ibn Majah. He died in A.H. 118 (*Taqrib al-tahdhib* (y16), 423).

x90   Anas (a4.1) is Anas ibn Malik ibn Nadar al-Khazraji (Allah be well
pleased with him), a Medinan Helper and Companion of the Prophet (Allah bless
him and give him peace). Born ten years before the Hijra (A.D. 612) in Medina,
he entered Islam while young, was the personal servant of the Prophet during the
last ten years of his life (Allah bless him and give him peace), and related over
2,200 hadiths. After the Prophet's death (Allah bless him and give him peace), he
travelled to Damascus and later settled in Basra. The Prophet (Allah bless him
and give him peace) prayed that Allah would bless him with abundance (baraka)
in his wealth, life, and offspring, and grant him forgiveness; and he became
among the wealthiest of men, had over 120 children and grandchildren at the time
of his death, an orchard that bore fruit twice a year, and he lived until he was tired
of living any longer, dying in Basra at one hundred years of age in 93/712, the last

of the Companions to die there (*al-A'lam* (y136), 2.24–25; and *al-Shifa* (y116), 1.47).

x91   The Antichrist (w9.9) is Ibn Sayyad al-Masih al-Dajjal of Bani Isra'il, according to Imam Nawawi alive at the present day among the Jews. He will come forth at the end of time, claim to be a deity, and work wonders, bringing forth a heaven, a hell, and mountains of bread, though he will be unable to enter Mecca or Medina. The prophet 'Isa (upon whom be peace) will slay him at his Final Coming (*al-Shifa* (y116); 1.663; and A).

x92   Ash'ari (*see* Abul Hasan Ash'ari, x47)

x93   (Imam) 'Asqalani (*see* Ibn Hajar 'Asqalani, x159)

x94   Asuf ibn Barkhiya (w30.1(3)) was the vizier of the prophet Sulayman (upon whom be peace), a *siddiq* (great-faithed one) who was steadfastly true to Allah and to his fellow men, a friend (wali) of Allah Most High to whom Allah vouchsafed many miracles (*al-Futuhat al-ilahiyya* (y65), 3.315).

x95   Ayyub (u3.5) is Ayyub ibn Amwas ibn Razih ibn 'Ays ibn Ishaq ibn Ibrahim (upon whom be peace), the prophet and messenger of Allah Most High, who mentions him in various places in the Holy Koran. He is best known for his proverbial steadfastness and patience in affliction (*al-Futuhat al-ilahiyya* (y65), 2.58; and *al-Shifa* (y116), 1.293).

x96   al-'Azizi (b7.5) is 'Ali ibn Ahmad ibn Muhammad al-'Azizi al-Bulaqi, born in al-'Aziziyya, Egypt. He was a scholar of Shafi'i jurisprudence and hadith who authored various works, of which his three-volume *al-Siraj al-munir sharh al-Jami' al-saghir* [The lightgiving lamp: an exegesis of "The minor compendium"], a commentary on a famous hadith collection by Suyuti, is perhaps the most well known. He died in Bulaq in 1070/1660 (*al-A'lam* (y136), 4.258).

x97   'Azra'il (u3.3) is not mentioned by name in the Koran, but referred to only as the "Angel of Death" (Malak al-Mawt). In reality it is Allah who reclaims the souls of men from their bodies, but He does so by means of the Angel of Death, whom He orders to take a person's soul when the time arrives. 'Azra'il has helpers in this from the angels of mercy and angels of torment, depending on whom the deceased is, and they draw out the spirit of the deceased until it reaches the throat, when 'Azra'il takes it himself. The whole world has been made as if it were the size of an open palm for him, and he takes the soul of anyone he wishes, from east to west, without difficulty (*al-Futuhat al-ilahiyya* (y65), 2.40, 3.415; and n).

x98   Badr al-Din al-Hasani (e14.1) is Muhammad Badr al-Din ibn Yusuf ibn Badr al-Din ibn 'Abd al-Rahman al-Hasani, born in Damascus in 1267/1850. The son of a Moroccan Maliki scholar, Badr al-Din followed the Hanafi school and became the hadith scholar of Damascus of his time. He memorized the Holy Koran, the *Sahih*s of Bukhari and Muslim with their texts and channels of transmission, and twenty thousand verses of the rhyming mnemonic texts (mutun) that

Islamic scholars formerly used to commit to memory to have a framework within which to remember and understand the more detailed works of the Islamic sciences that they would read with their sheikhs. After this, he devoted himself to worship and teaching, living an ascetic life of fasting and service to the Muslim community. He wrote works in many fields, including hadith, tenets of Islamic faith, Koranic exegesis, mathematics, logic, and Arabic grammar. The attribution to him of the formal legal opinion (fatwa) mentioned at e14.1 of the present volume was made by Sheikh Shu'ayb Arna'ut, Sheikh 'Abd al-Wakil Durubi, and others. He died in Damascus in 1354/1935 (*al-A'lam* (y136), 7.157–58; and n).

x99   (Imam) Baghawi (w4.3) is al-Husayn ibn Mas'ud ibn Muhammad ibn al-Farra', Abu Muhammad Muhyi al-Sunna al-Baghawi, born in Bagha, Persia, in 436/1044. Known to contemporaries as the Reviver of the Sunna, he was an Imam in Shafi'i jurisprudence, hadith, and Koranic exegesis, writing valuable works in each, among them his sixteen-volume *Sharh al-sunna* [The explanation of the sunna], which proceeds through the usual chapter arangement of works on Shafi'i jurisprudence, discussing the hadiths and Koranic verses upon which the rulings of the school are based, and how the various other Imams have understood them. His commentary on the Holy Koran *Lubab al-ta'wil fi ma'alam al-Tanzil* [The quintessence of interpretation: on features of the Revelation], has also proved very popular among scholars and been printed in several editions. He died in Merv (in present-day Turkmen S.S.R.) in 510/1117 (*al-A'lam* (y136), 2.259; and n).

x100   Bajuri (k1.1) is Ibrahim ibn Muhammad ibn Ahmad al-Bajuri, born in Bajur, Egypt, in 1198/1784. Educated at al-Azhar, he was one of the foremost Shafi'i scholars and theologians of his time, authoring over twenty works and commentaries in Sacred Law, tenets of faith, Islamic estate division, scholastic theology, logic, and Arabic. In A.H. 1263 he was appointed Sheikh of al-Azhar, an office he remained in until his death in Cairo in 1288/1860 (*al-A'lam* (y136), 1.71).

x101   Baqillani (*see* (Imam) Abu Bakr Baqillani, x32)

x102   Baydawi (r21.1) is 'Abdullah ibn 'Umar ibn Muhammad ibn 'Ali, Nasir al-Din al-Shirazi al-Baydawi, born in Bayda, near Shiraz, Persia. He was a Shafi'i scholar, judge, and Koranic exegete whose commentary *Anwar al-Tanzil wa asrar al-ta'wil* [The lights of the Revelation and secrets of interpretation] is so well known that whenever scholars mention "The Judge" (al-Qadi) in the context of Koranic commentary, it is Baydawi who is meant. He wrote a number of other scholarly works in tenets of faith, jurisprudence, and Arabic, as well as a history in Persian. After serving as a judge in Shiraz, he moved to Tabriz, where he died in 685/1286 (*al-A'lam* (y136), 4.110; and n).

x103   Bayhaqi (f8.44) is Ahmad ibn al-Husayn ibn 'Ali, Abu Bakr al-Bayhaqi, born in Khasrajand, a village around Bayhaq near Nishapur, Persia, in 384/994. A principle hadith master (hafiz) and Shafi'i Imam, he was raised in Bayhaq, but travelled to gain Sacred Knowledge to Baghdad, Kufa, Mecca, and other cities. Dhahabi was to say of him, "Had Bayhaqi wanted to found his own school of jurisprudence and be its *mujtahid*, he would have been able to, because of the vast

range of subjects of which he was a master, and his knowledge of scholarly differences.'' Bayhaqi's works amount to nearly one thousand volumes, treating the
sciences of hadith, Koranic exegesis, Sacred Law, tenets of faith, and other subjects. The Imam of the Two Sanctuaries Juwayni once observed, ''Every Shafi'i
scholar is indebted to Shafi'i except Bayhaqi, to whom Shafi'i is indebted for his
writing so many works strengthening the school, expanding questions on which
the Imam had been brief, and supporting his positions.'' He died in Nishapur in
458/1066 (*al-A'lam* (y136), 1.116).

x104   B.G. Martin (w9.4) is Bradford G. Martin, a professor who has taught
and written about Sufism and Muslim Africa since 1963. The preface to his *Muslim Brotherhoods in Nineteenth-Century Africa* was written in Bloomington,
Indiana, in 1976. The book accurately reports the names and dates of the events
it discusses, though its explanations of Muslim figures, their motives, and their
place within the Islamic world are observed through the lens of unbelief (kufr),
giving an inverted image of many of the realities thus beheld, and perhaps
calling for a word here on the literature that has been termed *Orientalism*, or in
the contemporary idiom, ''area studies.''
    It is a viewpoint requiring that scholarly description of something like ''Afri-
can Islam'' (Martin's phrase) be first and foremost *objective*. The premises of this
objectivity conform closely, upon reflection, to the lived and felt experience of a
post-religious, Western intellectual tradition in understanding religion; namely,
that comparing human cultural systems and societies in their historical succession
and multiplicity leads the open-minded observer to moral relativism, since no
moral value can be discovered which on its own merits is transculturally valid.
Here, human civilizations, with their cultural forms, religions, hopes, aims,
beliefs, prophets, sacred scriptures, and deities, are essentially plants that grow
out of the earth, springing from their various seeds and soils, thriving for a time,
and then withering away. The scholar's concern is only to record these elements
and propose a plausible relation between them.
    Such a point of departure, if *de rigueur* for serious academic works like *Mus-
lim Brotherhoods*, is of course non-Islamic and anti-Islamic. As a fundamental
incomprehension of Islam, it naturally distorts what it seeks to explain, yet with
an observable disparity in the *degree* of distortion in any given description that
seems to correspond roughly to how close the object of explanation is to the core
of Islam. In dealing with central issues like Allah, the Prophet (Allah bless him
and give him peace), the Koran, or hadith, it is at its worst; while the further it
proceeds to the periphery, such as historical details of trade concessions, treaties,
names of rulers, weights of coins, etc., the less distorted it becomes. In either
case, it is plainly superior for Muslims to rely on fellow Muslims when Islamic
sources are available on a subject (and there are few imaginable subjects that
Islamic scholars have not discussed in detail and written highly interesting and
professional works about), if only to avoid the subtle and not-so-subtle distortions
of non-Islamic works about Islam. One cannot help but feel that nothing bad
would happen to us if we were to abandon the trend of many contemporary Muslim writers of faithfully annotating our works with quotes from the founding
fathers of Orientalism, if only because to sleep with the dogs is generally to rise
with the fleas. And where Islamic works cannot be found and non-Islamic sources
are used, we should keep in mind that their premises are those of unbelief, and

how this colors the whole process of scholarly inquiry. We find in *Muslim Brotherhoods*, for example, a discussion of a hypothesized alteration in the "carbon dioxide-oxygen balance in the brain," resulting from communal remembrance of Allah (dhikr) and producing a susceptibility to visions, hallucinations, and intense emotional experiences that enabled African Sufi brotherhoods to "generate much love and devotion" between members, who could thereby be more successfully directed towards collective action. When one looks at the men being explained, however, those who risked their lives in jihad against the enemies of Allah for four, twelve, fifteen, twenty-one, or thirty-five years, an explanation of their motivations that downplays faith in Allah and His messenger (Allah bless him and give him peace) must surely need a great deal more to be convincing than this type of fatuous detail. Or the suggestion that a *mujahid* scholar who had memorized the Holy Koran and the *Sahih* collections of Bukhari and Muslim, and lived and taught the strictest adherence to Islam by precept and example for a lifetime of seventy years ('Umar Tal, x355) might have committed suicide after a defeat in battle—a report based on a single story told by a blacksmith of unknown veracity some twenty-six years after the event—such aspects show little appreciation of psychological absurdities in an Islamic context.

Though there is little doubt that B.G. Martin's work is a sincere attempt to understand its subject matter, and one that incidentally uses much original African source material, it should be understood by Muslims for what it is, an account of "African Islam"—of religious men, sacrifices, and motives—from a point of view that has been sanitized of anything religious to guard its "objectivity" (*Muslim Brotherhoods* (y86), preface and bibliography; Sharif 'Abdul-Karim; and n).

x105   Bilal (w29.2) is Bilal ibn Rabah, Abu 'Abdullah al-Habashi (Allah be well pleased with him), the muezzin of the Prophet (Allah bless him and give him peace) and his watchman over the Muslim common fund (bayt al-mal). A hadith says of him, "Bilal is the foremost of the Ethiopians." One of the earliest converts to Islam, he was present at every battle with the Prophet (Allah bless him and give him peace), and when the latter died, Bilal called the Muslims to prayer for his last time. He lived in Medina until Muslim armies were dispatched to Syria and then travelled with them, dying in Damascus in 20/641 (*al-'Alam* (y136), 2.73).

x106   Bint Harith (w30.1) is Zaynab bint al-Harith, the sister of 'Uqba ibn al-Harith, who killed Khubayb al-Ansari (x220) (*Fath al-Bari* (y17), 7.382).

x107   Bukhari (Introduction) is Muhammad ibn Isma'il ibn Ibrahim ibn Mughira, Abu 'Abdullah al-Bukhari, born in Bukhara (in present-day Uzbek S.S.R.) in 194/810. Raised as an orphan, he was a Shafi'i scholar who learned Sacred Law in Mecca from 'Abdullah ibn Zubayr al-Humaydi, the disciple of Shafi'i, and he became the greatest Imam in hadith that the world has ever known. He began his long travels in search of hadith in A.H. 210, visiting Khurasan, Iraq, Egypt, the Hijaz, and Syria, hearing hadiths from nearly a thousand sheikhs, gathering some 600,000 prophetic traditions from which he selected the approximately 4,400 (not counting those repeated) that compose his *Jami' al-Sahih* [Rigorously authenticated collection]. Choosing them for their authenticity, he was the first scholar in Islam to compile a work on this basis, and his book is the foremost of the six great hadith collections. Ibn Khuzayma said of him, "No one under the sky is more knowledgeable in hadith," and Abu 'Umar al-Khaffaf once referred to him as the "pure, godfearing scholar whom I have never seen anyone comparable to, Muhammad ibn Isma'il Bukhari, twenty times greater in knowledge of hadith than Ishaq [Rahawayh], Ahmad, or anyone else." At the end of his life some bigots attacked him for not agreeing with their misunderstanding of the uncreatedness of the Koran, and for his steadfastness in the convictions of Ahl al-Sunna they hounded him from Bukhara to Samarkand, where he died in the village of Khartan in 256/870 (*al-A'lam* (y136), 6.34; *Tabaqat al-Shafi'iyya al-Kubra* (y128), 2.212–14; *al-Targhib wa al-tarhib* (y9), 1.19; N; and n).

x108   Burayda (w18.3(2)) is Burayda ibn al-Husayb ibn 'Abdullah ibn al-Harith al-Aslami (Allah be well pleased with him), a Companion of the Prophet (Allah bless him and give him peace) who entered Islam before the battle of Badr and participated in the siege of Khaybar and conquest of Mecca. He related 167 hadiths. He lived in Medina, later moved to Basra, and finally to Merv (in present-day Turkmen S.S.R.), where he died in 63/683 (*al-A'lam* (y136), 2.50; and n).

x109   Darami (h8.8) is Muhammad ibn 'Abd al-Wahid ibn Muhammad ibn 'Umar, Abu al-Faraj al-Darami, born in Baghdad in 358/969. A gifted speaker in Arabic, he was a mathematician and legal scholar who did in-depth research in the Shafi'i school and produced a number of copious works including *Jami' al-jawami' wa muda' al-bada'i'* [The compendium of compendiums and storehouse of wonders], which details the positions of the school and evaluates the evidence for them, and *al-Istidhkar* [The reminding], which contains a large number of rare legal questions. He died in Damascus in 449/1057 (*al-A'lam* (y136), 6.254; and *Tabaqat al-Shafi'iyya al-kubra* (y128), 4.182–85).

x110   Daraqutni (m3.4) is 'Ali ibn 'Umar ibn Ahmad ibn Mahdi, Abu al-Hasan al-Daraqutni, born in Dar al-Qutn, a neighborhood in Baghdad, in 306/919. He was a Shafi'i scholar who was among the Imams of his time in hadith, and the first to record the canonical readings of the Holy Koran (qira'at) in a work. He travelled to Egypt, where he helped Ibn Hanzaba compose his *Musnad* [Ascribed traditions] and then returned to Baghdad. He wrote a number of works on hadith, the most famous of which is his *Sunan* [Sunnas]. He died in Baghdad in 385/995 (*al-A'lam* (y136), 4.314).

x111   David (*see next entry*)

x112   Dawud (u3.5) is Dawud ibn Isha (upon whom be peace), a prophet of Allah Most High to Bani Isra'il. He was the first to forge iron into chain mail, and is mentioned more than once in the Holy Koran. While still a boy, he slew the giant Jalut (Goliath), a deed for which King Talut (Saul) gave him his daughter in marriage and half his kingdom. Dawud lived with the king for forty years until the latter's death, after which he lived another seven years and then died too (*al-Futuhat al-ilahiyya* (y65), 1.204).

x113   (The) Devil (*see* Satan, x321)

x114   (Imam) Dhahabi (Introduction) is Muhammad ibn Ahmad ibn 'Uthman ibn Qaymaz, Abu 'Abdullah Shams al-Din al-Dhahabi, the great Shafi'i hadith master (hafiz) and historian of Islam, born in Damascus in 673/1274. Of Turkoman origin, he first studied in Damascus and then travelled to Cairo and other cities in pursuit of Sacred Knowledge. He authored nearly a hundred works, some of them of considerable size, like his twenty-three volume *Siyar a'lam al-nubala'* [The lives of noble figures], or his thirty-six volume *Tarikh al-Islam al-kabir* [Major history of Islam]. In addition to his mastery of hadith, he was also an Imam in canonical Koranic readings (qira'at) and textual criticism. He went blind about seven years before his death, and died in Damascus in 748/1348 (*al-A'lam* (y136), 5.326; *Kitab al-kaba'ir* (y36), 23–25; and *Tabaqat al-Shafi'iyya al-kubra* (y128), 9.100).

x115   Dhul Kifl (u3.5) is Hizqil (upon whom be peace), a prophet of Allah Most High to Bani Isra'il. He was the third prophet to succeed Musa (upon whom be peace), and commentators relate that he was nicknamed Dhul Kifl (lit. "He of the Guarantee") because he gave his guarantee to the wicked of Bani Isra'il that he would ensure the appearance on a particular day of seventy prophets whom they wished to kill, putting up his own life in forfeit, after which he told the prophets, "Go, it is that I should be killed than you." When the time for the execution arrived and Dhul Kifl was asked about them, he merely said he did not know where they had gone, after which Allah Most High saved him too (*al-Siraj al-munir* (y72), 1.158).

x116   Dhul Nun al-Misri (t1.9) is Thawban ibn Ibrahim, Abu al-Fayd al-Ikhmimi al-Misri, the famous Egyptian ascetic and saint. One of the greatest of the early Sufis, he was of Nubian origin and had a gift for expressive aphorisms, of which a large number have fortunately been preserved. He was the first in Egypt to speak of the states and spiritual stations of the way. The Abbasid caliph al-Mutawakkil charged him with heresy (zandaqa) and had him brought to him, but upon hearing Dhul Nun speak he realized his innocence and released him, whereupon he returned to Egypt. He died in Giza in 245/859 (*al-A'lam* (y136), 2.102; and n).

x117   Elias (*see* Ilyas, x186)

x118   Elisha (*see* al-Yasa', x374)

x119   Enoch (*see* Idris, x185)

x120   Eve (w32.1(4)) is Hawa', the wife of the prophet Adam (upon whom be peace), created from him to become the Mother of Mankind. She was named Hawa' because she was created directly from a living being (hayy), Adam, in his sleep without his being aware of it or feeling any pain therefrom (*al-Siraj al-munir* (y72), 1.49).

x121   Ezekial (*see* Dhul Kifl, x115)

x122 (a)   al-Fakhr al-Razi (w57.2) is Muhammad ibn 'Umar ibn al-Hasan ibn al-Husayn, Abu 'Abdullah Fakhr al-Din al-Razi, born in Rayy, Persia (just south of present-day Tehran, Iran), in 544/1150. A Shafi'i scholar of genius and a *mujtahid* Imam in tenets of faith, he was among the foremost figures of his time in mastery of the rational and traditional Islamic sciences, and preserved the religion of Ahl al-Sunna from the deviations of the Mu'tazilites, Shiites, Anthropomorphists, and other aberrant sects of his era by authoring a number of brilliant works that came to enjoy a wide readership among his contemporaries and have remained popular with scholars to this day. His thirty-two-volume Koranic exegesis *Mafatih al-ghayb* [The keys of the unseen] is one of the most famous of his works, though he also wrote on tenets of belief, heresiology, fundamentals of Islamic law and faith, scholastic theology, rhetoric, geometry, and poetry in Arabic and Persian, in both of which he was a preacher of considerable eloquence. His efforts to purify Islam from the heresies of anthropomorphists reached the point that when unable to answer his arguments against them, they resorted to writing ugly remarks and insinuations on scraps of paper and attaching them to the pulpit (minbar) from which he gave the Friday sermon. He arrived one day and read one of these, and then spoke to those present in an impassioned voice, saying: "This piece of paper says that my son does such and such. If it is true, he is but a youth and I hope he will repent. It also says that my wife does such and such. If it is true, she is a faithless woman. And it says that my servant does such and such. Servants are wont to commit every wrong, except for those Allah protects. But on none of these scraps of paper—and may Allah be praised!—is it written that my son says Allah is a corporeal body, or that he likens Him to created things, or that my wife believes that, or my servant—So which of the two groups is closer to guidance?" He travelled to Khawarzim and Khurasan, and finally to Herat, Afghanistan, where he died in 606/1210 (*al-A'lam* (y136), 6.313; and *Tabaqat al-Shafi'iyya al-kubra* (y128), 8.81–89).

x122 (b)   Fath Allah Ya Sin Jazar (Document 4) was born in Nahiya in the governorate of Giza, Egypt, in 1930. He memorized the Holy Koran at nine years of age and in 1946 entered al-Azhar, where he studied at the secondary level and then at the College of Arabic Language, from whence he received his first degree in 1959, after which he pursued his studies in the language to receive a master's degree in 1960. In 1965 he joined al-Azhar's Islamic Research Academy, which, according to the terms of its charter, is "the highest scholarly body for Islamic research" and is presided over by the Sheikh of al-Azhar. In addition to research, propagating Islam (da'wa), sending delegates to Muslim countries to teach, and checking and certifying new books for accuracy and conformity with the tenets of Islam, the academy also examines all Korans published in Egypt and those sent to it from abroad for authorization. Sheikh Fath Allah worked in the latter capacity until 1971, when he was sent as al-Azhar's delegate to Tripoli, Lebanon, to foster Islamic education through teaching and publishing. In 1977, he returned to the academy's General Department of Research as trustee, and was subsequently named as General Director of Research, Writing, and Translation in 1985, the position he currently holds. The present volume, *The Reliance of the Traveller*, was submitted to the academy for checking and authorization on 14 May 1990 and was certified on 11 February 1991 (n).

x123   Fatima (b7.6) is Fatima al-Zahra bint Muhammad (Allah be well pleased with her) born to the Messenger of Allah (Allah bless him and give him peace) and his wife Khadija eighteen years before the Hijra. With Maryam, the mother of the prophet 'Isa (upon whom be peace), Fatima is the purest and best of womenkind. The Prophet (Allah bless him and give him peace) gave her to 'Ali ibn Abi Talib in marriage when she was eighteen years old, and they had four children, al-Hasan, al-Husayn, Umm Kalthum, and Zaynab. She was the only one of the Prophet's children to survive him (Allah bless him and give him peace), though she died after him by only six months in A.H. 11, at twenty-nine years of age (*al-A'lam* (y136), 5.132; and *al-Shifa* (y116), 1.412).

x124   Furani (r40.4) is 'Abd al-Rahman ibn Muhammad ibn Ahmad ibn Furan, Abu al-Qasim al-Furani, born in Merv (in present-day Turkmen S.S.R.) in 388/998. He was a Shafi'i scholar in applications of Islamic jurisprudence and fundamentals of law and faith who authored works in Sacred Law, scholarly differences of opinion, tenets of faith, and heresiology. He died in Merv in 461/1069 (*al-A'lam* (y136), 3.326).

x125   (Sheikh al-Islam) Futuhi al-Hanbali (w25.1) is Muhammad ibn Ahmad ibn 'Abd al-'Aziz, Abu al-Baqa al-Futuhi al-Hanbali, also known as Ibn al-Najjar, born in 898/1492. He was an Egyptian Hanbali scholar, judge, and author. 'Abd al-Wahhab Sha'rani once said of him, "I kept his company for forty years, and never saw anything reprehensible in him, nor anyone who spoke better than he or showed more politeness to those he sat with." He died in 972/1564 (ibid., 6.6).

x126   Gabriel (u1.1) is Jibril (upon whom be peace), the chief of the angels, who descended to the prophets of Allah Most High bearing the divine revelation. He is also the angel entrusted with visiting Allah's punishments upon men, for which reason Bani Isra'il have traditionally feared him. A hadith relates that 'Umar once asked the Jews about Gabriel, and they said, "He is an enemy of ours, for he reveals our secrets to Muhammad and is the one entrusted with making the earth swallow (khasf) those to whom it happens, and with inflicting every divine punishment." Qurtubi records the position of some Koranic exegetes that Gabriel is meant by the verses, "Do you feel secure that he who is in the heavens [lit. "sky"] will not make the earth swallow you while it quakes? Or do you feel secure that he who is in the heavens will not send a storm of pebbles against you, that you shall know how My warning is?" (Koran 67:16–17). Allah Most High also describes Gabriel as "a noble messenger endowed with power, of station with Him of the Throne, obeyed there and trustworthy" (Koran 81:19–21) (*al-Jami' li ahkam al-Qur'an* (y117), 18.215; *al-Shifa* (y116), 1.710; and *al-Siraj al-munir* (y72), 1.79, 4.344).

x127   (Imam) Ghazali (a4.4) is Muhammad ibn Muhammad ibn Muhammad ibn Ahmad, Abu Hamid Hujjat al-Islam al-Ghazali al-Tusi, the Shafi'i Imam, Proof of Islam, and Sufi adept born in Tabiran, near Tus (just north of present-day Mashhad, Iran), in 450/1058. The Imam of his time, nicknamed Shafi'i the Second for his legal virtuosity, he was a brilliant intellectual who first studied jurisprudence at Tus, and then travelled the Islamic world, to Baghdad, Damascus, Jerusalem, Cairo, Alexandria, Mecca, and Medina, taking Sacred Knowledge from its masters, among them the Imam of the Two Sanctuaries Juwayni, with whom he studied until the Imam's death, becoming at his hands a scholar in

Shafi'i law, logic, tenets of faith, debate, and in the rationalistic doctrines of the philosophical schools of his time, which he was later called upon to refute. When Juwayni died, Ghazali debated the Imams and scholars of Baghdad in the presence of the vizier Nizam al-Mulk, who was so impressed that he appointed him to a teaching post at the Nizamiyya Academy in Baghdad, where word of his brilliance spread, and scholars journeyed to hear him.

His worldly success was something of a mixed blessing, and in mid-career, after considerable reflection, he was gripped by an intense fear for his soul and his fate in the afterlife, and he resigned from his post, travelling first to Jerusalem and then to Damascus to purify his heart by following the way of Sufism. In Damascus he lived in seclusion for some ten years, engaged in spiritual struggle and the remembrance of Allah, at the end of which he emerged to produce his master-piece *Ihya' 'ulum al-din* [Giving life to the religious sciences], a classic among the books of the Muslims about internalizing godfearingness (taqwa) in one's deal-ings with Allah, illuminating the soul through obedience to Him, and the levels of believers' attainments therein. The work shows how deeply Ghazali personally realized what he wrote about, and his masterly treatment of hundreds of ques-tions dealing with the inner life that no one had previously discussed or solved is a performance of sustained excellence that shows its author's well-disciplined legal intellect and profound appreciation of human psychology. He also wrote nearly two hundred other works, on the theory of government, Sacred Law, refu-tations of philosophers, tenets of faith, Sufism, Koranic exegesis, scholastic theol-ogy, and bases of Islamic jurisprudence. He died in Tabiran in 505/1111 (*al-A'lam* (y136), 7.22; *Ihya' 'ulum al-din* (y39), 1.330; *al-Munqidh min al-dalal* (y41), 46–50; *al-Shifa* (y116), 2.602; N; and n).

x128   ("al-Hajj ...") (*see under proper name*)

x129   Hakim (g1.1) is Muhammad ibn 'Abdullah ibn Hamdawayh ibn Na'im al-Dabi, Abu 'Abdullah al-Hakim al-Naysaburi, born in Nishapur, Persia, in 321/933. A Shafi'i scholar, hadith master, and Imam, he journeyed far in quest of knowledge of prophetic traditions, travelling to 'Iraq, to the Hijaz, and then to the lands beyond the Oxus, hearing hadiths from nearly two thousand sheikhs. He was appointed to the judiciary in Nishapur in A.H. 359, whence the nickname al-Hakim (the Magistrate), and subsequently in Jurjan, but refused the second posi-tion. He was among the most knowledgeable scholars in distinguishing rigorously authenticated from poorly authenticated hadiths, and among the most prolific. Ibn 'Asakir estimates that Hakim's works on hadith and other subjects amount to approximately fifteen hundred volumes, though he is most famous for his four-volume *al-Mustadrak 'ala al-Sahihayn* [The addendum to the two "Sahih" collec-tions of Bukhari and Muslim]. He died in Nishapur in 405/1014 (*al-A'lam* (y136), 6.227; and *Tabaqat al-Shafi'iyya al-kubra* (y128), 4.155).

x130   Hakim Tirmidhi (w9.4) is Muhammad ibn 'Ali ibn al-Hasan ibn Bishr, Abu 'Abdullah al-Hakim al-Tirmidhi, a muezzin and author originally from Ter-mez (in present-day Uzbek S.S.R.). A Sufi and Shafi'i scholar in Sacred Law, hadith, and tenets of faith, he was exiled from his native Termez over a book its inhabitants did not agree with, and went to Balkh (present-day Wazirabad, Afghanistan), where he was welcomed and honored. He wrote a number of works in hadith, Sacred Law, and Sufism, among which his *Nawadir al-usul* [Rare hadith sources] is perhaps the best known. He died in Balkh at ninety years of age, probably around A.H. 320 (*al-A'lam* (y136), 6.272; and *Tabaqat al-Shafi'iyya al-kubra* (y128), 2.245; and n).

x131   Haman (r38.2) was the vizier of Pharaoh (Fir'awn). Among his commissions was to build a tower of baked bricks so that Pharaoh, imagining Allah to be a corporeal entity in the sky, might climb up and look for him (*al-Futuhat al-ilahiyya* (y65), 3.349–50).

x132   Hammad ibn Salama (w40.5) is Hammad ibn Salama ibn Dinar, Abu Salama al-Basri, the mufti of Basra and a trustworthy memorizer and principle narrator of hadith, though his memory grew poor in his advanced years. Dhahabi relates that he was an Imam in the field of Arabic, and an author and scholar in Sacred Law who uncompromisingly opposed reprehensible innovations (bid'a). He died in 167/784 (*al-A'lam* (y136), 2.272).

x133   Harb Kirmani (w55.3) is Harb ibn Isma'il, Abu Muhammad al-Kirmani, a Hanbali scholar who studied under Imam Ahmad ibn Hanbal, Ishaq ibn Rahawayh, and others. Dhahabi states that his *Masa'il* [Legal questions] is among the most valuable works in the Hanbali school. He died in A.H. 280 at about ninety years of age (*Siyar a'lam al-nubala'* (y37), 13.244–45).

x134   Harith al-Muhasibi (t1.8) is al-Harith ibn Asad, Abu 'Abdullah al-Muhasibi, born in Basra. Notable for his abstinence and self-discipline, he was the teacher of most of the Sufis of Baghdad in his time, a scholar in fundamentals of law and faith who possessed considerable eloquence in giving sermons. Among his sayings is, "The finest people of this Community are those whose hereafter does not prevent them from attending to their this-worldly concerns, nor this world prevent from attending to their hereafter." He authored works on Sufism, asceticism, and rebuttals of the Mu'tazilites, and died in Baghdad in 243/857 (*al-A'lam* (y136), 2.153).

x135   Harun (u3.5) is Harun ibn 'Imran ibn Qahith ibn 'Azir ibn Lawi ibn Ya'qub ibn Ishaq ibn Ibrahim (upon whom be peace), the prophet of Allah Most High to Bani Isra'il and brother and vizier of the prophet Musa (upon whom be peace). Commentators relate that he died a year before the death of Musa during the forty years Bani Isra'il were wandering in the desert, having gone forth with his brother to some caves, where he died and was buried by him (*al-Futuhat al-ilahiyya* (y65), 1.56, 3.89).

x136   Harut (p3.2) was one of two Angels sent to the city of Babylon to teach sorcery to the wicked, as a temptation and trial from Allah, who commanded the two to warn people not to learn it from them. Ghazali explains *sorcery* as "a type of learning deduced from the knowledge of properties of substances and arithmetical relations concerning the positions of stars, from which properties a form is taken resembling the image of the victim, and the stars are observed for a particular time to come, when words of unbelief (kufr) and obscenity, violating the Sacred Law, are pronounced, whereby the help of devils is sought, and through which, by virtue of natural relations of instrumentality that Allah has disposed and arranged, strange states are brought about in the person ensorcelled." Another position is that the two angels were sent down to teach men sorcery so that the difference between sorcery and inimitable prophetic miracles (mu'jiza, def: w30.2) might be recognized, and people not be misled by sorcerers, of whom many existed at that time and some claimed to be prophets (*al-Futuhat al-ilahiyya* (y65), 1.87; and *al-Siraj al-munir* (y72), 1.82).

x137 **Hasanayn Muhammad Makhluf** (L10.2) is a contemporary Egyptian scholar, the son of the Maliki scholar Muhammad Makhluf. The former grand mufti of Egypt (mufti al-diyar al-Misriyya), he is a member of the Faculty of Outstanding Islamic Scholars at al-Azhar University, and a member of the founding council of the Islamic World League (*Mafahim yajibu an tusahhaha* (y83), 30).

x138 **Hasan al-Basri** (w26.1) is al-Hasan ibn Yasar, Abu Sa'id al-Basri, born in Medina in 21/642 and raised at the side of 'Ali ibn Abi Talib (Allah be well pleased with him). He was the Imam of Basra and scholar of the Islamic Community of his time; learned, eloquent, devout, courageous, and held in such awe by contemporaries that he could walk into the chambers of rulers and command the right and forbid the wrong, which he did on several occasions without fear of whoever might blame him. Ghazali said of him, "His speech was the closest of any to that of the prophets, and his guidedness the closest of any to that of the Companions." He died in Basra in 110/728 (*al-A'lam* (y136), 2.226).

x139 **Hasan Saqqaf** (w28.1) is Hasan ibn 'Ali ibn Hashim ibn Ahmad, Abu Hashim al-Saqqaf al-Husayni, a contemporary Shafi'i scholar who lives in Amman, Jordan. His sheikhs include Hashim Majdhub of Damascus in Shafi'i jurisprudence, Muti' Hammami in estate division, and Muhammad Hulayyil of Amman in Arabic grammar, and he has been given written authorizations in the Shadhili tariqa and hadith from Sheikh 'Abdullah Ghimari of Tangiers. He teaches a circle of students in Amman and has published over forty-five books and treatises on tenets of faith, jurisprudence, and heresiology (n).

x140 **Hashim al-Khatib** (w41.3) is Muhammad Hashim ibn Rashid ibn Muhammad ibn 'Abdullah al-Khatib, born in Damascus in 1304/1890. He was a Shafi'i scholar, public speaker, and teacher who studied under nearly twenty-eight of the foremost sheikhs of his time in Damascus and received written authorizations from each of them to teach the subjects he read with them. He knew the Holy Koran by heart and was a master of its recitation and exegesis. Of the Qadiri tariqa, he was one of the scholars who travelled the Syrian countryside during the French occupation and urged the Muslims to rise in jihad against it. He taught in the Umayyad Mosque, the Sulaymaniyya Takiya, and at the Qalbaqjiyya Mosque, where he devoted the latter part of his life to teaching students. He authored a number of treatises and pamphlets on contemporary religious issues, and died in Damascus in 1378/1958 (*Tarikh 'ulama' Dimashq* (y1), 2.710–14).

x141 **Hatib ibn Abi Balta'a** (p74.1) is Hatib ibn Abi Balta'a al-Lakhami (Allah be well pleased with him), born thirty-five years before the Hijra (A.D. 586), a Companion of the Prophet (Allah bless him and give him peace) who was present at every battle with him. Among the greatest archers of the Companions, an outstanding horseman of the Quraysh, and a poet from the pre-Islamic period of ignorance, he had extensive trade dealings, and the Prophet (Allah bless him and give him peace) selected him as his envoy to the Muqawqis of Alexandria. He died in 30/650 in Medina (*al-A'lam* (y136), 2.159).

x142   Haytami (*see* (Imam, Sheikh al-Islam) Ibn Hajar Haytami, x160)

x143   Haythami (w40.4) is 'Ali ibn Abu Bakr ibn Sulayman, Abu al-Hasan Nur al-Din al-Haythami, born in Cairo in 735/1335. He was a Shafi'i scholar, hadith master (hafiz), and Imam who compiled many hadith collections, among the most famous of which is his ten-volume *Majma' al-zawa'id wa manba' al-fawa'id* [Compendium of hadiths not mentioned in the six main collections, and wellspring of information], which has become a virtual necessity for modern students of hadith. He is sometimes confused with Ibn Hajar Haytami, whom he is unrelated to. He died in 807/1405 (*al-A'lam* (y136), 4.266; and Sheikh Shu'ayb Arna'ut).

x144   Hilal ibn al-'Ala' (p35.3) is Hilal ibn al-'Ala' ibn Hilal ibn 'Umar ibn Hilal, Abu 'Umar al-Bahili. A hadith master (hafiz) and Imam who was a reliable (saduq) transmitter, he died in A.H. 280 or 281 (*Siyar a'lam al-nubula'* (y37), 13.309–10).

x145   Hind (r2.19) is Hind bint 'Utba ibn Rabi'a ibn 'Abd al-Shams ibn 'Abd Manaf (Allah be well pleased with her), the mother of the caliph Mu'awiya and wife of Abu Sufyan, the Companion of the Prophet (Allah bless him and give him peace). She was an eloquent and courageous woman of the Quraysh who was noted for her outstanding poetry. At first a bitter foe of Islam and the Muslims, she entered Islam after the conquest of Mecca and made good her Islam. She had extensive trade dealings in the caliphate of 'Umar, was present at the battle of Yarmouk, and with her poetry inspired and encouraged the Muslim forces in their jihad against the unbelievers on the Syrian campaign. She died in 14/635 (*al-A'lam* (y136), 8.98).

x146   Hud (u3.5) is Hud ibn 'Abdullah ibn Rabah ibn al-Khulud ibn 'Ad (upon whom be peace), the Arabian prophet of Allah Most High to the people of 'Ad, in the northern part of what is now the Hadramawt region of South Yemen. They were idol worshippers and Hud called them to worship the one God, but they cried lies to him and were destroyed for their unbelief (*al-A'lam* (y136), 8.101; and Koran 26:123–40).

x147   Husayn ibn Mansur al-Hallaj (w9.11) is al-Husayn ibn Mansur, Abu al-Mughith al-Hallaj, originally from Bayda, Persia, but raised in Wasit, Iraq. He kept the company of Junayd, Abu al-Husayn al-Nuri, 'Amr al-Makki, and others of the Sufis. Sulami records that most of the sheikhs of his own time rejected al-Hallaj and denied that he had any standing in the Sufi way, though others praised him, among them Muhammad ibn Khafif (x166), who called him "a godly scholar." Allah knows best as to his spiritual state, but he was executed in Baghdad in 309/922 for saying "*Ana al-Haqq*" ("I am the Truth," i.e. God), and among the evidence that he wronged himself was that his former sheikh, Junayd, was among those who gave the verdict that he should die (*Tabaqat al-Sufiyya* (y129), 307–8; and n).

x148   Huyay (w27.1) is Huyay ibn Akhtab, one of the chiefs of the Medinan Jewish tribe of Bani Nadir. Huyay participated in their plan to invite the Prophet (Allah bless him and give him peace) to a meal to kill him, but Gabriel warned him of it and he got up and left, after which he sent a messenger telling them that they had vitiated their solemn covenant and would have to leave Medina. The tribe resettled in Khaybar, from whence they endeavored to recoup their losses by sending a delegation of their leaders, among them Huyay, to Mecca to enter into a pact with Abu Sufyan, Safwan ibn Umayya, and other leaders of the Quraysh to extirpate the Muslims. The pact culminated in the Battle of the Confederates, after which Huyay was captured and executed with the Medinan Jewish tribe of Bani Qurayza, whom he had also persuaded to violate their covenant with the Muslims by joining the hostilities against them (*Muhammad* (y75), 203, 215, and 268).

x149   Ibn 'Abbas (b3.2) is 'Abdullah ibn 'Abbas ibn 'Abd al-Muttalib (Allah be well pleased with him), born three years before the Hijra (A.D. 619) in Mecca. He was the cousin and Companion of the Prophet (Allah bless him and give him peace) and kept his company during his lifetime, relating some 1,660 hadiths from him. Among the most knowledgeable of the Companions, much Koranic exegesis is also related from him, and the caliph 'Umar used to call for Ibn 'Abbas when he could not reach a conclusion on a particular legal question, telling him, "This and the likes of it are what you are for," and he would adopt Ibn 'Abbas's judgement on the matter without consulting anyone else. His memory was phenomenal, and when the poet Ibn Abi Rabi' delivered an eighty- stanza ode in his presence, Ibn 'Abbas could recite it by heart upon hearing it the once. The scholar of the Muslims of his time, he was visited by many people seeking knowledge of the lawful and unlawful, poetry, Arabic, and geneology. He went blind in his later years and resided at Ta'if, where he died in 68/687 (*al-A'lam* (y136), 4.95).

x150   Ibn 'Abd al-Barr (w40.5) is Yusuf ibn 'Abdullah ibn Muhammad ibn 'Abd al-Barr, born in Cordova (in present-day Spain) in 368/978. A major hadith master (hafiz), Maliki scholar, and author, he was nicknamed the Hadith Master of the West, and was known for his travels throughout Andalusia in pursuit of hadith. He was appointed to the judiciary more than once, and authored works in hadith, Sacred Law, biographies of famous Muslims, canonical Koranic readings (qira'at), geneology, and history. He died in Shatiba in 463/1071 (*al-A'lam* (y136), 8.240).

x151   Ibn 'Abd al-Salam (*see* (Imam) 'Izz ibn 'Abd al-Salam, x199)

x152   Ibn Abi Khaythama (w40.5) is Ahmad ibn Zuhayr Abi Khaythama ibn Harb ibn Shidad, Abu Bakr al-Nasa'i, born in Baghdad in 185/801. A historian, hadith master (hafiz), and the Imam of his own now-extinct school of jurisprudence, he authored a fifty-volume history entitled *al-Tarikh al-kabir* [The major history], of which Daraqutni said, "I know of no work richer in notes (fawa'id) than his history," but of which only fragments remain. He died in Baghdad in 279/892 (*al-A'lam* (y136), 1.128).

x153   Ibn 'Ajiba (s4.5) is Ahmad ibn Muhammad ibn al-Mahdi ibn 'Ajiba al-Hasani, born in Morocco in 1160/1747. He was a Maliki scholar, Sufi, and Koranic exegete who authored works in Arabic grammar, Sufism, Maliki biographies, and history, as well as a mystical Koranic exegesis called *al-Bahr al-madid fi tafsir al-Qur'an al-Majid* [The far-stretching sea: an exegesis of the Noble Koran] in four volumes. He took the Shadhili tariqa from the Moroccan master al-'Arabi al-Darqawi by way of his deputy, Muhammad Buzaydi (not the Muhammad Buzidi who was the sheikh of Ahmad al-'Alawi), and Darqawi addresses him in various places of his *al-Rasa'il al-Darqawiyya* [The Darqawi letters]. He is said to have written some seventeen commentaries on the *Hikam* [Aphorisms] of Ibn 'Ata' Illah, of which his *Iqaz al-himam fi sharh al-Hikam* [The awakening of spiritual powers: a commentary on "The aphorisms"] is the most widely known. He died in 'Anjara, Morocco, in 1224/1809 (ibid., 1.245; Sheikh 'Abdullah Muhammad Ghimari; and n).

x154   Ibn 'Amr (w27.1) (*see* 'Abdullah ibn 'Amr, x20)

x155   Ibn 'Ata' (w9.11) is Ahmad ibn Muhammad ibn Sahl ibn 'Ata', Abu al-'Abbas al-Adami, of Baghdad. A Sufi ascetic and devotee, it is related that for a space of years he would recite the whole Koran daily, but later spent more than twenty years finishing it but once, for his pondering its meanings. He died in Baghdad in A.H. 309 (*Siyar a'lam al-nubala'* (y37), 14.255–56).

x156   Ibn 'Ata' Illah (t2.1) is Ahmad ibn Muhammad ibn 'Abd al-Karim, Abu al-Fadl Taj al-Din Ibn 'Ata' Illah al-Iskandari, Sufi Imam and author of *al-Hikam al-'Ata'iyya* [The aphorisms of 'Ata'], one of the greatest works of the Shadhili tariqa, in which he was the second successor to Imam Abul Hasan al-Shadhili himself. Originally from Alexandria, he moved to Cairo, where he attracted a large following and gave public lectures that were well attended. He was a scholar in Arabic grammar, hadith, Koranic exegesis, fundamentals of law and faith, and jurisprudence; and Dhahabi notes that when he spoke at al-Azhar Mosque, he would combine the words of the Sufis with hadiths, stories of the early Muslims, and scholarly topics. Among the words he conveyed from the founder of his order were, "This path is not monasticism, eating barley and bran, or the garrulousness of affectation, but rather perseverance in the divine commands and certainty in the divine guidance." He was also the sheikh of the Shafi'i Imam Taqi al-Din Subki, whose son Taj al-Din feels that Ibn 'Ata' Illah was more probably a Shafi'i than a Maliki, as others have held. But his true legacy lies in the path he served and the disciples he left to further it, their hearts opened to the knowledge of Allah Most High through his instruction in the mystic way, which his *Hikam* and other works amply attest to his profound mastery of. He died in Cairo in 709/1309 (*al-A'lam* (y136), 1.221–22; *al-Durar al-kamina* (y13), 1.273–74; *Tabaqat al-Shafi'iyya al-kubra* (y128), 9.23; and n).

x157   Ibn Daqiq al-'Eid (p75.27) is Muhammad ibn 'Ali ibn Wahb ibn Muti', Abu al-Fath Taqi al-Din al-Qushayri, born in Yanbu' on the Hijaz side of the Red Sea, and known, like his father and grandfather, as Ibn Daqiq al-'Eid. He was a Shafi'i *mujtahid* Imam who was educated in Damascus, Alexandria, and in Cairo, where he was appointed to the judiciary in A.H. 695. One of Islam's great scholars in fundamentals of law and belief, he authored *al-Ilmam bi ahadith al-ahkam* [An outline of the hadiths for the rulings of Sacred Law] and other works in law, principles of jurisprudence, hadith, tenets of faith, and poetry, and died in Cairo in 702/1302 (*al-A'lam* (y136), 6.283; and *Tabaqat al-Shafi'iyya al-kubra* (y128), 9.207).

x158   Ibn Hajar (m1.4) (*see* (Imam, Sheikh al-Islam) Ibn Hajar Haytami, x160)

x159   Ibn Hajar 'Asqalani (w29.2(1)) is Ahmad ibn 'Ali ibn Muhammad al-Kinani, Abu al-Fadl Shihab al-Din Ibn Hajar al-'Asqalani, born in Cairo in 773/1372. A Shafi'i Imam and hadith master (hafiz), he reached the level of Commander of the Faithful in Hadith, the only rank above that of hadith master (hafiz). He first learned literature and poetry, but then devoted his considerable talents to hadith, which he studied under the renowned African master al-Zayla'i and others in Cairo, Yemen, and the Hijaz. His works were popular in his own lifetime and were hand-copied by the greatest scholars of the era and given by kings to one another as gifts. Known as Sheikh al-Islam, scholars travelled to take knowledge from him, and he was appointed to the judiciary in Egypt several times. He authored a number of works on hadith, history, biography, Koranic exegesis, poetry, and Shafi'i jurisprudence, among the most famous of them his fourteen-volume *Fath al-Bari bi sharh Sahih al-Bukhari* [The victory of the Creator: a commentary on the "Sahih" of Bukhari] which few serious students of Islamic knowledge can do without. He died in Cairo in 852/1449 (*al-A'lam* (y136), 1.178; Sheikh Shu'ayb Arna'ut; Sheikh Hasan Saqqaf; and A).

x160   (Imam, Sheikh al-Islam) Ibn Hajar Haytami (o25.0) is Ahmad ibn Muhammad ibn 'Ali ibn Hajar, Abu al'Abbas Shihab al-Din al-Haytami al-Makki, born in 909/1504 in Abu Haytam, western Egypt. He was the Shafi'i Imam of his time, a brilliant scholar of in-depth applications of Sacred Law, and with Imam Ahmad al-Ramli, represents the foremost resource for legal opinion (fatwa) for the entire late Shafi'i school. He was educated at al-Azhar, but later moved to Mecca, where he authored major works in Shafi'i jurisprudence, hadith, tenets of faith, education, hadith commentary, and formal legal opinion. His most famous works include *Tuhfa al-muhtaj bi sharh al-Minhaj* [The gift of him in need: an explanation of "The road"], a commentary on Nawawi's *Minhaj al-talibin* [The seekers' road] whose ten volumes represent a high point in Shafi'i scholarship; the four-volume *al-Fatawa al-kubra al-fiqhiyya* [The major collection of legal opinions]; and *al-Zawajir 'an iqtiraf al-kaba'ir* [Deterrents from committing enormities], which with its detailed presentation of Koran and hadith evidence and masterful legal inferences, remains unique among Muslim works dealing with godfearingness (taqwa) and is even recognized by Hanafi scholars like Ibn 'Abidin as a source of authoritative legal texts (nusus) valid in their own school. After a lifetime of outstanding scholarship, the Imam died and was buried in Mecca in 974/1567 (*al-A'lam* (y136), 1.234; A; and n).

x161   Ibn Hazm (b3.2) is 'Ali ibn Ahmad ibn Sa'id, Abu Muhammad ibn Hazm al-Zahiri, born in Cordova (in present-day Spain) in 384/994. A gifted author, minister in government, poet, and the scholar of Andalusia in his era, he followed Imam Dawud al-Zahiri ("the literalist"), a student of Imam Shafi'i who accepted only the Koran, hadith, and scholarly consensus (ijma') as sources of evidence in Sacred Law, denying the validity of analogical reasoning (qiyas). As nothing remains of Dawud's writings, Ibn Hazm, with the Sufi Muhyiddin ibn al-'Arabi, remains virtually the only written representative of the Zahiri school.

Though he authored works on heresiology, poetry, logic, history, biography, grammar, and fundamentals of Islamic Law, Ibn Hazm is perhaps most famous for an eleven-volume work in his own school of jurisprudence entitled al-Muhalla [The embellished], whose good aspects are somewhat alloyed with bitter attacks on other Imams of jurisprudence, misrepresentations of their lines of evidence, and abuse of any who would disagree with his own methodological premises, none of which have traditionally been the hallmarks of Islamic scholars. Were one to eliminate these features from it, as Ibn al-'Arabi did in an unfortunately lost work, much would remain that would be valuable. Ibn Hajar 'Asqalani praises Ibn Hazm's accuracy in relating hadiths, and because of his extremism in restricting the validity of scholarly consensus (ijma') to the prophetic Companions exclusively, when he does report consensus on an issue, it carries particular weight. His acrimonious way of making a case against opponents has endeared him to some contemporary Muslim students, but few of the great scholars of Islam have accepted many of his premises or conclusions, not only because of his unfair attacks and misrepresentations, but also because of the inflexibility of the Zahiri school's method, whose inability to use analogy makes it something of a dinosaur in dealing with a changing world. The scholars of his time agreed that Ibn Hazm was misguided, warned their rulers against the strife he was causing, and the common people from approaching him, and he was exiled and fled to Labla in the Andalusian countryside, where he died in 456/1064 (al-A'lam (y136), 4.254; N; and n).

x162   Ibn Hibban (g1.1) is Muhammad ibn Hibban ibn Ahmad ibn Hibban ibn Mu'adh ibn Ma'bad, Abu Hatim al-Tamimi al-Busti, born in Bust (in present-day Afghanistan). A Shafi'i Imam and hadith master (hafiz), he was an extremely prolific author whom Yaqut once said "produced works in the sciences of hadith that no one else could have written." In his search for knowledge of hadith, he travelled to Khurasan, Syria, Egypt, Iraq, the Arabian Peninsula, and Nishapur, before returning to his native city, after which he served as a judge for a period in Samarkand. He authored al-Anwa' wa al-taqasim [Types and categories], also known as al-Musnad al-sahih [Authenticated ascribed traditions] and other voluminous works in hadith, encyclopediology, biography, and history, and died in Bust in 354/965 (al-A'lam (y136), 6.78; and Tabaqat al-Shafi'iyya al-kubra (y128), 3.131).

x163   Ibn Jawzi (see 'Abd al-Rahman ibn Jawzi, x12)

x164   (Imam) Ibn Juzayy (w57.2) is Muhammad ibn Ahmad ibn Muhammad ibn 'Abdullah, Abu al-Qasim Ibn Juzayy al-Kalbi of Granada (in present-day Spain), born in 693/1294. He was a Maliki scholar and Imam in Koranic exegesis and Arabic lexicology who also did research in fundamentals of Sacred Law and hadith. His Koranic commentary al-Tashil li 'ulum al-Tanzil [The facilitation of the sciences of the Revelation] enjoys a prodigious reputation and is widely quoted. He died in 741/1340 (al-A'lam (y136), 5.325; and n).

x165   Ibn Kathir (Introduction) is Isma'il ibn 'Umar ibn Kathir ibn Daww ibn Dara', Abu al-Fida' 'Imad al-Din, born in 701/1302 in a village outside of Damascus, where he moved with his brother at the age of five. He later travelled in pursuit of Sacred Knowledge, becoming a principle Shafi'i scholar, hadith master (hafiz), and historian who authored works in each of these fields, though he is perhaps best known for his four-volume *Tafsir al-Qur'an al-'Azim* [Commentary on the Mighty Koran], which reflects its author's magisterial command of the sciences of hadith. He died in Damascus in 774/1373 (*al-A'lam* (y136), 1.320).

x166   Ibn Khafif (w9.11) is Muhammad ibn Khafif ibn Isfikshar, Abu 'Abdullah al-Shirazi, born in 276/890. The son of a prince, he later turned to asceticism, wandered much, and became a Sufi of whom Sulami said, "He is today the Sheikh of Sheikhs.... No Sufi remains who is more advanced than he. He kept the company of Ruwaym ibn Ahmad and Ibn 'Ata', met al-Hallaj, and is among the most knowledgeable sheikhs in outward learning, strictly adhering to the Koran and sunna, a Shafi'i scholar." He lived in Shiraz, Persia, where he died at ninety-five years of age in 371/982 (ibid., 6.114; and *Siyar a'lam al-nubala'* (y37), 16.342–47).

x167   Ibn Khaldun (b3.1) is 'Abd al-Rahman ibn Muhammad ibn Muhammad, Abu Zayd Ibn Khaldun, born in Tunis in 732/1332. He was a philosopher and historian who grew up in Tunis and travelled to Tlemcen, Fez, Granada, and Andalusia, where he was appointed to various governmental positions, which he lost through the vicissitudes of the day and eventually returned to Tunis. He then set out for Egypt, where the sultan al-Zahir welcomed and honored him, appointing him to the Maliki judgeship, a position from which he was dismissed for preferring his native Tunisian dress during the hours of work over the customary judicial robes, but to which he was later reinstated. He is most famous for his seven-volume *al-'Ibar wa diwan al-mubtadi' wa al-khabar fi tarikh al-'arab wa al-'ajam wa al-barbar* [The reflections and record of subject and predicate: a history of the Arabs, Persians, and Berbers], whose *al-Muqaddima* [The prolegomenon] is considered the world's first work on social theory. He died in Cairo in 808/1406 (*al-A'lam* (136), 3.330).

x168   Ibn Khuzayma (w40.5) is Muhammad ibn Ishaq ibn Khuzayma, Abu Bakr al-Sulami, born in Nishapur, Persia, in 223/838. He was a Shafi'i scholar and *mujtahid*, the Imam of Nishapur in his time, a hadith specialist who travelled for Sacred Knowledge to Iraq, Syria, the Arabian Peninsula, and Egypt. He authored more than 140 works, among them his main contribution to the science of hadith, *Mukhtasar al-Mukhtasar* [The abridgement of "The abridgment"], also known as his *Sahih*. He died in Nishapur in 311/924 (ibid., 6.29; and *Tabaqat al-Shafi'iyya al-kubra* (y128), 3.109).

x169   Ibn Ma'in (w48.2) is Yahya ibn Ma'in ibn 'Awn ibn Ziyad, Abu Zakariyya al-Baghdadi, born in Niqya, a village near al-Anbar, Iraq, in 157/775. Among the greatest Imams of hadith and in knowledge of its narrators, Imam Ahmad referred to him as "the most knowledgeable of us in transmitters of hadith," and Dhahabi called him the "Master of Hadith Masters." His father left him a large fortune which he spent in learning and gathering hadiths. He once said, "I have written a million hadiths with my hand." He lived in Baghdad, authored a number of valuable works on the sciences of hadith, and died while on hajj in 233/848 (*al-A'lam* (y136), 8.172–73).

x170   Ibn Majah (Introduction) is Muhammad ibn Yazid al-Rub'i, Abu 'Abdullah Ibn Majah al-Qazwini, of Qazvin, Persia, born in 209/824. He was a hadith master (hafiz), Imam, and Koranic exegete whose travels in pursuit of knowledge of hadith led him to Basra, Baghdad, Syria, Cairo, the Hijaz, and Rayy, and enabled him to author his *Sunan* [Sunnas], one of the six principle collections of Sunni Islam. He died in 273/887 (ibid., 7.144; and *al-Targhib wa al-tarhib* (y9), 1.21).

x171   Ibn Mas'ud (b3.2) is 'Abdullah ibn Mas'ud ibn Ghafil ibn Habib, Abu 'Abd al-Rahman al-Hadhali (Allah be well pleased with him), of Mecca. One of the greatest of the Companions in virtue, intelligence, and in closeness to the Prophet (Allah bless him and give him peace), he was among the earliest converts to Islam, the first to recite the Holy Koran aloud in Mecca, and a trusted servant of the Prophet (Allah bless him and give him peace) who kept his secrets, carried his sandals, and accompanied him while travelling or at home. 'Umar once referred to him as "a vessel replete with knowledge." He made both the emigration to Ethiopia and to Medina, was present at the battle of Badr and all the others, and was put in charge of the Muslim common fund (bayt al-mal) at Kufa after the Prophet's death (Allah bless him and give him peace), though he returned to Medina during the caliphate of 'Uthman. He loved perfume and when he left home, people could tell where he had passed by the beautiful scent. Among the great scholars of the Companions, he related 848 hadiths, and died in Medina in 32/653 at about sixty years of age (*al-A'lam* (y136), 4.137; and *al-Shifa* (y116), 1.214).

x172   Ibn al-Mubarak (w18.2) is 'Abdullah ibn al-Mubarak ibn Wadih, Abu 'Abd al-Rahman al-Hanzali al-Tamimi, originally of Merv (in present-day Turkmen S.S.R), born in 118/736. He was a hadith master (hafiz) and scholar of Sacred Law and Arabic who spent nearly his whole life travelling, whether for hajj, jihad, or trade, and he joined in his person between learning, generosity, and courage. The first author in Islam to produce a work on jihad, he died in Hit, Iraq, after a battle with the Byzantines in 181/797 (*al-A'lam* (y136), 4.115).

x173   Ibn Naqib (*see* Ahmad ibn Naqib al-Misri, x76)

x174   Ibn al-Qayyim (w18.7) is Muhammad ibn Abu Bakr ibn Ayyub ibn Sa'd, Abu 'Abdullah al-Zura'i Ibn Qayyim al-Jawziyya, born in Damascus in 691/1292. He was a Hanbali hadith scholar and author who wrote a number of works, among them *Zad al-ma'ad* [The provision for the return] in hadith, and *I'lam al-mawaqqi'in* [The instruction of those who sign formal legal opinions] in fundamentals of Islamic law. His most significant contribution however, was his editing and preparing for publication the writings of Ibn Taymiya, whose devoted pupil he was. He went to prison with his sheikh in the citadel of Damascus and suffered with him until Ibn Taymiya's death in 728/1328, when he was released. He thereafter worked to spread and popularize the master's ideas, as dedicated to him after his death as he had been in life, supporting him in what was right and what was wrong. A specimen of the latter is Ibn al-Qayyim's *al-Qasida al-nuniyya* [Ode rhyming in the letter *n*], a lengthy poem on tenets of faith that is filled with corrupt suggestions about the attributes of God, which Imam Taqi al-Din Subki analyses in detail in his *al-Sayf al-saqil* [The burnished sword], giving the verdict that the poem's anthropomorphisms of the Divinity are beyond the pale of Islam. The poem could not be openly circulated in Ibn al-Qayyim's lifetime but only secretly, and it seems that he never abandoned it, for the Hanbali historian and biographer Ibn Rajab heard it from its author in the year of his death.

A second unfortunate peculiarity the poem shares with some of Ibn al-Qayyim's other works on Islamic faith is that it presents the reader with a false dilemma, namely that one must either believe that Allah has eyes, hands, a descending motion, and so forth, in a *literal* (haqiqi) sense, or else one has nullified ('attala) or negated (nafa) these attributes. And this is erroneous, for the *literal* is that which corresponds to an expression's primary lexical sense as ordinarily used in a language by the people who speak it, while the above words are clearly intended otherwise, in accordance with the Koranic verse, "There is nothing whatsoever like unto Him" (Koran 42:11), for if the above were intended literally, there would be innumerable things like unto Him in such respects as having eyes, hands, motion, and so forth, in the literal meaning of these terms. The would-be dilemma is also far from the practice of the early Muslims, who used only to accept such Koranic verses and hadiths as they have come, consigning the knowledge of what is meant by them—while affirming Allah's absolute transcendence above any resemblance to created things—to Allah Most High alone, without trying to determinately specify how they are meant (bi la kayf), let alone suggesting people understand them *literally* (haqiqatan) as Ibn al-Qayyim tried to do.

While granting that his other scholarly achievements are not necessarily compromised by his extreme aberrances in tenets of faith, it should not be forgotten that depicting the latter as a "reform" or "return to early Islam" represents a blameworthy innovation on his part that appeared more than seven centuries after the time of the Prophet (Allah bless him and give him peace) and his Companions. A particularly unsavory aspect of it is that in his attempts to vindicate the doctrine, Ibn al-Qayyim casts aspersions upon the Islam of anyone who does not subscribe to it, at their forefront the Ash'ari school, whom his books castigate as "Jahmiyya" or "Mu'attila," implying, by equating them with the most extreme factions of the Mu'tazilites, that they deny any significance to the divine attributes, a misrepresentation that has seen a lamentable recrudescence in parts of the Muslim world today. Whether such views are called "fundamentalism" or some other name, the scholars of the Muslims remember history, and that it was Abu Hanifa who first observed, "Two depraved opinions have reached us from the East, those of Jahm, the nullifier of the divine attributes [dis: x202], and those of Muqatil [n: ibn Sulayman al-Balkhi, d. ca. A.H. 150], the likener of Allah to His creation." To make of these two an either-or for Muslims, or depict the latter as "sunna" when it has been counted among heresies and rejected by the Muslim Community for the first seven centuries of Islam that preceded Ibn al-Qayyim and his mentor Ibn Taymiya, is to say the least difficult to accept, and it would seem fitter to simply acknowledge that Ibn al-Qayyim was a talented author in fundamentals of law, hadith, and other fields, but unfortunately enamored with his teacher to the extent of following him in innovations (bid'a) in tenets of faith and misrepresenting the positions of those who opposed them. He died in Damascus in 751/1350 (*al-A'lam* (y136), 6.56; *al-Sayf al-saqil* (y70), 2–192; *Sharh al-Qasida al-nuniyya* (y45), 1.268–88; *Siyar a'lam al-nubala'* (y37), 7.202; and n).

x175   Ibn Qudama (w18.2) is 'Abdullah ibn Muhammad ibn Qudama, Abu Muhammad Muwaffaq al-Din al-Jama'ili al-Maqdisi, born in Jama'il, Palestine, in 541/1146. A Hanbali scholar and Imam, he was educated in Damascus, and was the author of the nine-volume *al-Mughni* [The enricher] in Hanbali jurisprudence as well as other works in fundamentals of Sacred Law, tenets of faith, geneology, biography, and Koranic exegesis. He travelled to Baghdad in A.H. 561 and lived there four years before returning to Damascus, where he died in 620/1223. Both he and the subject of the next entry were called Ibn Qudama al-Maqdisi, as were others, all from a single family that was blessed with Hanbali scholars (*al-A'lam* (y136), 4.67; and n).

x176   Ibn Qudama al-Maqdisi (q0.1) is Ahmad ibn 'Abd al-Rahman ibn Muhammad ibn Ahmad ibn Muhammad ibn Qudama al-Maqdisi, born in Damascus in 651/1253. He studied hadith and Hanbali jurisprudence with his father, who was head of the judiciary (qadi al-qudah), and when he was himself appointed as a judge before thirty years of age, he performed the office diligently and well. A Hanbali scholar of great personal virtue and integrity, he taught at many schools in Damascus, and was a well-known preacher at Friday prayers on Mount Qasiyun. He participated in the campaign in which the sultan Malik Mansur liberated Tripoli, Lebanon, from foreign occupation, and died in Damascus at thirty-eight years of age in 689/1290 (*Mukhtasar Minhaj al-qasidin* (y62), 8).

x177   Ibn Salah (b7.6) is 'Uthman ibn 'Abd al-Rahman Salah al-Din ibn 'Uthman ibn Musa, Abu 'Amr Taqi al-Din al-Shahrazuri, born in Sharkhan of Kurdish descent in 577/1181. One of the greatest Shafi'i Imams in knowledge and godfearingness, he was a hadith master (hafiz) who studied in Mosul, Baghdad, Nishapur, Merv, and in Damascus under Hanbali Imam Muwaffaq al-Din Ibn Qudama al-Maqdisi. He taught for a period in the Salahiyya School in Jerusalem, after which he returned to Damascus, where he was appointed as the head of Dar al-Hadith. He authored a number of works in Shafi'i jurisprudence, Koranic exegesis, hadith, the methodology of formal legal opinion, and biography, and died in Damascus in 643/1245 (*al-A'lam* (y136), 4.207–8; *Tabaqat al-Shafi'iyya al-kubra* (y128), 8.326; and Sheikh Hasan Saqqaf).

x178   Ibn Taymiya (p75.23) is Ahmad ibn 'Abd al-Halim ibn 'Abd al-Salam ibn 'Abdullah, Abu al-'Abbas Taqi al-Din Ibn Taymiya al-Harrani, born in Harran, east of Damascus, in 661/1263. A famous Hanbali scholar in Koranic exegesis, hadith, and jurisprudence, Ibn Taymiya was a voracious reader and author of great personal courage who was endowed with a compelling writing style and a keen memory. Dhahabi wrote of him, "I never saw anyone faster at recalling the Koranic verses dealing with subjects he was discussing, or anyone who could remember hadith texts more vividly." Dhahabi estimates that his legal opinions on various subjects amount to three-hundred or more volumes.

    He was imprisoned during much of his life in Cairo, Alexandria, and Damascus for his writings, scholars of his time accusing him of believing Allah to be a corporeal entity because of what he mentioned in his *al-'Aqida al-Hamawiyya,* and *al-Wasitiyya* and other works, such as that Allah's 'hand', 'foot', 'shin', and 'face', are literal (haqiqi) attributes, and that He is upon the Throne in person. The error in this, as mentioned above at x174, is that suggesting such attributes are literal is an innovation and unjustifiable inference from the Koranic and hadith texts that mention them, for the way of the early Muslims was mere acceptance of such expressions on faith without saying how they are meant, and without additions, subtractions, or substituting meanings imagined to be synonyms, while acknowledging Allah's absolute transcendence beyond the characteristics of created things, in conformity with the Koranic verse, "There is nothing whatsoever like unto Him" (Koran 42:11). As for figurative interpretations that preserve the divine transcendence, scholars of tenets of faith have only had recourse to them in times when men of reprehensible innovations (bid'a), quoting hadiths and Koranic verses, have caused confusion in the minds of common Muslims as to whether Allah has attributes like those of His creation or whether He is transcendently beyond any image conceivable to the minds of men. Scholars' firmness in condemning those who have raised such confusions has traditionally been very uncompromising, and this is no doubt the reason that a number of the Imams of the Shafi'i school, among them Taqi al-Din Subki, Ibn Hajar Haytami, and al-'Izz Ibn Jama'a, gave formal legal opinions that Ibn Taymiya was misguided and misguiding in tenets of faith, and warned people from accepting his theories. The Hanafi scholar Muhammad Zahid al-Kawthari has written, "Whoever thinks that all the scholars of his time joined in a single conspiracy against him from personal envy should rather impugn their own intelligence and understanding, after studying the repugnance of his deviations in belief and works, for which he was asked to repent time after time and moved from prison to prison until he passed on to what he'd sent ahead."

While few deny that Ibn Taymiya was a copious and eloquent writer and hadith scholar, his career, like that of others, demonstrates that a man may be outstanding in one field and yet suffer from radical deficiencies in another, the most reliable index of which is how a field's Imams regard his work in it. By this measure, indeed, by the standards of all previous Ahl al-Sunna scholars, it is clear that despite a voluminous and influential written legacy, Ibn Taymiya cannot be considered an authority on tenets of faith, a field in which he made mistakes profoundly incompatible with the beliefs of Islam, as also with a number of his legal views that violated the scholarly consensus (ijma') of Sunni Muslims. It should be remembered that such matters are not the province of personal reasoning (ijtihad), whether Ibn Taymiya considered them to be so out of sincere conviction, or whether simply because, as Imam Subki said, "his learning exceeded his intelligence." He died in Damascus in 728/1328 (*al-A'lam* (y136), 1.144; *al-Durar al-kamina* (y13), 1.144–55; *al-Fatawa al-hadithiyya* (y48), 114; *al-Rasa'il al-Subkiyya* (y52), 151–52; *al-Sayf al-saqil* (y70), 6; Sheikh Hasan Saqqaf; and n).

x179   Ibn 'Umar (b3.2) is 'Abdullah ibn 'Umar ibn al-Khattab, Abu 'Abd al-Rahman al-'Adawi (Allah be well pleased with him), born to one of the noblest families of the Quraysh in Mecca ten years before the Hijra (A.D. 613). He was a Companion of the Prophet (Allah bless him and give him peace) who emigrated to Medina with his father 'Umar ibn Khattab and was raised in Islam. Though too young to fight at Badr, he was daring and courageous, and participated in the Battle of the Confederates and the conquest of Mecca. One of the most knowledgeable of the Companions, he gave formal legal opinions to Muslims for sixty years and related 2,630 hadiths. He fought in jihad in North Africa on two separate campaigns, lost his eyesight at the end of his life, and was the last of the Companions to die in Mecca, in 73/692 (*al-A'lam* (y136), 4.108; and n).

x180   Ibrahim (f8.45) is Ibrahim ibn Tarikh ibn Azar ibn Takhur ibn Sharukh ibn Arghu ibn Faligh (upon whom be peace), the prophet and messenger of Allah Most High. The blessing upon "Ibrahim and the *folk* of Ibrahim" in the final Testification of Faith (Tashahhud) of the prayer (salat) refers to the prophets, *siddiq*s (great-faithed ones), martyrs, and pious of his descendants, for all the prophets (upon whom peace) of Bani Isra'il were descended from Ishaq, Ibrahim's son by Sarah, while the only prophet descended from Isma'il, his son by Hajar, was the Prophet Muhammad (Allah bless him and give him peace). Ibrahim is mentioned in various places in the Holy Koran, which records how he built the Kaaba with his son Isma'il, how he smashed the idols of his people, and how he obeyed what he was bidden to do in a dream by going to sacrifice his son, who did not have to be sacrificed in the end, but for which Ibrahim became the Friend of the All-merciful (Khalil al-Rahman). He is buried in al-Khalil (Hebron) in Palestine (*al-Futuhat al-ilahiyya* (y65), 1.102; *al-Futuhat al-rabbaniyya* (y26), 2.348; and n).

x181   Ibrahim (g6.3) is Ibrahim ibn Muhammad ibn 'Abdullah, born to the Messenger of Allah (Allah bless him and give him peace) of Mariya the Copt, the Prophet's concubine who was given to him by the Muqawqis of Alexandria. Ibrahim was born in A.H. 8, and when he died before reaching two full years of age, the Prophet (Allah bless him and give him peace) said, "Verily, O Ibrahim, we are in deep sorrow over your departure" (Sheikh Yunus Hamdan; and n).

x182   Ibrahim ibn Adham (r2.13) is Ibrahim ibn Adham ibn Mansur, Abu Ishaq al-Tamimi al-Balkhi, an early Sufi saint and ascetic. Originally born into a wealthy family of Balkh (in present-day Afghanistan), he eschewed the comfortable life, studied Sacred Law, and then travelled to Baghdad, after which he wandered at length through Iraq, Syria, and the Hijaz, taking knowledge from many famous scholars while supporting himself by working as a reaper, porter, guard for orchards, and miller. He fought in jihad against the Byzantines, and when a slave brought him the news at Massisa (south of present-day Antakya, Turkey) that his father had died, leaving him a tremendous fortune in Balkh of which the slave was carrying ten thousand dirhams, Ibrahim freed him and gave him the dirhams, informing him that he had no desire for the rest. He used to fast whether travelling or not, always spoke faultless Arabic, and many of his sayings have been preserved. When he attended the homilies of Sufyan al-Thawri, the latter would curtail his words for fear of making a mistake. He died, probably at Sufnan on the southern Byzantine frontier, in 161/778 (*al-A'lam* (y136), 1.31; and n).

x183   (Sheikh) Ibrahim Bajuri (*see* Bajuri, x100)

x184   Ibrahim al-Ghazzi (Introduction) is Ibrahim ibn Tayyib al-Ghazzi, a teacher in the school of Islamic judiciary in Zabadani, northwest of Damascus, and the sheikh and mentor of Sheikh 'Abd al-Wakil Durubi, who was with him from approximately 1933 to 1950 (n).

x185   Idris (u3.5) is a prophet of Allah Most High whose true name, according to commentators, was Akhnukh ibn Shith ibn Adam (upon whom be peace). The grandfather of the prophet Nuh, he was called "Idris" for his devoted study (darasa) of Sacred Scripture, since when Allah made him a prophet, He revealed to him thirty-three pages. He was a tailor, and the first to write with a pen, sew, and wear cloth garments (skins were worn before him), the first to take weapons and fight unbelievers in jihad, and the first to study astronomy and mathematics. He is mentioned in the Holy Koran (19:56–57), where he is described as a *siddiq* (lit. "great-faithed one") and prophet, and Allah says, "We raised him to a high place," which refers to the fourth heaven where he presently is, having been seen there by the Prophet (Allah bless him and give him peace) on the night of his nocturnal ascent (mi'raj), as mentioned in a rigorously authenticated (sahih) hadith (*al-Futuhat al-ilahiyya* (y65), 3.67).

x186   Ilyas (u3.5) is Ilyas ibn Yasin ibn Fanhas ibn 'Izar ibn Harun ibn 'Imran (upon whom be peace), a prophet of Allah Most high who was a descendant of the prophet Harun, brother of Musa (upon whom be peace). Commentators relate that he was sent to a tribe of Bani Isra'il who lived around Baalbek (in present-day Lebanon) under King Arhab, who erected a huge gold statue with four faces that he called Baal and had them worship. Satan used to enter the statue and issue commands and prohibitions to its priests, who would memorize his directives and convey them to the people, while Ilyas called them to the worship of the one God. As Ilyas saw that the people but followed their king, he convinced the king to enter his religion, and there was a period of guidance, after which the king forsook the true path and returned to his former ways, with great anger and spite against Ilyas. He was forced to flee to the mountains and live in caves and ravines on herbs and fruits, while the people sought in vain to find and slay him. After living thus for seven years, Ilyas supplicated Allah Most High to relieve him of them, and Allah made his companion al-Yasa' a prophet in his stead (ibid., 2.58, 3.550).

x187   ("Imam ...") (*see under proper name*)

x188   al-'Iraqi (w12.2) is 'Abd al-Rahman ibn al-Husayn ibn 'Abd al-Rahman, Abu al-Fadl Zayn al-Din al-Hafiz al-'Iraqi, born in 725/1325 in Razanan, near Arbil, Iraq. A Shafi'i scholar of Kurdish origin, he moved with his father while still young to Cairo, where he was educated and became one of the greatest hadith masters (huffaz) of his time. He travelled to the Hijaz, Syria, and Palestine before returning to Egypt, where he settled and authored works in hadith, fundamentals of Islamic law and faith, principles of jurisprudence, prophetic biography, and biographies of Islamic scholars. He died in Cairo in 806/1404 (*al-A'lam* (y136), 3.344; and Sheikh Shu'ayb Arna'ut).

x189   'Isa (u3.5) is 'Isa ibn Maryam (upon whom be peace), the prophet and messenger of Allah Most High to Bani Isra'il, who denied him and plotted against him. He was known as the Word of God because Allah created him without a father by the mere word "be" (kun), whereupon his mother Maryam conceived him. Among the inimitable prophetic miracles (mu'jizat) vouchsafed to him was that by the leave of Allah he raised the dead, made the blind see, healed lepers, and when he molded a bird from clay and breathed into it, it became a living bird. It is related that when the Sacred Law was summarized before him by a lawyer in the words "It is that you love the Lord your God with your whole heart, whole soul, whole strength and whole mind; and that you love neighbor as yourself," 'Isa confirmed him in this. When Bani Isra'il wanted to kill him, Allah Most High saved him, as described in the words of the Holy Koran, "They did not slay him or crucify him, but thus was it made to seem to them" (Koran 4:157), referring to when Yahuda, chief of the Jews, met with a band of his people to kill 'Isa out of fear of his message, but Allah sent Gabriel to 'Isa to lead him to a covered alley-way that had a skylight, through which he was taken up to the sky. When Yahuda, in pursuit, ordered one of his companions to follow him into the passageway and murder him, Allah cast the likeness of 'Isa upon the man as he entered, and when he came out again after a fruitless search, the Jews attacked and killed him, think-ing him to be 'Isa, and hung him upon a cross (al-Shifa (y116), 1.192; al-Siraj al-munir (y72), 1.213, 1.216–17, 1.220; and n).

x190   Isaaq (*see next entry*)

x191   Ishaq (u3.5) is Ishaq ibn Ibrahim ibn Tarikh ibn Azar (upon whom be peace), the prophet of Allah Most High and son of the prophet Ibrahim and Sarah. All the prophets of Bani Isra'il were descended from Ibrahim through him, and commentators relate that he lived 180 years (al-Futuhat al-ilahiyya (y65), 1.102, 2.57).

x192   Ishaq (w55.3) (*see next entry*)

x193   Ishaq ibn Rahawayh (w18.2) is Ishaq ibn Ibrahim ibn Mukhallad, Abu Ya'qub Ibn Rahawayh al-Hanzali al-Tamimi, originally of Merv (in present-day Turkmen S.S.R.), born in 161/778. The scholar of Khurasan of his time, he is counted among the great hadith masters (huffaz) of Islam. He travelled in pursuit of knowledge to Iraq, the Hijaz, Syria, and Yemen, hearing hadiths from such sheikhs as Ahmad, Bukhari, Muslim, Tirmidhi, Nasa'i, and others, and he authored numerous works in the science, including his four-volume *Musnad* [As-cribed traditions]. Khatib Baghdadi once said of him, "He combined in his person hadith, Sacred Law, scholarship, truthfulness, piety, and abstinence," and Darami observed, "His sincerity was greater than the peoples of the east and west." He settled in Nishapur, and died there in 238/853 (al-A'lam (y136), 1.292).

x194   Ishmael (*see next entry*)

x195   Isma'il (u3.5) is Isma'il ibn Ibrahim ibn Tarikh ibn Azar (upon whom be peace), the prophet of Allah Most High. The son of Ibrahim and Hajar, he was born before the prophet Ishaq, and was eighty-nine years old when his father died, after which he lived another forty-one years. He is called the Father of the Arabs because he married into the tribe of Jurhum, from whom the Arabs are descended (al-Futuhat al-ilahiyya (y65), 1.102, 2.57; and al-Shifa (y116), 1.296).

x196   Isma'il Ansari (w48.3) is Isma'il ibn Muhammad al-Ansari, a contemporary Egyptian scholar of hadith and Sacred Law who works at the Department of Islamic Legal Opinion (Da'ira al-Ifta') in Riyadh, Saudi Arabia (A; and N).

x197   Israfil (u3.3) is one of the Archangels, and is responsible for blowing into the *Sur*, a horn-like trumpet whose call will usher in the events of the Last Day (*al-Shifa* (y116), 1.709; and n).

x198   Isra'il (w31.1) is Isra'il ibn Yunus ibn Abi Ishaq 'Amr ibn 'Abdullah, Abu Yusuf al-Hamdani al-Shaybi'i of Kufa, born in A.H. 100. He was a memorizer and trustworthy narrator whose hadiths appear in the works of both Bukhari and Muslim. It is related that he had a book of hadiths he memorized from. Shaqiq al-Balkhi said of him, "I learned awe (khushu') from Isra'il. We would be around him, and he would not know who was on his right or left, for his absorption in the hereafter, so I knew him for a pious man." He died in A.H. 160 (*Siyar a'lam al-nubala'* (y37), 7.355–60).

x199   (Imam) 'Izz ibn 'Abd al-Salam (p77.3) is 'Abd al-'Aziz ibn 'Abd al-Salam ibn Abu al-Qasim ibn al-Hasan, 'Izz al-Din al-Sulami, nicknamed the Sultan of Scholars, born in Damascus in 577/1181. A Shafi'i scholar and *mujtahid* Imam, he was educated in Damascus, went to Baghdad in A.H. 599, and then returned to his native city, where he first taught and gave the Friday sermon at the Zawiya of al-Ghazali, and then at the Great Umayyad Mosque. When the ruler al-Salih Isma'il ibn al-'Adal willingly surrendered the Palestinian citadel of Safad to the Franks, Ibn 'Abd al-Salam condemned him from the pulpit and omitted mentioning him in the post-sermon prayer, for which he was imprisoned. Upon his release, he moved to Cairo, where he was appointed as judge and imam of the Friday prayer, gaining such public influence that he could (and did) command the right and forbid the wrong with the force of law. He later resigned from the judiciary and remained at home to produce a number of brilliant works in Shafi'i jurisprudence, Koranic exegesis, methodological fundamentals of Sacred Law, formal legal opinion, government, and Sufism, though his main and enduring contribution was his masterpiece on Islamic legal principles *Qawa'id al-ahkam fi masalih al-anam* [The bases of legal rulings in the interests of mankind]. It is recorded that he kept the company of Imam Abul Hasan al-Shadhili, founder of the Shadhili tariqa, and his works on Sufism bespeak an understanding of the way. He died in Cairo at the age of eighty-one in 660/1262 (*al-A'lam* (y136), 4.21; *al-Imam al-'Izz ibn 'Abd al-Salam* (y38), 1.130–31; and n).

x200   Jabir (f10.12) is Jabir ibn 'Abdullah ibn 'Amr ibn Haram al-Khazraji (Allah be well pleased with him), a Medinan Helper and Companion of the Prophet (Allah bless him and give him peace) who was born sixteen years before the Hijra (A.D. 607). He participated in all the Muslims' battles except Badr. A prolific narrator of hadith, 1,540 traditions have been related from him by Bukhari, Muslim, and others. In later years he used to teach in the Prophet's mosque, and was the last of the Companions to die at Medina, in 78/697 (*al-A'lam* (y136), 2.104; and *al-Shifa* (y116), 1.154).

x201   Jabir ibn 'Abdullah (w53.1) (*see previous entry*)

x202   Jahm (w55.3) is Jahm ibn Safwan, Abu Muhriz al-Rasibi of Samarkand (in present-day Uzbek S.S.R.), a writer who inaugurated reprehensible innovations (bid‘a) in tenets of faith, founding the Jahmiyya school that bore his name. His doctrines first appeared in Termez, and represented among other things a denial of the Divine attributes affirmed by the Koran and hadith, claiming that Allah was beyond them; that man's acts were purely determined by Allah; that Allah was "everywhere"; and that the Koran was created. He was killed by Salam ibn Ahwaz in Merv (in present-day Turkmen S.S.R.) in 128/745 for denying that Allah spoke to Moses (*al-A‘lam* (y136), 2.141; *Sharh al-sunna* (y22), 1.172; and *Siyar a‘lam al-nubala’* (y37), 6.26–27).

x203   Jalal al-Din Suyuti (*see* Suyuti, x341)

x204   Jalal Bulqini (w12.3) is ‘Abd al-Rahman ibn ‘Umar ibn Ruslan, Abu al-Fadl Jalal al-Din al-Kinani al-Bulqini, born in 763/1362. He was an Egyptian Shafi‘i scholar and hadith specialist who succeeded his father Siraj al-Din as the foremost Shafi‘i authority of his time for formal legal opinion (fatwa). Appointed to the Islamic judiciary in Egypt several times, he served as a judge until the end of his life, and authored works in Sacred Law, Koranic exegesis, hadith commentary, and admonitions (wa‘z). He died in Cairo in 824/1421 (*al-A‘lam* (y136), 3.320).

x205   Jesus (*see* ‘Isa, x189)

x206   Jibril (*see* Gabriel, x126)

x207   Job (*see* Ayyub, x95)

x208   John (*see* Yahya, x371)

x209   Jonah (*see* Yunus, x376)

x210   Joseph (*see* Yusuf, x378)

x211   Junayd (*see* Abul Qasim al-Junayd, x51)

x212   (The Imam of the Two Sanctuaries) Juwayni (a2.7) is ‘Abd al-Malik ibn ‘Abdullah ibn Yusuf ibn Muhammad, Abu al-Ma‘ali Rukn al-Din Imam al-Haramayn al-Juwayni, a scholar in tenets of faith and the Imam of the Shafi‘i school of his time, originally from Juwain (in present-day Afghanistan), born in 419/1028. He was educated by his father, and after his death read his father's entire library and then took his place as teacher at Nishapur, though he was later forced to travel to Baghdad because of trouble between the Ash‘aris, Mu‘tazilites, and Shiites. After meeting the greatest scholars of Baghdad, he went on to Mecca, living in the Sacred Precinct for four years, after which he moved to Medina and taught and gave formal legal opinion (fatwa), gaining his nickname, the Imam of the Two Sanctuaries, i.e. of Mecca and Medina. At length he returned to Persia, where the vizier Nizam al-Mulk, having built a first Nizamiyya Academy in Baghdad for Abu Ishaq Shirazi to teach in, built a second one for al-

Juwayni at Nishapur. It was here the Imam wrote in earnest, completing his fifteen-volume *Nihaya al-matlab fi diraya al-madhhab* [The utmost of what is sought: on understanding the evidence of the Shafi'i school] which no one in the field of Islamic law had ever produced the like of, as well as other works in tenets of faith, Ash'ari theology, fundamentals of Islamic legal methodology, and Shafi'i law. Among his greatest legacies to Islam and the Muslims was his pupil Ghazali, who is said to have surpassed even the Imam at the end of his life. He died in Nishapur in 478/1085 (*al-A'lam* (y136), 4.160; *Introduction to Sharh al-Waraqat* (y64), 3–4; *Tabaqat al-Shafi'iyya al-kubra* (y128), 5.165; and n).

x213   Kamal 'Abd al-Majid Muhammad (Document 2) is Kamal ibn 'Abd al-Majid ibn Muhammad, Abu Muhammad, Abu Hudayb al-'Abbadi al-Balqawi, born in 1953 in Khilda, in the al-Balqa' region of Jordan to the northwest of Amman. He took the Shadhili tariqa from Sheikh 'Abd al-Rahman Shaghouri of Damascus in 1977, and has studied Arabic grammar, tenets of faith, Shafi'i jurisprudence, and hadith with Sheikh Yunus Hamdan. He lives in Khilda, where he presently manufactures and distributes concrete building blocks (n).

x214   Kamal ibn al-Humam (w43.3) is Muhammad ibn 'Abd al-Wahid ibn 'Abd al-Hamid ibn Mas'ud, Kamal al-Din Ibn al-Humam, born in Alexandria in 790/1388. He was among the foremost Imams of the Hanafi school, and a scholar in Sacred Law, hadith, tenets of faith, Koranic exegesis, estate division, mathematics, Arabic lexicology, and logic. He was educated in Cairo, and lived for a time in Aleppo, Mecca, and Medina before returning to Egypt, where the came to enjoy considerable prestige among the rulers and heads of state. His major work is the eight-volume *Fath al-Qadir* [Triumph of the Omnipotent], a commentary on Marghiyani's *al-Hidaya* [Guidance]. Though unfinished by its author, it ranks among the greatest Hanafi works for explaining primary textual evidence from the Koran and hadith and the reasoning of the school's Imams in deriving rulings from them. He died in Cairo in 861/1457 (*al-A'lam* (y136), 6.255; and Sheikh Shu'ayb Arna'ut).

x215   Khalil Nahlawi (r0.1) is Khalil ibn 'Abd al-Qadir al-Shaybani al-Nahlawi, a Hanafi scholar of Damascus. He did not live to publish his *al-Durar al-mubaha fi al-hazr wa al-ibaha* [The uncovered pearls: on the unlawful and lawful], but died in Damascus in 1350/1931, after which his sons printed the work (*al-Durar al-mubaha* (y99), 235; and *Mu'jam al-mu'allifin* (y69), 4.121).

x216   Khatib Baghdadi (w56.2) is Ahmad ibn 'Ali ibn Thabit, Abu Bakr al-Khatib al-Baghdadi, born in Ghuzayya, midway between Kufa and Mecca, in 392/1002. He was a Shafi'i scholar, hadith master (hafiz), and historian who was raised in Baghdad and travelled to Mecca, Basra, al-Dinawar, Kufa, and other cities in quest of hadith before returning to Baghdad, where his ability won recognition from the caliph's vizier Ibn Musallam. A turn in political fortunes toward the end of his career caused him to leave Baghdad for a period, during which he travelled to Syria and resided in Damascus, Sur, Tripoli, and Aleppo before returning. He authored some fifty-six works in hadith, Sacred Law, and history, though he is best known for his fourteen-volume *Tarikh Baghdad* [The history of Baghdad]. In his final illness he made a pious endowment of his entire library and distributed his money and property to charitable causes. He died in Baghdad in 463/1072 (*al-A'lam* (y136), 1.172; and *Tabaqat al-Shafi'iyya al-kubra* (y128), 4.29).

x217   (Sheikh) al-Khatib (*see* Muhammad Shirbini Khatib, x264(a))

x218   Khattabi (r4.2) is Hamd ibn Muhammad ibn Ibrahim ibn al-Khattab, Abu Sulayman al-Khattabi of Bust, Afghanistan, born in 319/931. An Imam in Shafi'i jurisprudence, hadith, and Arabic lexicology, he studied hadith in Mecca, Basra, Baghdad, and Nishapur, and later taught many students, including the hadith master (hafiz) al-Hakim. He wrote a number of works in Sacred Law and hadith, but is perhaps best known for his outstanding four-volume commentary on the *Sunan* of Abu Dawud, *Ma'alim al-Sunan* [The waymarks of "The sunnas"]. He died in Bust in 388/998 (*al-A'lam* (y136), 2.273; and *Tabaqat al-Shafi'iyya al-Kubra* (y128), 3.282).

x219   Khidr (w9.10), according to commentators, is Balya' ibn Malikan, Abu al-'Abbas al-Khidr (upon whom be peace), who is referred to in the story of Moses in sura al-Kahf of the Holy Koran (18:65). It is said that he was of Bani Isra'il, while others relate that he was a prince who left his this-worldly possessions for a life of asceticism and devotions. He was nicknamed al-Khidr (derived from "greenness") because when he sat on withered patch of vegetation it would become thriving and green. Scholars disagree as to whether he is presently alive, though most believe he is and will remain so until the Day of Judgement because of having drunk of the water of life—and also as to whether he is a prophet, angel, or friend of Allah (wali), the majority holding him to be a prophet (*al-Futuhat al-ilahiyya* (y65), 3.35; *al-Siraj al-munir* (y72), 2.391; and A).

x220   Khubayb al-Ansari (w30.1) is Khubayb ibn 'Adi ibn 'Amir ibn Majda'a ibn Jahjaba (Allah be well pleased with him), one of the Medinan Helpers and a Companion of the Prophet (Allah bless him and give him peace). Dispatched on the raid of al-Raji', Khubayb was captured and later sold in Mecca to the sons of al-Harith ibn 'Amir, whom he had previously slain at the battle of Badr. He remained their prisoner until his killers assembled, and they took him to Tan'im, outside the Sacred Precinct, where he asked to be allowed to pray two rak'as, after which he said, "By Allah, were I not afraid of your thinking I fear death, I would have prayed more." Then he supplicated, "O Allah, reckon them in number, kill them one by one, and let none of them remain alive." Then 'Uqba ibn al-Harith rose and killed him, Khubayb thus being the one to establish the sunna for Muslims being killed to pray two rak'as (*Siyar a'lam al-nubala'* (y37), 1.246–47).

x221   Kirmani (p75.2) is Muhammad ibn Yusuf ibn 'Ali ibn Sa'id, Shams al-Din al-Kirmani, born in 717/1317. A scholar of hadith and Sacred Law originally from Kirman, Persia, he became famous in Baghdad, where he taught for thirty years. He resided for a period in Mecca, where he devoted himself to writing his twenty-five-volume commentary on Bukhari's *Sahih* called *al-Kawakib al-darari fi sharh Sahih al-Bukhari* [The brilliant stars: an exegesis of "Sahih al-Bukhari"]. He also authored works on Koranic commentary and fundamentals of Islamic law and faith. He died in 786/1384 on his return from hajj to Baghdad, where he was buried (*al-A'lam* (y136), 7.153).

x222   Korah (w8.2) is Qarun ibn Yas-hur ibn Qahath ibn Lawi ibn Ya'qub ibn Ishaq ibn Ibrahim, a cousin of the prophet Musa (upon whom be peace), as his father Yas-hur and Musa's father 'Imran were brothers. He believed in Musa, though he later grew jealous of Musa's being sent as a prophet and Harun's being an Imam, and finally became an unbeliever because of his wealth, seeking to be superior to Musa by wearing his garments long and by oppressing Bani Isra'il when Pharaoh appointed him over them. Allah gave him such wealth that carrying the very keys to it weighed heavily on a group of strong men, and when his people told him not to exult in it but to seek the life of the next world by spending it in obedience to Allah, he replied that he had only been given it because of his knowledge, for he was the most learned of them in the Torah after Musa (upon whom be peace). One day, as he came out in his finery to the people, some of whom envied him for his wealth and success, Allah caused the earth to swallow both him and his house (*al-Futuhat al-ilahiyya* (y65), 3.359–62).

x223   Lot (*see next entry*)

x224   Lut (u3.5) is Lut ibn Haran ibn Tarikh (upon whom be peace), the prophet of Allah Most High to the people of Sadhum (Sodom). His father Haran was the brother of the prophet Ibrahim (upon whom be peace). Commentators relate that they lived in Babylon in Iraq, but emigrated west, Ibrahim settling in Palestine, and Lut in Jordan, from whence he was sent to Sadhum. The story of Lut and the people of Sadhum is told in the Holy Koran (7:80–84), and how Allah Most High rained down stones upon them and destroyed them for their wicked practice of sodomy (*al-Futuhat al-ilahiyya* (y65), 2.58–59, 2.161–62).

x225   Ma' al-'Aynayn al-Qalqami (w9.4) is Muhammad Mustafa ibn Muhammad Fadil ibn Muhammad May'man, Abu al-Anwar Ma' al-'Anayn al-Qalqami, born near Walata in the Hawd of southeastern Mauritania in 1831. Of Mauritanian and Moroccan descent, he was a traditional religious figure, Sufi sheikh of the Qadiri order, and a prolific writer who was also widely known as a digger of wells and energetic founder of Sufi hospices (zawaya). He participated, after making a personal alliance with the Sharifian dynasty of Morocco, in armed resistance to the French in which he lost several sons, dying in Tiznit in southern Morocco in 1910 (*al-A'lam* (y136), 7.243; and *Muslim Brotherhoods* (y86), 125).

x226   Mahmud ibn Rabi' (w31.1) is Mahmud ibn al-Rabi' ibn Suraqa ibn 'Amr, Abu Muhammad al-Khazraji (Allah be well pleased with him) of Medina, born in A.H. 6. He met the Prophet (Allah bless him and give him peace) when four years old in his family's home, where the Prophet (Allah bless him and give him peace) spat a mouthful of water from the family well upon his face for the blessing of it. An Imam and reliable transmitter, he related hadiths from Abu Ayyub al-Ansari, 'Ubada ibn al-Samit, and others; and among those who related hadiths from him were Anas ibn Malik, Makhul, and Zuhri. He died in A.H. 99 at ninety-three years of age (*Siyar a'lam al-nubala'* (y37), 3.519)

x227   Makhul (w43.3) is Makhul ibn Abi Muslim Shahrab ibn Shadhil, Abu 'Abdullah al-Shamil, born in Kabul, Afghanistan. The scholar of Syria of his time, he was a freed slave who learned Sacred Law and travelled to many places in search of knowledge, among them Iraq, Medina, and Damascus, where he settled. Imam Zuhri said of him, "No one of his time had more insight in giving formal legal opinions." He died in Damascus in 112/730 (*al-A'lam* (y136), 7.284).

x228   (Imam) Malik (b1.2) is Malik ibn Anas ibn Malik, Abu 'Abdullah al-Asbahi al-Himyari, the *mujtahid* Imam born in Medina in 93/712. The second of the four greatest Imams of Sacred Law, his school has more followers than that of anyone besides Abu Hanifa. He was known as the Scholar of Medina, and was as renowned for his sincerity, faith, piety, and godfearingness as for his command of the sciences of hadith and knowledge of Sacred Law.His generosity was legend-ary, as was his love for the Prophet (Allah bless him and give him peace), whom he held in such awe and respect that he would not mount his horse within the con-fines of Medina out of reverence for the ground that enclosed the Prophet's body (Allah bless him and give him peace). His piety was such that he was never too proud to say he did not know when asked about matters he was not sure of, and he would not relate a hadith without first performing ablution. He was the author of *al-Muwatta'* [The trodden path], the greatest hadith collection of its time, nearly every hadith of which was accepted by Bukhari in his *Sahih*. His disciple Imam Shafi'i used to say of it, "After the Book of Allah, no book has appeared on earth that is sounder than Malik's." He was uncompromising in his religion and kept far from the rulers and princes of his time. When he gave the opinion that the caliph al-Mansur should be removed and Muhammad ibn 'Abdullah of 'Ali's family be instated, the caliph's uncle Ja'far ibn Sulayman, governor of Medina, had Malik scourged seventy lashes, dislocating his shoulder. The only effect of this was to increase the Imam's highmindedness and dignity, and when al-Mansur learned of it, he apologized profusely and asked Malik to write a book of Islamic jurisprudence that he could enjoin with the force of law upon all Muslims regard-less of their school, but the Imam refused. He authored outstanding works in Sac-red Law, hadith, and Koranic exegesis, and left behind a host of brilliant scholars he had trained as part of his great legacy to Islam and the Muslims. He died in Medina in 179/795 (*al-A'lam* (y136), 5.257; *al-Muwatta'* (y82), introduction; *al-Targhib wa al-tarhib* (y9), 1.14; Sheikh Shu'ayb Arna'ut; and n).

x229   Malik (u3.3) is the keeper of hell and head of the angels of torment there, who receive his orders. His place in the midst of hell is connected to all parts of it by bridges which the angels of torment pass upon, above its inhabitants, and he sees the farthest reaches of it as easily as he sees the closest (*al-Futuhat al-ilahiyya* (y65), 4.96).

x230   Malik ibn Dinar (s5.1) is Malik ibn Dinar, Abu Yahya al-Basri, born in the time of Ibn 'Abbas. He was an early Sufi and scholar who studied under Hasan al-Basri, from whom he related hadiths, as well as from Anas ibn Malik, Ibn Sirin, and others. Pious and abstinent, he lived from the work of his own hands, copying out Korans for payment. Among his sayings is, "Since coming to know people I have not enjoyed their praise or disliked their blame, for those who praise exaggerate, and those who blame exaggerate." He died in Basra in 131/748 (*al-A'lam* (y136), 5.260–61; *Siyar a'lam al-nubala'* (y37), 5.362–64; and n).

x231   Malik al-Rahawi (p48.2) is Malik ibn Marara al-Rahawi (Allah be well pleased with him) of Yemen, a prophetic Companion. It is related that when he returned to his people after visiting the Prophet (Allah bless him and give him peace), the latter sent them a letter that said, "... I enjoin you to goodness towards him, for he is looked up to," and the Hamdan tribe gathered eighty-nine camels that they presented him as a gift (*al-Isaba fi tamyiz al-Sahaba* (y14), 3.334–35).

x232   Mansur 'Ali Nasif (w17.1) is Mansur ibn 'Ali Nasif, an Egyptian Shafi'i scholar and hadith specialist of the present century. A teacher in the Zaynabi Friday Mosque in Cairo, his most well known work is the five-volume *al-Taj al-jami' li al-usul fi ahadith al-Rasul* [The crown containing the fundamentals of Sacred Law from the hadiths of the Prophet], which, with its 5,887 hadiths, is among the best works on the primary texts for the rulings of the Shafi'i school. He died sometime after 1371/1951 (*al-A'lam* (y136), 7.301; and n).

x233   Martin Lings (w1.1) is a contemporary English Muslim author on Islam and Sufism. He took an English degree at Oxford and later lectured at Cairo University, mainly on Shakespeare, for twelve years. In 1952 he returned to England, took a degree in Arabic at London University, and was appointed in special charge of the Arabic manuscripts at the British Museum. Sheikh 'Abd al-Wakil remembers him visiting Sheikh Muhammad Hashimi in Damascus when researching his book on Sheikh Ahmad al-'Alawi, *A Sufi Saint of the Twentieth Century*. Among his other works are his outstanding prophetic biography *Muhammad,* as well as *What Is Sufism?, Shakespeare in the Light of of Sacred Art, Quranic Arts of Calligraphy and Illumination,* and *Ancient Beliefs and Modern Superstitions.*

    Despite many excellent passages of genuine insight, the latter work and parts of his others diverge from the teachings of Islam on such questions as the validity of non-Islamic religions (dis: w4, x348), and the suggestion that all the inhabitants of hell will enter paradise (*Muhammad* (y75), 94), adducing the words of the Koran referring to hell's eternality, "... except as your Lord wills" (Koran 6:128, 11:107, previously discussed in the twentieth paragraph of w55.3), together with a hadith to the effect that Allah will remove from hell a people (Ar. *qawm,* and in Bukhari's version "some peoples" (*aqwam*)) who did no good at all, and enter them into paradise (*Sahih al-Bukhari* (y30), 9.398–99; and *Sahih Muslim* (y92), 1.170). Some scholars understand the hadith as alluding to those who did no good in this life beyond mere acknowledgement of Allah and His messenger, even if this minimal amount of faith was not perceptible to the angels previously commanded to remove those with "a grain of faith in their hearts" from the fire; while others say it refers not to those who refused to believe in the prophetic messengers sent to them, but rather to those who lived in the times between the coming of successive messengers such that Allah's commands did not reach them. Both groups of scholars interpret the hadith in this way to reach an accord between it and the more than fifty Koranic verses mentioned above at w55.3 that clearly prove that unbelievers shall remain in hell forever, for it is understood among scholars that while abrogation (nasikh wa mansukh) enters into certain primary texts about rites and acts, it does not under any circumstances enter into texts about tenets of faith ('aqida), such that one Koranic text should be believed and another discarded. Rather, we look for a more comprehensive explanation that joins between all the texts, for all are the truth. Despite such interpretive shortcomings, Lings's works are generally of a high quality, and some, like his *What Is Sufism?* and *Muhammad* are unsurpassed in their genre, and seem destined to contribute much to the understanding of Islam in the West. He presently lives in England (*Muhammad* (y75), inside back cover; Sheikh Shu'ayb Arna'ut; N; and n).

x234   Marut (p3.2) is one of the two angels sent to Babylon to teach sorcery to the wicked, discussed above at x136 (n).

x235   Mary (*see next entry*)

x236   Maryam (w30.1) is Maryam bint 'Imran, the daughter of the priest 'Imran and his wife Hanna, who when pregnant with Maryam, vowed to dedicate the child she bore to the service of the Holy Temple in Jerusalem, and at her birth accordingly named her *Maryam,* meaning "servant of her Lord." The purest of womenkind, she was a *siddiqa* (lit. "great-faithed one"), and miraculously conceived the prophet 'Isa (upon whom be peace). Both she and her child were unfortunately later taken as objects of worship by some sects of Christians because of the strangeness of 'Isa's birth without a father, though as commentators point out, by such reasoning the prophet Adam (upon whom be peace) might better deserve to be worshipped, since he had neither father nor mother (*al-Futuhat al-ilahiyya* (y65), 1.262–63, 1.269; and n).

x237   al-Mawardi (*see* (Imam) Abul Hasan Mawardi, x48)

x238   Maydani (m2.8) is 'Abd al-Ghani ibn Talib ibn Hamada ibn Ibrahim al-Ghunaymi al-Maydani, of Damascus, born in 1222/1807. A Hanafi scholar who studied under Imam Muhammad Amin Ibn 'Abidin and authored works in Sacred Law, hadith commentary, tenets of faith, and Arabic grammar, his best known work is the four-volume *al-Lubab fi sharh al-Kitab* [The quintessence: an exegesis of "The book"], which expounds Ahmad Quduri's classic in Hanafi jurisprudence *Kitab al-Quduri*. He died in 1298/1881 (*al-A'lam* (y136), 4.33).

x239   Mika'il (u3.3) is the archangel of safety, fertility, and rain. He is mentioned together with Gabriel in the Holy Koran (at 2:98) because he is the angel of sustenance (rizq), the life of the body; just as Gabriel is the angel of revelation (wahy), the life of the spirit (*al-Futuhat al-ilahiyya* (y65), 1.84; *al-Shifa* (y116), 1.710; and *al-Siraj al-munir* (y72), 1.79).

x240   Moses (*see* Musa, x271)

x241   Mu'adh (*see next entry*)

x242   Mu'adh ibn Jabal (w26.1) is Mu'adh ibn Jabal ibn 'Amr ibn Aws, Abu 'Abd al-Rahman al-Khazraji (Allah be well pleased with him), born twenty years before the Hijra (A.D. 603). A Medinan Helper, he was among the greatest of the

Companions of the Prophet (Allah bless him and give him peace) in the knowledge of the lawful and unlawful, and one of the six who gathered the Koran in the lifetime of the Prophet (Allah bless him and give him peace). He participated in the battles of Badr, the Confederates, and all the others. After the campaign of Tabuk, he was sent as a judge and teacher to the people of Yemen, where he remained until Abu Bakr had been made caliph following the Prophet's death (Allah bless him and give him peace), when he returned to Medina. He went with Abu 'Ubayda ibn al-Jarrah on the Syrian jihad, which he assumed command of when Abu 'Ubayda died of the plague, and he was confirmed in the position by 'Umar. He died of the plague in the same year, 18/639, and was buried in the Jordan Rift Valley to the west of present-day Irbid, Jordan (al-A'lam (y136), 7.258; and n).

x243   Mu'awiya (r9.2) is Mu'awiya ibn Abu Sufyan Sakhr ibn Harb ibn Umayya ibn 'Abd al-Shams ibn 'Abd Manaf (Allah be well pleased with him), born in Mecca twenty years before the Hijra (A.D. 603). A noble of Quraysh, collected, eloquent, and dignified, he entered Islam the day Mecca was conquered (A.H. 8), and the Prophet (Allah bless him and give him peace) made him one of the scribes who recorded the Koran in writing. He later became the governor of Syria and in A.H. 41 assumed the Islamic caliphate, founding the Umayyad dynasty whose capital was Damascus. His reign was one that added great conquests to the domains of Islam, which was established in his time as the religion of peoples across North Africa to the Atlantic Ocean, as well as Sudan, many of the islands of Greece, and the Dardenelles. He was the first to use the Mediterranean for naval jihad, and the first to build mihrabs (niches) in mosques. He died in Damascus in 60/680 (al-A'lam (y136), 7.261–62).

x244   al-Mughira (m2.2) is al-Mughira ibn Shu'ba ibn Abu 'Amr ibn Mas'ud, Abu 'Abdullah al-Thaqafi (Allah be well pleased with him), born in Ta'if twenty years before the Hijra (A.D. 603). A Companion of the Prophet (Allah bless him and give him peace) who was noted for his keen intellect, he entered Islam in A.H. 5, was present at Hudaybiya, fought against the false prophet Musaylima at al-Yamama, and also took part in the northern jihads that opened Syria-Palestine for Islam, losing an eye at the battle of Yarmouk. The caliph 'Umar made him governor of Basra, and he conquered several new lands for Islam before 'Umar removed him from the position, though he later instated him as governor of Kufa, an office which the caliph 'Uthman first confirmed him in, but then removed him. He stayed aloof from the discord between 'Ali and Mu'awiya, and the latter afterwards made him governor of Kufa a second time, and he remained in the position the rest of his life. He related 136 hadiths from the Prophet (Allah bless him and give him peace), and died in Kufa in 50/670 (ibid., 7.277).

x245   Muhammad (Introduction) is Muhammad ibn 'Abdullah ibn 'Abd al-Muttalib ibn Hashim, Abu al-Qasim (Allah bless him and give him peace), the unlettered Qurayshite Arabian prophet of Allah Most High to the entire world, the greatest and most influential human being in the history of mankind, born on the twelfth of Rabi' Awwal, fifty-three years befor the Hijra (A.D. 571), in Mecca. The son of 'Abdullah ibn 'Abd al-Muttalib and Amina bint Wahb of Bani Zahra, his father died before his birth, leaving him an orphan. He first grew up in the desert, being nursed there for two years by Halima al-Sa'diyya, and when his mother died in his seventh year, his grandfather 'Abd al-Muttalib became his guardian. Despite being raised as an orphan, he developed the noblest character, and was known among his people as the Truthful and Trustworthy (al-Sadiq al-Amin). He first worked as a shepherd and then engaged in trade, travelling to Syria twice, and he married the owner of the goods he managed, the wealthy, beautiful, and virtuous Khadija bint Khuwaylid at her request when he was twenty-five years of age.

When he was forty, Allah Most High chose him to be the last of the succession of His prophets, sent to all mankind and jinn to teach them the religion of Islam, the most perfect and comprehensive system for felicity in this world and unending happiness in the next. The essence of the new religion was to proclaim that there was no god but the one living eternal God, Allah, who is without son, associate, or partner; to call to the worship of Him alone, obedience of His laws alone, and the recognition that the only superiority men possess over one another is in their godfearingness (taqwa) and sincerity in servanthood to Him; and to warn men that they would be accountable for their actions on a Day of Judgement, whence they would enter paradise or hell. In a word, it enjoined high-mindedness and nobility and forbade all that was contemptible and base, ordering man to use every means to realize the right and eliminate the wrong.

After thirteen years of calling people in Mecca to Islam and enduring the persecution of idolators there, the Prophet (Allah bless him and give him peace) was invited by a delegation of the notables of Medina (then called Yathrib) in the north to end their immemorial feuds by agreeing to rule them, and his emmigration (hijra) to them was to mark the beginning of the Islamic calendar. At Medina, a new phase began, deputations were sent to various peoples to invite them to Islam, and finally Allah ordered the Prophet (Allah bless him and give him peace) to fight to free mankind from the servitude of false gods and other men, and lead them to the light of revealed monotheism. In this undertaking, though a gentle and peaceable man, the Prophet (Allah bless him and give him peace) risked his person in some twenty-seven separate battles, including Badr in A.H. 2 and Uhud in A.H. 3, both against the idolators of Mecca; Bani Nadir in A.H. 4; the Confederates and Bani Qurayza in A.H. 5; Khaybar and the conquest of Mecca in A.H. 7; Hunayn in A.H. 8; and Tabuk in A.H. 9. Never in his life did the Prophet (Allah bless him and give him peace) flee from battle or turn his back to the enemy, even in the deadliest peril, and by ten years after the Hijra, Allah was worshipped in the Arabian peninsula, and the one true religion had been established.

While abrogating the laws of all prior religions regarding particular religious rites and works (furu'), it was equally the primordial religion, identical with the message of every previously sent prophet in tenets of faith (usul), in terms of enjoining belief and worship of the one Supreme Being alone, in which sense Muslims say, "We differentiate between none of His messengers" (Koran 2:285), for all taught pure monotheism. At the same time, Allah Most High mentions the prophets by saying, "Those are the messengers, We have favored some above others" (Koran 2:253), and He vouchsafed favors to Muhammad (Allah bless him and give him peace) that no prophet had previously been given; among them that he was sent to all mankind, not just a particular tribe or race; that he was the final prophet and messenger; that his followers are greater in number than those of any other prophet; that he was sent as a mercy unto the worlds; and that he was granted the magnificent and incomparable Arabic Koran, a living miracle which no one has ever been able to compose anything similar to, which remains in its textual purity as it was revealed, preserved from alteration by human hand until the end of time. By any standards, no one has so profoundly influenced so many, in day to day manners, speech, dress, worship, belief, and culture, as has the Prophet (Allah bless him and give him peace), who died in Medina, his message delivered and mission wonderfully accomplished, in 11/633 (*al-A'lam* (y136), 6.218–19; *al-Siraj al-munir* (y72), 1.166; *Sutur min hayat Muhammad* (y115), 2–4; and n).

x246   (Imam) Muhammad (*see* Muhammad ibn Hasan Shaybani, x257)

x247   Muhammad 'Abdullah Jurdani (j12.6) is Muhammad ibn 'Abdullah ibn 'Abd al-Latif al-Jurdani, born in Dumyat, Egypt. One of the great Shafi'i scholars of nineteenth-century Egypt, he studied under Sheikh Ibrahim Bajuri and authored a number of valuable works in hadith commentary, tenets of faith, and Sacred Law, in the latter field being best known for his four-volume *Fath al-'Allam bi sharh Murshid al-anam* [The victory of the All-knowing: an exegesis of "The people's guide"], a commentary on a shorter work by himself. He died in Dumyat in 1331/1913 (*al-A'lam* (y136), 6.244; and n).

x248   Muhammad Abul Mawahib (w9.4) is Muhammad, Abu al-Mawahib Jamal al-Din al-Shadhili of Cairo. He was an Islamic scholar, Sufi sage, and author of considerable eloquence in all aspects of the Sufi way. Among his works is *Qawanin hukm al-ishraq* [The laws of the dawning of illumination], which 'Abd al-Wahhab Sha'rani describes as "a marvelous work which no one else has produced anything comparable to, and which attests to the fullness of its author's experience in the path." He lived near al-Azhar Mosque in Cairo, and died sometime after A.H. 851 (*al-Tabaqat al-kubra* (y124), 2.67, 2.74).

x249   (al-Hajj) Muhammad al-Ahrash (w9.4), also known as Bu Dali, was a Moroccan Sufi of the Darqawi tariqa who went to the Hijaz on pilgrimage, and when he returned in 1799 via Egypt, which was under attack by the French, he gathered a force of Tunisians and Moroccans, many of whom lived in Cairo, to fight the invaders. He later fought the forces of the Bey of Constantine from the mountains of eastern Algeria, from which he was eventually dislodged and fled westward to the Oran region where he joined Muhammad ibn Sharif, after which history records nothing further of him (*Muslim Brotherhoods* (y86), 43–44).

x250   Muhammad 'Alawi Maliki (w47.1) is Muhammad al-Hasan ibn 'Alawi ibn 'Abbas ibn 'Abd al-'Aziz al-Maliki, a descendant of the Prophet (Allah bless him and give him peace). A contemporary Meccan scholar of hadith, Maliki jurisprudence, Koranic exegesis, tenets of faith, and prophetic biography, he was born to a family of traditional Maliki scholars of ancestral residence in the Holy City and educated by his father, al-Sayyid 'Alawi Maliki, who authorized him to teach every work he read with him, which he began to do while still in his childhood. He has a doctorate in hadith from al-Azhar, and has travelled to Morocco, Egypt, Pakistan, and India to learn hadiths, gather manuscripts, visit scholars, and record their knowledge. In A.H. 1390/1970 he was appointed full professor in the college of Sacred Law at Umm al-Qura University in Mecca, and after his father's death, the scholars of Mecca met in his home to ask him to accept his father's position as teacher in al-Masjid al-Haram, which he did. He has authored a number of works on the Prophet (Allah bless him and give him peace), Sacred Law, and tenets of faith, including *Muhammad al-insan al-kamil* [Muhammad, the perfect man], *Mafahim yajibu an tusahhaha* [Notions that should be corrected], and *Mawatta' al-Imam Malik ibn Anas riwaya Ibn al-Qasim* ["The trodden path" of Imam Malik ibn Anas in the transmission received from Ibn al-Qasim]. Currently prevented from teaching in both the Sacred Mosque and the university, he gives free traditional Islamic instruction in Arabic grammar, hadith, Maliki jurisprudence, and other subjects at his own residence and mosque on Maliki Street in the Rusayfa district of Mecca (*al-Ta'i' al-sa'id* (y84), 3–4; and n).

x251   Muhammad 'Ali Sanusi (w9.4) is Muhammad ibn 'Ali ibn al-Sanus, Abu 'Abdullah al-Sanusi al-Khattabi al-Hasani al-Idrisi, born in Mosteghanem, Algeria, in 1202/1787. The founder of the Sanusi tariqa, he was a scholar of the Koran, hadith, and Maliki jurisprudence, and a Sufi adept whose sheikhs included al-'Arabi al-Darqawi and Ahmad Tijani, the respective founders of the Darqawi and Tijani orders. He was a prolific writer who produced more than forty books, poems, and treatises in Sacred Law, hadith, fundamentals of jurisprudence, tenets of faith, history, geneology, and mathematics. He travelled to Fez, Tunis, Tripoli, Egypt, and Mecca, and in 1842 founded his main Sufi center (zawiya) near al-Bayda in Libya. His order worked continuously for the next fifteen years to proselytize for Islam in a sustained southerly movement along the trade routes to the interior of Africa, with considerable success in establishing the religion throughout the sub-Saharan region. Leaving the order's affairs in the hands of a deputy, he travelled to Mecca and remained there until 1853, when he returned to establish a new center in the east of Libya, at Jaghbub, where he spent the final productive years of his life, and died in 1286/1859 (*al-A'lam* (y136), 6.299; and *Muslim Brotherhoods* (y86), 101–14).

x252   Muhammad ibn 'Allan Bakri (j16.1) is Muhammad 'Ali ibn Muhammad 'Allan ibn Ibrahim ibn Muhammad ibn 'Allan al-Bakri al-Siddiqi, born in Mecca in 996/1588. He was a Shafi'i scholar of hadith, Sacred Law, Koranic exegesis, and other subjects, which he acquired from the sheikhs of his time, memorizing the Koran in all of its canonical readings (qira'at), and becoming learned enough in Shafi'i jurisprudence to be named mufti of Mecca at the age of twenty-four. Called the Suyuti of His Time, he authored works about the Prophet (Allah bless him and give him peace), as well as in Koranic exegesis, hadith, Sacred Law, formal legal opinion, Sufism, tenets of faith, history, and Arabic grammar. His two hadith commentaries, *al-Futuhat al-rabbaniyya 'ala al-adhkar al-Nawawiyya* [The godly victories: an exegesis of Nawawi's "Remembrances of Allah"], and *Dalil al-falihin li turuq Riyad al-salihin* [The guide of the successful to the ways of "The gardens of the righteous"], are both extremely professional and attest to his knowledge of Sacred Law and hadith. He died in Mecca in 1057/1647 and was buried near Sheikh al-Islam Ibn Hajar Haytami (*al-A'lam* (y136), 6.293; *al-Adhkar* (y102), 7–10; and n).

x253   (Imam) Muhammad Amin ibn 'Abidin (w9.4) is Muhammad Amin ibn 'Umar ibn 'Abd al-'Aziz 'Abidin, born in Damascus in 1198/1784. Originally a

Shafi'i, he changed his school and became the Hanafi Imam of his time. His most famous work, the eight-volume *Hashiya radd al-muhtar 'ala al-Durr al-mukhtar* [The enlightenment of the baffled: a commentary on "The choice pearls"], is highly thought of by Hanafi scholars, who consider every word of it an authoritative text (nass) in the school. He also authored works in fundamentals of Islamic law and faith, formal legal opinion, Koranic exegesis, and estate division, and died in Damascus in 1252/1836 (*al-A'lam* (y136), 6.42; A; and n).

x254   (Sheikh) Muhammad Amin Kurdi (w9.1) is Muhammad Amin ibn Fath Allah al-Irbali al-Kurdi, born in Arbil, Iraq. Of Kurdish origin, he was Shafi'i scholar who was among the greatest Naqshbandi masters of the last century. Instructed and authorized in the Sufi path in Iraq by Sheikh 'Umar Diya' al-Din ibn 'Uthman Siraj al-Din al-Naqshbandi, he travelled to the Hijaz on hajj and stayed in Mecca for a year before proceeding to Cairo, where he studied Sacred Law and other subjects at al-Azhar, an education he turned to good account in his *Tanwir al-qulub fi mu'amala 'Allam al-Ghuyub* [The enlightenment of hearts: on one's dealings with the Knower of the Unseen], a manual on tenets of faith, Shafi'i Law, and the path of Sufism as taught by his masters. Of great personal sincerity, sanctity, and spiritual will, he gained a large following in Cairo and became the sheikh of his time in guiding seekers to the truth, placing particular emphasis in his training on the insight that only Allah Most High has any effect in the world, and that He is beyond any resemblance to created things. He authored a number of works in Sacred Law, tenets of faith, and Sufism, and Allah vouchsafed many graces to him during his lifetime, the greatest of which was his firm adherence to the Koran and sunna. He died in Cairo in 1331/1914 (*al-A'lam* (y136), 6.43; *Tanwir al-qulub* (y74), 1–55; and n).

x255   Muhammad Bakhit al-Muti'i (e14.1) is Muhammad Bakhit ibn Husayn al-Muti'i, born in al-Muti'a, upper Egypt, in 1271/1854. The grand mufti of Egypt and one of the leading Hanafi scholars of his time, he was educated at al-Azhar, where he subsequently taught before being appointed first as judge in A.H. 1297, and then as mufti in 1333/1914, which office he held for seven years. After contact with Jamal al-Din al-Afghani, he became one of the bitterest foes of the "Islamic Reform" movement of Afghani and Afghani's pupil and fellow Mason, Muhammad 'Abduh. An author of works in Sacred Law, formal legal opinion, fundamentals of jurisprudence, tenets of faith, and Koranic exegesis, he was a godfearing traditional scholar who chose to lose his position as mufti rather than bow to government pressure to issue an opinion that a Muslim who had killed a Christian deserved to be executed for it (dis: o1.2(2)). His legal opinion on the purity (tahara) of alcohol (dis: e14.1(7)) appeared in the magazine *al-Islam*, published at al-Azhar in Cairo in 1938, while his opinion on the permissibility of photographs (dis: w50.9) was mentioned to the translator by Sheikh Shu'ayb Arna'ut, Sheikh 'Abdullah Muhammad Ghimari, and others. He died in Cairo in 1354/1935 (*al-A'lam* (y136), 6.50; Sheikh 'Abdullah Muhammad Ghimari; Sheikh Shu'ayb Arna'ut; and n).

x256   Muhammad Hamid (w8.1) is Muhammad ibn Mahmud al-Hamid, a prominent Hanafi scholar of the present century who was born in Hama, Syria, in 1328/1910. Orphaned while young, his brother the poet Badr al-Din al-Hamid sent him after primary school to the Dar al-'Ulum Islamic Secondary School, and then to Aleppo, where he enrolled in the Khusrawiyya School of Islamic Law, run at the time by a number of leading Hanafis such as Sheikh Ahmad Zarqa, Sheikh Ahmad al-Kurdi the Hanafi mufti of Aleppo, and others. Upon finishing, he returned to Hama and then travelled to Egypt where he attended al-Azhar, receiving a number of higher degrees in Sacred Law, specializing in judicial studies and taking a certification for the Islamic judgeship, though when he came home he preferred instead to teach and lead the Friday prayer at the Sultan Mosque, and to continue his education under the sheikhs of Hama of his time, including Muhammad Sa'id al-Jabi, Muhammad Tawfiq al-Sabbagh, and the mufti of Hama Muhammad Sa'id Na'sani. He also took the Sufi path from Sheikh Muhammad Abu al-Nasir al-Naqshbandi of Homs. He wrote a number of books and treatises on tenets of faith, Koranic exegesis, Sacred Law, and formal legal opinion, of which the best known is the two-volume *Rudud 'ala abatil wa rasa'il al-Shaykh Muhammad al-Hamid* [Rebuttals of falsehoods, and the letters of Sheikh Muhammad Hamid], comprising letters, articles, and answers to questions on Sacred Law sent to him from all parts of the Arab and Islamic world. When he died in 1389/1969, all of Hama joined his funeral procession, and his passing was mourned in Damascus and other cities by public figures and religious scholars alike (*Shuruh Risala al-Shaykh Arslan* (y51), 286–87).

x257   Muhammad ibn Hasan Shaybani (w43.1) is Muhammad ibn al-Hasan ibn Farqad, Abu 'Abdullah al-Shaybani, born in Wasit, Iraq, in 131/748. A *mujtahid* Imam of powerful intellect, prodigious mastery of Koranic and hadith primary texts, and the matchless legal training of being educated by Imams Abu Hanifa, Abu Yusuf, and Malik, he was among the greatest figures in the history of Islamic jurisprudence. He was raised in Kufa where he first met Abu Hanifa, joined his school of thought, and distinguished himself before moving to Baghdad, where he was appointed by Harun al-Rashid to the judiciary. He was among the sheikhs of Imam Shafi'i, who once observed, "If I wished to say that the Koran was revealed in the language of Muhammad ibn Hasan, I could say it, for the purity of his Arabic." He wrote a large number of works in Sacred Law and its methodology, as well as in the sciences of hadith, and it is related that when Imam Ahmad was once asked, "From whence did you acquire these legal subtleties?" he replied, "From the books of Muhammad ibn Hasan." He died in 189/804 in Rayy, Persia (*al-A'lam* (y136), 6.80; *Siyar a'lam al-nubala'* (y37), 9.134–36; Sheikh Shu'ayb Arna'ut; and n).

x258   (Sheikh) Muhammad Hashimi (w9.7) is Muhammad ibn Ahmad ibn Muhammad ibn Muhammad ibn 'Abd al-Rahman ibn Abu Jam'a al-Hashimi, born in Sabda near Tlemcen, Algeria, in 1298/1880. He was a Sufi, Maliki scholar, author in tenets of Islamic faith, and the successor in the East of Sheikh Ahmad al-'Alawi. Educated in Algeria before emigrating with his sheikh Muhammad ibn Yallis to Damascus, he completed his studies in Syria with a number of the sheikhs of his time, among them Badr al-Din al-Hasani, Muhammad Ja'far al-Kattani, Tawfiq al-Ayyubi, and others. Ibn Yallis authorized him to give the general litany (al-wird al-'amm) of the *tariqa* to those who wanted it, but it was not until after Ibn Yallis's death that the great renewer of the Shadhili tariqa Sheikh Ahmad al-'Alawi (who had had the same sheikh as Ibn Yallis's teacher) came to

Damascus on his way to hajj in 1350/1931 and authorized Hashimi as a sheikh in the order's 'Alawi-Darqawi branch that he had founded, giving him full authority in all aspects of the way, including the solitary retreat (khalwa) that al-'Alawi emphasized. Hashimi's spiritual presence, humility, and ability to guide seekers to the truth gained him many disciples, and whoever sought Allah did not go away disappointed. He taught Islam at all levels, in classes at his home and in mosques, and would not permit disciples' ignorance in Islamic law or tenets of faith, the latter of which he taught from traditional Ash'ari classics and his own *Miftah al-janna fi sharh 'aqida Ahl al-Sunna* [The key to paradise: an explanation of the faith of Ahl al-Sunna]. He gave written authorizations during his lifetime to a number of sheikhs in the path, among them 'Abd al-Qadir 'Isa of Aleppo, author of *Haqa'iq 'an al-Tasawuf* [Facts about Sufism]; Muhammad Sa'id Burhani, his immediate successor in Damascus; and Muhammad Sa'id al-Kurdi, who brought the Shadhili tariqa to Jordan. When he died in Damascus in 1381/1961, he left a legacy not only of his writings, but also the illumined hearts of those he had led to Allah, and it was they who, out of regard for the master, renamed the *tariqa* the Hashimi-Darqawi way after his death (*Tarikh 'ulama' Damashq* (y1), 2.747–51; Sheikh 'Abd al-Rahman Shaghouri; and n).

x259   Muhammad Jurdani (*see* Muhammad 'Abdullah Jurdani, x247)

x260   Muhammad Makhluf (w35.1) is Muhammad Hasanayn ibn Muhammad Makhluf al-'Adawi al-Maliki, born in Bani 'Adi, Egypt, in 1288/1871. He was a Maliki scholar who was educated at al-Azhar University, where he taught and became a member of its supervisory board, in which capacity he founded and organized al-Azhar Library. After later appointments, first as sheikh of the Ahmadi Mosque and then as general director of religious academies, he retired in A.H. 1334 to devote himself to teaching Islamic theology (tawhid), philosophy, and fundamentals of law and faith. He authored some thirty-seven works in Koranic exegesis, fundamentals of jurisprudence, and other subjects, and died in Cairo in 1355/1936 (*al-A'lam* (y136) 6.96).

x261   Muhammad Ma'ruf (w9.4) is Muhammad Ma'ruf ibn Ahmad ibn Abu Bakr, born is 1853 in Moroni on Grand Comoro Island, which lies between the northern tip of Madagascar and the East African Coast. He was a social reformer, preacher, and the sheikh of the Yashrutiyya branch of the Shadhili tariqa in East Africa, which is credited with contributing to a considerable expansion of Islam there, and is reported to have had, before the sheikh's death, many hospices (zawaya) along the islands and mainland of the East African Coast, including Madagascar, Mozambique, Zanzibar, Pemba, Mauritius, Mafia Island, and the Comoros, as well as in Kenya, Tanganyika, and even far-off New Guinea. He died in 1905 and was buried at his *zawiya* on Grand Comoro Island (*Muslim Brotherhoods* (y86), 152–58).

x262   Muhammad Sa'id Burhani (t3.1) is Muhammad Sa'id ibn 'Abd al-Rahman ibn Muhammad Sa'id ibn Mustafa ibn 'Ali al-Daghestani al-Burhani, a Hanafi scholar in fundamentals of law and faith, Sufi, and commentator who was born in Damascus in 1311/1894. He fought against the French at the outset of the foreign occupation of Syria in 1920, after which he returned to Damascus to study the Islamic sciences, first with his father, and then with scholars such as 'Abd al-Qadir al-Iskandari, Badr al-Din al-Hasani, the mufti of Damascus 'Ata Allah al-Kasam, and others. After first taking the Naqshbandi way from Sheikh Abu al-Khayr al-Maydani, he became a disciple of Sheikh Muhammad Hashimi. He taught at the Tawba and Umayyad Mosques, and upon his retirement devoted himself to helping Sheikh Hashimi, who was to appoint him as his successor. A voracious reader, he edited, annotated, and prepared indexes for a large number of books and treatises, among them 'Ala' al-Din 'Abidin's classic primer in Hanafi law, *al-Hadiyya al-'Ala'iyya* [The gift of 'Ala'], and Sheikh Muhammad Hashimi's *Sharh Shatranj al-'arifin* [Explanation of "The chess of the gnostics"], a mystical commentary on a chessboard-like diagram ascribed to Sheikh Muhyiddin ibn al-'Arabi. He died in 1386/1967 in Damascus (*Shuruh Risala al-Shaykh Arslan* (y51), 281–82; and *Tarikh 'ulama' Dimashq* (y1), 2.794).

x263   Muhammad Sa'id Buti (b1.1) is Muhammad Sa'id ibn al-Mulla Muhammad Ramadan al-Buti, born of Kurdish descent in 1350/1931 in Damascus. The son of one of the foremost Shafi'i scholars of his time, Mulla Ramadan, he studied Arabic grammar, logic, and philosophy with his father, as well as Shafi'i jurisprudence and fundamentals of Islamic law and faith, and after graduating from the al-Tawjih al-Islami Institute in Damascus, travelled to Cairo and took a degree from al-Azhar before returning to Syria, where he taught first in Homs and then in Damascus at the College of Sacred Law. He took a doctorate in principles of Islamic legal methodology from the University of Damascus in A.H. 1385, and was appointed as a professor there in the Faculty of Sacred Law and Arts. He has written many works, among them *Fiqh al-sira* [Sacred Law inferred from the prophetic biography], and *al-Lamadhhabiyya akhtar bid'a tuhaddidu al-shari'a al-Islamiyya* [Not following a school of jurisprudence is the most dangerous innovation threatening Islamic Sacred law], while his most recent work, *al-Salafiyya marhala zamaniyya mubaraka la madhhab Islami* [The "way of the early Muslims" was a blessed historical epoch, not an Islamic school of thought], has gained a wide readership. He lives in Damascus, where he writes, teaches at the university, and gives well-attended public lectures at several mosques (*Shuruh Risala al-Shaykh Arslan* (y51), 283; and n).

x264 (a)   Muhammad Shirbini Khatib (h1.0) is Muhammad ibn Ahmad, Shams al-Din al-Shirbini al-Khatib of Cairo. A Shafi'i Imam and Koranic exegete of knowledge and piety, he studied in Cairo under Imam Ahmad al-Ramli, as well as Nur al-Din Mahalli, Ahmad Burullusi, and others, who authorized him to give formal legal opinion and instruction. He educated a multitude of scholars, and his works won recognition in their author's lifetime for their outstanding clarity and reliability, among the most famous of them his four-volume *Mughni al-muhtaj ila ma'rifa ma'ani alfaz al-Minhaj* [The enricher of him in need of knowledge of the meanings of the words of "The seekers' road"], a commentary on Nawawi's *Minhaj al-talibin*; and his Koranic exegesis *al-Siraj al-munir fi al-i'ana 'ala ma'rifa ba'd kalam Rabbina al-Hakim al-Khabir* [The light-giving lamp: an aid in knowing some of the words of our Lord, the All-wise and All-knowing]. He died in Cairo in 977/1570 (*al-A'lam* (y136), 6.6; *Mughni al-muhtaj* (y73), 4.548; and n).

x264 (b)   **Muhammad 'Umar Muhammad 'Umar** (Document 4) was born in the Suwayd governorate of Egypt in about 1934 and was educated in Cairo, where he graduated from the College of Arts at Cairo University. In 1985 he was appointed to his current post as Director of the Department of Translation at al-Azhar's Islamic Research Academy (Sheikh Fath Allah Ya Sin Jazar).

x265   Muhyiddin ibn al-'Arabi (r20.3) is Muhammad ibn 'Ali ibn Muhammad ibn al-'Arabi, Abu Bakr Muhyi al-Din al-Hatimi al-Ta'i, The Greatest Sheikh (al-Shaykh al-Akbar), born in Murcia (in present-day Spain) in 560/1165. A *mujtahid* Imam in Sacred Law, Sufism, Koranic exegesis, hadith, and other Islamic sciences, and widely regarded as a friend (wali) of Allah Most High, he was the foremost representative of the Sufi school of the 'oneness of being' (wahdat al-wujud, dis: x5), as well as a Muslim of strict literal observance of the prescriptions of the Koran and sunna. He first took the way of Sufism in A.H. 580, and in the years that followed authored some six hundred books and treatises in the course of travels and residences in Fez, Tunis, Alexandria, Cairo, Mecca, Baghdad, Mosul, Konya, Aleppo, and finally Damascus, where he lived till the end of his life and completed his *al-Futuhat al-Makkiyya* [The Meccan revelations] and *Fusus al-hikam* [The precious stones of the ring-settings of the wisdoms]. Since interest in his work continues among even non-Muslim scholars, a number of hermeneutical obstacles are worth mentioning here that have in some measure so far hindered serious efforts to understand the sheikh's works, by friend and foe alike.

The first is lack of common ground with the author, who has written, "We are a group whose works are unlawful to peruse, since the Sufis, one and all, use terms in technical senses by which they intend other than what is customarily meant by their usage among scholars, and those who interpret them according to their usual significance commit unbelief." While this may not be particularly intimidating to someone who is already an unbeliever, it does at least implicitly deny the validity of a do-it-yourself approach to the sheikh's thought and point up the relevance of the traditional maxim, Knowledge is to be taken from those who possess it.

A related difficulty is that the context of much of Ibn al-'Arabi's *Futuhat* and other works is not only the outward Islamic sciences, but also their inner significance, not by any means an "esoteric symbolism" that nullifies the outward content of the sheikh's inquiries, but a dimension of depth, a reflective counterpart to their this-worldly significance whose place and existential context is the world of the spirit, to which the physical universe—in which many of his would-be interpreters are firmly enmeshed and know nothing besides, especially those who are atheists—is like a speck of dust in the sea. While the present discussion cannot adequately do justice to the topic, one may yet observe that the heart of someone familiar only with the "What will I eat," "What will I say," "Will it prove feasible," and other physical and intellectual relations of instrumentality that make up this world is no more capable of real insight into the world of someone like the sheikh than a person inches away from a giant Monet is capable of *seeing* the picture he believes is "before his very eyes." The way of Ibn al-'Arabi is precisely a *way*, and if one has not travelled it or been trained to see as Ibn al-'Arabi sees, one may well produce intelligent remarks about one's perceptions of the matter, as attested to by a whole literature of "historical studies" of Sufism, but the fact remains that one does not see.

A third difficulty is the problem of spurious interpolations by copyists, as once happened to 'Abd al-Wahhab Sha'rani, who had to bring his own handwritten manuscript to court to prove he was innocent of the unbelief that enemies had inserted into his work and published in his name. The *Hashiya* of Ibn 'Abidin notes that this has also happened to the *Fusus al-hikam* of Ibn al-'Arabi, the details being given in a promulgation by the Supreme Ottoman Sultanate exonerating the author of the statements of unbelief (kufr) it said that Jews had interpolated into the work. This is supported by the opinion of Mahmud Mahmud Ghurab, an Ibn al-'Arabi specialist of Damascus who has published more than twelve books on the sheikh's thought, among them *al-Fiqh 'ind al-Shaykh al-Akbar Muhyiddin ibn al-'Arabi* [Sacred Law according to the Greatest Sheikh, Muhyiddin ibn al-'Arabi], which clarifies Ibn al-'Arabi's position as a Zahiri Imam and *mujtahid* in Sacred Law; and *Sharh Fusus al-hikam* [Exegesis of "The precious stones of the ring-settings of the wisdoms"], in which Ghurab indicates eighty-six passages of the *Fusus* that he believes are spurious, adducing that they contradict the letter and spirit of *al-Futuhat al-Makkiyya,* which must be given precedence because we possess a manuscript copy in the author's own handwriting, while there are no such copies of the *Fusus.*

One may summarize the above-mentioned difficulties and others by the general observation that without a master with whom to read these texts, someone who has himself read them with a teacher aware of their place in the whole of the sheikh's work, one is in danger of projecting one's own limitations onto the author. This happens in our times to various groups of interpreters, among them non-Muslim "Sufis" who have posthumously made Ibn al-'Arabi an honorary Mason, saying that he believed all religions to be equally valid and acceptable—which Ghurab says is an ignorant misreading, and to which the sheikh himself furnishes a sufficient reply in his account of his convictions ('aqida) at the first of the *Futuhat* where he says, "Just as I charge Allah, His angels, His entire creation, and all of you to bear witness upon me that I affirm His unity, so too I charge Him Most Glorious, His angels, His entire creation, and all of you to bear witness upon me that I believe in the one He has elected, chosen, and selected from all His existence, Muhammad (Allah bless him and give him peace), whom He has sent to all mankind entirely (ila jami' al-nas kaffatan) to bring good tidings and to warn and to call to Allah by His leave" (*al-Futuhat al-Makkiyya* (y55), 1.38). It is fairly obvious that his being sent to all mankind would be pointless if all other religions were not now abrogated, as would jihad, something that Ibn al-'Arabi discusses, before going on to explain its spiritual side, in what is unmistakably a treatment of its outward military aspect and rules, believer against unbeliever, sword against sword, which Ghurab points out would be meaningless if both sides were upon guidance. Finally, in a chapter entitled "The Levels of the Inhabitants of Hell" (*al-Futuhat al-Makkiyya* (y55), 1.301), the sheikh clearly explains that while disobedient Muslims ('usat) will one day leave the hellfire, those who associated others with Allah (mushrikun) and the Jews and Christians (Ahl al-Kitab) who did not accept the Prophet (Allah bless him and give him peace) after his coming will remain in hell forever—which is as far from the universal validity of all religions as anything could be.

Other interpreters who error are well-meaning Muslims who do not and cannot understand the sheikh's work, which they read in their native Arabic as if it were a newspaper and then level accusations of unbelief against the author on the basis of what comes to their minds while doing so. For all groups of interpreters, there is a pressing need for scholarly modesty and candor about our exegetical limitations, and to draw attention to the fact that without a guide in reading the sheikh's thought, one is adrift in a sea of one's own guesswork.

Aside from these basic hermeneutic requirements for reading the work of Ibn al-'Arabi, other, existential qualifications are needed, for as mentioned above, the sheikh's method is a way, and as such entails not only curiosity, but commitment and most of all submission to Allah Most High as the sheikh had submission to Him, namely through Islam—as well as other conditions mentioned by Ibn Hajar Haytami in a legal opinion in which, after noting that it is permissible or even meritorious (mustahabb) to read the sheikh's works, but only for the qualified, he writes: "Imam Ibn al-'Arabi has explicitly stated: 'It is unlawful to read [the Sufis'] books unless one attains to their level of character and learns the meaning of their words in conformity with their technical usages, neither of which is found except in someone who has worked assiduously, rolled up his sleeves, abandoned the wrong, tightened his belt, filled himself replete with the outward Islamic sciences, and purified himself from every low trait connected with this world and the next. It is just such a person who comprehends what is being said and is allowed to enter when he stands at the door.' " The sheikh outlines what is entailed by *working assiduously* in a series of injunctions (wasaya) at the end of his *Futuhat* ((y55), 4.444–551) that virtually anyone can benefit from, and by which one may infer some of the outward details of the sheikh's way. By all accounts, he lived what he wrote in this respect, and his legacy bears eloquent testimony to it. He died in his home in Damascus, a copy of Ghazali's *Ihya' 'ulum al-din* on his lap, in 638/1240 (*al-A'lam* (y136), 6.281; *al-Fatawa al-hadithiyya* (y48), 296–97; *al-Futuhat al-Makkiyya* (y55), 1.38, 1.301, 2.425, 4.444–551; *Hashiya radd al-muhtar* (y47), 4.238; *Sharh Fusus al-hikam* (y42), 475–98; Mahmud Mahmud Ghurab; Sheikh 'Abd al-Rahman Shaghouri; A; and n).

x266   Muhyiddin Mahmalji (Document 1) is a friend of Sheikh 'Abd al-Wakil Durubi and Yasin 'Arafa who lives in Damascus. He frequently visits the Darwishiyya to sit with the circle that gathers there, and is about Sheikh 'Abd al-Wakil's age (n).

x267   Mujahid (a4.6) is Mujahid ibn Jabr, Abu al-Hajjaj al-Makki, of Mecca, born in 21/642. A Koranic exegete of the generation who followed that of the Companions, he is referred to by Dhahabi as "the sheikh of Koran reciters and interpreters" and took his knowledge of Koranic exegesis from Ibn 'Abbas, with whom he read the Koran three times, stopping at every verse and asking him how and in reference to what it was revealed. He moved from place of place and finally settled in Kufa. Unable to hear of anything strange or marvelous without personally going to investigate, he went to the Well of Barahut in Hadramawt, Yemen, which is said to contain the souls of unbelievers and hypocrites, and went to Babylon to look for Harut and Marut. It is said he died while prostrate in prayer, in 104/722 (*al-A'lam* (y136), 5.278; and *Mu'jam al-buldan* (y43), 1.405).

x268   Munawi (*see* 'Abd al-Ra'uf Munawi, x15)

x269   Mundhiri (w40.4) is 'Abd al-'Adhim ibn 'Abd al-Qawi ibn 'Abdullah ibn Salama, Abu Muhammad Zaki al-Din al-Mundhiri, born in Egypt in 581/1185. He was a Shafi'i scholar, historian, lexicographer, and the hadith master (hafiz) of his time, a saintly ascetic who was regarded by contemporaries as a friend (wali) of Allah Most High. He studied hadith under masters in Mecca, Damascus, Harran, al-Ruha, and Alexandria before returning to Cairo, where he was appointed as sheikh in the Dar al-Hadith al-Kamaliyya. He held this position for twenty years, teaching, writing, and not leaving the school except for the Friday prayer, and he authored a lexicon, a history, and a number of works on hadith, of which the four-volume *al-Targhib wa al-tarhib* [The instilling of desire and fear] is the most well known. He died in Cairo in 657/1258 (*al-A'lam* (y136), 4.30; and *Tabaqat al-Shafi'iyya al-kubra* (y128), 8.259).

x270   Munkar (u3.3) is one of the two fearsome angels who question the newly-buried in their graves, as discussed above at v2.2 and w32.1(2) (n).

x271   Musa (u3.5) is Musa ibn 'Imran ibn Qahith ibn 'Azir ibn Lawi ibn Ya'qub ibn Ishaq ibn Ibrahim (upon whom be peace), the prophet and messenger of Allah Most High to Bani Isra'il. He is mentioned in many places in the Holy Koran, among them sura al-A'raf, which tells of the two great signs that Allah vouchsafed to him to convince Pharaoh to let Bani Isra'il leave Egypt with him. The first of these was that when he cast his staff, it became a snake, while the second was that when Musa drew forth his hand from his bosom, it illumined the earth to the sky, after which he returned it to his bosom and it became as it had been. But the members of Pharaoh's council told him that Musa was merely a sorcerer, and Pharaoh refused to heed what he had been shown. The Koran describes the afflictions that were visited on Pharaoh's people in the wake of his refusal, how Musa left Egypt with Bani Isra'il, the drowning of Pharaoh and his host, and the wanderings of Bani Isra'il in the desert for forty years, during which Musa's brother Harun died, and then Musa a year later (*al-Futuhat al-ilahiyya* (y65), 1.56; *Qisas al-anbiya'* (y59), 296; *al-Siraj al-munir* (y72), 1.499; and n).

x272   Musaylima the Liar (w30.2) is Musaylima al-Kadhdhab ibn Thumama ibn Habib al-Hanafi al-Wa'ili, born in al-Yamama in a village now known as al-Jubayla in the Najd highlands of eastern Arabia. It is related that he wrote a letter to the Prophet (Allah bless him and give him peace) after the conquest of Mecca, saying: "From Musaylima the Messenger of Allah to Muhammad the Messenger of Allah. Peace be upon you. To commence: I have been given to share with you in the matter. We shall have half the earth and the Quraysh have half, though the Quraysh are a people who transgress." The Prophet (Allah bless him and give him peace) answered, "From Muhammad the Messenger of Allah to Musaylima the Liar. Peace be upon whoever follows guidance. To commence: the earth belongs to Allah, who bequeaths it to whomever He wills of His servants, and the outcome is to the godfearing." Musaylima composed rhyming verse in attempts to imitate the Koran, and the Prophet (Allah bless him and give him peace) died before he could finish him, though when Abu Bakr became caliph he gathered a large army he placed under the leadership of Khalid ibn al-Walid, who proceeded to Yamama and attacked Musaylima in A.H. 12 in a pitched battle that extirpated the false prophet and his followers, but at a cost of some 1,220 Muslim lives, 450 of whom were Companions (*al-A'lam* (y136), 7.226).

x273   Muslim (Introduction) is Muslim ibn al-Hajjaj ibn Muslim, Abu al-Husayn al-Qushayri al-Naysaburi, born in Nishapur, Persia, in 204/820. A Shafi'i scholar, and a hadith master (hafiz) and Imam second only to his mentor Bukhari, he was the author of the famous hadith collection *Sahih Muslim* [The rigorously authenticated collection of Muslim], which has inspired many commentaries and is considered among the greatest works on hadith in Islam. Besides studying with Bukhari, he travelled to the Hijaz, Egypt, Syria, and Iraq, learning hadiths from over 220 of the principle sheikhs of the time, including Ahmad and Ishaq ibn Rahawayh. While some scholars have considered Muslim's *Sahih* to be greater than Bukhari's because of the excellence of its arrangement and other editorial features, the truth is that Bukhari's collection is superior because of its additional strictures for a hadith's admissibility as "rigorously authenticated" (sahih). Imam Muslim also wrote a number of other works in hadith, and died in Nishapur in 261/875 (ibid., 7.221; *Sharh Sahih Muslim* (y93), 1.1–3; *Siyar a'lam al-nubala'* (y37), 12.557–61; *al-Taj al-jami' li al-usul* (y100), 1.16; and n).

x274   Mutawalli (m12.6) is 'Abd al-Rahman ibn Ma'mun ibn 'Ali ibn Ibrahim, Abu Sa'd al-Naysaburi al-Mutawalli, born in Nishapur, Persia, in 426/1035. A Shafi'i Imam and scholar in Sacred Law, principles of jurisprudence, and tenets of faith, he studied in Merv (in present-day Turkmen S.S.R.) under 'Abd al-Rahman Furani (x124) and authored *Tatimma al-Ibana* [The completion of "The explanation"], a voluminous commentary on a work by Furani. He also studied Shafi'i jurisprudence under the sheikh of Imam Baghawi, al-Qadi Husayn ibn Muhammad Marwazi, and took hadith from Abul Qasim Qushayri before succeeding Abu Ishaq Shirazi as the sheikh of the Nizamiyya Academy at Baghdad, where he died in 478/1087 (ibid., 3.323; and *Tabaqat al-Shafi'iyya al-kubra* (y128), 5.106–7).

x275   Muzani (o1.0) is Isma'il ibn Yahya ibn Isma'il, Abu Ibrahim al-Muzani of Egypt, born in 175/791. A Shafi'i scholar of Sacred Law and student of the Imam himself, he was so expert at arguing a case that Shafi'i once remarked of him, "Were he to debate the Devil, he would win." Abu Ishaq Shirazi described him as "an ascetic scholar and *mujtahid*, a debater of considerable skill at presenting an argument with an aptitude for subtle shades of meaning." He wrote a number of works in Sacred Law, of which his summary of the school's rulings, *al-Mukhtasar* [The epitome], is perhaps the most famous. Devoted to worship, if he missed a prescribed prayer in congregation he would pray it twenty-five times alone, and it was his practice to wash the dead without payment in hope of Allah's reward, saying, "I do it to soften my heart." He died in 264/878 (*al-A'lam* (y136), 1.329; and *Tabaqat al-Shafi'iyya al-kubra* (y128), 2.93).

x276   (N:) (*see* (Sheikh) Nuh 'Ali Salman, x290)

x277   (n:) (*see* Nuh Ha Mim Keller, x291)

x278   Nafi' (w28.1(3)) is Nafi', Abu 'Abdullah al-Qurashi. Originally taken prisoner by 'Abdullah ibn 'Umar, he grew up in Medina to become the mufti and Imam of the generation that followed the Companions. He was one of the sheikhs of Imam Malik, relating hadiths from Ibn 'Umar, 'A'isha, Abu Hurayra, Abu Sa'id al-Khudri, and others. Not a single mistake is known in all the hadiths he related, and Imam Bukhari was to say, "The most rigorously authenticated channel of transmission is that of Malik from Nafi' from Ibn 'Umar." He died in 117/735 (*al-A'lam* (y136), 8.5; and *Siyar a'lam al-nubala'* (y37), 5.95–97).

x279   Nahlawi (*see* Khalil Nahlawi, x215)

x280   Najm al-Ghazzi (r28.1) is Muhammad ibn Muhammad ibn Muhammad, Abu al-Makarim Najm al-Din al-Ghazzi, born in Damascus in 977/1570. He was a Shafi'i scholar, researcher, litterateur, biographer, and historian who composed a number of books and treatises, including his well-known biographical collection *al-Kawakib al-sa'ira fi tarajim a'yan al-mi'a al-'ashira* [The moving stars: on biographies of notables of the tenth century]. He died in Damascus in 1061/1651 (*al-A'lam* (y136), 7.63; and Sheikh Shu'ayb Arna'ut).

x281   Nakir (u3.3) is one of the two angels who question the dead in their graves after burial, as mentioned above at v2.2 and w32.1(2) (n).

x282   (Imam) Nasafi (w57.2) is 'Abdullah ibn Ahmad ibn Mahmud, Abu al-Barakat Hafiz al-Din al-Nasafi of Idhaj, a village near Isfahan, Persia. Among the great Hanafi Imams of his time, he authored major contributions in methodological fundamentals of Sacred Law, Hanafi jurisprudence, and tenets of faith, though he is most famous outside of his school for his three-volume Koranic commentary *Madarik al-Tanzil* [Realizations of the Revelation], which places particular emphasis on the lexical and grammatical dimensions of Koranic interpretation. He died in Idhaj in 710/1310 (*al-A'lam* (y136), 4.67).

x283   Nasa'i (Introduction) is Ahmad ibn 'Ali ibn Shu'ayb ibn 'Ali ibn Sinan ibn Bahr ibn Dinar, Abu 'Abd al-Rahman al-Nasa'i, originally of Nasa, Persia, born in 215/830. He was a Shafi'i scholar and judge, a hadith master (hafiz) and Imam. Educated in hadith by scholars like Ishaq ibn Rahawayh, Abu al-Qasim Tabarani, and others during travels to Khurasan, Iraq, Syria, the Hijaz, and the Arabian Peninsula, he eventually settled in Egypt. It is related that he used to fast every other day, and was fond of women, having four wives whom he took turns with as well as a number of concubines. While he authored works on the merits of the Companions and an outstanding volume on the excellences of Imam 'Ali ibn Abi Talib (Allah be well pleased with him), his main work is his *Sunan* [Sunnas], one of the six great hadith collections of Islam. Daraqutni said of him, "Abu 'Abd al-Rahman leads all others of his time who are mentioned in the field of hadith," and when Dhahabi was asked who was more learned, Nasa'i or Muslim, he replied that the former was, a verdict that Imam Taqi al-Din Subki concurred with. After a lifetime of worship and of devotion to Sacred Knowledge, Nasa'i was martyred in 303/915 in Damascus for his love of Imam 'Ali by remnants of the Kharijite sect, who gave him a beating from which he died (ibid., 1.171; and *Tabaqat al-Shafi'iyya al-kubra* (y128), 3.14–16).

x284   Nasir al-Mutarrizi (w42.2) is Nasir ibn 'Abd al-Sayyid Abi al-Makarim ibn 'Ali, Abu al-Fath Burhan al-Din al-Mutarrizi, born in Jurjaniyya, Khawarizm (in present-day Turkmen S.S.R.), in 538/1144. A Hanafi scholar and poet, he was a specialist in Arabic lexicology and grammar who wrote a number of works of which his *al-Mughrib fi tartib al-Mu'rib* [The causer of wonder: on the order of

"The clarifier"], an exposition of a shorter rhymed work on lexicology of his own composition, is still among the best books available for rare words appearing in Hanafi legal texts. He died in Khawarizm in 610/1213 (*al-A'lam* (y136), 7.348; and n).

x285   (Imam) Nawawi (Introduction) is Yahya ibn Sharaf ibn Murri ibn Hasan, Abu Zakariyya Muhyi al-Din al-Nawawi, born in the village of Nawa on the Horan Plain of southern Syria in 631/1233. He was the Imam of the later Shafi'i school, the scholar of his time in knowledge, piety, and abstinence, a hadith master (hafiz), biographer, lexicologist, and Sufi. When he first came to Damascus in A.H. 649, he memorized the text of Abu Ishaq Shirazi's *al-Tanbih* [The notice] in four and a half months, then the first quarter of Shirazi's *al-Muhadhdhab* [The rarefaction], after which he accompanied his father on hajj, then visited Medina, and then returned to Damascus, where he assidously devoted himself to mastering the Islamic sciences. He took Shafi'i Law, hadith, tenets of faith, fundamentals of jurisprudence, Arabic, and other subjects from more than twenty-two scholars of the time, including Abu Ibrahim Ishaq al-Maghribi, 'Abd al-Rahman ibn Qudama al-Maqdisi, and others, at a period of his life in which, as Dhahabi notes, "his dedication to learning, night and day, became proverbial." Spending all his time in either worship or gaining Sacred Knowledge, he took some twelve lessons a day, only dozed off in the night at moments when sleep overcame him, and drilled himself on the lessons he learned by heart while walking along the street. Fastidious in detail and deep in understanding of the subjects he thus mastered, he authored many great works in Shafi'i jurisprudence, hadith, history, and legal opinion, among the best known of which are his *Minhaj al-talibin* [The seekers' road], which has become a main reference for the Shafi'i school, *Riyad al-salihin* [The gardens of the righteous] and *Kitab al-adhkar* [The Book of remembrances of Allah] in hadith, and his eighteen-volume *Sharh Sahih Muslim* [Commentary on Muslim's "Sahih"]. He lived simply, and it is related that his entire wardrobe consisted of a turban and an ankle-length shirt (thawb) with a single button at the collar. After a residence in Damascus of twenty-seven years, he returned the books he had borrowed from charitable endowments, bade his friends farewell, visited the graves of his sheikhs who had died, and departed, going first to Jerusalem and then to his native Nawa, where he became ill at his father's home and died at forty-four years of age in 676/1277, young in years but great in benefit to Islam and the Muslims (*al-A'lam* (y136), 8.149; *Mughni al-muhtaj* (y73), 4.545–47; *Riyad al-salihin* (y107), introduction; Sheikh Hasan Saqqaf; A; and n).

x286   Nimrod (u3.8) is Nimrudh, the illegitimate son of King Kan'an. The first man to claim he was God, to tyrannize people, and to put a crown on his head, he was the enemy of the prophet Ibrahim (upon whom be peace), whom he threw into a fire and tried to burn, though Allah Most High commanded the fire to be cool and harmless to Ibrahim. After this, according to commentators, Nimrudh was killed when Allah sent an affliction of gnats upon his people as a punishment (*al-Futuhat al-ilahiyya* (y65), 1.210, 3.135).

x287   Noah (*see* Nuh, x289)

x288   Nu'aym ibn Hammad (w4.7) is Nu'aym ibn Hammad ibn Mu'awiya ibn al-Harith, Abu 'Abdullah al-Khuza'i, originally of Merv (in present-day Turkmen S.S.R.), who lived in Egypt. A scholar who knew the rules of Islamic estate division (fara'id), he is considered by Ibn Hajar 'Asqalani to be an honest hadith narrator who had a poor memory and made many mistakes in transmission, though Muhammad Zahid al-Kawthari and others have drawn attention to a number of hadiths he related containing corrupt convictions about basic tenets of faith. He died in A.H. 228 (*Taqrib al-tahdhib* (y16), 564; and n).

x289   Nuh (u3.5) is Nuh ibn Lamak ibn Matushalakh ibn Akhnukh (upon whom be peace), the first prophet sent by Allah Most High after Idris. The first to bring a revealed law (shari'a), to warn against polytheism (shirk), and the first whose people were punished for rejecting his message, he was a carpenter by trade who was sent to his people when fifty years old. Commentators relate that his true name was 'Abd al-Ghaffar, but he became known as Nuh for his copious weeping (naha) over his having prayed to Allah to extirpate his corrupt people, who, after rejecting his message for 950 years, were drowned in a flood. Allah preserved Nuh and the believers from the Deluge by inspiring him to build an Ark which carried them safely upon the waters. All the inimitable miracles (mu'jizat) that Allah vouchsafed to Nuh pertained to his person, for he lived a thousand years without loss of strength or his hair turning gray, even though he fasted perpetually, and no one ever bore the afflictions he endured from his people throughout his life (*al-Siraj al-munir* (y72) 1.345, 1.484; and n).

x290   (Sheikh) Nuh 'Ali Salman (Introduction) is Nuh ibn 'Ali ibn Salman al-Qudah, born in 1939 in 'Ayn Janna, near 'Ajlun, Jordan. His father was a Shafi'i scholar who was educated in Damascus under Sheikh 'Ali al-Daqar, and when he returned to Jordan, studied various works of the Islamic sciences (among them Ghazali's *Ihya 'ulum al-din,* which he read seven times) and taught his four sons Sacred Law, grammar, and tenets of faith before sending them, each in their turn, to Damascus for an Islamic education. Nuh went in 1954, spending seven years in the Islamic preparatory and secondary schools of al-Jama'iyya al-Ghurra' founded by his father's sheikh, where in addition to secular subjects, he studied tenets of faith and Shafi'i jurisprudence from works like *'Umdat al-salik* [The reliance of the traveller], *Matan Abi Shuja'* [The text of Abu Shuja'], and Nawawi's *Minhaj al-talibin* [The seekers' road] with such sheikhs as 'Abd al-Karim al-Rifa'i, Ahmad al-Basrawi, 'Abd al-Razzaq al-Himsi, Nayyif al-'Abbas, Mahmud al-Ranqusi, and the judge Muhammad Khayr al-Shamma', and during which time he also attended the lessons of Sheikh Muhammad Hashimi, from whom he took the daily *dhikr* (wird) of the Shadhili tariqa. After secondary school, he attended the College of Sacred Law at the University of Damascus for four years, much of his study devoted to Hanafi jurisprudence, under Mustafa al-Zarqa, Wahbi al-Zuhayli, 'Abd al-Rahman al-Sabuni, Amin al-Misri, 'Abd al-Fattah Abu Ghudda, Muhammad al-Mubarak, Fawzi Faydullah, and others. He graduated in 1965 and returned to Jordan, where he joined the armed forces and worked with Sheikh 'Abdullah Muhammad al-'Azam whom he succeeded as mufti in 1972. In 1977, he went to Cairo and spent three years in the master's degree program at al-Azhar, where he studied fundamentals of law and belief under Sheikh 'Abd al-Ghani 'Abd al-Khaliq, comparative jurisprudence with Sheikh Hasan al-Shadhili, and heard the late rector of al-Azhar Sheikh 'Abd al-Halim Mahmud lecture on Sufism. It was during this period that he wrote his *Qada' al-'ibadat wa al-niyaba fiha* [Making up acts of worship and performing them for others] with Sheikh Muhammad al-Anbadhi as his supervisor, for which he received his master's degree in 1980. The following year, he enrolled in the doctoral program at the University of Imam Muhammad ibn Sa'ud in Riyadh, and in 1986 took a doctorate for his second main work, *Ibra' al-dhimma min huquq al-'ibad* [Fulfilling one's obligation to give others their rights].

From the time of his appointment as mufti in 1972, Sheikh Nuh has discharged the duties of his office with energy and competence, writing hundreds of formal legal opinions in response to questions on all aspects of the religion of Islam, many of them published in the Armed Forces monthly religious journal *al-Tadhkira* [The reminder], in addition to lectures, books, and articles on Sacred Law, prophetic biography, tenets of faith, and other topics. During his tenure, the Jordanian Army has been distinguished by having an imam in every unit who is not only part of it wherever it goes, but leads the obligatory prayers, gives weekly religious lessons, answers questions about Islam, and is subject to regular refresher courses in Shafi'i jurisprudence, hadith, Koran, and tenets of faith. In the course of helping with the present volume, though busy with official duties, Sheikh Nuh generously spent his after-work hours with the translator in sessions often extending late into the night at his own home, never refusing any service he could render or declining to research any question connected with Sacred Law, and never asking for anything in return. He presently lives in Marj al-Hamam, near Amman, Jordan (n).

x291   Nuh Ha Mim Keller (Title Page) is from Odessa, Washington, in the northwestern United States. Born in 1954 and raised as a Roman Catholic, he worked as a commercial fisherman in the North Pacific for a space of years between travelling in the off-seasons and attending institutions of higher learning. He studied philosophy, concentrating mainly on the epistemology of ethical theory, with Andrew J. Bjelland at Gonzaga University and with the French philosopher Paul Ricoeur, author of *The Symbolism of Evil* and *The Conflict of Interpretations,* at the University of Chicago. It was at the latter that he first studied classical Arabic with Carolyn Killean and Galal Nahhal, then with Salim Hermis Yunus in Cairo—where he became a Muslim at al-Azhar by the mercy and grace of Allah in 1977—and then with Claude Audebert at UCLA, from which he received a degree in philosophy in 1980. Moving to Jordan, he pursued his learning of Arabic at the University of Jordan under Hala Nashif and later taught English at Yarmouk University. He took the Shadhili tariqa in 1982 in Damascus from Sheikh 'Abd al-Rahman Shaghouri, his teacher in the way of *tasawwuf* from that time. In need of a basic manual of Islamic law, in the fall of 1982 he bought the copy of *'Umdat al-salik wa 'uddat al-nasik* that with the help and instruction of Sheikh 'Abd al-Wakil Durubi and Sheikh Nuh 'Ali Salman was completed in annotated translation as the present work, *The Reliance of the Traveller,* in 1990. Among his other teachers is Sheikh Shu'ayb Arna'ut, with whom he studies Hanafi jurisprudence. He presently lives in Amman (n).

x292   (O:) (*see* (Sheikh) 'Umar Barakat, x352)

x293   P. Casanova (w15.2) is Paul Casanova, a French orientalist born in Algeria who went to Paris in 1879, studied at the School of Living Eastern Languages, and was appointed as secretary of the Department of Oriental Numismatics, after which he became a professor of Arabic at the University of France in 1909. He journeyed to Cairo three times and published works about Ibn Khaldun, Egypt, and studies on Islamic coinage, weights, and measures. He died in Cairo in 1334/1924 (*al-A'lam* (y136), 2.78).

x294   Pharaoh (q6.3) is Fir'awn, a title customarily borne by each of the Amalekite kings of ancient Egypt, though applied in the Koran to al-Walid ibn Mus'ab ibn Rayyan, the king at the time of the prophet Musa (upon whom be peace). Described in many places in the Holy Koran, Pharaoh was the personification of evil for his enmity towards the prophet Musa and crimes against God and man. He lived more than four hundred years and was drowned in the Red Sea at the head of his armies while pursuing Bani Isra'il (*al-Futuhat al-ilahiyya* (y65), 1.51; *al-Shifa* (y116), 1.211; and n).

x295   (The) Prophet (*see* Muhammad, x245)

x296   Qadi 'Iyad (o25.3(a)) is 'Iyad ibn Musa ibn 'Iyad ibn 'Imran, Abu al-Fadl al-Yahsabi, born in Sabta (present-day Ceuta, on the Strait of Gibraltar) in 476/1083. The Imam of western Muslimdom in hadith and Arabic lexicology, he was a gifted Maliki scholar and author who wrote a number of books in the sciences of hadith, Maliki jurisprudence, and history, though he is best remembered for his two-volume *al-Shifa bi ta'rif huquq al-Mustafa* [The cure, in outlining the attributes of the Chosen One], universally acknowledged as among the finest works ever written on the Prophet (Allah bless him and give him peace). He was appointed as the judge (Ar. *qadi,* whence the nickname) of Sabta, then Granada, and finally Marrakesh, where he died of poisoning, allegedly by a Jew, in 544/1149 (*al-A'lam* (y136), 5.99).

x297   (Sheikh) al-Qalyubi (w41.3) is Ahmad ibn Ahmad ibn Salama, Abu al-'Abbas Shihab al-Din al-Qalyubi, of Qalyub, Egypt. He was a Shafi'i scholar in Sacred Law and hadith, a physician, and the author of a number of books, commentaries, and treatises in Islamic jurisprudence, hadith, medicine, history, and geography. He died in 1069/1659 (ibid., (y136), 1.92; *Rudud 'ala abatil* (y44), 1.646; and Sheikh Shu'ayb Arna'ut).

x298   al-Qannad (w9.11) is probably 'Ali ibn 'Abd al-Rahim, Abu al-Hasan al-Qannad al-Sufi of Wasit, Iraq, who used to travel without any provisions, and met many of the sheikhs of his time. From the fact that he related some of the sayings of al-Hallaj, he may be supposed to have died after the latter's death in 309/922 (*Tabaqat al-Sufiyya* (y129), 165; and n).

x299   Qatada (a4.6) is Qatada ibn Da'ama ibn Qatada ibn 'Uzayr, Abu al-Khattab al-Sadusi, of Basra, Iraq, born in 61/680. Blind from birth, he was a hadith scholar and Imam of Koranic exegesis, Arabic, and geneology who met and related hadiths from many of the prophetic Companions and from those who came after them, including Anas ibn Malik, Abu al-Tufayl al-Kinani, Sa'id ibn al-

Musayyib, and others. Ahmad once called him "the most learned person in Basra." He died of the plague in Wasit in 118/736 (al-A'lam (y136), 5.189; and Siyar a'lam al-nubala' (y37), 5.269–70).

x300   (The) Queen of Sheba (w30.1) is Bilqis bint Sharahil, descended of Ya'rab ibn Qahtan. It is related that her father, the king of Yemen, was unable to find a suitable wife among the princesses of outlying kingdoms, so he instead wed Rayhan bint al-Sakan, a woman of the jinn, and from their marriage was born Bilqis, who inherited his kingdom. The Holy Koran tells how the hoopoe of Sulayman (upon whom be peace) went to her kingdom and saw the queen and her people prostrating to the sun, and describes the events that led to her accepting Islam from Sulayman. Commentators relate that Sulayman then married her and confirmed her in her kingdom, ordering the jinn to build three incomparable palaces for her in Yemen, where he would visit her each month for three days, and that her reign lasted as long as his (al-Futuhat al-ilahiyya (y65), 3.309–18).

x301   (Imam) Qurtubi (p75.23) is Muhammad ibn Ahmad ibn Abu Bakr ibn Farah, Abu 'Abdullah al-Ansari al-Qurtubi, of Cordova (in present-day Spain). A Maliki scholar and hadith specialist, he was one of the greatest Imams of Koranic exegesis, an ascetic who divided his days between worship and writing. Educated in hadith by masters like 'Ali ibn Muhammad al-Yahsabi and al-Hasan ibn Muhammad al-Bakri, he wrote works in the sciences of hadith and tenets of faith, though his enduring contribution is his twenty-volume al-Jami' li ahkam al-Qur'an [The compendium of the rules of the Koran], from which he mainly omitted the stories and histories customary in other commentaries, and recorded instead the legal rulings contained in the Koran and how scholars have inferred them, together with canonical readings (qira'at), Arabic grammar, and which verses abrogate others and which are abrogated (nasikh wa mansukh). Scholars have used it extensively ever since it was written. It is related that Qurtubi disdained airs, and used to walk about in a simple caftan with a plain cap (taqiyya) on his head. He travelled east and settled in Munya Abi al-Khusayb in upper Egypt, where he died in 671/1273 (al-A'lam (y136), 5.322; al-Jami' li ahkam al-Qur'an (y117), 1.6–7; Sheikh Shu'ayb Arna'ut; and n).

x302   Qushayri (see Abul Qasim Qushayri, x53)

x303   (Imam) Rafi'i (d1.2) is 'Abd al-Karim ibn Muhammad ibn 'Abd al-Karim ibn al-Fadl ibn al-Hasan, Abu al-Qasim al-Rafi'i of Qazvin, Persia, born in 557/1162. The Imam of his time in Sacred Law and Koranic exegesis, he represents, with Imam Nawawi, the principle reference of the late Shafi'i school. His main work, a commentary on Ghazali's al-Wajiz [The synopsis] entitled Fath al-'Aziz fi shurh al-Wajiz [The victory of the Invincible: an exegesis of "The synopsis"] was later to furnish the textual basis for Nawawi's Minhaj al-talibin [The seekers' road]. Taj al-Din Subki noted of its author: "Imam Rafi'i was steeped to repletion in the sciences of Sacred Law, Koranic exegesis, hadith, and fundamentals of Islamic legal methodology, towering above his contemporaries in the transmission of evidence, in research, guidance, and in attainment.... It was as if jurisprudence had been dead, and he revived it and spread it, raising its foundations after ignorance had killed and buried it." He authored works in Sacred Law and history, and taught Koranic exegesis and hadith in Qazvin, where the hadith master (hafiz) Mundhiri was among his students. Known as a pure-hearted ascetic who followed the mystic path, Nawawi observed of him that he "had a firm standing in righteousness, and many miracles were vouchsafed to him." He died in Qazvin in 623/1226 (*al-A'lam* (y136), 4.55; *Tabaqat al-Shafi'iyya al-kubra* (y128), 8.281–85; and n).

x304   Richard Doll (w41.2) is Sir Richard Doll, Emeritus Regius Professor of Medicine, University of Oxford, Green College, Oxford, U.K. (*Oxford Textbook of Medicine* (y76), xiv).

x305   Ridwan (u3.3) is the angel who guards the gates of paradise (n).

x306   (Sheikh) Ridwan al-'Adal Baybars (w15.2) is Ridwan ibn al-'Adal ibn Ahmad Baybars, Abu al-Na'im al-Jazari, born in 1264/1847 in Jazira al-Qibab, Egypt. He was a Shafi'i scholar and Sufi who authored works of litanies of the Blessings upon the Prophet (Allah bless him and give him peace), and Sacred Law, among the latter his *Rawda al-muhtajin li ma'rifa qawa'id al-din* [The garden of those in need of knowing the fundamentals of the religion], which is distinguished by its clear presentation and discussions of contemporary legal questions. He died sometime after 1323/1905 (*Mu'jam al-mu'allifin* (y69), 4.165; and n).

x307   Rifa'a ibn Rafi' (w29.2(2)) is Rifa'a ibn Rafi' ibn Malik ibn 'Ajlan, Abu Mu'adh al-Zuraqi (Allah be well pleased with him), a Medinan Helper and Companion of the Prophet (Allah bless him and give him peace). He was among those who fought at the battle of Badr, and related twenty-four hadiths from the Prophet (Allah bless him and give him peace). He died in 41/661 (*al-A'lam* (y136), 3.29).

x308   R. Peto (w41.2) is the Imperial Cancer Research Fund Reader in Cancer Studies, Nuffield Department of Clinical Medicine, University of Oxford, Radcliffe Infirmary, Oxford, U.K. (*Oxford Textbook of Medicine* (y76), xvi).

x309   Rukana (n3.5) is Rukana ibn 'Abd Yazid ibn Hashim ibn al-Muttalib ibn 'Abd Manaf (Allah be well pleased with him). A Companion of the Prophet (Allah bless him and give him peace) who entered Islam the day Mecca was conquered, he later settled in Medina, where he died in A.H. 42 (*al-Shifa* (y116), 1.165; and *Taqrib al-tahdhib* (y16), 210).

x310   Ruyani (m13.2) is 'Abd al-Wahid ibn Isma'il ibn Ahmad, Abu al-Mahasin Fakhr al-Islam al-Ruyani, of Ruyan in Tabaristan, Persia, born in 315/1025. He was a Shafi'i Imam who was educated under the sheikhs of his time in Bukhara, Ghazna, Nishapur, Rayy, and Isfahan, and founded a school in Amul, Tabaristan (just south of the Caspian seacoast northeast of present-day Tehran, Iran). He once said, "If all Shafi'i's books were burned, I could dictate them anew from memory." Renowned in his lifetime for his scholarship and honored by the vizier Nizam al-Mulk, he authored *Bahr al-madhhab* [The sea of the school], one of the most extensive works in Shafi'i jurisprudence. He died in 402/1108 (*al-A'lam* (y136), 4.175; and *Tabaqat al-Shafi'iyya al-kubra* (y128), 7.193–94).

x311   Sa'd ibn Abi Waqqas (o25.4) is Sa'd ibn Abi Waqqas Malik ibn Wuhayb ibn 'Abd Manaf, Abu Ishaq al-Zuhri al-Qurashi (Allah be well pleased with him), born twenty-three years before the Hijra (A.D. 600). Among the great Companions of the Prophet (Allah bless him and give him peace), he entered Islam at seventeen years of age, fought at the battle of Badr, and led the Muslims to victory at the battle of Qadisiyya, conquering Iraq and the cities of Persia for Islam. He was the first Muslim to release an arrow in the path of Allah, and was one of the ten informed he would enter paradise. Appointed as governor of Kufa during the caliphate of 'Umar, he was confirmed therein for a period by 'Uthman but then dismissed, after which he returned to Medina. He later lost his eyesight, and died at home in 'Aqiq, about ten miles from Medina, in 55/675 (al-A'lam (y136), 3.87; *Taqrib al-tahdhib*, (y16), 232; and n).

x312   Safiyya (w27.1) is the Mother of the Faithful, Safiyya bint Huyay ibn Akhtab ibn Sa'ya (Allah be well pleased with her), a descendant of the prophet Harun (upon whom be peace). The daughter of Huyay, a notable of the Jewish tribes of Bani Qurayza and Nadir, when her husband was killed at Khaybar, she fell the lot of Dihya al-Kalbi and was presented to the Prophet (Allah bless him and give him peace), who freed her and married her. Safiyya was a noble and religious woman who possessed beauty and intelligence, and it is related that she had a bondswoman during the caliphate of 'Umar who went to him and said, "Safiyya loves Saturday and has connections with the Jews," whereupon 'Umar sent for her and inquired about it, and she replied, "As for Saturday, I have not loved it since Allah gave me Friday in its place, and as for the Jews, I have kinfolk among them and maintain my family ties." When she asked her servant what made her do what she did, she was told, "The Devil," to which Safiyya responded, "You may go now, you are free." She died in Medina in 50/670 (al-A'lam (y136), 3.206; and *Siyar a'lam al-nubala'* (y37), 2.232–33).

x313   Safwan ibn Umayya (o9.16) is Safwan ibn Umayya ibn Khalaf ibn Wahb ibn Hudhafa (Allah be well pleased with him), of Mecca, a Companion of the Prophet (Allah bless him and give him peace). A noble of the Quraysh renowned for his eloquence and generosity, he entered Islam after the conquest of Mecca and made good his Islam, being among those who fought in the battle of Yarmouk. He related thirteen hadiths, and died in Mecca in A.H. 41 (al-A'lam (y136), 3.205; and *Siyar a'lam al-nubala'* (y37), 2.562–67).

x314   Sahl ibn 'Abdullah (t1.7) is Sahl ibn 'Abdullah ibn Yunus, Abu Muhammad al-Tustari, of Shushtar, Persia, born in 200/815. An Imam of the Sufis and scholar who wrote on Koranic exegesis and Sufism, no one of his time resembled him in piety, asceticism, and devotions, and he was vouchsafed many miracles. Fine aphorisms on sincerity and self-discipline are related from him, and it is recorded that he met Dhul Nun al-Misri in Mecca in the year of the latter's hajj. He died in 283/896 (al-A'lam (y136), 3.143; *al-Risala al-Qushayriyya* (y118), 400; and n).

x315   Salama ibn al-Akwa' (p15.2) is Salama ibn 'Amr ibn Sinan al-Akwa' al-Aslami (Allah be well pleased with him). Among the Companions who swore fealty to the Prophet (Allah bless him and give him) under the tree, he was a courageous archer and runner who participated in seven battles with the Prophet (Allah bless him and give him peace) including Khaybar and Hunayn, and fought in the Muslim jihad in North Africa during the caliphate of 'Uthman. He related some seventy-seven hadiths, and died in Medina in 74/693 (*al-A'lam* (y136), 3.113; and n).

x316   Salih (u3.5) is Salih ibn 'Ubayd ibn Asif ibn Masih ibn 'Ubayd ibn Hadhir ibn Tamud ibn Ghabir ibn Sam ibn Nuh (upon whom be peace), the prophet of Allah Most High to the people of Thamud, who carved homes in the rock of mountainsides. He lived before the time of Shu'ayb and Musa (upon whom be peace), and was sent to guide his people, though all but a very few denied him. When Allah enjoined them to allow a she-camel to graze and water freely as a sign to them, they hamstrung and killed it, and in punishment were taken by a great earthquake from beneath and a cry (sayha) from the sky, which slew them while sitting upon their knees in their homes (*al-A'lam* (y136), 3.188; *al-Futuhat al-ilahiyya* (y65), 2.158; and *al-Siraj al-munir* (y72), 1.488–90).

x317   Salih Mu'adhdhin (b6.1) is Salih ibn Muhammad Mu'adhdhin, born in Damascus in 1947. He is a contemporary Shafi'i scholar who studied Sacred Law with Sheikh 'Abd al-Karim al-Rifa'i, Sheikh Muhammad 'Awad, and Sheikh Jamal al-Din al-Sayrawan. In 1972 he took a degree in pharmacy from the University of Damascus, and now lives in Amman (n).

x318   Salman the Persian (w4.4) is Salman, Abu 'Abdullah al-Farisi (Allah be well pleased with him), a Companion of the Prophet (Allah bless him and give him peace). Originally a devout Zoroastrian from near Isfahan, Persia, he converted to Christianity and travelled to a series of ascetic masters, serving each in turn until their death, in Damascus, Mosul, Nusaybin, and Ammuriyya (in present-day Turkey), whence he was directed to seek out a new prophet from Mecca whose time was imminent. Enslaved on the way, he was sold to a Jew of Bani Qurayza, met the Prophet (Allah bless him and give him peace) in Medina, and three years later with the help of his fellow Muslims was able to purchase his freedom from his master. Digging the trench before the Battle of the Confederates was his idea. He was a physically strong man of wisdom and learning who was well acquainted with the books of the Persians, Greeks, and Jews; when 'Ali was once asked about him he said, "He was a man of us and for us, the line of the prophetic house, and in relation to you was as the sage Luqman, having learned the first knowledge and the last, read the first scripture and the last: an inexhaustible sea." He related some sixty hadiths, and died in 36/656 (*al-A'lam* (y136), 3.111–12; and *Siyar a'lam al-nubala'* (y37), 1.505–11).

x319   (Imam) Sarakhsi (w43.3) is Muhammad ibn Ahmad ibn Sahl, Abu Bakr Shams al-A'imma al-Sarakhsi of Serakhs (in present-day Turkmen S.S.R.). He was a great Hanafi Imam, *mujtahid*, judge, and the author of the encyclopedic *al-Mabsut* [The extensive], whose thirty volumes he dictated to students from an underground cell where he was imprisoned in Uzjand near Fergana (in present-day Uzbek S.S.R.) for advising a local chief in the matter of religion. He wrote a number of outstanding works in Hanafi jurisprudence and methodological principles of Sacred Law, and died in Fergana in 483/1090 (*al-A'lam* (y136), 5.315; and n).

x320   Sariya (w60.1) is Sariya ibn Zunaym ibn 'Abdullah ibn Jabir ibn Mahmiyya al-Kinani (Allah be well pleased with him). A physically powerful man who could outstrip horses for his fleetness of foot, he was a brigand in the pre-Islamic period of ignorance who participated in many raids, but afterwards became a Muslim who made good his Islam. Ibn 'Asakir believes him to have known the Prophet (Allah bless him and give him peace), though Ibn Hibban considers him among those (tabi'in) who met only the Companions. In 23 A.H., the caliph 'Umar (Allah be well pleased with him) placed Sariya at the head of an army which he dispatched to Persia, and when he was later giving the Friday prayer sermon in Medina, it came to his mind that the army was encountering the enemy in the middle of a valley near a mountain. They seemed to 'Umar to be on the verge of fleeing, so he called out in the midst of the sermon, "O Sariya, the mountain! the mountain!" raising his voice, which Allah miraculously caused to reach the hearing of Sariya and the army, and the Muslims rallied to the side of the mountain and fought the enemy from a united front until Allah gave them the victory. Imam Bayhaqi related this with a well-authenticated (hasan) chain of transmission from Nafi' from Ibn 'Umar, and the story is corroborated by a number of other parallel accounts of the event. It is said that Sariya also won Isfahan for Islam through peaceful negotiation (*al-Isaba fi tamyiz al-Sahaba* (y14), 2.2–3; and *Usud al-ghaba fi ma'rifa al-Sahaba* (y57), 2.306).

x321   Satan (r2.14) is the Devil, Iblis, the Accursed, a slave and creature of Allah Most High. Originally of the angels in kind but of the jinn in works, he was cast down from a high degree of obedience and faith through his pride and disobedience to Allah when ordered to prostrate out of respect to Adam (upon whom be peace). He was then respited until the Last Day, as a trial and affliction for those who would accept his misguidance, though he has no power except through Allah's will and no influence over Allah's righteous servants (*al-Siraj al-munir* (y72), 1.48; and n).

x322   Sayyid Muhammad 'Abdullah al-Somali (w9.4) is Muhammad ibn 'Abdullah ibn Hasan al-Somali, born in 1864 near Bohotle, in north central Somalia. A scholar in Shafi'i jurisprudence, the Koran, and hadith, he was an important Somali intellectual and religious leader who led resistance to the British and Italians in his country for more than two decades (1899–1920). He studied for five or six years in Mecca under Sheikh Muhammad ibn Salih al-Rashidi, founder of the Salihiyya tariqa of which he was made a sheikh before returning to Somalia via Aden in 1895. Among his recorded speeches are the words: "Unbelieving men of religion have assaulted our country from their remote homelands. They wish to corrupt our religion, to force us to accept Christianity, supported by the armed force of their governments, their weapons, their numbers. You have only your faith in God, your arms and your determination. Do not be frightened by their soldiers or armies: God is mightier than they ...." Bradford Martin relates that with the Salihiyya tariqa as an organizational basis, Sayyid Muhammad mounted a military movement that was perhaps longer sustained and more successful than any other movement led by an African Muslim leader of the nineteenth or early twentieth century, for twenty years tying the hands of the British and Italians and making them spend huge sums and many lives on purely military operations; through which means he maintained and defended traditional Somalian Muslim values and ways of life. He died, possibly of influenza, in 1920 at fifty-six years of age (*Muslim Brotherhoods* (y86), 179–200).

x323   Seyyed Hossein Nasr (Facing Title Page) was born in Tehran, Iran, where he received his early education. He later studied in the West and received his B.S. from the Massachusetts Institute of Technology and his M.A and Ph.D. from Harvard, where he studied the history of science and learning with special concentration on Islamic science and philosophy. He has taught at Tehran University, the American University in Beirut, Temple University, and George Washington University, and is the author of a number of works that are among the best available in English on the relevance of traditional Islamic sciences and mystical disciplines to the situation of modern man, including *Ideals and Realities of Islam, Man and Nature, Islamic Science: an Illustrated Study,* and *Sufi Essays.* The translator is indebted to his writings for being among the reasons he became a Muslim. While from a Shiite background, Hossein Nasr has a firmer footing in traditional Islamic knowledge than many other western interpreters of Islam, Muslim or non-Muslim, and his works are generally free of the mistakes in detail found in others' books, though some passages are occasionally colored by the comparative religions approach (dis: x348) that mars the writings of a number of contemporary Muslim intellectuals. He lives and teaches in the United States (*Ideals and Realities of Islam* (y101), 4; and n).

x324   (Imam) Shafi'i (Introduction) is Muhammad ibn Idris ibn al-'Abbas ibn 'Uthman ibn Shafi' ibn al-Sa'ib ibn 'Ubayd ibn 'Abd Yazid ibn Hashim ibn al-Muttalib ibn 'Abd Manaf, Abu 'Abdullah al-Qurashi al-Makki al-Shafi'i, descended from the great-grandfather of the Prophet (Allah bless him and give him peace). Born in 150/767 in Gaza, Palestine, Shafi'i was the Imam of the World, the *mujtahid* of his time, one of the most brilliant and original legal scholars mankind has ever known. An orphan brought to Mecca when two years old and raised there by his mother in circumstances of extreme poverty and want, he memorized the Holy Koran at age seven, the *Muwatta'* of Imam Malik at ten, and was authorized to give formal legal opinion (fatwa) at the age of fifteen by his sheikh, Muslim ibn Khalid al-Zinji, the mufti of Mecca. He travelled to Medina and studied under Imam Malik, and then to Baghdad, where he was the student of Imam Muhammad ibn Hasan Shaybani, the colleague of Abu Hanifa. In Baghdad, Imam Shafi'i produced his first school of jurisprudence (al-madhhab al-qadim), but when the persecution arose over the uncreatedness of the Koran (dis: x72), he spoke to Ahmad ibn Hanbal, and they mutually agreed that rather than risk the loss of both of Islam's living *mujtahid*s, they should part company, Shafi'i travelling with his books and belongings to Cairo, and Ahmad remaining in Iraq. It was in Cairo that in the astonishing space of only four years, Shafi'i conceived and edited a second, entirely new school of jurisprudence (al-madhhab al-jadid), embodied in his seven-volume *al-Umm* [The mother].

   The Imam and his legacy are monumental. His *al-Risala* [The letter] was the first work in the history of mankind to investigate the theoretical and practical bases of jurisprudence. In Koranic exegesis, he was the first to formulate the principles of the science of which verses abrogate others and which are abrogated ('ilm al-nasikh wa al-mansukh). His knowledge of the Koran and sunna and of the accord between the different elements of each and the conditionality and explanation of some by others were incomparable. His Arabic style and diction were recorded and used as lexical evidence by later grammarians and lexicologists, and despite his surpassing eloquence in the language, being Arabic in tongue, residence, and historical epoch, he studied it in depth for twenty years, and through the medium of it grasped the Koran and sunna. He paved the way for the enormous importance attached by subsequent generations of Muslims to the study of prophetic hadith, as reflected in the fact that most of the Imams in the field were of his school, including Bukhari, Muslim, Abu Dawud, Tirmidhi, Nasa'i. Ibn Majah, Bayhaqi, al-Hakim, Abu Nu'aym, Ibn Hibban, Daraqutni, Ibn Khuzayma, Ibn Salah, al-'Iraqi, Suyuti, Dhahabi, Ibn Kathir, Nur al-Din Haythami, Mundhiri, Nawawi, Taqi al-Din Subki, and others. Imam Muhammad ibn Hasan Shaybani said of him, "If the scholars of hadith speak, it is in the language of Shafi'i," and Hasan ibn Muhammad Za'frani observed, "The scholars of hadith were asleep and awoke when Shafi'i woke them." Imam Ahmad said, "No one touches an inkwell or pen with his hand, save that he owes a debt to Shafi'i."

By the time Shafi'i reached Cairo in A.H. 199, his fame had spread to the horizons, scholars from all parts of the Muslim world travelled to hear him, and his student and scribe Rabi' ibn Sulayman was to say, "I have seen seven hundred riding camels tethered at Shafi'i's door, belonging to those who came to hear him exposit his writings." The author of some 113 works, it was nonetheless Shafi'i's hope that "people would learn this knowledge without ascribing a single letter of it to me," and as Zakariyya Ansari remarked, "Allah granted his wish, for one seldom hears any position of his, save that it is ascribed to others of his school with the words, 'Rafi'i, or Nawawi, or Zarkashi says ...' and the like." Of proverbial generosity, it is recorded that when he once brought ten thousand dinars from Yemen, he pitched a tent outside of Mecca and had given it all away to passersby before the day ended. He was moderate in dress, and his ring bore the inscription, "Allah suffices Muhammad ibn Idris as a reliance." He once said, "Knowledge is not what is memorized, but only what benefits," and this conviction imbued his personal religious life, for he divided his night into three parts, in the first of which he would write, in the second pray, and in the third sleep. He recited the entire Koran each day at prayer, and twice a day in Ramadan. When a remark was once made to him about his using a walking stick, he said, "I do it to remind myself that I am on a journey out of this life." A man of intense spiritual presence who could truthfully say of himself, "I have never told a lie," his students were in such awe of him that they could not take a drink of water while he was looking on. Among his pupils were a number of the Imams of the time such as Ahmad, Rabi' ibn Sulayman, al-Muzani, Dawud ibn Khalaf al-Zahiri, and others. He studied and taught Sacred Law in Cairo until his death at fifty-three years of age in 204/820, the end of a lifetime of service to Islam and the Muslims by one of the greatest in knowledge of the Koran and sunna (al-A'lam (y136), 6.26; al-Majmu' (y108), 1.8–10, 'Umdat al-salik (y90), 9 10; al Tabaqat al kubra (y124) 1.50–52; and n)

x325   Shamil Daghestani (w9.4) is Shamil Muhammad al-Daghestani, a sheikh who helped spread the Naqshbandi tariqa throughout Caucasia and fought with the Muslim jihad there against Czarist Russia for some thirty-five years. His sheikh was Mulla Muhammad al-Ghazi al-Kamrawi, whose military career began when Russia declared protection for Christians in Khurjistan and then formal annexation of the region from Safavid Persia in 1215/1800. Al-Ghazi (lit. "the

Warrior") recruited hundreds of thousands of soldiers from his Naqshbandi der-
vishes and fought until his death in 1248/1832, when his successor al-Amir Hamza
al-Khanzaji took over but was martyred the same year, after which the jihad's
leadership devolved to Sheikh Shamil. He fought many pitched battles with the
Russians in the twenty-seven years of jihad that followed, in 1260/1844 freeing
Daghestan of the unbelievers and capturing thirty-five of their cannon, which pro-
voked Russia to send an even larger army to finish the *mujahidin*, who fought on
fifteen more years until 1279/1859, when the sheikh was captured. Advanced in
years, he was banished to Turkey, whence he travelled to Medina in hope of being
buried there with the Companions and early Muslims. He spent the last of his life
worshipping in the Rawda of the Mosque of the Prophet (Allah bless him and give
him peace) between the pulpit and the noble tomb, and when he died he was in-
terred, according to his wish, in al-Baqi' Cemetery (*al-Muslimun fi al-Ittihad al-
Sufyati 'abr al-tarikh* (y28), 1.65, 1.149, 1.154–55, 1.398).

x326   Shams al-Din ... Dhahabi (*see* (Imam) Dhahabi, x114)

x327   Shawkani (w40.5) is Muhammad ibn 'Ali ibn Muhammad ibn 'Abdullah
al-Shawkani, born in Shawkan near Khawlan, Yemen, in 1173/1760. A major
scholar in Sacred Law and hadith, he was educated in San'a, where he was
appointed as an Islamic judge in A.H. 1229, a position he held throughout his life.
He authored 114 works in hadith, biography, Sacred Law, Koranic exegesis, fundamentals of Islamic jurisprudence, and tenets of faith, though his greatest work
was his eight-volume hadith commentary *Nayl al-awtar min asrar muntaqa al-
akhbar* [The realization of desires, from the secrets of selected hadiths]. He died
in San'a in 1250/1834 (*al-A'lam* (y136), 6.298).

x328   ("Sheikh...," "Sheikh al-Islam...,") (*see under proper name*)

x329   (Imam, Sheikh) Shirbini (al-Khatib) (*see* Muhammad Shirbini Khatib,
x264(a))

x330   Shu'ayb (u3.5) is Shu'ayb ibn Mikil ibn Yashjar ibn Madyan (upon whom
be peace), a prophet of Allah Most High who was nicknamed the Speaker of the
Prophets for the fairness of his exhortations to the folk of Madyan, who were
unbelievers who cheated when weighing and measuring out goods to people. He
was descended of Ibrahim (upon whom be peace) and came after Hud and Salih,
only a short time before Musa. Commentators relate that when his people
repeatedly rejected his call to pure monotheism, Shu'ayb and those who believed
departed from them, and Allah opened up to them one of the gates of hell, afflict-
ing them with the most extreme heat. They entered tunnels to flee from it, but
found it the more unbearable, so some of them came out onto an open plain,
where they found a cloud above them and with it, a cool, pleasant breeze. They
called the others to come and join them until the entire people were assembled
under it, whereupon Allah caused the earth to quake, changed the cloud to fire,
and burned them to ashes (*al-A'lam* (y136), 3.165–66; and *al-Siraj al-munir* (y72),
1.495).

x331   (Sheikh) Shu'ayb Arna'ut (o22.1(d(II(end)))) is Shu'ayb ibn Muharram
ibn 'Ali, Abu Usama al-Arna'ut, born in Damascus in 1928, two years after his

father's emigration for religious reasons from Shköder, Albania. He is a scholar of hadith, Hanafi law, Koranic exegesis, and Arabic grammar and lexicology who has edited many classic Islamic works from old manuscripts. Educated in Damascus, he studied Hanafi jurisprudence with sheikhs such as 'Abd al-Razzaq al-Halabi, Nuh al-Albani, Sulayman al-Ghawji, and others, and hadith terminology under 'Abdullah al-Habashi, Sheikh al-Kallas, and Salih al-Farfur, with the latter of whom he also read the eight-volume Hanafi *Hashiya radd al-muhtar* of Ibn 'Abidin during the course of seven years, and the Koranic commentaries of Zamakhshari and Nasafi. Among the better known scholars of his profession, he has edited, annotated, and judged the hadiths of more than eighty works to date, of which the most famous is perhaps the five-volume *Zad al-ma'ad* [The provision for the return] by Ibn Qayyim al-Jawziyya, though he feels that his most important scholarly contribution lies in the editing of three works: *Sharh al-sunna* [The explanation of the sunna] by Imam Baghawi, which presents the primary Koranic and hadith textual evidence for rulings of Sacred Law; *Sharh mushkil al-athar* [The explanation of problematic hadiths] by Imam Tahawi, which explains the accord between ostensible contradictions among hadiths in terms of which ones are understood, abrogated, or conditioned by others or by the Koran; and *al-Ihsan fi taqrib Sahih Ibn Hibban* [The proficiency: on facilitating the "Rigorously authenticated hadith collection" of Ibn Hibban], whose basic text is 'Ala' al-Din Farisi's commentary on the *Sahih* of Ibn Hibban. The preparation of these works, each of which has sixteen volumes, was by no means a mere exercise in editing. With *Ibn Hibban*, for example, the original text consisted of eight volumes, to which Sheikh Shu'ayb supplied the equivalent of eight additional volumes of his own notes and commentary. In our times, as sheikhs qualified to teach the classic works of the Islamic sciences grow steadily fewer, Shu'ayb's hope is that such expanded and annotated editions will to some extent fulfill the educational needs of the Muslims who read them. Though he will probably be remembered for his work in hadith, he strongly believes that Muslims should take their religion from those with the best understanding of the primary texts of the Koran and prophetic traditions, at their forefront the Imams of the four schools. "They are explainers, not popes," he says, "but in each of their schools there afterwards followed a hundred or more scholars who refined and added to their work, men whose stature in Islamic knowledge was like mountains, any of whom could put fifteen of the scholars available today in his pocket." He presently lives in Amman, where he supervises the research staff and library of the Mu'assasa al-Risala publishing house (n).

x332   Shu'ba (w40.5) is Shu'ba ibn al-Hajjaj ibn al-Ward, Abu Bistam al-'Ataki, of Wasit, Iraq, and then of Basra, born in 82/701. A reliable narrator and proficient hadith scholar, he was the first to search in Iraq for knowledge of the reliability of various hadith transmitters and to defend the sunna. Imam Shafi'i said of him, "If not for Shu'ba, hadith would have been unknown in Iraq." He was noted for his devotions in his personal life, and died in 160/778 (*al-A'lam* (y136), 3.164; and *Taqrib al-tahdhib* (y16), 266).

x333   Siraj al-Din Bulqini (w12.3) is 'Umar ibn Ruslan ibn Nusayr ibn Salih, Abu Hafs Siraj al-Din al-Kinani al-Bulqini, born in Bulqina, Egypt, in 724/1324. A Shafi'i *mujtahid* Imam, hadith master (hafiz), and judge, he was educated in

Cairo and gained recognition as the foremost representative of the Shafi'i school in his time. In A.H. 769 he was appointed to the judiciary in Damascus. He authored a number of works in Shafi'i jurisprudence, hadith, and formal legal opinion, and died in Cairo in 805/1403 (*al-A'lam* (y136), 5.46; and n).

x334   Solomon (*see* Sulayman, x338)

x335   Subki (*see* (Imam) Taqi al-Din Subki, x345)

x336   Suddi (w4.4) is Isma'il ibn 'Abd al-Rahman ibn Abi Karima, Abu Muhammad al-Suddi, originally of the Hijaz and then of Kufa. An Imam of Koranic exegesis whom Ahmad ibn Hanbal names as a reliable narrator, he related hadiths from the Companions Anas ibn Malik, Ibn 'Abbas, and 'Abd Khayr al-Hamdani, while his hadiths were related by Shu'ba, Sufyan al-Thawri, Isra'il, and others. He died in A.H. 127 (*Siyar a'lam al-nubala'* (y37), 5.264–65).

x337   Sufyan al-Thawri (a2.6) is Sufyan ibn Sa'id ibn Masruq ibn Habib, Abu 'Abdullah al-Thawri of Kufa, born in 97/716. The Imam of hadith masters (huffaz) of his time and among the foremost in Sacred Knowledge and godfearingness, he possessed a phenomenal memory and was able to say, "I have never learned something and then forgot it." His father began educating him while young, and he studied under nearly six hundred sheikhs, the most important of whom were those who transmitted hadiths from Companions like Abu Hurayra, Jarir ibn 'Abdullah, Ibn 'Abbas, and others. A number of principle Imams took hadiths from him, such as Ja'far al-Sadiq, Abu Hanifa, al-Awza'i, Shu'ba, (all of whom died before he did) and a number of others. He once said, "I've never heard a hadith of the Prophet (Allah bless him and give him peace) without acting upon it, even if only once." He authored a number of works in hadith and Islamic estate division, and many of his aphorisms have been recorded, among them, "Asceticism is not eating coarse food or wearing poor clothes, but rather expecting life not to last, and being watchful for death." He died in 161/778 (*al-A'lam* (y136), 3.104–5; and *Siyar a'lam al-nubala'* (y37), 7.229–43).

x338   Sulayk Ghatafani (w28.1) is Sulayk ibn 'Amr al-Ghatafani (Allah be well pleased with him), of the Ghatafan tribe, a Companion of the Prophet (Allah bless him and give him peace). The incident mentioned in the hadith of the text (at w28.1) was related by Muslim and others, and is virtually the only information known about him (*Usud al-ghaba fi ma'rifa al-Sahaba* (y57), 2.441–42).

x339   Sulayman (u3.5) is Sulayman ibn Dawud ibn Isha (upon whom be peace), the prophet of Allah Most High and son of the prophet Dawud. He knew the language of birds, inherited the kingship of Bani Isra'il from his father, and had an army of birds, jinn, and men. Allah Most High subjected the winds to his command, and according to commentators, he possessed a great platform that could hold all he needed of palaces, tents, belongings, horses, camels, men, and jinn; and whenever he desired to make war, travel, or sojourn in any land on earth, he would laden it and command the winds to convey it there, and it would travel a month's journey in a single day. Many wonders are recorded of him in the Holy Koran and its commentaries, and he is said to have ruled for forty years before his death at the age of fifty-two (*Qisas al-anbiya'* (y59), 498–519).

x340   Sulayman Bujayrmi (w41.3) is Sulayman ibn Muhammad ibn 'Umar al-Bujayrmi, born in Bujayrm, Egypt, in 1331/1719. He was a Shafi'i scholar who moved to Cairo at a young age, was educated at al-Azhar, and later taught there. Though he lost this eyesight, he produced a number of famous commentaries on Shafi'i classics, among them his four-volume *al-Tajrid* [The abstract], and *Tuhfa al-Habib* [The gift of the beloved], a commentary on Shirbini's *al-Iqna'* [The persuading] also in four volumes. He died in the village of Mastiyya, near Bujayrm, in 1221/1806 (*al-A'lam* (y136), 3.133).

x341   Suyuti (b3.2) is 'Abd al-Rahman ibn Abu Bakr ibn Muhammad ibn Sabiq al-Din, Jalal al-Din al-Suyuti, born in 849/1445. He was a Shafi'i *mujtahid* Imam, Sufi, hadith master (hafiz), and historian, a prolific writer who authored works in virtually every Islamic science. Raised as an orphan in Cairo, he memorized the Koran at eight, then several complete works of Sacred Law, fundamentals of jurisprudence, and Arabic grammar; after which he devoted himself to studying the Sacred Sciences under some of the foremost sheikhs of the time in each discipline, among them Siraj al-Din Bulqini, with whom he studied Shafi'i jurisprudence until his death; Sharaf al-Din al-Munawi, with whom he read Koranic exegesis; Taqi al-Din al-Shamani in hadith and the sciences of Arabic; and others. He travelled to gain Sacred Knowledge to Damascus, the Hijaz, Yemen, India, Morocco, and the lands south of Morocco, as well as to centers of learning in Egypt such as Mahalla, Dumyat, and Fayyum.

When he reached forty years of age, he abandoned the company of men for the solitude of the Garden of al-Miqyas by the side of the Nile, avoiding his former colleagues as though he had never known them, and it was here that he authored most of his nearly six hundred books and treatises. Wealthy Muslims and princes would visit him with offers of money and gifts, but he put all of them off, and when the sultan requested his presence a number of times, he refused. Blessed with success in his years of solitude, it is difficult to name a field in which Suyuti did not make outstanding contributions, among them his ten-volume hadith work *Jam' al-jawami'* [The collection of collections]; his Koranic exegesis *Tafsir al-Jalalayn* [The commentary of the two Jalals], of which he finished the second half of an uncompleted manuscript by Jalal al-Din Mahalli in just forty days; his classic commentary on the sciences of hadith *Tadrib al-rawi fi sharh Taqrib al-Nawawi* [The training of the hadith transmitter: an exegesis of Nawawi's "The facilitation"]; and many others. A giant among contemporaries, he remained alone, producing a sustained output of scholarly writings until his death in Cairo at sixty years of age in 911/1505 (*al-A'lam* (y136), 3.301–2; *Tadrib al-rawi* (y109), 1.11–12; and n).

x342 (a)   Tabarani (w32.1) is Sulayman ibn Ahmad ibn Ayyub ibn Mutayr, Abu al-Qasim al-Lakhami al-Tabarani, born in Acre, Palestine, in 260/873. A great hadith master (hafiz) and Koranic commentator, he travelled to listen to hadith masters for sixteen years, to the Hijaz, Yemen, Egypt, Iraq, Persia, and the Arabian Peninsula, meeting approximately a thousand sheikhs. He finally settled in Isfahan, Persia, where he related hadiths for sixty years, was visited by scholars from all parts of the Muslim world, and authored his three main hadith collections, the largest of which is his twenty-five-volume *al-Mu'jam al-kabir* [The major lexicon], called a "lexicon" because of the alphabetical arrangement of its narrators. When once asked how he acquired such a prodigious store of hadith knowledge, he answered, "By sleeping on reed mats for thirty years." He died in Isfahan in 360/971 (*al-A'lam* (y136), 3.121; *Siyar a'lam al-nubala'* (y37), 16.119–23; *al-Targhib wa al-tarhib* (y9), 1.21; and Sheikh Shu'ayb Arna'ut).

x342 (b)   (Dr.) Taha Jabir al-'Alwani (Document 3) is a Shafi'i scholar and specialist in fundamentals of Islamic jurisprudence born of Kurdish parents in al-Falluja, to the west of Baghdad, in 1935. After receiving his elementary and secondary education in Iraq, he attended al-Azhar, where he studied under Sheikh 'Abd al-Ghani 'Abd al-Khaliq, author of *Hujjiya al-sunna* [The evidentiary character of the sunna], and other scholars and graduated in 1959 from theCollege of Sacred Law, then pursued his postgraduate studies to receive a master's degree and his doctorate in 1972. He has taught Islamic law and its principles at the University of Imam Muhammad ibn Sa'ud in Riyadh, Saudi Arabia, is a member of the founding council of the Muslim World League in Mecca, a member of the Organization of the Islamic Conference (OIC) Islamic Fiqh Academy at Jedda, and president of the Fiqh Council of North America. He has edited and annotated the six-volume *al-Mahsul fi 'ilm al-usul* [The summary: the science of the principles of Islamic jurisprudence] by al-Fakhr al-Razi, currently under preparation for its second printing, and has authored *Adab al-ikhtilaf fi al-Islam* [The proper way of scholarly disagreement in Islam], *Usul al-fiqh al-Islami* [The bases of Islamic jurisprudence], and *al-Ijtihad wa al-taqlid fi al-Islam* [Personal juridical reasoning versus following qualified scholarship in Islam], the latter two of which have been recently translated into English. The International Institute of Islamic Thought, which Dr. al-'Alwani helped found in 1981, is an autonomous, non-profit organization dedicated to articulating the relevance of Islam to the problems of thought and life of contemporary Muslims, and promoting and serving Islamic research throughout the world. From its headquarters in Washington D.C., and with offices from Cairo to Kuala Lumpur, it conducts specialized seminars, commissions the production of scholarly works, grants research scholarships, and disseminates an impressive array of publications to interested scholars around the globe. He has headed the institute as president since 1986 (n).

x343   Tahtawi (w24.2) is Ahmad ibn Muhammad ibn Isma'il al-Tahtawi, born in Tahta, near Asyut, Egypt. He was educated at al-Azhar, where he was later appointed sheikh of the Hanafi school. He is best known for his *Hashiya al-durr al-mukhtar* [The commentary on "The choice pearls"], a commentary on the basic text of Ibn 'Abidin's famous *Radd al-muhtar* [The enlightenment of the baffled]; and his *Hashiya 'ala Maraqi al-falah sharh Nur al-idah* [Commentary on "The ascents of felicity: an exegesis of 'The light of clarity' "]. He died in Cairo in 1231/1816 (*al-A'lam* (y136), 1.245).

x344   Talha (o25.4) is Talha ibn 'Ubayd Allah ibn 'Uthman, Abu Muhammad al-Tamimi al-Qurashi (Allah be well pleased with him), born twenty-eight years before the Hijra (A.D. 596) in Mecca. Among the most courageous and generous Companions of the Prophet (Allah bless him and give him peace), he was of the first eight men to enter Islam, of the ten informed that they would enter paradise, and one of the committee (shura) 'Umar chose to name his caliphal successor. Present with the Prophet (Allah bless him and give him peace) at the battle of Uhud, Talha stood unflinchingly by his side during the reverses suffered there, and swearing to remain with him to the death if need be, sustained twenty-four wounds from which he later recovered to fight in every subsequent battle. He had extensive trade dealings in Iraq, and never allowed a member of his clan to suffer want or debt save that he would pay for their needs at his own expense. He was killed at the Battle of al-Jamal at the side of 'A'isha in 36/656 and buried in Basra (ibid., 3.229).

x345   (Imam) Taqi al-Din Subki (Introduction) is 'Ali ibn 'Abd al-Kafi ibn 'Ali ibn Tamam, Abu al-Hasan Taqi al-Din al-Subki, born in Subk, Egypt, in 683/1284. The Shafi'i scholar and Imam of his time, he was a brilliant intellectual, hadith master (hafiz), Koranic exegete, and Islamic judge who was described by Ibn Hajar Haytami as "the *mujtahid* Imam whose imamate, greatness, and having reached the level of *ijtihad* are agreed upon," and by Dhahabi as "the most learned, eloquent, and wisest in judgement of all the sheikhs of the age." Educated in Cairo by such scholars as Ibn Rif'a in Sacred Law, 'Alam al-Din Iraqi in Koranic exegesis, and Sharaf al-Din al-Dimyati in hadith, he also travelled to acquire knowledge of hadith from the sheikhs of Syria, Alexandria, and the Hijaz, after which, as Suyuti records, "he devoted himself to writing and giving legal opinion, authoring more than 150 works, his writings displaying his profound knowledge of hadith and other fields and his magisterial command of the Islamic sciences. He educated the foremost scholars of the time, was a painstaking, accurate, and penetrating researcher, and a brilliant debater in the disciplines. No previous scholar attained to his achievements in Sacred Law, of masterful inferences, subtleties in detail, and carefully worked-out methodological principles." Salah al-Din Safadi said of him, "People say that no one like him had appeared since Ghazali, though in my opinion they thereby do him an injustice, for to my mind he does not resemble anyone less than Sufyan al-Thawri." With his vast erudition, he was at the same time a godfearing ascetic in his personal life who was devoted to worship and mysticism, though vigilant and uncompromising in matters of religion and ready to assail any innovation (bid'a) or departure from the tenets of faith of Ahl al-Sunna. In addition to *al-Takmila* [The completion], his eleven-volume supplement to Nawawi's *Sharh al-Muhadhdhab* [The exegesis of "The rarefaction"], he also authored the widely quoted *Fatawa al-Subki* [The legal opinions of Subki] in two volumes, as well as a number of other works on tenets of faith, Koranic exegesis, and fundamentals of Islamic law, in the latter of which his three-volume *al-Ibhaj fi sharh al-Minhaj* [The gladdening: an exegesis of "The road"], an exposition of Baydawi's *al-Minhaj* on the methodological bases of legal *ijtihad*, has won lasting recognition among scholars. In A.H. 739 he moved from Cairo to Damascus, where he was appointed to the judiciary and presided for seventeen years, at the end of which he became ill, was replaced by his son Taj al-Din, and returned to Cairo, where he died twenty days later in 756/1355 (ibid., 4.302; *al-Fatawa al-hadithiyya* (y48), 114; *al-Rasa'il al-Subkiyya* (y52), 9–13; Sheikh Hasan Saqqaf; and n).

x346   Tha'laba ibn Hatib (p75.15) is Tha'laba ibn Hatib (or ibn Abi Hatib) al-Ansari. Ibn Ishaq mentions him among those who helped build the Mosque of al-Dirar (Koran 9:107) by which they intended, out of hypocrisy and unbelief, to compete with the Mosque of Quba' and disunite the Muslims, and in hopes that the longtime enemy of Islam Abu 'Amir the Monk would return from Syria to defeat the Prophet (Allah bless him and give him peace) and make the mosque his center. This Tha'laba is sometimes confused with Tha'laba ibn Hatib ibn 'Amr ibn 'Ubayd ibn Umayya al-Aws, who fought at Badr and was martyred at Uhud. The hadith mentioned in the text (p75.15) of the former Tha'laba's nonpayment of zakat was researched by Ibn Hajar 'Asqalani, who said that its chains of transmission are weak, as they come through 'Ali ibn Yazid al-Alhani, an extremely unreliable (matruk) hadith narrator (*al-Isaba fi tamyiz al-Sahaba* (y14) 1.200–201; *al-Siraj al-munir* (y72), 1.649; and *Zad al-masir fi 'ilm al-tafsir* (y12), 3.474).

x347   Tirmidhi (Introduction) is Muhammad ibn 'Isa ibn Sura ibn Musa, Abu 'Isa al-Sulami al-Tirmidhi, of Termez (in present-day Uzbek S.S.R.), born in 209/824. A hadith master (hafiz) and Imam who was a student of Bukhari, Ishaq ibn Rahawayh, and others, he travelled in pursuit of knowledge to Khurasan, Iraq, Medina, and Mecca, and authored a number of works in history and hadith, among the most famous of which are his five-volume *al-Jami' al-kabir* [The major collection], also known as *Sahih al-Tirmidhi;* and his *al-Shama'il al-nabawiyya* [The prophetic traits], which describes in detail the person, manners, and appearance of the Prophet (Allah bless him and give him peace). 'Umar ibn 'Allak said of Tirmidhi, "Bukhari died without leaving anyone in Khurasan like Abu 'Isa in knowledge, memory, piety, and asceticism ...." In later life he became blind, and died in Termez in 279/892 (*al-A'lam* (y136), 6.322; and *Siyar a'lam al-nubala'* (y37), 13.270–73).

x348   Titus Burckhardt (w13.1) is a European Muslim writer of the present century who was born in Florence, Italy, the son of the Swiss sculptor Carl Burckhardt and a member of a patrician family of Basle. Although he first followed his father's profession, his strong attraction to oriental art led him to a theoretical study of eastern doctrines and repeated journeys to Islamic countries. After some years of studying the history of art and oriental languages, he became director of the Graf-Verlag publishing house, which specialized in facsimile editions of ancient manuscripts. In 1972 he was appointed to UNESCO for the preservation of the ancient city of Fez. He is the author of *The Moorish Culture in Spain,* one of the best and most sensitive works on an Islamic civilization; *Art of Islam: Language and Meaning; Sacred Art in East and West; An Introduction to Sufi Doctrine;* and *Letters of a Sufi Master,* a translation of the *Rasa'il* [Letters] of al-'Arabi al-Darqawi. His books on Sufism have a wide readership, both Muslim and non-Muslim, for which reason it is worth mentioning here two points of departure in them that occasionally obscure the spirit of what they are intended to explain.

The first is his transposition of Sufi theosophy to Platonic philosophical language, not only in ordinary, needful metaphysical distinctions such as 'being', 'act', and 'essence', but also in substantive doctrinal conceptions of the Platonic worldview such as 'immutable essences', 'archetypes', 'Ideas', and so forth, which at Burckhardt's hands often generate passages of philosophical interest, but whose connection with their *explanadum,* Sufism, is not clear or convincing. For Sufis, whatever vocabulary they may choose, behold the Truth by the sun of divine revelation, not the movements of human introspection, and in a word, are illumined, while Plato is unillumined.

The second point of departure is a *comparative religions* approach to Islam and Sufism which understands them according to the "essential unity" (and universal validity) of all religions. On this point, Islam clearly teaches that all true religions, as originally revealed, were identical in fundamentals of belief (usul) such as the oneness of God, the Final Judgement, and heaven and hell, in which sense "we make no distinction between any of His messengers" (Koran 2:285), though each prophetic messenger brought particular rules and rites (furu') that differed to some extent from those of previous messengers, and "to every nation We appointed a worship" (Koran 22:67). So while the anciently revealed religions that are found today naturally show some similarities to Islam, this fact does not prove their "essential unity" with it as they presently exist, for the One who revealed the religions informs us not only that their beliefs and scriptures have since been altered by the hands of men, who "changed the words from their places and forgot a share of what they were reminded of" (Koran 5:13), but also that their rites and laws have been abrogated by those revealed to the Final Messenger (Allah bless him and give him peace), which is why "whoever seeks other than Islam as a religion will never have it accepted from him" (Koran 3:85). This is how Allah Most High has explained the similarities and differences between religions, and any comparative approach beyond this can never lay claim to the truth.

Aside from such ideas, which are far from Islam, the works of Titus Burckhardt contain many original discussions of the meaning of Islamic art, a field which few westerners have equalled his depth in and appreciation of, and for which he is likely to be remembered. He died in Lausanne, Switzerland, in 1984 (*Art of Islam* (y31), inside back cover; and n).

x349　'Ubada ibn al-Samit (w18.4) is 'Ubada ibn al-Samit ibn Qays, Abu al-Walid al-Khazraji (Allah be well pleased with him), born thirty-eight years before the Hijra (A.D. 586). A Medinan Helper and Companion of the Prophet (Allah bless him and give him peace), he was known for his personal piety, and was among those who fought at the battle of Badr, as well as the others, and in the conquest of Egypt. He related 181 hadiths from the Prophet (Allah bless him and give him peace) and became the first person appointed as an Islamic judge in Palestine, where he died, in either Ramla or Jerusalem, in 34/654 (*al-A'lam* (y136), 3.258).

x350　Ubayy ibn Khalaf (o9.0) was one of the unbelievers of Mecca who used to injure the Prophet (Allah bless him and give him peace) and once even incited 'Uqba ibn Abi Mu'it to spit in his face. When he told the Prophet (Allah bless him and give him peace) after Badr that he was feeding a horse each day in Mecca upon which he would kill him, the Prophet (Allah bless him and give him peace) replied, "It is I who shall slay you, Allah willing," and kept his word the following year at the battle of Uhud, where he killed him with a stab from a short spear. A hadith declares, "The wretchedest of men is whoever kills a prophet, or a prophet kills" (*al Shifa* (y116), 1.238 39).

x351　'Umar (b3.2) is 'Umar ibn al-Khattab ibn Nufayl, Abu Hafs al-Qurashi al-'Adawi (Allah be well pleased with him), born forty years before the Hijra (A.D. 584) in Mecca. He was one of the greatest Companions of the Prophet (Allah bless him and give him peace), as renowned for his tremendous personal courage and steadfastness as for his fairness in giving judgements. Among the heroes of the Meccan nobles in the pre-Islamic period of ignorance, he entered Islam five years before the emigration to Medina, and Ibn Mas'ud was later to observe, "We were not able to pray by the Kaaba until 'Umar became Muslim." He fought in all the battles of the Prophet (Allah bless him and give him peace) and was sworn fealty to as the second caliph of Islam on the day of Abu Bakr's death. During his ten-and-a-half-year caliphate, Syria, Palestine, Iraq, Egypt, and all the Arabian Peninsula were added to the dominions of Islam, and about twelve thousand mosques were built. He related 537 hadiths from the Prophet (Allah bless him and give him peace) and was the first to date Islamic events from the year of the Hijra. His sayings, addresses, and letters were of great eloquence, and a memorable event seldom befell him without his composing a line of poetry about it. His ring was inscribed with the words, "Death suffices as an admonition, O 'Umar." Stabbed by a slave while performing the dawn prayer, he died three nights later in 23/644 (*al-A'lam* (y136), 5.45–46).

x352   (Sheikh) 'Umar Barakat (Introduction) is 'Umar Barakat ibn al-Sayyid Muhammad Barakat al-Shami al-Biqa'i, A scholar of Shafi'i jurisprudence and rhetoric, he was originally from al-Biqa', north of Damascus, Syria, and was educated at al-Azhar, where he studied under Sheikh Ibrahim Bajuri. He then moved to Mecca and authored his two-volume commentary on *'Umdat al-salik* [The reliance of the traveller] entitled *Fayd al-Ilah al-Malik fi hall alfaz 'Umdat al-salik wa 'uddat al-nasik* [The outpouring of the Sovereign Divinity in solving the words of "The reliance of the traveller and tools of the worshipper"], which he wrote because, in his words, "there was no explanatory work to solve its words and clarify its meanings except for one commentary by the great teacher al-Jawjari, which is a valuable exegesis of the familiar short work, but which contains interpolations and misprints unnoticable to any save someone with experience in authoring works of Sacred Law, as well as some obvious errors. It has remained thus because it was printed in Mallibar, there being no one in those lands to correct it ...." He also authored a work on rhetoric about types of metaphors, and died sometime after 1307/1890, the date he completed *Fayd al-Ilah al-Malik* (ibid., 5.65; and *Fayd al-Ilah al-Malik* (y27), 1.2–3, 2.224, 2.355).

x353   'Umar ibn Khattab (*see* 'Umar, x351)

x354   'Umar al-Maliki (w27.2) is someone about whom no other information was available than that he was a disciple of the early ascetic and mystic, Hasan al-Basri, as is mentioned in Suyuti's narrative at w27.2 (n).

x355   (al-Hajj) 'Umar Tal (w4.9) is 'Umar ibn Sa'id ibn 'Uthman, al-Futi al-Turi al-Kidiwi, born in Halwar, near Podor in the Gidi district of northern Senegal in 1794. A Tijani sheikh of impressive education, intellect, and remarkable organizational talents, he conducted jihad against French troops and pagan indigenous peoples in Guinea, Senegal, and Mali from 1852 to 1864. He first studied Arabic and Islamic subjects with his father, and by the time he left home to study elsewhere, had not only memorized the Koran, but also the two *Sahih*s of Bukhari and Muslim. He taught the Sacred Sciences in Satina for about twelve years, during which period he joined the Tijani tariqa, a new order founded only thirteen years before his birth which was then spreading through West Africa from

Mauritania. He first took the way from Sheikh 'Abd al-Karim ibn Ahmad al-Naqil, but in less than two years decided to perform the hajj, and made his way eastward across Africa to the Hijaz, where he fulfilled the pilgrimage and completed his training in the *tariqa* with the Moroccan sheikh Muhammad al-Ghali al-Tijani. He stayed with the latter for three years in Medina before being authorized as an independent sheikh. After performing hajj again, he returned first to Cairo, where he authored a Koranic commentary, and then set off in 1830 for West Africa. Enroute, he stopped for a series of residences in various cities, among them Sokoto, Nigeria, where he remained six years with Muhammad Bello, the son of the Fulani *mujahid* 'Uthman ibn Fodi (x364), writing and acquiring the firsthand military and administrative expertise that he was later to use in his jihad in West Africa, the plans for which he was beginning to formulate in his mind. Returning to his homeland after twenty years, he recruited many to the Tijani tariqa, which he marshalled for the purposes of jihad. In his military campaigns, which are too numerous to record in detail here, he fought occasional skirmishes with the French, but his main efforts were directed at spreading Islam eastward by fighting the pagan Bambara people of Karta and Segu, which he did with considerable success at the head of an army that at its peak numbered some thirty thousand men. His force was well disciplined and applied Islamic law, as for example at the surrender of Karta, where 'Umar ordered the indigenous idols be brought out to be smashed at his own hands with an iron mace. His opinions paralleled those of Ahmad ibn Idris al-Fasi and Muhammad 'Ali Sanusi on many issues, and he admired the writings of Sheikh 'Abd al-Wahhab Sha'rani. He died in Ghoro, Mali, in 1280/1864 after an escape from being besieged in Hamdallahi during an unsuccessful bid to take Masina (*Muslim Brotherhoods* (y86), 68–98).

x356   'Umayr ibn Yazid (*see* Abu Ja'far Khatmi, x44)

x357   Umm Kulthum (r8.2) is Umm Kulthum bint 'Uqba ibn Abi Mu'it al-Umawiyya (Allah be well pleased with her), not the Prophet's daughter (Allah bless him and give him peace) of that name, but the half-sister of the caliph 'Uthman from his mother. Among those who entered Islam very early, when she learned that the Prophet (Allah bless him and give him peace) had left for Medina, she set out on foot to follow him, refusing to return when her brothers caught up with her to take her back. She related hadiths from the Prophet (Allah bless him and give him peace) that are recorded in the collections of both Bukhari and Muslim, and died in about 33/653 (*al-A'lam* (y136), 5.231).

x358   Umm Salama (w31.1) is Hind bint Abi Umayya ibn al-Mughira ibn 'Abdullah ibn 'Umar, Umm Salama al-Makhzumiyya (Allah be well pleased with her), Mother of the Faithful, one of the wives of the Prophet (Allah bless him and give him peace). One of the most intelligent and refined of women, she entered Islam in the early years and emigrated with her first husband, Abu Salama, to Ethiopia before emigrating to Medina, where her husband died. Abu Bakr then asked for her hand in marriage but she refused, after which the Prophet (Allah bless him and give him peace) proposed to her and she accepted, marrying him in A.H. 4. She lived a long life, relating 378 hadiths from the Prophet (Allah bless him and give him peace), and died in Medina in 62/681 (ibid., 8.97–98; and *Taqrib al-tahdhib* (y16), 754).

x359   'Uqba ibn 'Amir (k29.0) is 'Uqba ibn 'Abas al-Juhani (Allah be well pleased with him). One of the Companions of the Prophet (Allah bless him and give him peace), he was an archer, poet, and reciter of the Koran who was knowledgeable in Sacred Law. He was one of those who helped gather the Holy Koran, and he related fifty-five hadiths from the Prophet (Allah bless him and give him peace). He participated in the Muslim conquest of Egypt with 'Amr ibn al-'As, and ruled it for a time before being relieved of command, after which he took charge of Muslim naval military expeditions, and later died in Egypt in 58/678 (*al-A'lam* (y136), 4.240).

x360   'Uthman (o25.4) is 'Uthman ibn 'Affan ibn Abi al-'As ibn Umayya al-Qurashi (Allah be well pleased with him), born in Mecca forty-seven years before the Hijra (A.D. 577). He was the third caliph of Islam and one of the ten whom the Prophet (Allah bless him and give him peace) informed they would enter paradise. Of noble lineage, wealthy, and extremely handsome, he entered Islam shortly after the prophetic mission began, and among his greatest works was to outfit the "army of hardship" for the expedition to Tabuk, donating three hundred camels with their equipage and one thousand gold dinars, whereupon the Prophet (Allah bless him and give him peace) said, "Nothing 'Uthman does after today will harm him." He accepted the caliphate after 'Umar's death in A.H. 23, and during His tenure, Armenia, Caucasia, Khurasan, Kirman, Sijistan, Cyprus, and much of North Africa were added to the dominions of Islam. He completed the gathering of the Koran begun by Abu Bakr, who had collected the written fragments of it that the Companions possessed, which 'Uthman now called for to be checked and collated with those who had memorized it, written into a single volume, and ordered everything else to be burned before he had the text copied and sent to all parts of the Muslim world. He related 146 hadiths from the Prophet (Allah bless him and give him peace), who married two of his daughters to him at different times, Ruqayya and Umm Kulthum, for which reason 'Uthman was called He of the Two Lights (Dhul Nurayn). At the end of his caliphate in 35/656, groups of men came from Egypt, Basra, and Kufa, complaining that 'Uthman had placed members of his clan, Bani Umayya, in prominent public offices, and demanded he remove them. When he refused, they surrounded his house in an attempt to force him to resign, but he would not, and finally some of them climbed over the walls of his home and murdered him as he sat reading the Koran (ibid., 4.210; and Sheikh Shu'ayb Arna'ut).

x361   'Uthman (w40.5) is 'Uthman ibn 'Umar ibn Faris al-Abadi of Basra, originally from Bukhara. He was a reliable transmitter (thiqa) whose hadiths were recorded in the works of Bukhari, Muslim, and in the other main collections. He died in A.H. 209 (*Taqrib al-tahdhib* (y16), 385).

x362   'Uthman ibn 'Abdullah (w31.1) is 'Uthman ibn 'Abdullah ibn Mawhab al-Tamimi, of Medina. A reliable hadith transmitter of the generation who came after the Companions, his hadiths were recorded in the collections of Bukhari, Muslim, Tirmidhi, and others. He died after A.H. 120 (ibid., 385; and *Siyar a'lam al-nubala* (y37), 5.187).

x363   'Uthman ibn 'Affan (*see* 'Uthman, x360)

x364   'Uthman ibn Fodi (w9.4), known as Usuman dan Fodio, was born in Maratta in northern Nigeria in 1754. An Islamic scholar and Qadiri sheikh from a family of learned Muslims, he led the Fulani jihad in northern Nigeria with his younger brother 'Abdallahi and son Muhammad Bello. Having memorized the Koran and learned Maliki jurisprudence, hadith, and Arabic grammar when young, he became an accomplished scholar, author, poet, and Sufi. He recorded his experience of a stage of the mystic way in the words, "When I reached the age of thirty-six, God stripped the veil from my sight, the imperfection from my hearing and sense of smell, the flatness from my taste, the knots from my hands, and the heaviness from my feet and body. I saw things far away like near things and heard distant sounds like close ones. I smelt the good smell of the worshipper of God, sweeter than any sweetness, and the bad odor of the sinful man, more repugnant than any putrefaction ...." Though he authored a number of works in Arabic on Sufism, theology, and Sacred Law, his particular concern was syncretism, the compromise of Islam by admixture of pagan elements indigenous to the Nigeria of his time. These aberrant practices led first to an emigration (hijra) by him and his Qadiri followers from the lands of Gobir to the north and west, and then galvanized them to undertake a jihad that would physically bring all the region to orthodox Islam. It began with a vision of 'Abd al-Qadir al-Jilani, who fastened upon him "the sword of Allah to draw against His foes," and 'Uthman and his army were to fight for four years, mainly against the Gobir and Habe peoples, their hardest campaign being the siege on the Gobir capital of Alkalawa in 1806, which lasted two years. With its surrender, the Habe will to resist also disappeared and 'Uthman and his forces had effectively won the war. He divided the leadership of the Islamic state between his brother and son, and then retired to study and to teach his many students until his death in Sifawa in 1817 (*Muslim Brotherhoods* (y86), 15–25).

x365   'Uthman ibn Hunayf (w40.3) is 'Uthman ibn Hunayf ibn Wahb, Abu 'Amr of Aws (Allah be well pleased with him). A Companion of the Prophet (Allah bless him and give him peace) who participated in the battle of Uhud and those after it, he was appointed during 'Umar's caliphate as governor of southern Iraq (al-Sawad), and in 'Ali's time as governor of Basra. After the Battle of al-Jamal he went to live in Kufa, where he died in the caliphate of Mu'awiya some time after 41/661 (*al-A'lam* (y136), 4.205).

x366   'Uthman ibn 'Isa Marani (m12.6) is 'Uthman ibn 'Isa ibn Dirbas ibn Khayr, Abu 'Amr Diya' al-Din al-Marani al-Kurdi al-Mawsuli, born near Mosul, Iraq, in 516/1123. A Shafi'i scholar of Kurdish descent described by Taj al-Din Subki as "the most learned Shafi'i of his time in jurisprudence and fundamentals of law and faith," he first studied Sacred Law in Arbil, Iraq, and then Damascus before moving to Cairo, where he settled. He was appointed as head of the Egyptian judiciary by Sultan Salah al-Din Ayyubi in A.H. 566, though he later left the position and devoted himself to teaching and writing. He authored a commentary on Abu Ishaq Shirazi's *al-Luma'* [The effulgences] in fundamentals of jurisprudence, but is best known for his twenty-volume work in Shafi'i law, *al-Istiqsa' li madhahib al-fuqaha'* [The comprehensive: on jurists' schools of thought], a commentary on Shirazi's *al-Muhadhdhab* [The rarefaction]. He died in Cairo in 602/

1206 (ibid., 4.212; *Siyar a'lam al-nubala'* (y37), 22.291; and *Tabaqat al-Shafi'iyya al-kubra* (y128), 8.337).

x367   Uways al-Barawi (w9.4) is Uways ibn Muhammad ibn Bashir al-Barawi, born in Brava on the southern Somalian coast in 1847. He studied Shafi'i jurisprudence, Koranic exegesis, Arabic grammar, and Sufism in his hometown before travelling to Baghdad, the headquarters of the Qadiri order to which he belonged, for fuller instruction in the way. After a number of years of study there with Sheikh Mustafa ibn al-Sayyid Salman al-Jaylani, he received authorization as a sheikh in the *tariqa* and returned home. Possessed of considerable organizational capacity, leadership, and spiritual gifts, he won numerous adherents, many of whom he trained for missionary activities, and his Uwaysi-Qadiri tariqa is credited with a considerable expansion of Islam in Tanganyika, southern Somalia, and eastern Zaire. He also founded agricultural settlements at Bilad al-Amin and at Biolay, 150 miles north of Brava, where he was assassinated at the age of sixty-three in 1909. B.G. Martin states: "In its spread from Brava to Zanzibar to the mainland of Tanganyika and then westward into the Congo, the Uwaysiya Qadiriya became a major Muslim movement in East Africa. Though it began as early as 1883, Qadiri proselytization is still continuing. In a region where adherence to a *tariqa* is synonymous with conversion to Islam, such a movement assumed more than ordinary significance" (*Muslim Brotherhoods* (y86), 152–65, 176).

x368   Wali al-Din al-'Iraqi (w28.1) is Ahmad ibn 'Abd al-Rahim ibn al-Husayn, Abu Zar'a Wali al-Din al-'Iraqi, born in Cairo in 762/1361. Of Kurdish descent, he was the son of Zayn al-Din al-'Iraqi (x188) and like him, was also a Shafi'i scholar and hadith master (hafiz). His father took him to Damascus, where he was educated, and when he returned to Cairo, he succeeded Jalal Bulqini as the head of the judiciary, though his uncompromising attitude towards rulers caused him to be later removed from office. He authored a number of works in Sacred Law, hadith and its sciences, Muslim biographies, and formal legal opinion, and died in Cairo in 826/1423 (*al-A'lam* (y136), 1.148).

x369   Wasiyyullah 'Abbas (w56.2) is a contemporary hadith scholar who edited and annotated Imam Ahmad ibn Hanbal's *Fada'il al-Sahaba* [The excellences of the prophetic Companions] as his doctoral thesis at Umm al-Qura University in Mecca. His two-volume dissertation was first published in Beirut in 1403/1983 (n).

x370   Ya'qub (u3.5) is Ya'qub ibn Ishaq ibn Ibrahim (upon whom be peace), a prophet of Allah Most High. Also known as Isra'il, the offspring of his twelve sons composed the twelve tribes of Bani Isra'il, who took their name from him. He is mentioned in the Holy Koran in various places, among them sura Yusuf, named for his son, who was also a prophet. Commentators record that he lived for 147 years (*al-Futuhat al-ilahiyya* (y65), 2.433; and n).

x371   Yahya (u3.5) is Yahya ibn Zakariyya (upon whom be peace), the prophet of Allah Most High born to the prophet Zakariyya and his wife, who was the maternal aunt of 'Isa (upon whom be peace), though Yahya was born before 'Isa. Commentators record that he was descended through Zakariyya from Sulayman (upon whom be peace), and that he was the last one sent before 'Isa to Bani Isra'il, who killed him when he was 120 years old, just as they had killed his father (*al-Shifa* (y116), 1.192).

x372   Yahya ibn Abi Kathir (a2.5) is Yahya ibn Salih, Abu Nasr Ibn Abi Kathir al-Ta'i al-Yamami. Originally of Basra, he lived in Medina for ten years, taking hadiths from the foremost of the generation that followed the Companions, and then moved to Yamama, in the Najd, where he was famous as a hadith scholar, though he later suffered for his outspoken condemnation of some of the policies of the Umayyad caliphs. One of the leading early hadith Imams, some have considered him even more learned than Zuhri. He died in 129/747 (*al-A'lam* (y136), 8.150).

x373   Yahya ibn Sa'id (w48.2) is Yahya ibn Sa'id ibn Qays, Abu Sa'id al-Ansari al-Najjari, originally of Medina. An Islamic judge first in Medina and later in Iraq, he was one of the main figures in the early science of hadith, and al-Jumhi said of him, "I have not seen anyone who resembled Zuhri more closely than Yahya ibn Sa'id. If not for the two of them, many sunnas would have been lost." He died in al-Hashimiyya, Iraq, in 143/760 (ibid., 8.147).

x374   al-Yasa' (u3.5) is al-Yasa' ibn Akhtub ibn al-'Ajuz (upon whom be peace), whom Allah Most High made a prophet and messenger to Bani Isra'il after Ilyas (x186) was raised up from among them. Allah inspired and aided him, and his people believed in him and honored him, applying the Sacred Law among themselves until his death (*al-Futuhat al-ilahiyya* (y65), 2.58, 3.550).

x375   Yasin 'Arafa (Document 1), a native of Damascus, is a friend of Sheikh 'Abd al-Wakil Durubi's of about his own age who has visited him almost daily for the past thirty-five years and been his business partner in editing and publishing a number of classic works on Sufism and Shafi'i jurisprudence (n).

x376   Yunus (u3.5) (upon whom be peace), also known as He of the Fish (Dhul Nun), was the prophet of Allah Most High to the people of Nineveh (in present-day Iraq) whom, as commentators relate, he called to the worship of Allah alone, but who rejected him and his message until he at length grew angry with them and departed, informing them that Allah's punishment would be visited upon them in three days. When he left them and boarded a ship, his people saw the seriousness of their plight and made a deep and sincere repentance, all of them coming forth from their dwellings to beg Allah to turn aside His punishment, and when it appeared above like a section of darkest night, Allah caused it to revolve harmlessly overhead. A storm at sea meanwhile assailed the ship carrying Yunus, and in the course of it, the passengers saw that their only hope was for one of their number to lighten ship by jumping overboard, but when they drew lots to see who it would be, the lot fell to Yunus. Unwilling to put him off, they cast lots again and again, but each time it fell to the prophet, and at length they saw that some great matter was afoot and let him go. As he took to the water, a great fish swallowed him and he remained in its belly for some days, regretting his anger towards his people, and expressing his abject humility towards Allah with the words, "There is no god but You, glory be to You, verily I was of the wrongdoers," and Allah saved him by causing the fish to cast him up on the shore (*Qisas al-anbiya'* (y59), 286–93).

x377   Yunus Hamdan (Document 2) is Yunus ibn Hamdan ibn Qublan Abu Jamus, Abu Anas, born in the Marka area east of Amman, Jordan, in 1944. Educated in Amman, he served as a teacher for four years in the Jordanian Army before becoming the imam of a mosque under the Ministry of Endowments (Wizara al-Awqaf) in 1968. He took the Shadhili tariqa from Sheikh Muhammad Sa'id Kurdi in the summer of 1967, and by the time of the sheikh's death five years later, was one of his most advanced disciples. He studied Shafi'i jurisprudence with both his sheikh and with the mufti of Irbid, Sheikh Barakat, and in 1982 took a degree from the University of Jordan in Sacred Law. He has been the translator's neighbor since 1983, and was one of those who generously agreed to check the Arabic of the present volume before it was submitted for publication. One of the signs of Allah in humility, kindness, and patience, he currently lives in Amman, where he teaches Arabic grammar, Shafi'i jurisprudence, and Koran recital to a small circle of students (n).

x378   Yusuf (u3.5) is Yusuf ibn Ya'qub (upon whom be peace), the prophet of Allah Most High whose story is recounted by the Holy Koran in the sura that bears his name; how his brothers, jealous of the love their father had for him, cast him into a well, how he was sold into slavery in Egypt, later rising to a high position there, and the forgiveness he showed them when they came to him in their hour of need (Koran 12; and n).

x379   Yusuf Ardabili (o22.1(d(II))) is Yusuf ibn Ibrahim, Jamal al-Din al-Ardabili, of Ardabil, Azerbaijan. He was a Shafi'i scholar whom Ibn Qadi Shuhba described as "tremendous in Sacred Knowledge," and who authored *Kitab al-anwar li a'mal al-abrar* [The book of lights for the works of the pious] in Sacred Law. He died in Ardabil in 799/1397 at over seventy years of age (*al-A'lam* (y136), 8.212).

x380   (Sheikh) Yusuf Nabahani (w52.1(60)) is Yusuf ibn Isma'il ibn Yusuf al-Nabahani, born in the village of Ijzim, Palestine, in 1265/1849. He was a Shafi'i scholar, Sufi, judge, poet, and the author of works in Sacred Law, tenets of faith, prophetic biography, hadith, heresiology, and Sufism, including his two-volume *Jami' karamat al-awliya'* [Compendium of the miracles of the friends of Allah], *Wasa'il al-wusul ila shama'il al-Rasul* [The means of knowing the attributes of the Prophet], *Sa'ada al-darayn fi al-salat 'ala Sayyid al-Kawnayn* [Felicity in this world and the next through the blessings upon the Liegelord of the Two Abodes], and forty-five others, among them some of the most beautiful works that exist in commemoration of the Prophet (Allah bless him and give him peace). He was educated at al-Azhar, edited a newspaper in Istanbul for a period and corrected the books it published, and then returned to be appointed to the judiciary in Beirut, a capacity in which he served for twenty years before moving to Medina. After the outbreak of the First World War, he returned to Ijzim, where he died in 1350/1932 (ibid., 8.218; *Wasa'il al-wusul* (y97), 11; and n).

x381   Yusuf Qaradawi (w46.1) was born in Egypt in 1926. A contemporary Islamic scholar, author, and poet, he memorized the Holy Koran before age ten and completed his education at al-Azhar, where he took a doctoral degree with highest honors in 1973. He has written more than twenty works which have gained a wide readership in the Islamic world, but is probably best known for his *al-Halal wa al-haram fi al-Islam* [The lawful and unlawful in Islam] which, although it contains some unreliable positions in Sacred Law, represents an original effort to make the comprehensive rules of Islam accessible and understandable to nonspecialists, and shows its author as a modern thinker concerned with joining between the principles of the religion and the problems of the times. He is currently the Dean of a college of Sacred Law in Qatar (*al-Sahwa al-Islamiyya* (y111), back cover; and n).

x382 (a)   (Sheikh) Yusuf al-Rifa'i (w40.2) is Yusuf ibn al-Sayyid Hashim al-Rifa'i, born in Kuweit in 1351/1932. A Shafi'i scholar, former minister of state, educator, Sufi, and author, he was given his primary education in the Holy Koran by Sheikh Ahmad al-'Aqil in Kuweit, and studied Sacred Law in Damascus and Shafi'i jurisprudence under Sheikh Muhammad Muhammad Salih of Kuweit and others. His father, al-Sayyid Hashim al-Rifa'i, was the captain of a pearl-harvesting sailing ship, then a state official, and finally an advocate in the Shari'a court of Kuweit. Sheikh Yusuf is descendant of the Prophet (Allah bless him and give him peace) through the friend (wali) of Allah Most High, Sheikh Ahmad al-Rifa'i. He was made a member of Parliament in Kuweit in 1963, minister of telecommunications and postage in 1964, and he served as the minister of state from 1965 to 1970. He is also a sheikh of the Rifa'i tariqa founded by his ancestor, having been authorized in Zabadani, near Damascus, by Sheikh Makki al-Kattani, whose teacher Ibrahim al-Rawi was the student of Sheikh Abu al-Huda al-Sayyadi, one of the outstanding recent figures in the Rifa'i way, which Yusuf notes is especially distinguished, like its founder, for its rigorous adherence to the Sacred Law, outwardly and inwardly. The value of Sufism in Islam, he believes, is not only as a means to spiritual sincerity, but as a powerful force to convey Islam (da'wa) to non-Muslims and to regenerate the religion in the Muslim heartlands from within. Among his written works are *Khawatir fi al-siyasa wa al-mujtama'* [Thoughts on politics and society], comprising articles on contemporary issues such as the need for Muslims to defend the rights of Muslim minorities in non-Muslim countries; *Adilla Ahl al-Sunna wa al-Jama'a aw al-Radd al-muhkam al-mani' 'ala munkarat wa shubuhat Ibn Mani'* [The evidences of the Sunni Community, or, The unassailably proficient rebuttal of the blameworthy and doubtful points of Ibn Mani'], which he wrote in response to a contemporary's attack on Sheikh Muhammad 'Alawi Maliki for the latter's having contradicted the tenets of the Wahhabi sect on a number of questions; and *Adilla al-qunut fi salat al-fajr* [The evidences for standing in supplication at the dawn prayer]. He takes a keen interest in the problems of Muslims today, and at a recent symposium in Amman with Sheikh 'Abdullah Muhammad Ghimari and Sheikh Hasan Saqqaf, he voiced his concern for the obstacles to the current Islamic revival and world propagation of Islam that are being put in its way by "fundamentalists" whose view of Allah is anthropomorphic, view of the Prophet (Allah bless him and give him peace) is that he is over-venerated and loved by Muslims, and view of Muslims is that they are unbelievers or immersed in unlawful innovations (bid'a). The unity of the Community and its future, he said, lie in holding fast to the agreed-upon schools of jurisprudence and tenets of faith, directing our efforts to non-Muslims; not in trying to convince Muslims that everything their forefathers believed was a mistake. He presently directs the al-Iman School, founded in 1973 in Kuweit, which provides Islamic and secular education patterned on the al-Azhar model at the elementary, preparatory, and secondary levels. He is a familiar figure at Islamic conferences around the world, and in 1988 was elected as president of the World Union of Islamic Propagation and Information at its London conference (n).

x382 (b)   Yusuf Talal DeLorenzo (Document 3) is an American Muslim scholar who was born in Plymouth, Massachusetts in 1947 and raised in Duxbury, where his family has lived for several generations. He entered Islam in 1970 in Beirut, and in 1971 became the student of the hadith expert Sheikh Muhammad Yusuf al-Bannuri of Pakistan. After six years of study, the sheikh, author of *Ma'arif al-Sunan* [The knowledges of "The sunnas"], a six-volume commentary on *Jami' al-Tirmidhi* [The hadith collection of Tirmidhi], and other works, authorized him to teach and relate   the hadiths he had read before him and on which he had commented. Yusuf has since taught hadith and principles of jurisprudence (usul al-fiqh) in Pakistan, served as advisor on Islamic education to the late President Zia al-Haqq (Allah have mercy on him), been headmaster of the only private Muslim college in Sri Lanka—where he taught *'Umdat al-salik*, the main text of the present volume—lectured at the International Islamic University in Islamabad, and served as Chief of the Translation Bureau at the Islamic Research Institute there. In June, 1989, after nearly twenty years abroad, he was appointed as research coordinator for the International Institute of Islamic Thought in Washington, D.C.
  A veteran Islamic translator, his more than ten works include English versions of a Hanafi manual of Sacred Law as well as *Kitab al-halal wa al-haram* [The book of the lawful and unlawful] from Imam Ghazali's *Ihya' 'ulum al-din* [Giving life to the religious sciences], *Usul al-fiqh al-Islami* [The bases of Islamic jurisprudence], and *al-Ijtihad wa al-taqlid fi al-Islam* [Personal juridical reasoning versus following qualified scholarship, in Islam], both by Dr. Taha Jabir al-'Alwani. His most recent effort, a pioneering translation of his own Arabic edition of Abu Bakr al-Jassas's multi-volume Koranic exegesis *Ahkam al-Qur'an* [Legal interpretations of the Koran], seems destined for wide recognition and use, representing the definitive Hanafi work on deducing legal rulings from the Holy Koran. He presently lives in Sterling, Virginia (n).

x383   Zacharias (*see next entry*)

x384   Zakariyya (u3.5) is Zakariyya ibn Ladun ibn Muslim ibn Saduq ibn Hashban ibn Dawud ibn Sulayman (upon whom be peace), a prophet of Allah Most High to Bani Isra'il. The Holy Koran mentions how Allah gave him a son, the prophet Yahya, in his old age to inherit his knowledge and prophethood, and how, when his wife's sister gave birth to Maryam and vowed her to the service of the Sacred Temple, Zakariyya undertook to care for her in a room in the temple, where he brought her food, drink, and other necessities. Allah Most High describes him and family as "vying in pious deeds, calling upon Us in hope and fear, and humble to Us" (Koran 21:90) (*Qisas al-anbiya'* (y59), 543–44).

x385   (Sheikh al-Islam) Zakariyya Ansari (o16.6) is Zakariyya ibn Muhammad ibn Ahmad ibn Zakariyya, Abu Yahya Sheikh al-Islam al-Ansari, born in Sanika,

Egypt, in 823/1420. Known as the Sheikh of Sheikhs, he was the Shafi'i scholar of his time, a hadith master (hafiz), judge, and Koranic exegete. He was educated in Cairo in circumstances of such poverty that he used to have to leave the mosque by night to look for watermelon rinds, which he would wash and eat. When his knowledge later won him fame and recognition, he was to receive so many gifts that his income before his appointment to the judiciary amounted to nearly three thousand dirhams a day, which he spent to gather books, teach, and give financial help to the students who studied with him. When Sultan Quytubay al-Jurkasi appointed him as head of the judiciary in Cairo, he accepted the post with reluctance after being repeatedly asked, but when the sultan later committed a wrong act and he sent him a letter upbraiding him, the sultan dismissed him and he returned to teaching. He authored works in Sacred Law, the sciences of Koran and hadith, logic, Arabic, fundamentals of jurisprudence, and Sufism, and was the sheikh of Imam Ibn Hajar Haytami. He died in 926/1520 at one hundred years of age (*al-A'lam* (y136), 3.46).

x386   Zarkashi (f5:1) is Muhammad ibn Bahadur ibn 'Abdullah, Abu 'Abdullah Badr al-Din al-Zarkashi, born in Egypt in 745/1344. Of Turkish origin, he was a scholar of Shafi'i jurisprudence, fundamentals of law, hadith, and literature, who wrote many works, among them his three-volume *al-Bahr al-Muhit* [The encompassing sea], on Islamic legal principles. He died in 794/1392 (ibid., 6.60).

x387   Zayd ibn 'Ali ibn Husayn (b7.6) is Zayd ibn 'Ali ibn Husayn ibn 'Ali ibn Abi Talib, Abu al-Husayn al-Shahid al-'Alawi al-Hashimi, born in 79/698. He was an Imam of Sacred Law who lived in Kufa, Iraq, where Imam Abu Hanifa knew him and once said, "I never saw anyone of his time more knowledgeable in Sacred Law, faster to answer, or clearer in discourse." Two works have been ascribed to him, the recently discovered *Majmu' fi al-fiqh* [Collection in Sacred Law], which if his, is the oldest recorded work in Islamic jurisprudence; and *Tafsir gharib al-Qur'an* [Explanation of rare words in the Koran], whose ascription likewise remains unestablished. At the end of his life he headed an uprising against the Umayyads, and was killed in Kufa in 122/740 (ibid., 3.59).

x388   Zayd ibn Thabit (b3.2) is Zayd ibn Thabit ibn al-Dahhak, Abu Kharija (Allah be well pleased with him), born in Medina eleven years before the Hijra (A.D. 611) and raised in Mecca. Among the great Companions of the Prophet (Allah bless him and give him peace), he was one of the scribes who recorded the Koran in writing. His father was killed when he was six years old, and he emigrated at age eleven to Medina, where he learned the religion of Islam and later became one of the Companions' principle scholarly resources in deciding cases, giving formal legal opinion, in Koranic recitation, and inheritance. When the caliph 'Umar used to travel from Medina, he would leave Zayd in his place until he returned. Ibn 'Abbas, with his immense erudition, used to visit him at home to take knowledge from him. He was among those who gathered the Koran in the time of the Prophet (Allah bless him and give him peace) and checked it with him, who wrote it in the time of Abu Bakr, and who copied out the Korans that 'Uthman sent to the cities of the outlying Islamic lands. He related ninety-two hadiths, and when he died in 45/665, Abu Hurayra said, "The scholar of this nation has died today; haply Allah will make Ibn 'Abbas his successor" (ibid., 3.57).

x389   Zayn al-Din Mallibari (w12.2) is Zayn al-Din ibn 'Abd al-'Aziz ibn Zayn al-Din ibn 'Ali ibn Ahmad al-Mallibari, originally of Mallibar, India. A Shafi'i scholar who studied under Imam Ibn Hajar Haytami, he authored *Qurra al-'ayn bi muhimmat al-din* [The gladdening of the eye with the essentials of the religion] and its commentary *Fath al-Mu'in* [The victory of the Helper]; as well as *Irshad al-'ibad ila sabil al-rashad* [The guidance of servants to the way of wisdom]. He died in 987/1579 (ibid. 3.64; *Mu'jam al-buldan* (y43), 5.196; and A).

x390   Zubayr (o25.4) is Zubayr ibn al-'Awwam ibn Khuwaylid, Abu 'Abdullah al-Asadi al-Qurashi (Allah be well pleased with him), born twenty-eight years before the Hijra in Mecca. One of the most courageous of the Companions of the Prophet (Allah bless him and give him peace), he entered Islam at the age of sixteen, was one of the ten informed they would enter paradise, and was the first to draw a sword for Islam, participating in the battles of Badr, Uhud, and others. He was the son of the paternal aunt of the Prophet (Allah bless him and give him peace), and 'Umar considered him one of those qualified to be caliph after him. A wealthy man with wide trade dealings, his property was sold after his death for forty million dirhams. He was assassinated by Ibn Jarmuz in 36/656 on the day of the Battle of al-Jamal, about twenty-one miles outside of Basra (*al-A'lam* (y136), 3.43).

x391   (Imam) Zuhri (w57.2) is Muhammad ibn Muslim ibn 'Abdullah ibn Shihab, Abu Bakr al-Zuhri of Medina, born in 58/678. Of the generation that met the Companions, Zuhri was reportedly the first to record prophetic traditions in writing, and one of the most important early scholars in hadith and Sacred Law. He visited Syria and settled there, and the caliph 'Umar ibn 'Abd al-'Aziz wrote to some of his officials, "See well to Ibn Shihab [Zuhri], for you will find no one more knowledgeable in the sunnas of the past than he." He died in 124/742 in Shaghb, at the northern extremity of the Hijaz where it becomes Palestine (ibid., 7.97).

*

BOOK Y
WORKS CITED

y1   Abaza, Nizar, and Muhammad Muti' al-Hafiz. *Tarikh 'ulama' Dimashq fi al-qarn al-rabi' 'ashar al-hijri*. 2 vols. Damascus: Dar al-Fikr, 1406/1986.

y2   al-'Abbadi, Ahmad ibn Qasim, Ibn Hajar al-Haytami, Yahya ibn Sharaf al-Nawawi, and 'Abd al-Hamid al-Sharwani. *Hawashi al-Shaykh 'Abd al-Hamid al-Sharwani wa al-Shaykh Ahmad ibn Qasim al-'Abbadi 'ala Tuhfa al-muhtaj bi sharh al-Minhaj* [Haytami's interlineal exegesis of Nawawi's *Minhaj al-talibin*, printed with it on the margins of its commentaries by Sharwani and (below him) 'Abbadi]. 10 vols. 1315/1898. Reprint. Cairo: Dar al-Fikr, n.d.

y3   'Abbas, Wasiyyullah Muhammad. Introduction to *Kitab fada'il al-Sahaba* by Ahmad ibn Hanbal. 2 vols. Beirut: Mu'assasa al-Risala, 1403/1983.

y4   'Abidin, Muhammad 'Ala' al-Din. *al-Hadiyya al-'Ala'iyya*. Edited and annotated by Muhammad Sa'id al-Burhani. Damascus: Dar al-Ma'arif, 1398/1978.

y5   Abu Shuja' al-Asfahani, Ahmad ibn al-Husayn, Ibrahim ibn Muhammad al-Bajuri, and Muhammad ibn Qasim al-Ghazzi. *Hashiya al-Shaykh Ibrahim al-Bayjuri* [sic] *'ala Sharh al-'Allama Ibn Qasim al-Ghazzi 'ala Matan al-Shaykh Abi Shuja'* [Ibn Qasim's interlineal exegesis of Abu Shuja''s *al-Ghaya fi al-ikhtisar*, printed with it on the margins of Bajuri's commentary on them]. 2 vols. 1344/1925. Reprint. Beirut: Dar al-Fikr, n.d.

y6   Abu Shuja' al-Asfahani, Ahmad ibn al-Husayn, Sulayman ibn Muhammad al-Bujayrmi, and Muhammad al-Shirbini al-Khatib. *Tuhfa al-Habib 'ala Sharh al-Khatib al-musamma bi al-Iqna' fi hall alfaz Abi Shuja'* [Khatib's interlineal exegesis of Abu Shuja''s *al-Ghaya fi al-ikhtisar*, printed with it on the margins of Bujayrmi's commentary on them]. 4 vols. Cairo: Mustafa al-Babi al-Halabi wa Awladuhu, 1338/1919–20.

y7   Abu Shuja al-Asfahani, Ahmad ibn al-Husayn', and Muhammad al-Shirbini al-Khatib. *al-Iqna' fi hall alfaz Abi Shuja'* [Khatib's interlineal exegesis of Abu Shuja''s *al-Ghaya fi al-ikhtisar* with a commentary by Ibrahim Bajuri, Sheikh

'Awad, and others printed on its margins]. 2 vols. N.d. Reprint (2 vols. in 1). Beirut and Damascus: Dar al-Khayr, n.d.

y8   al-'Alawi, Ahmad ibn Mustafa, and 'Abd al-Wahid ibn Ahmad ibn 'Ashir. *al-Minah al-quddusiyya fi sharh al-Murshid al-mu'in bi tariq al-Sufiyya* [a commentary by Sheikh al-'Alawi on Ibn 'Ashir's poem *al-Murshid al-mu'in 'ala al-daruri min 'ulum al-din*]. 1355/1936. Reprint. Damascus: 'Abd al-Wakil al-Durubi, n.d.

y9   'Amara, Mustafa Muhammad. Introduction to *al-Targhib wa al-tarhib* by 'Abd al-'Adhim al-Mundhiri, 4 vols. 1353/1934. Reprint. Cairo: Dar al-Hadith, 1407/1987.

y10   al-Ansari, Isma'il ibn Muhammad. *al-Isaba fi nusra al-Khulafa' al-Rashidin wa al-Sahaba fi tashih hadith Ibn Khusayfa fi al-tarawih,* pt. 11. Damascus: Muhammad Hamdi al-Jurayiati, 1390/1970.

y11   al-Ardabili, Yusuf ibn Ibrahim. *Kitab al-Anwar li a'mal al-abrar fi fiqh al-Imam al-Shafi'i.* Cairo: Mustafa al-Babi al-Halabi, 1326/1908.

y12   al-Arna'ut, 'Abd al-Qadir, and Shu'ayb al-Arna'ut, eds. Introduction and notes to *Zad al-masir fi 'ilm al-tafsir* by 'Abd al-Rahman ibn al-Jawzi. 9 vols. Damascus: al-Maktab al-Islami, 1384/1964.

y13   al-'Asqalani, Ibn Hajar. *al-Durar al-kamina fi a'yan al-mi'a al-thamina.* 4 vols. 1350/1931. Reprint. Beirut: Dar al-Jil, n.d.

y14   ———. *al-Isaba fi tamyiz al-Sahaba.* 4 vols. 1359/1940. Reprint. Beirut: Dar al-Turath al-'Arabi, n.d.

y15   ———. *Talkhis al-habir fi takhrij ahadith al-Rafi'i al-kabir.* 4 vols. in 2. Cairo: Maktaba al-Kulliyyat al-Azhariyya, 1399/1979.

y16   ———. *Taqrib al-tahdhib.* Edited by Muhammad 'Awwama. Aleppo: Dar al-Rashid, 1406/1986.

y17   al-'Asqalani, Ibn Hajar, and Muhammad ibn Isma'il al-Bukhari. *Fath al-Bari bi sharh Sahih al-Imam Abi 'Abdullah Muhammad ibn Isma'il al-Bukhari* [a commentary by 'Asqalani on the hadiths of Bukhari's *al-Jami' al-sahih*]. Edited by Muhammad Fu'ad 'Abd al-Baqi and Muhibb al-Din al-Khatib. 14 vols. Cairo: al-Maktaba al-Salafiyya, 1390/1970.

y18   al-'Azizi, 'Ali ibn Ahmad, and Jalal al-Din al-Suyuti. *al-Siraj al-munir sharh al-Jami' al-saghir* [a commentary by 'Azizi on the hadiths of Suyuti's *al-Jami' al-saghir*]. 3 vols. Cairo: Ahmad al-Babi al-Halabi, 1312/1894–95.

y19   Ba'alawi, 'Abd al-Rahman. *Bughya al-mustarshidin fi talkhis fatawa ba'd al-a'imma min al-muta'akhkhirin.* Cairo: Mustafa al-Babi al-Halabi wa Akhuwahu, 1325/1907.

y20   Ba'alawi, 'Abdullah ibn Mahfuz. *al-Sunna wa al-bid'a*. N.p. Sharika Matabi' al-Wazzan, n.d.

y21   al-Babarti, Akmal al-Din, Kamal al-Din ibn al-Humam, Burhan al-Din al-Marghiyani, Shams al-Din Ahmad al-Qadi Zada, and Sa'd Allah ibn 'Isa Sa'di al-Chalabi. *Sharh fath al-Qadir 'ala al-Hidaya sharh Bidaya al-mubtadi'* [Marghiyani's *Hidaya*, an interlineal exegesis of his own *Bidaya al-mubtadi'* printed with it at the top of the page above Ibn al-Humam's commentary *Fath al-Qadir* (unfinished but completed in its final volumes by al-Qadi Zada's supplement *Nata'ij al-afkar fi kashf al-ramuz wa al-asrar*), under which is Babarti's interlineal exegesis of the *Hidaya* called *Sharh al-'inaya 'ala al-Hidaya* with a commentary (*Hashiya*) below it by Sa'di al-Chalabi]. 10 vols. Cairo: Mustafa al-Babi al-Halabi wa Awladuhu, 1389/1970.

y22   al-Baghawi, al-Husayn ibn Mas'ud. *Sharh al-sunna*. Edited with notes by Shu'ayb al-Arna'ut. 16 vols. Damascus: al-Maktab al-Islami, 1400/1980.

y23   al-Baghdadi, 'Abd al-Qahir. *Usul al-din*. Istanbul: Matba'a al-Dawla, 1346/1928.

y24   al-Bajuri, Ibrahim ibn Muhammad, and Ibrahim ibn Hasan al-Laqqani. *Sharh Jawhara al-tawhid al-musamma bi Tuhfa al-murid* [Laqqani's poem *Jawhara al-tawhid* at the top of the page with Bajuri's commentary printed below it and annotated by Ahmad al-Ujhuri]. N.d. Reprint. Beirut: Dar al-Kutub al-'Ilmiyya, 1403/1983.

y25   al-Bakri, Muhammad ibn 'Allan, and Yahya ibn Sharaf al-Nawawi. *Dalil al-falihin li turuq Riyad al-salihin* [Nawawi's *Riyad al-salihin* printed above Bakri's interlineal commentary]. Edited by the Azhar Society for Publishing and Writing. 8 vols. N.d. Reprint (8 vols. in 4). Beirut: Dar al-Kitab al-'Arabi, n.d.

y26   ———. *al-Futuhat al-rabbaniyya 'ala al-Adhkar al-Nawawiyya* [Nawawi's *al-Adhkar* printed above Bakri's interlineal commentary]. Edited by the Azhar Society for Publishing and Writing. 7 vols. N.d. Reprint (7 vols. in 4). Beirut: Dar Ihya' al-Turath al-'Arabi, n.d.

y27   Barakat, 'Umar, and Ahmad ibn al-Naqib al-Misri. *Fayd al-Ilah al-Malik fi hall alfaz 'Umdat al-salik wa 'uddat al-nasik* [Ibn Naqib's *'Umdat al-salik* printed on the margins of 'Umar Barakat's interlineal commentary]. 2 vols. Cairo: Matba'a al-Istiqama, 1374/1955.

y28   al-Barr, Muhammad 'Ali. *al-Muslimun fi al-Ittihad al-Sufyati 'abr al-tarikh*. 2 vols. Jedda: Dar al-Shuruq, 1403/1984.

y29   Baybars, Ridwan al-'Adal. *Kitab rawda al-muhtajin li ma'rifa qawa'id al-din*. Bulaq: al-Mataba'a al-Kubra al-Amiriyya, 1323/1905.

y30   al-Bukhari, Muhammad ibn Isma'il, and Muhammad Muhsin Khan.

Sahih al-Bukhari [the Arabic text of Bukhari's *al-Jami' al-sahih* with Khan's prefatory matter and English translation]. 9 vols. Cairo: Dar al-Fikr, n.d.

y31   Burckhardt, Titus. *Art of Islam: Language and Meaning*. London: World of Islam Festival Publishing Company, 1976.

y32   ———. *Moorish Culture in Spain*. Translated by Alisa Jaffa. London: George Allen and Unwin, 1972.

y33   al-Buti, Muhammad Sa'id. *al-Lamadhhabiyya akhtar bid'a tuhaddidu al-shari'a al-Islamiyya*. Damascus: Maktaba al-Farabi, 1390/1970.

y34   ———. *al-Salafiyya marhala zamaniyya mubaraka la madhhab Islami*. Damascus: Dar al-Fikr, 1408/1988.

y35   al-Dardir, Ahmad ibn Muhammad, and Ahmad ibn Muhammad al-Sawi. *al-Sharh al-saghir 'ala Aqrab al-masalik ila madhhab al-Imam Malik* [Dardir's interlineal exegesis of his own *Aqrab al-masalik* printed with it above the commentary of Sawi]. Edited with introduction and appendices by Mustafa Kamal Wasfi. 4 vols. Cairo: Dar al-Ma'arif, 1394/1974.

y36   al-Dhahabi, Muhammad ibn Ahmad. *Kitab al-kaba'ir wa tabyin al-maharim*. Edited with introduction by Muhyiddin Mistu. Damascus: Mu'assasa 'Ulum al-Qur'an, 1404/1984.

y37   ———. *Siyar a'lam al-nubala'*. Editing supervised and hadiths researched by Shu'ayb al-Arna'ut. 23 vols. [with two additional vols. of indexes, 24 and 25, in 1989]. Beirut: Mu'assasa al-Risala, 1401/1981.

y38   al-Faqir, 'Ali Mustafa. *al-Imam al-'Izz ibn 'Abd al-Salam wa atharuhu fi al-fiqh al-Islami*. 2 vols. Amman: Mudiriyya al-Ifta' li al-Quwat al-Musallaha al-Urduniyya, 1399/1979.

y39   al-Ghazali, Abu Hamid. *Ihya' 'ulum al-din* [with notes on its hadiths by Zayn al-Din al-'Iraqi printed below it, and 'Umar Suhrawardi's *'Awarif al-ma'arif* on its margins]. 4 vols. 1347/1929. Reprint. Beirut: 'Alam al-kutub, n.d.

y40   ———. *al-Maqsad al-asna sharh asma' Allah al-husna*. Edited by Muhammad Mustafa Abu al-'Ula. Cairo: Maktaba al-Jundi, 1395/1975.

y41   ———. *al-Munqidh min al-dalal*. Edited by Muhammad Muhammad Jabir. Cairo: Maktaba al-Jundi, n.d.

y42   al-Ghurab, Mahmud Mahmud, and Muhyiddin ibn al-'Arabi. *Sharh Fusus al-hikam* [Ibn al-'Arabi's *Fusus al-hikam* printed above Ghurab's commentary]. Damascus: Matba'a Zayd ibn Thabit, 1405/1985.

y43   al-Hamawi, Yaqut ibn 'Abdullah. *Mu'jam al-buldan*. 5 vols. Beirut: Dar Ihya al-Turath al-'Arabi, 1399/1979.

y44   al-Hamid, Muhammad. *Rudud 'ala abatil wa rasa'il al-Shaykh Muham-mad al-Hamid.* Edited by 'Abdullah ibn Ibrahim al-Ansari. 2 vols. Sidon and Beirut: al-Maktaba al-'Asriyya, n.d.

y45   Harras, Muhammad Khalil, and Ibn Qayyim al-Jawziyya. *Sharh al-Qasida al-nuniyya al-musamma al-Kafiya al-shafiya fi al-intisar li al-firqa al-najiya* [Jawziyya's poem *al-Qasida al-nuniyya* in sections interspersed with Harras's commentary]. 2 vols. Cairo: Maktaba Ibn Taymiya, 1407/1986.

y46   al-Hashimi, Muhammad ibn Ahmad. *al-Hall al-sadid li ma astashkalahu al-murid.* Edited with appendices by Muhammad Sa'id al-Burhani. Damascus: Muhammad Sa'id al-Burhani, 1383/1963.

y47   al-Haskafi, Muhammad ibn 'Ali, Muhammad Amin ibn 'Abidin, and Muhammad ibn 'Abdullah al-Tumurtashi. *Hashiya radd al-muhtar 'ala al-Durr al-mukhtar sharh Tanwir al-absar* [Haskafi's *al-Durr al-mukhtar,* an interlineal exegesis of Tumurtashi's *Tanwir al-absar* printed with it above Ibn 'Abidin's commentary]. 8 vols. Beirut: Dar al-Fikr, 1399/1979.

y48   al-Haytami, Ibn Hajar. *al-Fatawa al-hadithiyya.* N.d. Reprint. Beirut: Dar al-Ma'rifa, n.d.

y49   ———. *al-Zawajir 'an iqtiraf al-kaba'ir* [containing *al-Zawajir* (vol. 1, and vol. 2 from beginning to page 264), *Kaff al-ra'a' 'an muharramat al-lahw wa al-sama'* (2.265–335), and *al-I'lam bi qawati' al-Islam* (2.337–406)]. 2 vols. 1398/1978. Reprint. Beirut: Dar al-Fikr, 1403/1983.

y50   Hinz, Walther. *al-Makayil wa al-awzan al-Islamiyya wa ma yu'adiluha fi al-nizam al-mitri.* Translated by Kamil al-'Asali. Amman: al-Jami'a al-Urduniyya, 1970.

y51   Husriyya, 'Izzat, ed. *Shuruh risala al-Shaykh Arslan fi 'ulum al-tawhid wa al-tasawwuf.* Damascus: Matba'a al-'Alam, 1389/1969.

y52   [al-Hut, Kamal Yusuf, ed.] *al-Rasa'il al-Subkiyya fi al-radd 'ala Ibn Taymiya wa tilmidhihi Ibn Qayyim al-Jawziyya* [documents, letters, and passages by Taqi al-Din al-Subki and others edited and commentated upon by al-Hut]. Beirut: 'Alam al-Kutub, 1403/1983.

y53   Ibn 'Abidin, Muhammad Amin. *al-'Uqud al-durriyya fi tanqih al-Fatawa al-hamidiyya.* Cairo: al-Matba'a al-Maymaniyya, 1310/1892.

y54   Ibn 'Ajiba, Ahmad ibn Muhammad, and Ahmad ibn Muhammad Ibn 'Ata' Illah. *Iqaz al-himam fi sharh al-Hikam* [Ibn 'Ata' Illah's *al-Hikam al-'Ata'iyya* printed with Ibn 'Ajiba's commentary]. Cairo: Mustafa al-Babi al-Halabi wa Awladuhu, 1392/1972.

y55   Ibn al-'Arabi, Muhyiddin. *al-Futuhat al-Makkiyya.* 4 vols. 1329/1911. Reprint. Beirut: Dar Sadir, n.d.

y56   Ibn 'Ata' Illah, Ahmad ibn Muhammad. *al-Hikam al-'Ata'iyya wa al-munajat al-ilahiyya*. Damascus: al-Maktaba al-'Arabiyya, 1393/1973.

y57   Ibn al-Athir, 'Izz al-Din. *Usud al-ghaba fi ma'rifa al-Sahaba*. Edited by Muhammad Ahmad 'Ashul, Muhammad Ibrahim al-Banna, and Mahmud 'Abd al-Wahhab Fayid. 7 vols. Beirut: Dar al-Sha'b, 1390/1970.

y58   Ibn Hazm, 'Ali ibn Ahmad. *al-Muhalla*. Edited by Ahmad Muhammad Shakir and Zaydan Abu al-Makarim Hasan. 13 vols. Cairo: Maktaba al-Jumhuriyya al-'Arabiyya, 1387/1967.

y59   Ibn Kathir, Isma'il ibn 'Umar. *Qisas al-anbiya'*. Beirut: al-Maktaba al-Thiqafiyya, 1407/1987.

y60   ———. *Tafsir al-Qur'an al-'Azim*. 4 vols. N.d. Reprint. Beirut: Dar al-Ma'rifa, 1403/1983.

y61   Ibn Kathir, Isma'il ibn 'Umar, and Ahmad ibn Muhammad Shakir. *al-Bahith al-hathith sharh Ikhtisar 'ulum al-hadith* [Ibn Kathir's *Ikhtisar 'ulum al-hadith* printed above Shakir's commentary]. 1370/1951. Reprint. Beirut: Dar al-Kutub al-'Ilmiyya, n.d.

y62   Ibn Qudama al-Maqdisi, Ahmad ibn 'Abd al-Rahman. *Mukhtasar Minhaj al-qasidin*. Edited and annotated by 'Abd al-Qadir al-Arna'ut and Shu'ayb al-Arna'ut with introduction by Muhammad Dahman. Damascus: Maktaba Dar al-Bayan, 1398/1978.

y63   Ibn Qudama al-Maqdisi, Muwaffaq al-Din. *al-Mughni*. Edited by 'Abd al-Qadir Ahmad 'Ata, Muhammad 'Abd al-Wahhab Fayid, and Taha Muhammad al-Zayni. 10 vols. Cairo: Maktaba al-Qahira, 1968–70.

y64   *Introduction to Sharh al-Waraqat*. 1379/1959–60. Reprint. Amman: Mudiriyya al-Ifta' li al-Quwat al-Musallaha al-Urduniyya, n.d.

y65   al-Jamal, Sulayman ibn 'Umar al-'Ajili, Jalal al-Din al-Mahalli, and Jalal al-Din al-Suyuti. *al-Futuhat al-ilahiyya bi tawdih Tafsir al-Jalalayn li al-daqa'iq al-khafiyya* [Mahalli and Suyuti's interlineal exegesis of the Holy Koran *Tafsir al-Jalalayn* printed on the margins of Jamal's commentary]. 4 vols. 1377/1958. Reprint. Beirut: Dar Ihya' al-Turath al-'Arabi, n.d.

y66   al-Jaziri, 'Abd al-Rahman. *al-Fiqh 'ala al-madhahib al-arba'a*. 5 vols. 1392/1972. Reprint. Beirut: Dar al-Fikr, n.d.

y67   al-Jurdani, Muhammad ibn 'Abdullah. *Mufid 'awam al-Muslimin ma yajibu 'alayhim min ahkam al-din* [a commentary on Jurdani's own *Murshid al-anam* that is printed below it]. Cairo: Matba'a Muhammad 'Ali Subayh wa Awladihi, 1373/1954.

y68   al-Jurdani, Muhammad ibn 'Abdullah, and Yahya ibn Sharaf al-Nawawi. *al-Jawahir al-lu'lu'iyya fi sharh al-Araba'in al-Nawawiyya* [the hadiths of

Nawawi's *al-Arba'un al-Nawawiyya* printed above Jurdani's commentary]. 1328/ 1910. Reprint. Damascus: 'Abd al-Wakil al-Durubi, n.d.

y69   Kahhala, 'Umar Rida. *Mu'jam al-mu'allifin*. 15 vols. 1376/1957. Reprint (15 vols. in 8). Beirut: Dar Ihya' al-Turath al-'Arabi, n.d.

y70   al-Kawthari, Muhammad Zahid, and Taqi al-Din al-Subki. *al-Sayf al-saqil fi al-radd 'ala Ibn Zafil* [Subki's *al-Sayf al-saqil* printed above the commentary of Kawthari and followed by the latter's addendum *Takmila al-radd 'ala Nuniyya Ibn al-Qayyim*]. Edited with an afterword by 'Abd al-Hafiz Sa'd 'Atiyya. 1356/1937. Reprint. Cairo: Maktaba Zahran, n.d.

y71   Khallaf, 'Abd al-Wahhab. *'Ilm usul al-fiqh*. Kuweit: Dar al-Qalam, 1361/ 1942.

y72   al-Khatib, Muhammad al-Shirbini. *al-Siraj al-munir fi al-i'ana 'ala ba'd ma'ani kalam Rabbina al-Hakim al-Khabir*. 4 vols. 1285/1868. Reprint. Beirut: Dar al-Ma'rifa, n.d.

y73   al-Khatib, Muhammad al-Shirbini, and Yahya ibn Sharaf al-Nawawi. *Mughni al-muhtaj ila ma'rifa ma'ani alfaz al-Minhaj* [Nawawi's *Minhaj al-talibin* with Khatib's commentary printed below it]. 4 vols. 1353/1933. Reprint. Beirut: Dar Ihya' al-Turath al-'Arabi, n.d.

y74   al-Kurdi, Muhammad Amin. *Tanwir al-qulub fi mu'amala 'Allam al-Ghuyub*. 1372/1953. Reprint. Beirut: Dar Ihya' al-Turath al-'Arabi, n.d.

y75   Lings, Martin. *Muhammad: His Life Based on the Earliest Sources*. London: Islamic Texts Society and George Allen and Unwin, 1983.

y76   Ledingham, J.G.G., D.A. Warrell, and D.J. Weatherall, eds. *Oxford Textbook of Medicine*. New York: Oxford University Press, 1984.

y77   al-Mahalli, Jalal al-Din, and Jalal al-Din al-Suyuti. *Tafsir al-Jalalayn* [the Holy Koran with Mahalli and Suyuti's interlineal exegesis printed on its margins]. Beirut: Dar al-Ma'rifa, 1403/1983.

y78   Majlisul Ulama of South Africa. *Islam and Television*. Benoni: Young Men's Muslim Association, n.d.

y79   Makhluf, Hasanayn Muhammad. *Fatawa shar'iyya wa buhuth Islamiyya*. 2 vols. Cairo: Dar al I'tisam, 1405/1985.

y80   ———. *al-Mawarith fi al-shari'a al-Islamiyya*. Cairo: Matba'a Lajna al-Bayan al-'Arabi, 1378/1958.

y81   al-Makki, Abu Talib. *Qut al-qulub fi mu'amala al-Mahbub wa wasf tariq al-murid ila maqam al-tawhid*. 2 vols. 1310/1893. Reprint (2 vols. in 1). Beirut: Dar Sadir, n.d.

y82   Malik ibn Anas. *al-Muwatta'*.Edited by Muhammad Fu'ad 'Abd al-Baqi. 2 vols. 1370/1951. Reprint (2 vols. in 1). Cairo: Dar al-Hadith, n.d.

y83   al-Maliki, Muhammad al-Hasan ibn 'Alawi. *Mafahim yajibu an tusah-haha*. Dubai: Hashr ibn Muhammad ibn al-Shaykh Ahmad Dalmuk, 1407/1986.

y84   ———. *al-Ta'i' al-sa'id al-muntakhab min al-musalsalat wa al-asanid*. Jedda: Matabi' Sahar, n.d.

y85   al-Mallibari, Zayn al-Din. *Kitab fath al-Mu'in bi sharh Qurra al-'ayn* [Mallibari's commentary on his own *Qurra al-'ayn*]. Cairo: Matba'a Muhammad 'Ali Subayh, 1346/1927–28.

y86   Martin, Bradford G. *Muslim Brotherhoods in Nineteenth-Century Africa*. New York: Cambridge University Press, 1976.

y87   al-Mawardi, Abu al-Hasan. *al-Ahkam al-sultaniyya wa al-wilayat al-diniyya*. Beirut: Dar al-Kutub al-'Ilmiyya, 1405/1985.

y88   al-Maydani, 'Abd al-Ghani al-Ghunaymi, and Ahmad ibn Muhammad al-Quduri. *al-Lubab fi sharh al-Kitab* [Quduri's *al-Kitab* with Maydani's commentary printed below it]. Edited by Mahmud Amin al-Nawawi and Muhammad Muhyiddin 'Abd al-Hamid. 4 vols. 1399/1979. Reprint (4 vols. in 2). Homs and Beirut: Dar al-Hadith, n.d.

y89   al-Misri, Ahmad ibn al-Naqib. *'Umdat al-salik wa 'uddat al-nasik*. 1367/1948. Reprint. Damascus: 'Abd al-Wakil al-Durubi wa Dar al-Karam, n.d.

y90   Mu'adhdhin, Salih, and Muhammad al-Sabbagh, eds. Introduction and notes to *'Umdat al-salik wa 'uddat al-nasik* by Ahmad ibn al-Naqib al-Misri. Damascus: Maktaba al-Ghazali, 1405/1985.

y91   al-Munawi, 'Abd al-Ra'uf, and Jalal al-Din al-Suyuti. *Fayd al-Qadir sharh al-Jami' al-saghir* [the hadiths of Suyuti's *al-Jami' al-saghir* printed above Munawi's commentary on them]. 6 vols. 1357/1938. Reprint. Beirut: Dar al-Ma'rifa, 1391/1972.

y92   Muslim ibn al-Hajjaj. *Sahih Muslim*. Edited and annotated by Muhammad Fu'ad 'Abd al-Baqi. 5 vols. 1376/1956. Reprint. Beirut: Dar al-Fikr, 1403/1983.

y93   Muslim ibn al-Hajjaj, and Yahya ibn Sharaf al-Nawawi. *Sahih Muslim bi Sharh al-Nawawi* [the hadiths of *Sahih Muslim* with Nawawi's commentary printed below them]. 18 vols. 1349/1930. Reprint (18 vols. in 9). Beirut: Dar al-Fikr, 1401/1981.

y94   al-Mutarrizi, Nasir ibn 'Abd al-Sayyid. *al-Mughrib fi tartib al-Mu'rib* [Mutarrizi's commentary on his own *al-Mu'rib*]. Edited by 'Abd al-Hamid

Mukhtar and Muhammad Fakhuri. 2 vols. Aleppo: Maktaba Usama ibn Zayd, 1399/1979.

y95   al-Nabahani, Yusuf ibn Isma'il. *Jami' karamat al-awliya'*. 2 vols. 1329/1911. Reprint (2 vols. in 1). Beirut: Dar Sadir, n.d.

y96   ———. *Sa'ada al-darayn fi al-salat 'ala Sayyid al-Kawnayn*. 1316/1898–99. Reprint. Cairo: n.p., n.d.

y97   ———. *Wasa'il al-wusul ila shama'il al-Rasul*. Edited by Hasan Tamim. Beirut: Maktaba al-Hayat, n.d.

y98   al-Nabulsi, 'Abd al-Ghani. *Idah al-maqsud min wahdat al-wujud* [with two appendices by Mustafa Kamal al-Sharif, *al-Irada al-juz'iyya – al-ikhtiyar – al-kasb*, and *Wahdat al-wujud – al-'ilal wa al-asbab*]. Edited with introduction by 'Izzat Husriyya. Damascus: Matba'a al-'Alam, 1398/1969.

y99   al-Nahlawi, Khalil ibn 'Abd al-Qadir al-Shaybani. *al-Durar al-mubaha fi al-hazr al-ibaha*. Edited and annotated by Muhammad Sa'id al-Burhani. Damascus: Matba'a al-Adab wa al-'Ulum, 1387/1967.

y100   Nasif, Mansur 'Ali. *al-Taj al-jami' li al-usul fi ahadith al-Rasul* [with the author's own commentary *Ghaya al-ma'mul sharh al-Taj al-jami' li al-usul* printed below it]. 5 vols. 1382/1962. Reprint. Beirut: Dar Ihya' al-Turath al-'Arabi, n.d.

y101   Nasr, Seyyed Hossein. *Ideals and Realities of Islam*. London: Allen and Unwin, Unwin Paperbacks, 1979.

y102   al-Nawawi, Yahya ibn Sharaf. *al-Adhkar al-muntakhaba min kalam Sayyid al-Abrar*. Edited by Muhammad Riyad Khurshid with notes from the commentary of Muhammad ibn 'Allan al-Bakri. Damascus: Maktaba al-Ghazali, 1401/1981.

y103   ———. *al-Arba'un al-Nawawiyya wa sharhuha* [Nawawi's commentary on the hadiths of his own *al-Arba'un al-Nawawiyya*]. Cairo: al-Maktaba al-Salafiyya, 1397/1977.

y104   ———. *Bustan al-'arifin*. Edited and annotated by Muhammad al-Hajjar. Beirut: Dar al-Da'wa, 1399/1979.

y105   ———. *Fatawa al-Imam al-Nawawi*. Recorded and arranged by his student 'Ala' al-Din ibn al-'Attar. Cairo: Matba'a al-Istiqama, 1352/1933–34

y106   ———. *al-Maqasid fi bayan ma yajibu ma'rifatuhu min al-din*. Damascus: Dar al-Iman, 1405/1985.

y107   ———. *Riyad al-salihin*. Edited and annotated by Shu'ayb al-Arna'ut, Ahmad Yusuf al-Daqqaq, and 'Abd al-'Aziz Rabah. Damascus: Dar al-Ma'mun li al-Turath, 1401/1981.

y108   al-Nawawi, Yahya ibn Sharaf, Abu Ishaq al-Shirazi, and Taqi al-Din al-Subki. *al-Majmu': sharh al-Muhadhdhab* [Shirazi's *al-Muhadhdhab* printed with Nawawi's interlineal commentary, which is completed by Subki's supplement (vols. 10–20) *Takmila al-Majmu'*]. 20 vols. N.d. Reprint. Medina: al-Maktaba al-Salafiyya, n.d.

y109   al-Nawawi, Yahya ibn Sharaf, and Jalal al-Din al-Suyuti. *Tadrib al-rawi fi sharh Taqrib al-Nawawi* [Nawawi's *al-Taqrib wa al-taysir li ma'rifa sunan al-Bashir wa al-Nadhir* printed above Suyuti's commentary]. Edited with introduction by 'Abd al-Wahhab 'Abd al-Latif. 2 vols. 1386/1966. Reprint (2 vols. in 1). Beirut: Dar al-Fikr, n.d.

y110   al-Qaradawi, Yusuf. *al-Halal wa al-haram fi al-Islam*. Hadiths researched by Nasir al-Din al-Albani, with introduction by Zuhayr al-Shawish. Beirut: al-Maktab al-Islami, 1400/1980.

y111   ———. *al-Sahwa al-Islamiyya bayn al-juhud wa al-tatarruq*. Doha: Ri'asa al-Mahakim al-Shar'iyya wa al-Shu'un al-Diniyya fi Dawla Qatar, 1402/1982.

y112   al-Qari, 'Ali ibn Sultan. *Risala al-mawdu'at*. Istanbul: Shariket Sahafet 'Uthmaniyyet, n.d.

y113   al-Qudah, Nuh 'Ali Salman. *Mudhakkirat fi al-tawhid*. Amman: Mudiriyya al-Ifta' li al-Quwat al-Musallaha al-Urduniyya, n.d.

y114   ———. *Qada' al-'ibadat wa al-niyaba fiha*. Amman: Maktaba al-Risala al-Haditha, 1403/1983.

y115   ———. *Sutur min hayat Muhammad salla Allah 'alayhi wa sallam*. Amman: Mudiriya al-Ifta' li al-Quwat al-Musallaha al-Urduniyya, n.d.

y116   Qurra 'Ali, Muhammad Amin, Nur al-Din Qurra 'Ali, Usama al-Rifa'i, Jamal al-Sayrawan, and 'Abd al-Fattah al-Sayyid, eds. Introduction and notes to *al-Shifa bi ta'rif huquq al-Mustafa* by al-Qadi 'Iyad. 2 vols. Damascus: Maktaba al-Farabi and Mu'assasa 'Ulum al-Quran, 1392/1972.

y117   al-Qurtubi, Muhammad ibn Ahmad. *al-Jami' li ahkam al-Quran*. Edited by Ahmad 'Abd al-'Alim al-Burduni, Bashandi Khalaf Allah, Ibrahim Atfish, and Muhammad Muhammad Hasanayn. 20 vols. 1387/1967. Reprint (20 vols. in 10). Beirut: Dar Ihya' al-Turath al-'Arabi, n.d.

y118   al-Qushayri, Abu al-Qasim. *al-Risala al-Qushayriyya fi 'ilm al-tasawwuf*. Edited with introduction, notes, and appendices by 'Ali 'Abd al-Hamid Baltaji and Ma'ruf Zurayq. Damascus: Dar al-Khayr, 1408/1988.

y119   al-Rifa'i, Yusuf al-Sayyid Hashim. *Adilla Ahl al-Sunna wa al-Jama'a aw al-Radd al-muhkam al-mani' 'ala munkarat wa shubuhat Ibn Mani' fi tahajjumihi 'ala al-Sayyid Muhammad 'Alawi al-Maliki al-Makki*. Kuweit: Dar al-Siyasa, 1404/1984.

y120   al-Saqqaf, Hasan ibn 'Ali. "al-Adilla al-jaliyya li sunna al-jumu'a al-qab-liyya." Photocopy. Amman: 1405/1985.

y121   al-Shadhili, Muhammad Abu al-Mawahib, Ahmad ibn Muhammad al-Sharishi, and Ahmad ibn Ahmad Zarruq. *Kitab qawanin hukm al-ishraq ila kaffa al-Sufiyya fi jami' al-afaq* [containing Shadhili's *Qawanin* followed by Sharishi's poem *Anwar al-sara'ir wa sara'ir al-anwar* and Zarruq's *Usul al-tariqa al-Shadhiliyya*]. Damascus: 'Abd al-Wakil al-Durubi, 1386/1966.

y122   al-Sha'rani, 'Abd al-Wahhab. *Lata'if al-minan wa al-akhlaq fi bayan wujub al-tahadduth bi ni'ma Allah 'ala al-itlaq.* 2 vols. 1311/1894. Reprint. Damascus: Dar al-Hikma, 1405/1985.

y123   ———. *al-Mizan al-kubra.* 2 vols. N.d. Reprint (2 vols. in 1). Beirut: Dar al-Fikr, n.d.

y124   ———. *al-Tabaqat al-kubra al-musamma bi Lawaqih al-anwar fi tabaqat al-akhyar.* 2 vols. 1374/1954. Reprint (2 vols in 1). Beirut: Dar al-Fikr, n.d.

y125   al-Shirazi, Abu Ishaq. *al-Muhadhdhab fi fiqh al-Imam al-Shafi'i* [with notes from *al-Nazm al-musta'badh fi sharh gharib al-Muhadhdhab* by Muhammad ibn Ahmad ibn Battal al-Rakbi]. 2 vols. 1379/1959. Reprint. Beirut: Dar al-Ma'rifa, n.d.

y126   al-Shurunbulali, Hasan ibn 'Ammar. *Maraqi al-falah sharh Nur al-idah* [the author's *Nur al-idah wa najat al-arwah* printed on the margins of his commentary on it]. Edited by Ahmad Sa'd 'Ali. 1367/1947. Reprint. Beirut: Dar al-Ma'rifa, n.d.

y127   al-Shurunbulali, Hasan ibn 'Ammar, and Ahmad ibn Muhammad al-Tahtawi. *Hashiya 'ala Maraqi al-Falah sharh Nur al-idah* [Shurunbulali's inter-lineal exegesis on his own *Nur al-idah wa najat al-arwah* printed with it on the margins of Tahtawi's commentary on them]. Beirut: Dar Ihya' al-Turath al-'Arabi, n.d.

y128   al-Subki, Taj al-Din. *Tabaqat al-Shafi'iyya al-kubra.* Edited by 'Abd al-Fattah Muhammad al-Hilu and Mahmud Muhammad al-Tanahi. 10 vols. Cairo: Matba'a 'Isa al-Babi al-Halabi, 1383/1964.

y129   al-Sulami, Abu 'Abd al-Rahman. *Tabaqat al-Sufiyya.* Edited by Nur al-Din Shariba. 1373/1953. Reprint. Cairo: Maktaba al-Khanji, 1406/1986.

y130   al-Suyuti, Jalal al-Din. *al-Hawi li al-fatawi fi al-fiqh wa 'ulum al-tafsir wa al-hadith wa al-usul wa al-nahw wa al-i'rab wa sa'ir al-funun.* 2 vols. 1352/1933–34. Reprint. Beirut: Dar al-Kutub al-'Ilmiyya, 1403/1983.

y131   al-Tabarani, Sulayman ibn Ahmad. *al-Mu'jam al-saghir.* Edited by 'Abd al-Rahman Muhammad 'Uthman. 2 vols. in 1. Medina: al-Maktaba al-Salafiyya, 1388/1968.

y132   al-Tirmidhi, al-Hakim. *Nawadir al-usul al-mulaqqab bi Silwa al-'arifin wa bustan al-muwahhidin*. 1293/1877. Reprint. Beirut: Dar Sadir, n.d.

y133   'Uyun al-Sud, 'Abd al-Ghaffar. *al-Riyad al-nadira fi tafsir suratayy al-Fatiha wa al-Baqara*. 3 vols. Homs: Matba'a Fata al-Sharq, 1342/1923–24.

y134   Wizarat al-Awqaf wa al-Shu'un al-Islamiyya li Dawla al-Kuweit. *Mawdu' al-ashriba*. Tab'a tamhidiyya li mawdu'at al-Mawsu'a al-fiqhiyya, no. 1. Kuweit: Wizara al-Awqaf wa al-Shu'un al-Islamiyya, n.d.

y135   al-Zayla'i, 'Abdullah ibn Yusuf. *Nasb al-raya li ahadith al-Hidaya* [with notes from Qasim ibn Qutlubugha's *Munya al-alma'i fi ma fata min takhrij ahadith al-Hidaya li al-Zayla'i* printed below it]. Edited by 'Abd al-Majid al-Dasuqi, Ibrahim al-Dasuqi, Ahmad al-Hanbuli al-Fayyumi, 'Abd al-Hamid Hijazi, and Amin 'Abd al-Rahman al-Jaziri. 4 vols. 1357/1938. Reprint. Cairo: Dar al-Hadith, n.d.

y136   al-Zirikly, Khayr al-Din. *al-A'lam qamus tarajim li ashhar al-rijal wa al-nisa' min al-'Arab wa al-musta'ribin wa al-mustashriqin*. 8 vols. Beirut: Dar al-'Ilm li al-Milayin, 1405/1984.

*

BOOK Z

INDEXES

I. SUBJECT INDEX

one was missed, f2.11

whether to recite aloud or to
oneself in, f8.25(end)

Makkah. *See* Mecca

Makr Allah. See Devising of Allah, the

Makruh. See Offensive, the

Mal al-haram. See Income, blameworthy;
Wrongfully gotten property

Ma la ya'ni. See Conversation, about
what does not concern one

Malice, as an enormity, w52.1(3)

Maliki school

on depicting animate life, w50.5(end)

on dogs and pigs, physical purity
of, e14.7(end), w14.1(6)

on donating the reward for acts
of worship to the dead, w35.2

on the end of children and others'
suspension from dealings,
k13.5(end)

on facing the direction of prayer
(qibla), criterion for, f6.7

on forgetting the Koran after
memorizing it, w52.1(68)

on those who miss prayers remaining
Muslims, w18.2

on passing in front of a person
praying, p75.27

on manual partnerships, k16.9(1)

on meat of animals hunted with
guns, lawfulness of, j17.9

on performing prescribed prayers
in a vehicle, w24.1

on positions of sitting for
prayer, f8.43

on postmarital waiting period ('idda)
when menstruation stops, n9.9

on praying behind in imam of a
different legal school, f12.29

on reusing water previously used
for purification, e1.9

on sales by or to the blind,
k2.6(end)

on stipulating the date of a loan's
repayment, validity of, k10.4

on taking turns with wives,

minimal turn, m10.5

on whispering to another in the
presence of a third, r6.2

on wiping the entire head in ablution,
obligatoriness of, w14.1(6)

on the zakat of livestock, h2.2(end)

Ma'lum min al-din bi al-darura. See
Necessarily known as being
of Islam

Mandub. See Recommended, the

Mani'. See Preventive, legal

Maniyy. See Sperm/ Sexual fluid

Manners (adab). *See* Decorum

Mansukh (Koranic ruling type),
o22.1(d(I)). *See also* Supersession

Manumission, k32.0

Maqam. See Spiritual stations

Marfu' hadiths, o22.1(d(II(6)))

Ma'rifa. See Gnosis

Marijuana. *See* Drugs; Hashish

Marine life. *See* Amphibians; Aquatic
animals; Fish

Marital intimacy. *See* Conjugal rights;
Sexual intercourse

Marksmanship

competitions involving, k29.0,
k29.3, w52.1(386)

neglect of after learning,
w52.1(387)

Marriage

annulment of (*see also* Annulment)

—, because of change of religion
or apostasy, m7.4, m8.7, o8.6

breast-feeding, unmarriageability
because of, m6.1(13), m6.2(10),
n12.1–4

bride's marriage payment (mahr)
(*see* Marriage payment)

choosing a bride for, m1.4

commissioning another to conduct,
k17.2, m3.10

contract of, integrals of, m3.1

—, marriage payment (mahr)
stipulated in, m8.1

—, presence of bride's guardian
for, m3.4–15

—, spoken versus written, m3.2(end)

—, witnesses for, m3.3

discipline of wife by husband in,
m10.12, o17.4

disrespect of wife to husband in,
unlawfulness of, r32.2

as not of this world, w5.1

rank of compared to the friends of Allah (awliya'), s4.8, w60.2

scholars as the heirs of, a2.2(5)

as the spiritual physicians of mankind, w3

Sufism as following the way of, w9.5

visiting the tombs of, g5.9, j13.1–5, w21

unity of the message of, t3.15, x245, x348

Proposing marriage. *See* Engagement for marriage

Prostitutes

marriage to, p12.1(n:)

sexual intercourse with, enormity of, w52.1(346)

Prostration

to other than Allah, as unbelief, o8.7(1)

in prayer, f8.33–36

—, sitting up between, f8.36–38

unlawfulness of without a valid reason, f11.20

Prostration of forgetfulness. *See* Forgetfulness prostration

Prostration of Koran recital, e8.1, f11.13–18, f11.21

Prostration of thanks, e8.1, f11.19

Protection, guarantee of, from Muslim to non-Muslim. *See* Safe-conduct

Protective words. *See* Amulets

Prying into others' affairs. *See* Other people; Privacy, invasion of

Psalms, as the word of Allah, u3.4, v1.8

Psi phenomena. *See* Miracles

Psychics. *See also* Astrology; Fortune-telling; Unseen (al-ghayb), the

belief in, enormity of, p41, w52.1(307–16)

Puberty

criteria for, k13.8

legal responsibility established by, c8.1

Pubic hair. *See* Hair, body

Pubs. *See* Alcohol; Bars

Punishment. *See* Death penalty; Disciplinary action; Prescribed legal penalty (hadd); Retaliation (qisas); *and names of particular offenses*

Punishment in the hereafter. *See also* Hell

kinds of (*see* Judgement Day)

subjects of threats of as enormities, p0.0

Purification (tahara), e1.1–e14.15. *See also* book e *Contents* p. 49

defined, e1.2

from filth (najasa) (*see* Filth, how to wash away)

water used in (*see* Water used in purification)

Purity

all things considered as having until existence of filth is made certain of, f4.8(N:)

of heart (*see* Heart, the)

ritual (*see* Ablution (wudu); Bath, purificatory (ghusl); *and following entry*)

Purity of body, clothes, and place of prayer, f4.1–15

amount of filth excusable on person praying, f4.3–4

filth considered nonexistent until presence is verified, f4.8

how to wash away filth to purify, e14.10–12, e14.14

inexcusable amounts of filth found after prayer, f4.7

losing track of filth on a garment etc., f4.10, f4.12

meaning of *filth* that negates, e14

neglecting, enormity of, f17.5, p31

purifying ground, floor, or carpet of filth, e14.12

when unable to purify person etc., f4.9

wearing clothes affected by filth when not praying, f17.5

Purse snatching, o14.6

Pus

amount excusable on person praying, f4.4

as filth (najasa), e14.1(4)

Qada' al-salat. See Makeup prayers

al-Qada' wa al-qadr. See Destiny

Qadhf. See Accusing another of adultery or sodomy

Qadi. See Judges, Islamic

Qadianis, o11.2(A:)

QADI 'IYAD, x296

AL-QALQAMI, MA' AL-'AYNAYN, x225

AL-QALYUBI, x297

AL-QANNAD, x298

a different school
TALHA, x344
Talion. *See* Retaliation
Talking. *See* Conversation; Speech
Talqin al-mayyit. See Instructing the dead
Tamattu' (style of performing hajj),
 j1.15, j1.17
 description of obligation to slaughter
 or fast for, j12.6(I)
 going between Safa and Marwa
 during, j6.1
Tambourines, permissibility of, r40.2
al-Tan'im, entering ihram for 'umra at,
 j1.14
Tanning. *See* Leather
Tape-recording the *dhikr* and
 supplications of the present
 volume, index for, w2
Taqiyya. See Head, covering
Taqlid. See Following qualified scholarship
Taqwa. See Godfearingness
Tarawih prayer, f10.5
Tariffs, p22.0(A:)
Tasbih. See Rosaries; "Subhan Allah"
Tasmiya. See Basmala
Tasriya, (fraud in sales of milk
 animals), k5.8, w52.1(197)
Tattletales. *See* Informing on others;
 Secrets
Tattooing, enormity of, p59, w52.1(81)
Taverns. *See* Bars
Tawaf. See Circumambulation
Tawaf al-ifada. See Circumambulation,
 the going-forth
Tawaf al-qudum. See Circumambulation,
 the arrival
Tawaf al-wada'. See Circumambulation,
 the farewell
Tawakkul, t2.2, w59
Tawarruk style of sitting in payer, f8.43
Tawassul, f21.2, j13.2, w40
Tawba. See Forgiveness; Repentance
Tawhid. See Allah
TAWHIDI, ABU HAYYAN, x39
Ta'wil. See Interpretation of Koran
 and hadith, figurative
Ta'wiz. See Amulets; Medicine
Tawrah. See Torah
Taxes, non-Islamic, p32
 citizens accepting proceeds of as
 wages for labor, w49
 disposing of unlawful wealth by
 paying, h9.2(end)
 enormity of, p20.2, p32, w52.1(131)

on estates, L4.3(1)
impermissibility of speaking of as
 a "right," r12
offensiveness of prayer in places
 where gathered, f4.14(6)
as unlawful innovation (bid'a), w29.3(2)
Tayammum. See Dry ablution
Ta'zir. See Disciplinary action
Ta'ziya. See Consoling
Teachers. *See also* Children, education
 of; Knowledge, Sacred; Sheikhs;
 Students
behavior of with students, r32.1–2
discipline of students by, o17.4
discussing others' mistakes for
 instruction, r23.1
looking at the opposite sex for
 teaching, m2.11
offensiveness of greeting with Salams
 during a lesson, r32.1, r33.1(2)
slander permissible in warning students
 about corrupt, r2.20(3)
of Sacred Knowledge, eligibility of
 for zakat, w36
toothstick (siwak) recommended before
 teaching, e3.2
using explicit language for sexual
 terms etc., r26.2
Teeth
 repairing with gold, f17.7
 sharpening, enormity of, w52.1(82)
Television, w50.10
Temporary marriage (mut'a), m6.12(2),
 w52.1(345)
Temptation (fitna) in dealing with
 the opposite sex. *See also*
 Men; Women
 defined, m2.3
 in mosques where both sexes
 pray, f12.4(N:)
Tenets of faith ('aqida). *See*
 also book u *Contents,* p. 807;
 book v *Contents,* p. 816
 about the afterlife, u3.6, v2.2–8, w6.1,
 w6.3–4
 about Allah, u3.2, v1
 about the finality of the
 messengerhood of the Prophet
 (Allah bless him and give
 him peace), w4
 about the Prophet (Allah bless
 him and give him peace),
 v2.1, x245
 about other religions, o8.7(20),

to perform the prayer or fast,
i2.6, j18.7–8
to perform spiritual retreat (i'tikaf),
i3.4–7
unfulfilled, enormity of, w52.1(395)
—, discharging of, paid for from
deceased's estate, L3.5
Vulgarity, r26
enormity of, p75.8, w52.1(64, 435)
as part of hypocrisy (nifaq), p64.2(6)
worse on fast-days than others, i1.27(1)

Wadi'a. See Deposits for safekeeping
Wady (nonsperm male discharge),
defined, e10.5–6
as filth (najasa), e14.1(9)
Wages
enormity of delaying, w52.1(225)
job (*see* Job wages)
Wahdat al-wujud, x5, x68, x265
Wahm. See Imagine
Waiting period, postmarital ('idda), n9
end of, n9.17–18, w52.1(292)
after husband's death, n9.11, n9.19
marrying during, unlawfulness of, m6.9
proposing marriage during,
unlawfulness of, m2.12–14
after release from marriage for
payment from wife (khul'), n9.10
sexual intercourse with wife during,
enormity of, w52.1(283)
taking back wife during (*see*
Taking back a divorced wife)
woman's deceit about, enormity of,
w52.1(292)
woman's housing and support during,
m11.10, n9.13–15, w52.1(293)
Wajib, contrasted with *fard,* c2.1(A:)
Wakala, Wakil. See Commissioning another
Wali. See Friends of Allah
Walima. See Wedding feast
Walking to prayers, recommendedness of,
f12.8, f18.14(2), f19.4(1)
Walking with a strutting gait, enormity
of, w52.1(110)
Waqf. See Endowment
Warfare. *See* Jihad
Wasiyya. See Bequests
Waste, bodily. *See* Excrement; Lavatory,
going to the; Urine
Wasting time, r13.3
Waswasa. See Doubts, obsessive
Water

when taking others' is permitted by
thirst, e12.6(end)
withholding one's surplus from those
in need, enormity of, p69,
w52.1(136, 229)
Watering place (hawd) before entering
paradise, the, v2.5
Water used in purification, e1
amount of, e5.25(1–2)
change in, defined, e1.17
—, from filth (najasa), e1.4
dipping hands in, e1.9
filth *discernible by eyesight* in,
defined, e1.15
less than 216 liters becomes
impure through mere contact
with filth, e1.15
less than 216 liters of used or
impure water becomes purifying
if increased to 216 liters
and no change remains, e1.16
216 liters or more becomes impure
only by change through
filth, e1.12
216 liters or more becomes purifying
again if change due to filth
disappears, e1.13
216 liters or more remains purifying
after use, e1.10
natural variations in, e1.5
when obligatory to clean oneself
with, after using the
lavatory, e9.5
purifying water distinguished from
pure or impure water, e1.1–4
purity of, after being used to wash
away filth (najasa), e14.14
not reusable, e1.5, e1.7(2–3)
reusable in Maliki school, e1.9
not usable if altered by a pure
substance, e1.7(1)
using earth in place of (*see*
Dry ablution)
Way of greater precaution. *See*
Precaution, the way of greater
Weak (da'if) hadiths, o22.1(d(II(2)))
not considered lies, p9.5
use of as legal evidence, w48
Wealth, unlawful. *See* Income,
blameworthy; Wrongfully gotten
property
Wealthy, the
admiring for their wealth, enormity
of, w52.1(13)

cutting hair by, e4.4, j9.7
defense of, o7.2–3
divorce of (*see* Divorce)
fasts by, without husband's permission,
    p42.2(3), w52.1(143)
following funeral processions,
    w52.1(123)
gold worn by, f17.11
group prayer of (*see also* Group prayer)
—, call to prayer (adhan) not
    given before, f3.4
—, clap hands to apprise imam of
    mistakes, f9.4
—, invalidity of leading men
    at, f12.27
—, at mosques, f12.4(N:), f18.14, f20.3
—, place of in relation to men, f12.32
—, sunna of, f12.2
hajj and 'umra of (*see also* Hajj;
    Ihram; 'Umra)
—, clothing for, j3.2(end), j3.24
—, cutting hair during, j9.7
—, entering ihram without husband's
    permission, m11.9(3), w52.1(151)
—, *mahram* etc. required to accompany
    on, j1.7
—, things prohibited to in ihram,
    j3.24
indemnity for death or injury of, o4.9
injury to, o3.3, o4.9, o7.2–3, o9.10
in jihad, o9.3(end), o9.10
leadership by, o25.3(d), p28.1(1)
leaving the house, m10.3–4, p42.2(4),
    w52.1(272)
marital obligations of (*see* Wife,
    duties of)
marital rights of (*see* Wife, rights of)
marriage payment (mahr) of (*see*
    Marriage payment)
marrying husband of choice, right of,
    m3.9
masculinity in, p28.1(2–3), w52.1(107)
men giving medical treatment to, m2.10
men being alone with, m2.3(end)
men imitating, p28, w52.1(107)
men looking at, f5.3, m2.2–11,
    w52.1(238–40)
men obeying, p28.1(1)
men speaking with when there is
    no need, r32.6
men touching, m2.9–10
menstruation of (*see* Menstruation)
nakedness of, defined, f5.3, w23
obedience of to husbands, m10.12(N:)

prayer of (*see also* Prayer
    (salat), the)
—, clothing recommended for, f5.6
—, joining two prayers because of
    chronic vaginal discharge, breast-
    feeding, etc., f15.18(3)
—, shortening or joining for travel,
    f15.4–5
not punished during pregnancy for
    fornication, o12.5–6
removing facial hair, w51
require husband's permission for
    spiritual retreat (i'tikaf), i3.9
retaliation (qisas) of against men, o3.3
sexual discharge of (*see* Sperm/
    sexual fluid)
sexual relations of (*see* Conjugal
    rights; Sexual intercourse, marital;
    Wife, duties of; Wife, rights of)
showing body to adolescents or non-
    Muslim women, m2.7
travelling alone by, m10.3, w52.1(100)
unmarriageable kinsmen (mahram) of,
    m6.2
veiling by (*see* Veils, face)
visiting of graves by, g5.9, w34,
    w52.1(122)
voices of, m2.3
working, n9.13(end)
Word, breaking one's, enormity of,
    p24.2(2), p75.15, w52.1(53)
Work, occupational, as an excuse to
    join two prayers, f15.18(5)
World, this (dunya). *See* This World
Worship, acts of
    claims to made from pride,
        enormity of, w52.1(46)
    donating the reward of to the
        dead, w35
    as medicine for the heart, w3.1
    offensiveness of preferring others to
        oneself in, f18.16
Worshippers, delusions of. *See* Devotees
Worshipping others with Allah. *See* Shirk
Wounds. *See* Injuries
Wrestling, k29.4
Writings
    beneficial, recommendedness of,
        w29.3(3)
    covert boasting by authors in,
        illness of, s2.2(end)
    embellishment of script with
        silver, f17.10
    slander in, unlawfulness of, r2.8

when ownership of property is
interrupted during the year, h1.11
payment of wife's to husband, h7.4
as a pillar of Islam, p10.1(3),
u2.1–2
prayer (du'a) of recipient for
giver, h8.4
relatives recommended to be given,
h8.22
unpaid is taken from deceased's
estate, L3.5, L4.2(1)
who is obliged to pay, h1.1–6
year of (hawl), h1.9–12
Zakat al-Fitr. *See* 'Eid al-Fitr, zakat of
Zann. See Think
Zamzam, drinking the water of, j11.6(3)
ZARKASHI, MUHAMMAD, x386
ZAYD IBN 'ALI IBN HUSAYN, x387
ZAYD IBN THABIT, x388
Zaydi school, impermissibility of following
the positions of, b7.6
Zealotry, for other than Allah's
religion, enormity of, w52.1(22)

Zihar. See Injurious comparison
Zikr. See Dhikr
Zina. See Fornication
*Zindiq*s (those with corrupt beliefs
on basic tenets of faith)
hadith forgery by, p9.4
meat slaughtered by, j17.2
Zoroastrians
indemnity for death or injury of, o4.9
jihad against, o9.8
meat slaughtered by, j17.2
Muslim marriages with, unlawfulness
of, m6.7
Muslims ordered to differentiate
themselves from, p75.16
as subjects of the Islamic state, o11
ZUBAYR, x390
Zuhd. See Abstinence; This world
Zuhr. See Noon prayer
ZUHRI, x391
Zulm. See Injustice; Oppressors
Zunnar, o11.5(2)
ZURRUQ, AHMAD, x78

*

II. SECTION INDEX

BOOK L: INHERITANCE

BOOK M: MARRIAGE

*

للإجـازة، فأجـازه مجمع البحوث الإسلامية في الأزهر الشريف، وكذلك المعهـد العالمي للفكر الإسلامي بواشنطن، وقد أثبت صورة عن كل من هاتين الإجازتين في أول الكتاب، والحمد لله أولاً وآخراً.

هذا؛ وقد وضعت النص العربي الأصيل للكتاب إلى يمين الترجمة الإنكليزية؛ راغباً من وراء ذلك بتحقيق غايتين:

الأولى: أن لا أفوّت على القارىء الذي نال قسطاً من المعرفة باللغة العربية أن يطّلع على النص الأصلي للمادة المترجمة.

والأخرى: أن يشعر القارىء بالراحة التامة والثقة الأكيدة بدقة الترجمة وصدق النقل.

وأسأل الله العلي القدير أن يكتب لعملي هذا قبولاً حسناً، وأن ينفع به، وأن يجعله ذخراً لكل من ساهم فيه بكثير أو قليل، وأن يجزيهم خير الجزاء؛ إنه نعم المولى ونعم الوكيل، والحمد لله رب العالمين، وصلى الله على سيدنا محمد وعلى آله وصحبه وسلم.

عمان في شهر رمضان سنة ١٤١١هـ
الموافق آذار سنة ١٩٩١م

وكتبه الطالب المسلم الأمريكي
نوح حا ميم كلر

*

والعشاءِ كذلكَ في كلِّ سفرٍ تُقْصَرُ الصلاةُ فيه .

time of either of them (N: or the Friday prayer (jumu'a) and midafternoon prayer in the time of the Friday prayer), and permissible to similarly join the sunset prayer (maghrib) and nightfall prayer ('isha) during the time of either, provided one joins them during a journey in which prayer may be shortened (def: f15.8(a,b,c,d)).

فالنص العربي المكتوب أعلاه يقابله من الإنكليزية ما معناه: «يجوز أن يجمع بين صلاة الظهر وصلاة العصر في وقت أي منهما (الشيخ نوح: وبين صلاة الجمعة وصلاة العصر في وقت صلاة الجمعة)، ويجوز كذلك أن يجمع بين صلاة المغرب وصلاة العشاء في وقت أي منهما؛ بشرط أن يجمعهما في سفرٍ يجوز أن تقصر الصلاة فيه (تعريفه f15.8 (a, b, c, d))»، وهذا الأخير هو رقم الفقرة التي تبيّن شروط السفر الذي تُقصر الصلاة فيه .

ويلاحظ أيضاً تعليق الشيخ نوح علي سلمان المشار إليه بالحرف (N:) المثبت (بين القوسين) بالإنكليزية فقط دون المتن العربي .

ولعل القارىء يستطيع أن يلمس هنا ما في هذا الأسلوب من اليسر والسهولة والبعد عن المصطلحات الفنية التي قد تحول دون فهم المقصود .

ثم إنني أضفت في الترجمة الإنكليزية في كثير من المواضع عناوين فرعية غير موجودة في الأصل العربي، وعندما نقلها الشيخ نوح علي سلمان إلى العربية؛ راعى فيها اصطلاح الفقهاء، ولذلك نجد أحياناً عدم المطابقة التامة بين العنوانين، وأمثّل لذلك بما جاء في باب الصيد والذبائح في الصفحة ٣٦٦، فقد عنونت له بالإنكليزية بكلمة (Hunting)؛ يعني الصيد، بينما وضع الشيخ نوح له عنواناً: أحكام الصيد. . . وهكذا .

دقة الترجمة :

ثم إنني عرضت هذا الكتاب على عدد ممن يتقنون العربية والإنكليزية معاً لمراجعته؛ زيادة في التوثيق، وتحرياً لمزيد من الدقة، وقدمته بعد ذلك

التفسيرية لا الحرفية، وهـذا الأمر ينسحب أيضاً على النصوص القرآنية، حيث كنت أولاً أقرأ النص القرآني باللغة العربية، ثم أنظر ما تيسر من كتب معاني القرآن المترجمة إلى اللغة الإنكليزية، ثم أراجع معاني هذا النص في التفاسير المختلفة؛ كـ «تفسير الجلالين بحاشية الجمل»، أو «تفسير ابن كثير»، أو «تفسير القرطبي»، ثم أنقـل إلى الإنكليزية أقرب المعاني إلى موضع الاستشهاد، ولعل من المفيد هنا أن أشير إلى أن ترجمة النص القرآني إلى أي لغة أجنبية تفقده ميزة احتماله للمعاني والوجوه المتعددة بآن واحد، فلا يمكن أن نأخذ إلا وجهاً واحداً من تلك الوجوه عند الترجمة؛ لأنه تفسير للقـرآن بتلك اللغـة وليس ترجمـة للقرآن، إذ لا يسمّى قرآناً بالمعنى الاصطلاحي إلا نصه العربي.

نصوص الحديث الشريف:

ثم إنني سلكت المسلك المذكور نفسه في ترجمة نصوص الحديث الشريف، ورجعت من أجل ذلك إلى واحدٍ أو أكثر من كتب السنّة التالية: «فتـح البـاري» للحافظ ابن حجر، و«شرح صحيح مسلم» للإمام النووي، و«النهـاية في غريب الحـديث» لابن الأثير، و«فيض القـدير شرح الجامع الصغير» لعبد الرؤوف المناوي، و«دليل الفالحين لطرق رياض الصالحين» لابن علان البكري، و«الفتوحات الربانية على الأذكار النووية» له أيضاً.

النصوص الفقهية:

وأما النصوص الفقهية؛ فإنني نسجت فيها على نفس المنوال؛ ساعياً قدر المستطاع إلى اليسـر والسهـولة اللتين تعينان القارىء على الفهم ثم التطبيق، ولعل المثال التالي (المأخوذ من الصفحة ١٩٣ و١٩٤) من الكتاب يوضح هٰذا الأمر بصورة جلية:

f15.9 It is permissible to join the noon prayer (zuhr) and midafternoon prayer ('asr) during the	f15.9 يجــوزُ الجمـعُ بين الظهـر والعصر في وقت أحدِهِمَا وبين المغرب

ما قالـه ، ثم عنـوان الكتـاب والجـزء والصفحة ، فإن كان هناك حذف في الكلام ؛ أشرت إلى موضعه بثلاث نقاط [. . .] ، ثم قلت في آخر الكلام : «محرَّر من المصدر الفلاني» ؛ وإن لم يكن هناك حذف ؛ استغنيت عن هذه النقـاط ، وقلت في آخره : «نُقل من المصدر الفلاني» ، وفي كلتا الحالتين أضفت في آخر النص المترجم بالإنكليزية رقم مصدره كـ (y29) في ثبت المـراجع المشار إليها في آخر الكتاب ، والتي تُبيِّن اسم الكتاب الكامل ، وأسماء حواشيه إن وُجدَت ، وأسماء المؤلف والمحشِّي والمحقِّق والناشر ، وعدد أجزائه ، ومتى طُبع ، وأين ، وإن كان مصوَّراً ؛ فمتى طُبع الأصل .

وبالجملة ؛ فليس في الكتاب من جهالة في نسبة النصوص إلى مصادرها .

وسيلاحظ القارىء أني قرنت كل فقرة من فقرات الكتاب بعلامة مؤلفة من حرف ورقم ؛ مثال ذلك : (e1.12) ، وهو حكم تنجس القلتين من الماء ، فحرف (e) يشير إلى كونه من كتاب الطهارة ، ورقم (1) يشير إلى أنه أول باب من هذا الكتاب ، وأما رقم (12) ؛ فيشير إلى أنه الموضوع الثاني عشر من هذا البـاب . وفائدة اقتران فقرات الكتاب بهذه العلامات هي تسهيل استعمال الفهارس ، وسهولة إحالة القارىء على مسائل الكتاب ، وسأبين ذٰلك فيما بعد .

منهج الترجمة :

أمـا طريقـة التـرجمة ؛ فهي تفسيرية كما سبق ذكره ، وسأوضح هذا بالنسبـة لتـرجمة ثلاثة أنواع من النصوص إلى معانيها بالإنكليزية ، وهي : نصوص القرآن الكريم ، ونصوص الحديث الشريف ، والنصوص الفقهية .

نصوص القرآن الكريم :

ذكرت فيما سبق أنني اعتمدت في نصوص كتابي هذا أسلوب الترجمة

وأخيراً وضعت بالإنكليزية قائمة بأسماء المراجع الواردة في الكتاب، وهي ١٣٦ مرجعاً.

طريقة تحرير النصوص، واصطلاحات ضبطها:

ذكرت أن المتن الفقهي الأساسي هو «عمدة السالك» الذي ألفه الشيخ أحمد بن النقيب المصري، وقد أثبتُّ كامل النص العربي، وضبطت أفعاله بالشكل التام، في حين ضبطت أواخر الكلمات الأخرى، وعند نقله إلى الإنكليزية تركت ترجمة بعض الأحكام نادرة الوقوع؛ إلا أن تكون مهمة، وقد وضعت ما لم أترجم من النص العربي بين معقوفتين [ ].

وأما شرح المتن ـ وهو «فيض الإله المالك»، تأليف الشيخ عمر بركات ـ؛ فقد أدخلت بعضه في ثنايا المتن، وميّزته في النص العربي بوضعه بين قوسين، وتركهِ من غير تشكيل، وأما في النص الإنكليزي؛ فوضعته بين قوسين وأشرت إليه بالحرف (O:) الكبير.

وأثبتُّ تعليقات الشيخ عبد الوكيل الدروبي في اللغتين بين قوسين، وأشرت إليها بالحرف (ع :) في النص العربي، وبالحرف (A:) في النص الإنكليزي.

وأما تعليقات الشيخ نوح علي سلمان؛ فقد أثبتها بين قوسين، وأشرت إليها بالحرف (ح :) في النص العربي، وبالحرف (N:) في النص الإنكليزي.

وكثيراً ما اقتصرت على ذكر ملاحظات الشيخين بالإنكليزية فقط.

وأما ملاحظاتي أنا المترجم؛ فقد وضعتها بين قوسين، وأشرت إليها بالحرف (n:) الصغير في الإنكليزية، وبالحرف (ت :) في العربية، وأحياناً قد توجد هذه الملاحظات في إحدى اللغتين دون الأخرى.

وأما ما أخذ من المصادر الأخرى؛ فقد ذكرت قبل كل قول قائله، ثم

وأضفت بعد المتن أبواباً؛ كملخص «كتاب الكبائر» للإمام الذهبي، الذي يلحق بباب الشهادة من «عمدة السالك»، حيث ورد فيه أنه لا تقبل شهادة صاحب كبيرة، فأردت أن أوضح للقارىء هذه المسألة بسرد الكبائر، و«كتاب حفظ اللسان» من «كتاب الأذكار» للإمام النووي؛ لأن الأحكام المتعلقة بالغيبة المحرمة ـ مثلاً ـ لها في حياة المسلم اليومية أهمية توازي أو تزيد على أهمية أحكام سنن الوضوء المتضمنة في «عمدة السالك». . . وهكذا، و«كتاب الأمر بالمعروف والنهي عن المنكر»، و«كتاب الغرور»؛ اللذان لخصهما ابن قدامة المقدسي من «منهاج القاصدين» لابن الجوزي، وهو تهذيب لـ «إحياء علوم الدين»، وفي العقيدة اخترت «ترجمة عقيدة أهل السنة في كلمتي الشهادة» لحجة الإسلام الإمام الغزالي، وبعده حديث جبريل عليه السلام؛ بشرحين: أحدهما للإمام النووي، والثاني للشيخ محمد بن عبد الله الجرداني (تلميذ العلامة الباجوري) يفسران معاني الإسلام والإيمان والإحسان.

وفي آخر الكتاب أضفت ملاحق تتعلق بأمور مذكورة في المتن احتاجت إلى زيادة التوضيح، وهي ستون مبحثاً مقتبسة من علماء أهل السنة؛ كالإمام النووي، والغزالي، والقرطبي، والسيوطي، والبغوي، وأبي اسحاق الشيرازي، والعز بن عبد السلام، وابن حجر العسقلاني، وابن كثير، وتقي الدين السبكي، وابن حجر الهيتمي، ومحمد أمين ابن عابدين، والحافظ المناوي، وابن علان البكري، وعبد الوهاب الشعراني، وغيرهم. وليس لهذه الملاحق ترتيب فيما بينها غير ترتيب ورودها في نصوص الكتاب التي تتعلق بها.

ثم أفردت باباً خاصّاً باللغة الإنكليزية في ترجمة الأعلام المذكورين في الكتاب، وهو يشتمل على ترجمة ٣٩٥ علماً.

بما رجحه النووي في «منهاج الطالبين».

ولما كان الفهم هو أول واجبات ناقل مثل هذه النصوص؛ شرح الله صدري أن أقرأه على الأستاذ الشيخ عبد الوكيل الدروبي بجامع درويش باشا بدمشق الشـام، وكـذلك راجعته مع الشيخ نوح علي سلمان مفتي القوات المسلحة الأردنية في عمّان، فنقّحت كامل النص العربي، واستعرضته كلمة كلمة مع كل من الشيخين جزاهما الله خيراً في مجالس متعددة على مدار خمس سنـوات، وأجـازني كل منهـما خطّياً بشرحه وترجمته، وقد صورت الإجازتين في الصفحات الأولى من مصنفي هذا.

ثم إنني بعد أن اطمأننت إلى تمكني من استيعاب مادة الكتاب وفهمها وهضمها على وجه أحسبه حسناً، عملت على توصيل هذا الفهم إلى القارىء باللغة الإنكليزية بطريقة سهلة عصرية تناسب القارىء الغربي، فاعتمدت في عملي هٰذا ترجمة تفسيرية لا حرفية للنصوص، أغنيتها بما استفدته من كتاب «فيض الإلٰه المالك في حل ألفاظ عمدة السالك وعدة الناسك» للشيخ عمر بركات تلميذ الشيخ العلامة إبراهيم الباجوري، وما استفدته أيضاً من الشيخ عبـد الـوكيل الـدروبي، والشيخ نوح علي سلمـان، وبهٰذا أغنيت القارىء الغربي عن الخوض في تعقيدات المصطلحات الفنية الفقهية التي قد يصعب عليه فهمها.

هٰذا؛ وقد أضفت إلى مباحث الكتاب أبواباً أخرى:

منهـا ثلاثـة قبـل ترجمـة المتن، وهي: «كتـاب العلم» مقتبس من «المجمـوع شرح المهذب» للإمام النووي، و«كتاب مشروعية التقليد» من كتاب «اللامذهبية أخطر بدعة تهدد الشريعة الإسلامية» للدكتور محمد سعيد البوطي، و«كتاب الحكم الشرعي» من كتب الأصول وبخاصة كتاب «علم أصول الفقه» للشيخ عبد الوهاب خلاف.

غير أنه من الضروري أن نشير في هذا المقام إلى أن هذه المكتبة الضخمة تنحصر الاستفادة منها بالمسلمين العرب دون غيرهم من الذين لا يجيدون العربية أو لا يتكلمونها، ولا سيما المسلمين في العالم الغربي، الذين لا يعرفون في معظم الأحيان عن هذا الدين العظيم إلا مبادىء وأوليات لا تفي بحاجتهم كمسلمين جدد ينتظرون أن يجدوا في الإسلام نظاماً شاملاً يستوعب كل مناحي الحياة، فإذا أراد أحدهم أن يتوسع في معرفة تفاصيل هذا الدين الحنيف؛ لم يجد أمامه إلا منشورات تخدم أغراض بعض الفئات المنحرفة؛ كالقاديانيين والمستشرقين وغيرهم.

ومن هنا أحببتُ أن أُقدم لإخواني المسلمين الذين يحسنون الإنكليزية مصنفاً يعينهم على معرفة الأحكام الفقهية التي تتوقف عليها صحة عباداتهم ومعاملاتهم بيسر ووضوح، فرأيت أن أقوم بترجمة كتاب فقهي معتَمد عند الشافعية هو «عمدة السالك وعدة الناسك»، مع إضافة بعض النصوص الأخرى؛ تكميلاً للفائدة؛ راجياً من الله تعالى أن يَسْلُكَني في عداد من أخبر عنهم رسول الله ﷺ بقوله: «من دعا إلى هدى؛ كان له من الأجر مثل أجور من تبعه لا ينقص ذلك من أجورهم شيئاً».

وصف مضمون الكتاب:

يعدّ المتن الأساسي «عمدة السالك» بحق من أرقى وأوثق المتون في مذهب الإمام الشافعي رضي الله عنه؛ ذلك أن المؤلف ـ وهو الشيخ العلامة أحمد بن النقيب المصري (المتوفى ٧٦٩هـ) رحمه الله ـ اقتصر على الصحيح من المذهب عند الرافعي والنووي؛ مقدماً لتصحيح النووي؛ لأنه العمدة في المذهب، وقد اتبع في ترتيبه موسوعة النووي «المجموع: شرح المهذب» مع «التكملة» التي كتبها شيخ ابن النقيب الإمام الحافظ تقي الدين السبكي؛ فـ «عمدة السالك» هو ملخص لأحكام «المجموع» تصحيحاً له

بسم الله الرحمن الرحيم

إن الحمد لله؛ نحمده، ونستعينه، ونستغفره، ونعوذ بالله من شرور أنفسنا وسيئات أعمالنا، من يهده الله؛ فلا مضلَّ له، ومن يضلل؛ فلا هادي له.

وأشهد أن لا إلٰه إلا الله وحده لا شريك له، وأشهد أنّ محمداً عبده ورسوله صلى الله عليه وعلى آله وصبحه وسلم تسليماً كثيراً.

أما بعد؛ فإن الله تعالى قد بعث خير الخلق بدين الحق لِيُظْهِرَهُ على الدين كله رحمة للعالمين، وحفظ القرآن العظيم، والسنة الشريفة، والشريعة المطهرة؛ برجال من العلماء العاملين، الذين وقفوا حياتهم على خدمة هٰذا الدين؛ طلباً لمرضاة رب العالمين.

وإن الله عز وجل جعل الفقه في الدين، والعلم بأحكام الشرع؛ سبباً لرضوانه، ومقياساً للتفاوت بين عباده المؤمنين، فقال سبحانه وتعالى: ﴿قُلْ هَلْ يَسْتَوِي الَّذِينَ يَعْلَمُونَ وَالَّذِينَ لا يَعْلَمُونَ﴾، وجعل سبحانه وتعالى خشْيَتَه حقَّ الخشية ثمرةً من ثمرات العلم، فقال جل وعلا: ﴿إِنَّما يَخْشَى اللَّهَ مِنْ عِبادِهِ العُلَماءُ﴾، وحث كذلك رسول الله ﷺ على السعي في طلب العلم والجد في أخذه، فقال ﷺ: «مَنْ يُرِدِ اللَّهُ بِهِ خَيْراً يفقِّهْهُ في الدِّين».

ومن ثم أقبل علماء هذه الأمة في كل العصور على كتاب الله عز وجل وسنة رسوله ﷺ؛ حفظاً، ودراسةً، واستنباطاً، فكان أن قدّموا هٰذا التراث الفقهي الضخم الذي تفخر به أمة الإسلام، وتزهو به على غيرها من الأمم، ولله الفضل والمنة.

المحتويات

١

Published 1991. Revised Edition 1994,

*This new edition 1997
published by amana publications
10710 Tucker Street, Suite B
Beltsville, Maryland 20705-2223 USA
Tel. (301) 595-5777 Fax (301) 595-5888
Website: www.amana-publications.com
Email: igamana@erols.com*

Printed in the United States of America

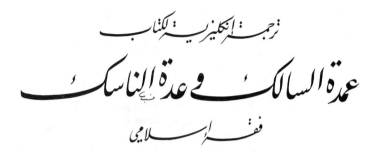

ترجمة إنكليزية لكتاب

عمدة السالك وعدة الناسك

فقـــه إســــلامي

تأليف

الشيخ أحمد ابن النقيب المصري

المتوفى سنة ٧٦٩ هجريَّة

النَّص العَرَبي مُقابل ترجمته بالإنكليزيَّة
مَعَ ملاحق في الفِـــقه والعَقيدة والأخلاق

تَرجَمَهُ وَعَلَّقَ عَليه

نوح حا ميم كلر

أمانه للنشر
amana publications
Beltsville, Maryland U.S.A

ترجمهٔ انگلیزیِ کتاب

عمدة السالك و عدة الناسك

فقه اسلامی